Rayden & Jackson on Divorce and Family Matters

Eighteenth edition

Volume 2(1)   Statutory materials

Statutes

Mark Everall MA (OXON)
One of Her Majesty's Counsel and of the Western Circuit

Nigel Dyer BA (DUNELM)
Barrister

Philip Waller LLB (EXON)
Senior District Judge of the Family Division

Rebecca Bailey-Harris
Barrister, Professor of Law, University of Bristol

Consulting Editors

The Rt Hon Sir Mathew Thorpe
One of Her Majesty's Lord Justices of Appeal

GJ Maple LLB (LOND)
District Judge of the Principal Registry of the Family Division

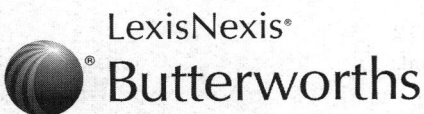

LexisNexis®
Butterworths

Members of the LexisNexis Group worldwide

United Kingdom	LexisNexis Butterworths, a Division of Reed Elsevier (UK) Ltd, Halsbury House, 35 Chancery Lane, LONDON, WC2A 1EL, and RSH, 1–3 Baxter's Place, Leith Walk EDINBURGH EH1 3AF
Argentina	LexisNexis Argentina, BUENOS AIRES
Australia	LexisNexis Butterworths, CHATSWOOD, New South Wales
Austria	LexisNexis Verlag ARD Orac GmbH & Co KG, VIENNA
Canada	LexisNexis Butterworths, MARKHAM, Ontario
Chile	LexisNexis Chile Ltda, SANTIAGO DE CHILE
Czech Republic	Nakladatelství Orac sro, PRAGUE
France	Editions du Juris-Classeur SA, PARIS
Germany	LexisNexis Deutschland GmbH, FRANKFURT and MUNSTER
Hong Kong	LexisNexis Butterworths, HONG KONG
Hungary	HVG-Orac, BUDAPEST
India	LexisNexis Butterworths, NEW DELHI
Italy	Giuffrè Editore, MILAN
Malaysia	Malayan Law Journal Sdn Bhd, KUALA LUMPUR
New Zealand	LexisNexis Butterworths, WELLINGTON
Poland	Wydawnictwo Prawnicze LexisNexis, WARSAW
Singapore	LexisNexis Butterworths, SINGAPORE
South Africa	LexisNexis Butterworths, DURBAN
Switzerland	Stämpfli Verlag AG, BERNE
USA	LexisNexis, DAYTON, Ohio

© Reed Elsevier (UK) Ltd 2004

Published by LexisNexis Butterworths

A CIP Catalogue record for this book is available from the British Library.

ISBN 0-406-94825-9

9 780406 948250

ISBN 0 406 94825 9
ISBN for the complete set of volumes 0 406 94823 2

Typeset by Columns Design Ltd, Reading, England.
Printed and bound in Great Britain by CPI Bath.

Visit LexisNexis Butterworths at www.lexisnexis.co.uk

Contents

Volume 2(1)   Statutory materials

Statutes

Appendix 1   Chronological table of statutes

Appendix 1   Alphabetical table of statutes

Volume 2(2)   Statutory materials

Statutory instruments, European material, Court fees

Appendix 2   Chronological table of rules, regulations and orders

Appendix 2   Alphabetical table of rules, regulations and orders

Appendix 3   European material

Appendix 4   Court fees

Statutes

Provisions repealed or prospectively repealed are printed in italics.

Statutes

Provisions repealed or prospectively repealed are printed in italics.

Note. The text follows the Acts as obtained from HM Printers. Chapter 1 (p 1) gives an account of the origin, background and jurisdiction of the courts in relation to matrimonial and family matters generally. It is sufficient here to point out that most of the provisions of the earlier Matrimonial Causes Acts were repealed and re-enacted by the Supreme Court of Judicature (Consolidation) Act 1952 (repealed finally by the Supreme Court Act 1981 (p 2821)) and sections of this Act in turn were substituted and considerably added to by the Matrimonial Causes Act 1937 (p 2095), which, as amended, was consolidated and replaced by the Matrimonial Causes Act 1950 (p 2130), itself amended and added to by later enactments, all of which were consolidated in the Matrimonial Causes Act 1965 (p 2237). New provisions relating to matrimonial causes were enacted by the Matrimonial Causes Act 1967 (p 2272). A major change in the law was effected by the Divorce Reform Act 1969 (p 2338)) and by the Matrimonial Proceedings and Property Act 1970 (p 2363), both of which came into force on 1 January 1971. The Act of 1969 and the bulk of the Act of 1970, together with most of the remaining unrepealed provisions of the Act of 1965 and the Nullity of Marriage Act 1971, were consolidated in the Matrimonial Causes Act 1973 (p 2495), which came into force on 1 January 1974. The main provisions relating to matrimonial causes are now to be found in the Act of 1973, as amended by subsequent legislation including the Matrimonial and Family Proceedings Act 1984. Nevertheless sections of the repealed Acts are retained for the purposes of reference and comparison. It is significant to trace how the law has been changed and to ascertain the 'mischief' to which such change is directed and the actual effect of such change. Statutes relating to marriage, status and relationships, including the Marriage Acts, the Legitimacy Acts, the Adoption Act 1976 and the Human Fertilisation and Embryology Act 1990, are also reproduced in whole or in part. The law relating to children has been radically altered by the Children Act 1989, so much so that it has been considered unnecessary to include such repealed statutes as the Guardianship Acts, the Affiliation Acts or the Children Act 1975, for all of which reference should be made to the 15th edition of this work. The Children Act 1989 is, however, printed in full. Statutes relevant to county court proceedings are reproduced in whole or in part, as are those which relate to matrimonial and other relevant proceedings in magistrates' courts. Those parts of the Courts and Legal Services Act 1990 which are relevant to this work are also reproduced. Appropriate cross-references are given.

Comparative Tables. For convenience, comparative tables are included for the following Acts, showing the relationship between them and the enactments consolidated in each case: Matrimonial Causes Act 1965 (p 2237); Matrimonial Causes Act 1973 (p 2495); Magistrates' Courts Act 1980 (p 2762); and Supreme Court Act 1981 (p 2821).

MATRIMONIAL CAUSES ACT 1857*

(20 & 21 Vict c 85)

An Act to amend the Law relating to divorce and matrimonial causes in England.
[28 August 1857]

WHEREAS it is expedient to amend the law relating to divorce, and to constitute a Court with exclusive jurisdiction in matters matrimonial in England, and with authority in certain cases to decree the dissolution of a marriage: Be it therefore enacted, etc

1. (*Commencement of Act*, 1 *January* 1858.)
Note. Partly repealed by Statute Law Revision Act 1875 and wholly by Statute Law Revision Act 1892.

2. Jurisdiction in matters matrimonial now vested in Ecclesiastical Courts to cease. *As soon as this Act shall come into operation, all jurisdiction now exerciseable by any Ecclesiastical Court in England in respect of divorces à mensâ et thoro, suits of nullity of marriage, suits of jactitation of marriage, suits for restitution of conjugal rights, and in all causes, suits and matters matrimonial, shall cease to be so exerciseable, except so far as relates to the granting of marriage licences, which may be granted as if this Act had not been passed.*
Note. Repealed in part by Statute Law Revision Act 1892 and wholly by Supreme Court of Judicature (Consolidation) Act 1925, Sch 6. See now Supreme Court Act 1981, s 26 (p 2832).

3. (*Power to enforce previous decrees and orders.*)
Note. Repealed by Statute Law Revision Act 1892.

4. (*As to suits pending at commencement of Act.*)
Note. Repealed by Statute Law Revision Act 1875.

5. (*Power to Judges whose jurisdiction is determined to deliver written judgments.*)
Note. Repealed by Statute Law Revision Act 1875.

6. Jurisdiction over causes matrimonial to be exercised by the Court for divorce and matrimonial causes. *As soon as this Act shall come into operation, all jurisdiction now vested in or exerciseable by any Ecclesiastical Court or person in England in respect of divorces à mensâ et thoro, suits of nullity of marriage, suits of restitution of conjugal rights, or jactitation of marriage, and in all causes, suits, and matters matrimonial, except in respect of marriage licences, shall belong to and be vested in Her Majesty, and such jurisdiction, together with the jurisdiction conferred by this Act, shall be exercised in the name of Her Majesty in a Court of Record to be called 'The Court for Divorce and Matrimonial Causes.'*
Note. Repealed in part by Statute Law Revision Act 1892, and wholly by Supreme Court of Judicature (Consolidation) Act 1925, Sch 6. See now Supreme Court Act 1981, ss 26, 61, Sch 1, para 3 (pp 2832, 2851, 2866).

7. No decree for divorce à mensâ et thoro to be made hereafter, but a judicial separation. *No decree shall hereafter be made for a divorce à mensâ et thoro, but in all cases in which a decree for a divorce à mensâ et thoro might now be pronounced the Court may pronounce a decree for a judicial separation, which shall have the same force and the same consequence as a divorce à mensâ et thoro now has.*
Note. Repealed by Supreme Court of Judicature (Consolidation) Act 1925, Sch 6. See now Matrimonial Causes Act 1973, s 17 (p 2506), replacing Matrimonial Causes Act 1965, s 12

---

* This Act, most of which had already been repealed, was finally and totally repealed by Administration of Justice Act 1965, s 34(1) and Sch 2.

(p 2245), replacing Matrimonial Causes Act 1950, s 14(1), (2) (p 2135), replacing Act of 1925, s 185, as substituted by Matrimonial Causes Act 1937, s 5.

8. Judges of the Court. *The Lord Chancellor, the Lord Chief Justice of the Court of Queen's Bench, the Lord Chief Justice of the Court of Common Pleas, the Lord Chief Baron of the Court of Exchequer, the senior puisne judge for the time being in each of the three last-mentioned Courts, and the Judge of Her Majesty's Court of Probate constituted by any Act of the present session, shall be the Judges of the said Court.*

Note. Repealed by Statute Law Revision Act 1892.

9. Judge of the Court of Probate to be the Judge Ordinary, and shall have full authority, &c. *The Judge of the Court of Probate shall be called the Judge Ordinary of the said Court, and shall have full authority, either alone or with one or more of the other Judges of the said Court, to hear and determine all matters arising therein, except petitions for the dissolving of or annulling marriage, and applications for new trials of questions or issues before a jury, bills of exception, special verdicts, and special cases, and, except as aforesaid, may exercise all the powers and authority of the said Court.*

Note. Partly repealed by Statute Law Revision Act 1875 and wholly by Statute Law Revision Act 1892.

10. Petitions for dissolution of a marriage, &c., to be heard by three Judges. *All petitions, either for the dissolution or for a sentence of nullity of marriage, and applications for new trials of questions or issues before a jury, shall be heard and determined by three or more Judges of the said Court, of whom the Judge of the Court of Probate shall be one.*

Note. Repealed by Statute Law Revision Act 1875, and also by Statute Law Revision Act 1892. See also Matrimonial Causes Act 1858, s 18 (repealed) (p 2017); Matrimonial Causes Act 1860, ss 1, 2 (repealed) (p 2019).

11. (*Who to act as Judge, during absence of the Judge Ordinary.*)

Note. Repealed by Statute Law Revision Act 1892.

12. Sittings of the Court. *The Court for divorce and matrimonial causes shall hold its sittings at such place or places in London or Middlesex or elsewhere as Her Majesty in Council shall from time to time appoint.*

Note. Repealed by Supreme Court of Judicature (Consolidation) Act 1925, Sch 6.

13. Seal of the Court. *The Lord Chancellor shall direct a seal to be made for the said Court, and may direct the same to be broken, altered, and renewed, at his discretion; and all decrees and orders, or copies of decrees or orders, of the said Court, sealed with the said seal, shall be received in evidence.*

Note. Repealed by Supreme Court of Judicature (Consolidation) Act 1925, Sch 6. See now Supreme Court Act 1981, s 132 (p 2862).

14. (*Officers of the Court.*)

Note. Repealed by Judicature (Officers) Act 1879, s 29, which Act was repealed by Supreme Court of Judicature (Consolidation) Act 1925.

15. (*Power to Advocates, barristers, &c. of Ecclesiastical and Superior Courts to practise in the Court.*)

Note. Repealed by Statute Law Revision Act 1892.

16. Sentence of judicial separation may be obtained by husband or wife for adultery, &c. *A sentence of judicial separation (which shall have the effect of a divorce à mensâ et thoro under the existing law, and such other legal effect as herein mentioned), may* *be obtained, either by the husband or the wife, on the grounds of adultery, or cruelty, or desertion without cause for two years and upwards.*

Note. Repealed by Supreme Court of Judicature (Consolidation) Act 1925, Sch 6. See now Matrimonial Causes Act 1973, s 17 (p 2506), replacing Matrimonial Causes Act 1965, s 12 (p 2245), replacing Matrimonial Causes Act 1950, s 14(1) (p 2135), replacing Act of 1925, s 185(1) (p 2060), as substituted by Matrimonial Causes Act 1937, s 5.

17. Application for restitution of conjugal rights or judicial separation may be made by husband or wife by petition to Court &c. *Application for restitution of conjugal rights or for judicial separation on any one of the grounds aforesaid may be made by either husband or wife, by petition to the Court, or to any Judge of Assize of the Assizes held for the county in which the husband and wife reside or last resided together, and which Judge of Assize is hereby authorized and required to hear and determine such petition, according to the rules and regulations which shall be made under the authority of this Act; and the Court or Judge to which such petition is addressed, on being satisfied of the truth of the allegation therein contained, and that there is no legal ground why the same should not be granted, may decree such restitution of conjugal rights or judicial separation accordingly, and where the application is by the wife may make any order for alimony which shall be deemed just: Provided always, that any Judge of Assize to whom such petition shall be presented may refer the same to any of Her Majesty's Counsel or Serjeant-at-Law named in the Commission of Assize or nisi prius, and such counsel or serjeant shall, for the purpose of deciding upon the matters of such petition, have all the powers that any such Judge would have had by virtue of this Act or otherwise.*

Note. Partly repealed by Matrimonial Causes Act 1858, s 19, and by Statute Law Revision Act 1875. Wholly repealed by Supreme Court of Judicature (Consolidation) Act 1925, Sch 6. See Matrimonial Proceedings and Property Act 1970, s 20 (repealed) (p 2376) which abolished the right to claim restitution of conjugal rights, and Matrimonial Causes Act 1973, s 17 (p 2506), replacing Matrimonial Causes Act 1965, s 12 (p 2245); and ss 22–24, 26(1), 40 of the 1973 Act (pp 2510–2515, 2528, 2549), replacing Matrimonial Proceedings and Property Act 1970, ss 1–4, 24(1), 26 (pp 2365–2366, 2377–2378), replacing Act of 1965, ss 13, 15, 16(3), 18(1), 19, 20(1), 30 and 34(6) (pp 2246–2249, 2256–2259), replacing Matrimonial Causes Act 1950, ss 14, 15, 19(4), 20(3), 27 and 29 (pp 2135, 2138, 2139, 2141, 2142), replacing Act of 1925, ss 185, 186 and 190(4) (pp 2060, 2063), and Matrimonial Causes Act 1937, s 10 (p 2098).

18. (*Powers of Judges of Assize for purposes of deciding applications under authority of this Act.*)

Note. This section introduced the system of appointment of what are now deputy High Court Judges: see Supreme Court Act 1981, s 9(4) (p 2828).

19. (*The Courts to regulate fees on proceedings before Judges, &c.*)

20. (*Orders may be reviewed.*)

Note. Sections 18, 19 and 20 repealed by Matrimonial Causes Act 1858, s 19; and also by Statute Law Revision Act 1875.

21. Wife deserted by her husband may apply to a police magistrate or justices in petty sessions for protection. *A wife deserted by her husband may at any time after such desertion, if resident within the metropolitan district, apply to a police magistrate, or if resident in the country to justices in petty sessions, or in either case to the Court, for an order to protect any money or property she may acquire by her own lawful industry, and property which she may become possessed of, after such desertion, against her husband or his creditors, or any person claiming under him: and such magistrate or justice or Court, if satisfied of the fact of such desertion, and that the same was without reasonable cause, and that the wife is maintaining herself by her own industry or property, may make and give to the wife an order protecting her earnings and property acquired since the commencement of such desertion, from her husband and all creditors and persons claiming under him, and such earnings and property shall belong to the wife as if she were a feme sole: Provided always, that every such order, if made by a police* *magistrate, or justices at petty sessions, shall, within ten days after the making thereof, be entered with the registrar of the County Court within whose jurisdiction the wife is resident; and that it shall be lawful for the husband, and any creditor or other person claiming under him, to apply to the Court, or to the magistrate or justices by whom such order was made, for the discharge thereof: Provided also, that if the husband or any creditor of or person claiming under the husband shall seize or continue to hold any property of the wife after notice of any such order, he shall be liable, at the suit of the wife (which she is hereby empowered to bring), to restore the specific property, and also for a sum equal to double the value of the property so seized or held after such notice as aforesaid: If any such order of protection be made, the wife shall during the continuance thereof be and be deemed to have been, during such desertion of her, in the like position in all respects, with regard to property and contracts, and suing and being sued, as she would be under this Act if she obtained a decree of judicial separation.*

Note. Partly repealed for all purposes and wholly repealed, so far as it related to the High Court, by Supreme Court of Judicature (Consolidation) Act 1925, Sch 6 and finally repealed by the Administration of Justice Act 1965, s 34 and Sch 2. This section was rendered obsolete by the Law Reform (Married Women and Tortfeasors) Act 1935 (p 2094), which enabled a married woman to acquire, hold, and dispose of property as if she were a single woman. See also Matrimonial Causes Act 1864, s 1 (repealed) (p 2021); Law Reform (Husband and Wife) Act 1962 (p 2231).

22. Court to act on principles of the Ecclesiastical Courts. *In all suits and proceedings, other than proceedings to dissolve any marriage, the said Court shall proceed and act and give relief on principles and rules which in the opinion of the said Court shall be as nearly as may be conformable to the principles and rules on which the Ecclesiastical Courts have heretofore acted and given relief, but subject to the provisions herein contained and to the rules and orders under this Act.*

Note. Repealed by Supreme Court of Judicature (Consolidation) Act 1925, Sch 6. See s 32 of that Act (p 2055) (repealed) replacing Supreme Court of Judicature Act 1873, s 23 (p 2027).

23. Decree of separation obtained during the absence of husband or wife may be reversed. *Any husband or wife, upon the application of whose wife or husband, as the case may be, a decree of judicial separation has been pronounced, may, at any time thereafter, present a petition to the Court praying for a reversal of such decree on the ground that it was obtained in his or her absence, and that there was reasonable ground for the alleged desertion, where desertion was the ground of such decree; and the Court may, on being satisfied of the truth of the allegations of such petition reverse the decree accordingly, but the reversal thereof shall not prejudice or affect the rights or remedies which any other person would have had in case such reversal had not been decreed, in respect of any debts, contracts, or acts of the wife incurred, entered into, or done between the times of the sentence of separation and of the reversal thereof.*

Note. Repealed by Supreme Court of Judicature (Consolidation) Act 1925, Sch 6. Cf Matrimonial Causes Act 1965, s 12(3) (p 2245) (repealed and not replaced), which replaced Matrimonial Causes Act 1950, s 14(3) (p 2135), which replaced Act of 1925, s 185 (p 2060), as amended by Matrimonial Causes Act 1937, s 5. The word 'and' in line 4 should be 'or'.

24. Court may direct payment of alimony to wife or to her trustee. *In all cases in which the Court shall make any decree or order for alimony, it may direct the same to be paid either to the wife herself or to any trustee on her behalf, to be approved by the Court, and may impose any terms or restrictions which to the Court may seem expedient, and may from time to time appoint a new trustee, if for any reason it shall appear to the Court expedient so to do.*

Note. Repealed by Supreme Court of Judicature (Consolidation) Act 1925, Sch 6. See Matrimonial Causes Act 1965, s 30(1) (p 2256), repealed, replacing Matrimonial Causes Act 1950, s 27(1) (p 2141), replacing Act of 1925, s 190(5) (p 2063).

25. In case of judicial separation the wife to be considered a feme sole with respect to property she may acquire, &c. *In every case of a judicial separation the wife shall, from the date of the sentence and whilst the separation shall continue, be considered as a* *feme sole with respect to property of every description which she may acquire or which may come to or devolve upon her; and such property may be disposed of by her in all respects as a feme sole, and on her decease the same shall, in case she shall die instestate, go as the same would have gone if her husband had been then dead: provided, that if any such wife should again cohabit with her husband, all such property as she may be entitled to when such cohabitation shall take place shall be held to her separate use, subject, however, to any agreement in writing made between herself and her husband whilst separate.*

Note. Repealed by Supreme Court of Judicature (Consolidation) Act 1925, Sch 6. See Matrimonial Causes Act 1973, s 18 (p 2507), replacing Matrimonial Proceedings and Property Act 1970, s 40 (p 2383), replacing Matrimonial Causes Act 1965, s 20(3) (p 2249), replacing Matrimonial Causes Act 1950, s 21 (p 2139), replacing Act of 1925, s 194 (p 2064), as amended by Law Reform (Married Women and Tortfeasors) Act 1935, s 5(1), Sch 1.

26. Also, for purposes of contract and suing. *In every case of a judicial separation the wife shall, whilst so separated, be considered as a feme sole for the purposes of contract, and wrongs and injuries, and suing and being sued in any civil proceeding; and her husband shall not be liable in respect of any engagement or contract she may have entered into, or for any wrongful act or omission by her, or for any costs she may incur as plaintiff or defendant; provided, that where upon any such judicial separation alimony has been decreed or ordered to be paid to the wife, and the same shall not be duly paid by the husband, he shall be liable for necessaries supplied for her use; provided also, that nothing shall prevent the wife from joining, at any time during such separation, in the exercise of any joint power given to herself and her husband.*

Note. Repealed by Supreme Court of Judicature (Consolidation) Act 1925, Sch 6. See Matrimonial Causes Act 1965, s 20(4) (p 2249), repealed, replacing Matrimonial Causes Act 1950, s 21 (p 2139), replacing Act of 1925, s 194 (p 2064), as amended by Law Reform (Married Women and Tortfeasors) Act 1935, s 5(1), Sch 1.

27. On adultery of wife or incest, &c., of husband, petition for dissolution of marriage may be presented. *It shall be lawful for any husband to present a petition to the said Court, praying that his marriage may be dissolved, on the ground that his wife has since the celebration thereof been guilty of adultery; and it shall be lawful for any wife to present a petition to the said Court, praying that her marriage may be dissolved, on the ground that since the celebration thereof her husband has been guilty of incestuous adultery, or of bigamy with adultery, or of rape, or of sodomy or bestiality, or of adultery coupled with such cruelty as without adultery would have entitled her to a divorce à mensâ et thoro, or of adultery coupled with desertion, without reasonable excuse, for two years or upwards; and every such petition shall state as distinctly as the nature of the case permits the facts on which the claim to have such marriage dissolved is founded: Provided that for the purposes of this Act incestuous adultery shall be taken to mean adultery committed by a husband with a woman with whom if his wife were dead he could not lawfully contract marriage by reason of her being within the prohibited degrees of consanguinity or affinity; and bigamy shall be taken to mean marriage of any person, being married, to any other person during the life of the former husband or wife, whether the second marriage shall have taken place within the dominions of Her Majesty or elsewhere.*

Note. Partly repealed by Matrimonial Causes Act 1923, s 2, Schedule. Wholly repealed by Supreme Court of Judicature (Consolidation) Act 1925, Sch 6. See now Matrimonial Causes Act 1973, s 1 (p 2497), replacing Divorce Reform Act 1969, ss 1, 2 (p 2338), replacing Matrimonial Causes Act 1965, s 1(1) (p 2239), replacing Matrimonial Causes Act 1950, s 1 (p 2130), replacing Act of 1925, s 176 (p 2056), as substituted by Matrimonial Causes Act 1937, s 2.

28. Adulterer to be a co-respondent. *Upon any such petition presented by a husband the petitioner shall make the alleged adulterer a co-respondent to the said petition, unless on special grounds, to be allowed by the Court, he shall be excused from so doing; and on every petition presented by a wife for dissolution of marriage the Court, if it see fit, may direct that the person with whom the husband is alleged to have committed adultery be made a respondent; and the parties or either of them may insist on having the contested matters of fact tried by a jury as herein-after mentioned.*

Note. Repealed by Supreme Court of Judicature (Consolidation) Act 1925, Sch 6. See now Matrimonial Causes Act 1973, s 49 (p 2557), replacing Matrimonial Causes Act 1965, s 4 (p 2236), replacing Matrimonial Causes Act 1950, s 4 (p 2132), replacing Act of 1925, ss 99(1)(h) and 177 (p 2056). See also Family Proceedings Rules 1991, r 2.32(1).

29. Court to be satisfied of absence of collusion. *Upon any such petition for the dissolution of a marriage, it shall be the duty of the Court to satisfy itself, so far as it reasonably can, not only as to the facts alleged, but also whether or not the petitioner has been in any manner accessory to or conniving at the adultery, or has condoned the same, and shall also inquire into any counter-charge which may be made against the petitioner.*

Note. Repealed by Supreme Court of Judicature (Consolidation) Act 1925, Sch 6. See now Matrimonial Causes Act 1973, s 1(3) (p 2497), replacing Divorce Reform Act 1969, s 2(2) (p 2338), replacing Matrimonial Causes Act 1965, s 5(1) (p 2236), replacing Matrimonial Causes Act 1950, s 4 (p 2132), replacing Act of 1925, s 178 (p 2057), as substituted by Matrimonial Causes Act 1937, s 4.

30. Dismissal of petition. *In case the Court, on the evidence in relation to any such petition, shall not be satisfied that the alleged adultery has been committed, or shall find that the petitioner has during the marriage been accessory to or conniving at the adultery of the other party to the marriage, or has condoned the adultery complained of, or that the petition is presented or prosecuted in collusion with either of the respondents, then and in any of the said cases the Court shall dismiss the said petition.*

Note. Repealed by Supreme Court of Judicature (Consolidation) Act 1925, Sch 6. See now Matrimonial Causes Act 1973, s 2(1) (p 2498), replacing Divorce Reform Act 1969, s 3(3) (p 2339), replacing Matrimonial Causes Act 1965, s 5(4) (p 2236), replacing Matrimonial Causes Act 1950, s 4 (p 2132), as amended by Matrimonial Causes Act 1963, s 4, replacing Supreme Court of Judicature (Consolidation) Act 1925, s 178 (p 2057), as substituted by Matrimonial Causes Act 1937, s 4.

31. Power of Court to pronounce decree for dissolving marriage. *In case the Court shall be satisfied on the evidence that the case of the petitioner has been proved, and shall not find that the petitioner has been in any manner accessory to or conniving at the adultery of the other party to the marriage, or has condoned the adultery complained of, or that the petition is presented or prosecuted in collusion with either of the respondents, then the Court shall pronounce a decree declaring such marriage to be dissolved: Provided always, that the Court shall not be bound to pronounce such decree if it shall find that the petitioner has during the marriage been guilty of adultery, or if the petitioner shall, in the opinion of the Court, have been guilty of unreasonable delay in presenting or prosecuting such petition, or of cruelty towards the other party to the marriage, or of having deserted or wilfully separated himself or herself from the other party before the adultery complained of, and without reasonable excuse, or of such wilful neglect or misconduct as has conduced to the adultery.*

Note. Repealed by Supreme Court of Judicature (Consolidation) Act 1925, Sch 6. See now Matrimonial Causes Act 1973, s 1(4) (p 2498), replacing Divorce Reform Act 1969, s 2(3) (p 2338), replacing Matrimonial Causes Act 1965, s 5(3), (4) (p 2236), replacing Matrimonial Causes Act 1950, s 4 (p 2132), as amended by Matrimonial Causes Act 1963, s 4, replacing the Act of 1925, s 178 (p 2057), as substituted by Matrimonial Causes Act 1937, s 4.

32. Alimony. *The Court may, if it shall think fit, on any such decree, order that the husband shall to the satisfaction of the Court secure to the wife such gross sum of money, or such annual sum of money for any term not exceeding her own life, as, having regard to her fortune (if any), to the ability of the husband, and to the conduct of the parties it shall deem reasonable, and for that purpose may refer it to any one of the conveyancing counsel of the Court of Chancery to settle and approve of a proper deed or instrument to be executed by all necessary parties; and the said Court may in such case, if it shall see fit, suspend the pronouncing of its decree until such deed shall have been duly executed; and upon any petition for dissolution of marriage the Court shall have the same power to make interim* *orders for payment of money, by way of alimony or otherwise, to the wife, as it would have in a suit instituted for judicial separation.*

Note. Repealed, with Matrimonial Causes Act 1866, s 1, by Matrimonial Causes Act 1907, s 2. See now Matrimonial Causes Act 1973, Part II (pp 2509 et seq), replacing Matrimonial Proceedings and Property Act 1970, Part I (pp 2365 et seq), which largely replaced Matrimonial Causes Act 1965, Parts II and III (pp 2246 et seq), replacing Matrimonial Causes Act 1950, ss 19–29 (pp 2138 et seq), replacing Supreme Court of Judicature (Consolidation) Act 1925, s 190 (p 2062), and Matrimonial Causes Act 1937, s 10 (p 2098).

33. Husband may claim damages from adulterers. *Any husband may, either in a petition for dissolution of marriage or for judicial separation, or in a petition limited to such object only, claim damages from any person on the ground of his having committed adultery with the wife of such petitioner, and such petition shall be served on the alleged adulterer and the wife, unless the Court shall dispense with such service, or direct some other service to be substituted; and the claim made by every such petition shall be heard and tried on the same principle, in the same manner, and subject to the same or the like rules and regulations as actions for criminal conversation are now tried and decided in Courts of Common Law; and all the enactments herein contained with reference to the hearing and decision of petitions to the Court shall, so far as may be necessary, be deemed applicable to the hearing and decision of petitions presented under this enactment; and the damages to be recovered on any such petition shall in all cases be ascertained by the verdict of a jury, although the respondents or either of them may not appear; and after the verdict has been given the Court shall have power to direct in what manner such damage shall be paid or applied, and to direct that the whole or any part thereof shall be settled for the benefit of the children (if any) of the marriage, or as a provision for the maintenance of the wife.*

Note. Repealed by Supreme Court of Judicature (Consolidation) Act 1925, Sch 6. See Law Reform (Miscellaneous Provisions) Act 1970, s 4 (p 2361) (which abolished the right to claim damages for adultery), replacing Matrimonial Causes Act 1965, s 41 (p 2263), replacing Matrimonial Causes Act 1950, s 30 (p 2142), replacing Act of 1925, s 189 (p 2062).

34. Power to Court to order adulterer to pay costs. *Whenever in any petition presented by a husband the alleged adulterer shall have been made a co-respondent, and the adultery shall have been established, it shall be lawful for the Court to order the adulterer to pay the whole or any part of the costs of the proceedings.*

Note. Repealed by Supreme Court of Judicature (Consolidation) Act 1925, Sch 6. See Law Reform (Miscellaneous Provisions) Act 1970, s 4 (p 2361).

35. Power to Court to make orders as to custody of children. *In any suit or other proceeding for obtaining a judicial separation or a decree of nullity of marriage, and on any petition for dissolving a marriage, the Court may from time to time, before making its final decree, make such interim orders, and may make such provision in the final decree, as it may deem just and proper with respect to the custody maintenance, and education of the children the marriage of whose parents is the subject of such suit or other proceeding, and may, if it shall think fit, direct proper proceedings to be taken for placing such children under the protection of the Court of Chancery.*

Note. Repealed by Supreme Court of Judicature (Consolidation) Act 1925, Sch 6. See now Matrimonial Causes Act 1973, s 42 and the notes thereto (p 2551), replacing Matrimonial Proceedings and Property Act 1970, s 18 (p 2376), replacing Matrimonial Causes Act 1965, ss 34(1), (4) and 46(2) (pp 2258, 2259, 2265), replacing Matrimonial Causes Act 1950, s 26 (p 2163), replacing Act of 1925, s 193 (p 2064), and Matrimonial Causes Act 1937, s 10 (p 2098).

36. Questions of fact may be tried before the Court. *In questions of fact arising in proceedings under this Act it shall be lawful for, but, except as herein-before provided, not obligatory upon, the Court to direct the truth thereof to be determined before itself, or before any one or more of the Judges of the said Court, by the verdict of a special or common jury.*

Note. Repealed by Administration of Justice Act 1925, s 29(4), Sch 5.

37. Where a question is ordered to be tried a jury may be summoned as in the Common Law Courts. *The Court, or any Judge thereof, may make all such rules and orders upon the sheriff or any other person for procuring the attendance of a special or common jury for the trial of such question as may now be made by any of the Superior Courts of Common Law at Westminster, and may also make any other orders which to such Court or Judge may seem requisite; and every such jury shall consist of persons possessing the like qualifications, and shall be struck, summoned, balloted for, and called in like manner, as if such jury were a jury for the trial of any cause in any of the said Superior Courts; and every juryman so summoned shall be entitled to the same rights, and subject to the same duties and liabilities, as if he had been duly summoned for the trial of any such cause in any of the said Superior Courts; and every party to any such proceeding shall be entitled to the same rights as to challenge and otherwise as if he were a party to any such cause.*

Note. Repealed by Administration of Justice Act 1925, s 27, Sch 4. (The *Rayden* editor of the time participated in one fully contested divorce trial, *Pearce v Pearce and McHugh* (October and November 1953, unreported), before a Judge and jury.)

38. Question to be reduced into writing, and a jury to be sworn to try it. Judge to have same powers as at nisi prius. *When any such question shall be so ordered to be tried such question shall be reduced into writing in such form as the Court shall direct, and at the trial the jury shall be sworn to try the said question, and a true verdict to give thereon according to the evidence; and upon every such trial the Court or Judge shall have the same powers, jurisdiction, and authority as any Judge of any of the said Superior Courts sitting at nisi prius.*

Note. Repealed by Administration of Justice Act 1925, s 27, Sch 4.

39. Bill of exceptions, special verdict, and special case. *Upon the trial of any such question or of any issue under this Act a bill of exceptions may be tendered, and a general or special verdict or verdicts, subject to a special case, may be returned, in like manner as in any cause tried in any of the said Superior Courts; and every such bill of exceptions, special verdict, and special case respectively shall be stated, settled, and sealed in like manner as in any cause tried in any of the said Superior Courts, and where the trial shall not have been had in the Court for Divorce and Matrimonial Causes shall be returned into such Court without any writ of error or other writ; and the matter of law in every such bill of exceptions, special verdict, and special cases shall be heard and determined by the full Court, subject to such rights of appeal as is hereinafter given in other cases.*

Note. Repealed by Matrimonial Causes Rules 1937, r 82(1).

40. Court may direct issues to try any fact. *It shall be lawful for the Court to direct one or more issue or issues to be tried in any Court of Common Law, and either before a Judge of Assize in any county or at the sittings for the trial of causes in London or Middlesex, and either by a special or common jury, in like manner as is now done by the Court of Chancery.*

Note. Repealed by Administration of Justice Act 1925, s 27, Sch 4; see Administration of Justice Act 1920, s 1, repealed and re-enacted by Supreme Court of Judicature (Consolidation) Act 1925, s 70(5), repealed by Courts Act 1971, s 56, Sch 11.

41. Affidavit in support of a petition. *Every person seeking a decree of nullity of marriage, or a decree of judicial separation, or a dissolution of marriage, or a decree in a suit of jactitation of marriage, shall, together with the petition or other application for the same, file an affidavit verifying the same so far as he or she is able to do so, and stating that there is not any collusion or connivance between the deponent and the other party to the marriage.*

Note. Repealed by Matrimonial Causes Rules 1937, r 82(1). As from 1 June 1966 the requirement as to affidavits in support of petitions was abolished: see SI 1966 No 560.

42. Service of petition. *Every such petition shall be served on the party to be affected thereby, either within or without Her Majesty's Dominions, in such manner as the Court shall by any general or special order from time to time direct, and for that purpose the Court shall have all the* *powers conferred by any statute on the Court of Chancery: Provided always, that the said Court may dispense with such service altogether in case it shall seem necessary or expedient so to do.*

Note. Repealed by Matrimonial Causes Rules 1950, r 82; see now Family Proceedings Rules 1991, r 2.9.

43. Examination of petitioner. *The Court may, if it shall think fit, order the attendance of the petitioner, and may examine him or her, or permit him or her to be examined or cross-examined on oath on the hearing of any petition, but no such petitioner shall be bound to answer any question tending to show that he or she has been guilty of adultery.*

Note. Repealed by Matrimonial Causes Rules 1937, r 82(1). See Matrimonial Causes Act 1859, s 6 (p 2019); Evidence Further Amendment Act 1869, s 3, repealed and re-enacted by the Supreme Court of Judicature (Consolidation) Act 1925, s 198 (p 2066), now replaced by Matrimonial Causes Act 1973, s 48(1) (p 2557), replacing Matrimonial Causes Act 1965, s 43(2) (p 2264), replacing Matrimonial Causes Act 1950, s 32(2) (p 2143). See also Matrimonial Causes Act 1973, s 48(2) (p 2557), replacing Matrimonial Causes Act 1965, s 43(3) (p 2265), replacing Act of 1950, s 32(4) (p 2143), replacing Supreme Court of Judicature (Consolidation) Act 1925, s 198A (p 2066), as inserted by Supreme Court of Judicature (Amendment) Act 1935, s 4.

44. Adjournment. *The Court may from time to time adjourn the hearing of any such petition, and may require further evidence thereon, if it shall see fit so to do.*

Note. Repealed by Statute Law Revision Act 1950, Sch 1.

45. Court may order settlement of property for benefit of innocent party and children of marriage. *In any case in which the Court shall pronounce a sentence of divorce or judicial separation for adultery of the wife, if it shall be made appear to the Court that the wife is entitled to any property either in possession or reversion, it shall be lawful for the Court, if it shall think proper, to order such settlement as it shall think reasonable to be made of such property or any part thereof, for the benefit of the innocent party, and of the children of the marriage, or either or any of them.*

Note. Repealed by Supreme Court of Judicature (Consolidation) Act 1925, Sch 6. See now Matrimonial Causes Act 1973, ss 24, 25 (pp 2515, 2519), replacing Matrimonial Proceedings and Property Act 1970, ss 4, 5 (pp 2366), replacing Matrimonial Causes Act 1965, ss 17(2) and 20(2) (pp 2248), replacing Matrimonial Causes Act 1950, s 24 (p 2140), replacing Matrimonial Causes Act 1937, s 10 (p 2098), which replaced Act of 1925, s 191 (p 2063).

46. Mode of taking evidence. *Subject to such rules and regulations as may be established as herein provided, the witnesses in all proceedings before the Court where their attendance can be had shall be sworn and examined orally in open Court: Provided that parties, except as hereinbefore provided, shall be at liberty to verify their respective cases in whole or in part by affidavit, but so that the deponent in every such affidavit shall, on the application of the opposite party or by direction of the Court, be subject to be cross-examined by or on behalf of the opposite party orally in open Court, and after such cross-examination may be re-examined orally in open Court as aforesaid by or on behalf of the party by whom such affidavit was filed.*

Note. Repealed by Matrimonial Causes Rules 1937, r 82(1). These Rules may be found in the 4th edition of this work. See now Supreme Court Act 1981, s 87(1) (p 2857).

47. Court may issue commissions or give orders for examination of witnesses abroad or unable to attend. *Provided, that where a witness is out of the jurisdiction of the Court, or where, by reason of his illness or from other circumstances, the Court shall not think fit to enforce the attendance of the witness in open Court, it shall be lawful for the Court to order a commission to issue for the examination of such witness on oath, upon interrogatories or otherwise, or if the witness be within the jurisdiction of the Court to order the examination of such witness on oath, upon interrogatories or otherwise, before any officer of the said Court, or other person to be named in such order for the purpose; and all the powers given to the Courts of Law at Westminster by the Acts of the Thirteenth Year of King George the Third, Chapter sixty-three (a), and of the First Year of King William the Fourth, Chapter Twenty-two (b), for* *enabling the Courts of Law at Westminster to issue commissions and give orders for the examination of witnesses in actions depending in such Courts, and to enforce such examination, and all the provisions of the said Acts, and of any other Acts for enforcing or otherwise applicable to such examination and the witnesses examined, shall extend and be applicable to the Court and to the examination of witnesses under the commissions and orders of the said Court, and to the witnesses examined, as if such Court were one of the Courts of Law at Westminster, and the matter before it were an action pending in such Court.*

Note. Repealed by Statute Law Revision Act 1892. See now Family Proceedings Rules 1991, r 2.28.

(a) Ie East India Company Act 1772 (repealed).
(b) Ie Evidence on Commission Act 1831 (repealed by Statute Law Revision Act 1963).

48. Rules of evidence in Common Law Courts to be observed. *The rules of evidence observed in the Superior Courts of Common Law at Westminster shall be applicable to and observed in the trial of all questions of fact in the Court.*

Note. Repealed by Statute Law Revision Act 1892.

49. Attendance of witnesses on the Court. *The Court may, under its seal, issue writs of subpœna or subpœna duces tecum, commanding the attendance of witnesses at such time and place as shall be therein expressed; and such writs may be served in any part of Great Britain or Ireland; and every person served with such writ shall be bound to attend, and to be sworn and give evidence in obedience thereto, in the same manner as if it had been a writ of subpœna or subpœna duces tecum issued from any of the said Superior Courts of Common Law in a cause pending therein, and served in Great Britain or Ireland, as the case may be: Provided that any petitioner required to be examined, or any person called as a witness or required or desiring to make an affidavit or deposition under or for the purposes of this Act, shall be permitted to make his solemn affirmation or declaration instead of being sworn in the circumstances and manner in which a person called as a witness or desiring to make an affidavit or deposition would be permitted so to do under the 'Common Law Procedure Act 1854,' in cases within the provisions of that Act.*

Note. The proviso was repealed by Statute Law Revision Act 1892; the remainder of the section by Statute Law Revision Act 1950, Sch 1. Common Law Procedure Act 1854, s 20, was repealed and replaced by Oaths Act 1888 (repealed). See now Oaths Act 1978 (p 2733).

50. Penalties for false evidence. *All persons wilfully deposing or affirming falsely in any proceeding before the Court shall be deemed to be guilty of perjury, and shall be liable to all the pains and penalties attached thereto.*

Note. Repealed by the Perjury Act 1911.

51. Costs. *The Court on the hearing of any suit, proceeding, or petition under this Act, and the House of Lords on the hearing of any appeal under this Act, may make such order as to costs as to such Court or House respectively may seem just: Provided always, that there shall be no appeal on the subject of costs only.*

Note. Repealed by Statute Law Revision Act 1892. See now Supreme Court Act 1981, s 51 (p 2846).

52. Enforcement of orders and decrees. *All decrees and orders to be made by the Court in any suit, proceeding, or petition to be instituted under authority of this Act shall be enforced and put in execution in the same or the like manner as the judgments, orders, and decrees of the High Court of Chancery may be now enforced and put in execution.*

Note. Repealed by Statute Law Revision Act 1892.

53. Power to make rules, &c., for procedure, and to alter them from time to time. *The Court shall make such rules and regulations concerning the practice and procedure* *under this Act as it may from time to time consider expedient, and shall have full power from time to time to revoke or alter the same.*

Note. Repealed by Administration of Justice Act 1925, s 29(4), Sch 5. See now Supreme Court Act 1981, s 84 (p 2855), and Matrimonial Causes Act 1973, s 50 (p 2557), replacing Matrimonial Causes Act 1967, s 7 (p 2275), and Family Proceedings Rules 1991.

54. Fees to be regulated. *The Court shall have full power to fix and regulate from time to time the fees payable upon all proceedings before it, all which fees shall be received, paid, and applied as herein directed: Provided always, that the said Court may make such rules and regulations as it may deem necessary and expedient for enabling persons to sue in the said Court in forma pauperis.*

Note. Partly repealed by Statute Law Revision Act 1892 and wholly, by Administration of Justice Act 1925, s 29(4), Sch 5. See now Supreme Court Act 1981, s 130 (p 2861).

55. Appeal from the Judge Ordinary to the full Court. *Either party dissatisfied with any decision of the Court in any matter which, according to the provisions aforesaid, may be made by the Judge Ordinary alone, may, within three calendar months after the pronouncing thereof, appeal therefrom to the full Court, whose decision shall be final.*

Note. Partly repealed by Statute Law Revision Act 1892; and, wholly, by Supreme Court of Judicature (Consolidation) Act 1925, Sch 6, which also repealed Supreme Court of Judicature Act 1881, s 9 ('Appeals under Divorce Act').

56. Appeal to the House of Lords in case of petition for dissolution of a marriage. *Either party dissatisfied with the decision of the full Court on any petition for the dissolution of a marriage may, within three months after the pronouncing thereof, appeal therefrom to the House of Lords if Parliament be then sitting, or if Parliament be not sitting at the end of such three months, then within fourteen days next after its meeting; and on the hearing of any such appeal the House of Lords may either dismiss the appeal or reverse the decree, or remit the case to the Court, to be dealt with in all respects as the House of Lords shall direct.*

Note. Repealed by Matrimonial Causes Act 1868, s 2; see also Matrimonial Causes Act 1858, s 17 (p 2017); Matrimonial Causes Act 1860, ss 2, 3 (pp 2019–2020); Supreme Court of Judicature Act 1881, s 9, and, now, Supreme Court Act 1981, s 16 (p 2830); Administration of Justice (Appeals) Act 1934, s 1 (p 2093), and Administration of Justice Act 1969, Part II (pp 2344 et seq).

57. Liberty to parties to marry again. *When the time hereby limited for appealing against any decree dissolving a marriage shall have expired, and no appeal shall have been presented against such decree, or when any such appeal shall have been dismissed, or when in the result of any appeal any marriage shall be declared to be dissolved, but not sooner, it shall be lawful for the respective parties thereto to marry again, as if the prior marriage had been dissolved by death: Provided always, that no clergyman in Holy Orders of the United Church of England and Ireland shall be compelled to solemnize the marriage of any person whose former marriage may have been dissolved on the grounds of his or her adultery, or shall be liable to any suit, penalty, or censure for solemnizing or refusing to solemnize the marriage of any such person.*

Note. Repealed by Supreme Court of Judicature (Consolidation) Act 1925, Sch 6. See now Matrimonial Causes Act 1965, s 8(2) (p 2244), replacing s 13(2) of the Matrimonial Causes Act 1950 (p 2135), replacing s 184 of the Act of 1925 (p 2059), as amended by s 12 of Matrimonial Causes Act 1937.

58. If minister of any Church, &c., refuses to perform marriage ceremony, any other minister may perform such service. *Provided always, that when any minister of any church or chapel of the United Church of England and Ireland shall refuse to perform such marriage service between any persons who but for such refusal would be entitled to have the same service performed in such church or chapel, such minister shall permit any other minister in*

Holy Orders of the said United Church, entitled to officiate within the diocese in which such church or chapel is situate, to perform such marriage service in such church or chapel.

Note. Repealed by Supreme Court of Judicature (Consolidation) Act 1925, Sch 6. See Matrimonial Causes Act 1965, s 8(2) (p 2244), replacing Matrimonial Causes Act 1950, s 13(2) (p 2135), replacing Act of 1925, s 184(2), (3) (p 2059), as substituted by Matrimonial Causes Act 1937, s 12 (no clergyman to be compelled to solemnise marriage of divorced person whose former spouse is living, or to permit marriage of such person in Church or Chapel of which he is minister).

59. No action in England for criminal conversation. *After this Act shall have come into operation no action shall be maintainable in England for criminal conversation.*

Note. Repealed by Statute Law Revision Act 1892.

60. (*All fees, except as herein provided, to be collected by stamps.*)

Note. Repealed by Statute Law Revision Act 1892.

61. (*Provisions concerning stamps for the Court of Probate to be applicable to the purposes of this Act.*)

Note. Repealed by Statute Law Revision Act 1892.

62. (*Expenses of the Court to be paid out of moneys to be provided by Parliament.*)

Note. Repealed by Supreme Court of Judicature (Officers) Act 1879.

63. (*Stamp duty on admission of Proctors, and annual certificates.*)

Note. Partly repealed by Statute Law Revision Act 1875; and, wholly, by Statute Law Revision Act 1892.

64. (*Compensation to Proctors: an annuity not exceeding half the annual loss sustained.*)

Note. Repealed by Statute Law Revision Act 1892.

65. (*Salary of Judge of Court of Probate, if appointed Judge of Court of Divorce, &c., £5,000.*)

Note. Partly repealed by Statute Law Revision Act 1875; and, wholly, by Statute Law Revision Act 1892.

66. Power to Secretary of State to order all letters patent, records &c., to be transmitted from all Ecclesiastical Courts. *Any one of Her Majesty's principal Secretaries of State may order every judge, registrar, or other officer of any Ecclesiastical Court in England or the Isle of Man, or any other person having the public custody of or control over any letters patent, records, deeds, processes, acts, proceedings, books, documents, or other instrument relating to marriages, or to suits for divorce, nullity of marriage, restitution of conjugal rights, or to any other matters or causes matrimonial, except marriage licences, to transmit the same, at such times and in such manner, to such places in London or Westminster, and under such regulations, as the said Secretary of State may appoint; and if any judge, registrar, officer, or other person shall wilfully disobey such order he shall for the first offence forfeit the sum of one hundred pounds, to be recoverable by any registrar of the Court of Probate as a debt under this Act in any of the Superior Courts at Westminster, and for the second and subsequent offences the Judge Ordinary may commit the person so offending to prison for any period not exceeding three calendar months, provided that the warrant of committal be countersigned by one of Her Majesty's principal Secretaries of State, and the said persons so offending shall forfeit all claim to compensation under this Act.*

Note. Repealed by Supreme Court of Judicature (Consolidation) Act 1925, Sch 6 and re-enacted by s 199 of that Act (p 2066) subsequently repealed by Public Records Act 1958.

67. Rules, &c., to be laid before Parliament. *All rules and regulations concerning practice or procedure, or fixing or regulating fees, which may be made by the Court under this Act, shall be laid before both Houses of Parliament within one month after the making thereof, if Parliament be then sitting, or if Parliament be not then sitting, within one month after the commencement of the then next session of Parliament.*

Note. Partly repealed by Statute Law Revision Act 1892; and wholly, by Administration of Justice Act 1925, s 29(4), Sch 5. See now Supreme Court Act 1981, s 84 (p 2855) and Matrimonial Causes Act 1973, s 50 (p 2557).

68. (*Yearly account of fees, &c., to be laid before Parliament.*)

Note. Repealed by Supreme Court of Judicature (Officers) Act 1879, s 29 as amended by Statute Law Revision Act 1894.

MATRIMONIAL CAUSES ACT 1858

(21 & 22 Vict c 108)

*An Act to amend the Act of the Twentieth and Twenty-first Victoria Chapter Eighty-five.**

[*2 August 1858*]

WHEREAS in the last session of Parliament an Act was passed, intituled an Act to amend the law relating to divorce and matrimonial causes in England, and whereas it is expedient to amend the same: Be it therefore enacted, etc.

Note. Preamble repealed by Statute Law Revision Act 1892.

1. The Judge Ordinary of the Court for Divorce and Matrimonial Causes may sit in Chambers. *It shall be lawful for the Judge Ordinary of the Court for Divorce and Matrimonial Causes for the time being to sit in Chambers for the despatch of such part of the business of the said Court as can in the opinion of the said Judge Ordinary, with advantage to the suitors, be heard in Chambers; and such sittings shall from time to time be appointed by the said Judge Ordinary.*

Note. Repealed by Statute Law Revision Act 1892.

2. (*The Treasury to cause Chambers to be provided.*)

Note. Partly repealed by Statute Law Revision Act 1875; and wholly, by Statute Law Revision Act 1892.

3. Powers of Judge when sitting in Chambers. *The said Judge Ordinary when so sitting in Chambers shall have and exercise the same power and jurisdiction in respect of the business to be brought before him as if sitting in open Court.*

Note. Repealed by Statute Law Revision Act 1892.

4. The registrars to do all acts heretofore done by surrogates. *The registrars of the principal registry of the Court of Probate shall be invested with and shall and may exercise with reference to proceedings in the Court of Divorce and Matrimonial Causes the same power and authority which surrogates of the Official Principal of the Court of Arches could or might before the passing of the twentieth and twenty-first Victoria, chapter seventy-seven† have exercised in chambers with reference to proceedings in that Court.*

Note. Repealed by Supreme Court of Judicature (Consolidation) Act 1925, Sch 6.

---

* Ie Matrimonial Causes Act 1857 (p 2002).
† Ie Court of Probate Act 1857.

5. Evidence on which divorce obtained prior to 20 & 21 Vict c 85,* may be used in support of petition in the Court for Divorce and Matrimonial Causes. *In every cause in which a sentence of divorce and separation from bed, board, and mutual cohabitation has been given by a competent Ecclesiastical Court before the Act of the twentieth and twenty-first Victoria, chapter eighty-five,* came into operation, the evidence in the cause in which such sentence was pronounced in such Ecclesiastical Court may, whenever from the death of a witness or from any other cause it may appear to the Court reasonable and proper, be received on the hearing of any petition which may be presented to the said Court for Divorce and Matrimonial Causes.*

Note. Repealed by Administration of Justice Act 1925, s 27, Sch 4.

6. Wives deserted by their husbands may apply to the judge for an order to protected property, &c., acquired by them. *Every wife deserted by her husband, wheresoever resident in England, may, at any time after such desertion, apply to the said Judge Ordinary for an order to protect any money or property in England she may have acquired or may acquire by her own lawful industry, and any property she may have become possessed of or may become possessed of after such desertion against her husband and his creditors, and any person claiming under him; and the Judge Ordinary shall exercise in respect of every such application all the powers conferred upon the Court for Divorce and Matrimonial Causes under the twentieth and twenty-first Victoria, chapter eighty-five,* section twenty-one.*

Note. Repealed by Supreme Court of Judicature (Consolidation) Act 1925, Sch 6, and not re-enacted. See Matrimonial Causes Act 1857, s 21, and note thereto (p 2004).

7. Provisions respecting property of wife to extend to property vested in her as executrix, &c. *The provisions contained in this Act and in the said Act of the twentieth and twenty-first Victoria, chapter eighty-five,* respecting the property of a wife who has obtained a decree for judicial separation or an order for protection, shall be deemed to extend to property to which such wife has become or shall become entitled as executrix, administratrix, or trustee since the sentence of separation or the commencement of the desertion (as the case may be); and the death of the testator or intestate shall be deemed to be the time when such wife became entitled as executrix or administratrix.*

Note. Repealed by Supreme Court of Judicature (Consolidation) Act 1925, Sch 6. See now Matrimonial Causes Act 1973, ss 24, 25 (pp 2515, 2520), replacing Matrimonial Proceedings and Property Act 1970, ss 4, 5 (pp 2366), replacing (with saving for sub-s (3) thereof) Matrimonial Causes Act 1965, s 20 (p 2248), replacing Matrimonial Causes Act 1950, s 21 (p 2139), replacing s 194 of the Act of 1925 (p 2064), and Law Reform (Married Women and Tortfeasors) Act 1935, s 5(1) and Sch 1.

8. Order for protection of earnings, &c., of wife to be deemed valid. *In every case in which a wife shall under this Act or under the said Act of the twentieth and twenty-first Victoria, chapter eighty-five,* have obtained an order to protect her earnings or property, or a decree for judicial separation, such order or decree shall, until reversed or discharged, so far as necessary for the protection of any person or corporation who shall deal with the wife, be deemed valid and effectual; and no discharge, variation, or reversal of such order or decree shall prejudice or affect any rights or remedies which any person would have had in case the same had not been so reversed, varied, or discharged in respect of any debts, contracts, or acts of the wife incurred, entered into, or done between the times of the making such order or decree and the discharge, variation, or reversal thereof; and property of or to which the wife is possessed or entitled for an estate in remainder or reversion at the date of the desertion or decree (as the case may be), shall be deemed to be included in the protection given by the order or decree.*

Note. Repealed by Supreme Court of Judicature (Consolidation) Act 1925, Sch 6. See now Matrimonial Causes Act 1973, ss 24, 25 (pp 2515, 2520), replacing Matrimonial Proceedings and Property Act 1970, ss 4, 5 (pp 2366), replacing (with saving for sub-s (3) thereof) Matrimonial Causes Act 1965, s 20 (p 2248), replacing Matrimonial Causes Act 1950, s 21

---

* Ie Matrimonial Causes Act 1857 (p 2002).

(p 2139), replacing s 194 of the Act of 1925 (p 2064), and see note to s 7 above. See also Act of 1925, s 195 (p 2065). This section was repealed by the Act of 1950, Schedule, and not re-enacted.

9. Order to state the time at which the desertion commenced. *Every order which shall be obtained by a wife under the said Act of the twentieth and twenty-first Victoria, chapter eighty-five,* or under this Act, for the protection of her earnings or property, shall state the time at which the desertion in consequence whereof the order is made commenced; and the order shall, as regards all persons dealing with such wife in reliance thereon, be conclusive as to the time when such desertion commenced.*

Note. Repealed by Supreme Court of Judicature (Consolidation) Act 1925, Sch 6, and not re-enacted.

10. Indemnity to corporations, &c., making payments under orders afterwards reversed. *All persons and corporations who shall, in reliance on any such order or decree as aforesaid, make any payment to, or permit any transfer or act to be made or done by, the wife who has obtained the same, shall, notwithstanding such order or decree may then have been discharged, reversed, or varied, or the separation of the wife from her husband may have ceased, or at some time since the making of the order or decree been discontinued, be protected and indemnified in the same way in all respects as if, at the time of such payment, transfer, or other act, such order or decree were valid and still subsisting without variation in full force and effect, and the separation of the wife from her husband had not ceased or been discontinued, unless at the time of such payment, transfer, or other act such persons or corporations had notice of the discharge, reversal, or variation of such order or decree, or of the cessation or discontinuance of such separation.*

Note. Repealed by Supreme Court of Judicature (Consolidation) Act 1925, Sch 6. See now Matrimonial Causes Act 1973, ss 24, 25 (pp 2515, 2520), replacing Matrimonial Proceedings and Property Act 1970, ss 4, 5 (pp 2366), replacing (with saving for sub-s (3) thereof) Matrimonial Causes Act 1965, s 20 (p 2248), replacing Matrimonial Causes Act 1950, s 21 (p 2139). See also s 195 of the Act of 1925 (p 2065): this section was repealed by the Act of 1950, Schedule, and not re-enacted.

11. Where alleged adulterer a co-respondent Court may order him to be dismissed from the suit. *In all cases now pending, or hereafter to be commenced in which, on the petition of a husband for a divorce, the alleged adulterer is made a co-respondent, or in which, on the petition of a wife, the person with whom the husband is alleged to have committed adultery is made a respondent, it shall be lawful for the Court, after the close of the evidence on the part of the petitioner, to direct such co-respondent or respondent to be dismissed from the suit, if it shall think there is not sufficient evidence against him or her.*

Note. Repealed by Supreme Court of Judicature (Consolidation) Act 1925, Sch 6. See now Matrimonial Causes Act 1973, s 49(3) (p 2557), replacing Matrimonial Causes Act 1965, s 4(3) (p 2241), replacing Matrimonial Causes Act 1950, s 5 (p 2132), replacing Act of 1925, s 179 (p 2057).

12. (*Persons who administer oaths under 20 & 21 Vict c 77,† to administer under 20 & 21 Vict c 85.**)

Note. Repealed by Statute Law Revision Act 1892.

13. Bills of proctors, attorneys, &c., to be subject to taxation. *The bill of any proctor, attorney, or solicitor, for any fees, charges, or disbursements in respect of any business transacted in the Court for Divorce and Matrimonial Causes, and whether the same was transacted before the full Court or before the Judge Ordinary, shall, as well between proctor or attorney or solicitor and client, as between party and party, be subject to taxation by any one of the registrars belonging to the principal registry of the Court of Probate, and the mode in*

---

† Court of Probate Act 1857.
* Matrimonial Causes Act 1857 (p 2002).

which any such bill shall be referred for taxation, and by whom the costs of taxation shall be paid, shall be regulated by the rules and orders to be made under the Act of the twentieth and twenty-first of Victoria, chapter eighty-five,* and the certificate of the registrar of the amount at which such bill is taxed shall be subject to appeal to the Judge of the said Court.

Note. Repealed by Statute Law Revision Act 1892.

14. Power to enforce decree as to costs. *The Judge Ordinary of the Court for Divorce and Matrimonial Causes, and the registrars of the principal registry of the Court of Probate, shall respectively, in any case where an Ecclesiastical Court having matrimonial jurisdiction had, previously to the commencement of the Act of the twentieth and twenty-first Victoria, chapter eighty-five,* made any order or decree in respect of costs, have the same power of taxing such costs, and enforcing payment thereof, or of otherwise carrying such order or decree into effect, as if the cause wherein such decree was made had been originally commenced and prosecuted in the said Court for Divorce and Matrimonial Causes: provided that in taxing any such costs, or any other costs incurred in causes depending in any Ecclesiastical Court previously to the commencement of the said recited Act, all fees, charges, and expenses shall be allowed which might have been legally made, charged, and enforced according to the practice of the Court of Arches.*

Note. Repealed by Administration of Justice Act 1925, s 27, Sch 4.

15. Judge to exercise power and authority over proctors, &c. *The Judge Ordinary of the Court for Divorce and Matrimonial Causes shall have and exercise, over proctors, solicitors, and attorneys practising in the said Court, the like authority and control as is now exercised by the judges of any Court of equity or of common law over persons practising therein as proctors, solicitors, or attorneys.*

Note. Repealed by Supreme Court of Judicature (Consolidation) Act 1925, Sch 6.

16. (*Commissioners may be appointed in the Isle of Man, &c.*)

Note. Repealed by Statute Law Revision Act 1892.

17. Appeal in cases of nullity of marriage to lie to the House of Lords. *Whereas doubts may be entertained whether the rights of appeal given by the Act of the twentieth and twenty-first Victoria, chapter eighty-five,* section fifty-six, extends to sentences on petitions for nullity of marriage: be it enacted and declared, that either party dissatisfied with any such sentence may appeal therefrom in the same manner, within the same time, and subject to the same regulations as affect appeals against sentences on petitions for the dissolution of marriage.*

Note. Repealed by Matrimonial Causes Act 1868, s 2. For Matrimonial Causes Act 1857, s 56, see p 2012.

18. Judge Ordinary may grant rule nisi for new trial, &c. *Where any trial shall have been heard by a jury before the full Court or before the Judge Ordinary, or upon any issue directed by the full Court or by the Judge Ordinary, it shall be lawful for the Judge Ordinary, subject to any rules to be hereafter made, to grant a rule nisi for a new trial, but no such rule shall be made absolute except by the full Court.*

Note. Partly repealed by Statute Law Revision Act 1875; and, wholly, by Statute Law Revision Act 1892.

19. So much of 20 & 21 Vict c 85* as to be applications to judges of assizes repealed. *So much of the Act of the twentieth and twenty-first Victoria, chapter eighty-five,* as authorises application to be made for restitution of conjugal rights or for judicial separation by petition to any judge of assize, and as relates to the proceedings on such petition, shall be and the same is hereby repealed.*

---

* Matrimonial Causes Act 1857 (p 2002).

Note. Repealed by Statute Law Revision Act 1875.

20. (*Affidavits, before whom to be sworn when parties making them reside in foreign parts.*)

21. (*Affidavits, before whom to be sworn.*)

22. (*Persons forging seal or signature guilty of felony.*)

23. (*Persons taking a false oath before a surrogate guilty of perjury.*)
Note. The above four sections were repealed by Commissioners for Oaths Act 1889, s 12.

MATRIMONIAL CAUSES ACT 1859†

(22 & 23 Vict c 61)

An Act to make further provision concerning the Court for Divorce and Matrimonial Causes.
[*13 August 1859*]
† The whole Act was repealed by Supreme Court of Judicature (Consolidation) Act 1925, Sch 6.

1. (*Judges of the Queen's Bench, &c., to be judges of the Court for Divorce.*)
Note. Repealed by Statute Law Revision Act 1892.

2. (*Judge Ordinary and eight of the other judges to appoint the sittings of the full Court.*)
Note. Repealed by Matrimonial Causes Act 1860, s 4, and also by Statute Law Revision Act 1892.

3. (*Precedence of the Judge Ordinary.*)
Note. Repealed by Statute Law Revision Act 1892.

4. The Court may make orders as to custody of children after a final decree of separation. *The Court after a final decree of judicial separation, nullity of marriage, or dissolution of marriage, may upon application (by petition) for this purpose make, from time to time, all such orders and provision with respect to the custody, maintenance, and education of the children the marriage of whose parents was the subject of the decree, or for placing such children under the protection of the Court of Chancery, as might have been made by such final decree or by interim orders in case the proceedings for obtaining such decree were still pending; and all orders under this enactment may be made by the Judge Ordinary alone or with one or more of the other judges of the Court.*
Note. Partly repealed by Statute Law Revision Act 1875; and, wholly, by Supreme Court of Judicature (Consolidation) Act 1925, Sch 6. See now Matrimonial Causes Act 1973, ss 42, 52(1) (pp 2551, 2559), replacing Matrimonial Proceedings and Property Act 1970, ss 18, 19, 27(1) (pp 2356, 2359), replacing Matrimonial Causes Act 1965, ss 34(1), (4), 46(2) (pp 2258, 2259, 2265), replacing Matrimonial Causes Act 1950, s 26 (p 2131), replacing Act of 1925, s 193 (p 2064), as extended by Matrimonial Causes Act 1937, s 10(4) (p 2099).

5. As to marriage settlements of parties after final decrees of nullity of marriage. *The Court after a final decree of nullity of marriage or dissolution of marriage may inquire into the existence of ante-nuptial or post-nuptial settlements made on the parties whose marriage is the subject of the decree, and may make such orders with reference to the application of the whole or a portion of the property settled either for the benefit of the children of the marriage, or of their respective parents as to the Court shall seem fit.*
Note. Extended by Matrimonial Causes Act 1878, s 3; and repealed by Supreme Court of Judicature (Consolidation) Act 1925, Sch 6 (p 2067). See now Matrimonial Causes Act 1973,

ss 24, 25, 52(1) (pp 2515, 2520, 2559), replacing Matrimonial Proceedings and Property Act 1970, ss 4, 5, 27(1) (pp 2336, 2378), replacing Matrimonial Causes Act 1965, ss 17(1), 19, 46(2) (pp 2247, 2248, 2265), replacing Matrimonial Causes Act 1950, s 25 (p 2141), replacing Act of 1925, s 192 (p 2063).

6. On a petition by wife on account of adultery, &c., both husband and wife competent, &c., to give evidence. *On any petition presented by a wife, praying that her marriage may be dissolved by reason of her husband having been guilty of adultery coupled with cruelty, or of adultery coupled with desertion, the husband and wife respectively shall be competent and compellable to give evidence of or relating to such cruelty or desertion.*

Note. Repealed by Supreme Court of Judicature (Consolidation) Act 1925, Sch 6. See now Matrimonial Causes Act 1973, s 48 (p 2557), replacing Matrimonial Causes Act 1965, s 43 (p 2264), replacing Matrimonial Causes Act 1950, s 32 (p 2143), replacing Act of 1925, s 198 (p 2064), which repealed and re-enacted Evidence Further Amendment Act 1869, s 3, and which was extended by Supreme Court of Judicature (Amendment) Act 1935, s 4 (p 2093).

7. Extension of right of appeal to House of Lords. *The right of appeal to the House of Lords given by the fifty-sixth section of the recited Act, shall extend to all sentences and final judgments on petitions under the Legitimacy Declaration Act 1858.*

Note. Repealed by Statute Law Revision Act 1892 and by Supreme Court of Judicature (Consolidation) Act 1925, Sch 6: see Administration of Justice (Appeals) Act 1934, s 1 (p 2093). For 'recited Act' (ie Matrimonial Causes Act 1857), s 56, see p 2012.

MATRIMONIAL CAUSES ACT 1860*

(23 & 24 Vict c 144)

An Act to amend the procedure and powers of the Court for Divorce and Matrimonial Causes.
[*28 August 1860*]

* The whole Act was repealed by Supreme Court of Judicature (Consolidation) Act 1925, Sch 6, although much of it had already been repealed, as indicated in the notes to the various sections. The preamble was repealed by Statute Law Revision Act 1892 (55 and 56 Vict c 19).

1. The Judge Ordinary may exercise powers now vested in the full Court. *It shall be lawful for the Judge Ordinary of the Court for Divorce and Matrimonial Causes alone to hear and determine all matters arising in the said Court, and to exercise all powers and authority whatever which may now be heard and determined and exercised respectively by the full Court or by three or more judges of the said Court, the Judge Ordinary being one, or where the Judge Ordinary shall deem it expedient in relation to any matter which he might hear and determine alone by virtue of this Act, to have the assistance of one other judge of the said Court, it shall be lawful for the Judge Ordinary to sit and act with such one other judge accordingly, and, in conjunction with such other judge, to exercise all the jurisdiction, powers, and authority of the said Court.*

Note. Repealed by Statute Law Revision Act 1892 and by Supreme Court of Judicature (Consolidation) Act 1925, Sch 6.

2. Judge may direct any matter to be heard by the full Court. *Provided always, that the Judge Ordinary may, where he shall deem it expedient, direct that any such matter as aforesaid shall be heard and determined by the full Court; and in addition to the cases in which an appeal to the full Court now lies from the decision of the Judge Ordinary, either party dissatisfied with the decision of such Judge sitting alone in granting or refusing any application for a new trial which by virtue of this Act he is empowered to hear and determine may, within fourteen days after the pronouncing thereof, appeal to the full Court, whose decision shall be final.*

Note. Repealed by Statute Law Revision Act 1892 and by Supreme Court of Judicature (Consolidation) Act 1925, Sch 6. The Supreme Court of Judicature Act 1881, s 9, is partly repealed and re-enacted by Supreme Court of Judicature (Consolidation) Act 1925, s 27.

3. Appeal to the House of Lords. *Where there is a right of appeal to the House of Lords from the decision of the full Court there shall be the like right of appeal to the said House from the decision of the Judge Ordinary alone, or with any other judge, under this Act.*
Note. Repealed by Matrimonial Causes Act 1868, s 2 and by Supreme Court of Judicature (Consolidation) Act 1925, Sch 6.

4. (*Regulation of the sittings of the full Court: Matrimonial Causes Act 1859, s 2, repealed.*)
Note. Partly repealed by Statute Law Revision Act 1875, and, wholly, by Statute Law Revision Act 1892 and by Supreme Court of Judicature (Consolidation) Act 1925, Sch 6: see Administration of Justice (Appeals) Act 1934 (p 2093).
For Matrimonial Causes Act 1859, s 2, see p 2018.

5. Court may, where one party only appears, require counsel to be appointed to argue on the other side. *In every case of a petition for a dissolution of marriage it shall be lawful for the Court, if it shall see fit, to direct all necessary papers in the matter to be sent to Her Majesty's Proctor, who shall, under the directions of the Attorney-General, instruct counsel to argue before the Court any question in relation to such matter, and which the Court may deem it necessary or expedient to have fully argued; and Her Majesty's Proctor shall be entitled to charge and be reimbursed the costs of such proceeding as part of the expense of his office.*
Note. Repealed by Supreme Court of Judicature (Consolidation) Act 1925, Sch 6. See now Matrimonial Causes Act 1973, s 8(1) (p 2501), replacing Matrimonial Causes Act 1965, s 6(1) (p 2243), replacing Matrimonial Causes Act 1950, s 10 (p 2134), replacing Act of 1925, s 181 (p 2058).

6. 20 & 21 Vict c 85, s 45, amended. *And whereas by section forty-five of the Act of the session holden in the twentieth and twenty-first year of her Majesty, chapter eighty-five, it was enacted, that 'In any case in which the Court should pronounce a sentence of divorce or judicial separation for adultery of the wife, if it should be made appear to the Court that the wife was entitled to any property, either in possession or reversion, it should be lawful for the Court, if it should think proper, to order such settlement as it should think reasonable to be made of such property, or any part thereof, for the benefit of the innocent party and of the children of the marriage, or either of them': Be it further enacted, that any instrument executed pursuant to any order of the Court made under the said enactment before or after the passing of this Act, at the time of or after the pronouncing of a final decree of divorce or judicial separation, shall be deemed valid and effectual in the law, notwithstanding the existence of the disability of coverture at the time of the execution thereof.*
Note. Partly repealed by Statute Law Revision Act 1892: and wholly, by Supreme Court of Judicature (Consolidation) Act 1925, Sch 6. See now Matrimonial Causes Act 1973, ss 24, 25 (pp 2516, 2520), replacing Matrimonial Proceedings and Property Act 1970, ss 4, 5 (pp 2366), replacing Matrimonial Causes Act 1965, ss 17(2), 20(2), 21(3) (pp 2248, 2249), replacing Matrimonial Causes Act 1950, s 24 (p 2140), replacing s 191 of the Act of 1925 (p 2063), and Matrimonial Causes Act 1937, s 10 (p 2098).
For Matrimonial Causes Act 1857, s 45, see p 2010.

7. Decrees. *Every decree for a divorce shall in the first instance be a decree nisi, not to be made absolute till after the expiration of such time, not less than three months from the pronouncing thereof, as the Court shall by general or special order from time to time direct; and during that period any person shall be at liberty, in such manner as the Court shall by general or special order in that behalf from time to time direct, to show cause why the said decree should not be made absolute by reason of the same having been obtained by collusion or by reason of material facts not brought before the Court; and, on cause being so shown, the Court shall deal with the case by making the decree absolute, or by reversing the decree nisi, or by requiring further inquiry, or otherwise as justice may require; and at any time during the progress of the cause or before the* *decree is made absolute any person may give information to Her Majesty's Proctor of any matter material to the due decision of the case, who may thereupon take such steps as the Attorney-General may deem necessary or expedient; and if from any such information or otherwise the said Proctor shall suspect that any parties to the suit are or have been acting in collusion for the purpose of obtaining a divorce contrary to the justice of the case, he may, under the direction of the Attorney-General, and by leave of the Court, intervene in the suit, alleging such case of collusion, and retain counsel and subpœna witnesses to prove it; and it shall be lawful for the Court to order the costs of such counsel and witnesses, and otherwise, arising from such intervention, to be paid by the parties or such of them as it shall see fit, including a wife if she have separate property; and in case the said Proctor shall not thereby be fully satisfied his reasonable costs, he shall be entitled to charge and be reimbursed the difference as part of the expense of his office.*

Note. Extended to decrees for nullity by Matrimonial Causes Act 1873, s 1 (p 2026); and repealed by Supreme Court of Judicature (Consolidation) Act 1925, Sch 6. See now Matrimonial Causes Act 1973, ss 1–10 (pp 2497–2502), replacing Divorce Reform Act 1969, ss 1–5 (pp 2338–2340), and Matrimonial Causes Act 1965, ss 5, 6, 7, 10 (pp 2241, 2243, 2245), replacing Matrimonial Causes Act 1950, ss 10, 11, 12 (p 2134), as amended by Matrimonial Causes Act 1963, s 4, replacing Act of 1925, ss 181, 182, 183 (pp 2058–2059): s 182 having been amended by Matrimonial Causes Act 1937, s 9.

8. Continuance of Act. *This Act shall continue in force until the thirty-first day of July one thousand eight hundred and sixty-two, and no longer.*

Note. 'Perpetuated' by Perpetuation of Matrimonial Causes Act 1860 Act 1862, passed expressly for that purpose; and wholly repealed by Supreme Court of Judicature (Consolidation) Act 1925, Sch 6.

MATRIMONIAL CAUSES ACT 1864*

(27 & 28 Vict c 44)

An Act to amend the Act relating to divorce and matrimonial causes in England, twentieth and twenty-first Victoria, chapter eighty-five.†

[*14 July 1864*]

1*. Amending provisions of 20 & 21 Vict c 85,† as to orders of protection of property of wife deserted by her husband. *Where under the provisions of section twenty-one of the said Act† a wife deserted by her husband shall have obtained or shall hereafter obtain an order protecting her earnings and property, from a police magistrate, or justices in petty sessions, or the Court for Divorce and Matrimonial Causes, as the case may be, the husband, and any creditor or other person claiming under him may apply to the Court or to the magistrate or justices by whom such order was made, for the discharge thereof as by the said Act authorised; and in case the said order shall have been made by a police magistrate and the said magistrate shall have died or been removed, or have become incapable of acting, then in every such case the husband or creditor, or such other person as aforesaid, may apply to the magistrate for the time being acting as the successor or in the place of the magistrate who made the order of protection, for the discharge of it, who shall have authority to make an order discharging the same; and an order for discharge of an order for protection may be applied for to and be granted by the Court, although the order for protection was not made by the Court, and an order for protection made at one petty sessions may be discharged by the justices of any later petty sessions, or by the Court.*

* Partly repealed for all purposes and wholly repealed, so far as it related to the High Court, by Supreme Court of Judicature (Consolidation) Act 1925, Sch 6 and finally repealed for all purposes by Administration of Justice Act 1965, s 34, Sch 2.

† Ie Matrimonial Causes Act 1857, s 21 (p 2004).

MATRIMONIAL CAUSES ACT 1866‡

(29 & 30 Vict c 32)

An Act further to amend the procedure and powers of the Court for Divorce and Matrimonial Causes.

[*11 June 1866*]

‡ This Act was repealed by Supreme Court of Judicature (Consolidation) Act 1925, Sch 6.

Whereas by the Act passed in the session of parliament holden in the twentieth and twenty-first years of the reign of her present Majesty intituled An Act to amend the laws relating to Divorce and Matrimonial Causes in England, it is by the thirty-second section enacted, 'that the Court may, on pronouncing any decree for a dissolution of marriage, order that the husband shall to the satisfaction of the Court secure to the wife such gross or annual sum of money as to the Court may seem reasonable, and for that purpose may refer it to one of the conveyancing counsel of the Court of Chancery to settle and approve of a proper deed to be executed by all necessary parties:'

And whereas it sometimes happens that a decree for a dissolution of marriage is obtained against a husband who has no property on which the payments of any such gross or annual sum can be secured, but nevertheless he would be able to make a monthly or weekly payment to the wife during their joint lives:

Be it therefore enacted, etc.

1. Power to order monthly or weekly payments to wife from husband on dissolution of marriage. *In every such case it shall be lawful for the Court to make an order on the husband for payment to the wife during their joint lives of such monthly or weekly sums for her maintenance and support as the Court may think reasonable: Provided always, that if the husband shall afterwards from any cause become unable to make such payments it shall be lawful for the Court to discharge or modify the order, or temporarily to suspend the same as to the whole or any part of the money so ordered to be paid and again to revive the same order, wholly or in part, as to the Court may seem fit.*

Note. Repealed by the Matrimonial Causes Act 1907, s 2. See now Matrimonial Causes Act 1973, ss 22, 23, 25, 27 (pp 2510, 2513, 2520, 2529), replacing Matrimonial Proceedings and Property Act 1970, ss 1, 3, 5, 7 (pp 2365, 2366, 2368), replacing Matrimonial Causes Act 1965, ss 15, 16, 19, 20(1), (2) (pp 2246, 2247, 2248), replacing Matrimonial Causes Act 1950, ss 19, 20, 22 (pp 2138, 2139), replacing Supreme Court of Judicature (Consolidation) Act 1925, s 190 (p 2062).

2. In cases of opposition on certain grounds. *In any suit instituted for dissolution of marriage, if the respondent shall oppose the relief sought on the ground in case of such a suit instituted by a husband of his adultery, cruelty, or desertion, or in case of such a suit instituted by a wife on the ground of her adultery or cruelty, the Court may in such suit give to the respondent, on his or her application, the same relief to which he or she would have been entitled in case he or she had filed a petition seeking such relief.*

Note. Repealed by Supreme Court of Judicature (Consolidation) Act 1925, Sch 6. See now Matrimonial Causes Act 1973, s 20 (p 2508), replacing Matrimonial Causes Act 1965, s 5(6) (p 2242), replacing Matrimonial Causes Act 1950, s 6 (p 2132), replacing Act of 1925, s 180 (p 2058).

3. Decree nisi not absolute till after 6 months. *No decree nisi for a divorce shall be made absolute until after the expiration of six calendar months from the pronouncing thereof, unless the Court shall under the power now vested in it fix a shorter time.*

Note. Extended to nullity decrees by Matrimonial Causes Act 1873, s 1 (p 2026); repealed by Supreme Court of Judicature (Consolidation) Act 1925, Sch 6. See now Matrimonial Causes Act 1973, s 1(5) (p 2498), replacing Matrimonial Causes Act 1965, s 5(7) (p 2242), replacing Matrimonial Causes Act 1950, s 12 (p 2134), replacing Act of 1925, s 183 (p 2059), as amended by Matrimonial Causes Act 1937, s 9.

MATRIMONIAL CAUSES ACT 1868*

(31 & 32 Vict c 77)

An Act to amend the law relating to appeals from the Court of Divorce and Matrimonial Causes in England.   [*31 July 1868*]

* This Act was repealed by Supreme Court of Judicature (Consolidation) Act 1925, Sch 6.

1. (*Interpretation.*)
Note. Repealed by Statute Law Revision Act 1893.

2. *Matrimonial Causes Act 1857 (20 & 21 Vict c 85), s 56; Matrimonial Causes Act 1858 (21 & 22 Vict c 108), s 17; and Matrimonial Causes Act 1860 (23 & 24 Vict c 144), s 3, repealed.*
Note. Repealed by Statute Law Revision Act 1875.
    For Matrimonial Causes Act 1857, s 56, see p 2012.
    For Matrimonial Causes Act 1858, s 17, see p 2017.
    For Matrimonial Causes Act 1860, s 3, see p 2020.

3. Appeals to House of Lords to be within one month. *Either party dissatisfied with the final decision of the Court on any petition for dissolution or nullity of marriage may, within one calendar month after the pronouncing thereof, appeal therefrom to the House of Lords, and on the hearing of any such appeal the House of Lords may either dismiss the appeal or reverse the decree, or remit the case to be dealt with in all respects as the House of Lords shall direct: Provided always, that in suits for dissolution of marriage no respondent or co-respondent, not appearing and defending the suit on the occasion of the decree nisi being made, shall have any right of appeal to the House of Lords against a decree when made absolute, unless the Court, upon application made at the time of the pronouncing of the decree absolute, shall see fit to permit an appeal.*
Note. Repealed by Statute Law Revision Act 1893. See Supreme Court of Judicature Act 1881, ss 9, 10; and, now, Supreme Court Act 1981, ss 16, 18(1)(d) (pp 2830).

4. Liberty to parties to marry again. *Section fifty-seven of the said Act of twenty-first Victoria, chapter eighty-five, shall be read and construed with reference to the time for appealing as varied by this Act; and in cases where under this Act there shall be no right of appeal, the parties respectively shall be at liberty to marry again at any time after the pronouncing of the decree absolute.*
Note. Partly repealed by Statute Law Revision Act 1893 and, wholly, by Supreme Court of Judicature (Consolidation) Act, 1925, Sch 6. See now Supreme Court Act 1981, ss 16, 18(1)(d) (pp 2775, 2776), and Matrimonial Causes Act 1965, s 8(2) (p 2244), replacing Matrimonial Causes Act 1950, s 13(2) (p 2135), replacing Matrimonial Causes Act 1937, s 12 (p 2100).
    For Matrimonial Causes Act 1857, s 57, see p 2012.

5. Short title. *This Act may be cited as 'the Divorce Amendment Act 1868.'*
Note. But, by the Matrimonial Causes Act 1873, s 2 (p 2027), it could be cited as the Matrimonial Causes Act 1868.

6. (*Qualified retrospective operation.*)
Note. Partly repealed by Statute Law Revision Act 1875, and, wholly, by Statute Law Revision Act 1893.

DEBTORS ACT 1869

32 & 33 Vict c 62

An Act for the Abolition of Imprisonment for Debt, for the punishment of fraudulent debtors, and for other purposes.   [9 August 1869]

Preliminary

1.   Short title. This Act may be cited for all purposes as 'The Debtors Act 1869'.

2.   Extent. This Act shall not extend to Scotland or Ireland.

3.   Construction. … Words and expressions defined or explained in the Bankruptcy Act 1869 shall have the same meaning in this Act.

Note. Words omitted repealed by Statute Law Revision (No 2) Act 1893.

PART I

ABOLITION OF IMPRISONMENT FOR DEBT

4.   Abolition of imprisonment for debt, with exceptions. With the exceptions herein-after mentioned, no person shall … be arrested or imprisoned for making default in payment of a sum of money.

There shall be excepted from the operation of the above enactment:

1.   Default in payment of a penalty, or sum in the nature of a penalty, other than a penalty in respect of any contract:

2.   Default in payment of any sum recoverable summarily before a justice or justices of the peace:

3.   Default by a trustee or person acting in a fiduciary capacity and ordered to pay by a court of equity any sum in his possession or under his control:

4.   Default by any attorney or solicitor in payment of costs when ordered to pay costs for misconduct as such, or in payment of a sum of money when ordered to pay the same in his character of an officer of the court making the order:

5.   Default in payment for the benefit of creditors of any portion of a salary or other income in respect of the payment of which any court having jurisdiction in bankruptcy is authorised to make an order:

6.   Default in payment of sums in respect of the payment of which orders are in this Act authorised to be made:

Provided, first, that no person shall be imprisoned in any case excepted from the operation of this section for a longer period than one year; and, secondly, that nothing in this section shall alter the effect of any judgment or order of any court for payment of money except as regards the arrest and imprisonment of the person making default in paying such money.

Note. Words omitted repealed by Statute Law Revision (No 2) Act 1893.

5.   Saving of power of committal for small debts. Subject to the provisions herein-after mentioned, and to the prescribed rules, any court may commit to prison for a term not exceeding six weeks, or until payment of the sum due, any person who makes default in payment of any debt or instalment of any debt due from him in pursuance of any order or judgment of that or any other competent court.

Provided—(1) That the jurisdiction by this section given of committing a person to prison shall, in the case of any court other than the superior courts of law and equity, be exercised only subject to the following restrictions; that is to say,

  (a) Be exercised only by a judge or his deputy, and by an order made in open court and showing on its face the ground on which it is issued:

  (b) …

  (c) Be exercised only as respects a judgment of a county court by a county court judge or his deputy.

(2) That such jurisdiction shall only be exercised where it is proved to the satisfaction of the court that the person making default either has or has had since the date of the order or judgment the means to pay the sum in respect of which he has made default, and has refused or neglected, or refuses or neglects, to pay the same.

Proof of the means of the person making default may be given in such manner as the court thinks just; and for the purposes of such proof the debtor and any witnesses may be summoned and examined on oath, according to the prescribed rules.

Any jurisdiction by this section given to the superior courts may be exercised by a judge sitting in chambers, or otherwise, in the prescribed manner.

For the purposes of this section any court may direct any debt due from any person in pursuance of any order or judgment of that or any other competent court to be paid by instalments, and may from time to time rescind or vary such order:

Persons committed under this section by a superior court may be committed to the prison in which they would have been confined if arrested on a writ of capias ad satisfaciendum, and every order of committal by any superior court shall, subject to the prescribed rules, be issued, obeyed, and executed in the like manner as such writ.

This section, so far as it relates to any county court, shall be deemed to be substituted for sections ninety-eight and ninety-nine of the County Courts Act 1846 and that Act and the Acts amending the same shall be construed accordingly, and shall extend to orders made by the county court with respect to sums due in pursuance of any order or judgment of any court other than a county court.

No imprisonment under this section shall operate as a satisfaction or extinguishment of any debt or demand or cause of action, or deprive any person of any right to take out execution against the lands, goods, or chattels of the person imprisoned, in the same manner as if such imprisonment had not taken place.

Any person imprisoned under this section shall be discharged out of custody upon a certificate signed in the prescribed manner to the effect that he has satisfied a debt or instalment of a debt in respect of which he was imprisoned, together with the prescribed costs (if any).

Note. Words omitted repealed by Bankruptcy Act 1883, s 169(1), Sch 5. Modified by Administration of Justice Act 1970, s 11, Sch 4.

Words in italics repealed by the Statute Law (Repeals) Act 2004, as from 22 July 2004.

6. Arrest of defendant about to quit England. ... Where the plaintiff in any action in any of Her Majesty's superior courts of law at Westminster in which, if brought before the commencement of this Act, the defendant would have been liable to arrest, proves at any time before final judgment by evidence on oath, to the satisfaction of a judge of one of those courts, that the plaintiff has good cause of action against the defendant to the amount of fifty pounds or upwards, and that there is probable cause for believing that the defendant is about to quit England unless he be apprehended, and that the absence of the defendant from England will materially prejudice the plaintiff in the prosecution of his action, such judge may in the prescribed manner order such defendant to be arrested and imprisoned for a period not exceeding six months, unless and until he has sooner given the prescribed security, not exceeding the amount claimed in the action, that he will not go out of England without the leave of the court.

Where the action is for a penalty or sum in the nature of a penalty other than a penalty in respect of any contract, it shall not be necessary to prove that the absence of the defendant from England will materially prejudice the plaintiff in the prosecution of his action, and the security given (instead of being that the defendant will not go out of England) shall be to the effect that any sum recovered against the defendant in the action shall be paid, or that the defendant shall be rendered to prison.

Note. Words omitted repealed by Statute Law Revision (No 2) Act 1893.

* * * * *

8. Saving for sequestration against property. Sequestration against the property of a debtor may ... be issued by any court of equity in the same manner as if such debtor had been actually arrested.

Note. Words omitted repealed by Statute Law Revision (No 2) Act 1893.

* * * * *

10.   Definition of 'prescribed'. In this part of this Act the term 'prescribed' means as follows:—

As respects the superior courts of common law, prescribed by general rules to be made in pursuance of the Common Law Procedure Act 1852;

As respects the superior courts of equity prescribed by general rules and orders to be made in pursuance of the Court of Chancery Act 1852;

As respects the county courts, prescribed by general rules to be made under the County Courts Act 1856; and

…

And general rules and orders may respectively be made by such authorities as aforesaid, for the purpose of carrying into effect this part of this Act.

Note. Words omitted repealed by Courts Act 1971, s 56(4), Sch 11, Part IV. This section repealed as respects courts of summary jurisdiction by Justices of the Peace Act 1949, s 46(2), Sch 7, Part II.

* * * * *

PART II

PUNISHMENT OF FRAUDULENT DEBTORS

13.   Penalty on fraudulently obtaining credit, etc. Any person shall in each of the cases following be deemed guilty of a misdemeanour, and on conviction thereof shall be liable to be imprisoned for any time not exceeding one year, with or without hard labour; that is to say,

(1) …

(2) If he has with intent to defraud his creditors, or any of them, made or caused to be made any gift, delivery, or transfer of or any charge on his property:

(3) If he has, with intent to defraud his creditors, concealed or removed any part of his property since or within two months before the date of any unsatisfied judgment or order for payment of money obtained against him.

Note. Words omitted repealed by Theft Act 1968, ss 33(3), 35, Sch 3, Part I.

EVIDENCE FURTHER AMENDMENT ACT 1869

(32 & 33 Vict c 68)

[*9 August 1869*]

3. Parties and their husbands and wives to be witnesses in suits for adultery.
The parties to any proceeding instituted in consequence of adultery, and the husbands and wives of such parties, shall be competent to give evidence in such proceeding; Provided that no witness in any proceeding, whether a party to the suit or not, shall be liable to be asked or bound to answer any question tending to show that he or she has been guilty of adultery, unless such witness shall have already given evidence in the same proceeding in disproof of his or her alleged adultery.

Note. Repealed by Supreme Court of Judicature (Consolidation) Act 1925, Sch 6 'so far as it relates to the High Court': see ibid s 198 (p 2066) and the note thereto. Wholly repealed except as to Northern Ireland, by Statute Law (Repeals) Act 1978, and as to Northern Ireland, by SI 1984 No 1984.

MATRIMONIAL CAUSES ACT 1873*

(36 & 37 Vict c 31)

An Act to extend to suits for nullity of marriage the law with respect to the intervention of Her Majesty's Proctor and others in suits in England for dissolving marriages.   [*16 June 1873*]

* This Act was repealed by the Supreme Court of Judicature (Consolidation) Act 1925, Sch 6.

Whereas under section seven of the Act of the session of the twenty-third and twenty-fourth years of the reign of Her present Majesty, chapter one hundred and forty-four, intituled 'An Act to amend the procedure and powers of the Court for Divorce and Matrimonial Causes' [ie the Matrimonial Causes Act, 1860 (23 & 24 Vict c 144), s 7], and under section three of the Act of the session of the twenty-ninth and thirtieth years of the reign of Her present Majesty, chapter thirty-two, intituled 'An Act further to amend the procedure and powers of the Court for Divorce and Matrimonial Causes' [ie the Matrimonial Causes Act, 1866 (29 & 30 Vict c 32), s 3], a decree for divorce is required in the first instance to be a decree nisi, and not to be made absolute until after the expiration of six months, unless the Court otherwise direct, and provision is made for any person showing cause why the decree should not be made absolute by reason of the same having been obtained by collusion, or of material facts not having been brought before the Court, and power is given to any person to give information to Her Majesty's Proctor, who is thereupon authorised to take such steps as the Attorney-General may deem necessary or expedient, and such Proctor, if he suspects that any parties to the suit are acting in collusion for the purpose of obtaining a divorce contrary to the justice of the case, is authorised under the direction of the Attorney-General and by leave of the Court to intervene in the suit, and otherwise proceed as therein mentioned, and provision is made for the payment of his costs in so acting:

And whereas it is expedient to extend such provisions to a suit for nullity of marriage:

Be it therefore enacted, etc.

Note. Preamble repealed by Statute Law Revision (No 2) Act 1893.
For Matrimonial Causes Act 1860, s 7, see p 2020.
For Matrimonial Causes Act 1866, s 3, see p 2022.

1. Extension of s 7 of [Matrimonial Causes Act 1860] 23 & 24 Vict c 144, and s 3 of [Matrimonial Causes Act 1866] 29 & 30 Vict c 32, to suits for nullity of marriage. *The above-mentioned sections of the said Acts shall extend to decrees and suits for nullity of marriage in like manner as they apply to decrees and suits for divorce, and shall be construed as if they were herein enacted, with the substitution of the words 'a decree for nullity of marriage' for the words 'decree for a divorce' or 'divorce,' as the case may require.*

Note. Repealed by Supreme Court of Judicature (Consolidation) Act 1925, Sch 6. See now Matrimonial Causes Act 1973, ss 1(5), 8, 9, 15 (pp 2498, 2501, 2502, 2505), replacing Matrimonial Causes Act 1965, ss 5(7), 6, 7, 10 (pp 2242, 2243, 2245), replacing Matrimonial Causes Act 1950, ss 10, 11, 12 (p 2143), replacing Act of 1925, ss 181, 182, 183 (pp 2058, 2059), and Matrimonial Causes Act 1937, s 9 (p 2502).

2. Short title. *This Act, together with the Acts specified in the schedule to this Act, may be cited as 'the Matrimonial Causes Acts, 1857 to 1873,' and each Act may be cited as the Matrimonial Causes Act of the year in which it was passed.*

Note. Partly repealed (together with the Schedule which detailed the previous Acts) by Statute Law Revision (No 2) Act 1893, and, wholly, by Supreme Court of Judicature (Consolidation) Act 1925, Sch 6.

SUPREME COURT OF JUDICATURE ACT 1873
(36 & 37 Vict c 66)

[*5 August 1873*]

23. Rules as to exercise of jurisdiction. *The jurisdiction by this Act transferred to the said High Court of Justice and the said Court of Appeal respectively shall be exercised (so far as regards procedure and practice) in the manner provided by this Act, or by such Rules and Orders of Court as may be made pursuant to this Act; and where no special provision is contained in this Act or in any such Rules or Orders of Court with reference thereto, it shall be exercised as nearly as may be in the same manner as the same might have been exercised by the respective Courts from which such jurisdiction shall have been transferred, or by any of such Courts.*

Note. Repealed and replaced by Supreme Court of Judicature Act 1925, s 32 (repealed: see note thereto).

MATRIMONIAL CAUSES ACT 1878*

(41 & 42 Vict c 19)

An Act to amend the Matrimonial Causes Acts.   [*27 May 1878*]

   * This Act was repealed by Supreme Court of Judicature (Consolidation) Act 1925, Sch 6.

1. Short title. *This Act may be cited as the Matrimonial Causes Act 1878.*

2. Costs of intervention. *Where the Queen's Proctor or any other person shall intervene or show cause against a decree nisi in any suit or proceedings for divorce or for nullity of marriage, the Court may make such order as to the costs of the Queen's Proctor, or of any other person who shall intervene or show cause as aforesaid, or of all and every party or parties thereto, occasioned by such intervention or showing cause as aforesaid, as may seem just; and the Queen's Proctor, any other person as aforesaid, and such party or parties shall be entitled to recover such costs in like manner as in other cases: Provided that the Treasury may, if it shall think fit, order any costs which the Queen's Proctor shall, by any order of the Court made under this section, pay to the said party or parties, to be deemed to be part of the expenses of his office.*

Note. Repealed by Supreme Court of Judicature (Consolidation) Act 1925, Sch 6. See now Matrimonial Causes Act 1973, ss 8, 15 (pp 2501, 2505), replacing Matrimonial Causes Act 1965, ss 6, 10 (pp 2243, 2245), replacing Matrimonial Causes Act 1950, s 11 (p 2134), replacing Act of 1925, s 182 (p 2058).

3. Extension of power given by [Matrimonial Causes Act, 1859]. *The Court may exercise the powers vested in it by the provisions of section five of the Act of the twenty-second and twenty-third years of Victoria, chapter sixty-one, notwithstanding that there are no children of the marriage.*

Note. Ie the power to vary ante-nuptial and post-nuptial settlements after a final decree of divorce or nullity. Repealed by Supreme Court of Judicature (Consolidation) Act 1925, Sch 6. See now Matrimonial Causes Act 1973, ss 24, 25, 51(1) (pp 2515, 2520, 2559), replacing Matrimonial Proceedings and Property Act 1970, ss 4, 5, 27(1) (pp 2132, 2141), replacing Matrimonial Causes Act 1965, ss 17(1), 19, 46(2) (pp 2247, 2248, 2265), replacing Matrimonial Causes Act 1950, s 25 (p 2141), replacing Act of 1925, s 192 (p 2063.)

   For Matrimonial Causes Act 1859, s 5, see p 2018.

4. If husband convicted of aggravated assault, Court may order that wife be not bound to cohabit, &c. *If a husband shall be convicted summarily or otherwise of an aggravated assault within the meaning of the statute twenty-fourth and twenty-fifth Victoria, chapter one hundred, section forty-three, upon his wife, the Court or magistrate before whom he shall be so convicted may, if satisfied that the future safety of the wife is in peril, order that the wife shall be no longer bound to cohabit with her husband; and such order shall have the force and effect in all respects of a decree of judicial separation on the ground of cruelty; and such order may further provide.*

   (*1*) *That the husband shall pay to his wife such weekly sum as the Court or magistrate may consider to be in accordance with his means, and with any means which the wife may have for her support, and the payment of any sum of money so ordered shall be enforceable and enforced against the husband in the same manner as the payment of money is enforced under an order of affiliation; and the Court or magistrate by whom any such order for payment of money shall be made shall have power from time to time to vary the same on the application of either the husband or the wife, upon proof that the means of the husband or wife have been altered in amount since the original order or any subsequent order varying it shall have been made;*

   (*2*) *That the legal custody of any children of the marriage under the age of ten years shall, in the discretion of the Court or magistrate be given to the wife.*

   Provided always, that no order for payment of money by the husband or for the custody of children by the wife, shall be made in favour of a wife who shall be proved to have committed adultery, unless such adultery has been condoned; and that any order for payment of money or for the custody of children may be discharged by the Court or magistrate by whom such order was made upon proof that the wife has since the making thereof been guilty of adultery; and provided also, that all orders made under this section shall be subject to appeal to the Probate and Admiralty Division [sic] *of the High Court of Justice.*

Note. Repealed by Summary Jurisdiction (Married Women) Act 1895, s 12.

BANKERS' BOOKS EVIDENCE ACT 1879

(42 & 43 Vict c 11)

An Act to amend the Law of Evidence with respect to Bankers' Books. [23 May 1879]

1. Short title. This Act may be cited as the Bankers' Books Evidence Act 1879.

2. ...

Note. This section repealed by Statute Law Revision Act 1894.

3. Mode of proof of entries in bankers' books. Subject to the provisions of this Act, a copy of any entry in a banker's book shall in all legal proceedings be received as primâ facie evidence of such entry, and of the matters, transactions, and accounts therein recorded.

4. Proof that book is a banker's book. A copy of an entry in a banker's book shall not be received in evidence under this Act unless it be first proved that the book was at the time of the making of the entry one of the ordinary books of the bank, and that the entry was made in the usual and ordinary course of business, and that the book is in the custody or control of the bank.

Such proof may be given by a partner or officer of the bank, and may be given orally or by an affidavit sworn before any commissioner or person authorised to take affidavits.

[*Where the proceedings concerned are proceedings before a magistrates' court inquiring into an offence as examining justices, this section shall have effect with the omission of the words 'orally or'.*]

Note. Words in square brackets added by Criminal Procedure and Investigations Act 1996, s 47, Sch 1, para 15, as from 4 July 1996, with effect in relation to any alleged offence into which no criminal investigation has begun before 1 April 1997.

Words in italics repealed (except in relation to Northern Ireland) by the Criminal Justice Act 2003, ss 41, 332, Sch 3, Pt 2, para 30(1), (2), Sch 37, Pt 4, as from a date to be appointed.

5. Verification of copy. A copy of an entry in a banker's book shall not be received in evidence under this Act unless it be further proved that the copy has been examined with the original entry and is correct.

Such proof shall be given by some person who has examined the copy with the original entry, and may be given either orally or by an affidavit sworn before any commissioner or person authorised to take affidavits.

[*Where the proceedings concerned are proceedings before a magistrates' court inquiring into an offence as examining justices, this section shall have effect with the omission of the words 'orally or'.*]

Note. Words in square brackets added by Criminal Procedure and Investigations Act 1996, s 47, Sch 1, para 16, as from 4 July 1996, with effect in relation to any alleged offence into which no criminal investigation has begun before 1 April 1997.

Words in italics repealed (except in relation to Northern Ireland) by the Criminal Justice Act 2003, ss 41, 332, Sch 3, Pt 2, para 30(1), (2), Sch 37, Pt 4, as from a date to be appointed.

6. Case in which banker, etc, not compellable to produce book, etc. A banker or officer of a bank shall not, in any legal proceeding to which the bank is not a party, be compellable to produce any banker's book the contents of which can be proved under this Act [or under the Civil Evidence (Scotland) Act 1988] [or Schedule 8 to the Criminal Procedure (Scotland) Act 1995] [or Schedule 3 to the

Prisoners and Criminal Proceedings (Scotland) Act 1993], or to appear as a witness to prove the matters, transactions, and accounts therein recorded, unless by order of a judge made for special cause.

Note. Words in first pair of square brackets inserted by Civil Evidence (Scotland) Act 1988, s 73, as from 3 April 1989. Words in second pair of square brackets inserted by Criminal Procedure (Consequential Provisions) (Scotland) Act 1995, s 5, Sch 4, para 2, as from 1 April 1996. Words in third pair of square brackets inserted by Prisoners and Criminal Proceedings (Scotland) Act 1993, s 29, Sch 3, para 7(3), as from 1 October 1993.

7. Court or judge may order inspection, etc. On the application of any party to a legal proceeding a court or judge may order that such party be at liberty to inspect and take copies of any entries in a banker's book for any of the purposes of such proceedings. An order under this section may be made either with or without summoning the bank or any other party, and shall be served on the bank three clear days before the same is to be obeyed, unless the court or judge otherwise directs.

8. Costs. The costs of any application to a court or judge or for the purposes of this Act, and the costs of anything done or to be done under an order of a court or judge made under or for the purposes of this Act shall be in the discretion of the court or judge, who may order the same or any part thereof to be paid to any party by the bank where the same have been occasioned by any default or delay on the part of the bank. Any such order against a bank may be enforced as if the bank was a party to the proceeding.

[9. Interpretation of 'bank', 'banker', and 'bankers' book'—(1) In this Act the expressions 'bank' and 'banker' mean—

[(a) *a recognised bank, licensed institution or municipal bank, within the meaning of the Banking Act 1979;*

[*(a) an institution authorised under the Banking Act 1987 or a municipal bank within the meaning of that Act;*]

[*(aa) a building society (within the meaning of the Building Societies Act 1986)*; [*and*]]

[(a) a deposit taker;]

[(b) *a trustee savings bank within the meaning of* [*the Trustee Savings Banks Act 1981*];

[(c) the National Savings Bank; and

[(d) the Post Office, in the exercise of its powers to provide banking services.

[(1A) 'Deposit taker' means—

(a) a person who has permission under Part 4 of the Financial Services and Markets Act 2000 to accept deposits; or

(b) an EEA firm of the kind mentioned in paragraph 5(b) of Schedule 3 to that Act which has permission under paragraph 15 of that Schedule (as a result of qualifying for authorisation under paragraph 12(1) of that Schedule) to accept deposits or other repayable funds from the public.

(1B) But a person is not a deposit-taker if he has permission to accept deposits only for the purpose of carrying on another regulated activity in accordance with that permission.

(1C) Subsections (1A) and (1B) must be read with—

(a) section 22 of the Financial Services and Markets Act 2000;

(b) any relevant order under that section; and

(c) Schedule 2 to that Act.]

(2) Expressions in this Act relating to 'bankers' books' include ledgers, day books, cash books, account books and other records used in the ordinary business of the bank, whether those records are in written form or are kept on microfilm, magnetic tape or any form of mechanical or electronic data retrieval mechanism.]

Note. This section substituted by Banking Act 1979, s 51(1), Sch 6, Part I, para 1, as from 19 February 1982, and sub-s (1)(b) further amended by Trustee Savings Bank Act 1981, s 55(1),

Sch 6. Sub-s (1)(b) repealed by Trustee Savings Banks Act 1985, ss 4(3), 7(4), Sch 4. Sub-s (1)(a) substituted by Banking Act 1987, s 108(1), Sch 6, para 1. Sub-s 1(aa) inserted by Building Societies Act 1986, s 120(1), Sch 18, Part I, para 1, as from 1 January 1987.

In sub-s (1)(aa) word 'and' inserted by the Postal Services Act 2000 (Consequential Modifications No 1) Order 2001, SI 2001/1149, Sch 1, para 3, as from 26 March 2001.

Sub-s (1)(a) substituted for sub-ss (1)(a), (aa) by the Financial Services and Markets Act 2000 (Consequential Amendments and Repeals) Order 2001, SI 2001/3649, art 265(1), (2), as from 1 December 2001.

Sub-ss (1A)–(1C) inserted by the Financial Services and Markets Act 2000 (Consequential Amendments and Repeals) Order 2001, SI 2001/3649, art 265(1), (3), as from 1 December 2001.

10. Interpretation of 'legal proceeding', 'court', 'judge'. In this Act—

The expression 'legal proceeding' means any civil or criminal proceeding or inquiry in which evidence is or may be given, and includes *an arbitration [and an application to, or an inquiry or other proceeding before the Solicitors Disciplinary Tribunal or any body exercising functions in relation to solicitors in Scotland or Northern Ireland corresponding to the functions of that Tribunal];*

[(a) an arbitration;

(b) an application to, or an inquiry or other proceeding before, the Solicitors Disciplinary Tribunal or any body exercising functions in relation to solicitors in Scotland or Northern Ireland corresponding to the functions of that Tribunal; and

(c) *an investigation of a complaint by the adjudicator of a recognised scheme for the purposes of section 83 of the Building Societies Act 1986.*]

[(c) an investigation, consideration or determination of a complaint by a member of the panel of ombudsmen for the purposes of the ombudsmen scheme within the meaning of the Financial Services and Markets Act 2000.]

The expression 'the court' means the court, judge, arbitrator, persons or person before whom a legal proceeding is held or taken;

The expression 'a judge' means with respect to England a judge of the High Court … , and with respect to Scotland a lord ordinary of the Outer House of the Court of Session, and with respect to Ireland a judge of the High Court … in Ireland;

The judge of a county court may with respect to any action in such court exercise the powers of a judge under this Act.

Note. The words omitted repealed by Statute Law Revision Act 1898. First words in square brackets inserted by Solicitors Act 1974, s 86. Words in italics repealed and subsequent words in square brackets substituted by the Building Societies Act 1997, s 45(1), as from 9 June 1997.

Para (c) substituted by the Financial Services and Markets Act 2000 (Consequential Amendments and Repeals) Order 2001, SI 2001/3649, art 266, as from 1 December 2001.

11. Computation of time. Sunday, Christmas Day, Good Friday, and any bank holiday shall be excluded from the computation of time under this Act.

MARRIED WOMEN'S PROPERTY ACT 1882

(45 & 46 Vict c 75)

12. Remedies of married woman for protection and security of separate property. *Every woman, whether married before or after this Act, shall have in her own name against all persons whomsoever, including her husband, the same civil remedies, and also (subject, as regards her husband, to the proviso hereinafter contained) the same remedies and redress by way of criminal proceedings, for the protection and security of her own separate property, as if such property belonged to her as [she were] a feme sole, but, except as aforesaid, no husband or wife shall be entitled to sue the other for a tort. In any indictment or other proceeding under this section it shall be sufficient to allege such property to be her property; and* *in any proceeding under this section a husband or wife shall be competent to give evidence against each other, any statute or rule of law to the contrary notwithstanding: Provided always, that no criminal proceeding shall be taken by any wife against her husband by virtue of this Act while they are living together, as to or concerning any property claimed by her, nor while they are living apart, as to or concerning any act done by the husband while they were living together, concerning property claimed by the wife, unless such property shall have been wrongfully taken by the husband when leaving or deserting, or about to leave or desert, his wife.*

Note. Words in square brackets substituted by Law Reform (Married Women and Tortfeasors) Act 1935, s 5(1), First Schedule, for the original words 'such property belonged to her as'.

The whole section repealed, except so far as related to criminal proceedings, by Law Reform (Husband and Wife) Act 1962, s 3(2), Schedule, and repealed for all purposes by Theft Act 1968, s 33(3), Sch 3, Part III.

17. Questions between husband and wife as to property to be decided in a summary way. In any question between husband and wife as to the title to or possession of property, either party, *or any such bank, corporation, company, public body, or society as aforesaid in whose books any stocks, funds, or share of either party are standing*, may apply by summons or otherwise in a summary way [to the High Court or such county court as may be prescribed and the court may, on such an application (which may be heard in private), make such order with respect to the property as it thinks fit.

In this section 'prescribed' means prescribed by rules of court and rules made for the purposes of this section may confer jurisdiction on county courts whatever the situation or value of the property in dispute.] *to any judge of the High Court of Justice in England or in Ireland, according as such property is in England or Ireland, or (at the option of the applicant irrespectively of the value of the property in dispute) in England to the judge of the county court of the district, or in Ireland to the chairman of the civil bill court of the division in which either party resides, and the judge of the High Court of Justice or of the county court, or the chairman of the civil bill court (as the case may be) may make such order with respect to the property in dispute, and as to the costs of and consequent on the application as he thinks fit, or may direct such application to stand over from time to time, and any inquiry touching the matters in question to be made in such manner as he shall think fit: Provided always, that any order of a judge of the High Court of Justice to be made under the provisions of this section shall be subject to appeal in the same way as an order made by the same judge in a suit pending or on an equitable plaint in the said court would be; and any order of a county or civil bill court under the provisions of this section shall be subject to appeal in the same way as any other order made by the same court would be, and all proceedings in a county court or civil bill court under this section in which, by reason of the value of the property in dispute, such court would not have had jurisdiction if this Act or the Married Women's Property Act 1870, had not passed, may, at the option of the defendant or respondent to such proceedings, be removed as of right into the High Court of Justice in England or Ireland (as the case may be) by writ of certiorari or otherwise as may be prescribed by any rule of such High Court; but any order made or act done in the course of such proceedings prior to such removal shall be valid, unless order shall be made to the contrary by such High Court: Provided also, that the judge of the High Court of Justice or of the county court, or the chairman of the civil bill court, if either party so require, may hear any such application in his private room: Provided also, that any such bank, corporation, company, public body, or society as aforesaid, shall, in the matter of any such application for the purposes of costs or otherwise, be treated as a stakeholder only.*

Note. Words in italics 'or any such bank ... are standing' and 'Provided also ... as a stakeholder only' repealed as to England and Wales by Statute Law (Repeals) Act 1969, s 1, Schedule.

Words in italics 'to any judge of the High Court ... in his private room' substituted by words in square brackets by Matrimonial and Family Proceedings Act 1984, s 43.

For the extension of the court's powers under this section, see Matrimonial Causes (Property and Maintenance) Act 1958, s 7 (p 2202) and Matrimonial Proceedings and Property Act 1970, s 39 (p 2383). See also Law Reform (Husband and Wife) Act 1962 (p 2231) and Married Women's Property Act 1964 (p 2237).

For the application of this section to engaged couples where the agreement to marry is terminated, see Law Reform (Miscellaneous Provisions) Act 1970, s 2(2) (p 2232).

MATRIMONIAL CAUSES ACT 1884*

(47 & 48 Vict c 68)

An Act to amend the Matrimonial Causes Acts. [*14 August 1884*]

   * This Act was repealed by Supreme Court of Judicature (Consolidation) Act 1925.

1. Short title. *This Act may be cited as the Matrimonial Causes Act 1884.*

Note. But it was not referred to in the Matrimonial Causes Act 1907, s 4 (p 2036), as a Matrimonial Causes Act.

2. Periodical payments in lieu of attachment. *From and after the passing of this Act a decree for restitution of conjugal rights shall not be enforced by attachment, but where the application is by the wife the Court may, at the time of making such decree, or at any time afterwards, order that in the event of such decree not being complied with within any time in that behalf limited by the Court, the respondent shall make to the petitioner such periodical payments as may be just, and such order may be enforced in the same manner as an order for alimony in a suit for judicial separation. The Court may, if it shall think fit, order that the husband shall, to the satisfaction of the Court, secure to the wife such periodical payment, and for that purpose may refer it to any one of the Conveyancing Counsel of the Court to settle and approve of a proper deed or instrument to be executed by all necessary parties.*

Note. See Matrimonial Proceedings and Property Act 1970, ss 20, 42(2), Sch 3 (repealed) (pp 2376, 2383, 2388), repealing but not replacing Matrimonial Causes Act 1965, s 21(1), (2), (p 2249), replacing Matrimonial Causes Act 1950, s 22(3), (4) (p 2139, 2140), replacing Supreme Court of Judicature (Consolidation) Act 1925, s 187 (p 2061).

3. Settlement of wife's property. *Where the application for restitution of conjugal rights is by the husband, if it shall be made to appear to the Court that the wife is entitled to any property, either in possession or reversion, or is in receipt of any profits of trade or earnings, the Court may, if it shall think fit, order a settlement to be made to the satisfaction of the Court of such property, or any part thereof, for the benefit of the petitioner and of the children of the marriage, or either or any of them, or may order such part as the Court may think reasonable of such profits of trade or earnings to be periodically paid by the respondent to the petitioner for his own benefit, or to the petitioner or any other person for the benefit of the children of the marriage, or either or any of them.*

Note. See Matrimonial Proceedings and Property Act 1970, ss 20 (abolition of right to claim restitution of conjugal rights), 42(2), Sch 3 (repealed) (pp 2376, 2383, 2388), repealing but not replacing Matrimonial Causes Act 1965, s 21(3) (p 2249), replacing Matrimonial Causes Act 1950, s 24 (p 2140), replacing Supreme Court of Judicature (Consolidation) Act 1925, s 191(2) (p 2063).

4. Power to vary orders. *The Court may from time to time vary or modify any order for the periodical payment of money, either by altering the times of payment or by increasing or diminishing the amount, or may temporarily suspend the same as to the whole or any part of the money so ordered to be paid and again revive the same order wholly or in part, as the Court may think just.*

Note. See now Matrimonial Causes Act 1973, s 31 (p 2536), replacing Matrimonial Proceedings and Property Act 1970, s 9 (p 2370), replacing Matrimonial Causes Act 1965, s 31 (p 2257), replacing Matrimonial Causes Act 1950, s 28 (p 2142).

5. Non-compliance with decree deemed to be desertion. *If the respondent shall fail to comply with a decree of the Court for restitution of conjugal rights such respondent shall thereupon be deemed to have been guilty of desertion without reasonable cause, and a suit for judicial separation may be forthwith instituted, and a sentence of judicial separation may be pronounced although the period of two years may have elapsed since the failure to comply with the decree for restitution of conjugal rights: and when any husband who has been guilty of desertion by failure on his part to comply with a decree for restitution of conjugal rights has also been guilty of adultery, the wife may forthwith present a petition for dissolution of her marriage, and the Court may pronounce a decree nisi for the dissolution of the marriage on the grounds of adultery* *coupled with desertion. Such decree nisi shall not be made absolute until after the expiration of six calendar months from the pronouncing thereof, unless the Court shall fix a shorter time.*

Note. See now Matrimonial Causes Act 1973, ss 1, 17 (pp 2471, 2479), replacing Divorce Reform Act 1969, ss 1, 2, 8 (pp 2338, 2341), replacing Matrimonial Causes Act 1965, ss 1(1), 12(1) (pp 2239, 2245), replacing Matrimonial Causes Act 1950, ss 1(1), 14(1) (pp 2130, 2135), replacing Supreme Court of Judicature (Consolidation) Act 1925, ss 176, 185(1) (pp 2095, 2097), as amended by Matrimonial Causes Act 1937, ss 2, 5. The right to claim restitution of conjugal rights was repealed by Matrimonial Proceedings and Property Act 1970, s 20 (p 2376).

6. Custody, &c. of children. *The Court may, at any time before final decree on any application for restitution of conjugal rights, or after final decree if the respondent shall fail to comply therewith, upon application for that purpose, make from time to time all such orders and provisions with respect to the custody, maintenance, and education of the children of the petitioner and respondent as might have been made by interim orders during the pendency of a trial for judicial separation between the same parties.*

Note. See now Matrimonial Causes Act 1973, ss 23, 42, 52(1) (pp 2513, 2551, 2559), replacing Matrimonial Proceedings and Property Act 1970, ss 3, 18, 19, 27(1) (pp 2365, 2375, 2376, 2378), replacing Matrimonial Causes Act 1965, ss 34(1), (4), 46(2) (pp 2258, 2259, 2265), replacing Matrimonial Causes Act 1950, s 26 (p 2141), replacing Supreme Court of Judicature (Consolidation) Act 1925, s 193 (p 2064), as extended by Matrimonial Causes Act 1937, s 10(4) (p 2099), and s 10(1) of that Act (p 2098).

7. (*Act to apply to England only.*)

MARRIED WOMEN'S PROPERTY ACT 1893

(56 & 57 Vict c 63)

An Act to amend the Married Women's Property Act 1882.   [5 December 1893]

1. Effect of contracts by married women. *Every contract hereafter entered into by a married woman, otherwise than as agent,*
   (*a*) *shall be deemed to be a contract entered into by her with respect to and to bind her separate property whether she is or is not in fact possessed of or entitled to any separate property at the time when she enters into such contract;*
   (*b*) *shall bind all separate property which she may at that time or thereafter be possessed of or entitled to; and*
   (*c*) *shall also be enforceable by process of law against all property which she may thereafter while discovert be possessed of or entitled to;*
   Provided that nothing in this section contained shall render available to satisfy any liability or obligation arising out of such contract any separate property which at that time or thereafter she is restrained from anticipating.

2. Costs may be ordered to be paid out of property subject to restraint on anticipation. *In any action or proceeding now or hereafter instituted by a woman or by a next friend on her behalf, the court before which such action or proceeding is pending shall have jurisdiction by judgment or order from time to time to order payment of the costs of the opposite party out of property which is subject to a restraint on anticipation, and may enforce such payment by the appointment of a receiver and the sale of the property or otherwise as may be just.*

3. Will of married woman. Section twenty-four of the Wills Act 1837, shall apply to the will of a married woman made during coverture whether she is or is not possessed of or entitled to any separate property at the time of making it, and such will shall not require to be re-executed or republished after the death of her husband.

4. Repeal. *Subsections (3) and (4) of section one of the Married Women's Property Act 1882 are hereby repealed.*

5. Short title. This Act may be cited as the Married Women's Property Act 1893.

6. Extent. This Act shall not apply to Scotland.

Note. Section 1 repealed by Law Reform (Married Women and Tortfeasors) Act 1935, ss 5(2), 8(2), Sch 2. Section 2 repealed by Married Women (Restraint Upon Anticipation) Act 1949, ss 1(4), 2(2), Sch 2. Section 4 repealed by Statute Law Revision Act 1908.

MATRIMONIAL CAUSES ACT 1907*

(7 Edw 7 c 12)

An Act to amend the Matrimonial Causes Act 1857 and 1866, by extending the powers of the Court in relation to Maintenance and Alimony, and leave to intervene.   [*9 August 1907*]

* This Act was repealed by Supreme Court of Judicature (Consolidation) Act 1925, Sch 6.

1. Power to grant maintenance and alimony [sic]—(*1*) *The Court may, if it thinks fit, on any decree for dissolution or nullity of marriage, order that the husband shall, to the satisfaction of the Court, secure to the wife such gross sum of money or such annual sum of money for any term not exceeding her life as, having regard to her fortune (if any), to the ability of the husband, and to the conduct of the parties, it may deem reasonable, and for that purpose may refer the matter to any one of the conveyancing counsel of the Court to settle and approve of a proper deed or instrument to be executed by all necessary parties, and the Court may, if it thinks fit, suspend the pronouncing of its decree until such deed shall have been duly executed.*

(*2*) *In any such case the Court may, if it thinks fit, make an order on the husband for payment to the wife during their joint lives of such monthly or weekly sum for her maintenance and support as the Court may think reasonable, and any such order may be made either in addition to or instead of an order under the last preceding subsection;*
Provided that—
(*a*) *If the husband afterwards from any cause becomes unable to make such payments it shall be lawful for the Court to discharge or modify the order or temporarily to suspend the same as to the whole or any part of the money so ordered to be paid and again to revive the order wholly or in part as the Court may think fit; and*
(*b*) *Where the Court has made any such order as is mentioned in this subsection and the Court is satisfied that the means of the husband have increased, the Court may, if it thinks fit, increase the amount payable under the order.*

(*3*) *Upon any petition for dissolution or nullity of marriage the Court shall have the same power to make interim orders for payment of money, by way of alimony or otherwise to the wife, as it has in a suit instituted for judicial separation.*

Note. See now Matrimonial Causes Act 1973, ss 22, 23, 31 (pp 2510, 2513, 2536), replacing Matrimonial Proceedings and Property Act 1970, ss 1, 2, 9 (pp 2365, 2370), replacing Matrimonial Causes Act 1965, ss 15, 16, 19, 31 (pp 2246, 2247, 2248, 2257), replacing Matrimonial Causes Act 1950, ss 19, 28 (pp 2138, 2142), replacing Supreme Court of Judicature (Consolidation) Act 1925, s 190 (p 2062), and Matrimonial Causes Act 1937, s 10 (p 2099).

2. Repeal of section 32 of 20 & 21 Vict c 85, and section 1 of 29 & 30 Vict c 32. *Section thirty-two of the Matrimonial Causes Act 1857, and section one of the Matrimonial Causes Act 1866, are hereby repealed.*

Note. For Matrimonial Causes Act 1857, s 32, see p 2007.
For Matrimonial Causes Act 1866, s 1, see p 2022.

3. Power to allow intervention on terms. *In every case, not already provided for by law, in which any person is charged with adultery with any party to a suit, or in which the Court may consider, in the interest of any person not already a party to the suit, that such person should be made a party to the suit, the Court may, if it thinks fit, allow that person to intervene upon such terms (if any) as the Court may think just.*

Note. See now Matrimonial Causes Act 1973, s 49(5) (p 2557), replacing Matrimonial Causes Act 1965, s 44 (p 2265), replacing Matrimonial Causes Act 1950, s 31 (p 2143), replacing Supreme Court of Judicature (Consolidation) Act 1925, s 197 (p 2066).

4. Short title. *This Act may be cited as the Matrimonial Causes Act 1907, and may be cited with the Matrimonial Causes Acts 1857 to 1878.*

MAINTENANCE ORDERS (FACILITIES FOR ENFORCEMENT) ACT 1920*

(10 & 11 Geo 5 c 33)

An Act to facilitate the enforcement in England and Ireland† of Maintenance Orders made in other parts of His Majesty's Dominions and Protectorates‡ and vice versa.

[*16 August 1920*]

  * This Act has been repealed by Maintenance Orders (Reciprocal Enforcement) Act 1972, s 22(2)(a), as from a day to be appointed (see note to s 49 of Act of 1972, p 2487). For provisions relating to maintenance orders registered in the High Court under Act of 1920 on the coming into force of s 1 of the Act of 1972, see s 23 of the Act of 1972 (p 2449).

1. Enforcement in England and Ireland† of maintenance orders made in His Majesty's dominions outside the United Kingdom—*(1) Where a maintenance order has, whether before or after the passing of this Act, been made against any person by any Court in any part of His Majesty's dominions outside the United Kingdom to which this Act extends, and a certified copy of the order has been transmitted by the governor of that part of His Majesty's dominions to the Secretary of State [Lord Chancellor], the Secretary of State [Lord Chancellor] shall send a copy of the order to the prescribed officer of a Court in England or Ireland† for registration; and on receipt thereof the order shall be registered in the prescribed manner, and shall, from the date of such registration, be of the same force and effect, and, subject to the provisions of this Act, all proceedings may be taken on such order as if it had been an order originally obtained in the Court in which it is so registered, and that Court shall have power to enforce the order accordingly.*

Note. Words 'Lord Chancellor' in square brackets substituted for words 'Secretary of State' by Transfer of Functions (Magistrates' Court and Family Law) Order 1992, SI 1992 No 709, art 4, as from 1 April 1992.

  (2) The Court in which an order is to be so registered as aforesaid shall, if the Court by which the order was made was a Court of superior jurisdiction, be the Probate, Divorce and Admiralty Division [Family Division] of the High Court, or in Ireland† the King's Bench Division (Matrimonial) of the High Court of Justice in Ireland, and, if the Court was not a Court of superior jurisdiction, be a Court of summary jurisdiction.

Note. Words in square brackets substituted for words 'Probate, Divorce and Admiralty Division' by Administration of Justice Act 1970, s 1(6)(a), Sch 2, para 2.

  Appeals are governed by RSC Ord 56, r 5(2).

  † The Act does *not* extend to the Republic of Ireland, and Orders made since the constitution of that State contain an express saving of the Irish Free State, when that was the appropriate designation for the Republic.

  ‡ The Maintenance Orders (Facilities for Enforcement) Order 1959 (SI 1959 No 377), as partially revoked by SI 1974 No 557, SI 1975 No 2188, SI 1979 No 116, SI 1983 No 1124 [and SI 2002 No 789] and amended by the Pakistan Act 1973, s 4(4), which now provides that this Act applies to the following countries and territories:

Antigua and Barbuda	Jamaica	St Vincent and the Grenadines
The Bahamas	Jersey	Seychelles
Belize	Kiribati	Sierra Leone
Botswana	Lesotho	Solomon Islands
Brunei	Malawi	Sri Lanka
Cayman Islands	Malaysia	Swaziland
Christmas Island	Mauritius	Trinidad and Tobago
Cocos (Keeling) Islands	Montserrat	Tuvalu

Cyprus	*Newfoundland*	Uganda
Dominica	Nigeria	Virgin Islands
The Gambia	Prince Edward Island	Yukon Territory
Grenada	St Kitts and Nevis	Zambia
Guernsey	St Lucia	Zanzibar*
Guyana		

* Ie that part of the United Republic of Tanzania to which the 1972 Act does not apply

2. Transmission of maintenance orders made in England or Ireland. *Where a Court in England or Ireland* has, whether before or after the commencement of this Act, made a maintenance order against any person, and it is proved to that Court that the person against whom the order was made is resident in some part of His Majesty's dominions outside the United Kingdom to which this Act extends,† the Court shall send to the Secretary of State [Lord Chancellor] for transmission to the governor of that part of His Majesty's dominions a certified copy of the order.*

Note. Words 'Lord Chancellor' in square brackets substituted for words 'Secretary of State' by virtue of Transfer of Functions (Magistrates' Courts and Family Law) Order 1992, SI 1992 No 709, art 4, as from 1 April 1992.

3. Power to make provisional orders of maintenance against persons resident in His Majesty's dominions outside the United Kingdom—(*1*) *Where an application is made to a court of summary jurisdiction in England or Ireland* for a maintenance order against any person, and it is proved that that person is resident in a part of His Majesty's dominions outside the United Kingdom to which this Act extends,† the Court may, in the absence of that person, if after hearing the evidence it is satisfied of the justice of the application, make any such order as it might have made if a summons had been duly served on that person and he [that person had been resident in England and Wales, had received reasonable notice of the date of the hearing of the application and] had failed to appear at the hearing, but in such case the order shall be provisional only, and shall have no effect unless and until confirmed by a competent Court in such part of His Majesty's dominions as aforesaid.*

(*2*) *The evidence of any witness who is examined on any such application shall be put into writing, and such deposition shall be read over to and signed by him.*

Note. Words in square brackets substituted for words 'a summons had been duly served on that person and he' by Maintenance Orders (Reciprocal Enforcement Act 1992, s 1(1), Sch 1, Part I, para 1(2), as from 5 April 1993.

(*3*) *Where such an order is made, the Court shall send to the Secretary of State [Lord Chancellor] for transmission to the governor of the part of His Majesty's dominions in which the persons against whom the order is made is alleged to reside the depositions so taken and a certified copy of the order, together with a statement of the grounds on which the making of the order might have been opposed if the person against whom the order is made had been duly served with a summons [resident in England and Wales, had received reasonable notice of the date of the hearing] and had appeared at the hearing, and such information as the Court possesses for facilitating the identification of that person, and ascertaining his whereabouts.*

Note. Words 'Lord Chancellor' in square brackets substituted for words 'Secretary of State' by virtue of Transfer of Functions (Magistrates' Courts and Family Law) Order 1992, SI 1992 No 709, art 4, as from 1 April 1992. Words in second pair of square brackets substituted for words 'duly served with a summons' by Maintenance Orders (Reciprocal Enforcement) Act 1992, s 1(1), Sch 1, Part I, para 1(3), as from 5 April 1993.

* See note † above.
† See note ‡ above.

(*4*) *Where any such provisional order has come before a Court in a part of His Majesty's dominions outside the United Kingdom to which this Act extends for confirmation, and the order has by that Court been remitted to the court of summary jurisdiction which made the order for the purpose of taking further evidence that Court or any other court of summary jurisdiction sitting and acting for the same place [appointed for the same commission area (within the meaning of section 1 of the Administration of Justice Act 1973 [the Justices of the Peace Act 1979 [the Justices of the Peace Act 1997]])] shall, after giving the prescribed notice, proceed to take evidence in like manner and subject to the like conditions as the evidence in support of the original application.*

　If upon the hearing of such evidence it appears to the Court that the order ought not to have been made, the Court may rescind [revoke] the order, but in any other case the depositions shall be sent to the Secretary of State [Lord Chancellor] and dealt with in like manner as the original depositions.

Note. Words in first pair of square brackets substituted for 'sitting and acting for the same place' by Domestic Proceedings and Magistrates' Courts Act 1978, s 89, Sch 2, para 2, as from 1 February 1981, and reference to Justices of the Peace Act 1979 substituted for reference to Act of 1973 by Act of 1979, s 71, Sch 2, para 1, as from the same date. Word 'revoke' substituted for word 'rescind' by Maintenance Orders (Reciprocal Enforcement) Act 1992, s 1, Sch 1, Part I, para 1, as from 5 April 1993. Words 'Lord Chancellor' in square brackets substituted for words 'Secretary of State' by virtue of Transfer of Functions (Magistrates' Courts and Family Law) Order 1992, SI 1992 No 709, art 4, as from 1 April 1992.

　Reference to Justices of the Peace Act 1997 substituted for reference to Act of 1979 by Act of 1997, s 73(2), Sch 5, para 2, as from 19 June 1997.

　Words from '(within to 1997)' repealed by the Access to Justices Act 1999, Sch 15, Pt V(1), as from 27 September 1999.

　Words 'appointed for the same commission area' repealed by the Courts Act 2003, s 109(1), (3), Sch 8, para 68, Sch 10, as from a date to be appointed.

　(5)　The confirmation of an order made under this section shall not affect any power of a court of summary jurisdiction to vary or rescind [revoke] that order: Provided that on the making of a varying or rescinding [revoking] order the Court shall send a certified copy thereof to the Secretary of State [Lord Chancellor] for transmission to the governor of the part of His Majesty's dominions in which the original order was confirmed, and that in the case of an order varying the original order the order shall not have any effect unless and until confirmed in like manner as the original order.

Note. Words 'revoke' and 'revoking' in square brackets substituted for words 'rescind' and 'rescinding' respectively by Maintenance Orders (Reciprocal Enforcement) Act 1992, s 1(1), Sch 1, Part I, para 1(5), as from 5 April 1993. Words 'Lord Chancellor' in square brackets substituted for words 'Secretary of State' by virtue of Transfer of Functions (Magistrates' Courts and Family Law) Order 1992, SI 1992 No 709, art 4, as from 1 April 1992.

　(6)　The applicant shall have the same right of appeal, if any, against a refusal to make a provisional order as he would have had against a refusal to make the order had a summons been duly served on the person against whom the order is sought to be made [the person against whom the order is sought to be made been resident in England and Wales and received reasonable notice of the date of the hearing of the application].

Note. Words in square brackets substituted for words 'a summons' to the end by Maintenance Orders (Reciprocal Enforcement) Act 1992, s 1(1), Sch 1, Part I, para 1(6), as from 5 April 1993.

　[(7)　Where subsection (1) of section 60 of the Magistrates' Courts Act 1980 (revocation, variation etc of orders for periodical payment) applies in relation to an order made under this section which has been confirmed, that subsection shall have effect as if for the words 'by order on complaint,' there were substituted 'on an application being made, by order'.

　(8)　In this section 'revoke' includes discharge.]

Note. Sub-ss (7), (8) added by Maintenance Orders (Reciprocal Enforcement) Act 1992, s 1, Sch 1, Part I, para 1, as from 5 April 1993.

4. Power of court of summary jurisdiction to confirm maintenance order made out of the United Kingdom—*(1)　Where a maintenance order has been made by a Court in a part of His Majesty's dominions outside the United Kingdom to which this Act extends,* * *and the order is provisional only and has no effect unless and until confirmed by a*

---

　* See note on p 2036, for places to which the Act extends.

court of summary jurisdiction in England or Ireland, and a certified copy of the order, together with the depositions of witnesses and a statement of the grounds on which the order might have been opposed has been transmitted to the Secretary of State [Lord Chancellor], and it appears to the Secretary of State [Lord Chancellor] that the person against whom the order was made is resident in England or Ireland, the Secretary of State [Lord Chancellor] may send the said documents to the prescribed officer of a court of summary jurisdiction, with a requisition that a summons be issued calling upon the person [notice be served on the person informing him that he may attend a hearing at the time and place specified in the notice] to show cause why that order should not be confirmed, and upon receipt of such documents and requisition the Court shall issue such a summons and cause it to be served upon such person.

Note. Words 'Lord Chancellor' in square brackets substituted for words 'Secretary of State' by virtue of Transfer of Functions (Magistrates' Courts and Family Law) Order 1992, SI 1992 No 709, art 4, as from 1 April 1992. Other words in square brackets substituted for words 'summons be issued calling upon the person' and 'issue such a summons and cause it' respectively, by Maintenance Orders (Reciprocal Enforcement) Act 1992, s 1(1), Sch 1, Part I, para 2(2), as from 5 April 1993.

(2) A summons so issued may be served in England or Ireland in the same manner as if it had been originally issued or subsequently endorsed by a court of summary jurisdiction having jurisdiction in the place where the person happens to be.

[(2) A notice required to be served under this section may be served by post.]

Note. Sub-s (2) in square brackets substituted by Maintenance Orders (Reciprocal Enforcement) Act 1992, s 1(1), Sch 1, Part I, para 2(3), as from 5 April 1993.

(3) At the hearing it shall be open to the person on whom the summons [notice] was served to raise any defence which he might have raised in the original proceedings had he been a party thereto, but no other defence [oppose the confirmation of the order on any grounds on which he might have opposed the making of the order in the original proceedings had he been a party to them, but on no other grounds], and the certificate from the Court which made the provisional order stating the grounds on which the making of the order might have been opposed if the person against whom the order was made had been a party to the proceedings shall be conclusive evidence that those grounds are grounds on which objection may be taken.

Note. Words in square brackets substituted for words 'notice' and words from 'raise any defence' to 'no other defence' respectively, by Maintenance Orders (Reciprocal Enforcement) Act 1992, s 1(1), Sch 1, Part I, para 2(4), as from 5 April 1993.

(4) If at the hearing the person served with the summons [notice] does not appear or, on appearing, fails to satisfy the Court that the order ought not to be confirmed, the Court may confirm the order either without modification or with such modifications as to the Court after hearing the evidence may seem just.

Note. Word in square brackets substituted for word 'summons' by Maintenance Orders (Reciprocal Enforcement) Act 1992, s 1(1), Sch 1, Part I, para 2(5), as from 5 April 1993.

(5) If the person against whom the summons was issued [served with the notice] appears at the hearing and satisfies the Court that for the purpose of any defence [establishing any grounds on which he opposes the confirmation of the order] it is necessary to remit the case to the Court which made the provisional order for the taking of any further evidence, the Court may so remit the case and adjourn the proceedings for the purpose.

Note. Words in square brackets substituted for words 'against whom the summons was issued' and 'any defence' respectively, by Maintenance Orders (Reciprocal Enforcement) Act 1992, s 1(1), Sch 1, Part I, para 2(6), as from 5 April 1993.

[(5A) Where a magistrates' court confirms a provisional order under this section, it shall at the same time exercise one of its powers under subsection (5B).

(5B) The powers of the court are—

(a) the power to order that payments under the order be made directly to the clerk of the court or the clerk of any other magistrates' court [a justices' chief executive] [the designated officer for the court or for any other magistrates' court];

(b)   the power to order that payments under the order be made to the clerk of the court, or to the clerk of any other magistrates' court [a justices' chief executive] [the designated officer for the court of for any other magistrates' court], by such method of payment falling within section 59(6) of the Magistrates' Courts Act 1980 (standing order, etc) as may be specified;

(c)   the power to make an attachment of earnings order under the Attachment of Earnings Act 1971 to secure payments under the order.

(5C)   In deciding which of the powers under subsection (5B) it is to exercise, the court shall have regard to any representations made by the person liable to make payments under the order.

(5D)   Subsection (4) of section 59 of the Magistrates' Courts Act 1980 (power of court to require debtor to open account) shall apply for the purposes of subsection (5B) as it applies for the purposes of that section but as if for paragraph (a) there were substituted—

'(a)   the court proposes to exercise its power under paragraph (b) of section 4(5B) of the Maintenance Orders (Facilities for Enforcement) Act 1920, and'.]

Note. Sub-ss (5A)–(5D) in square brackets inserted by Maintenance Enforcement Act 1991, s 10, Sch 1, para 1(1), as from 1 April 1992.

In sub-s (5B), words in square brackets substituted for words 'the clerk of the court or the clerk of any other magistrates' court' and 'the clerk of the court, or to the clerk of any other magistrates' court' by the Access to Justice Act 1999, ss 90, 106, Sch 13, para 7, Sch 15, Pt V (7), as from 1 April 2001 (SI 2001 No 916).

In sub-s (5B), words in square brackets substituted, in relation to England and Wales, for words 'a justices' chief executive' by the Courts Act 2003, s 109(1), Sch 8, para 69(1), (2), (4), as from a date to be appointed.

(6)   Where a provisional order has been confirmed under this section, it may be varied or rescinded in like manner as if it had originally been made by the confirming Court, and where on an application for rescission or variation the Court is satisfied that it is necessary to remit the case to the Court which made the order for the purpose of taking any further evidence, the Court may so remit the case and adjourn the proceedings for the purpose.

[(6)   Subject to subsection (6A), where a provisional order has been confirmed under this section, it may be varied or revoked in like manner as if it had originally been made by the confirming court.

(6A)   Where the confirming court is a magistrates' court, section 60 of the Magistrates' Courts Act 1980 (revocation, variation etc of orders for periodical payment) shall have effect in relation to a provisional order confirmed under this section—

(za)   as if in subsection (1) for the words 'by order on complaint' there were substituted 'on an application being made, by order']

(a)   as if in subsection (3) for the words 'paragraphs (a) to (d) of section 59(3) above' there were substituted 'section 4(5B) of the Maintenance Orders (Facilities for Enforcement) Act 1920';

(b)   as if in subsection (4) for paragraph (b) there were substituted—

'(b)   payments under the order are required to be made to the clerk of the court, or to the clerk of any other magistrates' court [a justices' chief executive] [the designated officer for the court or for any other magistrates' court], by any method of payment falling within section 59(6) above (standing order, etc)';

and as if after the words 'the court' there were inserted 'which made the order';

(c)   as if in subsection (5) for the words 'to the clerk' [justices' chief executive for the court] [designated officer for the court] there were substituted 'in accordance with paragraph (a) of section 4(5B) of the Maintenance Orders (Facilities for Enforcement) Act 1920';

(d)   as if in subsection (7), paragraph (c) and the word 'and' immediately preceding it were omitted;

(e)   as if in subsection (8) for the words 'paragraphs (a) to (d) of section 59(3) above' there were substituted 'section 4(5B) of the Maintenance Orders (Facilities for Enforcement) Act 1920';

(f)   as if for subsections (9) and (10) there were substituted the following subsections—

'(9)   In deciding, for the purposes of subsections (3) and (8) above, which of the *powers under section 4(5B) of the Maintenance Orders (Facilities for Enforcement) Act 1920 it is to exercise, the court shall have regard to any representations made by the debtor.*

(10) Subsection (4) of section 59 above (power of court to require debtor to open account) shall apply for the purposes of subsections (3) and (8) above as it applies for the purposes of that section but as if for paragraph (a) there were substituted—

"(a) the court proposes to exercise its power under paragraph (b) of section 4(5B) of the Maintenance Orders (Facilities for Enforcement) Act 1920, and".'

Note. Sub-s (6A)(za) inserted by Maintenance Orders (Reciprocal Enforcement) Act 1992, s 1(1), Sch 1, Part I, para 2(7), as from 5 April 1993.

In sub-s (6A)(b), first words in square brackets substituted for words 'the clerk of the court, or to the clerk of any other magistrates' court' by the Access to Justice Act 1999, ss 90, 106, Sch 13, para 7, Sch 15, Pt V(7), as from 1 April 2001, (SI 2001 No 916).

In sub-s (6A)(b), second words in square brackets substituted in relation to England and Wales for words 'a judges' chief executive' by the Courts Act 2003, s 109(1), Sch 8, para 69(1), (3)(a), (4), as from a date to be appointed.

In sub-s (6A)(b), words from 'and as it' to the end repealed by the Access to Justice Act 1999, ss 90, 106, Sch 13, para 7, Sch 15, Pt V(7), as from 1 April 2001, (SI 2001 No 916).

In sub-s (6A)(c), first words in square brackets substituted for the words 'clerk' by the Access to Justice Act 1999, ss 90, 106, Sch 13, para 7, Sch 15, Pt V(7), as from 1 April 2001 (SI 2001 No 916).

In sub-s (6A)(c), second words in square brackets substituted in relation to England and Wales for words 'justices' chief executive for the court' by the Courts Act 2003, s 109(1), Sch 8, para 69(1), (3)(b), (4), as from a date to be appointed.

(6B) Where on an application for variation or revocation the confirming court is satisfied that it is necessary to remit the case to the court which made the order for the purpose of taking any further evidence, the court may so remit the case and adjourn the proceedings for the purpose.]

Note. Sub-ss (6), (6A), (6B) in square brackets substituted for original sub-s (6) by Maintenance Enforcement Act 1991, s 10, Sch 1, para 1(2), as from 1 April 1992.

(7) Where an order has been so confirmed, the person bound thereby shall have the same right of appeal, if any, against the confirmation of the order as he would have had against the making of the order had the order been an order made by the Court confirming the order.

[4A. Variation and revocation of maintenance orders—(*1*) *This section applies to—*

(*a*) *any maintenance order made by virtue of section 3 of this Act which has been confirmed as mentioned in that section; and*

(*b*) *any maintenance order which has been confirmed under section 4 of this Act.*

(*2*) *Where the respondent to an application for the variation or revocation of a maintenance order to which this section applies is residing in a part of Her Majesty's dominions outside the United Kingdom to which this Act extends, a magistrates' court in England and Wales shall have jurisdiction to hear the application (where it would not have such jurisdiction apart from this subsection) if that court would have had jurisdiction to hear it had the respondent been residing in England and Wales.*

(*3*) *Where the defendant to a complaint [respondent to an application] for the variation or revocation of a maintenance order to which this section applies is residing in a part of Her Majesty's dominions outside the United Kingdom to which this Act extends, a court of summary jurisdiction in Northern Ireland shall have jurisdiction to hear the complaint [the application (where it would not have such jurisdiction apart from this subsection)] if that court would have had jurisdiction to hear it had the defendant [respondent] been residing in Northern Ireland.*

(*4*) *Where—*

(*a*) *the respondent to an application for the variation or revocation of a maintenance order to which this section applies does not appear at the time and place appointed for the hearing of the application by a magistrates' court in England and Wales, and*

    (*b*) *the court is satisfied that the respondent is residing in a part of Her Majesty's dominions outside the United Kingdom to which this Act extends,*
the court may proceed to hear and determine the application at the time and place appointed for the hearing or for any adjourned hearing in like manner as if the respondent had appeared at that time and place.

    (*5*) *Subsection (4) shall apply to Northern Ireland with the following modifications—*
    (*a*) *for the word 'respondent' (in each place where it occurs) there shall be substituted 'defendant',*
    (*b*) *for the words 'an application' and 'the application' (in each place where they occur) there shall be substituted 'a complaint' and 'the complaint' respectively, and*
    (*c*) *for the words 'a magistrates' court in England and Wales' there shall be substituted 'a court of summary jurisdiction in Northern Ireland'.*
    (*6*) *In this section 'revocation' includes discharge.*]

Note. This section inserted by Maintenance Orders (Reciprocal Enforcement) Act 1992, s 1, Sch 1, Part I, para 3, as from 5 April 1993. In sub-s (3) words in square brackets substituted for words 'defendant to a complaint', 'the complaint' and 'defendant', and sub-s (5)(a), (b) repealed, by Children (Northern Ireland) Order 1995, SI 1995 No 755, art 185, Sch 9, para 5, Sch 10, as from 4 November 1996.

5. Power of Secretary of State to make regulations for facilitating communications between Courts. *The Secretary of State [Lord Chancellor] may make regulations as to the manner in which a case can be remitted by a Court authorised to confirm a provisional order to the Court which made the provisional order, and generally for facilitating communications between such Courts.*

Note. Words 'Lord Chancellor' in square brackets substituted for words 'Secretary of State' by virtue of Transfer of Functions (Magistrates' Courts and Family Law) Order 1992, SI 1992 No 709, art 4, as from 1 April 1992.

6. Mode of enforcing orders—(*1*) *A court of summary jurisdiction in which an order has been registered under this Act or by which an order has been confirmed under this Act, and the officers of such Court, shall take all such steps for enforcing the order as may be prescribed.*

    (*2*) *Every such order shall be enforceable in like manner as if the order were for the payment of a civil debt recoverable summarily:*
    Provided that, if the order is of such a nature that if made by the Court in which it is so registered, or by which it is so confirmed, it would be enforceable in like manner as an order of affiliation [as a magistrates' court maintenance order], the order shall be so enforceable [the order shall, subject to the modifications of sections 76 and 93 of the Magistrates' Courts Act 1980 (enforcement of sums adjudged to be paid and complaint for arrears) specified in subsections (2ZA) and (2ZB) of section 18 of the Maintenance Orders Act 1950 (enforcement of registered orders), be so enforceable].
    [*In this subsection 'magistrates' court maintenance order' has the same meaning as in section 150(1) of the Magistrates' Courts Act 1980.*]
    (*3*) *A warrant of distress or commitment issued by a court of summary jurisdiction for the purpose of enforcing any order so registered or confirmed may be executed in any part of the United Kingdom in the same manner as if the warrant had been originally issued or subsequently endorsed by a court of summary jurisdiction having jurisdiction in the place where the warrant is executed.*

Note. First set of words in square brackets substituted for words 'in like manner as an order of affiliation' and third set of words inserted by Family Law Reform Act 1987, s 33(1), Sch 2, para 1, as from 1 April 1989; second set of words in square brackets substituted for words 'the order shall be so enforceable' by Maintenance Enforcement Act 1991, s 9, Sch 1, para 2, as from 1 April 1992.

7. Application of Summary Jurisdiction Acts[—(*1*)] *The Summary Jurisdiction Acts shall apply to proceedings before courts of summary jurisdiction under this Act in like manner as they apply to proceedings under those Acts, and the power of the Lord Chancellor to* *make rules under section twenty-nine of the Summary Jurisdiction Act 1879, shall include power to make rules regulating the procedure of courts of summary jurisdiction under this Act.*

[*(2) Without prejudice to the generality of the power to make rules under section 144 of the Magistrates' Courts Act 1980 (magistrates' courts rules), for the purpose of giving effect to this Act such rules [for the purpose of giving effect to this Act rules of court] may make, in relation to any proceedings brought under or by virtue of this Act, any provision which—*

    (a) falls within subsection (2) of section 93 of the Children Act 1989, and

    (b) may be made in relation to relevant proceedings under that section.]

Note. Sub-s (1) numbered as such, and sub-s (2) added, by Maintenance Orders (Reciprocal Enforcement) Act 1992, s 1, Sch 1, Part I, para 4, as from 5 April 1993. In sub-s (1) words from 'and the power' to end of the sub-section repealed by Justices of the Peace Act 1949, s 46(2), Seventh Schedule, Part II.

See Maintenance Orders (Facilities for Enforcement) Rules 1922 (SR & O 1922, No 1355): Maintenance Orders Act 1950 (p 2144), and Maintenance Orders Act 1958 (p 2204).

In sub-s (2), words in square brackets substituted in relation to England and Wales for words from 'Without prejudice' to 'such rules' by the Courts Act 2003, s 109(1), Sch 8, para 70, as from a date to be appointed.

8. Proof of documents signed by officers of Court. *Any document purporting to be signed by a judge or officer of a Court outside the United Kingdom shall, until the contrary is proved, be deemed to have been so signed without proof of the signature or judicial or official character of the person appearing to have signed it, and the officer of a Court by whom a document is signed shall, until the contrary is proved, be deemed to have been the proper officer of the Court to sign the document.*

9. Depositions to be evidence. *Depositions taken in a Court in a part of His Majesty's dominions outside the United Kingdom to which this Act extends* for the purposes of this Act, may be received in evidence in proceedings before courts of summary jurisdiction under this Act.*

  * See note on p 2036, for places to which the Act extends. The Act does not extend to the Republic of Ireland.

10. Interpretation. *For the purposes of this Act, the expression 'maintenance order' means an order other than an order of affiliation for the periodical payment of sums of money towards the maintenance of the wife or other dependants of the person against whom the order is made, and the expression 'dependants' means such persons as that person is, according to the law in force in the part of His Majesty's dominions in which the maintenance order was made, liable to maintain; the expression 'certified copy' in relation to an order of a Court means a copy of the order certified by the proper officer of the Court to be a true copy, and the expression 'prescribed' means prescribed by rules of Court.*

11. Application to Ireland. *In the application of this Act to Ireland the following modifications shall be made:*

[*(za) In section 3(1), (3) and (6) for the words 'England and Wales' there shall be substituted the words 'Northern Ireland' and for subsection (7) of that section there shall be substituted the following subsection—*

    '*(7) Where paragraph (1) of Article 86 of the Magistrates' Courts (Northern Ireland) Order 1981 (revocation, variation, etc, of orders for periodical payment) applies in relation to an order made under this section which has been confirmed, that paragraph shall have effect as if for the words "by order on complaint" there were substituted the words "on an application being made, by order". ';*]

Note. Para (za) inserted by Children (Northern Ireland) Order 1995, SI 1995 No 755, art 185, Sch 9, para 6, Sch 10, as from 4 November 1996.

    (a) The Lord Chancellor of Ireland may make rules regulating the procedure of courts of summary jurisdiction under this Act, and other matters incidental thereto:

Note. See Maintenance Orders (Facilities for Enforcement) Rules (Northern Ireland) 1925, SR & O 1925 No 254).

(*b*)   *Orders intended to be registered or confirmed in Ireland shall be transmitted by the Secretary of State* [*Lord Chancellor*] *to the prescribed officer of a Court in Ireland through the Lord Chancellor of Ireland:*

Note. Words 'Lord Chancellor' in square brackets substituted for words 'Secretary of State' by virtue of Transfer of Functions (Magistrates' Courts and Family Law) Order 1992, SI 1992 No 709, art 4, as from 1 April 1992.

(*c*)   *The expression 'maintenance order' includes an order or decree for the recovery or repayment of the cost of relief or maintenance made by virtue of the provisions of the Poor Relief (Ireland) Acts 1839 to 1914.*

[(*a*)   *In section 4 (power of court of summary jurisdiction to confirm maintenance order made out of UK) after subsection (5) there shall be inserted the following subsections—*
'(*5A*)   *Where a court of summary jurisdiction confirms a provisional order under this section, it shall at the same time exercise one of its powers under subsection (5B).*
(*5B*)   *The powers of the court are—*
(*a*)   *the power to order that payments under the order be made directly to the collecting officer;*
(*b*)   *the power to order that payments under the order be made to the collecting officer by such method of payment falling within Article 85(7) of the Magistrates' Courts (Northern Ireland) Order 1981 (standing order, etc) as may be specified;*
(*c*)   *the power to make an attachment of earnings order under Part IX of the Order of 1981 to secure payments under the order;*
and in this subsection "collecting officer" means the officer mentioned in Article 85(4) of the Order of 1981.*
(*5C*)   *In deciding which of the powers under subsection (5B) it is to exercise, the court shall have regard to any representations made by the person liable to make payments under the order.*
(*5D*)   *Paragraph (5) of Article 85 of the Magistrates' Courts (Northern Ireland) Order 1981 (power of court to require debtor to open account) shall apply for the purposes of subsection (5B) as it applies for the purposes of that Article but as if for sub-paragraph (a) there were substituted—*
"(*a*)   *the court proposes to exercise its power under paragraph (b) of section 4(5B) of the Maintenance Orders (Facilities for Enforcement) Act 1920, and";'*
(*b*)   *In section 4, for subsection (6) there shall be substituted the following subsections—*
'(*6*)   *Subject to subsection (6A), where a provisional order has been confirmed under this section, it may be varied or revoked in like manner as if it had originally been made by the confirming court.*
(*6A*)   *Where the confirming court is a court of summary jurisdiction, Article 86 of the Magistrates' Courts (Northern Ireland) Order 1981 (revocation, variation, etc, of orders for periodical payment) shall have effect in relation to a provisional order confirmed under this section—*
[(*za*) *as if in paragraph (1) for the words "by order on complaint" there were substituted "on an application being made, by order";*]
(*a*)   *as if in paragraph (3) for the words "sub-paragraphs (a) to (d) of Article 85(3)" there were substituted "section 4(5B) of the Maintenance Orders (Facilities for Enforcement) Act 1920";*
(*b*)   *as if in paragraph (4) for sub-paragraph (b) there were substituted—*
"(*b*)   *payments under the order are required to be made to the collecting officer by any method of payment falling within Article 85(7) (standing order, etc)";*
and as if after the words "petty sessions" there were inserted "for the petty sessions district for which the court which made the order acts";*
(*c*)   *as if in paragraph (5) for the words "to the collecting officer" there were substituted "in accordance with paragraph (a) of section 4(5B) of the Maintenance Orders (Facilities for Enforcement) Act 1920";*
(*d*)   *as if in paragraph (7), sub-paragraph (c) and the word "and" immediately preceding it were omitted;*

(*e*)   *as if in paragraph (8) for the words "sub-paragraphs (a) to (d) of Article 85(3)" there were substituted "section 4(5B) of the Maintenance Orders (Facilities for Enforcement) Act 1920";*

(*f*)   *as if for paragraphs (9) and (10) there were substituted the following paragraphs—*

"*(9)   In deciding, for the purposes of paragraphs (3) and (8), which of the powers under section 4(5B) of the Maintenance Orders (Facilities for Enforcement) Act 1920 it is to exercise, the court shall have regard to any representations made by the debtor.*

(10)   Paragraph (5) of Article 85 (power of court to require debtor to open account) shall apply for the purposes of paragraphs (3) and (8) as it applies for the purposes of that Article but as if for sub-paragraph (a) there were substituted—

'(*a*)   *the court proposes to exercise its power under paragraph (b) of section 4(5B) of the Maintenance Orders (Facilities for Enforcement) Act 1920, and'.*"

(*6B*)   *Where on an application for variation or revocation the confirming court is satisfied that it is necessary to remit the case to the court which made the order for the purpose of taking any further evidence, the court may so remit the case and adjourn the proceedings for the purpose.';*

(*c*)   *In section 6 (mode of enforcing orders registered or confirmed by courts under Act) in subsection (2) for the words 'the order shall be so enforceable' there shall be substituted 'the order shall, subject to the modifications of Article 98 of the Magistrates' Courts (Northern Ireland) Order 1981 (enforcement of sums adjudged to be paid and complaint for arrears) specified in subsection (3ZA) of section 18 of the Maintenance Orders Act 1950 (enforcement of registered orders), be so enforceable'.*]

[(*c*)   *In section 6 (mode of enforcing orders), in the proviso to subsection (2), for the words from 'in like manner' to the end substitute 'as an order to which Article 98 of the Magistrates' Courts (Northern Ireland) Order 1981 applies, the order shall be so enforceable subject to the modifications of that Article specified in subsection (3ZA) of section 18 of the Maintenance Orders Act 1950 (enforcement of registered orders)';*

(*cc*)   *In section 7 (application of Summary Jurisdiction Acts), after subsection (2) there shall be added the following subsection—*

'(*3*)   *Without prejudice to the generality of the power to make rules under Article 13 of the Magistrates' Courts (Northern Ireland) Order 1981 (magistrates' courts rules), for the purpose of giving effect to this Act such rules may make, in relation to any proceedings brought under or by virtue of this Act, any provision which—*

(*a*)   *falls within paragraph (2) of Article 165 of the Children (Northern Ireland) Order 1995, and*

(*b*)   *may be made in relation to relevant proceedings under that Article'.*]

Note. Paras (a)–(c) in square brackets substituted for original paras (a)–(c) by Family Law (Northern Ireland) Order 1993, SI 1993 No 1576, art 11, Sch 1, para 1, as from 4 November 1996. Para (b) amended, and para (c) further substituted by subsequent paras (c), (cc) in square brackets, by Children (Northern Ireland) Order 1995, SI 1995 No 755, art 185, Sch 9, para 6, Sch 10, as from 4 November 1996.

[(*d*)   *the amendments of section 3(1), (3) and (6) and section 4 made by the Maintenance Orders (Reciprocal Enforcement) Act 1992 shall be disregarded.*]

Note. Para (d) added by Maintenance Orders (Reciprocal Enforcement) Act 1992, s 1, Sch 1, Part I, para 5, as from 5 April 1993. Para (d) repealed by Children (Northern Ireland) Order 1995, SI 1995 No 755, art 185, Sch 9, para 6, Sch 10, as from 4 November 1996 (SR 1996 No 297).

12.   Extent of Act—(*1*)   *Where His Majesty is satisfied that reciprocal provisions have been made by the legislature of any part of His Majesty's dominions outside the United Kingdom for the enforcement within that part of maintenance orders made by Courts within England and*

Ireland, His Majesty may by Order in Council extend this Act to that part, and thereupon that part shall become a part of His Majesty's dominions to which this Act extends.*

(2) His Majesty may by Order in Council extend this Act to any British protectorate, and where so extended this Act shall apply as if any such protectorate was a part of His Majesty's dominions to which this Act extends.

Note. For power to revoke or vary an Order in Council made under this section, see Maintenance Orders Act 1958, s 19 (p 2217).

13. *This Act may be cited as the Maintenance Orders (Facilities for Enforcement) Act 1920.*
Note. See also Maintenance Orders Act 1950 (p 2144) and Maintenance Orders Act 1958 (p 2204), which deal with position within the United Kingdom.

MARRIED WOMEN (MAINTENANCE) ACT 1920*

(10 & 11 Geo 5 c 63)

An Act to provide for the inclusion in Orders made under the Summary Jurisdiction (Married Women) Act 1895, of a provision for the Maintenance of the Children of the Marriage under sixteen.   [*23 December 1920*]

* Whole Act repealed by Matrimonial Proceedings (Magistrates' Courts) Act 1960, s 18(1), Schedule.

1. Provision for maintenance of children—(*1*) *An order under section four of the Summary Jurisdiction (Married Women) Act 1895, whether as originally enacted or as extended by section five of the Licensing Act 1902, made on the application of a married woman, which contains a provision committing the legal custody of any children of the marriage to the applicant, may, in addition to any other provision authorised by the Act, include a provision that the husband shall pay to the applicant, or to any officer of the Court or third person on her behalf, a weekly sum not exceeding ten shillings for the maintenance of each such child until such child attains the age of sixteen years.*

(2) Any such order made before the passing of this Act may be varied, on the application of the married woman, so as to include from the date of the variation of the order such a provision for the maintenance of the children as aforesaid.

2. Short title. *This Act may be cited as the Married Women (Maintenance) Act, 1920, and the Summary Jurisdiction (Married Women) Act 1895, and this Act may be cited together as the Married Women (Maintenance) Acts 1895 and 1920.*

ADMINISTRATION OF JUSTICE ACT 1920

(10 & 11 Geo 5 c 81)

An Act to amend the law with respect to the administration of justice and with respect to the constitution of the Supreme Court, to facilitate the reciprocal enforcement of judgments and awards in the United Kingdom and other parts of His Majesty's Dominions or Territories under His Majesty's protection, and to regulate the fees chargeable by, and on the registration of, Commissioners for Oaths.
                                                                          [23 December 1920]

*   *   *   *   *

PART II

RECIPROCAL ENFORCEMENT OF JUDGMENTS IN THE UNITED KINGDOM AND IN OTHER PARTS
OF HIS MAJESTY'S DOMINIONS†

**9. Enforcement in the United Kingdom of judgments obtained in superior
courts in other British dominions**—(1) Where a judgment has been obtained in a
superior court in any part of His Majesty's dominions outside the United Kingdom to
which this Part of this Act extends,† the judgment creditor may apply to the High
Court in England or Ireland,† or to the Court of Session in Scotland, at any time
within twelve months after the date of the judgment, or such longer period as may be
allowed by the Court, to have the judgment registered in the Court, and on any such
application the Court may, if in all the circumstances of the case they think it is just
and convenient that the judgment should be enforced in the United Kingdom, and
subject to the provisions of this section, order the judgment to be registered
accordingly.

(2) No judgment shall be ordered to be registered under this section if—

(a) the original Court acted without jurisdiction; or

(b) the judgment debtor, being a person who was neither carrying on business
nor ordinarily resident within the jurisdiction of the original Court, did not
voluntarily appear or otherwise submit or agree to submit to the jurisdiction
of that Court; or

(c) the judgment debtor, being the defendant in the proceedings, was not duly
served with the process of the original Court and did not appear,
notwithstanding that he was ordinarily resident or was carrying on business
within the jurisdiction of that Court or agreed to submit to the jurisdiction
of that Court; or

(d) the judgment was obtained by fraud; or

(e) the judgment debtor satisfies the registering Court either that an appeal is
pending, or that he is entitled and intends to appeal, against the judgment; or

(f) the judgment was in respect of a cause of action which for reasons of public
policy or for some other similar reason could not have been entertained by
the registering Court.

(3) Where a judgment is registered under this section—

(a) the judgment shall, as from the date of registration, be of the same force and
effect, and proceedings may be taken thereon, as if it had been a judgment

---

† See Reciprocal Enforcement of Judgments (Administration of Justice Act 1920, Part II)
(Consolidation) Order 1984, SI 1984 No 129, as amended by SI 1985 No 1994, extending this
Part of this Act to the following countries and territories: Anguilla, Antigua and Barbuda,
Bahamas, Barbados, Belize, Bermuda, Botswana, British Indian Ocean Territory, Cayman
Islands, Christmas Island, Cocos (Keeling) Islands, Republic of Cyprus, Dominica, Falkland
Islands, Fiji, The Gambia, Ghana, Gibraltar, Grenada, Guyana, Hong Kong, Jamaica, Kenya,
Kiribati, Lesotho, Malawi, Malaysia, Malta, Mauritius, Montserrat, Newfoundland, New South
Wales, New Zealand, Nigeria, Territory of Norfolk Island, Northern Territory of Australia,
Papua New Guinea, Queensland, St Christopher and Nevis, St Helena, St Lucia, St Vincent
and the Grenadines, Saskatchewan, Seychelles, Sierra Leone, Singapore, Solomon Islands,
South Australia, Sovereign Base Areas of Akrotiri and Dhekelia in Cyprus, Sri Lanka,
Swaziland, Tanzania, Tasmania, Trinidad and Tobago, Turks and Caicos Islands, Tuvalu,
Uganda, Victoria, Western Australia, Zambia, Zimbabwe.

By Order in Council made under s 7(1) of the Foreign Judgments (Reciprocal Enforcement)
Act 1933 (SR & O 1933, No 1073), no further colonies or dominions are to be included under
the arrangement for reciprocal enforcement provided for in the 1920 Act, other than those
territories to which the Act was extended before 10 November 1933. Moreover, if, at any time,
any one of these territories is brought within the provisions of the Act of 1933, then the Act of
1920 will cease to apply to it (s 7(2) of the Act of 1933, p 2089). For procedure, see RSC, Ord
71.

† The operation of this part of the Act is confined to England, Scotland, and Northern
Ireland, and similar provision has not yet been made as regards the Republic of Ireland.

originally obtained or entered upon the date of registration in the registering Court;

Note. See Administration of Justice Act 1956, s 40(b) (p 2185), for effect of Debtors Act 1869, s 5.

(b) the registering Court shall have the same control and jurisdiction over the judgment as it has over similar judgments given by itself, but in so far only as relates to execution under this section;

(c) the reasonable costs of and incidental to the registration of the judgment (including the costs of obtaining a certified copy thereof from the original Court and of the application for registration) shall be recoverable in like manner as if they were sums payable under the judgment.

(4) Rules of Court shall provide—

(a) for service on the judgment debtor of notice of the registration of a judgment under this section; and

(b) for enabling the registering Court on an application by the judgment debtor to set aside the registration of a judgment under this section on such terms as the Court thinks fit; and

(c) for suspending the execution of a judgment registered under this section until the expiration of the period during which the judgment debtor may apply to have the registration set aside.

Note. In relation to Northern Ireland, for 'Rules of Court shall provide', read: 'Rules made under section seven of the Northern Ireland Act 1962, shall provide': Northern Ireland Act 1962, s 7, Sch 1.

(5) In any action brought in any Court in the United Kingdom on any judgment which might be ordered to be registered under this section, the plaintiff shall not be entitled to recover any costs of the action unless an application to register the judgment under this section has previously been refused, or unless the Court otherwise orders.

10. Issue of certificates of judgments obtained in the United Kingdom. *Where a judgment has been obtained in the High Court in England or Ireland,* or in the Court of Session in Scotland, against any person, the Court shall, on an application made by the judgment creditor and on proof that the judgment debtor is resident in some part of His Majesty's dominions outside the United Kingdom to which this Part of this Act extends, issue to the judgment creditor a certified copy of the judgment.*

* This Part of the Act does *not* extend to the Republic of Ireland.

[**10.**—(1) Where—

(a) a judgment has been obtained in the High Court in England or Northern Ireland, or in the Court of Session in Scotland, against any person; and

(b) the judgment creditor wishes to secure the enforcement of the judgment in a part of Her Majesty's dominions outside the United Kingdom to which this Part of this Act extends,

the court shall, on an application made by the judgment creditor, issue to him a certified copy of the judgment.

(2) The reference in the preceding subsection to Her Majesty's dominions shall be construed as if that subsection had come into force in its present form at the commencement of this Act.]

Note. Section 10 in square brackets substituted for s 10 in italics by Civil Jurisdiction and Judgments Act 1982, s 35(2), as from 1 January 1987.

11. Power to make rules. Provision may be made by rules of Court for regulating the practice and procedure (including scales of fees and evidence), in respect of proceedings of any kind under this Part of this Act.†

Note. In relation to Northern Ireland, for 'Provision may be made by rules of Court', read: 'Rules may be made under section seven of the Northern Ireland Act 1962, providing': Northern Ireland Act 1962, s 7, Sch 1.

† See RSC Ord 71 (p 3956).

12. Interpretation—(1) In this Part of this Act, unless the context otherwise requires—

The expression 'judgment' means any judgment or order given or made by a Court in any civil proceedings, whether before or after the passing of this Act, whereby any sum of money is made payable, and includes an award in proceedings on an arbitration if the award has, in pursuance of the law in force in the place where it was made, become enforceable in the same manner as a judgment given by a Court in that place:

The expression 'original Court' in relation to any judgment means the Court by which the judgment was given:

The expression 'registering Court' in relation to any judgment means the Court by which the judgment was registered:

The expression 'judgment creditor' means the person by whom the judgment was obtained, and includes the successors and assigns of that person:

The expression 'judgment debtor' means the person against whom the judgment was given, and includes any person against whom the judgment is enforceable in the place where it was given.

(2) Subject to rules of Court, any of the powers conferred by this Part of this Act on any Court may be exercised by a Judge of the Court.

Note. In relation to Northern Ireland, for 'rules of Court', read: 'rules made under section seven of the Northern Ireland Act 1962': Northern Ireland Act 1962, s 7, Sch 1.

13. Power to apply Part II of Act to territories under His Majesty's Protection. His Majesty may by Order in Council declare that this Part of this Act shall apply to any territory which is under His Majesty's protection, or in respect of which a mandate is being exercised by the Government of any part of His Majesty's dominions, as if that territory were part of His Majesty's dominions, and on the making of any such Order this Part of this Act shall, subject to the provisions of the Order, have effect accordingly.*

* See note on p 2045, for places to which the Act extends.

14. Extent of Part II of Act—(1) Where His Majesty is satisfied that reciprocal provisions have been made by the legislature of any part of His Majesty's dominions outside the United Kingdom for the enforcement within that part of His dominions of judgments obtained in the High Court in England, the Court of Session in Scotland, and the High Court in Ireland, His Majesty may by Order in Council declare that this Part of this Act shall extend to that part of His dominions, and on any such Order being made this Part of this Act shall extend accordingly.†

(2) An Order in Council under this section may be varied or revoked by a subsequent Order.

[(3) Her Majesty may by Order in Council under this section consolidate any Orders in Council under this section which are in force when the consolidating Order is made.]

Note. Sub-s (3) inserted by Civil Jurisdiction and Judgments Act 1982, s 35(3), as from 24 August 1982.

† See RSC Ord 71.

* * * * *

MATRIMONIAL CAUSES ACT 1923*

(13 & 14 Geo 5 c 19)

An Act to amend the Matrimonial Causes Act 1857.   [*18 July 1923*]

* This Act was repealed by Supreme Court of Judicature (Consolidation) Act 1925, Sch 6.

1. Right of wife to divorce husband for adultery. *It shall be lawful for any wife to present a petition to the Court praying that her marriage may be dissolved on the ground that her husband has, since the celebration thereof and since the passing of this Act, been guilty of adultery: Provided that nothing contained herein shall affect or take away any right of any wife existing immediately before the passing of this Act.*

Note. See now Matrimonial Causes Act 1973, s 1 (p 2497), replacing Divorce Reform Act 1969, ss 1, 2 (p 2338), replacing Matrimonial Causes Act 1965, s 1(1) (p 2239), replacing Matrimonial Causes Act 1950, s 1(1) (p 2130), replacing Supreme Court of Judicature (Consolidation) Act 1925, s 176 (p 2056), as substituted by Matrimonial Causes Act 1937, s 2.

2. Amendment of 20 & 21 Vict c 85, s 27. *The provisions of the Matrimonial Causes Act 1857, set out in the Schedule to this Act are hereby repealed.*

3. Short title. *This Act may be cited as the Matrimonial Causes Act 1923, and shall be construed as one with, and may be cited with, the Matrimonial Causes Acts 1857 to 1919.*

Note. The reference to the Act of 1919 is to the temporary Matrimonial Causes (Dominions Troops) Act 1919, repealed by Statute Law Revision Act 1927.

SCHEDULE
Section twenty-seven the words 'incestuous adultery or of bigamy with', and the words 'or of adultery coupled with such cruelty as, without adultery, would have entitled her to a divorce à mensâ et thoro, or of adultery coupled with desertion, without reasonable excuse, for two years or upwards'; and all the words in the proviso.

Note. For Matrimonial Causes Act 1857, s 27, see p 2006.

TRUSTEE ACT 1925

(15 & 16 Geo 5 c 19)

An Act to consolidate certain enactments relating to trustees in England and Wales.
                                                                      [9 April 1925]

*   *   *   *   *

PART II

GENERAL POWERS OF TRUSTEES AND PERSONAL REPRESENTATIVES

*   *   *   *   *

Maintenance, Advancement and Protective Trusts

31. Power to apply income for maintenance and to accumulate surplus income during a minority—(1) Where any property is held by trustees in trust for any person for any interest whatsoever, whether vested or contingent, then, subject to any prior interests or charges affecting that property—

(i)   during the infancy of any such person, if his interest so long continues, the trustees may, at their sole discretion, pay to his parent or guardian, if any, or otherwise apply for or towards his maintenance, education, or benefit, the whole or such part, if any, of the income of that property as may, in all the circumstances, be reasonable, whether or not there is—

(a)   any other fund applicable to the same purpose; or

(b)   any person bound by law to provide for his maintenance or education; and

   (ii) if such person on attaining the age of *twenty-one years* [eighteen years] has not a vested interest in such income, the trustees shall thenceforth pay the income of that property and of any accretion thereto under subsection (2) of this section to him, until he either attains a vested interest therein or dies, or until failure of his interest:

Provided that, in deciding whether the whole or any part of the income of the property is during a minority to be paid or applied for the purposes aforesaid, the trustees shall have regard to the age of the infant and his requirements and generally to the circumstances of the case, and in particular to what other income, if any, is applicable for the same purposes; and where trustees have notice that the income of more than one fund is applicable for those purposes, then, so far as practicable, unless the entire income of the funds is paid or applied as aforesaid or the court otherwise directs, a proportionate part only of the income of each fund shall be so paid or applied.

(2) During the infancy of any such person, if his interest so long continues, the trustees shall accumulate all the residue of that income *in the way of compound interest by investing the same and the resulting income thereof* [by investing it, and any profits from so investing it] from time to time in authorised investments, and shall hold those accumulations as follows—

   (i) If any such person—

      (a) attains the age of *twenty-one years* [eighteen years], or marries under that age, and his interest in such income during his infancy or until his marriage is a vested interest; or

      (b) on attaining the age of *twenty-one years* [eighteen years] or on marriage under that age becomes entitled to the property from which such income arose in fee simple, absolute or determinable, or absolutely, or for an entailed interest;

      the trustees shall hold the accumulations in trust for such person absolutely, but without prejudice to any provision with respect thereto contained in any settlement by him made under any statutory powers during his infancy, and so that the receipt of such person after marriage, and though still an infant, shall be a good discharge; and

   (ii) In any other case the trustees shall, notwithstanding that such person had a vested interest in such income, hold the accumulations as an accretion to the capital of the property from which such accumulations arose, and as one fund with such capital for all purposes, and so that, if such property is settled land, such accumulations shall be held upon the same trusts as if the same were capital money arising therefrom;

but the trustees may, at any time during the infancy of such person if his interest so long coninues, apply those accumulations, or any part thereof, as if they were income arising in the then current year.

(3) This section applies in the case of a contingent interest only if the limitation or trust carries the intermediate income of the property, but it applies to a future or contingent legacy by the parent of, or a person standing in loco parentis to, the legatee, if and for such period as, under the general law, the legacy carries interest for the maintenance of the legatee, and in any such case as last aforesaid the rate of interest shall (if the income available is sufficient, and subject to any rules of court to the contrary) be five pounds per centum per annum.

(4) This section applies to a vested annuity in like manner as if the annuity were the income of property held by trustees in trust to pay the income thereof to the annuitant for the same period for which the annuity is payable, save that in any case accumulations made during the infancy of the annuitant shall be held in trust for the annuitant or his personal representative absolutely.

(5) This section does not apply where the instrument, if any, under which the interest arises came into operation before the commencement of this Act.

Note. The words in square brackets in sub-ss (1)(ii), (2)(i)(a), (b) were substituted by Family Law Reform Act 1969, s 1(3), Sch 1, Part I, for the words 'twenty-one years' in italics but by virtue of s 1(4) of that Act and Sch 3, para 5(1) thereto (p 2321), the amendment does not affect this section in its application to interests under instruments made before 1970 or, in its application by virtue of Administration of Estates Act 1925, s 47(1)(ii), to the estate of an intestate dying before 1970, and, by virtue of s 1(4) of the 1969 Act and Sch 3, para 9 (p 2322), the amendment does not affect the construction of any statutory provision where it is incorporated in and has effect as part of any deed, will or other instrument not otherwise affected by s 1 of that Act.

In sub-s (2) words in square brackets substituted for words from 'in the way' to 'income thereof' by the Trustee Act 2000, s 40(1), Sch 2, Pt II, para 25, as from 1 February 2001 (SI 2001 No 49).

32. Power of advancement—(1) Trustees may at any time or times pay or apply any capital money subject to a trust, for the advancement or benefit, in such manner as they may, in their absolute discretion, think fit, of any person entitled to the capital of the trust property or of any share thereof, whether absolutely or contingently on his attaining any specified age or on the occurrence of any other event, or subject to a gift over on his death under any specified age or on the occurrence of any other event, and whether in possession or in remainder or reversion, and such payment or application may be made notwithstanding that the interest of such person is liable to be defeated by the exercise of a power of appointment or revocation, or to be diminished by the increase of the class to which he belongs:

Provided that—

(a)   the money so paid or applied for the advancement or benefit of any person shall not exceed altogether in amount one-half of the presumptive or vested share or interest of that person in the trust property; and

(b)   if that person is or becomes absolutely and indefeasibly entitled to a share in the trust property the money so paid or applied shall be brought into account as part of such share; and

(c)   no such payment or application shall be made so as to prejudice any person entitled to any prior life or other interest, whether vested or contingent, in the money paid or applied unless such person is in existence and of full age and consents in writing to such payment or application.

(2) *This section applies only where the trust property consists of money or securities or of property held upon trust for sale calling in and conversion, and such money or securities, or the proceeds of such sale calling in and conversion are not by statute or in equity considered as land, or applicable as capital money for the purposes of the Settled Land Act 1925.*

[(2) This section does not apply to capital money arising under the Settled Land Act 1925.]

Note. Sub-s (2) in square brackets substituted for sub-s (2) in italics by Trusts of Land and Appointment of Trustees Act 1996, s 25(1), Sch 3, para 3(8), as from 1 January 1997.

(3) This section does not apply to trusts constituted or created before the commencement of this Act.

*   *   *   *   *

PART V

GENERAL PROVISIONS

*   *   *   *   *

68. Definitions—[(1)] In this Act, unless the context otherwise requires, the following expressions have the meanings hereby assigned to them respectively, that is to say—

(1)   'Authorised investments' mean investments authorised by the instrument, if any, creating the trust for the investment of money subject to the trust, or by law:

(2)   'Contingent right' as applied to land includes a contingent or executory interest, a possibility coupled with an interest, whether the object of the gift or limitation of the interest, or possibility is or is not ascertained, also a right of entry, whether immediate or future, and whether vested or contingent:

*   *   *   *   *

(6)   'Land' includes land of any tenure, and mines and minerals, whether or not severed from the surface, buildings or parts of buildings, whether the division is horizontal, vertical or made in any other way, and other corporeal hereditaments; also a manor, an advowson, and a rent and other incorporeal hereditaments, and an easement, right, privilege, or benefit in, over, or derived from land, *but not an undivided share in land*; and in this definition 'mines and minerals' include any strata or seam of minerals or substances in or under any land, and powers of working and getting the same, *but not an undivided share thereof*; and 'hereditaments' mean real property which under an intestacy occurring before the commencement of this Act might have devolved on an heir;

Note. Words in italics repealed by Trusts of Land and Appointment of Trustees Act 1996, s 25(2), Sch 4, as from 1 January 1997.

*   *   *   *   *

(9)   'Personal representative' means the executor, original or by representation, or administrator for the time being of a deceased person;

(10)   'Possession' includes receipt of rents and profits or the right to receive the same, if any; 'income' includes rents and profits; and 'possessed' applies to receipt of income of and to any vested estate less than a life interest in possession or in expectancy in any land;

(11)   'Property' includes real and personal property, and any estate share and interest in any property, real or personal, and any debt, and any thing in action, and any other right or interest, whether in possession or not;

(12)   'Rights' include estates and interests;

(13)   'Securities' include stocks, funds, and shares; ... and 'securities payable to bearer' include securities transferable by delivery or by delivery and endorsement;

*   *   *   *   *

(15)   'Tenant for life,' 'statutory owner,' 'settled land,' 'settlement,' 'trust instrument,' 'trustees of the settlement' ... 'term of years absolute' and 'vesting instrument' have the same meanings as in the Settled Land Act 1925, and 'entailed interest' has the same meaning as in the Law of Property Act 1925;

*   *   *   *   *

(17)   'Trust' does not include the duties incident to an estate conveyed by way of mortgage, but with this exception the expressions 'trust' and 'trustee' extend to implied and constructive trusts, and to cases where the trustee has a beneficial interest in the trust property, and to the duties incident to the office of a personal representative, and 'trustee' where the context admits, includes a personal representative, and 'new trustee' includes an additional trustee;

*   *   *   *   *

(19)   'Trust for sale' in relation to land means an immediate *binding* trust for sale, whether or not exercisable at the request or with the consent of any person, *and with or without power at discretion to postpone the sale; 'trustees for sale' mean the persons (including a personal representative) holding land on trust for sale*;

*   *   *   *   *

Note. Only the definitions of expressions used in ss 31, 32 of this Act are reproduced above. Words omitted from para (13) repealed by Administration of Justice Act 1965, s 17(1), Sch 1. Words omitted from para (15) repealed by Mental Health Act 1959, s 142(2), Sch 8, Part I. Words in italics in para (19) repealed by Trusts of Land and Appointment of Trustees Act 1996, s 25(2), Sch 4, as from 1 January 1997.

*   *   *   *   *

71. Short title, commencement, extent—(1) This Act may be cited as the Trustee Act 1925.

(2) ...

(3) This Act, except where otherwise expressly provided, extends to England and Wales only.

(4) The provisions of this Act bind the Crown.

Note. Sub-s (2) repealed by SLR Act 1950.

*   *   *   *   *

LAW OF PROPERTY ACT 1925

(15 & 16 Geo 5 c 20)

*   *   *   *   *

30. Powers of court where trustees for sale refuse to exercise powers—[(*1*)] *If the trustees for sale refuse to sell or to exercise any of the powers conferred by either of the last two sections, or any requisite consent cannot be obtained, any person interested may apply to the court for a vesting or other order for giving effect to the proposed transaction or for an order directing the trustees for sale to give effect thereto, and the court may make such order as it thinks fit.*

[(*2*) *The county court has jurisdiction under this section where the land which is to be dealt with in the the court does not exceed the county court limit in capital value or net annual value for rating.*]

Note. This section, as originally enacted, numbered sub-s (1), and sub-s (2) added, by County Courts Act 1984, s 148(1), Sch 2, Part II, para 2, as from 1 August 1984. Words from 'where the land' to the end in sub-s (2) repealed by High Court and County Courts Jurisdiction Order 1991, SI 1991 No 724, art 2(1), Schedule, Part I, as from 1 July 1991. This section repealed by Trusts of Land and Appointment of Trustees Act 1996, s 25(2), Sch 4, as from 1 January 1997.

*   *   *   *   *

172. Voluntary conveyances to defraud creditors voidable—(*1*) *Save as provided in this section, every conveyance of property, made whether before or after the commencement of this Act, with intent to defraud creditors, shall be voidable, at the instance of any person thereby prejudiced.*

(*2*) *This section does not affect the operation of a disentailing assurance, or the law of bankruptcy for the time being in force.*

(*3*) *This section does not extend to any estate or interest in property conveyed for valuable consideration and in good faith or upon good consideration and in good faith to any person not having, at the time of the conveyance, notice of the intent to defraud creditors.*

Note. Repealed by Insolvency Act 1985, s 235(3), Sch 10.

*   *   *   *   *

198. Registration under the Land Charges Act 1925 to be notice—(1) The registration of any instrument or matter *under the provisions of the Land Charges Act 1925 or any enactment which it replaces, in any register kept at the land registry or elsewhere* [in any register kept under the Land Charges Act 1972 or any local land charges register], shall be deemed to constitute actual notice of such instrument or matter, and of the fact of such registration, to all persons and for all purposes connected with the land affected, as from the date of registration or other prescribed date and so long as the registration continues in force.

(2) This section operates without prejudice to the provisions of this Act respecting the making of further advances by a mortgagee, and applies only to instruments and matters required or authorised to be registered *under the Land Charges Act 1925* [in any such register].

Note. Words in square brackets substituted for words in italics by Local Land Charges Act 1975, s 17(2), Sch 1, as from 1 August 1977. The reference to the 1925 Act in the heading to the section is now inapposite.

199. Restrictions on constructive notice—(1) A purchaser shall not be prejudicially affected by notice of—
   (i) any instrument or matter capable of registration under the provisions of the Land Charges Act 1925, or any enactment which it replaces, which is void or not enforceable as against him under that Act or enactment, by reason of the non-registration thereof;
   (ii) any other instrument or matter or any fact or thing unless-
      (a) it is within his own knowledge, or would have come to his knowledge if such inquiries and inspections had been made as ought reasonably to have been made by him; or
      (b) in the same transaction with respect to which a question of notice to the purchaser arises, it has come to the knowledge of his counsel, as such, or of his solicitor or other agent, as such, or would have come to the knowledge of his solicitor or other agent, as such, if such inquiries and inspections had been made as ought reasonably to have been made by the solicitor or other agent.

(2) Paragraph (ii) of the last subsection shall not exempt a purchaser from any liability under, or any obligation to perform or observe, any covenant, condition, provision, or restriction contained in any instrument under which his title is derived, mediately or immediately; and such liability or obligation may be enforced in the same manner and to the same extent as if that paragraph had not been enacted.

(3) A purchaser shall not by reason of anything in this section be affected by notice in any case where he would not have been so affected if this section had not been enacted.

(4) This section applies to purchases made either before or after the commencement of this Act.

*   *   *   *   *

SUPREME COURT OF JUDICATURE (CONSOLIDATION) ACT 1925*

(15 & 16 Geo 5 c 49)

An Act to consolidate the Judicature Acts 1873 to 1910, and other enactments relating to the Supreme Court of Judicature in England and the administration of justice therein.

[*31 July 1925*]

* Whole Act, sections of which had already been repealed and some replaced, was repealed by Supreme Court Act 1981, s 152(4), Sch 7. Only those sections of the Act which related to divorce law and practice are printed here.

32. Rules as to exercise of jurisdiction. *The jurisdiction vested in the High Court and the Court of Appeal respectively shall, so far as regards procedure and practice, be exercised in the manner provided by this Act or by rules of court, and where no special provision is contained in this Act or in rules of court with reference thereto, any such jurisdiction shall be exercised as nearly as may be in the same manner as that in which it might have been exercised by the court to which it formerly appertained.*

Note. Supreme Court of Judicature Act 1873, s 23 (p 2026), and see Matrimonial Causes Act 1857, s 22 (p 2005).

This section was restricted by Divorce Reform Act 1969, s 9(3) (p 2342) (subsequently repealed), and then repealed by Supreme Court Act 1981, s 152(4), Sch 7.

*   *   *   *   *

43. Determination of matter completely and finally. *The High Court and the Court of Appeal respectively, in the exercise of the jurisdiction vested in them by this Act, shall, in every cause or matter pending before the court, grant, either absolutely or on such terms and conditions as the court thinks just, all such remedies whatsoever as any of the parties thereto may appear to be entitled to in respect of any legal or equitable claim property brought forward by them in the cause or matter, so that, as far as possible, all matters in controversy between the parties may be completely and finally determined, and all multiplicity of legal proceedings concerning any of those matters avoided.*

Note. Supreme Court of Judicature Act 1873, s 24(7). See now Supreme Court Act 1981, s 49 (p 2846).

*   *   *   *   *

PART VIII

MATRIMONIAL CAUSES AND MATTERS

Divorce and Nullity of Marriage

176. Grounds for petition for divorce. *A petition for divorce may be presented to the High Court (in this Part of this Act referred to as 'the court')—*

(*a*) *by a husband on the ground that his wife has since the celebration of the marriage been guilty of adultery; and*

(*b*) *by a wife on the ground that her husband has since the celebration of the marriage been guilty of rape, or of sodomy or bestiality, or that he has since the celebration of the marriage and since the seventeenth day of July, nineteen hundred and twenty-three, been guilty of adultery:*

    Provided that nothing in this Act shall affect the right of a wife to present a petition for divorce on any ground on which she might, if the Matrimonial Causes Act 1923, had not passed, have presented such a petition, and on any petition presented by a wife for divorce on the ground of the adultery and cruelty, or adultery and desertion, of her husband, the husband and wife shall be competent and compellable to give evidence with respect to the cruelty or desertion.

Note. A new s 176 was substituted for the section printed above by Matrimonial Causes Act 1937, s 2. The substituted section was repealed by Matrimonial Causes Act 1950, s 34(1), Schedule. See now Matrimonial Causes Act 1973, s 1(1), (2) (p 2497), replacing Divorce Reform Act 1969, ss 1, 2(1) (p 2338), replacing Matrimonial Causes Act 1965, s 1(1) (p 2239), replacing Matrimonial Causes Act 1950, s 1(1) (p 2130).

For former law, see Matrimonial Causes Act 1857, s 27 (p 2006); Matrimonial Causes Act 1859, s 6 (p 2019); Matrimonial Causes Act 1923 (p 2050).

177. Provision as to making adulterer co-respondent—(*1*) *On a petition for divorce presented by the husband or in the answer of a husband praying for divorce the petitioner or respondent, as the case may be, shall make the alleged adulterer a co-respondent unless he is excused by the court on special grounds from so doing.*

    (*2*) *On a petition for divorce presented by the wife the court may, if it thinks fit, direct that the person with whom the husband is alleged to have committed adultery be made a respondent.*

Note. Repealed by Matrimonial Causes Act 1950, s 34(1), Schedule. See now Matrimonial Causes Act 1973, s 49 (p 2557), replacing Matrimonial Causes Act 1965, s 4 (p 2241), replacing Matrimonial Causes Act 1950, s 3 (p 2132).

178. Duty of court on presentation of petition—[(*1*) *On a petition for divorce it shall be the duty of the court to satisfy itself so far as it reasonably can both as to the facts alleged and* *also as to whether the petitioner has been accessory to or has connived at or condoned the adultery or not, and also to enquire into any countercharge which is made against the petitioner.*

(*2*) *If on the evidence the court is not satisfied that the alleged adultery has been committed or finds that the petitioner has during the marriage been accessory to or has connived at or condoned the adultery complained of, or that the petition is presented or prosecuted in collusion with either of the respondents, the court shall dismiss the petition.*

(*3*) *If the court is satisfied on the evidence that the case for the petition has been proved and does not find that the petitioner has in any manner been accessory to or connived at or condoned the adultery or that the petition is presented or prosecuted in collusion with either of the respondents, the court shall pronounce a decree of divorce:*

Provided that the court shall not be bound to pronounce a decree of divorce if it finds that the petitioner has during the marriage been guilty of adultery, or if in the opinion of the court he has been guilty—

(*a*)   *of unreasonable delay in presenting or prosecuting the petition; or*

(*b*)   *of cruelty towards the other party to the marriage; or*

(*c*)   *of having without reasonable excuse deserted, or of having without reasonable excuse wilfully separated himself or herself from, the other party before the adultery complained of; or*

(*d*)   *of such wilful neglect or misconduct as has conduced to the adultery*].

178.—(*1*)   *On a petition for divorce it shall be the duty of the court to inquire, so far as it reasonably can into the facts alleged and whether there has been any connivance or condonation on the part of the petitioner and whether any collusion exists between the parties and also to inquire into any countercharge which is made against the petitioner.*

(*2*)   *If the court is satisfied on the evidence that—*

(*i*)   *the case for the petition has been proved; and*

(*ii*)   *where the ground of the petition is adultery, the petitioner has not in any manner been accessory to, or connived at, or condoned the adultery, or where the ground of the petition is cruelty the petitioner has not in any manner condoned the cruelty; and*

(*iii*)   *the petition is not presented or prosecuted in collusion with the respondent or either of the respondents,*

the court shall pronounce a decree of divorce, but if the court is not satisfied with respect to any of the aforesaid matters, it shall dismiss the petition:

Provided that the court shall not be bound to pronounce a decree of divorce and may dismiss the petition if it finds that the petitioner has during the marriage been guilty of adultery or if, in the opinion of the court, the petitioner has been guilty—

(*a*)   *of unreasonable delay in presenting or prosecuting the petition; or*

(*b*)   *of cruelty towards the other party to the marriage; or*

(*c*)   *where the ground of the petition is adultery or cruelty, of having without reasonable excuse deserted, or having without reasonable excuse wilfully separated himself or herself from, the other party before the adultery or cruelty complained of; or*

(*d*)   *where the ground of the petition is adultery or unsoundness of mind or desertion, of such wilful neglect or misconduct as has conduced to the adultery or unsoundness of mind or desertion.*

Note. Section 178 in square brackets substituted for section printed above by Matrimonial Causes Act 1937, s 4. The substituted section was repealed by Matrimonial Causes Act 1950, s 34(1), Schedule. See now Matrimonial Causes Act 1973, ss 1(3), (4), 2(1), (3) (p 2497), replacing Divorce Reform Act 1969, ss 2(2), (3), 3(3), (4) (pp 2338, 2339), replacing Matrimonial Causes Act 1965, s 5 (p 2241), replacing Matrimonial Causes Act 1950, s 4 (p 2132), as amended by Matrimonial Causes Act 1963, s 4.

For former statutory provisions, see Matrimonial Causes Act 1857, ss 29, 30, 31 (p 2007).

179.   Dismissal of respondent or co-respondent from proceedings. *In any case in which, on the petition of a husband for divorce, the alleged adulterer is made a co-respondent or in which, on the petition of a wife for divorce, the person with whom the husband is alleged to have* *committed adultery is made a respondent, the court may, after the close of the evidence on the part of the petitioner, direct the co-respondent or the respondent, as the case may be, to be dismissed from the proceedings if the court is of opinion that there is not sufficient evidence against him or her.*

Note. Repealed by Matrimonial Causes Act 1950, s 34(1), Schedule. See now Matrimonial Causes Act 1973, s 49(3) (p 2557), replacing Matrimonial Causes Act 1965, s 4(3) (p 2241), replacing Matrimonial Causes Act 1950, s 5 (p 2132).

For former statutory provision, see Matrimonial Causes Act 1858, s 11 (p 2016).

180. Relief to respondent on petition for divorce. *If in any proceedings for divorce the respondent opposes the relief sought, in the case of proceedings instituted by the husband, on the ground of his adultery, cruelty or desertion, or, in the case of proceedings instituted by the wife, on the ground of her adultery, cruelty or desertion, the court may give to the respondent the same relief to which he or she would have been entitled if he or she had presented a petition seeking such relief.*

Note. Repealed by Matrimonial Causes Act 1950, s 34(1), Schedule. See now Matrimonial Causes Act 1973, s 20 (p 2508), replacing Matrimonial Causes Act 1965, s 5(6) (p 2242), replacing Matrimonial Causes Act 1950, s 6 (p 2132).

For former statutory provision, see Matrimonial Causes Act 1866, s 2 (p 2022).

181. Duties of King's Proctor. *In the case of any petition for divorce or for nullity of marriage—*

(*1*) *The court may, if it thinks fit, direct all necessary papers in the matter to be sent to His Majesty's Proctor, who shall under the directions of the Attorney-General instruct counsel to argue before the court any question in relation to the matter which the court deems to be necessary or expedient to have fully argued, and His Majesty's Proctor shall be entitled to charge the costs of the proceedings as part of the expenses of his office:*

(*2*) *Any person may at any time during the progress of the proceedings or before the decree nisi is made absolute give information to His Majesty's Proctor of any matter material to the due decision of the case, and His Majesty's Proctor may thereupon take such steps as the Attorney-General considers necessary or expedient:*

(*3*) *If in consequence of any such information or otherwise His Majesty's Proctor suspects that any parties to the petition are or have been acting in collusion for the purpose of obtaining a decree contrary to the justice of the case, he may, under the direction of the Attorney-General, after obtaining the leave of the court, intervene and retain counsel and subpœna witnesses to prove the alleged collusion.*

Note. Repealed by Matrimonial Causes Act 1950, s 34(1), Schedule. See now Matrimonial Causes Act 1973, ss 8(1), 15 (pp 2501, 2505), replacing Matrimonial Causes Act 1965, ss 6(1), 10 (pp 2241, 2245), replacing Matrimonial Causes Act 1950, s 10 (p 2134).

For former statutory provisions, see Matrimonial Causes Act 1860, ss 5, 7 (p 2020); Matrimonial Causes Act 1873, s 1 (p 2027).

182. Provisions as to costs where King's Proctor intervenes or shows cause—

(*1*) *Where His Majesty's Proctor intervenes or shows cause against a decree nisi in any proceedings for divorce or for nullity of marriage, the court may make such order as to the payment by other parties to the proceedings of the costs incurred by him in so doing or as to the payment by him of any costs incurred by any of the said parties by reason of his so doing, as may seem just.*

(*2*) *So far as the reasonable costs incurred by His Majesty's Proctor in so intervening or showing cause are not fully satisfied by any order made under this section for the payment of his costs, he shall be entitled to charge the difference as part of the expenses of his office, and the Treasury may, if they think fit, order that any costs which under any order made by the court under this section His Majesty's Proctor pays to any parties shall be deemed to be part of the expenses of his office.*

Note. Repealed by Matrimonial Causes Act 1950, s 34(1), Schedule. See now Matrimonial Causes Act 1973, ss 8(2), (3), 15 (pp 2502, 2505), replacing Matrimonial Causes Act 1965, ss 6(2), (3), 10 (pp 2241, 2245), replacing Matrimonial Causes Act 1950, s 11 (p 2134).

For former statutory provisions, see Matrimonial Causes Act 1860, s 7 (p 2020); Matrimonial Causes Act 1878, s 2 (p 2028).

183. Decree nisi for divorce or nullity of marriage—(*1*) *Every decree for a divorce or for nullity of marriage shall, in the first instance, be a decree nisi not to be made absolute until after the expiration of six months from the pronouncing thereof, unless the court by general or special order from time to time fixes a shorter time.*

(*2*) *After the pronouncing of the decree nisi and before the decree is made absolute, any person may, in the prescribed manner, show cause why the decree should not be made absolute by reason of the decree having been obtained by collusion or by reason of material facts not having been brought before the court, and in any such case the court may make the decree absolute, reverse the decree nisi, require further inquiry or otherwise deal with the case as the court thinks fit.*

[(*3*) *Where a decree nisi has been obtained, whether before or after the passing of this Act, and no application for the decree to be made absolute has been made by the party who obtained the decree, then at any time after the expiration of three months from the earliest date on which that party could have made such an application, the party against whom the decree nisi has been granted shall be at liberty to apply to the court and the court shall, on such application, have power to make the decree absolute, reverse the decree nisi, require further inquiry or otherwise deal with the case as the court thinks fit.*]

Note. Sub-s (3) added by Matrimonial Causes Act 1937, s 9. The whole section, as amended, repealed by Matrimonial Causes Act 1950, s 34(1), Schedule. See now Matrimonial Causes Act 1973, ss 1(5), 9, 15 (pp 2498, 2502, 2505), replacing Matrimonial Causes Act 1965, ss 5(7), 7, 10 (pp 2242, 2243, 2245), replacing Matrimonial Causes Act 1950, s 12 (p 2134).

For former statutory provisions, see Matrimonial Causes Act 1860, s 7 (p 2020); Matrimonial Causes Act 1866, s 3 (p 2022); Matrimonial Causes Act 1873, s 1 (p 2027).

184. Re-marriage of divorced persons—(*1*) *As soon as any decree for divorce is made absolute, either of the parties to the marriage may, if there is no right of appeal against the decree absolute, marry again as if the prior marriage had been dissolved by death or, if there is such a right of appeal, may so marry again, if no appeal is presented against the decree, as soon as the time for appealing has expired, or, if an appeal is so presented, as soon as the appeal has been dismissed:*

Provided that it shall be lawful for a man to marry the sister or half-sister of his divorced wife or of his wife by whom he has been divorced during the lifetime of the wife, or the divorced wife of his brother or half-brother or the wife of his brother or half-brother who has divorced his brother during the lifetime of the brother or half-brother.

Note. The following proviso was substituted for the one printed above by Marriage (Prohibited Degrees of Relationship) Act 1931, s 2:

[*Provided that it shall not be unlawful for a man to contract any marriage which, upon the decease of any person, would be authorised by the Marriage (Prohibited Degrees of Relationship) Acts 1907 to 1931 (as amended by any subsequent enactment) but which would otherwise have been void or voidable by reason of affinity, during the lifetime of that person.*]

(*2*) *No clergyman of the Church of England shall be compelled to solemnise the marriage of any person whose former marriage has been dissolved on the ground of his or her adultery, or shall be liable to any proceedings, penalty or censure for solemnising or refusing to solemnise the marriage of any such person.*

(*3*) *If any minister of any church or chapel of the Church of England refuses to perform the marriage service between any persons who but for his refusal would be entitled to have the service performed in that church or chapel, he shall permit any other minister of the Church of England entitled to officiate within the diocese in which the church or chapel is situate to perform the marriage service in that church or chapel.*

[(*2*) *No clergyman of the Church of England or of the Church in Wales shall be compelled to solemnize the marriage of any person whose former marriage has been dissolved on any ground and whose former husband or wife is still living or to permit the marriage of any such person in the Church or Chapel of which he is the minister.*]

Note. Sub-ss (2), (3) repealed and replaced by new sub-s (2) in square brackets by Matrimonial Causes Act 1937, s 12. The section, as amended, repealed by Matrimonial Causes Act 1950, s 34(1), Schedule, and replaced by s 13 of that Act (p 2143). See Matrimonial Causes Act 1965, s 8 (p 2244).

For former statutory provisions, see Matrimonial Causes Act 1857, ss 57, 58 (p 2012); Matrimonial Causes Act 1868, s 4 (p 2023); Deceased Wife's Sister's Marriage Act 1907, ss 3(2), 5; Deceased Brother's Widow's Marriage Act 1921, s 1(2)(b), (4). See also Marriage Act 1949 (p 2107); and Marriage (Enabling) Act 1960.

Judicial Separation and Restitution of Conjugal Rights

185. Decree for judicial separation—(*1*) *A petition for judicial separation may be presented to the court either by the husband or the wife on the ground of adultery or cruelty, desertion without cause for not less than two years, failure to comply with a decree for restitution of conjugal rights, or on any ground on which a decree for divorce a mensa et thoro might have been pronounced immediately before the commencement of the Matrimonial Causes Act 1857.*

(*2*) *The court may, on being satisfied that the allegations contained in the petition are true and that there is no legal ground why the petition should not be granted, make a decree for judicial separation, and any such decree shall have the same force and effect as a decree for divorce a mensa et thoro had immediately before the commencement of the Matrimonial Causes Act 1857.*

[(*1*) *A petition for judicial separation may be presented to the court either by the husband or the wife on any grounds on which a petition for divorce might have been presented, or on the ground of failure to comply with a decree for restitution of conjugal rights or on any ground on which a decree for divorce a mensa et thoro might have been pronounced immediately before the commencement of the Matrimonial Causes Act 1857, and the foregoing provisions of this Part of the Act relating to the duty of the court on the presentation of a petition for divorce, and the circumstances in which such a petition shall or may be granted or dismissed, shall apply in like manner to a petition for judicial separation.*

(*2*) *Where the court in accordance with the said provisions grants a decree of judicial separation, it shall no longer be obligatory for the petitioner to cohabit with the respondent.*]

Note. Sub-ss (1), (2) replaced by new sub-ss (1), (2) in square brackets by Matrimonial Causes Act 1937, s 5.

(*3*) *The court may, on the application by petition of the husband or wife against whom a decree for judicial separation has been made, and on being satisfied that the allegations contained in the petition are true, reverse the decree at any time after the making thereof, on the ground that it was obtained in the absence of the person making the application, or, if desertion was the ground of the decree, that there was reasonable cause for the alleged desertion.*

(*4*) *The reversal of a decree for judicial separation shall not affect the rights or remedies which any other person would have had if the decree had not been reversed in respect of any debts, contracts or acts of the wife incurred, entered into or done between that date of the decree and of the reversal thereof.*

Note. As stated, sub-ss (1) and (2) repealed and replaced by Matrimonial Causes Act 1937, s 5. The substituted subsections and sub-s (3) repealed by Matrimonial Causes Act 1950, s 34(1), Schedule. See now Matrimonial Causes Act 1973, ss 17, 18 (pp 2506, 2507), replacing Matrimonial Causes Act 1965, s 12 (p 2245), replacing Matrimonial Causes Act 1950, s 14 (p 2135). Sub-s (4) repealed by the 1950 Act and not replaced.

For former statutory provisions, see Matrimonial Causes Act 1857, ss 7, 16, 17, 23 (pp 2002, 2003–2004, 2005); Matrimonial Causes Act 1884, s 5 (p 2033).

186. Decree for restitution of conjugal rights. *A petition for restitution of conjugal rights may be presented to the court either by the husband or the wife, and the court, on being satisfied that the allegations contained in the petition are true, and that there is no legal ground why a decree for restitution of conjugal rights should not be granted, may make the decree accordingly.*

Note. Repealed by Matrimonial Causes Act 1950, s 34(1), Schedule and re-enacted by ibid, s 15(1) (p 2135), which was replaced by Matrimonial Causes Act 1965, s 13(1) (p 2246), which was repealed but not replaced by Matrimonial Proceedings and Property Act 1970, s 42(2), Sch 3. See also Act of 1970, s 20 (p 2376).

For former statutory provision, see Matrimonial Causes Act 1857, s 17 (p 2004).

187. Periodical payments in lieu of attachment—(*1*) *A decree for restitution of conjugal rights shall not be enforced by attachment, but where the application is by the wife the court, at the time of making the decree or at any time afterwards, may, in the event of the decree not being complied with within any time in that behalf limited by the court, order the respondent to make to the petitioner such periodical payments as may be just, and the order may be enforced in the same manner as an order for alimony in proceedings for judicial separation.*

Note. Repealed by Matrimonial Causes Act 1950, s 34(1), Schedule, and re-enacted by ibid, ss 15(2), 22(3) (pp 2135, 2139), which were replaced by Matrimonial Causes Act 1965, ss 13(2), 21(1), (2) (pp 2246, 2249), which were repealed but not replaced by Matrimonial Proceedings and Property Act 1970, s 42(2), Sch 3.

(*2*) *The court may, if it thinks fit, order that the husband shall, to the satisfaction of the court, secure to the wife the periodical payments, and for that purpose may direct that it shall be referred to one of the conveyancing counsel of the court to settle and approve a proper deed or instrument to be executed by all necessary parties.*

Note. Repealed by Matrimonial Causes Act 1950, s 34(1), Schedule. See now Matrimonial Causes Act 1973, s 27 (p 2529), replacing Matrimonial Proceedings and Property Act 1970, s 6 (p 2367), replacing Matrimonial Causes Act 1965, s 22(2) (p 2250), replacing Matrimonial Causes Act 1950, s 22(4) (p 2140).

For former statutory provision, see Matrimonial Causes Act 1884, s 2 (p 2033). See also Administration of Justice (Miscellaneous Provisions) Act 1938, s 14.

Legitimacy Declarations

188. Declaration of legitimacy, &c.—(*1*) *Any person who is a natural-born subject of His Majesty, or whose right to be deemed a natural-born subject of His Majesty depends wholly or in part on his legitimacy or on the validity of any marriage, may, if he is domiciled in England or Northern Ireland or claims any real or personal estate situate in England, apply by petition to the court for a decree declaring that the petitioner is the legitimate child of his parents, and that the marriage of his father and mother or of the grandfather and grandmother was a valid marriage or that his own marriage was a valid marriage.*

(*2*) *Any person who is so domiciled or claims as aforesaid, may apply to the court for a decree declaring his right to be deemed a natural-born subject of His Majesty.*

(*3*) *Applications under subsections (1) and (2) of this section may be included in the same petition and on any such application the court shall make such decree as the court thinks just, and the decree shall be binding on His Majesty and all other persons whatsoever:*

Provided that the decree of the court shall not prejudice any person—

  (*i*) *if it is subsequently proved to have been obtained by fraud or collusion; or*

  (*ii*) *unless that person has been cited or made a party to the proceedings or is the heir-at-law, next of kin, or other real or personal representative of, or derives title under or through, a person so cited or made a party.*

(*4*) *A copy of every petition under this section and of any affidavit accompanying the petition shall be delivered to the Attorney-General at least one month before the petition is presented or filed, and the Attorney-General shall be a respondent on the hearing of the petition and on any subsequent proceedings relating thereto.*

(*5*) *In any application under this section such persons shall, subject to rules of court, be cited to see proceedings or otherwise summoned as the court shall think fit, and any such persons may be permitted to become parties to the proceedings and to oppose the application.*

(*6*) *The provisions of this Act relating to matrimonial causes shall, so far as applicable, extend to any proceedings under this section.*

(*7*) *No proceedings under this section shall affect any final judgment or decree already pronounced or made by any court of competent jurisdiction.*

Note. Words 'natural-born' in sub-ss (1), (2) repealed by British Nationality Act 1948, Sch IV. The whole section repealed by Matrimonial Causes Act 1950, s 34(1), Schedule. See now Matrimonial Causes Act 1973, s 45 (p 2554), replacing Matrimonial Causes Act 1965, s 39 (p 2262), replacing Matrimonial Causes Act 1950, s 17, as amended (p 2136).

For former statutory provision, see Legitimacy Declaration Act 1858, ss 1, 2, 4, 6–8. See also Legitimacy Act 1926, s 2(1), and Administration of Justice (Miscellaneous Provisions) Act 1933, s 7(1).

Miscellaneous

189. Damages—(*1*) *A husband may on a petition for divorce or for judicial separation or for damages only, claim damages from any person on the ground of adultery with the wife of the petitioner.*

(*2*) *A claim for damages on the ground of adultery shall, subject to the provisions of any enactment relating to trial by jury in the court, be tried on the same principles and in the same manner as actions for criminal conversation were tried immediately before the commencement of the Matrimonial Causes Act 1857, and the provisions of this Act with reference to the hearing and decision of petitions shall so far as may be necessary apply to the hearing and decision of petitions on which damages are claimed.*

(*3*) *The court may direct in what manner the damages recovered on any such petition are to be paid or applied, and may direct the whole or any part of the damages to be settled for the benefit of the children, if any, of the marriage, or as a provision for the maintenance of the wife.*

Note. Repealed by Matrimonial Causes Act 1950, s 34(1), Schedule and replaced by ibid, s 30 (p 2142), subsequently replaced by Matrimonial Causes Act 1965, s 41 (p 2263) and finally repealed by Law Reform (Miscellaneous Provisions) Act 1970, ss 4, 7(2), Schedule.

For former statutory provision, see Matrimonial Causes Act 1857, s 33 (p 2008).

190. Alimony [sic]—(*1*) *The court may, if it thinks fit, on any decree for divorce or nullity of marriage, order that the husband shall, to the satisfaction of the court, secure to the wife such gross sum of money or annual sum of money for any term, not exceeding her life, as having regard to her fortune, if any, to the ability of her husband and to the conduct of the parties, the court may deem to be reasonable, and the court may for that purpose order that it shall be referred to one of the conveyancing counsel of the court to settle and approve a proper deed or instrument, to be executed by all the necessary parties, and may, if it thinks fit, suspend the pronouncing of the decree until the deed or instrument has been duly executed.*

(*2*) *In any such case as aforesaid the court may, if it thinks fit by order, either in addition to or instead of an order under subsection (1) of this section, direct the husband to pay to the wife during the joint lives of the husband and wife such monthly or weekly sum for her maintenance and support as the court may think reasonable:*

Provided that—

    (*a*) *if the husband, after any such order has been made, becomes from any cause unable to make the payments, the court may discharge or modify the order, or temporarily suspend the order as to the whole or any part of the money ordered to be paid, and subsequently revive it wholly or in part as the court thinks fit; and*

    (*b*) *where the court has made any such order as is mentioned in this subsection and the court is satisfied that the means of the husband have increased, the court may, if it thinks fit, increase the amount payable under the order.*

Note. Words 'Provided that' to end of subsection repealed by Administration of Justice (Miscellaneous Provisions) Act 1938, s 20, Fourth Schedule.

Remainder of sub-s (2), and sub-s (1) repealed, and replaced by Matrimonial Causes Act 1950, s 34(1), Schedule. See now Matrimonial Causes Act 1973, s 23 (p 2513), replacing Matrimonial Proceedings and Property Act 1970, s 2 (p 2365), replacing Matrimonial Causes Act 1965, ss 16(1), (2), 19 (pp 2247, 2248), replacing Matrimonial Causes Act 1950, s 19(2), (3) (p 2138, 2139).

(*3*) *On any petition for divorce or nullity of marriage the court shall have the same power to make interim orders for the payment of money by way of alimony or otherwise to the wife as the court has in proceedings for judicial separation.*

Note. Repealed by Matrimonial Causes Act 1950, s 34(1), Schedule. See now Matrimonial Causes Act 1973, s 22 (p 2510) replacing Matrimonial Proceedings and Property Act 1970, s 1 (p 2365), replacing Matrimonial Causes Act 1965, s 15 (p 2246), replacing Matrimonial Causes Act 1950, ss 19(1), 20(1), 22(1) (pp 2138, 2139).

(4) *Where any decree for restitution of conjugal rights or judicial separation is made on the application of the wife, the court may make such order for alimony as the court thinks just.*

Note. Repealed by Matrimonial Causes Act 1950, s 34(1), Schedule and replaced by ibid, ss 20(2), 22(2) (p 2139), which were replaced by Matrimonial Causes Act 1965, s 20(1) (p 2248) (replaced by Matrimonial Proceedings and Property Act 1970, ss 2, 21(1) (pp 2365, 2376) (repealed but not replaced by ibid, ss 20, 42(2), Sch 3). See now Matrimonial Causes Act 1973, s 23 (p 2513).

(5) *In all cases where the court makes an order for alimony, the court may direct the alimony to be paid either to the wife or to a trustee approved by the court on her behalf, and may impose such terms or restrictions as the court thinks expedient, and may from time to time appoint a new trustee if for any reason it appears to the court expedient so to do.*

Note. Repealed by Matrimonial Causes Act 1950, s 34(1), Schedule and replaced by ibid, s 27(1) (p 2141), replaced by Matrimonial Causes Act 1965, s 30(1) (p 2256), which was repealed but not replaced by Matrimonial Proceedings and Property Act 1970, s 42(2), Sch 3.

For former statutory provisions, see Matrimonial Causes Act 1857, ss 17, 24 (pp 2004, 2005); Matrimonial Causes Act 1907, s 1 (p 2035). See also Matrimonial Causes Act 1937, s 10 (p 2098).

191. Power of court to order settlement of wife's property—(*1*) *If it appears to the court in any case in which the court pronounces a decree for divorce or for judicial separation by reason of the adultery, [desertion, or cruelty] of the wife that the wife is entitled to any property either in possession or reversion, the court may, if it thinks fit, order such settlement as it thinks reasonable to be made of the property, or any part thereof, for the benefit of the innocent party, and of the children of the marriage or any or either of them.*

Any instrument made under any order of the court made under this section shall be valid and effectual, notwithstanding the existence of coverture at the time of the execution thereof.

Note. Words in square brackets inserted by Matrimonial Causes Act 1937, s 10(3).

Repealed by Matrimonial Causes Act 1950, s 34(1), Schedule. See now Matrimonial Causes Act 1973, s 24 (p 2516), replacing Matrimonial Proceedings and Property Act 1970, s 4 (p 2366), replacing Matrimonial Causes Act 1965, ss 17(2), 20(2) (pp 2248, 2249), replacing Matrimonial Causes Act 1950, s 24(1) (p 2251).

For former statutory provisions, see Matrimonial Causes Act 1857, s 45 (p 2010); Matrimonial Causes Act 1860, ss 6, 7 (p 2020). See also Matrimonial Causes Act 1937, s 10 (p 2098), and Administration of Justice (Miscellaneous Provisions) Act 1938.

(*2*) *Where the application for restitution of conjugal rights is by the husband, and it appears to the court that the wife is entitled to any property, either in possession or reversion, or is in receipt of any profits of trade or earnings, the court may, if it thinks fit, order a settlement to be made to the satisfaction of the court of the property or any part thereof for the benefit of the petitioner and of the children of the marriage or either or any of them or may order such part of the profits of trade or earnings, as the court thinks reasonable, to be periodically paid by the respondent to the petitioner for his own benefit, or to the petitioner or any other person for the benefit of the children of the marriage, or either or any of them.*

Note. Repealed by Matrimonial Causes Act 1950, s 34(1), Schedule, and replaced by ibid, s 24(2) (p 2140), which was replaced by Matrimonial Causes Act 1965, s 21(3) (p 2249), which was finally repealed but not replaced by Matrimonial Proceedings and Property Act 1970, ss 20, 42(2), Sch 3.

For former statutory provision, see Matrimonial Causes Act 1884, s 3 (p 2033).

192. Power of court to make order as to application of settled property. *The court may after pronouncing a decree for divorce or for nullity of marriage inquire into the existence of ante-nuptial or post-nuptial settlements made on the parties whose marriage is the subject of the decree, and may make such orders with reference to the application of the whole or any part of the property settled either for the benefit of the children of the marriage or of the* *parties to the marriage, as the court thinks fit, and the court may exercise the powers conferred by this subsection notwithstanding that there are no children of the marriage.*

Note. Repealed by Matrimonial Causes Act 1950, s 34(1), Schedule. See now Matrimonial Causes Act 1973, ss 24, 52(1) (pp 2515, 2559), replacing Matrimonial Proceedings and Property Act 1970, ss 4, 27(1) (pp 2366, 2378), replacing Matrimonial Causes Act 1965, ss 17(1), 19, 46(2) (pp 2247, 2248, 2265), replacing Matrimonial Causes Act 1950, s 25 (p 2141).

For former statutory provisions, see Matrimonial Causes Act 1859, s 5 (p 2018); Matrimonial Causes Act 1878, s 3 (p 2028). See also Matrimonial Causes Act 1937, s 10 (p 2098).

193. Custody of children—(*1*) *In any proceedings for divorce or nullity of marriage or judicial separation, the court may from time to time, either before or by or after the final decree, make such provision as appears just with respect to the custody, maintenance and education of the children, the marriage of whose parents is the subject of the proceedings, or, if it thinks fit, direct proper proceedings to be taken for placing the children under the protection of the court.*

Note. Repealed by Matrimonial Causes Act 1950, s 34(1), Schedule. See now Matrimonial Causes Act 1973, ss 23, 42, 52(1) (pp 2512, 2551, 2559), replacing Matrimonial Proceedings and Property Act 1970, ss 3, 18, 27(1) (pp 2365, 2375, 2378), replacing Matrimonial Causes Act 1965, ss 34(1), (4), 46(2) (pp 2258, 2259, 2265), replacing Matrimonial Causes Act 1950, s 26(1) (p 2141).

For former statutory provisions, see Matrimonial Causes Act 1857, s 35 (p 2008); Matrimonial Causes Act 1859, s 4 (p 2018). See also Guardianship of Minors Act 1971, s 1 and Guardianship Act 1973.

(*2*) *On an application made in that behalf the court may, at any time before final decree, in any proceedings for restitution of conjugal rights, or, if the respondent fails to comply therewith, after final decree, make from time to time all such orders and provisions with respect to the custody, maintenance and education of the children of the petitioner and respondent as might have been made by interim orders if proceedings for judicial separation had been pending between the same parties.*

[(*3*) *The court may, if it thinks fit, on any decree of divorce or nullity of marriage, order the husband, or (in the case of a petition for divorce by a wife on the ground of her husband's insanity) order the wife, to secure for the benefit of the children such gross sum of money or annual sum of money as the court may deem reasonable, and the court may for that purpose order that it shall be referred to one of the conveyancing counsel of the court to settle and approve a proper deed or instrument to be executed by all necessary parties:*

Provided that the term for which any sum of money is secured for the benefit of a child shall not extend beyond the date when the child will attain twenty-one years of age.]

Note. Sub-s (3) added by Matrimonial Causes Act 1937, s 10(4). Section as amended repealed by Matrimonial Causes Act 1950, s 34(1), Schedule, re-enacted by ibid, s 26(2), (3) (p 2141), replaced by Matrimonial Causes Act 1965, ss 34(1), (3), (4), 46(2) (pp 2258, 2259, 2265). See Matrimonial Proceedings and Property Act 1970, ss 3, 18, 20 (abolition of right to claim restitution of conjugal rights), 27(1), 42(2), Sch 3 (pp 2365, 2375, 2376, 2378, 2383, 2388), replaced by Matrimonial Causes Act 1973, ss 23, 42, 52 and the notes thereto (pp 2513, 2551, 2559).

See also Matrimonial Causes Act 1973, s 10(1) (p 2502).

For former statutory provision, see Matrimonial Causes Act 1884, s 6 (p 2034). See also Guardianship of Minors Act 1971, s 1 and Guardianship Act 1973.

194. Wife's property in a case of judicial separation—(*1*) *In every case of judicial separation*—

(*a*) *the wife shall, as from the date of the decree and so long as the separation continue, be considered as a feme sole with respect to any property which she may acquire or which may devolve upon her, and any such property may be disposed of by her in all respects as a feme sole and if she dies intestate shall devolve as if her husband had been then dead; and*

(*b*) *the wife shall, during the separation, be considered as a feme sole for the purpose of contract and wrongs and injuries, and of suing and being sued, and the husband shall not be liable in respect of her contracts or for any wrongful act or omission by her or for any costs she incurs as plaintiff or defendant:*

Provided that—

   (*i*)   *where on any judicial separation alimony has been ordered to be paid and has not been duly paid by the husband, he shall be liable for necessaries supplied for the use of the wife;*

  (*ii*)   *if the wife returns to cohabitation with her husband, any property to which she is entitled at the date of her return shall, subject to any agreement in writing made between herself and her husband while separate, be her separate property;*

 (*iii*)   *nothing in this section shall prevent the wife from joining at any time during the separation in the exercise of any joint power given to herself and her husband.*

[(*1*) *In every case of judicial separation—*

   (*a*)   *as from the date of the decree and so long as the separation continues any property which is acquired by or devolves upon the wife shall not be affected by any restraint upon anticipation attached to the enjoyment by the wife of any property under any settlement, agreement for a settlement, will, or other instrument; and if she dies intestate shall devolve as if her husband had been then dead;*

   (*b*)   *if alimony has been ordered to be paid and has not been duly paid by the husband he shall be liable for necessaries supplied for the use of the wife.*]

Note. New sub-s (1) in square brackets substituted by Law Reform (Married Women and Tortfeasors) Act 1935, s 5(1), Sch 1, and para (a) of the substituted subsection replaced by Married Women (Restraint Upon Anticipation) Act 1949, s 1(2), Sch 1 (pp 2128, 2129): 'any property which is acquired by or devolves upon the wife on or after the date of the decree whilst the separation continues shall, if she dies intestate, devolve as if her husband had then been dead'.

The amended and substituted subsection repealed by Matrimonial Causes Act 1950, s 34(1), Schedule and replaced by ibid, s 21(1) (p 2139), replaced by Matrimonial Causes Act 1965, s 20(3), (4) (p 2249), which was repealed (with saving for s 20(3)) by Matrimonial Proceedings and Property Act 1970, s 42(2), Sch 3 (pp 2383, 2388). See now Matrimonial Causes Act 1973, s 18(2) (p 2507), replacing s 40(1) of the Act of 1970 (p 2389).

(*2*) *In any case where the decree for judicial separation is obtained by the wife, any property to which she is entitled for an estate in remainder or reversion at the date of the decree, and any property to which she becomes entitled as executrix, administratrix or trustee after the date of the decree, shall be deemed to be property to which this section applies, and for the purpose aforesaid the death of the testator or intestate shall be deemed to be the date when the wife became entitled as executrix or administratrix.*

Note. Repealed and replaced by Matrimonial Causes Act 1950, s 21(2) (p 2139), replaced by Matrimonial Causes Act 1965, s 20(3) (p 2249), which was repealed (with saving) by Matrimonial Proceedings and Property Act 1970, s 42(2), Sch 3 (pp 2383, 2388).

For former statutory provisions, see Matrimonial Causes Act 1857, ss 25, 26 (pp 2005, 2006); Matrimonial Causes Act 1858, ss 7, 8 (p 2015).

195. Protection of third parties—(*1*) *Where a wife obtains a decree for judicial separation, the decree shall, so far as may be necessary for the protection of any person dealing with the wife, be valid and effectual until discharged, and the discharge or variation of the decree shall not affect any rights or remedies which any person would have had, if the decree had not been discharged or varied, in respect of any debts, contracts or acts of the wife incurred, entered into or done during the period between the date of the decree and the discharge or variation thereof.*

(*2*) *Any person who, in reliance on any such decree as aforesaid, makes any payment to or permits any transfer or act to be made or done by the wife, shall, notwithstanding the subsequent discharge or variation of the decree, or the fact that the separation has ceased or has been discontinued, be protected and indemnified in the same way in all respects as if at the time of the payment, transfer or other act the decree were valid and still subsisting without variation in full force and effect, or the separation had not ceased or been discontinued, as the case may be, unless at that time that person had notice of the discharge or variation of the decree or that the separation had ceased or been discontinued.*

Note. Repealed by Matrimonial Causes Act 1950, Schedule.

For former statutory provisions, see Matrimonial Causes Act 1858, ss 8, 10 (pp 2133, 2134).

196. Power to vary orders. *The court may from time to time vary or modify any order for the periodical payment of money made under the provisions of this Act relating to matrimonial causes and matters either by altering the times of payment or by increasing or diminishing the amount, or may temporarily suspend the order as to the whole or any part of the money ordered to be paid, and subsequently revive it wholly or in part, as the court thinks just.*

Note. Repealed by Administration of Justice (Miscellaneous Provisions) Act 1938, s 20, Sch 4. See now Matrimonial Causes Act 1973, s 31 (p 2536), replacing Matrimonial Proceedings and Property Act 1970, s 9 (p 2370), replacing Matrimonial Causes Act 1965, s 31 (p 2257), replacing Matrimonial Causes Act 1950, s 28 (p 2142), replacing Administration of Justice (Miscellaneous Provisions) Act 1938, s 14.

For former statutory provision, see Matrimonial Causes Act 1884, s 4 (p 2033).

197. Power to allow intervention on terms. *In every case in which any person is charged with adultery with any party to a suit or in which the court may consider, in the interest of any person not already a party to the suit, that that person should be made a party to the suit, the court may, if it thinks fit, allow that person to intervene upon such terms, if any, as the court thinks just.*

Note. Repealed by Matrimonial Causes Act 1950, s 34(1), Schedule. See now Matrimonial Causes Act 1973, s 49(5) (p 2559), replacing Matrimonial Causes Act 1965, s 44 (p 2265), replacing Matrimonial Causes Act 1950, s 31 (p 2143).

For former statutory provision, see Matrimonial Causes Act 1907, s 3 (p 2036).

198. Evidence. *The parties to any proceedings instituted in consequence of adultery and the husbands and wives of the parties shall be competent to give evidence in the proceedings, but no witness in any such proceedings, whether a party thereto or not, shall be liable to be asked or be bound to answer any question tending to show that he or she has been guilty of adultery unless he or she has already given evidence in the same proceedings in disproof of the alleged adultery.*

Note. Repealed by Matrimonial Causes Act 1950, s 34(1), Schedule, replaced by ibid, s 32(3) (p 2143), replaced by Matrimonial Causes Act 1965, s 43(2) (p 2264) which was repealed by Matrimonial Causes Act 1973, s 54(1), Sch 3, and not replaced.

[198A. *In any proceedings for nullity of marriage, evidence on the question of sexual capacity shall be heard in camera unless in any case the judge is satisfied that in the interests of justice any such evidence ought to be heard in open court.*]

Note. Section 198A added by Supreme Court of Judicature (Amendment) Act 1935, s 4, and repealed and re-enacted by Matrimonial Causes Act 1950 (see ibid, s 32(4), p 2143), replaced by Matrimonial Causes Act 1965, s 43(3) (p 2265), and now replaced by Matrimonial Causes Act 1973, s 48(2) (p 2557).

199. Power of Secretary of State to order records to be transmitted from ecclesiastical courts—(*1*) *A Secretary of State may order any judge, registrar or other officer of any ecclesiastical court in England or the Isle of Man, or any other person having the public custody or control of any records, books, documents or other instruments relating to matrimonial causes and matters to transmit the same at such times, and in such manner, and to such places in London or Westminster, and subject to such regulations, as the Secretary of State may appoint.*

(*2*) *If any person wilfully disobeys an order made under this section he shall for the first offence forfeit the sum of one hundred pounds to be recoverable as a debt in the court by any registrar of the principal probate registry, and for a second or any subsequent offence the court may, by a warrant of committal countersigned by a Secretary of State, commit the person so offending to prison for any period not exceeding three months.*

Note. For former statutory provision, see Matrimonial Causes Act 1857, s 66 (p 2013).

Repealed by Public Records Act 1958, Sch 4: see now para 4(1)(n) of the First Schedule to that Act, which makes the records of the ecclesiastical courts, when exercising testamentary and matrimonial jurisdiction, 'public records'.

200. Seal of court for use in matrimonial causes—(*1*) *The seal of the court to be used in respect of its jurisdiction in matrimonial causes and matters shall be such as the Lord Chancellor may from time to time direct.*

(*2*) *All decrees and orders of the court, or copies thereof, made in pursuance of the said jurisdiction shall, if purporting to be sealed with the said seal, be received in evidence in all parts in the United Kingdom without further proof.*

Note. For former statutory provision, see Matrimonial Causes Act 1857, s 13 (p 2003).

* * * * *

SCHEDULES

FIRST SCHEDULE   Section 99

ENACTMENTS CONTAINING AND REGULATING MATTERS WITH RESPECT TO WHICH RULES OF COURT MAY BE MADE

Session and Chapter	Title or Short Title	Enactments affected
* * *	* * *	* * *
20 & 21 Vict c 85.	The Matrimonial Causes Act 1857.	Sections thirty-nine, forty-one to forty-four, forty-six and forty-nine.
21 & 22 Vict c 93.	The Legitimacy Declaration Act 1858.	Section three.
* * *	* * *	* * *
21 & 22 Vict c 108.	The Matrimonial Causes Act 1858.	Section thirteen.
* * *	* * *	* * *

Note. This Schedule repealed by Supreme Court Act 1981, s 152(4), Sch 7.

SIXTH SCHEDULE

Session and Chapter	Title or Short Title	Enactments affected
* * *	* * *	Sections two, six, seven, twelve, thirteen, sixteen and seventeen, and so far as it relates to the High Court section twenty-one, sections twenty-two to thirty-one, thirty-three to thirty-five, forty-five, fifty-five, fifty-seven, fifty-eight and sixty-six.
20 & 21 Vict c 85.	The Matrimonial Causes Act 1857.	
* * *	* * *	
20 & 22 Vict c 93.	The Legitimacy Declaration Act 1858.	
* * *	* * *	* * *
21 & 22 Vict c 108.	The Matrimonial Causes Act 1858.	The whole Act, except section three and except so far as the Act relates to Scotland.
* * *	* * *	* * *
22 & 23 Vict c 61.	The Matrimonial Causes Act 1859.	Sections four, six to eleven, and fifteen.
* * *	* * *	* * *
23 & 24 Vict c 144.	The Matrimonial Causes Act 1860.	The whole Act.
* * *	* * *	* * *

Session and Chapter	Title or Short Title	Enactments affected
27 & 28 Vict c 44.	The Matrimonial Causes Act 1864.	The whole Act so far as it relates to the High Court.
* * *	* * *	* * *
29 & 30 Vict c 22.	The Matrimonial Causes Act 1866.	The whole Act.
31 & 32 Vict c 77.	The Matrimonial Causes Act 1868.	The whole Act.
32 & 33 Vict c 68.	The Evidence Further Amendment Act 1869.	Section three so far as it relates to the High Court.
* * *	* * *	* * *
36 & 37 Vict c 31.	The Matrimonial Causes Act 1873.	The whole Act.
* * *	* * *	* * *
41 & 42 Vict c 19.	The Matrimonial Causes Act 1878.	The whole Act.
* * *	* * *	* * *
44 & 45 Vict c 68.	The Supreme Court of Judicature Act 1881.	The whole Act except section one and the third and fourth paragraphs of section 9.
* * *	* * *	* * *
47 & 48 Vict c 68.	The Matrimonial Causes Act 1884.	The whole Act.
* * *	* * *	* * *
7 Edw 7 c 12.	The Matrimonial Causes Act 1907.	The whole Act.
* * *	* * *	* * *
13 & 14 Geo 5 c 19.	The Matrimonial Causes Act 1923.	The whole Act.
* * *	* * *	* * *

Note. This Schedule repealed by Supreme Court Act 1981, s 152(4), Sch 7.

JUDICIAL PROCEEDINGS (REGULATION OF REPORTS) ACT 1926

(16 & 17 Geo 5 c 61)

An Act to regulate the publication of reports of judicial proceedings in such manner as to prevent injury to public morals.   [15 December 1926]

1. Restriction on publication of reports of judicial proceedings—(1) It shall not be lawful to print or publish, or cause or procure to be printed or published—
  (a) in relation to any judicial proceedings any indecent matter or indecent medical, surgical or physiological details being matter or details the publication of which would be calculated to injure public morals;
  (b) in relation to [any proceedings under Part II of the Family Law Act 1996 or otherwise in relation to] any judicial proceedings for dissolution of marriage, for nullity of marriage, or for judicial separation, or for restitution of conjugal rights, any particulars other than the following, that is to say—
     (i) the names, addresses and occupations of the parties and witnesses;
     (ii) a concise statement of the charges, defences and countercharges in support of which evidence has been given;

      (iii) submissions on any point of law arising in the course of the proceedings, and the decision of the court thereon;

      (iv) the summing-up of the judge and the finding of the jury (if any) and the judgment of the court and observations made by the judge in giving judgment:

Provided that nothing in this part of this subsection shall be held to permit the publication of anything contrary to the provisions of paragraph (a) of this subsection.

Note. Sub-s (1)(b) extended and modified by Domestic and Appellate Proceedings (Restriction of Publicity) Act 1968, s 2(3) (p 2283). Words in square brackets in sub-s (1)(b) inserted by Family Law Act 1996, s 66(1), Sch 8, Part I, para 2, as from a day to be appointed, subject to savings in s 66(2) of, and para 5 of Sch 9 to, the 1996 Act.

(2) If any person acts in contravention of the provisions of this Act, he shall in respect of each offence be liable, on summary conviction, to imprisonment for a term not exceeding *four months* [51 weeks], or to a fine not exceeding *five hundred pounds* [level 5 on standard scale], or to both such imprisonment and fine:

Provided that no person, other than a proprietor, editor, master printer or publisher, shall be liable to be convicted under this Act.

Note. Reference to level 5 effected by Criminal Justice Act 1982, ss 37, 38(1), (6), 46(1).

Words '51 weeks' in square brackets substituted for words 'four months' by the Criminal Justice Act 2003, s 280(2), (3), Sch 26, para 7, as from a date to be appointed.

(3) No prosecution for an offence under this Act shall be commenced in England and Wales by any person without the sanction of the Attorney-General.

(4) Nothing in this section shall apply to the printing of any pleading, transcript of evidence or other document for use in connection with any judicial proceedings or the communication thereof to persons concerned in the proceedings, or to the printing or publishing of any notice or report in pursuance of the directions of the court; or to the printing or publishing of any matter in any separate volume or part of any bonâ fide series of law reports which does not form part of any other publication and consists solely of reports of proceedings in courts of law, or in any publication of a technical character bonâ fide intended for circulation among members of the legal or medical professions.

(5) [Application to Scotland.]

Note. Cf Magistrates' Courts Act 1980, s 71 (p 2782); and see Administration of Justice Act 1960, s 12 (p 2229), as to publication of information relating to proceedings in private.

2. Short title and extent—(1) This Act may be cited as the Judicial Proceedings (Regulation of Reports) Act 1926.

(2) This Act does not extend to Northern Ireland.

EVIDENCE (FOREIGN, DOMINION AND COLONIAL DOCUMENTS) ACT 1933

(23 & 24 Geo 5 c 4)

An Act to make further and better provision with respect to the admissibility in evidence in the United Kingdom of entries contained in the public registers of other countries and with respect to the proof by means of duly authenticated official certificates of entries in such registers and in consular registers and of other matters.   [29 March 1933]

1. *Proof and effect of foreign, dominion and colonial registers and certain official certificates—*
(1) If, upon consideration of a report from the Lord Chancellor and a Secretary of State, His Majesty in Council is satisfied with respect to any country that, having regard to the law of that country as to the recognition therein of public registers of the United Kingdom as authentic

*records and as to the proof of the contents of such registers and other matters by means of duly authenticated certificates issued by public officers in the United Kingdom, it is desirable in the interests of reciprocity to make with respect to public registers of that country and certificates issued by public officers therein such an Order as is hereinafter mentioned, it shall be lawful for His Majesty in Council to make such an Order accordingly.**

(2) An Order in Council made under *this section* [section 5 of the Oaths and Evidence (Overseas Authorities and Countries) Act 1963] may provide that in all parts of the United Kingdom—

(a) a register of the country to which the Order relates, being such a register as is specified in the Order, shall be deemed to be a public register kept under the authority of the law of that country and recognised by the courts thereof as an authentic record, and to be a document of such a public nature as to be admissible as evidence of the matters regularly recorded therein;

(b) such matters as may be specified in the Order shall, if recorded in such a register, be deemed, until the contrary is proved, to be regularly recorded therein;

(c) subject to any conditions specified in the Order and to any requirements of rules of court a document purporting to be issued in the country to which the Order relates as an official copy of an entry in such a register as is so specified, and purporting to be authenticated as such in the manner specified in the Order as appropriate in the case of such a register, shall, without evidence as to the custody of the register or of inability to produce it and without any further or other proof, be received as evidence that the register contains such an entry;

(d) subject as aforesaid a certificate purporting to be given in the country to which the Order relates as an official certificate of any such class as is specified in the Order, and purporting to be signed by the officer, and to be authenticated in the manner, specified in the Order as appropriate in the case of a certificate of that class, shall be received as evidence of the facts stated in the certificate;

(e) no official document issued in the country to which the Order relates as proof of any matters for the proof of which provision is made by the Order shall, if otherwise admissible in evidence, be inadmissible by reason only that it is not authenticated by the process known as legislation.

(3) Official books of record preserved in a central registry and containing entries copied from original registers may, if those entries were copied by officials in the course of their duty, themselves be treated for the purposes of this section as registers.

(4) In this section the expression 'country' means a Dominion, the Isle of Man, any of the Channel Islands, a British colony or protectorate, a foreign country, a colony or protectorate of a foreign country, or any mandated territory:

Provided that where a part of a country is under both a local and a central legislature, an Order under this section may be made as well with respect to that

---

* The following Orders have been made: SR & O 1933 No 383 (Belgium); 1937 No 515 (France); 1938 No 739 (Australia); 1959 No 1306 (New Zealand); 1961 Nos 2041–2053 (Bahamas, Bermuda, British Guiana, British Honduras, Dominica, Fiji, Gibraltar, Mauritius, St Helena, Sarawak, Tanganyika, Uganda, Zanzibar); 1962 Nos 641–644 (Barbados, Hong Kong, Jamaica, Montserrat); 1962 Nos 2605–2609 (British Antarctic Territory, certain provinces of Canada, Falkland Islands, Seychelles, Sierra Leone); Guernsey (SI 1973 No 610); Isle of Man (SI 1973 No 611); Jersey (SI 1973 No 612); Italy (SI 1973 No 1894); Tonga (SI 1980 No 1523); and Surinam (SI 1981 No 735). SI 1933 No 1073 is amended by Zimbabwe (Independence and Membership of Commonwealth) (Consequential Provisions) Order 1980, SI 1980 No 701, art 7, Schedule, para 4(1). The validity of these Orders is not affected by the repeal of s 1(1): Oaths and Evidence (Overseas Authorities and Countries) Act 1963, s 5(2). See Appendix II (p 2233), where the requirements of the various Orders are set out. For Orders made under Oaths and Evidence (Overseas Authorities and Countries) Act 1963, s 5: see footnote on p 2233.

part, as with respect to all the parts under that central legislature.

(5) *His Majesty in Council may vary or revoke any Order previously made under this section.*

Note. Sub-ss (1), (5) repealed and words in square brackets in sub-s (2) substituted for words in italics by Oaths and Evidence (Overseas Authorities and Countries) Act 1963, s 5.

* * * * *

3. Short title. This Act may be cited as the Evidence (Foreign, Dominion and Colonial Documents) Act 1933.

CHILDREN AND YOUNG PERSONS ACT 1933

(23 & 24 Geo 5 c 12)

An Act to consolidate certain enactments relating to persons under the age of eighteen years. [13 April 1933]

* * * * *

36. Prohibition against children being present in court during trial of other persons. No child (other than an infant in arms) shall be permitted to be present in court during the trial of any other person charged with an offence, or during any proceedings preliminary thereto, except during such time as his presence is required as a witness or otherwise for the purposes of justice [or while the court consents to his presence]; and any child present in court when under this section he is not to be permitted to be so shall be ordered to be removed:

Provided that this section shall not apply to messengers, clerks, and other persons required to attend at any court for purposes connected with their employment.

Note. Words in square brackets inserted by the Access to Justice Act 1999, s 73(1) as from 27 September 1999.

Words from 'Provided that' to 'their employment' repealed by the Access to Justice Act 1999, s 106, Sch 15, Pt III, as from 27 September 1999.

37. Power to clear court while child or young person is giving evidence in certain cases—(1) Where, in any proceedings in relation to an offence against, or any conduct contrary to, decency or morality, a person who, in the opinion of the court is a child or young person is called as a witness, the court may direct that all or any persons, not being members or officers of the court or parties to the case, their counsel or solicitors, or persons otherwise directly concerned with the case, be excluded from the court during the taking of the evidence of that witness:

Provided that nothing in this section shall authorise the exclusion of bona fide representatives of a *newspaper or news agency* [news gathering or reporting organisation].

Note. Words in square brackets substituted for words 'newspaper or news agency' by the Youth Justice and Criminal Evidence Act 1999, s 67(1), Sch 4, para 2(1), (2) as from a date to be appointed.

(2) The powers conferred on a court by this section shall be in addition and without prejudice to any other powers of the court to hear proceedings in camera.

38. Evidence of child of tender years—(*1*) *Where, in any proceedings against any person for any offence, any child of tender years called as a witness does not in the opinion of the court understand the nature of an oath, his evidence may be received, though not given upon oath, if, in the opinion of the court, he is possessed of sufficient intelligence to justify the reception of the evidence, and understands the duty of speaking the truth; and his evidence, though not given on oath, but otherwise taken and reduced into writing in accordance with the provisions of section seventeen of the Indictable Offences Act 1848, or of this Part of this Act, shall be deemed to be a deposition within the meaning of that section and that Part respectively:*

Provided that where evidence admitted by virtue of this section is given on behalf of the prosecution the accused shall not be liable to be convicted of the offence unless that evidence is corroborated by some other material evidence in support thereof implicating him.

(2) If any child whose evidence is received as aforesaid [unsworn in any proceedings for an offence by virtue of section 52 of the Criminal Justice Act 1991] wilfully gives false evidence in such circumstances that he would, if the evidence had been given on oath, have been guilty of perjury, he shall be liable on summary conviction to be dealt with as if he had been summarily convicted of an indictable offence punishable in the case of an adult with imprisonment.

Note. Sub-s (1) repealed by Criminal Justice Act 1991, s 101(2), Sch 13, as from 1 October 1992. Proviso to sub-s (1) repealed by Criminal Justice Act 1988, ss 34(1), 170(2), Sch 16, except in relation to proceedings before a magistrates' court acting as examining justices, or to a trial, which began before 12 October 1988. Words in square brackets in sub-s (2) substituted for words in italics by Criminal Justice Act 1991, s 100, Sch 11, para 1, as from 1 October 1992.

Remainder repealed by the Youth Justice and Criminal Evidence Act 1999, s 67(3), Sch 6, as from a date to be appointed.

39. Power to prohibit publication of certain matter in newspapers—(1) In relation to any proceedings in any court ... the court may direct that—

(a) no newspaper report of the proceedings shall reveal the name, address, or school, or include any particulars calculated to lead to the identification, of any child or young person concerned in the proceedings, either as being the person [by or against] or in respect of whom the proceedings are taken, or as being a witness therein;

(b) no picture shall be published in any newspaper as being or including a picture of any child or young person so concerned in the proceedings as aforesaid; except in so far (if at all) as may be permitted by the direction of the court.

(2) Any person who publishes any matter in contravention of any such direction shall on summary conviction be liable in respect of each offence to a fine not exceeding *£500* [level 5 on the standard scale].

[(3) In this section 'proceedings' means proceedings other than criminal proceedings.]

Note. In sub-s (1) words omitted repealed by Children and Young Persons Act 1963, ss 57(1), 64(3), Sch 5, and words in square brackets substituted by s 57(1) of that Act. Reference to level 5 substituted by virtue of Criminal Justice Act 1982, ss 39, 46, Sch 3.

Sub-s (3) inserted by the Youth Justice and Criminal Evidence Act 1999, s 48, Sch 2, paras 1, 2, Sch 7, para 1(2) as from a date to be appointed.

Special Procedure with regard to Offences specified in First Schedule

40. Warrant to search for or remove a child or young person—(*1*) *If it appears to a justice of the peace on information on oath laid by any person who, in the opinion of the justice, is acting in the interests of a child or young person, that there is reasonable cause to suspect—*

(*a*) *that the child or young person has been or is being assaulted, ill-treated, or neglected in any place within the jurisdiction of the justice, in a manner likely to cause him unnecessary suffering, or injury to health; or*

(*b*) *that any offence mentioned in the First Schedule to this Act has been or is being committed in respect of the child or young person,*

the justice may issue a warrant authorising any constable named therein to search for the child or young person, and, if it is found that he has been or is being assaulted, ill-treated, or neglected in manner aforesaid, or that any such offence as aforesaid has been or is being committed in respect of him [to take him to a place of safety, or authorising any constable to remove him with or without search to a place of safety, and a child or young person taken to a place of safety in pursuance of such a warrant may be detained there] until he can be brought before a juvenile court.

(*2*) *A justice issuing a warrant under this section may by the same warrant cause any person accused of any offence in respect of the child or young person to be apprehended and brought before a court of summary jurisdiction, and proceedings to be taken against him according to law.*

(*3*) *Any constable authorised by warrant under this section to search for any child or young person, or to remove any child or young person with or without search, may enter (if need be by force) any house, building, or other place specified in the warrant, and may remove him therefrom.*

(*4*) *Every warrant issued under this section shall be addressed to and executed by a constable, who shall be accompanied by the person laying the information, if that person so desires, unless the justice by whom the warrant is issued otherwise directs, and may also, if the justice by whom the warrant is issued so directs, be accompanied by a duly qualified medical practitioner.*

(*5*) *It shall not be necessary in any information or warrant under this section to name the child or young person.*

Note. This section repealed by Children Act 1989, s 108(4), (7), Sch 12, para 3, Sch 15, as from 14 October 1991. For transitional provisions, see Sch 14, paras 1, 27, to that Act (pp 3427, 3438). Words 'named herein' in sub-s (1) and words 'addressed to and' in sub-s (4) repealed by Police and Criminal Evidence Act 1984, s 119(2), Sch 7, Part I. Words in square brackets in sub-s (1) substituted by Children and Young Persons Act 1963, s 64(1), Sch 3, para 11.

41. Power to proceed with case in absence of child or young person. Where in any proceedings with relation to any of the offences mentioned in the First Schedule to this Act, the court is satisfied that the attendance before the court of any child or young person in respect of whom the offence is alleged to have been committed is not essential to the just hearing of the case, the case may be proceeded with and determined in the absence of the child or young person.

42. Extension of power to take deposition of child or young person—(1) Where a justice of the peace is satisfied by the evidence of a duly qualified medical practitioner that the attendance before the court of any child or young person in respect of whom any of the offences mentioned in the First Schedule to this Act is alleged to have been committed would involve serious danger to his life or health, the justice may take in writing the deposition of the child or young person on oath, and shall thereupon subscribe the deposition and add thereto a statement of his reason for taking it and of the day when and place where it was taken, and of the names of the persons (if any) present at the taking thereof.

(2) The justice taking any such deposition shall transmit it with his statement—

(a) if the deposition relates to an offence for which any accused person is already *committed* [sent] for trial, to the proper officer of the court for trial at which the accused person has been *committed* [sent]; and

(b) in any other case, to the *clerk* [proper officer] of the court before which proceedings are pending in respect of the offence.

Note. Words in square brackets in sub-s (2)(a) substituted for words 'committed' in both places they occur by the Criminal Justice Act 2003, s 41, Sch 3, Pt 2, para 33, as from a date to be appointed.

Words in square brackets in sub-s (2)(b) substituted for word 'clerk' by the Access to Justice Act 1999, s 90, Sch 13, paras 8, 9, as from 1 April 2001 (SI 2001 No 916).

43. Admission of deposition of child or young person in evidence. Where, in any proceedings in respect of any of the offences mentioned in the First Schedule to this Act, the court is satisfied by the evidence of a duly qualified medical practitioner that the attendance before the court of any child or young person in respect of whom the offence is alleged to have been committed would involve serious danger to his life or health, any deposition of the child or young person taken under the Indictable Offences Act 1848, or this Part of this Act, shall be admissible in evidence either for or against the accused person without further proof thereof if it purports to be signed by the justice by or before whom it purports to be taken:

Provided that the deposition shall not be admissible in evidence against the accused person unless it is proved that reasonable notice of the intention to take the deposition has been served upon him and that he or his counsel or solicitor had, or might have had if he had chosen to be present, an opportunity of cross-examining the child or young person making the deposition.

Principles to be observed by all Courts in dealing with Children and Young Persons

44. General considerations—(1) Every court in dealing with a child or young person who is brought before it, either as ... an offender or otherwise, shall have regard to the welfare of the child or young person and shall in a proper case take steps for removing him from undesirable surroundings, and for securing proper provision is made for his education and training.

(2) ...

Note. Words omitted from sub-s (1) and whole of sub-s (2) repealed by Children and Young Persons Act 1969, s 72(4), Sch 6. Children Act 1989, s 1 (p 3205) provides that when a court determines any question with respect to the upbringing of a child or the administration of a child's property or the application of any income arising from it, the child's welfare shall be the court's paramount consideration.

Juvenile Courts

45. Constitution of juvenile courts—[(1)] *Courts of summary jurisdiction constituted in accordance with the provisions of the Second Schedule to this Act and sitting for the purpose of hearing any charge against a child or young person or for the purpose of exercising any other jurisdiction conferred on juvenile courts [youth courts] by or under this or any other Act, shall be known as juvenile courts [youth courts] and in whatever place sitting shall be deemed to be petty sessional courts.*

[(2) The justices' chief executive appointed by a magistrates' courts committee is the justices' chief executive for every youth court for their area].

Note. Sub-s (1) numbered as such by the Access to Justice Act 1999, s 90, Sch 13, paras 8, 9 as from 1 April 2001 (SI 2001 No 916).

In sub-s (1), words in square brackets substituted for words in italics by Criminal Justice Act 1991, s 100, Sch 11, para 40(1), (2)(a), as from 1 October 1991.

Sub-s (2) inserted by the Access to Justice Act 1999, s 90, Sch 13, paras 8, 10, as from 1 April 2001 (SI 2001 No 916).

[45. Youth courts—(1) Magistrates' courts—
  (a) constituted in accordance with this section or section 66 of the Courts Act 2003 (judges having powers of District Judges (Magistrates' Courts)), and
  (b) sitting for the purpose of—
    (i) hearing any charge against a child or young person, or
    (ii) exercising any other jurisdiction conferred on youth courts by or under this or any other Act,
are to be known as youth courts.

(2) A justice of the peace is not qualified to sit as a member of a youth court for the purpose of dealing with any proceedings unless he has an authorisation extending to the proceedings.

(3) He has an authorisation extending to the proceedings only if he has been authorised by the Lord Chancellor or a person acting on his behalf to sit as a member of the youth court to deal with—
  (a) proceedings of that description, or
  (b) all proceedings dealt with by youth courts.

(4) The Lord Chancellor may by rules make provision about—
  (a) the grant and revocation of authorisations,
  (b) the appointment of chairmen of youth courts, and
  (c) the composition of youth courts.

(5) Rules under subsection (4) may confer powers on the Lord Chancellor with respect to any of the matters specified in the rules.

(6) Rules under subsection (4) may be made only after consultation with the Criminal Procedure Rule Committee.

(7) Rules under subsection (4) are to be made by statutory instrument.

(8) A statutory instrument containing rules under subsection (4) is subject to annulment in pursuance of a resolution in either House of Parliament.]

Note. Section 45 in square brackets substituted for s 45 in italics by the Courts Act 2003, s 50(1), Sch 9, para 13, as from a date to be appointed.

* * * * *

49. Restrictions on newspaper reports of proceedings in juvenile courts—
(*1*) *Subject as hereinafter provided, no newspaper report of any proceedings in a juvenile court shall reveal the name, address or school, or include any particulars calculated to lead to the identification, of any child or young person concerned in those proceedings, either as being the person against or in respect of whom the proceedings are taken or as being a witness therein, nor shall any picture be published in any newspaper as being or including a picture of any child or young person so concerned in any such proceedings as aforesaid:*

Provided that the court or the Secretary of State may in any case, if satisfied that it is [*appropriate to do so for the purpose of avoiding injustice to a child or young person*]*, by order dispense with the requirements of this section* [*in relation to him*] *to such extent as may be specified in the order.*

(*2*) *Any person who publishes any matter in contravention of this section shall on summary conviction be liable in respect of each offence to a fine not exceeding £500* [*level 5 on the standard scale*].

Note. Words in square brackets in sub-s (1) substituted and inserted, respectively, by Children and Young Persons Act 1969, s 10(1). In sub-s (2) reference to level 5 substituted by virtue of Criminal Justice Act 1982, ss 39, 46, Sch 3. Fine previously increased to £500 by Criminal Law Act 1977, s 31, Sch 6.

[**49. Restrictions on reports of proceedings in which children or young persons are concerned—**(*1*) *The following prohibitions apply (subject to subsection (5) below) in relation to any proceedings to which this section applies, that is to say—*
  (*a*) *no report shall be published which reveals the name, address or school of any child or young person concerned in the proceedings or includes any particulars likely to lead to the identification of any child or young person concerned in the proceedings; and*
  (*b*) *no picture shall be published or included in a programme service as being or including a picture of any child or young person concerned in the proceedings.*

[(1) No matter relating to any child or young person concerned in proceedings to which this section applies shall while he is under the age of 18 be included in any publication if it is likely to lead members of the public to identify him as someone concerned in the proceedings.]

(2) The proceedings to which this section applies are—
  (a) proceedings in a youth court;
  (b) proceedings on appeal from a youth court (including proceedings by way of case stated);
  (c) proceedings under *section 15 or 16 of the Children and Young Persons Act 1969* [Schedule 7 to the Powers of Criminal Courts (Sentencing) Act 2000] (proceedings for varying or revoking supervision orders); and
  (d) proceedings on appeal from a magistrates' court arising out of proceedings under *section 15 or 16 of that Act* [Schedule 7 to that Act] (including proceedings by way of case stated).

(*3*) *The reports to which this section applies are reports in a newspaper and reports included in a programme service; and similarly as respects pictures.*

[(3) In this section 'publication' includes any speech, writing, relevant programme or other communication in whatever form, which is addressed to the public at large or any section of the public (and for this purpose every relevant programme shall be taken to be so addressed), but does not include an indictment or other document prepared for use in particular legal proceedings.

(3A) The matters relating to a person in relation to which the restrictions imposed by subsection (1) above apply (if their inclusion in any publication is likely to have the result mentioned in that subsection) include in particular—

    (a) his name,

    (b) his address,

    (c) the identity of any school or other educational establishment attended by him,

    (d) the identity of any place of work, and

    (e) any still or moving picture of him.]

(4) For the purposes of this section a child or young person is 'concerned' in any proceedings *whether as being the person against or in respect of whom the proceedings are taken or as being a witness in the proceedings* [if he is—

    (a) a person against or in respect of whom the proceedings are taken, or

    (b) a person called, or proposed to be called, to give evidence in the proceedings.]

[(4A) If a court is satisfied that it is in the public interest to do so, it may, in relation to a child or young person who has been convicted of an offence, by order dispense to any specified extent with the *requirements of this section* [restrictions imposed by subsection (1) above] in relation to any proceedings before it to which this section applies by virtue of subsection (2)(a) or (b) above, being proceedings relating to—

    (a) the prosecution or conviction of the offender for the offence;

    (b) the manner in which he, or his parent or guardian, should be dealt with in respect of the offence;

    (c) the enforcement, amendment, variation, revocation or discharge of any order made in respect of the offence;

    (d) where an attendance centre order is made in respect of the offence, the enforcement of any such rules made under *section 16(3) of the Criminal Justice Act 1982* [*section 62(3) of the Powers of Criminal Courts (Sentencing) Act 2000*] [section 222(1)(d) or (e) of the Criminal Justice Act 2003]; or

    (e) where a secure training order is so made, the enforcement of any requirements imposed under section 3(7) of the Criminal Justice and Public Order Act 1994;

    [(e) where a detention and training order is made, the enforcement of any requirements imposed under *section 76(6)(b) of the Crime and Disorder Act 1998* [section 103(6)(b) of the Powers of Criminal Courts (Sentencing) Act 2000].]

(4B) A court shall not exercise its power under subsection (4A) above without—

    (a) affording the parties to the proceedings an opportunity to make representations; and

    (b) taking into account any representations which are duly made.]

(5) Subject to subsection (7) below, a court may, in relation to proceedings before it to which this section applies, by order dispense to any specified extent with the requirements of this section in relation to a child or young person who is concerned in the proceedings if it is satisfied—

    (a) that it is appropriate to do so for the purpose of avoiding injustice to the child or young person; or

    (b) that, as respects a child or young person to whom this paragraph applies who is unlawfully at large, it is necessary to dispense with those requirements for the purpose of apprehending him and bringing him before a court or returning him to the place in which he was in custody.

(6) Paragraph (b) of subsection (5) above applies to any child or young person who is charged with or has been convicted of—

    (a) a violent offence,

    (b) a sexual offence,

    (c) an offence punishable in the case of a person aged *21* [18] or over with imprisonment for fourteen years or more.

(7) The court shall not exercise its power under subsection (5)(b) above—

(a) except in pursuance of an application by or on behalf of the Director of Public Prosecutions; and

(b) unless notice of the application has been given by the Director of Public Prosecutions to any legal representative of the child or young person.

(8) The court's power under subsection [(4A) or] (5) above may be exercised by a single justice.

(9) If a report or picture is published or included in a programme service in contravention of subsection (1) above, the following persons, that is to say—

(a) in the case of publication of a written report or a picture as part of a newspaper, any proprietor, editor or publisher of the newspaper;

(b) in the case of the inclusion of a report or picture in a programme service, any body corporate which provides the service and any person having functions in relation to the programme corresponding to those of an editor of a newspaper,

shall be liable on summary conviction to a fine not exceeding level 5 on the standard scale.

[(9) If a publication includes any matter in contravention of subsection (1) above, the following persons shall be guilty of an offence and liable on summary conviction to a fine not exceeding level 5 on the standard scale—

(a) where the publication is a newspaper or periodical, any proprietor, any editor and any publisher of the newspaper or periodical;

(b) where the publication is a relevant programme—

(i) any body corporate or Scottish partnership engaged in providing the programme service in which the programme is included; and

(ii) any person having functions in relation to the programme corresponding to those of an editor of a newspaper;

(c) in the case of any other publication, any person publishing it.

(9A) Where a person is charged with an offence under subsection (9) above it shall be a defence to prove that at the time of the alleged offence he was not aware, and neither suspected nor had reason to suspect, that the publication included the matter in question.

(9B) If an offence under subsection (9) above committed by a body corporate is proved—

(a) to have been committed with the consent or connivance of, or

(b) to be attributable to any neglect on the part of,

an officer, the officer as well as the body corporate is guilty of the offence and liable to be proceeded against and punished accordingly.

(9C) In subsection (9B) above 'officer' means a director, manager, secretary or other similar officer of the body, or a person purporting to act in any such capacity.

(9D) If the affairs of a body corporate are managed by its members, 'director' in subsection (9C) above means a member of that body.

(9E) Where an offence under subsection (9) above is committed but a Scottish partnership and is proved to have been committed with the consent or connivance of a partner, he as well as the partnership shall be guilty of the offence and shall be liable to be proceeded against and punished accordingly.]

(10) In any proceedings under *section 15 or 16 of the Children and Young Persons Act 1969* [Schedule 7 to the Powers of Criminal Courts (Sentencing) Act 2000] (proceedings for varying or revoking supervision orders) before a magistrates' court other than a youth court or on appeal from such a court it shall be the duty of the magistrates' court or the appellate court to announce in the course of the proceedings that this section applies to the proceedings; and if the court fails to do so this section shall not apply to the proceedings.

(11) In this section—

'legal representative' means an authorised advocate or authorised litigator, as defined by section 119(1) of the Courts and Legal Services Act 1990;

'programme' and 'programme service' have the same meaning as in the Broadcasting Act 1990;

['picture' includes a likeness however produced; 'relevant programme' means a programme included in a programme service, within the meaning of the Broadcasting Act 1990;]

'sexual offence' *has the same meaning as in section 31(1) of the Criminal Justice Act 1991* [*the Powers of Criminal Courts (Sentencing) Act 2000*] [means an offence listed in Part 2 of Schedule 15 to the Criminal Justice Act 2003];

'specified' means specified in an order under this section;

'violent offence' *has the same meaning as in section 31(1) of the Criminal Justice Act 1991* [*The Powers of Criminal Court (Sentencing) Act 2000*] [means an offence listed in Part 1 of Schedule 15 to the Criminal Justice Act 2003];

and a person who, having been granted bail, is liable to arrest (whether with or without a warrant) shall be treated as unlawfully at large.

[(12) This section extends to England and Wales, Scotland and Northern Ireland, but no reference in this section to any court includes a court in Scotland.

(13) In its application to Northern Ireland, this section has effect as if—

(a) in subsection (1) for the reference to the age of 18 there were substituted a reference to the age of 17;

(b) subsection (2)(c) and (d) were omitted;

(c) in subsection (4A)—

(i) in paragraph (d) for the reference to section 16(3) of the Criminal Justice Act 1982 [section 62(3) of the Powers of Criminal Courts (Sentencing) Act 2000] there were substituted a reference to Article 50(3) of the Criminal Justice (Children) (Northern Ireland) Order 1998; and

(ii) in paragraph (e) for the references to a detention and training order and to section 76(6)(b) of the Crime and Disorder Act 1998 [section 103(6)(b) of the Powers of Criminal Courts (Sentencing) Act 2000] there were substituted references to a juvenile justice centre order and to Article 40(2) of the Criminal Justice (Children) (Northern Ireland) Order 1998;

(d) in subsection (5) for references to a court (other than the reference in paragraph (b)) there were substituted references to a court or the Secretary of State;

(e) in subsection (7)—

(i) for the references to the Director of Public Prosecutions there were substituted references to the Director of Public Prosecutions for Northern Ireland; and

(ii) in paragraph (b) for the reference to any legal representative of the child or young person there were substituted a reference to any barrister or solicitor acting for the child or young person;

(f) subsections (8) and (10) were omitted; and

(g) in subsection (11)—

(i) the definition of 'legal representative' were omitted; and

(ii) for the references to section 31(1) of the Criminal Justice Act 1991 [the Powers of Criminal Courts (Sentencing) Act 2000] there were substituted references to Article 2(2) of the Criminal Justice (Northern Ireland) Order 1996.

(14) References in this section to a young person concerned in proceedings are, where the proceedings are in a court in Northern Ireland, to a person who has attained the age of 14 but is under the age of 17.]]

Note. Section 49 in square brackets substituted for s 49 in italics by Criminal Justice and Public Order Act 1994, s 49, as from 3 February 1995.

Sub-s (1) substituted by the Youth Justice and Criminal Evidence Act 1999, s 48, Sch 2, paras 1, 3(1), (2), as from a date to be appointed.

In sub-s (2)(c) words in square brackets substituted for words 'section 15 or 16 of the Children and Young Persons Act 1969' in italics by the Powers of Criminal Courts (Sentencing) Act 2000, s 165(1), Sch 9, para 2(1), (2)(a), as from 25 August 2000.

In sub-s (2)(d) words in square brackets substituted for words 'section 15 or 16 of that Act' in italics by the Powers of Criminal Courts (Sentencing) Act 2000, s 165(1), Sch 9, para 2(1), (2)(b), as from 25 August 2000.

Sub-ss (3), (3A) substituted for sub-ss (3) by the Youth Justice and Criminal Evidence Act 1999, s 48, Sch 2, paras 1, 3(1), (3), as from a date to be appointed.

In sub-s (4) words in square brackets substituted for words from 'whether as being' to 'in the proceedings' in italics by the Youth Justice and Criminal Evidence Act 1999, s 48, Sch 2, pras 1, 3(1), (4), as from a date to be a appointed.

Sub-ss (4A), (4B): inserted by the Crime (Sentences) Act 1997, s 45, as from 1 October 1997 (SI 1997 No 2200).

In sub-s (4A) words in square brackets substituted for words 'requirements of this section' in italics by the Youth Justice and Criminal Evidence Act 1999, s 48, Sch 2, paras 1, 3(1), (5), as from a date to be appointed.

In sub-s (4A)(d) words in square brackets substituted for words 'section 16(3) of the Criminal Justice Act 1982' in italics by the Powers of Criminal Courts (Sentencing) Act 2000, s 165(1), Sch 9, para 2(1), (3)(a), as from 25 August 2000.

In sub-s (4A)(d) words in square brackets substituted for words 'section 62(3) of the Powers of Criminal Courts (Sentencing) Act 2000' in italics by the Criminal Justice Act 2003, s 304, Sch 32, Pt 1, para 2(1), (2), as from a date to be appointed.

Sub-s (4A)(e) substituted by the Crime and Disorder Act 1998, s 119, Sch 8, para 1, as from 1 April 2000, (SI 1999/3426).

In sub-s (4A)(e) words in square brackets substituted for words 'section 76(6)(b) of the Crime and Disorder Act 1998' in italics by the Powers of Criminal Courts (Sentencing) Act 2000, s 165(1), Sch 9, para 2(1), (3)(b), as from 25 August 2000.

In sub-s (6)(c) number in square brackets substituted for number '21' in italics by the Criminal Justice and Court Services Act 2000, s 74, Sch 7, Pt II, para 5, as from a date to be appointed.

In sub-s (8) words in square brackets inserted by the Youth Justice and Criminal Evidence Act 1999, s 48, Sch 2, paras 1, 3(1), (6), as from a date to be appointed.

Sub-ss (9), (9A)–(9E) substituted for sub-s (9) by the Youth Justice and Criminal Evidence Act 1999, s 48, Sch 2, paras 1, 3(1), (7), as from a date to be appointed.

In sub-s (10) words in square brackets substituted for words 'section 15 or 16 of the Children and Young Persons Act 1969' in italics by the Powers of Criminal Courts (Sentencing) Act 2000, s 165(1), Sch 9, para 2(1), (4), as from 25 August 2000.

In sub-s (11) definitions 'picture' and 'relevant programme' in square brackets substituted for definition 'programme' and 'programme service' in italics by the Youth Justice and Criminal Evidence Act 1999, s 48, Sch 2, paras 1, 3(1), (8), as from a date to be appointed.

In sub-s (11) in definition 'sexual offence' second words in square brackets substituted for words 'has the same meaning as in the Powers of Criminal Courts (Sentencing) Act 2000' in italics by the Criminal Justice Act 2003, s 304, Sch 32, Pt 1, para 2(1), (3)(a), as from a date to be appointed.

In sub-s (11) in definition 'sexual offence' first words in square brckets substituted for words 'section 31(1) of the Criminal Justice Act 1991' initalics by the Powers of Criminal Courts (Sentencing) Act 2000, s 165(1), Sch 9, para 2(1), (5), as from 25 August 2000.

In sub-s (11) in definition 'violent offence' second words in square brackets substituted for words 'has the same meaning as in the Powers of Criminal Courts (Sentencing) Act 2000' in italics by the Criminal Justice Act 2003, s 304, Sch 32, Pt 1, para 2(1), (3)(b), as from a date to be appointed.

In sub-s (11) in definition 'violent offence' first words in square brackets substituted for words 'section 31(1) of the Criminal Justice Act 1991' in italics by the Powers of Criminal Courts (Sentencing) Act 2000, s 165(1), Sch 9, para 2(1), (5), as from 25 August 2000.

Sub-ss (12)–(14) inserted by the Youth Justice and Criminal Evidence Act 1999, s 48, Sch 2, paras 1, 3(1), (9) (as amended, in the case of sub-s (13), by the Powers of Criminal Courts (Sentencing) Act 2000, s 165(1), Sch 9, para 205, as from a date in force to be appointed.

Juvenile Offenders

50. Age of criminal responsibility. It shall be conclusively presumed that no child under the age of [ten] years can be guilty of any offence.

Note. Word in square brackets substituted by Children and Young Persons Act 1963, s 16(1).

Section as originally enacted provided that it should be conclusively presumed that no child under the age of eight could be guilty of any offence, thereby raising the then age of criminal responsibility by one year.

A similar presumption exists in the case of sexual and unnatural offences by boys under the age of fourteen years. In the case of other crimes by an infant between the ages of ten and fourteen years the presumption of incapacity may be rebutted.

Under Children and Young Persons Act 1963, s 16(2) in any proceedings for an offence committed by a person of or over the age of twenty-one any offence of which he was found guilty while under fourteen is to be disregarded for the purposes of any evidence relating to his previous convictions.

*   *   *   *   *

PART VI   SUPPLEMENTAL

Local Authorities

96. Provisions as to local authorities—(1) Subject to the modifications here-inafter contained as to the City of London, where any powers or duties are by [Part II of this Act] conferred or imposed on local authorities (by that description), those powers and duties shall ... be powers and duties of local education authorities ...

[(1A) The local authorities for the purposes of Parts III and IV of this Act shall be the councils of counties (other than metropolitan counties), of metropolitan districts and of London boroughs and the Common Council of the City of London [but, in relation to Wales, shall be the councils of counties and county boroughs].]

(2) ...

(3) Expenses incurred by a local authority in connection with powers and duties which are, under this Act, exercised and performed by them as local education authorities [shall be defrayed as expenses under the enactments relating to education].

(4) Expenses incurred under this Act by the council of a county or county borough, exclusive of any expenses to be defrayed [in accordance with] the last foregoing subsection ... shall be defrayed—

(a) ...

(b) ... as expenses for general county purposes or, as the case may be, out of the general rate.

[(4A) Subsection (4) does not apply in relation to the council of any Welsh county or county borough.]

(5), (6) ...

(7) [Subject to the provisions of [sections 2 and 3 of the Local Authority Social Services Act 1970 (which require certain matters to be referred to the social services committee and restrict the reference of other matters to that committee)]] a local authority may refer to a committee appointed for the purposes of this Act, or to any committee appointed for the purposes of any other Act, any matter relating to the exercise by the authority of any of their powers under this Act and may delegate any of the said powers (other than any power to borrow money) to any such committee.

(8) A local authority, or a committee to whom any powers of a local authority under this Act have been delegated, may by resolution empower the clerk or the chief education officer of the authority to exercise in the name of the authority in any case which appears to him to be one of urgency any powers of the authority or, as the case may be, of the committee with respect to the institution of proceedings under this Act.

Note. In sub-s (1) words in square brackets substituted by Children Act 1948, s 60(2), Sch 3, and words omitted repealed by Education Act 1944, s 121, Sch 9, Part I.

Sub-s (1A) inserted by Child Care Act 1980, s 89(2), Sch 5, para 1; sub-s (2) repealed and words in square brackets in sub-s (3) substituted by Education Act 1944, s 120, Sch 8, Part I.

Words in square brackets in sub-s (1A), and sub-s (4A), added by Local Government (Wales) Act 1994, s 22(4), Sch 10, para 1, as from 1 April 1996.

In sub-s (4) words in square brackets substituted by Education Act 1944, s 120, Sch 8, Part I; words omitted in the first place repealed by Education Act 1944, s 121, Sch 9, Part I, and in the second and third places by National Assistance Act 1948, s 62, Sch 7, Part III.

Sub-s (5) repealed by Acquisition of Land Act 1981, s 34(3), Sch 6, Part II, and sub-s (6) repealed by London Government Act 1963, s 93(1), Sch 18, Part II.

In sub-s (7) words from 'Subject to' to 'that committee' originally inserted by Children Act 1948, s 60(2), Sch 3, further amended by Local Authority Social Services Act 1970, s 14, Sch 2, para 1.

*   *   *   *   *

Supplementary Provisions as to Legal Proceedings

99. Presumption and determination of age—(1) Where a person, whether charged with an offence or not, is brought before any court otherwise than for the purpose of giving evidence, and it appears to the court that he is a child or young person, the court shall make due inquiry as to the age of that person, and for that purpose shall take such evidence as may be forthcoming at the hearing of the case, but an order or judgment of the court shall not be invalidated by any subsequent proof that the age of that person has not been correctly stated to the court, and the age presumed or declared by the court to be the age of the person so brought before it shall, for the purposes of this Act, be deemed to be the true age of that person, and, where it appears to the court that the person so brought before it has attained *the age of seventeen* [the age of eighteen] years, that person shall for the purposes of this Act be deemed not be be a child or young person.

(2) Where in any charge or indictment for any offence under this Act or any of the offences mentioned in the First Schedule to this Act, [except as provided in that Schedule], it is alleged that the person by or in respect of whom the offence was committed was a child or young person or was under or had attained any specified age, and he appears to the court to have been at the date of the commission of the alleged offence a child or young person, or to have been under or to have attained the specified age, as the case may be, he shall for the purposes of this Act be presumed at that date to have been a child or young person or to have been under or to have attained that age, as the case may be, unless the contrary is proved.

(3) Where, in any charge or indictment for any offence under this Act or any of the offences mentioned in the First Schedule to this Act, it is alleged that the person in respect of whom the offence was committed was a child or was a young person, it shall not be a defence to prove that the person alleged to have been a child was a young person or the person alleged to have been a young person was a child in any case where the acts constituting the alleged offence would equally have been an offence if committed in respect of a young person or child respectively.

(4) Where a person is charged with an offence under this Act in respect of a person apparently under a specified age it shall be a defence to prove that the person was actually of or over that age.

Note. Words in square brackets in sub-s (1) substituted for words in italics by Criminal Justice Act 1991, s 68, Sch 8, para 1(2), as from 1 October 1992. Words in square brackets in sub-s (2) substituted by Sexual Offences Act 1956, s 48, Sch 3.

*   *   *   *   *

101. Application of Summary Jurisdiction Acts—*(1) Subject to the provisions of this Act, all orders of a court of summary jurisdiction, whether a petty sessional court or not, under this Act shall be made, and all proceedings in relation to any such orders shall be taken, in manner provided by the Summary Jurisdiction Acts ...*
   (2) ...

Note. Words omitted from sub-s (1) and whole of sub-s (2) repealed by Justices of the Peace Act 1949, s 46(2), Sch 7, Part II. See now Magistrates' Courts Act 1980 (p 2762).
   Remainder repealed by the Courts Act 2003, s 109(1), (3), Sch 8, para 76, Sch 10, as from a date to be appointed.

＊   ＊   ＊   ＊   ＊

107. Interpretation—(1) In this Act, unless the context otherwise requires, the following expressions have the meanings hereby respectively assigned to them, that is to say,—

＊   ＊   ＊   ＊   ＊

   [*'Care order' and 'interim order' have the same meanings as in the Children and Young Persons Act 1969;*]
   'Chief officer of police' [*as regards England has the same meaning as in the Police Act 1964*], as regards Scotland has the same meaning as in [the Police (Scotland) Act 1967], and as regards Northern Ireland means a district inspector of the Royal Ulster Constabulary;
   'Child' means a person under the age of fourteen years;
   'Guardian', in relation to a child or young person, includes any person who, in the opinion of the court having cognisance of any case in relation to the child or young person or in which the child or young person is concerned, has for the time being the *charge of or control over* [care of] the child or young person;

＊   ＊   ＊   ＊   ＊

   'Intoxicating liquor' [has the same meaning as in the Licensing Act 1964];
   'Legal guardian' in relation to a child or young person, means a person appointed, according to law, to be his guardian by deed or will, or by order of a court of competent jurisdiction;
   ['Legal guardian', in relation to a child or young person, means a guardian of a child as defined in the Children Act 1989;]

＊   ＊   ＊   ＊   ＊

   'Place of safety' means [a community home provided by a local authority or a controlled community home] any police station, or any hospital, surgery, or any other suitable place, the occupier of which is willing temporarily to receive a child or young person;

＊   ＊   ＊   ＊   ＊

   'Prescribed' means prescribed by regulations made by the Secretary of State;
   'Public place' includes any public park, garden, sea beach or railway station, and any ground to which the public for the time being have or are permitted to have access, whether on payment or otherwise;

＊   ＊   ＊   ＊   ＊

   'Street' includes any highway and any public bridge, road, lane, footway, square, court, alley or passage, whether a thoroughfare or not;
   'Young person' means a person who has attained the age of fourteen years and is under the age of seventeen years.
   ['Young person' means a person who has attained the age of fourteen and is under the age of eighteen years.]
   (2) ...

(3) References in this Act to any enactment or to any provision in any enactment shall, unless the context otherwise requires, be construed as references to that enactment or provision as amended by any subsequent enactment including this Act.

Note. Definitions omitted from sub-s (1) repealed by National Assistance Act 1948, s 62, Sch 7, Part III; Children and Young Persons Act 1963, s 64(3), Sch 5; Police Act 1964, s 64(3), Sch 10; Children and Young Persons Act 1969, s 72(4), Sch 6; Child Care Act 1980, s 89(3), Sch 6; and Statute Law (Repeals) Act 1986.

Definitions 'care order' and 'interim order' inserted by Children and Young Persons Act 1969, s 72(3), Sch 5, para 12, repealed by Children Act 1989, s 108(7), Sch 15, as from 14 October 1991; in the definition 'chief officer of police' the words in the first square brackets substituted by Police Act 1964, s 63, Sch 9, repealed by Police Act 1996, s 103(3), Sch 9, Part I, as from 22 August 1996, and words in second square brackets substituted by Police (Scotland) Act 1967, ss 52, 53, Sch 4; words in square brackets in definition 'guardian' substituted for words in italics, and definition 'legal guardian' in square brackets substituted for that definition in italics by Children Act 1989, s 108(5), Sch 13, para 7, as from 14 October 1991; words in square brackets in definition 'intoxicating liquor' substituted by Finance Act 1967, s 5(1)(e); and words in square brackets in the definition 'place of safety' substituted by Children and Young Persons Act 1969, s 72(3), Sch 5, para 12. Definition 'young person' in square brackets substituted for that definition in italics by Criminal Justice Act 1991, s 68, Sch 8, para 1(3), as from 1 October 1992.

Sub-s (2) repealed by Children and Young Persons Act 1969, s 72(3), (4), Sch 5, para 12, Sch 6.

$$* \quad * \quad * \quad * \quad *$$

109. Short title, commencement, extent and repeals—(1) This Act may be cited as the Children and Young Persons Act 1933.

SCHEDULE 1

OFFENCES AGAINST CHILDREN AND YOUNG PERSONS WITH RESPECT TO WHICH SPECIAL PROVISIONS OF THIS ACT APPLY

Sections 13, 14, 15, 40, 41, 42, 43, 63, 67, 99, 108

The murder or manslaughter of a child or young person.

Infanticide.

Any offence under sections twenty-seven, ... or fifty-six of the Offences against the Person Act 1861, and any offence against a child or young person under sections five, ..., ... of that Act

[Common assault, or battery.]

Any offence under sections one, ... three, four, eleven or twenty-three of this Act.

[Any offence against a child or young person under any of the following sections of the Sexual Offences Act 1956, that is to say sections two to seven, ten to sixteen, nineteen, twenty, twenty-two to twenty-six and twenty-eight, and any attempt to commit against a child or young person an offence under section two, five, six, seven, ten, eleven, twelve, twenty-two or twenty-three of that Act:

Provided that for the purposes of subsection (2) of section ninety-nine of this Act this entry shall apply so far only as it relates to offences under sections ten, eleven, twelve, fourteen, fifteen, sixteen, twenty and twenty-eight of the Sexual Offences Act 1956, and attempts to commit offences under sections ten, eleven and twelve of that Act.]

[Any offence against a child or young person under any of sections 1 to 41, 47 to 53, 57 to 61, 66 and 67 of the Sexual Offences Act 2003, or any attempt to commit such an offence.

Any offence under section 62 or 63 of the Sexual Offences Act 2003 where the intended offence was an offence against a child or young person, or any attempt to commit such an offence.]

Any other offence involving bodily injury to a child or young person.

Note. First, third, fourth and final words omitted repealed by the Sexual Offences Act 1956, s 51, Sch 4.

Second words omitted repealed by the Criminal Justice Act 1988, s 170(2), Sch 16.

Words 'Common assault, or battery.' in square brackets inserted by the Criminal Justice Act 1988, s 170(1), Sch 15, para 8.

Words from 'Any offence against' to 'such an offence.' in square brackets substituted for words from 'Any offence against' to 'of that Act.' in italics by the Sexual Offences Act 2003, s 139, Sch 6, para 7, as from 1 May 2004, (SI 2004/874).

FOREIGN JUDGMENTS (RECIPROCAL ENFORCEMENT) ACT 1933

(23 & 24 Geo 5 c 13)

An Act to make provision for the enforcement in the United Kingdom of judgments given in foreign countries which accord reciprocal treatment to judgments given in the United Kingdom, for facilitating the enforcement in foreign countries of judgments given in the United Kingdom, and for other purposes in connection with the matters aforesaid.   [13 April 1933]

Note. For procedure under this Act, see RSC Ord 71, r 13.

For modification of Part I of this Act, see Administration of Justice Act 1956, s 51 (p 2186).

PART I*

Registration of Foreign Judgments

1. Power to extend Part I of Act to foreign countries giving reciprocal treatment—(*1*) *His Majesty, if he is satisfied that, in the event of the benefits conferred by this Part of this Act being extended to judgments given in the superior courts of any foreign country, substantial reciprocity of treatment will be assured as respects the enforcement in that foreign country of judgments given in the superior courts of the United Kingdom, may by Order in Council direct—*

    (*a*) *that this Part of this Act shall extend to that foreign country; and*

    (*b*) *that such courts of that foreign country as are specified in the Order shall be deemed superior courts of that country for the purposes of this Part of this Act.*

    (*2*) *Any judgment of a superior court of a foreign country to which this Part of this Act extends, other than a judgment of such a court given on appeal from a court which is not a superior court, shall be a judgment to which this Part of this Act applies, if—*

    (*a*) *it is final and conclusive as between the parties thereto; and*

    (*b*) *there is payable thereunder a sum of money, not being a sum payable in respect of taxes or other charges of a like nature or in respect of a fine or other penalty; and*

    (*c*) *it is given after the coming into operation of the Order in Council directing that this Part of this Act shall extend to that foreign country.*

[(1) If, in the case of any foreign country, Her Majesty is satisfied that, in the event of the benefits conferred by this Part of this Act being extended to, or to any

---

* Part I of the Act has been applied to the Dominions, etc, by Reciprocal Enforcement of Judgments (General Application to His Majesty's Dominions, etc) Order 1933 (SR & O 1933 No 1073); Pakistan (SI 1958 No 141); India (SI 1958 No 425); Norway (SI 1962 No 636); Austria (SI 1962 No 1339); Israel (SI 1971 No 1039); Guernsey (SI 1973 No 610); Isle of Man (SI 1973 No 611); Jersey (SI 1973 No 612); Italy (SI 1973 No 1894); Tonga (SI 1980 No 1523); Suriname (SI 1981 No 735); Canada (SI 1987 No 468, as amended by SI 1987 No 2211, SI 1988 No 1304, SI 1988 No 1853, SI 1989 No 987 and SI 1991 No 1724); Reciprocal Enforcement of Judgments (Australian) Order 1994 (SI 1994 No 1901).

particular class of, judgments given in the courts of that country or in any particular class of those courts, substantial reciprocity of treatment will be assured as regards the enforcement in that country of similar judgments given in similar courts of the United Kingdom, She may by Order in Council direct—

   (a) that this Part of this Act shall extend to that country;
   (b) that such courts of that country as are specified in the Order shall be recognised courts of that country for the purposes of this Part of this Act; and
   (c) that judgments of any such recognised court, or such judgments of any class so specified, shall, if within subsection (2) of this section, be judgments to which this Part of this Act applies.

   (2) Subject to subsection (2A) of this section, a judgment of a recognised court is within this subsection if it satisfies the following conditions, namely—

   (a) it is either final and conclusive as between the judgment debtor and the judgment creditor or requires the former to make an interim payment to the latter; and
   (b) there is payable under it a sum of money, not being a sum payable in respect of taxes or other charges of a like nature or in respect of a fine or other penalty; and
   (c) it is given after the coming into force of the Order in Council which made that court a recognised court.

   (2A) The following judgments of a recognised court are not within subsection (2) of this section—

   (a) a judgment given by that court on appeal from a court which is not a recognised court;
   (b) a judgment or other instrument which is regarded for the purposes of its enforcement as a judgment of that court but which was given or made in another country;
   (c) a judgment given by that court in proceedings founded on a judgment of a court in another country and having as their object the enforcement of that judgment.]

Note. Sub-ss (1), (2), (2A) in square brackets substituted for sub-ss (1), (2) in italics by Civil Jurisdiction and Judgments Act 1982, s 35(1), Sch 10, para 1(1), (2), as from 14 November 1986.

   (3) For the purposes of this section, a judgment shall be deemed to be final and conclusive notwithstanding that an appeal may be pending against it, or that it may still be subject to appeal, in the courts of the country of the original court.

   (4) His Majesty may by a subsequent Order in Council vary or revoke any Order previously made under this section.

   [(5) Any Order in Council made under this section before its amendment by the Civil Jurisdiction and Judgments Act 1982 which deems any court of a foreign country to be a superior court of that country for the purposes of this Part of this Act shall (without prejudice to subsection (4) of this section) have effect from the time of that amendment as if it provided for that court to be a recognised court of that country for those purposes, and for any final and conclusive judgment of that court, if within subsection (2) of this section, to be a judgment to which this Part of this Act applies.]

Note. Sub-s (5) added by Civil Jurisdiction and Judgments Act 1982, s 35(1), Sch 10, para 1(3), as from 1 January 1987.

2. Application for, and effect of, registration of foreign judgment—(1) A person, being a judgment creditor under a judgment to which this Part of this Act applies, may apply to the High Court at any time within six years after the date of the judgment, or, where there have been proceedings by way of appeal against the judgment, after the date of the last judgment given in those proceedings, to have the judgment registered in the High Court, and on any such application the court shall, subject to proof of the prescribed matters and to the other provisions of this Act, order the judgment to be registered:

Provided that a judgment shall not be registered if at the date of the application—

(a) it has been wholly satisfied; or

(b) it could not be enforced by execution in the country of the original court.

(2) Subject to the provisions of this Act with respect to the setting aside of registration—

(a) a registered judgment shall, for the purposes of execution, be of the same force and effect; and

(b) proceedings may be taken on a registered judgment; and

(c) the sum for which a judgment is registered shall carry interest; and

(d) the registering court shall have the same control over the execution of a registered judgment;

as if the judgment had been a judgment originally given in the registering court and entered on the date of registration:

Provided that execution shall not issue on the judgment so long as, under this Part of this Act and the Rules of Court made thereunder, it is competent for any party to make an application to have the registration of the judgment set aside, or, where such an application is made, until after the application has been finally determined.

(3) Where the sum payable under a judgment which is to be registered is expressed in a currency other than the currency of the United Kingdom, the judgment shall be registered as if it were a judgment for such sum in the currency of the United Kingdom as, on the basis of the rate of exchange prevailing at the date of the judgment of the original court, is equivalent to the sum so payable.

Note. Sub-s (3) repealed by Administration of Justice Act 1977, ss 4, 32(4), Sch 5.

(4) If at the date of the application for registration the judgment of the original court has been partly satisfied, the judgment shall not be registered in respect of the whole sum payable under the judgment of the original court, but only in respect of the balance remaining payable at that date.

(5) If, on an application for the registration of a judgment, it appears to the registering court that the judgment is in respect of different matters and that some, but not all, of the provisions of the judgment are such that if those provisions had been contained in separate judgments those judgments could properly have been registered, the judgment may be registered in respect of the provisions aforesaid but not in respect of any other provisions contained therein.

(6) In addition to the sum of money payable under the judgment of the original court, including any interest which by the law of the country of the original court becomes due under the judgment up to the time of registration, the judgment shall be registered for the reasonable costs of and incidental to registration, including the costs of obtaining a certified copy of the judgment from the original court.

3.—(1) The power to make *rules of court under section ninety-nine of the Supreme Court of Judicature (Consolidation) Act 1925 [84 of the Supreme Court Act 1981]* [Civil Procedure Rules], shall, subject to the provisions of this section, include power to make rules for the following purposes—

Note. Words in square brackets substituted in relation to England and Wales for words 'rules of court under section 84 of the Supreme Court Act 1981' in italics by the Courts Act 2003, s 109(1), Sch 8, para 78, as from a date to be appointed. Reference to 1981 Act substituted for reference to 1925 Act by Supreme Court Act 1981, s 152(1), Sch 5. For s 84 of that Act, see p 2798.

(a) For making provision with respect to the giving of security for costs by persons applying for the registration of judgments;

(b) For prescribing the matters to be proved on an application for the registration of a judgment and for regulating the mode of proving those matters;

(c) For providing for the service on the judgment debtor of notice of the registration of a judgment;

(d) For making provision with respect to the fixing of the period within which an application may be made to have the registration of the judgment set aside and with respect to the extension of the period so fixed;

(e) For prescribing the method by which any question arising under this Act whether a foreign judgment can be enforced by execution in the country of the original court, or what interest is payable under a foreign judgment under the law of the original court, is to be determined;

(f) For prescribing any matter which under this Part of this Act is to be prescribed.

(2) Rules made for the purposes of this Part of this Act shall be expressed to have, and shall have, effect subject to any such provisions contained in Orders in Council made under section one of this Act as are declared by the said Orders to be necessary for giving effect to the agreements made between His Majesty and foreign countries in relation to matters with respect to which there is power to make rules of court for the purposes of this Part of this Act.

4. Cases in which registered judgments must, or may, be set aside—(1) On an application in that behalf duly made by any party against whom a registered judgment may be enforced, the registration of the judgment—

(a) shall be set aside if the registering court is satisfied—

    (i) that the judgment is not a judgment to which this Part of this Act applies or was registered in contravention of the foregoing provisions of this Act; or

    (ii) that the courts of the country of the original court had no jurisdiction in the circumstances of the case; or

    (iii) that the judgment debtor, being the defendant in the proceedings in the original court, did not (notwithstanding that process may have been duly served on him in accordance with the law of the country of the original court) receive notice of those proceedings in sufficient time to enable him to defend the proceedings and did not appear; or

    (iv) that the judgment was obtained by fraud; or

    (v) that the enforcement of the judgment would be contrary to public policy in the country of the registering court; or

    (vi) that the rights under the judgment are not vested in the person by whom the application for registration was made;

(b) may be set aside if the registering court is satisfied that the matter in dispute in the proceedings in the original court had previously to the date of the judgment in the original court been the subject of a final and conclusive judgment by a court having jurisdiction in the matter.

(2) For the purposes of this section the courts of the country of the original court shall, subject to the provisions of subsection (3) of this section, be deemed to have had jurisdiction—

(a) in the case of a judgment given in an action in personam—

    (i) if the judgment debtor, being a defendant in the original court, submitted to the jurisdiction of that court by voluntarily appearing in the proceedings *otherwise than for the purpose of protecting, or obtaining the release of, property seized, or threatened with seizure, in the proceedings or of contesting the jurisdiction of that court*; or

    (ii) if the judgment debtor was plaintiff in, or counterclaimed in, the proceedings in the original court; or

    (iii) if the judgment debtor, being a defendant in the original court, had before the commencement of the proceedings agreed, in respect of the subject matter of the proceedings, to submit to the jurisdiction of that court or of the courts of the country of that court; or

  (iv) if the judgment debtor, being a defendant in the original court, was at the time when the proceedings were instituted resident in, or being a body corporate had its principal place of business in, the country of that court; or

  (v) if the judgment debtor, being a defendant in the original court, had an office or place of business in the country of that court and the proceedings in that court were in respect of a transaction effected through or at that office or place;

(b) in the case of a judgment given in an action of which the subject matter was immovable property or in an action in rem of which the subject matter was movable property, if the property in question was at the time of the proceedings in the original court situate in the country of that court;

(c) in the case of a judgment given in an action other than any such action as is mentioned in paragraph (a) or paragraph (b) of this subsection, if the jurisdiction of the original court is recognised by the law of the registering court.

(3) Notwithstanding anything in subsection (2) of this section, the courts of the country of the original court shall not be deemed to have had jurisdiction—

(a) if the subject matter of the proceedings was immovable property outside the country of the original court; or

(b) *except in the cases mentioned in sub-paragraphs (i), (ii) and (iii) of paragraph (a) and in paragraph (c) of subsection (2) of this section, if the bringing of the proceedings in the original court was contrary to an agreement under which the dispute in question was to be settled otherwise than by proceedings in the courts of the country of that court; or*

(c) if the judgment debtor, being a defendant in the original proceedings, was a person who under the rules of public international law was entitled to immunity from the jurisdiction of the courts of the country of the original court and did not submit to the jurisdiction of that court.

Note. Words in italics in sub-s (2)(a)(i), and sub-s (3)(b), repealed by Civil Jurisdiction and Judgments Act 1982, s 54, Sch 14, as from 24 August 1982 except in relation to judgments registered under Part I of that Act before that date: s 53(2), Sch 13, Part II, paras 8(2), 9(2).

5. Powers of registering court on application to set aside registration—(1) If, on an application to set aside the registration of a judgment, the applicant satisfies the registering court either that an appeal is pending, or that he is entitled and intends to appeal, against the judgment, the court, if it thinks fit, may, on such terms as it may think just, either set aside the registration or adjourn the application to set aside the registration until after the expiration of such period as appears to the court to be reasonably sufficient to enable the applicant to take the necessary steps to have the appeal disposed of by the competent tribunal.

(2) Where the registration of a judgment is set aside under the last foregoing subsection, or solely for the reason that the judgment was not at the date of the application for registration enforceable by execution in the country of the original court, the setting aside of the registration shall not prejudice a further application to register the judgment when the appeal has been disposed of or if and when the judgment becomes enforceable by execution in that country, as the case may be.

(3) Where the registration of a judgment is set aside solely for the reason that the judgment, notwithstanding that it had at the date of the application for registration been partly satisfied, was registered for the whole sum payable thereunder, the registering court shall, on the application of the judgment creditor, order judgment to be registered for the balance remaining payable at that date.

6. Foreign judgments which can be registered not to be enforceable otherwise. No proceedings for the recovery of a sum payable under a foreign judgment, being a judgment to which this Part of this Act applies, other than proceedings by way of registration of the judgment, shall be entertained by any court in the United Kingdom.

7. Power to apply Part I of Act to British dominions, protectorates and mandated territories—(1) His Majesty may by Order in Council direct that this Part of this Act shall apply to His Majesty's dominions outside the United Kingdom and to judgments obtained in the courts of the said dominions as it applies to foreign countries and judgments obtained in the courts of foreign countries, and, in the event of His Majesty so directing, this Act shall have effect accordingly and Part II of the Administration of Justice Act 1920 shall cease to have effect except in relation to those parts of the said dominions to which it extends at the date of the Order.

Note. See also Reciprocal Enforcement of Judgments (General Application to His Majesty's Dominions, etc) Order 1933 (SR & O 1933 No 1073), amended by Zimbabwe (Independence and Membership of Commonwealth) (Consequential Provisions) Order 1980, SI 1980 No 701, art 7, Schedule, para 4(1).

For Administration of Justice Act 1920, Part. II, see p 2047.

(2) If at any time after His Majesty has directed as aforesaid an Order in Council is made under section one of this Act extending Part I of this Act to any part of His Majesty's dominions to which the said Part II extends as aforesaid, the said Part II shall cease to have effect in relation to that part of His Majesty's dominions.

Note. For Administration of Justice Act 1920, Part II, see p 2047.

(3) References in this section to His Majesty's dominions outside the United Kingdom shall be construed as including references to any territories which are under His Majesty's protection and to any territories in respect of which a mandate under the League of Nations has been accepted by His Majesty.

PART II

Miscellaneous and General

8. General effect of certain foreign judgments—(1) Subject to the provisions of this section, a judgment to which Part I of this Act applies or would have applied if a sum of money had been payable thereunder, whether it can be registered or not, and whether, if it can be registered, it is registered or not, shall be recognised in any court in the United Kingdom as conclusive between the parties thereto in all proceedings founded on the same cause of action and may be relied on by way of defence or counterclaim in any such proceedings.

(2) This section shall not apply in the case of any judgment—

(a) where the judgment has been registered and the registration thereof has been set aside on some ground other than—
   (i) that a sum of money was not payable under the judgment; or
   (ii) that the judgment had been wholly or partly satisfied; or
   (iii) that at the date of the application the judgment could not be enforced by execution in the country of the original court; or

(b) where the judgment has not been registered, it is shown (whether it could have been registered or not) that if it had been registered the registration thereof would have been set aside on an application for that purpose on some ground other than one of the grounds specified in paragraph (a) of this subsection.

(3) Nothing in this section shall be taken to prevent any court in the United Kingdom recognising any judgment as conclusive of any matter of law or fact decided therein if that judgment would have been so recognised before the passing of this Act.

9. Power to make foreign judgments unenforceable in United Kingdom if no reciprocity—(1) If it appears to His Majesty that the treatment in respect of recognition and enforcement accorded by the courts of any foreign country to judgments given in the *superior* courts of the United Kingdom is substantially less favourable than that accorded by the courts of the United Kingdom to judgments of the *superior* courts of that country, His Majesty may by Order in Council apply this section to that country.

Note. 'Superior' repealed in both places where it occurs by Civil Jurisdiction and Judgments Act 1982, ss 35(1), 54, Sch 10, para 2, Sch 14, as from 14 November 1986.

(2) Except in so far as His Majesty may by Order in Council under this section otherwise direct, no proceedings shall be entertained in any court in the United Kingdom for the recovery of any sum alleged to be payable under a judgment given in a court of a country to which this section applies.

(3) His Majesty may by a subsequent Order in Council vary or revoke any Order previously made under this section.

10. Issue of certificates of judgments obtained in the United Kingdom. *Where a judgment under which a sum of money is payable, not being a sum payable in respect of taxes or other charges of a like nature or in respect of a fine or other penalty, has been entered in the High Court against any person and the judgment creditor is desirous of enforcing the judgment in a foreign country to which Part I of this Act applies, the court shall, on an application made by the judgment creditor and on payment of such fee as may be fixed for the purposes of this section under section two hundred and thirteen of the Supreme Court of Judicature (Consolidation) Act 1925 [130 of the Supreme Court Act 1981] issue to the judgment creditor a certified copy of the judgment, together with a certificate containing such particulars with respect to the action, including the causes of action, and the rate of interest, if any, payable on the sum payable under the judgment, as may be prescribed:*
Provided that, where execution of a judgment is stayed for any period pending an appeal or for any other reason, an application shall not be made under this section with respect to the judgment until the expiration of that period.

Note. Reference to Supreme Court Act 1981 substituted for reference to Act of 1925 by Supreme Court Act 1981, s 152(1), Sch 5.

[10. Provision for issue of copies of, and certificates in connection with, UK judgments—(1) Rules may make provision for enabling any judgment creditor wishing to secure the enforcement in a foreign country to which Part I of this Act extends of a judgment to which this subsection applies, to obtain, subject to any conditions specified in the rules—
    (a) a copy of the judgment; and
    (b) a certificate giving particulars relating to the judgment and the proceedings
        in which it was given.
(2) Subsection (1) applies to any judgment given by a court or tribunal in the United Kingdom under which a sum of money is payable, not being a sum payable in respect of taxes or other charges of a like nature or in respect of a fine or other penalty.
(3) In this section 'rules'—
    (a) in relation to judgments given by a court, means rules of court;
    (b) in relation to judgments given by any other tribunal, means rules or
        regulations made by the authority having power to make rules or regulations
        regulating the procedure of that tribunal.]

[10A. Arbitration awards. The provisions of this Act, except sections 1(5) and 6, shall apply, as they apply to a judgment, in relation to an award in proceedings on an arbitration which has, in pursuance of the law in force in the place where it was made, become enforceable in the same manner as a judgment given by a court in that place.]

Note. Section 10 substituted and s 10A inserted (both in square brackets) by Civil Jurisdiction and Judgments Act 1982, s 35(1), Sch 10, paras 3, 4, as from 14 November 1986.

11. Interpretation—(1) In this Act, unless the context otherwise requires, the following expressions have the meanings hereby assigned to them respectively, that is to say—

'Appeal' includes any proceedings by way of discharging or setting aside a judgment or an application for a new trial or a stay of execution;

'Country of the original court' means the country in which the original court is situated;

['Court', except in section 10 of this Act, includes a tribunal;]

'Judgment' means a judgment or order given or made by a court in any civil proceedings, or a judgment or order given or made by a court in any criminal proceedings for the payment of a sum of money in respect of compensation or damages to an injured party;

'Judgment creditor' means the person in whose favour the judgment was given and includes any person in whom the rights under the judgment have become vested by succession or assignment or otherwise;

'Judgment debtor' means the person against whom the judgment was given, and includes any person against whom the judgment is enforceable under the law of the original court;

'*Judgments given in the superior courts of the United Kingdom' means judgments given in the High Court in England, the Court of Session in Scotland, the High Court in Northern Ireland, the Court of Chancery of the County Palatine of Lancaster or the Court of Chancery of the County Palatine of Durham, and includes judgments given in any courts on appeals against any judgments so given;*

'Original court' in relation to any judgment means the court by which the judgment was given;

'Prescribed' means prescribed by rules of court;

'Registration' means registration under Part I of this Act, and the expressions 'register' and 'registered' shall be construed accordingly;

'Registered court' in relation to any judgment means the court to which an application to register the judgment is made.

Note. Words 'the Court of Chancery ... County Palatine of Durham' in definition 'Judgments given in the superior courts of the United Kingdom' repealed by Courts Act 1971, s 56(4), Sch 11, Part II.

Definition 'Court' inserted and definition 'Judgments given in the superior courts of the United Kingdom' repealed by Civil Jurisdiction and Judgments Act 1982, ss 35(1), 54, Sch 10, para 5, Sch 14, as from 14 November 1986.

(2) For the purposes of this Act, the expression 'action in personam' shall not be deemed to include any matrimonial cause or any proceedings in connection with any of the following matters, that is to say, matrimonial matters, administration of the estates of deceased persons, bankruptcy, winding up of companies, lunacy, or guardianship of infants.

12. Application to Scotland. This Act in its application to Scotland shall have effect subject to the following modifications—

(a) For any reference to the High Court (*except in section eleven of this Act*) there shall be substituted a reference to the Court of Session:

(b) The Court of Session shall, subject to the provisions of subsection (2) of section three of this Act, have power by Act of Sederunt to make rules for the purposes specified in subsection (1) of the said section:

(c) Registration under Part I of this Act shall be effected by registering in the Books of Council and Session or in such manner as the Court of Session may by Act of Sederunt prescribe:

(d) *For any reference to section two hundred and thirteen of the Supreme Court of Judicature (Consolidation) Act 1925, there shall be substituted a reference to the Courts of Law Fees (Scotland) Act 1895:*

(e) For any reference to the entering of a judgment there shall be substituted a reference to the signing of the interlocutor embodying the judgment.

Note. Words in italics in para (a) and whole of para (d) repealed by Civil Jurisdiction and Judgments Act 1982, s 54, Sch 14, as from 1 January 1987.

13. Application to Northern Ireland. This Act in its application to Northern Ireland shall have effect subject to the following modifications—

(a) References to the High Court shall, unless the context otherwise requires, be construed as references to the High Court in Northern Ireland:

(b) For the references to section ninety-nine *and section two hundred and thirteen* of the Supreme Court of Judicature (Consolidation) Act 1925, there shall be substituted [*respectively*, reference to sections 55 *and 116* of the Judicature (Northern Ireland) Act 1978].

Note. Words in square brackets substituted by Judicature (Northern Ireland) Act 1978, s 122(1), Sch 5. Words in italics repealed by Civil Jurisdiction and Judgments Act 1982, s 54, Sch 14, as from 1 January 1987.

14. Short title. This Act may be cited as the Foreign Judgments (Reciprocal Enforcement) Act 1933.

ADMINISTRATION OF JUSTICE (MISCELLANEOUS PROVISIONS) ACT 1933

(23 & 24 Geo 5 c 36)

*   *   *   *   *

7. Costs in Crown proceedings—(1) In any civil proceedings to which the Crown is a party in any court having power to award costs in cases between subjects, and in any arbitration to which the Crown is a party, the costs of and incidental to the proceedings shall be in the discretion of the court or arbitrator to be exercised in the same manner and on the same principles as in cases between subjects, and the court or arbitrator shall have power to make an order for the payment of costs by or to the Crown accordingly:

Provided that—

(a) in the case of proceedings to which by reason of any enactment or otherwise the Attorney-General, a Government department or any officer of the Crown as such is required to be made a party, the court or arbitrator shall have regard to the nature of the proceedings and the character and circumstances in which the Attorney-General, the department or officer of the Crown appears, and may in the exercise of its or his discretion order any other party to the proceedings to pay the costs of the Attorney-General, department or officer, whatever may be the result of the proceedings; and

(b) nothing in this section shall affect the power of the court or arbitrator to order, or any enactment providing for, the payment of costs out of any particular fund or property, or any enactment expressly relieving any department or officer of the Crown of the liability to pay costs.

(2) In this section the expression 'civil proceedings' includes *proceedings by petition of right and* proceedings by the Crown in the High Court or a county court for the recovery of fines or penalties, and references to proceedings to which the Crown is a party include references to proceedings to which the Attorney-General or any Government department or any officer of the Crown as such is a party, so, however, that the Crown shall not be deemed to be a party to any proceedings by reason only

that the proceedings are proceedings by the Attorney-General on the relation of some other person.

(*3*) *This section shall apply to proceedings pending at the commencement of this Act.*

*   *   *   *   *

Note. Proceedings by petition of right were abolished by Crown Proceedings Act 1947, s 23, Sch 1, and Petitions of Right Act 1860 was repealed by s 39 of, and Sch 2 to, that Act. Sub-s (3) repealed by Statute Law (Repeals) Act 1993, s 1(1), Sch 1, Part I, as from 5 November 1993.

ADMINISTRATION OF JUSTICE (APPEALS) ACT 1934

(24 & 25 Geo 5 c 40)

An Act to provide that no appeal shall lie from the Court of Appeal to the House of Lords except with the leave of that Court or the House of Lords, to make further provision as respects appeals from county courts, and for purposes connected with the matters aforesaid.   [25 July 1934]

1. Restriction on appeals from Court of Appeal to House of Lords—(1) No appeal shall lie to the House of Lords from any order or judgment made or given by the Court of Appeal after the first day of October nineteen hundred and thirty-four, except with the leave of that Court or of the House of Lords.

(2) The House of Lords may by order provide for the hearing and determination by a Committee of that House of petitions for leave to appeal from the Court of Appeal:

Provided that section five of the Appellate Jurisdiction Act 1876, shall apply to the hearing and determination of any such petition by a Committee of the House as it applies to the hearing and determination of an appeal by the House.

(3) Nothing in this section shall affect any restriction existing, apart from this section, on the bringing of appeals from the Court of Appeal to the House of Lords.

*   *   *   *   *

3. Short title and extent—(1) This Act may be cited as the Administration of Justice (Appeals) Act 1934.

(2) This Act shall not extend to Scotland or Northern Ireland.

SUPREME COURT OF JUDICATURE (AMENDMENT) ACT 1935

(25 Geo 5 c 2)

*   *   *   *   *

4. Certain evidence in nullity proceedings to be in camera. *The principal Act shall have effect as if the following section were inserted after section one hundred and ninety-eight thereof—*

'*198A. In any proceedings for nullity of marriage, evidence on the question of sexual capacity shall be heard in camera unless in any case the judge is satisfied that in the interests of justice any such evidence ought to be heard in open court.*'

Note. Repealed by Matrimonial Causes Act 1950, s 34, Schedule, and replaced by ibid, s 32(4) (p 2143). See now Matrimonial Causes Act 1973, s 48(2) (p 2557), replacing Matrimonial Causes Act 1965, s 43(3) (p 2265).

*   *   *   *   *

LAW REFORM (MARRIED WOMEN AND TORTFEASORS) ACT 1935

(25 & 26 Geo 5 c 30)

*   *   *   *   *

2. Property of married women—(1) Subject to the provisions of this Part of this Act all property which—

   (a)   immediately before the passing of this Act was the separate property of a married woman or held for her separate use in equity; or

   (b)   belongs at the time of her marriage to a woman married after the passing of this Act; or

   (c)   after the passing of this Act is acquired by or devolves upon a married woman,

shall belong to her in all respects as if she were a feme sole and may be disposed of accordingly:

Provided that nothing in this subsection shall interfere with or render inoperative any restriction upon anticipation or alienation attached to the enjoyment of any property by virtue of any provision attaching such a restriction, contained in any Act passed before the passing of this Act, or in any instrument executed before the first day of January, nineteen hundred and thirty-six.

(2) Any instrument executed on or after the first day of January, nineteen hundred and thirty-six, shall, in so far as it purports to attach to the enjoyment of any property by a woman any restriction upon anticipation or alienation which could not have been attached to the enjoyment of that property by a man, be void.

(3) For the purposes of the provisions of this section relating to restrictions upon anticipation or alienation—

   (a)   an instrument attaching such a restriction as aforesaid executed on or after the first day of January, nineteen hundred and thirty-six, in pursuance of an obligation imposed before that date to attach such a restriction shall be deemed to have been executed before the said first day of January;

   (b)   a provision contained in an instrument made in exercise of a special power of appointment shall be deemed to be contained in that instrument only and not in the instrument by which the power was created; and

   (c)   the will of any testator who dies after the thirty-first day of December, nineteen hundred and forty-five, shall (notwithstanding the actual date of the execution thereof) be deemed to have been executed after the first day of January, nineteen hundred and thirty-six.

Note. Word in italics repealed by Married Women (Restraint Upon Anticipation) Act 1949, s 1, Sch 2.

*   *   *   *

4. Savings—(1) Nothing in this Part of this Act shall—

   (a)   during coverture which began before the first day of January, eighteen hundred and eighty-three, affect any property to which the title (whether vested or contingent, and whether in possession, reversion, or remainder) of a married woman accrued before that date, except property held for her separate use in equity;

   (b)   affect any legal proceeding in respect of any tort if proceedings had been instituted in respect thereof before the passing of this Act;

   (c)   enable any judgment or order against a married woman in respect of a contract entered into, or debt or obligation incurred, before the passing of this Act, to be enforced in bankruptcy or to be enforced otherwise than against her property.

(2) For the avoidance of doubt it is hereby declared that nothing in this Part of this Act—

   (a)   renders the husband of a married woman liable in respect of any contract entered into, or debt or obligation incurred, by her after the marriage in respect of which he would not have been liable if this Act had not been passed;

(b) exempts the husband of a married woman from liability in respect of any contract entered into, or debt or obligation (not being a debt or obligation arising out of the commission of a tort) incurred, by her after the marriage in respect of which he would have been liable if this Act had not been passed;

(c) prevents a husband and wife from acquiring, holding, and disposing of, any property jointly or as tenants in common, or from rendering themselves, or being rendered, jointly liable in respect of any tort, contract, debt or obligation, and of suing and being sued either in tort or in contract or otherwise, in like manner as if they were not married;

(d) prevents the exercise of any joint power given to a husband and wife.

*   *   *   *   *

MATRIMONIAL CAUSES ACT 1937*

(1 Edw 8 & 1 Geo 6 c 57)

An Act to amend the law relating to marriage and divorce.   [*30 July 1937*]

* The whole Act, except s 11, repealed by Matrimonial Causes Act 1950, s 34(1), Schedule.

1. Restriction on petitions for divorce during first three years after marriage—
(*1*) *No petition for divorce shall be presented to the High Court unless at the date of the presentation of the petition three years have passed since the date of the marriage:*

Provided that a judge of the High Court may, upon application being made to him in accordance with rules of court, allow a petition to be presented before three years have passed on the ground that the case is one of exceptional hardship suffered by the petitioner or of exceptional depravity on the part of the respondent, but if it appears to the court at the hearing of the petition, that the petitioner obtained leave to present the petition by any misrepresentation or concealment of the nature of the case, the court may, if it pronounces a decree nisi, do so subject to the condition that no application to make the decree absolute shall be made until after the expiration of three years from the date of the marriage, or may dismiss the petition, without prejudice to any petition which may be brought after the expiration of the said three years upon the same, or substantially the same, facts as those proved in support of the petition so dismissed.

(*2*) *In determining any application under this section for leave to present a petition before the expiration of three years from the date of the marriage, the judge shall have regard to the interests of any children of the marriage and to the question whether there is reasonable probability of a reconciliation between the parties before the expiration of the said three years.*

(*3*) *Nothing in this section shall be deemed to prohibit the presentation of a petition based upon matters which have occurred before the expiration of three years from the date of the marriage.*

Note. See now Matrimonial Causes Act 1973, s 3 (p 2449), replacing Matrimonial Causes Act 1965, ss 2, 5(5) (pp 2240, 2242), replacing Matrimonial Causes Act 1950, s 2(1), (2), (3) (p 2131).

This section did not apply to petitions brought under Matrimonial Causes (War Marriages) Act 1944. See Matrimonial Causes Act 1950, s 2(4) (p 2131), repealed by Matrimonial Causes Act 1965.

2. Grounds of petition for divorce. *The following section shall be substituted for section one hundred and seventy-six of the Supreme Court of Judicature (Consolidation) Act 1925 (hereinafter called 'the principal Act')—*

'**176A.** *A petition for divorce may be presented to the High Court (in this part of this Act referred to as 'the Court') either by the husband or the wife on the ground that the respondent—*

(*a*) *has since the celebration of the marriage committed adultery; or*

(*b*) *has deserted the petitioner without cause for a period of at least three years immediately preceding the presentation of the petition; or*

(*c*) *has since the celebration of the marriage treated the petitioner with cruelty; or* (*d*) *is incurably of unsound mind and has been continuously under care and treatment for a period of at least five years immediately preceding the presentation of the petition, and by the wife on the ground that her husband has, since the celebration of the marriage, been guilty of rape, sodomy or bestiality.'*

Note. See now Matrimonial Causes Act 1973, s 1(1), (2) (p 2497), replacing Divorce Reform Act 1969, ss 1, 2(1) (p 2338), replacing Matrimonial Causes Act 1965, s 1(1) (p 2239), replacing Matrimonial Causes Act 1950, s 1(1) (p 2130).

3. Definition of 'care and treatment' in relation to insanity. *For the purposes of section one hundred and seventy-six of the principal Act, as amended by this Act, a person of unsound mind shall be deemed to be under care and treatment—*

Note. For Supreme Court of Judicature (Consolidation) Act 1925, s 176 (repealed), see p 2056.

    (*a*) *while he is detained in pursuance of any order or inquisition under the Lunacy and Mental Treatment Acts 1890 to 1930, or of any order or warrant under the Army Act, the Air Force Act, the Naval Discipline Act, the Naval Enlistment Act 1884 or the Yarmouth Naval Hospital Act 1931, or is being detained as a criminal lunatic or in pursuance of an order made under the Criminal Lunatics Act 1884;*

    (*b*) *while he is receiving treatment as a voluntary patient under the Mental Treatment Act 1930, being treatment which follows without any interval a period of such detention as aforesaid;*

and not otherwise.

Note. Extended by Law Reform (Miscellaneous Provisions) Act 1949, s 3 (repealed).

Repealed and re-enacted by Matrimonial Causes Act 1950, s 1(2) (p 2130), replaced by Matrimonial Causes Act 1965, s 1(3) (p 2240), repealed by Divorce Reform Act 1969, s 9(2), Sch 2 and not replaced.

4. Duty of Court on presentation of petition for divorce. *The following section shall be substituted for section one hundred and seventy-eight of the principal Act—*

    '**178**—(*1*) *On a petition for divorce it shall be the duty of the court to inquire, so far as it reasonably can into the facts alleged and whether there has been any connivance or condonation on the part of the petitioner and whether any collusion exists between the parties and also to inquire into any countercharge which is made against the petitioner.*

    (*2*) *If the court is satisfied on the evidence that—*

    (*i*) *the case for the petition has been proved; and*

    (*ii*) *where the ground of the petition is adultery, the petitioner has not in any manner been accessory to, or connived at, or condoned the adultery, or where the ground of the petition is cruelty the petitioner has not in any manner condoned the cruelty; and*

    (*iii*) *the petition is not presented or prosecuted in collusion with the respondent or either of the respondents,*

the court shall pronounce a decree of divorce, but if the court is not satisfied with respect to any of the aforesaid matters, it shall dismiss the petition:

    Provided that the court shall not be bound to pronounce a decree of divorce and may dismiss the petition if it finds that the petitioner has during the marriage been guilty of adultery or if, in the opinion of the court, the petitioner has been guilty—

    (*a*) *of unreasonable delay in presenting or prosecuting the petition; or*

    (*b*) *of cruelty towards the other party to the marriage; or*

    (*c*) *where the ground of the petition is adultery or cruelty, of having without reasonable excuse deserted, or having without reasonable excuse wilfully separated himself or herself from, the other party before the adultery or cruelty complained of; or*

    (*d*) *where the ground of the petition is adultery or unsoundness of mind or desertion, of such wilful neglect or misconduct as has conduced to the adultery or unsoundness of mind or desertion.'*

Note. Substituted s 178 repealed by Matrimonial Causes Act 1950, s 34(1), Schedule. See now Matrimonial Causes Act 1973, ss 1(3), (4), 2(1), (2) (p 2497, 2498), replacing Divorce Reform Act 1969, ss 2(2), (3), 3(3) (pp 2338, 2339), replacing Matrimonial Causes Act 1965, s 5(1), (3), (4) (p 2241, 2242), replacing Matrimonial Causes Act 1950, s 4 (p 2132), as amended by Matrimonial Causes Act 1963, s 4.

5. Decree of judicial separation. *The following subsections shall be substituted for subsections (1) and (2) of section one hundred and eighty-five of the principal Act:*

'(*1*) *A petition for judicial separation may be presented to the court either by the husband or the wife on any grounds on which a petition for divorce might have been presented, or on the ground of failure to comply with a decree for restitution of conjugal rights or on any ground on which a decree for divorce a mensa et thoro might have been pronounced immediately before the commencement of the Matrimonial Causes Act 1857, and the foregoing provisions of this Part of the Act relating to the duty of the court on the presentation of a petition for divorce, and the circumstances in which such a petition shall or may be granted or dismissed, shall apply in like manner to a petition for judicial separation.*

(*2*) *Where the court in accordance with the said provisions grants a decree of judicial separation, it shall no longer be obligatory for the petitioner to cohabit with the respondent.*'

Note. Repealed by Matrimonial Causes Act 1950, s 34(1), Schedule. See now Matrimonial Causes Act 1973, ss 17, 18 (pp 2506, 2507), replacing Matrimonial Causes Act 1965, s 12 (p 2245), replacing Matrimonial Causes Act 1950, s 14(1), (2) (p 2135).

6. Divorce proceedings after grant of judicial separation or other relief—(*1*) *A person shall not be prevented from presenting a petition for divorce, or the court from pronouncing a decree of divorce, by reason only that the petitioner has at any time been granted a judicial separation or an order under the Summary Jurisdiction (Separation and Maintenance) Acts 1895 to 1925, upon the same or substantially the same facts as those proved in support of the petition for divorce.*

Note. Summary Jurisdiction (Separation and Maintenance) Acts 1895 to 1925 are Summary Jurisdiction (Married Women) Act 1895, Licensing Act 1902, s 5, Married Women (Maintenance) Act 1920, and Summary Jurisdiction (Separation and Maintenance) Act 1925.

(*2*) *On any such petition for divorce, the court may treat the decree of judicial separation or the said order as sufficient proof of the adultery, desertion, or other ground on which it was granted, but the court shall not pronounce a decree of divorce without receiving evidence from the petitioner.*

(*3*) *For the purposes of any petition for divorce, a period of desertion immediately preceding the institution of proceedings for a decree of judicial separation or an order under the said Acts having the effect of such a decree shall, if the parties have not resumed cohabitation and the decree or order has been continuously in force since the granting thereof, be deemed immediately to precede the presentation of the petition for divorce.*

Note. See now Matrimonial Causes Act 1973, s 4 (p 2499), replacing Matrimonial Causes Act 1965, s 3 (p 2240), replacing Matrimonial Causes Act 1950, s 7 (p 2133).

7. New grounds for decree of nullity—(*1*) *In addition to any other grounds on which a marriage is by law void or voidable, a marriage shall be voidable on the ground*—

(*a*) *that the marriage has not been consummated owing to the wilful refusal of the respondent to consummate the marriage; or*

(*b*) *that either party to the marriage was at the time of the marriage of unsound mind or a mental defective within the meaning of the Mental Deficiency Acts 1913 to 1927, or subject to recurrent fits of insanity or epilepsy; or*

(*c*) *that the respondent was at the time of the marriage suffering from venereal disease in a communicable form; or*

(*d*) *that the respondent was at the time of the marriage pregnant by some other person other than the petitioner:*

Provided that, in the cases specified in paragraphs (b), (c) and (d) of this subsection, the court shall not grant a decree unless it is satisfied—

(*i*) *that the petitioner was at the time of the marriage ignorant of the facts alleged;*

(*ii*) *that proceedings were instituted within a year from the date of the marriage; and*

(*iii*) *that marital intercourse with the consent of the petitioner has not taken place since the discovery by the petitioner of the existence of the grounds for a decree.*

Note. Subsection (1) replaced by Matrimonial Causes Act 1950, s 8(1) (p 2133), replaced by Matrimonial Causes Act 1965, s 9(1), (2) (p 2244) which was repealed by Nullity of Marriage Act 1971, s 7(3), except in relation to marriages taking place before 1 August 1971.

(*2*) *Any child born of a marriage avoided pursuant to paragraphs* (*b*) *or* (*c*) *of the last foregoing subsection shall be a legitimate child of the parties thereto notwithstanding that the marriage is so avoided.*

Note. Subsection (2) repealed by Law Reform (Miscellaneous Provisions) Act 1949, s 4(2). See now Matrimonial Causes Act 1973, Sch 1, para 12 (p 2564), replacing Matrimonial Causes Act 1965, s 11 (p 2245), replacing Matrimonial Causes Act 1950, s 9 (p 2133).

(*3*) *Nothing in this section shall be construed as validating any marriage which is by law void, but with respect to which a decree of nullity has not been granted.*

Note. Subsection (3) repealed by Matrimonial Causes Act 1950, s 8(2), replaced by Matrimonial Causes Act 1965, s 9(3) (p 2244), which was repealed by Nullity of Marriage Act 1971, s 7(3), except in relation to marriages taking place before 1 August 1971.

For the grounds on which a marriage celebrated after 31 July 1971 is void or voidable, see Matrimonial Causes Act 1973, ss 11, 12 (pp 2503), replacing Nullity of Marriage Act 1971, ss 1, 2 (pp 2418, 2419).

8. Proceedings for decree of presumption of death and dissolution of marriage—(*1*) *Any married person who alleges that reasonable grounds exist for supposing that the other party to the marriage is dead may present a petition to the court to have it presumed that the other party is dead and to have the marriage dissolved, and the court, if satisfied that such reasonable grounds exist, may make a decree of presumption of death and of dissolution of the marriage.*

(*2*) *In any such proceedings the fact that for a period of seven years or upwards the other party to the marriage has been continually absent from the petitioner, and the petitioner has no reason to believe that the other party has been living within that time, shall be evidence that he or she is dead until the contrary is proved.*

(*3*) *Sections one hundred and eighty-one to one hundred and eighty-four inclusive of the principal Act shall apply to a petition and a decree under this section as they apply to a petition for divorce and a decree of divorce respectively.*

Note. See now Matrimonial Causes Act 1973, s 19 (p 2507), replacing Matrimonial Causes Act 1965, s 14 (p 2246), replacing Matrimonial Causes Act 1950, s 16 (p 2136).

For Supreme Court of Judicature (Consolidation) Act 1925, ss 181–184 (repealed), see pp 2058–2059.

9. Presentation of delay in application for decree absolute. *Section one hundred and eighty-three of the principal Act shall be amended by adding thereto a subsection as follows—*

'(*3*) *Where a decree nisi has been obtained, whether before or after the passing of this Act, and no application for the decree to be made absolute has been made by the party who obtained the decree, then at any time after the expiration of three months from the earliest date on which that party could have made such an application, the party against whom the decree nisi has been granted shall be at liberty to apply to the court and the court shall, on such application, have power to make the decree absolute, reverse the decree nisi, require further inquiry or otherwise deal with the case as the court thinks fit.'*

Note. Repealed by Matrimonial Causes Act 1950, s 34(1), Schedule. See now Matrimonial Causes Act 1973, ss 9(2), 15 (pp 2502, 2505), replacing Matrimonial Causes Act 1965, ss 7(2), 10 (pp 2244, 2245), replacing Matrimonial Causes Act 1950, s 12(3) (p 2134).

10. Amendments as to maintenance, settlement of property, &c.—(*1*) *When a petition for divorce or nullity of marriage has been presented, proceedings under section one hundred and ninety, section one hundred and ninety-one, section one hundred and ninety-two or subsection* (*3*) *of section one hundred and ninety-three of the principal Act* (*which, respectively, confer power on the court to order the provision of alimony, the settlement of the wife's property, the application of property which is the subject of marriage settlements, and the securing of money for the benefit of the children*) *may, subject to and in accordance with rules of court, be commenced at any time after the presentation of the petition:*

Note. For Supreme Court of Judicature (Consolidation) Act 1925, ss 190–192, 193(3) (repealed), see pp 2060–2062.

Provided that no order under any of the said sections or under the said subsection (other than an interim order for the payment of alimony under section one hundred and ninety) shall be made unless and until a decree nisi has been pronounced, and no such order, save in so far as it relates to the preparation, execution, or approval of a deed or instrument and no settlement made in pursuance of any such order, shall take effect unless and until the decree is made absolute.

Note. See now Matrimonial Causes Act 1973, ss 23, 24 (pp 2512, 2515), replacing Matrimonial Proceedings and Property Act 1970, ss 2, 4, 24 (pp 2365, 2366, 2377), replacing Matrimonial Causes Act 1965, ss 18, 19 (p 2248).

(2) The said section one hundred and ninety shall apply in any case where a petition for divorce or judicial separation is presented by the wife on the ground of her husband's insanity as if for the references to the husband there were substituted references to the wife, and for the references to the wife there were substituted references to the husband, and in any such case and in any case where a petition for divorce, nullity, or judicial separation, is presented by the husband on the ground of his wife's insanity or mental deficiency, the court may order the payments of alimony or maintenance under the said section to be made to such persons having charge of the respondent as the court may direct.

Note. See now Matrimonial Causes Act 1973, ss 22, 23, 40 (pp 2510, 2512, 2549), replacing Matrimonial Proceedings and Property Act 1970, ss 1, 2, 26 (pp 2365, 2378), replacing Matrimonial Causes Act 1965, ss 15, 16(3), 20(1), 30 (pp 2246, 2247, 2248, 22566), replacing Matrimonial Causes Act 1950, ss 19(4), 20(3), 27 (pp 2138, 2139, 2141).

For Supreme Court of Judicature (Consolidation) Act 1925, s 190 (repealed), see p 2062.

(3) In subsection (1) of the said section one hundred and ninety-one there shall be inserted after the word 'adultery' the words 'desertion, or cruelty.'

Note. For Supreme Court of Judicature (Consolidation) Act 1925, s 191(1) (repealed), see p 2063.

See now Matrimonial Causes Act 1973, s 24 (p 2516), replacing Matrimonial Proceedings and Property Act 1970, s 4 (p 2366), replacing Matrimonial Causes Act 1965, ss 17(2), 20(2) (pp 2247, 2249), replacing Matrimonial Causes Act 1950, s 24(1) (p 2140).

(4) The following subsection shall be added to section one hundred and ninety-three of the principal Act:

'(3) The court may, if it thinks fit, on any decree of divorce or nullity of marriage, order the husband, or (in the case of a petition for divorce by a wife on the ground of her husband's insanity) order the wife, to secure for the benefit of the children such gross sum of money or annual sum of money as the court may deem reasonable, and the court may for that purpose order that it shall be referred to one of the conveyancing counsel of the court to settle and approve a proper deed or instrument to be executed by all necessary parties:

Provided that the term for which any sum of money is secured for the benefit of a child shall not extend beyond the date when the child will attain twenty-one years of age.'

Note. Repealed by Matrimonial Causes Act 1950, s 34(1), Schedule, re-enacted by ibid, s 26(2), (3) (p 2141). See now Matrimonial Causes Act 1973, s 23 (p 2512), replacing Matrimonial Proceedings and Property Act 1970, s 3 (p 2365), replacing Matrimonial Causes Act 1965, s 34(3) (p 2259), replacing Matrimonial Causes Act 1950, s 26(3) (p 2141).

(5) Section three of the Supreme Court of Judicature (Amendment) Act 1935 shall cease to have effect.

Note. Repealed by Matrimonial Causes Act 1950, s 34, Schedule.

11. Extension of jurisdiction of courts of summary jurisdiction in matrimonial matters—*(1) Among the grounds on which a married woman may apply to a court of summary jurisdiction under the Summary Jurisdiction (Married Women) Act 1895, for an order or orders under that Act there shall be included the ground that her husband has been guilty of adultery.*

(*2*) *A husband shall be entitled to apply to a court of summary jurisdiction for an order on the ground that his wife has been guilty of adultery, and the powers of the court under the Summary Jurisdiction (Separation and Maintenance) Acts 1895 to 1925, shall include power to make, upon any such application, any one or more of the orders set out in section five of the Licensing Act 1902.*

Note. For Summary Jurisdiction (Separation and Maintenance) Acts 1895–1925, see note to s 6(1) (p 2097).

(*3*) *On any application made by virtue of this section, the court shall not make an order unless it is satisfied that the applicant has not condoned or connived at, or by his or her wilful neglect or misconduct conduced to, the adultery, and that the application is not made or prosecuted in collusion with the other party to the marriage or any person with whom it is alleged that adultery has been committed.*

Note. This section repealed by Matrimonial Proceedings (Magistrates' Courts) Act 1960, s 18(1), Schedule, that whole Act being repealed by Domestic Proceedings and Magistrates' Courts' Act 1978, Sch 3.

12. Relief for clergy of Church of England and of Church in Wales. *The following subsection shall be substituted for subsections (2) and (3) of section one hundred and eighty-four of the principal Act—*

'(*2*) *No clergyman of the Church of England or of the Church in Wales shall be compelled to solemnize the marriage of any person whose former marriage has been dissolved on any ground and whose former husband or wife is still living or to permit the marriage of any such person in the Church or Chapel of which he is the minister.*'

Note. Repealed by Matrimonial Causes Act 1950, s 34(1), Schedule. See now Matrimonial Causes Act 1965, s 8(2) (p 2244), replacing Matrimonial Causes Act 1950, s 13(2) (p 2135).

13. Jurisdiction under Part VII of principal Act in case of husband's change of domicile. *Where a wife has been deserted by her husband, or where her husband has been deported from the United Kingdom under any law for the time being in force relating to the deportation of aliens, and the husband was immediately before the desertion or deportation domiciled in England and Wales, the court shall have jurisdiction for the purpose of any proceedings under Part VIII of the principal Act, notwithstanding that the husband has changed his domicile since the desertion or deportation.*

Note. Amended by Law Reform (Miscellaneous Provisions) Act 1949, s 1(4). See now Matrimonial Causes Act 1973, s 46 (p 2555), replacing Matrimonial Causes Act 1965, s 40 (p 2263), replacing Matrimonial Causes Act 1950, s 18 (p 2137).

For Supreme Court of Judicature (Consolidation) Act 1925, Part VIII, see p 2056.

14. Short title, construction, commencement and application—(*1*) *This Act may be cited as the Matrimonial Causes Act 1937, and shall be construed as one with Part VIII of the principal Act, and this Act and that Part may be cited together as the Matrimonial Causes Acts 1925 and 1937.*

(*2*) *This Act shall come into operation on the first day of January, nineteen hundred and thirty-eight.*

(*3*) *This Act shall not apply to Scotland or Northern Ireland.*

EVIDENCE AND POWERS OF ATTORNEY ACT 1943

(6 & 7 Geo 6 c 18)

An Act to amend the Evidence and Powers of Attorney Act 1940, to provide for the proof of notarial acts of certain foreign, diplomatic and consular representatives, and for purposes connected therewith. [22 April 1943]

4. Evidence of notarial acts done by certain foreign diplomatic and consular representatives. The Secretary of State may by order direct that so much of subsection (2) of section six of the Commissioners for Oaths Act 1889, as relates to the proof of notarial acts done in foreign countries and places by British diplomatic and consular officers shall apply in relation to notarial acts done by such persons as may be specified in the order, being persons serving in the diplomatic, consular or other foreign service of a Power which, by arrangement with His Majesty, has undertaken to represent His interests in any country or place in which His Majesty has for the time being no diplomatic or consular representatives appointed on the advice of His Government in the United Kingdom.

5. Construction, short title and citation—(*1*) *References in this Act to the principal Act shall, except where the context otherwise requires, be construed as references to that Act as amended by this Act.*

(2) This Act may be cited as the Evidence and Powers of Attorney Act 1943, *and this Act and the principal Act may be cited together as the Evidence and Powers of Attorney Acts 1940 and 1943.*

Note. Words in italics repealed by Statute Law (Repeals) Act 1977.
See also Enduring Powers of Attorney Act 1985 (p 3048).

EDUCATION ACT 1944*

(7 & 8 Geo 6 c 31)

An Act to reform the law relating to education in England and Wales. [*3 August 1944*]

 * Whole Act repealed by Education Act 1996, s 582(2), Sch 38, Part I, as from 1 November 1996.

* * * * *

PART II

THE STATUTORY SYSTEM OF EDUCATION

* * * * *

Compulsory Attendance at Primary and Secondary Schools

35. Compulsory school age. *In this Act the expression 'compulsory school age' means any age between five years and fifteen* [*sixteen*] *years, and accordingly a person shall be deemed to be of compulsory school age if he has attained the age of five years and has not attained the age of fifteen* [*sixteen*] *years and a person shall be deemed to be over compulsory school age as soon as he has attained the age of fifteen* [*sixteen*] *years:*

 Provided that, as soon as the Minister [*the Secretary of State*] *is satisfied that it has become practicable to raise to sixteen the upper limit of the compulsory school age, he shall lay before Parliament the draft of an Order in Council directing that the foregoing provisions of this section shall have effect as if for references therein to the age of fifteen years there were substituted references to the age of sixteen years; and unless either House of Parliament, within the period of forty days beginning with the day on which any such draft as aforesaid is laid before it, resolves that the draft be not presented to His Majesty, His Majesty may by Order in Council direct accordingly.*

 In reckoning any such period of forty days, no account shall be taken of any time during which Parliament is dissolved or prorogued or during which both Houses are adjourned for more than four days.

Note. References to 'sixteen' substituted for references to 'fifteen' by virtue of Raising of the School Leaving Age Order 1972, SI 1972 No 444, art 2; as a consequence of that amendment the proviso is spent. Reference to 'the Secretary of State' substituted for the reference to 'the Minister' by virtue of Secretary of State for Education and Science Order 1964, SI 1964 No 490, art 3(2)(a).

36. Duty of parents to secure the education of their children. *It shall be the duty of the parent of every child of compulsory school age to cause him to receive efficent full-time education suitable to his age, ability, and aptitude,* [*and to any special educational needs he may have*] *either by regular attendance at school or otherwise.*

Note. Words in square brackets inserted by Education Act 1981, s 17, as from 1 April 1983.

37. School attendance orders—(*1*) *If it appears to a local education authority that the parent of any child of compulsory school age in their area is failing to perform the duty imposed on him by the last foregoing section, it shall be the duty of the authority to serve upon the parent a notice requiring him, within such time as may be specified in the notice not being less than fourteen days from the service thereof, to satisfy the authority that the child is receiving efficient full-time education suitable to his age, ability, and aptitude* [*and to any special educational needs he may have*] *either by regular attendance at school or otherwise.*

(*2*) *If, after such a notice has been served upon a parent by a local education authority, the parent fails to satisfy the authority in accordance with the requirements of the notice that the child to whom the notice relates is receiving efficient full-time education suitable to his age, ability, and aptitude,* [*and to any special educational needs he may have*] *then, if in the opinion of the authority it is expedient that he should attend school, the authority shall serve upon the parent an order in the prescribed form (hereinafter referred to as a 'school attendance order') requiring him to cause the child to become a registered pupil at a school named in the order:*

Provided that before serving such an order upon a parent the authority shall, where practicable, afford him an opportunity of selecting the school to be named in the order, and if a school is selected by him, that school shall, unless the Minister [*the Secretary of State*] *otherwise directs, be the school named in the order.*

[*Provided that—*

(*a*) *no such order shall be served by the authority upon the parent until the expiration of the period of fourteen days beginning with the day next following that on which they have served upon him a written notice of their intention to serve the order stating that if, before the expiration of that period, he selects a school at which he desires the child to become a registered pupil, that school will, unless the Minister* [*the Secretary of State*] *otherwise directs, be named in the order; and*

(*b*) *if, before the expiration of that period, the parent selects such a school as aforesaid, that school shall, unless the Minister* [*the Secretary of State*] *otherwise directs, be so named.*]

(*3*) *If the local education authority are of opinion that the school selected by the parent as the school to be named in a school attendance order is unsuitable to the age, ability or aptitude of the child with respect to whom the order is to be made, or that the attendance of the child at the school so selected would involve unreasonable expense to the authority, the authority may, after giving to the parent notice of their intention to do so, apply to the Minister* [*the Secretary of State*] *for a direction determining what school is to be named in the order.*

(*4*) *If at any time while a school attendance order is in force with respect to any child the parent of the child makes application to the local education authority by whom the order was made requesting that another school be substituted for that named in the order, or requesting that the order be revoked on the ground that arrangements have been made for the child to receive efficient full-time education suitable to his age, ability, and aptitude* [*and to any special educational needs he may have*] *otherwise than at school, the authority shall amend or revoke the order in compliance with the request unless they are of opinion that the proposed change of school is unreasonable or inexpedient in the interests of the child, or that no satisfactory arrangements have been made for the education of the child otherwise than at school, as the case may be; and if a parent is aggrieved by a refusal of the authority to comply with any such request, he may refer the question to the Minister* [*the Secretary of State*], *who shall give such direction thereon as he thinks fit.*

(*5*) *If any person upon whom a school attendance order is served fails to comply with the requirements of the order, he shall be guilty of an offence against this section unless he proves that he is causing the child to receive efficient full-time education suitable to his age, ability, and aptitude* [*and to any special educational needs he may have*] *otherwise than at school.*

(*6*) *If in proceedings against any person for a failure to comply with a school attendance order that person is acquitted, the court may direct that the school attendance order shall cease to be in force, but without prejudice to the duty of the local education authority to take further action under this section if at any time the authority are of opinion that having regard to any change of circumstances it is expedient so to do.*

(7) *Save as provided by the last foregoing subsection, a school attendance order made with respect to any child shall, subject to any amendment thereof which may be made by the local education authority, continue in force so long as he is of compulsory school age unless revoked by that authority.*

Note. This section repealed by Education Act 1993, s 307(1), (3), Sch 19, paras 3, 11, Sch 21, Part I, as from 1 October 1993. References throughout this section to 'the Secretary of State' substituted for those to 'the Minister' by virtue of Secretary of State for Education and Science Order 1964, SI 1964 No 490, art 3(2)(a). References to 'any special educational needs he may have' in sub-ss (1), (2), (4), (5), substituted by Education Act 1981, s 21(4), Sch 3, and the second proviso to sub-s (2) (that having been substituted for the first proviso by the Education (Miscellaneous Provisions) Act 1953, s 10), sub-s (3) and words 'requesting that another school ... in the order', 'shall amend', 'that the proposed change ... interests of the child, or', 'as the case may be' in sub-s (4), repealed by s 21(5) of, and Sch 4 to, the 1981 Act.

38. (*Repealed by the Education Act 1981, s 21, Sch 4.*)

39. Duty of parents to secure regular attendance of registered pupils—(*1*) *If any child of compulsory school age who is a registered pupil at a school fails to attend regularly thereat, the parent of the child shall be guilty of an offence against this section.*

(*2*) *In any proceedings for an offence against this section in respect of a child who is not a boarder at the school at which he is a registered pupil, the child shall not be deemed to have failed to attend regularly at the school by reason of his absence therefrom with leave or—*

(*a*) *at any time when he was prevented from attending by reason of sickness or any unavoidable cause;*

(*b*) *on any day exclusively set apart for religious observance by the religious body to which his parent belongs;*

(*c*) *if the parent proves that the school at which the child is a registered pupil is not within walking distance of the child's home, and that no suitable arrangements have been made by the local education authority either for his transport to and from the school or for boarding accommodation for him at or near the school or for enabling him to become a registered pupil at a school nearer to his home.*

(*3*) *Where in any proceedings for an offence against this section it is proved that the child has no fixed abode, paragraph (c) of the last foregoing subsection shall not apply, but if the parent proves that he is engaged in any trade or business of such a nature as to require him to travel from place to place and that the child has attended at a school at which he was a registered pupil as regularly as the nature of the trade or business of the parent permits, the parent shall be acquitted:*

Provided that, in the case of a child who has attained the age of six years, the parent shall not be entitled to be acquitted under this subsection unless he proves that the child has made at least two hundred attendances during the period of twelve months ending with the date on which the proceedings were instituted.

(*4*) *In any proceedings for an offence against this section in respect of a child who is a boarder at the school at which he is a registered pupil, the child shall be deemed to have failed to attend regularly at the school if he is absent therefrom without leave during any part of the school term at a time when he was not prevented from being present by reason of sickness or any unavoidable cause.*

(*5*) *In this section the expression 'leave' in relation to any school means leave granted by any person authorised in that behalf by the managers, governors or proprietor of the school, and the expression 'walking distance' means, in relation to a child who has not attained the age of eight years two miles, and in the case of any other child three miles, measured by the nearest available route.*

Note. This section repealed by Education Act 1993, s 307(1), (3), Sch 19, paras 3, 11, Sch 21, Part I, as from 1 October 1993. Word 'manager' in sub-s (5) repealed by Education Act 1980, s 1(3), Sch 1, para 10.

*   *   *   *   *

PART V

SUPPLEMENTAL

*   *   *   *   *

114. Interpretation—(*1*) *In this Act, unless the context otherwise requires, the following expressions have the meanings hereby respectively assigned to them, that is to say*—

*   *   *   *   *

'Local education authority' means, in relation to any area for which a joint education board is constituted as the local education authority under the provisions of Part I of the First Schedule to this Act, the board so constituted, and, save as aforesaid, means, in relation to a county, the council of the county, and, in relation to a county borough, the council of the county borough [*in relation to a non-metropolitan county, the council of the county* [*in relation to a county borough, the council of the county borough*], *and in relation to a metropolitan district, the council of the district*];

*   *   *   *   *

'Registered pupil' means, in relation to any school, a pupil registered as such [*person registered as a pupil*] *in the register kept in accordance with the reqirements of this Act, but does not include any child who has been withdrawn from the school in the prescribed manner;*

*   *   *   *   *

Note. Words in first pair of square brackets in definition 'Local education authority' substituted for words 'in relation to a county, the council of the county, and, in relation to a county borough, the council of the county borough' by Local Authority etc (Miscellaneous Provision) Order 1977, SI 1977 No 293, art 4(1). Words in second pair of square brackets in that definition inserted by Local Government (Wales) Act 1994, s 21, as from 1 April 1996. Words in square brackets in definition of 'Registered pupil' substituted for words 'pupil registered as such' by Education Act 1993, s 307(1), Sch 19, paras 3, 24, as from 1 October 1993. Words 'but does not include' to the end of that definition repealed by Education (Miscellaneous Provisions) Act 1948, s 11, Sch 2.

*   *   *   *   *

NATIONAL ASSISTANCE ACT 1948

(11 & 12 Geo 6 c 29)

*   *   *   *   *

42. Liability to maintain wife or husband and children—(1) For the purposes of this Act—
   (a) a man shall be liable to maintain his wife and his children, and
   (b) a woman shall be liable to maintain her husband and her children.
Note. For construction of s 42(1), see Family Law Reform Act 1987, s 2(1)(a) (p 3128), as from 1 April 1989.

(*2*) *The reference in paragraph* (*a*) *of the last foregoing subsection to a man's children includes a reference to children of whom he has been adjudged to be the putative father, and the reference in paragraph* (*b*) *of that subsection to a woman's children includes a reference to her illegitimate children.*

[(2) Any reference in subsection (1) of this section to a person's children shall be construed in accordance with section 1 of the Family Law Reform Act 1987.]

Note. Sub-s (2) in square brackets substituted for sub-s (2) in italics by Family Law Reform Act 1987, s 33(1), Sch 2, para 5, and see ibid, Sch 4 (p 3134) for repeal of sub-s (2), as from 1 April 1989.

(3) [Applies to Scotland.]

Note. 'Child' means a person under the age of sixteen (s 64(1)). He shall not be deemed to have attained the age of sixteen until the commencement of the sixteenth anniversary of the day of his birth (s 64(3)).

See also Ministry of Social Security Act 1966, s 23, p 2271.

43. Recovery of cost of assistance from persons liable for maintenance— (1) Where assistance is given or applied for by reference to the requirements of any person (in this section referred to as a person assisted), *the Board or* the local authority concerned may make a complaint to the court against any other person who for the purposes of this Act is liable to maintain the person assisted.

Note. Words in italics repealed by Ministry of Social Security Act 1966, s 39(3), Sch 8.

(2) On a complaint under this section the court shall have regard to all the circumstances and in particular to the resources of the defendant, and may order the defendant to pay such sum, weekly or otherwise, as the court may consider appropriate.

(3) For the purposes of the application of the last foregoing subsection to payments in respect of assistance given before the complaint was made, a person shall not be treated as having at the time when the complaint is heard any greater resources than he had at the time when the assistance was given.

(4) In this section the expression 'assistance' means *an assistance grant, assistance in kind or assistance given under section ten of this Act (hereinafter referred to as 'assistance under Part II of this Act'), or* the provision of accommodation under Part III of this Act (hereinafter referred to as 'assistance under Part III of this Act'); and the expression 'the court' means *the court of summary jurisdiction having jurisdiction in the place* [*appointed for the commission area (within the meaning of section 1 of the Administration of Justice Act 1973* [the Justices of the Peace Act 1979] [*the Justices of the Peace Act 1997*])] *where the assistance was given or applied for*—

(a) in England and Wales, a magistrates' court acting in the local justice area where the assistance was given or applied for;

(b) in Scotland, the sheriff having jurisdiction in the place where the assistance was given or applied for].

Note. First words in italics repealed by the Supplementary Benefit Act 1966, s 39(3), Sch 8.

Words in square brackets substituted for words from 'the court of' to 'or applied for' in italics by the Courts Act 2003, s 109(1), Sch 8, para 80, as from a date to be appointed.

Words in square brackets beginning with the words 'appointed for the' substituted for words 'having jurisdiction in the place' in italics by the Domestic Proceedings and Magistrates' Courts Act 1978, s 89(2), Sch 2, para 6, as from 1 February 1981.

Words from '(within' to '1997)' in italics repealed by the Access to Justice Act 1999, s 106, Sch 15, Pt V(1), as from 27 September 1999.

Words 'the Justices of the Peace Act 1979' in square brackets substituted for words 'section 1 of the Administration of Justice Act 1973' in italics by the Justices of the Peace Act 1979, s 71, Sch 2, para 3, as from 1 February 1981.

Words 'the Justices of the Peace Act 1997' in square brackets substituted for words 'the Justices of the Peace Act 1979' in italics by the Access to Justice Act 1999, s 103, Sch 15, Pt V(1), as from 27 September 1999.

Note. Words in square brackets substituted for words in italics by Domestic Proceedings and Magistrates Courts Act 1978, s 89, Sch 2, para 6, as from 1 February 1981, save that the reference to Justices of the Peace Act 1979 was substituted for the reference to Administration of Justice Act 1973, s 1, by Justices of the Peace Act 1979, s 71, Sch 2, para 3, as from the same date. Other words in italics repealed by Ministry of Social Security Act 1966, s 39(3), Sch 8.

(5) Payments under subsection (2) of this section shall be made—

(a) to *the Board or* the local authority concerned, in respect of the cost of assistance, whether given before or after the making of the order, or

(b) to the applicant for assistance or any other person being a person assisted, or

(c) to such other person as appears to the court expedient in the interests of
the person assisted,

or as to part in one such manner and as to part in another, as may be provided by
the order.

Note. Words in italics repealed by Ministry of Social Security Act 1966, s 39(3), Sch 8.

(*6*) *The payments to be made to the Board or a local authority under this section shall*
(*irrespective of the recipient thereof*) *be applied as follows, that is to say—*

(*a*) *payments in respect of any period during which the person assisted was in receipt of
assistance both under Part II of this Act and also under Part III thereof shall inure
for the benefit of the Board up to an amount equal to the cost of the assistance under
Part II of this Act, and the balance, if any, shall inure for the benefit of the local
authority giving the assistance under Part III of this Act;*

(*b*) *payments in respect of any other period shall inure for the benefit of the Board or local
authority giving assistance;*

*and such adjustments shall be made between the Board and the local authorities as may be
requisite for giving effect to the foregoing provisions of this subsection.*

Note. Sub-s (6)(b) repealed by Ministry of Social Security Act 1966, Sch 8.

[(*6*) *Any order made, whether before or after the commencement of the Supplementary
Benefits Act 1976, under this section shall be enforceable as an affiliation order, and accordingly
subsection (1) of section 56 of this Act shall not apply to any sum due under such an order.*

[(6) An order under this section shall be enforceable as a magistrates' court
maintenance order within the meaning of section 150(1) of the Magistrates'
Courts Act 1980.]

(*7*) *Any proceedings for such an order (but not proceedings for the enforcement, revocation
or variation of such an order) shall be included among the proceedings which are domestic
proceedings within the meaning of the Magistrates' Courts Act 1952; and section 56 of that
Act (definition of 'domestic proceedings') shall have effect accordingly.*

(8) Subsections (6) and (7) of this section do not extend to Scotland.]

Note. New sub-ss (6)–(8) added by Supplementary Benefits Act 1976, s 35(2), Sch 7, para 4.
Sub-s (7) repealed by Domestic Proceedings and Magistrates' Courts Act 1978, s 89(2)(b),
Sch 3, as from 1 November 1979. Further new sub-s (6) (in second square brackets)
substituted by Family Law Reform Act 1987, s 33(1), Sch 2, para 6, as from 1 April 1989.

44. Affiliation orders—(*1*) *The following provisions of this section shall have effect
where—*

(*a*) *assistance is given under Part II of this Act by reference to the requirements of an
illegitimate child, or*

(*b*) *accommodation is provided for an illegitimate child by, or by arrangement with, a
local authority under Part III of this Act,*

and the provisions of the last foregoing section shall not apply in relation to the father of the child.

Note. Sub-s 1(a) repealed by Ministry of Social Security Act 1966, s 39(3), Sch 8.

(*2*) *If no affiliation order is in force, the Board or local authority may within three years
from the time when the assistance was given or accommodation provided make application to a
court of summary jurisdiction having jurisdiction in the place [appointed for the commission
area (within the meaning of section 1 of the Administration of Justice Act 1973 [the Justices of
the Peace Act 1979])] where the mother of the child resides for a summons to be served under
section three of the Bastardy Laws Amendment Act 1872.*

Note. Words in square brackets substituted for preceding words 'having jurisdiction in the
place' by Domestic Proceedings and Magistrates' Courts Act 1978, s 89, Sch 2, para 7, as from 1
February 1981, save that the reference to Justices of the Peace Act 1979 substituted for the
reference to Administration of Justice Act 1973, s 1 by the Act of 1979, s 71, Sch 2, para 3, as
from the same date. Words 'Board or' and 'assistance was given or' repealed by Ministry of
Social Security Act 1966, s 39(3), Sch 8.

(*3*) *In any proceedings on an application under the last foregoing subsection the court shall hear such evidence as the Board or local authority may produce, in addition to the evidence required to be heard by section four of the said Act of 1872, and shall in all other respects, but subject to the provisions of the next following subsection, proceed as on an application made by the mother under the said section three.*

Note. Words 'Board or' repealed by Ministry of Social Security Act 1966, s 39(3), Sch 8. Words 'in addition ... of 1872' repealed by Affiliation Proceedings (Amendment) Act 1972, s 1(4).

(*4*) *An order under section four to the said Act of 1872 made on an application under subsection (2) of this section may be made so as to provide that the payments, or a part of the payments, to be made thereunder shall, in lieu of being made to the mother or a person appointed to have the custody of the child, be made to the Board or local authority or to such other person as the court may direct.*

(*5*) *On an application by the Board or local authority in any proceedings under the said section three brought by the mother of the child an order under the said section four may be made so as to provide as aforesaid.*

(*6*) *Any order under the said section four, whether made before or after the commencement of this Act, may on the application of the Board or local authority be varied so as to provide as aforesaid; and any order under the said section four which provides as aforesaid may on the application of the mother of the child be varied so as to provide that the payments thereunder shall be made to the mother or a person appointed to have the custody of the child.*

Note. Words 'Board or' in sub-ss (4)–(6) repealed by Ministry of Social Security Act 1966, s 39(3), Sch 8.

(*7*) (*Applies to Scotland.*)

(*8*) *Subsection (6) of the last foregoing section shall apply to payments recovered by the Board or local authority under an order made in pursuance of subsections (4) to (7) of this section as it applies to payments recovered by the Board or local authority under that section.*

(*9*) *The Secretary of State may issue such new or altered forms of proceedings as he may deem necessary or expedient for giving effect to the foregoing provisions of this section, so far as they apply to England and Wales.*

Note. Sub-s (8) repealed by Ministry of Social Security Act 1966, s 39(3), Sch 8. Sub-s (9) repealed by Justices of the Peace Act 1949, s 46(2), Sch 7, Part II. This section repealed by Family Law Reform Act 1987, s 33, Sch 2, para 7, Sch 4, as from 1 April 1989, but see ibid, Sch 3, para 6(2)(a) (p 3133).

MARRIAGE ACT 1949

(12, 13 & 14 Geo 6 c 76)

An Act to consolidate certain enactments relating to the solemnization and registration of marriages in England with such corrections and improvements as may be authorised under the Consolidation of Enactments (Procedure) Act 1949.

[24 November 1949]

PART I

RESTRICTIONS ON MARRIAGE

1. Marriages within prohibited degrees—(1) A marriage solemnised between a man and any of the persons mentioned in the first column of Part I of the First Schedule to this Act, or between a woman and any of the persons mentioned in the second column of the said Part I, shall be void.

(*2*) *A marriage solemnised between a man and any of the persons mentioned in the first column of Part II of the said First Schedule, or between a woman and any of the persons mentioned in the second column of the said Part II, shall not be void or voidable by reason only of affinity.*

(*3*) *A marriage which by virtue of the last foregoing subsection is not void or voidable if solemnised after the decease of any person shall be void if solemnised during the lifetime of that person.*

Note. Sub-ss (2), (3) repealed by Marriage (Enabling) Act 1960, s 1(4), Schedule.

[(2) Subject to subsection (3) of this section, a marriage solemnised between a man and any of the persons mentioned in the first column of Part II of the First Schedule to this Act, or between a woman and any of the persons mentioned in the second column of the said Part II, shall be void.

Note. See s 27B (p 2104).

(3) Any such marriage as is mentioned in subsection (2) of this section shall not be void by reason only of affinity if both the parties to the marriage have attained the age of twenty-one at the time of the marriage and the younger party has not at any time before attaining the age of eighteen been a child of the family in relation to the other party.

Note. See s 27B (p 2104).

(4) Subject to subsection (5) of this section, a marriage solemnised between a man and any of the persons mentioned in the first column of Part III of the First Schedule to this Act or between a woman and any of the persons mentioned in the second column of the said Part III shall be void.

Note. See s 27C (p 2105).

(5) Any such marriage as is mentioned in subsection (4) of this section shall not be void by reason only of affinity if both the parties to the marriage have attained the age of twenty-one at the time of the marriage and the marriage is solemnised—

(a) in the case of a marriage between a man and the mother of a former wife of his, after the death of both the former wife and the father of the former wife;

(b) in the case of a marriage between a man and the former wife of his son, after the death of both his son and the mother of his son;

(c) in the case of a marriage between a woman and the father of a former husband of hers, after the death of both the former husband and the mother of the former husband;

(d) in the case of a marriage between a woman and a former husband of her daughter, after the death of both her daughter and the father of her daughter.]

Note. Sub-ss (2)–(5) added by Marriage (Prohibited Degrees of Relationship) Act 1986, s 1, Sch 1, para 2, as from 1 November 1986. See s 27C (p 2114).

[(6) Subsection (5) of this section and Parts 2 and 3 of the First Schedule to this Act have effect subject to the following modifications in the case of a party to a marriage whose gender has become the acquired gender under the Gender Recognition Act 2004 ('the relevant person').

(7) Any reference in those provisions to a former wife or former husband of the relevant person includes (respectively) any former husband or former wife of the relevant person.

(8) And—

(a) the reference in paragraph (b) of subsection (5) of this section to the relevant person's son's mother is to the relevant person's father if the relevant person is the son's mother; and

(b) the reference in paragraph (d) of that subsection to the relevant person's daughter's father is to the relevant person's daughter's mother if the relevant person is the daughter's father.]

Note. Sub-ss (6)–(8) inserted by the Gender Recognition Act 2004, s 11, Sch 4, Pt 1, paras 1, 2, as from a date to be appointed.

2. Marriages of persons under sixteen. A marriage solemnised between persons either of whom is under the age of sixteen shall be void.

3. Marriages of persons under [eighteen]—(1) Where the marriage of *an infant* [a child], not being a widower or widow, is intended to be solemnised on the authority of *a certificate* [certificates] issued by a superintendent registrar under Part III of this Act, *whether by licence or without licence*, the consent of the *person or persons specified in the Second Schedule to this Act* [*subsection 1A of this section*] [appropriate persons] shall be required [*unless the infant* [*the child*] *is subject to a custodianship order, when the consent of the custodian and, where the custodian is the husband or wife of a parent of the infant* [*the child*], *of that parent shall be required*]:

Provided that—

(a) if the superintendent registrar is satisfied that the consent of any person whose consent is so required cannot be obtained by reason of absence or inaccessibility or by reason of his being under any disability, the necessity for the consent of that person shall be dispensed with, if there is any other person whose consent is also required; and if the consent of no other person is required, the Registrar General may dispense with the necessity of obtaining any consent, or the court may, on application being made, consent to the marriage, and the consent of the court so given shall have the same effect as if it had been given by the person whose consent cannot be so obtained;

(b) if any person whose consent is required refuses his consent, the court may, on application being made, consent to the marriage, and the consent of the court so given shall have the same effect as if it had been given by the person whose consent is refused.

Note. For the substitution of 'child' for 'infant', see Family Law Reform Act 1987, s 33(1), Sch 2, para 9, as from 4 April 1988. Words in second pair of square brackets substituted for words in italics by Children Act 1989, s 108(4), Sch 12, para 5, as from 14 October 1991. Words in third pair of square brackets, as originally inserted by Children Act 1975, s 108(1), Sch 3, as from 1 December 1985 repealed by s 108(7) of, and Sch 15 to, the 1989 Act, as from 14 October 1991. As for appointment of Registrar General, see Registration Service Act 1953, ss 1–4. As to the power of the superintendent registrar to require written evidence of consent, see Family Law Reform Act 1969, s 2(3) (p 2301).

[*(1A) The consents are*—
(a) *subject to paragraphs (b) to (d) of this subsection, the consent of*—
　(i) *each parent (if any) of the child who has parental responsibility for him; and*
　(ii) *each guardian (if any) of the child;*
(b) *where a residence order is in force with respect to the child, the consent of the person or persons with whom he lives, or is to live, as a result of the order (in substitution for the consents mentioned in paragraph (a) of this subsection);*
(c) *where a care order is in force with respect to the child, the consent of the local authority designated in the order (in addition to the consents mentioned in paragraph (a) of this subsection);*
(d) *where neither paragraph (b) nor (c) of this subsection applies but a residence order was in force with respect to the child immediately before he reached the age of sixteen, the consent of the person or persons with whom he lived, or was to live, as a result of the order (in substitution for the consents mentioned in paragraph (a) of this subsection).*
(1B) In this section 'guardian of a child', 'parental responsibility', 'residence order' and 'care order' have the same meaning as in the Children Act 1989.]

[(1A) The appropriate persons are—
(a) if none of the paragraphs (b) to (h) apply, each of the following—
　(i) any parent of the child who has parental responsibility for him; and
　(ii) any guardian of the child;
(b) where a special guardianship order is in force with respect to a child, each of the child's special guardians, unless any of paragraphs (c) to (g) applies;
(c) where a care order has effect with respect to the child, the local authority

designated in the order, and each parent, guardian or special guardian (in so far as their parental responsibility has not been restricted under section 33(3) of the Children Act 1989), unless paragraph (e) applies;

(d) where a residence order has effect with respect to the child, the persons with whom the child lives, or is to live, as a result of the order, unless paragraph (e) applies;

(e) where an adoption agency is authorised to place the child for adoption under section 19 of the Adoption and Children Act 2002, that agency or, where a care order has effect with respect to the child, the local authority designated in the order;

(f) where a placement order is in force with respect to the child, the appropriate local authority;

(g) where a child has been placed for adoption with prospective adopters, the prospective adopters (in so far as their parental responsibility has not been restricted under section 25(4) of the Adoption and Children Act 2002), in addition to those persons specified in paragraph (e) or (f);

(h) where none of paragraphs (b) to (g) apply but a residence order was in force with respect to the child immediately before he reached the age of sixteen, the persons with whom he lived, or was to live, as a result of the order.]

[(1B) In this section—

'guardian of a child', 'parental responsibility', 'residence order', 'special guardian', 'special guardianship order' and 'care order' have the same meaning as in the Children Act 1989;

'adoption agency', 'placed for adoption', 'placement order' and 'local authority' have the same meaning as in the Adoption and Children Act 2002;

'appropriate local authority' means the local authority authorised by the placement order to place the child for adoption.]

Note. Sub-ss (1A), (1B) inserted by Children Act 1989, s 108(4), Sch 12, para 5, as from 14 October 1991, but by s 108(6) of, and Sch 14, para 37(1) to, that Act, in the circumstances mentioned in Sch 14, para 37(2) to, that Act, this section and Sch 2 to, this Act (p 2122), are to continue to have effect, regardless of the amendment made to this section by Sch 12, para 5, to that Act.

Sub-ss (1A), (1B) substituted by the Adoption and Children Act 2002, Sch 3, paras 3, 4, as from a date to be appointed.

(2) *The last foregoing subsection* [subsection (1)] shall apply to marriages intended to be solemnised on the authority of a common licence, with the substitution of references to the ecclesiastical authority by whom the licence was granted for the reference to the superintendent registrar, and with the substitution of a reference to the Master of the Faculties for the reference to the Registrar General.

Note. Words in square brackets substituted for words 'The last foregoing subsection' in italics by the Adoption and Children Act 2002, Sch 3, para 5, as from a date to be appointed.

(3) Where the marriage of *an infant* [a child], not being a widower or widow, is intended to be solemnised after the publication of banns of matrimony then, if any person whose consent to the marriage would have been required under this section in the case of a marriage intended to be solemnised otherwise than after the publication of the banns, openly and publicly declares or causes to be declared, in the church or chapel in which the banns are published, at the time of the publication, his dissent from the intended marriage, the publication of banns shall be void.

(4) A clergyman shall not be liable to ecclesiastical censure for solemnising the marriage of *an infant* [a child] after the publication of banns without the consent of the parents or guardians of the infant unless he had notice of the dissent of any person who is entitled to give notice of dissent under the last foregoing subsection.

(5) For the purposes of this section, 'the court' means the High Court, *the county*

court of the district in which any respondent resides [the county court of the district in which any applicant or respondent resides] or a court of summary jurisdiction [*having jurisdiction in the place* [*appointed for the commission area* [acting in the local justice area] *(within the meaning of section 1 of the Administration of Justice Act 1973* [*the Justices of the Peace Act 1979*] [*the Justices of the Peace Act 1997*])], in which any applicant or respondent resides], and rules of court may be made for enabling applications under this section—

(a) if made to the High Court, to be heard in chambers;
(b) if made to the county court, to be heard and determined by the registrar subject to appeal to the judge;
(c) if made to a court of summary jurisdiction, to be heard and determined otherwise than in open court,

and shall provide that, where an application is made in consequence of a refusal to give consent, notice of the application shall be served on the person who has refused consent.

Note. For substitution of 'child' for 'infant', see Family Law Reform Act 1987, s 33(1), Sch 2, para 9, as from 4 April 1988. Words in square brackets added by Family Law Reform Act 1969, s 2(2) and altered as to the commission area by Domestic Proceedings and Magistrates' Courts Act 1978, s 89, Sch 2, para 9, as from 1 February 1981 and by Justices of the Peace Act 1979, s 71, Sch 2, para 5, as from the same date, and subsequently by Justices of the Peace Act 1997, s 73(2), Sch 5, para 6, as from 19 June 1997.

Words 'acting in the local justice area' in square brackets substituted for words 'appointed for the commission area' in italics by the Courts Act 2003, s 109(1), Sch 8, para 35, as from a date to be appointed.

Words from '(within' to 1997)' in italics repealed by the Access to Justice Act 1999, s 106, Sch 15, Pt V(1), as from 27 September 1999.

(6) Nothing in this section shall dispense with the necessity of obtaining the consent of the High Court to the marriage of a ward of court.

Note. This section is applied with modifications, by Marriage (Registrar General's Licence) Act 1970, s 6.

*   *   *   *   *

4. Hours for solemnisation of marriages. A marriage may be solemnised at any time between the hours of eight in the forenoon and six in the afternoon.

PART II

MARRIAGE ACCORDING TO RITES OF THE CHURCH OF ENGLAND

Preliminary

*   *   *   *   *

[5A. Marriages between certain persons related by affinity. No clergyman shall be obliged—

(a) to solemnise a marriage which, apart from the Marriage (Prohibited Degrees of Relationship) Act 1986, would have been void by reason of the relationship of the persons to be married; or
(b) to permit such a marriage to be solemnised in the church or chapel of which he is the minister.]

Note. This section inserted by Marriage (Prohibited Degrees of Relationship) Act 1986, s 3, as from 1 November 1986.

*   *   *   *   *

Miscellaneous Provisions

22. Witnesses. All marriages solemnised according to the rites of the Church of England shall be solemnised in the presence of two or more witnesses in addition to the clergyman by whom the marriage is solemnised.

*   *   *   *   *

24. Proof of residence not necessary to validity of marriage by banns or common licence—(1) Where any marriage has been solemnised after the publication of banns of matrimony, it shall not be necessary in support of the marriage to give any proof of the residence of the parties or either of them in any parish or other ecclesiastical district in which the banns were published, and no evidence shall be given to prove the contrary in any proceedings touching the validity of the marriage.

(2) Where any marriage has been solemnised on the authority of a common licence, it shall not be necessary in support of the marriage to give any proof that the usual place of residence of one of the parties was for fifteen days immediately before the grant of the licence in the parish or other ecclesiastical district in which the marriage was solemnised, and no evidence shall be given to prove the contrary in any proceedings touching the validity of the marriage.

25. Void marriages. If any persons knowingly and wilfully intermarry according to the rites of the Church of England (otherwise than by special licence)—

(a) [except in the case of a marriage in pursuance of section 26(1)(dd) of this Act] in any place other than a church or other building in which banns may be published;

(b) without banns having been duly published, a common licence having been obtained, or *a certificate* [certificates] having been duly issued under Part III of this Act by a superintendent registrar to whom due notice of marriage has been given; or

(c) on the authority of a publication of banns which is void by virtue of subsection (3) of section three or subsection (2) of section twelve of this Act, on the authority of a common licence which is void by virtue of subsection (3) of section sixteen of this Act, or on the authority of *a certificate of a superintendent registrar which is* [certificates of a superintendent registrar which are] void by virtue of subsection (2) of section thirty-three of this Act;

(d) in the case of a marriage on the authority of *a certificate* [certificates] of a superintendent registrar, in any place other than the church *or other building specified in the notice of marriage and certificate* [building or other place specified in the *notice of marriage and certificate* [notices of marriage and certificates] as the place where the marriage is to be solemnised];

or if they knowingly and wilfully consent to or acquiesce in the solemnisation of the marriage by any person who is not in Holy Orders, the marriage shall be void.

Note. Words in square brackets in para (a) inserted, and words in square brackets in para (d) substituted for words in italics by Marriage Act 1983, s 1(7), Sch 1, para 3, as from 1 May 1984.

In para (b) word in square brackets substituted for words 'a certificate' in italics by the Immigration and Asylum Act 1999, s 169(1), Sch 14, para 7, as from 1 January 2001 (SI 2000/2698).

In para (c) words in square brackets substituted for words 'a certificate of a superintendent registrar which is' in italics by the Immigration and Asylum Act 1999, s 169(1), Sch 14, para 7, as from 1 January 2001 (SI 2000/2698).

In para (d) word in square brackets substituted for words 'a certificate' in italics by the Immigration and Asylum Act 1999, s 169(1), Sch 14, para 7, as from 1 January 2001 (SI 2000/2698).

In para (d) words in square brackets substituted for words 'notice of marriage and certificate' in italics by the Immigration and Asylum Act 1999, s 169(1), Sch 14, para 7, as from 1 January 2001 (SI 2000/2698).

* * * * *

PART III

MARRIAGE UNDER SUPERINTENDENT REGISTRAR'S CERTIFICATE

Issue of certificates

27B. Provisions relating to section 1(3) marriages—(1) This section applies in relation to any marriage mentioned in subsection (2) of section 1 of this Act which is intended to be solemnised on the authority of *a certificate* [certificates] of a superintendent registrar.

(2) The superintendent registrar shall not enter notice of the marriage in the marriage notice book unless—

(a) he is satisfied by the production of evidence that both the persons to be married have attained the age of twenty-one; and

(b) he has received a declaration made in the prescribed form by each of those persons, each declaration having been signed and attested in the prescribed manner, specifying their affinal relationship and declaring that the younger of those persons has not at any time before attaining the age of eighteen been a child of the family in relation to the other.

(3) The fact that a superintendent registrar has received a declaration under subsection (2) of this section shall be entered in the marriage notice book together with the particulars given in the notice of marriage and any such declaration shall be filed and kept with the records of the office of the superintendent registrar or, where notice of marriage is required to be given to two superintendent registrars, of each of them.

(4) Where the superintendent registrar receives from some person other than the persons to be married a written statement signed by that person which alleges that the declaration made under subsection (2) of this section is false in a material particular, the superintendent registrar shall not issue a certificate *or licence* unless a declaration is obtained from the High Court under subsection (5) of this section.

(5) Either of the persons to be married may, whether or not any statement has been received by the superintendent registrar under subsection (4) of this section, apply to the High Court for a declaration that, both those persons having attained the age of twenty-one and the younger of those persons not having at any time before attaining the age of eighteen been a child of the family in relation to the other, there is no impediment of affinity to the solemnisation of the marriage; and where such a declaration is obtained the superintendent registrar may enter notice of the marriage in the marriage notice book and may issue a certificate, *or certificate and licence,* whether or not any declaration has been made under subsection (2) of this section.

(6) Section 29 of this Act shall not apply to a marriage to which this section applies, except so far as a caveat against the issue of a certificate *or licence* for the marriage is entered under that section on a ground other than the relationship of the persons to be married.

Note. This section inserted by Marriage (Prohibited Degrees of Relationship) Act 1986, s 1, Sch 1, para 5, as from 1 November 1986.

In sub-s (1) word in square brackets substituted for words 'a certificate' in italics by the Immigration and Asylum Act 1999, s 169(1), (3), Sch 14, para 10, Sch 16, as from 1 January 2001 (SI 2000/2698).

In sub-s (4) words 'or licence' in italics repealed by the Immigration and Asylum Act 1999, s 169(1), (3), Sch 14, para 10, Sch 16, as from 1 January 2001 (SI 2000/2698).

In sub-s (5) words ', or certificate and licence' in italics repealed by the Immigration and Asylum Act 1999, s 169(1), (3), Sch 14, para 10, Sch 16, as from 1 January 2001 (SI 2000/2698).

In sub-s (6) words 'or licence' in italics repealed by the Immigration and Asylum Act 1999, s 169(1), (3), Sch 14, para 10, Sch 16, as from 1 January 2001 (SI 2000/2698).

27C. Provisions relating to section 1(5) marriages. In the case of a marriage mentioned in subsection (4) of section 1 of this Act which by virtue of subsection (5) of that section is valid only if at the time of the marriage both the parties to the marriage have attained the age of twenty-one and the death has taken place of two other persons related to those parties in the manner mentioned in the said subsection (5), the superintendent registrar shall not enter notice of the marriage in the marriage notice book unless satisfied by the production of evidence—

    (a) that both the parties to the marriage have attained the age of twenty-one, and

    (b) that both those other persons are dead.]

Note. This section inserted by Marriage (Prohibited Degrees of Relationship) Act 1986, s 1, Sch 1, para 5, as from 1 November 1986.

*   *   *   *   *

Miscellaneous Provisions

48. Proof of certain matters not necessary to validity of marriages—(1) Where any marriage has been solemnised under the provisions of this Part of this Act, it shall not be necessary in support of the marriage to give any proof—

    (a) that before the marriage either of the parties thereto resided, or resided for any period, in the registration district stated in the *notice* [notices] of marriage to be that of his or her place of residence;

    (b) that any person whose consent to the marriage was required by section three of this Act had given his consent;

    (c) that the registered building in which the marriage was solemnised had been certified as required by law as a place of religious worship;

    (d) that the building was the usual place of worship of either of the parties to the marriage; or

    (e) that the facts stated in a declaration made under subsection (1) of section thirty-five of this Act were correct;

nor shall any evidence be given to prove the contrary in any proceedings touching the validity of the marriage.

(2) A marriage solemnised in accordance with the provisions of this Part of this Act in a registered building which has not been certified as required by law as a place of religious worship shall be as valid as if the building had been so certified.

Note. This section is applied by Marriage (Registrar General's Licence) Act 1970, s 12.

In sub-s (1)(a) word in square brackets substituted for word 'notice' in italics by the Immigration and Asylum Act 1999, s 169(1), Sch 14, para 26, as from 1 January 2001 (SI 2000/2698).

49. Void marriages. If any persons knowingly and wilfully intermarry under the provisions of this Part of this Act—

    (a) without having given due notice of marriage to the superintendent registrar;

    (b) without a certificate for marriage having been duly issued [, in respect of each of the persons to be married,] by the superintendent registrar to whom notice of marriage was given;

    (c) *without a licence having been so issued, in a case in which a licence is necessary;*

    (d) on the authority of *a certificate which is* [certificates which are] void by virtue of subsection (2) of section thirty-three of this Act;

(e)   in any place other than the church, chapel, registered building, office or other place specified in the *notice* [notices] of marriage and *certificate* [certificates] of the superintendent registrar;

[(ee) in the case of a marriage purporting to be in pursuance of section 26(1)(bb) of this Act, on any premises that at the time the marriage is solemnised are not approved premises;]

(f)   in the case of a marriage registered building (not being a marriage in the presence of an authorised person), in the absence of a registrar of the registration district in which the registered building is situated; *or*

(g)   in the case of a marriage in the office of a superintendent registrar, in the absence of the superintendent registrar or of a registrar of the registration district of that superintendent registrar; [*or*

[(gg) in the case of a marriage on approved premises, in the absence of the superintendent registrar of the registration district in which the premises are situated or in the absence of a registrar of that district; or]

(h)   in the case of a marriage to which section 45A of this Act applies, in the absence of any superintendent registrar or registrar whose presence at that marriage is required by that section;]

the marriage shall be void.

Note. This section is applied, with modifications, by Marriage (Registrar General's Licence) Act 1970, s 13. Paras (ee), (gg) inserted, and word 'or' in italics in both places repealed, by Marriage Act 1994, s 1(3), Schedule, paras 1, 3, as from 1 April 1995. Para (h) added by Marriage Act 1983, s 1(7), Sch 1, para 13, as from 1 May 1984.

In para (b) words in square brackets inserted by the Immigration and Asylum Act 1999, s 169(1), (3), Sch 14, para 27, Sch 16, as from 1 January 2001 (SI 2000/2698).

Para (c) repealed by the Immigration and Asylum Act 1999, s 169(1), (3), Sch 14, para 27, Sch 16, as from 1 January 2001 (SI 2000/2698).

In para (d) words in square brackets substituted for words 'a certificate which is' in italics by the Immigration and Asylum Act 1999, s 169(1), (3), Sch 14, para 27, Sch 16, as from 1 January 2001 (SI 2000/2698).

In para (c) words in square brackets substituted for words in italics by the Immigration and Asylum Act 1999, s 169(1), (3), Sch 14, para 27, Sch 16, as from 1 January 2001 (SI 2000/2698).

*   *   *   *   *

PART V

MARRIAGES IN NAVAL, MILITARY, AND AIR FORCE CHAPELS

71. Evidence of marriages under Part V. Where a marriage has been solemnised under this Part of this Act, it shall not be necessary, in support of the marriage, to give any proof—

(a)   that the chapel in which the marriage was solemnised was certified or licensed or registered in accordance with this Part of this Act; or

(b)   that either of the parties was a qualified person within the meaning of this Part of this Act; or

(c)   in the case of a marriage according to the rites of the Church of England, that the marriage was solemnised in the presence of a clergyman duly appointed under this Part of this Act for the purpose of registering marriages;

and no evidence shall be given to prove the contrary in any proceedings touching the validity of any such marriage.

*   *   *   *   *

PART VI

GENERAL

75. Offences relating to solemnisation of marriages—(1) Any person who knowingly and wilfully—

 (a) solemnises a marriage at any other time than between the hours of eight in the forenoon and six in the afternoon (not being a marriage by special licence, a marriage according to the usages of the Society of Friends or a marriage between two persons professing the Jewish religion according to the usages of the Jews);

 (b) solemnises a marriage according to the rites of the Church of England without banns of matrimony having been duly published (not being a marriage solemnised on the authority of a special licence, a common licence or a *certificate* [certificates] of a superintendent registrar);

 (c) solemnises a marriage according to the said rites (not being a marriage by special licence [or a marriage in pursuance of section 26(1)(dd) of this Act]) in any place other than a church or other building in which banns may be published;

 (d) solemnises a marriage according to the said rites falsely pretending to be in Holy Orders;

shall be guilty of felony and shall be liable to imprisonment for a term not exceeding fourteen years.

Note. Sub-s (1)(a) excluded by Marriage (Registrar General's Licence) Act 1970, s 16(4). Words in square brackets inserted by Marriage Act 1983, s 1(7), Sch 1, para 20(a), as from 1 May 1984.

In sub-s (1)(b) word in square brackets substituted for words 'a certificate' in italics by the Immigration and Asylum Act 1999, s 169(1), (3), Sch 14, para 30, Sch 16, as from 1 January 2001 (SI 2000/2698).

 (2) Any person who knowingly and wilfully—

 (a)   solemnises a marriage (not being a marriage by special licence, a marriage according to the usages of the Society of Friends or a marriage between two persons professing the Jewish religion according to the usages of the Jews) in any place other than—

  (i) a church or other building in which marriages may be solemnised according to the rites of the Church of England, or

  (ii) the registered building *or office specified* [office [, approved premises] or person's residence specified as the place where the marriage was to be solemnised] in the *notice of marriage and certificate* [notices of marriage and certificates] required under Part III of this Act;

 [(aa) solemnises a marriage purporting to be in pursuance of section 26(1)(bb) of this Act on premises that are not approved premises;]

 (b)   solemnises a marriage in any such registered building as aforesaid (not being a marriage in the presence of an authorised person) in the absence of a registrar of the district in which the registered building is situated;

 [(bb) solemnises a marriage in pursuance of section 26(1)(dd) of this Act, otherwise than according to the rites of the Church of England, in the absence of a registrar of the registration district in which the place where the marriage is solemnised is situated;]

 (c)   solemnises a marriage in the office of a superintendent registrar in the absence of a registrar of the district in which the office is situated;

 [(cc) solemnises a marriage on approved premises in pursuance of section 26(1)(bb) of this Act in the absence of a registrar of the district in which the premises are situated;]

 (d)   solemnises a marriage on the authority of *a certificate* [certificates] of a superintendent registrar *(not being a marriage by licence) within twenty-one days after the day on which the notice of marriage was entered in the marriage notice book* [before the expiry of the waiting period in relation to each notice of marriage]; or

(e) solemnises a marriage on the authority of *a certificate* [certificates] of a superintendent registrar after the expiration of [the period which is, in relation to that marriage, the applicable period for the purposes of section 33 of this Act];

shall be guilty of felony and shall be liable to imprisonment for a term not exceeding five years.

Note. Sub-s (2)(a) excluded by Marriage (Registrar General's Licence) Act 1970, s 16(4). Words in first pair of square brackets in sub-s (2)(a)(ii) substituted for words in italics, and sub-s (2)(bb) inserted by Marriage Act 1983, s 1(7), Sch 1, para 20(b), (c), as from 1 May 1984. Sub-s (2)(aa), (cc) and words ', approved premises' in sub-s (2)(a)(ii) inserted by Marriage Act 1994, s 1(3), Sch 1, paras 1, 7, as from 1 April 1995. Words in square brackets in sub-s (2)(e) substituted by the Deregulation (Validity of Civil Preliminaries to Marriage) Order 1997, SI 1997/986, art 2(4), as from 1 October 1997.

In sub-s (2)(a)(ii) third words in square brackets substituted for words in italics by the Immigration and Asylum Act 1999, s 169(1), (3), Sch 14, para 30, Sch 16, as from 1 January 2001 (SI 2000/2698).

In sub-s (2)(d), (e) words in square brackets substituted for words in italics by the Immigration and Asylum Act 1999, s 169(1), (3), Sch 14, para 30, Sch 16, as from 1 January 2001 (SI 2000/2698).

[(2A) In subsection (2)(d) 'the waiting period' has the same meaning as in section 31(4A).]

Note. Sub-s (2A) inserted by the Immigration and Asylum Act 1999, s 169(1), (3), Sch 14, para 30, Sch 16, as from 1 January 2001 (SI 2000/2698).

(3) A superintendent registrar who knowingly and wilfully—

(a) *issues any certificate for marriage (not being a marriage by licence) before the expiration of twenty-one days from the day on which the notice of marriage was entered in the marriage notice book, or issues a certificate for marriage by licence before the expiration of one whole day from the said day on which the notice was entered as aforesaid;*

[(a) issues any certificate for marriage before the expiry of 15 days from the day on which the notice of marriage was entered in the marriage notice book;]

(b) issues any certificate *or licence* for marriage after the expiration of [the period which is, in relation to that marriage, the applicable period for the purposes of section 33 of this Act];

(c) issues any certificate the issue of which has been forbidden under section thirty of this Act by any person entitled to forbid the issue of such a certificate; or

(d) solemnises or permits to be solemnised in his office [or, in the case of a marriage in pursuance of *section 26(1)(dd)* [section 26(1)(bb) or (dd)], in any other place] any marriage which is void by virtue of the provisions of Part III of this Act;

shall be guilty of felony and shall be liable to imprisonment for a term not exceeding five years.

Note. Words in square brackets in sub-s (3)(b) substituted by Deregulation (Validity of Civil Preliminaries to Marriage) Order 1997, SI 1997/986, art 2(4), as from 1 October 1997. In sub-s (3)(d) words in first pair square brackets inserted by Marriage Act 1983, s 1(7), Sch 1, para 20(d), as from 1 May 1984; words in second pair square brackets substituted for words in italics by Marriage Act 1994, s 1(3), Sch 1, paras 1, 7, as from 1 April 1995.

Sub-s (3)(a) substituted by the Immigration and Asylum Act 1999, s 169(1), (3), Sch 14, para 30, Sch 16, as from 1 January 2001 (SI 2000/2698).

In sub-s (3)(b) words in italics repealed by the Immigration and Asylum Act 1999, s 169(1), (3), Sch 14, para 30, Sch 16, as from 1 January 2001 (SI 2000/2698).

(4) No prosecution under this section shall be commenced after the expiration of three years from the commission of the offence.

(5) Any reference in subsection (2) of this section to a registered building shall be construed as including a reference to any chapel registered under section seventy of this Act.

76. Offences relating to registration of marriages—(1) Any person who refuses or without reasonable cause omits to register any marriage which he is required by this Act to register, and any person having the custody of a marriage register book or a certified copy of a marriage register book or part thereof who carelessly loses or injures the said book or copy or carelessly allows the said book or copy to be injured while in his keeping, shall be liable on summary conviction to a fine not exceeding *fifty pounds* [level 3 on the standard scale].

Note. Reference to level 3 substituted by virtue of Criminal Justice Act 1982, ss 38, 46.

(2) Where any person who is required under Part IV of this Act to make and deliver to a superintendent registrar a certified copy of entries made in the marriage register book kept by him, or a certificate that no entries have been made therein since the date of the last certified copy, refuses to deliver any such copy or certificate, or fails to deliver any such copy or certificate during any month in which he is required to do so, he shall be liable on summary conviction to a fine not exceeding *ten pounds* [*twenty pounds*] [level 1 on the standard scale].

Note. 'Twenty pounds' substituted for the words 'ten pounds' by Criminal Justice Act 1967, s 92(1), Sch 3, Part I and reference to level 1 substituted by Criminal Justice Act 1982, s 37(2), and see ibid, s 38(6).

(3) Any registrar who knowingly and wilfully registers any marriage which is void by virtue of any of the provisions of Part III of this Act shall be guilty of felony and shall be liable to imprisonment for a term not exceeding five years.

(4) The balance of any sum paid or recovered on account of a fine imposed under subsection (1) or subsection (2) of this section, after making any such payments in respect of court or police fees as are mentioned in paragraphs (a), (b) and (c) of subsection (1) of section five of the Criminal Justice Administration Act, 1914, shall be paid—

(a) in the case of a fine imposed under subsection (1) of this section, into the Exchequer; and

(b) in the case of a fine imposed under subsection (2) of this section, to the Registrar General or such other person as may be appointed by the Treasury, for the use of His Majesty.

(5) Subject as may be prescribed, a superintendent registrar may prosecute any person guilty of an offence under either of the said subsections committed within his district, and any costs incurred by the superintendent registrar in prosecuting such a person, being costs which are not otherwise provided for, shall be defrayed out of moneys provided by Parliament.

(6) No prosecution under subsection (3) of this section shall be commenced after the expiration of three years from the commission of the offence.

77. Offences by authorised persons. Any authorised person who refuses or fails to comply with the provisions of this Act or of any regulations made under section seventy-four thereof shall be guilty of an offence against this Act, and, unless the offence is one for which a specific penalty is provided under the foregoing provisions of this Part of this Act, shall be liable, on summary conviction, to a fine not exceeding *ten pounds* [the prescribed sum] or, on conviction on indictment, to imprisonment for a term not exceeding two years or to a fine *not exceeding fifty pounds*, and shall upon conviction cease to be an authorised person.

Note. Maximum fine on summary conviction now the prescribed sum under Magistrates' Courts Act 1980, s 32(2). The fine on conviction on indictment may now be of any amount; see Criminal Law Act 1977, s 32(1).

78. Interpretation—(1) In this Act, except where the context otherwise requires, the following expressions have the meanings hereby respectively assigned to them, that is to say—

'approved premises' means premises approved in accordance with regulations under section 46A of this Act as premises on which marriages may be solemnised in pursuance of section 26(1)(bb) of this Act;]

'authorised chapel' means—

   (a) in relation to a chapelry, a chapel of the chapelry in which banns of matrimony could lawfully be published immediately before the passing of the Marriage Act 1823, or in which banns may be published and marriages may be solemnised by virtue of section two of the Marriages Confirmation Act 1825, or of an authorisation given under section three of the Marriage Act 1823;

   (b) in relation to an extra-parochial place, a church or chapel of that place in which banns may be published and marriages may be solemnised by virtue of section two of the Marriages Confirmation Act, 1825, or of an authorisation given under section three of the Marriage Act, 1823, or section twenty-one of this Act;

   (c) in relation to a district specified in a licence granted under section twenty of this Act, the chapel in which banns may be published and marriages may be solemnised by virtue of that licence;

'authorised person' has the meaning assigned to it by section forty-three of this Act;

'brother' includes a brother of the half blood;

['child' means a person under the age of eighteen,]

['child of the family', in relation to any person, means a child who has lived in the same household as that person and been treated by that person as a child of his family];

'clergyman' means a clerk in Holy Orders of the Church of England;

'common licence' has the meaning assigned to it by section five of this Act;

'ecclesiastical district', in relation to a district other than a parish, means a district specified in a licence granted under section twenty of this Act, a chapelry or an extra-parochial place;

'*infant*' *means a person under the age of twenty-one years* [*eighteen years*];

Note. Definition 'approved premises' inserted by Marriage Act 1994, s 1(3), Schedule, paras 1, 8, as from 1 April 1995. Words 'eighteen years' substituted for words 'twenty-one years' by Family Law Reform Act 1969, s 2(1)(c). Definition 'child' substituted for definition 'infant' by Family Law Reform Act 1987, s 33(1), Sch 2, para 10(a), as from 4 April 1988. Definition 'child of the family' inserted by Marriage (Prohibited Degrees of Relationship) Act 1986, Sch 1, para 7.

'marriage notice book' has the meaning assigned to it by section twenty-seven of this Act;

'parish' means an ecclesiastical parish and includes a district constituted under the Church Building Acts 1818 to 1884, notwithstanding that the district has not become a new parish by virtue of section fourteen of the New Parishes Act 1856, or section five of the New Parishes Measure 1943, being a district to which Acts of Parliament relating to the publication of banns of matrimony and the solemnisation of marriages were applied by the said Church Building Acts as if the district had been an ancient parish, and the expression 'parish church' shall be construed accordingly;

'prescribed' means prescribed by regulations made under section seventy-four of this Act;

'registered building' means a building registered under Part III of this Act;

'registrar' means a registrar of marriages;

'Registrar General' means the Registrar General of Births, Deaths and Marriages in England;

'registration district' means the district of a superintendent registrar.

'sister' includes a sister of the half blood;

'special licence' has the meaning assigned to it by section five of this Act;

'superintendent registrar' means a superintendent registrar of births, deaths and marriages;

'trustees or governing body', in relation to Roman Catholic registered buildings, includes a bishop or vicar general of the diocese.

[(*1A*) *References in this Act to the parents of a child being or not being married to each other at the time of his birth shall be construed in accordance with section 1 of the Family Law Reform Act 1987.*]

Note. Sub-s (1A) inserted by Family Law Reform Act 1987, s 33(1), Sch 2, para 10(b), as from 4 April 1988 and repealed by Children Act 1989, s 108(7), Sch 15, as from 14 October 1991.

(2) Any reference in this Act to the Church of England shall, unless the context otherwise requires, be construed as including a reference to the Church in Wales.

[(3) For the purposes of this Act a person is house-bound if—

(a) *the notice* [each notice] of his or her marriage given in accordance with section 27 of this Act is accompanied by a medical statement (within the meaning of section 27A(7) of this Act) made, not more than fourteen days before the date on which that notice was given, in relation to that person; and

(b) he or she is not a detained person.

(4) For the purposes of this Act a person is a detained person if he or she is for the time being detained—

(a) otherwise than by virtue of section 2, 4, 35, 36 or 136 of the Mental Health Act 1983 (short term detentions), as a patient in a hospital; or

(b) in a prison or other place to which the Prison Act 1952 applies,

and in paragraph (a) above 'patient' and 'hospital' have the same meanings as in Part II of the Mental Health Act 1983.

(5) For the purposes of this Act a person who is house-bound or is a detained person shall be taken, if he or she would not otherwise be, to be resident and usually resident at the place where he or she is for the time being.]

Note. Sub-ss (3)–(5) added by Marriage Act 1983, s 1(7), Sch 1, para 21, as from 1 May 1984.

In sub-s (3)(a) words in square brackets substituted for words 'the notice' in italics by the Immigration and Asylum Act 1999, s 169(1), Sch 14, para 31, as from 1 January 2001 (SI 2000/2698).

79. Repeals and savings—(1) The Acts specified in Part I of the Fifth Schedule to this Act, and the Measures of the Church Assembly specified in Part II of that Schedule, are hereby repealed to the extent specified in relation thereto in the third column of that Schedule.

*   *   *   *   *

(4) Any document referring to an enactment repealed by this Act shall be construed as referring to the corresponding provision of this Act.

(5) Nothing in this Act shall affect any law or custom relating to the marriage of members of the Royal Family.

(6) Nothing in this Act shall affect the right of the Archbishop of Canterbury or

any other person by virtue of the Ecclesiastical Licences Act 1533, to grant special licences to marry at any convenient time or place, or affect the validity of any marriage solemnised on the authority of such a licence.

(7) Nothing in this Act shall affect the validity of any marriage solemnised before the commencement of this Act.

*   *   *   *   *

(13) Nothing in the foregoing provisions of this section shall be taken as prejudicing the operation of section thirty-eight of the Interpretation Act 1889 (which relates to the effect of repeals).

Note. Interpretation Act 1889, s 38, replaced by Interpretation Act 1978, ss 16, 17 (pp 2736).

80. Short title, extent and commencement—(1) This Act may be cited as the Marriage Act 1949.

(2) Save as is otherwise expressly provided, this Act shall not extend to Scotland or to Northern Ireland.

(3) The provisions of this Act specified in the Sixth Schedule to this Act shall not extend to Wales or Monmouthshire.

(4) This Act shall come into force on the first day of January nineteen hundred and fifty.

FIRST SCHEDULE   Section 1

KINDRED AND AFFINITY

PART I

Prohibited degrees of relationship

Mother [Adoptive mother or former adoptive mother]	Father [Adoptive father or former adoptive father]
Daughter [Adoptive daughter or former adoptive daughter]	Son [Adoptive son or former adoptive son]
Father's mother	Father's father
Mother's mother	Mother's father
Son's daughter	Son's son
Daughter's daughter	Daughter's son
Sister	Brother
Wife's mother	*Husband's father*
Wife's daughter	*Husband's son*
Father's wife	*Mother's husband*
Son's wife	*Daughter's husband*
Father's father's wife	*Father's mother's husband*
Mother's father's wife	*Mother's mother's husband*
Wife's father's mother	*Husband's father's father*
Wife's mother's mother	*Husband's mother's father*
Wife's son's daughter	*Husband's son's son*
Wife's daughter's daughter	*Husband's daughter's son*
Son's son's wife	*Son's daughter's husband*
Daughter's son's wife	*Daughter's daughter's husband*
Father's sister	Father's brother
Mother's sister	Mother's brother
Brother's daughter	Brother's son
Sister's daughter	Sister's son

Note. Words in square brackets inserted by Children Act 1975, s 108(1), Sch 3, para 8, as from 1 January 1976. Words in italics repealed by Marriage (Prohibited Degrees of Relationship) Act 1986, Sch 1, para 8(a), as from 1 November 1986.

PART II

Statutory exceptions from prohibited degrees of relationship

Deceased wife's sister	*Deceased sister's husband*
Deceased brother's wife	*Deceased husband's brother*
Deceased wife's brother's daughter	*Father's deceased sister's husband*
Deceased wife's sister's daughter	*Mother's deceased sister's husband*
Father's deceased brother's wife	*Deceased husband's brother's son*
Mother's deceased brother's wife	*Deceased husband's sister's son*
Deceased wife's father's sister	*Brother's deceased daughter's husband*
Deceased wife's mother's sister	*Sister's deceased daughter's husband*
Brother's deceased son's wife	*Deceased husband's father's brother*
Sister's deceased son's wife	*Deceased husband's mother's brother*

[PART II

Degrees of affinity referred to in section 1(2) and (3) of this Act

Daughter of former wife	Son of former husband
Former wife of father	Former husband of mother
Former wife of father's father	Former husband of father's mother
Former wife of mother's father	Former husband of mother's mother
Daughter of son of former wife	Son of son of former husband
Daughter of daughter of former wife	Son of daughter of former husband

PART III

Degrees of affinity referred to in section 1(4) and (5) of this Act

Mother of former wife	Father of former husband
Former wife of son	Former husband of daughter].

Note. Part II in italics repealed by Marriage (Enabling) Act 1960, s 1(4), Part II in square brackets and Part III added by Marriage (Prohibited Degrees of Relationship) Act 1986, s 1, Sch 1, para 8(b), as from 1 November 1986.

SECOND SCHEDULE

CONSENTS REQUIRED TO THE MARRIAGE OF *AN INFANT* [A CHILD] BY COMMON LICENCE OR SUPERINTENDENT REGISTRAR'S CERTIFICATE

I. WHERE THE INFANT [*THE CHILD*] *IS LEGITIMATE*

[*I. WHERE THE PARENTS OF THE CHILD WERE MARRIED TO EACH OTHER AT THE TIME OF HIS BIRTH*]

Note. Heading substituted by Family Law Reform Act 1987, s 33(1), Sch 2, para 11, as from 4 April 1988. For 'a child' replacing 'an infant', see ibid, Sch 2, para 9, as from 4 April 1988.

Circumstances	Person or Persons whose consent is required
1. *Where both parents are living:*	
(a) *if parents are living together;*	*Both parents.*
(b) *if parents are divorced or separated by order of any court or by agreement;*	*The parent to whom the custody of the infant is committed by order of the court or by the agreement, or, if the custody of the infant [the child] is so committed to one parent during part of the year and to the other parent during the rest of the year, both parents.*
(c) *if one parent has been deserted by the other;*	*The parent who has been deserted.*
(d) *if both parents have been deprived of custody of infant by order of any court.*	*The person to whose custody the infant [the child] is committed by order of the court.*
2. *Where one parent is dead:*	
(a) *if there is no other guardian;*	*The surviving parent.*
(b) *if a guardian has been appointed by the deceased parent [or by the court under section 3 of the Guardianship of Minors Act, 1971].*	*The surviving parent and the guardian if acting jointly, or the surviving parent or the guardian if the parent or guardian is the sole guardian of the infant [the child].*

Note. The words in square brackets in the first column of para 2 inserted by Children Act 1975, s 108(1), Sch 3, para 9, as from 1 January 1976.

3. *Where both parents are dead.*	*The guardians or guardian appointed by the deceased parents or by the court under [section 3 or 5 of the Guardianship of Minors Act 1971].*

Note. Words in square brackets substituted for 'section four of the Guardianship of Infants Act 1925' by Guardianship of Minors Act 1971, s 18(1), Sch 1.

II. WHERE THE INFANT IS ILLEGITIMATE

Circumstances	Person whose consent is required
If the mother of the infant is alive.	*The mother, or if she has by order of any court been deprived of the custody of the infant [the child], the person to whom the custody of the infant has been committed by order of the court.*
If the mother of the infant is dead.	*The guardian appointed by the mother.*

Note. See Family Law Reform Act 1987, Sch 2, para 9 for substitution of 'child' for 'infant', as from 4 April 1988.

Whole Schedule repealed, with savings, by Children Act 1989, s 108(7), Sch 1, as from 14 October 1991. For savings, see the note to s 3 of this Act (p 2109).

THIRD SCHEDULE   Section 68

CAPACITIES REFERRED TO IN SECTION 68(2)(d) OF THIS ACT

PART *I*

NAVAL FORCES

> *Employment with the medical branch of the Royal Navy as an officer.*
> *Member of the Women's Royal Naval Service.*
> *Member of Queen Alexandra's Royal Naval Nursing Service, or its reserve.*

PART *II*

MILITARY FORCES

> Employment with the Royal Army Medical Corps as an officer.
> Member of Queen Alexandra's Imperial Military Nursing Service, or its reserve.
> Member of the Auxiliary Territorial Service.*

* Now the Women's Royal Army Corps.

PART *III*

AIR FORCES

> Employment with the medical branch of the Royal Air Force as an officer.
> Member of Princess Mary's Royal Air Force Nursing Service, or its reserve.
> Member of the Women's Auxiliary Air Force.*

* Now the Women's Royal Air Force.

Note. Whole Schedule repealed, with savings, by Armed Forces Act 1981, s 28(2), Sch 5, Part I.

FOURTH SCHEDULE   Sections 69, 70

PROVISIONS OF ACT WHICH ARE EXCLUDED OR MODIFIED IN THEIR APPLICATION TO NAVAL, MILITARY AND AIR FORCE CHAPELS

PART I

EXCLUSION OF PROVISIONS RELATING TO MARRIAGES ACCORDING TO THE RITES OF THE CHURCH OF ENGLAND

> Subsection (4) of section six.
> Paragraph (b) of subsection (1) of section fifteen.
> The proviso to section seventeen.
> Section eighteen.
> Section twenty.
> Subsection (3) of section thirty-five.
> The proviso to subsection (1) of section forty-four.
> Sections fifty-three to fifty-seven, fifty-nine and sixty, so far as those sections relate
to the registration of marriages by clergymen and to the duties of incumbents in
relation to marriage register books.

PART II

MODIFICATION OF PROVISIONS RELATING TO MARRIAGE ACCORDING TO THE RITES OF THE CHURCH OF ENGLAND

Subsection (1) of section six shall apply as if the chapel were the parish church of the parish in which the chapel is situated.

Subsection (3) of section seven shall apply as if for the reference to the parochial church council there were substituted, in relation to a naval chapel, a reference to the Admiralty and, in relation to any other chapel, a reference to a Secretary of State.

Section eight shall apply as if it required the notice in writing mentioned therein to include a statement that one at least of the persons to be married is a qualified person within the meaning of Part V of this Act, and to specify the person so qualified and the nature of his qualification.

Paragraph (a) of subsection (1) of section fifteen shall apply as if the chapel were the parish church of the parish in which the chapel is situated.

Subsection (1) of section sixteen shall apply as if it required the oath, which is to be taken thereunder, to include a statement that one at least of the persons to be married is a qualified person within the meaning of Part V of this Act and to specify the person so qualified and the nature of his qualification.

Subsection (3) of section twenty-seven shall apply as if it required the notice of marriage to include a statement that one at least of the persons to be married is a qualified person within the meaning of Part V of this Act and to specify the person so qualified and the nature of his qualification.

Section fifty shall apply as if for the reference to the officiating clergyman there were substituted a reference to the clergyman appointed under section sixty-nine of this Act for the purpose of registering marriage, in whose presence the marriage is solemnised.

PART III

EXCLUSION OF PROVISIONS RELATING TO MARRIAGES OTHERWISE THAN ACCORDING TO THE RITES OF THE CHURCH OF ENGLAND

The proviso to section seventeen.
The proviso to subsection (2) of section twenty-six.
Section forty-one.
Section forty-two.
[The proviso to subsection (1) of section forty-three].
The proviso to subsection (1) of section forty-four.

Note. Words in square brackets inserted by Marriage Acts (Amendment) Act 1958, s 1(2).

Words in italics repealed by the Immigration and Asylum Act 1999, s 169(1), (3), Sch 14, para 32, Sch 16, as from 1 January 2001 (SI 2000/2698).

PART IV

MODIFICATION OF PROVISIONS RELATING TO MARRIAGES OTHERWISE THAN ACCORDING TO THE RITES OF THE CHURCH OF ENGLAND

Subsection (3) of section twenty-seven shall apply as if it required the notice of marriage to include a statement that one at least of the persons to be married is a qualified person within the meaning of Part V of this Act and to specify the person so qualified and the nature of his qualification.

Sections forty-three, forty-four and fifty-four shall apply as if for any reference to the trustees or governing body of a building there were substituted a reference to the Admiralty or any person authorised by them, in the case of a naval chapel, and a reference to a Secretary of State or any person authorised by him, in the case of any other chapel.

FIFTH SCHEDULE   Section 79

ENACTMENTS REPEALED

PART I

Acts of Parliament repealed

Session and Chapter	Short Title	Extent of Repeal
32 Hen 8 c 38	*The Marriage Act 1540*	*The whole Act.*
2 & 3 Edw 6 c 23	—	*The whole Act.*
4 Geo 4 c 76	*The Marriage Act 1823*	*The whole Act.*
5 Geo 4 c 32	*The Marriage Act 1824*	*The whole Act.*
11 Geo 4 & 1 Will 4 c 18	*The Marriage Confirmation Act 1830*	*Section two.*
11 Geo 4 & 1 Will 4 c 66	*The Forgery Act 1830*	*In section twenty-one the words 'marriage' and 'or of the parties married.'*
5 & 6 Will 4 c 54	*The Marriage Act 1835*	*The whole Act.*

Session and Chapter	Short Title	Extent of Repeal
6 & 7 Will 4 c 85	*The Marriage Act 1836*	*The whole Act except sections three, seventeen and forty-five.*
6 & 7 Will 4 c 86	*The Births and Deaths Registration Act 1836*	*Sections thirty, thirty-one, thirty-three, forty, forty-two and forty-four and Schedule C, and so much of sections seventeen, thirty-four, thirty-five, thirty-seven and thirty-eight as relates to registers of marriages or to certified copies thereof.*
7 Will 4 & 1 Vict c 22	*The Births and Deaths Registration Act 1837*	*Sections one, three, five, twenty-three, twenty-seven and thirty-three to thirty-six, and so much of sections twenty-six, twenty-eight and twenty-nine as relates to registers of marriages or to certified copies thereof.*
3 & 4 Vict c 72	*The Marriage Act 1840*	*The whole Act.*
19 & 20 Vict c 119	*The Marriage and Registration Act 1856*	*The whole Act except sections fifteen, sixteen, twenty-four and twenty-five.*
20 Vict c 19	*The Extra-Parochial Places Act 1857*	*Sections nine and ten.*
23 & 24 Vict c 18	*The Marriage (Society of Friends) Act 1860*	*The whole Act.*
23 & 24 Vict c 24	*The Marriage Confirmation Act 1860*	*The whole Act.*
35 & 36 Vict c 10	*The Marriage (Society of Friends) Act 1872*	*The whole Act.*
37 & 38 Vict c 88	*The Births and Deaths Registration Act 1874*	*Section thirty-two so far as it relates to the making of indexes of registers of marriages, section forty-one so far as it relates to documents relating to marriages, and the Second Schedule so far as it relates to fees payable for searches in marriage registers and for certified copies of entries therein.*
49 & 50 Vict c 3	*The Marriages Validity Act 1886*	*The whole Act.*
49 & 50 Vict c 14	*The Marriage Act 1886*	*The whole Act.*
61 & 62 Vict c 58	*The Marriage Act 1898*	*The whole Act.*
62 & 63 Vict c 27	The Marriages Validity Act 1899	The whole Act so far as it relates to marriages solemnised in England.
7 Edw 7 c 47	*The Deceased Wife's Sister's Marriage Act 1907*	*The whole Act.*

Session and Chapter	Short Title	Extent of Repeal
8 Edw 7 c 26	The Naval Marriages Act 1908	The whole Act so far as it relates to marriages solemnised in England.
11 & 12 Geo 5 c 24	*The Deceased Brother's Widow's Marriage Act 1921*	*The whole Act.*
15 & 16 Geo 5 c 45	*The Guardianship of Infants Act 1925*	*Section nine, in subsection (2) of section eleven the words 'except so far as it amends the law relating to the marriage of infants' and the Schedule.*
19 & 20 Geo 5 c 36	*The Age of Marriage Act 1929*	*In section one, in subsection (1) the words from the beginning to 'Provided that' and paragraph (a) of subsection (2).*
21 & 22 Geo 5 c 31	*The Marriage (Prohibited Degrees of Relationship) Act 1931*	*Section one and in subsection (1) of section three the words from 'and this Act' to the end of the subsection and subsections (2), (3) and (4) of that section.*
22 & 23 Geo 5 c 31	*The Marriage (Naval, Military, and Air Force Chapels) Act 1932*	*The whole Act.*
24 & 25 Geo 5 c 13	*The Marriage (Extension of Hours) Act 1934*	*In section one, subsection (1) and in subsection (2) the words 'the Marriage Act, 1886 and', section two, and in section three the words 'and this Act and the Marriage Acts 1811 to 1932, may be cited together as the Marriage Acts 1811 to 1934'.*
2 & 3 Geo 6 c 33	The Marriage Act 1939	Section one, so far as it relates to marriages solemnised in England, *in subsection (3) of section two the words 'section eight of the Marriage and Registration Act 1856, section three of the Naval Marriages Act 1908, and' and section three.*
2 & 3 Geo 6 c 35	*The Marriages Validity Act 1939*	*The whole Act.*
4 & 5 Geo 6 c 47	*The Marriage (Members of His Majesty's Forces) Act 1941*	*The whole Act.*

PART II

Church Assembly Measures repealed

Session and Chapter	Short Title	Extent of Repeal
14 & 15 Geo 5 No 2	The Union of Benefices Measure 1923	*Subsection (3) of section twenty-five.*
20 & 21 Geo 5 No 3	The Marriage Measure 1930	The whole Measure.
24 & 25 Geo 5 No 2	The Banns of Marriage Measure 1934	The whole Measure.
1 & 2 Geo 6 No 1	The Marriage (Licensing of Chapels) Measure 1938	The whole Measure.
4 & 5 Geo 6 No 1	The Diocesan Reorganisation Committees Measure 1941	Paragraph (iii) of subsection (3) of section three.
6 & 7 Geo 6 No 1	The New Parishes Measure 1943	Section twenty-five.
7 & 8 Geo 6 No 1	The Reorganisation Areas Measure 1944	In section twenty-four the words 'marriage registers and other' and the proviso to that section and subsection (2) of section twenty-eight.
12 & 13 Geo 6 No 3	The Pastoral Reorganisation Measure 1949	In subsection (1) of section six the words from 'and where banns' to the end of the subsection.

Words in italics repealed by Statute Law Revision Act 1953.

MARRIED WOMEN (RESTRAINT UPON ANTICIPATION) ACT 1949

(12, 13 & 14 Geo 6 c 78)

An Act to render inoperative any restriction upon anticipation or alienation attached to the enjoyment of property by a woman. [16 December 1949]

1. Abolition of restraint upon anticipation, and consequential amendments and repeals—(1) No restriction upon anticipation or alienation attached, or purported to be attached, to the enjoyment of any property by a woman which could not have been attached to the enjoyment of that property by a man shall be of any effect after the passing of this Act.

(2) The preceding subsection shall have effect whatever is the date of the passing, execution or coming into operation of the Act or instrument containing the provision by virtue of which the restriction was attached or purported to be attached, *and accordingly in section two of the Law Reform (Married Women and Tortfeasors) Act 1935 the proviso to subsection (1) and subsections (2) and (3) (which make provision differentiating as to the operation of such a restriction between an Act passed before the passing of that Act or an instrument executed before the date mentioned in the said proviso on the one hand and an instrument on or after that date on the other hand) are hereby repealed.*

Note. Words in italics repealed by the Statute Law (Repeals) Act 1975.

(3) The enactments mentioned in the first column of the First Schedule to this Act shall have effect subject to the amendments specified in the second column of that Schedule.

Note. Repealed by Statute Law (Repeals) Act 1969.

(4) The enactments mentioned in the Second Schedule to this Act are hereby repealed to the extent specified in the third column of that Schedule.

Note. Sub-s (4) repealed by Statute Law Revision Act 1953.

2. Short title and extent—(1) This Act may be cited as the Married Women (Restraint upon Anticipation) Act 1949.

(2) This Act shall not extend to Scotland or to Northern Ireland.

FIRST SCHEDULE   Section 1

CONSEQUENTIAL AMENDMENTS

The Married Woman's Property Act 1882.
(45 & 46 Vict c 75).

The Supreme Court of Judicature (Consolidation) Act 1925.
15 & 16 Geo 5 c 49).

In section nineteen, the words from 'or shall interfere' to 'before marriage' shall be repealed, and the word 'but' shall be substituted for the word 'and' where it occurs immediately after the said repealed words.

In section one hundred and ninety-four, in the subsection substituted for subsection (1) by the Law Reform (Married Women and Tortfeasors) Act 1935, the following paragraph shall be substituted for paragraph (a), that is to say—

(a) any property which is acquired by or devolves upon the wife on or after the date of the decree whilst the separation continues shall, if she dies intestate, devolve as if her husband had been then dead'.

Note. The part of this Schedule relating to Married Women's Property Act 1882 repealed by Statute Law (Repeals) Act 1969.

The part of this Schedule relating to Supreme Court of Judicature (Consolidation) Act 1925 repealed by Matrimonial Causes Act 1950, Schedule: see now Matrimonial Causes Act 1973, s 18(2) (p 2480), replacing Matrimonial Proceedings and Property Act 1970, s 40 (p 2383), replacing (with saving) Matrimonial Causes Act 1965, s 20(3), (4) (p 2248), replacing s 21 of the Matrimonial Causes Act 1950 (p 2130).

SECOND SCHEDULE   Section 1

ENACTMENTS REPEALED

Session and Chapter	Short Title	Extent of Repeal
20 & 21 Vict c 57	The Married Women's Reversionary Interests Act 1857	*In section one, the proviso.*
56 & 57 Vict c 63	The Married Women's Property Act 1893	*Section two.*
4 & 5 Geo 5 c 59	The Bankruptcy Act 1914	*Section fifty-two.*
15 & 16 Geo 5 c 18	The Settled Land Act 1925	*In section one, subsection (1), paragraph (iv). In section twenty, in subsection (1), paragraph (x). In section twenty-five, subsection (2).*
15 & 16 Geo 5 c 19	The Trustee Act 1925	*In section sixty-two, in subsection (1), the words from 'and notwithstanding' to 'anticipation'.*
15 & 16 Geo 5 c 20	The Law of Property Act 1925	*In section one hundred and fifty-three, in subsection (6), in paragraph (i), the words 'or is subject to a restraint on anticipation'.*

Session and Chapter	Short Title	Extent of Repeal
		In section one hundred and sixty-nine, the words 'is restrained from anticipation or from alienation' and the word 'or' where it occurs for the third time.
25 & 26 Geo 5 c 30	*The Law Reform (Married Women and Tortfeasors) Act 1935*	*In section two, in subsection (1), the proviso, and subsections (2) and (3).*
11 & 12 Geo 6 c 63	*The Agricultural Holdings Act 1948*	*In section eighty-five, in paragraph (a), the words 'and is not restrained from anticipation'.*

Note. Second Schedule repealed by Statute Law Revision Act 1953.

MATRIMONIAL CAUSES ACT 1950*

(14 Geo 6 c 25)

An Act to consolidate certain enactments relating to matrimonial causes in the High Court in England and to declarations of legitimacy and of validity of marriage and of British nationality, with such corrections and improvements as may be authorised by the Consolidation of Enactments (Procedure) Act 1949. [*28 July 1950*]

* Whole act repealed by Matrimonial Causes Act 1965, s 45, Sch 2.

Divorce and nullity of marriage

1. Grounds for petition for divorce—(*1*) *Subject to the provisions of the next following section, a petition for divorce may be presented to the court either by the husband or the wife on the ground that the respondent—*
  (*a*) *has since the celebration of the marriage committed adultery; or*
  (*b*) *has deserted the petitioner without cause for a period of at least three years immediately preceding the presentation of the petition; or*
  (*c*) *has since the celebration of the marriage treated the petitioner with cruelty; or*
  (*d*) *is incurably of unsound mind and has been continuously under care and treatment for a period of at least five years immediately preceding the presentation of the petition:*
and by the wife on the ground that her husband has, since the celebration of the marriage, been guilty of rape, sodomy or bestiality.

Note. This subsection replaced Supreme Court of Judicature (Consolidation) Act 1925, s 176, as substituted by Matrimonial Causes Act 1937, s 2 (p 2095). See now Matrimonial Causes Act 1973, s 1(1), (2) (p 2497), replacing Divorce Reform Act 1969 ss 1, 2(1) (p 2338), replacing Matrimonial Causes Act 1965, s 1(1) (p 2239).

  (*2*) *For the purposes of this section a person of unsound mind shall be deemed to be under care and treatment—*
  (*a*) *while he is detained in pursuance of any order or inquisition under the Lunacy and Mental Treatment Acts 1890 to 1930, or of any order or warrant under the Army Act, the Air Force Act, the Naval Discipline Act, the Naval Enlistment Act 1884, or the Yarmouth Naval Hospital Act 1931, or is being detained as a Broadmoor patient or in pursuance of an order made under the Criminal Lunatics Act 1884 [while he is liable to be detained in a hospital, mental nursing home or place of safety under the Mental Health Act 1959];*

Note. Words in square brackets replaced preceding provisions of para (a) except so far as related to any time before the commencement of Mental Health Act 1959; see Act of 1959, Sch 7.

(b) [*while he is liable to be detained in a hospital or place of safety under the Mental Health (Scotland) Act 1960*];

Note. Words in square brackets substituted for 'while he is detained in pursuance of any order or warrant for his detention or custody as a lunatic under the Lunacy (Scotland) Acts 1857 to 1919' by Mental Health (Scotland) Act 1960, Sch IV.

(c) *while he is detained in pursuance of any order for his detention or treatment as a person of unsound mind or a person suffering from mental illness made under any law for the time being in force in Northern Ireland, the Isle of Man or any of the Channel Islands (including any such law relating to criminal lunatics);*

(d) *while he is receiving treatment as a voluntary patient under the Mental Treatment Act 1930, or under any such law as is mentioned in paragraph (c) of this subsection, being treatment which follows without any interval a period during which he was detained as mentioned in paragraph (a), paragraph (b) or paragraph (c) of this subsection;*

Note. The words 'the Mental Treatment Act 1930, or under', except so far as related to any time before the commencement of Mental Health Act 1959 were omitted: see Act of 1959, Sch 7. The words 'being treatment . . . this subsection' were repealed by Divorce (Insanity and Desertion) Act 1958, s 4.

and not otherwise.

Note. This subsection replaced Matrimonial Causes Act 1937, s 3 (p 2096), as added to by Law Reform (Miscellaneous Provisions) Act 1949, s 3, subsequently amended by Divorce (Insanity and Desertion) Act 1958, s 4 and by Mental Health Act 1959, Schs 7, 8. Subsection as amended replaced by Matrimonial Causes Act 1965, s 1(3) repealed by Divorce Reform Act 1969, s 9(2), Sch 2 and not replaced.

2. Restriction on petitions for divorce during first three years after marriage—(*1*) *No petition for divorce shall be presented to the court unless at the date of the presentation of the petition three years have passed since the date of the marriage:*

Provided that a judge of the court, may upon application being made to him in accordance with rules of court, allow a petition to be presented before three years have passed on the ground that the case is one of exceptional hardship suffered by the petitioner or of exceptional depravity on the part of the respondent, but if it appears to the court at the hearing of the petition that the petitioner obtained leave to present the petition by any misrepresentation or concealment of the nature of the case, the court may, if it pronounces a decree nisi, do so subject to the condition that no application to make the decree absolute shall be made until after the expiration of three years from the date of the marriage, or may dismiss the petition, without prejudice to any petition which may be brought after the expiration of the said three years upon the same, or substantially the same, facts as those proved in support of the petition so dismissed.

(*2*) *In determining any application under this section for leave to present a petition before the expiration of three years from the date of the marriage, the judge shall have regard to the interests of any children of the marriage and to the question whether there is reasonable probability of a reconciliation between the parties before the expiration of the said three years.*

(*3*) *Nothing in this section shall be deemed to prohibit the presentation of a petition based upon matters which have occurred before the expiration of three years from the date of the marriage.*

Note. The first three subsections replaced Matrimonial Causes Act 1937, s 1 (p 2095). See now Matrimonial Causes Act 1973, s 3 (p 2499), replacing Matrimonial Causes Act 1965, ss 2, 5(5) (pp 2240, 2241).

(*4*) *This section shall not apply in the case of marriages to which section one of the Matrimonial Causes (War Marriages) Act 1944, applies (being certain marriages celebrated on or after the third day of September, nineteen hundred and thirty-nine, and before the first day of June nineteen hundred and fifty).*

3. Provision as to making adulterer co-respondent—(*1*) *On a petition for divorce presented by the husband on the ground of adultery or in the answer of a husband praying for divorce on the said ground, the petitioner or respondent, as the case may be, shall make the alleged adulterer a co-respondent unless he is excused by the court on special grounds from so doing.*

(*2*) *On a petition for divorce presented by the wife on the ground of adultery the court may, if it thinks fit, direct that the person with whom the husband is alleged to have committed adultery be made a respondent.*

Note. This section replaced Supreme Court of Judicature (Consolidation) Act 1925, s 177 (p 2056). See now Matrimonial Causes Act 1973, s 49 (p 2557), replacing Matrimonial Causes Act 1965, s 4(1), (2) (p 2241).

4. Duty of court on presentation of petition—(*1*) *On a petition for divorce it shall be the duty of the court to inquire, so far as it reasonably can, into the facts alleged and whether there has been any connivance or condonation on the part of the petitioner and whether any collusion exists between the parties, and also to inquire into any countercharge which is made against the petitioner.*

(*2*) *If the court is satisfied on the evidence that—*
(*a*) *the case for the petition has been proved; and*
(*b*) *where the ground of the petition is adultery, the petitioner has not in any manner been accessory to, or connived at, or condoned, the adultery, or, where the ground of the petition is cruelty, the petitioner has not in any manner condoned the cruelty; and*
(*c*) *the petition is not presented or prosecuted in collusion with the respondents;*
the court shall pronounce a decree of divorce, but if the court is not satisfied with respect to any of the aforesaid matters, it shall dismiss the petition:

Note. Sub-s 4(2)(c) repealed by Matrimonial Causes Act 1963, s 4(1)(a).

Provided that the court shall not be bound to pronounce a decree of divorce and may dismiss the petition if it finds [that the petition is presented or prosecuted in collusion with the respondent or either of the respondents or] that the petitioner has during the marriage been guilty of adultery or if, in the opinion of the court, the petitioner has been guilty—
(*i*) *of unreasonable delay in presenting or prosecuting the petition; or*
(*ii*) *of cruelty towards the other party to the marriage; or*
(*iii*) *where the ground of the petition is adultery or cruelty, of having without reasonable excuse deserted, or having without reasonable excuse wilfully separated himself or herself from, the other party before the adultery or cruelty complained of; or*
(*iv*) *where the ground of the petition is adultery or unsoundness of mind or desertion, of such wilful neglect or misconduct as has conduced to the adultery or unsoundness of mind or desertion.*

Note. Words in square brackets inserted by Matrimonial Causes Act 1963, s 4(1)(b).
This section replaced Supreme Court of Judicature (Consolidation) Act 1925, s 178 (p 2057), as substituted by Matrimonial Causes Act 1937, s 4. See now Matrimonial Causes Act 1973, ss 1(3), (4), 2(1), (3) (pp 2497, 2498), replacing Divorce Reform Act 1969, ss 2(2), (3), 3(3), (4) (pp 2338, 2339), replacing Matrimonial Causes Act 1965, s 5(1), (3), (4) (pp 2241, 2242).

5. Dismissal of respondent or co-respondent from proceedings. *In any case in which, on the petition of a husband for divorce on the ground of adultery, the alleged adulterer is made a co-respondent or in which, on the petition of a wife for divorce on the ground of adultery, the person with whom the husband is alleged to have committed adultery is made a respondent, the court may, after the close of the evidence on the part of the petitioner, direct the co-respondent or the respondent, as the case may be, to be dismissed from the proceedings if the court is of opinion that there is not sufficient evidence against him or her.*

Note. This section replaced Supreme Court of Judicature (Consolidation) Act 1925, s 179 (p 2057). See now Matrimonial Causes Act 1973, s 49(3) (p 2557), replacing Matrimonial Causes Act 1965, s 4(3) (p 2241).

6. Relief to respondent on petition for divorce. *If in any proceedings for divorce the respondent opposes the relief sought on the ground of the petitioner's adultery, cruelty or* *desertion, the court may give to the respondent the same relief to which he or she would have been entitled if he or she had presented a petition seeking such relief.*

Note. This section replaced Supreme Court of Judicature (Consolidation) Act 1925, s 180 (p 2058). See now Matrimonial Causes Act 1973, s 20 (p 2508), replacing Matrimonial Causes Act 1965, s 5(6) (p 2242).

7. Divorce proceedings after grant of judicial separation or other relief—(*1*)
A person shall not be prevented from presenting a petition for divorce, or the court from pronouncing a decree of divorce, by reason only that the petitioner has at any time been granted a judicial separation or an order under the Summary Jurisdiction (Separation and Maintenance) Acts 1895 to 1949, upon the same or substantially the same facts as those proved in support of the petition for divorce.

(*2*) *On any such petition for divorce, the court may treat the decree of judicial separation or the said order as sufficient proof of the adultery, desertion, or other ground on which it was granted, but the court shall not pronounce a decree of divorce without receiving evidence from the petitioner.*

(*3*) *For the purposes of any such petition for divorce, a period of desertion immediately preceding the institution of proceedings for a decree of judicial separation or an order under the said Acts having the effect of such decree shall, if the parties have not resumed cohabitation and the decree or order has been continuously in force since the granting thereof, be deemed immediately to precede the presentation of the petition for divorce.*

Note. This section replaced Matrimonial Causes Act 1937, s 6 (p 2097). See now Matrimonial Causes Act 1973, s 4 (p 2499), replacing Matrimonial Causes Act 1965, s 3 (p 2240).

8. Additional grounds for decree of nullity—(*1*) *In addition to any other grounds on which a marriage is by law void or voidable, a marriage shall be voidable on the ground—*
    (*a*) *that the marriage has not been consummated owing to the wilful refusal of the respondent to consummate the marriage; or*
    (*b*) *that either party of the marriage was at the time of the marriage of unsound mind or a mental defective within the meaning of the Mental Deficiency Acts 1913 to 1938 [was then suffering from mental disorder within the meaning of the Mental Health Act 1959, of such a kind or to such an extent as to be unfitted for marriage and the procreation of children], or subject to recurrent fits [attacks] of insanity or epilepsy; or*

Note. Words from 'a mental defective' to '1938' and 'fits' replaced by words in square brackets by Mental Health Act 1959, Sch 7 except so far as related to a marriage celebrated before the commencement of that Act.

    (*c*) *that the respondent was at the time of the marriage suffering from venereal disease in a communicable form; or*
    (*d*) *that the respondent was at the time of the marriage pregnant by some person other than the petitioner:*
Provided that, in the cases specified in paragraphs (b), (c) and (d) of this subsection, the court shall not grant a decree unless it is satisfied—
    (*i*) *that the petitioner was at the time of the marriage ignorant of the facts alleged;*
    (*ii*) *that proceedings were instituted within a year from the date of the marriage; and*
    (*iii*) *that marital intercourse with the consent of the petitioner has not taken place since the discovery by the petitioner of the existence of the grounds for a decree.*

(*2*) *Nothing in this section shall be construed as validating any marriage which is by law void, but with respect to which a decree of nullity has not been granted.*

Note. This section replaced Matrimonial Causes Act 1937, s 7(1), (3) (pp 2097, 2098) and was replaced by Matrimonial Causes Act 1965, s 9 (p 2244), repealed by Nullity of Marriage Act 1971, s 7(3) in relation to marriages celebrated after 31 July 1971. See now Matrimonial Causes Act 1973, ss 11, 12 (p 2503), replacing Nullity of Marriage Act 1971, ss 1, 2 (pp 2418–2419), in relation to marriages celebrated after 31 July 1971, and Matrimonial Causes Act 1973, Sch 1, para 11, (p 2563) in relation to marriages celebrated before 1 August 1971.

9. Legitimacy of children of voidable marriages. *Where a decree of nullity is granted in respect of a voidable marriage, any child who would have been the legitimate child*

of the parties to the marriage if it had been dissolved, instead of being annulled, at the date of the decree shall be deemed to be their legitimate child notwithstanding the annulment.

Note. This section replaced Matrimonial Causes Act 1937, s 7(2) (p 2098), as amended by Law Reform (Miscellaneous Provisions) Act 1949, s 4 and was replaced by Matrimonial Causes Act 1965, s 11 (p 2245): s 11 was repealed by Matrimonial Causes Act 1973, s 54(1), Sch 3 but was re-enacted by ibid, s 53, Sch 1, para 12 (pp 2561, 2564) in relation to decrees granted before 1 August 1971. For the corresponding provision in relation to decrees granted after 31 July 1971, see Matrimonial Causes Act 1973, s 16 (p 2506), replacing Nullity of Marriage Act 1971, s 5 (p 2420).

10. Duties of King's Proctor. *In the case of any petition for divorce or for nullity of marriage—*

 (1) *the court may, if it thinks fit, direct all necessary papers in the matter to be sent to His Majesty's Proctor, who shall under the directions of the Attorney-General instruct counsel to argue before the court any question in relation to the matter which the court deems to be necessary or expedient to have fully argued, and His Majesty's Proctor shall be entitled to charge the costs of the proceedings as part of the expenses of his office;*

 (2) *any person may at any time during the progress of the proceedings or before the decree nisi is made absolute give information to His Majesty's Proctor of any matter material to the due decision of the case, and His Majesty's Proctor may thereupon take such steps as the Attorney-General considers necessary or expedient;*

 (3) *if in consequence of any such information or otherwise His Majesty's Proctor suspects that any parties to the petition are or have been acting in collusion for the purpose of obtaining a decree contrary to the justice of the case, he may, under the direction of the Attorney-General, after obtaining the leave of the Court, intervene and retain counsel and subpœna witnesses to prove the alleged collusion.*

Note. This section replaced Supreme Court of Judicature (Consolidation) Act 1925, s 181 (p 2058). See now Matrimonial Causes Act 1973, ss 8(1), 15 (pp 2501, 2505), replacing Matrimonial Causes Act 1965, ss 6(1), 10 (pp 2243, 2245).

11. Provisions as to costs where King's Proctor intervenes or shows cause—(*1*) *Where His Majesty's Proctor intervenes or shows cause against a decree nisi in any proceedings for divorce or for nullity of marriage, the court may make such order as to the payment by other parties to the proceedings of the costs incurred by him in so doing or as to the payment by him of any costs incurred by any of the said parties by reason of his so doing, as may seem just.*

 (*2*) *So far as the reasonable costs incurred by His Majesty's Proctor in so intervening or showing cause are not fully satisfied by any order made under this section for the payment of his costs, he shall be entitled to charge the difference as part of the expenses of his office, and the Treasury may, if they think fit, order that any costs which under any order made by the court under this section His Majesty's Proctor pays to any parties shall be deemed to be part of the expenses of his office.*

Note. This section replaced Supreme Court of Judicature (Consolidation) Act 1925, s 182 (p 2058). See now Matrimonial Causes Act 1973, ss 8(2), (3), 15 (pp 2502, 2505), replacing Matrimonial Causes Act 1965, ss 6(2), (3), 10 (pp 2243, 2245).

12. Decree nisi for divorce or nullity of marriage—(*1*) *Every decree for a divorce or for nullity of marriage shall, in the first instance, be a decree nisi not to be made absolute until after the expiration of six months from the pronouncing thereof, unless the court by general or special order from time to time fixes a shorter time.*

 (*2*) *After the pronouncing of the decree nisi and before the decree is made absolute, any person may, in the prescribed manner, show cause why the decree should not be made absolute by reason of the decree having been obtained by collusion or by reason of material facts not having been brought before the court, and in any such case the court may make the decree absolute, reverse the decree nisi, require further inquiry or otherwise deal with the case as the court thinks fit.*

 (*3*) *Where a decree nisi has been obtained and no application for the decree to be made absolute has been made by the party who obtained the decree, then, at any time after the expiration of three months from the earliest date on which that party could have made such an application, the party against whom the decree nisi has been granted shall be at liberty to apply to the court and the court shall, on such application, have power to make the decree absolute, reverse the decree nisi, require further inquiry or otherwise deal with the case as the court thinks fit.*

Note. This section replaced Supreme Court of Judicature (Consolidation) Act 1925, s 183 (p 2059), as added to by Matrimonial Causes Act 1937, s 9. See now Matrimonial Causes Act 1973, ss 1(5), 9, 15 (pp 2498, 2502, 2505), replacing Matrimonial Causes Act 1965, ss 5(7), 7, 10 (pp 2242, 2243, 2245).

13. Re-marriage of divorced persons—(*1*) *Where a decree of divorce has been made absolute and either there is no right of appeal against the decree absolute, or if there is such a right of appeal, the time for appealing has expired without an appeal having been presented or an appeal has been presented but has been dismissed, either party to the marriage may marry again.*

(*2*) *No clergyman of the Church of England or of the Church in Wales shall be compelled to solemnise the marriage of any person whose former marriage has been dissolved on any ground and whose former husband or wife is still living, or to permit the marriage of any such person to be solemnised in the Church or Chapel of which he is the minister.*

Note. This section replaced Supreme Court of Judicature (Consolidation) Act 1925, s 184 (p 2057), as amended by Matrimonial Causes Act 1937, s 12. See now Matrimonial Causes Act 1965, s 8 (p 2244). Section 8(1) of the Act of 1965 (corresponding to s 13(1), above) was repealed by Matrimonial Causes Act 1973, s 54(1), Sch 3, and not replaced.

Judicial Separation and Restitution of Conjugal Rights

14. Decree for judicial separation—(*1*) *A petition for judicial separation may be presented to the court either by the husband or the wife on any grounds on which a petition for divorce might have been presented, or on the ground of failure to comply with a decree for restitution of conjugal rights, or on any ground on which a decree for divorce a mensa et thoro might have been pronounced immediately before the commencement of the Matrimonial Causes Act 1857, and the foregoing provisions of this Act relating to the duty of the court on the presentation of a petition for divorce, and the circumstances in which such a petition shall or may be granted or dismissed, shall apply in like manner to a petition for judicial separation.*

(*2*) *Where the court in accordance with the said provisions grants a decree for judicial separation, it shall no longer be obligatory for the petitioner to cohabit with the respondent.*

(*3*) *The court may, on the application by petition of the husband or wife against whom a decree for judicial separation has been made, and on being satisfied that the allegations contained in the petition are true, reverse the decree at any time after the making thereof, on the ground that it was obtained in the absence of the person making the application, or, if desertion was the ground of the decree, that there was reasonable cause for the alleged desertion.*

Note. This section replaced Supreme Court of Judicature (Consolidation) Act 1925, s 185(1), (2), (3) (p 2060), as amended by Matrimonial Causes Act 1937, s 5. See now Matrimonial Causes Act 1973, ss 17, 18 (pp 2506, 2507), replacing Matrimonial Causes Act 1965, s 12 (p 2245).

15. Decree for restitution of conjugal rights—(*1*) *A petition for restitution of conjugal rights may be presented to the court either by the husband or the wife, and the court, on being satisfied that the allegations contained in the petition are true, and that there is no legal ground why a decree for restitution of conjugal rights should not be granted, may make the decree accordingly.*

Note. This subsection replaced Supreme Court of Judicature (Consolidation) Act 1925, s 186 (p 2060). See Matrimonial Proceedings and Property Act 1970, ss 20 (abolition of right to claim restitution of conjugal rights), 42(2), Sch 3 (since repealed) (pp 2376, 2383, 2388) repealing Matrimonial Causes Act 1965, s 13(1) (p 2246).

(*2*) *A decree for restitution of conjugal rights shall not be enforced by attachment.*

Note. This subsection replaced part of Supreme Court of Judicature (Consolidation) Act 1925, s 187(1) (p 2061). See Matrimonial Proceedings and Property Act 1970, ss 20 (abolition of right to claim restitution of conjugal rights), 42(2), Sch 3 (since repealed) (pp 2376, 2383, 2388), repealing Matrimonial Causes Act 1965, s 13(2) (p 2246).

Presumption of death and dissolution of marriage

16. Proceedings for decree of presumption of death and dissolution of marriage—(*1*) *Any married person who alleges that reasonable grounds exist for supposing that the other party to the marriage is dead may, if he is domiciled in England, present a petition to the court to have it presumed that the other party is dead and to have the marriage dissolved, and the court, if satisfied that such reasonable grounds exist, may make a decree of presumption of death and of dissolution of the marriage.*

(*2*) *In any such proceedings the fact that for a period of seven years or upwards the other party to the marriage has been continually absent from the petitioner, and the petitioner has no reason to believe that the other party has been living within that time, shall be evidence that he or she is dead until the contrary is proved.*

(*3*) *Sections ten to thirteen of this Act shall apply to a petition and a decree under this section as they apply to a petition for divorce and a decree of divorce respectively.*

(*4*) *In determining for the purpose of this section whether a woman is domiciled in England, her husband shall be treated as having died immediately after the last occasion on which she knew or had reason to believe him to be living.*

Note. This section replaced Matrimonial Causes Act 1937, s 8 (p 2098), as amended by Law Reform (Miscellaneous Provisions) Act 1949, s 1(3). See now Matrimonial Causes Act 1973, s 19 (p 2507), replacing Matrimonial Causes Act 1965, s 14 (p 2246).

Declaration of Legitimacy, &c

17. Declaration of legitimacy, &c—(*1*) *Any person who is a British subject, or whose right to be deemed a British subject depends wholly or in part on his legitimacy or on the validity of any marriage, may, if he is domiciled in England or Northern Ireland or claims any real or personal estate situate in England, apply by petition to the court for a decree declaring that the petitioner is the legitimate child of his parents, and* [*or*] *that the marriage of his father and mother or of his grandfather and grandmother was a valid marriage or that his own marriage was a valid marriage.*

Note. This subsection replaced Supreme Court of Judicature (Consolidation) Act 1925, s 188(1) (p 2061), as amended by British Nationality Act 1948, Sch IV. The word 'and' was replaced by the word 'or' by Legitimacy Act 1959, s 2(6). See now Matrimonial Causes Act 1973, s 45(1) (p 2554), replacing Matrimonial Causes Act 1965, s 39(1) (p 2262).

(*2*) *Any person claiming that he or his parent or any remoter ancestor became or has become a legitimated person may apply by petition to the court* [*to the court by petition or to a county court*] *for a decree declaring that he or his parent or remoter ancestor, as the case may be, became or has become a legitimated person.*

In this subsection the expression 'legitimated person' means a person legitimated by the Legitimacy Act 1926, and includes a person recognised under section eight of that Act as legitimated.

Note. This subsection replaced s 2(1) of the Legitimacy Act 1926, and Administration of Justice Act 1928, s 19(3), Sch I, Part III. The words in square brackets were substituted for 'by petition to the court' by Administration of Justice Act 1956, s 31(2). See now Matrimonial Causes Act 1973, s 45(2) (p 2554), replacing Matrimonial Causes Act 1965, s 39(2) (p 2262).

(*3*) *A petition under the last foregoing subsection may be presented to a county court instead of to the High Court. Provided that, where a petition is presented to a county court* [*Where an application under the last foregoing subsection is made to a county court*] *the county court, if it considers that the case is one which owing to the value of the property involved or otherwise ought to be dealt with by the High Court, may, and if so ordered by the High Court shall, transfer the matter to the High Court, and on such transfer the proceeding shall be continued in the High Court as if it has been originally commenced therein* [*by a petition presented to the High Court*]*.*

Note. This subsection replaced Legitimacy Act 1926, s 2(2).

The words in the first set of square brackets were substituted for the words 'A petition under the last foregoing subsection may be presented to a county court instead of to the High Court. Provided that, where a petition is presented to a county court'; and the words in the second set of square brackets were substituted for the word 'therein': see Administration of Justice Act 1956, ss 31(2), 57, Sch 2. See now Matrimonial Causes Act 1973, s 45(3) (p 2554), replacing Matrimonial Causes Act 1965, s 39(3) (p 2262).

(*4*) *Any person who is domiciled in England or Northern Ireland or claims any real or personal estate situate in England may apply to the court for a decree declaring his right to be deemed a British subject.*

(*5*) *Applications to the court (but not to a county court) under the foregoing provisions of this section may be included in the same petition, and on any application under the foregoing provisions of this section (including an application to a county court) the court shall make such decree as the court thinks just, and the decree shall be binding on His Majesty and all other persons whatsoever:*

Provided that the decree of the court shall not prejudice any person—

(*a*) *if it is subsequently proved to have been obtained by fraud or collusion; or*

(*b*) *unless that person has been cited or made a party to the proceedings or claims through a person so cited or made a party.*

(*6*) *A copy of every petition [or other application] under this section and of any affidavit accompanying the petition [or other application] shall be delivered to the Attorney-General at least one month before the petition [or other application] is presented [or made], and the Attorney-General shall be a respondent on the hearing of the petition [or other application] and on any subsequent proceedings relating thereto.*

Note. Words in square brackets added by Administration of Justice Act 1956, s 31(2).

(*7*) *In any application under this section such persons shall, subject to rules of court, be cited to see proceedings or otherwise summoned as the court shall think fit, and any such persons may be permitted to become parties to the proceedings and to oppose the application.*

(*8*) *No proceedings under this section shall affect any final judgment or decree already pronounced or made by any court of competent jurisdiction.*

Note. Sub-ss (4)–(8) replaced Supreme Court of Judicature (Consolidation) Act 1925, s 188(1)–(5), (7) (p 2061). See now Matrimonial Causes Act 1973, s 45(4)–(8) (p 2555), replacing Matrimonial Causes Act 1965, s 39(4)–(8) (pp 2262, 2263).

18. Additional jurisdiction in proceedings by a wife—(*1*) *Without prejudice to any jurisdiction exercisable by the court apart from this section, the court shall by virtue of this section have jurisdiction to entertain proceedings by a wife in any of the following cases, notwithstanding that the husband is not domiciled in England, that is to say—*

(*a*) *in the case of any proceedings under this Act other than proceedings for presumption of death and dissolution of marriage, if the wife has been deserted by her husband, or the husband has been deported from the United Kingdom under any law for the time being in force relating to the deportation of aliens [to deportation] and the husband was immediately before the desertion or deportation domiciled in England;*

Note. The words 'to the deportation of aliens' were replaced by 'to deportation' by Commonwealth Immigrants Act 1962, s 20.

(*b*) *in the case of proceedings for divorce or nullity of marriage, if the wife is resident in England and has been ordinarily resident there for a period of three years immediately preceding the commencement of the proceedings, and the husband is not domiciled in any other part of the United Kingdom or in the Channel Islands or the Isle of Man.*

(*2*) *Without prejudice to the jurisdiction of the court to entertain proceedings under section sixteen of this Act in cases where the petitioner is domiciled in England, the court shall by virtue of this section have jurisdiction to entertain any such proceedings brought by a wife, if the wife is resident in England and has been ordinarily resident there for a period of three years immediately preceding the commencement of the proceedings.*

(*3*) *In any proceedings in which the court has jurisdiction by virtue of this section, the issues shall be determined in accordance with the law which would be applicable thereto if both parties were domiciled in England at the time of the proceedings.*

Note. This section replaced Matrimonial Causes Act 1937, s 13 (p 2100), and Law Reform (Miscellaneous Provisions) Act 1949, s 1, except so much of s 1(4) of the Act of 1949 as related to the Act of 1944. See now Matrimonial Causes Act 1973, ss 19(2), (5), 46 (pp 2507, 2555), replacing Matrimonial Causes Act 1965, ss 14(2), (5), 40 (pp 2246, 2263).

Alimony, Maintenance and Custody of Children

19. Alimony and maintenance in case of divorce and nullity of marriage—
(*1*) *On any petition for divorce or nullity of marriage, the court may make such interim orders for the payment of alimony to the wife as the court thinks just.*

Note. This subsection replaced in part Supreme Court of Judicature (Consolidation) Act 1925, s 190(3) (p 2062). See now Matrimonial Causes Act 1973, s 22 (p 2510), replacing Matrimonial Proceedings and Property Act 1970, s 1 (p 2365), replacing Matrimonial Causes Act 1965, s 15 (p 2246).

(*2*) *On any decree for divorce or nullity of marriage* [*Subject to the provisions of section twenty-nine of this Act, on pronouncing a decree nisi for divorce or nullity of marriage or at any time thereafter, whether before or after the decree has been made absolute*] *the court may, if it thinks fit, order that the husband shall, to the satisfaction of the court, secure to the wife such gross sum of money or annual sum of money for any term, not exceeding her life, as, having regard to her fortune, if any, to the ability of her husband and to the conduct of the parties, the court may deem to be reasonable; and the court may for that purpose order that it shall be referred to one of the conveyancing counsel of the court to settle and approve a proper deed or instrument to be executed by all necessary parties, and may, if it thinks fit, suspend the pronouncing of the decree until the deed or instrument has been duly executed.*

Note. This subsection replaced Supreme Court of Judicature (Consolidation) Act 1925, s 190(1) (p 2062). The words 'On any decree for divorce or nullity of marriage' were replaced by the words in square brackets by Matrimonial Causes (Property and Maintenance) Act 1958, s 1, Schedule (pp 2197, 2203). See now Matrimonial Causes Act 1973, ss 23, 30 (pp 2512, 2536), replacing Matrimonial Proceedings and Property Act 1970, ss 2, 25 (pp 2365, 2378), replacing Matrimonial Causes Act 1965, ss 16(1), (2), 19 (pp 2247, 2248).

As to power to order a lump sum payment, see Matrimonial Causes Act 1973, s 23(1)(c) (p 2512), replacing Matrimonial Proceedings and Property Act 1970, s 2(1)(c) (p 2365), replacing Matrimonial Causes Act 1965, s 16(1) (p 2247) which replaced Matrimonial Causes Act 1963, s 5(1) (p 2236).

(*3*) *On any decree for divorce or nullity of marriage* [*Subject to the provisions of the said section twenty-nine, on pronouncing a decree nisi for divorce or nullity of marriage or at any time thereafter, whether before or after the decree has been made absolute*] *the court may, if it thinks fit, by order direct the husband to pay to the wife, during their joint lives, such monthly or weekly sum for the maintenance and support of the wife as the court may think reasonable, and any such order may either be in addition to or be instead of an order made under the last foregoing subsection.*

Note. This subsection replaced Supreme Court of Judicature (Consolidation) Act 1925, s 190(2) (p 2062). The words 'On any decree for divorce or nullity of marriage' were replaced by the words in square brackets by Matrimonial Causes (Property and Maintenance) Act 1958, s 1, Schedule (pp 2197, 2203).

See now Matrimonial Causes Act 1973, ss 23, 30 (pp 2512, 2536), replacing Matrimonial Proceedings and Property Act 1970, ss 2, 25 (pp 2365, 2378), replacing Matrimonial Causes Act 1965, ss 16(1), 19 (pp 2247, 2248).

(*4*) *The foregoing provisions of this section shall have effect, in any case where a petition for divorce is presented by a wife on the ground of her husband's insanity, as if for the references to the husband there were substituted references to the wife, and for the references to the wife there were substituted references to the husband.*

Note. This subsection replaced Matrimonial Causes Act 1937, s 10(2) (p 2100). See now Matrimonial Causes Act 1973, ss 22, 23 (pp 2510, 2512), replacing Matrimonial Proceedings and Property Act 1970, ss 1, 2 (p 2365), replacing Matrimonial Causes Act 1965, ss 15, 16(3) (pp 2246, 2247) which replaced Matrimonial Causes Act 1950, s 19.

20. Alimony in case of judicial separation—(*1*) *On any petition for judicial separation, the court may make such interim orders for the payment of alimony to the wife as the court thinks just.*

Note. This subsection replaced in part Supreme Court of Judicature (Consolidation) Act 1925, s 190(3) (p 2062). See now Matrimonial Causes Act 1973, s 22 (p 2510), replacing Matrimonial Proceedings and Property Act 1970, s 1 (p 2365), replacing Matrimonial Causes Act 1965, s 20(1) (p 2248).

(*2*) *On any decree [On or at any time after a decree] for judicial separation, the court may make such order for the payment of alimony to the wife as the court thinks just.*

Note. This subsection replaced in part Supreme Court of Judicature (Consolidation) Act 1925, s 190(4) (p 2063). The words 'On any decree' were replaced by the words in square brackets by Matrimonial Causes (Property and Maintenance) Act 1958, s 1, Schedule (pp 2197, 2203).

See now Matrimonial Causes Act 1973, s 23 (p 2512), replacing Matrimonial Proceedings and Property Act 1970, s 2 (p 2365), replacing Matrimonial Causes Act 1965, s 20(1) (p 2248).

(*3*) *The foregoing provisions of this section shall have effect, in any case where a petition for judicial separation is presented by a wife on the ground of her husband's insanity, as if for the references to the wife there were substituted references to the husband.*

Note. This subsection replaced in part Matrimonial Causes Act 1937, s 10(2) (p 2099). See now Matrimonial Causes Act 1973, ss 22, 23 (pp 2510, 2512), replacing Matrimonial Proceedings and Property Act 1970, ss 1, 2 (p 2365), replacing Matrimonial Causes Act 1965, ss 15, 20(1) (pp 2246, 2248).

21. Wife's property and necessaries supplied to wife in case of judicial separation—(*1*) *In every case of judicial separation—*

(*a*) *any property which is acquired by or devolves upon the wife, on or after the date of the decree whilst the separation continues, shall if she dies intestate, devolve as if her husband had been then dead:*

(*b*) *if alimony has been ordered to be paid and has not been duly paid by the husband, he shall be liable for necessaries supplied for the use of the wife.*

(*2*) *In any case where the decree for judicial separation is obtained by the wife, any property to which she is entitled for an estate in remainder or reversion at the date of the decree shall be deemed to be property to which this section applies.*

Note. This subsection replaced Supreme Court of Judicature (Consolidation) Act 1925, s 194 (p 2064), as amended by Law Reform (Married Women and Tortfeasors) Act 1935, Schedule. See now Matrimonial Causes Act 1973, s 18(2) (p 2507), replacing Matrimonial Proceedings and Property Act 1970, s 40 (p 2383), replacing Matrimonial Causes Act 1965, s 20(3), (4) (p 2249).

22. Alimony and periodical payments in case of restitution of conjugal rights—(*1*) *On any petition for restitution of conjugal rights, the court may make such interim order for the payment of alimony to the wife as the court thinks just.*

Note. This subsection replaced in part Supreme Court of Judicature (Consolidation) Act 1925, s 190(3) (p 2062). See Matrimonial Proceedings and Property Act 1970, s 20 (abolition of right to claim restitution of conjugal rights) (p 2376).

(*2*) *Where any decree for restitution of conjugal rights is made on the application of the wife, the court may make such order for the payment of alimony to the wife as the court thinks just.*

Note. This subsection replaced in part Supreme Court of Judicature (Consolidation) Act 1925, s 190(4) (p 2063). See Matrimonial Proceedings and Property Act 1970, s 20 (abolition of right to claim restitution of conjugal rights) (p 2376).

(*3*) *Where any decree for restitution of conjugal rights is made on the application of the wife, the court, at the time of making of the decree or at any time afterwards may, in the event of the decree not being complied with within any time limited in that behalf by the court, order the respondent to make to the petitioner such periodical payments as the court thinks just, and the order may be enforced in the same manner as an order for alimony.*

Note. This subsection replaced in part Supreme Court of Judicature (Consolidation) Act 1925, s 187(1) (p 2061). See notes above to sub-ss (1) and (2).

(*4*) *Where the court makes an order under the last foregoing subsection, the court may, if it thinks fit, order that the husband shall, to the satisfaction of the court, secure to the wife the periodical payments, and for that purpose may direct that it shall be referred to one of the conveyancing counsel of the court to settle and approve a proper deed or instrument to be executed by all the necessary parties.*

Note. This subsection replaced in part Supreme Court of Judicature (Consolidation) Act 1925, s 187(2) (p 2061), itself replaced by Matrimonial Causes Act 1965, s 21(2) (p 2249). Cf Matrimonial Causes Act 1973, ss 23, 30 (pp 2512, 2536), replacing Matrimonial Proceedings and Property Act 1970, ss 2, 25 (pp 2365, 2376), replacing Matrimonial Causes Act 1965, s 21(2) (p 2249).

Matrimonial Proceedings and Property Act 1970, s 20 (p 2357) abolished the right to claim restitution of conjugal rights.

23. Additional power of court to make orders for maintenance—(*1*) *Where a husband has been guilty of wilful neglect to provide reasonable maintenance for his wife or the infant children of the marriage the court, if it would have jurisdiction to entertain proceedings by the wife for judicial separation, may, on the application of the wife, order the husband to make to her such periodical payments as may be just; and the order may be enforced in the same manner as an order for alimony in proceedings for judicial separation.*

Note. The words 'infant children of the marriage' included a reference to an illegitimate child of both parties to the marriage. See now Matrimonial Causes Act 1973, s 27 (p 2529), replacing Matrimonial Proceedings and Property Act 1970, s 6 (p 2367), replacing Matrimonial Causes Act 1965, s 22(2) (p 2250) which replaced this section.

(*2*) *Where the court makes an order under this section for periodical payments it may, if it thinks fit, order that the husband shall, to the satisfaction of the court, secure to the wife the periodical payments, and for that purpose may direct that a proper deed or instrument to be executed by all necessary parties shall be settled and approved by one of the conveyancing counsel of the court.*

Note. This section replaced Law Reform (Miscellaneous Provisions) Act 1949, s 5. See now Matrimonial Causes Act 1973, ss 23, 30 (pp 2512, 2536), replacing Matrimonial Proceedings and Property Act 1970, ss 2, 25 (pp 2365, 2371), replacing Matrimonial Causes Act 1965, s 22 (p 2250) which replaced this section.

24. Power of court to order settlement of wife's property—(*1*) *If it appears to the court in any case in which the court pronounces a decree for divorce or for judicial separation by reason of the adultery, desertion or cruelty of the wife that the wife is entitled to any property either in possession or reversion, the court may, if it thinks fit, order such settlement as it thinks reasonable to be made of the property, or any part thereof, for the benefit of the innocent party, and of the children of the marriage or either or any of them.*

(*2*) *Where a decree for restitution of conjugal rights is made on the application of the husband, and it appears to the court that the wife is entitled to any property, either in possession or reversion, or is in receipt of any profits of trade or earnings, the court may, if it thinks fit, order a settlement to be made to the satisfaction of the court of the property or any part thereof for the benefit of the petitioner and of the children of the marriage or either or any of them, or may order such part of the profits of trade or earnings as the court thinks reasonable to be periodically paid by the respondent to the petitioner for his own benefit, or to the petitioner or any other person for the benefit of the children of the marriage or either or any of them.*

Note. This section replaced Supreme Court of Judicature (Consolidation) Act 1925, s 191 (p 2063), as amended by Matrimonial Causes Act 1973, s 10(3), and was itself replaced by Matrimonial Causes Act 1965. See now Matrimonial Causes Act 1973, ss 23–25 (pp 2512–2519), replacing Matrimonial Proceedings and Property Act 1970, ss 2–5 (pp 2361–2366), replacing Matrimonial Causes Act 1965, ss 17(2), 20(2), 21(3) (pp 2248, 2249).

25. Power of court to make orders as to application of settled property. *The court may after pronouncing a decree for divorce or for nullity of marriage enquire into the existence of ante-nuptial or post-nuptial settlements made on the parties whose marriage is the subject of the decree, and may make such orders with reference to the application of the whole or any part of the property settled either for the benefit of the children of the marriage or of the parties to the marriage, as the court thinks fit, and the court may exercise the powers conferred by this section notwithstanding that there are no children of the marriage.*

Note. This section replaced Supreme Court of Judicature (Consolidation) Act 1925, s 192 (p 2063), and was itself replaced by Matrimonial Causes Act 1965 (ss 17(1), 19, 46(2), pp 2247, 2248, 2265). See now Matrimonial Causes Act 1973, ss 24, 52(1) (pp 2515, 2559), replacing Matrimonial Proceedings and Property Act 1970, ss 4, 27(1) (pp 2366, 2378), replacing Matrimonial Causes Act 1965, ss 17(1), 19, 46(2) (pp 2247, 2248, 2265).

26. Custody and maintenance of children—(*1*) *In any proceedings for divorce or nullity of marriage or judicial separation, the court may from time to time, either before or by or after the final decree, make such provision as appears just with respect to the custody, maintenance and education of the children the marriage of whose parents is the subject of the proceedings, or, if it thinks fit, direct proper proceedings to be taken for placing the children under the protection of the court.*

(*2*) *On an application made in that behalf, the court may, in any proceedings for restitution of conjugal rights, at any time before final decree, or, if the respondent fails to comply therewith, after final decree, make from time to time all such orders and provisions with respect to the custody, maintenance and education of the children of the petitioner and respondent as might have been made by interim orders if proceedings for judicial separation had been pending between the same parties.*

(*3*) *On any decree of divorce or nullity of marriage [Subject to the provisions of section twenty-nine of this Act, on pronouncing a decree nisi of divorce or nullity of marriage or at any time thereafter, whether before or after the decree has been made absolute], the court shall have power to order the husband, and on a decree of divorce, [where the decree is a decree of divorce and is] made on the ground of the husband's insanity, shall also have power to order the wife, to secure for the benefit of the children such gross sum of money or annual sum of money as the court may deem reasonable, and the court may for that purpose order that it shall be referred to one of the conveyancing counsel of the court to settle and approve a proper deed or instrument to be executed by all necessary parties:*

Note. The words 'on any decree of divorce or nullity' and 'on a decree of divorce' were replaced by the words in square brackets by Matrimonial Causes (Property and Maintenance) Act 1958, s 1, Schedule (pp 2197, 2203).

Provided that the term for which any sum of money is secured for the benefit of a child shall not extend beyond the date when the child will attain twenty-one years of age.

Note. This section replaced Supreme Court of Judicature (Consolidation) Act 1925, s 193 (p 2064), as amended by Matrimonial Causes Act 1937, s 10(4), and was itself replaced by Matrimonial Causes Act 1965, ss 34, 46(2) (pp 2258, 2265). For extended jurisdiction in regard to children, see Matrimonial Proceedings (Children) Act 1958, ss 1, 3, 5, 6 (pp 2223, 2225, 2226). See now Matrimonial Causes Act 1973, ss 23, 42, 52(1) (pp 2512, 2551, 2559), replacing Matrimonial Proceedings and Property Act 1970, ss 3, 18, 19, 27(1) (pp 2365, 2375, 2376, 2378), replacing Matrimonial Causes Act 1965, ss 34, 46(2) (pp 2258, 2265).

27. Payment of alimony and maintenance to trustees and persons having charge of respondent—(*1*) *In any case where the court makes an order for alimony, the court may direct the alimony to be paid either to the wife or the husband, as the case may be, or to a trustee approved by the court on her or his behalf, and may impose such terms or restrictions as the court thinks expedient, and may from time to time appoint a new trustee if for any reason it appears to the court expedient so to do.*

(*2*) *In any case where—*

(*a*) *a petition for divorce or judicial separation is presented by a wife on the ground of her husband's insanity; or* (*b*) *a petition for divorce, nullity or judicial separation is presented by a husband on the ground of his wife's insanity or mental deficiency* [*or disorder*],

and the court orders payments of alimony or maintenance under section nineteen or section twenty of this Act in favour of the respondent, the court may order the payments to be made to such persons having charge of the respondent as the court may direct.

Note. This section replaced Supreme Court of Judicature (Consolidation) Act 1925, s 190(5) (p 2063), as amended by Matrimonial Causes Act 1937, s 10(2), and was itself replaced by Matrimonial Causes Act 1965, s 30. The words in square brackets were added by Mental Health Act 1959, Sch 7. See now Matrimonial Causes Act 1973, s 40 (p 2549), replacing Matrimonial Proceedings and Property Act 1970, s 26 (p 2378), replacing Matrimonial Causes Act 1965, s 30 (p 2256).

28. Variation and discharge of orders for alimony and maintenance—(*1*) *Where the court has made an order under section nineteen, section twenty, section twenty-two, section twenty-three or subsection* (*2*) *of section twenty-four of this Act, the court shall have power to discharge or vary the order or to suspend any provision thereof temporarily and to revive the operation of any provisions so suspended:*

Provided that in relation to an order made before the sixteenth day of December, nineteen hundred and forty-nine, being an order which, by virtue of subsection (*2*) *of section thirty-four of this Act, is deemed to have been made under subsection* (*2*) *of section nineteen of this Act, the powers conferred by this section shall not be exercised unless the court is satisfied that the case is one of exceptional hardship which cannot be met by the discharge, variation or suspension of any order made, or deemed as aforesaid to have been made, under subsection* (*3*) *of the said section nineteen.*

(*2*) *The powers exercisable by the court under this section in relation to any order shall be exercisable also in relation to any deed or other instrument executed in pursuance of the order.*

(*3*) *In exercising the powers conferred by this section, the court shall have regard to all the circumstances of the case, including any increase or decrease in the means of either of the parties to the marriage.*

Note. This section replaced Administration of Justice (Miscellaneous Provisions) Act 1938, s 14, as amended by Law Reform (Miscellaneous Provisions) Act 1949, s 6, and was itself replaced by Matrimonial Causes Act 1965, s 31 (p 2257). See now Matrimonial Causes Act 1973, s 31 (p 2536), replacing Matrimonial Proceedings and Property Act 1970, s 9 (p 2370), replacing Matrimonial Causes Act 1965, s 31, Sch 1, para 9 (pp 2257, 2267).

29. Commencement of proceedings for maintenance, settlement of property, &c. *When a petition for divorce or nullity of marriage has been presented, proceedings under section nineteen, twenty-four, twenty-five or subsection* (*3*) *of section twenty-six of this Act may, subject to and in accordance with rules of court, be commenced at any time after the presentation of the petition:*

Provided that no order under any of the said sections or under the said subsection (*other than an interim order for the payment of alimony under section nineteen*) *shall be made unless and until a decree nisi has been pronounced, and no such order, save in so far as it relates to the preparation, execution, or approval of a deed or instrument, and no settlement made in pursuance of any such order, shall take effect unless and until the decree is made absolute.*

Note. This section replaced Matrimonial Causes Act 1937, s 10 (p 2098), and was itself replaced by Matrimonial Causes Act 1965, ss 18(1), 34(6) (pp 2248, 2259). See now Matrimonial Causes Act 1973, s 26 (p 2528), replacing Matrimonial Proceedings and Property Act 1970, s 24 (p 2378), replacing Matrimonial Causes Act 1965, ss 18(1), 34(6) (pp 2248, 2259).

Miscellaneous

30. Damages for adultery—(*1*) *A husband may, on a petition for divorce or for judicial separation, or for damages only, claim damages from any person on the ground of adultery with the wife of the petitioner.*

(*2*) *A claim for damages on the ground of adultery shall, subject to the provisions of any enactment relating to trial by jury in the court, be tried on the same principles and in the same manner as actions for criminal conversation were tried immediately before the commencement of the Matrimonial Causes Act 1857, and the provisions of this Act with reference to the hearing and decision of petitions shall so far as may be necessary apply to the hearing and decision of petitions on which damages are claimed.*

(3) The court may direct in what manner the damages recovered on any such petition are to be paid or applied, and may direct the whole or any part of the damages to be settled for the benefit of the children, if any, of the marriage, or as a provision for the maintenance of the wife.

Note. This section replaced Supreme Court of Judicature (Consolidation) Act 1925, s 189 (p 2062), and was itself replaced by Matrimonial Causes Act 1965, s 41 (p 2263). See Law Reform (Miscellaneous Provisions) Act 1970, ss 4, 7 (pp 2362, 2363), which repealed, and did not replace, Matrimonial Causes Act 1965, s 41 (p 2263).

31. Power to allow intervention on terms. *In every case in which any person is charged with adultery with any party to a suit or in which the court may consider, in the interest of any person not already a party to the suit, that that person should be made a party to the suit, the court may, if it thinks fit, allow that person to intervene upon such terms, if any, as the court thinks just.*

Note. This section replaced Supreme Court of Judicature (Consolidation) Act 1925, s 197 (p 2066), and was itself replaced by Matrimonial Causes Act 1965, s 44 (p 2265). See now Matrimonial Causes Act 1973, s 49(5) (p 2557), replacing Matrimonial Causes Act 1965, s 44 (p 2265).

32. Evidence—(*1*) *Notwithstanding any rule of law, the evidence of a husband or wife shall be admissible in any proceedings to prove that marital intercourse did or did not take place between them during any period.*

(2) Notwithstanding anything in this section or any rule of law, a husband or wife shall not be compellable in any proceedings to give evidence of the matters aforesaid.

(3) The parties to any proceedings instituted in consequence of adultery and the husband and wives of the parties shall be competent to give evidence in the proceedings, but no witness in any such proceedings, whether a party thereto or not, shall be liable to be asked or be bound to answer any question tending to show that he or she has been guilty of adultery unless he or she has already given evidence in the same proceedings in disproof of the alleged adultery.

(4) In any proceedings for nullity of marriage, evidence on the question of sexual capacity shall be heard in camera unless in any case the judge is satisfied that in the interests of justice any such evidence ought to be heard in open court.

Note. This section replaced Law Reform (Miscellaneous Provisions) Act 1949, s 7, amending Supreme Court of Judicature (Consolidation) Act 1925, s 198 (p 2066) and s 198A as added by Supreme Court of Judicature (Amendment) Act 1935, s 4. See now Matrimonial Causes Act 1973, s 48 (p 2557), replacing Matrimonial Causes Act 1965, s 43 (p 2264), which replaced this section.

Interpretation, repeal and short title

33. Interpretation. *In this Act the expression 'the court' means the High Court, except that in section seventeen, where the context so requires, it means or includes a county court, and the expression 'prescribed' means prescribed by rules of court.*

34. Repeal and savings—(*1*) *The enactments set out in the Schedule to this Act are hereby repealed to the extent specified in the third column of that Schedule.*

(2) Without prejudice to the provisions of section thirty-eight of the Interpretation Act 1889—

(a) nothing in this repeal shall effect any order made, direction given or thing done, under any enactment repealed by this Act or the Supreme Court of Judicature (Consolidation) Act 1925, or deemed to have been made, given or done respectively under any such enactment, and every such order, direction or thing shall if in force at the commencement of this Act continue in force, and, so far as it could have been made, given or done under this Act, shall be deemed to have been made, given or done under the corresponding provision of this Act

(b) any other order in force at the commencement of this Act which could have been made under any provision of this Act shall be deemed to have been so made;

(c) *any document referring to any Act or enactment repealed by this Act or the said Act of 1925 shall be construed as referring to this Act or to the corresponding enactment in this Act;*

(d) *for the purposes of the India (Consequential Provision) Act 1949 this Act shall be deemed to have been in force on the twenty-sixth day of January, nineteen hundred and fifty.*

35. Short title, commencement and extent—(*1*) *This Act may be cited as the Matrimonial Causes Act 1950.*

(*2*) *This Act shall come into operation on the first day of January, nineteen hundred and fifty-one.*

(*3*) *This Act shall not extend to Scotland or Northern Ireland.*

SCHEDULE

ENACTMENTS REPEALED

Session and Chapter	Short Title	Extent of Repeal
15 & 16 Geo 5 c 49	*The Supreme Court of Judicature (Consolidation) Act 1925*	*Sections one hundred and seventy-six to one hundred and ninety-eight A.*
16 & 17 Geo 5 c 60	*The Legitimacy Act 1926*	*Section two.*
18 & 19 Geo 5 c 26	*The Administration of Justice Act 1928*	*Subsection (3) of section nineteen, and Part III of the First Schedule.*
21 & 22 Geo 5 c 31	*The Marriage (Prohibited Degrees of Relationship) Act 1931*	*The whole Act.*
25 & 26 Geo 5 c 2	*The Supreme Court of Judicature (Amendment) Act 1935*	*Section four.*
25 & 26 Geo 5 c 30	*The Law Reform (Married Women and Tortfeasors) Act 1935*	*The First Schedule, so far as it relates to the Supreme Court of Judicature (Consolidation) Act 1925.*
1 Edw 8 & 1 Geo 6 c 57	*The Matrimonial Causes Act 1937*	*The whole Act, except section eleven.*
1 & 2 Geo 6 c 63	*The Administration of Justice (Miscellaneous Provisions) Act 1938*	*Section fourteen.*
7 & 8 Geo 6 c 43	*The Matrimonial Causes (War Marriages) Act 1944*	*In section one, paragraph (b) of subsection (1).*
12, 13 & 14 Geo 6 c 78	*The Married Women (Restraint upon Anticipation) Act 1949*	*The First Schedule, so far as it relates to the Supreme Court of Judicature (Consolidation) Act 1925.*

MAINTENANCE ORDERS ACT 1950

(14 Geo 6 c 37)

An Act to enable certain maintenance orders and other orders relating to married persons and children to be made and enforced throughout the United Kingdom.

[26 October 1950]

PART I

JURISDICTION

Jurisdiction of English Courts

1. Jurisdiction of English courts to make summary maintenance orders—(*1*) *Subject to the following provisions of this section, a court in England shall have jurisdiction in proceedings under section four of the Summary Jurisdiction (Married Women) Act 1895, against a man residing in Scotland or Northern Ireland, if the applicant in the proceedings resides in England and the parties last ordinarily resided together as a man and wife in England.*

(*2*) *It is hereby declared that a court in England has jurisdiction—*

(*a*) *in proceedings under the said section four by a woman residing in Scotland or Northern Ireland against a man residing in England;*

(*b*) *in proceedings by or against a person residing in Scotland or Northern Ireland for the revocation, revival or variation of any order made under that section.*

(*3*) *The reference in this section to the revocation of an order made under section four of the Summary Jurisdiction (Married Women) Act 1895, includes a reference to the making of a new order under paragraph (b) of the proviso to section seven of that Act.*

(*4*) *Nothing in this section shall be construed as enabling a court to make a separation order under paragraph (a) of section five of the Summary Jurisdiction (Married Women) Act 1895, against a person residing in Scotland or Northern Ireland.*

Note. This section repealed by Matrimonial Proceedings (Magistrates' Courts) Act 1960, s 18(1), Schedule: see ibid, ss 1(3), 19(2).

2. Jurisdiction of English summary courts to make orders for custody and maintenance of infants—(*1*) *An order under the Guardianship of Infants Acts 1886 and 1925, giving the custody of an infant to the mother, whether with or without an order requiring the father to make payments to the mother towards the infant's maintenance, may be made, if the father resides in Scotland or Northern Ireland and the mother and the infant in England, by a court of summary jurisdiction having jurisdiction in the place in which the mother resides.*

(*2*) *It is hereby declared that a court of summary jurisdiction in England has jurisdiction—*

(*a*) *in proceedings under the said Acts by a person residing in Scotland or Northern Ireland against a person residing in England for an order relating to the custody of an infant (including, in the case of proceedings by the mother, an order requiring the father to make payments to the mother towards the infant's maintenance);*

(*b*) *in proceedings by or against a person residing in Scotland or Northern Ireland for the revocation, revival or variation of any such order.*

(*3*) *Where proceedings for an order under section five of the Guardianship of Infants Act 1886, or section four of the Summary Jurisdiction (Married Women) Act 1895, relating to the custody of an infant are brought in a court of summary jurisdiction in England by a woman residing in Scotland or Northern Ireland, that court shall have jurisdiction to make any order in respect of the infant under the said section five upon the application of the defendant in the proceedings.*

Note. Sub-ss (1), (2) and the reference to Guardianship of Infants Act 1886 in sub-s (3) repealed by Guardianship of Minors Act 1971, s 18(2), Sch 2, and sub-s (3) repealed by Domestic Proceedings and Magistrates' Courts Act 1978, s 89, Sch 3, as from 1 February 1981. This section was replaced by Guardianship of Minors Act 1971, s 15(4)–(6).

3. Jurisdiction of English courts to make affiliation orders—(*1*) *A court in England shall have jurisdiction in proceedings under the Bastardy Laws Amendment Act 1872, or under section forty-four of the National Assistance Act 1948, or section twenty-six of the Children Act 1948 [or section 19 of the Supplementary Benefits Act 1976] [or section 25 of the Social Security Act 1986] for an affiliation order against a man residing in Scotland or Northern Ireland, if the act of intercourse resulting in the birth of the child or any act of intercourse between the parties which may have resulted therein took place in England.*

Note. Words 'or section twenty-six of the Children Act 1948' repealed by Child Care Act 1980, s 89, Sch 6, as from 1 April 1981. First words in square brackets inserted by Supplementary

Benefits Act 1976, s 36(3), Sch 7. Second words in square brackets inserted by Social Security
Act 1986, s 86, Sch 10, Part II, para 34, as from 11 April 1988. Whole section repealed by
Family Law Reform Act 1987, s 33(4), Sch 4, as from 1 April 1989.

* * * * *

5. Transfer of proceedings. *Rules made by the Lord Chancellor under section fifteen of
the Justices of the Peace Act 1949, may make provision for securing that where proceedings are
begun against a defendant residing in Scotland or Northern Ireland in a court having
jurisdiction by virtue of subsection (1) of section one of this Act, not being a court having
jurisdiction in the place where the parties last ordinarily resided together as man and wife, the
proceedings may be removed upon the application of the defendant into a court of summary
jurisdiction having jurisdiction in that place.*
Note. This section repealed by Matrimonial Proceedings (Magistrates' Courts) Act 1960,
s 18(1), Schedule.

* * * * *

Supplemental

15. Service of process—(1) *Where proceedings are begun in a court having jurisdiction
under or by virtue of this Part of this Act* [*or section 15 of the Guardianship of Minors Act
1971*] [*or section 41 of the Maintenance Orders (Reciprocal Enforcement) Act 1972*] *against a
person residing*
   [Where—
   (a) proceedings are begun in a court having jurisdiction under or by virtue of
        the following, namely—
        (i)   this Part of this Act; or
        (ii) *section 1(3) or 9(1) of the Matrimonial Proceedings (Magistrates' Courts)
              Act 1960* [sections 24(1) and 30(3) of the Domestic Proceedings and
              Magistrates' Courts Act 1978]; or
        (iii) *section 15 of the Guardianship of Minors Act, 1971; or*
        (iv) *section 41 of the Maintenance Orders (Reciprocal Enforcement) Act 1972* [*or
              sections 33 to 45 of the Children Act 1975*] [*or section 55 of the Child Care
              Act 1980*], *or*
   [(iii) section 92 of and Schedule 11 to the Children Act 1989; or
    (iv) section 93(2)(g) of that Act (including that provision as applied in
          relation to Northern Ireland by section 116(3) of the Courts and
          Legal Services Act 1990)]
Note. Sub-s (1)(a)(iii), (iv) substituted by Courts and Legal Services Act 1990, s 116(2), Sch
16, Part II, para 34, as from 14 October 1991.

   [(v) *Article 26(1) or 32(2) of the Domestic Proceedings (Northern Ireland) Order
         1980; or*]
   [(v) Article 164 of and Schedule 7 to the Children (Northern Ireland)
         Order 1995 or Article 165(2)(g) of that Order; or]
Note. Sub-s (1)(a)(v) added by Maintenance Orders (Northern Ireland Consequential
Amendments) Order 1980 (SI 1980 No 564). Sub-s (1)(a)(v) substituted by Children (Northern
Ireland Consequential Amendments) Order 1995, SI 1995 No 756, arts 2, 15, Schedule, as from
4 November 1996.

   [(vi) Article 5(2) of Schedule 4 to the Civil Jurisdiction and Judgments Act
         1982; or]
Note. Sub-s (1)(a)(vi) added by Civil Jurisdiction and Judgments Act 1982, s 53(1), Sch 13,
Part I, para 3, as from 1 January 1987.

   (b) an action *for separation and aliment* [which contains a conclusion for aliment
        not falling within the scope of paragraph (a)(i) above] is commenced in a
        sheriff court in Scotland, and the person against whom the action or other
        proceedings is or are brought resides] in another part of the United Kingdom

any summons or initial writ addressed to him in the proceedings may, if endorsed in accordance with the provisions of this section in that part of the United Kingdom, be served within that part of the United Kingdom as if it had been issued or authorised to be served, as the case may be, by the endorsing authority.

Note. Reference in square brackets to Guardianship of Minors Act 1971 inserted by Guardianship of Minors Act 1971, ss 18(1), 20(4)(a), Sch 1. Reference in square brackets to Maintenance Orders (Reciprocal Enforcement) Act 1972 inserted by ibid, s 41(3).

Words from 'where' to 'residing' in italics substituted by words from 'where' to 'resides' in square brackets by Administration of Justice Act 1977, s 3, Sch 3, para 11, as from 1 September 1977. In sub-s (1)(a)(ii), as so substituted, words in square brackets substituted for words in italics by Domestic Proceedings and Magistrates' Courts Act 1978, s 89, Sch 2, para 12, as from 1 November 1979. In sub-s (1)(a)(iv), reference to Children Act 1975 inserted by Children Act 1975, s 108(1), Sch 3, para 10, as from 1 December 1985, and reference to Child Care Act 1980 inserted by Child Care Act 1980, s 89, Sch 5, para 2, as from 1 April 1981.

Words from 'which' to 'above' in square brackets in para (b) substituted by Civil Jurisdiction and Judgments Act 1982, s 23(2), Sch 12, Part II, para 2, as from 1 January 1987.

(2) A summons or writ may be endorsed under this section, in England by a justice of the peace, in Scotland by a sheriff, and in Northern Ireland by a resident magistrate; and the endorsement shall be made in the form numbered 1 in the Second Schedule to this Act, or any form to the like effect.

(3) In any proceedings in which a summons or writ is served under this section, the service may be proved by means of a declaration made in the form numbered 2 in the Second Schedule to this Act, or any form to the like effect, before a justice of the peace, sheriff or resident magistrate, as the case may be.

(4) Nothing in this section shall be construed as authorising the service of a summons or writ otherwise than personally.

(5) Section four of the Summary Jurisdiction (Process) Act 1881, shall not apply to any process which may be served under this section; and nothing in this section or in any other enactment shall be construed as authorising the execution in one part of the United Kingdom of a warrant for the arrest of a person who fails to appear in answer to any such process issued in another part of the United Kingdom.

Note. This section has effect in relation to a complaint mentioned in Attachment of Earnings Act 1971, s 20, as it has effect in relation to proceedings mentioned in this section: see Attachment of Earnings Act 1971, s 20(2) (p 2405).

PART II*

ENFORCEMENT

16. Application of Part II—(1) Any order to which this section applies (in this Part of this Act referred to as a maintenance order) made by a court in any part of the United Kingdom may, if registered in accordance with the provisions of this Part of this Act in a court in another part of the United Kingdom, be enforced in accordance with those provisions in that other part of the United Kingdom.

(2) This section applies to the following orders, that is to say—

(a) an order for alimony, maintenance or other payment made or deemed to be made by a court in England under any of the following enactments—

　　(i) *sections nineteen to twenty-seven of the Matrimonial Causes Act 1950;*

　　[(i) sections 15 to 17, 19 to 22, 30, 34 and 35 of the Matrimonial Causes Act 1965 and sections 22, *23(1)*, *(2)* and *(4)* [22A, 23] and 27 of the Matrimonial Causes Act 1973;] [and section 14 or 17 of the Matrimonial and Family Proceedings Act 1984;]

---

* Part II of this Act does not apply to an order registered in a court in the United Kingdom under Part II of Maintenance Orders (Reciprocal Enforcement) Act 1972: see s 33(6) of Act of 1972 (p 2471).

Note. Sub-para (i) in square brackets substituted for original sub-para (i) by Matrimonial Causes Act 1973, s 54, Sch 2, para 3(1)(a), and amended by Matrimonial and Family Proceedings Act 1984, s 46(1), Sch 1, para 1(a), as from 16 September 1985 and by Family Law Act 1996, s 66(1), Sch 8, Part I, para 3, as from a day to be appointed, subject to savings in s 66(2) of, and para 5 of Sch 9 to, the 1996 Act.

> (*ii*)   *The Summary Jurisdiction (Separation and Maintenance) Acts, 1895 to 1949;*
> [(ii)   Part I of the Domestic Proceedings and Magistrates' Courts Act 1978];

Note. Sub-para (ii) in square brackets substituted for sub-para (ii) in italics by Domestic Proceedings and Magistrates' Courts Act 1978, s 89, Sch 2, para 13, as from 1 February 1981.

> (*iii*)   *subsection (2) of section three or subsection (4) of section five of the Guardianship of Infants Act 1925;*
> [(*iii*)   *section 9(2), 10(1) or 12(2) of the Guardianship of Minors Act 1971*] [*or section 2(3) or 2(4)(a) of the Guardianship Act 1973*];

Note. First words in square brackets in sub-para (iii) substituted for original sub-para (iii) by Guardianship of Minors Act 1971, s 18(1), Sch 1. Second words in square brackets added by Guardianship Act 1973, s 9(3).

> [(*iii*)   *section 11B, 11C(1) or 11D of the Guardianship of Minors Act 1971 or section 2(3) or 2(4A) of the Guardianship Act 1973;*]
> [(iii)   Schedule 1 to the Children Act 1989;]

Note. Sub-para (iii) substituted by Family Law Reform Act 1987, s 33(1), Sch 2, para 12(a), as from 1 April 1989. Sub-para (iii) further substituted by Courts and Legal Services Act 1990, s 116(2), Sch 16, para 35, as from 14 October 1991.

> (*iv*)   *section four of the Bastardy Laws Amendment Act 1872, section forty-four of the National Assistance Act, 1948 or section twenty-six of the Children Act 1948* [*section 50 of the Child Care Act 1980*];

Note. Words in square brackets substituted for reference to Act of 1948 by Child Care Act 1980, s 89, Sch 5, para 3, as from 1 April 1981.

Bastardy Laws Amendment Act 1872 is repealed by Affiliation Proceedings Act 1957, Schedule.

Sub-para (iv) repealed by Family Law Reform Act 1987, s 33, Sch 2, para 12(b), Sch 4.

> (v)   *section eighty-seven of the Children and Young Persons Act 1933* [*section 47 of the Child Care Act 1980*] [paragraph 23 of Schedule 2 to the Children Act 1989], or section forty-three of the National Assistance Act 1948;

Note. Words in first pair of square brackets substituted for words in italics by Child Care Act 1980, s 89, Sch 5, para 3, as from 1 April 1981. Reference to Children Act 1989 substituted by Courts and Legal Services Act 1990, s 116(2), Sch 16, para 35, as from 14 October 1991.

Orders under Family Law Reform Act 1969, ss 4(2), (6) are included in this section by virtue of ibid, ss 4(5), 6(7) (pp 2302, 2304).

> [(*vi*)   *section 4 of the Affiliation Proceedings Act 1957, on an application made under section 45 of the Children Act 1975;*
> (*vii*)   *section 34(1)(b) of the Children Act 1975;*]

Note. Sub-paras (vi), (vii) above inserted by Children Act 1975, s 108(1), Sch 3, para 11, as from 1 December 1985. See also sub-para (vi) infra. This sub-para (vi) repealed by Family Law Reform Act 1987, s 33, Sch 2, para 12(c), Sch. 4. Sub-para (vii) repealed by Courts and Legal Services Act 1990, s 125(7), Sch 20, as from 14 October 1991.

> [(vi)   section 18 of the Supplementary Benefits Act 1976 *or section 4 of the Affiliation Proceedings Act 1957 on an application made under section 19(2) of the Act of 1976;*]

Note. This sub-para (vi) inserted by Supplementary Benefits Act 1976, s 35(2), Sch 7, para 13: see also sub-para (vi) supra. Words in italics repealed by Family Law Reform Act 1987, s 33, Sch 2, para 12(d), Sch 4, as from 1 April 1989.

> [(viii)   *section 24 of the Social Security Act 1986* [section 106 of the Social Security Administration Act 1992] *or section 4 of the Affiliation Proceedings Act 1957 on an application made under section 25(1) of the Act of 1986;*]

Note. Sub-para (viii) inserted by Social Security Act 1986, s 86, Sch 10, Part II, para 39(a). Reference to Social Security Administration Act 1992 substituted by Social Security (Consequential Provisions) Act 1992, s 4, Sch 2, para 3(1), as from 1 July 1992. Words from 'or section 4' to 'Act of 1986' in italics repealed by Family Law Reform Act 1987, s 33(1), (4), Sch 2, para 12(e), Sch 4, as from 1 April 1989.

    (b) a decree for payment of aliment granted by a court in Scotland, including—

        (i) an order for the payment of an annual or periodical allowance under section two of the Divorce (Scotland) Act 1938 or [an order for the payment of a periodical allowance [or a capital sum] under section 26 of the Succession (Scotland) Act 1964 or section 5 of the Divorce (Scotland) Act 1976] [or section 29 of the Matrimonial and Family Proceedings Act 1984] [or an order for financial provision in the form of a monetary payment under s 8 of the Family Law (Scotland) Act 1985];

Note. Sub-para (i) amended by Divorce (Scotland) Act 1976, s 12(1), Sch 1, para 1, and Administration of Justice Act 1977, s 3, Sch 3, and by Matrimonial and Family Proceedings Act 1984, s 46(1), Sch 1, para 1(b), and by Family Law (Scotland) Act 1985, s 28(1), Sch 1, para 3.

       (ii) an order for the payment of weekly or periodical sums under subsection (2) of section three or subsection (4) of section five of the Guardianship of Infants Act, 1925;

      (iii) an order for the payment of sums in respect of aliment under subsection (3) of section one of the Illegitimate Children (Scotland) Act 1930;

      (iv) a decree for payment of aliment under section forty-four of the National Assistance Act 1948, or under section twenty-six of the Children Act 1948; and

Note. Proceedings under both these sections are now 'domestic proceedings': see Affiliation Proceedings (Amendment) Act 1972, s 3(1).

      (v) *a contribution order under section ninety-one of the Children and Young Persons (Scotland) Act 1937, or* an order under section forty-three of the National Assistance Act 1948;

Note. Words in italics repealed by Civil Jurisdiction and Judgments Act 1982, s 54, Sch 14, as from 1 January 1987.

      [(vi) a contribution order under section 80 of, or a decree or an order made under section 81 of, the Social Work (Scotland) Act 1968;]

Note. Sub-para (vi) added by Social Work (Scotland) Act 1968, s 95(1), Sch 8, para 34.

     [(vii) an order for the payment of weekly or other periodical sums under subsection (3) of section 11 of the Guardianship Act 1973;]

Note. Sub-para (vii) inserted by Guardianship Act 1973, s 14, Sch 5; Guardianship Act 1973, s 11(3), which applies only to Scotland, is in similar terms to Guardianship Act 1973, s 2(3) which applies to England and Wales.

    [(viii) an order made on an application under *section 19(8)(b)* [section 18 or 19(8)] of the Supplementary Benefits Act 1976;]

Note. Sub-para (viii) inserted by Supplementary Benefits Act 1976, s 35(2), Sch 7, para 13; amended by Social Security and Housing Benefits Act 1982, s 48(5), Sch 4, para 2, as from 28 June 1982.

     [(ix) an order made on an application under *section 24 of the Social Security Act 1986* [section 106 of the Social Security Administration Act 1992];]

Note. Sub-para (ix) inserted by Social Security Act 1986, s 86, Sch 10, Part II, para 39(b), as from 11 April 1988; amended by Social Security (Consequential Provisions) Act 1992, s 4, Sch 2, para 3(1), as from 1 July 1992.

    (c) an order for alimony, maintenance or other payments made by a court in Northern Ireland under or by virtue of any of the following enactments—

> (i) subsection (2) of section seventeen, subsections (2) to (7) of section nineteen, subsection (2) of section twenty, section twenty-two or subsection (1) of section twenty-eight of the Matrimonial Causes Act (Northern Ireland) 1939;
>
> (*ii*) *the Summary Jurisdiction (Separation and Maintenance Act (Northern Ireland) 1945;*
>
> [(ii) Schedule 1 to the Children (Northern Ireland) Order 1995;]

Note. Sub-para (ii) in square brackets substituted for sub-para (ii) in italics by Children (Northern Ireland Consequential Amendments) Order 1995, SI 1995 No 756, art 2(4)(a), as from 4 November 1996.

> (*iii*) *section one of the Illegitimate Children (Affiliation Orders) Act (Northern Ireland) 1924, section twenty-one of the National Assistance Act (Northern Ireland) 1948, section twelve of the Welfare Services Act (Northern Ireland) 1949, or section one hundred and twenty-four of the Children and Young Persons Act (Northern Ireland) 1950 [section 159 of the Children and Young Persons Act (Northern Ireland) 1968 or Article 102 of the Health and Personal Social Services (Northern Ireland) Order 1972];*

Note. Sub-para (iii) repealed by Children (Northern Ireland Consequential Amendments) Order 1995, SI 1995 No 756, art 15, Schedule, as from 4 November 1996. Words in square brackets substituted for words 'section twenty-one ... (Northern Ireland) 1950' by Supplementary Benefits etc (Consequential Provisions) (Northern Ireland) Order 1977, SI 1977 No 2158.

> (*iv*) *section one hundred and twenty-two of the Children and Young Persons Act (Northern Ireland) 1950, section twenty of the National Assistance Act (Northern Ireland) 1948, or section eleven of the Welfare Services Act (Northern Ireland) 1949;*
>
> [(iv) section 156 of the Children and Young Persons Act (Northern Ireland) 1968 [Article 41 of the Children (Northern Ireland) Order 1995] or Article 101 of the Health and Personal Social Services (Northern Ireland) Order 1972;]

Note. Sub-para (iv) in square brackets substituted for sub-para (iv) in italics by Supplementary Benefits etc (Consequential Provisions) (Northern Ireland) Order 1977, SI 1977 No 2158. Words in square brackets substituted for words in italics by Children (Northern Ireland Consequential Amendments) Order 1995, SI 1995 No 756, art 2(4)(b), as from 4 November 1996.

> (*v*) *any enactment of the Parliament of Northern Ireland containing provisions corresponding with subsection (1) of section twenty-three of the Matrimonial Causes Act 1950 [or section 12(2) of the Guardianship of Minors Act 1971].*
>
> [(v) any enactment of the Parliament of Northern Ireland containing provisions corresponding with section 22(1), 34 or 35 of the Matrimonial Causes Act 1965, with section 22, 23(1), (2), or (4) or 27 of the Matrimonial Causes Act 1973 [(as that Act had effect immediately before the passing of the Family Law Act 1996)], *or with section 12(2) of the Guardianship of Minors Act 1971*].

Note. Words in square brackets in original sub-para (v) (in italics) inserted by Guardianship of Minors Act 1971, s 18(1), Sch 1; new sub-para (v) in square brackets substituted by Matrimonial Causes Act 1973, s 54(1), Sch 2, para 3. Words in square brackets in new sub-para (v) inserted by Family Law Act 1996, s 66(1), Sch 8, para 3(b), as from a day to be appointed, subject to savings in s 66(2) of, and para 5 of Sch 9 to, the 1996 Act. Words in italics repealed by Children (Northern Ireland Consequential Amendments) Order 1995, SI 1995 No 746, art 15, Schedule, as from 4 November 1996.

> [(*vi*) *section 24 or 25 of the Supplementary Benefits etc Act (Northern Ireland) 1966.*]
>
> [(vi) Article 23 or 24 of the Supplementary Benefits (Northern Ireland) Order 1977.]

Note. Sub-para (vi) in italics added by Supplementary Benefits Act 1976, s 35(2), Sch 7, para 13, and substituted by Supplementary Benefits etc (Consequential Provisions) (Northern Ireland) Order 1977, SI 1977 No 2158.

[(vii) the Domestic Proceedings (Northern Ireland) Order 1980.]

Note. Sub-para (vii) added by the Maintenance Orders (Northern Ireland Consequential Amendments) Order 1980, SI 1980 No 564.

[(viii) any enactment applying in Northern Ireland and corresponding to *section 24 of the Social Security Act 1986* [section 106 of the Social Security Administration Act 1992];]

Note. Sub-para (viii) inserted by Social Security Act 1986, s 86, Sch 10, para 39(c), as from 11 April 1988; amended by Social Security (Consequential Provisions) Act 1992, s 4, Sch 2, para 3(1), as from 1 July 1992.

[(ix) Article 18 or 21 of the Matrimonial and Family Proceedings (Northern Ireland) Order 1989;]

Note. Sub-para (ix) added by Matrimonial and Family Proceedings (Northern Ireland Consequential Amendments) Order 1989, SI 1989 No 678, art 42, Sch 2.

(3) For the purposes of this section, any order made before the commencement of the Matrimonial Causes Act (Northern Ireland) 1939, being an order which, if that Act had been in force, could have been made under or by virtue of any provision of that Act, shall be deemed to be an order made by virtue of that provision.

Note. For the exclusion of orders registered under Part II of Maintenance Orders Act 1958, see the Act of 1958, s 1(2) (p 2204).

17. Procedure for registration of maintenance orders—(1) An application for the registration of a maintenance order under this Part of this Act shall be made in the prescribed manner to the appropriate authority, that is to say—

  (a) where the maintenance order was made by a court of summary jurisdiction in England, a justice or justices acting *for the same place* [acting in the same local justice area] as the court which made the order;
  (b) where the maintenance order was made by a court of summary jurisdiction in Northern Ireland, a resident magistrate acting for the same petty sessions district as the court which made the order;
  (c) in every other case, the prescribed officer of the court which made the order.

Note. In para (a) words 'acting in the same local justice area' in square brackets substituted for words 'for the same place' by the Courts Act 2003, s 109(1), Sch 8, para 87, as from a day to be appointed.

(2) If upon application made as aforesaid by or on behalf of the person entitled to payments under a maintenance order it appears that the person liable to make those payments resides in another part of the United Kingdom, and that it is convenient that the order should be enforceable there, the appropriate authority shall cause a certified copy of the order to be sent to the prescribed officer of a court in that part of the United Kingdom in accordance with the provisions of the next following subsection.

(3) The Court to whose officer the certified copy of a maintenance order is sent under this section shall be—

  (a) where the maintenance order was made by a superior court, the Supreme Court of Judicature in England, the Court of Session or the Supreme Court of Judicature of Northern Ireland, as the case may be;
  (b) in any other case, a court of summary jurisdiction acting for the place in England or Northern Ireland in which the defendant appears to be, or, as the case may be, the sheriff court in Scotland within the jurisdiction of which he appears to be.

(4) Where the prescribed officer of any court receives a certified copy of a maintenance order sent to him under this section, he shall cause the order to be

registered in that court in the prescribed manner, and shall give notice of the registration in the prescribed manner to the prescribed officer of the court which made the order.

(5) The officer to whom any notice is given under the last foregoing subsection shall cause particulars of the notice to be registered in his court in the prescribed manner.

(6) Where the sums payable under a maintenance order, being an order made by a court of summary jurisdiction in England or Northern Ireland, are payable to or through an officer of any court, that officer shall, if the person entitled to the payments so requests, make an application on behalf of that person for the registration of the order under this Part of this Act; but the person at whose request the application is made shall have the same liability for costs properly incurred in or about the application as if the application had been made by him.

(7) An order which is for the time being registered under this Part of this Act in any court shall not be registered thereunder in any other court.

18. Enforcement of registered orders—(1) Subject to the provisions of this section, a maintenance order registered under this Part of this Act in a court in any part of the United Kingdom may be enforced in that part of the United Kingdom in all respects as if it had been made by that court and as if that court had had jurisdiction to make it; and proceedings for or with respect to the enforcement of any such order may be taken accordingly.

[(1A) A maintenance order registered under this Part of this Act in a court of summary jurisdiction in England or Northern Ireland shall not carry interest; but where a maintenance order so registered is registered in the High Court under Part I of the Maintenance Orders Act 1958 or section 36 of the Civil Jurisdiction and Judgments Act 1982, this subsection shall not prevent any sum for whose payment the order provides from carrying interest in accordance with section 2A of the said Act of 1958 or section 11A of the Maintenance and Affiliation Orders Act (Northern Ireland) 1966.

(1B) A maintenance order made in Scotland which is registered under this Part of this Act in the Supreme Court in England or Northern Ireland shall, if interest is by the law of Scotland recoverable under the order, carry the like interest in accordance with subsection (1) of this section.]

Note. Sub-ss (1A), (1B) inserted by Civil Jurisdiction and Judgments Act 1982, s 37(1), Sch 11, para 5, as from 1 January 1987.

(*2*) *Every maintenance order registered under this Part of this Act in a court of summary jurisdiction in England (not being an order made in Scotland under section forty-three of the National Assistance Act 1948, or an order made under section twenty of the National Assistance Act (Northern Ireland) 1948, or section eleven of the Welfare Services Act (Northern Ireland) 1949) shall be enforceable as if it were an affiliation order made by that court under the Bastardy Laws Amendment Act 1872, and the provisions of any enactment with respect to the enforcement of affiliation orders (including enactments relating to the accrual of arrears and the remission of sums due) shall apply accordingly.*

Note. Words 'not being ... 1949' repealed by Ministry of Social Security Act 1966, s 39(3), Sch 8: whole sub-s substituted by sub-s in square brackets infra by Family Law Reform Act 1987, s 33(1), Sch 2, para 13. Bastardy Laws Amendment Act 1872 repealed by Affiliation Proceedings Act 1957, Schedule.

[(2) Every maintenance order registered under this Part of this Act in a magistrates' court in England and Wales *shall be enforceable* [shall, subject to the modifications of sections 76 and 93 of the Magistrates' Courts Act 1980 specified in subsections (2ZA) and (2ZB) of this section be enforceable] as a magistrates' court maintenance order within the meaning of section 150(1) of the Magistrates' Courts Act 1980.]

[(2ZA) Section 76 (enforcement of sums adjudged to be paid) shall have effect as if for subsections (4) to (6) there were substituted the following subsections—

'(4) Where proceedings are brought for the enforcement of a magistrates' court maintenance order under this section, the court may vary the order by exercising one of its powers under subsection (5) below.

(5) The powers of the court are—

(a) the power to order that payments under the order be made directly to *the clerk of the court or the clerk of any other magistrates' court* [*a justices' chief executive*] [the designated officer for the court or for any other magistrates' court];

(b) the power to order that payments under the order be made to the clerk of the court, *or to the clerk of any other magistrates' court* [*a justices' chief executive*] [the designated officer for the court or for any other magistrates' court], by such method of payment falling within section 59(6) above (standing order, etc) as may be specified;

(c) the power to make an attachment of earnings order under the Attachment of Earnings Act 1971 to secure payments under the order.

(6) In deciding which of the powers under subsection (5) above it is to exercise, the court shall have regard to any representations made by the debtor (within the meaning of section 59 above).

(7) Subsection (4) of section 59 above (power of court to require debtor to open account) shall apply for the purposes of subsection (5) above as it applies for the purposes of that section but as if for paragraph (a) there were substituted—

"(a) the court proposes to exercise its power under paragraph (b) of section 76(5) below, and".'

(2ZB) In section 93 (complaint for arrears), subsection (6) (court not to impose imprisonment in certain circumstances) shall have effect as if for paragraph (b) there were substituted—

'(b) if the court is of the opinion that it is appropriate—

(i) to make an attachment of earnings order; or

(ii) to exercise its power under paragraph (b) of section 76(5) above.'

Note. Words in square brackets in sub-s (2) substituted for words in italics, and sub-ss (2ZA), (2ZB) inserted, by Maintenance Enforcement Act 1991, s 10, Sch 1, para 3, as from 1 April 1992. In sub-s (2ZA) words 'a justices' chief executive' in square brackets in both places they occur substituted for words 'the clerk of the court or the clerk of any other magistrates' court,' by the Access to Justice Act 1999, s 90, Sch 13, paras 12, 13, as from 1 April 2001 (SI 2001 No 916). In sub-s (2ZA) words 'the designated officer for the court or for any other magistrates' court' in square brackets in both places they occur substituted for words 'a justices' chief executive' by the Courts Act 2003, s 108(1), Sch 8, para 88(1), (2), as from a day to be appointed.

[(2A) Any person under an obligation to make payments under a maintenance order registered under this Part of this Act in a court of summary jurisdiction in England [or Northern Ireland] shall give notice of any change of address to the *clerk* [proper officer] of the court; and any person who without reasonable excuse fails to give such a notice shall be liable on summary conviction to a fine not exceeding level 2 on the standard scale (*as defined in section 75 of the Criminal Justice Act 1982*).]

Note. Sub-s (2A) inserted by Matrimonial and Family Proceedings Act 1984, s 46(1), Sch 1, para 2. 'Standard Scale' is now defined in Interpretation Act 1978, s 5, Sch 1 (pp 2735, 2738). Words 'or Northern Ireland' in square brackets in sub-s (2A) inserted by Matrimonial and Family Proceedings (Northern Ireland) Order 1989, SI 1989 No 678, art 42, Sch 2. Words 'proper officer' in square brackets substituted for word 'clerk' by the Access to Justice Act 1999, s 90(1), Sch 13, paras 12, 13(1), (3), as from 1 April 2001 (SI 2000 No 916). Words in italics repealed by Statute Law (Repeals) Act 1993, s 1(1), Sch 1, Part XIV, as from 5 November 1993.

[(2B) In subsection (2A) of this section 'proper officer' means—

(a) in relation to a court of summary jurisdiction in England and Wales, the *justices' chief executive* [designated officer] for the court; and

(b) in relation to a court of summary jurisdiction in Northern Ireland, the clerk of the court.]

Note. Sub-s (2B) inserted by the Access to Justice Act 1999, s 90(1), Sch 13, paras 12, 13(1), (4), as from 1 April 2001 (SI 2001 No 916). In para (a) words 'designated officer' in square brackets substituted for words 'justices' chief executive' by the Courts Act 2003, s 109(1), Sch 8, para 88(1), (3), as from a day to be appointed.

(3) Every maintenance order registered under this Part of this Act in a court of summary jurisdiction in Northern Ireland (*not being an order made under section forty-three of the National Assistance Act 1948*) shall be enforceable as *if it were an order made by that court under the Summary Jurisdiction (Separation and Maintenance) Act (Northern Ireland) 1945, and the provisions of section six of that Act [section 110 of the Magistrates' Courts Act (Northern Ireland) 1964] shall apply accordingly [shall, subject to the modifications specified in subsection (3ZA) of this section, apply accordingly]* [an order made by that Court to which Article 98 of the Magistrates' Courts (Northern Ireland) Order 1981 applies, subject to the modifications of that Article specified in subsection (3ZA) of this section].

Note. Words '(not being ... 1948)' in italics repealed by Ministry of Social Security Act 1966, s 39(3), Sch 8. Words in first pair of square brackets substituted for words 'section six of that Act' by Magistrates' Courts Act (Northern Ireland) 1964, s 172, Sch 7. Words in second pair of square brackets substituted for words 'shall apply accordingly' by Family Law (Northern Ireland Consequential Amendments) Order 1993, SI 1993 No 1577, art 2, as from 4 November 1996 (SR 1996 No 454). Words in third pair of square brackets substituted for words 'if it were' to the end by Children (Northern Ireland Consequential Amendments) Order 1995, SI 1995 No 756, art 2, as from 4 November 1996.

[(3ZA) Article 98 (enforcement of sums adjudged to be paid) shall have effect—
(a) as if for paragraph (7)(a) there were substituted the following sub-paragraph—
'(a) if the court is of the opinion that it is appropriate—
(i) to make an attachment of earnings order; or
(ii) to exercise its power under paragraph (8C)(b)'.
(b) as if for paragraphs (8B) to (8D) there were substituted the following paragraphs—
'(8B) Upon the appearance of a person or proof of service of the summons on him as mentioned in paragraph (4) for the enforcement of an order to which this Article applies, the court or resident magistrate may vary the order by exercising one of the powers under paragraph (8C).
(8C) The powers mentioned in paragraph (8B) are—
(a) the power to order that payments under the order be made directly to the collecting officer;
(b) the power to order that payments under the order be made to the collecting officer by such method of payment falling within Article 85(7) (standing order, etc) as may be specified;
(c) the power to make an attachment of earnings order under Part IX to secure payments under the order.
(8D) In deciding which of the powers under paragraph (8C) is to be exercised, the court or, as the case may be, a resident magistrate shall have regard to any representations made by the debtor (within the meaning of Article 85).
(8E) Paragraph (5) of Article 85 (power of court to require debtor to open account) shall apply for the purposes of paragraph (8C) as it applies for the purposes of that Article but as if for sub-paragraph (a) there were substituted—
'(a) the court proposes to exercise its power under sub-paragraph (b) of Article 98(8C), and'.']

Note. Sub-s (3ZA) inserted by Family Law (Northern Ireland Consequential Amendments) Order 1993, SI 1993 No 1577, art 2, as from a day to be appointed.

[(3A) Notwithstanding subsection (1) above, no court in England in which a maintenance order is registered under this Part of this Act shall enforce that order *whilst it is registered* [to the extent that it is for the time being registered] in another court in England under Part I of the Maintenance Orders Act 1958].

Note. Sub-s (3A) inserted by Administration of Justice Act 1977, s 3, Sch 3, para 6, as from 1 January 1981, and amended by Civil Jurisdiction and Judgments Act 1982, s 37(1), Sch 11, para 1, as from 1 January 1987.

[(3B) Notwithstanding subsection (1) above, no court in Northern Ireland in which a maintenance order is registered under this Part of this Act shall enforce that order to the extent that it is for the time being registered in another court in Northern Ireland under section 36 of the Civil Jurisdiction and Judgments Act 1982.]

Note. Sub-s (3B) inserted by Civil Jurisdiction and Judgments Act 1982, s 36(6), Sch 12, Part III, para 1(1), (2), as from 1 January 1987.

(*4*) *Where an order made in Scotland under section forty-three of the National Assistance Act 1948, or made under section twenty of the National Assistance Act (Northern Ireland) 1948, or section eleven of the Welfare Services Act (Northern Ireland) 1949, is registered under this Part of this Act in a court in England, the order shall be enforceable as if it were an order made by that court under the said section forty-three.*

(*5*) *Where an order made under section forty-three of the National Assistance Act 1948, is registered under this Part of this Act in a court in Northern Ireland, the order shall be enforceable as if it were an order made by that court under section twenty of the National Assistance Act (Northern Ireland) 1948.*

(6) Except as provided by this section, no proceedings shall be taken for or with respect to the enforcement of a maintenance order which is for the time being registered in any court under this Part of this Act.

Note. Sub-ss (4), (5) repealed by Ministry of Social Security Act 1966, s 39(3), Sch 8.

19. Functions of collecting officer, etc—(1) Where a maintenance order made in England or Northern Ireland by a court of summary jurisdiction is registered in any court under this Part of this Act, any provision of the order by virtue of which sums payable thereunder are required to be paid through or to any officer or person on behalf of the person entitled thereto shall be of no effect so long as the order is so registered.

Note. See Maintenance Orders Act 1958, s 2(6) (p 2193).

(2) Where a maintenance order is registered under this Part of this Act in a court of summary jurisdiction in England or Northern Ireland, the court shall, *unless it is satisfied that it is undesirable to do so* [unless, in the case of a court of summary jurisdiction in Northern Ireland, it is satisfied that it is undesirable to do so], order that all payments to be made under the maintenance order (including any arrears accrued before the date of the registration) shall be made through the collecting officer of the court or the collecting officer of some other court of summary jurisdiction in England or Northern Ireland, as the case may be.

Note. See Maintenance Orders Act 1958, s 2(6) (p 2205).

Words in square brackets substituted for preceding words in italics by Maintenance Enforcement Act 1991, s 10, Sch 1, para 4(1), as from 1 April 1992. Words in square brackets repealed by Family Law (Northern Ireland Consequential Amendments) Order 1993, SI 1993 No 1577, art 2, as from a day to be appointed.

(*3*) *An order made by a court of summary jurisdiction under subsection (2) of this section may be varied or revoked by a subsequent order.*

[(3) An order made under subsection (2) of this section—

(a) by a court of summary jurisdiction in England may be varied or revoked by an exercise of the powers conferred by virtue of section 18(2ZA) or section 22(1A) or (1E) of this Act;

   (*b*) *by a court of summary jurisdiction in Northern Ireland may be varied or revoked by a subsequent order.*]

  [(b) by a court of summary jurisdiction in Northern Ireland may be varied or revoked by an exercise of the powers conferred by virtue of section 18(3ZA) or section 22(1F) or (1J) of this Act.]

Note. Sub-s (3) in square brackets substituted for sub-s (3) in italics by Maintenance Enforcement Act 1991, s 10, Sch 1, para 4(2), as from 1 April 1992. Sub-s (3)(b) in square brackets substituted for sub-s (3)(b) in italics by Family Law (Northern Ireland Consequential Amendments) Order 1993, SI 1993 No 1577, art 2, as from 4 November 1996 (SR 1996 No 454).

   (4) Where by virtue of the provisions of this section or any order made thereunder payments under a maintenance order cease to be or become payable through or to any officer or person, the person liable to make the payments shall, until he is given the prescribed notice to that effect, be deemed to comply with the maintenance order if he makes payments in accordance with the maintenance order and any order under this section of which he has received such notice.

Note. See Maintenance Orders Act 1958, s 2(6) (p 2205).

   (*5*) *In any case where, by virtue of an order made under this section by a court in Northern Ireland, payments under a maintenance order are required to be made through the collecting officer of any court—*

  [(*a*) *subsections (5) and (6) of section ninety-five of the Magistrates' Courts Act (Northern Ireland) 1964 (which regulate the functions of collecting officers in relation to orders for periodical payment), shall apply as if the order made under this section were made under the said section ninety-five; and*

   (*b*) *subsection (8) of the said section ninety-five shall have effect as if money paid in accordance with an order under this section were paid in pursuance of an order under the said section ninety-five.*]

  [(*a*) *paragraph (4) of Article 85 of the Magistrates' Courts (Northern Ireland) Order 1981 (which regulates the functions of collecting officers in relation to orders for periodical payment) shall apply as if the order made under this section were made under the said Article 85; and*

   (*b*) *paragraph (7) of the said Article 85 shall have effect as if money paid in accordance with an order under this section were paid in pursuance of an order under the said Article 85.*]

Note. Sub-s (5) repealed by Family Law (Northern Ireland Consequential Amendments) Order 1993, SI 1993 No 1577, art 2, as from 4 November 1996 (SR 1996 No 454). First paras (a), (b) in square brackets substituted by Magistrates' Courts Act (Northern Ireland) 1964, s 171(1), Sch 6. Second paras (a), (b) in square brackets substituted by Magistrates' Courts (Northern Ireland) Order 1981, SI 1981 No 1675, art 170(2), Sch 6, Part I, para 6.

20. Arrears under registered maintenance orders—(1) Where application is made for the registration of a maintenance order under this Part of this Act, the applicant may lodge with the appropriate authority—

   (a) if the payments under the order are required to be made to or through an officer of any court, a certificate in the prescribed form, signed by that officer, as to the amount of any arrears due under the order;

   (b) in any other case, a statutory declaration or affidavit as to the amount of those arrears;

and if a certified copy of the maintenance order is sent to the prescribed officer of any court in pursuance of the application, the certificate, declaration or affidavit shall also be sent to that officer.

   (2) In any proceedings for or with respect to the enforcement of a maintenance order which is for the time being registered in any court under this Part of this Act, a certificate, declaration or affidavit sent under this section to the appropriate officer of that court shall be evidence, and in Scotland sufficient evidence, of the facts stated therein.

(3) Where a maintenance order made by a court in England or Northern Ireland is registered in a court in Scotland, a person shall not be entitled, except with the leave of the last-mentioned court, to enforce, whether by diligence or otherwise, the payment of any arrears accrued and due under the order before the commencement of this Act; and on any application for leave to enforce the payment of any such arrears, the court may refuse leave, or may grant leave subject to such restrictions and conditions (including conditions as to the allowing of time for payment or the making of payment by instalments) as the court thinks proper, or may remit the payment of such arrears or of any part thereof.

21. Discharge and variation of maintenance orders registered in superior courts—(1) The registration of a maintenance order in a superior court under this Part of this Act shall not confer on that court any power to vary or discharge the order, or affect any jurisdiction of the court in which the order was made to vary or discharge the order.

(2) Where a maintenance order made in Scotland is for the time being *registered under this Part of this Act in a superior court*

[(a) registered under this Part of this Act in a superior court and not registered under Part I of the Maintenance Orders Act 1958 [or under section 36 of the Civil Jurisdiction and Judgments Act 1982], or

(b) registered in a court in England under that Part of that Act [of 1958] by virtue of section 1(2) of that Act [of 1958]]

[(c) registered in a court in Northern Ireland under section 36 of the Civil Jurisdiction and Judgments Act 1982]

the person liable to make payments under the order may, upon application made to that court in the prescribed manner, adduce before that court any evidence upon which he would be entitled to rely in any proceedings brought before the court by which the order was made for the variation or discharge of the order.

Note. Paras (a), (b) in square brackets substituted for words in italics by Administration of Justice Act 1977, s 3, Sch 3, para 7, as from 1 January 1981. In sub-s (2)(a) after '1958' the words 'or under section 36 of the Civil Jurisdiction and Judgments Act 1982' inserted, in sub-s (2)(b) after the words 'that Act' (in both places) the words 'of 1958' inserted, and para (c) inserted by Civil Jurisdiction and Judgments Act 1982, s 36(6), Sch 12, Part III, para 1(3), as from 1 January 1987.

(3) A court before which evidence is adduced in accordance with the foregoing subsection shall cause a transcript or summary of that evidence, signed by the deponent, to be sent to the prescribed officer of the court by which the order was made; and in any proceedings before the last-mentioned court for the variation or discharge of the order, the transcript or summary shall be evidence of the facts stated therein.

22. Discharge and variation of maintenance orders registered in summary or sheriff courts—(1) Where a maintenance order is for the time being registered under this Part of this Act in a court of summary jurisdiction or sheriff court, that court may, upon application made in the prescribed manner by or on behalf of the person liable to make [periodical] payments under the order or the person entitled to those payments, by order make such variation as the court thinks fit in the rate of the payments under the maintenance order; but no such variation shall impose on the person liable to make payments under the maintenance order a liability to make payments in excess of the maximum rate (if any) authorised by the law for the time being in force in the part of the United Kingdom in which the maintenance order was made.

Note. Word 'periodical' in square brackets inserted by Domestic Proceedings and Magistrates' Courts Act 1978, s 89, Sch 2, para 14, as from 1 February 1981.

[(1A) The power of a magistrates' court in England and Wales to vary a maintenance order under subsection (1) of this section shall include power, if the court is satisfied that payment has not been made in accordance with the order, to vary the order by exercising one of its powers under subsection (1B) of this section.

(1B) The powers of the court are—

(a) the power to order that payments under the order be made directly to *the clerk of the court or the clerk of any other magistrates' court in England and Wales* [*a justices' chief executive*] [the designated officer for the court or for any other magistrates' court in England and Wales];

(b) the power to order that payments under the order be made to *the clerk of the court, or to the clerk of any other magistrates' court in England and Wales* [*a justices' chief executive*] [the designated officer for the court or for any other magistrates' court in England and Wales], by such method of payment falling within section 59(6) of the Magistrates' Courts Act 1980 (standing order, etc) as may be specified;

(c) the power to make an attachment of earnings order under the Attachment of Earnings Act 1971 to secure payments under the order.

(1C) In deciding which of the powers under subsection (1B) of this section it is to exercise, the court shall have regard to any representations made by the person liable to make payments under the order.

(1D) Subsection (4) of section 59 of the Magistrates' Courts Act 1980 (power of court to require debtor to open account) shall apply for the purposes of subsection (1B) of this section as it applies for the purposes of that section but as if for paragraph (a) there were substituted—

'(a) the court proposes to exercise its power under paragraph (b) of section 22(1B) of the Maintenance Orders Act 1950, and'.

(1E) Subsections (4) to (11) of section 60 of the Magistrates' Courts Act 1980 (power of clerk and court to vary maintenance order) shall apply in relation to a maintenance order for the time being registered under this Part of this Act in a magistrates' court in England and Wales as they apply in relation to a maintenance order made by a magistrates' court in England and Wales, but—

(a) as if in subsection (4) for paragraph (b) there were substituted—

'(b) payments under the order are required to be made to *the clerk of the court, or to the clerk of any other magistrates' court* [*a justices' chief executive*] [the designated officer for the court or for any other magistrates' court], by any method of payment falling within section 59(6) above (standing order, etc)';

and as if after the words 'the court' there were inserted 'which made the order';

(b) as if in subsection (5) for the words 'to the *clerk*' [*justices' chief executive for the court*] [designated officer for the court'] there were substituted 'in accordance with paragraph (a) of section 22(1B) of the Maintenance Orders Act 1950';

(c) as if in subsection (7), paragraph (c) and the word 'and' immediately preceding it were omitted;

(d) as if in subsection (8) for the words 'paragraphs (a) to (d) of section 59(3) above' there were substituted 'section 22(1B) of the Maintenance Orders Act 1950';

(e) as if for subsections (9) and (10) there were substituted the following subsections—

'(9) In deciding which of the powers under section 22(1B) of the Maintenance Orders Act 1950 it is to exercise, the court shall have regard to any representations made by the debtor.

(10) Subsection (4) of section 59 above (power of court to require debtor to open account) shall apply for the purposes of subsection (8) above as it applies for the purposes of that section but as if for paragraph (a) there were substituted—

"(a) the court proposes to exercise its power under paragraph (b) of section 22(1B) of the Maintenance Orders Act 1950, and"'.]

Note. Sub-ss (1A)–(1E) inserted by Maintenance Enforcement Act 1991, s 10, Sch 1, para 5, as from 1 April 1992. In sub-s (1B) words 'a justices' chief executive' in square brackets in both places they occur substituted for words 'the clerk of … England and Wales', by the Access to Justice Act 1999, s 90(1), Sch 13, paras 12, 14(1), (2), as from 1 April 2001 (SI 2001 No 916). Words 'the designated officer … England and Wales' in square brackets in both places they occur substituted for words 'a justices' chief executive' by the Courts Act 2003, s 109(1), Sch 8, para 89(1), (2), as from a day to be appointed. In sub-s (1E) words 'a justices' chief executive' and 'justices' chief executive for the court' in square brackets substituted respectively for the words 'the clerk of … magistrates' court,' and 'clerk' by the Access to Justice Act 1999, s 90(1), Sch 13, paras 12, 14(1), (3)(a), as from 1 April 2001 (SI 2001 No 916). Words 'the designated … magistrates' court' and 'designated officer for the court' in square brackets substituted respectively for words 'a justices' chief executive' and 'justices' chief executive for the court' by the Courts Act 2003, s 109(1), Sch 8, para 89(1), (3)(a), (b), as from a day to be appointed. Words 'and as if … the order' in italics repealed by the Access to Justice Act 1999, s 106, Sch 15, Pt V, Table (7), as from 1 April 2001 (SI 2001 No 916).

[(1F) The power of a court of summary jurisdiction in Northern Ireland to vary a maintenance order under subsection (1) of this section shall include power, if the court is satisfied that payment has not been made in accordance with the order, to vary the order by exercising one of its powers under subsection (1G) of this section.

(1G) The powers of the court are—

(a) the power to order that payments under the order be made directly to the collecting officer;

(b) the power to order that payments under the order be made to the collecting officer by such method of payment falling within Article 85(7) of the Magistrates' Courts (Northern Ireland) Order 1981 (standing order, etc) as may be specified;

(c) the power to make an attachment of earnings order under Part IX of the Order of 1981 to secure payments under the order;

and in this subsection 'collecting officer' means the officer mentioned in Article 85(4) of the Order of 1981.

(1H) In deciding which of the powers under subsection (1G) of this section it is to exercise, the court shall have regard to any representations made by the person liable to make payments under the order.

(1I) Paragraph (5) of Article 85 of the Magistrates' Courts (Northern Ireland) Order 1981 (power of court to require debtor to open account) shall apply for the purposes of subsection (1G) of this section as it applies for the purposes of that Article but as if for sub-paragraph (a) there were substituted—

'(a) the court proposes to exercise its power under paragraph (b) of section 22(1G) of the Maintenance Orders Act 1950, and'.

(1J) Paragraphs (4) to (11) of Article 86 of the Magistrates' Courts (Northern Ireland) Order 1981 (power of clerk and court to vary maintenance order) shall apply in relation to a maintenance order for the time being registered under this Part of this Act in a court of summary jurisdiction in Northern Ireland as they apply in relation to a maintenance order made by a court of summary jurisdiction in Northern Ireland but—

(a) as if in paragraph (4) for sub-paragraph (b) there were substituted—

'(b) payments under the order are required to be made to the collecting officer by any method of payment falling within Article 85(7) (standing order, etc)';

and as if after the words 'petty sessions' there were inserted 'for the petty sessions district for which the court which made the order acts';

(b) as if in paragraph (5) for the words 'to the collecting officer' there were substituted 'in accordance with paragraph (a) of section 22(1G) of the Maintenance Orders Act 1950';

(c) as if in paragraph (7), sub-paragraph (c) and the word 'and' immediately preceding it were omitted;

(d) as if in paragraph (8) for the words 'sub-paragraphs (a) to (d) of Article 85(3)' there were substituted 'section 22(1G) of the Maintenance Orders Act 1950';

(e) as if for paragraphs (9) and (10) there were substituted the following paragraphs—

'(9) In deciding which of the powers under section 22(1G) of the Maintenance Orders Act 1950 it is to exercise, the court shall have regard to any representations made by the debtor.

(10) Paragraph (5) of Article 85 (power of court to require debtor to open account) shall apply for the purposes of paragraph (8) as it applies for the purposes of that Article but as if for sub-paragraph (a) there were substituted—

"(a) the court proposes to exercise its power under paragraph (b) of section 22(1G) of the Maintenance Orders Act 1950, and".'.]

Note. Sub-ss (1F)–(1J) inserted by Family Law (Northern Ireland Consequential Amendments) Order 1993, SI 1993 No 1577, art 2, as from 4 November 1996 (SR 1996 No 454).

(2) For the purposes of subsection (1) of this section, a court in any part of the United Kingdom may take notice of the law in force in any other part of the United Kingdom.

(3) Section fifteen of this Act shall apply to the service of process for the purposes of this section as it applies to the service of process in proceedings begun in a court having jurisdiction by virtue of Part I of this Act.

(4) Except as provided by subsection (1) of this section, no variation shall be made in the rate of the payments under a maintenance order which is for the time being registered under this Part of this Act in a court of summary jurisdiction or sheriff court, but without prejudice to any power of the court which made the order to discharge it or vary it otherwise than in respect of the rate of the payments thereunder.

(5) Where a maintenance order is for the time being registered under this Part of this Act in a court of summary jurisdiction or sheriff court—

(a) the person entitled to payments under the order or the person liable to make payments under the order may, upon application made in the prescribed manner to the court by which the order was made, or in which the order is registered, as the case may be, adduce in the prescribed manner before the court in which the application is made any evidence on which he would be entitled to rely in proceedings for the variation or discharge of the order;

(b) the court in which the application is made shall cause a transcript or summary of that evidence, signed by the deponent, to be sent to the prescribed officer of the court in which the order is registered or of the court by which the order was made, as the case may be; and in any proceedings for the variation or discharge of the order the transcript or summary shall be evidence of the facts stated therein.

23. Notice of variation, etc—(*1*) *Where a maintenance order registered under this Part of this Act in any court is varied by that court, the prescribed officer of that court shall give notice of the variation in the prescribed manner to the prescribed officer of the court by which the order was made.*

(*2*) *Where a maintenance order registered under this Part of this Act in any court is discharged or varied by any other court, the prescribed officer of the last-mentioned court shall give notice of the discharge or variation in the prescribed manner to the prescribed officer of the court in which the order is registered.*

(*3*) *The officer to whom any notice is given under this section shall cause particulars of the notice to be registered in his court in the prescribed manner.*

[**23.**—(1) Where a maintenance order registered under this Part of this Act is discharged or varied by any court, the prescribed officer of that court shall give notice of the discharge or variation in the prescribed manner—

    (a) to the prescribed officer of any court in which the order is registered; and

    (b) if the order was made by another court, to the prescribed officer of that court.

(2) Any officer to whom a notice is given under this section shall cause particulars of the notice to be registered in his court in the prescribed manner.]

Note. Section 23 in square brackets substituted for s 23 in italics by Administration of Justice Act 1977, s 3, Sch 3, as from 1 January 1981.

24. Cancellation of registration—(1) At any time while a maintenance order is registered under this Part of this Act in any court, an application for the cancellation of the registration may be made in the prescribed manner to the prescribed officer of that court by or on behalf of the person entitled to payments under the order; and upon any such application that officer shall (unless proceedings for the variation of the order are pending in that court), cancel the registration, and thereupon the order shall cease to be registered in that court.

(2) Where, after a maintenance order has been registered under this Part of this Act in a court of summary jurisdiction in England or Northern Ireland or a sheriff court in Scotland, it appears to the appropriate authority (as defined by section seventeen of this Act), upon application made in the prescribed manner by or on behalf of the person liable to make payments under the order, that that person has ceased to reside in England, Northern Ireland or Scotland, as the case may be, the appropriate authority may cause a notice to that effect to be sent to the prescribed officer *of the court* [of any court] in which the order is registered; and where such a notice is sent the prescribed officer shall cancel the registration of the maintenance order, and thereupon the order shall cease to be registered in that court.

Note. Words in square brackets substituted for words in italics by Administration of Justice Act 1977, s 3, Sch 3, para 9, as from 1 January 1981.

(3) Where the prescribed officer of any court cancels the registration of a maintenance order under this section, he shall give notice of the cancellation in the prescribed manner *to the prescribed officer of the court by which the order was made and the last-mentioned officer shall cause particulars of the notice to be registered in his court in the prescribed manner.*

  [(a) to the prescribed officer of the court by which the order was made; and

    (b) to the prescribed officer of any court in which it is registered under Part I of the Maintenance Orders Act 1958 [or section 36 of the Civil Jurisdiction and Judgments Act 1982]].

  [(3A) On receipt of a notice under subsection (3) above:

  (a) any such officer as is mentioned in paragraph (a) of that subsection shall cause particulars of the notice to be registered in his court in the prescribed manner; and

  (b) any such officer as is mentioned in paragraph (b) of that subsection shall cause particulars of the notice to be registered in his court in the prescribed manner and shall cancel the registration of the order.]

Note. Sub-s (3)(a), (b) in square brackets substituted for words in italics, and sub-s (3A) inserted by Administration of Justice Act 1977, s 3, Sch 3, para 9, as from 1 January 1981, and reference to Act of 1982 added by Civil Jurisdiction and Judgments Act 1982, s 36(6), Sch 12, Part III, para 1(4), as from 1 January 1987.

(4) Except as provided by subsection (5) of this section, the cancellation of the registration of a maintenance order shall not affect anything done in relation to the maintenance order while it was registered.

(5) On the cancellation of the registration of a maintenance order, any order made in relation thereto under subsection (2) of section nineteen of this Act shall cease to have effect; but until the person liable to make payments under the

maintenance order receives the prescribed notice of the cancellation, he shall be deemed to comply with the maintenance order if he makes payments in accordance with any order under the said subsection (2) which was in force immediately before the cancellation.

[(5A) On the cancellation of the registration of a maintenance order registered in a magistrates' court in England and Wales, any order—

(a) made in relation thereto by virtue of the powers conferred by section 18(2ZA) or section 22(1A) or (1E) of this Act, and

(b) requiring payment to *the clerk of a magistrates' court in England and Wales* [*a justices' chief executive*] [the designated officer for a magistrates' court in England and Wales] (whether or not by any method of payment falling within section 59(6) of the Magistrates' Courts Act 1980),

shall cease to have effect; but until the person liable to make payments under the maintenance order receives the prescribed notice of the cancellation, he shall be deemed to comply with the maintenance order if he makes payments in accordance with any such order which was in force immediately before the cancellation.]

Note. Sub-s (5A) inserted by Maintenance Enforcement Act 1991, s 10, Sch 1, para 6, as from 1 April 1992. In para (b) words 'a justices' chief executive' in square brackets substituted for words 'clerk of … and Wales' by the Access to Justice Act 1999, s 90, Sch 13, paras 12, 15, as from 1 April 2001 (SI 2001 No 916). Words 'the designated officer for a magistrates' court in England and Wales' in square brackets substituted for words 'a justices' chief executive' by the Courts Act 2003, s 109(1), Sch 8, para 90, as from a day to be appointed.

[(5B) On the cancellation of the registration of a maintenance order registered in a court of summary jurisdiction in Northern Ireland, any order—

(a) made in relation thereto by virtue of the powers conferred by section 18(3ZA) or section 22(1F) or (1J) of this Act, and

(b) requiring payment to the collecting officer in Northern Ireland (whether or not by any method of payment falling within Article 85(7) of the Magistrates' Courts (Northern Ireland) Order 1981),

shall cease to have effect; but until the person liable to make payments under the maintenance order receives the prescribed notice of the cancellation, he shall be deemed to comply with the maintenance order if he makes payments in accordance with any such order which was in force immediately before the cancellation.]

Note. Sub-s (5B) inserted by Family Law (Northern Ireland Consequential Amendments) Order 1993, SI 1993 No 1577, art 2, as from 4 November 1996 (SR 1996 No 454).

(6) Where, by virtue of an order made under subsection (2) of section nineteen of this Act, sums payable under a maintenance order registered in a court of summary jurisdiction in England or Northern Ireland are payable through the collecting officer of any court, that officer shall, if the person entitled to the payments so requests, make an application on behalf of that person for the cancellation of the registration.

25. Rules as to procedure of courts of summary jurisdiction—*(1) The power of the Lord Chancellor to make rules under section fifteen of the Justices of the Peace Act 1949* [section 144 of the Magistrates' Courts Act 1980] *shall include power to make rules for regulating the practice to be followed in courts of summary jurisdiction in England under this Part of this Act.*

Note. Words in square brackets substituted for words in italics by Magistrates' Courts Act 1980, s 154, Sch 7, para 8, as from 6 July 1981. Repealed by the Courts Act 2003, s 109(1), (3), Sch 8, para 91(1), (2), Sch 10, as from a day to be appointed.

(2) *The Lord Chief Justice of Northern Ireland shall have power to make rules for regulating* [Rules made under section 23 of the Magistrates' Courts Act (Northern Ireland) 1964 may regulate] the practice to be followed in courts of summary jurisdiction in Northern Ireland under this Part of this Act.

Note. Words in square brackets substituted for words in italics by Judicature (Northern Ireland) Act 1978, s 122, Sch 5.

[(2A) Without prejudice to the generality of the power to make rules under Article 13 of the Magistrates' Courts (Northern Ireland) Order 1981, for the purpose of giving effect to this Part of this Act such rules may make, in relation to any proceedings brought under or by virtue of this part of this Act, any provision not covered by subsection (2) above which—

(a) falls within paragraph (2) of Article 165 of the Children (Northern Ireland) Order 1995, and

(b) may be made in relation to relevant proceedings under that Article.]

Note. Sub-s (2A) inserted by Children (Northern Ireland Consequential Amendments) Order 1995, SI 1995 No 756, art 2, as from 4 November 1996.

(3) Rules [of court] made for the purposes of this Part of this Act may require that any order or other matter required under this Part of this Act to be registered in a court of summary jurisdiction in England or Northern Ireland shall be registered—

(a) in England, *by means of a memorandum entered and signed by the prescribed officer of the court in the register kept pursuant to section twenty-two of the Summary Jurisdiction Act 1879* [in accordance with the rules];

(b) in Northern Ireland, by means of an entry made and signed by the prescribed officer of the court in the order book kept pursuant to *section twenty-one of the Petty Sessions (Ireland) Act 1851* [magistrates' court rules made under section 23(4) of the Magistrates' Courts Act (Northern Ireland) 1964].

Note. First words in square brackets inserted, in relation to England, Scotland and Wales, by the Courts Act 2003, s 109(1), Sch 8, para 91(1), (3)(a), (4), as from a day to be appointed. Second words in square brackets substituted for words in italics, in relation to England, Scotland and Wales, by the Courts Act 2003, s 109(1), Sch 8, para 91(1), (3)(b), (4), as from a day to be appointed. Third words in square brackets substituted for words in italics by Supplementary Benefits, etc, (Consequential Provisions) (Northern Ireland) Order 1977, SI 1977 No 2158.

PART III

GENERAL

26. Proof of declarations, etc—(1) Any document purporting to be a declaration made under section fifteen of this Act, or to be a certified copy, statutory declaration, affidavit, certificate, transcript or summary made for the purposes of this Act or of any rules made thereunder shall, unless the contrary is shown, be deemed without further proof to be the document which it purports to be, and to have been duly certified, made or signed by or before the person or persons by or before whom it purports to have been certified, made or signed.

(2) Paragraph 7 of the Second Schedule to the Emergency Laws (Miscellaneous Provisions) Act 1947 (which relates to the proof of affiliation orders and maintenance orders and of orders for the discharge or variation of such orders), shall apply to the registration of orders under Part II of this Act, and to the cancellation of such registration, as it applies to the variation of orders: and for the purposes of that paragraph—

(a) a maintenance order registered under the said Part II in a court of summary jurisdiction; and

(b) any proceeding under the said Part II relating to a maintenance order made by or registered in such a court, being a proceeding of which a memorandum is required to be entered in the register kept by the clerk of that court pursuant to section twenty-two of the Summary Jurisdiction Act 1879,

shall be deemed to be an order made by that court.

27. General provisions as to jurisdiction—(1) Nothing in this Act shall be construed as derogating from any jurisdiction exercisable, apart from the provisions of this Act, by any court in any part of the United Kingdom.

(2) It is hereby declared that any jurisdiction conferred by Part I of this Act, or any enactment therein referred to, upon a court in any part of the United Kingdom is exercisable notwithstanding that any party to the proceedings is not domiciled in that part of the United Kingdom; and any jurisdiction so conferred in affiliation proceedings shall be exercisable notwithstanding that the child to whom the proceedings relate was not born in that part of the United Kingdom.

(3) For the avoidance of doubt it is hereby declared that in relation to proceedings in which the sheriff has jurisdiction by virtue of the provisions of this Act there are the same rights of appeal and of remit to the Court of Session as there are in relation to the like proceedings in which the sheriff has jurisdiction otherwise than by virtue of the said provisions.

28. Interpretation—(1) In this Act the following expressions have the meanings hereby assigned to them, that is to say—

'certified copy', in relation to an order of any court, means a copy certified by the proper officer of the court to be a true copy of the order or of the official record thereof;

'collecting officer', *in relation to a court of summary jurisdiction in England, means the person authorised to act as such under section twenty-one of the Justices of the Peace Act 1949, and* [in relation to a court of summary jurisdiction in England, means the designated officer for the court, and] in relation to a court of summary jurisdiction in Northern Ireland, means the officer *appointed under subsection (1) of section eight of the Illegitimate Children (Affiliation Orders) Act (Northern Ireland) 1924* [authorised to act as such for the purposes of section ninety-five of the Magistrates' Courts Act (Northern Ireland) 1964];

Note. Words 'in relation to ... Peace Act 1949, and' in italics repealed by the Access to Justice Act 1999, s 106, Sch 15, Pt V(7), as from 1 April 2001 (SI 2001 No 916). First words in square brackets inserted by the Courts Act 2003, s 109(1), Sch 8, para 92(1), (2), as from a day to be appointed. Second words in square brackets substituted for words in italics by Magistrates' Courts (Northern Ireland) Order 1981, SI 1981 No 1675, art 170(2), Sch 6, Part I, para 7.

'court of summary jurisdiction', in relation to Northern Ireland, means a court of summary jurisdiction constituted in accordance with the provisions of the Summary Jurisdiction and Criminal Justice Act (Northern Ireland) 1935, or any other Act of the Parliament of Northern Ireland, whether passed before or after this Act;

Note. Repealed by Northern Ireland Act 1962, s 30, Sch 4, Part IV.

'enactment' includes any order, rule or regulation made in pursuance of any Act;
'England' includes Wales;
'prescribed' means, in relation to a court of summary jurisdiction in *England or* Northern Ireland, prescribed *by rules made under section fifteen of the Justices of the Peace Act 1949, or* by rules made *by the Lord Chief Justice of Northern Ireland under this Act* [under section 23 of the Magistrates' Courts Act (Northern Ireland) 1964] *as the case may be,* and in relation to any other court means prescribed by rules of court.

Note. Words 'England or', 'by rules made ... Peace Act 1949, or' and 'as the case may be,' in italics repealed by the Courts Act 2003, s 109(1), (3), Sch 8, para 92(1), (3)(a)–(c), Sch 10, as from a day to be appointed. Words 'under section 23 ... 1964' in square brackets substituted for words in italics by Judicature (Northern Ireland) Act 1978, s 122, Sch 5, Part II.

(2) References in this Act to parts of the United Kingdom are references to England, Scotland and Northern Ireland.

(3) Any reference in this Act to any enactment shall be construed as a reference to that enactment as amended by any subsequent enactment, including this Act.

29. Publication of rules—(*1*) *The power of the Court of Session to prescribe anything which under this Act is to be prescribed shall be exercisable by statutory instrument, and the Statutory Instruments Act 1946 shall apply to a statutory instrument containing an act of sederunt made for that purpose by the Court in like manner as if the act of sederunt had been made by a minister of the Crown.*

(*2*) *It is hereby declared that the said Act applies to any rules made under section twenty-nine of the Summary Jurisdiction Act 1879, as amended by this Act.*

(*3*) *Any rule made under this Act by the Lord Chief Justice of Northern Ireland shall, whether or not it relates to a matter in respect of which the Parliament of Northern Ireland has power to make laws, be deemed to be a statutory rule to which the Rules Publication Act (Northern Ireland) 1925 applies, and shall be printed and published accordingly.*

Note. Sub-ss (1), (2) repealed by Law Reform (Miscellaneous Provisions) (Scotland) Act 1966, ss 10, 11(2), Schedule, Part I. Sub-s (3) repealed by Northern Ireland Act 1955, s 6(3), Schedule: see ibid, s 4.

30. Repeal and transitory provisions—(*1*) *Section six of the Summary Jurisdiction (Process) Act 1881 is hereby repealed.*

(*2*) *Until the date on which section fifteen of the Justices of the Peace Act 1949, comes into force references in this Act to that section shall be construed as references to section twenty-nine of the Summary Jurisdiction Act 1879.*

(*3*) *Until the date on which section nineteen of the Justices of the Peace Act 1949, comes into force*—

(*a*) *the reference to section twenty-one of that Act in section twenty-eight of this Act shall be construed as a reference to the Affiliation Orders Act 1914; and*

(*b*) *section four of the Married Women (Maintenance) Act 1949 (which requires collecting officers to take proceedings for enforcement in certain cases), shall apply to any order registered under Part II of this Act in a court of summary jurisdiction in England as it applies to an order made under the Summary Jurisdiction (Married Women) Act 1895, and references in the said section four to the married woman shall be construed accordingly.*

Note. Repealed by Statute Law Revision Act 1953.

Married Women (Maintenance) Act 1949, s 4 repealed by Magistrates' Courts Act 1952, s 132, Sch 6: see now Magistrates' Courts Act 1980, s 59 (p 2767). Affiliation Orders Act 1948 repealed by Affiliation Proceedings Act 1957, Schedule.

31. Special provisions relating to Northern Ireland—(*1*) *For the purposes of section six of the Government of Ireland Act 1920 (which relates to the power of the Parliament of Northern Ireland to make laws), the provisions of this Act, so far as they extend to Northern Ireland, shall be deemed to be provisions of an Act passed before the appointed day.*

Note. Sub-s (1) repealed by Northern Ireland Constitution Act 1973, s 41(1), Sch 6, Part I.

(2) Any reference in this Act to an enactment of the Parliament of Northern Ireland, or to an enactment which that Parliament has power to amend, shall be construed, in relation to Northern Ireland, as a reference to that enactment as amended by any Act of that Parliament, whether passed before or after this Act, and to any enactment of that Parliament passed after this Act and re-enacting the said enactment with or without modifications.

32. Short title and commencement—(1) This Act may be cited as the Maintenance Orders Act 1950.

(2) This Act shall come into force on the first day of January, nineteen hundred and fifty-one.

*   *   *   *   *

SECOND SCHEDULE   Section 15

FORMS

FORM NO 1: ENDORSEMENT OF SUMMONS

I, A. B., a justice of the peace [sheriff] [resident magistrate] for the [county] of   , hereby authorise the service of this summons [writ] in England [Scotland] [Northern Ireland] under section fifteen of the Maintenance Orders Act 1950.

Given under my hand this   day of   , 19   .

FORM NO 2: DECLARATION AS TO SERVICE

I, C. D. of   hereby declare that on the   day of   , 19   , I served E. F. of   with the summons [writ] now shown to me and marked 'A' by delivering a true copy to him.

                     (*Signed*) C. D.

Declared before me this   day of   , 19   .

                              A. B.

                Justice of the Peace [sheriff] [resident magistrate] for the [county] of

BIRTHS AND DEATHS REGISTRATION ACT 1953

(1 & 2 Eliz 2 c 20)   [14 July 1953]

10. Provision as to father of illegitimate child. *Notwithstanding anything in the foregoing provisions of this Act, in the case of an illegitimate child, no person shall as father of the child be required to give information concerning the birth of the child, and the registrar shall not enter in the register the name of any person as father of the child except at the joint request of the mother and the person acknowledging himself to be the father of the child, and that person shall in that case sign the register together with the mother [except—*

   (*a*)   *at the joint request of the mother and the person acknowledging himself to be the father of the child (in which case that person shall sign the register together with the mother); or*

   (*b*)   *at the request of the mother on production of—*

       (*i*)   *a declaration in the prescribed form made by the mother stating that the said person is the father of the child; and*

       (*ii*)   *a statutory declaration made by that person acknowledging himself to be the father of the child;] [or*

   (*c*)   *at the request of the mother (which shall be made in writing) on production of—*

       (*i*)   *a certified copy of an order made under section 4 of the Affiliation Proceedings Act 1957 naming that person as the putative father of the child, and*

       (*ii*)   *if the child has attained the age of 16 years, the written consent of the child to the registration of that person as his father].*

Note. Paras (a), (b) and word 'except' preceding them substituted for words 'except at … together with the mother' by Family Law Reform Act 1969, s 27(1). Para (c) and word 'or' preceding it added by Children Act 1975, s 93(1).

[10. Registration of father where parents not married—(1) Notwithstanding anything in the foregoing provisions of this Act [and subject to section 10ZA of this Act], in the case of a child whose father and mother were not married to each other at the time of his birth, no person shall as father of the child be required to give information concerning the birth of the child, and the registrar shall not enter in the register the name of any person as father of the child except—

   (a)   at the joint request of the mother and the person stating himself to be the father of the child (in which case that person shall sign the register together with the mother); or

(b) at the request of the mother on production of—
   (i) a declaration in the prescribed form made by the mother stating that that person is the father of the child; and
   (ii) a statutory declaration made by that person stating himself to be the father of the child; or
(c) at the request of that person on production of—
   (i) a declaration in the prescribed form by that person stating himself to be the father of the child; and
   (ii) a statutory declaration made by the mother stating that that person is the father of the child; or
(*d*) *at the request of the mother or that person (which shall in either case be made in writing) on production of—*
   (*i*) *a certified copy of a relevant order; and*
   (*ii*) *if the child has attained the age of sixteen, the written consent of the child to the registration of that person as his father.*
[(d) at the request of the mother or that person on production of—
   (i) a copy of *a parental responsibility agreement made between them in relation to the child* [any agreement made between them under section 4(1)(b) of the Children Act 1989 in relation to the child]; and
   (ii) a declaration in the prescribed form by the person making the request stating that the agreement was made in compliance with section 4 of *the Children Act 1989* [that Act] and has not been brought to an end by an order of a court; or
(e) at the request of the mother or that person on production of—
   (i) a certified copy of an order under section 4 of the Children Act 1989 giving that person parental responsibility for the child; and
   (ii) a declaration in the prescribed form by the person making the request stating that the order has not been brought to an end by an order of a court; or
(f) at the request of the mother or that person on production of—
   (i) a certified copy of an order under paragraph 1 of Schedule 1 to the Children Act 1989 which requires that person to make any financial provision for the child and which is not an order falling within paragraph 4(3) of that Schedule; and
   (ii) a declaration in the prescribed form by the person making the request stating that the order has not been discharged by an order of a court; or
(g) at the request of the mother or that person on production of—
   (i) a certified copy of any of the orders which are mentioned in subsection (1A) of this section which has been made in relation to the child; and
   (ii) a declaration in the prescribed form by the person making the request stating that the order has not been brought to an end or discharged by an order of a court.]

Note. Words 'and subject to section 10ZA of this Act' in square brackets inserted by the Human Fertilisation and Embryology (Deceased Fathers) Act 2003, s 2(1), Schedule, para 2, as from 1 December 2003 (SI 2003 No 3095), For retrospective, transitional and transitory provision see s 3(1) of the 2003 Act. Paras (d)–(g) in square brackets substituted for original para (d) in italics, by Children Act 1989, s 108(4), Sch 12, para 6(1), (2), as from 14 October 1991. In para (d) words in square brackets in both places substituted for words in italics by the Adoption and Children Act 2002, s 139(1), Sch 3, para 6(a), (b), as from 1 October 2003 (SI 2003 No 3079).

[(1A) The orders are—
(a) an order under section 4 of the Family Law Reform Act 1987 that that person shall have all the parental rights and duties with respect to the child;

(b) an order that that person shall have custody or care and control or legal custody of the child made under section 9 of the Guardianship of Minors Act 1971 at a time when such an order could only be made in favour of a parent;

(c) an order under section 9 or 11B of that Act which requires that person to make any financial provision in relation to the child;

(d) an order under section 4 of the Affiliation Proceedings Act 1957 naming that person as putative father of the child.]

Note. Sub-s (1A) inserted by Children Act 1989, s 108(4), Sch 12, para 6(1), (3), as from 14 October 1991.

(2) Where, in the case of a child whose father and mother were not married to each other at the time of his birth, a person stating himself to be the father of the child makes a request to the registrar in accordance with paragraph (c) *or* (d) [to (g)] of subsection (1) of this section—

(a) he shall be treated as a qualified informant concerning the birth of the child for the purposes of this Act; and

(b) the giving of information concerning the birth of the child by that person and the signing of the register by him in the presence of the registrar shall act as a discharge of any duty of any other qualified informant under section 2 of this Act.

(3) In this section and section 10A of this Act references to a child whose father and mother were not married to each other at the time of his birth shall be construed in accordance with section 1 of the Family Law Reform Act 1987 *and 'relevant order', in relation to a request under subsection (1)(d) that the name of any person be entered in the register as father of a child, means any of the following orders, namely—*

(a) an order under section 4 of the said Act of 1987 which gives that person all the parental rights and duties with respect to the child;

(b) an order under section 9 of the Guardianship of Minors Act 1971 which gives that person any parental right with respect to the child; and

(c) an order under section 11B of that Act which requires that person to make any financial provision for the child]

[*'parental responsibility agreement' has the same meaning as in the Children Act 1989.*]]

Note. Section 10 in square brackets substituted for original s 10 by Family Law Reform Act 1987, s 24, as from 1 April 1989. For transitional provisions, see Sch 3, paras 11, 12 to the 1987 Act (repealed) (p 3195, 3196).

Words in square brackets in sub-ss (2), (3) substituted for words in italics by Children Act 1989, s 108(4)), Sch 12, para 6(1), (4), (5), as from 14 October 1991. Words 'and 'relevant order' ... Children Act 1989' in italics repealed by the Adoption and Children Act 2002, s 139(1), (3), Sch 3, para 6(c), Sch 5, as from 1 December 2003 (SI 2003 No 3079).

[10A. Re-registration of births of illegitimate children—(*1*) *Where the birth of an illegitimate child has been registered under this Act but no person has been registered as the child's father, the registrar shall re-register the birth so as to show a person as the father—*

(a) at the joint request of the mother and of that person; or

(b) at the request of the mother on production of—

(i) a declaration in the prescribed form made by the mother stating that that person is the father of the child; and

(ii) a statutory declaration made by that person acknowledging himself to be the father of the child; or

(c) at the request of the mother (which shall be made in writing) on production of—

(i) a certified copy of an order made under section 4 of the Affiliation Proceedings Act 1957 naming that person as the putative father of that child, and

(ii) if the child has attained the age of 16 years, the written consent of the child to the registration of that person as his father;

but no birth shall be re-registered under this section except in the prescribed manner and with the authority of the Registrar General.

(*3*) On the re-registration of a birth under this section—
(*a*) the registrar and the mother shall sign the register;
(*b*) in the case of a request under paragraph (*a*) of subsection (*1*) of this section, the other person making the request shall also sign the register; and
(*c*) if the re-registration takes place more than three months after the birth, the superintendent registrar shall also sign the register.]

Note. This section inserted by Children Act 1975, s 93, as from 1 January 1977.

[10A. Re-registration where parents not married—(1) Where there has been registered under this Act the birth of a child whose father and mother were not married to each other at the time of the birth, but no person has been registered as the father of the child, the registrar shall re-register the birth so as to show a person as the father—

(a) at the joint request of the mother and that person; or
(b) at the request of the mother on production of—
    (i) a declaration in the prescribed form made by the mother stating that that person is the father of the child; and
    (ii) a statutory declaration made by that person stating himself to be the father of the child; or
(c) at the request of that person on production of—
    (i) a declaration in the prescribed form by that person stating himself to be the father of the child; and
    (ii) a statutory declaration made by the mother stating that that person is the father of the child; or
(*d*) at the request of the mother or that person (*which shall in either case be made in writing*) on production of—
    (*i*) a certified copy of a relevant order; and
    (*ii*) if the child has attained the age of sixteen, the written consent of the child to the registration of that person as his father;
but no birth shall be re-registered under this section except in the prescribed manner and with the authority of the Registrar General.

[(d) at the request of the mother or that person on production of—
    (i) a copy of *a parental responsibility agreement made between them in relation to the child* [any agreement made between them under section 4(1)(b) of the Children Act 1989 in relation to the child]; and
    (ii) a declaration in the prescribed form by the person making the request stating that the agreement was made in compliance with section 4 of *the Children Act 1989* [that Act] and has not been brought to an end by an order of a court; or
(e) at the request of the mother or that person on production of—
    (i) a certified copy of an order under section 4 of the Children Act 1989 giving that person parental responsibility for the child; and
    (ii) a declaration in the prescribed form by the person making the request stating that the order has not been brought to an end by an order of a court; or
(f) at the request of the mother or that person on production of—
    (i) a certified copy of an order under paragraph 1 of Schedule 1 to the Children Act 1989 which requires that person to make any financial provision for the child and which is not an order falling within paragraph 4(3) of that Schedule; and
    (ii) a declaration in the prescribed form by the person making the request stating that the order has not been discharged by an order of a court; or
[(ff) in the case of a man who is to be treated as the father of the child by virtue of section 28(5A), (5B), (5C) or (5D) of the Human Fertilisation and

Embryology Act 1990, if the condition in section 10ZA(2) of this Act is satisfied; or]

(g) at the request of the mother or that person on production of—

    (i) a certified copy of any of the orders which are mentioned in sub-section (1A) of this section which has been made in relation to the child; and

    (ii) a declaration in the prescribed form by the person making the request stating that the order has not been brought to an end or discharged by an order of a court.]

Note. Sub-s (1)(d)–(g) in square brackets substituted for sub-s (1)(d) in italics, by Children Act 1989, s 108(4), Sch 12, para 6(1), (2), as from 14 October 1991. In para (d) words in square brackets in both places substituted for words in italics by the Adoption and Children Act 2002, s 139(1), Sch 3, para 7(a), (b), as from 1 December 2003 (SI 2003 No 3079). Para (ff) inserted by the Human Fertilisation and Embryology (Deceased Fathers) Act 2003, s 2(1), Schedule, para 4, as from 1 December 2003 (SI 2003 No 3095). For retrospective, transitional and transitory provisions see s 3(1) to the 2003 Act.

[(1A) The orders are—

(a) an order under section 4 of the Family Law Reform Act 1987 that that person shall have all the parental rights and duties with respect to the child;

(b) an order that that person shall have custody or care and control or legal custody of the child made under section 9 of the Guardianship of Minors Act 1971 at a time when such an order could only be made in favour of a parent;

(c) an order under section 9 or 11B of that Act which requires that person to make any financial provision in relation to the child;

(d) an order under section 4 of the Affiliation Proceedings Act 1957 naming that person as putative father of the child.]

Note. Sub-s (1A) inserted by Children Act 1989, s 108(4), Sch 12, para 6(1), (3), as from 14 October 1991.

(2) On the re-registration of a birth under this section—

(a) the registrar shall sign the register;

(b) in the case of a request under paragraph (a) or (b) of subsection (1) of this section, or a request under *paragraph (d)* [any of paragraphs (d) to (g)] of that subsection made by the mother of the child, the mother shall also sign the register;

[(bb) in a case within paragraph (ff) of that subsection, the mother or (as the case may be) the qualified informant shall also sign the register;]

(c) in the case of a request under paragraph (a) or (c) of that subsection, or a request made under *paragraph (d)* [any of paragraphs (d) to (g)] of that subsection by the person requesting to be registered as the father of the child, that person shall also sign the register; and

(d) if the re-registration takes place more than three months after the birth, the superintendent registrar shall also sign the register.]

Note. Section 10A substituted for s 10A supra, as inserted by the 1975 Act, by Family Law Reform Act 1987, s 25, as from 1 April 1989.

Words in square brackets in sub-s (2)(b), (c) substituted for words in italics by Children Act 1989, s 108(4), Sch 12, para 6(1), (6), as from 14 October 1991. Para (bb) inserted by the Human Fertilisation and Embryology (Deceased Fathers) Act 2003, s 2(1), Schedule, para 5, as from 1 December 2003 (SI 2003 No 3095). For retrospective, transitional and transitory provision see s 3(1) of the 2003 Act.

EMERGENCY LAWS (MISCELLANEOUS PROVISIONS) ACT 1953

(1 & 2 Eliz 2 c 47)   [31 July 1953]

Note. This Act makes permanent provision for certain matters formerly dealt with under emergency legislation. It replaces, by s 10, the provisions of Evidence and Powers of Attorney Act 1940, relating to the power of naval officers to take affidavits and declarations outside the United Kingdom (the provisions relating to army and air force officers having previously been made permanent by Army and Air Force (Annual) Act 1952, s 5); and, by Sch I, para 3, it replaces regulation 17E of Defence (Administration of Justice) Regulations 1940. See now Army Act 1955 and Air Force Act 1955, s 204 (pp 2173, 2184).

1. Permanent enactment of provisions contained in certain Defence Regulations. The provisions set out in the First Schedule to this Act, which reproduce provisions contained in the Defence Regulations revoked by the Third Schedule to this Act, with minor modifications and adaptations and the addition of transitional provisions, shall have permanent effect.

*   *   *   *   *

10. Power of certain officers to take affidavits, etc—(1) An officer subject to the Naval Discipline Act who is of or above the rank of lieutenant-commander or equivalent rank or relative rank [or is of the rank of lieutenant and is specially appointed for the purposes of this section] may, at any place outside the United Kingdom, take affidavits and declarations from any of the following persons, that is to say, persons subject to that Act and persons not so subject who are employed by or are in the service of *the Admiralty or* [the Secretary of State for Defence for the naval purposes of his department, or are employed by or are in the service of] any of Her Majesty's naval forces, or accompany any of such forces.

[(1A) An officer of the rank of lieutenant shall not be appointed to take affidavits and declarations under subsection (1) above unless he is a barrister, solicitor or advocate.]

(2) A document purporting to have subscribed thereto the signature of any such officer as aforesaid in testimony of an affidavit or declaration being taken before him in pursuance of this section, and containing in the jurat or attestation a statement of the date on which and the place at which the affidavit or declaration was taken, and of the full name and rank of that officer, shall be admitted in evidence without proof of the signature being the signature of that officer or of the facts so stated.

(3) For the purposes of this section the relative ranks of officers shall be such as may be prescribed by the Queen's Regulations *and Admiralty Instructions* for the time being in force.

[(4) The power conferred by subsection (1) above may also be exercised by any officer empowered to take affidavits and declarations by section 204(1) of the Army Act 1955 or section 204(1) of the Air Force Act 1955.]

Note. Words in first pair of square brackets in sub-s (1) inserted by Armed Forces Act 1981, s 19(2)(a), and words in second pair of square brackets in that subsection substituted for words in italics by Defence (Transfer of Functions) (No 1) Order 1964, SI 1964 No 488, art 2, Sch 1, Part I. Sub-s (1A) inserted by Armed Forces Act 1981, s 19(2)(b). Words in italics in sub-s (3) repealed by Defence (Transfer of Functions) (No 1) Order 1964, SI 1964 No 488. Sub-s (4) inserted by Armed Forces Act 1971, s 70(4).

*   *   *   *   *

FIRST SCHEDULE

*   *   *   *   *

Extension of time for instituting proceedings under Separation and Maintenance Acts

3.—(*1*) *An application for an order under the Summary Jurisdiction (Separation and Maintenance) Acts 1895 to 1949, being an application made by virtue of section eleven of the Matrimonial Causes Acts 1937, on the ground of the adultery of the applicant's wife or husband, shall not be dismissed by reason only that it was not made within the six months allowed by section one hundred and four of the Magistrates' Courts Act 1952, if the court is satisfied that the applicant—*

> (*a*) *during the said six months or any part thereof was serving outside the United Kingdom in Her Majesty's forces or as the master or a member of the crew of a British ship or any other ship for the time being chartered on behalf of Her Majesty; and*

> (*b*) *on the date of the application, had not been in the United Kingdom for a continuous period of three months since the date of his first return to the United Kingdom after the expiration of the said six months or, if he was in the United Kingdom at the expiration of those six months, the date of his last return to the United Kingdom during those six months.*

(*2*) *For the purposes of this paragraph—*

> (*a*) *a certificate purporting to be signed by an officer designated for the purpose by the Admiralty, Army Council or Air Council that the applicant during any period or periods was serving outside the United Kingdom in Her Majesty's naval, military or air forces, as the case may be; and*

> (*b*) *a certificate purporting to be signed by a person designated for the purpose by the Minister of Transport that the applicant during any period or periods was serving outside the United Kingdom as the master or a member of the crew of a British ship or any other ship for the time being chartered on behalf of Her Majesty;*

shall be evidence of the facts so certified, and that the applicant was not in the United Kingdom during any such period or periods.

Note. This para repealed by Matrimonial Proceedings (Magistrates' Courts) Act 1960, s 18(1), Schedule.

* * * * *

THIRD SCHEDULE

* * * * *

PART II

DEFENCE REGULATIONS REVOKED

Year and Number	Short Title	Extent of Revocation
S R & O 1939 No 927	*The Defence (General) Regulations 1939*	*Paragraph (4) of Regulation 52.* *Regulation 60M.* *Regulations 68AB.* *Regulation 70A.* *Paragraph (1C) of Regulation 72.* *Regulation 76A.* *Regulation 79CA.*
S R & O 1939 No 1303	*The Defence (Agriculture and Fisheries) Regulations 1939*	*Regulation 28A.*
S R & O 1940 No 1028	*The Defence (Administration of Justice) Regulations 1940*	*The whole of the Regulations.*

Note. Repealed by Statute Law (Repeal) Acts 1974 and 1976.

ARMY ACT 1955

(3 & 4 Eliz 2 c 18)

As to the expiry date of this Act, see the Armed Forces Act 2001, s 1(1).

*   *   *   *   *

PART III

FORFEITURES AND DEDUCTIONS AND ENFORCEMENT OF MAINTENANCE LIABILITIES

150. Enforcement of maintenance and affiliation orders by deduction from pay—(1) Where any court in the United Kingdom has made an order against any person (hereinafter referred to as 'the defendant') for the payment of any periodical or other sum specified in the order for or in respect of—

(a)   the maintenance of his wife *or child* ...; or

[(aa) the maintenance of any child of his or his wife or of any other child who has been treated by them both as a child of their family; or]

(b)   any costs incurred in obtaining the order; or

(c)   any costs incurred in proceedings on appeal against, or for the variation, revocation or revival of, any such order,

[(d) ...]

and the defendant is an officer, warrant officer, non-commissioned officer or soldier of the regular forces, then (whether or not he was a member of those forces when the said order was made) [the Defence Council] or an officer authorised by them may order such sum to be deducted from the pay of the defendant and appropriated in or towards satisfaction of the payment due under the order of the court as [the Defence Council] or officer think fit.

Note. In sub-s (1)(a) words 'or child' in italics repealed by Armed Forces Act 1991, s 14(2), 26(2), Sch 3, as from 1 January 1992; words omitted repealed by Army and Air Force Act 1961, s 29(2). Sub-s (1)(aa) inserted by Armed Forces Act 1991, s 14(2), as from 1 January 1992. Sub-s (1)(d) inserted by Administration of Justice Act 1970, s 43(6), repealed by Armed Forces Act 1971, ss 59(1), 77(1), Sch 4, Part II. Other words in square brackets substituted by Defence (Transfer of Functions) (No 1) Order 1964, SI 1964 No 488, art 2, Sch 1, Part I.

[(1A) Without prejudice to any enactment or rule of law relating to adoption or legitimation, in subsection (1)(aa) above any reference to a child of the defendant or his wife shall be construed without regard to whether or not the father and mother of the child have or had been married to each other at any time.]

Note. Sub-s (1A) inserted by Armed Forces Act 1991, s 14(3), as from 1 January 1992.

(2) Where to the knowledge of the court making any such order as aforesaid, or an order varying, revoking or reviving any such order, the defendant is an officer, warrant officer, non-commissioned officer or soldier of the regular forces the court shall send a copy of the order to [the Defence Council] or an officer authorised by them.

Note. Words in square brackets substituted by Defence (Transfer of Functions) (No 1) Order 1964, SI 1964 No 488, art 2, Sch 1, Part I.

(3) Where such an order as is mentioned in subsection (1) of this section has been made by a court in Her Majesty's dominions outside the United Kingdom, and [the Defence Council] or an officer authorised by them are satisfied that the defendant has had a reasonable opportunity of appearing in person, or has appeared by a duly authorised legal representative, to defend the case before the court by which the order was made, [the Defence Council] or officer shall have the like power under subsection (1) of this section as if the order had been made by such a court as is mentioned in that subsection:

Provided that this subsection shall not apply to [an order adjudging a man to be the father of an illegitimate child, and ordering him to pay a sum of money for or in respect of the maintenance of that child or any order varying or reviving such an order, or any order] for the payment of costs incurred in obtaining such an order or in proceedings on appeal against, or for the variation, revocation or revival of, such an order.

Note. Words in first and second pairs of square brackets substituted by Defence (Transfer of Functions) (No 1) Order 1964, SI 1964 No 488, art 2, Sch 1, Part I. Words in third pair of square brackets substituted by Army and Air Force Act 1961, s 29(2).

(4) [The Defence Council] or an officer authorised by them may by order vary or revoke any order previously made under this section, and may treat any order made under this section as being in suspense at any time while the person against whom the order was made is absent as mentioned in paragraph (a) of subsection (1) of section one hundred and forty-five of this Act.

Note. Words in square brackets substituted by Defence (Transfer of Functions) (No 1) Order 1964, SI 1964 No 488, art 2, Sch 1, Part I.

(5) In this section—

references to an order made by a court in the United Kingdom include references to an order registered in or confirmed by such a court under the provisions of the Maintenance Orders (Facilities for Enforcement) Act 1920 [and to an order registered in such a court under Part I of the Maintenance Orders (Reciprocal Enforcement) Act 1972] [or Part I of the Civil Jurisdiction and Judgments Act 1982] [or Council Regulation (EC) No 44/2001 of 22nd December 2000 on jurisdiction and the recognition and enforcement of judgments in civil and commercial matters];

references to a wife *or child* include, in relation to an order made in proceedings in connection with the dissolution or annulment of a marriage, references to a person who would have been the wife *or child* of the defendant if the marriage had subsisted;

[*references to a child of a person include references to a child of his wife, and to an illegitimate … child of that person or of his wife, …;*]

references to a sum ordered to be paid for or in respect of the maintenance of an illegitimate child include references to any sum ordered to be paid by an order under section four of the Bastardy Laws Amendment Act 1872.

Note. Words in first pair of square brackets inserted by Maintenance Orders (Reciprocal Enforcement) Act 1972, s 22(1), Schedule, para 2, as from 1 April 1974. Words in second pair of square brackets inserted by Civil Jurisdiction and Judgments Act 1982, s 15(4), Sch 12, para 1, as from 1 January 1987. Words in third pair of square brackets inserted by the Civil Jurisdiction and Judgments Order 2001, SI 2001 No 3929, art 5, Sch 3, para 2, as from 1 March 2002. Words 'or child' in italics repealed by Armed Forces Act 1991, ss 14(4)(a), 26, Sch 3, as from 1 January 1992. Words in fourth pair of square brackets inserted by Army and Air Force Act 1961, s 29(1), repealed by Armed Forces Act 1991, ss 14(4)(b), 26, Sch 3, as from 1 January 1992. Words omitted repealed by Children Act 1975, s 108(1), Sch 4, Part I. Words 'references to a sum … 1872' repealed by Family Law Reform Act 1987, s 33(4), Sch 4, as from 1 April 1989, and, in relation to Northern Ireland, by Children (Northern Ireland) Order 1995, SI 1995 No 755, art 185(2), Sch 10, as from 4 November 1996.

[150A. Enforcement of *maintenance assessment* [maintenance calculation] by deductions from pay—(1) Subsection (2) applies where any officer, warrant officer, non-commissioned officer or soldier of the regular forces ('the liable person') is required to make periodical payments in respect of any child in accordance with a *maintenance assessment* [maintenance calculation] made under the Child Support Act 1991.

Note. Words in square brackets substituted for words 'maintenance assessment' by the Child Support, Pensions and Social Security Act 2000, s 26, Sch 3, para 1, as from 3 March 2003 (in relation to some cases: SI 2003 No 1192); for remaining purposes: to be appointed.

(2) The Defence Council or an officer authorised by them may order such sum to be deducted from the pay of the liable person and appropriated in or towards satisfaction of any obligation of his—

(a) to make periodical payments in accordance with the *maintenance assessment* [maintenance calculation]; *or*

(b) *to pay interest (by virtue of regulations made under section 41(3) of the Act of 1991) with respect to arrears of child support maintenance payable in accordance with the assessment,*

as they, or the authorised officer, thinks fit.

Note. In para (a) words in square brackets substituted for words 'maintenance assessment' by the Child Support, Pensions and Social Security Act 2000, s 26, Sch 3, para 1, as from 3 March 2003 (in relation to some cases: SI 2003 No 192); for remaining purposes: to be appointed. Para (b) and word 'or' immediately preceding it repealed by the Child Support, Pensions and Social Security Act 2000, s 85, Sch 9, Pt 1, as from 3 March 2003 (in relation to some cases: SI 2003 No 192); for remaining purposes: to be appointed.

(3) Where *a child support officer* [the Secretary of State]—

(a) makes *or cancels* a *maintenance assessment* [maintenance calculation] or a fresh *maintenance assessment* [maintenance calculation]; and

(b) has reason to believe that the person against whom *the assessment* [the calculation] is, or was, made is an officer, warrant officer, non-commissioned officer or soldier of the regular forces,

the Secretary of State shall inform the Defence Council or an officer authorised by them of the terms of the assessment *or (as the case may be) that it has been cancelled.*

Note. Words 'the Secretary of State' in square brackets substituted for words in italics by the Social Security Act 1998, s 86(1), Sch 7, para 1, as from 1 June 1999 (SI 1999 No 1510). Words 'maintenance calculation' in both places they occur and words 'the calculation' in square brackets substituted for words 'maintenance assessment' and 'the assessment' by the Child Support, Pensions and Social Security Act 2000, s 26, Sch 3, para 1, as from 3 March 2003 (in relation to some cases: SI 2003 No 192); for remaining purposes: to be appointed. Words 'or cancels' and 'or (as the ... been cancelled' in italics repealed by the Child Support, Pensions and Social Security Act 2000, s 85, Sch 9, Pt 1, as from 3 March 2003 (in relation to some cases: SI 2003 No 192); for remaining purposes: to be appointed.

(4) This section applies whether or not the liable person was a member of the regular forces when the *maintenance assessment* [maintenance calculation] was made.]

Note. This section inserted by Child Support Act 1991 (Consequential Amendments) Order 1993, SI 1993 No 785, art 2(1), as from 12 April 1993. Words in square brackets substituted for words 'maintenance assessment' by the Child Support, Pensions and Social Security Act 2000, s 26, Sch 3, para 1, as from 3 March 2003 (in relation to some cases: SI 2003 No 192); for remaining purposes: to be appointed.

[150AA. Enforcement of maintenance assessment by deductions from pay—
(1) Subsection (2) applies where any officer, warrant officer, non-commissioned officer or soldier of the regular forces ('the liable person') is required to make periodical payments in respect of any child in accordance with a maintenance assessment made under the Child Support (Northern Ireland) Order 1991.

(2) The Defence Council or an officer authorised by them may order such sum to be deducted from the pay of the liable person and appropriated in or towards satisfaction of any obligation of his—

(a) to make periodical payments in accordance with the maintenance assessment; or

(b) *to pay interest (by virtue of regulations made under Article 38(3) of the Order of 1991) with respect to arrests of child support maintenance payable in accordance with the assessment,*

as they, or the authorised officer, thinks fit.

Note. Para (b) and word 'or' immediately preceding it repealed by the Child Support, Pensions and Social Security Act (Northern Ireland) 2000, s 67, Sch 9, Pt 1, as from a day to be appointed.

(3) Where *a child support officer* [the Department of Health and Social Services for Northern Ireland]—

    (a) makes *or cancels* a maintenance assessment or a fresh maintenance assessment; and

    (b) has reason to believe that the person against whom the assessment is, or was, made is an officer, warrant officer, non-commissioned officer or soldier of the regular forces,

the Department of Health and Social Services for Northern Ireland [that Department] shall inform the Defence Council or an officer authorised by them of the terms of the assessment *or (as the case may be) that it has been cancelled.*

Note. Words 'the Department of Health and Social Services for Northern Ireland' in square brackets substituted for words 'a child support officer' by the Social Security (Northern Ireland) Order 1998, SI 1998 No 1506 (NI 10), art 78(1), Sch 6, para 1, as from a day to be appointed. Words 'that Department' in square brackets substituted for words 'the Department ... for Northern Ireland' in italics by the Social Security (Northern Ireland) Order 1998, SI 1998 No 1506 (NI 10), art 78(1), Sch 6, para 1, as from a day to be appointed. Words 'or cancels' and 'or (as the ... been cancelled' in italics repealed by the Child Support, Pensions and Social Security Act (Northern Ireland) 2000, s 67, Sch 9, Pt 1, as from a day to be appointed.

(4) This section applies whether or not the liable person was a member of the regular forces when the maintenance assessment was made.]

Note. This section inserted by Child Support (Northern Ireland) Order 1991 (Consequential Amendments) Order (Northern Ireland) 1993, SI 1993 No 157, art 2, as from 12 April 1993.

151. Deductions from pay for maintenance of wife or child—(1) Where [the Defence Council] or an officer authorised by them are satisfied that an officer, warrant officer, non-commissioned officer or soldier of the regular forces is neglecting, without reasonable cause, to maintain his wife or any child of his under the age of [seventeen or that such a child of his is in care] [the Defence Council] or officer may order such sum to be deducted from his pay and appropriated towards the maintenance of his wife or child as [the Defence Council] or officer think fit.

Note. Words in second pair of square brackets substituted by Armed Forces Act 1976, s 18, as from 1 July 1977. Other words in square brackets substituted by Defence (Transfer of Functions) (No 1) Order 1964, SI 1964, No 488, art 2, Sch 1, Part I.

[(1A) A child is in care for the purposes of this section at any time when by virtue of any enactment (including an enactment of the Parliament of Northern Ireland or a Measure of the Northern Ireland Assembly)—

    (a) he is *in the care of a local authority in England or Wales* [being looked after by a local authority in England or Wales (within the meaning of the Children Act 1989)]; or

    (b) ...; or

    (c) *he is in the care—*

        (i) *of the managers of a training school in Northern Ireland, or*

        (ii) *of a fit person in Northern Ireland, or*

        (iii) *of the Department of Health and Social Services for Northern Ireland.*

    [(c) he is being looked after by an authority (within the meaning of the Children (Northern Ireland) Order 1995).]]

Note. Sub-s (1A) inserted by Armed Forces Act 1976, s 18, as from 1 July 1977. In sub-s (1A)(a) words in square brackets substituted for words in italics by Children Act 1989, s 108(4), Sch 12, para 7, as from 14 October 1991. Sub-s (1A)(b) applies to Scotland only. Sub-s (1A)(c) in square brackets substituted for sub-s (1A)(c) in italics by Children (Northern Ireland Consequential Amendments) Order 1995, SI 1995 No 756, art 3, as from 4 November 1996.

(2) On an application made to [the Defence Council] or an officer authorised by them for an order under [subsection (1) of this section] [the Defence Council] or officer, if satisfied that a prima facie case has been made out for the making of such an order, may make an interim order for such deduction and appropriation as is mentioned in [subsection (1) of this section] to take effect pending the further examination of the case.

Note. Words in first and third pairs of square brackets substituted by Defence (Transfer of Functions) (No 1) Order 1964, SI 1964 No 488, art 2, Sch 1, Part I. Words in second and fourth pairs of square brackets substituted by Armed Forces Act 1981, s 11, Sch 2, para 8, as from 1 May 1992.

(3) Where an order is in force under subsection (1) or subsection (3) of the last foregoing section for the making of deductions in favour of any person from the pay of an officer, warrant officer, non-commissioned officer or soldier of the regular forces, no deductions from his pay in favour of the same person shall be ordered under the foregoing provisions of this section unless the officer, warrant officer, non-commissioned officer or soldier is in a place where process cannot be served on him in connection with proceedings for the variation of the order of the court in consequence of which the order under the last foregoing section was made.

[(3A) Where an order is in force under section 150A of this Act for deductions to be made from the pay of any member of the regular forces with respect to the maintenance of a child of his, no order may be made under this section for the deductions of any sums from the pay of that person with respect to the maintenance of that child.]

Note. Sub-s (3A) inserted by Child Support Act 1991 (Consequential Amendments) Order 1993, SI 1993 No 785, art 2(2), as from 12 April 1993.

[(3AA) Where an order is in force under section 150AA of this Act for deductions to be made from the pay of any member of the regular forces with respect to the maintenance of a child of his, no order may be made under this section for the deductions of any sums from the pay of that person with respect to the maintenance of that child.]

Note. Sub-s (3AA) inserted by Child Support (Northern Ireland) Order 1991 (Consequential Amendments) Order (Northern Ireland) 1993, SI 1993 No 157, art 2, as from 12 April 1993.

(4) [The Defence Council] or an officer authorised by them may by order vary or revoke any order previously made under this section, and may treat any order made under this section as being in suspense at any time while the person against whom the order was made is absent as mentioned in paragraph (a) of subsection (1) of section one hundred and forty-five of this Act.

Note. Words in square brackets substituted by Defence (Transfer of Functions) (No 1) Order 1964, SI 1964 No 488, art 2, Sch 1, Part I.

(5) The power to make an order under this section for the deduction of any sum and its appropriation towards the maintenance of a child shall include power—

(a) subject to the provisions of subsection (3) of this section, to make such an order after the child has attained the age of [seventeen], if an order in favour of the child is in force under subsection (1) or subsection (3) of the last foregoing section; or

(b) to make such an order after the child has attained the age of [seventeen] if—

(i) such an order of the court as is mentioned in subsection (1) of the last foregoing section was in force in favour of the child at the time when the child attained that age, and

(ii) the person from whose pay the deductions are ordered is in such a place as is mentioned in subsection (3) of this section, and

(iii) the child is for the time being engaged in a course of education or training; or

   (c) to continue such an order from time to time after the child has attained the age of [seventeen], if the child is for the time being engaged in a course of education or training;

but no order so made or continued shall remain in force after the child attains the age of twenty-one or shall, unless continued under paragraph (c) of this subsection, remain in force for more than two years.

Note. Words in square brackets substituted by Armed Forces Act 1976, s 18, as from 1 July 1977.

[(6) Without prejudice to any enactment or rule of law relating to adoption or legitimation, references in this section to a child of any person shall be construed without regard to whether the father and mother of the child have or had been married to each other at any time.]

Note. Sub-s (6) inserted with retrospective effect by Armed Forces Act 1991, s 14(5).

* * * * *

203. Avoidance of assignment of or charge on military pay, pensions, etc—
(1) Every assignment of or charge on, and every agreement to assign or charge, any pay, military award, grant, pension or allowance payable to any person in respect of his or any other person's service in Her Majesty's military forces shall be void.

(2) Save as expressly provided by this Act, no order shall be made by any court the effect of which would be to restrain any person from receiving anything which by virtue of this section he is precluded from assigning and to direct payment thereof to another person.

(3) Nothing in this section shall prejudice any enactment providing for the payment of any sum to a bankrupt's trustee in bankruptcy for distribution among creditors.

(4) This section shall have effect in the United Kingdom and in any colony.

204. Power of certain officers to take affidavits and declarations—(1) An officer of the regular forces *of a rank not below that of major* [who is of or above the rank of major or is of the rank of captain and is a member of the legal [services branch of any] corps of those forces] (hereinafter referred to as an 'authorised officer'), may, at a place outside the United Kingdom, take affidavits and declarations from any of the following persons, that is to say, persons subject to military law and persons not so subject who are of any description specified in the Fifth Schedule to this Act.

(2) A document purporting to have subscribed thereto the signature of an authorised officer in testimony of an affidavit or declaration being taken before him in pursuance of this section and containing in the jurat or attestation a statement of the date on which and the place at which the affidavit or declaration was taken and of the full name and rank of that officer shall be admitted in evidence without proof of the signature being the signature of that officer or of the facts so stated.

[(3) The power conferred by subsection (1) above may also be exercised by any officer empowered to take affidavits and declarations by section 204(1) of the Air Force Act 1955 or section 10(1) of the Emergency Laws (Miscellaneous Provisions) Act 1953.]

Note. Words in first pair of square brackets in sub-s (1) substituted for words in italics by Armed Forces Act 1981, s 19(3), as from 28 July 1981. Words in second pair of square brackets inserted by Armed Forces Act 1996, s 35(1), Sch 6, para 2, as from 1 October 1996. Sub-s (3) added by Armed Forces Act 1971, s 70(1), (2).

* * * * *

FIFTH SCHEDULE   Sections 204, 209

* * * * *

CIVILIANS OUTSIDE THE UNITED KINGDOM SUBJECT TO PART II ON ACTIVE SERVICE

1. Persons serving Her Majesty, or otherwise employed, in such capacities connected with Her Majesty's naval, military or air forces as may be specified for the purposes of this Schedule by regulations of [the Defence Council], being persons serving or employed under Her Majesty's Government in the United Kingdom.

Note. Words in square brackets substituted for the words 'the Army Council' by Defence (Transfer of Functions) (No 1) Order 1964, SI 1964 No 488.

2. Persons who are employed by, or in the service of, any naval, military or air force organisation so specified to which Her Majesty's Government in the United Kingdom is a party and are employed by or in the service of that organisation by reason of that Government being a party thereto.

3. Persons belonging to or employed by any other organisation so specified which operates in connection with Her Majesty's naval, military or air forces.

4. Persons who, for the purposes of their profession [business] or employment, are attached to or accompany any of Her Majesty's naval, military or air forces in pursuance of an authorisation granted by or on behalf of *the Admiralty*, [the Defence Council] *or the Air Council* [or by an officer authorised by the Defence Council].

Note. First word in square brackets inserted by the Armed Forces Act 2002, s 34, Sch 6, Pt 6, para 4(a), as from 1 October 2002 (SI 2002 No 3234). Second words in square brackets substituted for words 'the Army Council', and words in italics repealed, by Defence (Transfer of Functions) (No 1) Order 1964, SI 1964 No 488. Words 'or by an officer authorised by the Defence Council' in square brackets inserted by the Armed Forces Act 2001, s 34, Sch 6, Pt 6, para 44(b), as from 1 October 2001 (SI 2001 No 3234).

5. Persons forming part of the family of members of any of Her Majesty's naval, military or air forces and residing with them or about to reside or departing after residing with them.

6. Persons forming part of the family of persons falling within paragraphs 1 to 4 of this Schedule and residing with them or about to reside or departing after residing with them.

7. Persons employed by members of any of Her Majesty's naval, military or air forces.

8. Persons employed by persons falling within paragraphs 1 to 6 of this Schedule.

9. Persons forming part of the family of persons falling within either of the last two foregoing paragraphs and residing with them or about to reside or departing after residing with them.

AIR FORCE ACT 1955

(3 & 4 Eliz 2 c 19)

As to the expiry date of this Act, see the Armed Forces Act 2001, s 1(1).

* * * * *

PART III

FORFEITURES AND DEDUCTIONS AND ENFORCEMENT OF MAINTENANCE LIABILITIES

150. Enforcement of maintenance and affiliation orders by deduction from pay—(1) Where any court in the United Kingdom has made an order against any person (hereinafter referred to as 'the defendant') for the payment of any periodical or other sum specified in the order for or in respect of—

(a) the maintenance of his wife *or child* ...; or

[(aa) the maintenance of any child of his or his wife or of any other child who has been treated by them both as a child of their family; or]

(b) any costs incurred in obtaining the order; or

(c)   any costs incurred in proceedings on appeal against, or for the variation, revocation or revival of, any such order,

[(d) ...]

and the defendant is an officer, warrant officer, non-commissioned officer or airman of the regular air force, then (whether or not he was a member of that force when the said order was made) [the Defence Council] or an officer authorised by them may order such sum to be deducted from the pay of the defendant and appropriated in or towards satisfaction of the payment due under the order of the court as [the Defence Council] or officer think fit.

Note. In sub-s (1)(a) words 'or child' in italics repealed by Armed Forces Act 1991, ss 14(2), 26(2), Sch 3, as from 1 January 1992; words omitted repealed by Army and Air Force Act 1961, s 29(2). Sub-s (1)(aa) inserted by Armed Forces Act 1991, s 14(2), as from 1 January 1992. Sub-s (1)(d) inserted by Administration of Justice Act 1970, s 43(6), repealed by Armed Forces Act 1971, ss 59(1), 77(1), Sch 4, Part II. Other words in square brackets substituted by Defence (Transfer of Functions) (No 1) Order 1964, SI 1964 No 488, art 2, Sch 1, Part I.

[(1A) Without prejudice to any enactment or rule of law relating to adoption or legitimation, in subsection (1)(aa) above any reference to a child of the defendant or his wife shall be construed without regard to whether or not the father and mother of the child have or had been married to each other at any time.]

Note. Sub-s (1A) inserted by Armed Forces Act 1991, s 14(3), as from 1 January 1992.

(2) Where to the knowledge of the court making any such order as aforesaid, or an order varying, revoking or reviving any such order, the defendant is an officer, warrant officer, non-commissioned officer or airman of the regular air force, the court shall send a copy of the order to [the Defence Council] or an officer authorised by them.

Note. Words in square brackets substituted by Defence (Transfer of Functions) (No 1) Order 1964, SI 1964 No 488, art 2, Sch 1, Part I.

(3) Where such an order as is mentioned in subsection (1) of this section has been made by a court in Her Majesty's dominions outside the United Kingdom, and [the Defence Council] or an officer authorised by them are satisfied that the defendant has had a reasonable opportunity of appearing in person, or has appeared by a duly authorised legal representative, to defend the case before the court by which the order was made, [the Defence Council] or officer shall have the like power under subsection (1) of this section as if the order had been made by such a court as is mentioned in that subsection:

Provided that this subsection shall not apply to [an order adjudging a man to be the father of an illegitimate child, and ordering him to pay a sum of money for or in respect of the maintenance of that child or any order varying or reviving such an order, or any order] for the payment of costs incurred in obtaining such an order or in proceedings on appeal against, or for the variation, revocation or revival of, such an order.

Note. Words in first and second pairs of square brackets substituted by Defence (Transfer of Functions) (No 1) Order 1964, SI 1964 No 488, art 2, Sch 1, Part I. Words in third pair of square brackets substituted by Army and Air Force Act 1961, s 29(2).

(4) [The Defence Council] or an officer authorised by them may by order vary or revoke any order previously made under this section, and may treat any order made under this section as being in suspense at any time while the person against whom the order was made is absent as mentioned in paragraph (a) of subsection (1) of section one hundred and forty-five of this Act.

Note. Words in square brackets substituted by Defence (Transfer of Functions) (No 1) Order 1964, SI 1964 No 488, art 2, Sch 1, Part I.

(5) In this section—

references to an order made by a court in the United Kingdom include references to an order registered in or confirmed by such a court under the provisions of the Maintenance Orders (Facilities for Enforcement) Act 1920 [and to an order registered in such a court under Part I of the Maintenance Orders (Reciprocal Enforcement) Act 1972] [or Part I of the Civil Jurisdiction and Judgments Act 1982] [or Council Regulation (EC) No 44/2001 of 22nd December 2000 on jurisdiction and the recognition and enforcement of judgments in civil and commercial matters];

references to a wife *or child* include, in relation to an order made in proceedings in connection with the dissolution or annulment of a marriage, references to a person who would have been the wife *or child* of the defendant if the marriage had subsisted;

[*references to a child of a person include references to a child of his wife, and to an illegitimate ... child of that person or of his wife, ...;*]

references to a sum ordered to be paid for or in respect of the maintenance of an illegitimate child include references to any sum ordered to be paid by an order under section four of the Bastardy Laws Amendment Act 1872.

Note. Words in first pair of square brackets inserted by Maintenance Orders (Reciprocal Enforcement) Act 1972, s 22(1), Schedule, para 2, as from 1 April 1974. Words in second pair of square brackets inserted by Civil Jurisdiction and Judgments Act 1982, s 15(4), Sch 12, para 1, as from 1 January 1987. Words in third pair of square brackets inserted by the Civil Jurisdiction and Judgments Order 2001, SI 2001 No 3929, art 5, Sch 3, para 2, as from 1 March 2002. Words 'or child' in italics repealed by Armed Forces Act 1991, ss 14(4)(a), 26, Sch 3, as from 1 January 1992. Words in fourth pair of square brackets inserted by Army and Air Force Act 1961, s 29(1), repealed by Armed Forces Act 1991, ss 14(4)(b), 26, Sch 3, as from 1 January 1992. Words omitted repealed by Children Act 1975, s 108(1), Sch 4, Part I. Words 'references to a sum ... 1872' repealed by Family Law Reform Act 1987, s 33(4), Sch 4, as from 1 April 1989, and, in relation to Northern Ireland, by Children (Northern Ireland) Order 1995, SI 1995 No 755, art 185(2), Sch 10, as from 4 November 1996.

[150A. Enforcement of *maintenance assessment* [maintenance calculation] by deductions from pay—(1) Subsection (2) applies where any officer, warrant officer, non-commissioned officer or airman of the regular air force ('the liable person') is required to make periodical payments in respect of any child in accordance with a *maintenance assessment* [maintenance calculation] made under the Child Support Act 1991.

Note. Words in section heading and sub-s (1) in square brackets substituted for words in italics by the Child Support, Pensions and Social Security Act 2000, s 26, Sch 3, para 2(1), (2) as from in relation to certain cases: 3 March 2003 (SI 2003 No 192); for remaining purposes: to be appointed.

(2) The Defence Council or an officer authorised by them may order such sum to be deducted from the pay of the liable person and appropriated in or towards satisfaction of any obligation of his—

(a) to make periodical payments in accordance with the *maintenance assessment* [maintenance calculation]; *or*

(b) *to pay interest (by virtue of regulations made under section 41(3) of the Act of 1991) with respect of arrears of child support maintenance payable in accordance with the assessment,*

as they, or the authorised officer, thinks fit.

Note. In para (a) words in square brackets substituted for words in italics and para (b) and word 'or' in para (a) in italics repealed by the Child Support, Pensions and Social Security Act 2000, ss 26, 85, Sch 3, para 2(1), (2), Sch 9, Pt 1 as from in relation to certain cases: 3 March 2003 (SI 2003 No 192); for remaining purposes: to be appointed.

(3) Where *a child support officer* [the Secretary of State]—

(a) makes *or cancels* a *maintenance assessment* [maintenance calculation] or a fresh *maintenance assessment* [maintenance calculation]; and

(b) has reason to believe that the person against whom *the assessment* [the calculation] is, or was, made is an officer, warrant officer, non-commissioned officer or airman of the regular air force,

the Secretary of State shall inform the Defence Council or an officer authorised by them of the terms of the assessment *or (as the case may be) that it has been cancelled.*

Note. First words in square brackets substituted for words in italics by the Social Security Act 1998, s 86(1), Sch 7, para 2, as from 1 June 1999 (SI 1999 No 1510). Second, third and fourth words in square brackets substituted for words in italics and words 'or cancels' and 'or (as … been cancelled' in italics repealed by the Child Support, Pensions and Social Security Act 2000, ss 26, 85, Sch 3, para 2(1)–(3), Sch 9, Pt 1 as from in relation to certain cases: 3 March 2003 (SI 2003 No 192); for remaining purposes: to be appointed.

(4) This section applies whether or not the liable person was a member of the regular air force when the *maintenance assessment* [maintenance calculation] was made.]

Note. This section inserted by Child Support Act 1991 (Consequential Amendments) Order 1993, SI 1993 No 785, art 3(1), as from 12 April 1993. In sub-s (4) words in square brackets substituted for words in italics by the Child Support, Pensions and Social Security Act 2000, s 26, Sch 3, para 2(1), (2) as from in relation to certain cases: 3 March 2003 (SI 200 No 192); for remaining purposes: to be appointed.

[150AA. Enforcement of maintenance assessment by deductions from pay—
(1) Subsection (2) applies where any officer, warrant officer, non-commissioned officer or airman of the regular air force ('the liable person') is required to make periodical payments in respect of any child in accordance with a maintenance assessment made under the Child Support (Northern Ireland) Order 1991.

(2) The Defence Council or an officer authorised by them may order such sum to be deducted from the pay of the liable person and appropriated in or towards satisfaction of any obligation of his—

(a) to make periodical payments in accordance with the maintenance assessment; or

(b) to pay interest (by virtue of regulations made under Article 38(3) of the Order of 1991) with respect to arrests of child support maintenance payable in accordance with the assessment,

as they, or the authorised officer, thinks fit.

(3) Where *a child support officer* [the Department of Health and Social Services for Northern Ireland]—

(a) makes or cancels a maintenance assessment or a fresh maintenance assessment; and

(b) has reason to believe that the person against whom the assessment is, or was, made is an officer, warrant officer, non-commissioned officer or airman of the regular air force,

the Department of Health and Social Services for Northern Ireland [that Department] shall inform the Defence Council or an officer authorised by them of the terms of the assessment or (as the case may be) that it has been cancelled.

Note. Words in square brackets in both places substituted for words in italics by the Social Security (Northern Ireland) Order 1998, SI 1998 No 1506 (NI 10), art 78(1), Sch 6, para 2, as from a date to be appointed.

(4) This section applies whether or not the liable person was a member of the regular air force when the maintenance assessment was made.]

Note. This section inserted by Child Support (Northern Ireland) Order 1991 (Consequential Amendments) Order (Northern Ireland) 1993, SI 1993 No 157, art 3, as from 12 April 1993.

151. Deductions from pay for maintenance of wife or child—(1) Where [the Defence Council] or an officer authorised by them are satisfied that an officer, warrant officer, non-commissioned officer or airman of the regular air force is neglecting, without reasonable cause, to maintain his wife or any child of his under the age of [seventeen or that such a child of his is in care] [the Defence Council] or officer may order such sum to be deducted from his pay and appropriated towards the maintenance of his wife or child as [the Defence Council] or officer think fit.

Note. Words in second pair of square brackets substituted by Armed Forces Act 1976, s 18(1), (2). Other words in square brackets substituted by Defence (Transfer of Functions) (No 1) Order 1964, SI 1964 No 488, art 2, Sch 1, Part I.

[(1A) A child is in care for the purposes of this section at any time when by virtue of any enactment (including an enactment of the Parliament of Northern Ireland or a Measure of the Northern Ireland Assembly)—

(a) he is *in the care of a local authority in England or Wales* [being looked after by a local authority in England or Wales (within the meaning of the Children Act 1989)]; or

(b) ...; or

(c) *he is in the care—*
  (i) *of the managers of a training school in Northern Ireland, or*
  (ii) *of a fit person in Northern Ireland, or*
  (iii) *of the Department of Health and Social Services for Northern Ireland.*

[(c) he is being looked after by an authority (within the meaning of the Children (Northern Ireland) Order 1995).]]

Note. Sub-s (1A) inserted by Armed Forces Act 1976, s 18(3), as from 1 July 1977. In sub-s (1A)(a) words in square brackets substituted for words in italics by Children Act 1989, s 108(4), Sch 12, paras 7, 9, as from 14 October 1991. Sub-s (1A)(b) applies to Scotland only. Sub-s (1A)(c) in square brackets substituted for sub-s (1A)(c) in italics by Children (Northern Ireland Consequential Amendments) Order 1995, SI 1995 No 756, art 4, as from 4 November 1996.

(2) On an application made to [the Defence Council] or an officer authorised by them for an order under [subsection (1) of this section] [the Defence Council] or officer, if satisfied that a prima facie case has been made out for the making of such an order, may make an interim order for such deduction and appropriation as is mentioned in [subsection (1) of this section] to take effect pending the further examination of the case.

Note. Words in first and third pairs of square brackets substituted by Defence (Transfer of Functions) (No 1) Order 1964, SI 1964 No 488, art 2, Sch 1, Part I. Words in second and fourth pairs of square brackets substituted by Armed Forces Act 1981, s 11, Sch 2, para 8, as from 1 May 1992.

(3) Where an order is in force under subsection (1) or subsection (3) of the last foregoing section for the making of deductions in favour of any person from the pay of an officer, warrant officer, non-commissioned officer or airman of the regular air force, no deductions from his pay in favour of the same person shall be ordered under the foregoing provisions of this section unless the officer, warrant officer, non-commissioned officer or airman is in a place where process cannot be served on him in connection with proceedings for the variation of the order of the court in consequence of which the order under the last foregoing section was made.

[(3A) Where an order is in force under section 150A of this Act for deductions to be made from the pay of any member of the regular air force with respect to the maintenance of a child of his, no order may be made under this section for the deduction of any sums from the pay of that person with respect to the maintenance of that child.]

Note. Sub-s (3A) inserted by Child Support Act 1991 (Consequential Amendments) Order 1993, SI 1993 No 785, art 3(2), as from 12 April 1993.

[(3AA) Where an order is in force under section 150AA of this Act for deductions to be made from the pay of any member of the regular air force with respect to the maintenance of a child of his, no order may be made under this section for the deductions of any sums from the pay of that person with respect to the maintenance of that child.]

Note. Sub-s (3AA) inserted by Child Support (Northern Ireland) Order 1991 (Consequential Amendments) Order (Northern Ireland) 1993, SI 1993 No 157, art 3, as from 12 April 1993.

(4) [The Defence Council] or an officer authorised by them may by order vary or revoke any order previously made under this section, and may treat any order made under this section as being in suspense at any time while the person against whom the order was made is absent as mentioned in paragraph (a) of subsection (1) of section one hundred and forty-five of this Act.

Note. Words in square brackets substituted by Defence (Transfer of Functions) (No 1) Order 1964, SI 1964 No 488, art 2, Sch 1, Part I.

(5) The power to make an order under this section for the deduction of any sum and its appropriation towards the maintenance of a child shall include power—
(a) subject to the provisions of subsection (3) of this section, to make such an order after the child has attained the age of [seventeen], if an order in favour of the child is in force under subsection (1) or subsection (3) of the last foregoing section; or
(b) to make such an order after the child has attained the age of [seventeen] if—
    (i) such an order of the court as is mentioned in subsection (1) of the last foregoing section was in force in favour of the child at the time when the child attained that age, and
    (ii) the person from whose pay the deductions are ordered is in such a place as is mentioned in subsection (3) of this section, and
    (iii) the child is for the time being engaged in a course of education or training; or
(c) to continue such an order from time to time after the child has attained the age of [seventeen], if the child is for the time being engaged in a course of education or training;
but no order so made or continued shall remain in force after the child attains the age of twenty-one or shall, unless continued under paragraph (c) of this subsection, remain in force for more than two years.

Note. Words in square brackets substituted by Armed Forces Act 1976, s 18(1), as from 1 July 1977.

[(6) Without prejudice to any enactment or rule of law relating to adoption or legitimation, references in this section to a child of any person shall be construed without regard to whether the father and mother of the child have or had been married to each other at any time.]

Note. Sub-s (6) added with retrospective effect by Armed Forces Act 1991, s 14(5).

*   *   *   *   *

204. Power of certain officers to take affidavits and declarations—(1) An officer of the regular air force *of a rank not below that of squadron leader* [who is of or above the rank of squadron leader or is of the rank of flight lieutenant and is a member of the legal branch of that force] (hereinafter referred to as an 'authorised officer'), may, at a place outside the United Kingdom, take affidavits and declarations from any of the following persons, that is to say, persons subject to air force law and persons not so subject who are of any description specified in the Fifth Schedule to this Act.

(2) A document purporting to have subscribed thereto the signature of an authorised officer in testimony of an affidavit or declaration being taken before him

in pursuance of this section and containing in the jurat or attestation a statement of the date on which and the place at which the affidavit or declaration was taken and of the full name and rank of that officer shall be admitted in evidence without proof of the signature being the signature of that officer or of the facts so stated.

[(3) The power conferred by subsection (1) above may also be exercised by any officer empowered to take affidavits or declarations by section 204(1) of the Army Act, 1955 or section 10(1) of the Emergency Laws (Miscellaneous Provisions) Act 1953.]

Note. The words in square brackets in sub-s (1) were substituted for the words in italics by Armed Forces Act 1981, s 19(4). Sub-s (3) was added by Armed Forces Act 1971, s 70(1), (3).

* * * * *

CIVILIANS OUTSIDE THE UNITED KINGDOM SUBJECT TO PART II ON ACTIVE SERVICE

Note. The Fifth Schedule is in identical terms with the Fifth Schedule to Army Act 1955, supra.

ADMINISTRATION OF JUSTICE ACT 1956

(4 & 5 Eliz 2 c 46)

An Act to amend the law relating to Admiralty jurisdiction, legal proceedings in connection with ships and aircraft and the arrest of ships and other property, to make further provision as to the appointment, tenure of office, powers and qualifications of certain judges and officers, to make certain other amendments of the law relating to the Supreme Court and the county courts and of the law relating to the enforcement of certain judgments, orders and decrees, to enable certain funds in court in the Lancashire Chancery Court to be transferred to the official trustees of charitable funds or the Church Commissioners, and for purposes connected with the matters aforesaid. [5 July 1956]

Commencement. By Administration of Justice Act (Commencement) Order 1956, SI 1956 No 1065, ss 9–14, 16–25, 32(1)–(3), 33, 36, 38, 40, 42–44, 51–54, and repeals consequential on these provisions were brought into force on 16 July 1956. Likewise, by SI 1956 No 1979, ss 26, 27, 31, 35, 39, 41 were brought into force on 1 January 1957; and by SI 1957 No 1179, s 15 was brought into force on 1 October 1957.

* * * * *

PART IV

GENERAL PROVISIONS AS TO ENFORCEMENT OF JUDGMENTS AND ORDERS

* * * * *

40. Effect of registration of judgments of courts outside England and Wales—Section five of the Debtors Act 1869, as amended by any subsequent enactment, and *the Bankruptcy Act 1914*, as so amended, shall have effect as if—

(a) any judgment of the High Court of Northern Ireland or decree of the Court of Session a certificate of which has been registered in the High Court under section one or section three of the Judgment Extension Act 1868; and

(b) any judgment, as defined in Part II of the Administration of Justice Act 1920, which has been registered in the High Court under the said Part II; and

(c) any judgment, as defined in the Inferior Courts Judgments Extension Act, 1882, a certificate of which has been registered in the High Court or in a county court under that Act,

were a judgment of the High Court or, as the case may be, of that county court, and proceedings may be taken under *those Acts* [the said Act of 1869] accordingly.

Note. Words 'the Bankruptcy Act 1914' in italics repealed and words in square brackets substituted for words 'these Acts' in italics by Insolvency Act 1985, s 235(1), (3), Sch 8, para 11, Sch 10, Part III. For transitional provisions and savings as respects the amendment of this section by the 1985 Act, see Insolvency Act 1986, s 437, Sch 11, Part II.

*   *   *   *   *

PART VI

MISCELLANEOUS AND SUPPLEMENTAL

51. Modification of Foreign Judgments (Reciprocal Enforcement) Act 1933, in relation to certain parts of Her Majesty's dominions. Where an Order in Council is made extending Part I of the Foreign Judgments (Reciprocal Enforcement) Act 1933, to a part of Her Majesty's dominions or other territory to which Part II of the Administration of Justice Act 1920, extends, the said Part I shall, in relation to that part of Her Majesty's dominions or other territory, have effect as if—

(a) *the expression 'judgment' included an award in proceedings on an arbitration if the award has, in pursuance of the law in force in the place where it was made, become enforceable in the same manner as a judgment given by a court in that place;*

(b) the fact that a judgment was given before the coming into operation of the Order did not prevent it from being a judgment to which the said Part I applies, but the time limited for the registration of a judgment were, in the case of a judgment so given, twelve months from the date of the judgment or such longer period as may be allowed by the High Court in England and Wales, the Court of Session in Scotland, or the High Court in Northern Ireland;

(c) any judgment registered in any of the said courts under the said Part II before the coming into operation of the Order had been registered in that court under the said Part I and anything done in relation thereto under the said Part II or any rules of court or other provisions applicable to the said Part II had been done under the said Part I or the corresponding rules of court or other provisions applicable to the said Part I.

Note. Para (a) repealed by Civil Jurisdiction and Judgments Act 1982, s 54, Sch 14, as from 1 January 1987.

*   *   *   *   *

57. Short title, repeal, extent and commencement—(1) This Act may be cited as the Administration of Justice Act 1956.

(2) *Subject to any saving contained in this Act, the enactments mentioned in the Second Schedule to this Act are hereby repealed to the extent specified in the third column of that Schedule.*

Note. Sub-s (2) repealed by Statute Law (Repeals) Act 1974.

(3) This Act, except Part V and section fifty-one thereof, shall not extend to Scotland.

(4) The provisions of this Act, other than Part V thereof, section fifty-five thereof and the First Schedule thereto, shall come into force on such day as the Lord Chancellor may appoint by order made by statutory instrument, and he may appoint different days for different purposes.

*   *   *   *   *

MAINTENANCE AGREEMENTS ACT 1957*

(5 & 6 Eliz 2 c 35)

An Act to make provision with respect to the validity and alterations by the court of financial arrangements in connection with agreements between the parties to a marriage, whether made during the continuance or after dissolution or annulment of the marriage, for the purposes of those parties living separately; and for purposes connected therewith. [*17 July 1957*]

* The whole Act was repealed by Matrimonial Causes Act 1965, s 45, Sch 2.

1. Validity and alteration by court of maintenance agreements—(*1*) *This section applies to any agreement in writing made, whether before or after the commencement of this Act, between the parties to a marriage for the purposes of their living separately, being*—

(*a*) *an agreement containing financial arrangements, whether made during the continuance or after the dissolution or annulment of the marriage; or*

(*b*) *a separation agreement which contains no financial arrangements in a case where no other agreement in writing between the same parties contains such arrangements.*

Note. See now Matrimonial Causes Act 1973, s 34 (p 2543), replacing Matrimonial Proceedings and Property Act 1970, ss 13, 14 (p 2371), replacing Matrimonial Causes Act 1965, s 23(2) (p 2250) which replaced this section.

(*2*) *If an agreement to which this section applies includes a provision purporting to restrict any right to apply to a court for an order containing financial arrangements that provision shall be void but any other financial arrangements contained in the agreement shall not thereby be rendered void or unenforceable but, unless void or unenforceable for any other reason, and subject to the next following subsection, shall be binding on the parties to the agreement:*

Provided that—

(*a*) *where the party chargeable under the agreement has died before the date of the commencement of this Act*—

    (*i*) *this subsection shall not apply to that agreement unless there remain undistributed at that date assets of that party's estate (apart from any property in which he had only a life interest) representing not less than four-fifths of the value of that estate for probate after providing for the discharge of the funeral, testamentary and administrative expenses, debts and liabilities payable thereout (other than any liability arising by virtue of this subsection); and*

    (*ii*) *nothing in this subsection shall render liable to recovery, or impose any liability upon the personal representatives of that party in respect of, any part of that party's estate which has been distributed before that date;*

(*b*) *no right or liability shall attach by virtue of this subsection in respect of any sum payable under the agreement in respect of a period falling before the commencement of this Act.*

Note. This subsection was replaced by Matrimonial Causes Act 1965, s 23(1), Sch 1, paras 6, 7 (pp 2267), repealed by Matrimonial Proceedings and Property Act 1970, s 42(2), Sch 3.

(*3*) *Where an agreement to which this section applies is for the time being subsisting and the parties thereto are for the time being either both domiciled or both resident in England, and on an application by either party the High Court, or, subject to the next following subsection, a magistrates' court is satisfied either*—

(*a*) *that by reason of a change in the circumstances in the light of which any financial arrangements contained in the agreement were made or, as the case may be, financial arrangements were omitted therefrom, the agreement should be altered so as to make different, or, as the case may be, so as to contain, financial arrangements; or*

(*b*) *that the agreement does not contain proper financial arrangements with respect to any child of the marriage,*

the court may by order make such alterations in the agreement by varying or revoking any financial arrangements contained therein or by inserting therein financial arrangements for the benefit of one of the parties to the agreement or of a child of the marriage as may appear to the court to be just having regard to all the circumstances or, as the case may be, as may appear to the court to be just in all the circumstances in order to secure that the agreement contains proper financial arrangements with respect to any child of the marriage; and the agreement shall have effect thereafter as if any alteration made by the order had been made by agreement between the parties and for valuable consideration:

Provided that this subsection shall not apply to an agreement made more than six months after the dissolution or annulment of the marriage.

Note. See now Matrimonial Causes 1973, s 35(1), (2) (p 2544), replacing Matrimonial Proceedings and Property Act 1970, s 14(1), (2) (p 2372), replacing Matrimonial Causes Act 1965, s 24(1) (p 2251) which replaced this sub-s.

(4) A magistrates' court shall not entertain any application under the last foregoing subsection unless both the parties to the agreement are resident in England and at least one of the parties is resident in the petty sessions area for which that court acts, and shall not have power to make any order on such an application except—

(a) in a case where the agreement includes no provision for periodical payments by either of the parties, an order inserting provision for the making by one of the parties of periodical payments—

(i) for the maintenance of the other party, at a rate not exceeding five pounds a week;

(ii) for the maintenance of any child of the marriage, at a rate not exceeding thirty shillings a week in respect of each such child;

(b) in a case where the agreement includes provision for the making by one of the parties of periodical payments at rates not exceeding the appropriate rate aforesaid, or reducing the rate of, or terminating, any of those payments.

Note. See now Matrimonial Causes Act 1973, s 35(3) (p 2544), replacing Matrimonial Proceedings and Property Act 1970, s 14(3) (p 2372), replacing Matrimonial Causes Act 1965, s 24(2) (p 2251).

(5) For the avoidance of doubt it is hereby declared that nothing in this section affects any power of the court before which any proceedings between the parties to an agreement to which this section applies are brought under any other enactment to make an order containing financial arrangements or any right of either party to apply for such an order in such proceedings.

Note. See now Matrimonial Causes Act 1973, s 35(6) (p 2544), replacing Matrimonial Proceedings and Property Act 1970, s 14(6) (p 2373), replacing Matrimonial Causes Act 1965, ss 23(2), 24(2) (pp 2250, 2251).

(6) In this section—

(a) the expression 'financial arrangements' means provisions governing the rights and liabilities towards one another when living separately of the parties to a marriage (including a marriage which has been dissolved or annulled) in respect of the making or securing of payments or the disposition or use of any property, including such rights and liabilities with respect to the maintenance or education of any child, whether or not a child of the marriage;

(b) the expression 'child of marriage' includes any child of both parties of the marriage, whether or not born in lawful wedlock, and any child adopted by both parties to the marriage; and

(c) the expressions 'magistrates' court' and 'petty sessions area' have the same meanings as in the Magistrates' Courts Act 1952.

2. Alteration of maintenance agreement after death of one party—(*1*) *Where an agreement to which the foregoing section applies provides for the continuation of payments thereunder after the death of one of the parties and that party dies after the commencement of this Act domiciled in England, the surviving party may, at any time before the expiration of six months from the date when representation in regard to the deceased's estate is first taken out or, with the permission of the court, at any time thereafter before the administration and distribution of the estate is completed, make to the High Court any application for an order under subsection (3) of the foregoing section which the surviving party might have made immediately before the death; and, if any alteration in the agreement is made by the court on* *such an application, the like consequences shall ensue as if that alteration had been made immediately before the death by agreement between the parties and for valuable consideration.*

Note. Sub-s (1) replaced by Matrimonial Causes Act 1965, s 25(1), (2) (p 2252) itself repealed by Matrimonial Proceedings and Property Act 1970, s 42(2), Sch 3 and replaced by ibid, s 14 (p 2372). See now Matrimonial Causes Act 1973, s 36 (p 2545).

(*2*) *The provisions of this section shall not render the personal representatives of the deceased liable for having distributed any part of the estate of the deceased after the expiration of the said period of six months on the ground that they ought to have taken into account the possibility that the court might permit an application by virtue of this section after that period, but this subsection shall not prejudice any power to recover any part of the estate so distributed arising by virtue of the making of an order under this Act.*

(*3*) *In considering under subsection* (*1*) *of this section the question when representation was first taken out, a grant limited to settled land or to trust property shall be left out of account, and a grant limited to real estate or to personal estate shall be left out of account unless a grant limited to the remainder of the estate has previously been made or is made at the same time.*

(*4*) *For the purposes of subsection* (*1*) *of section one hundred and sixty-two of the Supreme Court of Judicature* (*Consolidation*) *Act 1925* (*which relates to the discretion of the court as to the persons to whom administration is to be granted*) *a person by whom an application under this Act is proposed to be made by virtue of this section shall be deemed to be a person interested in the deceased's estate.*

Note. See now Matrimonial Causes Act 1973, s 36 (p 2545), replacing Matrimonial Proceedings and Property Act 1970, s 15 (p 2373), replacing Matrimonial Causes Act 1965, s 25(3)–(5) (p 2252).

3. Short title, commencement and extent—(*1*) *This Act may be cited as the Maintenance Agreements Act 1957.*

(*2*) *This Act shall come into force at the expiration of the period of one month beginning with the date of its passing.*

(*3*) *This Act shall not extend to Scotland or to Northern Ireland.*

AFFILIATION PROCEEDINGS ACT 1957*

(5 & 6 Eliz 2 c 55)

An Act to consolidate the enactments relating to bastardy, with corrections and improvements made under the Consolidation of Enactments (Procedure) Act 1949.   [*31 July 1957*]

* Whole Act repealed by Family Law Reform Act 1987, ss 17, 33(4), Sch 4, as from 1 April 1989. For transitional provisions and savings see ibid, s 33(2), Sch 3, paras 1, 6, 11, 12 (pp 3194, 3195, 3196).

1. Commencement of affiliation proceedings. *A single woman who is with child, or who has been delivered of an illegitimate child, may apply by complaint to a justice of the peace for a summons to be served on the man alleged by her to be the father of the child.*

2. Time for application for summons—(*1*) *A complaint under section one of this Act, where the complainant has been delivered of an illegitimate child, may be made—*

(*a*) *at any time within twelve months* [*three years*] *from the child's birth, or*

(*b*) *at any subsequent time, upon proof that the man alleged to be the father of the child has within the twelve months* [*three years*] *next after the birth paid money for its maintenance, or*

(*c*) *at any time within the twelve months next after the man's return to England, upon proof that he ceased to reside in England within the twelve months* [*three years*] *next after the birth.*

Note. Words 'three years' in paras (a), (b) substituted for words 'twelve months' by Affiliation Proceedings (Amendment) Act 1972, s 2(1).

(*2*)   *A single woman who has been delivered of a child may, upon proof that—*

(*a*)   *before the birth she was a party to a marriage which would have been valid but for provisions of an Act of Parliament making it void on account of her, or the other party to the marriage, being under the age of sixteen, and*

(*b*)   *the said other party had access to her within twelve months before the birth,*

make at any time a complaint under section one of this Act against that party, notwithstanding that he may not within the twelve months [three years] next after the birth have paid money for the child's maintenance.

Note. Words 'three years' in para (b) substituted for words 'twelve months' by Affiliation Proceedings (Amendment) Act 1972, s 2(1).

3. Venue and procedure—(*1*)   *A complaint under section one of this Act—*

(*a*)   *shall not be made except to a justice of the peace acting for the petty sessions area (within the meaning of the Magistrates' Courts Act 1952) [appointed for the commission area (within the meaning of [the Justices of the Peace Act 1979])] in which the mother of the child resides,*

(*b*)   *if made before the birth of the child, shall be substantiated on oath.*

and the magistrates' court which, under the summons, is to hear the complaint shall be a magistrates' court for the said petty sessions area [appointed for the said area].

Note. Words in square brackets substituted for words 'acting for ... 1952' and 'for the said petty sessions area' by Domestic Proceedings and Magistrates' Courts Act 1978, s 49(a), as from 1 February 1981, save that words 'the Justices of the Peace Act 1979' substituted for words 'section 1 of the Administration of Justice Act 1973' by Justices of the Peace Act 1979, s 72, Sch 2, para 10, as from the same date.

(*2*)   *The foregoing subsection shall have effect subject to subsection (2) of section three of the Maintenance Orders Act 1950 (which relates to a complaint by a person residing in Scotland or Northern Ireland).*

(*3*)   *If the justice to whom a complaint under section one of this Act has been made dies, or ceases to be a justice, or is unable to act, the summons may be issued by any other justice acting for the same petty sessions area [appointed for the same commission area].*

Note. Words in square brackets substituted for words 'acting ... area' by Domestic Proceedings and Magistrates' Courts Act 1978, s 49(b), as from 1 February 1981.

4. Powers of court on hearing of complaint—(*1*)   *On the hearing of a complaint under section one of this Act the court shall hear the evidence of the mother (notwithstanding any consent or admission on the part of the defendant) and such other evidence as she may produce, and shall also hear any evidence tendered by or on behalf of the defendant.*

[(1)   On the hearing of a complaint under section 1 of this Act the court may adjudge the defendant to be the putative father of the child but shall not do so, in a case where evidence is given by the mother, unless her evidence is corroborated in some material particular by other evidence to the court's satisfaction.]

Note. Sub-s (1) in square brackets substituted for original sub-s (1) by Affiliation Proceedings (Amendment) Act 1972, s 1(1).

(*2*)   *If the evidence of the mother is corroborated in some material particular by other evidence to the court's satisfaction, the court may adjudge the defendant to be the putative father of the child and may also [Where the court has adjudged the defendant to be the putative father of the child it may also] if it thinks fit in all the circumstances of the case, proceed to make against him an order (referred to in this Act as 'an affiliation order') for the payment by him of—*

(*a*)   *a sum of money weekly, not exceeding thirty shillings [fifty shillings] a week, for the maintenance and education of the child,*

(*b*)   *the expenses incidental to the birth of the child, and*

(*c*)   *if the child has died before the making of the order, the child's funeral expenses.*

[containing one or both of the following provisions—

(*a*)   *provision for the making by him of such periodical payments for the maintenance and education of the child, and for such term, as may be specified in the order;*

(*b*)   *provision for the payment by him of such lump sum as may be so specified.]*

Note. Words 'Where the court has adjudged' to 'it may also' substituted for words 'If the evidence' to 'and may also' by Affiliation Proceedings (Amendment) Act 1972, s 1(2). Words 'fifty shillings' in para (a) substituted for words 'thirty shillings' by Matrimonial Proceedings (Magistrates' Courts) Act 1960, s 15(a) and words 'not exceeding fifty shillings a week' repealed by Maintenance Orders Act 1968, s 1, Schedule. Words 'containing one or both' to 'may be so specified' substituted for words 'for the payment' to 'funeral expenses' by Domestic Proceedings and Magistrates' Courts Act 1978, s 50(1), as from 1 February 1981.

(*3*) *Where a complaint under section one of this Act is made before or within two months after the birth of the child, any weekly sum ordered to be paid under paragraph* (*a*) *of the last foregoing subsection may, if the court thinks fit, be calculated from the date of the birth.*

[(*3*) *In deciding whether to exercise its powers under subsection* (*2*) *of this section and, if so, in what manner, the court shall, among the circumstances of the case, have regard to the following matters, that is to say—*

(*a*) *the income, earning capacity, property and other financial resources which the mother of the child and the person adjudged to be the putative father of the child have or are likely to have in the foreseeable future;*

(*b*) *the financial needs, obligations and responsibilities which the mother and that person have or are likely to have in the foreseeable future;*

(*c*) *the financial needs of the child;*

(*d*) *the income, earning capacity* (*if any*), *property and other financial resources of the child;*

(*e*) *any physical or mental disability of the child.*

(*4*) *Without prejudice to the generality of subsection* (*2*)(*b*) *of this section, an affiliation order may provide for the payment of a lump sum to be made for the purpose of enabling liabilities or expenses reasonably incurred before the making of the order to be met, being liabilities or expenses incurred in connection with the birth of the child or in maintaining the child or, if the child has died before the making of the order, being the child's funeral expenses.*

(*5*) *The amount of any lump sum required to be paid by an affiliation order shall not exceed £500 or such larger amount as the Secretary of State may from time to time by order fix for the purposes of this subsection.*

Any order made by the Secretary of State under this subsection shall be made by statutory instrument and shall be subject to annulment in pursuance of a resolution of either House of Parliament.]

Note. Sub-ss (3)–(5) in square brackets substituted for original sub-s (3) by Domestic Proceedings and Magistrates' Courts Act 1978, s 50(2), as from 1 February 1981.

See Family Law Reform Act 1987, s 33(2), Sch 3, paras 11(c), 12, as from 1 April 1989.

5. Persons entitled to payments under affiliation order—(*1*) *Subject to the provisions of this section and of the enactments mentioned in the following subsection, the person entitled to any payments to be made under an affiliation order shall be the child's mother* [*for the benefit of the child or the child himself*], *and the order shall make provision accordingly.*

Note. Words in square brackets added by Domestic Proceedings and Magistrates' Courts Act 1978, s 51(1), as from 1 February 1981.

(*2*) *The enactments referred to above are—*

(*a*) *section eighty-eight of the Children and Young Persons Act 1933* (*which provides that, where an illegitimate child is committed to the care of a* [*local authority*], *the person entitled to receive contributions in respect of the child under section eighty-six of that Act may be given the benefit of payments under an affiliation order in respect of the child*);

[(*a*) *section 49 of the Child Care Act 1980* (*which provides that, where an illegitimate child is in the care of a local authority, the authority entitled to receive contributions in respect of the child under section 45(2) of that Act may be given the benefit of payments under an affiliation order in respect of the child*);]

(*b*) *the said section eighty-eight as extended by section twenty-three of the Children Act 1948* (*which applies the former section to children received into the care of a local authority under section one of the Act of 1948*);

(*c*) *section forty-four of the National Assistance Act 1948* (*under which the National Assistance Board or a local authority giving assistance in respect of an illegitimate child may obtain an affiliation order providing for payments thereunder being made to the Board or authority, or may apply for an existing order to be varied so as to provide as aforesaid); and*

(d) *section twenty-six of the Children Act 1948 [section 50 of the Child Care Act 1980] (which makes provision corresponding to the said section forty-four for the benefit of a local authority having an illegitimate child in their care or maintaining an illegitimate child in an approved school),*

[(e) *section 45 of the Children Act 1975 (which enables the custodian of a child to apply for an affiliation order under this Act within three years after the making of the custodianship order).*]

Note. Sub-s (2)(a) in square brackets substituted for original sub-s (2)(a), sub-s (2)(b) repealed, and, in sub-s (2)(d), reference to Child Care Act 1980 substituted for reference to Children Act 1948, by Child Care Act 1980, s 89, Sch 5, para 6, as from 1 April 1981. In original sub-s (2)(a), words in square brackets substituted for words 'fit person or is ordered to be sent to an approved school', by Children and Young Persons Act 1969, s 72(3), Sch 5, para 28(1). In sub-s (2)(c), words 'the National Assistance Board or' repealed by Ministry of Social Security Act 1966, s 29(3), Sch 8. In sub-s (2)(d), final words 'or maintaining ... school' repealed by Children and Young Persons Act 1969, s 72(4), Sch 6.

Sub-s (2)(e) added by Children Act 1975, s 108(1), Sch 3, para 14, as from 1 December 1985.

(3) *An affiliation order may, on the application of a person other than the child's mother who for the time being has the custody of the child, either legally or by any arrangement approved by the court, be made or varied by a magistrates' court so as to entitle that person to any payments to be made under the order [provided that the person entitled to payments under the order shall be that person for the benefit of the child or the child himself].*

Note. Words in square brackets substituted for words 'entitle ... order' by Domestic Proceedings and Magistrates' Courts Act 1978, s 51(2), as from 1 February 1981.

(4) *Where an affiliation order for the time being provides for the child's mother to be entitled to any payments to be made under the order the payments shall be due under the order in respect of such time and so long as she is living and of sound mind and is not in prison, and if the mother has died, or is of unsound mind, or is in prison, any two justices of the peace may by order from time to time appoint some person (with his consent) to have the custody of the child; and a person appointed as guardian under this subsection shall be entitled to any payments to be made under the affiliation order and [where the court has appointed a person as guardian under this subsection the court may provide that the person entitled to any payments to be made under the affiliation order shall be that guardian for the benefit of the child or the child himself and the guardian] may make application for the recovery of any payments due thereunder in the same manner as the mother might have done.*

Any two justices of the peace may revoke an appointment made under this subsection and appoint another person thereunder in place of the person formerly appointed.

Note. Words in square brackets substituted for words 'a person appointed ... affiliation order and' by Domestic Proceedings and Magistrates' Courts Act 1978, s 51(3), as from 1 February 1981.

(5) *An affiliation order shall, in any case where payments to be made thereunder are not ordered to be made to the clerk of a magistrates' court under section fifty-two of the Magistrates' Courts Act 1952 [section 59 of the Magistrates' Courts Act 1980] provide for the payments to be made to the person for the time being entitled thereto in accordance with the provisions of this Act.*

Note. Reference to Act of 1980 substituted for reference to Act of 1952 by Magistrates' Courts Act 1980, s 154, Sch 7, para 20, as from 6 July 1981.

Subsection (5) does not apply to orders registered in a court in the United Kingdom under Part II of Maintenance Orders (Reciprocal Enforcement) Act 1972: see s 27(9) of that Act (p 2454).

6. Duration of orders. *Subject to the provisions of this Act, an affiliation order shall not, except for the purpose of recovering money previously due under the order, be of any force or validity after the child has attained the age of sixteen years or has died; and payments under the order shall not be required to be made in respect of any period after the child has* *attained the age of thirteen years unless the order contains a direction that payments to be made under it are to continue until the child attains the age of sixteen years.*

[6. Age limit on making of orders and duration of orders—(*1*) *No affiliation order shall be made in respect of a child who has attained the age of eighteen.*

(*2*) *The term to be specified in an affiliation order which requires the making of periodical payments in favour of a child may begin with the date of the making of an application for the summons under this Act or any later date, but—*

(*a*) *shall not in the first instance extend beyond the date of the birthday of the child next following his attaining the upper limit of the compulsory school age (that is to say, the age that is for the time being that limit by virtue of section 35 of the Education Act 1944, together with any Order in Council made under that section) unless the court thinks it right in the circumstances of the case to specify a later date; and*

(*b*) *shall not in any event, subject to subsection (4) of this section, extend beyond the date of the child's eighteenth birthday.*

(*3*) *Where a complaint under section 1 of this Act is made before or within two months after the birth of the child, the term to be specified in an affiliation order which requires the making of periodical payments may, if the court thinks fit, begin with the date of the birth.*

(*4*) *Paragraph (b) of subsection (2) of this section shall not apply in the case of a child if it appears to the court that—*

(*a*) *the child is, or will be, or if an order were made without complying with that paragraph would be, receiving instruction at an educational establishment or undergoing training for a trade, profession or vocation, whether or not he is also, or will also be, in gainful employment; or*

(*b*) *there are special circumstances which justify the making of an order without complying with that paragraph.*

(*5*) *An affiliation order requiring the making of periodical payments shall, notwithstanding anything in the order, cease to have effect on the death of the person liable to make payments under the order.*]

Note. Section 6 in square brackets substituted for original s 6 by Domestic Proceedings and Magistrates' Courts Act 1978, s 52(1), as from 1 February 1981.

6A. Variation and revocation of orders—(*1*) *The power of the court under section 53 of the Magistrates' Courts Act 1952 [section 60 of the Magistrates' Courts Act 1980], to vary an affiliation order which provides for the making of periodical payments shall include power to vary the order so that it makes provision for the payment of a lump sum (whether or not when the affiliation order was first made, or on an earlier variation, provision was made for the payment of a lump sum).*

(*2*) *In exercising its powers under the said section 53 [the said section 60] to revoke, vary or revive an affiliation order the court shall have regard to all the circumstances of the case, including any change in any of the matters to which the court was required to have regard when making the order.*

(*3*) *An application for the variation or revival of an affiliation order so as to require periodical payments to be made thereunder after the date mentioned in section 6(2)(a) of this Act may be made by the child's mother or by any person who for the time being has the custody of the child either legally or by an arrangement approved by the court, but not including a local authority in whose care the child is under section 1 of the Children Act 1948 [section 2 of the Child Care Act 1980], or by virtue of a care order (other than an interim order) within the meaning of the Children and Young Persons Act 1969; and, if the child has attained the age of sixteen, an application for the variation or revival of an affiliation order may be made by the child himself.*

(*4*) *Where on an application for the variation of an affiliation order the court decides to make provision for the payment of a lump sum, the court may provide for the payment of a sum not exceeding the maximum amount that may at that time be required to be paid under section 4(5) of this Act.*

(*5*) *Where in the exercise of its powers under section 63 of the Magistrates' Courts Act 1952* [*section 75 of the Magistrates' Courts Act 1980*], *the court orders that a lump sum required to be paid under an affiliation order shall be paid by instalments, the court, on an application made either by the person liable to pay or the person entitled to receive that sum, shall have power to vary that order by varying the number of instalments payable, the amount of any instalment payable and the date on which any instalment becomes payable.*]

Note. Section 6A added by Domestic Proceedings and Magistrates' Courts Act 1978, s 53, as from 1 February 1981.

In sub-ss (1), (2), (5), words in square brackets substituted for references to earlier statutes by Magistrates' Courts Act 1980, s 154, Sch 7, para 21, as from 6 July 1981. In sub-s (3) words in square brackets substituted for words 'section … 1948' by Child Care Act 1980, s 89, Sch 5, para 7, as from 1 April 1981.

7. Continuance of payments in certain cases—(*1*) *The power under section fifty-three of the Magistrates' Courts Act 1952, to vary or revive an affiliation order shall, notwithstanding anything in the last foregoing section, include power to vary or revive it in accordance with the following provisions of this section.*

(*2*) *If, on the application of the child's mother, it appears to the court that the child is or will be engaged in a course of education or training after attaining the age of sixteen years, and that it is expedient for that purpose for payments to be made under the order after the child attains that age, then subject to the two next following subsections the court may by order direct that payments shall be so made for such period, not exceeding two years from the date of the order, as may be specified in the order.*

(*3*) *Subject to the next following subsection, the period specified in an order made by virtue of the foregoing provisions of this section may from time to time be extended by a subsequent order so made, but shall not in any case extend beyond the date when the child attains the age of twenty-one.*

Note. Sub-ss (1)–(3) repealed by Domestic Proceedings and Magistrates' Courts Act 1978, ss 52(2), 89, Sch 3, as from 1 February 1981.

(*4*) *Notwithstanding anything in the foregoing provisions of this section or in any order made by virtue of this section* [*section 6 of this Act*], *an affiliation order shall not operate, after the child has attained the age of sixteen,*—

  (*a*) *so as to require payments thereunder to be made either*—

    (*i*) *in respect of any period during which the child is detained in an approved school, or*

    (*ii*) *subject to the next following subsection, in respect of any period during which the child is in the care of a local authority under section one of the Children Act, 1948, or there is in force an order under the Children and Young Persons Act, 1933, committing the child to the care of a fit person;*

  [(*a*) *subject to the next following subsection, so as to require payments thereunder to be made in respect of any period when the child is in the care of a local authority under section one of the Children Act 1948* [*section 2 of the Child Care Act 1980*], *or by virtue of a care order (other than an interim order) within the meaning of the Children and Young Persons Act 1969;*]

  (*b*) *so as to entitle any person other than the child's mother* [*or the child himself*] *to the payments.*

Note. Words in square brackets referring to section 6 and, in para (b), to the child himself substituted and inserted by Domestic Proceedings and Magistrates' Courts Act 1978, s 52(2), as from 1 February 1981.

Para (a) in square brackets substituted for original para (a) by Children and Young Persons Act 1969, s 72(3), Sch 5, para 28(2). In new para (a), reference to Child Care Act 1980 substituted for reference to Children Act 1948 by Child Care Act 1980, s 89, Sch 5, para 8(a), as from 1 April 1981.

(*5*) *Sub-paragraph (ii) of paragraph (a) of the last foregoing subsection shall not apply to any part of such a period as is there mentioned during which the child is permitted to reside with his mother.*

Note. Words 'Sub-paragraph (ii) of' repealed by Children and Young Persons Act 1969, s 72(4), Sch 6.

(*6*) *Any reference in this section to a child's mother shall be taken as including a reference to any person for the time being having the custody of the child either legally or by any arrangement approved by the court, except that it shall not be taken as referring to a local authority in whose care the child is under section one of the Children Act 1948 [section 2 of the Child Care Act 1980], or a person to whose care the child is committed by an order under the Children and Young Persons Act 1933 [by virtue of such a care order as aforesaid].*

Note. Reference to Child Care Act 1980 substituted for reference to Children Act 1948 by Child Care Act 1980, s 89, Sch 5, para 8(b), as from 1 April 1981. Final words in square brackets substituted for preceding reference to Act of 1933 by Children and Young Persons Act 1969, s 72(3), Sch 5, para 28(3).

8. Appeal—(*1*) *An appeal shall lie to [the Crown Court] from the making of an order under this Act, or from any refusal by a magistrates' court to make such an order, or from the revocation, revival or variation by a magistrates' court of such an order.*

Note. Words 'the Crown Court' substituted for 'a court of quarter sessions' by virtue of Courts Act 1971, s 56(2), Sch 9, Part I.

(*2*) *On an appeal against an order under section four of this Act by the person adjudged to be the putative father (as well as on an appeal against a refusal to make an order under that section) the court shall hear the evidence of the mother and such other evidence as she may produce, and shall also hear any evidence tendered by or on behalf of the other party, but the court shall not confirm the order appealed against (or reverse the refusal to make an order) unless the evidence of the mother is corroborated in some material particular by other evidence to the court's satisfaction [hear any evidence given by or on behalf of either party but shall not confirm the order appealed against (or reverse the refusal to make an order), in a case where evidence is given by the mother, unless her evidence is corroborated in some material particular by other evidence to the court's satisfaction].*

Note. Words in square brackets substituted for words 'hear ... satisfaction' by Affiliation Proceedings (Amendment) Act 1972, s 1(3).

9. Duty of putative father to notify change of address—(*1*) *A person against whom an affiliation order has been made—*

(*a*) *shall, if he changes his address and he is required to make any payment under the order to the clerk of a magistrates' court, give notice of the change to the clerk of that court;*

(*b*) *shall, in a case where the foregoing paragraph does not apply and he is required under the order to make any payments (including payments of costs) to any person, give notice of any change of address to such person (if any) as may be specified in the order.*

(*2*) *Any person failing without reasonable excuse to give a notice which he is required by this section to give shall be liable on summary conviction to a fine not exceeding [£50] [level 2 on the standard scale].*

Note. £10 substituted by virtue of Criminal Justice Act 1967, s 92(1), (9), Sch 3, and £50 by Domestic Proceedings and Magistrates' Courts Act 1978, s 89(2), Sch 2, para 16, as from 1 February 1981; and reference to level 2 substituted by Criminal Justice Act 1982, ss 37, 46(1).

10. Attachment of pension or income to satisfy affiliation order—(*1*) *Where an affiliation order has been made against a person and there is payable to him any pension or income which is capable of being attached, the justices who made the order or a magistrates' court may—*

(*a*) *after giving the person an opportunity of being heard, and*

(*b*) *on being satisfied that the person has without reasonable cause failed to make any payments which he is required by the order to make,*

order the pension or income to be attached as to the weekly amount payable under the affiliation order, or as to any lesser amount, and the amount attached to be paid to the person named by the court.

(*2*) *An order under this section shall be an authority to the person by whom the pension or income is payable to make the payment in accordance with the order, and the receipt of the person to whom the payment is ordered to be made shall be a good discharge to the payor.*

Note. This section repealed by Maintenance Orders Act 1958, s 23(4), except as respects orders in force or deemed to be in force at the commencement of that subsection, which orders may be discharged or varied.

11. Misconduct by guardian of illegitimate child. *If any person appointed under subsection (4) of section five of this Act to have the custody of an illegitimate child—*

(*a*) *misapplies any money paid by the putative father for the child's support, or*

(*b*) *withholds proper nourishment from, or otherwise abuses or maltreats, the child,*

he shall be liable on summary conviction to a fine not exceeding [£25] [*level 1 on the standard scale*].

Note. Fine increased to £25 by Criminal Law Act 1977, s 31(6), (9): reference to level 1 substituted by Criminal Justice Act 1982, ss 37, 46(1).

12. Repeals and savings—(*1*) *The enactments specified in the second column of the Schedule to this Act are hereby repealed to the extent specified in the third column of the Schedule.*

Note. Repealed by Statute Law (Repeals) Act 1974.

(*2*) *Any application, order, appointment or other thing made or having effect under or for the purposes of an enactment repealed by this Act and pending or in force immediately before the commencement of this Act shall be deemed to have been made under or for the purposes of the corresponding enactment in this Act; and any proceeding or other thing begun under any enactment so repealed may be continued under this Act, as if begun thereunder.*

(*3*) *So much of any enactment or document as refers expressly or by implication to any enactment repealed by this Act shall, if and so far as the nature of the subject-matter of the enactment or document permits, be construed as referring to this Act or the corresponding enactment therein, as the case may require.*

(*4*) *Nothing in this section shall be taken as prejudicing the general application of section thirty-eight of the Interpretation Act 1889 with regard to the effect of repeals.*

Note. Interpretation Act 1889, s 38 repealed by Interpretation Act 1978, s 25, Sch 3, and replaced by ss 16(1), 17(a) of, and Sch 2, para 3 to, that Act.

13. Short title, extent and commencement—(*1*) *This Act may be cited as the Affiliation Proceedings Act 1957.*

(*2*) *This Act shall not extend to Scotland or Northern Ireland.*

(*3*) *This Act shall come into force on the first day of April, nineteen hundred and fifty-eight.*

SCHEDULE   Section 12

Enactments Repealed

Session and Chapter	Short Title	Extent of Repeal
7 & 8 Vict c 101	The Poor Law Amendment Act 1844	Sections five and eight.
8 & 9 Vict c 10	The Bastardy Act 1845	The whole Act.
35 & 36 Vict c 65	The Bastardy Laws Amendment Act 1872	The whole Act.
4 & 5 Geo 5 c 6	The Affiliation Orders Act 1914	The whole Act.
13 & 14 Geo 5 c 23	The Bastardy Act 1923	The whole Act.
19 & 20 Geo 5 c 36	The Age of Marriage Act 1929	The whole Act.
15 & 16 Geo 6 & 1 Eliz 2 c 41	The Affiliation Orders Act 1952	The whole Act except section four.
15 & 16 Geo 6 & 1 Eliz 2 c 55	The Magistrates' Courts Act 1952	Section fifty-one; subsection (4) of section eighty-three.

Note. Repealed by Statute Law (Repeals) Act 1974.

MATRIMONIAL CAUSES (PROPERTY AND MAINTENANCE) ACT 1958

(6 & 7 Eliz 2 c 35)

An Act to enable the power of the court in matrimonial proceedings to order alimony, maintenance or the securing of a sum of money to be exercised at any time after a decree; to provide for the setting aside of dispositions of property made for the purpose of reducing the assets available for satisfying such an order; to enable the court after the death of a party to a marriage which has been dissolved or annulled to make provision out of his estate in favour of the other party; and to extend the powers of the court under section seventeen of the Married Women's Property Act 1882. [7 July 1958]

1. Time for making orders for maintenance or alimony—(*1*) *Any power of the court, under the enactments mentioned in the next following subsection, to make an order on a decree for divorce, nullity of marriage or judicial separation shall (subject as mentioned in subsection (3) of this section) be exercisable either on pronouncing such a decree or at any time thereafter.*

(*2*) *The said enactments are the following provisions of the Matrimonial Causes Act 1950 (in this Act referred to as 'the Act of 1950'), that is to say,—*

(*a*) *subsections (2) and (3) of section nineteen (whereby, on a decree for divorce or nullity of marriage, the court may order the husband to make a secured provision for the wife or to pay her a monthly or weekly sum), and those subsections as extended by subsection (4) of that section (whereby the like provision or payments may be ordered for a husband where a petition for divorce is presented by his wife on the ground of his insanity);*

(*b*) *subsection (3) of section twenty-six (whereby, on a decree of divorce or nullity of marriage, the court may order the husband, and, on a decree of divorce, made on the ground of the husband's insanity, may order the wife, to make a secured provision for the benefit of the children); and*

(*c*) *subsection (2) of section twenty (whereby, on a decree for judicial separation, a husband may be ordered to pay alimony to his wife), and that subsection as extended by subsection (3) of that section whereby the like payments may be ordered to be made by a wife where a petition for judicial separation is presented by her on the ground of her husband's insanity).*

Note. For Matrimonial Causes Act 1950, ss 19(2), (3), 20(2), (3), 26(3) see pp 2138, 2139, 2141.

(*3*) *In relation to the provisions of the Act of 1950 specified in paragraphs (a) and (b) of the last preceding subsection,—*

(*a*) *any reference to subsection (1) of this section to a decree shall be construed as a reference to a decree nisi, and the reference to any time after a decree shall be construed as a reference to any such time whether before or after the decree has been made absolute; but*

(*b*) *nothing in subsection (1) of this section shall be construed as affecting the provisions of section twenty-nine of the Act of 1950 as to the commencement of proceedings for an order under the provisions specified in those paragraphs or as to the making or effect of such an order.*

Note. For Matrimonial Causes Act 1950, s 29 see p 2142.

(*4*) *In accordance with the preceding provisions of this section, the provisions of the Act of 1950 specified in the Schedule to this Act shall have effect subject to the amendments specified in that Schedule.*

(*5*) *Nothing in this section, or in any amendment made by this section in any of the enactments referred to therein, shall be construed as requiring the court, in determining any application for an order under any of those enactments, to disregard any delay in making or proceeding with the application.*

Note. This section repealed by Matrimonial Causes Act 1965, s 45, Sch 2. See now Matrimonial Causes Act 1973, s 23(1) (p 2512), replacing Matrimonial Proceedings and Property Act 1970, s 2(1) (p 2365), replacing Matrimonial Causes Act 1965, s 16(1) (p 2247).

2. Avoidance of disposition made to defeat wife's claim for financial relief—
(*1*) *Where under any of the relevant provisions of the Act of 1950 proceedings are brought against a man (in this section referred to as 'the husband') by his wife or former wife (in this section referred to as 'the wife') for financial relief, the wife may make an application under this section to the court in those proceedings with respect to any disposition made by the husband within the period of three years ending with the date of the application under this section, whether the disposition was made before or after the commencement of those proceedings.*
(*2*) *Subject to the following provisions of this section, if on an application by the wife under this section it appears to the court—*
  (*a*) *that the disposition to which the application relates was made by the husband with the intention of defeating the wife's claim for financial relief, and*
  (*b*) *that, if the disposition were set aside, financial relief, or, as the case may be, different financial relief, would be granted to her,*
the court may by order set aside the disposition and may give such consequential directions (including directions requiring the making of any payment or the disposal of any property) as the court thinks fit for the purpose of giving effect to the order under this subsection.
(*3*) *The power conferred by the last preceding subsection shall not be exercisable in respect of a disposition made for valuable consideration to a person who, at the time of the disposition, acted in relation thereto in good faith and without notice of any intention on the part of the husband to defeat the wife's claim for financial relief.*
(*4*) *Where an application is made under this section with respect to a disposition, not being a disposition falling within the last preceding subsection, and the court is satisfied that the disposition would (apart from this section) have the consequence of defeating the wife's claim for financial relief, the disposition shall be presumed, unless the contrary is proved, to have been made by the husband with the intention of defeating the wife's claim for financial relief.*
(*5*) *The preceding provisions of this section shall have effect for enabling an application to the High Court to be made thereunder by a woman after she has obtained an order against her husband or former husband under any relevant provisions of the Act of 1950 as they apply for enabling an application to be made in proceedings for such an order:*
  Provided that for the purposes of the application of those provisions in accordance with this subsection—
  (*a*) *subsection (2) of this section shall apply as if paragraph (b) thereof were omitted, and*
  (*b*) *the presumption mentioned in the last preceding subsection shall apply (in the case of a disposition not falling within subsection (3) of this section) if the court is satisfied that in consequence of the disposition the wife's claim for financial relief was defeated.*
(*6*) *The provisions of this section do not apply to a disposition made before the commencement of this Act.*
(*7*) *In this section any reference to defeating the wife's claim for financial relief is a reference to preventing financial relief from being granted to her, or reducing the amount of any such relief which might be so granted, or frustrating or impeding the enforcement of any order which might be made on her application under any of the relevant provisions of the Act of 1950.*
(*8*) *In this section—*
'financial relief' means relief under any of the relevant provisions of the Act of 1950;
'the relevant provisions of the Act of 1950' means the following provisions of that Act, that is to say,—
  (*a*) *subsections (2) and (3) of section nineteen;*
  (*b*) *subsection (2) of section twenty;*
  (*c*) *subsections (2) to (4) of section twenty-two (whereby, in connection with a decree for restitution of conjugal rights, a husband may be ordered to pay alimony to his wife, or to make or secure periodical payments to her); and*
  (*d*) *section twenty-three (which confers additional power on the court to make orders for maintenance);*
'valuable consideration' does not include marriage.

Note. For Matrimonial Causes Act 1950, ss 19, 20, 22, 23 see pp 2138–2140.

This section repealed by Matrimonial Causes Act 1965, s 45, Sch 2. See now Matrimonial Causes Act 1973, s 37 (p 2546), replacing Matrimonial Proceedings and Property Act 1970, s 16 (p 2374), replacing Matrimonial Causes Act 1965, s 32 (p 2257).

3. Provision for former wife out of estate of deceased former husband—(*1*)

Where after the commencement of this Act a person dies domiciled in England and is survived by a former wife of his who has not re-married, the former wife may apply to the High Court for an order under this section on the ground that the deceased has not made reasonable provision for her maintenance after his death:

Provided that an application under this section shall not be made except—

(*a*) *before the end of the period of six months beginning with the date on which representation in regard to the estate of the deceased is first taken out, or*

(*b*) *with the permission of the court, after the end of that period but before the administration and distribution of the estate have been completed.*

(*2*) *If on an application by a former wife under this section the court is satisfied—*

(*a*) *that it would have been reasonable for the deceased to make provision for her maintenance and*

(*b*) *that the deceased has made no provision, or has not made reasonable provision, for her maintenance,*

the court may order that such reasonable provision for her maintenance as the court thinks fit shall be made out of the net estate of the deceased, subject to such conditions or restrictions (if any) as the court may impose.

(*3*) *Where the court makes an order under this section requiring provision to be made for the maintenance of a former wife, the order shall require that provision to be made by way of periodical payments terminating not later than her death and, if she re-married, not later than her re-marriage:*

Provided that if the value of the net estate of the deceased does not exceed five thousand pounds the order may require the provision for her maintenance to be made, wholly or in part, by way of a lump sum payment.

(*4*) *On any application under this section, the court shall have regard—*

(*a*) *to any past, present or future capital of the applicant and to any income of hers from any source;*

(*b*) *to her conduct in relation to the deceased and otherwise;*

(*c*) *to any application made by her during the lifetime of the deceased under the Act of 1950 or the enactments repealed by that Act, for such an order as is mentioned in subsection (2) or subsection (3) of section nineteen of that Act, and to the order (if any) made on any such application, or (if no such application was made by her, or such an application was made by her and no such order was made thereon) the circumstances appearing to the court to be the reasons why no such application was made, or no such order was made, as the case may be; and*

(*d*) *to any other matter or thing which, in the circumstances of the case, the court may consider relevant or material in relation to her, persons interested in the estate of the deceased, or otherwise.*

Note. For Matrimonial Causes Act 1950, s 19(2), (3), see p 2138.

(*5*) *In determining whether, and in what way, and as from what date, provision for maintenance ought to be made by an order under this section, the court shall have regard to the nature of the property representing the net estate of the deceased, and shall not order any such provision to be made as would necessitate a realisation that would be improvident having regard to the interests of the dependants of the deceased, of the applicant, and of the persons who, apart from the order, would be entitled to that property.*

(*6*) *In this and the next following section 'former wife', in relation to a deceased person, means a woman whose marriage with him was during his lifetime dissolved or annulled by a decree made under the Act of 1950 or under any of the enactments repealed by that Act, and 'net estate' and 'dependant' have the same meanings respectively as in the Inheritance (Family Provision) Act 1938.*

Note. This section repealed by Matrimonial Causes Act 1965, s 45, Sch 2, and replaced by ibid, s 26 (p 2253), repealed by Inheritance (Provision for Family and Dependants) Act 1975, s 26(2), Schedule.

4. Discharge and variation of orders under s 3—(*1*) *Subject to the following provisions of this section, where an order (in this section referred to as 'the original order') has been made under the last preceding section, the High Court, on an application under this section, shall have power by order to discharge or vary the original order or to suspend any provision thereof temporarily and to revive the operation of any provision so suspended.*

(*2*) *An application under this section may be made by or on behalf of any of the following persons that is to say,*—

   (*a*)   *the former wife on whose application the original order was made;*

   (*b*)   *any other former wife of the deceased;*

   (*c*)   *any dependant of the deceased;*

   (*d*)   *the trustee of any relevant property;*

   (*e*)   *any person who, under the will of the deceased or under the law relating to intestacy, is beneficially interested in any relevant property.*

(*3*) *An order under this section varying the original order, or reviving any suspended provision thereof, shall not be made so as to affect any property which, at the time of the application for the order under this section, is not relevant property.*

(*4*) *In exercising the powers conferred by this section, the court shall have regard to all the circumstances of the case, including any change in the circumstances to which the court was required to have regard in determining the application for the original order.*

(*5*) *In this section 'relevant property' means property the income of which, in accordance with the original order or any consequential directions given by the court in connection therewith, is applicable (wholly or in part) for the maintenance of the former wife on whose application the original order was made.*

Note. This section repealed by Matrimonial Causes Act 1965, s 45, Sch 2, and replaced by ibid, s 27 (p 2254), repealed by Inheritance (Provision for Family and Dependants) Act 1975, s 26(2), Schedule.

5. Extension of preceding provisions in favour of husband or former husband—(*1*) *Subject to the next following subsection, the provisions of section two of this Act shall have effect for enabling an application thereunder to be made by a man with respect to a disposition made by his wife or former wife, as those provisions have effect for enabling an application thereunder to be made by a woman with respect to a disposition made by her husband or former husband.*

Note. Sub-s (1) repealed by Matrimonial Causes Act 1965, s 45, Sch 2. See now Matrimonial Causes Act 1973, s 37 (p 2546), replacing Matrimonial Proceedings and Property Act 1970, s 16 (p 2374), replacing Matrimonial Causes Act 1965, s 32 (p 2257).

(*2*) *For the purposes of the application of those provisions in accordance with the preceding subsection*—

   (*a*)   *for references to a man and to a wife or former wife there shall be substituted respectively references to a woman and to a husband or former husband, and for references to a woman and to a husband or former husband there shall be substituted respectively references to a man and to a wife or former wife;*

   (*b*)   *'the relevant provisions of the Act of 1950' (instead of having the meaning assigned to it by subsection (8) of section two of this Act) means the following provisions of that Act, that is to say,*—

      (*i*)   *subsections (2) and (3) of section nineteen as extended by subsection (4) of that section,*

      (*ii*)   *subsection (2) of section twenty as extended by subsection (3) of that section,*

      (*iii*)   *subsection (1) of section twenty-four (which, in a case where the court pronounces a decree for divorce or judicial separation by reason of the adultery, desertion or cruelty of the wife, enables the court to order a settlement of property to which she is entitled), and* (*iv*) subsection (2) of section twenty-four (which enables the court, where a decree for restitution of conjugal rights is made on the application of the husband, to make an order for the settlement of property to which the wife is entitled or for periodical payments in respect of profits or earnings received by her).

Note. For Matrimonial Causes Act 1950, ss 19, 20, 24 see pp 2138–2140. Sub-s (2) repealed by Matrimonial Causes Act 1965, s 45, Sch 2. See now Matrimonial Causes Act 1973, s 37 (p 2513), replacing Matrimonial Proceedings and Property Act 1970, s 16 (p 2374), replacing Matrimonial Causes Act 1965, s 32 (p 2257).

(3) The provisions of sections three and four of this Act shall have effect in relation to a former husband of a deceased woman as they have effect in relation to a former wife of a deceased man, as if any reference in those sections to a former wife were a reference to a former husband:

Provided that, for the purposes of those provisions as applied by this subsection, the reference in paragraph (c) of subsection (4) of section three of this Act to such an order as is mentioned in subsection (2) or subsection (3) of section nineteen of the Act of 1950 shall be construed as a reference to any such order as could be made either—

(a) under the said subsection (2) or subsection (3) as extended by subsection (4) of the said section nineteen, or

(b) under subsection (1) of section twenty-four of that Act.

Note. For Matrimonial Causes Act 1950, ss 19, 24, see pp 2138, 2140. Sub-s (3) repealed by Matrimonial Causes Act 1965, s 45, Sch 2.

(4) In the last preceding subsection (but without prejudice to the generality of any reference to a former husband in subsection (1) or subsection (2) of this section) 'former husband', in relation to a deceased woman, means a man whose marriage with her was during her lifetime dissolved or annulled by a decree made under the Act of 1950 or under any of the enactments repealed by that Act.

Note. Sub-s (4) repealed by Matrimonial Causes Act 1965, s 45, Sch 2.

6. Supplementary provisions as to orders under ss 3 and 4—(1) The provisions of sections three and four of this Act shall not render the personal representatives of a deceased person liable for having distributed any part of the estate of the deceased after the end of the period of six months referred to in subsection (1) of section three of this Act, on the ground that they ought to have taken into account the possibility that the court might permit an application under that section after the end of that period, or that an order under that section might be varied under section four of this Act; but this subsection shall be without prejudice to any power to recover any part of the estate so distributed arising by virtue of the making of an order under section three or section four of this Act.

(2) In considering, under subsection (1) of section three of this Act, the question when representation was first taken out, a grant limited to settled land or to trust property shall be left out of account, and a grant limited to real estate or to personal estate shall be left out of account unless a grant limited to the remainder of the estate had previously been made or is made at the same time.

(3) For the purposes of subsection (1) of section one hundred and sixty-two of the Supreme Court of Judicature (Consolidation) Act 1925 (which relates to the discretion of the court as to the persons to whom administration is to be granted), a person by whom or on whose behalf an application under section three or section four of this Act is proposed to be made shall be deemed to be a person interested in the estate of the deceased.

Note. As to Supreme Court of Judicature (Consolidation) Act 1925, s 162(1) see now Supreme Court Act 1981, s 116.

(4) Section three of the Inheritance (Family Provision) Act 1938 (which relates to the effect and form of orders under that Act), shall have effect in relation to orders under sections three and four of this Act as it has effect in relation to orders under that Act.

(5) In this section any reference to any of the provisions of section three or section four of this Act shall be construed as including a reference to those provisions as applied by the last preceding section.

Note. This section repealed by Matrimonial Causes Act 1965, s 45, Sch 2, and replaced by ibid, s 28 (p 2255); repealed and not replaced by Matrimonial Proceedings and Property Act 1970, s 42(2), Sch 3.

7. Extension of s 17 of Married Women's Property Act 1882—(1) Any right of a wife, under section seventeen of the Married Women's Property Act 1882, to apply to a judge of the High Court or of a county court, in any question between husband and wife as to the title to or possession of property, shall include the right to make such an application where it is claimed by the wife that her husband has had in his possession or under his control—

    (a) money to which, or to a share of which, she was beneficially entitled (whether by reason that it represented the proceeds of property to which, or to an interest in which, she was beneficially entitled, or for any other reason), or

    (b) property (other than money) to which, or to an interest in which, she was beneficially entitled,

and that either that money or other property has ceased to be in his possession or under his control or that she does not know whether it is still in his possession or under his control.

Note. For Married Women's Property Act 1882, s 17 see p 2032.

(2) Where, on an application made to a judge of the High Court or of a county court under the said section seventeen, as extended by the preceding subsection, the judge is satisfied—

    (a) that the husband has had in his possession or under his control money or other property as mentioned in paragraph (a) or paragraph (b) of the preceding subsection, and

    (b) that he has not made to the wife, in respect of that money or other property, such payment or disposition as would have been appropriate in the circumstances,

the power to make orders under that section shall be extended in accordance with the next following subsection.

(3) Where the last preceding subsection applies, the power to make orders under the said section seventeen shall include power for the judge to order the husband to pay to the wife—

    (a) in a case falling within paragraph (a) of subsection (1) of this section, such sum in respect of the money to which the application relates, or the wife's share thereof, as the case may be, or

    (b) in a case falling within paragraph (b) of the said subsection (1), such sum in respect of the value of the property to which the application relates, or the wife's interest therein, as the case may be,

as the judge may consider appropriate.

(4) Where on an application under the said section seventeen as extended by this section it appears to the judge that there is any property which—

    (a) represents the whole or part of the money or property in question, and

    (b) is property in respect of which an order could have been made under that section if an application had been made by the wife thereunder in a question as to the title to or possession of that property,

the judge (either in substitution for or in addition to the making of an order in accordance with the last preceding subsection) may make any order under that section in respect of that property which he could have made on such an application as is mentioned in paragraph (b) of this subsection.

(5) The preceding provisions of this section shall have effect in relation to a husband as they have effect in relation to a wife, as if any reference to the husband were a reference to the wife and any reference to the wife were a reference to the husband.

(6) *Any power of a judge under the said section seventeen to direct inquiries or give any other directions in relation to an application under that section shall be exercisable in relation to an application made under that section as extended by this section; and the provisos to that section (which relate to appeals and other matters) shall apply in relation to any order made under the said section seventeen as extended by this section as they apply in relation to an order made under that section apart from this section.*

[(6) Any power of a judge which is exercisable on an application under the said section seventeen shall be exercisable in relation to an application made under that section as extended by this section.]

Note. Sub-s (6) in square brackets substituted for sub-s (6) in italics by Matrimonial and Family Proceedings Act 1984, s 46(1), Sch 1, para 3, as from 28 April 1986.

(7) For the avoidance of doubt it is hereby declared that any power conferred by the said section seventeen to make orders with respect to any property includes power to order a sale of the property.

Note. For the application of this section to engaged couples where the agreement to marry is terminated, see Law Reform (Miscellaneous Provisions) Act 1970, s 2(2) (p 2361). See also Matrimonial Proceedings and Property Act 1970, s 39 (p 2383).

8. Interpretation—(1) In this Act, except in so far as the context otherwise requires, the following expressions have the meanings hereby assigned to them respectively, that is to say:

'disposition' does not include any provision contained in a will, but, with that exception, includes any conveyance, assurance or gift of property of any description, whether made by an instrument or otherwise;

'property' means any real or personal property, any estate or interest in real or personal property, any money, any negotiable instrument, debt or other chose in action, and any other right or interest whether in possession or not;

'will' includes a codicil.

Note. See Matrimonial Causes Act 1965, ss 26(6), 27(2) (pp 2254), and see now Matrimonial Causes Act 1973, s 37(6) (p 2547), replacing Matrimonial Proceedings and Property Act 1970, s 16(4) (p 2374).

(2) Except in so far as the context otherwise requires, any reference in this Act to an enactment shall be construed as a reference to that enactment as amended by or under any other enactment.

9. Short title, commencement and extent—(1) This Act may be cited as the Matrimonial Causes (Property and Maintenance) Act 1958.

(2) This Act shall come into operation on such day as may be appointed by the Lord Chancellor by an order made by statutory instrument.

Commencement. The Act was brought into operation by Matrimonial Causes (Property and Maintenance) Act (Commencement) Order 1958, SI 1958 No 2080, on 1 January 1959.

(3) This Act shall not extend to Scotland or to Northern Ireland.

SCHEDULE

AMENDMENTS OF MATRIMONIAL CAUSES ACT 1950

In section nineteen, in subsection (2), for the words 'On any decree for divorce or nullity of marriage' there shall be substituted the words 'Subject to the provisions of section twenty-nine of this Act, on pronouncing a decree nisi for divorce or nullity of marriage or at any time thereafter, whether before or after the decree has been made absolute'; and in subsection (3), for the words 'On any decree for divorce or nullity of marriage', there shall be substituted the words 'Subject to the provisions of the said section twenty-nine, on pronouncing a decree nisi for divorce or nullity of marriage or at any time thereafter, whether before or after the decree has been made absolute'.

In section twenty, in subsection (2), for the words 'On any decree' there shall be substituted the words 'On or at any time after a decree'.

In section twenty-six, in subsection (3), for the words 'On any decree of divorce or nullity of marriage', there shall be substituted the words 'Subject to the provisions of section twenty-nine of this Act, on pronouncing a decree nisi of divorce or nullity of marriage or at any time thereafter, whether before or after the decree has been made absolute', and for the words 'on a decree of divorce' there shall be substituted the words 'where the decree is a decree of divorce and is'.

Note. For Matrimonial Causes Act 1950, ss 19, 20, 26, see pp 2138, 2139, 2141. The Schedule repealed by Matrimonial Causes Act 1965, s 45, Sch 2, and replaced by ibid, ss 16(1), 19, 20(1), 34(3) (pp 2247, 2248, 2259), repealed by Matrimonial Proceedings and Property Act 1970, s 42(2), Sch 3.

MAINTENANCE ORDERS ACT 1958

(6 & 7 Eliz 2 c 29)

An Act to make provision for the registration in the High Court or a magistrates' court of certain maintenance orders made by the order of those courts or a county court and with respect to the enforcement and variation of registered orders; to make provision for the attachment of sums falling to be paid by way of wages, salary or other earnings or by way of pension for the purpose of enforcing certain maintenance orders; to amend section seventy-four of the Magistrates' Courts Act 1952; to make provision for the review of committals to prison by magistrates' courts for failure to comply with maintenance orders; to enable Orders in Council under section twelve of the Maintenance Orders (Facilities for Enforcement) Act 1920, to be revoked or varied; and for purposes connected with the matters aforesaid.   [7 July 1958]

PART I

REGISTRATION, ENFORCEMENT AND VARIATION OF CERTAIN MAINTENANCE ORDERS

1. Application of Part I—(1) The provisions of this Part of this Act shall have effect for the purposes of enabling maintenance orders to which this Part of this Act applies to be registered—

(a) in the case of an order made by the High Court or a county court, in a magistrates' court; and

(b) in the case of an order made by a magistrates' court, in the High Court,

and, subject to those provisions, while so registered—

(i) to be enforced in like manner as an order made by the court of registration; and

(ii) in the case of an order registered in a magistrates' court, to be varied by a magistrates' court.

[(1A) In the following provisions of this Act 'maintenance order' means any order specified in Schedule 8 to the Administration of Justice Act 1970.]

Note. Sub-s (1A) inserted by Administration of Justice Act 1970, s 27(3), as from 2 August 1971. For Sch 8 of that Act, see p 2354.

(2) *This Part of this Act applies to maintenance orders made by the High Court, a county court or a magistrates' court, other than orders registered under Part II of the Maintenance Orders Act 1950.*

Note. For Maintenance Orders Act 1950, Part II, see pp 2147, et seq.

[(2) For the purposes of subsection (1) above, a maintenance order made by a court in Scotland or Northern Ireland and registered in England under Part II of the Maintenance Orders Act 1950 shall be deemed to have been made by the court in England in which it is so registered.

(2A) This Part of this Act applies—

(a) to maintenance orders made by the High Court or a county court or a magistrates' court, other than orders registered in Scotland or Northern Ireland under Part II of the Maintenance Orders Act 1950, and

(b) to maintenance orders made by a court in Scotland or Northern Ireland and registered in England under Part II of the Maintenance Orders Act 1950.]

Note. Sub-ss (2), (2A) in square brackets substituted for sub-s (2) in italics by Administration of Justice Act 1977, s 3, Sch 3, para 1, as from 1 January 1981.

(3) Without prejudice to the provisions of section twenty-one of this Act, in this Part of this Act, unless the context otherwise requires, the following expressions have the following meanings—

'High Court order', 'county court order' and 'magistrates' court order' mean an order made by the High Court, a county court or a magistrates' court, as the case may be;

'order' means a maintenance order to which this Part of this Act applies;

'original court' and 'court of registration', in relation to an order, mean the court by which the order was made or, as the case may be, the court in which the order is registered;

'registered' means registered in accordance with the provisions of this Part of this Act, and 'registration' shall be construed accordingly;

and for the purposes of this Part of this Act an order for the payment by the defendant of any costs incurred in proceedings relating to a maintenance order, being an order for the payment of costs made while the maintenance order is not registered, shall be deemed to form part of that maintenance order.

[(4) For the purposes of this section a maintenance order *within the meaning of Part I of the Maintenance Orders (Reciprocal Enforcement) Act 1972 which is registered in a magistrates' court under the said Part I* [which is registered in a magistrates' court under Part I of the Maintenance Orders (Reciprocal Enforcement) Act 1972 or Part I of the Civil Jurisdiction and Judgments Act 1982] [or Council Regulation (EC) No 44/2001 of 22nd December 2000 on jurisdiction and the recognition and enforcement of judgments in civil and commercial matters] shall be deemed to be a maintenance order made by that court.]

Note. Sub-s (4) added by Maintenance Orders (Reciprocal Enforcement) Act 1972, s 22(1), Schedule, as amended by Civil Jurisdiction and Judgments Act 1982, s 15(4), Sch 12, Part I, para 3, as from 1 January 1987. Words in square brackets inserted by the Civil Jurisdiction and Judgments Order 2001, SI 2001, No 3929, art 5, Sch 3, para 5, as from 1 March 2002.

2. Registration of orders—(1) A person entitled to receive payments under a High Court or county court order may apply for the registration of the order to the original court, and the court may, if it thinks fit, grant the application.

(2) Where an application for the registration of such an order is granted—

(a) no proceedings shall be begun, and no writ, warrant or other process shall be issued, for the enforcement of the order before the registration of the order or the expiration of the prescribed period from the grant of the application, whichever first occurs; and

(b) the original court shall, on being satisfied within the period aforesaid by the person who made the application that no such proceedings or process begun or issued before the grant of the application remain pending or in force, cause a certified copy of the order to be sent to *the clerk* [*justices' chief executive for*] of *the magistrates' court acting for the petty sessions area* [designated officer for the magistrates' court acting in the local justice area] in which the defendant appears to be;

but if at the expiration of the period aforesaid the original court has not been so satisfied, the grant of the application shall become void.

Note. In para (b) first words in square brackets substituted for words 'the clerk' by the Access to Justice Act 1999, s 90(1), Sch 13, paras 25, 26(1), (2), as from 1 April 2001 (SI 2001 No 916). Second words in square brackets substituted for words 'Justices' chief executive … sessions area' by the Courts Act 2003, s 109(1), Sch 8, para 98(1), (2), as from a day to be appointed.

(3) A person entitled to receive payments under a magistrates' court order who considers that the order could be more effectively enforced if it were registered may apply for the registration of the order to the original court, and the court *shall grant the application on being satisfied in the prescribed manner that, at the time when the application was made, an amount equal to not less, in the case of an order for weekly payments, than four or, in any other case, than two of the payments required by the order was due thereunder and unpaid* [may, if it thinks fit, grant the application].

[(3A) Without prejudice to subsection (3) of this section, where a magistrates' court order provides both for the payment of a lump sum and for the making of periodical payments, a person entitled to receive a lump sum under the order who considers that, so far as it relates to that sum, the order could be more effectively enforced if it were registered may apply to the original court for the registration of the order so far as it so relates, and the court may, if it thinks fit, grant the application.

(3B) Where an application under subsection (3A) of this section is granted in the case of a magistrates' court order, the provisions of this Part of this Act shall have effect in relation to that order as if so far as it relates to the payment of a lump sum it were a separate order.]

Note. Words in square brackets in sub-s (3) substituted for words in italics, and sub-ss (3A), (3B) inserted, by Civil Jurisdiction and Judgments Act 1982, s 37(1), Sch 11, Part I, para 2, as from 1 January 1987.

(4) Where an application for the registration of a magistrates' court order is granted—

(a) no proceedings for the enforcement of the order shall be begun before the registration takes place and no warrant or other process for the enforcement thereof shall be issued in consequence of any such proceedings begun before the grant of the application;

(b) *any warrant of commitment issued for the enforcement of the order shall cease to have effect when the person in possession of the warrant is informed of the grant of the application, unless the defendant has then already been detained in pursuance of the warrant;* and

(c) the original court shall, on being satisfied in the prescribed manner that no process for the enforcement of the order issued before the grant of the application remains in force, cause a certified copy of the order to be sent to the prescribed officer of the High Court.

Note. Para (b) repealed by the Access to Justice Act 1999, ss 97(1)(a), 106, Sch 15, Pt V, Table (8), as from 19 February 2001 (SI 2001 No 168). For transitional provisions relating to warrants issued before 8 January 2001 but not executed before 19 February 2001 see arts 2(a), (3) of SI 2001 No 168.

(5) The officer *or clerk of* [of, or *justices' chief executive for,*] [of, or for,] a court who receives a certified copy of an order sent to him under this section shall cause the order to be registered in that court.

Note. First words in square brackets substituted for words 'or clerk of' in italics by the Access to Justice Act 1999, s 90(1), Sch 13, paras 25, 26(1), (3), as from 1 April 2001 (SI 2001 No 916). Second words in square brackets substituted for words 'of, or justices' chief executive for,' in italics by the Courts Act 2003, s 109(1), Sch 8, para 98(1), (3), as from a day to be appointed,

(6) *Subsections (1) to (4) of section nineteen of the Maintenance Orders Act 1950 (which provide for the suspension, while a magistrates' court order is registered under Part II of that Act, of any provision of the order requiring payments to be made through a third party, for ordering payments under an order so registered in a magistrates' court to be paid through a collecting officer, and for authorising a person to make payments otherwise than in accordance with the requirements of that section until he has notice of those requirements) shall have effect for the purposes of this Part of this Act as if for any reference in that section to the said Part II and a maintenance order there were substituted a reference to this Part of this Act and a maintenance order to which this Part of this Act applies.*

[(*6*) Where a magistrates' court order is registered under this Part of this Act in the High Court, then—
  (a) if payments under the magistrates' court order are required to be made (otherwise than to *the clerk of a magistrates' court* [*a justices' chief executive*] [the designated officer for a magistrates' court]) by any method of payment falling within section 59(6) of the Magistrates' Courts Act 1980 (standing order, etc), any order requiring payment by that method shall continue to have effect after registration;
  (b) any order by virtue of which sums payable under the magistrates' court order are required to be paid to *the clerk of a magistrates' court* [*a justices' chief executive*] [the designated officer for a magistrates' court] (whether or not by any method of payment falling within section 59(6) of that Act) on behalf of the person entitled thereto shall cease to have effect.
(6ZA) Where a High Court or county court order is registered under this Part of this Act in a magistrates' court, then—
  (a) if a means of payment order (within the meaning of section 1(7) of the Maintenance Enforcement Act 1991) has effect in relation to the order in question, it shall continue to have effect after registration; and
  (b) in any other case, the magistrates' court shall order that all payments to be made under the order in question (including any arrears accrued before registration) shall be made to the *clerk of the court or the clerk of any other magistrates' court* [*a justices' chief executive*] [the designated officer for the court or for any other magistrates' court].
(6ZB) Any such order as to payment—
  (a) as is referred to in paragraph (a) of subsection (6) of this section may be revoked, suspended, revived or varied by an exercise of the powers conferred by section 4A of this Act; and
  (b) as is referred to in paragraph (a) or (b) of subsection (6ZA) of this section may be varied or revoked by an exercise of the powers conferred by section 3(2A) or (2B) or section 4(2A), (5A) or (5B) of this Act.
(6ZC) Where by virtue of the provisions of this section or any order under subsection (6ZA)(b) of this section payments under an order cease to be or become payable to *the clerk of a magistrates' court* [*a justices' chief executive*] [the designated officer for a magistrates' court], the person liable to make the payments shall, until he is given the prescribed notice to that effect, be deemed to comply with the order if he makes payments in accordance with the order and any order under subsection (6ZA)(b) of this section of which he has received such notice.]

Note. Sub-ss (6)–(6ZC) substituted for sub-s (6) in italics by Maintenance Enforcement Act 1991, s 10, Sch 1, para 7, as from 1 April 1992. In sub-ss (6), (6ZA), (6ZC) words 'a justices' chief executive' in square brackets in each place they occur substituted for words in italics by the Access to Justice Act 1999, s 90(1), Sch 13, paras 25, 26(1), (4)–(6), as from 1 April 2001 (SI 2001 No 916). In sub-ss (6), (6ZC) words 'the designated officer for a magistrates' court' in square brackets in each place they occur and in sub-s (6ZA) words 'the designated officer … magistrates' court' in square brackets substituted for words 'a justices' chief executive' by the Courts Act 2003, s 109(1), Sch 8, para 98(1), (4)–(6), as from a day to be appointed.

  [(6A) In this section—
  'High Court order' includes a maintenance order deemed to be made by the High Court by virtue of section 1(2) above, and 'magistrates' court order' includes a maintenance order deemed to be made by a magistrates' court by virtue of that subsection.]

Note. Sub-s (6A) inserted by Administration of Justice Act 1977, s 3, Sch 3, para 2, as from 1 January 1981.

  (7) In this section 'certified copy' in relation to an order of a court means a copy certified by the proper officer of the court to be a true copy of the order or of the official record thereof.

Note. For modifications of this section (except sub-s (6A)) for the purposes of an application under Civil Jurisdiction and Judgments Act 1982, s 36(1) for the registration of a maintenance order in Northern Ireland, see s 36(3) of the 1982 Act (p 2902), as from 1 January 1987.

[2A. Interest on sums recoverable under certain orders registered in the High Court—(1) Where, in connection with an application under section 2(3) of this Act for the registration of a magistrates' court order, the applicant shows in accordance with rules of court—

(a) that the order, though deemed for the purposes of section 1 of this Act to have been made by a magistrates' court in England, was in fact made in another part of the United Kingdom or in a country or territory outside the United Kingdom; and

(b) that, as regards any sum for whose payment the order provides, interest on that sum at a particular rate is, by the law of that part or of that country or territory, recoverable under the order from a particular date or time,

then, if the original court grants the application and causes a certified copy of the order to be sent to the prescribed officer of the High Court under section 2(4)(c) of this Act, it shall also cause to be sent to him a certificate in the prescribed form showing, as regards that sum, the rate of interest so recoverable and the date or time from which it is so recoverable.

(2) The officer of the court who receives a certificate sent to him under the preceding subsection shall cause the certificate to be registered in that court together with the order to which it relates.

(3) Where an order is registered together with a certificate under this section, then, subject to any provision made under the next following subsection, sums payable under the order shall carry interest at the rate specified in the certificate from the date or time so specified.

(4) Provision may be made by rules of court as to the manner in which and the periods by reference to which any interest payable by virtue of subsection (3) is to be calculated and paid, including provision for such interest to cease to accrue as from a prescribed date.

(5) Except as provided by this section sums payable under registered orders shall not carry interest.]

Note. This section inserted by Civil Jurisdiction and Judgments Act 1982, s 37(1), Sch 11, Part II, para 6(1), (2), as from 1 January 1987.

For modifications of s 2A for the purposes of an application under s 36(1) of the Act of 1982 for the registration of a maintenance order in Northern Ireland, see ibid, s 36(3) (p 2840), as from 1 January 1987.

3. Enforcement of registered orders—(1) Subject to the provisions of [section 2A of this Act and] this section, a registered order shall be enforceable in all respects as if it had been made by the court of registration and as if that court had jurisdiction to make it; and proceedings for or with respect to the enforcement of a registered order may be taken accordingly.

Note. Words in square brackets inserted by Civil Jurisdiction and Judgments Act 1982, s 37(1), Sch 11, Part II, para 6(3), as from 1 January 1987.

(2) Subject to the provisions of the next following subsection, an order registered in a magistrates' court shall be enforceable as if it were an affiliation order; and the provisions of any enactment with respect to the enforcement of affiliation orders (including enactments relating to the accrual of arrears and the remission of sums due) shall apply accordingly.

In this subsection 'enactment' includes any order, rule or regulation made in pursuance of any Act.

[(2) *Subject to the provisions of the next following subsection* [Subject to the provisions of subsections (2A) to (3) of this section], an order registered in magistrates' court shall be enforceable as a magistrates' court maintenance order within the meaning of section 150(1) of the Magistrates' Courts Act 1980.]

[(2A) Where an order registered in a magistrates' court is an order other than one deemed to be made by the High Court by virtue of section 1(2) of this Act, section 76 of the Magistrates' Courts Act 1980 (enforcement of sums adjudged to be paid) shall have effect as if for subsections (4) to (6) there were substituted the following subsections—

'(4) Where proceedings are brought for the enforcement of a magistrates' court maintenance order under this section, the court may vary the order by exercising one of its powers under paragraphs (a) to (d) of section 59(3) above.

(5) In deciding which of the powers under paragraphs (a) to (d) of section 59(3) above it is to exercise, the court shall have regard to any representations made by the debtor and the creditor (which expressions have the same meaning as they have in section 59 above).

(6) Subsection (4) of section 59 above shall apply for the purposes of subsection (4) above as it applies for the purposes of that section.'

(2B) Where an order registered in a magistrates' court is an order deemed to be made by the High Court by virtue of section 1(2) of this Act, sections 76 and 93 of the Magistrates' Courts Act 1980 (enforcement of sums adjudged to be paid and complaint for arrears) shall have effect subject to the modifications specified in subsections (2ZA) and (2ZB) of section 18 of the Maintenance Orders Act 1950 (enforcement of registered orders).]

Note. Sub-s (2) in square brackets substituted for sub-s (2) in italics by Family Law Reform Act 1987, s 33(1), Sch 2, para 18, as from 1 April 1989.

Words in square brackets in sub-s (2) substituted for words in italics and sub-ss (2A), (2B) inserted by Maintenance Enforcement Act 1991, s 10, Sch 1, para 8, as from 1 April 1992.

(3) Where an order remains or becomes registered after the discharge of the order, no proceedings shall be taken by virtue of that registration except in respect of arrears which were due under that order at the time of the discharge and have not been remitted.

[(3A) Any person under an obligation to make payments under an order registered in a magistrates' court shall give notice of any change of address to the *clerk of [justices' chief executive for]* [designated officer for] the court; and any person who without reasonable excuse fails to give such a notice shall be liable on summary conviction to a fine not exceeding level 2 on the standard scale (*as defined in section 75 of the Criminal Justice Act 1982*).]

Note. Sub-s (3A) inserted by Matrimonial and Family Proceedings Act 1984, s 46(1), Sch 1, para 4, as from 12 October 1984. Words in italics repealed by Statute Law (Repeals) Act 1993, s 1(1), Sch 1, Part XIV, as from 5 November 1993. For Criminal Justice Act 1982, s 75, see p 2931.

Words 'justices' chief executive for' in square brackets substituted for words in italics by the Access to Justice Act 1999, s 90(1), Sch 13, paras 25, 27, as from 1 April 2001 (SI 2001 No 916). Words 'designated officer for' in square brackets substituted for words 'justices' chief executive for' by the Courts Act 2003, s 109(1), Sch 8, para 99, as from a day to be appointed.

(4) Except as provided by this section, no proceedings shall be taken for or with respect to the enforcement of a registered order.

4. Variation of orders registered in magistrates' courts—(1) The provisions of this section shall have effect with respect to the variation of orders registered in magistrates' courts, and references in this section to registered orders shall be construed accordingly.

(2) Subject to the following provisions of this section—

(a) the court of registration may exercise the same jurisdiction to vary any rate of payments specified by a registered order (other than jurisdiction in a case where a party to the order is not present in England when the application for variation is made) as is exercisable, apart from this subsection, by the original court; and

(b) a rate of payments specified by a registered order shall not be varied except by the court of registration or any other magistrates' court to which the jurisdiction conferred by the foregoing paragraph is extended by rules of court.

[(2A) The power of a magistrates' court to vary a registered order under subsection (2) of this section shall include power, if the court is satisfied that payment has not been made in accordance with the order, to vary the order by exercising one of its powers under paragraphs (a) to (d) of section 59(3) of the Magistrates' Courts Act 1980.

(2B) Subsection (4) of section 59 of that Act shall apply for the purposes of subsection (2A) of this section as it applies for the purposes of that section.

(2C) In deciding which of the powers under paragraphs (a) to (d) of section 59(3) of that Act it is to exercise, the court shall have regard to any representations made by the debtor and the creditor (which expressions have the same meaning as they have in section 59 of that Act).]

Note. Sub-ss (2A)–(2C) inserted by Maintenance Enforcement Act 1991, s 10, Sch 1, para 9(1), as from 1 April 1992.

(3) A rate of payments specified by a registered order shall not be varied by virtue of the last foregoing subsection so as to exceed whichever of the following rates is the greater, that is to say—
   (a)   the rate of payments specified by the order as made or last varied by the original court; or
   (b)   in the case of payments for the maintenance of a person as a party to a marriage (including a marriage which has been dissolved or annulled) [seven pounds ten shillings] a week and, in the case of payments for the maintenance of a child or children in [fifty] shillings a week in respect of each child

[*the rate of payments specified by the order as made or last varied by the original court*].

Note. Words in square brackets at the end of sub-s (3) substituted for words 'whichever of the following rates' to 'in respect of each child' by Maintenance Orders Act 1968, s 1, Schedule. Words 'seven pounds ten shillings' and 'fifty' substituted for words 'five pounds' and 'thirty shillings' by Matrimonial Proceedings (Magistrates' Courts) Act 1960, s 15(b). Whole subsection repealed by Administration of Justice Act 1970, s 54, Sch 11, as from 1 September 1970; see also ibid, s 48(2) (p 2352).

(4) If it appears to the court to which an application is made by virtue of subsection (2) of this section for the variation of a rate of payments specified by a registered order *that, by reason of the limitations imposed on the court's jurisdiction by the last foregoing subsection or for any other reason, it is* [that it is for any reason] appropriate to remit the application to the original court, the first-mentioned court shall so remit the application and the original court shall thereupon deal with the application as if the order were not registered.

Note. Words in square brackets substituted for words in italics by Administration of Justice Act 1970, s 48(3), as from 1 September 1970.

(5) Nothing in subsection (2) of this section shall affect the jurisdiction of the original court to vary a rate of payments specified by a registered order if an application for the variation of that rate is made to that court—
   (a)   in proceedings for a variation of provisions of the order which do not specify a rate of payments; or
   (b)   at a time when a party to the order is not present in England.

[(5A) Subject to the following provisions of this section, subsections (4) to (11) of section 60 of the Magistrates' Courts Act 1980 (power of clerk and court to vary maintenance orders) shall apply in relation to a registered order (other than one deemed to be made by the High Court by virtue of section 1(2) of this Act) as they apply in relation to a maintenance order made by a magistrates' court (disregarding section 23(2) of the Domestic Proceedings and Magistrates' Courts Act 1978 and section 15(2) of the Children Act 1989) but

(a) as if in subsection (8) after the words 'the court which may' there were inserted 'subject to subsection (10) below'; and

(b) as if for subsections (9) and (10) there were substituted the following subsections—

'(9) Subsection (4) of section 59 above shall apply for the purposes of subsection (8) above as it applies for the purposes of that section.

(10) In deciding which of the powers under paragraphs (a) to (d) of section 59(3) above it is to exercise, the court shall have regard to any representations made by the debtor and the creditor.'

(5B) Subject to the following provisions of this section, subsections (4) to (11) of section 60 of the Magistrates' Courts Act 1980 (power of clerk and court to vary maintenance orders) shall apply in relation to a registered order deemed to be made by the High Court by virtue of section 1(2) of this Act as they apply in relation to a maintenance order made by a magistrates' court (disregarding section 23(2) of the Domestic Proceedings and Magistrates' Courts Act 1978 and section 15(2) of the Children Act 1989) but—

(a) as if in subsection (4) for paragraph (b) there were substituted—

'(b) payments under the order are required to be made to *the clerk of the court, or to the clerk of any other magistrates' court* [*a justices' chief executive*] [the designated officer for the court or for any other magistrates' court], by any method of payment falling within section 59(6) above (standing order, etc)';

and as if after the words 'the court' there were inserted 'which made the order';

(b) as if in subsection (5) for the words 'to the clerk' [*justices' chief executive for the court*] [designated officer for the court'] there were substituted 'in accordance with paragraph (a) of subsection (9) below';

(c) as if in subsection (7), paragraph (c) and the word 'and' immediately preceding it were omitted;

(d) as if in subsection (8) for the words 'paragraphs (a) to (d) of section 59(3) above' there were substituted 'subsection (9) below';

(e) as if for subsections (9) and (10) there were substituted the following subsections—

'(9) The powers of the court are—

(a) the power to order that payments under the order be made directly to *the clerk of the court, or to the clerk of any other magistrates' court* [*a justices' chief executive*] [the designated officer for the court or for any other magistrates' court];

(b) the power to order that payments under the order be made to *the clerk of the court, or to the clerk of any other magistrates' court* [*a justices' chief executive*] [the designated officer for the court or for any other magistrates' court], by such method of payment falling within section 59(6) above (standing order, etc) as may be specified;

(c) the power to make an attachment of earnings order under the Attachment of Earnings Act 1971 to secure payments under the order.

(10) In deciding which of the powers under subsection (9) above it is to exercise, the court shall have regard to any representations made by the debtor.]

(10A) Subsection (4) of section 59 above (power of court to require debtor to open account) shall apply for the purposes of subsection (9) above as it applies for the purposes of that section but as if for paragraph (a) there were substituted—

'(a) the court proposes to exercise its power under paragraph (b) of section 60(9) below'.]

Note. Sub-ss (5A), (5B) inserted by Maintenance Enforcement Act 1991, s 10, Sch 1, para 9(2), as from 1 April 1992. In sub-s (5B) words 'a justices' chief executive' in square brackets in each place they occur and words 'a justices' chief executive for the court' in square brackets substituted for words in italics by the Access to Justice Act 1999, s 90(1), Sch 13, paras 25, 28(1)–(4), as from 1 April 2001 (SI 2001 No 916). Words 'the designated ... court' in square brackets in each place they occur and 'designated officer for the court' in square brackets substituted for words 'a justices' chief executive' and 'justices' chief executive for the court' by the Courts Act 2003, s 109(1), Sch 8, para 100(a)–(c), as from a day to be appointed. In sub-s (5B)(a) words 'and as if ... the order' in italics repealed by the Access to Justice Act 1999, s 106, Sch 15, Pt V, Table (7), as from 1 April 2001 (SI 2001 No 916).

(6) No application for any variation of a registered order shall be made to any court while proceedings for any variation of the order are pending in any other court.

[(6A) [Except as provided by subsection (5B) of this section] No application for any variation in respect of a registered order shall be made to any court in respect of an order made by the Court of Session or the High Court in Northern Ireland and registered in that court in accordance with the provisions of this Part of this Act by virtue of section 1(2) above.]

Note. Sub-s (6A) inserted by Administration of Justice Act 1977, s 3, Sch 3, para 3, as from 1 January 1981. Words in square brackets inserted by Maintenance Enforcement Act 1991, s 10, Sch 1, para 9(3), as from 1 April 1992.

[(6B) No application for any variation of a registered order shall be made to any court in respect of an order for periodical or other payments made under Part III of the Matrimonial and Family Proceedings Act 1984.]

Note. Sub-s (6B) inserted by Matrimonial and Family Proceedings Act 1984, s 46(1), Sch 1, para 5, as from 16 September 1985.

(7) Where a magistrates' court, in exercise of the jurisdiction conferred by subsection (2) of this section, varies or refuses to vary a registered order, an appeal from the variation or refusal shall lie to the High Court: *and so much of subsection (1) of section sixty-three of the Supreme Court of Judicature (Consolidation) Act 1925, as requires an appeal from any court to the High Court to be heard and determined by a divisional court shall not apply to appeals under this subsection.*

Note. Words in italics repealed by Administration of Justice Act 1977, s 32, Sch 5, Part IV, as from 1 January 1981. Supreme Court of Judicature (Consolidation) Act 1925, s 63 replaced by Supreme Court Act 1981, s 66 (p 2852).

[4A. Variation etc of orders registered in the High Court—(1) The provisions of this section shall have effect with respect to orders registered in the High Court other than maintenance orders deemed to be made by a magistrates' court by virtue of section 1(4) of this Act, and the reference in subsection (2) of this section to a registered order shall be construed accordingly.

(2) The High Court may exercise the same powers in relation to a registered order as are exercisable by the High Court under section 1 of the Maintenance Enforcement Act 1991 in relation to a qualifying periodical maintenance order (within the meaning of that section) which has been made by the High Court, including the power under subsection (7) of that section to revoke, suspend, revive or vary—

(a) any such order as is referred to in paragraph (a) of section 2(6) of this Act which continues to have effect by virtue of that paragraph; and

(b) any means of payment order (within the meaning of section 1(7) of that Act of 1991) made by virtue of the provisions of this section.]

Note. This section inserted by Maintenance Enforcement Act 1991, s 10, Sch 1, para 10, as from 1 April 1992.

5. Cancellation of registration—(1) If a person entitled to receive payments under a registered order desires the registration to be cancelled, he may give notice under this section.

(2) Where the original court varies or discharges an order registered in a magistrates' court, the original court may, if it thinks fit, give notice under this section.

Note. See Note to sub-s (4A).

(3) Where *a magistrates' court* [the original court] discharges an order registered in the High Court and it appears to *the magistrates' court* [the original court], whether by reason of the remission of arrears by that court or otherwise, that no arrears under the order remain to be recovered, *the magistrates' court* [the original court] shall give notice under this section.

Note. Words in square brackets substituted for words in italics by Administration of Justice Act 1977, s 3, Sch 3, para 4, as from 1 January 1981. See Note to sub-s (4A).

(4) Notice under this section shall be given to the court of registration; and where such notice is given—

    (a) no proceedings for the enforcement of the registered order shall be begun before the cancellation of the registration and no writ, warrant or other process for the enforcement thereof shall be issued in consequence of any such proceedings begun before the giving of the notice;

    (b) *where the order is registered in a magistrates' court, any warrant of commitment issued for the enforcement of the order shall cease to have effect when the person in possession of the warrant is informed of the giving of the notice, unless the defendant has then already been detained in pursuance of the warrant;* and

    (c) the court of registration shall cancel the registration on being satisfied in the prescribed manner—

        (i) that no process for the enforcement of the registered order issued before the giving of the notice remains in force; and

        (ii) in the case of an order registered in a magistrates' court, that no proceedings for the variation of the order are pending in a magistrates' court.

Note. See Note to sub-s (4A). Para (b) repealed by the Access to Justice Act 1999, ss 97(1)(b), 106, Sch 15, Pt V, Table (8), as from 19 February 2001 (SI 2001 No 168). For transitional provisions relating to warrants issued before 8 January 2001 but not executed before 19 February 2001 see arts 2(a), 3 of SI 2001 No 168.

[(4A) For the purposes of a notice under subsection (2) or (3) above—

'court of registration' includes any court in which an order is registered under Part II of the Maintenance Orders Act 1950, and

'registration' includes registration under that Act.]

Note. Sub-s (4A) inserted by Administration of Justice Act 1977, s 3, Sch 3, para 4, as from 1 January 1981.

For modifications of sub-ss (2), (3), (4), (4A) for the purposes of an application under Civil Jurisdiction and Judgments Act 1982, s 36(1), for the registration of a maintenance order in Northern Ireland, see s 36(3) of the Act of 1982 (p 2902), as from 1 January 1987.

(5) *On the cancellation of the registration of a High Court or county court order, any order made in relation thereto under subsection (2) of section nineteen of the Maintenance Orders Act 1950, as applied by subsection (6) of section two of this Act, shall cease to have effect, but until the defendant receives the prescribed notice of the cancellation he shall be deemed to comply with the High Court or county court order if he makes payments in accordance with any order under the said subsection (2) as so applied which was in force immediately before the cancellation and of which he has notice.*

[(5) On the cancellation of the registration of a High Court or county court order—

    (a) any order which requires payments under the order in question to be made (otherwise than to *the clerk of a magistrates' court* [*a justices' chief executive*] [the designated officer for a magistrates' court]) by any method of payment falling within section 59(6) of the Magistrates' Courts Act 1980 or section 1(5) of the Maintenance Enforcement Act 1991 (standing order, etc) shall continue to have effect; and

    (b) any order made under section 2(6ZA)(b) of this Act or by virtue of the powers conferred by section 3(2A) or (2B) or section 4(2A), (5A) or (5B) of this Act and which requires payments under the order in question to be made to *the clerk of a magistrates' court* [*a justices' chief executive*] [the designated officer for a magistrates' court] (whether or not by any method of payment falling within section 59(6) of the Magistrates' Courts Act 1980) shall cease to have effect;

but, in a case falling within paragraph (b) of this subsection, until the defendant receives the prescribed notice of the cancellation he shall be deemed to comply with the High Court or county court order if he makes payment in accordance with any such order as is referred to in paragraph (b) of this subsection which was in force immediately before the cancellation and of which he has notice.

Note. Words 'a justices' chief executive' in square brackets in both places they occur substituted for words in italics by the Access to Justice Act 1999, s 90(1), Sch 13, paras 25, 29(1), (2), as from 1 April 2001 (SI 2001 No 916). Words 'the designated officer for a magistrates' court' in square brackets in both places they occur substituted for words 'a justices' chief executive' by the Courts Act 2003, s 109(1), Sch 8, para 10(1), (2), as from a day to be appointed.

(6) On the cancellation of the registration of a magistrates' court order—

(a) any order which requires payments under the magistrates' court order to be made by any method of payment falling within section 59(6) of the Magistrates' Courts Act 1980 or section 1(5) of the Maintenance Enforcement Act 1991 (standing order, etc) shall continue to have effect; and

(b) in any other case, payments shall become payable to the *clerk of* [*justices' chief executive*] [designated officer for] the original court;

but, in a case falling within paragraph (b) of this subsection, until the defendant receives the prescribed notice of the cancellation he shall be deemed to comply with the magistrates' court order if he makes payments in accordance with any order which was in force immediately before the cancellation and of which he has notice.

Note. In para (b) words 'justices' chief executive' in square brackets substituted for words in italics by the Access to Justice Act 1999, s 90(1), Sch 13, paras 25, 29(1), (3), as from 1 April 2001 (SI 2001 No 916). Words 'designated officer for' in square brackets substituted for words 'justices' chief executive' by the Courts Act 2003, s 109(1), Sch 8, para 101(1), (3), as from a day to be appointed.

(7) In subsections (5) and (6) of this section 'High Court order' and 'magistrates' court order' shall be construed in accordance with section 2(6A) of this Act.]

Note. Sub-ss (5)–(7) substituted for sub-s (5) in italics by Maintenance Enforcement Act 1991, s 10, Sch 1, para 11, as from 1 April 1992.

*   *   *   *   *

PART III

*   *   *   *   *

Note. This Part applied with modifications by Criminal Justice Act 1967, ss 46(2), 79(7), Sch 1.

17. Prohibition of committal more than once in respect of same arrears. Where a defendant has been imprisoned or otherwise detained under an order or warrant of commitment issued in respect of his failure to pay a sum due under a maintenance order, then, notwithstanding anything in this Act, no such order or warrant (other than a warrant of which the issue has been postponed under paragraph (ii) of subsection (5) of the next following section) shall thereafter be issued in respect of that sum or any part thereof.

18. Powers of magistrates to review committals, etc—(1) Where, for the purpose of enforcing a maintenance order, a magistrates' court has exercised its power under *subsection (2) of section sixty-five of the Magistrates' Courts Act 1952* [subsection (2) of section 77 of the Magistrates' Courts Act 1980], or this section to postpone the issue of a warrant of commitment and under the terms of the postponement the warrant falls to be issued, then—

(a) the warrant shall not be issued except in pursuance of subsection (2) or paragraph (a) of subsection (3) of this section; and

(b) the *clerk of [justices' chief executive for]* [designated officer for] the court shall give notice to the defendant stating that if the defendant considers there are grounds for not issuing the warrant he may make an application to the court in the prescribed manner requesting that the warrant shall not be issued and stating those grounds.

Note. Reference to Magistrates' Courts Act 1980 substituted for reference to Act of 1952 by Magistrates' Courts Act 1980, s 154, Sch 7, para 23. In para (b) words 'justices' chief executive for' in square brackets substituted for words in italics by the Access to Justice Act 1999, s 90(1), Sch 13, paras 25, 30, as from 1 April 2001 (SI 2001 No 916). Words 'designated officer for' in square brackets substituted for words 'justices' chief executive for' by the Courts Act 2003, s 109(1), Sch 8, para 102(1), (2), as from a day to be appointed.

(2) If no such application is received by the *clerk of [justices' chief executive for]* [designated officer for] the court within the prescribed period, any justice of the peace *acting for the same petty sessions area* [acting in the same local justice area] as the court may issue the warrant of commitment at any time after the expiration of that period; and if such an application is so received any such justice may, after considering the statements contained in the application—

(a) if he is of opinion that the application should be further considered, refer it to the court:

(b) if he is not of that opinion, issue the warrant forthwith;

and when an application is referred to the court under this subsection, the *clerk of [justices' chief executive for]* [designated officer for] the court shall give to the defendant and the person in whose favour the maintenance order in question was made notice of the time and place appointed for the consideration of the application by the court.

Note. Words 'justices' chief executive for' in square brackets in both places they occur substituted for words in italics by the Access to Justice Act 1999, s 90(1), Sch 13, paras 25, 30, as from 1 April 2001 (SI 2001 No 916). Words 'designated officer for' in square brackets in both places they occur substituted for words 'justices' chief executive for' by the Courts Act 2003, s 109(1), Sch 8, para 102(1), (2), as from a day to be appointed. Words 'acting in the same local justice area' in square brackets substituted for words in italics by the Courts Act 2003, s 109(1), Sch 8, para 102(1), (3), as from a day to be appointed.

(3) On considering an application referred to it under the last foregoing subsection the court shall, unless in pursuance of subsection (6) of this section it remits the whole of the sum in respect of which the warrant could otherwise be issued, either—

(a) issue the warrant; or

(b) further postpone the issue thereof until such time and on such conditions, if any, as the court thinks just; or

(c) if in consequence of any change in the circumstances of the defendant the court considers it appropriate so to do, order that the warrant shall not be issued in any event.

(4) A defendant who is for the time being imprisoned or otherwise detained under a warrant of commitment issued by a magistrates' court for the purpose of enforcing a maintenance order, and who is not detained otherwise than for the enforcement of such an order, may make an application to the court in the prescribed manner requesting that the warrant shall be cancelled and stating the grounds of the application; and thereupon any justice of the peace *acting for the same petty sessions area* [acting in the same local justice area] as the court may, after considering the statements contained in the application—

(a) if he is of opinion that the application should be further considered, refer it to the court;

(b) if he is not of that opinion, refuse the application;

and when an application is referred to the court under this subsection, the *clerk of* [*justices' chief executive for*] [designated officer for] the court shall give to the person in charge of the prison or other place in which the defendant is detained and the person in whose favour the maintenance order in question was made notice of the time and place appointed for the consideration of the application by the court.

Note. Words 'acting in the same local justice area' in square brackets substituted for words in italics by the Courts Act 2003, s 109(1), Sch 8, para 102(1), (3), as from a day to be appointed. Words 'justices' chief executive for' in square brackets substituted for words in italics by the Access to Justice Act 1999, s 90(1), Sch 13, paras 25, 30 as from 1 April 2001 (SI 2001 No 916). Words 'designated officer for, in square brackets substituted for words 'justices' chief executive for' by the Courts Act 2003, s 109(1), Sch 8, para 102(1), (2), as from a day to be appointed.

(5) On considering an application referred to it under the last foregoing subsection, the court shall, unless in pursuance of the next following subsection it remits the whole of the sum in respect of which the warrant was issued or such part thereof as remains to be paid, either—

(a) refuse the application; or

(b) if the court is satisfied that the defendant is unable to pay, or to make any payment or further payment towards, the sum aforesaid and if it is of opinion that in all the circumstances of the case the defendant ought not to continue to be detained under the warrant, order that the warrant shall cease to have effect when the person in charge of the prison or other place aforesaid is informed of the making of the order:

and where the court makes an order under paragraph (b) of this subsection, it may if it thinks fit also—

(i) fix a term of imprisonment in respect of the sum aforesaid or such part thereof as remains to be paid, being a term not exceeding so much of the term of the previous warrant as, after taking into account any reduction thereof by virtue of the next following subsection, remained to be served at the date of the order; and

(ii) postpone the issue of a warrant for the commitment of the defendant for that term until such time and on such conditions, if any, as the court thinks just.

(6) On considering an application under this section in respect of a warrant or a postponed warrant, the court may, if the maintenance order in question is an affiliation order or an order enforceable as an affiliation order, remit the whole or any part of the sum due under the order; and where the court remits the sum or part of the sum in respect of which the warrant was issued or the postponed warrant could have been issued, *section sixty-seven of the Magistrates' Courts Act 1952* [section 79 of the Magistrates' Courts Act 1980] (which provides that on payment of the sum for which imprisonment has been ordered by a magistrates' court the order shall cease to have effect and that on payment of part of that sum the period of detention shall be reduced proportionately) shall apply as if payment of that sum or part had been made as therein mentioned.

Note. Reference to Magistrates' Courts Act 1980 substituted for reference to Act of 1952 by Magistrates' Courts Act 1980, s 154, Sch 7, para 23.

(7) Where notice of the time and place appointed for the consideration of an application is required by this section to be given to the defendant or the person in whose favour the maintenance order in question was made and the defendant or, as the case may be, that person does not appear at that time and place, the court may proceed with the consideration of the application in his absence.

(8) A notice required by this section to be given by the *clerk of* [*justices' chief executive for*] [designated officer for] a magistrates' court to any person shall be deemed to be given to that person if it is sent by registered post addressed to

him at his last known address, notwithstanding that the notice is returned as undelivered or is for any other reason not received by that person.

Note. Words 'justices' chief executive for' in square brackets substituted for words in italics by the Access to Justice Act 1999, s 90(1), Sch 13, paras 25, 30, as from 1 April 2001 (SI 2001 No 916). Words 'designated officer for' in square brackets substituted for words 'justices' chief executive for' by the Courts Act 2003, s 109(1), Sch 8, para 102(1), (2), as from a day to be appointed.

19. Revocation and variation of Orders in Council under 10 & 11 Geo 5 c 55, s 12. *Her Majesty may by Order in Council revoke or vary any Order in Council made under section twelve of the Maintenance Orders (Facilities for Enforcement) Act 1920 (which provides for the extension of that Act by Order in Council to certain overseas territories), and an Order under this section may contain such incidental, consequential and transitional provisions as Her Majesty considers expedient for the purposes of that Act.*

Note. This section repealed by Maintenance Orders (Reciprocal Enforcement) Act 1972, s 22(2)(c), as from a day to be appointed.

Supplemental

20*. Special provisions as to magistrates' courts—(1) Notwithstanding anything in this Act [*or Part II of the Administration of Justice Act 1970*], *the clerk of a magistrates' court* [a justices' chief executive] *who* [the designated officer for a magistrates' court who] is entitled to receive payments under a maintenance order for transmission to another person shall not—

(a) apply for the registration of the maintenance order under Part I of this Act or give notice in relation to the order in pursuance of subsection (1) of section five thereof; *or*

(b) *apply for an attachment of earnings order, or (except as required by subsection (5) of section nine of this Act) an order discharging or varying an attachment of earnings order, in respect of those payments,*

[(b) *apply for an attachment of earnings order to secure payments under the maintenance order or (except as required by section 9(5) of this Act) an order discharging or varying such an attachment of earnings order; or*

(c) *apply for a determination under section 22 of the Administration of Justice Act 1970,*]

unless he is requested in writing to do so by a person entitled to receive the payments through him; and where *the clerk is* [*a justices' chief executive is*] [the designated officer is] requested as aforesaid—

(i) he shall comply with the request unless it appears to him unreasonable in the circumstances to do so;

(ii) the person by whom the request was made shall have the same liabilities for all the costs properly incurred in or about any proceedings taken in pursuance of the request as if the proceedings had been taken by that person;

and for the purposes of paragraph (ii) of this subsection any application made by the clerk as required by the said subsection (5) shall be deemed to be made on the request of the person in whose favour the attachment of earnings order in question was made.

Note. Paras (b), (c) in square brackets substituted for para (b) in italics, and words in square brackets added by Administration of Justice Act 1970, s 27, Sch 7, para 6(a); words 'or Part II of the Administration of Justice Act 1970', word 'or' at the end of para (a), paras (b), (c) and words 'and for the purposes' onwards, repealed by Attachment of Earnings Act 1971, s 29, Sch 6. Words 'a justices' chief executive' in square brackets substituted in both places they occur substituted for words 'the clerk of a magistrates' court' and 'the clerk' respectively by the Access to Justice Act 1999, s 90(1), Sch 13, paras 25, 31(a), (b), as from 1 April 2001 (SI 2001 No 916). Words 'the

---

* In consequence of the repeals effected by Attachment of Earnings Act 1971, this section, except sub-s (6), has effect as set out in Sch 5 to the Act of 1971 (p 2417); see s 27(1) of the Act of 1971 (p 2411).

designated officer for a magistrates' court who' in square brackets substituted for words 'a justices' chief executive who' by the Courts Act 2003, s 109(1), Sch 8, para 103(a), as from a day to be appointed. Words 'the designated officer is' in square brackets substituted for words 'a justices' chief executive is' by the Courts Act 2003, s 109(1), Sch 8, para 103(b), as from a day to be appointed.

(2) [*Subject to rules of court made by virtue of section 18(3)(c) of the Administration of Justice Act 1970*] an application to a magistrates' court by virtue of subsection (2) of section four of this Act for the variation of a maintenance order *and an application to a magistrates' court for an attachment of earnings order, or an order discharging or varying an attachment of earnings order,* shall be made by complaint.

Note. Words in square brackets added by Administration of Justice Act 1970, s 27, Sch 7, para 6(b); words in italics repealed by Attachment of Earnings Act 1971, s 29, Sch 6.

(*3*) *It is hereby declared that a magistrates' court has jurisdiction to hear a complaint by or against a person residing outside England for the discharge or variation of an attachment of earnings order made by a magistrates' court [to secure maintenance payments]; and where such a complaint is made against a person residing outside England, then—*

(a) *if he resides in Scotland or Northern Ireland, section fifteen of the Maintenance Orders Act 1950 (which relates to the service of process on persons residing in those countries) shall have effect in relation to the complaint as it had effect in relation to the proceedings therein mentioned; and*

(b) *if the said person resides outside the United Kingdom and does not appear at the time and place appointed for the hearing of the complaint but it is proved to the satisfaction of the court, on oath or in such other manner as may be prescribed, that the complainant has taken such steps as may be prescribed to give to the said person notice of the complaint and of the time and place aforesaid, the court may, if it thinks it reasonable in all the circumstances to do so, proceed to hear and determine the complaint at the time and place appointed for the hearing or for any adjourned hearing in like manner as if the said person had then appeared.*

Note. Sub-s (3) repealed by Attachment of Earnings Act 1971, s 29, Sch 6. Words in square brackets added by Administration of Justice Act 1970, s 27, Sch 7, para 6(c). For Maintenance Orders Act 1950, s 15, see p 2146.

(*4*) *For the purposes of section forty-three of the Magistrates' Courts Act 1952 (which provides for the issue of a summons directed to the person against whom an order may be made in pursuance of a complaint)—*

(a) *the power to make an order in pursuance of a complaint by the defendant for the discharge or variation of an attachment of earnings order shall be deemed to be a power to make an order against the person in whose favour the attachment of earnings order was made; and*

[(a) *the power to make an order in pursuance of a complaint by the debtor for an attachment of earnings order, or the discharge or variation of such an order, shall be deemed to be a power to make an order against the person to whom payment under the relevant adjudication is required to be made (whether directly or through an officer of the court)]; and*

(b) *the power to make an attachment of earnings order, or an order discharging or varying an attachment of earnings order, in pursuance of a complaint by any other person (including a complaint in proceedings to which paragraph (b) of section seven of this Act [section 14(4)(b) of the Administration of Justice Act 1970] applies) shall be deemed to be a power to make an order against the defendant [debtor].*

Note. Original para (a), words 'paragraph (b) of section seven of the Act' and 'defendant' in para (b) repealed and words in square brackets added by Administration of Justice Act 1970, s 27, Sch 7, para 6(d), (e); the whole subsection as amended repealed by Attachment of Earnings Act 1971, s 29, Sch 6.

(*5*) *Where the court referred to in subsection (1) of section twelve of this Act is a magistrates' court—*

(*a*) the power conferred by subsection (2) of section one hundred and twenty-two of the Magistrates' Courts Act 1952, to provide by rules for jurisdiction expressly conferred on a magistrates' court to hear a complaint to be extended to any other magistrates' court shall be exercisable, and

(*b*) subsection (1) of section seventy-seven of that Act (which relates to the attendance of witnesses) shall apply,

as if subsection (1) of the said section twelve required an application thereunder to be made by complaint; and on making a determination under that subsection the court may in its discretion make such order as it thinks just and reasonable as to the payment by any of the persons mentioned in that subsection of the whole or any part of the costs of the determination, and costs ordered to be paid under this subsection shall—

(*i*) in the case of costs to be paid by the defendant to the person in whose favour the attachment of earnings order in question is made, be deemed to be a sum due under the related maintenance order; and

(*ii*) in any other case, be enforceable as a civil debt.

[(5) An application to a magistrates' court for a determination under section 22 of the Administration of Justice Act 1970 shall be made by complaint; and on making a determination under that section a magistrates' court may in its discretion make such order as it thinks just and reasonable for the payment by any of the persons mentioned in subsection (2) of that section of the whole or any part of the costs of the determination (but subject to subsection (1)(ii) of this section); and costs ordered to be paid under this subsection shall—

(*a*) in the case of costs to be paid by the debtor to the person in whose favour the attachment of earnings order in question was made, be deemed to be—

(*i*) if the attachment of earnings order was made to secure maintenance payments, a sum due under the related maintenance order, and

(*ii*) otherwise, a sum due to the clerk of the court; and

(*b*) in any other case, be enforceable as a civil debt.]

Note. A new sub-s (5), set out in square brackets above, substituted for original sub-s (5) by Administration of Justice Act 1970, s 27, Sch 7, para 6(f) and subsequently repealed by Attachment of Earnings Act 1971, s 29, Sch 6.

(6) In subsection (3) of section fifty-two of the Magistrates' Courts Act 1952 (which provides for the clerk through whom payments under a magistrates' court order are required to be made to proceed in his own name for the recovery of arrears under the order) for the words 'Where an order under subsection (1) of this section requires the payments to be made weekly' there shall be substituted the words 'Where periodical payments under an order of any court are required to be paid to or through the clerk of a magistrates' court'; and in subsection (4) of that section (which provides that nothing in that section shall affect any right of a person to proceed in his own name for the recovery of sums payable on his behalf under any order under subsection (1) of that section) for the words 'any order under subsection (1) of this section' there shall be substituted the words 'an order of any court.'

Note. Sub-s (6) repealed by Magistrates' Courts Act 1980, s 154, Sch 9, and replaced by s 59 thereof (p 2767).

(7) A complaint for an attachment of earnings order may be heard notwithstanding that the complaint was not made within the six months allowed by section one hundred and four of the Magistrates' Courts Act 1952.

Note. Sub-s (7) repealed by Attachment of Earnings Act 1971, s 29, Sch 6.

(8) For the avoidance of doubt it is hereby declared that a complaint may be made to enforce payment of a sum due and unpaid under a maintenance order notwithstanding that a previous complaint has been made in respect of that sum or a part thereof and whether or not an order was made in pursuance of the previous complaint.

21. Interpretation, etc—(1) In this Act, unless the context otherwise requires, the following expressions have the following meanings—

'*affiliation order*', '*magistrates' court*' *and* '*petty sessions area*' *have the meanings assigned to them by the Magistrates' Courts Act 1952 [the Magistrates' Courts Act 1980] and for the purpose of the definition of a magistrates' court* [has the meaning assigned to it by the Magistrates' Courts Act 1980 and] the reference to that Act in *subsection (2) of section one hundred and twenty-four thereof* [subsection (2) of section 148] thereof shall be construed as including a reference to this Act;

Note. First and third words in square brackets substituted for words 'the Magistrates' Courts Act 1952' and 'subsection (2) … thereof' by the Magistrates' Courts Act 1980, s 154, Sch 7, para 24, as from 6 July 1981, save as to words 'affiliation order' which are repealed by Family Law Reform Act 1987, s 33(4), Sch 4, as from 1 April 1989. Second words in square brackets substituted for words 'and 'petty sessions area' … magistrates' court' by the Access to Justice Act 1999, s 76(2), Sch 10, para 22, as from 27 September 1999.

'*attachment of earnings order*' *has the meaning assigned to it by subsection (1) of section six of this Act;*

Note. Above definition repealed by Administration of Justice Act 1970, s 54, Sch 11.

'defendant', in relation to a maintenance order or a related attachment of earnings order, means the person liable to make payments under the maintenance order;

'*earnings*', *in relation to a defendant, means any sums (other than excepted sums) payable to him—*

    (*a*) *by way of wages or salary (including any fees, bonus, commission, overtime pay or other emoluments payable in addition to wages or salary by the person paying the wages or salary or payable under a contract of service);*

    (*b*) *by way of pension (including an annuity in respect of past services, whether or not the services were rendered to the person paying the annuity, and including periodical payments by way of compensation for the loss, abolition or relinquishment, or any diminution in the emoluments, of any office or employment);*

Note. Above definition repealed by Administration of Justice Act 1970, s 54, Sch 11.

'*employer*' *means a person by whom, as a principal and not as servant or agent, earnings fall to be paid to a defendant, and reference to payment of earnings shall be construed accordingly;*

Note. Above definition repealed by Administration of Justice Act 1970, s 54, Sch 11.

'England' includes Wales;

'*excepted sums*' *means—*

    (*a*) *sums payable by any public department of the government of any territory outside the United Kingdom or of Northern Ireland;*

    (*b*) *pay or allowances payable to the defendant as a member of Her Majesty's Forces;*

    (*c*) *pension, allowances or benefit payable by [the Secretary of State], other than such part of any pension as is so payable to the defendant in respect of his service to Her Majesty's forces or in respect of any employment of his;*

    (*d*) *pension or allowances payable to the defendant in respect of his disablement or disability; and*

    (*e*) *wages payable to the defendant as a seaman or apprentice, other than wages payable to him as a seaman or apprentice of a fishing boat;*

and in paragraph (e) of this definition expressions used in the Merchant Shipping Act 1894, have the same meanings as in that Act;

Note. Above definition repealed by Administration of Justice Act 1970, s 54, Sch 11. Words in square brackets substituted for words 'the Minister of Pensions and National Insurance' by virtue of Ministry of Social Security Act 1966, s 2(3), and SI 1968 No 1699, art 5(4).

'*maintenance order*' *means—*

    (*a*) *an order for alimony, maintenance or other payments made or deemed to be made by a court in England under any of the following enactments, that is to say—*

        (i) *sections nineteen to twenty-seven of the Matrimonial Causes Act 1950;*

Note. For Matrimonial Causes Act 1950, ss 19–27, see pp 2138–2141. See now Matrimonial Causes Act 1973, ss 22–24, 27, 40, 42, 52(1) (pp 2510 et seq), replacing Matrimonial Proceedings and Property Act 1970, ss 1–4, 6, 18, 19, 26, 27(1) (pp 2365 et seq), replacing Matrimonial Causes Act 1965, ss 15, 16, 17, 19, 20, 21, 22, 30, 34, 46(2) (pp 2246 et seq).

> (*ii*) the Summary Jurisdiction (Separation and Maintenance) Acts 1895 to 1949;
>
> (*iii*) [section 9(2), 10(1), 11 or 12(2) of the Guardianship of Minors Act 1971];

Note. Words in square brackets substituted for references to Guardianship of Infants Act 1925, ss 3(2), 5(4), 6 by Guardianship of Minors Act 1971, s 18(1), Sch 1.

> (*iv*) section four of the Affiliation Proceedings Act 1957, section forty-four of the National Assistance Act 1948, or section twenty-six of the Children Act 1948;

Note. For Affiliation Proceedings Act 1957, s 4, see p 2177; for National Assistance Act 1948, s 44, see p 2099; Children Act 1948, s 26, replaced by Child Care Act 1980, s 50.

> (*v*) section eighty-seven of the Children and Young Persons Act 1933, or section forty-three of the National Assistance Act 1948; or

Note. Children and Young Persons Act 1933, s 87, replaced by Child Care Act 1980, s 47; for National Assistance Act 1948, s 43, see p 2105.

> (*b*) an order registered in a court in England under Part II of the Maintenance Orders Act 1950, or the Maintenance Orders (Facilities for Enforcement) Act 1920, or an order confirmed by such a court under the last-mentioned Act,

Note. For Maintenance Orders Act 1950, Part II, see p 2147; for Maintenance Orders (Facilities for Enforcement) Act 1920, see p 2036.

> and includes any such order which has been discharged if any arrears are recoverable thereunder;

Note. Definition 'maintenance order' repealed by Administration of Justice Act 1970, s 54, Sch 11. See now Sch 8 to that Act (p 2354).

'prescribed' means prescribed by rules of court;

'proper officer', in relation to a magistrates' court, means the clerk of the court;

Note. Above definition repealed by the Access to Justice Act 1999, s 106, Sch 15, Pt V, Table (7), as from 1 April 2001 (SI 2001 No 916).

'rules of court', in relation to a magistrates' court, means rules under section fifteen of the Justices of the Peace Act 1949.

Note. Justices of the Peace Act 1949, s 15 replaced by Magistrates' Courts Act 1980, s 144. Above definition repealed by the Courts Act 2003, s 109(1), (3), Sch 8, para 104, Sch 10, as from a date to be appointed.

(2) Any reference in this Act to a person entitled to receive payments under a maintenance order is a reference to a person entitled to receive such payments either directly or through another person or for transmission to another person.

(3) Any reference in this Act to proceedings relating to an order includes a reference to proceedings in which the order may be made.

(4) Any reference in this Act to costs incurred in proceedings relating to a maintenance order shall be construed, in the case of a maintenance order made by the High Court, as a reference to such costs as are included in an order for costs relating solely to that maintenance order.

(5) Any earnings which, in pursuance of a scheme under the Dock Workers (Regulation of Employment) Act 1946, fall to be paid to a defendant by a body responsible for the local administration of the scheme acting as agent for the defendant's employer or as delegate of the body responsible for the general administration of the scheme shall be treated for the purposes of this Act as falling to be paid to the defendant by the last-mentioned body acting as a principal.

Note. Sub-s (5) repealed by Administration of Justice Act 1970, s 54, Sch 11.

(6) Any reference in this Act to any enactment is a reference to that enactment as amended by or under any subsequent enactment.

22. Legislative powers of Parliament of Northern Ireland. *No limitation on the powers of the Parliament of Northern Ireland imposed by the Government of Ireland Act 1920 shall preclude that Parliament from making laws for purposes similar to the purposes of this Act.*

Note. Repealed by Northern Ireland Constitution Act 1973, s 41(1), Sch 6, Part I.

23. Short title, extent, commencement and repeals—(1) This Act may be cited as the Maintenance Orders Act 1958.

(*2*) *This Act, except paragraph (a) of subsection (3) of section twenty, shall not extend to Scotland or, except section nineteen, the said paragraph (a) and the last foregoing section, to Northern Ireland.*

Note. Words 'except paragraph (a) of subsection (3) of section 20' repealed by Attachment of Earnings Act 1971, s 29, Sch 6, and words 'section nineteen' repealed by Maintenance Orders (Reciprocal Enforcement) Act 1972, s 22(2)(c), as from a day to be appointed.

[(2) The following provisions of this Act, namely—
    section 2;
    [section 2A];
    section 5(2), (3), (4) and (4A);
extend to Scotland and Northern Ireland.

(2A) Section 20(3)(a) above extends to Northern Ireland.

(2B) Subject to subsections (2) and (2A) above, this Act extends only to England.]

Note. Sub-ss (2), (2A), (2B) substituted for sub-s (2) in italics by Administration of Justice Act 1977, s 3, Sch 3, para 5, as from 1 January 1981. Reference to s 2A inserted by Civil Jurisdiction and Judgments Act 1982, s 36(6), Sch 12, Part III, para 2, as from 1 January 1987.

(3) This Act shall come into operation on such date as the Secretary of State may by order, made by statutory instrument, appoint; and different dates may be so appointed for the purposes of different provisions of this Act.

Note. Act brought into operation by Maintenance Orders Act 1958 (Commencement) Order 1958, SI 1958 No 2111, on 16 February 1959.

(4) Subsection (2) of section eight of the Guardianship of Infants Act 1925, and section ten of the Affiliation Proceedings Act 1957, are hereby repealed; but nothing in this subsection shall affect any order in force or deemed to be in force under either of those provisions at the commencement of this subsection, and any such order may be discharged or varied as if this subsection had not been passed.

Note. For Affiliation Proceedings Act 1957, s 10, see p 2195.

SCHEDULE

PAYMENTS UNDER ATTACHMENT OF EARNINGS ORDERS

1. The provisions of this Schedule shall have effect in respect of each occasion (in this Schedule referred to as a 'pay-day') on which earnings to which an attachment of earnings order relates fall to be paid.

2. In this Schedule, the following expressions have the following meanings respectively—
'*normal deduction*' *and* '*protected earnings*', *in relation to any pay-day, mean the amount which would represent a payment at the normal deduction rate specified by the order or, as the case may be, at the protected earnings rate so specified in respect of the period between the pay-day in question and either the last preceding pay-day or, where there is no last preceding pay-day, the date last before the pay-day in question on which the employer became the defendant's employer;*

'*relevant earnings*', *in relation to any pay-day, means the amount of the earnings aforesaid falling to be paid on the pay-day in question after the deductions from those earnings of any amount falling to be deducted therefrom by the employer by way of income tax or of contributions under the National Insurance (Industrial Injuries) Acts 1946 to 1957, the National Insurance Acts 1946 to 1957, or the National Health Service Contributions Act 1957, or of lawful deductions under any enactment, or in pursuance of a request in writing by the defendant, requiring or authorising deductions to be made for the purposes of a superannuation scheme within the meaning of the Wages Councils Act 1945.*

3. *If the relevant earnings exceed the sum of—*

(*a*) *the protected earnings; and*

(*b*) *so much of any amount by which the relevant earnings falling to be paid on any previous pay-day fell short of the protected earnings for the purposes of that pay-day as has not been made good by virtue of this sub-paragraph on any other previous pay-day,*

the employer shall, so far as that excess permits, pay to the officer designated for the purpose in the order—

(*i*) *the normal deductions; and*

(*ii*) *so much of the normal deduction for any previous pay-day as was not paid on that pay-day and has not been paid by virtue of this sub-paragraph on any other previous pay-day.*

Note. Schedule repealed by Administration of Justice Act 1970, s 54, Sch 11.

MATRIMONIAL PROCEEDINGS (CHILDREN) ACT 1958*

(6 & 7 Eliz 2 c 40)

An Act to extend the powers of courts to make orders in respect of children in connection with proceedings between husband and wife and to require arrangements with respect to children to be made to the satisfaction of the court before the making of a decree in such proceedings.   [7 July 1958]

'PART I

JURISDICTION IN ENGLAND AND WALES

1. Extension of jurisdiction of Divorce Court to further classes of children—
(*1*) *Subject to the provisions of this section, section twenty-six of the Matrimonial Causes Act 1950 (which enables the High Court to provide for the custody, maintenance and education of the children of the parties to matrimonial proceedings), shall apply in relation to a child of one party to the marriage (including an illegitimate or adopted child) who has been accepted as one of the family by the other party as it applies in relation to a child of both parties.*

Note. See now Matrimonial Causes Act 1973, ss 41, 42, 52(1) and the notes thereto (pp 2550, 2551, 2559), replacing Matrimonial Proceedings and Property Act 1970, ss 17, 18, 27(1) (pp 2375, 2378), replacing Matrimonial Causes Act 1965, ss 33(1), 34(1), 46(2) (pp 2258, 2265).

(*2*) *In considering whether any and what provision should be made by virtue of the foregoing subsection for requiring any party to make any payment towards the maintenance or education of a child who is not his own, the court shall have regard to the extent, if any, to which that party had, on or after the acceptance of the child as one of the family, assumed responsibility for the child's maintenance and to the liability of any person other than a party to the marriage to maintain the child.*

---

* With the exception of ss 17 (partly), 18 (partly), 'whole Act' repealed by Matrimonial Causes Act 1965, s 45, Sch 2.

'Whole Act' did not mean 'whole Act' presumably because the Act of 1965 'does not extend to Scotland or Northern Ireland': s 46(4) (p 2266), and so s 13 of the Act of 1958 (in Part II, Jurisdiction in Scotland) was repealed by Family Law Act 1986, Sch 2, as from 4 April 1988 (SI 1988 No 375).

Note. See now Matrimonial Causes Act 1973, s 25(3) (p 2519), replacing Matrimonial Proceedings and Property Act 1970, s 5(3) (p 2367), replacing Matrimonial Causes Act 1965, s 34(4) (p 2259). See also Matrimonial Causes Act 1973, s 3(3) and the notes thereto (p 2499).

   (3) It is hereby declared that the reference in subsection (2) of the said section twenty-six to the children of the petitioner and respondent includes a reference to any illegitimate child of the petitioner and respondent.

Note. See now Matrimonial Causes Act 1973, s 52(1) (p 2559), replacing Matrimonial Proceedings and Property Act 1970, s 27(1) (p 2378), replacing Matrimonial Causes Act 1965, ss 3(1), 46(2) (pp 2240, 2265).

   (4) In subsection (1) of section twenty-three of the said Act (under which a husband guilty of wilful neglect to maintain his wife or the infant children of the marriage may be ordered to make periodical payments to his wife) the reference to the infant children of the marriage shall be construed as including a reference to an illegitimate child of both parties to the marriage.

Note. See now Matrimonial Causes Act 1973, s 52(1), (p 2559), replacing Matrimonial Proceedings and Property Act 1970, s 27(1) (p 2378), replacing Matrimonial Causes Act 1965, s 22(2) (p 2250).

   (5) In this section 'adopted child' means a child adopted in pursuance of an adoption order made under the Adoption Act 1950, or any enactment repealed by that Act, or under any corresponding enactment of the Parliament of Northern Ireland.

Note. See now Matrimonial Causes Act 1973, s 52(1) (p 2559), replacing Matrimonial Proceedings and Property Act 1970, s 27(1) (p 2378), replacing Matrimonial Causes Act 1965, s 46(2) (p 2265).

   (6) This section shall not apply in relation to proceedings instituted before the commencement of this Part of this Act.

Note. Sub-s (6) replaced by Matrimonial Causes Act 1965, s 33(1) (p 2258), now repealed by Matrimonial Proceedings and Property Act 1970, s 42(2), Sch 3.

   For Matrimonial Causes Act 1950, ss 23, 26, see pp 2140, 2141. Adoption Act 1950 was replaced as from 1 April 1959 by Adoption Act 1958; see now Adoption Act 1976 (p 2620).

2. Restrictions on grant of relief in proceedings for divorce, etc., involving welfare of children—*(1) Subject to the provisions of this section, in any proceedings for divorce, nullity of marriage or judicial separation where the High Court has, by virtue of subsection (1) of section twenty-six of the Matrimonial Causes Act 1950, jurisdiction in relation to any child, the court shall not make absolute any decree for divorce or nullity of marriage or pronounce a decree of judicial separation unless and until the court is satisfied as respects every such child who has not attained the age of sixteen years—*

   (a)   that arrangements have been made for the care and upbringing of the child and that those arrangements are satisfactory or are the best which can be devised in the circumstances, or

   (b)   that it is impracticable for the party or parties appearing before the court to make any such arrangements.

   (2) The court may if it thinks fit proceed without observing the requirements of the foregoing subsection if it appears that there are circumstances making it desirable that the decree nisi should be made absolute, or, as the case may be, that the decree for judicial separation should be pronounced, without delay and if the court has obtained a satisfactory undertaking from either or both of the parties to bring the question of the arrangements for the children before the court within a specified time.

Note. See now Matrimonial Causes Act 1973, s 41 (p 2550), replacing Matrimonial Proceedings and Property Act 1970, s 17 (p 2375), replacing Matrimonial Causes Act 1965, s 33 (p 2258).

   (3) In subsection (2) of section two of the said Act (which requires the judge in determining an application for leave to present a petition for divorce before the expiration of three years from

the date of the marriage to have regard to the interests of any children of the marriage) the reference to any children of the marriage shall be construed as including a reference to any other child in relation to whom the court would have jurisdiction by virtue of subsection (1) of the said section twenty-six in proceedings instituted by the petition.

Note. For Matrimonial Causes Act 1950, s 2(2), see p 2131, and for ibid, s 26(1), see p 2141. See now Matrimonial Causes Act 1973, ss 41, 52(1) (pp 2550, 2559), replacing Matrimonial Proceedings and Property Act 1970, ss 17, 27(1) (pp 2374, 2378), replacing Matrimonial Causes Act 1965, ss 2(2), 46(2) (pp 2240, 2265).

(4) Subsection (1) of this section shall not apply in relation to proceedings instituted before the commencement of this Part of this Act.

Note. Sub-s (4) replaced by Matrimonial Causes Act 1965, s 33(1) (p 2258), repealed by Matrimonial Proceedings and Property Act 1970, s 42(2), Sch 3.

3. Power of Divorce Court to provide for children on dismissal of proceedings for divorce, etc—*(1) Where proceedings instituted after the commencement of this Part of this Act in the High Court for divorce, nullity of marriage or judicial separation are dismissed at any stage after the beginning of the trial, the court may, either forthwith or within a reasonable period after the proceedings have been dismissed, make such provision with respect to the custody, maintenance and education of any child as could be made in the case of that child under subsection (1) of section twenty-six of the Matrimonial Causes Act 1950, if the proceedings were still before the court.*

Note. For Matrimonial Causes Act 1950, s 2(1), see p 2131. See now Matrimonial Causes Act 1973, ss 23, 42(1) and the notes thereto (pp 2513, 2551), replacing Matrimonial Proceedings and Property Act 1970, ss 3, 18(1) (pp 2365, 2375), replacing Matrimonial Causes Act 1965, s 34(1) (p 2258).

(2) Where an order has been made under the foregoing subsection as respects a child, the court may from time to time make further provision with respect to his custody, maintenance and education.

Note. See now Matrimonial Causes Act 1973, s 42(6) (p 2552), replacing Matrimonial Proceedings and Property Act 1970, s 18(5) (p 2376), replacing Matrimonial Causes Act 1965, s 34(5) (p 2259).

4. Power of Divorce Court to provide for children in proceedings for maintenance—*(1) Where the court makes an order after the commencement of this Part of this Act under subsection (1) of section twenty-three of the Matrimonial Causes Act 1950, the court shall also have jurisdiction from time to time to make such provision as appears just with respect to the custody of any such child as is referred to in that subsection (and, as in a case, under the last foregoing section, with respect to access to the child), but the jurisdiction conferred by this subsection, and any order made in exercise of that jurisdiction, shall have effect only as respects any period when an order is in force under subsection (1) of the said section twenty-three.*

Note. For Matrimonial Causes Act 1950, s 23, see p 2140. See now Matrimonial Causes Act 1973, s 42 (repealed) (p 2551), replacing Matrimonial Proceedings and Property Act 1970, s 19 (p 2376), replacing Matrimonial Causes Act 1965, s 35(1), (4), Sch 1, para 11 (pp 2260, 2267).

(2) In any case where the court would have power, on an application made under subsection (1) of the said section twenty-three, to order the husband to make to the wife periodical payments for the maintenance of any such child as is referred to in that subsection, the court may, if it thinks fit, order those payments to be made to the child, or to any other person for the benefit of the child, instead of to the wife; and the reference to the wife in subsection (2) of that section (which relates to security for maintenance) shall be construed accordingly.

Note. For Matrimonial Causes Act 1950, s 23, see p 2140. See now Matrimonial Causes Act 1973, s 27 (p 2529), replacing Matrimonial Proceedings and Property Act 1970, s 6 (p 2367), replacing Matrimonial Causes Act 1965, s 35(2) (p 2260).

5. Power of Divorce Court to commit children to care of local authority—
(1) Where the court has jurisdiction to make provision as to the custody of a child, either by virtue of section twenty-six of the Matrimonial Causes Act 1950, or of this Part of this Act and it appears to the court that there are exceptional circumstances making it impracticable or undesirable for the child to be entrusted to either of the parties to the marriage or to any other individual, the court may if it thinks fit make an order committing the care of the child to the council of a county or county borough (hereinafter referred to as the local authority) and thereupon Part II of the Children Act 1948 (which relates to the treatment of children in the care of a local authority), shall, subject to the provisions of this section, apply as if the child had been received by the local authority into their care under section one of that Act.

Note. For Matrimonial Causes Act 1950, s 26(1), see p 2141.

(2) The authority specified in an order under this section shall be the council of the county or county borough in which the child was, in the opinion of the court, resident before the order was made to commit the child to the care of a local authority, and the court shall before making an order under this section hear any representations from the local authority, including any representations as to the making of an order for payments for the maintenance and education of the child.

(3) While an order made by virtue of this section is in force with respect to any child, the child shall continue in the care of the local authority notwithstanding any claim by a parent or other person.

(4) An order made by virtue of this section shall cease to have effect as respects any child when that child attains the age of eighteen years and the court shall not make an order committing a child to the care of a local authority under this section after he has attained the age of seventeen years.

(5) In the application of the said Part II of the Children Act 1948, under this section—
(a)   the exercise by the local authority of their powers under sections twelve to sixteen of that Act shall be subject to any directions given by the court, and
(b)   section seventeen of that Act (which relates to arrangements for the emigration of a child under the care of a local authority) shall not apply.

(6) If a child who is committed to the care of a local authority under this section comes under the control of any person or authority under the provisions of the Mental Deficiency Acts 1913 to 1938, or the Lunacy and Mental Treatment Acts 1890 to 1930, he shall thereupon cease to be committed to the care of the local authority under this section.

Note. This subsection repealed, as were the statutes referred to therein, by Mental Health Act 1959, Sch 8.

(7) It shall be the duty of any parent or guardian of a child committed to the care of a local authority under this section to secure that the local authority are informed of his address for the time being and a person who knowingly fails to comply with this subsection shall be liable on summary conviction to a fine not exceeding five pounds.

(8) The court shall have power from time to time by an order under this section to vary or discharge any provision made in pursuance of this section.

Note. See now Matrimonial Causes Act 1973, s 43 (p 2552), replacing Matrimonial Causes Act 1965, s 36 (p 2260).

6. Power of Divorce Court to provide for supervision of children—*(1) Where the court has jurisdiction to provide for the custody of a child under section twenty-six of the Matrimonial Causes Act 1950, or this Part of this Act and it appears to the court that there are exceptional circumstances making it desirable that the child should be under the supervision of an independent person, the court may, as respects any period during which the child is, in exercise of that jurisdiction, committed to the custody of any person, order that the child be under the supervision of an officer appointed under this section as a welfare officer or under the supervision of a local authority.*

Note. For Matrimonial Causes Act 1950, s 26, see p 2141. See now Matrimonial Causes Act 1973, s 44 (p 2553), replacing Matrimonial Causes Act 1965, s 37 (p 2261).

(2) *Where the court makes an order under this section for supervision by a welfare officer, the officer responsible for carrying out the order shall be such probation officer as may be selected under arrangements made by the Secretary of State and where an order is for supervision by a local authority, that authority shall be the council of a county or county borough selected by the court and specified in the order.*

(3) *This section shall be included among the enactments specified in subsection (1) of section thirty-nine of the Children Act 1948 (which lists the functions which are matters for the children's committee of a local authority and in respect of which grants are payable under section forty-seven of that Act), and a local authority shall discharge the duties conferred on them by an order under this section through an officer employed in connection with those functions.*

(4) *The court shall not have power to make an order under this section as respects a child who in pursuance of an order under the last foregoing section is in the care of a local authority.*

(5) *Where a child is under the supervision of any person in pursuance of this section the jurisdiction possessed by a court to vary any order made with respect to the child's custody, maintenance or education under section twenty-six of the Matrimonial Causes Act 1950, or this Part of this Act shall, subject to any rules of court, be exercisable at the instance of the court itself.*

Note. For Matrimonial Causes Act 1950, s 26, see p 2141.

(6) *The court shall have power from time to time by an order under this section to vary or discharge any provision made in pursuance of this section.*

Note. See now Matrimonial Causes Act 1973, s 44 (p 2553), replacing Matrimonial Causes Act 1965, s 37 (p 2261).

(Part II applies to Scotland only.)

PART III

GENERAL

16. Expenses. *There shall be paid out of moneys provided by Parliament any increase attributable to this Act in the sums payable out of moneys so provided—*
- (a) *under section forty-seven of the Children Act 1948, or*
- (b) *under Part I of the Local Government Act 1948, or the Local Government (Financial Provision) (Scotland) Act 1954, as amended by the Valuation and Rating (Scotland) Act 1956.*

Note. This section repealed and not replaced by Matrimonial Causes Act 1965, s 45, Sch 2.

17. Application of enactments regulating the enforcement of maintenance orders. Any order for maintenance or other payments made by virtue of this Act or any corresponding enactment of the Parliament of Northern Ireland shall be included among the orders to which section sixteen of the Maintenance Orders Act 1950, applies (which section specifies the maintenance orders which are enforceable under Part II of that Act) *and, in the case of an order made by virtue of Part I of this Act, shall be a maintenance order within the meaning of the Maintenance Orders Act 1958.*

Note. For Maintenance Orders Act 1950, s 16, see p 2147, and for Maintenance Orders Act 1958, see p 2204. Words in italics repealed by Matrimonial Causes Act 1965, s 45, Sch 2, and replaced by ibid, s 38(1) (p 2262) which was repealed, and not replaced, by Matrimonial Causes Act 1973, s 54(1), Sch 3.

18. Short title, extent and commencement—(1) This Act may be cited as the Matrimonial Proceedings (Children) Act 1958.

(2) Any reference in this Act to any enactment shall be construed as a reference to that enactment as amended or extended by any other Act, including this Act.

(3) This Act (except so far as it affects Part II of the Maintenance Orders Act 1950) shall not extend to Northern Ireland.

(4) Part I of this Act shall come into force on such a day as may be appointed by the Lord Chancellor by an order contained in a statutory instrument and Part II of this Act shall come into force on such day as may be appointed by the Secretary of State by such an order.

Note. Part I brought into operation on 1 January 1959 by Matrimonial Proceedings (Children) Act (Commencement) Order 1958, SI 1958 No 2081.

Sub-s (4) repealed by Matrimonial Causes Act 1965, s 45, Sch 2.

DIVORCE (INSANITY AND DESERTION) ACT 1958*

(6 & 7 Eliz 2 c 54)

An Act to amend the law as to the circumstances in which, for the purposes of proceedings for divorce in England or Scotland, a person is to be treated as having been continuously under care and treatment and as to the effect of insanity on desertion; and to enable a petition for divorce to be presented on the ground of desertion notwithstanding any separation agreement entered into before desertion became a ground for divorce in English law.

[*23 July 1958*]

* This Act was repealed by Matrimonial Causes Act 1965, s 45, Sch 2, and replaced as noted.

1. Care and treatment for purposes of divorce proceedings—*(1) Notwithstanding anything in subsection (2) of section one of the Matrimonial Causes Act 1950, or subsection (3) of section six of the Divorce (Scotland) Act 1938, a person shall be deemed to be under care and treatment for the purposes of the said section one, and under care and treatment as an insane person for the purposes of the said section six, at any time when he is receiving treatment for mental illness—*

(a)   as a resident in a hospital or other institution provided, approved, licensed, registered or exempted from registration by any Minister or other authority in the United Kingdom, the Isle of Man or the Channel Islands;

(b)   as a resident in a hospital or other institution in any other country, being a hospital or institution in which his treatment is comparable with the treatment provided in any such hospital or institution as is mentioned in paragraph (a) of this subsection.

Note. For Matrimonial Causes Act 1950, s 1(2), see p 2130. Sub-s (1) replaced by Matrimonial Causes Act 1965, s 1(3) (p 2240), repealed and not replaced by Divorce Reform Act 1969, s 9, Sch 2.

(2) For the purposes of the foregoing subsection a certificate by the Admiralty or a Secretary of State that a person was receiving treatment for mental illness during any period as a resident in any naval, military or air-force hospital under the direction of the Admiralty, the Army Council or the Air Council shall be conclusive evidence of the facts certified.

(3) In determining for the purposes of the said section one or the said section six whether any period of care and treatment has been continuous, any interruption of such a period for twenty-eight days or less shall be disregarded.

Note. Sub-s (2) replaced by Matrimonial Causes Act 1965, s 1(3), (4) (p 2240), repealed and not replaced by Divorce Reform Act 1969, s 9, Sch 2.

2. Power of court to treat desertion as continuing during period of incapacity.
For the purposes of any petition or action for divorce or judicial separation the court may treat a period of desertion as having continued at a time when the deserting party was incapable of continuing the necessary intention, if the evidence before the court is such that, had he not been so incapable, the court would have inferred that the intention continued at that time.

Note. This section replaced by Matrimonial Causes Act 1965, s 1(2) (p 2240), repealed and not replaced by Divorce Reform Act 1969, s 9, Sch 2.

3. Divorce for desertion notwithstanding separation agreement. *For the purposes of paragraph (b) of subsection (1) of section one of the Matrimonial Causes Act 1950* *(which provides that a petition for divorce may be presented to the High Court on the ground that the respondent has deserted the petitioner without cause for a period of at least three years immediately preceding the presentation of the petition), any agreement between the petitioner and the respondent to live separate and apart, whether or not in writing, shall be disregarded if the agreement was entered into before the first day of January, nineteen hundred and thirty-eight, and either—*

    (a) at the time when the agreement was made the respondent had deserted the petitioner without cause; or

    (b) the court is satisfied that the circumstances in which the agreement was made and the parties proceeded to live separate and apart were such as, but for the agreement, to amount to desertion of the petitioner by the respondent without cause.

Note. For Matrimonial Causes Act 1950, s 1(1), see p 2130.

4. Short title, extent and repeal—*(1) This Act may be cited as the Divorce (Insanity and Desertion) Act 1958.*

    (2) This Act does not extend to Northern Ireland.

    (3) In paragraph (d) of subsection (2) of section one of the Matrimonial Causes Act 1950, the words from 'being treatment' to 'this subsection', and in subsection (3) of section six of the Divorce (Scotland) Act 1938, the words 'other than treatment as a voluntary patient' are hereby repealed.

Note. This section, already repealed by Matrimonial Causes Act 1965, again repealed by Statute Law (Repeals) Act 1974.

ADMINISTRATION OF JUSTICE ACT 1960

(8 & 9 Eliz 2 c 65)

*   *   *   *   *

Contempt of court, habeas corpus and certiorari

*   *   *   *   *

12. Publication of information relating to proceedings in private—(1) The publication of information relating to proceedings before any court sitting in private shall not of itself be contempt of court except in the following cases, that is to say—

    (a) where the proceedings relate to the wardship or adoption of an infant or wholly or mainly to the guardianship, custody, maintenance or upbringing of an infant, or rights of access to an infant;

  [*(a) where the proceedings—*

        (i) *relate to the inherent jurisdiction of the High Court with respect to minors;*

        (ii) *are brought under the Children Act 1989; or*

        (iii) *otherwise relate wholly or mainly to the maintenance or upbringing of a minor.*]

Note. Sub-s (1)(a) in square brackets substituted for sub-s (1)(a) in italics by Children Act 1989, s 108(5), Sch 13, para 14, as from 14 October 1991.

*   *   *   *   *

(2) Without prejudice to the foregoing subsection, the publication of the text or a summary of the whole or part of an order made by a court sitting in private shall not of itself be contempt of court except where the court (having power to do so) expressly prohibits the publication.

*   *   *   *   *

(4) Nothing in this section shall be construed as implying that any publication is punishable as contempt of court which would not be so punishable apart from this section.

13. Appeal in cases of contempt of court—(1) Subject to the provisions of this section, an appeal shall lie under this section from any order or decision of a court in the exercise of jurisdiction to punish for contempt of court (including criminal contempt); and in relation to any such order or decision the provisions of this section shall have effect in substitution for any other enactment relating to appeals in civil or criminal proceedings.

(2) An appeal under this section shall lie in any case at the instance of the defendant and, in the case of an application for committal or attachment, at the instance of the applicant; and the appeal shall lie—

(a)   from an order or decision of any inferior court not referred to in the next following paragraph, to *a Divisional Court of* the High Court;

(b)   from an order or decision of a county court or any other inferior court from which appeals generally lie to the Court of Appeal, and from an order or *decision of the Chancery Court of a County Palatine, of a single* [decision (other than a decision on an appeal under this section) of a single] judge of the High Court, or of any court having the powers of the High Court or of a judge of that court, to the Court of Appeal;

[(bb) from an order or decision of the Crown Court to the Court of Appeal;]

(c)   [from a decision of a single judge of the High Court on an appeal under this section,] from an order or decision of a Divisional Court or the Court of Appeal (including a decision of either of those courts on an appeal under this section), and from an order or decision of the Court of Criminal Appeal or the Courts-Martial Appeal Court, to the House of Lords.

Note. Words 'a Divisional Court' in italics in para (a) repealed by the Access to Justice Act 1999, ss 64(1), (2), 106, Sch 15, Pt III, as from 27 September 1999. In para (b) words 'decision (other … of a single' in square brackets substituted for words 'decision …, of a single' by the Access to Justice Act 1999, s 64(1), (3), as from 27 September 1999. Words 'of the Chancery Court of a County Palatine' in italics in (b) repealed, and para (bb) inserted, by Courts Act 1971, s 56, Sch 8, para 40(1), Sch 11, Part II, as from 1 January 1972. In para (c) words 'from a decision … this section,' in square brackets inserted by the Access to Justice Act 1999, s 64(1), (4), as from 27 September 1999.

(3) The court to which an appeal is brought under this section may reverse or vary the order or decision of the court below, and make such other order as may be just; and without prejudice to the inherent power of any court referred to in subsection (2) of this section, provision may be made by rules of court for authorising the release on bail of an appellant under this section.

*   *   *   *   *

(5) In this section 'court' includes any tribunal or person having power to punish for contempt; and references in this section to an order or decision of a court in the exercise of jurisdiction to punish for contempt of court include references—

(a)   to an order or decision of the High Court [the Crown Court] or a county court under any enactment enabling that court to deal with an offence as if it were contempt of court;

(b)   to an order or decision of a county court, or of any court having the powers of a county court, under *section thirty, section one hundred and twenty-seven or section one hundred and fifty-seven of the County Courts Act 1959* [section 14, 92 or 118 of the County Courts Act 1984];

(c)   to an order or decision of a magistrates' court under *section fifty-four of the Magistrates' Courts Act 1952* [subsection (3) of section 63 of the Magistrates' Courts Act 1980],

but do not include references to orders under section five of the Debtors Act 1869, or under any provision of the Magistrates' Courts Act 1952 [Magistrates' Courts Act

1980], or the County Courts Act 1959 [1984], except those referred to in paragraphs (b) and (c) of this subsection and except *sections seventy-four and one hundred and ninety-five* [sections 38 and 142] of the last mentioned Act so far as those sections confer jurisdiction in respect of contempt of court.

Note. Words 'the Crown Court' inserted in sub-s (5)(a) by Courts Act 1971, s 56, Sch 8, para 40(2).

References to Magistrates' Courts Act 1980 substituted for references to Magistrates' Courts Act 1952 by Magistrates' Courts Act 1980, s 154, Sch 7, para 37, as from 6 July 1981.

References to the County Courts Act 1984 substituted for County Courts Act 1959 by County Courts Act 1984, s 148(1), Sch 2, Part V, para 25, as from 1 August 1984.

This section is applied to offences under Administration of Justice Act 1970, s 25 by ibid., s 25(9).

For the purposes of this section Attachment of Earnings Act 1971, s 23(3), is to be treated as an enactment enabling the High Court or county court to deal with an offence under Courts Act 1971, s 23(2) as if it were a contempt of court: see Courts Act 1971, s 23(9).

*   *   *   *   *

Supplementary

17. Interpretation—(1) In this Act any reference to the defendant shall be construed—

*   *   *   *   *

(b) in relation to any proceedings or order for or in respect of contempt of court, as a reference to the person against whom the proceedings were brought or the order was made;

and any reference to the prosecutor shall be construed accordingly.

*   *   *   *   *

(3) In this Act any reference to the court below shall, in relation to any function of a Divisional Court, be construed as a reference to the Divisional Court or to a judge according as the function is by virtue of rules of court exercisable by the Divisional Court or a judge.

*   *   *   *   *

LAW REFORM (HUSBAND AND WIFE) ACT 1962

(10 & 11 Eliz 2 c 48)

An Act to amend the law with respect to civil proceedings between husband and wife.

[1 August 1962]

1. Actions in tort between husband and wife—(1) Subject to the provisions of this section, each of the parties to a marriage shall have the like right of action in tort against the other as if they were not married.

(2) Where an action in tort is brought by one of the parties to a marriage against the other during the subsistence of the marriage, the court may stay the action if it appears—

(a) that no substantial benefit would accrue to either party from the continuation of the proceedings; or

(b) that the question or questions in issue could more conveniently be disposed of on an application made under section seventeen of the Married Women's Property Act 1882 (determination of questions between husband and wife as to the title to or possession of property);

and without prejudice to paragraph (b) of this subsection the court may, in such an action, either exercise any power which could be exercised on an application under the said section seventeen, or give such directions as it thinks fit for the disposal under that section of any question arising in the proceedings.

(3) Provision shall be made by rules of court for requiring the court to consider at an early stage of the proceedings whether the power to stay an action under subsection (2) of this section should or should not be exercised; and rules under the County Courts Act 1959, may confer on the registrar any jurisdiction of the court under that subsection.

Note. Sub-s (3) repealed by the Civil Procedure (Modification of Enactments) Order 1998, SI 1998 No 2940, art 4, as from 26 April 1999. In sub-s (3) words 'may confer ... that sub-section' repealed by County Courts Act 1984, s 148(3), Sch 4, as from 1 August 1984.

(4) (Applies to Scotland only.)

2. Proceedings between husband and wife in respect of delict—(1) Subject to the provisions of this section, each of the parties to a marriage shall have the like right to bring proceedings against the other in respect of a wrongful or negligent act or omission, or for the prevention of a wrongful act, as if they were not married.

(2) Where any such proceedings are brought by one of the parties to a marriage against the other during the subsistence of the marriage, the court may dismiss the proceedings if it appears that no substantial benefit would accrue to either party from the continuation thereof; and it shall be the duty of the court to consider at an early stage of the proceedings whether the power to dismiss the proceedings under this subsection should or should not be exercised.

(3) This section extends to Scotland only.

3. Short title, repeal, interpretation, saving and extent—(1) This Act may be cited as the Law Reform (Husband and Wife) Act 1962.

(2) The enactments described in the Schedule to this Act are hereby repealed to the extent specified in the third column of that Schedule.

(3) The references in subsection (1) of section one and subsection (1) of section two of this Act to the parties to a marriage include references to the persons who were parties to a marriage which has been dissolved.

(4) This Act does not apply to any cause of action which arose, or would but for the subsistence of a marriage have arisen, before the commencement of this Act.

(5) This Act does not extend to Northern Ireland.

Note. Sub-s (2) repealed by Statute Laws (Repeals) Act 1974.

SCHEDULE   Section 3

ENACTMENTS REPEALED

Session and Chapter	Short Title	Extent of Repeal
45 & 46 Vict c 75.	*The Married Women's Property Act 1882.*	*Section twelve, except so far as it relates to criminal proceedings. Section twenty-three.*
	* * * * *	

Note. Repealed by Statute Laws (Repeals) Act 1974.

OATHS AND EVIDENCE (OVERSEAS AUTHORITIES AND COUNTRIES) ACT 1963

(1963 c 27)

* * * * *

5. Amendment of 23 & 24 Geo 5 c 4—(1) If Her Majesty in Council is satisfied as respects any country that—
(a) there exist in that country public registers kept under the authority of the law of that country and recognised by the courts of that country as authentic records, and
(b) that the registers are regularly and properly kept,
Her Majesty may by Order in Council make in respect of that country* and all or any of those registers such provision as is specified in subsection (2) of section 1 of the Evidence (Foreign, Dominion and Colonial Documents) Act 1933.

(2) The foregoing subsection shall have effect in substitution for subsection (1) of the said section 1, and accordingly subsections (1) and (5) of the said section 1 are hereby repealed, in subsection (2) of that section for the words 'this section' there shall be substituted 'section 5 of the Oaths and Evidence (Overseas Authorities and Countries) Act 1963', and subsection (4) of that section (interpretation of 'country') shall apply for the interpretation of the foregoing subsection as it applies for the interpretation of the said section 1; but any Order in Council made under the said section 1 and in force at the commencement of this Act shall continue in force until revoked, or as varied, by an Order in Council under this section.

Note. For Evidence (Foreign, Dominion and Colonial Documents) Act 1933, see p 2068.

* In addition to the Orders made under Evidence (Foreign, Dominion and Colonial Documents) Act 1933, s 1 (which are listed in the footnote on p 2068) the following orders have been made under Oaths and Evidence (Overseas Authorities and Countries) Act 1963: 1965 Nos 312–313 (Antigua, Cayman Islands); 1965 No 1527 (Aden); 1965 No 1712 (Kenya); 1965 Nos 1719–1721 (Basutoland, Bechuanaland Protectorate, Saint Lucia); 1965 No 1865 (Swaziland); 1966 Nos 82–83 (Grenada, Turks and Caicos Islands); 1969 Nos 144–146 (Denmark, Italy, USA); 1969 No 1059 (Republic of Ireland); 1970 No 284 (Netherlands); 1970 No 819 (Federal Republic of Germany; 1972 No 116 (Luxembourg); 1984 No 857 (British Indian Ocean Territory).

CHILDREN AND YOUNG PERSONS ACT 1963

(1963 c 37)

An Act to amend the law relating to children and young persons; and for purposes connected therewith.

[31 July 1963]

* * * * *

23. Children and young persons detained in places of safety—*(1) A court or justice of the peace—*
(a) authorising any person under section 26(6) or section 6(1) of the principal Act to take a child or young person to a place of safety; or
(b) issuing a warrant under section 40 of that Act [the principal Act] authorising a constable to take a child or young person to a place of safety; or
(c) ordering the removal of a child or young person to a place of safety under section 7 of the Children Act 1958 [section 12 of the Foster Children Act 1980] or section 43 of the Adoption Act 1958 [section 34 of the Adoption Act 1976];

shall specify in the warrant, authority or order a period, which shall not exceed twenty-eight days, beyond which the child or young person must not be detained in a place of safety without being brought before a juvenile court; and accordingly the child or young person shall be brought before a juvenile court not later than the end of that period unless he has been released or received into the care of a local authority.

    (2)   Where a child or young person has taken refuge in a place of safety or has been taken there otherwise than under the authority of a court or justice of the peace, he shall be brought before a juvenile court or a justice of the peace within the period of eight days beginning with the day when he arrived at the place of safety, unless he has been released or received into the care of a local authority.

    (3)   A child or young person required to be brought before a juvenile court or a justice of the peace under subsection (1) or subsection (2) of this section shall (if not otherwise brought before the court or justice) be brought before the court or justice by the local authority in whose area the place of safety is situated; and the person occupying or in charge of a place of safety not provided by that local authority shall as soon as practicable notify that local authority whenever a child or young person takes refuge there or is taken there as mentioned in subsection (1) or subsection (2) of this section.

    (4)   Notwithstanding anything in the preceding provisions of this section, where the person to be brought before a court or justice is under the age of five or cannot be brought before the court or justice by reason of illness or accident, the duty to bring him before the court or justice may be discharged by the making of an application for an order under subsection (5) of this section.

    (5)   Where a person is brought before a juvenile court or justice of the peace in pursuance of subsection (3) of this section or an application is made in respect of any person to a juvenile court or justice of the peace in pursuance of subsection (4) thereof, the court or justice may either order him to be released or make an interim order for his detention in a place of safety, or for his committal to the care of a fit person, whether a relative or not, who is willing to undertake the care of him [within the meaning of the Children and Young Persons Act 1969].

    (6)   An interim order under this section shall cease to have effect—

      (a)   if made by a juvenile court, not later than twenty-eight days after it is made; and

      (b)   if made otherwise than by a juvenile court, not later than twenty-eight days after the person in respect of whom it is made arrived at the place of safety;

but if before the expiration of that period a juvenile court thinks it expedient to do so it may make a further interim order under this section, and, where the person concerned is under the age of five or cannot be brought before the court by reason of illness or accident, may do so in his absence.

    (7)   Subsections (2) to (4) of section 6 of the Children and Young Persons Act 1938 (which make provision for children and young persons needing medical treatment while in a place of safety) shall with the necessary modifications apply in relation to orders under this section as they apply in relation to such orders as are mentioned in subsection (2) of that section.

    (8)   In this section 'young person' includes a person of or over the age of seventeen who is about to be brought before a juvenile court under section 66 of the principal Act.

Note.   Sub-ss (1)(a), (2), (6)–(8), words 'authority' in sub-s (1), words 'or subsection (2)' in both places where they occur in sub-s (3) and words 'takes refuge there or' in the same subsection, repealed by Children and Young Persons Act 1969, s 72 (4), Sch 6. Words in square brackets in sub-ss (1)(b), (5) substituted for words 'that Act' and 'for his detention … undertake the care of him' respectively, by s 72(3), Sch 5, para 48 to, the 1969 Act. Words in first pair of square brackets in sub-s (1)(c) substituted for words 'section 7 of the Children Act 1958' by Foster Children Act 1980, s 23(2), Sch 2, Part I, and words in second pair of square brackets in that subsection substituted for words 'section 43 of the Adoption Act 1958', by Adoption Act 1976, s 73(2), Sch 3, para 8, as from 1 January 1988.

    This section repealed by Children Act 1989, s 108(7), Sch 15, as from 14 October 1991. For transitional provisions and savings in relation to pending proceedings, etc, and applying to place of safety orders and interim orders made under sub-s (5) above in force immediately before the commencement of Children Act 1989, Part IV (ss 31–42, Sch 3), see s 108(6) of, and Sch 14, paras 1, 27 to, that Act (pp 3288, 3373, 3384).

*   *   *   *   *

28. Form of oath for use in juvenile courts and by children and young people in other courts—(1) Subject to subsection (2) of this section, in relation to any oath administered to and taken by any person before a *juvenile court* [youth court] or administered to and taken by any child or young person before any other court, section 2 of the Oaths Act 1909 [section 1 of the Oaths Act 1978] shall have effect as if the words 'I promise before Almighty God' were set out in it instead of the words 'I swear by Almighty God'.

Note. Words 'youth court' in square brackets substituted for words 'juvenile court' in italics by Criminal Justice Act 1991, s 100, Sch 11, para 40, as from 1 October 1992. Reference to Oaths Act 1978 substituted for reference to Oaths Act 1909 by Oaths Act 1978, s 2, as from 1 August 1978.

(2) Where in any oath otherwise duly administered and taken, either of the forms mentioned in this section is used instead of the other, the oath shall nevertheless be deemed as have been duly administered and taken.

Note. For Oaths Act 1978, s 1, see p 2733.

MATRIMONIAL CAUSES ACT 1963*
(1963 c 45)

An Act to amend the law relating to matrimonial causes; to facilitate reconciliation in such causes; and for purposes connected with the matters aforesaid.

[*31 July 1963*]

* This Act was repealed by Matrimonial Causes Act 1965, s 45, Sch 2.

1. Presumption as to condonation by husband. *Any presumption of condonation which arises from the continuance or resumption of marital intercourse may be rebutted on the part of a husband, as well as on the part of a wife, by evidence sufficient to negative the necessary intent.*

Note. See Matrimonial Causes Act 1965, s 42(1) (p 2264) and cf Matrimonial Causes Act 1973, s 27(8) (p 2532).

2. Relief notwithstanding temporary cohabitation with a view to reconciliation—*(1) For the purposes of the Matrimonial Causes Act 1950, and of the Matrimonial Proceedings (Magistrates' Courts) Act 1960, adultery or cruelty shall not be deemed to have been condoned by reason only of a continuation or resumption of cohabitation between the parties for one period not exceeding three months, or of anything done during such cohabitation, if it is proved that cohabitation was continued or resumed, as the case may be, with a view to effecting a reconciliation.*

Note. See Matrimonial Causes Act 1965, s 42(2) (p 2264) and Matrimonial Causes Act 1973, s 2(1), (2) (p 2498), replacing Divorce Reform Act 1969, s 3(3), (4) (p 2339).

(2) In calculating for the purposes of section 1(1)(b) of the Matrimonial Causes Act 1950, the period for which the respondent has deserted the petitioner without cause, and in considering whether such desertion has been continuous, no account shall be taken of any one period (not exceeding three months) during which the parties resumed cohabitation with a view to a reconciliation.

Note. For Matrimonial Causes Act 1950, s 1(1)(b), see p 2120. Sub-s (2) was replaced by Matrimonial Causes Act 1965, s 1(2) (p 2239), repealed by Matrimonial Proceedings and Property Act 1970, s 42(2), Sch 3. Cf Matrimonial Causes Act 1973, s 2(5) (p 2498), replacing Divorce Reform Act 1969, s 3(5) (p 2339).

3. Adultery not to be revived. *Adultery which has been condoned shall not be capable of being revived.*

Note. See Matrimonial Causes Act 1965, s 4(3) (p 2241) and cf Matrimonial Causes Act 1973, s 27(8) (p 2532).

4. Amendment of law of collusion—*(1) Section 4 of the Matrimonial Causes Act 1950 (duty of court on presentation of petition), shall be amended as follows—*

(a) paragraph (c) of subsection (2) (proof of absence of collusion) together with the word 'and' immediately preceding that paragraph shall be omitted;

(b) in the proviso to that subsection, after the words 'if it finds' there shall be inserted the words 'that the petition is presented or prosecuted in collusion with the respondent or either of the respondents or'.

(2) Nothing in this section affects the duty of the court under the said section 4 to inquire whether any collusion exists between the parties, or any duty of the parties to disclose to the court any agreement or arrangement made between them in contemplation of or in connection with the proceedings, or any power or duty of Her Majesty's Proctor under the said Act.

(3) Provision may be made by rules of court for enabling the court, upon application made either before or after the presentation of a petition for divorce, to take into consideration for the purposes of the said section 4 as amended by this section any agreement or arrangement made or proposed to be made between the parties, and to give such directions in the matter as the court thinks fit.

Note. For Matrimonial Causes Act 1950, s 4 see p 2132, replaced by Matrimonial Causes Act 1965, ss 5, 12(1) (pp 2241, 2245), repealed and not replaced by Divorce Reform Act 1969, s 9(2), Sch 2.

5. Maintenance and alimony—*(1) In any case in which the court has power to make an order (other than an interim order) under section 19 or section 20 of the Matrimonial Causes Act 1950 (maintenance and alimony), the court may, in lieu of, or in addition to, making such an order, make an order for the payment of a lump sum.*

(2) Notwithstanding anything in the said Act of 1950 or in the Matrimonial Causes (Property and Maintenance) Act 1958, rules of court may provide, in such cases as may be prescribed by the rules—

(a) that applications for ancillary relief shall be made in the petition or answer; or

(b) that applications for ancillary relief which are not made as aforesaid shall be made only with the leave of the court.

(3) Any rules of court made before the commencement of this Act shall be deemed to have been validly made if such rules could be made after that date under the last foregoing subsection; but nothing in this subsection affects any order for ancillary relief made on or after 20 December 1962, and before the commencement of this Act.

(4) In subsections (2) and (3) of this section 'ancillary relief' means relief under section 19, section 20, section 22 and section 26 of the said Act of 1950.

Note. For Matrimonial Causes Act 1950, ss 19, 20, 26, see pp 2138, 2139, 2141. See now Matrimonial Causes Act 1973, ss 23, 26(2) (pp 2512, 2528), replacing Matrimonial Proceedings and Property Act 1970, ss 2, 24(2) (pp 2365, 2370), replacing Matrimonial Causes Act 1965, ss 16(1), 19, 20(1), 29, 34(6), Sch 1, para 8 (pp 2247, 2248, 2256, 2259, 2267).

6. Attempts to defeat claims for financial relief—*(1) Where proceedings are brought for financial relief and the court is satisfied, on an application under this section by the person bringing those proceedings—*

(a) that the person against whom the proceedings are brought is about to make any disposition with the intention of defeating the claim for financial relief made in the proceedings, or

(b) that the person is about to transfer any property out of the jurisdiction of the court, or otherwise to deal with any property, with that intention,

the court may make such order restraining that person from making the disposition or transferring or otherwise dealing with the property, as the case may be, or otherwise for protecting the claim, as the court thinks fit.

(2) In this section 'financial relief' means relief (otherwise than by way of an interim order) under section 19, section 20, section 22, section 23, section 24 or section 26 of the Matrimonial Causes Act 1950, or under subsection (1) of section 5 of this Act, and 'disposition' and 'property' have the same meanings as in the Matrimonial Causes (Property and Maintenance) Act 1958.

(3) Subsections (4) and (7) of section 2 of the said Act of 1958 (except so much of subsection (4) as refers to a disposition falling within subsection (3) of that section) shall apply to this section, and to any transaction or claim to which this section applies, as they apply to that section and to any disposition or claim to which that section applies.

(4) For the purposes of sections 2 and 5 of the said Act of 1958, 'financial relief' shall include relief under subsections (1) and (3) of section 26 of the said Act of 1950 and subsection (1) of section 5 of this Act.

Note. For Matrimonial Causes Act 1950, ss 19, 20, 22, 23, 24, 26, see pp 2138–2141. For Matrimonial Causes (Property and Maintenance) Act 1958, ss 2, 5, see pp 2198, 2200. See now Matrimonial Causes Act 1973, ss 23, 37 (pp 2512, 2546), replacing Matrimonial Proceedings and Property Act 1970, ss 3, 16 (pp 2365, 2374), replacing Matrimonial Causes Act 1965, ss 32(1), (3), (4), 34(7) (pp 2257, 2259).

7. Short title, construction and extent—*(1) This Act may be cited as the Matrimonial Causes Act 1963.*

(2) This Act shall be construed as one with the Matrimonial Causes Act 1950.

(3) This Act does not apply to Scotland or Northern Ireland.

MARRIED WOMEN'S PROPERTY ACT 1964

(1964 c 19)

An Act to amend the law relating to rights of property as between husband and wife.
[25 March 1964]

1. Money and property derived from housekeeping allowance. If any question arises as to the right of a husband or wife to money derived from any allowance made by the husband for the expenses of the matrimonial home or for similar purposes, or to any property acquired out of such money, the money or property shall, in the absence of any agreement between them to the contrary, be treated as belonging to the husband and the wife in equal shares.

2. Short title and extent—(1) This Act may be cited as the Married Women's Property Act 1964.

(2) This Act does not extend to Northern Ireland.

Note. For Married Women's Property Act 1882, see p 2031.

MATRIMONIAL CAUSES ACT 1965

(1965 c 72)

ARRANGEMENT OF SECTIONS

PART I

DIVORCE, NULLITY AND OTHER MATRIMONIAL SUITS

Divorce

PART IV

MISCELLANEOUS AND GENERAL

Miscellaneous

General

An Act to consolidate certain enactments relating to matrimonial causes, maintenance and declarations of legitimacy and British nationality, with corrections
and improvements made under the Consolidation of Enactments (Procedure)
Act 1949.

[8 November 1965]

PART I

DIVORCE, NULLITY AND OTHER MATRIMONIAL SUITS

Divorce

1. Grounds for petition—*(1) Subject to the next following section, a petition for divorce
may be presented to the High Court (hereafter in this Act referred to as 'the court')—*
   (a) by the husband or the wife on the ground that the respondent—
       (i) has since the celebration of the marriage committed adultery; or
       *(ii) has deserted the petitioner without cause for a period of at least three years
              immediately preceding the presentation of the petition; or*
       (iii) has since the celebration of the marriage treated the petitioner with cruelty; or
       *(iv) is incurably of unsound mind and has been continuously under care and
              treatment for a period of at least five years immediately preceding the presenta-
              tion of the petition;*
   *(b) by the wife on the ground that her husband has since the celebration of the marriage been
          guilty of rape, sodomy or bestiality.*

Note. This subsection replaced Matrimonial Causes Act 1950, s 1 (p 2130) which replaced
Supreme Court of Judicature (Consolidation) Act 1925, s 176 (p 2056), as substituted by
Matrimonial Causes Act 1937, s 2.
   The subsection repealed by Divorce Reform Act 1969, s 9(2), Sch 2. See now Matrimonial
Causes Act 1973, s 1(1), (2) (p 2497), replacing ss 1, 2(1) of the 1969 Act (p 2338).

   *(2) In calculating for the purposes of subsection (1)(a)(ii) of this section the period for which
the respondent has deserted the petitioner without cause, and in considering whether the desertion has been continuous, no account shall be taken of any one period (not exceeding three
months) during which the parties resumed cohabitation with a view to reconciliation; and, for
the purposes of a petition for divorce, the court may treat a period of desertion as having continued at a time when the deserting party was incapable of continuing the necessary intention if
the evidence before the court is such that, had that party not been so incapable, the court would
have inferred that that intention continued at that time.*

Note. This subsection replaced Matrimonial Causes Act 1963, s 2(2) (p 2235) and Divorce (Insanity and Desertion) Act 1958, s 2 (p 2228). It was repealed by Divorce Reform Act 1969, s 9(2), Sch 2. See now Matrimonial Causes Act 1973, ss 2(4), (5) (p 2498), replacing Divorce Reform Act 1969, ss 2(4), 3 (5) (pp 2339, 2340).

(3) For the purposes of subsection (1)(a)(iv) of this section, a person of unsound mind shall be deemed to be under care and treatment while, and only while—

(a)   he is liable to be detained in a hospital, mental nursing home or place of safety under the Mental Health Act 1959, or in a hospital or place of safety under the Mental Health (Scotland) Act 1960;

(b)   he is detained in pursuance of an order for his detention or treatment as a person of unsound mind or a person suffering from mental illness made under any law for the time being in force in Northern Ireland, the Isle of Man or any of the Channel Islands (including any such law relating to criminal lunatics) or is receiving treatment as a voluntary patient under any law so in force;

(c)   he is receiving treatment for mental illness as a resident in—

(i)   a hospital or other institution provided, approved, licensed, registered or exempted from registration by any Minister or other authority in the United Kingdom, the Isle of Man or the Channel Islands; or

(ii)   a hospital or other institution in any other country, being a hospital or institution in which his treatment is comparable with the treatment provided in any such hospital or institution as is mentioned in sub-paragraph (i) of this paragraph;

and, in determining for the purposes of the said subsection (1)(a)(iv) whether any period of care and treatment has been continuous, any interruption of the period for twenty-eight days or less shall be disregarded.

Note. This subsection replaced Divorce (Insanity and Desertion) Act 1958, s 1(1), (3), (pp 2228). It was repealed by Divorce Reform Act 1969, s 9(2), Sch 2 and was not replaced.

(4) A certificate by a Secretary of State that a person was receiving treatment for mental illness during any period as a resident in any naval, military or air force hospital under the direction of the Defence Council shall for the purposes of paragraph (c) of the last foregoing subsection be conclusive evidence of the facts certified.

Note. This subsection replaced Divorce (Insanity and Desertion) Act 1958, s 1(2) (p 2228). It was repealed by Divorce Reform Act 1969, s 9(2), Sch 2 and was not replaced.

2.   Restriction on petitions within three years of marriage—*(1) Subject to the next following subsection, no petition for divorce shall be presented to the court before the expiration of the period of three years from the date of the marriage (hereafter in this section referred to as 'the specified period').*

(2) A judge of the court may, on an application made to him, allow the presentation of a petition for divorce within the specified period on the ground that the case is one of exceptional hardship suffered by the petitioner or of exceptional depravity on the part of the respondent; but in determining the application the judge shall have regard to the interests of any [child of the family within the meaning of Part I of the Matrimonial Proceedings and Property Act 1970] and to the question whether there is reasonable probability of a reconciliation between the parties during the specified period.

(3) Nothing in this section shall be deemed to prohibit the presentation of a petition based upon matters which occurred before the expiration of the specified period.

Note. These three subsections replaced Matrimonial Causes Act 1950, s 2(1), (2) (p 2131) which replaced Matrimonial Causes Act 1937, s 1 (p 2095).

Words in square brackets in sub-s (2) substituted for 'relevant child' by Matrimonial Proceedings and Property Act 1970, s 35.

The whole section repealed by Matrimonial Causes Act 1973, s 54(1), Sch 3 and replaced by ibid, s 3 (p 2499).

3.   Divorce not precluded by previous judicial separation—*(1) A person shall not be prevented from presenting a petition for divorce, or the court from granting a decree of* *divorce, by reason only that the petitioner [or respondent] has at any time, on the same facts or substantially the same facts as those proved in support of the petition, been granted a decree of judicial separation or an order under, or having effect as if made under, the Matrimonial Proceedings (Magistrates' Courts) Act 1960 or any corresponding enactments in force in Northern Ireland, the Isle of Man or any of the Channel Islands.*

Note. Words in square brackets inserted by Divorce Reform Act 1969, s 9 (1), Sch 1, para 1.

(2) On a petition for divorce in such a case as is mentioned in the foregoing subsection, the court may treat the decree of judicial separation or the said order as sufficient proof of the adultery, desertion or other ground on which it was granted, but shall not grant a decree of divorce without receiving evidence from the petitioner.

(3) For the purposes of a petition for divorce in such a case, a period of desertion immediately preceding the institution of proceedings for a decree of judicial separation or for such an order as aforesaid having the effect of a decree of judicial separation shall, if the parties have not resumed cohabitation and the decree or order has been continuously in force since it was granted, be deemed immediately to precede the presentation of the petition.

Note. This section replaced Matrimonial Causes Act 1950, s 7 (p 2133). The whole section was repealed by Matrimonial Causes Act 1973, s 54(1), Sch 3 and replaced by ibid, s 4 (p 2499).

4. Alleged adulterer as a party—*(1) On a petition for divorce presented by the husband [in which adultery is alleged], or in the answer of a husband praying for divorce [and alleging adultery], the husband shall make the alleged adulterer a co-respondent unless excused by the court on special grounds from doing so.*

(2) On a petition for divorce presented by the wife [in which adultery is alleged] the court may, if it thinks fit, direct that the alleged adulteress be made a respondent.

Note. These two subsections replaced Matrimonial Causes Act 1950, s 3 (p 2132) which replaced Supreme Court of Judicature (Consolidation) Act 1925, s 177 (p 2056).

Words 'in which adultery is alleged' in sub-ss (1), (2) substituted for 'on the ground of adultery', and 'and alleging adultery' in sub-s (1) substituted for 'on that ground' by Divorce Reform Act 1969, s 9(1), Sch 1, para 2.

(3) Where an alleged adulterer is made a co-respondent on such a petition as is mentioned in subsection (1) of this section or an alleged adulteress is made a respondent on such a petition as is mentioned in the last foregoing subsection, the court may, after the close of the evidence on the part of the petitioner, direct that the co-respondent or, as the case may be, the respondent be dismissed from the suit if the court is of opinion that there is not sufficient evidence against him or her.

Note. This subsection replaced Matrimonial Causes Act 1950, s 5 (p 2132) which replaced Supreme Court of Judicature (Consolidation) Act 1925, s 179 (p 2057).

The whole section was repealed by Matrimonial Causes Act 1973, s 54(1), Sch 3.

For corresponding provisions, see Matrimonial Causes Act 1973, s 49 (p 2557).

5. Hearing of petition—*(1) On a petition for divorce it shall be the duty of the court—*

(a) to inquire, so far as it reasonably can, into the facts alleged and whether there has been any connivance or condonation on the part of the petitioner and whether any collusion exists between the parties; and

(b) to inquire into any countercharge made against the petitioner.

Note. This subsection replaced Matrimonial Causes Act 1950, s 4(1) (p 2132) which replaced in part Supreme Court of Judicature (Consolidation) Act 1925, s 178 (p 2056) as substituted by Matrimonial Causes Act 1937, s 4.

The subsection was repealed by Divorce Reform Act 1969, s 9 (2), Sch 2. See now Matrimonial Causes Act 1973, s 1(3) (p 2497), replacing Divorce Reform Act 1969, s 2(2) (p 2338).

(2) Provision may be made by rules of court for enabling the court, on application made either before or after the presentation of the petition, to take into consideration for the purposes of this section any agreement or arrangement made or proposed to be made between the parties and to give such directions in the matter as the court thinks fit; but nothing in this subsection affects any duty of the parties to disclose to the court any agreement or arrangement made between the parties in contemplation of or in connection with the proceedings.

Note. This subsection replaced Matrimonial Causes Act 1963, s 4(2), (3) (p 2236) and was repealed by Divorce Reform Act 1969, s 9(2), Sch 2. See now Matrimonial Causes Act 1973, s 7 (p 2501), replacing Divorce Reform Act 1969, s 7(1) (p 2341).

   (3) If the court is satisfied on the evidence that the case for the petition has been proved and—

   (a) where the ground of the petition is adultery, that the petitioner has not in any manner been accessory to or connived at or condoned the adultery;

   (b) where the ground of the petition is cruelty, that the petitioner has not in any manner condoned the cruelty,

the court shall, subject to subsections (4) and (5) of this section, grant a decree of divorce: and if the court is not satisfied with respect to any of the matters aforesaid, it shall dismiss the petition.

   (4) The court may dismiss a petition for divorce if—

   (a) it finds that the petition is presented or prosecuted in collusion with the respondent or either of the respondents; or

   (b) it finds that the petitioner has during the marriage been guilty of adultery; or

   (c) in its opinion the petitioner has been guilty—

      (i) of unreasonable delay in presenting or prosecuting the petition; or

      (ii) of cruelty towards the other party to the marriage; or

      (iii) where the ground of the petition is adultery or cruelty, of having without reasonable excuse either deserted or wilfully separated himself or herself from the other party before the adultery or cruelty; or

      (iv) where the ground of the petition is adultery or unsoundness of mind or desertion, of such wilful neglect or misconduct as conduced to the adultery or unsoundness of mind or desertion.

Note. Sub-ss (3), (4) replaced Matrimonial Causes Act 1950, s 4(2) (p 2132) as amended by Matrimonial Causes Act 1963, s 4(1)(a). Section 4 of the Act of 1950 replaced Supreme Court of Judicature (Consolidation) Act 1925, s 178 (p 2056), as substituted by Matrimonial Causes Act 1937, s 4. They were repealed by Divorce Reform Act 1969, s 9(2), Sch 2. For provisions corresponding to sub-s (3), see now Matrimonial Causes Act 1973, ss 1(4), 2(1), (3) (p 2498), replacing Divorce Reform Act 1969, ss 2(3), 3(3), (4) (pp 2338, 2339). Sub-s (4) was not replaced.

   (5) If it appears to the court, at the hearing of a petition for divorce presented in pursuance of leave granted under section 2(2) of this Act, that the leave was obtained by the petitioner by any misrepresentation or concealment of the nature of the case, the court may—

   (a) dismiss the petition, without prejudice to any petition which may be brought after the expiration of the period of three years from the date of the marriage upon the same facts, or substantially the same facts, as those proved in support of the dismissed petition; or

   (b) if it grants a decree, direct that no application to make the decree absolute shall be made during that period.

Note. This subsection replaced Matrimonial Causes Act 1950, s 2(1) (p 2131) which replaced Matrimonial Causes Act 1937, s 1 (p 2095) and was applied by Divorce Reform Act 1969, s 2(3) (p 2338). The subsection was repealed by Matrimonial Causes Act 1973, s 54(1), Sch 3 and replaced by ibid, s 3(3) (p 2499).

   (6) If in any proceedings for divorce the respondent [alleges against the petitioner and proves any such fact as is mentioned in section 2(1) of the Divorce Reform Act 1969], the court may give to the respondent the relief to which the respondent would have been entitled if the respondent had presented a petition seeking that relief.

Note. This subsection replaced Matrimonial Causes Act 1950, s 6 (p 2132) which replaced Supreme Court of Judicature (Consolidation) Act 1925, s 180 (p 2058).

   Words in square brackets substituted for 'opposes the relief sought on the ground of the petitioner's adultery, cruelty or desertion' by Divorce Reform Act 1969, s 9(1), Sch 1, para 3.

   The subsection was repealed by Matrimonial Causes Act 1973, s 54(1), Sch 3 and replaced by ibid, s 20 (p 2508).

   (7) Every decree of divorce shall in the first instance be a decree nisi and shall not be made absolute before the expiration of six months from its grant unless the court by general or special order from time to time fixes a shorter period.

Note. This subsection replaced Matrimonial Causes Act 1950, s 12(1) (p 2134) which replaced in part Supreme Court of Judicature (Consolidation) Act 1925, s 183 (p 2059) as added to by Matrimonial Causes Act 1937, s 9. These provisions also applied in the case of a decree of nullity: see s 10 (p 2245).

The subsection was repealed by Matrimonial Causes Act 1973, s 54(1), Sch 3 and replaced by ibid, s 1(5) (p 2498).

6. Intervention of Queen's Proctor—*(1) In the case of a petition for divorce—*

    (a)   *the court may, if it thinks fit, direct all necessary papers in the matter to be sent to Her Majesty's Proctor (hereafter in this and the next following section referred to as 'the Proctor'), who shall under the directions of the Attorney General instruct counsel to argue before the court any question in relation to the matter which the court deems it necessary or expedient to have fully argued;*

    (b)   *any person may at any time during the progress of the proceedings or before the decree nisi is made absolute give information to the Proctor on any matter material to the due decision of the case, and the Proctor may thereupon take such steps as the Attorney General considers necessary or expedient;*

    (c)   *if in consequence of any such information or otherwise the Proctor considers that any parties to the petition are or have been acting in collusion for the purpose of obtaining a decree contrary to the justice of the case, he may, under the direction of the Attorney General, and after obtaining the leave of the court, intervene and retain counsel and subpoena witnesses to prove the alleged collusion.*

Note. Para (c) was repealed by Divorce Reform Act 1969, s 9(2), Sch 2, except in so far as it was applied by ss 10, 14. Para (c) as applied by ss 10, 14 was repealed by Nullity of Marriage Act 1971, s 7(3).

    (2) Where the Proctor intervenes or shows cause against a decree nisi in any proceedings for divorce, the court may make such order as may be just as to the payment by other parties to the proceedings of the costs incurred by him in so doing or as to the payment by him of any costs incurred by any of those parties by reason of his so doing.

    (3) The Proctor shall be entitled to charge as part of the expenses of his office—

    (a)   *the costs of any proceedings under subsection (1)(a) of this section;*

    (b)   *where his reasonable costs of intervening or showing cause as mentioned in subsection (2) of this section are not fully satisfied by any order under that subsection, the amount of the difference;*

    (c)   *if the Treasury so directs, any costs which he pays to any parties under an order made under the said subsection (2).*

Note. This section replaced Matrimonial Causes Act 1950, s 11 (p 2134) which replaced Supreme Court of Judicature (Consolidation) Act 1925, s 182 (p 2058). These provisions also applied in the case of a decree nisi of nullity: see s 10 (p 2245).

The section was repealed by Matrimonial Causes Act 1973, s 54(1), Sch 3 and replaced by ibid, s 8 (p 2501).

7. Proceedings after decree nisi—*(1) Where a decree nisi of divorce has been granted but not made absolute, then, without prejudice to the last foregoing section, any person (excluding a party to the proceedings other than the Proctor) may show cause why the decree should not be made absolute either by reason of its having been obtained by collusion or by reason of material facts not having been brought before the court; and in such a case the court may—*

    (a)   *notwithstanding anything in section 5(7) of this Act, make the decree absolute; or*

    (b)   *rescind the decree nisi; or*

    (c)   *require further enquiry; or*

    (d)   *otherwise deal with the case as it thinks fit.*

Note. The words 'either by reason of its having been obtained by collusion or' were repealed by Divorce Reform Act 1969, s 9(2), Sch 2, except in so far as sub-s (1) was applied by ss 10, 14. Those words in sub-s (1) as applied by ss 10, 14 were repealed by Nullity of Marriage Act 1971, s 7(3).

(2) Where a decree nisi of divorce has been granted and no application for it to be made absolute has been made by the party to whom it was granted, then, at any time after the expiration of three months from the earliest date on which that party could have made such an application, the party against whom it was granted may make an application to the court, and on that application the court may exercise any of the powers mentioned in paragraphs (a) to (d) of the foregoing subsection.

Note. This section replaced Matrimonial Causes Act 1950, s 12(2), (3) (p 2134) which replaced in part Supreme Court of Judicature (Consolidation) Act 1925, s 183 (p 2059) as added to by Matrimonial Causes Act 1937, s 9. These provisions also applied in the case of a decree nisi of nullity: see s 10, infra.

The section was repealed by Matrimonial Causes Act 1973, s 5 (1), Sch 3 and replaced by ibid, s 9 (p 2502).

8. Remarriage of divorced persons—*(1) Where a decree has been made absolute and either—*

(a)   *there is no right of appeal against the decree absolute; or*

(b)   *the time for appealing against the decree absolute has expired without an appeal having been brought; or*

(c)   *an appeal against the decree absolute has been dismissed,*
either party to the former marriage may marry again.

Note. Sub-s (1) repealed by Matrimonial Causes Act 1973, s 54(1), Sch 3 and not replaced.

(2) No clergyman of the Church of England or the Church of Wales shall be compelled—

(a)   to solemnise the marriage of any person whose former marriage has been dissolved and whose former spouse is still living; or

(b)   to permit the marriage of such a person to be solemnised in the church or chapel of which he is the minister.

Note. This section replaced Matrimonial Causes Act 1950, s 13 (p 2135) which replaced Supreme Court of Judicature (Consolidation) Act 1925, s 184 (p 2059) as amended by Matrimonial Causes Act 1937, s 12.

Nullity

9. Additional grounds for decree of nullity—*(1) In addition to any other grounds on which a marriage is by law void or voidable, a marriage shall, subject to the next following subsection, be voidable on the ground—*

(a)   *that the marriage has not been consummated owing to the wilful refusal of the respondent to consummate it; or*

(b)   *that at the time of the marriage, either party to the marriage—*

(i)   *was of unsound mind, or*

(ii)   *was suffering from mental disorder within the meaning of the Mental Health Act 1959, of such a kind or to such an extent as to be unfitted for marriage and the procreation of children, or*

(iii)   *was subject to recurrent attacks of insanity or epilepsy; or*

(c)   *that the respondent was at the time of the marriage suffering from venereal disease in a communicable form; or*

(d)   *that the respondent was at the time of the marriage pregnant by some person other than the petitioner.*

(2) The court shall not grant a decree of nullity in a case falling within paragraph (b), (c) or (d) of the foregoing subsection unless it is satisfied that—

(a)   *the petitioner was at the time of the marriage ignorant of the facts alleged; and*

(b)   *proceedings were instituted within a year from the date of the marriage; and*

(c)   *marital intercourse with the consent of the petitioner has not taken place since the petitioner discovered the existence of the grounds for a decree.*

(3) Nothing in this section shall be construed as validating a marriage which is by law void but with respect to which a decree of nullity has not been granted.

Note. This section replaced Matrimonial Causes Act 1950, s 8 (p 2133) as amended by Mental Health Act 1959 which replaced Matrimonial Causes Act 1937, s 7(1), (3) (pp 2097, 2098).

The section was repealed by Nullity of Marriage Act 1971, s 7(3), except in relation to marriages taking place before 1 August 1971 and was re-enacted in relation to marriages before that date by Matrimonial Causes Act 1973, s 53, Sch 1, para 11 (pp 2561, 2563). For the grounds on which a marriage celebrated after 31 June 1971 is void or voidable, see now Matrimonial Causes Act 1973, ss 11, 12 (pp 2503) replacing Nullity of Marriage Act 1971, ss 1, 2 (pp 2418, 2419).

10. Application of ss 5(7), 6 and 7 to nullity proceedings. *Sections 5(7), 6 and 7 of this Act shall apply in relation to proceedings for nullity of marriage as if for any reference in those provisions to divorce there were substituted a reference to nullity of marriage.*
Note. This section was repealed by Matrimonial Causes Act 1973, s 54(1), Sch 3 and was replaced by ibid, s 15 (p 2505).

11. Legitimacy of children of annulled marriages. *Where a decree of nullity is granted in respect of a voidable marriage, any child who would have been the legitimate child of the parties to the marriage if at the date of the decree it had been dissolved instead of being annulled shall be deemed to be their legitimate child.*
Note. This section replaced Matrimonial Causes Act 1950, s 9 (p 2133) which replaced Matrimonial Causes Act 1937, s 7(2) (p 2090) as amended by Law Reform (Miscellaneous Provisions) Act 1949, s 4.

This section repealed by Matrimonial Causes Act 1973, s 54(1), Sch 3 but was re-enacted by ibid, s 53, Sch 1, para 12 (pp 2561, 2564) in respect of decrees of nullity granted before 1 August 1971. For the corresponding provision in respect of decrees granted after 31 July 1971, see Matrimonial Causes Act 1973, s 16 (p 2506), replacing Nullity of Marriage Act 1971, s 5 (p 2420).

Other matrimonial suits

12. Judicial separation—*(1) A petition for judicial separation may be presented to the court by the husband or the wife—*
  (a) on any of the grounds specified in section 1 of this Act; or
  (b) on the ground of failure to comply with a decree for restitution of conjugal rights; or
  (c) on any ground on which a decree of divorce a mensa et thoro might have been pronounced immediately before the commencement of the Matrimonial Causes Act 1857;
and sections 1 and 5(1) to (4) of this Act and paragraphs 2 and 3 of Schedule 1 to this Act shall apply in relation to such a petition as they apply in relation to a petition for divorce but as if the reference in section 5(3) to section 5(5) were omitted.

[(1) A petition for judicial separation may be presented to the court by either party to a marriage on the ground that any such fact as is mentioned in section 2(1) of the Divorce Reform Act 1969 exists, and sections 2(2), (4), (5) and (6), 3 and 7 of that Act and paragraph 2 of Schedule 1 to this Act shall, with the necessary modifications, apply in relation to such a petition as they apply in relation to a petition for divorce.]
Note. Sub-s (1) in square brackets substituted for original sub-s (1) by Divorce Reform Act 1969, s 8(2).

 (2) Where the court grants a decree of judicial separation it shall no longer be obligatory for the petitioner to cohabit with the respondent.
 (3) The court may, on an application by petition of the spouse against whom a decree of judicial separation has been made and on being satisfied that the allegations in the petition are true, rescind the decree at any time on the ground that it was obtained in the absence of the applicant or, if desertion was the ground of the decree, that there was reasonable cause for the alleged desertion.
Note. This section replaced Matrimonial Causes Act 1950, s 14 (p 2135) which replaced Supreme Court of Judicature Act 1925, s 185(1), (2) (p 2060) as amended by Matrimonial Causes Act 1937, s 5.

The section was repealed by Matrimonial Causes Act 1973, s 54 (1), Sch 3; sub-s (1) was replaced by ibid, s 17(1) (p 2506) and sub-s (2) by ibid, s 18(1) (p 2507); sub-s (3) was not replaced.

13. Restitution of conjugal rights—*(1) A petition for restitution of conjugal rights may be presented to the court by the husband or the wife; and the court, on being satisfied that—*

   (a)   the allegations contained in the petition are true; and

   (b)   there is no legal ground why a decree for restitution of conjugal rights should not be granted,

may grant the decree accordingly.

   (2)   A decree for restitution of conjugal rights shall not be enforced by imprisonment.

Note. This section replaced Matrimonial Causes Act 1950, s 15 (p 2135) which replaced part of Supreme Court of Judicature (Consolidation) Act 1925, s 187(1) (p 2061). The section was repealed by Matrimonial Proceedings and Property Act 1970, s 42(2), Sch 3. See also ibid, s 20 (p 2376) which abolished the right to claim restitution of conjugal rights.

14. Presumption of death and dissolution of marriage—*(1) Any married person who alleges that reasonable grounds exist for supposing that the other party to the marriage is dead may, subject to the next following subsection, present a petition to the court to have it presumed that the other party is dead and to have the marriage dissolved, and the court may, if satisfied that such reasonable grounds exist, make a decree of presumption of death and dissolution of the marriage.*

   (2)   A petition may be presented in pursuance of the foregoing subsection—

   (a)   in any case, if the petitioner is domiciled in England; and

   (b)   in the case of a petition presented by a wife, if she is resident in England and has been ordinarily resident there for a period of three years immediately preceding the commencement of the proceedings.

   (3)   In any proceedings under this section the fact that for a period of seven years or more the other party to the marriage has been continually absent from the petitioner and the petitioner has no reason to believe that the other party has been living within that time shall be evidence that the other party is dead until the contrary is proved.

   (4)   Sections 5(7) and 6 to 8 of this Act apply to a petition and a decree under this section as they apply to a petition for divorce and a decree of divorce respectively.

   (5)   In determining for the purposes of this section whether a woman is domiciled in England, her husband shall be treated as having died immediately after the last occasion on which she knew or had reason to believe him to be living; and in any proceedings brought in pursuance of subsection (2)(b) of this section the issues shall be determined in accordance with the law which would be applicable thereto if both parties to the marriage were domiciled in England at the time of the proceedings.

Note. This section replaced Matrimonial Causes Act 1950, s 16 (p 2136) which replaced Matrimonial Causes Act 1937, s 8 (p 2098) as amended by Law Reform (Miscellaneous Provisions) Act 1949, s 1(3).

   Section 6(1)(c) which was otherwise repealed was applied in respect of this section and as so applied was repealed by Nullity of Marriage Act 1971, s 7(3).

   Section 14 was repealed by Matrimonial Causes Act 1973, s 54(1), Sch 3 and replaced by ibid, s 19(1)–(5) (pp 2507–2508).

PART II*

ANCILLARY RELIEF

   * Jurisdiction under this Part was extended to divorce county courts by Matrimonial Causes Act 1967, s 2 (p 2273).

Interim orders for alimony

15. Interim orders for alimony.   *On a petition for divorce, nullity of marriage, judicial separation or restitution of conjugal rights, the court may make such interim orders as it thinks just for the payment of alimony—*

(a)   *in any case other than a case falling within paragraph (b) of this section, to the wife; and*

(b)   *in the case of a petition for divorce or judicial separation presented by a wife [and alleging any such fact as is mentioned in section 2(1)(e) of the Divorce Reform Act 1969 where the court is satisfied on proof of such facts as may be prescribed by rules of court that her husband is insane], to the husband.*

Note. This section replaced Matrimonial Causes Act 1950, ss 19(1), (4), 20(1), (3) and 22(1) (pp 2138, 2139).

Words in square brackets substituted for 'on the ground of her husband's insanity' by Divorce Reform Act 1969, s 9(1), Sch 1, para 4, with effect from 1 January 1971, but the whole section was simultaneously repealed by Matrimonial Proceedings and Property Act 1970, s 42(2), Sch 3, both statutes coming into operation on 1 January 1971 (some of the Act of 1970 came into force on 1 August 1970). See now Matrimonial Causes Act 1973, s 22 (p 2510), replacing s 1 of the Act of 1970 (p 2365).

Maintenance and application of property in cases of divorce

16. Maintenance orders—*(1) On granting a decree of divorce or at any time thereafter (whether before or after the decree is made absolute), the court may if it thinks fit and subject to subsection (3) of this section, make one or more of the following orders—*

(a)   *an order requiring the husband to secure to the wife, to the satisfaction of the court, such lump or annual sum for any term not exceeding her life as the court thinks reasonable having regard to her fortune (if any), his ability and the conduct of the parties;*

(b)   *an order requiring the husband to pay to the wife during their joint lives such monthly or weekly sum for her maintenance as the court thinks reasonable;*

(c)   *an order requiring the husband to pay to the wife such lump sum as the court thinks reasonable.*

Note. This subsection replaced Matrimonial Causes Act 1950, s 19(2), (3) (p 2128) which replaced Supreme Court of Judicature (Consolidation) Act 1925, s 190(1), (2) (p 2060) as amended by Matrimonial Causes (Property and Maintenance) Act 1958, s 1, Schedule. It further replaced Matrimonial Causes Act 1963, s 5(1) (p 2220). Repealed and replaced as noted to sub-s (3) below.

(2) Where the court decides to make an order under paragraph (a) of the foregoing subsection, it may—

(a)   *direct that the matter be referred to one of the conveyancing counsel of the court for him to settle a proper instrument to be executed by all necessary parties; and*

(b)   *if it thinks fit, defer the grant of the decree until the instrument has been duly executed.*

Note. This subsection replaced Matrimonial Causes Act 1950, s 19(2) (p 2138) which replaced part of Supreme Court of Judicature Act 1925, s 190(1) (p 2062). Repealed and replaced as noted to sub-s (3) below.

(3) [Where on a petition for divorce presented by a wife the court granted her a decree and held that the only fact mentioned in section 2(1) of the Divorce Reform Act 1969 on which she was entitled to rely was that mentioned in paragraph (e), then if the court is satisfied on proof of such facts as may be prescribed by rules of court that the husband is insane], subsection (1) of this section shall have effect with the substitution of references to the wife for references to the husband and of references to the husband for references to the wife.

Note. This subsection replaced Matrimonial Causes Act 1950, s 19(4) (p 2138) which replaced Matrimonial Causes Act 1937, s 10(2) (p 2099).

Words in square brackets in sub-s (3) substituted for 'Where a petition for divorce is presented by the wife on the ground of her husband's insanity' by Divorce Reform Act 1969, s 9(1), Sch 1, para. 5, with effect from 1 January 1971, but the whole section was simultaneously repealed by Matrimonial Proceedings and Property Act 1970, s 42(2), Sch 3. See now Matrimonial Causes Act 1973, ss 29, 30 (pp 2534, 2536), replacing ss 2, 25 of the Act of 1970 (pp 2365, 2378).

17. Application of settled and other property—*(1) The court may, after granting a decree of divorce—*

(a) inquire into the existence of ante-nuptial or post-nuptial settlements made on the parties whose marriage is the subject of the decree; and

(b) make such orders as the court thinks fit as respects the application, for the benefit of the children of the marriage or the parties to the marriage, of the whole or any part of the property settled;

and the court may exercise its powers under the foregoing provisions of this section notwithstanding that there are no children of the marriage.

Note. This subsection replaced Matrimonial Causes Act 1950, s 25 (p 2141) which replaced Supreme Court of Judicature (Consolidation) Act 1925, s 192 (p 2063). Repealed and replaced as noted to sub-s (2) below.

(2) [Where on a petition for divorce presented by the husband he satisfies the court of any such fact as is mentioned in section 2 (1) (a), (b) or (c) of the Divorce Reform Act 1969, and the court grants him a decree of divorce, then if it appears to the court that the wife] is entitled to any property either in possession or reversion, the court may if it thinks fit order such settlement as it thinks reasonable to be made of the property, or of any part of it, for the benefit of the [husband] and of the children of the marriage or either or any of them.

Note. This subsection replaced Matrimonial Causes Act 1950, s 24(1) (p 2140) which replaced Supreme Court of Judicature (Consolidation) Act 1925, s 191(1) (p 2063). These provisions also applied in the case of judicial separation: see s 20(2), infra.

Words in first square brackets in sub-s (2) substituted for 'Where the court grants a decree of divorce by reason of the adultery, desertion or cruelty of the wife and it appears to the court that she', and word in second square brackets substituted for 'innocent party' by Divorce Reform Act 1969, s 9(1), Sch 1, para 6, with effect from 1 January 1971, but the whole section was simultaneously repealed by Matrimonial Proceedings and Property Act 1970, s 42(2), Sch 3. See now Matrimonial Causes Act 1973, s 24 (p 2515) replacing s 4 of the Act of 1970 (p 2366).

18. Commencement of proceedings with respect to maintenance and settlements—(1) Where a petition for divorce has been presented, proceedings under the foregoing provisions of this Part of this Act may be begun, subject to and in accordance with rules of court, at any time after the presentation of the petition; but—

(a) no order under section 16 or 17 of this Act shall be made unless a decree nisi has been granted;

(b) without prejudice to the power to give directions under section 16(2)(a) of this Act, no such order and no settlement made in pursuance of such an order shall take effect unless the decree has been made absolute.

Note. This subsection replaced s 29 of the Act of 1950 (p 2142) which replaced s 10 of Matrimonial Causes Act 1937 (p 2098). Repealed and replaced as noted to sub-s (2) below.

(2) Subsection (1) of this section shall have effect notwithstanding anything in the foregoing provisions of this Part of this Act but subject to section 29 of this Act.

Note. The whole section repealed by Matrimonial Proceedings and Property Act 1970, s 42(2), Sch 3. See now Matrimonial Causes Act 1973, s 26 (p 2528), replacing s 24 of the Act of 1970 (p 2377).

Maintenance, etc. in other cases

19. Nullity. Sections 16(1) and (2) and 17(1) of this Act and, so far as it relates to those provisions, section 18 of this Act shall apply in relation to nullity of marriage as they apply in relation to divorce but as if the reference in section 16(1) to section 16(3) were omitted.

Note. Repealed by Matrimonial Proceedings and Property Act 1970, s 42(2), Sch 3. See now Matrimonial Causes Act 1973, ss 23, 24 (pp 2512, 2515), replacing ss 2, 4 of the Act of 1970 (pp 2365, 2366).

20. Judicial separation—(1) On granting a decree of judicial separation or at any time thereafter the court may make such order as it thinks just for the payment of alimony or a lump sum or both—

(a)   in any case other than a case falling within paragraph (b) of this subsection, to the wife; and

(b)   in a case where the petition was presented by the wife [and the court held that the only fact mentioned in section 2(1) of the Divorce Reform Act 1969 on which she was entitled to rely was that mentioned in paragraph (e) and the court is satisfied on proof of such facts as may be prescribed by rules of court that the husband is insane], to the husband.

Note. This subsection replaced Matrimonial Causes Act 1950, s 20(2), (3) (p 2139) which replaced in part Matrimonial Causes Act 1937, s 10(2) (p 2099). It further replaced Matrimonial Causes Act 1963, s 5(1) (p 2236).

Words in square brackets in para (b) substituted for 'on the ground of her husband's insanity' by Divorce Reform Act 1969, s 9(1), Sch 1, para 7, with effect from 1 January 1971, but the whole of sub-s (1) was simultaneously repealed by Matrimonial Proceedings and Property Act 1970, s 42(2), Sch 3. See now Matrimonial Causes Act 1973, s 23 (p 2512), replacing s 2 of the Act of 1970 (p 2365).

(2)   Section 17(2) of this Act shall apply in relation to judicial separation as it applies in relation to divorce.

Note. Repealed by Matrimonial Proceedings and Property Act 1970, s 42(2), Sch 3.

(3)   In a case of judicial separation—
(a)   any property which is acquired by or devolves upon the wife on or after the date of the decree whilst the separation continues; and
(b)   where the decree is obtained by the wife, any property to which she is entitled for an estate in remainder or reversion on the date of the decree,
shall, if she dies intestate, devolve as if her husband had then been dead.

Note. Repealed by Matrimonial Proceedings and Property Act 1970, s 42(2), Sch 3, as from 1 August 1970 (see ibid, ss 40(3), 43(2), pp 2383, 2384) except in relation to a case where the death occurred before 1 January 1971. See now Matrimonial Causes Act 1973, s 18(2) (p 2507), replacing s 40(1) of the Act of 1970 (p 2383).

(4)   If in a case of judicial separation alimony has been ordered to be paid under the foregoing provisions of this Part of this Act and has not been duly paid by the husband, he shall be liable for necessaries supplied for the use of the wife.

Note. Sub-s (4) repealed by Matrimonial Proceedings and Property Act 1970, ss 41(2), 42(2), Sch 3, and ceased to have effect from 1 August 1970 (see ibid, ss 40(3), 43(2), pp 2383, 2384). Sub-ss (2)–(4) replaced Matrimonial Causes Act 1950, s 21 (p 2139) which replaced Supreme Court of Judicature (Consolidation) Act 1925, s 194 (p 2064) as amended by Law Reform (Married Women and Tortfeasors) Act 1935, Schedule.

21. Restitution of conjugal rights—(1) Where a decree for restitution of conjugal rights is made on the application of the wife, the court may—
(a)   make such order as it thinks just for the payment of alimony to the wife;
(b)   on making the decree or at any time thereafter, order the husband to pay to the wife, if the decree is not complied with within the time specified by the court, such periodical payments as the court thinks just.
(2)   Where the court makes an order under paragraph (b) of the foregoing subsection—
(a)   the order may be enforced in the same manner as an order for alimony; and
(b)   the court may, if it thinks fit, order that the husband shall to the satisfaction of the court, secure the periodical payments to the wife, and may for that purpose give such a direction as is mentioned in section 16(2)(a) of this Act.

Note. These subsections replaced Matrimonial Causes Act 1950, s 22(2), (3) (p 2129) which replaced in part Supreme Court of Judicature (Consolidation) Act 1925, ss 187(1), 190(4) (pp 2061, 2063). Repealed as noted to sub-s (3) below.

(3)   Where a decree for restitution of conjugal rights is made on the application of the husband and it appears to the court that the wife is entitled to any property, either in possession or reversion, or is in receipt of any profits of trade or earnings, the court may—

    (a)   *order a settlement of the property or any part of it to be made to the satisfaction of the court for the benefit of the husband and of the children of the marriage or either or any of them; or*

    (b)   *order such part of the profits or earnings as the court thinks reasonable to be paid periodically by the wife to the husband for his own benefit, or to him or another person for the benefit of the children of the marriage or either or any of them.*

Note. This subsection replaced Matrimonial Causes Act 1950, s 24(2) (p 2130) which replaced Supreme Court of Judicature Act 1925, s 191(2) (p 2063) as amended by Matrimonial Causes Act 1937, s 10(3).

    The whole section was repealed by Matrimonial Proceedings and Property Act 1970, s 42(2), Sch 3. See also ibid, s 20 (p 2376) which abolished the right to claim restitution of conjugal rights.

22. Neglect to maintain—*(1) Where—*

    (a)   *a husband has been guilty of wilful neglect to provide reasonable maintenance for his wife or any child to whom this subsection applies; and*

    (b)   *the court would have jurisdiction to entertain proceedings by the wife for judicial separation, then, without prejudice to the provisions of section 35(2) of this Act, the court may on the application of the wife order the husband to make to her such periodical payments as may be just.*

    (2)   *The foregoing subsection applies to [any child of the marriage who is under twenty-one and any illegitimate child of both parties to the marriage who is under that age].*

Note. The original version of this section was Law Reform (Miscellaneous Provisions) Act 1949, s 5, when there could have been an 'infant illegitimate child of both parties to the marriage'. See also Domestic and Appellate Proceedings (Restriction of Publicity) Act 1968, s 2(1) (p 2282).

    Words in square brackets in sub-s (2) substituted for 'any infant child of the marriage in question and any infant illegitimate child of both parties to the marriage' by Family Law Reform Act 1969, s 5(3).

    The whole section was repealed and replaced as noted to sub-s (3) below.

    (3)   *Where the court makes an order under subsection (1) of this section—*

    (a)   *the order may be enforced in the same manner as an order for alimony in proceedings for judicial separation; and*

    (b)   *the court may, if it thinks fit, order that the husband shall, to the satisfaction of the court, secure the periodical payments to the wife and may for that purpose give such a direction as is mentioned in section 16(2)(a) of this Act.*

Note. This section replaced Matrimonial Causes Act 1950, s 23 (p 2140) which replaced Law Reform (Miscellaneous Provisions) Act 1949, s 5.

    The whole section was repealed by Matrimonial Proceedings and Property Act 1970, s 42(2), Sch 3. See now Matrimonial Causes Act 1973, s 27 (p 2529), replacing s 6 of the Act of 1970 (p 2367).

Maintenance agreements

23. Validity of maintenance agreements—*(1) If a maintenance agreement includes a provision purporting to restrict any right to apply to a court for an order containing financial arrangements, then—*

    (a)   *that provision shall be void; but*

    (b)   *any other financial arrangements contained in the agreement shall not thereby be rendered void or unenforceable and shall, unless they are void or unenforceable for any other reason (and subject to the next two following sections), be binding on the parties to the agreement.*

Note. This subsection together with Sch 1, paras 6, 7 (p 2267) replaced Maintenance Agreements Act 1957, s 1(2) (p 2187). Repealed and replaced as noted to sub-s (2) below.

    (2)   *In this and the next following section—*

    'maintenance agreement' means any agreement in writing made, whether before or after the

commencement of this Act, between the parties to a marriage for the purposes of their living separately, being—

    (a) *an agreement containing financial arrangements, whether made during the continuance or after the dissolution or annulment of the marriage; or*

    (b) *a separation agreement which contains no financial arrangements in a case where no other agreement in writing between the same parties contains such arrangements;*

'*financial arrangements*' *means provisions governing the rights and liabilities towards one another when living separately of the parties to a marriage (including a marriage which has been dissolved or annulled) in respect of the making or securing of payments or the disposition or use of any property, including such rights and liabilities with respect to the maintenance or education of any child, whether or not a child of the marriage; and*

'*child of the marriage*' *includes any child of both parties to the marriage, whether legitimate or not, and any child adopted by both parties to the marriage.*

Note. This subsection replaced Maintenance Agreements Act 1957, s 1(1), (p 2187).

The whole section was repealed by Matrimonial Proceedings and Property Act 1970, s 42(2), Sch 3. See now Matrimonial Causes Act 1973, s 34 (p 2543), replacing Matrimonial Proceedings and Property Act 1970, s 13 (p 2371).

24. Alteration of agreements by court during lives of parties—*(1) Where a maintenance agreement (other than an agreement made more than six months after the dissolution or annulment of the marriage) is for the time being subsisting and the parties to the agreement are for the time being both domiciled or both resident in England and on an application by either party the High Court or, subject to the next following subsection, a magistrates' court is satisfied either—*

    (a) *that by reason of a change in the circumstances in the light of which any financial arrangements contained in the agreement were made or, as the case may be, financial arrangements were omitted from it, the agreement should be altered so as to make different or as the case may be so as to contain, financial arrangements; or*

    (b) *that the agreement does not contain proper financial arrangements with respect to any child of the marriage.*

the court to which the application is made may by order make such alterations in the agreement by varying or revoking any financial arrangements contained in it or by inserting in it financial arrangements for the benefit of one of the parties to the agreement or of a child of the marriage as may appear to that court to be just having regard to all the circumstances or, as the case may be, as may appear to that court to be just in all the circumstances in order to secure that the agreement contains proper financial arrangements with respect to any child of the marriage: and the agreement shall have effect thereafter as if any alteration made by the order had been made by agreement between the parties and for valuable consideration.

Note. This subsection replaces Maintenance Agreements Act 1957, s 1(3) (p 2187). Repealed and replaced as noted to sub-s (3) below.

(2) A magistrates' court shall not entertain an application under the foregoing subsection unless both the parties to the agreement are resident in England and at least one of the parties is resident in the petty sessions area (within the meaning of the Magistrates' Courts Act 1952) for which that court acts, and shall not have power to make any order on such an application except—

    (a) *in a case where the agreement includes no provision for periodical payments by either of the parties, an order inserting provision for the making by one of the parties of periodical payments—*

        (i) *for the maintenance of the other party ...;*

        (ii) *for the maintenance of any child of the marriage . . .;*

Note. In para (i) at the place indicated by dots the words 'at a rate not exceeding seven pounds ten shillings a week', and in para (ii) at the place indicated by dots the words 'at a rate not exceeding fifty shillings a week in respect of each such child' repealed by Maintenance Orders Act 1968, s 1, Schedule.

(b)   *in a case where the agreement includes provision for the making by one of the parties of periodical payments* [*an order increasing*], *or reducing the rate of, or terminating, any of those payments.*

Note. Words in square brackets in para (b) substituted for 'at rates not exceeding those aforesaid, an order increasing to such higher rate not exceeding the appropriate rate aforesaid' by Maintenance Orders Act 1968, s 1, Schedule.

This subsection replaced Maintenance Agreements Act 1957, s 1(4), (5) (p 2188). Repealed and replaced as noted to sub-s (3) below.

(3)   For the avoidance of doubt it is hereby declared that nothing in this or the last foregoing section affects any power of the court before which any proceedings between the parties to a maintenance agreement are brought under any other enactment (including a provision of this Act) to make an order containing financial arrangements or any right of either party to apply for such an order in such proceedings.

Note. The whole section repealed by Matrimonial Proceedings and Property Act 1970, s 42(2), Sch 3. See now Matrimonial Causes Act 1973, s 35 (p 2544), replacing Matrimonial Proceedings and Property Act 1970, s 14 (p 2383).

25. Alteration of agreements by court after death of one party—*(1) Where a maintenance agreement within the meaning of section 23 of this Act provides for the continuation of payments under the agreement after the death of one of the parties and that party dies after 16 August 1957 domiciled in England, the surviving party may—*

(a)   *before the end of the period of six months from the date when representation in regard to the deceased's estate is first taken out; or*

(b)   *with the permission of the court, after the end of that period but before the administration and distribution of the estate is completed,*

apply to the High Court for any order under subsection (1) of the last foregoing section for which the surviving party might have applied immediately before the death.

[*An application under this section shall not, except with the permission of the court, be made after the end of the period of six months from the date on which representation in regard to the estate of the deceased is first taken out.*]

(2)   If a maintenance agreement is altered by the court on an application made in pursuance of the foregoing subsection, the like consequences shall ensue as if the alteration had been made immediately before the death by agreement between the parties and for valuable consideration.

Note. These two subsections replaced Maintenance Agreements Act 1957, s 2(1) (p 2188).

Paras (a), (b) of sub-s (1) repealed by Family Provision Act 1966, ss 5(3), 10(2), Sch 2, and the words in square brackets at the end of that subsection added by ibid, s 5(3).

Whole section repealed with savings for sub-ss (4), (5) as noted to sub-s (5) below.

(3)   The provisions of this section shall not render the personal representatives of the deceased liable for having distributed any part of the estate of the deceased after the expiration of the said period of six months on the ground that they ought to have taken into account the possibility that the court might permit an application by virtue of this section after that period; but this subsection shall not prejudice any power to recover any part of the estate so distributed arising by virtue of the making of an order in pursuance of this section.

(4)   In considering for the purposes of subsection (1) of this section the question when representation was first taken out, a grant limited to settled land or to trust property shall be left out of account, and a grant limited to real estate or to personal estate shall be left out of account unless a grant limited to the remainder of the estate has previously been made or is made at the same time.

(5)   For the purposes of section 162(1) of the Supreme Court of Judicature (Consolidation) Act 1925 (which relates to the direction of the court as to the persons to whom administration is to be granted) a person by whom an application is proposed to be made by virtue of this section shall be deemed to be a person interested in the deceased's estate.

Note. These three subsections replaced Maintenance Agreements Act 1957, s 2(2), (3), (4) (p 2188).

The whole section except sub-ss (4), (5) as applied by s 28(2) repealed by Matrimonial Proceedings and Property Act 1970, s 42(2), Sch 3. Sub-ss (4), (5) as applied by s 28(2) repealed by Inheritance (Provision for Family and Dependants) Act 1975, s 26, Schedule. See now Matrimonial Causes Act 1973, s 36 (p 2545), replacing Matrimonial Proceedings and Property Act 1970, s 15 (p 2373).

Maintenance from estate of deceased former spouse

26. Orders for maintenance from deceased's estate—*(1) Where after 31 December 1958 a person dies domiciled in England and is survived by a former spouse of his or hers (hereafter in this section referred to as 'the survivor') who has not remarried, the survivor may—*

(a) *before the end of the period of six months beginning with the date on which representation in regard to the estate of the deceased is first taken out; or*

(b) *with the permission of the court, after the end of that period but before the administration and distribution of the estate is completed,*

apply to the court for an order under this section on the ground that the deceased has not made reasonable provision for the survivor's maintenance after the deceased's death.

[An application under this section shall not, except with the permission of the court, be made after the end of the period of six months from the date on which representation in regard to the estate of the deceased is first taken out.]

Note. Paras (a), (b) of sub-s (1) repealed by Family Provision Act 1966, ss 5(3), 10(2), Sch 2, and the words in square brackets at the end of that subsection added by ibid, s 5(3).

(2) If on an application under this section the court is satisfied—

(a) *that it would have been reasonable for the deceased to make provision for the survivor's maintenance; and*

(b) *that the deceased has made no provision, or has not made reasonable provision, for the survivor's maintenance,*

the court may order that such reasonable provision for the survivor's maintenance as the court thinks fit shall be made out of the net estate of the deceased, subject to such conditions or restrictions (if any) as the court may impose.

(3) Where the court makes an order under this section requiring provision to be made for the maintenance of the survivor, the order shall require that provision to be made by way of periodical payments terminating not later than the survivor's death and, if the survivor remarries, not later than the remarriage, so however that [if the court sees fit] the order may require that provision to be made wholly or in part by way of a lump sum payment.

Note. Words in square brackets in sub-s (3) substituted for 'if the value of the net estate of the deceased does not exceed five thousand pounds' by Family Provision Act 1966, s 4.

(4) On an application under this section the court shall have regard—

(a) *to the past, present or future capital of the survivor and to any income of the survivor from any source;*

(b) *to the survivor's conduct in relation to the deceased and otherwise;*

(c) *to any application made or deemed to be made by the survivor during the lifetime of the deceased—*

(i) *where the survivor is a former wife of the deceased, of such an order as is mentioned in section 16(1) of this Act or that subsection as applied by section 19 of this Act;*

(ii) *where the survivor is a former husband of the deceased, for such an order as could be made either under the said section 16(1) as applied by subsection (3) of that section or under section 17(2) of this Act;*

[(iii) *where the survivor is a former wife or a former husband of the deceased, for an order under section 2 or 4 of the Matrimonial Proceedings and Property Act 1970,]*

[(iii) *where the survivor is a former wife or a former husband of the deceased, for an order under section 2 or 4 of the Matrimonial Proceedings and Property Act 1970 or under section 23(1)(a), (b) or (c) or 24 of the Matrimonial Causes Act 1973]*

and to the order (if any) made on any such application, of (if no such application was made by the survivor, or such an application was made by the survivor and no order was made on the application) to the circumstances appearing to the court to be the reasons why no such application was made, or no such order was made, as the case may be; and

Note. Sub-para (iii) where first appearing inserted by Matrimonial Proceedings and Property Act 1970, s 42(1), Sch 2, para 1(1); new sub-para (iii) substituted by Matrimonial Causes Act 1973, s 54(1), Sch 2, para 5.

> (d)   *to any matter or thing which, in the circumstances of the case, the court may consider relevant or material in relation to the survivor, to persons interested in the estate of the deceased, or otherwise.*
>
> *(5) In determining whether, and in what way, and as from what date, provision for mainte-nance ought to be made by an order under this section, the court shall have regard to the nature of the property representing the net estate of the deceased and shall not order any such provision to be made as would necessitate a realisation that would be imprudent having regard to the interests of the dependants of the deceased, of the survivor, and of the persons who apart from the order would be entitled to that property.*
>
> *[(5A) For the avoidance of doubt it is hereby declared that references in this section to remar-riage include references to a marriage which is by law void and voidable.]*

Note. Sub-s (5A) inserted by Matrimonial Proceedings and Property Act 1970, s 36.

> *(6) In this and [the three next following sections]—*
>
> *['court' [means the High Court and] includes a county court in relation to cases in which a county court has jurisdiction];*
>
> *'former spouse', in relation to a deceased person, means a person whose marriage with the deceased was during the deceased's lifetime dissolved or annulled by a decree made or deemed to be made under [the Matrimonial Causes Act 1973] and 'former wife' and 'for-mer husband' shall be construed accordingly;*
>
> *'net estate' and 'dependant' have the same meaning as in the Inheritance (Family Provision) Act 1938 [as amended by the Family Provision Act 1966] [and the Family Law Reform Act 1969] [the Family Law Reform Act 1969 and the Law Reform (Miscellaneous Provisions) Act 1970]; and*
>
> *'property' means any real or personal property, any estate or interest in real or personal prop-erty, any money, any negotiable instrument, debt or other chose in action, or any other right or interest whether in possession or not.*

Note. Words in the first square brackets in sub-s (6) substituted for 'the next following section' by Family Provision Act 1966, s 6(2).

Definition of 'court' inserted by Family Provision Act 1966, s 7(4) and words 'means the High Court and' inserted by Divorce Reform Act 1969, s 9 (1), Sch 1, para 8; those words con-tinued to have effect notwithstanding the repeal of Divorce Reform Act 1969 by Matrimonial Causes Act 1973: see Act of 1973, s 54(1), Sch 2, para 5(1)(b) (pp 2561, 2568).

Words in square brackets in definition 'former spouse' substituted for 'this Act' by Matrimonial Causes Act 1973, s 54 (1), Sch 2, para 5(1)(c).

Words in the first square brackets in definition of 'net estate' and 'dependant' inserted by Family Provision Act 1966, s 8(2), and words in the second square brackets inserted by Family Law Reform Act 1969, s 18 (2), and replaced by the words in the last square brackets by Law Reform (Miscellaneous Provisions) Act 1970, s 6(5) (p 2362).

This section replaced Matrimonial Causes (Property and Maintenance) Act 1958, s 3 (p 2199).

The section extended by Family Provision Act 1966, s 7.

The whole section repealed by Inheritance (Provision for Family and Dependants) Act 1975, s 26, Schedule.

27. Discharge and variation of orders under s 26—*(1) Subject to the following pro-visions of this section, where an order (in this section referred to as 'the original order') has been made under the last foregoing section, the court, on an application under this section, shall have power by order to discharge or vary the original order or to suspend any provision of it tem-porarily and to revive the operation of any provision so suspended.*

> *(2) An application under this section may be made by any of the following persons, that is to say,—*
>
> *(a)   the former spouse on whose application the original order was made;*
>
> *(b)   any other former spouse of the deceased;*

(c)   any dependant of the deceased;

(d)   the trustees of any relevant property;

(e)   any person who, under the will or codicil of the deceased or under the law relating to intestacy, is beneficially interested in any relevant property.

(3) An order under this section varying the original order, or reviving any suspended provision of it, shall not be made so as to affect any property which, at the time of the application for the order under this section is not relevant property.

(4) In exercising the powers conferred by this section, the court shall have regard to all the circumstances of the case, including any change in the circumstances to which the court was required to have regard in determining the application for the original order.

(5) In this section 'relevant property' means property the income of which, in accordance with the original order or any consequential directions given by the court in connection with it, is applicable wholly or in part for the maintenance of the former spouse on whose application the original order was made.

Note. This section replaced Matrimonial Causes (Property and Maintenance) Act 1958, s 4 (p 2200). The whole section repealed by Inheritance (Provision for Family and Dependants) Act 1975, s 26, Schedule.

28. Additional provisions as to orders under ss 26 and 27—*(1) The provisions of the last two foregoing sections shall not render the personal representatives of a deceased person liable for having distributed any part of the estate of the deceased after the end of the period mentioned in subsection (1) of section 26 of this Act on the ground that they ought to have taken into account the possibility that the court might permit an application under that section after the end of that period, or that an order under that section might be varied under section 27 of this Act; but this subsection shall not prejudice any power to recover any part of the estate so distributed arising by virtue of the making of an order under section 26 or section 27 of this Act.*

(2) Section 25(4) of this Act shall apply for the purposes of section 26(1) of this Act as it applies for the purposes of subsection (1) of the said section 25; and section 25(5) of this Act shall apply in relation to an application under section 26 or section 27 of this Act as it applies in relation to an application in pursuance of the said section 25.

(3) Section 3 of the Inheritance (Family Provision) Act 1938 [as amended by the Family Provision Act 1966] (which relates to the effect and form of orders under that Act) shall have effect in relation to orders under sections 26 and 27 of this Act as it has effect in relation to orders under that Act.

Note. This section replaced Matrimonial Causes (Property and Maintenance) Act 1958, s 6 (p 2201).

Words in square brackets in sub-s (3) added by Family Provision Act 1966, s 3(2).

The whole section repealed by Inheritance (Provision for Family and Dependants) Act 1975, s 26, Schedule.

[28A. Interim orders—*(1) Where on an application for maintenance under section 26 of this Act it appears to the court—*

(a)   *that the applicant is in immediate need of financial assistance, but it is not yet possible to determine what order (if any) should be made on the application for the provision of maintenance for the applicant; and*

(b)   *that property forming part of the net estate of the deceased is or can be made available to meet the need of the applicant;*

the court may order that, subject to such conditions or restrictions, if any, as the court may impose and to any further order of the court, there shall be paid to or for the benefit of the applicant out of the deceased's net estate such sum or sums and (if more than one) at such intervals as the court thinks reasonable.

(2) In determining what order, if any, should be made under this section the court shall, so far as the urgency of the case admits, take account of the same considerations as would be relevant in determining what order should be made on the application for the provision of maintenance for the applicant; and any subsequent order for the provision of maintenance may provide that sums paid to or for the benefit of the applicant by virtue of this section shall be treated to

such extent, if any, and in such manner as may be provided by that order as having been paid on account of the maintenance provided for by that order.

(3) Subject to subsection (2) above, section 3 of the Inheritance (Family Provision) Act 1938 as applied by section 28 of this Act shall apply in relation to an order under this section as it applies in relation to an order providing for maintenance.

(4) Where the deceased's personal representative pays any sum directed by an order under this section to be paid out of the deceased's net estate, he shall not be under any liability by reason of that estate not being sufficient to make the payment, unless at the time of making the payment he has reasonable cause to believe that the estate is not sufficient.]

Note. Section added by Family Provision Act 1966, s 6(2), and repealed by Inheritance (Provision for Family and Dependants) Act 1975, s 26, Schedule.

Supplemental

29. Applications for ancillary relief—*(1) Rules of court may provide, in such cases as may be prescribed by the rules,—*

(a)   *that all applications for ancillary relief shall be made in the petition or answer; or*

(b)   *that applications for ancillary relief which are not so made shall be made only with the leave of the court.*

Note. This subsection replaced s 5(2) of the Matrimonial Causes Act 1963 (p 2236). Repealed as noted to sub-s (2) below.

(2) In the foregoing subsection 'ancillary relief' means relief under any of the following provisions of this Act, that is to say, section 15, section 16 (1), that subsection as applied by section 16 (3) and by section 19, section 20 (1), and section 21 (1) and (2).

Note. This subsection replaced Matrimonial Causes Act 1963, s 5(4) (p 2236).

The whole section repealed by Matrimonial Proceedings and Property Act 1970, s 42(2), Sch 3. See now Matrimonial Causes Act 1973, s 26(2) (p 2528), replacing Matrimonial Proceedings and Property Act 1970, s 24(2) (p 2378).

30. Payment of alimony or maintenance to trustees, etc—*(1) Where the court makes an order for alimony, it may—*

(a)   *direct the alimony to be paid either to the wife or husband, as the case may be, or to a trustee approved by the court on her or his behalf; and*

(b)   *impose such terms or restrictions as the court thinks expedient; and*

(c)   *from time to time appoint a new trustee if for any reason it appears to the court expedient to do so.*

(2) *Where—*

(a)   *a petition for divorce or judicial separation is presented by a wife [and the court is satisfied on proof of such facts as may be prescribed by rules of court that her husband is insane]; or*

[(aa)   *a petition for divorce or judicial separation is presented by a husband and the court is satisfied on proof of such facts as may be prescribed by rules of court that his wife is insane; or]*

(b)   *a petition for . . . nullity . . . is presented by a husband on the ground of his wife's insanity or mental deficiency or disorder,*

and the court orders payments, other than a lump sum payment, in favour of the respondent under section 15, section 16(1), that subsection as applied by section 16(3) or by section 19, or under section 20(1) of this Act, the court may order the payments to be made to such persons having charge of the respondent as the court may direct.

Note. This section replaced Matrimonial Causes Act 1950, s 27 (p 2141) which replaced Supreme Court of Judicature (Consolidation) Act 1925, s 190(5) (p 2063) as amended by Matrimonial Causes Act 1937, s 10(2), and by Mental Health Act 1959, Sch 7.

Words in square brackets in sub-s (2) (a) substituted for 'on the ground of her husband's insanity' and sub-s (1)(aa) added by Divorce Reform Act 1969, s 9(1), Sch 1, para 9, and at the first place indicated by dots the word 'divorce' and at the second place indicated by dots the words 'or judicial separation' repealed by ibid, s 9(1), (2), Sch 1, para 9, Sch 2, all with effect from 1 January 1971, but the whole section simultaneously repealed by Matrimonial Proceedings and Property Act 1970, s 42(2), Sch 3. See now Matrimonial Causes Act 1973, s 40 (p 2549), replacing Matrimonial Proceedings and Property Act 1970, s 26 (p 2378).

31. Variation and discharge of certain orders for relief—*(1) Where the court has made an order under section 21(3) or section 22 or any of the provisions mentioned in section 29(2) of this Act (other than an order for the payment of a lump sum), the court shall have power to discharge or vary the order or to suspend any provision thereof temporarily and to revive the operation of any provision so suspended.*

(2) The powers exercisable by the court under this section in relation to an order shall be exercisable also in relation to any instrument executed in pursuance of the order.

(3) In exercising the powers conferred by this section the court shall have regard to all the circumstances of the case, including any increase or decrease in the means of either of the parties to the marriage.

Note. This section, together with Sch 1, para 9, replaced Matrimonial Causes Act 1950, s 28 (p 2142) which replaced Administration of Justice (Provisions) Act 1938, s 14, as amended by Law Reform (Miscellaneous Provisions) Act 1949, s 6.

The whole section repealed by Matrimonial Proceedings and Property Act 1970, s 42(2), Sch 3. See now Matrimonial Causes Act 1973, s 31 (p 2536), replacing Matrimonial Proceedings and Property Act 1970, s 9 (p 2370).

32. Avoidance of transactions intended to prevent relief—*(1) Where proceedings for relief under any of the relevant provisions of this Act (hereafter in this section referred to as 'financial relief') are brought by a person against his or her spouse or former spouse (hereafter in this section referred to as 'the other party'), the court may, on an application by that person—*

(a) *if it is satisfied that the other party is, with the intention of defeating the claim for financial relief, about to make any disposition or to transfer out of the jurisdiction or otherwise deal with any property, make such order as it thinks fit for restraining the other party from so doing or otherwise for protecting the claim;*

(b) *if it is satisfied that the other party has, with the intention aforesaid, made a disposition to which this paragraph applies and that if the disposition were set aside financial relief or different financial relief would be granted to the applicant, make an order setting aside the disposition and give such consequential directions as it thinks fit for giving effect to the order (including directions requiring the making of any payment or the disposal of any property);*

(c) *if it is satisfied, in a case where an order under the relevant provisions of this Act has been obtained by the applicant against the other party, that the other party has, with the intention aforesaid, made a disposition to which this paragraph applies, make such an order and give such directions as are mentioned in the last foregoing paragraph.*

and an application for the purposes of paragraph (b) of this subsection shall be made in the proceedings for the financial relief in question.

(2) Paragraphs (b) and (c) of the foregoing subsection apply respectively to a disposition made by the other party (whether before or after the commencement of the proceedings for financial relief) within the period of three years ending with the date of the application made for the purposes of the paragraph in question, not being a disposition made for valuable consideration (other than marriage) to a person who, at the time of the disposition, acted in relation to it in good faith and without notice of any such intention as aforesaid on the part of the other party.

(3) Where an application is made under this section with respect to a disposition or other transaction and the court is satisfied—

(a) *in a case falling within subsection (1)(a) or (b) of this section, that the disposition or other transaction would (apart from this section) have the consequence, or*

(b) *in a case falling within subsection (1)(c) of this section, that the disposition has had the consequence,*

of defeating the applicant's claim for financial relief, the disposition shall be presumed, unless the contrary is shown, to have been made by the other party with the intention aforesaid.

(4) In this section—

'disposition' does not include any provision contained in a will or codicil but, with that

exception, includes any conveyance, assurance or gift of property of any description, whether made by an instrument or otherwise;
'property' has the same meaning as in section 26 of this Act; and
'the relevant provisions of this Act' means any of the provisions of the following enactments, that is to say, sections 16, 17(2), 20(1), 21 and 22 of this Act and section 16(1) as applied by section 19 and section 17(2) as applied by section 20(2) of this Act;
and any reference to defeating an applicant's claim for financial relief is a reference to preventing financial relief from being granted to the applicant or reducing the amount of any financial relief which might be so granted, or frustrating or impeding the enforcement of any order which might be made at the instance of the applicant under the relevant provisions of this Act.

Note. This section replaced Matrimonial Causes (Property and Maintenance) Act 1958, ss 2, 5(1), (2) (pp 2224, 2226) and further replaced Matrimonial Causes Act 1963, s 6 (p 2220).

The whole section repealed by Matrimonial Proceedings and Property Act 1970, s 42(2), Sch 3. See now Matrimonial Causes Act 1973, s 37 (p 2546), replacing Matrimonial Proceedings and Property Act 1970, s 16 (p 2374).

PART III*

PROTECTION OF CHILDREN
* Jurisdiction under this Part was extended to divorce county courts by Matrimonial Causes Act 1967, s 2 (p 2273).

33. Restrictions on decrees for dissolution or separation affecting children—
(1) Notwithstanding anything in Part I of this Act but subject to the following subsection, the court shall not make absolute a decree of divorce or nullity of marriage in any proceedings begun after 31 December 1958, or make a decree of judicial separation in any such proceedings, unless it is satisfied as respects every relevant child who is under sixteen that—

(a) *arrangements for his care and upbringing have been made and are satisfactory or are the best that can be devised in the circumstances; or*

(b) *it is impracticable for the party or parties appearing before the court to make any such arrangements.*

(2) The court may if it thinks fit proceed without observing the requirements of the foregoing subsection if—

(a) *it appears that there are circumstances making it desirable that the decree should be made absolute or should be made, as the case may be, without delay; and*

(b) *the court has obtained a satisfactory undertaking from either or both of the parties to bring the question of the arrangements for the children before the court within a specified time.*

Note. This section replaced Matrimonial Proceedings (Children) Act 1958, ss 1(1), (6), 2(1), (2), (4) (pp 2223, 2224).

The whole section repealed by Matrimonial Proceedings and Property Act 1970, s 42(2), Sch 3. See now Matrimonial Causes Act 1973, s 41 (p 2550), replacing Matrimonial Proceedings and Property Act 1970, s 17 (p 2375).

34. Custody and maintenance of children affected by matrimonial suits—*(1)*
Subject to subsection (6) of this section, the court may make such order as it thinks just for the custody, maintenance and education of any relevant child—

(a) *in any proceedings for divorce, nullity of marriage or judicial separation, before, by or after the final decree;*

(b) *where such proceedings are dismissed after the beginning of the trial, either forthwith or within a reasonable period after the dismissal;*

(c) *in any proceedings for restitution of conjugal rights, before the decree or, if the respondent fails to comply with the decree, after the decree;*

and in any case in which the court has power by virtue of paragraph (a) of this subsection to make an order in respect of a child it may instead, if it thinks fit, direct that proper proceedings be taken for placing the child under the protection of the court.

Note. This subsection replaced Matrimonial Causes Act 1950, s 26(1) (p 2141) which replaced Supreme Court of Judicature (Consolidation) Act 1925, s 193 (p 2064) as amended by

Matrimonial Causes Act 1937, s 10(4). The subsection further replaced Matrimonial Proceedings (Children) Act 1958, ss 1(1), (3), 3(1) (pp 2223, 2225). Repealed and replaced as noted to sub-s (7) below.

(2) Where the court makes or makes absolute a decree of divorce or makes a decree of judicial separation, it may include in the decree a declaration that the parent by reason of whose misconduct the decree is made is unfit to have the custody of the children of the marriage; and the parent to whom the declaration relates shall not, on the death of the other parent, be entitled as of right to the custody or the guardianship of the children of the marriage.

Note. This subsection replaced Guardianship of Infants Act 1886, s 7. Repealed and replaced as noted to sub-s (7) below.

(3) Subject to subsection (6) of this section, on granting a decree of divorce or nullity of marriage or at any time thereafter (whether before or after the decree is made absolute) the court may make an order—

(a) in any case, requiring the husband; and

(b) in the case of a decree of divorce made [in favour of a wife where the court held that the only fact mentioned in section 2(1) of the Divorce Reform Act 1969 on which she was entitled to rely was that mentioned in paragraph (e) and the court is satisfied on proof of such facts as may be prescribed by rules of court that the husband is insane], requiring the wife,

to secure for the benefit of the relevant children such lump or annual sum as the court thinks reasonable, and may for that purpose give such a direction as is mentioned in section 16(2)(a) of this Act; but the term for which any sum is secured for the benefit of a child in pursuance of this subsection shall not extend beyond the date when the child will become twenty-one.

Note. This subsection replaced Matrimonial Causes Act 1950, s 26(3) (p 2141) which replaced Supreme Court of Judicature (Consolidation) Act 1925, s 193 (p 2064) as amended by Matrimonial Causes Act 1937, s 10(4).

Words in square brackets in sub-s (3)(b) substituted for 'on the ground of the husband's insanity' by Divorce Reform Act 1969, s 9(1), Sch 1, para 10, with effect from 1 January 1971, but the whole section was simultaneously repealed and replaced as noted to sub-s (7) below.

(4) In considering whether any and what order shall be made under this section for requiring any party to make any payment, by virtue of paragraph (b) in section 46(2) of this Act, towards the maintenance or education of a child who is not his own, the court shall have regard—

(a) to the extent (if any) to which that party had, on or after the acceptance of the child as one of the family, assumed responsibility for the children's maintenance; and

(b) to the liability of any person other than a party to the marriage to maintain the child.

Note. This subsection replaced Matrimonial Causes Act 1950, s 26(1) (p 2141) and further replaced Matrimonial Proceedings (Children) Act 1958, s 1(2) (p 2223). Repealed and replaced as noted to sub-s (7) below.

(5) While the court has power to make an order in any proceedings by virtue of paragraph (a) or (c) of subsection (1) of this section, it may exercise that power from time to time; and where the court makes an order by virtue of paragraph (b) of that subsection with respect to a child it may from time to time make a further order with respect to his custody, maintenance and education.

Note. This subsection replaced Matrimonial Proceedings (Children) Act 1958, s 3(2) (p 2225). Repealed and replaced as noted to sub-s (7) below.

(6) Section 18 of this Act (including that section as applied by section 19 of this Act) shall apply to proceedings and orders under subsection (3) of this section as it applies to such proceedings and orders as are mentioned in the said section 18; and section 29(1) of this Act shall apply to relief under subsections (1) and (3) of this section (other than relief under subsection (1)(b)) as it applies to ancillary relief within the meaning of the said section 29.

(7) Section 32 of this Act shall apply to relief under this section as if for references in that section to the relevant provisions of this Act there were substituted references to this section.

Note. The whole section was repealed by Matrimonial Proceedings and Property Act 1970, s 42(2), Sch 3. See now Matrimonial Causes Act 1973, ss 23, 42 and the notes thereto (pp 2512, 2551), replacing Matrimonial Proceedings and Property Act 1970, ss 3, 18 (pp 2365, 2375).

35. Custody, etc. of children in cases of neglect—*(1) Where the court makes an order under section 22(1) of this Act, the court shall also have jurisdiction from time to time to make such order as appears just with respect to the custody of any child to whom that subsection applies [who is under eighteen]; but the jurisdiction conferred by this subsection and any order made in exercise of that jurisdiction shall have effect only as respects any period when an order is in force under that subsection [and the child is under that age].*
Note. This sub-s together with sub-s (4), replaced Matrimonial Proceedings (Children) Act 1958, s 4(1) (p 2225). Words in square brackets inserted by Family Law Reform Act 1969, s 5(3), and the whole subsection repealed and replaced as noted to sub-s (4) below.

(2) In any case where the court would have power, on an application made under the said section 22(1), to order the husband to make to the wife periodical payments for the maintenance of a child to whom that subsection applies, the court may, if it thinks fit, order those payments to be made to the child, or to any other person for the benefit of the child, instead of to the wife; and the reference to the wife in subsection (3) of that section shall be construed accordingly.
Note. This subsection replaced Matrimonial Proceedings (Children) Act 1958, s 4(2) (p 2225). Repealed and replaced as noted to sub-s (4) below.

(3) Section 32 of this Act shall apply to relief under this section as if for references in that section to the relevant provisions of this Act there were substituted references to this section.
(4) Without prejudice to any power to include, in any order under this Act for the custody, maintenance and education of a child, provision for access to him, the reference to custody of a child in subsection (1) of this section includes a reference to access to the child.
Note. These subsections replaced Matrimonial Proceedings (Children) Act 1958, s 4(1) (p 2225).
   The whole section repealed by Matrimonial Proceedings and Property Act 1970, s 42(2), Sch 3. See now Matrimonial Causes Act 1973, s 42 and the notes thereto (p 2551), replacing Matrimonial Proceedings and Property Act 1970, s 19 (p 2376).

36. Power to commit children to care of local authority—*(1) Where the court has jurisdiction by virtue of this Part of this Act [or of the Matrimonial Proceedings and Property Act 1970] to make an order for the custody of a child and it appears to the court that there are exceptional circumstances making it impracticable or undesirable for the child to be entrusted to either of the parties to the marriage or to any other individual, the court may if it thinks fit make an order committing the care of the child to the council of a county, county borough or London borough or the Common Council of the City of London (hereafter in this section referred to as 'the local authority'); and thereupon Part II of the Children Act 1948 (which relates to the treatment of children in the care of a local authority) shall, subject to the provisions of this section, apply as if the child had been received by the local authority into their care under section 1 of that Act.*
Note. Words in square brackets inserted by Matrimonial Proceedings and Property Act 1970, s 42(1), Sch 2, para 1(2).

(2) The authority specified in an order under this section shall be the local authority for the area in which the child was, in the opinion of the court, resident before the order was made to commit the child to the care of a local authority, and the court shall before making an order under this section hear any representations from the local authority, including any representations as to the making of an order for payments for the maintenance and education of the child.
(3) While an order made by virtue of this section is in force with respect to a child, the child shall continue in the care of the local authority notwithstanding any claim by a parent or other person.
(4) An order made by virtue of this section shall cease to have effect as respects any child when he becomes eighteen, and the court shall not make an order committing a child to the care of a local authority under this section after he has become seventeen.

(5) *In the application of Part II of the Children Act 1948 by virtue of this section—*

(a) *the exercise by the local authority of their powers under sections 12 to 16 of that Act (which among other things relate to the accommodation and welfare of a child in the care of a local authority) shall be subject to any directions given by the court; and*

(b) *section 17 of that Act (which relates to arrangements for the emigration of such a child) shall not apply.*

Note. These five subsections replaced Matrimonial Proceedings (Children) Act 1958, s 5(1)–(5) (p 2226). Part II of Children Act 1948 repealed by Child Care Act 1980, s 89(3), Sch 6.

(6) *It shall be the duty of any parent or guardian of a child committed to the care of a local authority under this section to secure that the local authority are informed of his address for the time being, and a person who knowingly fails to comply with this subsection shall be liable on summary conviction to a fine not exceeding [ten pounds].*

Note. Words in square brackets substituted for 'five pounds' by Criminal Justice Act 1967, s 92, Sch 3, Part I.

(7) *The court shall have power from time to time by an order under this section to vary or discharge any provision made in pursuance of this section.*

Note. These two subsections replaced Matrimonial Proceedings (Children) Act 1958, s 5(7), (8) (p 2226). See also Family Law Reform Act 1969, s 7(3) (p 2306).

Section 36 repealed by Matrimonial Causes Act 1973, s 54(1), Sch 3 and replaced by ibid, s 43 (p 2552).

37. Power to provide for supervision of children—*(1) Where the court has jurisdiction by virtue of this Part of this Act [or of the Matrimonial Proceedings and Property Act 1970] to make an order for the custody of a child and it appears to the court that there are exceptional circumstances making it desirable that the child should be under the supervision of an independent person, the court may, as respects any period during which the child is, in exercise of that jurisdiction, committed to the custody of any person, order that the child be under the supervision of an officer appointed under this section as a welfare officer or under the supervision of a local authority.*

Note. Words in square brackets inserted by Matrimonial Proceedings and Property Act 1970, s 42(1), Sch 2, para 1(2).

(2) *Where the court makes an order under this section for supervision by a welfare officer, the officer responsible for carrying out the order shall be such probation officer as may be selected under arrangements made by the Secretary of State; and where the order is for supervision by a local authority, that authority shall be the council of a county, county borough, or London borough selected by the court and specified in the order or, if the Common Council of the City of London is so selected and specified, that Council.*

(3) *This section shall be included among the enactments specified in subsection (1) of section 39 of the Children Act 1948 (which lists the functions which are matters for the children's committee of a local authority), and a local authority shall discharge the duties conferred on them by an order under this section through an officer employed in connection with those functions.*

Note. Subsection (3) repealed by Local Authority Social Services Act 1970, s 14, Sch 3. Children Act 1948, s 39(1) repealed by Child Care Act 1980, s 89(3), Sch 6. See also Family Law Reform Act 1969, s 7(4) (p 2306).

(4) *The court shall not have power to make an order under this section as respects a child who in pursuance of an order under the last foregoing section is in the care of a local authority.*

(5) *Where a child is under the supervision of any person in pursuance of this section the jurisdiction possessed by a court to vary any order made with respect to the child's custody, maintenance or education under this Part of this Act [or under the Matrimonial Proceedings and Property Act 1970] shall, subject to any rules of court, be exercisable at the instance of that court itself.*

Note. Words in square brackets inserted by Matrimonial Proceedings and Property Act 1970, s 42(1), Sch 2, para 1(3).

(6) The court shall have power from time to time by an order under this section to vary or discharge any provision made in pursuance of this section.

Note. This section replaced Matrimonial Proceedings (Children) Act 1958, s 6 (p 2226). The whole section, so far as unrepealed, repealed by Matrimonial Causes Act 1973, s 54(1), Sch 3 and replaced by ibid, s 44 (p 2553).

38. Application of Maintenance Orders Acts to orders under Part III—*(1) Without prejudice to the operation of section 38(1) of the Interpretation Act 1889 (which provides for references to enactments which are repealed and re-enacted to be construed as references to those enactments as re-enacted), any order for maintenance or other payments made by virtue of this Part of this Act or any corresponding enactment of the Parliament of Northern Ireland shall be included among the orders to which section 16 of the Maintenance Orders Act 1950 applies (which section specifies the orders enforceable under Part II of that Act); and any order for maintenance or other payments made by virtue of this Part of this Act shall be a maintenance order within the meaning of the Maintenance Orders Act 1968.*

Note. Interpretation Act 1889, s 38(1) repealed by Interpretation Act 1978, s 25, Sch 3, and replaced by ss 16(1), 17(a) of, and Sch 2, para 3 to, that Act. This subsection replaced Matrimonial Proceedings (Children) Act 1958, s 17 (p 2227).

The words 'and any order for maintenance' to the end of the subsection repealed by Administration of Justice Act 1970, s 54, Sch 11.

(2) This section, so far as it affects Part II of the Maintenance Orders Act 1950, shall extend to Scotland and Northern Ireland.

Note. Section 38 repealed by Matrimonial Causes Act 1973, s 54(1), Sch 3.

PART IV

MISCELLANEOUS AND GENERAL

Miscellaneous

39. Declarations of legitimacy, etc—*(1) Any person who is a British subject, or whose right to be deemed a British subject depends wholly or in part on his legitimacy or on the validity of any marriage, may, if he is domiciled in England or Northern Ireland or claims any real or personal estate situate in England, apply by petition to the court for a decree declaring that he is the legitimate child of his parents, or that the marriage of his father and mother or of his grandfather and grandmother was a valid marriage or that his own marriage was a valid marriage.*

(2) Any person claiming that he or his parent or any remoter ancestor became or has become a legitimated person may apply by petition to the court, or may apply to a county court in the manner prescribed by county court rules, for a decree declaring that he or his parent or remoter ancestor, as the case may be, became or has become a legitimated person.

In this subsection 'legitimated person' means a person legitimated by the Legitimacy Act 1926, and includes a person recognised under section 8 of that Act as legitimated.

(3) Where an application under the last foregoing subsection is made to a county court, the county court, if it considers that the case is one which owing to the value of the property involved or otherwise ought to be dealt with by the High Court, may, and if so ordered by the High Court shall, transfer the matter to the High Court; and on such a transfer the proceeding shall be continued in the High Court as if it had been originally commenced by petition to the court.

(4) Any person who is domiciled in England or Northern Ireland or claims any real or personal estate situate in England may apply to the court for a decree declaring his right to be deemed a British subject.

(5) Applications to the court (but not to a county court) under the foregoing provisions of this section may be included in the same petition, and on any application under the foregoing provisions of this section (including an application to a county court) the court or the county court shall make such decree as it thinks just, and the decree shall be binding on Her Majesty and all other persons whatsoever, so however that the decree shall not prejudice any person—

(a)   if it is subsequently proved to have been obtained by fraud or collusion; or

(b)   unless that person has been given notice of the application in the manner prescribed by rules of court or made a party to the proceedings or claims through a person so given notice or made a party.

(6)   A copy of every application under this section and of any affidavit accompanying it shall be delivered to the Attorney-General at least one month before the application is made, and the Attorney-General shall be a respondent on the hearing of the application and on any subsequent proceedings relating thereto.

(7)   Where any application is made under this section, such persons as the court or county court thinks fit shall, subject to rules of court, be given notice of the application in the manner prescribed by rules of court, and any such persons may be permitted to become parties to the proceedings and to oppose the application.

(8)   No proceedings under this section shall affect any final judgment or decree already pronounced or made by any court of competent jurisdiction.

[(9)   The court (including a county court) by which any proceedings under this section are heard may direct that the whole or any part of the proceedings shall be heard in camera, and an application for a direction under this subsection shall be heard in camera unless the court otherwise directs.]

Note. This section replaced Matrimonial Causes Act 1950, s 17 (p 2136) which replaced Legitimacy Act 1926, s 2 and Supreme Court of Judicature (Consolidation) Act 1925, s 188 (1)–(5), (7) (p 2061). For details of amendments to the earlier Acts, see Matrimonial Causes Act 1950, s 17 (p 2136).

Sub-s (9) added by Domestic and Appellate Proceedings (Restriction of Publicity) Act 1968, s 2(1), (2). The whole section repealed by Matrimonial Causes Act 1973, s 54(1), Sch 3 and replaced by ibid, s 45 (p 2554).

40. Additional jurisdiction in proceedings by a wife—*(1) Without prejudice to any jurisdiction exercisable by the court apart from this section, the court shall have jurisdiction to entertain proceedings by a wife, notwithstanding that the husband is not domiciled in England,—*

(a)   in the case of any proceedings under this Act (other than proceedings under section 14 or sections 23 to 28) [or under the Nullity of Marriage Act 1971], if—

(i)   the wife has been deserted by her husband, or

(ii)   the husband has been deported from the United Kingdom under any law for the time being in force relating to deportation,

and the husband was immediately before the desertion or deportation domiciled in England;

(b)   in the case of proceedings for divorce or nullity of marriage, if—

(i)   the wife is resident in England and has been ordinarily resident for a period of three years immediately preceding the commencement of the proceedings, and

(ii)   the husband is not domiciled in any other part of the United Kingdom or in the Channel Islands or the Isle of Man.

Note. Words in square brackets inserted by Nullity of Marriage Act 1971, s 7(2).

This subsection replaced Matrimonial Causes Act 1950, s 18(1) (p 2137) which replaced Matrimonial Causes Act 1937, s 13 (p 2100) as amended by Law Reform (Miscellaneous Provisions) Act 1949, s 3, and by Commonwealth Immigrants Act 1962, s 20.

(2)   In any proceedings in which the court has jurisdiction by virtue of the foregoing subsection the issues shall be determined in accordance with the law which would be applicable thereto if both parties were domiciled in England at the time of the proceedings.

Note. Sub-s (2) replaced Matrimonial Causes Act 1950, s 18(3) (p 2137)

The whole section repealed by Matrimonial Causes Act 1973, s 54(1), Sch 3 and replaced by ibid, s 46 (p 2555).

41. Damages for adultery—*(1) A husband may, on a petition for divorce or for judicial separation or for damages only, claim damages from any person on the ground of adultery with the wife of the petitioner.*

(2) A claim for damages on the grounds of adultery shall, subject to the provisions of any enactment relating to trial by jury in the court, be tried on the same principles and in the same manner as actions for criminal conversation were tried immediately before the commencement of the Matrimonial Causes Act 1857, and the provisions of this Act with reference to the hearing and decision of petitions shall so far as may be necessary apply to the hearing and decision of petitions on which damages are claimed.

(3) The court may direct in what manner the damages recovered on any such petition are to be paid or applied, and may direct the whole or any part of the damages to be settled for the benefit of the children, if any, of the marriage, or as a provision for the maintenance of the wife.

Note. This section replaced Matrimonial Causes Act 1950, s 30 (p 2142) which replaced Supreme Court of Judicature (Consolidation) Act 1925, s 189 (p 2062).

The whole section repealed by Law Reform (Miscellaneous Provisions) Act 1970, ss 4, 7(2), Schedule, and was not replaced; see also Matrimonial Causes Act 1973, Sch 1, para 4 (p 2562).

42. Condonation—*(1) [For the purposes of the Matrimonial Proceedings (Magistrates' Courts) Act 1960] any presumption of condonation which arises from the continuance or resumption of marital intercourse may be rebutted by evidence sufficient to negative the necessary intent.*

Note. This subsection replaced s 1 of the Matrimonial Causes Act 1963 (p 2219).

The subsection repealed so far as it applied in relation to proceedings for divorce or judicial separation by Divorce Reform Act 1969, s 9(2), Sch 2. Words in square brackets inserted by Matrimonial Causes Act 1973, s 54(1), Sch 2, para 5(2).

Repealed by Domestic Proceedings and Magistrates' Courts Act 1978, s 89(2), Sch 3, as from 1 February 1981.

(2) For the purposes of [this Act and] the Matrimonial Proceedings (Magistrates' Courts) Act 1960, adultery or cruelty shall not be deemed to have been condoned by reason only of a continuation or resumption of cohabitation between the parties for one period not exceeding three months, or of anything done during such cohabitation, if it is proved that cohabitation was continued or resumed, as the case may be, with a view to effecting a reconciliation.

Note. This subsection replaced Matrimonial Causes Act 1963, s 2(1) (p 2235). Words in square brackets repealed by Divorce Reform Act 1969, s 9(2), Sch 2.

Repealed by Domestic Proceedings and Magistrates' Courts Act 1978, s 89(2), Sch 3, as from 1 February.

(3) [For the purposes of the Matrimonial Proceedings (Magistrates' Courts) Act 1960] adultery which has been condoned shall not be capable of being revived.

Note. This subsection replaced Matrimonial Causes Act 1963, s 3 (p 2235).

The subsection was repealed so far as it applied in relation to proceedings for divorce or judicial separation by Divorce Reform Act 1969, s 9(2), Sch 2. Words in square brackets inserted by Matrimonial Causes Act 1973, s 54(1), Sch 2, para 5(2).

Repealed by Domestic Proceedings and Magistrates' Courts Act 1978, s 89(2), Sch 3, as from 1 February 1981.

43. Evidence—*(1) The evidence of a husband or wife shall be admissible in any proceedings to prove that marital intercourse did or did not take place between them during any period; but a husband or wife shall not be compellable in any proceedings to give evidence of the matters aforesaid.*

Note. This subsection replaced Matrimonial Causes Act 1950, s 32(1), (2) (p 2143) which replaced Law Reform (Miscellaneous Provisions) Act 1949, s 7 amending Supreme Court of Judicature (Consolidation) Act 1925, s 198 (p 2066) and s 198A added by Supreme Court of Judicature (Amendment) Act 1935, s 4. The words 'The evidence of a husband' to 'during any period' were repealed by Matrimonial Causes Act 1973, s 54(1), Sch 3 and replaced by ibid, s 48(1) (p 2557). The words 'but a husband' to 'the matters aforesaid' were repealed except in relation to criminal proceedings by Civil Evidence Act 1968, s 16(4).

(2) The parties to any proceedings instituted in consequence of adultery and the husbands and wives of the parties shall be competent to give evidence in the proceedings; but no witness in any such proceedings, whether a party to the proceedings or not, shall be liable to be asked or be

bound to answer any question tending to show that he or she has been guilty of adultery unless he or she has already given evidence in the same proceedings in disproof of the alleged adultery.

Note. The words 'The parties to any proceedings' to 'evidence in the proceedings' repealed by Matrimonial Causes Act 1973, s 54(1), Sch 3 and not replaced. The words 'but no witness' to the end of the subsection repealed by Civil Evidence Act 1968, s 16(5).

(3) In any proceedings for nullity of marriage, evidence on the question of sexual capacity shall be heard in camera unless in any case the judge is satisfied that in the interests of justice any such evidence ought to be heard in open court.

Note. Sub-ss (2), (3) replaced Matrimonial Causes Act 1950, s 32(3), (4) (p 2143).

Sub-s (3) repealed by Matrimonial Causes Act 1973, s 54(1), Sch 3 and replaced by ibid, s 48(2) (p 2557).

44. Power to allow intervention on terms. *In every case in which any person is charged with adultery with any party to a suit or in which the court may consider, in the interest of any person not already a party to the suit, that that person should be made a party to the suit, the court may if it thinks fit allow that person to intervene upon such terms, if any, as the court thinks just.*

Note. This section replaced Matrimonial Causes Act 1950, s 31 (p 2143) which replaced Supreme Court of Judicature (Consolidation) Act 1925, s 197 (p 2066).

The section repealed by Matrimonial Causes Act 1973, s 54(1), Sch 3 and replaced by ibid, s 49(5) (p 2557).

General

45. Transitional provisions and repeals. *The foregoing provisions of this Act shall have effect subject to the provisions of Schedule 1 to this Act (which contains transitional provisions required in consequence of the repeals made by this Act); and, subject to the provisions of the said Schedule 1, the enactments mentioned in the first and second columns of Schedule 2 to this Act are hereby repealed to the extent shown in the third column of that Schedule.*

Note. This section repealed by Matrimonial Causes Act 1973, s 54(1), Sch 3.

46. Short title, interpretation, commencement and extent—*(1)* This Act may be cited as the Matrimonial Causes Act 1965.

(2) In this Act—
'*adopted*', *except in section 23(2), means adopted in pursuance of an adoption order made under the Adoption Act 1958, any previous enactment relating to the adoption of children or any corresponding enactment of the Parliament of Northern Ireland or made in the Isle of Man or any of the Channel Islands; and*
['*the court*' *(except in sections 26, 27, 28 and 28A means the High Court or, where a county court has jurisdiction by virtue of the Matrimonial Causes Act 1967, a county court; and*]
'*relevant child*' *means a child who is—*
   (a) a child of both parties to the marriage in question: or
   (b) a child of one party to the marriage who has been accepted as one of the family by the other party,
and in paragraphs (a) and (b) of this definition '*child*' *includes illegitimate child and adopted child;*
and references to a child of the marriage in sections 17, 21(3), 22(2), 34(2) and 41(3) of this Act include reference to a child adopted by both parties to the marriage.

Note. Definition 'the court' inserted by Divorce Reform Act 1969, s 9(1), Sch 1, para 11, with effect from 1 January 1971, but the whole of sub-s (2) simultaneously repealed, so far as it applies for the interpretation of s 41(3), by Law Reform (Miscellaneous Provisions) Act 1970, and, so far as unrepealed, by Matrimonial Proceedings and Property Act 1970, s 42(2), Sch 3. See now Matrimonial Causes Act 1973, s 52(1) (p 2559) replacing Matrimonial Causes Act 1950, s 27(1) (p 2141).

(3) This Act shall come into force on such day as the Lord Chancellor may appoint by order made by statutory instrument.

Note. The appointed day was 1 January 1966.

(4) Subject to the provisions of section 38(2) of this Act, this Act does not extend to Scotland or Northern Ireland.

Note. Sub-ss (2), (3) and words in italics in sub-s (4) repealed by Matrimonial Causes Act 1973, s 54(1), Sch 3.

Words in italics in sub-s (4) repealed again by Statute Law (Repeals) Act 1977.

SCHEDULES

SCHEDULE 1

TRANSITIONAL PROVISIONS

1. *Without prejudice to the provisions of section 38 of the Interpretation Act 1889 (which relates to the effect of repeals)—*
  (a) *nothing in any repeal made by this Act shall affect any order or rule made, direction given or thing done, or deemed to have been made, given or done, under any enactment repealed by this Act, and every such order, rule, direction or thing shall, if in force at the commencement of this Act, continue in force and, so far as it could have been made, given or done under this Act, be deemed to have been made, given or done under the corresponding provisions of this Act; and*
  (b) *any reference in any document (including an enactment) to any enactment repealed by this Act, whether a specific reference or a reference to provisions of a description which includes, or apart from any repeal made by this Act includes, the enactment so repealed, shall be construed as a reference to the corresponding enactment in this Act.*

2. *Any agreement between the petitioner and the respondent to live separate and apart, whether or not made in writing, shall be disregarded for the purposes of section 1(1)(a)(ii) of this Act [or of section 2(1)(c) of the Divorce Reform Act 1969] if the agreement was entered into before 1 January 1938 and either—*
  (a) *at the time when the agreement was made the respondent had deserted the petitioner without cause; or*
  (b) *the court is satisfied that the circumstances in which the agreement was made and the parties proceeded to live separate and apart were such as, but for the agreement, to amount to desertion of the petitioner by the respondent without cause.*

Note. Words in square brackets inserted by Divorce Reform Act 1969, s 9(1), Sch 1, para 12.

3. *Without prejudice to the provisions of section 38 of the said Act of 1889 and notwithstanding anything in section 1(3) of this Act, a person of unsound mind shall be deemed to have been under care and treatment for the purposes of subsection (1)(a)(iv) of section 1 of this Act while—*
  (a) *at any time before 1 November 1960 he was—*
      (i) *detained in pursuance of an order or inquisition under the Lunacy and Mental Treatment Acts 1890 to 1930 or of an order or warrant under the Army Act, the Air Force Act, the Naval Discipline Act, the Naval Enlistment Act 1884 or the Yarmouth Naval Hospital Act 1931, or*
      (ii) *detained as a Broadmoor patient or in pursuance of an order made under the Criminal Lunatics Act 1884, or*
      (iii) *receiving treatment as a voluntary patient under the Mental Treatment Act 1930;*
  (b) *at any time before 1 June 1962 he was detained in pursuance of an order or warrant for his detention or custody as a lunatic under the Lunacy (Scotland) Acts 1857 to 1919.*

4. *In relation to a marriage celebrated before 1 November 1960, for sub-paragraphs (ii) and (iii) of section 9(1)(b) of this Act there shall be substituted the following sub-paragraphs—*
  '(ii) *was a mental defective within the meaning of the Mental Deficiency Acts 1913 to 1938, or*
  (iii) *was subject to recurrent fits of insanity or epilepsy; or'.*

5. *In relation to proceedings under section 23 of the Matrimonial Causes Act 1950 begun before 1 January 1959 and deemed by virtue of paragraph 1 of this Schedule to be proceedings under section 22(1) of this Act, that sub-section shall have effect as if the reference to any illegitimate child of both parties to the marriage in section 22(2) of this Act were omitted.*

Note. For Matrimonial Causes Act 1950, s 23, see p 2140; for Matrimonial Causes Act 1965, s 22, see p 2250.

6. *Where the party chargeable under a maintenance agreement within the meaning of section 23 of this Act died before 17 August 1957, then—*

(a) *subsection (1) of that section shall not apply to the agreement unless there remained undistributed at that date assets of that party's estate (apart from any property in which he had only a life interest) representing not less than four-fifths of the value of that estate for probate after providing for the discharge of the funeral, testamentary and administrative expenses, debts and liabilities payable thereout (other than any liability arising by virtue of that subsection); and*

(b) *nothing in that subsection shall render liable to recovery, or impose any liability upon the personal representatives of that party in respect of, any part of that party's estate which had been distributed before that date.*

Note. For Matrimonial Causes Act 1965, s 23, see p 2250.

7. *No right or liability shall attach by virtue of section 23(1) of this Act in respect of any sum payable under a maintenance agreement within the meaning of that section in respect of a period before 17 August 1957.*

8. *Any rules of court made before 31 July 1963 shall be deemed to have been validly made if they could have been made after the commencement of this Act under section 29(1) of this Act or that subsection as applied by section 34(6) of this Act; but nothing in this paragraph affects any order for ancillary relief (as defined by section 5(4) of the Matrimonial Causes Act 1963) made after 19 December 1962 and before 31 July 1963.*

Note. For Matrimonial Causes Act 1965, ss 29, 34(6), see pp 2256, 2259; for Matrimonial Causes Act 1963, s 5(4), see p 2236.

9. *In relation to an order made before 16 December 1949 which, by virtue of paragraph 1 of this Schedule is deemed to have been made under section 16(1)(a) of this Act or the said paragraph (a) as applied by section 19 of this Act, the powers conferred by section 31 of this Act shall not be exercised unless the court is satisfied that the case is one of exceptional hardship which cannot be met by the discharge, variation or suspension of any order made, or deemed as aforesaid to have been made, under section 16(1)(b) of this Act, or that paragraph as so applied, as the case may be.*

Note. For Matrimonial Causes Act 1965, ss 16, 34, see pp 2247, 2258.

10. *In relation to such proceedings as are mentioned in section 34(1) of this Act which were begun before 1 January 1959, that subsection shall have effect as if paragraph (b) were omitted; and, in relation to any such proceedings and in the application of section 34(3) of this Act to any proceedings so begun, subsections (1) and (3) of that section shall have effect respectively as if paragraph (b) in section 46(2) of this Act were omitted.*

Note. For Matrimonial Causes Act 1965, ss 34, 46, see pp 2258, 2265.

11. *Section 35(1) of this Act shall not apply in relation to an order made under section 23(1) of the Matrimonial Causes Act 1950 before 1 January 1959 and deemed by virtue of paragraph 1 of this Schedule to be made under section 22(1) of this Act.*

Note. For Matrimonial Causes Act 1965, ss 22, 35, see pp 2250, 2260; for Matrimonial Causes Act 1950, s 23(1), see p 2140.

Paras 5–7, 9–11 repealed by Matrimonial Proceedings and Property Act 1970, s 42(2), Sch 3. The whole Schedule, so far as unrepealed, repealed by Matrimonial Causes Act 1973, s 54(1), Sch 3.

SCHEDULE 2

REPEALS

Chapter	Short Title	Extent of Repeal
49 & 50 Vict c 27	The Guardianship of Infants Act 1886	Section 7
14 Geo 6 c 25	The Matrimonial Causes Act 1950	The whole Act
4 & 5 Eliz 2 c 46	The Administration of Justice Act 1956	Section 31(2)
5 & 6 Eliz. 2 c 35	The Maintenance Agreements Act 1957	The whole Act
6 & 7 Eliz 2 c 35	The Matrimonial Causes (Property and Maintenance) Act 195	Sections 1 to 6 and the Schedule
6 & 7 Eliz 2 c 40	The Matrimonial Proceedings (Children) Act 1958	The whole Act, except sections 17 and 18 In section 17, the words from 'and in' onward Section 18(4)
6 & 7 Eliz 2 c 54	The Divorce (Insanity and Desertion) Act 1958	The whole Act
7 & 8 Eliz 2 c 72	The Mental Health Act 1959	In Schedule 7, the entry relating to the Matrimonial Causes Act 1950
7 & 8 Eliz 2 c 73	The Legitimacy Act 1959	Section 2(6)
8 & 9 Eliz 2 c 61	The Mental Health (Scotland) Act 1960	In Schedule 4, the entry relating to the Matrimonial Causes Act 1950
10 & 11 Eliz 2 c 21	The Commonwealth Immigrants Act 1962	In section 20(1), the words from the beginning to '1950 and'
1963 c 45	The Matrimonial Causes Act 1963	The whole Act

Note. Sch 2 repealed by Matrimonial Causes Act 1973, s 54 (1), Sch 3.

TABLE OF COMPARISON BETWEEN PREVIOUS ENACTMENTS AND THE MATRIMONIAL CAUSES ACT 1965

This table shows in column (1) the enactments repealed by Matrimonial Causes Act 1965 (c 72) and in column (2) the provisions of that Act corresponding thereto.

In some cases the enactment in column (1), though having a corresponding provision in column (2), was not, or was not wholly, repealed as it was still wholly or partly required for the purposes of other legislation.

(1)	(2)	(1)	(2)
Guardianship of Infants Act 1886 (c 27)	Matrimonial Causes Act 1965 (c 72)	Matrimonial Causes Act 1950 (c 25)	Matrimonial Causes Act 1965 (c 72)
		s 1(1) (2)	s 1(1) (3)
s 7	s 34(2)		

(1) Matrimonial Causes Act 1950 (c 25)	(2) Matrimonial Causes Act 1965 (c 72)
s 2(1)	ss 2(1), (2), 5(5)
(2)	2(2), 46(2)
(3)	s 2(3)
(4)	Not reproduced
3	s 4(1), (2)
4(1)	5(1)
(2)	(3), (4)
5	4(3)
6	5(6)
7	3
8(1)	9(1), (2)
(2)	(3)
9	11
10	ss 6(1), 10
11(1)	6(1), (2), 10
(2)	6(1), (3), 10
12(1)	5(7), 10
(2), (3)	7, 10
13	s 8
ss 14, 15	ss 12, 13
s 16(1)	s 14(1), (2)
(2), (3)	(3), (4)
(4)	(5)
17	39
18(1)	s 40(1)
(2)	14(2)
(3)	ss 14(5), 40(2)
19(1)	s 15
(2)	ss 16(1), (2), 19
(3)	16(1), 19
(4)	15, 16(3)
20(1)	s 15
(2)	20(1)
(3)	ss 15, 20(1)
21(1)	s 20(3), (4)
(2)	(3)
22(1)	15
(2)	21(1)
(3)	(1), (2)
(4)	(2)
23(1)	22
(2)	(3)
24(1)	17(2), 20(2)
(2)	s 21(3)
25	ss 17(1), 19, 46(2)
26(1)	34(1), (4), 46(2)
(2)	
(3)	s 34(3)
27	30
28(1)	31(1), Sch 1, para 9
(2), (3)	31(2), (3)
29	ss 18(1), 19, 34(6)
30	s 41
31	44
32(1), (2)	43(1)

(1) Matrimonial Causes Act 1950 (c 25)	(2) Matrimonial Causes Act 1965 (c 72)
s 32(3), (4)	s 43(2), (3)
33	1(1)
34(1)	Not reproduced
(2)	See Sch 1, para 1
35(2)	Not reproduced
(3)	s 46(4)
Schedule	Not reproduced
Administration of Justice Act 1956 (c 46)	
s 31(2)	s 39(2), (3), (6)
Maintenance Agreements Act 1957 (c 35)	
s 1(1)	s 23(2)
(2)	23(1), Sch 1, paras 6 and 7
(3)	24(1)
(4)	(2)
(5)	ss 23(2), 24(2)
2(1)	s 25(1), (2)
(2)–(4)	(3)–(5)
3(1)	Not reproduced
(2)	s 25(2), Sch 1, paras 6, 7
(3)	46(4)
Matrimonial Causes (Property and Maintenance) Act 1958 (c 35)	
s 1(1)	See ss 16(1), 19, 20(1) and 34(3)
(2)	
(3)	
(4), (5)	Not reproduced
2(1)	s 32(1), (2)
(2)	(1)
(3)	(2)
(4)	(3)
(5)	(1), (3)
(6)	Not reproduced
(7)	s 32(4)
(8)	(1), (2), (4)
ss 3, 4	ss 26, 27
s 5(1)	s 32
(2)	(1), (4)
(3)	ss 26, 27
(4)	s 26(6)
6(1)	28(1)
(2), (3)	(2)

(1)	(2)	(1)	(2)
Matrimonial Causes (Property and Maintenance) Act 1958 (c 35)	Matrimonial Causes Act 1965 (c 72) ———	Mental Health Act 1959 (c 72) ——— Sch 7†	Matrimonial Causes Act 1965 (c 72) ss 1(3), 9(1), 30(2)
s 6(4)	s 28(3)	Legitimacy Act 1959 (c 73)	
(5)	(1)–(3)	———	
8(1)	ss 26(6), 27(2), 32 (4)	s 2(6)	s 39(1)
9(3)*	s 46(34)	6(1)*	46(4)
Schedule	ss 16(1), 19, 20(1), 34(3)	Mental Health (Scotland) Act 1960 (c 61)	
Matrimonial Proceedings (Children) Act 1958 (c 40)		——— Sch 4	s 1(3)
———		Commonwealth Immigrants Act 1962 (c 21)	
s 1(1)	ss 33(1), 34(1), 46 (2)	———	
(2)	s 34(4); and see s 2(2)	s 20(1)	s 40(1)
(3)	ss 34(1), 46(2)	Matrimonial Causes Act 1963 (c 45)	
(4)	s 22(2)	———	
(5)	46(2)	s 1	s 42(1)
(6)	33(1)	2(1)	(2)
2(1), (2)	33	(2)	1(2)
(3)	ss 2(2)†, 46(2)	3	42(3)
(4)	s 33(1)	4(1)	5(4)
3(1)	34(1)	(2)	(2)
(2)	34(5)	(3)	ss 5(2), 12(1)
4(1)	35(1), (4), Sch 1, para 11	5(1)	16(1), 19, 20(1)
(2)	35(2)	(2)	29(1), 34(6)
5(1)–(5)	36(1)–(5)	(3)	Sch 1, para 8
(6)	Rep. 1959 c 72, ss 10(2), 149(2), Sch 8, Part I	(4)	ss 29(2), 34(6), Sch 1, para 8
(7), (8)	s 36(6), (7)	6(1)	s 32(1)
6	37	(2)	ss 32(1), (4), 34(7)
16	Not reproduced	(3)	s 32(3), (4)
17	s 38(1)	(4)	ss 32(1), (4), 34(7)
18(3)	46(4); and see s 38(2)	7(1)	Not reproduced
(4)	Not reproduced	(2)	
		(3)	s 40(4)
Divorce (Insanity and Desertion) Act 1958 (c 54)	Matrimonial Causes Act 1965 (c 72) ———		
s 1(1)	s 1(3)		
(2)	(4)		
(3)	(3)		
2	(2)		
3	Sch para 2		
4(1)	Not reproduced		
(2)	s 46(4)		
(3)	Not reproduced		

*Not repealed.   †Repealed only in part.

MINISTRY OF SOCIAL SECURITY ACT 1966*

(1966 c 20)

An Act to provide for the appointment of a Minister of Social Security and the transfer to him of the functions of the Minister of Pensions and National Insurance and of certain functions of the National Assistance Board; to replace Part II of the National Assistance Act 1948 by provisions giving rights to non-contributory benefit; and for purposes connected with those matters.

[3 August 1966]

* Whole Act (in so far as not already repealed) repealed by Supplementary Benefits Act 1976, Sch 8.

*   *   *   *

PART III

RECOVERY OF EXPENSES

22. Liability to maintain—*(1) For the purposes of this Act—*
   (a) *a man shall be liable to maintain his wife and his children, and*
   (b) *a woman shall be liable to maintain her husband and her children;*
and in this subsection the reference to a man's children includes a reference to children of whom he has been adjudged to be the putative father and the reference to a woman's children a reference to her illegitimate children.
   (2) [Applies to Scotland.]

23. Recovery of cost of benefit from persons liable for maintenance—*(1) The following provisions of this section shall apply where benefit is paid or claimed to meet requirements which are or include those of a person (in this section referred to as 'the dependant') whom another person is for the purpose of this Act liable to maintain, except where the dependant is an illegitimate child and the other person his father.*
   (2) The Commission may make a complaint against that other person to a magistrates' court and on such a complaint the court shall have regard to all the circumstances and, in particular, to the other person's resources and may order him to pay such sum, weekly or otherwise, as the court may consider appropriate.
   (3) In determining whether to order any payments to be made in respect of benefit for any period before the complaint was made or the amount of any such payments the court shall disregard any excess of that other person's resources over what they were during that period.
   (4) Any payments ordered to be made under this section shall be made—
   (a) *to the Minister in so far as they are attributable to any benefit (whether paid before or after the making of the order);*
   (b) *to the person claiming benefit or (if different) the dependant; or*
   (c) *to such other person as appears to the court expedient in the interests of the dependant;*
and where the payments are ordered to be made to the Minister the Commission shall be a party to any proceedings with respect to the enforcement, revocation or variation of the order to which, but for this provision, the Minister would be a party.
   (5) An order under this section shall be enforceable as an affiliation order, and any proceedings for such an order (but not proceedings for the enforcement, revocation or variation of such an order) shall be included among the proceedings which are domestic proceedings within the meaning of the Magistrates' Courts Act 1952; and section 56 of that Act (which defines 'domestic proceedings') shall have effect accordingly.
   (6) The Maintenance Orders Act 1950 shall have effect as if an order under this section were included among the orders referred to in subsections (1) and (2) of section 4 and subsections (1) and (2) of section 9 and were a maintenance order within the meaning of Part II of that Act, that is to say, an order to which section 16 thereof applies; and the Maintenance Orders Act 1958 shall have effect as if such an order were included in the definition of 'maintenance order' in section 21 of that Act.
   (7) [Applies to Scotland.]

24. Affiliation orders—*(1) The following provisions of this section shall apply where benefit is paid to meet requirements which include those of an illegitimate child.*

(2) If no affiliation order is in force the Commission may within three years from the time when any payment by way of benefit was made make application to a justice of the peace acting for the petty sessions area in which the mother of the child resides for a summons to be served under section 1 of the Affiliation Proceedings Act 1957.

(3) In any proceedings on an application under the preceding subsection the court shall hear such evidence as the Commission may produce, in addition to the evidence required to be heard by section 4 of the said Act of 1957, and shall in all other respects, subject to the provisions of subsection (4) of this subsection, proceed as on an application made by the mother under the said section 1.

(4) An affiliation order made on an application under subsection (2) of this section may be made so as to provide that the payments, or a part of the payments, to be made thereunder shall, in lieu of being made to the mother or a person having the custody of the child, be made to the Minister or to such other person as the court may direct; and where the order provides for the payments to be made to the Minister the Commission shall be a party to any proceedings with respect to the enforcement, revocation or variation of the order to which, but for this provision, the Minister would be a party.

(5) On an application by the Commission in any proceedings under the said section 1 brought by the mother of the child an affiliation order may be made so as to provide as mentioned in subsection (4) of this section.

(6) Any affiliation order, whether made before or after the commencement of this Act, may on the application of the Commission be varied so as to provide as mentioned in subsection (4) of this section and any affiliation order which provides as mentioned in that subsection may on the application of the mother of the child be varied so as to provide that the payments thereunder shall be made to the mother or a person having the custody of the child.

(7) An application by the Commission under the preceding subsection may be made notwithstanding that the mother has died and no person has been appointed to have the custody of the child; and may, where the child is not in her care and she is not contributing to his maintenance, be made without making her a party to the proceedings.

(8) Proceedings on an application under subsection (2) of this section shall be included among the proceedings which are domestic proceedings within the meaning of the Magistrates' Courts Act 1952; and section 56 of that Act (which defines 'domestic proceedings') shall have effect accordingly.

(9) The Maintenance Orders Act 1950 shall have effect as if this section were included in the enactments referred to in section 3(1) of that Act and as if an order made on an application under subsection (2) of this section were a maintenance order within the meaning of Part II of that Act, that is to say, an order to which section 16 thereof applies; and the Maintenance Orders Act 1958 shall have effect as if such an order were included in the definition of 'maintenance order' in section 21 of that Act.

MATRIMONIAL CAUSES ACT 1967*

(1967 c 56)

An Act to confer jurisdiction on county courts in certain matrimonial proceedings; and for purposes connected therewith. [*21 July 1967*]

*This Act repealed by Matrimonial and Family Proceedings Act 1984, s 46(3), Sch 3, as from 28 April 1986. See now Part V of the Act of 1984.

1. Jurisdiction of county courts in undefended matrimonial causes—*(1) The Lord Chancellor may by order designate any county court as a divorce county court, and any court so designated shall have jurisdiction to hear and determine any undefended matrimonial cause, except that it shall have jurisdiction to try such a cause only if it is also designated in the order as a court of trial.*

(2) The jurisdiction conferred by this Act on a divorce county court shall be exercisable throughout England and Wales, but rules of court may provide for a matrimonial cause pending in one such court to be heard and determined in another or partly in that and partly in another.

(3) Every matrimonial cause shall be commenced in a divorce county court, but rules of court—

    (a) shall provide for the transfer to the High Court of any matrimonial cause which ceases to be undefended; and

    (b) may provide for the transfer to that court of matrimonial causes which remain undefended.

Note. Under Courts Act 1971, s 45(3) (p 2391) (repealed) the power conferred by sub-s (3)(b) is to be construed as including power to provide for the removal of proceedings at the direction of the High Court.

(4) Rules of court may provide for the transfer or retransfer from the High Court to a divorce county court of any matrimonial cause which is or again becomes undefended.

(5) Rules of court shall define the circumstances in which any matrimonial cause is to be treated for the purposes of this Act as undefended, and may make different provision with respect to matrimonial causes of different descriptions.

(6) The power to make an order under this section shall be exercisable by statutory instrument and includes power to vary or revoke such an order by a subsequent order.

2. Ancillary relief and protection of children—*(1) Subject to the following provisions of this section, a divorce county court shall have jurisdiction to exercise any power exercisable under Part II or Part III of the Matrimonial Causes Act 1965 [Part II or III of the Matrimonial Causes Act 1973] [or Part I of the Matrimonial Proceedings and Property Act 1970] in connection with any petition, decree or order pending in or made by such a court and to exercise any power under section 22 or section 24 of that Act [section 6 or section 14 of the said Act of 1970] [section 27 or 35 of that Act].*

Note. The reference to Parts II and III of Matrimonial Causes Act 1973 substituted for the reference to Parts II and III of Matrimonial Causes Act 1965 by Matrimonial Causes Act 1973, s 54(1), Sch 2, para 6(1) and the reference to Part I of Matrimonial Proceedings and Property Act 1970 inserted by Matrimonial Proceedings and Property Act 1970, s 42(1), Sch 2, para 2(1); Part I of Matrimonial Proceedings and Property Act 1970 repealed by Matrimonial Causes Act 1973, s 54(1), Sch 3.

The reference to Matrimonial Proceedings and Property Act 1970, ss 6, 14, substituted for the reference to Matrimonial Causes Act 1965, ss 22, 24, by Matrimonial Proceedings and Property Act 1970, s 42(1), Sch 2, para 2(1) and the reference to Matrimonial Causes Act 1973, ss 27, 35 substituted therefor by Matrimonial Causes Act 1973, s 54(1), Sch 2, para 6(1).

(2) Any proceedings for the exercise of a power which a divorce county court has jurisdiction to exercise by virtue of this section shall be commenced in such divorce county court as may be prescribed by rules of court; but rules of court shall provide for the transfer to the High Court of any proceedings pending in a county court by virtue of this section in any case where the transfer appears to the county court to be desirable, and may so provide in such other cases as may be specified in the rules.

Note. The words 'and may so provide ... the rules' repealed by Courts Act 1971, s 56(4), Sch 11, Part IV.

(3) A divorce county court shall not by virtue of this section have jurisdiction to exercise any power under sections 25 to 27 of the Matrimonial Causes Act 1965 but without prejudice to the exercise by virtue of section 7 of the Family Provision Act 1966 of any power exercisable by a county court under section 26 or 27 of the said Act of 1965.

[(3) A divorce county court shall not by virtue of this section have jurisdiction to exercise any power under—

    (a) section 26 or 27 of the Matrimonial Causes Act 1965; or

    (b) section 10, 11, 15 or 22 of the Matrimonial Proceedings and Property Act 1970 or paragraph 5 of Schedule 1 thereto;

but without prejudice to the exercise by virtue of section 7 of the Family Provision Act 1966 of any power exercisable by a county court under the said section 26 or 27 or to the exercise by virtue of any such provision of the said Act of 1970 as is mentioned in paragraph (b) of this subsection of any power exercisable by a county court under that provision.]

[*(3) A divorce county court shall not by virtue of this section have jurisdiction to exercise any power under section 32, 33, 36 or 38 of the Matrimonial Causes Act 1973; but nothing in this section shall prejudice the exercise by a county court of any jurisdiction conferred on county courts by any of those sections.*]

Note. Sub-s (3) was replaced by a new subsection (the second version, in square brackets) by Matrimonial Proceedings and Property Act 1970, s 42(1), Sch 2, para 2(1)(b), in turn replaced by a new subsection (the third version, in square brackets) by Matrimonial Causes Act 1973, s 54(1), Sch 2, para 6(1).

(4) Nothing in this section shall affect the jurisdiction of a magistrates' court under section 24 of the Matrimonial Causes Act 1965 [section 14 of the Matrimonial Proceedings and Property Act 1970] [section 35 of the Matrimonial Causes Act 1973].

Note. The reference to Matrimonial Causes Act 1965, s 24, replaced by the reference to Matrimonial Proceedings and Property Act 1970, s 14, by Matrimonial Proceedings and Property Act 1970, s 42(1), Sch 2, para 2(1) which was in turn replaced by the reference to Matrimonial Causes Act 1973, s 35, by Matrimonial Causes Act 1973, s 54(1), Sch 2, para 6(1).

3. Consideration of agreements or arrangements. *Any provision to be made by rules of court for the purposes of section 5(2) of the Matrimonial Causes Act 1965 [section 7 of the Matrimonial Causes Act 1973] [or of section 7 of the Divorce Reform Act 1969] with respect to any power exercisable by the court on an application made before the presentation of a petition shall confer jurisdiction to exercise the power on divorce county courts.*

Note. The reference to Matrimonial Causes Act 1973, s 7 substituted for the reference to Matrimonial Causes Act 1965, s 5(2), by Matrimonial Causes Act 1973, s 54(1) and Sch 2, para 6(2), and the reference to Divorce Reform Act 1969, s 7 inserted by Divorce Reform Act 1969, s 7(2); s 7 repealed by Matrimonial Causes Act 1973, s 54(1), Sch 3.

4. County court proceedings in principal probate registry—*(1) Sections 1 to 3 of this Act shall not prevent the commencement of any proceedings in the principal probate registry [divorce registry], except where rules of court under section 2(2) of this Act otherwise provide; and the following provisions of this section shall have effect for the purpose of enabling proceedings to be dealt with in that registry as in a divorce county court.*

(2) The jurisdiction conferred by this Act on divorce county courts shall be exercised in the principal probate registry [divorce registry]—

(a) *so far as it is exercisable by judges of such courts, at such sittings and in such places as the Lord Chancellor may direct; and*

(b) *so far as it is exercisable by registrars of such courts, by such registrars or by registrars and other officers of the principal probate registry [divorce registry], according as rules of court may provide;*

and rules of court may make provision for treating, for any purposes specified in the rules, proceedings pending in that registry with respect to which that jurisdiction is exercisable as pending in a divorce county court and for the application of section 73(4) of the Solicitors Act 1957 [section 74(3) of the Solicitors Act 1974] (amount of costs allowed on taxation in connection with proceedings in a county court) with respect to any proceedings so treated.

(3) The principal probate registry [divorce registry] shall be treated as a divorce county court—

(a) *for the purpose of any provision to be made by rules of court under section 1(2) of this Act; and*

(b) *for the purpose of any provision to be made under section 2(2) of this Act prescribing the county court in which any proceedings are to be commenced.*

(4) Rules of court shall make provision for securing, with respect to proceedings dealt with under this section, that, as nearly as may be, the same consequences shall follow—

(a) *as regards service of process, as if proceedings commenced in the principal probate registry [divorce registry] had been commenced in a divorce county court; and*

(b) *as regards enforcement of orders, as if orders made in that registry in the exercise of the jurisdiction conferred by this Act on divorce county courts were orders made by such a court.*

(5) *The provision to be made by rules of court for the purposes of this Act for the transfer of proceedings between a divorce county court and the High Court shall, in the case of proceedings pending in the principal probate registry [divorce registry] and dealt with or to be dealt with under this section, be provision for the proceedings to be treated, or as the case may be no longer to be treated, for any purposes specified in the rules, as pending in a divorce county court; and any provision so made for the transfer of proceedings between divorce county courts shall include provision for the transfer to or from the principal probate registry [divorce registry] or proceedings falling to be treated as pending in a divorce county court.*

Note. Words 'divorce registry' substituted for 'principal probate registry' in each case where they occur by Administration of Justice Act 1970, s 1, Sch 2.

In sub-s (2) reference to Solicitors Act 1974 substituted for reference to Solicitors Act 1957 by Solicitors Act 1974, s 89(1), Sch 3, para 8.

5. Assignment of county court judges to matrimonial proceedings. *The jurisdiction conferred by this Act on divorce county courts, so far as it is exercisable by judges of such courts, shall be exercised by such county court judges as the Lord Chancellor may direct.*

6. Appeals on questions of fact. *Section 109 of the County Courts Act 1959 (appeals on questions of fact) shall have effect as if the proceedings mentioned in subsection (2) of that section included any proceedings with respect to which jurisdiction is conferred by this Act on divorce county courts.*

Note. This section repealed by Supreme Court Act 1981, s 152(4), Sch 7, as from 1 January 1982.

7. Matrimonial causes rules—*(1) The authority having power to make rules of court for the purposes of*—

   (a) the Matrimonial Causes Act 1965, except proceedings in the county court under section 26 or section 27 (where the county court has jurisdiction by virtue of section 7 of the Family Provision Act 1966) and proceedings under section 39 (declarations of legitimacy, etc);

   (b) this Act; or

   (c) any enactment passed after this Act which relates to any matter dealt with in the Matrimonial Causes Act 1965 or this Act, other than such proceedings as are specified in paragraph (a) of this subsection; [or

   (d) without prejudice to the generality of paragraph (c) of this subsection, Part I of the Matrimonial Proceedings and Property Act 1970, and Schedule 1 thereto, except proceedings in the county court under section 10, 11, 15 or 22 or paragraph 5 of Schedule 1]

shall be the Lord Chancellor together with any four or more of the following persons, namely, the President of the [Family Division], one puisne judge attached to that division, one registrar of the [divorce registry], two [Circuit judges], one registrar appointed under the County Courts Act 1959, two practising barristers being members of the General Council of the Bar and two practising solicitors of whom one shall be a member of the Council of the Law Society and the other a member of the Law Society and also of a local law society.

   The said puisne judge, [Circuit judges], registrars, barristers and solicitors shall be appointed by the Lord Chancellor for such time as he may think fit.

Note. Under Courts Act 1971, s 45(7) (p 2391) (repealed), the reference in para (b) above to this Act included a reference to Courts Act 1971, s 45.

Word 'or' at the end of para (b) omitted, and words in square brackets following para (c) inserted, by Matrimonial Proceedings and Property Act 1970, s 42(1), Sch 2, para 2(2).

Words 'Family Division' and 'divorce registry' substituted for 'Probate, Divorce and Admiralty Division' and 'principal probate registry' by Administration of Justice Act 1970, s 1, Sch 2, para 27. 'Circuit judges' substituted for 'county court judges' by Courts Act 1971, s 56, Sch 8, para 47.

   (2) The power to make such rules of court shall be exercisable by statutory instrument, which shall be subject to annulment in pursuance of a resolution of either House of Parliament.

   (3) Rules of court made under this section may apply, with or without modification, any rules of court made under the Supreme Court of Judicature (Consolidation) Act 1925, the County Courts Act 1959 or any other enactment and—

   (a)   *may modify or exclude the application of any such rules or of any provision of the said Act of 1959;*

   (b)   *may provide for the enforcement in the High Court of orders made in a divorce county court;*

and, without prejudice to the generality of the following provisions, may make with respect to proceedings in a divorce county court any provision regarding the Official Solicitor or any solicitor of the Supreme Court which could be made by rules of court with respect to proceedings in the High Court.

Note. This section repealed by Matrimonial Causes Act 1973, s 54(1), Sch 3 and replaced by ibid, s 50 (p 2557).

8. Fees.   *The fees to be taken in any proceedings to which rules under section 7 of this Act apply shall be such as the Lord Chancellor with the concurrence of the Treasury may from time to time by order made by statutory instrument prescribe.*

Note. This section repealed by Matrimonial Causes Act 1973, s 54(1), Sch 3, replaced by ibid, s 51 (p 2559).

9. Remuneration of persons giving legal aid.   *Rules of court may provide that the sums payable under [section 10(1) of the Legal Aid Act 1974] to a solicitor or counsel acting in an undefended matrimonial cause shall, at his election, be either—*

   (a)   *such fixed amount specified in the rules as may be applicable under the rules; or*

   (b)   *an amount ascertained on taxation or assessment of costs as provided by [Schedule 2] to that Act;*

and may provide for modifying the said Schedule in relation to any proceedings which by virtue of this Act are at any stage treated as pending in a divorce county court.

Note. References to Legal Aid Act 1974, s 10 and Sch 2 substituted for references to Legal Aid and Advice Act 1949, by Legal Aid Act 1974, s 41, Sch 4, para 2.

10. Interpretation—*(1) In this Act—*

   'divorce county court' means a county court designated under section 1 of this Act;

   ['*divorce registry' means the principal registry of the Family Division of the High Court;*]

   ['*matrimonial cause' means an action for divorce, nullity of marriage, judicial separation, or jactitation of marriage or an application under section 3 of the Matrimonial Causes Act 1973;*]

   'undefended matrimonial cause' has the meaning assigned to it by section 1(5) of this Act.

Note. Definition 'divorce registry' added by Administration of Justice Act 1970, s 1, Sch 2.

Definition 'matrimonial cause' substituted by Supreme Court Act 1981, s 152(1), Sch 5, as from 1 January 1982.

   (2) References in this Act to a transfer to the High Court include references to a transfer to a district registry.

11. Short title, commencement and extent—*(1) This Act may be cited as the Matrimonial Causes Act 1967.*

   (2) This Act shall come into force on such day as the Lord Chancellor may by order made by statutory instrument appoint.

   (3) This Act does not extend to Scotland or to Northern Ireland.

ABORTION ACT 1967

(1967 c 87)

An Act to amend and clarify the law relating to termination of pregnancy by registered medical practitioners.

[27 October 1967]

1. Medical termination of pregnancy—*(1)* Subject to the provisions of this section, a person shall not be guilty of an offence under the law relating to abortion when a pregnancy is terminated by a registered medical practitioner if two registered medical practitioners are of the opinion, formed in good faith—

(a) *that the continuance of the pregnancy would involve risk to the life of the pregnant woman, or of injury to the physical or mental health of the pregnant woman or any existing children of her family, greater than if the pregnancy were terminated; or*

(b) *that there is a substantial risk that if the child were born it would suffer from such physical or mental abnormalities as to be seriously handicapped.*

[(a) that the pregnancy has not exceeded its twenty-fourth week and that the continuance of the pregnancy would involve risk, greater than if the pregnancy were terminated, of injury to the physical or mental health of the pregnant woman or any existing children of her family; or

(b) that the termination is necessary to prevent grave permanent injury to the physical or mental health of the pregnant woman; or

(c) that the continuance of the pregnancy would involve risk to the life of the pregnant woman, greater than if the pregnancy were terminated; or

(d) that there is a substantial risk that if the child were born it would suffer from such physical or mental abnormalities as to be seriously handicapped.]

Note. Sub-s (1)(a)–(d) in square brackets substituted for sub-s (1)(a), (b) in italics by Human Fertilisation and Embryology Act 1990, s 37(1), as from 1 April 1991.

(2) In determining whether the continuance of a pregnancy would involve such risk of injury to health as is mentioned in paragraph (a) [or (b)] of subsection (1) of this section, account may be taken of the pregnant woman's actual or reasonably foreseeable environment.

Note. Words in square brackets inserted by Human Fertilisation and Embryology Act 1990, s 37(2), as from 1 April 1991.

(3) Except as provided by subsection (4) of this section, any treatment for the termination of pregnancy must be carried out in a hospital vested in [the Secretary of State for the purposes of his functions under the National Health Service Act 1977 or the National Health Service (Scotland) Act 1978 [or in a hospital vested in [a Primary Care Trust or] a National Health Service trust] [or an NHS foundation trust] or in a place approved for the purposes of this section by the Secretary of State].

Note. Words 'the Secretary of State ... Secretary of State' in square brackets substituted by Health Services Act 1980, ss 1, 2, Sch 1, para 17(1). Words 'or in a ... Service trust' in square brackets inserted by the National Health Service and Community Care Act 1990, s 66(1), Sch 9, para 8, as from 2 July 1990. Words 'a Primary Care Trust or' in square brackets inserted by the Health Act 1999 (Supplementary, Consequential etc Provisions) Order 2000, SI 2000 No 90, art 3(1), Sch 1, para 6, as from 8 February 2000. Words 'or an NHS foundation trust' in square brackets inserted by the Health and Social Care (Community Health and Standards) Act 2003, s 34, Sch 4, paras 9, 10, as from in relation to England and Wales: 1 April 2004 (SI 2004 No 759); in relation to Scotland: to be appointed.

[(3A) The power under subsection (3) of this section to approve a place includes power, in relation to treatment consisting primarily in the use of such medicines as may be specified in the approval and carried out in such manner as may be so specified, to approve a class of places.]

Note. Sub-s (3A) inserted by Human Fertilisation and Embryology Act 1990, s 37(3), as from 1 April 1991.

(4) Subsection (3) of this section, and so much of subsection (1) as relates to the opinion of two registered medical practitioners, shall not apply to the termination of a pregnancy by a registered medical practitioner in a case where he is of the opinion, formed in good faith, that the termination is immediately necessary to save the life or to prevent grave permanent injury to the physical or mental health of the pregnant woman.

2. Notification—(1) The [Secretary of State] in respect of England and Wales and the Secretary of State in respect of Scotland, shall by statutory instrument make regulations to provide—

(a) for requiring any such opinion as is referred to in section 1 of this Act to be certified by the practitioners or practitioner concerned in such form and at such time as may be prescribed by the regulations, and for requiring the preservation and disposal of certificates for the purposes of the regulations;

(b) for requiring any registered medical practitioner who terminates a pregnancy to give notice of the termination and such other information relating to the termination as may be so prescribed;

(c) for prohibiting the disclosure, except to such persons or for such purpose as may be so prescribed, of notices given or information furnished pursuant to the regulations.

(2) The information furnished in pursuance of regulations made by virtue of paragraph (b) of subsection (1) of this section shall be notified solely to the [Chief Medical Officer of the *Department of Health and Social Security* [Department of Health], or of the Welsh Office, or of the Scottish Home and Health Department].

(3) Any person who wilfully contravenes or wilfully fails to comply with the requirements or regulations under subsection (1) of this section shall be liable on summary conviction to a fine not exceeding [level 5 on the standard scale].

(4) Any statutory instrument made by virtue of this section shall be subject to annulment in pursuance of a resolution of either House of Parliament.

Note. Words in square brackets in sub-s (1) substituted by virtue of Secretary of State for Social Services Order 1968, SI 1968 No 1699, art 5(4).

Words in outer pair of square brackets in sub-s (2) substituted by Transfer of Functions (Wales) Order 1969, SI 1969 No 388, art 2, Sch 1. Words in inner pair of square brackets in sub-s (2) substituted for words in italics by Transfer of Functions (Health and Social Security) Order 1988, SI 1988 No 1843, art 5(4), Sch 3, para 3(a), as from 28 November 1988.

Reference to level 5 on the standard scale in sub-s (3) substituted by virtue of Criminal Justice Act 1982, s 46. Maximum fine previously increased to £1,000 by Criminal Law Act 1977, s 31(1), Sch 6.

3. Application of Act to visiting forces etc—(1) In relation to the termination of a pregnancy in a case where the following conditions are satisfied, that is to say—

(a) the treatment for termination of the pregnancy was carried out in a hospital controlled by the proper authorities of a body to which this section applies; and

(b) the pregnant woman had at the time of the treatment a relevant association with that body; and

(c) the treatment was carried out by a registered medical practitioner or a person who at the time of the treatment was a member of that body appointed as a medical practitioner for that body by the proper authorities of that body,

this Act shall have effect as if any reference in section 1 to a registered medical practitioner and to a hospital vested in [the Secretary of State] under the National Health Service Acts included respectively a reference to such a person as is mentioned in paragraph (c) of this subsection and to a hospital controlled as aforesaid, and as if section 2 were omitted.

(2) The bodies to which this section applies are any force which is a visiting force within the meaning of any of the provisions of Part I of the Visiting Forces Act 1952 and any headquarters within the meaning of the Schedule to the International Headquarters and Defence Organisations Act 1964; and for the purposes of this section—

(a) a woman shall be treated as having a relevant association at any time with a body to which this section applies if at that time—

(i) in the case of such a force as aforesaid, she had a relevant association within the meaning of the said Part I with the force; and

(ii) in the case of such a headquarters as aforesaid, she was a member of the headquarters or a dependant within the meaning of the Schedule aforesaid of such a member; and

(b) any reference to a member of a body to which this section applies shall be construed—

(i) in the case of such a force as aforesaid, as a reference to a member of or of a civilian component of that force within the meaning of the said Part I; and

(ii) in the case of such a headquarters as aforesaid, as a reference to a member of that headquarters within the meaning of the Schedule aforesaid.

Note. Words in square brackets in sub-s (1) substituted by Health Services Act 1980, ss 1, 2, Sch 1, para 17(2).

4. Conscientious objection to participation in treatment—(1) Subject to subsection (2) of this section, no person shall be under any duty, whether by contract or by any statutory or other legal requirement, to participate in any treatment authorised by this Act to which he has a conscientious objection:

Provided that in any legal proceedings the burden of proof of conscientious objection shall rest on the person claiming to rely on it.

(2) Nothing in subsection (1) of this section shall affect any duty to participate in treatment which is necessary to save the life or to prevent grave permanent injury to the physical or mental health of a pregnant woman.

(3) In any proceedings before a court in Scotland, a statement on oath by any person to the effect that he has a conscientious objection to participating in any treatment authorised by this Act shall be sufficient evidence for the purpose of discharging the burden of proof imposed upon him by subsection (1) of this section.

5. Supplementary provisions—(*1*) *Nothing in this Act shall effect the provisions of the Infant Life (Preservation) Act 1929 (protecting the life of the viable foetus).*

[(1) No offence under the Infant Life (Preservation) Act 1929 shall be committed by a registered medical practitioner who terminates a pregnancy in accordance with the provisions of this Act.]

(2) For the purposes of the law relating to abortion, anything done with intent to procure *the miscarriage of a woman is unlawfully done unless authorised by section 1 of this Act* [a woman's miscarriage (or, in the case of a woman carrying more than one foetus, her miscarriage of any foetus) is unlawfully done unless authorised by section 1 of this Act and, in the case of a woman carrying more than one foetus, anything done with intent to procure her miscarriage of any foetus is authorised by that section if:

(a) the ground for termination of the pregenancy specified in subsection (1)(d) of that section applies in relation to any foetus and the thing is done for the purpose of procuring the miscarriage of that foetus, or

(b) any of the other grounds for termination of the pregnancy specified in that section applies].

Note. Words in square brackets substituted for words in italics by Human Fertilisation and Embryology Act 1990, s 37(4), (5), as from 1 April 1991.

6. Interpretation.   In this Act, the following expressions have meanings hereby assigned to them;

'the law relating to abortion' means sections 58 and 59 of the Offences against the Persons Act 1861, and any rule of law relating to the procurement of abortion;

*   *   *   *   *

Note. Words omitted repealed by Health Services Act 1980, s 25(4), Sch 7.

7. Short title, commencement and extent—(1) This Act may be cited as the Abortion Act 1967.

(2) This Act shall come into force on the expiration of the period of six months beginning with the date on which it is passed.

(3) This Act does not extend to Northern Ireland.

MAINTENANCE ORDERS ACT 1968

(1968 c 36)

An Act to amend the enactments relating to matrimonial, guardianship and affiliation proceedings so far as they limit the weekly rate of the maintenance payments which may be ordered by magistrates' courts.

[3 July 1968]

*   *   *   *   *

1. Increase of maximum payments for children. *The enactments described in the Schedule to this Act shall have effect subject to the amendments specified in the second column of that Schedule, being amendments removing the limits of fifty shillings and seven pounds ten shillings imposed by those enactments upon the weekly rate of the payments for the maintenance of a child, and for the maintenance of a party to a marriage, which may be required by order of a magistrates' court thereunder.*

Note. This section repealed by Statute Law (Repeals) Act 1993, s 1(1), Sch 1, Part VIII, as from 5 November 1993.

2. Supplementary. Any order made by a magistrates' court before the date of the commencement of this Act may be varied so as to include, from the date of the variation, provision for the payment of such increased sums as would have been lawful if the order had been made after the first mentioned date.

3. Short title, extent, commencement and repeal—(1) This Act may be cited as the Maintenance Orders Act 1968.

(2) This Act does not extend to Scotland or Northern Ireland.

(3) This Act shall come into force at the expiration of the period of one month beginning with the day on which it is passed.

(4) Section 15 of the Matrimonial Proceedings (Magistrates' Courts) Act 1960 is hereby repealed.

Note. Sub-s 4 repealed by Statute Law (Repeals) Act 1993, s 1(1), Sch 1, Part VIII, as from 5 November 1993.

SCHEDULE

ENACTMENTS AMENDED

The Guardianship of Infants Act 1925   *In section 7, in subsection (1), paragraph (c) of*
(15 & 16 Geo 5 c 45)   *the proviso shall be omitted.*

Note. Guardianship of Infants Act 1925, s 7(1) repealed by Guardianship of Minors Act 1971, s 18(2), Sch 2 (repealed by Children Act 1989, s 108(7), Sch 15). Reference to Guardianship of Infants Act 1925 in the Schedule repealed by Statute Law (Repeals) Act 1977.

The Affiliation Proceedings Act   *In section 4, in paragraph (a) of subsection*
1957 (5 & 6 Eliz 2 c 55)   *(2), the words 'not exceeding fifty shillings a week'*
                                                shall be omitted.

The Maintenance Orders Act 1958   *In section 4, in subsection (3), for the words from*
(6 & 7 Eliz 2 c 39)   *'whichever' to the end there shall be substituted the*
                                                words 'the rate of payments specified by the order
                                                as made or last varied by the original court'.

Note. Entry relating to Maintenance Orders Act 1958 repealed by Administration of Justice Act 1970, s 54, Sch 11, as from 1 September 1970.

The Matrimonial Proceedings (*Magistrates' Courts*) *Act 1960* (*8 & 9 Eliz 2 c* 48)	*In section 2, in paragraphs* (*b*) *and* (*c*) *of subsection* (*1*), *the words* '*not exceeding seven pounds ten shillings*' *shall be omitted; and in paragraph* (*h*) *of that subsection for the words from* '*payments by way of a weekly sum*' *to* '*fifty shillings*' *there shall be substituted the words* '*weekly payments*'.

Note. Entry relating to the 1960 Act repealed by Domestic Proceedings and Magistrates' Courts Act 1978, s 89(2), Sch 3, as from 1 February 1981.

The Matrimonial Causes Act 1965 (*1965 c 72*)	*In section 24, in paragraph* (*a*) *of subsection* (*2*), *the words* '*at a rate not exceeding seven pounds ten shillings a week*' *and the words* '*at a rate not exceeding fifty shillings a week in respect of each such child*' *shall be omitted; and in paragraph* (*b*) *of that subsection for the words from* '*at rates*' *to* '*rate aforesaid*' *there shall be substituted the words* '*an order increasing*'.

Note. Entry relating to Matrimonial Causes Act 1965 repealed by Matrimonial Proceedings and Property Act 1970, s 42(2), Sch 3. Schedule repealed by Statute Law (Repeals) Act 1993, s 1(1), Sch 1, Part VIII, as from 5 November 1993.

DOMESTIC AND APPELLATE PROCEEDINGS (RESTRICTION OF PUBLICITY) ACT 1968

(1968 c 63)

An Act to make further provision for enabling courts to sit in private and for preventing or restricting publicity for certain proceedings.

[25 October 1968]

1. Power of court hearing certain appeals and applications to sit in private—
(1) Where an appeal is brought against a decision of any of the courts mentioned in subsection (4) below, or an application is made for leave to appeal against a decision of any of those courts, and that court had power to sit in private during the whole or any part of the proceedings in which the decision was given, then, subject to subsections (2) and (3) below, the court hearing the appeal or application shall have power to sit in private during the whole or any part of the proceedings on the appeal or application.

(2) Without prejudice to the next following subsection, the court hearing the appeal or application shall give its decision and the reason for its decision in public unless there are good and sufficient grounds for giving them in private and in that case the court shall state those grounds in public.

(3) Where the decision of any of the courts mentioned in subsection (4) below against which an appeal is brought—
   (a) is a conviction, or a sentence or other order made on conviction, or
   (b) was given in the exercise of jurisdiction to punish for contempt of court,
the court hearing the appeal or any further appeal arising out of the same proceedings shall, notwithstanding that it sat in private during the whole or any part of the proceedings on the appeal, state in open court the order made by it on the appeal.

(4) The courts referred to in subsections (1) and (3) above are the Court of Appeal, the High Court, [the Crown Court] *the Chancery Court of a County Palatine,* the Restrictive Practices Court, *the Crown Court at Liverpool, the Crown Court at Manchester, a court of quarter sessions,* a county court and a magistrates' court.

Note. Words 'the Crown Court' inserted and words in italics repealed by Courts Act 1971, s 56(1), Sch 8, para 58, Sch 11, Part IV.

(5) An application to a court to sit in private during the whole or any part of the proceedings on such an appeal or application as is mentioned in subsection (1) above shall be heard in private unless the court otherwise directs.

(6) The powers conferred on a court by this section shall be in addition to any other power of the court to sit in private.

(7) In this section references to a power to sit in private are references to a power to sit in camera or in chambers, but the power conferred by this section on a court which has no power to sit in chambers is a power to sit in camera only.

(8) In this section 'appeal' includes appeal by case stated, and references to a court include references to a judge exercising the powers of a court.

2. Restriction of publicity for legitimacy proceedings, etc, and certain proceedings by a wife for maintenance—(1) The following provisions of this section shall have effect with a view to preventing or restricting publicity for—

    (a) *proceedings under section 39 of the Matrimonial Causes Act 1965 [section 45 of the Matrimonial Causes Act 1973] (which relates to declaration of legitimacy and the like), including any proceedings begun before the commencement of that Act and carried on under that section; and*

    (b) *proceedings under section 22 of that Act (which relates to proceedings by a wife against her husband for maintenance), including any proceedings begun before the said commencement and carried on under that section and any proceedings for the discharge or variation of an order made or deemed to have been made under that section or for the temporary suspension of any provision of any such order or the revival of the operation of any provision so suspended; [and*

    (c) *proceedings under section 6 of the Matrimonial Proceedings and Property Act 1970 (which relates to proceedings by a wife against her husband, or by a husband against his wife, for financial provision) and any proceedings for the discharge or variation of an order made under that section or for the temporary suspension of any provision of any such order or the revival of the operation of any provision so suspended.]*

    [(c) proceedings under section 27 of the Matrimonial Causes Act 1973 (which relates to proceedings by a wife against her husband, or by a husband against his wife, for financial provision) and any proceedings for the discharge or variation of an order made under that section or for the temporary suspension of any provision of any such order or the revival of the operation of any provision so suspended].

    [(d) proceedings under Part III of the Family Law Act 1986;]

    [*(e) proceedings under section 56 (1) of the Family Law Act 1986 (declarations of parentage;]*

Note. Words in square brackets in para (a) substituted for words 'section 39 of the Matrimonial Causes Act 1965' by Matrimonial Causes Act 1973, s 54(1), Sch 2, para 7(1) and whole sub-s (1)(a) repealed by Family Law Act 1986, s 68(1), (2) Sch 1, para 9(a), Sch 2, as from 4 April 1988. Para (b) repealed by Family Law Act 1996, s 66(3), Sch 10, as from a day to be appointed, subject to savings in s 66(2) of, and para 5 of Sch 9 to, the 1996 Act. The word 'and' and para (c) in italics inserted by Matrimonial Proceedings and Property Act 1970, s 42(1), Sch 2, para 3, and a new para (c) in square brackets substituted by Matrimonial Causes Act 1973, s 54(1), Sch 2, para 7(1). Para (d) added by Family Law Act 1986, s 68(1), Sch 1, para 9(a), as from 4 April 1988. Para (e) added by Family Law Reform Act 1987, s 33(1), Sch 2, para 19(a) which also provides that 'and' at the end of (b) repealed by ibid, s 33(4), Sch 4, both amendments as from 4 April 1988. Para (e) repealed by the Child Support, Pensions and Social Security Act 2000, s 85, Sch 9, Pt IX, as from 1 April 2001 (SI 2001 No 774).

    (2) At the end of the said section 39 there shall be added the following subsection:

    '(9) The court (including a county court) by which any proceedings under this section are heard may direct that the whole or any part of the proceedings shall be heard in camera, and an application for a direction under this subsection shall be heard in camera unless the court otherwise directs.'

Note. Sub-s (2) repealed by Matrimonial Causes Act 1973, s 54(1), Sch 2, para 7(1), Sch 3.

(3) Section 1(1)(b) of the Judicial Proceedings (Regulation of Reports) Act 1926 (which restricts the reporting of matrimonial causes) shall extend to any such proceedings as are mentioned in subsection (1) above subject, in the case of the proceedings mentioned in subsection (1)(a) [*subsection (1)(d)*] [subsection 1(d) *or (e)*] above, to the modification that the matters allowed to be printed or published by virtue of subparagraph (ii) of the said section 1(1)(b) shall be particulars of the declaration sought by a petition (instead of a concise statement of the charges, defences and counter charges in support of which evidence has been given).

Note. References in sub-s (3) above to sub-s (1) and to sub-s (1)(a) to be construed as references to sub-s (1) and sub-s (1)(a) as they respectively have effect by virtue of Matrimonial Causes Act 1973, Sch 2, para 7(1); see ibid, para 7(1) to this effect (p 2568). The reference to sub-s (1)(d) in square brackets substituted by Family Law Act 1986, s 68(1), Sch 1, para 9(b), as from 4 April 1988. The reference to sub-s (1)(d) or (e) in square brackets substituted by Family Law Reform Act 1987, s 33(1), Sch 2, para 19(b), as from 4 April 1988. Words 'or (e)' in italics repealed by the Child Support, Pensions and Social Security Act 2000, s 85, Sch 9, Pt IX, as from 1 April 2001 (SI 2001 No 774).

3. Provisions relating to Scotland—(1) Section 1 of this Act shall not extend to Scotland; but nothing in this subsection shall be construed as limiting the powers of the Court of Session in relation to appeals against decisions of the Restrictive Practices Court.

(2) For avoidance of doubt it is hereby declared that, in relation to proceedings on appeals against decisions of the Court of Session, the appellate court has the like power to sit in private as has the Court of Session in relation to proceedings before it.

(3) Subsection (2) above applies to proceedings on applications for leave to appeal as it applies to proceedings on appeals.

(4) In the application to Scotland of section 2 of this Act, subsection (2) thereof shall be omitted.

Note. Sub-s (4) repealed by Matrimonial Causes Act 1973, s 54(1), Sch 3.

4. Provisions relating to Northern Ireland—(1) So much of section 1 of this Act as relates to an appeal against a decision of the Restrictive Practices Court shall extend to Northern Ireland.

(2) The said section 1 shall apply in relation to an appeal, and an application for leave to appeal, against a decision of the Court of Appeal in Northern Ireland and, where the appeal is to the House of Lords, of *a Divisional Court of the Queen's Bench Division of* the High Court of Justice in Northern Ireland as if each of those courts were a court mentioned in subsection (4) of that section.

Note. Words in italics repealed by Judicature (Northern Ireland) Act 1978, s 122(2), Sch 7, Part I.

(3) No limitation on the powers of the Parliament of Northern Ireland imposed by the Government of Ireland Act 1920 shall apply so as to preclude that Parliament from enacting a provision corresponding to section 1 or 2(2) of this Act [of this Act or to section 45(9) of the Matrimonial Causes Act 1973].

Note. Words in square brackets substituted for the words 'or 2(2) of this Act' by Matrimonial Causes Act 1973, s 54(1), Sch 2, para 7(2). Sub-s (3) repealed by Northern Ireland Constitution Act 1973, s 41(1), Sch 6, Part I.

(4) This section and so much of this Act as is applied by this section shall extend to Northern Ireland but save as aforesaid this Act shall not extend to Northern Ireland.

5. Short title. This act may be cited as the Domestic and Appellate Proceedings (Restriction of Publicity) Act 1968.

CIVIL EVIDENCE ACT 1968

(1968 c 64)

An Act to amend the law of evidence in relation to civil proceedings, and in respect of the privilege against self-incrimination to make corresponding amendments in relation to statutory powers of inspection or investigation.   [25 October 1968]

PART I

HEARSAY EVIDENCE

1. Hearsay evidence to be admissible only by virtue of this Act and other statutory provisions, or by agreement—*(1) In any civil proceedings a statement other than one made by a person while giving oral evidence in those proceedings shall be admissible as evidence of any fact stated therein to the extent that it is so admissible by virtue of any provision of this Part of this Act or by virtue of any other statutory provision or by agreement of the parties, but not otherwise.*

(2) In this section 'statutory provision' means any provision contained in, or in an instrument made under, this or any other Act, including any Act passed after this Act.

Note. This section repealed by Civil Evidence Act 1995, s 15(2), Sch 2, as from 31 January 1997. As to persons suffering from defect of speech or of hearing, see s 18(6) (p 2298). For definition of 'statement' see s 10(1) (p 2290) and of 'civil proceedings' see s 18(1) (p 2297).

2. Admissibility of out-of-court statements as evidence of facts stated—*(1) In any civil proceedings a statement made, whether orally or in a document or otherwise, by any person, whether called as a witness in those proceedings or not, shall, subject to this section and to rules of court, be admissible as evidence of any fact stated therein of which direct oral evidence by him would be admissible.*

(2) Where in any civil proceedings a party desiring to give a statement in evidence by virtue of this section has called or intends to call as a witness in the proceedings the person by whom the statement was made, the statement—

(a) shall not be given in evidence by virtue of this section on behalf of that party without the leave of the court; and

(b) without prejudice to paragraph (a) above, shall not be given in evidence by virtue of this section on behalf of that party before the conclusion of the examination-in-chief of the person by whom it was made, except—

    (i) where before that person is called the court allows evidence of the making of the statement to be given on behalf of that party by some other person; or

    (ii) in so far as the court allows the person by whom the statement was made to narrate it in the course of his examination-in-chief on the ground that to prevent him from doing so would adversely affect the intelligibility of his evidence.

(3) Where in any civil proceedings a statement which was made otherwise than in a document is admissible by virtue of this section, no evidence other than direct oral evidence by the person who made the statement or any person who heard or otherwise perceived it being made shall be admissible for the purposes of proving it:

Provided that if the statement was made by a person while giving oral evidence in some other legal proceedings (whether civil or criminal), it may be proved in any manner authorised by the court.

Note. This section repealed by Civil Evidence Act 1995, s 15(2), Sch 2, as from 31 January 1997. For definitions of 'document' and 'statement', see s 10(1) (p 2290), and for definitions of 'civil proceedings', 'court' and 'legal proceedings', see s 18(1), (2) (p 2297).

3. Witness's previous statement, if proved, to be evidence of facts stated—*(1) Where in any civil proceedings—*

(a) a previous inconsistent or contradictory statement made by a person called as a witness in those proceedings is proved by virtue of section 3, 4 or 5 of the Criminal Procedure Act 1865; or

(b) *a previous statement made by a person called as aforesaid is proved for the purpose of rebutting a suggestion that his evidence has been fabricated,*
that statement shall by virtue of this subsection be admissible as evidence of any fact stated therein of which direct oral evidence by him would be admissible.

(2) *Nothing in this Act shall affect any of the rules of law relating to the circumstances in which, where a person called as a witness in any civil proceedings is cross-examined on a document used by him to refresh his memory, that document may be made evidence in those proceedings; and where a document or any part of a document is received in evidence in any such proceedings by virtue of any such rule of law, any statement made in that document or part by the person using the document to refresh his memory shall by virtue of this subsection be admissible as evidence of any fact stated therein of which direct oral evidence by him would be admissible.*

Note. This section repealed by Civil Evidence Act 1995, s 15(2), Sch 2, as from 31 January 1997. For definitions of 'document' and 'statement', see s 10(1) (p 2290), and of 'civil proceedings' see s 18(1) (p 2297).

4. Admissibility of certain records as evidence of facts stated—(1) *Without prejudice to section 5 of this Act, in any civil proceedings a statement contained in a document shall, subject to this section and to rules of court, be admissible as evidence of any fact stated therein of which direct oral evidence would be admissible, if the document is, or forms part of, a record compiled by a person acting under a duty from information which was supplied by a person (whether acting under a duty or not) who had, or may reasonably be supposed to have had, personal knowledge of the matters dealt with in that information and which, if not supplied by that person to the compiler of the record directly, was supplied by him to the compiler of the record indirectly through one or more intermediaries each acting under a duty.*

(2) *Where in any civil proceedings a party desiring to give a statement in evidence by virtue of this section has called or intends to call as a witness in the proceedings the person who originally supplied the information from which the record containing the statement was compiled, the statement—*

(a) *shall not be given in evidence by virtue of this section on behalf of that party without the leave of the court; and*

(b) *without prejudice to paragraph (a) above, shall not without the leave of the court be given in evidence by virtue of this section on behalf of that party before the conclusion of the examination-in-chief of the person who originally supplied the said information.*

(3) *Any reference in this section to a person acting under a duty includes a reference to a person acting in the course of any trade, business, profession or other occupation in which he is engaged or employed or for the purposes of any paid or unpaid office held by him.*

Note. This section repealed by Civil Evidence Act 1995, s 15(2), Sch 2, as from 31 January 1997. For definitions of 'document' and 'statement', see s 10(1) (p 2290), and of 'civil proceedings' see s 18(1) (p 2297).

5. Admissibility of statements produced by computers—(1) *In any civil proceedings a statement contained in a document produced by a computer shall, subject to rules of court, be admissible as evidence of any fact stated therein of which direct oral evidence would be admissible, if it is shown that the conditions mentioned in subsection (2) below are satisfied in relation to the statement and computer in question.*

(2) *The said conditions are—*

(a) *that the document containing the statement was produced by the computer during a period over which the computer was used regularly to store or process information for the purposes of any activities regularly carried on over that period, whether for profit or not, by any body, whether corporate or not, or by any individual;*

(b) *that over that period there was regularly supplied to the computer in the ordinary course of those activities information of the kind contained in the statement or of the kind from which the information so contained is derived;*

 (c) *that throughout the material part of that period the computer was operating properly or, if not, that any respect in which it was not operating properly or was out of operation during that part of that period was not such as to affect the production of the document or the accuracy of its contents; and*

 (d) *that the information contained in the statement reproduces or is derived from information supplied to the computer in the ordinary course of those activities.*

 (3) Where over a period the function of storing or processing information for the purposes of any activities regularly carried on over that period as mentioned in subsection (2) (a) above was regularly performed by computers, whether—

 (a) *by a combination of computers operating over that period; or*

 (b) *by different computers operating in succession over that period; or*

 (c) *by different combinations of computers operating in succession over that period; or*

 (d) *in any other manner involving the successive operation over that period, in whatever order, of one or more computers and one or more combinations of computers,*

all the computers used for that purpose during that period shall be treated for the purposes of this Part of this Act as constituting a single computer; and references in this Part of this Act to a computer shall be construed accordingly.

 (4) In any civil proceedings where it is desired to give a statement in evidence by virtue of this section, a certificate doing any of the following things, that is to say—

 (a) *identifying the document containing the statement and describing the manner in which it was produced;*

 (b) *giving such particulars of any device involved in the production of that document as may be appropriate for the purpose of showing that the document was produced by a computer;*

 (c) *dealing with any of the matters to which the conditions mentioned in subsection (2) above relate,*

and purporting to be signed by a person occupying a responsible position in relation to the operation of the relevant device or the management of the relevant activities (whichever is appropriate) shall be evidence of any matter stated in the certificate; and for the purposes of this subsection it shall be sufficient for a matter to be stated to the best of the knowledge and belief of the person stating it.

 (5) For the purposes of this Part of this Act—

 (a) *information shall be taken to be supplied to a computer if it is supplied thereto in any appropriate form and whether it is so supplied directly or (with or without human intervention) by means of any appropriate equipment;*

 (b) *where, in the course of activities carried on by any individual or body, information is supplied with a view to its being stored or processed for the purposes of those activities by a computer operated otherwise than in the course of those activities, that information, if duly supplied to that computer, shall be taken to be supplied to it in the course of those activities;*

 (c) *a document shall be taken to have been produced by a computer whether it was produced by it directly or (with or without human intervention) by means of any appropriate equipment.*

 (6) Subject to subsection (3) above, in this Part of this Act 'computer' means any device for storing and processing information, and any reference to information being derived from other information is a reference to its being derived therefrom by calculation, comparison or any other process.

Note. This section repealed by Civil Evidence Act 1995, s 15(2), Sch 2, as from 31 January 1997.

6. Provisions supplementary to ss 2 to 5—*(1) Where in any civil proceedings a statement contained in a document is proposed to be given in evidence by virtue of section 2, 4 or 5 of this Act it may, subject to any rules of court, be proved by the production of that document or (whether or not that document is still in existence) by the production of a copy of that document, or of the material part thereof, authenticated in such manner as the court may approve.*

(2) For the purpose of deciding whether or not a statement is admissible in evidence by virtue of section 2, 4 or 5 of this Act, the court may draw any reasonable inference from the circumstances in which the statement was made or otherwise came into being or from any other circumstances, including, in the case of a statement contained in a document, the form and contents of that document.

(3) In estimating the weight, if any, to be attached to a statement admissible in evidence by virtue of section 2, 3, 4 or 5 of this Act regard shall be had to all the circumstances from which any inference can reasonably be drawn as to the accuracy or otherwise of the statement and, in particular—

(a) in the case of a statement falling within section 2(1) or 3(1) or (2) of this Act, to the question whether or not the statement was made contemporaneously with the occurrence or existence of the facts stated, and to the question whether or not the maker of the statement had any incentive to conceal or misrepresent the facts;

(b) in the case of a statement falling within section 4(1) of this Act, to the question whether or not the person who originally supplied the information from which the record containing the statement was compiled did so contemporaneously with the occurrence or existence of the facts dealt with in that information, and to the question whether or not that person, or any person concerned with compiling or keeping the record containing the statement, had any incentive to conceal or misrepresent the facts; and

(c) in the case of a statement falling within section 5(1) of this Act, to the question whether or not the information which the information contained in the statement reproduces or is derived from was supplied to the relevant computer, or recorded for the purpose of being supplied thereto, contemporaneously with the occurrence or existence of the facts dealt with in that information, and to the question whether or not any person concerned with the supply of information to that computer, or with the operation of that computer any equipment by means of which the document containing the statement was produced by it, had any incentive to conceal or misrepresent the facts.

(4) For the purpose of any enactment or rule of law or practice requiring evidence to be corroborated or regulating the manner in which uncorroborated evidence is to be treated—

(a) a statement which is admissible in evidence by virtue of section 2 or 3 of this Act shall not be capable of corroborating evidence given by the maker of the statement; and

(b) a statement which is admissible in evidence by virtue of section 4 of this Act shall not be capable of corroborating evidence given by the person who originally supplied the information from which the record containing the statement was compiled.

(5) If any person in a certificate tendered in evidence in civil proceedings by virtue of section 5(4) of this Act wilfully makes a statement material in those proceedings which he knows to be false or does not believe to be true, he shall be liable on conviction on indictment to imprisonment for a term not exceeding two years or a fine or both.

Note. This section repealed by Civil Evidence Act 1995, s 15(2), Sch 2, as from 31 January 1997. For definitions of 'document' and 'statement', see s 10(1) (p 2290), and of 'civil proceedings' see s 18(1) (p 2297).

7. Admissibility of evidence as to credibility of maker etc of statement admitted under s 2 or 4—(1) Subject to rules of court, where in any civil proceedings a statement made by a person who is not called as a witness in those proceedings is given in evidence by virtue of section 2 of this Act—

(a) any evidence which, if that person had been so called, would be admissible for the purpose of destroying or supporting his credibility as a witness shall be admissible for that purpose in those proceedings; and

(b) evidence tending to prove that, whether before or after he made that statement, that person made (whether orally or in a document or otherwise) another statement inconsistent therewith shall be admissible for the purpose of showing that that person has contradicted himself:

2288 Civil Evidence Act 1968, s 7

Provided that nothing in this subsection shall enable evidence to be given of any matter of which, if the person in question had been called as a witness and had denied that matter in cross-examination, evidence could not have been adduced by the cross-examining party.

(2) Subsection (1) above shall apply in relation to a statement given in evidence by virtue of section 4 of this Act as it applies in relation to a statement given in evidence by virtue of section 2 of this Act, except that references to the person who made the statement and to his making the statement shall be construed respectively as references to the person who originally supplied the information from which the record containing the statement was compiled and to his supplying that information.

(3) Section 3(1) of this Act shall apply to any statement proved by virtue of subsection (1)(b) above as it applies to a previous inconsistent or contradictory statement made by a person called as a witness which is proved as mentioned in paragraph (a) of the said section 3(1).

Note. This section repealed by Civil Evidence Act 1995, s 15(2), Sch 2, as from 31 January 1997. For definitions of 'document' and 'statement', see s 10(1) (p 2290), and of 'civil proceedings', see s 18(1) (p 2297).

8. Rules of court—*(1) Provision shall be made by rules of court as to the procedure which, subject to any exceptions provided for in the rules, must be followed and the other conditions which, subject as aforesaid, must be fulfilled before a statement can be given in evidence in civil proceedings by virtue of section 2, 4 or 5 of this Act.*

(2) Rules of court made in pursuance of subsection (1) above shall in particular, subject to such exceptions (if any) as may be provided for in the rules—

(a) *require a party to any civil proceedings who desires to give in evidence any such statement as is mentioned in that subsection to give to every other party to the proceedings such notice of his desire to do so and such particulars of or relating to the statement as may be specified in the rules, including particulars of such one or more of the persons connected with the making or recording of the statement or, in the case of a statement falling within section 5(1) of this Act, such one or more of the persons concerned as mentioned in section 6(3)(c) of this Act as the rules may in any case require; and*

(b) *enable any party who receives such notice as aforesaid by counter-notice to require any person of whom particulars were given with the notice to be called as a witness in the proceedings unless that person is dead, or beyond the seas, or unfit by reason of his bodily or mental condition to attend as a witness, or cannot with reasonable diligence be identified or found, or cannot reasonably be expected (having regard to the time which has elapsed since he was connected or concerned as aforesaid and to all the circumstances) to have any recollection of matters relevant to the accuracy or otherwise of the statement.*

(3) Rules of court made in pursuance of subsection (1) above—

(a) *may confer on the court in any civil proceedings a discretion to allow a statement falling within section 2(1), 4(1) or 5(1) of this Act to be given in evidence notwithstanding that any requirement of the rules affecting the admissibility of that statement has not been compiled with, but except in pursuance of paragraph (b) below shall not confer on the court a discretion to exclude such a statement where the requirements of the rules affecting its admissibility have been complied with;*

(b) *may confer on the court power, where a party to any civil proceedings has given notice that he desires to give in evidence—*

    (i) *a statement falling within section 2(1) of this Act which was made by a person, whether orally or in a document, in the course of giving evidence in some other legal proceedings (whether civil or criminal); or*

    (ii) *a statement falling within section 4(1) of this Act which is contained in a record of any direct oral evidence given in some other legal proceedings (whether civil or criminal)* to give directions on the application of any party to the proceedings as to whether, and if so on what conditions, the party desiring to give the statement in evidence will be permitted to do so and (whether applicable) as to the manner in which that statement and any other evidence given in those other proceedings is to be proved; and

(c)   may make different provision for different circumstances, and in particular may make different provision with respect to statements falling within sections 2(1), 4(1) and 5(1) of this Act respectively;

and any discretion conferred on the court by rules of court made as aforesaid may be either a general discretion or a discretion exercisable only in such circumstances as may be specified in the rules.

(4)   Rules of court may make provision for preventing a party to any civil proceedings (subject to any exceptions provided for in the rules) from adducing in relation to a person who is not called as a witness in those proceedings any evidence which could otherwise be adduced by him by virtue of section 7 of this Act unless that party has in pursuance of the rules given in respect of that person such a counter-notice as is mentioned in subsection (2)(b) above.

(5)   In deciding for the purposes of any rules of court made in pursuance of this section whether or not a person is fit to attend as a witness, a court may act on a certificate purporting to be a certificate of a fully registered medical practitioner.

(6)   Nothing in the foregoing provisions of this section shall prejudice the generality of section 99 of the Supreme Court of Judicature (Consolidation) Act 1925, section 102 of the County Courts Act 1959, [section 75 of the County Courts Act 1984], section 15 of the Justices of the Peace Act 1949 [section 144 of the Magistrates' Courts Act 1980] or any other enactment conferring power to make rules of court; and nothing in section 101 of the Supreme Court of Judicature (Consolidation) Act 1925, section 102(2) of the County Courts Act 1959 [section 75(2) of the County Courts Act 1984] or any other enactment restricting the matters with respect to which rules of court may be made shall prejudice the making of rules of court with respect to any matter mentioned in the foregoing provisions of this section or the operation of any rules of court made with respect to any such matter.

Note. This section repealed by Civil Evidence Act 1995, s 15(2), Sch 2, as from 31 January 1997. References to Supreme Court of Judicature (Consolidation) Act 1925 in both places repealed by Supreme Court Act 1981, s 152(4), Sch 7.

Reference to Magistrates' Courts Act 1980 substituted for reference to Justices of the Peace Act 1949 by Magistrates' Courts Act 1980, s 154, Sch 7, para 76, as from 6 July 1981.

References to County Courts Act 1984 substituted for references to County Courts Act 1959 by County Courts Act 1984, s 148(1), Sch 2, Part V, para 33, as from 1 August 1984. For definitions of 'statement', see s 10(1) (p 2290), and of 'civil proceedings', 'court' and 'legal proceedings', see s 18(1), (2) (p 2297).

9. Admissibility of certain hearsay evidence formerly admissible at common law—(1) In any civil proceedings a statement which, if this Part of this Act had not been passed, would by virtue of any rule of law mentioned in subsection (2) below have been admissible as evidence of any fact stated therein shall be admissible as evidence of that fact by virtue of this subsection.

(2)   The rules of law referred to in subsection (1) above are the following, that is to say any rule of law—

(a)   whereby in any civil proceedings an admission adverse to a party to the proceedings, whether made by that party or by another person, may be given in evidence against that party for the purpose of proving any fact stated in the admission;

(b)   whereby in any civil proceedings published works dealing with matters of a public nature (for example, histories, scientific works, dictionaries and maps) are admissible as evidence of facts of a public nature stated therein;

(c)   whereby in any civil proceedings public documents (for example, public registers, and returns made under public authority with respect to matters of public interest) are admissible as evidence of facts stated therein; or

    (d)   *whereby in any civil proceedings records (for example, the records of certain courts, treaties, Crown grants, pardons and commissions) are admissible as evidence of facts stated therein.*

In this subsection 'admission' includes any representation of fact, whether made in words or otherwise.

    (3) *In any civil proceedings a statement which tends to establish reputation or family tradition with respect to any matter and which, if this Act had not been passed, would have been admissible in evidence by virtue of any rule of law mentioned in subsection (4) below—*

    (a)   *shall be admissible in evidence by virtue of this paragraph in so far as it is not capable of being rendered admissible under section 2 or 4 of this Act; and*

    (b)   *if given in evidence under this Part of this Act (whether by virtue of paragraph (a) above or otherwise) shall by virtue of this paragraph be admissible as evidence of the matter reputed or handed down;*

and, without prejudice to paragraph (b) above, reputation shall for the purposes of this Part of this Act be treated as a fact and not as a statement or multiplicity of statements dealing with the matter reputed.

    (4) *The rules of law referred to in subsection (3) above are the following, that is to say any rule of law—*

    (a)   *whereby in any civil proceedings evidence of a person's reputation is admissible for the purpose of establishing his good or bad character;*

    (b)   *whereby in any civil proceedings involving a question of pedigree or in which the existence of a marriage is in issue evidence of reputation or family tradition is admissible for the purpose of proving or disproving pedigree or the existence of the marriage, as the case may be; or*

    (c)   *whereby in any civil proceedings evidence of reputation or family tradition is admissible for the purpose of proving or disproving the existence of any public or general right or of identifying any person or thing.*

    (5) *It is hereby declared that in so far as any statement is admissible in any civil proceedings by virtue of subsection (1) or (3)(a) above, it may be given in evidence in those proceedings not withstanding anything in sections 2 to 7 of this Act or in any rules of court made in pursuance of section 8 of this Act.*

    (6) *The words in which any rule of law mentioned in subsection (2) or (4) above is there described are intended only to identify the rule in question and shall not be construed as altering that rule in any way.*

Note. This section repealed by Civil Evidence Act 1995, s 15(2), Sch 2, as from 31 January 1997. For definitions of 'statement', see s 10(1), and of 'civil proceedings', see s 18(1) (p 2297).

10. Interpretation of Part I, and application to arbitrations, etc—*(1) In this Part of this Act—*

    'computer' has the meaning assigned by section 5 of this Act;

    'document' includes, in addition to a document in writing—

    (a)   *any map, plan, graph or drawing;*

    (b)   *any photograph;*

    (c)   *any disc, tape, sound track or other device in which sounds or other data (not being visual images) are embodied so as to be capable (with or without the aid of some other equipment) of being reproduced therefrom; and*

    (d)   *any film, negative, tape or other device in which one or more visual images are embodied so as to be capable (as aforesaid) of being reproduced therefrom;*

    'film' includes a microfilm;

    'statement' includes any representation of fact, whether made in words or otherwise.

    (2) *In this Part of this Act any reference to a copy of a document includes—*

    (a)   *in the case of a document falling within paragraph (c) but not (d) of the definition of 'document' in the foregoing subsection, a transcript of the sounds or other data embodied therein;*

(b)   in the case of a document falling within paragraph (d) but not (c) of that definition, a reproduction or still reproduction of the image or images embodied therein, whether enlarged or not;

(c)   in the case of a document falling within both those paragraphs, such a transcript together with such a still reproduction; and

(d)   in the case of a document not falling within the said paragraph (d) of which a visual image is embodied in a document falling within that paragraph, a reproduction of that image, whether enlarged or not,

and any reference to a copy of the material part of a document shall be construed accordingly.

(3) For the purposes of the application of this Part of this Act in relation to any such civil proceedings as are mentioned in section 18(1)(a) and (b) of this Act [other than civil proceedings on a reference to arbitration under section 64 of the County Courts Act 1984], any rules of court made for the purposes of this Act under section 99 of the Supreme Court of Judicature (Consolidation) Act 1925 shall (except in so far as their operation is excluded by agreement) apply, subject to such modifications as may be appropriate, in like manner as they apply in relation to civil proceedings in the High Court:

Provided that in the case of a reference under section 92 of the County Courts Act 1959 this subsection shall have effect as if for the references to the said section 99 and to civil proceedings in the High Court there were substituted respectively references to section 102 of the County Courts Act 1959 and to proceedings in a county court.

[(3A) For the purposes of the application of this Part of this Act in relation to proceedings on an arbitration under section 64 of the County Courts Act 1984 any rules made for the purposes of this Act under section 75 of that Act shall (except in so far as their operation is excluded by agreement) apply, subject to such modifications as may be appropriate, in like manner as they apply in relation to proceedings in the county court.]

Note. Reference to County Courts Act 1984 in square brackets in sub-s (3) inserted and sub-s (3A) substituted for proviso to sub-s (3) by County Courts Act 1984, s 148(1), Sch 2, Part V, para 34, as from 1 August 1984. Supreme Court of Judicature (Consolidation) Act 1925 repealed by Supreme Court Act 1981, s 152(4), Sch 7.

As for sub-ss (3), (4), see Civil Evidence Act 1972, s 5(2) (p 2490).

(4) If any question arises as to what are, for the purposes of any such civil proceedings as are mentioned in section 18(1)(a) or (b) of this Act, the appropriate modifications of any such rule of court as is mentioned in subsection (3) above, that question shall, in default of agreement, be determined by the tribunal or the arbitrator or umpire, as the case may be.

Note. This section repealed by Civil Evidence Act 1995, s 15(2), Sch 2, as from 31 January 1997.

PART II

MISCELLANEOUS AND GENERAL

Convictions, etc, as evidence in civil proceedings

11. Convictions as evidence in civil proceeding—(1) In any civil proceedings the fact that a person has been convicted of an offence by or before any court in the United Kingdom or by a court-martial there or elsewhere shall (subject to subsection (3) below) be admissible in evidence for the purpose of proving, where to do so is relevant to any issue in those proceedings, that he committed that offence, whether he was so convicted upon a plea of guilty or otherwise and whether or not he is a party to the civil proceedings; but no conviction other than a subsisting one shall be admissible in evidence by virtue of this section.

(2) In any civil proceedings in which by virtue of this section a person is proved to have been convicted of an offence by or before any court in the United Kingdom or by a court-martial there or elsewhere—

(a)   he shall be taken to have committed that offence unless the contrary is proved; and

(b) without prejudice to the reception of any other admissible evidence for the purpose of identifying the facts on which the conviction was based, the contents of any document which is admissible as evidence of the conviction, and the contents of the information, complaint, indictment or charge-sheet on which the person in question was convicted, shall be admissible in evidence for that purpose.

(3) Nothing in this section shall prejudice the operation of section 13 of this Act or any other enactment whereby a conviction or a finding of fact in any criminal proceedings is for the purposes of any other proceedings made conclusive evidence of any fact.

(4) Where in any civil proceedings the contents of any document are admissible in evidence by virtue of subsection (2) above, a copy of that document, or of the material part thereof, purporting to be certified or otherwise authenticated by or on behalf of the court or authority having custody of that document shall be admissible in evidence and shall be taken to be a true copy of that document or part unless the contrary is shown.

(5) Nothing in any of the following enactments, that is to say—

(a) *section 12 of the Criminal Justice Act 1948* [*section 13* [*section 1C*] *of the Powers of Criminal Courts Act 1973*] [section 14 of the Powers of Criminal Courts (Sentencing) Act 2000] (under which a conviction leading to *probation or* discharge is to be disregarded except as therein mentioned);

(b) section 9 of the Criminal Justice (Scotland) Act 1949 (which makes similar provision in respect of convictions on indictment in Scotland); and

(c) section 8 of the Probation Act (Northern Ireland) 1950 (which corresponds to the said section 12) or any corresponding enactment of the Parliament of Northern Ireland for the time being in force,

shall affect the operation of this section; and for the purposes of this section any order made by a court of summary jurisdiction in Scotland under section 1 or section 2 of the said Act of 1949 shall be treated as a conviction.

Note. Reference to Powers of Criminal Courts Act 1973 substituted for reference to Criminal Justice Act 1948 by Act of 1973, ss 56(1), 60(2), Sch 5, para 31. Words 'section 1C' in square brackets in sub-s (5)(a) substituted for words 'section 13' in italics and words 'probation or' in italics repealed, by Criminal Justice Act 1991, ss 100, 101(2), Sch 11, para 5, Sch 13, as from 1 October 1992. Reference to the Powers of Criminal Courts (Sentencing) Act 2000 substituted for reference to the Powers of Criminal Courts Act 1973 by the Powers of Criminal Courts (Senencing) Act 2000, s 165(1), Sch 9, para 36, as from 25 August 2000.

(6) In this section 'court-martial' means a court-martial constituted under the Army Act 1955, the Air Force Act 1955 or the Naval Discipline Act 1957 or a disciplinary court constituted under *section 50* [section 52G] of the said Act of 1957, and in relation to a court-martial 'conviction', *as regards a court-martial constituted under either of the said Acts of 1955, means a finding of guilty which is, or falls to be treated as, a finding of the court duly confirmed, and as regards a court-martial or disciplinary court constituted under the said Act of 1957,* means a finding of guilty which is, or falls to be treated as, the finding of the court, and 'convicted' shall be construed accordingly.

Note. Words 'section 52G' in square brackets substituted for words 'section 50' in italics, and words 'as regards . . . Act of 1957' in italics repealed by Armed Forces Act 1996, ss 5, 35(2), Sch 1, Part IV, para 100, Sch 7, Part II, as from 1 April 1997. For definitions of 'civil proceedings', see s 18(1) (p 2297), and of 'court', see s 18(2) (p 2297).

12. Findings of adultery and paternity as evidence in civil proceedings—(1)
In any civil proceedings—

(a) the fact that a person has been found guilty of adultery in any matrimonial proceedings; and

(b) *the fact that a person has been adjudged to be the father of a child in affiliation proceedings before any court in the United Kingdom,* [(b) the fact that a person has been found to be the father of a child in relevant proceedings before any court in England and Wales [or Northern Ireland] or has been adjudged to be the father of a child in affiliation proceedings before any court in the United Kingdom;]

shall (subject to subsection (3) below) be admissible in evidence for the purpose of proving, where to do so is relevant to any issue in those civil proceedings, that he committed the adultery to which the finding relates or, as the case may be, is (or was) the father of that child, whether or not he offered any defence to the allegation of adultery or paternity and whether or not he is a party to the civil proceedings; but no finding or adjudication other than a subsisting one shall be admissible in evidence by virtue of this section.

Note. Sub-s (1)(b) in square brackets substituted for sub-s (1)(b) in italics by Family Law Reform Act 1987, s 29(2), as from 4 April 1988. Words 'or Northern Ireland' in square brackets inserted by Children (Northern Ireland Consequential Amendments) Order 1995, SI 1995 No 756, art 6, as from 4 November 1996.

(2) In any civil proceedings in which by virtue of this section a person is proved to have been found guilty of adultery as mentioned in subsection (1)(a) above or *to have been adjudged* [to have been found or adjudged] to be the father of a child as mentioned in subsection (1)(b) above—

(a) he shall be taken to have committed the adultery to which the finding relates or, as the case may be, to be (or have been) the father of that child, unless the contrary is proved; and

(b) without prejudice to the reception of any other admissible evidence for the purpose of identifying the facts on which the finding or adjudication was based, the contents of any document which was before the court, or which contains any pronouncement of the court, in the *matrimonial or affiliation proceedings* [other proceedings] in question shall be admissible in evidence for that purpose.

Note. Words in square brackets substituted for words in italics by Family Law Reform Act 1987, s 29(3), as from 4 April 1988.

(3) Nothing in this section shall prejudice the operation of any enactment whereby a finding of fact in any matrimonial or affiliation proceedings is for the purposes of any other proceedings made conclusive evidence of any fact.

(4) Subsection (4) of section 11 of this Act shall apply for the purposes of this section as if the reference to subsection (2) were a reference to subsection (2) of this section.

(5) In this section—

'matrimonial proceedings' means any matrimonial cause in the High Court or a county court in England and Wales or in the High Court in Northern Ireland, any consistorial action in Scotland, or any appeal arising out of any such cause or action;

[*'relevant proceedings' means*—

(a) *proceedings on a complaint under section 42 of the National Assistance Act 1948 or section 26 of the Social Security Act 1986;*

(b) *proceedings on an application for an order under any of the following, namely*—

(i) *section 6 of the Family Law Reform Act 1969;*

(ii) *the Guardianship of Minors Act 1971;*

(iii) *section 34(1)(a), (b) or (c) of the Children Act 1975;*

(iv) *section 47 of the Child Care Act 1980; and*

[*(iv) paragraph 23 of Schedule 2 to the Children Act 1989*]

(v) *section 4 of the Family Law Reform Act 1987;*

(c) *proceedings on an application under section 35 of the said Act of 1975 for the revocation of a custodianship order;*]

['relevant proceedings' means—
  (a) proceedings on a complaint under section 42 of the National Assistance Act 1948 or section 26 of the Social Security Act 1986;
  (b) proceedings under the Children Act 1989;
  (c) proceedings which would have been relevant proceedings for the purposes of this section in the form in which it was in force before the passing of the Children Act 1989;
  [*(d) section 27 of the Child Support Act 1991;*]
  [(e) proceedings which are relevant proceedings as defined in section 8(5) of the Civil Evidence Act (Northern Ireland) 1971];
  'affiliation proceedings' means, in relation to Scotland, any action of affiliation and aliment;
and in this subsection 'consistorial action' does not include an action of aliment only between husband and wife raised in the Court of Session or an action of interim aliment raised in the sheriff court.

Note. Note definition of 'matrimonial proceedings' in sub-s (5), and for 'civil proceedings' and 'court', see s 18(2) (p 2297). Definition of 'relevant proceedings' in italics inserted by Family Law Reform Act 1987, s 29(4), as from 4 April 1988. Sub-para (iv) in square brackets in definition 'relevant proceedings' in italics substituted by Children Act 1989, s 108(5), Sch 13, para 24, as from 14 October 1991. Definition 'relevant proceedings' in square brackets substituted for definition in italics by Courts and Legal Services Act 1990, s 116, Sch 16, para 2(1), as from 14 October 1991. In definition 'relevant proceedings' para (d) added by Child Support Act 1991, s 27(5), as from 5 April 1993, para (e) added by Children (Northern Ireland Consequential Amendments) Order 1995, SI 1995 No 756, art 6, as from 4 November 1996. In definition 'relevant proceedings' para (d) repealed by the Child Support, Pensions and Social Security Act 2000, s 85, Sch 9, Pt IX, as from 1 April 2001 (SI 2001 No 774).

13. Conclusiveness of convictions for purposes of defamation actions—(1) In an action for libel or slander in which the question whether *a person* [the plaintiff] did or did not commit a criminal offence is relevant to an issue arising in the action, proof that, at the time when that issue falls to be determined, *that person* [he] stands convicted of that offence shall be conclusive evidence that he committed that offence; and his conviction thereof shall be admissible in evidence accordingly.

(2) In any such action as aforesaid in which by virtue of this section *a person* [the plaintiff] is proved to have been convicted of an offence, the contents of any document which is admissible as evidence of the conviction, and the contents of the information, complaint, indictment or charge-sheet on which *that person* [he] was convicted, shall, without prejudice to the reception of any other admissible evidence for the purpose of identifying the facts on which the conviction was based, be admissible in evidence for the purpose of identifying those facts.

Note. Words in square brackets in sub-ss (1), (2) substituted for words in italics by Defamation Act 1996, s 12(1), as from 4 September 1996, in relation to trials of actions beginning after that date.

(2A) In the case of an action for libel or slander in which there is more than one plaintiff—
  (a) the references in subsections (1) and (2) above to the plaintiff shall be construed as references to any of the plaintiffs, and
  (b) proof that any of the plaintiffs stands convicted of an offence shall be conclusive evidence that he committed that offence so far as that fact is relevant to any issue arising in relation to his cause of action or that of any other plaintiff.]

Note. Sub-s (2A) inserted by Defamation Act 1996, s 12(1), as from 4 September 1996, in relation to trials of actions beginning after that date.

(3) For the purposes of this section a person shall be taken to stand convicted of an offence if but only if there subsists against him a conviction of that offence by or before a court in the United Kingdom or by a court-martial there or elsewhere.

(4) Subsections (4) to (6) of section 11 of this Act shall apply for the purposes of this section as they apply for the purposes of that section, but as if in the said subsection (4) the reference to subsection (2) were a reference to subsection (2) of this section.

(5) The foregoing provisions of this section shall apply for the purposes of any action begun after the passing of this Act, whenever the cause of action arose, but shall not apply for the purposes of any action begun before the passing of this Act or any appeal or other proceedings arising out of any such action.

Note. For definitions of 'court martial', 'convicted' and 'conviction', see s 11(6) (p 2292), and of 'court' see s 18(2) (p 2297).

Privilege

14. Privilege against incrimination of self or spouse—(1) The right of a person in any legal proceedings other than criminal proceedings to refuse to answer any question or produce any document or thing if to do so would tend to expose that person to proceedings for an offence or for the recovery of a penalty—

    (a) shall apply only as regards criminal offences under the law of any part of the United Kingdom and penalties provided for by such law; and

    (b) shall include a like right to refuse to answer any question or produce any document or thing if to do so would tend to expose the husband or wife of that person to proceedings for any such criminal offence or for the recovery of any such penalty.

(2) In so far as any existing enactment conferring (in whatever words) powers of inspection or investigation confers on a person (in whatever words) any right otherwise than in criminal proceedings to refuse to answer any question or give any evidence tending to incriminate that person, subsection (1) above shall apply to that right as it applies to the right described in that subscription; and every such existing enactment shall be construed accordingly.

(3) In so far as any existing enactment provides (in whatever words) that in any proceedings other than criminal proceedings a person shall not be excused from answering any question or giving any evidence on the ground that to do so may incriminate that person, that enactment shall be construed as providing also that in such proceedings a person shall not be excused from answering any question or giving any evidence on the ground that to do so may incriminate the husband or wife of that person.

(4) Where any existing enactment (however worded) that—

    (a) confers powers of inspection or investigation; or

    (b) provides as mentioned in subsection (3) above,

further provides (in whatever words) that any answer or evidence given by a person shall not be admissible in evidence against that person in any proceedings or class of proceedings (however described, and whether criminal or not), that enactment shall be construed as providing also that any answer or evidence given by that person shall not be admissible in evidence against the husband or wife of that person in the proceedings or class of proceedings in question.

(5) In this section 'existing enactment' means any enactment passed before this Act; and the references to giving evidence are references to giving evidence in any manner, whether by furnishing information, making discovery, producing documents or otherwise.

Note. For definition of 'legal proceedings' and meaning of 'husband' and 'wife', see s 18(2) (p 2297).

15. Privilege for certain communications relating to patent proceedings.

Note. Repealed by Patents Act 1977, s 132, Sch 6.

16. Abolition of certain privileges—(1) The following rules of law are hereby abrogated except in relation to criminal proceedings, that is to say—

    (a) the rule whereby, in any legal proceedings, a person cannot be compelled to answer any question or produce any document or thing if to do so would tend to expose him to a forfeiture; and

    (b) the rule whereby, in any legal proceedings, a person other than a party to the proceedings cannot be compelled to produce any deed or other document relating to his title to any land.

(2) The rule of law whereby, in any civil proceedings, a party to the proceedings cannot be compelled to produce any document relating solely to his own case and in no way tending to impeach that case or support the case of any opposing party is hereby abrogated.

(3) Section 3 of the Evidence (Amendment) Act 1853 (which provides that a husband or wife shall not be compellable to disclose any communication made to him or her by his or her spouse during the marriage) shall cease to have effect except in relation to criminal proceedings.

(4) In section 43(1) of the Matrimonial Causes Act 1965 (under which the evidence of a husband or wife is admissible in any proceedings to prove that marital intercourse did or did not take place between them during any period, but a husband or wife is not compellable in any proceedings to give evidence of the matters aforesaid), the words from 'but a husband or wife' to the end of the subsection shall cease to have effect except in relation to criminal proceedings.

Note. For Matrimonial Causes Act 1965, s 43, see p 2248. Remaining words in s 43(1) repealed by Matrimonial Causes Act 1973, s 54(1), Sch 3 and replaced by ibid, s 48(1) (p 2551).

(5) A witness in any proceedings instituted in consequence of adultery, whether a party to the proceedings or not, shall not be excused from answering any question by reason that it tends to show that he or she has been guilty of adultery; and accordingly the proviso to section 3 of the Evidence Further Amendment Act 1869 and, in section 43(2) of the Matrimonial Causes Act 1965, the words from 'but' to the end of the subsection shall cease to have effect.

Note. For Matrimonial Causes Act 1965, s 43, see p 2552. Unrepealed part of s 43(2) repealed by Matrimonial Causes Act 1973, s 54(1), Sch 3 and not replaced. For definitions of 'civil proceedings' and 'legal proceedings', see s 18(1), (2) (p 2297).

17. Consequential amendments relating to privilege—(1) In relation to England and Wales—

    (a) section 1(3) of the Tribunals of Inquiry (Evidence) Act 1921 (under which a witness before a tribunal to which that Act has been applied is entitled to the same privileges as if he were a witness before the High Court) shall have effect as if after the word 'witness', in the second place where it occurs, there were inserted the words 'in civil proceedings'; and

    (b) section 8(5) of the Parliamentary Commissioner Act 1967 (which provides that, subject as there mentioned, no person shall be compelled for the purposes of an investigation under that Act to give any evidence or produce any document which he could not be compelled to give or produce in proceedings before the High Court) shall have effect as if before the word 'proceedings' there were inserted the word 'civil';

and, so far as it applies to England and Wales, any other existing enactment, however framed or worded, which in relation to any tribunal, investigation or inquiry (however described) confers on persons required to answer questions or give evidence any privilege described by reference to the privileges of witnesses in proceedings before any court shall, unless the contrary intention appears, be construed as referring to the privileges of witnesses in civil proceedings before that court.

(2) Where a person is examined by virtue of an order under section 1 of the Foreign Tribunals Evidence Act 1856 or section 1 of the Evidence by Commission Act 1859 made by a

court or judge in England and Wales for the purpose of obtaining his testimony in relation to any legal proceedings pending before a court or tribunal outside England and Wales, then for the purpose of determining his rights under section 5 of the said Act of 1856 or section 4 of the said Act of 1859 to refuse to answer questions or produce documents—

(a) *if those proceedings are criminal proceedings, the provisions of sections 14 to 16 of this Act and the amendments provided for by the Schedule to this Act shall be disregarded; but*

(b) *in any other case the references in the said section 5 of the said section 4, as the case may be, to any cause pending as mentioned in that section shall be construed as references to any civil cause so pending.*

Note. Sub-s (2) repealed by Evidence (Proceedings in Other Jurisdictions) Act 1975, s 8(2), Sch 2, as from 4 May 1976, and extended to Sovereign Base Areas of Akrotiri and Dhekalia in Cyprus by Evidence (Proceedings in Other Jurisdictions) (Sovereign Base Areas of Akrotiri and Dhekelia) Order 1978, SI 1978 No 1920, art 2, Schedule.

(3) Without prejudice to the generality of subsections (2) to (4) of section 14 of this Act, the enactments mentioned in the Schedule to this Act shall have effect subject to the amendments provided for by that Schedule (being verbal amendments to bring those enactments into conformity with the provisions of that section).

(4) Subsection (5) of section 14 of this Act shall apply for the purposes of this section as it applies for the purposes of that section.

General

18. General interpretation, and savings—(1) In this Act 'civil proceedings' includes, in addition to civil proceedings in any of the ordinary courts of law—

(a) civil proceedings before any other tribunal, being proceedings in relation to which the strict rules of evidence apply; and

(b) an arbitration or reference, whether under an enactment or not, but does not include civil proceedings in relation to which the strict rules of evidence do not apply.

(2) In this Act—

'court' does not include a court-martial, and, in relation to an arbitration or reference, means the arbitrator or umpire and, in relation to proceedings before a tribunal (not being one of the ordinary courts of law), means the tribunal;

'legal proceedings' includes an arbitration or reference, whether under an enactment or not;

and for the avoidance of doubt it is hereby declared that in this Act, and in any amendment made by this Act in any other enactment, references to a person's husband or wife do not include references to a person who is no longer married to that person.

(3) Any reference in this Act to any other enactment is a reference thereto as amended, and includes a reference thereto as applied, by or under any other enactment.

(4) Nothing in this Act shall prejudice the operation of any enactment which provides (in whatever words) that any answer or evidence given by a person in specified circumstances shall not be admissible in evidence against him or some other person in any proceedings or class of proceedings (however described).

In this subsection the reference to giving evidence is a reference to giving evidence in any manner, whether by furnishing information, making discovery, producing documents or otherwise.

(5) Nothing in this Act shall prejudice—

(a) any power of a court, in any legal proceedings, to exclude evidence (whether by preventing questions from being put or otherwise) at its discretion; or

(b) the operation of any agreement (whenever made) between the parties to any legal proceedings as to the evidence which is to be admissible (whether generally or for any particular purpose) in those proceedings.

(6) It is hereby declared that where, by reason of any defect of speech or hearing from which he is suffering, a person called as a witness in any legal proceedings gives his evidence in writing or by signs, that evidence is to be treated for the purposes of this Act as being given orally.

Note. See Civil Evidence Act 1972, s 5(1) (p 2464) and Children Act 1989, s 96(7) (p 3280).

19. Northern Ireland.

Note. *Repealed by Northern Ireland Constitution Act 1973, s 41, Sch 6, Part I.*

20. Short title, repeals, extent and commencement—(1) This Act may be cited as the Civil Evidence Act 1968.

(2) Sections 1, 2, 6(1) (except the words from 'Proceedings' to 'references') and 6(2)(b) of the Evidence Act 1938 are hereby repealed.

(3) This Act shall not extend to Scotland or, *except in so far as it enlarges the powers of the Parliament of Northern Ireland*, to Northern Ireland.

Note. Words in italics repealed by Northern Ireland Constitution Act 1973, s 41(1), Sch 6, Part I.

(4) The following provisions of this Act, namely section 13 to 19, this section (except subsection (2)) and the Schedule, shall come into force on the day this Act is passed, and the other provisions of this Act shall come into force on such day as the Lord Chancellor may by order made by statutory instrument appoint; and different days may be so appointed for different purposes of this Act or for the same purposes in relation to different circumstances.

Note. The whole Act brought into force save that Part I (ss 1–10) and s 20(2) not brought into force as regards proceedings in magistrates' courts: see SI 1968 No 1734, SI 1969 No 1104 and SI 1970 No 18.

SCHEDULE   Section 17

CONSEQUENTIAL AMENDMENTS

Act amended	Amendment
The Hop (Prevention of Frauds) Act 1866 (29 & 30 Vict c 37)	*In section 12 (answers to be inadmissible against person giving them), after the words 'such person' shall there be inserted the words 'or the husband or wife of such person'.*

Note. Entry repealed by Statute Law (Repeals) Act 1981, as from 21 May 1981.

The Explosive Substances Act 1883 (46 & 47 Vict c 3)	In section 6(2) (answers to be inadmissible against person giving them), for the word 'himself' there shall be substituted the words 'that witness or the husband or wife of that witness', after the word 'him', where it first occurs, there shall be inserted the words 'or her', and for the words 'against him' there shall be substituted the words 'against that person or the husband or wife of that person'.
The Land Registration Act 1925 (15 & 16 Geo 5 c 21)	*In section 119(2) (answers to be inadmissible against person giving them), after the words 'such person' there shall be inserted the words 'or the husband or wife of such person'.*

Note. Entry repealed by the Land Registration Act 2002, s 135, Sch 13, as from a day to be appointed.

The Borrowing (Control and Guarantees) Act 1946 (9 & 10 Geo 6 c 58)	*In the Schedule, in paragraph 2(1) (privilege against self- substituted the words 'that person or the husband or wife of that person, that person'.*

Note. Entry repealed by Government Trading Act 1990, s 4, Sch 2, Part I, as from 11 February 1991.

The Representation of the People Act 1949 (12, 13 & 14 Geo 6 c 68)	In section *123(7)* (*answers to be inadmissible against person giving them*), *for the words 'himself' and 'him' respectively there shall be substituted the words 'that person or the husband or wife of that person'.*

Note. Entry repealed by Representation of the People Act 1983, s 206, Sch 9, Part II, as from 15 March 1983.

The Baking Industry (Hours of Work) Act 1954 (2 & 3 Eliz 2 c 57)	In section *6(2)* (*privilege against self-incrimination*), *after the words 'himself' there shall be added the words 'or, in the case of a person who is married, his or her wife or husband'.*

Note. Entry repealed by Sex Discrimination Act 1986, s 9(2), Schedule, Part III, as from 27 February 1987.

The Wages Councils Act 1959 (7 & 8 Eliz 2 c 69)	In section *19(3)* (*privilege against self-incrimination*), *after the word 'himself' there shall be added the words 'or, in the case of a person who is married, his or her wife or husband'.*

Note. Entry repealed by Wages Councils Act 1979, s 31(3), Sch 7.

The Factories Act 1961 (9 & 10 Eliz 2 c 34)	In section 146(1)(f) (privilege against self-incrimination), after the word 'himself' there shall be inserted the words 'or, in the case of a person who is married, his or her wife or husband'.
The Offices, Shops and Railway Premises Act 1963 (1963 c 41)	In section 53(1)(d) (answers to be inadmissible against person giving them), for the words against him' there shall be substituted the words 'against that person or the husband or wife of that person'.
The National Insurance Act 1965 (1965 c 51)	In section *90(4)* (*privilege against self-incrimination*), *after the word 'himself' there shall be added the words 'or, in the case of a person who is married, his or her wife or husband'.*
The National Insurance (Industrial Injuries) Act 1965 (1965 c 52)	In section *64(4)* (*privilege against self-incrimination*), *after the word 'himself' there shall be added the words 'or, in the case of a person who is married, his or her wife or husband'.*

Note. Entries in italics repealed by Social Security Act 1973, ss 100, 101, Sch 28, as from 6 April 1975.

The Selective Employment Payments Act 1966 (1966 c 32)	In section 8(3) (privilege against self-incrimination), after the words 'him' there shall be added the words or, in the case of a person who is married, his or her wife or husband'.

FAMILY LAW REFORM ACT 1969

(1969 c 46)

ARRANGEMENT OF SECTIONS

PART I

REDUCTION OF AGE OF MAJORITY AND RELATED PROVISIONS

PART II

PROPERTY RIGHTS OF ILLEGITIMATE CHILDREN

PART III

PROVISIONS FOR USE OF BLOOD TESTS IN DETERMINING PATERNITY

PART IV

MISCELLANEOUS AND GENERAL

An Act to amend the law relating to the age of majority, to persons who have not attained that age and to the time when a particular age is attained; to amend the law relating to the property rights of illegitimate children and of other persons whose relationship is traced through an illegitimate link; to make provisions for the use of blood tests for the purpose of determining the paternity of any person in civil proceedings; to make provision with respect to the evidence required to rebut a presumption of legitimacy and illegitimacy; to make further provision, in connection with the registration of the birth of an illegitimate child, for entering the name of the father; and for connected purposes. [25 July 1969]

PART I

REDUCTION OF AGE OF MAJORITY AND RELATED PROVISIONS

1. Reduction of age of majority from 21 to 18—(1) As from the date on which this section comes into force a person shall attain full age on attaining the age of eighteen instead of on attaining the age of twenty-one; and a person shall attain full age on that date if he has then already attained the age of eighteen but not the age of twenty-one.

(2) The foregoing subsection applies for the purposes of any rule of law, and, in the absence of a definition or of any indication of a contrary intention, for the construction of 'full age', 'infant', 'infancy', 'minor', 'minority' and similar expressions in—

(a) any statutory provision, whether passed or made before, on or after the date on which this section comes into force; and

(b) any deed, will or other instrument of whatever nature (not being a statutory provision) made on or after that date.

(3) In the statutory provisions specified in Schedule 1 to this Act for any reference to the age of twenty-one years there shall be substituted a reference to the age of eighteen years; but the amendment by this subsection of the provisions specified in Part II of that Schedule shall be without prejudice to any power of amending or revoking those provisions.

(4) This section does not affect the construction of any such expression as is referred to in subsection (2) of this section in any of the statutory provisions described in Schedule 2 to this Act, and the transitional provisions and savings contained in Schedule 3 to this Act shall have effect in relation to this section.

(5) The Lord Chancellor may by order made by statutory instrument amend any provision in any local enactment passed on or before the date on which this section comes into force (not being a provision decribed in paragraph 2 of Schedule 2 to this Act) by substituting a reference to the age of eighteen years for any reference therein to the age of twenty-one years; and any statutory instrument containing an order under this subsection shall be subject to annulment in pursuance of a resolution of either House of Parliament.

(6) In this section 'statutory provision' means any enactment (including, except where the context otherwise requires, this Act) and any order, rule, regulation, byelaw or other instrument made in the exercise of a power conferred by any enactment.

(7) Notwithstanding any rule of law, a will or codicil executed before the date on which this section comes into force shall not be treated for the purposes of this section as made on or after that date by reason only that the will or codicil is confirmed by a codicil executed on or after that date.

2. Provisions relating to marriage—(1) In the following enactments, that is to say—

(a) *section 7(c) of the Foreign Marriage Act 1892 (persons under 21 intending to be married by a marriage officer to swear that necessary consents have been obtained);*

(b) paragraph 2(c) of Part I of the Schedule to the Marriage with Foreigners Act, 1906 (persons under 21 seeking certificate to swear that necessary consents have been obtained);

(c) section 78(1) of the Marriage Act 1949 (definition of 'infant' as person under
the age of 21),

for the words 'twenty-one years' there shall be substituted the words 'eighteen years'.

Note. Sub-s (1)(a) repealed by Foreign Marriage (Amendment) Act 1988, s 7(2), Schedule, as
from 12 April 1990. For Marriage Act 1949, s 78, see p 2119.

(2) In subsection (5) of section 3 of the said Act of 1949 (which defines the courts
having jurisdiction to consent to the marriage of an infant)—

(a) for the words 'the county court of the district in which any respondent
resides' there shall be substituted the words 'the county court of the district in
which any applicant or respondent resides'; and

(b) after the words 'or a court of summary jurisdiction' there shall be inserted
the words 'having jurisdiction in the place in which any applicant or respondent resides'.

Note. For Marriage Act 1949, s 3(5), see p 2108.

(3) Where for the purposes of obtaining a certificate *or licence* for marriage under
Part III of the said Act of 1949 a person declares that the consent of any person or
persons whose consent to the marriage is required under the said section 3 has been
obtained, the superintendent registrar may refuse to issue the certificate *or licence* for
marriage unless satisfied by the production of written evidence that the consent of
that person or of those persons has in fact been obtained.

Note. Words in italics repealed by the Immigration and Asylum Act 1999, s 169(1), (3), Sch 14,
para 37, Sch 16, as from 1 January 2001 (SI 2001 No 2698).

(4) In this section any expression which is also used in the said Act of 1949 has
the same meaning as in that Act.

3. Provisions relating to wills and intestacy—(1) In the following enactments,
that is to say—

(a) section 7 of the Wills Act 1837 (invalidity of wills made by persons under 21);

(b) section 1 and 3(1) of the Wills (Soldiers and Sailors) Act 1918 (soldier etc. eligible to make will and dispose of real property although under 21),

in their application to wills made after the coming into force of this section, for the
words 'twenty-one years' there shall be substituted the words 'eighteen years'.

(2) In section 47(1)(i) of the Administration of Estates Act 1925 (statutory trusts
on intestacy), in its application to the estate of an intestate dying after the coming
into force of this section, for the words 'twenty-one years' in both places where they
occur there shall be substituted the words 'eighteen years'.

(3) Any will which—

(a) has been made, whether before or after the coming into force of this section,
by a person under the age of eighteen; and

(b) is valid by virtue of the provisions of section 11 of the said Act of 1837 and the
said Act of 1918,

may be revoked by that person notwithstanding that he is still under that age
whether or not the circumstances are then such that he would be entitled to make a
valid will under those provisions.

(4) In this section 'will' has the same meaning as in the said Act of 1837 and
'intestate' has the same meaning as in the said Act of 1925.

**4. Maintenance for children under Guardianship of Infants Acts to continue
to age of 21**—*(1) An order under section 3(2), 5(4) or 6 of the Guardianship of Infants Act
1925 for the payment of sums towards the maintenance or education of a minor may require
such sums to continue to be paid in respect of any period after the date on which he ceases to be a
minor but not extending beyond the date on which he attains the age of twenty-one; and any
order which is made as aforesaid may provide that any sum which is payable thereunder for the
benefit of a person who has ceased to be a minor shall be paid to that person himself.*

(2) *Subject to subsections (3) and (4) of this section, where a person who has ceased to be a minor but has not attained the age of twenty-one has, while a minor, been the subject of an order under any of the provisions of the Guardianship of Infants Acts 1886 and 1925, the court may, on the application of either parent of that person or of that person himself, make an order requiring either parent to pay to the other parent, to anyone else for the benefit of that person or to that person himself, in respect of any period not extending beyond the date when he attains the said age, such weekly or other periodical sums towards his maintenance or education as the court thinks reasonable having regard to the means of the person on whom the requirement is imposed.*

(3) *No order shall be made under subsection (2) of this section, and no liability under such an order shall accrue, at a time when the parents of the person in question are residing together, and if they so reside for a period of three months after an order has been made it shall cease to have effect.*

(4) *No order shall be made under subsection (2) of this section requiring any person to pay any sum towards the maintenance or education of an illegitimate child of that person.*

(5) *Subsection (2) of this section shall be construed as one with the said Acts of 1886 and 1925, and—*

(a) *any order under that subsection, or under any corresponding enactment of the Parliament of Northern Ireland, shall be included among the orders to which section 16 of the Maintenance Orders Act 1950 applies;*

(b) *any order under that subsection shall be included among the orders mentioned in section 2(1)(d) of the Reserve and Auxiliary Forces (Protection of Civil Interests) Act 1951 and be deemed to be a maintenance order within the meaning of the Maintenance Orders Act 1958.*

Note. This section repealed by Guardianship of Minors Act 1971, s 18(2), Sch 2. In sub-s (5), the words 'and be deemed' to the end of sub-s (5)(b) repealed by Administration of Justice Act 1970, s 54, Sch 11.

5. Modification of other enactments relating to maintenance of children so as to preserve benefits up to age of 21—(1) *For the purposes of the Inheritance (Family Provision) Act 1938, the dependants of a deceased person shall continue to include any son who has not attained the age of twenty-one; and accordingly—*

(a) *in subsection (1)(c) of that Act for the words 'infant son' there shall be substituted the words 'a son who has not attained the age of twenty-one years';*

(b) *in subsection (2)(c) of that Act for the words 'in the case of an infant son, his attaining the age of twenty-one years' there shall be substituted the words 'in the case of a son who has not attained the age of twenty-one years, his attaining that age'.*

Note. Sub-s (1) repealed by Inheritance (Provision for Family and Dependants) Act 1975, s 26(2), Schedule.

(2) *Where a child in respect of whom an affiliation order has been made under the Affiliation Proceedings Act 1957 has attained the age of eighteen and his mother is dead, of unsound mind or in prison—*

(a) *any application for an order under subsection (2) or (3) of section 7 of that Act directing that payments shall be made under the affiliation order for any period after he has attained that age may be made by the child himself; and*

(b) *the child himself shall be the person entitled to any payments directed by an order under that section to be so made for any such period as aforesaid.*

Note. Sub-s (2) repealed by Domestic Proceedings and Magistrates' Courts Act 1978, s 89(2), Sch 3, as from 1 February 1981.

(3) *Section 22 of the Matrimonial Causes Act 1965 (power to order maintenance for infant children in cases of wilful neglect) shall continue to apply to children up to the age of twenty-one, but not so as to enable an order for custody to be made under section 35(1) of that Act (custody of children where maintenance is ordered under section 22) in respect of any child who has attained the age of eighteen; and accordingly—*

(a)   in subsection (2) of the said section 22 for the words 'any infant child of the marriage in question and any infant illegitimate child of both parties to the marriage' there shall be substituted the words 'any child of the marriage who is under twenty-one and any illegitimate child of both parties to the marriage who is under that age';

(b)   in the said section 35(1) after the words 'any child to whom that subsection applies' there shall be inserted the words 'who is under eighteen', and at the end there shall be added the words 'and the child is under that age'.

Note. Sub-s (3) repealed by Matrimonial Proceedings and Property Act 1970, s 42(2), Sch 3.

6. Maintenance for wards of court—*(1)   In this section 'the court' means any of the following courts in the exercise of its jurisdiction relating to the wardship of children, that is to say, the High Court, the Court of Chancery of the County Palatine of Lancaster and the Court of Chancery of the County Palatine of Durham, and 'ward of court' means a ward of the court in question [and references (however expressed) to any relationship between two persons shall be construed in accordance with section 1 of the Family Law Reform Act 1987].*

Note. Words 'the Court of Chancery ... Durham' repealed by Courts Act 1971, s 56(4), Sch 11, Part II. Words in square brackets added by Family Law Reform Act 1987, s 33(1), Sch 2, para 20(2), as from 1 April 1989.

(2)   Subject to the provisions of this section, the court may make an order—

(a)   requiring either parent of a ward of court to pay to the other parent; or

(b)   requiring either parent or both parents of a ward of court to pay to any other person having the care and control of the ward [or to the ward],

such weekly or other periodical sums towards the maintenance and education of the ward as the court thinks reasonable having regard to the means of the person or persons on whom the requirement is imposed.

Note. Words in square brackets inserted by Administration of Justice Act 1982, s 50, as from 1 January 1983.

(3)   An order under subsection (2) of this section may require such sums as are mentioned in that subsection to continue to be paid in respect of any period after the date on which the person for whose benefit the payments are to be made ceases to be a minor but not beyond the date on which he attains the age of twenty-one, and any order made as aforesaid may provide that any sum which is payable thereunder for the benefit of that person after he has ceased to be a minor shall be paid to that person himself.

[(3)   Section 12 of the Guardianship of Minors Act 1971 (duration of orders for maintenance) and subsections (4), (5) and (6) of section 12C of that Act (variation and revival of orders for periodical payments) shall apply in relation to an order made under subsection (2) of this section as they apply in relation to an order made by the High Court under section 11B of that Act.]

Note. Sub-s (3) in square brackets substituted for original sub-s (3) by Family Law Reform Act 1987, s 33(1), Sch 2, para 20(3), as from 1 April 1989.

(4)   Subject to the provisions of this section, where a person who has ceased to be a minor but has not attained the age of twenty-one has at any time been the subject of an order making him a ward of court, the court may, on the application of either parent of that person or of that person himself, make an order requiring either parent to pay to the other parent, to anyone else for the benefit of that person or to that person himself, in respect of any period not extending beyond the date when he attains the said age, such weekly or other periodical sums towards his maintenance or education as the court thinks reasonable having regard to the means of the person on whom the requirement in question is imposed.

(5)   No order shall be made under this section, and no liability under such an order shall accrue, at a time when the parents of the ward or former ward, as the case may be, are residing together, and if they so reside for a period of three months [six months] after such an order has been made it shall cease to have effect; but the foregoing provisions of this subsection shall not apply to any order made by virtue of subsection (2)(b) of this section.

Note. Words in square brackets substituted for words 'three months' by Family Law Reform Act 1987, s 33(1) Sch 2, para 20(3), as from 1 April 1989.

(6) No order shall be made under this section requiring any person to pay any sum towards the maintenance or education of an illegitimate child of that person.

Note. Sub-s (6) repealed by Family Law Reform Act 1987, s 33(1), Sch 2, para 20(5), as from 1 April 1989.

(7) Any order under this section, or under any corresponding enactment of the Parliament of Northern Ireland [or under section 27 of the Judicature (Northern Ireland) Act 1978] shall be included among the orders to which section 16 of the Maintenance Orders Act 1950 applies; and any order under this section shall be included among the orders mentioned in section 2(1)(d) of the Reserve and Auxiliary Forces (Protection of Civil Interests) Act 1951 and be deemed to be a maintenance order within the meaning of the Maintenance Orders Act 1958.

Note. For Maintenance Orders Act 1950, s 16, see p 2147.

Words 'or under any corresponding enactment of the Parliament of Northern Ireland' substituted by words in square brackets by Judicature (Northern Ireland) Act 1978, s 122(1), Sch 5, Part II. Words 'and be deemed …' to end repealed by Administration of Justice Act 1970, s 54, Sch 11.

(8) The court shall have power from time to time by an order under this section to vary or discharge any previous order thereunder.

Note. For construction of s 6, see Family Law Reform Act 1987, s 2(1)(b), as from 1 April 1989. See also Civil Evidence Act 1968, s 12 (p 2292); Children Act 1989, s 15(1), Sch 1, para 2 (p 2147).

Whole section repealed by Courts and Legal Services Act 1990, s 125(7), Sch 20, as from 14 October 1991.

7. Commital of wards of court to care of local authority and supervision of wards of court—*(1) In this section 'the court' means any of the following courts in the exercise of its jurisdiction relating to the wardships of children, that is to say, the High Court, the Court of Chancery of the County Palatine of Lancaster and the Court of Chancery of the County Palatine of Durham, and 'ward of court' means a ward of the court in question.*

Note. Words 'the Court of Chancery … Durham' repealed by Courts Act 1971, s 56(4), Sch 11, Part II.

(2) Where it appears to the court that there are exceptional circumstances making it impracticable or undesirable for a ward of court to be, or to continue to be, under the care of either of his parents or of any other individual the court may, if it thinks fit, make an order committing the care of the ward to a local authority; and thereupon [Part II of the Children Act 1948] [Part III of the Child Care Act 1980] (which relates to the treatment of children in the care of a local authority) shall, subject to the next following subsection, apply as if the child has been received by the local authority into their care under [section 1] [section 2] of that Act.
[and thereupon—

(a) Part III of the Child Care Act 1980 (which relates to the treatment of children in the care of a local authority); and

(b) for the purposes only of contributions by the child himself at a time when he has attained the age of 16, Part V of that Act (which relates to contributions towards the maintenance of children in the care of a local authority),

shall apply subject to the next following subsection, as if the child had been received by the local authority into their care under section 2 of that Act.]

Note. References to Act of 1980 substituted for references to Act of 1948 by Child Care Act 1980, s 89, Sch 5, para 23, as from 1 April 1981. Words 'and thereupon' to end of sub-s (2) substituted by Health and Social Services and Social Security Adjudications Act 1983, s 9, Sch 2, para 9, as from 1 January 1984.

(3) In subsection (2) of this section 'local authority' means one of the local authorities referred to in subsection (1) of section 36 of the Matrimonial Causes Act 1965 [section 43 of the Matrimonial Causes Act 1973] (under which a child may be committed to the care of a local authority by a court having jurisdiction to make an order for its custody); and subsections (2) to (6) of that section (ancillary provisions) shall have effect as if any reference therein to that section included a reference to subsection (2) of this section [and as if, in relation to a ward of court, the reference in subsection (5)(b) to sections 24 and 28 of the Child Care Act 1980 included a reference to section 23 of that Act (guarantee of apprenticeship deeds) and section 29 of that Act (visiting and assistance of persons formerly in care).]

Note. First words in square brackets substituted for words in italics by Matrimonial Causes Act 1973, s 54(1), Sch 2, para 8. Words in square brackets at end of sub-s (3) added by Child Care Act 1980, s 89, Sch 5, para 23, as from 1 April 1981.

(4) Where it appears to the court that there are exceptional circumstances making it desirable that a ward of court (not being a ward who in pursuance of an order under subsection (2) of this section is in the care of a local authority) should be under the supervision of an independent person, the court may, as respects such period as the court thinks fit, order that the ward be under the supervision of a welfare officer or of a local authority; and subsections (2) and (3) of section 37 of the said Act of 1965 [section 44(2) of the Matrimonial Causes Act 1973] (ancillary provisions where a child is placed under supervision by a court having jurisdiction to make an order for its custody) shall have effect as if any reference therein to that section included a reference to this subsection.

Note. Words 'and (3)' repealed by Local Authority Social Services Act 1970, s 14, Sch 3. Words in square brackets substituted for words from 'subsections (2)' to '1965' by Matrimonial Causes Act 1973, s 54(1), Sch 2, para 8.

See Family Law Act 1986, s 6(6)(a) as to cessation of effect of supervision order in circumstances there stated.

(5) The court shall have power from time to time by an order under this section to vary or discharge any previous order thereunder.

Note. This section repealed by Children Act 1989, ss 100(1), 108(7), Sch 15, as from 14 October 1991. See ibid s 108(6), Sch 14, paras 1, 15, 26 (pp 3346, 3427, 3432, 3437).

8. Consent by persons over 16 to surgical medical and dental treatment—(1) The consent of a minor who has attained the age of sixteen years to any surgical, medical or dental treatment which, in the absence of consent, would constitute a trespass to his person, shall be as effective as it would be if he were of full age; and where a minor has by virtue of this section given an effective consent to any treatment it shall not be necessary to obtain any consent for it from his parent or guardian.

(2) In this section 'surgical, medical or dental treatment' includes any procedure undertaken for the purposes of diagnosis, and this section applies to any procedure (including, in particular, the administration of an anaesthetic) which is ancillary to any treatment as it applies to that treatment.

Note. As for 'full age', see s 1(1), (2) (p 2301).

(3) Nothing in this section shall be construed as making ineffective any consent which would have been effective if this section had not been enacted.

9. Time at which a person attains a particular age—(1) The time at which a person attains a particular age expressed in years shall be the commencement of the relevant anniversary of the date of his birth.

(2) This section applies only where the relevant anniversary falls on a date after that on which this section comes into force, and, in relation to any enactment, deed, will or other instrument, has effect subject to any provision therein.

10. Modification of enactments relating to Duke of Cornwall and other children of Her Majesty—(1) Section 1(1) of this Act shall apply for the construction of the expression 'minor' in section 2(2) of the Civil List Act 1952 (which relates to the amount payable for the Queen's Civil List while the Duke of Cornwall is for the time being a minor) and accordingly—

(a) section 2(2)(b) of that Act (which relates to the three years during which the Duke is over 18 but under 21): and

(b) in section 2(2)(a) of that Act the words 'for each year whilst he is under the age of eighteen years'.

are hereby repealed except in relation to any period falling before section 1 of this Act comes into force.

(2) In section 4(1)(a) of the said Act of 1952 (under which benefits are provided for the children of Her Majesty, other than the Duke of Cornwall, who attain the age of 21 or marry) for the words 'twenty-one years' there shall be substituted the words 'eighteen years' but no sum shall be payable by virtue of this subsection in respect of any period falling before section 1 of this Act comes into force.

(3) In section 38 of the Duchy of Cornwall Management Act 1863 (under which certain rights and powers of the Duke of Cornwall may, while he is under 21, be exercised on his behalf by the Sovereign or persons acting under Her authority) for the words 'twenty-one years' wherever they occur there shall be substituted the words 'eighteen years'.

11. Repeal of certain enactments relating to minors.   The following enactments are hereby repealed—

(a) the Infant Settlements Act 1855 (which enables a male infant over 20 and a female infant over 17 to make a marriage settlement), together with section 27(3) of the Settled Land Act 1925, except in relation to anything done before the coming into force of this section:

(b) in section 6 of the Employers and Workmen Act 1875 (powers of justices in respect of apprentices)—

   (i) the paragraph numbered (1) (power to direct apprentice to perform his duties), and

   (ii) the sentence following the paragraph numbered (2) (power to order imprisonment of an apprentice who fails to comply with direction);

(c) in the Sexual Offences Act 1956, section 18 and paragraph 5 of Schedule 2 (fraudulent abduction of heiress).

12. Persons under full age may be described as minors instead of infants.   A person who is not of full age may be described as a minor instead of as an infant and accordingly in this Act 'minor' means such a person as aforesaid.

13. Powers of Parliament of Northern Ireland.   *Notwithstanding anything in the Government of Ireland Act 1920 the Parliament of Northern Ireland shall have power to make laws for purposes similar to any of the purposes of this Part of this Act [as amended by the Finance Act 1969].*

Note. Words in square brackets inserted by Finance Act 1969, s 16(2).
   This section repealed by Northern Ireland Constitution Act 1973, s 41(1), Sch 6, Part I.

PART II

PROPERTY RIGHTS OF ILLEGITIMATE CHILDREN

14. Right of illegitimate child to succeed on intestacy of parents, and of parents to succeed on intestacy of illegitimate child—(*1*) *Where either parent of an illegitimate child dies intestate, as respects all or any of his or her real or personal property, the illegitimate child or, if he is dead, his issue, shall be entitled to take any interest therein to which he or such issue would have been entitled if he had been born legitimate.*

(2) *Where an illegitimate child dies intestate in respect of all or any of his real or personal property, each of his parents, if surviving, shall be entitled to take any interest therein to which that parent would have been entitled if the child had been born legitimate.*

(3) *In accordance with the foregoing provisions of this section, Part IV of the Administration of Estates Act 1925 (which deals with the distribution of the estate of an intestate) shall have effect as if—*

(a) *any reference to the issue of the intestate included a reference to any illegitimate child of his and to the issue of any such child;*

(b) *any reference to the child or children of the intestate included a reference to any illegitimate child or children of his; and*

(c) *in relation to an intestate who is an illegitimate child, any reference to the parent, parents, father or mother of the intestate were a reference to his natural parent, parents, father or mother.*

(4) *For the purposes of subsection (2) of this section and of the provisions amended by subsection (3)(c) thereof, an illegitimate child shall be presumed not to have been survived by his father unless the contrary is shown.*

(5) *This section does not apply to or affect the right of any person to take any entailed interest in real or personal property.*

(6) *The reference in section 50(1) of the said Act of 1925 (which relates to the construction of documents) to Part IV of that Act, or to the foregoing provisions of that Part, shall in relation to an instrument inter vivos made, or a will or codicil coming into operation, after the coming into force of this section (but not in relation to instruments inter vivos made or wills or codicils coming into operation earlier) be construed as including references to this section.*

(7) *Section 9 of the Legitimacy Act 1926 (under which an illegitimate child and his issue are entitled to succeed on the intestacy of his mother if she leaves no legitimate issue, and the mother of an illegitimate child is entitled to succeed on his intestacy as if she were the only surviving parent) is hereby repealed.*

(8) *In this section 'illegitimate child' does not include an illegitimate child who is—*

(a) *a legitimated person within the meaning of the said Act of 1926 or a person recognised by virtue of that Act or at common law as having been legitimated; or*

(b) *an adopted person under an adoption order made in any part of the United Kingdom, the Isle of Man or the Channel Islands or under an overseas adoption as defined in section 4(3) of the Adoption Act 1968.*

Note. Sub-s (8) repealed by Children Act 1975, s 108(1), Sch 4, Part II, as from 1 January 1976.

(9) *This section does not affect any rights under the intestacy of a person dying before the coming into force of this section.*

Note. This section repealed by Family Law Reform Act 1987, s 33(4), Sch 4, as from 4 April 1988, but see ibid, Sch 3, para 8.

15. Presumption that in dispositions of property references to children and other relatives include references to, and to persons related through, illegitimate children—*(1) In any disposition made after the coming into force of this section—*

(a) *any reference (whether express or implied) to the child or children of any person shall, unless the contrary intention appears, be construed as, or as including, a reference to any illegitimate child of that person; and*

(b) *any reference (whether express or implied) to a person or persons related in some other manner to any person shall, unless the contrary intention appears, be construed as, or as including, a reference to anyone who would be so related if he, or some other person through whom the relationship is deduced, had been born legitimate.*

(2) *The foregoing subsection applies only where the reference in question is to a person who is to benefit or to be capable of benefiting under the disposition or, for the purpose of designating such a person, to someone else to or through whom that person is related; but that subsection does not affect the construction of the word 'heir' or 'heirs' or of any expression which is used to create an entailed interest in real or personal property.*

(3) In relation to any disposition made after the coming into force of this section, section 33 of the Trustee Act 1925 (which specifies the trusts implied by a direction that income is to be held on protective trusts for the benefit of any person) shall have effect as if—

(a) *the reference to the children or more remote issue of the principal beneficiary included a reference to any illegitimate child of the principal beneficiary and to anyone who would rank as such issue if he, or some other person through whom he is descended from the principal beneficiary, had been born legitimate; and*

(b) *the reference to the issue of the principal beneficiary included a reference to anyone who would rank as such issue if he, or some other person through whom he is descended from the principal beneficiary, had been born legitimate.*

(4) In this section references to an illegitimate child include references to an illegitimate child who is or becomes a legitimated person within the meaning of the Legitimacy Act 1926 or a person recognised by virtue of that Act or at common law as having been legitimated; and in section 3 of that Act—

(a) *subsection (1)(b) (which relates to the effect of dispositions where a person has been legitimated) shall not apply to a disposition made after the coming into force of this section except as respects any interest in relation to which the disposition refers only to persons who are, or whose relationship is deduced through, legitimate persons; and*

(b) *subsection (2) (which provides that, where the right to any property depends on the relative seniority of the children of any person, legitimated persons shall rank as if born on the date of legitimation) shall not apply in relation to any right conferred by a disposition made after the coming into force of this section unless the terms of the disposition are such that the children whose relative seniority is in question cannot include any illegitimate children who are not either legitimated persons within the meaning of that Act or persons recognised by virtue of that Act as having been legitimated.*

Note. Sub-s (4) repealed by Children Act 1975, s 108(1), Sch 4, Part II, as from 1 January 1976.

(5) Where under any disposition any real or personal property or any interest in such property is limited (whether subject to any preceding limitation or charge or not) in such a way that it would, apart from this section, devolve (as nearly as the law permits) along with a dignity or title of honour, then, whether or not the disposition contains an express reference to the dignity or title of honour, and whether or not the property or some interest in the property may in some event become severed therefrom, nothing in this section shall operate to sever the property or any interest therein from the dignity or title, but the property or interest shall devolve in all respects as if this section had not been enacted.

(6) This section is without prejudice to sections 16 and 17 of the Adoption Act 1958 (which relate to the construction of dispositions in cases of adoption).

Note. Sub-s (6) repealed by Children Act 1975, s 108(1), Sch 4, Part II, as from 1 January 1976.

(7) There is hereby abolished, as respects dispositions made after the coming into force of this section, any rule of law that a disposition in favour of illegitimate children not in being when the disposition takes effect is void as contrary to public policy.

(8) In this section 'disposition' means a disposition, including an oral disposition, of real or personal property whether inter vivos or by will or codicil; and, notwithstanding any rule of law, a disposition made by will or codicil executed before the date on which this section comes into force shall not be treated for the purposes of this section as made on or after that date by reason only that the will or codicil is confirmed by a codicil executed on or after that date.

Note. This section repealed by Family Law Reform Act 1987, s 33(4), Sch 4, as from 4 April 1988, but see ibid, Sch 3, para 9.

16. Meaning of 'child' and 'issue' in s 33 of Wills Act 1837—*(1) In relation to a testator who dies after the coming into force of this section, section 33 of the Wills Act 1837 (gift to children or other issue of testator not to lapse if they pre-decease him but themselves leave issue) shall have effect as if—*

(a) *the reference to a child or other issue of the testator (that is, the intended beneficiary) included a reference to any illegitimate child of the testator and to anyone who would*

rank as such issue if he, or some other person through whom he is descended from the testator, had been born legitimate; and

(b)   the reference to the issue of the intended beneficiary included a reference to anyone who
would rank as such issue if he, or some other person through whom he is descended from
the intended beneficiary, had been born legitimate.

(2) In this section 'illegitimate child' includes an illegitimate child who is a legitimated person within the meaning of the Legitimacy Act 1926 or a person recognised by virtue of that Act
or at common law as having been legitimated.

Note. Sub-s (2) repealed by Legitimacy Act 1976, s 11, Sch 2. Whole section repealed by
Administration of Justice Act 1982, s 75(1), Sch 9, Part I, as from 1 January 1983, except in
relation to testators who died before that date (s 73(6)).

17. Protection of trustees and personal representatives. *Notwithstanding the
foregoing provisions of this Part of this Act, trustees or personal representatives may convey or
distribute any real or personal property to or among the persons entitled thereto without having ascertained that there is no person who is or may be entitled to any interest therein by
virtue of—*

(a)   section 14 of this Act so far as it confers any interest on illegitimate children or their
issue or on the father of an illegitimate child; or

(b)   section 15 or 16 of this Act,

and shall not be liable to any such person of whose claim they have not had notice at the time of
the conveyance or distribution; but nothing in this section shall prejudice the right of any such
person to follow the property, or any property representing it, into the hands of any person, other
than a purchaser, who may have received it.

Note. This section repealed by Family Law Reform Act 1987, ss 20, 33(4), Sch 4, as from
4 April 1988, but see ibid, Sch 3, para 10.

**18. Illegitimate children to count as dependants under Inheritance (Family
Provision) Act 1938**—*(1) For the purposes of the Inheritance (Family Provision) Act 1938,
a person's illegitimate son or daughter shall be treated as his dependant in any case in which a
legitimate son or daughter of that person would be so treated, and accordingly in the definition
of the expressions 'son' and 'daughter' in section 5(1) of that Act, as amended by the Family
Provision Act 1966, after the words 'respectively include' there shall be inserted the words 'an
illegitimate son or daughter of the deceased'.*

*(2) In section 26(6) of the Matrimonial Causes Act 1965 (which provides, among other
things, for the word 'dependant' to have the same meaning as in the said Act of 1938 as
amended by the said Act of 1966), after the words 'as amended by the Family Provision Act
1966' there shall be inserted the words 'and the Family Law Reform Act 1969'.*

*(3) This section does not affect the operation of the said Acts of 1938 and 1965 in relation
to a person dying before the coming into force of this section.*

Note. For Matrimonial Causes Act 1965, s 26, see p 2253.

This section repealed by Inheritance (Provision for Family and Dependants) Act 1975,
s 26(2), Schedule.

19. Policies of assurance and property in industrial and provident societies—
(1) In section 11 of the Married Women's Property Act 1882 *and section 2 of the
Married Women's Policies of Assurance (Scotland) Act 1880* (policies of assurance effected
for the benefit of children) the expression 'children' shall include illegitimate
children.

(2) In section 25(2) of the Industrial and Provident Societies Act 1965 (application of property in registered society where member was illegitimate and is not survived by certain specified relatives) for the words 'and leaves no widow, widower or
issue, and his mother does not survive him' there shall be substituted the words 'and
leaves no widow, widower or issue (including any illegitimate child of the member)
and neither of his parents survives him'.

(3) Subsection(1) of this section does not affect the operation of the said Acts of 1882 *and 1880* in relation to a policy effected before the coming into force of that subsection; and subsection (2) of this section does not affect the operation of the said Act of 1965 in relation to a member of a registered society who dies before the coming into force of the said subsection (2).

Note. Words in italics in sub-ss (1), (3) repealed by Married Women's Policies of Assurance (Scotland) (Amendment) Act 1980, s 5, as from 29 October 1980.

PART III

PROVISIONS FOR USE OF BLOOD TESTS IN DETERMINING PATERNITY

20. Power of court to require use of blood tests—*(1) In any civil proceedings in which the paternity of any person falls to be determined by the court hearing the proceedings, the court may, on an application by any party to the proceedings, give a direction for the use of blood tests to ascertain whether such tests show that a party to the proceedings is or is not thereby excluded from being the father of that person and for the taking, within a period to be specified in the direction, of blood samples from that person, the mother of that person and any party alleged to be the father of that person or from any, or any two, of those persons.*

A court may at any time revoke or vary a direction previously given by it under this section.

(2) The person responsible for carrying out blood tests taken for the purpose of giving effect to a direction under this section shall make to the court by which the direction was given a report in which he shall state—

   (a)   the results of the tests;

   (b)   whether the party to whom the report relates is or is not excluded by the results from being the father of the person whose paternity is to be determined; and

   (c)   if that party is not so excluded, the value, if any, of the results in determining whether that party is that person's father;

and the report shall be received by the court as evidence in the proceedings of the matters stated therein.

[(1) In any civil proceedings in which the parentage of any person falls to be determined, the court may, either of its own motion or on an application by any party to the proceedings, give a direction—

   (a)   for the use of scientific tests to ascertain whether such tests show that a party to the proceedings is or is not the father or mother of that person; and

   (b)   for the taking, within a period specified in the direction, of bodily samples from all or any of the following, namely, that person, any party who is alleged to be the father or mother of that person and any other party to the proceedings;

and the court may at any time revoke or vary a direction previously given by it under this subsection.

   [*(1A) Where—*

   (a)   an application is made for a direction under this section; and

   (b)   the person whose paternity is in issue is under the age of eighteen when the application is made,

the application shall specify who is to carry out the tests.

   (1B) In the case of a direction made on an application to which subsection (1A) applies the court shall—

   [*(1A) An application for a direction under this section shall specify who is to carry out the tests.*

   (1B) A direction under this section shall]

   (a)   specify, as the person who is to carry out the tests, the person specified in the application; or

   (b)   where the court considers that it would be inappropriate to specify that person (whether because to specify him would be incompatible with any provision made by or under regulations made under section 22 of this Act or for any other reason), decline to give the direction applied for.]

[(1A) Tests required by a direction under this section may only be carried out by a body which has been accredited for the purposes of this section by—

(a) the Lord Chancellor, or

(b) a body appointed by him for the purpose.]

Note. Sub-ss (1A), (1B) inserted by Children Act 1989, s 89, as from 16 November 1989. Second sub-s (1A) and words preceding para (a) in sub-s (1B) substituted for words in italics by Courts and Legal Services Act 1990, s 116, Sch 16, para 3, as from 14 October 1991. Third sub-s (1A) substituted for preceding sub-ss (1A), (1B) by Child Support, Pensions and Social Security Act 2000, s 82(1), (2)(a), as from 1 April 2001 *SI 2001 No 774), except in relation to any poceedings pending at that date.

(2) The *person responsible for* [individual] carrying out scientific tests in pursuance of a direction under subsection (1) above shall make to the court a report in which he shall state—

(a) the results of the tests;

(b) whether any party to whom the report relates is or is not excluded by the results from being the father or mother of the person whose parentage is to be determined; and

(c) in relation to any party who is not so excluded, the value, if any, of the results in determining whether that party is the father or mother of that person;

and the report shall be received by the court as evidence in the proceedings of the matters stated in it.

(2A) Where the proceedings in which the parentage of any person falls to be determined are proceedings on an application under section 56 [55A or 56] of the Family Law Act 1986, any reference in subsection (1) or (2) of this section to any party to the proceedings shall include a reference to any person named in the application.]

Note. Sub-ss (1), (2), (2A) in square brackets substituted for sub-ss (1), (2) in italics by Family Law Reform Act 1987, s 23(1), as from 1 April 2001 (SI 2001 No 777). Original sub-s (2) further amended by the Child Support, Pensions and Social Security Act 2000, s 83(5), Sch 8, para 9(a). In new sub-s (2) word 'individual' in square brackets substituted for words in italics by virtue of the Child Support, Pensions and Social Security Act 2000, Sch 8, para 9(a), as from 1 April 2001 (SI 2001 No 774), except in relation to any proceecings pending at that date. In sub-s (2A) references to '55A or 56' in square brackets substituted for reference in italics by virtue of the Child Support, Pensions and Social Security Act 2000, s 83(5), Sch 8, para 9(b), as from 1 April 2001 (SI 2001 No 774).

(3) A report under subsection (2) of this section shall be in the form prescribed by regulations made under section 22 of this Act.

(4) Where a report has been made to a court under subsection (2) of this section, any party may, with the leave of the court, or shall, if the court so directs, obtain from *the person who made the report* [the tester] a written statement explaining or amplifying any statement made in the report, and that statement shall be deemed for the purposes of this section (except subsection (3) thereof) to form part of the report made to the court.

Note. Words 'the tester' in square brackets substituted for words in italics by the Child Support, Pensions and Social Security Act 2000, s 82(1), (2)(c), as from 1 April 2001 (SI 2001 No 774), except in relation to any proceedings pending at that date.

(5) Where a direction is given under this section in any proceedings, a party to the proceedings, unless the court otherwise directs, shall not be entitled to call as a witness *the person responsible for carrying out the tests taken for the purpose of giving effect to the direction, or any* [the tester, or any other] person by whom any thing necessary for the purpose of enabling those tests to be carried out was done, unless within fourteen days after receiving a copy of the report he serves notice on the other parties to the proceedings, or on such of them as the court may direct, of his intention to call that person [the tester or that person] ; and where [the tester or] any such person is called as a witness the party who called him shall be entitled to cross-examine him.

Note. Words 'the tester, or any other' and 'the tester or that person' in square brackets substituted for words in italics, and words 'the tester or' in square brackets inserted by the Child Support, Pensions and Social Security Act 2000, s 82(1), (2)(d), as from 1 April 2001 (SI 2001 No 774), except in relation to any proceedings pending at that date.

(6) Where a direction is given under this section the party on whose application the direction is given shall pay the cost of taking and testing *blood samples* [bodily samples] for the purpose of giving effect to the direction (including any expenses reasonably incurred by any person in taking any steps required of him for the purpose), and of making a report to the court under this section, but the amount paid shall be treated as costs incurred by him in the proceedings.

Note. This section does not apply to proceedings under Maintenance Orders (Reciprocal Enforcement) Act 1972: see ibid, s 44(1) (p 2427). Words 'bodily samples' in square brackets substituted for words 'blood samples' in italics by Family Law Reform Act 1987, s 33(1), Sch 2, para 21, as from 1 April 2001 (SI 2001 No 777).

21. Consents, etc, required for taking of *blood samples* [bodily samples]—(1) Subject to the provisions of subsections (3) and (4) of this section, a *blood sample* [bodily sample] which is required to be taken from any person for the purpose of giving effect to a direction under section 20 of this Act shall not be taken from that person except with his consent.

(2) The consent of a minor who has attained the age of sixteen years to the taking from himself of a *blood sample* [bodily sample] shall be as effective as it would be if he were of full age; and where a minor has by virtue of this subsection given an effective consent to the taking of a *blood sample* [bodily sample] it shall not be necessary to obtain any consent for it from any other person.

(3) A *blood sample* [bodily sample] may be taken from a person under the age of sixteen years, not being such person as is referred to in subsection (4) of this section, *if the person who has the care and control of him consents*
 [(a) if the person who has the care and control of him consents; or
 (b) where that person does not consent, if the court considers that it would be in his best interests for the sample to be taken.]

Note. Paras (a), (b) substituted for words 'if the ... him consents' in italics by the Child Support, Pensions and Social Security Act 2000, s 82(1), (3), (5) as from 1 April 2001 (SI 2001 No 774), except in relation to any proceedings pending at that date.

(4) A *blood sample* [bodily sample] may be taken from a person who is suffering from mental disorder within the meaning of *the Mental Health Act 1959* [the Mental Health Act 1983] and is incapable of understanding the nature and purpose of *blood tests* [scientific tests] if the person who has the care and control of him consents and the medical practitioner in whose care he is has certified that the taking of a blood sample from him will not be prejudicial to his proper care and treatment.

Note. References to Mental Health Act 1983 substituted by ibid, s 148, Sch 4, para 25.

(5) The foregoing provisions of this section are without prejudice to the provisions of section 23 of this Act.

Note. References to 'bodily sample' and 'scientific tests' substituted by Family Law Reform Act 1987, s 33(1), Sch 2, para 22, as from 1 April 2001 (SI 2001 No 777).

22. Power to provide for manner of giving effect to direction for use of blood test—(1) The *Secretary of State* [Lord Chancellor] may by regulations make provision as to the manner of giving effect to directions under section 20 of this Act and, in particular, any such regulations may—
 (a) provide that *blood samples* [bodily samples] shall not be taken except by *such medical practitioners as may be appointed by the Secretary of State [Lord Chancellor]* [registered medical practitioners or members of such professional bodies as may be prescribed by the regulations];
 [(aa) prescribe the bodily samples to be taken;]

(b) regulate the taking, identification and transport of *blood samples* [bodily samples];

(c) require the production at the time when a *blood sample* [bodily sample] is to be taken of such evidence of the identity of the person from whom it is to be taken as may be prescribed by the regulations;

(d) require any person from whom a *blood sample* [bodily sample] is to be taken, or, in such cases as may be prescribed by the regulations, such other person as may be so prescribed, to state in writing whether he or the person from whom the sample is to be taken, as the case may be, has during such period as may be specified in the regulations suffered from any such illness [or condition or undergone any such treatment] as may be so specified or received a transfusion of blood;

(*e*) *provide that blood tests [scientific tests] shall not be carried out except by such persons, and at such places, as may be appointed by the Secretary of State [Lord Chancellor];*

[(e) prescribe conditions which a body must meet in order to be eligible for accreditation for the purposes of section 20 of this Act;]

(f) prescribe the *blood tests* [scientific tests] to be carried out and the manner in which they are to be carried out;

(g) regulate the charges that may be made for the taking and testing of *blood samples* [bodily samples] and for the making of a report to a court under section 20 of this Act;

(h) make provision for securing that so far as practicable the *blood samples* [bodily samples] to be tested for the purpose of giving effect to a direction under section 20 of this Act are tested by the same person;

(i) prescribe the form of the report to be made to a court under section 20 of this Act.

[(j) make different provision for different cases or for different descriptions of case.]

(2) The power to make regulations under this section shall be exercisable by statutory instrument which shall be subject to annulment in pursuance of a resolution of either House of Parliament.

Note. References to 'bodily sample', 'bodily samples' and 'scientific tests' substituted by Family Law Reform Act 1987, s 33(1), Sch 2, para 23(2), as from 1 April 2001 (SI 2001 No 777). Sub-s (1)(aa), words in second pair of square brackets in sub-s (1)(d), and sub-s (1)(j) added by Family Law Reform Act 1987, s 33(1), para 23(3), (4), as from 1 April 2001 (SI 2001 No 777). References to 'Lord Chancellor' in sub-s (1) substituted by virtue of Transfer of Functions (Magistrates' Courts and Family Law) Order 1992, SI 1992 No 709, art 3(2), Sch 2, as from 1 April 1992. In sub-s (1)(a) words 'registered medical … the regulations' in square brackets substituted for words 'such medical … Lord Chancellor' and sub-s (1)(e) substituted by the Child Support, Pensions and Social Security Act 2000, s 82(1), (4)(a), (b), as from 1 April 2001 (SI 2001 No 774), except in relation to any poceedings pending at that date.

23. Failure to comply with direction for taking blood tests—(1) Where a court gives a direction under section 20 of this Act and any person fails to take any step required of him for the purpose of giving effect to the direction, the court may draw such inferences, if any, from the fact as appear proper in the circumstances.

(2) Where in any proceedings in which the *paternity* [parentage] of any person falls to be determined by the court hearing the proceedings there is a presumption of law that that person is legitimate, then if—

(a) a direction is given under section 20 of this Act in those proceedings, and

(b) any party who is claiming any relief in the proceedings and who for the purpose of obtaining that relief is entitled to rely on the presumption fails to take any step required of him for the purpose of giving effect to the direction,

the court may adjourn the hearing for such period as it thinks fit to enable that party to take that step, and if at the end of that period he has failed without reasonable cause to take it the court may, without prejudice to subsection (1) of this section, dismiss his claim for relief notwithstanding the absence of evidence to rebut the presumption.

Note. 'Parentage' substituted for 'paternity' by Family Law Reform Act 1987, s 33(1), Sch 2, para 24, as from 1 April 2001 (SI 2001 No 777).

(3) Where any person named in a direction under section 20 of this Act fails to consent to the taking of a *blood sample* [bodily sample] from himself or from any person named in the direction of whom he has the care and control, he shall be deemed for the purposes of this section to have failed to take a step required of him for the purpose of giving effect to the direction.

Note. 'Bodily sample' substituted for 'blood sample' by Family Law Reform Act 1987, s 33(1), Sch 2, para 24, as from 1 April 2001 (SI 2001 No 777).

24. Penalty for personating another, etc, for purpose of providing *blood sample* [bodily sample]. If for the purpose of providing a *blood sample* [bodily sample] for a test required to give effect to a direction under section 20 of this Act any person personates another, or proffers a child knowing that it is not the child named in the direction, he shall be liable—

(a) on conviction on indictment, to imprisonment for a term not exceeding two years, or

(b) on summary conviction, to a fine not exceeding [the prescribed sum].

Note. The maximum fine is now the prescribed sum under Magistrates' Courts Act 1980, s 32(2). 'Bodily sample' substituted for 'blood sample' by Family Law Reform Act 1987, s 33(1), Sch 2, para 25, as from 1 April 2001 (SI 2001 No 777).

25. Interpretation of Part III. In this Part of this Act the following expressions have the meanings hereby respectively assigned to them, that is to say—

'*blood samples*' *means blood taken for the purpose of blood tests;*

'*blood tests*' *means blood tests carried out under this Part of this Act and includes any test made with the object of ascertaining the inheritable characteristics of blood;*

['bodily sample' means a sample of bodily fluid or bodily tissue taken for the purpose of scientific tests;]

'excluded' means excluded subject to the occurrence of mutation, [to section 27 of the Family Law Reform Act 1987 and to sections 27 to 29 of the Human Fertilisation and Embryology Act 1990].

['scientific tests' means scientific tests carried out under this Part of this Act and made with the object of ascertaining the inheritable characteristics of bodily fluids or bodily tissue.]

Note. Definition 'bodily sample' substituted for definitions 'blood samples' and 'blood tests', and definition of 'scientific tests' inserted by Family Law Reform Act 1987, s 23(2), as from 1 April 2001 (SI 2001 No 777). Words in square brackets at end of definition of 'excluded' added by Human Fertilisation and Embryology Act 1990, s 49(5), Sch 4, para 1, as from 1 August 1991; for transitional provisions, see arts 3, 4 of that Order, as amended by SI 1991 No 1781, art. 2.

PART IV

MISCELLANEOUS AND GENERAL

26. Rebuttal of presumption as to legitimacy and illegitimacy. Any presumption of law as to the legitimacy or illegitimacy of any person may in any civil proceedings be rebutted by evidence which shows that it is more probable than not that that person is illegitimate or legitimate, as the case may be, and it shall not be necessary to prove that fact beyond reasonable doubt in order to rebut the presumption.

27. Entry of father's name on registration of birth of illegitimate child—*(1) In section 10 of the Births and Deaths Registration Act 1953 (which provides that the registrar* *shall not enter the name of any person as the father of an illegitimate child except at the joint request of the mother and the person acknowledging himself to be the father and requires that person to sign the register together with the mother) for the words from 'except' onwards there shall be substituted the words 'except—*

(a)   *at the joint request of the mother and the person acknowledging himself to be the father of the child (in which case that person shall sign the register together with the mother); or*

(b)   *at the request of the mother on production of—*

  (i)   *a declaration in the prescribed form made by the mother stating that the said person is the father of the child; and*

  (ii)   *a statutory declaration made by that person acknowledging himself to be the father of the child.'*

(2)   *If on the registration under Part I of the said Act of 1953 of the birth of an illegitimate child no person has been entered in the register as the father, the registrar may re-register the birth so as to show a person as the father—*

(a)   *at the joint request of the mother and of that person (in which case the mother and that person shall both sign the register in the presence of the registrar); or*

(b)   *at the request of the mother on production of—*

  (i)   *a declaration in the prescribed form made by the mother stating that the person in question is the father of the child; and*

  (ii)   *a statutory declaration made by that person acknowledging himself to be the father of the child;*

but no birth shall be re-registered as aforesaid except with the authority of the Registrar General and any such re-registration shall be effected in such manner as may be prescribed.

(3)   *A request under paragraph (a) or (b) of section 10 of the said Act of 1953 as amended by subsection (1) of this section may be included in a declaration under section 9 of that Act (registration of birth pursuant to a declaration made in another district) and, if a request under the said paragraph (b) is included in such a declaration, the documents mentioned in that paragraph shall be produced to the officer in whose presence the declaration is made and sent by him, together with the declaration, to the registrar.*

(4)   *A request under paragraph (a) or (b) of subsection (2) of this section may, instead of being made to the registrar, be made by making and signing in the presence of and delivering to such officer as may be prescribed a written statement in the prescribed form and, in the case of a request under the said paragraph (b), producing to that officer the documents mentioned in that paragraph, and the officer shall send the statement together with the documents, if any, to the registrar; and thereupon that subsection shall have effect as if the request had been made to the registrar and, if the birth is re-registered pursuant to the request, the person or persons who signed the statement shall be treated as having signed the register as required by that subsection.*

(5)   *This section shall be construed as one with the said Act of 1953; and in section 14 (1) (a) of that Act (re-registration of birth of legitimated person) the reference to section 10 of that Act shall include a reference to subsection (2) of this section.*

Note. Sub-ss (2)–(5) repealed by Children Act 1975, s 108(1), Sch 4, Part VI, as from 1 January 1977. Whole section repealed by Family Law Reform Act 1987, s 33(4), Sch 4, as from 1 April 1989.

28.   Short title, interpretation, commencement and extent—(1) This Act may be cited as the Family Law Reform Act 1969.

(2)   Except where the context otherwise requires, any reference in this Act to any enactment shall be construed as a reference to that enactment as amended, extended or applied by or under any other enactment, including this Act.

(3)   This Act shall come into force on such date as the Lord Chancellor may appoint by order made by statutory instrument, and different dates may be appointed for the coming into force of different provisions.

(4)   In this Act—

(a)   *section 1 and Schedule 1, so far as they amend the British Nationality Act 1948, have the same extent as that Act and are hereby declared for the purposes of section 3(3) of the West Indies Act 1967 to extend to all the associated states;*

(b) section 2, so far as it amends any provision of *the Foreign Marriage Act 1892 or* the Marriage with Foreigners Act 1906, has the same extent as that provision;

(c) sections *4(5) and* 6(7), so far as they affect Part II of the Maintenance Orders Act 1950, extend to Scotland and Northern Ireland;

(d) section 10, so far as it relates to the Civil List Act 1952, extends to Scotland and Northern Ireland;

(e) section 11, so far as it relates to the Employers and Workmen Act 1875, extends to Scotland;

(f) *section 13 extends to Northern Ireland;*

(g) section 19 extends to Scotland;

but, save as aforesaid, this Act shall extend to England and Wales only.

Note. Sub-s (4)(a) repealed by British Nationality Act 1981, s 52(8), Sch 9. Words in italics in sub-s (4)(b) repealed by Foreign Marriage (Amendment) Act 1988, s 7(2), Schedule, as from 12 April 1990. Words '4(5) and' in sub-s (4)(c) repealed by Guardianship of Minors Act 1971, s 18(2), Sch 2.

Sub-s (4)(f) repealed by Northern Ireland Constitution Act 1973, s 41(1), Sch 6, Part I.

SCHEDULES

SCHEDULE 1   Section 1(3)

STATUTORY PROVISIONS AMENDED BY SUBSTITUTING 18 FOR 21 YEARS

PART I

ENACTMENTS

	Short title	Section	Subject matter
c 24.	The Tenures Abolition Act 1660.	Sections 8 and 9.	Custody of children under 21.
c 22.	The Trade Union Act Amendment Act 1876.	Section 9.	Persons under 21 but above 16 eligible as members of trade union but not of committee of management etc.
c 25.	The Friendly Societies Act 1896.	Section 36.	Persons under 21 eligible as members of society and branches but not of committee etc.
c 18.	The Settled Land Act 1925.	Section 102(5).	Management of land during minority.
c 19.	The Trustee Act 1925.	Section 31(1)(ii), (2)(i)(a) and (b).	Power to apply income for maintenance and to accumulate surplus income during a minority.
c 20.	The Law of Property Act 1925.	Section 134(1).	Restrictions on executory limitations.
c 49.	The Supreme Court of Judicature (Consolidation) Act 1925.	Section 165(1).	Probate not to be granted to infant if appointed sole executor until he attains the age of 21 years.
c 56.	The British Nationality Act 1948.	Section 32(1) and (9).	Definition of 'minor' and 'full age' by reference to age of 21.
c 44.	The Customs and Excise Act 1952.	Section 244(2)(a).	Entry invalid unless made by persons over 21.
c 46.	The Hypnotism Act 1952.	Section 3.	Persons under 21 not to be hypnotised at public entertainment.

Short title	Section	Subject matter
c 63. The Trustee Savings Banks Acts 1954.	Section 23.	Payments to persons under 21.
c 69. The Sexual Offences Act 1956.	Section 38.	Power of court where person convicted of incest with girl under 21.
c 5. The Adoption Act 1958.	Section 57(1).	Definition of 'infant' by reference to age of 21.
c 22. The County Courts Act 1959.	Section 80.	Persons under 21 may sue for wages in same manner as if of full age.
c 72. The Mental Health Act 1959.	Section 49(4)(c).	Provision where nearest relative of patient is under 21.
	Section 51(1).	Meaning of 'nearest relative' of patient who has not attained the age of 21.
	Section 127(2).	Rescinding order under s 38 of Sexual Offences Act 1956 in case of girl under 21 who is a defective.
c 37. The Building Societies Act 1962.	Section 9	Persons under 21 eligible as members of building society but cannot vote or hold office.
	Section 47.	Receipt given to building society by persons under 21 to be valid.
c 2. The Betting, Gaming and Lotteries Act 1963	Section 22(1) and (3).	Offence of sending betting advertisements to persons under 21.
c 12. The Industrial and Provident Societies Act 1965.	Section 20.	Persons under 21 but above 16 eligible as members of society but not of committee etc.

Note. Entries relating to Tenures Abolition Act 1660, Trade Union Act Amendment Act 1876, Trustee Savings Banks Act 1954 and Adoption Act 1958 repealed by Statute Law (Repeals) Act 1993, s 1(1), Sch 1, Part VIII, as from 5 November 1993.

Entry relating to Friendly Societies Act 1896 repealed by Friendly Societies Act 1974, s 116(4), Sch 11.

Entry relating to Supreme Court of Judicature (Consolidation) Act 1925 repealed by Supreme Court Act 1981, s 152(4), Sch 7.

Entry relating to British Nationality Act 1948 repealed by British Nationality Act 1981, s 52(8), Sch 9.

Entries relating to Sexual Offences Act 1956 and Mental Health Act 1959 repealed by Guardianship Act 1973, s 9(1), Sch 3.

Entry relating to Customs and Excise Act 1952 repealed by Customs and Excise Management Act 1979, s 177(3), Sch 6, Part I.

Entries relating to Mental Health Act 1959 repealed again by Mental Health Act 1983, s 148, Sch 6, as from 30 September 1983.

Entry relating to County Courts Act 1959, s 80, repealed by County Courts Act 1984, s 148(3), Sch 4, as from 1 August 1984. See now Act of 1984, s 47.

Entry relating to Building Societies Act 1962 repealed by Building Societies Act 1986, s 120(2), Sch 19, Part I.

PART **II**

RULES, REGULATIONS ETC

	Title	Provision	Subject matter
1927 SR & O 1184; 1953 SI 264.	*The Supreme Court Funds Rules 1927 as amended by the Supreme Court Funds Rules 1953.*	*Rule 97(1)(i).*	*Unclaimed moneys in court.*
1929 SR & O 1048.	*The Trustee Savings Banks Regulations 1929.*	*Regulation 28(2).*	*Payments to persons under 21.*
1933 SR & O 1149.	*The Savings Certificates Regulations 1933.*	*Regulation 2(1)(a).*	*Persons entitled to purchase and hold certificates.*
		Regulation 21(2).	*Persons under disability.*
1946 SR & O 1156.	*The North of Scotland Hydro-Electric Board (Borrowing and Stock) Regulations 1946.*	*Regulation 36(1) and (2).*	*Stock held by persons under 21.*
1949 SI 751.	*The Gas (Stock) Regulations 1949.*	*Regulation 19(1) and (2).*	*Stock held by person under 21.*
1954 SI 796.	*The Non-contentious Probate Rules 1954.*	*Rules 31 and 32.*	*Grants of probate on behalf of infant and where infant is coexecutor.*
1955 SI 1752.	*The South of Scotland Electricity Board (Borrowing and Stock) Regulations 1955.*	*Regulation 30(1) and (2).*	*Stock held by persons under 21.*
1956 SI 1657.	*The Premium Savings Bonds Regulations 1956.*	*Regulation 2(1).*	*Persons entitled to purchase and hold bonds.*
		Regulation 12(2).	*Persons under disability.*
1957 SI 2228.	*The Electricity (Stock) Regulations 1957.*	*Regulation 22(1) and (2).*	*Stock held by persons under 21.*
1963 SI 935.	*The Exchange of Securities (General) Rules 1963.*	*Rule 1(1).*	*Definition of 'minor'.*
1965 SI 1420.	*The Government Stock Regulations 1965.*	*Regulation 14(1), (2), (3) and (5).*	*Stock held by persons under 21.*

Title	Provision	Subject matter
1965 SI 1500. *The County Court Funds Rules 1965.*	*Rule 36(1)(b).*	*Unclaimed moneys in court.*
1965 SI 1707. *The Mayor's and City of London Court Funds Rules 1965.*	*Rule 25(1)(b).*	*Unclaimed moneys in court.*
1968 SI 2049. *The Registration of Births, Deaths and Marriages Regulations 1968.*	*Regulation 63 and, in Schedule 1, Forms 15 to 18.*	*Forms of notice of marriage.*

Note. Entries in italics repealed by Statute Law (Repeals) Act 1993, s 1(1), Sch 1, Part VIII, as from 5 November 1993. Entry 'The Government Stock Regulations 1965' in italics repealed by the Government Stock (Consequential and Transitional Provision) (No 2) Order 2004, SI 2004, No 1662, as from 1 July 2004. For transitional provisions see art 3 of SI 2004 No 1662.

SCHEDULE 2   Section 1(4)

STATUTORY PROVISIONS UNAFFECTED BY SECTION 1

1. The Regency Acts 1937 to 1953.

2. *The Representation of the People Acts (and any regulations, rules or other instruments thereunder),* section 7 of the Parliamentary Elections Act 1695, *section 57 of the Local Government Act 1933 and any statutory provision relating to municipal elections in the City of London within the meaning of section 167(1)(a) of the Representation of the People Act 1949.*

Note. Words from the beginning to 'thereunder)' and words from 'and any statutory provision' to '1949' in italics repealed by Representation of the People Act 1983, s 206, Sch 9, Part I, as from 15 March 1983. Words 'section 57 of the Local Government Act 1933' repealed by Statute Law (Repeals) Act 1993, s 1(1), Sch 1, Part VIII, as from 5 November 1993.

3. *Any statutory provision relating to income tax (including surtax) capital gains tax, corporation tax or estate duty.*

Note. Para 3 repealed by Finance Act 1969, ss 16(1), 61(6), Sch 21, Part IV.

SCHEDULE 3   Section 1(4)

TRANSITIONAL PROVISIONS AND SAVINGS

Interpretation

1. (1) In this Schedule 'the principal section' means section 1 of this Act and 'the commencement date' means the date on which that section comes into force.

(2) Subsection (7) of the principal section shall apply for the purposes of this Schedule as it applies for the purposes of that section.

Funds in court

2. Any order or direction in force immediately before the commencement date by virtue of—

    (a) any rules of court or other statutory provision (including, in particular, section 174 of the County Courts Acts 1959) relating to the control of money recovered by or otherwise payable to an infant in any proceedings; or

    (b) section 19 of the Administration of Justice Act 1965 (control of money recovered by widow in fatal accident proceedings which are also brought for the benefit of an infant), shall have effect as if any reference therein to the infant's attaining the age of twenty-one were a reference to his attaining the age of eighteen or, in relation to a person who by virtue of the principal section attains full age on the commencement date, to that date.

Wardship and custody orders

3.   (1) Any order in force immediately before the commencement date—
  (a)   making a person a ward of court; or
  (b)   under the Guardianship of Infants Acts 1886 and 1925, or under the Matrimonial Causes Act 1965 or any enactment repealed by that Act, for the custody of, or access to, any person,
which is expressed to continue in force until the person who is the subject of the order attains the age of twenty-one, or any age between eighteen and twenty-one, shall have effect as if the reference to his attaining that age were a reference to his attaining the age of eighteen or, in relation to a person who by virtue of the principal section attains full age on the commencement date, to that date.
  (2)   *This paragraph is without prejudice to so much of any order as makes provision for the maintenance or education of a person after he has attained the age of eighteen.*

Adoption orders

4.   The principal section shall not prevent the making of an adoption order or provisional adoption order under the Adoption Act 1958 in respect of a person who has attained the age of eighteen if the application for the order was made before the commencement date, and in relation to any such case that Act shall have effect as if the principal section had not been enacted.

Power of trustees to apply income for maintenance of minor

5.   (1) The principal section shall not affect section 31 of the Trustee Act 1925—
  (a)   in its application to any interest under an instrument made before the commencement date; or
  (b)   in its application, by virtue of section 47(1)(ii) of the Administration of Estates Act 1925 to the estate of an intestate (within the meaning of that Act) dying before that date.
  (2)   In any case in which (whether by virtue of this paragraph or paragraph 9 of this Schedule) trustees have power under subsection (1)(i) of the said section 31 to pay income to the parent or guardian of any person who has attained the age of eighteen, or to apply it for or towards the maintenance, education or benefit of any such person, they shall also have power to pay it to that person himself.

Personal representatives' powers during minority of beneficiary

6.   The principal section shall not affect the meaning of 'minority' in sections 33(3) and 39(1) of the Administration of Estates Act 1925 in the case of a beneficiary whose interest arises under a will or codicil made before the commencement date or on the death before that date of an intestate (within the meaning of that Act).

Accumulation periods

7.   The change, by virtue of the principal section, in the construction of—
  (a)   sections 164 to 166 of the Law of Property Act 1925.
  (b)   section 13(1) of the Perpetuities and Accumulations Act 1964,
(which lay down permissible periods for the accumulation of income under settlements and other dispositions) shall not invalidate any direction for accumulation in a settlement or other disposition made by a deed, will or other instrument which was made before the commencement date.

Limitation of actions

8. The change, by virtue of the principal section, in the construction of section 31(2) of the Limitation Act 1939 (limitation in case of person under disability) shall not affect the time for bringing proceedings in respect of a cause of action which arose before the commencement date.

Note. Limitation Act 1939, s 31(2) replaced by Limitation Act 1980, s 38(2), as from 1 May 1981.

Statutory provisions incorporated in deeds, wills, etc

9. The principal section shall not affect the construction of any statutory provision where it is incorporated in and has effect as part of any deed, will or other instrument the construction of which is not affected by that section.

CHILDREN AND YOUNG PERSONS ACT 1969

(1969 c 54)

An Act to amend the law relating to children and young persons; and for purposes connected therewith.   [22 October 1969]

PART I

CARE AND OTHER TREATMENT OF JUVENILES THROUGH COURT PROCEEDINGS

Care of children and young persons through juvenile courts

1. Care proceedings in juvenile courts—*(1) Any local authority, constable or authorised person who reasonably believes that there are grounds for making an order under this section in respect of a child or young person may, subject to section 2(3) and (8) of this Act, bring him before a juvenile court.*

   (2)   If the court before which a child or young person is brought under this section is of opinion that any of the following conditions is satisfied with respect to him, that is to say—

   (a)   his proper development is being avoidably prevented or neglected or his health is being avoidably impaired or neglected or he is being ill-treated; or

   (b)   it is probable that the condition set out in the preceding paragraph will be satisfied in his case, having regard to the fact that the court or another court has found that that condition is or was satisfied in the case of another child or young person who is or was a member of the household to which he belongs; or

   [(bb)   it is probable that the condition set out in paragraph (a) of this subsection will be satisfied in his case, having regard to the fact that a person who has been convicted of an offence mentioned in Schedule 1 to the Act of 1933, including a person convicted of such an offence on whose conviction for the offence an order was made under Part I of the Powers of Criminal Courts Act 1973 placing him on probation or discharging him absolutely or conditionally is, or may become, a member of the same household as the child or young person;]

   (c)   he is exposed to moral danger; or

   (d)   he is beyond the control of his parent or guardian; or

   (e)   he is of compulsory school age within the meaning of the Education Act 1944 and is not receiving efficient full-time education suitable to his age, ability and aptitude [and to any special educational needs he may have]; or

   (f)   he is guilty of an offence, excluding homicide,

and also that he is in need of care or control which he is unlikely to receive unless the court makes an order under this section in respect of him, then, subject to the following provisions of this section and sections 2 and 3 of this Act, the court may if it thinks fit make such an order.

   (3)   The order which a court may make under this section in respect of a child or young person is—

(a) *an order requiring his parent or guardian to enter into a recognisance to take proper care of him and exercise proper control over him; or*

(b) *a supervision order; or*

(c) *a care order (other than an interim order); or*

(d) *a hospital order within the meaning of [Part III of the Mental Health Act 1983]; or*

(e) *a guardianship order within the meaning of that Act.*

(4) *In any proceedings under this section the court may make orders in pursuance of paragraphs (c) and (d) of the preceding subsection but subject to that shall not make more than one of the orders mentioned in the preceding subsection, without prejudice to any power to make a further order in subsequent proceedings of any description; and if in proceedings under this section the court makes one of those orders and an order so mentioned is already in force in respect of the child or young person in question, the court may discharge the earlier order unless it is a hospital or guardianship order.*

(5) *An order under this section shall not be made in respect of a child or young person—*

(a) *in pursuance of paragraph (a) of subsection (3) of this section unless the parent or guardian in question consents;*

(b) *in pursuance of paragraph (d) or (e) of that subsection unless the conditions which, under [section 37 of the said Act of 1983], are required to be satisfied for the making of a hospital or guardianship order in respect of a person convicted as mentioned in that section are satisfied in his case so far as they are applicable;*

(c) *if he has attained the age of sixteen and is or has been married.*

(6) *In this section 'authorised person' means a person authorised by order of the Secretary of State to bring proceedings in pursuance of this section and any officer of a society which is so authorised, and in sections 2 and 3 of this Act 'care proceedings' means proceedings in pursuance of this section and 'relevant infant' means the child or young person in respect of whom such proceedings are brought or proposed to be brought.*

Note. In sub-s (2), para (bb) inserted by Children Act 1975, s 108(1)(a), Sch 3, para 67, and subsequently substituted by Health and Social Services and Social Security Adjudications Act 1983, s 9, Sch 2, para 10, and words in square brackets in para (e) inserted by Education Act 1981, s 21(4), Sch 3, para 9.

In sub-ss (3), (5) words in square brackets substituted by Mental Health Act 1983, s 148, Sch 4, para 26(a), (b).

This section repealed by Children Act 1989, s 108(7), Sch 15, as from 14 October 1991; see ibid, s 108(6), Sch 14, paras 1, 15, 25, 36. See now ibid, ss 31–42, Sch 3 (pp 3268–3279, 3369).

2. Provisions supplementary to section 1—(1) *If a local authority receive information suggesting that there are grounds for bringing care proceedings in respect of a child or young person who resides or is found in their area, it shall be the duty of the authority to cause enquiries to be made into the case unless they are satisfied that such enquiries are unnecessary.*

(2) *If it appears to a local authority that there are grounds for bringing care proceedings in respect of a child or young person who resides or is found in their area, it shall be the duty of the authority to exercise their power under the preceding section to bring care proceedings in respect of him unless they are satisfied that it is neither in his interest nor the public interest to do so or that some other person is about to do so or to charge him with an offence.*

(3) *No care proceedings shall be begun by any person unless that person has given notice of the proceedings to the local authority for the area in which it appears to him that the relevant infant resides or, if it appears to him that the relevant infant does not reside in the area of a local authority, to the local authority for any area in which it appears to him that any circumstances giving rise to the proceedings arose; but the preceding provisions of this subsection shall not apply where the person by whom the notice would fall to be given is the local authority in question.*

(4) *Without prejudice to any power to issue a summons or warrant apart from this subsection, a justice may issue a summons or warrant for the purpose of securing the attendance of the relevant infant before the court in which care proceedings are brought or proposed to be brought in respect of him; but [subsections (3) and (4) of section 55 of the Magistrates' Courts Act 1980] (which among other things restrict the circumstances in which a warrant may be issued)*

shall apply with the necessary modifications to a warrant under this subsection as they apply to a warrant under that section and as if in subsection (3) after the word 'summons' there were inserted the words 'cannot be served or'.

 (5) Where the relevant infant is arrested in pursuance of a warrant issued by virtue of the preceding subsection and cannot be brought immediately before the court aforesaid, the person in whose custody he is—

  (a) *may make arrangements for his detention in a place of safety for a period of not more than seventy-two hours from the time of the arrest (and it shall be lawful for him to be detained in pursuance of the arrangements); and*

  (b) *shall within that period, unless within it the relevant infant is brought before the court aforesaid, bring him before a justice;*

and the justice shall either make an interim order in respect of him or direct that he be released forthwith.

 (6) [Section 97 of the Magistrates' Courts Act 1980] (under which a summons or warrant may be issued to secure the attendance of a witness) shall apply to care proceedings as it applies to the hearing of a complaint.

 (7) In determining whether the condition set out in subsection (2)(b) of the preceding section is satisfied in respect of the relevant infant, it shall be assumed that no order under that section is to be made in respect of him.

 (8) In relation to the condition set out in subsection (2)(e) of the preceding section the references to a local authority in that section and subsections (1), (2) and (11)(b) of this section shall be construed as references to a local education authority; and in any care proceedings—

  (a) *the court shall not entertain an allegation that the condition is satisfied unless the proceedings are brought by a local education authority; and*

  (b) *the said condition shall be deemed to be satisfied if the relevant infant is of the age mentioned in that condition and it is proved that he—*

   (i) *is the subject of a school attendance order which is in force under section 37 of the Education Act 1944 and has not been complied with, or*

   (ii) *is a registered pupil at a school which he is not attending regularly within the meaning of section 39 of that Act, or*

   (iii) *is a person whom another person habitually wandering from place to place takes with him,]*

unless it is also proved that he is receiving the education mentioned in that condition; but nothing in paragraph (a) of this subsection shall prevent any evidence from being considered in care proceedings for any purpose other than that of determining whether that condition is satisfied in respect of the relevent infant.

 (9) If on application under this subsection to the court in which it is proposed to bring care proceedings in respect of a relevant infant who is not present before the court it appears to the court that he is under the age of five and either—

  (a) *it is proved to the satisfaction of the court, on oath or in such other manner as may be prescribed by rules under section 15 of the Justices of the Peace Act 1949, that notice of the proposal to bring the proceedings at the time and place at which the application is made was served on the parent or guardian of the relevant infant at what appears to the court to be a reasonable time before the making of the application; or*

  (b) *it appears to the court that his parent or guardian is present before the court*

the court may if it thinks fit, after giving the parent or guardian if he is present an opportunity to be heard, give a direction under this subsection in respect of the relevant infant; and a relevant infant in respect of whom such a direction is given by a court shall be deemed to have been brought before the court under section 1 of this Act at the time of the direction, and care proceedings in respect of him may be continued accordingly.

 (10) If the court before which the relevant infant is brought in care proceedings is not in a position to decide what order, if any, ought to be made under the preceding section in respect of him, [the court may make—

  (a) *an interim order; or*

(b) an interim hospital order within the meaning of [section 38 of the Mental Health Act 1983],

in respect of him; but an order shall not be made in respect of the relevant infant in pursuance of paragraph (b) of this subsection unless the conditions which, under [the said section 38], are required to be satisfied for the making of an interim hospital order in respect of a person convicted as mentioned in that section are satisfied in his case so far as they are applicable].

(11) If it appears to the court before which the relevant infant is brought in care proceedings that he resides in a petty sessions area other than that for which the court acts, the court shall, unless it dismisses the case and subject to subsection (5) of the following section, direct that he be brought under the preceding section before a juvenile court acting for the petty sessions area in which he resides; and where the court so directs—

(a) it may make an interim order in respect of him and, if it does so, shall cause the clerk of the court to which the direction relates to be informed of the case;

(b) if the court does not make such an order it shall cause the local authority in whose area it appears to the court that the relevant infant resides to be informed of the case, and it shall be the duty of that authority to give effect to the direction within twenty-one days.

(12) The relevant infant [or, in a case where a parent or guardian of his was a party to the care proceedings by virtue of an order under section 32A of this Act, the parent or guardian] may appeal to [the Crown Court] against any order made in respect of him [the relevant infant] under the preceding section except such an order as is mentioned in subsection (3)(a) of that section.

(13) Such an order as is mentioned in subsection (3)(a) of the preceding section shall not require the parent or guardian in question to enter into a recognisance for an amount exceeding [£1,000] or for a period exceeding three years or, where the relevant infant will attain the age of eighteen in a period shorter than three years, for a period exceeding that shorter period; and [section 120 of the Magistrates' Courts Act 1980] (which relates to the forfeiture of recognisances) shall apply to a recognisance entered into in pursuance of such an order as it applies to a recognisance to keep the peace.

(14) For the purposes of this Act, care proceedings in respect of a relevant infant are begun when he is first brought before a juvenile court in pursuance of the preceding section in connection with the matter to which the proceedings relate.

Note. Words in square brackets in sub-ss (4), (6) substituted by Magistrates' Courts Act 1980, s 154, Sch 7, para 78: in sub-s (10) words from 'the court may make' to the end substituted by Mental Health (Amendment) Act 1982, s 65(1), Sch 3, Part I, para 44, and words in square brackets within that amendment substituted by Mental Health Act 1983, s 148, Sch 4, para 26(c): words in second square brackets in sub-s (12) substituted by Courts Act 1971, s 56(2), Sch 9, Part I, and in first and third square brackets inserted and substituted respectively by Children and Young Persons (Amendment) Act 1986, s 2(1), as from 1 August 1988: and in sub-s (13) sum in first square brackets substituted by SI 1984 No 447, and words in second pair of square brackets substituted by Magistrates' Courts Act 1980, s 154, Sch 7, para 78.

This section repealed by Children Act 1989, s 108(7), Sch 15, as from 14 October 1991; see ibid s 108(6), Sch 14, paras 1, 36. See now ibid, ss 31–42, Sch 3 (pp 3268–3279, 3369).

3. Further supplementary provisions relating to s 1(2)(f)—(1) In any care proceedings, no account shall be taken for the purposes of the condition set out in paragraph (f) of subsection (2) of section 1 of this Act (hereafter in this section referred to as 'the offence condition') of an offence alleged to have been committed by the relevant infant if—

(a) in any previous care proceedings in respect of him it was alleged that the offence condition was satisfied in consequence of the offence; or

(b) the offence is a summary offence … and, disregarding section 4 of this Act, the period for beginning summary proceedings in respect of it expired before the care proceedings were begun; or

(c) disregarding section 4 of this Act, he would if charged with the offence be entitled to be discharged under any rule of law relating to previous acquittal or conviction.

(2) In any care proceedings the court shall not entertain an allegation that the offence condition is satisfied in respect of the relevant infant unless the proceedings are brought by a local authority or a constable [and, in the case of proceedings brought by a constable, the Director of Public Prosecutions has consented to the allegation being made]; but nothing in this or the preceding subsection shall prevent any evidence from being considered in care proceedings for any purpose other than that of determining whether the offence condition is satisfied in respect of the relevant infant.

(3) If in any care proceedings the relevant infant is alleged to have committed an offence in consequence of which the offence condition is satisfied with respect to him, the court shall not find the offence condition satisfied in consequence of the offence unless, disregarding section 4 of this Act, it would have found him guilty of the offence if the proceedings had been in pursuance of an information duly charging him with the offence and the court had had jurisdiction to try the information; and without prejudice to the preceding provisions of this subsection the same proof shall be required to substantiate or refute an allegation that the offence condition is satisfied in consequence of an offence as is required to warrant a finding of guilty, or as the case may be, of not guilty of the offence.

(4) A person shall not be charged with an offence if in care proceedings previously brought in respect of him it was alleged that the offence condition was satisfied in consequence of that offence.

(5) If in any care proceedings in which it is alleged that the offence condition is satisfied in respect of the relevant infant it appears to the court that the case falls to be remitted to another court in pursuance of subsection (11) of the preceding section but that it is appropriate to determine whether the condition is satisfied before remitting the case, the court may determine accordingly; and any determination under this subsection shall be binding on the court to which the case is remitted.

[(6) Where in any care proceedings the court finds the offence condition satisfied with respect to the relevant infant, then, whether or not the court makes an order under section 1 of this Act—

    (a)   section 35 of the Powers of Criminal Courts Act 1973 (which relates to compensation for personal injury and loss of or damage to property) shall apply as if the finding were a finding of guilty of the offence; and

    (b)   it shall be the duty of the court, subject to subsections (6A) and (6B) of this section, to order that any sum awarded by virtue of this section be paid by the relevant infant's parent or guardian instead of by the relevant infant, unless the court is satisfied—

        (i)   that the parent or guardian cannot be found; or

        (ii)   that it would be unreasonable to make an order for payment, having regard to the circumstances of the case.

(6A) An order shall not be made in pursuance of the preceding subsection unless the parent or guardian has been given an opportunity of being heard or has been required to attend the proceedings and failed to do so.

(6B) Where the finding that the offence condition is satisfied is made in pursuance of subsection (5) of this section, the powers conferred by subsection (6) of this section shall be exercisable by the court to which the case is remitted instead of by the court which made the finding.]

(7) Where in any care proceedings the court finds the offence condition satisfied with respect to the relevant infant and he is a young person, the court may if it thinks fit and he consents, instead of making such an order as is mentioned in section 1(3) of this Act, order him to enter into a recognisance for an amount not exceeding [£50] and for a period not exceeding one year to keep the peace or to be of good behaviour; and such an order shall be deemed to be an order under section 1 of this Act but no appeal to [the Crown Court] may be brought against an order under this subsection.

(8) Where in any care proceedings the court finds the offence condition satisfied with respect to the relevant infant in consequence of an offence which was not admitted by him before the court, then—

    (a)   if the finding is made in pursuance of subsection (5) of this section and the court to which the case is remitted decides not to make any order under section 1 of this Act in respect of the relevant infant; or

    (b)   if the finding is not made in pursuance of that subsection and the court decides as aforesaid,

the relevant infant may appeal to [*the Crown Court*] *against the finding, and in a case falling within paragraph* (*a*) *of this subsection any notice of appeal shall be given within* [*twenty-one days*] *after the date of the decision mentioned in that paragraph; and a person ordered to pay compensation by virtue of subsection* (*6*) *of this section may appeal to* [*the Crown Court*] *against the order.*

(*9*) ...

Note. Amended by Courts Act, 1971, s 56(2), Sch 9, Part I, Criminal Law Act 1977, ss 58(3), 65(5), Sch 13, Criminal Justice Act 1982, s 27, Crown Court Rules 1982, SI 1982 No 1109, Prosecution of Offences Act 1985, s 27.

This section repealed by Children Act 1989, s 108(7), Sch 15, as from 14 October 1991; see ibid, s 108(6), Sch 14, paras 1, 36. See now ibid, ss 31–42, Sch 3 (pp 3268–3279, 3369). Words 'disregarding section 4 of this Act' in italics repealed by Criminal Justice Act 1991, s 101(2), Sch 13, as from 1 October 1992.

*   *   *   *   *

Committal to care of local authorities

20. Orders for committal to care of local authorities—(*1*) *Any provision of this Act authorising the making of a care order in respect of any person shall be construed as authorising the making of an order committing him to the care of a local authority; and in this Act 'care order' shall be construed accordingly and 'interim order' means a care order containing provision for the order to expire with the expiration of twenty-eight days, or of a shorter period specified in the order beginning—*

(*a*)   *if the order is made by a court, with the date of the making of the order; and*

(*b*)   *if it is made by a justice, with the date when the person to whom it relates was first in legal custody in connection with the matter in consequence of which the order is made.*

(*2*) *The local authority to whose care a person is committed by a care order shall be—*

(*a*)   *except in the case of an interim order, the local authority in whose area it appears to the court making the order that that person resides or, if it does not appear to the court that he resides in the area of a local authority, any local authority in whose area it appears to the court that any offence was committed or any circumstances arose in consequence of which the order is made; and*

(*b*)   *in the case of an interim order, such one of the local authorities mentioned in paragraph* (*a*) *of this subsection as the court or justice making the order thinks fit* (*whether or not the person in question appears to reside in their area*).

[(*2A*) *In determining the place of residence of any person for the purposes of this section, any period shall be disregarded during which, while in the care of a local authority* (*whether by virtue of a care order or not*), *he resided outside the local authority's area.*]

(*3*) *Subject to the provisions of the following section, a care order other than an interim order shall cease to have effect—*

(*a*)   *if the person to whom it relates had attained the age of sixteen when the order was originally made, when he attains the age of nineteen; and*

(*b*)   *in any other case, when that person attains the age of eighteen.*

(*4*) *A care order shall be sufficient authority for the detention by any local authority or constable of the person to whom the order relates until he is received into the care of the authority to whose care he is committed by the order.*

Note. Sub-s (2A) inserted by Health and Social Services and Social Security Adjudications Act 1983, s 9, Sch 2, para 12.

This section repealed by Children Act 1989, s 108(7), Sch 15, as from 14 October 1991; see ibid, s 108(6), Sch 14, paras 1, 16, 36. See now ibid, ss 31–42, Sch 3 (pp 3268–3279, 3369).

20A. Power of court to add condition as to charge and control of offender in care—(*1*) *Where a person to whom a care order relates which was made—*

(*a*)   *by virtue of subsection* (*3*) *of section 1 of this Act in a case where the court which made the order was of the opinion that the condition mentioned in subsection* (*2*)(*f*) *of that section was satisfied; or*

(b)   *by virtue of section 7(7) of this Act, [or*
(c)   *by virtue of section 15(1) of this Act in a case where—*

   (i)   *the supervision order for which the care order was substituted was made under section 7(7) of this Act; and*
   (ii)   *the offence in respect of which the supervision order was made was punishable with imprisonment in the case of a person over 21,]*

is convicted or found guilty of an offence punishable with imprisonment in the case of a person over 21, the court which convicts or finds him guilty of that offence may add to the care order a condition under this section that the power conferred by section 21(2) of the Child Care Act 1980 (power of local authority to allow a parent, guardian, relative or friend charge and control) shall for such period not exceeding 6 months as the court may specify in the condition—

(a)   *not be exercisable; or*
(b)   *not be exercisable except to allow the person to whom the order relates to be under the charge and control of a specified parent, guardian, relative or friend.*

(2) Where—

(a)   *the power conferred by subsection (1) above has been exercised; and*
(b)   *before the period specified in the condition has expired the person to whom the care order relates is convicted or found guilty of another offence punishable with imprisonment in the case of a person over 21,*

the court may replace the condition with another condition under this section.

(3) A court shall not exercise the powers conferred by this section unless the court is of opinion that it is appropriate to exercise those powers because of the seriousness of the offence and that no other method of dealing with the person to whom the care order relates is appropriate; and for the purpose of determining whether any other method of dealing with him is appropriate the court shall obtain and consider information about the circumstances.

(4) A court shall not exercise the said powers in respect of a person who is not legally represented in that court unless either—

(a)   *he applied for legal aid and the application was refused on the ground that it did not appear his means were such that he required assistance; or*
(b)   *having been informed of his right to apply for legal aid and had the opportunity to do so, he refused or failed to apply.*

(5) Before adding a condition under this section to a care order a court shall explain to the person to whom the care order relates the purpose and effect of the condition.

(6) At any time when a care order includes a condition under this section—

(a)   *the person to whom the order relates;*
(b)   *his parent or guardian, acting on his behalf; or*
(c)   *the local authority in whose care he is,*

may apply to a juvenile court for the revocation or variation of the condition.

(7) The local authority may appeal to the Crown Court against the imposition of a condition under this section by a magistrates' court or against the terms of such a condition.

(8) For the purposes of this section a person is to be treated as legally represented in a court if, but only if, he has the assistance of counsel or a solicitor to represent him in the proceedings in that court at some time after he is convicted or found guilty and before any power conferred by this section is exercised, and in this section 'legal aid' means legal aid for the purposes of proceedings in that court, whether the whole proceedings or the proceedings on or in relation to the exercise of the power; but in the case of a person committed to the Crown Court for sentence or trial, it is immaterial whether he applied for legal aid in the Crown Court to, or was informed of his right to apply by, that court or the court which committed him.]

Note. This section inserted by Criminal Justice Act 1982, s 22. Words in square brackets in sub-s (1) inserted by Criminal Justice Act 1988, s 170(1), Sch 15, para 35, as from 1 October 1988.

This section repealed by Children Act 1989, s 108(7), Sch 15, as from 14 October 1991; see ibid, s 108(6), Sch 14, paras 1, 36. See now ibid, ss 31–42, Sch 3 (pp 3268–3279, 3369).

21. Variation and discharge of care orders—*(1) If it appears to a juvenile court, on the application of a local authority to whose care a person is committed by a care order which* *would cease to have effect by virtue of subsection (3)(b) of the preceding section, that he is accommodated in a community home or a home provided by the Secretary of State and that by reason of his mental condition or behaviour it is in his interest or the public interest for him to continue to be so accommodated after he attains the age of eighteen, the court may order that the care order shall continue in force until he attains the age of nineteen; but the court shall not make an order under this subsection unless the person in question is present before the court.*

(2) If it appears to a juvenile court, on the application of a local authority to whose care a person is committed by a care order or on the application of that person, that it is appropriate to discharge the order, the court may discharge it and on discharging it may, unless it was an interim order and unless the person to whom the discharged order related has attained the age of eighteen, make a supervision order in respect of him.

[(2A) A juvenile court shall not make an order under subsection (2) of this section in the case of a person who has not attained the age of 18 and appears to the court to be in need of care or control unless the court is satisfied that, whether through the making of a supervision order or otherwise, he will receive that care or control.]

(3) Where an application under [subsection (2) of this section] for the discharge of a care order is dismissed, then—

    (a) in the case of an interim order, no further application for its discharge shall be made under that subsection except with the consent of a juvenile court (without prejudice to the power to make an application under subsection (4) of the following section); and

    (b) in any other case, no further application for its discharge shall be made under this subsection by any person during the period of three months beginning with the date of the dismissal except with the consent of a juvenile court.

(4) The person to whom the relevant care order relates or related may appeal to [the Crown Court] against an order under subsection (1) of this section or a supervision order made in pursuance of subsection (2) of this section or the dismissal of an application under the said subsection (2) for the discharge of the care order.

[(4A) In a case where a parent or guardian is a party to the proceedings on an application under subsection (2) of this section by virtue of an order under section 32A of this Act, the parent or guardian may appeal to the Crown Court against the making of a supervision order or the refusal of the court to discharge the care order.]

(5) The local authority to whose care a person is committed by a care order (other than an interim order) may, within the period of three months beginning with the date of the order, appeal to [the Crown Court] against the provision of the order naming their area on the ground that at the time the order was made the person aforesaid resided in the area of another local authority named in the notice of appeal; but no appeal shall be brought by a local authority under this subsection unless they give notice in writing of the proposal to bring it to the other local authority in question before giving notice of appeal.

(6) References in this section to a juvenile court, in relation to a care order, are references to a juvenile court acting for any part of the area of the local authority to whose care a person is committed by the order or for the place where that person resides.

Note. Sub-s (2A) inserted and words in square brackets in sub-s (3) substituted by Children Act 1975, s 108(1)(a), Sch 3, para 69; and words in square brackets in sub-ss (4), (5) substituted by Courts Act 1971, s 56(2), Sch 9, Part I. Sub-s (4A) inserted by Children and Young Persons (Amendment) Act 1986, s 2(3), as from 1 August 1988.

This section repealed by Children Act 1989, s 108(7), Sch 15, as from 14 October 1991; see ibid, s 108(6), Sch 14, paras 1, 16, 25, 36. See now ibid, ss 31–42, Sch 3 (pp 3268–3279, 3369).

21A. Termination of care order on adoption etc—*(1) A care order relating to a person under the age of 18 shall cease to have effect—*

    (a) on his adoption;

    (b) if any order under an enactment to which this paragraph applies is made in relation to him;

    (c) if an order similar to an order under section 25 of the Children Act 1975 is made in relation to him in Northern Ireland, the Isle of Man or any of the Channel islands.

(2) Subsection (1)(b) above applies to the following enactments—

    (a)   sections 14 and 25 of the Children Act 1975;

    (b)   sections 18 and 55 of the Adoption Act 1976; and

    (c)   (applies to Scotland only).

(3) After the commencement of section 55 of the Adoption Act 1976 subsection (1)(c) above shall have effect with the substitution of '55 of the Adoption Act 1976' for '25 of the Children Act 1975'].

Note. This section inserted by Children Act 1975, s 108(1)(a), Sch 3, para 70, and subsequently substituted by Health and Social Services and Social Security Adjudications Act 1983, s 9, Sch 2, para 13.

This section repealed by Children Act 1989, s 108(7), Sch 15, as from 14 October 1991; see ibid, s 108(6), Sch 14, paras 1, 36. See now ibid, ss 31–42, Sch 3 (pp 3268–3279, 3369).

22. Special provisions relating to interim orders—*(1) A juvenile court or a justice shall not make an interim order in respect of any person unless either—*

    (a)   that person is present before the court or justice; or

    (b)   the court or justice is satisfied that he is under the age of five or cannot be present as aforesaid by reason of illness or accident.

(2) An interim order shall contain provision requiring the local authority to whose care a person is committed by the order to bring that person before a court specified in the order on the expiration of the order or at such earlier time as the specified court may require, so however that the said provision shall, if the court making the order considers it appropriate so to direct by reason of the fact that that person is under the age of five [or is legally represented] or by reason of illness or accident, require the local authority to bring him before the specified court on the expiration of the order only if the specified court so requires.

(3) A juvenile court acting for the same area as a juvenile court by which or a justice by whom an interim order has been made in respect of any person may, at any time before the expiration of the order, make a further interim order in respect of him; and the power to make an interim order conferred by this subsection is without prejudice to any other power to make such an order.

(4) The High Court may, on the application of a person to whom an interim order relates[, or, in a case where the order was made in proceedings to which a parent or guardian was a party by virtue of an order under section 32A of this Act, of the parent or guardian,] discharge the order on such terms as the court thinks fit; but if on such an application the discharge of the order is refused, the local authority to whose care he is committed by the order shall not exercise in his case their powers under [section 21(2) of the Child Care Act 1980] (which enables them to allow a parent or other person to be in charge of him) except with the consent and in accordance with any directions of the High Court.

(5) If a court which has made or, apart from this subsection, would make an interim order in respect of a person who has attained the age of fourteen certifies that he is of so unruly a character that he cannot safely be committed to the care of a local authority and has been notified by the Secretary of State that a remand centre is available for the reception from the court of persons of his class or description, then, subject to the following provisions of this section, the court shall commit him to a remand centre for twenty-eight days or such shorter period as may be specified in the warrant; but in a case where an interim order is in force in respect of the person in question, a warrant under this subsection shall not be issued in respect of him except on the application of the local authority to whose care he is committed by the order and shall not be issued for a period extending beyond the date fixed for the expiration of the order, and on the issue of a warrant under this subsection in such a case the interim order shall cease to have effect.

In this subsection 'court' includes a justice.

(6) Subsections (1), (3) and (4) of this section, so much of section 2(11)(a) as requires the clerk to be informed and section 21(2) to (4) of this Act shall apply to a warrant under subsection (5) of this section as they apply to an interim order but as if the words 'is under the age of five or' in subsection (1) of this section were omitted.

Note. Words in square brackets in sub-s (2) inserted by Health and Social Services and Social Security Adjudications Act 1983, s 9, Sch 2, para 14, and words in first square brackets in sub-s (4) by Children and Young Persons (Amendment) Act 1986, s 2(4), as from 1 August 1988, and in second square brackets in sub-s (4) substituted by Child Care Act 1980, s 89(3), Sch 5, para 24. Sub-s (5) repealed by Criminal Justice Act 1988, ss 125, 170(2), Sch 16, as from 1 October 1988.

This section repealed by Children Act 1989, s 108(7), Sch 15, as from 14 October 1991; see ibid, s 108(6), Sch 14, paras 1, 36. See now ibid, ss 31–42, Sch 3 (pp 3268–3279, 3369).

*   *   *   *   *

Detention

28. Detention of child or young person in place of safety—*(1) If, upon an application to a justice by any person for authority to detain a child or young person and take him to a place of safety, the justice is satisfied that the applicant has reasonable cause to believe that—*

   (a)   any of the conditions set out in section 1(2)(a) to (e) of this Act is satisfied in respect of the child or young person; or

   (b)   an appropriate court would find the condition set out in section 1(2)(b) of this Act satisfied in respect of him; or

   (c)   the child or young person is about to leave the United Kingdom in contravention of section 25 of the Act of 1933 (which regulates the sending abroad of juvenile entertainers),

the justice may grant the application; and the child or young person in respect of whom an authorisation is issued under this subsection may be detained in a place of safety by virtue of the authorisation for twenty-eight days beginning with the date of authorisation, or for such shorter period beginning with that date as may be specified in the authorisation.

(2) Any constable may detain a child or young person as respects whom the constable has reasonable cause to believe that any of the conditions set out in section 1(2)(a) to (d) of this Act is satisfied or that an appropriate court would find the condition set out in section 1(2)(b) of this Act satisfied or that an offence is being committed under section 10(1) of the Act of 1933 (which penalises a vagrant who takes a juvenile from place to place).

(3) A person who detains any person in pursuance of the preceding provisions of this section shall, as soon as practicable after doing so, inform him of the reason for his detention and take such steps as are practicable for informing his parent or guardian of his detention and of the reason for it.

(4) A constable who detains any person in pursuance of subsection (2) of this section or who arrests a child without a warrant otherwise than for homicide shall as soon as practicable after doing so secure that the case is enquired into by a police officer not below the rank of inspector or by the police officer in charge of [the custody officer at] a police station, and that officer shall on completing the enquiry either—

   (a)   release the person in question; or

   (b)   if the officer considers that he ought to be further detained in his own interests or, in the case of an arrested child, because of the nature of the alleged offence, make arrangements for his detention in a place of safety and inform him, and take such steps as are practicable for informing his parent or guardian, of his right to apply to a justice under subsection (5) of this section for his release;

and subject to the said subsection (5) it shall be lawful to detain the person in question in accordance with any such arrangements.

(5) It shall not be lawful for a child arrested without a warrant otherwise than for homicide to be detained in consequence of the arrest or such arrangements as aforesaid, or for any person to be detained by virtue of subsection (2) of this section or any such arrangements, after the expiration of the period of eight days beginning with the day on which he was arrested or, as the case may be, on which his detention in pursuance of the said subsection (2) began; and if during that period the person in question applies to a justice for his release, the justice shall direct that he be released forthwith unless the justice considers that he ought to be further detained in his own interests or, in the case of an arrested child, because of the nature of the alleged offence.

(6) If while a person is detained in pursuance of this section an application for an interim order in respect of him is made to a magistrates' court or a justice, the court or justice shall either make or refuse to make the order and, in the case of a refusal, may direct that he be released forthwith.

Note. Words 'police officer not below ... charge of' in sub-s (4) substituted by words 'the custody officer at' by Police and Criminal Evidence Act 1984, s 19(1), Sch 6, Part I, para 19(a).

This section repealed by Children Act 1989, s 108(7), Sch 15, as from 14 October 1991; see ibid, s 108(6), Sch 4, paras 1, 36. See now ibid, ss 31–42, Sch 3 (pp 3268–3279, 3369).

*   *   *   *   *

30. Detention of young offenders in community homes—(1) The power to give directions under *section 53 of the Act of 1933* [section 92 of the Powers of Criminal Courts (Sentencing) Act 2000] (under which young offenders convicted on indictment of certain grave crimes may be detained in accordance with directions given by the Secretary of State) shall include power to direct detention by a local authority specified in the directions in a home so specified which is a community home provided by the authority or a controlled community home for the management, equipment and maintenance of which the authority are responsible; but a person shall not be liable to be detained in the manner provided by this section after he attains the age of nineteen.

Note. Words 'section 92 of the Powers of Criminal Courts (Sentencing) Act 2000' in square brackets substituted for words in italics by the Powers of Criminal Courts (Sentencing) Act 2000, s 165(1), Sch 9, para 40, as from 25 August 2000.

(2) It shall be the duty of a local authority specified in directions given in pursuance of this section to detain the person to whom the directions relate in the home specified in the directions subject to and in accordance with such instructions relating to him as the Secretary of State may give to the authority from time to time; and the authority shall be entitled to recover from the Secretary of State any expenses reasonably incurred by them in discharging that duty.

*   *   *   *   *

[*Conflict of interest between parent and child or young person*]

[32A. Conflict of interest between parent and child or young person—*(1) If before or in the course of proceedings in respect of a child or young person—*

    (a)   *in pursuance of section 1 of this Act; or*

    (b)   *on an application under section 15(1) of this Act for the discharge of a relevant supervision order or a supervision order made under section 21(2) of this Act on the discharge of a relevant care order; or*

    (c)   *on an application under section 21(2) of this Act for the discharge of a relevant care order or a care order made under section 15(1) of this Act on the discharge of a relevant supervision order; or*

    (d)   *on an appeal to the Crown Court under section 2(12) of this Act; or*

    (e)   *on an appeal to the Crown Court under section 16(8) of this Act against the dismissal of an application for the discharge of a relevant supervision order or against a care order made under section 15(1) on the discharge of—*

        (i) *a relevant supervision order; or*

        (ii) *a supervision order made under section 21(2) on the discharge of a relevant care order; or*

    (f)   *on an appeal to the Crown Court under section 21(4) of this Act against the dismissal of an application for the discharge of a relevant care order or against a supervision order made under section 21(2) on the discharge of—*

        (i) *a relevant care order; or*

        (ii) *a care order made under section 15(1) on the discharge of a relevant supervision order, it appears to the court that there is or may be a conflict, on any matter relevant to the proceedings, between the interests of the child or young person and those of his parent or guardian, the court may order that in relation to the proceeding the parent or guardian is not to be treated as representing the child or young person or as otherwise authorised to act on his behalf.*

(2) If an application such as is referred to in subsection (1)(b) or (c) of this section is unopposed, the court, unless satisfied that to do so is not necessary for safeguarding the interests of the child or young person, shall order that in relation to proceedings on the application no parent or guardian of his shall be treated as representing him or as otherwise authorised to act on his behalf; but where the application was made by a parent or guardian on his behalf the order shall not invalidate the application.

(3) Where an order is made under subsection (1) or (2) of this section for the purposes of proceedings on an application within subsection (1)(a), (b) or (c) of this section, that order shall also have effect for the purposes of any appeal to the Crown Court arising out of those proceedings.

(4) The power of the court to make orders for the purposes of an application within subsection (1)(a), (b) or (c) of this section shall also be exercisable, before the hearing of the application, by a single justice.

[(4A) Where an order is made under this section in respect of a parent or guardian in relation to any proceedings he shall by virtue of the order be made a party to the proceedings.]

(5) In this section—

'relevant care order' means a care order made under section 1 of this Act;

'relevant supervision order' means a supervision order made under section 1 of this Act.]

Note. This section inserted by Children Act 1975, s 64. Sub-s (4A) inserted by Children and Young Persons (Amendment) Act 1986, s 3(1), as from 1 August 1988: see ibid, s 4(2).

Whole section repealed by Children Act 1989, s 108(7), Sch 15, as from 14 October 1991; see ibid, 108(6), Sch 14, paras 1, 36. See now ibid, ss 31–42, Sch 3 (pp 3268–3279, 3369).

[32B. Safeguarding of interests of child or young person where section 32A order made—*(1) Where the court makes an order under section 32A(2) of this Act the court, unless satisfied that to do so is not necessary for safeguarding the interests of the child or young person, shall in accordance with rules of court appoint a guardian ad litem of the child or young person for the purposes of the proceedings.*

In this subsection 'court' includes a single justice.

(2) Rules of court shall provide for the appointment of a guardian ad litem of the child or young person for the purposes of any proceedings to which an order under section 32A(1) of this Act relates.

(3) A guardian ad litem appointed in pursuance of this section shall be under a duty to safeguard the interests of the child or young person in the manner prescribed by rules of court.]

Note. This section inserted by Children Act 1975, s 64.

Whole section repealed by Children Act 1989, s 108(7), Sch 15, as from 14 October 1991; see ibid, 108(6), Sch 14, paras 1, 36. See now ibid, ss 31–42, Sch 3 (pp 3268–3279, 3369).

[32C. Applications by grandparents to be parties to proceedings—*(1) Where in any such proceedings as are mentioned in the section 32A(1) of this Act any grandparent of the child or young person in respect of whom the proceedings are brought makes an application to the court under this section, the court may, in such circumstances as may be specified in rules of court, give leave for the grandparent to be made a party to the proceedings.*

(2) Rules of court shall make provision as to the circumstances in which the court may give leave under subsection (1) above.

(3) In this section 'the court' includes a single justice.]

Note. This section inserted by Children and Young Persons (Amendment) Act 1986, s 3(2), as from 1 August 1988: see ibid, s 4(2).

Whole section repealed by Children Act 1989, s 108(7), Sch 15, as from 14 October 1991; see ibid, s 108(6), Sch 14, paras 1, 36. See now ibid, ss 31–42, Sch 3 (pp 3268–3279, 3369).

2334   Children and Young Persons Act 1969, s 34

Transitional modifications of Part I for persons of specified ages

34. Transitional modifications of Part I for persons of specified ages—(1)
The Secretary of State may by order provide—

  (a) *that any reference to a child in section 4, 13(2) or 28(4) or (5) [or 13(2)] of this Act
       shall be construed as excluding a child who has attained such age as may be specified
       in the order;*

  (b) *that any reference to a young person in section 5 of this Act (except subsection (8)) shall
       be construed as including a child, or excluding a young person, who has attained such
       age as may be so specified;*

  (c) that any reference to a young person in section 5(8), *7(7), 7(8),* 9(1), 23(1) or
       29(1) of this Act shall be construed as including a child who has attained
       such age as may be so specified;

  (d) ...

  (e) that *section 23(2) or (3)* [section 23(4) to (6)] of this Act shall effect as if the
       references to a young person excluded a young person who has not attained
       such age as may be so specified;

  (f) *that section 22(5) of this Act shall have effect as if for the reference to the age of fourteen
       ... there were substituted a reference to such greater age as may be so specified.*

Note. Para (a) repealed and in para (c) reference to '7(7), 7(8),' in italics repealed by the
Crime and Disorder Act 1998, ss 106, 120(2), Sch 7, para 8, Sch 10, as from 30 September 1998
(SI 1998 No 2327). Number '4' in para (a), and para (b) repealed by Criminal Justice Act 1991,
s 101(2), Sch 13, as from 1 October 1992. Words in square brackets in paras (a), (e) substituted
for words '13(2) or 28(4) or (5)' and 'section 23(2) or (3)' by Children Act 1989, s 108(4),
Sch 12, para 28, as from 14 October 1991. Para (d) and words omitted from para (f) repealed
by Criminal Justice Act 1982, s 78, Sch 16. Whole of para (f) repealed by Criminal Justice Act
1988, s 170(2), Sch 16, as from 1 October 1988.

  (2) In the case of a person who has not attained *the age of seventeen* [the age of
eighteen] but has attained such lower age as the Secretary of State may by order
specify, no proceedings *under section 1 of this Act or for an offence shall be begun in any
court unless the person proposing to begin the proceedings has, in addition to any notice falling
to be given by him to a local authority in pursuance of section 2(3) or 5(8) of this Act, given
notice of the proceedings to *a probation officer* [an officer of a local probation board]
for the area for which the court acts; *and accordingly in the case of such a person the reference in section 1(1) of this Act to the said section 2(3) shall be construed as including a reference to this subsection.*

Note. Words 'the age of eighteen' in square brackets substituted for words 'the age of seventeen' in italics by the Criminal Justice and Public Order Act 1994, s 168(1), Sch 9, para 9,
as from 3 February 1995. Words 'an officer of a local probation board' in square brackets
substituted for words 'a probation officer' in italics by the Criminal Justice and Court
Services Act 2000, s 74, Sch 7, Pt 1, para 4(1)(a), (2), as from 1 April 2001 (SI 2001 No 919).
Words 'under section 1 ... section 2(3) or' and 'and accordingly ... this subsection' in italics
repealed by the Children Act 1989, s 108(7), Sch 15, as from 14 October 1991.

  (3) In the case of a person who has attained such age as the Secretary of State
may by order specify, an authority shall, without prejudice to subsection (2) of
section 9 of this Act, not be required by virtue of subsection (1) of that section
to make investigations or provide information which it does not already possess
with respect to his home surroundings if, by direction of the justice or [*probation
committee*] [local probation board] acting for any relevant area, arrangements
are in force for information with respect to his home surroundings to be
furnished to the court in question by *a probation officer* [an officer of a local
probation board].

Note. Words 'probation committee' in square brackets substituted by the Criminal Justice
Act 1982, s 65(1). Words 'local probation board' and 'an officer of a local probation board'
in square brackets substituted for words in italics by the Criminal Justice and Court Services
Act 2000, s 74, Sch 7, Pt 1, para 4(1)(a), (2), as from 1 April 2001 (SI 2001 No 919).

(4) Except in relation to section 13(2) of this Act references to a child in subsection (1) of this section do not include references to a person under the age of ten.

(5) ...

Note. Repealed by the Criminal Law Act 1977, s 65(5), Sch 13.

(6) Without prejudice to the generality of section 69(4) of this Act, an order under the section may specify different ages for the purposes of different provisions of this Act specified in the order.

(7) A draft of any order proposed to be made under this section shall be laid before Parliament and, in the case of an order of which the effect is that the reference to a child in section 4 of this Act includes a child who has attained an age of more than twelve, shall not be made unless the draft has been approved by a resolution of each House of Parliament.

Note. Words 'probation committee' in square brackets substituted by Criminal Justice Act 1982, s 65(1).

PART II

ACCOMMODATION ETC FOR CHILDREN IN CARE, AND FOSTER CHILDREN

Community homes

46. Discontinuance of approved schools etc on establishment of community homes—(1) If in the case of any approved school, [or remand home within the meaning of the Criminal Justice Act 1948 or approved probation hostel *or approved probation home within the meaning of the Powers of Criminal Courts Act 1973 [within the meaning of the Probation Service Act 1993]* (hereafter in this section referred to as an 'approved institution') it appears to the Secretary of State that in consequence of the establishment of community homes for a planning area the institution as such is no longer required, he may by order provide that is shall cease to be an approved institution on a date specified in the order.

(2) The provisions of Schedule 3 to this Act should have effect in relation to institutions which are, or by virtue of this section have ceased to be, approved institutions.

Note. Words from 'or remand home' to '1973' in square brackets substituted by Powers of Criminal Courts Act 1973, s 56(1), Sch 5, para 36. Words 'within the meaning of the Probation Service Act 1993' in square brackets substituted for words in italics by Probation Service Act 1993, s 32(2), Sch 3, para 3, as from 3 February 1994. Words 'within the meaning of the Probation Services Act 1993' in italics repealed by the Criminal Justice and Court Services Act 2000, s 74, 75, Sch 7, Pt II, paras 38, 41, Sch 8, as from 1 April 2001 (SI 2001 No 919).

*　　*　　*　　*　　*

70. Interpretation and ancillary provisions—(1) In this Act, unless the contrary intention appears, the following expressions have the following meanings:—

'the Act of 1933' means the Children and Young Persons Act 1933;

'the Act of 1963' means the Children and Young Persons Act 1963;

'approved school order', 'guardian' and 'place of safety' have the same meanings as in the Act of 1933;

'care order' has the meaning assigned to it by section 20 of this Act;

'child', except in Part II (including Schedule 3) and sections 27, 63, 64 and 65 of this Act, means a person under the age of fourteen, and in that Part (including that Schedule) and those sections means a person under the age of eighteen and a person who has attained the age of eighteen and is the subject of a care order;

*　　*　　*　　*　　*

'interim order' has the meaning assigned to it by section 20 of this Act;

'local authority' [except in relation to proceedings under section 1 of this Act instituted by a local education authority, means the council of a non-metropolitan county or of a [county borough,] metropolitan district] or London borough or the Common Council of the City of London;

['local authority accommodation' means accommodation provided by or on behalf of a local authority (within the meaning of the Children Act 1989)]

['local probation board' means a local probation board established under section 4 of the Criminal Justice and Court Services Act 2000;]

'petty sessions area' has the same meaning as in [the Magistrates' Courts Act 1980] except that, in relation to a juvenile court [youth court] constituted for a metropolitan area within the meaning of Part II of Schedule 2 to the Act of 1963, it means such a division of that area as is mentioned in paragraph 14 of that Schedule;

* * * * *

'police officer' means a member of a police force;

* * * * *

'reside' means habitually reside, and cognate expressions shall be construed accordingly *except in section 12(4) and (5) [12B(1) and (2)] of this Act;*

'supervision order', 'supervised person' and 'supervisor' have the meanings assigned to them by section 11 of this Act;

['supervision order' has the same meaning as in the Powers of Criminal Courts (Sentencing) Act 2000;]

* * * * *

'young person' means a person who has attained the age of fourteen and is under the age of seventeen;

['young person' means a person who has attained the age of fourteen and is under the age of eighteen years;]

['youth offending tream' means a team established under s 39 of the Crime and Disorder Act 1998;]

and it is hereby declared that, in the expression 'care or control', 'care' includes protection and guidance and 'control' includes discipline.

Note. Definition 'young person' in square brackets substituted for that definition in italics by Criminal Justice Act 1991, s 68, Sch 8, para 4(2), as from 1 October 1992.

[*(1A) Where, in the case of a child whose father and mother were not married to each other at the time of his birth, an order of any court is in force giving the right to the actual custody of the child to the father, any reference in this Act to the parent of the child includes, unless the contrary intention appears, a reference to the father.*

In this subsection 'actual custody', in relation to a child, means actual possession of his person.]

Note. Sub-s (1A) added by Family Law Reform Act 1987, s 8(1), as from 1 April 1989.

[*(1B) In subsection (1A) of this section the reference to a child whose father and mother were not married to each other at the time of his birth shall be construed in accordance with section 1 of the Family Law Reform Act 1987 and 'actual custody', in relation to a child, means actual possession of his person.*]

Note. Sub-s (1B) added by Family Law Reform Act 1987, s 33(1), Sch 2, para 26, as from 1 April 1989.

[(1A) In the case of a child or young person—

(a) whose father and mother were not married to each other at the time of his birth, and

(b) with respect to whom a residence order is in force in favour of the father,

any reference in this Act to the parent of the child or young person includes (unless the contrary intention appears) a reference to the father.

(1B) In subsection (1A) of this section, the reference to child or young person whose father and mother were not married to each other at the time of his birth shall be construed in accordance with section 1 of the Family Law Reform Act 1987 and 'residence order' has the meaning given by section 8(1) of the Children Act 1989.]

Note. Sub-ss (1A), (1B) substituted for sub-ss (1A), (1B) in italics by the Crime and Disorder Act 1998, s 106, Sch 7, para 10, as from 30 September 1998 (SI 1998 No 2327).

(2) Without prejudice to any power apart from this subsection to bring proceedings on behalf of another person, any power to make an application which is exercisable by a child or young person by virtue of section 15(1), 21(2), 22(4) or (6) or 28 (5) of this Act shall also be exercisable on his behalf by his parent or guardian; and in this subsection 'guardian' includes any person who was a guardian of the child or young person in question at the time when any supervision order, *care order or warrant* to which the application relates was originally made.

(3) In section 99(1) of the Act of 1933 (under which the age which a court presumes or declares to be the age of a person brought before it is deemed to be his true age for the purposes of that Act) the references to that Act shall be construed as including references to this Act.

(4) Subject to the following subsection, any reference in this Act to any enactment is a reference to it as amended, and includes a reference to it as applied, by or under any other enactment including this Act.

(5) Any reference in this Act to an enactment of the Parliament of Northern Ireland shall be construed as a reference to that enactment as amended by any Act of that Parliament, whether passed before or after this Act, and to any enactment of that Parliament for the time being in force which re-enacts the said enactment with or without modifications.

Note. Definitions omitted repealed by Child Care Act 1980, s 89(3), Sch 6 and Children Act 1989, s 108(7), Sch 15. Words from 'except in relation to' to 'metropolitan district' in square brackets in definition of 'local authority' substituted by Local Government Act 1972, s 195(6), Sch 23, para 16 and words 'county borough,' in square brackets in that definition inserted by Local Government (Wales) Act 1994, s 22(4), Sch 10, para 6, as from 1 October 1992. Definition 'local probation board' added by the Criminal Justice and Court Services Act 2000, s 74, Sch 7, Pt II, paras 38, 42, as from 1 April 2001 (SI 2001 No 919). Words in square brackets in the definition of 'petty sessions area' substituted by Magistrates' Courts Act 1980, s 154, Sch 7, para 85; words 'youth court' in square brackets in that definition substituted for words 'juvenile court' in italics by Criminal Justice Act 1991, s 100 Sch 11, para 40, as from 1 October 1992.

Definitions of 'care order' and 'interim order' in sub-s (1), and words '21(2), 22(4) or (6) or 28' in sub-s (2) repealed by Children Act 1989, s 108(7), Sch 15, as from 14 October 1991. Definition of 'local authorities accommodation' inserted and words in square brackets in definition of 'reside' substituted for words in italics, by ibid, s 108(4), Sch 12, para 29, as from 14 October 1991. In definition 'reside' words 'except in ... of this Act' in italics repealed by the Powers of Criminal Cours (Sentencing) Act 2000, s 165(4), Sch 12, Pt 1, as from 25 August 2000. Definition 'supervision order' substituted for definitions 'supervision order', 'supervised person' and supervisor' by the Powers of Criminal Courts (Sentencing) Act 2000, s 165(1), Sch 9, para 42, as from 25 August 2000. Definition 'youth offending team' added by the Crime and Disorder Act 1998, s 119, Sch 8, para 23, as from 30 September 1998 for certain purposes (SI 1998 No 2327), In definition 'petty sessions area' words 'has the ... except that' and 'it' repealed by the Access to Justice Act 1999, s 106, Sch 15, Pt V(1), as from 27 September 1999. Whole definition 'petty sessions area' repealed by the Access to Justice Act 1999, s 106, Sch 15, Pt V(2), as from a day to be appointed.

Sub-s (2) repealed by the Powers of Criminal Courts (Sentencing) Act 2000, s 165(4), Sch 12, Pt 1, as from 25 August 2000.

*   *   *   *

73. Citation, commencement and extent—(1) This Act may be cited as the Children and Young Persons Act 1969, and this Act and the Children and Young Persons Acts 1933 to 1963 may be cited together as the Children and Young Persons Acts 1933 to 1969.

*   *   *   *

DIVORCE REFORM ACT 1969*

(1969 c 55)

> * Whole Act repealed by Matrimonial Causes Act 1973, s 54(1), Sch 3.

ARRANGEMENT OF SECTIONS

An Act to amend the grounds for divorce and judicial separation; to facilitate reconciliation in matrimonial causes; and for purposes connected with the matters aforesaid.

[*22 October 1969*]

1. Breakdown of marriage to be sole ground for divorce.   *After the commencement of this Act the sole ground on which a petition for divorce may be presented to the court by either party to a marriage shall be that the marriage has broken down irretrievably.*

Note. This section, with s 2(1) below, replaced Matrimonial Causes Act 1965, s 1(1) (p 2239). See now Matrimonial Causes Act 1973, s 1(1) (p 2471).

2. Proof of breakdown—(*1*) *The court hearing a petition for divorce shall not hold the marriage to have broken down irretrievably unless the petitioner satisfies the court of one or more of the following facts, that is to say*—

(a)   *that the respondent has committed adultery and the petitioner finds it intolerable to live with the respondent;*

(b)   *that the respondent has behaved in such a way that the petitioner cannot reasonably be expected to live with the respondent;*

(c)   *that the respondent has deserted the petitioner for a continuous period of at least two years immediately preceding the presentation of the petition;*

(d)   *that the parties to the marriage have lived apart for a continuous period of at least two years immediately preceding the presentation of the petition and the respondent consents to a decree being granted;*

(e)   *that the parties to the marriage have lived apart for a continuous period of at least five years immediately preceding the presentation of the petition.*

Note. Sub-s (1), with s 1 above, replaced Matrimonial Causes Act 1965, s 1(1) (p 2239). See now Matrimonial Causes Act 1973, s 1(2) (p 2497).

(*2*) *On a petition for divorce it shall be the duty of the court to inquire, so far as it reasonably can, into the facts alleged by the petitioner and into any facts alleged by the respondent.*

Note. Sub-s (2) replaced in part Matrimonial Causes Act 1965, s 5(1) (p 2241). See now Matrimonial Causes Act 1973, s 1(3) (p 2497).

(*3*) *If the court is satisfied on the evidence of any such fact as is mentioned in subsection (1) of this section, then, unless it is satisfied on all the evidence that the marriage has not broken down irretrievably, it shall, subject to section 4 of this Act and section 5(5) of the Matrimonial Causes Act 1965, grant a decree nisi of divorce.*

Note. Sub-s (3) replaced Matrimonial Causes Act 1965, s 5(3) (p 2242). See now Matrimonial Causes Act 1973, s 1(4) (p 2498).

(4) For the purposes of subsection (1)(c) of this section the court may treat a period of desertion as having continued at a time when the deserting party was incapable of continuing the necessary intention if the evidence before the court is such that, had that party not been so incapable, the court would have inferred that his desertion continued at that time.

Note. Sub-s (4) replaced in part Matrimonial Causes Act 1965, s 1(2) (p 2239). See now Matrimonial Causes Act 1973, s 2(4) (p 2498).

(5) For the purposes of this Act a husband and wife shall be treated as living apart unless they are living with each other in the same household.

Note. See now Matrimonial Causes Act 1973, s 2(6) (p 2498).

(6) Provision shall be made by rules of court for the purpose of ensuring that where in pursuance of subsection (1)(d) of this section the petitioner alleges that the respondent consents to a decree being granted the respondent has been given such information as will enable him to understand the consequences to him of his consenting to a decree being granted and the steps which he must take to indicate that he consents to the grant of a decree.

Note. See now Matrimonial Causes Act 1973, s 2(7) (p 2499).

3. Provisions designed to encourage reconciliation—*(1) Provision shall be made by rules of court for requiring the solicitor acting for a petitioner for divorce to certify whether he has discussed with the petitioner the possibility of a reconciliation and given him the names and addresses of persons qualified to help effect a reconciliation between parties to a marriage who have become estranged.*

Note. See now Matrimonial Causes Act 1973, s 6(1) (p 2501).

(2) If at any stage of proceedings for divorce it appears to the court that there is a reasonable possibility of a reconciliation between the parties to the marriage, the court may adjourn the proceedings for such period as it thinks fit to enable attempts to be made to effect such a reconciliation.

The power conferred by the foregoing provision is additional to any other power of the court to adjourn proceedings.

Note. See now Matrimonial Causes Act 1973, s 6(2) (p 2501).

(3) Where the parties to the marriage have lived with each other for any period or periods after it became known to the petitioner that the respondent had, since the celebration of the marriage, committed adultery, then,—

(a) *if the length of that period or those periods together was six months or less, their living with each other during that period or those periods shall be disregarded in determining for the purposes of section 2(1)(a) of this Act whether the petitioner finds it intolerable to live with the respondent; but*

(b) *if the length of that period or of those periods together exceeded six months, the petitioner shall not be entitled to rely on that adultery for the purposes of the said section 2(1)(a).*

Note. Sub-s (3) replaced in part Matrimonial Causes Act 1965, s 5(3) (p 2242). See now Matrimonial Causes Act 1973, s 2(1), (2) (p 2498).

(4) Where the petitioner alleges that the respondent has behaved in such a way that the petitioner cannot reasonably be expected to live with him, but the parties to the marriage have lived with each other for a period or periods after the date of the occurrence of the final incident relied on by the petitioner and held by the court to support his allegations that fact shall be disregarded in determining for the purposes of section 2(1)(b) of this Act whether the petitioner cannot reasonably be expected to live with the respondent if the length of that period or of those periods together was six months or less.

Note. Sub-s (4) replaced in part Matrimonial Causes Act 1965, s 5(3) (p 2242). See now Matrimonial Causes Act 1973, s 2(3) (p 2498).

(5) In considering for the purposes of section 2(1) of this Act whether the period for which the respondent has deserted the petitioner or the period for which the parties to a marriage have lived apart has been continuous, no account shall be taken of any one period (not exceeding six months) or of any two or more periods (not exceeding six months in all) during which the

parties resumed living with each other, but no period during which the parties lived with each other shall count as part of the period of desertion or of the period for which the parties to the marriage lived apart, as the case may be.

Note. Sub-s (5) replaced in part Matrimonial Causes Act 1965, s 1(2) (p 2239). See now Matrimonial Causes Act 1973, s 2(5) (p 2498).

(6) References in this section to the parties to a marriage living with each other shall be construed as references to their living with each other in the same household.

Note. See now Matrimonial Causes Act 1973, s 2(6) (p 2498).

4. Decree to be refused in certain circumstances—*(1) The respondent to a petition for divorce in which the petitioner alleges any such fact as is mentioned in paragraph (e) of section 2(1) of this Act may oppose the grant of a decree nisi on the ground that the dissolution of the marriage will result in grave financial or other hardship to him and that it would in all the circumstances be wrong to dissolve the marriage.*

(2) Where the grant of a decree nisi is opposed by virtue of this section, then—

(a) if the court is satisfied that the only fact mentioned in the said section 2(1) on which the petitioner is entitled to rely in support of his petition is that mentioned in the said paragraph (e), and

(b) if apart from this section it would grant a decree nisi,

the court shall consider all the circumstances, including the conduct of the parties to the marriage and the interests of those parties and of any children or other persons concerned, and if the court is of opinion that the dissolution of the marriage will result in grave financial or other hardship to the respondent and that it would in all the circumstances be wrong to dissolve the marriage it shall dismiss the petition.

(3) For the purposes of this section hardship shall include the loss of the chance of acquiring any benefit which the respondent might acquire if the marriage were not dissolved.

Note. Section 4 replaced by Matrimonial Causes Act 1973, s 5 (p 2500).

5. Power to rescind decree nisi in certain cases. *Where the court on granting a decree of divorce held that the only fact mentioned in section 2(1) of this Act on which the petitioner was entitled to rely in support of his petition was that mentioned in paragraph (d), it may, on an application made by the respondent at any time before the decree is made absolute, rescind the decree if it is satisfied that the petitioner misled the respondent (whether intentionally or unintentionally) about any matter which the respondent took into account in deciding to consent to the grant of a decree.*

Note. Section 5 replaced by Matrimonial Causes Act 1973, s 10(1) (p 2502).

6. Financial protection for respondent in certain cases—*(1) The following provisions of this section shall have effect where—*

(a) the respondent to a petition for divorce in which the petitioner alleged any such fact as is mentioned in paragraph (d) or (e) of section 2(1) of this Act has applied to the court under this section for it to consider for the purposes of subsection (2) hereof the financial position of the respondent after the divorce; and

(b) a decree nisi of divorce has been granted on the petition and the court has held that the only fact mentioned in the said section 2(1) on which the petitioner was entitled to rely in support of his petition was that mentioned in the said paragraph (d) or (e).

Note. Sub-s (1) replaced by Matrimonial Causes Act 1973, s 10(2) (p 2502).

(2) The court hearing an application by the respondent under this section shall consider all the circumstances, including the age, health, conduct, earning capacity, financial resources and financial obligations of each of the parties, and the financial position of the respondent as, having regard to the divorce, it is likely to be after the death of the petitioner should the petitioner die first; and notwithstanding anything in the foregoing provisions of this Act but subject to subsection (3) of this section, the court shall not make absolute the decree of divorce unless it is satisfied—

(a) that the petitioner should not be required to make any financial provision for the respondent, or

(b) that the financial provision made by the petitioner for the respondent is reasonable and fair or the best that can be made in the circumstances.

Note. Sub-s (2) replaced by Matrimonial Causes Act 1973, s 10(3) (p 2503).

(3) The court may if it thinks fit proceed without observing the requirements of subsection (2) of this section if—

(a) it appears that there are circumstances making it desirable that the decree should be made absolute without delay, and

(b) the court has obtained a satisfactory undertaking from the petitioner that he will make such financial provision for the respondent as the court may approve.

Note. Sub-s (3) replaced by Matrimonial Causes Act 1973, s 10(4) (p 2503).

7. Rules may enable certain agreements or arrangements to be referred to the court—(1) Provision may be made by rules of court for enabling the parties to a marriage, or either of them, on application made either before or after the presentation of a petition for divorce, to refer to the court any agreement or arrangement made or proposed to be made between them, being an agreement or arrangement which relates to, arises out of, or is connected with, the proceedings for divorce which are contemplated or, as the case may be, have begun, and for enabling the court to express an opinion, should it think it desirable to do so, as to the reasonableness of the agreement or arrangement and to give such directions, if any, in the matter as it thinks fit.

Note. Sub-s (1) replaced Matrimonial Causes Act 1965, s 5(2) (p 2241). See now Matrimonial Causes Act 1973, s 7 (p 2501).

(2) In section 3 of the Matrimonial Causes Act 1967 (consideration of agreements or arrangements by divorce county courts) after the word '1965' there shall be inserted the words 'or of section 7 of the Divorce Reform Act 1969'.

8. Judicial separation—(1) After the commencement of this Act the existence of any such fact as is mentioned in section 2(1) of this Act shall be a ground on which either party to a marriage may present a petition for judicial separation; and the ground of failure to comply with a decree for restitution of conjugal rights and any ground on which a decree of divorce a mensa et thoro might have been pronounced immediately before the commencement of the Matrimonial Causes Act 1857 shall cease to be a ground on which such a petition may be presented.

(2) Accordingly for subsection (1) of section 12 of the Matrimonial Causes Act 1965 there shall be substituted the following subsection:—

'(1) A petition for judicial separation may be presented to the court by either party to a marriage on the ground that any such fact as is mentioned in section 2(1) of the Divorce Reform Act 1969 exists, and sections 2(2), (4), (5) and (6), 3 and 7 of that Act and paragraph 2 of Schedule 1 to this Act shall, with the necessary modifications, apply in relation to such a petition as they apply in relation to a petition for divorce.'

(3) The court hearing a petition for judicial separation shall not be concerned to consider whether the marriage has broken down irretrievably, and if it is satisfied on the evidence of any such fact as is mentioned in section 2(1) of this Act, it shall, subject to [section 17 of the Matrimonial Proceedings and Property Act 1970] (restrictions on decrees for dissolution or separation affecting children), grant a decree of judicial separation.

Note. The words in square brackets substituted for the words 'section 33 of the Matrimonial Causes Act 1965' by Matrimonial Proceedings and Property Act 1970, s 42, Sch 2, para 4. See now Matrimonial Causes Act 1973, s 17 (p 2506).

9. Consequential amendments, repeals and saving—(1) The provisions of the Matrimonial Causes Act 1965 specified in Schedule 1 to this Act shall have effect subject to the amendments set out in that Schedule, being amendments consequential on the foregoing provisions of this Act.

Note. Cf Matrimonial Causes Act 1973, ss 4(1), 20, 49, Sch 1, para 8 (pp 2499, 2508, 2557, 2562).

(2) Each of the provisions of the Matrimonial Causes Act 1965 specified in column 1 of Schedule 2 to this Act is, to the extent specified in relation to it in column 2 of that Schedule, hereby repealed.

(3) Without prejudice to any provision of this Act or of the Matrimonial Causes Act 1965, as amended by this Act, which empowers or requires the court to dismiss a petition for divorce or judicial separation or to dismiss an application for a decree nisi of divorce to be made absolute, nothing in section 32 of the Supreme Court of Judicature (Consolidation) Act 1925 (rules as to exercise of jurisdiction) or in any rule of law shall be taken as empowering or requiring the court to dismiss such a petition or application on the ground of collusion between the parties in connection with the presentation or prosecution of the petition or the obtaining of the decree nisi or on the ground of any conduct on the part of the petitioner.

Note. Sub-ss (2), (3) not replaced.

10. Saving for petitions presented before commencement of Act. *This Act (including the repeals and amendments made by it) shall not have effect in relation to any petition for divorce or judicial separation presented before the commencement of this Act.*

11. Short title, construction, commencement and extent—(1) *This Act may be cited as the Divorce Reform Act 1969.*

(2) This Act shall be construed as one with the Matrimonial Causes Act 1965.

(3) This Act shall come into operation on 1 January 1971.

(4) This Act does not extend to Scotland or Northern Ireland.

SCHEDULES

SCHEDULE 1   Section 9(1)

CONSEQUENTIAL AMENDMENTS OF THE MATRIMONIAL CAUSES ACT 1965

1. *In section 3(1) after the word 'petitioner' there shall be inserted the words 'or respondent'.*

2. *In section 4(1) and (2) for the words 'on the ground of adultery' there shall be substituted the words 'in which adultery is alleged' and in section 4(1) for the words 'on that ground' there shall be substituted the words 'and alleging adultery'.*

3. *In section 5(6) for the words from 'opposes' to 'desertion' there shall be substituted the words 'alleges against the petitioner and proves any such fact as is mentioned in section 2(1) of the Divorce Reform Act 1969.*

4. *In section 15(b) for the words 'on the ground of her husband's insanity' there shall be substituted the words 'and alleging any such fact as is mentioned in section 2(1)(e) of the Divorce Reform Act 1969 where the court is satisfied on proof of such facts as may be prescribed by rules of court that her husband is insane'.*

5. *In section 16(3) for the words from the beginning to 'insanity' there shall be substituted the words 'Where on a petition for divorce presented by a wife the court granted her a decree and held that the only fact mentioned in section 2(1) of the Divorce Reform Act 1969 on which she was entitled to rely was that mentioned in paragraph (e), then if the court is satisfied on proof of such facts as may be prescribed by rules of court that the husband is insane'.*

6. *In section 17(2) for the words from the beginning to 'she' there shall be substituted the words 'Where on a petition for divorce presented by the husband he satisfies the court of any such fact as is mentioned in section 2(1)(a), (b) or (c) of the Divorce Reform Act 1969 and the court grants him a decree of divorce, then if it appears to the court that the wife' and for the words 'innocent party' there shall be substituted the word 'husband'.*

7. *In section 20(1)(b) for the words 'on the ground of her husband's insanity' there shall be substituted the words 'and the court held that the only fact mentioned in section 2(1) of the Divorce Reform Act 1969 on which she was entitled to rely was that mentioned in paragraph (e) and the court is satisfied on proof of such facts as may be prescribed by rules of court that the husband is insane'.*

Note. Paras 4–7 repealed by Matrimonial Proceedings and Property Act 1970, s 42(2), Sch 3.

8. *In section 26(6), as amended by the Family Provision Act 1966, in the definition of 'court', after the word 'court', where first occurring, there shall be inserted the words 'means the High Court and'.*

9. *In section 30(2)—*
   (a) *in paragraph (a) for the words 'on the ground of her husband's insanity' there shall be substituted the words 'and the court is satisfied on proof of such facts as may be prescribed by rules of court that her husband is insane';*
   (b) *in paragraph (b) the word 'divorce' and the words 'or judicial separation' shall be omitted; and*
   (c) *after paragraph (a) there shall be inserted the following paragraph:—*
      '(aa) a petition for divorce or judicial separation is presented by a husband and the court is satisfied on proof of such facts as may be prescribed by rules of court that his wife is insane; or'.

10. *In section 34(3) for the words 'on the ground of the husband's insanity' there shall be substituted the words 'in favour of a wife where the court held that the only fact mentioned in section 2(1) of the Divorce Reform Act 1969 on which she was entitled to rely was that mentioned in paragraph (e) and the court is satisfied on proof of such facts as may be prescribed by rules of court that the husband is insane'.*
Note. Paras 9, 10 repealed by Matrimonial Proceedings and Property Act 1970, s 42(2), Sch 3.

11. *In section 46(2) after the definition of 'adopted' there shall be inserted the following definition—*
   ' "the Court" (except in sections 26, 27, 28 and 28A) means the High Court or, where a county court has jurisdiction by virtue of the Matrimonial Causes Act 1967, a county court; and'.

12. *In Schedule 1, in paragraph 2 after the word 'Act' there shall be inserted the words 'or of section 2(1)(c) of the Divorce Reform Act 1969'.*

SCHEDULE 2   Section 9(2)

REPEALS IN THE MATRIMONIAL CAUSES ACT 1965

Provision	Extent of Repeal
Section 1	*The whole section.*
Section 5	*Subsections (1), (2), (3) and (4).*
Section 6	*In subsection (1), except as applied by section 10 or 14 of the said Act of 1965, paragraph (c).*
Section 7	*In subsection (1), except as applied by the said section 10 or 14, the words from 'either' to 'collusion or'.*
Section 30	*In subsection (2)(b), the word 'divorce' and the words 'or judicial separation'.*
Section 42	*Subsections (1) and (3) so far as they apply in relation to proceedings for divorce or judicial separation.*
	In subsection (2), the words 'this Act and'.

ADMINISTRATION OF JUSTICE ACT 1969

(1969 c 58)

An Act to increase the jurisdiction of county courts and to amend the County Courts Act 1959; to make further provision for appeals from the High Court (whether in England and Wales or in Northern Ireland) to the House of Lords; to enable wills and codicils to be made for mentally disordered persons; to make provision for interim payments to be made where proceedings are pending, and for conferring powers to be exercisable by the court before the commencement of an action, and to make further provision with respect to interest on damages; to enable any jurisdiction of the High Court to be assigned to two or more Divisions concurrently; to enable the Appeal Tribunals under the Patents Act 1949 and the Registered Designs Act 1949 to consist of two or more judges; to change the title and qualification of clerks to registrars of the Chancery Division; to make further provision with respect to miscellaneous matters, that is to say, certain employments in the offices of the Supreme Court, records of grants of probate and grants of administration and the making of second and subsequent grants, admission as a public notary, pension rights and related matters in connection with certain judicial offices, and the stipend and fees of the Chancellor of the County Palatine of Durham; to extend the legislative power of the Parliament of Northern Ireland with respect to grand juries and indictments; and for purposes connected with the matters aforesaid.

[22 October 1969]

*   *   *   *   *

PART II

APPEAL FROM HIGH COURT TO HOUSE OF LORDS

12. Grant of certificate by trial judge—(1) Where on the application of any of the parties to any proceedings to which this section applies the judge is satisfied—
- (a) that the relevant conditions are fulfilled in relation to his decision in those proceedings, and
- (b) that a sufficient case for an appeal to the House of Lords under this Part of this Act has been made out to justify an application for leave to bring such an appeal, and
- (c) that all the parties to the proceedings consent to the grant of a certificate under this section,

the judge, subject to the following provisions of this Part of this Act may grant a certificate to that effect.

(2) This section applies to any civil proceedings in the High Court which are either—
- (a) proceedings before a single judge of the High Court (*including a person acting as such a judge under section 3 of the Judicature Act 1925*), or
- (b) *proceedings before a commissioner acting under a commission issued under section 70 of the Judicature Act 1925, or*
- (c) proceedings before a Divisional Court.

Note. In sub-s (2)(a), words in italics repealed in relation to England and Wales by Supreme Court Act 1981, s 152(4), Sch 7, as from 1 January 1982.

Sub-s (2)(b) repealed in relation to England and Wales by Courts Act 1971, s 56(4), Sch 11, Part IV as from 1 January 1972, and repealed in relation to Northern Ireland by Judicature (Northern Ireland) Act 1978, s 122(2), Sch 7, Part I, as from 18 April 1979.

(3) Subject to any Order in Council made under the following provisions of this section, for the purposes of this section the relevant conditions, in relation to a decision of the judge in any proceedings, are that a point of law of general public importance is involved in that decision and that that point of law either—

(a) relates wholly or mainly to the construction of an enactment or of a statutory instrument, and has been fully argued in the proceedings and fully considered in the judgment of the judge in the proceedings, or

(b) is one in respect of which the judge is bound by a decision of the Court of Appeal or of the House of Lords in previous proceedings, and was fully considered in the judgments given by the Court of Appeal or the House of Lords (as the case may be) in those previous proceedings.

(4) Any application for a certificate under this section shall be made to the judge immediately after he gives judgment in the proceedings:

Provided that the judge may in any particular case entertain any such application made at any later time before the end of the period of fourteen days beginning with the date on which the judgment is given or such other period as may be prescribed by rules of court.

(5) No appeal shall lie against the grant or refusal of a certificate under this section.

(6) Her Majesty may by Order in Council amend subsection (3) of this section by altering, deleting, or substituting one or more new paragraphs for, either or both of paragraphs (a) and (b) of that subsection, or by adding one or more further paragraphs.

(7) Any Order in Council made under this section shall be subject to annulment in pursuance of a resolution of either House of Parliament.

(8) In this Part of this Act 'civil proceedings' means any proceedings other than proceedings in a criminal cause or matter, and 'the judge', in relation to any proceedings to which this section applies, means the judge *or commissioner* referred to in paragraph (a) *or paragraph (b)* of subsection (2) of this section, or the Divisional Court referred to in paragraph (c) of that subsection, as the case may be.

Note. In sub-s (8) words in italics repealed in relation to England and Wales by Courts Act 1971, s 56(4), Sch 11, Part IV as from 1 January 1972, and repealed in relation to Northern Ireland by Judicature (Northern Ireland) Act 1978, s 122(2), Sch 7, Part I, as from 18 April 1979.

13. Leave to appeal to House of Lords—(1) Where in any proceedings the judge grants a certificate under section 12 of this Act, then, at any time within one month from the date on which that certificate is granted or such extended time as in any particular case the House of Lords may allow, any of the parties to the proceedings may make an application to the House of Lords under this section.

(2) Subject to the following provisions of this section, if on such an application it appears to the House of Lords to be expedient to do so, the House may grant leave for an appeal to be brought directly to the House; and where leave is granted under this section—

(a) no appeal from the decision of the judge to which the certificate relates shall lie to the Court of Appeal, but

(b) an appeal shall lie from that decision to the House of Lords.

(3) Applications under this section shall be determined without a hearing.

(4) Any order of the House of Lords which provides for applications under this section to be determined by a committee of the House—

(a) shall direct that the committee shall consist of or include not less than three of the persons designated as Lords of Appeal in accordance with section 5 of the Appellate Jurisdiction Act 1876, and

(b) may direct that the decision of the committee on any such application shall be taken on behalf of the House.

(5) Without prejudice to subsection (2) of this section, no appeal shall lie to the Court of Appeal from a decision of the judge in respect of which a certificate is granted under section 12 of this Act until—

(a) the time within which an application can be made under this section has expired, and

(b) where such an application is made, that application has been determined in accordance with the preceding provisions of this section.

14. Appeal where leave granted.   In relation to any appeal which lies to the House of Lords by virtue of subsection (2) of section 13 of this Act—

   (a) section 4 of the Appellate Jurisdiction Act 1876 (which provides for the bringing of appeals to the House of Lords by way of petition).

   (b) section 5 of that Act (which regulates the composition of the House for the hearing and determination of appeals), and

   (c) except in so far as those orders otherwise provide, any orders of the House of Lords made with respect to the matters specified in section 11 of that Act (which relates to the procedure on appeals),

shall have effect as they have effect in relation to appeals under that Act.

15. Cases excluded from s 12—(1) No certificate shall be granted under section 12 of this Act in respect of a decision of the judge in any proceedings where by virtue of any enactment, apart from the provisions of this Part of this Act, no appeal would lie from that decision to the Court of Appeal, with or without the leave of the judge or of the Court of Appeal.

   (2) No certificate shall be granted under section 12 of this Act in respect of a decision of the judge where—

   (a) the decision is in proceedings other than proceedings under the Matrimonial Causes Act 1965, and

   (b) by virtue of any enactment, apart from the provisions of this Part of this Act, no appeal would (with or without the leave of the Court of Appeal or of the House of Lords) lie from any decision of the Court of Appeal or an appeal from the decision of the judge.

Note. Sub-s (2)(a) repealed by Administration of Justice Act 1977, s 32(4), Sch 5, Part IV. Civil Jurisdiction and Judgments Act 1982, s 6(1)(a) (further appeal on point of law, referred to in two Articles in relation to the recognition or enforcement of a judgment other than a maintenance order, to Court of Appeal or to House of Lords) has effect notwithstanding s 15(2): s 6(2) of Act of 1982 (p 2891).

   (3) Where by virtue of any enactment, apart from the provisions of this Part of this Act, no appeal would lie to the Court of Appeal from the decision of the judge except with the leave of the judge or of the Court of Appeal, no certificate shall be granted under section 12 of this Act in respect of that decision unless it appears to the judge that apart from the provisions of this Part of this Act it would be a proper case for granting such leave.

   (4) No certificate shall be granted under section 12 of this Act where the decision of the judge, or any order made by him in pursuance of that decision, is made in the exercise of jurisdiction to punish for contempt of court.

16. Application of Part II to Northern Ireland—(1) In the application of this Part of this Act to Northern Ireland—

   'the Court of Appeal' means Her Majesty's Court of Appeal in Northern Ireland;

   'the High Court' means the High Court of Justice in Northern Ireland;

   'statutory instrument' includes an instrument made under an enactment of the Parliament of Northern Ireland;

   for the references in section 12(2) to *sections 3 and 70 of the Judicature Act 1925 there shall be substituted respectively references to section 5(1) of the Northern Ireland Act 1962 and to sections 29 and 41 of the Supreme Court of Judicature Act (Ireland) 1877* [section 3 of the Judicature Act 1925 there shall be substituted a reference to sections 6 and 7 of the Judicature (Northern Ireland) Act 1978]; and

   for the reference in section 15(2)(a) to the Matrimonial Causes Act 1965 there shall be substituted a reference to *the Matrimonial Causes Act (Northern Ireland) 1939* [the Matrimonial Causes (Northern Ireland) Order 1978] or any enactment re-enacting *that Act* [that Order] (whether with or without modifications).

(2) Nothing in this Part of this Act shall affect the operation of—

(a) any enactment of the Parliament of Northern Ireland having effect after the commencement of this Act by virtue of section 1 (8) or section 2 (3) of the Northern Ireland Act 1962, or

(b) paragraph 6 (2) of Schedule 1 to the Irish Free State (Consequential Provisions) Act 1922 (Session 2) (appeals to the Court of Appeal in Northern Ireland where validity of Acts of the Northern Ireland Parliament is involved and an appeal would not otherwise lie).

Note. Words 'section 3 of the Judicature Act 1925' to '1978' in square brackets in sub-s (1) substituted for words in italics by Judicature (Northern Ireland) Act 1978, s 122(1), Sch 5, Part II, as from 18 April 1979. Words 'the Matrimonial Causes (Northern Ireland) Order 1978' and 'that Order' in square brackets in sub-s (1) substituted for words in italics by Matrimonial Causes (Northern Ireland) Order 1978, SI 1978 No 1045, art 63, Sch 4, para 13. Sub-s (2) repealed by Judicature (Northern Ireland) Act 1978, s 122(2), Sch 7, Part I, as from 18 April 1979.

By virtue of the Northern Ireland Act 1998, any referenee in this section to the Parliament of Northern Ireland or the Assembly established under the Northern Ireland Assembly Act 1973, s 1, certain office-holders and ministers, and any legislative act and certain financial dealings thereof, shall, for the period specified, be construed in accordance with Sch 12, paras 1–11 to the 1998 Act.

*   *   *   *   *

21. Powers of court exercisable before commencement of action—*(1) On the application of any person in accordance with rules of court, the High Court shall, in such circumstances as may be specified in the rules, have power to make an order providing for any one or more of the following matters, that is to say—*

(a) *the inspection, photographing, preservation, custody and detention of property which appears to the court to be property which may become the subject-matter of subsequent proceedings in the court, or as to which any question may arise in any such proceedings, and*

(b) *the taking of samples of any such property as is mentioned in the preceding paragraph and the carrying out of any experiment on or with any such property.*

(2) The power to make rules of court under section 99 of the Judicature Act 1925 shall include power to make rules of court as to the manner in which an application for such an order can be made, and as to the circumstances in which such an order can be made; and any such rules may include such incidental, supplementary and consequential provisions as the authority making the rules may consider necessary or expedient.

(3) The preceding provisions of this section shall have effect in relation to county courts in England and Wales as they have effect in relation to the High Court, as if in those provisions references to rules of court and to section 99 of the Judicature Act 1925 included references to county court rules and to section 102 of the County Courts Act 1959.

(4) In the application of this section to Northern Ireland, 'the High Court' means the High Court of Justice in Northern Ireland, the reference in subsection (2) to section 99 of the Judicature Act 1925 shall be construed as a reference to *section 7 of the Northern Ireland Act 1962* [section 55 of the Judicature (Northern Ireland) Act 1978] and subsection (3) shall be omitted.

(5) In this section 'property' includes any land, chattel or other corporeal property of any description.

Note. Reference to Judicature (Northern Ireland) Act 1978 substituted for reference to Northern Ireland Act 1962 by Judicature (Northern Ireland) Act 1978, s 122(1), Sch 5, Part II, Sch 6, para 13, as from 2 January 1979.

Sub-ss (1)–(3), (5) repealed in relation to England and Wales by Supreme Court Act 1981, s 152(4), Sch 7, as from 1 January 1982.

ADMINISTRATION OF JUSTICE ACT 1970
(1970 c 31)

ARRANGEMENTS OF SECTIONS

PART I

COURTS AND JUDGES

High Court

An Act to make further provision about the courts (including assizes), their business, jurisdiction and procedure; to enable a High Court judge to accept appointment as arbitrator or umpire under an arbitration agreement; to amend the law respecting the enforcement of debt and other liabilities; to amend section 106 of the Rent Act 1968; and for miscellaneous purposes connected with the administration of justice.   [29   May 1970]

PART I

COURTS AND JUDGES

High Court

1. Redistribution of business among divisions of the High Court—*(1) The Probate, Divorce and Admiralty Division of the High Court shall be re-named the Family Division; and the principal probate registry shall be re-named the principal registry of the Family Division.*

(2) *There shall be assigned to the Family Division all causes and matters involving the exercise of the High Court's jurisdiction in proceedings specified in Schedule 1 to this Act.*

(3) *Causes and matters involving the exercise of the High Court's Admiralty jurisdiction, or its jurisdiction as a prize court, shall be assigned to the Queen's Bench Division.*

(4) *As respects the exercise of the High Court's probate jurisdiction—*

(a) *non-contentious or common form probate business shall continue to be assigned to the Family Division; and*

(b) *all other probate business shall be assigned to the Chancery Division.*

(5) *In section 5 of the Supreme Court of Judicature (Consolidation) Act 1925 (which enables Her Majesty, on the recommendation of the judges, by Order in Council to alter the number of divisions of the High Court or of puisne judges to be attached to any division) for the reference to a report or recommendation of the council of judges there shall be substituted a reference to a recommendation of the Lord Chancellor, the Lord Chief Justice, the Master of the Rolls, the President of the Family Division and the Vice-Chancellor.*

(6) In accordance with the foregoing subsections—

(a) the enactments specified in Schedule 2 to this Act (*that is to say, the said Act of 1925 and other* enactments relative to the High Court, its jurisdiction, judges, divisions and business) shall be amended as shown in that Schedule; and

(b) references in any other enactment or document to the Probate, Divorce and Admiralty Division, the President of that division, the principal probate registry, the principal (or senior) probate registrar and a probate registrar shall, so far as may be necessary to preserve the effect of the enactment or document, be construed respectively as references to the Family Division and to the President, principal registry, principal registrar and a registrar of that division.

(7) *This section is not to be taken as affecting any of the following provisions of the said Act of 1925—*

(a) *section 55 (which provides for the distribution of business in the High Court to be regulated by rules);*

(b) *section 57 (which enables the Lord Chancellor to assign or re-assign the jurisdiction of the court among divisions and judges);*

(c) *section 58 (which provides for the assignment of causes and matters);*

(d) *section 59 (which enables an action to be transferred at any stage from one division to another).*

(8) *Notwithstanding anything in section 114(3) of the said Act of 1925 (appointment of officers attached to a division), the right of filling any vacancy in the office of the Admiralty registrar or assistant Admiralty registrar shall be vested in the Lord Chancellor; and any other officer of the Supreme Court who is to be employed in the Admiralty registry shall be appointed by the Lord Chancellor.*

Note. Sub-ss (1)–(5), (6)(a) in part, (7), (8) repealed by Supreme Court Act 1981, s 152(4), Sch 7, as from 1 January 1982.

2. Admiralty Court—(1) *There shall be constituted, as part of the Queen's Bench Division of the High Court, an Admiralty Court to take Admiralty business, that is to say causes and matters assigned to that division and involving the exercise of the High Court's Admiralty jurisdiction, or its jurisdiction as a prize court.*

(2) *The judges of the Admiralty Court shall be such of the puisne judges of the High Court as the Lord Chancellor may from time to time nominate to be Admiralty Judges.*

(3) *Nothing in this section is to be taken as prejudicing provisions of the Supreme Court of Judicature (Consolidation) Act 1925 which enable the whole jurisdiction of the High Court to be exercised by any judge of that court.*

(4) *In section 1(1) of the Administration of Justice Act 1956 (which defines the Admiralty jurisdiction of the High Court) for the words 'which for the time being assigned by rules of court to the Probate, Divorce and Admiralty Division' there shall be substituted the words 'which is for the time being assigned by rules of court to the Queen's Bench Division and directed by the rules to be exercised by the Admiralty Court'.*

Note. Sub-ss (1)–(4) repealed by Supreme Court Act 1981, s 152(4), Sch 7, as from 1 January 1982.

(5) In the Prize Act 1948—

(a) in section 7(2) (determination of form and manner of advertising for claims in relation to the Supreme Court Prize Deposit Account), for the words 'the President of the Probate Division of the High Court' there shall be substituted the words 'such one of the Admiralty Judges of the High Court as the Lord Chancellor may nominate for the purposes of this section' and for the words 'the said President' there shall be substituted the words 'the said Admiralty Judge'; and

(b) in section 8 (regulation of payments into and out of the said Account) for the words from 'the President' onwards there shall be substituted the words 'such one of the Admiralty Judges of the High Court as the Lord Chancellor may nominate for the purposes of this section'.

Note. Sub-s (5) repealed by Statute Law (Repeals) Act 1977.

* * * * *

4. Power of judges of Commercial Court to take arbitrations—*(1) A judge of the Commercial Court may, if in all the circumstances he thinks fit, accept appointment as sole arbitrator, or as umpire, by or by virtue of an arbitration agreement within the meaning of the Arbitration Act 1950, where the dispute appears to him to be of a commercial character.*

(2) A judge of the Commercial Court shall not accept appointment as arbitrator or umpire unless the Lord Chief Justice has informed him that, having regard to the state of business in the High Court and at assizes [in the Crown Court], he can be made available to do so.

Note. Words 'in the Crown Court' substituted for 'at assizes' by Courts Act 1971, s 56, Sch 8, para 60(1).

(3) The fees payable for the services of a judge as arbitrator or umpire shall be taken in the High Court.

(4) Schedule 3 to this Act shall have effect for modifying, and in certain cases replacing, provisions of the Arbitration Act 1950 in relation to arbitration by judges and, in particular, for substituting the Court of Appeal for the High Court in provisions of that Act whereby arbitrators and umpires, their proceedings and awards, are subject to control and review by the court.

(5) Any jurisdiction which is exercisable by the High Court in relation to arbitrators and umpires otherwise than under the Arbitration Act 1950 shall, in relation to a judge of the Commercial Court appointed as arbitrator or umpire, be exercisable instead by the Court of Appeal

Note. This section repealed by Arbitration Act 1996, s 107(2), Sch 4, as from 31 January 1997.

* * * * *

PART II

ENFORCEMENT OF DEBT

Provisions restricting sanction of imprisonment

11. Restriction on power of committal under Debtors Act 1869. The jurisdiction given by section 5 of the Debtors Act 1869 to commit to prison a person who makes default in payment of a debt, or instalment of a debt, due from him in pursuance of an order or judgment shall be exercisable only—

(a) by the High Court in respect of a High Court maintenance order; and

(b) by a county court in respect of—

    (i) A High Court or a county court maintenance order; or

    (ii) a judgment or order which is enforceable by a court in England and Wales and is for the payment of any of the taxes, contributions [premiums] or liabilities specified in Schedule 4 to this Act.

Note. Word 'premiums' inserted by Social Security Act 1973, s 10(2)(a), Sch 27, para 85, as from a day to be appointed.

* * * * *

28. Other provisions for interpretation of Part II—(1) In this Part of this Act, except where the context otherwise requires—

*   *   *   *   *

'High Court maintenance order' and 'county court maintenance order' . . . mean respectively a maintenance order enforceable by the High Court and a county court . . . ;

*   *   *   *   *

'maintenance order' means any order specified in Schedule 8 to this Act and includes such an order which has been discharged, if any arrears are recoverable therunder;

*   *   *   *   *

(2)–(5) . . .

Note. Words omitted from sub-s (1) repealed by Attachment of Earnings Act 1971, s 29(2), Sch 6, as from 2 August 1971, and by Magistrates' Courts Act 1980, s 154, Sch 9, as from 6 July 1981. Sub-ss (2)–(5) repealed by Attachment of Earnings Act 1971, s 29(2), Sch 6, as from 2 August 1971.

*   *   *   *   *

30. Consequential and transitional provisions—*(1) Sections 11 and 12 of this Act shall not affect the validity of an order made, or warrant issued, by a court before the coming into force of those sections for the committal of a person to prison in respect of any description of liability for which there remains power under either of those sections for that or any other court to commit, nor affect the continuance of any proceedings, or the exercise of any power, in connection with such an order or warrant; but subject to this any order or warrant of committal made or issued by any court before the appointed day shall on that day cease to have effect if it is one which, in consequence of the said sections 11 and 12, that court would, on and after that day, have no jurisdiction to make.*

(2) Any person who immediately before the appointed day was in custody under an order or warrant which ceases to have effect by virtue of subsection (1) above shall be discharged.

Note. Sub-ss (1), (2) repealed as respects s 12 of this Act by Magistrates' Courts Act 1980, s 154, Sch 9, as from 6 July 1981.

(3) As from the appointed day, an attachment of earnings order made before that day under Part II of the Act of 1958 (including an order made under that Part of that Act as applied by section 46 or 79 of the Criminal Justice Act 1967) shall take effect as an attachment of earnings order made under the corresponding power of this Part of this Act, and the provisions of this Part of this Act shall apply to it accordingly so far as they are capable of doing so.

(4) Rules of court may make such provision as the rule-making authority considers requisite—

(a) for enabling an attachment of earnings order to which subsection (3) above applies to be varied so as to bring it into conformity, as from the appointed day, with the provisions of this Part of this Act, or to be replaced by an attachment of earnings order having effect as if made under the corresponding power in this Part of this Act;

(b) to secure that anything required or authorised by this Part of this Act to be done in relation to an attachment of earnings order made thereunder is required or, as the case may be, authorised to be done in relation to an attachment of earnings order to which the said subsection (3) applies.

Note. Sub-ss (3), (4) repealed by Attachment of Earnings Act 1971, s 29, Sch 6, as from 2 August 1971.

(5) In this section, 'the appointed day' means the day appointed under section 54 of this Act for the coming into force of this Part of this Act.

Note. This section repealed by Statute Law (Repeals) Act 1989, s 1(1), Sch 1, Part I.

*   *   *   *   *

PART V

MISCELLANEOUS PROVISIONS

*   *   *   *   *

44. Interest on judgment debts—(1) The Lord Chancellor may by order made with the concurrence of the Treasury direct that section 17 of the Judgments Act 1838 (as that enactment has effect for the time being whether by virtue of this subsection or otherwise) shall be amended so as to substitute for the rate specified in that section as the rate at which judgment debts shall carry interest such rates as may be specified in the order.

(2) An order under this section shall be made by statutory instrument which shall be laid before Parliament after being made.

44A. Interest on judgment debts expressed in currencies other than sterling—(1) Where a judgment is given for a sum expressed in a currency other than sterling and the judgment debt is one to which section 17 of the Judgments Act 1838 applies, the court may order that the interest rate applicable to the debt shall be such rate as the court thinks fit.

(2) Where the court makes such an order, section 17 of the Judgments Act 1838 shall have effect in relation to the judgment debt as if the rate specified in the order were substituted for the rate specified in that section.

Note. This section inserted by Private International Law (Miscellaneous Provisions) Act 1995, s 1(1), as from 1 November 1996.

*   *   *   *   *

48. Variation in rate of payments in maintenance order registered in magistrates' court—(1) Section 4 of the Maintenance Orders Act 1958 (which enables the rate of payments in a maintenance order registered in a magistrates' court under that Act to be varied by the court of registration) shall be amended in accordance with this section.

(2) Subsection (3) of that section (rate of payments not to be varied upwards) shall cease to have effect in relation to any maintenance order as defined by section 28(1) of this Act, whether made or registered before or after the coming into force of this section.

(3) In subsection (4) of that section (power of magistrates' court, on application for variation, to remit to the court which made the order), for the words 'that, by reason of the limitations imposed on the court's jurisdiction by the last foregoing subsection or for any other reason, it is' there shall be substituted the words 'that is for any reason'.

Note. For Maintenance Orders Act 1958, s 4, see p 2209.

49. Amendments relating to guardianship of minors—*(1) Any order made under section 4(2) of the Family Law Reform Act 1969 (maintenance for persons between 18 and 21 who have been subject to an order under the Guardianship of Infants Acts) may be varied or discharged by a subsequent order made on the application of any person by or to whom payments were required to be made under the previous order.*

(2) In the Guardianship of Infants Act 1886—
(a) in section 5, the words from 'and in every case' onwards (costs in custody proceedings); and
(b) in section 11 (rules of procedure) paragraph (a) and, in paragraph (c), the words 'England or',
shall cease to have effect.

(3) Subsection (1) of this section shall be deemed to have come into operation at the same time as section 4 of the said Act of 1969.

Note. For Family Law Reform Act 1969, s 4, see p 2302.
This section repealed by Guardianship of Minors Act 1971, s 18(2), Sch 2.

51. Minor amendments of Children and Young Persons Act 1969—*(1) In sections 2(4) and 104 of the Act of 1952 the references to sections 20 and 21 of that Act (which are repealed by the Act of 1969 and replaced by section 6 of that Act) shall be construed as references to the said section 6; and for the purposes of section 126(5) of the Act of 1952 and section 70(3) of the Act of 1969 (which relate to proof of age) the said section 6 shall be deemed to be a provision of the Act of 1952 and not the Act of 1969.*

Note. Sub-s (1) repealed by Magistrates' Courts Act 1980, s 154, Sch 9, as from 6 July 1981.

(2) (*Adds para 1A to Sch 4 to the Children and Young Persons Act 1969 (not printed in this work*).)

(3) In this section '*the Act of 1952*' and 'the Act of 1969' mean respectively *the Magistrates' Courts Act 1952* and the Children and Young Persons Act 1969.

Note. Words in italics repealed by Magistrates' Courts Act 1980, s 154, Sch 9, as from 6 July 1981.

* * * * *

PART VI

GENERAL

* * * * *

54. Citation, interpretation, repeals, commencement and extent—(1) This Act may be cited as the Administration of Justice Act 1970.

(2) References in this Act to any enactment include references to that enactment as amended or extended by or under any other enactment, including this Act.

(3) The enactments specified in Schedule 11 of this Act are hereby repealed to the extent specified in the third column of that Schedule.

(4) *This Act shall come into force on such day as the Lord Chancellor may appoint by order made by statutory instrument, and different days may be so appointed for different provisions of this Act, or for different purposes.*

Note. Repealed by the Statute Law (Repeals) Act 2004, as from 22 July 2004.

(5) Except insofar as it amends, or authorises the amendment of, any enactment which extends to Scotland, this Act shall not extend to Scotland.

(6) This section (except subsection (3)) and the following provisions only of this Act extend to Northern Ireland, that is to say—

(a) sections 1(6) *and 27* and Schedules 2 *and 7*, so far as they relate to any enactment which extends to Northern Ireland, *and section 2(5)*;

(b) Part III; and

(c) sections 36 [38A], 39, *43(6) and 53*,

and the amendment of section 25 of the Court of Probate Act (Ireland) 1859 made by the said section 1(6) and Schedule 2 shall be treated for the purposes of section 6 of the Government of Ireland Act 1920 (which restricts the power of the Parliament of Northern Ireland to alter Acts of the Parliament of the United Kingdom passed after the day appointed for the purposes of that section) as having been made by an Act passed before that day.

Note. Words 'and 27' and 'and 7' repealed by Attachment of Earnings Act 1971, s 29, Sch 6, as from 2 August 1971. Words from 'and the amendment' to the end of sub-s (6) repealed by Administration of Estates Act 1971, s 12, Sch 2, Part I, as from 1 January 1972. Words 'and 53' repealed by Northern Ireland Constitution Act 1973, s 41(1), Sch 6, Part I, as from 18 July 1973. Words '38A' added by Consumer Credit Act 1974, s 192(3)(a), Sch 4, para 31, as from 19 May 1985. Words ', and section 2(5)' and reference to ', 43(6)' in italics repealed by the Statute Law (Repeals) Act 2004, as from 22 July 2004.

SCHEDULES

* * * * *

(*Sch 2 makes amendment of enactments consequential on s 1 of this Act; those which are relevant, have been incorporated in this work.*)

* * * * *

SCHEDULE 8

Section 28

MAINTENANCE ORDERS FOR PURPOSES OF 1958 ACT AND PART II OF THIS ACT

1. An order for alimony, maintenance or other payments made, or having effect as if made, under Part II of the Matrimonial Causes Act 1965 (ancillary relief in actions for divorce etc).

2. An order for payments to or in respect of a child being an order made, or having effect as if made, under Part III of the said Act of 1965 (maintenance of children following divorce, etc).

[**2A.** An order for periodical or other payments made, or having effect as if made, under Part II of the Matrimonial Causes Act 1973.]
Note. Para 2A inserted by Matrimonial Causes Act 1973, s 54(1), Sch 2, para 10(2), as from 1 January 1974.

3. An order for maintenance or other payments to or in respect of a spouse or child being an order made, *or having effect as if made, under the Matrimonial Proceedings* (*Magistrates' Courts*) *Act 1960* [under Part I of the Domestic Proceedings and Magistrates' Courts Act 1978].
Note. Words in square brackets substituted for words in italics by Domestic Proceedings and Magistrates' Courts Act 1978, s 89(2), Sch 2, para 26, as from 1 February 1981.

4. *An order under—*
[*(a)* *section 9(2), 10(1), 11 or 12(2) of the Guardianship of Minors Act 1971* [*or section 2(3) or 2(4)(a) of the Guardianship Act 1973*] (*payments for maintenance of persons who are or have been in guardianship*);] *or*
[*(a)* *section 11B, 11C or 11D of the Guardianship of Minors Act 1971 or section 2(3) or 2(4A) of the Guardianship Act 1973* (*payments for maintenance of persons who are or have been in guardianship*);]
  (c) *section 6 of the said Act of 1969* [*the Family Law Reform Act 1969*] (*payment for maintenance of ward of court*).

[**4.** An order for periodical or other payments made or having effect as if made under Schedule 1 to the Children Act 1989.]
Note. Para (a) in first square brackets in italics substituted for previous paras (a), (b), containing references to Guardianship of Infants Act 1925, ss 3(2), 5(4), 6 and to Family Law Reform Act 1969, s 4(2); and words in square brackets in para (c) substituted for 'the said Act of 1969', by Guardianship of Minors Act 1971, s 18(1), Sch 1. Reference to Guardianship Act 1973 in para (a) inserted by Guardianship Act 1973, s 9(3).
  Para (a) in second square brackets substituted for first para (a) in italics by Family Law Reform Act 1987, s 33(1), Sch 2, para 27(a), as from 1 April 1989.
  Para 4 in square brackets substituted for para 4 in italics by Courts and Legal Services Act 1990, s 116, Sch 16, para 37(1), as from 14 October 1991.

5. *An affiliation order* (*that is to say an order under section 4 of the Affiliation Proceedings Act 1957, section 44 of the National Assistance Act 1948, section 26 of the Children Act 1948* [*section 50 of the Child Care Act 1980*] *or section 24 of the Ministry of Social Security Act 1966* [*or section 19 of the Supplementary Benefits Act 1976*]) [*or section 45 of the Children Act 1975*] [*or section 25 of the Social Security Act 1986*].
Note. First words in square brackets substituted for preceding reference to 1948 Act by Child Care Act 1980, s 89, Sch 5, para 20, as from 1 April 1981. Second words in square brackets added by Supplementary Benefit Act 1976, s 35(2), Sch 7, as from 15 November 1976. Third words in square brackets added by Children Act 1975, s 108(1), Sch 3, para 73(2), as from 1 December 1985. Fourth words in square brackets added by Social Security Act 1986, s 86, Sch 10, Part I, para 42, as from 11 April 1988. Whole para repealed by Family Law Reform Act 1987, s 33(1), (4), Sch 2, para 27(b), Sch 4, as from 1 April 1989.

6. An order *under section 87 of the Children and Young Persons Act 1933, section 30 of the Children and Young Persons Act 1963* [*section 47 or 51 of the Child Care Act 1980*] [—
   (a) made or having effect as if made under paragraph 23 of Schedule 2 to the Children Act 1989; or
   (b) made under] *or*
section 23 of the Ministry of Social Security Act 1966 [*or* section 18 of the Supplementary Benefits Act 1976] [*or* section 24 of the Social Security Act 1986] [or section 106 of the Social Security Administration Act 1992] (various provisions for obtaining contributions from a person whose dependants are assisted or maintained out of public funds).

Note. First words in square brackets substituted for preceding words in italics by Child Care Act 1980, s 89, Sch 5, para 28, as from 1 April 1981. Second words in square brackets substituted by Courts and Legal Services Act 1990, s 116, Sch 16, para 6(1), as from 14 October 1991 (and superseding similar amendment made by Children Act 1989, s 108(5), Sch 13, para 25). Third words in square brackets added by Supplementary Benefits Act 1976, s 35(2), Sch 7, as from 15 November 1976. Fourth words in square brackets inserted by Social Security Act 1986, s 86, Sch 10, Part I, para 42, as from 11 April 1988. Fifth words in square brackets inserted by Social Security (Consequential Provisions) Act 1992, s 4, Sch 2, para 7, as from 1 July 1992.

7. An order under section 43 of the National Assistance Act 1948 (recovery of costs of maintaining assisted person).

8. An order to which section 16 of the Maintenance Orders Act 1950 applies by virtue of subsection (2)(b) or (c) of that section (that is to say an order made by a court in Scotland or Northern Ireland and corresponding to one of those specified in the foregoing paragraphs) and which has been registered in a court in England and Wales under Part II of that Act.

Note. The reference to Maintenance Orders Act 1950, s 16(2)(c) is to be construed as a reference to s 16(2)(c) as amended: see Matrimonial Causes Act 1973, s 54(1), Sch 2, para 3(2) (pp 2561, 2567).

9. A maintenance order within the meaning of the Maintenance Orders (Facilities for Enforcement) Act 1920 (Commonwealth orders enforceable in the United Kingdom) registered in, or confirmed by, a court in England and Wales under that Act.

[**10.** An order for periodical or other payments made under Part I of the Matrimonial Proceedings and Property Act 1970.]

Note. Para 10 added by Matrimonial Proceedings and Property Act 1970, s 42, Sch 2, para 5.

[**11.** A maintenance order within the meaning of Part I of the Maintenance Orders (Reciprocal Enforcement) Act 1972 registered in a magistrates' court under the said Part I.]

Note. Para 11 added by Maintenance Orders (Reciprocal Enforcement) Act 1972, s 22(1), Schedule, para 6, as from 1 April 1974.

[**12.** *An order under section 34(1)(b) of the Children Act 1975 (payments of maintenance in respect of a child to his custodian).*]

Note. Para 12 added by Children Act 1975, s 108(1), Sch 3, para 73(2), as from 1 December 1985; repealed by Courts and Legal Services Act 1990, ss 116, 125(7), Sch 16, para 37(2), Sch 20, as from 14 October 1991.

[**13.** A maintenance order within the meaning of Part I of the Civil Jurisdiction and Judgments Act 1982 which is registered in a magistrates' court under that Part.]

Note. Para 13 added by Civil Jurisdiction and Judgments Act 1982, s 15(4), Sch 12, Part I, para 5, as from 1 January 1987.

[**13A.** A maintenance judgment within the meaning of Council Regulation (EC) No 44/2001 of 22nd December 2000 on jurisdiction and the recognition and enforcement of judgments in civil and commercial matters, which is registered in a magistrates' court under that Regulation.]

Note. Para 13A added by the Civil Jurisdiction and Judgments Order 2001, SI 2001 No 3929, as from 1 March 2002.

[**14.** An order for periodical or other payments made under Part III of the Matrimonial and Family Proceedings Act 1984].

Note. Para 14 added by Matrimonial and Family Proceedings Act 1984, s 46(1), Sch 1, para 8, as from 16 September 1985.

SCHEDULE 9

ENFORCEMENT OF ORDERS FOR COSTS, COMPENSATION, ETC

PART I

CASES WHERE PAYMENT ENFORCEABLE AS ON SUMMARY CONVICTION

Costs awarded by magistrates

1. Where a magistrates' court, on the summary trial of an information, makes an order as to costs to be paid by the accused to the prosecutor.

[**1A.** Where a magistrates' court makes an order as to costs to be paid by the accused in exercise of any power in that behalf conferred by regulations made under section 19(1) of the Prosecution of Offences Act 1985.]

2. Where an appellant to *quarter sessions* [the Crown Court] against conviction or sentence by a magistrates' court abandons his appeal and the magistrates' court orders him to pay costs to the other party to the appeal.

Costs awarded by assizes and quarter sessions

3. Where a person appeals to *quarter sessions* [the Crown Court] against conviction or sentence by a magistrates' court, and *quarter sessions* [the Crown Court] makes an order as to costs to be paid by him.

4. Where a person is prosecuted or tried on indictment *or inquisition* before *a court of assize or quarter sessions* [the Crown Court] and is convicted, and the court *orders him to pay the whole or part of the costs incurred in or about the prosecution and conviction* [makes an order as to costs to be paid by him].

Note. Words in italics in first place repealed by Criminal Law Act 1977, s 65, Sch 13, as from 1 January 1978.

[**4A.** Where the Crown Court makes an order as to costs to be paid by the accused in exercise of any power in that behalf conferred by regulations made under section 19(1) of the Prosecution of Offences Act 1985.]

*   *   *   *   *

Costs awarded by Court of Appeal (criminal division) or House of Lords

6. *Where the criminal division of the Court of Appeal dismisses an appeal or application for leave to appeal and orders the appellant or applicant to pay the whole or part of the costs of the appeal or application.*

7. *Where the criminal division of the Court of Appeal or the House of Lords dismisses an application for leave to appeal to that House (being an application made by the person who was the appellant before the criminal division) and orders him to pay the whole or part of the costs of the application.*

[**6.** Where the criminal division of the Court of Appeal makes an order as to costs to be paid by—
(a) an appellant;
(b) an applicant for leave to appeal to that court; or

(c) in the case of an application for leave to appeal to the House of Lords, an applicant who was the appellant before the criminal division.]

* * * * *

Miscellaneous orders for costs, compensation, damage etc

[**9.** Where a court makes an order by virtue of *section 18 of the Costs in Criminal Cases Act 1973* [regulations made under section 19(5) of the Prosecution of Offences Act 1985] for the payment of costs by an offender.]

Note. Para 9 substituted by Costs in Criminal Cases Act 1973, s 21(1), Sch 1, para 6.

[*10. Where under section 35 of the Powers of Criminal Courts Act 1973 a court orders the payment of compensation.*]

[**10.** Where under section 130 of the Powers of Criminal Courts (Sentencing) Act 2000 a court orders the payment of compensation.]

Note. Para 10 substituted by Powers of Criminal Courts Act 1973, s 56(1), Sch 5, para 40, as from 1 July 1974. Further sunbstituted by the Powers of Criminal Courts (Sentencing) Act 2000, s 165(1), Sch 9, para 43(1), (2), as from 25 August 2000.

12. Where under *section 55 of the Children and Young Persons Act 1933* [section 137 of the Powers of Criminal Courts (Senencing) Act 2000] a court orders any fine, *damages,* compensation or costs, or any sum awarded by way of satisfaction or compensation to be paid by the parent or guardian of a child or young person.

Note. Word 'section 137 of the Powers of Criminal Courts (Sentencing) Act 2000' in square brackets substituted for words 'section 55 of the Children and Young Persons Act 1933' by the Powers of Criminal Courts (Sentencing) Act 2000, s 165(1), Sch 9, para 43(1), (3), as from 25 August 2000. Word 'damages' repealed by Criminal Justice Act 1972, s 64(2), Sch 6, Part II, as from 1 January 1973.

PART II

CASES WHERE COSTS ENFORCEABLE SUMMARILY AS CIVIL DEBT

Costs awarded by magistrates

13. *Where a magistrates' court, on the summary trial of an information, makes an order as to costs to be paid by the prosecutor to the accused.*

[**13.** Where a magistrates' court makes an order as to costs to be paid by the prosecutor in exercise of any power in that behalf conferred by regulations made under section 19(1) of the Prosecution of Offences Act 1985.]

14. Where an appellant to *quarter sessions* [the Crown Court] from a magistrates' court (otherwise than against conviction or sentence) abandons his appeal and the magistrates' court order him to pay costs to the other party to the appeal.

15. *Where examining justices determine not to commit a person for trial and order the prosecutor to pay the whole or part of the costs incurred in or about the defence.*

Note. Words 'the Crown Court' in paras 1–15 substituted for preceding words in italics by Courts Act 1971, s 56(1), Sch 8, para 60(3), as from 1 January 1972, and para 16 below in square brackets was substituted for original paras 16–20 by ibid, para 60(4).

Costs awarded by [the Crown Court]

[**16.** Any order for the payment of costs made by the Crown Court, other than an order falling within Part I above, or an order for costs to be paid out of money provided by Parliament.]

Note. See Note to para 15, supra.

[Costs awarded by Court of Appeal (criminal division)

16A. Where the criminal division of the Court of Appeal makes an award as to costs to be paid by the respondent or, in the case of an application for leave to appeal to the House of Lords, an applicant who was the respondent before the criminal division, and does so in exercise of any power in that behalf conferred by regulations made under section 19(1) of the Prosecution of Offences Act 1985.]

Note. Paras 1A, 4A, 16A inserted, words in square brackets in paras 4, 9 substituted for words in italics, para 6 in square brackets substituted for paras 6, 7 in italics, para 13 in square brackets substituted for para 13 in italics, and para 15 repealed by Prosecution of Offences Act 1985, s 31(5), (6), Sch 1, Part II, para 7, Sch 2, as from 1 October 1986.

*   *   *   *   *

SCHEDULE 11

ENACTMENTS REPEALED

Chapter	Short Title	Extent of Repeal
33 & 34 Vict c 23.	The Forfeiture Act 1870.	In section 4, the words from 'and the amount' onwards.
49 & 50 Vict c 27.	*The Guardianship of Infants Act 1886.*	In section 5 the words from 'and in every case' onwards. *In section 6, the words 'in any divisions thereof'. In section 9, the words from 'Any application' to 'Rules of Court'. In section 10, the words 'before a judge of the Chancery Division' and the words from 'and, subject to any' to 'as he shall direct'.* In section 11, paragraph (a) and, in paragraph (c), the words 'England or'.
4 & 5 Geo 5 c 59.	The Bankruptcy Act 1914.	Section 107(1) to (3).
15 & 16 Geo 5 c 23.	The Administration of Estates Act 1925.	In section 30(3), the words 'the Probate, Divorce and Admiralty Division of '.
15 & 16 Geo 5 c 49.	The Supreme Court of Judicature (Consolidation) Act 1925.	In section 5(1), the words 'report or'. In section 58, the words from 'and (4) Subject to rules of court' onwards. In section 63, in paragraph (b) of the proviso to subsection (6), the words 'with the concurrence of the other judges of the Division or a majority thereof, or in the case of the King's Bench Division'. In section 225, the definition of 'Probate Division'.
23 & 24 Geo 5 c 12.	The Children and Young Persons Act 1933.	Section 55(4).
23 & 24 Geo 5 c 38.	The Summary Jurisdiction (Appeals) Act 1933.	Section 5(2).
11 & 12 Geo 6 c 58.	The Criminal Justice Act 1948.	Section 11(3).
12, 13 and 14 Geo 6 c 87.	The Patents Act 1949.	Section 85(6).
12, 13 and 14 Geo 6 c 88.	The Registered Designs Act 1949.	Section 28(6).

Chapter	Short Title	Extent of Repeal
15 & 16 Geo 6 & 1 Eliz 2 c 48.	The Costs in Criminal Cases Act 1952.	Section 10(1) to (3); and in section 10(5) the words 'under this section', wherever occurring.
15 & 16 Geo 6 & 1 Eliz 2 c 55.	The Magistrates' Courts Act 1952.	In section 34, the words from I'and any sum' onwards. In section 74(6)(a), the words 'under the Maintenance Orders Act 1958'. Section 85(3).
6 & 7 Eliz 2 c 39.	The Maintenance Orders Act 1958.	Section 4(3). Sections 6 to 8. Sections 9(1), (3) and (6). Sections 10 to 15. In section 21(1), the definitions of 'attachment of earnings order', 'earnings', 'employer', 'excepted sums' and 'maintenance order'; and section 21(5). The Schedule.
1959 c 22.	The County Courts Act 1959.	Section 153(a). Section 154.
1964 c 42.	The Administration of Justice Act 1964.	Section 5(2). In Schedule 3, paragraph 25(2).
1965 c 72.	The Matrimonial Causes Act 1965.	In section 38(1), the words from 'and any order' onwards.
1966 c 20.	The Ministry of Social Security Act 1966.	In section 23(6), the words from 'and the Maintenance Orders Act 1958' onwards. In section 24(9), the words from 'and the Maintenance Orders Act 1958' onwards.
1966 c 31.	The Criminal Appeal Act 1966.	Section 1(4) and (6)(b). Section 2(2).
1967 c 80.	The Criminal Justice Act 1967.	Section 46. Section 79(3) to (7). In section 84, the definition of 'appropriate authority'. Schedule 1.
1968 c 19.	The Criminal Appeal Act 1968.	In Section 45(2), the words 'of the Queen's Bench Division of'. In Schedule 5, the entry relating to section 10(2) of the Costs in Criminal Cases Act 1952.
1968 c 36.	The Maintenance Orders Act 1968.	In the Schedule, the entry relating to section 4 of the Maintenance Orders Act 1958.
1969 c 46.	The Family Law Reform Act 1969.	In section 4(5)(b), the words from 'and be deemed' onwards. In section 6(7) the words from 'and be deemed' onwards.

Chapter	Short Title	Extent of Repeal
1969 c 54.	The Children and Young Persons Act 1969.	In section 3(6), the word 'and' at the end of paragraph (b), and paragraph (c).

Note. This Schedule, so far as it relates to Guardianship of Infants Act 1886, ss 6, 9, 10, repealed by Guardianship of Minors Act 1971, s 18(2), Sch 2.

LAW REFORM (MISCELLANEOUS PROVISIONS) ACT 1970

(1970 c 33)

ARRANGEMENT OF SECTIONS

An Act to abolish actions for breach of promise of marriage and make provision with respect to the property of, and gifts between, persons who have been engaged to marry; to abolish the right of a husband to claim damages for adultery with his wife; to abolish actions for the enticement or harbouring of a spouse, or for the enticement, seduction or harbouring of a child; to make provision with respect to the maintenance of survivors of void marriages; and for purposes connected with the matters aforesaid. [29 May 1970]

Legal consequences of termination of contract to marry

1. Engagements to marry not enforceable at law—(1) An agreement between two persons to marry one another shall not under the law of England and Wales have effect as a contract giving rise to legal rights and no action shall lie in England and Wales for breach of such an agreement, whatever the law applicable to the agreement.

(2) This section shall have effect in relation to agreements entered into before it comes into force, except that it shall not affect any action commenced before it comes into force.

2. Property of engaged couples—(1) Where an agreement to marry is terminated, any rule of law relating to the rights of husbands and wives in relation to property in which either or both has or have a beneficial interest, including any such rule as explained by section 37 of the Matrimonial Proceedings and Property Act 1970, shall apply, in relation to any property in which either or both of the parties to the agreement had a beneficial interest while the agreement was in force, as it applies in relation to property in which a husband or wife has a beneficial interest.

Note. For Matrimonial Proceedings and Property Act 1970, s 37, see p 2382.

(2) Where an agreement to marry is terminated, section 17 of the Married Women's Property Act 1882 and section 7 of the of the Matrimonial Causes (Property and Maintenance) Act 1958 (which sections confer power on a judge of the High Court or a county court to settle disputes between husband and wife about property) shall apply, as if the parties were married, to any dispute between, or claim by, one of them in relation to property in which either or both had a beneficial interest while the agreement was in force; but an application made by virtue of this section to the judge under the said section 17, as originally enacted or as extended by the said section 7, shall be made within three years of the termination of the agreement.

Note. For Married Women's Property Act 1882, s 17, see p 2032.

For Matrimonial Causes (Property and Maintenance) Act 1958, s 7, see p 2202.

3. Gifts between engaged couples—(1) A party to an agreement to marry who makes a gift of property to the other party to the agreement on the condition (express or implied) that it shall be returned if the agreement is terminated shall not be prevented from recovering the property by reason only of his having terminated the agreement.

(2) The gift of an engagement ring shall be presumed to be an absolute gift; this presumption may be rebutted by proving that the ring was given on the condition, express or implied, that it should be returned if the marriage did not take place for any reason.

Damages for adultery

4. Abolition of right to claim damages for adultery. *After this Act comes into force no person shall be entitled to petition any court for, or include in a petition a claim for, damages from any other person on the ground of adultery with the wife of the first-mentioned person.*

Note. This section repealed by Matrimonial Causes Act 1973, s 54(1), Sch 3.

Enticement of spouse, etc

5. Abolition of actions for enticement, seduction and harbouring of spouse or child. No person shall be liable in tort under the law of England and Wales—

  (a) to any other person on the ground only of his having induced the wife or husband of that other person to leave or remain apart from the other spouse;

  (b) to a parent (or person standing in the place of a parent) on the ground only of his having deprived the parent (or other person) of the services of his or her child by raping, seducing or enticing that child; or

  (c) to any other person for harbouring the wife or child of that other person,

except in the case of a cause of action accruing before this Act comes into force if an action in respect thereof has been begun before this Act comes into force.

Maintenance for survivor of void marriage

6. Orders for maintenance of surviving party to void marriage from estate of other party—*(1) Where a person domiciled in England and Wales dies after the commencement of this Act and is survived by someone (hereafter referred to as 'the survivor') who, whether before or after the commencement of this Act, had in good faith entered into a void marriage with the deceased, then subject to subsections (2) and (3) below the survivor shall be treated for purposes of the Inheritance (Family Provision) Act 1938 as a dependant of the deceased within the meaning of that Act.*

(2) An order shall not be made under the Inheritance (Family Provision) Act 1938 in favour of the survivor unless the court is satisfied that it would have been reasonable for the deceased to make provision for the survivor's maintenance; and if an order is so made requiring provision for the survivor's maintenance by way of periodical payments, the order shall provide

for their termination not later than the survivor's death and, if the survivor remarries, not later than the remarriage.

(3) This section shall not apply if the marriage of the deceased and the survivor was dissolved or annulled during the deceased's lifetime and the dissolution or annulment is recognised by the law of England and Wales, or if the survivor has before the making of the order entered into a later marriage.

(4) It is hereby declared that the reference in subsection (2) above to remarriage and the reference in subsection (3) above to a later marriage include references to a marriage which is by law void or voidable.

(5) In section 26 of the Matrimonial Causes Act 1965 (orders for maintenance from deceased's estate following dissolution or annulment of a marriage), in the definition of 'net estate' and 'dependant' in subsection (6) (as amended by subsequent enactments) for the words 'and the Family Law Reform Act 1969' there shall be substituted the words 'the Family Law Reform Act 1969 and the Law Reform (Miscellaneous Provisions) Act 1970'.

Note. This section repealed by Inheritance (Provision for Family and Dependants) Act 1975, s 26(2), (3), Schedule, as from 1 April 1976.

For Matrimonial Causes Act 1965, s 26, see p 2243.

Supplemental

7. Citation, repeal, commencement and extent—(1) This Act may be cited as the Law Reform (Miscellaneous Provisions) Act 1970.

(2) The enactments specified in the Schedule to this Act are hereby repealed to the extent specified in the third column of that Schedule, but the repeal of those enactments shall not affect any action commenced or petition presented before this Act comes into force or any claim made in any such action or on any such petition.

(3) This Act shall come into force on 1 January 1971.

(4) This Act does not extend to Scotland or Northern Ireland.

SCHEDULE   Section 7

ENACTMENTS REPEALED

Chapter	Short Title	Extent of Repeal
32 & 33 Vict c 68.	The Evidence Further Amendment Act 1869.	Section 2.
23 & 24 Geo 5 c 36.	The Administration of Justice (Miscellaneous Provisions) Act 1933.	In section 6(1)(b), the words 'or breach of promise of marriage'.
24 & 25 Geo 5 c 41	The Law Reform (Miscellaneous Provisions) Act 1934.	In section 1(1), the words from 'or for inducing' to the end; and section 1(2)(b).
12, 13 & 14 Geo 6 c 51.	The Legal Aid and Advice Act 1949.	In Part II of Schedule 1, paragraph 1(b) and (d).
7 & 8 Eliz 2 c 22.	The County Courts Act 1959.	In section 39(1)(c), and in section 94(3)(b), the words 'or breach of promise of marriage'.
1965 c 72.	The Matrimonial Causes Act 1965.	Section 41. Section 46(2) so far as i applies for the interpretation of section 41(3) of that Act.

MATRIMONIAL PROCEEDINGS AND PROPERTY ACT 1970*
(1970 c 45)

* The Act was passed on 27 July 1971. Whole Act repealed, as amended, by Family Law Act 1986, s 68(2), Sch 2, as from 4 April 1988.

ARRANGEMENT OF SECTIONS

PART I

PROVISIONS WITH RESPECT TO ANCILLARY AND OTHER RELIEF IN MATRIMONIAL CAUSES AND TO CERTAIN OTHER MATRIMONIAL PROCEEDINGS

Maintenance pending suit in cases of divorce, etc

PART II

MISCELLANEOUS PROVISIONS

PART III

SUPPLEMENTARY

An Act to make fresh provision for empowering the court in matrimonial proceedings to make orders ordering either spouse to make financial provision for, or transfer property to, the other spouse or a child of the family, orders for the variation of ante-nuptial and post-nuptial settlements, orders for the custody and education of children and orders varying, discharging or suspending orders made in such proceedings; to make other amendments of the law relating to matrimonial proceedings; to abolish the right to claim restitution of conjugal rights; to declare what interest in property is acquired by a spouse who contributes to its improvements;

to make provision as to a spouse's rights of occupation under section 1 of the Matrimonial Homes Act 1967 in certain cases; to extend section 17 of the Married Women's Property Act 1882 and section 7 of the Matrimonial Causes (Property and Maintenance) Act 1958; to amend the law about the property of a person whose marriage is the subject of a decree of judicial separation dying intestate; to abolish the agency of necessity of a wife; and for purposes connected with the matters aforesaid. [*29 May 1970*]

PART I*

PROVISIONS WITH RESPECT TO ANCILLARY AND OTHER RELIEF IN MATRIMONIAL CAUSES AND TO CERTAIN OTHER MATRIMONIAL PROCEEDINGS

* Part I repealed by Matrimonial Causes Act 1973, s 54(1), Sch 3 and was replaced as noted to each section.

Maintenance pending suit in cases of divorce, etc

1. Maintenance pending suit in cases of divorce, etc. *On a petition for divorce, nullity of marriage or judicial separation, the court may order either party to the marriage to make to the other such periodical payments for his or her maintenance and for such term, being a term beginning not earlier than the date of the presentation of the petition and ending with the date of the determination of the suit, as the court thinks reasonable.*

Note. Section 1 replaced Matrimonial Causes Act 1965, s 15 (p 2230). See now Matrimonial Causes Act 1973, s 22 (p 2510).

Powers of court in cases of divorce, etc, to make orders with respect to financial provision for parties to the marriage and children of the family

2. Financial provision for party to a marriage in cases of divorce, etc—*(1) On granting a decree of divorce, a decree of nullity of marriage or a decree of judicial separation or at any time thereafter (whether, in the case of a decree of divorce or of nullity of marriage, before or after the decree is made absolute), the court may, subject to the provisions of section 24(1) of this Act, make any one or more of the following orders, that is to say—*

    (a) an order that either party to the marriage shall make to the other such periodical payments and for such term as may be specified in the order;

    (b) an order that either party to the marriage shall secure to the other to the satisfaction of the court, such periodical payments and for such term as may be so specified;

    (c) an order that either party to the marriage shall pay to the other such lump sum or sums as may be so specified.

Note. Section 2(1) replaced Matrimonial Causes Act 1965, ss 16(1), 19, 20(1) (pp 2247, 2248). See now Matrimonial Causes Act 1973, s 23(1) (p 2513).

    (2) Without prejudice to the generality of subsection (1)(c) above, an order under this section that a party to a marriage shall pay a lump sum to the other party—

    (a) may be made for the purposes of enabling that other party to meet any liabilities or expenses reasonably incurred by him or her in maintaining himself or herself or any child of the family before making an application for an order under this section;

    (b) may provide for the payment of that sum by instalments of such amount as may be specified in the order and may require the payment of the instalments to be secured to the satisfaction of the court.

3. Financial provision for child of the family in cases of divorce, etc—*(1) Subject to the provisions of section 8 of this Act, in proceedings for divorce, nullity of marriage or judicial separation, the court may make any one or more of the orders mentioned in subsection (2) below—*

    (a) before or on granting the decree of divorce, of nullity of marriage or of judicial separation, as the case may be, or at any time thereafter;

    (b) where any such proceedings are dismissed after the beginning of the trial, either forthwith or within a reasonable period after the dismissal.

(2) The orders referred to in subsection (1) above are—

(a) an order that a party to the marriage shall make to such person as may be specified in the order for the benefit of a child of the family, or to such a child, such periodical payments and for such term as may be so specified;

(b) an order that a party to the marriage shall secure to such person as may be so specified for the benefit of such a child, to the satisfaction of the court, such periodical payments and for such term as may be so specified;

(c) an order that a party to the marriage shall pay to such person as may be so specified for the benefit of such child, or to such a child, such lump sum as may be so specified.

(3) Without prejudice to the generality of subsection (2)(c) above, an order under this section for the payment of a lump sum to any person for the benefit of a child of the family, or to such a child, may be made for the purpose of enabling any liabilities or expenses reasonably incurred by or for the benefit of that child before the making of an application for an order under this section to be met.

(4) An order under this section for the payment of a lump sum may provide for the payment of that sum by instalments of such amount as may be specified in the order and may require the payment of the instalments to be secured to the satisfaction of the court.

(5) While the court has power to make an order in any proceedings by virtue of subsection (1)(a) above, it may exercise that power from time to time; and where the court makes an order by virtue of subsection (1)(b) above in relation to a child it may from time to time make a further order under this section in relation to him.

Note. Section 3 replaced Matrimonial Causes Act 1965, s 34(3), (4), (6) (p 2258). See now Matrimonial Causes Act 1973, s 23 (p 2513).

4. Orders for transfer and settlement of property and for variation of settlements in cases of divorce, etc. *On granting a decree of divorce, a decree of nullity of marriage or a decree of judicial separation, or at any time thereafter (whether, in the case of a decree of divorce or of nullity of marriage, before or after the decree is made absolute), the court may, subject to the provisions of sections 8 and 24(1) of this Act, make any one or more of the following orders, that is to say—*

(a) an order that a party to the marriage shall transfer to the other party, to any child of the family or to such person as may be specified in the order for the benefit of such a child such property as may be so specified, being property to which the first-mentioned party is entitled, either in possession or reversion;

(b) an order that a settlement of such property as may be so specified, being property to which a party to the marriage is so entitled, be made to the satisfaction of the court for the benefit of the other party to the marriage and of the children of the family or either or any of them;

(c) an order varying for the benefit of the parties to the marriage and of the children of the family or either or any of them any ante-nuptial or post-nuptial settlement (including such a settlement made by will or codicil) made on the parties to the marriage;

(d) an order extinguishing or reducing the interest of either of the parties to the marriage under any such settlement;

and the court may make an order under paragraph (c) above notwithstanding that there are no children of the family.

Note. Section 4 in part replaced Matrimonial Causes Act 1965, ss 17, 19 (pp 2247, 2248). See now Matrimonial Causes Act 1973, s 24(1), (2) (p 2515).

5. Matters to which court is to have regard in deciding what orders to make under ss 2, 3 and 4—(1) It shall be the duty of the court in deciding whether to exercise its powers under section 2 or 4 of this Act in relation to a party to the marriage and, if so, in what manner, to have regard to all the circumstances of the case including the following matters, that is to say—

(a) the income, earning capacity, property and other financial resources which each of the parties to the marriage has or is likely to have in the foreseeable future;

(b) the financial needs, obligations and responsibilities which each of the parties to the marriage has or is likely to have in the foreseeable future;

(c)   the standard of living enjoyed by the family before the breakdown of the marriage;

(d)   the age of each party to the marriage and the duration of the marriage;

(e)   any physical or mental disability of either of the parties to the marriage;

(f)   the contributions made by each of the parties to the welfare of the family, including any contribution made by looking after the home or caring for the family;

(g)   in the case of proceedings for divorce or nullity of marriage, the value to either of the parties to the marriage of any benefit (for example, a pension) which, by reason of the dissolution or annulment of the marriage, that party will lose the chance of acquiring;

and so to exercise those powers as to place the parties, so far as it is practicable and, having regard to their conduct, just to do so, in the financial position in which they would have been if the marriage had not broken down and each had properly discharged his or her financial obligations and responsibilities to the other.

(2)   Without prejudice to subsection (3) below, it shall be the duty of the court in deciding whether to exercise its powers under section 3 or 4 of this Act in relation to a child of the family and, if so, in what manner, to have regard to all the circumstances of the case including the following matters, that is to say—

(a)   the financial needs of the child;

(b)   the income, earning capacity (if any), property and other financial resources of the child;

(c)   any physical or mental disability of the child;

(d)   the standard of living enjoyed by the family before the breakdown of the marriage;

(e)   the manner in which he was being and in which the parties to the marriage expected him to be educated or trained;

and so to exercise those powers as to place the child, so far as it is practicable and, having regard to the considerations mentioned in relation to the parties to the marriage in paragraphs (a) and (b) of subsection (1) above, just to do so, in the financial position in which the child would have been if the marriage had not broken down and each of those parties had properly discharged his or her financial obligations and responsibilities towards him.

(3)   It shall be the duty of the court in deciding whether to exercise its powers under the said section 3 or 4 against a party to a marriage in favour of a child of the family who is not the child of that party and, if so, in what manner, to have regard (among the circumstances of the case)—

(a)   to whether that party has assumed any responsibility for the child's maintenance and, if so, to the extent to which, and the basis upon which, that party assumed such responsibility and to the length of time for which that party discharged such responsibility;

(b)   to whether in assuming and discharging such responsibility that party did so knowing that the child was not his or her own;

(c)   to the liability of any other person to maintain the child.

Note.   Section 5 replaced by Matrimonial Causes Act 1973, s 25 (p 2519).

Additional powers of court to make orders requiring party to marriage to make payments to other party, etc

6. Neglect by party to marriage to maintain other party or child of the family—

(1)   Either party to a marriage may apply to the court for an order under this section on the ground that the other party to the marriage (in this section referred to as the respondent)—

(a)   being the husband, has wilfully neglected—

(i)   to provide reasonable maintenance for the applicant, or

(ii)   to provide, or to make a proper contribution towards, reasonable maintenance for any child of the family to whom this section applies;

(b)   being the wife, has wilfully neglected to provide, or to make a proper contribution towards, reasonable maintenance—

(i)   for the applicant in a case where, by reason of the impairment of the applicant's earning capacity through age, illness or disability of mind or body, and having regard to any resources of the applicant and the respondent respectively which are, or should properly be made, available for the purpose, it is reasonable in all the circumstances to expect the respondent so to provide or contribute, or

(ii)   for any child of the family to whom this section applies.

(2) *The court shall not entertain an application under this section unless it would have jurisdiction to entertain proceedings by the applicant for judicial separation.*

(3) *This section applies to any child of the family for whose maintenance it is reasonable in all the circumstances to expect the respondent to provide or towards whose maintenance it is reasonable in all the circumstances to expect the respondent to make a proper contribution.*

(4) *Where the child of the family to whom the application under this section relates is not the child of the respondent, then, in deciding—*

(a) *whether the respondent has been guilty of wilful neglect to provide, or to make a proper contribution towards, reasonable maintenance for the child, and*

(b) *what order, if any, to make under this section in favour or for the benefit of the child, the court shall have regard to the matters mentioned in section 5(3) of this Act.*

(5) *Where on an application under this section it appears to the court that the applicant or any child of the family to whom the application relates is in immediate need of financial assistance, but it is not yet possible to determine what order, if any, should be made on the application, the court may order the respondent to make to the applicant until the determinatiion of the application such periodical payments as the court thinks reasonable.*

(6) *Where on an application under this section the applicant satisfies the court of any ground mentioned in subsection (1) above, then, subject to the provisions of section 8 of this Act, the court may make such one or more of the following orders as it thinks just, that is to say—*

(a) *an order that the respondent shall make to the applicant such periodical payments and for such term as may be specified in the order;*

(b) *an order that the respondent shall secure to the applicant, to the satisfaction of the court, such periodical payments and for such term as may be so specified;*

(c) *an order that the respondent shall pay to the applicant such lump sum as may be so specified;*

(d) *an order that the respondent shall make to such person as may be specified in the order for the benefit of the child to whom the application relates, or to that child, such periodical payments and for such term as may be so specified;*

(e) *an order that the respondent shall secure to such person as may be so specified for the benefit of that child, or to that child, to the satisfaction of the court, such periodical payments and for such term as may be so specified;*

(f) *an order that the respondent shall pay to such person as may be so specified for the benefit of that child, or to that child, such lump sum as may be so specified.*

(7) *Without prejudice to the generality of subsection (6)(c) and (f) above, an order under this section that the respondent shall pay a lump sum—*

(a) *may be made for the purpose of enabling any liabilities or expenses reasonably incurred in maintaining the applicant or any child of the family to whom the application relates before the making of the application to be met;*

(b) *may provide for the payment of that sum by instalments of such amount as may be specified in the order and may require the payment of the instalments to be secured to the satisfaction of the court.*

Note. Section 6 replaced Matrimonial Causes Act 1965, s 22 (p 2250). See now Matrimonial Causes Act 1973, s 27 (p 2529).

Further provisions relating to orders under sections 2, 3, 4 and 6

7. Duration of certain orders made in favour of party to marriage and effect of remarriage—(1) *The term to be specified in any order made by virtue of section 2(1)(a) or (b) of this Act or section 6(6)(a) or (b) thereof shall be such term, being a term beginning not earlier than the date of the making of an application for the order in question and lasting not longer than the maximum term, as the court thinks fit.*

(2) *In subsection (1) above 'the maximum term' means—*

(a) *in the case of an order made by virtue of the said section 2(1)(a) in proceedings for divorce or nullity of marriage, the joint lives of the parties to the marriage or a term ending with the date of the remarriage of the party in whose favour the order is made, whichever is the shorter;*

(b)   in the case of an order made by virtue of the said section 2(1)(b) in any such proceedings, the life of that party or a term ending with the date of the remarriage of that party, whichever is the shorter;

(c)   in the case of an order made by virtue of the said section 2(1)(a) in proceedings for judicial separation or made by virtue of the said section 6(6)(a), the joint lives of the parties to the marriage;

(d)   in the case of an order made by virtue of the said section 2(1)(b) in proceedings for judicial separation or made by virtue of the said section 6(6)(b), the life of the party in whose favour the order is made.

(3)   Where an order is made by virtue of the said section 2(1)(a) or (b) in proceedings for judicial separation or by virtue of the said section 6(6)(a) or (b) and the marriage of the parties affected by the order is subsequently dissolved or annulled but the order continues in force, the order shall, notwithstanding anything in it, cease to have effect on the remarriage of the party in whose favour it was made, except in relation to any arrears due under it on the date of such remarriage.

(4)   If after the grant of a decree dissolving or annulling a marriage either party to that marriage remarries, that party shall not be entitled to apply for an order under section 2 or 4 of this Act against the person to whom he or she was married immediately before the grant of that decree unless the remarriage is with that person and that marriage is also dissolved or annulled or a decree of judicial separation is made on a petition presented by either party to that marriage.

Note. Section 7 replaced by Matrimonial Causes Act 1973, s 28 (p 2532).

8. Provisions as to powers of court to make orders in favour of children and duration of such orders—(1) Subject to subsection (3) below—

(a)   no order under section 3, 4(a) or 6 of this Act shall be made in favour of a child who has attained the age of eighteen; and

(b)   the term for which by virtue of an order under the said section 3 or 6 any payments are to be made or secured to or for the benefit of a child may begin with the date of the making of an application for the order in question or any later date but shall not extend beyond the date when the child will attain the age of eighteen.

(2)   The term for which by virtue of an order under the said section 3 or 6 any payments are to be made or secured to or for the benefit of a child shall not in the first instance extend beyond the date of the birthday of the child next following his attaining the upper limit of the compulsory school age unless the court which makes the order thinks it right in the circumstances of the case to specify a later date therein.

For the purposes of this subsection the upper limit of the compulsory school age means the age that is for the time being that limit by virtue of section 35 of the Education Act 1944 together with any Order in Council made under that section.

(3)   The court may make such an order as is mentioned in subsection (1)(a) above in favour of a child who has attained the age of eighteen, and may include in an order made under the said section 3 or 6 in relation to a child who has not attained that age a provision extending beyond the date when the child will attain that age the term for which by virtue of the order any payments are to be so made or secured to or for the benefit of that child, if it appears to the court that—

(a)   that child is, or will be, or if such an order or provision were made would be, receiving instruction at an educational establishment or undergoing training for a trade, profession or vocation, whether or not he is also, or will also be, in gainful employment; or

(b)   there are special circumstances which justify the making of the order or provision.

(4)   Any order made by virtue of section 3(2)(a) of this Act or section 6(6)(d) thereof shall, notwithstanding anything in the order, cease to have effect on the death of the person liable to make payments under the order, except in relation to any arrears due under the order on the date of such death.

Note. Section 8 replaced by Matrimonial Causes Act 1973, s 29 (p 2534).

Provisions as to variations, discharge and enforcement of certain orders

9. Variation, discharge, etc, of orders for financial provision—*(1) Where the court has made an order to which this section applies, then, subject to the provisions of this section, the court shall have power to vary or discharge the order or to suspend any provision thereof temporarily and to revive the operation of any provision so suspended.*

(2) This section applies to the following orders, that is to say—

(a)   any order under section 1 of this Act;

(b)   any order made by virtue of section 2(1)(a) or (b) or 2(2)(b) of this Act;

(c)   any order made by virtue of section 3(2)(a) or (b) or 3(4) of this Act;

(d)   any order made by virtue of section 4(b), (c) or (d) of this Act on or after granting a decree of judicial separation; and

(e)   any order made by virtue of section 6(5), 6(6)(a), (b), (d) or (e) or 6(7)(b) of this Act.

(3) The powers exercisable by the court under this section in relation to an order shall be exercisable also in relation to any instrument executed in pursuance of the order.

(4) The court shall not exercise the powers conferred by this section in relation to any order made by virtue of the said section 4(b), (c) or (d) on or after granting a decree of judicial separation except on an application made in the proceedings—

(a)   for the rescission of that decree, or

(b)   for the dissolution of the marriage of the parties to the proceedings in which that decree was made.

(5) No such order as is mentioned in section 4 of this Act shall be made on an application for the variation of an order made by virtue of the said section 2(1)(a) or (b) or the said section 3(2)(a) or (b), and no order for the payment of a lump sum shall be made on an application for the variation of an order made by virtue of the said section 2(1)(a) or (b) or of the said section 6(6)(a) or (b).

(6) Where the person liable to make payments under an order made by virtue of the said section 2(1)(b), the said section 3(2)(b) or the said section 6(6)(b) or (e) has died, an application under this section relating to that order may be made by the person entitled to payments under the order or by the personal representatives of the deceased person, but no such application shall, except with the permission of the court, be made after the end of the period of six months from the date on which representation in regard to the estate of that person is first taken out.

(7) In exercising the powers conferred by this section the court shall have regard to all the circumstances of the case, including any change in any of the matters to which the court was required to have regard when making the order to which the application relates and, where the party against whom that order was made has died, the changed circumstances resulting from his or her death.

(8) The personal representatives of a deceased person against whom any such order as is referred to in subsection (6) above was made shall not be liable for having distributed any part of the estate of the deceased after the expiration of the period of six months referred to in that subsection on the ground that they ought to have taken into account the possibility that the court might permit an application under this section to be made after that period by the person entitled to payments under the order; but this subsection shall not prejudice any power to recover any part of the estate so distributed arising by virtue of the making of an order in pursuance of this section.

(9) In considering for the purposes of subsection (6) above the question when representation was first taken out, a grant limited to settled land or to trust property shall be left out of account and a grant limited to real estate or to personal estate shall be left out of account unless a grant limited to the remainder of the estate has previously been made or is made at the same time.

Note. Section 9 replaced Matrimonial Causes Act 1965, s 31 (p 2257). See now Matrimonial Causes Act 1973, s 31 (p 2536).

10. Payment of certain arrears unenforceable without the leave of the court—
(1) A person shall not be entitled to enforce through the High Court or any county court the payment of any arrears due under an order made by virtue of section 1, 2(1), 3(2), 6(5) or 6(6) of this Act without the leave of that court if those arrears became due more than twelve months before proceedings to enforce the payment of them are begun.

(2) *The court hearing an application for the grant of leave under this section may refuse leave, or may grant leave subject to such restrictions and conditions (including conditions as to the allowing of time for payment or the making of payment by instalments) as that court thinks proper, or may remit the payment of such arrears or of any part thereof.*

(3) *Any application for the grant of leave under this section shall be made in such manner as may be prescribed by rules of court.*

Note. Section 10 replaced by Matrimonial Causes Act 1973, s 32 (p 2542).

11. Power of court to order sums paid under certain orders to be repaid in certain cases—(1) *Where on an application made under this section in relation to an order to which this section applies it appears to the court that by reason of—*

(a) *a change in the circumstances of the person entitled to, or liable to make, payments under the order since the order was made, or*

(b) *the changed circumstances resulting from the death of the person so liable.*

the amount received by the person entitled to payments under the order in respect of a period after those circumstances changed or after the death of the person liable to make payments under the order, as the case may be, exceeds the amount which the person so liable or his or her personal representatives should have been required to pay, the court may order the respondent to the application to pay to the applicant such sum, not exceeding the amount of the excess, as the court thinks just.

This section applies to an order made by virtue of section 1, 2(1)(a) or (b), 3(2)(a) or (b), 6(5) or 6(6)(a), (b), (d) or (e) of this Act.

(2) *An application under this section may be made by the person liable to make payments under an order to which this section applies or his personal representatives and may be made against the person entitled to payments under the order or her or his personal representatives.*

(3) *An application under this section may be made in proceedings in the High Court or a county court for—*

(a) *the variation or discharge of the order to which this section applies, or*

(b) *leave to enforce, or the enforcement of, the payment of arrears under that order;*

but except as aforesaid such an application shall be made to a county court, and accordingly references in this section to the court are references to the High Court or a county court, as the circumstances require.

(4) *Any order under this section for the payment of any sum may provide for the payment of that sum by instalments of such amount as may be specified in the order.*

Note. Section 11 replaced by Matrimonial Causes Act 1973, s 11 (p 2503).

12. Application of Maintenance Orders Acts to orders under ss 1, 2, 3 and 6—(1) *Any order made by virtue of section 1, 2, 3 or 6 of this Act or any corresponding enactment of the Parliament of Northern Ireland shall be included among the orders to which section 16 of the Maintenance Orders Act 1950, applies (which section specifies the orders enforceable under Part II of that Act); and any order made by virtue of the said section 1, 2, 3 or 6 shall be a maintenance order within the meaning of the Maintenance Orders Act 1958.*

(2) *This section, so far as it affects Part II of the Maintenance Orders Act 1950, shall extend to Scotland and Northern Ireland.*

Note. For Maintenance Orders Act 1950, s 16, see p 2136.

Maintenance agreements

13. Validity of maintenance agreements—(1) *If a maintenance agreement includes a provision purporting to restrict any right to apply to a court for an order containing financial arrangements, then—*

(a) *that provision shall be void; but*

(b) *any other financial arrangements contained in the agreement shall not thereby be rendered void or unenforceable and shall, unless they are void or unenforceable for any other reason (and subject to sections 14 and 15 of this Act), be binding on the parties to the agreement.*

(2) In this and the next following section—
'maintenance agreement' means any agreement in writing made, whether before or after the commencement of this Act, between the parties to a marriage, being—

    (a) an agreement containing financial arrangements, whether made during the continuance or after the dissolution or annulment of the marriage; or

    (b) a separation agreement which contains no financial arrangements in a case where no other agreement in writing between the same parties contains such arrangements:

'financial arrangements' means provisions governing the rights and liabilities towards one another when living separately of the parties to a marriage (including a marriage which has been dissolved or annulled) in respect of the making or securing of payments or the disposition or use of any property, including such rights and liabilities with respect to the maintenance or education of any child, whether or not a child of the family.

Note. Section 13 replaced Matrimonial Causes Act 1965, s 23 (p 2250). See now Matrimonial Causes Act 1973, s 34 (p 2543).

14. Alteration of agreements by court during lives of parties—*(1) Where a maintenance agreement is for the time being subsisting and each of the parties to the agreement is for the time being either domiciled or resident in England and Wales, then, subject to subsection (3) below, either party may apply to the court or to a magistrates' court for an order under this section.*

(2) If the court to which the application is made is satisfied either—

    (a) that by reason of a change in the circumstances in the light of which any financial arrangements contained in the agreement were made or, as the case may be, financial arrangements were omitted from it (including a change foreseen by the parties when making the agreement), the agreement should be altered so as to make different, or, as the case may be, so as to contain, financial arrangements, or

    (b) that the agreement does not contain proper financial arrangements with respect to any child of the family,

then, subject to subsections (3), (4) and (5) below, that court may by order make such alterations in the agreement—

    (i) by varying or revoking any financial arrangements contained in it, or

    (ii) by inserting in it financial arrangements for the benefit of one of the parties to the agreement or of a child of the family,

as may appear to that court to be just having regard to all the circumstances, including, if relevant, the matters mentioned in section 5(3) of this Act; and the agreement shall have effect thereafter as if any alteration made by the order had been made by agreement between the parties and for valuable consideration.

(3) A magistrates' court shall not entertain an application under subsection (1) above unless both the parties to the agreement are resident in England and Wales and at least one of the parties is resident in the petty sessions area (within the meaning of the Magistrates' Court Act 1952) for which the court acts, and shall not have power to make any order on such an application except—

    (a) in a case where the agreement includes no provision for periodical payments by either of the parties, an order inserting provision for the making by one of the parties of periodical payments for the maintenance of the other party or for the maintenance of any child of the family;

    (b) in a case where the agreement includes provision for the making by one of the parties of periodical payments, an order increasing or reducing the rate of, or terminating, any of those payments.

(4) Where a court decides to alter, by order under this section, an agreement by inserting provision for the making or securing by one of the parties to the agreement of periodical payments for the maintenance of the other party or by increasing the rate of the periodical payments which the agreement provides shall be made by one of the parties for the maintenance of the other, the term for which the payments or, as the case may be, so much of the payments as is attributable to the increase are or is to be made under the agreement as altered by the order shall be such term as the court may specify, but that term shall not exceed—

(a)   where the payments will not be secured, the joint lives of the parties to the agreement or a term ending with the remarriage of the party to whom the payments are to be made, whichever is the shorter;

(b)   where the payment will be secured, the life of that party or a term ending with the remarriage of that party, whichever is the shorter.

(5)   Where a court decides to alter, by order under this section, an agreement by inserting provision for the making or securing by one of the parties to the agreement of periodical payments for the maintenance of a child of the family or by increasing the rate of the periodical payments which the agreement provides shall be made or secured by one of the parties for the maintenance of such a child, then, in deciding the term for which under the agreement as altered by the order the payments or, as the case may be, so much of the payments as is attributable to the increase are or is to be made or secured for the benefit of the child, the court shall apply the provisions of section 8(1), (2) and (3) of this Act as if the order to which this subsection relates were an order under section 3 of this Act.

(6)   For the avoidance of doubt it is hereby declared that nothing in this or the last foregoing section affects any power of a court before which any proceedings between the parties to a maintenance agreement are brought under any other enactment (including a provision of this Act) to make an order containing financial arrangements or any right of either party to apply for such an order in such proceedings.

Note. Section 14 replaced Matrimonial Causes Act 1965, s 24 (p 2251). See now Matrimonial Causes Act 1973, s 35 (p 2544).

15.   Alteration of agreements by court after death of one party—(1) *Where a maintenance agreement within the meaning of section 13 of this Act provides for the continuation of payments under the agreement after the death of one of the parties and that party dies domiciled in England and Wales, the surviving party or the personal representatives of the deceased party may, subject to subsections (2) and (3) below, apply to the High Court or a county court for an order under section 14 of this Act.*

(2)   *An application under this section shall not, except with the permission of the High Court or a county court, be made after the end of the period of six months from the date on which representation in regard to the estate of the deceased is first taken out.*

(3)   *A county court shall not entertain an application under this section, or an application for permission to make an application under this section, unless it would have jurisdiction by virtue of section 7 of the Family Provision Act 1966 (which confers jurisdiction on county courts in proceedings under the Inheritance (Family Provision) Act 1938 or section 26 of the Matrimonial Causes Act 1965 if the value of the deceased's net estate does not exceed £5,000 or such larger sum as may be fixed by order of the Lord Chancellor) to hear and determine proceedings for an order under the said section 26 (application for maintenance out of deceased's estate by former spouse) in relation to the deceased's estate.*

(4)   *If a maintenance agreement is altered by a court on an application made in pursuance of subsection (1) above, the like consequences shall ensue as if the alteration had been made immediately before the death by agreement between the parties and for valuable consideration.*

(5)   *The provisions of this section shall not render the personal representatives of the deceased liable for having distributed any part of the estate of the deceased after the expiration of the said period of six months on the ground that they ought to have taken into account the possibility that a court might permit an application by virtue of this section to be made by the surviving party after that period; but this subsection shall not prejudice any power to recover any part of the estate so distributed arising by virtue of the making of an order in pursuance of this section.*

(5)   *Section 9(9) of this Act shall apply for the purposes of subsection (2) of this section as it applies for the purposes of subsection (6) of the said section 9.*

Note. This subsection is numbered (5) in the Queen's Printer's copy.

(6)   *Subsection (3) of section 7 of the Family Provision Act 1966 (transfer to county courts of proceedings commenced in the High Court) and paragraphs (a) and (b) of subsection (5) thereof (provisions relating to proceedings commenced in county court before coming into force of order of the Lord Chancellor under that section) shall apply in relation to proceedings consisting*

of any such application as is referred to in subsection (3) above as they apply in relation to any such proceedings as are referred to in subsection (1) of the said section 7.

Note. Section 15 replaced Matrimonial Causes Act 1965, s 25 (p 2252). See now Matrimonial Causes Act 1973, s 36 (p 2545).

Avoidance of transactions intended to defeat certain claims

16. Avoidance of transactions intended to defeat certain claims—*(1) Where proceedings for relief under any of the relevant provisions of this Act (hereafter in this section referred to as 'financial provision') are brought by a person (hereafter in this section referred to as 'the applicant') against any other person (hereafter in this section referred to as 'the other party'), the court may, on an application by the applicant—*

(a) *if it is satisfied that the other party is, with the intention of defeating the claim for financial provision, about to make any disposition or to transfer out of the jurisdiction or otherwise deal with any property, make such order as it thinks fit for restraining the other party from so doing or otherwise for protecting the claim;*

(b) *if it is satisfied that the other party has, with the intention aforesaid, made a disposition to which this paragraph applies and that if the disposition were set aside financial provision or different financial provision would be granted to the applicant, make an order setting aside the disposition and give such consequential directions as it thinks fit for giving effect to the order (including directions requiring the making of any payment or the disposal of any property);*

(c) *if it is satisfied, in a case where an order under the relevant provisions of this Act has been obtained by the applicant against the other party, that the other party has, with the intention aforesaid, made a disposition to which this paragraph applies, make such an order and give such directions as are mentioned in paragraph (b) above;*

and an application for the purposes of paragraph (b) above shall be made in the proceedings for the financial provision in question.

(2) Paragraphs (b) and (c) of subsection (1) above apply respectively to any disposition made by the other party (whether before or after the commencement of the proceedings for financial provision), not being a disposition made for valuable consideration (other than marriage) to a person who, at the time of the disposition, acted in relation to it in good faith and without notice of any such intention as aforesaid on the part of the other party.

(3) Where an application is made under this section with respect to a disposition which took place less than three years before the date of the application or to a disposition or other dealing with property which is about to take place and the court is satisfied—

(a) *in a case falling within subsection (1)(a) or (b) above, that the disposition or other dealing would (apart from this section) have the consequence, or*

(b) *in a case falling within subsection (1)(c) above, that the disposition has had the consequence,*

of defeating the applicant's claim for financial provision, it shall be presumed, unless the contrary is shown, that the other party disposed of the property with the intention aforesaid, or, as the case may be, is, with that intention, about to dispose of or deal with the property.

(4) In this section—

'*disposition*' *does not include any provision contained in a will or codicil but, with that exception, includes any conveyance, assurance or gift of property of any description, whether made by an instrument or otherwise;*

'*the relevant provisions of this Act*' *means any of the provisions of the following enactments, that is to say, sections 1, 2, 3, 4, 6, 9 (except subsection (6)) and 14 of this Act;*

and any reference to defeating an applicant's claim for financial provision is a reference to preventing financial provision from being granted to the applicant, or to the applicant for the benefit of a child of the family, or reducing the amount of any financial provision which might be so granted, or frustrating or impeding the enforcement of any order which might be or has been made at the instance of the applicant under the relevant provisions of this Act.

(5) The provisions of this section shall not apply to a disposition made more than three years before the commencement of this Act.

Note. Section 16 replaced Matrimonial Causes Act 1965, s 32 (p 2257). See now Matrimonial Causes Act 1973, s 37 (p 2546).

Protection, custody, etc, of children

17. Restrictions on decrees for dissolution, annulment or separation affecting children—*(1) The court shall not make absolute a decree of divorce or of nullity of marriage, or make a decree of judicial separation, unless the court, by order, has declared that it is satisfied—*

(a) *that for the purposes of this section there are no children of the family to whom this section applies; or*

(b) *that the only children who are or may be children of the family to whom this section applies are the children named in the order and that—*

    (i) *arrangements for the welfare of every child so named have been made and are satisfactory or are the best that can be devised in the circumstances; or*

    (ii) *it is impracticable for the party or parties appearing before the court to make any such arrangements; or*

(c) *that there are circumstances making it desirable that the decree should be made absolute or should be made, as the case may be, without delay notwithstanding that there are or may be children of the family to whom this section applies and that the court is unable to make a declaration in accordance with paragraph (b) above.*

(2) The court shall not make an order declaring that it is satisfied as mentioned in subsection (1)(c) above unless it has obtained a satisfactory undertaking from either or both of the parties to bring the question of the arrangements for the children named in the order before the court within a specified time.

(3) If the court makes absolute a decree nisi of divorce or of nullity of marriage, or makes a decree of judicial separation, without having made an order under subsection (1) above the decree shall be void but, if such an order was made, no person shall be entitled to challenge the validity of the decree on the ground that the conditions prescribed by subsections (1) and (2) above were not fulfilled.

(4) If the court refuses to make an order under subsection (1) above in any proceedings for divorce, nullity of marriage or judicial separation, it shall, on an application by either party to the proceedings, make an order declaring that it is not satisfied as mentioned in that subsection.

(5) This section applies to the following children of the family, that is to say—

(a) *any minor child of the family who at the date of the order under subsection (1) above is—*

    (i) *under the age of sixteen, or*

    (ii) *receiving instruction at an educational establishment or undergoing training for a trade, profession or vocation, whether or not he is also in gainful employment; and*

(b) *any other child of the family to whom the court by an order under that subsection directs that this section shall apply:*

and the court may give such a direction if it is of opinion that there are special circumstances which make it desirable in the interest of the child that this section should apply to it.

(6) In this section 'welfare', in relation to a child, includes the custody and education of the child and financial provision for him.

Note. Section 17 replaced Matrimonial Causes Act 1965, s 33 (p 2258). See now Matrimonial Causes Act 1973, s 41 (p 2550).

18. Orders for custody and education of children affected by matrimonial suits—*(1) The court may make such order as it thinks fit for the custody and education of any child of the family who is under the age of eighteen—*

(a) *in any proceedings for divorce, nullity of marriage or judicial separation, before, by or after the final decree;*

(b) *where such proceedings are dismissed after the beginning of the trial, either forthwith or within a reasonable period after the dismissal;*

and in any case in which the court has power by virtue of this subsection to make an order in respect of a child it may instead, if it thinks fit, direct that proper proceedings be taken for making the child a ward of court.

(2) When an order in respect of a child is made under this section, the order shall not affect the rights over or with respect to the child of any person, other than a party to the marriage in question, unless the child is the child of one or both of the parties to that marriage and that person was a party to the proceedings on the application for an order under this section.

(3) Where the court makes or makes absolute a decree of divorce or makes a decree of judicial separation, it may include in the decree a declaration that either party to the marriage in question is unfit to have the custody of the children of the family.

(4) Where a decree of divorce or of judicial separation contains such a declaration as is mentioned in subsection (3) above, then, if the party to whom the declaration relates is a parent of any child of the family, that party shall not, on the death of the other parent, be entitled as of right to the custody or the guardianship of that child.

(5) While the court has power to make an order in any proceedings by virtue of paragraph (a) of subsection (1) above, it may exercise that power from time to time; and where the court makes an order by virtue of paragraph (b) of that subsection with respect to a child it may from time to time until that child attains the age of eighteen make a further order with respect to his custody and education.

(6) The court shall have power to discharge or vary an order made under this section or to suspend any provision thereof temporarily and to revive the operation of any provision so suspended.

Note. Section 18 replaced Matrimonial Causes Act 1965, s 34(1), (2), (5) (p 2258). See now Matrimonial Causes Act 1973, s 42 (repealed) (p 2551).

19. Orders for custody of children in cases of neglect to maintain—*(1) Where the court makes an order under section 6 of this Act, the court shall also have the power from time to time to make such orders as it thinks fit with respect to the custody of any child of the family who is for the time being under the age of eighteen; but the power conferred by this section and any order made in exercise of that power shall have effect only as respects any period when an order is in force under that section and the child is under that age.*

(2) Section 18(2) and (6) of this Act shall apply in relation to an order made under this section as they apply in relation to an order made under that section.

Note. Section 19 replaced Matrimonial Causes Act 1965, s 33 (p 2258). See now Matrimonial Causes Act 1973, s 42(2), (5)–(7) (repealed) (p 2551).

Abolition of right to claim restitution of conjugal rights

20. Abolition of right to claim restitution of conjugal rights. *No person shall after the commencement of this Act be entitled to petition the High Court or any county court for restitution of conjugal rights.*

Remarriage of party entitled to payments under certain orders, etc

21. Orders for maintenance of party to marriage under Matrimonial Causes Act 1965 to cease to have effect on remarriage of that party—*(1) An order made, or deemed to have been made, under section 16(1)(a) or (b) of the Matrimonial Causes Act 1965 shall, notwithstanding anything in the order, cease to have effect on the remarriage after the commencement of this Act of the person in whose favour the order was made, except in relation to any arrears due under it on the date of such remarriage.*

(2) An order for the payment of alimony made, or deemed to have been made, under section 20 of the said Act of 1965, and an order made, or deemed to have been made, under section 21 or 22 of that Act, shall, if the marriage of the parties to the proceedings in which the order was made was or is subsequently dissolved or annulled but the order continues in force, cease to have effect on the remarriage after the said commencement of the party in whose favour the order was made, except in relation to any arrears due under it on the date of such remarriage.

Note. See now Matrimonial Causes Act 1973, s 53, Sch 1, para 15 (pp 2561, 2564).

22. Orders for repayment in certain cases of sums paid after cessation of order by reason of remarriage—*(1) Where*—

    (a)   *an order to which this section applies has ceased to have effect by reason of the remarriage of the person entitled to payments under the order, and*

    (b)   *the person liable to make payments under the order or his or her personal representatives made payments in accordance with it in respect of a period after the date of such remarriage in the mistaken belief that the order was still subsisting,*

no proceedings in respect of a cause of action arising out of the circumstances mentioned in paragraphs (a) and (b) above shall be maintainable by the person so liable or his or her personal representatives against the person so entitled or her or his personal representatives; but on an application made under this section the court may exercise the powers conferred on it by subsection (2) below.

    This section applies to an order made by virtue of section 2(1)(a) or (b) or 6(6)(a) or (b) of this Act and to any such order as is referred to in subsection (1) or (2) of section 21 thereof.

    (2) The court may order the respondent to an application made under this section to pay to the applicant a sum equal to the amount of the payments made in respect of the period mentioned in subsection (1)(b) above or, if it appears to the court that it would be unjust to make that order, it may either order the respondent to pay to the applicant such lesser sum as it thinks fit or dismiss the application.

    (3) Subsections (2) to (4) of section 11 of this Act shall apply to an application made under this section and to an order made on such an application as they apply to an application made under that section and to an order made on the last mentioned application, and the references to the court in this section shall be construed in accordance with subsection (3) of that section as applied by this subsection.

    (4) The clerk of a magistrates' court to whom any payments under an order to which this section applies are required to be made, and the collecting officer under an attachment of earnings order made to secure payments under the first mentioned order, shall not be liable—

    (a)   *in the case of that clerk, for any act done by him in pursuance of the first mentioned order after the date on which that order ceased to have effect by reason of the remarriage of the person entitled to payments under it, and*

    (b)   *in the case of the collecting officer, for any act done by him after that date in accordance with any enactment or rule of court specifying how payments made to him in compliance with the attachment of earnings order are to be dealt with,*

if, but only if, the act was one which he would have been under a duty to do had the first mentioned order not ceased to have effect as aforesaid and the act was done before notice in writing of the fact that the person so entitled had remarried was given to him by or on behalf of that person, the person liable to make payments under the first mentioned order or the personal representatives of either of those persons.

    (5) In this section 'collecting officer', in relation to an attachment of earnings order, means the officer of the High Court, the registrar of a county court or the clerk of a magistrates' court to whom a person makes payments in compliance with the order.

Note. Section 22 replaced by Matrimonial Causes Act 1973, s 38 (p 2514).

Miscellaneous and supplemental

23. Settlement, etc, made in compliance with order under s 4 may be avoided on bankruptcy of settlor.   *The fact that a settlement or transfer of property had to be made in order to comply with an order of the court under section 4 of this Act shall not prevent that settlement or transfer from being a settlement of property to which section 42(1) of the Bankruptcy Act 1914 (avoidance of certain settlements) applies.*

Note. Section 23 replaced by Matrimonial Causes Act 1973, s 23 (p 2513).

24. Commencement of proceedings for financial provision orders, etc—*(1) Where a petition for divorce, nullity of marriage or judicial separation has been presented, then, subject to subsection (2) below, proceedings under section 1, 2, 3 or 4 of this Act may be begun, subject to and in accordance with rules of court, at any time after the presentation of the petition; but—*

    (a)   *no order under section 2 or 4 of this Act shall be made unless a decree nisi of divorce or of nullity of marriage or a decree of judicial separation, as the case may be, has been granted;*

    (b)   *without prejudice to the power to give a direction under section 25 of this Act, no such order made on or after granting a decree nisi of divorce or of nullity of marriage, and no settlement made in pursuance of such an order, shall take effect unless the decree has been made absolute.*

Note. Sub-s (1) replaced Matrimonial Causes Act 1965, s 18 (p 2248). See now Matrimonial Causes Act 1973, s 26(1) (p 2528).

    (2) *Rules of court may provide, in such cases as may be prescribed by the rules—*

    (a)   *that applications for ancillary relief shall be made in the petition or answer; and*

    (b)   *that applications for ancillary relief which are not so made, or are not made until after the expiration of such period following the presentation of the petition or filing of the answer as may be so prescribed, shall be made only with the leave of the court.*

In this subsection 'ancillary relief' means relief under any of the following provisions of this Act, that is to say, sections 1, 2, 3 and 4.

Note. Sub-s (2) replaced Matrimonial Causes Act 1965, s 29 (p 2256). See now Matrimonial Causes Act 1973, s 26(2) (p 2528).

25. Direction for instrument to be settled by conveyancing counsel.   *Where the court decides to make an order under this Part of this Act requiring any payments to be secured or an order under section 4 of this Act—*

    (a)   *it may direct that the matter be referred to one of the conveyancing counsel of the court for him to settle a proper instrument to be executed by all necessary parties; and*

    (b)   *in the case of an order under section 2, 3 or 4 of this Act, it may, if it thinks fit, defer the grant of the decree in question until the instrument has been duly executed.*

Note. Section 25 replaced Matrimonial Causes Act 1965, s 16(2) (p 2247). See now Matrimonial Causes Act 1973, s 30 (p 2536).

26. Payments etc, under order made in favour of person suffering from mental disorder.   *Where the court makes an order under this Part of this Act requiring payments (including a lump sum payment) to be made, or property to be transferred, to a party to a marriage and the court is satisfied that the person in whose favour the order is made is incapable, by reason of mental disorder within the meaning of the Mental Health Act 1959, of managing and administering his or her property and affairs, then, subject to any order, direction or authority made or given in relation to that person under Part VIII of the said Act of 1959, the court may order the payments to be made, or, as the case may be, the property to be transferred, to such persons having charge of that person as the court may direct.*

Note. Section 26 replaced Matrimonial Causes Act 1965, s 30(2) (p 2256). See now Matrimonial Causes Act 1973, s 40 (p 2549).

27. Interpretation—(*1*)   *In this Part of this Act—*

'adopted' means adopted in pursuance of—

    (a)   *an adoption order made under the Adoption Act 1958, any previous enactment relating to the adoption of children, the Adoption Act 1968 or any corresponding enactment of the Parliament of Northern Ireland; or*

    (b)   *an adoption order made in the Isle of Man or any of the Channel Islands; or*

    (c)   *subject to sections 5 and 6 of the Adoption Act 1968, an overseas adoption within the meaning of section 4 of that Act;*

'child', in relation to one or both of the parties to a marriage, includes an illegitimate or adopted child of that party or, as the case may be, of both parties;

'child of the family', in relation to the parties to a marriage, means—

    (a)   *a child of both those parties; and*

    (b)   *any other child, not being a child who has been boarded-out with those parties by a local authority or voluntary organisation, who has been treated by both of those parties as a child of their family;*

'*the court*' (*except where the context otherwise requires*) *means the High Court, or, where a county court has jurisdiction by virtue of the Matrimonial Causes Act 1967, a county court;*

'*custody*', *in relation to a child, includes access to the child;*

'*education*' *includes training.*

    (2) *For the avoidance of doubt it is hereby declared that references in this Part of this Act to remarriage include references to a marriage which is by law void or voidable.*

    (3) *Any reference in this Part of this Act to any enactment is a reference to that enactment as amended by or under any subsequent enactment, including this Act.*

Note. Section 27 replaced by Matrimonial Causes Act 1973, s 52 (p 2559).

Transitional provisions, savings, etc

28. Transitional provisions and savings.   *Schedule 1 to this Act shall have effect for the purpose of the transition to the provisions of this Part of this Act from the law in force before the commencement of this Act and with respect to the application of certain provisions of this Part of this Act to orders made, or deemed to have been made, under the Matrimonial Causes Act 1965.*

29. Validation of certain void or voidable decrees.   *Any decree of divorce, nullity of marriage or judicial separation which, apart from this section, would be void or voidable on the ground only that the provisions of section 33 of the Matrimonial Causes Act 1965 (which restricts the making of decrees of dissolution or separation where children are affected) or of section 2 of the Matrimonial Proceedings (Children) Act 1958 (corresponding provision replaced by the said section 33) had not been complied with when the decree was made absolute or granted, as the case may be, shall be deemed always to have been valid unless—*

    (a) *before the commencement of this Act the court declared the decree to be void; or*

    (b) *in proceedings for the annulment of the decree pending at the said commencement the court declares the decree to be void.*

Note. See now Matrimonial Causes Act 1973, s 53, Sch 1 (p 2561).

PART II

MISCELLANEOUS PROVISIONS

Provisions relating to orders made by magistrates' courts in matrimonial proceedings

30. Order for maintenance of party to marriage made by magistrates' court to cease to have effect on remarriage of that party—(1) *At the end of section 7 of the Matrimonial Proceedings (Magistrates' Courts) Act 1960 there shall be added the following subsections—*

    '*(4) Where after the making by a magistrates' court of a matrimonial order consisting of or including a provision such as is mentioned in paragraph (b) or (c) of section 2(1) of this Act the marriage of the parties to the proceedings in which that order was made is dissolved or annulled but the order continues in force, then, subject to subsection (5) of this section, that order or, as the case may be, that provision thereof shall cease to have effect on the remarriage of the party in whose favour it was made, except in relation to any arrears due under it on the date of such remarriage and shall not be capable of being revived.*

    (5) *Subsection (4) of this section shall not apply where a party in whose favour such an order as is therein mentioned was made remarried before the commencement of the Matrimonial Proceedings and Property Act 1970.*

    (6) *For the avoidance of doubt it is hereby declared that references in this section to remarriage include references to a marriage which is by law void or voidable.*'

Note. Sub-s (1) repealed by Domestic Proceedings and Magistrates' Courts Act 1978, s 89(2), Sch 3, as from 1 February 1981.

(2) Subsections (4), (5) and (6) of section 7 of the Matrimonial Proceedings (Magistrates' Courts) Act 1960 [section 4(2) of the Domestic Proceedings and Magistrates' Courts Act 1978] shall apply in relation to an order consisting of or including a provision such as is mentioned in section 2(1)(b) or (c) [section 2(1)(a)] of that Act made by a magistrates' court and confirmed in accordance with section 3 of the Maintenance Orders (Facilities for Enforcement) Act 1920 (which enables a magistrates' court to make a maintenance order against a person resident in a part of Her Majesty's dominions outside the United Kingdom but provides that the order shall have no effect unless and until confirmed by a competent court in that part) as they apply in relation to such an order as is referred to in the said subsection (4) [as it applies in relation to an order made under section 2(1)(a) of the Domestic Proceedings and Magistrates' Courts Act 1978], but with the modification that for the reference to the making of such an order as is referred to in that subsection there shall be substituted a reference to the confirmation in accordance with the said section 3 of the order referred to in this subsection.

Note. Words from 'but with the modification' to the end of the subsection repealed by Maintenance Orders (Reciprocal Enforcement) Act 1972, s 42(3), as from 1 April 1974. Words in square brackets substituted for, respectively, 'Subsections (4) ... 1960', 'section 2(1)(b) or (c)' and 'as they apply ... subsection (4)' by Domestic Proceedings and Magistrates' Courts Act 1978, s 89(2), Sch 2, para 28, as from 1 February 1981.

31. Sums paid after cessation of order of magistrates' court by reason of remarriage may be ordered to be repaid in certain cases. *After section 13 of the Matrimonial Proceedings (Magistrates' Courts) Act 1960 there shall be inserted the following section—*

'*13A. Orders for repayment in certain cases of sum paid after cessation of order by reason of remarriage—*

(1) Where—

(a) an order to which this section applies or a provision thereof has ceased to have effect by reason of the remarriage of the person entitled to payments under the order, and

(b) the person liable to make payments under the order made payments in accordance with it in respect of a period after the date of such remarriage in the mistaken belief that the order or provision was still subsisting,

no proceedings in respect of a cause of action arising out of the circumstances mentioned in paragraphs (a) and (b) above shall be maintainable by the person so liable or his or her personal representatives against the person so entitled on her or his personal representatives, but on an application made under this section the court may exercise the powers conferred on it by the following subsection.

This section applies to an order in relation to which subsection (4) of section 7 of this Act, as amended by the Matrimonial Proceedings and Property Act 1970, applies.

(2) The court may order the respondent to an application made under this section to pay to the applicant a sum equal to the amount of the payments made in respect of the period mentioned in subsection (1)(b) of this section or, if it appears to the court that it would be unjust to make the order, it may either order the respondent to pay to the applicant such lesser sum as it thinks fit or dismiss the application.

(3) An application under this section may be made by the person to make payments under an order to which this section applies or his or her personal representatives and may be made against the person entitled to payments under the order or her or his personal representatives.

(4) An application under this section may be made in proceedings in the High Court or a county court for leave to enforce, or the enforcement of, the payment of arrears under an order to which this section applies, but except as aforesaid such an application shall be made to a county court, and accordingly references in this section to the court are references to the High Court or a county court, as the circumstances require.

(5) An order under this section for the payment of any sum may provide for the payment of that sum by instalments of such amount as may be specified in the order.

(6) The jurisdiction conferred on a county court by this section shall be exercisable by a county court notwithstanding that by reason of the amount claimed in an application under this section the jurisdiction would not but for this subsection be exercisable by a county court.

(7) Section 13(1) and (2) of this Act shall not apply to an order under this section.

(8) The clerk of a magistrates' court to whom any payments under an order to which this section applies are required to be made, and the collecting officer under an attachment of earnings order made to secure payments under the first mentioned order shall not be liable—

(a) *in the case of that clerk, for any act done by him in pursuance of the first mentioned order after the date on which that order or a provision thereof ceased to have effect by reason of the remarriage of the person entitled to payments under it, and*

(b) *in the case of the collecting officer, for any act done by him after that date in accordance with any enactment or rule of court specifying how payments made to him in compliance with the attachment of earnings order are to be dealt with,*

if, but only if, the act was one which he would have been under a duty to do had the first mentioned order or a provision thereof not ceased to have effect as aforesaid and the act was done before notice in writing of the fact that the person so entitled had remarried was given to him by or on behalf of that person, the person liable to make payments under the first mentioned order or the personal representatives of either of those persons.

(9) In this section "collecting office", in relation to an attachment of earnings order, means the officer of the High Court, the registrar of a county court or the clerk of a magistrates' court to whom a person makes payments in compliance with the order.'

Note. This section repealed by Domestic Proceedings and Magistrates' Courts Act 1978, s 89(2), Sch 3, as from 1 February 1981.

32. Restriction on enforcement in High Court or county court of certain orders of magistrates' courts. *At the end of section 13 of the Matrimonial Proceedings (Magistrates' Courts) Act 1960 there shall be added the following subsections:—*

'(5) A person shall not be entitled to enforce through the High Court or any county court the payment of any arrears due under an order made by virtue of this Act without the leave of that court if those arrears became due more than twelve months before proceedings to enforce the payment of them are begun.

(6) The court hearing an application for the grant of leave under subsection (5) of this section may refuse leave, or may grant leave subject to such restrictions and conditions (including conditions as to the allowing of time for payment or the making of payment by instalments) as that court thinks proper, or may remit the payment of such arrears or any part thereof.

(7) An application for the grant of leave under the said subsection (5) shall be made in such manner as may be prescribed by rules of court.'

Note. This section repealed by Domestic Proceedings and Magistrates' Courts Act 1978, s 89(2), Sch 3, as from 1 February 1981.

33. Minor corrections of Matrimonial Proceedings (Magistrates' Courts) Act 1960, s 7(3). *Section 7(3) of the Matrimonial Proceedings (Magistrates' Courts) Act 1960 (which provides that where after the making by a magistrates' court of a matrimonial or interim order proceedings between, and relating to the marriage of, the parties to the proceedings in which the order was made have been begun in the High Court, the High Court may direct that the order shall cease to have effect on a date specified by that court) shall be amended as follows—*

(a) *after the words 'the High Court', where first occurring, there shall be inserted the words 'or a county court';*

(b) *for the words 'the High Court', where next occurring, there shall be substituted the words 'the court in which the proceedings or any application made therein are or is pending'; and*

(c) *for the words 'the High Court may specify' there shall be substituted the words 'may be specified in the direction'.*

Note. This section repealed by Domestic Proceedings and Magistrates' Courts Act 1978, s 89(2), Sch 3, as from 1 February 1981.

Provisions relating to certain proceedings in county courts

34. Jurisdiction of, and appeal on question of fact from, county courts—*(1) The jurisdiction conferred on a county court by section 11 or section 22 of this Act or paragraph 5 of Schedule 1 thereto shall be exercisable by a county court notwithstanding that by reason of the amount claimed in an application made under either of those sections or the said paragraph 5, as the case may be, the jurisdiction would not but for this subsection be exercisable by a county court.*

(2) At the end of subsection (2) of section 109 of the County Courts Act 1959 (appeals on questions of fact) there shall be inserted the following paragraph:—

'*(g)   any proceedings on an application for an order under section 13A of the Matrimonial Proceedings (Magistrates' Courts) Act 1960, section 11 of the Matrimonial Proceedings and Property Act 1970, section 15 of that Act, section 22 thereof or paragraph 5 of Schedule 1 thereto.*'

Note. This section repealed by Matrimonial Causes Act 1973, s 54(1), Sch 3. See now ibid, ss 33(5), 38(4), Sch 2, para 4 (pp 2543, 2548, 2568).

Amendments of the Matrimonial Causes Act 1965

35. Amendment of reference to child in 1965, c 72, s 2.   *In section 2(2) of the Matrimonial Causes Act 1965 (which provides that in determining an application to allow the presentation of a petition for divorce within three years from the date of the marriage the judge shall have regard to the interests of any relevant child) for the words 'relevant child' there shall be substituted the words 'child of the family within the meaning of Part I of the Matrimonial Proceedings and Property Act 1970'.*

Note. This section repealed by Matrimonial Causes Act 1973, s 54(1), Sch 3, as was Matrimonial Causes Act 1965, s 2(2); see now Matrimonial Causes Act 1973, s 3(2) (p 2499).

36. Construction of references to remarriage in 1965, c 72, s 26.   *Section 26 of the Matrimonial Causes Act 1965 (which authorises the making of orders for maintenance out of a deceased's estate for a former spouse who has not remarried and provides that maintenance by way of periodical payments out of the estate shall terminate not later than his or her death or remarriage) shall have effect, and be deemed always to have had effect, as if after subsection (5) there were inserted the following subsection—*

'*(5A) For the avoidance of doubt it is hereby declared that references in this section to remarriage include references to a marriage which is by law void or voidable.*'

Note. This section repealed by Inheritance (Provision for Family and Dependants) Act 1975, s 26(2), (3), Schedule, as from 1 April 1976. For Matrimonial Causes Act 1965, s 26, see p 2253.

Provisions relating to property of married persons

37. Contributions by spouse in money or money's worth to the improvement of property.   *It is hereby declared that where a husband or wife contributes in money or money's worth to the improvement of real or personal property in which or in the proceeds of sale of which either or both of them has or have a beneficial interest, the husband or wife so contributing shall, if the contribution is of a substantial nature and subject to any agreement between them to the contrary express or implied, be treated as having then acquired by virtue of his or her contribution a share or an enlarged share, as the case may be, in that beneficial interest of such an extent as may have been then agreed or, in default of such agreement, as may seem in all the circumstances just to any court before which the question of the existence or extent of the beneficial interest of the husband or wife arises (whether in proceedings between them or in any other proceedings).*

38. Rights of occupation under Matrimonial Homes Act 1967 of spouse with equitable interest in home, etc.   *There shall be inserted in section 1 of the Matrimonial Homes Act 1967 (which protects against eviction from the home the spouse not entitled by virtue of any estate or interest, etc, to occupy it) a new subsection—*

'(9) It is hereby declared that a spouse who has an equitable interest in a dwelling house or in the proceeds of sale thereof, not being a spouse in whom is vested (whether solely or as a joint tenant) a legal estate in fee simple or a legal term of years absolute in the dwelling house, is to be treated for the purpose only of determining whether he or she has rights of occupation under this section as not being entitled to occupy the dwelling house by virtue of that interest'.

Note. This section repealed by Matrimonial Homes Act 1983, s 12, Sch 3, as from 9 August 1983. See now Act of 1983, s 1(11) (p 2935).

39. Extension of s 17 of Married Women's Property Act 1882. *An application may be made to the High Court or a county court under section 17 of the Married Women's Property Act 1882 (powers of the court in disputes between husband and wife about property) (including that section as extended by section 7 of the Matrimonial Causes (Property and Maintenance) Act 1958) by either of the parties to a marriage notwithstanding that their marriage has been dissolved or annulled so long as the application is made within the period of three years beginning with the date on which the marriage was dissolved or annulled; and references in the said section 17 and the said section 7 to a husband or a wife shall be construed accordingly.*

Note. For Married Women's Property Act 1882, s 17, see p 2032. For Matrimonial Causes (Property and Maintenance) Act 1958, s 7, see p 2202.

40. Judically separated spouses not entitled to claim in intestacy of each other—*(1) If while a decree of judicial separation is in force and the separation is continuing either of the parties whose marriage is the subject of the decree dies after the commencement of this Act intestate as respects all or any of his or her real or personal property, the property of that party as respects which he or she died intestate shall devolve as if the other party to the marriage had then been dead.*

(2) Notwithstanding anything in section 2(1)(a) of the Matrimonial Proceedings (Magistrates' Courts) Act 1960, a provision in force in an order made, or having effect as if made, under that section that a party to a marriage be no longer bound to cohabit with the other party to the marriage shall not have effect as a decree of judicial separation for the purposes of this section.

(3) Section 20(3) of the Matrimonial Causes Act 1965 (which provides that in a case of judicial separation certain property of the wife shall, if she dies intestate, devolve as if her husband had then been dead) shall cease to have effect except in relation to a case where the death occurred before the commencement of this Act.

Note. This section replaced Matrimonial Causes Act 1965, s 20(3) (p 2249); repealed by Matrimonial Causes Act 1973, s 54(1), Sch 3. See now ibid, s 18(2), (3) (p 2507).

Abolition of wife's agency of necessity

41. Abolition of wife's agency of necessity—(1) *Any rule of law or equity conferring on a wife authority, as agent of necessity of her husband, to pledge his credit or to borrow money on his credit is hereby abrogated.*

(2) Section 20(4) of the Matrimonial Causes Act 1965 (which provides that if in a case of judicial separation alimony has been ordered but has not been paid by the husband he shall be liable for necessaries supplied for the use of the wife) shall cease to have effect.

Note. This section repealed by Matrimonial Causes Act 1973, s 54(1), Sch 3.

PART III

SUPPLEMENTARY

42. Minor and consequential amendments and repeals—*(1) The enactments specified in Schedule 2 to this Act shall have effect subject to amendments specified in that Schedule.*

(2) Subject to the provisions of Schedule 1 to this Act, the enactments specified in Schedule 3 to this Act are hereby repealed to the extent specified in the third column of that Schedule.

Note. This section repealed by Matrimonial Causes Act 1973, s 54(1), Sch 3.

43. Citation, commencement and extent—*(1) This Act may be cited as the Matrimonial Proceedings and Property Act 1970.*

(2) The following provisions of this Act, that is to say, this section, sections 33, 36 to 41 and 42(2), so far as it repeals section 20(3) and (4) of the Matrimonial Causes Act 1965, shall come into force on 1 August 1970 and the other provisions of this Act shall come into force on 1 January 1971.

(3) Any reference in any provision of this Act, or in any enactment amended by a provision of this Act, to the commencement of this Act shall be construed as a reference to the date on which that provision comes into force.

(4) Subject to the provisions of section 12(2) of this Act, this Act does not extend to Scotland or Northern Ireland.

Note. Sub-s (2) and words preceding comma in sub-s (4) repealed by Matrimonial Causes Act 1973, s 54(1), Sch 3. Words preceding comma in sub-s (4) repealed again by Statute Law (Repeals) Act 1977.

SCHEDULES

SCHEDULE 1   Section 28

TRANSITIONAL PROVISIONS AND SAVINGS

General provisions

1. *Without prejudice to the provisions of section 38 of the Interpretation Act 1889 (which relates to the effect of repeals), nothing in any repeal made by this Act shall affect any application made, proceeding begun, order made or deemed to have been made, or direction given or deemed to have been given, under any enactment repealed by this Act, and subject to the provisions of this Act—*

    (a) every such application or proceeding which is pending at the commencement of this Act shall have effect as if made or begun under the corresponding provision of this Act; and

    (b) every such order or direction shall, if in force at the commencement of this Act, continue in force.

Provisions relating to proceedings for restitution of conjugal rights

2.—*(1) Sections 13, 15, 21, 30(1), 31, 34(1), (4) and (5) and 46(2) of the Matrimonial Causes Act 1965 (hereinafter referred to as 'the Act of 1965') shall continue to apply in relation to proceedings for restitution of conjugal rights begun before the commencement of this Act and in relation to decrees and orders made in such proceedings so begun.*

(2) In subsection (2) of the said section 21, as applied by sub-paragraph (1) above, the reference to such a direction as is mentioned in section 16(2)(a) of the Act of 1965 shall be construed as a reference to such a direction as is mentioned in section 25(a) of this Act.

(3) Notwithstanding the repeal by this Act of section 29 of the Act of 1965, rules of court made by virtue of that section, in so far as they apply to applications for relief under subsection (1) or (2) of the said section 21 or for relief under subsection (1)(c) of the said section 34, shall continue to have effect.

Variation, etc of certain orders made, etc, under the Act of 1965

3.—*(1) Subject to the provisions of this paragraph, section 9 of this Act shall apply to an order (other than an order for the payment of a lump sum) made or deemed to have been made under any of the following provisions of the Act of 1965, that is to say—*

    (a) section 15, except in its application to proceedings for restitution of conjugal rights,

    (b) section 16(1), that subsection as applied by section 16(3) and by section 19,

    (c) section 20(1) and section 17(2) as applied by section 20(2),

    (d) section 22,

    (e) section 34(1)(a) or (b), in so far as it relates to the maintenance of a child, and section 34(3),

as it applies to the orders mentioned in subsection (2) of the said section 9.

(2) Subject to the provisions of this paragraph, the court hearing an application for the variation of an order made or deemed to have been made under any of the provisions of the Act of 1965 mentioned in sub-paragraph (1) above shall have power to vary that order in any way in which it would have power to vary it had the order been made under the corresponding provision of Part I of this Act.

(3) The said section 9, as applied by sub-paragraph (1) above, shall have effect as if for subsections (4), (5) and (6) thereof there were substituted the following subsections—

'(4) The court shall not exercise the powers conferred by this section in relation to an order made or deemed to have been made under section 17(2) of the Act of 1965, as applied by section 20(2) thereof, in proceedings for judicial separation except on an application made in proceedings—

(a) for the rescission of the decree of judicial separation, or

(b) for the dissolution of the marriage of the parties to the proceedings in which that decree was made.

(5) The court hearing on application for the variation of any order made or deemed to have been made under section 16(1), 20(1), 22, 34(1)(a) or (b) or 34(3) of the Act of 1965 or under the said section 16(1) as applied by section 16(3) of that Act or by section 19 thereof shall not have power to vary that order by making an order for the payment of a lump sum or any such order as is mentioned in section 4 of this Act.

(6) Where the person liable to make payments under a secured periodical payments order made or deemed to have been made under the said section 16(1), 22 or 34(3) or under the said section 16(1), as applied by the said section 16(3) or by the said section 19, has died, an application under this section relating to that order may be made by the person entitled to payments under the order or by the personal representatives of the deceased person, but no such application shall, except with permission of the court, be made after the end of the period of six months from the date on which representation in regard to the estate of that person is first taken out.

In this subsection "secured periodical payments order" means an order requiring a person to secure an annual sum or periodical payments to some other person.'

(4) In relation to an order made before 16 December 1949 which, by virtue of paragraph 1 of Schedule 1 to the Act of 1965, is deemed to have been made under section 16(1)(a) of that Act or the said paragraph (a) as applied by section 19 of that Act, the powers conferred by this paragraph shall not be exercised unless the court is satisfied that the case is one of exceptional hardship which cannot be met by discharge, variation or suspension of any order made, or deemed as aforesaid to have been made, under section 16(1)(b) of that Act or that paragraph, as so applied, as the case may be.

(5) Section 9(1) and (3) of this Act shall apply to an order made or deemed to have been made under section 15 of the Act of 1965 in its application to proceedings for restitution of conjugal rights, under section 21 of that Act or under section 34(1)(c) thereof as they apply to the orders mentioned in subsection (2) of the said section 9, and in exercising the powers conferred by virtue of this paragraph the court shall have regard to all the circumstances of the case, including any change in any of the matters to which the court was required to have regard when making the order to which the application relates.

4. Section 10 of this Act shall apply in relation to the enforcement of the payment of arrears due under an order made, or deemed to have been made, under any of the following provisions of the Act of 1965, that is to say, sections 15, 16, 20, 21, 22 and 34 and section 16, as applied by section 19, where proceedings to enforce through the High Court or any county court the payment of such arrears are begun after the commencement of this Act as it applies in relation to the enforcement of the payment of arrears due under any such order as is mentioned in that section.

5. An application may be made under this paragraph in relation to an order to which this paragraph applies in the like circumstances as those in which an application may be made under section 11 of this Act, and the provisions of that section shall apply to such an application and to an order made on such an application as they apply to an application made under that section and to an order made on the last mentioned application.

This paragraph applies to an order made, or deemed to have been made, under any of the following provisions of the Act of 1965, that is to say, sections 15, 16(1)(a) and (b), 20(1), 21 and 22, section 16(1)(a) and (b) as applied by section 16(3) and by section 19, section 34(1), in so far as it applies to maintenance, and section 34(3).

6. *Section 18(6) of this Act shall apply in relation to an order for the custody or education of a child made or deemed to have been made under section 34 of the Act of 1965, and in relation to an order for the custody of a child made or deemed to have been made under section 35 of that Act, as it applies in relation to an order made under the said section 18.*

Provisions with respect to certain maintenance agreements

7. *Where the party chargeable under a maintenance agreement within the meaning of section 13 of this Act died before 17 August 1957, then—*

    (a) *subsection (1) of that section shall not apply to the agreement unless there remained undistributed at that date assets of that party's estate (apart from any property in which he had only a life interest) representing not less than four-fifths of the value of that estate for probate after providing for the discharge of the funeral, testamentary and administrative expenses, debts and liabilities payable thereout (other than any liability arising by virtue of that subsection); and*

    (b) *nothing in that subsection shall render liable to recovery, or impose any liability upon the personal representatives of that party in respect of, any part of that party's estate which had been distributed before that date.*

8. *No right or liability shall attach by virtue of section 13(1) of this Act in respect of any sum payable under a maintenance agreement within the meaning of that section in respect of a period before 17 August 1957.*

Avoidance of transactions intended to defeat claims for relief under the Act of 1965

9.—*(1) Section 16 of this Act shall apply in relation to proceedings for relief under any of the following provisions of the Act of 1965, that is to say, sections 16, 17(2), 20(1), 22, 24, 31, 34(1)(a) or (b), 34(3) and 35, section 16(1) as applied by section 19 and section 17(2) as applied by section 20(2), where the proceedings are pending at the commencement of this Act, and in relation to proceedings for relief under section 21 or 34(1)(c) of the Act of 1965, as it applies in relation to proceedings for relief under any of the provisions of this Act specified in section 16(4) of this Act.*

    (2) Without prejudice to sub-paragraph (1) above, the said section 16 shall apply in a case where an order has been obtained under any of the provisions of the Act of 1965 mentioned in sub-paragraph (1) above as it applies in a case where an order has been obtained under any of the provisions of this Act specified in the said section 16(4).

Protection, custody, etc, of children

10. *Section 33 of the Act of 1965 shall continue to apply, and section 17 of this Act shall not apply, in relation to any proceedings for divorce or nullity of marriage in which a decree nisi has been granted but not made absolute before the commencement of this Act.*

11. *Where in any such proceedings the court has made an order by virtue of section 34(1) of the Act of 1965 in relation to a child, the court shall have the like power to make a further order from time to time in relation to that child under section 3 or 18 of this Act as it has where it makes an order in relation to a child under subsection (1) of the said section 3 or 18, but nothing in the foregoing provision shall be taken as affecting the power of the court in any such proceedings to make an order under either of those sections in relation to any other child, being a child of the family.*

12. *Where the court has made an order under section 22 of the Act of 1965 the court shall have the like power to make orders under section 19 of this Act with respect to the custody of any child of the family as it has where it makes an order under section 6 of this Act.*

Note. Sch 1 repealed by Matrimonial Causes Act 1973, s 54(1), Sch 3.

SCHEDULE 2   Section 42

MINOR AND CONSEQUENTIAL AMENDMENTS

1—*(1) In section 26(4) of the Matrimonial Causes Act 1965 (matters to which court is to have regard on application for maintenance from estate of deceased spouse), after sub-paragraph (ii) there shall be inserted the following sub-paragraph—*

'*(iii)   where the survivor is a former wife or a former husband of the deceased, for an order under section 2 or 4 of the Matrimonial Proceedings and Property Act 1970*'.

(2) In subsection (1) of section 36 of the said Act of 1965 (power to commit children to care of local authority), and in subsection (1) of section 37 of that Act (power to provide for supervision of children), after the words 'this Act' there shall be inserted the words 'or of the Matrimonial Proceedings and Property Act 1970'.

(3) In subsection (5) of the said section 37 after the words 'this Act' there shall be inserted the words 'or under the Matrimonial Proceedings and Property Act 1970'.

2.—*(1) Section 2 of the Matrimonial Causes Act 1967 (jurisdiction of divorce county court to exercise powers exercisable under certain provisions of the Matrimonial Causes Act 1965 relating to ancillary relief and the protection of children) shall be amended as follows—*

(a)   in subsection (1), after the words 'Matrimonial Causes Act 1965' there shall be inserted the words 'or Part I of the Matrimonial Proceedings and Property Act 1970' and for the words from 'section 22' onwards there shall be substituted the words 'section 6 or section 14 of the said Act of 1970'; and

(b)   for subsection (3) there shall be substituted the following subsection—

'*(3)   A divorce county court shall not by virtue of this section have jurisdiction to exercise any power under—*

(a)   section 26 or 27 of the Matrimonial Causes Act 1965; or

(b)   section 10, 11, 15 or 22 of the Matrimonial Proceedings and Property Act 1970 or paragraph 5 of Schedule 1 thereto;

but without prejudice to the exercise by virtue of section 7 of the Family Provision Act 1966 of any power exercisable by a county court under the said section 26 or 27 or to the exercise by virtue of any such provision of the said Act of 1970 as is mentioned in paragraph (b) of this subsection of any power exercisable by a county court under that provision'; and

(c)   in subsection (4), for the words from 'section 24' onwards there shall be substituted the words 'section 14 of the Matrimonial Proceedings and Property Act 1970'.

(2) In section 7(1) of the said Act of 1967 (which specifies the authority having power to make rules of court for the purposes of certain enactments) the word 'or' at the end of paragraph (b) shall be omitted and after paragraph (c) there shall be inserted the words 'or

(d)   without prejudice to the generality of paragraph (c) of this subsection, Part I of the Matrimonial Proceedings and Property Act 1970, and Schedule 1 thereto, except proceedings in the county court under section 10, 11, 15 or 22 or paragraph 5 of Schedule 1'.

3. *At the end of paragraph (b) of subsection (1) of section 2 of the Domestic and Appellate Proceedings (Restriction of Publicity) Act 1968 (restriction of publicity for certain proceedings) there shall be inserted the word 'and' and the following paragraph shall be added at the end of that subsection—*

'*(c)   proceedings under section 6 of the Matrimonial Proceedings and Property Act 1970 (which relates to proceedings by a wife against her husband, or by a husband against his wife, for financial provision) and any proceedings for the discharge or variation of an order made under that section or for the temporary suspension of any provision of any such order or the revival of the operation of any provision so suspended'.*

4. *In section 8(3) of the Divorce Reform Act 1969 (grant of decree of judicial separation) for the words 'section 33 of the Matrimonial Causes Act 1965' there shall be substituted the words 'section 17 of the Matrimonial Proceedings and Property Act 1970'.*

5. *At the end of Schedule 8 to the Administration of Justice Act 1970 (maintenance order to which Part II of that Act applies) there shall be inserted the following paragraph:—*

'*10.   An order for periodical or other payments made under Part I of the Matrimonial Proceedings and Property Act 1970.*'

Note. Sch 2 repealed by Matrimonial Causes Act 1973, s 54(1), Sch 3.

SCHEDULE 3

REPEALS

Chapter	Short Title	Extent of Repeal
1965 c 72.	*The Matrimonial Causes Act 1965.*	*Section 13.* *Sections 15 to 19.* *In section 20, subsections (1) and (2), subsection (3) except in relation to a case where the death occurred before the commencement of this Act and subsection (4).* *Sections 21 to 25 except section 25(4) and (5) as applied by section 28(2) of that Act.* *Sections 29 to 35.* *Section 46(2) except so far as it applies for the interpretation of section 41(3) of that Act.* *In Schedule 1, paragraphs 5, 6, 7, 9, 10 and 11.*
1966 c 35.	*The Family Provision Act 1966.*	*In section 5(3), the words 'section 25(1) and in'.*
1968 c 36.	*The Maintenance Orders Act 1968.*	*In the Schedule, the entry relating to the Matrimonial Causes Act 1965.*
1969 c 46.	*The Family Law Reform Act 1969.*	*Section 5(3).*
1969 c 55.	*The Divorce Reform Act 1969.*	*In Schedule 1, paragraphs 4, 5, 6, 7, 9 and 10.*

Note. Sch 3 repealed by Matrimonial Causes Act 1973, s 54(1), Sch 3.

COURTS ACT 1971

(1971 c 23)

An Act to make further provision as respects the Supreme Court and county courts, judges and juries, to establish a Crown Court as part of the Supreme Court to try indictments and exercise certain other jurisdiction, to abolish courts of assize and certain other courts and to deal with their jurisdiction and other consequential matters, and to amend in other respects the law about courts and court proceedings. [12 May 1971]

*   *   *   *   *

PART III

JUDGES

16. Appointment of Circuit judges—(1) Her Majesty may from time to time appoint as Circuit judges, to serve in the Crown Court and county courts and to carry out such other judicial functions as may be conferred on them under this or any other enactment, such qualified persons as may be recommended to Her by the Lord Chancellor.

(2) The maximum number of Circuit judges shall be such as may be determined from time to time by the Lord Chancellor with the concurrence of the Minister for the Civil Service.

(3) No person shall be qualified to be appointed a Circuit judge *unless he is a barrister of at least ten years' standing or a Recorder who has held that office for at least five* [*three*] *years* [unless—

(a) he has a 10 year Crown Court or 10 year county court qualification within the meaning of section 71 of the Courts and Legal Services Act 1990;

(b) he is a Recorder; or

(c) he has held as a full-time appointment for at least 3 years one of the offices listed in Part 1A of Schedule 2.]

Note. Word 'three' substituted for 'five' by Administration of Justice Act 1977, s 12. Words in second pair of square brackets substituted for words in italics by Courts and Legal Services Act 1990, s 71(2), Sch 10, para 31(1), as from 1 January 1991.

(4) Before recommending any person to Her Majesty for appointment as a Circuit judge, the Lord Chancellor shall take steps to satisfy himself that that person's health is satisfactory.

(5) The provisions of Part I of Schedule 2 to this Act shall have effect with respect to the appointment as Circuit judges of the holders of certain judicial offices, and the supplementary provisions in Part II of that Schedule shall have effect.

*   *   *   *   *

20. Judges of county courts—(*1*) *Every Circuit judge shall, by virtue of his office, be capable of sitting as a judge for any county court district in England and Wales, and the Lord Chancellor shall assign one or more Circuit judges to each district and may from time to time vary the assignment of Circuit judges among the districts.*

(*2*) *Subject to any directions given by or on behalf of the Lord Chancellor, in any case where more than one Circuit judge is assigned to a district under subsection (1) above, any function conferred by or under the County Courts Act 1959 on the judge for a district may be exercised by any of the Circuit judges for the time being assigned to that district.*

(*3*) *The following, that is—*

every judge of the Court of Appeal,
every judge of the High Court,
every Recorder,

shall, by virtue of his office, be capable of sitting as a judge for any county court district in England and Wales and if he consents to do so, shall sit as such a judge at such times and on such occasions as the Lord Chancellor considers desirable.

(*4*) *Notwithstanding that he is not for the time being assigned to a particular district, a Circuit judge—*

(*a*) *shall sit as a judge of that district at such times and on such occasions as the Lord Chancellor may direct; and*

(*b*) *may sit as a judge of that district in any case where it appears to him that the judge of that district is not, or none of the judges of that district is, available to deal with the case.*

Note. Sub-ss (1)–(4) repealed by County Courts Act 1984, s 148(3), Sch 4, as from 1 August 1984. See now County Courts Act 1984, s 5.

(*5*) *So much of Part I of the County Courts Act 1959 as makes special provision in relation to county court districts within the Duchy of Lancaster shall cease to have effect.*

(*6*) *On the appointed day all appointments of temporary and deputy judges of county courts shall terminate and the provisions of the County Courts Act 1959 relating to such temporary and deputy judges shall cease to have effect.*

Note. Sub-ss (5), (6) repealed by the Statute Law (Repeals) Act 2004, as from 22 July 2004.

(7) Nothing in this Act shall affect the operation, in relation to the superannuation and other benefits payable to or in respect of persons who ceased to be judges of county courts before the day appointed for the coming into force of section 16(5) of this Act, of any enactment repealed or amended by this Act.

* * * * *

[24. Deputy Circuit judges and assistant Recorders—(1) If it appears to the Lord Chancellor it is expedient as a temporary measure to make an appointment under this section in order to facilitate the disposal of business in the Crown Court or a county court or official referees' business in the High Court, he may—

    (a) appoint to be a deputy Circuit judge, during such period or on such occasions as he thinks fit, any person who has held office as a judge of the Court of Appeal or of the High Court or as a Circuit judge; or

    (b) appoint to be an assistant Recorder, during such period or on such occasions as he thinks fit, *any barrister or solicitor of at least ten years' standing* [any person who has a 10 year Crown Court or 10 year county court qualification, within the meaning of section 71 of the Courts and Legal Services Act 1990].

Note. Words in square brackets substituted for words in italics by Courts and Legal Services Act 1990, s 71(2), Sch 10, para 32(2), as from 1 January 1991.

[(1A) No appointment of a person under subsection (1) above shall be such as to extend—

    (a) in the case of appointment as a deputy Circuit judge, beyond the day on which he attains the age of seventy-five; or

    (b) in the case of appointment as an assistant Recorder, beyond the day on which he attains the age of seventy;

but paragraph (b) above is subject to section 26(4) to (6) of the Judicial Pensions and Retirement Act 1993 (Lord Chancellor's power to authorise continuance in office up to the age of 75).]

Note. Sub-s (1A) inserted by Judicial Pensions and Retirement Act 1993, s 26(10), Sch 6, para 9(2), as from 31 March 1995, subject to transitional provisions in s 27 of, and Sch 7 to, the 1993 Act.

(2) Except as provided by subsection (3) below, during the period or on the occasions for which a deputy Circuit judge or assistant Recorder is appointed under this section he shall be treated for all purposes as, and accordingly may perform any of the functions of, a Circuit judge or a Recorder, as the case may be.

(3) A deputy Circuit judge appointed under this section shall not be treated as a Circuit judge for the purpose of any provision made by or under any enactment and relating to the appointment, retirement, removal or disqualification of Circuit judges, the tenure of office and oaths to be taken by such judges, or the remuneration, allowances or pensions of such judges; and section 21 of this Act shall not apply to an assistant Recorder appointed under this section.

(4) Notwithstanding the expiry of any period for which a person is appointed under this section a deputy Circuit judge or an assistant Recorder, he may attend at the Crown Court or a county court or, as regards any [in the case of a deputy Circuit judge, as regards] official referees' business, at the High Court for the purpose of continuing to deal with, giving judgment in, or dealing with any ancillary matter relating to, any case which may have been begun before him when sitting as a deputy Circuit judge or an assistant Recorder, and for that purpose and for the purpose of any proceedings subsequent thereon he shall be treated as a Circuit judge or a Recorder, as the case may be.

Note. Words in square brackets substituted for words 'as regards any' by Administration of Justice Act 1982, s 59(3), as from 1 January 1983. Sub-s (4) repealed by Judicial Pensions and Retirement Act 1993, s 31, Sch 9, as from 31 March 1995.

(5) There shall be paid out of money provided by Parliament to deputy Circuit judges and assistant Recorders appointed under this section such remuneration and allowances as the Lord Chancellor may, with the approval of the Minister for the Civil Service, determine.]

Note. Section 24 in square brackets substituted by Supreme Court Act 1981, s 146, as from 1 January 1982.

* * * * *

PART VI

MISCELLANEOUS AND SUPPLEMENTAL

* * * * *

Matrimonial jurisdiction and patent appeals

45. Matrimonial jurisdiction—(*1*) *This section has effect as respects any proceedings for the exercise of a power under—*
  (*a*) *Part II or Part III of the Matrimonial Causes Act 1965;*
  (*b*) *Part I of the Matrimonial Proceedings and Property Act 1970;*
 [(*a*) *section 26 to 28A of the Matrimonial Causes Act 1965;*
  (*b*) *Part II or Part III of the Matrimonial Causes Act 1973;*]
  (*c*) *section 17 of the Married Women's Property Act 1882.*

Note. Paras (a), (b) (in square brackets) substituted for original paras (a), (b) (above them) by Matrimonial Causes Act 1973, s 54(1), Sch 2, para 12, and the substituted para (a) repealed by Inheritance (Provision for Family and Dependants) Act 1975, s 26(2), Schedule.

Whole section repealed by Matrimonial and Family Proceedings Act 1984, s 46(3), Sch 3, as from 28 April 1986. See now Matrimonial and Family Proceedings Act 1984, Part V.

(*2*) *Rules of court may provide for the transfer or retransfer from a county court to the High Court, or from the High Court to a divorce county court, of any such proceedings.*

(*3*) *The power conferred by subsection (2) above and the power conferred by section 1(3)(b) of the Matrimonial Causes Act 1967 (transfer of matrimonial causes) shall be construed as including power to provide for the removal of proceedings at the direction of the High Court.*

Note. As to repeal of section, see second paragraph of note to sub-s (1) above.

(*4*) *A court shall have jurisdiction to entertain any proceedings transferred to the court by virtue of rules made in pursuance of subsection (2) above.*

(*5*) *Rules of court may, as respects any of the jurisdiction conferred by the enactments referred to in paragraphs (a), (b) and (c) of subsection (1) above—*
  (*a*) *provide for its exercise in the principal probate registry,*
  (*b*) *make any such provision as section 4 of the Matrimonial Causes Act 1967 (assimilation of proceedings in the principal probate registry to proceedings in divorce county courts) makes, or authorises rules of court to make, as respects any jurisdiction.*

Note. As to repeal of section, see second paragraph of note to sub-s (1) above.

(*6*) *Where, in pursuance of rules of court made under [section 50 of the Matrimonial Causes Act 1973 for the purposes of] this section or the said Act of 1967, any proceedings are removed into the High Court section 76 of the County Courts Act 1959 (costs) shall apply as if the proceedings had been transferred.*

Note. Words in square brackets inserted by Matrimonial Causes Act 1973, s 54(1), Sch 2, para 12. As to repeal of section, see second paragraph of note to sub-s (1) above.

(*7*) *This section is without prejudice to any power of making rules of court conferred by the said Act of 1967, and in section 7(1)(b) of that Act (matrimonial causes rules) the reference to that Act shall include a reference to this section.*

Note. Sub-s (7) repealed by Matrimonial Causes Act 1973, s 54(1), Sch 2, para 12, Sch 3. As to repeal of section, see second paragraph of note to sub-s (1) above.

(*8*) *Any reference in this section to section 17 of the Married Women's Property Act 1882 is a reference to that Act as originally enacted, or as extended by section 7 of the Matrimonial Causes (Property and Maintenance) Act 1958 or by section 2 of the Law Reform (Miscellaneous Provisions) Act 1970 or by section 39 of the Matrimonial Proceedings and Property Act 1970.*

Note. As to repeal of section, see second paragraph of note to sub-s (1) above. For Married Women's Property Act 1882, s 17, see p 2032.

For Matrimonial Causes (Property and Maintenance) Act 1958, s 7, see p 2202.

*   *   *   *   *

59. Short title, commencement and extent—(1) This Act may be cited as the Courts Act 1971.

(2) *This Act shall come into force on such date as the Lord Chancellor may by order in a statutory instrument appoint, and different dates may be appointed for different provisions of this Act, or for different purposes.*

Note. Sub-s (2) repealed by the Statute Law (Repeals) Act 2004, as from 22 July 2004.

Certain provisions of the Act, including ss 20(3) (so far as it relates to judges of the Court of Appeal and High Court) and 59 above, came into force 1 October 1971; the remainder of the Act came into force 1 January 1972: see SI 1971 No 1151.

ATTACHMENT OF EARNINGS ACT 1971

(1971 c 32)

ARRANGEMENT OF SECTIONS

An Act to consolidate the enactments relating to the attachment of earnings as a
means of enforcing the discharge of monetary obligations.   [12 May 1971]

Cases in which attachment is available

1. Courts with power to attach earnings—(1) The High Court may make an attachment of earnings order to secure payments under a High Court maintenance order.

(2) A county court may make an attachment of earnings order to secure—

(a) payments under a High Court or a county court maintenance order;

(b) the payment of a judgment debt, other than a debt of less than £5 or such
other sum as may be prescribed by county court rules; or

(c) payments under an administration order.

(3) A magistrates' court may make an attachment of earnings order to secure—

(a) payments under a magistrates' court maintenance order;

(b) the payment of any sum adjudged to be paid by a conviction or treated (by
any enactment relating to the collection and enforcement of fines, costs,
compensation or forfeited recognisances) as so adjudged to be paid; or

(c) the payment of any sum required to be paid by a *legal aid contribution order*
[order under section 17(2) of the Access to Justice Act 1999].

Note. Words in square brackets substituted for words in italics by the Access to Justice Act
1999, s 24, Sch 4, para 8, as from 2 April 2001.

(4) The following provisions of this Act apply, except where otherwise stated, to
attachment of earnings orders made, or to be made, by any court.

(5) Any power conferred by this Act to make an attachment of earnings order
includes a power to make such an order to secure the discharge of liabilities arising
before the coming into force of this Act.

Note. Section modified, in respect of a person aged 18 or over liable to pay a sum to which
the Courts Act 2003, Sch 5 applies: see the Fines Collection Regulations 2004, SI 2004/176,
regs 2, 3, 4(a), (b).

2. Principal definitions.   In this Act—
   (a) 'maintenance order' means any order specified in Schedule 1 to this Act and includes such an order which has been discharged if any arrears are recoverable thereunder;
   (b) 'High Court maintenance order', 'county court maintenance order' and 'magistrates' court maintenance order' mean respectively a maintenance order enforceable by the High Court, a county court and a magistrates' court;
   (c) 'judgment debt' means a sum payable under—
      (i) a judgment or order enforceable by a court in England and Wales (not being a magistrates' court);
      (ii) an order of a magistrates' court for the payment of money recoverable summarily as a civil debt; or
      (iii) an order of any court which is enforceable as if it were for the payment of money so recoverable,
   but does not include any sum payable under a maintenance order or an administration order;
   (d) 'the relevant adjudication', in relation to any payment secured or to be secured by an attachment of earnings order, means the conviction, judgment, order or other adjudication from which there arises the liability to make the payment; and
   (e) 'the debtor', in relation to an attachment of earnings order, or to proceedings in which a court has power to make an attachment of earnings order, or to proceedings arising out of such an order, means the person by whom payment is required by the relevant adjudication to be made.

3. Application for order and conditions of court's power to make it—(1) The following persons may apply for an attachment of earnings order—
   (a) the person to whom payment under the relevant adjudication is required to be made (whether directly or through an officer of any court);
   (b) where the relevant adjudication is an administration order, any one of the creditors scheduled to the order;
   (c) without prejudice to paragraph (a) above, where the application is to a magistrates' court for an order to secure maintenance payments, and there is in force an order under *section 52(1) of the Magistrates' Courts Act 1952* [*section 59(1)* [section 59] of the Magistrates' Courts Act 1980], or section 19(2) of the Maintenance Orders Act 1950, that those payments be made to *the clerk of a magistrates' court, the clerk of that court* [*a justices' chief executive, that justices' chief executive*] [the designated officer for a magistrates' court, that officer];
   (d) in the following cases the debtor—
      (i) where the application is to a magistrates' court; or
      (ii) where the application is to the High Court or a county court for an order to secure maintenance payments.

Note. Words in outer pair of square brackets substituted for words 'section 52(1) of the Magistrates' Courts Act 1952' by Magistrates' Courts Act 1980, s 154, Sch 7, para 97, as from 6 July 1981. Words 'section 59' substituted for 'section 59(1)' by Maintenance Enforcement Act 1991, s 11(1), Sch 2, para 1(1), as from 1 April 1992.

Words 'a justices' chief executive, that justices' chief executive' in square brackets substituted for words 'the clerk of a magistrates' court, the clerk of that court' by the Access to Justice Act 1999, s 90, Sch 13, paras 64, 65, as from 1 April 2001. Words 'the designated officer for a magistrates' court, that officer' in square brackets substituted for words 'a justices' chief executive, that justices' chief executive' by the Courts Act 2003, s 109(1), Sch 8, para 141, as from a day to be appointed.

   (*2*) *An application for an attachment of earnings order to secure maintenance payments shall not be made, except by the debtor, unless at least fifteen days have elapsed since the making of the related maintenance order.*

Note. Sub-s (2) repealed by Maintenance Enforcement Act 1991, s 11, Sch 2, para 1(2), Sch 3, as from 1 April 1991.

(3) [Subject to subsection (3A) below] for an attachment of earnings order to be made on the application of any person other than the debtor it must appear to the court that the debtor has failed to make one or more payments required by the relevant adjudication.

Note. Words in square brackets inserted by Maintenance Enforcement Act 1991, s 11(1), Sch 2, para 1(3), as from 1 April 1991.

[(3A) Subsection (3) above shall not apply where the relevant adjudication is a maintenance order.]

Note. Sub-s (3A) inserted by Maintenance Enforcement Act 1991, s 11(1), Sch 2, para 1(4), as from 1 April 1992.

[(3B) Where—
(a) a magistrates' court imposes a fine on a person in respect of an offence, and
(b) that person consents to an order being made under this subsection,
the court may at the time it imposes the fine, and without the need for an application, make an attachment of earnings order to secure the payment of the fine.

(3C) Where—
(a) a magistrates' court makes in the case of a person convicted of an offence an order under *section 35 of the Powers of Criminal Courts Act 1973* [section 130 of the Powers of Criminal Courts (Sentencing) Act 2000] (a compensation order) requiring him to pay compensation or to make other payments, and
(b) that person consents to an order being made under this subsection,
the court may at the time it makes the compensation order, and without the need for an application, make an attachment of earnings order to secure the payment of the compensation or other payments.]

Note. Sub-ss (3B), (3C) inserted by Criminal Procedure and Investigations Act 1996, s 53(1), as from 4 July 1996, in relation to offences committed on or after 1 October 1996.

Words in square brackets in sub-s (3C) substituted for words in italics by the Powers of Criminal Courts (Sentencing) Act 2000, s 165(1), Sch 9, para 44, as from 25 August 2000.

(4) Where proceedings are brought—
(a) in the High Court or a county court for the enforcement of a maintenance order by committal under section 5 of the Debtors Act 1869; or
(b) in a magistrates' court for the enforcement of a maintenance order under *section 64 of the Magistrates' Courts Act 1952* [section 76 of the Magistrates' Courts Act 1980] (distress or committal).
then, *subject to subsection (5) below,* the court may make an attachment of earnings order to secure payments under the maintenance order, instead of dealing with the case under section 5 of the said Act of 1869 or, as the case may be, *section 64 of the said Act of 1952* [section 76 of the said Act of 1980].

Note. Words in square brackets substituted for preceding words in italics by Magistrates' Courts Act 1980, s 154, Sch 7, para 97, as from 6 July 1981. Words 'subject to subsection (5) below' repealed by Maintenance Enforcement Act 1991, s 11, Sch 2, para 1(5), Sch 3, as from 1 April 1991.

(5) The court shall not, except on the application of the debtor, make an attachment of earnings order to secure payments under a maintenance order if it appears to it that the debtor's failure to make payments in accordance with the maintenance order is not due to his wilful refusal or culpable neglect.

Note. Sub-s (5) repealed by Maintenance Enforcement Act 1991, s 11, Sch 2, para 1(6), Sch 3, as from 1 April 1992.

(6) Where proceedings are brought in a county court for an order of committal under section 5 of the Debtors Act 1869 in respect of a judgment debt for any of the taxes, contributions [premiums] or liabilities specified in Schedule 2 to this

Act, the court may, in any circumstances in which it has power to make such an order, make instead an attachment of earnings order to secure the payment of the judgment debt.

Note. Word 'premiums' inserted by Social Security Act 1973, ss 100, 101, Sch 27, para 88, as from a day to be appointed.

(7) A county court shall not make an attachment of earnings order to secure the payment of a judgment debt if there is in force an order or warrant for the debtor's committal, under section 5 of the Debtors Act 1869, in respect of that debt; but in any such case the court may discharge the order or warrant with a view to making an attachment of earnings order instead.

Note. Section modified, in respect of a person aged 18 or over liable to pay a sum to which the Courts Act 2003, Sch 5 applies: see the Fines Collection Regulations 2004, SI 2004/176, regs 2, 3, 4(c).

Administration orders in the county court

4. Extension of power to make administration order—(1) Where, on an application to a county court for an attachment of earnings order to secure the payment of a judgment debt, it appears to the court that the debtor also has other debts, the court—

    (a)　shall consider whether the case may be one in which all the debtor's liabilities should be dealt with together and that for that purpose *an order should be made for the administration of his estate* [an administration order should be made]; and

    (b)　if of opinion that it may be such a case, shall have power (whether or not it make the attachment of earnings order applied for), with a view to making an administration order, to order the debtor to furnish to the court a list of all his creditors and the amounts which he owes to them respectively.

Note. Words in square brackets substituted for words in italics by Insolvency Act 1976, s 13(2), as from 20 December 1976. See also, in respect of the continued effect of the amendment to sub-s (1)(a) above, the Statute Law (Repeals) Act 2004, Sch 2, para 10.

(2) If, on receipt of the list referred to in subsection (1)(b) above, it appears to the court that the debtor's whole indebtedness amounts to not more than the amount *for the time being specified in section 148(1)(b) of the County Courts Act 1959* [which for the time being is the county court limit for the purposes of section 112 of the County Courts Act 1984] (limit of total indebtedness governing county court's power to make administration order on application of debtor), the court may make such an order in respect of the debtor's estate.

This subsection is subject to section 20(3) of the Administration of Justice Act 1965 (which requires that, before an administration order is made, notice is to be given to all the creditors and thereafter restricts the right of any creditor to institute bankruptcy proceedings).

[(2A) Subsection (2) above is subject to section 112(3) and (4) of the County Courts Act 1984 (which require that, before an administration order is made, notice is to be given to all the creditors and thereafter restricts the right of any creditor to institute bankruptcy proceedings).]

Note. Words in square brackets in first paragraph substituted for words in italics by County Courts Act 1984, s 148(1), Sch 2, Part V, para 40(a), as from 1 August 1984.

New sub-s (2A) substituted for the second paragraph by County Courts Act 1984, s 148(1), Sch 2, Part V, para 40(b), as from 1 August 1984.

(3) *Where under subsection (1) above a county court orders a person to furnish to it a list of all his creditors, the making of the order shall, for the purposes of the Bankruptcy Act 1914, be an act of bankruptcy by him.*

Note. Sub-s (3) repealed by Insolvency Act 1976, ss 13(1), 14(4), Sch 3, as from 20 December 1976.

(4) Nothing in this section is to be taken as prejudicing any right of a debtor to apply, under *section 148 of the County Courts Act 1959* [section 112 of the County Courts Act 1984], for an administration order.

Note. Words in square brackets substituted for words in italics by County Courts Act 1984, s 148(1), Sch 2, Part V, para 40(c), as from 1 August 1984.

5. Attachment of earnings to secure payments under administration order—
(1) Where a county court makes an administration order in respect of a debtor's estate, it may also make an attachment of earnings order to secure the payments required by the administration order.

(2) At any time when an administration order is in force a county court may (with or without an application) make an attachment of earnings order to secure the payments required by the administration order, if it appears to the court that the debtor has failed to make any such payment.

(3) The power of a county court under this section to make an attachment of earnings order to secure the payments required by an administration order shall, where the debtor is already subject to an attachment of earnings order to secure the payment of a judgment debt, include power to direct that the last-mentioned order shall take effect (with or without variation under section 9 of this Act) as an order to secure the payments required by the administration order.

Consequences of attachment order

6. Effect and contents of order—(1) An attachment of earnings order shall be an order directed to a person who appears to the court to have the debtor in his employment and shall operate as an instruction to that person—

(a) to make periodical deductions from the debtor's earnings in accordance with Part I of Schedule 3 to this Act; and

(b) at such times as the order may require, or as the court may allow, to pay the amounts deducted to the collecting officer of the court, as specified in the order.

(2) For the purposes of this Act, the relationship of employer and employee shall be treated as subsisting between two persons if one of them, as a principal and not as a servant or agent, pays to the other any sums defined as earnings by section 24 of this Act.

(3) An attachment of earnings order shall contain prescribed particulars enabling the debtor to be identified by the employer.

(4) Except where it is made to secure maintenance payments, the order shall specify the whole amount payable under the relevant adjudication (or so much of that amount as remains unpaid), including any relevant costs.

(5) The order shall specify—

(a) the normal deduction rate, that is to say, the rate (expressed as a sum of money per week, month or other period) at which the court thinks it reasonable for the debtor's earnings to be applied to meeting his liability under the relevant adjudication; and

(b) the protected earnings rate, that is to say the rate (so expressed) below which, having regard to the debtor's resources and needs, the court thinks it reasonable that the earnings actually paid to him should not be reduced.

(6) In the case of an order made to secure payments under a maintenance order (not being an order for the payment of a lump sum), the normal deduction rate—

(a) shall be determined after taking account of any right or liability of the debtor to deduct income tax when making the payments; and

(b) shall not exceed the rate which appears to the court necessary for the purpose of—

(i) securing payment of the sums falling due from time to time under the maintenance order, and

        (ii) securing payment within a reasonable period of any sums already due and unpaid under the maintenance order.

(7) For the purposes of an attachment of earnings order, the collecting officer of the court shall be (subject to later variation of the order under section 9 of this Act)—

    (a) in the case of an order made by the High Court, either—

        (i) the proper officer of the High Court, or

        (ii) the *registrar* [appropriate officer] of such county court as the order may specify;

    (b) in the case of an order made by a county court, the *registrar* [appropriate officer] of that court; and

    (c) in the case of an order made by a magistrates' court, the *clerk either of that court or of* [*justices' chief executive for that court or for*] [designated officer for that court or for] another magistrates' court specified in the order.

[(8) In subsection (7) above 'appropriate officer' means an officer designated by the Lord Chancellor.]

Note. Words in square brackets in sub-s (7)(a)(ii) substituted for words in italics, words 'justices' chief executive for that court or for' in square brackets substituted for words 'clerk either of that court or of' by the Access to Justice Act 1999, s 90, Sch 13, paras 64, 66, as from 2 April 2001. Words 'designated officer for that court or for' in square brackets substituted for words 'justices' chief executive for that court or for' by the Courts Act 2003, s 109(1), Sch 8, para 142, as from a day to be appointed, and sub-s (8) added by Administration of Justice Act 1977, s 19(5), as from 3 July 1978.

[(9) The Lord Chancellor may by order make such provision as he considers expedient (including transitional provision) with a view to providing for the payment of amounts deducted under attachment of earnings orders to be made to such officers as may be designated by the order rather than to collecting officers of the court.

(10) Any such order may make such amendments in this Act, in relation to functions exercised by or in relation to collecting officers of the court as he considers expedient in consequence of the provision made by virtue of subsection (9) above.

(11) The power to make such an order shall be exercisable by statutory instrument.

(12) Any such statutory instrument shall be subject to annulment in pursuance of a resolution of either House of Parliament.]

Note. Sub-ss (9)–(12) added by Courts and Legal Services Act 1990, s 125(2), Sch 17, para 5, as from a day to be appointed.

Section modified, in respect of a person aged 18 or over liable to pay a sum to which the Courts Act 2003, Sch 5 applies: see the Fines Collection Regulations 2004, SI 2004/176, regs 2, 3, 4(d)–(f), 12(a).

7. Compliance with order by employer—(1) Where an attachment of earnings order has been made, the employer shall, if he has been served with the order, comply with it; but he shall be under no liability for non-compliance before seven days have elapsed since the service.

(2) Where a person is served with an attachment of earnings order directed to him and he has not the debtor in his employment, or the debtor subsequently ceases to be in his employment, he shall (in either case), within ten days from the date of service or, as the case may be, the cesser, give notice of that fact to the court.

(3) Part II of Schedule 3 to this Act shall have effect with respect to the priority to be accorded as between two or more attachment of earnings orders directed to a person in respect of the same debtor.

(4) On any occasion when the employer makes, in compliance with the order, a deduction from the debtor's earnings—

    (a) he shall be entitled to deduct, in addition, five new pence, or such other sum as may be prescribed by order made by the Lord Chancellor, towards his clerical and administrative costs; and

    (b) he shall give to the debtor a statement in writing of the total amount of the deduction.

(5) An order of the Lord Chancellor under subsection (4)(a) above—

(a) may prescribe different sums in relation to different classes of cases;

(b) may be varied or revoked by a subsequent order made under that paragraph; and

(c) shall be made by statutory instrument subject to annulment by resolution of either House of Parliament.

Note. The employer's deduction under sub-s (4)(a) increased from 1 June 1980 to 50 pence: SI 1980 No 558, and further increased to £1.00 by Attachment of Earnings (Employer's Deduction) Order 1991, SI 1991 No 356, art 2, as from 1 April 1991.

Section modified, in respect of a person aged 18 or over liable to pay a sum to which the Courts Act 2003, Sch 5 applies: see the Fines Collection Regulations 2004, SI 2004/176, regs 2, 3, 4(d).

8. Interrelation with alternative remedies open to creditor—(1) Where an attachment of earnings order has been made to secure maintenance payments, no order or warrant of commitment shall be issued in consequence of any proceedings for the enforcement of the related maintenance order begun before the making of the attachment of earnings order.

(2) Where a county court has made an attachment of earnings order to secure the payment of a judgment debt—

(a) no order or warrant of commitment shall be issued in consequence of any proceedings for the enforcement of the debt begun before the making of the attachment of earnings order; and

(b) so long as the order is in force, no execution for the recovery of the debt shall issue against any property of the debtor without the leave of the county court.

(3) An attachment of earnings order made to secure maintenance payments shall cease to have effect upon the making of an order of commitment or the issue of a warrant of commitment for the enforcement of the related maintenance order, or upon the exercise for that purpose of the power conferred on a magistrates' court by *section 65(2) of the Magistrates' Courts Act 1952* [section 77(2) of the Magistrates' Courts Act 1980] to postpone the issue of such a warrant.

Note. Words in square brackets substituted for words in italics by Magistrates' Courts Act 1980, s 154, Sch 7, para 98, as from 6 July 1981.

(4) An attachment of earnings order made to secure the payment of a judgment debt shall cease to have effect on the making of an order of commitment or the issue of a warrant of commitment for the enforcement of the debt.

(5) An attachment of earnings order made to secure any payment specified in section 1(3)(b) or (c) of this Act shall cease to have effect on the issue of a warrant committing the debtor to prison for default in making that payment.

Note. Section modified, in respect of a person aged 18 or over liable to pay a sum to which the Courts Act 2003, Sch 5 applies: see the Fines Collection Regulations 2004, SI 2004/176, regs 2, 3, 4(g).

Subsequent proceedings

9. Variation, lapse and discharge of orders—(1) The court may make an order discharging or varying an attachment of earnings order.

(2) Where an order is varied, the employer shall, if he has been served with notice of the variation, comply with the order as varied; but he shall be under no liability for non-compliance before seven days have elapsed since the service.

(3) Rules of court may make provision—

(a) as to the circumstances in which an attachment of earnings order may be varied or discharged by the court of its own motion;

(b) in the case of an attachment of earnings order made by a magistrates' court, for enabling a single justice, on an application made by the debtor on the ground of a material change in his resources and needs since the order was made or last varied, to vary the order for a period of not more than four weeks by an increase of the protected earnings rate.

(4) Where an attachment of earnings order has been made and the person to whom it is directed ceases to have the debtor in his employment, the order shall lapse (except as respects deduction from earnings paid after the cesser and payment to the collecting officer of amounts deducted at any time) and be of no effect unless and until the court again directs it to a person (whether the same as before or another) who appears to the court to have the debtor in his employment.

(5) The lapse of an order under subsection (4) above shall not prevent its being treated as remaining in force for other purposes.

Note. Section modified, in respect of a person aged 18 or over liable to pay a sum to which the Courts Act 2003, Sch 5 applies: see the Fines Collection Regulations 2004, SI 2004/176, regs 2, 3, 4(d),(h).

10. Normal deduction rate to be reduced in certain cases—(1) The following provisions shall have effect, in the case of an attachment of earnings order made to secure maintenance payments, where it appears to the collecting officer of the court that—

    (a) the aggregate of the payments made for the purposes of the related maintenance order by the debtor (whether under the attachment of earnings order or otherwise) exceeds the aggregate of the payments required up to that time by the maintenance order; and

    (b) the normal deduction rate specified by the attachment of earnings order (or, where two or more such orders are in force in relation to the maintenance order, the aggregate of the normal deduction rates specified by those orders) exceeds the rate of payments required by the maintenance order; and

    (c) no proceedings for the variation or discharge of the attachment of earnings order are pending.

(2) In the case of an order made by the High Court or a county court, the collecting officer shall give the prescribed notice to the person to whom he is required to pay sums received under the attachment of earnings order, and to the debtor; and the court shall make the appropriate variation order, unless the debtor requests it to discharge the attachment of earnings order, or to vary it in some other way, and the court thinks fit to comply with the request.

(3) In the case of an order made by a magistrates' court, the collecting officer shall apply to the court for the appropriate variation order; and the court shall grant the application unless the debtor appears at the hearing and requests the court to discharge the attachment of earnings order, or to vary it in some other way, and the court thinks fit to comply with the request.

(4) In this section, 'the appropriate variation order' means an order varying the attachment of earnings order in question by reducing the normal deduction rate specified thereby so as to secure that that rate (or, in the case mentioned in subsection (1)(b) above, the aggregate of the rates therein mentioned)—

    (a) is the same as the rate of payments required by the maintenance order; or

    (b) is such lower rate as the court thinks fit having regard to the amount of the excess mentioned in subsection (1)(a).

11. Attachment order in respect of maintenance payments to cease to have effect on the occurrence of certain events—(1) An attachment of earnings order made to secure maintenance payments shall cease to have effect—

    (a) upon the grant of an application for registration of the related maintenance order under section 2 of the Maintenance Orders Act 1958 (which provides for the registration in a magistrates' court of a High Court or county court maintenance order, and for registration in the High Court of a magistrates' court maintenance order);

(b) where the related maintenance order is registered under Part I of the said Act of 1958, upon the giving of notice with respect thereto under section 5 of that Act (notice with view to cancellation of registration);

(c) subject to subsection (3) below, upon the discharge of the related maintenance order while it is not registered under Part I of the said Act of 1958;

(d) upon the related maintenance order ceasing to be registered in a court in England or Wales, or becoming registered in a court in Scotland or Northern Ireland, under Part II of the Maintenance Orders Act 1950.

(2) Subsection (1)(a) above shall have effect, in the case of an application for registration under section 2(1) of the said Act of 1958, notwithstanding that the grant of the application may subsequently become void under subsection (2) of that section.

(3) Where the related maintenance order is discharged as mentioned in subsection (1)(c) above and it appears to the court discharging the order that arrears thereunder will remain to be recovered after the discharge, that court may, if it thinks fit, direct that subsection (1) shall not apply.

12. Termination of employer's liability to make deductions—(1) Where an attachment of earnings order ceases to have effect under section 8 or 11 of this Act, the proper officer of the prescribed court shall give notice of the cesser to the person to whom the order was directed.

(2) Where, in the case of an attachment of earnings order made otherwise than to secure maintenance payments, the whole amount payable under the relevant adjudication has been paid, and also any relevant costs, the court shall give notice to the employer that no further compliance with the order is required.

(3) Where an attachment of earnings order—

(a) ceases to have effect under section 8 or 11 of this Act; or

(b) is discharged under section 9,

the person to whom the order has been directed shall be under no liability in consequence of his treating the order as still in force at any time before the expiration of seven days from the date on which the notice required by subsection (1) above or, as the case may be, a copy of the discharging order is served on him.

Note. Section modified, in respect of a person aged 18 or over liable to pay a sum to which the Courts Act 2003, Sch 5 applies: see the Fines Collection Regulations 2004, SI 2004/176, regs 2, 3, 4(d).

Administrative provisions

13. Application of sums received by collecting officer—(1) Subject to subsection (3) below, the collecting officer to whom a person makes payments in compliance with an attachment of earnings order shall, after deducting such court fees, if any, in respect of proceedings for or arising out of the order, as are deductible from those payments, deal with the sums paid in the same way as he would if they had been paid by the debtor to satisfy the relevant adjudication.

(2) Any sums paid to the collecting officer under an attachment of earnings order made to secure maintenance payments shall, when paid to the person entitled to receive those payments, be deemed to be payments made by the debtor (with such deductions, if any, in respect of income tax as the debtor is entitled or required to make) so as to discharge—

(a) first, any sums for the time being due and unpaid under the related maintenance order (a sum due at an earlier date being discharged before a sum due at a later date); and

(b) secondly, any costs incurred in proceedings relating to the related maintenance order which were payable by the debtor when the attachment of earnings order was made or last varied.

(3) Where a county court makes an attachment of earnings order to secure the payment of a judgment debt and also, under section 4(1) of this Act, orders the debtor to furnish to the court a list of all his creditors, sums paid to the collecting officer in compliance with the attachment of earnings order shall not be dealt with by him as mentioned in subsection (1) above, but shall be retained by him pending the decision of the court whether or not to make an administration order and shall then be dealt with by him as the court may direct.

14. Power of court to obtain statements of earnings etc—(1) Where in any proceedings a court has power to make an attachment of earnings order, it may—
  (a) order the debtor to give to the court, within a specified period, a statement signed by him of—
     (i) the name and address of any person by whom earnings are paid to him;
     (ii) specified particulars as to his earnings and anticipated earnings, and as to his resources and needs; and
     (iii) specified particulars for the purpose of enabling the debtor to be identified by any employer of his;
  (b) order any person appearing to the court to have the debtor in his employment to give to the court, within a specified period, a statement signed by him or on his behalf of specified particulars of the debtor's earnings and anticipated earnings.
  (2) Where an attachment of earnings order has been made, the court may at any time thereafter while the order is in force *make such an order as is described in subsection (1)(a) or (b) above.*
  [(a) make such an order as is described in subsection (1)(a) or (b) above; and
  (b) order the debtor to attend before it on a day and at a time specified in the order to give the information described in subsection (1)(a) above.]

Note. Words in square brackets substituted for words in italics by Administration of Justice Act 1982, s 53(1), as from 1 January 1983.

  (3) In the case of an application to a magistrates' court for an attachment of earnings order, or for the variation or discharge of such an order, the power to make an order under subsection (1) or (2) above shall be exercisable also, before the hearing of the application, by a single justice.
  (4) Without prejudice to subsections (1) to (3) above, rules of court may provide that where notice of an application for an attachment of earnings order is served on the debtor, it shall include a requirement that he shall give to the court, within such period and in such manner as may be prescribed, a statement in writing of the matters specified in subsection (1)(a) above and of any other prescribed matters which are, or may be, relevant under section 6 of this Act to the determination of the normal deduction rate and the protected earnings rate to be specified in any order made on the application.
  (5) In any proceedings in which a court has power to make an attachment of earnings order, and in any proceedings for the making, variation or discharge of such an order, a document purporting to be a statement given to the court in compliance with an order under subsection (1)(a) or (b) above, or with any such requirement of a notice of application for an attachment of earnings order as is mentioned in subsection (4) above, shall, in the absence of proof to the contrary, be deemed to be a statement so given and shall be evidence of the facts stated therein.

Note. Section modified, in respect of a person aged 18 or over liable to pay a sum to which the Courts Act 2003, Sch 5 applies: see the Fines Collection Regulations 2004, SI 2004/176, regs 2, 3, 4(i),(j).

15. Obligation of debtor and his employers to notify changes of employment and earnings.   While an attachment of earnings order is in force—

(a) the debtor shall from time to time notify the court in writing of every occasion on which he leaves any employment, or becomes employed or re-employed, not later (in each case) than seven days from the date on which he did so;

(b) the debtor shall, on any occasion when he becomes employed or re-employed, include in his notification under paragraph (a) above particulars of his earnings and anticipated earnings from the relevant employment; and

(c) any person who becomes the debtor's employer and knows that the order is in force and by what court it was made shall, within seven days of his becoming the debtor's employer or of acquiring that knowledge (whichever is the later) notify that court in writing that he is the debtor's employer, and include in his notification a statement of the debtor's earnings and anticipated earnings.

Note. Section modified, in respect of a person aged 18 or over liable to pay a sum to which the Courts Act 2003, Sch 5 applies: see the Fines Collection Regulations 2004, SI 2004/176, regs 2, 3, 4(k).

16. Power of court to determine whether particular payments are earnings—
(1) Where an attachment of earnings order is in force, the court shall, on the application of a person specified in subsection (2) below, determine whether payments to the debtor of a particular class or description specified by the application are earnings for the purposes of the order; and the employer shall be entitled to give effect to any determination for the time being in force under this section.

(2) The persons referred to in subsection (1) above are—

(a) the employer;

(b) the debtor;

(c) the person to whom payment under the relevant adjudication is required to be made (whether directly or through an officer of any court); and

(d) without prejudice to paragraph (c) above, where the application is in respect of an attachment of earnings order made to secure payments under a magistrates' court maintenance order, the collecting officer.

(3) Where an application under this section is made by the employer, he shall not incur any liability for non-compliance with the order as respects any payments of the class or description specified by the application which are made by him to the debtor while the application, or any appeal in consequence thereof, is pending; but this subsection shall not, unless the court otherwise orders, apply as respects such payments if the employer subsequently withdraws the application or, as the case may be, abandons the appeal.

17. Consolidated attachment orders—(1) The powers of a county court under sections 1 and 3 of this Act shall include power to make an attachment of earnings order to secure the payment of any number of judgment debts; and the powers of a magistrates' court under those sections shall include power to make an attachment of earnings order to secure the discharge of any number of such liabilities as are specified in section 1(3).

(2) An attachment of earnings order made by virtue of this section shall be known as a consolidated attachment order.

(3) The power to make a consolidated attachment order shall be exercised subject to and in accordance with rules of court; and rules made for the purposes of this section may provide—

(a) for the transfer from one court to another—

(i) of an attachment of earnings order, or any proceedings for or arising out of such an order; and

(ii) of functions relating to the enforcement of any liability capable of being secured by attachment of earnings;

(b) for enabling a court to which any order, proceedings or functions have been transferred under the rules to vary or discharge an attachment of earnings order made by another court and to replace it (if the court thinks fit) with a consolidated attachment order;

(c) for the cases in which any power exercisable under this section or the rules may be exercised by a court of its own motion or on the application of a prescribed person;

(d) for requiring the *clerk or registrar* [officer] of a court who receives payments made to him in compliance with an attachment of earnings order, instead of complying with section 13 of this Act, to deal with them as directed by the court or the rules; and

(e) for modifying or excluding provisions of this Act or *Part III of the Magistrates' Courts Act 1952* [Part III of the Magistrates' Courts Act 1980] but only so far as may be necessary or expedient for securing conformity with the operation of rules made by virtue of paragraphs (a) to (d) of this subsection.

Note. Word 'officer' in square brackets in sub-s (3)(d) substituted for words in italics by the Access to Justice Act 1999, s 90, Sch 13, paras 64, 67, as from 1 April 2001. Words 'Part III of the Magistrates' Courts Act 1980' in square brackets in sub-s (3)(e) substituted for words in italics by Magistrates' Courts Act 1980, s 154, Sch 7, para 99, as from 6 July 1981.

Section modified, in respect of a person aged 18 or over liable to pay a sum to which the Courts Act 2003, Sch 5 applies: see the Fines Collection Regulations 2004, SI 2004/176, regs 2, 3, 4(l).

Special provisions with respect to magistrates' courts

18. Certain action not to be taken by collecting officer except on request—

(1) *The clerk of a magistrates' court* [*A justices' chief executive*] [A designated officer for a magistrates' court] who is entitled to receive payments under a maintenance order for transmission to another person shall not—

(a) apply for an attachment of earnings order to secure payments under the maintenance order; or

(b) except as provided by section 10(3) of this Act, apply for an order discharging or varying such an attachment of earnings order; or

(c) apply for a determination under section 16 of this Act,

unless he is requested in writing to do so by a person entitled to receive the payments through him.

Note. Words 'A justices' chief executive' in square brackets substituted for words 'The clerk of a magistrates' court' by the Access to Justice Act 1999, s 90, Sch 13, paras 64, 68, as from 1 April 2001. Words 'A designated officer for a magistrates' court' in square brackets substituted for words 'A justices' chief executive' by the Courts Act 2003, s 109(1), Sch 8, para 143(1), (2), as from a day to be appointed.

(2) Where *the clerk* [*a justices' chief executive*] [the designated officer for a magistrates' court] is so requested—

(a) he shall comply with the request unless it appears to him unreasonable in the circumstances to do so; and

(b) the person by whom the request was made shall have the same liabilities for all the costs properly incurred in or about any proceedings taken in pursuance of the request as if the proceedings had been taken by that person.

(3) For the purposes of subsection (2)(b) above, any application made by *the clerk* [*a justices' chief executive*] [the designated officer for a magistrates' court] as required by section 10(3) of this Act shall be deemed to be made on the request of the person in whose favour the attachment of earnings order in question was made.

Note. In sub-ss (2), (3) words 'a justices' chief executive' in square brackets substituted for words 'the clerk' by the Access to Justice Act 1999, s 90, Sch 13, paras 64, 68, as from 1 April 2001. In sub-ss (2), (3) words 'the designated officer for a magistrates' court' in square brackets substituted for words 'a justices' chief executive' by the Courts Act 2003, s 109(1), Sch 8, para 143(1), (3), as from a day to be appointed.

19. Procedure on applications—(1) Subject to rules of court made by virtue of the following subsection, an application to a magistrates' court for an attachment of earnings order, or an order discharging or varying an attachment of earnings order, shall be made by complaint.

(2) Rules of court may make provision excluding subsection (1) in the case of such an application as is referred to in section 9(3)(b) of this Act.

(3) An application to a magistrates' court for a determination under section 16 of this Act shall be made by complaint.

(4) For the purposes of *section 43 of the Magistrates' Courts Act 1952* [section 51 of the Magistrates' Courts Act 1980] (which provides for the issue of a summons directed to the person against whom an order may be made in pursuance of a complaint)—

(a) the power to make an order in pursuance of a complaint by the debtor for an attachment of earnings order, or the discharge or variation of such an order, shall be deemed to be a power to make an order against the person to whom payment under the relevant adjudication is required to be made (whether directly or through an officer of any court); and

(b) the power to make an attachment of earnings order, or an order discharging or varying an attachment of earnings order, in pursuance of a complaint by any other person (including a complaint in proceedings to which section 3(4)(b) of this Act applies) shall be deemed to be a power to make an order against the debtor.

(5) A complaint for an attachment of earnings order may be heard not-withstanding that it was not made within the six months allowed by *section 104 of the Magistrates' Courts Act 1952* [section 127(1) of the Magistrates' Courts Act 1980].

Note. In sub-ss (4), (5) words in square brackets substituted for words in italics by Magistrates' Courts Act 1980, s 154, Sch 7, para 100, as from 6 July 1981.

20. Jurisdiction in respect of persons residing outside England and Wales—(1) It is hereby declared that a magistrates' court has jurisdiction to hear a complaint by or against a person residing outside England and Wales for the discharge or variation of an attachment of earnings order made by a magistrates' court to secure maintenance payments; and where such a complaint is made, the following provisions shall have effect.

(2) If the person resides in Scotland or Northern Ireland, section 15 of the Maintenance Orders Act 1950 (which relates to the service of process on persons residing in those countries) shall have effect in relation to the complaint as it has effect in relation to the proceedings therein mentioned.

(3) Subject to the following subsection, if the person resides outside the United Kingdom and does not appear at the time and place appointed for the hearing of the complaint, the court may, if it thinks it reasonable in all the circumstances to do so, proceed to hear and determine the complaint at the time and place appointed for the hearing, or for any adjourned hearing, in like manner as if the person had then appeared.

(4) Subsection (3) above shall apply only if it is proved to the satisfaction of the court, on oath or in such other manner as may be prescribed, that the complainant has taken such steps as may be prescribed to give to the said person notice of the complaint and of the time and place appointed for the hearing of it.

21. Costs on application under s 16—(1) On making a determination under section 16 of this Act, a magistrates' court may in its discretion make such order as it thinks just and reasonable for payment by any of the persons mentioned in subsection (2) of that section of the whole or any part of the costs of the determination (but subject to section 18(2)(b) of this Act).

(2) Costs ordered to be paid under this section shall—

(a) in the case of costs to be paid by the debtor to the person in whose favour the attachment of earnings order in question was made, be deemed—

    (i) if the attachment of earnings order was made to secure maintenance payments, to be a sum due under the related maintenance order, and

    (ii) otherwise, to be a sum due to the *clerk of* [*justices' chief executive* for] *the* [designated officer for the magistrates] court; and

(b) in any other case, be enforceable as a civil debt.

Note. Words 'the justices' chief executive for' in square brackets substituted for words 'clerk of' by the Access to Justice Act 1999, s 90, Sch 13, paras 64, 69, as from 1 April 2001. Words 'designated officer for the magistrates' in square brackets substituted for words 'justices' chief executive for the' by the Courts Act 2003, s 109(1), Sch 8, para 144, as from a day to be appointed.

Miscellaneous provisions

22. Persons employed under the Crown—(1) The fact that an attachment of earnings order is made at the suit of the Crown shall not prevent its operation at any time when the debtor is in the employment of the Crown.

(2) Where a debtor is in the employment of the Crown and an attachment of earnings order is made in respect of him, then for the purposes of this Act—

(a) the chief officer for the time being of the department, office or other body in which the debtor is employed shall be treated as having the debtor in his employment (any transfer of the debtor from one department, office or body to another being treated as a change of employment); and

(b) any earnings paid by the Crown or a Minister of the Crown, or out of the public revenue of the United Kingdom, shall be treated as paid by the said chief officer.

(3) If any question arises, in proceedings for or arising out of an attachment of earnings order, as to what department, office or other body is concerned for the purposes of this section, or as to who for those purposes is the chief officer thereof, the question shall be referred to and determined by the Minister for the Civil Service; but that Minister shall not be under any obligation to consider a reference under this subsection unless it is made by the court.

(4) A document purporting to set out a determination of the said Minister under subsection (3) above and to be signed by an official of the *Civil Service Department* [*Management and Personnel Office*] [*Office of the said Minister*] [Office of Public Service *and Science*] shall, in any such proceedings as are mentioned in that subsection, be admissible in evidence and be deemed to contain an accurate statement of such a determination unless the contrary is shown.

Note. Words in first pair of square brackets substituted for preceding words in italics by Transfer of Functions (Minister for the Civil Service and Treasury) Order 1981, SI 1981 No 1670. Words in second pair of square brackets substituted for words in italics by Transfer of Functions (Minister for the Civil Service and Treasury) Order 1987, SI 1987 No 2039, as from 25 December 1987. Words in third pair of square brackets substituted for words in italics in second pair of square brackets by Transfer of Functions (Science) Order 1992, SI 1992 No 1296, Schedule, para 4. Words 'and Science' in italics repealed by Transfer of Functions (Science) Order 1995, SI 1995 No 2985, art 5(1), Schedule, para 3, as from 1 January 1996.

(5) This Act shall have effect notwithstanding any enactment passed before 29 May 1970 and preventing or avoiding the attachment or diversion of sums due to a person in respect of service under the Crown, whether by way of remuneration, pension or otherwise.

23. Enforcement provisions—(1) If, after being served with notice of an application to a county court for an attachment of earnings order or for the variation of such an order [or with an order made under section 14(2)(b) above], the debtor fails to attend on the day and at the time specified for any hearing of the application [or specified in the order], the court may adjourn the hearing and order him to attend at a specified time on another day; and if the debtor—

(a) fails to attend at that time on that day; or

(b) attends, but refuses to be sworn or give evidence,

he may be ordered by the judge to be imprisoned for not more than fourteen days.

Note. Words in square brackets inserted by Administration of Justice Act 1982, s 53(2), as from 1 January 1983.

[(1A) In any case where the judge has power to make an order of imprisonment under subsection (1) for failure to attend, he may, in lieu of or in addition to making that order, order the debtor to be arrested and brought before the court either forthwith or at such time as the judge may direct.]

Note. Sub-s (1A) inserted by Contempt of Court Act 1981, s 14, Sch 2, Part III, para 6, as from 27 August 1981.

(2) Subject to this section, a person commits an offence if—

(a) being required by section 7(1) or 9(2) of this Act to comply with an attachment of earnings order, he fails to do so; or

(b) being required by section 7(2) of this Act to give a notice for the purposes of that subsection, he fails to give it, or fails to give it within the time required by that subsection; or

(c) he fails to comply with an order under section 14(1) of this Act or with any such requirement of a notice of application for an attachment of earnings order as is mentioned in section 14(4), or fails (in either case) to comply within the time required by the order or notice; or

(d) he fails to comply with section 15 of this Act; or

(e) he gives a notice for the purposes of section 7(2) of this Act, or a notification for the purposes of section 15, which he knows to be false in a material particular, or recklessly gives such a notice or notification which is false in a material particular; or

(f) in purported compliance with section 7(2) or 15 of this Act, or with an order under section 14(1), or with any such requirement of a notice of application for an attachment of earnings order as is mentioned in section 14(4), he makes any statement which he knows to be false in a material particular, or recklessly makes any statement which is false in a material particular.

(3) Where a person commits an offence under subsection (2) above in relation to proceedings in, or to an attachment of earnings order made by the High Court or a county court, he shall be liable on summary conviction to a fine of not more than £25 [level 2 on the standard scale] or he may be ordered by a judge of the High Court or the county court judge (as the case may be) to pay a fine of not more than £25 [£100] [£250] or, in the case of an offence specified in subsection (4) below, to be imprisoned for not more than fourteen days; and where a person commits an offence under subsection (2) otherwise than as mentioned above in this subsection, he shall be liable on summary conviction to a fine of not more than £25 [level 2 on the standard scale].

Note. The maximum fines of £25 on summary conviction are increased to the current amount at level 2 on the standard scale by virtue of the Criminal Justice Act 1982, ss 38(1), (6), 46(1); as to the standard scale, see s 37 of the 1982 Act.

The maximum fine which a person may be ordered by a judge to pay under sub-s (3) was increased to £50 by ibid, s 39(3), Sch 4. This fine has been further increased to £100 as from 1 May 1984 by Order (SI 1984 No 447) made under Magistrates' Courts Act 1980, s 143, as amended by s 48 of the Act of 1982: see ibid, s 143(2)(f) and Sch 6A as inserted by s 48(1)(b)(iii), Sch 5. The maximum fine was further increased to £250 by Criminal Justice Act 1991, s 17(3), Sch 4, Part I, as from 1 October 1992.

For the purposes of the Criminal Justice Act 1982, s 9(1) (detention of persons aged 17 to 20 for default or contempt), the power of a court to order a person to be imprisoned under this section is taken to be a power to commit him to prison: see ibid, s 9(2).

(4) The offences referred to above in the case of which a judge may impose imprisonment are—

(a) an offence under subsection (2)(c) or (d), if committed by the debtor; and

(b) an offence under subsection (2)(e) or (f), whether committed by the debtor or any other person.

(5) It shall be a defence—

(a) for a person charged with an offence under subsection (2)(a) above to prove that he took all reasonable steps to comply with the attachment of earnings order in question;

(b) for a person charged with an offence under subsection (2)(b) to prove that he did not know, and could not reasonably be expected to know, that the debtor was not in his employment, or (as the case may be) had ceased to be so, and that he gave the required notice as soon as reasonably practicable after the fact came to his knowledge.

(6) Where a person is convicted or dealt with for an offence under subsection (2)(a), the court may order him to pay, to whoever is the collecting officer of the court for the purposes of the attachment of earnings order in question, any sums deducted by that person from the debtor's earnings and not already paid to the collecting officer.

(7) Where under this section a person is ordered by a judge of the High Court or a county court to be imprisoned, the judge may at any time revoke the order and, if the person is already in custody, order his discharge.

(8) Any fine imposed by a judge of the High Court under subsection (3) above and any sums ordered by the High Court to be paid under subsection (6) above shall be recoverable in the same way as a fine imposed by that court in the exercise of its jurisdiction to punish for contempt of court; *section 179 of the County Courts Act 1959* [section 129 of the County Courts Act 1984] (enforcement of fines) shall apply to payment of a fine imposed by a county court judge under subsection (3) and of any sums ordered by a county court judge to be paid under subsection (6); and any sum ordered by a magistrates' court to be paid under subsection (6) shall be recoverable as a sum adjudged to be paid on a conviction by that court.

Note. Words in square brackets substituted for words in italics by County Courts Act 1984, s 148(1), Sch 2, Part V, para 41, as from 1 August 1984.

(9) For the purposes of section 13 of the Administration of Justice Act 1960 (appeal in cases of contempt of court), subsection (3) above shall be treated as an enactment enabling the High Court or a county court to deal with an offence under subsection (2) above as if it were contempt of court.

(10) In this section references to proceedings in a court are to proceedings in which that court has power to make an attachment of earnings order or has made such an order.

[(11) A district judge, assistant district judge or deputy district judge shall have the same powers under this section as a judge of a county court.]

Note. Sub-s (11) added by Courts and Legal Services Act 1990, s 125(2), Sch 7, para 6, as from 1 July 1991.

24. Meaning of 'earnings'—(1) For the purposes of this Act, but subject to the following subsection, 'earnings' are any sums payable to a person—

(a) by way of wages or salary (including any fees, bonus, commission, overtime pay or other emoluments payable in addition to wages or salary or payable under a contract of service);

(b) by way of pension (including an annuity in respect of past services, whether or not rendered to the person paying the annuity, and including periodical payments by way of compensation for the loss, abolition or relinquishment, or diminution in the emoluments, of any office or employment).

[(c) by way of statutory sick pay].

Note. Para (c) added by Social Security Act 1985, s 21, Sch 4, para 1, as from 16 September 1985.

(2) The following shall not be treated as earnings—

(a) sums payable by any public department of the Government of Northern Ireland or of a territory outside the United Kingdom;

(b) pay or allowances payable to the debtor as a member of Her Majesty's forces [other than pay or allowances payable by his employer to him as a special member of a reserve force (within the meaning of the Reserve Forces Act 1996)];

(ba) a tax credit (within the meaning of the Tax Credits Act 2002);

(c) pension, allowances or benefit payable under any *of the enactments specified in Schedule 4 to this Act (being enactments relating to social security)* [enactment relating to social security];

(d) pension or allowances payable in respect of disablement or disability;

(e) [except in relation to a maintenance order] wages payable to a person as a seaman, other than wages payable to him as a seaman of a fishing boat.

[(f) guaranteed minimum pension within the meaning of the *Social Security Pensions Act 1975* [Pension Schemes Act 1993].]

Note. Words in square brackets in para (b) added by SI 1998/3086, reg 6(1), as from 1 January 1999. Para (ba) added by the Tax Credits Act 2002, s 47, Sch 3, para 1, as from 6 April 2003. Words in square brackets in para (c) substituted for words in italics by Social Security Act 1986, s 86(1), Sch 10, Part VI, para 102, as from 26 June 1987. Words in square brackets in para (e) added by Merchant Shipping Act 1979, s 39(1), as from 1 August 1979. Para (f) added by Social Security Pensions Act 1975, s 65(1), Sch 4, para 15 and words in square brackets in para (f) substituted for words in italics by Pension Schemes Act 1993, s 190, Sch 8, para 4, as from 7 February 1994.

(3) In subsection (2)(e) above, *expressions used in the Merchant Shipping Act 1894 have the same meanings as in that Act.*

['fishing boat' means a vessel of whatever size, and in whatever way propelled, which is for the time being employed in sea fishing or in the sea-fishing service;

'seamen' includes every person (except masters and pilots) employed or engaged in any capacity on board any ship; and

'wages' includes emoluments.]

Note. Words in square brackets substituted for words in italics by Merchant Shipping Act 1995, s 314(2), Sch 13, para 46, as from 1 January 1996.

25. General interpretation—(1) In this Act, except where the context otherwise requires—

'administration order' means an order made under, and so referred to in, *Part VII of the County Courts Act 1959* [Part VI of the County Courts Act 1984];

Note. Words in square brackets substituted for words in italics by County Courts Act 1984, s 148(1), Sch 2, Part V, para 42, as from 1 August 1984.

'the court', in relation to an attachment of earnings order, means the court which made the order, subject to rules of court as to the venue for, and the transfer of, proceedings in county courts and magistrates' courts;

'debtor' and 'relevant adjudication' have the meanings given by section 2 of this Act;

'the employer', in relation to an attachment of earnings order, means the person who is required by the order to make deductions from earnings paid by him to the debtor;

'judgment debt' has the meaning given by section 2 of this Act;

'legal aid contribution order' means an order under section 76 of the Criminal Justice Act 1967 [*section 32 of the Legal Aid Act 1974*] [*section 7 or 8(2) of the Legal Aid Act 1982*] [section 23 of the Legal Aid Act 1988];

Note. Words in first square brackets substituted for words in italics by Legal Aid Act 1974, s 41, Sch 4, and words in second pair of square brackets by Legal Aid Act 1982, s 14(3), as from 1 March 1984, and words in third pair of square brackets substituted by Legal Aid Act

1988, s 45(1), (3), Sch 5, para 3, as from 1 April 1989. Definition 'legal aid contribution order' repealed by the Access to Justice Act 1999, s 106, Sch 15, Pt I, as from 2 April 2001 (with savings in relation to existing cases).

> 'maintenance order' has the meaning given by section 2 of this Act;
> 'maintenance payments' means payments required under a maintenance order;
> 'prescribed' means prescribed by rules of court; *and*
> *'rules of court', in relation to a magistrates' court, means rules under section 15 of the Justices of the Peace Act 1949 [section 144 of the Magistrates' Courts Act 1980]*;

Note. Words in square brackets substituted for words in italics by Magistrates' Courts Act 1980, s 154, Sch 7, para 101, as from 6 July 1981. Definition 'rules of court' and word 'and' in italics immediately preceding it repealed by the Courts Act 2003, s 109(1), (3) Sch 8, para 145, Sch 10, as from 1 September 2004 (except in relation to the operation of this section in relation to rules of court other than Criminal Procedure Rules during the period between that date and the coming into force of the first Criminal Procedure Rules made under the Courts Act 2003, s 69).

and, in relation to a magistrates' court, references to a single justice are to a justice of the peace acting for the same petty sessions area as the court.

Note. Words from 'and, in relation to' to the end in italics repealed by the Access to Justice Act 1999, s 106, Sch 15, Pt V(7), as from 2 April 2001.

(2) Any reference in this Act to sums payable under a judgment or order, or to the payment of such sums, includes a reference to costs and the payment of them; and the references in sections 6(4) and 12(2) to relevant costs are to any costs of the proceedings in which the attachment of earnings order in question was made, being costs which the debtor is liable to pay.

(3) References in sections 6(5)(b), 9(3)(b) and 14(1)(a) of this Act to the debtor's needs includes references to the needs of any person for whom he must, or reasonably may, provide.

(4) Earnings which, in pursuance of a scheme under the Dock Workers (Regulation of Employment) Act 1946, are paid to a debtor by a body responsible for the local administration of the scheme acting as agent for the debtor's employer or as delegate of the body responsible for the general administration of the scheme shall be treated for the purposes of this Act as paid to the debtor by the last-mentioned body acting as principal.

Note. Sub-s (4) repealed by Dock Work Act 1989, s 7(1), Sch 1, Part I, as from 3 July 1989.

(5) Any power to make rules which is conferred by this Act is without prejudice to any other power to make rules of court.

(6) This Act, so far as it relates to magistrates' courts, and *Part III of the Magistrates' Courts Act 1952* [Part III of the Magistrates' Courts Act 1980] shall be construed as if this Act were contained in that Part.

Note. Reference to Magistrates' Courts Act 1980 substituted for reference to Magistrates' Courts Act 1952 by Magistrates' Courts Act 1980, s 154, Sch 7, para 101, as from 6 July 1981.

(7) References in this Act to any enactment include references to that enactment as amended by or under any other enactment, including this Act.

Note. Section modified, in respect of a person aged 18 or over liable to pay a sum to which the Courts Act 2003, Sch 5 applies: see the Fines Collection Regulations 2004, SI 2004/176, regs 2, 3, 4(m).

General

26. Transitional provision—(1) As from the appointed day, an attachment of earnings order made before that day under Part II of the Maintenance Orders Act 1958 (including an order made under that Part of that Act as applied by section 46 or 79 of the Criminal Justice Act 1967) shall take effect as an attachment of earnings order made under the corresponding power in this Act, and the provisions of this Act shall apply to it accordingly, so far as they are capable of doing so.

(2) Rules of court may make such provision as the rule-making authority considers requisite—

(a) for enabling an attachment of earnings order to which subsection (1) above applies to be varied so as to bring it into conformity, as from the appointed day, with the provisions of this Act, or to be replaced by an attachment of earnings order having effect as if made under the corresponding power in this Act;

(b) to secure that anything required or authorised by this Act to be done in relation to an attachment of earnings order made thereunder is required or, as the case may be, authorised to be done in relation to an attachment of earnings order to which the said subsection (1) applies.

(3) In this section, 'the appointed day' means the day appointed under section 54 of the Administration of Justice Act 1970 for the coming into force of Part II of that Act.

27. Consequential amendment of enactments—(1) In consequence of the repeals effected by this Act, section 20 of the Maintenance Orders Act 1958 (which contains certain provisions about magistrates' courts and their procedure), except subsection (6) of that section (which amends section 52(3) of the Magistrates' Courts Act 1952), shall have effect as set out in Schedule 5 to this Act.

(2) In section 156(1) of the County Courts Act 1959 (which confers power to make rules of court with respect to administration orders), for the words 'section 29 of the Administration of Justice Act 1970' there shall be substituted the words 'section 4 of the Attachment of Earnings Act 1971'.

Note. Sub-s (2) repealed by Insolvency Act 1976, s 14(4), Sch 3, as from 1 March 1978.

(3) In section 95(4) of the Merchant Shipping Act 1970 (saving, in relation to fishermen's wages, of provisions in Part II of the Administration of Justice Act 1970) for the words 'Part II of the Administration of Justice Act 1970' there shall be substituted the words 'the Attachment of Earnings Act 1971'.

28. Northern Ireland. *Notwithstanding anything in the Government of Ireland Act 1920, the Parliament of Northern Ireland shall have power to make laws for purposes similar to those of section 22 of this Act.*

Note. This section repealed by Northern Ireland Constitution Act 1973, s 41(1), Sch 6, Part I.

29. Citation, repeal, extent and commencement—(1) This Act may be cited as the Attachment of Earnings Act 1971.

(2) The enactments specified in Schedule 6 to this Act are hereby repealed to the extent specified in the third column of that Schedule.

(3) This Act, except section 20(2), does not extend to Scotland and, except sections 20(2) *and 28*, does not extend to Northern Ireland.

Note. Words in italics repealed by Northern Ireland Constitution Act 1973, s 41(1), Sch 6, Part I.

(4) This Act shall come into force on the day appointed under section 54 of the Administration of Justice Act 1970 for the coming into force of Part II of that Act.

Note. The Act came into force on 2 August 1971: SI 1971 No 834.

SCHEDULES

SCHEDULE 1   Section 2

MAINTENANCE ORDERS TO WHICH THIS ACT APPLIES

1. An order for alimony, maintenance or other payments made, or having effect as if made, under Part II of the Matrimonial Causes Act 1965 (ancillary relief in actions for divorce etc).

Note. Part II of Matrimonial Causes Act 1965 has been repealed. See now Matrimonial Causes Act 1973, Part II.

2. An order for payments to or in respect of a child, being an order made, or having effect as if made, under Part III of the said Act of 1965 (maintenance of children following divorce, etc).

Note. Part III of Matrimonial Causes Act 1965 has been repealed. See now Matrimonial Causes Act 1973, s 23.

3. *An order for periodical or other payments made under Part I of the Matrimonial Proceedings and Property Act 1970.*

[**3.** An order for periodical or other payments made, or having effect as if made, under Part II of the Matrimonial Causes Act 1973.]

Note. Para 3 in square brackets substituted for para 3 in italics by Matrimonial Causes Act 1973, s 54(1), Sch 2, para 13, as from 1 January 1974.

4. An order for maintenance or other payments to or in respect of a spouse or child, being an order made, *or having effect as if made, under the Matrimonial Proceedings (Magistrates' Courts) Act 1960* [under Part I of the Domestic Proceedings and Magistrates' Courts Act 1978].

Note. Words in square brackets substituted for words in italics by Domestic Proceedings and Magistrates' Courts Act 1978, s 89(2)(a), Sch 2, para 32, as from 1 February 1981.

5. *An order under—*
   (*a*) *section 9(2), 10(1), 11 or 12(2) of the Guardianship of Minors Act 1971* [*or section 2(3) or 2(4)(a) of the Guardianship Act 1973*] (*payments for maintenance of persons who are, or have been, in guardianship*); or
   [(*a*) *section 11B, 11C or 11D of the Guardianship of Minors Act 1971 or section 2(3) or 2(4A) of the Guardianship Act 1973 (payments for maintenance of persons who are or have been in guardianship);*]
   (*b*) *section 6 of the Family Law Reform Act 1969* (*payments for maintenance of ward of court*).

[**5.** An order for periodical or other payments made or having effect as if made under Schedule 1 of the Children Act 1989.]

Note. Words in square brackets in original sub-para (a) in italics inserted by Guardianship Act 1973, s 9(3).

Sub-para (a) substituted by sub-para (a) in square brackets by Family Law Reform Act 1987, s 33(1), Sch 2, para 44(a), as from 1 April 1989.

Para 5 in square brackets substituted for para 5 in italics by Courts and Legal Services Act 1990, s 116, Sch 16, para 38, as from 14 October 1991.

6. *An affiliation order* (*that is to say an order under section 4 of the Affiliation Proceedings Act 1957, section 44 of the National Assistance Act 1948, section 26 of the Children Act 1948* [*section 50 of the Child Care Act 1980*] *or section 24 of the Ministry of Social Security Act 1966* [*or section 19 of the Supplementary Benefits Act 1976*] [*or section 45 of the Children Act 1975*] [*or section 25 of the Social Security Act 1986*]).

Note. Words in first square brackets substituted for preceding words by Child Care Act 1980, s 89, Sch 5, para 32, as from 1 April 1981. Words in second square brackets added by Supplementary Benefits Act 1976, s 35(2), Sch 7, para 20. Words in third square brackets added by Children Act 1975, s 108(1)(a), Sch 3, para 76, as from 1 December 1985. Words in fourth square brackets added by Social Security Act 1986, s 86(1), Sch 10, Part II, para 43(a), as from 11 April 1988.

Para 6 repealed by Family Law Reform Act 1987, s 33, Sch 2, para 44(b), Sch 4, as from 1 April 1989.

7. An order under *section 87 of the Children and Young Persons Act 1933, section 30 of the Children and Young Persons Act 1963* [*section 47 or 51 of the Child Care Act 1980*] [paragraph 23 of Schedule 2 to the Children Act 1989] *or* section 23 of the Ministry of Social Security Act 1966 [*or* section 18 of the Supplementary Benefits Act 1976] [*or* section 24 of the Social Security Act 1986] [or section 106 of the Social Security Administration Act 1992] (various provisions for obtaining contributions from a person whose dependants are assisted or maintained out of public funds).

Note. Words in first pair of square brackets substituted for preceding words in italics by Child Care Act 1980, s 89, Sch 5, para 32, as from 1 April 1981.

Words in second pair of square brackets substituted for words in italics in square brackets by Children Act 1989, s 108(5), Sch 13, para 29, as from 14 October 1991.

Words in third pair of square brackets inserted by Supplementary Benefits Act 1976, s 36(3), Sch 7, para 20, as from 15 November 1976.

Words in fourth pair of square brackets added by Social Security Act 1986, s 86(1), Sch 10, Part II, para 43(6), as from 11 April 1988. Words in fifth pair of square brackets inserted by Social Security (Consequential Provisions) Act 1992, s 4, Sch 2, para 7, as from 1 July 1992.

8. An order under section 43 of the National Assistance Act 1948 (recovery of costs of maintaining assisted person).

9. An order to which section 16 of the Maintenance Orders Act 1950 applies by virtue of subsection (2)(b) or (c) of that section (that is to say an order made by a court in Scotland or Northern Ireland and corresponding to one of those specified in the foregoing paragraphs) and which has been registered in a court in England and Wales under Part II of that Act.

Note. The reference to Maintenance Orders Act 1950, s 16(2)(c) is to be construed as a reference to s 16(2)(c) as amended: see Matrimonial Causes Act 1973, s 54(1), Sch 2, para 3(2).

10. A maintenance order within the meaning of the Maintenance Orders (Facilities for Enforcement) Act 1920 (Commonwealth orders enforceable in the United Kingdom) registered in, or confirmed by, a court in England and Wales under that Act.

[**11.** A maintenance order within the meaning of Part I of the Maintenance Orders (Reciprocal Enforcement) Act 1972 registered in a magistrates' court under the said Part I.]

Note. Para 11 added by Maintenance Orders (Reciprocal Enforcement) Act 1972, s 22(1), Schedule, as from 1 April 1974.

[**12.** An order under section 34(1)(b) of the Children Act 1975 (payments of maintenance in respect of a child to his custodian).]

Note. Para 12 added by Children Act 1975, s 108(1)(a), Sch 3, para 76, as from 1 December 1985.

[**13.** A maintenance order within the meaning of Part I of the Civil Jurisdiction and Judgments Act 1982 which is registered in a magistrates' court under that Part].

Note. Para 13 added by Civil Jurisdiction and Judgments Act 1982, s 15(4), Sch 12, Part I, para 6, as from 1 January 1987.

[**14.** A maintenance judgment within the meaning of Council Regulation (EC) No 44/2001 of 22nd December 2000 on jurisdiction and the recognition and enforcement of judgments in civil and commercial matters, which is registered in a magistrates' court under that Regulation.]

Note. Para 14 added by the Civil Jurisdiction and Judgments Order 2001, SI 2001/3929, art 5, Sch 3, para 9, as from 1 March 2002.

This part modified, in respect of a person aged 18 or over liable to pay a sum to which the Courts Act 2003, Sch 5 applies: see the Fines Collection Regulations 2004, SI 2004/176, regs 2, 3, 4(e), 12(a).

SCHEDULE 2 Section 3

TAXES, SOCIAL SECURITY CONTRIBUTIONS ETC RELEVANT FOR PURPOSES OF SECTION 3(6)

1. Income tax or any other tax or liability recoverable under section 65, 66 or 68 of the Taxes Management Act 1970.

2. *Selective employment tax under section 44 of the Finance Act 1966.*

Note. Para 2 repealed by Statute Law (Repeals) Act 1989, s 1(1), Sch 1, Part I.

3. *Contributions under—*
section 3 (flat-rate) or section 4 (graduated) of the National Insurance Act 1965;
section 1 of the National Health Service Contributions Act 1965; or
section 2 of the National Insurance (Industrial Injuries) Act 1965.

[**3.** *Reserve scheme premiums and contributions under Part III of the Social Security Act 1973.*]

[**3.** *State scheme premiums* [Contributions equivalent premiums] under Part III of the *Social Security Pensions Act 1975* [Pension Schemes Act 1993].]

Note. Para 3 in italics and square brackets substituted for original para 3 in italics by Social Security (Consequential Provisions) Act 1975, s 1(3), Sch 2, para 42. Para 3 in roman and square brackets substituted for para 3 in italics and square brackets by Social Security Pensions Act 1975, s 65(1), Sch 4, para 16. Words 'Contributions equivalent premiums' substituted for preceding words in italics by Pensions Act 1995, s 151, Sch 5, para 3, as from 6 April 1997. Words 'Pension Schemes Act 1993' substituted for preceding words in italics by Pension Schemes Act 1993, s 190, Sch 8, as from 7 February 1994.

[**3A.** Class 1, 2 and 4 contributions under Part I of the *Social Security Act 1975* [Social Security Contributions and Benefits Act 1992].]

Note. Para 3A added by Social Security (Consequential Provisions) Act 1975, s 1(3), Sch 2, para 42. Words in square brackets substituted for words in italics by Social Security (Consequential Provisions) Act 1992, s 4, Sch 2, para 6, as from 1 July 1992.

4. *Redundancy Fund contributions under section 27 of the Redundancy Payments Act 1965.*
Note. Para 4 repealed by Social Security Act 1973, ss 100, 101, Sch 26, Sch 28, Part I.

SCHEDULE 3   Sections 6 and 7

DEDUCTIONS BY EMPLOYER UNDER ATTACHMENT OF EARNINGS ORDER

PART I

SCHEME OF DEDUCTIONS

Preliminary definitions

1. The following three paragraphs have effect for defining and explaining, for purposes of this Schedule, expressions used therein.

2. 'Pay-day', in relation to earnings paid to a debtor, means an occasion on which they are paid.

3. 'Attachable earnings', in relation to a pay-day, are the earnings which remain payable to the debtor on that day after deduction by the employer of—
  (a) income tax,
  (b) *contributions under any of the following enactments—*
       the National Insurance Act 1965,
       the National Insurance (Industrial Injuries) Act 1965, or
       the National Health Service Contributions Act 1965;
  [(b) *primary reserve scheme contributions under Part III of the Social Security Act 1973,*
  (bb) primary Class I contributions under Part I of the Social Security Act 1975.]
  (c) *amounts deductible under any enactment, or in pursuance of a request in writing by the debtor, for the purposes of a superannuation scheme within the meaning of the Wages Councils Act 1959 [Wages Councils Act 1979].*
  [(c) amounts deductible under any enactment, or in pursuance of a request in writing by the debtor, for the purposes of a superannuation scheme, namely any enactment, rules, deed or other instrument providing for the payment of annuities or lump sums—
       (i) to the persons with respect to whom the instrument has effect on their retirement at a specified age or on becoming incapacitated at some earlier age, or

(ii) to the personal representatives or the widows, relatives or dependants of such persons on their death or otherwise, whether with or without any further or other benefits.]

Note. Paras (b), (bb) in square brackets substituted for first para (b) in italics by Social Security (Consequential Provisions) Act 1975, s 1(3), Sch 2, para 43. Second para (b) in italics repealed by Social Security Pensions Act 1975, s 65(3), Sch 5. In first para (c) words in square brackets substituted for words 'Wages Councils Act 1959' by Wages Councils Act 1979, s 31(2), Sch 6, para 3; para (c) in square brackets substituted for para (c) in italics by Wages Act 1986, s 32(1), Sch 4, para 4, as from 25 September 1986. The substitution of para 3(c) is to continue to have effect by virtue of Employment Rights Act 1996, s 240, Sch 1, para 3.

4. *On any pay-day—*
- (a) *'the normal deduction' is arrived at by applying the normal deduction rate (as specified in the relevant attachment of earnings order) with respect to the period since the past pay-day or, if it is the first pay-day of the debtor's employment with the employer, since the employment began; and*
- (b) *'the protected earnings' are arrived at by applying the protected earnings rate (as so specified) with respect to the said period.*

[**4.**—(1) On any pay-day—
- (a) 'the normal deduction' is arrived at by applying the normal deduction rate (as specified in the relevant attachment of earnings order) with respect to the relevant period; and
- (b) 'the protected earnings' are arrived at by applying the protected earnings rate (as so specified) with respect to the relevant period.

(2) For the purposes of this paragraph the relevant period in relation to any pay-day is the period beginning—
- (a) if it is the first pay-day of the debtor's employment with the employer, with the first day of the employment; or
- (b) if on the last pay-day earnings were paid in respect of a period falling wholly or partly after that pay-day, with the first day after the end of that period; or
- (c) in any other case, with the first day after the last pay-day, and ending—
  - (i) where earnings are paid in respect of a period falling wholly or partly after the pay-day, with the last day of that period; or
  - (ii) in any other case, with the pay-day.]

Note. Para 4 in square brackets substituted for para 4 in italics by Administration of Justice Act 1982, s 54, as from 1 April 1983.

Employer's deduction (judgment debts and administration orders)

5. In the case of an attachment of earnings order made to secure the payment of a judgment debt or payments under an administration order, the employer shall on any pay-day—
- (a) if the attachable earnings exceed the protected earnings, deduct from the attachable earnings the amount of the excess or the normal deduction, whichever is the less;
- (b) make no deduction if the attachable earnings are equal to, or less than, the protected earnings.

Employer's deduction (other cases)

6.—(1) The following provision shall have effect in the case of an attachment of earnings order to which paragraph 5 above does not apply.
(2) If on a pay-day the attachable earnings exceed the sum of—
- (a) the protected earnings; and
- (b) so much of any amount by which the attachable earnings on any previous pay-day fell short of the protected earnings as has not been made good by virtue of this sub-paragraph on another previous pay-day,

then, in so far as the excess allows, the employer shall deduct from the attachable earnings the amount specified in the following sub-paragraph.

(3) The said amount is the sum of—

(a) the normal deduction; and

(b) so much of the normal deduction on any previous pay-day as was not deducted on that day and has not been paid by virtue of this sub-paragraph on any other previous pay-day.

(4) No deduction shall be made on any pay-day when the attachable earnings are equal to, or less than, the protected earnings.

PART II

PRIORITY AS BETWEEN ORDERS

7. Where the employer is required to comply with two or more attachment of earnings orders in respect of the same debtor, all or none of which orders are made to secure either the payment of judgment debts or payments under an administration order, then on any pay-day the employer shall, for the purpose of complying with Part I of this Schedule,—

(a) deal with the orders according to the respective dates on which they were made, disregarding any later order until an earlier one has been dealt with;

(b) deal with any later order as if the earnings to which it relates were the residue of the debtor's earnings after the making of any deduction to comply with any earlier order.

8. Where the employer is required to comply with two or more attachment of earnings orders, and one or more (but not all) of those orders are made to secure either the payment of judgment debts or payments under an administration order, then on any pay-day the employer shall, for the purpose of complying with Part I of this Schedule—

(a) deal first with any order which is not made to secure the payment of a judgment debt or payments under an administration order (complying with paragraph 7 above if there are two or more such orders); and

(b) deal thereafter with any order which is made to secure the payment of a judgment debt or payments under an administration order as if the earnings to which it relates were the residue of the debtor's earnings after the making of any deduction to comply with an order having priority by virtue of sub-paragraph (a) above; and

(c) if there are two or more orders to which sub-paragraph (b) above applies, comply with paragraph 7 above in respect of those orders.

SCHEDULE 4   Section 24

ENACTMENTS PROVIDING BENEFITS WHICH ARE NOT TO BE TREATED AS DEBTOR'S EARNINGS

The National Insurance Act 1965.

The National Insurance (Industrial Injuries) Act 1965.

The Family Allowances Act 1965.

The Ministry of Social Security Act 1966.

The Industrial Injuries and Diseases (Old Cases) Act 1967.

The Family Income Supplement Act 1970.

[The Child Benefit Act 1975.

The Family Incomes Supplement Act 1970 (c 55).

The Social Security Act 1975 (c 14 and 60).

The Industrial Injuries and Diseases (old cases) Act 1975 (c 16).

The Supplementary Benefits Act 1976].

Note. Words in square brackets substituted for preceding words in italics by Social Security (Consequential Provisions) Act 1975, s 1(3), Sch 2, para 44, and further amended by Child Benefit Act 1975, s 21(1), Sch 4, para 6, Social Security Pensions Act 1975, s 65(1), Sch 4, para 17, and Supplementary Benefits Act 1976, s 35(2), Sch 7, para 21. Whole Schedule repealed by Social Security Act 1986, s 86(2), Sch 11, as from 26 June 1987.

SCHEDULE 5   Section 27

SECTION 20 OF MAINTENANCE ORDERS ACT 1958 AS HAVING EFFECT IN CONSEQUENCE OF THIS ACT

20. Special provision as to Magistrates' Courts—(1) Notwithstanding anything in this Act, the clerk of a magistrates' court who is entitled to receive payments under a maintenance order for transmission to another person shall not apply for the registration of the maintenance order under Part I of this Act or give notice in relation to the order in pursuance of subsection (1) of section five thereof unless he is requested in writing to do so by a person entitled to receive the payments through him; and where the clerk is requested as aforesaid—

  (i) he shall comply with the request unless it appears to him unreasonable in the circumstances to do so;

  (ii) the person by whom the request was made shall have the same liabilities for all the costs properly incurred in or about any proceedings taken in pursuance of the request as if the proceedings had been taken by that person.

(2) An application to a magistrates' court by virtue of subsection (2) of section four of this Act for the variation of a maintenance order shall be made by complaint.

*   *   *   *   *

(8) For the avoidance of doubt it is hereby declared that a complaint may be made to enforce payment of a sum due and unpaid under a maintenance order notwithstanding that a previous complaint has been made in respect of that sum or a part thereof and whether or not an order was made in pursuance of the previous complaint.

SCHEDULE 6   Section 32

ENACTMENTS REPEALED

Chapter	Short Title	Extent of Repeal
6 & 7 Eliz 2 c 39.	The Maintenance Orders Act 1958.	Section 9. In section 20, in subsection (1) the words 'or Part II of the Administration of Justice Act 1970', the word 'or' at the end of paragraph (a), paragraphs (b) and (c) and the words from 'and for the purposes' onwards; in subsection (2), the words 'Subject to rules of court made by virtue of section 18(3)(c) of the Administration of Justice Act 1970', and the words 'and an application to a magistrates' court for an

Chapter	Short Title	Extent of Repeal
		attachment of earnings order, or an order discharging or varying an attachment of earnings order'; and subsections (3), (4), (5) and (7). In section 23(2), the words 'except paragraph (a) of subsection (3) of section 20'.
1970 c 31.	The Administration of Justice Act 1970.	Sections 13 to 26. Section 27(1) and (2). In section 28— in subsection (1), the definitions of 'Act of 1958', 'administration order', 'the court', 'debtor', 'judgment debt', 'relevant adjudication', 'the employer', 'legal aid contribution order', and the words from '"maintenance payments"' onwards; and subsections (2) to (5). Section 29(1) to (4). Section 30(3) and (4). In section 53, the words '24 or'. In section 54(6), the words 'and 27' and 'and 7'. Schedules 5, 6 and 7.
1970 c 55.	The Family Income Supplements Act 1970.	Section 14.

NULLITY OF MARRIAGE ACT 1971*

(1971 c 44)

An Act to restate, with certain alterations, the grounds on which a marriage is void or voidable and the bars to the grant of a decree of nullity on the ground that a marriage is voidable; to alter the effect of decrees of nullity in respect of voidable marriages; and to abolish certain remaining bars to the grant of matrimonial relief. [*1 July 1971*]

* Whole Act was repealed by Matrimonial Causes Act 1973, s 54(1), Sch 3 and replaced as noted to each section.

1. Grounds on which a marriage is void. *A marriage which takes place after the commencement of this Act shall be void on the following grounds only, that is to say—*
  (*a*) *that it is not a valid marriage under the provisions of the Marriages Acts 1949 to 1970 (that is to say where—*
    (*i*) *the parties are within the prohibited degrees of relationship;*
    (*ii*) *either party is under the age of sixteen; or*

(*iii*) the parties have intermarried in disregard of certain requirements as to the formation of marriage);

(*b*) that at the time of the marriage either party was already lawfully married;

(*c*) that the parties are not respectively male and female;

[(*d*) in the case of a polygamous marriage entered into outside England and Wales, that either party was at the time of the marriage domiciled in England and Wales.

For the purposes of paragraph (*d*) of this section a marriage may be polygamous although at its inception neither spouse has any spouse additional to the other.]

Note. Words in square brackets added by Matrimonial Proceedings (Polygamous Marriages) Act 1972, s 4. Section 1 replaced by Matrimonial Causes Act 1973, s 11 (p 2503).

2. Grounds on which a marriage is voidable. *A marriage which takes place after the commencement of this Act shall be voidable on the following grounds only, that is to say*—

(*a*) that the marriage has not been consummated owing to the incapacity of either party to consummate it;

(*b*) that the marriage has not been consummated owing to the wilful refusal of the respondent to consummate it;

(*c*) that either party to the marriage did not validly consent to it, whether in consequence of duress, mistake, unsoundness of mind or otherwise;

(*d*) that at the time of the marriage either party, though capable of giving a valid consent, was suffering (whether continuously or intermittently) from mental disorder within the meaning of the Mental Health Act 1959 of such a kind or to such an extent as to be unfitted for marriage;

(*e*) that at the time of the marriage the respondent was suffering from venereal disease in a communicable form;

(*f*) that at the time of the marriage the respondent was pregnant by some person other than the petitioner.

Note. Section 2 replaced Matrimonial Causes Act 1965, s 9 in respect of marriages taking place on or after 1 August 1971. See now Matrimonial Causes Act 1973, s 12 (p 2503).

3. Bars to relief where marriage is voidable—(*1*) *The court shall not, in proceedings instituted after the commencement of this Act, grant a decree of nullity on the ground that a marriage is voidable (whether the marriage took place before or after the commencement of this Act) if the respondent satisfies the court*—

(*a*) that the petitioner, with knowledge that it was open to him to have the marriage avoided, so conducted himself in relation to the respondent as to lead the respondent reasonably to believe that he would not seek to do so; and

(*b*) that it would be unjust to the respondent to grant the decree.

(*2*) Without prejudice to subsection (*1*) of this section, the court shall not grant a decree of nullity by virtue of section 2 of this Act on the grounds mentioned in paragraph (*c*), (*d*), (*e*) or (*f*) of that section unless it is satisfied that proceedings were instituted within three years from the date of the marriage.

(*3*) Without prejudice to subsections (*1*) and (*2*) of this section, the court shall not grant a decree of nullity by virtue of section 2 of this Act on the grounds mentioned in paragraph (*e*) or (*f*) of that section unless it is satisfied that the petitioner was at the time of the marriage ignorant of the facts alleged.

(*4*) Subsection (*1*) of this section replaces, in relation to any decree to which it applies, any rule of law whereby a decree may be refused by reason of approbation, ratification or lack of sincerity on the part of the petitioner or on similar grounds, but in relation to a marriage which took place before the commencement of this Act, is without prejudice to section 9(*2*) of the Matrimonial Causes Act 1965.

(*5*) In this section 'the court' has the same meaning as in the Matrimonial Causes Act 1965.

Note. Sub-ss (1)–(3) replaced by Matrimonial Causes Act 1973, s 13 (p 2504).

4. Marriages governed by foreign law or celebrated abroad under English law—(*1*) *Where, apart from this Act, any matter affecting the validity of a marriage would fall to be determined (in accordance with the rules of private international law) by reference to the law of a country outside England and Wales, nothing in section 1, 2 or 3(1) of this Act shall*—

(*a*) *preclude the determination of that matter as aforesaid; or*

(*b*) *require the application to the marriage of the grounds or bar there mentioned except so far as applicable in accordance with those rules.*

(*2*) *In the case of a marriage which purports to have been celebrated under the Foreign Marriages Acts 1892 to 1947 or has taken place outside England and Wales and purports to be a marriage under common law, section 1 of this Act is without prejudice to any ground on which the marriage may be void under those Acts or, as the case may be, by virtue of the rules governing the celebration of marriages outside England and Wales under common law.*

Note. Section 4 replaced by Matrimonial Causes Act 1973, s 14 (p 2505).

5. Effect of decree of nullity in case of voidable marriage. *A decree of nullity granted after the commencement of this Act on the ground that a marriage is voidable shall operate to annul the marriage only as respects any time after the decree has been made absolute, and the marriage shall, notwithstanding the decree, be treated as if it had existed up to that time.*

Note. Section 5 replaced by Matrimonial Causes Act 1973, s 16 (p 2506).

6. Collusion etc, not to be bar to relief in cases of nullity or under s 14 of Act of 1965—(*1*) *Collusion shall not be a bar to the granting of a decree of nullity whether the marriage took place, or the proceedings were instituted, before or after the commencement of this Act.*

(*2*) *It is hereby declared that neither collusion nor any other conduct on the part of the petitioner which has at any time been a bar to relief in matrimonial proceedings constitutes a bar to the grant of a decree under section 14 of the Matrimonial Causes Act 1965 (presumption of death and dissolution of marriage).*

Note. Sub-s (2) replaced by Matrimonial Causes Act 1973, s 19(6) (p 2508).

7. Short title, consequential amendments and repeals, saving, commencement and extent—(*1*) *This Act may be cited as the Nullity of Marriage Act 1971.*

(*2*) *In section 40(1)(a) of the Matrimonial Causes Act 1965 (additional jurisdiction in proceedings under that Act by wife) after the words in brackets there shall be inserted the words 'or under the Nullity of Marriage Act 1971'; and in section 2 of the Limitation (Enemies and War Prisoners) Act 1945, at the end of the definition of 'statute of limitation', there shall be added the words 'section 3(2) of the Nullity of Marriage Act 1971'.*

(*3*) *The following provisions of the said Act of 1965 are hereby repealed, that is to say*—

section 6(1)(c) as applied by sections 10 and 14;

in section 7, as applied by sections 10 and 14, the words from 'either' to 'collusion or';

section 9, except in relation to marriages taking place before the commencement of this Act.

(*4*) *Nothing in this Act affects any law or custom relating to the marriage of members of the Royal Family.*

Note. Sub-s (4) replaced by Matrimonial Causes Act 1973, Sch 1, para 6 (p 2562).

(*5*) *This Act shall come into force at the expiration of the period of one month beginning with the day on which it is passed.*

Note. The Act came into force on 1 August 1971.

(*6*) *This Act does not extend to Scotland or Northern Ireland.*

MAINTENANCE ORDERS (RECIPROCAL ENFORCEMENT) ACT 1972

(1972 c 18)

ARRANGEMENT OF SECTIONS

PART I

RECIPROCAL ENFORCEMENT OF MAINTENANCE ORDERS MADE IN UNITED KINGDOM OR
RECIPROCATING COUNTRY

PART II

RECIPROCAL ENFORCEMENT OF CLAIMS FOR THE RECOVERY OF MAINTENANCE

PART III

MISCELLANEOUS AND SUPPLEMENTAL

Further provisions relating to enforcement of maintenance orders and to applications for recovery of maintenance

Provisions with respect to certain orders of magistrates' courts

Supplemental provisions

An Act to make new provision, applying throughout the United Kingdom, in place of the Maintenance Orders (Facilities for Enforcement) Act 1920; to make provision with a view to the accession by the United Kingdom to the United Nations Convention on the Recovery Abroad of Maintenance done at New York on 20 June 1956; to make other provision for facilitating the recovery of maintenance by or from persons in the United Kingdom from or by persons in other countries; to extend the jurisdiction of magistrates' courts to hear complaints by or against persons outside England and Wales; and for the purposes connected with the matters aforesaid.   [23 March 1972]

PART I

RECIPROCAL ENFORCEMENT OF MAINTENANCE ORDERS MADE IN UNITED KINGDOM OR RECIPROCATING COUNTRY

Note. For modification of Part I in relation to Hague Convention countries, see SI 1979 No 1317.

Designation of reciprocating countries

1. Orders in Council designating reciprocating countries—(1) Her Majesty, if satisfied that, in the event of the benefits conferred by this Part of this Act being applied, to, or to particular classes of, maintenance orders made by the courts of any country or territory outside the United Kingdom, similar benefits will in that country or territory be applied to, or to those classes of, maintenance orders made by the courts of the United Kingdom, may by Order in Council designate that country or territory as a reciprocating country for the purposes of this Part of this Act; and, subject to subsection (2) below, in this Part of this Act 'reciprocating country' means a country or territory that is for the time being so designated.

(2) A country or territory may be designated under subsection (1) above as a reciprocating country either as regards maintenance orders generally, or as regards maintenance orders other than those of any specified class, or as regards maintenance orders of one or more specified classes only; and a country or territory which is for the time being so designated otherwise than as regards maintenance orders generally shall for the purposes of this Part of this Act be taken to be a reciprocating country only as regards maintenance orders of the class to which the designation extends.

Note. The following orders have been made under this section: Reciprocal Enforcement of Maintenance Orders (Designation of Reciprocating Countries) Order 1974, SI 1974 No 556, as amended by SI 1979 No 115, SI 1983 No 1125; and Reciprocal Enforcement of Maintenance Orders (Designation of Reciprocating Countries) Order 1975, SI 1975 No 2187; Reciprocal Enforcement of Maintenance Orders (Designation of Reciprocating Countries) Order 1979, SI 1979 No 115; and Reciprocal Enforcement of Maintenance Orders (Designation of Reciprocating Countries) Order 1983, SI 1983 No 1125. See also SI 1979 No 1317 for the Hague Convention countries to which Part I applies.

Orders made by courts in the United Kingdom

2. Transmission of maintenance order made in United Kingdom for enforcement in reciprocating country—(1) Subject to subsection (2) below, where the payer under a maintenance order made, whether before or after the commencement of this Part of this Act, by a court in the United Kingdom is residing [or has assets] in a reciprocating country, the payee under the order may apply for the order to be sent to that country for enforcement.

Note. Words in square brackets inserted by Civil Jurisdiction and Judgments Act 1982, s 37(1), Sch 11, Part III, para 9, as from 1 January 1987.

(2) Subsection (1) above shall not have effect in relation to a provisional order or to an order made by virtue of a provision of Part II of this Act.

(3) Every application under this section shall be made in the prescribed manner to the prescribed officer of the court which made the maintenance order to which the application relates.

(4) If, on an application duly made under this section to the prescribed officer of a court in the United Kingdom, that officer is satisfied that the payer under the maintenance order to which the application relates is residing [or has assets] in a reciprocating country, the following documents, that is to say—

(a) a certified copy of the maintenance order;

(b) a certificate signed by that officer certifying that the order is enforceable in the United Kingdom;

(c) a certificate of arrears so signed;

(d) a statement giving such information as the officer possesses as to the whereabouts of the payer [and the nature and location of his assets in that country];

(e) a statement giving such information as the officer possesses for facilitating the identification of the payer; and

(f) where available, a photograph of the payer;

shall be sent by that officer to the *Secretary of State* [Lord Chancellor] with a view to their being transmitted by the *Secretary of State* [Lord Chancellor] to the responsible authority in the reciprocating country if he is satisfied that the statement relating to the whereabouts of the payer [and the nature and location of his assets in that country] gives sufficient information to justify that being done.

Note. Words 'or has assets' and 'and the nature and location of his assets in that country' in square brackets inserted by Civil Jurisdiction and Judgments Act 1982, s 37(1), Sch 11, Part III, paras 8, 9(a), as from 1 January 1987. Words 'Lord Chancellor' in square brackets substituted for words 'Secretary of State' in italics by virtue of Transfer of Functions (Magistrates' Courts and Family Law) Order 1992, SI 1992 No 709, art 4, as from 1 April 1992.

(5) Nothing in this section shall be taken as affecting any jurisdiction of a court in the United Kingdom with respect to a maintenance order to which this section applies, and any such order may be enforced, varied or revoked accordingly.

3. Power of magistrates' court to make provisional maintenance order against person residing in reciprocating country—(*1*) *Where a complaint is made to a magistrates' court against a person residing in a reciprocating country and the complaint is one on which the court would have jurisdiction by virtue of any enactment to make a maintenance order if—*

(*a*) *that person were residing in England and Wales;*

(*b*) *a summons to appear before the court to answer to the complaint had been duly served on him,*

the court shall have jurisdiction to hear the complaint and may, subject to subsection (2) below, make a maintenance order on the complaint.

[(1) Where an application is made to a magistrates' court for a maintenance order against a person residing in a reciprocating country and the court would have jurisdiction to determine the application under the Domestic Proceedings and Magistrates' Courts Act 1978 or the Children Act 1989 if that person—

(a) were residing in England and Wales, and

(b) received reasonable notice of the date of the hearing of the application,

the court shall (subject to subsection (2) below) have jurisdiction to determine the application.]

Note. Sub-s (1) substituted by Maintenance Orders (Reciprocal Enforcement) Act 1992, s 1(2), Sch 1, Part II, para 6, as from 5 April 1993.

(2) A maintenance order made by virtue of this section shall be a provisional order.

(*3*) *If the court hearing a complaint to which subsection (1) above applies is satisfied—*

(*a*) *that there are grounds on which a maintenance order containing a provision requiring the making of payments for the maintenance of a child may be made on that complaint, but*

(*b*) *that it has no jurisdiction to make that order unless it also makes an order providing for the legal custody of that child,*

then, for the purpose of enabling the court to make the maintenance order, the complainant shall be deemed to be the person to whom the legal custody of that child has been committed by an order of the court which is for the time being in force.

Note. Sub-s (3) repealed by Family Law Reform Act 1987, s 33(4), Sch 4, as from 1 April 1989, and repealed in relation to Northern Ireland by Children (Northern Ireland) Order 1995, SI 1995 No 755, art 185(2), Sch 10, as from 4 November 1996.

(*4*) *No enactment empowering a magistrates' court to refuse to make an order on a complaint on the ground that the matter in question is one which would be more conveniently dealt with by the High Court shall apply in relation to a complaint to which subsection (1) above applies.*

[(4) No enactment (or provision made under an enactment) requiring or enabling—

(a) a court to transfer proceedings from a magistrates' court to a county court or the High Court, or

(b) a magistrates' court to refuse to make an order on an application on the ground that any matter in question is one that would be more conveniently dealt with by the High Court,

shall apply in relation to an application to which subsection (1) above applies.]

Note. Sub-s (4) in square brackets substituted for sub-s (4) in italics by Maintenance Orders (Reciprocal Enforcement) Act 1992, s 1(2), Sch 1, Part II, para 6, as from 5 April 1993.

(5) Where a court makes a maintenance order which is by virtue of this section a provisional order, the following documents, that is to say—

(a) a certified copy of the maintenance order;

(b) a document, authenticated in the prescribed manner, setting out or summarising the evidence given in the proceedings;

(c) a certificate by the prescribed officer of the court certifying that the grounds stated in the certificate are the grounds on which the making of the order might have been opposed by the payer under the order;

(d) a statement giving such information as was available to the court as to the whereabouts of the payer;

(e) a statement giving such information as the officer possesses for facilitating the identification of the payer; and

(f) where available, a photograph of the payer;

shall be sent by that officer to the *Secretary of State* [Lord Chancellor] with a view to their being transmitted by the *Secretary of State* [Lord Chancellor] to the responsible authority in the reciprocating country in which the payer is residing if he is satisfied that the statement relating to the whereabouts of the payer gives sufficient information to justify that being done.

Note. Words 'Lord Chancellor' in square brackets substituted for words 'Secretary of State' in italics by virtue of Transfer of Functions (Magistrates' Courts and Family Law) Order 1992, SI 1992 No 709, art 4, as from 1 April 1992.

(6) A maintenance order made by virtue of this section which has been confirmed by a competent court in a reciprocating country shall be treated for all purposes as if the magistrates' court which made the order had made it in the form in which it was confirmed and as if the order had never been a provisional order, and subject to section 5 of this Act, any such order may be enforced, varied or revoked accordingly.

(7) *In the application of this section to Northern Ireland, in subsection (1), for the reference to England and Wales there shall be substituted a reference to Northern Ireland and in subsection (4), for the reference to the High Court there shall be substituted a reference to the High Court of Justice in Northern Ireland.*

[(7) *In the application of this section to Northern Ireland—*

(a) *for subsection (1) there shall be substituted—*

'(1) *Where a complaint is made to a magistrates' court against a person residing in a reciprocating country and the complaint is one on which the court would have jurisdiction by virtue of any enactment to make a maintenance order if—*

(a) *that person were residing in Northern Ireland, and*

(b) *a summons to appear before the court to answer the complaint had been duly served on him,*

the court shall have jurisdiction to hear the complaint and may (subject to subsection (2) below) make a maintenance order on the complaint.', and

(b) *for subsection (4) there shall be substituted—*

'(4) *No enactment empowering a magistrates' court to refuse to make an order on a complaint on the ground that any matter in question is one which would be more conveniently dealt with by the High Court of Justice in Northern Ireland shall apply in relation to a complaint to which subsection (1) above applies.'*]

[(7) In the application of this section to Northern Ireland—

(a) for subsection (1) there shall be substituted—

'(1) Where an application is made to a magistrates' court against a person residing in a reciprocating country and the court would have jurisdiction to determine the application under the Domestic Proceedings (Northern Ireland) Order 1980 or the Children (Northern Ireland) Order 1995 if that person—

(a) were residing in Northern Ireland, and

(b) received reasonable notice of the date of the hearing of the application, the court shall (subject to subsection (2) below) have jurisdiction to determine the application.';

(b) in subsection (4), for references to the High Court there shall be substituted references to the High Court of Justice in Northern Ireland.]

Note. First sub-s (7) in square brackets substituted for sub-s (7) in italics by Maintenance Orders (Reciprocal Enforcement) Act 1992, s 1(2), Sch 1, Part II, para 6, as from 5 April 1993. Second sub-s (7) in square brackets substituted for preceding sub-s (7) in square brackets by Children (Northern Ireland) Order 1995, SI 1995 No 755, art 185(1), Sch 9, para 66, as from 4 November 1996.

4. Power of sheriff to make provisional maintenance order against person residing in reciprocating country—(*1*) *The sheriff shall have jurisdiction in any action to which this section applies if—*

(*a*) *the pursuer resides within the jurisdiction of the sheriff; and*

(*b*) *the sheriff is satisfied that, to the best of the information or belief of the pursuer, the defender is residing in a reciprocating country; and*

(*c*) *the sheriff would not, apart from this subsection, have jurisdiction in that action;*
but a maintenance order granted by the sheriff in an action in which he has jurisdiction by virtue of this subsection shall be a provisional order.

(*2*) *This section applies to any action for the payment of aliment which is competent in the sheriff court, and includes an action of affiliation and aliment, but does not include an action of separation and aliment or adherence and aliment, or any action containing a crave for the custody of a child.*

[(1) In any action where the sheriff has jurisdiction by virtue of Rule 2(5) of Schedule 8 to the Civil Jurisdiction and Judgments Act 1982 and the defender resides in a reciprocating country, any maintenance order granted by the sheriff shall be a provisional order.]

Note. Sub-ss (1), (2) in italics substituted by sub-s (1) in square brackets by Civil Jurisdiction and Judgments Act 1982, s 23(2), Sch 12, Part II, para 3(1), as from 1 January 1987.

(3) Where in any action in which the payment of aliment in respect of a child is claimed, being an action *in which the sheriff has jurisdiction by virtue of* [referred to in] subsection (1) above, the sheriff is satisfied—

(a) that there are grounds on which a maintenance order containing a provision requiring the payment of aliment in respect of that child may be made in that action, but

(b) that he has no power to make that order unless he also makes an order providing for the custody of the child,

then, for the purpose of enabling the sheriff to make the maintenance order, the pursuer shall be deemed to be a person to whom the custody of the child has been committed by a decree of the sheriff which is for the time being in force.

Note. Words in square brackets substituted for words in italics by Civil Jurisdiction and Judgments Act 1982, s 23(2), Sch 12, Part II, para 3(2), as from 1 January 1987.

(4) In any action *in which the sheriff has jurisdiction by virtue of* [referred to in] subsection (1) above—

(a) it shall not be necessary for the pursuer to obtain a warrant for the citation of any person, and the action may commence and proceed without such citation;

(b) no decree shall be granted in favour of the pursuer unless the grounds of action have been substantiated by sufficient evidence and section 36(3) of the Sheriff Courts (Scotland) Act 1971 shall not apply in relation to any such action which is a summary cause.

Note. See Note to sub-s (3) above.

(5) No enactment empowering the sheriff to remit an action to the Court of Session shall apply in relation to proceedings *in which the sheriff has jurisdiction by virtue of* [referred to in] subsection (1) above.

Note. See Note to sub-s (3) above.

(6) Section 3(5) and (6) of this Act shall apply for the purposes of this section as they apply for the purposes of that section, with the substitution, for references to a magistrates' court, of references to the sheriff.

5. Variation and revocation of maintenance order made in United Kingdom—
(1) This section applies to a maintenance order a certified copy of which has been sent to a reciprocating country in pursuance of section 2 of this Act and to a maintenance order made by virtue of section 3 or 4 thereof which has been confirmed by a competent court in such a country.

(2) A court in the United Kingdom having power to vary a maintenance order to which this section applies shall have power to vary that order by a provisional order.

(3) Where the court hearing an application for the variation of a maintenance order to which this section applies proposes to vary it by increasing the rate of the payments under the order then, unless either—

(a) both the payer and the payee under the order appear in the proceedings, or

(b) the applicant appears and the appropriate process has been duly served on the other party,

the order varying the order shall be a provisional order.

[(3A) Where subsection (1) of section 60 of the Magistrates' Courts Act 1980 (revocation, variation, etc of orders for periodical payment) applies in relation to a maintenance order to which this section applies, that subsection shall have effect as if for the words 'by order on complaint,' there were substituted 'on an application being made, by order'.]

Note. Sub-s (3A) inserted by Maintenance Orders (Reciprocal Enforcement) Act 1992, s 1(2), Sch 1, Part II, para 7, as from 5 April 1993.

[(3B) Where paragraph (1) of Article 86 of the Magistrates' Courts (Northern Ireland) Order 1981 applies in relation to a maintenance order to which this section applies, that paragraph shall have effect as if for the words 'by order on complaint,' there were substituted 'on an application being made, by order'.]

Note. Sub-s (3B) inserted by Children (Northern Ireland) Order 1995, SI 1995 No 755, art 185(1), Sch 9, para 67, as from 4 November 1996.

(4) Where a court in the United Kingdom makes a provisional order varying a maintenance order to which this section applies, the prescribed officer of the court shall send in the prescribed manner to the court in a reciprocating country having power to confirm the provisional order a certified copy of the provisional order together with a document, authenticated in the prescribed manner, setting out or summarising the evidence given in the proceedings.

(5) Where a certified copy of a provisional order made by a court in a reciprocating country, being an order varying or revoking a maintenance order to which this section applies, together with a document, duly authenticated, setting out or summarising the evidence given in the proceedings in which the provisional order was made, is received by the court in the United Kingdom which made the maintenance order, that court may confirm or refuse to confirm the provisional order and, if that order is an order varying the maintenance order, confirm it either without alteration or with such alterations as it thinks reasonable.

(6) For the purpose of determining whether a provisional order should be confirmed under subsection (5) above, the court shall proceed as if an application for the variation or revocation, as the case may be, of the maintenance order in question had been made to it.

(7) Where a maintenance order to which this section applies has been varied by an order (including a provisional order which has been confirmed) made by a court in the United Kingdom or by a competent court in a reciprocating country, the maintenance order shall, as from *the date on which the order was made* [the date on which under the provisions of the order the variation is to take effect], have effect as varied by that order and, where that order was a provisional order, as if that order had been made in the form in which it was confirmed, and as if it had never been a provisional order.

Note. Words in square brackets substituted for words in italics by Domestic Proceedings and Magistrates' Courts Act 1978, s 54(a), as from 1 February 1981.

(8) Where a maintenance order to which this section applies has been revoked by an order made by a court in the United Kingdom or by a competent court in a reciprocating country, including a provisional order made by the last-mentioned court which has been confirmed by a court in the United Kingdom, the maintenance order shall, as from the *date on which the order was made* [the date on which under the provisions of the order the revocation is to take effect], be deemed to have ceased to have effect except as respects any arrears due under the maintenance order at that date.

Note. Words in square brackets substituted for words in italics by Domestic Proceedings and Magistrates' Courts Act 1978, s 54(b), as from 1 February 1981.

(9) Where before a maintenance order made by virtue of section 3 or 4 of this Act is confirmed a document, duly authenticated, setting out or summarising evidence taken in a reciprocating country for the purpose of proceedings relating to the confirmation of the order is received by the court in the United Kingdom which made the order, or that court, in compliance with a request made to it by a court in such a country, takes the evidence of a person residing in the United Kingdom for the purpose of such proceedings, the court in the United Kingdom which made the order shall consider that evidence and if, having done so, it appears to it that the order ought not to have been made—

(a) it shall, in such manner as may be prescribed, give to the person on whose application the maintenance order was made an opportunity to consider that evidence, to make representations with respect to it and to adduce further evidence; and

(b) after considering all the evidence and any representations made by that person, it may revoke the maintenance order.

(10) In the application of this section to Scotland—

(a) for subsection (3) there shall be substituted the following subsections:—

'(3) Where the payer under a maintenance order to which this section applies is for the time being residing in a reciprocating country, the court shall not, on an application made by the payee under the order for the variation of the order, vary the order by increasing the rate of the payments thereunder otherwise than by a provisional order.

(3A) It shall not be necessary for the payee under a maintenance order to which this section applies to intimate to any person the making by him of an application for a provisional order varying the said maintenance order by increasing the rate of the payments thereunder.';

(b) for subsection (6) there shall be substituted the following subsection:—

'(6) Where a certified copy of a provisional order varying or revoking a maintenance order to which this section applies is received by a court as mentioned in subsection (5) above, the prescribed officer of that court shall intimate to the payee under the maintenance order, in the prescribed manner, that the provisional order has been received as aforesaid and that unless the payee enters appearance within the prescribed period, the court will confirm the provisional order under this section.'

Orders made by courts in reciprocating countries

6. Registration in United Kingdom court of maintenance order made in reciprocating country—(1) This section applies to a maintenance order made, whether before or after the commencement of this Part of this Act, by a court in a reciprocating country, including such an order made by such a court which had been confirmed by a court in another reciprocating country but excluding a provisional order which has not been confirmed.

(2) Where a certified copy of an order to which this section applies is received by the *Secretary of State* [Lord Chancellor] from the responsible authority in a

reciprocating country, and it appears to the *Secretary of State* [Lord Chancellor] that the payer under the order is residing [or has assets] in the United Kingdom, he shall send the copy of the order to the prescribed officer of the appropriate court.

Note. Words 'Lord Chancellor' in square brackets substituted for words 'Secretary of State' in italics by virtue of Transfer of Functions (Magistrates' Courts and Family Law) Order 1992, SI 1992 No 709, art 4, as from 1 April 1992. Words 'or has assets' in square brackets added by Civil Jurisdiction and Judgments Act 1982, s 37(1), Sch 11, para 10(a), (b), as from 1 January 1987.

(3) Where the prescribed officer of the appropriate court receives from the *Secretary of State* [Lord Chancellor] a certified copy of an order to which this section applies, he shall, subject to subsection (4) below, register the order in the prescribed manner in that court.

Note. Words 'Lord Chancellor' in square brackets substituted for words 'Secretary of State' in italics by virtue of Transfer of Functions (Magistrates' Courts and Family Law) Order 1992, SI 1992 No 709, art 4, as from 1 April 1992.

(4) Before registering an order under this section an officer of a court shall take such steps as he thinks fit for the purpose of ascertaining whether the payer under the order is residing [or has assets] within the jurisdiction of the court, and if after taking those steps he is satisfied that the payer is not *so residing* [residing and has no assets within the jurisdiction of the court] he shall return the certified copy of the order to the *Secretary of State* [Lord Chancellor] with a statement giving such information as he possesses as to the whereabouts of the payer [and the nature and location of his assets.]

Note. Words 'or has assets', 'and the nature and location of his assets' in square brackets inserted, and words from 'residing' to 'jurisdiction of the court' in square brackets substituted for words 'so residing' in italics by Civil Jurisdiction and Judgments Act 1982, s 37(1), Sch 11, para 10, as from 1 January 1987. Words 'Lord Chancellor' in square brackets substituted for words 'Secretary of State' in italics by virtue of Transfer of Functions (Magistrates' Courts and Family Law) Order 1992, SI 1992 No 709, art 4, as from 1 April 1992.

7. Confirmation by United Kingdom court of provisional maintenance order made in reciprocating country—(1) This section applies to a maintenance order made, whether before or after the commencement of this Part of this Act, by a court in a reciprocating country being a provisional order.

(2) Where a certified copy of an order to which this section applies together with—

(a) a document duly authenticated, setting out or summarising the evidence given in the proceedings in which the order was made; and

(b) a statement of the grounds on which the making of the order might have been opposed by the payer under the order,

is received by the *Secretary of State* [Lord Chancellor] from the responsible authority in a reciprocating country, and it appears to the *Secretary of State* [Lord Chancellor] that the payer under the order is residing in the United Kingdom, he shall send the copy of the order and documents which accompanied it to the prescribed officer of the appropriate court, and that court shall—

(i) if the payer under the order establishes *any such defence as he might have raised* [any grounds on which he might have opposed the making of the order] in the proceedings in which the order was made, refuse to confirm the order; and

(ii) in any other case, confirm the order either without alteration or with such alterations as it thinks reasonable.

Note. Words 'Lord Chancellor' in square brackets substituted for words 'Secretary of State' in italics by virtue of Transfer of Functions (Magistrates' Courts and Family Law) Order 1992, SI 1992 No 709, art 4, as from 1 April 1992. Words from 'any grounds' to 'making of the order' in square brackets substituted for preceding words in italics by Maintenance Orders (Reciprocal Enforcement) Act 1992, s 1(2), Sch 1, Part II, para 8, as from 5 April 1993.

(3) In any proceedings for the confirmation under this section of a provisional order, the statement received from the court which made the order of the grounds on which the making of the order might have been opposed by the payer under the order shall be conclusive evidence that the payer might have *raised a defence on any of those grounds in the proceedings in which the order was made* [opposed the making of the order on any of those grounds].

Note. Words in square brackets substituted for words in italics by Maintenance Orders (Reciprocal Enforcement) Act 1992, s 1(2), Sch 1, Part II, para 8, as from 5 April 1993.

(4) For the purpose of determining whether a provisional order should be confirmed under this section *the court* [a magistrates' court in Northern Ireland] shall proceed as if an application for a maintenance order against the payer under the provisional order had been made to it.

Note. Words in square brackets substituted for words in italics by Maintenance Orders (Reciprocal Enforcement) Act 1992, s 1(2), Sch 1, Part II, para 8, as from 5 April 1993.

(5) The prescribed officer of a court having power under this section to confirm a provisional order shall, if the court confirms the order, register the order in the prescribed manner in that court, and shall, if the court refuses to confirm the order, return the certified copy of the order and the documents which accompanied it to the Secretary of State.

[(5A) Where a magistrates' court in England and Wales confirms a provisional order under this section, it shall at the same time exercise one of its powers under subsection (5B) below.

(5B) The powers of the court are—

(a) the power to order that payments under the order be made directly to the *clerk of the court or the clerk of any other magistrates' court in England and Wales* [*a justices' chief executive*] [the designated officer for the court or for any other magistrates' court in England and Wales];

(b) the power to order that payments under the order be made to *the clerk of the court, or to the clerk of any other magistrates' court in England and Wales* [*a justices' chief executive*] [the designated officer for the court or for any other magistrates' court in England and Wales], by such method or payment falling within section 59(6) of the Magistrates' Courts Act 1980 (standing order, etc) as may be specified;

(c) the power to make an attachment of earnings order under the Attachment of Earnings Act 1971 to secure payments under the order.

Note. Words 'a justices' chief executive' in square brackets in paras (a), (b) substituted for words 'the clerk of the court or the clerk of any other magistrates' court in England and Wales' in italics in para (a) and words 'the clerk of the court, or to the clerk of any other magistrates' court in England and Wales,' in italics in para (b) by the Access to Justice Act 1999, s 90, Sch 13, paras 71, 72, as from 1 April 2001. Words 'the designated officer for the court or for any other magistrates' court in England and Wales' in square brackets in paras (a), (b) substituted for words 'a justices' chief executive' in italics in paras (a), (b), by the Courts Act 2003, s 109(1), Sch 8, para 151, as from a day to be appointed.

(5C) In deciding which of the powers under subsection (5B) above it is to exercise, the court shall have regard to any representations made by the payer under the order.

(5D) Subsection (4) of section 59 of the Magistrates' Courts Act 1980 (power of court to require debtor to open account) shall apply for the purposes of subsection (5B) above as it applies for the purposes of that section but as if for paragraph (a) there were substituted—

'(a) the court proposes to exercise its power under paragraph (b) of section 7(5B) of the Maintenance Orders (Reciprocal Enforcement) Act 1972, and'.]

Note. Sub-ss (5A)–(5D) inserted by Maintenance Enforcement Act 1991, s 10, Sch 1, para 12, as from 1 April 1992.

[(5E) Where a court of summary jurisdiction in Northern Ireland confirms a provisional order under this section, it shall at the same time exercise one of its powers under subsection (5F) below.

(5F) The powers of the court are—

(a) the power to order that payments under the order be made directly to the collecting officer;

(b) the power to order that payments under the order be made to the collecting officer, by such method of payment falling within Article 85(7) of the Magistrates' Courts (Northern Ireland) Order 1981 (standing order, etc) as may be specified;

(c) the power to make an attachment of earnings order under Part IX of the Order of 1981 to secure payments under the order;

and in this subsection 'collecting officer' means the officer mentioned in Article 85(4) of the Order of 1981.

(5G) In deciding which of the powers under subsection (5F) above it is to exercise, the court shall have regard to any representations made by the payer under the order.

(5H) Paragraph (5) of Article 85 of the Magistrates' Courts (Northern Ireland) Order 1981 (power of court to require debtor to open account) shall apply for the purposes of subsection (5F) above as it applies for the purposes of that Article but as if for sub-paragraph (a) there were substituted—

'(a) the court proposes to exercise its power under paragraph (b) of section 7(5F) of the Maintenance Orders (Reciprocal Enforcement) Act 1972, and'.]

Note. Sub-ss (5E)–(5H) inserted by Family Law (Northern Ireland) Order 1993, SI 1993 No 1576, art 11, Sch 1, para 7, as from 4 November 1996.

(6) If *a summons to appear in* [notice of] the proceedings for the confirmation of the provisional order cannot be duly served on the payer under that order the officer by whom the certified copy of the order was received shall return that copy and the documents which accompanied it to the Secretary of State with a statement giving such information as he possesses as to the whereabouts of the payer.

Note. Words 'notice of' in square brackets substituted for words 'a summons to appear in' in italics by Maintenance Orders (Reciprocal Enforcement) Act 1992, s 1(2), Sch 1, Part II, para 8, as from 5 April 1993.

(7) This section shall apply to Scotland subject to the following modifications—

(a) for subsection (4) there shall be substituted the following subsection—

'(4) On receiving a certified copy of a provisional order sent to him in pursuance of subsection (2) above the prescribed officer of the appropriate court shall intimate to the payer under the order, in the prescribed manner, that the order has been received as aforesaid and that, unless the payer enters appearance within the prescribed period, the court will confirm the order under this section.';

(b) in subsection (6), for the words from the beginning to 'that order' there shall be substituted the words 'If such intimation as is mentioned in subsection (4) above cannot be given to the payer under a provisional order in pursuance of that subsection'; and

(c) in any proceedings for the confirmation under this section of a provisional order made by a court in a reciprocating country, the sheriff shall apply the law in force in that country with respect to the sufficiency of evidence.

[(8) *In the application of this section to Northern Ireland—*

(a) *in subsection (2)(i), for the words from 'any grounds' to 'making of the order' there shall be substituted 'any such defence as he might have raised',*

(b) *in subsection (3), for the words from 'opposed the making' to the end there shall be substituted 'raised a defence on any of those grounds in the proceedings in which the order was made.', and* (*c*) in subsection (*6*), for the words 'notice of' there shall be substituted 'a summons to appear in'.

Note. Sub-s (8) added by Maintenance Orders (Reciprocal Enforcement) Act 1992, s 1(2), Sch 1, Part II, para 8, as from 5 April 1993; repealed by Children (Northern Ireland) Order 1995, SI 1995 No 755, art 185(2), Sch 10, as from 4 November 1996.

8. Enforcement of maintenance order registered in United Kingdom court—
(1) Subject to subsection (2) below, a registered order may be enforced in the United Kingdom as if it has been made by the registering court and as if that court had had jurisdiction to make it; and proceedings for or with respect to the enforcement of any such order may be taken accordingly.

(2) Subsection (1) above does not apply to an order which is for the time being registered in the High Court under Part I of the Maintenance Orders Act 1958 or to an order which is for the time being registered in the High Court of Justice in Northern Ireland under Part II of the Maintenance and Affiliation Orders Act (Northern Ireland) 1966.

(3) Any person for the time being under an obligation to make payments in pursuance of a registered order shall give notice of any change of address to the *clerk* [appropriate officer] of the registered court, and any person failing without reasonable excuse to give such a notice shall be liable on summary conviction to a fine not exceeding [*£50*] [level 2 on the standard scale].

Note. Words 'appropriate officer' in square brackets substituted for word 'clerk' in italics by the Access to Justice Act 1999, s 90, Sch 13, paras 71, 73, as from 1 April 2001. £50 substituted for £10 by Domestic Proceedings and Magistrates' Courts Act 1978, s 89(2), Sch 2, para 33, as from 1 February 1981. Reference to level 2 substituted by Criminal Justice Act 1982, ss 37, 46(1).

[(3A) in subsection (3) above 'appropriate officer' means—
(a) in relation to a magistrates' court in England and Wales, the *justices' chief executive* [designated officer] for the court; and
(b) in relation to a court elsewhere, the clerk of the court.]

Note. Sub-s (3A) added by the Access to Justice Act 1999, s 90, Sch 13, paras 71, 73, as from 1 April 2001. Words 'designated officer' in square brackets substituted for words in italics by the Courts Act 2003, s 109(1), Sch 8, para 152(1), (2), as from a day to be appointed.

(*4*) An order which by virtue of this section is enforceable by a magistrates' court shall be enforceable as if it were an affiliation order made by that court; and the provisions of any enactment with respect to the enforcement of affiliation orders (including enactments relating to the accrual of arrears and the remission of sums due) shall apply accordingly.
In this subsection 'enactment' includes any order, rule or regulation made in pursuance of any Act. [an order made by that court to which that Article applies.]

Note. Words in square brackets substituted for words 'if it were ... any Act.' in relation to Northern Ireland by Children (Northern Ireland) Order 1995, SI 1995 No 755, art 185(1), Sch 9, para 68, as from 4 November 1996.

[(4) An order which by virtue of this section is enforceable by a magistrates' court shall [subject to the modifications of Article 98 of the Magistrates' Courts (Northern Ireland) Order 1981 specified in subsection (4C) below] [subject to the modifications of sections 76 and 93 of the Magistrates' Courts Act 1980 specified in subsections (4A) and (4B) below] be enforceable as if it were a magistrates' court maintenance order made by that court.
In this subsection 'magistrates' court maintenance order' has the same meaning as in section 150(1) of the Magistrates' Courts Act 1980.]

Note. Sub-s (4) in square brackets substituted for sub-s (4) in italics by Family Law Reform Act 1987, s 33(1), Sch 2, para 45, in relation to England and Wales, as from 1 April 1989. Words in first pair of square brackets inserted by Family Law (Northern Ireland) Order 1993, SI 1993 No 1576, art 11, Sch 1, para 8, as from 4 November 1996. Words in second pair of square brackets in new sub-s (4) inserted by Maintenance Enforcement Act 1991, s 10, Sch 1, para 13(1), as from 1 April 1992.

[(4A) Section 76 (enforcement of sums adjudged to be paid) shall have effect as if for subsections (4) to (6) there were substituted the following subsections—

'(4) Where proceedings are brought for the enforcement of a magistrates' court maintenance order under this section, the court may vary the order by exercising one of its powers under subsection (5) below.

(5) The powers of the court are—

(a) the power to order that payments under the order be made directly to the *clerk of the court or the clerk of any other magistrates' court* [*a justices' chief executive*] [the designated officer for the court or for any other magistrates' court];

(b) the power to order that payments under the order be made to *the clerk of the court, or to the clerk of any other magistrates' court* [*a justices' chief executive*] [the designated officer for the court or for any other magistrates' court], by such method of payment falling within section 59(6) above (standing order, etc) as may be specified;

(c) the power to make an attachment of earnings order under the Attachment of Earnings Act 1971 to secure payments under the order.

(6) In deciding which of the powers under subsection (5) above it is to exercise, the court shall have regard to any representations made by the debtor (within the meaning of section 59 above).

(7) Subsection (4) of section 59 above (power of court to require debtor to open account) shall apply for the purposes of subsection (5) above as it applies for the purposes of that section but as if for paragraph (a) there were substituted—

"(a) the court proposes to exercise its power under paragraph (b) of section 76(5) below, and"'

Note. Words 'a justices' chief executive' in square brackets in both places they occur substituted for words 'the clerk of the court or the clerk of any other magistrates' court' in italics and words 'the clerk of the court, or to the clerk of any other magistrates' court,' in italics by the Access to Justice Act 1999, s 90, Sch 13, paras 71, 73, as from 1 April 2001. Words 'the designated officer for the court or for any other magistrates' court' in square brackets in both places they occur substituted for words 'a justices' chief executive' in italics in both places they occur by the Courts Act 2003, s 109(1), Sch 8, para 152(1), (3), as from a day to be appointed.

(4B) In section 93 (complaint for arrears), subsection (6) (court not to impose imprisonment in certain circumstances) shall have effect as if for paragraph (b) there were substituted—

'(b) if the court is of the opinion that it is appropriate—

(i) to make an attachment of earnings order; or

(ii) to exercise its power under paragraph (b) of section 76(5) above.']

Note. Sub-ss (4A), (4B) inserted by Maintenance Enforcement Act 1991, s 10, Sch 1, para 13(2), as from 1 April 1992.

[(4C) Article 98 of the Magistrates' Courts (Northern Ireland) Order 1981 (enforcement of sums adjudged to be paid) shall have effect—

(a) as if for paragraph (7)(a) there were substituted the following paragraph—

'(a) if the court is of the opinion that it is appropriate—

(i) to make an attachment of earnings order; or

(ii) to exercise its power under paragraph (8C)(b)';

(b) as if for paragraphs (8B) to (8D) there were substituted the following paragraphs—

'(8B) Upon the appearance of a person or proof of service of the summons on him as mentioned in paragraph (4) for the enforcement of an order to which this Article applies, the court or resident magistrate may vary the order by exercising one of the powers under paragraph (8C).

(8C) The powers mentioned in paragraph (8B) are—

(a) the power to order that payments under the order be made directly to the collecting officer;

(b) the power to order that payments under the order be made to the collecting officer, by such method of payment falling within Article 85(7) (standing order, etc) as may be specified;

(c) the power to make an attachment of earnings order under Part IX to secure payments under the order.

(8D) In deciding which of the powers under paragraph (8C) is to be exercised, the court or, as the case may be, a resident magistrate shall have regard to any representations made by the debtor (within the meaning of Article 85).

(8E) Paragraph (5) of Article 85 (power of court to require debtor to open account) shall apply for the purposes of paragraph (8C) as it applies for the purposes of that Article but as if for sub-paragraph (a) there were substituted—

"(a) the court proposes to exercise its power under sub-paragraph (b) of Article 98(8C), and".'

Note. Sub-s (4C) inserted by Family Law (Northern Ireland) Order 1993, SI 1993 No 1576, art 11, Sch 1, para 8, as from 4 November 1996.

(5) The magistrates' court by which an order is enforceable by virtue of this section, and the officers thereof, shall take all such steps for enforcing [or facilitating the enforcement of] the order as may be prescribed.

Note. Words in square brackets inserted by Civil Jurisdiction and Judgments Act 1982, s 37(1), Sch 11, para 11, as from 1 January 1987.

(6) In any proceedings for or with respect to the enforcement of an order which is for the time being registered in any court under this Part of this Act a certificate of arrears sent to the prescribed officer of the court shall be evidence of the facts stated therein.

(7) Subject to subsection (8) below, sums of moneys payable under a registered order shall be payable in accordance with the order as from *the date on which the order was made* [the date on which they are required to be paid under the provisions of the order].

Note. Words in square brackets substituted for words in italics by Domestic Proceedings and Magistrates' Courts Act 1978, s 54(c), as from 1 February 1981.

(8) The court having power under section 7 of this Act to confirm a provisional order may, if it decides to confirm the order, direct that the sums of money payable under it shall be deemed to have been payable in accordance with the order as from *such date, being a date later than the date on which the order was made* [the date on which they are required to be paid under the provisions of the order or such later date], as it may specify; and subject to any such direction, a maintenance order registered under the said section 7 shall be treated as if it had been made in the form in which it was confirmed and as if it had never been a provisional order.

Note. Words in square brackets substituted for words in italics by Domestic Proceedings and Magistrates' Courts Act 1978, s 54(d), as from 1 February 1981.

(9) In the application of this section to Scotland—

(a) subsections (2) to (5) shall be omitted; and

(b) in subsection (6), for the word 'evidence' there shall be substituted the words 'sufficient evidence'.

(*10*) *For the purposes of the application of this section to Northern Ireland, in section 110(9) of the Magistrates' Courts Act (Northern Ireland) 1964 (orders for periodical payment of money), after paragraph (a) there shall be inserted the following paragraph:—*

'*(aa)   maintenance orders made outside the United Kingdom and registered in a court of summary jurisdiction in Northern Ireland under Part I of the Maintenance Orders (Reciprocal Enforcement) Act 1972;*'.

Note. Sub-s (10) repealed by Magistrates' Courts (Northern Ireland) Order 1981, SI 1981 No 1675, art 170(3), Sch 7.

9. Variation and revocation of maintenance order registered in United Kingdom court—(1) Subject to the provisions of this section, the registering court—

(a) shall have the like power, on an application made by the payer or payee under a registered order, to vary or revoke the order as if it had been made by the registering court and as if that court had had jurisdiction to make it; and

(b) shall have power to vary or revoke a registered order by a provisional order.

[(1ZA) Where the registering court is a magistrates' court in England and Wales, section 60 of the Magistrates' Courts Act 1980 (revocation, variation etc of orders for periodical payment) shall have effect in relation to the registered order—

[(za) as if in subsection (1) for the words 'by order on complaint,' there were substituted 'on an application being made, by order';]

(a) as if in subsection (3) for the words 'paragraphs (a) to (d) of section 59(3) above' there were substituted 'subsection (3A) below' and after that subsection there were inserted—

'(3A) The powers of the court are—

(a) the power to order that payments under the order be made directly to *the clerk of the court or the clerk of any other magistrates' court* [*a justices' chief executive*] [the designated officer for the court or for any other magistrates' court];

(b) the power to order that payments under the order be made to *the clerk of the court, or to the clerk of any other magistrates' court* [*a justices' chief executive*] [the designated officer for the court or for any other magistrates' court], by such method of payment falling within section 59(6) above (standing order, etc) as may be specified;

(c) the power to make an attachment of earnings order under the Attachment of Earnings Act 1971 to secure payments under the order.';

(b) as if in subsection (4) for paragraph (b) there were substituted—

'(b) payments under the order are required to be made to *the clerk of the court, or to the clerk of any other magistrates' court* [*a justices' chief executive*] [the designated officer for the court or for any other magistrates' court], by any method of payment falling within section 59(6) above (standing order, etc)';

and as if after the words 'the court' there were inserted 'which made the order';

(c) as if in subsection (5) for the words 'to the *clerk*' [*justices' chief executive for the court*] [designated officer for the court] there were substituted 'in accordance with paragraph (a) of subsection (3A) above';

(d) as if in subsection (7), paragraph (c) and the word 'and' immediately preceding it were omitted;

(e) as if in subsection (8) for the words 'paragraphs (a) to (d) of section 59(3) above' there were substituted 'subsection (3A) above';

(f) as if for subsections (9) and (10) there were substituted the following subsections—

'(9) In deciding, for the purposes of subsections (3) and (8) above, which of the powers under subsection (3A) above it is to exercise, the court shall have regard to any representations made by the debtor.

(10) Subsection (4) of section 59 above (power of court to require debtor to open account) shall apply for the purposes of subsection (3A) above as it applies for the purposes of that section but as if for paragraph (a) there were substituted—

"(a) the court proposes to exercise its power under paragraph (b) of section 60(3A) below, and" '.]

Note. Sub-s (1ZA) inserted by Maintenance Enforcement Act 1991, s 10, Sch 1, para 14, as from 1 April 1992. Sub-s (1ZA)(za) inserted by Maintenance Orders (Reciprocal Enforcement) Act 1992, s 1(2), Sch 1, Part II, para 9, as from 5 April 1993. Words 'a justices' chief executive' in square brackets in both places they occur substituted for words 'the clerk of the court or the clerk of any other magistrates' court' in italics and words 'the clerk of the court, or to the clerk of any other magistrates' court,' in italics in both places they occur by the Access for Justice Act 1999, s 90, Sch 13, paras 71, 74, as from 1 April 2001. Words 'the designated officer for the court or for any other magistrates' court' in square brackets in each place they occur substituted for words 'a justices' chief executive' in italics in each place they occur by the Courts Act 2003, s 109(1), Sch 8, para 153, as from a day to be appointed.

Words from 'and as if' to the end in italics repealed by the Access to Justice Act 1999, ss 90, 106, Sch 13, paras 71, 74, Sch 15, Pt V(7), as from 1 April 2001.

Words 'justices' chief executive for the court' in square brackets substituted for word 'clerk' in italics by the Access to Justice Act 1999, s 90, Sch 13, paras 71, 74, as from 1 April 2001.

Words 'designated officer for the court' in square brackets substituted for words 'justices' chief executive for the court' in italics by the Courts Act 2003, s 109(1), Sch 8, para 153, as from a day to be appointed.

[(1ZB) Where the registering court is a court of summary jurisdiction in Northern Ireland, Article 86 of the Magistrates' Courts (Northern Ireland) Order 1981 (revocation, variation etc, of orders for periodical payment) shall have effect in relation to the registered order—

[(za) as if in paragraph (1) for the words 'by order on complaint,' there were substituted 'on an application being made, by order';]

(a) as if in paragraph (3) for the words 'sub-paragraphs (a) to (d) of Article 85(3)' there were substituted 'paragraph (3A)' and after that paragraph there were inserted—

'(3A) The powers of the court are—

(a) the power to order that payments under the order be made directly to the collecting officer;

(b) the power to order that payments under the order be made to the collecting officer by such method of payment falling within Article 85(7) (standing order, etc) as may be specified;

(c) the power to make an attachment of earnings order under Part IX to secure payments under the order.';

(b) as if in paragraph (4) for sub-paragraph (b) there were substituted—

'(b) payments under the order are required to be made to the collecting officer by any method of payment falling within Article 85(7) (standing order, etc)';

and as if after the words 'petty sessions' there were inserted 'for the petty sessions district for which the court which made the order acts';

(c) as if in paragraph (5) for the words 'to the collecting officer' there were substituted 'in accordance with sub-paragraph (a) of paragraph (3A)';

(d) as if in paragraph (7), sub-paragraph (c) and the word 'and' immediately preceding it were omitted;

(e) as if in paragraph (8) for the words 'sub-paragraphs (a) to (d) of Article 85(3)' there were substituted 'paragraph (3A)';

(f) as if for paragraphs (9) and (10) there were substituted the following paragraphs—

'(9) In deciding, for the purposes of paragraphs (3) and (8), which of the powers under paragraph (3A) it is to exercise, the court shall have regard to any representations made by the debtor.

(10) Paragraph (5) of Article 85 (power of court to require debtor to open account) shall apply for the purposes of paragraph (3A) as it applies for the purposes of that Article but as if for sub-paragraph (a) there were substituted—

"(a) the court proposes to exercise its power under sub-paragraph (b) of Article 86(3A), and".'.]

Note. Sub-s (1ZB) inserted by Family Law (Northern Ireland) Order 1993, SI 1993 No 1576, art 11, Sch 1, para 9, as from 4 November 1996. Sub-s (1ZB)(za) inserted by Children (Northern Ireland) Order 1995, SI 1995 No 755, art 185(1), Sch 9, para 69, as from 4 November 1996.

[(1A) The powers conferred by subsection (1) above are not exercisable in relation to so much of a registered order as provides for the payment of a lump sum.]

Note. Sub-s (1A) added by Civil Jurisdiction and Judgments Act 1982, s 37(1), Sch 11, para 4(1), as from 1 January 1987.

[(1B) The registering court shall not vary or revoke a registered order if neither the payer nor the payee under the order is resident in the United Kingdom.]

Note. Sub-s (1B) added by Civil Jurisdiction and Judgments Act 1982 s 37(1), Sch 11, para 12, as from 1 January 1987.

(2) The registering court shall not vary a registered order otherwise than by a provisional order unless—

(a) both the payer and the payee under the registered order are for the time being residing in the United Kingdom; or
(b) the application is made by the payee under the registered order; or
(c) the variation consists of a reduction in the rate of payments under the registered order and is made solely on the ground that there has been a change in the financial circumstances of the payer since the registered order was made or, in the case of an order registered under section 7 of this Act, since the registered order was confirmed, and the courts in the reciprocating country in which the maintenance order in question was made do not have power, according to the law in force in that country, to confirm provisional orders varying maintenance orders.

(3) The registering court shall not revoke a registered order otherwise than by a provisional order unless both the payer and the payee under the registered order are for the time being residing in the United Kingdom.

(4) On an application for the revocation of a registered order the registering court shall, unless both the payer and the payee under the registered order are for the time being residing in the United Kingdom, apply the law applied by the reciprocating country in which the registered order was made; but where by virtue of this subsection the registering court is required to apply that law, that court may make a provisional order if it has reason to believe that the ground on which the application is made is a ground on which the order could be revoked according to the law applied by the reciprocating country, notwithstanding that it has not been established that it is such a ground.

(5) Where the registering court makes a provisional order varying or revoking a registered order the prescribed officer of the court shall send in the prescribed manner to the court in the reciprocating country which made the registered order a certified copy of the provisional order together with a document, authenticated in the prescribed manner, setting out or summarising the evidence given in the proceedings.

(6) Where a certified copy of a provisional order made by a court in a reciprocating country, being an order varying a registered order, together with a document, duly authenticated, setting out or summarising the evidence given in the proceedings in which the provisional order was made, is received by the registering court, that court may confirm the order either without alteration or with such alterations as it thinks reasonable or refuse to confirm the order.

(7) For the purpose of determining whether a provisional order should be confirmed under subsection (6) above the court shall proceed as if an application for the variation of the registered order had been made to it.

(8) Where a registered order has been varied by an order (including a provisional order which has been confirmed) made by a court in the United Kingdom or by a competent court in a reciprocating country, the registered order shall, as from *the date on which the order was made* [the date on which under the provisions of the order the variation is to take effect], have effect as varied by that order and, where that order was a provisional order, as if that order had been made in the form in which it was confirmed and as if it had never been a provisional order.

Note. Words in square brackets substituted for words in italics by Domestic Proceedings and Magistrates' Courts Act 1978, s 54(e), as from 1 February 1981.

(9) Where a registered order has been revoked by an order made by a court in the United Kingdom or by a competent court in a reciprocating country, including a provisional order made by the first-mentioned court which has been confirmed by a competent court in a reciprocating country, the registered order shall, as from *the date on which the order was made* [the date on which under the provisions of the order the revocation is to take effect], be deemed to have ceased to have effect except as respects any arrears due under the registered order at that date.

Note. Words in square brackets substituted for words in italics by Domestic Proceedings and Magistrates' Courts Act 1978, s 54(f), as from 1 February 1981.

(10) The prescribed officer of the registering court shall register in the prescribed manner any order varying a registered order other than a provisional order which is not confirmed.

(11) In the application of this section to Scotland—

(a) after subsection (4) there shall be inserted the following subsection:—

'(4A) It shall not be necessary for the payer under a registered order to intimate to any person the making by him of an application for a provisional order varying or revoking the registered order.'; and

(b) for subsection (7) there shall be substituted the following subsection:—

'(7) Where a certified copy of a provisional order varying a registered order is received by the registering court as mentioned in subsection (6) above, the prescribed officer of that court shall intimate to the payer under the registered order, in the prescribed manner, that the provisional order has been received as aforesaid and that, unless the payer enters appearance within the prescribed period, the court will confirm the provisional order under this section.'

10. Cancellation of registration and transfer of order—(1) Where—

(a) a registered order is revoked by an order made by the registering court; or

(b) a registered order is revoked by a provisional order made by that court which has been confirmed by a court in a reciprocating country and notice of the confirmation is received by the registering court; or

(c) a registered order is revoked by an order made by a court in such a country and notice of the revocation is received by the registering court,

the prescribed officer of the registering court shall cancel the registration; but any arrears due under the registered order at the date when its registration is cancelled by virtue of this subsection shall continue to be recoverable as if the registration had not been cancelled.

(2) Where the prescribed officer of the registering court is of opinion that the payer under a registered order *has ceased to reside within the jurisdiction of that court* [is not residing within the jurisdiction of that court and has no assets within that jurisdiction against which the order can be effectively enforced], he shall cancel the registration of the order and, subject to subsection (3) below, shall send the certified copy of the order to the *Secretary of State* [Lord Chancellor].

(3) Where the prescribed officer of the registering court, being a magistrates' court, is of opinion that the payer is residing [or has assets] within the jurisdiction of another magistrates' court in that part of the United Kingdom in which the registering court is, he shall transfer the order to that other court by sending the certified copy of the order to the prescribed officer of that other court.

(4) On the transfer of an order under subsection (3) above the prescribed officer of the court to which it is transferred shall, subject to subsection (6) below, register the order in the prescribed manner in that court.

(5) Where the certified copy of an order is received by the *Secretary of State* [Lord Chancellor] under this section and it appears to him that the payer under the order is *still residing* [residing or has assets] in the United Kingdom, he shall transfer the order to the appropriate court by sending the certified copy of the order together with the related documents to the prescribed officer of the appropriate court and, subject to subsection (6) below, that officer shall register the order in the prescribed manner in that court.

(6) Before registering an order in pursuance of subsection (4) or (5) above an officer of a court shall take such steps as he thinks fit for the purpose of ascertaining whether the payer is residing [or has assets] within the jurisdiction of the court, and if after taking those steps he is satisfied that the payer is not *so residing* [residing and has no assets within the jurisdiction of the court] he shall send the certified copy of the order to the *Secretary of State* [Lord Chancellor].

(7) The officer of a court who is required by any of the foregoing provisions of this section to send to the *Secretary of State* [Lord Chancellor] or to the prescribed officer of another court the certified copy of an order shall send with that copy—

   (a) a certificate of arrears signed by him;
   (b) a statement giving such information as he possesses as to the whereabouts of the payer [and the nature and location of his assets]; and
   (c) any relevant documents in his possession relating to the case.

(8) In the application of this section to Scotland—

   (a) in subsection (2), for the words 'within the jurisdiction of that court' there shall be substituted the words 'in Scotland'; and
   (b) subsections (3) and (4) shall be omitted.

Note. In sub-ss (2), (5), (6), (7), references to Lord Chancellor substituted for references to Secretary of State by virtue of Transfer of Functions (Magistrates' Courts and Family Law) Order 1992, SI 1992 No 709, art 4, as from 1 April 1992. In sub-ss (2), (3), (5), (6), (7) other words in square brackets substituted for words in italics or added by Civil Jurisdiction and Judgments Act 1982, s 37(1), Sch 11, Part III, para 13, as from 1 January 1987.

11. Steps to be taken by Secretary of State where payer under certain orders is not residing in the United Kingdom—(1) If [at any time] it appears to the *Secretary of State* [Lord Chancellor] that the payer under a maintenance order, a certified copy of which has been received by him from a reciprocating country, is not residing *in the United Kingdom or, in the case of an order which subsequently became a registered order, has ceased to reside therein* [and has no assets in the United Kingdom], he shall send to the responsible authority in that country or, if having regard to all the circumstances he thinks it proper to do so, to the responsible authority in another reciprocating country—

   (a) the certified copy of the order in question and a certified copy of any order varying that order;
   (b) if the order has at any time been a registered order, a certificate of arrears signed by the prescribed officer;
   (c) a statement giving such information as the *Secretary of State* [Lord Chancellor] possesses as to the whereabouts of the payer [and the nature and location of his assets]; and
   (d) any other relevant documents in his possession relating to the case.

Note. Words 'at any time', 'and the nature and location of his assets' in square brackets inserted, and words 'and has no assets in the United Kingdom' in square brackets substituted for preceding words in italics by Civil Jurisdiction and Judgments Act 1982, s 37(1), Sch 11, Part III, para 14, as from 1 January 1987. Words 'Lord Chancellor' in square brackets substituted for words 'Secretary of State' in italics by virtue of Transfer of Functions (Magistrates' Courts and Family Law) Order 1992, SI 1992 No 709, art 4, as from 1 April 1992.

(2) Where the documents mentioned in subsection (1) above are sent to the responsible authority in a reciprocating country other than that in which the order in question was made, the *Secretary of State* [Lord Chancellor] shall inform the responsible authority in the reciprocating country in which that order was made of what he has done.

Note. Words 'Lord Chancellor' in square brackets substituted for words 'Secretary of State' in italics by virtue of Transfer of Functions (Magistrates' Courts and Family Law) Order 1992, SI 1992 No 709, art 4, as from 1 April 1992.

Appeals

12. Appeals—(1) No appeal shall lie from a provisional order made in pursuance of any provision of this Part of this Act by a court in the United Kingdom.

(2) Where in pursuance of any such provision any such court confirms or refuses to confirm a provisional order made by a court in a reciprocating country, whether a maintenance order or an order varying or revoking a maintenance order, the payer or payee under the maintenance order shall have the like right of appeal (if any) from the confirmation of, or refusal to confirm, the provisional order as he would have if that order were not a provisional order and the court which confirmed or refused to confirm it had made or, as the case may be, refused to make it.

(3) Where in pursuance of any such provision any such court makes, or refuses to make, an order varying or revoking a maintenance order made by a court in a reciprocating country, then, subject to subsection (1) above, the payer or payee under the maintenance order shall have the like right of appeal (if any) from that order or from the refusal to make it as he would have if the maintenance order had been made by the first-mentioned court.

(4) Nothing in this section (except subsection (1)) shall be construed as affecting any right of appeal conferred by any other enactment.

Evidence

13. Admissibility of evidence given in reciprocating country—(1) A statement contained in—

(a) a document, duly authenticated, which purports to set out or summarise evidence given in proceedings in a court in a reciprocating country; or

(b) a document, duly authenticated, which purports to set out or summarise evidence taken in such a country for the purpose of proceedings in a court in the United Kingdom under this Part of this Act, whether in response to a request made by such a court or otherwise; or

(c) a document, duly authenticated, which purports to have been received in evidence in proceedings in a court in such a country or to be a copy of a document so received,

shall in any proceedings in a court in the United Kingdom relating to a maintenance order to which this Part of this Act applies be admissible as evidence of any fact stated therein to the same extent as oral evidence of that fact is admissible in those proceedings.

(2) A document purporting to set out or summarise evidence given as mentioned in subsection (1)(a) above, or taken as mentioned in subsection (1)(b) above, shall be deemed to be duly authenticated for the purposes of that subsection if the

document purports to be certified by the judge, magistrate or other person before whom the evidence was given, or, as the case may be, by whom it was taken, to be the original document containing or recording, or, as the case may be, summarising, that evidence or a true copy of that document.

(3) A document purporting to have been received in evidence as mentioned in subsection (1)(c) above, or to be a copy of a document so received, shall be deemed to be duly authenticated for the purposes of that subsection if the document purports to be certified by a judge, magistrate or officer of the court in question to have been, or to be a true copy of a document which has been, so received.

(4) It shall not be necessary in any such proceedings to prove the signature or official position of the person appearing to have given such a certificate.

(5) Nothing in this section shall prejudice the admission in evidence of any document which is admissible in evidence apart from this section.

14. Obtaining of evidence needed for purpose of certain proceedings—(1) Where for the purpose of any proceedings in a court in a reciprocating country relating to a maintenance order to which this Part of this Act applies a request is made by or on behalf of that court for the taking in the United Kingdom of the evidence of a person residing therein relating to matters specified in the request, such court in the United Kingdom as may be prescribed shall have power to take that evidence and, after giving notice of the time and place at which the evidence is to be taken to such persons and in such manner as it thinks fit, shall take the evidence in such manner as may be prescribed.

Evidence taken in compliance with such a request shall be sent in the prescribed manner by the prescribed officer of the court to the court in the reciprocating country by or on behalf of which the request was made.

(2) Where any person, not being the payer or the payee under the maintenance order to which the proceedings in question relate, is required by virtue of this section to give evidence before a court in the United Kingdom, the court may order that there shall be paid—

(a) if the court is a court in England, Wales or Scotland, out of moneys provided by parliament; and

(b) if the court is a court in Northern Ireland, out of moneys provided by the *Parliament of Northern Ireland* [Parliament],

such sums as appear to the court reasonably sufficient to compensate that person for the expense, trouble or loss of time properly incurred in or incidental to his attendance.

Note. 'Parliament' substituted for 'Parliament of Northern Ireland' by Northern Ireland (Modification of Enactments—No 1) Order 1973, SI 1973 No 2163, art 14(1), Sch 5, para 22.

(3) *Section 77(1), (3) and (4) of the Magistrates' Courts Act 1952* [section 97(1), (3) and (4) of the Magistrates' Courts Act 1980] (which provide for compelling the attendance of witnesses, etc) shall apply in relation to a magistrates' court having power under subsection (1) above to take the evidence of any person as if the proceedings in the court in a reciprocating country for the purpose of which a request for the taking of the evidence has been made were proceedings in the magistrates' court and had been begun by complaint.

Note. Words in square brackets substituted for words in italics by Magistrates' Courts Act 1980, s 154, Sch 7, para 105, as from 6 July 1981.

(4) Paragraphs 71 and 73 of Schedule 1 to the Sheriff Courts (Scotland) Act 1907 (which provide for the citation of witnesses, etc) shall apply in relation to a sheriff having power under subsection (1) above to take the evidence of any person as if the proceedings in the court in a reciprocating country for the purpose of which a request for the taking of the evidence has been made were proceedings in the sheriff court.

(5) A court in the United Kingdom may for the purpose of any proceedings in that court under this Part of this Act relating to a maintenance order to which this part of this Act applies request a court in a reciprocating country to take or provide evidence relating to such matters as may be specified in the request and may remit the case to that court for that purpose.

(6) In the application of this section to Northern Ireland, in subsection (3), for the reference to *section 77(1), (3) and (4) of the Magistrates' Courts Act 1952* [section 97(1), (3) and (4) of the Magistrates' Courts Act 1980] there shall be substituted a reference to *sections 120(1), (3) and (4), 121 and 122 of the Magistrates' Courts Act (Northern Ireland) 1964* [Articles 118(1), (3) and (4), 119 and 120 of the Magistrates' Courts (Northern Ireland) Order 1981].

Note. Words in first pair of square brackets substituted for words in italics by Magistrates' Courts Act 1980, s 154, Sch 7, para 105, as from 6 July 1981. Words in second pair of square brackets substituted for preceding words in italics by Magistrates' Courts (Northern Ireland) Order 1981, SI 1981 No 1675, art 170(2), Sch 6, Part I, para 21.

15. Order, etc made abroad need not be proved.   For the purposes of this Part of this Act, unless the contrary is shown—

(a) any order made by a court in a reciprocating country purporting to bear the seal of that court or to be signed by any person in his capacity as a judge, magistrate or officer of the court, shall be deemed without further proof to have been duly sealed or, as the case may be, to have been signed by that person;

(b) the person by whom the order was signed shall be deemed without further proof to have been a judge, magistrate or officer, as the case may be, of that court when he signed it and, in the case of an officer, to have been authorised to sign it; and

(c) a document purporting to be a certified copy of an order made by a court in a reciprocating country shall be deemed without further proof to be such a copy.

Supplemental

16. Payment of sums under orders made abroad: conversion of currency—
(1) Payment of sums due under a registered order shall, while the order is registered in a court in England, Wales or Northern Ireland, be made in such manner and to such person as may be prescribed.

(2) Where the sums required to be paid under a registered order are expressed in a currency other than the currency of the United Kingdom, then, as from the relevant date, the order shall be treated as if it were an order requiring the payment of such sums in the currency of the United Kingdom as, on the basis of the rate of exchange prevailing at that date, are equivalent to the sums so required to be paid.

(3) Where the sum specified in any statement, being a statement of the amount of any arrears due under a maintenance order made by a court in a reciprocating country, is expressed in a currency other than the currency of the United Kingdom, that sum shall be deemed to be such sum in the currency of the United Kingdom as, on the basis of the rate of exchange prevailing at the relevant date, is equivalent to the sum so specified.

(4) For the purposes of this section a written statement purporting to be signed by an officer of any bank in the United Kingdom certifying that a specified rate of exchange prevailed between the currencies at a specified date and that at such a rate a specified sum in the currency of the United Kingdom is equivalent to a specified sum in another specified currency shall be evidence of the rate of exchange so prevailing on that date and of the equivalent sums in terms of the respective currencies.

(5) In this section 'the relevant date' means—

(a) in relation to a registered order or to a statement of arrears due under a maintenance order made by a court in a reciprocating country, the date on which the order first becomes a registered order or (if earlier) the date on which it is confirmed by a court in the United Kingdom;

(b) in relation to a registered order which has been varied, the date on which the last order varying that order is registered in a court in the United Kingdom or (if earlier) the date on which the last order varying that order is confirmed by such a court.

(6) In the application of this section to Scotland:—

(a) subsection (1) shall not apply;

(b) in subsection (4), for the word 'evidence' there shall be substituted the words 'sufficient evidence'.

17. Proceedings in magistrates' courts—(*1*) *Subject to subsection (2) below, the proceedings which are domestic proceedings within the meaning of the Magistrates' Courts Act 1952 shall include all proceedings in a magistrates' court under this Part of this Act other than proceedings for the variation or enforcement of a maintenance order.*

(2) The magistrates' court before which there fall to be heard any proceedings for the variation of a maintenance order to which this Part of this Act applies may, if it thinks fit, order that those proceedings and any other proceedings being heard therewith shall be treated for the purposes of the said Act of 1952 as domestic proceedings.

(3) The said Act of 1952 shall have effect in accordance with subsections (1) and (2) above notwithstanding anything in subsection (1) of section 56 thereof or section 5 of the Legitimacy Act 1959 (definition of 'domestic proceedings').

Note. Words 'or section 5 of the Legitimacy Act 1959' repealed by Affiliation Proceedings (Amendment) Act 1972, s 3(3), and sub-ss (1)–(3) repealed by Domestic Proceedings and Magistrates' Courts Act 1978, Sch 3, as from 1 November 1979.

(4) Anything authorised or required by this Part of this Act to be done by, to or before the magistrates' court by, to or before which any other thing was done may be done by, to or before any magistrates' court acting for *the same petty sessions area* [in the same local justice area] (or, in Northern Ireland, [acting for the same] petty sessions district) as that court.

Note. Words 'in the same local justice area' in square brackets substituted for words in italics and words 'acting for the same' in square brackets added by the Courts Act 2003, s 109(1), Sch 8, para 154, as from a day to be appointed.

(5) Any application which by virtue of a provision of this Part of this Act is made to a magistrates' court [in Northern Ireland] shall be made by complaint.

Note. Words 'in Northern Ireland' in square brackets inserted by Maintenance Orders (Reciprocal Enforcement) Act 1992, s 1(2), Sch 1, Part II, para 10, as from 5 April 1993. Sub-s (5) repealed by Children (Northern Ireland) Order 1995, SI 1995 No 755, art 185(2), Sch 9, para 70, Sch 10, as from 4 November 1996.

[(5A) Where the respondent to an application for the variation or revocation of—

(a) a maintenance order made by a magistrates' court in England and Wales, being an order to which section 5 of this Act applies; or

(b) a registered order which is registered in such a court,

is residing in a reciprocating country, a magistrates' court in England and Wales shall have jurisdiction to hear the application (where it would not have such jurisdiction apart from this subsection) if it would have had jurisdiction to hear it had the respondent been residing in England and Wales.]

Note. Sub-s (5A) inserted by Maintenance Orders (Reciprocal Enforcement) Act 1992, s 1(2), Sch 1, Part II, para 10, as from 5 April 1993.

(6) A magistrates' court in Northern Ireland shall have jurisdiction to hear a complaint for the variation or revocation—

   (a) *of a maintenance order made by such a court, being an order to which section 5 of this Act applies; or*
   (b) *of a registered order which is registered in that court.*
if the defendant to the complaint is residing in a reciprocating country and the court would have jurisdiction to hear the complaint had the defendant been residing in Northern Ireland.
   [(6) Where the respondent to an application for the variation or revocation of—
   (a) a maintenance order made by a magistrates' court in Northern Ireland, being an order to which section 5 of this Act applies; or
   (b) a registered order which is registered in such a court,
is residing in a reciprocating country, a magistrates' court in Northern Ireland shall have jurisdiction to hear the application (where it would not have jurisdiction apart from this subsection) if it would have had jurisdiction to hear it had the respondent been residing in Northern Ireland.]

Note. Sub-s (6) in square brackets substituted for sub-s (6) in italics by Children (Northern Ireland) Order 1995, SI 1995 No 755, art 185(2), Sch 9, para 70, Sch 10, as from 4 November 1996.

   (7) Where the *defendant* [respondent] to *a complaint* [an application] for the variation or revocation—
   (a) of a maintenance order made by a magistrates' court, being an order to which section 5 of this act applies; or
   (b) of a registered order registered in a magistrates' court,
does not appear at the time and place appointed for the hearing of *the complaint* [the application], but the court is satisfied that the *defendant* [respondent] is residing in a reciprocating country, the court may proceed to hear and determine *the complaint* [the application] at the time and place appointed for the hearing or for any adjourned hearing in like manner as if the *defendant* [respondent] had appeared at that time and place.

Note. Words in square brackets substituted for words in italics by Maintenance Orders (Reciprocal Enforcement) Act 1992, s 1(2), Sch 1, Part II, para 10, as from 5 April 1993.

   [(7A) *In the application of this section to Northern Ireland, in subsection (7)—*
   (a) *for the word 'respondent', in each place where it occurs, there shall be substituted 'defendant'; and*
   (b) *for the words 'an application' and 'the application', in each place where they occur, there shall be substituted 'a complaint' and 'the complaint' respectively.*]

Note. Sub-s (7A) added by Maintenance Orders (Reciprocal Enforcement) Act 1992, s 1(2), Sch 1, Part II, para 10, as from 5 April 1993; repealed by Children (Northern Ireland) Order 1995, SI 1995 No 755, art 185, Sch 9, para 70, Sch 10, as from 4 November 1996.

   (8) *At the end of paragraph (a) of section 98 of the Magistrates' Courts Act (Northern Ireland) 1964 (definition of 'domestic proceedings') there shall be inserted the words 'or Part I of the Maintenance Orders (Reciprocal Enforcement) Act 1972'.*

Note. Sub-s (8) repealed by Magistrates' Courts (Northern Ireland) Order 1981, SI 1981 No 1675, art 170(3), Sch 7.

18. Magistrates' courts rules—(1) *Without prejudice to the generality of the power to make rules under section 15 of the Justices of the Peace Act 1949* [*section 144 of the Magistrates' Courts Act 1980*] *(magistrates' courts rules), provision may be made by such rules with respect to any of the following matters, namely—* [Rules of court may make provision with respect to—]
   (a) the circumstances in which anything authorised or required by this Part of this Act to be done by, to or before a magistrates' court acting *for a particular petty sessions area* [in a particular local justice area] or by, to or before an officer of that court may be done by, to or before a magistrates' court acting *for such other petty sessions area* [in such other local justice area] as the rules may provide or by, to or before an officer of that court;

(b) the orders made, or other things done, by a magistrates' court, or an officer of such a court, under this Part of this Act, or by a court in a reciprocating country, notice of which is to be given to such persons as the rules may provide and the manner in which such notices shall be given;

(c) the cases and manner in which courts in reciprocating countries are to be informed of orders made, or other things done, by a magistrates' court under this Part of this Act;

(d) the cases and manner in which a justices' clerk may take evidence needed for the purpose of proceedings in a court in a reciprocating country relating to a maintenance order to which this Part of this Act applies;

(e) the circumstances and manner in which cases may be remitted by magistrates' courts to courts in reciprocating countries;

(f) the circumstances and manner in which magistrates' courts may for the purposes of this Part of this Act communicate with courts in reciprocating countries.

Note. Words 'section 144 of the Magistrates' Court Act 1980' in square brackets substituted for words 'section 15 of the Justices of the Peace Act 1949' in italics by Magistrates' Courts Act 1980, s 154, Sch 7, para 106, as from 6 July 1981. Words from 'Rules of court' to 'with respect to—' in square brackets substituted for words from 'without prejudice to' to 'matters, namely—' in italics and in para (a) words 'in a particular local justice area' and 'in such other local justice area' in square brackets substituted for words in italics by the Courts Act 2003, s 109(1), Sch 8, para 155, as from a day to be appointed.

[(1A) For the purpose of giving effect to this Part of this Act, *rules made under section 144 of the Magistrates' Courts Act 1980* [rules of court] may make, in relation to any proceedings brought under or by virtue of this Part of this Act, any provision not covered by subsection (1) above which—

(a) falls within subsection (2) of section 93 of the Children Act 1989, and

(b) may be made in relation to relevant proceedings under that section.]

Note. Sub-s (1A) inserted by Maintenance Orders (Reciprocal Enforcement) Act 1992, s 1(2), Sch 1, Part II, para 11, as from 5 April 1993.

Words 'rules of court' in square brackets substituted for words in italics by the Courts Act 2003, s 109(1), Sch 8, para 155, as from a day to be appointed.

(2) Rules with respect to the matters mentioned in subsection (1) above may be made in accordance with *section 23 of the Magistrates' Courts Act (Northern Ireland) 1964* [Article 13 of the Magistrates' Courts (Northern Ireland) Order 1981] in relation to proceedings or matters in magistrates' courts in Northern Ireland under this Part of this Act.

Note. Words in square brackets substituted for words in italics by Magistrates' Courts (Northern Ireland) Order 1981, SI 1981 No 1675, art 170(2), Sch 6, Part I, para 22.

[(2A) For the purpose of giving effect to this Part of this Act, rules made in accordance with Article 13 of the Magistrates' Courts (Northern Ireland) Order 1981 may make, in relation to any proceedings brought under or by virtue of this Part of this Act, any provision not covered by subsection (2) above which—

(a) falls within paragraph (2) of Article 165 of the Children (Northern Ireland) Order 1995, and

(b) may be made in relation to relevant proceedings under that Article.]

Note. Sub-s (2A) inserted by Children (Northern Ireland) Order 1995, SI 1995 No 755, art 185, Sch 9, para 71, as from 4 November 1996.

19. Rules for sheriff court. Without prejudice to the generality of the powers conferred on the Court of Session by section 32 of the Sheriff Courts (Scotland) Act 1971 to regulate by act of sederunt the procedure of the sheriff court, the said powers shall include power—

(a) to prescribe the decrees granted, or other things done, by the sheriff, or an officer of the sheriff court, under this Part of this Act, or by a court in a reciprocating country, notice of which is to be given to such persons as the act of sederunt may provide and the manner in which such notice shall be given;

(b) to provide that evidence needed for the purpose of proceedings in a court in a reciprocating country relating to a maintenance order to which this Part of this Act applies may, in such cases and manner as the act of sederunt may provide, be taken by a sheriff clerk or sheriff clerk depute;

(c) to prescribe the cases and manner in which courts in reciprocating countries are to be informed of decrees granted, or other things done, by the sheriff under this Part of this Act;

(d) to prescribe the circumstances and manner in which cases may be remitted by the sheriff to courts in reciprocating countries;

(e) to prescribe the circumstances and manner in which the sheriff may for the purposes of this Part of this Act communicate with courts in reciprocating countries.

20. Restriction on enforcement of arrears under maintenance order registered in Scotland.   Where a maintenance order is for the time being registered in the sheriff court under this Part of this Act, a person shall not be entitled, except with the leave of the sheriff, to enforce, whether by diligence or otherwise, the payment of any arrears due under the order, if either—

(a) the sheriff has made a provisional order under section 9 of this Act revoking the said maintenance order and the arrears accrued after the making of the said provisional order, or

(b) the arrears accrued before the commencement of this Part of this Act;

and on any application for leave to enforce the payment of any such arrears, the sheriff may refuse leave, or may grant leave subject to such restrictions and conditions (including conditions as to the allowing of time for payment or the making of payment by instalments) as he thinks appropriate, or may remit the payment of such arrears or of any part thereof.

21. Interpretation of Part I—(1) In this Part of this Act—

'affiliation order' means an order (however described) adjudging, finding or declaring a person to be the father of a child, whether or not it also provides for the maintenance of the child;

'the appropriate court' in relation to a person residing [or having assets] in England and Wales or in Northern Ireland means a magistrates' court, and in relation to a person residing [or having assets] in Scotland means *the sheriff court* [a sheriff court] within the jurisdiction of which that person is residing [or has assets];

Note. Words in square brackets substituted or inserted by Civil Jurisdiction and Judgments Act 1982, s 37(1), Sch 11, para 15, as from 1 January 1987.

'certificate of arrears', in relation to a maintenance order, means a certificate certifying that the sum specified in the certificate is to the best of the information or belief of the officer giving the certificate the amount of the arrears due under the order at the date of the certificate or, as the case may be, that to the best of his information or belief there are no arrears due thereunder at that date;

'certified copy', in relation to an order of a court, means a copy of the order certified by the proper officer of the court to be a true copy;

'court' includes any tribunal or person having power to make, confirm, enforce, vary or revoke a maintenance order;

'*maintenance*', *as respects Scotland, means aliment;*

'maintenance order' means an order (however described) of any of the following descriptions, that is to say—

(a) an order (including an affiliation order or order consequent upon an affiliation order) which provides for the *periodical payment of sums of money* [payment of a lump sum or the making of periodical payments] towards the maintenance of any person, being a person whom the person liable to make payments under the order is, according to the law applied in the place where the order was made, liable to maintain; and

[(aa) an order which has been made in Scotland, on or after the granting of a decree of divorce, for the payment of a periodical allowance by one party to the marriage to the other party; and]

Note. Definition 'maintenance' repealed and para (aa) in definition 'maintenance order' added by Domestic Proceedings and Magistrates' Courts Act 1978, s 55(a), as from 1 February 1981.

Words in square brackets in para (a) of definition 'maintenance order' substituted for words in italics by Civil Jurisdiction and Judgments Act 1982, s 37(1), Sch 11, para 4(2)(a), as from 1 January 1987.

(b) an affiliation order or order consequent upon an affiliation order, being an order which provides for the payment by a person adjudged, found or declared to be a child's father of expenses incidental to the child's birth or, where the child has died, of his funeral expenses,

and, in the case of a maintenance order which has been varied, means that order as varied;

'order', as respects Scotland, includes any interlocutor and any decree or provision contained in an interlocutor;

'payee', in relation to a maintenance order, means the person entitled to the payments for which the order provides;

'payer', in relation to a maintenance order, means the person liable to make payments under the order;

'prescribed', in relation to a magistrates' court *in England and Wales or* in Northern Ireland, means prescribed *by rules made under section 15 of the Justices of the Peace Act 1949* [*section 144 of the Magistrates' Courts Act 1980*] *or* by rules made in accordance with *section 23 of the Magistrates' Courts Act (Northern Ireland) 1964* [Article 13 of the Magistrates' Courts (Northern Ireland) Order 1981], *as the case may be,* and in relation to any other court means prescribed by rules of court;

Note. Words in first pair of square brackets substituted for words in italics by Magistrates' Courts Act 1980, s 154, Sch 7, para 107, as from 6 July 1981. Words in second pair of square brackets substituted for words in italics by Magistrates' Courts (Northern Ireland) Order 1981, SI 1981 No 1675, art 170(2), Sch 6, Part I, para 23. Words 'in England and Wales or', words from 'by rules made' to 'Magistrates' Courts Act 1980 or' and words 'as the case may be,' in italics repealed by the Courts Act 2003, s 109(1), (3), Sch 8, para 156, Sch 10, as from a day to be appointed.

'provisional order' means (according to the context)—

(a) an order made by a court in the United Kingdom which is provisional only and has no effect unless and until confirmed, with or without alteration, by a competent court in a reciprocating country; or

(b) an order made by a court in a reciprocating country which is provisional only and has no effect unless and until confirmed, with or without alteration, by a court in the United Kingdom having power under this Part of this Act to confirm it;

'reciprocating country' has the meaning assigned to it by section 1 of this Act;

'registered order' means a maintenance order which is for the time being registered in a court in the United Kingdom under this Part of this Act;

'registering court', in relation to a registered order, means the court in which that order is for the time being registered under this Part of this Act;

'the responsible authority', in relation to a reciprocating country, means any person who in that country has functions similar to those of the *Secretary of State* [Lord Chancellor] under this Part of this Act.

Note. Words 'Lord Chancellor' in square brackets substituted for words in italics by Transfer of Functions (Magistrates' Court and Family Law) Order 1992, SI 1992 No 709, art 4, as from 1 April 1992.

['revoke' and 'revocation' include discharge.]

Note. Definition 'revoke' and 'revocation' added by Maintenance Orders (Reciprocal Enforcement) Act 1992, s 1(2), Sch 1, Part II, para 12, as from 5 April 1993.

(2) For the purposes of this Part of this Act an order shall be taken to be a maintenance order so far (but only so far) as it relates to the *periodical payment of sums of money* [payment of a lump sum or the making of periodical payments] as mentioned in paragraph (a) of the definition of 'maintenance order' in subsection (1) above [, to the payment of a periodical allowance as mentioned in paragraph (aa) of that definition] or to the payment by a person adjudged, found or declared to be a child's father of any such expenses as are mentioned in paragraph (b) of that definition.

Note. Words 'to the payment ... that definition' in square brackets added by Domestic Proceedings and Magistrates' Courts Act 1978, s 55(b), as from 1 February 1981. Words 'payment of a lump sum ... payments' substituted for the words in italics by Civil Jurisdiction and Judgments Act 1982, s 37(1), Sch 11, para 4(2)(b), as from 1 January 1987.

(3) Any reference in this Part of this Act to the payment of money for the maintenance of a child shall be construed as including a reference to the payment of money for the child's education.

Amendments, repeals and transitional provisions

22. Amendments and repeals—(1) The enactments mentioned in the Schedule to this Act shall have effect subject to the minor and consequential amendments specified therein.

(2) The following are hereby repealed—

(a) the Maintenance Orders (Facilities for Enforcement) Act 1920;
(b) *in the Magistrates' Courts Act 1952, in section 56(1), paragraph (c) and the words from 'or in an order' to the end;*
(c) in the Maintenance Orders Act 1958, section 19 and, in section 23(2), the words 'section nineteen';
(d) *in the South Africa Act 1962, paragraph 2 of Schedule 2.*

Note. Sub-s (2) in force on a date to be appointed.

Sub-s (2)(b) repealed by Magistrates' Courts Act 1980, s 154, Sch 9, as from 6 July 1981. Sub-s (2)(d) repealed by South Africa Act 1995, s 1, Schedule, para 7(2), as from 23 March 1995.

23. Maintenance order registered in High Court under the Maintenance Orders etc Act 1920—(1) Where a country or territory, being a country or territory to which at the commencement of section 1 of this Act the Maintenance Orders (Facilities for Enforcement) Act 1920 extended, becomes a reciprocating country, then, if immediately before the Order in Council made under section 12 of that Act extending that Act to that country or territory was revoked any maintenance order made by a court in that country or territory was registered in the High Court under Section 1 of that Act, the High Court may, on an application by the payer or the payee under the order or of its own motion, transfer the order to such magistrates' court as having regard to the place where the payer is residing and to all the circumstances it thinks most appropriate, with a view to the order being registered in that court under this Part of this Act.

(2) Where the High Court transfers an order to a magistrates' court under this section it shall—

(a) cause a certified copy of the order to be sent to the *clerk* [appropriate officer] of that court, and
(b) cancel the registration of the order in the High Court.

(3) The *clerk* [appropriate officer] of the court who receives a certified copy of an order sent to him under this section shall register the order in the prescribed manner in that court.

(4) On registering a maintenance order in a magistrates' court by virtue of this section the *clerk* [appropriate officer] of the court shall, if the order is registered in that court under Part I of the Maintenance Orders Act 1958, cancel that registration.

Note. Words 'appropriate officer' in square brackets in sub-ss (2)–(4) substituted for words in italics by the Access to Justice Act 1999, s 90, Sch 13, paras 71, 75, as from 1 April 2001.

(5) In the application of this section to Northern Ireland, for references to the High Court there shall be substituted references to the High Court of Justice in Northern Ireland.

[(6) in this section 'appropriate officer' means—

(a) in relation to a magistrates' court in England and Wales, the *justices' chief executive* [designated officer] for the court; and

(b) in relation to a magistrates' court in Northern Ireland, the clerk of the court.]

Note. Sub-s (6) added by the Access to Justice Act 1999, s 90, Sch 13, paras 71, 75, as from 1 April 2001. Words 'designated officer' in square brackets substituted for words in italics by the Courts Act 2003, s 109(1), Sch 8, para 157, as from a day to be appointed.

24. Application of Part I to certain orders and proceedings under the Maintenance Orders etc Act 1920. Where Her Majesty proposes by an Order in Council under section 1 of this Act to designate as a reciprocating country a country or territory to which at the commencement of that section the Maintenance Orders (Facilities for Enforcement) Act 1920 extended, that Order in Council may contain such provisions as Her Majesty considers expedient for the purpose of securing—

(a) that the provisions of this Part of this Act apply, subject to such modifications as may be specified in the Order, to maintenance orders, or maintenance orders of a specified class—

(i) made by a court in England, Wales or Northern Ireland against a person residing [or having assets] in that country or territory, or

(ii) made by a court in that country or territory against a person residing [or having assets] in England, Wales or Northern Ireland,

being orders to which immediately before the date of the coming into operation of the Order in Council the said Act of 1920 applied, except any order which immediately before that date is registered in the High Court or the High Court of Justice in Northern Ireland under section 1 of that Act;

(b) that any maintenance order, or maintenance order of a specified class, made by a court in that country or territory which has been confirmed by a court in England, Wales or Northern Ireland under section 4 of the said Act of 1920 and is in force immediately before that date is registered under section 7 of this Act;

(c) that any proceedings brought under or by virtue of a provision of the said Act of 1920 in a court in England, Wales or Northern Ireland which are pending at that date, being proceedings affecting a person resident in that country or territory, are continued as if they had been brought under or by virtue of the corresponding provision of this Part of this Act.

Note. Words in square brackets in para (a) inserted by Civil Jurisdiction and Judgments Act 1982, s 37(1), Sch 11, para 16, as from 1 January 1987.

application shall be treated for the purposes of any enactment as if it were a complaint [made at the time when the application was received by the Secretary of State or the Lord Chancellor] and references in this section and in sections 28, 29 [sections 28, 28A, 29, 29A] and 30 of this Act to the complaint, the complainant and the defendant shall be construed accordingly.

Note. Words in first pair of square brackets inserted by Civil Jurisdiction and Judgments Act 1982, s 37(2), as from 1 January 1987. Words in second pair of square brackets substituted for words 'sections 28, 29' by Domestic Proceedings and Magistrates' Courts Act 1978, s 89(2), Sch 2, para 34, as from 1 February 1981.

(*2*) *Where the complaint is for an affiliation order, a magistrates' court [appointed for the commission area (within the meaning of section 1 of the Administration of Justice Act 1973 [the Justices of the Peace Act 1979]) or] acting for the petty sessions area or petty sessions district, as the case may be, [acting for the petty session district], in which the defendant is residing shall have jurisdiction to hear the complaint.*

Note. Words in first square brackets inserted, and words 'petty sessions area or' repealed by Domestic Proceedings and Magistrates' Courts Act 1978, s 56, as from 1 February 1981, save that reference to Justices of the Peace Act 1979 substituted for reference to Administration of Justice Act 1973 by Justices of the Peace Act 1979, s 71, Sch 2, para 18, as from the same date. Words in second square brackets substituted for 'appointed for … as the case may be' by Family Law Reform Act 1987, s 33(1), Sch 2, para 46(a), as from 1 April 1989.

(*3*) *Section 15(2)(a) of the Guardianship of Minors Act 1971 (which restricts the power of a magistrates' court to entertain an application under that Act relating to a minor who has attained the age of sixteen) shall not apply to the complaint.*

Note. Sub-s (3) repealed by Domestic Proceedings and Magistrates' Courts Act 1978, s 89(2), Sch 3, as from 1 February 1981.

(*4*) *If a summons to appear before a magistrates' court having jurisdiction to hear the complaint cannot be duly served on the defendant, the clerk of the court shall, subject to subsection (5) below, return the complaint and the accompanying documents to the Secretary of State with a statement giving such information as he possesses as to the whereabouts of the defendant, and unless the Secretary of State is satisfied that the defendant is not residing in the United Kingdom he shall deal with the complaint in accordance with subsection (1) above or section 31 of this Act, as the circumstances of the case require.*

(*5*) *If the clerk of a magistrates' court to whom the complaint is sent in pursuance of a provision of this section is satisfied that the defendant is residing within the jurisdiction of another magistrates' court in that part of the United Kingdom in which the first-mentioned court is he shall send the complaint and accompanying documents to the clerk of that other court and shall inform the Secretary of State that he has done so.*

(*6*) *The clerk of a court to whom the complaint is sent under subsection (5) above shall proceed as if it had been sent to him under subsection (1) above.*

(*7*) *When hearing the complaint a magistrates' court shall proceed as if the complainant were before the court.*

[(*7A*) *Where a magistrates' court in England and Wales makes an order on the complaint, section 59 of the Magistrates' Courts Act 1980 (orders for periodical payment: means of payment) and subsection (2) of section 32 of the Domestic Proceedings and Magistrates' Courts Act 1978 (extension of section 59) shall not apply, but the court shall, at the same time that it makes the order, exercise one of its powers under subsection (7B) below.*

(*7B*) *The powers of the court are—*

(*a*) *the power to order that payments under the order be made directly to the clerk of the court or the clerk of any other magistrates' court in England and Wales;*

(*b*) *the power to order that payments under the order be made to the clerk of the court, or to the clerk of any other magistrates' court in England and Wales, by such method of payment falling within section 59(6) of the Magistrates' Courts Act 1980 (standing order, etc) as may be specified;*

(*c*) *the power to make an attachment of earnings under the Attachment of Earnings Act 1971 to secure payments under the order.*

(*7C*) *In deciding which of the powers under subsection (7B) above it is to exercise, the court shall have regard to any representations made by the person liable to make payments under the order.*

(*7D*) *Subsection (4) of section 59 of the Magistrates' Courts Act 1980 (power of court to require debtor to open account) shall apply for the purposes of subsection (7B) above as it applies for the purposes of that section but as if for paragraph (a) there were substituted—*

> *'(a)   the court proposes to exercise its power under paragraph (b) of section 27(7B) of the Maintenance Orders (Reciprocal Enforcement) Act 1972, and'.*]

Note. Sub-ss (7A)–(7D) inserted by Maintenance Enforcement Act 1991, s 10, Sch 1, para 15(1), as from date to be appointed under s 12(2).

(*8*) *If a magistrates' court makes an order on the complaint, the clerk of the court shall register the order in the prescribed manner in that court.*

(*9*) *Payment of sums due under a registered order shall, while the order is registered in a magistrates' court, be made in such manner and to such person as may be prescribed, and none of the following enactments relating to the power of a magistrates' court to direct payments to be made to or through the collecting officer of the court or some other person, that is to say, section 52 of the Magistrates' Courts Act 1952 [section 59 of the Magistrates' Courts Act 1980], section 5(5) of the Affiliation Proceedings Act 1957, section 13(2) of the Matrimonial Proceedings (Magistrates' Courts) Act 1960 [section 32(2) of the Domestic Proceedings and Magistrates' Courts Act 1978] and subsections (1) to (8) of section 95 of the Magistrates' Courts Act (Northern Ireland) 1964, [paragraphs (1) to (7) of Article 85 of the Magistrates' Courts (Northern Ireland) Order 1981], [and Article 36(1) of the Domestic Proceedings (Northern Ireland) Order 1980] shall apply in relation to a registered order.*

Note. Reference to Magistrates' Courts Act 1980 substituted for reference to Magistrates' Courts Act 1952 by the Magistrates' Courts Act 1980, s 154, Sch 7, para 108, as from 6 July 1981.

Reference to Domestic Proceedings and Magistrates' Courts Act 1978 substituted for reference to Matrimonial Proceedings (Magistrates' Courts) Act 1960 by Domestic Proceedings and Magistrates' Courts Act 1978, s 89(2), Sch 2, para 34, as from 1 February 1981. Reference to Magistrates' Courts (Northern Ireland) Order 1981 substituted for reference to Magistrates' Courts Act (Northern Ireland) 1964 by SI 1981 No 1675. Reference to Domestic Proceedings (Northern Ireland) Order 1980 inserted by SI 1980 No 564.

Reference to Affiliation Proceedings Act 1957 repealed by Family Law Reform Act 1987, s 33, Sch 2, para 46(b), Sch 4, as from 1 April 1989.

Sub-s (9) repealed by Maintenance Enforcement Act 1991, ss 10, 11(2), Sch 1, para 15(2), Sch 3, as from date to be appointed under s 12(2).

(*10*) *Without prejudice to the generality of the power to make rules under section 15 of the Justices of the Peace Act 1949 [section 144 of the Magistrates' Courts Act 1980] (magistrates' courts rules), the said power shall include power to prescribe the orders made or other things done by a magistrates' court, or an officer of such a court, under this Part of this Act, notice of which is to be given to such persons as the rules may provide and the manner in which such notice shall be given.*

Note. Reference to Magistrates' Courts Act 1980 substituted for reference to Justices of the Peace Act 1949 by Magistrates' Courts Act 1980, s 154, Sch 7, para 108, as from 6 July 1981.

(*11*) *In the application of this section to Northern Ireland, in subsection (10), for the reference to section 15 of the Justices of the Peace Act 1949 there shall be substituted a reference to section 23 of the Magistrates' Courts Act (Northern Ireland) 1964 [Article 13 of the Magistrates' Courts (Northern Ireland) Order 1981].*

Note. Reference to Magistrates' Courts (Northern Ireland) Order 1981 substituted by SI 1981 No 1675. This section substituted as noted to s 27C.

As this section is no longer effective the prospective amendments made by the Maintenance Enforcement Act 1991, ss 10, 11, Sch 1, will not be brought into force. (The amending provisions have been repealed).

[27A. Applications for recovery of maintenance in England and Wales—(1) This section applies to any application which—

(a) is received by the Lord Chancellor from the appropriate authority in a convention country, and

(b) is an application by a person in that country for the recovery of maintenance from another person who is for the time being residing in England and Wales.

(2) Subject to sections 27B to 28B of this Act, an application to which this section applies shall be treated for the purposes of any enactment as if it were an application for a maintenance order under the relevant Act, made at the time when the application was received by the Lord Chancellor.

(3) In the case of an application for maintenance for a child (or children) alone, the relevant Act is the Children Act 1989.

(4) In any other case, the relevant Act is the Domestic Proceedings and Magistrates' Courts Act 1978.

(5) In subsection (3) above, 'child' means the same as in Schedule 1 to the Children Act 1989.

27B. Sending application to the appropriate magistrates' court—(1) On receipt of an application to which section 27A of this Act applies, the Lord Chancellor shall send it, together with any accompanying documents, to the *clerk of* [*justices' chief executive for*] a *magistrates' court acting for the petty sessions* [designated officer for a magistrates' court which is acting in the local justice] area in which the respondent is residing.

Note. Words 'justices' chief executive for' in square brackets substituted for words 'clerk of' in italics by the Access to Justice Act 1999, s 90, Sch 13, paras 71, 77, as from 1 April 2001. Words 'designated officer for a magistrates' court which is acting in the local justice' in square brackets substituted for words in italics by the Courts Act 2003, s 109(1), Sch 8, para 159(1), (2), as from a day to be appointed.

(2) Subject to subsection (4) below, if notice of the hearing of the application by a magistrates' court having jurisdiction to hear it cannot be duly served on the respondent, the *clerk of* [*justices' chief executive for*] [designated officer for] the court shall return the application and the accompanying documents to the Lord Chancellor with a statement giving such information as he possesses as to the whereabouts of the respondent.

Note. Words 'a justices' chief executive for' in square brackets substituted for words 'clerk of' in italics by the Access to Justice Act 1999, s 90, Sch 13, paras 71, 77, as from 1 April 2001. Words 'designated officer for' in square brackets substituted for words 'justices' chief executive for' by the Courts Act 2003, s 109(1), Sch 8, para 159(1), (3), as from a day to be appointed.

(3) If the application is returned to the Lord Chancellor under subsection (2) above, then, unless he is satisfied that the respondent is not residing in the United Kingdom, he shall deal with it in accordance with subsection (1) above or section 28C [28D(1)] of this Act or send it to the Secretary of State to be dealt with in accordance with section 31 of this Act (as the circumstances of the case require).

Note. Reference to '28D(1)' in square brackets substituted by Children (Northern Ireland Consequential Amendments) Order 1995, SI 1995 No 756, art 8, as from 4 November 1996.

(4) If the clerk of [*justices' chief executive for*] *a court to whom the application is sent under this section is satisfied that the respondent is residing within the petty sessions area for which another magistrates' court acts, he shall send the application and accompanying documents to the clerk of* [*justices' chief executive for*] *that other court and shall inform the Lord Chancellor that he has done so.*

Note. Words 'justices' chief executive for' in square brackets substituted for words 'clerk of' by the Access to Justice Act 1999, s 90, Sch 13, paras 71, 77, as from 1 April 2001. Sub-s (4) substituted for sub-s (4) in square brackets by the Courts Act 2003, s 109(1), Sch 8, para 159(1), (4), as from a day to be appointed.

(5) If the application is sent to the *clerk of* [*justices' chief executive for*] [designated

officer for] a court under subsection (4) above, he shall proceed as if it had been sent to him under subsection (1) above.

Note. Words 'justices' chief executive for' in square brackets substituted for words 'clerk of' in italics by the Access to Justice Act 1999, s 90, Sch 13, paras 71, 77, as from 1 April 2001. Words 'designated officer for' in square brackets substituted for words 'justices' chief executive for' in italics by the Courts Act 2003, s 109(1), Sch 8, para 159(1), (5), as from a day to be appointed.

27C. Applications to which section 27A applies: general—(1) This section applies where a magistrates' court makes an order on an application to which section 27A of this Act applies.

(2) Section 59 of the Magistrates' Courts Act 1980 (orders for periodical payment: means of payment) shall not apply.

(3) The court shall, at the same time that it makes the order, exercise one of its powers under subsection (4) below.

(4) Those powers are—

(a) the power to order that payments under the order be made directly to *the clerk of the court or the clerk of any other magistrates' court in England and Wales [a justices' chief executive]* [the designated officer for the court or for any other magistrates' court in England and Wales];

(b) the power to order that payments under the order be made to *the clerk of the court, or to the clerk of any other magistrates' court in England and Wales [a justices' chief executive]* [the designated officer for the court or for any other magistrates' court in England and Wales], by such method of payment falling within section 59(6) of the Magistrates' Courts Act 1980 (standing order, etc) as may be specified;

(c) the power to make an attachment of earnings order under the Attachment of Earnings Act 1971 to secure payments under the order.

Note. Words in first pair of square brackets in paras (a), (b) substituted for words in italics by the Access to Justice Act 1999, s 90(1), Sch 13, paras 71, 78, as from 1 April 2001. Words in second pair of square brackets substituted for words in first pair of square brackets by the Courts Act 2003, s 109(1), Sch 8, para 160(1), (2), as from a day to be appointed.

(5) In deciding which of the powers under subsection (4) above it is to exercise, the court shall have regard to any representations made by the person liable to make payments under the order.

(6) Subsection (4) of section 59 of the Magistrates' Courts Act 1980 (power of court to require debtor to open account) shall apply for the purposes of subsection (4) above as it applies for the purposes of that section, but as if for paragraph (a) there were substituted—

'(a) the court proposes to exercise its power under paragraph (b) of section 27C(4) of the Maintenance Orders (Reciprocal Enforcement) Act 1972, and'.

(7) The *clerk of [justices' chief executive for]* [designated officer for] the court shall register the order in the prescribed manner in the court.]

Note. Words 'justices' chief executive for' in square brackets substituted for words ' clerk of' in italics by the Access to Justice Act 1999, s 90, Sch 13, paras 71, 78, as from 1 April 2001. Words 'designated officer for' in square brackets substituted for words 'justices' chief executive for' in italics by the Courts Act 2003, s 109(1), Sch 8, para 160(1), (3), as from a day to be appointed.

Sections 27A–27C substituted for s 27 by Maintenance orders (Reciprocal Enforcement) Act 1992, s 1(2), Sch 1, Part II, para 13, as from 5 April 1993.

28. Complaint by spouse in convention country for recovery in England and Wales of maintenance from other spouse—(*1*) *Where the complaint is a complaint* *under section 1 of the Matrimonial Proceedings (Magistrates' Courts) Act 1960, the provisions of this section shall have effect.*

(2) *Where the complainant is the wife of the defendant, the only provisions which the court hearing the complaint may include in an order under section 2(1) of the said Act of 1960, or in an interim order under section 6 thereof, are either or both of the following provisions, namely—*

(a) *a provision such as is mentioned in paragraph (b) of the said section 2(1); and*

(b) *a provision for the making by the defendant for the maintenance of any child of the family of weekly payments, being—*

    (i) *if and for so long as the child is under the age of sixteen years, payments to the complainant;*

    (ii) *if it appears to the court that the child is, or will be, or if such payments were made would be, a dependant though over the age of sixteen years, and that it is expedient that such payments should be made in respect of that child while such a dependant, payments to such person (who may be the child or the complainant) as may be specified in the order, for such period during which the child is over that age, but under the age of twenty-one years as may be so specified.*

(3) *Where the complainant is the husband of the defendant, the only provisions which the court hearing the complaint may include in an order under the said section 2(1), or in an interim order under the said section 6 are either or both of the following provisions, namely—*

(a) *where, by reason of the impairment of the husband's earning capacity through age, illness or disability of mind or body, it appears to the court reasonable in all the circumstances so to do, a provision such as is mentioned in paragraph (c) of the said section 2(1); and*

(b) *a provision such as is mentioned in subsection (2)(b) above.*

(4) *Where the court has begun to hear the complaint, being a complaint for maintenance for the complainant and for a child of the family, then, whether or not the court makes an order containing a provision such as is mentioned in paragraph (b) or (c) of the said section 2(1), it may, subject to section 2(5) of the said Act of 1960 (order for payments by a party in respect of child who is not a child of that party), make a matrimonial order containing a provision such as is mentioned in sub-section (2)(b) above; and the court shall not dismiss or make its final order on the complaint until it has decided whether or not, and if so how, the power conferred on it by this subsection should be exercised.*

(5) *For the avoidance of doubt it is hereby declared that the power of a magistrates' court under section 53 of the Magistrates' Courts Act 1952 to vary an order for the periodical payment of money includes power to vary an order made under the said Act of 1960 on the complaint by adding to that order any provision authorised by this section to be included in such an order.*

(6) *Subject to subsections (2) and (3) above, the said Act of 1960 shall, in its application to the complaint and to a matrimonial order or interim order made on the complaint, have effect subject to the following modifications, that is to say—*

(a) *in sections 2(5), 6(2), 7(3) and 8(2), for references to section 2(1)(h) of that Act there shall be substituted references to subsection (2)(b) above;*

(b) *in sections 6(3) and (4), 7(2) and 11(2), and in the definitions of those orders in section 16, references to section 8 of that act shall be construed as including references to section 53 of the Magistrates' Courts Act 1952;*

(c) *in section 13(4), the reference to that Act shall be construed as including references to this Part of this Act; and*

(d) *sections 3, 4, 5, 8(1), 9, 10 and 13(2) shall be omitted.*

[28. Complaint by spouse in convention country for recovery in England and Wales of maintenance from other spouse. *Where the complaint is a complaint made for an order under section 2 of the Domestic Proceedings and Magistrates' Courts Act 1978, the court hearing the complaint may make any order which it has power to make under section 2 or 19(1)(i) of that Act; and Part I of that Act, except sections 6 to 18, [20ZA], 19(1)(ii), [20A], 21, 23(1), 24 to 27, 28(2), 32(2), 33 and 34, shall apply in relation to the complaint and to any order made on the complaint.]*

Note. Section 28 in square brackets substituted for original s 28 by Domestic Proceedings and Magistrates' Courts Act 1978, s 57, as from 1 February 1981.

Reference to s 20ZA inserted by Maintenance Enforcement Act 1991, s 10, Sch 1, para 16, as from date to be appointed under s 12(2).

Reference to s 20A added by Family Law Reform Act 1987, s 33(1), Sch 2, para 47, as from 1 April 1989. This section further substituted as noted to current s 28 below.

As this section is no longer effective the prospective amendments made by the Maintenance Enforcement Act 1991, ss 10, 11, Sch 1, will not be brought into force. (The amending provisions have been repealed).

[28. Applications by spouses under the Domestic Proceedings and Magistrates' Courts Act 1978—(1) The magistrates' court hearing an application which by virtue of section 27A of this Act is to be treated as if it were an application for a maintenance order under the Domestic Proceedings and Magistrates' Courts Act 1978 may make any order on the application which it has power to make under section 2 or 19(1) of that Act.

(2) Part I of that Act shall apply in relation to such an application, and to any order made on such an application, with the following modifications—

    (a) sections 6 to 8, 16 to 18, 20ZA, 25 to 27 and 28(2) shall be omitted,

    (b) in section 30(1), for the words 'either the applicant or the respondent ordinarily resides' there shall be substituted 'the respondent resides', and

    (c) section 32(2) shall be omitted.

(3) Subsections (1) and (2) above do not apply where section 28A of this Act applies.]

Note. Section 28 further substituted by Maintenance Orders (Reciprocal Enforcement) Act 1992, s 1(2), Sch 1, Part II, para 13, as from 1 April 1993.

[28A. Complaint of former spouse in convention country for recovery in England and Wales of maintenance from other spouse—(*1*) *Where on an application under section 27(1) of this Act for the recovery of maintenance from a person who is residing in England and Wales—*

    (*a*) *that person is a former spouse of the applicant in a convention country who is seeking to recover maintenance, and*

    (*b*) *the marriage between the applicant and the former spouse has been dissolved by a divorce granted in a convention country which is recognised as valid by the law of England and Wales, and*

    (*c*) *an order for the payment of maintenance for the benefit of the applicant or a child of the family has, by reason of the divorce proceedings in the convention country, been made by the court which granted the divorce or by any other court in that country,*

the application shall, notwithstanding that the marriage has been dissolved, be treated as a complaint for an order under section 2 of the Domestic Proceedings and Magistrates' Courts Act 1978, and the provisions of this section shall have effect.

    [(*1*) *Where an application under section 27(1) of this Act for the recovery of maintenance from a person who is residing in England and Wales—*

    (*a*) *that person is a former spouse of the applicant in a convention country who is seeking to recover maintenance, and*

    (*b*) *the marriage between the applicant and the former spouse has been dissolved or annulled in a country or territory outside the United Kingdom by a divorce or annulment which is recognised as valid by the law of England and Wales, and*

    (*c*) *an order for the payment of maintenance for the benefit of the applicant or a child of the family has, by reason of the divorce or annulment, been made by a court in a convention country, and*

    (*d*) *in a case where the order for the payment of maintenance was made by a court of a different country from that in which the divorce or annulment was obtained, either the applicant or his or her former spouse was resident in the convention country whose court made the maintenance order at the time the application for that order was made, the application shall, notwithstanding that the marriage has been dissolved or annulled, be treated as a complaint for an order under section 2 of the Domestic Proceedings and Magistrates' Courts Act 1978, and the provisions of this section shall have effect.*]

Note. Sub-s (1) in square brackets substituted for original sub-s (1) by Matrimonial and Family Proceedings Act 1984, s 26(2), as from 16 September 1985.

(2) *On hearing a complaint by virtue of this section the magistrates' court may, if satisfied that the defendant has failed to comply with the provisions of any such order as is mentioned in subsection (1)(c) above, make any order which it has power to make under section 2 or section 19(1)(i) of the Domestic Proceedings and Magistrates' Courts Act 1978 except that—*

(a) *an order for the making of periodical payments for the benefit of the applicant or any child of the family shall not be made unless the order made in the convention country provides for the making of periodical payments for the benefit of the applicant or, as the case may be, that child, and*

(b) *an order for the payment of a lump sum for the benefit of the applicant or any child of the family shall not be made unless the order made in the convention country provides for the payment of a lump sum to the applicant or, as the case may be, to that child.*

(3) *Part I of the Domestic Proceedings and Magistrates' Courts Act 1978 shall apply in relation to any application which is treated by virtue of this section as a complaint for an order under section 2 of that Act, and in relation to any order made on the complaint, subject to the following modifications, that is to say—*

(a) *section 1 shall be omitted;*

(b) *for the reference in section 2(1) to any ground mentioned in section 1 of that Act there shall be substituted a reference to non-compliance with any such order as is mentioned in sub-section (1)(c) of this section;*

(c) *in section 3(1) [sections 3(2) and (3)] for the reference to the occurrence of the conduct which is alleged as the ground of the application there shall be substituted a reference to the breakdown of the marriage;*

Note. Words in square brackets substituted for words 'section 3(1)' by Matrimonial and Family Proceedings Act 1984, s 46(1), Sch 1, para 9, as from 12 October 1984.

(d) *in section 4(2) the reference to the subsequent dissolution or annulment of the marriage of the parties affected by the order shall be omitted;*

(e) *sections 6 to 18, [20ZA], 19(1)(ii), [20A], 21, 23(1), 24 to 28, 33 and 34 shall be omitted.*

Note. Reference to s 20ZA inserted by Maintenance Enforcement Act 1991, s 10, Sch 1, para 17, as from date to be appointed under s 12(2). Reference to s 20A added by Family Law Reform Act 1987, s 33(1), Sch 2, para 48, as from 1 April 1989.

(4) *A divorce obtained in a convention country shall be presumed for the purposes of this section to be one the validity of which is recognised by the law of England and Wales, unless the contrary is proved by the defendant.*

[(4) *A divorce or annulment obtained in a country or territory outside the United Kingdom shall be presumed for the purpose of this section to be one the validity of which is recognised by the law of England and Wales, unless the contrary is proved by the defendant.*]

Note. Sub-s (4) in square brackets substituted for original sub-s (4) by Matrimonial and Family Proceedings Act 1984, s 26(3), as from 16 September 1985.

(5) *The reference in subsection (1)(b) above to the dissolution of a marriage by divorce shall be construed as including a reference to the annulment of the marriage and any reference in this section to a divorce or to divorce proceedings shall be construed accordingly.*

Note. Sub-s (5) repealed by Matrimonial and Family Proceedings Act 1984, s 26(4), as from 16 September 1985.

(6) *In this section the expression 'child of the family' has the same meaning as in section 88 of the Domestic Proceedings and Magistrates' Courts Act 1978.*

Note. Section 28A added by Domestic Proceedings and Magistrates' Courts Act 1978, s 58, as from 1 February 1981. This section substituted as noted to s 28C.

As this section is no longer effective the prospective amendments made by the Maintenance Enforcement Act 1991, ss 10, 11, Sch 1, will not be brought into force. (The amending provisions have been repealed).

28A. Applications by former spouses under the Domestic Proceedings and Magistrates' Courts Act 1978—(1) This section applies where in the case of any application which by virtue of section 27A of this Act is to be treated as if it were an application for a maintenance order under the Domestic Proceedings and Magistrates' Courts Act 1978 ('the 1978 Act')—

(a) the applicant and respondent were formerly married,

(b) their marriage was dissolved or annulled in a country or territory outside the United Kingdom by a divorce or annulment which is recognised as valid by the law of England and Wales,

(c) an order for the payment of maintenance for the benefit of the applicant or a child of the family has, by reason of the divorce or annulment, been made by a court in a convention country, and

(d) where the order for the payment of maintenance was made by a court of a different country from that in which the divorce of annulment was obtained, either the applicant or the respondent was resident in the convention country whose court made that order at the time that order was applied for.

(2) Any magistrates' court that would have jurisdiction to hear the application under section 30 of the 1978 Act (as modified in accordance with subsection (6) below) if the applicant and the respondent were still married shall have jurisdiction to hear it notwithstanding the dissolution or annulment of the marriage.

(3) If the magistrates' court hearing the application is satisfied that the respondent has failed to comply with the provisions of any order such as is mentioned in subsection (1)(c) above, it may (subject to subsections (4) and (5) below) make any order which it has power to make under section 2 or 19(1) of the 1978 Act.

(4) The court shall not make an order for the making of periodical payments for the benefit of the applicant or any child of the family unless the order made in the convention country provides for the making of periodical payments for the benefit of the applicant or, as the case may be, that child.

(5) The court shall not make an order for the payment of a lump sum for the benefit of the applicant or any child of the family unless the order made in the convention country provides for the payment of a lump sum to the applicant or, as the case may be, to that child.

(6) Part I of the 1978 Act shall apply in relation to the application, and to any order made on the application, with the following modifications—

(a) section 1 shall be omitted,

(b) for the reference in section 2(1) to any ground mentioned in section 1 of that Act there shall be substituted a reference to non-compliance with any such order as is mentioned in subsection (1)(c) of this section,

(c) for the references in section 3(2) and (3) to the occurrence of the conduct which is alleged as the ground of the application there shall be substituted references to the breakdown of the marriage,

(d) the reference in section 4(2) to the subsequent dissolution or annulment of the marriage of the parties affected by the order shall be omitted,

(e) sections 6 to 8, 16 to 18, 20ZA and 25 to 28 shall be omitted,

(f) in section 30(1), for the words 'either the applicant or the respondent ordinarily resides' there shall be substituted 'the respondent resides', and

(g) section 32(2) shall be omitted.

(7) A divorce or annulment obtained in a country or territory outside the United Kingdom shall be presumed for the purposes of this section to be one the validity of which is recognised by the law of England and Wales, unless the contrary is proved by the respondent.

(8) In this section, 'child of the family' has the meaning given in section 88 of the 1978 Act.

28B. Applications under the Children Act 1989. No provision of an order made under Schedule 11 to the Children Act 1989 requiring or enabling a court to transfer proceedings from a magistrates' court to a county court or the High Court shall apply in relation to an application which by virtue of section 27A of this Act is to be treated as if it were an application for a maintenance order under that Act.

28C. Applications for recovery of maintenance in Northern Ireland—(*1*) *This section applies where the Lord Chancellor receives from the appropriate authority in a convention country an application by a person in that country for the recovery of maintenance from another person who is for the time being residing in Northern Ireland.*

(*2*) *The Lord Chancellor shall send the application, together with any accompanying documents, to the clerk of a magistrates' court acting for the petty sessions district in which that other person is residing.*

(*3*) *The application shall be treated for the purposes of any enactment as if it were a complaint made at the time when the application was received by the Lord Chancellor, and references in this section and in sections 29, 29A and 30 of this Act to the complaint, the complainant and the defendant shall be construed accordingly.*

(*4*) *Where the complaint is for an affiliation order, a magistrates' court acting for the petty sessions district in which the defendant is residing shall have jurisdiction to hear the complaint.*

(*5*) *If a summons to appear before a magistrates' court having jurisdiction to hear the complaint cannot be duly served on the defendant, the clerk of the court shall (subject to subsection (7) below) return the complaint and the accompanying documents to the Lord Chancellor with a statement giving such information as he possesses as to the whereabouts of the defendant.*

(*6*) *If the complaint is returned to the Lord Chancellor under subsection (5) above, then, unless he is satisfied that the respondent is not residing in the United Kingdom, he shall deal with it in accordance with subsection (2) above or section 27B of this Act or send it to the Secretary of State to be dealt with in accordance with section 31 of this Act (as the circumstances of the case require).*

(*7*) *If the clerk of a court to whom the complaint is sent under this section is satisfied that the defendant is residing within the jurisdiction of another magistrates' court in Northern Ireland, he shall send the complaint and accompanying documents to the clerk of that other court and shall inform the Lord Chancellor that he has done so.*

(*8*) *If the complaint is sent to the clerk of a court under subsection (7) above, he shall proceed as if it had been sent to him under subsection (2) above.*

(*9*) *When hearing the complaint, a magistrates' court shall proceed as if the complainant were before the court.*

(*10*) *If a magistrates' court makes an order on the complaint, the clerk of the court shall register the order in the prescribed manner in that court.*

(*11*) *Payment of sums due under a registered order shall, while the order is registered in a magistrates' court in Northern Ireland, be made in such manner and to such person as may be prescribed, and neither Article 36(1) of the Domestic Proceedings (Northern Ireland) Order 1980 nor Article 85(1) to (7) of the Magistrates' Courts (Northern Ireland) Order 1981 (which relate to the power of a magistrates' court to direct payments to be made to or through the collecting officer of the court or some other person) shall apply in relation to a registered order.*]

Note. Sections 28A, 28B, 28C in square brackets substituted for preceding s 28A by Maintenance Orders (Reciprocal Enforcement) Act 1992, s 1(2), Sch 1, Part II, para 13, as from 5 April 1993.

This section further substituted as noted to s 28E.

[28C. Applications for recovery of maintenance in Northern Ireland—(1) This section applies to any application which—

    (a) is received by the Lord Chancellor from the appropriate authority in a convention country, and

    (b) is an application by a person in that country for the recovery of maintenance from another person who is for the time being residing in Northern Ireland.

(2) Subject to sections 28D to 29B of this Act, an application to which this section applies shall be treated for the purposes of any enactment as if it were an

application for a maintenance order under the relevant Order, made at the time when the application was received by the Lord Chancellor.

(3) In the case of an application for maintenance for a child (or children) alone, the relevant Order is the Children (Northern Ireland) Order 1995.

(4) In any other case, the relevant Order is the Domestic Proceedings (Northern Ireland) Order 1980.

(5) In subsection (3) above, 'child' means the same as in Schedule 1 to the Children (Northern Ireland) Order 1995.

28D. Sending application to the appropriate magistrates' court—(1) On receipt of an application to which section 28C of this Act applies, the Lord Chancellor shall send it, together with any accompanying documents, to the clerk of a magistrates' court acting for the petty sessions district in which the respondent is residing.

(2) Subject to subsection (4) below, if notice of the hearing of the application by a magistrates' court having jurisdiction to hear it cannot be duly served on the respondent, the clerk of the court shall return the application and the accompanying documents to the Lord Chancellor with a statement giving such information as he possesses as to the whereabouts of the respondent.

(3) If the application is returned to the Lord Chancellor under subsection (2) above, then, unless he is satisfied that the respondent is not residing in the United Kingdom, he shall deal with it in accordance with subsection (1) above or section 27B of this Act or send it to the Secretary of State to be dealt with in accordance with section 31 of this Act (as the circumstances of the case require).

(4) If the clerk of a court to whom the application is sent under this section is satisfied that the respondent is residing within the petty sessions district for which another magistrates' court acts, he shall send the application and accompanying documents to the clerk of that other court and shall inform the Lord Chancellor that he has done so.

(5) If the application is sent to the clerk of a court under subsection (4) above, he shall proceed as if it had been sent to him under subsection (1) above.

28E. Applications to which section 28C applies: general—(1) This section applies where a magistrates' court makes an order on an application to which section 28C of this Act applies.

(2) Article 85 of the Magistrates' Courts (Northern Ireland) Order 1981 ('the 1981 Order') (orders for periodical payment: means of payment) shall not apply.

(3) The court shall, at the same time that it makes the order, exercise one of its powers under subsection (4) below.

(4) Those powers are—

(a) the power to order that payments under the order be made directly to the collecting officer;

(b) the power to order that payments under the order be made to the collecting officer, by such method of payment falling within Article 85(7) of the 1981 Order (standing order, etc) as may be specified;

(c) the power to make an attachment of earnings order under Part IX of the 1981 Order to secure payments under the order;

and in this subsection 'collecting officer' means the officer mentioned in Article 85(4) of the 1981 Order.

(5) In deciding which of the powers under subsection (4) above it is to exercise, the court shall have regard to any representations made by the person liable to make payments under the order.

(6) Paragraph (5) of Article 85 of the 1981 Order (power of court to require debtor to open account) shall apply for the purposes of subsection (4) above as it applies for the purposes of that Article but as if for sub-paragraph (a) there were substituted—

'(a) the court proposes to exercise its power under paragraph (b) of section 28E(4) of the Maintenance Orders (Reciprocal Enforcement) Act 1972, and'.

(7) The clerk of the court shall register the order in the prescribed manner in the court.

Note. Sections 28C–28E substituted for previous s 28C, by Children (Northern Ireland) Order 1995, SI 1995/755, art 185, Sch 9, para 72, as from 4 November 1996.

29. Complaint by woman in convention country for recovery in Northern Ireland of maintenance from her husband—(*1*) *Where the complaint is a complaint under section 1 of the Summary Jurisdiction (Separation and Maintenance) Act (Northern Ireland) 1945, the provisions of this section shall have effect.*

(*2*) *The only provisions which the court hearing the complaint may include in an order under section 3(1) of the said Act of 1945, or in an interim order under section 4 thereof, are either or both of the following provisions, namely—*

 (*a*) *a provision such as is mentioned in paragraph (c) of the said section 3(1); and*

 (*b*) *a provision such as is mentioned in paragraph (d) of that subsection;*

but in determining whether to include in any such order a provision such as is mentioned in the said paragraph (d) as respects a child the legal custody of whom has not been committed to any person, the court shall proceed as if it had made an order under the said section 3(1) committing the child to the custody of the wife.

(*3*) *Section 5(2) of the said Act of 1945 (power to make new order where order made on application of a married woman is discharged) shall have effect where an order made on the complaint is discharged as if the words 'that the legal custody of the children of the marriage shall continue to be committed to such married woman and' were omitted.*

(*4*) *Section 8 of the said Act of 1945 (power to refuse order in case more suitable for High Court) shall not apply in relation to the complaint.*

[29. Complaint by spouse in convention country for recovery in Northern Ireland of maintenance from other spouse. *Where the complaint is a complaint made for an order under Article 4 of the Domestic Proceedings (Northern Ireland) Order 1980, the court hearing the complaint may make any order which it has power to make under Article 4 or 20(1)(i) of that Order; and that Order except Articles 8 to 19, 20(1)(ii), 21, [22A] 23, 25(1), 26 to 29, 36(1), 37 and 38 shall apply in relation to the complaint and to any order made on the complaint.*]

Note. Section 29 in square brackets substituted for original s 29 by Maintenance Orders (Northern Ireland Consequential Amendments) Order 1980, SI 1980 No 564. Reference to '22A' in square brackets inserted by Family Law (Northern Ireland) Order 1993, SI 1993 No 1576, art 11, Sch 1, para 11, which was revoked by Children (Northern Ireland) Order 1995, SI 1995 No 755, art 185(2), Sch 10 before a day was appointed for its commencement; therefore this amendment will not take effect. This section further substituted as noted to current s 29 below.

[29. Applications by spouses under the Domestic Proceedings (Northern Ireland) Order 1980—(1) The magistrates' court hearing an application which by virtue of section 28C of this Act is to be treated as if it were an application for a maintenance order under the Domestic Proceedings (Northern Ireland) Order 1980 may make any order on the application which it has power to make under Article 4 or 20(1) of that Order.

(2) That Order shall apply in relation to such an application, and to any order made on such an application, with the following omissions—

 (a) Articles 8 to 10, 18, 19, 21, 22A, 25(1), 27 to 29 and 30(1A),

 (b) in Article 32(1) the words 'either the applicant or', and

 (c) Article 36(1).

(3) Subsections (1) and (2) above do not apply where section 29A of this Act applies.]

Note. Section 29 further substituted by Children (Northern Ireland) Order 1995, SI 1995/755, art 185, Sch 9, para 72, as from 4 November 1996.

[29A. Complaint by former wife in convention country for recovery in Northern Ireland of maintenance from former husband—(*1*) *Where on an application under section 27(1) of this Act for the recovery of maintenance from a person who is residing in Northern Ireland—*

(a) *that person is a former husband of the applicant in a convention country who is seeking to recover maintenance, and*

(b) *the marriage between the applicant and the former husband has been dissolved by a divorce granted in a convention country which is recognised as valid by the law of Northern Ireland, and*

(c) *an order for the payment of maintenance for the benefit of the applicant or a child of the marriage has, by reason of the divorce proceedings in the convention country, been made by the court which granted the divorce or by any other court in that country.*

the application shall, notwithstanding that the marriage has been dissolved, be treated as a complaint for an order under section 3 of the Summary Jurisdiction (Separation and Maintenance) Act (Northern Ireland) 1945, and the provisions of this section shall have effect.

(2) Subject to subsection (3) below, on hearing a complaint by virtue of this section the magistrates' court may, if satisfied that the defendant has failed to comply with the provisions of any such order as is mentioned in subsection (1)(c) above, make any order which it has power to make under section 3(1)(c) or (d) (payment of weekly sum for benefit of wife, or of a child committed to her custody) or section 4 (interim payments) of the Summary Jurisdiction (Separation and Maintenance) Act (Northern Ireland) 1945, treating, for the purposes of the said section 3(1)(d), a child whose legal custody has not been committed to any person as a child committed to the custody of the applicant.

(3) An order shall not be made by virtue of subsection (2) above for the payment of a weekly sum for the benefit of the applicant unless the order made in the convention country provides for the making of periodical payments for her benefit; nor shall an order be made by virtue of that subsection for the payment of a weekly sum for the benefit of a child of the marriage unless the order made in the convention country provides for the making of periodical payments for the benefit of that child.

(4) The Summary Jurisdiction (Separation and Maintenance) Act (Northern Ireland) 1945 shall apply in relation to any application which is treated by virtue of this section as a complaint for an order under section 3 of that Act, and in relation to any order made on the complaint, subject to the following modifications, that is to say—

(a) *references to the husband or the wife shall be construed as references to, respectively, the former husband or the former wife, and references to the parties to the marriage shall be construed accordingly;*

(b) *sections 1 and 2 shall be omitted;*

(c) *for the reference in section 3(1) to an application under the foregoing provisions of that Act there shall be substituted a reference to an application such as is mentioned in subsection (1) above;*

(d) *in section 3, subsection (1)(a) and (b) and subsections (2) to (4) shall be omitted;*

(e) *payments under section 3(1)(c) or (d) or section 4 shall be made in the prescribed manner to the prescribed person, instead of to such a person as is mentioned in those provisions (and accordingly subsection (9) of section 27 of this Act shall have effect as if those provisions were included among the enactments mentioned in that subsection);*

(f) *section 5(2) to (5) shall be omitted;*

(g) *section 8 shall be omitted;*

(h) *proviso (b) to section 13(1) shall be omitted.*

(5) A divorce obtained in a convention country shall be presumed for the purposes of this section to be one the validity of which is recognised by the law of Northern Ireland, unless the contrary is proved by the defendant.

(6) The reference in subsection (1)(b) above to the dissolution of a marriage by divorce shall be construed as including a reference to the annulment of the marriage and any reference in this section to a divorce or to divorce proceedings shall be construed accordingly.

(7) In this section the expression 'child of the marriage' shall be construed in accordance with section 8 of the Maintenance and Affiliation Orders Act (Northern Ireland) 1966.]

[29A. Complaint by former spouse in convention country for recovery in Northern Ireland of maintenance from other spouse—(*1*) *Where on an application under section 27(1) of this Act for the recovery of maintenance from a person who is residing in Northern Ireland*—

(*a*) *that person is a former spouse of the applicant in a convention country who is seeking to recover maintenance, and*

(*b*) *the marriage between the applicant and the former spouse has been dissolved by a divorce granted in a convention country which is recognised as valid by the law of Northern Ireland, and*

(*c*) *an order for the payment of maintenance for the benefit of the applicant or a child of the family has, by reason of the divorce proceedings in the convention country, been made by the court which granted the divorce or by any other court in the country,*

the application shall, notwithstanding that the marriage has been dissolved, be treated as a complaint for an order under Article 4 of the Domestic Proceedings (Northern Ireland) Order 1980, and the provisions of this section shall have effect.

[(*1*) *Where on an application under section 27(1)* [*section 28C(1)*] *of this Act for the recovery of maintenance from a person who is residing in Northern Ireland*—

(*a*) *that person is a former spouse of the applicant in a convention country who is seeking to recover maintenance, and*

(*b*) *the marriage between the applicant and the former spouse has been dissolved or annulled in a country or territory outside the United Kingdom by a divorce or annulment which is recognised as valid by the law of Northern Ireland, and*

(*c*) *an order for the payment of maintenance for the benefit of the applicant or a child of the family has, by reason of the divorce or annulment, been made by a court in a convention country, and*

(*d*) *in a case where the order for the payment of maintenance was made by a court of a different country from that in which the divorce or annulment was obtained, either the applicant or his or her former spouse was resident in the convention country whose court made the maintenance order at the time the application for that order was made,*

the applicant shall, notwithstanding that the marriage has been dissolved or annulled, be treated as a complaint for an order under Article 4 of the Domestic Proceedings (Northern Ireland) Order 1980, and the provisions of this section shall have effect.]

Note. Sub-s (1) in square brackets substituted for original sub-s (1) by Matrimonial and Family Proceedings Act 1984, s 45, as from a day to be appointed. Reference to 'section 28C(1)' substituted by Maintenance Orders (Reciprocal Enforcement) Act 1992, s 1(2), Sch 1, Part II, para 14, as from 5 April 1993.

(*2*) *On hearing a complaint by virtue of this section the magistrates' court may, if satisfied that the defendant has failed to comply with the provisions of any such order as is mentioned in subsection (1)(c) above, make any order which it has power to make under Article 4 or 20(1)(i) of the Domestic Proceedings (Northern Ireland) Order 1980, except that*—

(*a*) *an order for the making of periodical payments for the benefit of the applicant or any child of the family shall not be made unless the order made in the convention country provides for the making of periodical payments for the benefit of the applicant or, as the case may be, that child, and*

(*b*) *an order for the payment of a lump sum for the benefit of the applicant or any child of the family shall not be made unless the order made in the convention country provides for the payment of a lump sum to the applicant or, as the case may be, to that child.*

(*3*) *The Domestic Proceedings (Northern Ireland) Order 1980 shall apply in relation to any application which is treated by virtue of this section as a complaint for an order under Article 4 of that Order, and in relation to any order made on the complaint, subject to the following modifications, that is to say*—

(*a*) *Article 3 shall be omitted;*

(*b*) *for the reference in Article 4(1) to any ground mentioned in Article 3 of that Order there shall be substituted a reference to non-compliance with any such order as is mentioned in subsection (1)(c) of this section;*

(c) *in Article 5(1)(c) [Article 5(2) and (3)] for the reference to the occurrence of the conduct which is alleged as the ground of the application there shall be substituted a reference to the breakdown of the marriage;*

(d) *in Article 6(2) the reference to the subsequent dissolution or annulment of the marriage of the parties affected by the order shall be omitted;*

(e) *Articles 8 to 19, 20(1)(ii), 21, [22A] 23, 25(1), 26 to 30, 36(1), 37 and 38 shall be omitted.*

Note. In sub-s (3)(c) words 'Article 5(2) and (3)' in square brackets substituted for words 'Article 5(1)(c)' by Matrimonial and Family Proceedings (Northern Ireland) Order 1989, SI 1989 No 677, art 42(1), Sch 2. In sub-s (3)(e) reference to '22A' inserted by Family Law (Northern Ireland) Order 1993, SI 1993 No 1576, art 11, Sch 1, para 12, which was revoked by Children (Northern Ireland) Order 1995, SI 1995 No 755, art 185(2), Sch 10 before a day was appointed for its commencement; therefore this amendment will not take effect.

(4) *A divorce obtained in a convention country shall be presumed for the purposes of this section to be one the validity of which is recognised by the law of Northern Ireland, unless the contrary is proved by the defendant.*

[(4) *A divorce or annulment obtained in a country or territory outside the United Kingdom shall be presumed for the purposes of this section to be one the validity of which is recognised by the law of Northern Ireland unless the contrary is proved by the defendant.*]

Note. Sub-s (4) in square brackets substituted for original sub-s (4) by Matrimonial and Family Proceedings Act 1984, s 45, as from a day to be appointed.

(5) *The reference in subsection (1)(b) above to the dissolution of a marriage by divorce shall be construed as including a reference to the annulment of the marriage and any reference in this section to a divorce or to divorce proceedings shall be construed accordingly.*

Note. Sub-s (5) repealed by Matrimonial and Family Proceedings Act 1984, s 45, as from a day to be appointed.

(6) *In this section the expression 'child of the family' has the same meaning as in the Domestic Proceedings (Northern Ireland) Order 1980.*]

Note. Section 29A inserted by Domestic Proceedings and Magistrates' Courts Act 1978, s 59, as from 1 February 1981. Section 29A in square brackets substituted for original s 29A by Maintenance Order (Northern Ireland Consequential Amendments) Order 1980, SI 1980 No 564. Section 29A further substituted as noted to current s 29A below.

As this section is no longer effective the prospective amendments made by the Matrimonial and Family Proceedings Act 1984, s 45 will not be brought into force. (The amending provisions have been repealed).

[29A. Applications by former spouses under the Domestic Proceedings (Northern Ireland) Order 1980—(1) This section applies where in the case of any application which by virtue of section 28C of this Act is to be treated as if it were an application for a maintenance order under the Domestic Proceedings (Northern Ireland) Order 1980 ('the 1980 Order')—

(a) the applicant and respondent were formerly married,

(b) their marriage was dissolved or annulled in a country or territory outside the United Kingdom by a divorce or annulment which is recognised as valid by the law of Northern Ireland;

(c) an order for the payment of maintenance for the benefit of the applicant or a child of the family has, by reason of the divorce or annulment, been made by a court in a convention country, and

(d) where the order for the payment of maintenance was made by a court of a different country from that in which the divorce or annulment was obtained, either the applicant or the respondent was resident in the convention country whose court made that order at the time that order was applied for.

(2) Any magistrates' court that would have jurisdiction to hear the application under Article 32 of the 1980 Order (as modified in accordance with subsection (6)

below) if the applicant and the respondent were still married shall have jurisdiction to hear it notwithstanding the dissolution or annulment of the marriage.

(3) If the magistrates' court hearing the application is satisfied that the respondent has failed to comply with the provisions of any order such as is mentioned in subsection (1)(c) above, it may (subject to subsections (4) and (5) below) make any order which it has power to make under Article 4 or 20(1) of the 1980 Order.

(4) The court shall not make an order for the making of periodical payments for the benefit of the applicant or any child of the family unless the order made in the convention country provides for the making of periodical payments for the benefit of the applicant or, as the case may be, that child.

(5) The court shall not make an order for the payment of a lump sum for the benefit of the applicant or any child of the family unless the order made in the convention country provides for the payment of a lump sum to the applicant or, as the case may be, to that child.

(6) The 1980 Order shall apply in relation to the application, and to any order made on the application, with the following modifications—

(a) Article 3 shall be omitted,
(b) for the reference in Article 4(1) to any ground mentioned in Article 3 there shall be substituted a reference to non-compliance with any such order as is mentioned in subsection (1)(c) of this section,
(c) for the references in Article 5(2) and (3) to the occurrence of the conduct which is alleged as the ground of the application there shall be substituted references to the breakdown of the marriage,
(d) the reference in Article 6(2) to the subsequent dissolution or annulment of the marriage of the parties affected by the order shall be omitted,
(e) Articles 8 to 10, 18, 19, 21, 22A, 25(1) and 27 to 30 shall be omitted,
(f) in Article 32(1), the words 'either the applicant or' shall be omitted, and
(g) Article 36(1) shall be omitted.

(7) A divorce or annulment obtained in a country or territory outside the United Kingdom shall be presumed for the purposes of this section to be one the validity of which is recognised by the law of Northern Ireland, unless the contrary is proved by the respondent.

(8) In this section 'child of the family' has the meaning given in Article 2(2) of the 1980 Order.]

Note. Section 29A further substituted by Children (Northern Ireland) Order 1995, SI 1995/755, art 185, Sch 9, para 72, as from 4 November 1996.

[29B. Applications under the Children (Northern Ireland) Order 1995. No provision of an order made under Schedule 7 to the Children (Northern Ireland) Order 1995 requiring or enabling a court to transfer proceedings from a magistrates' court to a county court or the High Court shall apply in relation to an application which by virtue of section 28C of this Act is to be treated as if it were an application for a maintenance order under that Order.]

Note. Section 29B inserted by Children (Northern Ireland) Order 1995, SI 1995 No 755, art 185, Sch 9, para 72, as from 4 November 1996.

30. Further provisions relating to recovery in England, Wales and Northern Ireland of maintenance for children—(*1*) *Where the complaint is for an order under section 9(2) of the Guardianship of Minors Act 1971, and the court hearing the complaint is satisfied that, if it made an order under subsection (1) of that section giving the custody of the minor to whom the complaint relates to the complainant, it would have power to make an order under subsection (2) of that section for the payment of sums towards the maintenance of the minor, it shall in determining whether to make an order on the complaint proceed as if it had made an order under subsection (1) of that section giving the custody of the minor to the complainant.*

[(*1*) *Section 12C(5) of the Guardianship of Minors Act 1971 (revival by High Court or county court of orders for periodical payments) shall not apply in relation to an order made on a complaint for an order under section 11B of that Act.*]

Note. Sub-s (1) in square brackets substituted for original sub-s (1) by Family Law Reform Act 1987, s 33(1), Sch 2, para 49(2), as from 1 April 1989.

Sub-s (1) repealed by Courts and Legal Services Act 1990, s 125(7), Sch 20, as from 14 October 1991.

(*2*) *Section 16(4) of the said Act of 1971 (refusal of order in case more suitable for the High Court) shall not apply in relation to a complaint to which subsection (1) above applies [for an order under section 11B of that Act] or in relation to an application for the variation or revocation of an order made on such a complaint.*

Note. Words in square brackets substituted for words 'to which subsection (1) above applies' by Family Law Reform Act 1987, s 33(1), Sch 2, para 49(3), as from 1 April 1989.

Sub-s (2) repealed by Courts and Legal Services Act 1990, s 125(7), Sch 20, as from 14 October 1991.

(*3*) *Where the complaint is for an affiliation order under the Affiliation Proceedings Act 1957 or the Illegitimate Children (Affiliation Orders) Act (Northern Ireland) 1924—*

(*a*) *it shall be sufficient for the purposes of paragraph (b) of section 2(1) of the said Act of 1957 (time for making complaint) or paragraph (c) of section 2(3) of the said Act of 1924 (provision to the like effect), as the case may be, to prove that the defendant has within the twelve months [three years (or twelve months in the case of a complaint under the said Act of 1924)] next after the birth of the child to whom the complaint relates paid money for its maintenance in pursuance of a requirement of the law applied by a court outside the United Kingdom; and*

(*b*) *any evidence of the complainant in support of the complaint given in a convention country a record or summary of which is received by the court hearing the complaint, or the court hearing an appeal against an affiliation order made on the complaint or against the refusal to make such an order, shall be treated by the court hearing the complaint or the court hearing such an appeal, as the case may be, as if it had been given by the complainant in person before that court.*

Note. In para (a) words in square brackets substituted for words 'twelve months', and para (b) and the word 'and' preceding it repealed by Affiliation Proceedings (Amendment) Act 1972, ss 1(4), 2(2); further amended by Family Law Reform Act 1987, s 33(1), (4), Sch 2, para 49(4), Sch 4, as from 1 April 1989. Sub-s (3) repealed by Children (Northern Ireland) Order 1995, SI 1995 No 755, art 185, Sch 10, as from 4 November 1996.

(*4*) *Where the complaint is for an affiliation order under the said Act of 1924, a summons may be issued on the complaint notwithstanding that the complainant has not made the information mentioned in section 2(4) of that Act.*

Note. Sub-s (4) repealed by Children (Northern Ireland) Order 1995, SI 1995 No 755, art 185, Sch 10, as from 4 November 1996.

(*5*) *Without prejudice to any other enactment empowering a magistrates' court to vary an affiliation order made by it, an affiliation order made under the said Act of 1957 or the said Act of 1924, as the case may be, on the complaint may be varied by such a court so as to entitle any person, other than the complainant, who for the time being has the custody of the child to whom the order relates to any payments to be made under the order.*

Note. Words 'the said Act of 1957', 'as the case may be' repealed by Family Law Reform Act 1987, s 33(1), (4), Sch 2, para 49(5), Sch 4, as from 1 April 1989. Sub-s (5) repealed by Children (Northern Ireland) Order 1995, SI 1995 No 755, art 185, Sch 10, as from 4 November 1996.

(*6*) *Section 41 of this Act shall not apply in relation to an order under section 9(2) of the said Act of 1971, or an affiliation order under the said Act of 1957, made on the complaint.*

Note. Words 'or an affiliation order under the said Act of 1957' repealed by Family Law Reform Act 1987, s 33(1), (4), Sch 2, para 49(6), Sch 4, as from 1 April 1989.

Sub-s (6) repealed by Courts and Legal Services Act 1990, s 125(7), Sch 20, as from 14 October 1991.

Application by person in convention country for recovery of maintenance in Scotland

31. Application by person in convention country for recovery of maintenance in Scotland—(1) Where the Secretary of State receives from the appropriate authority in a convention country an application by a person in that country for the recovery of maintenance from another person who is for the time being residing in Scotland, he shall send the application, together with any accompanying documents, to the secretary of the committee established under Article 5 of the Legal Aid (Scotland) Scheme 1958, or under the corresponding provision of any scheme amending or having effect in place of that Scheme; and the secretary shall thereupon send the application and any accompanying documents to a solicitor practising in the sheriff court within the jurisdiction of which that other person is residing, with a view to the solicitor's taking on behalf of the applicant such steps as appear to the solicitor appropriate in respect of the application.

[(1A) In any proceedings arising out of such an application as aforesaid the sheriff may subject to subsection (4) below make, with respect to an application under subsection (1) above, such order as he thinks fit having regard to the respective means of the applicant and the person from whom recovery of maintenance is sought and to all the circumstances of the case.]

(2) Where in any proceedings arising out of such an application as aforesaid the sheriff [, or (on appeal or remit) the Court of Session] makes an order containing a provision requiring the payment of maintenance, *the sheriff clerk or sheriff clerk depute shall register the order in the prescribed manner in the court* [the order shall be registered forthwith in the prescribed manner in the appropriate sheriff court by the sheriff clerk or sheriff clerk depute of that sheriff court; and where an order of the Court of Session varies or revokes a registered order of the sheriff, the said sheriff clerk or sheriff clerk depute shall amend the register accordingly].

[(2A) In subsection (2) above 'the appropriate sheriff court' means the sheriff court making the order or (where the order is an order of the Court of Session) from which the remit or appeal has come.]

(3) Without prejudice to the generality of the powers conferred on the Court of Session by section 32 of the Sheriff Courts (Scotland) Act 1971 to regulate by act of sederunt the procedure of the sheriff court, the said powers shall include power to prescribe the decrees granted, or other things done, by the sheriff, or an officer of the sheriff court, under this Part of this Act, notice of which is to be given to such persons as the act of sederunt may provide and the manner in which such notice shall be given.

[(4) Where an application under subsection (1) above is for the recovery of maintenance from a person who is a former spouse of the applicant an order containing a provision requiring the payment of such maintenance for the benefit of the applicant shall not be made in respect of that application unless—

(i) the marriage between the applicant and the said former spouse has been dissolved by a divorce which has been granted in a convention country and which is recognised as valid by the law of Scotland;

(ii) an order for the payment of maintenance for the benefit of the applicant has, in or by reason of the divorce proceedings in the convention country, been made by the court which granted the divorce or by any other court in that country; and

(iii) the court making the order under this section is satisfied that the former spouse of the applicant has failed to comply with the order mentioned in paragraph (ii) above.

(5) Without prejudice to any existing power of variation or revocation but subject to section 34(1) of this Act, subsections (4) and (5) of section 5 of the Divorce (Scotland) Act 1976 shall, where an order with respect to an application under subsection (1) above requires the payment of maintenance by a person to a

former spouse of that person, apply to that order as they apply to an order under section 5 of the said Act of 1976.

(6) Section 8 of the Law Reform (Miscellaneous Provisions) (Scotland) Act 1966 (which relates to the variation and recall by the sheriff of certain orders made by the Court of Session) shall not apply to an order of the Court of Session registered under subsection (2) above.]

Note. Words in italics repealed and words in square brackets inserted by Domestic Proceedings and Magistrates' Courts Act 1978, s 60, as from 1 February 1981.

For amendments in relation to Scotland, see Legal Aid (Scotland) Act 1986, s 45(1), Sch 3, para 1(1).

Transfer, enforcement, variation and revocation of registered orders

32. Transfer of orders—(1) Where the prescribed officer of the registering court is of opinion that the payer under a registered order has ceased to reside within the jurisdiction of that court, then, unless he is of opinion that the payer has ceased to reside in the United Kingdom, he shall, subject to subsection (2) below, send a certified copy of the order and the related documents to the *Secretary of State* [Lord Chancellor], and if he is of opinion that the payer has ceased to reside in the United Kingdom he shall send a notice to that effect to the *Secretary of State* [Lord Chancellor].

(2) Where *the clerk* [the appropriate officer] of the registering court, being a magistrates' court, is of opinion that the payer is residing within the jurisdiction of another magistrates' court in that part of the United Kingdom in which the registering court is, he shall transfer the order to that other court by sending a certified copy of the order and the related documents to *the clerk* [the appropriate officer] of that other court and, subject to subsection (4) below, *that clerk* [the appropriate officer] shall register the order in the prescribed manner in that court.

Note. Words 'the appropriate officer' in each place it occurs substituted for words in italics by the Access to Justice Act 1999, s 90, Sch 13, paras 71, 79, as from 1 April 2001.

[(2A) In subsection (2) above the 'appropriate officer' means—
   (a) in relation to a court in England and Wales, the *justices' chief executive* [designated officer] for the court; and
   (b) in relation to a court in Northern Ireland, the clerk of the court.]

Note. Sub-s (2A) added by the Access to Justice Act 1999, s 90, Sch 13, paras 71, 79, as from 1 April 2001. Words 'designated officer' in square brackets in para (a) substituted for words in italics by the Courts Act 2003, s 109(1), Sch 8, para 161, as from a day to be appointed.

(3) Where a certified copy of an order is received by the *Secretary of State* [Lord Chancellor] under this section and it appears to him that the payer under the order is still residing in the United Kingdom, he shall transfer the order to the appropriate court by sending the copy of the order and the related documents to the prescribed officer of the appropriate court and, subject to subsection (4) below, that officer shall register the order in the prescribed manner in that court.

(4) Before registering an order in pursuance of subsection (2) or (3) above an officer of a court shall take such steps as he thinks fit for the purpose of ascertaining whether the payer under the order is residing within the jurisdiction of the court, and if after taking those steps he is satisfied that the payer is not so residing he shall return the certified copy of the order and the related documents to the officer of the court or the *Secretary of State* [Lord Chancellor], as the case may be, from whom he received them, together with a statement giving such information as he possesses as to the whereabouts of the payer.

(5) Where a certified copy of an order is received by the *Secretary of State* [Lord Chancellor] under this section and it appears to him that the payer under the order has ceased to reside in the United Kingdom he shall return the copy of the order and the related documents to the registering court.

Note. In sub-ss (1), (3)–(5) words 'Lord Chancellor' in square brackets substituted for words 'Secretary of State' in italics by virtue of Transfer of Functions (Magistrates' Courts and Family Law) Order 1992, SI 1992 No 709, art 4, as from 1 April 1992.

(6) An officer of a court on registering an order in the court in pursuance of subsection (2) or (3) above shall give notice of the registration in the prescribed manner to the prescribed officer of the court in which immediately before its registration under this section the order was registered.

(7) The officer to whom notice is given under subsection (6) above shall on receiving the notice cancel the registration of the order in that court.

(8) In this section—

'the appropriate court', in relation to a person residing in England and Wales or in Northern Ireland, means a magistrates' court within the jurisdiction of which that person is residing;

'certificate of arrears' and 'certified copy' have the same meanings respectively as in Part I of this Act;

'payer', in relation to a registered order, means the person liable to make payments under the order; and

'related documents' means—

(a) the application on which the order was made;

(b) a certificate of arrears signed by the prescribed officer of the registering court;

(c) a statement giving such information as he possesses as to the whereabouts of the payer; and

(d) any relevant documents in his possession relating to the case.

(9) In the application of this section to Scotland—

(a) in subsection (1), for the words 'within the jurisdiction of that court' there shall be substituted the words 'in Scotland';

(b) subsection (2) shall be omitted;

(c) in subsection (4), for the words 'the officer of the court or the Secretary of State, as the case may be, from whom he received them' there shall be substituted the words 'the Secretary of State';

(d) at the end of subsection (6) there shall be inserted the words 'and to the Secretary of State';

(e) after subsection (7) there shall be inserted the following subsections:—

'(7A) The Secretary of State on receiving notice under subsection (6) above shall send a copy of the registered order and of the related documents to the secretary of the committee mentioned in section 31(3) of this Act, and the secretary shall thereupon send the copy of the order and of the related documents to a solicitor practising in the registering court, with a view to the solicitor's taking on behalf of the person entitled to the payments for which the order provides such steps as appear to the solicitor appropriate to enforce the order.

(7B) Where an order is registered in the sheriff court by virtue of subsection (3) above, any provision of the order by virtue of which the payments for which the order provides are required to be made through or to any officer or person on behalf of the person entitled thereto shall be of no effect so long as the order is so registered.':

(f) 'appropriate court', in relation to a person residing in Scotland, means the sheriff court within the jurisdiction of which that person is residing.

Note. For amendments in relation to Scotland, see Legal Aid (Scotland) Act 1986, s 45(1), Sch 3, para 1(2)(a).

33. Enforcement of orders—(1) Subject to subsection (2) below, a registered order which is registered in a court other than the court by which the order was made may be enforced as if it had been made by the registering court and as if that court had had jurisdiction to make it; and proceedings for or with respect to the enforcement of any such order may be taken in accordance with this subsection but not otherwise.

(2) Subsection (1) above does not apply to an order which is for the time being registered in the High Court under Part I of the Maintenance Orders Act 1958 or to an order which is for the time being registered in the High Court of Justice in Northern Ireland under Part II of the Maintenance and Affiliation Orders Act (Northern Ireland) 1966.

(3) An order which by virtue of subsection (1) above is enforceable by a magistrates' court shall be enforceable as if it were an affiliation order made by that court; and the provisions of any enactment with respect to the enforcement of affiliation orders (including enactments relating to the accrual of arrears and the remission of sums due) shall apply accordingly.

In this subsection 'enactment' includes any order, rule or regulation made in pursuance of any Act. [an order made by that court to which that Article applies.]

Note. Words in square brackets substituted for words 'if it were ... any Act', in relation to Northern Ireland, by Children (Northern Ireland) Order 1995, SI 1995 No 755, art 185(1), Sch 9, para 73, as from 4 November 1996.

[(3) An order which by virtue of subsection (1) above is enforceable by a magistrates' court *shall be enforceable* [shall, subject to the modifications of sections 76 and 93 of the Magistrates' Courts Act 1980 (enforcement of sums adjudged to be paid and complaint for arrears) specified in subsections (4A) and (4B) of section 8 of this Act, be enforceable] [shall, subject to the modifications of Article 98 of the Magistrates' Courts (Northern Ireland) Order 1981 (enforcement of sums adjudged to be paid and complaint for arrears) specified in subsection (4C) of section 8 of this Act, be enforceable] as if it were a magistrates' court maintenance order made by that court.

In this subsection 'magistrates' court maintenance order' has the same meaning as in section 150(1) of the Magistrates' Courts Act 1980.]

Note. Sub-s (3) in square brackets substituted for sub-s (3) in italics in relation to England and Wales by Family Law Reform Act 1987, s 33(1), Sch 2, para 50, as from 1 April 1989. First words in square brackets in new sub-s (3) substituted for words in italics in relation to England and Wales by Maintenance Enforcement Act 1991, s 10, Sch 1, para 18(1), as from 1 April 1992. Second words in square brackets substituted for words 'shall be enforceable' in italics in relation to Northern Ireland by Family Law (Northern Ireland) Order 1993, SI 1993 No 1576, art 11, Sch 1, para 13, as from 4 November 1996.

[(3A) Where, by virtue of being registered in the magistrates' court in which it was made, a registered order is enforceable as a magistrates' court maintenance order, sections 76 and 93 of the Magistrates' Courts Act 1980 shall have effect subject to the modifications specified in subsections (4A) and (4B) of section 8 of this Act.]

Note. Sub-s (3A) inserted by Maintenance Enforcement Act 1991, s 10, Sch 1, para 18(2), as from 1 April 1992.

[(3B) Where, by virtue of being registered in the court of summary jurisdiction in which it was made, a registered order is enforceable as a maintenance order made by a court of summary jurisdiction, Article 98 of the Magistrates' Courts (Northern Ireland) Order 1981 shall have effect subject to the modifications specified in subsection (4C) of section 8 of this Act.]

Note. Sub-s (3B) inserted by Family Law (Northern Ireland) Order 1993, SI 1993 No 1576, art 11, Sch 1, para 13, as from 4 November 1996.

(4) A magistrates' court in which an order is registered under this Part of this Act, and the officers thereof, shall take all such steps for enforcing the order as may be prescribed.

(5) In any proceedings for or with respect to the enforcement of an order which is for the time being registered in any court under this Part of this Act a certificate of arrears sent under section 32 of this Act to the prescribed officer of the court shall be evidence of the facts stated therein.

(6) Part II of the Maintenance Orders Act 1950 (enforcement of certain orders throughout the United Kingdom) shall not apply to a registered order.

(7) In the application of this section to Scotland—

(a) subsections (2) and (4) shall be omitted; and

(b) in subsection (5), for the word 'evidence' there shall be substituted the words 'sufficient evidence'.

34. Variation and revocation of orders—(1) [Subject to [subsection (3A) below and] section 34A of this Act] [Subject to [subsection (3B) below and] section 34B of this Act] where a registered order is registered in a court other than the court by which the order was made, the registering court shall have the like power to vary or revoke the order as if it had been made by the registering court and as if that court had had jurisdiction to make it; and no court other than the registering court shall have power to vary or revoke a registered order.

Note. Words 'Subject to section 34A of this Act' in square brackets inserted by Maintenance Enforcement Act 1991, s 10, Sch 1, para 19(1), as from 1 April 1992. Words 'subsection (3A) below and' in square brackets inserted by Maintenance Orders (Reciprocal Enforcement) Act 1992, s 1(2), Sch 1, Part II, para 15, as from 5 April 1993. Words 'Subject to section 34B of this Act' in square brackets inserted in relation to Northern Ireland by Family Law (Northern Ireland) Order 1993, SI 1993 No 1576, art 11, Sch 1, para 14, as from 4 November 1996. Words 'subsection (3B) below and' in square brackets inserted in relation to Northern Ireland by Children (Northern Ireland) Order 1995, SI 1995 No 755, art 185, Sch 9, para 74, as from 4 November 1996.

(2) Where the registering court revokes a registered order it shall cancel the registration.

(3) Where the Secretary of State receives from the appropriate authority in a convention country an application by a person in that country for the variation of a registered order, he shall, if the registering court is a magistrates' court, send the application together with any documents accompanying it to *the clerk of that court*

[(a) *the justices' chief executive* [designated officer] for the court, if the court is in England and Wales; or

(b) the clerk of the court, if the court is in Northern Ireland.]

Note. Paras (a), (b) in square brackets substituted for words in italics by the Access to Justice Act 1999, s 90(1), Sch 13, paras 71, 80, as from 1 April 2001. Words 'designated officer' in square brackets in para (a) substituted for words in italics by the Courts Act 2003, s 109(1), Sch 8, para 162, as from a day to be appointed.

[(3A) Where subsection (1) of section 60 of the Magistrates' Courts Act 1980 (revocation, variation etc of orders for periodical payment) applies in relation to a registered order, that subsection shall have effect as if for the words 'by order on complaint,' there were substituted 'on an application being made, by order'.]

Note. Sub-s (3A) inserted by Maintenance Orders (Reciprocal Enforcement) Act 1992, s 1(2), Sch 1, Part II, para 15, as from 5 April 1993.

[(3B) Where paragraph (1) of Article 86 of the Magistrates' Courts (Northern Ireland) Order 1981 (revocation, variation etc of orders for periodical payment) applies in relation to a registered order, that paragraph shall have effect as if for the words 'by order on complaint,' there were substituted the words 'on application being made, by order'.]

Note. Sub-s (3B) inserted by Children (Northern Ireland) Order 1995, SI 1995 No 755, art 185, Sch 9, para 74, as from 4 November 1996.

(4) Where a court in a part of the United Kingdom makes, or refuses to make, an order varying or revoking a registered order made by a court in another part thereof, any person shall have the like right of appeal (if any) against the order or refusal as he would have if the registered order had been made by the first-mentioned court.

(5) In the application of this section to Scotland [—

(a)   the words 'and no court other than the registering court shall have power to vary or revoke a registered order' in subsection (1) above are subject to any power of the Court of Session on appeal; and

(b)]   for subsection (3) there shall be substituted the following subsection:—

'(3) Where the Secretary of State receives from the appropriate authority in a convention country an application by a person in that country for the variation of a registered order, he shall, if the registering court is a sheriff court, send the application, together with any documents accompanying it, to the secretary of the committee mentioned in section 31(1) of this Act, and the secretary shall thereupon send the application and any accompanying documents to a solicitor practising in the registering court, with a view to the solicitor's taking on behalf of the applicant such steps as appear to the solicitor appropriate in respect of the application.'

Note. Words in square brackets inserted by Domestic Proceedings and Magistrates' Courts Act 1978, s 60(2), as from 1 February 1982.

For amendments in relation to Scotland, see Legal Aid (Scotland) Act 1986, s 45(1), Sch 3, para 1(3).

[34A. Variation of orders by magistrates' courts in England and Wales—(1) The provisions of this section shall have effect in relation to a registered order which is registered in a magistrates' court in England and Wales (whether or not the court made the order) in place of the following enactments, that is to say—

(a)   subsections (3) to (11) of section 60 of the Magistrates' Courts Act 1980;

(b)   section 20ZA of the Domestic Proceedings and Magistrates' Courts Act 1978; and

(c)   paragraph 6A of Schedule 1 to the Children Act 1989.

(2) The power of a magistrates' court in England and Wales to vary a registered order shall include power, if the court is satisfied that payment has not been made in accordance with the order, to exercise one of its powers under subsection (3) below.

(3) The powers of the court are—

(a)   the power to order that payments under the order be made directly to *the clerk of the court or the clerk of any other magistrates' court in England and Wales* [*a justices' chief executive*] [the designated officer for the court or for any other magistrates' court in England and Wales];

(b)   the power to order that payments under the order be made to *the clerk of the court, or to the clerk of any other magistrates' court in England and Wales* [*a justices' chief executive*] [the designated officer for the court or for any other magistrates' court in England and Wales], by such method of payment falling within section 59(6) of the Magistrates' Courts Act 1980 (standing order, etc) as may be specified;

(c)   the power to make an attachment of earnings order under the Attachment of Earnings Act 1971 to secure payments under the order.

Note. Words 'a justices' chief executive' in square brackets in both places they occur substituted for words in italics by the Access to Justice Act 1999, s 90, Sch 13, paras 71, 81, as from 1 April 2001. Words from 'the designated officer' to 'England and Wales' in italics by the Courts Act 2003, s 109(1), Sch 8, para 163(1), (2), as from a day to be appointed.

(4) In any case where—

(a)   a registered order is registered in a magistrates' court in England and Wales, and

(b)   payments under the order are required to be made to *the clerk of the court, or to the clerk of any other magistrates' court in England and Wales* [*a justices' chief executive*] [the designated officer for the court or for any other magistrates' court in England and Wales], by any method of payment falling within section 59(6) of the Magistrates' Courts Act 1980 (standing order, etc), an interested party may apply in writing to *the clerk of* the court in which the order is registered for the order to be varied as mentioned in subsection (5) below.

Note. Words 'a justices' chief executive' in square brackets substituted for words in italics by the Access to Justice Act 1999, s 90, Sch 13, paras 71, 81, as from 1 April 1001. Words from 'the designated officer' to 'England and Wales' in square brackets substituted for words in italics by the Courts Act 2003, s 109(1), Sch 8, para 163(1), (5)(a), as from a day to be appointed. Words 'the clerk of' in italics repealed by the courts Act 2003, s 109(1), (3), Sch 8, para 163(1), (3)(b), Sch 10, as from a day to be appointed.

(5) Subject to subsection (8) below, where an application has been made under subsection (4) above, *the clerk* [a justices' clerk], after giving written notice (by post or otherwise) of the application to any other interested party and allowing that party, within the period of 14 days beginning with the date of the giving of that notice, an opportunity to make written representations, may vary the order to provide that payments under the order shall be made in accordance with paragraph (a) of subsection (3) above.

Note. Words 'a justices' clerk' in square brackets substituted for words in italics by the Courts Act 2003, s 109(1), Sch 8, para 163(1), (4), as from a day to be appointed.

(6) The clerk may proceed with an application under subsection (4) above notwithstanding that any such interested party as is referred to in subsection (5) above has not received written notice of the application.

(7) In subsections (4) to (6) above 'interested party', in relation to an order, means the debtor or the creditor.

(8) Where an application has been made under subsection (4) above, the clerk may, if he considers it inappropriate to exercise his power under subsection (5) above, refer the matter to the court which may vary the order by exercising one of its powers under subsection (3) above.

(9) In deciding, for the purposes of subsections (2) and (8) above, which of the powers under subsection (3) above it is to exercise, the court shall have regard to any representations made by the debtor.

(10) Subsection (4) of section 59 of the Magistrates' Courts Act 1980 (power of court to require debtor to open account) shall apply for the purposes of subsection (3) above as it applies for the purposes of that section but as if for paragraph (a) there were substituted—

'(a) the court proposes to exercise its power under paragraph (b) of section 34A(3) of the Maintenance Orders (Reciprocal Enforcement) Act 1972, and'.

(11) In this section 'creditor' and 'debtor' have the same meaning as they have in section 59 of the Magistrates' Courts Act 1980.]

Note. Section 34A inserted by Maintenance Enforcement Act 1991, s 10, Sch 1, para 19(2), as from 1 April 1992.

[34B. Variation of orders by courts of summary jurisdiction in Northern Ireland—(1) The provisions of this section shall have effect in relation to a registered order which is registered in a court of summary jurisdiction in Northern Ireland (whether or not the court made the order) in place of the following enactments, that is to say—

(a) paragraphs (3) to (11) of Article 86 of the Magistrates' Courts (Northern Ireland) Order 1981; and

(b) Article 22A of the Domestic Proceedings (Northern Ireland) Order 1980.

(2) The power of a court of summary jurisdiction in Northern Ireland to vary a registered order shall include power, if the court is satisfied that payment has not been made in accordance with the order, to exercise one of its powers under subsection (3) below.

(3) The powers of the court are—

(a) the power to order that payments under the order be made directly to the collecting officer;

(b) the power to order that payments under the order be made to the collecting officer by such method of payment falling within Article 85(7) of the Magistrates' Courts (Northern Ireland) Order 1981 (standing order, etc) as may be specified;

(c) the power to make an attachment of earnings order under Part IX of the Order of 1981 to secure payments under the order;

and in this subsection 'collecting officer' means the officer mentioned in Article 85(4) of the Order of 1981.

(4) In any case where—

(a) a registered order is registered in a court of summary jurisdiction in Northern Ireland, and

(b) payments under the order are required to be made to the collecting officer in Northern Ireland, by any method of payment falling within Article 85(7) of the Magistrates' Courts (Northern Ireland) Order 1981 (standing order, etc),

an interested party may apply in writing to the clerk of petty sessions in which the order is registered for the order to be varied as mentioned in subsection (5) below.

(5) Subject to subsection (8) below, where an application has been made under subsection (4) above, the clerk, after giving written notice (by post or otherwise) of the application to any other interested party and allowing that party, within the period of 14 days beginning with the date of the giving of that notice, an opportunity to make written representations, may vary the order to provide that payments under the order shall be made in accordance with paragraph (a) of subsection (3) above.

(6) The clerk may proceed with an application under subsection (4) above notwithstanding that any such interested party as is referred to in subsection (5) above has not received written notice of the application.

(7) In subsections (4) to (6) above 'interested party', in relation to an order, means the debtor or the creditor.

(8) Where an application has been made under subsection (4) above, the clerk may, if he considers it inappropriate to exercise his power under subsection (5) above, refer the matter to the court which may vary the order by exercising one of its powers under subsection (3) above.

(9) In deciding, for the purposes of subsections (2) and (8) above, which of the powers under subsection (3) above it is to exercise, the court shall have regard to any representations made by the debtor.

(10) Paragraph (5) of Article 85 of the Magistrates' Courts (Northern Ireland) Order 1981 (power of court to require debtor to open account) shall apply for the purposes of subsection (3) above as it applies for the purposes of that Article but as if for sub-paragraph (a) there were substituted—

'(a) the court proposes to exercise its power under paragraph (b) of section 34B(3) of the Maintenance Orders (Reciprocal Enforcement) Act 1972, and'.

(11) In this section 'creditor' and 'debtor' have the same meaning as they have in Article 85 of the Magistrates' Courts (Northern Ireland) Order 1981.]

Note. Section 34B inserted by Family Law (Northern Ireland) Order 1993, SI 1993 No 1576, art 11, Sch 1, para 14(b), as from 4 November 1996.

35. Further provisions with respect to variation, etc of orders by magistrates' courts—(*1*) *Notwithstanding anything in section 28(6)(d)* [*sections 28, 28A(3)(e)*] *or 30(6) of this Act, a magistrates' court shall have jurisdiction to hear an application for the variation or revocation of a registered order registered in that court, being—*

(*a*) *an application made by the person against whom or on whose application the order was made, or*

(*b*) *an application made by some other person in pursuance of section 30(5) of this Act for the variation of an affiliation order.*

notwithstanding that the person by or against whom the application is made is residing outside England and Wales [but none of the powers of the court, or of the clerk of the court, conferred by section 34A of this Act shall be exercisable in relation to such an application].

Note. Words in first pair of square brackets substituted for words 'section 28(6)(d)' by Domestic Proceedings and Magistrates' Courts Act 1978, s 89(2), Sch 2, para 35, as from 1 February 1981. Words in second pair of square brackets added by Maintenance Enforcement Act 1991, s 10, Sch 1, para 20, as from 1 April 1992.

(*2*) *Where an application by a person in a convention country for the variation of a registered order is received from the Secretary of State by the clerk of a magistrates' court, he shall treat the application as if it were a complaint for the variation of the order to which the application relates, and the court hearing the application shall proceed as if the application were a complaint and the applicant were before the court.*

(*3*) *Without prejudice to subsection (2) above, an application to a magistrates' court for the variation or revocation of a registered order shall be made by complaint.*

(*4*) *Where the defendant to a complaint for the variation or revocation of a registered order, being an order registered in a magistrates' court does not appear at the time and place appointed for the hearing of the complaint, but the court is satisfied—*

(*a*) *that the defendant is residing outside England and Wales; and*
(*b*) *that such notice of the making of the complaint and of the time and place aforesaid as may be prescribed has been given to the defendant in the prescribed manner,*

the court may proceed to hear and determine the complaint at the time and place appointed for the hearing or for any adjourned hearing in like manner as if the defendant had appeared at that time and place.

(*5*) *This section shall have effect in Northern Ireland with the substitution of references to Northern Ireland for references to England and Wales [and with the substitution in subsection (1) for the references to sections 28 and 28A(3)(e) of references to sections 29 and 29A(3)(a)].*

Note. Words in square brackets added by Maintenance Orders (Northern Ireland Consequential Amendments) Order 1980, SI 1980, No 564.

[35. Further provisions with respect to variation etc of orders by magistrates' courts in England and Wales—(1) Notwithstanding anything in section 28(2) or 28A(6)(e) of this Act, a magistrates' court in England and Wales shall have jurisdiction to hear an application—

(a) for the variation or revocation of a registered order registered in that court, and
(b) made by the person against whom or on whose application the order was made,

notwithstanding that the person by or against whom the application is made is residing outside England and Wales.

(2) None of the powers of the court, or of the clerk of the court, under section 34A of this Act shall be exercisable in relation to such an application.

(3) Where the respondent to an application for the variation or revocation of a registered order which is registered in a magistrates' court in England and Wales does not appear at the time and place appointed for the hearing of the application, but the court is satisfied—

(a) that the respondent is residing outside England and Wales [but none of the powers of the court, or of the clerk, conferred by section 34B of this Act shall be exercisable in relation to such an application], and
(b) that the prescribed notice of the making of the application and of the time and place appointed for the hearing has been given to the respondent in the prescribed manner,

the court may proceed to hear and determine the application at the time and place appointed for the hearing or for any adjourned hearing in like manner as if the respondent had appeared at that time and place.

Note. Words in square brackets inserted by Family Law (Northern Ireland) Order 1993, SI 1993 No 1576, art 11, Sch 1, para 15, as from a day to be appointed.

The amendment made to sub-s (3)(a) by the Family Law (Northern Ireland) Order 1993, SI 1993/1576, art 11, Sch 1, para 15 will not be brought into force, as the amending provisions have been revoked by the Children (Northern Ireland) Order, SI 1995/755.

35A. Further provisions with respect to variation etc of orders by magistrates' courts in Northern Ireland—(*1*) *Notwithstanding anything in section 29 or 29A(3)(e) of this Act, a magistrates' court in Northern Ireland shall have jurisdiction to hear an application for the variation or revocation of a registered order registered in that court, being—*

(*a*) *an application made by the person against whom or on whose application the order was made, or*

(*b*) *an application made by some other person in pursuance of section 30(5) of this Act for the variation of an affiliation order,*

notwithstanding that the person by or against whom the application is made is residing outside Northern Ireland.

(*2*) *Where an application by a person in a convention country for the variation of a registered order is received from the Lord Chancellor by the clerk of a magistrates' court in Northern Ireland, he shall treat the application as if it were a complaint for the variation of the order to which the application relates, and the court hearing the application shall proceed as if the application were a complaint and the applicant were before the court.*

(*3*) *Without prejudice to subsection (2) above, an application to a magistrates' court in Northern Ireland for the variation or revocation of a registered order shall be made by complaint.*

(*4*) *Where the defendant to a complaint for the variation or revocation of a registered order which is registered in a magistrates' court in Northern Ireland does not appear at the time and place appointed for the hearing of the complaint, but the court is satisfied—*

(*a*) *that the defendant is residing outside Northern Ireland, and*

(*b*) *that the prescribed notice of the making of the complaint and of the time and place appointed for the hearing has been given to the defendant in the prescribed manner,*

the court may proceed to hear and determine the complaint at the time and place appointed for the hearing or for any adjourned hearing in like manner as if the defendant had appeared at that time and place.]

Note. Sections 35, 35A in square brackets substituted for previous s 35 in italics by Maintenance Orders (Reciprocal Enforcement) Act 1992, s 1(2), Sch 1, Part II, para 16, as from 5 April 1993.

[**35A. Further provisions with respect to variation etc of orders by magistrates' courts in Northern Ireland**—(1) Notwithstanding anything in section 29(2) or 29A(6)(e) of this Act, a magistrates' court in Northern Ireland shall have jurisdiction to hear an application—

(a) for the variation or revocation of a registered order registered in that court, and

(b) made by the person against whom or on whose application the order was made,

notwithstanding that the person by or against whom the application is made is residing outside Northern Ireland.

(2) None of the powers of the court, or of the clerk, under section 34B of this Act shall be exercisable in relation to such an application.

(3) Where the respondent to an application for the variation or revocation of a registered order which is registered in a magistrates' court in Northern Ireland does not appear at the time and place appointed for the hearing of the application, but the court is satisfied—

(a) that the respondent is residing outside Northern Ireland, and

(b) that the prescribed notice of the making of the application and of the time and place appointed for the hearing has been given to the respondent in the prescribed manner, the court may proceed to hear and determine the application at the time and place appointed for the hearing or for any adjourned hearing in like manner as if the respondent had appeared at that time and place.]

Note. Section 35A in square brackets substituted for previous s 35A in italics by Children (Northern Ireland) Order 1995, SI 1995 No 755, art 185, Sch 9, para 75, as from 4 November 1996.

Supplemental

36. Admissibility of evidence given in convention country—(1) A statement contained in—

(a) a document, duly authenticated, which purports to set out or summarise evidence given in proceedings in a court in a convention country; or

(b) a document, duly authenticated, which purports to set out or summarise evidence taken in such a country for the purpose of proceedings in a court in the United Kingdom under this Part of this Act, whether in response to a request made on behalf of such a court or otherwise; or

(c) a document, duly authenticated, which purports to have been received in evidence in proceedings in a court in such a country, or to be a copy of a document so received,

shall, in any proceedings in a magistrates' court or [in, or remitted from, a] sheriff court arising out of an application *received by the Secretary of State as mentioned in section 27(1) or 31(1) of this Act or out of* [to which section 27A(1) of this Act applies, an application *received by the Lord Chancellor as mentioned in section 28C(1) of this Act* [to which section 28C(1) of this Act applies], an application received by the Secretary of State as mentioned in section 31(1) of this Act or] an application made by any person for the variation or revocation of a registered order or in proceedings on appeal from any such proceedings, be admissible as evidence of any fact stated therein to the same extent as oral evidence of that fact is admissible in those proceedings.

Note. Words 'in, or remitted from, a' in square brackets inserted by Domestic Proceedings and Magistrates' Courts Act 1978, s 60(3), as from 1 February 1981. Words from 'to which section 27A(1)' to 'of this Act or' in square brackets substituted for previous words in italics by Maintenance Orders (Reciprocal Enforcement) Act 1992, s 1(2), Sch 1, Part II, para 17, as from 5 April 1993. Words 'to which section 28C(1) of this Act applies' in square brackets substituted for words 'received by the Lord Chancellor ... of this Act' in italics by Children (Northern Ireland) Order 1995, SI 1995 No 755, art 185, Sch 9, para 76, as from 4 November 1996.

(2) A document purporting to set out or summarise evidence given as mentioned in subsection (1)(a) above, or taken as mentioned in subsection (1)(b) above, shall be deemed to be duly authenticated for the purposes of that subsection if the document purports to be certified by the judge, magistrate or other person before whom the evidence was given or, as the case may be, by whom it was taken, to be the original document containing or recording, or, as the case may be, summarising, that evidence or a true copy of that document.

(3) A document purporting to have been received in evidence as mentioned in subsection (1)(c) above, or to be a copy of a document so received, shall be deemed to be duly authenticated for the purposes of that subsection if the document purports to be certified by a judge, magistrate or officer of the court in question to have been, or to be a true copy of a document which has been, so received.

(4) It shall not be necessary in any such proceedings to prove the signature or official position of the person appearing to have given such a certificate.

(5) Nothing in this section shall prejudice the admission in evidence of any document which is admissible in evidence apart from this section.

37. Obtaining of evidence for purpose of proceedings in United Kingdom court—(1) A court in the United Kingdom may for the purpose of any proceedings in that court under this Part of this Act arising out of an application received by the

Secretary of State from a convention country request the Secretary of State to make to the appropriate authority or court in the convention country a request for the taking in that country of the evidence of a person residing therein relating to matters connected with the application.

(2) A request made by a court under this section shall—

(a) give details of the application in question;

(b) state the name and address of the person whose evidence is to be taken; and

(c) specify the matters relating to which the evidence of that person is required.

(3) If the Secretary of State is satisfied that a request made to him under this section contains sufficient information to enable the evidence of the person named in the request relating to the matters specified therein to be taken by a court or person in the convention country, he shall transmit the request to the appropriate authority or court in that country.

38. Taking of evidence at request of court in convention country—(1) Where a request is made to the Secretary of State by or on behalf of a court in a convention country to obtain the evidence of a person residing in the United Kingdom relating to matters connected with an application to which section 26 of this Act applies, the Secretary of State shall request such court, or such officer of a court, as he may determine to take the evidence of that person relating to such matters connected with that application as may be specified in the request.

(2) The court by which or officer by whom a request under subsection (1) above is received from the Secretary of State shall have power to take the evidence and, after giving notice of the time and place at which the evidence is to be taken to such persons and in such manner as it or he thinks fit, shall take the evidence of the person named in the request relating to the matters specified therein in such manner as may be prescribed; and the evidence so taken shall be sent in the prescribed manner by the prescribed officer to the court in the convention country by or on behalf of which the request referred to in subsection (1) above was made.

(3) Where any person, not being the person by whom the application mentioned in subsection (1) above was made, is required by virtue of this section to give evidence before a court in the United Kingdom, the court may order that there shall be paid—

(a) if the court is a court in England, Wales or Scotland, out of moneys provided by Parliament; and

(b) if the court is a court in Northern Ireland, out of moneys provided by *the Parliament of Northern Ireland* [Parliament],

such sums as appear to the court reasonably sufficient to compensate that person for the expense, trouble or loss of time properly incurred in or incidental to his attendance.

Note. 'Parliament' substituted for 'the Parliament of Northern Ireland' by Northern Ireland (Modification of Enactments—No 1) Order 1973, SI 1973 No 2163, art 14, Sch 5, para 22.

(4) *Section 77(1), (3) and (4) of the Magistrates' Courts Act 1952* [Section 97(1), (3) and (4) of the Magistrates' Courts Act 1980] (which provide for compelling the attendance of witnesses, etc) shall apply in relation to a magistrates' court to which a request under subsection (1) above is made as if the application to which the request relates were a complaint to be heard by that court.

Note. Reference to Magistrates' Courts Act 1980 substituted for reference to Magistrates' Courts Act 1952 by Magistrates' Courts Act 1980, s 154, Sch 7, para 109, as from 6 July 1981.

(5) Paragraphs 71 and 73 of Schedule 1 to the Sheriff Courts (Scotland) Act 1907 (which provide for the citation of witnesses, etc) shall apply in relation to a sheriff court to which a request under subsection (1) above is made as if the application to which the request relates were proceedings in that court.

(6) In the application of this section to Northern Ireland, in subsection (4), for the reference to *section 77(1)*, *(3) and (4) of the Magistrates' Courts Act 1952* [section 97(1), (3) and (4) of the Magistrates' Courts Act 1980] there shall be substituted a reference to *section 120(1)*, *(3) and (4)*, *121 and 122 of the Magistrates' Courts Act (Northern Ireland) 1964* [Articles 118(1), (3) and (4), 119 and 120 of the Magistrates' Courts (Northern Ireland) Order 1981].

Note. Reference to Magistrates' Court Act 1980 substituted for reference to Magistrates' Courts Act 1952 by Magistrates' Courts Act 1980, s 154, Sch 7, para 109, as from 6 July 1981. Reference to Magistrates' Courts (Northern Ireland) Order 1981 substituted for reference to Magistrates' Courts Act (Northern Ireland) 1964 by Magistrates' Courts (Northern Ireland) Order 1981, SI 1981 No 1675, art 170, Sch 6, Part I, para 25.

[*38A. Magistrates' courts rules* [**38A. Rules of court**]—(1) *Without prejudice to the generality of the power to make rules under section 144 of the Magistrates' Courts Act 1980 (magistrates' courts rules), such rules* [rules of court] may make provision with respect to the orders made or other things done by a magistrates' court, or an officer of such a court, by virtue of this Part of this Act, notice of which is to be given to such persons as the rules may provide and the manner in which such notice shall be given.

Note. Section heading substituted and words in square brackets substituted for words in italics by SI 2004/2035, art 3, Schedule, para 2(1), (2), (5), as from 1 September 2004.

(2) For the purpose of giving effect to this Part of this Act, *rules made under section 144 of the Magistrates' Courts Act 1980* [rules of court] may make, in relation to any proceedings brought under or by virtue of this Part of this Act, any provision not covered by subsection (1) above which—

(a) falls within subsection (2) of section 93 of the Children Act 1989, and

(b) may be made in relation to relevant proceedings under that section.

Note. Words in square brackets substituted for words in italics by SI 2004/2035, art 3, Schedule, para 2(1), (3), as from 1 September 2004.

(3) In the application of this section to Northern Ireland—

(a) in subsection (1), for the reference to section 144 of the Magistrates' Courts Act 1980 there shall be substituted a reference to Article 13 of the Magistrates' Courts (Northern Ireland) Order 1981, and

(b) subsection (2) shall be omitted.

Note. Sub-s (3) repealed by SI 2004/2035, art 3, Schedule, para 2(1), (4), as from 1 September 2004.

[(4) For the purpose of giving effect to this Part of the Act, rules made under Article 13 of the Magistrates' Courts (Northern Ireland) Order 1981 may make, in relation to any proceedings brought under or by virtue of this Part of this Act, any provision not covered by subsection (1) above which—

(a) falls within paragraph (2) of Article 165 of the Children (Northern Ireland) Order 1995, and

(b) may be made in relation to relevant proceedings under that Article.]]

Note. Section 38A inserted by Maintenance Orders (Reciprocal Enforcement) Act 1992, s 1(2), Sch 1, Part II, para 18, as from 5 April 1993. Sub-s (3)(b) repealed and sub-s (4) added by Children (Northern Ireland) Order 1995, SI 1995 No 755, art 185, Sch 9, para 77, Sch 10, as from 4 November 1996.

39. Interpretation of Part II. In this Part of this Act—

'maintenance', as respects Scotland, *means aliment* [includes aliment and any sums which are payable, following divorce, as a periodical allowance];

['maintenance order' has the same meaning as in Part I of this Act;]

'order', as respects Scotland, includes any interlocutor, and any decree or provision contained in an interlocutor;

2482   Maintenance Orders (Reciprocal Enforcement) Act 1972, s 39

'prescribed' has the same meaning as in Part I of this Act;

'registered order' means an order which is for the time being registered in a court in the United Kingdom under this Part of this Act;

'registering court', in relation to a registered order, means the court in which that order is for the time being registered under this Part of this Act.

['revoke' and 'revocation' include discharge.]

Note. In definition 'maintenance' words in square brackets substituted for words in italics by Domestic Proceedings and Magistrates' Courts Act 1978, s 60(4), as from 1 February 1981. Definitions 'maintenance order', 'revoke' and 'revocation' added by Maintenance Orders (Reciprocal Enforcement) Act 1992, s 1(2), Sch 1, Part II, para 19, as from 5 April 1993.

PART III

MISCELLANEOUS AND SUPPLEMENTAL

Further provisions relating to enforcement of maintenance orders and to applications for recovery of maintenance

40. Power to apply Act to maintenance orders and applications for recovery of maintenance made in certain countries. Where Her Majesty is satisfied—

   (a) that arrangements have been or will be made in a country or territory outside the United Kingdom to ensure that maintenance orders made by courts in the United Kingdom *against persons in that country or territory* can be enforced in that country or territory or that applications by persons in the United Kingdom for the recovery of maintenance from persons in that country or territory can be entertained by courts in that country or territory; and

   (b) that in the interest of reciprocity it is desirable to ensure that maintenance orders made by courts in that country or territory *against persons in the United Kingdom* can be enforced in the United Kingdom or, as the case may be, that applications by persons in that country or territory for the recovery of maintenance from persons in the United Kingdom can be entertained by courts in the United Kingdom,

Her Majesty may by Order in Council make provision for applying the provisions of this Act, with such exceptions, adaptations and modifications as may be specified in the Order, to such orders or applications as are referred to in paragraphs (a) and (b) above and to maintenance and other orders made in connection with such applications by courts in the United Kingdom or in that country or territory.

Note. Words in paras (a), (b) in italics repealed by Civil Jurisdiction and Judgments Act 1982, ss 37(1), 54, Sch 11, para 17, Sch 14, as from 1 January 1987.

Provisions with respect to certain orders of magistrates' courts

41. Complaint for variation, etc of certain orders by or against persons outside England and Wales—(*1*) *The jurisdiction to revoke, revive or vary an order for the periodical payment of money conferred on magistrates' courts by section 53 of the Magistrates' Courts Act 1952* [*section 60 of the Magistrates' Courts Act 1980*] *shall, in the case of—*

   (*a*) *an affiliation order, or*

   (*b*) *an order under section 9, 10 or 11 of the Guardianship of Minors Act 1971 for the payment of sums towards the maintenance of a minor,*

[*an affiliation order*] *be exercisable notwithstanding that the proceedings for the revocation, revival or variation, as the case may be, of the order are brought by or against a person residing outside England and Wales.*

Note. Reference to Magistrates' Courts Act 1980 substituted for reference to Magistrates' Courts Act 1952 by Magistrates' Courts Act 1980, s 154, Sch 7, para 110, as from 6 July 1981.

Words 'an affiliation order' substituted for preceding words by Domestic Proceedings and Magistrates' Courts Act 1978, s 89(2), Sch 2, para 36(a), as from 1 February 1981.

Sub-s (1) repealed by Family Law Reform Act 1987, s 33(1), (4), Sch 2, para 51(2), Sch 4, as from 1 April 1989.

(2) Subsections (2) to (5) of section 9 of the Matrimonial Proceedings (Magistrates' Courts) Act 1960 (which relates to the procedure to be followed in the case of a complaint by or against a person outside England and Wales for variation, etc, of an order made under that Act) shall, for the purposes of subsection (1) above, apply in respect of any such order as is mentioned in paragraph (a) or (b) of that subsection as they apply in respect of a matrimonial or interim order, but with the substitution of references to section 53 of the said Act of 1952 for references to section 8 of the said Act of 1960.

[(2) The jurisdiction to revoke or vary an order for the periodical payment of money conferred on magistrates' courts by sections 9, 10 or 11 [section 11B or 11C] of the Guardianship of Minors Act 1971 shall be exercisable notwithstanding that the proceedings for the revocation or variation of the order are brought by or against a person residing outside England and Wales.

Note. Words 'section 11B or 11C' substituted for words 'sections 9, 10 or 11' by Family Law Reform Act 1987, s 33(1), Sch 2, para 51(3), as from 1 April 1989.

(2A) Subject to subsection (2B) below, a magistrates' court may, if it is satisfied that the respondent has been outside the United Kingdom during such period as may be prescribed by rules made under section 15 of the Justices of the Peace Act 1949 [section 144 of the Magistrates' Courts Act 1980] proceed on—

(a) an application made under section 53 of the Magistrates' Courts Act 1952 [section 60 of the Magistrates' Courts Act 1980] for the revocation, revival or variation of an affiliation order, or

Note. Sub-s (2A)(a) repealed by Family Law Reform Act 1987, s 33(1), (4), Sch 2, para 51(4), Sch 4, as from 1 April 1989.

(b) an application made under section 9, 10, 11 or 12C(5) of the Guardianship of Minors Act 1971 for the revocation or variation of an order for the periodical payment of money made under the said section 9, 10 or 11,

[(b) an application made under section 11B or 11C of the Guardianship of Minors Act 1971 for the revocation or variation of an order for the periodical payment of money made under the said section 11B or 11C.]

Note. Sub-s (2A)(b) in square brackets substituted for preceding sub-s (2A)(b) by Family Law Reform Act 1987, s 33(1), Sch 2, para 51(4), as from 1 April 1989.

notwithstanding that the respondent has not been served with the summons; and rules may prescribe any other matters as to which the court is to be satisfied before proceeding in such a case.

(2B) A magistrates' court shall not—

(a) exercise its powers under section 53 of the Magistrates' Courts Act 1952 [section 60 of the Magistrates' Courts Act 1980] so as to increase the amount of any periodical payments required to be made by any person under an affiliation order; or

Note. Sub-s (2B)(a) repealed by Family Law Reform Act 1987, s 33(1), (4), Sch 4, para 51(5), Sch 4, as from 1 April 1989.

(b) exercise its powers under section 9, 10 or 11 [section 11B or 11C] of the Guardianship of Minors Act 1971 so as to increase the amount of any periodical payments required to be made by any person by an order under one of those sections,

unless those powers are exercised at a hearing at which the person required to make the periodical payment appears or the requirements of section 47(3) of the Magistrates' Courts Act 1952 [section 55(3) of the Magistrates' Courts Act 1980] with respect to proof of service of summons or appearance on a previous occasion are satisfied in respect of that person.]

Note. Sub-ss (2), (2A), (2B) in square brackets substituted for original sub-s (2) by Domestic Proceedings and Magistrates' Courts Act 1978, s 89(2), Sch 2, para 36(b), as from 1 February 1981.

References to Magistrates' Courts Act 1980 substituted for references to 1952 Act by ibid, s 154, Sch 7, para 110, as from 6 July 1981.

References to s 11B or 11C in sub-s (2B)(b) substituted by Family Law Reform Act 1987, s 33(1), Sch 2, para 51(5), as from 1 April 1989.

(*3*) *In section 15(1) of the Maintenance Orders Act 1950 (service of process on a person residing in Scotland or Northern Ireland), after the words 'Act 1971' there shall be inserted the words 'or section 41 of the Maintenance Orders (Reciprocal Enforcement) Act 1972'.*

(*4*) *Section 3(2) of the said Act of 1950 (jurisdiction in proceedings by or against a person residing in Scotland or Northern Ireland for the revocation, etc, of an affiliation order) is hereby repealed.*

Note. This section repealed by Children Act 1989, s 108(7), Sch 15, as from 14 October 1991.

42. Provisional order for maintenance of party to marriage made by magistrates' court to cease to have effect on remarriage of party—(1) Where a magistrates' court has, by virtue of section 3 of this Act, made a provisional maintenance order consisting of, or including, a provision such as is mentioned in *section 2(1)(b) or (c) of the Matrimonial Proceedings (Magistrates' Courts) Act 1960 (payment of weekly sums by husband or wife)* [section 2(1)(a) of the Domestic Proceedings and Magistrates' Courts Act 1978 (making of periodical payments by husband or wife)] [or Article 4(1)(a) of the Domestic Proceedings (Northern Ireland) Order 1980] and the order has been confirmed by a competent court in a reciprocating country, then, if after the making of that order the marriage of the parties to the proceedings in which the order was made is dissolved or annulled but the order continues in force, that order or, as the case may be, that provision thereof shall cease to have effect on the remarriage of the party in whose favour it was made, except in relation to any arrears due under it on the date of such remarriage and shall not be capable of being revived.

Note. First words in square brackets substituted for preceding words in italics by Domestic Proceedings and Magistrates' Courts Act 1978, s 89(2), Sch 2, para 37, as from 1 February 1981. Second words in square brackets inserted by Maintenance Orders (Northern Ireland Consequential Amendments) Order 1980, SI 1980 No 564, art 4(6).

(2) For the avoidance of doubt it is hereby declared that references in this section to remarriage include references to a marriage which is by law void or voidable.

(3) In section 30(2) of the Matrimonial Proceedings and Property Act 1970 (which makes, in relation to such an order as is referred to in subsection (1) above which was confirmed in accordance with section 3 of the Maintenance Orders (Facilities for Enforcement) Act 1920, provision to the like effect as that subsection) the words from 'but which the modification' to the end are hereby repealed.

Supplemental provisions

43. Extension of legal aid—(*1*) *At the end of paragraph 3 of Part I of Schedule 1 to the Legal Aid and Advice Act 1949 (which specified the proceedings in a magistrates' court or the Crown Court for which legal aid may be given under section 1 of that Act) there shall be inserted the following sub-paragraph—*

'(*a*) *proceedings under Part I of the Maintenance Orders (Reciprocal Enforcement) Act 1972 relating to a maintenance order made by a court of a country outside the United Kingdom.'*

Note. Sub-s (1) repealed by Legal Aid Act 1974, s 42(1), Sch 5, Part I.

(*2*) *At the end of paragraph 3 of Part I of Schedule 1 to the Legal Aid and Advice Act (Northern Ireland) 1965 (which specifies the proceedings in magistrates' court in Northern Ireland for which legal aid may be given under section 1 of that Act) there shall be inserted the following sub-paragraph—*

'(*a*) *proceedings under Part I of the Maintenance Orders (Reciprocal Enforcement) Act 1972 relating to a maintenance order made by a court of a country outside the United Kingdom, and any such proceedings as are referred to in sub-paragraph (a) above brought by virtue of Part II of the said Act of 1972'.*

(*3*) *The amendment made by subsection (2) above shall have effect notwithstanding anything in paragraph (b) of section 1(6) of the said Act of 1965.*

Note. Sub-ss (2), (3) repealed by Legal Aid, Advice and Assistance (Northern Ireland) Order 1981, SI 1981 No 228, Sch 4.

[43A. Eligibility for legal aid in Scotland—(1) In connection with proceedings under Part I of this Act in relation to a maintenance order made by a court in a reciprocating country, where there is produced a certificate from the responsible authority in that country to the effect that the payee would, in that country, be financially eligible for complete or partial—
  (i) legal aid; or
  (ii) exemption from costs or expenses,
in proceedings there in relation to that maintenance order, sections 2(1) and (6)(c), 3 and 4 of the Legal Aid (Scotland) Act 1967 shall not apply in respect of the payee and, subject to the other provisions of that Act, legal aid shall under that Act be available to the payee without inquiry into the payee's resources.
  (2) In connection with proceedings under Part II of this Act—
  (a) arising out of an application received from a convention country for the recovery of maintenance; or
  (b) relating to an order made in respect of such an application,
where there is produced a certificate from the appropriate authority in that country to the effect that the applicant would, in that country, be financially eligible for complete or partial—
  (i) legal aid; or
  (ii) exemption from costs or expenses,
in proceedings there for the recovery of maintenance, sections 2(1) and (6)(c), 3 and 4 of the said Act of 1967 shall not apply in respect of the applicant and, subject to the other provisions of that Act, legal aid shall under that Act be available to the applicant without inquiry into the applicant's resources.
  (3) Where, in connection with proceedings under Part I or II of this Act, a person has received legal aid by virtue of subsection (1) or (2) above, legal advice and assistance under the Legal Advice and Assistance Act 1972 shall, notwithstanding—
  (i) any financial conditions imposed by, or by virtue of, sections 1 and 4(2), (3) and (4); and
  (ii) in relation to the effect of subsections (1) to (4) and (7) of section 4 of the said Act of 1967, the provisions of section 6(1)(b),
of the said Act of 1972 (but subject otherwise to the provisions of the said Act of 1972), be available in Scotland for that person, without inquiry into his resources, in connection with any matter incidental to, or arising out of, those proceedings.
  (4) In subsection (1) above 'maintenance order', 'reciprocating country', 'responsible authority' and 'payee' have the same meanings respectively as in Part I of this Act; and in subsection (2) above 'convention country' means a country or territory specified in an Order in Council under section 25(1) of this Act, 'maintenance' has the same meaning as in Part II of this Act, and 'appropriate authority' means the authority from which the Secretary of State received the application.]
Note. Section 43A added by Domestic Proceedings and Magistrates' Courts Act 1978, s 61, as from 1 February 1981.
  For amendments in relation to Scotland, see Legal Aid (Scotland) Act 1986, s 45(1), Sch 3, para 2.

44. Exclusion of certain enactments relating to evidence—(1) Section 20 of the Family Law Reform Act 1969 (power of court hearing certain proceedings to require use of blood tests to determine paternity) and any corresponding enactment of the Parliament of Northern Ireland shall not apply to any proceedings under this Act, but the foregoing provision is without prejudice to the power of a court to allow the report of any person who has carried out such tests to be given in evidence in those proceedings.

(2) *The Foreign Tribunals Evidence Act 1856 (which relates to the taking of evidence in the United Kingdom for the purpose of proceedings before a foreign tribunal) and the Evidence by Commission Act 1859 (which relates to the taking of evidence in the United Kingdom for the purpose of proceedings before a court in Her Majesty's dominions)* [The Evidence (Proceedings in other Jurisdictions) Act 1975] shall not apply to the taking of evidence in the United Kingdom for the taking of which section 14 or section 38 of this Act provides.

Note. Words in square brackets substituted for words in italics by Evidence (Proceedings in Other Jurisdictions) Act 1975, s 8(1), Sch 1.

45. Orders in Council—(1) An Order in Council under section 1, section 25 or section 40 of this Act may be varied or revoked by a subsequent Order in Council thereunder, and an Order made by virtue of this section may contain such incidental, consequential and transitional provisions as Her Majesty considers expedient for the purposes of that section.

(2) An Order in Council made under the said section 1 or the said section 40 shall be subject to annulment in pursuance of a resolution of either House of Parliament.

46. Financial provisions.   There shall be paid out of moneys provided by Parliament—

    (a) any sums ordered by a court under section 14(2) or 38(3) of this Act to be paid out of moneys so provided; and

    (b) any increase attributable to the provisions of this Act in the sums payable under the Legal Aid and Advice Act 1949 or the Legal Aid (Scotland) Act 1967 out of moneys so provided.

47. Interpretation: general—(1) In this Act—

    'enactment' includes an enactment of the Parliament of Northern Ireland;

    'magistrates' court', in relation to Northern Ireland, means a court of summary jurisdiction within the meaning of *section 1(1) of the Magistrates' Courts Act (Northern Ireland) 1964* [Article 2(2)(a) of the Magistrates' Courts (Northern Ireland) Order 1981].

Note. Words in square brackets substituted for words in italics by Magistrates' Courts (Northern Ireland) Order 1981, SI 1981 No 1675, art 170(2), Sch 6, Part I, para 26.

(2) References in this Act to a part of the United Kingdom are references to England and Wales, to Scotland, or to Northern Ireland.

(3) Any reference in this Act to the jurisdiction of a court, where the reference is [to assets being located or] to a person residing, *or having ceased to reside,* within the jurisdiction of a court, shall be *construed in relation to a magistrates' court in England and Wales as a reference to the petty sessions area, and in relation to a magistrates' court in Northern Ireland as a reference to the petty sessions district, for which the court acts* [construed—

    (a) in relation to a magistrates' court in England and Wales as a reference to the local justice area in which the court acts, and

    (b) in relation to a magistrates' court in Northern Ireland as a reference to the petty sessions district for which the court acts]

Note. Words in square brackets inserted and words in italics repealed by Civil Jurisdiction and Judgments Act 1982, ss 37(1), 54, Sch 11, para 18, Sch 14, as from 1 January 1987.

Word 'construed' and paras (a), (b) in square brackets substituted for words from 'construed in relation' to 'the court acts' in italics by the Courts Act 2003, s 109(1), Sch 8, para 164, as from a day to be appointed.

(4) Any reference in this Act to any other enactment is a reference thereto as amended, and includes a reference thereto as extended or applied, by or under any other enactment.

48. Special provisions relating to Northern Ireland—(1) Nothing in this Act shall authorise any Department of the Government of Northern Ireland to incur any expenses attributable to the provisions of this Act until provision has been made by the Parliament of Northern Ireland for those expenses to be defrayed out of moneys provided by that Parliament.

(2) *For the purposes of section 6 of the Government of Ireland Act 1920 (which relates to the power of the Parliament of Northern Ireland to make laws), the provisions of this Act, so far as they extend to Northern Ireland, shall be deemed to be provisions of an Act passed before the appointed day.*

Note. Sub-s (2) repealed by Northern Ireland Constitution Act 1973, s 41(1), Sch 6, Part I.

(3) Any reference in this Act to an enactment of the Parliament of Northern Ireland or to an enactment which that Parliament has power to amend, shall be construed in relation to Northern Ireland, as a reference to that enactment as amended or extended by any Act of that Parliament, whether passed before or after this Act, and to any enactment of that Parliament passed after this Act and re-enacting the said enactment with or without modifications.

(4) If the Parliament of Northern Ireland passes any enactment for purposes similar to those of any enactment in force in England and Wales which is referred to in this Act, Her Majesty may by order in Council direct that this Act shall have effect subject to such modifications or adaptations as may be specified in the Order for the purpose of ensuring the continued operation of this Act in, or in relation to, Northern Ireland.

(5) Section 45 of this Act shall apply in relation to an Order in Council under subsection (4) above as it applies in relation to an Order in Council under section 1 or 40 of this Act.

49. Short title and commencement—(1) This Act may be cited as the Maintenance Orders (Reciprocal Enforcement) Act 1972.

(2) This Act shall come into force on such day as the Secretary of State may by order made by statutory instrument appoint, and different days may be so appointed for different provisions of this Act, or for different purposes.

Commencement. Parts I and III of and the Schedule to Maintenance Orders (Reciprocal Enforcement) Act 1972 with the exception of s 22(2), came into force on 1 April 1974 (SI 1974 No 517). Part II came into force on 12 April 1975 (SI 1975 No 377).

(*Schedule: Para 1 (which amended Magistrates' Courts Act 1952, s 57(4)) repealed by Domestic Proceedings and Magistrates' Courts Act 1978, s 89(2), Sch 3, as from 1 February 1980; para 2 amends Army Act 1955, s 150 (p 2161), Air Force Act 1955, s 150(5) (p 2174); para 3 amends Naval Discipline Act 1957, s 101(5) (not printed in this work); para 4 (which amended Maintenance Orders Act 1958, s 1) repealed by Civil Jurisdiction and Judgments Act 1982, s 54, Sch 14, as from 1 January 1987; para 5 amends Maintenance and Affiliation Orders Act (Northern Ireland) 1966, s 10 (not printed in this work); para 6 inserts Administration of Justice Act 1970, Sch 8, para 11 (p 2355); para 7 inserts Attachment of Earnings Act 1971, Sch 1, para 11 (p 2413)*).

CIVIL EVIDENCE ACT 1972

(1972 c 30)

ARRANGEMENT OF SECTIONS

An Act to make, for civil proceedings in England and Wales, provision as to the admissibility in evidence of statements of opinion and the reception of expert evidence; and to facilitate proof in such proceedings of any law other than that of England and Wales. [12 June 1972]

1. Application of Part I of Civil Evidence Act 1968 to statements of opinion—
(*1*) *Subject to the provisions of this section, Part I (hearsay evidence) of the Civil Evidence Act 1968, except section 5 (statements produced by computers), shall apply in relation to statements of opinion as it applies in relation to statements of fact, subject to the necessary modifications and in particular the modification that any reference to a fact stated in a statement shall be construed as a reference to a matter dealt with therein.*

(*2*) *Section 4 (admissibility of certain records) of the Civil Evidence Act 1968, as applied by subsection (1) above, shall not render admissible in any civil proceedings a statement of opinion contained in a record unless that statement would be admissible in those proceedings if made in the course of giving oral evidence by the person who originally supplied the information from which the record was compiled; but where a statement of opinion contained in a record deals with a matter on which the person who originally supplied the information from which the record was compiled is (or would if living be) qualified to give oral expert evidence, the said section 4, as applied by subsection (1) above, shall have effect in relation to that statement as if so much of subsection (1) of that section as requires personal knowledge on the part of that person were omitted.*

Note. This section repealed by Civil Evidence Act 1995, s 15(2), Sch 2, as from 31 January 1997. For Civil Evidence Act 1968, s 4 see p 2285.

2. Rules of court with respect to expert reports and oral expert evidence—(*1*) *If and so far as rules of court so provide, subsection (2) of section 2 of the Civil Evidence Act 1968 (which imposes restrictions on the giving of a statement in evidence by virtue of that section on behalf of a party who has called or intends to call as a witness the maker of the statement) shall not apply to statements (whether of fact or opinion) contained in expert reports.*

(*2*) *In so far as they relate to statements (whether of fact or opinion) contained in expert reports, rules of court made in pursuance of subsection (1) of section 8 of the Civil Evidence Act 1968 as to the procedure to be followed and the other conditions to be fulfilled before a statement can be given in evidence in civil proceedings by virtue of section 2 of that Act (admissibility of out-of-court statements) shall not be subject to the requirements of subsection (2) of the said section 8 (which specifies certain matters of procedure for which provision must ordinarily be made by rules of court made in pursuance of the said subsection (1)).*

Note. Sub-ss (1), (2) repealed by Civil Evidence Act 1995, s 15(2), Sch 2, as from 31 January 1997.

(3) Notwithstanding any enactment or rule of law by virtue of which documents prepared for the purpose of pending or contemplated civil proceedings or in connection with the obtaining or giving of legal advice are in certain circumstances privileged from disclosure, provision may be made by rules of court—
   (a) for enabling the court in any civil proceedings to direct, with respect to medical matters or matters of any other class which may be specified in the direction, that the parties or some of them shall each by such date as may be so specified (or such later date as may be permitted or agreed in accordance with the rules) disclose to the other or others in the form of one or more expert reports the evidence on matters of that class which he proposes to adduce as part of his case at the trial; and
   (b) for prohibiting a party who fails to comply with a direction given in any such proceedings under rules of court made by virtue of paragraph (a) above from adducing in evidence *by virtue of section 2 of the Civil Evidence Act 1968 (admissibility of out-of-court statements)*, except with the leave of the court, any statement (whether of fact or opinion) contained in any expert report whatsoever in so far as that statement deals with matters of any class specified in the direction.

Note. Words in italics in sub-s (3)(b) repealed by Civil Evidence Act 1995, s 15(2), Sch 2, as from 31 January 1997.

(4) Provision may be made by rules of court as to the conditions subject to which oral expert evidence may be given in civil proceedings.

(5) Without prejudice to the generality of subsection (4) above, rules of court made in pursuance of that subsection may make provision for prohibiting a party who fails to comply with a direction given as mentioned in subsection (3)(b) above from adducing, except with the leave of the court, any oral expert evidence whatsoever with respect to matters of any class specified in the direction.

(6) Any rules of court made in pursuance of this section may make different provision for different classes of cases, for expert reports dealing with matters of different classes, and for other different circumstances.

(7) References in this section to an expert report are references to a written report by a person dealing wholly or mainly with matters on which he is (or would if living be) qualified to give expert evidence.

(8) Nothing in the foregoing provisions of this section shall prejudice the generality of section 99 of the Supreme Court of Judicature (Consolidation) Act 1925, section 102 of the County Courts Act 1959 [section 75 of the County Courts Act 1984], section 15 of the Justices of the Peace Act 1949 [section 144 of the Magistrates' Courts Act 1980] or any other enactment conferring power to make rules of court; and nothing in section 101 of the said Act of 1925, section 102(2) of the County Courts Act 1959 [section 75(2) of the County Courts Act 1984] or any other enactment restricting the matters with respect to which rules of court may be made shall prejudice the making of rules of court in pursuance of this section or the operation of any rules of court so made.

Note. Reference to Magistrates' Courts Act 1980 substituted for reference to Justices of the Peace Act 1949 by Magistrates' Courts Act 1980, s 154, Sch 7, para 114, as from 6 July 1981. References to County Courts Act 1984 substituted for references to County Courts Act 1959 by County Courts Act 1984, s 148(1), Sch 2, Part V, para 43, as from 1 August 1984. Other words in italics repealed by Supreme Court Act 1981, s 152(4), Sch 7.

Sub-s(8) repealed by the Courts Act 2003, s 109(1), (3), Sch 8, para 165, Sch 10, as from a day to be appointed.

3. Admissibility of expert opinion and certain expressions of non-expert opinion—(1) Subject to any rules of court made in pursuance of *Part I of the Civil Evidence Act 1968 or* this Act, where a person is called as a witness in any civil proceedings, his opinion on any relevant matter on which he is qualified to give expert evidence shall be admissible in evidence.

Note. Words in italics repealed by Civil Evidence Act 1995, s 15(2), Sch 2, as from 31 January 1997.

(2) It is hereby declared that where a person is called as a witness in any civil proceedings, a statement of opinion by him on any relevant matter on which he is not qualified to give expert evidence, if made as a way of conveying relevant facts personally perceived by him, is admissible as evidence of what he perceived.

(3) In this section 'relevant matter' includes an issue in the proceedings in question.

Note. For Civil Evidence Act 1968, Part I, see p 2284.

4. Evidence of foreign law—(1) It is hereby declared that in civil proceedings a person who is suitably qualified to do so on account of his knowledge or experience is competent to give expert evidence as to the law of any country or territory outside the United Kingdom, or of any part of the United Kingdom other than England and Wales, irrespective of whether he has acted or is entitled to act as a legal practitioner there.

(2) Where any question as to the law of any country or territory outside the United Kingdom, or of any part of the United Kingdom other than England and

2490 Civil Evidence Act 1972, s 4

Wales, with respect to any matter has been determined (whether before or after the passing of this Act) in any such proceedings as are mentioned in subsection (4) below, then in any civil proceedings (not being proceedings before a court which can take judicial notice of the law of that country, territory or part with respect to that matter)—

(a) any finding made or decision given on that question in the first-mentioned proceedings shall, if reported or recorded in citable form, be admissible in evidence for the purpose of proving the law of that country, territory or part with respect to that matter; and

(b) if that finding or decision, as so reported or recorded, is adduced for that purpose, the law of that country, territory or part with respect to that matter shall be taken to be in accordance with that finding or decision unless the contrary is proved:

Provided that paragraph (b) above shall not apply in the case of a finding or decision which conflicts with another finding or decision on the same question adduced by virtue of this subsection in the same proceedings.

(3) Except with the leave of the court, a party to any civil proceedings shall not be permitted to adduce any such finding or decision as is mentioned in subsection (2) above by virtue of that subsection unless he has in accordance with rules of court given to every other party to the proceedings notice that he intends to do so.

(4) The proceedings referred to in subsection (2) above are the following, whether civil or criminal, namely—

(a) proceedings at first instance in any of the following courts, namely the High Court, the Crown Court, a court of quarter sessions, the Court of Chancery of the county palatine of Lancaster and the Court of Chancery of the county palatine of Durham;

(b) appeals arising out of any such proceedings as are mentioned in paragraph (a) above;

(c) proceedings before the Judicial Committee of the Privy Council on appeal (whether to Her Majesty in Council or to the Judicial Committee as such) from any decision of any court outside the United Kingdom.

(5) For the purposes of this section a finding or decision on any such question as is mentioned in subsection (2) above shall be taken to be reported or recorded in citable form if, but only if, it is reported or recorded in writing in a report transcript or other document which, if that question had been a question as to the law of England and Wales, could be cited as an authority in legal proceedings in England and Wales.

Note. For 'civil proceedings', 'court', 'legal proceedings', see Civil Evidence Act 1968, s 18(1), (2) (p 2297).

5. Interpretation, application to arbitrations etc and savings—(1) *In this Act 'civil proceedings' and 'court' have the meanings assigned by section 18(1) and (2) of the Civil Evidence Act 1968.*

(2) *Subsections (3) and (4) of section 10 of the Civil Evidence Act 1968 shall apply for the purposes of the application of sections 2 and 4 of this Act in relation to any such civil proceedings as are mentioned in section 18(1)(a) and (b) of that Act (that is to say civil proceedings before a tribunal other than one of the ordinary courts of law, being proceedings in relation to which the strict rules of evidence apply, and an arbitration or reference, whether under an enactment or not) as they apply for the purposes of the application of Part I of that Act in relation to any such civil proceedings.*

[(1) In this Act 'civil proceedings' means civil proceedings, before any tribunal, in relation to which the strict rules of evidence apply, whether as a matter of law or by agreement of the parties; and references to 'the court' shall be construed accordingly.

(2) The rules of court made for the purposes of the application of sections 2 and 4 of this Act to proceedings in the High Court apply, except in so far as their

application is excluded by agreement, to proceedings before tribunals other than the ordinary courts of law, subject to such modifications as may be appropriate.

Any question arising as to what modifications are appropriate shall be determined, in default of agreement, by the tribunal.]

Note. Sub-ss (1), (2) substituted by Civil Evidence Act 1995, s 15(1), Sch 1, para 7, as from 31 January 1997.

(3) Nothing in this Act shall prejudice—

(a) any power of a court, in any civil proceedings, to exclude evidence (whether by preventing questions from being put or otherwise) at its discretion; or

(b) the operation of any agreement (whenever made) between the parties to any civil proceedings as to the evidence which is to be admissible (whether generally or for any particular purpose) in those proceedings.

Note. For Civil Evidence Act 1968, ss 10, 18, see pp 2290, 2297.

6. Short title, extent and commencement—(1) This Act may be cited as the Civil Evidence Act 1972.

(2) This Act shall not extend to Scotland or Northern Ireland.

(3) This Act, except sections *1 and* 4(2) to (5), shall come into force on 1 January 1973, and sections *1 and* 4(2) to (5) shall come into force on such day as the Lord Chancellor may by order made by statutory instrument appoint; and different days may be so appointed for different purposes or for the same purposes in relation to different courts or proceedings or otherwise in relation to different circumstances.

Commencement. Sections 1, 4(2)–(5) came into force for the purposes of civil proceedings in the Supreme Court (except bankruptcy) on 1 June 1974: SI 1974 No 280. Sections 1, 4(2)–(5) came into force on 1 September 1974, for the purposes of proceedings in county courts (except bankruptcy): SI 1974 No 1137.

Note. In sub-s (3), words in italics repealed by Civil Evidence Act 1995, s 15(2), Sch 2, as from 31 January 1997.

MATRIMONIAL PROCEEDINGS (POLYGAMOUS MARRIAGES) ACT 1972

(1972 c 38)

An Act to enable matrimonial relief to be granted, and declarations concerning the validity of a marriage to be made, notwithstanding that the marriage in question was entered into under a law which permits polygamy, and to make a consequential amendment in the Nullity of Marriage Act 1971. [29 June 1972]

1. Matrimonial relief and declarations of validity in respect of polygamous marriages: England and Wales—(*1*) *A court in England and Wales shall not be precluded from granting matrimonial relief or making a declaration concerning the validity of a marriage by reason only that the marriage in question was entered into under a law which permits polygamy.*

(*2*) *In this section 'matrimonial relief' means—*

(*a*) *a decree of divorce, nullity of marriage or judicial separation;*

(*b*) *a decree under section 14 of the Matrimonial Causes Act 1965 (presumption of death and dissolution of marriage);*

(*c*) *an order under section 6 of the Matrimonial Proceedings and Property Act 1970 (wilful neglect to maintain);*

(*d*) *an order under section 14 of the said Act of 1970 (alteration of maintenance agreements);*

(*e*) *an order under any provision of the said Acts of 1965 and 1970 or the Divorce Reform Act 1969 which confers a power exercisable in connection with, or in connection with proceedings for, any such decree or order as is mentioned in the foregoing paragraphs;*

(f) an order under the Matrimonial Proceedings (Magistrates' Courts) Act 1960.

(3) In this section 'a declaration concerning the validity of a marriage' means—

    (a) a declaration that a marriage is valid or invalid; and

    (b) any other declaration involving a determination as to the validity of a marriage,

being a declaration in a decree granted under section 39 of the said Act of 1965 or a declaration made in proceedings brought by virtue of rules of court relating to declaratory judgments.

(4) This section has effect whether or not either party to the marriage in question has for the time being any spouse additional to the other party; and provision may be made by rules of court—

    (a) for requiring notice of proceedings brought by virtue of this section to be served on any such other spouse; and

    (b) for conferring on any other spouse the right to be heard in any such proceedings,

in such cases as may be specified in the rules.

Note. Section 1 repealed by Matrimonial Causes Act 1973, s 54(1), Sch 3 and replaced by ibid, s 47 (p 2556).

2. [*Applies to Scotland.*]

3. [*Applies to Northern Ireland.*]

4. (*Amends Nullity of Marriage Act 1971, s 1 (p 2418); s 4 repealed by Matrimonial Causes Act 1973, s 54(1), Sch 3 as was s 1 of the 1971 Act; see now Matrimonial Causes Act 1973, s 11 (p 2503).*)

5. Short title, interpretation and powers of Parliament of Northern Ireland—
(1) This Act may be cited as the Matrimonial Proceedings (Polygamous Marriages) Act 1972.

(2) References in this Act to any enactment shall be construed as references to that enactment as amended, and as including references thereto as extended or applied, by any subsequent enactment.

(3) In subsection (2) of this section 'enactment' includes an enactment of the Parliament of Northern Ireland; and for the purposes of section 6 of the Government of Ireland Act 1920 this Act shall, so far as it relates to matters within the powers of the Parliament of Northern Ireland, be deemed to be an act passed before the appointed day within the meaning of that section.

Commencement. The Act came into force on 29 July 1972.

Note. Sub-s (3) repealed by Northern Ireland Constitution Act 1973, s 41(1), Sch 6, Part I, and SI 1978 No 1045, art 63(b), Sch 5.

LAND CHARGES ACT 1972

(1972 c 61)

An Act to consolidate enactments relating to the registration of land charges and other instruments and matters affecting land.   [9 August 1972]

1. The registers and the index—(1) The registrar shall continue to keep at the registry in the prescribed manner the following registers, namely—

    (a) a register of land charges;

    (b) a register of pending actions;

    (c) a register of writs and orders affecting land;

    (d) a register of deeds of arrangement affecting land;

    (e) a register of annuities,

and shall also continue to keep there an index whereby all entries made in any of those registers can readily be traced.

*   *   *   *   *

(5) An office copy of an entry in any register kept under this section shall be admissible in evidence in all proceedings and between all parties to the same extent as the original would be admissible.

*   *   *   *   *

5. The register of pending actions—(1) There may be registered in the register of pending actions—

(a) a pending land action;

(b) a petition in bankruptcy filed on or after 1 January 1926.

(2) Subject to general rules under section 16 of this Act, every application for registration under this section shall contain particulars of the title of the proceedings and the name, address and description of the estate owner or other person whose estate or interest is intended to be affected.

(3) An application for registration shall also state—

(a) if it relates to a pending land action, the court in which and the day on which the action was commenced; and

(b) if it relates to a petition in bankruptcy, the court in which and the day on which the petition was filed.

(4) The registrar shall forthwith enter the particulars in the register, in the name of the estate owner or other person where estate or interest is intended to be affected.

[(4A) Where a person has died and a pending land action would apart from his death have been registered in his name, it shall be so registered notwithstanding his death.]

Note. Sub-s (4A) inserted by Law of Property (Miscellaneous Provisions) Act 1994, s 15(1), (3), as from 1 July 1995, in relation to applications for registration made on or after 1 July 1995 (but without prejudice to a person's right to make a new application after commencement).

(5) An application to register a petition in bankruptcy against a firm shall state the names and addresses of the partners, and the registration shall be effected against each partner as well as against the firm.

(6) No fee shall be charged for the registration of a petition in bankruptcy if the application for registration is made by the registrar of the court in which the petition is filed.

(7) A pending land action shall not bind a purchaser without express notice of it unless it is for the time being registered under this section.

(8) A petition in bankruptcy shall not bind a purchaser of a legal estate in good faith, for money or money's worth, *without notice of an available act of bankruptcy,* unless it is for the time being registered under this section.

(*9*) *As respects any transfer or creation of a legal estate, a petition in bankruptcy which is not for the time being registered under this section shall not be notice or evidence of any act of bankruptcy alleged in the petition.*

(10) The court, if it thinks fit, may, upon the determination of the proceedings, or during the pendency of the proceedings if satisfied that they are not prosecuted in good faith, make an order vacating a registration under this section, and direct the party on whose behalf it was made to pay all or any of the costs and expenses occasioned by the registration and by its vacation.

[(11) The county court has jurisdiction under subsection (10) of this section where the action was brought or the petition in bankruptcy was filed in that court.]

Note. Words in italics in sub-s (8) and sub-s (9) repealed by Insolvency Act 1985, s 235(1), (3), Sch 8, para 21(2), Sch 10, Part III, as from 29 December 1986. Sub-s (11) added by County Courts Act 1984, s 148(1), Sch 2, para 17, as from 1 August 1984.

*   *   *   *   *

17. Interpretation—(1) In this Act, unless the context otherwise requires,—

'annuity' means a rentcharge or an annuity for a life or lives or for any term of years or greater estate determinable on a life or on lives and created after 25 April 1855 and before 1 January 1926, but does not include an annuity created by a marriage settlement or will;

'the Board' means the Commissioners of Inland Revenue;

'conveyance' includes a mortgage, charge, lease, assent, vesting declaration, vesting instrument, release and every other assurance of property, or of an interest in property, by any instrument except a will, and 'convey' has a corresponding meaning;

'court' means the High Court, or the county court in a case where that court has jurisdiction;

'deed of arrangement' has the same meaning as in the Deeds of Arrangement Act 1914;

'estate owner', 'legal estate', 'equitable interest', '*trust for sale*', 'charge by way of legal mortgage', *'will' and 'death duties'* [and 'will'] have the same meanings as in the Law of Property Act 1925;

'judgment' includes any order or decree having the effect of a judgment;

'land' includes land of any tenure and mines and minerals, whether or not severed from the surface, buildings or parts of buildings (whether the division is horizontal, vertical or made in any other way) and other corporeal hereditaments, also a manor, advowson and a rent and other incorporeal hereditaments, and an easement right, privilege or benefit in, over or derived from land, but not an undivided share in land, and 'hereditament' means real property which, on an intestacy occurring before 1 January 1926, might have devolved on an heir;

'land improvement charge' means any charge under the Improvement of Land Act 1864 or under any special improvement Act within the meaning of the Improvement of Land Act 1899;

'pending land action' means any action or proceeding pending in court relating to land or any interest in or charge on land;

'prescribed' means prescribed by rules made pursuant to this Act;

'purchaser' means any person (including a mortgagee or lessee) who, for valuable consideration, takes any interest in land or in a charge on land, and 'purchase' has a corresponding meaning;

'registrar' means the Chief Land Registrar, 'registry' means Her Majesty's Land Registry, and 'registered land' has the same meaning as in the *Land Registration Act 1925* [Land Registration Act 2002];

'tenant for life', 'statutory owner', 'vesting instrument' and 'settlement' have the same meanings as in the Settled Land Act 1925.

Note. Definition 'trust for sale' repealed, except in relation to any entailed interest created before 1 January 1997, by Trusts of Land and Appointment of Trustees Act 1996, s 25(2), Sch 4, as from 1 January 1997. Words in square brackets substituted for words in italics by Finance Act 1975, s 52(1), Sch 12, paras 2, 18(1), (6). Words 'Land Registration Act 2002' in square brackets substituted for words in italics by the Land Registration Act 2002, s 133, Sch 11, para 10(1), (14), as from 13 October 2003.

MATRIMONIAL CAUSES ACT 1973

(1973 c 18)

ARRANGEMENT OF SECTIONS

An Act to consolidate certain enactments relating to matrimonial proceedings, maintenance agreements, and declarations of legitimacy, validity of marriage and British nationality, with amendments to give effect to recommendations of the Law Commission.   [23 May 1973]

Note. Proceedings under this Act are 'family proceedings' for the purposes of Children Act 1989; see ibid, s 8(3)(b), (4)(b) (p 3296, 3297).

PART I

DIVORCE, NULLITY AND OTHER MATRIMONIAL SUITS

Divorce

1. Divorce on breakdown of marriage—(*1*) *Subject to section 3 below, a petition for divorce may be presented to the court by either party to a marriage on the ground that the marriage has broken down irretrievably.*

Note. Sub-s (1) replaced Divorce Reform Act 1969, s 1 (p 2338).

(*2*) *The court hearing a petition for divorce shall not hold the marriage to have broken down irretrievably unless the petitioner satisfies the court of one or more of the following facts, that is to say—*

    (*a*) *that the respondent has committed adultery and the petitioner finds it intolerable to live with the respondent;*

    (*b*) *that the respondent has behaved in such a way that the petitioner cannot reasonably be expected to live with the respondent;*

    (*c*) *that the respondent has deserted the petitioner for a continuous period of at least two years immediately preceding the presentation of the petition;*

    (*d*) *that the parties to the marriage have lived apart for a continuous period of at least two years immediately preceding the presentation of the petition (hereafter in this Act referred to as 'two years' separation') and the respondent consents to a decree being granted;*

    (*e*) *that the parties to the marriage have lived apart for a continuous period of at least five years immediately preceding the presentation of the petition (hereafter in this Act referred to as 'five years' separation').*

Note. Sub-s (2) replaced Divorce Reform Act 1969, s 2(1) (p 2338).

(*3*) *On a petition for divorce it shall be the duty of the court to inquire, so far as it reasonably can, into the facts alleged by the petitioner and into any facts alleged by the respondent.*

Note. Sub-s (3) replaced Divorce Reform Act 1969, s 2(2) (p. 2338).

(*4*) *If the court is satisfied on the evidence of any such fact as is mentioned in subsection (2) above, then, unless it is satisfied on all the evidence that the marriage has not broken down irretrievably, it shall, subject to sections 3(3) and 5 [section 5] below, grant a decree of divorce.*

Note. Sub-s (4) replaced Divorce Reform Act 1969, s 2(3) (p 2338). The reference in square brackets to s 5 substituted for reference to sections 3(3) and 5 by Matrimonial and Family Proceedings Act 1984, s 46(1), Sch 1, para 10, as from 12 October 1984.

(*5*) *Every decree of divorce shall in the first instance be a decree nisi and shall not be made absolute before the expiration of six months from its grant unless the High Court by general order from time to time fixes a shorter period, or unless in any particular case the court in which the proceedings are for the time being pending from time to time by special order fixes a shorter period than the period otherwise applicable for the time being by virtue of this subsection.*

Note. Sub-s (5) replaced Matrimonial Causes Act 1965, s 5(7) (p 2242). This section repealed by Family Law Act 1996, s 66(3), Sch 10, as from a day to be appointed, subject to savings in s 66(2) of, and para 5 of Sch 9 to, the 1996 Act.

2. Supplemental provisions as to facts raising presumption of breakdown—

(*1*) *One party to a marriage shall not be entitled to rely for the purposes of section 1(2)(a) above on adultery committed by the other if, after it became known to him that the other had committed that adultery, the parties have lived with each other for a period exceeding, or periods together exceeding, six months.*

(*2*) *Where the parties to a marriage have lived with each other after it became known to one party that the other had committed adultery, but subsection (1) above does not apply, in any proceedings for divorce in which the petitioner relies on that adultery the fact that the parties have lived with each other after that time shall be disregarded in determining for the purposes of section 1(2)(a) above whether the petitioner finds it intolerable to live with the respondent.*

Note. Sub-ss (1), (2) replaced Divorce Reform Act 1969, s 3(3) (p 2339).

(*3*) *Where in any proceedings for divorce the petitioner alleges that the respondent has behaved in such a way that the petitioner cannot reasonably be expected to live with him, but the parties to the marriage have lived with each other for a period or periods after the date of the occurrence of the final incident relied on by the petitioner and held by the court to support his allegation, that fact shall be disregarded in determining for the purposes of section 1(2)(b) above whether the petitioner cannot reasonably be expected to live with the respondent if the length of that period or of those periods together was six months or less.*

Note. Sub-s (3) replaced Divorce Reform Act 1969, s 3(4) (p 2319).

(*4*) *For the purposes of section 1(2)(c) above the court may treat a period of desertion as having continued at a time when the deserting party was incapable of continuing the necessary intention if the evidence before the court is such that, had that party not been so incapable, the court would have inferred that his desertion continued at that time.*

Note. Sub-s (4) replaced Divorce Reform Act 1969, s 2(4) (p 2339).

(*5*) *In considering for the purposes of section 1(2) above whether the period for which the respondent has deserted the petitioner or the period for which the parties to a marriage have lived apart has been continuous, no account shall be taken of any one period (not exceeding six months) or of any two or more periods (not exceeding six months in all) during which the parties resumed living with each other, but no period during which the parties lived with each other shall count as part of the period of desertion or of the period for which the parties to the marriage lived apart, as the case may be.*

Note. Sub-s (5) replaced Divorce Reform Act 1969, s 3(5) (p 2339).

(*6*) *For the purposes of section 1(2)(d) and (e) above and this section a husband and wife shall be treated as living apart unless they are living with each other in the same household, and references in this section to the parties to a marriage living with each other shall be construed as references to their living with each other in the same household.*

Note. Sub-s (6) replaced Divorce Reform Act 1969, ss 2(5), 3(6) (pp 2339, 2340).

(*7*) *Provision shall be made by rules of court for the purpose of ensuring that where in pursuance of section 1(2)(d) above the petitioner alleges that the respondent consents to a decree being granted the respondent has been given such information as will enable him to understand the consequences to him of his consenting to a decree being granted and the steps which he must take to indicate that he consents to the grant of a decree.*

Note. Sub-s (7) replaced Divorce Reform Act 1969, s 2(6) (p 2339). This section repealed by Family Law Act 1996, s 66(3), Sch 10, as from a day to be appointed, subject to savings in s 66(2) of, and para 5 of Sch 9 to, the 1996 Act.

3. Restriction on petitions for divorce within three years of marriage—(*1*) *Subject to subsection (2) below, no petition for divorce shall be presented to the court before the expiration of the period of three years from the date of the marriage (hereafter in this section referred to as 'the specified period').*

Note. Sub-s (1) replaced Matrimonial Causes Act 1965, s 2(1) (p 2240).

(*2*) *A judge of the court may, on an application made to him, allow the presentation of a petition for divorce within the specified period on the ground that the case is one of exceptional hardship suffered by the petitioner or of exceptional depravity on the part of the respondent; but in determining the application the judge shall have regard to the interests of any child of the family and to the question whether there is reasonable probability of a reconciliation between the parties during the specified period.*

Note. Sub-s (2) replaced Matrimonial Causes Act 1965, s 2(2) (p 2240).

(*3*) *If it appears to the court, at the hearing of a petition for divorce presented in pursuance of leave granted under subsection (2) above, that the leave was obtained by the petitioner by any misrepresentation or concealment of the nature of the case, the court may—*
   (*a*) *dismiss the petition, without prejudice to any petition which may be brought after the expiration of the specified period upon the same facts, or substantially the same facts, as those proved in support of the dismissed petition; or*
   (*b*) *if it grants a decree, direct that no application to make the decree absolute shall be made during the specified period.*

Note. Sub-s (3) replaced Matrimonial Causes Act 1965, s 5(5) (p 2242).

(*4*) *Nothing in this section shall be deemed to prohibit the presentation of a petition based upon matters which occurred before the expiration of the specific period.*

Note. Sub-s (4) replaced Matrimonial Causes Act 1965, s 2(3) (p 2240).

[**3. Bar on petitions for divorce within one year of marriage—**(*1*) *No petition for divorce shall be presented to the court before the expiration of the period of one year from the date of the marriage.*
   (*2*) *Nothing in this section shall prohibit the presentation of a petition based on matters which occurred before the expiration of that period.*]

Note. Section 3 in square brackets substituted for previous s 3 in italics by Matrimonial and Family Proceedings Act 1984, s 1, as from 12 October 1984. This section repealed by Family Law Act 1996, s 66(3), Sch 10, as from a day to be appointed, subject to savings in s 66(2) of, and para 5 of Sch 9 to, the 1996 Act.

4. Divorce not precluded by previous judicial separation—(*1*) *A person shall not be prevented from presenting a petition for divorce, or the court from granting a decree of divorce, by reason only that the petitioner or respondent has at any time, on the same facts or substantially the same facts as those proved in support of the petition, been granted a decree of judicial separation or an order under, or having effect as if made under, the Matrimonial Proceedings (Magistrates' Courts) Act 1960 [or Part I of the Domestic Proceedings and Magistrates' Courts Act 1978] or any corresponding enactments in force in Northern Ireland, the Isle of Man or any of the Channel Islands.*

Note. Words in square brackets inserted by Domestic Proceedings and Magistrates' Courts Act 1978, s 89(2), Sch 2, para 38, as from 1 November 1979.

(*2*) *On a petition for divorce in such a case as is mentioned in subsection (1) above, the court may treat the decree or order as sufficient proof of any adultery, desertion or other fact by reference to which it was granted, but shall not grant a decree of divorce without receiving evidence from the petitioner.*

(*3*) *Where a petition for divorce in such a case follows a decree of judicial separation or* [(*subject to subsection* (*5*) *below*)] *an order containing a provision exempting one party to the marriage from the obligation to cohabit with the other, for the purposes of that petition a period of desertion immediately preceding the institution of the proceedings for the decree or order shall, if the parties have not resumed cohabitation and the decree or order has been continuously in force since it was granted, be deemed immediately to precede the presentation of the petition.*

Note. Words in square brackets inserted by Domestic Proceedings and Magistrates' Courts Act 1978, s 62(a), as from 1 February 1981.

[(*4*) *For the purposes of section 1(2)(c) above the court may treat as a period during which the respondent has deserted the petitioner any of the following periods, that is to say—*
- (*a*) *any period during which there is in force an injunction granted by the High Court or a county court which excludes the respondent from the matrimonial home;*
- (*b*) *any period during which there is in force an order made by the High Court or a county court under—*
  - (*i*) *section 1 of the Matrimonial Homes Act 1967, or*
  - (*ii*) *section 4 of the Domestic Violence and Matrimonial Proceedings Act 1976,*
  [*section 1 or 9 of the Matrimonial Homes Act 1983*] *which prohibits the exercise by the respondent of the right to occupy a dwelling-house in which the applicant and the respondent have or at any time have had a matrimonial home;*
- (*c*) *any period during which there is in force an order made by a magistrates' court under section 16(3) of the Domestic Proceedings and Magistrates' Courts Act 1978 which requires the respondent to leave the matrimonial home or prohibits the respondent from entering the matrimonial home.*
- (*5*) *Where—*
- (*a*) *a petition for divorce is presented after the date on which Part I of the Domestic Proceedings and Magistrates' Courts Act 1978 comes into force, and*
- (*b*) *an order made under the Matrimonial Proceedings (Magistrates' Courts) Act 1960 containing a provision exempting the petitioner from the obligation to cohabit with the respondent is in force on that date,*

then, *for the purposes of section 1(2)(c) above, the court may treat a period during which such a provision was included in that order (whether before or after that date) as a period during which the respondent has deserted the petitioner.*]

Note. Section 4 replaced Matrimonial Causes Act 1965, s 3 (p 2240).

Sub-ss (4), (5) added by Domestic Proceedings and Magistrates' Courts Act 1978, s 62, as from 1 February 1981.

Words in square brackets in sub-s (4)(b) substituted for sub-paras (i), (ii) by Matrimonial Homes Act 1983, s 12, Sch 2, as from 9 August 1983.

This section repealed by Family Law Act 1996, s 66(3), Sch 10, as from a day to be appointed, subject to savings in s 66(2) of, and para 5 of Sch 9 to, the 1996 Act.

5. Refusal of decree in five year separation cases on grounds of grave hardship to respondent—(*1*) *The respondent to a petition for divorce in which the petitioner alleges five years' separation may oppose the grant of a decree on the ground that the dissolution of the marriage will result in grave financial or other hardship to him and that it would in all the circumstances be wrong to dissolve the marriage.*

(*2*) *Where the grant of a decree is opposed by virtue of this section, then—*
- (*a*) *if the court finds that the petitioner is entitled to rely in support of his petition on the fact of five years' separation and makes no such finding as to any other fact mentioned in section 1(2) above, and*
- (*b*) *if apart from this section the court would grant a decree on the petition,*

the court shall consider all the circumstances, including the conduct of the parties to the marriage and the interests of those parties and of any children or other persons concerned, and if of opinion that the dissolution of the marriage will result in grave financial or other hardship to the respondent and that it would in all the circumstances be wrong to dissolve the marriage it shall dismiss the petition.

(*3*) *For the purposes of this section hardship shall include the loss of the chance of acquiring any benefit which the respondent might acquire if the marriage were not dissolved.*

Note. Section 5 replaced Divorce Reform Act 1969, s 4 (p 2340). This section repealed by Family Law Act 1996, s 66(3), Sch 10, as from a day to be appointed, subject to savings in s 66(2) of, and para 5 of Sch 9 to, the 1996 Act.

6. Attempts at reconciliation of parties to marriage—(*1*) *Provision shall be made by rules of court for requiring the solicitor acting for a petitioner for divorce to certify whether he has discussed with the petitioner the possibility of a reconciliation and given him the names and addresses of persons qualified to help effect a reconciliation between parties to a marriage who have become estranged.*

(*2*) *If at any stage of proceedings for divorce it appears to the court that there is a reasonable possibility of a reconciliation between the parties to the marriage, the court may adjourn the proceedings for such period as it thinks fit to enable attempts to be made to effect such a reconciliation.*

The power conferred by the foregoing provision is additional to any other power of the court to adjourn proceedings.

Note. Section 6 replaced Divorce Reform Act 1969, s 3(1), (2) (p 2339). This section repealed by Family Law Act 1996, s 66(3), Sch 10, as from a day to be appointed, subject to savings in s 66(2) of, and para 5 of Sch 9 to, the 1996 Act.

7. Consideration by the court of certain agreements or arrangements. *Provision may be made by rules of court for enabling the parties to a marriage, or either of them, on application made either before or after the presentation of a petition for divorce, to refer to the court any agreement or arrangement made or proposed to be made between them, being an agreement or arrangement which relates to, arises out of, or is connected with, the proceedings for divorce which are contemplated or, as the case may be, have begun, and for enabling the court to express an opinion, should it think it desirable to do so, as to the reasonableness of the agreement or arrangement and to give such directions, if any, in the matter as it thinks fit.*

Note. Section 7 replaced Divorce Reform Act 1969, s 7(1) (p 2341). This section repealed by Family Law Act 1996, s 66(3), Sch 10, as from a day to be appointed, subject to savings in s 66(2) of, and para 5 of Sch 9 to, the 1996 Act.

8. Intervention of Queen's Proctor—(1) In the case of *a petition for divorce* [proceedings for a divorce order]—

(a) the court may, if it thinks fit, direct all necessary papers in the matter to be sent to the Queen's Proctor, who shall under the directions of the Attorney-General instruct counsel to argue before the court any question in relation to the matter which the court considers it necessary or expedient to have fully argued;

(b) any person may at any time during the progress of the proceedings *or before the decree nisi is made absolute* give information to the Queen's Proctor on any matter material to the due decision of the case, and the Queen's Proctor may thereupon take such steps as the Attorney-General considers necessary or expedient.

Note. Words 'proceedings for a divorce order' in square brackets substituted for words 'a petition for divorce', and words 'or before the decree nisi is made absolute' repealed by Family Law Act 1996, s 66, Sch 8, Part I, para 5, Sch 10, as from a day to be appointed, subject to savings in s 66(2) of, and para 5 of Sch 9 to, the 1996 Act.

(2) Where the Queen's Proctor intervenes or shows cause against *a decree nisi in any proceedings for divorce* [the making of a divorce order], the court may make such order as may be just as to the payment by other parties to the proceedings of the costs incurred by him in so doing or as to the payment by him of any costs incurred by any of those parties by reason of his so doing.

Note. Words in square brackets substituted for words in italics by Family Law Act 1996, s 66(1), Sch 8, Part I, para 5, as from a day to be appointed, subject to savings in s 66(2) of, and para 5 of Sch 9 to, the 1996 Act.

(3) The Queen's Proctor shall be entitled to charge as part of the expenses of his office—

    (a) the costs of any proceedings under subsection (1)(a) above;

    (b) where his reasonable costs of intervening or showing cause as mentioned in subsection (2) above are not fully satisfied by any order under that subsection, the amount of the difference;

    (c) if the Treasury so directs, any costs which he pays to any parties under an order made under subsection (2).

Note. Section 8 replaced Matrimonial Causes Act 1965, s 6 (p 2243).

9. Proceedings after decree nisi: general powers of court—(*1*) *Where a decree of divorce has been granted but not made absolute, then, without prejudice to section 8 above, any person (excluding a party to the proceedings other than the Queen's Proctor) may show cause why the decree should not be made absolute by reason of material facts not having been brought before the court; and in such a case the court may*—

    (*a*) *notwithstanding anything in section 1(5) above (but subject to sections 10(2) to (4) and 41 below) make the decree absolute; or*

    (*b*) *rescind the decree; or*

    (*c*) *require further inquiry; or*

    (*d*) *otherwise deal with the case as it thinks fit.*

    (*2*) *Where a decree of divorce has been granted and no application for it to be made absolute has been made by the party to whom it was granted, then, at any time after the expiration of three months from the earliest date on which that party could have made such an application, the party against whom it was granted may make an application to the court, and on that application the court may exercise any of the powers mentioned in paragraphs (a) to (d) of subsection (1) above.*

Note. Section 9 replaced Matrimonial Causes Act 1965, s 7 (p 2243). This section repealed by Family Law Act 1996, s 66(3), Sch 10, as from a day to be appointed, subject to savings in s 66(2) of, and para 5 of Sch 9 to, the 1996 Act.

10. Proceedings after decree nisi: special protection for respondent in separation cases—(*1*) *Where in any case the court has granted a decree of divorce on the basis of a finding that the petitioner was entitled to rely in support of his petition on the fact of two years' separation coupled with the respondent's consent to a decree being granted and has made no such finding as to any other fact mentioned in section 1(2) above, the court may, on an application made by the respondent at any time before the decree is made absolute, rescind the decree if it is satisfied that the petitioner misled the respondent (whether intentionally or unintentionally) about any matter which the respondent took into account in deciding to give his consent.*

Note. Sub-s (1) replaced Divorce Reform Act 1969, s 5 (p 2340).

    (*2*) *The following provisions of this section apply where*—

    (*a*) *the respondent to a petition for divorce in which the petitioner alleged two years' or five years' separation coupled, in the former case, with the respondent's consent to a decree being granted, has applied to the court for consideration under subsection (3) below of his financial position after the divorce; and*

    (*b*) *the court has granted a decree on the petition on the basis of a finding that the petitioner was entitled to rely in support of his petition on the fact of two years' or five years' separation (as the case may be) and has made no such finding as to any other fact mentioned in section 1(2) above.*

    (*3*) *The court hearing an application by the respondent under subsection (2) above shall consider all the circumstances, including the age, health, conduct, earning capacity, financial resources and financial obligations of each of the parties, and the financial position of the respondent as, having regard to the divorce, it is likely to be after the death of the petitioner should the petitioner die first; and, subject to subsection (4) below, the court shall not make the decree absolute unless it is satisfied*—

    (*a*) *that the petitioner should not be required to make any financial provision for the respondent, or*

    (*b*) *that the financial provision made by the petitioner for the respondent is reasonable and fair or the best that can be made in the circumstances.*

    (*4*) *The court may if it thinks fit make the decree absolute notwithstanding the requirements of subsection (3) above if*—

(a) it appears that there are circumstances making it desirable that the decree should be made absolute without delay, and

(b) the court has obtained a satisfactory undertaking from the petitioner that he will make such financial provision for the respondent as the court may approve.

Note. Sub-ss (2)–(4) replaced Divorce Reform Act 1969, s 6 (p 2340).

This section repealed by Family Law Act 1996, s 66(3), Sch 10, as from a day to be appointed, subject to savings in s 66(2) of, and para 5 of Sch 9 to, the 1996 Act.

10A. Proceedings after decree nisi: religious marriage. (1) This section applies if a decree of divorce has been granted but not made absolute and the parties to the marriage concerned—

(a) were married in accordance with—

(i) the usages of the Jews, or

(ii) any othe4r prescribed religious usages; and

(b) must co-operate if the marriage is to be dissolved in accordanc with those usages.

(2) On the occasion of either party, the court may order that a decree of divorce is not to be made absolute until a declaration made by both parties that they have taken such steps as are required to dissolve the marriage in accordance with those usages is produced to the court.

(3) An order under subsection (2)—

(a) may be made only if the court is satisfied that in all the circumstances of the case it is just and reasonable to do so; and

(b) may be revoked at any time.

(4) A declaration of a kind mentioned in subsection (2)—

(a) must be in a specified form;

(b) must, in specified cases, be accompanied by such documents as may be specified; and

(c) must, in specified cases, satisfy such other requirements as may be specified.

(5) The validity of a decree of divorce made by reference to such a declaration is not to be affected by any inaccuracy in that declaration.

(6) 'Prescribed' means prescribed in an order made by the Lord Chancellor and such an order—

(a) must be made by statutory instrument;

(b) shall be subject to annulment in pursuance of a resolution of either House of Parliament.

(7) 'Specified' means specified in rules of court.

Note. Inserted by the Divorce (Religious Marriages) Act 2002, s 1 as from 24 February 2003.

Nullity

11. Grounds on which a marriage is void. A marriage celebrated after 31 July 1971 shall be void on the following grounds only, that is to say—

(a) that it is not a valid marriage under the provisions of *the Marriage Acts 1949 to 1970* [*the Marriage Acts 1949 to 1983*] [the Marriage Acts 1949 to 1986] (that is to say where—

(i) the parties are within the prohibited degrees of relationship;

(ii) either party is under the age of sixteen; or

(iii) the parties have intermarried in disregard of certain requirements as to the formation of marriage);

(b) that at the time of the marriage either party was already lawfully married;

(c) that the parties are not respectively male and female;

(d) in the case of a polygamous marriage entered into outside England and Wales, that either party was at the time of the marriage domiciled in England and Wales.

For the purposes of paragraph (d) of this subsection a marriage *may be polygamous although* [is not polygamous if] at its inception neither party has any spouse additional to the other.

Note. Section 11 replaced Nullity of Marriage Act 1971, s 1 (p 2418), as amended by Matrimonial Proceedings (Polygamous Marriages) Act 1972, s 4.

Words in first square brackets in (a) substituted for words in italics by Marriage Act 1983, s 2(4), as from 1 May 1984, and words in second square brackets substituted by Marriage (Prohibited Degrees of Relationship) Act 1986, s 6(4), as from 1 November 1986. Words 'is not polygamous if' in square brackets substituted for words 'may be polygamous although' in italics by Private International Law (Miscellaneous Provisions) Act 1995, s 8(2), Schedule, para 2, as from 8 January 1996.

12. Grounds on which a marriage is voidable. A marriage celebrated after 31 July 1971 shall be voidable on the following grounds only, that is to say—

(a) that the marriage has not been consummated owing to the incapacity of either party to consummate it;

(b) that the marriage has not been consummated owing to the wilful refusal of the respondent to consummate it;

(c) that either party to the marriage did not validly consent to it, whether in consequence of duress, mistake, unsoundness of mind or otherwise;

(d) that at the time of the marriage either party, though capable of giving a valid consent, was suffering (whether continuously or intermittently) from mental disorder within the meaning of *the Mental Health Act 1959* [the Mental Health Act 1983] of such a kind or to such an extent as to be unfitted for marriage;

(e) that at the time of the marriage the respondent was suffering from venereal disease in a communicable form;

(f) that at the time of the marriage the respondent was pregnant by some person other than the petitioner;

[(g) that an interim gender recognition certificate under the Gender Recognition Act 2004 has after the time of the marriage, been issued to either party to the marriage];

[(h) that the respondent is a person whose gender at the time of the marriage had become the acquired gender under the Gender Recognition Act 2004].

Note. Section 12 replaced Nullity of Marriage Act 1971, s 2 (p 2419).

Words in square brackets in para (d) substituted for words in italics by Mental Health Act 1983, s 148, Sch 4, para 34, as from 30 September 1983. Sub-ss (g), and (h) added by the Gender Recognition Act 2004, ss 4(4), 11, Sch 2, Pt 1, paras 1, 2, Sch 4, Pt 1, paras 4, 5, as from a day to be appointed.

13. Bars to relief where marriage is voidable—(1) The court shall not, in proceedings instituted after 31 July 1971, grant a decree of nullity on the ground that a marriage is voidable if the respondent satisfies the court—

(a) that the petitioner, with knowledge that it was open to him to have the marriage avoided, so conducted himself in relation to the respondent as to lead the respondent reasonably to believe that he would not seek to do so; and

(b) that it would be unjust to the respondent to grant the decree.

(*2*) *Without prejudice to subsection (1) above, the court shall not grant a decree of nullity by virtue of section 12 above on the grounds mentioned in paragraph (c), (d), (e) or (f) of that section unless it is satisfied that proceedings were instituted within three years from the date of marriage.*

[(2) Without prejudice to subsection (1) above, the court shall not grant a decree of nullity by virtue of section 12 above on the grounds mentioned in paragraph (c), (d), (e) *or (f)* [, (f) or (h)] of that section unless—

(a) it is satisfied that proceedings were instituted within the period of three years from the date of the marriage, or

(b) leave for the institution of proceedings after the expiration of that period has been granted under subsection (4) below.]

Note. Sub-s (2) in square brackets substituted for sub-s (2) in italics by Matrimonial and Family Proceedings Act 1984, s 2(2), as from 12 October 1984. Words ', (f) or (h)' in square brackets substituted for words in italics by the Gender Recognition Act 2004, s 11, Sch 4, Pt 1, paras 4, 6, as from a date to be appointed.

[(2A) Without prejudice to subsection (1) above, the court shall not grant a decree of nullity by virtue of section 12 above on the ground mentioned in paragraph (g) of that section unless it is satisfied that proceedings were instituted within the period of six months from the date of issue of the interim gender recognition certificate.]

Note. Sub-s (2A) added by the Gender Recognition Act 2004, s 4(4), Sch 2, Pt 1, paras 1, 3, as from a day to be appointed.

(3) Without prejudice to subsections (1) and (2) above, the court shall not grant a decree of nullity by virtue of section 12 above on the grounds mentioned in paragraph (e) *or (f)* [, (f) or (h)] of that section unless it is satisfied that the petitioner was at the time of the marriage ignorant of the facts alleged.

Note. Section 13 replaced Nullity of Marriage Act 1971, s 3 (p 2397). Words ', (f) or (h)' in square brackets substituted for words in italics by the Gender Recognition Act 2004, s 11, Sch 4, Pt 1, paras 4, 6, as from a day to be appointed.

[(4) In the case of proceedings for the grant of a decree of nullity by virtue of section 12 above on the grounds mentioned in paragraph (c), (d), (e) *or (f)* [, (f) or (h)] of that section, a judge of the court may, on an application made to him, grant leave for the institution of proceedings after the expiration of the period of three years from the date of the marriage if—

   (a) he is satisfied that the petitioner has at some time during that period suffered from mental disorder within the meaning of the Mental Health Act 1983, and

   (b) he considers that in all the circumstances of the case it would be just to grant leave for the institution of proceedings.

(5) An application for leave under subsection (4) above may be made after the expiration of the period of three years from the date of the marriage.]

Note. Sub-ss (4), (5) added by Matrimonial and Family Proceedings Act 1984, s 2(3), as from 12 October 1984. Words ', (f) or (h)' in square brackets in sub-s (4) substituted for words in italics by the Gender Recognition Act 2004, s 11, Sch 13, paras 4, 6, as from a day to be appointed.

14. Marriages governed by foreign law or celebrated abroad under English law—(1) Where, apart from this Act, any matter affecting the validity of a marriage would fall to be determined (in accordance with the rules of private international law) by reference to the law of a country outside England and Wales, nothing in section 11, 12 or 13(1) above shall—

   (a) preclude the determination of that matter as aforesaid; or

   (b) require the application to the marriage of the grounds or bar there mentioned except so far as applicable in accordance with those rules.

(2) In the case of a marriage which purports to have been celebrated under the Foreign Marriage Acts 1892 to 1947 or has taken place outside England and Wales and purports to be a marriage under common law, section 11 above is without prejudice to any ground on which the marriage may be void under those Acts or, as the case may be, by virtue of the rules governing the celebration of marriages outside England and Wales under common law.

Note. Section 14 replaced Nullity of Marriage Act 1971, s 4 (p 2420).

15. Application of ss 1(5), 8 and 9 to nullity proceedings. *Sections 1(5), 8 and 9 above shall apply in relation to proceedings for nullity of marriage as if for any reference in those provisions to divorce there were substituted a reference to nullity of marriage.*

[**15. Decrees of nullity to be decrees nisi.** Every decree of nullity of marriage shall in the first instance be a decree nisi and shall not be made absolute before the end of six weeks from its grant unless—

   (a) the High Court by general order from time to time fixes a shorter period; or

   (b) in any particular case, the court in which the proceedings are for the time being pending from time to time by special order fixes a shorter period than the period otherwise applicable for the time being by virtue of this section.

15A. Intervention of Queen's Proctor—(1) In the case of a petition for nullity of marriage—

   (a) the court may, if it thinks fit, direct all necessary papers in the matter to be sent to the Queen's Proctor, who shall under the directions of the Attorney-General instruct counsel to argue before the court any question in relation to the matter which the court considers it necessary or expedient to have fully argued;

   (b) any person may at any time during the progress of the proceedings or before the decree nisi is made absolute give information to the Queen's Proctor on any matter material to the due decision of the case, and the Queen's Proctor may thereupon take such steps as the Attorney-General considers necessary or expedient.

(2) If the Queen's Proctor intervenes or shows cause against a decree nisi in any proceedings for nullity of marriage, the court may make such order as may be just as to the payment by other parties to the proceedings of the costs incurred by him in so doing or as to the payment by him of any costs incurred by any of those parties by reason of his so doing.

(3) Subsection (3) of section 8 above applies in relation to this section as it applies in relation to that section.

15B. Proceedings after decree nisi: general powers of court—(1) Where a decree of nullity of marriage has been granted under this Act but not made absolute, then, without prejudice to section 15A above, any person (excluding a party to the proceedings other than the Queen's Proctor) may show cause why the decree should not be made absolute by reason of material facts not having been brought before the court; and in such a case the court may—

   (a) notwithstanding anything in section 15 above (but subject to section 41 below) make the decree absolute; or

   (b) rescind the decree; or

   (c) require further inquiry; or

   (d) otherwise deal with the case as it thinks fit.

(2) Where a decree of nullity of marriage has been granted under this Act and no application for it to be made absolute has been made by the party to whom it was granted, then, at any time after the expiration of three months from the earliest date on which that party could have made such an application, the party against whom it was granted may make an application to the court, and on that application the court may exercise any of the powers mentioned in paragraphs (a) to (d) of subsection (1) above.]

Note. Section 15 replaced Matrimonial Causes Act 1965, s 10 (p 2245).

Sections 15, 15A, 15B in square brackets substituted for s 15 in italics by Family Law Act 1996, s 66(1), Sch 8, Part I, para 6, as from a day to be appointed, subject to savings in s 66(2) of, and para 5 of Sch 9 to, the 1996 Act.

16. Effect of decree of nullity in case of voidable marriage.   A decree of nullity granted after 31 July 1971 in respect of a voidable marriage shall operate to annul the marriage only as respects any time after the decree has been made absolute, and the marriage shall, notwithstanding the decree, be treated as if it had existed up to that time.

Note. Section 16 replaced Nullity of Marriage Act 1971, s 5 (p 2420).

Other matrimonial suits

17. Judicial separation—(*1*) *A petition for judicial separation may be presented to the court by either party to a marriage on the ground that any such fact as is mentioned in section 1(2) above exists, and the provisions of section 2 above shall apply accordingly for the purposes of a petition for judicial separation alleging any such fact, as they apply in relation to a petition for divorce alleging that fact.*

Note. Sub-s (1) replaced Matrimonial Causes Act 1965, s 12(1) (p 2245) and Divorce Reform Act 1969, s 8(1), (2) (p 2341).

(*2*) *On a petition for judicial separation it shall be the duty of the court to inquire, so far as it reasonably can, into the facts alleged by the petitioner and into any facts alleged by the respondent, but the court shall not be concerned to consider whether the marriage has broken down irretrievably, and if it is satisfied on the evidence of any such fact as is mentioned in section 1(2) above it shall, subject to section 41 below, grant a decree of judicial separation.*

Note. Sub-s (2) replaced Divorce Reform Act 1969, s 8(3) (p 2341).

(*3*) *Sections 6 and 7 above shall apply for the purpose of encouraging the reconciliation of parties to proceedings for judicial separation and of enabling the parties to a marriage to refer to the court for its opinion an agreement or arrangement relevant to actual or contemplated proceedings for judicial separation, as they apply in relation to proceedings for divorce.*

Note. This section repealed by Family Law Act 1996, s 66(3), Sch 10, as from a day to be appointed, subject to savings in s 66(2) of, and para 5 of Sch 9 to, the 1996 Act.

18. Effects of judicial separation—(*1*) *Where the court grants a decree of judicial separation it shall no longer be obligatory for the petitioner to cohabit with the respondent.*

Note. Sub-s (1) replaced Matrimonial Causes Act 1965, s 12(2) (p 2245).

(*2*) *If while a decree of judicial separation is in force and the separation is continuing either of the parties to the marriage dies intestate as respects all or any of his or her real or personal property, the property as respects which he or she died intestate shall devolve as if the other party to the marriage had then been dead.*

Note. Sub-s (2) replaced Matrimonial Proceedings and Property Act 1970, s 40(1) (p 2383).

(*3*) *Notwithstanding anything in section 2(1)(a) of the Matrimonial Proceedings (Magistrates' Courts) Act 1960, a provision in force under an order made, or having effect as if made, under that section exempting one party to a marriage from the obligation to cohabit with the other shall not have effect as a decree of judicial separation for the purposes of subsection (2) above.*

Note. Sub-s (3) replaced Matrimonial Proceedings and Property Act 1970, s 40(2) (p 2383).
This section repealed by Family Law Act 1996, s 66(3), Sch 10, as from a day to be appointed, subject to savings in s 66(2) of, and para 5 of Sch 9 to, the 1996 Act.

19. Presumption of death and dissolution of marriage—(1) Any married person who alleges that reasonable grounds exist for supposing that the other party to the marriage is dead may, *subject to subsection (2) below,* present a petition to the court to have it presumed that the other party is dead and to have the marriage dissolved, and the court may, if satisfied that such reasonable grounds exist, grant a decree of presumption of death and dissolution of the marriage.

Note. Words in italics repealed by Domicile and Matrimonial Proceedings Act 1973, s 17(2), Sch 6, as from 1 January 1974.

(*2*) *A petition may be presented in pursuance of subsection (1) above—*
(*a*) *in any case, if the petitioner is domiciled in England and Wales; and*
(*b*) *in the case of a petition presented by a wife, if she is resident in England and Wales and has been ordinarily resident there for a period of three years immediately preceding the commencement of the proceedings.*

Note. Sub-s (2) repealed by Domicile and Matrimonial Proceedings Act 1973, s 17(2), Sch 6, as from 1 January 1974; see now s 5(4) of that Act (p 2575).

(3) In any proceedings under this section the fact that for a period of seven years or more the other party to the marriage has been continually absent from the petitioner and the petitioner has no reason to believe that the other party has been living within that time shall be evidence that the other party is dead until the contrary is proved.

(4) Sections *1(5), 8 and 9* [15, 15A and 15B] above shall apply to a petition and a decree under this section as they apply to a petition for *divorce* [nullity of marriage] and a decree of *divorce* [nullity of marriage] respectively.

Note. Words in square brackets substituted for words in italics by Family Law Act 1996, s 66(1), Sch 8, Part I, para 7, as from a day to be appointed, subject to savings in s 66(2) of, and para 5 of Sch 9 to, the 1996 Act.

(5) *In determining for the purposes of this section whether a woman is domiciled in England and Wales, her husband shall be treated as having died immediately after the last occasion on which she knew or had reason to believe him to be living; and in any proceedings brought in pursuance of subsection (2)(b) above the issues shall be determined in accordance with the law which would be applicable thereto if both parties to the marriage were domiciled in England and Wales at the time of the proceedings.*

Note. Sub-s (5) repealed by Domicile and Matrimonial Proceedings Act 1973, s 17(2), Sch 6, as from 1 January 1974.

Sub-ss (1)–(5) replaced Matrimonial Causes Act 1965, s 14 (p 2246).

(6) It is hereby declared that neither collusion nor any other conduct on the part of the petitioner which has at any time been a bar to relief in matrimonial proceedings constitutes a bar to the grant of a decree under this section.

Note. Sub-s (6) replaced Nullity of Marriage Act 1971, s 6(2) (p 2420).

General

20. Relief for respondent in divorce proceedings.   *If in any proceedings for divorce the respondent alleges and proves any such fact as is mentioned in subsection (2) of section 1 above (treating the respondent as the petitioner and the petitioner as the respondent for the purposes of that subsection) the court may give to the respondent the relief to which he would have been entitled if he had presented a petition seeking that relief.*

Note. Section 20 replaced Matrimonial Causes Act 1965, s 5(6) (p 2242). This section repealed by Family Law Act 1996, s 66(3), Sch 10, as from a day to be appointed, subject to savings in s 66(2) of, and para 5 of Sch 9 to, the 1996 Act.

PART II

FINANCIAL RELIEF FOR PARTIES TO MARRIAGE AND CHILDREN OF FAMILY

Financial provision and property adjustment orders

21. Financial provision and property adjustment orders—(*1*) *The financial provision orders for the purposes of this Act are the orders for periodical or lump sum provision available (subject to the provisions of this Act) under section 23 below for the purpose of adjusting the financial position of the parties to a marriage and any children of the family in connection with proceedings for divorce, nullity of marriage or judicial separation and under section 27(6) below on proof of neglect by one party to a marriage to provide, or to make a proper contribution towards, reasonable maintenance for the other or a child of the family, that is to say—*

(*a*) *any order for periodical payments in favour of a party to a marriage under section 23(1)(a) or 27(6)(a) or in favour of a child of the family under section 23(1)(d), (2) or (4) or 27(6)(d);*

(*b*) *any order for secured periodical payments in favour of a party to a marriage under section 23(1)(b) or 27(6)(b) or in favour of a child of the family under section 23(1)(e), (2) or (4) or 27(6)(e); and*

(*c*) *any order for lump sum provision in favour of a party to a marriage under section 23(1)(c) or 27(6)(c) or in favour of a child of the family under section 23(1)(f), (2) or (4) or 27(6)(f);*

and references in this Act (except in paragraphs 17(1) and 23 of Schedule 1 below) to periodical payments orders, secured periodical payments orders, and orders for the payment of a lump sum are references to all or some of the financial provision orders requiring the sort of financial provision in question according as the context of each reference may require.

(2) The property adjustment orders for the purposes of this Act are the orders dealing with property rights available (subject to the provisions of this Act) under section 24 below for the purpose of adjusting the financial position of the parties to a marriage and any children of the family on or after the grant of a decree of divorce, nullity of marriage or judicial separation, that is to say—

   (a) any order under subsection (1)(a) of that section for a transfer of property;
   (b) any order under subsection (1)(b) of that section for a settlement of property; and
   (c) any order under subsection (1)(c) or (d) of that section for a variation of settlement.

[21. Financial provision and property adjustment orders—(1) For the purposes of this Act, a financial provision order is—

   (a) an order that a party must make in favour of another person such periodical payments, for such term, as may be specified (a 'periodical payments order');

   (b) an order that a party must, to the satisfaction of the court, secure in favour of another person such periodical payments, for such term, as may be specified (a 'secured periodical payments order');

   (c) an order that a party must make a payment in favour of another person of such lump sum or sums as may be specified (an 'order for the payment of a lump sum').

   (2) For the purposes of this Act, a property adjustment order is—

   (a) an order that a party must transfer such of his or her property as may be specified in favour of the other party or a child of the family;

   (b) an order that a settlement of such property of a party as may be specified must be made, to the satisfaction of the court, for the benefit of the other party and of the children of the family, or either or any of them;

   (c) an order varying, for the benefit of the parties and of the children of the family, or either or any of them, any marriage settlement;

   (d) an order extinguishing or reducing the interest of either of the parties under any marriage settlement.

   (3) Subject to section 40 below, where an order of the court under this Part of this Act requires a party to make or secure a payment in favour of another person or to transfer property in favour of any person, that payment must be made or secured or that property transferred—

   (a) if that other person is the other party to the marriage, to that other party; and

   (b) if that other person is a child of the family, according to the terms of the order—

      (i) to the child; or
      (ii) to such other person as may be specified, for the benefit of that child.

   (4) References in this section to the property of a party are references to any property to which that party is entitled either in possession or in reversion.

   (5) Any power of the court under this Part of this Act to make such an order as is mentioned in subsection (2)(b) to (d) above is exercisable even though there are no children of the family.

   (6) In this section—

'marriage settlement' means an ante-nuptial or post-nuptial settlement made on the parties (including one made by will or codicil);

'party' means a party to a marriage; and

'specified' means specified in the order in question.]

Note. This section substituted, together with s 21A, by new s 21, by the Family Law Act 1996, s 15, Sch 2, para 2 (as amended by the Welfare Reform and Pensions Act 1999, s 84(1), Sch 12, Pt 1, paras 64, 65(1)–(8)), as from a day to be appointed, subject to savings in s 66(2) of, and para 5 of Sch 9 to, the 1996 Act.

[21A. Pension sharing orders] [*(1) For the purpose of this Act, a pension sharing order is an order which—*
 (a)   *provides that one party's—*
   (i)   *shareable rights under a specified pension arrangement, or*
   (ii) *shareable state scheme rights,*
   be subject to pension sharing for the benefit of the other party, and
 (b)   *specified the percentage value to be transferred.*
 (2) *In subsection (1) above—*
 (a)   *the reference to shareable rights under a pension arrangement is to rights in relation to which pension sharing is available under Chapter 1 of Part IV of the Welfare Reform and Pensions Act 1999, or under corresponding Northern Ireland legislation.*
 (b)   *the reference to shareable state scheme rights is to rights in relation to which pension sharing is available under Chapter II of Part IV of the Welfare Reform and Pensions Act 1999, or under corresponding Northern Ireland legislation, and*
 (c)   *'party' means a party to a marriage.*]

Note. This section inserted by the Welfare Reform and Pensions Act 1999, s 19, Sch 3, paras 1, 2, as from 1 December 2000.

Ancillary relief in connection with divorce proceedings, etc

22. Maintenance pending suit.   *On a petition for divorce, nullity of marriage or judicial separation, the court may make an order for maintenance pending suit, that is to say, an order requiring either party to the marriage to make to the other such periodical payments for his or her maintenance and for such term, being a term beginning not earlier than the date of the presentation of the petition and ending with the date of the determination of the suit, as the court thinks reasonable.*

Note. Section 22 replaced Matrimonial Proceedings and Property Act 1970, s 66(3), Sch 10, as from a day to be appointed, subject to savings in s 66(2) of, and para 5 of Sch 9 to, the 1996 Act.

[22A. Financial provision orders: divorce and separation—(1) On an application made under this section, the court may at the appropriate time make one or more financial provision orders in favour of—
 (a)   a party to the marriage to which the application relates; or
 (b)   any of the children of the family.
 (2) The 'appropriate time' is any time—
 (a)   after a statement of marital breakdown has been received by the court and before any application for a divorce order or for a separation order is made to the court by reference to that statement;
 (b)   when an application for a divorce order or separation order has been made under section 3 of the 1996 Act and has not been withdrawn;
 (c)   when an application for a divorce order has been made under section 4 of the 1996 Act and has not been withdrawn;
 (d)   after a divorce order has been made;
 (e)   when a separation order is in force.
 (3) The court may make—
 (a)   a combined order against the parties on one occasion,
 (b)   separate orders on different occasions,
 (c)   different orders in favour of different children,
 (d)   different orders from time to time in favour of the same child,
but may not make, in favour of the same party, more than one periodical payments order, or more than one order for payment of a lump sum, in relation to any marital proceedings, whether in the course of the proceedings or by reference to a divorce order or separation order made in the proceedings.

(4) If it would not otherwise be in a position to make a financial provision order in favour of a party or child of the family, the court may make an interim periodical payments order, an interim order for the payment of a lump sum or a series of such orders, in favour of that party or child.

(5) Any order for the payment of a lump sum made under this section may—

(a) provide for the payment of the lump sum by instalments of such amounts as may be specified in the order; and

(b) require the payment of the instalments to be secured to the satisfaction of the court.

(6) Nothing in subsection (5) above affects—

(a) the power of the court under this section to make an order for the payment of a lump sum; or

(b) the provisions of this Part of this Act as to the beginning of the term specified in any periodical payments order or secured periodical payments order.

(7) Subsection (8) below applies where the court—

(a) makes an order under this section ('the main order') for the payment of a lump sum; and

(b) directs—

(i) that payment of that sum, or any part of it, is to be deferred; or

(ii) that that sum, or any part of it, is to be paid by instalments.

(8) In such a case, the court may, on or at any time after making the main order, make an order ('the order for interest') for the amount deferred, or the instalments, to carry interest (at such rate as may be specified in the order for interest)—

(a) from such date, not earlier than the date of the main order, as may be so specified;

(b) until the date when the payment is due.

(9) This section is to be read subject to any restrictions imposed by this Act and to section 19 of the 1996 Act.

22B. Restrictions affecting section 22A—(1) No financial provision order, other than an interim order, may be made under section 22A above so as to take effect before the making of a divorce order or separation order in relation to the marriage, unless the court is satisfied—

(a) that the circumstances of the case are exceptional; and

(b) that it would be just and reasonable for the order to be so made.

(2) Except in the case of an interim periodical payments order, the court may not make a financial provision order under section 22A above at any time while the period for reflection and consideration is interrupted under section 7(8) of the 1996 Act.

(3) No financial provision order may be made under section 22A above by reference to the making of a statement of marital breakdown if, by virtue of section 5(3) or 7(9) of the 1996 Act (lapse of divorce or separation process), it has ceased to be possible—

(a) for an application to be made by reference to that statement; or

(b) for an order to be made on such an application.

(4) No financial provision order may be made under section 22A after a divorce order has been made, or while a separation order is in force, except—

(a) in response to an application made before the divorce order or separation order was made; or

(b) on a subsequent application made with the leave of the court.

(5) In this section, 'period for reflection and consideration' means the period fixed by section 7 of the 1996 Act.]

Note. Sections 22A, 22B inserted by Family Law Act 1996, s 15, Sch 2, para 3, as from a day to be appointed, subject to savings in s 66(2) of, and para 5 of Sch 9 to, the 1996 Act.

23. Financial provision orders in connection with divorce proceedings, etc—

(*1*) On granting a decree of divorce, a decree of nullity of marriage or a decree of judicial separation or at any time thereafter (whether, in the case of a decree of divorce or of nullity of marriage, before or after the decree is made absolute), the court may make any one or more of the following orders, that is to say—

(*a*)   an order that either party to the marriage shall make to the other such periodical payments, for such term, as may be specified in the order;

(*b*)   an order that either party to the marriage shall secure to the other to the satisfaction of the court such periodical payments, for such term, as may be so specified;

(*c*)   an order that either party to the marriage shall pay to the other such lump sum or sums as may be so specified;

(*d*)   an order that a party to the marriage shall make to such person as may be specified in the order for the benefit of a child of the family, or to such a child, such periodical payments, for such term, as may be so specified;

(*e*)   an order that a party to the marriage shall secure to such person as may be so specified for the benefit of such a child, or to such a child, to the satisfaction of the court, such periodical payments, for such term, as may be so specified;

(*f*)   an order that a party to the marriage shall pay to such person as may be so specified for the benefit of such a child, or to such a child, such lump sum as may be so specified;

subject, however, in the case of an order under paragraph (*d*), (*e*) or (*f*) above, to the restrictions imposed by section 29(1) and (3) below on the making of financial provision orders in favour of children who have attained the age of eighteen.

Note. Sub-s (1) replaced Matrimonial Proceedings and Property Act 1970, ss 2(1), 3(1) (p 2365).

(*2*) The court may also, subject to those restrictions, make any one or more of the orders mentioned in subsection (*1*)(*d*), (*e*) and (*f*) above—

(*a*)   in any proceedings for divorce, nullity of marriage or judicial separation, before granting a decree; and

(*b*)   where any such proceedings are dismissed after the beginning of the trial, either forthwith or within a reasonable period after the dismissal.

Note. Sub-s (2) replaced Matrimonial Proceedings and Property Act 1970, s 3(1) (p 2346).

(*3*) Without prejudice to the generality of subsection (*1*)(*c*) or (*f*) above—

(*a*)   an order under this section that a party to a marriage shall pay a lump sum to the other party may be made for the purpose of enabling that other party to meet any liabilities or expenses reasonably incurred by him or her in maintaining himself or herself or any child of the family before making an application for an order under this section in his or her favour;

(*b*)   an order under this section for the payment of a lump sum to or for the benefit of a child of the family may be made for the purpose of enabling any liabilities or expenses reasonably incurred by or for the benefit of that child before the making of an application for an order under this section in his favour to be met; and

(*c*)   an order under this section for the payment of a lump sum may provide for the payment of that sum by instalments of such amount as may be specified in the order and may require the payment of the instalments to be secured to the satisfaction of the court.

Note. Sub-s (3) replaced Matrimonial Proceedings and Property Act 1970, ss 2(2), 3(3), (4) (pp 2365, 2366).

(*4*) The power of the court under subsection (*1*) or (*2*)(*a*) above to make an order in favour of a child of the family shall be exercisable from time to time; and where the court makes an order in favour of a child under subsection (*2*)(*b*) above, it may from time to time, subject to the restrictions mentioned in subsection (*1*) above, make a further order in his favour of any of the kinds mentioned in subsection (*1*)(*d*), (*e*) or (*f*) above.

Note. Sub-s (4) replaced Matrimonial Proceedings and Property Act 1970, s 3(5) (p 2366).

(5) *Without prejudice to the power to give a direction under section 30 below for the settlement of an instrument by conveyancing counsel, where an order is made under subsection (1)(a), (b) or (c) above on or after granting a decree of divorce or nullity of marriage, neither the order nor any settlement made in pursuance of the order shall take effect unless the decree has been made absolute.*

[(6) *Where the court—*
(a) *makes an order under this section for the payment of a lump sum; and*
(b) *directs—*
    (i) *that payment of that sum or any part of it shall be deferred; or*
    (ii) *that the sum or any part of it shall be paid by instalments,*
the court may order that the amount deferred or the instalments shall carry interest at such rate as may be specified by the order from such date, not earlier than the date of the order, as may be so specified, until the date when payment of it is due.]

Note. Sub-s (6) added by Administration of Justice Act 1982, s 16, as from 1 April 1983.
    Sub-s (5) replaced in part Matrimonial Proceedings and Property Act 1970, s 24(1) (p 2377).

[23. Financial provision orders: nullity—(1) On or after granting a decree of nullity of marriage (whether before or after the decree is made absolute), the court may, on an application made under this section, make one or more financial provision orders in favour of—
(a) either party to the marriage; or
(b) any child of the family.
(2) Before granting a decree in any proceedings for nullity of marriage, the court may make against either or each of the parties to the marriage—
(a) an interim periodical payments order, an interim order for the payment of a lump sum, or a series of such orders, in favour of the other party;
(b) an interim periodical payments order, an interim order for the payment of a lump sum, a series of such orders or any one or more other financial provision orders in favour of each child of the family.
(3) Where any such proceedings are dismissed, the court may (either immediately or within a reasonable period after the dismissal) make any one or more financial provision orders in favour of each child of the family.
(4) An order under this section that a party to a marriage must pay a lump sum to the other party may be made for the purpose of enabling that other party to meet any liabilities or expenses reasonably incurred by him or her in maintaining himself or herself or any child of the family before making an application for an order under this section in his or her favour.
(5) An order under this section for the payment of a lump sum to or for the benefit of a child of the family may be made for the purpose of enabling any liabilities or expenses reasonably incurred by or for the benefit of that child before the making of an application for an order under this section in his favour to be met.
(6) An order under this section for the payment of a lump sum may—
(a) provide for the payment of that sum by instalments of such amount as may be specified in the order; and
(b) require the payment of the instalments to be secured to the satisfaction of the court.
(7) Nothing in subsections (4) to (6) above affects—
(a) the power under subsection (1) above to make an order for the payment of a lump sum; or
(b) the provisions of this Act as to the beginning of the term specified in any periodical payments order or secured periodical payments order.
(8) The powers of the court under this section to make one or more financial provision orders are exercisable against each party to the marriage by the making of—

(a) a combined order on one occasion, or

(b) separate orders on different occasions,

but the court may not make more than one periodical payments order, or more than one order for payment of a lump sum, in favour of the same party.

(9) The powers of the court under this section so far as they consist in power to make one or more orders in favour of the children of the family—

(a) may be exercised differently in favour of different children; and

(b) except in the case of the power conferred by subsection (3) above, may be exercised from time to time in favour of the same child; and

(c) in the case of the power conferred by that subsection, if it is exercised by the making of a financial provision order of any kind in favour of a child, shall include power to make, from time to time, further financial provision orders of that or any other kind in favour of that child.

(10) Where an order is made under subsection (1) above in favour of a party to the marriage on or after the granting of a decree of nullity of marriage, neither the order nor any settlement made in pursuance of the order takes effect unless the decree has been made absolute.

(11) Subsection (10) above does not affect the power to give a direction under section 30 below for the settlement of an instrument by conveyancing counsel.

(12) Where the court—

(a) makes an order under this section ('the main order') for the payment of a lump sum; and

(b) directs—

  (i) that payment of that sum or any part of it is to be deferred; or

  (ii) that that sum or any part of it is to be paid by instalments,

it may, on or at any time after making the main order, make an order ('the order for interest') for the amount deferred or the instalments to carry interest at such rate as may be specified by the order for interest from such date, not earlier than the date of the main order, as may be so specified, until the date when payment of it is due.

(13) This section is to be read subject to any restrictions imposed by this Act.]

Note. Section 23 in square brackets substituted for s 23 in italics by Family Law Act 1996, s 15, Sch 2, para 4, as from a day to be appointed, subject to savings in s 66(2) of, and para 5 of Sch 9 to, the 1996 Act.

[23A. Property adjustment orders: divorce and separation—(1) On an application made under this section, the court may, at any time mentioned in section 22A(2) above, make one or more property adjustment orders.

(2) If the court makes, in favour of the same party to the marriage, more than one property adjustment order in relation to any marital proceedings, whether in the course of the proceedings or by reference to a divorce order or separation order made in the proceedings, each order must fall within a different paragraph of section 21(2) above.

(3) The court shall exercise its powers under this section, so far as is practicable, by making on one occasion all such provision as can be made by way of one or more property adjustment orders in relation to the marriage as it thinks fit.

(4) Subsection (3) above does not affect section 31 or 31A below.

(5) This section is to be read subject to any restrictions imposed by this Act and to section 19 of the 1996 Act.

23B. Restrictions affecting section 23A—(1) No property adjustment order may be made under section 23A above so as to take effect before the making of a divorce order or separation order in relation to the marriage unless the court is satisfied—

(a) that the circumstances of the case are exceptional; and

(b) that it would be just and reasonable for the order to be so made.

(2) The court may not make a property adjustment order under section 23A above at any time while the period for reflection and consideration is interrupted under section 7(8) of the 1996 Act.

(3) No property adjustment order may be made under section 23A above by virtue of the making of a statement of marital breakdown if, by virtue of section 5(3) or 7(5) of the 1996 Act (lapse of divorce or separation process), it has ceased to be possible—

(a) for an application to be made by reference to that statement; or

(b) for an order to be made on such an application.

(4) No property adjustment order may be made under section 23A above after a divorce order has been made, or while a separation order is in force, except—

(a) in response to an application made before the divorce order or separation order was made; or

(b) on a subsequent application made with the leave of the court.

(5) In this section, 'period for reflection and consideration' means the period fixed by section 7 of the 1996 Act.]

Note. Sections 23A, 23B inserted by Family Law Act 1996, s 15, Sch 2, para 5, as from a day to be appointed, subject to savings in s 66(2) of, and para 5 of Sch 9 to, the 1996 Act.

24. Property adjustment orders in connection with divorce proceedings, etc—

(*1*) *On granting a decree of divorce, a decree of nullity of marriage or a decree of judicial separation or at any time thereafter (whether, in the case of a decree of divorce or of nullity of marriage, before or after the decree is made absolute), the court may make any one or more of the following orders, that is to say—*

(*a*) *an order that a party to the marriage shall transfer to the other party, to any child of the family or to such person as may be specified in the order for the benefit of such a child such property as may be so specified, being property to which the first-mentioned party is entitled, either in possession or reversion;*

(*b*) *an order that a settlement of such property as may be so specified, being property to which a party to the marriage is so entitled, be made to the satisfaction of the court for the benefit of the other party to the marriage and of the children of the family or either or any of them;*

(*c*) *an order varying for the benefit of the parties to the marriage and of the children of the family or either or any of them any ante-nuptial or post-nuptial settlement (including such a settlement made by will or codicil) made on the parties to the marriage [, other than one in the form of a pension arrangement (within the meaning of section 25D below)];*

(*d*) *an order extinguishing or reducing the interest of either of the parties to the marriage under any such settlement [, other than one in the form of a pension arrangement (within the meaning of section 25D below)];*

subject, however, in the case of an order under paragraph (a) above, to the restrictions imposed by section 29(1) and (3) below on the making of orders for a transfer of property in favour of children who have attained the age of eighteen.

(*2*) *The court may make an order under subsection (1)(c) above notwithstanding that there are no children of the family.*

Note. Sub-ss (1), (2) replaced Matrimonial Proceedings and Property Act 1970, s 4 (p 2346). Words in square brackets in sub-s (1)(c), (d) inserted by the Welfare Reform and Pensions Act 1999, s 19, Sch 3, paras 1, 3, as from 1 December 2000.

(*3*) *Without prejudice to the power to give a direction under section 30 below for the settlement of an instrument by conveyancing counsel, where an order is made under this section on or after granting a decree of divorce or nullity of marriage, neither the order nor any settlement made in pursuance of the order shall take effect unless the decree has been made absolute.*

Note. Sub-s (3) replaced in part Matrimonial Proceedings and Property Act 1970, s 24(1) (p 2377).

[24. Property adjustment orders: nullity of marriage—(1) On or after granting a decree of nullity of marriage (whether before or after the decree is made absolute), the court may, on an application made under this section, make one or more property adjustment orders in relation to the marriage.

(2) The court shall exercise its powers under this section, so far as is practicable, by making on one occasion all such provision as can be made by way of one or more property adjustment orders in relation to the marriage as it thinks fit.

(3) Subsection (2) above does not affect section 31 or 31A below.

(4) Where a property adjustment order is made under this section on or after the granting of a decree of nullity of marriage, neither the order nor any settlement made in pursuance of the order is to take effect unless the decree has been made absolute.

(5) That does not affect the power to give a direction under section 30 below for the settlement of an instrument by conveyancing counsel.

(6) This section is to be read subject to any restrictions imposed by this Act.]

Note. Section 24 in square brackets substituted for s 24 in italics by Family Law Act 1996, s 15, Sch 2, para 6, as from a day to be appointed, subject to savings in s 66(2) of, and para 5 of Sch 9 to, the 1996 Act.

[24A. Orders for sale of property—(1) Where the court makes under *section 23 or 24 of this Act* [any of sections 22A to 24 above] a secured periodical payments order, an order for the payment of a lump sum or a property adjustment order, then, on making that order or at any time thereafter, the court may make a further order for the sale of such property as may be specified in the order, being property in which or in the proceeds of sale of which either or both of the parties to the marriage has or have a beneficial interest, either in possession or reversion.

Note. Words 'any of sections 22A to 24 above' in square brackets substituted for words 'section 23 or 24 of this Act' in italics by Family Law Act 1996, s 66(1), Sch 8, Part I, para 8, as from a day to be appointed, subject to savings in s 66(2) of, and para 5 of Sch 9 to, the 1996 Act.

(2) Any order made under subsection (1) above may contain such consequential or supplementary provisions as the court thinks fit and, without prejudice to the generality of the foregoing provision, may include—

(a) provision requiring the making of a payment out of the proceeds of sale of the property to which the order relates, and

(b) provision requiring any such property to be offered for sale to a person, or class of persons, specified in the order.

(3) Where an order is made under subsection (1) above on or after the grant of a decree of *divorce or* nullity of marriage, the order shall not take effect unless the decree has been made absolute.

Note. Words 'divorce or' in italics repealed by Family Law Act 1996, s 66(3), Sch 10, as from a day to be appointed, subject to savings in s 66(2) of, and para 5 of Sch 9 to, the 1996 Act.

(4) Where an order is made under subsection (1) above, the court may direct that the order, or such provision thereof as the court may specify, shall not take effect until the occurrence of an event specified by the court or the expiration of a period so specified.

(5) Where an order under subsection (1) above contains a provision requiring the proceeds of sale of the property to which the order relates to be used to secure periodical payments to a party to the marriage, the order shall cease to have effect on the death or re-marriage of that person.]

[(6) Where a party to a marriage has a beneficial interest in any property, or in the proceeds of sale thereof, and some other person who is not a party to the marriage also has a beneficial interest in that property or in the proceeds of the sale thereof, then, before deciding whether to make an order under this section in relation to that property, it shall be the duty of the court to give that other person an opportunity to make representations with respect to the order; and any representations made by that other person shall be included among the circumstances to which the court is required to have regard under section 25(1) below.]

Note. This section inserted by Matrimonial Homes and Property Act 1981, s 7, as from 1 October 1981.

Sub-s (6) added by Matrimonial and Family Proceedings Act 1984, s 46(1), Sch 1, para 11, as from 12 October 1984.

[24B Pension sharing orders in connection with divorce proceedings etc—(1) On granting a decree of divorce or a decree of nullity of marriage or at any time thereafter (whether before or after the decree is made absolute), the court may, on an application made under this section, make one or more pension sharing orders in relation to the marriage.

(2) A pension sharing order under this section is not to take effect unless the decree on or after which it is made has been made absolute.

(3) A pension sharing order under this section may not be made in relation to a pension arrangement which—

(a) is the subject of a pension sharing order in relation to the marriage, or

(b) has been the subject of pension sharing between the parties to the marriage.

(4) A pension sharing order under this section may not be made in relation to shareable state scheme rights if—

(a) such rights are the subject of a pension sharing order in relation to the marriage, or

(b) such rights have been the subject of pension sharing between the parties to the marriage.

(5) A pension sharing order under this section may not be made in relation to the rights of a person under a pension arrangement if there is in force a requirement imposed by virtue of section 25B or 25C below which relates to benefits or future benefits to which he is entitled under the pension arrangement.]

Note. This section inserted by the Welfare Reform and Pensions Act 1999, s 19, Sch 3, paras 1, 4, as from 1 December 2000.

[24BA Restrictions affecting section 24B—(1) No pension sharing order may be made under section 24B above so as to take effect before the making of a divorce order in relation to the marriage.

(2) The court may not make a pension sharing order under section 24B above at any time while the period for reflection and consideration is interrupted under section 7(8) of the 1996 Act.

(3) No pension sharing order may be made under section 24B above by virtue of a statement of marital breakdown if, by virtue of section 5(3) or 7(9) of the 1996 Act (lapse of divorce process), it has ceased to be possible—

(a) for an application to be made by reference to that statement, or

(b) for an order to be made on such an application.

(4) No pension sharing order may be made under section 24B above after a divorce order has been made, except—

(a) in response to an application made before the divorce order was made, or

(b) on a subsequent application made with the leave of the court.

(5) A pension sharing order under section 24B above may not be made in relation to a pension arrangement which—

(a) is the subject of a pension sharing order in relation to the marriage, or

(b) has been the subject of pension sharing between the parties to the marriage.

(6) A pension sharing order under section 24B above may not be made in relation to shareable state scheme rights if—

(a) such rights are the subject of a pension sharing order in relation to the marriage, or

(b) such rights have been the subject of pension sharing between the parties to the marriage.

(7) A pension sharing order under section 24B above may not be made in relation to the rights of a person under a pension arrangement if there is in force a requirement imposed by virtue of section 25B or 25C below which relates to benefits or future benefits to which he is entitled under the pension arrangement.

(8) In this section, 'period for reflection and consideration' means the period fixed by section 7 of the 1996 Act.]

Note. This section substituted, together with sections 24B, 24BB, 24BC, for section 24B (as inserted by the Welfare Reform and Pensions Act 1999, s 19, Sch 3, paras 1, 4), by the Family Law Act 1996, s 15, Sch 2, para 6A (as inserted by the Welfare Reform and Pensions Act 1999, s 84(1), Sch 12, Pt I, paras 64, 65(1), (9)), as from a day to be appointed.

[24BB Pension sharing orders: nullity of marriage—(1) On or after granting a decree of nullity of marriage (whether before or after the decree is made absolute), the court may, on an application made under this section, make one or more pension sharing orders in relation to the marriage.

(2) The court shall exercise its powers under this section, so far as is practicable by making on one occasion all such provision as can be made by way of one or more pension sharing orders in relation to the marriage as it thinks fit.

(3) Where a pension sharing order is made under this section on or after the granting of a decree of nullity of marriage, the order is not to take effect unless the decree has been made absolute.

(4) This section is to be read subject to any restrictions imposed by this Act.]

Note. This section substituted, together with sections 24B, 24BA, 24BC, for section 24B (as inserted by the Welfare Reform and Pensions Act 1999, s 19, Sch 3, paras 1, 4), by the Family Law Act 1996, s 15, Sch 2, para 6A (as inserted by the Welfare Reform and Pensions Act 1999, s 84(1), Sch 12, Pt I, paras 64, 65(1), (9)), as from a day to be appointed.

[24BC Restrictions affecting section 24BB—(1) A pension sharing order under section 24BB above may not be made in relation to a pension arrangement which—

(a) is the subject of a pension sharing order in relation to the marriage, or

(b) has been the subject of pension sharing between the parties to the marriage.

(2) A pension sharing order under section 24BB above may not be made in relation to shareable state scheme rights if—

(a) such rights are the subject of a pension sharing order in relation to the marriage, or

(b) such rights have been the subject of pension sharing between the parties to the marriage.

(3) A pension sharing order under section 24BB above may not be made in relation to the rights of a person under a pension arrangement if there is in force a requirement imposed by virtue of section 25B or 25C below which relates to benefits or future benefits to which he is entitled under the pension arrangement.]

Note. This section substituted, together with sections 24B, 24BA, 24BB, for section 24B (as inserted by the Welfare Reform and Pensions Act 1999, s 19, Sch 3, paras 1, 4), by the Family Law Act 1996, s 15, Sch 2, para 6A (as inserted by the Welfare Reform and Pensions Act 1999, s 84(1), Sch 12, Pt I, paras 64, 65(1), (9)), as from a day to be appointed.

[24C Pension sharing orders: duty to stay—(1) No pension sharing order may be made so as to take effect before the end of such period after the making of the order as may be prescribed by regulations made by the Lord Chancellor.

(2) The power to make regulations under this section shall be exercisable by statutory instrument which shall be subject to annulment in pursuance of a resolution of either House of Parliament.]

Note. This section inserted by the Welfare Reform and Pensions Act 1999, s 19, Sch 3, paras 1, 4, as from 1 December 2000.

[24D Pension sharing orders: apportionment of charges—If a pension sharing order relates to rights under a pension arrangement, the court may include in the order provision about the apportionment between the parties of any charge under section 41 of the Welfare Reform and Pensions Act 1999 (charges in respect of pension sharing cost), or under corresponding Northern Ireland legislation.]

Note. This section inserted by the Welfare Reform and Pensions Act 1999, s 19, Sch 3, paras 1, 4, as from 1 December 2000.

25. Matters to which court is to have regard in deciding how to exercise its powers under sections 23 and 24—(*1*) *It shall be the duty of the court in deciding whether to exercise its powers under section 23(1)(a), (b) or (c) or 24 [24 or 24A] above in relation to a party to the marriage and, if so, in what manner, to have regard to all the circumstances of the case including the following matters, that is to say—*
- (*a*) *the income, earning capacity, property and other financial resources which each of the parties to the marriage has or is likely to have in the foreseeable future;*
- (*b*) *the financial needs, obligations and responsibilities which each of the parties to the marriage has or is likely to have in the foreseeable future;*
- (*c*) *the standard of living enjoyed by the family before the breakdown of the marriage;*
- (*d*) *the age of each party to the marriage and the duration of the marriage;*
- (*e*) *any physical or mental disability of either of the parties to the marriage;*
- (*f*) *the contributions made by each of the parties to the welfare of the family, including any contribution made by looking after the home or caring for the family;*
- (*g*) *in the case of proceedings for divorce or nullity of marriage, the value to either of the parties to the marriage of any benefit (for example, a pension) which, by reason of the dissolution or annulment of the marriage, that party will lose the chance of acquiring;*
and so to exercise those powers as to place the parties, so far as it is practicable and, having regard to their conduct, just to do so, in the financial position in which they would have been if the marriage had not broken down and each had properly discharged his or her financial obligations and responsibilities towards the other.

(*2*) *Without prejudice to subsection (3) below, it shall be the duty of the court in deciding whether to exercise its powers under section 23(1)(d), (e) or (f), (2) or (4) or 24 [24 or 24A] above in relation to a child of the family and, if so, in what manner, to have regard to all the circumstances of the case including the following matters, that is to say—*
- (*a*) *the financial needs of the child;*
- (*b*) *the income, earning capacity (if any), property and other financial resources of the child;*
- (*c*) *any physical or mental disability of the child;*
- (*d*) *the standard of living enjoyed by the family before the breakdown of the marriage;*
- (*e*) *the manner in which he was being and in which the parties to the marriage expected him to be educated or trained;*
and so to exercise those powers as to place the child, so far as it is practicable and, having regard to the considerations mentioned in relation to the parties to the marriage in paragraphs (a) and (b) of subsection (1) above, just to do so, in the financial position in which the child would have been if the marriage had not broken down and each of those parties had properly discharged his or her financial obligations and responsibilities towards him.

(*3*) *It shall be the duty of the court in deciding whether to exercise its powers under section 23(1)(d), (e) or (f), (2) or (4) or 24 [24 or 24A] above against a party to a marriage in favour of a child of the family who is not the child of that party and, if so, in what manner, to have regard (among the circumstances of the case)—*

(a) to whether that party had assumed any responsibility for the child's maintenance and, if so, to the extent to which, and the basis upon which, that party assumed such responsibility and to the length of time for which that party discharged such responsibility;

(b) to whether in assuming and discharging such responsibility that party did so knowing that the child was not his or her own;

(c) to the liability of any other person to maintain the child.

[(4) Where a party to a marriage has a beneficial interest in any property, or in the proceeds of sale thereof, and some other person who is not a party to the marriage also has a beneficial interest in that property or in the proceeds of sale thereof, then, before deciding whether to make an order under section 24A above in relation to that property, it shall be the duty of the court to give that other person an opportunity to make representations with respect to the order; and any representations made by that other person shall be included among the circumstances to which the court is required to have regard under this section.]

Note. Section 25 replaced Matrimonial Proceedings and Property Act 1970, s 5 (p 2366).

Words in square brackets substituted for words 'or 24' and sub-s (4) added by Matrimonial Homes and Property Act 1981, s 8(1), as from 1 October 1981.

[25. Matters to which court is to have regard in deciding how to exercise its powers under ss 23, 24 and 24A—(1) It shall be the duty of the court in deciding whether to exercise its powers under *section 23, 24 or 24A [, 24A or 24B]* [any of sections 22A to 24BB] above and, if so, in what manner, to have regard to all the circumstances of the case, first consideration being given to the welfare while a minor of any child of the family who has not attained the age of eighteen.

Note. Words ', 24A or 24B' in square brackets substituted, for words 'or 24A' in italics by the Welfare Reform and Pensions Act 1999, s 19, Sch 3, paras 1, 5, as from 1 December 2000. Words 'any of sections 22A to 24BB' in square brackets substituted for words in italics by Family Law Act 1996, s 66(1), Sch 8, Part I, para 9, as from a day to be appointed, subject to savings in s 66(2) of, and para 5 of Sch 9 to, the 1996 Act.

(2) As regards the exercise of the powers of the court under *section 23(1)(a), (b) or (c),* [section 22A or 23 above to make a financial provision order in favour of a party to a marriage or the exercise of its powers under section 23A,] 24 *or 24A [, 24A or 24B [, 24B or 24BB]]* above in relation to a party to the marriage, the court shall in particular have regard to the following matters—

(a) the income, earning capacity, property and other financial resources which each of the parties to the marriage has or is likely to have in the foreseeable future, including in the case of earning capacity any increase in that capacity which it would in the opinion of the court be reasonable to expect a party to the marriage to take steps to acquire;

(b) the financial needs, obligations and responsibilities which each of the parties to the marriage has or is likely to have in the foreseeable future;

(c) the standard of living enjoyed by the family before the breakdown of the marriage;

(d) the age of each party to the marriage and the duration of the marriage;

(e) any physical or mental disability of either of the parties to the marriage;

(f) the contributions which each of the parties has made or is likely in the foreseeable future to make to the welfare of the family, including any contribution by looking after the home or caring for the family;

(g) the conduct of each of the parties [, whatever the nature of the conduct and whether it occurred during the marriage or after the separation of the parties or (as the case may be) dissolution or annulment of the marriage], if that conduct is such that it would in the opinion of the court be inequitable to disregard it;

(h) *in the case of proceedings for divorce or nullity of marriage,* the value to each of the parties to the marriage of any benefit (*for example, a pension*) which, by reason of the dissolution or annulment of the marriage, that party will lose the chance of acquiring.

Note. First words in square brackets substituted for previous words in italics, words ', 24A or 24B' in square brackets substituted for words 'or 24A' in italics by the Welfare Reform and Pensions Act 1999, s 19, Sch 3, paras 1, 5, as from 1 December 2000, words ', 24B or 24BB' in square brackets substituted for words 'or 24B' in italics, words in square brackets in sub-s (2)(g) inserted, and first words in italics in sub-s (2)(h) repealed by Family Law Act 1996, s 66, Sch 8, Part I, para 9 (including para 9(3)(aa) as inserted by the Welfare Reform and Pensions Act 1999, s 84(1), Sch 12, Pt I, Paras 64, 66(1), (2)(b)), Sch 10, as from a day to be appointed, subject to savings in s 66(2) of, and para 5 of Sch 9 to, the 1996 Act. Words '(for example, a pension)' repealed by Pensions Act 1995, s 166(1), as from 1 August 1996.

(3) As regards the exercise of the powers of the court under *section 23(1)(d)*, *(e)* *or (f)*, *(2) or (4)*, *24 or 24A* [section 22A or 23 above to make a financial provision order in favour of a child of the family or the exercise of its powers under section 23A,] above in relation to a child of the family, the court shall in particular have regard to the following matters—

(a) the financial needs of the child;

(b) the income, earning capacity (if any), property and other financial resources of the child;

(c) any physical or mental disability of the child;

(d) the manner in which he was being and in which the parties to the marriage expected him to be educated or trained;

(e) the considerations mentioned in relation to the parties to the marriage in paragraphs (a), (b), (c) and (e) of subsection (2) above.

(4) As regards the exercise of the powers of the court under *section 23(1)(d)*, *(e)* *or (f)*, *(2) or (4)*, *24 or 24A* [any of sections 22A to 24A] above against a party to a marriage in favour of a child of the family who is not the child of that party, the court shall also have regard—

(a) to whether that party assumed any responsibility for the child's maintenance, and, if so, to the extent to which, and the basis upon which, that party assumed such responsibility and to the length of time for which that party discharged such responsibility;

(b) to whether in assuming and discharging such responsibility that party did so knowing that the child was not his or her own;

(c) to the liability of any other person to maintain the child.

Note. Words in square brackets in sub-ss (3), (4) substituted for words in italics by Family Law Act 1996, s 66(1), Sch 8, Part I, para 9, as from a day to be appointed, subject to savings in s 66(2) of, and para 5 of Sch 9 to, the 1996 Act.

[(5) In relation to any power of the court to make an interim periodical payments order or an interim order for the payment of a lump sum, the preceding provisions of this section, in imposing any obligation on the court with respect to the matters to which it is to have regard, shall not require the court to do anything which would cause such a delay as would, in the opinion of the court, be inappropriate having regard—

(a) to any immediate need for an interim order;

(b) to the matters in relation to which it is practicable for the court to inquire before making an interim order; and

(c) to the ability of the court to have regard to any matter and to make appropriate adjustments when subsequently making a financial provision order which is not interim.]

Note. Sub-s (5) added by Family Law Act 1996, s 66(1), Sch 8, Part I, para 9, as from a day to be appointed, subject to savings in s 66(2) of, and para 5 of Sch 9 to, the 1996 Act.

25A. Exercise of court's powers in favour of party to marriage on decree of divorce or nullity of marriage—(1) *Where on or after the grant of a decree of divorce or nullity of marriage the court decides to exercise its powers under section 23(1)(a)*, *(b) or (c)*, *24 or 24A [, 24A or 24B] above in favour of a party to the marriage* [If the court decides to exercise any of its powers under any of sections 22A to 24A above in favour of a party to a marriage (other than its power to make an interim periodical payments order or an interim order for the payment of a lump sum)], it shall be the duty of the court to consider whether it would be appropriate so to exercise those powers that the financial obligations of each party towards the other will be terminated as soon after the grant of *the decree* [a divorce order or decree of nullity] as the court considers just and reasonable.

Note. First words in square brackets substituted for words 'or 24A' in italics. Second words in square brackets substituted for words in italics by Family Law Act 1996, s 66(1), Sch 8, Part I, para 10, as from a day to be appointed, subject to savings in s 66(2) of, and para 5 of Sch 9 to, the 1996 Act.

(2) Where the court decides in such a case to make a periodical payments or secured periodical payments order in favour of a party to the marriage, the court shall in particular consider whether it would be appropriate to require those payments to be made or secured only for such term as would in the opinion of the court be sufficient to enable the party in whose favour the order is made to adjust without undue hardship to the termination of his or her financial dependence on the other party.

(3) Where on or after the grant of a decree of divorce or nullity of marriage an application is made by a party to the marriage for a periodical payments or secured periodical payments order in his or her favour, then, if the court considers that no continuing obligation should be imposed on either party to make or secure periodical payments in favour of the other, the court may dismiss the application with a direction that the applicant shall not be entitled to make any further application in relation to that marriage for an order under section 23(1)(a) or (b) above.

[(3) If the court—

(a) would have power under section 22A or 23 above to make a financial provision order in favour of a party to a marriage ('the first party'), but

(b) considers that no continuing obligation should be imposed on the other party to the marriage ('the second party') to make or secure periodical payments in favour of the first party,

it may direct that the first party may not at any time after the direction takes effect, apply to the court for the making against the second party of any periodical payments order or secured periodical payments order and, if the first party has already applied to the court for the making of such an order, it may dismiss the application.

(3A) If the court—

(a) exercises, or has exercised, its power under section 22A at any time before making a divorce order, and

(b) gives a direction under subsection (3) above in respect of a periodical payments order or a secured periodical payments order,

it shall provide for the direction not to take effect until a divorce order is made.]]

Note. New ss 25, 25A substituted by Matrimonial and Family Proceedings Act 1984, s 3, as from 12 October 1984. Sub-ss (3), (3A) in square brackets substituted for sub-s (3) in italics by Family Law Act 1996, s 66(1), Sch 8, Part I, para 10, as from a day to be appointed, subject to savings in s 66(2) of, and para 5 of Sch 9 to, the 1996 Act.

[25B. Pensions—(1) The matters to which the court is to have regard under section 25(2) above include—

(a) in the case of paragraph (a), any benefits under a pension *scheme* [arrangement] which a party to the marriage has or is likely to have, and

(b) in the case of paragraph (h), any benefits under a pension *scheme* [arrangement] which, by reason of the dissolution or annulment of the marriage, a party to the marriage will lose the chance of acquiring, and, accordingly, in relation to benefits under a pension *scheme* [arrangement], section 25(2)(a) above shall have effect as if 'in the foreseeable future' were omitted.

Note. Word 'arrangement' in square brackets in each place it occurs substituted for words in italics by the Welfare Reform and Pensions Act 1999, s 21, Sch 4, para 1, as from 1 December 2000.

(2) In any proceedings for a financial provision order under section 23 [section 22A or 23] above in a case where a party to the marriage has, or is likely to have, any benefit under a pension scheme the court shall, in addition to considering any other matter which it is required to consider apart from this subsection, consider—

  (a) *whether, having regard to any matter to which it is required to have regard in the proceedings by virtue of subsection (1) above, such an order (whether deferred or not) should be made, and*

  (b) *where the court determines to make such an order, how the terms of the order should be affected, having regard to any such matter.*

  [(c) *in particular, where the court determines to make such an order, whether the order should provide for the accrued rights of the party with pension rights ('the pension rights') to be divided between that party and the other party in such a way as to reduce the pension rights of the party with those rights and to create pension rights for the other party.]*

Note. Words 'section 22A or 23' in square brackets substituted for words 'section 23' in italics, and para (c) added, by Family Law Act 1996, ss 16(2), 66(1), Sch 8, Part I, para 11, as from a day to be appointed, subject to savings in s 66(2) of, and para 5 of Sch 9 to, the 1996 Act.

Sub-s (2) repealed by the Welfare Reform and Pensions Act 1999, ss 21, 88, Sch 4, para 1, Sch 13, Pt II, as from 1 December 2000.

(3) The following provisions apply where, having regard to any benefits under a pension *scheme* [arrangement], the court determines to make an order under *section 23* [section 22A or 23] above.

Note. Word 'arrangement' in square brackets substituted for word in italics by the Welfare Reform and Pensions Act 1999, s 21, Sch 4, para 1, as from 1 December 2000. Words 'section 22A or 23' substituted for words 'section 23' in italics by Family Law Act 1996, s 66(1), Sch 8, Part I, para 11, as from a day to be appointed, subject to savings in s 66(2) of, and para 5 of Sch 9 to, the 1996 Act.

(4) To the extent to which the order is made having regard to any benefits under a pension *scheme* [arrangement], the order may require the *trustees or managers of* [person responsible for] the pension *scheme* [arrangement] in question, if at any time any payment in respect of any benefits under the *scheme* [arrangement] becomes due to the party with pension rights, to make a payment for the benefit of the other party.

Note. Word 'arrangement' in square brackets in each place it occurs substituted for words in italics and words 'person responsible for' in square brackets substituted for words 'trustees or managers of' in italics by the Welfare Reform and Pensions Act 1999, s 21, Sch 4, para 1, as from 1 December 2000.

(5) The amount of any payment which, by virtue of subsection (4) above, the trustees or managers are required to make under the order at any time shall not exceed the amount of the payment which is due at that time to the party with pension rights.

[(5) The Order must express the amount of any payment required to be made by virtue of subsection (4) above as a percentage of the payment which becomes due to the party with pension rights.]

Note. Sub-s (5) substituted by the Welfare Reform and Pensions Act 1999, s 21, Sch 4, para 1, as from 1 December 2000.

(6) Any such payment by the *trustees or managers* [person responsible for the arrangement]—

(a) shall discharge so much of *the trustees or managers* [his] liability to the party with pension rights as corresponds to the amount of the payment, and
(b) shall be treated for all purposes as a payment made by the party with pension rights in or towards the discharge of his liability under the order.

Note. First and second words in square brackets substituted for first and second words in italics by the Welfare Reform and Pensions Act 1999, s 21, Sch 4, para 1, as from 1 December 2000.

(7) Where the party with pension rights *may require any benefits which he has or is likely to have under the scheme to be commuted, the order may require him to commute the whole or part of those benefits* [has a right of commutation under the arrangement, the order may require him to exercise it to any extent], and this section applies to the *payment of any amount commuted* [any payment due in consequence of commutation] in pursuance of the order as it applies to other payments in respect of benefits under the *scheme* [arrangement].

Note. First, second and final words in square brackets substituted for preceding words in italics by the Welfare Reform and Pensions Act 1999, s 21, Sch 4, para 1, as from 1 December 2000.

[(7A) The power conferred by subsection (7) above may not be exercised for the purpose of commuting a benefit payable to the party with pension rights to a benefit payable to the other party.

(7B) The power conferred by subsection (4) or (7) above may not be exercised in relation to a pension arrangement which—
(a) is the subject of a pension sharing order in relation to the marriage, or
(b) has been the subject of pension sharing between the parties to the marriage.

(7C) In subsection (1) above, references to benefits under a pension arrangement include any benefits by way of pension, whether under a pension arrangement or not.]

Note. Sub-ss (7A)–(7C) inserted by the Welfare Reform and Pensions Act 1999, s 21, Sch 4, para 1(1), (9), as from 1 December 2000.

[(8) If a pensions adjustment order under subsection (2)(c) above is made, the pension rights shall be reduced and pension rights of the other party shall be created in the prescribed manner with benefits payable on prescribed conditions, except that the court shall not have the power—
(a) to require the trustees or managers of the scheme to provide benefits under their own scheme if they are able and willing to create the rights for the other party by making a transfer payment to another scheme and the trustees and managers of that other scheme are able and willing to accept such a payment and to create those rights; or
(b) to require the trustees or managers of the scheme to make a transfer to another scheme—
  (i) if the scheme is an unfunded scheme (unless the trustees or managers are able and willing to make such a transfer payment); or
  (ii) in prescribed circumstances.
(9) No pensions adjustment order may be made under subsection (2)(c) above—
(a) if the scheme is a scheme of a prescribed type, or
(b) in prescribed circumstances, or
(c) insofar as it would affect benefits of a prescribed type.]

Note. Sub-ss (8), (9) added by Family Law Act 1996, s 16(3), as from a day to be appointed, subject to savings in s 66(2) of, and para 5 of Sch 9 to, the 1996 Act.

25C. Pensions: lump sums—(1) The power of the court under *section 23* [section 22A or 23] above to order a party to a marriage to pay a lump sum to the other party includes, where the benefits which the party with pension rights has or is likely to have under a pension *scheme* [arrangement] include any lump sum payable in respect of his death, power to make any of the following provision by the order.

Note. Words 'section 22A or 23' in square brackets substituted for words 'section 23' in italics by Family Law Act 1996, s 66(1), Sch 8, Part I, para 11, as from a day to be appointed, subject to savings in s 66(2) of, and para 5 of Sch 9 to, the 1996 Act. Word 'arrangement' in square brackets substituted for word 'scheme' in italics by the Welfare Reform and Pensions Act 1999, s 21, Sch 4, para 2, as from 1 December 2000.

(2) The court may—

(a) if the *trustees or managers of the pension scheme in question have* [person responsible for the pension arrangement in question has] power to determine the person to whom the sum or any part of it, is to be paid, require *them* [him] to pay the whole or part of that sum, when it becomes due, to the other party,

(b) if the party with pension rights has power to nominate the person to whom the sum, or any part of it, is to be paid, require the party with pension rights to nominate the other party in respect of the whole or part of that sum,

(c) in any other case, require the *trustees or managers of the pension scheme* [person responsible for the pension arrangement] in question to pay the whole or part of that sum, when it becomes due, for the benefit of the other party instead of to the person to whom, apart from the order, it would be paid.

Note. First, second and final words in square brackets substituted for words in italics by the Welfare Reform and Pensions Act 1999, s 21, Sch 4, para 2, as from 1 December 2000.

(3) Any payment by the *trustees or managers* [person responsible for the arrangement] under an order made under *section 23* [section 22A or 23] above by virtue of this section shall discharge so much of *the trustees, or managers* [his], liability in respect of the party with pension rights as corresponds to the amount of the payment.

Note. Words 'section 22A or 23' in square brackets substituted for words 'section 23' in italics by Family Law Act 1996, s 66(1), Sch 8, Part I, para 11, as from a day to be appointed, subject to savings in s 66(2) of, and para 5 of Sch 9 to, the 1996 Act. Words 'person responsible for the arrangement' in square brackets substituted for preceding words in italics and word 'his" in square brackets substituted for preceding words in italics by the Welfare Reform and Pensions Act 1999, s 21, Sch 4, para 2, as from 1 December 2000.

[(4) The powers conferred by this section may not be exercised in relation to a pension arrangement which—

(a) is the subject of a pension sharing order in relation to the marriage, or

(b) has been the subject of pension sharing between the parties to the marriage.]

Note. Sub-s (4) inserted by the Welfare Reform and Pensions Act 1999, s 21, Sch 4, para 2, as from 1 December 2000.

25D. Pensions: supplementary—(*1*) *Where*—

(a) *an order made under section 23 [section 22A or 23] above by virtue of section 25B or 25C above imposes any requirement on the trustees or managers of a pension scheme ('the first scheme') and the party with pension rights acquires transfer credits under another pension scheme ('the new scheme') which are derived (directly or indirectly) from a transfer from the first scheme of all his accrued rights under that scheme (including transfer credits allowed by that scheme), and*

(b) *the trustees or managers of the new scheme have been given notice in accordance with regulations,*

the order shall have effect as if it has been made instead in respect of the trustees or managers of the new scheme; and in this subsection 'transfer credits' has the same meaning as in the Pension Schemes Act 1993.

[(1) Where—

(a) an order made under section 23 above by virtue of section 25B or 25C above imposes any requirement on the person responsible for a pension arrangement ('the first arrangement') and the party with pension rights acquires rights under another pension arrangement ('the new arrangement') which are derived (directly or indirectly) from the whole of his rights under the first arrangement, and

(b) the person responsible for the new arrangement has been given notice in accordance with regulations made by the Lord Chancellor,

the order shall have effect as if it had been made instead in respect of the person responsible for the new arrangement.]

Note. Sub-s (1) in square brackets substituted for sub-s (1) in italics by the Welfare Reform and Pensions Act 1999, s 21, Sch 4, para 3, as from 1 December 2000.

(2) *Regulations may* [The Lord Chancellor may by regulations]—

(a) in relation to any provision of sections 25B or 25C above which authorises the court making an order under *section 23* [section 22A or 23] above to require the *trustees or managers of a pension scheme* [person responsible for a pension arrangement] to make a payment for the benefit of the other party, make provision as to the person to whom, and the terms on which, the payment is to be made, [or prescribe the rights of the other party under the pension scheme,]

[(aa) make such consequential modifications of any enactment or subordinate legislation as appear to the Lord Chancellor necessary or expedient to give effect to the provisions of section 25B; and an order under this paragraph may make provision applying generally in relation to enactments and subordinate legislation of a description specified in the order,]

[(ab) make, in relation to payment under a mistaken belief as to the continuation in force of a provision included by virtue of section 25B or 25C above in an order under section 23 above, provIsion about the rights or liabilities of the payer, the payee or the person to whom the payment was due,]

(b) require notices to be given in respect of changes of circumstances relevant to such orders which include provision made by virtue of sections 25B and 25C above,

[(ba) make provision for the person responsible for a pension arrangement to be discharged in prescribed circumstances from a requirement imposed by virtue of section 25B or 25C above,]

(c) *make provision for the trustees or managers of any pension scheme to provide, for the purposes of orders under section 23 [section 22A or 23] above, information as to the value of any benefits under the scheme,*

(d) *make provision for the recovery of the administrative expenses of—*

    (i) *complying with such orders, so far as they include provision made by virtue of sections 25B and 25C above, and*

    (ii) *providing such information,*

    from the party with pension rights or the other party,

(e) *make provision for the value of any benefits under a pension scheme to be calculated and verified, for the purposes of orders under* section 23 *[section 22A or 23] above, in a prescribed manner,*

and regulations made by virtue of paragraph (e) above may provide for that value to be calculated and verified in accordance with guidance which is prepared and from time to time revised by a prescribed person and approved by the Secretary of State.

[(e) make provision about calculation and verification in relation to the valuation of—

    (i) benefits under a pension arrangement, or

    (ii) shareable state scheme rights,

for the purposes of the court's functions in connection with the exercise of any of its powers under this Part of this Act,]

Note. Words 'section 22A or 23' in square brackets in sub-ss (1), (2) substituted for words 'section 23' in italics, and other words in square brackets inserted, by Family Law Act 1996, ss 16(4), 66(1), Sch 8, Part I, para 11, as from a day to be appointed, subject to savings in s 66(2) of, and para 5 of Sch 9 to, the 1996 Act. Words 'The Lord Chancellor may by regulations' in square brackets substituted for preceding words in italics in sub-s (2), words 'person responsible for a pension arrangement' in square brackets substituted for preceding words in italics in sub-s (2)(a), paras (ab) and (ba) inserted, paras (c), (d) and words from 'and regulations made' to the end in para (e) repealed and para (e) substituted by the Welfare Reform and Pensions Act 1999, s 21, Sch 4, para 3, as from 1 December 2000.

[(2A) Regulations under subsection (2)(e) above may include—

(a) provision for calculation or verification in accordance with guidance from time to time prepared by a prescribed person, and

(b) provision by reference to regulations under section 30 or 49(4) of the Welfare Reform and Pensions Act 1999.

(2B) Regulations under subsection (2) above may make different provision for different cases.

(2C) Power to make regulations under this section shall be exercisable by statutory instrument which shall be subject to annulment in pursuance of a resolution of either House of Parliament.]

Note. Sub-ss (2A)–(2C) inserted by the Welfare Reform and Pensions Act 1999, s 21, Sch 4, para 3, as from 1 December 2000.

(3) In this section and sections 25B and 25C above—

(a) references to a pension scheme include—

(i) a retirement annuity contract, or

(ii) an annuity, or insurance policy, purchased or transferred for the purpose of giving effect to rights under a pension scheme,

(b) in relation to such a contract or annuity, references to the trustees or managers shall be read as references to the provider of the annuity,

(c) in relation to such a policy, references to the trustees or managers shall be read as references to the insurer,

and in section 25B(1) and (2) above, references to benefits under a pension scheme include any benefits by way of pension, whether under a pension scheme or not.

(4) In this section and sections 25B and 25C above—

['funded scheme' means a scheme under which the benefits are provided for by setting aside resources related to the value of the members' rights as they accrue (and 'unfunded scheme' shall be construed accordingly);]

'the party with pension rights' means the party to the marriage who has or is likely to have benefits under a pension scheme and 'the other party' means the other party to the marriage,

'pension scheme' means an occupational pension scheme or a personal pension scheme (applying the definitions in section 1 of the Pension Schemes Act 1993, but as if the reference to employed earners in the definition of 'personal pension scheme' were to any earners),

'prescribed' means prescribed by regulations, and

'regulations' means regulations made by the Lord Chancellor;

['subordinate legislation' has the same meaning as in the Interpretation Act 1978;]

and the power to make regulations under this section shall be exercisable by statutory instrument, which shall be subject to annulment in pursuance of a resolution of either House of Parliament.

[(3) In this section and sections 25B and 25C above—

'occupational pension scheme' has the same meaning as in the Pension Schemes Act 1993;

'the party with pension rights' means the party to the marriage who has or is likely to have benefits under a pension arrangement and 'the other party" means the other party to the marriage;

'pension arrangement' means—

(a) an occupational pension scheme,

(b) a personal pension scheme,

(c) a retirement annuity contract,

(d) an annuity or insurance policy purchased, or transferred, for the purpose of giving effect to rights under an occupational pension scheme or a personal pension scheme, and

(e) an annuity purchased, or entered into, for the purpose of discharging liability in respect of a pension credit under section 29(1)(b) of the Welfare Reform and Pensions Act 1999 or under corresponding Northern Ireland legislation;

'personal pension scheme' has the same meaning as in the Pension Schemes Act 1993;

'prescribed' means prescribed by regulations;

'retirement annuity contract' means a contract or scheme approved under Chapter III of Part XIV of the Income and Corporation Taxes Act 1988;

'shareable state scheme rights' has the same meaning as in section 21A(1) above; and

'trustees or managers', in relation to an occupational pension scheme or a personal pension scheme, means—

(a) in the case of a scheme established under a trust, the trustees of the scheme, and

(b) in any other case, the managers of the scheme,

(4) In this section and sections 25B and 25C above, references to the person responsible for a pension arrangement are—

(a) in the case of an occupational pension scheme or a personal pension scheme, to the trustees or managers of the scheme,

(b) in the case of a retirement annuity contract or an annuity falling within paragraph (d) or (e) of the definition of 'pension arrangement' above, the provider to the annuity,

and

(c) in the case of an insurance policy falling within paragraph (d) of the definition of that expression, the insurer,]

Note. Definitions 'funded scheme', 'subordinate legislation' inserted by Family Law Act 1996, s 16(4), as from a day to be appointed, subject to savings in s 66(2) of, and para 5 of Sch 9 to, the 1996 Act. Sub-ss (3), (4) in square brackets substituted for sub-ss (3), (4) in italics by the Welfare Reform and Pensions Act 1999, s 21, Sch 4, para 3, as from 1 December 2000.

[(4A) Other expressions used in section 25B above shall be construed in accordance with section 124 (interpretation of Part I) of the Pensions Act 1995.]]

Note. Sections 25B–25D inserted by Pensions Act 1995, s 166(1), as from 27 June 1996, in relation to s 25D(2)–(4), and as from 1 August 1996, otherwise.

Sub-s (4A) inserted by Family Law Act 1996, s 16(4), as from a day to be appointed, subject to savings in s 66(2) of, and para 5 to Sch 9 to, the 1996 Act.

26. Commencement of proceedings for ancillary relief, etc—(*1*) *Where a petition for divorce, nullity of marriage or judicial separation has been presented, then, subject to subsection (2) below, proceedings for maintenance pending suit under section 22 above* [(1) If a petition for nullity of marriage has been presented, then, subject to subsection (2) below, proceedings] for a financial provision order under section 23 above, or for a property adjustment order may be begun, subject to and in accordance with rules of court, at any time after the presentation of the petition.

Note. Sub-s (1) replaced in part Matrimonial Proceedings and Property Act 1970, s 24(1) (p 2377). Words in square brackets substituted for words in italics by Family Law Act 1996, s 66(1), Sch 8, Part I, para 12, as from a day to be appointed, subject to savings in s 66(2) of, and para 5 of Sch 9 to, the 1996 Act.

(2) Rules of court may provide, in such cases as may be prescribed by the rules—

(a) that applications for any such relief as is mentioned in subsection (1) above shall be made in the petition or answer; and

(b) that applications for any such relief which are not so made, or are not made until after the expiration of such period following the presentation of the petition or filing of the answer as may be so prescribed, shall be made only with the leave of the court.

Note. Sub-s (2) replaced Matrimonial Proceedings and Property Act 1970, s 24(2) (p 2358).

Financial provision in case of neglect to maintain

27. Financial provision orders, etc in case of neglect by party to marriage to maintain other party or child of the family—(*1*) *Either party to a marriage may apply to the court for an order under this section on the ground that the other party to the marriage* (*in this section referred to as the respondent*)—
  (*a*) *being the husband, has wilfully neglected*—
    (*i*) *to provide reasonable maintenance for the applicant, or*
    (*ii*) *to provide, or to make a proper contribution towards, reasonable maintenance for any child of the family to whom this section applies;*
  (*b*) *being the wife, has wilfully neglected to provide, or to make a proper contribution towards, reasonable maintenance*—
    (*i*) *for the applicant in a case where, by reason of the impairment of the applicant's earning capacity through age, illness or disability of mind or body, and having regard to any resources of the applicant and the respondent respectively which are, or should properly be made, available for the purpose, it is reasonable in all the circumstances to expect the respondent so to provide or contribute, or*
    (*ii*) *for any child of the family to whom this section applies.*

[(1) Either party to a marriage may apply to the court for an order under this section on the ground that the other party to the marriage (in this section referred to as the respondent)—
  (a) has failed to provide reasonable maintenance for the applicant, or
  (b) has failed to provide, or to make a proper contribution towards, reasonable maintenance for any child of the family.]

Note. Sub-s (1) substituted by Domestic Proceedings and Magistrates' Courts Act 1978, s 63(1), as from 1 February 1981.

(2) The court shall not entertain an application under this section *unless it would have jurisdiction to entertain proceedings by the applicant for judicial separation* [unless—
  (a) the applicant or the respondent is domiciled in England and Wales at the date of the application; or
  (b) the applicant has been habitually resident there throughout the period of one year ending with that date; or
  (c) the respondent is resident there on that date.]

Note. Words in square brackets substituted for words in italics by Domicile and Matrimonial Proceedings Act 1973, s 6(1), as from 1 January 1974.

  (*3*) *This section applies to any child of the family for whose maintenance it is reasonable in all the circumstances to expect the respondent to provide or towards whose maintenance it is reasonable in all the circumstances to expect the respondent to make a proper contribution.*
  (*4*) *Where the child of the family to whom the application under this section relates is not the child of the respondent, then, in deciding*—
    (*a*) *whether the respondent has been guilty of wilful neglect to provide, or to make a proper contribution towards, reasonable maintenance for the child, and*
    (*b*) *what order, if any, to make under this section in favour of the child, the court shall have regard to the matters mentioned in section 25(3) above.*

[(*3*) *Where an application under this section is made on the ground mentioned in subsection (1)(a) above then, in deciding*—
  (*a*) *whether the respondent has failed to provide reasonable maintenance for the applicant, and*

    (*b*) *what order, if any, to make under this section in favour of the applicant,*
the court shall have regard to all the circumstances of the case including the matters
mentioned in section 25(1)(a) to (f) above, and so far as it is just to take it into account,
the conduct of each of the parties in relation to the marriage.]

    [(3) Where an application under this section is made on the ground mentioned
in subsection (1)(a) above, then, in deciding—
    (a) whether the respondent has failed to provide reasonable maintenance for
        the applicant, and
    (b) what order, if any, to make under this section in favour of the applicant,
the court shall have regard to all the circumstances of the case including the
matters mentioned in section 25(2) above and where an application is also made
under this section in respect of a child of the family who has not attained the age
of eighteen, first consideration shall be given to the welfare of the child while a
minor.]

Note. Sub-ss (3), (4) as first printed in italics substituted by sub-s (3) in italics in square
brackets together with sub-ss (3A), (3B) below, by Domestic Proceedings and Magistrates'
Courts Act 1978, s 63(2), as from 1 February 1981: sub-s (3) in square brackets substituted for
sub-s (3) in italics in square brackets by Matrimonial and Family Proceedings Act 1984, s 4, as
from 12 October 1984.

    [(3A) Where an application under this section is made on the ground mentioned
in subsection (1)(b) above then, in deciding—
    (a) whether the respondent has failed to provide, or to make a proper
        contribution towards, reasonable maintenance for the child of the family to
        whom the application relates, and
    (b) what order, if any, to make under this section in favour of the child.
the court shall have regard to all the circumstances of the case including the
matters mentioned in *section 25(1)(a) and (b) and (2)(a) to (e)* [section 25(3)(a) to
(e)] above, and where the child of the family to whom the application relates is not
the child of the respondent, including also the matters mentioned in *section 25(3)*
[section 25(4)] above.

    (3B) In relation to an application under this section on the ground mentioned
in subsection (1)(a) above, *section 25(1)(c)* [section 25(2)(c)] shall have effect as if
for the reference therein to the breakdown of the marriage there were substituted
a reference to the failure to provide reasonable maintenance for the applicant,
and in relation to an application under this section on the ground mentioned in
subsection (1)(b) above, *section 25(2)(d)* [section 25(2)(c) above (as it applies by
virtue of section 25(3)(e) above)] shall have effect as if for the reference therein to
the breakdown of the marriage there were substituted a reference to the failure to
provide, or to make a proper contribution towards, reasonable maintenance for
the child of the family to whom the application relates.]

Note. Sub-ss (3A), (3B) substituted together with sub-s (3), for original sub-ss (3), (4), by
Domestic Proceedings and Magistrates' Courts Act 1978, s 63(2), as from 1 February 1981.
Words in square brackets in sub-ss (3A), (3B) substituted for words in italics by Matrimonial and
Family Proceedings Act 1984, s 46(1), Sch 1, para 12(b), as from 12 October 1984.

    (5) Where on an application under this section it appears to the court that the
applicant or any child of the family to whom the application relates is in immediate
need of financial assistance, but it is not yet possible to determine what order, if
any, should be made on the application, the court may make an interim order for
maintenance, that is to say, an order requiring the respondent[—
    (a)] to make to the applicant until the determination of the application such
        periodical payments as the court thinks reasonable
    [(b) to pay the applicant such lump sum or sums as the court thinks reasonable].

Note. Words in square brackets inserted by Family Law Act 1996, s 66(1), Sch 8, Part I, para
13, as from a day to be appointed, subject to savings in s 66(2) of, and para 5 of Sch 9 to, the
1996 Act.

(*6*) *Where on an application under this section the applicant satisfies the court of any ground mentioned in subsection* (*1*) *above, the court may make such one or more of the following orders* [*any one or more of the following orders*] *as it thinks just, that is to say—*

> (*a*) *an order that the respondent shall make to the applicant such periodical payments, for such term, as may be specified in the order;*
> (*b*) *an order that the respondent shall secure to the applicant, to the satisfaction of the court, such periodical payments, for such term, as may be so specified;*
> (*c*) *an order that the respondent shall pay to the applicant such lump sum as may be so specified;*
> (*d*) *an order that the respondent shall make to such person as may be specified in the order for the benefit of the child to whom the application relates, or to that child, such periodical payments, for such term, as may be so specified;*
> (*e*) *an order that the respondent shall secure to such person as may be so specified for the benefit of that child, or to that child, to the satisfaction of the court, such periodical payments, for such term, as may be so specified;*
> (*f*) *an order that the respondent shall pay to such person as may be so specified for the benefit of that child, or to that child, such lump sum as may be so specified;*

subject, however, in the case of an order under paragraph (*d*), (*e*) *or* (*f*) *above, to the restrictions imposed by section 29*(*1*) *and* (*3*) *below on the making of financial provision orders in favour of children who have attained the age of eighteen.*

Note. Words in square brackets substituted for words 'such one or more of the following orders' by Domestic Proceedings and Magistrates' Courts Act 1978, s 63(3), as from 1 February 1981.

[(6) Subject to the restrictions imposed by the following provisions of this Act, if on an application under this section the applicant satisfies the court of any ground mentioned in subsection (1) above, the court may make one or more financial provision orders against the respondent in favour of the applicant or a child of the family.]

Note. Sub-s (6) in square brackets substituted for sub-s (6) in italics by Family Law Act 1996, s 66(1), Sch 8, Part I, para 13, as from a day to be appointed, subject to savings in s 66(2) of, and para 5 of Sch 9 to, the 1996 Act.

[(6A) An application for the variation under section 31 of this Act of a periodical payments order or secured periodical payments order made under this section in favour of a child may, if the child has attained the age of sixteen, be made by the child himself.

(*6B*) *Where a periodical payments order made in favour of a child under this section ceases to have effect on the date on which the child attains the age of sixteen or at any time after that date but before or on the date on which he attains the age of eighteen, then, if at any time before he attains the age of twenty-one an application is made by the child for an order under this subsection, the court shall have power by order to revive the first mentioned order from such date as the court may specify, not being earlier than the date of the making of the application, and to exercise its powers under section 31 of this Act in relation to any order so revived.*]

[(6B) Where a periodical payments order made in favour of a child under this section ceases to have effect on the date on which the child attains the age of sixteen or at any time after that date but before or on the date on which he attains the age of eighteen, then if, on an application made to the court for an order under this subsection, it appears to the court that—

> (a) the child is, will be or (if an order were made under this subsection) would be receiving instruction at an educational establishment or undergoing training for a trade, profession or vocation, whether or not he also is, will be or would be in gainful employment; or
> (b) there are special circumstances which justify the making of an order under this subsection,

the court shall have power by order to revive the first mentioned order from such date as the court may specify, not being earlier than the date of the making of the application, and to exercise its power under section 31 of this Act in relation to any order so revived.]

Note. Sub-ss (6A) and original sub-s (6B) added by Domestic Proceedings and Magistrates' Courts Act 1978, s 63(4), as from 1 February 1981.

Sub-s (6B) in square brackets substituted for sub-s (6B) in italics by Family Law Reform Act 1987, s 33(1), Sch 2, para 52, as from 1 April 1989.

(7) Without prejudice to the generality of subsection (6)(*c*) *or* (*f*) [(6)] above, an order under this section for the payment of a lump sum—

    (a)   may be made for the purpose of enabling any liabilities or expenses reasonably incurred in maintaining the applicant or any child of the family to whom the application relates before the making of the application to be met;

    (b)   may provide for the payment of that sum by instalments of such amount as may be specified in the order and may require the payment of the instalments to be secured to the satisfaction of the court.

Note. Reference to '(6)' in square brackets substituted by Family Law Act 1996, s 66(1), Sch 8, Part I, para 13, as from a day to be appointed, subject to savings in s 66(2) of, and para 5 of Sch 9 to, the 1996 Act.

(*8*) *For the purpose of proceedings on an application under this section adultery which has been condoned shall not be capable of being revived, and any presumption of condonation which arises from the continuance or resumption of marital intercourse may be rebutted by evidence sufficient to negative the necessary intent.*

Note. Section 27(1)–(7) replaced Matrimonial Proceedings and Property Act 1970, s 6 (p 2367). Sub-s (8) corresponded to Matrimonial Causes Act 1965, s 42(1), (3) (p 2264), repealed by Domestic Proceedings and Magistrates' Courts Act 1978, ss 63(5), 89(2), Sch 3, as from 1 February 1981.

Additional provisions with respect to financial provision and property adjustment orders

28. Duration of continuing financial provision orders in favour of party to marriage, and effect of remarriage—(1) *The term to be specified in a periodical payments or secured periodical payments order in favour of a party to a marriage shall be such term as the court thinks fit, subject to the following limits* [Subject in the case of an order made on or after the grant of a decree of divorce or nullity of marriage to the provisions of sections 25A(2) above and 31(7) below, the term to be specified in a periodical payments or secured periodical payments order in favour of a party to a marriage shall be such term as the court thinks fit, except that the term shall not begin before or extend beyond the following limits], *that is to say*—

    (*a*)   *in the case of a periodical payments order, the term shall begin not earlier than the date of the making of an application for the order, and shall be so defined as not to extend beyond the death of either of the parties to the marriage or, where the order is made on or after the grant of a decree of divorce or nullity of marriage, the remarriage of the party in whose favour the order is made; and*

    (*b*)   *in the case of a secured periodical payments order, the term shall begin not earlier than the date of the making of an application for the order, and shall be so defined as not to extend beyond the death or, where the order is made on or after the grant of such a decree, the remarriage of the party in whose favour the order is made.*

[(a)   a term specified in the order which is to begin before the making of the order shall begin no earlier—

    (i)   where the order is made by virtue of section 22A(2)(a) or (b) above, unless sub-paragraph (ii) below applies, than the beginning of the day on which the statement of marital breakdown in question was received by the court;

(ii) where the order is made by virtue of section 22A(2)(b) above and the application for the divorce order was made following cancellation of an order preventing divorce under section 10 of the 1996 Act, than the date of the making of that application;

(iii) where the order is made by virtue of section 22A(2)(c) above, than the date of the making of the application for the divorce order; or

(iv) in any other case, than the date of the making of the application on which the order is made;

(b) a term specified in a periodical payments order or secured periodical payments order shall be so defined as not to extend beyond—

(i) in the case of a periodical payments order, the death of the party by whom the payments are to be made; or

(ii) in either case, the death of the party in whose favour the order was made or the remarriage of that party following the making of a divorce order or decree of nullity.]

Note. First words in square brackets substituted for words in italics by Matrimonial and Family Proceedings Act 1984, s 5(1), as from 12 October 1984. Words 'in the case of an order … nullity of marriage' repealed, and sub-s (1)(a), (b) in square brackets substituted for sub-s (1)(a), (b) in italics by Family Law Act 1996, ss 15, 66, Sch 2, para 7, Sch 10, as from a day to be appointed, subject to savings in s 66(2) of, and para 5 of Sch 9 to, the 1996 Act.

[*(1A) Where a periodical payments or secured periodical payments order in favour of a party to a marriage is made on or after the grant of a decree of divorce or nullity of marriage,*

[(1A) At any time when—

(a) the court exercises, or has exercised, its power under section 22A or 23 above to make a financial provision order in favour of a party to a marriage,

(b) but for having exercised that power, the court would have power under one of those sections to make such an order, and

(c) an application for a divorce order or a petition for a decree of nullity of marriage is outstanding or has been granted in relation to the marriage,]

the court may direct that that party shall not be entitled to apply under section 31 below for the extension of the term specified in the order.]

Note. Sub-s (1A) inserted by Matrimonial and Family Proceedings Act 1984, s 5(2), as from 12 October 1984. Words in square brackets substituted for words in italics by Family Law Act 1996, s 66(1), Sch 8, Part I, para 14, as from a day to be appointed, subject to savings in s 66(2) of, and para 5 of Sch 9 to, the 1996 Act.

[(1B) If the court—

(a) exercises, or has exercised, its power under section 22A at any time before making a divorce order, and

(b) gives a direction under subsection (1A) above in respect of a periodical payments order or a secured periodical payments order,

it shall provide for the direction not to take effect until a divorce order is made.]

Note. Sub-s (1B) inserted by Family Law Act 1996, s 66(1), Sch 8, Part I, para 14, as from a day to be appointed, subject to savings in s 66(2) of, and para 5 of Sch 9 to, the 1996 Act.

(2) Where a periodical payments or secured periodical payments order in favour of a party to a marriage is made otherwise than *on or after the grant of a decree of divorce or nullity of marriage* [at such a time as is mentioned in subsection (1A)(c) above], and the marriage in question is subsequently dissolved or annulled but the order continues in force, the order shall, notwithstanding anything in it, cease to have effect on the remarriage of that party, except in relation to any arrears due under it on the date of the remarriage.

Note. Words in square brackets substituted for words in italics by Family Law Act 1996, s 66(1), Sch 8, Part I, para 14, as from a day to be appointed, subject to savings in s 66(2) of, and para 5 of Sch 9 to, the 1996 Act.

(3) If after the grant of *a decree* [an order or decree] dissolving or annulling a marriage either party to that marriage remarries [whether at any time before or after the commencement of this Act], that party shall not be entitled to apply, by reference to the grant of *that decree* [that order or decree], for a financial provision order in his or her favour, or for a property adjustment order, against the other party to that marriage.

Note. Section 28 replaced Matrimonial Proceedings and Property Act 1970, s 7 (p 2368).

Words 'an order or decree' in square brackets substituted for words 'a decree' in italics, and words 'that order or decree' in square brackets substituted for words 'that decree' in italics by Family Law Act 1996, s 66(1), Sch 8, para 14, as from a day to be appointed, subject to savings in s 66(2) of, and para 5 of Sch 9 to, the 1996 Act.

Words 'Whether at … of this Act' in square brackets inserted by Matrimonial and Family Proceedings Act 1984, s 5(3), as from 12 October 1984.

29. Duration of continuing financial provision orders in favour of children, and age limit on making certain orders in their favour—(1) Subject to subsection (3) below, no financial provision order and no order for a transfer of property *under section 24(1)(a)* [such as is mentioned in section 21(2)(a)] above shall be made in favour of a child who has attained the age of eighteen.

Note. Words in square brackets substituted for words in italics by Family Law Act 1996, s 66(1), Sch 8, Part I, para 15, as from a day to be appointed, subject to savings in s 66(2) of, and para 5 of Sch 9 to, the 1996 Act.

[(1A) The term specified in a periodical payments order or secured periodical payments order made in favour of a child shall be such term as the court thinks fit.

(1B) If that term is to begin before the making of the order, it may do so no earlier than—

(a) in the case of an order made by virtue of section 22A(2)(a) or (b) above, except where paragraph (b) below applies, the beginning of the day on which the statement of marital breakdown in question was received by the court;

(b) in the case of an order made by virtue of section 22A(2)(b) above where the application for the divorce order was made following cancellation of an order preventing divorce under section 10 of the 1996 Act, the date of the making of that application;

(c) in the case of an order made by virtue of section 22A(2)(c) above, the date of the making of the application for the divorce order; or

(d) in any other case, the date of the making of the application on which the order is made.]

Note. Sub-ss (1A), (1B) inserted by Family Law Act 1996, s 15, Sch 2, para 7, as from a day to be appointed, subject to savings in s 66(2) of, and para 5 of Sch 9 to, the 1996 Act.

(2) The term to be specified in a periodical payments or secured periodical payments order in favour of a child *may begin with the date of the making of an application for the order in question or any later date* [*or a date ascertained in accordance with subsection (5) or (6) below*] *but*—

(a) shall not in the first instance extend beyond the date of the birthday of the child next following his attaining the upper limit of the compulsory school age (*that is to say, the age that is for the time being that limit by virtue of section 35 of the Education Act, 1944 together with any Order in Council made under that section*) [(construed in accordance with section 8 of the Education Act 1996)], *unless the court thinks it right in the circumstances of the case to specify a later date* [unless the court considers that in the circumstances of the case the welfare of the child requires that it should extend to a later date]; and

(b) shall not in any event, subject to subsection (3) below, extend beyond the date of the child's eighteenth birthday.

Note. Words 'or a date ... below' in square brackets added by Maintenance Orders (Back-dating) Order 1993, SI 1993 No 623, art 2, Sch 1, para 1, as from 5 April 1993. Words 'may begin with ... but' in italics repealed by Family Law Act 1996, s 66(3), Sch 10, as from a day to be appointed, subject to savings in s 66(2) of, and para 5 of Sch 9 to, the 1996 Act. Words '(construed in ... Act 1996)' in square brackets substituted for words '(that is to say ... section)' in italics by Education Act 1996, s 582(1), Sch 37, para 136, as from 1 September 1997. Words 'unless the court ... later date' in square brackets substituted for words 'unless the court ... later date' in italics by Matrimonial and Family Proceedings Act 1984, s 5(4), as from 12 October 1984.

(3) Subsection (1) above, and paragraph (b) of subsection (2), shall not apply in the case of a child, if it appears to the court that—

(a) the child is, or will be, or if an order were made without complying with either or both of those provisions would be, receiving instruction at an educational establishment or undergoing training for a trade, profession or vocation, whether or not he is also, or will also be, in gainful employment; or

(b) there are special circumstances which justify the making of an order without complying with either or both of those provisions.

(4) Any periodical payments order in favour of a child shall, notwithstanding anything in the order, cease to have effect on the death of the person liable to make payments under the order, except in relation to any arrears due under the order on the date of the death.

Note. Section 29 replaced Matrimonial Proceedings and Property Act 1970, s 8 (p 2369).

[(5) Where—

(a) a *maintenance assessment* [maintenance calculation] ('the *current assessment* [current calculation]') is in force with respect to a child; and

(b) an application is made under Part II of this Act for a periodical payments or secured periodical payments order in favour of that child—

(i) in accordance with section 8 of the Child Support Act 1991, and

(ii) before the end of the period of 6 months beginning with the making of the *current assessment* [current calculation]

the term to be specified in any such order made on that application may be expressed to begin on, or at any time after, the earliest permitted date.

(6) For the purposes of subsection (5) above, 'the earliest permitted date' is whichever is the later of—

(a) the date 6 months before the application is made; or

(b) the date on which the *current assessment* [current calculation] took effect or, where successive *maintenance assessments* [maintenance calculations] have been continuously in force with respect to a child, on which the first of *those assessments* [those calculations] took effect.

(7) Where—

(a) a *maintenance assessment* [maintenance calculation] ceases to have effect *or is cancelled* by or under any provision of the Child Support Act 1991; and

(b) an application is made, before the end of the period of 6 months beginning with the relevant date, for a periodical payments or secured periodical payments order in favour of a child with respect to whom that maintenance assessment was in force immediately before it ceased to have effect *or was cancelled,*

the term to be specified in any such order made on that application may begin with the date on which that maintenance assessment ceased to have effect *or, as the case may be, the date with effect from which it was cancelled,* or any later date.

(8) In subsection (7)(b) above—

(a) where the *maintenance assessment* [maintenance calculation]ceased to have effect, the relevant date is the date on which it so ceased; *and*

(*b*)   where the maintenance assessment was cancelled, the relevant date is the later of—
    (*i*)   the date on which the person who cancelled it did so, and
    (*ii*)   the date from which the cancellation first had effect.]

Note. Sub-ss (5)–(8) added by Maintenance Orders (Backdating) Order 1993, SI 1993 No 623, art 2, Sch 1, para 2, as from 5 April 1993. Words 'maintenance calculation' in square brackets in each place they occur in sub-ss (5)–(8) substituted for preceding words in italics, words 'current calculation' in square brackets in each place they occur in sub-ss (5)–(7) substituted for preceding words in italics, words 'maintenance calculations' in square brackets substituted for preceding words in italics and words 'those calculations' in square brackets substituted for preceding words in italics in sub-s (6)(b), words in italics in sub-s (7) repealed and sub-s (8)(b) and word 'and' in italics immediately preceding it repealed by the Child Support, Pensions and Social Security Act 2000, ss 26, 85, Sch 3, para 3(1), (2), Sch 9, Pt I, as from 3 March 2003 in relation to certain cases and as from a day to be appointed for remaining purposes.

30.   Direction for settlement of instrument for securing payments or effecting property adjustment.   Where the court decides to make a financial provision order requiring any payments to be secured or a property adjustment order—
  (a)   it may direct that the matter be referred to one of the conveyancing counsel of the court for him to settle a proper instrument to be executed by all necessary parties; and
  (b)   where the order is to be made in proceedings for *divorce*, nullity of marriage *or judicial separation* it may, if it thinks fit, defer the grant of the decree in question until the instrument has been duly executed.

Note. Section 30 replaced Matrimonial Proceedings and Property Act 1970, s 25 (p 2371). Words in italics repealed by Family Law Act 1996, s 66(3), Sch 10, as from a day to be appointed, subject to savings in s 66(2) of, and para 5 of Sch 9 to, the 1996 Act.

Variation, discharge and enforcement of certain orders, etc.

31.   Variation, discharge, etc of certain orders for financial relief—(1) Where the court has made an order to which this section applies, then, subject to the provisions of this section [and of section 28(1A) above], the court shall have power to vary or discharge the order or to suspend any provision thereof temporarily and to revive the operation of any provision so suspended.

Note. Words in square brackets inserted by Matrimonial and Family Proceedings Act 1984, s 6(2), as from 12 October 1984.

(2)   This section applies to the following orders [under this Part of this Act], that is to say—
  (a)   any *order for maintenance pending suit and any* interim order for maintenance;
  (b)   any periodical payments order;
  (c)   any secured periodical payments order;
  (d)   *any order made by virtue of section 23(3)(c) or 27(7)(b) above (provision for payment of a lump sum by instalments);*
  [(d)   an order for the payment of a lump sum in a case in which the payment is to be by instalments;]
  [(dd) any deferred order made by virtue of section *23(1)(c)* [21(1)(c)] (lump sums) which includes provision made by virtue of—
    (i)   section 25B(4), or
    (ii)   section 25C,
    (provision in respect of pension rights);]
  [(de) any other order for the payment of a lump sum, if it is made at a time when no divorce order has been made, and no separation order is in force, in relation to the marriage;]
  (e)   *any order for a settlement of property under section 24(1)(b) or for a variation of settlement under section 24(1)(c) or (d) above, being an order made on or after the grant of a decree of judicial separation;*

[(e) any order under section 23A of a kind referred to in section 21(2)(b), (c) or (d) which is made on or after the making of a separation order;

(ea) any order under section 23A which is made at a time when no divorce order has been made, and no separation order is in force, in relation to the marriage;]

[(f) any order made under section 24A(1) above for the sale of property;]

(g) a pension sharing order under section 24B above which is made at a time before the decree has been made absolute.]

Note. Words 'under this Part of this Act' in square brackets inserted, words in italics in sub-s (2)(a) repealed, sub-s (2)(d) substituted, reference to '21(1)(c)' in square brackets in sub-s (2)(dd) substituted, sub-s (2)(de) inserted, sub-s (2)(e), (ea) substituted for sub-s (2)(e) by Family Law Act 1996, s 66, Sch 8, Part I, para 16, Sch 10, as from a day to be appointed, subject to savings in s 66(2) of, and para 5 of Sch 9 to, the 1996 Act. Sub-s (2)(dd) inserted by Pensions Act 1995, s 166(3)(a), as from 1 August 1996. Sub-s (2)(f) inserted by Matrimonial Homes and Property Act 1981, s 8(2), as from 1 October 1981. Sub-s (2)(g) inserted by the Welfare Reform and Pensions Act 1999, s 19, Sch 3, paras 1, 7, as from 1 December 2000.

[(2A) Where the court has made an order referred to in subsection (2)(a), (b) or (c) above, then subject to the provisions of this section, the court shall have power to remit the payment of any arrears due under the order or of any part thereof.]

Note. Sub-s (2A) inserted by Administration of Justice Act 1982, s 51, as from 1 January 1983.

[(2B) Where the court has made an order referred to in subsection (2)(dd)(ii) above, this section shall cease to apply to the order on the death of either of the parties to the marriage.]

Note. Sub-s (2B) inserted by Pensions Act 1995, s 166(3)(b), as from 1 August 1996.

(3) The powers exercisable by the court under this section in relation to an order shall be exercisable also in relation to any instrument executed in pursuance of the order.

(4) The court shall not exercise the powers conferred by this section in relation to an order *for a settlement under section 24(1)(b) or for a variation of settlement under section 24(1)(c) or (d)* [referred to in subsection (2)(e)] above except on an application made in proceedings—

(a) *for the rescission of the decree of judicial separation by reference to which the order was made, or*

(b) *for the dissolution of the marriage in question* [on an application for a divorce order in relation to the marriage].

Note. Words in square brackets substituted for words in italics by Family Law Act 1996, s 66(1), Sch 8, Part I, para 16, as from a day to be appointed, subject to savings in s 66(2) of, and para 5 of Sch 9 to, the 1996 Act.

[(4A) In relation to an order which falls within subsection (2)(de) or (ea) above ('the subsection (2) order')—

(a) the powers conferred by this section may be exercised—

(i) only on an application made before the subsection (2) order has or, but for paragraph (b) below, would have taken effect; and

(ii) only if, at the time when the application is made, no divorce order has been made in relation to the marriage and no separation order has been so made since the subsection (2) order was made; and

(b) an application made in accordance with paragraph (a) above prevents the subsection (2) order from taking effect before the application has been dealt with.

[(4AA) No variation—

(a) of a financial provision order made under section 22A above, other than an interim order, or

(b) of a property adjustment order made under section 23A above,
shall be made so as to take effect before the making of a divorce order or
separation order in relation to the marriage, unless the court is satisfied that the
circumstances of the case are exceptional, and that it would be just and reasonable
for the variation to be so made.

(4AB) No variation of a pension sharing order under section 24B above shall be
made so as to take effect before the making of a divorce order in relation to the
marriage.]

(4B) No variation of a pension sharing order [under section 24BB above] shall
be made so as to take effect before the decree is made absolute.

(4C) The variation of a pension sharing order prevents the order taking effect
before the end of such period after the making of the variation as may be
prescribed by regulations made by the Lord Chancellor.]

Note. Sub-ss (4A)–(4C): inserted by the Welfare Reform and Pensions Act 1999, s 19, Sch 3,
para 7(3), as from 1 December 2000.

Sub-ss (4AA), (4AB): inserted by the Family Law Act 1996, s 66(1), Sch 8, Pt I, para 16(4) (as
amended by the Welfare Reform and Pensions Act 1999, s 84(1), Sch 12, Pt I, paras 64, 66(1),
(7)), as from a day to be appointed, subject to savings in s 66(2) of, and para 5 of Sch 9 to, the
1996 Act.

(5) [Subject to subsections (7A) to *(7F)* [(7G)] below and without prejudice to
any power exercisable by virtue of subsection (2)(d), (dd) *or (e)* [, (e) or (g)] above
or otherwise than by virtue of this section,] no property adjustment order [or
pension sharing order] shall be made on an application for the variation of a
periodical payments or secured periodical payments order made (whether in favour
of a party to a marriage or in favour of a child of the family) under *section 23* [section
22A or 23] above, and no order for the payment of a lump sum shall be made on an
application for the variation of a periodical payments or secured periodical payments
order in favour of a party to a marriage (whether made under *section 23* [section 22A
or 23] or under section 27 above).

Note. Words 'Subject to … section' in square brackets inserted, and words 'section 22A or 23'
in square brackets substituted for words 'section 23' in italics by Family Law Act 1996, s 66(1),
Sch 8, Part I, para 16, as from 1 November 1998, subject to savings in s 66(2) of, and para 5 of
Sch 9 to, the 1996 Act. Reference to '(7G)' in square brackets substituted for preceding
reference in italics, words ', (e) or (g)' in square brackets substituted for preceding words in
italics and words 'or person sharing order' in square brackets inserted by the Welfare Reform
and Pensions Act 1999, s 19, Sch 3, paras 1, 7, as from 1 December 2000.

(6) Where the person liable to make payments under a secured periodical
payments order has died, an application under this section relating to that order
may be made by the person entitled to payments under the order [(and to any order made
under section 24A(1) above which requires the proceeds of sale of property to be
used for securing those payments) may be made by the person entitled to
payments under the periodical payments order] or by the personal representatives
of the deceased person, but no such application shall, except with the permission
of the court, be made after the end of the period of six months from the date on
which representation in regard to the estate of that person is first taken out.

Note. Words in square brackets substituted for words in italics by Matrimonial Homes and
Property Act 1981, s 8(2), as from 1 October 1981. The forfeiture rule (as defined by Forfeiture
Act 1982, s 1(1) (p 2927)) shall not be taken to preclude any person from making any
application under this subsection or the making of any order on the application: see Forfeiture
Act 1982, s 3(1), (2)(b) (p 2928), as from 13 October 1982.

(7) *In exercising the powers conferred by this section the court shall have regard to all the
circumstances of the case, including any change in any of the matters to which the court was
required to have regard when making the order to which the application relates and, where the
party against whom that order was made has died, the changed circumstances resulting from
his or her death.*

[(7) In exercising the powers conferred by this section the court shall have regard to all the circumstances of the case, first consideration being given to the welfare while a minor of any child of the family who has not attained the age of eighteen, and the circumstances of the case shall include any change in any of the matters to which the court was required to have regard when making the order to which the application relates, and—

(a) in the case of a periodical payments or secured periodical payments order made *on or after the grant of a decree of divorce or nullity of marriage, the court shall consider* [in favour of a party to a marriage, the court shall, if the marriage has been dissolved or annulled, consider] whether in all the circumstances and after having regard to any such change it would be appropriate to vary the order so that payments under the order are required to be made or secured only for such further period as will in the opinion of the court be sufficient [(in the light of any proposed exercise by the court, where the marriage has been dissolved, of its powers under subsection (7B) below)] to enable the party in whose favour the order was made to adjust without undue hardship to the termination of those payments;

(b) in a case where the party against whom the order was made has died, the circumstances of the case shall also include the changed circumstances resulting from his or her death].

Note. Sub-s (7) in square brackets substituted for sub-s (7) in italics by Matrimonial and Family Proceedings Act 1984, s 6(3), as from 12 October 1984. Words '(in the light of ... below)' in square brackets inserted, as from 1 November 1998 and words 'in favour of ... consider' in square brackets substituted for words 'on or after ... consider' in italics, as from a day to be appointed by Family Law Act 1996, s 66(1), Sch 8, Part I, para 16. These amendments apply to orders made before their commencement; see para 6 of Sch 9 to the 1996 Act.

[(7A) Subsection (7B) below applies where, after the dissolution of a marriage, the court—

(a) discharges a periodical payments order or secured periodical payments order made in favour of a party to the marriage; or

(b) varies such an order so that payments under the order are required to be made or secured only for such further period as is determined by the court.

(7B) The court has power, in addition to any power it has apart from this subsection, to make supplemental provision consisting of any of—

(a) an order for the payment of a lump sum in favour of a party to the marriage;

(b) one or more property adjustment orders in favour of a party to the marriage;

[(ba) one or more pension sharing orders;]

(c) a direction that the party in whose favour the original order discharged or varied was made is not entitled to make any further application for—

(i) a periodical payments or secured periodical payments order, or

(ii) an extension of the period to which the original order is limited by any variation made by the court.

(7C) An order for the payment of a lump sum made under subsection (7B) above may—

(a) provide for the payment of that sum by instalments of such amount as may be specified in the order; and

(b) require the payment of the instalments to be secured to the satisfaction of the court.

(7D) Subsections (7) and (8) of section 22A above apply where the court makes an order for the payment of a lump sum under subsection (7B) above as they apply where it makes such an order under section 22A above.

(7E) If under subsection (7B) above the court makes more than one property adjustment order in favour of the same party to the marriage, each of those orders must fall within a different paragraph of section 21(2) above.

2540 Matrimonial Causes Act 1973, s 31

(7F) Sections 24A and 30 above apply where the court makes a property adjustment order under subsection (7B) above as they apply where it makes such an order under section 23A above.]

[(7G) *Subsections (3) to (5) of section 24B* [Section 24BA(5) to (7)] above apply in relation to a pension sharing order under subsection (7B) above as they apply in relation to a pension sharing order under *that section* [section 24B above].]

Note. Sub-ss (7A)–(7F) inserted by Family Law Act 1996, s 66(1), Sch 8, Part I, para 16, as from 1 November 1998. Insertion of sub-ss (7A)–(7F) applies to orders made before their commencement; see para 6 of Sch 9 to the 1996 Act. Sub-s (7G) inserted by the Welfare Reform and Pensions Act 1999, s 19, Sch 3, paras 1, 7, as from 1 December 2000. Words 'section 24BA(5) to (7)' and 'section 24B above' in square brackets substituted for preceding words in italics by the Family Law Act 1996, s 66(1), Sch 8, Pt I, para 16(9) (as inserted by the Welfare Reform and Pensions Act 1999, s 84(1), Sch 12, Pt I, paras 64, 66(1), (9)), as from a day to be appointed, subject to savings in s 66(2) of, and para 5 of Sch 9 to, the 1996 Act.

(8) The personal representatives of a deceased person against whom a secured periodical payments order was made shall not be liable for having distributed any part of the estate of the deceased after the expiration of the period of six months referred to in subsection (6) above on the ground that they ought to have taken into account the possibility that the court might permit an application under this section to be made after that period by the person entitled to payments under the order; but this subsection shall not prejudice any power to recover any part of the estate so distributed arising by virtue of the making of an order in pursuance of this section.

(9) In considering for the purposes of subsection (6) above the question when representation was first taken out, a grant limited to settled land or to trust property shall be left out of account and a grant limited to real estate or to personal estate shall be left out of account unless a grant limited to the remainder of the estate has previously been made or is made at the same time.

[(10) Where the court, in exercise of its powers under this section, decides to vary or discharge a periodical payments or secured periodical payments order, then, subject to section 28(1) and (2) above, the court shall have power to direct that the variation or discharge shall not take effect until the expiration of such period as may be specified in the order.]

Note. Sub-s (10) added by Matrimonial and Family Proceedings Act 1984, s 6(4), as from 12 October 1984.

Section 31 replaced Matrimonial Proceedings and Property Act 1970, s 9 (p 2370).

[(11) Where—
(a) a periodical payments or secured periodical payments order in favour of more than one child ('the order') is in force;
(b) the order requires payments specified in it to be made to or for the benefit of more than one child without apportioning those payments between them;
(c) *a maintenance assessment* [maintenance calculation] ('*the assessment* [the calculation]') is made with respect to one or more, but not all, of the children with respect to whom those payments are to be made; and
(d) an application is made, before the end of the period of 6 months beginning with the date on which *the assessment* [the calculation] was made, for the variation or discharge of the order,

the court may, in exercise of its powers under this section to vary or discharge the order, direct that the variation or discharge shall take effect from the date on which the assessment took effect or any later date.

(12) Where—
(a) an order ('the child order') of a kind prescribed for the purposes of section 10(1) of the Child Support Act 1991 is affected by a *maintenance assessment* [maintenance calculation];

(b) on the date on which the child order became so affected there was in force a periodical payments or secured periodical payments order ('the spousal order') in favour of a party to a marriage having the care of the child in whose favour the child order was made; and

(c) an application is made, before the end of the period of 6 months beginning with the date on which the *maintenance assessment* [maintenance calculation] was made, for the spousal order to be varied or discharged,

the court may, in exercise of its powers under this section to vary or discharge the spousal order, direct that the variation or discharge shall take effect from the date on which the child order became so affected or any later date.

(13) For the purposes of subsection (12) above, an order is affected if it ceases to have effect or is modified by or under section 10 of the Child Support Act 1991.

(14) Subsections (11) and (12) above are without prejudice to any other power of the court to direct that the variation or discharge of an order under this section shall take effect from a date earlier than that on which the order for variation or discharge was made.]

[(15) The power to make regulations under subsection (4C) above shall be exercisable by statutory instrument which shall be subject to annulment in persuance of a resolution of either House of Parliament.]

Note. Sub-ss (11)–(14) added by Maintenance Orders (Backdating) Order 1993, SI 1993 No 623, art 2, Sch 1, para 3, as from 5 April 1993. Words 'maintenance calculation' in square brackets in each place they occur in sub-ss (11), (12) substituted for preceding words in italics and words 'the calculation' in both places they occur in sub-s (11) substituted for preceding words in italics by the Child Support, Pensions and Social Security Act 2000, s 26, Sch 3, para 3(1), (3), as from a day to be appointed. Sub-s (15) inserted by the Welfare Reform and Pensions Act 1999, s 19, Sch 3, paras 1, 7, as from 1 December 2000.

[31A. Variation etc following reconciliations—(1) Where, at a time before the making of a divorce order—

(a) an order ('a paragraph (a) order') for the payment of a lump sum has been made under section 22A above in favour of a party,

(b) such an order has been made in favour of a child of the family but the payment has not yet been made, or

(c) a property adjustment order ('a paragraph (c) order') has been made under section 23A above,

the court may, on an application made jointly by the parties to the marriage, vary or discharge the order.

(2) Where the court varies or discharges a paragraph (a) order, it may order the repayment of an amount equal to the whole or any part of the lump sum.

(3) Where the court varies or discharges a paragraph (c) order, it may (if the order has taken effect)—

(a) order any person to whom property was transferred in pursuance of the paragraph (c) order to transfer—
  (i) the whole or any part of that property, or
  (ii) the whole or any part of any property appearing to the court to represent that property,
  in favour of a party to the marriage or a child of the family; or

(b) vary any settlement to which the order relates in favour of any person or extinguish or reduce any person's interest under that settlement.

(4) Where the court acts under subsection (3) it may make such supplemental provision (including a further property adjustment order or an order for the payment of a lump sum) as it thinks appropriate in consequence of any transfer, variation, extinguishment or reduction to be made under paragraph (a) or (b) of that subsection.

(5) Sections 24A and 30 above apply for the purposes of this section as they apply where the court makes a property adjustment order under section 23A or 24 above.

(6) The court shall not make an order under subsection (2), (3) or (4) above unless it appears to it that there has been a reconciliation between the parties to the marriage.

(7) The court shall also not make an order under subsection (3) or (4) above unless it appears to it that the order will not prejudice the interests of—

   (a) any child of the family; or

   (b) any person who has acquired any right or interest in consequence of the paragraph (c) order and is not a party to the marriage or a child of the family.]

Note. Section 31A inserted by Family Law Act 1996, s 15, Sch 2, para 8, as from a day to be appointed, subject to savings in s 66(2) of, and para 5 of Sch 9 to, the 1996 Act.

32. Payment of certain arrears unenforceable without the leave of the court—
(1) A person shall not be entitled to enforce through the High Court or any county court the payment of any arrears due under *an order for maintenance pending suit, an interim order for maintenance or any financial provision order* [any financial provision order under this Part of this Act or any interim order for maintenance] without the leave of that court if those arrears became due more than twelve months before proceedings to enforce the payment of them are begun.

Note. Words in square brackets substituted for words in italics by Family Law Act 1996, s 66(1), Sch 8, Part I, para 17, as from a day to be appointed, subject to savings in s 66(2) of, and para 5 of Sch 9 to, the 1996 Act.

(2) The court hearing an application for the grant of leave under this section may refuse leave, or may grant leave subject to such restrictions and conditions (including conditions as to the allowing of time for payment or the making of payment by instalments) as that court thinks proper, or may remit the payment of the arrears or of any part thereof.

(3) An application for the grant of leave under this section shall be made in such manner as may be prescribed by rules of court.

Note. Section 32 replaced Matrimonial Proceedings and Property Act 1970, s 10 (p 2370).

33. Orders for repayment in certain cases of sums paid under certain orders—(1) Where on an application made under this section in relation to an order to which this section applies it appears to the court that by reason of—

   (a) a change in the circumstances of the person entitled to, or liable to make, payments under the order since the order was made, or

   (b) the changed circumstances resulting from the death of the person so liable.

the amount received by the person entitled to payments under the order in respect of a period after those circumstances changed or after the death of the person liable to make payments under the order, as the case may be, exceeds the amount which the person so liable or his or her personal representatives should have been required to pay, the court may order the respondent to the application to pay to the applicant such sum, not exceeding the amount of the excess, as the court thinks just.

   (2) *This section applies to the following orders, that is to say—*

   (a) *any order for maintenance pending suit and any interim order for maintenance;*

   (b) *any periodical payments order; and*

   (c) *any secured periodical payments order.*

   [(2) This section applies to the following orders under this Part of this Act—

   (a) any periodical payments order;

   (b) any secured periodical payments order; and

   (c) any interim order for maintenance, so far as it requires the making of periodical payments.]

Note. Sub-s (2) substituted by Family Law Act 1996, s 66(1), Sch 8, Part I, para 18, as from a day to be appointed, subject to savings in s 66(2) of, and para 5 of Sch 9 to, the 1996 Act.

(3) An application under this section may be made by the person liable to make payments under an order to which this section applies or his or her personal representatives and may be made against the person entitled to payments under the order or her or his personal representatives.

(4) An application under this section may be made in proceedings in the High Court or a county court for—

(a) the variation or discharge of the order to which this section applies, or

(b) leave to enforce, or the enforcement of, the payment of arrears under that order;

but when not made in such proceedings shall be made to a county court, and accordingly references in this section to the court are references to the High Court or a county court, as the circumstances require.

(5) The jurisdiction conferred on a county court by this section shall be exercisable notwithstanding that by reason of the amount claimed in the application the jurisdiction would not but for this subsection be exercisable by a county court.

(6) An order under this section for the payment of any sum may provide for the payment of that sum by instalments of such amount as may be specified in the order.

Note. Section 33(1)–(4), (6) replaced Matrimonial Proceedings and Property Act 1970, s 11 (p 2371) and sub-s (5) replaced in part ibid, s 34(1) (p 2382).

[Consent orders

33A. Consent orders for financial provision or property adjustment—(1) Notwithstanding anything in the preceding provisions of this Part of this Act, on an application for a consent order for financial relief the court may, unless it has reason to think that there are other circumstances into which it ought to inquire, make an order in the terms agreed on the basis only of the prescribed information furnished with the application.

(2) Subsection (1) above applies [(subject, in the case of the powers of the court under section 31A above, to subsections (6) and (7) of that section)] to an application for a consent order varying or discharging an order for financial relief as it applies to an application for an order for financial relief.

(3) In this section—

'consent order', in relation to an application for an order, means an order in the terms applied for to which the respondent agrees;

'order for financial relief' means *an order under any of sections 23, 24, 24A* [, 24B] *or 27 above* [any of the following orders under this Part of this Act, that is to say, any financial provision order, any property adjustment order, any order for the sale of property or any interim order for maintenance]; and

'prescribed' means prescribed by rules of court.]

Note. Section 33A inserted by Matrimonial and Family Proceedings Act 1984, s 7, as from 12 October 1984. Words in square brackets in sub-s (2) inserted, and second words in square brackets in sub-s (3) substituted for words in italics by Family Law Act 1996, s 66(1), Sch 8, Part I, para 19, as from a day to be appointed, subject to savings in s 66(2) of, and para 5 of Sch 9 to, the 1996 Act. Reference to ', 24B' in square brackets in sub-s (3) inserted by the Welfare Reform and Pensions Act 1999, s 19, Sch 3, paras 1, 8, as from 1 December 2000.

Maintenance agreements

34. Validity of maintenance agreements—(1) If a maintenance agreement includes a provision purporting to restrict any right to apply to a court for an order containing financial arrangements, then—

(a) that provision shall be void; but

(b) any other financial arrangements contained in the agreement shall not thereby be rendered void or unenforceable and shall, unless they are void or enenforceable for any other reason (and subject to sections 35 and 36 below), be binding on the parties to the agreement.

(2) In this section and in section 35 below—

'maintenance agreement' means any agreement in writing made, whether before or after the commencement of this Act, between the parties to a marriage, being—

(a) an agreement containing financial arrangements, whether made during the continuance or after the dissolution or annulment of the marriage; or

(b) a separation agreement which contains no financial arrangements in a case where no other agreement in writing between the same parties contains such arrangements;

'financial arrangements' means provisions governing the rights and liabilities towards one another when living separately of the parties to a marriage (including a marriage which has been dissolved or annulled) in respect of the making or securing of payments or the disposition or use of any property, including such rights and liabilities with respect to the maintenance or education of any child, whether or not a child of the family.

Note. Section 34 replaced Matrimonial Proceedings and Property Act 1970, s 13 (p 2371).

35. Alteration of agreements by court during lives of parties—(1) Where a maintenance agreement is for the time being subsisting and each of the parties to the agreement is for the time being either domiciled or resident in England and Wales, then, subject to subsection (3) below, either party may apply to the court or to a magistrates' court for an order under this section.

(2) If the court to which the application is made is satisfied either—

(a) that by reason of a change in the circumstances in the light of which any financial arrangements contained in the agreement were made or, as the case may be, financial arrangements were omitted from it (including a change foreseen by the parties when making the agreement), the agreement should be altered so as to make different, or, as the case may be, so as to contain, financial arrangements, or

(b) that the agreement does not contain proper financial arrangements with respect to any child of the family,

then subject to subsections (3), (4) and (5) below, that court may by order make such alterations in the agreement—

(i) by varying or revoking any financial arrangements contained in it, or

(ii) by inserting in it financial arrangements for the benefit of one of the parties to the agreement or of a child of the family,

as may appear to that court to be just having regard to all the circumstances, including, if relevant, the matters mentioned in *section 25(3)* [section 25(4)] above; and the agreement shall have effect thereafter as if any alteration made by the order had been made by agreement between the parties and for valuable consideration.

Note. Words in square brackets substituted for words in italics by Matrimonial and Family Proceedings Act 1984, s 46(1), Sch 1, para 13(a), as from 12 October 1984.

(3) A magistrates' court shall not entertain an application under subsection (1) above unless both the parties to the agreement are resident in England and Wales and *at least one of the parties is resident in the petty sessions area (within the meaning of the Magistrates' Courts Act 1952) for which the court acts [within the commission area (within the meaning of the Justices of the Peace Act 1979 [the Justices of the Peace Act 1997]) for which the court is appointed]* [the court acts in, or is authorised by the Lord Chancellor to act for, a local justice area in which at least one of the parties is resident], and shall not have power to make any order on such an application except—

(a) in a case where the agreement includes no provision for periodical payments by either of the parties, an order inserting provision for the making by one of the parties of periodical payments for the maintenance of the other party or for the maintenance of any child of the family;

(b) in a case where the agreement includes provision for the making by one of the parties of periodical payments, an order increasing or reducing the rate of, or terminating, any of those payments.

Note. Words 'within the commission area (within the meaning of the Justices of the Peace Act 1979) for which the court is appointed' in square brackets substituted for words in italics by Matrimonial and Family Proceedings Act 1984, s 46(1), Sch 1, para 13(b), as from 12 October 1984. Words 'the Justices of the Peace Act 1997' in square brackets substituted for words 'the Justices of the Peace Act 1979' in italics by the Justices of the Peace Act 1997, s 73(2), Sch 5, para 14, as from 19 June 1997. Words from '(within' to '1997)' in italics repealed by the Access to Justice Act 1999, s 106, Sch 15, Pt V(1), as from 27 September 1999. Words from 'the court acts' to 'parties is resident' in square brackets substituted for words from 'at least one' to 'court is appointed' in italics by the Courts Act 2003, s 109(1), Sch 8, para 169, as from a day to be appointed.

(4) Where a court decides to alter, by order under this section, an agreement by inserting provision for the making or securing by one of the parties to the agreement of periodical payments for the maintenance of the other party or by increasing the rate of the periodical payments which the agreement provides shall be made by one of the parties for the maintenance of the other, the term for which the payments or, as the case may be, the additional payments attributable to the increase are to be made under the agreement as altered by the order shall be such term as the court may specify, subject to the following limits, that is to say—

(a) where the payments will not be secured, the term shall be so defined as not to extend beyond the death of either of the parties to the agreement or the remarriage of the party to whom the payments are to be made;

(b) where the payments will be secured, the term shall be so defined as not to extend beyond the death or remarriage of that party.

(5) Where a court decides to alter, by order under this section, an agreement by inserting provision for the making or securing by one of the parties to the agreement of periodical payments for the maintenance of a child of the family or by increasing the rate of the periodical payments which the agreement provides shall be made or secured by one of the parties for the maintenance of such a child, then, in deciding the term for which under the agreement as altered by the order the payments, or as the case may be, the additional payments attributable to the increase are to be made or secured for the benefit of the child, the court shall apply the provisions of section 29(2) and (3) above as to age limits as if the order in question were a periodical payments or secured periodical payments order in favour of the child.

(6) For the avoidance of doubt it is hereby declared that nothing in this section or in section 34 above affects any power of a court before which any proceedings between the parties to a maintenance agreement are brought under any other enactment (including a provision of this Act) to make an order containing financial arrangements or any right of either to apply for such an order in such proceedings.

[(7) Subject to subsection (5) above, references in this Act to any such order as is mentioned in section 21 above shall not include references to any order under this section.]

Note. Section 35 replaced Matrimonial Proceedings and Property Act 1970, s 14 (p 2372). Sub-s (7) inserted by Family Law Act 1996, s 66(1), Sch 8, Part I, para 20, as from a day to be appointed, subject to savings in s 66(2) of, and para 5 of Sch 9 to, the 1996 Act.

36. Alteration of agreements by court after death of one party—(1) Where a maintenance agreement within the meaning of section 34 above provides for the continuation of payments under the agreement after the death of one of the parties and that party dies domiciled in England and Wales, the surviving party or the personal representatives of the deceased party may, subject to subsections (2) and (3) below, apply to the High Court or a county court for an order under section 35 above.

Note. The forfeiture rule (as defined by Forfeiture Act 1982, s 1(1) (p 2927)) shall not be taken to preclude any person from making any application under this subsection or the making of any order on the application: see Forfeiture Act 1982, s 3(1), (2)(b) (p 2928) as from 13 October 1982.

(2) An application under this section shall not, except with the permission of the High Court or a county court, be made after the end of the period of six months from the date on which representation in regard to the estate of the deceased is first taken out.

(3) A county court shall not entertain an application under this section, or an application for permission to make an application under this section, unless it would have jurisdiction by virtue of *section 7 of the Family Provision Act 1966* [section 22 of the Inheritance (Provision for Family and Dependants) Act 1975] (which confers jurisdiction on county courts in proceedings under *the Inheritance (Family Provision) Act 1938 or section 26 of the Matrimonial Causes Act 1965 if the value of the deceased's net estate* [that Act if the value of the property mentioned in that section] does not exceed £5,000 or such larger sum as may be fixed by order of the Lord Chancellor) to hear and determine proceedings for an order under *section 26 of the Matrimonial Causes Act 1965 (application for maintenance out of deceased's estate by former spouse)* [section 2 of that Act] in relation to the deceased's estate.

Note. Words in square brackets substituted for words in italics by Inheritance (Provision for Family and Dependants) Act 1975, s 26(1), as from 1 April 1976.

(4) If a maintenance agreement is altered by a court on an application made in pursuance of subsection (1) above, the like consequences shall ensue as if the alteration had been made immediately before the death by agreement between the parties and for valuable consideration.

(5) The provisions of this section shall not render the personal representatives of the deceased liable for having distributed any part of the estate of the deceased after the expiration of the period of six months referred to in subsection (2) above on the ground that they ought to have taken into account the possibility that a court might permit an application by virtue of this section to be made by the surviving party after that period; but this subsection shall not prejudice any power to recover any part of the estate so distributed arising by virtue of the making of an order in pursuance of this section.

(6) Section 31(9) above shall apply for the purposes of subsection (2) above as it applies for the purposes of subsection (6) of section 31.

(7) Subsection (3) of *section 7 of the Family Provision Act 1966 (transfer to county court proceedings commenced in the High Court) and paragraphs (a) and (b) of subsection (5)* [section 22 of the Inheritance (Provision for Family and Dependants) Act 1975 (which enables rules of court to provide for the transfer from a county court to the High Court or from the High Court to a county court of proceedings for an order under section 2 of that Act) and paragraphs (a) and (b) of subsection (4)] of that section (provisions relating to proceedings commenced in county court before coming into force of order of the Lord Chancellor under that section) shall apply in relation to proceedings consisting of any such application as is referred to in subsection (3) above as they apply in relation to *any such proceedings as are referred to in subsection (1) of that section* [proceedings for an order under section 2 of that Act.]

Note. Words in square brackets substituted for words in italics by Inheritance (Provision for Family and Dependants) Act 1975, s 26(1), as from 1 April 1976. Section 36 replaced Matrimonial Proceedings and Property Act 1970, s 15 (p 2373).

Miscellaneous and supplemental

37. Avoidance of transactions intended to prevent or reduce financial relief—
(1) For the purposes of this section 'financial relief' means relief under any of the provisions of sections *22, 23, 24,* [24B,] *27, 31 (except subsection (6))* [22A to 24, 27,

31 (except subsection (6)), 31A] and 35 above, and any reference in this section to defeating a person's claim for financial relief is a reference to preventing financial relief from being granted to that person, or to that person for the benefit of a child of the family, or reducing the amount of any financial relief which might be so granted, or frustrating or impeding the enforcement of any order which might be or has been made at his instance under any of those provisions.

Note. Words in square brackets substituted for words in italics by Family Law Act 1996, s 66(1), Sch 8, Part I, para 21, as from a day to be appointed, subject to savings in s 66(2) of, and para 5 of Sch 9 to, the 1996 Act. Reference to '24B,' in square brackets inserted by the Welfare Reform and Pensions Act 1999, s 19, Sch 3, paras 1, 9, as from 1 December 2000.

(2) Where proceedings for financial relief are brought by one person against another, the court may, on the application of the first-mentioned person—
  (a) if it is satisfied that the other party to the proceedings is, with the intention of defeating the claim for financial relief, about to make any disposition or to transfer out of the jurisdiction or otherwise deal with any property, make such order as it thinks fit for restraining the other party from so doing or otherwise for protecting the claim;
  (b) if it is satisfied that the other party has, with that intention, made a reviewable disposition and that if the disposition were set aside financial relief or different financial relief would be granted to the applicant, make an order setting aside the disposition;
  (c) if it is satisfied, in a case where an order has been obtained under any of the provisions mentioned in subsection (1) above by the applicant against the other party, that the other party has, with that intention, made a reviewable disposition, make an order setting aside the disposition;
and an application for the purposes of paragraph (b) above shall be made in the proceedings for the financial relief in question.

(3) Where the court makes an order under subsection (2)(b) or (c) above setting aside a disposition it shall give such consequential directions as it thinks fit for giving effect to the order (including directions requiring the making of any payments or the disposal of any property).

(4) Any disposition made by the other party to the proceedings for financial relief in question (whether before or after the commencement of those proceedings) is a reviewable disposition for the purposes of subsection (2)(b) and (c) above unless it was made for valuable consideration (other than marriage) to a person who, at the time of the disposition, acted in relation to it in good faith and without notice of any intention on the part of the other party to defeat the applicant's claim for financial relief.

(5) Where an application is made under this section with respect to a disposition which took place less than three years before the date of the application or with respect to a disposition or other dealing with property which is about to take place and the court is satisfied—
  (a) in a case falling within subsection (2)(a) or (b) above, that the disposition or other dealing would (apart from this section) have the consequence, or
  (b) in a case falling within subsection (2)(c) above, that the disposition has had the consequence,
of defeating the applicant's claim for financial relief, it shall be presumed, unless the contrary is shown, that the person who disposed of or is about to dispose of or deal with the property did so or, as the case may be, is about to do so, with the intention of defeating the applicant's claim for financial relief.

(6) In this section 'disposition' does not include any provision contained in a will or codicil but, with that exception, includes any conveyance, assurance or gift of property of any description, whether made by an instrument or otherwise.

(7) This section does not apply to a disposition made before 1 January 1968.

Note. Section 37 replaced Matrimonial Proceedings and Property Act 1970, s 16 (p 2354).

38. Orders for repayment in certain cases of sums paid after cessation of order by reason of remarriage—(1) Where—

    (a) a periodical payments or secured periodical payments order in favour of a party to a marriage (hereafter in this section referred to as 'a payments order') has ceased to have effect by reason of the remarriage of that party, and

    (b) the person liable to make payments under the order or his or her personal representatives made payments in accordance with it in respect of a period after the date of the remarriage in the mistaken belief that the order was still subsisting,

the person so liable or his or her personal representatives shall not be entitled to bring proceedings in respect of a cause of action arising out of the circumstances mentioned in paragraphs (a) and (b) above against the person entitled to payments under the order or her or his personal representatives, but may instead make an application against that person or her or his personal representatives under this section.

(2) On an application under this section the court may order the respondent to pay to the applicant a sum equal to the amount of the payments made in respect of the period mentioned in subsection (1)(b) above or, if it appears to the court that it would be unjust to make that order, it may either order the respondent to pay to the applicant such lesser sum as it thinks fit or dismiss the application.

(3) An application under this section may be made in proceedings in the High Court or a county court for leave to enforce, or the enforcement of, payment of arrears under the order in question, but when not made in such proceedings shall be made to a county court; and accordingly references in this section to the court are references to the High Court or a county court, as the circumstances require.

(4) The jurisdiction conferred on a county court by this section shall be exercisable notwithstanding that by reason of the amount claimed in the application the jurisdiction would not but for this subsection be exercisable by a county court.

(5) An order under this section for the payment of any sum may provide for the payment of that sum by instalments of such amount as may be specified in the order.

(6) *The clerk of a magistrates' court* [*A justices' chief executive*] [The designated officer for a magistrates' court] to whom any payments under a payments order are required to be made, and the collecting officer under an attachment of earnings order made to secure payments under a payments order, shall not be liable—

    (a) in the case of *the clerk* [*the justices' chief executive*] [the designated officer], for any act done by him in pursuance of the payments order after the date on which that order ceased to have effect by reason of the remarriage of the person entitled to payments under it, and

    (b) in the case of the collecting officer, for any act done by him after that date in accordance with any enactment or rule of court specifying how payments made to him in compliance with the attachment of earnings order are to be dealt with,

if, but only if, the act was one which he would have been under a duty to do had the payments order not so ceased to have effect and the act was done before notice in writing of the fact that the person so entitled had remarried was given to him by or on behalf of that person, the person liable to make payments under the payments order or the personal representatives of either of those persons.

(7) In this section 'collecting officer', in relation to an attachment of earnings order, means the officer of the High Court, the registrar of a county court or *the clerk of a magistrates' court* [*a justices' chief executive*] [the designated officer for a magistrates court] to whom a person makes payments in compliance with the order.

Note. Section 38 replaced Matrimonial Proceedings and Property Act 1970, s 22 (p 2377). Words 'A justices' chief executive' in square brackets substituted for words 'The clerk of a magistrates' court' in italics and words 'the justices' chief executive' in square brackets substituted for words 'the clerk' in italics in sub-s (6) and words in square brackets substituted for words in italics in sub-s (70 by the Access to Justice Act 1999, s 90, Sch 13, para 82, as from 1 April 2001. Words 'The designated officer for a magistrates' court' and 'the designated officer' in square brackets in sub-s (6) substituted for preceding words in italics and words 'the designated officer for a magistrates' court' in square brackets substituted for preceding words in italics by the Courts Act 2003, s 109(1), Sch 8, para 170(1)–(3), as from a day to be appointed.

39. Settlement, etc, made in compliance with a property adjustment order may be avoided on bankruptcy of settlor. The fact that a settlement or transfer of property had to be made in order to comply with a property adjustment order shall not prevent that settlement or transfer from being *a settlement of property to which section 42(1) of the Bankruptcy Act 1914 (avoidance of certain settlements) applies* [a transaction in respect of which an order may be made under section 339 or 340 of the Insolvency Act 1986 (transfers at an undervalue and preferences)].

Note. Section 39 replaced Matrimonial Proceedings and Property Act 1970, s 23 (p 2358). Words in square brackets substituted for words in italics by Insolvency Act 1985, s 235(1), Sch 8, para 23, and Insolvency Act 1986, s 439(2), Sch 14. For a transitional provision, see s 437 of, and Part II, para 10 of Sch 11 to, the 1986 Act.

40. Payments, etc, under order made in favour of person suffering from mental disorder. Where the court makes an order under this Part of this Act requiring payments (including a lump sum payment) to be made, or property to be transferred, to a party to a marriage and the court is satisfied that the person in whose favour the order is made is incapable, by reason of mental disorder within the meaning of the Mental Health Act 1959, of managing and administering his or her property and affairs then, subject to any order, direction or authority made or given in relation to that person under Part VIII of that Act, the court may order the payments to be made, or as the case may be, the property to be transferred, to such persons having charge of that person as the court may direct.

Note. Section 40 replaced Matrimonial Proceedings and Property Act 1970, s 26 (p 2378).
 For the definition and classification of 'mental disorder', see Mental Health Act 1983, s 1(2).

[40A Appeals relating to pension sharing orders which have taken effect—(1) Subsections (2) and (3) below apply where an appeal against a pension sharing order is begun on or after the day on which the order takes effect.

(2) If the pension sharing order relates to a person's rights under a pension arrangement, the appeal court may not set aside or vary the order if the person responsible for the pension arrangement has acted to his detriment in reliance on the taking effect of the order.

(3) If the pension sharing order relates to a person's shareable state scheme rights, the appeal court may not set aside or vary the order if the Secretary of State has acted to his detriment in reliance on the taking effect of the order.

(4) In determining for the purposes of subsection (2) or (3) above whether a person has acted to his detriment in reliance on the taking effect of the order, the appeal court may disregard any detriment which in its opinion is insignificant.

(5) Where subsection (2) or (3) above applies, the appeal court may make such further orders (including one or more pension sharing orders) as it thinks fit for the purpose of putting the parties in the position it considers appropriate.

(6) Section 24C above only applies to a pension sharing order under this section if the decision of the appeal court can itself be the subject of an appeal.

(7) In subsection (2) above, the reference to the person responsible for the pension arrangement is to be read in accordance with section 25D(4) above.]

Note. This section inserted by the Welfare Reform and Pensions Act 1999, s 19, Sch 3, paras 1, 10, as from 1 December 2000.

PART **III**

PROTECTION, CUSTODY, ETC, OF CHILDREN

41. Restrictions on decrees for dissolution, annulment or separation affecting children—(*1*) *The Court shall not make absolute a decree of divorce or of nullity of marriage, or grant a decree of judicial separation, unless the court, by order, has declared that it is satisfied—*

> (*a*) *that for the purposes of this section there are no children of the family to whom this section applies; or*
>
> (*b*) *that the only children who are or may be children of the family to whom this section applies are the children named in the order and that—*
>
>> (*i*) *arrangements for the welfare of every child so named have been made and are satisfactory or are the best that can be devised in the circumstances; or*
>>
>> (*ii*) *it is impracticable for the party or parties appearing before the court to make any such arrangements; or*
>>
>> [(*iii*) *such arrangements have been made in respect of every child named in the order except any child with respect to whom the court has made an order under section 4(5) or 5(2) of the Family Law Act 1986 (orders precluding or staying proceedings for a custody order), or*]

Note. Sub-s (1)(b)(iii) inserted by Family Law Act 1986, s 68(1), Sch 1, para 13, as from 4 April 1988.

> (*c*) *that there are circumstances making it desirable that the decree should be made absolute or should be granted, as the case may be, without delay notwithstanding that there are or may be children of the family to whom this section applies and that the court is unable to make a declaration in accordance with paragraph (b) above.*

(*2*) *The court shall not make an order declaring that it is satisfied as mentioned in subsection (1)(c) above unless it has obtained a satisfactory undertaking from either or both of the parties to bring the question of the arrangements for the children named in the order before the court within a specified time.*

(*3*) *If the court makes absolute a decree of divorce or of nullity of marriage, or grants a decree of judicial separation, without having made an order under subsection (1) above the decree shall be void but, if such an order was made, no person shall be entitled to challenge the validity of the decree on the ground that the conditions prescribed by subsections (1) and (2) above were not fulfilled.*

(*4*) *If the court refuses to make an order under subsection (1) above in any proceedings for divorce, nullity of marriage or judicial separation, it shall, on an application by either party to the proceedings, make an order declaring that it is not satisfied as mentioned in that subsection.*

(*5*) *This section applies to the following children of the family, that is to say—*

> (*a*) *any minor child of the family who at the date of the order under subsection (1) above is—*
>
>> (*i*) *under the age of sixteen, or*
>>
>> (*ii*) *receiving instruction at an educational establishment or undergoing training for a trade, profession or vocation, whether or not he is also in gainful employment; and*
>
> (*b*) *any other child of the family to whom the court by an order under that subsection directs that this section shall apply;*

and the court may give such a direction if it is of opinion that there are special circumstances which make it desirable in the interest of the child that this section should apply to him.

(*6*) *In this section 'welfare', in relation to a child, includes the custody and education of the child and financial provision for him.*

Note. Section 41 replaced Matrimonial Proceedings and Property Act 1970, s 17 (p 2375).

[**41. Restrictions on decrees for dissolution, annulment or separation affecting children**—(1) In any proceedings for a decree of *divorce or* nullity of marriage, *or a decree of judicial separation,* the court shall consider—

(a) whether there are any children of the family to whom this section applies; and

(b) where there are any such children, whether (in the light of the arrangements which have been, or are proposed to be, made for their upbringing and welfare) it should exercise any of its powers under the Children Act 1989 with respect to any of them.

(2) Where, in any case to which this section applies, it appears to the court that—

(a) the circumstances of the case require it, or are likely to require it, to exercise any of its powers under the Act of 1989 with respect to any such child;

(b) it is not in a position to exercise that power or (as the case may be) those powers without giving further consideration to the case; and

(c) there are exceptional circumstances which make it desirable in the interests of the child that the court should give a direction under this section,

it may direct that the decree of *divorce or* nullity is not to be made absolute, *or that the decree of judicial separation is not to be granted,* until the court orders otherwise.

Note. Words in italics in sub-ss (1), (2) repealed by Family Law Act 1996, s 66(3), Sch 10, as from a day to be appointed, subject to savings in s 66(2) of, and Sch 9 to, the 1996 Act.

(3) This section applies to—

(a) any child of the family who has not reached the age of sixteen at the date when the court considers the case in accordance with the requirements of this section: and

(b) any child of the family who has reached that age at that date and in relation to whom the court directs that this section shall apply.]

Note. Section 41 in square brackets substituted for s 41 in italics by Children Act 1989, s 108(4), Sch 12, para 31, as from 14 October 1991.

42. Orders for custody and education of children in cases of divorce, etc, and for custody in cases of neglect—(*1*) *The court may make such order as it thinks fit for the custody and education of any child of the family who is under the age of eighteen—*

(*a*) *in any proceedings for divorce, nullity of marriage or judicial separation, before or on granting a decree or at any time thereafter (whether, in the case of a decree of divorce or nullity of marriage, before or after the decree is made absolute);*

(*b*) *where any such proceedings are dismissed after the beginning of the trial, either forthwith or within a reasonable period* [(*if an application for the order is made on or before the dismissal*)] *after the dismissal;*

and in any case in which the court has power by virtue of this subsection to make an order in respect of a child it may instead, if it thinks fit, direct that proper proceedings be taken for making the child a ward of court.

Note. Words in square brackets substituted for words 'within a reasonable period' by Family Law Act 1986, s 4(2), as from 4 April 1988. See Family Law Act 1986, ss 1(1)(a), 2(1), 4(1)–(3), (5), (6), 5(3) (pp 3148, 3151, 3153, 3154).

(*2*) *Where the court makes an order under section 27 above, the court shall also have power to make such order as it thinks fit with respect to the custody of any child of the family who is for the time being under the age of eighteen; but the power conferred by this subsection and any order made in exercise of that power shall have effect only as respects any period when an order is in force under that section and the child is under that age.*

Note. See Family Law Act 1986, s 1(1)(a) (p 3148).

(*3*) *Where the court grants or makes absolute a decree of divorce or grants a decree of judicial separation, it may include in the decree a declaration that either party to the marriage in question is unfit to have the custody of the children of the family.*

Note. Sub-s (3) repealed by Children Act 1989, s 108(4), Sch 12, para 32, as from 14 October 1991.

(*4*) *Where a decree of divorce or of judicial separation contains such a declaration as is mentioned in subsection* (*3*) *above, then, if the party to whom the declaration relates is a parent of any child of the family, that party shall not, on the death of the other parent, be entitled as of right to the custody or the guardianship of that child.*

(*5*) *Where an order in respect of a child is made under this section, the order shall not affect the rights over or with respect to the child of any person, other than a party to the marriage in question, unless the child is the child of one or both of the parties to that marriage and that person was a party to the proceedings on the application for an order under this section.*

(*6*) *The power of the court under subsection* (*1*)(*a*) *or* (*2*) *above to make an order with respect to a child shall be exercisable from time to time; and where the court makes an order under subsection* (*1*)(*b*) *above with respect to a child it may from time to time until that child attains the age of eighteen make a further order with respect to his custody and education.*

(*7*) *The court shall have power to vary or discharge an order made under this section or to suspend any provision thereof temporarily and to revive the operation of any provision so suspended.*

Note. Section 42 replaced Matrimonial Proceedings and Property Act 1970, ss 18, 19 (pp 2375, 2376). Section 42 repealed by Children Act 1989, s 108(7), Sch 15, as from 14 October 1991. See ibid, s 108(6), Sch 14, paras 1, 3, 5–11, 15, 16, 26 (pp 3408, 3489–3495, 3499, 3500).

43. Power to commit children to care of local authority—(*1*) *Where the court has jurisdiction by virtue of this Part of this Act to make an order for the custody of a child and it appears to the court that there are exceptional circumstances making it impracticable or undesirable for the child to be entrusted to either of the parties to the marriage or to any other individual, the court may if it thinks fit make an order committing the care of the child to the council of a county other than a metropolitan county, or of a metropolitan district or London borough or the Common Council of the City of London* (*hereafter in this section referred to as 'the local authority'*)*; and thereupon Part II of the Children Act 1948* [*Part III of the Child Care Act 1980*] (*which relates to the treatment of children in the care of a local authority*) *shall, subject to the provisions of this section, apply as if the child had been received by the local authority into their care under section 1 of that Act* [*section 2 of that Act*] [*and thereupon—*

(*a*) *Part III of the Child Care Act 1980* (*which relates to the treatment of children in the care of a local authority*)*; and*

(*b*) *for the purposes only of contributions by the child himself at a time when he has attained the age of 16, Part V of that Act* (*which relates to contributions towards the maintenance of children in the care of a local authority*),

shall apply, subject to the provisions of this section, as if the child had been received by the local authority into their care under section 2 of that Act.]

Note. Words 'other than a metropolitan county', repealed by the Local Government Act 1985, s 102, Sch 17. Words in square brackets substituting references to Act of 1980 for references to Act of 1948 substituted by Child Care Act 1980, s 89(2), Sch 5, para 34, as from 1 April 1981. Words in final square brackets ('and thereupon ... section 2 of that Act') substituted by Health and Social Services and Social Security Adjudications Act 1983, s 9, Sch 2, para 20, as from 1 January 1984.

As this section is no longer effective the prospective amendments made by the Children and Young Persons (Amendment) Act 1986, s 1(3) will not be brought into force. (The amending provisions have been repealed).

(*2*) *The authority specified in an order under this section shall be the local authority for the area in which the child was, in the opinion of the court, resident before the order was made to commit the child to the care of the local authority, and the court shall before making an order under this section hear any representations from the local authority, including any representations as to the making of a financial provision order in favour of the child.*

(*3*) *While an order made by virtue of this section is in force with respect to a child, the child shall continue in the care of the local authority notwithstanding any claim by a parent or other person.*

(4) An order made by virtue of this section shall cease to have effect as respects any child when he becomes eighteen, and the court shall not make an order committing a child to the care of a local authority under this section after he has become seventeen.

(5) In the application of Part II of the Children Act 1948 by virtue of this section—

(a) the exercise by the local authority of their powers under sections 12 to 14 of that Act (which among other things relate to the accommodation and welfare of a child in the care of a local authority) shall be subject to any directions given by the court; and

(b) section 17 of that Act (which relates to arrangements for the emigration of such a child) shall not apply.

[(5) In the application of Part III of the Child Care Act 1980 by virtue of this section—

(a) the exercise by the local authority of their powers under sections 18, 21 and 22 [, 22 and 22A] of that Act (which among other things relate to the accommodation and welfare of a child in the care of a local authority) shall be subject to any directions given by the court; and

(b) section 24 of that Act (which relates to arrangements for the emigration of such a child) and section 28 of that Act (which relates to the aftercare of a child in the care of a local authority under section 2 of that Act) shall not apply.]

Note. Sub-s (5) in square brackets substituted by Child Care Act 1980, s 89(2), Sch 5, para 34, as from 1 April 1981.

Words ', 22 and 22A' substituted for 'and 22' by Children and Young Persons (Amendment) Act 1986, s 1(3), to come into force on date to be appointed under ibid, s 5(1).

(6) It shall be the duty of any parent or guardian of a child committed to the care of a local authority under this section to secure that the local authority are informed of his address for the time being, and a person who knowingly fails to comply with this subsection shall be liable on summary conviction to a fine not exceeding ten pounds.

(7) The court shall have power from time to time by an order under this section to vary or discharge any provision made in pursuance of this section.

(8) So long as by virtue of paragraph 13 of Schedule 4 to the Children and Young Persons Act 1969 sections 15 and 16 of the Children Act 1948 continue to apply in relation to a local authority, subsection (5)(a) above shall have effect in relation to that authority as if for the reference to sections 12 to 14 of the last-mentioned Act there were substituted a reference to sections 12 to 16 of that Act.

Note. Sub-s (8) repealed by Child Care Act 1980, s 89(3), Sch 6, as from 1 April 1981.

(9) Subject to the following provisions of this subsection, until 1 April 1974 subsection (1) above shall have effect as if for the words 'other than a metropolitan county, or of a metropolitan district' there were substituted the words 'county borough'.

An order (or orders) made under section 273(2) of the Local Government Act 1972 (orders bringing provisions of that Act into force before 1 April 1974) may appoint an earlier date (or, as the case may be, different dates for different purposes or areas) on which subsection (1) above shall cease to have effect as mentioned above.

Note. Section 43 replaced Matrimonial Causes Act 1965, s 36 (p 2260). Sub-s (9) repealed by Matrimonial and Family Proceedings Act 1984, s 46(3), Sch 3, as from 12 October 1984. Section 43 repealed by Children Act 1989, s 108(7), Sch 15, as from 14 October 1991. See ibid, s 108(6), Sch 14, paras 1, 3, 5–11, 15, 16, 26 (pp 3346, 3427–3437).

44. Power to provide for supervision of children—(1) Where the court has jurisdiction by virtue of this Part of this Act to make an order for the custody of a child and it appears to the court that there are exceptional circumstances making it desirable that the child should be under the supervision of an independent person, the court may, as respects any period during which the child is, in exercise of that jurisdiction, committed to the custody of any person [care of any person], order that the child be under the supervision of an officer appointed under this section as a welfare officer or under the supervision of a local authority.

Note. Words in square brackets substituted for words 'custody of any person' by Children Act 1975, s 108(1)(a), Sch 3, para 18, as from 1 January 1976.

(*2*) *Where the court makes an order under this section for supervision by a welfare officer, the officer responsible for carrying out the order shall be such probation officer as may be selected under arrangements made by the Secretary of State; and where the order is for supervision by a local authority, that authority shall be the council of a county other than a metropolitan county, or of a metropolitan district or London borough selected by the court and specified in the order or, if the Common Council of the City of London is so selected and specified, that Council.*

Note. Words 'other than a metropolitan county' repealed by Local Government Act 1985, s 102, Sch 17.

(*3*) *The court shall not have power to make an order under this section as respects a child who in pursuance of an order under section 43 above is in the care of a local authority.*

(*4*) *Where a child is under the supervision of any person in pursuance of this section the jurisdiction possessed by a court to vary any financial provision order in the child's favour or any order made with respect to his custody or education under this Part of this Act shall, subject to any rules of court, be exercisable at the instance of that court itself.*

(*5*) *The court shall have power from time to time by an order under this section to vary or discharge any provision made in pursuance of this section.*

(*6*) *Subject to the following provisions of this subsection, until 1 April 1974 subsection* (*2*) *above shall have effect as if for the words 'other than a metropolitan county, or of a metropolitan district' there were substituted the words 'county borough'.*

An order (*or orders*) *made under section 273*(*2*) *of the Local Government Act 1972 may appoint an earlier date* (*or, as the case may be, different dates for different purposes or areas*) *on which subsection* (*2*) *above shall cease to have effect as mentioned above.*

Note. Section 44 replaced Matrimonial Causes Act 1965, s 37 (p 2261). Sub-s (6) repealed by Matrimonial and Family Proceedings Act 1984, s 46(3), Sch 3, as from 12 October 1984. See Family Law Act 1986, s 6(6)(b) as to cessation of effect of supervision orders made under s 44 in the circumstances there stated. Section 44 repealed by Children Act 1989, s 108(7), Sch 15, as from 14 October 1991. See ibid, s 108(6), Sch 14, paras 1, 3, 5–11, 15, 16, 26, (pp 3408, 3489–3495, 3499, 3500).

PART IV

MISCELLANEOUS AND SUPPLEMENTAL

45. Declarations of legitimacy, etc—(*1*) *Any person who is a British subject, or whose right to be deemed a British subject depends wholly or in part on his legitimacy or on the validity of any marriage, may, if he is domiciled in England and Wales or in Northern Ireland or claims any real or personal estate situate in England and Wales, apply by petition to the High Court for a decree declaring that he is the legitimate child of his parents, or that the marriage of his father and mother or of his grandfather and grandmother was a valid marriage or that his own marriage was a valid marriage.*

(*2*) *Any person claiming that he or his parent or any remoter ancestor became or has become a legitimated person may apply by petition to the High Court, or may apply to a county court in the manner prescribed by* [*county court rules*] [*rules of court*], *for a decree declaring that he or his parent or remoter ancestor as the case may be, became or has become a legitimated person.*

In this subsection 'legitimated person' means a person legitimated by the Legitimacy Act 1926, and includes a person recognised under section 8 of that Act as legitimated.

Note. The relevant provisions of Legitimacy Act 1926 were repealed and replaced by Legitimacy Act 1976, ss 2, 3. Note, however, the saving in Legitimacy Act 1976, Sch 1 (p 2618).

Words in second square brackets substituted for words in first square brackets by Matrimonial and Family Proceedings Act 1984, s 46(1), Sch 1, para 14.

(*3*) *Where an application under subsection* (*2*) *above is made to a county court, the county court, if it considers that the case is one which owing to the value of the property involved or otherwise ought to be dealt with by the High Court, may, and if so ordered by the High Court shall, transfer the matter to the High Court; and on such a transfer the proceeding shall be continued in the High Court as if it had been originally commenced by petition to the court.*

Note. Sub-s (3) repealed by Matrimonial and Family Proceedings Act 1984, s 46(3), Sch 3, as from 28 April 1986.

(*4*) *Any person who is domiciled in England and Wales or in Northern Ireland or claims any real or personal estate situate in England and Wales may apply to the High Court for a decree declaring his right to be deemed a British subject.*

(*5*) *Applications to the High Court under the preceding provisions of this section may be included in the same petition, and on any application under the preceding provisions of this section the High Court or, as the case may be, the county court shall make such decree as it thinks just, and the decree shall be binding on Her Majesty and all other persons whatsoever, so however that the decree shall not prejudice any person—*

 (*a*) *if it is subsequently proved to have been obtained by fraud or collusion; or*

 (*b*) *unless that person has been given notice of the application in the manner prescribed by rules of court or made a party to the proceedings or claims through a person so given notice or made a party.*

(*6*) *A copy of every application under this section and of any affidavit accompanying it shall be delivered to the Attorney-General at least one month before the application is made, and the Attorney-General shall be a respondent on the hearing of the application and on any subsequent proceedings relating thereto.*

(*7*) *Where any application is made under this section, such persons as the court hearing the application thinks fit shall, subject to rules of court, be given notice of the application in the manner prescribed by rules of court, and any such persons may be permitted to become parties to the proceedings and to oppose the application.*

(*8*) *No proceedings under this section shall affect any final judgment or decree already pronounced or made by any court of competent jurisdiction.*

(*9*) *The court hearing an application under this section may direct that the whole or any part of the proceedings shall be heard in camera, and an application for a direction under this subsection shall be heard in camera unless the court otherwise directs.*

Note. Section 45 replaced Matrimonial Causes Act 1965, s 39 (p 2262). Whole section repealed by Family Law Act 1986, s 68(2), Sch 2, as from 4 April 1988. See also ibid, s 68(3)(a) (as to proceedings begun before the date of commencement of ibid, Part III) (p 3185).

46. Additional jurisdiction in proceedings by a wife—(*1*) *Without prejudice to any jurisdiction exercisable by the court apart from this section, the court shall have jurisdiction to entertain proceedings by a wife, notwithstanding that the husband is not domiciled in England and Wales,—*

 (*a*) *in the case of any proceedings under this Act (other than proceedings under section 19 or sections 34 to 36), if—*

  (*i*) *the wife has been deserted by her husband, or*

  (*ii*) *the husband has been deported from the United Kingdom under any law for the time being in force relating to deportation, and the husband was immediately before the desertion or deportation domiciled in England and Wales;*

 (*b*) *in the case of proceedings for divorce or nullity of marriage, if—*

  (*i*) *the wife is resident in England and Wales and has been ordinarily resident there for a period of three years immediately preceding the commencement of the proceedings, and*

  (*ii*) *the husband is not domiciled in any other part of the United Kingdom or in the Channel Islands or the Isle of Man.*

(*2*) *In any proceedings in which the court has jurisdiction by virtue of subsection (1) above the issues shall be determined in accordance with the law which would be applicable thereto if both parties were domiciled in England and Wales at the time of the proceedings.*

Note. Section 46 replaced Matrimonial Causes Act 1965, s 40 (p 2263) and was repealed by Domicile and Matrimonial Proceedings Act 1973, s 17(2), Sch 6; see now ibid, s 5 (p 2574).

47. Matrimonial relief and declarations of validity in respect of polygamous marriages—(1) A court in England and Wales shall not be precluded from granting matrimonial relief or making a declaration concerning the validity of a marriage by reason only that *the marriage in question was entered into under a law which permits polygamy* [either party to the marriage is, or has during the subsistence of the marriage been, married to more than one person].

(2) In this section 'matrimonial relief' means—

(a) any [divorce order, any separation order under the 1996 Act or any] decree under Part I of this Act;

(b) a financial provision order under section 27 above;

(c) an order under section 35 above altering a maintenance agreement;

(d) an order under any provision of this Act [or the 1996 Act] which confers a power exercisable in connection with, or in connection with proceedings for, *such decree or order* [a statement of marital breakdown or any such order or decree] as is mentioned in paragraphs (a) to (c) above;

[(dd) an order under Part III of the Matrimonial and Family Proceedings Act 1984;]

(e) an order under *the Matrimonial Proceedings (Magistrates' Courts) Act 1960* [Part I of the Domestic Proceedings and Magistrates' Courts Act 1978].

Note. Words in square brackets in sub-s (1) substituted for words in italics by Private International Law (Miscellaneous Provisions) Act 1995, s 8(2), Schedule, para 2, as from 8 January 1996. Words in square brackets in sub-s (2)(a) substituted for words in italics, words 'or the 1996 Act' in square brackets in sub-s (2)(d) inserted, and words 'a statement … decree' in square brackets in sub-s (2)(d) substituted for words 'such decree or order' in italics by Family Law Act 1996, s 66(1), Sch 8, Part I, para 22, as from a day to be appointed, subject to savings in s 66(2) of, and para 5 of Sch 9 to, the 1996 Act. Words in square brackets in sub-s (2)(e) substituted by Domestic Proceedings and Magistrates' Courts Act 1978, s 89(2)(a), Sch 2, para 39, as from 1 November 1979. Sub-s (2)(dd) inserted by Matrimonial and Family Proceedings Act 1984, s 46(1), Sch 1, para 15, as from 16 September 1985.

(3) In this section 'a declaration concerning the validity of a marriage' means—

(a) a declaration that a marriage is valid or invalid; and

(b) any other declaration involving a determination as to the validity of a marriage;

being a declaration in a decree granted under section 45 above or a declaration made in the exercise by the High Court of its jurisdiction to grant declaratory relief in any proceedings notwithstanding that a declaration is the only substantive relief sought in those proceedings.

[(3) In this section 'a declaration concerning the validity of a marriage' means any declaration under Part III of the Family Law Act 1986 involving a determination as to the validity of a marriage.]

Note. Sub-s (3) in square brackets substituted for sub-s (3) in italics by Family Law Act 1986, s 68(1), Sch 1, para 14, as from 4 April 1988.

(4) This section has effect whether or not either party to the marriage in question has for the time being any spouse additional to the other party; and provision may be made by rules of court—

(a) for requiring notice of proceedings brought by virtue of this section to be served on any such other spouse; and

(b) for conferring on any such other spouse the right to be heard in any such proceedings, in such cases as may be prescribed by the rules.

[(4) Provision may be made by rules of court—

(a) for requiring notice of proceedings brought by virtue of this section to be served on any additional spouse of a party to the marriage in question; and

(b) for conferring on any such additional spouse the right to be heard in the proceedings,

in such cases as may be specified in the rules.]

Note. Sub-s (4) in square brackets substituted for sub-s (4) in italics by Private International Law (Miscellaneous Provisions) Act 1995, s 8(2), Schedule, para 2, as from 8 January 1996. Section 47 replaced Matrimonial Proceedings (Polygamous Marriages) Act 1972, s 1 (p 2491).

48. Evidence—(1) The evidence of a husband or wife shall be admissible in any proceedings to prove that marital intercourse did or did not take place between them during any period.

Note. Sub-s (1) replaced Matrimonial Causes Act 1965, s 13(1) (p 2246).

(2) In any proceedings for nullity of marriage, evidence on the question of sexual capacity shall be heard in camera unless in any case the judge is satisfied that in the interests of justice any such evidence ought to be heard in open court.

Note. Sub-s (2) replaced Matrimonial Causes Act 1965, s 43(3) (p 2248).

49. Parties to proceedings under this Act—(*1*) *Where in a petition for divorce or judicial separation, or in any other pleading praying for either form of relief, one party to a marriage alleges that the other has committed adultery, he or she shall make the person alleged to have committed adultery with the other party to the marriage a party to the proceedings unless excused by the court on special grounds from doing so.*

Note. Sub-s (1) replaced Matrimonial Causes Act 1965, s 4(1), (2) (p 2241).

(*2*) *Rules of court may, either generally or in such cases as may be prescribed by the rules, exclude the application of subsection (1) above where the person alleged to have committed adultery with the other party to the marriage is not named in the petition or other pleading.*

(*3*) *Where in pursuance of subsection (1) above a person is made a party to proceedings for divorce or judicial separation, the court may, if after the close of the evidence on the part of the person making the allegation of adultery it is of opinion that there is not sufficient evidence against the person so made a party, dismiss him or her from the suit.*

Note. Sub-s (3) replaced Matrimonial Causes Act 1965, s 4(3) (p 2241).

(*4*) *Rules of court may make provision, in cases not falling within subsection (1) above, with respect to the joinder as parties to proceedings under this Act of persons involved in allegations of adultery or other improper conduct made in those proceedings, and with respect to the dismissal from such proceedings of any parties so joined; and rules of court made by virtue of this subsection may make different provision for different cases.*

(*5*) *In every case in which adultery with any party to a suit is alleged against any person not made a party to the suit or in which the court considers, in the interest of any person not already a party to the suit, that that person should be made a party to the suit, the court may if it thinks fit allow that person to intervene upon such terms, if any, as the court thinks just.*

Note. Sub-s (5) replaced Matrimonial Causes Act 1965, s 44 (p 2265). This section repealed by Family Law Act 1996, s 66, Sch 8, Part I, para 23, Sch 10, as from a day to be appointed, subject to savings in s 66(2) of, and para 5 of Sch 9 to, the 1996 Act.

50. Matrimonial causes rules—(*1*) *The authority having power to make rules of court for the purposes of*—

(*a*) *this Act, the Matrimonial Causes Act 1967 (which confers jurisdiction on county courts in certain matrimonial proceedings), section 45 of the Courts Act 1971 (transfer of matrimonial proceedings between High Court and county court, etc) and sections 26 to 28A of the Matrimonial Causes Act 1965 (maintenance of survivor from estate of deceased former spouse)* [*and Part III of the Family Law Act 1986*];

Note. Amended by Family Law Act 1986, s 68(1), Sch 1, para 15(a), as from 4 April 1988.

(*b*) *proceedings in the High Court or a divorce county court for an order under section 7 of the Matrimonial Homes Act 1967 (transfer of protected or statutory tenancy under Rent Act 1968 on dissolution or annulment of marriage)* [*Schedule 1 to the Matrimonial Homes Act 1983 (transfer of certain tenancies on divorce, etc)*];

(*c*) *certain other proceedings in the High Court, that is to say*—

(*i*) *proceedings in the High Court under section 17 of the Married Women's Property Act 1882, not being proceedings in the divorce registry treated by virtue of rules made under this section for the purposes of section 45 of the Courts Act 1971 as pending in a county court;*

      (*ii*) *proceedings in the High Court under section 1 of the Matrimonial Homes Act 1967* [*Matrimonial Homes Act 1983*] *(rights of occupation of matrimonial home for spouse not otherwise entitled)*;

      (*iii*) *proceedings in which the only substantive relief sought is a declaration with respect to a person's matrimonial status; or*

  (*d*) *any enactment passed after this Act which relates to any matter dealt with in this Act, the Matrimonial Causes Act 1967 or sections 26 to 28A of the Matrimonial Causes Act 1965;* [*or*

  (*e*) *any enactment contained in Part II of or Schedule 1 to the Domicile and Matrimonial Proceedings Act 1973 which does not fall within paragraph (d) above*]*;* [*or*

  (*f*) *proceedings to which section 100(7)(d) of the Children Act 1975 applies (certain applications for revocation and variation of custodianship etc, orders)*]

shall, subject to the exceptions listed in subsection (2) below, be the Lord Chancellor together with any four or more of the following persons, namely, the President of the Family Division, one puisne judge attached to that division, one registrar of the divorce registry, two Circuit judges, one registrar appointed under the County Courts Act 1959 [*1984*]*, two practising barristers being members of the General Council of the Bar and two practising solicitors of whom one shall be a member of the Council of the Law Society and the other a member of the Law Society and also of a local law society.* [*one district judge of the principal registry of the Family Division, two Circuit judges, one district judge appointed under the County Courts Act 1984, two persons who have a Supreme Court qualification (within the meaning of section 71 of the Courts and Legal Services Act 1990), and two persons who have been granted by an authorised body, under Part II of that Act, the right to conduct litigation in relation to all proceedings in the Supreme Court.*]

    All the members of the authority, other than the Lord Chancellor himself and the President of the Family Division, shall be appointed by the Lord Chancellor for such time as he may think fit.

Note. Words 'and sections ... former spouse' in para (a) and 'or sections ... 1965' in para (d) repealed by Inheritance (Provision for Family and Dependants) Act 1975, s 26(2), Schedule. Word 'or' in para (c)(iii) repealed, and para (e) and word 'or' immediately preceding it added by Domicile and Matrimonial Proceedings Act 1973, s 6(2).

Para (f) and word 'or' immediately preceding it added by Children Act 1975, s 108(1), Sch 3, para 79, as from 1 December 1985.

Words 'being members of the General Council of the Bar' repealed by Administration of Justice Act 1977, s 32(4), Sch 5, Part VI.

In para (b) for the words from 'section 7' to the end of paragraph the words 'Schedule 1 to the Matrimonial Homes Act 1983 (transfer of certain tenancies on divorce, etc)' are substituted, and in (c) for the words 'Matrimonial Homes Act 1967' the words 'Matrimonial Homes Act 1983' are substituted by Matrimonial Homes Act 1983, s 12, Sch 2, as from 9 August 1983.

In sub-ss (1), (3) references to County Courts Act 1984 substituted by ibid, s 148(1), Sch 2, Part V, para 44, as from 1 August 1984.

Words in square brackets substituted for words 'one registrar of the divorce registry ... local law society' by Courts and Legal Services Act 1990, s 125(3), Sch 18, para 3, as from 1 January 1991.

  (2) *The following shall be excepted from the purposes mentioned in subsection (1) above—*

  (*a*) *proceedings in a county court in the exercise of a jurisdiction exercisable by any county court whether or not it is a divorce county court, that is to say, proceedings in a county court under section 32, 33, 36,* [*38 or 45 above*] [*or 38*] *or under section 26 or 27 of the Matrimonial Causes Act 1965;*

  (*b*) *section 47 above, in so far as it relates to* [*proceedings in a county court under section 45 above or to*] *proceedings for an order under the Matrimonial Proceedings (Magistrates' Courts) Act 1960* [*Part I of the Domestic Proceedings and Magistrates' Courts Act 1978*]*;*

  (*c*) *any enactment passed after this Act in so far as it relates to proceedings in a county court in the exercise of any such jurisdiction as is mentioned in paragraph (a) above* [*or to any aspect of section 47 above which is excepted by paragraph (b) above.*]

Note. Reference to Act of 1965 in para (a) repealed and replaced by Inheritance (Provision for Family and Dependants) Act 1975, s 26(2), Schedule (p 2613). Reference to Act of 1960 in para (b) repealed and replaced by Domestic Proceedings and Magistrates' Courts Act 1978, s 89(2), Sch 2, para 40, as from 1 November 1979. Words 'or 38' substituted for '38 or 45 above', words 'proceedings in a county court under section 45 above or to', and words 'or to any aspect of section 47 above which is excepted by paragraph (b) above' repealed by Family Law Act 1986, s 68(1), (2), Sch 1, para 15(b) and by ibid, Sch 2, as from 4 April 1988.

(*3*) *Rules of court made under this section may apply, with or without modification, any rules of court made under the Supreme Court of Judicature (Consolidation) Act 1925, the County Courts Act 1959 [1984] or any other enactment and—*

(*a*) *may modify or exclude the application of any such rules or of any provision of the County Courts Act 1959;*

(*b*) *may provide for the enforcement in the High Court of orders made in a divorce county court;*

and, without prejudice to the generality of the preceding provisions, may make with respect to proceedings in a divorce county court any provision regarding the Official Solicitor or any solicitor of the Supreme Court which could be made by rules of court with respect to proceedings in the High Court.

Note. Supreme Court of Judicature (Consolidation) Act 1925, s 99, replaced by Supreme Court Act 1981, s 84 (p 2855).

(*4*) *The power to make rules of court by virtue of subsection (1) above shall be exercisable by statutory instrument, which shall be subject to annulment in pursuance of a resolution of either House of Parliament.*

(*5*) *In this section 'divorce county court' means a county court designated under section 1 of the Matrimonial Causes Act 1967 and 'divorce registry' means the principal registry of the Family Division of the High Court.*

Note. Section 50 replaced Matrimonial Causes Act 1967, s 7 (p 2275).

For Matrimonial Causes Act 1967, s 1, see p 2272.

This section repealed by Matrimonial and Family Proceedings Act 1984, s 46(3), Sch 3, as from 14 October 1991. See now Matrimonial and Family Proceedings Act 1984, s 40 (p 3038) and the Family Proceedings Rules 1991, SI 1991 No 1247 (see Div C of the Service to this Edition).

51. Fees in matrimonial proceedings. *The fees to be taken in any proceedings to which rules under section 50 above shall be such as the Lord Chancellor with the concurrence of the Treasury may from time to time by order made by statutory instrument prescribe.*

Note. Section 51 replaced Matrimonial Causes Act 1967, s 8 (p 2276).

This section repealed by Matrimonial and Family Proceedings Act 1984, s 46(3), Sch 3, as from 14 October 1991. See now Matrimonial and Family Proceedings Act 1984, s 41 (p 3039).

52. Interpretation—(1) In this Act—

['the 1996 Act' means the Family Law Act 1996;]

'adopted' means adopted in pursuance of—

(*a*) *an adoption order made under the Adoption Act 1958, any previous enactment relating to the adoption of children, the Adoption Act 1968 or any corresponding enactment of the Parliament of Northern Ireland; or*

(*b*) *an adoption order made in the Isle of Man or any of the Channel Islands; or*

(*c*) *subject to sections 5 and 6 of the Adoption Act 1968, an overseas adoption within the meaning of section 4 of that Act;*

'child', in relation to one or both of the parties to a marriage, includes an illegitimate *or adopted* child of that party, or as the case may be, of both parties;

'child of the family', in relation to the parties to a marriage, means—

    (a) a child of both of those parties; and

    (b) any other child, not being a child who *has been boarded-out with those parties* [is placed with those parties as foster parents] by a local authority or voluntary organisation, who has been treated by both of those parties as a child of their family;

'the court' (except where the context otherwise requires) means the High Court or, where a county court has jurisdiction by virtue of *the Matrimonial Causes Act 1967* [Part V of the Matrimonial and Family Proceedings Act 1984], a county court;

'*custody*', *in relation to a child, includes access to the child;*

'education' includes training.

['*maintenance assessment* [maintenance calculation]' has the same meaning as it has in the Child Support Act 1991 by virtue of section 54 of that Act as read with any regulations in force under that section;]

['statement of marital breakdown' has the same meaning as in the Family Law Act 1996.]

Note. Sub-s (1) replaced Matrimonial Proceedings and Property Act 1970, s 27(1) (p 2378). Definitions 'the 1996 Act' and 'statement of marital breakdown' inserted by Family Law Act 1996, s 66(1), Sch 8, Part I, para 24, as from a day to be appointed, subject to savings in s 66(2) of, and para 5 of Sch 9 to, the 1996 Act. Definition 'adopted' and words 'or adopted' in definition 'child' repealed by Children Act 1975, s 108(1), Sch 4, Part I, as from 1 January 1976. Definition 'the court' amended by Matrimonial and Family Proceedings Act 1984, s 46(1), Sch 1, para 16, as from 28 April 1986. Definition 'child of the family' amended by Children Act 1989, s 108(4), Sch 12, para 33, as from 14 October 1991. Definition 'custody' repealed by s 108(7) of, and Sch 15 to, the 1989 Act, as from the same date. Definition 'maintenance assessment' added by Maintenance Orders (Backdating) Order 1993, SI 1993 No 623, art 2, Sch 1, para 4, as from 5 April 1993. Words 'maintenance calculation' in square brackets substituted for words 'maintenance assessment' by the Child Support, Pensions and Social Security Act 2000, s 26, Sch 3, para 3(1), (4), as from 3 March 2003 in relation to certain cases and as from a day to be appointed for remaining purposes.

    (2) In this Act—

    (a) references to financial provision orders, periodical payments and secured periodical payments orders and orders for the payment of a lump sum, and references to property adjustment orders, shall be construed in accordance *with section 21 above* [(subject to section 35(7) above) with section 21 above and—

        (i) in the case of a financial provision order or periodical payments order, as including (except where the context otherwise requires) references to an interim periodical payments order under section 22A or 23 above; and

       (ii) in the case of a financial provision order or order for the payment of a lump sum, as including (except where the context otherwise requires) references to an interim order for the payment of a lump sum under section 22A or 23 above;] *and*

[(aa) references to pension sharing orders shall be construed in accordance with s 21A above; and]

    (b) references *to orders for maintenance pending suit and* to interim orders for maintenance shall be construed *respectively* in accordance with *section 22 and* section 27(5) above.

Note. Words in square brackets in sub-s (2)(a) substituted for words in italics and words in italics in sub-s (2)(b) repealed by Family Law Act 1996, s 66, Sch 8, Part I, para 25, Sch 10, as from a day to be appointed, subject to savings in s 66(2) of, and para 5 of Sch 9 to, the 1996 Act. Para (aa) substituted for word 'and' in italics immediately preceding it by the Welfare Reform and Pensions Actg 1999, s 19, Sch 3, paras 1, 11, as from 1 December 2000.

    (3) For the avoidance of doubt it is hereby declared that references in this Act to remarriage include references to a marriage which is by law void or voidable.

    (4) Except where the contrary intention is indicated, references in this Act to any enactment include references to that enactment as amended, extended or applied by or under any subsequent enactment, including this Act.

Note. Sub-ss (3), (4) replaced Matrimonial Proceedings and Property Act 1970, s 27(2), (3) (p 2379).

53. Transitional provisions and savings.   Schedule 1 to this Act shall have effect for the purpose of—
- (a) the transition to the provisions of this Act from the law in force before the commencement of this Act;
- (b) the preservation for limited purposes of certain provisions superseded by provisions of this Act or by enactments repealed and replaced by this Act; and
- (c) the assimilation in certain respects to orders under this Act of orders made, or deemed to have been made, under the Matrimonial Causes Act 1965.

54. Consequential amendments and repeals—(1) Subject to the provisions of Schedule 1 to this Act—
- (a) the enactments specified in Schedule 2 to this Act shall have effect subject to the amendments specified in that Schedule, being amendments consequential on the provisions of this Act or on enactments repealed by this Act; and
- (*b*) *the enactments specified in Schedule 3 to this Act are hereby repealed to the extent specified in the third column of that Schedule.*

Note. Words in italics repealed by Statute Law (Repeals) Act 1977, Sch 1, Part VII.

(2) The amendment of any enactment by Schedule 2 to this Act shall not be taken as prejudicing the operation of section 38 of the Interpretation Act 1889 (which relates to the effect of repeals).

Note. See now Interpretation Act 1978, ss 16(1), 17(2)(a) (p 2736).

55. Citation, commencement and extent—(1) This Act may be cited as the Matrimonial Causes Act 1973.

(2) This Act shall come into force on such day as the Lord Chancellor may appoint by order made by statutory instrument.

Commencement. The Act came into force on 1 January 1974 (SI 1973 No 1972).

(3) Subject to the provisions of paragraphs 3(2) *and* 7(3) of Schedule 2 below, this Act does not extend to Scotland or Northern Ireland.

Note. Words 'and 7(3)' repealed by Statute Law (Repeals) Act 1977, Sch 1, Part VII.

SCHEDULES

SCHEDULE 1

TRANSITIONAL PROVISIONS AND SAVINGS

PART I

MISCELLANEOUS AND GENERAL

General transitional provisions and savings

1. Without prejudice to the provisions of section 38 of the Interpretation Act 1889 (which relates to the effect of repeals)—
- (a) nothing in any repeal made by this Act shall affect any order or rule made, direction given or thing done, or deemed to have been made, given or done, under any enactment repealed by this Act, and every such order, rule, direction or thing shall, if in force at the commencement of this Act, continue in force and, so far as it could have been made, given or done under this Act, be deemed to have been made, given or done under the corresponding provisions of this Act; and
- (b) any reference in any document (including an enactment) to any enactment repealed by this Act, whether a specific reference or a reference to provisions of a description which includes, or apart from any repeal made by this Act includes, the enactment so repealed, shall be construed as a reference to the corresponding enactment in this Act.

2. Without prejudice to paragraph 1 above, but subject to paragraph 3 below, any application made or proceeding begun, or deemed to have been made or begun, under any enactment repealed by this Act, being an application or proceeding which is pending at the commencement of this Act, shall be deemed to have been made or begun under the corresponding provisions of this Act.

3. Nothing in Part I of this Act shall apply in relation to any petition for divorce or judicial separation presented before 1 January 1971 and notwithstanding any repeal or amendment made by this Act the Matrimonial Causes Act 1965 (hereafter in this Schedule referred to as the Act of 1965) and any rules of court made for the purposes of that Act shall continue to have effect in relation to proceedings on any such petition which are pending at the commencement of this Act as they had effect immediately before the commencement of this Act.

4. Notwithstanding any repeal or amendment made by this Act, the Act of 1965 and any rules of court made for the purposes of that Act shall continue to have effect in relation to—

  (a) any proceedings on a petition for damages for adultery or for restitution of conjugal rights presented before 1 January 1971 which are pending at the commencement of this Act, and

  (b) any proceedings for relief under section 21 or 34(1)(c) of the Act of 1965 brought in connection with proceedings on a petition for restitution of conjugal rights so presented, being proceedings for relief which are themselves pending at the commencement of this Act,

as they had effect immediately before the commencement of this Act; and nothing in Schedule 2 below shall affect the operation of any other enactment in relation to any such proceedings.

5. Nothing in any repeal made by this Act shall affect any order made, or deemed to have been made, under the Act of 1965 which was continued in force by paragraph 1 of Schedule 1 to the Matrimonial Proceedings and Property Act 1970 notwithstanding the repeal by the last-mentioned Act of the provision of the Act of 1965 under which the order had effect, and every such order shall, if in force at the commencement of this Act, continue in force subject to the provisions of this Act.

6. Nothing in sections 11 to 14 or 16 of this Act affects any law or custom relating to the marriage of members of the Royal Family.

7. Nothing in section 50(1)(a) or (c) above affects—

  (a) any rules of court made under the Supreme Court of Judicature (Consolidation) Act 1925 for the purposes of proceedings under section 39 of the Act of 1965 and having effect by virtue of paragraph 1(b) above in relation to proceedings under section 45 above;

  (b) any rules of court so made for the purposes of proceedings under section 17 of the Married Women's Property Act 1882 or under section 1 of the Matrimonial Homes Act 1967; or

  (c) any rules of court so made for the purposes of the exercise by the High Court of its jurisdiction to grant declaratory relief in proceedings in which the only substantive relief sought is a declaration with respect to a person's matrimonial status;

but rules of court made under section 50 may revoke any rules of court made under the said Act of 1925 in so far as they apply for any such purposes.

Transitional provisions derived from the Act of 1965

8. *Any agreement between the petitioner and the respondent to live separate and apart, whether or not made in writing, shall be disregarded for the purposes of section 1(2)(c) above (including that paragraph as it applies, by virtue of section 17 above, to proceedings for judicial separation) if the agreement was entered into before 1 January 1938 and either—*

  (a) *at the time when the agreement was made the respondent had deserted the petitioner without cause; or* (*b*)   the court is satisfied that the circumstances in which the agreement was made and the parties proceeded to live separate and apart were such as, but for the agreement, to amount to desertion of the petitioner by the respondent.

Note. Para 8 repealed by Family Law Act 1996, s 66(3), Sch 10, as from a day to be appointed, subject to savings in s 66(2) of, and para 5 of Sch 9 to, the 1996 Act.

9. Where the party chargeable under a maintenance agreement within the meaning of section 34 above died before 17 August 1957, then—

  (a)   subsection (1) of that section shall not apply to the agreement unless there remained undistributed on that date assets of that party's estate (apart from any property in which he had only a life interest) representing not less than four-fifths of the value of that estate for probate after providing for the discharge of the funeral, testamentary and administrative expenses, debts, and liabilities payable thereout (other than any liability arising by virtue of that subsection); and

  (b)   nothing in that subsection shall render liable to recovery, or impose any liability upon the personal representatives of that party in respect of, any part of that party's estate which had been distributed before that date.

10. No right or liability shall attach by virtue of section 34(1) above in respect of any sum payable under a maintenance agreement within the meaning of that section in respect of a period before 17 August 1957.

PART II

PRESERVATION FOR LIMITED PURPOSES OF CERTAIN PROVISIONS OF PREVIOUS ENACTMENTS

Nullity

11. (1) Subject to sub-paragraphs (2) and (3) below, a marriage celebrated before 1st August 1971 shall (without prejudice to any other grounds on which a marriage celebrated before that date is by law void or voidable) be voidable on the ground—

  (a)   that the marriage has not been consummated owing to the wilful refusal of the respondent to consummate it; or

  (b)   that at the time of the marriage either party to the marriage—

      (i)   was of unsound mind, or

      (ii)   was suffering from mental disorder within the meaning of the Mental Health Act 1959 of such a kind or to such an extent as to be unfitted for marriage and the procreation of children, or

      (iii)   was subject to recurrent attacks of insanity or epilepsy; or

  (c)   that the respondent was at the time of the marriage suffering from venereal disease in a communicable form; or

  (d)   that the respondent was at the time of the marriage pregnant by some person other than the petitioner [; or

  (e)   that an interim gender recognition certificate under the Gender Recognition Act 2004 has been issued to either party to the marriage].

  (2) In relation to a marriage celebrated before 1 November 1960, for heads (ii) and (iii) of sub-paragraph (1)(b) above there shall be substituted the following heads—

      '(ii)   was a mental defective within the meaning of the Mental Deficiency Acts 1913 to 1938, or

      (iii)   was subject to recurrent fits of insanity or epilepsy; or'.

  (3) The court shall not grant a decree of nullity in a case falling within sub-paragraph (1)(b), (c) or (d) above unless it is satisfied that—

  (a)   the petitioner was at the time of the marriage ignorant of the facts alleged; and

  (b)   proceedings were instituted within a year from the date of the marriage; and

  (c)   marital intercourse with the consent of the petitioner has not taken place since the petitioner discovered the existence of the grounds for a decree;

and where the proceedings with respect to the marriage are instituted after 31 July 1971 the application of section 13(1) above in relation to the marriage shall be without prejudice to the preceding provisions of this sub-paragraph.

(3A) The Court shall not grant a decree of nullity in a case falling within sub-paragraph (1)(e) above unless it is satisfied that proceedings werre instituted within six months from the date of issue of the interim gender recognition certificate.]

(4) Nothing in this paragraph shall be construed as validating a marriage which is by law void but with respect to which a decree of nullity has not been granted.

Note. Para 11(2)(e) and word '; or' immediately preceding it, and para 11(3A) inserted by the Gender Recognition Act 2004, s 4(4), Sch 2, Pt 1, paras 1, 4(1)–(3), as from a day to be appointed.

12. Where a decree of nullity was granted on or before 31 July 1971 in respect of a voidable marriage, any child who would have been the legitimate child of the parties to the marriage if at the date of the decree it had been dissolved instead of being annulled shall be deemed to be their legitimate child.

Succession on intestacy in case of judicial separation

13. Section 18(2) above shall not apply in a case where the death occurred before 1 August 1970, but section 20(3) of the Act of 1965 (which provides that certain property of a wife judicially separated from her husband shall devolve, on her death intestate, as if her husband had then been dead) shall continue to apply in any such case.

Validation of certain void or voidable decrees

14. Any decree of divorce, nullity of marriage or judicial separation which, apart from this paragraph, would be void or voidable on the ground only that the provisions of section 33 of the Act of 1965 (restriction on the making of decrees of dissolution or separation where children are affected) or of section 2 of the Matrimonial Proceedings (Children) Act 1958 (corresponding provision replaced by section 33) had not been complied with when the decree was made absolute or granted, as the case may be, shall be deemed always to have been valid unless—

(a) the court declared the decree to be void before 1 January 1971, or

(b) in proceedings for the annulment of the decree pending at that date the court has before the commencement of this Act declared or after that commencement declares the decree to be void.

PART III

ASSIMILATION IN CERTAIN RESPECTS TO ORDERS UNDER THIS ACT OF ORDERS MADE, ETC, UNDER THE ACT OF 1965, ETC

Cesser on remarriage of orders made, etc, under the Act of 1965 and recovery of sums mistakenly paid thereunder

15. (1) An order made, or deemed to have been made, under section 16(1)(a) or (b) of the Act of 1965 (including either of those paragraphs as applied by section 16(3) or by section 19) shall, notwithstanding anything in the order, cease to have effect on the remarriage after the commencement of this Act of the person in whose favour the order was made, except in relation to any arrears due under it on the date of the remarriage.

(2) An order for the payment of alimony made, or deemed to have been made, under section 20 of the Act of 1965, and an order made, or deemed to have been made, under section 21 or 22 of that Act shall, if the marriage of the parties to the proceedings in which the order was made was or is subsequently dissolved or annulled but the order continues in force, cease to have effect on the remarriage after the commencement of this Act of the party in whose favour the order was made, except in relation to any arrears due under it on the date of the remarriage.

16. Section 38 above shall apply in relation to an order made or deemed to have been made under section 16(1) (including that subsection as applied by section 16(3) and by section 19), 20(1), 21 or 22 of the Act of 1965 as it applies in relation to a periodical payments or secured periodical payments order in favour of a party to a marriage.

Variation, etc, of certain orders made, etc, under the Act of 1965

17. (1) Subject to the provisions of this paragraph, section 31 above shall apply, as it applies to the orders mentioned in subsection (2) thereof, to an order (other than an order for the payment of a lump sum) made or deemed to have been made under any of the following provisions of the Act of 1965, that is to say—

(a) section 15 (except in its application to proceedings for restitution of conjugal rights);

(b) section 16(1) (including that subsection as applied by section 16(3) and by section 19);

(c) section 20(1) and section 17(2) as applied by section 20(2);

(d) section 22;

(e) section 34(1)(a) or (b), in so far as it relates to the maintenance of a child, and section 34(3).

(2) Subject to the provisions of this paragraph, the court hearing an application for the variation of an order made or deemed to have been made under any of the provisions of the Act of 1965 mentioned in sub-paragraph (1) above shall have power to vary that order in any way in which it would have power to vary it had the order been made under the corresponding provision of Part II of this Act.

(3) Section 31, as it applies by virtue of sub-paragraph (1) above, shall have effect as if for subsections (4), (5) and (6) there were substituted the following subsections—

'(4) The court shall not exercise the powers conferred by this section in relation to an order made or deemed to have been made under section 17(2) of the Act of 1965, as applied by section 20(2) of that Act, in connection with the grant of a decree of judicial separation except on an application made in proceedings—

(a) for the rescission of that decree, or

(b) for the dissolution of the marriage in question.

(5) No order for the payment of a lump sum and no property adjustment order shall be made on an application for the variation of any order made or deemed to have been made under section 16(1) (including that subsection as applied by section 16(3) or by section 19), 20(1), 22, 34(1)(a) or (b) or 34(3) of the Act of 1965.

(6) In the case of an order made or deemed to have been made under section 16(1) (including that subsection as applied by section 16(3) or by section 19), 22 or 34(3) of the Act of 1965 and requiring a party to a marriage to secure an annual sum or periodical payments to any other person, an application under this section relating to that order may be made after the death of the person liable to make payments under the order by the person entitled to the payments or by the personal representatives of the deceased person, but no such application shall, except with the permission of the court, be made after the end of the period of six months from the date on which representation in regard to the estate of that person is first taken out';

and in that section, as it so applies, the reference in subsection (8) to a secured periodical payments order shall be construed as a reference to any such order as is mentioned in subsection (6).

(4) In relation to an order made before 16 December 1949 on or after granting a decree of divorce or nullity of marriage and deemed, by virtue of paragraph 1 of Schedule 1 to the Act of 1965, to have been made under section 16(1)(a) of that Act (secured provision), the powers conferred by this paragraph shall not be exercised unless the court is satisfied that the case is one of exceptional hardship which cannot

be met by discharge, variation or suspension of any other order made by reference to that decree, being an order made, or deemed by virtue of that paragraph to have been made, under section 16(1)(b) of that Act (unsecured periodical payments).

18. (1) Subsections (1) and (3) of section 31 above shall apply to an order made or deemed to have been made under section 15 of the Act of 1965 in its application to proceedings for restitution of conjugal rights, or under section 21 or 34(1)(c) of that Act, as they apply to the orders mentioned in subsection (2) of section 31.

(2) In exercising the powers conferred by virtue of this paragraph the court shall have regard to all the circumstances of the case, including any change in any of the matters to which the court was required to have regard when making the order to which the application relates.

19. Section 42(7) above shall apply in relation to an order for the custody or education of a child made or deemed to have been made under section 34 of the Act of 1965, and in relation to an order for the custody of a child made or deemed to have been made under section 35 of that Act, as it applies in relation to an order made under section 42.

Orders made under the Act of 1965 to count as orders under this Act for certain purposes

20. The power of the court under section 23(1) or (2)(a) or 42(1)(a) above to make from time to time a financial provision order or, as the case may be, an order for custody or education in relation to a child of the family shall be exercisable notwithstanding the making of a previous order or orders in relation to the child under section 34(1)(a) of the Act of 1965; and where the court has made an order in relation to a child under section 34(1)(b) of that Act sections 23(4) and 42(6) above shall apply respectively in relation to that child as if the order were an order made under section 23(2)(b) or section 42(1)(b), as the case may be.

21. Where the court has made an order under section 22 of the Act of 1965 the court shall have the like power to make orders under section 42 above with respect to the custody of any child of the family as it has where it makes an order under section 27 above.

Application of provisions of this Act with respect to enforcement of arrears and recovery of excessive payments to certain orders made, etc, under the Act of 1965

22. Section 32 above shall apply in relation to the enforcement, by proceedings begun after 1 January 1971 (whether before or after the commencement of this Act), of the payment of arrears due under an order made, or deemed to have been made, under any of the following provisions of the Act of 1965, that is to say—

(a) section 15;
(b) section 16(1) (including that subsection as applied by section 16(3) and by section 19);
(c) section 20(1);
(d) section 21;
(e) section 22;
(f) section 34(1), in so far as it relates to the maintenance of a child, and section 34(3);

as it applies in relation to the enforcement of the payment of arrears due under any such order as is mentioned in that section.

23. Section 33 above shall apply to an order (other than an order for the payment of a lump sum) made or deemed to have been made under any of the provisions of the Act of 1965 mentioned in paragraph 22 above as it applies to the orders mentioned in section 33(2).

Avoidance under this Act of transactions intended to defeat claims for relief and relief granted under the Act of 1965

24. (1) Section 37 above shall apply in relation to proceedings for relief under section 21 or 34(1)(c) of the Act of 1965 continuing by virtue of paragraph 4(b) above as it applies in relation to proceedings for relief under any of the provisions of this Act specified in section 37(1).

(2) Without prejudice to sub-paragraph (1) above, section 37 shall also apply where an order has been obtained under any of the following provisions of the Act of 1965, that is to say—

(a) section 16(1) (including that subsection as applied by section 16(3) and by section 19);
(b) section 17(2) (including that subsection as applied by section 20(2));
(c) section 20(1);
(d) section 21;
(e) section 22;
(f) section 24;
(g) section 31;
(h) section 34(1), in so far as it relates to the maintenance of a child, and section 34(3);
(i) section 35;

as it applies where an order has been obtained under any of the provisions of this Act specified in section 37(1).

Care and supervision of children

25. (1) Sections 43 and 44 above shall apply where the court has jurisdiction by virtue of paragraph 4(b) above to make an order for the custody of a child under section 34(1)(c) of the Act of 1965 as they apply where the court has jurisdiction to make an order for custody under Part III of this Act, but as if the reference in section 43(2) to a financial provision order in favour of the child were a reference to an order for payments for the maintenance and education of the child.

(2) Without prejudice to the effect of paragraph 1(a) of this Schedule in relation to an order made under section 36 or 37 of the Act of 1965 which could have been made under section 43 or, as the case may be, section 44 above, any order made under section 36 or 37 of that Act by virtue of the jurisdiction of the court to make an order for the custody of a child under section 34(1)(c) of that Act shall be deemed to have been made under section 43 or 44 above, as the case may require.

26. Section 44(4) above shall apply in relation to the jurisdiction possessed by a court to vary an order made or deemed to have been made with respect to a child's custody, maintenance or education under Part III of the Act of 1965 as it applies in relation to the jurisdiction possessed by a court to vary any financial provision order in a child's favour and any order made with respect to a child's custody or education under Part III of this Act.

SCHEDULE 2

CONSEQUENTIAL AMENDMENTS

1., 2., 3. (*1*) (*Para 1 repealed by Supreme Court Act 1981, s 152(4), Sch 7; para 2 amends the definition of 'statute of limitation' in Limitation (Enemies and War Prisoners) Act 1945, s 2(1); para 3(1) substitutes Maintenance Orders Act 1950, s 16(2)(a)(i), (c)(v).*)

3. (2) Sub-paragraph (1) above extends to Scotland and Northern Ireland, and the references to section 16(2)(c) of the Maintenance Orders Act 1950 in paragraph 8 of Schedule 8 to the Administration of Justice Act 1970 and paragraph 9 of Schedule 1 to the Attachment of Earnings Act 1971 shall be construed as references to section 16(2)(c) as amended by sub-paragraph (1)(b) above.

4.–6. (*Para 4 inserts para (g) in County Courts Act 1959, s 109(2) (repealed); para 5(1) was repealed by Inheritance (Provision for Family Dependants) Act 1975, s 26(2), Schedule; para 5(2) amends Matrimonial Causes Act 1965, s 42 (repealed) (p 2264); para 6(1), (2) repealed by Matrimonial and Family Proceedings Act 1984, s 46(3), Sch 3; para 6(3) repealed by Supreme Court Act 1981, s 152(4), Sch 7.*)

7. (*1*) (*Amends Domestic and Appellate Proceedings (Restriction of Publicity) Act 1968, s 2(1) (p 2282) and repeals s 2(2) of that Act.*)

... and the references in subsection (3) of that section to subsection (1) and to subsection (1)(a) thereof shall be construed as references to subsection (1) and to subsection (1)(a) as they respectively have effect by virtue of this sub-paragraph.

(*2*), (*3*) (*Repealed by Statute Law (Repeals) Act 1977, Schedule, Part VII.*)

8.–13. (*Para 8 amends Family Law Reform Act 1969, s 7(3), (4) (p 2306); para 9 repealed by Child Care Act 1980, s 89(3), Sch 6; para 10(1) repealed by Supreme Court Act 1981, s 152(4), Sch 7; para 10(2) inserts para 2A in Administration of Justice Act 1970, Sch 8 (p 2354); para 11 repealed by Children Act 1989, s 108(7), Sch 15; para 12 partly repealed by Inheritance (Provision for Family and Dependants) Act 1975, s 26(2), Schedule, and wholly repealed by Matrimonial and Family Proceedings Act 1984, s 46(3), Sch 3; para 13 substitutes Attachment of Earnings Act 1971, Sch 1, para 3.*)

SCHEDULE 3

ENACTMENTS REPEALED

Chapter	Short Title	Extent of Repeal
1965 c 72.	The Matrimonial Causes Act 1965.	*The whole Act, except section 8(2); sections 26 to 28A and section 25(4) and (5) as applied by section 28(2); section 42; in section 43(1) the words from 'but a husband' to the end of the subsection; in subsection 46, subsection (1) and in subsection (4) the words from 'this Act does not' to the end of the subsection.*
1967 c 56.	The Matrimonial Causes Act 1967.	*Sections 7 and 8.*
1967 c 80.	The Criminal Justice Act 1967.	*In Part I of Schedule 3, the entry relating to section 36(6) of the Matrimonial Causes Act 1965.*
1968 c 63.	The Domestic and Appellate Proceedings (Restriction of Publicity) Act 1968.	*Sections 2(2) and 3(4).*
1969 c 55.	The Divorce Reform Act 1969.	*The whole Act.*
1970 c 31.	The Administration of Justice Act 1970.	*In Schedule 1, the paragraphs relating respectively to proceedings for a declaration, to proceedings under section 17 of the Married Women's Property Act 1882, and to proceedings under section 1 of the Matrimonial Homes Act 1967. In Schedule 2, paragraph 27.*

Chapter	Short Title	Extent of Repeal
1970 c 33.	*The Law Reform (Miscellaneous Provisions) Act 1970.*	Section 4.
1970 c 42.	*The Local Authority Social Services Act 1970.*	In Schedule 1, the entry relating to section 37 of the Matrimonial Causes Act 1965.
1970 c 45.	*The Matrimonial Proceedings and Property Act 1970.*	The whole of Part I. Sections 34, 35, 40, 41, and 42. In section 43, subsection (2) and, in subsection (4), the words from the beginning to 'of this Act'. The Schedules.
1971 c 3.	*The Guardianship of Minors Act 1971.*	In Schedule 1, in the entry relating to section 16(2) of the Maintenance Orders Act 1950, the words from 'and' to '1971'.
1971 c 23.	*The Courts Act 1971.*	Section 45(7). In Schedule 8, paragraph 47.
1971 c 44.	*The Nullity of Marriage Act 1971.*	The whole Act.
1972 c 38.	*The Matrimonial Proceedings (Polygamous Marriages) Act 1972.*	Sections 1 and 4.
1972 c 70.	*The Local Government Act 1972.*	In Schedule 23, paragraph 13.

Note. This Schedule repealed by Statute Law (Repeals) Act 1977.

COMPARATIVE TABLE

This Table shows in column (1) the enactments repealed by the Matrimonial Causes Act 1973 and in column (2) the provisions of that Act corresponding thereto.

In certain cases the enactment in column (1), though having a corresponding provision in column (2), is not, or is not wholly, repealed as it is still required, or partly required, for the purposes of other legislation.

(1)	(2)	(1)	(2)
Matrimonial Causes Act 1965 (c 72)	Matrimonial Causes Act 1973 (c 18)	Matrimonial Causes Act 1965 (c 72)	Matrimonial Causes Act 1973 (c 18)
s 1	Rep, 1969 c 55, s 9(2), Sch 2	s 8(1)	Omitted as recommended by the
2(1), (2)	3(1), (2)		Law Commission
(3)	(4)		in Cmnd 5167,
3	4		para 8
4	Cf 49(1)–(4)	9	Sch 1, para 11(1),
5(1)–(4)	Rep, 1969 c 55, s 9(2), Sch 2	10	(3), (4) s 15
(5)	3(3)	11	Sch 1, para 12
(6)	20	12(1)	s 17, Sch 1,
(7)	1(5)		para 8
ss 6, 7	ss 8, 9	(2)	s 18(1)

* Not repealed.   † Repealed in part.

(1)	(2)	(1)	(2)
Matrimonial Causes Act 1965 (c 72)	Matrimonial Causes Act 1973 (c 18)	Matrimonial Causes Act 1967 (c 56)	Matrimonial Causes Act 1973 (c 18)
s 12(3)	Omitted as recommended by the Law Commission in Cmnd 5167, para 9	s 7(1) (2) (3) 8 10(1)* Sch 3, Part I†	s 50(1), (2) (4) (3) 51 50(5) 43(6)
13	Rep, 1970 c 45, ss 28, 42(2), Sch 1, para 1, Sch 3		
14	s 19(1)–(5)	**Domestic and Appellate Proceedings (Restriction of Publicity) Act 1968 (c 63)**	
ss 15–24, 25(1), (3), 29–35	Rep, 1970 c 45, ss 28, 42(2), Sch 1, para 1, Sch 3		
s 36	s 43, Sch 1, para 25		
37(1), (2), (4)–(6)	44, Sch 1, paras 25, 26	s 2(2) 3(4)	s 45(9) Applied to Scotland
(3)	Rep, 1970 c 42, s 14, Sch 3	**Divorce Reform Act 1969 (c 55)**	
38	Sch 2, para 3		
39	s 45		
40	46	s 1	s 1
41	Rep, 1970 c 33, s 7, Sch	2(1)–(3) (4)–(6)	(2)–(4) 2 (4), (6), (7)
42(1)*, (3)*	s 27(8)	3(1), (2)	6
43(1)†	48(1)	(3)	2(1), (2)
(2)	Omitted as recommended by the Law Commission in Cmnd 5167, para 10	(4)–(6) 4 5 6 7(1)	(3), (5), (6) 5 10(1) (2)–(4) 7
(3)	s 48(2)	(2)	Sch 2, para 6(2)
44	49(5)	8(1)	
45	—	(2)	s 17, Sch 1, para 8
46(2)	Rep, 1970 c 45, ss 28, 42(2), Sch 1, para 1, Sch 3	(3) 9(1)	(2) ss 4(1), 20, 49, Sch 1, para 8
46(3)	—	(2), (3)	Sch 1, para 3
(4)†	s 55(3)	10	
Sch 1, para 1	Cf Sch 1, para 1	11(1)–(3)	s 55(3)
2	Sch 1, para 8	(4)	4(1)
3	—	Sch 1, para 1	Cf s 49
4	Sch 1, para 11(2)	2	s 20
paras 5–7, 9–11	Rep, 1970 c 45, ss 28, 42(2), Sch 1, para 1, Sch 3	3 paras 4–7	Rep, 1970 c 45, s 42(2), Sch 3
para 8	—	para 8	Sch 2, para 5(1)(b)
		paras 9–11	Rep, 1970 c 45, s 42(2), Sch 3

* Not repealed.   † Repealed in part.

(1)	(2)	(1)	(2)
Divorce Reform Act 1969 (c 55)	Matrimonial Causes Act 1973 (c 18)	Matrimonial Proceedings and Property Act 1970 (c 45)	Matrimonial Causes Act 1973 (c 18)
Sch 1, para 12	Sch 1, para 8	s 16	s 37
Sch 2	———	17	41
		18(1)	42(1)
Administration of Justice Act 1970 (c 31)		(2)	(5)
Sch 1†		(3), (4)	(3), (4)
Sch 2, para 27	s 50(1)	(5), (6)	(6), (7)
28*	(5)	19(1)	(2), (6)
		(2)	(5), (7)
Law Reform (Miscellaneous Provisions) Act 1970 (c 33)		20	———
		21	Sch 1, para 15
		22	s 38(1)–(3), (5)–(7), Sch 1, para 16
s 4	———	23	39
7(2)*	Sch 1, para 4	24	ss 23(5), 24(3), 26
		25	s 30
		26	40
Local Authority Social Services Act 1970 (c 42)		27	52(1), (3), (4)
		28	———
Sch 1†	———	29	Sch 1, para 14
		34(1)	ss 33(5), 38(4), Sch 1, para 23
Matrimonial Proceedings and Property Act 1970 (c 45)		(2)	Sch 2, para 4
		35	s 3(2)
		40(1), (2)	18(2), Sch 1, para 13
s 1	s 22	(2)	18(3)
2(1), (2)	23(1), (3)	(3)	Sch 1, para 13
3	(1)–(4)	41	———
4	24(1), (2)	42(1)	ss 17(2), 43(1), 44, 50(1), (2)
5	25	(2)	———
6	27(1)–(7)	43(2)	———
7	28	(4)†	s 55(3)
8	29	Sch 1, para 1	Sch 1, paras 2, 5
9	31	2	para 4
10	32	3(1)–	17
11	33(1)–(4), (6)	(4)	
12(1)	Sch 2, paras 3(1), 10(2)	(5)	18
(2)	para 3(2)	paras 4, 5	paras 22, 23
13	s 34	para 6	para 19
14	35	paras 7, 8	paras 9, 10
15	36	9	para 24
		10	———
		paras 11, 12	paras 20, 21
		Sch 2, para 1	ss 43(1), 44, Sch 2, para 5(1)(a)
		2(1)	Sch 2, para 6(1)

* Not repealed. † Repealed in part.

(1)	(2)	(1)	(2)
Matrimonial Proceedings and Property Act 1970 (c 45)	Matrimonial Causes Act 1973 (c 18)	Nullity of Marriage Act 1971 (c 44)	Matrimonial Causes Act 1973 (c 18)
Sch 2, para 2(2)	s 50(1), (2)	7(1)	————
3	Sch 2, para 7	(2)	46(1), Sch 2,
4	s 17(2)		para 2
5	Sch 2, para 10(2)	(3)	
Sch 3	————	(4)	Sch 1, para 6
Sch 1†	Sch 2, para 3(1)	(5)	————
		(6)	s 55(3)
Courts Act 1971 (c 23)		Matrimonial Proceedings (Polygamous Marriages) Act 1972 (c 38)	
————		————	
s 45(7)	s 50(1)(a)	s 1	s 47
Sch 8, para 47	(1)	4	11
		5(2)*	52(4)
Nullity of Marriage Act 1971 (c 44)		Local Government Act 1972 (c 70)	
————		————	
s 1	s 11	Sch 23, para 13(1)	43(1), (9)
2	12	(2)	44(2), (6)
3(1)–(3)	13		
(4)	Sch 1, para 11(3)		
4	s 14		
5	16		
6(1)	————		
(2)	19(6)		

* Not repealed.   † Repealed in part.

DOMICILE AND MATRIMONIAL PROCEEDINGS ACT 1973

(1973 c 45)

ARRANGEMENT OF SECTIONS

PART I

DOMICILE

Husband and wife

An Act to amend the law relating to the domicile of married women and persons not of full age, to matters connected with domicile and to jurisdiction in matrimonial proceedings including actions for reduction of consistorial decrees; to make further provision about the recognition of divorces and legal separations; and for purposes connected therewith.   [25 July 1973]

PART I

DOMICILE

Husband and wife

1. Abolition of wife's dependent domicile—(1) Subject to subsection (2) below, the domicile of a married woman as at any time after the coming into force of this section shall, instead of being the same as her husband's by virtue only of marriage, be ascertained by reference to the same factors as in the case of any other individual capable of having an independent domicile.

(2) Where immediately before this section came into force a woman was married and then had her husband's domicile by dependence, she is to be treated as retaining that domicile (as a domicile of choice, if it is not also her domicile of origin) unless and until it is changed by acquisition or revival of another domicile either on or after the coming into force of this section.

(3) This section extends to England and Wales, Scotland and Northern Ireland.

2. Amendments of Recognition Act consequent on s 1.   (*Repealed by Family Law Act 1986, s 68(2), Sch 2, as from 4 April 1988.*)

Minors and pupils

3. Age at which independent domicile can be acquired—(1) The time at which a person first becomes capable of having an independent domicile shall be when he attains the age of sixteen or marries under that age; and in the case of a person who immediately before 1 January 1974 was incapable of having an independent domicile, but had then attained the age of sixteen or been married, it shall be that date.

(2) This section extends to England and Wales and Northern Ireland (but not to Scotland).

4. Dependent domicile of child not living with his father—(1) Subsection (2) of this section shall have effect with respect to the dependent domicile of a child as at any time after the coming into force of this section when his father and mother are alive but living apart.

(2) The child's domicile as at that time shall be that of his mother if—

(a) he then has his home with her and has no home with his father; or

(b) he has at any time had her domicile by virtue of paragraph (a) above and has not since had a home with his father.

(3) As at any time after the coming into force of this section, the domicile of a child whose mother is dead shall be that which she last had before she died if at her death he had her domicile by virtue of subsection (2) above and he has not since had a home with his father.

(4) Nothing in this section prejudices any existing rule of law as to cases in which a child's domicile is regarded as being, by dependence, that of his mother.

(5) In this section, 'child' means a person incapable of having an independent domicile; *and in its application to a child who has been adopted, references to his father and his mother shall be construed as references to his adoptive father and mother.*

Note. Words in italics repealed by Children Act 1975, s 108(1)(b), Sch 4, Part I, as from 1 January 1976.

(6) This section extends to England and Wales, Scotland and Northern Ireland.

PART II

JURISDICTION IN MATRIMONIAL PROCEEDINGS (ENGLAND AND WALES)

5. Jurisdiction of High Court and county courts—(1) Subsections (2) to (5) below shall have effect, *subject to section 6(3) and (4) of this Act*, with respect to the jurisdiction of the court to entertain—

(a) proceedings for *divorce, judicial separation or* nullity of marriage; and

(b) proceedings for death to be presumed and a marriage to be dissolved in pursuance of section 19 of the Matrimonial Causes Act 1973;

and in this Part of this Act 'the court' means the High Court and a divorce county court within the meaning of the Matrimonial Causes Act 1967 [Part V of the Matrimonial and Family Proceedings Act 1984].

Note. For Matrimonial Causes Act 1973, s 19, see p 2507. Words 'subject to section 6(3) and (4) of this Act' and 'divorce, judicial separation or' in italics repealed by Family Law Act 1996, s 66(3), Sch 10, as from a day to be appointed, subject to savings in s 66(2) of, and para 5 of Sch 9 to, the 1996 Act. Words 'Part V ... Act 1984' in square brackets substituted for words in italics by Matrimonial and Family Proceedings Act 1984, s 46(1), Sch 1, para 17, as from 28 April 1986. Words 'and in this ... Family Proceedings Act 1984' in italics repealed by the European Communities (Matrimonial Jurisdiction and Judgments) Regulations 2001, SI 2001/310, reg 3(1), (2), as from 1 March 2001.

[(1A) In this Part of this Act—

'the Council Regulation' means Council Regulation (EC) No 1347/2000 of 29th May 2000 on jurisdiction and the recognition and enforcement of judgments in matrimonial matters and in matters of parental responsibility for children of both spouses;

'Contracting State' means—

(a) one of the original parties to the Council Regulation, that is to say Belgium, Germany, Greece, Spain, France, Ireland, Italy, Luxembourg, the Netherlands, Austria, Portugal, Finland, Sweden and the United Kingdom, and

(b) a party which has subsequently adopted the Council Regulation; and

'the court' means the High Court and a divorce county court within the meaning of Part V of the Matrimonial and Family Proceedings Act 1984.]

Note. Sub-s (3A) inserted by the European Communities (Matrimonial Jurisdiction and Judgments) Regulations 2001 SI 2001/310, reg 3(1), (3), as from 1 March 2001.

(*2*) *The court shall have jurisdiction to entertain proceedings for divorce or judicial separation if (and only if) either of the parties to the marriage—*
  (*a*) *is domiciled in England and Wales on the date when the proceedings are begun; or*
  (*b*) *was habitually resident in England and Wales throughout the period of one year ending with that date.*

Note. Sub-s (2) repealed by Family Law Act 1996, s 66(3), Sch 10, as from a day to be appointed, subject to savings in s 66(2) of, and para 5 of Sch 9 to, the 1996 Act.

(*3*) *The court shall have jurisdiction to entertain proceedings for nullity of marriage if (and only if) either of the parties to the marriage—*
  (*a*) *is domiciled in England and Wales on the date when the proceedings are begun; or*
  (*b*) *was habitually resident in England and Wales throughout the period of one year ending with that date; or*
  (*c*) *died before that date and either—*
      (*i*) *was at death domiciled in England and Wales, or*
      (*ii*) *had been habitually resident in England and Wales throughout the period of one year ending with the date of death.*

[(2) The court shall have jurisdiction to entertain proceedings for divorce or judicial separation if (and only if)—
  (a) the court has jurisdiction under the Council Regulation; or
  (b) no court of a Contracting State has jurisdiction under the Council Regulations and either of the parties to the marriage is domiciled in England and Wales on the date when the proceedings are begun.]

[(3) The court shall have jurisdiction to entertain proceedings for nullity of marriage if (and only if)—
  (a) the court has jurisdiction under the Council Regulation; or
  (b) no court of a Contracting State has jurisdiction under the Council Regulation and either of the parties to the marriage—
      (i) is domiciled in England and Wales on the date when the proceedings are begun; or
      (ii) died before that date and either was at death domiciled in England and Wales or had been habitually resident in England and Wales throughout the period of one year ending with the date of death.]

Note. Sub-ss (2), (3) in square brackets substituted for sub-ss (2), (3) in italics by the European Communities (Matrimonial Jurisdiction and Judgments) Regulations 2001, SI 2001/310, reg 3(1), (4)–(6), as from 1 March 2001.

[(3A) Subsections (21) and (3) above do not give the court jurisdiction to entertain proceedings in contravention of Article 7 of the Council Regulation.]

Note. Sub-s (3A) inserted by the European Communities (Matrimonial Jurisdiction and Judgments) Regulations 2001, SI 2001/310, reg 3(1), (4)–(6), as from 1 March 2001.

(4) The court shall have jurisdiction to entertain proceedings for death to be presumed and a marriage to be dissolved if (and only if) the petitioner—
  (a) is domiciled in England and Wales on the date when the proceedings are begun; or
  (b) was habitually resident in England and Wales throughout the period of one year ending with that date.

(*5*) *The court shall, at any time when proceedings are pending in respect of which it has jurisdiction by virtue of subsection (2) or (3) above (or of this subsection), also have jurisdiction to entertain other proceedings, in respect of the same marriage, for divorce, judicial separation or nullity of marriage, notwithstanding that jurisdiction would not be exercisable under subsection (2) or (3).*

[(5) The court shall have jurisdiction to entertain proceedings for nullity of marriage (even though it would not otherwise have jurisdiction) at any time when marital proceedings, as defined by section 20 of the Family Law Act 1996, are pending in relation to the marriage.]

Note. Sub-s (5) substituted by Family Law Act 1996, s 66(1), Sch 8, Part I, para 26, as from a day to be appointed, subject to savings in s 66(2) of, and para 5 of Sch 9 to, the 1996 Act.

(6) Schedule 1 to this Act shall have effect as to the cases in which matrimonial proceedings in England and Wales are to be, or may be, stayed by the court where there are concurrent proceedings elsewhere in respect of the same marriage, and as to the other matters dealt with in that Schedule; but nothing in the Schedule—

(a) requires or authorises a stay of proceedings which are pending when this section comes into force; or

(b) prejudices any power to stay proceedings which is exercisable by the court apart from the Schedule.

6. Miscellaneous amendments, transitional provision and savings—(1), (2) *(Sub-ss (1), (2) amend Matrimonial Causes Act 1973, ss 27(2), 50(1) respectively, pp 2529, 2557.*

(3) *No proceedings for divorce shall be entertained by the court by virtue of section 5(2) or (5) of this Act while proceedings for divorce or nullity of marriage, begun before the commencement of this Act, are pending (in respect of the same marriage) in Scotland, Northern Ireland, the Channel Islands or the Isle of Man; and provision may be made by rules of court as to when for the purposes of this subsection proceedings are to be treated as begun or pending in any of those places.*

(4) *Nothing in this Part of this Act—*

(a) *shall be construed to remove any limitation imposed on the jurisdiction of a county court by section 1 of the Matrimonial Causes Act 1967;*

(b) *affects the court's jurisdiction to entertain any proceedings begun before the commencement of this Act.*

Note. Sub-s (4)(a) repealed by Matrimonial and Family Proceedings Act 1984, s 46(3), Sch 3, as from 28 April 1986. Sub-ss (3), (4) repealed by Family Law Act 1996, s 66(3), Sch 10, as from a day to be appointed, subject to savings in s 66(2) of, and para 5 of Sch 9 to, the 1996 Act. For Matrimonial Causes Act 1967, s 1, see p 2272.

*   *   *   *   *

PART V

MISCELLANEOUS AND GENERAL

15, 16.   *(Repealed by Family Law Act 1986, s 68(2), Sch 2, as from 4 April 1988.)*

17. Citation, etc—(1) This Act may be cited as the Domicile and Matrimonial Proceedings Act 1973.

(2) Subject to sections 6(4), 12(6) and 14(3) of this Act, the enactments specified in Schedule 6 to this Act (including certain enactments of the Parliament of Northern Ireland) are hereby repealed to the extent specified in the third column of that Schedule.

(3) *So long as section 2 of the Southern Rhodesia Act 1965 remains in force, this Act shall have effect subject to such provision as may (before or after this Act comes into force) be made by Order in Council under and for the purposes of that section.*

Note. Sub-s (3) repealed by Zimbabwe Act 1979, s 6(3), Sch 3.

(4) Part II of this Act extends to England and Wales only; Part III extends to Scotland only; *Part IV extends to Northern Ireland only;* and this Part extends to the whole of the United Kingdom.

(5) This Act shall come into force on 1 January 1974.

Note. Words in italics in sub-s (4) repealed by Matrimonial Causes (Northern Ireland) Order 1978, SI 1978 No 1045, art 63(b), Sch 5.

SCHEDULES

SCHEDULE 1   Section 5(6)

STAYING OF MATRIMONIAL PROCEEDINGS (ENGLAND AND WALES)

Interpretation

1. *The following five paragraphs* [Paragraphs 2 to 6 below] have effect for the interpretation of this Schedule.

Note. Words in square brackets substituted for words in italics by Family Law Act 1996, s 19(5), Sch 3, para 2, as from a day to be appointed, subject to savings in s 66(2) of, and para 5 of Sch 9 to, the 1996 Act.

2. *'Matrimonial proceedings' means any proceedings so far as they are one or more of the five following kinds, namely, proceedings for—*
   divorce,
   judicial separation,
   nullity of marriage,
   a declaration as to the validity of a marriage of the petitioner, and
   a declaration as to the subsistence of such a marriage.
[**2.**   (1) 'Matrimonial proceedings' means—
   (a) marital proceedings;
   (b) proceedings for nullity of marriage;
   (c) proceedings for a declaration as to the validity of a marriage of the petitioner; or
   (d) proceedings for a declaration as to the subsistence of such a marriage.
   (2) 'Marital proceedings' has the meaning given by section 20 of the Family Law Act 1996.
   (3) 'Divorce proceedings' means marital proceedings that are divorce proceedings by virtue of that section.

Note. Para 2 substituted by Family Law Act 1996, s 19(5), Sch 3, para 3, as from a day to be appointed, subject to savings in s 66(2) of, and para 5 of Sch 9 to, the 1996 Act.

3.   (1) 'Another jurisdiction' means any country outside England and Wales.
   (2) 'Related jurisdiction' means any of the following countries, namely, Scotland, Northern Ireland, Jersey, Guernsey and the Isle of Man (the reference to Guernsey being treated as including Alderney and Sark).
4.   (1) References to the trial or first trial in any proceedings do not include references to the separate trial of an issue as to jurisdiction only.
   (2) For purposes of this Schedule, proceedings in the court are continuing if they are pending and not stayed.
[**4A.**   (1) 'Statement of marital breakdown' has the same meaning as in the Family Law Act 1996.
   (2) 'Relevant statement' in relation to any marital proceedings, means—
   (a) the statement of marital breakdown with which the proceedings commenced; or
   (b) if the proceedings are for the conversion of a separation order into a divorce order under section 4 of the Family Law Act 1996, the statement of marital breakdown by reference to which the separation order was made.]

Note. Para 4A inserted by Family Law Act 1996, s 19(5), Sch 3, para 4, as from a day to be appointed, subject to savings in s 66(2) of, and para 5 of Sch 9 to, the 1996 Act.

5. Any reference in this Schedule to proceedings in another jurisdiction is to proceedings in a court of that jurisdiction, and to any other proceedings in that jurisdiction, which are of a description prescribed for the purposes of this paragraph; and provision may be made by rules of court as to when proceedings of any description in another jurisdiction are continuing for the purposes of this Schedule.
6. 'Prescribed' means prescribed by rules of court.

Duty to furnish particulars of concurrent proceedings in another jurisdiction

7. *While matrimonial proceedings are pending in the court in respect of a marriage and the trial or first trial in those proceedings has not begun, it shall be the duty of any person who is a petitioner in the proceedings, or is a respondent and has in his answer included a prayer for relief, to furnish, in such manner and to such persons and on such occasions as may be prescribed, such particulars as may be prescribed of any proceedings which—*

    (*a*) *he knows to be continuing in another jurisdiction; and*

    (*b*) *are in respect of that marriage or capable of affecting its validity or subsistence.*

[**7.**   (1) While marital proceedings are pending in the court with respect to a marriage, this paragraph applies—

    (a) to the party or parties to the marriage who made the relevant statement; and

    (b) in prescribed circumstances where the statement was made by only one party, to the other party.

    (2) While matrimonial proceedings of any other kind are pending in the court with respect to a marriage and the trial or first trial in those proceedings has not begun, this paragraph applies—

    (a) to the petitioner; and

    (b) if the respondent has included a prayer for relief in his answer, to the respondent.

    (3) A person to whom this paragraph applies must give prescribed information about any proceedings which—

    (a) he knows to be continuing in another jurisdiction; and

    (b) are in respect of the marriage or capable of affecting its validity or subsistence.

    (4) The information must be given in such manner, to such persons and on such occasions as may be prescribed.]

Note. Para 7 substituted by Family Law Act 1996, s 19(5), Sch 3, para 5, as from a day to be appointed, subject to savings in s 66(2) of, and para 5 of Sch 9 to, the 1996 Act.

Obligatory stays

8.   (*1*) *Where before the beginning of the trial or first trial in any proceedings for divorce which are continuing in the court it appears to the court on the application of a party to the marriage* [(1) This paragraph applies where divorce proceedings are continuing in the court with respect to a marriage.

    (2) Where it appears to the court, on the application of a party to the marriage]—

    (a) that in respect of the same marriage proceedings for divorce or nullity of marriage are continuing in a related jurisdiction; and

    (b) that the parties to the marriage have resided together after its celebration; and

    (c) that the place where they resided together when the proceedings in the court were begun or, if they did not then reside together, where they last resided together before those proceedings were begun, is in that jurisdiction; and

    (d) that either of the said parties was habitually resident in that jurisdiction throughout the year ending with the date on which they last resided together before the date on which the proceedings in the court were begun,

it shall be the duty of the court, subject to paragraph 10(2) below, to order that the *proceedings* [divorce proceedings] in the court be stayed.

    (*2*) *References in sub-paragraph* (*1*) *above to the proceedings in the court are, in the case of proceedings which are not only proceedings for divorce, to the proceedings so far as they are proceedings for divorce.*

    [(3) The effect of such an order is that, while it is in force—

    (a) no application for a divorce order in relation to the marriage may be made either by reference to the relevant statement or by reference to any subsequent statement of marital breakdown; and

    (b) if such an application has been made, no divorce order may be made on that application.]

Note. Words in square brackets in para 8(1) substituted for words in italics, and para 8(3) in square brackets substituted for para 8(2) in italics by Family Law Act 1996, s 19(5), Sch 3, para 6, as from a day to be appointed, subject to savings in s 66(2) of, and para 5 of Sch 9 to, the 1996 Act.

Discretionary stays

9. (*1*) *Where before the beginning of the trial or first trial in any matrimonial proceedings* [, *other than proceedings governed by Council Regulation,*] *which are continuing in the court it appears to the court—*
  (*a*) *that any proceedings in respect of the marriage in question, or capable of affecting its validity or subsistence, are continuing in another jurisdiction; and*
  (*b*) *that the balance of fairness* (*including convenience*) *as between the parties to the marriage is such that it is appropriate for the proceedings in that jurisdiction to be disposed of before further steps are taken in the proceedings in the court or in those proceedings so far as they consist of a particular kind of matrimonial proceedings,*
the court may then, if it thinks fit, order that the proceedings in the court be stayed or, as the case may be, that those proceedings be stayed so far as they consist of proceedings of that kind.
[(1) Sub-paragraph (1A) below applies where—
  (a) marital proceedings are continuing in the court; or
  (b) matrimonial proceedings of any other kind are continuing in the court, if the trial or first trial in the proceedings has not begun.
  (1A) The court may make an order staying the proceedings if it appears to the court—
  (a) that proceedings in respect of the marriage, or capable of affecting its validity or subsistence, are continuing in another jurisdiction; and
  (b) that the balance of fairness (including convenience) as between the parties to the marriage is such that it is appropriate for proceedings in that jurisdiction to be disposed of before further steps are taken in the proceedings to which the order relates.]
  (2) In considering the balance of fairness and convenience for the purposes of sub-paragraph (1)(b) above, the court shall have regard to all factors appearing to be relevant, including the convenience of witnesses and any delay or expense which may result from the proceedings being stayed, or not being stayed.
  (*3*) *In the case of any proceedings so far as they are proceedings for divorce, the court shall not exercise the power conferred on it by sub-paragraph* (*1*) *above while an application under paragraph 8 above in respect of the proceedings is pending.*
  [(3) Where an application for a stay is pending under paragraph 8 above, the court shall not make an order under sub-paragraph (1A) staying marital proceedings in relation to the marriage.]
  (4) If, at any time after the beginning of the trial or the first trial in any matrimonial proceedings which are pending in the court [other than marital proceedings], the court declares by order that it is satisfied that a person has failed to perform the duty imposed on him in respect of the proceedings by paragraph 7 above, sub-paragraph (1) above shall have effect in relation to those proceedings and, to the other proceedings by reference to which the declaration is made, as if the words 'before the beginning of the trial or first trial' were omitted; but no action shall lie in respect of the failure of a person to perform such a duty.
  [(5) The effect of an order under sub-paragraph (1A) for a stay of marital proceedings is that, while it is in force—
  (a) no application for a divorce order or separation order in relation to the marriage may be made either by reference to the relevant statement or by reference to any subsequent statement of marital breakdown; and
  (b) if such an application has been made, no divorce order or separation order shall be made on that application.]

Note. Sub-paras (1), (1A) in square brackets substituted for sub-para (1) in italics, sub-para (3) in square brackets substituted for sub-para (3) in italics, words in square brackets in sub-para (4) inserted, and sub-para (5) inserted, by Family Law Act 1996, s 19(5), Sch 3, para 7, as from a day to be appointed. Words in square brackets in sub-s (1) inserted by the European Communities (Matrimonial Jurisdiction and Judgments) Regulations 2001, SI 2001/310, reg 4, as from 1 March 2001.

Supplementary

10. (1) Where an order staying any proceedings is in force in pursuance of paragraph 8 or 9 above, the court may, if it thinks fit, on the application of a party to the proceedings, discharge the order if it appears to the court that the other proceedings by reference to which the order was made are stayed or concluded, or that a party to those proceedings has delayed unreasonably in prosecuting them.

(*2*) *If the court discharges an order staying any proceedings and made in pursuance of paragraph 8 above, the court shall not again stay those proceedings in pursuance of that paragraph.*

[(1A) Where the court discharges an order staying any proceedings, it may direct that the whole or a specified part of any period while the order has been in force—

(a) is not to count towards any period specified in section 5(3) or 7(9) of the Family Law Act 1996; or

(b) is to count towards any such period only for specified purposes.

(2) Where the court discharges an order under paragraph 8 above, it shall not again make such an order in relation to the marriage except in a case where the obligation to do so arises under that paragraph following receipt by the court of a statement of marital breakdown after the discharge of the order.]

Note. Sub-paras (1A), (2) in square brackets substituted for sub-para (2) in italics by Family Law Act 1996, s 19(5), Sch 3, para 8, as from a day to be appointed.

11. (*1*) *The provisions of sub-paragraphs* (*2*) *and* (*3*) *below shall apply* (*subject to sub-paragraph* (*4*)) *where proceedings for divorce, judicial separation or nullity of marriage are stayed by reference to proceedings in a related jurisdiction for divorce, judicial separation or nullity of marriage; and in this paragraph—*

'custody' includes access to the child in question;

'education' includes training;

'lump sum order' means such an order as is mentioned in paragraph (*f*) *of section 23(1) of the Matrimonial Causes Act 1973* (*lump sum payment for children*), *being an order made under section 23(1) or* (*2*)(*a*) [*or an order made in equivalent circumstances under Schedule 1 to the Children Act 1989 and of a kind mentioned in paragraph 1(2)(c) of that Schedule*];

'the other proceedings', in relation to any stayed proceedings, means the proceedings in another jurisdiction by reference to which the stay was imposed;

'relevant order' means—

(*a*) *an order under section 22 of the Matrimonial Causes Act 1973* (*maintenance for spouse pending suit*),

(*b*) *such an order as is mentioned in paragraph* (*d*) *or* (*e*) *of section 23(1) of that Act* (*periodical payments for children*) *being an order made under section 23(1) or* (*2*)(*a*) [*or an order made in equivalent circumstances under Schedule 1 to the Children Act 1989 and of a kind mentioned in paragraph 1(2)(a) or* (*6*) *of that Schedule*],

(*c*) *an order under section 42(1)(a) of that Act* (*orders for the custody and education of children*) [*or a section 8 order under the Children Act 1989*], *and*

(*d*) *except for the purposes of sub-paragraph* (*3*) *below, any order restraining a person from removing a child out of England and Wales or out of the custody, care and control* [*care*] *of another person; and*

'stayed' means stayed in pursuance of this Schedule.

Note. In para 11(1), definitions 'custody' and 'education' repealed by Children Act 1989, s 108(7), Sch 15, as from 14 October 1991; in definition 'lump sum' words in square brackets added by s 108(5) of, and Sch 13, para 33(1)(a) to, the 1989 Act, as from the same date; and in definition 'relevant order' words in square brackets in paras (b)–(d) inserted or substituted by s 108(5) of, and Sch 13, para 33(b)–(d) to, the 1989 Act, as from the same date.

For Matrimonial Causes Act 1973, ss 22, 23, 42 and the notes thereto, see pp 2510, 2512, 2551.

For Children Act 1989, s 8, Sch 1, para 1(2)(a)–(c), see pp 3296, 3409.

[(1) Sub-paragraphs (2) and (3) below apply where a stay of marital proceedings or proceedings for nullity of marriage—

(a) has been imposed by reference to proceedings in a related jurisdiction for divorce, separation or nullity of marriage, and

(b) is in force.

(1A) In this paragraph—

'lump sum order', in relation to a stay, means an order—

(a) under section 22A or 23, 31 or 31A of the Matrimonial Causes Act 1973 which is an order for the payment of a lump sum for the purposes of Part II of that Act, or

(b) made in any equivalent circumstances under Schedule 1 to the Children Act 1989 and of a kind mentioned in paragraph 1(2)(a) or (b) of that Schedule,

so far as it satisfies the condition mentioned in sub-paragraph (1C) below;

'the other proceedings', in relation to a stay, means the proceedings in another jurisdiction by reference to which the stay was imposed;

'relevant order', in relation to a stay, means—

(a) any financial provision order (including an interim order), other than a lump sum order;

(b) any order made in equivalent circumstances under Schedule 1 to the Children Act 1989 and of a kind mentioned in paragraph 1(2)(a) or (b) of that Schedule;

(c) any section 8 order under the Act of 1989; and

(d) except for the purposes of sub-paragraph (3) below, any order restraining a person from removing a child out of England and Wales or out of the care of another person,

so far as it satisfies the condition mentioned in sub-paragraph (1C) below.

(1C) The condition is that the order is, or (apart from this paragraph) could be, made in connection with the proceedings to which the stay applies.]

Note. Sub-paras (1), (1A), (1C) in square brackets substituted for sub-para (1) in italics by Family Law Act 1996, s 19(5), Sch 3, para 9(2), as from a day to be appointed.

(2) Where *any proceedings are stayed* [this paragraph applies in relation to a stay], then, without prejudice to the effect of the stay apart from this paragraph—

(a) the court shall not have power to make a relevant order or a lump sum order *in connection with the stayed proceedings* except in pursuance of paragraph (c) below; and

(b) subject to paragraph (c) below, any relevant order *made in connection with the stayed proceedings* [already made] shall, unless the stay is previously removed or the order previously discharged, cease to have effect on the expiration of the period of three months beginning with the date on which the stay was imposed; but

(c) if the court considers that, for the purpose of dealing with circumstances needing to be dealt with urgently, it is necessary during or after that period to make a relevant order or a lump sum order *in connection with the stayed proceedings* or to extend or further extend the duration of a relevant order *made in connection with the stayed proceedings* [already made], the court may do so and the order shall not cease to have effect by virtue of paragraph (b) above.

Note. Words in square brackets substituted for words in italics, and other words in italics repealed by Family Law Act 1996, ss 19(5), 66(3), Sch 3, para 9(3), Sch 10, as from a day to be appointed.

(3) Where *any proceedings are stayed* [this paragraph applies in relation to a stay] and at the time when the stay is imposed an order is in force, or at a subsequent time an order comes into force, which was made in connection with the other proceedings and provides for any of the *four* following matters, namely, periodical payments for a spouse of the marriage in question, periodical payments for a child, *the custody of a child and the education of a child* [or any provision which could be made by a section 8 order under the Children Act 1989] then, on the imposition of the stay in a case where the order is in force when the stay is imposed and on the coming into force of the order in any other case—

(a)   any relevant order *made in connection with the stayed proceedings* [already made] shall cease to have effect in so far as it makes for a spouse or child any provision for any of those matters as respects which the same or different provision for that spouse or child is made by the other order;

(b)   the court shall not have power *in connection with the stayed proceedings* to make a relevant order containing for a spouse or child provision for any of those matters as respects which any provision for that spouse or child is made by the other order; and

(c)   if the other order contains provision for periodical payments for a child, the court shall not have power *in connection with the stayed proceedings* to make a lump sum order for that child.

[(3A) *Where any such order as is mentioned in paragraph (e) of section 23(1) of the Matrimonial Causes Act 1973, being an order made under section 23(1) or (2)(a) of that Act, ceases to have effect by virtue of sub-paragraph (2) or (3) above,* [Where a secured periodical payments order within the meaning of the Matrimonial Causes Act 1973—

(a)   has been made under section 22A(1)(b) or 23(1)(b) or (2)(b) of that Act, but

(b)   ceases to have effect by virtue of sub-paragraph (2) or (3) above,]

any order made under section 24A(1) of that Act which requires the proceeds of sale of property to be used for securing periodical payments under the first mentioned order shall also cease to have effect.]

Notes. In sub-para (3) word 'four' repealed by Children Act 1989, s 108(7), Sch 15, and words 'or any provision … 1989' in square brackets substituted for words in italics by s 108(5) of, and Sch 13, para 33(2) to, the 1989 Act, as from 14 October 1991.

Words in first pair of square brackets and words in sub-para (3)(a) in square brackets substituted for words in italics, and words in italics in sub-para (3)(b), (c), repealed, by Family Law Act 1996, ss 19(5), 66(3), Sch 3, para 9(4), Sch 10, as from a day to be appointed.

Sub-para (3A) added by Matrimonial Homes and Property Act 1981, s 8(3), as from 1 October 1981.

(4) *If any proceedings are stayed so far as they consist of matrimonial proceedings of a particular kind but are not stayed so far as they consist of matrimonial proceedings of a different kind, sub-paragraphs (2) and (3) above shall not apply to the proceedings but, without prejudice to the effect of the stay apart from this paragraph, the court shall not have power to make a relevant order or a lump sum order in connection with the proceedings so far as they are stayed; and in this sub-paragraph references to matrimonial proceedings do not include proceedings for a declaration.*

[(4) Nothing in sub-paragraphs (2) and (3) above affects any relevant order or lump sum order or any power to make such an order in so far as—

(a)   where the stay applies to matrimonial proceedings other than marital proceedings, the order has been made or the power may be exercised following the receipt by the court of a statement of marital breakdown;

(b)   where the stay is of marital proceedings, the order has been made or the power may be exercised in matrimonial proceedings of any other kind; or

(c)   where the stay is of divorce proceedings only, the order has been made or the power may be exercised—

(i)   in matrimonial proceedings which are not marital proceedings, or

(ii)   in marital proceedings in which an application has been made for a separation order.]

Note. Sub-para (4) in square brackets substituted for sub-para (4) in italics by Family Law Act 1996, s 19(5), Sch 3, para 9(6), as from a day to be appointed.

(5) Nothing in this paragraph affects any power of the court—

(a) to vary or discharge a relevant order so far as the order is for the time being in force; or

(b) to enforce a relevant order as respects any period when it is or was in force; or

(c) to make a relevant order or a lump sum order *in connection with proceedings which were but are no longer stayed* [where a stay no longer applies].

Note. Words in square brackets substituted for words in italics by Family Law Act 1996, s 19(5), Sch 3, para 9(7), as from a day to be appointed.

*   *   *   *   *

SCHEDULE 6   Section 17

REPEALS

Chapter	Short Title	Extent of Repeal
* * *	* * *	* * *
7 & 8 Geo 6 c 43.	The Matrimonial Causes (War Marriages) Act 1944.	Section 3.
* * *	* * *	* * *
12, 13 & 14 Geo 6 c 100.	The Law Reform (Miscellaneous Provisions) Act 1949.	In section 2, subsections (1), (2) and (3).
14 Geo 6 c 37.	The Maintenance Orders Act 1950.	In section 6(2), the words 'an action of separation and aliment'.
* * *	* * *	* * *
10 & 11 Eliz 2 c 21.	The Commonwealth Immigrants Act 1962.	Section 20.
1973 c 18.	The Matrimonial Causes Act 1973.	In section 19, in subsection (1) the words 'subject to subsection (2) below', subsections (2) and (5). Section 46.

EVIDENCE (PROCEEDINGS IN OTHER JURISDICTIONS) ACT 1975

(1975 c 34)

An Act to make new provision for enabling the High Court, the Court of Session and the High Court of Justice in Northern Ireland to assist in obtaining evidence required for the purposes of proceedings in other jurisdictions; to extend the powers of those courts to issue process effective throughout the United Kingdom for securing the attendance of witnesses; and for purposes connected with those matters.   [22 May 1975]

Evidence for civil proceedings

1. Application to United Kingdom court for assistance in obtaining evidence for civil proceedings in other court.   Where an application is made to the High Court, the Court of Session or the High Court of Justice in Northern Ireland for an order for evidence to be obtained in the part of the United Kingdom in which it exercises jurisdiction, and the court is satisfied—

(a) that the application is made in pursuance of a request issued by or on behalf of a court or tribunal ('the requesting court') exercising jurisdiction in any other part of the United Kingdom or in a country or territory outside the United Kingdom; and

(b) that the evidence to which the application relates is to be obtained for the purposes of civil proceedings which either have been instituted before the requesting court or whose institution before that court is contemplated,

the High Court, Court of Session or High Court of Justice in Northern Ireland, as the case may be, shall have the powers conferred on it by the following provisions of this Act.

Note. For definition of 'United Kingdom', see Interpretation Act 1978, s 5, Sch 1; for definition of 'civil proceedings', see s 9(1) of this Act (p 2586).

2. Power of United Kingdom court to give effect to application for assistance—(1) Subject to the provisions of this section, the High Court, the Court of Session and the High Court of Justice in Northern Ireland shall each have power, on any such application as is mentioned in section 1 above, by order to make such provision for obtaining evidence in the part of the United Kingdom in which it exercises jurisdiction as may appear to the court to be appropriate for the purpose of giving effect to the request in pursuance of which the application is made; and any such order may require a person specified therein to take such steps as the court may consider appropriate for that purpose.

(2) Without prejudice to the generality of subsection (1) above but subject to the provisions of this section, an order under this section may, in particular, make provision—

(a) for the examination of witnesses, either orally or in writing;

(b) for the production of documents;

(c) for the inspection, photographing, preservation, custody or detention of any property;

(d) for the taking of samples of any property and the carrying out of any experiments on or with any property;

(e) for the medical examination of any person;

(f) without prejudice to paragraph (e) above, for the taking and testing of samples of blood from any person.

(3) An order under this section shall not require any particular steps to be taken unless they are steps which can be required to be taken by way of obtaining evidence for the purposes of civil proceedings in the court making the order (whether or not proceedings of the same description as those to which the application for the order relates); but this subsection shall not preclude the making of an order requiring a person to give testimony (either orally or in writing) otherwise than on oath where this is asked for by the requesting court.

Note. For definition of 'oath', see Interpretation Act 1978, s 5, Sch 1.

(4) An order under this section shall not require a person—

(a) to state what documents relevant to the proceedings to which the application for the order relates are or have been in his possession, custody or power; or

(b) to produce any documents other than particular documents specified in the order as being documents appearing to the court making the order to be, or likely to be, in his possession, custody or power.

(5) A person who, by virtue of an order under this section, is required to attend at any place shall be entitled to the like conduct money and payment for expenses and loss of time as on attendance as a witness in civil proceedings before the court making the order.

3. Privilege of witnesses—(1) A person shall not be compelled by virtue of an order under section 2 above to give any evidence which he could not be compelled to give—

(a) in civil proceedings in the part of the United Kingdom in which the court that made the order exercises jurisdiction; or

(b) subject to subsection (2) below, in civil proceedings in the country or territory in which the requesting court exercises jurisdiction.

(2) Subsection (1)(b) above shall not apply unless the claim of the person in question to be exempt from giving evidence is either—

(a) supported by a statement contained in the request (whether it is so supported unconditionally or subject to conditions that are fulfilled); or

(b) conceded by the applicant for the order;

and where such a claim made by any person is not supported or conceded as aforesaid he may (subject to the provisions of this section) be required to give the evidence to which the claim relates but that evidence shall not be transmitted to the requesting court if that court, on the matter being referred to it, upholds the claim.

(3) Without prejudice to subsection (1) above, a person shall not be compelled by virtue of an order under section 2 above to give any evidence if his doing so would be prejudicial to the security of the United Kingdom; and a certificate signed by or on behalf of the Secretary of State to the effect that it would be so prejudicial for that person to do so shall be conclusive evidence of that fact.

(4) In this section references to giving evidence include references to answering any question and to producing any document and the reference in subsection (2) above to the transmission of evidence by a person shall be construed accordingly.

4. Extension of powers of High Court etc in relation to obtaining evidence for proceedings in that court.   *Section 49 of the Supreme Court of Judicature (Consolidation) Act 1925 (which enables the High Court to order the issue of a subpoena in special form, enforceable throughout the United Kingdom, for the attendance of a witness at a trial) and the Attendances of Witnesses Act 1854 (corresponding provisions for Court of Session and High Court of Justice in Northern Ireland) shall* [The Attendance of Witnesses Act 1854 (which enables the Court of Session to order the issue of a warrant of citation in special form, enforceable throughout the United Kingdom, for the attendance of a witness at a trial) shall] have effect as if references to attendance at a trial included references to attendance before an examiner or commissioner appointed by the court or a judge thereof in any cause or matter in that court, including an examiner or commissioner appointed to take evidence outside the jurisdiction of the court.

Note. Words in square brackets substituted for words in italics by Supreme Court Act 1981, s 152(1), Sch 5, as from 1 January 1982.

*   *   *   *   *

Evidence for international proceedings

6. Power of United Kingdom court to assist in obtaining evidence for international proceedings—(1) Her Majesty may by Order in Council direct that, subject to such exceptions, adaptations or modifications as may be specified in the Order, the provisions of sections 1 to 3 above shall have effect in relation to international proceedings of any description specified in the order.

(2) An Order in Council under this section may direct that section 1(4) of the Perjury Act 1911 or *section 1(4) of the Perjury Act (Northern Ireland) 1946* [article 3(4) of the Perjury (Northern Ireland) Order 1979] shall have effect in relation to international proceedings to which the Order applies as it has effect in relation to a judicial proceeding in a tribunal of a foreign state.

Note. Words in square brackets substituted for words in italics by Perjury (Northern Ireland) Order 1979, SI 1979 No 1714, art 19(1), Sch 1, para 26.

(3) In this section 'international proceedings' means proceedings before the International Court of Justice or any other court, tribunal, commission, body or authority (whether consisting of one or more persons) which, in pursuance of any international agreement or any resolution of the General Assembly of the United Nations, exercises any jurisdiction or performs any functions of a judicial nature or by way of arbitration, conciliation or inquiry or is appointed (whether permanently or temporarily) for the purpose of exercising any jurisdiction or performing any such functions.

Supplementary

7. Rules of Court.   *The power to make rules of court under section 99 of the Supreme Court of Judicature (Consolidation) Act 1925* [*84 of the Supreme Court Act 1981*] [Civil Procedure Rules or rules of court under] section 7 of the Northern Ireland Act 1962 *shall include power to make rules of court* [may make provision]—
  (a) as to the manner in which any such application as is mentioned in section 1 above is to be made;
  (b) subject to the provisions of this Act, as to the circumstances in which an order can be made under section 2 above; and
  (c) as to the manner in which any such reference as is mentioned in section 3(2) above is to be made;
and any such rules may include such incidental, supplementary and consequential provision as to the authority making the rules may consider necessary or expedient.

Note. Words '84 of the Supreme Court Act 1981' in square brackets substituted for words '99 of the Supreme Court of Judicature (Consolidation) Act 1925' in italics by Supreme Court Act 1981, s 152(1), Sch 5, as from 1 January 1982. For ibid, s 84, see p 2855. Words 'Civil Procedure Rules or rules of court under' and 'may make provision' in square brackets substituted for preceding words in italics by the Courts Act 2003, s 109(1), Sch 8, para 177, as from a day to be appointed.

8. Consequential amendments and repeals—(1) The enactments mentioned in Schedule 1 to this Act shall have effect subject to the amendments there specified, being amendments consequential on the provisions of this Act.

(2) The enactments mentioned in Schedule 2 to this Act are hereby repealed to the extent specified in the third column of that Schedule.

(3) Nothing in this section shall affect—
  (a) any application to any court or judge which is pending at the commencement of this Act;
  (b) any certificate given for the purposes of any such application;
  (c) any power to make an order on such an application; or
  (d) the operation or enforcement of any order made on such an application.

(4) Subsection (3) above is without prejudice to section 38(2) of the Interpretation Act 1889 (effect of repeals).

9. Interpretation—(1) In this Act—
  'civil proceedings', in relation to the requesting court, means proceedings in any civil or commercial matter;
  'requesting court' has the meaning given in section 1 above;
  'property' includes any land, chattel or other corporeal property of any description;
  'request' includes any commission, order or other process issued by or on behalf of the requesting court.

(2) In relation to any application made in pursuance of a request issued by the High Court under *section 85 of the County Courts Act 1959* [section 56 of the County Courts Act 1984] or the High Court of Justice in Northern Ireland under *section 58 of*

the County Courts Act (Northern Ireland) 1959 [Article 43 of the County Courts (Northern Ireland) Order 1980], the reference in section 1(b) above to proceedings instituted before the requesting court shall be construed as a reference to the relevant proceedings in the county court.

Note. Words in first pair of square brackets substituted for preceding words in italics by County Courts Act 1984, s 148(1), Sch 2, Part V, para 53, as from 1 August 1984. Words in second pair of square brackets substituted for preceding words in italics by County Courts (Northern Ireland) Order 1980, SI 1980 No 397, art 68(2), Sch 1, Part II.

(3) Any power conferred by this Act to make an Order in Council includes power to revoke or vary any such Order by a subsequent Order in Council.

(4) Nothing in this Act shall be construed as enabling any court to make an order that is binding on the Crown or on any person in his capacity as an officer or servant of the Crown.

(5) Except so far as the context otherwise requires, any reference in this Act to any enactment is a reference to that enactment as amended or extended by or under any other enactment.

10. Short title, commencement and extent—(1) This Act may be cited as the Evidence (Proceedings in Other Jurisdictions) Act 1975.

(2) This Act shall come into operation on such a day as Her Majesty may by Order in Council appoint.

(3) Her Majesty may by Order in Council make provision for extending any of the provisions of this Act (including section 6 or any Order in Council made thereunder), with such exceptions, adaptations or modifications as may be specified in the Order, to any of the Channel Islands, the Isle of Man, any colony (other than a colony for whose external relations a country other than the United Kingdom is responsible) or any country or territory outside Her Majesty's dominions in which Her Majesty has jurisdiction in right of Her Majesty's Government in the United Kingdom.

Commencement. This Act came into force on 4 May 1976 (SI 1976 No 429). For rules under s 7 see RSC Ord 70, rules 1–6.

Note. Orders in Council have been made in respect of the Cayman Islands, the Falkland Islands and Dependencies, Gibraltar, the Sovereign Base Areas of Akrotiri and Dhekelia, the Isle of Man, Guernsey, Jersey, Hong Kong, Aguilla, Bermuda, Turks and Caicos Islands.

SCHEDULES

(Sch 1 repealed in part by Perjury (Northern Ireland) Order 1979, SI 1979 No 1714, art 19(2), Sch 2. The remainder inserts Perjury Act 1911, s 1A, amends Maintenance Orders (Reciprocal Enforcement) Act 1972, s 44(2), p 2486 or applies to Scotland only.)

SCHEDULE 2   Section 8(2)

REPEALS

Chapter	Short Title	Extent of Repeal
19 & 20 Vict c 113.	The Foreign Tribunals Evidence Act 1856.	The whole Act.
22 Vict c 20.	The Evidence by Commission Act 1859.	The whole Act
33 & 34 Vict c 52.	The Extradition Act 1870.	Section 24.
48 & 49 Vict c 74.	The Evidence by Commission Act 1885.	The whole Act.
53 & 54 Vict c 37.	The Foreign Jurisdiction Act 1890.	In Schedule 1 the entries relating to the Foreign

Chapter	Short Title	Extent of Repeal
		Tribunals Evidence Act 1856, the Evidence by Commission Act 1859 and the Evidence by Commission Act 1885 but without prejudice to any Order in Council made in respect of any of those Acts before the commencement of this Act.
4 & 5 Eliz 2 c 2.	The German Conventions Act 1955.	Section 1(3).
10 & 11 Eliz 2 c 30.	The Northern Ireland Act 1962.	In Schedule 1 the entry relating to the Evidence by Commission Act 1859.
1963 c 27.	The Oaths and Evidence (Over-seas Authorities and Countries) Act 1963.	Section 4.
1966 c 41.	The Arbitration (International Investment Disputes) Act 1966.	In section 3(1), paragraph (b) together with the word 'and' immediately preceding that paragraph. In section 7(e), subsection (2) of the section 3 there set out.
1968 c 64.	The Civil Evidence Act 1968.	Section 17(2).
1971 c 36 (NI).	The Civil Evidence Act (Northern Ireland) 1971.	Section 13(2).

LITIGANTS IN PERSON (COSTS AND EXPENSES) ACT 1975

(1975 c 47)

An Act to make further provision as to the costs or expenses recoverable by litigants in person in civil proceedings.   [1 August 1975]

1. Costs or expenses recoverable—(1) Where, in any proceedings to which this subsection applies, any costs of a litigant in person are ordered to be paid by any other party to the proceedings or in any other way, there may, subject to rules of court, be allowed on the taxation or other determination of those costs sums in respect of any work done, and any expenses and losses incurred, by the litigant in or in connection with the proceedings to which the order relates.

This subsection applies to civil proceedings—
(a) in a county court, in the Supreme Court or in the House of Lords on appeal from the High Court or the Court of Appeal.
(b) before the Lands Tribunal or the Lands Tribunal for Northern Ireland, or
(c) in or before any other court or tribunal specified in an order made under this subsection by the Lord Chancellor.

(2) (*Applies to Scotland*).

(3) An order under subsection (1) or (2) above shall be made by statutory instrument and shall be subject to annulment in pursuance of a resolution of either House of Parliament.

(4) In this section 'rules of court'—

(a) in relation to the Lands Tribunal or the Lands Tribunal for Scotland, means rules made under section 3 of the Lands Tribunal Act 1949,

(b) in relation to the Lands Tribunal for Northern Ireland, means rules made under section 9 of the Lands Tribunal and Compensation Act (Northern Ireland) 1964, and

(c) in relation to any other tribunal specified in an order made under subsection (1) or (2) above, shall have the meaning given by the order as respects that tribunal.

(5) In the application of subsection (1) above to Northern Ireland, the expressions 'county court', 'the Supreme Court', 'the High Court' and 'the Court of Appeal' shall have the meanings respectively assigned to them by section 29(1) of the Northern Ireland Act 1962.

2. Short title, commencement and extent—(1) This Act may be cited as the Litigants in Person (Costs and Expenses) Act 1975.

(2) This Act shall come into operation—

(a) in relation to England and Wales and Northern Ireland, on such day as the Lord Chancellor may by order made by statutory instrument appoint, and

(b) (applies to Scotland).

(3) An order under subsection (2) above—

(a) may appoint different days for different purposes, and

(b) may make such transitional provision as appears to the Lord Chancellor, or as the case may be the Lord Advocate, to be necessary or expedient.

Note. Sub-ss (2), (3) repealed by the Statute Law (Repeals) Act 2004, Sch 1, Pt 1, as from 22 July 2004.

(4) This Act extends to Northern Ireland.

CHILD BENEFIT ACT 1975*

(1975 c 61)

* This Act was repealed by Social Security (Consequential Provisions) Act 1992, s 3, Sch 1, as from 1 July 1992. The provisions of the Child Benefit Act 1975 printed in this work are replaced by provisions of the Social Security Contributions and Benefits Act 1992 and Social Security Administration Act 1992.

Note. The operation of this Act was extended to territorial waters of the United Kingdom by Social Security and Housing Benefits Act 1982, s 44, as from 28 June 1982.

PART I

CHILD BENEFIT

Entitlement and amount

1. Child benefit—(*1*) *Subject to the provisions of this Part of this Act, a person who is responsible for one or more children in any week on or after the appointed day shall be entitled to a benefit (to be known as 'child benefit') for that week in respect of the child or each of the children for whom he is responsible.*

(*2*) *Child benefit shall be paid by the Secretary of State out of moneys provided by Parliament.*

(*3*) *No allowances shall be payable under the Family Allowances Act 1965 for any period beginning on or after the appointed day.*

2. Meaning of 'child'—(*1*) *For the purposes of this Part of this Act a person shall be treated as a child for any week in which—*

(*a*) *he is under the age of sixteen; or*

[(*aa*)   he is under the age of eighteen and not receiving full-time education and prescribed
conditions are satisfied in relation to him; or]

(*b*)   he is under the age of nineteen and receiving full-time education by attendance at a
recognised educational establishment [*either by attendance at a recognised educational
establishment or, if the education is recognised by the Secretary of State, elsewhere*].

[(*1A*)   The Secretary of State may recognise education provided otherwise than at a
recognised educational establishment for a person who, in the opinion of the Secretary of
State, could reasonably be expected to attend such an establishment only if the Secretary of
State is satisfied that education was being so provided for that person immediately before he
attained the age of sixteen.

(*1B*)   Regulations may prescribe the circumstances in which education is or is not to be
treated for the purposes of this Act as full-time.]

(*2*)   In determining for the purposes of paragraph (*b*) of subsection (*1*) above whether a
person is receiving full-time education as mentioned in that paragraph, no account shall be
taken of such interruptions as may be prescribed.

(*3*)   Regulations may provide that a person who in any week ceases to fall within
subsection (*1*) above shall be treated as continuing to do so for a prescribed period ending not
more than thirteen weeks after the end of that week; *but no person shall by virtue of any such
regulations be treated as continuing to fall within that subsection for any week after that in
which he attains the age of nineteen.*

Note. Words in square brackets in sub-s (1) substituted for words 'by attendance ...
establishment' and sub-ss (1A), (1B) inserted by Social Security Act 1986, s 70(1), as from 25
July 1986. Words in italics in sub-s (3) repealed by Social Security Act 1980, ss 4(5), 8, 21, Sch
5, Part I, as from 23 May 1980. Sub-s (1)(aa) inserted by Social Security Act 1988, s 4(3), as
from 12 September 1988.

3. Meaning of 'person responsible for child'—(*1*) *For the purposes of this Part of
this Act a person shall be treated as responsible for a child in any week if*—

(*a*)   he has the child living with him in that week; or

(*b*)   he is contributing to the cost of providing for the child at a weekly rate which is not
less than the weekly rate of child benefit payable in respect of the child for that week.

(*2*)   Where a person has had a child living with him for some time before a particular week
he shall be treated for the purposes of this section as having the child living with him in that
week notwithstanding their absence from one another unless, in the sixteen weeks preceding
that week, they were absent from one another for more than fifty-six days not counting any day
which is to be disregarded under subsection (*3*) below.

(*3*)   Subject to subsection (*4*) below, a day of absence shall be disregarded for the purposes
of subsection (*2*) above if it is due solely to the child's—

(*a*)   receiving full-time education by attendance at a recognised educational establishment;

(*b*)   undergoing medical or other treatment as an in-patient in a hospital or similar
institution; or

(*c*)   being, in such circumstances as may be prescribed, in residential accommodation
pursuant to arrangements made under [*section 21 of the National Assistance Act
1948, the Children Act 1989 or the Social Work (Scotland) Act 1968*] section 12 of
the Health Services and Public Health Act 1968 [*paragraph 2 of Schedule 8 to the
National Health Service Act 1977*] [*, the Children Act 1989*] or section 27(*1*) of the
National Health Service (Scotland) Act 1947.

Note. Words in first pair of square brackets substituted for words 'section 12 ... Act 1947' by
National Health Service and Community Care Act 1990, s 66(1), Sch 9, para 15, as from a day
to be appointed under s 67(2) of that Act. Words in second pair of square brackets substituted
for words 'section 12 of the Health Services and Public Health Act 1968' by National Health
Service Act 1977, s 129, Sch 15, para 67. Words ', the Children Act 1989' inserted by Children
Act 1989 (Consequential Amendments of Enactments) Order 1991, SI 1991 No 1881, art 2, as
from 14 October 1991.

(*4*)   The number of days that may be disregarded by virtue of subsection (*3*)(*b*) or (*c*) above
in the case of any child shall not exceed such number as may be prescribed unless the person
claiming to be responsible for the child regularly incurs expenditure in respect of the child.

(5) Regulations may prescribe the circumstances in which a person is or is not to be treated—
(a) as contributing to the cost of providing for a child as required by subsection (1)(b) above; or
(b) as regularly incurring expenditure in respect of a child as required by subsection (4) above;

and such regulations may in particular make provision whereby a contribution made or expenditure incurred by two or more persons is to be treated as made or incurred by one of them or whereby a contribution made or expenditure incurred by one of two spouses residing together is to be treated as made or incurred by the other.

4. Exclusions and priority—(1) Regulations may provide that child benefit shall not be payable by virtue of section 2(1)(b) above [or by virtue of section 2(1)(aa) above and regulations made under that paragraph] in such cases as may be prescribed; and Schedule 1 to this Act shall have effect for excluding entitlement to child benefit in other cases.

(2) Where, apart from this subsection, two or more persons would be entitled to benefit in respect of the same child for the same week, one of them only shall be entitled; and the question which of them is entitled shall be determined in accordance with Schedule 2 to this Act.

Note. Words in square brackets in sub-s (1) inserted by the Social Security Act 1988, s 4(4), as from 12 September 1988.

[4A. Overlap with benefits under legislation of other member States. Regulations may provide for adjusting child benefit payable in respect of any child in respect of whom any benefit is payable under the legislation of any member State other than the United Kingdom.]

Note. This section inserted by Social Security Act 1979, s 15(3).

* * * * *

Administration and enforcement

6. Claims and payment—(1) Subject to the provisions of this Act, no person shall be entitled to child benefit unless he claims it in the prescribed manner [and within the prescribed time] [in the manner, and within the time, prescribed in relation to child benefit by regulations under section 51 of the Social Security Act 1986].

Note. Words in first pair of square brackets added by Social Security Act 1986, s 86(1), Sch 10, Part V, para 96, as from 11 April 1988. Words in second pair of square brackets substituted for words 'in the prescribed ... time' by Social Security Act 1989, s 26, Sch 7, para 22, as from 1 October 1989.

(2) Unless regulations otherwise provide, no person shall be entitled to child benefit for any week more than fifty-two weeks before that in which it is claimed.

Note. Sub-s (2) repealed by Social Security Act 1986, s 86(2), Sch 11, as from 11 April 1988.

(3) Except where regulations otherwise provide, no person shall be entitled to child benefit for any week on a claim made by him after that week if child benefit in respect of the same child has already been paid for that week to another person, whether or not that other person was entitled to it.

* * * * *

Persons outside Great Britain and reciprocal arrangements with other countries

13. Persons outside Great Britain—(1) Regulations may modify the provisions of this Part of this Act in their application to persons who are or have been outside Great Britain at any prescribed time or in any prescribed circumstances.

(2) Subject to any regulations under subsection (1) above, no child benefit shall be payable in respect of a child for any week unless—
(a) he is in Great Britain in that week; and
(b) either he or at least one of his parents has been in Great Britain for more than one hundred and eighty-two days in the past fifty-two weeks preceding that week.

(3) Subject to any regulations under subsection (1) above, no person shall be entitled to child benefit for any week unless—

  (a) he is in Great Britain in that week; and

  (b) he has been in Great Britain for more than one hundred and eighty-two days in the fifty-two weeks preceding that week.

* * * * *

PART II

OTHER BENEFITS

16. Interim benefit for unmarried or separated parents with children—(1)
Subject to the provisions of this section, a person who is the parent of one or more children shall be entitled to a benefit under this section for any week in the interim period in which—

  (a) he has the child or any of the children living with him; and

  (b) either he has no spouse or is not residing with his spouse; and

  (c) he is not cohabiting with any other person as his spouse.

(2) In subsection (1) above 'the interim period' means the period ending immediately before the appointed day and beginning with such earlier day (being a Monday) as the Secretary of State may by order specify.

(3) The benefit to which a person is entitled under this section for any week shall be of an amount equal to that for the time being specified under section 1 of the Family Allowances Act 1965 as the weekly rate of an allowance under that Act for one child.

(4) Benefit under this section shall be paid by the Secretary of State out of moneys provided by Parliament.

(5) Subject to the provisions of this Act, no person shall be entitled to benefit under this section unless he claims it in the prescribed manner; and, unless regulations otherwise provide, no person shall be entitled to such benefit for any week before that in which it is claimed.

(6) Regulations may—

  (a) prescribe the circumstances in which a person is or is not to be treated for the purposes of this section as having a child living with him;

  (b) make provision for excluding entitlement to benefit under this section in the case of a person who is entitled to any such other payment out of public funds as may be prescribed and in a case where the child or all the children living with a person are included in another person's family for the purposes of the Family Allowances Act 1965;

  (c) make provision, in a case where a person is entitled to benefit under this section, for reducing by the amount of that benefit the amount of any such other payment out of public funds as may be prescribed.

(7) Any question as to the right under this section shall be determined by the Secretary of State but regulations shall make provision for an appeal to lie—

  (a) to such tribunal as may be constituted for that purpose by the regulations from any decision given by the Secretary of State on any such question, and

  (b) to such person as may be appointed for that purpose by the Lord Chancellor after consultation with the Lord Advocate from any decision given by such a tribunal.

(8) The chairman of any tribunal constituted for the purposes of subsection (7)(a) above shall be a barrister, advocate or solicitor.

(9) Regulations may also make provision—

  (a) for the review of decisions given under or by virtue of subsection (7) above;

  (b) for any purpose corresponding to the purposes of the provisions mentioned in sub-section (1) of section 8 above or to the purposes of subsection (2) of that section.

(10) The Secretary of State may out of moneys provided by Parliament—

  (a) pay to members of such tribunal as may be constituted by regulations under this section, and to any such person as may be appointed under this section, such fees and allowances; and

  (b) make such other payments to any other persons for the purpose of, or in connection with, their attendance before such a tribunal or such a person,

as the Secretary of State may with the consent of the Minister for the Civil Service determine.

(*11*)   Sections 2, 6(*4*) and (*5*), 9, 11, 12, 13 and 14 above shall have effect in relation to this section and benefit thereunder as they have effect in relation to Part I of this Act and child benefit.

*   *   *   *   *

18.   Provisions as to the exclusion from a family for family allowances purposes of children entitled to non-contributory invalidity pension—(*1*)   *In section 11 (which provides that certain children are not to be included in a family for family allowances purposes) of the Family Allowances Act 1965 after subsection (7) there shall be inserted*—

'(*8*)   *Where a person is entitled to a non-contributory invalidity pension under section 36 of the Social Security Act 1975, he shall not be treated as included in any family as being a child for the purposes of this Act as respects any period during which he is so entitled.'*

(*2*)   *In section 13(1) (regulations) of the said Act of 1965 after paragraph (e) there shall be inserted*—

'(*f*)   *for treating an allowance as having been paid on account of a non-contributory invalidity pension in cases where in consequence of a subsequent decision under the Social Security Act 1975 a child who had been treated as included in a family for the purposes of this Act is entitled to a non-contributory invalidity pension for any period for which the allowance was paid, and for reducing or withholding accordingly any arrears payable by virtue of the subsequent decision;*

(*g*)   *for treating a non-contributory invalidity pension paid to a child which it is subsequently decided was not payable as having been paid on account of an allowance in cases where in consequence of a subsequent decision under this Act he is treated as included in a family for any period for which the non-contributory invalidity pension was paid, and for reducing or withholding accordingly any arrears payable by virtue of that subsequent decision.'*

*   *   *   *   *

24.   Interpretation—(*1*)   *In this Act*—

'*the appointed day*' *means such day (being a Monday) as the Secretary of State may by order appoint;*

'*insurance officer*' *means an insurance officer appointed under section 97 of the Social Security Act 1975;*

'*local tribunal*' *means a tribunal appointed under section 97 of that Act;*

Note. Definitions 'insurance officer' and 'local tribunal' repealed by Health and Social Services and Social Security Adjudications Act 1983, s 30(1), Sch 10, Part I, as from 23 April 1984.

'*prescribed*', *except where the context otherwise requires, means prescribed by regulations under this Act;*

'*recognised educational establishment*' *means an establishment recognised by the Secretary of State as being, or as comparable to, a university, college or school, and regulations may prescribe the circumstances in which a person is or is not to be treated for the purposes of this Act as receiving full-time education by attendance at such an establishment;*

Note. Words 'and regulations may ... establishment' repealed by Social Security Act 1986, s 86(2), Sch 11, as from 6 April 1987.

'*voluntary organisation*' *means a body, other than a public or local authority, the activities of which are carried on otherwise than for profit;*

'*week*' *means a period of seven days beginning with a Monday.*

(*2*)   *Subject to any provision made by regulations, references in this Act to any condition being satisfied or any facts existing in a week shall be construed as references to the condition being satisfied or the facts existing at the beginning of that week.*

(*3*)   *References in this Act to a parent, father or mother of a child shall be construed*—

(*a*)   as including references to the natural parent, father or mother of an illegitimate child;
(*b*)   as including references to a step-parent, step-father or step-mother;
(*c*)   ...

Note. Sub-s (3)(c) repealed by Children Act 1975, s 108(1), (4), Sch 4, Part I.

(*4*)   *Regulations may prescribe the circumstances in which persons are or are not to be treated for the purposes of this Act as residing together.*

(*5*)   *Nothing in this Act shall be construed as conferring a right to child benefit on any body corporate; but regulations may confer such modifications of any provision of this Act as the Secretary of State thinks fit.*

(*6*)   *Except where the context otherwise requires, any reference in this Act to any enactment is a reference to that enactment as amended or extended by or under any other enactment, including this Act.*

25. Short title and extent—(*1*)   *This Act may be cited as the Child Benefit Act 1975.*
(*2*)   *This Act does not extend to Northern Ireland.*

SCHEDULE 1   Section 4(1)

EXCLUSIONS FROM ENTITLEMENT

Children in detention, care etc

1.   *Except where regulations otherwise provide, no person shall be entitled to child benefit in respect of a child for any week if in that week the child is—*
(*a*)   *undergoing imprisonment or detention in legal custody;*
(*b*)   *subject to a supervision requirement made under section 44 of the Social Work (Scotland) Act 1968 and residing in a residential establishment within the meaning of that section; or*
(*c*)   *in the care of a local authority in such circumstances as may be prescribed.*

Employed trainees, etc

2.   (*1*)   *No person shall be entitled to child benefit by virtue of section 2(1)(b) of this Act in respect of a child if the education in question is received by that child by virtue of his employment or at any office held by him.*
(*2*)   *Regulations may specify the circumstances in which a child is or is not to be treated as receiving education as mentioned in sub-paragraph (1) above.*

Married children

3.   *Except where regulations otherwise provide, no person shall be entitled to child benefit in respect of a child who is married.*

Persons exempt from tax

4.   *Except where regulations otherwise provide, no person shall be entitled to child benefit in respect of a child if either that person or such other person as may be prescribed is exempt from tax under such provisions as may be prescribed.*

Children entitled to non-contributory invalidity pension

5.   *Except where regulations otherwise provide, no person shall be entitled to child benefit in respect of a child for any week in which the child is entitled to a non-contributory invalidity pension [severe disablement allowance] under the Social Security Act 1975.*

Note. Words in square brackets substituted for words 'non-contributory invalidity pension' by Health and Social Security Act 1984, s 11(2), Sch 4, Part I, para 13.

SCHEDULE 2   Section 4(2)

PRIORITY BETWEEN PERSONS ENTITLED

Person with prior award

1. (*1*) Subject to sub-paragraph (*2*) below, as between a person claiming child benefit in respect of a child for any week and a person to whom child benefit in respect of that child for that week has already been awarded when the claim is made, the latter shall be entitled.

(*2*) Sub-paragraph (*1*) above shall not confer any priority where the week to which the claim relates is later than the third week following that in which the claim is made.

Person having child living with him

2. Subject to paragraph 1 above, as between a person entitled for any week by virtue of paragraph (*a*) of subsection (*1*) of section 3 of this Act and a person entitled by virtue of paragraph (*b*) of that subsection the former shall be entitled.

Husband and wife

3. Subject to paragraphs 1 and 2 above, as between a husband and wife residing together the wife shall be entitled.

Parents

4. (*1*) Subject to paragraphs 1 to 3 above, as between a person who is and one who is not a parent of the child the parent shall be entitled.

(*2*) Subject as aforesaid, as between two persons residing together who are parents of the child but not husband and wife, the mother shall be entitled.

Other cases

5. As between persons not falling within paragraphs 1 to 4 above, such one of them shall be entitled as they may jointly elect or, in default of election, as the Secretary of State may in his discretion determine.

Supplementary

6. (*1*) Any election under this Schedule shall be made in the prescribed manner.

(*2*) Regulations may provide for exceptions from and modifications of the provisions of paragraphs 1 to 5 above in relation to such cases as may be prescribed.

INHERITANCE (PROVISION FOR FAMILY AND DEPENDANTS) ACT 1975

(1975 c 63)

ARRANGEMENT OF SECTIONS

Powers of court to order financial provision from deceased's estate

An Act to make fresh provision for empowering the court to make orders for the making out of the estate of a deceased person of provision for the spouse, former spouse, child, child of the family or dependant of that person; and for matters connected therewith. [12 November 1975]

Note. Except in relation to a liability to tax arising before 25 July 1986 capital transfer tax shall be known as inheritance tax, by virtue of Finance Act 1986, s 100.

Powers of court to order financial provision from deceased's estate

1. Application for financial provision from deceased's estate—(1) Where after the commencement of this Act a person dies domiciled in England and Wales and is survived by any of the following persons—

(a) the wife or husband of the deceased;
(b) a former wife or former husband of the deceased who has not remarried;
[(ba) any person (not being a person included in paragraph (a) or (b) above) to whom subsection (1A) below applies;]
(c) a child of the deceased;
(d) any person (not being a child of the deceased) who, in the case of any marriage to which the deceased was at any time a party, was treated by the deceased as a child of the family in relation to that marriage;
(e) any person (not being a person included in the foregoing paragraphs of this subsection) who immediately before the death of the deceased was being maintained, either wholly or partly, by the deceased;

that person may apply to the court for an order under section 2 of this Act on the ground that the disposition of the deceased's estate effected by his will or the law relating to intestacy, or the combination of his will and that law, is not such as to make reasonable financial provision for the applicant.

Note. Sub-s (1)(ba) inserted by Law Reform (Succession) Act 1995, s 2(2), as from 8 November 1995.

[(1A) This subsection applies to a person if the deceased died on or after 1st January 1996 and, during the whole of the period of two years ending immediately before the date when the deceased died, the person was living—

   (a) in the same household as the deceased, and

   (b) as the husband or wife of the deceased.]

Note. Sub-s (1A) inserted by Law Reform (Succession) Act 1995, s 2(3), as from 8 November 1995.

   (2) In this Act 'reasonable financial provision'—

   (a) in the case of an application made by virtue of subsection (1)(a) above by the husband or wife of the deceased (except where *the marriage with the deceased was the subject of a decree of judicial separation and at the date of death the decree was in force* [, at the date of death, a separation order under the Family Law Act 1996 was in force in relation to the marriage] and the separation was continuing), means such financial provision as it would be reasonable in all the circumstances of the case for a husband or wife to receive, whether or not that provision is required for his or her maintenance;

   (b) in the case of any other application made by virtue of subsection (1) above, means such financial provision as it would be reasonable in all the circumstances of the case for the applicant to receive for his maintenance.

Note. Words in square brackets substituted for words in italics by Family Law Act 1996, s 66(1), Sch 8, Part I, para 27, as from a day to be appointed, subject to savings in s 66(2) of, and para 5 of Sch 9 to, the 1996 Act.

   (3) For the purposes of subsection (1)(e) above, a person shall be treated as being maintained by the deceased, either wholly or partly, as the case may be, if the deceased, otherwise than for full valuable consideration, was making a substantial contribution in money or money's worth towards the reasonable needs of that person.

Note. The forfeiture rule (as defined by the Forfeiture Act 1982, s 1(1) (p 2927)) shall not be taken to preclude any person from making any application under any provision of this Act or the making of any order on the application: see Forfeiture Act 1982, s 3(1), (2)(a) (p 2928), as from 13 October 1982.

2. Powers of court to make orders—(1) Subject to the provisions of this Act, where an application is made for an order under this section, the court may, if it is satisfied that the disposition of the deceased's estate effected by his will or the law relating to intestacy, or the combination of his will and that law, is not such as to make reasonable financial provision for the applicant, make any one or more of the following orders—

   (a) an order for the making to the applicant out of the net estate of the deceased of such periodical payments and for such term as may be specified in the order;

   (b) an order for the payment to the applicant out of that estate of a lump sum of such amount as may be so specified;

   (c) an order for the transfer to the applicant of such property comprised in that estate as may be so specified;

   (d) an order for the settlement for the benefit of the applicant of such property comprised in that estate as may be so specified;

   (e) an order for the acquisition out of property comprised in that estate of such property as may be so specified and for the transfer of the property so acquired to the applicant or for the settlement thereof for his benefit;

   (f) an order varying any ante-nuptial or post-nuptial settlement (including such a settlement made by will) made on the parties to a marriage to which the deceased was one of the parties, the variation being for the benefit of the surviving party to that marriage, or any child of that marriage, or any person who was treated by the deceased as a child of the family in relation to that marriage.

(2) An order under subsection (1)(a) above providing for the making out of the net estate of the deceased of periodical payments may provide for—

(a) payment of such amount as may be specified in the order,

(b) payments equal to the whole of the income of the net estate or of such portion thereof as may be so specified,

(c) payments equal to the whole of the income of such part of the net estate as the court may direct to be set aside or appropriated for the making out of the income thereof of payments under this section,

or may provide for the amount of the payments or any of them to be determined in any other way the court thinks fit.

(3) Where an order under subsection (1)(a) above provides for the making of payments of an amount specified in the order, the order may direct that such part of the net estate as may be so specified shall be set aside or appropriated for the making out of the income thereof of those payments; but no larger part of the net estate shall be so set aside or appropriated than is sufficient, at the date of the order, to produce by the income thereof the amount required for the making of those payments.

(4) An order under this section may contain such consequential and supplemental provisions as the court thinks necessary or expedient for the purpose of giving effect to the order or for the purpose of securing that the order operates fairly as between one beneficiary of the estate of the deceased and another and may, in particular, but without prejudice to the generality of this subsection—

(a) order any person who holds any property which forms part of the net estate of the deceased to make such payment or transfer such property as may be specified in the order;

(b) vary the disposition of the deceased's estate effected by the will or the law relating to intestacy, or by both the will and the law relating to intestacy, in such manner as the court thinks fair and reasonable having regard to the provisions of the order and all the circumstances of the case;

(c) confer on the trustees of any property which is the subject of an order under this section such powers as appear to the court to be necessary or expedient.

Note. See Family Law Reform Act 1987, s 16(3).

3. Matters to which court is to have regard in exercising powers under s 2—
(1) Where an application is made for an order under section 2 of this Act, the court shall, in determining whether the disposition of the deceased's estate effected by his will or the law relating to intestacy, or the combination of his will and that law, is such as to make reasonable financial provision for the applicant and, if the court considers that reasonable financial provision has not been made, in determining whether and in what manner it shall exercise its power under that section, have regard to the following matters, that is to say—

(a) the financial resources and financial needs which the applicant has or is likely to have in the foreseeable future;

(b) the financial resources and financial needs which any other applicant for an order under section 2 of this Act has or is likely to have in the foreseeable future;

(c) the financial resources and financial needs which any beneficiary of the estate of the deceased has or is likely to have in the foreseeable future;

(d) any obligations and responsibilities which the deceased had towards any applicant for an order under the said section 2 or towards any beneficiary of the estate of the deceased;

(e) the size and nature of the net estate of the deceased;

(f) any physical or mental disability of any applicant for an order under the said section 2 or any beneficiary of the estate of the deceased;

(g) any other matter, including the conduct of the applicant or any other person, which in the circumstances of the case the court may consider relevant.

(2) Without prejudice to the generality of paragraph (g) of subsection (1) above, where an application for an order under section 2 of this Act is made by virtue of section 1(1)(a) or 1(1)(b) of this Act, the court shall, in addition to the matters specifically mentioned in paragraphs (a) to (f) of that subsection, have regard to—

    (a)   the age of the applicant and the duration of the marriage;

    (b)   the contribution made by the applicant to the welfare of the family of the deceased, including any contribution made by looking after the home or caring for the family;

and, in the case of an application by the wife or husband of the deceased, the court shall also, unless at the date of death a *decree of judicial separation* [separation order under the Family Law Act 1996] was in force and the separation was continuing, have regard to the provision which the applicant might reasonably have expected to receive if on the day on which the deceased died the marriage, instead of being terminated by death, had been terminated by *a decree of divorce* [a divorce order].

Note. Words in square brackets substituted for words in italics by Family Law Act 1996, s 66(1), Sch 8, Part I, para 27, as from a day to be appointed, subject to savings in s 66(2) of, and para 5 of Sch 9 to, the 1996 Act.

[(2A) Without prejudice to the generality of paragraph (g) of subsection (1) above, where an application for an order under section 2 of this Act is made by virtue of section 1(1)(ba) of this Act, the court shall, in addition to the matters specifically mentioned in paragraphs (a) to (f) of that subsection, have regard to—

    (a)   the age of the applicant and the length of the period during which the applicant lived as the husband or wife of the deceased and in the same household as the deceased;

    (b)   the contribution made by the applicant to the welfare of the family of the deceased, including any contribution made by looking after the home or caring for the family.]

Note. Sub-s (2A) inserted by Law Reform (Succession) Act 1995, s 2(4), as from 8 November 1995.

(3) Without prejudice to the generality of paragraph (g) of subsection (1) above, where an application for an order under section 2 of this Act is made by virtue of section 1(1)(c) or 1(1)(d) of this Act, the court shall, in addition to the matters specifically mentioned in paragraphs (a) to (f) of that subsection, have regard to the manner in which the applicant was being or in which he might expect to be educated or trained, and where the application is made by virtue of section 1(1)(d) the court shall also have regard—

    (a)   to whether the deceased had assumed any responsibility for the applicant's maintenance and, if so, to the extent to which and the basis upon which the deceased assumed that responsibility and to the length of time for which the deceased discharged that responsibility;

    (b)   to whether in assuming and discharging that responsibility the deceased did so knowing that the applicant was not his own child;

    (c)   to the liability of any other person to maintain the applicant.

(4) Without prejudice to the generality of paragraph (g) of subsection (1) above, where an application for an order under section 2 of this Act is made by virtue of section 1(1)(e) of this Act, the court shall, in addition to the matters specifically mentioned in paragraphs (a) to (f) of that subsection, have regard to the extent to which and the basis upon which the deceased assumed responsibility for the maintenance of the applicant and to the length of time for which the deceased discharged that responsibility.

(5) In considering the matters to which the court is required to have regard under this section, the court shall take into account the facts as known to the court at the date of the hearing.

(6) In considering the financial resources of any person for the purposes of this section the court shall take into account his earning capacity and in considering the financial needs of any person for the purposes of this section the court shall take into account his financial obligations and responsibilities.

4. Time-limit for applications. An application for an order under section 2 of this Act shall not, except with the permission of the court, be made after the end of the period of six months from the date on which representation with respect to the estate of the deceased is first taken out.

5. Interim orders—(1) Where on an application for an order under section 2 of this Act it appears to the court—

(a) that the applicant is in immediate need of financial assistance, but it is not yet possible to determine what order (if any) should be made under that section; and

(b) that property forming part of the net estate of the deceased is or can be made available to meet the need of the applicant;

the court may order that, subject to such conditions or restrictions, if any, as the court may impose and to any further order of the court, there shall be paid to the applicant out of the net estate of the deceased such sum or sums and (if more than one) at such intervals as the court thinks reasonable; and the court may order that, subject to the provisions of this Act, such payments are to be made until such date as the court may specify, not being later than the date on which the court either makes an order under the said section 2 or decides not to exercise its powers under that section.

(2) Subsections (2), (3) and (4) of section 2 of this Act shall apply in relation to an order under this section as they apply in relation to an order under that section.

(3) In determining what order, if any, should be made under this section the court shall, so far as the urgency of the case admits, have regard to the same matters as those to which the court is required to have regard under section 3 of this Act.

(4) An order made under section 2 of this Act may provide that any sum paid to the applicant by virtue of this section shall be treated to such an extent and in such manner as may be provided by that order as having been paid on account of any payment provided for by that order.

6. Variation, discharge, etc of orders for periodical payments—(1) Subject to the provisions of this Act, where the court has made an order under section 2(1)(a) of this Act (in this section referred to as 'the original order') for the making of periodical payments to any person (in this section referred to as 'the original recipient'), the court, on an application under this section, shall have power by order to vary or discharge the original order or to suspend any provision of it temporarily and to revive the operation of any provision so suspended.

(2) Without prejudice to the generality of subsection (1) above, an order made on an application for the variation of the original order may—

(a) provide for the making out of any relevant property of such periodical payments and for such term as may be specified in the order to any person who has applied, or would but for section 4 of this Act be entitled to apply, for an order under section 2 of this Act (whether or not, in the case of any application, an order was made in favour of the applicant);

(b) provide for the payment out of any relevant property of a lump sum of such amount as may be so specified to the original recipient or to any such person as is mentioned in paragraph (a) above;

(c) provide for the transfer of the relevant property, or such part thereof as may be so specified, to the original recipient or to any such person as is so mentioned.

(3) Where the original order provides that any periodical payments payable thereunder to the original recipient are to cease on the occurrence of an event specified in the order (other than the remarriage of a former wife or former

husband) or on the expiration of a period so specified, then, if, before the end of the period of six months from the date of the occurrence of that event or of the expiration of that period, an application is made for an order under this section, the court shall have power to make any order which it would have had power to make if the application had been made before that date (whether in favour of the original recipient or any such person as is mentioned in subsection (2)(a) above and whether having effect from that date or from such later date as the court may specify).

(4) Any reference in this section to the original order shall include a reference to an order made under this section and any reference in this section to the original recipient shall include a reference to any person to whom periodical payments are required to be made by virtue of an order under this section.

(5) An application under this section may be made by any of the following persons, that is to say—

(a) any person who by virtue of section 1(1) of this Act has applied, or would but for section 4 of this Act be entitled to apply, for an order under section 2 of this Act,

(b) the personal representatives of the deceased,

(c) the trustees of any relevant property, and

(d) any beneficiary of the estate of the deceased.

(6) An order under this section may only affect—

(a) property the income of which is at the date of the order applicable wholly or in part for the making of periodical payments to any person who has applied for an order under this Act, or

(b) in the case of an application under subsection (3) above in respect of payments which have ceased to be payable on the occurrence of an event or the expiration of a period, property the income of which was so applicable immediately before the occurrence of that event or the expiration of that period, as the case may be,

and any such property as is mentioned in paragraph (a) or (b) above is in subsections (2) and (5) above referred to as 'relevant property'.

(7) In exercising the powers conferred by this section the court shall have regard to all the circumstances of the case, including any change in any of the matters to which the court was required to have regard when making the order to which the application relates.

(8) Where the court makes an order under this section, it may give such consequential directions as it thinks necessary or expedient having regard to the provisions of the order.

(9) No such order as is mentioned in section 2(1)(d), (e) or (f), 9, 10 or 11 of this Act shall be made on an application under this section.

(10) For the avoidance of doubt it is hereby declared that, in relation to an order which provides for the making of periodical payments which are to cease on the occurrence of an event specified in the order (other than the remarriage of a former wife or former husband) or on the expiration of a period so specified, the power to vary an order includes power to provide for the making of periodical payments after the expiration of that period or the occurrence of that event.

7. Payment of lump sums by instalments—(1) An order under section 2(1)(b) or 6(2)(b) of this Act for the payment of a lump sum may provide for the payment of that sum by instalments of such amount as may be specified in the order.

(2) Where an order is made by virtue of subsection (1) above, the court shall have power, on an application made by the person to whom the lump sum is payable, by the personal representatives of the deceased or by the trustees of the property out of which the lump sum is payable, to vary that order by varying the number of instalments payable, the amount of any instalment and the date on which any instalment becomes payable.

Property available for financial provision

8. Property treated as part of 'net estate'—(1) Where a deceased person has in accordance with the provisions of any enactment nominated any person to receive any sum of money or other property on his death and that nomination is in force at the time of his death, that sum of money, after deducting therefrom any capital transfer tax payable in respect thereof, or that other property, to the extent of the value thereof at the date of the death of the deceased after deducting therefrom any capital transfer tax so payable, shall be treated for the purposes of this Act as part of the net estate of the deceased; but this subsection shall not render any person liable for having paid that sum or transferred that other property to the person named in the nomination in accordance with the directions given in the nomination.

(2) Where any sum of money or other property is received by any person as a donatio mortis causa made by a deceased person, that sum of money, after deducting therefrom any capital transfer tax payable thereon, or that other property, to the extent of the value thereof at the date of the death of the deceased after deducting therefrom any capital transfer tax so payable, shall be treated for the purposes of this Act as part of the net estate of the deceased; but this subsection shall not render any person liable for having paid that sum or transferred that other property in order to give effect to that donatio mortis causa.

(3) The amount of capital transfer tax to be deducted for the purposes of this section shall not exceed the amount of that tax which has been borne by the person nominated by the deceased or, as the case may be, the person who has received a sum of money or other property as a donatio mortis causa.

9. Property held on a joint tenancy—(1) Where a deceased person was immediately before his death beneficially entitled to a joint tenancy of any property, then, if, before the end of the period of six months from the date on which representation with respect to the estate of the deceased was first taken out, an application is made for an order under section 2 of this Act, the court for the purpose of facilitating the making of financial provision for the applicant under this Act may order that the deceased's severable share of that property, at the value thereof immediately before his death, shall, to such extent as appears to the court to be just in all the circumstances of the case, be treated for the purposes of this Act as part of the net estate of the deceased.

(2) In determining the extent to which any severable share is to be treated as part of the net estate of the deceased by virtue of an order under subsection (1) above, the court shall have regard to any capital transfer tax payable in respect of that severable share.

(3) Where an order is made under subsection (1) above, the provisions of this section shall not render any person liable for anything done by him before the order was made.

(4) For the avoidance of doubt it is hereby declared that for the purposes of this section there may be a joint tenancy of a chose in action.

Powers of court in relation to transactions intended to defeat applications for financial provision

10. Dispositions intended to defeat applications for financial provision—(1) Where an application is made to the court for an order under section 2 of this Act, the applicant may, in the proceedings on that application, apply to the court for an order under subsection (2) below.

(2) Where on an application under subsection (1) above the court is satisfied—
(a) that, less than six years before the date of the death of the deceased, the deceased with the intention of defeating an application for financial provision under this Act made a disposition, and

(b) that full valuable consideration for that disposition was not given by the person to whom or for the benefit of whom the disposition was made (in this section referred to as 'the donee') or by any other person, and

(c) that the exercise of the powers conferred by this section would facilitate the making of financial provision for the applicant under this Act,

then, subject to the provisions of this section and of sections 12 and 13 of this Act, the court may order the donee (whether or not at the date of the order he holds any interest in the property disposed of to him or for his benefit by the deceased) to provide, for the purpose of the making of that financial provision, such sum of money or other property as may be specified in the order.

(3) Where an order is made under subsection (2) above as respects any disposition made by the deceased which consisted of the payment of money to or for the benefit of the donee, the amount of any sum of money or the value of any property ordered to be provided under that subsection shall not exceed the amount of the payment made by the deceased after deducting therefrom any capital transfer tax borne by the donee in respect of that payment.

(4) Where an order is made under subsection (2) above as respects any disposition made by the deceased which consisted of the transfer of property (other than a sum of money) to or for the benefit of the donee, the amount of any sum of money or the value of any property ordered to be provided under that subsection shall not exceed the value at the date of the death of the deceased of the property disposed of by him to or for the benefit of the donee (or if that property has been disposed of by the person to whom it was transferred by the deceased, the value at the date of that disposal thereof) after deducting therefrom any capital transfer tax borne by the donee in respect of the transfer of that property by the deceased.

(5) Where an application (in this subsection referred to as 'the original application') is made for an order under subsection (2) above in relation to any disposition, then, if on an application under this subsection by the donee or by the applicant for an order under section 2 of this Act the court is satisfied—

(a) that, less than six years before the date of the death of the deceased, the deceased with the intention of defeating an application for financial provision under this Act made a disposition other than the disposition which is the subject of the original application, and

(b) that full valuable consideration for that other disposition was not given by the person to whom or for the benefit of whom that other disposition was made or by any other person,

the court may exercise in relation to the person to whom or for the benefit of whom that other disposition was made the powers which the court would have had under subsection (2) above if the original application had been made in respect of that other disposition and the court had been satisfied as to the matters set out in paragraphs (a), (b) and (c) of that subsection; and where any application is made under this subsection, any reference in this section (except in subsection (2)(b) to the donee shall include a reference to the person to whom or for the benefit of whom that other disposition was made.

(6) In determining whether and in what manner to exercise its powers under this section, the court shall have regard to the circumstances in which any disposition was made and any valuable consideration which was given therefor, the relationship, if any, of the donee to the deceased, the conduct and financial resources of the donee and all the other circumstances of the case.

(7) In this section 'disposition' does not include—

(a) any provision in a will, any such nomination as is mentioned in section 8(1) of this Act or any donatio mortis causa, or

(b) any appointment of property made, otherwise than by will, in the exercise of a special power of appointment, but, subject to these exceptions, includes any payment of money (including the payment of a premium under a policy of assurance) and any conveyance, assurance, appointment or gift of property of any description, whether made by an instrument or otherwise.

(8) The provisions of this section do not apply to any disposition made before the commencement of this Act.

11. Contracts to leave property by will—(1) Where an application is made to a court for an order under section 2 of this Act, the applicant may, in the proceedings on that application, apply to the court for an order under this section.

(2) Where on an application under subsection (1) above the court is satisfied—

(a) that the deceased made a contract by which he agreed to leave by his will a sum of money or other property to any person or by which he agreed that a sum of money or other property would be paid or transferred to any person out of his estate, and

(b) that the deceased made that contract with the intention of defeating an application for financial provision under this Act, and

(c) that when the contract was made full valuable consideration for that contract was not given, or promised by the person with whom or for the benefit of whom the contract was made (in this section referred to as 'the donee') or by any other person, and

(d) that the exercise of the powers conferred by this section would facilitate the making of financial provision for the applicant under this Act,

then, subject to the provisions of this section and of sections 12 and 13 of this Act, the court may make any one or more of the following orders, that is to say—

(i) if any money has been paid or any other property has been transferred to or for the benefit of the donee in accordance with the contract, an order directing the donee to provide, for the purpose of the making of that financial provision, such sum of money or other property as may be specified in the order;

(ii) if the money or all the money has not been paid or the property or all the property has not been transferred in accordance with the contract, an order directing the personal representatives not to make any payment or transfer any property, or not to make any further payment or transfer any further property, as the case may be, in accordance therewith or directing the personal representatives only to make such payment or transfer such property as may be specified in the order.

(3) Notwithstanding anything in subsection (2) above, the court may exercise its powers thereunder in relation to any contract made by the deceased only to the extent that the court considers that the amount of any sum of money paid or to be paid or the value of any property transferred or to be transferred in accordance with the contract exceeds the value of any valuable consideration given or to be given for that contract, and for this purpose the court shall have regard to the value of property at the date of the hearing.

(4) In determining whether and in what manner to exercise its powers under this section, the court shall have regard to the circumstances in which the contract was made, the relationship, if any, of the donee to the deceased, the conduct and financial resources of the donee and all the other circumstances of the case.

(5) Where an order has been made under subsection (2) above in relation to any contract, the rights of any person to enforce that contract or to recover damages or to obtain other relief for the breach thereof shall be subject to any adjustment made by the court under section 12(3) of this Act and shall survive to such extent only as is consistent with giving effect to the terms of that order.

(6) The provisions of this section do not apply to a contract made before the commencement of this Act.

12. Provisions supplementary to ss 10 and 11—(1) Where the exercise of any of the powers conferred by section 10 or 11 of this Act is conditional on the court being satisfied that a disposition or contract was made by a deceased person with the intention of defeating an application for financial provision under this Act, that condition shall be fulfilled if the court is of the opinion that, on a balance of probabilities, the intention of the deceased (though not necessarily his sole intention) in making the disposition or contract was to prevent an order for financial provision being made under this Act or to reduce the amount of the provision which might otherwise be granted by an order thereunder.

(2) Where an application is made under section 11 of this Act with respect to any contract made by the deceased and no valuable consideration was given or promised by any person for that contract then, notwithstanding anything in subsection (1) above, it shall be presumed, unless the contrary is shown, that the deceased made that contract with the intention of defeating an application for financial provision under this Act.

(3) Where the court makes an order under section 10 or 11 of this Act it may give such consequential directions as it thinks fit (including directions requiring the making of any payment or the transfer of any property) for giving effect to the order or for securing a fair adjustment of the rights of the persons affected thereby.

(4) Any power conferred on the court by the said section 10 or 11 to order the donee, in relation to any disposition or contract, to provide any sum of money or other property shall be exercisable in like manner in relation to the personal representative of the donee, and—

(a) any reference in section 10(4) to the disposal of property by the donee shall include a reference to disposal by the personal representative of the donee, and

(b) any reference in section 10(5) to an application by the donee under that subsection shall include a reference to an application by the personal representative of the donee;

but the court shall not have power under the said section 10 or 11 to make an order in respect of any property forming part of the estate of the donee which has been distributed by the personal representative; and the personal representative shall not be liable for having distributed any such property before he has notice of the making of an application under the said section 10 or 11 on the ground that he ought to have taken into account the possibility that such an application would be made.

13. Provisions as to trustees in relation to ss 10 and 11—(1) Where an application is made for—

(a) an order under section 10 of this Act in respect of a disposition made by the deceased to any person as a trustee, or

(b) an order under section 11 of this Act in respect of any payment made or property transferred, in accordance with a contract made by the deceased, to any person as a trustee,

the powers of the court under the said section 10 or 11 to order that trustee to provide a sum of money or other property shall be subject to the following limitation (in addition, in a case of an application under section 10, to any provision regarding the deduction of capital transfer tax) namely, that the amount of any sum of money or the value of any property ordered to be provided—

(i) in the case of an application in respect of a disposition which consisted of the payment of money or an application in respect of the payment of money in accordance with a contract, shall not exceed the aggregate of so much of that money as is at the date of the order in the hands of the trustee and the value at that date of any property which represents that money or is derived therefrom and is at that date in the hands of the trustee;

(ii) in the case of an application in respect of a disposition which consisted of the transfer of property (other than a sum of money) or an application in respect of the transfer of property (other than a sum of money) in accordance with a contract, shall not exceed the aggregate of the value at the date of the order of so much of that property as is at that date in the hands of the trustee and the value at that date of any property which represents the first- mentioned property or is derived therefrom and is at that date in the hands of the trustee.

(2) Where any such application is made in respect of a disposition made to any person as a trustee or in respect of any payment made or property, transferred in pursuance of a contract to any person as a trustee, the trustee shall not be liable for having distributed any money or other property on the ground that he ought to have taken into account the possibility that such an application would be made.

(3) Where any such application is made in respect of a disposition made to any person as a trustee or in respect of any payment made or property transferred in accordance with a contract to any person as a trustee, any reference in the said section 10 or 11 to the donee shall be construed as including a reference to the trustee or trustees for the time being of the trust in question and any reference in subsection (1) or (2) above to a trustee shall be construed in the same way.

Special provisions relating to cases of divorce, separation etc

14. Provision as to cases where no financial relief was granted in divorce proceedings etc—(1) Where, within twelve months from the date on which *a decree of divorce or nullity of marriage has been made absolute or a decree of judicial separation has been granted* [a divorce order or separation order has been made under the Family Law Act 1996 in relation to a marriage or a decree of nullity of marriage has been made absolute], a party to the marriage dies and—

(a) an application for a financial provision order under *section 23* [section 22A or 23] of the Matrimonial Causes Act 1973 or a property adjustment order under *section 24* [section 23A or 24] of that Act has not been made by the other party to that marriage, or

(b) such an application has been made but the proceedings thereon have not been determined at the time of the death of the deceased,

then, if an application for an order under section 2 of this Act is made by that other party, the court shall, notwithstanding anything in section 1 or section 3 of this Act, have power, if it thinks it just to do so, to treat that party for the purposes of that application as if *the decree of divorce or nullity of marriage had not been made absolute or the decree of judicial separation had not been granted, as the case may be* [, as the case may be, the divorce order or separation order had not been made or the decree of nullity had not been made absolute].

(2) This section shall not apply in relation to a *decree of judicial separation* [separation order] unless at the date of the death of the deceased *the decree* [the order] was in force and the separation was continuing.

Note. Words in square brackets substituted for words in italics by Family Law Act 1996, s 66(1), Sch 8, Part I, para 27, as from a day to be appointed, subject to savings in s 66(2) of, and para 5 of Sch 9 to, the 1996 Act.

15. Restriction imposed in divorce proceedings etc on application under this Act—(*1*) *On granting a decree of divorce, a decree of nullity of marriage or a decree of judicial separation or at any time thereafter, the court may, if the court considers it just to do so and the parties to the marriage agree, order that either party to the marriage shall not be entitled on the death of the other party to apply for an order under section 2 of this Act.*

[(1) *On the grant of a decree of divorce, a decree of nullity of marriage or a decree of judicial separation or at any time thereafter* [At any time when the court—

(a) has jurisdiction under section 23A or 24 of the Matrimonial Causes Act 1973 to make a property adjustment order in relation to a marriage; or

(b) would have such jurisdiction if either the jurisdiction had not already been exercised or an application for such an order were made with the leave of the court,]

the court, if it considers it just to do so, may, on the application of either party to the marriage, order that the other party to the marriage shall not on the death of the applicant be entitled to apply for an order under section 2 of this Act.

In this subsection 'the court' means the High Court or, where a county court has jurisdiction by virtue of Part V of the Matrimonial and Family Proceedings Act 1984, a county court.]

Note. Sub-s (1) in square brackets substituted for sub-s (1) in italics by Matrimonial and Family Proceedings Act 1984, s 8(1), as from 12 October 1984. Words in square brackets substituted for words in italics by Family Law Act 1996, s 66(1), Sch 8, Part I, para 27, as from a day to be appointed, subject to savings in s 66(2) of, and para 5 of Sch 9 to, the 1996 Act.

(2) In the case of a decree of divorce or nullity of marriage an order may be made under subsection 1(1) above before or after the decree is made absolute, but if it is made before the decree is made absolute it shall not take effect unless the decree is made absolute.

(3) Where an order made under subsection (1) above on the grant of a decree of divorce or nullity of marriage has come into force with respect to a party to a marriage, then, on the death of the other party to that marriage, the court shall not entertain any application for an order under section 2 of this Act made by the first-mentioned party.

(4) Where an order made under subsection (1) above on the grant of a decree of judicial separation has come into force with respect to any party to a marriage, then, if the other party to that marriage dies while the decree is in force and the separation is continuing, the court shall not entertain any application for an order under section 2 of this Act made by the first-mentioned party.

[(2) An order made under subsection (1) above with respect to any party to a marriage has effect in accordance with subsection (3) below at any time—

(a) after the marriage has been dissolved;

(b) after a decree of nullity has been made absolute in relation to the marriage; and

(c) while a separation order under the Family Law Act 1996 is in force in relation to the marriage and the separation is continuing.

(3) If at any time when an order made under subsection (1) above with respect to any party to a marriage has effect the other party to the marriage dies, the court shall not entertain any application made by the surviving party to the marriage for an order under section 2 of this Act.]

Note. Sub-ss (2), (3) in square brackets substituted for sub-ss (2)–(4) in italics by Family Law Act 1996, s 66(1), Sch 8, Part I, para 27, as from a day to be appointed, subject to savings in s 66(2) of, and para 5 of Sch 9 to, the 1996 Act.

[15A. Restriction imposed in proceedings under Matrimonial and Family Proceedings Act 1984 on application under this Act—(1) On making an order under section 14 of the Matrimonial and Family Proceedings Act 1984 (orders for financial provision and property adjustment following overseas divorces, etc) the court, if it considers it just to do so, may, on the application of either party to the marriage, order that the other party to the marriage shall not on the death of the applicant be entitled to apply for an order under section 2 of this Act.

In this subsection 'the court' means the High Court or, where a county court has jurisdiction by virtue of Part V of the Matrimonial and Family Proceedings Act 1984, a county court.

(2) Where an order under subsection (1) above has been made with respect to a party to a marriage which has been dissolved or annulled, then, on the death of the other party to that marriage, the court shall not entertain an application under section 2 of this Act made by the first-mentioned party.

(3) Where an order under section (1) above has been made with respect to a party to a marriage the parties to which have been legally separated, then, if the other party to the marriage dies while the legal separation is in force, the court shall not entertain an application under section 2 of this Act made by the first-mentioned party.]

Note. This section inserted by Matrimonial and Family Proceedings Act 1984, s 25, as from 16 September 1985.

16. Variation and discharge of secured periodical payments orders made under Matrimonial Causes Act 1973—(1) Where an application for an order under section 2 of this Act is made to the court by any person who was at the time of the death of the deceased entitled to payments from the deceased under a secured periodical payments order made under the Matrimonial Causes Act 1973, then, in the proceedings on that application, the court shall have power, if an application is made under this section by that person or by the personal representative of the deceased, to vary or discharge that periodical payments order or to revive the operation of any provision thereof which has been suspended under section 31 of that Act.

(2) In exercising the powers conferred by this section the court shall have regard to all the circumstances of the case, including any order which the court proposes to make under section 2 or section 5 of this Act and any change (whether resulting from the death of the deceased or otherwise) in any of the matters to which the court was required to have regard when making the secured periodical payments order.

(3) The powers exercisable by the court under this section in relation to an order shall be exercisable also in relation to any instrument executed in pursuance of the order.

17. Variation and revocation of maintenance agreements—(1) Where an application for an order under section 2 of this Act is made to the court by any person who was at the time of the death of the deceased entitled to payments from the deceased under a maintenance agreement which provided for the continuation of payments under the agreement after the death of the deceased, then, in the proceedings on that application, the court shall have power, if an application is made under this section by that person or by the personal representative of the deceased, to vary or revoke that agreement.

(2) In exercising the powers conferred by this section the court shall have regard to all the circumstances of the case, including any order which the court proposes to make under section 2 or section 5 of this Act and any change (whether resulting from the death of the deceased or otherwise) in any of the circumstances in the light of which the agreement was made.

(3) If a maintenance agreement is varied by the court under this section the like consequences shall ensue as if the variation had been made immediately before the death of the deceased by agreement between the parties and for valuable consideration.

(4) In this section 'maintenance agreement', in relation to a deceased person, means any agreement made, whether in writing or not and whether before or after the commencement of this Act, by the deceased with any person with whom he entered into a marriage, being an agreement which contained provisions governing the rights and liabilities towards one another when living separately of the parties to that marriage (whether or not the marriage has been dissolved or annulled) in respect of the making or securing of payments or the disposition or use of any property, including such rights and liabilities with respect to the maintenance or education of any child, whether or not a child of the deceased or a person who was treated by the deceased as a child of the family in relation to that marriage.

18. Availability of court's powers under this Act in applications under ss 31 and 36 of the Matrimonial Causes Act 1973—(1) Where—

(a) a person against whom a secured periodical payments order was made under the Matrimonial Causes Act 1973 has died and an application is made under section 31(6) of that Act for the variation or discharge of that order or for the revival of the operation of any provision thereof which has been suspended, or

(b) a party to a maintenance agreement within the meaning of section 34 of that Act has died, the agreement being one which provides for the continuation of payments thereunder after the death of one of the parties, and an application is made under section 36(1) of that Act for the alteration of the agreement under section 35 thereof,

the court shall have power to direct that the application made under the said section 31(6) or 36(1) shall be deemed to have been accompanied by an application for an order under section 2 of this Act.

(2) Where the court gives a direction under subsection (1) above it shall have power, in the proceedings on the application under the said section 31(6) or 36(1), to make any order which the court would have had power to make under the provisions of this Act if the application under the said section 31(6) or 36(1), as the case may be, had been made jointly with an application for an order under the said section 2; and the court shall have power to give such consequential directions as may be necessary for enabling the court to exercise any of the powers available to the court under this Act in the case of an application for an order under section 2.

(3) Where an order made under section 15(1) of this Act is in force with respect to a party to a marriage, the court shall not give a direction under subsection (1) above with respect to any application made under the said section 31(6) or 36(1) by that party on the death of the other party.

Miscellaneous and supplementary provisions

19. Effect, duration and form of orders—(1) Where an order is made under section 2 of this Act then for all purposes, including the purposes of the enactments relating to capital transfer tax, the will or the law relating to intestacy, or both the will and the law relating to intestacy, as the case may be, shall have effect and be deemed to have had effect as from the deceased's death subject to the provisions of the order.

(2) Any order made under section 2 or 5 of this Act in favour of—

(a) an applicant who was the former husband or former wife of the deceased, or

(b) an applicant who was the husband or wife of the deceased in a case where *the marriage with the deceased was the subject of a decree of judicial separation and at the date of death the decree was in force* [, at the date of death, a separation order under the Family Law Act 1996 was in force in relation to the marriage with the deceased] and the separation was continuing,

shall, in so far as it provides for the making of periodical payments, cease to have effect on the remarriage of the applicant, except in relation to any arrears due under the order on the date of the remarriage.

Note. Words in square brackets in sub-s (2)(b) substituted for words in italics by Family Law Act 1996, s 66(1), Sch 8, Part I, para 27, as from a day to be appointed, subject to savings in s 66(2) of, and para 5 of Sch 9 to, the 1996 Act.

(3) A copy of every order made under this Act [other than an order made under section 15(1) of this Act] shall be sent to the principal registry of the Family Division for entry and filing, and a memorandum of the order shall be endorsed on, or permanently annexed to, the probate or letters of administration under which the estate is being administered.

Note. Words in square brackets in sub-s (3) inserted by Administration of Justice Act 1982, s 52, as from 28 October 1982. Despite the marginal note, this section does not deal with the form of orders.

20. Provisions as to personal representatives—(1) The provisions of this Act shall not render the personal representatives of a deceased person liable for having distributed any part of the estate of the deceased, after the end of the period of six months from the date on which representation with respect to the estate of the deceased is first taken out, on the ground that he ought to have taken into account the possibility—

(a) that the court might permit the making of an application for an order under section 2 of this Act after the end of that period, or

(b) that, where an order has been made under the said section 2, the court might exercise in relation thereto the powers conferred on it by section 6 of this Act,

but this subsection shall not prejudice any power to recover, by reason of the making of an order under this Act, any part of the estate so distributed.

(2) Where the personal representative of a deceased person pays any sum directed by an order under section 5 of this Act to be paid out of the deceased's net estate, he shall not be under any liability by reason of that estate not being sufficient to make the payment, unless at the time of making the payment he has reasonable cause to believe that the estate is not sufficient.

(3) Where a deceased person entered into a contract by which he agreed to leave by his will any sum of money or other property to any person or by which he agreed that a sum of money or other property would be paid or transferred to any person out of his estate, then, if the personal representative of the deceased has reason to believe that the deceased entered into the contract with the intention of defeating an application for financial provision under this Act, he may, notwithstanding anything in that contract, postpone the payment of that sum of money or the transfer of that property until the expiration of the period of six months from the date on which representation with respect to the estate of the deceased is first taken out or, if during that period an application is made for an order under section 2 of this Act, until the determination of the proceedings on that application.

21. Admissibility as evidence of statements made by deceased. *In any proceedings under this Act a statement made by the deceased, whether orally or in a document or otherwise, shall be admissible under section 2 of the Civil Evidence Act 1968 as evidence of any fact stated therein in like manner as if the statement were a statement falling within section 2(1) of that Act; and any reference in that Act to a statement admissible, or given or proposed to be given, in evidence under section 2 thereof or to the admissibility or the giving in evidence of a statement by virtue of that section or to any statement falling within section 2(1) of that Act shall be construed accordingly.*

Note. This section repealed by Civil Evidence Act 1995, s 15(2), Sch 2, as from 31 January 1997.

22. Jurisdiction of county courts—*(1) A county court shall have jurisdiction to hear and determine any application for an order under section 2 of this Act (including any application for permission to apply for such an order and any application made, in the proceedings on an application for an order under the said section 2, for an order under any other provision of this Act) where it is shown to the satisfaction of the court that the value at the date of the death of the deceased of all property included in his net estate for the purposes of this Act by virtue of paragraph (a) of the definition thereof in section 25(1) of this Act does not exceed the sum of [£30,000] or such larger sum as may from time to time be fixed for this purpose by order of the Lord Chancellor.*

Note. '£30,000' substituted by County Courts Jurisdiction (Inheritance—Provision for Family and Dependants) Order 1981, SI 1981 No 1636.

(2) *Where a county court makes an order under section 2 of this Act, the court shall have all the jurisdiction of the High Court for the purpose of any further proceedings in relation thereto under section 6 of this Act.*

(3) *Rules of court may provide for the transfer from a county court to the High Court, or from the High Court to a county court, of any proceedings for an order under section 2 of this Act.*

(4) *Any order of the Lord Chancellor under subsection (1) above shall be made by statutory instrument, and a draft of the statutory instrument shall be laid before Parliament; and—*

(a) *in relation to proceedings commenced in a county court after the making but before the coming into force of any such order the court may, if it thinks fit, refuse to make an order under section 66 of the County Courts Act 1959 (transfer to High Court of proceedings outside the jurisdiction of county court) if the proceedings are within the jurisdiction of the county court as extended by the order of the Lord Chancellor; but*

(b) *the coming into force of any such order of the Lord Chancellor shall not be taken to affect any order previously made under the said section 66.*

Note. This section repealed by Administration of Justice Act 1982, s 75(1), Sch 9, Part I, as from 1 January 1983. See now County Courts Act 1984, s 25, which provides:
'**25. Jurisdiction under Inheritance (Provision for Family and Dependants) Act 1975.** A county court shall have jurisdiction to hear and determine any application for an order under section 2 of the Inheritance (Provision for Family and Dependants) Act 1975 (including any application for permission to apply for such an order and any application made, in the proceedings on application for such an order, for an order under any other provision of that Act) where it is shown to the satisfaction of the court that the value at the date of the death of the deceased of all property included in his net estate for the purposes of that Act by virtue of paragraph (a) of the definition of 'net estate' in section 25(1) of that Act does not exceed the county court limit.'

23. Determination of date on which representation was first taken out. In considering for the purposes of this Act when representation with respect to the estate of a deceased person was first taken out, a grant limited to settled land or to trust property shall be left out of account, and a grant limited to real estate or to personal estate shall be left out of account unless a grant limited to the remainder of the estate has previously been made or is made at the same time.

24. Effect of this Act on s 46(1)(vi) of Administration of Estates Act 1925. Section 46(1)(vii) of the Administration of Estates Act 1925, in so far as it provides for the devolution of property on the Crown, the Duchy of Lancaster or the Duke of Cornwall as bona vacantia, shall have effect subject to the provisions of this Act.

25. Interpretation—(1) In this Act—
'beneficiary', in relation to the estate of a deceased person, means—
   (a) a person who under the will of the deceased or under the law relating to intestacy is beneficially interested in the estate or would be so interested if an order had not been made under this Act; and
   (b) a person who has received any sum of money or other property which by virtue of section 8(1) or 8(2) of this Act is treated as part of the net estate of the deceased or would have received that sum or other property if an order had not been made under this Act;
'child' includes an illegitimate child and a child en ventre sa mere at the death of the deceased;
'the court' means [unless the context otherwise requires] the High Court, or where a county court has jurisdiction by virtue of section 22 of this Act, a county court;
'former wife' or 'former husband' means a person whose marriage with the deceased was during the deceased's lifetime dissolved or annulled by a decree of divorce or of nullity of marriage made under the Matrimonial Causes Act 1973;
['former wife' or 'former husband' means a person whose marriage with the deceased was during the lifetime of the deceased either—

(a) dissolved or annulled by *a decree* [an order or decree] of divorce or a decree of nullity of marriage granted under the law of any part of the British Islands, or

(b) dissolved or annulled in any country or territory outside the British Islands by a divorce or annulment which is entitled to be recognised as valid by the law of England and Wales;]

Note. In definition 'the court' words in square brackets inserted by Matrimonial and Family Proceedings Act 1984, s 8(2), as from 12 October 1984. Definition of 'former wife' and 'former husband' in square brackets substituted for that in italics by Matrimonial and Family Proceedings Act 1984, s 25(2), as from 16 September 1985. Words in square brackets in that definition substituted for words in italics by Family Law Act 1996, s 66(1), Sch 8, Part I, para 27, as from a day to be appointed, subject to savings in s 66(2) of, and para 5 of Sch 9 to, the 1996 Act.

'net estate', in relation to a deceased person, means—

(a) all property of which the deceased had power to dispose by his will (otherwise than by virtue of a special power of appointment) less the amount of his funeral, testamentary and administration expenses, debts and liabilities, including any capital transfer tax payable out of his estate on his death;

(b) any property in respect of which the deceased held a general power of appointment (not being a power exercisable by will) which has not been exercised;

(c) any sum of money or other property which is treated for the purposes of this Act as part of the net estate of the deceased by virtue of section 8(1) or (2) of this Act;

(d) any property which is treated for the purposes of this Act as part of the net estate of the deceased by virtue of an order made under section 9 of the Act;

(e) any sum of money or other property which is, by reason of a disposition or contract made by the deceased, ordered under section 10 or 11 of this Act to be provided for the purpose of the making of financial provision under this Act;

'property' includes any chose in action;

'reasonable financial provision' has the meaning assigned to it by section 1 of this Act;

'valuable consideration' does not include marriage or a promise of marriage;

'will' includes codicil.

(2) For the purposes of paragraph (a) of the definition of 'net estate' in subsection (1) above a person who is not of full age and capacity shall be treated as having power to dispose by will of all property of which he would have had power to dispose by will if he had been of full age and capacity.

(3) Any reference in this Act to provision out of the net estate of a deceased person includes a reference to provision extending to the whole of that estate.

(4) For the purposes of this Act any reference to a wife or husband shall be treated as including a reference to a person who in good faith entered into a void marriage with the deceased unless either—

(a) the marriage of the deceased and that person was dissolved or annulled during the lifetime of the deceased and the dissolution or annulment is recognised by the law of England and Wales, or

(b) that person has during the lifetime of the deceased entered into a later marriage.

(5) Any reference in this Act to remarriage or to a person who has remarried includes a reference to a marriage which is by law void or voidable or to a person who has entered into such a marriage, as the case may be, and a marriage shall be treated for the purposes of this Act as a remarriage, in relation to any party thereto, notwithstanding that the previous marriage of that party was void or voidable.

(6) Any reference in this Act to an order or decree made under the Matrimonial Causes Act 1973 or under any section of that Act shall be construed as including a reference to an order or decree which is deemed to have been made under that Act or under that section thereof, as the case may be.

(7) Any reference in this Act to any enactment is a reference to that enactment as amended by or under any subsequent enactment.

26. Consequential amendments, repeals and transitional provisions—(1) (*Amends Matrimonial Causes Act 1973, s 36 (p 2545), and the words omitted from sub-s (2) below amend Sch 2, para 5(2) to, that Act.*)

(2) Subject to the provisions of this section, the enactments specified in the Schedule to this Act are hereby repealed to the extent specified in the third column of the Schedule; ...

(3) The repeal of the said enactments shall not affect their operation in relation to any application made thereunder (whether before or after the commencement of this Act) with reference to the death of any person who died before the commencement of this Act.

(4) Without prejudice to the provisions of section 38 of the Interpretation Act 1889 (which relates to the effect of repeals) nothing in any repeal made by this Act shall affect any order made or direction given under any enactment repealed by this Act, and, subject to the provisions of this Act, every such order or direction (other than an order made under section 4A of the Inheritance (Family Provision) Act 1938 or section 28A of the Matrimonial Causes Act 1965) shall, if it is in force at the commencement of this Act or is made by virtue of subsection (3) above, continue in force as if it had been made under section 2(1)(a) of this Act, and for the purposes of section 6(7) of this Act the court in exercising its powers under that section in relation to an order continued in force by this subsection shall be required to have regard to any change in any of the circumstances to which the court would have been required to have regard when making that order if the order had been made with reference to the death of any person who died after the commencement of this Act.

Note. Interpretation Act 1889, s 38 is replaced by Interpretation Act 1978, ss 17(2)(a) and 16(1).

27. Short title, commencement and extent—(1) This Act may be cited as the Inheritance (Provision for Family and Dependants) Act 1975.

(2) This Act does not extend to Scotland or Northern Ireland.

(3) This Act shall come into force on 1 April 1976.

SCHEDULE

ENACTMENTS REPEALED

Chapter	Short Title	Extent of Repeal
1938 c 72	The Inheritance (Family Provision) Act 1938	The whole Act.
1952 c 64	The Intestates' Estates Act 1952	Section 7 and Schedule 3.
1965 c 72	The Matrimonial Causes Act 1965	Sections 26 and 28A and section 25(4) and (5) as applied by section 28(2).
1966 c 35	The Family Provision Act 1966	The whole Act, except section 1 and subsection (1) and (3) of section 10.
1969 c 46	The Family Law Reform Act 1969	Sections 5(1) and 18.

Chapter	Short Title	Extent of Repeal
1970 c 31	The Administration of Justice Act 1970	In Schedule 2, paragraph 16.
1970 c 33	The Law Reform (Miscellaneous Provisions) Act 1970	Section 6.
1970 c 45	The Matrimonial Proceedings and Property Act 1970	Section 36.
1971 c 23	The Courts Act 1971	Section 45(1)(a).
1973 c 18	The Matrimonial Causes Act 1973	In section 50, in subsection (1)(a) the words from 'and sections 26' to the end of the paragraph, in subsection (1)(d) the words 'or sections 26 to 28A of the Matrimonial Causes Act 1965' and in subsection (2)(a) the words 'or under section 26 or 27 of the Matrimonial Causes Act 1965'. In Schedule 2, paragraph 5(1) and in paragraph 12 the words '(a) sections 26 to 28A of the Matrimonial Causes Act 1965'.
1975 c 7	The Finance Act 1975	In Schedule 12, paragraph 6.

LEGITIMACY ACT 1976

(1976 c 31)

An Act to consolidate certain enactments relating to legitimacy.   [22 July 1976]

1. Legitimacy of children of certain void marriages—(1) The child of a void marriage, whenever born, shall, subject to subsection (2) below, and Schedule 1 to this Act, be treated as the legitimate child of his parents if at the time of *the act of intercourse resulting in the birth* [the insemination resulting in the birth or, where there was no such insemination, the child's conception] (or at the time of the celebration of the marriage if later) both or either of the parties reasonably believed that the marriage was valid.

(2) This section only applies where the father of the child was domiciled in England and Wales at the time of the birth or, if he died before the birth, was so domiciled immediately before his death.

[(3) It is hereby declared for the avoidance of doubt that subsection (1) above applies notwithstanding that the belief that the marriage was valid was due to a mistake as to law.

(4) In relation to a child after the coming into force of section 28 of the Family Law Reform Act 1987, it shall be presumed for the purposes of subsection (1) above, unless the contrary is shown, that one of the parties to the void marriage reasonably believed at the time of the insemination resulting in the birth or, where there was no such insemination, the child's conception (or at the time of the celebration of the marriage if later) that the marriage was valid.]

Note. For definition of 'void marriage', see s 10(1) (p 2617). See Family Law Reform Act 1987, s 1(3)(a). Words in square brackets in sub-s (1) substituted for words in italics, and sub-ss (3), (4), added by Family Law Reform Act 1987, s 28(1), (2), as from 4 April 1988.

2. Legitimation by subsequent marriage of parents. Subject to the following provisions of this Act, where the parents of an illegitimate person marry one another, the marriage shall, if the father of the illegitimate person is at the date of marriage domiciled in England and Wales, render that person, if living, legitimate from the date of the marriage.

Note. See Family Law Act 1986, s 56(4) (p 3182).

3. Legitimation by extraneous law. Subject to the following provisions of this Act, where the parents of an illegitimate person marry one another and the father of the illegitimate person is not at the time of the marriage domiciled in England and Wales but is domiciled in a country by the law of which the illegitimate person became legitimated by virtue of such subsequent marriage, that person, if living, shall in England and Wales be recognised as having been so legitimated from the date of the marriage notwithstanding that, at the time of his birth, his father was domiciled in a country the law of which did not permit legitimation by subsequent marriage.

Note. See Family Law Act 1986, s 56(4) (p 3182).

4. Legitimation of adopted child—(1) *Paragraph 3 of Schedule 1 to the Children Act 1975* [Section 39 of the Adoption Act 1976] [or section 67 of the Adoption and Children Act 2002] does not prevent an adopted child being legitimated under section 2 or 3 above if either natural parent is the sole adoptive parent.

    (2) Where an adopted child (with a sole adoptive parent) is legitimated—

    (a) *sub-paragraph (2) of the said paragraph 3* [subsection (2) of the said section 39] [or subsecton (3)(b) of the said section 67] shall not apply after the legitimation to the natural relationship with the other natural parent, and

    (b) revocation of the adoption order in consequence of the legitimation shall not affect *Part II of the said Schedule 1* [section 39, 41 or 42 of the Adoption Act 1976] [or section 67, 68, 69 of the Adoption and Children Act 2002] as it applies to any instrument made before the date of legitimation.

Note. Words in square brackets substituted for words in italics by Adoption Act 1976, s 73(2), Sch 3, para 23, as from 1 January 1988. Words 'or section 67 of the Adoption and Children Act 2002', 'or subsection (3)(b) of the said section 67' and 'or section 67, 68 or 69 of the Adoption and Children Act 2002' in square brackets inserted by the Adoption and Children Act 2002, s 139(1), Sch 3, paras 16, 17, as from a day to be appointed.

5. Rights of legitimated persons and others to take interests in property—(1) Subject to any contrary indication, the rules of construction contained in this section apply to any instrument other than an existing instrument, so far as the instrument contains a disposition of property.

    (2) For the purposes of this section, provision of the law of intestate succession applicable to the estate of a deceased person shall be treated as if contained in an instrument executed by him (while of full capacity) immediately before his death.

    (3) A legitimated person, and any other person, shall be entitled to take any interest as if the legitimated person had been born legitimate.

    (4) A disposition which depends on the date of birth of a child or children of the parent or parents shall be construed as if—

    (a) a legitimated child had been born on the date of legitimation,

    (b) two or more legitimated children legitimated on the same date had been born on that date in the order of their actual births,

but this does not affect any reference to the age of a child.

    (5) Examples of phrases in wills on which subsection (4) above can operate are—

1. Children of A 'living at my death or born afterwards'.
2. Children of A 'living at my death or born afterwards before any one of such children for the time being in existence attains a vested interest, and who attain the age of 21 years'.
3. As in example 1 or 2, but referring to grandchildren of A, instead of children of A.
4. A for life 'until he has a child' and then to his child or children.

Note. Subsection (4) above will not affect the reference to the age of 21 years in example 2.

(6) If an illegitimate person or a person adopted by one of his natural parents dies, or has died before the commencement of this Act, and—

(a) after his death his parents marry or have married; and
(b) the deceased would, if living at the time of the marriage, have become a legitimated person,

this section shall apply for the construction of the instrument so far as it relates to the taking of interests by, or in succession to, his spouse, children and remoter issue as if he had been legitimated by virtue of the marriage.

(7) In this section 'instrument' includes a private Act settling property, but not any other enactment.

6. Dispositions depending on date of birth—(1) Where a disposition depends on the date of birth of a child who was born illegitimate and who is legitimated (or, if deceased, is treated as legitimated), section 5(4) above does not affect entitlement under Part II of the Family Law Reform Act 1969 (illegitimate children).

(2) Where a disposition depends on the date of birth of an adopted child who is legitimated (or, if deceased, is treated as legitimated) section 5(4) above does not affect entitlement by virtue of *paragraph 6(2) of Schedule 1 to the Children Act 1975* [section 42(2) of the Adoption Act 1976] [or section 69(2) of the Adoption and Children act 2002].

Note. Words in square brackets substituted for words in italics by Adoption Act 1976, s 73, Sch 3, para 24, as from 1 January 1988. Words 'or section 69(2) of the Adoption and Children Act 2002' in square brackets inserted by the Adoption and Children Act 2002, s 139(1), Sch 3, paras 16, 18, as from a day to be appointed.

(3) This section applies for example where—
(a) a testator dies in 1976 bequeathing a legacy to his eldest grandchild living at a specified time,
(b) his daughter has an illegitimate child in 1977 who is the first grandchild,
(c) his married son has a child in 1978,
(d) subsequently the illegitimate child is legitimated,

and in all those cases the daughter's child remains the eldest grandchild of the testator throughout.

7. Protection of trustees and personal representatives—(1) A trustee or personal representative is not under a duty, by virtue of the law relating to trusts or the administration of estates, to enquire, before conveying or distributing any property, whether any person is illegitimate or has been adopted by one of his natural parents, and could be legitimated (or if deceased be treated as legitimated), if that fact could affect entitlement to the property.

(2) A trustee or personal representative shall not be liable to any person by reason of a conveyance or distribution of the property made without regard to any such fact if he has not received notice of the fact before the conveyance or distribution.

(3) This section does not prejudice the right of a person to follow the property, or any property representing it, into the hands of another person, other than a purchaser, who has received it.

8. Personal rights and obligations. A legitimated person shall have the same rights, and shall be under the same obligations in respect of the maintenance and support of himself or of any other person as if he had been born legitimate, and, subject to the provisions of this Act, the provisions of any Act relating to claims for damages, compensation, allowance, benefit or otherwise by or in respect of a legitimate child shall apply in like manner in the case of a legitimated person.

9. Re-registration of birth of legitimated person—(1) It shall be the duty of the parents of a legitimated person or, in cases where re-registration can be effected on information furnished by one parent and one of the parents is dead, of the surviving parent to furnish to the Registrar General information with a view to obtaining the re-registration of the birth of that person within 3 months after the date of the marriage by virtue of which he was legitimated.

(2) The failure of the parents or either of them to furnish information as required by subsection (1) above in respect of any legitimated person shall not affect the legitimation of that person.

(3) This section does not apply in relation to a person who was legitimated otherwise than by virtue of the subsequent marriage of his parents

(4) Any parent who fails to give information as required by this section shall be liable on summary conviction to a fine not exceeding £2 [level 1 on the standard scale].

Note. Reference to level 1 substituted by virtue of Criminal Justice Act 1982, ss 38, 46.

10. Interpretation—(1) In this Act, except where the context otherwise requires—
  'disposition' includes the conferring of a power of appointment and any other disposition of an interest in or right over property;
  'existing', in relation to an instrument, means one made before 1 January 1976;
  'legitimated person' means a person legitimated or recognised as legitimated—
    (a) under section 2 or 3 above; or
    (b) under section 1 or 8 of the Legitimacy Act 1926; or
    (c) except in section 8, by a legitimation (whether or not by virtue of the subsequent marriage of his parents) recognised by the law of England and Wales and effected under the law of any other country;
    and cognate expressions shall be construed accordingly;
  'power of appointment' includes any discretionary power to transfer a beneficial interest in property without the furnishing of valuable consideration;
  'void marriage' means a marriage, not being voidable only, in respect of which the High Court has or had jurisdiction to grant a decree of nullity, or would have or would have had such jurisdiction if the parties were domiciled in England and Wales

(2) For the purposes of this Act 'legitimated person' includes, where the context admits, a person legitimated, or recognised as legitimated, before the passing of the Children Act 1975.

(3) For the purposes of this Act, except where the context otherwise requires—
  (a) the death of the testator is the date at which a will or codicil is to be regarded as made;
  (b an oral disposition of property shall be deemed to be contained in an instrument made when the disposition was made.

(*4*) *It is hereby declared that references in this Act to dispositions of property include references to a disposition by the creation of an entailed interest.*

Note. Sub-s (4) repealed by Trusts of Land and Appointment of Trustees Act 1996, s 25(2), Sch 4, as from 1 January 1997.

(5) Except in so far as the context otherwise requires, any reference in this Act to an enactment shall be construed as a reference to that enactment as amended by or under any other enactment, including this Act.

Note. See Family Law Reform Act 1987, s 1(3)(b) (p 3136).

11. Savings, amendments and repeals—(1) Schedule 1 to this Act, which contains savings and amendments to enactments consequential upon the provisions of this Act, shall have effect.

(2) The enactments mentioned in Schedule 2 to this Act are hereby repealed to the extent specified in column 3 of that Schedule.

12. Short title, commencement and extent—(1) This Act may be cited as the Legitimacy Act 1976.

(2) This Act shall come into force at the end of the period of one month beginning with the date on which it is passed.

(3) This Act does not extend to Scotland or to Northern Ireland.

SCHEDULES

SCHEDULE 1   Section 11

SAVINGS AND CONSEQUENTIAL AMENDMENTS

SAVINGS

1. (1) Notwithstanding the repeal by this Act of sections 1 and 8 of the Legitimacy Act 1926 persons legitimated or recognised as legitimated under that Act shall continue to be legitimated or recognised as legitimated by virtue of section 1 or, as the case may be, section 8 of that Act.

(2) In any enactment whether passed before or after this Act references to persons legitimated or recognised as legitimated under section 1 or section 8 of the Legitimacy Act 1926 or under section 2 or section 3 of this Act shall be construed as including references to persons legitimated or recognised as legitimated under section 2 or section 3 of this Act or under section 1 or section 8 of the said Act of 1926 respectively.

2. (1) The enactments repealed by Part II of Schedule 4 to the Children Act 1975 (which are superseded by section 5 of this Act) shall, notwithstanding those repeals, continue to have effect as respects existing instruments

In this sub-paragraph 'instrument' has the same meaning as in section 5 of this Act.

(2) Subject to paragraph (3)(b) below, nothing in this Act or in the Legitimacy Act 1926 (in so far as the effect of that Act is preserved by sub-paragraph (1) above) shall affect the operation or construction of any disposition coming into operation before 1 January 1927 or affect any rights under this intestacy of a person dying before that date.

(3) Sub-paragraph (2) above shall apply in relation to a person to whom the said Act of 1926 applied by virtue of section 1(1) of the Legitimacy Act 1959 with the substitution for '1 January 1927' of '29 October 1959'.

3. Section 1 does not—

(a) affect any rights under the intestacy of a person who died before 29 October 1959, or

(b) affect the operation or construction of any disposition coming into operation before 29 October 1959 except so far as may be necessary to avoid the severance from a dignity or title of honour of property limited (expressly or not) to devolve (as nearly as the law permits) along with the dignity or title of honour.

4. (1) Section 1 of this Act, so far as it affects the succession to a dignity or title of honour, or the devolution of property limited as aforesaid, only applies to children born after 28 October 1959.

(2) Apart from section 1, nothing in this Act shall affect the succession to any dignity or title of honour or render any person capable of succeeding to or transmitting a right to succeed to any such dignity or title.

(3) Apart from section 1, nothing in this Act shall affect the devolution of any property limited (expressly or not) to devolve (as nearly as the law permits) along with any dignity or title of honour.

This sub-paragraph applies only if and so far as a contrary intention is not expressed in the instrument, and shall have effect subject to the instrument.

5. It is hereby declared that nothing in this Act affects the Succession to the Throne.

CONSEQUENTIAL AMENDMENTS

(*Para 6 adds Births and Deaths Registration Act 1953, s 14(5)* (*not printed in this work*).)

Children Act 1975 (*c 72*)

7. *In paragraph 1(4) of Schedule 1 to the Children Act 1975 for the words 'These definitions of adoption and legitimation include' and 'those effected' there are substituted respectively the words 'This definition of adoption includes' and 'an adoption effected'.*

Note. Para 7 repealed by Adoption Act 1976, s 73, Sch 4, as from 1 January 1988.

SCHEDULE 2   Section 11

ENACTMENTS REPEALED

Chapter	Short Title	Extent of Repeal
16 & 17 Geo 5 c 60.	Legitimacy Act 1926.	Sections 1(1) and (4). Sections 6, 7 and 8. Sections 10, 11 and 12. The Schedule.
5 & 6 Eliz 2 c 39.	Legitimation (Re-registration of Birth) Act 1957.	Section 1(1). Section 2.
7 & 8 Eliz 2 c 73.	Legitimacy Act 1959.	Section 1. In section 2, subsection (1) to (5). Section 6(4).
1969 c 46.	Family Law Reform Act 1969.	Section 16(2).
1975 c 72.	Children Act 1975.	In section 8(9) the words from 'and related' to the end. In Schedule 1, paragraphs 1(3), 12 and 13; in paragraph 14, sub-paragraph(1)(b) and (2), and words 'or is legitimated' in sub-paragraphs (3)(d); and paragraph 15(1)(b).

ADOPTION ACT 1976

(1976 c 36)

ARRANGEMENT OF SECTIONS

PART I

THE ADOPTION SERVICE

PART II

ADOPTION ORDERS

PART III

CARE AND PROTECTION OF CHILDREN AWAITING ADOPTION

An Act to consolidate the enactments having effect in England and Wales in relation to adoption. [22 July 1976]

Note. Proceedings under this Act are 'family proceedings' for the purposes of Magistrates' Courts Act 1980, ss 66–74 (pp 2778–2784); see ibid s 65(1) (p 2776). See also Children Act 1989, s 92, Sch 11, Part I (pp 3395, 3459).

The Adoption Act 1976 is repealed by the Adoption and Children Act 2002, s 139(3), Sch 5, except Part 4 (ss 38–49) (status of adopted children) and Sch 2, para 6 as from a date to be appointed.

PART I

THE ADOPTION SERVICE

The Adoption Service

1. Establishment of Adoption Service—(1) It is the duty of every local authority to establish and maintain within their area a service designed to meet the needs, in relation to adoption, of—

(a) children who have been or may be adopted,

(b) parents and guardians of such children, and

(c) persons who have adopted or may adopt a child,

and for that purpose to provide the requisite facilities, or secure that they are provided by *approved adoption societies* [appropriate voluntary organisation].

(2) The facilities to be provided as part of the service maintained under subsection (1) include—

(a) temporary board and lodging where needed by pregnant women, mothers or children;

(b) arrangements for assessing children and prospective adopters, and placing children for adoption;

(c) counselling for persons with problems relating to adoption.

(3) The facilities of the service maintained under subsection (1) shall be provided in conjunction with the local authority's other social services and with *approved adoption societies* [appropriate voluntary organisations] in their area, so that help may be given in a co-ordinated manner without duplication, omission or avoidable delay.

[(3A) In this Part, references to adoption are to the adoption of children, wherever they may be habitually resident, effected under the law of any country or territory, whether within or outside the British Islands.]

Note. Sub-s (3A) inserted by the Adoption (Intercountry Aspects) Act 1999, s 9, as from 30 April 2001.

(4) The services maintained by local authorities under subsection (1) may be collectively referred to as 'the Adoption Service', and a local authority or *approved adoption society* [approved voluntary organisation] may be referred to as an adoption agency.

Note. Words 'appropriate voluntary organisation' and 'appropriate voluntary organisations' in square brackets in sub-ss (1), (3), (4) substituted for preceding words in italics by the Care Standards Act 2000, s 116, Sch 4, para 5(1), (2)(a), as from (in relation to Wales) 30 January 2003 and (in relation to England) 30 April 2003.

[(5) In this Act 'appropriate voluntary organisation' means a voluntary organisation which is an adoption society in respect of which a person is registered under Part II of the Care Standards Act 2000.]

Note. Sub-s (5) inserted by the Care Standards Act 2000, s 116, Sch 4, para 5(1), (2)(b), as from (in relation to Wales) 30 January 2003, (in relation to England for the purpose of making regulations) 24 February 2003 and (in relation to England for remaining purposes) 30 April 2003.

2. Local authorities' social services. The social services referred to in section 1(3) are the functions of a local authority which *stand referred to the authority's social services committee* [are social services functions within the meaning of the Local Authority Social Services Act 1970], including, in particular but without prejudice to the generality of the foregoing, a local authority's functions *relating to—*

(a) *the promotion of the welfare of children by diminishing the need to receive children into care or keep them in care, including (in exceptional circumstances) the giving of assistance in cash;*

(b) *the welfare of children in the care of a local authority;*

(c) *the welfare of children who are foster children within the meaning of the Children Act 1958* [Foster Children Act 1980];

(d) *children who are subject to supervision orders made in matrimonial proceedings;*

(e) *the provision of residential accommodation for expectant mothers and young children and of day-care facilities;*

(f) *the regulation and inspection of nurseries and child minders;*

(g) *care and other treatment of children through court proceedings*

[(a) under the Children Act 1989, relating to family assistance orders, local authority support for children and families, care and supervision and emergencey protection of children, community homes, voluntary homes and organisations, *registered* [private] children's homes, private arrangements for fostering children, child minding and day care for young children and children accommodated by *health authorities* [Health Authorities, Special Health Authorities'] [Primary Care Trusts], [National Health Service trusts] and local education authorities or in *residential care, nursing or mental nursing homes or in independent schools* [care homes, independent hospitals or schools]; and

(b) under the National Health Service Act 1977, relating to the provision of care for expectant and nursing mothers.]

Note. Words in square brackets in para (c) substituted for words 'Children Act 1958' by Foster Children Act 1980, s 23(2), Sch 2, as from 1 April 1981.

Paras (a), (b) in square brackets substituted for words in italics by Children Act 1989, s 88(1), Sch 10, Part I, para 1, as from 14 October 1991. Words 'Health Authorities, Special Health Authorities' in square brackets substituted for words 'health authorities' in italics by Health Authorities Act 1995, s 2(1), Sch 1, Part III, para 101, as from 28 June 1995, in so far as is necessary for enabling the making of any regulations, orders, directiuons, schemes or appointments, and as from 1 April 1996 otherwise. Words 'National Health Service Trusts' in square brackets in new para (a) inserted by National Health Service and Community Care Act 1990, s 66(1), Sch 9, para 17, as from 5 July 1990.

Words 'are social services ... 1970' in square brackets substituted for preceding words in italics by the Local Government Act 2000, s 107, Sch 5, para 16, as from 26 October 2000 in relation to England and 28 July 2001 in relation to Wales (unless the National Assembly for Wales by order provides for this amendment to come into force before that date). Words 'private' and 'care homes, independent hospitals or schools' in square brackets substituted for previous words in italics by the Care Standards Act 2000, s 116, Sch 4, para 5(1), (3), as from 1 April 2002. Words 'Primary Care Trusts,' in square brackets inserted by the Health Act

1999 (Supplementary, Consequential etc Provisions) Order 2000, SI 2000/90, art 3(1), Sch 1, para 12, as from 8 February 2000.

Adoption Societies

3. Approval of adoption societies—*(1) Subject to regulations under section 9(1), a body desiring [which is a voluntary organisation and desires] to act as an adoption society or, if it is already an adoption society, desiring [desires] to continue to act as such may, in the manner specified by regulations made by the Secretary of State, apply to the Secretary of State for his approval to its doing so.*

Note. Words in square brackets substituted for words in italics by Health and Social Services and Social Security Adjudications Act 1983, s 9, Sch 2, para 29, as from 15 August 1983.

(2) On an application under subsection (1), the Secretary of State shall take into account the matters relating to the applicant specified in subsections (3) to (5) and any other relevant considerations, and if, but only if, he is satisfied that the applicant is likely to make, or, if the applicant is an approved adoption society, is making, an effective contribution to the Adoption Service he shall by notice to the applicant give his approval, which shall be operative from a date specified in the notice or, in the case of a renewal of approval, from the date of the notice.

(3) In considering the application, the Secretary of State shall have regard, in relation to the period for which approval is sought, to the following—

    (a)   the applicant's adoption programme, including, in particular, its ability to make provision for children who are free for adoption,

    (b)   the number and qualification of its staff,

    (c)   its financial resources, and

    (d)   the organisation and control of its operations.

(4) Where it appears to the Secretary of State that the applicant is likely to operate extensively within the area of a particular local authority he shall ask the authority whether they support the application, and shall take account of any views about it put to him by the authority.

(5) Where the applicant is already an approved adoption society or, whether before or after the passing of this Act, previously acted as an adoption society, the Secretary of State, in considering the application shall also have regard to the record and reputation of the applicant in the adoption field, and the areas within which and the scale on which it is currently operating or has operated in the past.

(6) If after considering the application the Secretary of State is not satisfied that the applicant is likely to make or, as the case may be, is making an effective contribution to the Adoption Service, the Secretary of State shall, subject to section 5(1) and (2), by notice inform the applicant that its application is refused.

[(6A) Approval under this section may be given on terms that the applicant may act as an adoption society either—

    (a)   in relation to facilities provided in respect of adoptions other than those mentioned in subsection (6B); or

    (b)   in relation to facilities provided in respect of any adoptions, including those so mentioned.

(6B) The adoptions are—

    (a)   a Convention adoption;

    (b)   an adoption effected by a Convention adoption order;

    (c)   an overseas adoption;

    (d)   an adoption of a child habitually resident in the British Islands which is not a Convention adoption and is effected under the law of a country or territory outside the British Islands; and

    (e)   an adoption of a child habitually resident outside the British Islands which is effected by an adoption order other than a Convention adoption order.]

(7) *If not withdrawn earlier under section 4, approval given under this section shall last for a period of three years from the date on which it becomes operative, and shall then expire or, in the case of an approved adoption society whose further application for approval is pending at that time, shall expire on the date that application is granted or, as the case may be, refused.*

Note. Sub-ss (6A), (6B) inserted by the Adoption (Intercountry Aspects) Act 1999, s 10, as from a date to be appointed.

This section repealed by the Care Standards Act 2000, s 117(2), Sch 6, as from (in relation to Wales) 30 January 2003 and (in relation to England) 30 April 2003.

4. Withdrawal of approval—*(1) If, while approval of a body under section 3 is operative, it appears to the Secretary of State that the body is not making an effective contribution to the Adoption Service he shall, subject to section 5(3) and (4), by notice to the body withdraw the approval from a date specified in the notice.*

(2) If an approved adoption society fails to provide the Secretary of State with information required by him for the purpose of carrying out his functions under subsection (1), or fails to verify such information in the manner required by him, he may by notice to the society withdraw the approval from a date specified in the notice.

Note. Sub-ss (1), (2) repealed by the Care Standards Act 2000, s 117(2), Sch 6, as from (in relation to Wales) 30 January 2003 and (in relation to England) 30 April 2003.

(3) Where approval is withdrawn under subsection (1) or (2) or expires [Where, by virtue of the cancellation of the registration of any person under Part II of the Care Standards Act 2000, a body has ceased to be an appropriate voluntary organisation] the Secretary of State may direct the body *concerned* to make such arrangements as to children who are in its care and other transitional matters as seem to him expedient.

Note. Words 'Where, by virtue ... organisation' in square brackets substituted for preceding words in italics and word 'concerned' in italics repealed by the Care Standards Act 2000, ss 116, 117(2), Sch 4, para 5(1), (4), Sch 6, as from (in relation to Wales) 30 January 2003 and (in relation to England) 30 April 2003.

5. Procedure on refusal to approve, or withdrawal of approval from, adoption societies—*(1) Before notifying a body which has applied for approval that the application is refused in accordance with section 3(6) the Secretary of State shall serve on the applicant a notice—*

    (a) setting out the reasons why he proposes to refuse the application;

    (b) informing the applicant that it may make representations in writing to the Secretary of State within 28 days of the date of service of the notice.

(2) If any representations are made by the applicant in accordance with subsection (1), the Secretary of State shall give further consideration to the application taking into account those representations.

(3) The Secretary of State shall, before withdrawing approval of an adoption society in accordance with section 4(1), serve on the society a notice—

    (a) setting out the reasons why he proposes to withdraw the approval; and

    (b) informing the society that it may make representations in writing to the Secretary of State within 28 days of the date of service of the notice.

(4) If any representations are made by the society in accordance with subsection (3), the Secretary of State shall give further consideration to the withdrawal of approval under section 4(1) taking into account those representations.

(5) This section does not apply where the Secretary of State, after having considered any representations made by the applicant in accordance with this section, proposes to refuse approval or, as the case may be, to withdraw approval for reasons which have already been communicated to the applicant in a notice under this section.

Note. This section repealed by the Care Standards Act 2000, s 117(2), Sch 6, as from (in relation to Wales) 30 January 2003 and (in relation to England) 30 April 2003.

Welfare of children

6. Duty to promote welfare of child. In reaching any decision relating to the adoption of a child a court or adoption agency shall have regard to all the circumstances, first consideration being given to the need to safeguard and promote the welfare of the child throughout his childhood; and shall so far as practicable ascertain the wishes and feelings of the child regarding the decision and give due consideration to them, having regard to his age and understanding.

7. Religious upbringing of adopted child. An adoption agency shall in placing a child for adoption have regard (so far as is practicable) to any wishes of a child's parents and guardians as to the religious upbringing of the child.

Supplemental

8. Inactive or defunct adoption societies—(1) If it appears to the Secretary of State that *an approved adoption society, or one in relation to which approval has been withdrawn under section 4 or has expired* [a body which is or has been an appropriate voluntary organisation], is inactive or defunct he may, in relation to any child who is or was in the care of the *society* [organisation], direct what appears to him to be the appropriate local authority to take any such action as might have been taken by the *society* [organisation] or by the *society* [organisation] jointly with the authority; and if apart from this section the authority would not be entitled to take that action, or would not be entitled to take it without joining the *society* [organisation] in the action, it shall be entitled to do so.

(2) Before giving a direction under subsection (1) the Secretary of State shall, if practicable, consult both the *society* [organisation] and the authority.

Note. Words 'a body which ... organisation' in square brackets substituted for preceding words in italics and word 'organisation' in each place it occurs in square brackets substituted for preceding words in italics by the Care Standards Act 2000, s 116, Sch 4, para 5(1), (5)(b), as from (in relation to Wales) 30 January 2003 and (in relation to England) 30 April 2003.

9. Regulation of adoption agencies—*(1) The Secretary of State may by regulations prohibit unincorporated bodies from applying for approval under section 3; and he shall not approve any unincorporated body whose application is contrary to regulations made under this subsection.*

Note. Sub-s (1) repealed by the Care Standards Act 2000, s 117(2), Sch 6, as from (in relation to Wales) 30 January 2003 and (in relation to England) 30 April 2003.

(2) The *Secretary of State* [appropriate Minister] may make regulations for any purpose relating to the exercise of its functions by an *approved adoption society* [an appropriate voluntary organisation].

[(2A) The power under subsection (2) includes in particular power to make in relation to an appropriate voluntary organisation any provision which regulations under section 22(2) or (7) of the Care Standards Act 2000 (regulation of establishments and agencies) may make in relation to a fostering agency (within the meaning of that Act).]

Note. Sub-s (2A) inserted by the Care Standards Act 2000, s 116, Sch 4, para 5(1), (6)(c), as from (in relation to England for the purpose of making regulations) 24 February 2003, (in relation to England for remaining purposes) 30 April 2003 and (in relation to Wales) as from a day to be appointed.

(3) The *Secretary of State* [appropriate Minister] may make regulations with respect to the exercise by local authorities of their functions of making or participating in arrangements for the adoption of children.

Note. In sub-ss (2), (3) words 'appropriate minister' in both places they occur in square brackets substituted for preceding words in italics by the Adoption and Children Act 2002, Sch 4, para 4, as from 3 February 2003. Words 'an appropriate voluntary organisation' in square brackets in sub-s (2) substituted for preceding words in italics by the Care Standards Act 2000, s 116, Sch 4, para 5(1), (6)(a), as from (in relation to England for the purpose of making regulations) 24 February 2003, (in relation to England for remaining purposes) 30 April 2003 and (in relation to Wales) as from a date to be appointed.

[(3A) The power under subsection (3) includes in particular power to make in relation to the functions there mentioned any provision which regulations under section 48 of the Care Standards Act 2000 (regulation of the exercise of relevant fostering functions) may make in relation to relevant fostering functions (within the meaning of Part III of that Act).]

Note. Sub-s (3A) inserted by the Care Standards Act 2000, s 116, Sch 4, para 5(1), (6)(c), as from (in relation to England for the purpose of making regulations) 24 February 2003 (in relation to England for remaining purposes) 30 April 2003 and (in relation to Wales) as from day to be appointed.

(4) Any person who contravenes or fails to comply with regulations made under subsection (2) shall be guilty of an offence and liable on summary conviction to a fine not exceeding *£400* [level 5 on the standard scale].

Note. Reference to level 5 substituted by virtue of Criminal Justice Act 1982, ss 38, 46.

[(5) In this section and section 9A, 'the appropriate Minister' means—
(a) in relation to England, the Secretary of State,
(b) in relation to Wales, the National Assembly for Wales,
and in relation to England and Wales, means the Secretary of State and the Assembly acting jointly.]

Note. Sub-s (5) inserted by the Adoption and Children Act 2002, s 139(2), Sch 4, para 4(1)(b), as from 3 February 2003.

[9A. Independent review of determinations—(1) Regulations under section 9 may establish a procedure under which any person in respect of whom a qualifying determination has been made by an adoption agency may apply to a panel constituted by the appropriate Minister for a review of that determination.

(2) The regulations must make provision as to the description of determinations which are qualifying determinations for the purposes of subsection (1).

(3) The regulations may include provision as to—
(a) the duties and powers of a panel (including the power to recover the costs of a review from the adoption agency by which the determination reviewed was made),
(b) the administration and procedures of a panel,
(c) the appointment of members of a panel (including the number, or any limit on the number, of members who may be appointed and any conditions for appointment),
(d) the payment of expenses of members of a panel,
(e) the duties of adoption agencies in connection with reviews conducted under the regulations,
(f) the monitoring of any such reviews.

(4) The appropriate Minister may make an arrangement with an organisation under which functions in relation to the panel are performed by the organisation on his behalf.

(5) If the appropriate Minister makes such an arrangement with an organisation, the organisation is to perform its functions under the arrangement in accordance with any general or special directions given by the appropriate Minister.

(6) The arrangement may include provision for payments to be made to the organisation by the appropriate Minister.

(7) Where the appropriate Minister is the National Assembly for Wales, subsections (4) and (6) also apply as if references to an organisation included references to the Secretary of State.

(8) In this section, 'organisation' includes a public body and a private or voluntary organisation.]

Note. This section inserted by the Adoption and Children Act 2002, s 139(2), Sch 4, para 5, as from (in relation to England for the purposes of making regulations) 1 December 2003, (in relation to Wales) 7 February 2004 and (in relation to England for remaining purposes) 1 April 2004.

10. Inspection of books, etc, of approved adoption societies—(*1*) *A local authority may at any time give notice in writing to an approved adoption society, or to any officer of such a society, requiring that society or officer to produce to the authority such books, accounts and other documents relating to the performance by the society of the function of making arrangements for the adoption of children as the authority may consider necessary for its own information or that of the Secretary of State.*

(*2*) *Any such notice may contain a requirement that any information to be furnished in accordance with the notice shall be verified in a manner specified in the notice.*

(*3*) *Any person who fails to comply with the requirements of a notice under this section shall be guilty of an offence and liable on summary conviction to imprisonment for a term not exceeding 3 months or to a fine not exceeding £50 or to both.*

Note. This section repealed by Health and Social Services and Social Security Adjudications Act 1983, ss 9, 30, Sch 2, para 30, Sch 10, Part I, as from 15 August 1983.

11. Restriction on arranging adoptions and placing of children—(1) A person other than an adoption agency shall not make arrangements for the adoption of a child, or place a child for adoption, unless—
(a) the proposed adopter is a relative of the child, or
(b) he is acting in pursuance of an order of the High Court.

(2) *An adoption society approved as respects Scotland under section 4 of the Children Act 1975, but which is not approved under section 3 of this Act, shall not act as an adoption society in England and Wales except to the extent that the society considers it necessary to do so in the interests of a person mentioned in section 1 of that Act.*

[(2) An adoption society which is—
(a) approved as respects Scotland under section 3 of the Adoption (Scotland) Act 1978; or
(b) registered as respects Northern Ireland under Article 4 of the Adoption (Northern Ireland) Order 1987,
but which is not *approved under section 3 of this Act* [an appropriate voluntary organisation], shall not act as an adoption society in England and Wales except to the extent that the society considers it necessary to do so in the interests of a person mentioned in section 1 of the Act of 1978 or Article 3 of the Order of 1987.]

Note. Sub-s (2) in square brackets substituted for sub-s (2) in italics by Children Act 1989, s 88(1), Sch 10, Part I, para 2, as from 14 October 1991.

Words 'an appropriate voluntary organisation' in square brackets substituted for preceding words in italics by the Care Standards Act 2000, s 116, Sch 4, para 5(1), (7)(a), as from (in relation to Wales) 30 January 2003 and (in relation to England) 30 April 2003.

(3) A person who—
(a) takes part in the management or control of a body of persons which exists wholly or partly for the purpose of making arrangements for the adoption of children and *which is not an adoption agency* [which is not—
  (i) *a local authority; or*
  (ii) *a voluntary adoption agency within the meaning of the Care Standards Act 2000 in respectg of which he is registered*]; or
(b) contravenes subsection (1); or
(c) receives a child placed with him in contravention of subsection (1),

shall be guilty of an offence and liable on summary conviction to imprisonment for a term not exceeding 3 months or to a fine not exceeding £400 [level 5 on the standard scale] or to both.

Note. Words 'which is not ... is registered' in square brackets substituted for words in italics by the Care Standards Act 2000, s 116, Sch 4, para 5(1), (7)(b), as from a date to be appointed. Reference to level 5 substituted by virtue of Criminal Justice Act 1982, ss 38, 46.

(4) In any proceedings for an offence under paragraph (a) of subsection (3), proof of things done or of words written, spoken or published (whether or not in the presence of any party to the proceedings) by any person taking part in the management or control of a body of persons, or in making arrangements for the adoption of children on behalf of the body, shall be admissible as evidence of the purpose for which that body exists.

(5) *Section 26 shall apply where a person is convicted of a contravention of subsection (1) as it applies where an application for an adoption order is refused.*

Note. Sub-s (5) repealed by Children Act 1989, s 108(7), Sch 15, as from 14 October 1991.

PART II

ADOPTION ORDERS

The making of adoption orders

12. Adoption orders—(1) An adoption order is an order *vesting the parental rights and duties relating to a child in* [giving parental responsibility for a child to] the adopters, made on their application by an authorised court.

Note. Words in square brackets substituted for words in italics by Children Act 1989, s 88(1), Sch 10, Part I, para 3(1), as from 14 October 1991.

(2) The order does not affect *the parental rights and duties so far as they relate* [parental responsibility so far as it relates] to any period before the making of the order.

Note. Words in square brackets substituted for words in italics by Children Act 1989, s 88(1), Sch 10, Part I, para 3(2), as from 14 October 1991.

(3 The making of an adoption order operates to extinguish—
(*a*) *any parental right or duty relating to the child which—*
    (*i*) *is vested in a person (not being one of the adopters) who was the parent or guardian of the child immediately before the making of the order, or*
    (*ii*) *is vested in any other person by virtue of the order of any court; and*
[(a) the parental responsibility which any person has for the child immediately before the making of the order;
(aa) any order under the Children Act 1989]
(b) any duty arising by virtue of an agreement or the order of a court to make payments, so far as the payments are in respect of the child's maintenance *for any period after the making of the order or any other matter comprised in the parental duties and relating to such a period* [or upbringing for any period after the making of the order].

Note. Sub-s(3)(a), (aa) in square brackets substituted for sub-s (3)(a) in italics and words in square brackets in sub-s (3)(b) substituted for words in italics by Children Act 1989, s 88(1), Sch 10, Part I, para 3(3), as from 14 October 1991.

(4) Subsection (3)(b) does not apply to a duty arising by virtue of an agreement—
(a) which constitutes a trust, or
(b) which expressly provides that the duty is not to be extinguished by the making of an adoption order.

(5) An adoption order may not be made in relation to a child who is or has been married.

(6) An adoption order may contain such terms and conditions as the court thinks fit.

(7) An adoption order may be made notwithstanding that the child is already an adopted child.

13. Child to live with adopters before order made—(1) Where—
  (a) [(subject to sub-section (1A))] the applicant, or one of the applicants, is a parent, step-parent or relative of the child, or
  (b) the child was placed with the applicants by an adoption agency or in pursuance of an order of the High Court,
an adoption order shall not be made unless the child is at least 19 weeks old and at all times during the preceding 13 weeks had his home with the applicants or one of them.

Note. Words in square brackets in para (a) inserted by the Adoption and Children Act 2002, s 139(2), Sch 4, para 10(a), as from 1 June 2003.

[(1A) Where an adoption is proposed to be effected by a Convention adoption order, the order shall not be made unless at all times during the preceding six months the child had his home with the applicants or one of them.]

Note. Sub-s (1A) inserted by the Adoption and Children Act 2002, s 139(2), Sch 4, para 10(b), as from 1 June 2003.

(2) Where subsection (1) [or (1A)] does not apply, an adoption order shall not be made unless the child is at least 12 months old and at all times during the preceding 12 months had his home with the applicants or one of them.

Note. Words 'or (1A)' in square brackets inserted by the Adoption and Children Act 2002, s 139(2), Sch 4, para 10(c), as from 1 June 2003.

(3) An adoption order shall not be made unless the court is satisfied that sufficient opportunities to see the child with the applicant, or, in the case of an application by a married couple, both applicants together in the home environment have been afforded—
  (a) where the child was placed with the applicant by an adoption agency, to that agency, or
  (b) in any other case, to the local authority within whose area the home is
  [*(4) In relation to*—
  (a) *an adoption proposed to be effected by a Convention adoption order; or*
  (b) *an adoption of a child habitually resident outside the British Islands which is proposed to be effected by an adoption order other than a Convention adoption order,*
subsection (1) shall have effect as if the reference to the preceding 13 weeks were a reference to the preceding six months.]

Note. Sub-s (4) inserted by the Adoption (Intercountry Aspects) Act 1999, s 11, as from a date to be appointed. Sub-s (4) repealed by the Adoption and Children Act 2002, s 139(2), (3), Sch 4, para 10(d), Sch 5, as from 1 June 2003.

14. Adoption by married couple—(*1*) *Subject to section 37(1) of the Children Act 1975 (which provides for the making of a custodianship order instead of an adoption order in certain cases) an adoption order may be made on the application of a married couple where each has attained the age of 21 years but an adoption order shall not otherwise be made on the application of more than one person.*

[(1) An adoption order shall not be made on the application of more than one person except in the circumstances specified in subsections (1A) and (1B).

(1A) An adoption order may be made on the application of a married couple where both the husband and the wife have attained the age of 21 years

(1B) An adoption order may be made on the application of a married couple where—
  (a) the husband or the wife—
      (i) is the father or mother of the child; and
      (ii) has attained the age of 18 years; and
  (b) his or her spouse has attained the age of 21 years.]

Note. Sub-ss (1), (1A), (1B) in square brackets substituted for sub-s (1) in italics by Children Act 1989, s 88(1), Sch 10, Part I, para 3(4), as from 14 October 1991.

(2) An adoption order shall not be made on the application of a married couple unless—
  (a) at least one of them is domiciled in a part of the United Kingdom, or in the Channel Islands or the Isle of Man, or
  (b) the application is for a Convention adoption order and *section 17 is* [the requirements of regulations under section 17 are] complied with.

Note. Words 'the requirements of regulations under section 17 are' in square brackets substituted for words in italics by the Adoption (Intercountry Aspects) Act 1999, Sch 2, as from 1 June 2003 except in relation to a 1965 Convention adoption order (or an application for such an order) or a 1965 Convention adoption (as defined in s 17(2) of the 1999 Act.

(3) If the married couple consist of a parent and step-parent of the child, the court shall dismiss the application if it considers the matter would be better dealt with under section 42 (orders for custody etc) of the Matrimonial Causes Act 1973.

Note. Sub-s (3) repealed by Children Act 1989, s 108(7), Sch 15, as from 14 October 1991.

15. Adoption by one person—(1) *Subject to section 37(1) of the Children Act 1975 (which provides for the making of a custodianship order instead of an adoption order in certain cases)* an adoption order may be made on the application of one person where he has attained the age of 21 years and—
  (a) is not married, or
  (b) is married and the court is satisfied that—
      (i) his spouse cannot be found, or
      (ii) the spouses have separated and are living apart, and the separation is likely to be permanent, or
      (iii) his spouse is by reason of ill-health, whether physical or mental, incapable of making an application for an adoption order.

Note. Words in italics repealed by Children Act 1989, s 108(7), Sch 15, as from 14 October 1991.

(2) An adoption order shall not be made on the application of one person unless—
  (a) he is domiciled in a part of the United Kingdom, or in the Channel Islands or the Isle of Man, or
  (b) the application is for a Convention adoption order and *section 17 is* [the requirements of regulations under section17 are] complied with.

Note. Words 'the requirements of regulations under section 17 are' in square brackets substituted for words in italics by the Adoption (Intercountry Aspects) Act 1999, Sch 2, as from 1 June 2003 except in relation to a 1965 Convention adoption order (or an application for such an order) or a 1965 Convention adoption (as defined in s 17(2) of the 1999 Act).

(3) An adoption order shall not be made on the application of the mother or father of the child alone unless the court is satisfied that—
  (a) the other natural parent is dead or cannot be found [or, by virtue of section 28 of the Human Fertilisation and Embryology Act 1990 [(disregarding subsections (5A) to (5I) of that section)], there is no other parent], or
  (b) there is some other reason justifying the exclusion of the other natural parent,

and where such an order is made the reason justifying the exclusion of the other natural parent shall be recorded by the court.

Note. First words in square brackets inserted by Human Fertilisation and Embryology Act 1990, s 49(5), Sch 4, para 4, as from 1 August 1991. Second words in square brackets inserted by the Human Fertilisation and Embryology (Deceased Fathers) Act 2003, s 3(7), as 1 December 2003. (For further effect see s 3(1), (8) of the 2003 Act).

(4) If the applicant is a step-parent of the child, the court shall dismiss the application if it considers the matter would be better dealt with under section 42 (orders for custody etc) of the Matrimonial Causes Act 1973.

Note. Sub-s (4) repealed by Children Act 1989, s 108(7), Sch 15, as from 14 October 1991.

16. Parental agreement—(1) An adoption order shall not be made unless—

(a) the child is free for adoption by virtue of an order made *in England and Wales under section 18 or made in Scotland under section 14 of the Children Act 1975 (freeing children for adoption in Scotland)*
    [(i)   in England and Wales, under section 18;
    (ii)   in Scotland, under section 18 of the Adoption (Scotland) Act 1978; or
    (iii) in Northern Ireland, under Article 17(1) or 18(1) of the Adoption (Northern Ireland) Order 1987]; or

(b) in the case of each parent or guardian of the child the court is satisfied that—
    (i)   he freely, and with full understanding of what is involved, agrees unconditionally to the making of an adoption order (whether or not he knows the identity of the applicants), or
    (ii) his agreement to the making of the adoption order should be dispensed with on a ground specified in subsection (2).

Note. Words in square brackets substituted for words in italics by Children Act 1989, s 88(1), Sch 10, Part I, para 5(1), as from 14 October 1991.

(2) The grounds mentioned in subsection (1)(b)(ii) are that the parent or guardian—

(a) cannot be found or is incapable of giving agreement;
(b) is withholding his agreement unreasonably;
(c) has persistently failed without reasonable cause to discharge *the parental duties in relation to* [his parental responsibility for] the child;
(d) has abandoned or neglected the child;
(e) has persistently ill-treated the child;
(f) has seriously ill-treated the child (subject to subsection (5)).

Note. Words in square brackets in sub-s (2)(c) substituted for words in italics by Children Act 1989, s 88(1), Sch 10, Part I, para 5(2), as from 14 October 1991.

(3) Subsection (1) does not apply in any case where the child is not a United Kingdom national and the application for the adoption order is for a Convention adoption order.

Note. Sub-s (3) repealed by the Adoption (Intercountry Aspects) Act 1999, Sch 2, as from 1 June 2003 except in relation to a 1965 Convention adoption order (or an application for such an order) or a 1965 Convention adoption (as defined in s 17(2) of the 1999 Act).

(4) Agreement is ineffective for the purposes of subsection (1)(b)(i) if given by the mother less than six weeks after the child's birth.

(5) Subsection (2)(f) does not apply unless (because of the ill-treatment or for other reasons) the rehabilitation of the child within the household of the parent or guardian is unlikely.

17. Convention adoption orders—*(1) An adoption order shall be made as a Convention adoption order if the application is for a Convention adoption order and the following conditions are satisfied both at the time of the application and when the order is made.*

(2) The child—
(a) must be a United Kingdom national or a national of a Convention country, and
(b) must habitually reside in British territory or a Convention country.

(3) The applicant or applicants and the child must not all be United Kingdom nationals living in British territory.

(4) If the application is by a married couple, either—
(a) each must be a United Kingdom national or a national of a Convention country, and both must habitually reside in Great Britain, or
(b) both must be United Kingdom nationals, and each must habitually reside in British territory or a Convention country,

and if the applicants are nationals of the same Convention country the adoption must not be prohibited by a specified provision (as defined in subsection (8)) of the internal law of that country.

(5) If the application is by one person, either—
(a) he must be a national of a Convention country, and must habitually reside in Great Britain, or
(b) he must be a United Kingdom national and must habitually reside in British territory or a Convention country,

and if he is a national of a Convention country the adoption must not be prohibited by a specified provision (as defined in subsection (8)) of the internal law of that country.

(6) If the child is not a United Kingdom national the order shall not be made—
(a) except in accordance with the provisions, if any, relating to consents and consultations of the internal law relating to adoption of the Convention country of which the child is a national, and
(b) unless the court is satisfied that each person who consents to the order in accordance with that internal law does so with full understanding of what is involved.

(7) The reference to consents and consultations in subsection (6) does not include a reference to consent by and consultation with the applicant and members of the applicant's family (including his or her spouse), and for the purposes of subsection (6) consents may be proved in the manner prescribed by rules and the court shall be treated as the authority by whom, under the law mentioned in subsection (6), consents may be dispensed with and the adoption in question may be effected; and where the provisions there mentioned require the attendance before that authority of any person who does not reside in Great Britain, that requirement shall be treated as satisfied for the purposes of subsection (6) if—
(a) that person has been given a reasonable opportunity of communicating his opinion on the adoption in question to the proper officer or clerk of the court, or to an appropriate authority of the country in question, for transmission to the court; and
(b) where he has availed himself of that opportunity, his opinion has been transmitted to the court.

(8) In subsections (4) and (5) 'specified provision' means a provision specified in an order of the Secretary of State as one notified to the Government of the United Kingdom in pursuance of the provisions of the Convention which relate to prohibitions on an adoption contained in the national law of the Convention country in question.

[17 Convention adoption orders—An adoption order shall be made as a Convention adoption order if—
(a) the application is for a Convention adoption order, and
(b) such requirements as may be prescribed by regulations made by the Secretary of State are complied with.]

Note. This section substituted by Adoption (Intercountry Aspects) Act 1999, Sch 2, as from 1 June 2003 except in relation to a 1965 Convention adoption order (or an application for such an order) or a 1965 Convention adoption (as defined in s 17(2) of the 1999 Act).

Freeing for adoption

18. Freeing child for adoption—(1) Where, on an application by an adoption agency, an authorised court is satisfied, in the case of each parent or guardian of the child that—

(a) he freely, and with full understanding of what is involved, agrees generally and unconditionally to the making of an adoption order, or

(b) his agreement to the making of an adoption order should be dispensed with on a ground specified in section 16(2),

the court shall make an order declaring the child free for adoption.

(2) No application shall be made under subsection (1) unless—

(a) it is made with the consent of a parent or guardian of a child, or

(b) the adoption agency is applying for dispensation under subsection (1)(b) of the agreement of each parent or guardian of the child, and the child is in the care of the adoption agency.

[(2A) For the purposes of subsection (2) a child is in the care of an adoption agency if the adoption agency is a local authority and he is in their care.]

Note. Sub-s (2A) inserted by Children Act 1989, s 88(1), Sch 10, Part I, para 6(1), as from 14 October 1991.

(3) No agreement required under subsection (1)(a) shall be dispensed with under subsection (1)(b) unless the child is already placed for adoption or the court is satisfied that it is likely that the child will be placed for adoption.

(4) An agreement by the mother of the child is ineffective for the purposes of this section if given less than 6 weeks after the child's birth.

(5) On the making of an order under this section, *the parental rights and duties relating to the child vest in* [parental responsibility for the child is given to] the adoption agency, and subsections (2) *and (3)* [to (4)] of section 12 apply as if the order were an adoption order and the agency were the adopters.

Note. Words in square brackets substituted for words in italics by Children Act 1989, s 88(1), Sch 10, Part I, para 6(2), as from 14 October 1991.

(6) Before making an order under this section, the court shall satisfy itself, in relation to each parent or guardian *who agrees to the adoption of the child* [of the child who can be found], that he has been given an opportunity of making, if he so wishes, a declaration that he prefers not to be involved in future questions concerning the adoption of the child; and any such declaration shall be recorded by the court.

Note. Words in square brackets substituted for words in italics by Health and Social Services and Social Security Adjudications Act 1983, s 9, Sch 2, para 31, as from 15 August 1983. In relation to any time before the coming into force of s 18 (1 January 1988), see Family Law Reform Act 1987, Sch 3, para 3 (p 3114).

(*7*) *Before making an order under this section in the case of an illegitimate child whose father is not its guardian, the court shall satisfy itself in relation to any person claiming to be the father that either—*

(*a*) *he has no intention of applying for custody of the child under section 9 of the Guardianship of Minors Act 1971, or*

(*b*) *if he did apply for custody under that section the application would be likely to be refused.*

[(*7*) *Before making an order under this section in the case of a child whose father and mother were not married to each other at the time of his birth and whose father is not his guardian, the court shall satisfy itself in relation to any person claiming to be the father that either—*

(*a*) *he has no intention of making—*

(*i*) *an application under section 4 of the Family Law Reform Act 1987 for an order giving him all the parental rights and duties with respect to the child; or* (*ii*)   *an application under any other enactment for an order giving him a right to custody, legal or actual custody or care and control of the child; or*

(*b*) *if he did make such an application, the application would be likely to be refused.*]

[(7) Before making an order under this section in the case of a child whose father does not have parental responsibility for him, the court shall satisfy itself in relation to any person claiming to be the father that—

  (a) he has no intention of applying for—

      (i) an order under section 4(1) of the Children Act 1989, or

      (ii) a residence order under section 10 of that Act, or

  (b) if he did make any such application, it would be likely to be refused.]

Note. Sub-s (7) in square brackets and italics substituted for original sub-s (7) in italics by Family Law Reform Act 1987, s 7(1), as from 1 April 1989. Sub-s (7) in square brackets substituted for sub-s (7) in square brackets and italics by Children Act 1989, s 88(1), Sch 10, Part I, para 6(3), as from 14 October 1991.

[(*8*) *In subsection* (*7*) *the reference to a child whose father and mother were not married to each other at the time of his birth shall be construed in accordance with section 1 of the Family Law Reform Act 1987.*]

[(8) Subsections (5) and (7) of section 12 apply in relation to the making of an order under this section as they apply in relation to the making of an order under that section.]

Note. Sub-s (8) in italics added by Family Law Reform Act 1987, s 33(1), Sch 2, para 67, as from 1 April 1989. Sub-s (8) in square brackets substituted for sub-s (8) in italics by Children Act 1989, s 88(1), Sch 10, Part I, para 6(3), as from 14 October 1991.

19. Progress reports to former parent—(1) This section and section 20 apply to any person ('the former progress parent') who was required to be given an opportunity of making a declaration under section 18(6) but did not do so.

(2) Within the 14 days following the date 12 months after the making of the order under section 18 the adoption agency *in which the parental rights and duties were vested* [to which parental responsibility was given] on the making of the order, unless it has previously by notice to the former parent informed him that an adoption order has been made in respect of the child, shall by notice to the former parent inform him—

  (a) whether an adoption order has been made in respect of the child, and (if not)

  (b) whether the child has his home with a person with whom he has been placed for adoption.

Note. Words in square brackets substituted for words in italics by Children Act 1989, s 88(1), Sch 10, Part I, para 7, as from 14 October 1991.

(3) If at the time when the former parent is given notice under subsection (2) an adoption order has not been made in respect of the child, it is thereafter the duty of the adoption agency to give notice to the former parent of the making of an adoption order (if and when made), and meanwhile to give the former parent notice whenever the child is placed for adoption or ceases to have his home with a person with whom he has been placed for adoption.

(4) If at any time the former parent by notice makes a declaration to the adoption agency that he prefers not to be involved in future questions concerning the adoption of the child—

  (a) the agency shall secure that the declaration is recorded by the court which made the order under section 18, and

  (b) the agency is released from the duty of complying further with subsection (3) as respects that former parent.

20. Revocation of s 18 order—(1) The former parent, at any time more than 12 months after the making of the order under section 18 when—

(a) no adoption order has been made in respect of the child, and
(b) the child does not have his home with a person with whom he has been placed for adoption,

may apply to the court which made the order for a further order revoking it on the ground that he wishes to resume *the parental rights and duties* [parental responsibility].

Note. Words in square brackets substituted for words in italics by Children Act 1989, s 88(1), Sch 10, Part I, para 8(1), as from 14 October 1991.

(2) While the application is pending the adoption agency having *the parental rights and duties* [parental responsibility] shall not place the child for adoption without the leave of the court.

Note. Words in square brackets substituted for words in italics by Children Act 1989, s 88(1), Sch 10, Part I, para 8(1), as from 14 October 1991.

(*3*) *Where an order freeing a child for adoption is revoked under this section—*
(*a*) *the parental rights and duties relating to the child are vested in the individual or, as the case may be, the individuals in whom they vested immediately before that order was made;*
(*b*) *if the parental rights and duties, or any of them, vested in a local authority or voluntary organisation immediately before the order freeing the child for adoption was made, those rights and duties are vested in the individual, or as the case may be, the individuals in whom they vested immediately before they were vested in the authority or organisation; and*
(*c*) *any duty extinguished by virtue of section 12(3)(b) is forthwith revived,*
but the revocation does not affect any right or duty so far as it relates to any period before the date of the revocation.

[(3) The revocation of an order under section 18 ('a section 18 order') operates—
(a) to extinguish the parental responsibility given to the adoption agency under the section 18 order;
(b) to give parental responsibility for the child to—
    (i) the child's mother; and
    (ii) where the child's father and mother were married to each other at the time of his birth, the father; and
(c) to revive—
    (i) any parental responsiblity agreement,
    (ii) any order under section 4(1) of the Children Act 1989, and
    (iii) any appointment of a guardian in respect of the child (whether made by a court or otherwise),
    extinguished by the making of the section 18 order.
(3A) Subject to subsection (3)(c), the revocation does not—
(a) operate to revive—
    (i) any order under the Children Act 1989, or
    (ii) any duty referred to in section 12(3)(b).
    extinguished by the making of the section 18 order; or
(b) affect any person's parental responsibility so far as it relates to the period between the making of the section 18 order and the date of revocation of that order.]

Note. Sub-ss (3), (3A) in square brackets substituted for sub-s (3) in italics by Children Act 1989, s 88(1), Sch 10, Part I, para 8(2), as from 14 October 1991.

(4) Subject to subsection (5), if the application is dismissed on the ground that to allow it would contravene the principle embodied in section 6—
(a) the former parent who made the application shall not be entitled to make any further application under subsection (1) in respect of the child, and

(b) the adoption agency is released from the duty of complying further with section 19(3) as respects that parent.

(5) Subsection (4)(a) shall not apply where the court which dismissed the application gives leave to the former parent to make a further application under subsection (1), but such leave shall not be given unless it appears to the court that because of a change in circumstances or for any other reason it is proper to allow the application to be made.

21. Transfer of parental rights and duties between adoption agencies. *On the joint application of an adoption agency in which the parental rights and duties relating to a child who is in England or Wales are vested under section 18(5) of this Act or under Part I of the Children Act 1975 (adoption in Scotland), and any other adoption agency, an authorised court may if it thinks fit by order transfer the parental rights and duties to the latter agency.*

[21. Variation of section 18 order so as to substitute one adoption agency for another—(1) On an application to which this section applies, an authorised court may vary an order under section 18 so as to give parental responsibility for the child to another adoption agency ('the substitute agency') in place of the agency for the time being having parental responsibility for the child under the order ('the existing agency').

(2) This section applies to any application made jointly by—

(a) the existing agency; and

(b) the would-be substitute agency.

(3) Where an order under section 18 is varied under this section, section 19 shall apply as if the substitute agency had been given responsiblity for the child on the making of the order.]

Note. Section 21 in square brackets substituted for s 21 in italics by Children Act 1989, s 88(1), Sch 10, Part I, para 9, as from 14 October 1991.

Supplemental

22. Notification to local authority of adoption application—(1) An adoption order shall not be made in respect of a child who was not placed with the applicant by an adoption agency unless the applicant has, at least 3 months before the date of the order, given notice to the local authority within whose area he has his home of his intention to apply for the adoption order.

[(1A) An application for such an adoption order shall not be made unless the person wishing to make the application has, within the period of two years preceding the making of the application, given notice as mentioned in subsection (1).

(1B) In subsections (1) and (1A) the references to the area in which the applicant or person has his home are references to the area in which he has his home at the time of giving notice.]

Note. Sub-ss (1A), (1B) inserted by Children Act 1989, s 88(1), Sch 10, Part I, para 10(1), as from 14 October 1991.

(2) On receipt of such a notice the local authority shall investigate the matter and submit to the court a report of their investigation.

(3) Under subsection (2), the local authority shall in particular investigate,—

(a) so far as is practicable, the suitability of the applicant, and any other matters relevant to the operation of section 6 in relation to the application; and

(b) whether the child was placed with the applicant in contravention of section 11.

(4) A local authority which *receives* [receive] notice under subsection (1) in respect of a child whom the authority know to be *in the care of* [looked after by] another local authority shall, not more than 7 days after the receipt of the notice, inform that other local authority in writing, that they have received the notice.

Note. Words in square brackets substituted for words in italics by Children Act 1989, s 88(1), Sch 10, Part I, para 10(2), as from 14 October 1991.

23. Reports where child placed by agency. Where an application for an adoption order relates to a child placed by an adoption agency, the agency shall submit to the court a report on the suitability of the applicants and any other matters relevant to the operation of section 6, and shall assist the court in any manner the court may direct.

24. Restrictions on making adoption orders—(1) The court shall not proceed to hear an application for an adoption order in relation to a child where a previous application for a British adoption order made in relation to the child by the same persons was refused by any court unless—
(a) in refusing the previous application the court directed that this subsection should not apply, or
(b) it appears to the court that because of a change in circumstances or for any other reason it is proper to proceed with the application.
(2) The court shall not make an adoption order in relation to a child unless it is satisfied that the applicants have not, as respects the child, *made any payment or given any reward to a person in contravention of* [contravened] section 57.

Note. Word in square brackets substituted for words in italics by Health and Social Services and Social Security Adjudications Act 1983, s 9, Sch 2, para 32, as from 15 August 1983.

25. Interim orders—(1) Where on an application for an adoption order the requirements of sections 16(1) and 22(1) are complied with, the court may postpone the determination of the application and make an order *vesting the legal custody of the child in* [giving parental responsibility for the child to] the applicants for a probationary period not exceeding 2 years upon such terms for the maintenance of the child and otherwise as the court thinks fit.

Note. Words in square brackets substituted for words in italics by Children Act 1989, s 88(1), Sch 10, Part I, para 11, as from 14 October 1991.

(2) Where the probationary period specified in an order under subsection (1) is less than 2 years, the court may by a further order extend the period to a duration not exceeding 2 years in all.

26. Care etc of child on refusal of adoption order—*(1) Where on an application for an adoption order in relation to a child under the age of 16 years the court refuses to make the adoption order then—*
(a) if it appears to the court that there are exceptional circumstances making it desirable that the child should be under the supervision of an independent person, the court may order that the child shall be under the supervision of a specified local authority or under the supervision of a probation officer;
(b) if it appears to the court that there are exceptional circumstances making it impracticable or undesirable for the child to be entrusted to either of the parents or to any other individual, the court may by order commit the child to the care of a specified local authority.
(2) Where the court makes an order under subsection (1)(b) the order may require the payment by either parent to the local authority, while it has the care of the child, of such weekly or other periodical sum towards the maintenance of the child as the court thinks reasonable.
(3) Sections 3 and 4 of the Guardianship Act 1973 (which contain supplementary provisions relating to children who are subject to supervision, or in the care of local authorities, by virtue of orders made under section 2 of that Act) apply in relation to an order under this section as they apply in relation to an order under section 2 of that Act.

Note. Words 'under the age of 16 years' in sub-s (1) repealed by Domestic Proceedings and Magistrates' Courts Act 1978, s 72, as from 1 February 1981. Whole section repealed by Children Act 1989, s 108(7), Sch 15, as from 14 October 1991. In relation to orders in force before commencement of Children Act 1989 (14 October 1991: SI 1991 No 828), see ibid, s 108(6), Sch 14, paras 15, 24, 26.

PART **III**

CARE AND PROTECTION OF CHILDREN AWAITING ADOPTION

Restrictions on removal of children

27. Restrictions on removal where adoption agreed or application made under s 18—(1) While an application for an adoption order is pending in a case where a parent or guardian of the child has agreed to the making of the adoption order (whether or not he knows the identity of the applicant), the parent or guardian is not entitled, against the will of the person with whom the child has his home, to remove the child from the [*actual*] *custody* [home] of that person except with the leave of the court.

(2) While an application is pending for an order freeing a child for adoption and—

(a) the child is in the care of the adoption agency making the application, and

(b) the application was not made with the consent of each parent or guardian of the child,

no parent or guardian of the child is entitled, against the will of the person with whom the child has his home, to remove the child from the [*actual*] *custody* [home] of that person except with the leave of the court.

Note. Word 'actual' inserted before word 'custody' in sub-ss (1), (2) by Health and Social Services and Social Security Adjudications Act 1983, s 9, Sch 2, para 60(c), as from 15 August 1983. Word 'home' substituted for words 'actual custody' by Children Act 1989, s 88(1), Sch 10, Part I, para 12(a), as from 14 October 1991.

[(2A) For the purposes of subsection (2) a child is in the care of an adoption agency if the adoption agency is a local authority and he is in their care.]

Note. Sub-s (2A) inserted by Children Act 1989, s 88(1), Sch 10, Part I, para 13, as from 14 October 1991.

(3) Any person who contravenes subsection (1) or (2) shall be guilty of an offence and liable on summary conviction to imprisonment for a term not exceeding 3 months or a fine not exceeding £400 [level 5 on the standard scale] or both.

Note. Reference to level 5 substituted by virtue of Criminal Justice Act 1982, ss 38, 46.

(4) *This section, except subsection (3), applies notwithstanding that the child is in Scotland at the time he is removed.*

(5) *Any person who removes a child from the custody of any other person while the child is in England or Wales, contrary to section 34 of the Adoption Act 1958 (which makes for Scotland provision similar to this section), shall be guilty of an offence and liable on summary conviction to imprisonment for a term not exceeding 3 months or a fine not exceeding £400 or both.*

Note. Sub-ss (4), (5) repealed by Health and Social Services and Social Security Adjudications Act 1983, ss 9, 30(1), Sch 2, para 33, Sch 10, Part I, as from 15 August 1983.

28. Restrictions on removal where applicant has provided home for 5 years—(1) While an application for an adoption order in respect of a child made by the person with whom the child has had his home for the 5 years preceding the application is pending, no person is entitled, against the will of the applicant, to remove the child from the applicant's [*actual*] *custody* [home] except with the leave of the court or under authority conferred by any enactment or on the arrest of the child.

(2) Where a person ('the prospective adopter') gives notice to the local authority within whose area he has his home that he intends to apply for an

adoption order in respect of a child who for the preceding 5 years has had his home with the prospective adopter, no person is entitled, against the will of the prospective adopter, to remove the child from the prospective adopter's [*actual*] *custody* [home], except with the leave of a court or under authority conferred by any enactment or on the arrest of the child before—

(a) the prospective adopter applies for the adoption order, or

(b) the period of 3 months from the receipt of the notice by the local authority expires,

whichever occurs first.

Note. In sub-ss (1), (2), word 'actual' inserted before word 'custody' by Health and Social Services and Social Security Adjudications Act 1983, s 9, Sch 2, para 60(c), as from 15 August 1983. Word 'home' substituted for words 'actual custody' by Children Act 1989, s 88(1), Sch 10, Part I, para 12(b), as from 14 October 1991.

[(2A) The reference in subsections (1) and (2) to any enactment does not include a reference to section 20(8) of the Children Act 1989.]

Note. Sub-s (2A) inserted by Children Act 1989, s 88(1), Sch 10, Part I, para 14(1), as from 14 October 1991.

(*3*) *In any case where subsection (1) or (2) applies and—*

(*a*) *the child was in the care of a local authority before he began to have his home with the applicant or, as the case may be, the prospective adopter, and*

(*b*) *the child remains in the care of the local authority [a local authority],*

the authority [in whose care the child is] shall not remove the child from the actual custody of the applicant or of the prospective adopter except in accordance with section 30 or 31 or with leave of a court.

[(3) In any case where subsection (1) or (2) applies and—

(a) the child was being looked after by a local authority before he began to have his home with the applicant or, as the case may be, the prospective adopter, and

(b) the child is still being looked after by a local authority,

the authority which are looking after the child shall not remove him from the home of the applicant or the prospective adopter except in accordance with section 30 or 31 or with the leave of a court.]

Note. Words in first pair of square brackets in original sub-s (3) (italicised) substituted for words 'the local authority', and words in second pair of square brackets inserted by Domestic Proceedings and Magistrates' Courts Act 1978, Sch 2, para 50, as from 20 October 1978. Sub-s (3) in square brackets substituted for sub-s (3) in italics by Children Act 1989, s 88(1), Sch 10, Part I, para 14(2), as from 14 October 1991.

(4) In subsections (2) and (3) 'a court' means a court with jurisdiction to make adoption orders.

(5) A local authority which *receives* [receive] such notice as is mentioned in subsection (2) in respect of a child whom the authority know to be *in the care of another local authority or of a voluntary organisation* [looked after by another local authority] shall, not more than 7 days after the receipt of the notice, inform that other authority *or the organisation*, in writing, that they have received the notice.

Note. Words in square brackets substituted for words in italics in first two places, and words in italics in third place repealed by Children Act 1989, ss 88(1), 108(7), Sch 10, Part I, para 14(3), Sch 15, as from 14 October 1991.

(6) Subsection (2) does not apply to any further notice served by the prospective adopter on any local authority in respect of the same child during the period referred to in paragraph (b) of that subsection or within 28 days after its expiry.

(7) Any person who contravenes subsection (1) or (2) shall be guilty of an offence and liable on summary conviction to imprisonment for a term not exceeding 3 months or a fine not exceeding £400 [level 5 on the standard scale] or both.

Note. Reference to level 5 substituted by virtue of Criminal Justice Act 1982, ss 38, 46.

(*8*) This section, except subsection (*6*) [*subsection* (*7*)], applies notwithstanding that the child is in Scotland at the time he is removed.

Note. Words in square brackets in sub-s (8) substituted for 'subsection (6)' by Criminal Law Act 1977, s 65, Sch 12, as from 8 September 1977. Sub-s (8) repealed by Health and Social Services and Social Security Adjudications Act 1983, s 9, Sch 2, para 33, as from 15 August 1983.

(*9*) Any person who removes a child from the custody of any other person while the child is in England or Wales, contrary to section 34A of the Adoption Act 1958 (which makes for Scotland provision similar to this section), shall be guilty of an offence and liable on summary conviction to imprisonment for a term not exceeding 3 months or a fine not exceeding £400 or both.

Note. Sub-s (9) repealed by Health and Social Services and Social Security Adjudications Act 1983, s 9, Sch 2, para 33, as from 15 August 1983.

(10) The Secretary of State may by order amend subsection (1) or (2) to substitute a different period for the period of 5 years mentioned in that subsection (or the period which, by a previous order under this subsection, was substituted for that period).

29. Return of child taken away in breach of s 27 or 28—(*1*) An authorised court may on the application of a person from whose [actual] custody a child has been removed in breach of section 27 or 28 [or section 27 or 28 of the Adoption (Scotland) Act 1978] order the person who has so removed the child to return the child to the applicant.

(*2*) An authorised court may on the application of a person who has reasonable grounds for believing that another person is intending to remove a child from the applicant's [actual] custody in breach of section 27 or 28 [or section 27 or 28 of the Adoption (Scotland) Act 1978] by order direct that other person not to remove the child from the applicant's [actual] custody in breach of section 27 or 28 [or section 27 or 28 of the Adoption (Scotland) Act 1978].

[(1) An authorised court may, on the application of a person from whose home a child has been removed in breach of—

(a) section 27 or 28,

(b) section 27 or 28 of the Adoption (Scotland) Act 1978, or

(c) Article 28 or 29 of the Adoption (Northern Ireland) Order 1987,

order the person who has so removed the child to return the child to the applicant.

(2) An authorised court may, on the application of a person who has reasonable grounds for believing that another person is intending to remove a child from his home in breach of—

(a) section 27 or 28,

(b) section 27 or 28 of the Adoption (Scotland) Act 1978, or

(c) Article 28 or 29 of the Adoption (Northern Ireland) Order 1987,

by order direct that other person not to remove the child from the applicant's home in breach of any of those provisions.]

Note. In original sub-ss (1), (2) (italicised) words in square brackets inserted by Health and Social Services and Social Security Adjudications Act 1983, s 9, Sch 2, paras 34, 60(c), as from 15 August 1983. Sub-ss (1), (2) in square brackets substituted for sub-ss (1), (2) in italics by Children Act 1989, s 88(1), Sch 10, Part I, para 15, as from 14 October 1991.

(3) If, in the case of an order made by the High Court under subsection (1), the High Court or, in the case of an order made by a county court under subsection (1), a county court is satisfied that the child has not been returned to the applicant, the court may make an order authorising an officer of the court to search such premises as may be specified in the order for the child and, if the officer finds the child, to return the child to the applicant.

(4) If a justice of the peace is satisfied by information on oath that there are reasonable grounds for believing that a child to whom an order under subsection

(1) relates is in premises specified in the information, he may issue a search warrant authorising a constable to search the premises for the child; and if a constable acting in pursuance of a warrant under this section finds the child, he shall return the child to the person on whose application the order under subsection (1) was made.

(5) An order under subsection (3) may be enforced in like manner as a warrant for committal.

30. Return of children placed for adoption by adoption agencies—(1) Subject to subsection (2), at any time after a child has been *delivered into the actual custody of* [placed with] any person in pursuance of arrangements made by an adoption agency for the adoption of the child by that person, and before an adoption order has been made on the application of that person in respect of the child—

    (a) that person may give notice to the agency of his intention not to *retain the [actual] custody of the child* [give the child a home]; or

    (b) the agency may cause notice to be given to that person of their intention not to allow the child to remain in his [*actual*] *custody* [home].

Note. In sub-s (1)(a), (b) word 'actual' inserted before the word 'custody' by Health and Social Services and Social Security Adjudications Act 1983, s 9, Sch 2, para 60(c), as from 15 August 1983. Words in square brackets in first, third and fifth places substituted for words in italics by Children Act 1989, s 88(1), Sch 10, Part I, para 16(1), as from 14 October 1991.

(2) No notice under paragraph (b) of subsection (1) shall be given in respect of a child in relation to whom an application has been made for an adoption order except with the leave of the court to which the application has been made.

(3) Where a notice is given to an adoption agency by any person or by an adoption agency to any person under subsection (1), or where an application for an adoption order made by any person in respect of a child placed *in his actual custody* [with him] by an adoption agency is refused by the court or withdrawn, that person shall, within 7 days after the date on which notice was given or the application refused or withdrawn, as the case may be, cause the child to be returned to the agency, who shall receive the child.

Note. Words in square brackets substituted for words in italics by Children Act 1989, s 88(1), Sch 10, Part I, para 16(2), as from 14 October 1991.

(4) Where the period specified in an interim order made under section 25 (whether as originally made or as extended under subsection (2) of that section) expires without an adoption order having been made in respect of the child, subsection (3) shall apply as if the application for an adoption order upon which the interim order was made, had been refused at the expiration of that period.

(5) It shall be sufficient compliance with the requirements of subsection (3) if the child is delivered to, and is received by, a suitable person nominated for the purpose by the adoption agency.

(6) Where an application for an adoption order is refused the court may, if it thinks fit at any time before the expiry of the period of 7 days mentioned in subsection (3), order that period to be extended to a duration, not exceeding 6 weeks, specified in the order.

(7) Any person who contravenes the provisions of this section shall be guilty of an offence and liable on summary conviction to imprisonment for a term not exceeding 3 months or to a fine not exceeding £*400* [level 5 on the standard scale] or to both; and the court by which the offender is convicted may order the child in respect of whom the offence is committed to be returned to his parent or guardian or to the adoption agency which made the arrangements referred to in subsection (1).

Note. Reference to level 5 substituted by virtue of Criminal Justice Act 1982, ss 38, 46.

31. Application of s 30 where child not placed for adoption—(1) Where a person gives notice in pursuance of section 22(1) to the local authority within whose area he has his home of his intention to apply for an adoption order in respect of a *child who is for the time being in the care of a local authority, not being a child who was delivered into the actual custody of that person in pursuance of such arrangements as are mentioned in section 30(1), that section shall apply as if the child had been so delivered,* [child—

    (a) who is (when the notice is given) being looked after by a local authority; but

    (b) who was placed with that person otherwise than in pursuance of such arrangements as are mentioned in section 30(1),

that section shall apply as if the child had been placed in pursuance of such arrangements] except that where the application is refused by the court or withdrawn the child need not be returned to the local authority in whose care he is unless that authority so require.

Note. Words in square brackets substituted for words in italics by Children Act 1989, s 88(1), Sch 10, Part I, para 17(1), as from 14 October 1991.

(2) Where notice of intention is given as aforesaid in respect of any child who is *for the time being in the care of* [(when the notice is given) being looked after by] a local authority then, until the application for an adoption order has been made and disposed of, any right of the local authority to require the child to be returned to them otherwise than in pursuance of section 30 shall be suspended.

Note. Words in square brackets substituted for words in italics by Children Act 1989, s 88(1), Sch 10, Part I, para 17(2), as from 14 October 1991.

(3) While the child *remains in the actual custody of* [has his home with] the person by whom the notice is given no contribution shall be payable (whether under a contribution order or otherwise) in respect of the child by any person liable under *section 86 of the Children and Young Persons Act 1933* [*section 45 of the Child Care Act 1980*] [Part III of Schedule 2 to the Children Act 1989] to make contributions in respect of him (but without prejudice to the recovery of any sum due at the time the notice is given), unless 12 weeks have elapsed since the giving of the notice without the application being made or the application has been refused by the court or withdrawn.

Note. Words in first pair of square brackets substituted for words in italics by Children Act 1989, s 88(1), Sch 10, Part I, para 17(3), as from 14 October 1991. Words 'section 45 of the Child Care Act 1980' substituted for words 'section 86 of the Children and Young Persons Act 1933' by Child Care Act 1980, ss 89(2), 90(1), Sch 5, para 38, as from 1 April 1981. Words in third pair of square brackets substituted for words 'section 45 of the Child Care Act 1980' by Children Act 1989, s 88(1), Sch 10, Part I, para 17(3), as from 14 October 1991.

[(4) Nothing in this section affects the right of any person who has parental responsibility for a child to remove him under section 20(8) of the Children Act 1989.]

Note. Sub-s (4) added by Children Act 1989, s 88(1), Sch 10, Part I, para 17(4), as from 14 October 1991.

Protected children

32. Meaning of 'protected child'—(1) Where a person gives notice in pursuance of section 22(1) to the local authority within whose area he lives of his intention to apply for an adoption order in respect of a child, the child is for the purposes of this Part a protected child while he has his home with that person.

(2) A child shall be deemed to be a protected child for the purposes of this Part if he is a protected child within the meaning of *section 37 of the Adoption Act 1958*

    [(a) section 32 of the Adoption (Scotland) Act 1978; or

    (b) Article 33 of the Adoption (Northern Ireland) Order 1987.]

Note. Sub-s (2)(a), (b) in square brackets substituted for words in italics by Children Act 1989, s 88(1), Sch 10, Part I, para 18(1), as from 14 October 1991.

(3) A child is not a protected child by reason of any such notice as is mentioned in subsection (1) while—

(*a*) *he is in the care of any person in any such school, home or institution as is mentioned in subsection (3) or (5) of section 2 of the Children Act 1958 [section 2(2) of the Foster Children Act 1980]*; or

[(a) he is in the care of any person—

(i) in any *community home, voluntary home or registered children's home* [children's home in respect of which a person is registered under Part II of the Care Standards Act 2000];

(ii) in any school in which he is receiving full-time education;

(iii) in any health service hospital]

(*b*) *he is resident in a residential home for mentally disordered persons as defined by section 19 of the Mental Health Act 1959 [section 1(3) of the Residential Homes Act 1980]*

[(b) he is—

(i) suffering from mental disorder within the meaning of the Mental Health Act 1983; and

(ii) resident in a residential care home, within the meaning of Part I of Schedule 4 to the Health and Social Services and Social Security Adjudications Act 1983]; or

(c) he is liable to be detained or subject to guardianship under *the said Act of 1959 [the Mental Health Act 1959 or the Mental Health (Amendment) Act 1982]* [the Mental Health Act 1983].

[(d) he is in the care of any person in any home or institution not specified in this section but provided, equipped and maintained by the Secretary of State.]

Note. Words in square brackets in original para (a) (italicised) substituted for words 'subsection (3) or (5) of section 2 of the Children Act 1958' by Foster Children Act 1980, s 23(2), Sch 2, as from 1 April 1981. Para (a) in square brackets substituted by Children Act 1989, s 88(1), Sch 10, Part I, para 18(2), as from 14 October 1991. Words in square brackets in new para (a) in square brackets substituted for preceding words in italics by the Care Standards Act 2000, s 116, Sch 4, para 5(1), (8)(b), as from 1 April 2002. Words in square brackets in original (italicised) para (b) substituted for reference to 1959 Act by Residential Homes Act 1980, s 11(4), Sch 1, as from 1 August 1980. Para (b) in square brackets substituted by Health and Social Services and Social Security Adjudications Act 1983, s 29(1), Sch 9, para 19, as from 1 January 1985. In para (c) for words 'the said Act of 1959' words 'the Mental Health Act 1959 or the Mental Health (Amendment) Act 1982' substituted by Mental Health (Amendment) Act 1982, s 65(1), Sch 3, Part I, para 54, as from 30 September 1983; and for words as substituted, words 'the Mental Health Act 1983' substituted by Mental Health Act 1983, s 148, Sch 4, para 45, as from the same date. Para (d) added by Children Act 1989, s 88(1), Sch 10, Part I, para 18(2), as from 14 October 1991.

[(3A) In subsection (3), *'community home', 'voluntary home', 'registered children's home'* ['children's home'], 'school' and 'health service hospital' have the same meaning as in the Children Act 1989.]

Note. Sub-s (3A) inserted by Children Act 1989, s 88(1), Sch 10, Part I, para 18(3), as from 14 October 1991. Words in square brackets substituted for words in italics by the Care Standards Act 2000, s 116, Sch 4, para 5(1), (8)(b), as from 1 April 2002.

(*4*) *A protected child ceases to be a protected child—*

(*a*) *on the appointment of a guardian for him under the Guardianship of Minors Act 1971;*

(*b*) *on the notification to the local authority for the area where the child has his home that the application for an adoption order has been withdrawn;*

(c)   on the making of any of the following orders in respect of the child—
  (i)   an adoption order;
  (ii)   an order under section 26;
  (iii)   a custodianship order;
  (iv)   an order under section 42, 43 or 44 of the Matrimonial Causes Act 1973; or
(d)   on his attaining the age of 18 years,
whichever first occurs.

[(4)   A protected child ceases to be a protected child—
(a)   on the grant or refusal of the application for an adoption order;
(b)   on the notification to the local authority for the area where the child has his home that the application for an adoption order has been withdrawn;
(c)   in a case where no application is made for an adoption order, on the expiry of the period of two years from the giving of the notice;
(d)   on the making of a residence order, a care order or a supervision order under the Children Act 1989 in respect of the child;
(e)   on the appointment of a guardian for him under that Act;
(f)   on his attaining the age of 18 years; or
(g)   on his marriage,
whichever first occurs.

(5)   In subsection (4)(d) the references to a care order and a supervision order do not include references to an interim care order or interim supervision order.]

Note. Sub-ss (4), (5) in square brackets substituted for sub-s (4) in italics by Children Act 1989, s 88(1), Sch 10, Part I, para 18(4), as from 14 October 1991.

33. Duty of local authorities to secure well-being of protected children—(1) It shall be the duty of every local authority to secure that protected children within their area are visited from time to time by officers of the authority, who shall satisfy themselves as to the well-being of the children and give such advice as to their care and maintenance as may appear to be needed.

(2)   Any officer of a local authority authorised to visit protected children may, after producing, if asked to do so, some duly authenticated document showing that he is so authorised, inspect any premises in the area of the authority in which such children are to be or are being kept.

34. Removal of protected children from unsuitable surroundings—(1) If a juvenile court is satisfied, on the complaint of a local authority, that a protected child is being kept or is about to be received by any person who is unfit to have his care or in any premises or any environment detrimental or likely to be detrimental to him, the court may make an order for his removal to a place of safety until he can be restored to a parent, relative or guardian of his, or until other arrangements can be made with respect to him; and on proof that there is imminent danger to the health or well-being of the child the power to make an order under this section may be exercised by a justice of the peace acting on the application of a person authorised to visit protected children.

(2)   An order under this section may be executed by any person authorised to visit protected children or by any constable.

(3)   A local authority may receive into their care under section 1 of the Children Act 1948 [section 2 of the Child Care Act 1980] any child removed under this section, whether or not the circumstances of the child are such that they fall within paragraphs (a) to (c) of subsection (1) of that section and notwithstanding that he may appear to the local authority to be over the age of 17 years.

Note. Words in square brackets substituted for words 'section 1 of the Children Act 1948' by Child Care Act 1980, ss 89(2), 90(1), Sch 5, para 39, as from 1 April 1981.

(4)   Where a child is removed under this section the local authority shall, if practicable, inform a parent or guardian of the child, or any person who acts as his guardian.

Note. Whole section repealed by Children Act 1989, s 108(7), Sch 15, as from 14 October 1991. In relation to orders in force before commencment of Children Act 1989, Part IV, see ibid, s 108(6), Sch 14, para 27 (pp 3408, 3500).

35. Notices and information to be given to local authorities—(1) Where a person *who has a protected child in his actual custody* [with whom a protected child has his home] changes his permanent address he shall, not less than 2 weeks before the change, or, if the change is made in an emergency, not later than one week after the change, give notice specifying the new address to the local authority in whose area his permanent address is before the change, and if the new address is in the area of another local authority, the authority to whom the notice is given shall inform that other local authority and give them such of the following particulars as are known to them, that is to say—

    (a) the name, sex and date and place of birth of the child;

    (b) the name and address of every person who is a parent or guardian or acts as a guardian of the child or from whom the child was received.

    (2) If a protected child dies, the person *in whose actual custody he was* [with whom he had his home] at his death shall within 48 hours give notice of the child's death to the local authority.

Note. Words in square brackets in sub-ss (1), (2) substituted for words in italics by Children Act 1989, s 88(1), Sch 10, Part I, para 19, as from 14 October 1991.

36. Offences relating to protected children—(1) A person shall be guilty of an offence if—

    (a) being required, under section 35 to give any notice or information, he fails to give the notice within the time specified in that provision or fails to give the information within a reasonable time, or knowingly makes or causes or procures another person to make any false or misleading statement in the notice of information;

    (b) he refuses to allow the visiting of a protected child by a duly authorised officer of a local authority or the inspection, under the power conferred by section 33(2) of any premises;

    (c) *he refuses to comply with an order under section 34 for the removal of any child or obstructs any person in the execution of such an order.*

Note. Sub-s (1)(c) repealed by Children Act 1989, s 108(7), Sch 15, as from 14 October 1991.

    (2) A person guilty of an offence under this section shall be liable on summary conviction to imprisonment for a term not exceeding 3 months or a fine not exceeding *£400* [level 5 on the standard scale] or both.

Note. Reference to level 5 substituted by virtue of Criminal Justice Act 1982, ss 38, 46.

37. Miscellaneous provisions relating to protected children—*(1) For the purposes of section 40 of the Children and Young Persons Act 1933, under which a warrant authorising the search for and removal of a child may be issued on suspicion of unnecessary suffering caused to, or certain offences committed against, the child, any refusal to allow the visiting of a protected child or the inspection of any premises by a person authorised to do so under section 33 shall be treated as giving reasonable cause for such a suspicion.*

    (2) A person who maintains a protected child shall be deemed for the purposes of the Life Assurance Act 1774 to have no interest in the life of the child.

    (3) An appeal shall lie to the Crown Court against any order made under section 34 by a juvenile court or a justice of the peace.

    (4) Subsection (2) of section 47 of the Children and Young Persons Act 1933 (which restricts the time and place at which a sitting of a juvenile court may be held and the persons who may be present at such a sitting) shall not apply to any sitting of a juvenile court in any proceedings under section 34.

Note. Sub-ss (1), (3), (4) repealed by Children Act 1989, s 108(7), Sch 15, as from 14 October 1991.

PART **IV**

Note. As to Part IV, see Family Law Reform Act 1987, s 1(3)(c) (p 3190).

STATUS OF ADOPTED CHILDREN

38. Meaning of 'adoption' in Part IV—(1) In this Part 'adoption' means adoption—

    (a) by an adoption order;

    (b) by an order made under the Children Act 1975, the Adoption Act 1958, the Adoption Act 1950 or any enactment repealed by the Adoption Act 1950;

    (c) by an order made in Scotland, Northern Ireland, the Isle of Man or in any of the Channel Islands;

    [(cc) which is a Convention adoption;]

    (d) which is an overseas adoption; or

    (e) which is an adoption recognised by the law of England and Wales and effected under the law of any other country,

and cognate expressions shall be construed accordingly.

    (2) The definition of adoption includes, where the context admits, an adoption effected before the passing of the Children Act 1975 [but does not include an adoption of a kind mentioned in paragraphs (c) to (e) of sub-section (1) effected on or after the day which is the appointed day for the purposes of Chapter 4 of Part 1 of the Adoption and Children Act 2002], and the date of an adoption effected by an order is the date of the making of the order.

Note. In relation to any time before the coming into force of s 38 (1 January 1988), see Family Law Reform Act 1987, Sch 3, para 2 (p 3194). Words in square brackets in sub-s (2) inserted by the Adoption and Children Act 2002, s 139(1), Sch 3, para 19, as from a day to be appointed.

39. Status conferred by adoption—(1) An adopted child shall be treated in law—

    (a) where the adopters are a married couple, as if he had been born as a child of the marriage (whether or not he was in fact born after the marriage was solemnized);

    (b) in any other case, as if he had been born to the adopter in wedlock (but not as a child of any actual marriage of the adopter).

    (2) An adopted child shall, subject to *subsection (3)* [subsections (3) and (3A)], be treated in law as if he were not the child of any person other than the adopters or adopter.

Note. Words 'subsections (3) and (3A)' in square brackets substituted for words in italics by the Adoption (Intercountry Aspects) Act 1999, ss 4(2), 17, as from 1 June 2003 except in relation to a 1965 Convention adoption order (or an application for such an order) or a 1965 Convention adoption (as defined in s 17(2) of the 1999 Act).

    [(3A) Where, in the case of a Convention adoption, the High Court is satisfied, on an application under this subsection—

    (a) that under the law of the country in which the adoption was effected the adoption is not a full adoption;

    (b) that the consents referred to in Article 4(c) and (d) of the Convention have not been given for a full adoption, or that the United Kingdom is not the receiving State (within the meaning of Article 2 of the Convention); and

    (c) that it would be more favourable to the adopted child for a direction to be given under this subsection.

The Court may direct that subsection (2) shall not apply, or shall not apply to such extent as may be specified in the direction.

    In this subsection 'full adoption' means an adoption by virtue of which the adopted child falls to be treated in law as if he were not the child of any person other than the adopters or adopter.

(3B) The following provisions of the Family Law 1986—
  (a) section 59 (provisions relating to the Attorney General); and
  (b) section 60 (supplementary provision as to declarations), shall apply in relation to, and to an application for, a direction under subsection (3A) as they apply in relation to, and to an application for, a declaration under Part III of that Act.]

Note. Sub-ss (3A), (3B) inserted by the Adoption (Intercountry Aspects) Act 1999, ss 4(3), 17, as from 1 June 2003 except in relation to a 1965 Convention adoption order (or an application for such an order) or a 1965 Convention adoption (as defined in s 17(2) of the 1999 Act).

(3) In the case of a child adopted by one of its natural parents as sole adoptive parent, subsection (2) has no effect as respects entitlement to property depending on relationship to that parent, or as respects anything else depending on that relationship.

(4) It is hereby declared that this section prevents an adopted child from being illegitimate.

(5) This section has effect—
  (a) in the case of an adoption before 1 January 1976, from that date, and
  (b) in the case of any other adoption, from the date of the adoption.

(6) Subject to the provisions of this Part, this section—
  (a) applies for the construction of enactments or instruments passed or made before the adoption or later, and so applies subject to any contrary indication; and
  (b) has effect as respects things done, or events occurring, after the adoption, or after 31 December 1975, whichever is the later.

Note. See Family Law Act 1986, s 57(2) (p 3183).

40. Citizenship—(*1*) *Where an adoption order is made in relation to a child who is not a citizen of the United Kingdom and Colonies, but the adopter or, in the case of a joint adoption, the adoptive father is a citizen of the United Kingdom and Colonies, the child shall be a citizen of the United Kingdom and Colonies as from the date of the adoption.*

(*2*) *In subsection (1) the reference to an adoption order includes a reference to an order authorising the adoption of a child in Scotland, Northern Ireland, the Isle of Man or in any of the Channel Islands.*

(*3*) *Where a Convention adoption order, or a specified order ceases to have effect, either on annulment or otherwise, the cesser shall not affect the status as a citizen of the United Kingdom and Colonies of any person who, by virtue of this section or section 19 of the Adoption Act 1958, became such a citizen in consequence of the order.*

Note. This section repealed by British Nationality Act 1981, s 52(8), Sch 9, as from 1 January 1983.

41. Adoptive relatives—A relationship existing by virtue of section 39 may be referred to as an adoptive relationship, and—
  (a) a male adopter may be referred to as the adoptive father;
  (b) a female adopter may be referred to as the adoptive mother;
  (c) any other relative of any degree under an adoptive relationship may be referred to as an adoptive relative of that degree,
but this section does not prevent the term 'parent', or any other term not qualified by the word 'adoptive' being treated as including an adoptive relative.

42. Rules of construction for instruments concerning property—(1) Subject to any contrary indication, the rules of construction contained in this section apply to any instrument, other than an existing instrument, so far as it contains a disposition of property.

(2) In applying section 39(1) to a disposition which depends on the date of birth of a child or children of the adoptive parent or parents, the disposition shall be construed as if—

(a) the adopted child had been born on the date of adoption,

(b) two or more children adopted on the same date had been born on that date in the order of their actual births,

but this does not affect any reference to the age of a child.

(3) Examples of phrases in wills on which subsection (2) can operate are—

1. Children of A 'living at my death or born afterwards'.

2. Children of A 'living at my death or born afterwards before any one of such children for the time being in existence attains a vested interest and who attain the age of 21 years'.

3. As in example 1 or 2, but referring to grandchildren of A instead of children of A.

4. A for life 'until he has a child', and then to his child or children.

Note. Subsection (2) will not affect the reference to the age of 21 years in example 2.

(4) Section 39(2) does not prejudice any interest vested in possession in the adopted child before the adoption, or any interest expectant (whether immediately or not) upon an interest so vested.

(5) Where it is necessary to determine for the purposes of a disposition of property effected by an instrument whether a woman can have a child, it shall be presumed that once a woman has attained the age of 55 years she will not adopt a child after execution of the instrument, and, notwithstanding section 39, if she does so that child shall not be treated as her child or as the child of her spouse (if any) for the purposes of the instrument.

(6) In this section, 'instrument' includes a private Act settling property, but not any other enactment.

Note. In relation to any time before the coming into force of s 42 (1 January 1988), see Family Law Reform Act 1987, Sch 3, para 5 (p 3195). See also s 19(5) of that Act (p 3191).

43. Dispositions depending on date of birth—(1) Where a disposition depends on the date of birth of a child who was born illegitimate and who is adopted by one of the natural parents as sole adoptive parent, section 42(2) does not affect entitlement under Part II of the Family Law Reform Act 1969 (illegitimate children).

(2) Subsection (1) applies for example where—

(a) a testator dies in 1976 bequeathing a legacy to his eldest grandchild living at a specified time,

(b) his daughter has an illegitimate child in 1977 who is the first grandchild,

(c) his married son has a child in 1978,

(d) subsequently the illegitimate child is adopted by the mother as sole adoptive parent,

and in all those cases the daughter's child remains the eldest grandchild of the testator throughout.

44. Property devolving with peerages etc—(1) An adoption does not affect the descent of any peerage or dignity or title of honour.

(2) An adoption shall not affect the devolution of any property limited (expressly or not) to devolve (as nearly as the law permits) along with any peerage or dignity or title of honour.

(3) Subsection (2) applies only if and so far as a contrary intention is not expressed in the instrument, and shall have effect subject to the terms of the instrument.

45. Protection of trustees and personal representatives—(1) A trustee or personal representative is not under a duty, by virtue of the law relating to trusts or the administration of estates, to enquire, before conveying or distributing any property, whether any adoption has been effected or revoked if that fact could affect entitlement to the property.

(2) A trustee or personal representative shall not be liable to any person by reason of a conveyance or distribution of the property made without regard to any such fact if he has not received notice of the fact before the conveyance or distribution.

(3) This section does not prejudice the right of a person to follow the property, or any property representing it, into the hands of another person, other than a purchaser, who has received it.

46. Meaning of 'disposition'—(1) In this Part, unless the context otherwise requires,—

'disposition' includes the conferring of a power of appointment and any other disposition of an interest in or right over property;

'power of appointment' includes any discretionary power to transfer a beneficial interest in property without the furnishing of valuable consideration.

(2) This Part applies to an oral disposition as if contained in an instrument made when the disposition was made.

(3) For the purposes of this Part, the death of the testator is the date at which a will or codicil is to be regarded as made.

(4) For the purposes of this Part, provisions of the law of intestate succession applicable to the estate of a deceased person shall be treated as if contained in an instrument executed by him (while of full capacity) immediately before his death.

(5) *It is hereby declared that references in this Part to dispositions of property include references to a disposition by the creation of an entailed interest.*

Note. Sub-s (5) repealed by Trusts of Land and Appointment of Trustees Act 1996, s 25(2), Sch 4, as from 1 Janaury 1997.

47. Miscellaneous enactments—(1) Section 39 does not apply for the purposes of the table of kindred and affinity in Schedule 1 to the Marriage Act 1949 or sections 10 and 11 (incest) of the Sexual Offences Act 1956.

(2) *Without prejudice to section 40,* section 39 does not apply for the purposes of any provision of—

(a) [the British Nationality Act 1981],

(b) the Immigration Act 1971,

(c) any instrument having effect under an enactment within paragraph (a) or (b), or

(d) any other provision of the law for the time being in force which determines [British citizenship, British Dependent Territories citizenship[, the status of a British National (Overseas)] or British Overseas citizenship].

Note. Words in italics in sub-s (2) repealed and words in first and second pairs of square brackets substituted by British Nationality Act 1981, s 52(6), (8), Schs 7, 9, as from 1 January 1983. Words ', the status of a British National (Overseas)' in square brackets inserted by Hong Kong (British Nationality) Order 1986, SI 1986 No 948, art 8, Schedule.

(3) *Section 39 shall not prevent a person being treated as a near relative of a deceased person for the purposes of section 32 of the Social Security Act 1975 (payment of death grant), if apart from section 39 he would be so treated.*

Note. Sub-s (3) repealed by Social Security Act 1986, s 86(2), Sch 11, as from 6 April 1987.

(4) *Section 39 does not apply for the purposes of section 70(3)(b) or section 73(2) of the Social Security Act 1975 (payment of industrial death benefit to or in respect of an illegitimate child of the deceased and the child's mother).*

(5) *Subject to regulations made under section 72 of the Social Security Act 1975 (entitlement of certain relatives of deceased to industrial death benefit), section 39 shall not*

affect the entitlement to an industrial death benefit of a person who would, apart from section 39, be treated as a relative of a deceased person for the purposes of the said section 72.

Note. Sub-ss (4), (5) repealed by Social Security Act 1988, s 16, Sch 5, as from 4 July 1988.

48. Pensions. Section 39(2) does not affect entitlement to a pension which is payable to or for the benefit of a child and is in payment at the time of his adoption.

49. Insurance. Where a child is adopted whose natural parent has effected an insurance with a friendly society or a collecting society or an industrial insurance company for the payment on the death of the child of money for funeral expenses, the rights and liabilities under the policy shall by virtue of the adoption be transferred to the adoptive parents who shall for the purposes of the enactments relating to such societies and companies be treated as the person who took out the policy.

PART V

REGISTRATION AND REVOCATION OF ADOPTION ORDERS AND CONVENTION ADOPTIONS

50. Adopted Children Register—(1) The Registrar General shall maintain at the General Register Office a register, to be called the Adopted Children Register, in which *shall be made such entries as may be directed to be made therein by adoption orders, but no other entries* [such entries as may be—

(a) directed to be made in it by adoption orders, or

(b) required to be made under Schedule 1 to this Act.

and no other entries, shall be made]

Note. Word 'such entries … be made' in square brackets substituted for words in italics by the Adoption (Intercountry Aspects) Act 1999, s 12(1), as from (for the purposes of making regulations) 23 January 2003 and (for remaining purposes) 1 June 2003 except in relation to a 1965 Convention adoption order (or an application for such an order) or a 1965 Convention adoption (as defined in s 17(2) of the 1999 Act).

(2) A certified copy of an entry in the Adopted Children Register, if purporting to be sealed or stamped with the seal of the General Register Office, shall, without any further or other proof of that entry, be received as evidence of the adoption to which it relates and, where the entry contains a record of the date of the birth or the country or the district and sub-district of the birth of the adopted person, shall also be received as aforesaid as evidence of that date or country or district and sub-district in all respects as if the copy were a certified copy of an entry in the Registers of Births.

(3) The Registrar General shall cause an index of the Adopted Children Register to be made and kept in the General Register Office; and every person shall be entitled to search that index and to have a certified copy of any entry in the Adopted Children Register in all respects upon and subject to the same terms, conditions and regulations as to payment of fees and otherwise as are applicable under the Births and Deaths Registration Act 1953, and the Registration Service Act 1953, in respect of searches in other indexes kept in the General Register Office and in respect of the supply from that office of certified copies of entries in the certified copies of the Registers of Births and Deaths.

(4) The Registrar General shall, in addition to the Adopted Children Register and the index thereof, keep such other registers and books, and make such entries therein, as may be necessary to record and make traceable the connection between any entry in the Registers of Births which has been marked 'Adopted' and any corresponding entry in the Adopted Children Register.

(5) The registers and books kept under subsection (4) shall not be, nor shall any index thereof be, open to public inspection or search, and the Registrar General shall not furnish any person with any information contained in or with

any copy or extract from any such registers or books except in accordance with section 51 or under an order of any of the following courts, that is to say—

    (a)   the High Court;

    (b)   the Westminster County Court or such other county court as may be prescribed; and

    (c)   the court by which an adoption order was made in respect of the person to whom the information, copy or extract relates

    (6) In relation to an adoption order made by a magistrates' court, the reference in paragraph (c) of subsection (5) to the court by which the order was made includes a reference to a court acting for the same petty sessions area.

    (7) Schedule 1 to this Act, which, among other things, provides for the registration of adoptions and the amendment of adoption orders, shall have effect.

51. Disclosure of birth records of adopted children—(1) Subject to *subsections (4) and (6)* [what follows], the Registrar General shall on an application made in the prescribed manner by an adopted person a record of whose birth is kept by the Registrar General and who has attained the age of 18 years supply to that person on payment of the prescribed fee (if any) such information as is necessary to enable that person to obtain a certified copy of the record of his birth.

Note. Words in square brackets substituted for words in italics by Children Act 1989, s 88(1), Sch 10, Part I, para 20(1), as from 14 October 1991.

    (2) On an application made in the prescribed manner by an adopted person under the age of 18 years, a record of whose birth is kept by the Registrar General and who is intending to be married in England or Wales, and on payment of the prescribed fee (if any), the Registrar General shall inform the applicant whether or not it appears from information contained in the registers of live births or other records that the applicant and the person whom he intends to marry may be within the prohibited degrees of relationship for the purposes of the Marriage Act 1949.

    (3) It shall be the duty of the Registrar General and each local authority and approved adoption society to provide counselling for adopted persons who apply for information under subsection (1).

    (4) Before supplying any information to an applicant under subsection (1) the Registrar General shall inform the applicant that counselling services are available to him—

      (a)   at the General Register Office; or

      (b)   from the local authority for the area where the applicant is at the time the application is made; or

      (c)   from the local authority for the area where the court sat which made the adoption order relating to the applicant; or

      (d)   if the applicant's adoption was arranged by an adoption society which is approved under section 3 of this Act under section 4 of the Children Act 1975, from that society.

    (5) If the applicant chooses to receive counselling from a local authority or an adoption society under subsection (4) the Registrar General shall send to the authority or society of the applicant's choice the information to which the applicant is entitled under subsection (1).

    (6) The Registrar General shall not supply a person who was adopted before 12 November 1974 with any information under subsection (1) unless that person has attended an interview with a counsellor either at the General Register Office or in pursuance of arrangements made by the local authority or adoption society from whom the applicant is entitled to receive counselling in accordance with subsection (4).

    (7) In this section, 'prescribed' means prescribed by regulations made by the Registrar General.

    [(3) Before supplying any information to an applicant under subsection (1), the Register General shall inform the applicant that counselling services are available to him—

(a) if he is in England and Wales—
  (i) at the General Register Office;
  (ii) from the local authority in whose area he is living;
  (iii) where the adoption order relating to him was made in England and Wales, from the local authority in whose area the court which made the order sat; or
  (iv) from any other local authority;
(b) if he is in Scotland—
  (i) from the regional or islands council in whose area he is living;
  (ii) where the adoption order relating to him was made in Scotland, from the council in whose area the court which made the order sat; or
  (iii) from any other regional or islands council;
(c) if he is in Northern Ireland—
  (i) from the Board in whose area he is living;
  (ii) where the adoption order relating to him was made in Northern Ireland, from the Board in whose area the court which made the order sat; or
  (iii) from any other Board;
(d) if he is in the United Kingdom and his adoption was arranged by an adoption society—
  (i) *approved under section 3,*
  (i) which is an appropriate voluntary organisation,
  (ii) approved under section 3 of the Adoption (Scotland) Act 1978,
  (iii) registered under Article 4 of the Adoption (Northern Ireland) Order 1987,
  from that society.

Note. Sub-s (3)(d)(i) substituted by the Care Standards Act 2000, s 116, Sch 4, para 5(1), (9), as from (in relation to Wales) 30 January 2003 and (in relation to England) 30 April 2003.

(4) Where an adopted person who is in England and Wales—
(a) applies for information under—
  (i) subsection (1), or
  (ii) Article 54 of the Adoption (Northern Ireland) Order 1987, or
(b) is supplied with information under section 45 of the Adoption (Scotland) Act 1978,
it shall be the duty of the persons and bodies mentioned in subsection (5) to provide counselling for him if asked by him to do so.

(5) The persons and bodies are—
(a) the Registrar General;
(b) any local authority falling within subsection (3)(a)(ii) to (iv);
(c) any adoption society falling within subsection (3)(d) in so far as it is acting as an adoption society in England and Wales

(6) If the applicant chooses to receive counselling from a person or body falling within subsection (3), the Registrar General shall send to the person or body the information to which the applicant is entitled under subsection (1).

(7) Where a person—
(a) was adopted before 12 November 1975, and
(b) applies for information under subsection (1),
the Registrar General shall not supply the information to him unless he has attended an interview with a counsellor arranged by a person or body from whom counselling services are available as mentioned in subsection (3).

(8) Where the Registrar General is prevented by subsection (7) from supplying information to a person who is not living in the United Kingdom, he may supply the information to any body which—
(a) the Registrar General is satisfied is suitable to provide counselling to that person, and

(b) has notified the Registrar General that it is prepared to provide such counselling.

(9) In this section—

'a Board' means a Health and Social Services Board established under Article 16 of the Health and Personal Social Services (Northern Ireland) Order 1972; and

'prescribed' means prescribed by regulations made by the Registrar General.]

Note. Sub-ss (3)–(9) in square brackets substituted for sub-ss (3)–(7) in italics by Children Act 1989, s 88(1), Sch 10, Part I, para 20(2), as from 14 October 1991.

There is no absolute right for an applicant under this section to obtain a copy of his birth certificate; see *R v Registrar General, ex p Smith* [1990] 2 All ER 170, [1990] 2 WLR 980.

[51A. Adoption Contact Register—(1) The Registrar General shall maintain at the General Register Office a register to be called the Adoption Contact Register.

(2) The register shall be in two parts—

(a) Part I: Adopted Persons; and

(b) Part II: Relatives

(3) The Registrar General shall, on payment of such fee as may be prescribed, enter in Part I of the register the name and address of any adopted person who fulfils the conditions in subsection (4) and who gives notice that he wishes to contact any relative of his.

(4) The conditions are that—

(a) a record of the adopted person's birth is kept by the Registrar General; and

(b) the adopted person has attained the age of 18 years and—

(i) has been supplied by the Registrar General with information under section 51; or

(ii) has satisfied the Registrar General that he has such information as is necessary to enable him to obtain a certified copy of the record of his birth.

(5) The Registrar General shall, on payment of such fee as may be prescribed, enter in Part II of the register the name and address of any person who fulfils the conditions in subsection (6) and who gives notice that he wishes to contact an adopted person.

(6) The conditions are that—

(a) a record of the adopted person's birth is kept by the Registrar General; and

(b) the person giving notice under subsection (5) has attained the age of 18 years and has satisfied the Registrar General that—

(i) he is a relative of the adopted person; and

(ii) he has such information as is necessary to enable him to obtain a certified copy of the record of the adopted person's birth.

(7) The Registrar General shall, on receiving notice from any person named in an entry in the register that he wishes the entry to be cancelled, cancel the entry.

(8) Any notice given under this section must be in such form as may be determined by the Registrar General.

(9) The Registrar General shall transmit to an adopted person whose name is entered in Part I of the register the name and address of any relative in respect of whom there is an entry in Part II of the register.

(10) Any entry cancelled under subsection (7) ceases from the time of cancellation to be an an entry for the purposes of subsection (9).

(11) The register shall not be open to public inspection or search and the Registrar General shall not supply any person with information entered in the register (whether in an uncancelled or a cancelled entry) except in accordance with this section.

(12) The register may be kept by means of a computer.

(13) In this section—

(a) 'relative' means any person (other than an adoptive relative) who is related to the adopted person by blood (including half-blood) or marriage;

(b) 'address' includes any address at or through which the person concerned may be contacted; and

(c) 'prescribed' means prescribed by the Secretary of State.]

Note. This section inserted by Children Act 1989, s 88(1), Sch 10, Part I, para 21, as from 14 October 1991.

52. Revocation of adoptions on legitimation—(1) Where any person adopted by his father or mother alone has subsequently became a legitimated person on the marriage of his father and mother, the court by which the adoption order was made may, on the application of any of the parties concerned, revoke that order.

(2) Where any person legitimated by virtue of section 1 of the Legitimacy Act 1959, had been adopted by his father and mother before the commencement of that Act, the court by which the adoption order was made may, on the application of any of the parties concerned, revoke that order.

(3) Where a person adopted by his father or mother alone by virtue of a regulated adoption has subsequently become a legitimated person on the marriage of his father and mother, the High Court may, upon an application under this subsection by the parties concerned, by order revoke the adoption.

Note. Sub-s (3) repealed by the Adoption (Intercountry Aspects) Act 1999, Sch 2, as from 1 June 2003 except in relation to a 1965 Convention adoption order (or an application for such an order) or a 1965 Convention adoption (as defined in s 17(2) of the 1999 Act).

(4) In relation to an adoption order made by a magistrates' court, the reference in subsections (1) and (2) to the court by which the order was made includes a reference to a court acting for the same petty sessions area.

53. Annulment etc of overseas adoptions—*(1) The High Court may, upon an application under this subsection, by order annul a regulated adoption [or an adoption effected by a Convention adoption order]—*

(a) *on the ground that at the relevant time the adoption was prohibited by a notified provision, if under the internal law then in force in the country of which the adopter was then a national or the adopters were then nationals the adoption could have been impugned on that ground;*

(b) *on the ground that at the relevant time the adoption contravened provisions relating to consents of the internal law relating to adoption of the country of which the adopted person was then a national, if under that law the adoption could then have been impugned on that ground;*

(c) *on any other ground on which the adoption can be impugned under the law for the time being in force in the country in which the adoption was effected.*

[(1) The High Court may, on an application under this subsection, by order annul a Convention adoption or a Convention adoption order on the ground that the adoption or order is contrary to public policy.]

Note. Words in square brackets inserted by Domestic Proceedings and Magistrates' Courts Act 1978, s 74(2), as from 20 November 1978. Sub-s (1) substituted by the Adoption (Intercountry Aspects) Act 1999, s 6(1) as from 1 June 2003 except in relation to a 1965 Convention adoption order (or an application for such an order) or a 1965 Convention adoption (as defined in s 17(2) of the 1999 Act).

(2) The High Court may, upon an application under this subsection—

(a) order that an overseas adoption or a determination shall cease to be valid in Great Britain on the ground that the adoption or determination is contrary to public policy or that the authority which purported to authorise the adoption or make the determination was not competent to entertain the case;

(b) decide the extent, if any, to which a determination has been affected by a subsequent determination.

(3) Any court in Great Britain may, in any proceedings in that court, decide that an overseas adoption or a determination shall, for the purposes of those proceedings, be treated as invalid in Great Britain on either of the grounds mentioned in subsection (2).

(4) An order or decision of the Court of Session on an application under subsection (3) of section 6 of the Adoption Act 1968 shall be recognised and have effect as if it were an order or decision of the High Court on an application under subsection (3) of this section.

(5) Except as provided by this section *and section 52(3)* the validity of an overseas adoption or a determination shall not be impugned in England and Wales in proceedings in any court.

Note. Words 'and section 52(3)' in italics repealed by the Adoption (Intercountry Aspects) Act 1999, Sch 2, as from 1 June 2003 except in relation to a 1965 Convention adoption order (or an application for such an order) or a 1965 Convention adoption (as defined in s 17(2) of the 1999 Act).

54. Provisions supplementary to ss 52(3) and 53—(1) Any application for an order under section *52(3) or* 53 or a decision under section 53(3) shall be made in the prescribed manner and with such period, if any, as may be prescribed.

(2) No application shall be made under *section 52(3) or* section 53(1) in respect of an adoption unless immediately before the application is made the person adopted or the adopted habitually resides in England and Wales or, as the case may be, both adopters habitually reside there.

Note. Words in italics repealed by the Adoption (Intercountry Aspects) Act 1999, ss 15, 17, Sch 3, as from 1 June 2003 except in relation to a 1965 Convention adoption order (or an application for such an order) or a 1965 Convention adoption (as defined in s 17(2) of the 1999 Act).

(3) In deciding in pursuance of section 53 whether such an authority as is mentioned in section 59 was competent to entertain a particular case, a court shall be bound by any finding of fact made by the authority and stated by the authority to be so made for the purpose of determining whether the authority was competent to entertain the case.

(4) In section 53—

'determination' means such a determination as is mentioned in section 59 of this Act;

'notified provision' means a provision specified in an order of the Secretary of State as one in respect of which a notification to or by the Government of the United Kingdom was in force at the relevant time in pursuance of the provisions of the Convention relating to prohibitions contained in the national laws of the adopter; and

'relevant time' means the time when the adoption in question purported to take effect under the law of the country in which it purports to have been effected.

Note. Definitions 'notified provision' and 'relevant time' cease to have effect by virtue of the Adoption (Intercountry Aspects) Act 1999, ss 6(3), 15(2), 17, Sch 3, as from 1 June 2003 except in relation to a 1965 Convention adoption order (or an application for such an order) or a 1965 Convention adoption (as defined in s 17(2) of the 1999 Act).

PART VI

MISCELLANEOUS AND SUPPLEMENTAL

55. Adoption of children abroad—(1) Where on an application made in relation to a child by a person who is not domiciled in England and Wales or Scotland [or Northern Ireland] an authorised court is satisfied that he intends to adopt the child under the law of or within the country in which the applicant is domiciled, the court may, subject to the following provisions of this section, make an order *vesting in him the parental rights and duties relating to the child* [giving him parental responsibility for the child].

Note. Words in first pair of square brackets inserted, and words in second pair of square brackets substituted for words in italics by Children Act 1989, s 88(1), Sch 10, Part I, para 22(1), as from 14 October 1991.

(2) The provisions of Part II relating to adoption orders, except sections 12(1), 14(2), 15(2), 17 to 21 and 25, shall apply in relation to orders under this section as they apply in relation to adoption orders subject to the modification that in section 13(1) for '19' and '13' there are substituted '32' and '26' respectively.

(3) Sections 50 and 51 and paragraphs 1 and 2(1) of Schedule 1 shall apply in relation to an order under this section as they apply in relation to an adoption order except that any entry in the Registers of Births, or the Adopted Children Register which is required to be marked in consequence of the making of an order under this section shall, in lieu of being marked with the word 'Adopted' or 'Re-adopted' (with or without the addition of the *word* '(*Scotland*)' [words '(Scotland)' or '(Northern Ireland)'], be marked with the words 'Proposed foreign adoption' or 'Proposed foreign re-adoption', as the case may require.

Note. Words in square brackets substituted for words in italics by Children Act 1989, s 88(1), Sch 10, Part I, para 22(2), as from 14 October 1991.

(*4*) *References in sections 27, 28, 30, 31 and 32 to an adoption order include references to an order under this section or under section 25 of the Children Act 1975 (orders in Scotland authorising adoption abroad).*

Note. Sub-s (4) repealed by Children Act 1989, s 108(7), Sch 15, as from 14 October 1991.

56. Restriction on removal of children for adoption outside Great Britain—(1) Except under the authority of an order under section 55, *or under section 25 of the Children Act 1975 (orders in Scotland authorising adoption abroad)* [section 49 of the Adoption (Scotland) Act 1978 or Article 57 of the Adoption (Northern Ireland) Order 1987] it shall not be lawful for any person to take or send a child who is a British subject or a citizen of the Republic of Ireland out of Great Britain to any place outside the *British Islands* [United Kingdom, the Channel Islands and the Isle of Man] with a view to the adoption of the child by any person *not being a parent or guardian or relative of the child*; and any person who takes or sends a child out of Great Britain to any place in contravention of this subsection, or makes or takes part in any arrangements for *transferring the actual custody of a child to* [placing a child with] any person for that purpose, shall be guilty of an offence and liable on summary conviction to imprisonment for a term not exceeding 3 months or to a fine not exceeding *£400* [level 5 on the standard scale] or to both.

Note. Words in first three pairs of square brackets substituted for words in italics by Children Act 1989, s 88(1), Sch 10, Part I, para 23(1)(a), (2), as from 14 October 1991. Reference to level 5 substituted by virtue of Criminal Justice Act 1982, ss 38, 46. Words 'not being a parent or guardian or relative of the child' in italics repealed by the Adoption and Children Act 2002, s 139(2), (3), Sch 4, para 11(a), Sch 5, as from 1 June 2003.

(2) In any proceedings under this section, a report by a British consular officer or a deposition made before a British consular officer and authenticated under the signature of that officer shall, upon proof that the officer or the deponent cannot be found in the United Kingdom, be admissible as evidence of the matters stated therein, and it shall not be necessary to prove the signature or official character of the person who appears to have signed any such report or deposition.

(3) A person shall be deemed to take part in arrangements for *transferring the actual custody of a child to* [placing a child with] a person for the purpose referred to in subsection (1) if—

    (a) he facilitates the placing of the child *in the actual custody of* [with] that person; or

    (b) he initiates or takes part in any negotiations of which the purpose or effect is the conclusion of any agreement or the making of any arrangement therefor, and if he causes another person to do so.

Note. Words in square brackets substituted for words in italics by Children Act 1989, s 88(1), Sch 10, Part I, para 23(1), as from 14 October 1991.

    See Children Act 1989, s 23(9), Sch 2, Part II, para 19(6) (pp 3221, 3306).

    [(4) Regulations may provide for subsection (1) to apply with modifications, or not to apply, if—

    (a) the prospective adopters are parents, relatives or guardians of the child in question (or one of them is), or

    (b) the prospective adopter is a step-parent of the child,

and any prescribed conditions are met.

    (5) On the occasion of the first exercise of the power to make regulations under subsection (4)—

    (a) the regulations shall not be made unless a draft of the regulations has been approved by a resolution of each House of Parliament, and

    (b) accordingly section 67(2) does not apply to the statutory instrument containing the regulations.

    (6) In this section, 'prescribed' means prescribed by regulations and 'regulations' means regulations made by the Secretary of State, after consultation with the National Assembly for Wales.]

Note. Sub-ss (4)–(6) inserted by the Adoption and Children Act 2002, s 139(2), Sch 4, para 11 (b), as from a date to be appointed.

[56A Restriction on bringing children into the United Kingdom for adoption—*(1) A person habitually resident in the British Islands who at any time brings into the United Kingdom for the purpose of adoption a child who is habitually resident outside those Islands shall be guilty of an offence unless such requirements as may be prescribed by regulations made by the Secretary of State are satisfied either—*

    (a) before that time; or

    (b) within such period beginning with that time as may be so prescribed.

    (2) Subsection (1) does not apply where the child is brought into the United Kingdom for the purpose of adoption by a parent, guardian or relative.

    (3) A person guilty of an offence under this section is liable on summary conviction to imprisonment for a term not exceeding three months, or a fine not exceeding level 5 on the standard scale, or both.

    (4) Proceedings for an offence under this section may be brought within a period of six months from the date on which evidence sufficient in the opinion of the prosecutor to warrant the proceedings came to his knowledge; but no such proceedings shall be brought by virtue of this subsection more than three years after the commission of the offence.]

[56A Restriction on bringing children into the United Kingdom for adoption—(1) This section applies where a person who is habitually resident in the British Islands (the 'British resident')—

    (a) brings, or causes another to bring, a child who is habitually resident outside the British Islands into the United Kingdom for the purpose of adoption by the British resident, or

    (b) at any time brings, or causes another to bring, into the United Kingdom a child adopted by the British resident under an external adoption effected within the period of six months ending with that time.

The references to adoption, or to a child adopted, by the British resident include a reference to adoption, or to a child adopted, by the British resident and another person.

(2) But this section does not apply if the child is intended to be adopted under a Convention adoption order.

(3) An external adoption means an adoption, other than a Convention adoption, of a child effected under the law of any country or territory outside the British Islands, whether or not the adoption is—

    (a) an adoption within the meaning of Part IV of this Act, or

    (b) a full adoption (within the meaning of section 39(3A)).

(4) Regulations may require a person intending to bring, or to cause another to bring, a child into the United Kingdom in circumstances where this section applies—

    (a) to apply to an adoption agency (including an adoption agency within the meaning of section 1 of the Adoption (Scotland) Act 1978 or Article 3 of the Adoption (Northern Ireland) Order 1987) in the prescribed manner for an assessment of his suitability to adopt the child, and

    (b) to give the agency any information it may require for the purpose of the assessment.

(5) Regulations may require prescribed conditions to be met in respect of a child brought into the United Kingdom in circumstances where this section applies.

(6) In relation to a child brought into the United Kingdom for adoption in circumstances where this section applies, regulations may provide for any provision of Part II to apply with modifications or not to apply.

(7) If a person brings, or causes another to bring, a child into the United Kingdom at any time in circumstances where this section applies, he is guilty of an offence if—

    (a) he has not complied with any requirement imposed by virtue of subsection (4), or

    (b) any condition required to be met by virtue of subsection (5) is not met,

before that time, or before any later time which may be prescribed.

(8) A person guilty of an offence under this section is liable—

    (a) on summary conviction to imprisonment for a term not exceeding six months, or a fine not exceeding the statutory maximum, or both,

    (b) on conviction on indictment, to imprisonment for a term not exceeding twelve months, or a fine, or both.

(9) Regulations may provide for the preceding provisions of this section not to apply if—

    (a) the adopters or (as the case may be) prospective adopters are natural parents, natural relatives or guardians of the child in question (or one of them is), or

    (b) the British resident in question is a step-parent of the child,

and any prescribed conditions are met.

(10) On the occasion of the first exercise of the power to make regulations under subsection (9)—

    (a) the regulations shall not be made unless a draft of the regulations has been approved by a resolution of each House of Parliament, and

    (b) accordingly section 67(2) does not apply to the statutory instrument containing the regulations.

(11) In this section, 'prescribed' means prescribed by regulations and 'regulations' means regulations made by the Secretary of State, after consultation with the National Assembly for Wales.]

Note. This section inserted by the Adoption (Intercountry Aspects) Act 1999, s 14, as from 30 April 2001. This section substituted by the Adoption and Children Act 2002, s 139(2), Sch 4, para 12, as from (for the purposes of sub-ss (1)–(8), (11) for the purposes of making regulations) 1 April 2003, (for the purposes of sub-ss (1)–(8), (11) for remaining purposes) 1 June 2003 and (for the purposes of sub-ss (9), (10)) as from a date to be appointed.

57. Prohibition on certain payments—(1) Subject to the provisions of this section, it shall not be lawful to make or give to any person any payment or reward for or in consideration of—

    (a) the adoption by that person of a child;

    (b) the grant by that person of any agreement or consent required in connection with the adoption of a child;

    (c) the *transfer by that person of the actual custody of a child* [handing over a child by that person] with a view to the adoption of the child; or

    (d) the making by that person of any arrangements for the adoption of a child.

Note. Words in square brackets substituted for words in italics by Children Act 1989, s 88(1), Sch 10, Part I, para 24(1), as from 14 October 1991.

(2) Any person who makes or gives, or agrees or offers to make or give, any payment or reward prohibited by this section, or who receives or agrees to receive or attempts to obtain any such payment or reward, shall be guilty of an offence and liable on summary conviction to imprisonment for a term not exceeding 3 months or to a fine not exceeding *£400* [level 5 on the standard scale] or to both; *and the court may order any child in respect of whom the offence was committed to be removed to a place of safety until he can be restored to his parents or guardian or until other arrangements can be made for him.*

Note. Reference to level 5 substituted by virtue of Criminal Justice Act 1982, ss 38, 46. Words in italics repealed by Children Act 1989, s 108(7), Sch 5, as from 14 October 1991.

(3) This section does not apply to any payment made to an adoption agency by a parent or guardian of a child or by a person who adopts or proposes to adopt a child, being a payment in respect of expenses reasonably incurred by the agency in connection with the adoption of the child, or to any payment or reward authorised by the court to which an application for an adoption order in respect of a child is made.

[(3A) This section does not apply to—

    (a) any payment made by an adoption agency to a person who has applied or proposes to apply to a court for an adoption order or an order under section 55 (adoption of children abroad), being a payment of or towards any legal or medical expenses incurred or to be incurred by that person in connection with the application; or

    (b) any payment made by an adoption agency to another adoption agency in consideration of the placing of a child *in the actual custody of* [with] any person with a view to the child's adoption; or

    (c) any payment made by an adoption agency to a voluntary organisation for the time being approved for the purposes of this paragraph by the Secretary of State as a fee for the services of that organisation in putting that adoption agency into contact with another adoption agency with a view to the making of arrangements between the adoption agencies for the adoption of a child.

In paragraph (c) 'voluntary organisation' means a body, other than a public or local authority, the activities of which are not carried on for profit.]

Note. Sub-s (3A) inserted by Criminal Law Act 1977, s 65, Sch 12, as from 8 September 1977. Word in square brackets in sub-s (3A)(b) substituted for words in italics by Children Act 1989, s 88(1), Sch 10, Part I, para 24(2), as from 14 October 1991.

(4) If an adoption agency submits to the Secretary of State a scheme for the payment by the agency of allowances to persons who have adopted or intend to adopt a child where arrangements for the adoption were made, or are to be made, by that agency, and the Secretary of State approves the scheme, this section shall not apply to any payment made in accordance with the scheme.

(5) The Secretary of State, in the case of a scheme approved by him under subsection (4), may at any time—

    (a) make or approve the making by the agency of alterations to the scheme;

    (b) revoke the scheme.

(6) *The Secretary of State shall, within seven years of the date on which section 32 of the Children Act 1975 came into force and, thereafter, every five years, publish a report on the operation of the schemes since that date or since the publication of the last report.*

(7) *Subject to the following subsection, subsection (4) of this section shall expire on the seventh anniversary of the date on which section 32 of the Children Act 1975 came into force.*

Note. Sub-s (7) repealed by Adoption Allowance Schemes Order 1989, SI 1989 No 166, as from 14 February 1989.

(8) *The Secretary of State may by order made by statutory instrument at any time before the said anniversary repeal subsection (7) of this section.*

(9) *An order under subsection (8) of this section shall not be made unless a report has been published under subsection (6) of this section.*

(10) *Notwithstanding the expiry of subsection (4) of this section or the revocation of a scheme approved under this section, subsection (1) of this section shall not apply in relation to any payment made, whether before or after the expiry of subsection (4) or the revocation of the scheme, in accordance with a scheme which was approved under this section to a person to whom such payments were made—*

(a) *where the scheme was not revoked, before the expiry of subsection (4), or*

(b) *if the scheme was revoked, before the date of its revocation.*

Note. Sub-ss (4)–(6), (8)–(10) repealed by Children Act 1989, s 108(7), Sch 15, as from 14 October 1991.

[57A. Permitted allowances—(1) The Secretary of State may make regulations for the purpose of enabling adoption agencies to pay allowances to persons who have adopted, or intend to adopt, children in pursuance of arrangements made by the agencies.

(2) Section 57(1) shall not apply to any payment made by an adoption agency in accordance with the regulations

(3) The regulations may, in particular, make provision as to—

(a) the procedure to be followed by any agency in determining whether a person should be paid an allowance;

(b) the circumstances in which an allowance may be paid;

(c) the factors to be taken into account in determining the amount of an allowance;

(d) the procedure for review, variation and termination of allowances; and

(e) the information about allowances to be supplied by any agency to any person who is intending to adopt a child.

(4) Any scheme approved under section 57(4) shall be revoked as from the coming into force of this section.

(5) Section 57(1) shall not apply in relation to any payment made—

(a) in accordance with a scheme revoked under subsection (4) or section 57(5)(b); and

(b) to a person to whom such payments were made before the revocation of the scheme.

(6) Subsection (5) shall not apply where any person to whom any payments may lawfully be made by virtue of subsection (5) agress to receive (instead of such payments) payments complying with regulations made under this section.]

Note. This section inserted by Children Act 1989, s 88(1), Sch 10, Part I, para 25, as from 14 October 1991.

58. Restriction on advertisements—(1) It shall not be lawful for any advertisement to be published indicating—

(a) that the parent or guardian of a child desires to cause a child to be adopted; or

(b) that a person desires to adopt a child; or

(c) that any person (not being an adoption agency) is willing to make arrangements for the adoption of a child.

[(1A) Publishing an advertisement includes doing so by electronic means (for example, by means of the Internet).]

Note. Sub-s (1A) inserted by the Adoption and Children Act 2002, s 139(2), Sch 4, para 14(a), as from 1 June 2003.

(2) Any person who causes to be published or knowingly publishes an advertisement in contravention of the provisions of this section shall be guilty of an offence and liable on summary conviction *to a fine not exceeding £400 [level 5 on the standard scale]* [to imprisonment for a term not exceeding three months, or a fine not exceeding level 5 on the standard scale, or both].

Note. Reference to level 5 substituted by virtue of Criminal Justice Act 1982, ss 38, 46. Words 'to imprisonment ..., or both' in square brackets substituted for words 'to a fine ... standard scale' in italics by the Adoption and Children Act 2002, s 139(1), Sch 4, para 14(b), as from 1 June 2003.

[**58A. Information concerning adoption**—(1) Every local authority and every *approved adoption society* [appropriate voluntary organisation] shall transmit to the Secretary of State, at such times and in such form as he may direct, such particulars as he may require with respect—

    (a) to their performance of all or any of their functions under the enactments mentioned in subsection (2) below; and

    (b) to the children and other persons in relation to whom they have exercised those functions.

Note. Words 'appropriate voluntary organisation' in square brackets substituted for words in italics by the Care Standards Act 2000, s 116, Sch 4, para 5(1), (10), as from (in relation to Wales) 30 January 2003 and (in relation to England) 30 April 2003.

(2) The enactments referred to in subsection (1) above are—

    (a) the Adoption Act 1958;

    (b) Part I of the Children Act 1975; and

    (c) this Act.

(3) The *clerk of* [justices' chief executive for] each magistrates' court shall transmit to the Secretary of State, at such times and in such form as he may direct, such particulars as he may require with respect to the proceedings of the court under the enactments mentioned in subsection (2) above.

Note. Words 'justices' chief executive for' in square brackets substituted for words in italics by the Access to Justice Act 1999, s 90, Sch 13, para 88, as from 1 April 2001.

(4) The Secretary of State shall publish from time to time abstracts of the particulars transmitted to him under subsections (1) and (3) above.]

Note. This section inserted by Health and Social Services and Social Security Adjudications Act 1983, s 9, Sch 2, para 35, as from 15 August 1983.

This section and s 74 (p 2628) brought into force 27 May 1984 (SI 1983 No 1946, art 2(2)).

59. Effect of determination and orders made in Scotland and overseas in adoption proceedings—*(1) Where an authority of a Convention country or any British territory other than Great Britain [the United Kingdom] having power under the law of that country or territory—*

    (a) to authorise or review the authorisation of a regulated adoption or a specified order; or

    (b) to give or review a decision revoking or annulling a regulated adoption, a specified order or a Convention adoption order,

makes a determination in the exercise of that power, then, subject to sections 52(3) and 53 and any subsequent determination having effect under this subsection, the determination shall have effect in England and Wales for the purpose of effecting, confirming or terminating the adoption in question or confirming its termination, as the case may be.

[(1) Where—
(a) an authority of a Convention country (other than the United Kingdom) having power under the law of that country—
  (i) to authorise, or review the authorisation of, a Convention adoption; or
  (ii) to give or review a decision revoking or annulling such an adoption or a Convention adoption order; or
(b) an authority of any of the Channel Islands, the Isle of Man or any colony having power under the law of that territory—
  (i) to authorise, or review the authorisation of, a Convention adoption or an adoption effected in that territory; or
  (ii) to give or review a decision revoking or annulling such an adoption or a Convention adoption order,

makes a determination in the exercise of that power, then, subject to section 53 and any subsequent determination having effect under this subsection, the determination shall have effect in England and Wales for the purpose of effecting, confirming or terminating the adoption in question or confirming its termination as the case may be.]

Note. Words in square brackets substituted for words in italics by Children Act 1989, s 88(1), Sch 10, Part I, para 26(1), as from 14 October 1991. Sub-s (1) substituted by the Adoption (Intercountry Aspects) Act 1999, ss 6(4),17, except in relation to a 1965 Convention adoption order (or an application for such an order) or a 1965 Convention adoption (as defined in s 17(2) of the 1999 Act).

(2) Subsections (2) and (3) of section 12 shall apply in relation to an order under section 14 of the Children Act 1975 (freeing children for adoption in Scotland) as if the order were an adoption order; and, on the revocation of the order under section 16 of that Act, any duty extinguished by section 12(3)(b) is forthwith revived but the revival does not have the effect as respects anything done or not done before the revival.

[(2) Subsections (2) to (4) of section 12 shall apply in relation to an order freeing a child for adoption (other than an order under section 18) as if it were an adoption order; and, on the revocation in Scotland or Northern Ireland of an order freeing a child for adoption, subsections (3) and (3A) of section 20 shall apply as if the order had been revoked under that section.]

Note. Sub-s (2) in square brackets substituted for sub-s (2) in italics by Children Act 1989, s 88(1), Sch 10, Part I, para 26(2), as from 14 October 1991.

(3) Sections 12(3) and (4) and 49 apply in relation to a child who is the subject of an order which is similar to an order under section 55 and is made (whether before or after this Act has effect) in Scotland, Northern Ireland, the Isle of Man or any of the Channel Islands, as they apply in relation to a child who is the subject of an adoption order.

60. Evidence of adoption in Scotland and Northern Ireland. Any document which is receivable as evidence of any matter—
(a) in Scotland under *section 22(2) of the Adoption Act 1958* [section 45(2) of the Adoption (Scotland) Act 1978]; or
(b) in Northern Ireland under *section 23(4) of the Adoption Act (Northern Ireland) 1967 or any corresponding provision contained in a Measure of the Northern Ireland Assembly for the time being in force* [Article 63(1) of the Adoption (Northern Ireland) Order 1987],

shall also be so receivable in England and Wales.

Note. Words in square brackets substituted for words in italics by Children Act 1989, s 88(1), Sch 10, Part I, para 27, as from 14 October 1991.

61. Evidence of agreement and consent—(1) Any agreement or consent which is required by this Act to be given to the making of an order or application for an order *(other than an order to which section 17(6) applies)* may be given in writing, and, if the document signifying for agreement or consent is witnessed in accordance with *rules* [Family Procedure Rules], it shall be admissible in evidence without further proof of the signature of the person by whom it was executed.

(2) A document signifying such agreement or consent which purports to be witnessed in accordance with *rules* [Family Procedure Rules] shall be presumed to be so witnessed, and to have been executed and witnessed on the date and at the place specified in the document, unless the contrary is proved.

Note. Words '(other than ... applies)' in italics repealed by the Adoption (Intercountry Aspects) Act 1999, Sch 2, as from 1 June 2003 except in relation to a 1965 Convention adoption order (or an application for such an order) or a 1965 Convention adoption (as defined in s 17(2) of the 1999 Act). Words 'Family Procedure Rules' in square brackets in both places they occur substituted for words in italics by the Courts Act 2003 (Consequential Amendments) Order 2004, SI 2004/2035, art 3, Schedule, paras 4, 5, as from 1 September 2004.

62. Courts—(1) In this Act, 'authorised court', as respects an application for an order relating to a child, shall be construed as follows.

(2) Subject to subsections (4) to (6), if the child is in England or Wales when the application is made, the following are authorised courts—

  (a) the High Court;

  (b) *the county court within whose district the child is, and, in the case of an application for an order freeing a child for adoption, any county court within whose district a parent or guardian of the child is;*

  (c) any other county court prescribed by *rules* [Family Procedure Rules] made under [*section 102 of the County Courts Act 1959*] [*section 75 of the County Courts Act 1984*] [section 66(1) of this Act];

  (d) a magistrates' court within whose area the child is, and, in the case of an application for an order freeing the child for adoption, a magistrates' court within whose area a parent or guardian of the child is.

Note. Sub-s (2)(b) repealed by Children (Allocation of Proceedings) (Amendment) (No 2) Order 1994, SI 1994 No 1338, art 6, as from 3 January 1995. Words in second square brackets substituted for words in first square brackets by County Courts Act 1984, s 148(1), Sch 2, Part V, para 58, as from 1 August 1984. Words in second square brackets substituted by words in third square brackets by Matrimonial and Family Proceedings Act 1984, s 46(1), Sch 1, para 20(a), as from a day to be appointed. Words 'Family Procedure Rules' in square brackets substituted for word 'rules' in italics by the Courts Act 2003 (Consequential Amendments) Order 2004, SI 2004/2035, art 3, Schedule, paras 4, 6, as from 1 September 2004.

(3) If, in the case of an application for an adoption order or for an order freeing a child for adoption, the child is not in Great Britain when the application is made, the High Court is the authorised court.

(4) In the case of an application for a Convention adoption order, *paragraphs (b), (c) and (d) of subsection (2) do not apply* [paragraph (d) of subsection (2) does not apply].

Note. Words 'paragraph (d) of subsection (2) does not apply' in square brackets substituted for words in italics by the Adoption (Intercountry Aspects) Act 1999, Sch 2, as from 1 June 2003 except in relation to a 1965 Convention adoption order (or on application for such an order) or a 1965 Convention adoption (as defined in s 17(2) of the 1999 Act).

(5) Subsection (2) does not apply in the case of an application under section 29 but for the purposes of such an application the following are authorised courts—

  (a) if there is pending in respect of the child an application for an adoption order or an order freeing him for adoption, the court in which that application is pending;

(b) if paragraph (a) does not apply and there is no application for an order
under *section 8 or 14 of the Children Act 1975 (which make provision in Scotland for
adoption orders and orders freeing children for adoption pending in respect of the child)*
[(i)   section 12 or 18 of the Adoption (Scotland) Act 1978; or
(ii)   Article 12, 17 or 18 of the Adoption (Northern Ireland) Order 1987],
the High Court, the county court within whose district the applicant lives
and the magistrates' court within whose area the applicant lives.

Note. Words in square brackets substituted for words in italics by Children Act 1989, s 88(1),
Sch 10, Part I, para 28, as from 14 October 1991.

(6) In the case of an order under section 55, paragraph (d) of subsection (2)
does not apply.

[(7) Any court to which the proceedings on an application are transferred under
any enactment is, as regards the transferred proceedings, an authorised court if it is
not an authorised court under the preceding provisions of this section.]

Note. Sub-s (7) inserted by Matrimonial and Family Proceedings Act 1984, s 46(1), Sch 1,
para 20(b), as from 28 April 1986.

63. Appeals etc—*(1) Subject to subsection (4), where any application has been made
under this Act to a county court, the High Court may, at the instance of any party to the
application, order the application to be removed to the High Court and there proceedings with
on such terms as the costs as it thinks proper.*

(2) Subject to subsections (3) *and (4)*, where on an application to a magistrates'
court under this Act the court makes or refuses to make an order, an appeal shall
lie to the High Court.

(3) *Subject to subsection (4)*, where an application is made to a magistrates' court
under this Act, and the court considers that the matter is one which would more
conveniently be dealt with by the High Court, the magistrates' court shall refuse to
make an order, and in that case no appeal shall lie to the High Court.

(4) [*This section does not apply in relation to an application for leave of the court* [*to
remove a child from a person's custody under section 27 or 28*] *or to serve a notice under
section 30 (1) or in relation to an appeal*] [No appeal shall lie to the High Court]
against an order made under section 34.

Note. Words in interior square brackets in sub-s (4) 'to remove … or 28' repealed by
Domestic Proceedings and Magistrates' Courts Act 1978, s 89(2), Sch 2, para 51, as from 20
November 1978. Words 'Subject to subsection (4)' in sub-s (1) repealed by Health and Social
Services and Social Security Adjudications Act 1983, s 30(1), Sch 10, Part I, as from 15 August
1983. In sub-s (2) the words 'and (4)' and in sub-s (3) the words 'Subject to subsection (4),'
repealed by Health and Social Services and Social Security Adjudications Act 1983, s 30(1),
Sch 10, Part I, as from 15 August 1983.
In sub-s (4) for the words from the beginning to 'appeal' the words 'No appeal shall lie to
the High Court' substituted by Health and Social Services and Social Security Adjudications
Act 1983, s 9, Sch 2, para 36, as from 15 August 1983.
Sub-s (1) repealed by Matrimonial and Family Proceedings Act 1984, s 46(3), Sch 3, as
from 28 April 1986.
See now Matrimonial and Family Proceedings Act 1984, s 39 (p 3038).

64. Proceedings to be in private. Proceedings under *Part II, section 29 or section
55* [this Act]—
(a) in the High Court, may be disposed of in chambers;
(b) in a county court, shall be heard and determined in camera;
(c) *in a magistrates' court shall be domestic proceedings for the purposes of the
Magistrates' Courts Act 1952, but section 57(2)(d) of that Act shall not apply in
relation thereto.*

Note. Words in square brackets substituted for words in italics by Domestic Proceedings and
Magistrates' Courts Act 1978, s 73(2), as from 20 November 1978. Sub-s (1)(c) repealed by
Domestic Proceedings and Magistrates' Courts Act 1978, s 89, Sch 3, as from 1 November
1979.

65. *Guardians ad litem and reporting officers* [Duties of officers of the Service]—(1) For the purpose of any application for an adoption order or an order freeing a child for adoption or an order under section 20 or 55 *rules shall* [Family Procedure Rules shall] provide for the appointment, in such cases as are prescribed [or an officer of the Service]—

(a) *of a person to act as guardian ad litem* [to act on behalf] of the child upon the hearing of the application, with the duty of safeguarding the interests of the child in the prescribed manner;

(b) *of a person to act as reporting officer* for the purpose of witnessing agreements to adoption and performing such other duties as the rules may prescribe.

Note. Section heading in square brackets substituted for section heading in italics by the Criminal Justice and Court Services Act 2000, s 74, Sch 7, Pt II, para 51, 52(d), as from 1 April 2003. Words 'of an officer of the Service' in square brackets inserted, words 'to act on behalf' in square brackets in para (a) substituted for words in italics and words 'of a person to act as reporting officer' in italics repealed by the Criminal Justice and Court Services Act 2000, ss 74, 75, Sch 7, Pt II, paras 51, 52(a), Sch 8, as from 1 April 2001. Words 'Family Procedure Rules shall' in square brackets substituted for word 'rules' in italics by the Courts Act 2003 (Consequential Amendments) Order 2004, SI 2004/2035, art 3, Schedule, paras 4, 6, as from 1 September 2004.

(2) A person who is employed—

(a) in the case of an application for an adoption order, by the adoption agency by whom the child was placed; or

(b) in the case of an application for an order freeing a child for adoption, by the adoption agency by whom the application was made; or

(c) in the case of an application under section 20, by the adoption agency with the parental rights and duties relating to the child,

shall not be appointed to act *as guardian ad litem or reporting officer* [under subsection (1)] for the purposes of the application but, subject to that, the same person may if the court thinks fit *be both guardian ad litem and reporting officer* [act under both paragraphs (a) and (b) of subsection (1)].

Note. Words 'under subsection (1)' and words 'act under both paragraphs (a) and (b) of subsection (1)' in square brackets substituted for words in italics by the Criminal Justice and Court Services Act 2000, s 74, Sch 7, Pt II, paras 51, 52(b), as from 1 April 2001.

[(3) *Rules* [Family Procedure Rules] may make provision as to the assistance which an officer of the Service may be required by the court to give to it.

(4) In this section 'officer of the Service' has the same meaning as in the Criminal Justice and Court Services Act 2000.]

Note. Sub-ss (3), (4): inserted by the Criminal Justice and Court Services Act 2000, s 74, Sch 7, Pt II, paras 51, 52(c), as from 1 April 2001. Words 'Family Procedure Rules' in square brackets in sub-s (3) substituted for word 'Rules' in italics by the Courts Act 2003 (Consequential Amendments) Order 2004, SI 2004/2035, art 3, Schedule, paras 4, 7(1), (3), as from 1 September 2004.

[65A. Panels for selection of guardians ad litem and reporting officers—*(1) The Secretary of State may by regulations provide for the establishment of panels of persons from whom guardians ad litem and reporting officers appointed under rules made under section 65 must be selected.*

(2) The regulations may, in particular, make provision—

(a) as to the constitution, administration and procedures of panels;

(b) requiring two or more specified local authorities to make arrangements for the joint management of a panel;

(c) for the defrayment by local authorities of expenses incurred by members of panels;

(d) for the payment by local authorities of fees and allowances for members of panels;

(e) as to the qualifications for membership of a panel;

(f) as to the training to be given to members of panels;

(g)   as to the co-operation required of specified local authorities in the provision of panels in specified areas; and

(h)   for monitoring the work of guardians ad litem and reporting officers.

(3)   Rules of court may make provision as to the assistance which any guardian ad litem or reporting officer may be required by the court to give to it.]

[(4)   The Secretary of State may, with the consent of the Treasury, make such grants with respect to expenditure of any local authority—

(a)   *in connection with the establishment and administration of guardian ad litem and reporting officer panels in accordance with section 65;*

(b)   *in paying expenses, fees, allowances and in the provision of training for members of such panels,*

as he considers appropriate.]

Note. Section 65A(1)–(3) inserted by Children Act 1989, s 88(1), Sch 10, Part I, para 29, as from 14 October 1991. Sub-s (4) added by Courts and Legal Services Act 1990, s 116, Sch 16, para 7, as from the same date. This section repealed by the Criminal Justice and Court Services Act 2000, ss 74, 75, Sch 7, Pt II, paras 51, 53, Sch 8, as from 1 April 2001.

66.   Rules of procedure—(1)   Rules *in regard to any matter to be prescribed under this Act and* dealing generally with *all matters of procedure and* incidental matters arising out of this Act and for carrying this Act into effect shall be made by the Lord Chancellor.

Note. Words in italics repealed by the Courts Act 2003 (Consequential Amendments) Order 2004, SI 2004/2035, art 3, Schedule, paras 4, 8(1), (2), as from 1 September 2004.

(2)   Subsection (1) does not apply in relation to proceedings before magistrates' courts, but the power to make rules conferred by section 15 of the Justices of the Peace Act 1949 [section 144 of the Magistrates' Courts Act 1980] shall include power to make provision as to any of the matters mentioned in that subsection.

Note. Words in square brackets substituted for words in italics by Magistrates' Courts Act 1980, s 154, Sch 7, para 142, as from 6 July 1981. Sub-s (2) repealed by the Courts Act 2003 (Consequential Amendments) Order 2004, SI 2004/2035, art 3, Schedule, paras 4, 8(1), (3), as from 1 September 2004.

(3)   In the case of—

(a)   an application for an adoption order in relation to a child who is not free for adoption;

(b)   an application for an order freeing a child for adoption;

rules [Family Procedure Rules] shall require every person who can be found and whose agreement or consent to the making of the order is required under this Act to be notified of a date and place where he will be heard on the application and of the fact that, unless he wishes or the court requires, he need not attend.

(4)   In the case of an application under section 55, *rules* [Family Procedure Rules] shall require every parent and guardian of the child who can be found to be notified as aforesaid.

(5)   *Rules* [Family Procedure Rules] made as respects magistrates' courts may provide for enabling any fact tending to establish the identity of a child with a child to whom a document relates to be proved by affidavit and for excluding or restricting in relation to any facts that may be so proved the power of a justice of the peace to compel the attendance of witnesses.

Note. Words 'Family Procedure Rules' in square brackets in sub-ss (3)–(5) substituted for words in italics by the Courts Act 2003 (Consequential Amendments) Order 2004, SI 2004/2035, art 3, Schedule, paras 4, 8(1), (4), (5), as from 1 September 2004.

(6)   This section does not apply in relation to sections 9, 10, 11 and 32 to 37.

67.   Orders, rules and regulations—(1)   Any power to make orders, rules or regulations conferred by this Act on the Secretary of State, the Lord Chancellor or the Registrar General shall be exercisable by statutory instrument.

(2) A statutory instrument containing rules or regulations made under any provision of this Act, except section 3(1), shall be subject to annulment in pursuance of a resolution of either House of Parliament.

(3) An order under section 28(10) or 57(8) shall not be made unless a draft of the order has been approved by resolution of each House of Parliament.

(4) An order made under any provision of this Act, except section 74, may be revoked or varied by a subsequent order under that provision.

(5) Orders and regulations made under this Act may make different provision in relation to different cases or classes of cases and may exclude certain cases or classes of cases.

(6) The Registrar General shall not make regulations under section 51 or paragraph 1(1) [or 3] of Schedule 1 except with the approval of the *Secretary of State* [Chancellor of the Exchequer].

Note. Words 'or 3' in square brackets inserted by the Adoption (Intercountry Aspects) Act 1999, Sch 2, as from 1 June 2003 except in relation to a 1965 Convention adoption order (or an application for such an order) or a 1965 Convention adoption (as defined in s 17(2) of the 1999 Act). Words 'Chancellor of the Exchequer' in square brackets substituted for words 'Secretary of State' in italics by Transfer of Functions (Registration and Statistics) Order 1996, SI 1996 No 273, art 5, Sch 2, para 19, as from 1 April 1996

68. Offences by bodies corporate. Where an offence under this Act committed by a body corporate is proved to have been committed with the consent or connivance of or to be attributable to any neglect on the part of, any director, manager, member of the committee, secretary or other officer of the body, he as well as the body shall be deemed to be guilty of that offence and shall be liable to be proceeded against and punished accordingly.

69. Service of notices etc. Any notice or information required to be given under this Act may be given by post.

70. Nationality—*(1) If the Secretary of State by order declares that a description of person specified in the order has, in pursuance of the Convention, been notified to the Government of the United Kingdom as the description of person who are deemed to possess the nationality of a particular Convention country, persons of that description shall, subject to the following provisions of this section, be treated for the purposes of this Act as nationals of that country.*

(2) Subject to section 54(3) and subsection (3) of this section, where it appears to the court in any proceedings under this Act, or to any court by which a decision in pursuance of section 53(3) falls to be given, that a person is or was at a particular time a national of two or more countries, then—

(a) if it appears to the said court that he is or was then a United Kingdom national he shall be treated for the purposes of those proceedings or that decision as if he were or had then been a United Kingdom national only;

(b) if, in a case not falling within paragraph (a), it appears to the said court that one only of those countries is or was then a Convention country, he shall be treated for those purposes as if he were or had then been a national of that country only;

(c) if, in a case not falling within paragraph (a), it appears to the said court that two or more of those countries are or were then Convention countries, he shall be treated for those purposes as if he were or had then been a national of such one only of those Convention countries as the said court considers is the country with which he is or was then most closely connected;

(d) in any other case, he shall be treated for those purposes as if he were or had then been a national of such one only of those countries as the said court considers is the country with which he is or was then most closely connected.

(3) A court in which proceedings are brought in pursuance of section 17, 52(3) or 53 shall be entitled to disregard the provisions of subsection (2) in so far as it appears to that court

appropriate to do so for the purposes of those proceedings; but nothing in this subsection shall be construed as prejudicing the provisions of section 54(3).

(4) Where, after such inquiries as the court in question considers appropriate, it appears to the court in any proceedings under this Act, or to any court by which such a decision as aforesaid falls to be given, that a person has no nationality or no ascertainable nationality, he shall be treated for the purposes of those proceedings or that decision as a national of the country in which he resides or, where that country is one of two or more countries having the same law of nationality, as a national of those countries.

Note. This section repealed by the Adoption (Intercountry Aspects) Act 1999, Sch 2, as from 1 June 2003 except in relation to a 1965 Convention adoption order (or an application for such an order) or a 1965 Convention adoption (as defined in s 17(2) of the 1999 Act).

71. Internal law of a country—(1) In this Act 'internal law' in relation to any country means the law applicable in a case where no question arises as to the law in force in any other country.

(2) In any case where the internal law of a country falls to be ascertained for the purposes of this Act by any court and there are in force in that country two or more systems of internal law, the relevant system shall be ascertained in accordance with any rule in force throughout that country indicating which of the systems is relevant in the case in question or, if there is no such rule, shall be the system appearing to that court to be most closely connected with the case.

72. Interpretation—(1) In this Act, unless the context otherwise requires—
'adoption agency' in section 11, 13, 18 to 23 and 27 to 31 includes an adoption agency within the meaning of *section 1 of the Children Act 1975* (*adoption agencies in Scotland*) [—
   (a) section 1 of the Adoption (Scotland) Act 1978; and
   (b) Article 3 of the Adoption (Northern Ireland) Order 1987].

Note. Words in square brackets substituted for words in italics by Children Act 1989, s 88(1), Sch 10, Part I, para 30(1), (2), as from 14 October 1991.

'adoption order' means an order under section 12(1) and, in section 12(3) and (4), 18 to 21 [, 27 and 28] and 30 to 32 includes an order under section 8 of the Children Act 1975 (*adoption orders in Scotland*);
   ['adoption order'—
   (a) means an order under section 12(1); and
   (b) in sections 12(3) and (4), 18 to 20, 27, 28 and 30 to 32 and in the definition of 'British adoption order' in this subsection includes an order under section 12 of the Adoption (Scotland) Act 1978 and Article 12 of the Adoption (Northern Ireland) Order 1987 (adoption orders in Scotland and Northern Ireland respectively); and
   (c) in sections 27, 28 and 30 to 32 includes an order under section 55, section 49 of the Adoption (Scotland) Act 1978 and Article 57 of the Adoption (Northern Ireland) Order 1987 (orders in relation to children being adopted abroad).]

Note. Words in square brackets in original definition 'adoption order' in italics inserted by Health and Social Services and Social Security Adjudications Act 1983, s 9, Sch 2, para 37(a), (b), as from 15 August 1983. Definition 'adoption order' in square brackets substituted for definition in italics by Children Act 1989, s 88(1), Sch 10, Part I, para 30(1), (3,) as from 14 October 1991.

'adoption society' means a body of persons whose functions consist of or include the making of arrangements for the adoption of children;
   'approved adoption society' means an adoption society approved under Part I;
['appropriate voluntary organisation' has the meaning assigned by section 1(5);]

Note. Definition 'appropriate voluntary organisation' in square brackets substituted for definition 'approved adoption society' in italics by the Care Standards Act 2000, s 116, Sch 4, para 5(1), (11), as from (in relation to Wales) 30 January 2003 and (in relation to England) 30 April 2003.

'authorised court' shall be construed in accordance with section 62;

'body of person' means any body of person, whether incorporated or unincorporated;

'British adoption order' means an adoption order, an order under section 8 of the Children Act 1975 (adoption orders in Scotland), or any provision for the adoption of a child affected under the law of Northern Ireland or any British territory outside the United Kingdom;

['British adoption order' means—
  (a) an adoption order as defined in this subsection, and
  (b) an order under any provision for the adoption of a child effected under the law of any British territory outside the United Kingdom.]

Note. Definition 'British adoption order' in square brackets substituted for definition in italics by Children Act 1989, s 88(1), Sch 10, Part I, para 30(1), (4), as from 14 October 1991.

'British territory' means, for the purposes of any provision of this Act, any of the following countries, that is to say, Great Britain, Northern Ireland, the Channel Islands, the Isle of Man and a colony, being a country designated for the purposes of that provision by order of the Secretary of State or, if no country is so designated, any of those countries;

'child', except where used to express a relationship, means a person who has not attained the age of 18 years;

'the Convention' means the Convention relating to the adoption of children concluded at the Hague on 15 November 1965 and signed on behalf of the United Kingdom on that date;

'Convention adoption order' means an adoption order made in accordance with section 17(1);

'Convention country' means any country outside British territory, being a country for the time being designated by an order of the Secretary of State as a country in which, in his opinion, the Convention is in force;

['the Convention' means the Convention on Protection of Children and Co-operation in respect of Intercountry Adoption, concluded at the Hague on 29th May 1993;

'Convention adoption' means an adoption effected under the law of a Convention country outside the British Islands, and certified in pursuance of Article 23(1) of the Convention;

'Convention adoption order' means an adoption order made in accordance with section 17;

'Convention country' means any country or territory in which the Convention is in force;]

Note. Definitions 'the Convention', 'Convention adoption', 'Convention adoption order' and 'Convention country' substituted, for definitions 'the Convention', 'Convention adoption order' and 'Convention country' as originally enacted, by the Adoption (Intercountry Aspects) Act 1999, ss 8, 17, except in relation to a 1965 Convention adoption order (or an application for such an order) or a 1965 Convention adoption (as defined in s 17(2) of the 1999 Act), as from (in relation to definitions 'Convention adoption' and 'Convention adoption order' for the purposes of making regulations) 23 January 2003, (in relation to definitions 'Convention adoption' and Convention adoption order' for remaining purposes) 1 June 2003 and (in relation to definitions 'the Convention' and 'Convention country') 1 June 2003.

'existing', in relation to an enactment or other instrument, means one passed or made at any time before 1 January 1976;

'guardian' means—

(*a*) a person appointed by deed or will in accordance with the provisions of the Guardianship of Infants Act 1886 and 1925 or the Guardianship of Minors Act 1971 or by a court of competent jurisdiction to be the guardian of the child, and

(*b*) in the case of an illegitimate child, includes the father where he has custody of the child by virtue of an order under section 9 of the Guardianship of Minors Act 1971, or under section 2 of the Illegitimate Children (Scotland) Act 1930;

[(*b*) in the case of a child whose father and mother were not married to each other at the time of his birth, includes the father where—

(*i*) an order is in force under section 4 of the Family Law Reform Act 1987 giving him all the parental rights and duties with respect to the child; or

(*ii*) he has a right to custody, legal or actual custody or care and control of the child by virtue of an order made under any enactment.]

['guardian' has the same meaning as in the Children Act 1989].

Note. Para (b) in square brackets in original definition 'guardian' in italics substituted for para (b) by Family Law Reform Act 1987, s 7(2), as from 1 April 1989. Definition 'guardian' in square brackets substituted for definition in italics by Children Act 1989, s 88(1), Sch 10, Part I, para 30(1), (5), as from 14 October 1991.

'internal law' has the meaning assigned by section 71;

'local authority' means the council of a county (other than a metropolitan county), a metropolitan district, a London borough or the Common Council of the City of London[but, in relation to Wales, means the council of a county or county borough] *and, in sections 13, 22, 28 to 31, 35(1) and 51, includes a regional or islands council;*

Note. Words in square brackets inserted by Local Government (Wales) Act 1994, s 22(4), Sch 10, para 9, as from 1 April 1996. Words in italics repealed by Children Act 1989, s 108(7), Sch 15, as from 14 October 1991.

'notice' means a notice in writing;

'order freeing a child for adoption' means an order under section 18 [and in *section 27(2) includes an order under section 18 of the Adoption (Scotland) Act 1978 (order freeing a child for adoption made in Scotland)*] [sections 27(2) and 59 includes an order under—

(a) section 18 of the Adoption (Scotland) Act 1978; and

(b) Article 17 or 18 of the Adoption (Northern Ireland) Order 1987];

Note. Words in first pair of square brackets added by Health and Social Services and Social Security Adjudications Act 1983, s 9, Sch 2, para 37(a), (b), as from 15 August 1983. Words in second pair of square brackets substituted for words in italics by Children Act 1989, s 88(1), Sch 10, Part I, para 30(1), (6), as from 14 October 1991.

'overseas adoption' has the meaning assigned by sub-section (2);

['parent' means, in relation to a child, any parent who has parental responsibility for the child under the Children Act 1989;

'parental responsibility' and 'parental responsibility agreement' have the same meaning as in the Children Act 1989;]

Note. Definitions 'parent', 'parental responsibility' and 'parental responsibility agreement' inserted by Children Act 1989, s 88(1), Sch 10, Part I, para 30(1), (7), as from 14 October 1991.

'place of safety' means a community home provided by a local authority, a controlled community home, police station, or any hospital, surgery or other suitable place the occupier of which is willing temporarily to receive a child;

Note. Definition 'place of safety' repealed by Children Act 1989, s 108(7), Sch 15, as from 14 October 1991.

'prescribed' means prescribed by *rules* [Family Procedure Rules];

Note. Words 'Family Procedure Rules' in square brackets substituted for word 'rules' in italics by the Courts Act 2003 (Consequential Amendments) Order 2004, SI 2004/2035, art 3, Schedule, paras 4, 9(a), as from 1 September 2004.

'*regulated adoption*' *means an overseas adoption of a description designated by an order under subsection (2) as that of an adoption regulated by the Convention;*

Note. Definition 'regulated adoption' repealed by the Adoption (Intercountry Aspects Act 1999, ss 15(1), 17, Sch 2, para 3(8), as from 1 June 2003 except in relation to a 1965 Convention adoption order (or an application for such an order) or a 1965 Convention adoption (as defined in s 17(2) of the 1999 Act).

'relative' in relation to a child means a grandparent, brother, sister, uncle or aunt, whether of the full blood or half-blood or by affinity and includes, where the child is illegitimate, the father of the child and any person who would be a relative within the meaning of this definition if the child were the legitimate child of his mother and father;

'*rules*' *means rules made under section 66(1) or made by virtue of section 66(2) under section 15 of the Justices of the Peace Act 1949 [section 144 of the Magistrates' Courts Act 1980];*

Note. Words in square brackets substituted for words in italics by Magistrates' Courts Act 1980, s 154, Sch 7, para 143, as from 6 July 1981. Definition 'rules' repealed by the Courts Act 2003 (Consequential Amendments) Order 2004, SI 2004/2035, art 3, Schedule, paras 4, 9(b), as from 1 September 2004.

'*specified order*' *means any provision for the adoption of a child effected under enactments similar to section 12(1) and 17 in force in Northern Ireland or any British territory outside the United Kingdom;*

Note. Words in italics repealed by Children Act 1989, s 108(7), Sch 15, as from 14 October 1991. Definition 'specified order' repealed by the Adoption (Intercountry Aspects) Act 1999, ss 15(2), 17, Sch 3, as from 1 June 2003 except in relation to a 1965 Convention adoption order (or an application for such an order) or a 1965 Convention adoption (as defined in s 17(2) of the 1999 Act).

'United Kingdom national' means, for the purposes of any provision of this Act, a citizen of the United Kingdom and colonies satisfying such conditions, if any, as the Secretary of State may by order specify for the purposes of that provision;

['upbringing' has the same meaning as in the Children Act 1989;]

Note. Definition 'upbringing' inserted by Children Act 1989, s 88(1), Sch 10, Part I, para 30(1), (8), as from 14 October 1991.

'voluntary organisation' means a body other than a public or local authority the activities of which are not carried on for profit.

Note. In relation to any time before the coming into force of s 72(1) (1 January 1988), see Family Law Reform Act 1987, Sch 3, para 4.

[*(1A) In the definition of 'guardian' in subsection (1) the reference to a child whose father and mother were not married to each other at the time of his birth shall be construed in accordance with section 1 of the Family Law Reform Act 1987.*]

[(1A) In this Act, in determining with what person, or where, a child has his home, any absence of the child at a hospital or boarding school and any other temporary absence shall be disregarded.

(1B) In this Act, references to a child who is in the care of or looked after by a local authority have the same meaning as in the Children Act 1989.]

Note. Sub-s (1A) in italics inserted by Family Law Reform Act 1987, s 33(1), Sch 2, para 68, as from 1 April 1989. Sub-ss (1A), (1B) in square brackets substituted for sub-s (1A) in italics by Children Act 1989, s 88(1), Sch 10, Part I, para 30(1), (9), as from 14 October 1991.

(2) In this Act 'overseas adoption' means an adoption of such a description as the Secretary of State may by order specify, being a description of adoptions of children appearing to him to be effected under the law of any country outside *Great Britain* [the British Islands]; and an order under this subsection may contain provision as to the manner in which evidence of an overseas adoption may be given.

Note. See Family Law Act 1986, s 57(1). Words in square brackets substituted for words in italics by the Adoption (Intercountry Aspects) Act 1999, ss 15(1), 17, Sch 2, para 3(8), as from 1 June 2003 except in relation to a 1965 Convention adoption order (or an application for such an order) or a 1965 Convention adoption (as defined in s 17(2) of the 1999 Act).

(3) For the purposes of this Act, a person shall be deemed to make arrangements for the adoption of a child if he enters into or makes any agreement or arrangement for, or for facilitating, the adoption of any child by any other person, whether the adoption is effected, or is intended to be effected, in Great Britain or elsewhere, or if he initiates or takes part in any negotiations of which the purpose or effect is the conclusion of any agreement or the making of any arrangements therefor, and if he causes another person to do so.

[(3A) In this Act, in relation to the proposed adoption of a child resident outside the British Islands, references to arrangements for the adoption of a child include references to arrangements for an assessment for the purpose of indicating whether a person is suitable to adopt a child or not.

(3B) In this Act, in relation to—

(a) an adoption proposed to be effected by a Convention adoption order; or

(b) an adoption of a child habitually resident outside the British Islands which is proposed to be effected by an adoption order other than a Convention adoption order,

references to a child placed with any persons by an adoption agency include references to a child who, in pursuance of arrangements made by such an agency, has been adopted by or placed with those persons under the law of a country or territory outside the British Islands.]

Note. Sub-ss (3A), (3B) inserted by the Adoption (Intercountry Aspects) Act 1999, s 13, as from (in relation to sub-s (3A)) 31 January 2000 and (in relation to sub-s (3B)) as from a date to be appointed. Sub-s (3B) repealed by the Adoption and Children Act 2002, s 139(2), (3), Sch 4, para 13, Sch 5, as from 1 June 2003.

(4) Except so far as the context otherwise requires, any reference in this Act to an enactment shall be construed as a reference to that enactment as amended by or under any other enactment, including this Act.

(5) In this Act, except where otherwise indicated—

(a) a reference to a numbered Part, section or Schedule is a reference to the Part or section of, or the Schedule to, this Act so numbered, and

(b) a reference in a section to a numbered subsection is a reference to the subsection of that section so numbered, and

(c) a reference in a section, subsection or Schedule to a numbered paragraph is a reference to the paragraph of that section, subsection or Schedule so numbered.

73. Transitional provisions, amendments and repeals—(1) The transitional provisions contained in Schedule 2 shall have effect.

(2) The enactments specified in Schedule 3 shall have effect subject to the amendments specified in that Schedule, being amendments consequential upon the provisions of this Act.

(3) The enactments specified in Schedule 4 are hereby repealed to the extent specified in column 3 of that Schedule.

74. Short title, commencement and extent—(1) This Act may be cited as the Adoption Act 1976.

(2) This Act shall come into force on such date as the Secretary of State may by order appoint and different dates may be appointed for different provisions.

(3) This Act, except sections 22, 23, 51 and 73(2), this section and Part II of Schedule 3, shall not extend to Scotland and the said Part II shall not extend to England and Wales.

(4) This Act, except section 40 and Schedule 4 so far as it repeals section 19 of the Adoption Act 1958, section 1(3) of the Adoption Act 1964 and sections 9(5) and 14 of the Adoption Act 1968, shall not extend to Northern Ireland.

[(3) This Act extends to England and Wales only.]

Commencement. The provisions of this Act, except insofar as they have been repealed or superseded, came into force as follows:

15 August 1983: Sch 4 (repeal of Adoption Act 1958, s 33 only) (SI 1983 No 674);

27 May 1984: ss 58A, 74 (SI 1983 No 1946);

1 January 1988: remainder of Act (SI 1987 No 1242).

Note. Words 'except section 40 ... Adoption Act 1968' in sub-s (4) repealed by British Nationality Act 1981, s 52(8), Sch 9. Sub-s (3) in square brackets substituted for original sub-ss (3), (4) in italics by Children Act 1989, s 88(1), Sch 10, Part I, para 31, as from 14 October 1991.

SCHEDULES

SCHEDULE 1   Section 50

REGISTRATION OF ADOPTIONS

Registration of adoption orders

1. (1) Every adoption order shall contain a direction to the Registrar General to make in the Adopted Children Register an entry in such form as the Registrar General may by regulations specify.

(2) The direction contained in a Convention adoption order in pursuance of this paragraph shall include an instruction that the entry made in that register in consequence of the order shall be marked with the words 'Convention order'.

(3) Where on an application to a court for an adoption order in respect of a child (not being a child who has previously been the subject of an adoption order made by a court in England or Wales under this Act or any enactment at the time in force) there is proved to the satisfaction of the court the identity of the child with a child to whom an entry in the Registers of Births relates, any adoption order made in pursuance of the application shall contain a direction to the Registrar General to cause the entry in the Registers of Births to be marked with the word 'Adopted'.

(4) Where an adoption order is made in respect of a child who has previously been the subject of an adoption order made by a court in England or Wales under this Act or any enactment at the time in force, the order shall contain a direction to the Registrar General to cause the previous entry in the Adopted Children Register to be marked with the word 'Re-adopted'.

(5) Where an adoption order is made, the prescribed officer of the court which made the order shall cause the order to be communicated in the prescribed manner to the Registrar General, and upon receipt of the communication the Registrar General shall cause compliance to be made with the directions contained in the order.

Note. Para 1(2) repealed by the Adoption (Intercountry Aspects) Act 1999, s 12, as from 1 June 2003 except in relation to a 1965 Convention adoption order (or an application for such an order) or a 1965 Convention adoption (as defined in s 17(2) of the 1999 Act).

Registration of adoptions in Scotland, Northern Ireland, the Isle of Man and the Channel Islands

2. (1) Where the Registrar General is notified by the Registrar General for Scotland that an adoption order has been made by a court in Scotland in respect of a child to whom an entry in the Registers of Births or the Adopted Children Register relates, the Registrar General shall cause the entry to be marked 'Adopted (Scotland)' or, as the case may be, 'Re-adopted (Scotland)'; and where after an entry has been so marked, the Registrar General is notified as aforesaid that the adoption order has been quashed, or that an appeal against the adoption order has been allowed, he shall cause the marking to be cancelled.

(2) Where the Registrar General is notified by the authority maintaining a register of adoptions in Northern Ireland, the Isle of Man or any of the Channel Islands that an order has been made in that country authorising the adoption of a child to whom an entry in the Registers of Births or the Adopted Children Register relates, he shall cause the entry to be marked with the word 'Adopted' or 'Re-adopted', as the case may require, followed by the name, in brackets, of the country in which the order was made.

(3) Where, after an entry has been so marked, the Registrar General is notified as aforesaid that the order has been quashed, that an appeal against the order has been allowed or that the order has been revoked, he shall cause the marking to be cancelled; and a copy or extract of an entry in any register, being an entry the marking of which is cancelled under this sub-paragraph, shall be deemed to be an accurate copy if and only if both the marking and the cancellation are omitted therefrom.

(4) The preceding provisions of this paragraph shall apply in relation to orders corresponding to orders under section 55 as they apply in relation to orders authorising the adoption of a child; but any marking of an entry required by virtue of this sub-paragraph shall consist of the words 'proposed foreign adoption' or as the case may require, 'proposed foreign re-adoption' followed by the name in brackets of the country in which the order was made.

(5) Without prejudice to sub-paragraphs (2) and (3) where, after an entry in the Registers of Births has been marked in accordance with this paragraph, the birth is re-registered under section 14 of the Births and Deaths Registration Act 1953 (re-registration of births of legitimated children) the entry made on the re-registration shall be marked in the like manner.

Registration of overseas adoptions

3. If the Registrar General is satisfied that an entry in the Registers of Births relates to a person adopted under an overseas adoption and that he has sufficient particulars relating to that person to enable an entry, in the form specified for the purposes of this sub-paragraph in regulations made under paragraph 1(1), to be made in the Adopted Children Register in respect of that person, he shall—

    (a) make such an entry in the Adopted Children Register; and

    (b) if there is a previous entry in respect of that person in that register, mark the entry (or if there is more than one such entry the last of them) with the word 'Re-adopted' followed by the name in brackets of the country in which the adoption was effected; and

    (c) unless the entry in the Registers of Births is already marked with the word 'Adopted' (whether or not followed by other words), mark the entry with that word followed by the name in brackets of the country aforesaid.

[Registration of foreign adoptions

3. (1) If the Registrar General is satisfied, on an application under this paragraph, that he has sufficient particulars relating to a child adopted under a registrable foreign adoption to enable an entry to be made in the Adopted Children Register for the child—

    (a) he must make the entry accordingly, and

    (b) if he is also satisfied that an entry in the Registers of Births relates to the child, he must secure that the entry in those Registers is marked 'Adopted' or 'Re-adopted', as the case may be, followed by the name in brackets of the country in which the adoption was effected.

(2) An entry made in the Adopted Children Register by virtue of this paragraph must be made in the specified form.

(3) An application under this paragraph must be made, in the specified manner, by a specified person and give the specified particulars.

(4) In this paragraph—

'registrable foreign adoption' means a Convention or overseas adoption which satisfies specified requirements;

'specified' means specified by regulations made by the Registrar General.]

Note. Para 3 substituted by the Adoption (Intercountry Aspects) Act 1999, s 12(3), as from (for the purposes of making regulations) 23 January 2003 and (for remaining purposes) 1 June 2003.

Amendment of orders and rectification of Registers

4. (1) The court by which an adoption order has been made may, on the application of the adopter or of the adopted person, amend the order by the correction of any error in the particulars contained therein, and may—

    (a) if satisfied on the application of the adopter or the adopted person that within one year beginning with the date of the order any new name has been given to the adopted person (whether in baptism or otherwise), or taken by him, either in lieu of or in addition to a name specified in the particulars required to be entered in the Adopted Children Register in pursuance of the order, amend the order by substituting or adding that name in those particulars, as the case may require;

    (b) if satisfied on the application of any person concerned that a direction for the marking of an entry in the Registers of Births or the Adopted Children Register included in the order in pursuance of sub-paragraph (3) or (4) of paragraph 1 was wrongly so included, revoke that direction.

(2) Where an adoption order is amended or a direction revoked under sub-paragraph (1), the prescribed officer of the court shall cause the amendment to be communicated in the prescribed manner to the Registrar General who shall as the case may require—

    (a) cause the entry in the Adopted Children Register to be amended accordingly; or

    (b) cause the marking of the entry in the Registers of Births or the Adopted Children Register to be cancelled.

(3) Where an adoption order is quashed or an appeal against an adoption order allowed by any court, the court shall give directions to the Registrar General to cancel any entry in the Adopted Children Register, and any marking of an entry in that Register, or the Registers of Births as the case may be, which was effected in pursuance of the order.

(4) Where an adoption order has been amended, any certified copy of the relevant entry in the Adopted Children Register which may be issued pursuant to subsection (3) of section 50 shall be a copy of the entry as amended, without the reproduction of any note or marking relating to the amendment or of any matter cancelled pursuant thereto; and a copy or extract of an entry in any register, being an entry the marking of which has been cancelled, shall be deemed to be an accurate copy if and only if both the marking and the cancellation are omitted therefrom.

(5) If the Registrar General is satisfied—

    (a) that [a Convention adoption,] a Convention adoption order or an overseas adoption has ceased to have effect, whether on annulment or otherwise; or

    (b) that any entry or mark was erroneously made in pursuance of paragraph 3 in any register mentioned in that paragraph,

he may cause such alterations to be made in any such register as he considers are required in consequence of the cesser or to correct the error; and where an entry in such a register is amended in pursuance of this sub-paragraph, any copy or extract of the entry shall be deemed to be accurate if and only if it shows the entry as amended but without indicating that it has been amended.

(6) In relation to an adoption order made by a magistrates' court, the reference in sub-paragraph (1) to the court by which the order has been made includes a reference to a court acting for the same petty sessions area.

Note. Words 'a Convention adoption,' in square brackets in sub-para (5)(a) inserted by the Adoption (Intercountry Aspects) Act 1999, s 12(4), as from (for the purposes of making regulations) 23 January 2003 and (for remaining purposes) 1 June 2003.

Marking of entries on re-registration of birth on legitimation

5. (1) Without prejudice to section 52, where, after an entry in the Registers of Births has been marked with the word 'Adopted' (with or without the addition of the word '(Scotland)', the birth is re-registered under section 14 of the Births and Deaths Registration Act 1953 (re-registration of births of legitimated persons) the entry made on the re-registration shall be marked in the like manner.

(2) Without prejudice to paragraph 4(5), where an entry in the Registers of Births is marked in pursuance of paragraph 3 and the birth in question is subsequently re-registered under the said section 14, the entry made on re-registration shall be marked in the like manner.

Cancellation in Registers on legitimation

6. Where an adoption order, *other than a Convention adoption order*, is revoked under section 52(1) or (2) the prescribed officer of the court shall cause the revocation to be communicated in the prescribed manner to the Registrar General who shall cause to be cancelled—

(a) the entry in the Adopted Children Register relating to the adopted person; and

(b) the marking with the word 'Adopted' (or, as the case may be, with that word and the word '(Scotland)' of any entry relating to him in the Registers of Births;

and a copy of extract of any entry in any register, being an entry the marking of which is cancelled under this section, shall be deemed to be an accurate copy if and only if both the marking and the cancellation are omitted therefrom.

Note. Words in italics repealed by Domestic Proceedings and Magistrates' Courts Act 1978, ss 74(4), 89(2), Sch 3, as from 20 November 1978.

SCHEDULE 2

Section 73

TRANSITIONAL PROVISIONS AND SAVINGS

General

1. In so far as anything done under an enactment repealed by this Act could have been done under a corresponding provision of this Act it shall not be invalidated by the repeal but shall have effect as if done under that provision.

2. Where any period of time specified in an enactment repealed by this Act is current at the commencement of this Act, this Act shall have effect as if the corresponding provision thereof had been in force when that period began to run.

3. Nothing in this Act shall affect the enactments repealed by this Act in their operation in relation to offences committed before the commencement of this Act.

4. Any reference in any document, whether express or implied, to any enactment repealed by this Act shall, unless the context otherwise requires, be construed as a reference to the corresponding enactment of this Act.

Existing adoption orders

5. (1) Without prejudice to paragraph 1, an adoption order made under an enactment at any time before this Act comes into force shall not cease to have effect by virtue only of a repeal effected by this Act.

(2) Paragraph 4(1) and (2) of Schedule 1 shall apply in relation to an adoption order made before this Act came into force as if the order had been made under section 12, but as if, in sub-paragraph (1)(b) of the said paragraph 4, there were substituted for the reference to paragraph 1(3) and (4) a reference—

    (a) in the case of an entry under the Adoption of Children Act 1926, to section 12(3) and (4) of the Adoption of Children Act 1949,

    (b) in the case of an order under the Adoption Act 1950, to section 18(3) and (4) of that Act,

    (c) in the case of an order under the Adoption Act 1958, to section 21(4) and (5) of that Act.

(3) The power of the court under the said paragraph 4(1) to amend an order includes power, in relation to an order made before 1 April 1959, to make on the application of the adopter or adopted person any such amendment of the particulars contained in the order as appears to be required to bring the order into the form in which it would have been made if paragraph 1 of Schedule 1 had applied to the order.

(4) Section 52(1) and paragraph 6 of Schedule 1 shall apply in relation to an adoption order made under an enactment at any time before this Act came into force as they apply in relation to an adoption order made under this Act.

Rights relating to property

6. (1) Section 39—

    (a) does not apply to an existing instrument or enactment in so far as it contains a disposition of property, and

    (b) does not apply to any public general Act in its application to any disposition of property in an existing instrument or enactment.

(2) Sections 16 and 17 of the Adoption Act 1958, and provisions containing references to those sections shall continue to apply in relation to dispositions of property effected by existing instruments notwithstanding the repeal of those sections, and such provisions, by the Children Act 1975.

(3) Section 46 shall apply in relation to this paragraph as if it were contained in Part IV.

Payments relating to adoptions

7. Section 57(7), (8) and (9) shall not have effect if, immediately before section 57 comes into force, there is in force in England and Wales an order under section 50(8) of the Adoption Act 1958.

Registers of adoptions

8. Any register, or index to a register kept under the Adoption Act 1958, or any register or index deemed to be part of such a register, shall be deemed to be part of the register kept under section 50.

SCHEDULE 3   Section 73

Note. Paras 8–11, 15–19, 22–24 of this Schedule came into force on 1 January 1988 (SI 1987 No 1242).

CONSEQUENTIAL AMENDMENTS

PART I

AMENDMENTS EXTENDING ONLY TO ENGLAND AND WALES

Children Act 1948 (c 43)

1. *In section 2 of the Children Act 1948—*

    (a) *in subsection (8)(b), after the words 'section 14 or 25 of the Children Act 1975' there are added the words 'section 18 or 55 of the Adoption Act 1976';*

(*b*) in subsection (*11*), for the words 'section 14 of the Children Act 1975' and 'section 25' there are substituted respectively the words 'section 18 of the Adoption Act 1976' and 'section 55'.

2. In section 43(*1*) of the said Act of 1948, for the words from 'Adoption Act 1958' to the end there are substituted the words 'the Children Act 1975 and the Adoption Act 1976'.

3. In section 51(*1*) of the said Act of 1948, for the words 'Part IV of the Adoption Act 1958' there are substituted the words 'section 34 of the Adoption Act 1976'.

Note. Paras 1–3 repealed by Child Care Act 1980, s 89(3), Sch 6, as from 1 April 1981.

Magistrates' Courts Act 1952 (*c 55*)

4. In section 56(1) of the Magistrates' Courts Act 1952, for paragraph (*f*) there is substituted the following paragraph—

'(*f*) under Part II of the Children Act 1975 or under the provisions (other than section 34) of the Adoption Act 1976'.

Note. Para 4 repealed by Domestic Proceedings and Magistrates' Courts Act 1978, s 89(2), Sch 3, as from 1 November 1979.

Children Act 1958 (*c 65*)

5. In section 2(4A) of the Children Act 1958, for the words from 'by such' to the end there are substituted the words 'by an adoption agency within the meaning of section 1 of the Adoption Act 1976 or section 1 of the Children Act 1975 or while he is a protected child within the meaning of Part III of the said Act of 1976 '.

6. In section 6(1) of the said Act of 1958, in paragraph (*f*), after the words 'section 43 of the Adoption Act 1958' there are added the words 'or section 34 of the Adoption Act 1976 '.

Note. Paras 5, 6 repealed by Foster Children Act 1980, s 23(3), Sch 3, as from 1 April 1981.

County Courts Act 1959 (c 22)

7. In section 109(2) of the County Courts Act 1959, after paragraph (h) there is added the following paragraph—

'(*i*) any proceedings under Part II or section 29 or 55 of the Adoption Act 1976'.

Note. See now County Courts Act 1984, Sch 4 (p 3038), repealing County Courts Act 1959, s 109(2).

Children and Young Persons Act 1963 (c 37)

8. In section 23(*1*)(*c*) of the Children and Young Persons Act 1963 for the words 'section 43 of the Adoption Act 1958' there are substituted the words 'section 34 of the Adoption Act 1976'.

Note. Para 8 repealed by Children Act 1989, s 108(7), Sch 15, as from 14 October 1989.

Health Services and Public Health Act 1968 (*c 46*)

9. In section 64(3)(a) of the Health Services and Public Health Act 1968 there is added at the end the following paragraph—

'(xviii) the Adoption Act 1976.'

10. In section 65(3)(b) of the said Act of 1968 there is added at the end the following paragraph—

'(xix) the Adoption Act 1976'.

Children and Young Persons Act 1969 (c 54)

11. In section 21A of the Children and Young Persons Act 1969 for the references to sections 14 and 25 of the Children Act 1975 there are substituted references to sections 18 and 55 respectively of this Act.

Note. Para 11 repealed by Children Act 1989, s 108(7), Sch 15, as from 14 October 1989.

12. In section 58(1) of the said Act of 1969—

(*a*) in paragraph (*bb*) after the words 'Children Act 1975' there are inserted the words 'or section 1 of the Adoption Act 1976';

(b) in paragraph (c) for the words 'Part IV of the Adoption Act 1958' there are substituted the words 'Part III of the Adoption Act 1976'.

13. In section 63(6) of the said Act of 1969 at the end there is added the following paragraph—

'(j) the Adoption Act 1976.'

Note. Paras 12, 13 repealed by Child Care Act 1980, s 89(3), Sch 6, as from 1 April 1981.

Administration of Justice Act 1970 (c 31)

14. In Schedule 1 to the Administration of Justice Act 1970 for the words 'Adoption Acts 1958 and 1968' there are substituted the words 'Adoption Act 1976', and at the end of that Schedule there is added the following paragraph—

'Proceedings on appeal under Part II or section 29 or 55 of the Adoption Act 1976.'

Note. Para 14 repealed by Supreme Court Act 1981, s 152(4), Sch 7, as from 1 January 1982.

Local Authority Social Services Act 1970 (c 42)

15. In Schedule 1 to the Local Authority Social Services Act 1970, the following is added at the end—

'Adoption Act 1976 (c 36)   Maintenance of Adoption Service; functions of local authority as adoption agency; applications for orders freeing children for adoption; inquiries carried out by local authorities in adoption cases; care, possession and supervision of children awaiting adoption.'

Guardianship of Minors Act 1971 (c 3)

16. In section 9(6) of the Guardianship of Minors Act 1971, for the words from 'within' to the end there are substituted the following words 'by virtue of an order under section 18 of the Adoption Act 1976 (orders in England and Wales) or section 14 of the Children Act 1975 (orders in Scotland)'.

Note. Para 16 repealed by Family Law Reform Act 1987, s 33(4), Sch 4, as from 1 April 1989.

Immigration Act 1971 (c 77)

17. In section 33(1) of the Immigration Act 1971, in the definition of 'legally adopted', for the words 'section 4 of the Adoption Act 1968' there are substituted the words 'section 72(2) of the Adoption Act 1976'.

Legal Aid Act 1974 (c 4)

18. In Schedule 1 to the Legal Aid Act 1974 in paragraph 3(d) [for the words 'section 34 or 34A of the Adoption Act 1958' there are substituted the words 'section 27 or 28 of the Adoption Act 1976' and] for the words 'Part I of the Children Act 1975' there are substituted the words 'Part II or section 29 or 55 of the Adoption Act 1976'.

Note. Words in square brackets inserted by Domestic Proceedings and Magistrates' Courts Act 1978, s 89(2), Sch 2, para 52, as from 20 November 1978. Para 18 repealed by Legal Aid Act 1988, s 45(2), (3), Sch 6, as from 1 April 1989.

Children Act 1975 (c 72)

19. In section 37(1) of the Children Act 1975 for the words 'section 12' and 'section 24(6)' there are substituted respectively the words 'section 16 of the Adoption Act 1976' and 'section 17(6) of that Act'.

Note. Para 19 repealed by Children Act 1989, s 108(7), Sch 15, as from 14 October 1989.

20. In section 60(6) of the said Act of 1975 after the words 'section 14' and 'section 25' there are added the words 'section 18 of the Adoption Act 1976' and 'section 55 of that Act' respectively.

Note. Para 20 repealed by Child Care Act 1980, s 89(3), Sch 6, as from 1 April 1981.

21. *In section 98(1)(b) of the said Act of 1975 at the end there are added the words 'within the meaning of section 1 of the Adoption Act 1976'.*
Note. Para 21 repealed by Children Act 1989, s 108(7), Sch 15, as from 14 October 1991.

22. *In section 103(1)(a) of the said Act of 1975 for paragraph (i) there is substituted the following paragraph—*
'(*i*) *section 65 of the Adoption Act 1976;'.*
Note. Para 22 repealed by Children Act 1989, s 108(7), Sch 15, as from 14 October 1991.

Legitimacy Act 1976 (c 31)

23. In section 4 of the Legitimacy Act 1976.
(a) in subsection (1), for the words 'Paragraph 3 of Schedule 1 to the Children Act 1975' there are substituted the words 'Section 39 of the Adoption Act 1976';
(b) in subsection (2)(a), for the words 'sub-paragraph (2) of the said paragraph 3' there are substituted the words 'subsection (2) of the said section 39';
(c) in subsection (2)(b), for the words 'Part II of the said Schedule I' there are substituted the words 'section 39, 41 or 42 of the Adoption Act 1976'.

24. In section 6(2) of the said Act of 1976, for the words 'paragraph 6(2) of Schedule 1 to the Children Act 1975' there are substituted the words 'section 42(2) of the Adoption Act 1976'.

PART II

AMENDMENTS EXTENDING ONLY TO SCOTLAND

* * * *

SCHEDULE 4

REPEALS

Chapter	Short Title	Extent of Repeal
1958 c 5 (7 & 8 Eliz 2)	Adoption Act 1958.	The whole Act so far as unrepealed.
1959 c 72	Mental Health Act 1959.	In section 19(3), the words 'of a protected child within the meaning of Part IV of the Adoption Act 1958'.
1960 c 59	Adoption Act 1960.	The whole Act.
1964 c 57	Adoption Act 1964.	The whole Act.
1968 c 46	Health Services and Public Health Act 1968.	In section 64(3)(a), paragraphs(v) and (xii). In section 65(3)(b), paragraphs (v) and (xiii).
1968 c 53	Adoption Act 1968.	The whole Act.
1969 c 54	Children and Young Persons Act 1969.	In Schedule 5, paragraphs 33 to 36.
1970 c 31	Administration of Justice Act 1970.	In Schedule 1, the paragraphs relating to appeals under section 10 of the Adoption Act 1958.
1970 c 42	Local Authorities Social Services Act 1970.	In Schedule 1, the paragraphs relating to the Adoption Act 1958 and Part I of the Children Act 1975.

Chapter	Short Title	Extent of Repeal
1971 c 3	Guardianship of Minors Act 1971.	In Schedule 1, the paragraph relating to the Adoption Act 1958.
1972 c 70	Local Government Act 1972.	In Schedule 23, paragraph 8.
1975 c 72	Children Act 1975.	Part I.
1976 c 31	Legitimacy Act 1976.	Section 100(4), (5) and (6). In section 102(1), the words Part I except section 24(6) or' and paragraph (a). In section 107(1), the definitions of 'adoption order', 'adoption society', 'approved adoption society', 'British adoption order', 'British territory', 'the Convention', 'Convention adoption order, 'Convention country' and 'United Kingdom national', and, in the definition of 'guardian', paragraph (b). Schedules 1 and 2. In Schedule 3, paragraphs 6, 16(b), 17, 21, to 40, 44, 45, 61 to 65, and 74(a). In Schedule 1, paragraph 7.

DOMESTIC VIOLENCE AND MATRIMONIAL PROCEEDINGS ACT 1976*
(1976 c 50)

An Act to amend the law relating to matrimonial injunction; to provide the police with powers of arrest for the breach of injunction in cases of domestic violence; to amend section 1(2) of the Matrimonial Homes Act 1967; to make provision for varying rights of occupation where both spouses have the same rights in the matrimonial home; and for purposes connected therewith. [26 October 1976]

Note. *Whole Act repealed by Family Law Act 1996, s 66(3), Sch 10, as from 1 October 1997 (SI 1997/1892) subject to savings in s 66(2) of, and paras 5, 8, 10 of Sch 9 to, the 1996 Act.

1. Matrimonial injunctions in the county court—(*1*) *Without prejudice to the jurisdiction of the High Court, on an application by a party to a marriage a county court shall have jurisdiction to grant an injunction containing one or more of the following provisions, namely,—*
  (*a*) *a provision restraining the other party to the marriage from molesting the applicant;*
  (*b*) *a provision restraining the other party from molesting a child living with the applicant;*
  (*c*) *a provision excluding the other party from the matrimonial home or a part of the matrimonial home or from a specified area in which the matrimonial home is included;*
  (*d*) *a provision requiring the other party to permit the applicant to enter and remain in the matrimonial home or a part of the matrimonial home;*
whether or not any other relief is sought in the proceedings.

(2) Subsection (1) above shall apply to a man and a woman who are living with each other in the same household as husband and wife as it applies to the parties to a marriage and any reference to the matrimonial home shall be construed accordingly.

2. Arrest for breach of injunction—(1) Where, on an application by a party to a marriage, a judge grants an injunction containing a provision (in whatever terms)—

(a) restraining the other party to the marriage from using violence against the applicant, or

(b) restraining the other party from using violence against a child living with the applicant, or

(c) excluding the other party from the matrimonial home or from a specified area in which the matrimonial home is included,

the judge may, if he is satisfied that the other party has caused actual bodily harm to the applicant or, as the case may be, to the child concerned and considers that he is likely to do so again, attach a power of arrest to the injunction.

(2) References in subsection (1) above to the parties to a marriage include references to a man and a woman who are living with each other in the same household as husband and wife and any reference in that subsection to the matrimonial home shall be construed accordingly.

(3) If, by virtue of subsection (1) above, a power of arrest is attached to an injunction, a constable may arrest without warrant a person whom he has reasonable cause for suspecting of being in breach of such a provision of that injunction as falls within paragraphs (a) to (c) of subsection (1) above by reason of that person's use of violence or, as the case may be, of his entry into any premises or area.

(4) Where a power of arrest is attached to an injunction and a person to whom the injunction is addressed is arrested under subsection (3) above,—

(a) he shall be brought before a judge within the period of 24 hours beginning at the time of his arrest, and

(b) he shall not be released within that period except on the direction of the judge,

but nothing in this section shall authorise his detention at any time after the expiry of that period.

[In reckoning for the purposes of this subsection any period of 24 hours, no account shall be taken of Christmas Day, Good Friday, or any Sunday.]

Note. Words in square brackets added by Domestic Proceedings and Magistrates' Courts Act 1978, s 89(2), Sch 2, para 53, as from 20 November 1978.

(5) Where, by virtue of a power of arrest attached to an injunction, a constable arrests any person under subsection (3) above, the constable shall forthwith seek the directions—

(a) in a case where the injunction was granted by the High Court, of that court, and

(b) in any other case, of a county court,

as to the time and place at which that person is to be brought before a judge.

3. Amendment of Matrimonial Homes Act 1967. In section 1(2) of the Matrimonial Homes Act 1967 (which provides for applications for orders of the court declaring, enforcing, restricting or terminating rights of occupation under the Act or regulating the exercise by either spouse of the right to occupy the dwelling-house),—

(a) for the word 'regulating' there shall be substituted the words 'prohibiting, suspending or restricting'; and

(b) at the end of the subsection there shall be added the words 'or requiring either spouse to permit the exercise by the other of that right'.

Note. This section repealed by Matrimonial Homes Act 1983, s 12, Sch 3, as from 9 August 1983. See now Matrimonial Homes Act 1983, s 1(2) (p 2926).

4. Order restricting occupation of matrimonial home—(1) Where each of two spouses is entitled, by virtue of a legal estate vested in them jointly, to occupy a dwelling-house in which they have or at any time have had a matrimonial home, either of them may apply to the court, with respect to the exercise during the subsistence of the marriage of the right to *occupy the dwelling-house, for an order prohibiting, suspending or restricting its exercise by the other or requiring the other to permit its exercise by the applicant.*

(2) In relation to orders under this section, section 1(3), (4) and (6) of the Matrimonial Homes Act 1967 (which relate to the considerations relevant to and the contents of, and to the jurisdiction to make, orders under that section) shall apply as they apply in relation to orders under that section; and in this section 'dwelling-house' has the same meaning as in that Act.

(3) Where each of two spouses is entitled to occupy a dwelling-house by virtue of a contract, or by virtue of any enactment giving them the right to remain in occupation, this section shall apply as it applies where they are entitled by virtue of a legal estate vested in them jointly.

[(4) In the determining for the purposes of this section whether two spouses are entitled to occupy a dwelling-house there shall be disregarded any right to possession of the dwelling-house conferred on a mortgagee of the dwelling-house under or by virtue of his mortgage, whether the mortgagee is in possession or not.

In this subsection—

(a) 'mortgage' includes a charge and 'mortgagee' shall be construed accordingly;

(b) 'mortgagee' includes any person deriving title under the original mortgagee.]

Note. Sub-s (4) inserted by Matrimonial Homes and Property Act 1981, s 5(3), as from 14 February 1983.

Whole section repealed by Matrimonial Homes Act 1983, s 12, Sch 3, as from 9 August 1983. See now Matrimonial Homes Act 1983, s 9 (p 2940).

5. Short title, commencement and extent—*(1) This Act may be cited as the Domestic Violence and Matrimonial Proceedings Act 1976.*

(2) This Act shall come into force on such day as the Lord Chancellor may appoint by order made by statutory instrument, and different days may be so appointed for different provisions of this Act:

Provided that if any provisions of this Act are not in force on 1st April 1977, the Lord Chancellor shall then make an order by statutory instrument bringing such provisions into force.

(3) This Act shall not be extended to Northern Ireland or Scotland.

Commencement. Whole Act in force 1 June 1977 (SI 1977 No 559).

SUPPLEMENTARY BENEFITS ACT 1976

(1976 c 71)

PART II

LIABILITY TO MAINTAIN, RECOVERY OF EXPENDITURE AND OFFENCES

Liability to maintain

17. Liability to maintain—*(1) For the purposes of this Act—*

(a) a man shall be liable to maintain his wife and his children; and

(b) a woman shall be liable to maintain her husband and her children [; and

(c) a person shall be liable to maintain another person throughout any period in respect of which the first-mentioned person has, on or after the date of the passing of the Social Security Act 1980 and either alone or jointly with a further person, given an undertaking in writing in pursuance of immigration rules within the meaning of the Immigration Act 1971 to be responsible for the maintenance and accommodation of the other person.]

(2) In subsection (1) above—

(a) the reference to a man's children includes a reference to children of whom he has been adjudged to be the putative father, or, ...; and

(b) the reference to a woman's children includes a reference to her illegitimate children.

*   *   *   *   *

[(*3*) A document bearing a certificate which—
  (*a*) is signed by a person authorised in that behalf by the Secretary of State; and
  (*b*) states that the document apart from the certificate is, or is a copy of, such an undertaking as is mentioned in subsection (*1*)(*c*) of this section,
shall be conclusive evidence for the purposes of this Act of the undertaking in question; and a certificate purporting to be signed as aforesaid shall be deemed to be so signed until the contrary is proved.]

Note. Sections 17–19 repealed by Social Security Act 1986, s 86(2), Sch 11, as from 11 April 1988. Words in square brackets inserted by Social Security Act 1980, ss 6, 8, 21, Sch 2, Part I, para 16.

Recovery of expenditure

18. Recovery of expenditure on supplementary benefits from persons liable for maintenance—(*1*) Where supplementary benefit is paid or claimed to meet requirements which are, or include, those of a person whom another person is, for the purposes of this Act, liable to maintain (in this section referred to respectively as 'the dependant' and 'the liable relative') the Commission [person'] the Secretary of State] may make a complaint against the liable relative to [person to] a magistrates' court for an order under this section.

  (*2*) No [Except in a case falling within section 17(*1*)(*c*) of this Act, no] complaint under subsection (*1*) above shall be made where the dependant is an illegitimate child and the liable relative [person] is his father.

  (*3*) On the hearing of a complaint under subsection (*1*) above the court shall have regard to all the circumstances and, in particular, to the resources of the liable relative [person], and may order him to pay such sum, weekly or otherwise, as it may consider appropriate [, except that in a case falling within section 17(*1*)(*c*) of this Act that sum shall not include any amount which is not attributable to supplementary benefit (whether paid before or after the making of the order).]

  (*4*) In determining whether to order any payments to be made in respect of supplementary benefit for any period before the complaint was made, or the amount of any such payments, the court shall disregard any amount by which the liable relative's [person's] resources exceed the resources which were his during that period.

  (*5*) Any payments ordered to be made under this section shall be made—
  (*a*) to the Secretary of State in so far as they are attributable to any supplementary benefit (whether paid before or after the making of the order);
  (*b*) to the person claiming supplementary benefit or (if different) the dependant; or
  (*c*) to such other person as appears to the court expedient in the interests of the dependant.

  (*6*) Where the order provides for the making of payments to the Secretary of State, the Commission shall be a party to any proceedings with respect to the enforcement, revocation or variation of the order to which, but for this subsection, the Secretary of State would be a party.

Note. In sub-ss (1)–(4), words in square brackets substituted for preceding words, and sub-s (6) repealed by Social Security Act 1980, ss 6, 8, 21, Sch 2, Part I, para 17, Sch 5, Part II.

  (*7*) An order under this section shall be enforceable as an affiliation order, and any proceedings for such an order (but not proceedings for the enforcement, revocation or variation of such an order) shall be included among the proceedings which are domestic proceedings within the meaning of the Magistrates' Courts Act 1952, and section 56 of that Act (definition of 'domestic proceedings') shall have effect accordingly.

Note. In sub-s (7), words 'and any … accordingly' repealed by Domestic Proceedings and Magistrates' Courts Act 1978, s 89(2), Sch 3.

  (*8*), (*9*) (*Apply to Scotland.*)

Note. This section repealed as from 11 April 1988 as noted to s 17 ante.

19. Affiliation orders—(*1*) The provisions of this section apply in any case in which supplementary benefit is paid to meet requirements which include those of an illegitimate child.

(2) If no affiliation order is in force the Commission [Secretary of State] may, within three years from the time when any payment by way of supplementary benefit was made, make application to a justice of the peace acting for the petty sessions area [appointed for the commission area (within the meaning of [the Justices of the Peace Act 1979])] in which the mother of the child resides for a summons to be served under section 1 of the Affiliation Proceedings Act 1957.

(3) In any proceedings on an application under subsection (2) above the court shall hear such evidence as the Commission [Secretary of State] may produce, and shall in all other respects, subject to the provisions of subsection (4) below, proceed as on an application made by the mother under section 1 of the said Act of 1957.

(4) An affiliation order—

(a)   made on an application made by the Commission [Secretary of State] under subsection (2) above; or

(b)   made on an application made by the Commission [Secretary of State] in proceedings brought by the mother of the child under section 1 of the said Act of 1957;

may be made so as to provide that the payments, or a part of the payments, to be made under the order shall, instead of being made to the mother or a person having custody of the child [a person entitled under section 5 of the said Act of 1957], be made to the Secretary of State or to such other person as the court may direct.

(5) Any affiliation order, whether made before or after the commencement of this Act, may, on the application of the Commission [Secretary of State], be varied so as to provide for the making of payments, or part thereof, as mentioned in subsection (4) above; and an application by the Commission [Secretary of State] under this subsection may be made—

(a)   notwithstanding that the mother has died and no person has been appointed to have the custody of the child; and

(b)   where the child is not in the care of the mother and she is not contributing to his maintenance, without making her a party to the proceedings.

(6) Any affiliation order which provides for the making of payments, or part thereof, as mentioned in subsection (4) above may, on the application of the mother of the child, be varied so as to provide that the payments shall be made to the mother or a person having the custody of the child [a person entitled under section 5 of the said Act of 1957].

(7) Where an affiliation order provides for the making of payments, or part thereof, to the Secretary of State, the Commission shall be a party to any proceedings with respect to the enforcement, revocation or variation of the order to which, but for this subsection, the Secretary of State would be a party.

(8) (Applies to Scotland.)

Note. This section repealed as from 11 April 1988 as noted to s 17 ante. 'Secretary of State' substituted for 'Commission' and sub-s (7) repealed by Social Security Act 1980, ss 6, 8, 21, Sch 2, Part I, Sch 5, Part II. In sub-s (2), words in square brackets from 'appointed' to '1979' substituted for preceding words by Domestic Proceedings and Magistrates' Courts Act 1978, s 89, Sch 2, para 54, as from 1 February 1981, save that the reference to Justices of the Peace Act 1979 was substituted for a reference to Administration of Justice Act 1973, s 1 by Justices of the Peace Act 1979, s 71, Sch 2, para 30, from the same date. In sub-ss (4), (6) words in square brackets substituted for preceding words by Social Security and Housing Benefits Act 1982, s 48(5), Sch 4, para 25, as from 28 June 1982.

See Family Law Reform Act 1987, s 33(2), Sch 3, para 6(2)(a) (pp 3193, 3195).

ADMINISTRATION OF JUSTICE ACT 1977

(1977 c 38)

An Act to make further provision with respect to the administration of justice and matters connected therewith, to alter the method of protecting mortgages of registered land and to amend the law relating to oaths and affirmations and to the interest of a surviving spouse in an intestate's estate.   [29 July 1977]

PART I

GENERAL

*   *   *   *   *

3. Enforcement of maintenance orders. Schedule 3 to this Act shall have effect in relation to the enforcement in one part of the United Kingdom of maintenance orders made in another part.

*   *   *   *   *

PART II

ENGLAND AND WALES

*   *   *   *   *

Other provisions about courts

22. Membership of Rule Committees. *It shall cease to be a requirement that the practising barristers included among the persons empowered to make rules of court under section 99 of the Supreme Court of Judicature (Consolidation) Act 1925 and section 50 of the Matrimonial Causes Act 1973 be members of the General Council of the Bar.*

Note. Words in italics repealed by Supreme Court Act 1981, s 152(4), Sch 7, as from 1 January 1982. This section repealed by the Courts act 2003, s 109(1), (3), Sch 8, para 188, Sch 10, as from a day to be appointed.

*   *   *   *   *

32. *(5) The following provisions of this Act shall come into force at the expiration of a period of one month beginning with the date on which it is passed—*

*   *   *   *   *

section 22;

*   *   *   *   *

(6) The provisions of this Act, except section 31 above, this section and the sections mentioned in subsection (5) above, shall come into force on such a day as the Lord Chancellor may by order made by statutory instrument appoint.

Note. Sub-ss (5), (6) repealed by the Statute Law (Repeals) Act 2004, as from 22 July 2004.

*   *   *   *   *

Commencement. Sch 3, paras 1–10 in force 1 January 1981 (SI 1980 No 1981). Paras 11, 12 in force 1 September 1977 (SI 1977 No 1405).

*   *   *   *   *

SCHEDULE 3   Section 3

*   *   *   *   *

MAINTENANCE ORDERS

Registration etc of maintenance orders in England and Wales

1. The following subsections shall be substituted for subsection (2) of section 1 of the Maintenance Orders Act 1958 (introductory provisions relating to registration in one court of a maintenance order made by another)—

    '(2) For the purposes of subsection (1) above, a maintenance order made by a court in Scotland or Northern Ireland and registered in England under Part II of the Maintenance Orders Act 1950 shall be deemed to have been made by the court in England in which it is so registered.

    (2A) This Part of this Act applies—

(a) to maintenance orders made by the High Court or a county court, or a magistrates' court, other than orders registered in Scotland or Northern Ireland under Part II of the Maintenance Orders Act 1950, and

(b) to maintenance orders made by a court in Scotland or Northern Ireland and registered in England under Part II of the Maintenance Orders Act 1950'.

Note. For Maintenance Orders Act 1958, see p 2204.

2. The following subsection shall be inserted after subsection (6) of section 2 of the said Act of 1958 (registration of maintenance orders)—

'(6A) in this section—

"High Court order" includes a maintenance order deemed to be made by the High Court by virtue of section 1(2) above, and

"magistrates' court order" includes a maintenance order deemed to be made by a magistrates' court by virtue of that subsection'.

3. After subsection (6) of section 4 of the said Act of 1958 (variation of orders registered in magistrates' courts) there shall be inserted the following subsection—

'(6A) No application for any variation in respect of a registered order shall be made to any court in respect of an order made by the Court of Session or the High Court in Northern Ireland and registered in that court in accordance with the provisions of this Part of this Act by virtue of section 1(2) above'.

4. In section 5 of the said Act of 1958 (cancellation of registration)—

(a) in subsection (3) for the words 'a magistrates' court' and 'the magistrates' court', wherever they occur, there shall be substituted the words 'the original court'; and

(b) the following subsection shall be inserted after subsection (4)—

'(4A) For the purposes of a notice under subsection (2) or (3) above—

"court of registration" includes any court in which an order is registered under Part II of the Maintenance Orders Act 1950, and

"registration" includes registration under that Act'.

5. The following subsections shall be substituted for section 23(2) of the said Act of 1958 (extent)—

'(2) The following provisions of this Act, namely—

section 2;

section 5(2), (3), (4) and (4A);

extend to Scotland and Northern Ireland.

(2A) Section 20(3) (a) above extends to Northern Ireland.

(2B) Subject to subsections (2) and (2A) above, this Act extends only to England.'

6. The following subsection shall be inserted after section 18(3) of the Maintenance Orders Act 1950 (enforcement of registered orders)—

'(3A) Notwithstanding subsection (1) above, no court in England in which a maintenance order is registered under this Part of this Act shall enforce that order whilst it is registered in another court in England under Part I of the Maintenance Orders Act 1958'.

Note. For Maintenance Orders Act 1950, see p 2144.

7. In section 21(2) of the said Act of 1950 (evidence admissible before court where order registered) for the words from 'registered' to 'superior court' there shall be substituted the words—

'(a) registered under this Part of this Act in a superior court and not registered under Part I of the Maintenance Orders Act 1958, or

'(b) registered in a court in England under that Part of that Act by virtue of section 1(2) of that Act'.

8. The following section shall be substituted for section 23 of the said Act of 1950 (notice of variation, etc)—

'**23.**—(1) Where a maintenance order registered under this Part of this Act is discharged or varied by any court, the prescribed officer of that court shall give notice of the discharge or variation in the prescribed manner—

  (a) to the prescribed officer of any court in which the order is registered; and

  (b) if the order was made by another court, to the prescribed officer of that court.

(2) Any officer to whom a notice is given under this section shall cause particulars of the notice to be registered in his court in the prescribed manner'.

9. In section 24 of the said Act of 1950 (cancellation of registration)—

  (a) in subsection (2), for the words 'of the court' there shall be substituted the words 'of any court'; and

  (b) in subsection (3), for the words from 'to' in the first place where it occurs to the end of the subsection there shall be substituted the words—

    '(a) to the prescribed officer of the court by which the order was made; and

     (b) to the prescribed officer of any court in which it is registered under Part I of the Maintenance Orders Act 1958.

(3A) On receipt of a notice under subsection (3) above—

  (a) any such officer as is mentioned in paragraph (a) of that subsection shall cause particulars of the notice to be registered in his court in the prescribed manner; and

  (b) any such officer as is mentioned in paragraph (b) of that subsection shall cause particulars of the notice to be registered in his court in the prescribed manner and shall cancel the registration of the order'.

10. Maintenance orders made by the Court of Session or the High Court in Northern Ireland which were registered in the High Court and purportedly thereafter registered in a magistrates' court before the coming into force of this Schedule shall be deemed to be and always to have been validly registered in the magistrates' court, and accordingly the provisions of Part I of the Maintenance Orders Act 1958 shall apply to them.

Service of process

11. In section 15 of the Maintenance Orders Act 1950 (service of process), for the words in subsection (1) from the beginning to 'residing' there shall be substituted the words—

  'Where—

    (a) proceedings are begun in a court having jurisdiction under or by virtue of the following, namely—

      (i) this Part of this Act; or

      (ii) section 1(3) or 9(1) of the Matrimonial Proceedings (Magistrates' Courts) Act 1960; or

      (iii) section 15 of the Guardianship of Minors Act 1971; or

      (iv) section 41 of the Maintenance Orders (Reciprocal Enforcement) Act 1972, or

    (b) an action for separation and aliment is commenced in a sheriff court in Scotland,

  and the person against whom the action or other proceedings is or are brought resides'.

Enforcement of payment of capital sums in Scottish divorce actions

12. In section 16 of that Act (which provides for the enforcement of maintenance orders throughout the United Kingdom and includes in the orders which may be enforced orders for the payment of periodical allowances under section 26 of the

Succession (Scotland) Act 1964 and section 5 of the Divorce (Scotland) Act 1976), in subsection (2)(b)(i), after the words 'periodical allowance', in the second place where they occur, there shall be inserted the words 'or a capital sum'.

CRIMINAL LAW ACT 1977
(1977 c 45)

* * * * *

SCHEDULE 12

* * * *

Adoption Act 1958 (7 & 8 Eliz 2 c 5)
In section 50 (prohibition of certain payments), after subsection (3) insert—
'*(3A)   This section does not apply to—*
  (a)   any payment made by an adoption agency to a person who has applied or proposes to apply to a court for an adoption order or an order under section 53 of this Act (provisional adoption orders), being a payment of or towards any legal or medical expenses incurred or to be incurred by that person in connection with the application; or
  (b)   any payment made by an adoption agency to another adoption agency in consideration of the placing of a child in the actual custody of any person with a view to the child's adoption; or
  (c)   any payment made by an adoption agency to a voluntary organisation for the time being approved for the purposes of this paragraph by the putting that adoption agency into contact with another adoption agency with a view to the making of arrangements between the adoption agencies for the adoption of a child,
and never has applied to payments of the kinds mentioned in paragraphs (a) and (b) of this subsection.
  In paragraph (c) of this subsection "voluntary organisation" means a body, other than a public or local authority, the activities of which are not carried on for profit.'

Note. The amendment set out above became spent on the coming into force of the Adoption Act 1976 (p 2620) on 1 January 1988. See now s 57(3A) of that Act (p 2660).

DOMESTIC PROCEEDINGS AND MAGISTRATES' COURTS ACT 1978
(1978 c 22)

ARRANGEMENT OF SECTIONS

PART I

MATRIMONIAL PROCEEDINGS IN MAGISTRATES' COURTS

Powers of court to make orders for financial provision for parties to a marriage and children of the family

An Act to make fresh provision for matrimonial proceedings in magistrates' courts; to amend enactments relating to other proceedings so as to eliminate certain differences between the law relating to those proceedings and the law relating to matrimonial proceedings in magistrates' courts; to extend section 15 of the Justices of the Peace Act 1959; to amend Part II of the Magistrates' Courts Act 1952; to amend section 2 of the Administration of Justice Act 1964; to amend the Maintenance Orders (Reciprocal Enforcement) Act 1972; to amend certain enactments relating to adoption; and for purposes connected with those matters.

[30 June 1978]

Note. Proceedings under this Act are 'family proceedings' for the purposes of the Children Act 1989: see ibid s 8(3)(b), (4)(c) (p 3297). See also Magistrates' Courts Act 1980, s 65 (p 2776).

PART I

MATRIMONIAL PROCEEDINGS IN MAGISTRATES' COURTS

Note. As to application of Part I of this Act, see Magistrates' Courts Act 1980, s 59 (p 2767); Maintenance Orders (Reciprocal Enforcement) Act 1972, ss 27, 28, 28A, 34A (pp 2452, 2454, 2456, 2474); and Children Act 1989, Sch 1, para 2 (p 3410).

Powers of court to make orders for financial provision for parties to a marriage and children of the family

1. Grounds of application for financial provision. Either party to a marriage may apply to a magistrates' court for an order under section 2 of this Act on the ground that the other party to the marriage (*in this part of this Act referred to as 'the respondent'*)—

  (a) has failed to provide reasonable maintenance for the applicant; or

  (b) has failed to provide, or to make proper contribution towards, reasonable maintenance for any child of the family; *or*

  (*c*) *has behaved in such a way that the applicant cannot reasonably be expected to live with the respondent; or*

  (*d*) *has deserted the applicant.*

Note. Words 'in this part of . . . the "respondent"' in italics repealed by Matrimonial and Family Proceedings Act 1984, s 46(1), Sch 1, para 21, as from 1 October 1986. Paras (c), (d) and word 'or' repealed by Family Law Act 1996, ss 18(1), 66(3), Sch 10, as from a day to be appointed, subject to savings in s 66(2) of, and para 5 of Sch 9 to, the 1996 Act.

2. Powers of court to make orders for financial provision—(1) Where on an application for an order under this section the applicant satisfies the court of any ground mentioned in section 1 of this Act, the court may, subject to the provisions of this Part of this Act, make any one or more of the following orders, that is to say—

  (a) an order that the respondent shall make to the applicant such periodical payments, and for such term, as may be specified in the order;

  (b) an order that the respondent shall pay to the applicant such lump sum as may be so specified;

  (c) an order that the respondent shall make to the applicant for the benefit of a child of the family to whom the application relates, or to such a child, such periodical payments, and for such term, as may be so specified;

  (d) an order that the respondent shall pay to the applicant for the benefit of a child of the family to whom the application relates, or to such a child, such lump sum as may be so specified.

(2) Without prejudice to the generality of subsection (1)(b) or (d) above, an order under this section for the payment of a lump sum may be made for the purpose of enabling any liability or expenses reasonably incurred in maintaining the applicant, or any child of the family to whom the application relates, before the making of the order to be met.

(3) The amount of any lump sum required to be paid by an order under this section shall not exceed £500 or such larger amount as the *Secretary of State* [Lord Chancellor] may from time to time by order fix for the purposes of this subsection.

Any order made by the *Secretary of State* [Lord Chancellor] under this subsection shall be made by statutory instrument and shall be subject to annulment in pursuance of a resolution of either House of Parliament.

Note. Words 'Lord Chancellor' in square brackets substituted for words 'Secretary of State' in italics by Transfer of Functions (Magistrates' Courts and Family Law) Order 1992, SI 1992 No 709, art 3(2), Sch 2, as from 1 April 1992.

3. Matters to which court is to have regard in exercising its powers under s 2—(*1*) *Where an application is made for an order under section 2 of this Act, the court, in deciding whether to exercise its powers under subsection (1)(a) or (b) of that section and, if so, in what manner, shall have regard to the following matters, that is to say—*

(*a*) *the income, earning capacity, property and other financial resources which each of the parties to the marriage has or is likely to have in the foreseeable future;*

(*b*) *the financial needs, obligations and responsibilities which each of the parties to the marriage has or is likely to have in the foreseeable future;*

(*c*) *the standard of living enjoyed by the parties to the marriage before the occurrence of the conduct which is alleged as the ground of the application;*

(*d*) *the age of each party to the marriage and the duration of the marriage;*

(*e*) *any physical or mental disability of either of the parties to the marriage;*

(*f*) *the contributions made by each of the parties to the welfare of the family, including any contribution made by looking after the home or caring for the family;*

(*g*) *any other matter which in the circumstances of the case the court may consider relevant, including, so far as it is just to take it into account, the conduct of each of the parties in relation to the marriage.*

(*2*) *Where an application is made for an order under section 2 of this Act, the court, in deciding whether to exercise its powers under subsection (1)(c) or (d) of that section and, if so, in what manner, shall have regard to all the circumstances of the case including the following matters, that is to say—*

(*a*) *the financial needs of the child;*

(*b*) *the income, earning capacity (if any), property and other financial resources of the child;*

(*c*) *any physical or mental disability of the child;*

(*d*) *the standard of living enjoyed by the family before the occurrence of the conduct which is alleged as the ground of the application;*

(*e*) *the manner in which the child was being and in which the parties to the marriage expected him to be educated or trained;*

(*f*) *the matters mentioned in relation to the parties to the marriage in paragraphs (a) and (b) of subsection (1) above.*

(*3*) *The court, in deciding whether to exercise its powers under section 2(1)(c) or (d) of this Act in favour of a child of the family who is not the child of the respondent and, if so, in what manner, shall in addition to the matters mentioned in subsection (2) above have regard (among the circumstances of the case)—*

(*a*) *to whether the respondent had assumed any responsibility for the child's maintenance and, if he did, to the extent to which, and the basis on which he assumed that responsibility and to the length of time during which he discharged that responsibility;*

(*b*) *to whether in assuming and discharging that responsibility the respondent did so knowing that the child was not his own child;*

(*c*) *to the liability of any other person to maintain the child.*

[3. Matters to which court is to have regard in exercising its powers under s 2—(1) Where an application is made for an order under section 2 of this Act, it shall be the duty of the court, in deciding whether to exercise its powers under that section and, if so, in what manner, to have regard to all the circumstances of the case, first consideration being given to the welfare while a minor of any child of the family who has not attained the age of eighteen.

(2) As regards the exercise of its powers under subsection (1)(a) or (b) of section 2, the court shall in particular have regard to the following matters—

(a) the income, earning capacity, property and other financial resources which each of the parties to the marriage has or is likely to have in the foreseeable future, including in the case of earning capacity any increase in that capacity which it would in the opinion of the court be reasonable to expect a party to the marriage to take steps to acquire;

(b) the financial needs, obligations and responsibilities which each of the parties to the marriage has or is likely to have in the foreseeable future;

(c) the standard of living enjoyed by the parties to the marriage before the occurrence of the conduct which is alleged as the ground of the application;

(d) the age of each party to the marriage and the duration of the marriage;

(e) any physical or mental disability of either of the parties to the marriage;

(f) the contributions which each of the parties has made or is likely in the foreseeable future to make to the welfare of the family, including any contributions by looking after the home or caring for the family;

(g) the conduct of each of the parties, if that conduct is such that it would in the opinion of the court be inequitable to disregard it.

(3) As regards the exercise of its powers under subsection (1)(c) or (d) of section 2, the court shall in particular have regard to the following matters—

(a) the financial needs of the child;

(b) the income, earning capacity (if any), property and other financial resources of the child;

(c) any physical or mental disability of the child;

(d) the standard of living enjoyed by the family before the occurrence of the conduct which is alleged as the ground of the application;

(e) the manner in which the child was being and in which the parties to the marriage expected him to be educated or trained;

(f) the matters mentioned in relation to the parties to the marriage in paragraph (a) and (b) of subsection (2) above.

(4) As regards the exercise of its powers under section 2 in favour of a child of the family who is not the child of the respondent, the court shall also have regard—

(a) to whether the respondent has assumed any responsibilities for the child's maintenance and, if he did, to the extent to which, and the basis on which, he assumed that responsibility and to the length of time during which he discharged that responsibility;

(b) to whether in assuming and discharging that responsibility the respondent did so knowing that the child was not his own child;

(c) to the liability of any other person to maintain the child.]

Note. Section 3 in square brackets substituted for section 3 in italics by Matrimonial and Family Proceedings Act 1984, s 9(1), as from 12 October 1984: see ibid, s 47 (p 3040).

4. Duration of orders for financial provision for a party to a marriage—(1) The term to be specified in any order made under section 2(1)(a) of this Act shall be such term as the court thinks fit except that the term shall not begin earlier than the date of the making of the application for the order and shall not extend beyond the death of either of the parties to the marriage.

(2) Where an order is made under the said section 2(1)(a) and the marriage of the parties affected by the order is subsequently dissolved or annulled but the order continues in force, the order shall, notwithstanding anything in it, cease to have effect on the remarriage of the party in whose favour it was made, except in relation to any arrears due under the order on the date of the remarriage.

5. Age limit on making orders for financial provision for children and duration of such orders—(1) Subject to subsection (3) below, no order shall be made under section 2(1)(c) or (d) of this Act in favour of a child who has attained the age of eighteen.

(2) The term to be specified in an order made under section 2(1)(c) of this Act in favour of a child may begin with the date of the making of an application for the order in question or any later date [or a date ascertained in accordance with subsection (5) or (6) below] but—

    (a) shall not in the first instance extend beyond the date of the birthday of the child next following his attaining the upper limit of the compulsory school age (*that is to say, the age that is for the time being that limit by virtue of section 35 of the Education Act 1944 together with any Order in Council made under that section*) [(construed in accordance with section 8 of the Education Act 1996)] *unless the court thinks it right in the circumstances of the case to specify a later date* [unless the court considers that in the circumstances of the case the welfare of the child requires that it should extend to a later date]; and

    (b) shall not in any event, subject to subsection (3) below, extend beyond the date of the child's eighteenth birthday.

Note. Words 'or a date . . . below' in square brackets inserted by Maintenance Orders (Backdating) Order 1993, SI 1993 No 623, art 2, Sch 1, para 4, as from 5 April 1993. Words '(construed . . . Act 1996)' in square brackets substituted for words '(that is to say . . . section)' by Education Act 1996, s 582(1), Sch 37, Part II, para 138, as from 1 September 1997. Words 'unless the court . . . later date' in square brackets substituted for words 'unless the court . . . later date' in italics by Matrimonial and Family Proceedings Act 1984, s 9(2), as from 12 October 1984: see ibid, s 47 (p 3040).

(3) The court—

    (a) may make an order under section 2(1)(c) or (d) of this Act in favour of a child who has attained the age of eighteen, and

    (b) may include in an order made under section 2(1)(c) of this Act in relation to a child who has not attained that age a provision for extending beyond the date when the child will attain that age the term for which by virtue of the order any payments are to be made to or for the benefit of that child,

if it appears to the court—

    (i) that the child is, or will be, or if such an order or provision were made would be, receiving instruction at an educational establishment or undergoing training for a trade, profession or vocation, whether or not he is also, or will also be, in gainful employment, or

    (ii) that there are special circumstances which justify the making of the order or provision.

(4) Any order made under section 2(1)(c) of this Act in favour of a child shall, notwithstanding anything in the order, cease to have effect on the death of the person liable to make payments under the order.

[(5) Where—

    (a) a *maintenance assessment* [maintenance calculation] ('the *current assessment* [current calculation]') is in force with respect to a child; and

    (b) an application is made for an order under section 2(1)(c) of this Act—

        (i) in accordance with section 8 of the Child Support Act 1991; and

        (ii) before the end of the period of 6 months beginning with the making of the *current assessment* [current calculation],

the term to be specified in any such order made on that application may be expressed to begin on, or at any time after, the earliest permitted date.

Note. Words 'maintenance calculation' and words' current calculation' in both places they occur in square brackets substituted for preceding words in italics by the Child Support, Pensions and Social Security Act 2000, s 26, Sch 3, para 4(1), (2), as from (in relation to certain cases) 3 March 2003 and (for remaining purposes) as from a day to be appointed.

(6) For the purposes of subsection (5) above, 'the earliest permitted date' is whichever is the later of—

(a) the date 6 months before the application is made; or

(b) the date on which the *current assessment* [current calculation] took effect or, where successive maintenance assessments have been continuously in force with respect to a child, on which the first of *those assessments* [those calculations] took effect.

Note. Words 'current calculation' and 'those calculations' in square brackets substituted for words in italics by the Child Support, Pensions and Social Security Act 2000, s 26, Sch 3, para 4(1), (2), as from (in relation to certain cases) 3 March 2003 and (for remaining purposes) as from a day to be appointed.

(7) Where—

(a) a *maintenance assessment* [maintenance calculation] ceases to have effect *or is cancelled* by or under any provision of the Child Support Act 1991; and

(b) an application is made, before the end of the period of 6 months beginning with the relevant date, for an order under section 2(1)(c) of this Act in relation to a child with respect to whom that *maintenance assessment* [maintenance calculation] was in force immediately before it ceased to have effect *or was cancelled*,

the term to be specified in any such order, or in any interim order under section 19 of this Act, made on that application, may begin with the date on which that *maintenance assessment* [maintenance calculation] ceased to have effect *or, as the case may be, the date with effect from which it was cancelled*, or any later date.

Note. Words 'maintenance calculation' in each place they occur in square brackets substituted for words in italics by the Child Support, Pension and Social Security Act 2000, s 26, Sch 3, para 4(1), (2), as from (in relation to certain cases) 3 March 2003 and (for remaining purposes) as from a day to be appointed. Words 'or is cancelled', 'or was cancelled' and 'or as the case... cancelled' in italics repealed by the Child Support, Pensions and Social Security Act 2000, s 85, Sch 9, Pt I, as from (in relation to certain cases) 3 March 2003 and (for remaining purposes) as from a day to be appointed.

(8) In subsection (7)(b) above—

(a) where the *maintenance assessment* [maintenance calculation] ceased to have effect, the relevant date is the date on which it so ceased; *and*

(b) *where the maintenance assessment was cancelled, the relevant date is the later of—*

(i) *the date on which the person who cancelled it did so, and*

(ii) *the date from which the cancellation first had effect.]*

Note. Sub-ss (5)–(8) added by Maintenance Orders (Backdating) Order 1993, SI 1993 No 623, art 2, Sch 1, para 5, as from 5 April 1993.

Words 'maintenance calculation' in square brackets substituted for words in italics and sub-s (8)(b) and word 'and' immediately preceding it in italics repealed by the Child Support, Pensions and Social Security Act 2000, ss 26, 85, Sch 3, para 4(1), (2), Sch 9, Pt I, as from (in relation to certain cases) 3 March 2003 and (for remaining purposes) as from a day to be appointed.

6. Orders for payments which have been agreed by the parties—*(1) Either party to a marriage may apply to a magistrates' court for an order under this section on the ground that the other party to the marriage has agreed to make such financial provision as may be specified in the application and, subject to subsection (3) below, the court on such an application may if—*

(a) *it is satisfied that the respondent has agreed to make that provision, and*

(b) *it has no reason to think that it would be contrary to the interests of justice to exercise its powers hereunder,*

order that the respondent shall make the financial provision specified in the application.

(2) In this section 'financial provision' means the provision mentioned in any one or more of the following paragraphs, that is to say—

(a) *the making of periodical payments to the applicant,*

(b) *the payment of a lump sum to the applicant,*

(c) the making of periodical payments to a child of the family or to the applicant for the
benefit of such a child,

(d) the payment of a lump sum to a child of the family or to the applicant for the benefit of
such a child,

and any reference in this section to the financial provision specified in an application made
under subsection (1) above or specified by the court under subsection (5) below is a reference
to the type of provision specified in the application or by the court, as the case may be, to the
amount so specified as the amount of any payment to be made thereunder and, in the case of
periodical payments, to the term so specified as the term for which the payments are to be made.

(3) Where the financial provision specified in an application under subsection (1) above
includes or consists of provision in respect of a child of the family, the court shall not make an
order under that subsection unless it considers that the provision which the respondent has
agreed to make in respect of that child provides for, or makes a proper contribution towards,
the financial needs of the child.

(4) Where a party to a marriage has applied for an order under section 2 of this Act then,
at any time before the determination of that application, he may apply for an order under this
section; and if an order is made under this section the application made for an order under
the said section 2 shall be treated as if it had been withdrawn.

(5) Where on an application under subsection (1) above the court decides—

(a) that it would be contrary to the interests of justice to make an order for the making of
the financial provision specified in the application, or

(b) that any financial provision which the respondent has agreed to make in respect of a
child of the family does not provide for, or make a proper contribution towards, the
financial needs of that child,

but is of the opinion—

(i) that it would not be contrary to the interests of justice to make an order for the making
of some other financial provision specified by the court, and

(ii) that, in so far as that other financial provision contains any provision for a child of
the family, it provides for, or makes a proper contribution towards, the financial needs
of that child,

then, if the applicant and the respondent agree, the court may order that the respondent shall
make that other financial provision.

(6) The provisions of section 4 of this Act shall apply in relation to an order under this
section which requires periodical payments to be made to the applicant for his own benefit as
they apply in relation to an order under section 2(1)(a) of this Act.

(7) The provisions of section 5 of this Act shall apply in relation to an order under this
section for the making of financial provision in respect of a child of the family as they apply in
relation to an order under section 2(1)(c) or (d) of this Act.

(8) Where the respondent is not present or represented by counsel or solicitor at the hearing
of an application for an order under subsection (1) above, the court shall not make an order
under this section unless there is produced to the court such evidence as may be prescribed by
rules of—

(a) the consent of the respondent to the making of the order, and

(b) the financial resources of the respondent.

[6. Orders for payments which have been agreed by the parties—(1) Either
party to a marriage may apply to a magistrates' court for an order under this
section on the ground that either the party making the application or the other
party to the marriage has agreed to make such financial provision as may be
specified in the application and, subject to subsection (3) below, the court on such
an application may if—

(a) it is satisfied that the applicant or the respondent, as the case may be, has
agreed to make that provision, and

(b) it has no reason to think that it would be contrary to the interests of justice
to exercise its powers hereunder,

order that the applicant or the respondent, as the case may be, shall make the financial provision specified in the application.

(2) In this section 'financial provision' means the provision mentioned in any one or more of the following paragraphs, that is to say—

(a) the making of periodical payments by one party to the other,

(b) the payment of a lump sum by one party to the other,

(c) the making of periodical payments by one party to a child of the family or to the other party for the benefit of such a child,

(d) the payment by one party of a lump sum to a child of the family or to the other party for the benefit of such a child,

and any reference in this section to the financial provision specified in an application made under subsection (1) above or specified by the court under subsection (5) below is a reference to the type of provision specified in the application or by the court, as the case may be, to the amount so specified as the amount of any payment to be made thereunder and, in the case of periodical payments, to the term so specified as the term for which the payments are to be made.

(3) Where the financial provision specified in an application under subsection (1) above includes or consists of provision in respect of a child of the family, the court shall not make an order under that subsection unless it considers that the provision which the applicant or the respondent, as the case may be, has agreed to make in respect of that child provides for, or makes a proper contribution towards, the financial needs of the child.

(4) A party to a marriage who has applied for an order under section 2 of this Act shall not be precluded at any time before the determination of that application from applying for an order under this section; but if an order is made under this section on the application of either party and either of them has also made an application for an order under section 2 of this Act, the application made for the order under section 2 shall be treated as if it had been withdrawn.

(5) Where on an application under subsection (1) above the court decides—

(a) that it would be contrary to the interests of justice to make an order for the making of the financial provision specified in the application, or

(b) that any financial provision which the applicant or the respondent, as the case may be, has agreed to make in respect of a child of the family does not provide for, or make a proper contribution towards, the financial needs of that child,

but is of the opinion—

(i) that it would not be contrary to the interests of justice to make an order for the making of some other financial provision specified by the court, and

(ii) that, in so far as that other financial provision contains any provision for a child of the family, it provides for, or makes a proper contribution towards, the financial needs of that child,

then if both parties agree, the court may order that the applicant or the respondent, as the case may be, shall make that other financial provision.

(6) Subject to subsection (8) below, the provisions of section 4 of this Act shall apply in relation to an order under this section which requires periodical payments to be made to a party to a marriage for his own benefit as they apply in relation to an order under section 2(1)(a) of this Act.

(7) Subject to subsection (8) below, the provisions of section 5 of this Act shall apply in relation to an order under this section for the making of financial provision in respect of a child of the family as they apply in relation to an order under section 2(1)(c) or (d) of this Act.

(8) Where the court makes an order under this section which contains provision for the making of periodical payments and, by virtue of subsection (4) above, an application for an order under section 2 of this Act is treated as if it had been withdrawn, then the term which may be specified as the term for which the payments are to be made may begin with the date of the making of the application

for the order under section 2 or any later date.

(9) Where the respondent is not present or represented by counsel or solicitor at the hearing of an application for an order under subsection (1) above, the court shall not make an order under this section unless there is produced to the court such evidence as may be prescribed by *rules* [rules of court] of—

(a) the consent of the respondent to the making of the order,

(b) the financial resources of the respondent, and

(c) in a case where the financial provision specified in the application includes or consists of provision in respect of a child of the family to be made by the applicant to the respondent for the benefit of the child or to the child, the financial resources of the child.]

Note. Section 6 in square brackets substituted for section 6 in italics by Matrimonial and Family Proceedings Act 1984, s 10, as from 1 October 1986.

Words 'rules of court' in square brackets in sub-s (9) substituted for words in italics by the Courts Act 2003, s 109(1), Sch 8, para 191, as from a day to be appointed.

7. Powers of court where parties are living apart by agreement—(1) Where the parties to a marriage have been living apart for a continuous period, exceeding three months, *neither party having deserted the other*, and one of the parties has been making periodical payments for the benefit of the other party or of a child of the family, that other party may apply to a magistrates' court for an order under this section, and any application made under this subsection shall specify the aggregate amount of the payments so made during the period of three months immediately preceding the date of the making of the application.

Note. Words in italics repealed by Family Law Act 1996, ss 18(2), 66(3), Sch 10, as from a day to be appointed, subject to savings in s 66(2) of, and para 5 of Sch 9 to, the 1996 Act.

(2) Where on an application for an order under this section the court is satisfied that the respondent has made the payments specified in the application, the court may, subject to the provisions of this Part of this Act, make one or both of the following orders, that is to say—

(a) an order that the respondent shall make to the applicant such periodical payments, and for such term, as may be specified in the order;

(b) an order that the respondent shall make to the applicant for the benefit of a child of the family to whom the application relates, or to such a child, such periodical payments, and for such term, as may be so specified.

(3) The court in the exercise of its powers under this section—

(a) shall not require the respondent to make payments which exceed in aggregate during any period of three months the aggregate amount paid by him for the benefit of the applicant or a child of the family during the period of three months immediately preceding the date of the making of the application;

(b) shall not require the respondent to make payments to or for the benefit of any person which exceed in amount the payments which the court considers that it would have required the respondent to make to or for the benefit of that person on an application under section 1 of this Act;

(c) shall not require payments to be made to or for the benefit of a child of the family who is not a child of the respondent unless the court considers that it would have made an order in favour of that child on an application under section 1 of this Act.

(4) Where on an application under this section the court considers that the orders which it has the power to make under this section—

(a) would not provide reasonable maintenance for the applicant, or

(b) if the application relates to a child of the family, would not provide, or make a proper contribution towards reasonable maintenance for that child, the court shall refuse to make an order under this section, but the court may treat the application as if it were an application for an order under section 2 of this Act.

(5) The provisions of section 3 of this Act shall apply in relation to an application for an order under this section as they apply in relation to an application for an order under section 2 of this Act subject to the modification that for the reference in *subsection (1)* [subsection (2)(c)] of the said section 3 to the occurrence of the conduct which is alleged as the ground of the application there shall be substituted a reference to the living apart of the parties to the marriage.

Note. Words in square brackets substituted for words in italics by Matrimonial and Family Proceedings Act 1984, s 46(1), Sch 1, para 22, as from 12 October 1984.

(6) The provisions of section 4 of this Act shall apply in relation to an order under this section which requires periodical payments to be made to the applicant for his own benefit as they apply in relation to an order under section 2(1)(a) of this Act.

(7) The provisions of section 5 of this Act shall apply in relation to an order under this section for the making of periodical payments in respect of a child of the family as they apply in relation to an order under section 2(1)(c) of this Act.

Powers of court as to the custody etc of children

8. Orders for the custody of children—(*1*) *Where an application is made by a party to a marriage for an order under section 2, 6 or 7 of this Act, then, if there is a child of the family who is under the age of eighteen, the court shall not dismiss or make a final order on the application until it has decided whether to exercise its powers under this section and, if so, in what manner.*

(*2*) *On an application for an order under section 2, 6 or 7 [but subject to section 2 of the Family Law Act 1986] of this Act the court, whether or not it makes an order under the said section 2, 6 or 7, shall have power to make such order regarding—*

(*a*)   *the legal custody of any child of the family who is under the age of eighteen, and*

(*b*)   *access to any such child by either of the parties to the marriage or any other person who is a parent of that child,*

as the court thinks fit.

Note. Words in square brackets inserted by Family Law Act 1986, s 68(1), Sch 1, para 23, as from 4 April 1988: see also ibid, s 1(3)(a) (p 3067).

(*3*) *An order shall not be made under subsection (2) above giving the legal custody of a child to a person other than a party to the marriage or a parent of the child; but, where the court is of opinion that legal custody should be given to a person who is not a party to the marriage or a parent of the child, it may direct that that person shall be treated as if he had applied for a custodianship order under section 33 of the Children Act 1975.*

Where a direction is given under this subsection in respect of a person who is not qualified to apply for a custodianship order under the said section 33, that person shall be treated as if he were so qualified and Part II of that Act (except section 40) shall have effect accordingly.

Note. In relation to an application for an order under ss 2, 6 or 7 of this Act made before the commencement of Children Act 1975, s 33, the original s 8 had effect as if sub-s (3) were omitted (SI 1980 No 1478, Sch 2, para 2). Children Act 1975, s 33, in force on 1 December 1985.

(*4*) *An order shall not be made under this section giving the legal custody of a child to more than one person; but where the court makes an order giving the legal custody of a child to any person under this section, it may order that a party to the marriage in question who is not given the legal custody of the child shall retain all or such as the court may specify of the parental rights and duties comprised in legal custody (other than the right to the actual custody of the child) and shall have those rights and duties jointly with the person who is given the legal custody of the child.*

(5) An order made under subsection (2) above shall cease to have effect as respects any child when he attains the age of eighteen.

(6) Where an order is made under subsection (2) above the court may direct that the order, or such provision thereof as the court may specify, shall not have effect until the occurrence of an event specified by the court or the expiration of a period so specified; and where the court has directed that the order, or any provision thereof, shall not have effect until the expiration of a specified period, the court may, at any time before the expiration of that period, direct that the order, or that provision thereof, shall not have effect until the expiration of such further period as the court may specify.

(7) The court shall not have power to make—

(a) an order under subsection (2) above with respect to a child in respect of whose custody an order made by a court in England and Wales is for the time being in force;

(b) an order under subsection (2)(b) above with respect to a child who is already for the purposes of Part II of the Children Act 1948 [Part III of the Child Care Act 1980] in the care of a local authority.

Note. Words in square brackets substituted for words 'Part II of the Children Act 1948' by Child Care Act 1980, s 89(2), Sch 5, para 40, as from 1 April 1981.

(8) In any proceedings in which the powers conferred on the court by subsection (2) above are or may be exercisable, the question whether, and if so in what manner, those powers should be exercised shall be excepted from the issues arising in the proceedings which, under the proviso to section 60(1) of the Magistrates' Courts Act 1952 [section 72 (1) of the Magistrates' Courts Act 1980] must be determined by the court before the court may direct a probation officer to make to the court under that section a report on the means of the parties.

Note. Words in square brackets in sub-s (8) substituted for words 'section 60(1) of the Magistrates' Courts Act 1952' by Magistrates' Courts Act 1980, s 154, Sch 7, para 157, as from 6 July 1981.

[8. Restrictions on making of orders under this Act: welfare of children.
Where an application is made by a party to a marriage for an order under section 2, 6 or 7 of this Act, then, if there is a child of the family who is under the age of eighteen, the court shall not dismiss or make a final order on the application until it has decided whether to exercise any of its powers under the Children Act 1989 with respect to the child.]

Note. Section in square brackets substituted for s 8 in italics by Children Act 1989, s 108(5), Sch 13, para 36, as from 14 October 1991.

9. Powers of court to provide for supervision of children—(1) Where the court makes an order under section 8(2) of this Act regarding the legal custody of a child and it appears to the court that there are exceptional circumstances which make it desirable that the child should be under the supervision of an independent person, the court may order that the child shall be under the supervision of a local authority specified by the court or under the supervision of a probation officer.

(2) Where the court decides to make an order under this section providing for supervision by a probation officer, it shall provide for supervision by a probation officer appointed for or assigned to the petty sessions area, in which in the opinion of the court, the child is or will be resident, and the officer responsible for carrying out the order shall be selected in like manner as if the order were a probation order.

(3) An order made under this section shall cease to have effect as respects any child when he attains the age of eighteen.

(4) The court shall not have power to make an order under this section in respect of any child who is already for the purposes of Part II of the Children Act 1948 [Part III of the Child Care Act 1980] in the care of a local authority.

Note. Words in square brackets substituted for words 'Part III of the Children Act 1948' by Child Care Act 1980, s 89(2), Sch 5, para 41, as from 1 April 1981.

(*5*) *Without prejudice to section 21 of this Act, for the purposes of any order made under this section providing for a child to be under the supervision of a local authority or a probation officer, provision may be made by rules for substituting from time to time a different local authority or, as the case may be, a probation officer appointed for or assigned to a different petty sessions area, if in the opinion of the court the child is or will be resident in the area of that authority or, as the case may be, that petty sessions area.*

Note. Section repealed by Children Act 1989, s 108(7), Sch 15, as from 14 October 1991. See Family Law Act 1986, s 6(8)(e) (p 3156). In relation to any time before commencement of Children Act 1989 (14 October 1991), see ibid, s 108(6), Sch 14, paras 1, 5–11, 26 (pp 3408, 3489–3493, 3499, et seq).

10. Powers of court to commit children to care of local authority—(*1*) *Where a court has power by virtue of section 8(2) of this Act to make an order regarding the legal custody of a child and it appears to the court that there are exceptional circumstances which make it impracticable or undesirable for the child to be entrusted to either of the parties to the marriage or to any other individual, the court may, if it thinks fit, make an order committing the care of the child to such local authority as may be specified in the order.*

(*2*) *The authority specified in an order under this section shall be the local authority for the area in which the child was, in the opinion of the court, resident immediately before the order committing the child to the care of a local authority was made.*

(*3*) *Before making an order under this section the court shall—*

(*a*) *notify the local authority of their intention to make such an order, and*

(*b*) *hear any representations from the local authority, including any representations as to the making of an order under section 11(4) of this Act for the making of periodical payments,*

but the court shall not be required to give any notification to the local authority under paragraph (a) above if an officer of the authority has already made to the court under section 12(3) of this Act a report which contains a recommendation that an order should be made under this section.

(*4*) *On the making of an order under this section—*

(*a*) *Part II of the Children Act 1948 (which relates to the treatment of children in the care of a local authority) except section 17 thereof (which relates to arrangements for the emigration of such children); and*

(*b*) *for the purposes only of contributions by the child himself at a time when he has attained the age of sixteen and is engaged in remunerative full-time work, Part III of that Act (which relates to contributions towards the maintenance of children in the care of a local authority),*

shall apply as if the child had been received by the local authority into their care under section 1 of that Act.

[(*4*) *On the making of an order under this section:—*

(*a*) *Part III of the Child Care Act 1980 (which relates to the treatment of children in the care of a local authority), except section 24 (which relates to arrangements for the emigration of such children) and section 28 (which relates to the after-care of children who have been in the care of a local authority under section 2 of that Act); and*

(*b*) *for the purposes only of contributions by the child himself at a time when he has attained the age of 16 and is engaged in remunerative full-time work, Part V of that Act (which relates to contributions towards the maintenance of children in the care of a local authority) shall apply as if the child had been received by the local authority into their care under section 2 of that Act.*]

Note. Sub-s (4) in square brackets substituted for original sub-s (4) by Child Care Act 1980, s 89(2), Sch 5, para 42, as from 1 April 1981. The words 'and is engaged in remunerative full-time work' repealed by Health and Social Services and Social Security Adjudications Act 1983, s 30(1), Sch 10, Part I, as from 1 January 1984.

(*5*) *While an order made under this section is in force with respect to a child, the child shall continue in the care of the local authority notwithstanding any claim by a parent or other person.*

(*6*) *An order made under this section shall cease to have effect as respects any child when he attains the age of eighteen.*

(*7*) *The court shall not have power to make an order under this section with respect to a child who has attained the age of seventeen.*

(*8*) *The court shall not have power to make an order under this section with respect to a child who is already for the purposes of Part II of the Children Act 1948* [*Part III of the Child Care Act 1980*] *in the care of a local authority.*

Note. Words in square brackets substituted for words 'Part II of the Children Act 1948' by Child Care Act 1980, s 89(2), Sch 5, para 42, as from 1 April 1981.

(*9*) *Where the court makes an order under this section with respect to a child, the court shall not have power to make an order under section 8(2)(b) of this Act with respect to that child.*

(*10*) *Each parent or guardian of a child for the time being in the care of a local authority by virtue of an order made under this section shall give notice to the authority of any change of address of that parent or guardian, and any person who without reasonable excuse fails to comply with this subsection shall be liable on summary conviction to a fine not exceeding £50* [*level 2 on the standard scale*].

Note. Reference to level 2 substituted by Criminal Justice Act 1982, s 46(1), and see s 37 thereof (p 2929).

(*11*) *The Secretary of State may by order repeal subsection (7) above, and any such order shall be made by statutory instrument and shall be subject to annulment in pursuance of a resolution of either House of Parliament.*

Note. This section repealed by Children Act 1989, s 108(7), Sch 15, as from 14 October 1991. In relation to any time before commencement of Children Act 1989 (14 October 1991), see ibid, s 108(6), Sch 14, para 15.

11. Provision for maintenance for children in case of certain orders under ss 8 and 10—(*1*) *Where on an application under section 1 of this Act the court, although not satisfied of any ground mentioned in that section, makes an order under section 8(2) of this Act giving to the applicant the right to the actual custody of a child of the family, the court shall have the same powers to make an order in respect of that child under section 2(1)(c) and (d) of this Act as the court would have it were so satisfied.*

(*2*) *Where by an order made under section 8(2) of this Act* [*on an application for an order under section 2 or 7 of this Act,*] *the right to the actual custody of a child is given to the respondent, the court may make one or both of the following orders, that is to say—*

    (*a*) *an order that the applicant shall make to the respondent for the benefit of the child or to the child such periodical payments, and for such term, as may be specified in the order;*

    (*b*) *an order that the applicant shall pay to the respondent for the benefit of the child or to the child such lump sum as may be so specified.*

Note. Words in square brackets added by Matrimonial and Family Proceedings Act 1984, s 46(1), Sch 1, para 23.

[(*2A*) *Where by an order made under section 8(2) of this Act on an application for an order under section 6 of this Act, the right to the actual custody of a child is given to the party to the marriage who has agreed to make the financial provision specified in the application, the court may make one or both of the following orders, that is to say—*

    (*a*) *an order that the other party to the marriage shall make to that party for the benefit of the child or to the child such periodical payments, and for such term, as may be specified in the order;*

    (*b*) *an order that the other party to the marriage shall pay to that party for the benefit of the child or to the child such lump sum as may be so specified.*]

Note. Sub-s (2A) inserted by Matrimonial and Family Proceedings Act 1984, s 46(1), Sch 1, para 23.

(*3*) *Where by an order made under section 8(2) of this Act the legal custody of a child is given to a person who is a parent of that child but not a party to the marriage in question, the court may make one or more of the following orders, that is to say—*

(*a*) *an order that a party to the marriage shall make to that parent [that person] for the benefit of the child or to the child such periodical payments, and for such term, as may be specified in the order;*

(*b*) *an order that a party to the marriage shall make to that parent [that person] for the benefit of the child or to the child such lump sum as may be so specified.*

Note. In relation to applications for orders under ss 2, 6 or 7 of this Act made before the commencement of Children Act 1975, s 33, sub-s (3) had effect as if the words 'a parent of that child', 'that parent' and 'that parent' were omitted and the words in square brackets inserted (SI 1980 No 1478, Sch 2, para 3). Children Act 1975, s 33, in force on 1 December 1985.

(*4*) *Where an order under section 10(1) of this Act commits the care of a child to a local authority the court may make a further order requiring a party to the marriage in question to make to that authority or to the child such periodical payments, and for such term, as may be specified in the order.*

(*5*) *The court in deciding whether to exercise its powers under subsection (2), [(2A)], (3) or (4) above in relation to any child and, if so, in what manner, shall have regard to all the circumstances of the case including the matters to which the court is required to have regard under section 3(2) [section 3(3)] of this Act, and, in deciding whether to make an order against a party to the marriage who is not a parent of that child, shall also have regard (among the circumstances of the case)—*

(*a*) *to whether that party had assumed any responsibility for the child's maintenance and, if so, to the extent to which, and the basis upon which, that party assumed that responsibility and to the length of time for which he discharged that responsibility;*

(*b*) *to whether in assuming and discharging that responsibility that party did so knowing that the child was not his own child;*

(*c*) *to the liability of any other person to maintain the child.*

Note. Words in first pair of square brackets inserted and words in second pair of square brackets substituted for words 'section 3(2)' by Matrimonial and Family Proceedings Act 1984, s 46(1), Sch 1, para 23.

(*6*) *The provisions of section 5 of this Act (other than subsection (3)(a)) shall apply in relation to an order under subsection (2)(a), [(2A)(a)], (3)(a) or (4) above as they apply in relation to an order under section 2(1)(c) of this Act.*

Note. Words in square brackets inserted by Matrimonial and Family Proceedings Act 1984, s 46(1), Sch 1, para 23.

(*7*) *The provisions of section 2(2) and (3) of this Act shall apply in relation to an order under subsection (2)(b), [(2A)(b)] or (3)(b) above as they apply in relation to an order under section 2(1)(d) of this Act and no order shall be made under subsection (2)(b), [(2A)(b)] or (3) above in respect of a child who has attained the age of eighteen.*

Note. See Note to subsection (6) above.

(*8*) *Where the court, by virtue of subsection (6) of section 8 of this Act, directs that an order made under subsection (2) of that section in respect of a child, or the provision thereof providing for the custody of the child, shall not have effect until the expiration of a specified period or the occurrence of a specified event, an order made in respect of that child under subsection (2)(a) or (3) above shall only require payments to be made from the date on which the order made under section 8(2) of this Act, or that provision thereof, takes effect.*

Note. This section repealed by Children Act 1989, s 108(7), Sch 15, as from 14 October 1991. In relation to any time before commencement of Children Act 1989 (14 October 1991), see ibid s 108(6), Sch 14, para 24 (pp 3408, 3498).

12. Supplementary provisions with respect to powers of court under ss 8 to 10—(*1*) *Where an application is made by a party to a marriage for an order under section 2, 6 or 7 of this Act the court, before exercising its powers under sections 8 to 10 of this Act in respect of any child of the family, shall give each party to the marriage and any other person who, as a parent of that child, is present or represented by counsel or solicitor at the hearing, an opportunity of making representations; and any reference in this section to a party to the proceedings shall include a reference both to a party to the marriage and to any other such person who is present or represented.*

(*2*) *Where in the case of such an application there is a child of the family who is not the child of both parties to the marriage in question, the court shall not exercise its powers under the said sections 8 to 10 in relation to that child unless either—*

(*a*) *any person who is a parent of that child, though not a party to the marriage, is present or represented by counsel or solicitor at the hearing; or*

(*b*) *it is proved to the satisfaction of the court, on oath or in such other manner as may be prescribed by rules, that such steps have been taken as may be so prescribed with a view to giving notice to that person of the making of the application and of the time and place appointed for the hearing;*

except that notice shall not be required to be given under paragraph (*b*) above to any person as the father of an illegitimate child unless that person has been adjudged by a court to be the father of that child.

(*3*) *Where the court on such an application is of the opinion that it has not sufficient information to decide whether to exercise its powers under the said sections 8 to 10 and, if so, in what manner, the court may, at any stage of the proceedings on that application, request a local authority to arrange for an officer of the authority to make to the court a report, orally or in writing, with respect to any such matter as the court may specify (being a matter appearing to the court to be relevant to the decision) or may request a probation officer to make such a report to the court; and it shall be the duty of the local authority or probation officer to comply with the request.*

(*4*) *Any report made in pursuance of subsection (*3*) above shall be made or, if in writing, furnished to the court at the hearing of the application, and, if the report is in writing—*

(*a*) *a copy of the report shall be given to each party to the proceedings or to his counsel or solicitor either before or during the hearing, and*

(*b*) *the court may, if it thinks fit, require that the report, or such part thereof as the court may specify, shall be read aloud at the hearing.*

(*5*) *The court may, and if requested to do so at the hearing by a party to the proceedings or his counsel or solicitor shall, require the officer by whom the report was made to give evidence on or with respect to the matters referred to in the report, and, if the officer gives such evidence, any party to the proceedings may give or call evidence with respect to any matter referred to either in the report or in the evidence given by the officer.*

(*6*) *Subject to subsection (*7*) below, the court may take account of—*

(*a*) *any statement contained in a report made or furnished to the court under subsection (*4*) above, and*

(*b*) *any evidence given under subsection (*5*) above by the officer by whom the report was made,*

so far as that statement or evidence relates to any of the matters specified by the court under subsection (*3*) above, notwithstanding any enactment or rule of law relating to the admissibility of evidence.

(*7*) *A report made in pursuance of subsection (*3*) above shall not include anything said by either of the parties to a marriage in the course of an interview which took place with, or in the presence of, a probation officer with a view to the reconciliation of those parties, unless both parties have consented to its inclusion; and if anything so said is included without the consent of both those parties in any such report then, unless both those parties agree otherwise, that part of the report shall, for the purposes of the giving of evidence under subsection (*5*) above and for the purposes of subsection (*6*) above, be treated as not forming part of the report.*

(*8*) *Where for the purposes of this section the court adjourns the hearing of any application, then, subject to section 46(2) of the Magistrates' Courts Act 1952 [section 54(2) of the Magistrates' Courts Act 1980] (which requires adequate notice of the time and place of the resumption of the hearing to be given to the parties), the court may resume the hearing at the time and place appointed notwithstanding the absence of any or all of the parties*

Note. Words in square brackets substituted for words 'section 46(2) of the Magistrates' Courts Act 1952' by Magistrates' Courts Act 1980, s 154, Sch 7, para 158, as from 6 July 1981.

(9) The power of the court under subsection (3) above to request a report may, at any time before the hearing of the application, be exercised by a single justice, and, if any such request is made by a single justice, the report shall be made or furnished to the court which hears the application and the foregoing provisions of this section shall apply accordingly.

Note. This section repealed by Children Act 1989, s 108(7), Sch 15, as from 14 October 1991.

13. Disputes between persons holding parental rights and duties jointly—(*1*)
Where two persons who have a parental right or duty jointly by virtue of an order under section 8(2) of this Act disagree on any question affecting the child's welfare, either of them may apply to a magistrates' court for its direction, and the court may make such order regarding the matters in difference as it thinks fit.

(2) Where the court makes an order under subsection (1) above with respect to any child, the court may, on an application made by either of the persons who have a parental right or duty jointly, by order vary or revoke that order.

(3) The power of the court under section 12(3) of this Act to request a local authority to arrange for an officer of the authority to make a report, or to request a probation officer to make a report, shall apply in relation to the exercise by the court of its powers under this section as it applies in relation to the exercise by the court of its powers under sections 8 to 10 of this Act, and the provisions of subsections (4) to (9) of the said section 12 shall apply accordingly.

Note. This section repealed by Children Act 1989, s 108(7), Sch 15, as from 14 October 1991.

14. Access to children by grandparents—(*1*)
A magistrates' court, on making an order under section 8(2) of this Act regarding the legal custody of a child or at any time while such an order is in force, shall have power, on an application made by a grandparent of the child, to make such order requiring access to the child to be given to that grandparent as the court thinks fit.

(2) Subsections (5), (6), (7)(b) and (8) of section 8 and subsection (9) of section 10 of this Act shall apply in relation to an order under this section as they apply in relation to an order under section 8(2)(b) of this Act.

(3) Where a magistrates' court has made an order under subsection (1) above requiring access to a child to be given to a grandparent, the court shall have power to vary or revoke that order on an application made—
  (a) by that grandparent, or
  (b) by either party to the marriage in question, or
  (c) if the child is not a child of both the parties to the marriage, by any person who though not a party to the marriage is a parent of that child, [or
  (d) any other person who has the legal custody of the child].

Note. Sub-s (3)(d) added in relation to an application under sub-s (3) made before the commencement of Children Act 1975, s 33 (SI 1980 No 1478, Sch 2, para 4). Children Act 1975, s 33 in force on 1 December 1985.

(4) Section 12 of this Act shall apply in relation to the exercise by a court of its powers under this section on an application under subsection (1) or (3) above as it applies in relation to the exercise by the court of its powers under sections 8 to 10 of this Act on an application under section 1 of this Act, and any reference to a party to the proceedings in subsection (4) or (5) of section 12 of this Act shall include—
  (a) in the case of an application under subsection (1) above, a reference to the grandparent who has made an application under that subsection; and

(*b*) in the case of an application under subsection (*3*) above, a reference to the grandparent who has access to the child under the order for the variation or revocation of which the application is made.

(*5*) Where an order made under section 8(2)(*a*) of this Act in relation to a child ceases to have effect, whether by virtue of an order or direction of a magistrates' court or by virtue of any provision of this Part of this Act, any order made under this section regarding access to the child by a grandparent shall also cease to have effect.

(*6*) A court shall have power to make an order under this section in favour of a grandparent of a child notwithstanding that the child is illegitimate.

Note. This section repealed by Children Act 1989, s 108(7), Sch 15, as from 14 October 1991.

15. Principle on which questions relating to custody and upbringing of children are to be decided. *For the avoidance of doubt it is hereby declared that the provisions of section 1 of the Guardianship of Minors Act 1971 (which require a court in deciding any question relating to the custody or upbringing of a minor to have regard to the welfare of the minor as the first and paramount consideration) apply in relation to the exercise by a magistrates' court of its powers under this Part of this Act.*

Note. This section repealed by Children Act 1989, s 108(7), Sch 15, as from 14 October 1991.

Powers of the court to make orders for the protection of a party to a marriage or a child of the family

16. Powers of court to make orders for the protection of a party to a marriage or a child of the family—(*1*) *Either party to a marriage may, whether or not an application is made by that party for an order under section 2 of this Act, apply to a magistrates' court for an order under this section.*

(*2*) Where on an application for an order under this section the court is satisfied that the respondent has used, or threatened to use, violence against the person of the applicant or a child of the family and that it is necessary for the protection of the applicant or a child of the family that an order should be made under this subsection, the court may make one or both of the following orders, that is to say—

(*a*) an order that the respondent shall not use, or threaten to use, violence against the person of the applicant;

(*b*) an order that the respondent shall not use, or threaten to use, violence against the person of a child of the family.

(*3*) Where on an application for an order under this section the court is satisfied—

(*a*) that the respondent has used violence against the person of the applicant or a child of the family, or

(*b*) that the respondent has threatened to use violence against the person of the applicant or a child of the family and has used violence against some other person, or

(*c*) that the respondent has in contravention of an order made under subsection (*2*) above threatened to use violence against the person of the applicant or a child of the family,

and that the applicant or a child of the family is in danger of being physically injured by the respondent (or would be in such danger if the applicant or child were to enter the matrimonial home) the court may make one or both of the following orders, that is to say—

(*i*) an order requiring the respondent to leave the matrimonial home;

(*ii*) an order prohibiting the respondent from entering the matrimonial home.

(*4*) Where the court makes an order under subsection (*3*) above, the court may, if it thinks fit, make a further order requiring the respondent to permit the applicant to enter and remain in the matrimonial home.

(*5*) Where on an application for an order under this section the court considers that it is essential that the application should be heard without delay, the court may hear the application notwithstanding—

(*a*) that the court does not include both a man and a woman, (*b*)   *that any member of the court is not a member of a domestic court panel [family panel], or*

    (*c*)   *that the proceedings on the application are not separated from the hearing and determination of proceedings which are not domestic proceedings [family proceedings].*

Note. Words in square brackets substituted for words 'domestic court panel' and 'domestic proceedings' by Children Act 1989, s 92(1), (11), Sch 11, Part II, para 6, as from 14 October 1991.

    (*6*) *Where on an application for an order under this section the court is satisfied that there is imminent danger of physical injury to the applicant or a child of the family, the court may make an order under subsection (2) above notwithstanding—*

    (*a*)   *that the summons has not been served on the respondent or has not been served on the respondent within a reasonable time before the hearing of the application, or*

    (*b*)   *that the summons requires the respondent to appear at some other time or place, [that the respondent has not been given such notice of the proceedings as may be prescribed by rules]*

       and any order made by virtue of this subsection is in this section and in section 17 of this Act referred to as an 'expedited order'

Note. Words in square brackets substituted for paras (a), (b) by Courts and Leagal Services Act 1990, s 125(3), Sch 18, para 21, as from 14 October 1991.

    (*7*) *The power of the court to make, by virtue of subsection (6) above, an expedited order under subsection (2) above may be exercised by a single justice.*

Note. Sub-s (7) repealed by Courts and Legal Services Act 1990, s 125(7), Sch 20, as from 14 October 1991.

    (*8*) *An expedited order shall not take effect until the date on which notice of the making of the order is served on the respondent in such manner as may be prescribed or, if the court specifies a later date as the date on which the order is to take effect, that later date, and an expedited order shall cease to have effect on whichever of the following dates occurs first, that is to say—*

    (*a*)   *the date of the expiration of the period of 28 days beginning with the date of the making of the order; or*

    (*b*)   *the date of the commencement of the hearing, in accordance with the provisions of Part II of the Magistrates' Courts Act 1952 [Part II of the Magistrates' Courts Act 1980], of the application for an order under this section.*

Note. Words in square brackets substituted for words 'Part II of the Magistrates' Courts Act 1952' by Magistrates' Courts Act 1980, s 154, Sch 7, para 159, as from 6 July 1981.

    (*9*) *An order under this section may be made subject to such exceptions or conditions as may be specified in the order and, subject in the case of an expedited order to subsection (8) above, may be made for such terms as may be so specified.*

    (*10*) *The court in making an order under subsection (2)(a) or (b) above may include provision that the respondent shall not incite or assist any other person to use, or threaten to use, violence against the person of the applicant or, as the case may be, the child of the family.*

Note. This section repealed by Family Law Act 1996, s 66(3), Sch 10, as from 1 October 1997 (SI 1997/1892), subject to savings in s 66(2) of, and paras 5, 8, 10 of Sch 9 to, the 1996 Act.

17. Supplementary provisions with respect to orders under s 16—(*1*) *A magistrates' court shall, on an application made by either party to the marriage in question, have power by order to vary or revoke any order made under section 16 of this Act.*

    (*2*) *Rules may be made for the purpose of giving effect to the provision of section 16 of this Act and any such rules may in particular, but without prejudice to the generality of this subsection, make provision for the hearing without delay of any application for an order under subsection (3) of that section.*

Note. Sub-s (2) repealed by Courts and Legal Services Act 1990, s 125(7), Sch 20, as from 14 October 1991.

(*3*) *The expiry by virtue of subsection (8) of section 16 of this Act of an expedited order shall not prejudice the making of a further expedited order under that section.*

(*4*) *Except so far as the exercise by the respondent of a right to occupy the matrimonial home is suspended or restricted by virtue of an order made under subsection (3) of section 16 of this Act an order made under that section shall not affect any estate or interest in the matrimonial home of the respondent or any other person.*

Note. This section repealed by Family Law Act 1996, s 66(3), Sch 10, as from 1 October 1997 (SI 1997/1892), subject to savings in s 66(2) of, and paras 5, 8, 10 of Sch 9 to, the 1996 Act.

18. Powers of arrest for breach of s 16 order—(*1*) *Where a magistrates' court makes an order under section 16 of this Act which provides that the respondent—*

(*a*) *shall not use violence against the person of the applicant, or*

(*b*) *shall not use violence against a child of the family, or*

(*c*) *shall not enter the matrimonial home,*

the court may, if it is satisfied that the respondent has physically injured the applicant or a child of the family and considers that he is likely to do so again, attach a power of arrest to the order.

(*2*) *Where by virtue of subsection (1) above a power of arrest is attached to an order, a constable may arrest without warrant a person whom he has reasonable cause for suspecting of being in breach of any such provision of the order as is mentioned in paragraph (a), (b) or (c) of subsection (1) above by reason of that person's use of violence or, as the case may be, his entry into the matrimonial home.*

(*3*) *Where a power of arrest is attached to an order under subsection (1) above and the respondent is arrested under subsection (2) above—*

(*a*) *he shall be brought before a justice of the peace within a period of 24 hours beginning at the time of his arrest and*

(*b*) *the justice of the peace before whom he is brought may remand him.*

In reckoning for the purposes of this subsection any period of 24 hours, no account shall be taken of Christmas Day, Good Friday or any Sunday.

(*4*) *Where a court has made an order under section 16 of this Act but has not attached to the order a power of arrest under subsection (1) above, then, if at any time the applicant for that order considers that the other party to the marriage in question has disobeyed the order, he may apply for the issue of a warrant for the arrest of that other party to a justice of the peace for the commission area in which either party to the marriage ordinarily resides; but a justice of the peace shall not issue a warrant on such an application unless—*

(*a*) *the application is substantiated on oath, and*

(*b*) *the justice has reasonable grounds for believing that the other party to the marriage has disobeyed that order.*

(*5*) *The magistrates' court before whom any person is brought by virtue of a warrant issued under subsection (4) above may remand him.*

Note. This section repealed by Family Law Act 1996, s 66(3), Sch 10, as from 1 October 1997 (SI 1997/1892), subject to savings in s 66(2) of, and paras 5, 8, 10 of Sch 9 to, the 1996 Act.

Interim orders

19. Interim orders—(1) Where an application is made for an order under section 2, 6 or 7 of this Act—

(a) the magistrates' court at any time before making a final order on, or dismissing, the application or on refusing to make an order on the application by virtue of section 27 of this Act, and

(b) the High Court on ordering the application to be reheard by a magistrates' court (either after the refusal of an order under section 27 of this Act or on an appeal under section 29 of this Act),

shall, subject to the provisions of this Part of this Act, have the *following powers, that is to say*—

(i) power to make an order (in this Part of this Act referred to as an 'interim maintenance order') which requires the respondent to make to the applicant or to any child of the family who is under the age of eighteen, or to the applicant for the benefit of such a child, such periodical payments as the court thinks reasonable;

(*ii*) *power if the court is of the opinion that there are special circumstances which make it desirable that provision should be made for the legal custody of any child of the family who is under the age of eighteen, to make an order (in this Part of this Act referred to as an 'interim custody order') which makes any such provision with respect to the legal custody of, and access to, the child as the court has power to make under section 8(2) of this Act.*

Note. Words in italics repealed by Children Act 1989, s 108(7), Sch 15, as from 14 October 1991. See Family Law Act 1986, s 1(3)(a) (p 3067).

(*2*) *The power of the court under subsection (1)(i) above to make an interim maintenance order shall, if the person with whom the child has his home is a parent of the child but not a party to the marriage, include power to require the respondent to make periodical payments to that parent [that person] for the benefit of the child.*

Note. In relation to applications made before the commencement of Children Act 1975, s 33, sub-s (2) had effect as if the words 'a parent of the child but' and 'that parent' were omitted and the words in square brackets inserted (SI 1980 No 1478, Sch 2, para 5). Children Act 1975, s 33, in force on 1 December 1985. Sub-s (2) repealed by Children Act 1989, s 108(7), Sch 15, as from 14 October 1991.

(3) An interim maintenance order may provide for payments to be made from such date as the court may specify, *not being* [except that, subject to section 5(5) and (6) of this Act, the date shall not be] earlier than the date of the making of the application for an order under section 2, 6 or 7 of this Act; and where such an order made by the High Court on an appeal under section 29 of this Act provides for payments to be made from a date earlier than the date of the making of the order, the interim order may provide that payments made by the respondent under an order made by a magistrates' court shall, to such extent and in such manner as may be provided by the interim order, be treated as having been paid on account of any payment provided for by the interim order.

Note. Words in square brackets substituted for words in italics by Maintenance Orders (Backdating) Order 1993, SI 1993 No 623, art 2, Sch 1, para 6, as from 5 April 1993.

[(3A) Where an application is made for an order under section 6 of this Act by the party to the marriage who has agreed to make the financial provision specified in the application—

(a) subsection (1) shall apply as if the reference in paragraph (i) to the respondent were a reference to the applicant and the references to the applicant were references to the respondent; and

(b) *subsections (2) and* [subsection] (3) shall apply accordingly.]

Note. Sub-s (3A) inserted by Matrimonial and Family Proceedings Act 1984, s 46(1), Sch 1, para 24, as from 1 October 1986. Word in square brackets in sub-s (3A)(b) substituted for words in italics by Children Act 1989, s 108(5), Sch 13, para 37, as from 14 October 1991.

(*4*) *Section 8(6) of this Act shall apply in relation to an interim custody order as it applies in relation to an order made under subsection (2) of that section.*

Note. Sub-s (4) repealed by Children Act 1989, s 108(7), Sch 15, as from 14 October 1991.

(5) Subject to subsection (6) below, an interim order made on an application for an order under section 2, 6 or 7 of this Act shall cease to have effect on whichever of the following dates occurs first, that is to say—

(a) the date, if any, specified for the purpose in the interim order;

(b) the date of the expiration of the period of three months beginning with the date of the making of the interim order;

(c) the date on which a magistrates' court either makes a final order on or dismisses the application.

(6) Where an interim order made under subsection (1) above would, but for

this subsection, cease to have effect by virtue of subsection (5)(a) or (b) above, the magistrates' court which made the order or, in the case of an interim order made by the High Court, the magistrates' court by which the application for an order under section 2, 6 or 7 of this Act is to be reheard, shall have power by order to provide that the interim order shall continue in force for a further period, and any order continued in force under this subsection shall cease to have effect on whichever of the following dates occurs first, that is to say—

(a) the date, if any, specified for the purpose in the order made under this subsection;

(b) the date of the expiration of the period of three months beginning with the date of the making of the order under this subsection or, if more than one order has been made under this subsection with respect to the application, beginning with the date of the making of the first of those orders;

(c) the date on which the court either makes a final order on, or dismisses, the application.

(7) Not more than one interim maintenance order *and one interim custody order* may be made with respect to any application for an order under section 2, 6 or 7 of this Act, but without prejudice to the powers of a court under this section on any further such application.

Note. Words in italics repealed by Children Act 1989, s 108(7), Sch 15, as from 14 October 1991.

(8) No appeal shall lie from the making of or refusal to make, the variation of or refusal to vary, or the revocation of or refusal to revoke, an interim maintenance order.

(9) An interim order made by the High Court under this section on ordering that an application be reheard by a magistrates' court shall, for the purpose of its enforcement and for the purposes of section 20 *or 21* of this Act, be treated as if it were an order of that magistrates' court and not of the High Court.

Note. Words in italics repealed by Children Act 1989, s 108(7), Sch 15, as from 14 October 1991.

Variation, revocation and cessation of orders etc

20. Variation, revival and revocation of orders for periodical payments—(1) Where a magistrates' court has made an order under section 2(1)(a) or (c) of this Act for the making of periodical payments the court shall have power, on an application made under this section, to vary or revoke that order and also to make an order under section 2(1)(b) or (d) of this Act.

(*2*) *Where a magistrates' court has made an order under section 6 of this Act for the making of periodical payments, the court shall have power, on an application made under this section, to vary or revoke that order so far as it relates to the making of periodical payments and, if that order also provided for the payment of a lump sum by one of the parties to the marriage in question, the court shall also have power on such an application to make an order for the payment of a further lump sum by that party either—*

(*a*) *to the other party to the marriage, or*

(*b*) *to a child of the family or to that other party for the benefit of that child.*

[(2) Where a magistrates' court has made an order under section 6 of this Act for the making of periodical payments by a party to a marriage the court shall have power, on an application made under this section, to vary or revoke that order and also to make an order for the payment of a lump sum by that party either—

(a) to the other party to the marriage, or

(b) to a child of the family or to that other party for the benefit of that child.]

Note. Sub-s (2) in square brackets substituted for sub-s (2) in italics by Matrimonial and Family Proceedings Act 1984, s 11, as from 12 October 1984.

(3) Where a magistrates' court has made an order under section 7 of this Act for the making of periodical payments, the court shall have power, on an application made under this section to vary or revoke that order.

(*4*) *Where a magistrates' court has made an order under section 11(2)(a), (3)(a) or (4) of this Act for the making of periodical payments, the court shall have power, on an application made under this section, to vary or revoke that order and also, in the case of an application relating to an order under section 11(2)(a) or (3)(a) of this Act, to make an order under section 11(2)(b) or 11(3)(b) of this Act, as the case may be.*

Note. Sub-s (4) repealed by Children Act 1989, s 108(7), Sch 15, as from 14 October 1991.

(5) Where a magistrates' court has made an interim maintenance order under section 19 of this Act, the court, on an application made under this section, shall have power to vary or revoke that order, except that the court shall not by virtue of this subsection extend the period for which the order is in force.

(6) The power of the court under this section to vary an order for the making of periodical payments shall include power to suspend any provision thereof temporarily and to revive any provision so suspended.

(7) Where the court has power by virtue of this section to make an order for the payment of a lump sum, the amount of the lump sum shall not exceed the maximum amount that may at that time be required to be paid under section 2(3) of this Act, but the court may make an order for the payment of a lump sum not exceeding that amount notwithstanding that the person required to pay the lump sum was required to pay a lump sum by a previous order under this Part of this Act.

(8) Where the court has power by virtue of subsection (2) above to make an order for the payment of a lump sum and the respondent [or the applicant, as the case may be] has agreed to pay a lump sum of an amount exceeding the maximum amount that may at that time be required to be paid under section 2(3) of this Act, the court may, notwithstanding anything in subsection (7) above, make an order for the payment of a lump sum of that amount.

Note. Words in square brackets inserted by Matrimonial and Family Proceedings Act 1984, s 46(1), Sch 1, para 25, as from 1 October 1986.

(9) An order made by virtue of this section which varies an order for the making of periodical payments may, *subject to the provisions of section 11(8) of this Act*, provide that the payments as so varied shall be made from such date as the court may specify, *not being* [except that, subject to subsections (9A) and (9B) below, the date shall not be]earlier than the date of the making of the application under this section.

Note. Words in italics repealed by Children Act 1989, s 108(7), Sch 15, as from 14 October 1991. Words in squrae brackets substituted for words ', not being' in italics by Maintenance Orders (Backdating) Order 1993, SI 1993 No 623, art 2, Sch 1, para 7, as from 5 April 1993.

[(9A) Where—
   (a) there is in force an order ('the order')—
      (i) under section 2(1)(c) of this Act,
      (ii) under section 6(1) of this Act making provision of a kind mentioned in paragraph (c) of section 6(2) of this Act (regardless of whether it makes provision of any other kind mentioned in that paragraph),
      (iii) under section 7(2)(b) of this Act, or
      (iv) which is an interim maintenance order under which the payments are to be made to a child or to the applicant for the benefits of a child;
   (b) the order requires payments specified in it to be made to or for the benefit of more than one child without apportioning those payments between them;
   (c) a *maintenance assessment* [maintenance calculation] ('*the assessment* [the calculation]') is made with respect to one or more, but not all, of the children with respect to whom those payments are to be made; and
   (d) an application is made, before the end of the period of 6 months beginning with the date on which *the assessment* [the calculation] was made, for the variation or revocation of the order,
the court may, in exercise of its powers under this section to vary or revoke the

order, direct that the variation or revocation shall take effect from the date on which *the assessment* [the calculation] took effect or any later date.

(9B) Where—

(a) an order ('the child order') of a kind prescribed for the purposes of section 10(1) of the Child Support Act 1991 is affected by a *maintenance assessment* [maintenance calculation];

(b) on the date on which the child order became so affected there was in force an order ('the spousal order')—

   (i) under section 2(1)(a) of this Act,

   (ii) under section 6(1) of this Act making provision of a kind mentioned in section 6(2)(a) of this Act (regardless of whether it makes provision of any other kind mentioned in that paragraph),

   (iii) under section 7(2)(a) of this Act, or

   (iv) which is an interim maintenance order under which the payments are to be made to the applicant (otherwise than for the benefit of ta child); and

(c) an application is made, before the end of the period of 6 months beginning with the date on which the [maintenance calculation] was made, for the spousal order to be varied or revoked,

the court may, in exercise of its powers under this section to vary or revoke the spousal order, direct that the variation or revocation shall take effect from the date on which the child order became so affected or any later date.

(9C) For the purposes of subsection (9B) above, an order is affected if it ceases to have effect or is modified by or under section 10 of the Child Support Act 1991.]

Note. Sub-ss (9A)–(9C) inserted by Maintenance Orders (Backdating) Order 1993, SI 1993 No 623, art 2, Sch 1, para 8, as from 5 April 1993.

Words 'maintenance calculation in square brackets in each place they occur in sub-ss (9A) and (9B) substituted for words 'maintenance assessment' in italics and words 'the calculation' in square brackets in each place they occur in sub-s (9A) substituted for words 'the assessment' in italics by the Child Support, Pensions and Social Security Act 2000, s 26, Sch 3, para 4(1), (3) as from (in relation to certain cases) 3 March 2003 and (for remaining purposes) as from a day to be appointed.

(10) Where an order made by a magistrates' court under this Part of this Act for the making of periodical payments to or in respect of a child ceases to have effect on the date on which the child attains the age of sixteen or at any time after that date but before or on the date on which he attains the age of eighteen, then, if at any time before he attains the age of twenty-one an application is made by the child for an order under this subsection, the court shall have power by order to revive the first mentioned order from such date as the court may specify, not being earlier than the date of the making of the application.

Note. Sub-s (10) repealed by Family Law Reform Act 1987, s 33(4), Sch 4, as from 1 April 1989, except in relation to the revival of orders made under Part I of this Act before 1 April 1989.

(11) In exercising the powers conferred by this section, the court shall, so far as it appears to the court just to do so, give effect to any agreement which has been reached between the parties in relation to the application and, if there is no such agreement or if the court decides not to give effect to the agreement, the court shall have regard to all the circumstances of the case, *including any change* [first consideration being given to the welfare while a minor of any child of the family who has not attained the age of eighteen, and the circumstances of the case shall include any change] in any of the matters to which the court was required to have regard when making the order to which the application relates or, in the case of an application for the variation or revocation of an order made under section 6 of this Act or on an appeal under section 29 of this Act, to which the court would have been required to have regard if that order had been made under section 2 of this Act.

Note. Words in square brackets substituted for words in italics by Matrimonial and Family Proceedings Act 1984, s 9(3), as from 12 October 1984.

(*12*) *An application under this section for the variation or revocation of an order for periodical payments may be made by the following persons, that is to say—*
  (*a*) *in the case of an order under section 2, 6, 7, 11(2)(a) or 19 of this Act, by either party to the marriage in question,*
  (*b*) *in the case of an order under section 11(3)(a) of this Act for the making of periodical payments where the legal custody of a child of the family is given to a person who is a parent of that child but not a party to the marriage in question, by that parent [that person] or by the party to the marriage by whom the payments are required to be made, and*
  (*c*) *in the case of an order under section 11(4) of this Act for the making of periodical payments where a child of the family is committed to the care of a local authority, by that local authority or by the party to the marriage by whom the payments are required to be made,*
and an application for the variation of an order made under section 2(1)(c), 6, 7 or 11(2), (3) or (4) of this Act for the making of periodical payments to or in respect of a child may, if the child has attained the age of sixteen, be made by the child himself.

[(12) An application under this section may be made—
  (a) where it is for the variation or revocation of an order under section 2, 6, 7 or 19 of this Act for periodical payments, by either party to the marriage in question; and
  (b) where it is for the variation of an order under section 2(1)(c), 6, or 7 of this Act for periodical payments to or in respect of a child, also by the child himself, if he has attained the age of sixteen.]

Note. In original sub-s (12)(b) (in italics) words 'a parent of that child but' and 'that parent' omitted and words in square brackets inserted in relation to an application under sub-s (12)(b) made before the commencement of Children Act 1975, s 33. Children Act 1975, s 33, in force on 1 December 1985. Sub-s (12) in square brackets substituted for sub-s (12) in italics by Children Act 1989, s 108(5), Sch 13, para 38, as from 14 October 1991.

(*13*) *Any reference in this section to an order made under section 2, 6, 7 or 11 of this Act for the making of periodical payments includes a reference to such an order made under the said section 2, 6, 7 or 11 as the case may be, and revived under subsection (10) above.*

Note. Sub-s (13) repealed by Family Law Reform Act 1987, s 33(4), Sch 4, as from 1 April 1989 except in relation to revival of orders made under Part I of this Act before 1 April 1989.

[20ZA. Variation of orders for periodical payments: further provisions—(1) Subject to subsections (7) and (8) below, the power of the court under section 20 of this Act to vary an order for the making of periodical payments shall include power, if the court is satisfied that payment has not been made in accordance with the order, to exercise one of its powers under paragraphs (a) to (d) of section 59(3) of the Magistrates' Courts Act 1980.
  (2) In any case where—
  (a) a magistrates' court has made an order under this Part of this Act for the making of periodical payments, and
  (b) payments under the order are required to be made by any method of payment falling within section 59(6) of the Magistrates' Courts Act 1980 (standing order, etc),
an application may be made under this subsection to the *clerk to the justices for the petty sessions area for which the court is acting* [court] for the order to be varied as mentioned in subsection (3) below.

Note. Word 'court' in square brackets substituted for words in italics by the Courts Act 2003, s 109(1), Sch 8, para 192(1), (2), as from a day to be appointed.

  (3) Subject to subsection (5) below, where an application is made under subsection (2) above, *the clerk* [a justices' clerk], after giving written notice (by post or otherwise) of the application to the respondent and allowing the respondent,

within the period of 14 days beginning with the date of the giving of that notice, an opportunity to make written representations, may vary the order to provide that payments under the order shall be made *to the clerk* [*to the justices' chief executive for the court*] [to the designated officer for the court].

Note. Words 'a justices' clerk' in square brackets substituted for words 'the clerk' in italics by the Courts Act 2003, s 109(1), Sch 8, para 192(1), (3)(a), as from a day to be appointed. Words 'to the justices' chief executive for the court' in square brackets substituted for words 'to the clerk' in italics by the Access to Justice Act 1999, s 90, Sch 13, paras 90, 91, as from 1 April 2001. Words ' to the designated officer for the court' in square brackets substituted for words 'to the justices' chief executive for the court' in italics by the Courts Act 2003, s 109(1), Sch 8, para 192(1), (3)(b), as from a day to be appointed.

(4) The clerk may proceed with an application under subsection (2) above notwithstanding that the respondent has not received written notice of the application.

(5) Where an application has been made under subsection (2) above, the clerk may, if he considers it inappropriate to exercise his power under subsection (3) above, refer the matter to the court which, subject to subsections (7) and (8) below, may vary the order by exercising one of its powers under paragraphs (a) to (d) of section 59(3) of the Magistrates' Courts Act 1980.

(6) Subsection (4) of section 59 of the Magistrates' Courts Act 1980 (power of court to order that account be opened) shall apply for the purposes of subsections (1) and (5) above as it applies for the purposes of that section.

(7) Before varying the order by exercising one of its powers under paragraphs (a) to (d) of section 59(3) of the Magistrates' Courts Act 1980, the court shall have regard to any representations made by the parties to the application.

(8) If the court does not propose to exercise its power *under paragraph (c) or (d)* [under paragraph (c), (cc) or (d)] of subsection (3) of section 59 of the Magistrates' Courts Act 1980, the court shall, unless upon representations expressly made in that behalf by the person to whom payments under the order are required to be made it is satisfied that it is undesirable to do so, exercise its power under paragraph (b) of that subsection.

Note. Words in square brackets substituted for words in italics by Child Support Act 1991 (Consequential Amendments) Order 1994, SI 1994 No 731, art 2, as from 11 April 1994.

(9) Subsection (12) of section 20 of this Act shall have effect for the purposes of applications under subsection (2) above as it has effect for the purposes of applications under that section.

(10) None of the powers of the court, or of *the clerk to the justices* [a justices' clerk], conferred by this section shall be exercisable in relation to an order under this Part of this Act for the making of periodical payments which is not a qualifying maintenance order (within the meaning of section 59 of the Magistrates' Courts Act 1980).]

Note. This section inserted by Maintenance Enforcement Act 1991, s 5, as from 1 April 1992. Words 'a justices' clerk' in square brackets substituted for words in italics by the Courts Act 2003, s 109(1), Sch 8, para 192(1), (4), as from a day to be appointed.

[20A. Revival of orders for periodical payments—(*1*) *Where an order made by a magistrates' court under this Part of this Act for the making of periodical payments to or in respect of a child (other than an interim maintenance order) ceases to have effect on the date on which the child attains the age of 16 or at any time after that date but before or on the date on which he attains the age of 18, the child may apply to the High Court or a county court for an order for the revival of the order of the magistrates' court, and if, on such an application, it appears to the High Court or county court that—*

(*a*) *the child is, will be or (if an order were made under this subsection) would be receiving instruction at an educational establishment or undergoing training for a*

trade, profession or vocation, whether or not he also is, will be or would be in gainful
employment; or

  (*b*) *there are special circumstances which justify the making of an order under this*
subsection,

the court shall have power by order to revive the first mentioned order from such date as the
court may specify, not being earlier than the date of the making of the application.

  (*2*) *Where an order made by a magistrates' court is revived by an order of the High Court*
or a county court under subsection (1) above, then—

  (*a*) *for the purposes of the variation and discharge of the revived order, that order shall be*
treated as an order of the court by which it was revived and may be varied or
discharged by that court on the application of any person by whom or to whom
payments are required to be made under the order, and

  (*b*) *for the purposes of the enforcement of the revived order, that order shall be treated as*
an order of the magistrates' court by which the order was originally made.]

[20A. Revival of orders for periodical payments—(1) Where an order by a
magistrates' court under this Part of this Act for the making of periodical payments
to or in respect of a child (other than an interim maintenance order) ceases to
have effect—

  (a) on the date on which the child attains the age of sixteen, or

  (b) at any time after that date but before or on the date on which he attains the
age of eighteen,

the child may apply to the court which made the order for an order for its revival.

  (2) If on such an application it appears to the court that—

  (a) the child is, will be or (if an order were made under this subsection) would
be receiving instruction at an educational establishment or undergoing
training for a trade, profession or vocation, whether or not while in gainful
employment, or

  (b) there are special circumstances which justify the making of an order under
this subsection,

the court shall have power by order to revive the order from such date as the court
may specify, not being earlier than the date of the making of the application.

  (3) Any order revived under this section may be varied or revoked under section
20 in the same way as it could have been varied or revoked had it continued in being.]

Note. Original s 20A in italics inserted by Family Law Reform Act 1987, s 33(1), Sch 2, para
69, as from 1 April 1989 except in relation to revival of orders made under Part I of this Act
before 1 April 1989. New s 20A substituted for original s 20A in italics by Children Act 1989,
s 108(5), Sch 13, para 39, as from 14 October 1991.

21. Variation and revocation of orders relating to the custody of children—
(*1*) *Where on an application under section 1, 6 or 7 of this Act by a party to a marriage a*
magistrates' court has made an order in respect of a child of the family under section 8, 9 or
10 of this Act, either party to the marriage may apply to the court—

  (*a*) *in the case of an order under section 8 of this Act, for the variation or revocation of*
that order,

  (*b*) *in the case of an order under section 9 of this Act, for the variation or revocation of*
that order, and

  (*c*) *in the case of an order under section 10 of this Act, for the revocation of that order,*

and, on such an application, the court shall have power to make the order for which
application is made and also to make such other order with respect to that child under section
8, 9 or 10 of this Act as it thinks fit.

  (*2*) *Where on an application made by a party to a marriage a magistrates' court has*
made an order under section 2, 6 or 7 of this Act but has not exercised its powers under
section 8, 9 or 10 of this Act with respect to a child of the family, either party to the marriage

may, at any time while an order under section 2, 6 or 7 of this Act is in force, apply to the court for an order under section 8 of this Act and, on such an application, the court shall have power to make such order under section 8, 9 or 10 of this Act with respect to that child as the court thinks fit.

(3) Where a magistrates' court has made an interim custody order under section 19 of this Act, the court shall have power, on an application made under this section by either party to the marriage in question, to vary or revoke that order, except that the court shall not by virtue of this subsection extend the period for which the order is in force.

(4) On an application for an order under subsection (1) or (2) above the court shall not dismiss the application or make the order for which the application is made until it has decided whether to exercise its other powers under subsection (1) or (2) above, and if so, in what manner.

(5) Section 12 of this Act shall apply in relation to the exercise by the court of its powers under this section on an application under subsection (1) or (2) above as it applies in relation to the exercise by the court of its powers under sections 8 to 10 of this Act on an application under section 1, 6 or 7 of this Act.

(6) Any reference in section 11(2), (3) or (8) of this Act to an order made under section 8(2) of this Act includes a reference to an order made under the said section 8(2) by virtue of this section and to an order made under the said section 8(2) which is varied under this section, and any reference in section 11(4) of this Act to an order made under section 10(1) of this Act includes a reference to an order made under the said section 10(1) by virtue of this section, and where by virtue of an order under this section the right to the actual custody of a child is given to the person who made the original application for an order under section 1 or 6 of this Act, the court shall have power to make an order under section 2(1)(c) and (d) of this Act in respect of that child.

(7) An application under this section may be made in the following cases by the following persons, in addition to the parties to the marriage in question, that is to say—

(a) where a child of the family is not a child of both the parties to the marriage, an application under subsection (1), (2) or (3) above may be made by any person who, though not one of the parties to the marriage, is a parent of that child [or has the legal custody of that child];

(b) where by virtue of an order under section 9 of this Act a child of the family is under the supervision of a local authority or a probation officer, an application under subsection (1)(b) above may be made by that local authority or probation officer;

(c) where by virtue of an order under section 10 of this Act a child of the family is in the care of a local authority, an application under subsection (1)(c) above may be made by that local authority.

Note. In relation to an application under this section for the variation or revocation of an order under ss 8, 9, 10 or 19 of this Act made before the commencement of Children Act 1975, s 33, sub-s (7)(a) had effect as if the words 'or has the legal custody of the child' were added. Children Act 1975, s 33, in force 1 December 1985.

This section repealed by Children Act 1989, s 108(7), Sch 15, as from 14 October 1991.

22. Variation of instalments of lump sum. Where in the exercise of its powers under *section 63 of the Magistrates' Courts Act 1952* [section 75 of the Magistrates' Courts Act 1980] a magistrates' court orders that a lump sum required to be paid under this Part of this Act shall be paid by instalments, the court, on an application made by either the person liable to pay or the person entitled to receive that sum, shall have power to vary that order by varying the number of instalments payable, the amount of any instalment payable and the date on which any instalment becomes payable.

Note. Words in square brackets substituted for words in italics by Magistrates' Courts Act 1980, s 154, Sch 7, para 160, as from 6 July 1981.

23. Supplementary provisions with respect to variation and revocation of orders—(*1*) *Provision may be made by rules as to the persons who are to be made respondents on an application for the variation or revocation of an order under section 14(3), 20 or 21 [20] of this Act; and if on an application under section 20 of this Act [that section] there are two or more respondents, the powers of the court under section 55(1) of the Magistrates' Courts Act 1952 [section 64(1) of the Magistrates' Courts Act 1980], shall be deemed to include power, whatever adjudication the court makes on the application, to order any of the parties to pay the whole or part of the costs of all or any of the other parties*

Note. Words in first two pairs of square brackets substituted for words '14(3), 20 or 21' and 'section 20 of this Act' respectively by Children Act 1989, s 108(5), Sch 13, para 40, as from 14 October 1991. Words in third pair of square brackets substituted for words 'section 55(1) of the Magistrates' Courts Act 1952' by Magistrates' Courts Act 1980, s 154, Sch 7, para 161, as from 6 July 1981. Sub-s (1) repealed by Courts and Legal Services Act 1990, s 125(7), Sch 20, as from 14 October 1991.

(2)   The powers of a magistrates' court to revoke, revive or vary an order for the periodical payment of money [and the power of the clerk of a magistrates' court to vary such an order] under *section 53 of the Magistrates' Courts Act 1952* [section 60 of the Magistrates' Courts Act 1980] and [the power of a magistrates' court] to suspend or rescind certain other orders under *section 54(2) of that Act* [section 63(2) of that Act] shall not apply in relation to an order made under this Part of this Act.

Note. Words in first and third pairs of square brackets inserted by Maintenance Enforcement Act 1991, s 11(1), Sch 2, para 2, as from 1 April 1992. Words in second and fourth pairs of square brackets substituted for words in italics by Magistrates' Courts Act 1980, s 154, Sch 7, para 161, as from 6 July 1981.

24. Proceedings by or against a person outside England and Wales for variation or revocation of orders—(*1*) *It is hereby declared that any jurisdiction conferred on a magistrates' court by virtue of section 20 or 21 of this Act is exercisable notwithstanding that the proceedings are brought by or against a person residing outside England and Wales.*

Note. Words 'or 21' repealed by Children Act 1989, s 108(7), Sch 15, as from 14 October 1991.

(*2*) *Subject to subsection (3) below, a magistrates' court may, if it is satisfied that the respondent has been outside the United Kingdom during such period as may be prescribed by rules, proceed on an application made under section 20 or 21 of this Act notwithstanding that the respondent has not been served with the summons; and rules may prescribe any other matters as to which the court is to be satisfied before proceeding in such a case.*

Note. Words 'or 21' repealed by Children Act 1989, s 108(7), Sch 15, as from 14 October 1991.

(*3*) *A magistrates' court shall not exercise its powers under section 20 of this Act so as to increase the amount of any periodical payments required to be made by any person under this Part of this Act unless the order under that section is made at a hearing at which that person appears or the requirements of section 47(3) of the Magistrates' Courts Act 1952* [*section 55(3) of the Magistrates' Courts Act 1980*] *with respect to proof of service of summons or appearance on a previous occasion are satisfied in respect of that person.*

Note. Words in square brackets substituted for words 'section 47(3) of the Magistrates' Courts Act 1952' by Magistrates' Courts Act 1980, s 154, Sch 7, para 162, as from 6 July 1981. Section 24 repealed by Courts and Legal Services Act 1990, s 125(7), Sch 20, as from 14 October 1991.

25. Effect on certain orders of parties living together—(1) Where—
(a) periodical payments are required to be made to one of the parties to a marriage (whether for his own benefit or for the benefit of a child of the family) by an order made under section 2, *6 or 11(2)* [or 6] of this Act or by an interim maintenance order made under section 19 of this Act (otherwise than on an application under section 7 of this Act), *or*

(*b*)   *the right to the actual custody of a child is given to one of the parties to a marriage by an order made under section 8(2) of this Act or by an interim custody order made under section 19 of this Act,*

the order shall be enforceable notwithstanding that the parties to the marriage are living with each other at the date of the making of the order or that, although they are not living with each other at that date, they subsequently resume living with each other; but the order shall cease to have effect if after that date the parties continue to live with each other, or resume living with each other, for a continuous period exceeding six months.

Note. Words in square brackets in sub-s (1)(a) substituted for words in italics, and sub-s (1)(b) and the word 'or' preceding it repealed, by Children Act 1989, s 108(5), (7), Sch 13, para 41(1), Sch 15, as from 14 October 1991.

(2)   Where any of the following orders is made under this Part of this Act, that is to say—

(a)   an order under section 2, *6 or 11(2)* [or 6] of this Act which requires periodical payments to be made to a child of the family, [or]

(b)   an interim maintenance order under section 19 of this Act (otherwise than on an application under section 7 of this Act) which requires periodical payments to be made to a child of the family,

(*c*)   *an order under section 8(2) of this Act which gives legal custody of a child to a person who is a parent of that child but not a party to the marriage in question, or*

(*d*)   *an order under section 9, 10 or 11(3) or (4) of this Act,*

then, unless the court otherwise directs, the order shall continue to have effect and be enforceable notwithstanding that the parties to the marriage in question are living with each other at the date of the making of the order or that, although they are not living with each other at that date, they subsequently resume living with each other.

Note. In relation to an order under s 8(2) of this Act pursuant to an application made before the commencement of Children Act 1975, s 33, sub-s (2)(c) had effect as if the words 'a parent of that child' were omitted. Children Act 1975, s 33, in force 1 December 1985. Words 'or 6' in square brackets in sub-s (2)(a) substituted for words in italics, word 'or' inserted after that paragraph, and sub-s (2)(c), (d) repealed by Children Act 1989, s 108(5), (7), Sch 13, para 41(2), Sch 15, as from 14 October 1991.

(3)   Any order made under section 7 of this Act, and any interim maintenance order made on an application for an order under that section, shall cease to have effect if the parties to the marriage resume living with each other.

(4)   Where an order made under this Part of this Act ceases to have effect by virtue of subsection (1) or (3) above or by virtue of a direction given under subsection (2) above, a magistrates' court may, on an application made by either party to the marriage, make an order declaring that the first mentioned order ceased to have effect from such date as the court may specify.

Reconciliation

26. Reconciliation—(1) Where an application is made for an order under section 2 of this Act the court, before deciding whether to exercise its powers under that section, shall consider whether there is any possibility of reconciliation between the parties to the marriage in question; and if at any stage of the proceedings on that application it appears to the court that there is a reasonable possibility of such a reconciliation the court may adjourn the proceedings for such period as it thinks fit to enable attempts to be made to effect a reconciliation.

(2)   Where the court adjourns any proceedings under subsection (1) above, it may request *a probation officer* [an officer of the Service (within the meaning of the Criminal Justice and Court Services Act 2000)] or any other person to attempt to

effect a reconciliation between the parties to the marriage, and where any such request is made, *the probation officer or that* [that officer or] other person shall report in writing to the court whether the attempt has been successful or not, but shall not include in that report any other information.

Note. Words 'an officer of... 2000)' and 'that officer or' in square brackets substituted for words in italics by the Criminal Justice and Court Services Act 2000, s 74, Sch 7, Pt II, para 57, as from 1 April 2001.

Provisions relating to High Court and county court

27. Refusal of order in case more suitable for High Court. Where on hearing an application for an order under section 2 of this Act a magistrates' court is of the opinion that any of the matters in question between the parties would be more conveniently dealt with by the High Court, the magistrates' court shall refuse to make any order on the application, and no appeal shall lie from the refusal; but if in any proceedings in the High Court relating to or comprising the same subject matter as that application the High Court so orders, the application shall be reheard and determined by a magistrates' court acting *for the same petty sessions* [in the same local justice] area as the first mentioned court.

Note. Words 'in the same local justice' in square brackets substituted for words in italics by the Courts Act 2003, s 109(1), Sch 8 para 193, as from a day to be appointed.

28. Powers of High Court and county court in relation to certain orders under Part I—(1) Where after the making by a magistrates' court of an order under this Part of this Act

[(a) a statement of marital breakdown under section 5 of the Family Law Act 1996 with respect to the marriage has been received by the court but no application has been made under that Act by reference to that statement, or

(b)] proceedings between, and relating to the marriage of, the parties to the proceedings in which that order was made have been commenced in the High Court or a county court,

then, except in the case of an order for the payment of a lump sum, [then, except in the case of an order for the payment of a lump sum, any court to which an application may be made under that Act by reference to that statement or, as the case may be,] the court in which the proceedings or any application made therein are or is pending may, if it thinks fit direct that the order made by a magistrates' court shall cease to have effect on such date as may be specified in the direction.

Note. Words in first pair of square brackets inserted, and words in second pair of square brackets substituted for words in italics by Family Law Act 1996, s 66(1), Sch 8, Part I, para 28, as from a day to be appointed, subject to savings in s 66(2) of, and para 5 of Sch 9 to, the 1996 Act.

(2) Where after the making by a magistrates' court of an order under subsection (3) of section 16 of this Act in relation to a matrimonial home, one of the parties to the marriage in question applies for an order to be made in relation to that matrimonial home under—

(a) section 1(2) of the Matrimonial Homes Act 1967 [*Matrimonial Homes Act 1983*] *(which enables an application to be made for an order relating to rights of occupation under that Act or relating to the exercise by either spouse of a right to occupy a dwelling house), or*

(b) section 4 of the Domestic Violence and Matrimonial Proceedings Act 1976 [*section 9 of the Matrimonial Homes Act 1983*] *(which enables an application to be made for an order relating to the exercise of the right to occupy a dwelling house where both spouses have joint rights),*

the High Court or county court by which that application is heard may, if it thinks fit, direct that the order made under subsection (3) of section 16 of this Act, and any order made under subsection (4) of that section in relation to that matrimonial home, shall cease to have effect on such date as may be specified in the direction.

Note. Words in square brackets substituted for words 'Matrimonial Homes Act 1967' in sub-s (3)(a) and for words 'section 4 of the Domestic Violence and Matrimonial Proceedings Act 1976' in sub-s (3)(b) by Matrimonial Homes Act 1983, s 12, Sch 2, as from 9 August 1983. Sub-s (2) repealed by Family Law Act 1996, s 66(3), Sch 10, as from 1 October 1997 (SI 1997/1892), subject to savings in s 66(2) of, and para 5 of Sch 9 to, the 1996 Act.

(3) Nothing in this section shall be taken as prejudicing the effect of any order made by the High Court or a county court so far as it implicitly supersedes or revokes an order or part of an order made by a magistrates' court.

29. Appeals—(1) Subject to section 27 of this Act, where a magistrates' court makes or refuses to make, varies or refuses to vary, revokes or refuses to revoke an order (other than an interim maintenance order) under this Part of this Act, an appeal shall lie to the High Court.

(2) On an appeal under this section the High Court shall have power to make such orders as may be necessary to give effect to its determination of the appeal, including such incidental or consequential orders as appear to the court to be just, and, in the case of an appeal from a decision of a magistrates' court made on an application for or in respect of an order for the making of periodical payments, the High Court shall have power to order that its determination of the appeal shall have effect from such date as the court thinks fit, not being earlier than the date of the making of the application to the magistrates' court [or, in a case where there was made to the magistrates' court an application for an order under section 2 and an application under section 6 and the term of the periodical payments was or might have been ordered to begin on the date of the making of the application for an order under section 2, the date of the making of that application.]

Note. Words in square brackets added by Matrimonial and Family Proceedings Act 1984, s 46(1), Sch 1, para 26, as from 1 October 1986.

(3) Without prejudice to the generality of subsection (2) above where, on an appeal under this section in respect of an order of a magistrates' court requiring any person to make periodical payments, the High Court reduces the amount of those payments or discharges the order, the High Court shall have power to order the person entitled to payments under the order of the magistrates' court to pay to the person liable to make payments under that order such sum in respect of payments already made in compliance with the order as the court thinks fit and, if any arrears are due under the order of the magistrates' court, the High Court shall have power to remit the payment of those arrears or any part thereof.

(4) Where on an appeal under this section in respect of an interim custody order made by a magistrates' court the High Court varies or revokes that order, the High Court shall have power to vary or revoke any interim maintenance order made in connection with that order by the magistrates' court.

Note. Sub-s (4) repealed by Children Act 1989, s 108(7), Sch 15, as from 14 October 1991.

(5) Any order of the High Court made on an appeal under this section (other than an order directing that an application shall be reheard by a magistrates' court) shall for the purposes of the enforcement of the order and for the purposes of *sections 14(3), 20 and 21* [section 20] of this Act be treated as if it were an order of the magistrates' court from which the appeal was brought and not of the High Court.

Note. Words in square brackets substituted for words in italics by Children Act 1989, s 108(5), Sch 13, para 42, as from 14 October 1991.

Provisions relating to procedure, jurisdiction and enforcement

30. Provisions as to jurisdiction and procedure—(1) A magistrates' court shall, subject to [section 2 of the Family Law Act 1986 and] *section 11 of the Administration of Justice Act 1964* [section 70 of the Magistrates' Courts Act 1980] and any determination of *the committee of magistrates* [*a magistrates' courts committee*] {the Lord Chancellor] thereunder, have jurisdiction to hear an application for an order under this Part of this Act if *at the date of the making of the application either the applicant or the respondent ordinarily resides within the commission area for which the court is appointed* [it acts in, or is authorised by the Lord Chancellor to act for, a local justice area in which either the applicant or the respondent ordinarily resides at the date of the making of the application].

Note. Reference to Family Law Act 1986 inserted by ibid, s 68(1), Sch 1, para 24, as from 4 April 1988, and reference to Magistrates' Courts Act 1980 substituted by ibid, s 154, Sch 7, para 163, as from 6 July 1981. Words 'a magistrates' courts committee' in square brackets substituted for words 'the committee of magistrates' in italics by Police and Magistrates' Courts Act 1994, s 91(1), Sch 8, Part II, para 29, as from 1 April 1995.

Words 'the Lord Chancellor' in square brackets substituted for words ' a magistrates' courts committee' in italics and words 'it acts in, … application' in square brackets substituted for words 'at the date… appointed' in italics by the Courts Act 2003, s 109(1), Sch 8, para 194, as from a day to be appointed.

(*2*) *Any application for an order under this Part of this Act, including an application for the variation or revocation of such an order, shall be made by way of complaint.*

(*3*) *In relation to an application for an order under this Part of this Act (other than an application in relation to which jurisdiction is exercisable by virtue of section 24 of this Act) the jurisdiction conferred by subsection (1) above—*

  (*a*) *shall be exercisable notwithstanding that the respondent resides in Scotland or Northern Ireland if the applicant resides in England and Wales and the parties last ordinarily resided together as man and wife in England and Wales, and*

  (*b*) *is hereby declared to be exercisable where the applicant resides in Scotland or Northern Ireland if the respondent resides in England and Wales.*

(*4*) *Nothing in either subsection (3) above or subsection (1) of section 24 of this Act shall be construed as derogating from any jurisdiction exercisable by any court apart from the provisions of those subsections.*

Note. Sub-ss (2)–(4) repealed by Courts and Legal Services Act 1990, s 125(7), Sch 20, as from 14 October 1991.

(5) It is hereby declared that any jurisdiction conferred on a magistrate's court by this Part of this Act is exercisable notwithstanding that any party to the proceedings is not domiciled in England.

31. Constitution of courts—(1) Where the hearing of an application under section 1 of this Act is adjourned after the court has decided that it is satisfied of any ground mentioned in that section, the court which resumes the hearing of that application may include justices who were not sitting when the hearing began if—

  (a) the parties to the proceedings agree; and

  (b) at least one of the justices composing the court which resumes the hearing was sitting when the hearing of the application began.

(2) Where, by virtue of subsection (1) above, among the justices composing the court which resumes the hearing of an application under section 1 of this Act there are any justices who were not sitting when the hearing of the application began, the court which resumes the hearing shall before making any order on the application make such inquiry into the facts and circumstances of the case as will enable the justices who were not sitting when the hearing began to be fully acquainted with those facts and circumstances

32. Enforcement etc of orders for payment of money—(*1*) *An order for the payment of money made by a magistrates' court under this Part of this Act may be enforced in the same manner as an affiliation order, and the enactments relating to affiliation orders shall apply accordingly with the necessary modifications.*

  [(1) An order for the payment of money made by a magistrates' court under this Part of this Act shall be enforceable as a magistrates' court maintenance order.]

Note. Sub-s (1) in square brackets substituted for sub-s (1) in italics by Family Law Reform Act 1987, s 33(1), Sch 2, para 70, as from 1 April 1989.

(2) Without prejudice to *section 52 of the Magistrates' Courts Act 1952* [section 59 of the Magistrates' Courts Act 1980] (which relates to the power of a magistrates' court to direct periodical payments to be made through *the clerk of a magistrates' court* [*a justices' chief executive*] [the designated officer for a magistrates' court]), a magistrates' court making an order under this Part of this Act for the making of a periodical payment by one person to another may direct that it shall be made to some third party on that other person's behalf instead of directly to that other person; and, for the purposes of any order made under this Part of this Act, *the said section 52* [the said section 59] shall have effect as if, in *subsection (2)* [subsection (7)] thereof, for the words *'the applicant for the order'* ['the person who applied for the maintenance order'] there were substituted the words 'the person to whom the payments under the order fall to be made'.

Note. Words in first and second pairs of square brackets substituted for words in italics by Magistrates' Courts Act 1980, s 154, Sch 7, para 164, as from 6 July 1981. Words in third and fourth pairs of square brackets substituted for words in italics by Maintenance Enforcement Act 1991, s 11(1), Sch 2, para 3, as from 1 April 1992.

Words 'a justices' chief executive' in square brackets substituted for words 'the clerk of a magistrates' court' in italics by the Access to Justice Act 1999, s 90, Sch 12, paras 90, 92, as from 1 April 2001. Words 'the designated officer for a magistrates' court' in square brackets substituted for words 'a justices' chief executive' in italics by the Courts Act 2003, s 109(1), Sch 8, para 195(1), (2), as from a day to be appointed.

(3) Any person for the time being under an obligation to make payments in pursuance of any order for the payment of money made under this Part of this Act shall give notice of any change of address to such person, if any, as may be specified in the order; and any person who without reasonable excuse fails to give such a notice shall be liable on summary conviction to a fine not exceeding *£50* [level 2 on the standard scale].

Note. Words in square brackets substituted for words in italics by virtue of Criminal Justice Act 1982, s 46(1).

(4) A person shall not be entitled to enforce through the High Court or any county court the payment of any arrears due under an order made by virtue of this Part of this Act without the leave of that court if those arrears became due more than twelve months before proceedings to enforce the payment of them are begun.

(5) The court hearing an application for the grant of leave under subsection (4) above may refuse leave, or may grant leave subject to such restrictions and conditions (including conditions as to the allowing of time for payment or the making of payment by instalments) as that court thinks proper, or may remit the payment of such arrears or any part thereof.

(6) An application for the grant of leave under subsection (4) above shall be made in such manner as may be prescribed by *rules* [rules of court].

Note. Words 'rules of court' in square brackets substituted for words 'rules' in italics by the Courts Act 2003, s 109(1), Sch 8, para 195(1), (3), as from a day to be appointed.

33. Enforcement of orders for custody. *Where at a time when any person is entitled to the actual custody of a child, or a local authority is entitled to the care of a child, by virtue of an order made under this Part of this Act another person has the actual custody of the child, a copy of the order may be served on that other person, and thereupon the order may, without prejudice to any other remedy which may be available, be enforced under section 54(3) of the Magistrates' Courts Act 1952* [section 63(3) of the Magistrates' Courts Act 1980] *as if it were an order of a magistrates' court requiring that other person to give up the* *child to the person entitled by virtue of the order to actual custody or, as the case may be, to the local authority.*

Note. Words in square brackets substituted for words 'section 54(3) of the Magistrates' Courts Act 1952' by Magistrates' Courts Act 1980, s 154, Sch 7, para 165. Section repealed by Children Act 1989, s 108(7), Sch 15, as from 14 October 1991. In relation to orders in force before commencement of Children Act 1989, Parts I, II (14 October 1991), see ibid s 108(6), Sch 14, paras 5, 10 (pp 3408, 3490, 3492).

34. Restriction on removal of child from England and Wales—(*1*) *Where a magistrates' court makes*—

    (*a*) *an order under section 8(2) of this Act regarding the legal custody of a child, or*

    (*b*) *an interim custody order under section 19 of this Act in respect of a child,*

the court, on making the order or at any time while the order is in force, may, if an application is made for an order under this section, by order direct that no person shall take the child out of England and Wales [the United Kingdom, or any part of the United Kingdom specified in the order] while the order made under this section is in force, except with the leave of the court.

Note. Words in square brackets substituted for words 'England and Wales' by Family Law Act 1986, s 35(1)(c), as from 4 April 1988.

    (*2*) *A magistrates' court may by order vary or revoke any order made under this section.*

    (*3*) *An application for an order under subsection (1) above, or for the variation or revocation of such an order, may be made by either party to the marriage in question and also, in the case of an order made under section 8(2) or 19 of this Act with respect to a child of the family who is not a child of both the parties to the marriage, by any person who, though not one of the parties to the marriage, is a parent of that child [or has the legal custody of that child].*

Note. In relation to an order under s 8(2) or 19 of this Act pursuant to an application made before the commencement of Children Act 1975, s 33, sub-s (3) had effect as if the words in square brackets were added. Children Act 1975, s 33, in force on 1 December 1985.

    Whole section repealed by Children Act 1989, s 108(7), Sch 15, as from 14 October 1991.

35. Orders for repayment in certain cases of sums paid after cessation of order by reason of remarriage—(1) Where—

    (a) an order made under section 2(1)(a), 6 or 7 of this Act has, by virtue of section 4(2) of this Act, ceased to have effect by reason of the remarriage of the party in whose favour it was made, and

    (b) the person liable to make payments under the order made payments in accordance with it in respect of a period after the date of that remarriage in the mistaken belief that the order was still subsisting,

no proceedings in respect of a cause of action arising out of the circumstances mentioned in paragraphs (a) and (b) above shall be maintainable by the person so liable or his personal representatives against the person so entitled or his personal representatives, but on an application made under this section the court may exercise the powers conferred on it by subsection (2) below.

    (2) The court may order the respondent to an application made under this section to pay to the applicant a sum equal to the amount of the payments made in respect of the period mentioned in subsection (1)(b) above, or if it appears to the court that it would be unjust to make that order, it may either order the respondent to pay to the applicant such lesser sum as it thinks fit or dismiss the application.

    (3) An application under this section may be made by the person liable to make payments under the order made under section 2(1)(a), 6 or 7 of this Act or his personal representatives and may be made against the person entitled to payments under that order or his personal representatives.

(4) An application under this section shall be made to a county court, except that such an application may be made in proceedings in the High Court or a county court for leave to enforce, or the enforcement of, the payment of arrears under an order made under section 2(1)(a), 6 or 7 of this Act; and accordingly references in this section to the court are references to the High Court or a county court, as the circumstances require.

(5) An order under this section for the payment of any sum may provide for the payment of that sum by instalments of such amount as may be specified in the order.

(6) The jurisdiction conferred on a county court by this section shall be exercisable by a county court notwithstanding that by reason of the amount claimed in an application under this section the jurisdiction would not but for this subsection be exercisable by a county court.

(7) *The clerk of a magistrates' court* [*A Justices' chief executive*] [The designated officer for a magistrates' court] to whom any payments under an order made under section 2(1)(c), 6 or 7 of this Act are required to be made, and the collecting officer under an attachment of earnings order made to secure payments under the first mentioned order, shall not be liable—

(a) in the case of *the clerk* [*the justices' chief executive*] [the designated officer], for any act done by him in pursuance of the first mentioned order after the date on which that order ceased to have effect by reason of the remarriage of the person entitled to payments under it, and

(b) in the case of the collecting officer, for any act done by him after that date in accordance with any enactment or rule of court specifying how payments made to him in compliance with the attachment of earnings order are to be dealt with,

if, but only if, the act was one which he would have been under a duty to do had the first mentioned order not ceased to have effect by reason of the remarriage and the act was done before notice in writing of the fact that the person so entitled had remarried was given to him by or on behalf of that person, the person liable to make payments under the first mentioned order or the personal representatives of either of those persons.

Note. Words 'A justices' chief executive' and 'the justices' chief executive' in square brackets substituted for words 'The Clerk of a magistrates' court' and 'the clerk' respectively in italics by the Access to Justice Act 1999, s 90(1), Sch 13, paras 90, 93(1), (2), as from 1 April 2001. Words 'The designated office for a magistrates' court' and 'the designated officer' in square brackets substituted for words in italics by the Courts Act 2003, s 109(1), Sch 8, para 196(1), (2), as from a day to be appointed.

(8) In this section 'collecting officer', in relation to an attachment of earnings order, means the officer of the High Court, *the officer designated by the Lord Chancellor or the clerk of a magistrates' court* [*justices' chief executive*] [or the officer designated by the Lord Chancellor] to whom a person makes payments in compliance with the order.

Note. Words 'justices' chief executive' in square brackets substituted for words ' clerk of a magistrates' court' in italics by the Access to Justice Act 1999, s 90, Sch 13, paras 90, 93, as from 1 April 2001. Words 'or the officer designated by the Lord Chancellor' in square brackets substituted for words ', the officer designated by the Lord Chancellor or the justices' chief executive' in italics by the Courts Act 2003, s 109(1), Sch 8, para 196(1), (3), as from a day to be appointed.

PART II

AMENDMENTS OF THE GUARDIANSHIP OF MINORS ACTS 1971 AND 1973

Amendment of provisions relating to the custody of minors

36.–40.   (*Repealed by Children Act 1989, s 108(7), Sch 15, as from 14 October 1991*).
   41.   (*Repealed by Family Law Reform Act 1987, s 33(4), Sch 4, as from 1 April 1989*).
42.–44.   (*Repealed by Children Act 1989, s 108(7), Sch 15, as from 14 October 1991*).

General provisions

45.–48.   (*Repealed by Children Act 1989, s 108(7), Sch 15, as from 14 October 1991*).

PART III

AMENDMENTS OF OTHER ENACTMENTS RELATING TO DOMESTIC PROCEEDINGS

49.–53.   (*Repealed by Children Act 1989, s 108(7), Sch 15, as from 14 October 1991*).
54.–63.   (*Sections 54, 56, 59 amend Maintenance Orders (Reciprocal Enforcement) Act 1972 as noted to that Act; ss 57, 58 repealed by Maintenance Orders (Reciprocal Enforcement) Act 1992, s 2(2), Sch 3, as from 5 April 1993; ss 55, 60, 61 apply to Scotland only; ss 62, 63 amend Matrimonial Causes Act 1973, ss 4, 27 as noted to that Act; s 63(3) repealed by Family Law Act 1996, s 66(3), Sch 10, as from a day to be appointed, subject to savings in s 66(2) of, and para 5 of Sch 9 to, the 1996 Act*).
64.–71.   (*Repealed by Children Act 1989, s 108(7), Sch 15, as from 14 October 1991*).

Amendments of enactments relating to adoption

72.–74.   (*Ss 72, 73(1), 74(1), (3) repealed by Children Act 1989, s 108(7), Sch 15, as from 14 October 1991; ss 73(2), 74(2) amend Adoption 1976, ss 64, 53(1), respectively (pp 2665, 2655)*.)

PART IV

* * * * *

PART V

SUPPLEMENTARY PROVISIONS

* * * * *

87. Expenses   There shall be defrayed out of moneys provided by Parliament any increase attributable to this Act in the sums payable out of moneys so provided under any other enactment.

88. Interpretation—(1) In this Act—
   '*actual custody*', *in relation to a child, means the actual possession of his person;*
   'child', in relation to one or both of the parties to a marriage, includes *an illegitimate child of that party or, as the case may be, of both parties;* [a child whose father and mother were not married to each other at the time of his birth];
   'child of the family', in relation to the parties to a marriage, means—
      (a) a child of both of those parties; and
      (b) any other child, not being a child who is *being boarded-out with those parties* [placed with those parties as foster parents] by a local authority or voluntary organisation, who has been treated by both of those parties as a child of their family;
   '*commission area' has the same meaning as in section 1 of the Administration of Justice Act 1973* [*the Justices of the Peace Act 1979*] [*the Justices of the Peace Act 1997*];
   '*domestic proceedings*' [family proceedings] has the meaning assigned to it by *section 56 of the Magistrates' Courts Act 1952* [section 65 of the Magistrates' Courts Act 1980];
   'local authority' means the council of a county (other than a metropolitan county), of a metropolitan district or of a London borough, or the Common Council of the City of London;

['magistrates' court maintenance order' has the same meaning as in section 150(1) of the Magistrates' Courts Act 1980;]

['*maintenance assessment* [maintenance calculation]' has the same meaning as it has in the Child Support Act 1991 by virtue of section 54 of that Act as read with any regulations in force under that section.]

'*petty sessions area' means any of the following areas, that is to say, a non-metropolitan county which is not divided into petty sessional divisions, a petty sessional division of a non-metropolitan county, a metropolitan district which is not divided into petty sessional divisions, a petty sessional division of a metropolitan district, a London commission area which is not divided into petty sessional divisions, a petty sessional division of a London commission area and the City of London;*

['*petty sessions area' has the same meaning as in the Justices of the Peace Act 1979.*]

['*petty sessions area' has the same meaning as in the Justices of the Peace Act 1997;*]

'*rules' means rules made under section 15 of the Justices of the Peace Act 1949 [section 144 of the Magistrates' Courts Act 1980].*

Note. Definition 'actual custody' repealed, words in square brackets in definitions 'child' and 'child of the family' substituted for words in italics, and words 'family proceedings' substituted for words 'domestic proceedings', by Children Act 1989, ss 92(1), (11), 108(5), (7), Sch 11, Part II, para 6(a), Sch 13, para 43, Sch 15, as from 14 October 1991. Words in square brackets substituted for words in italics, in the case of the definition 'commission area', by Justices of the Peace Act 1979, s 71, Sch 2, para 31, as from 6 March 1980, and subsequently by Justices of the Peace Act 1997, s 73(2), Sch 5, para 18(a), as from 19 June 1997 and in definitions 'family proceedings' and 'rules', by Magistrates' Courts Act 1980, s 154, Sch 7, para 167, as from 6 July 1981. Definition 'commission area' repealed by the Access to Justice Act 1999, s 106, Sch 15, Pt V(1), as from 27 September 1999. Definition 'magistrates' court maintenance order' inserted by Family Law Reform Act 1987, s 33(1), Sch 2, para 71, as from 1 April 1989. Definition 'maintenance assessment' inserted by Maintenance Orders (Backdating) Order 1993, SI 1993 No 623, art 2, Sch 1, para 9, as from 5 April 1993. Words 'maintenance calculation' in square brackets substituted for words 'maintenance assessment' in italics by the Child Support, Pensions and Social Security Act 2000, s 26, Sch 3, para 4(1), (4), as from 3 March 2003 (in relation to certain cases) and as from a day to be appointed (for remaining purposes). Definition 'petty sessions area' in square brackets substituted for definition in italics by Local Government Act 1985, s 12(11), further substituted by Justices of the Peace Act 1997, s 73(2), Sch 5, para 18(b), as from 19 June 1997. Definition 'petty sessions area' repealed by the Access to Justice Act 1999, s 106, Sch 15, Pt V(1), as from 27 September 1999. Definition 'rules' repealed by the Courts Act 2003, s 109(1), (3), Sch 8, paras 197(1), (2), Sch 10, as from a day to be appointed.

(2) References in this Act to the parties to a marriage living with each other shall be construed as references to their living with each other in the same household.

(3) For the avoidance of doubt it is hereby declared that references in this Act to remarriage include references to a marriage which is by law void or voidable.

(4) Anything authorised or required by this Act to be done by, to or before the magistrates' court by, to or before which any other thing was done, or is to be done, may be done by, to or before any magistrates' court acting *for the same petty sessions* [in the same local justice] area as the court.

Note. Words 'in the same local justice' in square brackets substituted for words in italics by the Courts Act 2003, s 109(1), Sch 8, para 197(1), (3), as from a day to be appointed.

(5) Any reference in this Act to an enactment shall be construed as a reference to that enactment as amended or extended by or under any subsequent enactment, including this Act.

89. Transitional provisions, amendments, repeals and commencement—(1) The transitional provisions contained in Schedule 1 to this Act shall have effect.

(2) Subject to the transitional provisions contained in Schedule 1 to this Act—

(a) the enactments specified in Schedule 2 to this Act shall have effect subject to the amendments specified in that Schedule (being minor amendments and amendments consequential on the preceding provisions of this Act), and

(b) the enactments specified in Schedule 3 to this Act are hereby repealed to the extent specified in the third column of that Schedule.

(3) This Act shall come into force on such date as the Secretary of State may by order made by statutory instrument appoint and different dates may be appointed for, or for different purposes of, different provisions.

(4) Without prejudice to the transitional provisions contained in Schedule 1 to this Act, an order under subsection (3) above may make such further transitional provision as appears to the Secretary of State to be necessary or expedient in connection with the provisions thereby brought into force, including such adaptations of the provisions thereby brought into force or any provision of this Act then in force as appear to him to be necessary or expedient in consequence of the partial operation of this Act or the Children Act 1975.

(5) An order under subsection (3) above may repeal any provision of this Act which has ceased to have effect by reason of the coming into force of the Adoption Act 1976.

(6) The inclusion in this Act of any express transitional provision or amendment shall not be taken as prejudicing the general application of section 38 of the Interpretation Act 1889 with regard to the effect of repeals.

Commencement. The relevant provisions of this Act, except in so far as they have been superseded came into force as follows:
18 July 1978: ss 88(5), 89 except sub-s (2)(a), 90, Sch 1 (SI 1978 No 997);
20 November 1978: ss 87, (89)(2)(a) (SI 1978 No 1489);
1 November 1979: ss 16–18, 28, 29(1), (2), (5), 30, 88(1)–(4) (SI 1979 No 731);
1 February 1981: ss 1–15, 19–27, 29(3), (4), 31–35 (SI 1980 No 1478).

Note. Interpretation Act 1889, s 38 is replaced by Interpretation Act 1978, ss 17(2)(a), 16(1) (p 2736).

90. Short title and extent—(1) This Act may be cited as the Domestic Proceedings and Magistrates' Courts Act 1978.
(2) Except for the following provisions, that is to say—
(a) sections 54, 55, 60, 61, 74(1) and (3), 87, 88(5), 8(2)(a), (3) and (4) and this section, and
(b) paragraphs 1, 12, 13, 14, 17 and 18 of Schedule 2
this Act does not extend to Scotland.
(3) Except for the following provisions, that is to say—
(a) sections 54, 59, 74(5), 88(5), 89(2), (3) and (4) and this section, and
(b) *paragraphs 12, 13, 14, 33 and 34(a)* [paragraphs 12, 13, 14 and 33] of Schedule 2 and Schedule 3,
this Act does not extend to Northern Ireland, and in section 88(5) of this Act any reference to an enactment includes a reference to an enactment contained in an Act of Parliament of Northern Ireland or a Measure of the Northern Ireland Assembly.

Note. Words in square brackets substituted for words in italics by Maintenance Orders (Reciprocal Enforcement) Act 1992, s 2(1), Sch 2, para 1, as from 5 April 1993.

SCHEDULES

SCHEDULE 1   Section 89

TRANSITIONAL PROVISIONS

1. This Act (including the repeals and amendments made by it) shall not have effect in relation to any application made under any enactment repealed or amended by this Act if that application is pending at the time when the provision of this Act which repeals or amends that enactment comes into force.

2. Any order made or other thing done under the Matrimonial Proceedings (Magistrates' Courts) Act 1960 which is in force immediately before the coming into force of Part I of this Act shall not be affected by the repeal by this Act of that

Act, and the provisions of that Act shall after the coming into force of the said Part I apply in relation to such an order, and to an order made under that Act by virtue of paragraph 1 above, subject to the following modifications—

(a) on a complaint for the revocation of the order the court shall not be bound under section 8 of that Act to revoke the order by reason of an act of adultery committed by the person on whose complaint the order was made;

(b) on a complaint for the variation, revival or revocation of the order, the court, in exercising its powers under the said section 8 in relation to a provision of the order requiring the payment of money, shall have regard to any change in any of the matters to which the court would have been required to have regard when making that order if the order had been made on an application under section 2 of this Act;

[(bb) on a complaint after the coming into force of paragraph 21 of Schedule 1 to the Matrimonial and Family Proceedings Act 1984 for the variation, revival or revocation of the order, the court, in exercising its powers under the said section 8 in relation to any provision of the order requiring the payment of money, shall have power to order that payments required to be made for the maintenance of a child of the family shall be made to the child himself.]

Note. Sub-para (bb) inserted by Matrimonial and Family Proceedings Act 1984, s 46(1), Sch 1, para 27(a), as from 12 October 1984.

(c) where the order contains a provision for the legal custody of a child, the court shall have power, on a complaint made by a grandparent of the child, to vary that order under the said section 8 by the addition to the order of a provision requiring access to the child to be given to that grandparent;

(d) where the court, by virtue of paragraph (c) above, varies the order by the addition of a provision requiring access to a child to be given to a grandparent, the court shall have power to vary or revoke that provision on a complaint made—

(i) by that grandparent, or

(ii) by either party to the marriage in question, or

(iii) where the child is not a child of both the parties to the marriage, by any person who though not a party to the marriage is a parent of the child, or

(iv) where under the order a child is for the time being committed to the legal custody of some person other than one of the parents or a party to the marriage, by the person to whose legal custody the child is committed by the order.

3. The amendment by this Act of any enactment shall not affect the operation of that enactment in relation to any order made or having effect as if made under the Matrimonial Proceedings (Magistrates' Courts) Act 1960 (including an order made under that Act by virtue of paragraph 1 above) or in relation to any decision of a magistrates' court made on an application for such order or for the variation, revival or revocation of such an order [but as respects enactments amended by this Act in their application in relation to orders made or decisions on applications for orders or for the variation, revival or revocation of orders made or having effect as if made under other Acts those enactments shall apply as amended by this Act.]

Note. Words in square brackets added by Matrimonial and Family Proceedings Act 1984, s 46(1), Sch 1, para 27(b), as from 12 October 1984.

[**3A.** Any order for the payment of money in force under the Matrimonial Proceedings (Magistrates' Courts) Act 1960 (including any such order made under that Act by virtue of paragraph 1 above) shall be enforceable as a magistrates' court maintenance order.]

Note. Para 3A added by Family Law Reform Act 1987, s 33(1), Sch 2, para 72(a), as from 1 April 1989.

4. Any reference in paragraph 1 above to an application made under an enactment repealed by this Act shall be construed as including a reference to an application which is treated as a complaint under section 1 of the Matrimonial Proceedings (Magistrates' Courts) Act 1960 by virtue of section 27 of the Maintenance Orders (Reciprocal Enforcement) Act 1972 and any reference in *paragraph 2 or 3* [paragraph 2, 3 or 3A] above to an order made under the Matrimonial Proceedings (Magistrates' Courts) Act 1960 shall be construed as including a reference to an order which is made under that Act by virtue of section 28 of the Maintenance Orders (Reciprocal Enforcement) Act 1972.

Note. Words in square brackets substituted for words in italics by Family Law Reform Act 1987, s 33(1), Sch 2, para 72(b), as from 1 April 1989.

5. *A provision contained in section 72 or in any of sections 79 to 82 of this Act shall not apply in relation to proceedings commenced before the coming into force of that provision.*

Note. Words 'or in any of sections 79 to 82' repealed by Magistrates' Courts Act 1980, s 154, Sch 9, as from 6 July 1981. Whole para is spent as a result of the repeal of s 72 of this Act.

6. *The amendment by subsection (1) of section 78 of this Act of section 54(3) of the Magistrates' Courts Act 1952 shall not affect the punishment for disobeying an order of magistrates' court if the default occurred before the date on which the said subsection (1) comes into force.*

7. *The amendment by subsection (3) of section 82 of this Act of section 58(2) of the Magistrates' Courts Act 1952 shall not affect the punishment for an offence under the said section 58 which is committed before the date on which the said subsection (3) comes into force, except that a person shall not be liable to imprisonment in respect of an offence for which proceedings are commenced after that date even if the offence was committed before that date.*

Note. Paras 6, 7 repealed by Magistrates' Courts Act 1980, s 154, Sch 9, as from 6 July 1981.

8. A provision of Schedule 2 to this Act which relates to the punishment by way of fine which may be imposed for any offence shall not affect the punishment which may be imposed for an offence which is committed before the date on which that provision comes into force.

SCHEDULE 2   Section 89

MINOR AND CONSEQUENTIAL AMENDMENTS

(Para 1 applies to Scotland only; para 2 amends Maintenance Orders (Facilities for Enforcement) Act 1920, s 3(4) (p 2037); paras 2, 6, 9 repealed by the Courts Act 2003, s 109(3), Sch 10, as from a day to be appointed; paras 3–5, 8, 20, 24 repealed by Child Care Act 1980, s 89(3), Sch 6; paras 6, 7 amend National Assistance Act 1948, ss 43(4), 44(2) (not printed in this work); para 9 amends Marriage Act 1949, s 3(5) (p 2110); para 10 amends Justices of the Peace Act 1949, s 13(4) (repealed); para 11 amends Maintenance Orders Act 1950, s 3(2); paras 12–14 amend ss 15(1)(a), 16(2)(a), 22(1) of the 1950 Act, (pp 2146, 2147, 2157); paras 15, 21 repealed by Magistrates' Courts Act 1980, s 154, Sch 9; para 16 amends Affiliation Proceedings Act 1957, s 9(2) (p 2195); paras 17, 18 amend Adoption Act 1958, ss 32(2), 34A(3) (repealed); para 19 amends County Courts Act 1959, s 109(2) (repealed); paras 22, 23, 27, 29, 31, 36, 41–43, 46–48, 50, 52 repealed by Children Act 1989, s 108(7), Sch 15, as from 14 October 1991; para 25 repealed by Supreme Court Act 1981, s 152(4), Sch 7; para 26 amends Administration of Justice Act 1970, Sch 8, para 3 (p 2354); para 28 amends Matrimonial Proceedings and Property Act 1970, s 30(2) (p 2360); paras 30, 44 repealed by Family Law Reform Act 1987, s 33(4), Sch 4, as from 1 April 1989; para 32 amends Attachment of Earnings Act 1971, Sch 1, para 4 (p 2412); paras 33, 37 amend Maintenance Orders (Reciprocal Enforcement) Act 1972, ss 8(3), 41, 42(1) (pp 2433, 2482, 2484); paras 34, 35 repealed by Maintenance Orders (Reciprocal Enforcement) Act 1992, s 2(2), Sch 3, as from 5 April 1993; para 38 amends Matrimonial Causes Act 1973, s 4, repealed by Family Law Act 1996, s 66(3), Sch 10, as

from a day to be appointed, subject to savings in s 66(2) of, and para 5 of Sch 9 to, the 1996 Act; paras 39, 40 amend Matrimonial Causes Act 1973, ss 47(2)(e), 50(2)(b), (pp 2556, 2558); para 45 repealed by Legal Aid Act 1988, s 45(2), (3), Sch 6, as from 1 April 1989; para 49 repealed by Matrimonial and Family Proceedings Act 1984, s 46(3), Sch 3, and Children Act 1989, s 108(7), Sch 15, as from 14 October 1991; para 51 amends Adoption Act 1976, s 63(4) (p 2665); para 53 amends Domestic Violence and Matrimonial Proceedings Act 1976, s 2(4) (p 2683), repealed by Family Law Act 1996, s 66(3), Sch 10, as from 1 October 1997 (SI 1997/1892), subject to savings in s 66(2) of, and para 5 of Sch 9 to, the 1996 Act; para 54 amends Supplementary Benefits Act 1976, s 19(2) (not printed in this work).)

SCHEDULE 3 Section 89

ENACTMENTS REPEALED

Chapter	Short Title	Extent of Repeal
1948 c 29	The National Assistance Act 1948	In section 43, subsection (7).
1950 c 37	The Maintenance Orders Act 1950	In section 2, subsection (3).
1952 c 55	The Magistrates' Courts Act 1952	In section 57, subsection (4). Section 59. In section 60, in subsection (1) the word 'periodical' and the words 'or in any proceedings in any matter of bastardy' and in subsection (2)(a) the words from 'which shall be read aloud' to 'at the hearing'. In section 61, the words 'or in proceedings in any matter of bastardy.' Section 62. In section 121, subsection (2).
1957 c 55	The Affiliation Proceedings Act 1957	In section 7, subsections (1) to (3).
1960 c 48	The Matrimonial Proceedings (Magistrates' Courts Act 1960	The whole Act.
1961 c 39	The Criminal Justice Act 1961	In Schedule 4, the entry relating to section 54 of the Magistrates' Courts Act 1952.
1964 c 42	The Administration of Justice Act 1964	In section 2, subsection (3A). In Schedule 3, paragraph 27.
1965 c 72	The Matrimonial Causes Act 1965	Section 42.
1967 c 80	The Criminal Justice Act 1967	In Schedule 3, the entry relating to the Matrimonial Proceedings (Magistrates' Courts) Act 1960.

Chapter	Short Title	Extent of Repeal
1968 c 36	The Maintenance Orders Act 1968	In the Schedule, the entry relating to the Matrimonial Proceedings (Magistrates' Courts) Act 1960.
1969 c 46	The Family Law Reform Act 1969	In section 5, subsection (2).
1969 c 22 (NI)	The Adoption (Hague Convention) Act (Northern Ireland) 1969	In section 7(2) the words 'in respect of a foreign convention adoption'.
1970 c 42	The Local Authority Social Services Act 1970	In Schedule 1, the entry relating to the Matrimonial Proceedings (Magistrates' Courts) Act 1960.
1970 c 45	The Matrimonial Proceedings and Property Act 1970	In section 30, subsection (1). Sections 31 to 33.
1971 c 3	The Guardianship of Minors Act 1971	In section 9, subsection (3). In section 14, subsection (4).
1971 c 38	The Misuse of Drugs Act 1971	Section 34.
1972 c 18	The Maintenance Orders (Reciprocal Enforcement) Act 1972	In section 17, subsections (1) to (3). In section 27, subsection (3).
1972 c 49	The Affiliation Proceeedings (Amendment) Act 1972	In the Schedule, paragraph 1.
1972 c 70	The Local Government Act 1972	In section 3, subsections (1) and (2). In Schedule 23, paragraph 10.
1973 c 18	The Matrimonial Causes Act 1973	In section 27, subsection (8).
1973 c 29	The Guardianship Act 1973	In section 2, in subsection (5) the words from 'but an interim order' to the end of the subsection. In section 3, in subsection (2) the words from 'and where a supervision order' to the end of the subsection. Section 8. In Schedule 2, paragraph 1(2).
1974 c 4	The Legal Aid Act 1974	In Schedule 1, paragraph 3(a).
1975 c 72	The Children Act 1975	In section 17(1) the words 'under the age of 16'. In section 21, subsection (3). Section 91. In Schedule 3, paragraphs 12 and 26.
1976 c 36	The Adoption Act 1976	In section 26(1) the words 'under the age of 16 years'. In section 64, paragraph (c). In Schedule 1, in paragraph 6 the words 'other than a

Chapter	Short Title	Extent of Repeal
1976 c 71	The Supplementary Benefits Act 1976	Convention adoption order'. In Schedule 3, paragraph 4. In section 18(7) the words from 'and any proceedings for such an order' to the end of the subsection. In Schedule 7, the entry relating to section 43(7) of the National Assistance Act 1948.

Note. All previously unimplemented repeals in force on 1 February 1981 (SI 1980 No 1478). For earlier orders bringing repeals into force, see SI 1978 No 997, 1978 No 1489, SI 1979 No 731.

OATHS ACT 1978

(1978 c 19)

An Act to consolidate the Oaths Act 1838 and the Oaths Acts 1888 to 1977, and to repeal, as obsolete, section 13 of the Circuit Courts (Scotland) Act 1828.

[30 June 1978]

PART I

ENGLAND, WALES AND NORTHERN IRELAND

1. Manner of administration of oaths—(1) Any oath may be administered and taken in England, Wales or Northern Ireland in the following form and manner:—

The person taking the oath shall hold the New Testament, or, in the case of a Jew, the Old Testament, in his uplifted hand, and shall say or repeat after the officer administering the oath the words 'I swear by Almighty God that . . .', followed by the words of the oath prescribed by law.

(2) The officer shall (unless the person about to take the oath voluntarily objects thereto, or is physically incapable of so taking the oath) administer the oath in the form and manner aforesaid without question.

(3) In the case of a person who is neither a Christian nor a Jew, the oath shall be administered in any lawful manner.

(4) In this section 'officer' means any person duly authorised to administer oaths.

2. Consequential amendments. *In the following provisions, namely—*

(a) section 28(1) of the Children and Young Persons Act 1963; and

(b) section 56(1) of the Children and Young Persons Act (Northern Ireland) 1968

(each of which prescribes the form of oath for use in juvenile courts and by children and young persons in other courts) for the words 'section 2 of the Oaths Act 1909' there shall be substituted the words 'section 1 of the Oaths Act 1978'.

Note. This section repealed by SI 1998/1504, art 65(2), Sch 6.

PART II

UNITED KINGDOM

Oaths

3. Swearing with uplifted hand. If any person to whom an oath is administered desires to swear with uplifted hand, in the form and manner in which an oath is usually administered in Scotland, he shall be permitted so to do, and the oath shall be administered to him in such form and manner without further question.

4. Validity of oaths—(1) In any case in which an oath may lawfully be and has been administered to any person, if it has been administered in a form and manner other than that prescribed by law, he is bound by it if it has been administered in such form and with such ceremonies as he may have declared to be binding.

(2) Where an oath has been duly administered and taken, the fact that the person to whom it was administered had, at the time of taking it, no religious belief, shall not for any purpose affect the validity of the oath.

Solemn affirmations

5. Making of solemn affirmations—(1) Any person who objects to being sworn shall be permitted to make his solemn affirmation instead of taking an oath.

(2) Subsection (1) above shall apply in relation to a person to whom it is not reasonably practicable without inconvenience or delay to administer an oath in the manner appropriate to his religious belief as it applies in relation to a person objecting to be sworn.

(3) A person who may be permitted under subsection (2) above to make his solemn affirmation may also be required to do so.

(4) A solemn affirmation shall be of the same force and effect as an oath.

6. Form of affirmation—(1) Subject to subsection (2) below, every affirmation shall be as follows:—

'I,   do solemnly, sincerely and truly declare and affirm.'
and then proceed with the words of the oath prescribed by law, omitting any words of imprecation or calling to witness.

(2) Every affirmation in writing shall commence:—

'I,   of   , do solemnly and sincerely affirm,'
and the form in lieu of jurat shall be 'Affirmed at   this   day of 19 , Before me.'

Supplementary

7. Repeals and savings—(1) The enactments specified in Part I of the Schedule to this Act (consequential repeals) and Part II of that Schedule (enactment obsolete since the Oaths Act 1888) are hereby repealed to the extent specified in the third column of that Schedule.

(2) In so far as anything done under an enactment repealed by this Act could have been done under a corresponding provision of this Act, it shall not be invalidated by the repeal but shall have effect as if done under that provision.

(3) Where any instrument or document refers, either expressly or by implication, to an enactment repealed by this Act, the reference shall, except where the context otherwise requires, be construed as, or as including, a reference to the corresponding provision of this Act.

(4) The court-martial enactments (which make provision in relation to the use of affirmations at courts-martial corresponding to that made by subsection (2) of section 1 of the Oaths Act 1961) shall not be affected by the repeal of subsection (3) of that section (by virtue of which each of them was inserted in the section in which it appears).

(5) In this Act 'the court-martial enactments' means—

section 102(2) of the Army Act 1955;]
section 102(2) of the Air Force Act 1955; and]
section 60(6) of the Naval Discipline Act 1957.

(6) Nothing in this Act shall be taken as prejudicing the operation of section 38 of the Interpretation Act 1889 (which relates to the effect of repeals).

Note. Interpretation Act 1889, s 38, replaced by Interpretation Act 1978, ss 16, 17 (p 2688).

8. Short title, extent and commencement—(1) This Act may be cited as the Oaths Act 1978.

(2) Part I of this Act does not extend to Scotland.

(3) It is hereby declared that this Act extends to Northern Ireland.

(4) In their application to each of the court-martial enactments subsections (4) and (5) of section 7 above extend to any territory to which that enactment extends.

(5) This Act shall come into force on the expiration of the period of one month from the date on which it is passed.

SCHEDULE   Section 7

REPEALS

PART I

CONSEQUENTIAL REPEALS

Chapter	Short Title	Extent of Repeal
1 & 2 Vict c 105	Oaths Act 1838	The whole Act.
51 & 52 Vict c 46	Oaths Act 1888	The whole Act.
9 Edw 7 c 39	Oaths Act 1909	The whole Act.
9 & 10 Eliz 2 c 21	Oaths Act 1961	The whole Act.
1977 c 38	Administration of Justice Act 1977	Section 8. Section 32(2)

PART II

[*Applies to Scotland.*]

INTERPRETATION ACT 1978

(1978 c 30)

An Act to consolidate the Interpretation Act 1889 and certain other enactments relating to the construction and operation of Acts of Parliament and other instruments, with amendments to give effect to recommendations of the Law Commission and the Scottish Law Commission.   [20 July 1978]

General provisions as to enactment and operation

*   *   *   *   *

4. Time of commencement. An Act or provision of an Act comes into force—
  (a) where provision is made for it to come into force on a particular day, at the beginning of that day;
  (b) where no provision is made for its coming into force, at the beginning of the day on which the Act receives the Royal Assent.

Interpretation and construction

5. Definitions. In any Act, unless the contrary intention appears, words and expressions listed in Schedule 1 to this Act are to be construed according to that Schedule.

6. Gender and number. In any Act, unless the contrary intention appears—
(a) words importing the masculine gender include the feminine;
(b) words importing the feminine gender include the masculine;
(c) words in the singular include the plural and words in the plural include the singular.

7. References to service by post. Where an Act authorises or requires any document to be served by post (whether the expression 'serve' or the expression 'give' or 'send' or any other expression is used) then, unless the contrary intention appears, the service is deemed to be effected by properly addressing, prepaying and posting a letter containing the document and, unless the contrary is proved, to have been effected at the time at which the letter would be delivered in the ordinary course of post.

*   *   *   *   *

9. References to time of day. Subject to section 3 of the Summer Time Act 1972 (construction of references to points of time during the period of summer time), whenever an expression of time occurs in an Act, the time referred to shall, unless it is otherwise specifically stated, be held to be Greenwich mean time.

*   *   *   *   *

11. Construction of subordinate legislation. Where an Act confers power to make subordinate legislation, expressions used in that legislation have, unless the contrary intention appears, the meaning which they bear in the Act.

*   *   *   *   *

Repealing enactments

15. Repeal of repeal. Where an Act repeals a repealing enactment, the repeal does not revive any enactment previously repealed unless words are added reviving it.

16. General savings—(1) Without prejudice to section 15, where an Act repeals an enactment, the repeal does not, unless the contrary intention appears—
(a) revive anything not in force or existing at the time at which the repeal takes effect;
(b) affect the previous operation of the enactment repealed or anything duly done or suffered under that enactment;
(c) affect any right, privilege, obligation or liability acquired, accrued or incurred under that enactment;
(d) affect any penalty, forfeiture or punishment incurred in respect of any offence committed against that enactment;
(e) affect any investigation, legal proceeding or remedy in respect of any such right, privilege, obligation, liability, penalty, forfeiture or punishment;
and any such investigation, legal proceeding or remedy may be instituted, continued or enforced, and any such penalty, forfeiture or punishment may be imposed, as if the repealing Act had not been passed.
(2) This section applies to the expiry of a temporary enactment as if it were repealed by an Act.

17. Repeal and re-enactment—(1) Where an Act repeals a previous enactment and substitutes provisions for the enactment repealed, the repealed enactment remains in force until the substituted provisions come into force.
(2) Where an Act repeals and re-enacts, with or without modification, a previous enactment then, unless the contrary intention appears—
(a) any reference in any other enactment to the enactment so repealed shall be construed as a reference for the provision re-enacted;
(b) in so far as any subordinate legislation made or other thing done under the enactment so repealed, or having effect as if so made or done, could have been made or done under the provision re-enacted, it shall have effect as if made or done under that provision.

*   *   *   *   *

Supplementary

21. Interpretation etc—(1) In this Act 'Act' includes a local and personal or private Act; and 'subordinate legislation' means Orders in Council, orders, rules, regulations, schemes, warrants, byelaws and other instruments made or to be made under any Act.

(2) This Act binds the Crown.

22. Application to Acts and Measures—(1) This Act applies to itself, to any Act passed after the commencement of this Act and, to the extent specified in Part I of Schedule 2, to Acts passed before the commencement of this Act.

*   *   *   *   *

23. Application to other instruments—(1) The provisions of this Act, except sections 1 to 3 and 4(b), apply, so far as applicable and unless the contrary intention appears, to subordinate legislation made after the commencement of this Act and, to the extent specified in Part II of Schedule 2, to subordinate legislation made before the commencement of this Act, as they apply to Acts.

(2) In the application of this Act to Acts passed or subordinate legislation made after the commencement of this Act, all references to an enactment include an enactment comprised in subordinate legislation whenever made, and references to the passing or repeal of an enactment are to be construed accordingly.

(3) Sections 9 and 19(1) also apply to deeds and other instruments and documents as they apply to Acts and subordinate legislation; and in the application of section 17(2)(a) to Acts passed or subordinate legislation made after the commencement of this Act, the reference to any other enactment includes any deed or other instrument or document.

(4) Subsections (1) and (2) of this section do not apply to Orders in Council made under section 5 of the Statutory Instruments Act 1946, section 1(3) of the Northern Ireland (Temporary Provisions) Act 1972 or Schedule 1 to the Northern Ireland Act 1974.

*   *   *   *   *

[23A. Acts of the Scottish Parliament etc.—(1) This Act applies in relation to an Act of the Scottish Parliament and an instrument made under such an Act only to the extent provided in this section.

(2) Except as provided in subsection (3) below, sections 15 to 18 apply to—

(a) an Act of the Scottish Parliament as they apply to an Act,

(b) an instrument made under an Act of the Scottish Parliament as they apply to subordinate legislation.

(3) In the application of those sections to an Act and to subordinate legislation—

(a) references to an enactment include an enactment comprised in, or in an instrument made under, an Act of the Scottish Parliament, and

(b) the reference in section 17(2)(b) to subordinate legislation includes an instrument made under an Act of the Scottish Parliament.

(4) In the application of section 20 to an Act and to subordinate legislation, references to an enactment include an enactment comprised in, or in an instrument made under, an Act of the Scottish Parliament.]

Note. This section inserted by the Scotland Act 1998, s 125, Sch 8, para 16(2), as from 1 July 1999 (SI 1998 No 3178).

*   *   *   *   *

25. Repeals and savings—(1) The enactments described in Schedule 3 are repealed to the extent specified in the third column of that Schedule.

(2) Without prejudice to section 17(2)(a), a reference to the Interpretation Act 1889, to any provision of that Act or to any other enactment repealed by this Act, whether occurring in another Act, in subordinate legislation, in Northern Ireland legislation or in any deed or other instrument or document, shall be construed as referring to this Act, or to the corresponding provision of this Act, as it applies to Acts passed at the time of the reference.

(3) The provisions of this Act relating to Acts passed after any particular time do not affect the construction of Acts passed before that time, though continued or amended by Acts passed thereafter.

26. Commencement. This Act shall come into force on 1 January 1979.

27. Short title. This Act may be cited as the Interpretation Act 1978.

SCHEDULES

SCHEDULE 1   Section 5

WORDS AND EXPRESSIONS DEFINED

Note: The years or dates which follow certain entries in this Schedule are relevant for the purposes of paragraph 4 of Schedule 2 (application to existing enactments).

Definitions

*   *   *   *   *

['Act' means an Act of Parliament.]

Note. Definition 'Act' inserted by the Scotland Act 1998, s 125, Sch 8, para 16, as from 1 July 1999.

*   *   *   *   *

'British Islands' means the United Kingdom, the Channel Islands and the Isle of Man. [1889]

*   *   *   *   *

'British subject' and 'Commonwealth citizen' have the same meaning, that is—

(*a*)   *a person who under the British Nationality Act 1948 is a citizen of the United Kingdom and Colonies or who under any enactment for the time being in force in a country mentioned in section 1(3) of that Act is a citizen of that country; and*

(*b*)   *any other person who has the status of a British subject under that Act or any subsequent enactment.*

Note. Definition 'British subject' and 'Commonwealth citizen' repealed by British Nationality Act 1981, s 52(8), Sch 9, as from 1 January 1983.

*   *   *   *   *

['Enactment' does not include an enactment comprised in, or in an instrument made under, an Act of the Scottish Parliament.]

Note. Definition inserted by the Scotland Act 1998, s 125, Sch 8, para 16, as from 1 July 1999.

'England' means, subject to any alteration of boundaries under Part IV of the Local Government Act 1972, the area consisting of the counties established by section 1 of that Act, Greater London and the Isles of Scilly. [1 April 1974]

*   *   *   *   *

'Month' means calendar month. [1850]

'National Debt Commissioners' means the Commissioners for the Reduction of the National Debt.

'Northern Ireland legislation' has the meaning assigned by section 24(5) of this Act. [1 January 1979]

'Oath' and 'affidavit' include affirmation and declaration, and 'swear' includes affirm and declare.

*   *   *   *   *

'Rules of Court' in relation to any court means rules made by the authority having power to make rules or orders regulating the practice and procedure of that court, and in Scotland includes Acts of Adjournal and Acts of Sederunt; and the power of the authority to make rules of court (as above defined) includes power to make such rules for the purpose of any Act which directs or authorises anything to be done by rules of court. [1889]

*   *   *   *   *

[The 'standard scale', with reference to a fine or penalty for an offence triable only summarily,—
(a) in relation to England and Wales, has the meaning given by section 37 of the Criminal Justice Act 1982;
(b) (applies to Scotland);
(c) in relation to Northern Ireland, has the meaning given by Article 5 of the Fines and Penalties (Northern Ireland) Order 1984.]

Note. Definition 'standard scale' inserted by Criminal Justice Act 1988, s 170(1), Sch 15, para 58(a), as from 29 July 1988.

'Statutory declaration' means a declaration made by virtue of the Statutory Declarations Act 1835.

*   *   *   *   *

[*'Transfer for trial'* means the transfer of proceedings against an accused to the Crown Court for trial under section 7 of the Magistrates' Courts Act 1980.]

Note. Definition 'Transfer for trial' inserted by Criminal Justice and Public Order Act 1994, s 44(3), Sch 4, Pt II, para 28(6) repealed by virtue of the Criminal Procedure and Investigations Act 1996, s 80, Sch 5.

*   *   *   *   *

['Trust of land' and 'trustees of land', in relation to England and Wales, have the same meanings as in the Trusts of Land and Appointment of Trustees Act 1996.]

Note. Definitions 'Trust of land' and 'trustees of land' inserted by the Trusts of Land and Appointment of Trustees Act 1996, s 25(1), Sch 3, para 16.

*   *   *   *   *

'United Kingdom' means Great Britain and Northern Ireland. [12 April 1927]
['Wales' means the combined area of the counties which were created by section 20 of the Local Government Act 1972, as originally enacted, but subject to any alteration made under section 73 of that Act (consequential alteration of boundary following alteration of watercourse).]

Note. Definition 'Wales' substituted by the Local Government (Wales) Act 1994, s 1(3), Sch 2, para 9.

*   *   *   *   *

Construction of certain expressions relating to children

In relation to England and Wales the following expressions and references, namely—
(a) the expression 'the parental rights and duties';
(b) the expression 'legal custody' in relation to a child (as defined in the Children Act 1975); and
(c) any reference to the person with whom a child (as so defined) has his home,
are to be construed in accordance with Part IV of that Act. [12 November 1975]

Note. Repealed by Children Act 1989, s 108(7), Sch 15, as from 14 October 1991.

*   *   *   *   *

[*Construction of certain references to relationships*

In relation to England and Wales—
(a) references (however expressed) to any relationship between two persons;
(b) references to a person whose father and mother were or were not married to each other at the time of his birth; and
(c) references cognate with references falling within paragraph (b) above,
shall be construed in accordance with section 1 of the Family Law Reform Act 1987. [4 April 1988].]

Note. Inserted by Family Law Reform Act 1987, s 33(1), Sch 2, para 73, as from 4 April 1988. Section 1 of 1987 Act in force 4 April 1988.

SCHEDULE 2   Sections 22, 23

APPLICATION OF ACT TO EXISTING ENACTMENTS

PART I

ACTS

1. The following provisions of this Act apply to Acts whenever passed—
Section 6(a) and (c) so far as applicable to enactments relating to offences
    punishable on indictment or on summary conviction
Section 9
Section 10
Section 11 so far as it relates to subordinate legislation made after the year 1889
Section 18
Section 19(2).

2. The following apply to Acts passed after the year 1850—
Section 1
Section 2
Section 3
Section 6(a) and (c) so far as not applicable to such Acts by virtue of paragraph 1
Section 15
Section 17(1).

3. The following apply to Acts passed after the year 1889—
Section 4
Section 7
Section 8
Section 12
Section 13
Section 14 so far as it relates to rules, regulations or byelaws
Section 16(1)
Section 17(2)(a)
Section 19(1)
Section 20(1).

4.   (1) Subject to the following provisions of this paragraph—
  (a) paragraphs of Schedule 1 at the end of which a year or date *earlier than the
       commencement of this Act* is specified [or described] apply, so far as applicable, to
       Acts passed on or after the date, or after the year, so specified [or described]; and
  (b) paragraphs of that Schedule at the end of which no year or date is specified
       [or described] apply, so far as applicable, to Acts passed at any time.

Note. Words in italics repealed by Family Law Reform Act 1987, s 33, Sch 2, para 74, Sch 4,
and words in square brackets inserted by ibid, Sch 2, para 74, as from 4 April 1988.

  (2) The definition of 'British Islands', in its application to Acts passed after the
establishment of the Irish Free State but before the commencement of this Act,
includes the Republic of Ireland.

                                    *   *   *   *   *

5. The following definitions shall be treated as included in Schedule 1 for the
purposes specified in this paragraph—
  (a) in any Act passed before 1 April 1974, a reference to England includes
       Berwick upon Tweed and Monmouthshire and, in the case of an Act passed
       before the Welsh Language Act 1967, Wales;

                                    *   *   *   *   *

PART II

SUBORDINATE LEGISLATION

6. Sections 4(a), 9 and 19(1), and so much of Schedule 1 as defines the following
expression, namely—

British subject and Commonwealth citizen;
England;
Local land charges register and appropriate local land charges register;
Police area (and related expressions) in relation to Scotland;
United Kingdom;
Wales,

apply to subordinate legislation made at any time before the commencement of this Act as they apply to Acts passed at that time.

Note. Words in italics repealed by British Nationality Act 1981, s 52(8), Sch 9, as from 1 January 1983.

7. The definition in Schedule 1 of 'county court', in relation to England and Wales, applies to Orders in Council made after the year 1846.

*   *   *   *   *

CAPITAL GAINS TAX ACT 1979*

(1979 c 14)

ARRANGEMENT OF SECTIONS

*Whole Act repealed by Taxation of Chargeable Gains Act 1992, s 290(3), Sch 12. The provisions printed in this work are replaced by provisions of the 1992 Act printed at p 3560A.

An Act to consolidate Part III of the Finance Act 1965 with related provisions in that Act and subsequent Acts. [*22 March 1979*]

PART I

GENERAL

Capital gains tax and corporation tax

1. Taxation of capital gains—(*1*) Tax shall be charged in accordance with this Act in respect of capital gains, that is to say chargeable gains computed in accordance with this Act and accruing to a person on the disposal of assets.

(*2*) In the circumstances prescribed by the provisions of Part XI of the Taxes Act [*Taxes Act 1970 and Part VIII of the Taxes Act 1988*] (*taxation of companies and certain other bodies and associations*) the tax shall be chargeable in accordance with those provisions, and all the provisions of this Act have effect subject to those provisions.

Note. Words in square brackets substituted for words 'Taxes Act' by Income and Corporation Taxes Act 1988, s 844, Sch 29, para 32, as from 6 April 1988.

(*3*) Subject to the said provisions, capital gains tax shall be charged for all years of assessment in accordance with the following provisions of this Act.

Note. Replaces Finance Act 1965, s 19.

Capital gains tax

2. Persons chargeable—(*1*) Subject to any exceptions provided by this Act, a person shall be chargeable to capital gains tax in respect of chargeable gains accruing to him in a *year of assessment during any part of which he is resident in the United Kingdom, or during which he is ordinarily resident in the United Kingdom.*

(*2*) *This section is without prejudice to the provisions of section 12 below (non-resident with UK branch or agency), and of section 38 of the Finance Act 1973 (territorial sea of the United Kingdom).*

Note. Replaces Finance Act 1965, s 20(1). See Income and Corporation Taxes Act 1988, s 761(2) (offshore income gains).

3. Rate of tax. *The rate of capital gains tax shall be 30 per cent.*

Note. Repealed by Finance Act 1988, s 148, Sch 14, Part VII, in relation to disposals made on or after 6 April 1988. As to rates of capital gains tax, see now the Finance Act 1988, ss 98–100 (pp 3241, 3242).

4. Gains chargeable to tax—(*1*) *Capital gains tax shall be charged on the total amount of chargeable gains accruing to the person chargeable in the year of assessment, after deducting—*

(*a*) *any allowable losses accruing to that person in that year of assessment, and*

(*b*) *so far as they have not been allowed as a deduction from chargeable gains accruing in any previous year of assessment, any allowable losses accruing to that person in any previous year of assessment (not earlier than the year 1965–66).*

(*2*) *In the case of a woman who in a year of assessment is a married woman living with her husband any allowable loss which, under subsection (1) above, would be deductible from the chargeable gains accruing in that year of assessment to the one but for an insufficiency of chargeable gains shall, for the purposes of that subsection, be deductible from chargeable gains accruing in that year of assessment to the other:*

Provided that this subsection shall not apply in relation to losses accruing in a year of assessment to either if, before 6 July in the year next following that year of assessment, an application is made by the man or the wife to the inspector in such form and manner as the Board may prescribe.

Note. Sub-s (2) repealed by Finance Act 1988, ss 104(1)(a), (2), 148, Sch 14, Part VIII, with effect for the year 1990–91 and subsequent years of assessment.

5. Exemption for first [£3,000] of gains—(*1*) *An individual shall not be chargeable to capital gains tax in respect of so much of his taxable amount for any year of assessment as does not exceed £3,000 [the exempt amount for the year].]*

[(*1A*) *Subject to subsection (1B) below, the exempt amount for any year of assessment shall be £5,000.*

(*1B*) *If the retail prices index for the month of December preceding the year 1983–84 or any subsequent year of assessment is higher than it was for the previous December, then, unless Parliament otherwise determines, subsection (1A) above shall have effect for that year as if for the amount specified in that subsection as it applied for the previous year (whether by virtue of this subsection or otherwise) there were substituted an amount arrived at by increasing the amount for the previous year by the same percentage as the percentage increase in the retail prices index and, if the result is not a multiple of £100, rounding it up to the nearest amount which is such a multiple.*

(*1C*) *The Treasury shall, before the year 1983–84 and each subsequent year, make an order specifying the amount which by virtue of this section is the exempt amount for that year; and any such order shall be made by statutory instrument.]*

(*2*), (*3*) . . .

Note. For original sub-ss (1)–(3) there were substituted a new section heading and sub-s (1) by Finance Act 1980, s 77(1), (2), (5). The sum mentioned in the section heading is no longer apposite. Sub-ss (1A)–(1C) were inserted by Finance Act 1982, s 80(2), (5), and the words in square brackets in sub-ss (1), (4), (5) were substituted for the words in italics by s 80(1), (5) of that Act. The sum of '£5,000' in square brackets in sub-s (1A) is that substituted for the year 1988–89 by Finance Act 1988, s 108. For the year 1989–90 the capital gains tax basic annual exemption is fixed at £5,000, by Finance Act 1989, s 122 and sub-s (1B) above (indexation) does not apply for the year 1990–91; see Finance Act 1990, s 72. By Finance Act 1990, s 72, the capital gains tax basic annual exemption for 1990–91 is £5,000, ie the same as was fixed for 1989–90 by Finance Act 1989, s 122. In the absence of s 122 of the 1989 Act, the exemption would have been indexed at £5,400 by virtue of Capital Gains Tax (Annual Exempt Amount) Order 1990, SI 1990 No 681. As a result of independent taxation, a husband and wife are now each entitled to the full £5,000 fixed by s 72 of the 1990 Act.

(*4*) *For the purposes of this section an individual's taxable amount for a year of assessment is the amount on which he is chargeable under section 4(1) above for that year but—*
  (*a*) *where the amount of chargeable gains less allowable losses accruing to an individual in any year of assessment does not exceed [£3,000] [the exempt amount for the year], no deduction from that amount shall be made for that year in respect of allowable losses carried forward from a previous year or carried back from a subsequent year in which the individual dies, and*
  (*b*) *where the amount of chargeable gains less allowable losses accruing to an individual in any year of assessment exceeds [£3,000] [the exempt amount for the year], the deduction from that amount for that year in respect of allowable losses carried forward from a previous year or carried back from a subsequent year in which the individual dies shall not be greater than the excess.*
(*5*) *Where in a year of assessment—*
  (*a*) *the amount of chargeable gains accruing to an individual does not exceed [£3,000] [the exempt amount for the year], and*
  (*b*) *the aggregate amount or value of the consideration for all the disposals of assets made by him (other than disposals gains accruing on which are not chargeable gains) does not exceed £5,000 [an amount equal to twice the exempt amount for the year],*
a statement to the effect of paragraphs (a) and (b) above shall, unless the inspector otherwise requires, be sufficient compliance with any notice under section 8 of the Taxes Management Act 1970 requiring the individual to make a return of the chargeable gains accruing to him in that year.
Note. See Note at end of section.

(*6*) *Schedule 1 to this Act shall have effect as respect the application of this section to husbands and wives, personal representatives and trustees.*
Note. This section and Sch 1 replace Finance Act 1978, ss 44(1)–(6), Sch 7.
  Words 'husbands and wives' in sub-s (6) repealed by Finance Act 1988, s 148, Sch 14, Part VIII, with effect for the year 1990–91 and subsequent years of assessment.
  This section has been amended for the year 1980–81 and subsequent years of assessment by Finance Act 1980, s 77(2), (3). For further amendments for the year 1982–83 and subsequent years of assessment, see Finance Act 1982, s 80(1), (2).
  In subsection (5), the sum of £3,000, whenever it occurs, and the sum of £5,000 are replaced by the words in square brackets with effect for the year 1981–82 and subsequent years of assessment by Finance Act 1982, s 80(1)(a), (b). The exempt amount for 1983–84 is £5,600 (SI 1984 No 343); for 1985–86 is £5,900 (SI 1985 No 428); for 1986–87 is £6,300 (SI 1986 No 527); for 1987–88 is £6,600 (SI 1987 No 436); for 1988–89 is £6,900 (SI 1988 No 506); for 1989–90 is £5,000 (Finance Act 1990, s 72); for 1990–91 is £5,400 (SI 1990 No 681).

*   *   *   *   *

12. Non-resident with United Kingdom branch or agency—(*1*) *Subject to any exceptions provided by this Act, a person shall be chargeable to capital gains tax in respect of chargeable gains accruing to him in a year of assessment in which he is not resident and not ordinarily resident in the United Kingdom but is carrying on a trade in the United Kingdom through a branch or agency, and shall be so chargeable on chargeable gains accruing on the disposal—*
  (*a*) *of assets situated in the United Kingdom and used in or for the purposes of the trade at or before the time when the capital gain accrued, or*
  (*b*) *of assets situated in the United Kingdom and used or held for the purposes of the branch or agency at or before that time, or assets acquired for use by or for the purposes of the branch or agency.*
[(*1A*) *In the case of a disposal made on or after 14 March 1989, subsection (1) above only applies—*
  (*a*) *if it is made at a time when the person is carrying on the trade in the United Kingdom through a branch or agency, or*

(*b*) if he ceased to carry on the trade in the United Kingdom through a branch or agency before 14 March 1989.]

Note. Sub-s (1A) inserted for the year 1988–89, by Finance Act 1989, s 128(1), and another sub-s (1A) is inserted for the year 1989–90 and subsequent years of assessment, by s 128(2) of the 1989 Act, as set out below.

[(*1A*) *Subsection (1) above does not apply unless the disposal is made at a time when the person is carrying on the trade in the United Kingdom through a branch or agency.*]

(*2*) *This section shall not apply to a person who, by virtue of Part VIII of the Taxes Act [the Taxes Act 1988] (double taxation agreements), is exempt from income tax chargeable for the year of assessment in respect of the profits or gains of the branch or agency.*

Note. The words in square brackets in sub-s (2) were substituted for words 'the Taxes Act' by Income and Corporation Taxes Act 1988, s 844, Sch 29, para 15(a).

[(*2A*) *In the case of a disposal made on or after 14 March 1989, this section shall apply as if references to a trade included references to a profession or vocation, but not so as to make a person chargeable to capital gains tax by virtue of a profession or vocation which he ceased to carry on in the United Kingdom through a branch or agency before 14 March 1989.*]

Note. Sub-s (2A) inserted for the year 1988–89, by Finance Act 1989, s 126(1), and another sub-s (2A) is inserted, for the year 1989–90 and subsequent years of assessment, by s 126(2) of that Act.

[(*2A*) *This section shall apply as if references to a trade included references to a profession or vocation.*]

(*3*) *In this Act, unless the context otherwise requires, 'branch or agency' means any factorship, agency, receivership, branch or management, but does not include any person within the exemptions in section 82 of the Taxes Management Act 1970 (general agents and brokers).*

Note. Replaces Finance Act 1965, s 20(2). See Income and Corporation Taxes Act 1988, s 761(2), (3) (offshore income gains).

*   *   *   *   *

18. Residence etc and location of assets—(*1*) *In this Act 'resident' and 'ordinarily resident' have the same meanings as in the Income Tax Acts.*

Note. Replaces Finance Act 1965, s 43(1).

(*2*) *Section 207 of the Taxes Act [the Taxes Act 1988] (disputes as to domicile or ordinary residence) shall apply in relation to capital gains tax as it applies for the purposes mentioned in that section.*

Note. Replaces Income and Corporation Taxes Act 1970, Sch 15, para 7. Words in square brackets substituted for words 'the Taxes Act' by Income and Corporation Taxes Act 1988, s 844, Sch 29, para 15(a), as from 6 April 1988.

(*3*) *Subject to section 12(1) above, an individual who is in the United Kingdom for some temporary purpose only and not with any view or intent to establish his residence in the United Kingdom shall be charged to capital gains tax on chargeable gains accruing in any year of assessment if and only if the period (or the sum of the periods) for which he is resident in the United Kingdom in that year of assessment exceeds six months.*

Note. Replaces Finance Act 1965, s 43(2).

(*4*) *For the purposes of this Act—*

(*a*)   *the situation of rights or interests (otherwise than by way of security) in or over immovable property is that of the immovable property.*

(*b*)   *subject to the following provisions of this subsection, the situation of rights or interests (otherwise than by way of security) in or over tangible movable property is that of the tangible movable property,*

(*c*)   *subject to the following provisions of this subsection, a debt, secured or unsecured, is situated in the United Kingdom if and only if the creditor is resident in the United Kingdom,* (*d*)   *shares or securities issued by any municipal or governmental authority, or by any body created by such an authority, are situated in the country of that authority,*

   (*e*)   *subject to paragraph (d) above, registered shares or securities are situated where they are registered and, if registered in more than one register, where the principal register is situated,*

   (*f*)   *a ship or aircraft is situated in the United Kingdom if and only if the owner is then resident in the United Kingdom, and an interest or right in or over a ship or aircraft is situated in the United Kingdom if and only if the person entitled to the interest or right is resident in the United Kingdom,*

   (*g*)   *the situation of good-will as a trade, business or professional asset is at the place where the trade, business or profession is carried on,*

   (*h*)   *patents, trade-marks and designs are situated where they are registered, and if registered in more than one register, where each register is situated, and copyrights, franchises, rights and licences to use any copyright material, patent, trade-mark or design are situated in the United Kingdom if they, or any rights derived from them, are exercisable in the United Kingdom,*

 [(*ha*) *patents, trade marks, service marks and registered designs are situated where they are registered, and if registered in more than one register, where each register is situated, and rights or licences to use a patent, trade mark, service mark or registered design are situated in the United Kingdom if they or any right derived from them are exercisable in the United Kingdom*

 (*hb*) *copyright, design right and franchises, and rights or licences to use any copyright work or design in which design right subsists, are situated in the United Kingdom if they or any right derived from them are exercisable in the United Kingdom,*]

   (*i*)   *a judgment debt is situated where the judgment is recorded.*

 [(*j*)   *a debt which—*

      (*i*)   *is owed by a bank, and*

     (*ii*) *is not in sterling, and*

    (*iii*) *is represented by a sum standing to the credit of an account in the bank of an individual who is not domiciled in the United Kingdom,*

    is situated in the United Kingdom if and only if that individual is resident in the United Kingdom and the branch or other place of business of the bank at which the account is maintained is itself situated in the United Kingdom.]

Note. Sub-s (4)(ha), (hb) substituted for original sub-s (4)(h) by Copyright, Designs and Patents Act 1988, s 303(1), Sch 7, para 26, as from 1 August 1989. Sub-s (4)(j) added by Finance Act 1984, s 69. Replaces Finance Act, s 43(3).

   [(*5*) *A period during which a member of a visiting force to whom section 323(1) of the Taxes Act 1988 applies is in the United Kingdom by reason solely of his being a member of that force shall not be treated for the purposes of capital gains tax either as a period of residence in the United Kingdom or as creating a change in his residence or domicile.*

   This subsection shall be construed as one with subsection (2) of section 323 and subsections (4) to (8) of that section shall apply accordingly.

   (*6*) *An Agent-General who is resident in the United Kingdom shall be entitled to the same immunity from capital gains tax as that to which the head of a mission so resident is entitled under the Diplomatic Privileges Act 1964.*

   (*7*) *Any person having or exercising any employment to which section 320(2) of the Taxes Act 1988 applies (not being a person employed in any trade, business or other undertaking carried on for the purposes of profit) shall be entitled to the same immunity from capital gains tax as that to which a member of the staff of a mission is entitled under the Diplomatic Privileges Act 1964.*

   (*8*) *Subsections (6) and (7) above shall be construed as one with section 320 of the Taxes Act 1988.*]

Note. Sub-ss (5)–(8) added by Income and Corporation Taxes Act 1988, s 844, Sch 29, para 16, as from 6 April 1988.

*   *   *   *   *

PART III

PERSONS AND TRUSTS

Married persons

44. Husband and wife—(*1*) *If, in any year of assessment, and in the case of a woman who in that year of assessment is a married woman living with her husband, the man disposes of an asset to the wife, or the wife disposes of an asset to the man, both shall be treated as if the asset was acquired from the one making the disposal for a consideration of such amount as would secure that on the disposal neither a gain nor a loss would accrue to the one making the disposal.*

(*2*) *This section shall not apply—*

(*a*) *if until the disposal the asset formed part of trading stock of a trade carried on by the one making the disposal, or if the asset is acquired as trading stock for the purposes of a trade carried on by the one acquiring the asset, or*

(*b*) *if the disposal is by way of a donatio mortis causa,*

but this section shall have effect notwithstanding the provisions of section 62 (transactions between connected persons) or section 122 (appropriations to and from stock in trade) below, or of any other provisions of this Act fixing the amount of the consideration deemed to be given on a disposal or acquisition.

Note. Replaces Finance Act 1965, Sch 7, para 20. See also Finance Act 1982, ss 86, 88, Sch 13, Part I, para 3(3) (calculation of indexation allowance to be subtracted from the capital gains accruing to husband or wife on an initial disposal of an asset following a transfer between them); Finance Act 1983, Sch 5, para 16(1) (relief for investment in corporate trades; effect of the relief in the computation of capital gains or losses on disposals between husband and wife); Finance Act 1984, Sch 13, para 10(2)(a) (disposals of qualifying corporate bonds between husband and wife); Finance Act 1985, s 68(7), (7A) (modification of indexation allowance) and Finance Act 1988, Sch 8, para 1(1), (2), (3)(a), Sch 9, para 6. Where there is a disposal between spouses of an asset acquired on or after 6 April 1988, see s 96 of, and Sch 8, para 2 to, the 1988 Act.

45. Tax on married woman's gains—(*1*) *Subject to this section, the amount of capital gains tax on chargeable gains accruing to a married woman in—*

(*a*) *a year of assessment, or*

(*b*) *any part of a year of assessment, being a part beginning with 6 April,*

during which she is a married woman living with her husband shall be assessed and charged on the husband and not otherwise but this subsection shall not affect the amount of capital gains tax chargeable on a man apart from this subsection nor result in the additional amount of capital gains tax charged on a man by virtue of this subsection being different from the amount which would otherwise have remained chargeable on the married woman.

(*2*) *Subsection (1) above shall not apply in relation to a husband and wife in any year of assessment if, before 6 July in the year next following that year of assessment, an application is made by either the husband or wife, and such an application duly made shall have effect not only as respects the year of assessment for which it is made but also for any subsequent year of assessment:*

Provided that the applicant may give, for any subsequent year of assessment, a notice to withdraw that application and where such a notice is given the application shall not have effect with respect to the year for which the notice is given or any subsequent year.

A notice of withdrawal under this proviso shall not be valid unless it is given within the period for making, for the year for which the notice is given, an application similar to that to which the notice relates.

(*3*) *Returns under section 8 or 42(5) of the Taxes Management Act 1970 as respects chargeable gains accruing to a married woman may be required either from her or, if her husband is liable under subsection (1) above, from him.*

(*4*) *Section 40 (collection from wife of tax assessed on husband attributable to her income) and section 41 (right of husband to disclaim liability for tax on deceased wife's income) of the Taxes Act shall apply with any necessary modifications in relation to capital gains tax as they apply in relation to income tax.*

(*5*)　*An application or notice of withdrawal under this section shall be in such form and made in such manner as may be prescribed by the Board.*

Note. Replaces Finance Act 1965, Sch 10, para 3 as amended. See Finance Act 1984, Sch 14, para 1(3) (postponement of tax due from husband on gains of non-resident trustees). This section repealed by Finance Act 1988, ss 104(1), (2), 148, Sch 14, Part VIII, with effect for the year 1990–91 and subsequent years of assessment.

* * * * *

Other cases

* * * * *

62. Transactions between connected persons—(*1*)　*This section shall apply where a person acquires an asset and the person making the disposal is connected with him.*

(*2*)　*Without prejudice to the generality of* [*section 29A(1)*] *above the person acquiring the asset and the person making the disposal shall be treated as parties to a transaction otherwise than by way of a bargain made at arm's length.*

(*3*)　*If on the disposal a loss accrues to the person making the disposal, it shall not be deductible except from a chargeable gain accruing to him on some other disposal of an asset to the person acquiring the asset mentioned in subsection (1) above, being a disposal made at a time when they are connected persons:*

Provided that this subsection shall not apply to a disposal by way of gift in settlement if the gift and the income from it is wholly or primarily applicable for educational, cultural or recreational purposes, and the persons benefiting from the application for those purposes are confined to members of an association of persons for whose benefit the gift was made, not being persons all or most of whom are connected persons.

(*4*)　*Where the asset mentioned in subsection (1) above is an option to enter into a sale or other transaction given by the person making the disposal a loss accruing to the person acquiring the asset shall not be an allowable loss unless it accrues on a disposal of the option at arm's length to a person who is not connected with him.*

(*5*)　*In a case where the asset mentioned in subsection (1) above is subject to any right or restriction enforceable by the person making the disposal, or by a person connected with him, then* ([*where the amount of the consideration for the acquisition is*], *in accordance with subsection (2) above, deemed to be equal to the market value of the asset) that market value shall be—*

　　(*a*)　*what its market value would be if not subject to the right or restriction, minus—*

　　(*b*)　*the market value of the right or restriction or the amount by which its extinction would enhance the value of the asset to its owner, whichever is the less:*

Provided that if the right or restriction is of such a nature that its enforcement would or might effectively destroy or substantially impair the value of the asset without bringing any countervailing advantage either to the person making the disposal or a person connected with him or is an option or other right to acquire the asset or, in the case of incorporeal property, is a right to extinguish the asset in the hands of the person giving the consideration by forfeiture or merger or otherwise, that market value of the asset shall be determined, and the amount of the gain accruing on the disposal shall be computed, as if the right or restriction did not exist.

(*6*)　*Subsection (5) above shall not apply to a right of forfeiture or other right exercisable on breach of a covenant contained in a lease of land or other property, and shall not apply to any right or restriction under a mortgage or other charge.*

Note. Sub-ss (1)–(4) replace Finance Act 1965, Sch 7, para 17(1)–(4); sub-ss (5), (6) replace ibid, para 17(5).

Sub-ss (2), (5) printed as amended, in relation to acquisitions and disposals on or after 10 March 1981, by Finance Act 1981, s 90(3), (4).

63. Connected persons: interpretation—(*1*)　*Any question whether a person is connected with another shall for the purposes of this Act be determined in accordance with the following subsections of this section (any provision that one person is connected with another being taken to mean that they are connected with one another).*

(*2*)　*A person is connected with an individual if that person is the individual's husband or wife, or is a relative, or the husband or wife of a relative, of the individual or of the individual's husband or wife.*

(*3*) *A person, in his capacity as trustee of a settlement, is connected with any individual who in relation to the settlement is a settlor, with any person who is connected with such an individual and with a body corporate which, under section 454 [681] of the Taxes Act [the Taxes Act 1988], is deemed to be connected with that settlement ('settlement' and 'settlor' having for the purposes of this subsection the meanings assigned to them by subsection (3) [4] of the said section 454 [681]).*

Note. Words in square brackets substituted for words '454', 'the Taxes Act', '(3)', '454' by Income and Corporation Taxes Act 1988, s 844, Sch 29, paras 15(a), 32, as from 6 April 1988.

(*4*) *Except in relation to acquisitions or disposals of partnership assets pursuant to bona fide commercial arrangements, a person is connected with any person with whom he is in partnership, and with the husband or wife or a relative of any individual with whom he is in partnership.*

(*5*) *A company is connected with another company—*

(*a*) *if the same person has control of both, or a person has control of one and persons connected with him, or he and persons connected with him, have control of the other, or*

(*b*) *if a group of two or more persons has control of each company, and the groups either consist of the same persons or could be regarded as consisting of the same persons by treating (in one or more cases) a member of either group as replaced by a person with whom he is connected.*

(*6*) *A company is connected with another person, if that person has control of it or if that person and persons connected with him together have control of it.*

(*7*) *Any two or more persons acting together to secure or exercise control of a company shall be treated in relation to that company as connected with one another and with any person acting on the directions of any of them to secure or exercise control of the company.*

(*8*) *In this section 'relative' means brother, sister, ancestor or lineal descendant.*

Note. Replaces Finance Act 1965, Sch 7, para 21(1) to (8). See also s 155.

* * * * *

PART V

LAND

Private residences

101. Relief on disposal of private residence—(*1*) *This section applies to a gain accruing to an individual so far as attributable to the disposal of, or of an interest in—*

(*a*) *a dwelling-house or part of a dwelling-house which is or has at any time in his period of ownership been, his only or main residence, or*

(*b*) *land which he has for his own occupation and enjoyment with that residence as its garden or grounds up to the permitted area.*

(*2*) *In this section 'the permitted area' means, subject to subsections (3) and (4) below, an area (inclusive of the site of the dwelling-house) of one acre.*

(*3*) *In any particular case the permitted area shall be such area, larger than one acre, as the Commissioners concerned may determine if satisfied that, regard being had to the size and character of the dwelling-house, that larger area is required for the reasonable enjoyment of it (or of the part in question) as a residence.*

(*4*) *Where part of the land occupied with a residence is and part is not within subsection (1) above, then (up to the permitted area) that part shall be taken to be within subsection (1) above which, if the remainder were separately occupied, would be the most suitable for occupation and enjoyment with the residence.*

Note. Sub-ss (1)–(4) replace Finance Act 1965, s 29(1).

(*5*) *So far as it is necessary for the purposes of this section to determine which of two or more residences is an individual's main residence for any period—*

(*a*) the individual may conclude that question by notice in writing to the inspector given within two years from the beginning of that period, or given by the end of the year 1966–67, if that is later, but subject to a right to vary that notice by a further notice in writing to the inspector as respects any period beginning not earlier than two years before the giving of the further notice,

(*b*) subject to paragraph (*a*) above, the question shall be concluded by the determination of the inspector, which may be as respects either the whole or specified parts of the period of ownership in question,

and notice of any determination of the inspector under paragraph (*b*) above shall be given to the individual who may appeal to the General Commissioners or the Special Commissioners against that determination within thirty days of service of the notice.

Note. Sub-s 5 replaces Finance Act 1965, s 29(7).

(*6*) In the case of a man and his wife living with him—
(*a*) there can only be one residence or main residence for both, so long as living together, and, where a notice under subsection (5)(*a*) above affects both the husband and the wife, it must be given by both, and
(*b*) any notice under subsection (5)(*b*) above which affects a residence owned by the husband and a residence owned by the wife shall be given to each and either may appeal under that subsection.

Note. Paras (a), (b) replace Finance Act 1965, s 29(8)(a), (c) respectively.

(*7*) In this section, and sections 102 to 105 below, 'the period of ownership' where the individual has had different interests at different times shall be taken to begin from the first acquisition taken into account in arriving at the expenditure which under Chapter II of Part II of this Act is allowable as a deduction in computing under that Chapter the amount of the gain to which this section applies, and in the case of a man and his wife living with him—
(*a*) if one disposes of, or of his or her interest in, the dwelling-house or part of a dwelling-house which is their only or main residence to the other, and in particular if it passes on death to the other as legatee, the other's period of ownership shall begin with the beginning of the period of ownership of the one making the disposal, and
(*b*) if paragraph (*a*) above applies, but the dwelling-house or part of a dwelling-house was not the only or main residence of both throughout the period of ownership of the one making the disposal, account shall be taken of any part of that period during which it was his only or main residence as if it was also that of the other.

Note. Sub-s (7) replaces Finance Act 1965, s 29(8)(b), (bb), s 29(13)(a).

(*8*) If at any time (being a time after 30 July 1978) during an individual's period of ownership of a dwelling-house or part of a dwelling-house he—
(*a*) resides in living accommodation which is for him job-related within the meaning of paragraph 4A of Schedule 1 to the Finance Act 1974 [section 356 of the Taxes Act 1988], and
(*b*) intends in due course to occupy the dwelling-house or part of a dwelling-house as his only or main residence,
this section, and sections 102 to 105 below, shall apply as if the dwelling-house or part of a dwelling-house were at that time occupied by him as a residence.

Note. Sub-s (8) replaces Finance Act 1978, s 50. Words '(being a time after 30 July 1978)' repealed, and words in square brackets substituted for words 'paragraph 4A of Schedule 1 to the Finance Act 1974', by Income and Corporation Taxes Act 1988, s 844, Sch 29, para 21, as from 6 April 1988.

[(*8A*) Section 356(3)(*b*) and (5) of the Taxes Act 1988 shall apply for the purposes of subsection (8) above only in relation to residence on or after 6 April 1983 in living accommodation which is job-related within the meaning of that section.]

Note. Sub-s (8A) inserted by Income and Corporation Taxes Act 1988, s 844, Sch 29, para 32, as from 6 April 1988.

(*9*) *Apportionments of consideration shall be made wherever required by this section or sections 102 to 105 below and, in particular, where a person disposes of a dwelling-house only part of which is his only or main residence.*

Note. Sub-s (9) replaces Finance Act 1965, s 29(12).

See further the Inland Revenue concessions of 22 October 1973, printed in volume 1.

In relation to disposals after 5 April 1980 where a dwelling-house or part of it is or has been let, see Finance Act 1980, s 80(1). See also Finance Act 1984, s 50(10), Sch 11, para 5.

102. Amount of relief—(*1*) *No part of a gain to which section 101 above applies shall be a chargeable gain if the dwelling-house or part of a dwelling-house has been the individual's only or main residence throughout the period of ownership, or throughout the period of ownership except for all or any part of the last twelve* [*twenty-four*] *months of that period.*

(*2*) *Where subsection* (*1*) *above does not apply, a fraction of the gain shall not be a chargeable gain, and that fraction shall be—*

(*a*) *the length of the part or parts of the period of ownership during which the dwelling-house or the part of the dwelling-house was the individual's only or main residence, but inclusive of the last twelve* [*twenty-four*] *months of the period of ownership in any event, divided by*

(*b*) *the length of the period of ownership.*

(*3*) *For the purposes of subsections* (*1*) *and* (*2*) *above—*

(*a*) *a period of absence not exceeding three years* (*or periods of absence which together did not exceed three years*), *and in addition*

(*b*) *any period of absence throughout which the individual worked in an employment or office all the duties of which were performed outside the United Kingdom, and in addition*

(*c*) *any period of absence not exceeding four years* (*or periods of absence which together did not exceed four years*) *throughout which the individual was prevented from residing in the dwelling-house or part of the dwelling-house in consequence of the situation of his place of work or in consequence of any condition imposed by his employer requiring him to reside elsewhere, being a condition reasonably imposed to secure the effective performance by the employee of his duties,*

shall be treated as if in that period of absence the dwelling-house or the part of the dwelling-house was the individual's only or main residence if both before and after the period there was a time when the dwelling-house was the individual's only or main residence.

In this subsection 'period of absence' means a period during which the dwelling-house or part of the dwelling-house was not the individual's only or main residence and throughout which he had no residence or main residence eligible for relief under this section.

(*4*) *In this section 'period of ownership' does not include any period before 6 April 1965* [*31 March 1982*].

Note. Sub-ss (1)–(3) replace Finance Act 1965, s 29(2)–(4). Sub-s (4) replaces ibid, s 29(13)(b).

In relation to disposals after 5 April 1980 in sub-ss (1), (2)(a) 'twenty-four' is substituted for 'twelve': Finance Act 1980, s 80(2), (3).

Words in square brackets in sub-s (4) substituted for words '6 April 1965' by Finance Act 1988, s 96, Sch 8, para 8, in relation to disposals on or after 6 April 1988.

103. Amount of relief: further provisions—(*1*) *If the gain accrues from the disposal of a dwelling-house or part of a dwelling-house part of which is used exclusively for the purposes of a trade or business, or of a profession or vocation, the gain shall be apportioned and section 102 above shall apply in relation to the part of the gain apportioned to the part which is not exclusively used for those purposes.*

(*2*) *If at any time in the period of ownership there is a change in what is occupied as the individual's residence, whether on account of a reconstruction or conversion of a building or for any other reason, or there have been changes as regards the use of part of the dwelling-house for the purpose of a trade or business, or of a profession or vocation, or for any other purpose, the relief given by section 102 above may be adjusted in such manner as the Commissioners concerned may consider to be just and reasonable.*

(*3*) Section 102 above shall not apply in relation to a gain if the acquisition of, or of the interest in, the dwelling-house or the part of a dwelling-house was made wholly or partly for the purpose of realising a gain from the disposal of it, and shall not apply in relation to a gain so far as attributable to any expenditure which was incurred after the beginning of the period of ownership and was incurred wholly or partly for the purpose of realising a gain from the disposal.

Note. Sub-ss (1), (2) replace Finance Act 1965, s 29(5), (6). Sub-s (3) replaces Finance Act 1968, Sch 12, para 2(1).

104. Private residence occupied under terms of settlement. *Sections 101 to 103 above shall also apply in relation to a gain accruing to a trustee on a disposal of settled property being an asset within section 101(1) above where during the period of ownership of the trustee the dwelling-house or part of the dwelling-house mentioned in that subsection has been the only or main residence of a person entitled to occupy it under the terms of the settlement, and in those sections as so applied—*

(*a*) *references to the individual shall be taken as references to the trustee except in relation to the occupation of the dwelling-house or part of the dwelling-house, and*

(b) *the notice which may be given to the inspector under section 101(5)(a) above shall be a joint notice by the trustee and the person entitled to occupy the dwelling-house or part of the dwelling-house.*

Note. Replaces Finance Act 1965, s 29(9).

105. Private residence occupied by dependent relative—(*1*) *This section applies to a gain accruing to an individual so far as attributable to the disposal of, or of an interest in, a dwelling-house or part of a dwelling-house which is, or has at any time in his period of ownership been, the sole residence of a dependent relative of the individual, provided rent-free and without any other consideration.*

(*2*) *If the individual so claims, such relief shall be given in respect of it and its garden or grounds as would be given under sections 101 to 103 above if the dwelling-house (or part of the dwelling-house) had been the individual's only or main residence in the period of residence by the dependent relative, and shall be so given in addition to any relief available under those sections apart from this section.*

(*3*) *Not more than one dwelling-house (or part of a dwelling-house) may qualify for relief as being the residence of a dependent relative of the claimant at any one time nor, in the case of a man and his wife living with him, as being the residence of a dependent relative of the claimant or of the claimant's husband or wife at any one time.*

(*4*) *The inspector, before allowing a claim, may require the claimant to show that the giving of the relief claimed will not under subsection (3) above preclude the giving of relief to the claimant's wife or husband or that a claim to any such relief has been relinquished.*

(*5*) *In this section 'dependent relative' means, in relation to an individual—*

(*a*) *any relative of his or of his wife who is incapacitated by old age or infirmity from maintaining himself, or*

(b) *his or his wife's mother who, whether or not incapacitated, is either widowed, or living apart from her husband, or a single woman in consequence of dissolution or annulment of marriage.*

(*6*) *If the individual mentioned in subsection (5) above is a woman the references in that subsection to the individual's wife shall be construed as references to the individual's husband.*

Note. Replaces Finance Act 1965, s 29(10). By virtue of the Finance Act 1988 s 111(1), this section does not apply to disposals on or after 6 April 1988, but by s 111(2) of that Act, the disapplication does not have effect where, on 5 April 1988 or at any earlier time during the period of ownership of the individual making the disposal, the dwelling-house or part in question was the sole residence (provided rent-free and without any other consideration) of a dependent relative of his. See further s 111(3) of that Act.

＊　　＊　　＊　　＊　　＊

＊　　＊　　＊　　＊　　＊

PROPERTY: FURTHER PROVISIONS

Movable property

128. Chattel exemption—(*1*) *Subject to this section a gain accruing on a disposal of an asset which is tangible movable property shall not be a chargeable gain if the amount or value of the consideration for the disposal does not exceed £2,000 [£3,000] [£6,000].*

(*2*) *Where the amount or value of the consideration for the disposal of an asset which is tangible movable property exceeds £2,000 [£3,000] [£6,000], there shall be excluded from any chargeable gain accruing on the disposal so much of it as exceeds five-thirds of the difference between—*

(*a*) *the amount or value of the consideration, and*

(*b*) *£2,000 [£3,000] [£6,000].*

(*3*) *Subsections (1) and (2) above shall not affect the amount of an allowable loss accruing on the disposal of an asset, but for the purposes of computing under this Act the amount of a loss accruing on the disposal of tangible movable property the consideration for the disposal shall, if less than £2,000 [£3,000] [£6,000], be deemed to be £2,000 [£3,000] [£6,000] and the losses which are allowable losses shall be restricted accordingly.*

(*4*) *If two or more assets which have formed part of a set of articles of any description all owned at one time by one person are disposed of by that person, and—*

(*a*) *to the same person, or*

(*b*) *to persons who are acting in concert or who are connected persons*

whether on the same or different occasions, the two or more transactions shall be treated as a single transaction disposing of a single asset, but with any necessary apportionments of the reductions in chargeable gains, and in allowable losses, under subsection (2) and (3) above.

(*5*) *If the disposal is of a right or interest in or over tangible movable property—*

(*a*) *in the first instance subsections (1), (2) and (3) above shall be applied in relation to the asset as a whole, taking the consideration as including the market value of what remains undisposed of, in addition to the actual consideration,*

(*b*) *where the sum of the actual consideration and that market value exceeds £2,000 [£3,000] [£6,000], the part of any chargeable gain that is excluded from it under subsection (2) above shall be so much of the gain as exceeds five-thirds of the difference between that sum and £2,000 [£3,000] [£6,000] multiplied by the fraction equal to the actual consideration divided by the said sum, and*

(*c*) *where that sum is less than £2,000 [£3,000] [£6,000] any loss shall be restricted under subsection (3) above by deeming the consideration to be the actual consideration plus the fraction of the difference between the said sum and £2,000 [£3,000] [£6,000].*

(*6*) *This section shall not apply—*

(*a*) *in relation to a disposal of commodities of any description by a person dealing on a terminal market or dealing with or through a person ordinarily engaged in dealing on a terminal market, or*

(*b*) *in relation to a disposal of currency of any description.*

Note. Replaces Finance Act 1978, s 45. Figures '£3,000' replace figures '£2,000' in relation to disposals on or after 6 April 1982: see Finance Act 1982, s 81. Figures '£6,000' replace figure '£3,000', as so replaced, by Finance Act 1989, s 123(1)(a), (2), in relation to disposals on or after 6 April 1989.

* * * * *

PART VII

OTHER PROVISIONS

Insurance

* * * * *

143. Life assurance and deferred annuities—(*1*) *This section has effect as respects any policy of assurance or contract for a deferred annuity on the life of any person.*

(*2*) *No chargeable gain shall accrue on the disposal of, or of an interest in, the rights under any such policy of assurance or contract except where the person making the disposal is not the original beneficial owner and acquired the rights or interest for a consideration in money or money's worth.*

(*3*) *Subject to subsection* (*2*) *above, the occasion of—*

(*a*) *the payment of the sum or sums assured by a policy of assurance, or*

(*b*) *the transfer of investments or other assets to the owner of a policy of assurance in accordance with the policy,*

and the occasion of the surrender of a policy of assurance, shall be the occasion of a disposal of the rights under the policy of assurance.

(*4*) *Subject to subsection* (*2*) *above, the occasion of the payment of the first instalment of a deferred annuity, and the occasion of the surrender of the rights under a contract for a deferred annuity, shall be the occasion of a disposal of the rights under the contract for a deferred annuity and the amount of the consideration for the disposal of a contract for a deferred annuity shall be the market value at that time of the right to that and further instalments of the annuity.*

Note. Replaces Finance Act 1965, s 28(1)–(3) and Finance Act 1967, s 35(2).

Superannuation funds, annuities and annual payments

144. Superannuation funds, annuities and annual payments—*No chargeable gain shall accrue to any person on the disposal of a right to, or to any part of—*

(*a*) *any allowance, annuity or capital sum payable out of any superannuation fund, or under any superannuation scheme, established solely or mainly for persons employed in a profession, trade, undertaking or employment, and their dependants,*

(*b*) *an annuity granted otherwise than under a contract for a deferred annuity by a company as part of its business of granting annuities on human life, whether or not including instalments of capital, or an annuity granted or deemed to be granted under the Government Annuities Act 1929, or*

(*c*) *annual payments which are due under a covenant made by any person and which are not secured on any property.*

Note. Replaces Finance Act 1967, Sch 7, para 12.

* * * * *

PART VIII

SUPPLEMENTAL

Valuation

* * * * *

152. Unquoted shares and securities—(*1*) *The provisions of subsection* (*3*) *below shall have effect in any case where, in relation to any asset to which this section applies, there falls to be determined by virtue of section 150(1) above the price which the asset might reasonably be expected to fetch on a sale in the open market.*

(*2*) *The assets to which this section applies are shares and securities which are not quoted on a recognised stock exchange, within the meaning of section 535 [841] of the Taxes Act [the Taxes Act 1988], at the time as at which their market value for the purposes of tax or chargeable gains falls to be determined.*

Note. Words in square brackets substituted for words 'the Taxes Act' by Income and Corporation Taxes Act 1988, s 844, Sch 29, paras 15(a), 32, as from 6 April 1988.

(*3*) *For the purposes of a determination falling within subsection* (*1*) *above, it shall be assumed that, in the open market which is postulated for the purposes of that determination, there is available to any prospective purchaser of the asset in question all the information which a prudent prospective purchaser of the asset might reasonably require if he were proposing to purchase it from a willing vendor by private treaty and at arm's length.*

Note. Replaces Finance Act 1973, s 51(1)–(3).

Other provisions

* * * * *

155. Interpretation.

* * * * *

(*2*) *References in this Act to a married woman living with her husband shall be construed in accordance with section 42(1) (2) [282] of the Taxes Act [the Taxes Act 1988].*

Note. Replaces Finance Act 1965, s 45(3) as amended. Words in square brackets substituted for words '421(1) (2)', 'the Taxes Act' by Income and Corporation Taxes Act 1988, s 844, Sch 29, paras 15(a), 32, as from 6 April 1988.

* * * * *

PART IX

GENERAL

156. Commencement—(*1*) *Except as otherwise provided by this Part of this Act, this Act shall come into force in relation to tax for the year 1979–80 and subsequent years of assessment, and tax for other chargeable periods beginning after 5 April 1979.*

(*2*) *The following provisions of this Act, that is—*

(*a*) *so much of any provision of this Act as authorises the making of any order or other instrument,*

(*b*) *except where the tax concerned is all tax for chargeable periods to which this Act does not apply, so much of any provision of this Act as confers any power or imposes any duty the exercise or performance of which operates or may operate in relation to tax for more than one chargeable period,*

shall come into force for all purposes on 6 April 1979 to the exclusion of the corresponding enactments repealed by this Act.

* * * * *

SCHEDULES

SCHEDULE 1   Section 5

[APPLICATION OF EXEMPT AMOUNT IN PARTICULAR CASES]

Preliminary

1. *In this Schedule references to any subsections not otherwise identified are references to subsections of section 5 of this Act.*

Husband and wife

2. (*1*) *For any year of assessment during which a married woman is living with her husband [subsections (1) and (4)] shall apply to them as if [the amount of £3,000] [the exempt amount for the year] were divided between them—*

(*a*) *in proportion to their respective taxable amounts for that year (disregarding for this purpose paragraphs (a) and (b) of subsection (4)), or*

(*b*) *where the aggregate of those amounts does not exceed [£3,000] [the exempt amount for the year] and allowable losses accruing to either of them in a previous year are carried forward from that year, in such other proportion as they may agree.*

(*2*) *Sub-paragraph (1) above shall also apply for any year of assessment during a part of which (being a part beginning with 6 April) a married woman is living with her husband but—*

(*a*) *her taxable amount for that year shall not include chargeable gains or allowable losses accruing to her in the remainder of the year, and*

(*b*) *[subsections (1) and (4)] shall apply to her (without the modification in sub-paragraph (1) above) for the remainder of the year as if it were a separate year of assessment.*

3. (*1*) *For any year of assessment during which or during a part of which (being a part beginning with 6 April) the individual is a married man whose wife is living with him and in relation to whom section 45(1) of this Act applies subsection (5) shall apply as if—*

(*a*)　the chargeable gains accruing to him in the year included those accruing to her in the year or the part of the year, and

(*b*)　all the disposals of assets made by her in the year or the part of the year were made by him.

(2)　Subsection (5) shall not apply for any year of assessment during which or during part of which (being a part beginning with 6 April)—

(*a*)　the individual is a married man whose wife is living with him but in relation to whom the said section 45(1) does not apply, or

(*b*)　the individual is a married woman living with her husband.

Note. Heading to this Schedule in square brackets substituted by Finance Act 1982, s 80(3)(a), (5). In para 2, words in first pair of square brackets in sub-para (1) and words in square brackets in sub-para (2)(b) substituted by Finance Act 1980, ss 77(1), (4)(b), (5), and words in second and third pairs of square brackets in sub-para (1) substituted by s 80(3)(b), (5) of the 1982 Act. Paras 2, 3 repealed by Finance Act 1988, s 104(1), (2), 148, Sch 14, Part VIII, with effect for the year 1990–91 and subsequent years of assessment.

*　　*　　*　　*　　*

CHARGING ORDERS ACT 1979

(1979 c 53)

ARRANGEMENT OF SECTIONS

Charging orders

An Act to make provision for imposing charges to secure payment of money due, or to become due, under judgments or orders of court; to provide for restraining and prohibiting dealings with, and the making of payments in respect of, certain securities; and for connected purposes.　　　　　　　　　　[6 December 1979]

Charging orders

1. Charging orders—(1) Where, under a judgment or order of the High Court or a county court, a person (the 'debtor') is required to pay a sum of money to another person (the 'creditor') then, for the purpose of enforcing that judgment or order, the appropriate court may make an order in accordance with the provisions of this Act imposing on any such property of the debtor as may be specified in the order a charge for securing the payment of any money due or to become due under the judgment or order.

(2)　The appropriate court is—

(a)　in a case where the property to be charged is a fund in court, the court in which that fund is lodged;

(b)　in a case where paragraph (a) above does not apply and the order to be enforced is a maintenance order of the High Court, the High Court or a county court;

(c) in a case where neither paragraph (a) nor paragraph (b) above applies and the judgment or order to be enforced is a judgment or order of the High Court for a sum exceeding £2,000 [£5,000] [the county court limit], the High Court [or a county court]; and

(d) in any other case, a county court.

In this section ['county court limit' means the county court limit for the time being specified in an Order in Council under *section 192 of the County Courts Act 1959* [section 145 of the County Courts Act 1984], as the county court limit for the purposes of this section and] 'maintenance order' has the same meaning as in section 2(a) of the Attachment of Earnings Act 1971.

Note. '£5,000' substituted for '£2,000' by SI 1981 No 1123 and 'county court limit' for '£5,000' by Administration of Justice Act 1982, s 37, Sch 3, paras 2, 3(b)(iv), as from 1 January 1983. Definition 'county court limit' inserted by Administration of Justice Act 1982, s 37, Sch 3, para 6, as from 1 January 1983, and amended by County Courts Act 1984, s 148(1), Sch 2, Part V, para 71, as from 1 August 1984.

(3) An order under subsection (1) above is referred to in this Act as a 'charging order'.

(4) Where a person applies to the High Court for a charging order to enforce more than one judgment or order, that court shall be the appropriate court in relation to the application if it would be the appropriate court, apart from this subsection, on an application relating to one or more of the judgments or orders concerned.

(5) In deciding whether to make a charging order the court shall consider all the circumstances of the case and, in particular, any evidence before it as to—

(a) the personal circumstances of the debtor, and

(b) whether any other creditor of the debtor would be likely to be unduly prejudiced by the making of the order.

2. Property which may be charged—(1) Subject to subsection (3) below, a charge may be imposed by a charging order only on—

(a) any interest held by the debtor beneficially—
    (i) in any asset of a kind mentioned in subsection (2) below, or
    (ii) under any trust; or

(b) any interest held by a person as trustee of a trust ('the trust'), if the interest is in such an asset or is an interest under another trust and—
    (i) the judgment or order in respect of which a charge is to be imposed was made against that person as trustee of the trust, or
    (ii) the whole beneficial interest under the trust is held by the debtor unencumbered and for his own benefit, or
    (iii) in a case where there are two or more debtors all of whom are liable to the creditor for the same debt, they together hold the whole beneficial interest under the trust unencumbered and for their own benefit.

(2) The assets referred to in subsection (1) above are—

(a) land,

(b) securities of any of the following kinds—
    (i) government stock,
    (ii) stock of any body (other than a building society) incorporated within England and Wales,
    (iii) stock of any body incorporated outside England and Wales or of any state or territory outside the United Kingdom, being stock registered in a register kept at any place within England and Wales,
    (iv) units of any unit trust in respect of which a register of the unit holders is kept at any place within England and Wales, or

(c) funds in court.

(3) In any case where a charge is imposed by a charging order on any interest in an asset of a kind mentioned in paragraph (b) or (c) of subsection (2) above, the court making the order may provide for the charge to extend to any interest or dividend payable in respect of the asset.

3. Provisions supplementing sections 1 and 2—(1) A charging order may be made either absolutely or subject to conditions as to notifying the debtor or as to the time when the charge is to become enforceable, or as to other matters

(2) The Land Charges Act 1972 and the *Land Registration Act 1925* [Land Registration Act 2002] shall apply in relation to charging orders as they apply in relation to other orders or writs issued or made for the purpose of enforcing judgments.

(3) In section 49 of the Land Registration Act 1925 (protection of certain interests by notice) there is inserted at the end of subsection (1) the following paragraph—

'*(g)   charging orders (within the meaning of the Charging Orders Act 1979) which in the case of unregistered land may be protected by registration under the Land Charges Act 1972 and which, notwithstanding section 59 of this Act, it may be deemed expedient to protect by notice instead of by caution.*'

(4) Subject to the provisions of this Act, a charge imposed by a charging order shall have the like effect and shall be enforceable in the same courts and in the same manner as an equitable charge created by the debtor by writing under his hand.

(5) The court by which a charging order was made may at any time, on the application of the debtor or of any person interested in any property to which the order relates, make an order discharging or varying the charging order.

(6) Where a charging order has been protected by an entry registered under the Land Charges Act 1972 or the *Land Registration Act 1925* [Land Registration Act 2002], an order under subsection (5) above discharging the charging order may direct that the entry be cancelled.

(7) The Lord Chancellor may by order made by statutory instrument amend section 2(2) of this Act by adding to, or removing from, the kinds of asset for the time being referred to there, any asset of a kind which in his opinion ought to be so added or removed.

(8) Any order under subsection (7) above shall be subject to annulment in pursuance of a resolution of either House of Parliament.

Note. Words in square brackets substituted for words in italics by the Land Registration Act 2002, s 133, Sch 11, para 15, as from 13 October 2003. Sub-s (3) repealed by the Land Registration Act 2002, s 135, Sch 13, as from 13 October 2003.

4. Completion of execution. *In section 40 of the Bankruptcy Act 1914 and in section 325 of the Companies Act 1948 (which restrict the rights of creditors under execution or attachment) there is substituted, in each case for subsection (2), the following subsection—*

'*(2) For the purposes of this Act—*

(*a*)   *an execution against goods is completed by seizure and sale or by the making of a charging order under section 1 of the Charging Orders Act 1979;*

(*b*)   *an attachment of a debt is completed by the receipt of the debt; and*

(*c*)   *an execution against land is completed by seizure, by the appointment of a receiver, or by the making of a charging order under the said section 1.*'

Note. This section repealed by Insolvency Act 1985, s 235, Sch 10, Part III, as from 29 December 1986. See also Insolvency Act 1986, s 437, Sch 11, Part II.

Stop orders and notices

5. Stop orders and notices—(1) In this section—

'stop order' means an order of the court prohibiting the taking, in respect of any of the securities specified in the order, of any of the steps mentioned in subsection (5) below;

'stop notice' means a notice requiring any person or body on whom it is duly served to refrain from taking, in respect of any of the securities specified in the notice, any of those steps without first notifying the person by whom, or on whose behalf, the notice was served; and

'prescribed securities' means securities (including funds in court) of a kind prescribed by rules of court made under this section.

(2) The power to make rules of court under section 99 of the Supreme Court of Judicature (Consolidation) Act 1925 [84 of the Supreme Court Act 1981] shall include power by any such rules to make provision—

    (a) for the court to make a stop order on the application of any person claiming to be entitled to an interest in prescribed securities;

    (b) for the service of a stop notice by any person claiming to be entitled to an interest in prescribed securities.

[(2) The power to make rules of court under section 1 of, and Schedule 1 to, the Civil Procedure Act 1997 shall include power by any such rules to make provision—

    (a) for the High Court to make a stop order on the application of any person claiming to be entitled to an interest in prescribed securities; and

    (b) for the service of a stop notice by any person claiming to be entitled to an interest in prescribed securities.]

Note. Words in square brackets substituted for words '99 of the Supreme Court of Judicature (Consolidation) Act 1925' by Supreme Court Act 1981, s 152(1), Sch 5, as from 1 January 1982. Sub-s (2) substituted by SI 2002 No 439, arts 2, 5(a) as from 25 March 2002.

(3) The power to make rules of court under section 102 of the County Courts Act 1959 [section 75 of the County Courts Act 1984] shall include power by any such rules to make provision for the service of a stop notice by any person entitled to an interest in any securities by virtue of a charging order made by a county court.

Note. Words in square brackets substituted for words in italics by County Courts Act 1984, s 148(1), Sch 2, Part V, para 72, as from 1 August 1984. Sub-s (3) repealed by SI 2002 No 439, arts 2, 5(b), as from 25 March 2002.

(4) Rules of court made by virtue of subsection (2) *or (3)* above shall prescribe the person or body on whom a copy of any stop order or a stop notice is to be served.

Note. Words in italics repealed by SI 2002 No 439, arts 2, 5(c), as from 25 March 2002.

(5) The steps mentioned in subsection (1) above are—

    (a) the registration of any transfer of the securities;

    (b) in the case of funds in court, the transfer, sale, delivery out, payment or other dealing with the funds, or of the income thereon;

    (c) the making of any payment by way of dividend, interest or otherwise in respect of the securities; and

    (d) in the case of units of a unit trust, any acquisition of or other dealing with the units by any person or body exercising functions under the trust.

(6) Any rules of court made by virtue of this section may include such incidental, supplemental and consequential provisions as the authority making them consider necessary or expedient, and may make different provision in relation to different cases or classes of case.

Supplemental

6. Interpretation—(1) In this Act—

    'building society' has the same meaning as in the Building Societies Act *1962* [1986];

    'charging order' means an order made under section 1(1) of this Act;

    'debtor' and 'creditor' have the meanings given by section 1(1) of this Act;

    'dividend' includes any distribution in respect of any unit of a unit trust;

    'government stock' means any stock issued by Her Majesty's government in the United Kingdom or any funds of, or annuity granted by, that government;

    'stock' includes shares, debentures and any securities of the body concerned, whether or not constituting a charge on the assets of that body;

    'unit trust' means any trust established for the purpose, or having the effect, of providing, for persons having funds available for investment, facilities for the participation by them, as beneficiaries under the trust, in any profits or income arising from the acquisition, holding, management or disposal of any property whatsoever.

Note. '1986' in square brackets substituted for '1962' in italics by Building Societies Act 1986, s 120(1), Sch 18, Part I, para 14, as from 1 October 1987.

(2) For the purposes of section 1 of this Act references to a judgment or order of the High Court or a county court shall be taken to include references to a judgment, order, decree or award (however called) of any court or arbitrator (including any foreign court or arbitrator) which is or has become enforceable (whether wholly or to a limited extent) as if it were a judgment or order of the High Court or a county court.

(3) References in section 2 of this Act to any securities include references to any such securities standing in the name of the Accountant General.

7. Consequential amendment, repeals and transitional provisions—(*1*) *In section 192 of the County Courts Act 1959 (power to raise limits of jurisdiction) subsection (2) (as substituted by section 10 of the Administration of Justice Act 1969) is amended by inserting, at the end, the following paragraph—*

'(*e*) *section 1(2)(c) of the Charging Orders Act 1979*'.

Note. Sub-s (1) repealed by County Courts Act 1984, s 148(3), Sch 4.

(*2*) *Section 35 of the Administration of Justice Act 1956 and section 141 of the County Courts Act 1959 (which relate to the powers of courts to make charging orders) are hereby repealed; and in section 36(2) and (3) of the Act of 1956 and section 142(2) and (3) of the Act of 1959 for the words 'the last preceding section' (in section 36) and 'the last foregoing section' (in section 142) there are substituted, in each case, the words 'section 1 of the Charging Orders Act 1979*'.

Note. Sub-s (2) repealed in part by Supreme Court Act 1981, s 152(4), Sch 7 and in part by County Courts Act 1984, s 148(3), Sch 4.

(3) Any order made or notice given under any enactment repealed by this Act or under any rules of court revoked by rules of court made under this Act (the 'new rules') shall, if still in force when the provisions of this Act or, as the case may be, the new rules come into force, continue to have effect as if made under this Act or, as the case may be, under the new rules.

(*4*) *Any notice of such an order registered in the register maintained under the Land Registration Act 1925 which would have been registrable by virtue of the paragraph inserted in section 49(1) of that Act by section 3(3) of this Act, if section 3(3) had been in force when the notice was registered, shall have effect as if registered by virtue of that paragraph.*

Note. Sub-s (4) repealed by the Land Registration Act 2002, s 135, Sch 13, as from 13 October 2003 (SI 2003 No 1725).

8. Short title, commencement and extent—(1) This Act may be cited as the Charging Orders Act 1979.

(2) This Act comes into force on such day as the Lord Chancellor may appoint by order made by statutory instrument.

(3) This Act does not extend to Scotland or Northern Ireland.

Commencement. Act in force 3 June 1980: (SI 1980 No 627).

JUSTICES OF THE PEACE ACT 1979

(1979 c 55)

An Act to consolidate certain enactments relating to justices of the peace (including stipendiary magistrates), justices' clerks and the administrative and financial arrangements for magistrates' courts, and to matters connected therewith, with amendments to give effect to recommendations of the Law Commission.

[6 December 1979]

The whole Act was repealed by the Justices of the Peace Act 1997, s 73(3), Sch 6, Part I, as from 19 June 1997.

PART I

GENERAL

Areas and commissions of the peace

1. Commission areas. [*Subject to any order made under section 17 of the Local Government Act 1992*] [*or section 55 of the Local Government (Wales) Act 1994*] *There shall in England and Wales be a commission of the peace for the following areas (in this Act referred to as 'commission areas') and no others, that is to say—*
- (*a*)   *every county* [*in England*];
- [(*a*)   *every metropolitan county or relevant area in England;*]
- [(*aa*)   *every preserved county in Wales;*]
- (*b*)   *every London commission area; and*
- (*c*)   *the City of London*

[*and in this Act 'commission area' means an area for which there is a commissioner of the peace.*]

Note. Words 'Subject to any ... 1992' and 'and in this Act ... the peace' in square brackets added, words '(in this Act ... others' repealed, and sub-s (1)(a) in square brackets substituted for preceding sub-s (1)(a) by Local Government Changes for England (Magistrates' Courts) Regulations 1996, SI 1996 No 674, reg 2, Schedule, Part I, para 1(1), as from 1 April 1996. Words 'or section 55 ... Act 1994' inserted by Magistrates' Courts (Wales) (Consequences of Local Government Changes) Order 1996, SI 1996 No 675, art 2, Schedule, Part I, para 1, as from 1 April 1996. Words 'in England' in square brackets and sub-s (1)(aa) inserted by Local Government (Wales) Act 1994, s 1(3), Sch 2, para 10(1), as from 1 April 1996. See Family Law Reform Act 1987, s 15(4) and Children Act 1989, s 15(1), Sch 1, para 10(6) (pp 3214, 3297).

2. London commission areas—(*1*) *Subject to the provisions of section 3 of this Act, the following areas of Greater London, that is to say—*
- (*a*)   *an area to be known as the 'inner London area', consisting of the inner London boroughs;*
- (*b*)   *an area to be known as the 'north-east London area', consisting of the London boroughs of Barking, Havering, Newham, Redbridge and Waltham Forest;*
- (*c*)   *an area to be known as the 'south-east London area', consisting of the London boroughs of Bexley, Bromley and Croydon;*
- (*d*)   *an area to be known as the 'south-west London area', consisting of the London boroughs of Kingston upon Thames, Merton, Richmond upon Thames and Sutton; and*
- (*e*)   *an area to be known as the 'Middlesex area', consisting of the London boroughs of Barnet, Brent, Ealing, Enfield, Haringey, Harrow, Hillingdon and Hounslow,*

are in this Act referred to as 'London commission areas', and the areas specified in paragraphs (b) to (e) above are in this Act referred to as the 'outer London areas'.

(*2*) *Subject to the provisions of this Act, a London commission area shall be deemed to be a non-metropolitan county for all purposes of the law relating to commissions of the peace, justices of the peace, magistrates' courts, magistrates' courts committees, the keeper of the rolls, justices' clerks and matters connected with any of those matters; and references to a county in any enactment passed or instrument made before the 10 June 1964, and references to a non-metropolitan county in any enactment or instrument as amended or modified by or under the Local Government Act 1972, shall be construed accordingly.*

(*3*) *Subsection (2) above shall not apply to any enactment (including any enactment contained in this Act) to which apart from this subsection it would apply and which expressly refers in the same context both—*
- (*a*)   *to a county or counties or to a non-metropolitan county or non-metropolitan counties, and*
- (*b*)   *to a London commission area or London commission areas or any of those areas;*

and the generality of subsection (2) above shall not be taken to be prejudiced by any enactment to which by virtue of this subsection that subsection does not apply.

Note. Sub-ss (2), (3) repealed by Local Government Act 1985, s 102(2), Sch 17.

3. Power to adjust London commission areas—(*1*) *Her Majesty may by Order in Council substitute for any one or more of the areas specified in section 2(1) above any other area or areas comprising the whole or part of Greater London, or alter the boundaries of any area so specified; but the City of London shall not by virtue of any such Order be included in a London commission area.*

(*2*) *An Order in Council made under this section may contain such incidental, consequential, transitional or supplementary provisions as may be necessary or expedient for the purposes of the Order (including provisions amending this Act or any other enactment).*

(*3*) *Any statutory instrument made by virtue of this section shall be subject to annulment in pursuance of a resolution of either House of Parliament.*

4. Petty sessions areas—(*1*) *The following areas outside Greater London are petty sessions areas, that is to say—*

 (*a*) *every non-metropolitan county which is not divided into petty sessional divisions;*

 (*b*) *every petty sessional division of a non-metropolitan county;*

 (*c*) *every metropolitan district which is not divided into petty sessional divisions; and*

 (*d*) *every petty sessional division of a metropolitan district.*

 [(*1A*) *In subsection (1) above, any reference to a non-metropolitan county is to be construed [, in relation to England, as a reference to a relevant area and], in relation to Wales, as a reference to a preserved county.*]

Note. Sub-s (1A) inserted by Local Government (Wales) Act 1994, s 1(3), Sch 2, para 10(2), as from 1 April 1996. Words in square brackets inserted by Local Government Changes for England (Magistrates' Courts) Regulations 1996, SI 1996 No 674, reg 2, Schedule, Part I, para 1(2), as from 1 April 1996.

(*2*) *In the following provisions of this Act 'petty sessions area' means any of the following, that is to say—*

 (*a*) *any of the areas outside Greater London specified in subsection (1) above;*

 (*b*) *any London commission area which is not divided into petty sessional divisions;*

 (*c*) *any petty sessional division of the London commission area; and*

 (*d*) *the City of London.*

 [(*b*) *the inner London area if it is not divided into petty sessional divisions;*

 (*c*) *any petty sessional division of the inner London area;*

 (*d*) *any outer London borough which is not divided into petty sessional divisions;*

 (*e*) *any petty sessional division of an outer London borough; and*

 (*f*) *the City of London.*]

Note. Sub-s (2)(b)–(f) in square brackets substituted for preceding sub-s (2)(b)–(d) by Local Government Act 1985, s 12(2).

* * * * *

MAGISTRATES' COURTS ACT 1980*

(1980 c 43)

ARRANGEMENT OF SECTIONS

PART II

CIVIL JURISDICTION AND PROCEDURE

Jurisdiction to issue summons and deal with complaints

---

* For Table of derivations and destinations see pp 2804–2806.

An Act to consolidate certain enactments relating to the jurisdiction of, and the practice and procedure before, magistrates' courts and the functions of justices' clerks, and to matters connected therewith, with amendments to give effect to recommendations of the Law Commission.   [1 August 1980]

PART II

CIVIL JURISDICTION AND PROCEDURE

Jurisdiction to issue summons and deal with complaints

51. Issue of summons on complaint. *Subject to the provisions of this Act, where a complaint is made to a justice of the peace acting for any petty sessions area upon which a magistrates' court acting for that area has power to make an order against any person, the justice may issue a summons directed to that person requiring him to appear before a magistrates court acting for that area to answer to the complaint.*

[51. Issue of summons on complaint. Where a complaint relating to a person is made to a justice of the peace, the justice of the peace may issue a summons to the person requiring him to appear before a magistrates' court to answer the complaint.]

Notes. Section 51 as originally enacted in italics. Substituted by the Courts Act 2003, s 47(1), as from a date to be appointed.

52. Jurisdiction to deal with complaints. Where no express provision is made by any Act or the rules specifying what magistrates' courts shall have jurisdiction to hear a complaint, a magistrates' court shall have such jurisdiction if the complaint relates to anything done within the commission area for which the court is appointed or anything left undone that ought to have been done there, or ought to have been done either there or elsewhere, or relates to any other matter arising within that area.

In this section 'commission area' has the same meaning as in the Justices of the Peace Act 1979 [the Justices of the Peace Act 1997].

Note. Words in square brackets substituted for words 'the Justices of the Peace Act 1979' by Justices of the Peace Act 1997, s 73(2), Sch 5, para 19(3)(a), as from 19 June 1997. For Justices of the Peace Act 1979, s 1, see p 2761 Final sentence repealed by the Access to Justice Act 1999, s 106, Sch 15, Pt V.

[52. Jurisdiction to deal with complaints. (1) A magistrates' court has jurisdiction to hear any complaint.

(2) But subsection (1) is subject to provision made by any enactment.]

Note. Section 52 as originally enacted with amendments in italics. Substituted by the Courts Act 2003, s 47(2), as from a date to be appointed.

Hearing of complaint

53. Procedure on hearing—(1) On the hearing of a complaint, the court shall, if the defendant appears, state to him the substance of the complaint.

(2) The court, after hearing the evidence and the parties, shall make the order for which the complaint is made or dismiss the complaint.

(3) Where a complaint is for an order for the payment of a sum recoverable summarily as a civil debt, or for the variation of the rate of any periodical payments ordered by a magistrates' court to be made, or for such other matter as may be prescribed, the court may make the order with the consent of the defendant without hearing evidence.

54. Adjournment—(1) A magistrates' court may at any time, whether before or after beginning to hear a complaint, adjourn the hearing, and may do so, notwithstanding anything in this Act, when composed of a single justice.

(2) The court may when adjourning either fix the time and place at which the hearing is to be resumed or, unless it remands the defendant under section 55 below, leave the time and place to be determined later by the court; but the hearing shall not be resumed at that time and place unless the court is satisfied that the parties have had adequate notice thereof.

55. Non-appearance of defendant—(1) Where at the time and place appointed for the hearing or adjourned hearing of a complaint the complainant appears but the defendant does not, the court may, subject to subsection (3) below, proceed in his absence.

(2) Where the court, instead of proceeding in the absence of the defendant, adjourns, or further adjourns, the hearing, the court may, if the complaint has been substantiated on oath, and subject to the following provisions of this section, issue a warrant for his arrest.

(3) The court shall not begin to hear the complaint in the absence of the defendant or issue a warrant under this section unless either it is proved to the satisfaction of the court, on oath or in such other manner as may be prescribed, that the summons was served on him within what appears to the court to be a

reasonable time before the hearing or adjourned hearing or the defendant has appeared on a previous occasion to answer to the complaint.

(4) Where the defendant fails to appear at an adjourned hearing, the court shall not issue a warrant under this section unless it is satisfied that he has had adequate notice of the time and place of the adjourned hearing.

(5) Where the defendant is arrested under a warrant issued under this section, the court may, on any subsequent adjournment of the hearing, but subject to the provisions of subsection (6) below, remand him.

(6) The court shall not issue a warrant or remand a defendant under this section or further remand him by virtue of section 128(3) below after he has given evidence in the proceedings.

(7) Where the court remands the defendant, the time fixed for the resumption of the hearing shall be that at which he is required to appear or be brought before the court in pursuance of the remand.

(8) A warrant under this section shall not be issued in any proceedings for the recovery or enforcement of a sum recoverable summarily as a civil debt or in proceedings in any matter of bastardy.

56. Non-appearance of complainant. Where at the time and place appointed for the hearing or adjourned hearing of a complaint the defendant appears but the complainant does not, the court may dismiss the complaint or, if evidence has been received on a previous occasion, proceed in the absence of the complainant.

57. Non-appearance of both parties. Where at the time and place appointed for the hearing or adjourned hearing of a complaint neither the complainant nor the defendant appears, the court may dismiss the complaint.

* * * * *

Civil debt

58. Money recoverable summarily as civil debt—(1) A magistrates' court shall have power to make an order on complaint for the payment of any money recoverable summarily as a civil debt.

(2) Any sum payment of which may be ordered by a magistrates' court shall be recoverable summarily as a civil debt except—

(a) a sum recoverable on complaint for *an affiliation order or order enforceable as an affiliation order* [a magistrates' court maintenance order]; or

(b) a sum that may be adjudged to be paid by a summary conviction or by an order enforceable as if it were a summary conviction.

Note. Words in square brackets substituted for words in italics by Family Law Reform Act 1987, s 33(1), Sch 2, para 80, as from 1 April 1989.

Orders for periodical payment

59. Periodical payment through justices' clerk—(*1*) *Where a magistrates' court orders money to be paid periodically by one person to another, the court may order that the payment shall be made to the clerk of the court or the clerk of any other magistrates' court.*

(*2*) *Where the order is an affiliation order, an order under the Guardianship of Minors Acts 1971 and 1973* [(*or having effect as if made under*) *Schedule 1 to the Children Act 1989*] *or an order under Part I of the Domestic Proceedings and Magistrates' Courts Act 1978, the court shall, unless upon representations expressly made in that behalf by the applicant for the order it is satisfied that it is undesirable to do so, exercise its power under subsection (1) above.*

Note. Words 'an affiliation order' repealed by Family Law Reform Act 1987, s 33(4), Sch 4, as from 1 April 1989. Words in square brackets substituted for words 'the Guardianship of Minors Act 1971 and 1973' by Children Act 1989, s 108(5), Sch 13, para 44(1), as from 14 October 1991.

(*3*) *Where periodical payments under an order of any court are required to be paid to or through the clerk of a magistrates' court and any sums payable under the order are in arrear, the clerk shall, if the person for whose benefit the payment should have been made so requests in writing, and unless it appears to the clerk that it is unreasonable in the circumstances to do so, proceed in his own name for the recovery of those sums; but the said person shall have the same liability for all the costs properly incurred in or about the proceedings as if the proceedings had been taken by him.*

(4) Nothing in this section shall affect any right of a person to proceed in his own name for the recovery of sums payable on his behalf under an order of any court.

Note. Section 59 as originally enacted (in italics) replaced Magistrates' Courts Act 1952, s 52, as amended, which replaced Married Women's (Maintenance) Act 1949, s 4.

See also Maintenance Orders (Facilities for Enforcement) Act 1920, s 4 (p 2038); Maintenance Orders Act 1950, ss 8, 22, 24 (pp 2145, 2146, 2157, 2161); Attachment of Earnings Act 1971, s 3 (p 2394); Maintenance Orders (Reciprocal Enforcement) Act 1972, ss 7–9, 27, 34A (pp 2430–2436, 2452, 2474); Domestic Proceedings and Magistrates' Courts Act 1978, ss 20ZA, 32(2) (pp 2714, 2723); Civil Jurisdiction and Judgments Act 1982, s 5 (p 2889); Social Security Act 1986, s 24A; Children Act 1989, Sch 1, para 6A. See also ss 75, 76 of this Act (p 2785).

[59. Orders for periodical payment: means of payment—(1) In any case where a magistrates' court orders money to be paid periodically by one person (in this section referred to as 'the debtor') to another (in this section referred to as 'the creditor'), then—

    (a) if the order is a qualifying maintenance order, the court shall at the same time exercise one of its powers under paragraphs (a) to (d) of subsection (3) below;

    (b) if the order is not a maintenance order, the court shall at the same time exercise one of its powers under paragraphs (a) and (b) of that subsection.

(2) For the purposes of subsection (1)(a) above a maintenance order is a 'qualifying maintenance order' if, at the time it is made, the debtor is ordinarily resident in England and Wales.

(3) The powers of the court are—

    (a) the power to order that payments under the order be made directly by the debtor to the creditor;

    (b) the power to order that payments under the order be made to *the clerk of the court or to the clerk of any other magistrates' court* [*a justices' chief executive*] [the designated officer for the court or for any other magistrates' court];

    (c) the power to order that payments under the order be made by the debtor to the creditor by such method of payment falling within subsection (6) below as may be specified;

    [(cc) the power to order that payments under the order be made in accordance with arrangements made by the Secretary of State for their collection;]

    (d) the power to make an attachment of earnings order under the Attachment of Earnings Act 1971 to secure payments under the order.

Note. Sub-s (3)(cc) inserted by Child Support Act 1991 (Consequential Amendments) Order 1994, SI 1994 No 731, art 3, as from 11 April 1994. First words in italics repealed and words 'a justices' chief executive' in square brackets substituted by the Access to Justice Act 1999, s 90, Sch 13, paras 95, 99, as from 1 April 2001 (SI 2001 No 916). Words 'a justices' chief executive' substituted by subsequent words in square brackets by the Courts Act 2003, s 109(1), Sch 8, para 208(1), (2), as from a date to be appointed.

[(3A) No order made by a magistrates' court under paragraphs (a) to (d) of subsection (3) above (other than one made under paragraph (cc)) shall have effect at any time when the Secretary of State is arranging for the collection of payments under the qualifying maintenance order concerned.]

Note. Sub-s (3A) inserted by Child Support Act 1991 (Consequential Amendments) Order 1994, SI 1994 No 731, art 3, as from 11 April 1994.

    (4) In any case where—

    (a) the court proposes to exercise its power under paragraph (c) of subsection (3) above, and

(b) having given the debtor an opportunity of opening an account from which payments under the order may be made in accordance with the method of payment proposed to be ordered under that paragraph, the court is satisfied that the debtor has failed, without reasonable excuse, to open such an account,

the court in exercising its power under that paragraph may order that the debtor open such an account.

(5) In deciding, in the case of a maintenance order, which of the powers under paragraphs (a) to (d) of subsection (3) above [(other than paragraph (cc))] it is to exercise, the court having (if practicable) given them an opportunity to make representations shall have regard to any representations made—

(a) by the debtor,
(b) by the creditor, and
(c) if the person who applied for the maintenance order is a person other than the creditor, by that other person.

Note. Words in square brackets inserted by Child Support Act 1991 (Consequential Amendments) Order 1994, SI 1994 No 731, art 3, as from 11 April 1994.

(6) The methods of payment referred to in subsection (3)(c) above are the following, that is to say—

(a) payment by standing order; or
(b) payment by any other method which requires one person to give his authority for payments of a specific amount to be made from an account of his to an account of another's on specific dates during the period for which the authority is in force and without the need for any further authority from him.

(7) Where the maintenance order is an order—

(a) under the Guardianship of Minors Acts 1971 and 1973,
(b) under Part I of the Domestic Proceedings and Magistrates' Courts Act 1978, or
(c) under, or having effect as if made under, Schedule 1 to the Children Act 1989,

and the court does not propose to exercise its power under *paragraph (c) or (d)* [paragraph (c), (cc) or (d)] of subsection (3) above, the court shall, unless upon representations expressly made in that behalf by the person who applied for the maintenance order it is satisfied that it is undesirable to do so, exercise its power under paragraph (b) of that subsection.

Note. Words in square brackets substituted for words in italics by Child Support Act 1991 (Consequential Amendments) Order 1994, SI 1994 No 731, art 3, as from 11 April 1994.

(8) The *Secretary of State* [Lord Chancellor] may by regulations confer on magistrates' courts, in addition to their powers under paragraphs (a) to (d) of subsection (3) above, the power (the 'additional power') to order that payments under a qualifying maintenance order be made by the debtor to the creditor or *the clerk of a magistrates' court* [*a justices' chief executive*] [the designated officer for a magistrates' court] (as the regulations may provide) by such method of payment as may be specified in the regulations.

Note. Words 'Lord Chancellor' in square brackets substituted for words 'Secretary of State' in italics by Transfer of Functions (Magistrates' Courts and Family Law) Order 1992, SI 1992 No 709, art 3(2), Sch 2, as from 1 April 1992. First words in italics repealed and words 'a justices' chief executive' in square brackets substituted by the Access to Justice Act 1999, s 90, Sch 13, paras 95, 99, as from 1 April 2001 (SI 2001 No 916). Words 'a justices' chief executive' substituted by subsequent words in square brackets by the Courts Act 2003, s 109(1), Sch 8, para 208(1), (2), as from a date to be appointed.

(9) Any reference in any enactment to paragraphs (a) to (d) of subsection (3) above (but not a reference to any specific paragraph of that subsection) shall be taken to include a reference to the additional power, and the reference in subsection (10) below to the additional power shall be construed accordingly.

(10) Regulations under subsection (8) above may make provision for any enactment concerning, or connected with, payments under maintenance orders to apply, with or without modifications, in relation to the additional power.

(11) The power of the *Secretary of State* [Lord Chancellor] to make regulations under subsection (8) above shall be exercisable by statutory instrument and any such statutory instrument shall be subject to annulment in pursuance of a resolution of either House of Parliament.

Note. Words 'Lord Chancellor' in square brackets substituted for words 'Secretary of State' in italics by Transfer of Functions (Magistrates' Courts and Family Law) Order 1992, SI 1992 No 709, art 3(2), Sch 2, as from 1 April 1992.

(12) For the purposes of this section the reference in subsection (1) above to money paid periodically by one person to another includes, in the case of a maintenance order, a reference to a lump sum paid by instalments by one person to another.

[(12) For the purposes of this section—
(a) the reference in subsection (1) above to money paid periodically by one person to another includes, in the case of a maintenance order, a reference to a lump sum paid by instalments by one person to another; and
(b) references to arrangements made by the Secretary of State for the collection of payments are to arrangements made by him under section 30 of the Child Support Act 1991 and regulations made under that section.]]

Note. Section 59 in square brackets substituted for s 59 in italics by Maintenance Enforcement Act 1991, s 2, as from 1 April 1992. Sub-s (12) in square brackets substituted for sub-s (12) in italics by Child Support Act 1991 (Consequential Amendments) Order 1994, SI 1994 No 731, art 3, as from 11 April 1994.

[59A. Orders for periodical payment: proceedings by *clerk* [*justices' chief executive*] [designated officer]—(1) Where payments under a relevant UK order are required to be made periodically—
(a) to or through *the clerk of a magistrates' court* [*a justices' chief executive*] [the designated officer for a magistrates' court], or
(b) by any method of payment falling within section 59(6) above,
and any sums payable under the order are in arrear, *the clerk of the relevant court* [*the relevant justices' chief executive*] [the relevant designated officer] shall, if the person for whose benefit the payments are required to be made so requests in writing, and unless it appears *to the clerk* [*to that justices' chief executive*] [to that designated officer] that it is unreasonable in the circumstances to do so, proceed in his own name for the recovery of those sums.

Note. First words in italics repealed and subsequent words in square brackets substituted by the Access to Justice Act 1999, s 90, Sch 13, paras 95, 100 as from 1 April 2001 (SI 2001 No 916). Words in italics and in square brackets repealed and subsequent words underlined and in square brackets substituted by the Courts Act 2003, s 109(1), Sch 8, para 209, as from a day to be appointed.

(2) Where payments under a relevant UK order are required to be made periodically to or through *the clerk of a magistrates' court* [*a justices' chief executive*] [the designated officer for a magistrates' court], the person for whose benefit the payments are required to be made may, at any time during the period in which the payments are required to be so made, give authority in writing to *the clerk of the relevant court for the clerk* [*the relevant justices' chief executive for him*] [the relevant designated officer for him] to proceed as mentioned in subsection (3) below.

Note. First words in italics repealed and subsequent words in square brackets substituted by the Access to Justice Act 1999, s 90, Sch 13, paras 95, 100 as from 1 April 2001 (SI 2001 No 916). Words in italics and in square brackets repealed and subsequent words underlined and in square brackets substituted by the Courts Act 2003, s 109(1), Sch 8, para 209, as from a day to be appointed.

(3) Where authority under subsection (2) above is given to *the clerk of the relevant court, the clerk* [*the relevant justices' chief executive, he*] [the relevant designated officer, he] shall, unless it appears to him that it is unreasonable in the circumstances to do so, proceed in his own name for the recovery of any sums payable to or through

him under the order in question which, on or after the date of the giving of the authority, fall into arrear.

Note. First words in italics repealed and subsequent words in square brackets substituted by the Access to Justice Act 1999, s 90, Sch 13, paras 95, 100 as from 1 April 2001 (SI 2001 No 916). Words in italics and in square brackets repealed and subsequent words underlined and in square brackets substituted by the Courts Act 2003, s 109(1), Sch 8, para 209, as from a day to be appointed.

(4) In any case where—

(a)   authority under subsection (2) above has been given to *the clerk of a relevant court* [*a justices' chief executive*] [the relevant designated officer], and

(b)   the person for whose benefit the payments are required to be made gives notice in writing to the *clerk cancelling* [*justices' chief executive cancelling*] [relevant designated officer cancelling] the authority,

the authority shall cease to have effect and, accordingly, the *clerk shall* [*justices' chief executive shall*] [relevant designated officer shall] not continue any proceedings already commenced by virtue of the authority.

Note. First words in italics repealed and subsequent words in square brackets substituted by the Access to Justice Act 1999, s 90, Sch 13, paras 95, 100 as from 1 April 2001 (SI 2001 No 916). Words in italics and in square brackets repealed and subsequent words underlined and in square brackets substituted by the Courts Act 2003, s 109(1), Sch 8, para 209, as from a day to be appointed.

(5) The person for whose benefit the payments are required to be made shall have the same liability for all the costs properly incurred in or about proceedings taken under subsection (1) above at his request or under subsection (3) above by virtue of his authority (including any costs incurred as a result of any proceedings commenced not being continued) as if the proceedings had been taken by him.

(6) Nothing in subsection (1) or (3) above shall affect any right of a person to proceed in his own name for the recovery of sums payable on his behalf under an order of any court.

(7) In this section—

'the relevant court', in relation to an order, means—

    (a)   *in a case where payments under the order are required to be made to or through the clerk of a magistrates' court, that magistrates' court; and*

    (b)   *in a case where such payments are required to be made by any method of payment falling within section 59(6) above, the magistrates' court which made the order or, if the order was not made by a magistrates' court, the magistrates' court in which the order is registered;*

[*'the relevant justices' chief executive', in relation to an order, means—*

    (a)   *in a case where payments under the order are required to be made to or through a justices' chief executive, that justices' chief executive;*

    (b)   *in a case where such payments are required to be made by any method of payment falling within section 59(6) above and the order was made by a magistrates' court, the justices' chief executive for that magistrates' court; and*

    (c)   *in a case where such payments are required to be made by any method of payment falling within section 59(6) above and the order was not made by a magistrates' court, the justices' chief executive for the magistrates' court in which the order is registered;*]

['the relevant designated officer', in relation to an order, means—

    (a)   in a case where payments under the order are required to be made to or through a designated officer for a magistrates' court, the designated officer for that magistrates' court;

    (b)   in a case where such payments are required to be made by any method of payment falling within section 59(6) and the order was made by a magistrates' court, the designated officer for that magistrates' court; and

(c) in a case where such payments are required to be made by any method of payment falling within section 59(6) and the order was not made by a magistrates' court, the designated officer for the magistrates' court in which the order is registered;]

'relevant UK order' means—

(a) an order made by a magistrates' court, other than an order made by virtue of Part II of the Maintenance Orders (Reciprocal Enforcement) Act 1972;

(b) an order made by the High Court or a county court (including an order deemed to be made by the High Court by virtue of section 1(2) of the Maintenance Orders Act 1958) and registered under Part I of that Act of 1958 in a magistrates' court; or

(c) an order made by a court in Scotland or Northern Ireland and registered under Part II of the Maintenance Orders Act 1950 in a magistrates' court;

and any reference to payments required to be made periodically includes, in the case of a maintenance order, a reference to instalments required to be paid in respect of a lump sum payable by instalments.

Note. Definition 'the relevant court' substituted by definition 'the relevant justices' chief executive' by the Access to Justice Act 1999, s 90, Sch 13, paras 95, 99, as from 1 April 2001 (SI 2001 No 916). Definition 'the relevant justices' chief executive' substituted by definition 'the relevant designated officer' by the Courts Act 2003, s 109(1), Sch 8, para 209, as from a day to be appointed.

59B. Maintenance orders: penalty for breach—(1) In any case where—

(a) payments under a relevant English maintenance order are required to be made periodically in the manner mentioned in paragraph (a) or (b) of section 59A(1) above, and

(b) the debtor fails, on or after the date of commencement of this section, to comply with the order in so far as the order relates to the manner of payment concerned,

the person for whose benefit the payments are required to be made may make a complaint to a relevant justice giving details of the failure to comply.

(2) If the relevant justice is satisfied that the nature of the alleged failure to comply may be such as to justify the relevant court in exercising its power under subsection (3) below, he shall issue a summons directed to the debtor requiring him to appear before the relevant court to answer the complaint.

(3) On the hearing of the complaint, the relevant court may order the debtor to pay a sum not exceeding £1,000.

(4) Any sum ordered to be paid under subsection (3) above shall for the purposes of this Act be treated as adjudged to be paid by the conviction of a magistrates' court.

(5) In this section—

'debtor' has the same meaning as it has in section 59 above;

'the relevant court' has the same meaning as it has in section 59A above;

['the relevant court', in relation to an order, means—

(a) in a case where payments under the order are required to be made to or through the designated officer for a magistrates' court, that magistrates' court;

(b) in a case where such payments are required to be made by any method of payment falling within section 59(6) and the order was made by a magistrates' court, that magistrates' court; and

(c) in a case where such payments are required to be made by any method of payment falling within section 59(6) and the order was not made by a magistrates' court, the magistrates' court in which the order is registered;]

'relevant English maintenance order' means—
  (a) a maintenance order made by a magistrates' court, other than an order made by virtue of Part II of the Maintenance Orders (Reciprocal Enforcement) Act 1972; or
  (b) an order made by the High Court or a county court (other than an order deemed to be made by the High Court by virtue of section 1(2) of the Maintenance Orders Act 1958) and registered under Part I of that Act of 1958 in a magistrates' court;
'relevant justice,' in relation to a relevant court means a justice of the peace *for the petty sessions area for* [acting in the local justice area in] which the relevant court is acting;
and any reference to payments required to be made periodically includes a reference to instalments required to be paid in respect of a lump sum payable by instalments.]

Note. Sections 59A, 59B inserted by Maintenance Enforcement Act 1991, s 3, as from 1 April 1992. Definition 'the relevant court' substituted by the Courts Act 2003, s 109(1), Sch 8, para 210, as from a day to be appointed. In definition 'relevant justice' words in italics repealed and substituted words in square brackets substituted by the Courts Act 2003, s 109(1), Sch 8, para 210, as from a day to be appointed.

60. Revocation, variation, etc, of orders for periodical payment. *Where a magistrates' court has made an order for the periodical payment of money, the court may, by order on complaint, revoke, revive or vary the order.*

The power to vary an order by virtue of this section shall include power to suspend the operation of any provision of that order temporarily and to revive the operation of any provision so suspended.

[**60. Revocation, variation, etc, of orders for periodical payment**—(1) Where a magistrates' court has made an order for money to be paid periodically by one person to another, the court may, by order on complaint, revoke, revive or vary the order.

(2) The power under subsection (1) above to vary an order shall include power to suspend the operation of any provision of the order temporarily and to revive the operation of any provision so suspended.

(3) Where the order mentioned in subsection (1) above is a maintenance order, the power under that subsection to vary the order shall include power, if the court is satisfied that payment has not been made in accordance with the order, to exercise one of its powers under paragraphs (a) to (d) of section 59(3) above.

(4) In any case where—
  (a) a magistrates' court has made a maintenance order, and
  (b) payments under the order are required to be made by any method of payment falling within section 59(6) above,
an interested party may apply in writing to the clerk of the court for the order to be varied as mentioned in subsection (5) below.

(5) Subject to subsection (8) below, where an application has been made under subsection (4) above, *the clerk* [a justices' clerk], after giving written notice (by post or otherwise) of the application to any other interested party and allowing the party, within the period of 14 days beginning with the date of the giving of that notice, an opportunity to make written representations, may vary the order to provide that payments under the order shall be made *to the clerk* [*to the justices' chief executive for the court*] [to the designated officer for the court].

Note. First words in italics repealed and subsequent words in square brackets substituted by the Access to Justice Act 1999, s 90, Sch 13, paras 95, 100, as from 1 April 2001 (SI 2001 No 916). Words in italics and in square brackets repealed and subsequent words in square brackets substituted by the Courts Act 2003, s 109, Sch 8, para 211, as from a day to be appointed.

(6) The clerk may proceed with an application under subsection (4) above notwithstanding that any such interested party as is referred to in subsection (5) above has not received written notice of the application.

(7) In subsections (4) to (6) above 'interested party', in relation to a maintenance order, means—
  (a) the debtor;
  (b) the creditor; and
  (c) if the person who applied for the maintenance order is a person other than the creditor, that other person.
  (8) Where an application has been made under subsection (4) above, the clerk may, if he considers it inappropriate to exercise his power under subsection (5) above, refer the matter to the court which may vary the order by exercising one of its powers under paragraphs (a) to (d) of section 59(3) above.
  (9) Subsections (4), (5) and (7) of section 59 above shall apply for the purposes of subsections (3) and (8) above as they apply for the purposes of that section.
  (10) None of the powers of the court, or of *the clerk of the court* [a justices' clerk], conferred by subsections (3) to (9) above shall be exercisable in relation to a maintenance order which is not a qualifying maintenance order (within the meaning of section 59 above).

Note. Words in italics repealed and subsequent words in square brackets substituted by the Courts Act 2003, s 109, Sch 8, para 211, as from a day to be appointed.

  (11) For the purposes of this section—
  (a) 'creditor' and 'debtor' have the same meaning as they have in section 59 above; and
  (b) the reference in subsection (1) above to money paid periodically by one person to another includes, in the case of a maintenance order, a reference to a lump sum paid by instalments by one person to another.]

Note. Section 60 in square brackets substituted for s 60 in italics by Maintenance Enforcement Act 1991, s 4, as from 1 April 1992.
  Powers to revive, revoke or vary do not apply to orders made under Domestic Proceedings and Magistrates' Courts Act 1978: see ibid, s 23(2) (p 2718); nor to orders made under Children Act 1989, Sch 1; see ibid, s 15(2).
  As to application of s 60, see Maintenance Orders (Facilities for Enforcement) Act 1920, s 4 (p 2038); Maintenance Orders Act 1950, s 22 (p 2157); Maintenance Orders Act 1958, s 4 (p 2209); Maintenance Orders (Reciprocal Enforcement) Act 1972, ss 9, 34A (pp 2436, 2474); and s 75 of this Act (p 2785).
  Proceedings under this section are 'family proceedings'; see s 65 of this Act (p 2776).

61. Periodical payments payable by one person under more than one order—(1) *The power to make rules conferred by section 144 below shall, without prejudice to the generality of subsection (1) of that section, include power to* [Rules of court may] make provision—
  (a) for enabling a person to make one complaint for the recovery of payments required to be made to him by another person under more than one periodical payments order; and
  (b) for apportioning between two or more periodical payments orders, in such manner as may be prescribed by the rules, any sum paid to a *clerk to a magistrates' court* [*justices' chief executive*] [the designated officer for a magistrates' court] on any date by the person liable to make payments under the orders which is less than the total sum required to be paid on that date to *that clerk* [*that justices' chief executive*] [that designated officer] by that person in respect of those orders (being orders one of which requires payments to be made for the benefit of a child to the person with whom the child has his home and one or more of which requires payments to be made to that person either for his own benefit or for the benefit of another child who has his home with him).

Note. First words in italics repealed and subsequent words in square brackets substituted by the Access to Justice Act 1999, s 90, Sch 13, paras 95, 100, as from 1 April 2001 (SI 2001 No 916). Words in italics in square brackets repealed and subsequent words in square brackets substituted by the Courts Act 2003, s 109, Sch 8, para 212, as from a day to be appointed.

(2) In this section—

'child' means a person who has not attained the age of 18;

'periodical payments order' means an order made by a magistrates' court, or registered in a magistrates' court under Part II of the Maintenance Orders Act 1950 or Part I of the Maintenance Orders Act 1958, which requires the making of periodical payments,

and any payments required under a periodical payments order to be made to a child shall for the purposes of subsection (1) above be treated as if they were required to be made to the person with whom the child has his home.

Payments to children

62. Provisions as to payments required to be made to a child, etc—(1) Where—

(a) periodical payments are required to be made, or a lump sum is required to be paid, to a child under an order made by a magistrates' court, or

(b) periodical payments are required to be made to a child under an order which is registered in a magistrates' court,

any sum required under the order to be paid to the child may be paid to the person with whom the child has his home, and that person—

(i) may proceed in his own name for the variation, revival or revocation of the order, and

(ii) may either proceed in his own name for the recovery of any sum required to be paid under the order or *request the clerk to the magistrates' court, under subsection (3) of section 59 above* [request or authorise the *clerk of* [*justices' chief executive for*] [designated officer for] the magistrates' court under subsection (1) or subsection (2) respectively of section 59A above], to proceed for the recovery of that sum.

Note. Words in square brackets substituted for words in italics by Maintenance Enforcement Act 1991, s 11(1), Sch 2, para 5, as from 1 April 1992.

Further amended by the Access to Justice Act 1999, s 90, Sch 13, paras 95, 103, as from 1 April 2001 (SI 2001 No 916); and the Courts Act 2003, s 109, Sch 8, para 213, as from a day to be appointed.

(2) Where a child has a right under any enactment to apply for the revival of an order made by a magistrates' court which provided for the making of periodical payments to or for the benefit of the child, the person with whom the child has his home may proceed in his own name for the revival of that order.

(3) Where any person by whom periodical payments are required to be paid to a child under an order made by or registered in a magistrates' court makes a complaint for the variation or revocation of that order, the person with whom the child has his home may answer the complaint in his own name.

(4) Nothing in subsections (1) and (2) above shall affect any right of a child to proceed in his own name for the variation, revival or revocation of an order or for the recovery of any sum payable thereunder.

(5) *In this section references to the person with whom a child has his home shall be construed in accordance with Part IV of the Children Act 1975, except that, in the case of any child in the care of a local authority, the local authority shall be treated for the purposes of this section as the person with whom the child has his home.*

[(5) In this section references to the person with whom a child has his home—

(a) in the case of any child who is being looked after by a local authority (within the meaning of section 22 of the Children Act 1989), are references to that local authority; and

(b) in any other case, are references to the person who, disregarding any absence of the child at a hospital or boarding school and any other temporary absence, has care of the child.]

Note. Sub-s (5) in square brackets substituted for sub-s (5) in italics by Children Act 1989, s 108(5), Sch 13, para 44(2), as from 14 October 1991.

(6) In this section any reference to an order registered in a magistrates' court is a reference to an order registered in a magistrates' court under Part II of the Maintenance Orders Act 1950 or Part I of the Maintenance Orders Act 1958.

(7) In this section 'child' means a person who has not attained the age of 18.

Orders other than for payment of money

63. Orders other than for payment of money—(1) Where under any Act passed after 31 December 1879 a magistrates' court has power to require the doing of anything other than payment of money, or to prohibit the doing of anything, any order of the court for the purpose of exercising that power may contain such provisions for the manner in which anything is to be done, for the time within which anything is to be done, or during which anything is not to be done, and generally for giving effect to the order, as the court thinks fit.

(2) The court may by order made on complaint suspend or rescind any such order as aforesaid.

(3) Where any person disobeys an order of a magistrates' court made under an Act passed after 31 December 1879 to do anything other than the payment of money or to abstain from doing anything the court may—

(a) order him to pay a sum not exceeding £50 for every day during which he is in default or a sum not exceeding *£1,000* [*£2,000*] [£5,000]; or

(b) commit him to custody until he has remedied his default or for a period not exceeding 2 months;

but a person who is ordered to pay a sum for every day during which he is in default or who is committed to custody until he has remedied his default shall not by virtue of this section be ordered to pay more than £1,000 or be committed for more than 2 months in all for doing or abstaining from doing the same thing contrary to the order (without prejudice to the operation of this section in relation to any subsequent default).

Note. Sum £2,000 in square brackets in sub-s (3)(a) substituted for sum £1,000 in italics by Criminal Penalties etc (Increase) Order 1984, SI 1984 No 447, art 2(3), Sch 3. Sum £5,000 in square brackets substituted for sum £2,000 in italics by Criminal Justice Act 1991, s 17(3), Sch 4, Part I, as from 1 October 1992.

(4) Any sum ordered to be paid under subsection (3) above shall for the purposes of this Act be treated as adjudged to be paid by a conviction of a magistrates' court.

(5) The preceding provisions of this section shall not apply to any order for the enforcement of which provision is made by any other enactment.

Note. The power to suspend or rescind does not apply in relation to orders under Domestic Proceedings and Magistrates' Courts Act 1978, Part I: ibid, s 23(2), as amended (p 2690) nor to orders under Children Act 1989: ibid, s 92(3) (p 3395). As to application of sub-s (3), see Children Act 1989, ss 14(1), 108(6), Sch 14, paras 5, 10 (pp 3301, 3408, 3490, 3492).

Costs

64. Power to award costs and enforcement of costs—(1) On the hearing of a complaint, a magistrates' court shall have power in its discretion to make such order as to costs—

(a) on making the order for a which the complaint is made, to be paid by the defendant to the complainant;

(b) on dismissing the complaint, to be paid by the complainant to the defendant, as it thinks just and reasonable; but if the complaint is for an order for the periodical payment of money, or for the revocation, revival or variation of such an order, or for the enforcement of such an order, the court may, whatever adjudication it makes, order either party to pay the whole or any part of the other's costs.

(2) The amount of any sum ordered to be paid under subsection (1) above shall be specified in the order, or order of dismissal, as the case may be.

(3) Subject to subsection (4) below, costs ordered to be paid under this section shall be enforceable as a civil debt.

(*4*) *Any costs awarded on a complaint for an affiliation order or order enforceable as an affiliation order, or for the enforcement, variation, revocation, discharge or revival of such an order, against the person liable to make payments under the order shall be enforceable as a sum ordered to be paid by an affiliation order.*

[(4) Any costs awarded on a complaint for a maintenance order, or for the enforcement, variation, revocation, discharge or revival of such an order, against the person liable to make payments under the order shall be enforceable as a sum ordered to be paid by a magistrates' court maintenance order.]

Note. Sub-s (4) in square brackets substituted for sub-s (4) in italics by Family Law Reform Act 1987, s 33(1), Sch 2, para 81, as from 1 April 1989.

(5) The preceding provisions of this section shall have effect subject to any other Act enabling a magistrates' court to order a successful party to pay the other party's costs.

Note. For extended meaning to be given to the proviso to s 64(1) on applications to vary or revoke orders under Domestic Proceedings and Magistrates' Courts Act 1978, s 20, where there are two or more respondents, see ibid, s 23(1), as amended (p 2671).

[*Family proceedings*

65. Meaning of domestic proceedings [family proceedings]—(1) In this Act '*domestic proceedings*' [family proceedings] means proceedings under any of the following enactments, that is to say—

(a) the Maintenance Orders (Facilities for Enforcement) Act 1920;
(b) section 43 *or section 44* of the National Assistance Act 1948;
(c) section 3 of the Marriage Act 1949;
(d) *the Affiliation Proceedings Act 1957;*
(e) *the Guardianship of Minors Acts 1971 and 1973;*
[(ee) section 35 of the Matrimonial Causes Act 1973;]
(f) Part I of the Maintenance Orders (Reciprocal Enforcement) Act 1972;
(g) *Part II of the Children Act 1975;*
(h) *the Adoption Act 1976, except proceedings under section 34 of that Act;*
[(h) the Adoption and Children Act 2002;]
(i) section 18 *or section 19* of the Supplementary Benefits Act 1976;
(j) Part I of the Domestic Proceedings and Magistrates' Courts Act 1978;
(k) *section 47, 49 or 50 of the Child Care Act 1980;*
(l) section 60 of this Act;
[(m) Part I of the Civil Jurisdiction and Judgments Act 1982, so far as that Part relates to the recognition or enforcement of maintenance orders;]
[(*m*) *section 4 or 15 of the Family Law Reform Act 1987;*]
[(mm) section 55A of the Family Law Act 1986;]
[(n) the Children Act 1989;]
[(na) section 30 of the Human Fertilisation and Embryology Act 1990;]
[(*n*) [(nb)] section 106 of the Social Security Administration Act 1992;]
[(o) section 20 (so far as it provides, by virtue of an order under section 45, for appeals to be made to a court) *or section 27* of the Child Support Act 1991;]
[(p) Part IV of the Family Law Act 1996;]
[(q) sections 11 and 12 of the Crime and Disorder Act 1998;]
[(r) Council Regulation (EC) No 44/2001 of 22nd December 2000 on jurisdiction and the recognition and enforcement of judgments in civil and commercial matters, so far as that Regulation relates to the recognition or enforcement of maintenance orders;]

except that, subject to subsection (2) below, it does not include—

(i) proceedings for the enforcement of any order made, confirmed or registered under any of those enactments;
(ii) proceedings for the variation of any provision for the periodical payment of money contained in an order made, confirmed or registered under any of those enactments; or

(iii) proceedings on an information in respect of the commission of an offence under any of those enactments.

Note. Para (ee) inserted by Matrimonial and Family Proceedings Act 1984, s 44, as from 12 October 1984. First para (m) inserted by Civil Jurisdiction and Judgments Act 1982, s 15(4), Sch 12, Part I, para 7(a), as from 1 January 1987. Second para (m) inserted by Family Law Reform Act 1987, s 33(1), Sch 2, para 82, as from 1 April 1989. Repeals of part of (b), of (d), of part of (i) and words '49 or 50' in (k) effected by Family Law Reform Act 1987, s 33(4), Sch 4, as from 1 April 1989. Words 'family proceedings' substituted for words 'domestic proceedings', sub-paras (e) and (g) and second para (m) in italics repealed, and first para (n) inserted, by Children Act 1989, ss 92(11), 108(7), Sch 11, Part II, para 8(a)–(c), Sch 15, as from 14 October 1991. Para (k) repealed by Courts and Legal Services Act 1990, ss 116, 125(7), Sch 16, para 40, Sch 20, as from 14 October 1991. Second para (n) inserted by Social Security (Consequential Provisions) Act 1992, s 4, Sch 2, para 60, as from 1 July 1992. Para (o) inserted by Maintenance Orders (Backdating) Order 1992, SI 1992 No 623, art 3, Sch 2, as from 5 April 1993. Para (p) added by Family Law Act 1996, s 66(1), Sch 8, Part III, para 49, as from 1 October 1997. Further amended by the Adoption and Children Act 2002, as from a day to be appointed; the Child Support, Pensions and Social Security Act 2000, s 83(5), Sch 8, para 2, as from 1 April 2001 (SI 2001 No 774); SI 1997 No 1897, as from 1 October 1997; SI 2001 No 3929, as from 1 March 2002; the Courts Act 2003, s 109, Sch 8, para 214, as from a day to be appointed.

See Children Act 1989, s 92 (p 3395), and Sch 11, Part I (p 3459).

(2) The court before which there fall to be heard any of the following proceedings, that is to say—

(a) proceedings (whether under this Act or any other enactment) for the enforcement of any order made, confirmed or registered under any of the enactments specified in paragraphs (a) to (k) [*and (m)*] [(m) and (n) [, (p) and (r)]] of subsection (1) above;

(b) proceedings (whether under this Act or any other enactment) for the variation of any provision for the making of periodical payments contained in an order made, confirmed or registered under any of those enactments;

(c) proceedings for an attachment of earnings order to secure maintenance payments within the meaning of the Attachment of Earnings Act 1971 or for the discharge or variation of such an order; or

(d) proceedings for the enforcement of a maintenance order which is registered in a magistrates' court under Part II of the Maintenance Orders Act 1950 or Part I of the Maintenance Orders Act 1958 or for the variation of the rate of payments specified by such an order,

[(e) section 20 (so far as it provides, by virtue of an order under section 45, for appeals to be made to a court) *or section 27* of the Child Support Act 1991.]

may if it thinks fit order that those proceedings and any other proceedings being heard therewith shall, notwithstanding anything in subsection (1) above, be treated as *domestic proceedings* [family proceedings] for the purposes of this Act.

Note. Words 'and (m)' in italics in square brackets in para (a) inserted by Civil Jurisdiction and Judgments Act 1982, s 15(4), Sch 12, Part I, para 7(b), as from 1 January 1987. Words '(m) and (n)' substituted for 'and (m)' and words 'family proceedings' substituted for 'domestic proceedings' by Children Act 1989, s 92(11), Sch 11, Part II, para 8(b), (c), as from 14 October 1991. Sub-s (2)(e) added by Maintenance Orders (Backdating) Order 1993, SI 1993 No 623, art 3, Sch 2, as from 5 April 1993.

(3) Where the same parties are parties—

(a) to proceedings which are *domestic proceedings* [family proceedings] by virtue of subsection (1) above, and

(b) to proceedings which the court has power to treat as *domestic proceedings* [family proceedings] by virtue of subsection (2) above,

and the proceedings are heard together by a magistrates' court, the whole of those proceedings shall be treated as *domestic proceedings* [family proceedings] for the purposes of this Act.

Note. Words in square brackets substituted for words in italics by Children Act 1989, s 92(11), Sch 11, Part II, para 8(c), as from 14 October 1991.

(4) No appeal shall lie from the making of, or refusal to make, an order under subsection (2) above.

(5) Until the Adoption Act 1976 comes into force subsection (1) above shall have effect as if the paragraph (h) thereof there were substituted the following paragraph—

'(h) the Adoption Act 1958, the Adoption Act 1960 or Part I of the Children Act 1975, except proceedings under section 42 or 43 of the Adoption Act 1958.'

(6) Until the Child Care Act 1980 comes into force subsection (1) above shall have effect as if for paragraph (k) thereof there were substituted the following paragraph—

'(k) section 87 or section 88 of the Children and Young Persons Act 1933 or section 26 of the Children Act 1948.'

66. Composition of magistrates' courts for domestic proceedings: general—*(1) Subject to the provisions of this section, a magistrates' court when hearing* domestic proceedings *[family proceedings] shall be composed of not more than 3 justices of the peace, including, so far as practicable, both a man and a woman.*

Note. Words in square brackets substituted for words in non-italics by Children Act 1989, s 92(11), Sch 11, Part II, para 8(c), as from 14 October 1991.

(2) Subsection (1) above shall not apply to a magistrates' court for an inner London petty sessions area, and, notwithstanding anything in section 67 below, for the purpose of exercising jurisdiction to hear domestic proceedings *[family proceedings] such a court shall be composed of—*

(a) a metropolitan stipendiary magistrate as chairman and one or 2 lay justices who are members of the domestic court panel *[family panel] for that area; or*

(b) 2 or 3 lay justices who are members of that panel;

or, if it is not practicable for such a court to be so composed, the court shall for that purpose be composed of a metropolitan stipendiary magistrate sitting alone.

Note. Words in square brackets substituted for words in non-italics by Children Act 1989, s 92(11), Sch 11, Part II, para 8(c), (d), as from 14 October 1991.

(3) Where in pursuance of subsection (2) above a magistrates' court includes lay justices it shall, so far as practicable, include both a man and a woman.

(4) In the preceding provisions of this section 'lay justices' means justices of the peace for the inner London area who are not metropolitan stipendiary magistrates.

(5) In this section 'inner London petty sessions area' means the City of London or any petty sessional division of the inner London area.

[66. Composition of magistrates' courts for family proceedings: general]

[(1) A magistrates' court when hearing family proceedings shall be composed of—

(a) two or three lay justices; or

(b) a District Judge (Magistrates' Courts) as chairman and one or two lay justices; or, if it is not practicable for such a court to be so composed, a District Judge (Magistrates' Courts) sitting alone.

(2) Except where such a court is composed of a District Judge (Magistrates' Courts) sitting alone, it shall, so far as practicable, include both a man and a woman.

(3) In this section *and section 67 below 'lay justices' means justices of the peace who are not District Judges (Magistrates' Courts)* [']lay justice' has the same meaning as in the Courts Act 2003].

Note. Substituted by the Access to Justice Act 1999, s 78(2), Sch 11, paras 26, 27, as from 31 August 2000 (see SI 2000 No 1920). Sub-s (3) amended by the Courts Act 2003, s 109, Sch 8, para 215, as from a day to be appointed.

67. Domestic courts [Family proceedings courts] and panels—(1) *Magistrates' courts constituted in accordance with the provisions of this section and sitting for the purpose of hearing domestic proceedings [family proceedings] shall be known as domestic courts [family proceedings courts].*

(2) *A justice shall not be qualified to sit as a member of a domestic court [family proceedings court] unless*
[(a) *he is a District Judge (Magistrates' Courts) nominated by the Lord Chancellor to do so; or*
(b) *he is a member of a family panel, that is to say a panel of lay justices]* specially appointed to deal with *he is a member of a domestic court panel [family panel], that is to say a panel of justices specially appointed to deal with domestic proceedings [family proceedings].*

(3) *Without prejudice to the generality of the power to make rules under section 144 below relating to the procedure and practice to be followed in magistrates' courts, provision may be made by such rules with respect to any of the following matters, that is to say—*
   (a) *the formation and revision of* domestic court panels *[family panels] and the eligibility of justices to be members of such panels;*
   (b) *the appointment of persons as chairmen of* domestic courts *[family proceedings courts]; and*
   (c) *the composition of* domestic courts *[family proceedings courts].*

(4) *Any provision made by rules by virtue of subsection (3) above for the formation of* domestic court panels *[family panels] shall include provision for the formation of at least one* domestic court panel *[family panel] for each commission area, but provision shall not be made by the rules for the formation of more than one* domestic court panel *[family panel] for any petty sessions area.*

In this subsection 'commission area' has the same meaning as in the Justices of the Peace Act 1979.

Note. For Justices of the Peace Act 1979, s 1, see p 2761.

(5) *Rules made by virtue of subsection (3) above may confer powers on the Lord Chancellor with respect to any of the matters specified in the rules and may, in particular, provide for the appointment of* domestic court panels *[family panels] by him and for the removal from a* domestic court panel *[family panel] of any justice who, in his opinion, is unsuitable to serve on a* domestic court *[family proceedings court].*

(6) *Rules made by virtue of subsection (3) above may make different provision in relation to different areas for which* domestic court panels *[family panels] are formed; and in the application of this section to the counties of Greater Manchester, Merseyside and Lancashire for any reference in subsection (5) above to the Lord Chancellor there shall be substituted a reference to the Chancellor of the Duchy of Lancaster.*

(7) *A stipendiary magistrate who is a member of a* domestic court panel *[family panel] may, notwithstanding anything in section 66(1) above, hear and determine* domestic proceedings *[family proceedings] when sitting alone.*

(8) *Nothing in this section shall require the formation of a* domestic court panel *[family panel] for the City of London.*

Note. Words in square brackets substituted for words in non-italics by Children Act 1989, s 92(11), Sch 11, Part II, para 8(d)–(g), as from 14 October 1991.

Further amended and repealed in part by the Access to Justice Act 1999, ss 78, 106, Sch 11, Sch 15, as from 30 August 2000 (SI 2000 No 1920).

[**67. Family proceedings courts**
   (1) Magistrates' courts—
      (a) constituted in accordance with this section or section 66 of the Courts Act 2003 (judges having powers of District Judges (Magistrates' Courts)), and
      (b) sitting for the purpose of hearing family proceedings,
   are to be known as family proceedings courts.
   (2) A justice of the peace is not qualified to sit as a member of a family proceedings court to hear family proceedings of any description unless he has an authorisation extending to the proceedings.

(3) He has an authorisation extending to the proceedings only if he has been authorised by the Lord Chancellor or a person acting on his behalf to sit as a member of a family proceedings court to hear—
  (a) proceedings of that description, or
  (b) all family proceedings.
(4) The Lord Chancellor may by rules make provision about—
  (a) the grant and revocation of authorisations,
  (b) the appointment of chairmen of family proceedings courts, and
  (c) the composition of family proceedings courts.
(5) Rules under subsection (4) may confer powers on the Lord Chancellor with respect to any of the matters specified in the rules.
(6) Rules under subsection (4) may be made only after consultation with the Family Procedure Rule Committee.
(7) Rules under subsection (4) are to be made by statutory instrument.
(8) A statutory instrument containing rules under subsection (4) is subject to annulment in pursuance of a resolution of either House of Parliament.]

Note. Substituted by the Courts Act 2003, s 49(1), as from a day to be appointed.

68. Combined domestic court family panels—*(1) Where the* Secretary of State *[Lord Chancellor] considers—*
  (a) *that a combined* domestic court panel *[family panel] should be formed for 2 or more petty sessions areas, or*
  (b) *that any combined* domestic court panel *[family panel] which has been so formed should be dissolved,*
he may direct the magistrates' courts committee for the area concerned to review the functioning of domestic courts *[family proceedings courts] in their area and on completion of the review to submit a report to the* Secretary of State *[Lord Chancellor].*
  (2) Where the Secretary of State *[Lord Chancellor] gives a direction under subsection (1) above, then—*
  (a) *after consideration of any report submitted to him under that subsection, or*
  (b) *if the committee fail to comply with the direction within 6 months from the giving thereof, after the expiration of that period of 6 months,*
the Secretary of State *[Lord Chancellor] may, if he thinks fit, make an order for the formation of a combined* domestic court panel *[family panel] for the petty sessions areas concerned or, as the case may be, for the dissolution of the combined* domestic court panel *[family panel] concerned.*
  (3) Where the Secretary of State *[Lord Chancellor] proposes to make an order under subsection (2) above, he shall send a copy of the proposed order to the magistrates' courts committee for any area the whole or part of which is concerned and to any* domestic court panel *[family panel] which is concerned.*
  (4) Where a copy of the proposed order is required to be sent under subsection (3) above to any committee or panel, the Secretary of State *[Lord Chancellor] shall, before making an order, consider any representations made to him by the committee or panel within one month from the time the copy of the proposed order was sent.*
  (5) An order of the Secretary of State *[Lord Chancellor] under subsection (2) above shall be made by statutory instrument and may be revoked or varied by a subsequent order thereunder.*
  (6) Any order made under subsection (2) above may contain supplementary, incidental and consequential provisions.
  (7) In the application of this section to the inner London area any reference to the magistrates' courts committee shall be treated as a reference to the committee of magistrates.

Note. Sub-s (7) repealed by Police and Magistrates' Courts Act 1994, s 93, Sch 9, Part II, as from 1 April 1995. References to 'Lord Chancellor' in square brackets substituted for references to 'Secretary of State' in non-italics by Transfer of Functions (Magistrates' Courts and Family Law) Order 1992, SI 1992 No 709, art 3(2), Sch 2, as from 1 April 1992. Other words in square brackets substituted for words in non-italics by Children Act 1989, s 92(11), Sch 11, Part II, para 8(d), (f), as from 14 October 1991.

Repealed by the Courts Act 2003, s 49(2), as from a day to be appointed.

69. Sittings of magistrates' courts for domestic proceedings [family proceedings]—(1) The business of magistrates' courts shall, so far as is consistent with the due dispatch of business, be arranged in such manner as may be requisite for separating the hearing and determination of *domestic proceedings* [family proceedings] from other business.

Note. Words in square brackets substituted for words in italics by Children Act 1989, s 92(11), Sch 11, Part II, para 8(c), as from 14 October 1991.

(2) In the case of *domestic proceedings* [family proceedings] in a magistrates' court other than proceedings under *the Adoption Act 1976* [the Adoption and Children Act 2002], no person shall be present during the hearing and determination by the court of the proceedings except—

(a) officers of the court;

(b) parties to the case before the court, their *solicitors and counsel* [legal representatives], witnesses and other persons directly concerned in the case;

(c) representatives of newspapers or news agencies;

(d) any other person whom the court may in its discretion permit to be present, so, however, that permission shall not be withheld from a person who appears to the court to have adequate grounds for attendance.

Note. Words in first pair of square brackets substituted for words in italics by Children Act 1989, s 92(11), Sch 11, Part II, para 8(c), as from 14 October 1991. Words in third pair of square brackets substituted for words in italics by Courts and Legal Services Act 1990, s 125(3), Sch 18, para 25(1)(b), as from 1 January 1991. Further amended by the Adoption and Children Act 2002, s 139, Sch 3, paras 36, 38, as from a day to be appointed.

(3) In relation to any *domestic proceedings* [family proceedings] under *the Adoption Act 1976* [the Adoption and Children Act 2002], subsection (2) above shall apply with the omission of paragraphs (c) and (d).

Note. Words in first pair of square brackets substituted for words in italics by Children Act 1989, s 92(11), Sch 11, Part II, para 8(c), as from 14 October 1991. Further amended by the Adoption and Children Act 2002, s 139, Sch 3, paras 36, 38, as from a day to be appointed.

(4) When hearing *domestic proceedings* [family proceedings], a magistrates' court may, if it thinks it necessary in the interest of the administration of justice or of public decency, direct that any persons, not being officers of the court or parties to the case, the parties' *solicitors or counsel* [legal representatives], or other persons directly concerned in the case, be excluded during the taking of any indecent evidence.

Note. Words in first pair of square brackets substituted for words in italics by Children Act 1989, s 92(11), Sch 11, Part II, para 8(c), as from 14 October 1991. Words in second pair of square brackets substituted for words in italics by Courts and Legal Services Act 1990, s 125(3), Sch 18, para 25(1)(b), as from 1 January 1991.

(5) The powers conferred on a magistrates' court by this section shall be in addition and without prejudice to any other powers of the court to hear proceedings in camera.

(6) Nothing in this section shall affect the exercise by a magistrates' court of the power to direct that witnesses shall be excluded until they are called for examination.

(7) Until the coming into operation of the Adoption Act 1976 this section shall have effect as if for any reference to that Act there were substituted a reference to the Adoption Act 1958, the Adoption Act 1960 and Part I of the Children Act 1975.

70. Jurisdiction of magistrates' courts in inner London for domestic proceedings [family proceedings]—(1) A relevant court for an *inner London petty sessions* [acting in an inner London local justice] area shall, in addition to hearing proceedings which (apart from subsection (2) below) may be heard by a relevant court *for that* [acting in that] area, have jurisdiction to hear proceedings which could be heard before a relevant court *for any* [acting in any] other such area, but shall not exercise the jurisdiction conferred by this subsection except in such cases or classes of case as may be determined by the *committee of magistrates* [*magistrates' courts committee whose area consists of or includes that petty sessions area*] [<u>Lord Chancellor</u>].

Note. Words in penultimate pair of square brackets substituted for words in italics by Police and Magistrates' Courts Act 1994, s 91(1), Sch 8, Part II, para 30, as from 1 April 1995. Further amended by the Courts Act 2003, s 109, Sch 8, para 216, as from a day to be appointed.

(2) A magistrates' court for *an inner London petty sessions* [<u>acting in an inner London local justice</u>] area shall not hear any *domestic proceedings* [family proceedings] if the *committee of magistrates* [*magistrates' courts committee whose area consists of or includes that petty sessions area*] *so determine* [<u>Lord Chancellor so determines</u>].

Note. Words 'family proceedings' in square brackets substituted for words 'domestic proceedings' in italics by Children Act 1989, s 92(11), Sch 11, Part II, para 8(c), as from 14 October 1991. Words 'magistrates' courts ... area' in square brackets substituted for words 'committee of magistrates' in italics by Police and Magistrates' Courts Act 1994, s 91(1), Sch 8, Part II, para 30, as from 1 April 1995. Further amended by the Courts Act 2003, s 109, Sch 8, para 216, as from a day to be appointed.

(3) In this section—
'relevant court' means a magistrates' court when composed for the purpose of exercising jurisdiction to hear *domestic proceedings* [family proceedings];
'inner London petty sessions area' means [*any petty sessions* ['<u>inner London local justice area' means any local justice</u>] area falling wholly or partly within the area consisting of the inner London boroughs and the City of London].

Note. Words in first pair of square brackets substituted for words in italics by Children Act 1989, s 92(11), Sch 11, Part II, para 8(c), as from 14 October 1991. Definition 'inner London petty sessions area' amended by the Access to Justice Act 1999, s 76, Sch 10, as from 27 September 1999; the Courts Act 2003, s 109, Sch 8, para 216, as from a day to be appointed.

71. Newspaper reports of domestic proceedings [family proceedings]—(*1*) *In the case of domestic proceedings [family proceedings] in a magistrates' court (other than proceedings under the Adoption Act 1976) it shall not be lawful for the proprietor, editor or publisher of a newspaper or periodical to print or publish, or cause or procure to be printed or published, in it any particulars of the proceedings other than the following, that is to say—*
(*a*) *the names, addresses and occupations of the parties and witnesses;*
(*b*) *the grounds of the application, and a concise statement of the charges, defences and counter-charges in support of which evidence has been given;*
(*c*) *submissions on any point of law arising in the course of the proceedings and the decision of the court on the submissions;*
(*d*) *the decision of the court, and any observations made by the court in giving it.*

[(1) In the case of *domestic proceedings* [family proceedings] in a magistrates' court (*other than proceedings under the Adoption Act 1976*) it shall not be lawful for a person to whom this subsection applies—
(a) to print or publish, or cause or procure to be printed or published, in a newspaper or periodical, or
(b) to include, or cause or procure to be included, in a programme included in a programme service (within the meaning of the Broadcasting Act 1990) for reception in Great Britain,
any particulars of the proceedings other than such particulars as are mentioned in subsection (1A) below.

Note. Words in italics repealed by the Adoption and Children Act 2002, as from a day to be appointed.

(1A) The particulars referred to in subsection (1) above are—
(a) the names, addresses and occupations of the parties and witnesses;
(b) the grounds of the application, and a concise statement of the charges, defences and counter-charges in support of which evidence has been given;
(c) submissions on any point of law arising in the course of the proceedings and the decision of the court on the submissions;

(d) the decision of the court, and any observations made by the court in giving it.

(1B) Subsection (1) above applies—

(a) in relation to paragraph (a) of that subsection, to the proprietor, editor or publisher of the newspaper or periodical, and

(b) in relation to paragraph (b) of that subsection, to any body corporate which provides the service in which the programme is included and to any person having functions in relation to the programme corresponding to those of an editor of a newspaper.]

Note. Sub-ss (1), (1A), (1B) in square brackets substituted for sub-s (1) in italics by Broadcasting Act 1990, s 203(1), Sch 20, para 29(2), as from 1 January 1991. Words 'family proceedings' in square brackets in sub-s (1) substituted for words 'domestic proceedings' by Children Act 1989, s 92(11), Sch 11, Part II, para 8(c), as from 14 October 1991.

(2) In the case of *domestic proceedings* [family proceedings] in a magistrates' court under *the Adoption Act 1976* [the Adoption and Children Act 2002], *subsection (1)* [subsection 1A] above shall apply with the omission of paragraphs (a) and (b) *and the reference in that subsection to the particulars of the proceedings shall, in relation to any child concerned in the proceedings, include—*

(a) the name, address or school of the child,

(b) any picture as being, or including, a picture of the child, and

(c) any other particulars calculated to lead to the identification of the child.

Note. Words in first pair of square brackets substituted for words in italics by Children Act 1989, s 92(11), Sch 11, Part II, para 8(c), as from 14 October 1991. Words in third pair of square brackets substituted for words in italics by Broadcasting Act 1990, s 203(1), Sch 20, para 29(2), as from 1 January 1991. Further amended by the Adoption and Children Act 2002, s 139, Sch 3, paras 36, 39, Sch 5.

(3) Any person acting in contravention of this section shall be liable on summary conviction to a fine not exceeding £500 [level 4 on the standard scale].

Note. Reference to level 4 substituted by virtue of Criminal Justice Act 1982, ss 37, 46(1).

(4) No prosecution for an offence under this section shall be begun without the consent of the Attorney General.

(5) Nothing in this section shall prohibit the printing or publishing of any matter in a newspaper or periodical of a technical character bona fide intended for circulation among members of the legal or medical professions.

(6) Until the coming into operation of the Adoption Act 1976 this section shall have effect as if for any reference to that Act there were substituted a reference to the Adoption Act 1958, the Adoption Act 1960 and Part I of the Children Act 1975.

Note. See also Judicial Proceedings (Regulation of Reports) Act 1926 (p 2068) as extended and modified by Domestic and Appellate Proceedings (Restriction of Publicity) Act 1968, s 2(3) (p 2283), and Administration of Justice Act 1960, s 12 (p 2229).

As to application of section, see Children Act 1989, s 97(8) (p 3399).

72. *Report by probation officer on means of parties*—(*1*) *Where in any* domestic proceedings *[family proceedings] in which an order may be made for the payment of money by any person, or in any proceedings for the enforcement or variation of any such order, a magistrates' court has requested a probation officer to investigate the means of the parties to the proceedings, the court may direct the probation officer to report the result of his investigation to the court in accordance with the provisions of this section; but in the case of any such* domestic proceedings *[family proceedings] no direction to report to the court shall be given to a probation officer under this subsection until the court had determined all issues arising in the proceedings other than the amount to be directed to be paid by such an order.*

Note. Words in square brackets substituted for words in non-italics by Children Act 1989, s 92(11), Sch 11, Part II, para 8(c), as from 14 October 1991.

(2) Where the court directs a probation officer under this section to report to the court the result of any such investigation as aforesaid, the court may require him—

(a) to furnish to the court a statement in writing about his investigation; or

(b) to make an oral statement to the court about his investigation.

(3) Where the court requires a probation officer to furnish a statement in writing under subsection (2) above—

(a) a copy of the statement shall be given to each party to the proceedings or to his counsel or solicitor *[legal representative]* at the hearing; and

(b) the court may, if it thinks fit, require that the statement, or such part of the statement as the court may specify, shall be read aloud at the hearing.

Note. Words in square brackets substituted for words in non-italics by Courts and Legal Services Act 1990, s 125(3), Sch 18, para 25(1), (4)(b), as from 1 January 1991.

(4) The court may and, if requested to do so at the hearing by a party to the proceedings or his counsel or solicitor *[legal representative]* shall, require the probation officer to give evidence about his investigation, and if the officer gives such evidence, any party to the proceedings may give or call evidence with respect to any matter referred to either in the statement or in the evidence given by the officer.

Note. Words in square brackets substituted for words in non-italics by Courts and Legal Services Act 1990, s 125(3), Sch 18, para 25(1), (4)(b), as from 1 January 1991.

(5) Any statement made by a probation officer in a statement furnished or made by him under subsection (2) above, or any evidence which he is required to give under subsection (4) above, may be received by the court as evidence, notwithstanding anything to the contrary in any enactment or rule of law relating to the admissibility of evidence.

Note. Section 72 repealed by the Criminal Justice and Court Services Act 2000, ss 74, 75, Sch 7, Pt II, paras 58, 61, Sch 8, as from 1 April 2001 (SI 2001 No 919).

73. Examination of witnesses by court. Where in any *domestic proceedings* [family proceedings], or in any proceedings for the enforcement or variation of an order made in *domestic proceedings* [family proceedings], it appears to a magistrates' court that any party to the proceedings who is not legally represented is unable effectively to examine or cross-examine a witness, the court shall ascertain from that party what are the matters about which the witness may be able to depose or on which the witness ought to be cross-examined, as the case may be, and shall put, or cause to be put, to the witness such questions in the interests of that party as may appear to the court to be proper.

Note. Words in square brackets substituted for words in italics by Children Act 1989, s 92(11), Sch 11, Part II, para 8(c), as from 14 October 1991.

74. Reasons for decisions in domestic proceedings [family proceedings]—(1) *The power to make rules conferred by section 144 below shall, without prejudice to the generality of subsection (1) of that section, include power to* [Rules of court may] make provision for the recording by a magistrates' court, in such manner as may be prescribed by the rules, of reasons for a decision made in such *domestic proceedings* [family proceedings] or class of *domestic proceedings* [family proceedings] as may be so prescribed, and for making available a copy of any record made in accordance with those rules of the reasons for a decision of a magistrates' court to any person who requests a copy thereof for the purposes of an appeal against that decision or for the purpose of deciding whether or not to appeal against that decision.

Note. Words in second and third pair of square brackets substituted for words in italics by Children Act 1989, s 92(11), Sch 11, Part II, para 8(c), as from 14 October 1991. First words in italics repealed and subsequent words in square brackets substituted by the Courts Act 2003, s 109, Sch 8, para 217, as from a day to be appointed.

(2) A copy of any record made by virtue of this section of the reasons for a decision of a magistrates' court shall, if certified by such officer of the court as may be prescribed, be admissible as evidence of those reasons.

PART III

SATISFACTION AND ENFORCEMENT

General provisions

75. Power to dispense with immediate payment—(1) A magistrates' court by whose conviction or order a sum is adjudged to be paid may, instead of requiring immediate payment, allow time for payment, or order payment by instalments.

(2) Where a magistrates' court has allowed time for payment, the court may, on application by or on behalf of the person liable to make the payment, allow further time or order payment by instalments.

[(2A) An order under this section that a lump sum required to be paid under a maintenance order shall be paid by instalments (a 'maintenance instalments order') shall be treated for the purposes of sections 59, 59B and 60 above as a maintenance order.

(2B) Subsections (5) and (7) of section 59 above (including those subsections as they apply for the purposes of section 60 above) shall have effect in relation to a maintenance instalments order—

(a) as if in subsection (5), paragraph (c) and the word 'and' immediately preceding it were omitted; and
(b) as if in subsection (7)—
  (i) the reference to the maintenance order were a reference to the maintenance order in respect of which the maintenance instalments order in question is made;
  (ii) for the words 'the person who applied for the maintenance order' there were substituted 'the debtor'.

(2C) Section 60 above shall have effect in relation to a maintenance instalments order as if in subsection (7), paragraph (c) and the word 'and' immediately preceding it were omitted.]

Note. Sub-ss (2A), (2B), (2C) inserted by Maintenance Enforcement Act 1991, s 11(1), Sch 2, para 6, as from 1 April 1992.

(3) Where a court has ordered payment by instalments and default is made in the payment of any one instalment, proceedings may be taken as if the default has been made in the payment of all the instalments then unpaid.

76. Enforcement of sums adjudged to be paid—(1) Subject to the following provisions of this Part of this Act, and to section 132 below *and section 19 of the Powers of Criminal Courts Act 1973*, where default is made in paying a sum adjudged to be paid by a conviction or order of a magistrates' court, the court may issue a warrant of distress for the purpose of levying the sum or issue a warrant committing the defaulter to prison.

Note. Words in italics repealed by Criminal Justice Act 1982, s 78, Sch 16, as from 24 May 1983.

(2) A warrant of commitment may be issued as aforesaid either—

(a) where it appears on the return to a warrant of distress that the money and goods of the defaulter are insufficient to satisfy the sum with the costs and charges of levying the sum; or
(b) instead of a warrant of distress.

(3) The period for which a person may be committed to prison under such a warrant as aforesaid shall not, subject to the provisions of any enactment passed after 31 December 1879, exceed the period applicable to the case under Schedule 4 to this Act.

[(4) Where proceedings are brought for the enforcement of a magistrates' court maintenance order under this section, the court may vary the order by exercising one of its powers under paragraphs (a) to (d) of section 59(3) above.

(5) Subsections (4), (5) and (7) of section 59 above shall apply for the purposes of subsection (4) above as they apply for the purposes of that section.

(6) Subsections (4) and (5) above shall not have effect in relation to a maintenance order which is not a qualifying maintenance order (within the meaning of section 59 above).]

Note. Sub-ss (4)–(6) added by Maintenance Enforcement Act 1991, s 7, as from 1 April 1992.

See also Maintenance Orders (Facilities for Enforcement) Act 1920, s 6 (p 2042); Maintenance Orders Act 1950, s 18 (p 2214); Maintenance Orders Act 1958, s 3 (p 2194); Maintenance Orders (Reciprocal Enforcement) Act 1972, ss 8, 33 (pp 2433, 2471); Civil Jurisdiction and Judgments Act 1982, s 5 (p 2889); and ss 92, 93 of this Act (p 2788).

77. Postponement of issue of warrant—(1) Where a magistrates' court has power to issue a warrant of distress under this Part of this Act, it may, if it thinks it expedient to do so, postpone the issue of the warrant until such time and on such conditions, if any, as the court thinks just.

(2) Where a magistrates' court has power to issue a warrant of commitment under this Part of this Act, it may, if it thinks it expedient to do so, fix a term of imprisonment [*or detention under* section 9 of the Criminal Justice Act 1982 [section 108 of the Powers of Criminal Courts (Sentencing) Act 2000] *(detention of persons aged* 17 *[18] to 20 for default)*] and postpone the issue of the warrant until such time and on such conditions, if any, as the court thinks just.

Note. Words in square brackets inserted by Criminal Justice Act 1982, s 77, Sch 14, para 50, as from 24 May 1983. Further amended by the Criminal Justice and Court Services Act 2000, ss 74, 75, Sch 7, Pt II, paras 58, 62, Sch 8, as from a day to be appointed; the Powers of Criminal Courts (Sentencing) Act 2000, s 165, Sch 9, para 66, as from 25 August 2000.

[(3) A magistrates' court shall have power at any time to do either or both of the following—

(a) to direct that the issue of the warrant of commitment shall be postponed until a time different from that to which it was previously postponed;

(b) to vary any of the conditions on which its issue is postponed,

but only if it thinks it just to do so having regard to a change of circumstances since the relevant time.

(4) In this section 'the relevant time' means—

(a) where neither of the powers conferred by subsection (3) above has been exercised previously, the date when the issue of the warrant was postponed under subsection (2) above; and

(b) in any other case, the date of the exercise or latest exercise of either or both of the powers.

(5) Without prejudice to the generality of subsection (3) above, if on an application by a person in respect of whom issue of a warrant has been postponed it appears to a justice of the peace acting *for the petty sessions* [in the local justice] area in which the warrant has been or would have been issued that since the relevant time there has been a change of circumstances which would make it just for the court to exercise one or other or both of the powers conferred by that subsection, he shall refer the application to the court.

(6) *Where such an application is referred to the court, it shall be the duty of the clerk of the court—*

(a) *to fix a time and place for the application to be heard; and*

(b) *to give the applicant notice of the time and place which he fixes.*

[(6) *Where such an application is referred to the court—*

(a) *the clerk of the court shall fix a time and place for the application to be heard; and*

(b) *the justices' chief executive for the court shall give the applicant notice of that time and place.*]

[(6) Where such an application is referred to the court—

(a) the clerk of the court shall fix a time and place for the application to be heard; and

(b) the designated officer for the court shall give the applicant notice of the time and place.]

Note. Sub-s (6) substituted by SI 2001 No 618, art 3, as from 1 April 2001. Further substituted by the Courts Act 2003, s 109, Sch 8, para 218, as from a day to be appointed.

(7) Where such a notice has been given but the applicant does not appear at the time and place specified in the notice, the court may proceed with the consideration of the application in his absence.

(8) If a warrant of commitment in respect of the sum adjudged to be paid has been issued before the hearing of the application, the court shall have power to order that the warrant shall cease to have effect and, if the applicant has been arrested in pursuance of it, to order that he shall be released, but it shall only make an order under this subsection if it is satisfied that the change of circumstances on which the applicant relies was not put before the court when it was determining whether to issue the warrant.]

Note. Sub-ss (3)–(8) added by Criminal Justice Act 1988, s 61(1), (2), as from 5 January 1989.

*   *   *   *   *

79. Release from custody and reduction of detention on payment—(1) Where imprisonment or other detention has been imposed on any person by the order of a magistrates' court in default of payment of any sum adjudged to be paid by the conviction or order of a magistrates' court or for want of sufficient distress to satisfy such a sum, then, on the payment of the sum, together with the costs and charges, if any, of the commitment and distress, the order shall cease to have effect; and if the person has been committed to custody he shall be released unless he is in custody for some other cause.

(2) Where, after a period of imprisonment or other detention has been imposed on any person in default of payment of any sum adjudged to be paid by the conviction or order of a magistrates' court or for want of sufficient distress to satisfy such a sum, payment is made in accordance with *the rules* [rules of court] of part of the sum, the period of detention shall be reduced by such number of days as bears to the total number of days in that period less one day the same proportion as the amount so paid bears to so much of the said sum, and the costs and charges of any distress levied to satisfy that sum, as was due at the time the period of detention was imposed.

(3) In calculating the reduction required under subsection (2) above any fraction of a day shall be left out of account.

Note. Words in italics repealed and subsequent words in square brackets substituted by the Courts Act 2003, s 109, Sch 8, para 219, as from 1 September 2004 (for effect see SI 2004 No 2066).

80. Application of money found on defaulter to satisfy sum adjudged—(1) Where a magistrates' court has adjudged a person to pay a sum by a conviction or has ordered the enforcement of a sum due from a person under *an affiliation order or an order enforceable as an affiliation order* [a magistrates' court maintenance order], the court may order him to be searched.

Note. Words in square brackets substituted for words in italics by Family Law Reform Act 1987, s 33(1), Sch 2, para 83, as from 1 April 1989.

(2) Any money found on the arrest of a person adjudged to pay such a sum as aforesaid, or on a search as aforesaid, or on his being taken to a prison or other place of detention in default of payment of such a sum or for want of sufficient distress to satisfy such a sum, may, unless the court otherwise directs, be applied towards payment of the said sum; and the balance, if any, shall be returned to him.

(3) A magistrates' court shall not allow the application as aforesaid of any money found on a person if it is satisfied that the money does not belong to him or that the loss of the money would be more injurious to his family than would be his detention.

*   *   *   *   *

Sums adjudged to be paid by an order

92. Restriction on power to impose imprisonment for default—(1) A magistrates' court shall not exercise its power under section 76 above to issue a warrant to commit to prison a person who makes default in paying a sum adjudged to be paid by an order of such a court except where the default is under—

(a) a magistrates' court maintenance order;

(b) an order under *section 32 of the Legal Aid Act 1974* [*section 7 or 8(2) of the Legal Aid Act 1982*] [*section 23 of the Legal Aid Act 1988*] *(contribution by legally assisted person to* [section 17(2) of the Access to Justice Act 1999 (payment by individual in respect of] cost of his defence in a criminal case); or

(c) an order for the payment of any of the taxes, contributions, premiums or liabilities specified in Schedule 4 to the Administration of Justice Act 1970.

Note. Words in first pair of square brackets in italics substituted for words 'section 32 of the Legal Aid Act 1974' by Legal Aid Act 1982, s 14(3), as from 1 March 1984. Words in second pair of square brackets substituted for words 'section 7 or 8(2) of the Legal Aid Act 1982' by Legal Aid Act 1988, s 45(1), (3), Sch 5, para 9, as from 1 April 1989. Further amended by the Access to Justice Act 1999, s 24, Sch 4, paras 15, 17, as from 2 April 2001 (SI 2001 No 916).

(2) This section does not affect the power of a magistrates' court to issue such a warrant as aforesaid in the case of default in paying a sum adjudged to be paid by a conviction, or treated (by any enactment relating to the collection or enforcement of fines, costs, compensation or forfeited recognizances) as so adjudged to be paid.

(*3*) *In this section—*

'*magistrates' court maintenance order*' *means a maintenance order enforceable by a magistrates' court;*

'*maintenance order*' *means any order specified in Schedule 8 to the Administration of Justice Act 1970 and includes such an order which has been discharged, if any arrears are recoverable thereunder.*

Note. Sub-s (3) repealed by Family Law Reform Act 1987, s 33(4), Sch 4, as from 1 April 1989. See now s 150(1) of this Act (p 2800).

93. Complaint for arrears—(1) Where default is made in paying a sum ordered to be paid by an affiliation order or order enforceable as *an affiliation order* [a magistrates' court maintenance order], the court shall not enforce payment of the sum under section 76 above except by an order made on complaint.

Note. Words in square brackets substituted for words in italics by Family Law Reform Act 1987, s 33(1), Sch 2, para 84, as from 1 April 1989.

(2) A complaint under this section shall be made not earlier than the fifteenth day after the making of the order for the enforcement of which it is made; but subject to this such a complaint may be made at any time notwithstanding anything in this or any other Act.

(3) In relation to complaints under this section, section 55 above shall not apply and section 56 above shall have effect as if the words 'if evidence has been received on a previous occasion' were omitted.

(4) Where at the time and place appointed for the hearing or adjourned hearing of a complaint under this section the complainant appears but the defendant does not, the court may proceed in his absence; but the court shall not begin to hear the complaint in the absence of the defendant unless either it is proved to the satisfaction of the court, on oath or in such other manner as may be prescribed, that the summons was served on him within what appears to the court to be a reasonable time before the hearing or adjourned hearing or the defendant has appeared on a previous occasion to answer the complaint.

(5) If a complaint under this section is substantiated on oath, any justice of the peace acting for *the same petty sessions* [in the same local justice] area as a court having jurisdiction to hear the complaint may issue a warrant for the defendant's arrest, whether or not a summons has been previously issued.

Note. Amended by the Courts Act 2003, s 109, Sch 8, para 228, as from a day to be appointed.

(6) A magistrates' court shall not impose imprisonment in respect of a default to which a complaint under this section relates unless the court has inquired in the presence of the defendant whether the default was due to the defendant's wilful refusal or culpable neglect, and shall not impose imprisonment as aforesaid if it is of opinion that the default was not so due; and, without prejudice to the preceding provisions of this subsection, a magistrates' court shall not impose imprisonment as aforesaid—

(*a*) *in a case in which the court has power to make an attachment of earnings order unless the court is of opinion that it is inappropriate to make such an order;*

(*b*) *in any case, in the absence of the defendant.*

[(a) in the absence of the defendant; or

(b) in a case where the court has power to do so, if it is of the opinion that it is appropriate—

(i) to make an attachment of earnings order; or

(ii) to order that payments under the order be made by any method of payment falling within section 59(6) above; or

(c) where the sum to which the default relates comprises only interest which the defendant has been ordered to pay by virtue of section 94A(1) below.]

Note. Sub-ss (6)(a)–(c) in square brackets substituted for sub-ss (6)(a), (b) in italics by Maintenance Enforcement Act 1991, s 11(1), Sch 2, para 7, as from 1 April 1992.

(7) Notwithstanding anything in section 76(3) above, the period for which a defendant may be committed to prison under a warrant of commitment issued in pursuance of a complaint under this section shall not exceed 6 weeks.

(8) The imprisonment or other detention of a defendant under a warrant of commitment issued as aforesaid shall not operate to discharge the defendant from his liability to pay the sum in respect of which the warrant was issued.

Note. See Maintenance Orders (Facilities for Enforcement) Act 1920, s 6 (p 2042); Maintenance Orders Act 1950, s 18 (p 2214); Maintenance Orders Act 1958, s 3 (p 2208); Maintenance Orders (Reciprocal Enforcement) Act 1972, ss 8, 33 (pp 2433, 2471); Civil Jurisdiction and Judgments Act 1982, s 5 (p 2828); and also s 59 of this Act (p 2788).

94. Effect of committal on arrears.   Where a person is committed to custody under this Part of this Act for failure to pay a sum due under *an affiliation order or order enforceable as an affiliation order* [a magistrates' court maintenance order], then unless the court that commits him otherwise directs, no arrears shall accrue under the order while he is in custody.

Note. Words in square brackets substituted for words in italics by Family Law Reform Act 1987, s 33(1), Sch 2, para 85, as from 1 April 1989.

[**94A. Interest on arrears**—(1) The *Secretary of State* [Lord Chancellor] may by order provide that a magistrates' court, on the hearing of a complaint for the enforcement, revocation, revival, variation or discharge of an English maintenance order, may order that interest of an amount calculated at the prescribed rate shall be paid on so much of the sum due under the order as they may determine.

(2) In subsection (1) above 'the prescribed rate' means such rate of interest as the *Secretary of State* [Lord Chancellor] may by order prescribe.

Note. Words 'Lord Chancellor' in square brackets in sub-ss (1), (2), substituted for words 'Secretary of State' in italics by Transfer of Functions (Magistrates' Courts and Family Law) Order 1992, SI 1992 No 709, art 3(2), Sch 2, as from 1 April 1992.

(3) An order under this section may make provision for the manner in which and the periods by reference to which interest is to be calculated.

(4) Where, by virtue of subsection (1) above, a magistrates' court orders the payment of interest on any sum due under a maintenance order—

(a) then if it orders that the whole or any part of the interest be paid by instalments that order shall be regarded as an instalments order for the purposes of section 95 below and that section shall accordingly apply in relation to it; and

(b) the whole of the interest shall be enforceable as a sum adjudged to be paid by the maintenance order.

(5) In this section—

'English maintenance order' means—]

    (a) a qualifying maintenance order made by a magistrates' court, other than an order made by virtue of Part II of the Maintenance Orders (Reciprocal Enforcement) Act 1972; or

    (b) an order made by the High Court or a county court (other than an order deemed to be made by the High Court by virtue of section 1(2) of the Maintenance Orders Act 1958) and registered under Part I of that Act of 1958 in a magistrates' court;

'qualifying maintenance order' has the same meaning as it has in section 59 above.

(6) The power of the *Secretary of State* [Lord Chancellor] to make an order under this section shall be exercisable by statutory instrument made with the concurrence of the Treasury and any such statutory instrument shall be subject to annulment in pursuance of a resolution of either House of Parliament.]

Note. This section inserted by Maintenance Enforcement Act 1991, s 8, as from 1 April 1992. Words 'Lord Chancellor' in square brackets in sub-s (6) substituted for words 'Secretary of State' in italics by Transfer of Functions (Magistrates' Courts and Family Law) Order 1992, SI 1992 No 709, art 3(2), Sch 2, as from 1 April 1992.

95. Power to remit arrears. *On the hearing of a complaint for the enforcement, revocation, revival, variation or discharge of an affiliation order or an order enforceable as an affiliation order [a magistrates' court maintenance order], the court may remit the whole or any part of the sum due under the order.*

[**95. Remission of arrears and manner in which arrears to be paid**—(1) On the hearing of a complaint for the enforcement, revocation, revival, variation or discharge of a magistrates' court maintenance order, a magistrates' court may remit the whole or any part of the sum due under the order.

(2) If, on the hearing of a complaint for the enforcement, revocation, revival, variation or discharge of a magistrates' court maintenance order, a magistrates' court orders that the whole or any part of the sum due under the order be paid by instalments (an 'instalments order'), then—

    (a) if the maintenance order is an English maintenance order, the court shall at the same time exercise one of its powers under paragraphs (a) to (d) of section 59(3) above in relation to the instalments order;

    (b) if the maintenance order is a non-English maintenance order, the court shall at the same time exercise one of its powers under subsection (3) below in relation to the instalments order.

(3) The powers of the court referred to in subsection (2)(b) above are—

    (a) the power to order that payments under the order be made directly to *the clerk of the court or the clerk of any other magistrates' court [a justices' chief executive]* [the designated officer for the court or for any other magistrates' court];

    (b) the power to order that payments under the order be made to *the clerk of the court, or to the clerk of any other magistrates' court [a justices' chief executive]* [the designated officer for the court or for any other magistrates' court], by such method of payment falling within section 59(6) above as may be specified;

    (c) the power to make an attachment of earnings order under the Attachment of Earnings Act 1971 to secure payments under the order.

Note. Amended by the Access to Justice Act 1999, s 90, Sch 13, paras 95, 110, as from 1 April 2001 (SI 2001 No 916); the Courts Act 2003, s 109, Sch 8, para 229, as from a day to be appointed.

(4) The court may in the course of any proceedings concerning an instalments order or the magistrates' court maintenance order to which it relates vary the instalments order by exercising—
- (a) in respect of an English maintenance order, one of the powers referred to in subsection (2)(a) above;
- (b) in respect of a non-English maintenance order, one of its powers under subsection (3) above.

(5) In respect of an English maintenance order, subsections (4), (5) and (7) of section 59 above shall apply for the purposes of subsections (2)(a) and (4)(a) above as they apply for the purposes of that section.

(6) In respect of a non-English maintenance order—
- (a) subsection (4) of section 59 above shall apply for the purposes of subsections (2)(b) and (4)(b) above as it applies for the purposes of that section but as if for paragraph (a) there were substituted—
  '(a) the court proposes to exercise its power under paragraph (b) of section 95(3) below;'; and
- (b) in deciding which of the powers under subsection (3) above it is to exercise the court shall have regard to any representations made by the debtor (within the meaning of section 59 above).

(7) In this section—
'English maintenance order' has the same meaning as it has in section 94A above;
'non English maintenance order' means—
- (a) a maintenance order registered in, or confirmed by, a magistrates' court—
  - (i) under the Maintenance Orders (Facilities for Enforcement) Act 1920;
  - (ii) under Part II of the Maintenance Orders Act 1950;
  - (iii) under Part I of the Maintenance Orders (Reciprocal Enforcement) Act 1972; *or*
  - (iv) under Part I of the Civil Jurisdiction and Judgments Act 1982; [or]
  - [(v) under Council Regulation (EC) No 44/2001 of 22nd December 2000 on jurisdiction and the recognition and enforcement of judgments in civil and commercial matters;]
- (b) an order deemed to be made by the High Court by virtue of section 1(2) of the Maintenance Orders Act 1958 and registered under Part I of that Act in a magistrates' court; or
- (c) a maintenance order made by a magistrates' court by virtue of Part II of the Maintenance Orders (Reciprocal Enforcement) Act 1972.]

Note. Words in square brackets in original s 95 in italics substituted for words 'an affiliation order or an order enforceable as an affiliation order' by Family Law Reform Act 1987, s 33(1), Sch 2, para 86, as from 1 April 1989. Section 95 in square brackets substituted for s 95 in italics by Maintenance Enforcement Act 1991, s 11(1), Sch 2, para 8, as from 1 April 1992. Further amended by SI 2001 No 3929, art 5, Sch 3, paras 10, 12, as from 1 March 2002.
  See also s 59 of this Act (p 2718).

96. Civil debt: complaint for non-payment—(1) A magistrates' court shall not commit any person to prison or other detention in default of payment of a sum enforceable as a civil debt or for want of sufficient distress to satisfy such a sum except by an order made on complaint and on proof to the satisfaction of the court that that person has, or has had since the date on which the sum was adjudged to be paid, the means to pay the sum or any instalment of it on which he has defaulted, and refuses or neglects or, as the case may be, has refused or neglected to pay it.

(2) A complaint under this section may be made at any time notwithstanding anything in this or any other Act.

(3) Where on any such complaint the defendant is committed to custody, such costs incurred by the complainant in proceedings for the enforcement of the sum as the court may direct shall be included in the sum on payment of which the defendant may be released from custody.

**[*96A.   Application of Part III to persons* aged 17 *[aged 18] to 20.   This Part of this Act shall have effect in relation to a person* aged 17 *[aged 18] or over but less than 21 as if any reference to committing a person to prison, or fixing a term of imprisonment for a default, were a reference to committing the person to, or, as the case may be, to fixing a term of, detention under* section 9 of the Criminal Justice Act 1982 *[section 108 of the Powers of Criminal Courts (Sentencing) Act 2002]; and any reference to warrants of commitment, or to periods of imprisonment imposed for default, shall be construed accordingly.]*

Note. This section inserted by Criminal Justice Act 1982, s 77, Sch 14, para 54, as from 24 May 1983. Words 'aged 18' in square brackets substituted for words 'aged 17' in non-italics by Criminal Justice Act 1991, s 68, Sch 8, para 6(3), as from 1 October 1992. Further amended by the Powers of Criminal Courts (Sentencing) Act 2000, s 165, Sch 9, para 70, as from 25 August 2000. Repealed by the Criminal Justice and Court Services Act 2000, ss 74, 75, Sch 7, Pt II, paras 58, 65, Sch 8, as from a day to be appointed.

PART IV

WITNESSES AND EVIDENCE

Procuring attendance of witness

97.   Summons to witness and warrant for his arrest—(1) Where a justice of the peace for *any county, any London commission area or the City of London* [*any commission area in England or any county in Wales*] is satisfied that any person in England and Wales is likely to be able to give material evidence, or produce any document or thing likely to be material evidence, *at an inquiry into an indictable offence by a magistrates' court for that county, that London commission area or the City* [that commission area *or county*] (*as the case may be*) *or* at the summary trial of an information or hearing of a complaint by *such a court* [a magistrates' court *for that commission area*] and that that person will not voluntarily attend as a witness or will not voluntarily produce the document or thing, the justice shall issue a summons directed to that person requiring him to attend before the court at the time and place appointed in the summons to give evidence or to produce the document or thing.

Note. Words in first and second pairs of square brackets substituted for preceding words in italics by Local Government Changes for England (Magistrates' Courts) Regulations 1996, SI 1996 No 674, reg 2, Schedule, Part I, para 2(4), (5), as from 1 April 1996. Words 'in England or any county in Wales' and 'or county (as the case may be)' repealed by Magistrates' Courts (Wales) (Consequences of Local Government Changes) Order 1996, SI 1996 No 675, art 2, Schedule, Part I, para 2(4), as from 1 April 1996. Words 'at an inquiry into ... or' repealed, and words in third pair of square brackets substituted for words 'such a court' in italics by Criminal Procedure and Investigations Act 1996, ss 47, 80, Sch 1, para 7, Sch 5, in relation to alleged offences into which no criminal investigation was begun before 1 April 1997. Further repealed in part by the Courts Act 2003, s 109, Sch 8, para 230, Sch 10, as from a day to be appointed.

(2) If a justice of the peace is satisfied by evidence on oath of the matters mentioned in subsection (1) above, and also that it is probable that a summons under that subsection would not procure the attendance of the person in question, the justice may instead of issuing a summons issue a warrant to arrest that person and bring him before such a court as aforesaid at a time and place specified in the warrant; but a warrant shall not be issued under this subsection where the attendance is required for the hearing of a complaint.

[(2A) A summons may also be issued under subsection (1) above if the justice is satisfied that the person in question is outside the British Islands but no warrant shall be issued under subsection (2) above unless the justice is satisfied by evidence on oath that the person in question is in England or Wales.]

Note. Sub-s (2A) inserted by Criminal Justice (International Co-operation) Act 1990, s 31(1), Sch 4, para 2, as from 10 June 1991.

[(2B) A justice may refuse to issue a summons under subsection (1) above in relation to the summary trial of an information if he is not satisfied that an application for the summons was made by a party to the case as soon as reasonably practicable after the accused pleaded not guilty.

(2C) In relation to the summary trial of an information, subsection (2) above shall have effect as if the reference to the matters mentioned in subsection (1) above included a reference to the matter mentioned in subsection (2B) above.]

Note. Sub-ss (2B), (2C) inserted by Criminal Procedure and Investigations Act 1996, s 51(1), as from 4 July 1996 in relation to any proceedings for the purposes of which no summons has been issued under s 97(1), and no warrant has been issued under s 97(2), before 1 April 1997.

(3) On the failure of any person to attend before a magistrates' court in answer to a summons under this section, if—

(a) the court is satisfied by evidence on oath that he is likely to be able to give material evidence or produce any document or thing likely to be material evidence in the proceedings; and

(b) it is proved on oath, or in such other manner as may be prescribed, that he has been duly served with the summons, and that a reasonable sum has been paid or tendered to him for costs and expenses; and

(c) it appears to the court that there is no just excuse for the failure,

the court may issue a warrant to arrest him and bring him before the court at a time and place specified in the warrant.

(4) If any person attending or brought before a magistrates' court refuses without just excuse to be sworn or give evidence, or to produce any document or thing, the court may commit him to custody until the expiration of such period not exceeding *7 days* [one month] as may be specified in the warrant or until he sooner gives evidence or produces the document or thing [or impose on him a fine not exceeding *£500* [*£1,000*] [£2,500], or both].

Note. Section 97(1), (3) and (4) are applied by Maintenance Orders (Reciprocal Enforcement) Act 1972, s 14(3), as amended (p 2442), for the purpose of obtaining evidence under that section.

Words in first pair of square brackets substituted for words in italics and words 'or impose ... both' in square brackets inserted by Contempt of Court Act 1981, s 14, Sch 2, Part III, para 7. '£1,000' substituted for '£500' by Criminal Penalties etc (Increase) Order 1984, SI 1984 No 447, art 2(3), Sch 3. '£2,500' substituted for '£1,000' by Criminal Justice Act 1991, s 17(3), Sch 4, Part I, as from 1 October 1992.

[*(5) Section 18 of the Criminal Justice Act 1991 (fixing of certain fines by reference to units) shall apply for the purposes of subsection (4) above as if the failure to attend before the magistrates' court were a summary offence punishable by a fine not exceeding level 4 on the standard scale; and a fine imposed under that subsection shall be deemed for the purposes of any enactment to be a sum adjudged to be paid by a conviction.*]

[(5) A fine imposed under subsection (4) above shall be deemed, for the purposes of any enactment, to be a sum adjudged to be paid by a conviction.]

Note. Sub-s (5) in italics added by Criminal Justice Act 1991, s 17(3), Sch 4, Part V, para 2, as from 1 October 1992. Sub-s (5) in square brackets substituted for sub-s (5) in italics by Criminal Justice Act 1993, s 65(3), Sch 3, para 6(3), as from 20 September 1993, subject to s 65(4) of the 1993 Act.

[**97A. Summons or warrant as to committal proceedings**—*(1) Subsection (2) below applies where a justice of the peace for any commission area is satisfied that—*

(a) any person in England or Wales is likely to be able to make on behalf of the prosecutor a written statement containing material evidence, or produce on behalf of the prosecutor

a document or other exhibit likely to be material evidence, for the purposes of proceedings before a magistrates' court inquiring into an offence as examining justices, [*and*]

(b)   the person will not voluntarily make the statement or produce the document or other exhibit, and

(c)   the magistrates' court mentioned in paragraph (a) above is a court for the commission area concerned.

(2)   In such a case the justice shall issue a summons directed to that person requiring him to attend before a justice at the time and place appointed in the summons to have his evidence taken as a deposition or to produce the document or other exhibit.

(3)   If a justice of the peace is satisfied by evidence on oath of the matters mentioned in subsection (1) above, and also that it is probable that a summons under subsection (2) above would not procure the result required by it, the justice may instead of issuing a summons issue a warrant to arrest the person concerned and bring him before a justice at the time and place specified in the warrant.

(4)   A summons may also be issued under subsection (2) above if the justice is satisfied that the person concerned is outside the British Islands, but no warrant may be issued under subsection (3) above unless the justice is satisfied by evidence on oath that the person concerned is in England or Wales.

(5)   If—

(a)   a person fails to attend before a justice in answer to a summons under this section,

(b)   the justice is satisfied by evidence on oath that he is likely to be able to make a statement or produce a document or other exhibit as mentioned in subsection (1)(a) above,

(c)   it is proved on oath, or in such other manner as may be prescribed, that he has been duly served with the summons and that a reasonable sum has been paid or tendered to him for costs and expenses, and

(d)   it appears to the justice that there is no just excuse for the failure,

the justice may issue a warrant to arrest him and bring him before a justice at a time and place specified in the warrant.

(6)   Where—

(a)   a summons is issued under subsection (2) above or a warrant is issued under subsection (3) or (5) above, and

(b)   the summons or warrant is issued with a view to securing that a person has his evidence taken as a deposition,

the time appointed in the summons or specified in the warrant shall be such as to enable the evidence to be taken as a deposition before a magistrates' court begins to inquire into the offence concerned as examining justices.

(7)   If any person attending or brought before a justice in pursuance of this section refuses without just excuse to have his evidence taken as a deposition, or to produce the document or other exhibit, the justice may do one or both of the following—

(a)   commit him to custody until the expiration of such period not exceeding one month as may be specified in the summons or warrant or until he sooner has his evidence taken as a deposition or produces the document or other exhibit;

(b)   impose on him a fine not exceeding £2,500.

(8)   A fine imposed under subsection (7) above shall be deemed, for the purposes of any enactment, to be a sum adjudged to be paid by a conviction.

(9)   If in pursuance of this section a person has his evidence taken as a deposition, the clerk of [*chief executive to*] [*designated officer for*] the justice concerned shall as soon as is reasonably practicable send a copy of the deposition to the prosecutor.

(10)   If in pursuance of this section a person produces an exhibit which is a document, the clerk of [*designated officer for*] the justice concerned shall as soon as is reasonably practicable send a copy of the document to the prosecutor.

(11)   If in pursuance of this section a person produces an exhibit which is not a document, the clerk of [*designated officer for*] the justice concerned shall as soon as is reasonably practicable inform the prosecutor of the fact and of the nature of the exhibit.]

Note. This section inserted by Criminal Procedure and Investigations Act 1996, s 47, Sch 1, Part II, para 8, in relation to alleged offences into which no criminal investigation was begun before 1 April 1997. Amended by the Access to Justice Act 1999, s 90, Sch 13, paras 95, 111, as from 1 April 2001 (SI 2001 No 916); the Courts Act 2003, s 109, Sch 8, para 231, as from a day to be appointed. Repealed by the Criminal Justice Act 2003, ss 41, 332, Sch 3, Pt 2, para 51, Sch 37, Pt 4.

Evidence generally

98. Evidence on oath. Subject to the provisions of any enactment or rule of law authorising the reception of unsworn evidence, evidence given before a magistrates' court shall be given on oath.

99. Proof of non-payment of sum adjudged. Where a magistrates' court has ordered one person to pay to another any sum of money, and proceedings are taken before that or any other magistrates' court to enforce payment of that sum, then—

(a) if the person to whom the sum is ordered to be paid is a *clerk of a magistrates' court*, [*justices' chief executive*] [the designated officer for a magistrates' court] a certificate purporting to be signed by *the clerk* [*the justices' chief executive*] [the designated officer] that the sum has not been paid to him; and

(b) in any other case a document purporting to be a statutory declaration by the person to whom the sum is ordered to be paid that the sum has not been paid to him,

shall be admissible as evidence that the sum has not been paid to him, unless the court requires *the clerk* [*the justices' chief executive*] [the designated officer] or other person to be called as a witness.

Note. Amended by the Access to Justice Act 1999, s 90, Sch 13, paras 95, 112, as from 1 April 2001; the Courts Act 2003, s 109, Sch 8, para 232, as from a day to be appointed.

100. Statement of wages to be evidence. A statement in writing to the effect that wages of any amount have been paid to a person during any period, purporting to be signed by or on behalf of his employer, shall be evidence of the facts therein stated in any proceedings taken before a magistrates' court—

(a) for enforcing payment by the person to whom the wages are stated to have been paid of a sum adjudged to be paid by a summary conviction or order; or

(*b*) *on any application made by or against that person for the making of an order in any matter of bastardy or an order enforceable as an affiliation order, or for the variation, revocation, discharge or revival of such an order.*

[(b) on any application made by or against that person for the making of a magistrates' court maintenance order, or for the variation, revocation, discharge or revival of such an order.]

Note. Para (b) in square brackets substituted for para (b) in italics by Family Law Reform Act 1987, s 33(1), Sch 2, para 87, as from 1 April 1989.

101. Onus of proving exceptions, etc. Where the defendant to an information or complaint relies for his defence on any exception, exemption, proviso, excuse or qualification, whether or not it accompanies the description of the office or matter of complaint in the enactment creating the offence or on which the complaint is founded, the burden of proving the exception, exemption, proviso, excuse or qualification shall be on him; and this notwithstanding that the information or complaint contains an allegation negativing the exception, exemption, proviso, excuse or qualification.

*   *   *   *   *

PART V

APPEAL AND CASE STATED

*   *   *   *   *

Case stated

111. Statement of case by magistrates' court—(1) Any person who was a party to any proceeding before a magistrates' court or is aggrieved by the conviction, order, determination or other proceeding of the court may question the proceeding on the ground that it is wrong in law or is in excess of jurisdiction by applying to the justices composing the court to state a case for the opinion of the High Court on the question of law or jurisdiction involved; but a person shall not make an application under this section in respect of a decision against which he has a right of appeal to the High Court or which by virtue of any enactment passed after 31 December 1879 is final.

(2) An application under subsection (1) above shall be made within 21 days after the day on which the decision of the magistrates' court was given.

(3) For the purpose of subsection (2) above, the day on which the decision of the magistrates' court is given shall, where the court has adjourned the trial of an information after conviction, be the day on which the court sentences or otherwise deals with the offender.

(4) On the making of an application under this section in respect of a decision any right of the applicant to appeal against the decision to the Crown Court shall cease.

(5) If the justices are of opinion that an application under this section is frivolous, they may refuse to state a case, and, if the applicant so requires, shall give him a certificate stating that the application has been refused; but the justices shall not refuse to state a case if the application is made by or under the direction of the Attorney General.

(6) Where justices refuse to state a case, the High Court may, on the application of the person who applied for the case to be stated, make an order of mandamus requiring the justices to state a case.

112. Effect of decision of High Court on case stated by magistrates' court.
Any conviction, order, determination or other proceeding of a magistrates' court varied by the High Court on an appeal by case stated, and any judgment or order of the High Court on such an appeal, may be enforced as if it were a decision of the magistrates' court from which the appeal was brought.

* * * * *

PART VII

MISCELLANEOUS AND SUPPLEMENTARY

Constitution and place of sitting of magistrates' courts

121. Constitution and place of sitting of court—(1) A magistrates' court shall not try an information summarily or hear a complaint except when composed of at least 2 justices unless the trial or hearing is one that by virtue of any enactment may take place before a single justice.

* * * * *

(6) Subject to the provisions of subsection (7) below, the justices composing the court before which any proceedings take place shall be present during the whole of the proceedings; but, if during the course of the proceedings any justice absents himself, he shall cease to act further therein and, if the remaining justices are enough to satisfy the requirements of the preceding provisions of this section, the proceedings may continue before a court composed of those justices.

* * * * *

(8) This section shall have effect subject to the provisions of this Act relating to *domestic proceedings* [family proceedings].

Note. Words in square brackets substituted for words in italics by Children Act 1989, s 92(11), Sch 11, Part II, para 8(c), as from 14 October 1991.

Appearance by counsel or solicitor

122. Appearance by counsel or solicitor—(1) A party to any proceedings before a magistrates' court may be represented by *counsel or solicitor* [a legal representative].

(2) Subject to subsection (3) below, an absent party so represented shall be deemed not to be absent.

(3) Appearance of a party by *counsel or solicitor* [a legal representative] shall not satisfy any provision of any enactment or any condition of a recognizance expressly requiring his presence.

Note. Words in square brackets in sub-ss (1), (3) substituted for words in italics by Courts and Legal Services Act 1990, s 125(3), Sch 18, para 25(1), (3)(b), as from 1 January 1991.

*   *   *   *   *

Limitation of time

127. Limitation of time—(1) Except as otherwise expressly provided by any enactment and subject to subsection (2) below, a magistrates' court shall not try an information or hear a complaint unless the information was laid, or the complaint made, within 6 months from the time when the offence was committed, or the matter of complaint arose.

*   *   *   *   *

Fees, fines, forfeitures, etc

138. Remission of fees. A magistrates' court may on the ground of poverty or for other reasonable cause remit in whole or in part any fee payable in proceedings before the court.

Note. Repealed by the Courts Act 2003, s 109, Sch 8, para 242, Sch 10, as from a day to be appointed.

*   *   *   *   *

Rules

144. Rule committee and rules of procedure—(1) The Lord Chancellor may appoint a rule committee for magistrates' courts, and may on the advice of or after consultation with the rule committee make rules for regulating and prescribing, [except in relation to—
   (a) any criminal cause or matter, or
   (b) family proceedings,]
the procedure and practice to be followed in magistrates' courts and by justices' clerks [and justices' chief executives].

Note. Amended by the Courts Act 2003, s 109, Sch 8, para 245, as from a day to be appointed; the Access to Justice Act 1999, s 90, Sch 13, paras 95, 116, as from 1 April 2001 (SI 2001 No 916).

(2) The rule committee shall consist of the Lord Chief Justice, *the President of the Family Division of the High Court, the [Senior District Judge (Chief Magistrate)] chief metropolitan stipendiary magistrate* and such number of other persons appointed by the Lord Chancellor as he may determine.

Note. Amended by the Courts Act 2003, s 109, Sch 8, para 245, as from a day to be appointed; the Access to Justice Act 1999, s 90, Sch 13, paras 95, 116, as from 1 April 2001 (SI 2001 No 916).

(3) Among the members of the committee appointed by the Lord Chancellor there shall be at least *one justices' clerk*
   [(za) one District Judge (Magistrates' Courts);]
   [(a) one justices' clerk;
   (b) one person who has a Supreme Court qualification (within the meaning of section 71 of the Courts and Legal Services Act 1990); and
   (c) one person who has been granted by an authorised body, under Part II of that Act, the right to conduct litigation in relation to all proceedings in the Supreme Court.]
one practising barrister and one practising solicitor of the Supreme Court.

Note. Paras (a)–(c) in square brackets substituted for words in italics by Courts and Legal Services Act 1990, s 125(3), Sch 18, para 25(1), (7), as from 1 January 1991. Further amended by the Courts Act 2003, s 109, Sch 8, para 245, as from a day to be appointed.

(4) The power to make rules conferred by this section shall be exercisable by statutory instrument which shall be subject to annulment by resolution of either House of Parliament.

(5) In this section the expression 'justices' clerk' means a clerk to the justices for a petty sessions area.

Note. Repealed by the Courts Act 2003, s 109, Sch 8, para 245, Sch 10, as from a day to be appointed.

145. Rules: supplementary provisions—(1) The power to make rules conferred by section 144 above shall, without prejudice to the generality of subsection (1) of that section, include power to make provision—

(a)   as to the practice and procedure of justices in exercising functions preliminary or incidental to proceedings before a magistrates' court;

[*(aa)   as to the determination of applications under section 3B above (including provision for their determination by justices' clerks);*]

(b)   as to the service and execution of process issued by or for the purposes of a magistrates' court, including the service and execution in England and Wales of process issued in other parts of the United Kingdom;

(c)   as to the keeping of records of proceedings before magistrates' courts and the manner in which things done in the course of, or as preliminary or incidental to, any such proceedings, or any proceedings on appeal from a magistrates' court to the Crown Court, may be proved in any legal proceedings;

(d)   *as to the extent to which a justices' clerk may engage in practice as a solicitor or barrister* [*legal representative*];

(e)   *as to the functions of officers of the Crown Court for the purposes of securing the attendance at a trial on indictment of persons in respect of whom conditional witness orders, or orders treated as conditional witness orders, have been made under section 1 of the Criminal Procedure (Attendance of Witnesses) Act 1965;*

(f)   *as to the furnishing by any person having custody of the depositions of copies thereof, and of copies of the information if it is in writing, to a person committed for trial;*

(g)   as to what magistrates' court shall have jurisdiction to hear any complaint;

(h)   as to the matters additional to those specified in section 53 above on complaint for which a magistrates' court shall have power to make an order with the consent of the defendant without hearing evidence;

(i)   *as to any other matters as to which immediately before the coming into force of section 15 of the Justices of the Peace Act 1949 provision was or could have been made by virtue of the enactments and parts of enactments repealed by Part II of Schedule 7 to the said Act of 1949.*

Note. Words in square brackets in sub-s (1)(d) substituted for words 'solicitor or barrister' by Courts and Legal Services Act 1990, s 125(3), Sch 18, para 25(1), (4)(c), as from 1 January 1991. Sub-s (1)(d) repealed by Police and Magistrates' Courts Act 1994, ss 91(1), 93, Sch 8, Part II, para 31, Sch 9, Part II, as from 1 April 1995. Sub-s (1)(e) repealed by Criminal Procedure and Investigations Act 1996, ss 65(3), 80, Sch 5(6), in relation to alleged offences into which no criminal investigation was begun before 1 April 1997.

Further amended by the Access to Justice Act 1999, s 80, as from a day to be appointed. Repealed in part by the Criminal Justice Act 2003, ss 41, 332, Sch 3, Pt 2, para 51, Sch 37, Pt 4; the Courts Act 2003, s 109, Sch 8, para 246, Sch 10, as from a day to be appointed.

(2) Where any Act expressly confers jurisdiction on any magistrates' court to hear a complaint, rules made under subsection (1)(g) above shall not take away that jurisdiction, but may extend it to any other magistrates' court.

(3) Any Act passed before 16 December 1949, in so far as that Act relates to matters about which rules may be made under section 144 above, shall have effect subject to any rules so made and may be amended or repealed by the rules

accordingly; but nothing in the said section shall authorise the rules to reduce the number of justices required for any purpose by any Act.

(*4*) *No provision included in rules under section 144 above which dispenses with the need to prove that a summons issued under section 1 above and served in accordance with the rules has come to the knowledge of the accused shall apply to a summons for an indictable offence.*

Note. Repealed by the Courts Act 2003, s 109, Sch 8, para 246, Sch 10, in part on 1 September 2004 (SI 2004 No 2066).

(5) Any rules, directions, forms or other instrument having effect immediately before this subsection comes into force as if contained in rules made under section 15 of the Justices of the Peace Act 1949 by virtue of section 15(8) of that Act (rules etc which previously had effect under the enactments repealed by Part II of Schedule 7 to that Act) shall have effect as if contained in rules made under section 144 above.

[145A. Rules: costs order against legal representative—(1) In any civil proceedings, a magistrates' court may disallow or (as the case may be) order the legal or other representative concerned to meet the whole of any wasted costs or such part of them as may be determined in accordance with rules.

(2) In subsection (1), 'wasted costs' means any costs incurred by a party—
- (a) as a result of any improper, unreasonable or negligent act or omission on the part of any legal or other representative or any employee of such a representative; or
- (b) which, in the light of any such act or omission occurring after they were incurred, the court considers it is unreasonable to expect that party to pay.

(3) In this section 'legal or other representative', in relation to any proceedings, means any person who is exercising a right of audience, or a right to conduct litigation, on behalf of any party to the proceedings.

(4) Rules made by virtue of this section may, in particular, make provision as to the destination of any payment required to be made under the rules (including provision for the reimbursement of sums paid by the *Legal Aid Board* [Legal Services Commission]).

Note. Amended by the Access to Justice Act 1999, s 24, Sch 4, paras 15, 19, as from 1 April 2000 (SI 2000 No 774).

(5) Rules made by virtue of this section—
- (a) shall require a magistrates' court which proposes to act under the rules against a legal or other representative to allow him a reasonable opportunity to appear before it and show cause why it should not do so.
- (b) shall provide that action may be taken under the rules either on the application of any party to the proceedings or on the motion of the court.
- (c) shall provide that no such action shall be taken after the end of the period of six months beginning with the date on which the proceedings are disposed of by the court; and
- (d) shall provide that a legal or other representative against whom action is taken under the rules may appeal to the Crown Court.]

Note. This section inserted by Courts and Legal Services Act 1990, s 112, as from 1 October 1991.

*   *   *   *   *

Interpretation

148. 'Magistrates' court'—(1) In this Act the expression 'magistrates' court' means any justice or justices of the peace acting under any enactment or by virtue of his or their commission or under the common law.

(2) Except where the contrary is expressed, anything authorised or required by this Act to be done by, to or before the magistrates' court by, to or before which any other thing was done, or is to be done, may be done by, to or before any magistrates' court acting for the same petty sessions area as that court.

*   *   *   *   *

150. Interpretation of other terms—(1) In this Act, unless the context otherwise requires, the following expressions have the meaning hereby assigned to them, that is to say—

'Act' includes local Act;

'affiliation order' has the same meaning as in the Affiliation Proceedings Act 1957;

'bail in criminal proceedings' has the same meaning as in the Bail Act 1976;

[*'commission area', in relation to England, has the meaning given by section 1 of the Justices of the Peace Act 1979 [the Justices of the Peace Act 1997];*]

'commit to custody' means commit to prison or, where any enactment authorises or requires committal to some other place of detention instead of committal to prison, to that other place;

'committal proceedings' means proceedings before a magistrates' court acting as examining justices;

'domestic proceedings' [family proceedings] has the meaning assigned to it by section 65 above;

'enactment' includes an enactment contained in a local Act or in any order, regulation or other instrument having effect by virtue of an Act;

'fine', except for the purposes of any enactment imposing a limit on the amount of any fine, includes any pecuniary penalty or pecuniary forfeiture or pecuniary compensation payable under a conviction;

'impose imprisonment' means pass a sentence of imprisonment or fix a term of imprisonment for failure to pay any sum of money, or for want of sufficient distress to satisfy any sum of money, or for failure to do or abstain from doing anything required to be done or left undone;

['legal representative' means an authorised advocate or authorised litigator, as defined by section 119(1) of the Courts and Legal Services Act 1990;]

'London commission area' has the same meaning as in the Justices of the Peace Act 1979 [the Justices of the Peace Act 1997];

['magistrates' court maintenance order' means a maintenance order enforceable by a magistrates' court;

'maintenance order' means any order specified in Schedule 8 to the Administration of Justice Act 1970 and includes such an order which has been discharged, if any arrears are recoverable thereunder;]

'petty-sessional court-house' means any of the following, that is to say—

(a) *a court-house or place at which justices are accustomed to assemble for holding special or petty sessions or for the time being appointed as a substitute for such a court-house or place (including, where justices are accustomed to assemble for either special or petty sessions at more than one court-house or place in a petty sessional division [petty sessions area], any such court-house or place);*

(b) *a court-house or place at which a stipendiary magistrate [District Judge (Magistrates' Courts)] is authorised by law to do alone any act authorised to be done by more than one justice of the peace;*

'petty sessions area' means any of the following areas, that is to say, a non-metropolitan county which is not divided into petty sessional divisions, a petty sessional division of a non-metropolitan county, a metropolitan district which is not divided into petty sessional divisions, a petty sessional division of a metropolitan district, a London commission area which is not divided into petty sessional divisions, a petty sessional division of a London commission area and the City of London;

[*'petty sessions area' has the same meaning as in the Justices of the Peace Act 1979;*]

['petty sessions area' has the same meaning as in the Justices of the Peace Act 1997;]

'prescribed' means prescribed by the rules;

[*'preserved county' has the meaning given by section 64 of the Local Government (Wales) Act 1994;*]

['public prosecutor', 'requisition' and 'written charge' have the same meaning as in section 29 of the Criminal Justice Act 2003;]

'the register' means the register of proceedings before a magistrates' court required by the rules to be kept by the clerk of the court;

'the rules' means rules made under section 144 above;

'sentence' does not include a committal in default of payment of any sum of money, or for want of sufficient distress to satisfy any sum of money, or for failure to do or abstain from doing anything required to be done or left undone;

'sum enforceable as a civil debt' means—

(a) any sum recoverable summarily as a civil debt which is adjudged to be paid by the order of a magistrates' court;

(b) any other sum expressed by this or any other Act to be so enforceable;

'transfer of fine order' has the meaning assigned to it by section 89 above.

Note. Definition 'affiliation order' repealed, and definitions 'magistrates' court maintenance order' and 'maintenance order' inserted by Family Law Reform Act 1987, s 33, Sch 2, para 88, Sch 4, as from 1 April 1989. Definition 'commission area' inserted by Local Government Changes for England (Magistrates' Courts) Regulations 1996, SI 1996 No 674, reg 2, Schedule, Part I, para 2(7), first words in italics repealed by Magistrates' Courts (Wales) (Consequences of Local Government Changes) Order 1996, SI 1996 No 675, art 2, Schedule, Part I, para 2(7), as from 1 April 1996, words in square brackets substituted for preceding words in italics by Justices of the Peace Act 1997, s 73(2), Sch 5, para 19(5), as from 19 June 1997. Words 'family proceedings' in square brackets substituted for words 'domestic proceedings' by Children Act 1989, s 92(11), Sch 11, Part II, para 8(c), as from 14 October 1991. Definition 'legal representative' inserted by Courts and Legal Services Act 1990, s 125(3), Sch 18, para 25(1), (2), as from 1 January 1991. In definition 'London commission area' words in square brackets substituted for words in italics by Justices of the Peace Act 1997, s 73(2), Sch 5, para 19(5), as from 19 June 1997. Definition 'petty sessions area' substituted for definition in italics by Local Government Act 1985, s 12(11), further substituted by Justices of the Peace Act 1997, s 73(2), Sch 5, para 19(5), as from 19 June 1997. Definition 'preserved county' inserted by Local Government (Wales) Act 1994, s 1(3), Sch 2, para 11(4), repealed by Magistrates' Courts (Wales) Consequences of Local Government Changes) Order 1996, SI 1996 No 675, art 2, Schedule, Part I, para 2(7), as from 1 April 1996. Further amended by the Access to Justice Act 1999, s 106, Sch 15, Pt V; the Criminal Justice Act 2003, ss 41, 331, 332, Sch 3, Pt 2, para 51, Sch 36, Pt 2, paras 7, 9, Sch 37, Pt 4, as from a day to be appointed; the Courts Act 2003, s 109, Sch 8, para 250, Sch 10, as from a day to be appointed.

(2) Except where the contrary is expressed or implied anything required or authorised by this Act to be done by justices may, where two or more justices are present, be done by one of them on behalf of the others.

(3) Any reference in this Act to a sum adjudged to be paid by a conviction or order of a magistrates' court shall be construed as including a reference to any costs, damages or compensation adjudged to be paid by the conviction or order of which the amount is ascertained by the conviction or order; but this subsection does not prejudice the definition of 'sum adjudged to be paid by a conviction' contained in subsection (8) of section 81 above for the purposes of that section.

(4) Where the age of any person at any time is material for the purposes of any provision of this Act regulating the powers of a magistrates' court, his age at the material time shall be deemed to be or to have been that which appears to the court after considering any available evidence to be or to have been his age at that time.

(5) Except where the context otherwise requires, any reference in this Act to an offence shall be construed as including a reference to an alleged offence; and any reference in this Act to an offence committed, completed or begun anywhere shall be construed as including a reference to an offence alleged to have been committed, completed or begun there.

(6) References in this Act to an offence punishable with imprisonment or punishable on summary conviction with imprisonment shall be construed without regard to any prohibition or restriction imposed by or under this or any other Act on imprisonment of young offenders.

(7) The provisions of this Act authorising a magistrates' court on conviction of an offender to pass a sentence or make an order instead of dealing with him in any other way shall not be construed as taking away any power to order him to pay costs, damages or compensation.

* * * * *

Repeals, short title, etc

154. Consequential amendments, transitional provisions, repeals, etc—(1) Subject to subsection (2) below, the enactments mentioned in Schedule 7 to this Act shall have effect subject to the amendments specified in that Schedule, being amendments consequential on the provisions of this Act.

(2) The transitional provisions and savings in Schedule 8 to this Act shall have effect.

(3) Subject to subsection (2) above, the enactments specified in Schedule 9 to this Act (which include enactments which were spent before the passing of this Act) are hereby repealed to the extent specified in the third column of that Schedule.

(4) Nothing in this Act shall be taken as prejudicing the operation of sections 16 and 17 of the Interpretation Act 1978 (which relate to the effect of repeals).

155. Short title, extent and commencement—(1) This Act may be cited as the Magistrates' Courts Act 1980.

* * * * *

(7) This Act shall come into force on such date as the Secretary of State may appoint by order made by statutory instrument.

Commencement. This Act was brought into force on 6 July 1981 (SI 1981 No 457).

SCHEDULE 4   Section 76

MAXIMUM PERIODS OF IMPRISONMENT IN DEFAULT OF PAYMENT

1. Subject to the following provisions of this Schedule, the periods set out in the second column of the following Table shall be the maximum periods applicable respectively to the amounts set out opposite thereto, being amounts due at the time the imprisonment [or detention] is imposed.

TABLE

An amount not exceeding £25 [£50]	*7 days*
An amount exceeding £25 [£50] but not exceeding £50 [£100]	*14 days*
An amount exceeding £50 [£100] but not exceeding £200 [£400]	*30 days*
An amount exceeding £200 [£400] but not exceeding £500 [£1,000]	*60 days*
An amount exceeding £500 [£1,000] but not exceeding £1,000 [£2,000]	*90 days*
An amount exceeding £1,000 [£2,000] but not exceeding £2,500 [£5,000]	*6 months*
An amount exceeding £2,500 [£5,000] but not exceeding £5,000 [£10,000]	*9 months*
An amount exceeding £5,000 [£10,000]	*12 months*
[An amount not exceeding £50	*5 days*
An amount exceeding £50 but not exceeding £100	*7 days*
An amount exceeding £100 but not exceeding £400	*14 days*
An amount exceeding £400 but not exceeding £1,000	*30 days*
An amount exceeding £1,000 but not exceeding £2,000	*45 days*
An amount exceeding £2,000 but not exceeding £5,000	*3 months*
[An amount not exceeding £200	7 days
An amount exceeding £200 but not exceeding £500	14 days
An amount exceeding £500 but not exceeding £1,000	28 days
An amount exceeding £1,000 but not exceeding £2,500	45 days
An amount exceeding £2,500 but not exceeding £5,000	3 months]
An amount exceeding £5,000 but not exceeding £10,000	6 months
An amount exceeding £5,000 [£10,000]	12 months]

2. (1) Where the amount due at the time imprisonment [or detention] is imposed is so much of a sum adjudged to be paid by a summary conviction as remains due after part payment, then, subject to sub-paragraph (2) below, the maximum period applicable to the amount shall be the period applicable to the whole sum reduced by such number of days as bears to the total number of days therein the same proportion as the part paid bears to the whole sum.

(2) In calculating the reduction required under sub-paragraph (1) above any fraction of a day shall be left out of account and the maximum period shall not be reduced to less than *5 days* [seven days].

3. The maximum period applicable to a sum of any amount enforceable as a civil debt shall be 6 weeks.

Note. Words in square brackets in paras 1, 2(1) added by Criminal Justice Act 1982, s 77, Sch 14, para 59, as from 24 May 1983. Words in square brackets in para 2(2) substituted for words in italics by Criminal Justice Act 1991, s 100, Sch 11, para 28, as from 1 October 1992. Figures in square brackets in italics substituted for figures in italics by Criminal Penalties, etc (Increase) Order 1984, SI 1984 No 447, and first Table in square brackets substituted for Table in italics by Criminal Justice Act 1988, s 60(1), as from 5 January 1989. Second Table in square brackets substituted for entries in italics in first Table in square brackets by Criminal Justice Act 1991, s 23(1), as from 1 October 1992.

SCHEDULE 8   Section 154

TRANSITIONAL PROVISIONS AND SAVINGS

Interpretation

1. In this Schedule references to the old enactments are to enactments repealed or amended by this Act and references to the appointed day are to the day on which this Act comes into force.

Proceedings commenced before appointed day

2. (1) Where proceedings were commenced before the appointed day, the old enactments relating to the proceedings continue to apply and nothing in this Act affects those enactments.

(2) Without prejudice to the generality of sub-paragraph (1) above, the old enactments relating to proceedings which continue in force by virtue of it include any provision of those enactments which creates an offence, which relates to civil or criminal procedure, which relates to the punishment for an offence, or which relates to enforcing, appealing against, questioning, varying or rescinding anything ordered or done in the proceedings.

*   *   *   *   *

Other matters: general

4. Paragraphs 5 and 6 below have effect subject to paragraphs 2 and 3 above.

5. Without prejudice to any express amendment made by this Act, a reference in an enactment or other document, whether express or implied, to an enactment repealed by this Act shall, unless the context otherwise requires, be construed as, or as including, a reference to this Act or to the corresponding provision of this Act.

6. Where a period of time specified in an enactment repealed by this Act is current at the commencement of this Act, this Act shall have effect as if the corresponding provision of it had been in force when that period began to run.

Saving for transitionals in orders

7. (1) This paragraph applies where any provision of an old enactment—
  (a) was brought into force by order which made transitional provision in connection with the provision brought into force, or

(b) fell to be brought into force by order which could have made transitional provision in connection with the provision brought into force, if this Act had not been passed.

(2) In that case, an order under section 155(7) of this Act may make corresponding transitional provision in connection with any provision of this Act corresponding to that of the old enactment.

Savings of amendments

8. Notwithstanding the repeal by this Act of the Magistrates' Courts Act 1952, the amendments made in other enactments ('the amended enactments') by that Act shall, to the extent that they had effect immediately before the coming into force of this Act, continue to have effect subject to any amendment of any of the amended enactments by this Act.

DESTINATION TABLE

This Table shows in column (1) the enactments repealed by the Magistrates' Courts Act 1980 and in column (2) the provisions of that Act corresponding to the repealed provisions.

In certain cases the enactment in column (1), though having a corresponding provision in column (2), is not, or is not wholly, repealed, as it is still required, or partly required, for the purposes of other legislation.

The Table is restricted to sections of earlier legislation printed ante, and to sections of the Magistrates' Courts Act 1980 printed in this work.

(1)	(2)	(1)	(2)
Justices of the Peace Act 1949 (c 101)	Magistrates' Courts Act 1980 (c 43)	Magistrates' Courts Act 1952 (c 55)	Magistrates' Courts Act 1980 (c 43)
s 15(1)–(3)	s 144(1)–(3)	s 49	s 57
(7)	Sch 7, para 5	50	58
(8)	145(5)	51	Rep, 1957 c 55, s 12, Sch
(9)	144(4)		
44(1)†	(5)	52	s 59
		53	60
Magistrates' Courts Act 1952 (c 55)		53A	62
		54	63
		55	64
		56(1)	65(1), (6)
s 1(1)	1(1), (3), (8)	(1A)–(1D)	(2)–(5)
(2)	(2), (5), (8)	(2)	66(1)
(3)	(6)	56A	67
(4)	Rep, 1971 c 23, s (4), Sch 11, Part IV	56B	68
		57(1), (2)	69(1), (2)
		(2A)	(3)
(5)	1(7)	(2B)	(7)
43	s 51	(3)	(4)
44	52	(4)	Rep, 1978 c 22, s 89(2), Sch 3
45	53		
46	54	(5), (6)	s 69(5), (6)
47	55	58(1)	71(1)
48	56	(1A)	(2)

* Not repealed.	† Repealed in part.

(1)	(2)	(1)	(2)
Magistrates' Courts Act 1952 (c 55)	Magistrates' Courts Act 1980 (c 43)	Magistrates' Courts Act 1952 (c 55)	Magistrates' Courts Act 1980 (c 43)
s 58(1B)	s 71(6)	s 26(7)	Rep, 1967 c 58, s 10(2), Sch 3, Part III
(2)–(5)	(3)–(5)		
59	Rep, 1978 c 22, s 89(2), Sch 3	(8), (9)	s 150(6),(7)
60(1)–(3)	s 72(1)–(3)	(10)	————
(3A)	(4)	133(2)	s 155(3), (4), (6)
(4)	(5)	3, paras 1, 2	4, paras 1, 2
61	73	para 4	4, para 3
62	Rep, 1978 c 22, s 89(2), Sch 3	5	See Sch 8, para 8
63	s 75	Maintenance Orders Act 1958 (c 39)	
64	76		
65	77		
66	78	————	
67	79	s 16(1)	93(3)–(8)
68	80	(2)	————
70(1)	Rep, 1967 c 80, s 103(2), Sch 7, Part I	20(6)	59(3), (4)
		23(2)*	155(6)
(2)–(5)	s 83	Administration of Justice Act 1964 (c 42)	
73	96		
74	93		
75	94	————	
76	95	s 11(1), (2)	66(2), (3)
77	97	(3), (4)	70(1), (2)
78	98	(5)	66(5), 70(3)
79	99	38(1)*	66(5), 70(3)
80	100	41(7)*	155(6)
81	101	Sch 3, para 20(2)	144(2)
84	Rep, 1971 c 23, s 56(4), Sch 11, Part IV	s 1(6)(b)	144(2)
		12(1)	92(1)
		(2)	(1),(2)
87	s 111	28(1)†	(3)
88	112	30(1)†, (2)†	————
98	121	41(6)	89(1), (2)
99	122	42	87(1)
104	127(1)	50	150(4)
113(1)	138	51(1)	(4)
(2)	Rep, 1967 c 80, s 103(2), Sch 7, Part I	(3)†	————
		54(6)*	155(6)
122	s 145(1)–(3)	Guardianship Act 1973 (c 29)	
124	148		
126(1)–(3)	150(1)–(3)	————	
(4)	Rep, 1972 c 70, s 272(1), Sch 30	s 9(2)(b)	59(2)
(5), (6)	s 150(4), (5)		

* Not repealed.	† Repealed in part.

(1)	(2)	(1)	(2)
Social Security Act 1973 (c 38)	Magistrates' Courts Act 1980 (c 43)	Criminal Law Act 1977 (c 45)	Magistrates' Courts Act 1980 (c 43)
Sch 27, para 85†	s 92(1)	s 85	61
s 92(1)	Sch 4, para 3	90(3)*	155(6)
		Sch 1, para 5†	See Sch 8
Criminal Law Act 1977 (c 45)		para 6, 7	
		2, para 15	s 59(2)
		para 21	66(2)
s 18	s 127(2)–(4)		
75	52, 67(4)	Justices of the Peace Act 1979 (c 55)	
76	60		
77	62		
78	63(3), (4)		
79	65	s 2(1)*	150(1)
80	67, 68	33(1)*	66(4)
81(1)	69(2)	Sch 2, para 7	52, 67(4)
(2)	(3), (7)		
82(1)	71(1)	Child Care Act 1980 (c 5)	
(2)	(2), (6)		
(3)	(3)		
83	72	Sch 5, para 5	65(1)
84	74		

* Not repealed.   † Repealed in part.

CONTEMPT OF COURT ACT 1981

(1981 c 49)

ARRANGEMENT OF SECTIONS

Strict liability

An act to amend the laws relating to contempt of court and related matters.

[27 July 1981]

Strict liability

1. The strict liability rule. In this Act 'the strict liability rule' means the rule of law whereby conduct may be treated as a contempt of court as tending to interfere with the course of justice in particular legal proceedings regardless of intent to do so.

2. Limitation of scope of strict liability—(1) The strict liability rule applies only in relation to publications, and for this purpose 'publication' includes any speech, writing, *broadcast* [*cable programme*] [programme included in a programme service] or other communication in whatever form, which is addressed to the public at large or any section of the public.

Note. Words 'programme included in a programme service' in square brackets substituted for words in italics by Broadcasting Act 1990, s 203(1), Sch 20, para 31, as from 1 January 1991. Words 'cable programme' in square brackets inserted by Cable and Broadcasting Act 1984, s 57(1), Sch 5, para 39(1).

(2) The strict liability rule applies only to a publication which creates a substantial risk that the course of justice in the proceedings in question will be seriously impeded or prejudiced.

(3) The strict liability rule applies to a publication only if the proceedings in question are active within the meaning of this section at the time of the publication.

(4) Schedule 1 applies for determining the times at which proceedings are to be treated as active within the meaning of this section.

[(5) In this section 'programme service' has the same meaning as in the Broadcasting Act 1990.]

Note. Sub-s (5) inserted by Broadcasting Act 1990, s 203(1), Sch 20, para 31, as from 1 January 1991.

3. Defence of innocent publication or distribution—(1) A person is not guilty of contempt of court under the strict liability rule as the publisher of any matter to which that rule applies if at the time of publication (having taken all reasonable care) he does not know and has no reason to suspect that relevant proceedings are active.

(2) A person is not guilty of contempt of court under the strict liability rule as the distributor of a publication containing any such matter if at the time of distribution (having taken all reasonable care) he does not know that it contains such matter and has no reason to suspect that it is likely to do so.

(3) The burden of proof of any fact tending to establish a defence afforded by this section to any person lies upon that person.

(4) ...

Note. Sub-s (4) repeals Administration of Justice Act 1960, s 11. Repealed by the Statute Law (Repeals) Act 2004, as from 22 July 2004.

4. Contemporary reports of proceedings—(1) Subject to this section a person is not guilty of contempt of court under the strict liability rule in respect of a fair and accurate report of legal proceedings held in public, published contemporaneously and in good faith.

(2) In any such proceedings the court may, where it appears to be necessary for avoiding a substantial risk of prejudice to the administration of justice in those proceedings, or in any other proceedings pending or imminent, order that the publication of any report of the proceedings, or any part of the proceedings, be postponed for such period as the court thinks necessary for that purpose.

[(2A) Where in proceedings for any offence which is an administration of justice offence for the purposes of section 54 of the Criminal Procedure and Investigations Act 1996 (acquittal tainted by an administration of justice offence) it appears to the court that there is a possibility that (by virtue of that section) proceedings may be taken against a person for an offence of which he has been acquitted, subsection (2) of this section shall apply as if those proceedings were pending or imminent.]

Note. Sub-s (2A) inserted by Criminal Procedure and Investigations Act 1996, s 57(3), as from 4 July 1996, in relation to acquittals in respect of offences alleged to be committed on or after 15 April 1997.

(3) For the purposes of subsection (1) of this section *and of section 3 of the Law of Libel Amendment Act 1888 (privilege)* a report of proceedings shall be treated as published contemporaneously—

(a) in the case of a report of which publication is postponed pursuant to an order under subsection (2) of this section, if published as soon as practicable after that order expires;

(b) *in the case of a report of committal proceedings of which publication is permitted by virtue only of subsection (3) of section 8 of the Magistrates' Courts Act 1980, if published as soon as practicable after publication is so permitted.*

[(b) in the case of a report of allocation or sending proceedings of which publication is permitted by virtue only of subsection (6) of section 52A of the Crime and Disorder Act 1998 ('the 1998 Act'), if published as soon as practicable after publication is so permitted;

(c) in the case of a report of an application of which publication is permitted by virtue only of sub-paragraph (5) or (7) of paragraph 3 of Schedule 3 to the 1998 Act, if published as soon as practicable after publication is so permitted].

Note. Words in italics repealed by Defamation Act 1996, s 16, Sch 2, as from a day to be appointed. Further amended by the Criminal Justice Act 2003, s 41, as from a date to be appointed.

(4) ...

Note. Sub-s (4) repeals Magistrates' Courts Act 1980, s 8(9). Repealed by the Statute Law (Repeals) Act 2004, as from 22 July 2004.

5. Discussion of public affairs. A publication made as or as part of a discussion in good faith of public affairs or other matters of general public interest is not to be treated as a contempt of court under the strict liability rule if the risk of impediment or prejudice to particular legal proceedings is merely incidental to the discussion.

6. Savings. Nothing in the foregoing provisions of this Act—
  (a) prejudices any defence available at common law to a charge of contempt of court under the strict liability rule;
  (b) implies that any publication is punishable as contempt of court under that rule which would not be so punishable apart from those provisions;
  (c) restricts liability for contempt of court in respect of conduct intended to impede or prejudice the administration of justice.

7. Consent required for institution of proceedings. Proceedings for a contempt of court under the strict liability rule (other than Scottish proceedings) shall not be instituted except by or with the consent of the Attorney General or on the motion of a court having jurisdiction to deal with it.

Other aspects of law and procedure

8. Confidentiality of jury's deliberations—(1) Subject to subsection (2) below, it is a contempt of court to obtain, disclose or solicit any particulars of statements made, opinions expressed, arguments advanced or votes cast by members of a jury in the course of their deliberations in any legal proceedings.
  (2) This section does not apply to any disclosure of any particulars—
  (a) in the proceedings in question for the purpose of enabling the jury to arrive at their verdict, or in connection with the delivery of that verdict, or
  (b) in evidence in any subsequent proceedings for an offence alleged to have been committed in relation to the jury in the first mentioned proceedings,
or to the publication of any particulars so disclosed.
  (3) Proceedings for a contempt of court under this section (other than Scottish proceedings) shall not be instituted except by or with the consent of the Attorney General or on the motion of a court having jurisdiction to deal with it.

9. Use of tape recorders—(1) Subject to subsection (4) below, it is a contempt of court—
  (a) to use in court, or bring into court for use, any tape recorder or other instrument for recording sound, except with the leave of the court;
  (b) to publish a recording of legal proceedings made by means of any such instrument, or any recording derived directly or indirectly from it, by playing it in the hearing of the public or any section of the public, or to dispose of it or any recording so derived, with a view to such publication;
  (c) to use any such recording in contravention of any conditions of leave granted under paragraph (a).
  (2) Leave under paragraph (a) of subsection (1) may be granted or refused at the discretion of the court, and if granted may be granted subject to such conditions as

the court thinks proper with respect to the use of any recording made pursuant to the leave; and where leave has been granted the court may at the like discretion withdraw or amend it either generally or in relation to any particular part of the proceedings.

(3) Without prejudice to any other power to deal with an act of contempt under paragraph (a) of subsection (1), the court may order the instrument, or any recording made with it, or both, to be forfeited; and any object so forfeited shall (unless the court otherwise determines on application by a person appearing to be the owner) be sold or otherwise disposed of in such manner as the court may direct.

(4) This section does not apply to the making or use of sound recordings for purposes of official transcripts of proceedings.

10. Sources of information. No court may require a person to disclose, nor is any person guilty of contempt of court for refusing to disclose, the source of information contained in a publication for which he is responsible, unless it be established to the satisfaction of the court that disclosure is necessary in the interests of justice or national security or for the prevention of disorder or crime.

11. Publication of matters exempted from disclosure in court. In any case where a court (having power to do so) allows a name or other matter to be withheld from the public in proceedings before the court, the court may give such directions prohibiting the publication of that name or matter in connection with the proceedings as appear to the court to be necessary for the purpose for which it was so withheld.

Note. See *R v Arundel Justices, ex p Westminster Press Ltd* [1985] 2 All ER 390, [1985] 1 WLR 708, DC. See also *R v Westminster City Council, ex p Castelli: R v Same, ex p Tristran-Garcia* (1995) Times, 14 August. *R v Westminster CC, ex p Castelli* is also reported at [1996] 1 FLR 534, [1996] 2 FCR 49.

12. Offences of contempt of magistrates' courts—(1) A magistrates' court has jurisdiction under this section to deal with any person who—
  (a) wilfully insults the justice or justices, any witness before or officer of the court or any solicitor or counsel having business in the court, during his or their sitting or attendance in court or in going to or returning from the court; or
  (b) wilfully interrupts the proceedings of the court or otherwise misbehaves in court.

(2) In any such case the court may order any officer of the court, or any constable, to take the offender into custody and detain him until the rising of the court; and the court may, if it thinks fit, commit the offender to custody for a specified period not exceeding one month or impose on him a fine not exceeding £500 [£1,000] [£2,500], or both.

Note. '£1,000' substituted for '£500' by Criminal Penalties etc (Increase) Order 1984, SI 1984 No 447, art 2(3), Sch 3, as from 1 May 1984. '£2,500' substituted for '£1,000' by Criminal Justice Act 1991, s 17(3), Sch 4, Part I, as from 1 October 1992.

[(2A) *Section 18 of the Criminal Justice Act 1991 (fixing of certain fines by reference to units) shall apply for the purposes of subsection (2) above as if the failure to attend before the magistrates' court were a summary offence punishable by a fine not exceeding level 4 on the standard scale; and a fine imposed under that subsection shall be deemed for the purposes of any enactment to be a sum adjudged to be paid by a conviction.*]

[(2A) A fine imposed under subsection (2) above shall be deemed, for the purposes of any enactment, to be a sum adjudged to be paid by a conviction.]

Note. Sub-s (2A) in italics inserted by Criminal Justice Act 1991, s 17(3), Sch 4, Part V, para 3, as from 1 October 1992. Sub-s (2A) in square brackets substituted for sub-s (2A) in italics by Criminal Justice Act 1993, s 65(3), Sch 3, para 6(4), as from 20 September 1993.

(3) *The court shall not deal with the offender by making an order under section 19 of the Criminal Justice Act 1948 (an attendance centre order) if it appears to the court, after considering any available evidence, that he is under 17 years of age.*

Note. Sub-s (3) repealed by Criminal Justice Act 1982, s 78, Sch 16, as from 24 May 1983.

(4) A magistrates' court may at any time revoke an order of committal made under subsection (2) and, if the offender is in custody, order his discharge.

(5) [Section 135 of the Powers of Criminal Courts (Sentencing) Act 2000 (limit on fines in respect of young persons) and] the following provisions of the Magistrates' Courts Act 1980 apply in relation to an order under this section as they apply in relation to a sentence on conviction or finding of guilty of an offence, *namely: section 36 (restriction on fines in respect of young persons);* [; and those provisions of the Magistrates' Courts Act 1980 are] sections 75 to 91 (enforcement); section 108 (appeal to Crown Court); section 136 (overnight detention in default of payment); and section 142(1) (power to rectify mistakes).

Note. Amended by the Powers of Criminal Courts (Sentencing) Act 2000, s 165, Sch 9, para 83, as from 25 August 2000.

13. Legal aid—(*1*) *In any case where a person is liable to be committed or fined—*

    (*a*) *by a magistrates' court under section 12 of this Act;*

    (*b*) *by a county court under section 30, 127 or 157 of the County Courts Act 1959* [*section 14, 92 or 118 of the County Courts Act 1984*]; *or*

    (*c*) *by any superior court for contempt in the face of that or any other court,*

the court may order that he shall be given legal aid for the purposes of the proceedings.

    (*2*) *Where an order under subsection (1) is made by any court, the court may order that the legal aid to be given shall consist of representation by counsel only or, in any court where solicitors have a right of audience, by a solicitor only; and the court may assign for the purpose any counsel or solicitor who is within the precincts of the court at the time when the order is made.*

    (*3*) *Part II of the Legal Aid Act 1974 shall have effect subject to the amendments set out in Part I of Schedule 2, being amendments consequential on the foregoing provisions of this section.*

    (*4*) (*Applies to Scotland.*)

    (*5*) *This section is without prejudice to any other enactment by virtue of which legal aid may be granted in or for purposes of civil or criminal proceedings.*

Note. Words in square brackets in sub-s (1)(b) substituted for words 'section 30, 127 or 157 of the County Courts Act 1959' by County Courts Act 1984, s 148(1), Sch 2, Part V, para 76. Whole section repealed by Legal Aid Act 1988, s 45(2), (3), Sch 6, as from 1 April 1989. For transitional provisions, see s 45(4) of, and Sch 7 to, the 1988 Act (pp 3273, 3282). Remainder repealed by SI 2003 No 435, art 49(2), Sch 5, as from a date to be appointed.

Penalties for contempt and kindred offences

14. Proceedings in England and Wales—(1) In any case where a court has power to commit a person to prison for contempt of court and (apart from this provision) no limitation applies to the period of committal, the committal shall (without prejudice to the power of the court to order his earlier discharge) be for a fixed term, and that term shall not on any occasion exceed two years in the case of committal by a superior court, or one month in the case of committal by an inferior court.

(2) In any case where an inferior court has power to fine a person for contempt of court and (apart from this provision) no limit applies to the amount of the fine, the fine shall not on any occasion exceed £500 [*£1,000*] [£2,500].

Note. '£1,000' substituted for '£500' by Criminal Penalties etc (Increase) Order 1984, SI 1984 No 447, art 2(3), Sch 3, as from 1 May 1984. '£2,500' substituted for '£1,000' by Criminal Justice Act 1991, s 17(3), Sch 4, Part I, as from 1 October 1992, and by Criminal Justice (Northern Ireland) Order 1994, SI 1994 No 2795, art 3(5), Sch 1, as from 9 January 1995, in relation to Northern Ireland.

    [(*2A*) *Section 18 of the Criminal Justice Act 1991 (fixing of certain fines by reference to units) shall apply for the purposes of subsection (2) above as if the failure to attend before the magistrates' court were a summary offence punishable by a fine not exceeding level 4 on the standard scale; and a fine imposed under that subsection shall be deemed for the purposes of any enactment to be a sum adjudged to be paid by a conviction.*]

[(2A) A fine imposed under subsection (2) above shall be deemed, for the purposes of any enactment, to be a sum adjudged to be paid by a conviction.]

Note. Sub-s (2A) in italics inserted by Criminal Justice Act 1991, s 17(3), Sch 4, Part V, para 4, as from 1 October 1992. Sub-s (2A) in square brackets substituted for sub-s (2A) in italics by Criminal Justice Act 1993, s 65(3), Sch 3, para 6(5), as from 20 September 1993.

[(2A) In the exercise of jurisdiction to commit for contempt of court or any kindred offence the court shall not deal with the offender by making an order under *section 17 of the Criminal Justice Act 1982* [section 60 of the Powers of Criminal Courts (Sentencing) Act 2000] (an attendance order) if it appears to the court, after considering any available evidence, that he is under 17 years of age.]

Note. This sub-s (2A) inserted by Criminal Justice Act 1982, s 77, Sch 14, para 60, as from 24 May 1983. Amended by the Powers of Criminal Courts (Sentencing) Act 2000, s 165, Sch 9, para 84.

(3) In relation to the exercise of jurisdiction to commit for contempt of court or any kindred offence, subsection (1) of section 19 of the Powers of Criminal Courts Act 1973 (prohibition of imprisonment of persons under seventeen years of age) shall apply to all courts having that jurisdiction as it applies to the Crown Court and magistrates' courts.

Note. Sub-s (3) repealed by Criminal Justice Act 1982, s 78, Sch 16 as from 24 May 1983.

(4) Each of the superior courts shall have the like power to make a hospital order or guardianship order under *section 60 of the Mental Health Act 1959* [section 37 of the Mental Health Act 1983] [or an interim hospital order under *section 31 of the Mental Health (Amendment) Act 1982* [section 38 of that Act]] in the case of a person suffering from mental illness or *severe subnormality* [severe mental impairment] who could otherwise be committed to prison for contempt of court as the Crown Court has under that section in the case of a person convicted of an offence.

Note. Words 'or an interim hospital order under section 31 of the Mental Health (Amendment) Act 1982' inserted, and for the words 'severe subnormality' words 'severe mental impairment' substituted by Mental Health (Amendment) Act 1982, s 65(1), Sch 3, para 59, as from 30 September 1983. Words 'section 60 of the Mental Health Act 1959' and 'section 31 of the Mental Health (Amendment) Act 1982' substituted by words 'section 37 of the Mental Health Act 1983' and 'section 38 of that Act' by Mental Health Act 1983, s 148, Sch 4, para 57(a), as from 30 September 1983.

[(4A) Each of the superior courts shall have the like power to make an order under *section 29 of the said Act of 1982* [section 35 of the said Act of 1983] (remand for report on accused's mental condition) where there is reason to suspect that a person who could be committed to prison for contempt of court is suffering from mental illness or severe mental impairment as the Crown Court has under that section in the case of an accused person within the meaning of that section.]

Note. This sub-s (4A) inserted by Mental Health (Amendment) Act 1982, s 65(1), Sch 3, para 60, as from 30 September 1983. Words 'section 29 of the said Act of 1982' substituted by words 'section 35 of the said Act of 1983' by Mental Health Act 1983, s 148, Sch 4, para 57(b), as from 30 September 1983.

[(4A) For the purposes of the preceding provisions of this section a county court shall be treated as a superior court and not as an inferior court.]

Note. This sub-s (4A) inserted by County Courts (Penalties for Contempt) Act 1983, s 1, as from 13 May 1983.

(5) The enactments specified in Part III of Schedule 2 shall have effect subject to the amendments set out in that Part, being amendments relating to the penalties and procedure in respect of certain offences of contempt of coroners' courts, county courts and magistrates' courts.

15. (*Applies to Scotland only.*)

16. Enforcement of fines imposed by certain superior courts—(1) Payment of a fine for contempt of court imposed by a superior court, other than the Crown Court or one of the courts specified in subsection (4) below, may be enforced upon the order of the court—

(a) in like manner as a judgment of the High Court for the payment of money; or

(b) in like manner as a fine imposed by the Crown Court.

(2) Where payment of a fine imposed by any court falls to be enforced as mentioned in paragraph (a) of subsection (1)—

(a) the court shall, if the fine is not paid in full forthwith or within such time as the court may allow, certify to Her Majesty's Remembrancer the sum payable;

(b) Her Majesty's Remembrancer shall thereupon proceed to enforce payment of that sum as if it were due to him as a judgment debt; *and*

(c) *any payment received in respect of the fine shall be dealt with by him in the manner for the time being prescribed under section 28 of the Fines Act 1833 for receipts within that section.*

Note. Sub-s (2)(c) and the word 'and' preceding it repealed by Supreme Court Act 1981, s 154, Sch 7, as from 1 January 1982.

(3) Where payment of a fine imposed by any court falls to be enforced as mentioned in paragraph (b) of subsection (1), the provisions of *section 31 and 32 of the Powers of Criminal Courts Act 1973* [sections 139 and 140 of the Powers of Criminal Courts (Sentencing) Act 2000] shall apply as they apply to a fine imposed by the Crown Court.

Note. Amended by the Powers of Criminal Courts (Sentencing) Act 2000, s 165, Sch 9, para 85, as from 25 August 2000.

(4) Subsection (1) of this section does not apply to fines imposed by the criminal division of the Court of Appeal or by the House of Lords on appeal from that division.

(5) The Fines Act 1833 shall not apply to a fine to which subsection (1) of this section applies.

(6) *Paragraph 23(1) of Schedule 11 to the Employment Protection (Consolidation) Act 1978 and paragraph 30 of Schedule 1 to the Employment Act 1980 (which relate to the enforcement of fines imposed by the Employment Appeal Tribunal) are repealed.*

Note. Sub-s (6) repealed by Industrial Tribunals Act 1996, s 45, Sch 3, Part I, as from 22 August 1996.

17. Disobedience to certain orders of magistrates' courts—(1) The powers of a magistrates' court under subsection (3) of section 63 of the Magistrates' Courts Act 1980 (punishment by fine or committal for disobeying an order to do anything other than the payment of money or to abstain from doing anything) may be exercised either of the court's own motion or by order on complaint.

(2) In relation to the exercise of those powers the provisions of the Magistrates' Courts Act 1980 shall apply subject to the modifications set out in Schedule 3 to this Act.

Supplemental

18. Northern Ireland—(1) In the application of this Act to Northern Ireland references to the Attorney General shall be construed as references to the Attorney General for Northern Ireland.

(2) In their application to Northern Ireland, sections 12, 13, 14 and 16 of this Act shall have effect as set out in Schedule 4.

19. Interpretation. In this Act—

[*'cable programme' means a programme included in a cable programme service;*]

'court' includes any tribunal or body exercising the judicial power of the State and 'legal proceedings' shall be construed accordingly;

'publication' has the meaning assigned by subsection (1) of section 2, and 'publish' (except in section 9) shall be construed accordingly;

'Scottish proceedings' means proceedings before any court, including the Courts-Martial Appeal Court, the Restrictive Practices Court and the Employment Appeal Tribunal, sitting in Scotland, and includes proceedings before the House of Lords in the exercise of any appellate jurisdiction over proceedings in such a court;

'the strict liability rule' has the meaning assigned by section 1;

'superior court' means the Court of Appeal, the Restrictive Practices Court, the Employment Appeal Tribunal and any other court exercising in relation to its proceedings powers equivalent to those of the High Court, and includes the House of Lords in the exercise of its appellate jurisdiction.

Note. Definition 'cable programme' inserted by Cable and Broadcasting Act 1984, s 57(1), Sch 5, para 39(2), repealed by Broadcasting Act 1990, s 203, Sch 20, para 31, Sch 21, as from 1 January 1991.

20. Tribunals of Inquiry—(1) In relation to any tribunal to which the Tribunals of Inquiry (Evidence) Act 1921 applies, and the proceedings of such a tribunal, the provisions of this Act (except subsection (3) of section 9) apply as they apply in relation to courts and legal proceedings; and references to the course of justice or the administration of justice in legal proceedings shall be construed accordingly.

(2) The proceedings of a tribunal established under the said Act shall be treated as active within the meaning of section 2 from the time when the tribunal is appointed until its report is presented to Parliament.

21. Short title, commencement and extent—(1) This Act may be cited as the Contempt of Court Act 1981.

(2) The provisions of this Act relating to legal aid in England and Wales shall come into force on such day as the Lord Chancellor may appoint by order made by statutory instrument; and the provisions of this Act relating to legal aid in Scotland and Northern Ireland shall come into force on such day or days as the Secretary of State may so appoint.

Different days may be appointed under this subsection in relation to different courts.

(3) Subject to subsection (2), this Act shall come into force at the expiration of the period of one month beginning with the day on which it is passed.

(4) Sections 7, 8(3), 12, 13(1) to (3), 14, 16, 17, and 18, Parts I and III of Schedule 2 and Schedules 3 and 4 of this Act do not extend to Scotland.

(5) This Act, except sections 15 and 17 of Schedules 2 and 3, extends to Northern Ireland.

Commencement. Provisions relating to legal aid (namely s 13, Sch 2, Parts I, II) were repealed before being brought into force in England, Wales and Scotland.

SCHEDULES

SCHEDULE 1   Section 2

TIMES WHEN PROCEEDINGS ARE ACTIVE FOR PURPOSES OF SECTION 2

Preliminary

1. In this Schedule 'criminal proceedings' means proceedings against a person in respect of an offence, not being appellate proceedings or proceedings commenced by motion for committal or attachment in England and Wales or Northern Ireland, and 'appellate proceedings' means proceedings on appeal from or for the review of the decision of a court in any proceedings.

2. Criminal, appellate and other proceedings are active within the meaning of section 2 at the times respectively prescribed by the following paragraphs of this Schedule; and in relation to proceedings in which more than one of the steps described in any of those paragraphs is taken, the reference in that paragraph is a reference to the first of those steps.

Criminal proceedings

3. Subject to the following provisions of this Schedule, criminal proceedings are active from the relevant initial step specified in paragraph 4 [or 4A] until concluded as described in paragraph 5.

Note. Words in square brackets inserted by Criminal Procedure and Investigations Act 1996, s 57(4), as from 4 July 1996, in relation to acquittals in respect of offences alleged to be committed on or after 15 April 1997.

4. The initial steps of criminal proceedings are—
    (a) arrest without warrant;
    (b) the issue, or in Scotland the grant, of a warrant for arrest;
    (c) the issue of a summons to appear, or in Scotland the grant of a warrant to cite;
    (d) the service of an indictment or other document specifying the charge;
    (e) except in Scotland, oral charge.

[**4A.** Where as a result of an order under section 54 of the Criminal Procedure and Investigations Act 1996 (acquittal tainted by an administration of justice offence) proceedings are brought against a person for an offence of which he has previously been acquitted, the initial step of the proceedings is a certification under subsection (2) of that section; and paragraph 4 has effect subject to this.]

Note. Para 4A inserted by Criminal Procedure and Investigations Act 1996, s 57(4), as from 4 July 1996, in relation to acquittals in respect of offences alleged to be committed on or after 15 April 1997.

5. Criminal proceedings are concluded—
    (a) by acquittal or, as the case may be, by sentence;
    (b) by any other verdict, finding, order or decision which puts an end to the proceedings;
    (c) by discontinuance or by operation of law.

6. The reference in paragraph 5(a) to sentence includes any order or decision consequent on conviction or finding of guilt which disposes of the case, either absolutely or subject to future events, and a deferment of sentence under *section 1 of the Powers of Criminal Courts Act 1973* [section 1 of the Powers of Criminal Courts (Sentencing) Act 2000], section 219 or 432 of the Criminal Procedure (Scotland) Act 1975 or Article 14 of the Treatment of Offenders (Northern Ireland) Order 1976.

Note. Amended by the Powers of Criminal Courts (Sentencing) Act 2000, s 165(1), Sch 9, para 86, as from 25 August 2000.

7. Proceedings are discontinued within the meaning of paragraph 5(c)—
    (a) in England and Wales or Northern Ireland, if the charge or summons is withdrawn or a *nolle prosequi* entered;
  [(aa) in England and Wales, if they are discontinued by virtue of section 23 of the Prosecution of Offences Act 1985;]
    (b) (*applies to Scotland*);
    (c) in the case of proceedings in England and Wales or Northern Ireland commenced by arrest without warrant, if the person arrested is released, otherwise than on bail, without having been charged.

Note. Para 7(aa) inserted by Prosecution of Offences Act 1985, s 31(5), Sch 1, Part I, para 4, as from 1 April 1986.

8. Criminal proceedings before a court-martial or standing civilian court are not concluded until the completion of any review of finding or sentence.

9. Criminal proceedings in England and Wales or Northern Ireland cease to be active if an order is made for the charge to lie on the file, but become active again if leave is later given for the proceedings to continue.

[**9A.** Where proceedings in England and Wales have been discontinued by virtue of section 23 of the Prosecution of Offences Act 1985, but notice is given by the accused under subsection (7) of that section to the effect that he wants the proceedings to continue, they become active again with the giving of that notice.]

Note. Para 9A inserted by Prosecution of Offences Act 1985, s 31(5), Sch 1, Part I, para 5, as from 1 April 1986.

10. Without prejudice to paragraph 5(b) above, criminal proceedings against a person cease to be active—
- (a) if the accused is found to be under a disability such as to render him unfit to be tried or unfit to plead or, in Scotland, is found to be insane in bar of trial; or
- (b) if a hospital order is made in his case under *paragraph (b) of subsection (2) of section 76 of the Mental Health Act 1959* [section 51(5) of the Mental Health Act 1983] or *paragraph (b) of section (2) of section 62 of the Mental Health Act (Northern Ireland) 1961* [Article 57(5) of the Mental Health (Northern Ireland) Order 1986] or, in Scotland, where a transfer order ceases to have effect by virtue of *section 68(1) of the Mental Health (Scotland) Act 1960* [section 73(1) of the Mental Health (Scotland) Act 1984],

but become active again if they are later resumed.

Note. First words in square brackets substituted for words in italics by Mental Health Act 1983, s 148, Sch 4, para 57(c), as from 30 September 1983. Second words so substituted by Mental Health (Northern Ireland) Order 1986, SI 1986 No 594, art 136(1), Sch 5, Part II. Third words so substituted by Mental Health (Scotland) Act 1984, s 127(1), Sch 3, para 48.

11. Criminal proceedings against a person which become active on the issue or the grant of a warrant for his arrest cease to be active at the end of the period of twelve months beginning with the date of the warrant unless he has been arrested within that period, but become active again if he is subsequently arrested.

Other proceedings at first instance

12. Proceedings other than criminal proceedings and appellate proceedings are active from the time when arrangements for the hearing are made or, if no such arrangements are previously made, from the time the hearing begins, until the proceedings are disposed of or discontinued or withdrawn; and for the purposes of this paragraph any motion or application made in or for the purposes of any proceedings, and any pre-trial review in the county court, is to be treated as a distinct proceeding.

13. In England and Wales or Northern Ireland arrangements for the hearing of proceedings to which paragraph 12 applies are made within the meaning of that paragraph—
- (a) in the case of proceedings in the High Court for which provision is made by rules of court for settling down for trial, when the case is set down;
- (b) in the case of any proceedings, when a date for the trial or hearing is fixed.

14. (*Applies to Scotland only.*)

Appellate proceedings

15. Appellate proceedings are active from the time when they are commenced—
- (a) by application for leave to appeal or apply for review, or by notice of such an application;
- (b) by notice of appeal or of application for review;
- (c) by other originating process,

until disposed of or abandoned, discontinued or withdrawn.

16. Where, in appellate proceedings relating to criminal proceedings, the court—
- (a) remits the case to the court below; or
- (b) orders a new trial or a *venire de novo*, or in Scotland grants authority to bring a new prosecution,

any further or new proceedings which result shall be treated as active from the conclusion of the appellate proceedings.

SCHEDULE 2   Sections 13, 14

AMENDMENTS

PART *I*

LEGAL AID ACT *1974 (c 4)*

1. *In section 28, after subsection (11) there shall be inserted the following subsection—*
'*(11A) In any case where a person is liable to be committed or fined—*
      (a) *by a magistrates' court under section 12 of the Contempt of Court Act 1981;*
      (b) *by a county court under sections 30, 127 or 157 of the County Courts Act 1959;*
      or
      (c) *by any superior court for contempt in the face of that or any other court or tribunal,*
the court may order that he shall be given legal aid for the purposes of the proceedings.'
2. *In section 30, after subsection (4) there shall be inserted the following subsection—*
'*(4A) Where a court makes a legal aid order under section 28(11A) above, the court may order that the legal aid to be given shall consist of representation by counsel only or, in any court where solicitors have a right of audience, by a solicitor only; and the court may assign for the purpose any counsel or solicitor who is within the precincts of the court at the time when the order is made.'*

Note. Part I repealed by Legal Aid Act 1988, s 45(2), (3), Sch 6. For transitional provisions, see s 45(4) of, and Sch 7 to, that Act (pp 3273, 3282).

(Part II repealed by Legal Aid (Scotland) Act 1986, s 45(3), Sch 5 (not printed in this work).

PART III

CORONERS ACT 1887, COUNTY COURTS ACT 1959, ATTACHMENT OF EARNINGS ACT 1971 AND MAGISTRATES' COURT ACT 1980

Coroners Act 1887 (c 71)

1. *In subsections (1) and (2) of section 19 and in section 23, for the words 'five pounds' there shall be substituted '£200'.*

Note. Repealed by the Statute Law (Repeals) Act 2004, as from 22 July 2004.

County Courts Act 1959 (c 22)

2. *In section 30, in paragraph (a) of subsection (1), for the words and figures 'one month' and '£50' there shall be substituted respectively 'three months' and '£1,000, or both'; in paragraph (b) for the words 'one month' there shall be substituted 'three months'; and at the end of that paragraph there shall be added the words 'or to be so committed and to such a fine'.*
3. *In section 127, in paragraph (a) of subsection (1), for the words 'twenty pounds' there shall be substituted '£500, or both'; and at the end of paragraph (b) of that subsection there shall be added the words 'or to be so committed and to such a fine'.*
4. *In section 144, after subsection (2) there shall be inserted the following subsection—*
'*(2A) In any case where the judge has power to make an order of committal under subsection (2) for failure to attend, he may in lieu of or in addition to making that order, order the debtor to be arrested and brought before the court either forthwith or at such time as the judge may direct'.*
5. *In section 157, in paragraph (ii) of subsection (1), for the words 'twenty pounds' there shall be substituted '£500'; and after that paragraph there shall be added the words 'or may both make such an order and impose such a fine'.*

Note. Paras 2–5 repealed by County Courts Act 1984, s 148(3), Sch 4, as from 1 August 1984.

6, 7. (*Para 6 inserts Attachment of Earnings Act 1971, s 23(1A) (p 2407); para 7 amends Magistrates' Courts Act 1980, s 97(4) (p 2793).*)

SCHEDULE 3   Section 17

APPLICATION OF MAGISTRATES' COURTS ACT 1980 TO CIVIL CONTEMPT PROCEEDINGS UNDER SECTION 63(3)

1. (1) Where the proceedings are taken of the court's own motion the provisions of the Act listed in this sub-paragraph shall apply as if a complaint had been made against the person against whom the proceedings are taken, and subject to the modifications specified in sub-paragraphs (2) and (3) below. The enactments so applied are—

section 51 (issue of summons)
section 53(1) and (2) (procedure on hearing)
section 54 (adjournment)
section 55 (non-appearance of defendant)
section 97(1) (summons to witness)
section 101 (onus of proving exceptions etc)
section 121(1) and (3)(a) (constitution and place of sitting of court)
section 123 (defect in process)

(2) (*Sub-para (2) and para 3, amend Magistrates' Courts Act 1980, s 55(1)–(3) respectively (p 2765); sub-para (3) amends s 123 of the 1980 Act (not printed in this work).*)

2. Where the proceedings are taken by way of complaint for an order, section 127 of the Act (limitation of time) shall not apply to the complaint.

3. ...

SCHEDULE 4   Section 18

SECTIONS 12, 13, 14 AND 16 AS APPLIED TO NORTHERN IRELAND

12. Offences of contempt of magistrates' courts—(*1*) *In the Magistrates' Courts Act (Northern Ireland) 1964 the following shall be substituted for section 161—*

'**161. Misbehaviour in court**—(*1*) *A magistrates' court has jurisdiction under this section to deal with any person who—*

(*a*) *wilfully insults a resident magistrate or justice of the peace, any witness before or officer of the court or any solicitor or counsel having business in the court, during his sitting or attendance in court or in going to or returning from the court; or*

(*b*) *wilfully interrupts the proceedings of the court or otherwise misbehaves in court.*

(*2*) *In any such case the court may order any officer of the court, or any constable, to take the offender into custody and detain him until the rising of the court; and the court may, if it thinks fit, commit the offender to prison for a specified period not exceeding one month or impose on him a fine not exceeding £500 or both.*

(*3*) *A magistrates' court may at any time revoke an order of committal made under subsection (2) and, if the offender is in prison, order his discharge.*

(*4*) *An order under subsection (2) for the payment of a fine may be enforced as though the fine were a sum adjudged to be paid by a conviction.*'

(2) Paragraph 26 of Schedule 1 to the Criminal Justice (Northern Ireland) Order 1980 is repealed.

Note. Section 12(1) repealed by Magistrates' Courts (Northern Ireland) Order 1981, SI 1981 No 1675, art 170(3).

13. Legal aid—(*1*) *In any case where—*

(*a*) *a person is liable to be committed or fined—*

(*i*) *by a magistrates' court under section 161 of the Magistrates' Courts Act (Northern Ireland) 1964 [Article 160 of the Magistrates' Courts (Northern Ireland) Order 1981];*

(*ii*) *by a county court under Article 55 of the County Courts (Northern Ireland) Order 1980; or* [(iia)   *by a magistrates' court or the Crown Court under section 18 of the Criminal Procedure and Investigations Act 1996; or*]

   (iii)   *by any superior court for contempt in the face of that or any other court; and*
(b)   *it appears to the court that it is desirable in the interests of justice that he should have legal aid and that he has not sufficient means to enable him to obtain that aid;*
the court may order that he shall be given legal aid for the purposes of the proceedings.

   (2)   Unless the court orders that the legal aid to be given under this section shall consist of representation by counsel only or, in any court where solicitors have a right of audience, by a solicitor only, legal aid under this section shall consist of representation by a solicitor and counsel assigned by the court; and the court may assign for the purpose any counsel or solicitor who is within the precincts of the court at the time when the order is made.

   (3)   If on a question of granting a person legal aid under this section there is a doubt whether his means are sufficient to enable him to obtain legal aid or whether it is desirable in the interests of justice that he should have legal aid, the doubt shall be resolved in favour of granting him legal aid.

   (4)   Articles 32, 33, 36 and 40 of the Legal Aid, Advice and Assistance (Northern Ireland) Order 1981 shall apply in relation to legal aid under this section as they apply in relation to legal aid under Part III of that Order as if any legal aid under this section were given in pursuance of a certificate under Article 29 of that Order.

   (5)   This section is without prejudice to any other enactment by virtue of which legal aid may be granted in or for purposes of civil or criminal proceedings.

Note. This section repealed, without having been brought into force, by Legal Aid Act 1988, s 45(2), (3), Sch 6 and Legal Aid (Scotland) Act 1986, s 45(3), Sch 5.

Words in square brackets in s 13(1)(a)(i) substituted for words 'section 161 … 1964' by Magistrates' Courts (Northern Ireland) Order 1981, SI 1981 No 1675, art 170(2), Sch 6, para 61. Sub-s (1)(a)(iia) inserted by Criminal Procedure and Investigations Act 1996, ss 18(11), 79(4), Sch 4, para 11, as from 4 July 1996.

14.   Proceedings in Northern Ireland—(1)   In any case where a court has power to commit a person to prison for contempt of court and (apart from this provision) no limitation applies to the period of committal, the committal shall (without prejudice to the power of the court to order his earlier discharge) be for a fixed term, and that term shall not on any occasion exceed two years in the case of committal by a superior court, or one month in the case of committal by an inferior court.

   (2)   In any case where an inferior court has power to fine a person for contempt of court and (apart from this provision) no limit applies to the amount of the fine, the fine shall not on any occasion exceed £500.

   (3)   Section 72 of the Children and Young Persons Act (Northern Ireland) 1968 shall be amended by inserting the words 'for contempt of court or' after 'prison' in subsection (2), and after 'such a centre' in subsection (3).

   (4)   Each of the superior courts shall have the like power to make a hospital order or guardianship order under *section 48 of the Mental Health Act (Northern Ireland) 1961* [Article 44 of the Mental Health (Northern Ireland) Order 1986 or an interim hospital order under Article 45 of that Order] in the case of a person suffering from mental disorder who could otherwise be committed to prison for contempt of court as the Crown Court has under *that section* [that Article] in the case of a person convicted of an offence.

Note. Words in square brackets substituted for words in italics by Mental Health (Northern Ireland) Order 1986, SI 1986 No 595, art 136(1), Sch 5, Part II.

   [(4A)   Each of the superior courts shall have the like power to make an order under Article 42 of the said Order of 1986 where there is reason to suspect that a person who could be committed to prison for contempt of court is suffering from mental illness or severe mental impairment as the Crown Court has under that Article in the case of an accused person within the meaning of that Article.]

Note. This sub-s (4A) added by Mental Health (Northern Ireland) Order 1986, SI 1986 No 595, art 136(1), Sch 5, Part II.

[(4A) For the purposes of the preceding provisions of this section a county court shall be treated as a superior court and not as an inferior court.]

Note. This sub-s (4A) added by County Courts (Penalties for Contempt) Act 1983, ss 1, 2, as from 13 May 1983.

(5) In subsections (1) and (2) of section 20 of the Coroners Act (Northern Ireland) 1959, for the words 'ten pounds' there shall be substituted '£200' and in section 34 of that Act for the words 'twenty-five pounds' there shall be substituted '£500'.

(6) In section 122 of the Magistrates' Courts Act (Northern Ireland) 1964, in subsection (1), for the words 'eight days' there shall be substituted 'one month', and at the end of the subsection there shall be added the words 'or impose on him a fine not exceeding £500, or both'; and subsection (3) is repealed.

Note. Section 14(6) repealed by Magistrates' Courts (Northern Ireland) Order 1981, SI 1981 No 1675, art 170(3).

(7) In Article 55 of the County Courts (Northern Ireland) Order 1980, in paragraph (2), for the words 'not exceeding £50' there shall be substituted 'not exceeding £500' and for the words 'any period' there shall be substituted 'a specified period'.

16. Enforcement of fines imposed by superior courts. Section 35 of the Criminal Justice Act (Northern Ireland) 1945 shall apply to fines imposed for contempt of court by any superior court other than the Crown Court as it applies to fines imposed by the Crown Court.

SUPREME COURT ACT 1981*

(1981 c 54)

*A comparative table showing the principal enactments replaced by the provisions of this Act printed in this work is set out at p 2876.

ARRANGEMENT OF SECTIONS

PART I

CONSTITUTION OF SUPREME COURT

An Act to consolidate with amendments the Supreme Court of Judicature (Consolidation) Act 1925 and other enactments relating to the Supreme Court in England and Wales and the administration of justice therein; to repeal certain obsolete or unnecessary enactments so relating; to amend Part VIII of the Mental Health Act 1959, the Courts-Martial (Appeals) Act 1968, the Arbitration Act 1979 and the law relating to county courts; and for connected purposes.

[28 July 1981]

PART I

CONSTITUTION OF SUPREME COURT

The Supreme Court

1. The Supreme Court—(1) The Supreme Court of England and Wales shall consist of the Court of Appeal, the High Court of Justice and the Crown Court, each having such jurisdiction as is conferred on it by or under this or any other Act.

(2) The Lord Chancellor shall be president of the Supreme Court.

The Court of Appeal

2. The Court of Appeal—(1) The Court of Appeal shall consist of ex-officio judges and not more than *eighteen* [*twenty-three*] [*twenty-eight*] [*twenty-nine*] [*thirty-two*] [*thirty-five*] [thirty-seven] ordinary judges.

(2) The following shall be ex-officio judges of the Court of Appeal—

(a) the Lord Chancellor;

(b) any person who has been Lord Chancellor;

(c) any Lord of Appeal in Ordinary who at the date of his appointment was, or was qualified for appointment as, an ordinary judge of the Court of Appeal or held an office within paragraphs (d) to (g);

(d) the Lord Chief Justice;

(e) the Master of the Rolls;

(f) the President of the Family Division; and

(g) the Vice-Chancellor;

but a person within paragraph (b) or (c) shall not be required to sit and act as a judge of the Court of Appeal unless at the Lord Chancellor's request he consents to do so.

(3) The ordinary judges of the Court of Appeal (including the vice-president, if any, of either division) shall be styled 'Lords Justices of Appeal'.

[(3) An ordinary judge of the Court of Appeal (including the vice-president, if any, of either division) shall be styled 'Lord Justice of Appeal' or 'Lady Justice of Appeal'.]

Note. Substituted by the Courts Act 2003, s 63(1), as from 26 January 2004 (SI 2003 No 3345).

(4) Her Majesty may by Order in Council from time to time amend subsection (1) so as to increase or further increase the maximum number of ordinary judges of the Court of Appeal.

(5) No recommendation shall be made to Her Majesty in Council to make an Order under subsection (4) unless a draft of the Order has been laid before Parliament and approved by resolution of each House of Parliament.

(6) The Court of Appeal shall be taken to be duly constituted notwithstanding any vacancy in the office of Lord Chancellor, Lord Chief Justice, Master of the Rolls, President of the Family Division or Vice-Chancellor.

Note. Words 'twenty-three' in square brackets substituted for 'eighteen' by SI 1983 No 1705. Words 'twenty-eight' substituted for words 'twenty-three' by SI 1987 No 2059, as from 26 November 1987. Words 'twenty-nine' substituted for words 'twenty-eight' by virtue of Maximum Number of Judges Order 1993, SI 1993 No 605, as from 11 March 1993. Words 'thirty-two' substituted for words 'twenty-nine' by virtue of Maximum Number of Judges

Order 1994, SI 1994 No 3217, art 3, as from 15 December 1994. Words 'thirty-five' substituted for words 'thirty-two' by virtue of Maximum Number of Judges Order 1996, SI 1996 No 1142, art 2, as from 25 April 1996. Words 'thirty-seven' in square brackets substituted for words 'thirty-five' by virtue of SI 2002 No 2837, art 2, as from 21 November 2002.

3. Divisions of Court of Appeal—(1) There shall be two divisions of the Court of Appeal, namely the criminal division and the civil division.

(2) The Lord Chief Justice shall be president of the criminal division of the Court of Appeal, and the Master of the Rolls shall be president of the civil division of that court.

(3) The Lord Chancellor may appoint one of the ordinary judges of the Court of Appeal as vice-president of both divisions of that court, or one of those judges as vice-president of the criminal division and another of them as vice-president of the civil division.

(4) When sitting in a court of either division of the Court of Appeal in which no ex-officio judge of the Court of Appeal is sitting, the vice-president (if any) of that division shall preside.

(5) Any number of courts of either division of the Court of Appeal may sit at the same time.

The High Court

4. The High Court—(1) The High Court shall consist of—
    (a)   the Lord Chancellor;
    (b)   the Lord Chief Justice;
    (c)   the President of the Family Division;
    (d)   the Vice-Chancellor;
    [(dd) the Senior Presiding Judge;]
and
    [(ddd) the vice-president of the Queen's Bench Division;]
    (e)   not more than *eighty* [*eighty-five*] [*ninety-eight*] [108] puisne judges of that court.

(2) The puisne judges of the High Court shall be styled 'Justices of the High Court'.

(3) All the judges of the High Court shall, except where this Act expressly provides otherwise, have in all respects equal power, authority and jurisdiction.

(4) Her Majesty may by Order in Council from time to time amend subsection (1) so as to increase or further increase the maximum number of puisne judges of the High Court.

(5) No recommendation shall be made to Her Majesty in Council to make an Order under subsection (4) unless a draft of the Order has been laid before Parliament and approved by resolution of each House of Parliament.

(6) The High Court shall be taken to be duly constituted notwithstanding any vacancy in the office of Lord Chancellor, Lord Chief Justice, President of the Family Division *or Vice-Chancellor* [Vice Chancellor or Senior Presiding Judge]. [and whether or not an appointment has been made to the office of vice-president of the Queen's Bench Division].

Note. Sub-s (1)(dd) inserted, and words in square brackets in sub-s (6) substituted for words in italics by Courts and Legal Services Act 1990, s 72(6), as from 1 January 1991. Sub-s (1)(ddd) inserted by the Access to Justice Act 1999, s 69(2)(a), as from 27 September 1999. In sub-s (1)(e) 'eighty-five' substituted for 'eighty' by SI 1987 No 2059, as from 26 November 1987; 'ninety-eight' substituted for 'eighty-five' by Maximum Number of Judges (No 2) Order 1993, SI 1993 No 1255, as from 13 May 1993; '108' substituted for 'ninety-eight' by SI 2003 No 775, art 2, as from 21 March 2003. Sub-s(6) final words in square brackets inserted by the Access to Justice Act 1999, s 69(2)(b), as from 27 September 1999.

5. Divisions of High Court—(1) There shall be three divisions of the High Court namely—

   (a) the Chancery Division, consisting of the Lord Chancellor, who shall be president thereof, the Vice-Chancellor, who shall be vice-president thereof, and such of the puisne judges as are for the time being attached thereto in accordance with this section;

   (b) the Queen's Bench Division, consisting of the Lord Chief Justice, who shall be president thereof, [the vice-president of the Queen's Bench Division] and such of the puisne judges as are for the time being so attached thereto; and

   (c) the Family Division, consisting of the President of the Family Division and such of the puisne judges as are for the time being so attached thereto.

Note. Amended by the Access to Justice Act 1999, S 69(3), as from 27 September 1999.

(2) The puisne judges of the High Court shall be attached to the various Divisions by direction of the Lord Chancellor; and any such judge may with his consent be transferred from one Division to another by direction of the Lord Chancellor, but shall be so transferred only with the concurrence of the senior judge of the Division from which it is proposed to transfer him.

(3) Any judge attached to any Division may act as an additional judge of any other Division at the request of the *Lord Chancellor made with the concurrence of the senior judge of each of those Divisions* [Lord Chief Justice made with the concurrence of the President of the Family Division or the Vice-Chancellor, or both, as appropriate].

(4) Nothing in this section shall be taken to prevent a judge of any Division (whether nominated under section 6(2) or not) from sitting, whenever required, in a divisional court of another Division or for any judge of another Division.

(5) Without prejudice to the provisions of this Act relating to the distribution of business in the High Court, all jurisdiction vested in the High Court under this Act shall belong to all the Divisions alike.

Note. Words in square brackets in sub-s (3) substituted for words in italics by Courts and Legal Services Act 1990, s 125(2), Sch 17, para 12, as from 1 January 1991.

*   *   *   *   *

7. Power to alter Divisions or transfer certain courts to different Divisions— (1) Her Majesty may from time to time, on a recommendation of the judges mentioned in subsection (2), by Order in Council direct that—

   (a) any increase or reduction in the number of Divisions of the High Court; or

   (b) the transfer of any of the courts mentioned in section 6(1) to a different Division,

be carried into effect in pursuance of the recommendation.

(2) Those judges are the Lord Chancellor, the Lord Chief Justice, the Master of the Rolls, the President of the Family Division and the Vice-Chancellor.

(3) An Order in Council under this section may include such incidental, supplementary or consequential provisions as appear to Her Majesty necessary or expedient, including amendments of provisions referring to particular Divisions contained in this Act or any other statutory provision.

(4) Any Order in Council under this section shall be subject to annulment in pursuance of a resolution of either House of Parliament.

The Crown Court

8. The Crown Court—(1) The jurisdiction of the Crown Court shall be exercisable by—

   (a) any judge of the High Court; or

   (b) any Circuit judge or *Recorder* [, Recorder or District Judge (Magistrates' Courts)]; or

   (c) subject to and in accordance with the provisions of sections 74 and 75(2), a judge of the High Court, Circuit judge or Recorder sitting with not more than four justices of the peace,

and any such persons when exercising the jurisdiction of the Crown Court shall be judges of the Crown Court.

Note. Amended by the Courts Act 2003, s 65(1), as from a date to be appointed.

(2) A justice of the peace shall not be disqualified from acting as a judge of the Crown Court for the reason that the proceedings are not at a place within the area for which he was appointed as a justice, or because the proceedings are not related to that area in any other way.

[(2). A justice of the peace is not disqualified from acting as a judge of the Crown Court merely because the proceedings are not at a place within the local justice area to which he is assigned or because the proceedings are not related to that area in any other way.]

Note. Substituted by the Courts Act 2003, s 109, Sch 8, para 259, as from a date to be appointed.

(3) When the Crown Court sits in the City of London it shall be known as the Central Criminal Court; and the Lord Mayor of the City and any Alderman of the City shall be entitled to sit as judges of the Central Criminal Court with any judge of the High Court *or any Circuit judge or Recorder* [, Circuit judge, Recorder or District Judge (Magistrates' Courts)].

Note. Amended by the Courts Act 2003, s 109, Sch 8, para 259, as from a date to be appointed.

Other provisions

9. Assistance for transaction of judicial business of Supreme Court—(1) A person within any entry in column 1 of the following Table may [, subject to the proviso at the end of that Table,] at any time, at the request of the appropriate authority act—

(a) as a judge of a relevant court specified in the request; or

(b) if the request relates to a particular division of a relevant court so specified, as a judge of that court in that division.

TABLE

1 *Judge or ex-judge*	2 *Where competent to act on request*
1. A judge of the Court of Appeal.	The High Court and the Crown Court.
2. A person who has been a judge of the Court of Appeal.	The Court of Appeal, the High Court and the Crown Court.
3. A puisne judge of the High Court.	The Court of Appeal.
4. A person who has been a puisne judge of the High Court.	The Court of Appeal, the High Court and the Crown Court.
5. A Circuit judge.	The High Court [and the Court of Appeal].
[6. A Recorder.	The High Court.]

[The entry in column 2 specifying the Court of Appeal in relation to a Circuit judge only authorises such a judge to act as a judge of a court in the criminal division of the Court of Appeal.]

Note. Words ', subject to ... Table,' in square brackets, words 'and the Court of Appeal' in square brackets, and proviso in square brackets added by Criminal Justice and Public Order Act 1994, s 52(2), as from 11 January 1995. Entry 6 in square brackets added by Administration of Justice Act 1982, s 58, as from 1 January 1983.

[(1A) A person shall not act as a judge by virtue of subsection (1) after the day on which he attains the age of 75.]

Note. Sub-s (1A) inserted by Judicial Pensions and Retirement Act 1993, s 26(10), Sch 6, para 5(1), as from 31 March 1995.

(2) In subsection (1)—
'the appropriate authority'—
    (a) in the case of a request to a judge of the High Court [or a Circuit judge] to act in the criminal division of the Court of Appeal as a judge of that court, means the Lord Chief Justice or, at any time when the Lord Chief Justice is unable to make such a request himself or there is a vacancy in the office of Lord Chief Justice, the Master of the Rolls;
    (b) in any other case means the Lord Chancellor;
'relevant court', in the case of a person within any entry in column 1 of the Table, means a court specified in relation to that entry in column 2 of the Table.
[but no request shall be made to a Circuit judge to act as a judge of a court in the criminal division of the Court of Appeal unless he is approved for the time being by the Lord Chancellor for the purpose of acting as a judge of that division.]

Note. Words in square brackets inserted by Criminal Justice and Public Order Act 1994, s 52(3), as from 11 January 1995.

(3) In the case of—
    (a) a request under subsection (1) to a Lord Justice of Appeal to act in the High Court; or
    (b) any request under that subsection to a puisne judge of the High Court or a Circuit judge,
it shall be the duty of the person to whom the request is made to comply with it.

(4) Without prejudice to section 24 of the Courts Act 1971 (temporary appointment of deputy Circuit judges and assistant Recorders), if it appears to the Lord Chancellor that it is expedient as a temporary measure to make an appointment under this subsection in order to facilitate the disposal of business in the High Court or the Crown Court, he may appoint a person qualified for appointment as a puisne judge of the High Court to be a deputy judge of the High Court during such period or on such occasions as the Lord Chancellor thinks fit; and during the period or on the occasions for which a person is appointed as a deputy judge under this subsection, he may act as a puisne judge of the High Court.

[(4A) No appointment of a person as a deputy judge of the High Court shall be such as to extend beyond the day on which he attains the age of 70, but this subsection is subject to section 26(4) to (6) of the Judicial Pensions and Retirement Act 1993 (Lord Chancellor's power to authorise continuance in office up to the age of 75).]

Note. Sub-s (4A) inserted by Judicial Pensions and Retirement Act 1993, s 26(10), Sch 6, para 5(1), as from 31 March 1995.

(5) Every person while acting under this section shall, subject to *subsection (6)* [subsections (6) and (6A)], be treated for all purposes as, and accordingly may perform any of the functions of, a judge of the court in which he is acting.

Note. Words in square brackets substituted for words in italics by Criminal Justice and Public Order Act 1994, s 52(4), as from 11 January 1995.

(6) A person shall not by virtue of subsection (5)—
    (a) be treated as a judge of the court in which he is acting for the purposes of section 98(2) or of any statutory provision relating to—
        (i) the appointment, retirement, removal or disqualification of judges of that court;
        (ii) the tenure of office and oaths to be taken by such judges; or
        (iii) the remuneration, allowances or pensions of such judges; or
    (b) *subject to subsection (7)* [subject to section 27 of the Judicial Pensions and Retirement Act 1993], be treated as having been a judge of a court in which he has acted only under this section.

Note. Words in square brackets substituted for words in italics by Judicial Pensions and Retirement Act 1993, s 26(10), Sch 6, para 5(3), as from 31 March 1995.

[(6A) A Circuit judge or recorder shall not by virtue of subsection (5) exercise any of the powers conferred on a single judge by sections 31 [, 31B, 31C] and 44 of the Criminal Appeal Act 1968 (powers of single judge in connection with appeals to the Court of Appeal and appeals from the Court of Appeal to the House of Lords).]

Note. Sub-s (6A) inserted by Criminal Justice and Public Order Act 1994, s 52(5), as from 11 January 1995.

Amended by the Courts Act 2003, s 109, Sch 8, para 260, as from a date to be appointed.

(7) *Notwithstanding the expiry of any period for which a person is authorised by virtue of subsection (1) or (4) to act as a judge of a particular court—*

(a) *he may attend at that court for the purpose of continuing to deal with, giving judgment in, or dealing with any ancillary matter relating to, any case begun before him while acting as a judge of that court; and*

(b) *for that purpose, and for the purpose of any proceedings arising out of any such case or matter, he shall be treated as being or, as the case may be, having been a judge of that court.*

Note. Sub-s (7) repealed by Judicial Pensions and Retirement Act 1993, s 31(4), Sch 9, as from 31 March 1995.

(8) Such remuneration and allowances as the Lord Chancellor may, with the concurrence of the Minister for the Civil Service, determine may be paid out of money provided by Parliament—

(a) to any person who has been—

(i) a Lord of Appeal in Ordinary; or

(ii) a judge of the Court of Appeal; or

(iii) a judge of the High Court,

and is by virtue of subsection (1) acting as mentioned in that subsection;

(b) to any deputy judge of the High Court appointed under subsection (4).

* * * * *

13. Precedence of judges of Supreme Court—(1) When sitting in the Court of Appeal—

(a) the Lord Chief Justice and the Master of the Rolls shall rank in that order; and

(b) Lords of Appeal in Ordinary and persons who have been Lord Chancellor shall rank next after the Master of the Rolls and, among themselves, according to the priority of the dates on which they respectively became Lords of Appeal in Ordinary or Lord Chancellor, as the case may be.

(2) Subject to subsection (1)(b), the President of the Family Division shall rank next after the Master of the Rolls.

* * * * *

(6) The puisne judges of the High Court shall rank next after the judges of the Court of Appeal and, among themselves, according to the priority of the dates on which they respectively became judges of the High Court.

* * * * *

PART II

JURISDICTION

THE COURT OF APPEAL

15. General jurisdiction of Court of Appeal—(1) The Court of Appeal shall be a superior court of record.

(2) Subject to the provisions of this Act, there shall be exercisable by the Court of Appeal—

(a) all such jurisdiction (whether civil or criminal) as is conferred on it by this or any other Act; and

(b) all such other jurisdiction (whether civil or criminal) as was exercisable by it immediately before the commencement of this Act.

(3) For all purposes of or incidental to—

(a) the hearing and determination of any appeal to the civil division of the Court of Appeal; and

(b) the amendment, execution and enforcement of any judgment or order made on such an appeal,

the Court of Appeal shall have all the authority and jurisdiction of the court or tribunal from which the appeal was brought.

(4) It is hereby declared that any provision in this or any other Act which authorises or requires the taking of any steps for the execution or enforcement of a judgment or order of the High Court applies in relation to a judgment or order of the civil division of the Court of Appeal as it applies in relation to a judgment or order of the High Court.

16. Appeals from High Court—(1) Subject as otherwise provided by this or any other Act (and in particular to the provision in section 13(2)(a) of the Administration of Justice Act 1969 excluding appeals to the Court of Appeal in cases where leave to appeal from the High Court directly to the House of Lords is granted under Part II of that Act), [or as provided by any order made by the Lord Chancellor under section 56(1) of the Access to Justice Act 1999,] the Court of Appeal shall have jurisdiction to hear and determine appeals from any judgment or order of the High Court.

Note. Amended by SI No 1071, art 7, as from 2 May 2000.

(2) An appeal from a judgment or order of the High Court when acting as a prize court shall not be to the Court of Appeal, but shall be to Her Majesty in Council in accordance with the Prize Acts 1864 to 1944.

17. Applications for new trial—(1) Where any cause or matter, or any issue in any cause or matter, has been tried in the High Court, any application for a new trial thereof, or to set aside a verdict, finding or judgment therein, shall be heard and determined by the Court of Appeal except where rules of court made in pursuance of subsection (2) provide otherwise.

(2) As regards cases where the trial was by a judge alone and no error of the court at the trial is alleged, or any prescribed class or such cases rules of court may provide that any such application as is mentioned in subsection (1) shall be heard and determined by the High Court.

Note. See Family Proceedings Rules 1991, r 2.42.

(3) Nothing in this section shall alter the practice in bankruptcy.

18. Restrictions on appeals to Court of Appeal—(1) No appeal shall lie to the Court of Appeal—

(a) except as provided by the Administration of Justice Act 1960, from any judgment of the High Court in any criminal cause or matter;

(b) from any order of the High Court or any other court or tribunal allowing an extension of time for appealing from a judgment or order;

(c) from any order, judgment or decision of the High Court or any other court or tribunal which, by virtue of any provision (however expressed) of this or any other Act, is final;

(d) from a decree absolute of *divorce or* nullity of marriage, by a party who, having had time and opportunity to appeal from the decree nisi on which that decree was founded, has not appealed from the decree nisi;

[(dd) from a divorce order]

(*e*) *without the leave of the divisional court in question or of the Court of Appeal, from the determination by a divisional court of any appeal to the High Court;*

(*f*) *without the leave of the court or tribunal in question, from any order of the High Court or any other court or tribunal made with the consent of the parties or relating only to costs which are by law left to the discretion of the court or tribunal;*

(*g*) *except as provided by the Arbitration Act 1979, from any decision of the High Court—*

    (*i*) *on an appeal under section 1 of that Act on a question of law arising out of an arbitration award; or*

    (*ii*) *under section 2 of that Act on a question of law arising in the course of a reference;*

[(g) except as provided by Part I of the Arbitration Act 1996, from any decision of the High Court under that Part;]

(*h*) *without the leave of the court or tribunal in question or of the Court of Appeal, from any interlocutory order or interlocutory judgment made or given by the High Court or any other court or tribunal, except in the following cases, namely—*

    (*i*) *where the liberty of the subject or the custody [residence], education or welfare of a minor is concerned;*

    (*ii*) *where an applicant for access to [contact with] a minor is refused all access to [contact with] the minor;*

    (*iii*) *where an injunction or the appointment of a receiver is granted or refused;*

    (*iv*) *in the case of a decision determining the claim of any creditor, or the liability of any contributory or of any director or other officer, under the law relating to companies;*

    (*v*) *in the case of a decree nisi in a matrimonial cause, or a judgment or order in an admiralty action determining liability;*

    (*vi*) *in such other cases as may be prescribed.*

Note. Words in italics in sub-s (1)(d) repealed and sub-s (1)(dd) inserted by Family Law Act 1996, s 66, Sch 8, Part I, para 30, Sch 10, as from a day to be appointed, subject to savings in s 66(2) of, and para 5 of Sch 9 to, the 1996 Act. Sub-s (1)(e), (f), (h) repealed by Courts and Legal Services Act 1990, ss 7(1), (2), 125(7), Sch 20, as from 1 October 1993. Sub-s (1)(g) in square brackets substituted for sub-s (1)(g) in italics by Arbitration Act 1996, s 107(1), Sch 3, para 37, as from 31 January 1997. Words in square brackets in sub-s (1)(h)(i), (ii) substituted for words 'custody' and 'access to', by Children Act 1989, s 108(5), Sch 13, para 45(1), as from 14 October 1991.

[*(1A) In any such class of case as may be prescribed by Rules of the Supreme Court [rules of court], an appeal shall lie to the Court of Appeal only with the leave of the Court of Appeal or such court or tribunal as may be specified by the rules in relation to that class.*

(1B) Any enactment which authorises leave to appeal to the Court of Appeal being given by a single judge, or by a court consisting of two judges, shall have effect subject to any provision which—

    (*a*) *is made by Rules of the Supreme Court [rules of court]; and*

    (*b*) *in such classes of case as may be prescribed by the rules, requires leave to be given by such greater number of judges (not exceeding three) as may be so specified.]*

Note. Sub-ss (1A), (1B) inserted by Courts and Legal Services Act 1990, s 7(3), as from 23 July 1993; words in square brackets substituted for words in italics by Civil Procedure Act 1997, s 10, Sch 2, para 1(1), (2), as from 27 April 1997. Repealed by the Access to Justice Act 1999, S 106, Sch 15, Pt III, as from 27 September 1999.

(2) For the purposes of subsection (1)(h)—

    (*a*) *an order refusing unconditional leave to defend an action shall not be treated as an interlocutory order; and*

    (*b*) *'education' includes training and religious instruction.*

Note. Sub-s (2) repealed by Courts and Legal Services Act 1990, s 125(7), Sch 20, as from 1 October 1993.

THE HIGH COURT

General jurisdiction

19. General jurisdiction of High Court—(1) The High Court shall be a superior court of record.

(2) Subject to the provisions of this Act, there shall be exercisable by the High Court—

(a) all such jurisdiction (whether civil or criminal) as is conferred on it by this or any other Act; and

(b) all such other jurisdiction (whether civil or criminal) as was exercisable by it immediately before the commencement of this Act (including jurisdiction conferred on a judge of the High Court by any statutory provision).

(3) Any jurisdiction of the High Court shall be exercised only by a single judge of that court, except in so far as it is—

(a) by or by virtue of rules of court or any other statutory provision required to be exercised by a divisional court; or

(b) by rules of court made exercisable by a master, registrar or other officer of the court, or by any other person.

(4) The specific mention elsewhere in this Act of any jurisdiction covered by subsection (2) shall not derogate from the generality of that subsection.

*   *   *   *   *

Other particular fields of jurisdiction

25. Probate jurisdiction of High Court—(1) Subject to the provisions of Part V, the High Court shall, in accordance with section 19(2), have the following probate jurisdiction, that is to say all such jurisdiction in relation to probates and letters of administration as it had immediately before the commencement of this Act, and in particular all such contentious and non-contentious jurisdiction as it then had in relation to—

(a) testamentary causes or matters;

(b) the grant, amendment or revocation of probates and letters of administration; and

(c) the real and personal estate of deceased persons.

(2) Subject to the provisions of Part V, the High Court shall, in the exercise of its probate jurisdiction, perform all such duties with respect to the estate of deceased persons as fell to be performed by it immediately before the commencement of this Act.

26. Matrimonial jurisdiction of High Court. The High Court shall, in accordance with section 19(2), have all such jurisdiction in relation to matrimonial causes and matters as was immediately before the commencement of the Matrimonial Causes Act 1857 vested in or exercisable by any ecclesiastical court or person in England or Wales in respect of—

(a) divorce a mensa et thoro (renamed judicial separation by that Act);

(b) nullity of marriage *or jactitation of marriage;* and

(c) any matrimonial cause or matter except marriage licences.

Note. Words in s 26(b) repealed by Family Law Act 1986, s 68(1), (2), Sch 1, para 25, Sch 2, as from 4 April 1988.

*   *   *   *   *

28. Appeals from Crown court and inferior courts—(1) Subject to subsection (2), any order, judgment or other decision of the Crown court may be questioned by any party to the proceedings, on the ground that it is wrong in law or is in excess of jurisdiction, by applying to the Crown Court to have a case stated by that court for the opinion of the High Court.

(2) Subsection (1) shall not apply to—
    (a) a judgment or other decision of the Crown Court relating to trial on indictment; or
    (b) any decision of that court under the Betting, Gaming and Lotteries Act 1963, *the Licensing Act 1964 or the Gaming Act 1968* [, the Gaming Act 1968 or the Local Government (Miscellaneous Provisions) Act 1982] which, by any provision of any of those Acts, is to be final.
(3) Subject to the provisions of this Act and to rules of court, the High Court shall, in accordance with section 19(2), have jurisdiction to hear and determine—
    (a) any application, or any appeal (whether by way of case stated or otherwise), which it has power to hear and determine under or by virtue of this or any other Act; and
    (b) all such other appeals as it had jurisdiction to hear and determine immediately before the commencement of this Act.

Note. Sub-s (2)(b) amended by Local Government (Miscellaneous Provisions) Act 1982, s 2, Sch 3, para 27(6). Repealed in part by the Licensing Act 2003, s 199, Sch 7, as from a date to be appointed.

[(4) In subsection (2)(a) the reference to a decision of the Crown Court relating to trial on indictment does not include a decision relating to an order under section 17 of the Access to Justice Act 1999.]

Note. Inserted by the Access to Justice Act 1999, s 24, Sch 4, paras 21, 22 as from 2 April 2001 (SI 2001 No 916).

[**28A. Proceedings on case stated by magistrates' court**—*(1) The following provisions apply where a case is stated for the opinion of the High Court under section 111 of the Magistrates' Courts Act 1980 (case stated on question of law or jurisdiction).*

(2) The High Court may, if it thinks fit, cause the case to be sent back for amendment, whereupon it shall be amended accordingly.

(3) The High Court shall hear and determine the question arising on the case (or the case as amended) and shall—
    (a) reverse, affirm or amend the determination in respect of which the case has been stated, or
    (b) remit the matter to the justice or justices with the opinion of the court,
and may make such other order in relation to the matter (including as to costs) as it thinks fit.

(4) Except as provided by the Administration of Justice Act 1960 (right of appeal to House of Lords in criminal cases), a decision of the High Court under this section is final and conclusive on all parties.]

Note. This section inserted by Statute Law (Repeals) Act 1993, s 1(2), Sch 2, para 9, as from 5 November 1993.

[**28A Proceedings on case stated by magistrates' court or Crown Court**]—
[(1) This section applies where a case is stated for the opinion of the High Court—
    (a) by a magistrates' court under section 111 of the Magistrates' Courts Act 1980; or
    (b) by the Crown Court under section 28(1) of this Act.
(2) The High Court may, if it thinks fit, cause the case to be sent back for amendment and, where it does so, the case shall be amended accordingly.
(3) The High Court shall hear and determine the question arising on the case (or the case as amended) and shall—
    (a) reverse, affirm or amend the determination in respect of which the case has been stated; or
    (b) remit the matter to the magistrates' court, or the Crown Court, with the opinion of the High Court, and may make such other order in relation to the matter (including as to costs) as it thinks fit.

(4) Except as provided by the Administration of Justice Act 1960 (right of appeal to House of Lords in criminal cases), a decision of the High Court under this section is final.]

Note. Substituted by the Access to Justice Act 1999, s 61, as from 27 September 1999.

29. Orders of mandamus, prohibition and certiorari [[Mandatory, prohibiting and quashing orders]—*(1) The High Court shall have jurisdiction to make orders of mandamus, prohibition and certiorari in those classes of cases in which it had power to do so immediately before the commencement of this Act.*

[(1) The orders of mandamus, prohibition and certiorari shall be known instead as mandatory, prohibiting and quashing orders respectively.

(1A) The High Court shall have jurisdiction to make mandatory, prohibiting and quashing orders in those classes of case in which, immediately before 1st May 2004, it had jurisdiction to make orders of mandamus, prohibition and certiorari respectively.]

(2) Every such order shall be final, subject to any right of appeal therefrom.

(3) In relation to the jurisdiction of the Crown Court, other than its jurisdiction in matters relating to trial on indictment, the High Court shall have all such jurisdiction to make orders of *mandamus, prohibition or certiorari* [mandatory, prohibiting or quashing orders] as the High Court possesses in relation to the jurisdiction of an inferior court.

[(3A) The High Court shall have no jurisdiction to make [mandatory, prohibiting or quashing orders] in relation to the jurisdiction of a court-martial in matters relating to—

(a) trial by court-martial for an offence, or

(b) appeals from a Standing Civilian Court.

and in this subsection 'court-martial' means a court-martial under the Army Act 1955, the Air Force Act 1955 or the Naval Discipline Act 1957.]

(4) The power of the High Court under any enactment to require justices of the peace or a judge or officer of a county court to do any act relating to the duties of their respective offices, or to require a magistrates' court to state a case for the opinion of the High Court, in any case where the High Court formerly had by virtue of any enactment jurisdiction to make a rule absolute, or an order, for any of those purposes, shall be exercisable by *order of mandamus* [mandatory order].

(5) In any enactment—

(a) references to a writ of mandamus, of prohibition or of certiorari shall be read as references to the corresponding order; and

(b) references to the issue or award of any such writ shall be read as references to the making of the corresponding order.

[(5) In any statutory provision—

(a) references to mandamus or to a writ or order of mandamus shall be read as references to a mandatory order;

(b) references to prohibition or to a writ or order of prohibition shall be read as references to a prohibiting order;

(c) references to certiorari or to a writ or order of certiorari shall be read as references to a quashing order; and

(d) references to the issue or award of a writ of mandamus, prohibition or certiorari shall be read as references to the making of the corresponding mandatory, prohibiting or quashing order.]

[(6) In subsection (3) the reference to the Crown Court's jurisdiction in matters relating to trial on indictment does not include its jurisdiction relating to orders under section 17 of the Access to Justice Act 1999.]

Note. Amended by SI 2004 No 1033, arts 2, 3, as from 1 May 2004; the Armed Forces Act 2001, s 23(1), (3) as from 28 February 2002 (SI 2002 No 345); the Access to Justice Act 1999, s 24, Sch 4, paras 21, 23, as from 2 April 2001 (SI 2001 No 916).

30. Injunctions to restrain persons from acting in offices in which they are not entitled to act—(1) Where a person not entitled to do so acts in an office to which this section applies, the High Court may—

(a) grant an injunction restraining him from so acting; and

(b) if the case so requires, declare the office to be vacant.

(2) This section applies to any substantive office of a public nature and permanent character which is held under the Crown or which has been created by any statutory provision or royal charter.

31. Application for judicial review—(1) An application to the High Court for one or more of the following forms of relief, namely—

(a) *an order of mandamus, prohibition or certiorari;*

[(a) a mandatory, prohibiting or quashing order;]

(b) a declaration or injunction under subsection (2); or

(c) an injunction under section 30 restraining a person not entitled to do so from acting in an office to which that section applies,

shall be made in accordance with rules of court by a procedure to be known as an application for judicial review.

(2) A declaration may be made or an injunction granted under this subsection in any case where an application for judicial review, seeking that relief, has been made and the High Court considers that, having regard to—

(a) the nature of the matters in respect of which relief may be granted by *orders of mandamus, prohibition or certiorari* [mandatory, prohibiting or quashing orders];

(b) the nature of the persons and bodies against whom relief may be granted by such orders; and

(c) all the circumstances of the case,

it would be just and convenient for the declaration to be made or the injunction to be granted, as the case may be.

(3) No application for judicial review shall be made unless the leave of the High Court has been obtained in accordance with rules of court; and the court shall not grant leave to make such an application unless it considers that the applicant has a sufficient interest in the matter to which the application relates.

(4) On an application for judicial review the High Court may award damages to the applicant if—

(a) he has joined with his application a claim for damages arising from any matter to which the application relates; and

(b) the court is satisfied that, if the claim had been made in an action begun by the applicant at the time of making his application, he would have been awarded damages.

[(4) On an application for judicial review the High Court may award to the applicant damages, restitution or the recovery of a sum due if—

(a) the application includes a claim for such an award arising from any matter to which the application relates; and

(b) the court is satisfied that such an award would have been made if the claim had been made in an action begun by the applicant at the time of making the application.]

(5) If, on an application for judicial review seeking *an order of certiorari* [a quashing order], the High Court quashes the decision to which the application relates, the High Court may remit the matter to the court, tribunal or authority concerned, with a direction to reconsider it and reach a decision in accordance with the findings of the High Court.

(6) Where the High Court considers that there has been undue delay in making an application for judicial review, the court may refuse to grant—

(a) leave for the making of the application; or

(b) any relief sought on the application,

if it considers that the granting of the relief sought would be likely to cause substantial hardship to, or substantially prejudice the rights of, any person or would be detrimental to good administration.

(7) Subsection (6) is without prejudice to any enactment or rule which has the effect of limiting the time within which an application for judicial review may be made.

Note. See RSC Ord 53. Amended by SI 2004 No 1033, arts 2, 4, as from 1 May 2004.

Powers

32. Orders for interim payment—(1) As regards proceedings pending in the High Court, provision may be made by rules of court for enabling the court, in such circumstances as may be prescribed, to make an order requiring a party to the proceedings to make an interim payment of such amount as may be specified in the order, with provision for the payment to be made to such other party to the proceedings as may be so specified or, if the order so provides, by paying it into court.

(2) Any rules of court which make provision in accordance with subsection (1) may include provision for enabling a party to any proceedings who, in pursuance of such an order, has made an interim payment to recover the whole or part of the amount of the payment in such circumstances, and from such other party to the proceedings, as may be determined in accordance with the rules.

(3) Any rules made by virtue of this section may include such incidental, supplementary and consequential provisions as the rule-making authority may consider necessary or expedient.

(4) Nothing in this section shall be construed as affecting the exercise of any power relating to costs, including any power to make rules of court relating to costs.

(5) In this section 'interim payment', in relation to a party to any proceedings, means a payment on account of any damages, debt or other sum (excluding any costs) which that party may be held liable to pay to or for the benefit of another party to the proceedings if a final judgment or order of the court in the proceedings is given or made in favour of that other party.

[32A. Orders for provisional damages for personal injuries—(1) This section applies to an action for damages for personal injuries in which there is proved or admitted to be a chance that at some definite or indefinite time in the future the injured person will, as a result of the act or omission which gave rise to the cause of action, develop some serious disease or suffer some serious deterioration in his physical or mental condition.

(2) Subject to subsection (4) below, as regards any action for damages to which this section applies in which a judgment is given in the High Court, provision may be made by rules of court for enabling the court, in such circumstances as may be prescribed, to award the injured person—

(a) damages assessed on the assumption that the injured person will not develop the disease or suffer the deterioration in his condition; and

(b) further damages at a future date if he develops the disease or suffers the deterioration.

(3) Any rules made by virtue of this section may include such incidental, supplementary and consequential provisions as the rule-making authority may consider necessary or expedient.

(4) Nothing in this section shall be construed—

(a) as affecting the exercise of any power relating to costs, including any power to make rules of court relating to costs; or

(b) as prejudicing any duty of the court under any enactment or rule of law to reduce or limit the total damages which would have been recoverable apart from any such duty.]

Note. This section inserted by Administration of Justice Act 1982, ss 6(1), 73(2), as from 1 July 1985.

* * * * *

33. Powers of High Court exercisable before commencement of action—(1) On the application of any person in accordance with rules of court, the High Court shall, in such circumstances as may be specified in the rules, have power to make an order providing for any one or more of the following matters, that is to say—
  - (a) the inspection, photographing, preservation, custody and detention of property which appears to the court to be property which may become the subject-matter of subsequent proceedings in the High Court, or as to which any question may arise in any such proceedings; and
  - (b) the taking of samples of any such property as is mentioned in paragraph (a), and the carrying out of any experiment on or with any such property.
(2) On the application, in accordance with rules of court, of a person who appears to the High Court to be likely to be a party to subsequent proceedings in that court *in which a claim in respect of personal injuries to a person, or in respect of a person's death, is likely to be made*, the High Court shall, in such circumstances as may be specified in the rules, have power to order a person who appears to the court to be likely to be a party to the proceedings and to be likely to have or to have had in his possession, custody or power any documents which are relevant to an issue arising or likely to arise out of that claim—
  - (a) to disclose whether those documents are in his possession, custody or power; and
  - (b) to produce such of those documents as are in his possession, custody or power to the applicant or, on such conditions as may be specified in the order—
    - (i) to the applicant's legal advisers; or
    - (ii) to the applicant's legal advisers and any medical or other professional adviser of the applicant; or
    - (iii) if the applicant has no legal adviser, to any medical or other professional adviser of the applicant.

Note. This section repealed so far as relates to county courts by County Courts Act 1984, s 148(3), Sch 4, as from 1 August 1984: see now County Courts Act 1984, s 52. Repealed in part by SI 1998 No 2940, art 5(a), as from 26 April 1999.

* * * * *

[35A. Power of High Court to award interest on debts and damages—(1) Subject to rules of court, in proceedings (whenever instituted) before the High Court for the recovery of a debt or damages there may be included in any sum for which judgment is given simple interest, at such rate as the court thinks fit or as rules of court may provide, on all or any part of the debt or damages in respect of which judgment is given, or payment is made before judgment, for all or any part of the period between the date when the cause of action arose and—
  - (a) in the case of any sum paid before judgment, the date of the payment; and
  - (b) in the case of the sum for which judgment is given, the date of the judgment.
(2) In relation to a judgment given for damages for personal injuries or death which exceed £200 subsection (1) shall have effect—
  - (a) with the substitution of 'shall be included' for 'may be included'; and
  - (b) with the addition of 'unless the court is satisfied that there are special reasons to the contrary' after 'given', where first occurring.
(3) Subject to rules of court, where—
  - (a) there are proceedings (whenever instituted) before the High Court for the recovery of a debt; and
  - (b) the defendant pays the whole debt to the plaintiff (otherwise than in pursuance of a judgment in the proceedings),

the defendant shall be liable to pay the plaintiff simple interest at such rate as the court thinks fit or as rules of court may provide on all or any part of the debt for all or any part of the period between the date when the cause of action arose and the date of the payment.

(4) Interest in respect of a debt shall not be awarded under this section for a period during which, for whatever reason, interest on the debt already runs.

(5) Without prejudice to the generality of section 84, rules of court may provide for a rate of interest by reference to the rate specified in section 17 of the Judgments Act 1838 as that section has effect from time to time or by reference to a rate for which any other enactment provides.

(6) Interest under this section may be calculated at different rates in respect of different periods.

(7) In this section 'plaintiff' means the person seeking the debt or damages and 'defendant' means the person from whom the plaintiff seeks the debt or damages and 'personal injuries' includes any disease and any impairment of a person's physical or mental condition.

(8) Nothing in this section affects the damages recoverable for the dishonour of a bill of exchange.]

Note. This section inserted by Administration of Justice Act 1982, s 15(1), Sch 1, Part I, as from 1 April 1983.

36. Subpoena issued by High Court to run throughout United Kingdom—(1) If in any cause or matter in the High Court it appears to the court that it is proper to compel the personal attendance at any trial of a witness who may not be within the jurisdiction of the court, it shall be lawful for the court, if in the discretion of the court it seems fit so to do, to order that a writ of subpoena ad testificandum or writ of subpoena duces tecum shall issue in special form commanding the witness to attend the trial wherever he shall be within the United Kingdom; and the service of any such writ in any part of the United Kingdom shall be as valid and effectual for all purposes as if it had been served within the jurisdiction of the High Court.

(2) Every such writ shall have at its foot a statement to the effect that it is issued by the special order of the High Court, and no such writ shall issue without such a special order.

(3) If any person served with a writ issued under this section does not appear as required by the writ, the High Court, on proof to the satisfaction of the court of the service of the writ and of the default, may transmit a certificate of the default under the seal of the court or under the hand of a judge of the court—

(a) if the service was in Scotland, to the Court of Session at Edinburgh; or

(b) if the service was in Northern Ireland, to the High Court of Justice in Northern Ireland at Belfast;

and the court to which the certificate is sent shall thereupon proceed against and punish the person in default in like manner as if that person had neglected or refused to appear in obedience to process issued out of that court.

(4) No court shall in any case proceed against or punish any person for having made such default as aforesaid unless it is shown to the court that a reasonable and sufficient sum of money to defray *the expenses of coming and attending to give evidence and of returning from giving evidence was tendered to that person at the time when the writ was served upon him* [—

(a) the expenses of coming and attending to give evidence and of returning from giving evidence; and

(b) any other reasonable expenses which he has asked to be defrayed in connection with his evidence,

was tendered to him at the time when the unit was served upon him.]

Note. Words in square brackets substituted for words in italics by Courts and Legal Services Act 1990, s 125(2), Sch 17, para 13, as from 1 April 1991.

(5) Nothing in this section shall affect—

(a) the power of the High Court to issue a commission for the examination of witnesses out of the jurisdiction of the court in any case in which, notwithstanding this section, the court thinks fit to issue such a commission; or

(b) the admissibility at any trial of any evidence which, if this section had not been enacted, would have been admissible on the ground of a witness being outside the jurisdiction of the court.

(6) In this section references to attendance at a trial include references to attendance before an examiner or commissioner appointed by the High Court in any cause or matter in that court, including an examiner or commissioner appointed to take evidence outside the jurisdiction of the court.

37. Powers of High Court with respect to injunctions and receivers—(1) The High Court may by order (whether interlocutory or final) grant an injunction or appoint a receiver in all cases in which it appears to the court to be just and convenient to do so.

(2) Any such order may be made either unconditionally or on such terms and conditions as the court thinks just.

(3) The power of the High Court under subsection (1) to grant an interlocutory injunction restraining a party to any proceedings from removing from the jurisdiction of the High Court, or otherwise dealing with, assets located within the jurisdiction shall be exercisable in cases where that party is, as well as in cases where he is not, domiciled, resident or present within that jurisdiction.

(4) The power of the High Court to appoint a receiver by way of equitable execution shall operate in relation to all legal estates and interests in land; and that power—

(a) may be exercised in relation to an estate or interest in land whether or not a charge has been imposed on that land under section 1 of the Charging Orders Act 1979 for the purpose of enforcing the judgment, order or award in question; and

(b) shall be in addition to, and not in derogation of, any power of any court to appoint a receiver in proceedings for enforcing such a charge.

(5) Where an order under the said section 1 imposing a charge for the purpose of enforcing a judgment, order or award has been, or has effect as if, registered under section 6 of the Land Charges Act 1972, subsection (4) of the said section 6 (effect of non-registration of writs and orders registrable under that section) shall not apply to an order appointing a receiver made either—

(a) in proceedings for enforcing the charge; or

(b) by way of equitable execution of the judgment, order or award or, as the case may be, of so much of it as requires payment of moneys secured by the charge.

*   *   *   *   *

39. Execution of instrument by person nominated by High Court—(1) Where the High Court has given or made a judgment or order directing a person to execute any conveyance, contract or other document, or to indorse any negotiable instrument, then, if that person—

(a) neglects or refuses to comply with the judgment or order; or

(b) cannot after reasonable inquiry be found,

the High Court may, on such terms and conditions, if any, as may be just, order that the conveyance, contract or other document shall be executed, or that the negotiable instrument shall be indorsed, by such person as the court may nominate for that purpose.

(2) A conveyance, contract, document or instrument executed or indorsed in pursuance of an order under this section shall operate, and be for all purposes available, as if it had been executed or indorsed by the person originally directed to execute or indorse it.

40. Attachment of debts—(1) Subject to any order for the time being in force under subsection (4), this section applies to *the following accounts, namely*—
  (a) *any deposit account with a bank or other deposit-taking institution; and*
  (b) *any withdrawable share account with any deposit-taking institution* [any deposit account, and any withdrawable share account, with a deposit-taker].
  (2) In determining whether, for the purposes of the jurisdiction of the High Court to attach debts for the purpose of satisfying judgments or orders for the payment of money, a sum standing to the credit of a person in an account to which this section applies is a sum due or accruing to that person and, as such, attachable in accordance with rules of court, any condition mentioned in subsection (3) which applies to the account shall be disregarded.
  (3) Those conditions are—
  (a) any condition that notice is required before any money or share is withdrawn;
  (b) any condition that a personal application must be made before any money or share is withdrawn;
  (c) any condition that a deposit book or share-account book must be produced before any money or share is withdrawn; or
  (d) any other prescribed condition.
  (4) The Lord Chancellor may by order make such provision as he thinks fit, by way of amendment of this section or otherwise, for all or any of the following purposes, namely—
  (a) including in, or excluding from, the accounts to which this section applies accounts of any description specified in the order;
  (b) excluding from the accounts to which this section applies all accounts with any particular *deposit-taking institution* [deposit-taker] so specified or with any *deposit-taking institution* [deposit-taker] of a description so specified.
  (5) Any order under subsection (4) shall be made by statutory instrument subject to annulment in pursuance of a resolution of either House of Parliament.
  (6) In this section 'deposit-taking institution' means any person carrying on a business which is a deposit-taking business for the purposes of the Banking Act 1979 [the Banking Act 1987].
  [(6) 'Deposit-taker' means a person who may, in the course of his business, lawfully accept deposits in the United Kingdom.]
  [(7) Subsection (6) must be read with—
  (a) section 22 of the Financial Services and Markets Act 2000;
  (b) any relevant order under that section; and
  (c) Schedule 2 to that Act.]
Note. Reference to 1987 Act substituted for reference to 1979 Act by Banking Act 1987, s 108(1), Sch 6, para 11, as from 1 October 1987. Further amended by SI 2001/3649, art 290, as from 1 December 2001.

[40A. Administrative and clerical expenses of garnishees—*(1) A sum may be prescribed which, before complying with an order made in the exercise of the jurisdiction mentioned in section 40(2)—*
  (a) any deposit-taking institution; or
  (b) any such institution of a prescribed description,
may deduct, subject to subsection (2) below, towards the clerical and administrative expenses of complying with the order, from any money which, but for the deduction, would be attached by the order.
  [(1) Where an *order nisi* [interim third party debt order] made in the exercise of the jurisdiction mentioned in subsection (2) of the preceding section is served on *any deposit-taking institution, the institution* [a deposit-taker, it] may, subject to the provisions of this section, deduct from the relevant debt or debts an amount not exceeding the prescribed sum towards *the administrative and clerical expenses of the institution* [its administrative and clerical expenses] in complying with the order; and the right *of an institution* to make a deduction under this subsection shall be

exercisable as from the time the *order nisi* [interim third party debt order] is served on it.

(1A) In subsection (1) 'the relevant debt or debts', in relation to an *order nisi* [interim third party debt order] served on *any such institution as is mentioned in that subsection* [deposit-takers], means the amount, as at the time the order is served on *the institution* [it], of the debt or debts of which the whole or a part is expressed to be attached by the order.

(1B) A deduction may be made under subsection (1) in a case where the amount referred to in subsection (1A) is insufficient to cover both the amount of the deduction and the amount of the judgment debt and costs in respect of which the attachment was made, notwithstanding that the benefit of the attachment to the creditor is reduced as a result of the deduction.]

Note. Sub-ss (1), (1A), (1B) in square brackets substituted for sub-s (1) in italics by Administration of Justice Act 1985, s 52, as from 30 December 1985. For transitional provisions and savings, see s 69(5) of, and Sch 9, para 11 to, that Act (pp 3131, 3134).

(2) *The prescribed sum may not* [An amount may not in pursuance of subsection 1] be deducted or, as the case may be, retained in a case where, by virtue of *section 40 of the Bankruptcy Act 1914* [*section 179 of the Insolvency Act 1985*] [section 346 of the Insolvency Act 1986] or *section 325 of the Companies Act 1948* [section *621 of the Companies Act 1985*] [183 of the Insolvency Act 1986] or otherwise, the creditor is not entitled to retain the benefit of the attachment.

Note. Sub-s (2) amended by Administration of Justice Act 1985, s 52(3) (substitution of first words in italics by succeeding words in square brackets) and by Companies Consolidation (Consequential Provisions) Act 1985, s 30, Sch 2, Insolvency Act 1985, s 235(1), Sch 8, para 35, and Insolvency Act 1986, s 439(2), Sch 14. For transitional provisions and savings, see s 437 of, and Sch 11 to, that Act.

(3) In this section—
'*deposit-taking institution' has the meaning assigned to it by section 40(6)* ['deposit-taker' has the meaning given by section 40(6);]; and
'prescribed' means prescribed by an order made by the Lord Chancellor.

(4) An order under this section—
(a) may make different provision for different cases; *and*
(b) without prejudice to the generality of paragraph (a) of this subsection, may prescribe sums differing according to the amount due under the judgment or order to be satisfied;
[(c) may provide for this section not to apply to *deposit-taking institutions* [deposit-takers] of any prescribed description.]

Note. Word 'and' repealed and para (c) added by Administration of Justice Act 1985, ss 52(4), 67(2), Sch 8, Part II, as from 30 December 1985.

(5) Any such order shall be made by statutory instrument subject to annulment in pursuance of a resolution of either House of Parliament.]

Note. Section 40A inserted by Administration of Justice Act 1982, s 55(1), Sch 4, Part I, as from 1 January 1983. Further amended by SI 2001 No 3649, art 291, as from 1 December 2001; SI 2002 No 439, arts 2, 6, as from 25 March 2002.

41. Wards of court—(1) Subject to the provisions of this section, no minor shall be made a ward of court except by virtue of an order to that effect made by the High Court.

(2) Where an application is made for such an order in respect of a minor, the minor shall become a ward of court on the making of the application, but shall cease to be a ward of court at the end of such period as may be prescribed unless within that period an order has been made in accordance with the application.

[(2A) Subsection (2) does not apply with respect to a child who is the subject of a care order (as defined by section 105 of the Children Act 1989).]

Note. Sub-s (2A) inserted by Children Act 1989, s 108(5), Sch 13, para 45(2), as from 14 October 1991.

(3) The High Court may, either upon an application in that behalf or without such an application, order that any minor who is for the time being a ward of court shall cease to be a ward of court.

42. Restriction of vexatious legal proceedings—(1) If, on an application made by the Attorney General under this section, the High Court is satisfied that any person has habitually and persistently and without any reasonable ground—

(a) instituted vexatious *legal* [civil] proceedings, whether in the High Court or any inferior court, and whether against the same person or against different persons; or

(b) made vexatious applications in any *legal* [civil] proceedings, whether in the High Court or any inferior court, and whether instituted by him or another, [or

(c) instituted vexatious prosecutions (whether against the same person or different persons),]

the court may, after hearing that person or giving him an opportunity of being heard, order—

(i) *that no legal proceedings shall without the leave of the High Court be instituted by him in any court; and*

(ii) *that any legal proceedings instituted by him in any court before the making of the order shall not be continued by him without the leave of the High Court; and*

(iii) *that no application (other than an application for leave under this section) shall without the leave of the High Court be made by him in any legal proceedings instituted, whether by him or another, in any court.*

[make a civil proceedings order, a criminal proceedings order or an all proceedings order.]

[(1A) In this section—

'civil proceedings order' means an order that—

(a) no civil proceedings shall without the leave of the High Court be instituted in any court by the person against whom the order is made;

(b) any civil proceedings instituted by him in any court before the making of the order shall not be continued by him without the leave of the High Court; and

(c) no application (other than one for leave under this section) shall be made by him, in any civil proceedings instituted in any court by any person, without the leave of the High Court;

'criminal proceedings order' means an order that—

(a) no information shall be laid before a justice of the peace by the person against whom the order is made without the leave of the High Court; and

(b) no application for leave to prefer a bill of indictment shall be made by him without the leave of the High Court; and

'all proceedings order' means an order which has the combined effect of the two other orders.]

(2) An order under subsection (1) may provide that it is to cease to have effect at the end of a specified period, but shall otherwise remain in force indefinitely.

(3) Leave for the institution or continuance of, or for the making of an application in, any *legal* [civil] proceedings by a person who is the subject of an order for the time being in force under subsection (1) shall not be given unless the High Court is satisfied that the proceedings or application are not an abuse of the process of the court in question and that there are reasonable grounds for the proceedings or application.

[(3A) Leave for the laying of an information or for an application for leave to prefer a bill of indictment by a person who is the subject of an order for the time being in force under subsection (1) shall not be given unless the High Court is satisfied that the institution of the prosecution is not an abuse of the criminal process and that there are reasonable grounds for the institution of the prosecution by the applicant.]

(4) No appeal shall lie from a decision of the High Court refusing leave *for the institution or continuance of, or for the making of an application in, legal proceedings by a person who is the subject of an order for the time being in force under subsection (1)* [required by virtue of this section].

(5) A copy of any order made under subsection (1) shall be published in the London Gazette.

Note. Words in square brackets substituted for words in italics and sub-ss (1)(c), (1A), (3A) inserted by Prosecution of Offences Act 1985, s 24, as from 1 April 1986.

* * * * *

Other provisions

44. Extraordinary functions of judges of High Court—(1) Subject to the provisions of this Act, every judge of the High Court shall be—

(a) liable to perform any duty not incident to the administration of justice in any court of law which a judge of the High Court was, as the successor of any judge formerly subject to that duty, liable to perform immediately before the commencement of this Act by virtue of any statute, law or custom; and

(b) empowered to exercise any authority or power not so incident which a judge of the High Court was, as the successor of any judge formerly possessing that authority or power, empowered to exercise immediately before that commencement by virtue of any statute, law or custom.

(2) Any such duty, authority or power which immediately before the commencement of this Act was imposed or conferred by any statute, law or custom on the Lord Chancellor, the Lord Chief Justice or the Master of the Rolls shall continue to be performed and exercised by them respectively.

THE CROWN COURT

45. General Jurisdiction of Crown Court—(1) The Crown Court shall be a superior court of record.

(2) Subject to the provisions of this Act, there shall be exercisable by the Crown Court—

(a) all such appellate and other jurisdiction as is conferred on it by or under this or any other Act; and

(b) all such other jurisdiction as was exercisable by it immediately before the commencement of this Act.

(3) Without prejudice to subsection (2), the jurisdiction of the Crown Court shall include all such powers and duties as were exercisable or fell to be performed by it immediately before the commencement of this Act.

(4) Subject to section 8 of the Criminal Procedure (Attendance of Witnesses) Act 1965 (substitution in criminal cases of procedure in that Act for procedure by way of subpoena) and to any provision contained in or having effect under this Act, the Crown Court shall, in relation to the attendance and examination of witnesses, any contempt of court, the enforcement of its orders and all other matters incidental to its jurisdiction, have the like powers, rights, privileges and authority as the High Court.

(5) The specific mention elsewhere in this Act of any jurisdiction covered by subsections (2) and (3) shall not derogate from the generality of those subsections.

46. Exclusive jurisdiction of Crown Court in trial on indictment—(1) All proceedings on indictment shall be brought before the Crown Court.

(2) The jurisdiction of the Crown Court with respect to proceedings on indictment shall include jurisdiction in proceedings on indictment for offences wherever

committed, and in particular proceedings on indictment for offences within the jurisdiction of the Admiralty of England.

[46A. Offences committed on ships and abroad. Sections 280, 281 and 282 of the Merchant Shipping Act 1995 (offences on ships and abroad by British citizens and others) apply in relation to other offences under the laws of England and Wales as they apply in relation to offences under that Act or instruments under that Act.]

Note. This section inserted by Merchant Shipping Act 1995, s 314(2), Sch 13, para 59(4), as from 1 January 1996.

47. Sentences and other orders of Crown Court when dealing with offenders—(1) A sentence imposed, or other order made, by the Crown Court when dealing with an offender shall take effect from the beginning of the day on which it is imposed, unless the court otherwise directs.

[(1A) The power to give a direction under sub-s(1) above has effect subject to section 102 of the Crime and Disorder Act 1998.]

(2) Subject to the following provisions of this section, a sentence imposed, or other order made, by the Crown Court when dealing with an offender may be varied or restricted by the Crown Court within the period of twenty-eight days beginning with the day on which the sentence or other order was imposed or made or, where subsection (3) applies, within the time allowed by that subsection.

(3) Where two or more persons are jointly tried on an indictment, then, subject to the following provisions of this section, a sentence imposed, or other order made, by the Crown Court on conviction of any of those persons on the indictment may be varied or rescinded by the Crown Court not later than the expiration of whichever is the shorter of the following periods, that is—

(a) the period of twenty-eight days beginning with the date of conclusion of the joint trial;

(b) the period of fifty-six days beginning with the day on which the sentence or other order was imposed or made.

For the purposes of this subsection the joint trial is concluded on the latest of the following dates, that is any date on which any of the persons jointly tried is sentenced, or is acquitted, or on which a special verdict is brought in.

(4) A sentence or other order shall not be varied or rescinded under this section except by the court constituted as it was when the sentence or other order was imposed or made, or, where the court comprised one or more justices of the peace, a court so constituted except for the omission of any one or more of those justices.

(5) Where a sentence or other order is varied under this section, the sentence or other order, as so varied, shall take effect from the beginning of the day on which it was originally imposed or made, unless the court otherwise directs:

Provided that for the purposes of section 18(2) of the Criminal Appeal Act 1968 (time limit for notice of appeal or of application for leave to appeal) [and for the purposes of paragraph 1 of Schedule 3 to the Criminal Justice Act 1988 (time limit for notice of an application for leave to refer a case under section 36 of that Act)] the sentence or other order shall be regarded as imposed or made on the day on which it is so varied.

Note. Words in square brackets inserted by Criminal Justice Act 1988, s 170(1), Sch 15, para 79, as from 1 February 1989.

(6) Crown Court Rules—

(a) may, as respects cases where two or more persons are tried separately on the same or related facts alleged in one or more indictments, provide for extending the period fixed by subsection (2);

(b) may, subject to the preceding provisions of this section, prescribe the cases and circumstances in which, and the time within which, any order or other decision made by the Crown Court may be varied or rescinded by that court.

(7) In this section—

'order' does not include a legal aid *contribution order made under [section 7 or 8(2) of the Legal Aid Act 1982] [contribution order made under section 23 of the Legal Aid Act 1988]* [an order under section 17(2) of the Access to Justice Act 1999];

'sentence' includes a recommendation for deportation made when dealing with an offender.

Note. Words in first pair of square brackets substituted for words 'section 32 of the Legal Aid Act 1974' by Legal Aid Act 1982, s 14(3). Words in second pair of square brackets substituted for words in italics by Legal Aid Act 1988, s 45(1), (3), Sch 5, para 10, as from 1 April 1989.

Further amended by the Crime and Disorder Act 1998, s 119, Sch 8, para 47, as from 30 September 1998; the Access to Justice Act 1999, s 24, Sch 4, paras 21, 24, as from a date to be appointed. Repealed by the powers of Criminal Courts (Sentencing) Act 2000, s 165(4), Sch 12, Pt I, as from 25 August 2000.

48. Appeals to Crown Court—(1) The Crown Court may, in the course of hearing any appeal, correct any error or mistake in the order or judgment incorporating the decision which is the subject of the appeal.

(2) On the termination of the hearing of an appeal the Crown Court—

(a) may confirm, reverse or vary *the decision appealed against* [any part of the decision appealed against including a determination not to impose a separate penalty in respect of an offence]; or

(b) may remit the matter with its opinion thereon to the authority whose decision is appealed against; or

(c) may make such other order in the matter as the court thinks just, and by such order exercise any power which the said authority might have exercised.

(3) Subsection (2) has effect subject to any enactment relating to any such appeal which expressly limits the powers of the court on the appeal.

(4) *If* [Subject to section 11(6) of the Criminal Appeal Act 1995, if] the appeal is against a conviction or a sentence, the preceding provisions of this section shall be construed as including power to award any punishment, whether more or less severe than that awarded by the magistrates' court whose decision is appealed against, if that is a punishment which that magistrates' court might have awarded.

Note. Words in square brackets substituted for words in italics by Criminal Appeal Act 1995, s 29(1), Sch 2, para 14, as from 1 January 1997.

(5) This section applies whether or not the appeal is against the whole of the decision.

(6) In this section 'sentence' includes any order made by a court when dealing with an offender, including—

(a) a hospital order under [Part III of the Mental Health Act 1983], with or without [a restriction order, and an interim hospital order under [that Act]]; and

(b) a recommendation for deportation made when dealing with an offender.

[(7) The fact that an appeal is pending against an interim hospital order under [the said Act of 1983] shall not effect the power of the magistrates' court that made it to renew or terminate the order or to deal with the appellant on its termination; and where the Crown Court quashes such an order but does not pass any sentence or make any other order in its place the Court may direct the appellant to be kept in custody or released on bail pending his being dealt with by that magistrates' court.

(8) Where the Crown Court makes an interim hospital order by virtue of subsection (2)—

(a) the power of renewing or terminating the order and of dealing with the appellant on its termination shall be exercisable by the magistrates' court whose decision is appealed against and not by the Crown Court; and

(b) that magistrates' court shall be treated for the purposes of [section 38(7) of the said Act of 1983] (absconding offenders) as the court that made the order.]

Note. Words in square brackets in sub-s (2)(a) substituted for words in italics by Criminal Justice Act 1988, s 156, as from 12 October 1988. In sub-s (6)(a) words in first pair of square brackets, together with words 'that Act' substituted by Mental Health Act 1983, s 148, Sch 4, para 58, as from 30 September 1983, and words in second (outer) pair of square brackets substituted by Mental Health (Amendment) Act 1982, s 65(1), Sch 3, Part I, para 61, as from 30 September 1983. Sub-ss (7), (8) added by Mental Health (Amendment) Act 1982, s 65(1), Sch 3, Part I, para 61, as from 30 September 1983, and words in square brackets within those subsections substituted by Mental Health Act 1983, s 148, Sch 4, para 58, as from 30 September 1983.

GENERAL PROVISIONS

Law and equity

49. Concurrent administration of law and equity—(1) Subject to the provisions of this or any other Act, every court exercising jurisdiction in England or Wales in any civil cause or matter shall continue to administer law and equity on the basis that, wherever there is any conflict or variance between the rules of equity and the rules of the common law with reference to the same matter, the rules of equity shall prevail.

(2) Every such court shall give the same effect as hitherto—

(a) to all equitable estates, titles, rights, reliefs, defences and counterclaims, and to all equitable duties and liabilities; and

(b) subject thereto, to all legal claims and demands and all estates, titles, rights, duties, obligations and liabilities existing by the common law or by any custom or created by any statute,

and, subject to the provisions of this or any other Act, shall so exercise its jurisdiction in every cause or matter before it as to secure that, as far as possible, all matters in dispute between the parties are completely and finally determined, and all multiplicity of legal proceedings with respect to any of those matters is avoided.

(3) Nothing in this Act shall affect the power of the Court of Appeal or the High Court to stay any proceedings before it, where it thinks fit to do so, either of its own motion or on the application of any person, whether or not a party to the proceedings.

50. Power to award damages as well as, or in substitution for, injunction or specific performance. Where the Court of Appeal or the High Court has jurisdiction to entertain an application for an injunction or specific performance, it may award damages in addition to, or in substitution for, an injunction or specific performance.

Costs

51. Costs in civil division of Court of Appeal and High Court—(*1*) *Subject to the provisions of this or any other Act and to rules of court, the costs of and incidental to all proceedings in the civil division of the Court of Appeal and in the High Court, including the administration of estates and trusts, shall be in the discretion of the court, and the court shall have full power to determine by whom and to what extent the costs are to be paid.*

(*2*) *Nothing in subsection (1) shall alter the practice in any criminal cause or matter, or in bankruptcy.*

(*3*) *Provision may be made by rules of court for regulating any matters relating to the costs of proceedings in the civil division of the Court of Appeal or in the High Court, including the administration of estates and trusts.*

[**51. Costs in civil division of Court of Appeal, High Court and county courts**—(1) Subject to the provisions of this or any other enactment and to rules of court, the costs of and incidental to all proceedings in—

(a) the civil division of the Court of Appeal;

(b) the High Court; and

(c) any county court,

shall be in the discretion of the court.

(2) Without prejudice to any general power to make rules of court, such rules may make provision for regulating matters relating to the costs of those proceedings including, in particular, prescribing scales of costs to be paid to legal or other representatives [or for securing that the amount awarded to a party in respect of the costs to be paid by him to such representatives is not limited to what would have been payable by him to them if he had not been awarded costs.]

Note. Amended by the Access to Justice Act 1999, s 31, as from 2 June 2003 (SI 2003 No 1241).

(3) The court shall have full power to determine by whom and to what extent the costs are to be paid.

(4) In subsections (1) and (2) 'proceedings' includes the administration of estates and trusts.

(5) Nothing in subsection (1) shall alter the practice in any criminal cause, or in bankruptcy.

(6) In any proceedings mentioned in subsection (1), the court may disallow, or (as the case may be) order the legal or other representative concerned to meet, the whole of any wasted costs or such part of them as may be determined in accordance with rules of court.

(7) In subsection (6), 'wasted costs' means any costs incurred by a party—

(a) as a result of any improper, unreasonable or negligent act or omission on the part of any legal or other representative or any employee of such a representative; or

(b) which, in the light of any such act or omission occurring after they were incurred, the court considers it is unreasonable to expect that party to pay.

(8) Where—

(a) a person has commenced proceedings in the High Court; but

(b) those proceedings should, in the opinion of the court, have been commenced in a county court in accordance with any provision made under section 1 of the Courts and Legal Services Act 1990 or by or under any other enactment,

the person responsible for determining the amount which is to be awarded to that person by way of costs shall have regard to those circumstances.

(9) Where, in complying with subsection (8), the responsible person reduces the amount which would otherwise be awarded to the person in question—

(a) the amount of that reduction shall not exceed 25 per cent; and

(b) on any taxation of the costs payable by that person to his legal representative, regard shall be had to the amount of the reduction.

(10) The Lord Chancellor may by order amend subsection (9)(a) by substituting, for the percentage for the time being mentioned there, a different percentage.

(11) Any such order shall be made by statutory instrument and may make such transitional or incidental provision as the Lord Chancellor considers expedient.

(12) No such statutory instrument shall be made unless a draft of the instrument has been approved by both Houses of Parliament.

(13) In this section 'legal or other representative', in relation to a party to proceedings, means any person exercising a right of audience or right to conduct litigation on his behalf.]

Note. Section 51 in square brackets substituted for s 51 in italics by Courts and Legal Services Act 1990, s 4(1), as from 1 October 1991.

*   *   *   *   *

PART III

PRACTICE AND PROCEDURE

THE COURT OF APPEAL

Distribution of business

53. Distribution of business between civil and criminal divisions—(1) Rules of court may provide for the distribution of business in the Court of Appeal between the civil and criminal divisions, but subject to any such rules business shall be distributed in accordance with the following provisions of this section.

(2) The criminal division of the Court of Appeal shall exercise—

(a) all jurisdiction of the Court of Appeal under Parts I and II of the Criminal Appeal Act 1968;

(b) the jurisdiction of the Court of Appeal under section 13 of the Administration of Justice Act 1960 (appeals in cases of contempt of court) in relation to appeals from orders and decisions of the Crown Court;

(c) all other jurisdictions expressly conferred on that division by this or any other Act; and

(d) the jurisdiction to order the issue of writs of venire de novo.

(3) The civil division of the Court of Appeal shall exercise the whole of the jurisdiction of that court not exercisable by the criminal division.

(4) Where any class of proceedings in the Court of Appeal is by any statutory provision assigned to the criminal division of that court, rules of court may provide for any enactment relating to—

(a) appeals to the Court of Appeal under Part I of the Criminal Appeal Act 1968; or

(b) any matter connected with or arising out of such appeals,

to apply in relation to proceedings of that class or, as the case may be, to any corresponding matter connected with or arising out of such proceedings, as it applies in relation to such appeals or, as the case may be, to the relevant matter within paragraph (b), with or without prescribed modifications in either case.

Composition of court

54. Court of civil division—(1) This section relates to the civil division of the Court of Appeal; and in this section 'court', except where the context otherwise requires, means a court of that division.

(2) A court shall be duly constituted for the purpose of exercising any of its jurisdiction if it consists of an uneven number of judges not less than three.

(3) Where—

(a) part of any proceedings before a court has been heard by an uneven number of judges greater than three; and

(b) one or more members of the court are unable to continue,

the court shall remain duly constituted for the purpose of those proceedings so long as the number of members (whether even or uneven) is not reduced to less than three.

(4) A court shall, if it consists of two judges, be duly constituted for the purpose of—

(a) hearing and determining any appeal against an interlocutory order or interlocutory judgment;

[(aa) hearing and determining any application for leave to appeal;]

(b) hearing and determining any appeal against a decision of a single judge acting by virtue of section 58(1);

(c) hearing and determining any appeal where all the parties have before the hearing filed a consent to the appeal being heard and determined by two judges;

(d) hearing the remainder of, and determining, any appeal where part of it has been heard by three or more judges of whom one or more are unable to continue and all the parties have consented to the remainder of the appeal being heard, and the appeal being

determined, by two remaining judges; or

(e)   *hearing and determining an appeal of any such description or in any such circumstances not covered by paragraphs (a) to (d) as may be prescribed for the purposes of this subsection by an order made by the Lord Chancellor with the concurrence of the Master of the Rolls.*

[(2) Subject as follows, a court shall be duly constituted for the purpose of exercising any of its jurisdiction if it consists of one or more judges.

(3) The Master of the Rolls may, with the concurrence of the Lord Chancellor, give (or vary or revoke) directions about the minimum number of judges of which a court must consist if it is to be duly constituted for the purpose of any description of proceedings.

(4) The Master of the Rolls, or any Lord Justice of Appeal designated by him, may (subject to any directions under subsection (3)) determine the number of judges of which a court is to consist for the purpose of any particular proceedings.

(4A) The Master of the Rolls may give directions as to what is to happen in any particular case where one or more members of a court which has partly heard proceedings are unable to continue.]

(5) Where—

(a)   an appeal has been heard by a court consisting of an even number of judges; and

(b)   the members of the court are equally divided,

the case shall, on the application of any party to the appeal, be re-argued before and determined by an uneven number of judges not less than three, before an appeal to the House of Lords.

(6) An application to the civil division of the Court of Appeal for leave to appeal to that court may be determined by a single judge of that court, and no appeal shall lie from a decision of a single judge acting under this subsection.

(7) In any cause or matter pending before the civil division of the Court of Appeal a single judge of that court may at any time during vacation make an interim order to prevent prejudice to the claims of any parties pending an appeal.

(8) Subsections (1) and (2) of section 70 (assessors in the High Court shall apply in relation to causes and matters before the civil division of the Court of Appeal as they apply in relation to causes and matters before the High Court.

(9) Subsections (3) and (4) of section 70 (scientific advisers to assist the Patents Court in proceedings under the Patents Act 1949 and the Patents Act 1977) shall apply in relation to the civil division of the Court of Appeal and proceedings on appeal from any decision of the Patents Court in proceedings under those Acts as they apply in relation to the Patents Court and proceedings under those Acts.

(10) Any order under subsection (4) shall be made by statutory instrument subject to annulment in pursuance of a resolution of either House of Parliament.

Note. Sub-s (4)(aa) inserted by Courts and Legal Services Act 1990, s 7(4), as from 23 July 1993. Amended and repealed in part by the Access to Justice Act 1999, ss 59, 106, Sch 15, Pt III, as from 27 September 1999.

*   *   *   *   *

56. Judges not to sit on appeal from their own judgments, etc—(1) No judge shall sit as a member of the civil division of the Court of Appeal on the hearing of, or shall determine any application in proceedings incidental or preliminary to, an appeal from a judgment or order made in any case by himself or by any court of which he was a member.

(2) No judge shall sit as a member of the criminal division of the Court of Appeal on the hearing of, or shall determine any application in proceedings incidental or preliminary to, an appeal against—

(a) a conviction before himself or a court of which he was a member; or

(b) a sentence passed by himself or such a court.

*[**56A. Circuit judges not to sit on certain appeals.** No Circuit judge shall act in the criminal division of the Court of Appeal as a judge of that court under section 9 on the hearing of, or shall determine any application in proceedings incidental or preliminary to, an appeal against—*

(a) a conviction before a judge of the High Court; or

(b) a sentence passed by a judge of the High Court.

Note. Repealed by the Courts Act 2003, ss 67, 109, Sch 10, as from 26 January 2004 (SI 2003 No 3345).

56B. Allocation of cases in criminal division—(1) The appeals or classes of appeals suitable for allocation to a court of the criminal division of the Court of Appeal in which a Circuit judge is acting under section 9 shall be determined in accordance with directions given by or on behalf of the Lord Chief Justice with the concurrence of the Lord Chancellor.

(2) In subsection (1) 'appeal' includes the hearing of, or any application in proceedings incidental or preliminary to, an appeal.]

Note. Sections 56A, 56B inserted by Criminal Justice and Public Order Act 1994, s 52(8), (9), as from 11 January 1995.

Sittings and vacations

57. Sittings and vacations—(1) Sittings of the Court of Appeal may be held, and any other business of the Court of Appeal may be conducted, at any place in England or Wales.

(2) Subject to rules of court—

(a) the places at which the Court of Appeal sits outside the Royal Courts of Justice; and

(b) the days and times at which the Court of Appeal sits at any place outside the Royal Courts of Justice,

shall be determined in accordance with directions given by the Lord Chancellor.

(3) Rules of court may make provision for regulating the vacations to be observed by the Court of Appeal and in the offices of that court.

(4) Rules of court—

(a) may provide for securing such sittings of the civil division of the Court of Appeal during vacation as the Master of the Rolls may with the concurrence of the Lord Chancellor determine;

(b) without prejudice to paragraph (a), shall provide for the transaction during vacation by judges of the Court of Appeal of all such business in the civil division of that court as may require to be immediately or promptly transacted; and

(c) shall provide for securing sittings of the criminal division of that court during vacation if necessary.

Other provisions

58. Exercise of incidental jurisdiction in civil division—*(1) Any jurisdiction exercisable in any proceedings incidental to any cause or matter pending before the civil division of the Court of Appeal and not involving the determination of an appeal may, if and so far as rules of court so provide, be exercised (with or without a hearing) by a single judge of that court, whether in court or in chambers, or by the registrar of civil appeals.*

(2) Rules of court may provide for decisions of a single judge or the registrar of civil appeals acting by virtue of subsection (1) to be called in question in such manner as may be prescribed; but, except as may be provided by rules of court, no appeal shall lie from a decision of a single judge or that registrar so acting.

(3) For the purposes of subsection (1) the making of an interlocutory order having the effect of preventing an appeal from reaching the stage of being heard and determined shall not be treated as a determination of the appeal.

[58 Calling into question of incidental decisions in civil division]—[(1) Rules of court may provide that decisions of the Court of Appeal which—
  (a) are taken by a single judge or any officer or member of staff of that court in proceedings incidental to any cause or matter pending before the civil division of that court; and
  (b) do not involve the determination of an appeal or of an application for permission to appeal,
may be called into question in such manner as may be prescribed.

(2) No appeal shall lie to the House of Lords from a decision which may be called into question pursuant to rules under subsection (1).]

Note. Substituted by the Access to Justice Act 1999, s 60, as from 27 September 1999.

*   *   *   *   *

60. Rules of court, and decisions of Court of Appeal, as to whether judgment or order is final or interlocutory—(1) Rules of court may provide for orders or judgments of any prescribed descriptions to be treated for any prescribed purpose connected with appeals to the Court of Appeal as final or as interlocutory.

(2) No appeal shall lie from a decision of the Court of Appeal as to whether a judgment or order is, for any purpose connected with an appeal to that court, final or interlocutory.

THE HIGH COURT

Distribution of business

61. Distribution of business among Divisions—(1) Subject to any provisions made by or under this or any other Act (and in particular to any rules of court made in pursuance of subsection (2) and any order under subsection (3)), business in the High Court of any description mentioned in Schedule 1, as for the time being in force, shall be distributed among the Divisions in accordance with that Schedule.

(2) Rules of court may provide for the distribution of business in the High Court among the Divisions; but any rules made in pursuance of this subsection shall have effect subject to any orders for the time being in force under subsection (3).

(3) Subject to subsection (5), the Lord Chancellor may by order—
  (a) direct that any business in the High Court which is not for the time being assigned by or under this or any other Act to any Division be assigned to such Division as may be specified in the order;
  (b) if at any time it appears to him desirable to do so with a view to the more convenient administration of justice, direct that any business for the time being assigned by or under this or any other Act to any Division be assigned to such other Division as may be specified in the order; and
  (c) amend Schedule 1 so far as may be necessary in consequence of provision made by order under paragraph (a) or (b).

(4) The powers conferred by subsection (2) and subsection (3) include power to assign business of any description to two or more Divisions concurrently.

(5) No order under subsection (3)(b) relating to any business shall be made without the concurrence of the senior judge of—
  (a) the Division or each of the Divisions to which the business is for the time being assigned; and
  (b) the Division or each of the Divisions to which the business is to be assigned by the order.

(6) Subject to rules of court, the fact that a cause or matter commenced in the High Court falls within a class of business assigned by or under this Act to a particular Division does not make it obligatory for it to be allocated or transferred to that Division.

(7) Without prejudice to subsections (1) to (5) and section 63, rules of court may provide for the distribution of the business (other than business required to be heard by a divisional court) in any Division of the High Court among the judges of that Division.

(8) Any order under subsection (3) shall be made by statutory instrument, which shall be laid before Parliament after being made.

*　　*　　*　　*　　*

63. Business assigned to specially nominated judges—(1) Any business assigned, in accordance with this or any other Act or rules of court, to one or more specially nominated judges of the High Court may—

(a) during vacation; or

(b) during the illness or absence of that judge or any of those judges; or

(c) for any other reasonable cause,

be dealt with by any judge of the High Court named for that purpose by the Lord Chancellor.

(2) If at any time it appears to the Lord Chancellor desirable to do so with a view to the more convenient administration of justice, he may by order direct that business of any description which is for the time being assigned, in accordance with this or any other Act or rules of court, to one or more specially nominated judges of the High Court shall cease to be so assigned and may be dealt with by any one or more judges of the High Court.

(3) An order under subsection (2) shall not be made in respect of any business without the concurrence of the senior judge of the Division to which the business is for the time being assigned.

64. Choice of Division by plaintiff—(1) Without prejudice to the power of transfer under section 65, the person by whom any cause or matter is commenced in the High Court shall in the prescribed manner allocate it to whichever Division he thinks fit.

(2) Where a cause or matter is commenced in the High Court, all subsequent interlocutory or other steps or proceedings in the High Court in that cause or matter shall be taken in the Division to which the cause or matter is for the time being allocated (whether under subsection (1) or in consequence of its transfer under section 65).

65. Power of transfer—(1) Any cause or matter may at any time and at any stage thereof, and either with or without application from any of the parties, be transferred, by such authority and in such manner as rules of court may direct, from one Division or judge of the High Court to another Division or judge thereof.

(2) The transfer of a cause or matter under subsection (1) to a different Division or judge of the High Court shall not affect the validity of any steps or proceedings taken or order made in that cause or matter before the transfer.

Divisional courts

66. Divisional courts of High Court—(1) Divisional courts may be held for the transaction of any business in the High Court which is, by or by virtue of rules of court or any other statutory provision, required to be heard by a divisional court.

(2) Any number of divisional courts may sit at the same time.

(3) A divisional court shall be constituted of not less than two judges.

(4) Every judge of the High Court shall be qualified to sit in any divisional court.

(5) The judge who is, according to the order of precedence under this Act, the senior of the judges constituting a divisional court shall be the president of the court.

Mode of conducting business

67. Proceedings in court and in chambers. Business in the High Court shall be heard and disposed of in court except in so far as it may, under this or any other Act, under the rules of court or in accordance with the practice of the court, be dealt with in chambers.

68. Exercise of High Court jurisdiction otherwise than by judges of that court—(1) Provision may be made by rules of court as to the cases in which jurisdiction of the High Court may be exercised by—

    (a) such *of the Circuit judges* [Circuit judges, deputy Circuit judges or Recorders] as the Lord Chancellor may from time to time nominate to deal with official referees' business; or

    (b) special referees; *or*

    (c) masters, registrars, district registrars or other officers of the court.

Note. Words in square brackets substituted for words "of the Circuit judges" in italics by Administration of Justice Act 1982, s 59(1), as from 1 January 1983. Second words in italics repealed by Civil Procedure Act 1997, s 10, Sch 2, para 1(1), (3)(a), as from 14 March 1997.

(2) Without prejudice to the generality of subsection (1), rules of court may in particular—

    (a) authorise the whole of any cause or matter, or any question or issue therein, to be tried before any such person as is mentioned in that subsection; or

    (b) authorise any question arising in any cause or matter to be referred to *any such person* [a special referee] for inquiry and report.

(3) Rules of court shall not authorise the exercise of powers of attachment and committal by *any such person as is mentioned in subsection (1)(b) or (c)* [a special referee or any officer or other staff of the court].

(4) Subject to subsection (5), the decision of

    (a) any such person as is mentioned in subsection (1) [or

    (b) any officer or other staff of the court]

may be called in question in such manner as may be prescribed by rules of court, whether by appeal to the Court of Appeal, or by an appeal or application to a divisional court or a judge in court or a judge in chambers, or by an adjournment to a judge in court or a judge in chambers.

Note. Sub-s (2)(a) repealed, in sub-ss (2)(b), (3) words in square brackets substituted for words in italics, and in sub-s (4) words in square brackets inserted, by Civil Procedure Act 1997, s 10, Sch 2, para 1(1), (3)(b)–(d), 26 April 1999 (SI 1999 No 1009).

(5) Rules of court may provide either generally or to a limited extent for decisions of *Circuit judges* [persons] nominated under subsection (1)(a) being called in question only by appeal on a question of law.

(6) The cases in which jurisdiction of the High Court may be exercised by *Circuit judges* [persons] nominated under subsection (1)(a) shall be known as 'official referees' business'; and, subject to rules of court, the distribution of official referees' business among *judges* [persons] so nominated shall be determined in accordance with directions given by the Lord Chancellor.

(7) Any reference to an official referee in any enactment, whenever passed, or in rules of court or any other instrument or document, whenever made, shall, unless the context otherwise requires, be construed as, or (where the context requires) as including, a reference to a *Circuit judge* [person] nominated under subsection (1)(a).

Note. In sub-ss (5), (6), (7) words in square brackets substituted for words in italics by Administration of Justice Act 1982, s 59(2), as from 1 January 1983.

*   *   *   *   *

70. Assessors and scientific advisers—(1) In any cause or matter before the High Court the court may, if it thinks it expedient to do so, call in the aid of one or more assessors specially qualified, and hear and dispose of the cause or matter wholly or partially with their assistance.

(2) The remuneration, if any, to be paid to an assessor for his services under subsection (1) in connection with any proceedings shall be determined by the court, and shall form part of the costs of the proceedings.

Note. See Administration of Justice Act 1985, s 53(6) (p 3130).

*   *   *   *   *

Sittings and vacations

71. Sittings and vacations—(1) Sittings of the High Court may be held, and any other business of the High Court may be conducted, at any place in England or Wales.

(2) Subject to rules of court—

(a) the places at which the High Court sits outside the Royal Courts of Justice; and

(b) the days and times when the High Court sits at any place outside the Royal Courts of Justice,

shall be determined in accordance with directions given by the Lord Chancellor.

(3) Rules of court may make provision for regulating the vacations to be observed by the High Court and in the offices of that court.

(4) Rules of court—

(a) may provide for securing such sittings of any Division of the High Court during vacation as the senior judge of that Division may with the concurrence of the Lord Chancellor determine; and

(b) without prejudice to paragraph (a), shall provide for the transaction during vacation by judges of the High Court of all such business in the High Court as may require to be immediately or promptly transacted.

(5) Different provision may be made in pursuance of subsection (3) for different parts of the country.

Other provisions

72. Withdrawal of privilege against incrimination of self or spouse in certain proceedings—(1) In any proceedings to which this subsection applies a person shall not be excused, by reason that to do so would tend to expose that person, or his or her spouse, to proceedings for a related offence or for the recovery of a related penalty—

(a) from answering any question put to that person in the first-mentioned proceedings; or

(b) from complying with any order made in those proceedings.

(2) Subsection (1) applies to the following civil proceedings in the High Court, namely—

(a) proceedings for infringement of rights pertaining to any intellectual property or for passing off;

(b) proceedings brought to obtain disclosure of information relating to any infringement of such rights or to any passing off; and

(c) proceedings brought to prevent any apprehended infringement of such rights or any apprehended passing off.

(3) Subject to subsection (4), no statement or admission made by a person—

(a) in answering a question put to him in any proceedings to which subsection (1) applies; or

(b) in complying with any order made in such proceedings,

shall, in proceedings for any related offence or for the recovery of any related penalty, be admissible in evidence against that person or (unless they married after the making of the statement or admission) against the spouse of that person.

(4) Nothing in subsection (3) shall render any statement or admission made by a person as there mentioned inadmissible in evidence against that person in proceedings for perjury or contempt of court.

(5) In this section—

'intellectual property' means any patent, trade mark, copyright[, design right], registered design, technical or commercial information or other intellectual property;

'related offence', in relation to any proceedings to which subsection (1) applies, means—

(a) in the case of proceedings within subsection (2)(a) or (b)—

　(i) any offence committed by or in the course of the infringement or passing off to which those proceedings relate; or

　(ii) any offence not within sub-paragraph (i) committed in connection with that infringement or passing off, being an offence involving fraud or dishonesty;

(b) in the case of proceedings within subsection (2)(c), any offence revealed by the facts on which the plaintiff relies in those proceedings;

'related penalty', in relation to any proceedings to which subsection (1) applies means—

(a) in the case of proceedings within subsection (2)(a) or (b), any penalty incurred in respect of anything done or omitted in connection with the infringement or passing off to which those proceedings relate;

(b) in the case of proceedings within subsection (2)(c), any penalty incurred in respect of any act or omission revealed by the facts on which the plaintiff relies in those proceedings.

Note. Words in square brackets inserted by Copyright, Designs and Patents Act 1988, s 303(1), Sch 7, para 28(1), (2), as from 1 August 1989. By the Trade Marks Act 1994, s 106(1), Sch 4, para 1, the reference to a trade mark is to be construed as a reference to a trade mark within the meaning of that Act.

(6) Any reference in this section to civil proceedings in the High Court of any description includes a reference to proceedings on appeal arising out of civil proceedings in the High Court of that description.

*　　*　　*　　*　　*

RULES OF COURT

84. Power to make rules of court—(1) Rules of court may be made for the purpose of regulating and prescribing [, except in relation to any criminal cause or matter,] the practice and procedure to be followed in the *Supreme Court* [Crown Court *and the criminal division of the Court of Appeal*].

Note. Words in square brackets in sub-s (1) substituted for words in italics by Civil Procedure Act 1997, s 10, Sch 2, para 1(1), (4)(a), as from a day to be appointed. Further amended by SI 2004 No 2035, as from 1 September 2004.

(2) Without prejudice to the generality of subsection (1), the matters about which rules of court may be made under this section include all matters of practice and procedure in the Supreme Court which were regulated or prescribed by rules of court immediately before the commencement of this Act.

(3) No provision of this or any other Act, or contained in any instrument made under any Act, which—

(a) authorises or requires the making of rules of court about any particular matter or for any particular purpose; or

(b) provides (in whatever words) that the power to make rules of court under this section is to include power to make rules about any particular matter or for any particular purpose,

shall be taken as derogating from the generality of subsection (1).

(*4*) *Rules made under this section shall have effect subject to any special rules for the time being in force in relation to proceedings in the Supreme Court of any particular kind.*

Note. Sub-s (4) repealed by Civil Procedure Act 1997, s 10, Sch 2, para 1(1), (4)(b), as from 26 April 1999 (SI 1999/1009).

(*5*) *Special rules may, to any extent and with or without modifications, apply any rules made under this section to proceedings to which the special rules apply; and rules under this section may, to any extent and with or without modifications, apply any special rules to proceedings in the Supreme Court to which those special rules would not otherwise apply.*

(*6*) *Special rules which apply any rules made under this section may apply them as amended from time to time; and rules under this section which apply any special rules may apply them as amended from time to time.*

[(5) Special rules may apply—

(a) any rules made under this section, *or*

(b) Civil Procedure Rules,

[(c) Criminal Procedure Rules, or

(d) Family Procedure Rules]

to proceedings to which the special rules apply.

(5A) Rules made under this section may apply—

(a) any special rules, or

(b) Civil Procedure Rules,

[(c) Criminal Procedure Rules, or

(d) Family Procedure Rules]

to proceedings to which rules made under this section apply.

(6) Where rules may be applied under subsection (5) or (5A), they may be applied—

(a) to any extent,

(b) with or without modification, and

(c) as amended from time to time.]

Note. Sub-ss (5), (5A), (6) in square brackets substituted for sub-ss (5), (6) in italics by Civil Procedure Act 1997, s 10, Sch 2, para 1(1), (4)(c), as from 27 April 1997. Further amended by SI 2004 No 2035, art 3, Schedule, as from 1 September 2004.

(7) No rules which may involve an increase of expenditure out of public funds may be made under this section except with the concurrence of the Treasury, but the validity of any rule made under this section shall not be called in question in any proceedings in any court either by the court or by any party to the proceedings on the ground only that it was a rule as to the making of which the concurrence of the Treasury was necessary and that the Treasury did not concur or are not expressed to have concurred.

(8) Rules of court under this section shall be made by statutory instrument subject to annulment in pursuance of a resolution of either House of Parliament; and the Statutory Instruments Act 1946 shall apply to a statutory instrument containing such rules in like manner as if the rules had been made by a Minister of the Crown.

(9) In this section 'special rules' means rules applying to proceedings of any particular kind in the Supreme Court, being rules made by authority other than the *Supreme Court Rule Committee* [Civil Procedure Rule Committee] [, the Family Procedure Rule Committee, the Criminal Procedure Rule Committee,] or the Crown Court Rule Committee under any provision of this or any other Act which (in whatever words) confers on that authority power to make rules in relation to proceedings of that kind in the Supreme Court.

Note. Words in square brackets in sub-s (9) substituted for words in italics by Civil Procedure Act 1997, s 10, Sch 2, para 1(1), (4)(d), as from 26 April 1999 (SI 1999 No 1009).

Further amended by SI 2004 No 2035, art 3, Schedule, as from 1 September 2004.

85. The Supreme Court Rule Committee—*(1) The power to make rules of court under section 84 in relation to the High Court and civil division of the Court of Appeal shall be exercisable by the Lord Chancellor together with any four or more of the following persons, namely—*

(a) *the Lord Chief Justice,*

(b) *the Master of the Rolls,*

(c) *the President of the Family Division,*

(d) *the Vice-Chancellor,*

(e) *three other judges of the Supreme Court,*

(f) *two practising barristers, and*

(g) *two practising solicitors, of whom one shall be a member of the Council of the Law Society.*

[(f) *two persons who have a Supreme Court qualification (within the meaning of section 71 of the Courts and Legal Services Act 1990); and*

(g) *two persons who have been granted by an authorised body, under Part II of that Act, the right to conduct litigation in relation to all proceedings in the Supreme Court.*]

Note. Sub-ss (1)(f), (g) in square brackets substituted for preceding sub-ss (1)(f), (g) by Courts and Legal Services Act 1990, s 125(3), Sch 18, para 36(1)(a), as from 1 January 1991.

(2) The persons mentioned in subsection (1), acting in pursuance of that subsection, shall be known as 'the Supreme Court Rule Committee'.

(3) The persons to act in pursuance of subsection (1) with the Lord Chancellor, other than those eligible to act by virtue of their office, shall be appointed by the Lord Chancellor for such time as he may think fit.

(4) Before appointing a barrister under subsection (1)(f) the Lord Chancellor shall consult the Chairman of the Senate of the Inns of Court and the Bar, and before appointing a solicitor under subsection (1)(g) he shall consult the President of the Law Society.

[(4) *Before appointing a person under paragraph (f) or (g) of subsection (1), the Lord Chancellor shall consult any authorised body with members who are eligible for appointment under that paragraph.*]

Note. Sub-s (4) in square brackets substituted for preceding sub-s (4) by Courts and Legal Services Act 1990, s 125(3), Sch 18, para 36(1)(b), as from 1 January 1991.

This section repealed by Civil Procedure Act 1997, s 10, Sch 2, para 1(1), (5), as from 26 April 1999 (SI 1999 No 1009).

*   *   *   *   *

87. Particular matters for which rules of court may provide—*(1) Rules of court may make provision for regulating the means by which particular facts may be proved, and the mode in which evidence thereof may be given, in any proceedings in the High Court or in the civil division of the Court of Appeal or on any application in connection with or at any stage of any such proceedings.*

(2) Rules of court may make provision—

(a) *for enabling proceedings to be commenced in the High Court against the estate of a deceased person (whether by the appointment of a person to represent the estate or otherwise) where no grant of probate or administration has been made;*

(b) *for enabling proceedings purporting to have been commenced in that court against a person to be treated, if he was dead at their commencement, as having been commenced against his estate, whether or not a grant of probate or administration was made before their commencement; and*

(c) *for enabling any proceedings commenced or treated as commenced in that court against the estate of a deceased person to be maintained (whether by substitution of parties, amendment or otherwise) against a person appointed to represent the estate or, if a grant of probate or administration is or has been made, against the personal representative.*

Note. Sub-ss (1), (2) repealed by Civil Procedure Act 1997, s 10, Sch 2, para 1(1), (6)(a), as from 26 April 1999 (SI 1999 No 1009).

(3) Rules of court [made under section 84] may amend or repeal any statutory provision relating to the practice and procedure of the *Supreme Court* [Crown Court *or the criminal division of the Court of Appeal* [(except so far as relating to criminal causes or matters)] so far as may be necessary in consequence of provision made by the rules.

Note. Words in square brackets in sub-s (3) substituted for words in italics by Civil Procedure Act 1997, s 10, Sch 2, para 1(1), (6)(b), as from 26 April 1999 (SI 1999 No 1009).

Further amended by SI 2004 No 2035, art 3, Schedule, as from 1 September 2004.

* * * * *

PART IV

OFFICERS AND OFFICES

Appointment of certain officers of Supreme Court

* * * * *

89. Masters and registrars.

* * * * *

(3) The Lord Chancellor shall appoint—

* * * * *

(*e*) *one of the registrars of the Principal Registry of the Family Division as Senior Registrar of that Division; and*

[(e) one of the district judges of the Principal Registry of the Family Division as Senior District Judge of that Division; and]

Note. Sub-s (3)(e) in square brackets substituted for sub-s (3)(e) in italics by Courts and Legal Services Act 1990, s 125(3), Sch 18, para 38, as from 1 January 1991.

* * * * *

with, in each case, such additional salary in respect of that appointment as the Lord Chancellor may, with the concurrence of the Minister for the Civil Service, determine.

* * * * *

90. Official Solicitor—(1) There shall continue to be an Official Solicitor to the Supreme Court, who shall be appointed by the Lord Chancellor.

(2) There shall be paid to the Official Solicitor out of money provided by Parliament such salary as the Lord Chancellor may, with the concurrence of the Minister for the Civil Service, determine.

(3) The Official Solicitor shall have such powers and perform such duties as may for the time being be conferred or imposed on the holder of that office—

(a) by or under this or any other Act; or

(b) by or in accordance with any direction given (before or after the commencement of this Act) by the Lord Chancellor.

[(3A) The holder for the time being of the office of Official Solicitor shall have the right to conduct litigation in relation to any proceedings.

(3B) When acting as Official Solicitor a person who would otherwise have the right to conduct litigation by virtue of section 28(2)(a) of the Courts and Legal Services Act 1990 shall be treated as having acquired that right solely by virtue of subsection (3A).]

Note. Sub-ss (3A), (3B) inserted by Courts and Legal Services Act 1990, s 125(3), Sch 18, para 39, as from 1 January 1991.

(4) If—

(a) the Official Solicitor is not available because of his absence or for some other reason; or

(b) his office is vacant,

then, during such unavailability or vacancy, any powers or duties of the Official Solicitor shall be exercisable or fall to be performed by any person for the time being appointed by the Lord Chancellor as deputy to the Official Solicitor (and any property vested in the Official Solicitor may accordingly be dealt with by any such person in all respects as if it were vested in him instead).

*   *   *   *   *

District registries and district registrars

99. District registries—(1) The Lord Chancellor may by order direct that there shall be district registries of the High Court at such places and for such districts as are specified in the order.

(2) Any order under this section shall be made by statutory instrument, which shall be laid before Parliament after being made.

100. District registrars—(1) Subject to subsection (2), for each district registry the Lord Chancellor shall appoint a person who is a *county court registrar as a district registrar of the High Court* [district judge for a county court district, appointed under section 6 of the County Courts Act 1984, as a district judge of the High Court].

(2) The Lord Chancellor may, if he thinks fit, appoint two or more persons who are *county court registrars* [district judges for a county court district] to execute jointly the office of *district registrar* [district judge] in any district registry.

(3) Where joint *district registrars* [district judges] are appointed under subsection (2), the Lord Chancellor may—

(a) give directions with respect to the division between them of the duties of the office of *district registrar* [district judge]; and

(b) as he thinks fit, on the death, resignation or removal of one of them, either appoint in place of that person another person to be joint *district registrar* [district judge], or give directions that the continuing *registrar* [district judge] shall execute jointly the office of *district registrar* [district judge].

(4) Subsections (4) to (6) of section 92 shall apply in relation to a person appointed as a *district registrar* [district judge] as they apply in relation to a person appointed to an office to which subsection (1) of that section applies, except that he shall vacate his office as *district registrar* [district judge] at such time as, for any cause whatever, he vacates his office as *county court registrar* [district judge for a county court district].

(5) A district registrar who is a part-time registrar within the meaning of subsection (3) of section 22 of the County Courts Act 1959 [section 10 of the County Courts Act 1984] (restrictions on practice) shall not, either by himself or by any partner of his, be directly or indirectly engaged as a solicitor or agent for a party to any proceedings in the registry of which he is district registrar.

Note. Words in square brackets in sub-ss (1)–(4) substituted for words in italics, and whole of sub-s (5) repealed, by Courts and Legal Services Act 1990, s 125(3), (7), Sch 18, para 40(1), (2)(a), (b), Sch 20, as from 1 January 1991. Words in square brackets in sub-s (5) substituted for words 'section 22 of the County Courts Act 1959' by County Courts Act 1984, s 148(1), Sch 2, Part V, para 77, as from 1 August 1984.

101. Power of one district registrar to act for another—(1) A *district registrar* [district judge] of any registry shall be capable of acting in any other district registry for a *district registrar* [district judge] of that registry; and, where a *registrar* [district judge] is so acting, the *registrar* [district judge] of the other registry may divide the duties of his office as he thinks fit between himself and the *registrar* [district judge] acting for him.

(*2*) *Subsection* (*5*) *of the preceding section shall not apply to a person acting as district registrar of a registry by virtue of this section, but* (*in the case of a person who is a part-time registrar within the meaning of the said section 22(3)*) *he shall not so act as district registrar in relation to any proceedings in which he is, either by himself or by any partner of his, directly or indirectly engaged as a solicitor or agent for any party.*

Note. Words in square brackets substituted for words in italics and whole of sub-s (2) repealed, by Courts and Legal Services Act 1990, s 125(3), (7), Sch 18, para 40(2)(b), Sch 20, as from 1 January 1991.

102. Deputy district registrars—(1) If it appears to the Lord Chancellor that it is expedient to do so in order to facilitate the disposal of business in the High Court, he may appoint a person to be a *deputy district registrar* [deputy district judge] in any district registry during such period or on such occasions as the Lord Chancellor thinks fit.

(2) Subject to subsection (3), a person shall not be qualified for appointment as a *deputy district registrar* [deputy district judge] unless he is, or is qualified for appointment as, a *county court registrar* [district judge for a county court district].

Note. Words in square brackets in sub-ss (1), (2) substituted for words in italics by Courts and Legal Services Act 1990, s 125(3), Sch 18, para 40, as from 1 January 1991.

(3) A person may be appointed as a *deputy district registrar* [deputy district judge] if he would, but for his age, be qualified for appointment as a *county court registrar* [district judge for a county court district] and he has previously held the office of *county court registrar* [district judge for a county court district] [; but no appointment by virtue of this subsection shall be such as to extend beyond the day on which the person in question attains the age of seventy-five years.]

Note. Words 'deputy district judge' and 'district judge for a county court district' substituted for words 'deputy district registrar' and 'county court registrar' respectively by Courts and Legal Services Act 1990, s 125(3), Sch 18, para 40, as from 1 January 1991. Words '; but no appointment ... years' in square brackets added by Judicial Pensions and Retirement Act 1993, s 26(10), Sch 6, para 16, as from 31 March 1995.

(4) A *deputy district registrar* [deputy district judge], while acting under this section, shall have the same jurisdiction as the *district registrar* [district judge].

Note. Words in square brackets substituted for words in italics by Courts and Legal Services Act 1990, s 125(3), Sch 18, para 40, as from 1 January 1991.

(*5*) *Subsections* (*5*) *and* (*6*) *of section 91 apply in relation to a deputy district registrar* [*deputy district judge*] *appointed under this section as they apply in relation to a person appointed under that section.*

Note. Words 'deputy district judge' and 'district judge' substituted for words 'deputy district registrar' and 'district registrar' respectively by Courts and Legal Services Act 1990, s 125(3), Sch 18, para 40, as from 1 January 1991.

[(5) Subsection 6 of section 91 applies in relation to a deputy district judge appointed under this section as it applies in relation to a person appointed under that section.]

Note. Sub-s (5) in square brackets substituted for sub-s (5) in italics by Judicial Pensions and Retirement Act 1993, s 31(3), Sch 8, para 15(3), as from 31 March 1995.

(*6*) *A deputy district registrar shall not act as such in relation to any proceedings in which he is, either by himself or by any partner of his, directly or indirectly engaged as a solicitor or agent for any party.*

Note. Sub-s (6) repealed by Courts and Legal Services Act 1990, s 125(7), Sch 20, as from 1 January 1991.

103. Assistant district registrars—(*1*) *The Lord Chancellor may appoint assistant district registrars* [*assistant district judges*] *of the High Court in aid of district registrars* [*district judges*].

(*2*) *A person shall not be qualified for appointment as an assistant district registrar* [*assistant district judge*] *unless he is a county court registrar* [*district judge for a county court district*] *or an assistant county court registrar* [*district judge for a county court district*].

(*3*) *An assistant district registrar* [*assistant district judge*] *of any district registry shall be capable of discharging any of the functions of the district registrar* [*district judge*], *and in so doing shall have the same jurisdiction as the district registrar* [*district judge*].

(*4*) *A district registrar* [*district judge*] *of any registry where there is an assistant district registrar* [*assistant district judge*] *may divide the duties of his office as he thinks fit between himself and the assistant district registrar* [*assistant district judge*].

(*5*) *Subsections* (*4*) *to* (*6*) *of section 92 shall apply in relation to a person appointed as an assistant district registrar* [*assistant district judge*] *as they apply in relation to a person appointed to an office to which subsection* (*1*) *of that section applies, except that he shall vacate his office as assistant district registrar* [*assistant district judge*] *at such time as, for any cause whatever, he vacates his office as county court registrar* [*district judge for a county court district*] *or, as the case may be, assistant county court registrar* [*district judge for a county court district*] (*unless in the latter case he is thereupon appointed a county court registrar* [*district judge for a county court district*]).

(*6*) *Section 100(5) shall apply to an assistant district registrar as it applies to a district registrar, but as if 'a part-time registrar' included a part-time assistant registrar.*

Note. Words in square brackets in sub-ss (1)–(5) substituted for words 'assistant district registrars', 'district registrars', 'county court registrar', and whole of sub-s (6) repealed, by Courts and Legal Services Act 1990, s 125(3), (7), Sch 18, para 40(2)(a)–(c), Sch 20, as from 1 January 1991. Whole section repealed by Judicial Pensions and Retirement Act 1993, s 31(4), Sch 9, as from 31 March 1995.

*   *   *   *   *

PART VI

MISCELLANEOUS AND SUPPLEMENTARY

Miscellaneous provisions

*   *   *   *   *

130. Fees to be taken in Supreme Court—(*1*) *The Lord Chancellor may by order under this section prescribe the fees to be taken in the Supreme Court, other than fees which he or some other authority has power to prescribe apart from this section.*

(*2*) *The concurrence of the Treasury shall be required for the making of any order under this section; and in addition*—

   (*a*) *the concurrence of the Lord Chief Justice, the Master of the Rolls, the President of the Family Division and the Vice-Chancellor, or of any three of them, shall be required for the making of any such order not relating exclusively to fees to be taken in connection with proceedings in the Crown Court; and*

   (*b*) *the concurrence of the Lord Chief Justice shall be required for the making of any such order relating exclusively to fees to be taken in connection with proceedings in the Crown Court.*

(*3*) *Nothing in subsection* (*1*) *shall be taken to prevent any authority having power apart from this section to prescribe fees to be taken in the Supreme Court from applying to any extent any provisions contained in any order made under this section; and where any instrument made in the exercise of any such power applies any provisions so contained, then, unless the contrary intention appears, it shall be taken to apply those provisions as amended from time to time.*

2862 Supreme Court Act 1981, s 130

(4) Any order under this section shall be made by statutory instrument, which shall be laid before Parliament after being made.

Note. Repealed by the Courts Act 2003, s 109, Sch 8, para 263, Sch 10, as from a date to be appointed.

131. Conveyancing counsel of Supreme Court—(1) The conveyancing counsel of the Supreme Court shall be *conveyancing counsel in actual practice who have practised as such for not less than ten years* [persons who have a 10 year High Court qualification, within the meaning of section 71 of the Courts and Legal Services Act 1990].

(2) The conveyancing counsel of the court shall be not more than six, nor less than three, in number, and shall be appointed by the Lord Chancellor.

Note. Words in square brackets substituted for words in italics by Courts and Legal Services Act 1990, s 71(2), Sch 10, para 48, as from 1 January 1991.

132. Proof of documents bearing seal or stamp of Supreme Court or any office thereof. Every document purporting to be sealed or stamped with the seal or stamp of the Supreme Court or of any office of the Supreme Court shall be received in evidence in all parts of the United Kingdom without further proof.

133. Enrolment and engrossment of instruments—(1) The Master of the Rolls may make regulations for authorising and regulating the enrolment or filing of instruments in the Supreme Court, and for prescribing the form in which certificates of enrolment or filing are to be issued.

(2) Regulations under subsection (1) shall not affect the operation of any enactment requiring or authorising the enrolment of any instrument in the Supreme Court or prescribing the manner in which any instrument is to be enrolled there.

(3) Any instrument which is required or authorised by or under this or any other Act to be enrolled or engrossed in the Supreme Court shall be deemed to have been duly enrolled or engrossed if it is written on material authorised or required by regulations under subsection (1) and has been filed or otherwise preserved in accordance with regulations under that subsection.

(4) The Lord Chancellor may, with the concurrence of the Master of the Rolls and of the Treasury, make regulations prescribing the fees to be paid on the enrolment or filing of any instrument in the Supreme Court, including any additional fees payable on the enrolment or filing of any instrument out of time.

(5) Any regulations under this section shall be made by statutory instrument, which shall be laid before Parliament after being made; and the Statutory Instruments Act 1946 shall apply to a statutory instrument containing regulations under sub-section (1) in like manner as if the regulations had been made by a Minister of the Crown.

* * * * *

135. Bonds given under order of court—(1) A bond to be given by any person under or for the purposes of any order of the High Court or the civil division of the Court of Appeal shall be given in such form and to such officer of the court as may be prescribed and, if the court so requires, with one or more sureties.

(2) An officer of the court to whom a bond is given in accordance with subsection (1) shall as such have power to enforce it or to assign it, pursuant to an order of the court under subsection (4), to some other person.

(3) Where by rules of court made for the purposes of this section another officer is at any time substituted for the officer previously described as the officer to whom bonds of any class are to be given, the rules may provide that bonds of that class given before the rules come into operation shall have effect as if references in

the bonds to the officer previously prescribed were references to the substituted officer.

(4) Where it appears to the court that the condition of a bond given in accordance with subsection (1) had been broken, the court may, on an application in that behalf, order the bond to be assigned to such person as may be specified in the order.

(5) A person to whom a bond is ordered to be assigned under subsection (4) shall be entitled by virtue of the order to sue on the bond in his own name as if it had been originally given to him, and to recover on it as trustee for all persons interested the full amount recoverable in respect of the breach of condition.

136. Production of documents filed in, or in custody of, Supreme Court— (1) The Lord Chancellor may, with the concurrence of the Lord Chief Justice, the Master of the Rolls, the President of the Family Division and the Vice-Chancellor, or of any three of them, make rules for providing that, in any case where a document filed in, or in the custody of, any office of the Supreme Court is required to be produced to any court or tribunal (including an umpire or arbitrator) sitting elsewhere than at the Royal Courts of Justice—

(a) it shall not be necessary for any officer, whether served with a subpoena in that behalf or not, to attend for the purpose of producing the document; but

(b) the document may be produced to the court or tribunal by sending it to the court or tribunal, in the manner prescribed in the rules, together with a certificate, in the form so prescribed, to the effect that the document has been filed in, or is in the custody of, the office;

and any such certificate shall be prima facie evidence of the facts stated in it.

(2) Rules under this section may contain—

(a) provisions for securing the safe custody and return to the proper office of the Supreme Court of any document sent to a court or tribunal in pursuance of the rules; and

(b) such incidental and supplementary provisions as appear to the Lord Chancellor to be necessary or expedient.

(3) Rules under this section shall be made by statutory instrument, which shall be laid before Parliament after being made.

* * * * *

138. Effect of writs of execution against goods—*(1) Subject to subsection (2), a writ of fieri facias or other writ of execution against goods issued from the High Court shall bind the property in the goods of the execution debtor as from the time when the writ is delivered to the sheriff to be executed.*

(2) Such a writ shall not prejudice the title to any goods of the execution debtor acquired by a person in good faith and for valuable consideration unless he had, at the time when he acquired his title—

(a) notice that that writ or any other such writ by virtue of which the goods of the execution debtor might be seized or attached had been delivered to and remained unexecuted in the hands of the sheriff; or

(b) notice that an application for the issue of a warrant of execution against the goods of the execution debtor had been made to the registrar of a county court and that the warrant issued on the application either—

(i) remained unexecuted in the hands of the registrar of the court from which it was issued; or

(ii) had been sent for execution to, and received by, the registrar of another county court, and remained unexecuted in the hands of the registrar of that court.

(3) For the better manifestation of the time mentioned in subsection (1), it shall be the duty of the sheriff (without fee) on receipt of any such writ as is there mentioned to endorse on its back the hour, day, month and year when he received it.

[(3A) Every sheriff or officer executing any writ of execution issued from the High Court against the goods of any person may by virtue of it seize:—

(a) *any of that person's goods except:—*

    (i) *such tools, books, vehicles and other items of equipment as are necessary to that person for use personally by him in his employment, business or vocation;*

    (ii) *such clothing, bedding, furniture, household equipment and provisions as are necessary for satisfying the basic domestic needs of that person and his family; and*

(b) *any money, banknotes, bills of exchange, promissory notes, bonds, specialties or securities for money belonging to that person.]*

Note. Sub-s (3A) inserted by Courts and Legal Services Act 1990, s 15(1), as from 1 July 1991.

(4) For the purposes of this section—

(a) *'property' means the general property in goods, and not merely a special property;*

(b) *'sheriff' includes any officer charged with the enforcement of a writ of execution;*

(c) *any reference to the goods of the execution debtor includes a reference to anything else of his that may lawfully be seized in execution; and*

(d) *a thing shall be treated as done in good faith if it is in fact done honestly, whether it is done negligently or not.*

Note. Repealed by the Courts Act 2003, s 109, Sch 8, para 264, Sch 10, as from 15 March 2004 (SI 2004 No 401).

* * * * *

140. Enforcement of fines and forfeited recognisances—(1) Payment of a fine imposed, or sum due under a recognisance forfeited, by the High Court or the civil division of the Court of Appeal may be enforced upon the order of the court—

(a) in like manner as a judgment of the High Court for the payment of money; or

(b) in like manner as a fine imposed by the Crown Court.

(2) Where payment of a fine or other sum falls to be enforced as mentioned in paragraph (a) of subsection (1) upon an order of the High Court or the civil division of the Court of Appeal under that subsection—

(a) the court shall, if the fine or other sum is not paid in full forthwith or within such time as the court may allow, certify to Her Majesty's Remembrancer the sum payable; and

(b) Her Majesty's Remembrancer shall thereupon proceed to enforce payment of that sum as if it were due to him as a judgment debt.

(3) Where payment of a fine or other sum falls to be enforced as mentioned in paragraph (b) of subsection (1) upon an order of the High Court or the civil division of the Court of Appeal under that subsection, the provisions of *sections 31 and 32 of the Powers of Criminal Courts Act 1973* [sections 139 and 140 of the Powers of Criminal Courts (Sentencing) Act 2000] shall apply to that fine or other sum as they apply to a fine imposed by the Crown Court.

(4) Where payment of a fine or other sum has become enforceable by Her Majesty's Remembrancer by virtue of this section or section 16 of the Contempt of Court Act 1981, and payment received by him in respect of that fine or other sum shall be dealt with by him in such manner as the Lord Chancellor may direct.

(5) In this section, and in *sections 31 and 32 of the Powers of Criminal Courts Act 1973* [sections 139 and 140 of the Powers of Criminal Courts (Sentencing) Act 2000] as extended by this section, 'fine' includes a penalty imposed in civil proceedings.

Note. Amended by the Powers of Criminal Courts (Sentencing) Act 2000, s 165, Sch 9, para 88, as from 25 August 2000.

141. Abolition of certain writs. Writs of elegit (the issue of which was ended by the Administration of Justice Act 1956) and writs of capias and satisfaciendum are hereby abolished.

*   *   *   *   *

Supplementary

*   *   *   *   *

151. Interpretation of this Act, and rules of construction for other Acts and documents—(1) In this Act, unless the context otherwise requires—

'action' means any civil proceedings commenced by writ or in any other manner prescribed by rules of court;

'appeal', in the context of appeals to the civil division of the Court of Appeal, includes—

(a) an application for a new trial, and

(b) an application to set aside a verdict, finding or judgment in any cause or matter in the High Court which has been tried, or in which any issue has been tried, by a jury;

['arbitration agreement' has the same meaning as it has in *the Arbitration Act 1950 by virtue of section 32 of that Act*; [Part I of the Arbitration Act 1996;]]

'cause' means any action or any criminal proceedings;

'Division', where it appears with a capital letter, means a division of the High Court;

'judgment' includes a decree;

'jurisdiction' includes powers;

'matter' means any proceedings in court not in a cause;

'party', in relation to any proceedings, includes any person who pursuant to or by virtue of rules of court or any other statutory provision has been served with notice of, or has intervened in, those proceedings;

'prescribed' means—

(a) except in relation to fees, prescribed by rules of court; *and*

(b) *in relation to fees, prescribed by an order under section 130*;

'senior judge', where the reference is to the senior judge of a Division, means—

(a) in the case of the Chancery Division, the Vice-Chancellor;

(b) in any other case, the president of the Division in question;

'solicitor' means a solicitor of the Supreme Court;

'statutory provision' means any enactment, whenever passed, or any provision contained in subordinate legislation (as defined in section 21(1) of the Interpreta- tion Act 1978), whenever made;

'this or any other Act' includes an Act passed after this Act.

Note. Definition 'arbitration agreement' inserted by Courts and Legal Services Act 1990, s 125(5), Sch 18, para 41, as from 1 April 1991. Words in square brackets substituted for words in italics by Arbitration Act 1996, s 107(1), Sch 3, para 37, as from 31 January 1997. Repealed in part by the Courts Act 2003, s 109, Sch 8, para 265, Sch 10, as from a day to be appointed.

(2) Section 128 contains definitions of expressions used in Part V and in the other provisions of this Act relating to probate causes and matters.

(3) Any reference in this Act to rules of court under section 84 includes a reference to rules of court [in relation to the Supreme Court] under any provision of this or any other Act which confers on the *Supreme Court Rule Committee* [Civil Procedure Rule Committee] or the Crown Court Rule Committee power to make rules of court.

Note. First words in square brackets in sub-s (3) inserted and second words in square brackets substituted for words in italics by Civil Procedure Act 1997, s 10, Sch 2, para 1(1), (7), as from a day to be appointed.

(4) Except where the context otherwise requires, in this or any other Act—

'Criminal Appeal Rules' means rules of court made by the Crown Court Rule Committee in relation to the criminal division of the Court of Appeal;

'Crown Court Rules' means rules of court made by the Crown Court Rule Committee in relation to the Crown Court;

'divisional court' (with or without capital letters) means a divisional court constituted under section 66;

'judge of the Supreme Court' means—

    (a) a judge of the Court of Appeal other than an ex-officio judge within paragraph (b) or (c) of section 2(2), or

    (b) a judge of the High Court,

    and accordingly does not include, as such, a judge of the Crown Court;

'official referees' business' has the meaning given by section 68(6);

'Rules of the Supreme Court' means rules of court made of the Supreme Court Rule Committee.

Note. Words in italics in sub-s (4) repealed by Civil Procedure Act 1997, s 10, Sch 2, para 1(1), (7), as from 26 April 1999 (SI 1999 No 1009).

Further repealed in part by SI 2004 No 2035, art 3, Schedule, as from 1 September 2004.

(5) The provisions of Schedule 4 (construction of references to superseded courts and officers) shall have effect.

152. Amendments of other Acts, transitional provisions, savings and repeals—
(1) The enactments specified in Schedule 5 shall have effect subject to the amendments there specified, being amendments consequential on the provisions of this Act.

* * * * *

(4) The enactments mentioned in Schedule 7 (which include certain obsolete or unnecessary provisions) are hereby repealed to the extent specified in the third column of that Schedule.

* * * * *

153. Citation, commencement and extent—(1) This Act may be cited as the Supreme Court Act 1981.

(2) This Act, except the provisions mentioned in subsection (3), shall come into force on 1 January 1982; and references to the commencement of this Act shall be construed as references to the beginning of that day.

(3) Sections 72, 143 and 152(2) and this section shall come into force on the passing of this Act.

* * * * *

SCHEDULES

SCHEDULE 1   Section 61(1), (3)

DISTRIBUTION OF BUSINESS IN HIGH COURT

* * * * *

Family Division

3. To the Family Division are assigned—

    (a) all matrimonial causes and matters (whether at first instance or on appeal);

    (b) all causes and matters (whether at first instance or on appeal) relating to—

(i) legitimacy;

(*ii*) *the wardship, guardianship, custody or maintenance of minors (including proceedings about access) except proceedings solely for the appointment of a guardian of a minor's estate;*

[(ii) the exercise of the inherent jurisdiction of the High Court with respect to minors, the maintenance of minors and any proceedings under the Children Act 1989, except proceedings solely for the appointment of a guardian of a minor's estate;]

(iii) *affiliation or* adoption;

Note. Para 3(b)(ii) in square brackets substituted for para 3(b)(ii) in italics by Children Act 1989, ss 92(11), 108(5), Sch 11, Part II, para 9, Sch 13, para 45(3), as from 14 October 1991. Words 'affiliation or' in italics repealed by Family Law Reform Act 1987, s 33(4), Sch 4, as from 1 April 1989.

(iv) non-contentious or common form probate business;

(c) applications for consent to the marriage of a minor [or for a declaration under section 27B(5) of the Marriage Act 1949];

Note. Words in square brackets inserted by Marriage (Prohibited Degrees of Relationship) Act 1986, s 5, as from 1 November 1986.

(d) proceedings on appeal under section 13 of the Administration of Justice Act 1960 from an order or decision made under section 63(3) of the Magistrates' Courts Act 1980 to enforce an order of a magistrates' court made in matrimonial proceedings [or proceedings under Part IV of the Family Law Act 1996] or with respect to the guardianship of a minor;

Note. Words in square brackets inserted by Family Law Act 1996, s 66(1), Sch 8, Part III, para 51, as from 1 October 1997.

[(e) applications under Part III of the Family Law Act 1986]

[(e) proceedings under the Children Act 1989].

Note. First para 3(e) added by Family Law Act 1986, s 68(1), Sch 1, para 26, as from 4 April 1988. Second para 3(e) added by Children Act 1989, s 92(11), Sch 11, Part II, para 9, as from 14 October 1991.

[(f) all proceedings under—

(i) the *Domestic Violence and Matrimonial Proceedings Act 1976* [Part IV of the Family Law Act 1996];

(ii) the Child Abduction and Custody Act 1985;

(iii) the Family Law Act 1986;

(iv) section 30 of the Human Fertilisation and Embryology Act 1990; and

[(fa) all proceedings relating to a debit or credit under section 29(1) or 49(1) of the Welfare Reform and Pensions Act 1999;]

(g) all proceedings for the purpose of enforcing an order made in any proceedings of a type described in this paragraph.]

Note. Para 3(f), (g) added by High Court (Distribution of Business) Order 1991, SI 1991 No 1210, art 3, Schedule, as from 14 October 1991. Words in square brackets in para 3(f)(i) substituted for words in italics by Family Law Act 1996, s 66(1), Sch 8, Part III, para 51, as from 1 October 1997. Para 3(fa) inserted by the Welfare Reform and Pensions Act 1999, s 84, Sch 12, para 1, as from 1 December 2000 (SI 2000/1116).

[(h) all proceedings under the Child Support Act 1991.]

Note. Para 3(h) added by High Court (Distribution of Business) Order 1993, SI 1993 No 622, art 3, as from 5 April 1993.

SCHEDULE 2   Sections 88 to 95

LIST OF OFFICES IN SUPREME COURT FOR PURPOSES OF PART IV

*   *   *   *   *

PART II

1. *Office*   2. *Persons qualified*

*   *   *   *   *

7. *Registrar, Principal Registry of the Family Division.*

7. (*1*) *Barrister or solicitor of not less than 10 years' standing.*
(*2*) *District probate registrar who either—*
(*a*) *is of not less than 5 years' standing; or*
(*b*) *has, during so much of the 10 years immediately preceding his appointment as he has not been a district probate registrar, served as a clerk in the Principal Registry or a district probate registry.*
(*3*) *Clerk who has served not less than 10 years in the Principal Registry or a district probate registry.*

Note. The whole of this Schedule was substituted by Courts and Legal Services Act 1990, s 71(2), Sch 10, para 49, as from 1 January 1991 and para 9 set out below replaces para 7 above.

[**9.** District judge of the principal registry of the Family Division.

9. (1) A person who has a 7 year general qualification.
(2) A district probate registrar who either—
(a) is of at least 5 years' standing; or
(b) has, during so much of the 10 years immediately preceding his appointment as he has not been a district probate registrar, served as a civil servant in the principal registry or a district probate registry.
(3) A civil servant who has served at least 10 years in the principal registry or a district probate registry.]

*   *   *   *   *

(*Sch 3 repealed by County Courts Act 1984, s 148(3), Sch 4.*)

SCHEDULE 4   Section 151(5)

CONSTRUCTION OF REFERENCES TO SUPERSEDED COURTS AND OFFICERS

General

1. (1) So much of any enactment as refers or relates to any former court or judge whose jurisdiction is vested in the Court of Appeal or the High Court shall be construed and have effect as if any reference to that court or judge were a reference to the Court of Appeal or the High Court, as the case may be.

(2) All Acts, charters and other instruments which refer to Westminster as the locality of any former court, being a court whose jurisdiction is vested in the Court of

Appeal or the High Court, shall be construed as referring instead to the Royal Courts of Justice and other places at which the Court of Appeal or the High Court sits.

*　　*　　*　　*　　*

Principal registrar of Family Division

4. In any enactment or document passed or made before the commencement of this Act any reference to the principal registrar of the Family Division shall be read as a reference to the Senior Registrar of that Division.

SCHEDULE 5   Section 152(1)

CONSEQUENTIAL AMENDMENTS

(*The amendments made by this Schedule in so far as they affect provisions printed in this work have been incorporated.*)

*　　*　　*　　*　　*

SCHEDULE 6   Section 152(3)

TRANSITIONAL PROVISIONS AND SAVINGS

*　　*　　*　　*　　*

Scheme for establishment of district probate registries

6. *The scheme for the establishment of district probate registries as set out in Schedule 2 to the 1925 Act and in force immediately before the commencement of this Act shall continue to have effect, but as if it were contained in an order under section 104 of this Act; and accordingly it may be amended or revoked by an order under that section.*

Note. Para 6 repealed by Statute Law (Repeals) Act 1989, Sch 1, Part I, as from 16 November 1989.

*　　*　　*　　*　　*

Appeals from certain orders and decisions under section 54(3) of Magistrates' Courts Act 1952

12. In paragraph 3(d) of Schedule 1, the reference to an order or decision made under section 63(3) of the Magistrates' Courts Act 1980 includes a reference to an order or decision made under section 54(3) of the Magistrates' Courts Act 1952.

*　　*　　*　　*　　*

SCHEDULE 7 Section 152(4)

REPEALS

Chapter	Short Title	Extent of Repeal
* * * * *		
54 & 55 Vict c 53	Supreme Court of Judicature Act 1891	In section 5, the words from 'and' onwards.
* * * * *		
15 & 16 Geo 5 c 49	Supreme Court of Judicature (Consolidation) Act 1925	The whole Act.
* * * * *		
25 & 26 Geo 5 c 2	Supreme Court of Judicature (Amendment) Act 1935	The whole Act.
* * * * *		
1 & 2 Geo 6 c 28	Evidence Act 1938	Section 5.
* * * * *		
1 & 2 Geo 6 c 67	Supreme Court of Judicature (Amendment) Act 1938	The whole Act.
* * * * *		
7 & 8 Geo 6 c 9	Supreme Court of Judicature (Amendment) Act 1944	The whole Act.
* * * * *		
12, 13 & 14 Geo 6 c 100	Law Reform (Miscellaneous Provisions) Act 1949	Section 9.
* * * * *		
4 & 5 Eliz 2 c 46	Administration of Justice Act 1956	Parts I and II. Sections 34 and 36. Section 38. Sections 42 to 44. Section 54. Section 56.
* * * * *		
7 & 8 Eliz 2 c 22	County Courts Act 1959	Section 31. In section 39(1)(c), the word 'seduction'. Sections 43 to 45. In section 47(1) and (3), the words from 'or a judge' to 'that referee or officer'. Section 48(2). Sections 49 and 50. Section 51A(4). Section 52(2). Section 54. Sections 58 and 59.

Chapter	Short Title	Extent of Repeal
7 & 8 Eliz 2 c 22	*County Courts Act 1959*	In section 60, in subsections (2), (3) and (4), the words 'or a judge' and, in subsection (5), the words 'or a judge thereof'. Section 63. Section 65. Section 67. In section 68, the words 'or a judge thereof' and 'or judge'. In section 71, the words 'or of any other court in England and Wales.' Section 72. In section 74(1)(b), the words '(subject to the provisions of section sixty-five of this Act)'. In section 76, in paragraph (ii) of the proviso, the words 'or judge thereof' and 'or the judge by whom the transfer was ordered'. Section 77. In section 78(2), the proviso. Section 79. Section 83. In section 85(1), the words 'on application made in manner prescribed by rules of the Supreme Court'. Section 85(2). In section 90, the proviso. Section 94(4). In section 106(1), the words 'or a judge thereof'. Section 107. Section 109. Section 110(1) and (2). Section 115. In section 116(1), the words 'or a judge thereof'. In section 117(1), the words 'or a judge thereof' and, in both places where they occur, the words 'or judge thereof'. Section 118. Section 119. In section 120, in subsections (1) and (2), the words 'and chattels'. In section 122, in subsection (1), the words 'or chattels' and, in subsection (2), the

Chapter	Short Title	Extent of Repeal
7 & 8 Eliz 2 c 22	*County Courts Act 1959*	words 'and chattels' and 'and chattels of the first-mentioned person'. In section 124(1), the words 'or chattels' and 'and chattels'. In section 130(1), the words 'chattels or effects'. In section 131(1), the words 'chattels or effects'. Section 134. In section 136(1), the words 'or chattels'. In section 138, in subsection (1), the words 'and chattels', in both places where they occur, and, in subsection (3), the words 'or chattels'. In section 146, in subsection (1), the words 'or a judge thereof' and 'or judge' and in subsection (2), the words 'or judge'. In section 150(2), the words 'or other inferior court'. Section 172(1). Section 173. In section 174, in subsection (1), the words 'or a judge thereof' and 'or judge' and, in subsection (2), the words 'or a judge thereof'. Section 175. Section 194. In section 201, the definitions of 'Lord Chancellor', 'whole-time registrar' and 'whole-time assistant registrar'. Section 203. Section 205(3), (5), (6) and (9). Section 206. In Schedule 2, paragraph 5. Schedule 4.
7 & 8 Eliz 2 c 39	Supreme Court of Judicature (Amendment) Act 1959	The whole Act.
7 & 8 Eliz 2 c 72	Mental Health Act 1959	In section 111(2), the words from 'and' onwards. Section 115(2). In Schedule 7, in Part I, the entry relating to the Supreme Court of Judicature (Consolidation) Act 1925.

Chapter	Short Title	Extent of Repeal
	* * * * *	
8 & 9 Eliz. 2 c. 65	Administration of Justice Act 1960	In section 13(6), the words from 'and for' onwards. Section 16.
	* * * * *	
1967 c 56	Matrimonial Causes Act 1967	Section 6.
	* * * * *	
1968 c 64	Civil Evidence Act 1968	In section 8(6), the words 'section 99 of the Supreme Court of Judicature (Consolidation) Act 1925' and 'section 101 of the Supreme Court of Judicature (Consolidation) Act 1925'.
1969 c 46	Family Law Reform Act 1969	In Schedule 1, in Part I, the entry relating to the Supreme Court of Judicature (Consolidation) Act 1925.
	* * * * *	
1969 c 58	Administration of Justice Act 1969	In section 12(2)(a), the words from '(including' to '1925)'.
	* * * * *	In section 20(a), the words from the beginning to '1925, and' and the word 'each'. Section 21(1) to (3) and (5). Section 23. Sections 25, 26 and 27(1). In section 34(3), the words from the beginning to '1947, and' in their application to section 20 as regards rules of court under section 99 of the Supreme Court of Judicature (Consolidation) Act 1925.
	* * * * *	
1970 c 31	Administration of Justice Act 1970	In section 1— (a) subsections (1) to (5), (7) and (8), and (b) in subsection (6)(a), the words from 'that is' to 'other'. Section 2(1) to (4).

Chapter	Short Title	Extent of Repeal
1970 c 31	Administration of Justice Act 1970	Section 3. Sections 5 and 6. Section 9. Sections 31 to 33 so far as they relate to the High Court and county courts in England and Wales. Section 34(1). Section 35 so far as it relates to the High Court and county courts in England and Wales. Section 37(3). Section 45(3). Schedule 1. In Schedule 2, paragraphs 6 to 15, 18, 20 and 22, and in paragraph 23, the words 'and section 63 thereof (transfer of probate proceedings from High Court to county court),' and , 'in each place where they occur.'
1971 c 3	Guardianship of Minors Act 1971	In Schedule 1, in the entry relating to the Administration of Justice Act 1970, the amendments of Schedule 1 to that Act.
1971 c 23	Courts Act 1971	Parts I and II. Section 23. Sections 25 and 26. Section 50. In section 57, in subsection (1), the definition of 'the Judicature Act 1925', and subsection (3)(a). Schedule 1. In Schedule 8, paragraphs 18, 35(1), 40(3), 44, 46 and 57(2).
*	*	*	*	*
1972 c 30	Civil Evidence Act 1972	In section 2(8), the words 'section 99 of the Supreme Court of Judicature (Consolidation) Act 1925' and 'section 101 of the said Act of 1925'.
*	*	*	*	*
1973 c 18	Matrimonial Causes Act 1973	In Schedule 2, paragraphs 1, 6(3) and 10(1).

Chapter	Short Title	Extent of Repeal
1973 c 29	Guardianship Act 1973	Section 9(2)(c).
	* * * * *	
1975 c 72	Children Act 1975	In Schedule 3, paragraph 73(1).
1976 c 36	Adoption Act 1976	In Schedule 3, paragraph 14.
	* * * * *	
1977 c 38	Administration of Justice Act 1977	Sections 9 and 10. In section 22, the words and'. Section 27.
1978 c 22	Domestic Proceedings and Magistrates' Courts Act 1978	In Schedule 2, paragraph 25.
	* * * * *	
1979 c 53	Charging Orders Act 1979	Section 7(2), so far as it repeals section 35 or amends section 36 of the Administration of Justice Act 1956.
	* * * * *	
1981 c 49	Contempt of Court Act 1981	In section 16(2), paragraph (c) and the word 'and' preceding it.

Note. Entries relating to County Courts Act 1959 repealed by County Courts Act 1984, s 148(3), Sch 4, as from 1 August 1984.

COMPARATIVE TABLE

This table shows in column (1) the principal enactments replaced by the Supreme Court Act 1981, and in column (2) the provisions of that Act which replace (whether or not in amended form) the provisions in column (1). The table is not an exhaustive list of the enactments repealed and replaced by the Act of 1981.

In certain cases, the enactment in column (1) has not, or has not been wholly, repealed by the Act of 1981 as it is still required, or partly required, for the purposes of other legislation.

(1)	(2)	(1)	(2)
Chancery Amendment Act 1858 (c 27)	Supreme Court Act 1981 (c 54)	Supreme Court of Judicature (Consolidation) Act 1925 (c 49)	Supreme Court Act 1981 (c 54)
s 2	s 50	s 58, proviso (1)	s 64
		(2)	65(1)
Sale of Goods Act 1893 (c 71)		(3)	(2)
		59	65(1)
s 26	138	60	19(3)
		60A	63(2), (3)
Bankruptcy Act 1914 (c 59)		61	67
s 97(2), proviso	63(1)	63(1)	66(1)
		(2)	Cf s 5(5)
Supreme Court of Judicature (Consolidation) Act 1925 (c 49)		(3)	66(2)
		(4), (5)	(4), (5)
		(6)	(3)
s 2(1)	4(1)	68(1)	54(2), (4)(a)
(3)	(3)	(2)	60(2)
(4)	(2)	(4)	56(1)
4(1), (2)	5(1), (2)	(5)	54(4)(c)
(3), (4)	(4), (5)	proviso (6)	(5)
5(1)	7(1)–(3)	69(1)	54(7)
(2)	(4)	84(1)	99
16(1), (2)	13(1), (2)	(2)	100(1)
(4)	(6)	(3)	(2), (3)
17	14	(5)	(1)
18(1), (2)	19(1), (2)	(7)	(5)
20	25	85(2)	132
21(a)	26	98	54(8), 70(1), (2)
24	28(3)	99(1)	84(1)–(3), 87
26	15(1), (2)		(1)
27(1)	15(3), 16		(1), (3)
30(1)	17(1)	(2)	(7)
(2)	(3)	(4)	85(1)–(3)
31	18, 42(4)	(5)	84(8)
34	44	(6)	(4)–(6), (9)
36–44	49	101, proviso (a)	87(1)
45(1), (2)	37(1), (2)	174(2)	132
47	39	200(2)	132
49	36	219A	135
50	51(1), (20	220	136
51(1)	42(1), (3)	224(1)	Sch 4, para 1
(3)	(5)	225	151(1)
53	57(3), 71(3)		
54	57(4)(b), 71(4)(b)	Administration of Justice Act 1828 (c 26)	
55	61(2), (7)	s 6	s 5(5)
56	(1), Sch 1	7	63(2), (3)
57(1)	(3)(a), (b), (5)	12	135

* Not repealed.   † Repealed in part.

(1)	(2)	(1)	(2)
Administration of Justice (Miscellaneous Provisions) Act 1938 (c 63)	Supreme Court Act 1981 (c 54)	Criminal appeal Act 1968 (c 19)	Supreme Court Act 1981 (c 54)
s 7 8 9	s 29(1), (2), (5) 29(4) 30	s 46(1) Sch 5, Part 1†	s 84(1)–(3) 53(2)
Law Reform (Miscellaneous Provisions) Act 1949 (c 100)		Administration of Justice Act 1969 (c 58)	
s 9	41	s 20† 21(1)	32 33(1)
Administration of Justice Act 1956 (c 46)		Proceedings Against Estates Act 1970 (c 17)	
s 12 13 15 36 38 42	103 101 68(1)–(5) 37(4), (5) 40 15(4)	s 2	87(2)
		Administration of Justice Act 1970 (c 31)	
Supreme Court of Judicature (Amendment) Act 1959 (c 39)		s 31 45(3)	33(2) 100(3)
		Courts Act 1971 (c 23)	
s 1	42	s 2(1) (2) 4(2) (7) 5(3) (9) 10(1)–(3) (5) 14(1) (2)(e) (3) 15(5) 25(1), (2) (3)	71(1) (2) 8(1) (3) 8(1) (2) 28(1), (2) 29(3) 84(1)–(3) 74(7) 84(7) 84(8) 68(1), (2) (1), (2), (6), (7)
Administration of Justice Act 1965 (c 2)			
s 22(1), (2)	138		
Criminal Appeal Act 1966 (c 31)			
s 1(5) (6) 2(3) (5) 3(3) 1(2)* (3)*	53(1), (3) 51(1) 56(2) 57(4)(c) Sch 2 s 4(4) (5)	(4) 57(3)†	(6) 151(4)

* Not repealed.　　† Repealed in part.

(1)	(2)	(1)	(2)
Administration of Justice Act1973 (c 15)	Supreme Court Act 1981 (c 54)	Evidence (Proceedings in Other Jurisdictions) Act 1975 (c 34)	Supreme Court Act 1981 (c 54)
s 16(1) (3)† (4)† (5)†, (6)†	s 102(1), (4) (2), (3) (6) (5)	s 4	s 36(6)
		Administration of Justice Act 1977 (c 38)	
		s 22† 27	s 85(1) 87(2)

* Not repealed.   † Repealed in part.

BRITISH NATIONALITY ACT 1981

(1981 c 61)

An Act to make fresh provision about citizenship and nationality, and to amend the Immigration Act 1971 as regards the right of abode in the United Kingdom.

[30 October 1981]

1. Acquisition by birth or adoption.

*   *   *   *   *

(5) Where after commencement an order authorising the adoption of a minor who is not a British citizen is made by any court in the United Kingdom, he shall be a British citizen as from the date on which the order is made if the adopter or, in the case of a joint adoption, one of the adopters is a British citizen on that date.

[(5) Where—

(a) any court in the United Kingdom [or, on or after the appointed day, any court in a qualifying territory] makes an order authorising the adoption of a minor who is not a British citizen; or

(b) a minor who is not a British citizen is adopted under a Convention adoption, [effected under the law of a country or territory outside the United Kingdom.]

that minor shall, if the requirements of subsection (5A) are met, be a British citizen as from the date on which the order is made or the Convention adoption is effected, as the case may be.

(5A) Those requirements are that on the date on which the order is made or the Convention adoption is effected (as the case may be)—

(a) the adopter or, in the case of a joint adoption, one of the adopters is a British citizen; and

(b) in a case within subsection (5)(b), the adopter or, in the case of a joint adoption, both of the adopters are habitually resident in the United Kingdom [or in a designated territory.]

Note. Sub-ss (5), (5A) substituted for sub-s (5) as originally enacted, by the Adoption (Intercountry Aspects) Act 1999, s 7(1), as from 1 June 2003 (SI 2003 No 362). Further amended by the Adoption and Children Act 2002, s 137(3), (4)(a), as from a date to be appointed; and the British Overseas Territories Act 2002, s 5, Sch 1, para 1(1), (4), as from 21 May 2002 (SI 2002 No 1252).

*   *   *   *   *

8. Registration by virtue of marriage—*(1) A woman who immediately before commencement was the wife of a citizen of the United Kingdom and Colonies shall be entitled, on an application for her registration as a British citizen made within five years after commencement, to be registered as a British citizen if—*

(a) *immediately before commencement she would (if she had applied for it) have been entitled under section 6(2) of the 1948 Act to be registered as a citizen of the United Kingdom and Colonies by virtue of her marriage to the man who was then her husband; and*

(b) *that man became a British citizen at commencement and did not at any time in the period from commencement to the date of the application under this subsection cease to be such a citizen as a result of a declaration of renunciation; and*

(c) *she remained married to him throughout that period.*

(2) On an application for her registration as a British citizen made within five years after commencement, the Secretary of State may, if he thinks fit, cause a woman to be registered as such a citizen if—

(a) *immediately before commencement she would (if she had applied for it) have been entitled under section 6(2) of the 1948 Act to be registered as a citizen of the United Kingdom and Colonies by virtue of having been married to a man to whom she is no longer married on the date of the application under this subsection; and*

(b) *that man became a British citizen at commencement or would have done so but for his death.*

(3) On an application for her registration as a British citizen made within five years after commencement by a woman who at the time of the application is married, the Secretary of State may, if he thinks fit, cause her to be registered as such a citizen if—

(a) *immediately before commencement she would (if she had applied for it) have been entitled under section 6(2) of the 1948 Act to be registered as a citizen of the United Kingdom and Colonies by virtue of her being or having been married to the man who is her husband on the date of the application under this subsection; and*

(b) *that man either—*

(i) *became a British citizen at commencement but has ceased to be such a citizen as a result of a declaration of renunciation; or*

(ii) *would have become a British citizen at commencement but for his having ceased to be a citizen of the United Kingdom and Colonies as a result of a declaration of renunciation.*

Note. Section 8 in force on 1 January 1983 (SI 1982 No 933).

Repealed by the Nationality, Immigration and Asylum Act 2002, ss 15, 161, Sch 2, para 1(b), Sch 9, as from 7 November 2002 (but see s 162(2)(e), Sch 2, para 2).

*   *   *   *   *

15 Acquisition by birth or adoption.

*   *   *   *   *

(5) Where after commencement an order authorising the adoption of a minor who is not a British Dependent Territories citizen is made by a court in any *dependent territory* [British Overseas Territory], he shall be a *British Dependent Territories citizen* [British Overseas territories citizen] as from the date on which the order is made if the adopter or, in the case of a joint adoption, one of the adopters, is a British Dependent Territories citizen on that date.

Note. Amended by the British Overseas Territories Act 2002, ss 1(1)(b), 2(2)(b), as from 26 February 2002.

*   *   *   *   *

20. Registration by virtue of marriage—*(1) A woman who immediately before commencement was the wife of a citizen of the United Kingdom and Colonies shall be entitled, on an application for her registration as a British Dependent Territories citizen [British* *overseas territories citizen] made within five years after commencement, to be registered as a British Dependent Territories citizen [British overseas territories citizen] if—*

(a) *immediately before commencement she would (if she had applied for it) have been entitled under section 6(2) of the 1948 Act to be registered as a citizen of the United Kingdom and Colonies by virtue of her marriage to the man who was then her husband; and*

(b) *that man became a British Dependent Territories citizen [British overseas territories citizen] at commencement and did not at any time in the period from commencement to the date of the application under this subsection cease to be such a citizen as a result of a declaration of renunciation; and*

(c) *she remained married to him throughout that period.*

(2) *On such an application for her registration as a British Dependent Territories citizen [British overseas territories citizen] made within five years after commencement the Secretary of State may, if he thinks fit, cause a woman to be registered as such a citizen if—*

(a) *immediately before commencement she would (if she had applied for it) have been entitled under section 6(2) of the 1948 Act to be registered as a citizen of the United Kingdom and Colonies by virtue of having been married to a man to whom she is no longer married on the date of the application under this subsection; and*

(b) *that man became a British Dependent Territories citizen [British overseas territories citizen] at commencement or would have done so but for his death.*

(3) *On an application for her registration as a British Dependent Territories citizen [British overseas territories citizen] made within five years after commencement by a woman who at the time of the application is married, the Secretary of State shall, if he thinks fit, cause her to be registered as such a citizen if—*

(a) *immediately before commencement she would (if she had applied for it) have been entitled under section 6(2) of the 1948 Act to be registered as a citizen of the United Kingdom and Colonies by virtue of her being or having been married to the man who is her husband on the date of the application under this subsection; and*

(b) *that man either—*

(i) *became a British Dependent Territories citizen [British overseas territories citizen] at commencement but has ceased to be such a citizen as a result of a declaration of renunciation; or*

(ii) *would have become a British Dependent Territories citizen [British overseas territories citizen] at commencement but for his having ceased to be a citizen of the United Kingdom and Colonies as a result of a declaration of renunciation.*

Note. Section 20 in force on 1 January 1983 (SI 1982 No 933).

Repealed by the Nationality Immigration and Asylum Act 2002, ss 15, 161, Sch 2, para 1(e), Sch 9 as from 7 November 2002 (but see s 162(2)(e), Sch 2, para 2).

*   *   *   *   *

28. Registration by virtue of marriage—*(1) A woman who immediately before commencement was the wife of a citizen of the United Kingdom and Colonies shall be entitled, on an application for her registration as a British Overseas citizen made within five years after commencement, to be registered as a British Overseas citizen if—*

(a) *immediately before commencement she would (if she had applied for it) have been entitled under section 6(2) of the 1948 Act to be registered as a citizen of the United Kingdom and Colonies by virtue of her marriage to the man who was then her husband; and*

(b) *that man became a British Overseas citizen at commencement and did not at any time in the period from commencement to the date of the application under this subsection cease to be such a citizen as a result of a declaration of renunciation; and*

(c) *she remained married to him throughout that period.*

(2) *On an application for her registration as a British Overseas citizen made within five years after commencement, the Secretary of State may, if he thinks fit, cause a woman to be registered as such a citizen if—*

(a) immediately before commencement she would (if she had applied for it) have been entitled under section 6(2) of the 1948 Act to be registered as a citizen of the United Kingdom and Colonies by virtue of having been married to a man to whom she is no longer married on the date of the application under this subsection; and

(b) that man became a British Overseas citizen at commencement or would have done so but for his death.

(3) On an application for her registration as a British Overseas citizen made within five years after commencement by a woman who at the time of the application is married, the Secretary of State may, if he thinks fit, cause her to be registered as such a citizen if—

(a) immediately before commencement she would (if she had applied for it) have been entitled under section 6(2) of the 1948 Act to be registered as a citizen of the United Kingdom and Colonies by virtue of her being or having been married to the man who is her husband on the date of the application under this subsection; and

(b) that man either—

(i) became a British Overseas citizen at commencement but has ceased to be such a citizen as a result of a declaration of renunciation; or

(ii) would have become a British Overseas citizen at commencement but for his having ceased to be a citizen of the United Kingdom and Colonies as a result of a declaration of renunciation.

Note. Section 28 in force on 1 January 1983 (SI 1982 No 933).

Repealed by the Nationality Immigration and Asylum Act 2002, ss 15, 161, Sch 2, para 1(e), Sch 9 as from 7 November 2002 (but see s 162(2)(e), Sch 2, para 2).

CIVIL JURISDICTION AND JUDGMENTS ACT 1982

(1982 c 27)

ARRANGEMENT OF SECTIONS

PART I

IMPLEMENTATION OF THE CONVENTIONS

Main implementing provisions

An Act to make further provision about the jurisdiction of courts and tribunals in the United Kingdom and certain other territories and about the recognition and enforcement of judgments given in the United Kingdom or elsewhere; to provide for the modification of certain provisions relating to legal aid; and for connected purposes. [13 July 1982]

PART I

IMPLEMENTATION OF THE CONVENTIONS

Main implementing provisions

1. Interpretation of references to the Conventions and Contracting States—
(1) In this Act—
'the 1968 Convention' means the Convention on jurisdiction and the enforcement of judgments in civil and commercial matters (including the Protocol annexed to that Convention), signed at Brussels on 27 September 1968;
'the 1971 Protocol' means the Protocol on the interpretation of the 1968 Convention by the European Court, signed at Luxembourg on 3 June 1971;
'the Accession Convention' means the Convention on the accession to the 1968 Convention and the 1971 Protocol of Denmark, the Republic of Ireland and the United Kingdom, signed at Luxembourg on 9 October 1978;
['the 1982 Accession Convention' means the Convention on the accession of the Hellenic Republic to the 1968 Convention and the 1971 Protocol, with the adjustments made to them by the Accession Convention, signed at Luxembourg on 25 October 1982;]
['the 1989 Accession Convention' means the Convention on the accession of the Kingdom of Spain and the Portuguese Republic to the 1968 Convention and the 1971 Protocol, with the adjustments made to them by the Accession Convention and the 1982 Accession Convention, signed at Donostia—San Sebastián on 26 May 1989;]
['the 1996 Accession Convention' means the Convention on the accession of the Republic of Austria, the Republic of Finland and the Kingdom of Sweden to the 1968 Convention and the 1971 Protocol, with the adjustments made to them by the Accession Convention, the 1982 Accession Convention and the 1989 Accession Convention, signed at Brussels on 29th November 1996.]

Note. Definition 'the 1982 Accession Convention' inserted by Civil Jurisdiction and Judgments Act 1982 (Amendment) Order 1989, SI 1989 No 1346, art 3. Definition 'the 1989 Accession Convention' inserted by Civil Jurisdiction and Judgments Act 1982 (Amendment) Order 1990, SI 1990 No 2591, art 3. Definition 'the 1996 Convention' inserted by SI 2000 No 1824, art 3.

'the Conventions' means the 1968 Convention, the 1971 Protocol and the Accession Convention.
[*'the Conventions' means the 1968 Convention, the 1971 Protocol, the Accession Convention and the 1982 Accession Convention*].
[*'the Conventions'* ['the Brussels Conventions'] means the 1968 Convention, the 1971 Protocol, the Accession Convention, the 1982 Accession Convention *and the 1989 Accession Convention* [, the 1989 Accession Convention and the 1996 Accession Convention]].
['the Lugano Convention' means the Convention on jurisdiction and the enforcement of judgments in civil and commercial matters (including the Protocols annexed to that Convention) opened for signature at Lugano on 16 September 1988 and signed by the United Kingdom on 18 September 1989.]
['the Regulation' means Council Regulation (EC) No 44/2001 of 22nd December 2000 on jurisdiction and the recognition and enforcement of judgments in civil and commercial matters].

Note. Definition 'the Conventions' in square brackets substituted by Civil Jurisdiction and Judgments Act 1982 (Amendment) Order 1989, SI 1989 No 1346, art 4. Words in the fourth pair of square brackets substituted by Civil Jurisdiction and Judgments Act 1982 (Amendment) Order 1990, SI 1990 No 2591, art 4. Words 'the Brussels Conventions' in square brackets substituted for words 'the Conventions' in italics by Civil Jurisdiction and Judgments Act 1991, s 2(1), (2), as from 1 May 1992, and definition 'the Lugano Convention' added by s 2(1), (3) of the 1991 Act, as from 1 May 1992. Further definitions amended and added by SI 2000 No 1824, art 3, SI 2001 No 3929, art 4, Sch 2, Pt I, para 1(a) as from 25 January 2002.

(2) In this Act, unless the context otherwise requires—

(*a*) *references to, or to any provision of, the 1968 Convention or the 1971 Protocol are references to that Convention, Protocol or provision as amended by the Accession Convention; and*

[(*a*) *references to, or any provision of, the 1968 Convention or the 1971 Protocol are references to that Convention, Protocol or provision as amended by the Accession Convention and the 1982 Accession Convention; and*]

[(a) references to, or to any provision of, the 1968 Convention or the 1971 Protocol are references to that Convention, Protocol or provision as amended by the Accession Convention, the 1982 Accession Convention *and the 1989 Accession Convention* [, the 1989 Accession Convention and the 1996 Accession Convention]; and]

Note. Sub-s (2)(a) in first pair of square brackets originally substituted for sub-s (2)(a) in italics by Civil Jurisdiction and Judgments Act 1982 (Amendment) Order 1989, SI 1989 No 1346, art 5. Sub-s (2)(a) in second pair of square brackets substituted for sub-s (2)(a) in italics in square brackets by Civil Jurisdiction and Judgments Act 1982 (Amendment) Order 1990, SI 1990 No 2591, art 5. Further amended by SI 2000/1824, art 4. Sub-s (2)(aa) inserted by SI 2000/1824, art 9.

(*b*) *any reference to a numbered Article is a reference to the Article so numbered of the 1968 Convention, and any reference to a sub-division of a numbered Article shall be construed accordingly.*

[(b) any reference in any provision to a numbered Article without more is a reference—

   (i) to the Article so numbered of the 1968 Convention, in so far as the provision applies in relation to that Convention, and

   (ii) to the Article so numbered of the Lugano Convention, in so far as the provision applies in relation to that Convention,

and any reference to a sub-division of a numbered Article shall be construed accordingly.]

Note. Sub-s (2)(b) in square brackets substituted for sub-s (2)(b) in italics by Civil Jurisdiction and Judgments Act 1991, s 2(1), (4), as from 1 May 1992.

[(*3*) *In this Act 'Contracting State' means—*

(*a*) *one of the original parties to the 1968 Convention (Belgium, the Federal Republic of Germany, France, Italy, Luxembourg and the Netherlands); or*

(*b*) *one of the parties acceding to that Convention under the Accession Convention (Denmark, the Republic of Ireland and the United Kingdom),*

being a state in respect of which the Accession Convention has entered into force in accordance with Article 39 of that Convention.

[(*3*) *In this Act 'Contracting State' means—*

(*a*) *one of the original parties to the 1968 Convention (Belgium, the Federal Republic of Germany, France, Italy, Luxembourg and The Netherlands); or*

(*b*) *one of the parties acceding to that Convention under the Accession Convention (Denmark, the Republic of Ireland and the United Kingdom), or under the 1982 Accession Convention (the Hellenic Republic),*

being a state in respect of which the Accession Convention has entered into force in accordance with Article 39 of that Convention, or being a state in respect of which the 1982 Accession Convention has entered into force in accordance with Article 15 of that Convention, as the case might be.]

[(3) *In this Act 'Contracting State' means—*[In this Act—

'Contracting State', without more, in any provision means—

(a) in the application of the provision in relation to the Brussels Conventions, a Brussels Contracting State; and

(b) in the application of the provision in relation to the Lugano Convention, a Lugano Contracting State;

'Brussels Contracting State' means—

(a) one of the original parties to the 1968 Convention (Belgium, the Federal Republic of Germany, France, Italy, Luxembourg and The Netherlands); or

(b) one of the parties acceding to that Convention under the Accession Convention (Denmark, the Republic of Ireland and the United Kingdom), or under the 1982 Accession Convention (the Hellenic Republic), or under the 1989 Accession Convention (Spain and Portugal),

being a state in respect of which the Accession Convention has entered into force in accordance with Article 39 of that Convention, or being a state in respect of which the 1982 Accession Convention has entered into force in accordance with Article 15 of that Convention, or being a state in respect of which the 1989 Accession Convention has entered into force in accordance with Article 32 of that Convention, as the case might be.]

['Brussels Contracting State' means Denmark (which is not bound by the Regulation, but was one of the parties acceding to the 1968 Convention under the Accession Convention);]

[*'Lugano Contracting State' means one of the original parties to the Lugano Convention, that is to say—*

Austria, Belgium, Denmark, Finland, France, the Federal Republic of Germany, the Hellenic Republic, Iceland, the Republic of Ireland, Italy, Luxembourg, the Netherlands, Norway, Portugal, Spain, Sweden, Switzerland and the United Kingdom,

[['Lugano Contracting State' means—

(a) one of the original parties to the Lugano Convention, that is to say Austria, Belgium, Denmark, Finland, France, the Federal Republic of Germany, the Hellenic Republic, Iceland, the Republic of Ireland, Italy, Luxembourg, the Netherlands, Norway, Portugal, Spain, Sweden, Switzerland and the United Kingdom; or

(b) a party who has subsequently acceded to that Convention, that is to say, Poland],

being a State in relation to which that Convention has taken effect in accordance with paragraph 3 or 4 of Article 61.]

['Regulation State' in any provision, in the application of that provision in relation to the Regulation, has the same meaning as 'Member State' in the Regulation, that is all Members States except Denmark].]

[(4) Any question aarising as to whether it is the Regulation, any of the Brussels Conventions, or the Lugano Convention which applies in the circumstances of a particular case shall be determined as follows—

(a) in accordance with Articles 54B of the Lugano convention (which determines the relationship between the Brussels Conventions and the Lugano Convention); and

(b) In accordance with Article 68 of the Regulation (which determines the relationship between the Brussels Conventions and the Regulation).]

Note. Sub-s (3) in first pair of square brackets originally substituted for sub-s (3) in italics by Civil Jurisdiction and Judgments Act 1982 (Amendment) Order 1989, SI 1989 No 1346, art 6. Sub-s (3) in second pair of square brackets substituted for sub-s (3) in italics by Civil Jurisdiction and Judgments Act 1982 (Amendment) Order 1990, SI 1990 No 2591, art 6. Words 'In this Act ...' in square brackets substituted for words in italics by Civil Jurisdiction and Judgments Act 1991, s 2(1), (5), as from 1 May 1992. Definition 'Lugano Contracting State' in square brackets added by s 2(1), (6) of the 1991 Act, as from 1 May 1992. Further amended by SI 2001/3929, art 4, Sch 2, Pt 1; SI 2000/1824, art 10.

2. The Conventions to have the force of law—(1) The *Conventions* [Brussels Conventions] shall have the force of law in the United Kingdom, and judicial notice shall be taken of them.

Note. Words in square brackets substituted for words in italics by Civil Jurisdiction and Judgments Act 1991, s 3, Sch 2, para 1, as from 1 May 1992.

(*2*) *For convenience of reference there are set out in Schedules 1, 2 and 3 respectively the English texts of*—
   (*a*) *the 1968 Convention as amended by Titles II and III of the Accession Convention;*
   (*b*) *the 1971 Protocol as amended by Title IV of the Accession Convention; and*
   (*c*) *Titles V and VI of the Accession Convention (transitional and final provisions),*
being texts prepared from the authentic English texts referred to in Articles 37 and 41 of the Accession Convention.

[(*2*) *For convenience of reference there are set out in Schedules 1, 2, 3 and 3A respectively the English texts of*—
   (*a*) *the 1968 Convention as amended by Titles II and III of the Accession Convention and by Titles II and III of the 1982 Accession Convention;*
   (*b*) *the 1971 Protocol as amended by Title IV of the Accession Convention and by Title IV of the 1982 Accession Convention;*
   (*c*) *Titles V and VI of the Accession Convention (transitional and final provisions); and*
   (*d*) *Titles V and VI of the 1982 Accession Convention (transitional and final provisions),*
being texts prepared from the authentic English texts referred to in Articles 37 and 41 of the Accession Convention and in Article 17 of the Accession Convention.]

[(2) For convenience of reference there are set out in Schedules 1, 2, 3, 3A *and 3B* [, 3B and 3C] respectively the English texts of—
   (a) the 1968 Convention as amended by Titles II and III of the Accession Convention, by Titles II and III of the 1982 Accession Convention *and* by Titles II and III of, and Annex 1(d) to, the 1989 Accession Convention [and by Titles II and III of the 1996 Accession Convention];
   (b) the 1971 Protocol as amended by Title IV of the Accession Convention, by Title IV of the 1982 Accession Convention *and* by Title IV of the 1989 Accession Convention [and by Title IV of the 1996 Accession Convention];
   (c) Titles V and VI of the Accession Convention (transitional and final provisions) as amended by Title V of the 1989 Accession Convention;
   (d) Titles V and VI of the 1982 Accession Convention (transitional and final provisions); and
   (e) Titles VI and VII of the 1989 Accession Convention (transitional and final provisions),
   [(f) Titles V and VI of the 1996 Accession Convention (transitional and final provisions),]
being texts prepared from the authentic English texts referred to in Articles 37 and 41 of the Accession Convention, in Article 17 of the 1982 Accession Convention *and in Article 34 of the 1989 Accession Convention* [, in Article 34 of the 1989 Accession Convention and in Article 18 of the 1996 Convention].]

Note. Sub-s (2) in first pair of square brackets originally substituted for sub-s (2) in italics by Civil Jurisdiction and Judgments Act 1982 (Amendment) Order 1989, SI 1989 No 1346, art 7. Sub-s (2) in second pair of square brackets substituted for sub-s (2) in italics by Civil Jurisdiction and Judgments Act 1982 (Amendment) Order 1990, SI 1990 No 2591, art 7, as from 1 December 1991. Further amended by SI 2000 No 1824.

3. Interpretation of the Conventions—(1) Any question as to the meaning or effect of any provision of the *Conventions* [Brussels Conventions] shall, if not referred to the European Court in accordance with the 1971 Protocol, be determined in accordance with the principles laid down by and any relevant decision of the European Court.
   (2) Judicial notice shall be taken of any decision of, or expression of opinion by, the European Court on any such question.
   (3) Without prejudice to the generality of subsection (1), the following reports (which are reproduced in the Official Journal of the Communities), namely—

(a) the reports by Mr P Jenard on the 1968 Convention and the 1971 Protocol; and

(b) the report by Professor Peter Schlosser on the Accession Convention[; and

(c) the report by Professor Demetrios I Eurigerris and Professor KD Kerameus on the 1982 Accession Convention,][; and

(d) the report by Mr Martinho de Almeida Cruz, Mr Manuel Desantes Real and Mr P Jenard on the 1989 Accession Convention,]

may be considered in ascertaining the meaning or effect of any provision of the *Conventions* [Brussels Conventions] and shall be given such weight as is appropriate in the circumstances.

Note. Words in square brackets in sub-ss (1), (3) substituted for words in italics by Civil Jurisdiction and Judgments Act 1991, s 3, Sch 2, para 1, as from 1 May 1992. Sub-s (3)(c) and the word 'and' immediately preceding it inserted by Civil Jurisdiction and Judgments Act 1982 (Amendment) Order 1989, SI 1989 No 1346, art 8. Sub-s (3)(d) and the word 'and' immediately preceding it inserted by Civil Jurisdiction and Judgments Act 1982 (Amendment) Order 1990, SI 1990 No 2591, art 8, as from 1 December 1991.

Supplementary provisions as to recognition and enforcement of judgments

[3A. The Lugano Convention to have the force of law—(1) The Lugano Convention shall have the force of law in the United Kingdom, and judicial notice shall be taken of it.

(2) For the convenience of reference there is set out in Schedule 3C the English text of the Lugano Convention [as amended on the accession of Poland to that Convention].]

Note. This section inserted by Civil Jurisdiction and Judgments Act 1991, s 1(1), as from 1 May 1992. Amended by SI 2000 No 1824.

[3B. Interpretation of the Lugano Convention—(1) In determining any question as to the meaning or effect of a provision of the Lugano Convention, a court in the United Kingdom shall, in accordance with Protocol No 2 to that Convention, take account of any principles laid down in any relevant decision delivered by a court of any other Lugano Contracting State concerning provisions of the Convention.

(2) Without prejudice to any practice of the courts as to the matters which may be considered apart from this section, the report on the Lugano Convention by Mr P Jenard and Mr G Möller (which is reproduced in the Official Journal of the Communities of 28 July 1990) may be considered in ascertaining the meaning or effect of any provision of the Convention and shall be given such weight as is appropriate in the circumstances.]

Note. This section inserted by Civil Jurisdiction and Judgments Act 1991, s 1(1), as from 1 May 1992.

4. Enforcement of judgments other than maintenance orders—(1) A judgment, other than a maintenance order, which is the subject of an application under Article 31 [of the 1968 Convention or of the Lugano Convention] for its enforcement in any part of the United Kingdom shall, to the extent that its enforcement is authorised by the appropriate court, be registered in the prescribed manner in that court.

In this subsection 'the appropriate court' means the court to which the application is made in pursuance of Article 32 (that is to say, the High Court or the Court of Session).

(2) Where a judgment is registered under this section, the reasonable costs or expenses of and incidental to its registration shall be recoverable as if they were sums recoverable under the judgment.

(3) A judgment under this section shall, for the purposes of its enforcement, be of the same force and effect, the registering court shall have in relation to its enforcement the same powers, and proceedings for or with respect to its enforcement

may be taken, as if the judgment had been originally given by the registering court and had (where relevant) been entered.

(4) Subsection (3) is subject to Article 39 (restriction on enforcement where appeal pending or time for appeal unexpired), to section 7 and to any provision made by rules of court as to the manner in which and conditions subject to which a judgment registered under this section may be enforced.

Note. Words in square brackets in sub-s (1) inserted by Civil Jurisdiction and Judgments Act 1991, s 3, Sch 2, para 2, as from 1 May 1992.

5. Recognition and enforcement of maintenance orders—(1) The function of transmitting to the appropriate court an application under Article 31 [of the 1968 Convention or of the Lugano Convention] for the recognition or enforcement in the United Kingdom of a maintenance order shall be discharged—

(*a*) *as respects England and Wales and Scotland, by the Secretary of State;*
(*b*) *as respects Northern Ireland, by the Lord Chancellor.*
[(a) as respects England and Wales and Northern Ireland, by the Lord Chancellor, and
(b) as respects Scotland, by the Secretary of State.]

In this subsection 'the appropriate court' means the magistrates' court or sheriff court having jurisdiction in the matter in accordance with the second paragraph of Article 32.

Note. Words 'of the 1968 ... Convention' in square brackets inserted by Civil Jurisdiction and Judgments Act 1991, s 3, Sch 2, para 2, as from 1 May 1992. Paras (a), (b) in square brackets substituted for paras (a), (b) in italics by Transfer of Functions (Magistrates' Courts and Family Law) Order 1992, SI 1992 No 709, art 4(7), as from 1 April 1992.

(2) Such an application shall be determined in the first instance by the prescribed officer of that court.

(3) Where on such an application the enforcement of the order is authorised to any extent, the order shall to that extent be registered in the prescribed manner in that court.

(4) A maintenance order registered under this section shall, for the purposes of its enforcement, be of the same force and effect, the registering court shall have in relation to its enforcement the same powers, and proceedings for or with respect to its enforcement may be taken, as if the order had been originally made by the registering court.

(5) Subsection (4) is subject to Article 39 (restriction on enforcement where appeal pending or time for appeal unexpired), to section 7 and to any provision made by rules of court as to the manner in which and conditions subject to which an order registered under this section may be enforced.

[(5A) A maintenance order which by virtue of this section is enforceable by a magistrates' court in England and Wales *shall be enforceable* [shall, subject to the modifications of sections 76 and 93 of the Magistrates' Court Act 1980 specified in subsections (5B) and (5C) below, be enforceable] in the same manner as a magistrates' court maintenance order made by that court.

In this subsection 'magistrates' court maintenance order' has the same meaning as in section 150(1) of the Magistrates' Courts Act 1980.]

[(5B) Section 76 (enforcement of sums adjudged to be paid) shall have effect as if for subsections (4) to (6) there were substituted the following subsections—

'(4) Where proceedings are brought for the enforcement of a magistrates' court maintenance order under this section, the court may vary the order by exercising one of its powers under subsection (5) below.

(5) The powers of the court are—
(a) the power to order that payments under the order be made directly to *the clerk of the court or the clerk of any other magistrates' court* [*a justices' chief executive*] [the designated officer for the court or for any other magistrates' court];

(b)   the power to order that payments under the order be made to *the clerk of the court, or to the clerk of any other magistrates' court* [*a justices' chief executive*] [the designated officer for the court or for any other magistrates' court], by such method of payment falling within section 59(6) above (standing order, etc) as may be specified;

(c)   the power to make an attachment of earnings order under the Attachment of Earnings Act 1971 to secure payments under the order.

(6) In deciding which of the powers under subsection (5) above it is to exercise, the court shall have regard to any representations made by the debtor (within the meaning of section 59 above).

Note. Amended by the Access to Justice Act 1999, S 90, Sch 13, para 122, as from 1 April 2001; the Courts Act 2003, s 109, Sch 8, para 268, as from a day to be appointed.

(7) Subsection (4) of section 59 (power of court to require debtor to open account) shall apply for the purposes of subsection (5) above as it applies for the purposes of that section but as if for paragraph (a) there were substituted—

"(a) the court proposes to exercise its power under paragraph (b) of section 76(5) below, and".'

(5C) In section 93 (complaint for arrears), subsection (6) (court not to impose imprisonment in certain circumstances) shall have effect as if for paragraph (b) there were substituted—

'(b) if the court is of the opinion that it is appropriate—

(i)   to make an attachment of earnings order; or

(ii)   to exercise its power under paragraph (b) of section 76(5) above.']

Note. Sub-s (5A) inserted by Family Law Reform Act 1987, s 33(1), Sch 2, para 89, as from 1 April 1989. Words in square brackets in sub-s (5A) substituted for words in italics and sub-ss (5B), (5C) inserted by Maintenance Enforcement Act 1991, s 10, Sch 1, para 21, as from 1 April 1992.

(6) A maintenance order which by virtue of this section is enforceable by a magistrates' court in *England and Wales or* Northern Ireland *shall be enforceable* [shall, subject to the modifications of Article 98 of the Magistrates' Courts (Northern Ireland) Order 1981 specified in sub-s (6A) below, be enforceable] *in the same manner as an affiliation order made by that court* [as an order made by that court to which that Article applies].

Note. Words 'England and Wales or' in italics repealed by Family Law Reform Act 1987, s 33(1), Sch 2, para 89(3), as from 1 April 1989. Words 'shall, subject to ... enforceable' in square brackets substituted for words 'shall be enforceable' in italics by Family Law (Northern Ireland) Order 1993, SI 1993 No 1576, art 11, Sch 1, para 16, as from 4 November 1996. Words 'as an order ... Article applies' in square brackets substituted for words 'in the same ... court' in italics by Children (Northern Ireland) Order 1995, SI 1995 No 755, art 185, Sch 9, para 116, as from 4 November 1996.

[(6A) Article 98 (enforcement of sums adjudged to be paid) shall have effect—

(a)   as if for paragraph (7)(a) there were substituted the following paragraph—

'(a) if the court is of the opinion that it is appropriate—

(i)   to make an attachment of earnings order; or

(ii)   to exercise its power under paragraph (8C)(b)';

(b)   as if for paragraphs (8B) to (8D) there were substituted the following paragraphs—

'(8B) Upon the appearance of a person or proof of service of the summons on him as mentioned in paragraph (4) for the enforcement of an order to which this Article applies, the court or resident magistrate may vary the order by exercising one of the powers under paragraph (8C).

(8C) The powers mentioned in paragraph (8B) are—

(a) the power to order that payments under the order be made directly to the collecting officer;

(b) the power to order that payments under the order be made to the collecting officer by such method of payment falling within Article 85(7) (standing order, etc) as may be specified;
(c) the power to make an attachment of earnings order under Part IX to secure payments under the order.

(8D) In deciding which of the powers under paragraph (8C) is to be exercised, the court or, as the case may be, a resident magistrate shall have regard to any representations made by the debtor (within the meaning of Article 85).

(8E) Paragraph (5) of Article 85 (power of court to require debtor to open account) shall apply for the purposes of paragraph (8C) as it applies for the purposes of that Article but as if for sub-paragraph (a) there were substituted—

"(a) the court proposes to exercise its power under sub-paragraph (b) of Article 98(8C), and".'.]

Note. Sub-s (6A) inserted by Family Law (Northern Ireland) Order 1993, SI 1993 No 1576, art 11, Sch 1, para 16, as from 4 November 1996.

(7) The payer under a maintenance order registered under this section in a magistrates' court in England and Wales or Northern Ireland shall give notice of any change of address to the *clerk* [proper officer] of that court.

A person who without reasonable excuse fails to comply with this subsection shall be guilty of an offence and liable on summary conviction to a fine not exceeding *£50* [level 2 on the standard scale].

Note. Reference to level 2 substituted by virtue of Criminal Justice Act 1982, s 46. Further amended by the Access to Justice Act 1999, s 90, Sch 13, para 122, as from 1 April 2001 (SI 2001 No 916).

[(8) In subsection (7) 'proper officer' means—
(a) in relation to a magistrates' court in England and Wales, the justices' chief executive [designated officer] for the court; and
(b) in relation to a magistrates' court in Northern Ireland, the clerk of the court.]

Note. Inserted by the Access to Justice Act 1999, s 90, Sch 13, para 122, as from 1 April 2001 (SI 2001 No 916); amended by the Courts Act 2003, s 109, Sch 8, para 268, as from a date to be appointed.

6. Appeals under Article 37, second paragraph and Article 41—(1) The single further appeal on a point of law referred to [in the 1968 Convention and the Lugano Convention] in Article 37, second paragraph and Article 41 in relation to the recognition or enforcement of a judgment other than a maintenance order lies—
(a) in England and Wales or Northern Ireland, to the Court of Appeal or to the House of Lords in accordance with Part II of the Administration of Justice Act 1969 (appeals direct from the High Court to the House of Lords);
(b) (*applies to Scotland only*).

(2) Paragraph (a) of subsection (1) has effect notwithstanding section 15(2) of the Administration of Justice Act 1969 (exclusion of direct appeal to the House of Lords in cases where no appeal to that House lies from a decision of the Court of Appeal).

(3) The single further appeal on a point of law referred to [in each of those Conventions] in Article 37, second paragraph and Article 41 in relation to the recognition or enforcement of a maintenance order lies—
(a) in England and Wales, to the High Court by way of case stated in accordance with section 111 of the Magistrates' Court Act 1980;
(b) (*applies to Scotland only*);
(c) in Northern Ireland, to the Court of Appeal.

Note. Words in square brackets in sub-ss (1), (3) inserted by Civil Jurisdiction and Judgments Act 1991, s 3, Sch 2, para 3, as from 1 May 1992.

7. Interest on registered judgments—(1) Subject to subsection (4), where in connection with an application for registration of a judgment under section 4 or 5 the applicant shows—

(a) that the judgment provides for the payment of a sum of money; and

(b) that in accordance with the law of the Contracting State in which the judgment was given interest on that sum is recoverable under the judgment from a particular date or time,

the rate of interest and the date or time from which it is so recoverable shall be registered with the judgment and, subject to any provision made under subsection (2), the debt resulting, apart from section 4(2), from the registration of the judgment shall carry interest in accordance with the registered particulars.

(2) Provision may be made by rules of court as to the manner in which and the periods by reference to which any interest payable by virtue of subsection (1) is to be calculated and paid, including provision for such interest to cease to accrue as from a prescribed date.

(3) Costs or expenses recoverable by virtue of section 4(2) shall carry interest as if they were the subject of an order for the payment of costs or expenses made by the registering court on the date of registration.

(4) Interest on arrears of sums payable under a maintenance order registered under setion 5 in a magistrates' court in England and Wales or Northern Ireland shall not be recoverable in that court, but without prejudice to the operation in relation to any such order of section 2A of the Maintenance Orders Act 1958 or section 11A of the Maintenance and Affiliation Orders Act (Northern Ireland) 1966 (which enable interest to be recovered if the order is re-registered for enforcement in the High Court).

(5) Except as mentioned in subsection (4), debts under judgments registered under section 4 or 5 shall carry interest only as provided by this section.

8. Currency of payment under registered maintenance orders—(1) Sums payable in the United Kingdom under a maintenance order by virtue of its registration under section 5, including any arrears so payable, shall be paid in the currency of the United Kingdom.

(2) Where the order is expressed in any other currency, the amounts shall be converted on the basis of the exchange rate prevailing on the date of registration of the order.

(3) For the purposes of this section, a written certificate purporting to be signed by an officer of any bank in the United Kingdom and stating the exchange rate prevailing on a specified date shall be evidence, and in Scotland sufficient evidence, of the facts stated.

Other supplementary provisions

9. Provisions supplementary to Title VII of 1968 Convention—(1) The provisions of Title VII of the 1968 Convention [and, apart from Article 54B, of Title VII of the Lugano Convention] (relationship between *that convention* [the Convention in question] and other conventions to which Contracting States are or may become parties) shall have effect in relation to—

(a) any statutory provision, whenever passed or made, implementing any such other convention in the United Kingdom; and

(b) any rule of law so far as it has the effect of so implementing any such other convention,

as they have effect in relation to that other convention itself.

[*(1A) Any question arising as to whether it is the Lugano Convention or any of the Brussels Conventions which applies in the circumstances of a particular case falls to be determined in accordance with the provisions of Article 54B of the Lugano Convention.]*

Note. Repealed by SI 2001 No 3929, art 4, Sch 2, Pt I, para 2, as from 1 March 2002.

(2) Her Majesty may by Order in Council declare a provision of a convention entered into by the United Kingdom to be a provision whereby the United Kingdom assumed an obligation of a kind provided for in Article 59 (which allows a Contracting State to agree with a third State to withhold recognition in certain cases from a judgment given by a court in another Contracting State which took jurisdiction on one of the grounds mentioned in the second paragraph of Article 3).

Note. Words in first pair of square brackets in sub-s (1) inserted and words in second pair of square brackets substituted for words in italics, and the whole of sub-s (1A) inserted, by Civil Jurisdiction and Judgments Act 1991, ss 1(2), 3, Sch 2, para 4, as from 1 May 1992.

* * * * *

11. Proof and admissibility of certain judgments and related documents—
(1) For the purposes of the 1968 Convention [and the Lugano Convention]—
   (a) a document, duly authenticated, which purports to be a copy of a judgment given by a court of a Contracting State other than the United Kingdom shall without further proof be deemed to be a true copy, unless the contrary is shown; and
   (b) the original or a copy of any such document as is mentioned in Article 46(2) or 47 (supporting documents to be produced by a party seeking recognition or enforcement of a judgment) shall be evidence, and in Scotland sufficient evidence, of any matter to which it relates.

Note. Words in square brackets inserted by Civil Jurisdiction and Judgments Act 1991, s 3, Sch 2, para 6, as from 1 May 1992.

(2) A document purporting to be a copy of a judgment given by any such court as is mentioned in subsection (1)(a) is duly authenticated for the purposes of this section if it purports—
   (a) to bear the seal of that court; or
   (b) to be certified by any person in his capacity as a judge or officer of that court to be a true copy of a judgment given by that court.
(3) Nothing in this section shall prejudice the admission in evidence of any document which is admissible apart from this section.

12. Provision for issue of copies of, and certificates in connection with, UK judgments. Rules of court may make provision for enabling any interested party wishing to secure under the 1968 Convention [or the Lugano Convention] the recognition or enforcement in another Contracting State of a judgment given by a court in the United Kingdom to obtain, subject to any conditions specified in the rules—
   (a) a copy of the judgment; and
   (b) a certificate giving particulars relating to the judgment and the proceedings in which it was given.

Note. Words in square brackets inserted by Civil Jurisdiction and Judgments Act 1991, s 3, Sch 2, para 7, as from 1 May 1992.

13. Modifications to cover authentic instruments and court settlements—(1) Her Majesty may by Order in Council provide that—
   (a) any provision of this Act relating to the recognition or enforcement in the United Kingdom or elsewhere of judgments to which the 1968 Convention [or the Lugano Convention] applies; and
   (b) any other statutory provision, whenever passed or made, so relating,
shall apply, with such modifications as may be specified in the Order, in relation to documents and settlements within Title IV of the 1968 Convention [or, as the case may be, Title IV of the Lugano Convention] (authentic instruments and court settlements enforceable in the same manner as judgments) as if they were judgments to which *that Convention* [the Convention in question] applies.

Note. Words in first and second pairs of square brackets inserted, and words in third pair of square brackets substituted for words in italics by Civil Jurisdiction and Judgments Act 1991, s 3, Sch 2, para 8, as from 1 May 1992.

(2) An Order in Council under this section may make different provision in relation to different descriptions of documents and settlements.

(3) Any Order in Council under this section shall be subject to annulment in pursuance of a resolution of either House of Parliament.

14. Modifications consequential on revision of the Conventions—(1) If at any time it appears to Her Majesty in Council that Her Majesty's Government in the United Kingdom have agreed to a revision of *any of the Conventions* [the Lugano Convention or any of the Brussels Conventions], including in particular any revision connected with the accession to [the Lugano Convention or] the 1968 Convention of one or more further states, Her Majesty may by Order in Council make such modifications of this Act or any other statutory provision, whenever passed or made, as Her Majesty considers appropriate in consequence of the revision.

(2) An Order in Council under this section shall not be made unless a draft of the Order has been laid before Parliament and approved by a resolution of each House of Parliament.

(3) In this section 'revision' means an omission from, addition to or alteration of *any of the Conventions* [the Lugano Convention or any of the Brussels Conventions] and includes replacement of *any of the Conventions* [the Lugano Convention or any of the Brussels Conventions] to any extent by another convention, protocol or other description of international agreement.

Note. Words in first pair of square brackets in sub-s (1) and words in square brackets in sub-s (3) substituted for words in italics by Civil Jurisdiction and Judgments Act 1991, s 3, Sch 2, para 9(a), as from 1 May 1992. Words in second pair of square brackets in sub-s (1) inserted by s 3 of, and Sch 2, para 9(b) to, the 1991 Act, as from 1 May 1992.

15. Interpretation of Part I and consequential amendments—(1) In this Part, unless the context otherwise requires—

'judgment' has the meaning given by Article 25;

'maintenance order' means a maintenance judgment within the meaning of the 1968 Convention [or, as the case may be, the Lugano Convention];

'payer', in relation to a maintenance order, means the person liable to make the payments for which the order provides;

'prescribed' means prescribed by rules of court.

(2) References in this Part to a judgment registered under section 4 or 5 include, to the extent of its registration, references to a judgment so registered to a limited extent only.

(3) Anything authorised or required by the 1968 Convention [the Lugano Convention] or this Part to be done by, to or before a particular magistrates' court may be done by, to or before any magistrates' court acting *for the same petty sessions area (or, in Northern Ireland* [in the same local justice area (or, in Northern Ireland, for the same], petty sessions district) as that court.

(4) The enactments specified in Part 1 of Schedule 12 shall have effect with the amendments specified there, being amendments consequential on this Part.

Note. Words in square brackets in sub-ss (1), (3) inserted by Civil Jurisdiction and Judgments Act 1991, s 3, Sch 2, para 10, as from 1 May 1992. Further amended by the Courts Act 203, ss 109, Sch 8, para 269, as from a date to be appointed.

   (b)   an order which is enforceable in the same manner as a judgment of the
High Court in England and Wales by virtue of section 16 of the Contempt
of Court Act 1981 or section 140 of the Supreme Court Act 1981 (which
relate to fines for contempt of court and forfeiture of recognisances).

  [(*4A*) *This section does not apply as respects the enforcement in Scotland of orders made by
the High Court* [*or a county court*] *in England and Wales under or for the purposes of the Drug
Trafficking Offences Act 1986* [*or Part VI of the Criminal Justice Act 1988* (*confiscation of the
proceeds of offences*)] [; *or as respects the enforcement in England and Wales of orders made by
the Court of Session under or for the purposes of Part I of the Criminal Justice* (*Scotland*) *Act
1987*].]

  [(4A) This section does not apply as respects—
   (a)   the enforcement in Scotland of orders made by the High Court or a county
court in England and Wales under or for the purposes of Part VI of the
Criminal Justice Act 1988 or the Drug Trafficking Act 1994 (confiscation of
the proceeds of certain offences or of drug trafficking); or
   (b)   the enforcement in England and Wales of orders made by the Court of Session
[or by the sheriff] or for the purposes of *Part I of the Criminal Justice* (*Scotland*)
Act 1987 (*confiscation of the proceeds of drug trafficking*) [*or Part II of the Criminal
Justice* (*Scotland*) *Act 1995*] [the Proceeds of Crime (Scotland) Act 1995].]

Note. Sub-s (4A) in italics inserted by Drug Trafficking Offences Act 1986, s 39(4), words in
first pair of square brackets in that subsection inserted by Criminal Justice Act 1988, s 170(1),
Sch 15, para 82, and words in second pair of square brackets in that subsection added by
Criminal Justice (Scotland) Act 1987, s 45(3). Sub-s (4A) in square brackets substituted for sub-s
(4A) in italics by Drug Trafficking Act 1994, s 65(1), Sch 1, para 6, as from 3 February 1995.
First and second words in square brackets inserted by Criminal Justice (Scotland) Act 1995,
s 117, Sch 6, para 183, as from 31 March 1996. Words 'the Proceeds of Crime (Scotland) Act
1995' in square brackets substituted for words 'Part I of the Criminal Justice ... 1995' in italics by
Criminal Procedure (Consequential Provisions) (Scotland) Act 1995, s 5, Sch 4, para 42, as
from 1 April 1996.

  (5) This section does not apply to so much of any judgment as—
   (a)   is an order to which section 16 of the Maintenance Orders Act 1950 applies
(and is therefore an order for whose enforcement in another part of the
United Kingdom provision is made by Part II of that Act);
   (b)   concerns the status or legal capacity of an individual;
   (c)   relates to the management of the affairs of a person not capable of managing
his own affairs;
   (d)   is a provisional (including protective) measure other than an order for the
making of an interim payment;
and except where otherwise stated references to a judgment to which this section
applies are to such a judgment exclusive of any such provisions.

  (6) The following are within subsection (5)(b), but are without prejudice to the
generality of that provision—
   (a)   *a decree* [an order or decree] of judicial separation or of separation;
   (*b*)   *any provision relating to guardianship or custody.*
  [(b) any order which is a Part I order for the purposes of the Family Law Act 1986.]

Note. Words in square brackets in sub-s (6)(a) substituted for words in italics by Family Law
Act 1996, s 66(1), Sch 8, para 31, as from a day to be appointed, subject to savings in s 66(2)
of, and para 5 of Sch 9 to, the 1996 Act. Sub-s (6)(b) in square brackets substituted for sub-s
(6)(b) in italics by Courts and Legal Services Act 1990, s 116, Sch 16, para 41, as from
14 October 1991.

  (7) This section does not apply to a judgment of a court outside the United
Kingdom which falls to be treated for the purposes of its enforcement as a
judgment of a court of law in the United Kingdom by virtue of registration under
Part II of the Administration of Justice Act 1920, Part I of the Foreign Judgments
(Reciprocal Enforcement) Act 1933, Part I of the Maintenance Orders (Reciprocal
Enforcement) Act 1972 or section 4 or 5 of this Act.

(8) A judgment to which this section applies, other than a judgment within paragraph (e) of subsection (2), shall not be enforced in another part of the United Kingdom except by way of registration under Schedule 6 or 7.

* * * * *

PART III

JURISDICTION IN SCOTLAND

20-22. (*Apply to Scotland only.*)

23. Savings and consequential amendments—(1) Nothing in Schedule 8 shall affect—

(a) the power of any court to vary or recall a maintenacnce order granted by that court;

(b) the power of a sheriff court under section 22 of the Maintenance Orders Act 1950 (discharge and variation of maintenance orders registered in sheriff courts) to vary or discharge a maintenance order registered in that court under Part II of that Act; or

(c) the power of a sheriff court under section 9 of the Maintenance Orders (Reciprocal Enforcement) Act 1972 (variation and revocation of maintenance orders registered in United Kingdom courts) to vary or revoke a registered order within the meaning of Part I of that Act.

(2) The enactments specified in Part II of Schedule 12 shall have effect with the amendments specified there, being amendments consequential on Schedule 8.

PART IV

MISCELLANEOUS PROVISIONS

Provisions relating to jurisdiction

24. Interim relief and protective measures in cases of doubtful jurisdiction—(1) Any power of a court in England and Wales or Northern Ireland to grant interim relief pending trial or pending the determination of an appeal shall extend to a case where—

(a) the issue to be tried, or which is the subject of the appeal, relates to the jurisdiction of the court to entertain the proceedings; or

(b) the proceedings involve the reference of any matter to the European Court under the 1971 Protocol [; or

[(c) the proceedings involve a reference of any matter relating to the Regulation to the European Court under Article 68 of the Treaty establishing the European Community].

(2) (*Applies to Scotland only.*)

(3) Subsections (1) and (2) shall not be construed as restricting any power to grant interim relief or protective measures which a court may have apart from this section.

Note. Amended by SI 2003 no 3929, art 4, Sch 2, Pt II, as from 1 March 2002.

25. Interim relief in England and Wales and Northern Ireland in the absence of substantive proceedings—(1) The High Court in England and Wales or Northern Ireland shall have power to grant interim relief where—

(a) proceedings have been or are to be commenced in a *Contracting State* [Brussels or Lugano Contracting State] [or a Regulation State] other than the United Kingdom or in a part of the United Kingdom other than that in which the High Court in question exercises jurisdiction; and

(b) *they are or will be proceedings whose subject-matter is within the scope of the 1968 Convention as determined by Article 1 (whether or not the Convention [that or any other Convention] has effect in relation to the proceedings).*

[(b) they are or will be proceedings whose subject-matter is within the scope of the Regulation as determined by Article 1 of the Regulation (whether or not the Regulation has effect in relation to the proceedings)].

(2) On an application for any interim relief under subsection (1) the court may refuse to grant that relief if, in the opinion of the court, the fact that the court has no jurisdiction apart from this section in relation to the subject-matter of the proceedings in question makes it inexpedient for the court to grant it.

(3) Her Majesty may by Order in Council extend the power to grant interim relief conferred by subsection (1) so as to make it exercisable in relation to proceedings of any of the following descriptions, namely—

(a) proceedings commenced or to be commenced otherwise than in a *Contracting State* [Brussels or Lugano Contracting State [or Regulation State]];

(b) *proceedings whose subject-matter is not within the scope of the 1968 Convention as determined by Article 1;*

[(b) proceedings whose subject-matter is not within the scope of the Regulation as determined by Article 1 of the Regulation;]

(c) *arbitration proceedings.*

(4) An Order in Council under subsection (3)—

(a) may confer power to grant only specified descriptions of interim relief;

(b) may make different provision for different classes of proceedings, for proceedings pending in different countries or courts outside the United Kingdom or in different parts of the United Kingdom, and for other different circumstances; and

(c) may impose conditions or restrictions on the exercise of any power conferred by the Order.

(5) *An Order in Council under subsection (3) which confers power to grant interim relief in relation to arbitration proceedings may provide for the repeal of any provision of section 12(6) of the Arbitration Act 1950 or section 21(1) of the Arbitration Act (Northern Ireland) 1937 to the extent that it is superseded by the provisions of the Order.*

(6) Any Order in Council under subsection (3) shall be subject to annulment in pursuance of a resolution of either House of Parliament.

(7) In this section 'interim relief', in relation to the High Court in England and Wales or Northern Ireland, means interim relief of any kind which that court has power to grant in proceedings relating to matters within its jurisdiction, other than—

(a) a warrant for the arrest of property; or

(b) provision for obtaining evidence.

Note. Words in square brackets in sub-ss (1), (3) substituted for words in italics by Civil Jurisdiction and Judgments Act 1991, s 3, Sch 2, para 12, as from 1 May 1992. Sub-ss (3)(c), (5) repealed by Arbitration Act 1996, s 107(2), Sch 4, as from 31 January 1997.

Further amended by SI 2001 No 3929, art 4, Sch 2, Pt IV, as from 1 March 2002.

*   *   *   *   *

27. Provisional and protective measures in Scotland in the absence of substantive proceedings—(1) The Court of Session may, in any case to which this subsection applies—

(a) subject to subsection (2)(c), grant a warrant for the arrestment of any assets situated in Scotland;

(b) subject to subsection (2)(c), grant a warrant of inhibition over any property situated in Scotland; and

(c) grant interim interdict.

(2) Subsection (1) applies to any case in which—

(a) proceedings have been commenced but not concluded, or, in relation to paragraph (c) of that subsection, are to be commenced, in another *Contracting State* [Brussels or Lugano Contracting State] [, in another Regulation State] or in England and Wales or Northern Ireland;

(b) *the subject-matter of the proceedings is within the scope of the 1968 Convention as determined by Article 1; and*

[(b) the subject-matter of the proceedings is within the scope of the Regulation as determined by Article 1 of the Regulation; and]

(c) in relation to paragraphs (a) and (b) of subsection (1), such a warrant could competently have been granted in equivalent proceedings before a Scottish court;

but it shall not be necessary, in determining whether proceedings have been commenced for the purpose of paragraph (a) of this subsection, to show that any document has been served on or notice given to the defender.

(3) Her Majesty may by Order in Council confer on the Court of Session power to do anything mentioned in subsection (1) or in section 28 in relation to proceedings of any of the following descriptions, namely—

(a) proceedings commenced otherwise than in a *Contracting State* [Brussels or Lugano Contracting State] [or Regulation State];

(b) *proceedings whose subject-matter is not within the scope of the 1968 Convention as determined by Article 1;*

[(b) proceedings whose subject-matter is not within the scope of the Regulation as determined by Article 1 of the Regulation;]

(c) arbitration proceedings;

(d) in relation to subsection (1)(c) or section 28, proceedings which are to be commenced otherwise than in a *Contracting State* [Brussels or Lugano Contracting State] [or Regulation State].

(4) An Order in Council under subsection (3)—

(a) may confer power to do only certain of the things mentioned in subsection (1) or in section 28;

(b) may make different provision for different classes of proceedings, for proceedings pending in different countries or courts outside the United Kingdom or in different parts of the United Kingdom, and for other different circumstances; and

(c) may impose conditions or restrictions on the exercise of any power conferred by the Order.

(5) Any Order in Council under subsection (3) shall be subject to annulment in pursuance of a resolution of either House of Parliament.

Note. Words in square brackets in sub-ss (2)(a), (3)(a), (d) substituted for words in italics by Civil Jurisdiction and Judgments Act 1991, s 3, Sch 2, para 12, as from 1 May 1992.
  Further amended by SI 2002 No 3929, art 4, Sch 2, Pt IV, as from 1 March 2002.

28. Application of s 1 of Administration of Justice (Scotland) Act 1972. When any proceedings have been brought, or are likely to be brought, in another *Contracting State* [Brussels or Lugano Contracting State] [, in a Regulation State] or in England and Wales or Northern Ireland in respect of any matter which is within the scope of the *1968 Convention* [Regulation] as determined in Article 1, the Court of Session shall have the like power to make an order under section 1 of the Administration of Justice (Scotland) Act 1972 [as amended by the Law Reform (Miscellaneous Provisions) (Scotland) Act 1985] as if the proceedings in question had been brought, or were likely to be brought, in that court.

Note. Words 'Brussels or Lugano Contracting State' in square brackets substituted for words in italics by Civil Jurisdiction and Judgments Act 1991, s 3, Sch 2, para 12, as from 1 May 1992. Words 'as amended … Act 1985' in square brackets inserted by Law Reform (Miscellaneous Provisions) (Scotland) Act 1985, s 59(1), Sch 2, para 24. Further amended by SI 2001 No 3929, art 4, Sch 2, Pt IV, as from 1 March 2002.

29. (*Amends County Courts (Northern Ireland) Order 1980, SI 1980 No 397.*)

30. Proceedings in England and Wales or Northern Ireland for torts to immovable property—(1) The jurisdiction of any court in England and Wales or

Northern Ireland to entertain proceedings for trespass to, or any other tort affecting, immovable property shall extend to cases in which the property in question is situated outside that part of the United Kingdom unless the proceedings are principally concerned with a question of the title to, or the right to possession of, that property.

(2) Subsection (1) has effect subject to the 1968 Convention [and the Lugano Convention] [and the Regulation] and to the provisions set out in Schedule 4.

Note. Words in square brackets inserted by Civil Jurisdiction and Judgments Act 1991, s 3, Sch 2, para 13, as from 1 May 1992. Further amended by SI 2001 No 3929, art 4, Sch 2, Pt IV, as from 1 March 2002.

Provisions relating to recognition and enforcement of judgments

*   *   *   *   *

32. Overseas judgments given in proceedings brought in breach of agreement for settlement of disputes—(1) Subject to the following provisions of this section, a judgment given by a court of an overseas country in any proceedings shall not be recognised or enforced in the United Kingdom if—

   (a) the bringing of those proceedings in that court was contrary to an agreement under which the dispute in question was to be settled otherwise than by proceedings in the courts of that country; and
   (b) those proceedings were not brought in that court by, or with the agreement of, the person against whom the judgment was given; and
   (c) that person did not counterclaim in the proceedings or otherwise submit to the jurisdiction of that court.

(2) Subsection (1) does not apply where the agreement referred to in paragraph (a) of that subsection was illegal, void or unenforceable or was incapable of being performed for reasons not attributable to the fault of the party bringing the proceedings in which the judgment was given.

(3) In determining whether a judgment given by a court of an overseas country should be recognised or enforced in the United Kingdom, a court in the United Kingdom shall not be bound by any decision of the overseas court relating to any of the matters mentioned in subsection (1) or (2).

(4) Nothing in subsection (1) shall affect the recognition or enforcement in the United Kingdom of—

   (a) a judgment which is required to be recognised or enforced there under the 1968 Convention [or the Lugano Convention] [or the Regulation];
   (b) a judgment to which Part I of the Foreign Judgments (Reciprocal Enforcement) Act 1933 applies by virtue of section 4 of the Carriage of Goods by Road Act 1965, section 17(4) of the Nuclear Installations Act 1965, *section 13(3) of the Merchant Shipping (Oil Pollution) Act 1971, section 5 of the Carriage by Railway Act 1972* [section 6 of the International Transport Conventions Act 1983], *section 5 of the Carriage of Passengers by Road Act 1974 or section 6(4) of the Merchant Shipping Act 1974* [section 177(4) of the Merchant Shipping Act 1995].

Note. Words in square brackets in sub-s (4)(a) inserted by Civil Jurisdiction and Judgments Act 1991, s 3, Sch 2, para 14, as from 1 May 1992. Words 'section 13(3) of the Merchant Shipping (Oil Pollution) Act 1971' in italics repealed, and words 'section 177(4) of the Merchant Shipping Act 1995' in square brackets substituted for words 'section 6(4) of the Merchant Shipping Act 1974' in italics by Merchant Shipping Act 1995, s 314, Sch 12, Sch 13, para 66(b), as from 1 January 1996. Words 'section 6 of the International Transport Conventions Act 1983' in square brackets substituted for words 'section 5 of the Carriage by Railway Act 1972' in italics by International Transport Conventions Act 1983, s 11(2), as from 1 May 1985. Amended by SI 2001 No 3929, art 4 Sch 2, Pt IV, as from 1 March 2002. Repealed in part by the Statue Law Repeals Act 2004.

33. Certain steps not to amount to submission to jurisdiction of overseas court—(1) For the purposes of determining whether a judgment given by a court of an overseas country should be recognised or enforced in England and Wales or Northern Ireland, the person against whom the judgment was given shall not be regarded as having submitted to the jurisdiction of the court by reason only of the fact that he appeared (conditionally or otherwise) in the proceedings for all or any one or more of the following purposes, namely—

(a) to contest the jurisdiction of the court;

(b) to ask the court to dismiss or stay the proceedings on the ground that the dispute in question should be submitted to arbitration or to the determination of the courts of another country;

(c) to protect, or obtain the release of, property seized or threatened with seizure in the proceedings.

(2) Nothing in this section shall affect the recognition or enforcement in England and Wales or Northern Ireland of a judgment which is required to be recognised or enforced there under the 1968 Convention [or the Lugano Convention] [or the Regulation].

Note. Words in square brackets inserted by Civil Jurisdiction and Judgments Act 1991, s 3, Sch 2, para 15, as from 1 May 1992. Further amended by SI 2001/3929, art 4, Sch 2, Pt IV, as from 1 March 2002.

34. Certain judgments a bar to further proceedings on the same cause of action. No proceedings may be brought by a person in England and Wales or Northern Ireland on a cause of action in respect of which a judgment has been given in his favour in proceedings between the same parties, or their privies, in a court in another part of the United Kingdom or in a court of an overseas country, unless that judgment is not enforceable or entitled to recognition in England and Wales or, as the case may be, in Northern Ireland.

35. Minor amendments relating to overseas judgments—(1) The Foreign Judgments (Reciprocal Enforcement) Act 1933 shall have effect with the amendments specified in Schedule 10, being amendments whose main purpose is to enable Part I of that Act to be applied to judgments of courts other than superior courts, to judgments providing for interim payments and to certain arbitration awards.

(2), (3) *(Sub-s (2) substitutes Administration of Justice Act 1920, s 10 (p 2048), and sub-s (3) adds s 14(3) of that Act (p 2049)).*

36. Registration of maintenance orders in Northern Ireland—(1) Where—

(a) a High Court order or a Court of Session order has been registered in the High Court of Justice in Northern Ireland ('the Northern Ireland High Court') under Part II of the Maintenance Orders Act 1950; or

(b) a county court order, a magistrates' court order or a sheriff court order has been registered in a court of summary jurisdiction in Northern Ireland under that Part,

an application may be made to the original court for the registration of the order in, respectively, a court of summary jurisdiction in Northern Ireland or the Northern Ireland High Court.

(2) In subsection (1) 'the original court', in relation to an order, means the court by which the order was made.

(3) Section 2 (except subsection (6A)) and section 2A of the Maintenance Orders Act 1958 shall have effect for the purposes of an application under subsection (1), and subsections (2), (3), (4) and (4A) of section 5 of that Act shall have effect for the purposes of the cancellation of a registration made on such an application, as if—

(a) 'registration' in those provisions included registration in the appropriate Northern Ireland court ('registered' being construed accordingly);

(b) any reference in those provisions to a High Court order or a magistrates' court order included, respectively, a Court of Session order or a sheriff court order; and

(c) any other reference in those provisions to the High Court or a magistrates' court included the Northern Ireland High Court or a court of summary jurisdiction in Northern Ireland;

[(d) for section 2(6), there were substituted the following subsections—

'(6) Where a magistrates' court order is registered under this Part of this Act in the High Court, then—

(a) if payments under the magistrates' court order are required to be made (otherwise than to a collecting officer) by any method of payment falling within Article 85(7) of the Magistrates' Courts (Northern Ireland) Order 1981 (standing order, etc), any order requiring payment by that method shall continue to have effect after registration;

(b) any order by virtue of which sums payable under the magistrates' court order are required to be paid to the collecting officer (whether or not by any method of payment falling within Article 85(7) of that Order) on behalf of the person entitled thereto shall cease to have effect.

(6ZA) Where a High Court or county court order is registered under this Part of this Act in a magistrates' court, then—

(a) if a means of payment order (within the meaning of Article 96A(7) of the Judgments Enforcement (Northern Ireland) Order 1981) has effect in relation to the order in question, it shall continue to have effect after registration; and

(b) in any other case, the magistrates' court shall order that all payments to be made under the order in question (including any arrears accrued before registration) shall be made to the collecting officer.

(6ZB) Any such order as to payment—

(a) as is referred to in paragraph (a) of subsection (6) of this section may be revoked, suspended, revived or varied by an exercise of the powers conferred by section 13A of the Maintenance and Affiliation Orders Act (Northern Ireland) 1966; and

(b) as is referred to in paragraph (a) or (b) of subsection (6ZA) of this section may be varied or revoked by an exercise of the powers conferred by section 12(2) or 13(2A) or (5A) of that Act of 1966.

(6ZC) Where by virtue of the provisions of this section or any order under subsection (6ZA)(b) of this section payments under an order cease to be or become payable to the collecting officer, the person liable to make the payments shall, until he is given the prescribed notice to that effect, be deemed to comply with the order if he makes payments in accordance with the order and any order under subsection (6ZA)(b) of this section of which he has received such notice.

(6ZD) In subsections (6), (6ZA) and (6ZC) of this section "collecting officer" means the officer mentioned in Article 85(4) of the Magistrates' Courts (Northern Ireland) Order 1981.'.]

Note. Sub-s (3)(d) inserted by Family Law (Northern Ireland) Order 1993, SI 1993 No 1576, art 11, Sch 1, para 17(a), as from 4 November 1996.

(4) Where an order is registered in Northern Ireland under this section, Part II of the Maintenance and Affiliation Orders Act (Northern Ireland) 1966, except sections 11, 11A and 14(2) and (3), shall apply as if the order had been registered in accordance with provisions of that Part [, as if—

(a) in section 12(2), for modifications of Article 98(8B) to (8D) of the Magistrates' Courts (Northern Ireland) Order 1981 specified in that subsection there were substituted the modifications specified in section 18(3ZA) of the Maintenance Orders Act 1950 (enforcement of registered orders); and

(b) for section 13(5A), there were substituted the following subsection—

'(5A) Subject to the following provisions of this section, paragraphs (4) to (11) of Article 86 of the Magistrates' Courts (Northern Ireland) Order 1981 (power of clerk and court to vary maintenance orders) shall apply in relation to a registered order as they apply in relation to a maintenance order made by a court of summary jurisdiction (disregarding Article 25(2) of the Domestic Proceedings (Northern Ireland) Order 1980) but—

(a) as if for paragraph (4)(b) there were substituted—

"(b) payments under the order are required to be made to the collecting officer, by any method of payment falling within Article 85(7) (standing order, etc)",

and as if after the words "petty sessions" there were inserted "for the petty sessions district for which the court which made the order acts";

(b) as if in paragraph (5) for the words "to the collecting officer" there were substituted "in accordance with sub-paragraph (a) of paragraph (9)",

(c) as if in paragraph (7), sub-paragraph (c) and the word "and" immediately preceding it were omitted;

(d) as if in paragraph (8) for the words "sub-paragraphs (a) to (d) of Article 85(3)" there were substituted "paragraph (9)";

(e) as if for paragraphs (9) and (10) there were substituted the following paragraphs—

"(9) The powers of the court are—

(a) the power to order that payments under the order be made directly to the collecting officer;

(b) the power to order that payments under the order be made to the collecting officer, by such method of payment falling within Article 85(7) (standing order, etc) as may be specified;

(c) the power to make an attachment of earnings order under Part IX to secure payments under the order.

(10) In deciding which of the powers under paragraph (9) above it is to exercise, the court shall have regard to any representations made by the debtor.

(10A) Paragraph (5) of Article 85 (power of court to require debtor to open account) shall apply for the purposes of paragraph (9) as it applies for the purposes of that Article but as if for sub-paragraph (a) there were substituted—

'(a) the court proposes to exercise its power under sub-paragraph (b) of Article 86(9)'.".'.]

Note. Words in square brackets added by Family Law (Northern Ireland) Order 1993, SI 1993 No 1576, art 11, Sch 1, para 17(b), as from 4 November 1996.

(5) A court of summary jurisdiction in Northern Ireland shall have jurisdiction to hear *a complaint* [an application] by or against a person residing outside Northern Ireland for the discharge or variation of an order registered in Northern Ireland under this section; and where such *a complaint* [an application] is made against a person residing outside Northern Ireland, then, if he resides in England and Wales or Scotland, section 15 of the Maintenance Orders Act 1950 (which relates to the service of process on persons residing in those countries) shall have effect in relation to *the complaint* [the application] as it has effect in relation to the proceedings therein mentioned.

Note. Words in square brackets substituted for words in italics by Children (Northern Ireland) Order 1995, SI 1995 No 755, art 185(1), Sch 9, para 117, as from 4 November 1996.

[(5A) Article 165 of the Children (Northern Ireland) Order 1995 (provision which may be made by magistrates' courts rules, etc) shall apply for the purpose of giving effect to subsection (5) above as it applies for the purpose of giving effect to that Order, except that in the application of that Article by virtue of this subsection 'relevant proceedings' means any application made, or proceedings brought, by virtue of that subsection and any part of such proceedings.]

Note. Sub-s (5A) inserted by Children (Northern Ireland) Order 1995, SI 1995 No 755, art 185(1), Sch 9, para 117, as from 4 November 1996.

(6) The enactments specified in Part III of Schedule 12 shall have effect with the amendments specified there, being amendments consequential on this section.

37. Minor amendments relating to maintenance orders—(1) The enactments specified in Schedule 11 shall have effect with the amendments specified there, being amendments whose main purpose is as follows—

    Part I—to extend certain enforcement provisions to lump sum maintenance orders;

    Part II—to provide for the recovery of interest according to the law of the country of origin in the case of maintenance orders made in other jurisdictions and registered in the High Court;

    Part III—to extend the Maintenance Orders (Reciprocal Enforcement) Act 1972 to cases where the payer under a maintenance order is not resident within the jurisdiction but has assets there.

(2) In section 27(1) of the Maintenance Orders (Reciprocal Enforcement) Act 1972 (application by person in convention country for recovery of maintenance in England and Wales or Northern Ireland to be treated as a complaint), after 'as if it were a complaint' there shall be inserted 'made at the time when the application was received by the Secretary of State or the Lord Chancellor'.

Note. Sub-s (2) repealed by Maintenance Orders (Reciprocal Enforcement) Act 1992, s 2(2), Sch 3, as from 5 April 1993.

    *   *   *   *   *

Jurisdiction, and recognition and enforcement of judgments, as between United Kingdom and certain territories

39. Application of provisions corresponding to 1968 Convention in relation to certain territories—(1) Her Majesty may by Order in Council make provision corresponding to the provision made by the 1968 Convention as between the Contracting States to that Convention, with such modifications as appear to Her Majesty to be appropriate, for regulating, as between the United Kingdom and any of the territories mentioned in subsection (2), the jurisdiction of courts and the recognition and enforcement of judgments.

(2) The territories referred to in subsection (1) are—

    (a) the Isle of Man;

    (b) any of the Channel Islands;

    (*c*) *Gibraltar;*

    (*d*) *the Sovereign Base Areas of Akrotiri and Dhekelia (that is to say the areas mentioned in section 2(1) of the Cyprus Act 1960).*

  [(c) any colony]

(3) An Order in Council under this section may contain such supplementary and incidental provisions as appear to Her Majesty to be necessary or expedient, including in particular provisions corresponding to or applying any of the provisions of Part I with such modifications as may be specified in the Order.

(4) Any Order in Council under this section shall be subject to annulment in pursuance of a resolution of either House of Parliament.

Note. Sub-s (2)(c) in square brackets substituted for sub-s (2)(c), (d) in italics by Civil Jurisdiction and Judgments Act 1982 (Amendment) Order 1990, SI 1990 No 2591, art 10, as from 1 December 1991.

40.   (*Sub-s (1) repealed by Legal Aid Act 1988, s 45(2), Sch 6; sub-s (2) repealed by Legal Aid (Scotland) Act 1986, s 45(3), Sch 5; sub-s (3) inserts para (4A) in Legal Aid, Advice and Assistance (Northern Ireland) Order 1981, SI 1981 No 228, art 22. Sub-s (3) repealed by SI 2003 No 435, art 49, Sch 5, as from a date to be appointed.*)

PART V

SUPPLEMENTARY AND GENERAL PROVISIONS

Domicile

41. Domicile of individuals—(1) Subject to Article 52 (which contains provisions for determining whether a party is domiciled in a Contracting State), the following provisions of this section determine, for the purposes of the 1968 Convention [the Lugano Convention] and this Act, whether an individual is domiciled in the United Kingdom or in a particular part of, or place in, the United Kingdom or in a state other than a Contracting State.

(2) An individual is domiciled in the United Kingdom if and only if—
(a) he is resident in the United Kingdom; and
(b) the nature and circumstances of his residence indicate that he has a substantial connection with the United Kingdom.

(3) Subject to subsection (5), an individual is domiciled in a particular part of the United Kingdom if and only if—
(a) he is resident in that part; and
(b) the nature and circumstances of his residence indicate that he has a substantial connection with that part.

(4) An individual is domiciled in a particular place in the United Kingdom if and only if he—
(a) is domiciled in the part of the United Kingdom in which that place is situated; and
(b) is resident in that place.

(5) An individual who is domiciled in the United Kingdom but in whose case the requirements of subsection (3)(b) are not satisfied in relation to any particular part of the United Kingdom shall be treated as domiciled in the part of the United Kingdom in which he is resident.

(6) In the case of an individual who—
(a) is resident in the United Kingdom, or in a particular part of the United Kingdom; and
(b) has been so resident for the last three months or more,
the requirements of subsection (2)(b) or, as the case may be, subsection (3)(b) shall be presumed to be fulfilled unless the contrary is proved.

(7) An individual is domiciled in a state other than a Contracting State if and only if—
(a) he is resident in that state; and
(b) the nature and circumstances of his residence indicate that he has a substantial connection with that state.

Note. Words in square brackets in sub-s (1) inserted by Civil Jurisdiction and Judgments Act 1991, s 3, Sch 2, para 16, as from 1 May 1992.

*   *   *   *   *

Other supplementary provisions

47. Modifications occasioned by decisions of European Court as to meaning or effect of Conventions—(1) Her Majesty may by Order in Council—
(a) make such provision as Her Majesty considers appropriate for the purpose of bringing the law of any part of the United Kingdom into accord with the *Conventions* [Brussels Conventions] as affected by any principle laid down by

the European Court in connection with the *Conventions* [Brussels Conventions] or by any decision of that court as to the meaning or effect of any provision of the *Conventions* [Brussels Conventions]; or

(b) make such modifications of Schedule 4 or Schedule 8, or of any other statutory provision affected by any provision of either of those Schedules, as Her Majesty considers appropriate in view of any principle laid down by the European Court in connection with Title II of the 1968 Convention or of any decision of that court as to the meaning or effect of any provision of that Title.

(2) The provision which may be made by virtue of paragraph (a) of subsection (1) includes such modifications of this Act or any other statutory provision, whenever passed or made, as Her Majesty considers appropriate for the purpose mentioned in that paragraph.

(3) The modifications which may be made by virtue of paragraph (b) of subsection (1) include modifications designed to produce divergence between any provision of Schedule 4 or Schedule 8 and a corresponding provision of Title II of the 1968 Convention as affected by any such principle or decision as is mentioned in that paragraph.

(4) An Order in Council under this section shall not be made unless a draft of the Order has been laid before Parliament and approved by a resolution of each House of Parliament.

Note. Words in square brackets in sub-s (1)(a) substituted for words in italics by Civil Jurisdiction and Judgments Act 1991, s 3, Sch 2, para 22, as from 1 May 1992.

48. Matters for which rules of court may provide—(1) Rules of court may make for regulating the procedure to be followed in any court in connection with any provision of this Act *or the Conventions* [the Lugano Convention or the Brussels Conventions] [or the Regulation].

(2) Rules of court may make provision as to the manner in which and the conditions subject to which a certificate or judgment registered in any court under any provision of this Act [or the Regulation] may be enforced, including provision for enabling the court or, in Northern Ireland the Enforcement of Judgments Office, subject to any conditions specified in the rules, to give directions about such matters.

(3) Without prejudice to the generality of subsections (1) and (2), the power to make rules of court for magistrates' courts, and in Northern Ireland the power to make Judgment Enforcement Rules, shall include power to make such provision as the rule-making authority considers necessary or expedient for the purposes of the provisions of *the Conventions* [the Lugano Convention, the Brussels Conventions] [, the Regulation] and this Act relating to maintenance proceedings and the recognition and enforcement of maintenance orders, and shall in particular include power to make provision as to any of the following matters—

(a) authorising the service in another Contracting State [or Regulation State] of process issued by or for the purposes of a magistrates' court and the service and execution in England and Wales or Northern Ireland of process issued in another Contracting State [or Regulation State];

(b) requesting courts in other parts of the United Kingdom or in other Contracting States [or Regulation States] to take evidence there for the purposes of proceedings in England and Wales or Northern Ireland;

(c) the taking of evidence in England and Wales or Northern Ireland in response to similar requests received from such courts;

(d) the circumstances in which and the conditions subject to which any powers conferred under paragraphs (a) to (c) are to be exercised;

(e) the admission in evidence, subject to such conditions as may be prescribed in the rules, of statements contained in documents purporting to be made or authenticated by a court in another part of the United Kingdom or in another

Contracting State [or Regulation States], or by a judge or official of such court, which purport—

   (i) to set out or summarise evidence given in proceedings in that court or to be documents received in evidence in such proceedings or copies of such documents; or

   (ii) to set out or summarise evidence taken for the purposes of proceedings in England and Wales or Northern Ireland, whether or not in response to any such request as is mentioned in paragraph (b); or

   (iii) to record information relating to the payments made under an order of that court;

  (f) the circumstances and manner in which a magistrates' court may or must vary or revoke a maintenance order registered in that court, cancel the registration of, or refrain from enforcing, such an order or transmit such an order for enforcement in another part of the United Kingdom;

  (g) the cases and manner in which courts in other parts of the United Kingdom or in other Contracting States [or Regulation States] are to be informed of orders made, or other things done, by or for the purposes of a magistrates' court;

  (h) the circumstances and manner in which a magistrates' court may communicate for other purposes with such courts;

  (i) the giving of notice of such matters as may be prescribed in the rules to such persons as may be so prescribed and the manner in which such notice is to be given.

(4) Nothing in this section shall be taken as derogating from the generality of any power to make rules of court conferred by any other enactment.

Note. Words in square brackets in sub-ss (1), (3) substituted for words in italics by Civil Jurisdiction and Judgments Act 1991, s 3, Sch 2, para 23, as from 1 May 1992. Further amended by SI 2001 No 3929, art 4, Sch 2, Pt V, as from 2 March 2002.

49. Saving for powers to stay, sist, strike out or dismiss proceedings. Nothing in this Act shall prevent any court in the United Kingdom from staying, sisting, striking out or dismissing any proceedings before it, on the ground of *forum non conveniens* or otherwise, where to do so is not inconsistent with the 1968 Convention [or, as the case may be, the Lugano Convention].

Note. Words in square brackets inserted by Civil Jurisdiction and Judgments Act 1991, s 3, Sch 2, para 24, as from 1 May 1992.

General

50. Interpretation: general. In this Act, unless the context otherwise requires—

'the Accession Convention' has the meaning given by section 1(1);

['the Accession Convention', *'the 1982 Accession Convention' and 'the 1989 Accession Convention'* ['the 1982 Accession Convention', the 1989 Accession Convention' and 'the 1996 Accession Convention'] have the meaning given by section 1(1);]

'Article' and references to sub-divisions of numbered Articles are to be construed in accordance with section 1(2)(b);

'association' means an unincorporated body of persons;

['Brussels Contracting State' has the meaning given by section 1(3);

'the Brussels Conventions' has the meaning given by section 1(1);]

'Contracting State' has the meaning given by section 1(3);

'the 1968 Convention' has the meaning given by section 1(1), and references to that Convention and to provisions of it are to be construed in accordance with section 1(2)(a);

'the Conventions' has the meaning given by section 1(1);

'corporation' means a body corporate, and includes a partnership subsisting under the law of Scotland;

'court', without more, includes a tribunal;

'court of law', in relation to the United Kingdom, means any of the following courts, namely—

(a) the House of Lords,

(b) in England and Wales or Northern Ireland, the Court of Appeal, the High Court, the Crown Court, a county court and a magistrates' court,

(c) in Scotland the Court of Session and a sheriff court;

'the Crown' is to be construed in accordance with section 51(2);

'enactment' includes an enactment comprised in Northern Ireland legislation;

'judgment', subject to sections 15(1) and 18(2) and to paragraph 1 of Schedules 6 and 7, means any judgment or order (by whatever name called) given or made by a court in any civil proceedings;

['Lugano Contracting State' has the meaning given by section 1(3);

'the Lugano Convention' has the meaning given by section 1(1);]

'magistates' court', in relation to Northern Ireland, means a court of summary jurisdiction;

'modifications' includes additions, omissions and alterations;

'overseas country' means any country or territory outside the United Kingdom;

'part of the United Kingdom' means England and Wales, Scotland or Northern Ireland;

'the 1971 Protocol' has the meaning given by section 1(1), and references to that Protocol and to provisions of it are to be construed in accordance with section 1(2)(a);

['the Regulation' has the meaning given by section 1(1);]

['Regulation State' has the meaning given by section 1(3);]

'rules of court', in relation to any court, means rules, orders or regulations made by the authority having power to make rules, orders or regulations regulating the procedure of that court, and includes—

(a) in Scotland, Acts of Sederunt;

(b) in Northern Ireland, Judgment Enforcement Rules;

'statutory provision' means any provision contained in an Act, or in any Northern Ireland legislation, or in—

(a) subordinate legislation (as defined in section 21(1) of the Interpretation Act 1978); or

(b) any instrument of a legislative character made under any Northern Ireland legislation;

'tribunal'—

(a) means a tribunal of any description other than a court of law;

(b) in relation to an overseas country, includes as regards matters relating to maintenance within the meaning of the 1968 Convention, any authority having power to give, enforce, vary or revoke a maintenance order.

Note. Entry relating to 'the Accession Convention' in square brackets substituted for words in italics by Civil Jurisdiction and Judgments Act 1982 (Amendment) Order 1990, SI 1990 No 2591, art 9, as from 1 December 1991. Entry relating to 'the Conventions' repealed and other entries in square brackets inserted by Civil Jurisdiction and Judgments Act 1991, s 3, Sch 2, para 25, as from 1 May 1992.

Further amended by SI 2000 No 1824; SI 2001 No 3929, art 4 Sch 2, Pt V, as from 1 March 2002.

51. Application to Crown—(1) This Act binds the Crown.

(2) In this section and elsewhere in this Act references to the Crown do not include references to Her Majesty in Her private capacity or to Her Majesty in right of Her Duchy of Lancaster or to the Duke of Cornwall.

52. Extent—(1) This Act extends to Northern Ireland.

(2) Without prejudice to the power conferred by section 39, Her Majesty may by Order in Council direct that all or any of the provisions of this Act apart from that

section shall extend, subject to such modifications as may be specified in the Order, to any of the following territories, that is to say—

    (a) the Isle of Man;

    (b) any of the Channel Islands;

    (*c*) *Gibraltar,*

    (*d*) *the Sovereign Base Areas of Akrotiri and Dhekelia (that is to say the areas mentioned in section 2(1) of the Cyprus Act 1960).*

  [(c) any colony.]

Note. Sub-s (2)(c) in square brackets substituted for sub-s (2)(c), (d) in italics by Civil Jurisdiction and Judgments Act 1982 (Amendment) Order 1990, SI 1990 No 2591, art 11, as from 1 December 1991.

53. Commencement, transitional provisions and savings—(1) This Act shall come into force in accordance with the provisions of Part I of Schedule 13.

(2) The transitional provisions and savings contained in Part II of that Schedule shall have effect in relation to the commencement of the provisions of this Act mentioned in that Part.

Commencement. The provisions of this Act, so far as not already in force, were brought into force on 1 January 1987 by virtue of SI 1986 No 2044.

54. Repeals. The enactments mentioned in Schedule 14 are hereby repealed to the extent specified in the third column of that Schedule.

55. Short title. This Act may be cited as the Civil Jurisdiction and Judgments Act 1982.

SCHEDULES

SCHEDULE 1   *Section 2(2).*

TEXT OF *1968* CONVENTION, AS AMENDED

ARRANGEMENT OF PROVISIONS

TITLE	*I.*	SCOPE (*Article 1*)
TITLE	*II.*	JURISDICTION
Section	1.	*General provisions (Articles 2–4)*
Section	2.	*Special jurisdiction (Articles 5–6A)*
Section	3.	*Jurisdiction in matters relating to insurance (Articles 7–12A)*
Section	4.	*Jurisdiction over consumer contracts (Articles 13–15)*
Section	5.	*Exclusive jurisdiction (Article 16)*
Section	6.	*Prorogation of jurisdiction (Articles 17–18)*
Section	7.	*Examination as to jurisdiction and admissibility (Articles 19–20)*
Section	8.	*Lis pendens—Related actions (Articles 21–23)*
Section	9.	*Provisional, including protective, measures (Article 24)*
TITLE	*III.*	RECOGNITION AND ENFORCEMENT

Definition of 'judgment' (Article 25)

Section	1.	*Recognition (Articles 26–30)*
Section	2.	*Enforcement (Articles 31–45)*
Section	3.	*Common provisions (Articles 46–49)*
TITLE	*IV.*	AUTHENTIC INSTRUMENTS AND COURT SETTLEMENTS (*Articles 50–51*)
TITLE	*V.*	GENERAL PROVISIONS (*Articles 52–53*)
TITLE	*VI.*	TRANSITIONAL PROVISIONS (*Article 54*)
TITLE	*VII.*	RELATIONSHIP TO OTHER CONVENTIONS (*Articles 55–59*)
TITLE	*VIII.*	FINAL PROVISIONS (*Articles 60–68*)

Note. As to the substitution of this Schedule, see the note to Art 1 (p 2912).

CONVENTION ON JURISDICTION AND THE ENFORCEMENT OF JUDGMENTS IN CIVIL AND COMMERCIAL MATTERS

Preamble

The High Contracting Parties to the Treaty establishing the European Economic Community.

Desiring to implement the provisions of Article 220 of that Treaty by virtue of which they undertook to secure the simplification of formalities governing the reciprocal recognition and enforcement of judgments of courts or tribunals;

Anxious to strengthen in the Community the legal protection of persons therein established;

Considering that it is necessary for this purpose to determine the international jurisdiction of their courts, to facilitate recognition and to introduce an expeditious procedure for securing the enforcement of judgments, authentic instruments and court settlements;

Have decided to conclude this Convention and to this end have designated as their Plenipotentiaries:

(Designations of Plenipotentiaries of the original six Contracting States)

Who, meeting within the Council, having exchanged their Full Powers, found in good and due form,
Have agreed as follows:

TITLE I

SCOPE

ARTICLE 1

This Convention shall apply in civil and commercial matters whatever the nature of the court or tribunal. It shall not extend, in particular, to revenue, customs or administrative matters.

The Convention shall not apply to:
(1) the status or legal capacity of natural persons, rights in property arising out of a matrimonial relationship, wills and succession;
(2) bankruptcy, proceedings relating to the winding-up of insolvent companies or other legal persons, judical arrangements, compositions and analogous proceedings;
(3) social security;
(4) arbitration.

[SCHEDULE 1   Section 2(2)

TEXT OF 1968 CONVENTION, AS AMENDED

ARRANGEMENT OF PROVISIONS

TITLE IV.   AUTHENTIC INSTRUMENTS AND COURT SETTLEMENTS
(Articles 50–51).
TITLE V.   GENERAL PROVISIONS (Articles 52 and 53).
TITLE VI.   TRANSITIONAL PROVISIONS (Articles 54 and 54A).
TITLE VII.   RELATIONSHIP TO OTHER CONVENTIONS (Articles 55–59).
TITLE VIII.   FINAL PROVISIONS (Articles 60–68).

CONVENTION ON JURISDICTION AND THE ENFORCEMENT OF JUDGMENTS IN CIVIL AND COMMERCIAL MATTERS

Preamble

The High Contracting Parties to the Treaty establishing the European Economic Community,

Desiring to implement the provisions of Article 220 of that Treaty by virtue of which they undertook to secure the simplification of formalities governing the reciprocal recognition and enforcement of judgments of courts or tribunals;

Anxious to strengthen in the Community the legal protection of persons therein established;

Considering that it is necessary for this purpose to determine the international jurisdiction of their courts, to facilitate recognition and to introduce an expeditious procedure for securing the enforcement of judgments, authentic instruments and court settlements;

Have decided to conclude this Convention and to this end have designated as their Plenipotentiaries:

(Designations of Plenipotentiaries of the original six Contracting States)

Who, meeting within the Council, having exchanged their Full Powers, found in good and due form,

Have agreed as follows:]

TITLE I

SCOPE

ARTICLE 1

This Convention shall apply in civil and commercial matters whatever the nature of the court or tribunal. It shall not extend, in particular, to revenue, customs or administrative matters.
The Convention shall not apply to:
(1) the status or legal capacity of natural persons, rights in property arising out of a matrimonial relationship, wills and succession;
(2) bankruptcy, proceedings relating to the winding-up of insolvent companies or other legal persons, judicial arrangements, compositions and analogous proceedings;
(3) social security;
(4) arbitration.

Note. The whole of this Schedule was substituted by Civil Jurisdiction and Judgments Act 1982 (Amendment) Order 1989, SI 1989 No 1346, art 9(1), Sch 1. Further substituted by SI 2000 No 1824, art 8(1), Sch 1.
The whole of this Schedule was again substituted by Civil Jurisdiction and Judgments Act 1982 (Amendment) Order 1990, SI 1990 No 2591, art 12(1), Sch 1, as from 1 December 1991. The text of this Article remains unchanged.

TITLE II

JURISDICTION

Section 1

General provisions

ARTICLE 2

Subject to the provisions of this Convention, persons domiciled in a Contracting State, shall, whatever their nationality, be sued in the courts of that State.

Persons who are not nationals of the State in which they are domiciled shall be governed by the rules of jurisdiction applicable to nationals of that State.

ARTICLE 3

Persons domiciled in a Contracting State may be sued in the courts of another Contracting State only by virtue of the rules set out in Sections 2 to 6 of this Title.

In particular the following provisions shall not be applicable as against them:

—in Belgium:	Article 15 of the civil code (Code civil—Burgerlijk Wetboek) and Article 638 of the Judicial code (Code judiciaire—Gerechtelijk Wetboek);
—in Denmark:	Article 248(2) of the law on civil procedure (Lov om rettens pleje) and Chapter 3, Article 3 of the Greenland law on civil procedure (Lov for Grønland om rettens pleje);
—in the Federal Republic of Germany:	Article 23 of the code of civil procedure (Zivilprozessordnung);
—in France:	Articles 14 and 15 of the civil code (Code civil);
—in Ireland:	the rules which enable jurisdiction to be founded on the document instituting the proceedings having been served on the defendant during his temporary presence in Ireland;
—in Italy:	Article 2 and Article 4, Nos 1 and 2 of the code of civil procedure (Codice di procedura civile);
—in Luxembourg:	Articles 14 and 15 of the civil code (Code civil);
—in the Netherlands:	Article 126(3) and Article 127 of the code of civil procedure (Wetboek van Burgerlijke Rechtsvordering);
—in the United Kingdom:	the rules which enable jurisdiction to be founded on:

(a) the document instituting the proceedings having been served on the defendant during his temporary presence in the United Kingdom; or
(b) the presence within the United Kingdom of property belonging to the defendant; or
(c) the seizure by the plaintiff of property situated in the United Kingdom.

ARTICLE 4

If the defendant is not domiciled in a Contracting State, the jurisdiction of the courts of each Contracting State shall, subject to the provisions of Article 16, be determined by the law of that State.

As against such a defendant any person domiciled in a Contracting State may, whatever his nationality, avail himself in that State of the rules of jurisdiction there in force, and in particular those specified in the second paragraph of Article 3, in the same way as the nationals of that State.

Section 2

Special jurisdiction

ARTICLE 5

A person domiciled in a Contracting State may, in another Contracting State, be sued:

*   *   *   *   *

(2) in matters relating to maintenance, in the courts for the place where the maintenance creditor is domiciled or habitually resident or, if the matter is ancillary to proceedings concerning the status of a person, in the court which, according to its own law, has jurisdiction to entertain those proceedings, unless that jurisdiction is based solely on the nationality of one of the parties;

*   *   *   *   *

ARTICLE 6

A person domiciled in a Contracting State may also be sued:
(1) where he is one of a number of defendants, in the courts for the place where any one of them is domiciled;
(2) as a third party in an action on a warranty or guarantee or in any other third party proceedings, in the court seised of the original proceedings, unless these were instituted solely with the object of removing him from the jurisdiction of the court which would be competent in his case;
(3) on a counterclaim arising from the same contract or facts on which the original claim was based, in the court in which the original claim is pending.

*   *   *   *   *

Section 5

Exclusive jurisdiction

ARTICLE 16

The following courts shall have exclusive jurisdiction, regardless of domicile:

*   *   *   *   *

(5) in proceedings concerned with the enforcement of judgments, the courts of the Contracting State in which the judgment has been or is to be enforced.

Section 6

Prorogation of jurisdiction

*   *   *   *   *

ARTICLE 18

Apart from jurisdiction derived from other provisions of this Convention, a court of a Contracting State before whom a defendant enters an appearance shall have jurisdiction. This rule shall not apply where appearance was entered solely to contest the jurisdiction, or where another court has exclusive jurisdiction by virtue of Article 16.

Section 7

Examination as to jurisdiction and admissibility

ARTICLE 19

Where a court of a Contracting State is seised of a claim which is principally concerned with a matter over which the courts of another Contracting State have exclusive jurisdiction by virtue of Article 16, it shall declare of its own motion that it has no jurisdiction.

ARTICLE 20

Where a defendant domiciled in one Contracting State is sued in a court of another Contracting State and does not enter an appearance, the court shall declare of its own motion that it has no jurisdiction unless its jurisdiction is derived from the provisions of this Convention.

The court shall stay the proceedings so long as it is not shown that the defendant has been able to receive the document instituting the proceedings or an equivalent document in sufficient time to enable him to arrange for his defence, or that all necessary steps have been taken to this end.

The provisions of the foregoing paragraph shall be replaced by those of Article 15 of the Hague Convention of 15 November 1965 on the service abroad of judicial and extrajudicial documents in civil or commercial matters, if the document instituting the proceedings or notice thereof had to be transmitted abroad in accordance with that Convention.

Section 8

Lis pendens—related actions

ARTICLE 21

Where proceedings involving the same cause of action and between the same parties are brought in the courts of different Contracting States, any court other than the court first seised shall of its own motion decline jurisdiction in favour of that court.

A court which would be required to decline jurisdiction may stay its proceedings if the jurisdiction of the other court is contested.

ARTICLE 22

Where related actions are brought in the courts of different Contracting States, any court other than the court first seised may, while the actions are pending at first instance, stay its proceedings.

A court other than the court first seised may also, on the application of one of the parties, decline jurisdiction if the law of that court permits the consolidation of related actions and the court first seised has jurisdiction over both actions.

For the purposes of this Article, actions are deemed to be related where they are so closely connected that it is expedient to hear and determine them together to avoid the risk of irreconcilable judgments resulting from separate proceedings.

ARTICLE 23

Where actions come within the exclusive jurisdiction of several courts, any court other than the court first seised shall decline jurisdiction in favour of that court.

Section 9

Provisional, including protective, measures

ARTICLE 24

Application may be made to the courts of a Contracting State for such provisional, including protective, measures as may be available under the law of that State, even if, under this Convention, the courts of another Contracting State have jurisdiction as to the substance of the matter.

[TITLE II

JURISDICTION

Section 1

General provisions

ARTICLE 2

Subject to the provisions of this Convention, persons domiciled in a Contracting State shall, whatever their nationality, be sued in the courts of that State.

Persons who are not nationals of the State in which they are domiciled shall be governed by the rules of jurisdiction applicable to nationals of that State.

ARTICLE 3

Persons domiciled in a Contracting State may be sued in the courts of another Contracting State only by virtue of the rules set out in Sections 2 to 6 of this Title.
In particular the following provisions shall not be applicable as against them—
— in Belgium: Article 15 of the civil code (Code civil—Burgerlijk Wetboek) and Article 638 of the judicial code (Code judiciaire—Gerechtelijk Wetboek),
— *in Denmark: Article 248(2) of the law on civil procedure (Lov om rettens pleje) and Chapter 3, Article 3 of the Greenland law on civil procedure (Lov for Grønland om rettens pleje),*
[— in Denmark: Article 246(2) and (3) of the law on civil procedure (Lov om rettens pleje),]
— in the Federal Republic of Germany: Article 23 of the code of civil procedure (Zivilprozeβordnung),
— in Greece: Article 40 of the code of civil procedure (Κωδικας Πολιτικης Δικομιας,
— in France: Articles 14 and 15 of the civil code (Code civil),
— in Ireland: the rules which enable jurisdiction to be founded on the document instituting the proceedings having been served on the defendant during his temporary presence in Ireland,
— in Italy: Articles 2 and 4, nos 1 and 2 of the code of civil procedure (Codice di procedura civile),
— in Luxembourg: Articles 14 and 15 of the civil code (Code civil),
— in the Netherlands: Articles 126(3) and 127 of the code of civil procedure (Wetboek van Burgerlijke Rechtsvordering),
[— in Portugal: Article 65(1)(c), article 65(2) and Article 65A(c) of the code of civil procedure (Córdigo de Processo Civil) and Article 11 of the code of labour procedure (Córdigo de Processo de Trabalho),]
— in the United Kingdom: the rules which enable jurisdiction to be founded on:
  (a) the document instituting the proceedings having been served on the defendant during his temporary presence in the United Kingdom; or
  (b) the presence within the United Kingdom of property belonging to the defendant; or
  (c) the seizure by the plaintiff of property situated in the United Kingdom.

Note. The text of art 3 remains unchanged, except for the substitution of the entry relating to Denmark and the addition of the entry relating to Portugal.

ARTICLE 4

If the defendant is not domiciled in a Contracting State, the jurisdiction of the courts of each Contracting State shall, subject to the provisions of Article 16, be determined by the law of that State.
As against such a defendant, any person domiciled in a Contracting State may, whatever his nationality, avail himself in that State of the rules of jurisdiction there in force, and in particular those specified in the second paragraph of Article 3, in the same way as the nationals of that State.

Section 2

Special jurisdiction

ARTICLE 5

A person domiciled in a Contracting State may, in another Contracting State, be sued—

*   *   *   *   *

2. In matters relating to maintenance, in the courts for the place where the maintenance creditor is domiciled or habitually resident or, if the matter is ancillary to proceedings concerning the status of a person, in the court which, according to its own law, has jurisdiction to entertain those proceedings, unless that jurisdiction is based solely on the nationality of one of the parties.

* * * * *

ARTICLE 6

A person domiciled in a Contracting State may also be sued—
1. Where he is one of a number of defendants, in the courts for the place where any one of them is domiciled.
2. As a third party in an action on a warranty or guarantee or in any other third party proceedings, in the court seised of the original proceedings, unless these were instituted solely with the object of removing him from the jurisdiction of the court which would be competent in his case.
3. On a counter-claim arising from the same contract or facts on which the original claim was based, in the court in which the original claim is pending.
[4. In matters relating to a contract, if the action may be combined with an action against the same defendant in matters relating to rights in rem in immovable property, in the court of the Contracting State in which the property is situated.]

Note. The text of art 6 remains unchanged, except for the addition in square brackets.

* * * * *

Section 5

Exclusive jurisdiction

ARTICLE 16

The following courts shall have exclusive jurisdiction, regardless of domicile:

* * * * *

5. In proceedings concerned with the enforcement of judgments, the courts of the Contracting State in which the judgment has been or is to be enforced.

Section 6

Prorogation of jurisdiction

* * * * *

ARTICLE 18

Apart from jurisdiction derived from other provisions of this Convention, a court of a Contracting State before whom a defendant enters an appearance shall have jurisdiction. This rule shall not apply where appearance was entered solely to contest the jurisdiction, or where another court has exclusive jurisdiction by virtue of Article 16.

Section 7

Examination as to jurisdiction and admissibility

ARTICLE 19

Where a court of a Contracting State is seised of a claim which is principally concerned with a matter over which the courts of another Contracting State have exclusive jurisdiction by virtue of Article 16, it shall declare of its own motion that it has no jurisdiction.

ARTICLE 20

Where a defendant domiciled in one Contracting State is sued in a court of another Contracting State and does not enter an appearance, the court shall declare of its own motion that it has no jurisdiction unless its jurisdiction is derived from the provisions of the Convention.

The court shall stay the proceedings so long as it is not shown that the defendant has been able to receive the document instituting the proceedings or an equivalent document in sufficient time to enable him to arrange for his defence, or that all necessary steps have been taken to this end.

The provisions of the foregoing paragraph shall be replaced by those of Article 15 of the Hague Convention of 15th November 1965 on the service abroad of judicial and extrajudicial documents in civil or commercial matters, if the document instituting the proceedings or notice thereof had to be transmitted abroad in accordance with that convention.

Section 8

Lis pendens—related actions

ARTICLE 21

Where proceedings involving the same cause of action and between the same parties are brought in in the courts of different Contracting States, any court other than the court first seised shall of its own motion decline jurisdiction in favour of that court.

A court which would be required to decline jurisdiction may stay its proceedings if the jurisdiction of the other court is contested.

[Where proceedings involving the same cause of action and between the same parties are brought in the courts of different Contracting States, any court other than the court first seised shall of its own motion stay its proceedings until such time as the jursidiction of the court first seised is established.

Where the jurisdiction of the court first seised is established, any court other than the court first seised shall decline jurisdiction in favour of that court.]

Note. See the note to art 1 (p 2912). The text of new art 21 is as shown in square brackets.

ARTICLE 22

Where related actions are brought in the courts of different Contracting States, any court other than the court first seised may, while the actions are pending at first instance, stay its proceedings.

A court other than the court first seised may also, on the application of one of the parties, decline jurisdiction if the law of that court permits the consolidation of related actions and the court first seised has jurisdiction over both actions.

For the purposes of this Article, actions are deemed to be related where they are so closely connected that it is expedient to hear and determine them together to avoid the risk of irreconcilable judgments resulting from separate proceedings.

ARTICLE 23

Where actions come within the exclusive jurisdiction of several courts, any court other than the court first seised shall decline jurisdiction in favour of that court.

Section 9

Provisional, including protective, measures

ARTICLE 24

Application may be made to the courts of a Contracting State for such provisional, including protective, measures as may be available under the law of that State, even if, under this Convention, the courts of another Contracting State have jurisdiction as to the substance of the matter.]

TITLE III

RECOGNITION AND ENFORCEMENT

ARTICLE 25

For the purposes of this Convention, 'judgment' means any judgment given by a court or tribunal of a Contracting State, whatever the judgment may be called, including a decree, order, decision or writ of execution, as well as the determination of costs or expenses by an officer of the court.

Section 1

Recognition

ARTICLE 26

A judgment given in a Contracting State shall be recognised in the other Contracting States without any special procedure being required.

Any interested party who raises the recognition of a judgment as the principal issue in a dispute may, in accordance with the procedures provided for in Sections 2 and 3 of this Title, apply for a decision that the judgment be recognised.

If the outcome of proceedings in a court of a Contracting State depends on the determination of an incidental question of recognition that court shall have jurisdiction over that question.

ARTICLE 27

A judgment shall not be recognised:
(1) if such recognition is contrary to public policy in the State in which recognition is sought;
(2) where it was given in default of appearance, if the defendant was not duly served with the document which instituted the proceedings or with an equivalent document in sufficient time to enable him to arrange for his defence;
(3) if the judgment is irreconcilable with a judgment given in a dispute between the same parties in the State in which recognition is sought;
(4) if the court of the State in which the judgment was given, in order to arrive at its judgment, has decided a preliminary question concerning the status or legal capacity of natural persons, rights in property arising out of a matrimonial relationship, wills or succession in a way that conflicts with a rule of the private international law of the State in which the recognition is sought, unless the same result would have been reached by the application of the rules of private international law of that State;
(5) if the judgment is irreconcilable with an earlier judgment given in a non-Contracting State involving the same cause of action and between the same parties, provided that this latter judgment fulfils the conditions necessary for its recognition in the State addressed.

ARTICLE 28

Moreover, a judgment shall not be recognised if it conflicts with the provisions of Sections 3, 4 or 5 of Title II, or in a case provided for in Article 59.

In its examination of the grounds of jurisdiction referred to in the foregoing paragraph, the court or authority applied to shall be bound by the findings of fact on which the court of the State in which the judgment was given based its jurisdiction.

Subject to the provisions of the first paragraph, the jurisdiction of the court of the State in which the judgment was given may not be reviewed; the test of public policy referred to in Article 27(1) may not be applied to the rules relating to jurisdiction.

ARTICLE 29

Under no circumstances may a foreign judgment be reviewed as to its substance.

ARTICLE 30

A court of a Contracting State in which recognition is sought of a judgment given in another Contracting State may stay the proceedings if an ordinary appeal against the judgment has been lodged.

A court of a Contracting State in which recognition is sought of a judgment given in Ireland or the United Kingdom may stay the proceedings if enforcement is suspended in the State in which the judgment was given by reason of an appeal.

Section 2

Enforcement

ARTICLE 31

A judgment given in a Contracting State and enforceable in that State shall be enforced in another Contracting State when, on the application of any interested party, the order for its enforcement has been issued there.

However, in the United Kingdom, such a judgment shall be enforced in England and Wales, in Scotland or in Northern Ireland when, on the application of any interested party, it has been registered for enforcement in that part of the United Kingdom.

ARTICLE 32

The application shall be submitted:
— *in Belgium, to the tribunal de première instance or rechtbank van eerste aanleg;*
— *in Denmark, to the underret;*
— *in the Federal Republic of Germany, to the presiding judge of a chamber of the Landgericht;*
— *in France, to the presiding judge of the tribunal de grande instance;*
— *in Ireland, to the High Court;*
— *in Italy, to the corte d'appello;*
— *in Luxembourg, to the presiding judge of the tribunal d'arrondissement;*
— *in the Netherlands, to the presiding judge of the arrondissementsrechtbank;*
— *in the United Kingdom.*
  (1) in England and Wales, to the High Court of Justice, or in the case of a maintenance judgment to the Magistrates' Court on transmission by the Secretary of State;
  (2) in Scotland, to the Court of Session, or in the case of a maintenance judgment to the Sheriff Court on transmission by the Secretary of State;
  (3) in Northern Ireland, to the High Court of Justice, or in the case of a maintenance judgment to the Magistrates' Court on transmission by the Secretary of State.
The jurisdiction of local courts shall be determined by reference to the place of domicile of the party against whom enforcement is sought. If he is not domiciled in the State in which enforcement is sought, it shall be determined by reference to the place of enforcement.

ARTICLE 33

The procedure for making the application shall be governed by the law of the State in which enforcement is sought.

The applicant must give an address for service of process within the area of jurisdiction of the court applied to. However, if the law of the State in which enforcement is sought does not provide for the furnishing of such an address, the applicant shall appoint a representative ad litem.

The documents referred to in Articles 46 and 47 shall be attached to the application.

ARTICLE 34

The court applied to shall give its decision without delay; the party against whom enforcement is sought shall not at this stage of the proceedings be entitled to make any submissions on the application.

The application may be refused only for one of the reasons specified in Articles 27 and 28. Under no circumstances may the foreign judgment be reviewed as to its substance.

ARTICLE 35

The appropriate officer of the court shall without delay bring the decision given on the application to the notice of the applicant in accordance with the procedure laid down by the law of the State in which enforcement is sought.

ARTICLE 36

If enforcement is authorised, the party against whom enforcement is sought may appeal against the decision within one month of service thereof.

If that party is domiciled in a Contracting State other than that in which the decision authorising enforcement was given, the time for appealing shall be two months and shall run from the date of service, either on him in person or at his residence. No extension of time may be granted on account of distance.

ARTICLE 37

An appeal against the decision authorising enforcement shall be lodged in accordance with the rules governing procedure in contentious matters:
— *in Belgium, with the tribunal de première instance or rechtbank van eerste aanleg;*
— *in Denmark, with the landsret;*
— *in the Federal Republic of Germany, with the Oberlandesgericht;*
— *in France, with the cour d'appel;*
— *in Ireland, with the High Court;*
— *in Italy, with the corte d'appello;*
— *in Luxembourg, with the Cour supérieure de justice sitting as a court of civil appeal;*
— *in the Netherlands, with the arrondissementsrechtbank;*
— *in the United Kingdom:*
  (1) in England and Wales, with the High Court of Justice, or in the case of a maintenance judgment with the Magistrates' Court;
  (2) in Scotland, with the Court of Session, or in the case of a maintenance judgment with the Sheriff Court;
  (3) in Northern Ireland, with the High Court of Justice, or in the case of a maintenance judgment with the Magistrates' Court.
The judgment given on the appeal may be contested only:
— *in Belgium, Greece, France, Italy, Luxembourg and the Netherlands by an appeal in cassation;*
— *in Denmark, by an appeal to the højesteret, with the leave of the Minister of Justice;*
— *in the Federal Republic of Germany, by a Rechtsbeschwerde;*
— *in Ireland, by an appeal on a point of law to the Supreme Court;*
— *in the United Kingdom, by a single further appeal on a point of law.*

ARTICLE 38

The court with which the appeal under the first paragraph of Article 37 is lodged may, on the application of the appellant, stay the proceedings if an ordinary appeal has been lodged against the judgment in the State in which that judgment was given or if the time for such an appeal has not yet expired; in the latter case, the court may specify the time within which such an appeal is to be lodged.

Where the judgment was given in Ireland or the United Kingdom, any form of appeal available in the State in which it was given shall be treated as an ordinary appeal for the purposes of the first paragraph.

The court may also make enforcement conditional on the provision of such security as it shall determine.

ARTICLE 39

During the time specified for an appeal pursuant to Article 36 and until any such appeal has been determined, no measures of enforcement may be taken other than protective measures taken against the property of the party against whom enforcement is sought.

The decision authorising enforcement shall carry with it the power to proceed to any such protective measures.

ARTICLE 40

If the application for enforcement is refused, the applicant may appeal:
— in Belgium, to the cour d'appel or hof van beroep;
— in Denmark, to the landsret;
— in the Federal Republic of Germany to the Oberlandesgericht;
— in France, to the cour d'appel;
— in Ireland, to the High Court;
— in Italy, to the corte d'appello;
— in Luxembourg, to the Cour supérieure de justice sitting as a court of civil appeal;
— in the Netherlands, to the gerechtshof;
— in the United Kingdom:
  (1) in England and Wales, to the High Court of Justice, or in the case of a maintenance judgment to the Magistrates' Court;
  (2) in Scotland, to the Court of Session, or in the case of a maintenance judgment to the Sheriff Court;
  (3) in Northern Ireland, to the High Court of Justice, or in the case of a maintenance judgment to the Magistrates' Court.

The party against whom enforcement is sought shall be summoned to appear before the appellate court. If he fails to appear, the provisions of the second and third paragraphs of Article 20 shall apply even where he is not domiciled in any of the Contracting States.

ARTICLE 41

A judgment given on an appeal provided for in Article 40 may be contested only:
— in Belgium, Greece, France, Italy, Luxembourg and the Netherlands, by an appeal in cassation;
— in Denmark, by an appeal to the højesteret, with the leave of the Minister of Justice;
— in the Federal Republic of Germany, by a Rechtsbeschwerde;
— in Ireland, by an appeal on a point of law to the Supreme Court;
— in the United Kingdom, by a single further appeal on a point of law.

ARTICLE 42

Where a foreign judgment has been given in respect of several matters and enforcement cannot be authorised for all of them, the court shall authorise enforcement for one or more of them.

An applicant may request partial enforcement of a judgment.

ARTICLE 43

A foreign judgment which orders a periodic payment by way of a penalty shall be enforceable in the State in which enforcement is sought only if the amount of the payment has been finally determined by the courts of the State in which the judgment was given.

ARTICLE 44

An applicant who, in the State in which the judgment was given, has benefited from complete or partial legal aid or exemption from costs or expenses, shall be entitled, in the procedures provided for in Articles 32 to 35, to benefit from the most favourable legal aid or the most extensive exemption from costs or expenses provided for by the law of the State addressed.

However, an applicant who requests the enforcement of a decision given by an administrative authority in Denmark in respect of a maintenance order may, in the State addressed, claim the benefits referred to in the first paragraph if he presents a statement from the Danish Ministry of Justice to the effect that he fulfils the economic requirements to qualify for the grant of complete or partial legal aid or exemption from costs or expenses.

ARTICLE 45

No security, bond or deposit, however described, shall be required of a party who in one Contracting State applies for enforcement of a judgment given in another Contracting State on the ground that he is a foreign national or that he is not domiciled or resident in the State in which enforcement is sought.

Section 3

Common provisions

ARTICLE 46

A party seeking recognition or applying for enforcement of a judgment shall produce:
(1)   a copy of the judgment which satisfies the conditions necessary to establish its authenticity;
(2)   in the case of a judgment given in default, the original or a certified true copy of the document which establishes that the party in default was served with the document instituting the proceedings or with an equivalent document.

ARTICLE 47

A party applying for enforcement shall also produce:
(1)   documents which establish that, according to the law of the State in which it has been given, the judgment is enforceable and has been served;
(2)   where appropriate, a document showing that the applicant is in receipt of legal aid in the State in which the judgment was given.

ARTICLE 48

If the documents specified in Article 46(2) and Article 47(2) are not produced, the court may specify a time for their production, accept equivalent documents or, if it considers that it has sufficient information before it, dispense with their production.

If the court so requires, a translation of the documents shall be produced; the translation shall be certified by a person qualified to do so in one of the Contracting States.

ARTICLE 49

No legalisation or other similar formality shall be required in respect of the documents referred to in Articles 46 or 47 or the second paragraph of Article 48, or in respect of a document appointing a representative ad litem.

[TITLE III

RECOGNITION AND ENFORCEMENT

ARTICLE 25

For the purposes of this Convention, 'judgment' means any judgment given by a court or tribunal of a Contracting State, whatever the judgment may be called, including a decree, order, decision or writ of execution, as well as the determination of costs or expenses by an officer of the court.

Section 1

Recognition

ARTICLE 26

A judgment given in a Contracting State shall be recognized in the other Contracting States without any special procedure being required.

Any interested party who raises the recognition of a judgment as the principal issue in a dispute may, in accordance with the procedures provided for in Sections 2 and 3 of this Title, apply for a decision that the judgment be recognized.

If the outcome of proceedings in a court of a Contracting State depends on the determination of an incidental question of recognition that court shall have jurisdiction over that question.

ARTICLE 27

A judgment shall not be recognized—
(1) If such recognition is contrary to public policy in the State in which recognition is sought.
(2) Where it was given in default of appearance, if the defendant was not duly served with the document which instituted the proceedings or with an equivalent document in sufficient time to enable him to arrange for his defence.
(3) If the judgment is irreconcilable with a judgment given in a dispute between the same parties in the State in which recognition is sought.
(4) If the court of the State of origin, in order to arrive at its judgment, has decided a preliminary question concerning the status or legal capacity of natural persons, rights in property arising out of a matrimonial relationship, wills or succession in way that conflicts with a rule of the private international law of the State in which the recognition is sought, unless the same result would have been reached by the application of the rules of private international law of that State.
(5) If the judgment is irreconcilable with an earlier judgment given in a non-contracting State involving the same cause of action and between the same parties, provided that this latter judgment fulfils the conditions necessary for its recognition in the state addressed.

ARTICLE 28

Moreover, a judgment shall not be recognized if it conflicts with the provisions of Sections 3, 4 or 5 of Title II, or in a case provided for in Article 59.

In its examination of the grounds of jurisdiction referred to in the foregoing paragraph, the court or authority applied to shall be bound by the findings of fact on which the court of the State of origin based its jurisdiction.

Subject to the provisions of the first paragraph, the jurisdiction of the court of the State of origin may not be reviewed; the test of public policy referred to in point 1 of Article 27 may not be applied to the rules relating to jurisdiction.

ARTICLE 29

Under no circumstances may a foreign judgment be reviewed as to its substance.

ARTICLE 30

A court of a Contracting State in which recognition is sought of a judgment given in another Contracting State may stay the proceedings if an ordinary appeal against the judgment has been lodged.

A court of a Contracting State in which recognition is sought of a judgment given in Ireland or the United Kingdom may stay the proceedings if enforcement is suspended in the State in which the judgment was given by reason of an appeal.

[A court of a Contracting State in which recognition is sought of a judgment given in another Contracting State may stay the proceedings if an ordinary appeal against the judgment has been lodged.

A court of a Contracting State in which recognition is sought of a judgment given in Ireland or the United Kingdom may stay the proceedings if enforcement is suspended in the State of origin, by reason of an appeal.]

Note. The text of the new art 30 reads as substituted in square brackets above; see the note to art 1 (p 2912).

Section 2

Enforcement

ARTICLE 31

A judgment given in a Contracting State and enforceable in that State shall be enforced in another Contracting State when, on the application of any interested party, the order for its enforcement has been issued there.

However, in the United Kingdom, such a judgment shall be enforced in England and Wales, in Scotland, or in Northern Ireland when, on the application of any interested party, it has been registered for enforcement in that part of the United Kingdom.

[A judgment given in a Contracting State and enforceable in that State shall be enforced in another Contracting State when, on the application of any interested party, it has been declared enforceable there.

However, in the United Kingdom, such a judgment shall be enforced in England and Wales, in Scotland, or in Northern Ireland when, on the application of any interested party, it has been registered for enforcement in that part of the United Kingdom.]

Note. The text of the new art 31 reads as in square brackets; see the note to art 1 (p 2912).

ARTICLE 32

The application shall be submitted:
— *in Belgium, to the tribunal de première instance or rechtbank van eerste aanleg;*
— *in Denmark, to the underret;*
— *in the Federal Republic of Germany, to the presiding judge of a chamber of the Landgericht;*
— *in Greece, to the Μονομελεζ Πρωτοδικείο;*
— *in France, to the presiding judge of the tribunal de grande instance;*
— *in Ireland, to the High Court;*
— *in Italy, to the corte d'appello;*
— *in Luxembourg, to the presiding judge of the tribunal d'arrondissement;*
— *in the Netherlands, to the presiding judge of the arrondissementsrechtbank;*
— *in the United Kingdom;*
    (1) *in England and Wales, to the High Court of Justice, or in the case of a maintenance judgment to the Magistrates' Court on transmission by the Secretary of State;*
    (2) *in Scotland, to the Court of Session, or in the case of a maintenance judgment to the Sheriff Court on transmission by the Secretary of State;*
    (3) *in Northern Ireland, to the High Court of Justice, or in the case of a maintenance judgment to the Magistrates' Court on transmission by the Secretary of State.*
The jurisdiction of local courts shall be determined by reference to the place of domicile of

the party against whom enforcement is sought. If he is not domiciled in the State in which enforcement is sought, it shall be determined by reference to the place of enforcement.

[1. The application shall be submitted—
— in Belgium, to the tribunal de première instance or rechtbank van eerste aanleg,
— in Denmark, to the byret,
— in the Federal Republic of Germany, to the presiding judge of a chamber of the Landgericht,
— in Greece, to the Μονομελεζ Πρϖτοδικείο;
— in Spain, to the Juzgado de Primer Instancia,
— in France, to the presiding judge of the tribunal de grande instance,
— in Ireland, to the High Court,
— in Italy, to the corte d'appello,
— in Luxembourg, to the presiding judge of the tribunal d'arrondissement,
— in the Netherlands, to the presiding judge of the arrondissementsrechtbank,
— in Portugal, to the Tribunal Judicial de Circulo,
— in the United Kingdom—
  (a) in England and Wales, to the High Court of Justice, or in the case of maintenance judgment to the Magistrates' Court on transmission by the Secretary of State;
  (b) in Scotland, to the Court of Session, or in the case of a maintenance judgment to the Sheriff Court on transmission by the Secretary of State;
  (c) in Northern Ireland, to the High Court of Justice, or in the case of a maintenance judgment to the Magistrates' Court on transmission by the Secretary of State.

2. The jurisdiction of local courts shall be determined by reference to the place of domicile of the party against whom enforcement is sought. If he is not domiciled in the State in which enforcement is sought, it shall be determined by reference to the place of enforcement.]

Note. The text of the new art 32 reads as in square brackets above; see the note to art 1 (p 2912).

ARTICLE 33

The procedure for making the application shall be governed by the law of the State in which enforcement is sought.

The applicant must give an address for service of process within the area of jurisdiction of the court applied to. However, if the law of the State in which enforcement is sought does not provide for the furnishing of such an address, the applicant shall appoint a representative ad litem.

The documents referred to in Articles 46 and 47 shall be attached to the application.

ARTICLE 34

The court applied to shall give its decision without delay; the party against whom enforcement is sought shall not at this stage of the proceedings be entitled to make any submissions on the application.

The application may be refused only for one of the reasons specified in Articles 27 and 28.

Under no circumstances may the foreign judgment be reviewed as to its substance.

ARTICLE 35

The appropriate officer of the court shall without delay bring the decision given on the application to the notice of the applicant in accordance with the procedure laid down by the law of the State in which enforcement is sought.

ARTICLE 36

If enforcement is authorized, the party against whom enforcement is sought may appeal against the decision within one month of service thereof.

If that party is domiciled in a Contracting State other than that in which the decision authorizing enforcement was given, the time for appealing shall be two months and shall run from the date of service, either on him in person or at his residence. No extension of time may be granted on account of distance.

ARTICLE 37

An appeal against the decision authorizing enforcement shall be lodged in accordance with the rules governing procedure in contentious matters:
— *in Belgium, with the tribunal de première instance or rechtbank van eerste aanleg;*
— *in Denmark, with the landsret;*
— *in the Federal Republic of Germany, with the Oberlandesgericht;*
— *in Greece, with the Εφετείο;*
— *in France, with the cour d'appel;*
— *in Ireland, with the High Court;*
— *in Italy, with the corte d'appello;*
— *in Luxembourg, with the Cour supérieure de justice sitting as a court of civil appeal;*
— *in the Netherlands, with the arrondissementsrechtbank;*
— *in the United Kingdom;*
　(1) in England and Wales, with the High Court of Justice or in the case of a maintenance judgment with the Magistrates' Court;
　(2) in Scotland, with the Court of Session, or in the case of a maintenance judgment with the Sheriff Court;
　(3) in Northern Ireland, with the High Court of Justice, or in the case of a maintenance judgment with the Magistrates' Court.
The judgment given on the appeal may be contested only:
— *in Belgium, Greece, France, Italy, Luxembourg and the Netherlands, by an appeal on cassation;*
— *in Denmark, by an appeal to the højesteret, with the leave of the Minister of Justice;*
— *in the Federal Republic of Germany, by a Rechtsbeschwerde;*
— *in Ireland, by an appeal on a point of law to the Supreme Court;*
— *in the United Kingdom, by a single further appeal on a point of law.*

[**1.** An appeal against the decision authorizing enforcement shall be lodged in accordance with the rules governing procedure in contentious matters—
— in Belgium, with the tribunal de première instance or rechtbank van eerste aanleg,
— in Denmark, with the landsret,
— in the Federal Republic of Germany, with the Oberlandesgericht,
— in Greece, with the Εφετείο,
— in Spain, with the Audiencia Provincial,
— in France, with the cour d'appel,
— in Ireland, with the High Court,
— in Italy, with the corte d'appello,
— in Luxembourg, with the Cour supérieure de justice sitting as a court of civil appeal,
— in the Netherlands, with the arrondissementsrechtbank,
— in Portugal, with the Tribunal de Relação.
— in the United Kingdom—
　(a) in England and Wales, with the High Court of Justice, or in the case of a maintenance judgment with the Magistrates' Court;
　(b) in Scotland, with the Court of Session, or in the case of a maintenance judgment with the Sheriff Court;
　(c) in Northern Ireland, with the High Court of Justice, or in the case of a maintenance judgment with the Magistrates' Court.

2. The judgment given on the appeal may be contested only—
— in Belgium, Greece, Spain, France, Italy, Luxembourg and in the Netherlands, by an appeal in cassation,
— in Denmark, by an appeal to the højesteret, with the leave of the Minister of Justice,
— in the Federal Republic of Germany, by a Rechtsbeschwerde,
— in Ireland, by an appeal on a point of law to the Supreme Court,
— in Portugal, by an appeal on a point of law,
— in the United Kingdom, by a single further appeal on a point of law.]
Note. The text of the new art 37 reads as in square brackets above; see the note to art 1 (p 2912).

ARTICLE 38

The court with which the appeal under the first paragraph of Article 37 is lodged may, on the application of the appellant, stay the proceedings if an ordinary appeal has been lodged against the judgment in the State in which that judgment was given or if the time for such an appeal has not yet expired; in the latter case, the court may specify the time within which such an appeal is to be lodged.

Where the judgment was given in Ireland or the United Kingdom, any form of appeal available in the State in which it was given shall be treated as an ordinary appeal for the purposes of the first paragraph.

The court may also make enforcement conditional on the provision of such security as it shall determine.

[The court with which the appeal under Article 37(1) is lodged may, on the application of the appellant, stay the proceedings if an ordinary appeal has been lodged against the judgment in the State of origin or if the time for such an appeal has not yet expired; in the latter case, the court may specify the time within which such an appeal is to be lodged.

Where the judgment was given in Ireland or the United Kingdom, any form of appeal available in the State of origin shall be treated as an ordinary appeal for the purposes of the first paragraph.

The court may also make enforcement conditional on the provision of such security as it shall determine.]

Note. The text of art 38 reads as in square brackets above; see the note to art 1 (p 2912).

ARTICLE 39

During the time specified for an appeal pursuant to Article 36 and until any such appeal has been determined, no measures of enforcement may be taken other than protective measures taken against the property of the party against whom enforcement is sought.

The decision authorizing enforcement shall carry with it the power to proceed to any such protective measures.

ARTICLE 40

If the application for enforcement is refused, the applicant may appeal;
— *in Belgium, to the cour d'appel or hof van beroep;*
— *in Denmark, to the landsret;*
— *in the Federal Republic of Germany, to the Oberlandesgericht;*
— *in Greece, to the Εφετειο;*
— *in France, to the cour d'appel;*
— *in Ireland, to the High Court;*
— *in Italy, to the corte d'appello;*
— *in Luxembourg, to the Cour supérieure de justice sitting as a court of civil appeal;*
— *in the Netherlands, to the gerechtshof;*
— *in the United Kingdom;*

(*1*) in England and Wales, to the High Court of Justice, or in the case of a maintenance judgment to the Magistrates' Court;
(*2*) in Scotland, to the Court of Session, or in the case of a maintenance judgment to the Sheriff Court;
(*3*) in Northern Ireland, to the High Court of Justice, or in the case of a maintenance judgment to the Magistrates' Court.

The party against whom enforcement is sought shall be summoned to appear before the appellate court. If he fails to appear, the provisions of the second and third paragraphs of Article 20 shall apply even where he is not domiciled in any of the Contracting States.

[**1.** If the application for enforcement is refused, the applicant may appeal—
— in Belgium, to the cour d'appel or hof van beroep,
— in Denmark, to the landsret,
— in the Federal Republic of Germany, to the Oberlandesgericht,
— in Greece, to the Εφετειο,
— in Spain, to the Audiencia Provincial,
— in France, to the cour d'appel,
— in Ireland, to the High Court,
— in Italy, to the corte d'appello,
— in Luxembourg, to the Cour supérieure de justice sitting as a court of civil appeal,
— in the Netherlands, to the gerechtshof,
— in Portugal, to the Tribunal da Relação,
— in the United Kingdom—
  (a) in England and Wales, to the High Court of Justice, or in the case of a maintenance judgment to the Magistrates' Court;
  (b) in Scotland, to the Court of Session, or in the case of a maintenance judgment to the Sheriff Court;
  (c) in Northern Ireland, to the High Court of Justice, or in the case of a maintenance judgment to the Magistrates' Court.

2. The party against whom enforcement is sought shall be summoned to appear before the appellate court. If he fails to appear, the provisions of the second and third paragraphs of Article 20 shall apply even where he is not domiciled in any of the Contracting States.]

Note. The text of art 40 reads as in square brackets above; see the note to art 1 (p 2912).

ARTICLE 41

A judgment given on an appeal provided for in Article 40 may be contested only:
— in Belgium, Greece, France, Italy, Luxembourg and in the Netherlands, by an appeal in cassation;
— in Denmark, by an appeal to the højesteret, with the leave of the Minister of Justice;
— in the Federal Republic of Germany by a Rechtsbeschwerde;
— in Ireland, by an appeal on a point of law to the Supreme Court;
— in the United Kingdom, by a single further appeal on a point of law.

[A judgment given on appeal provided for in Article 40 may be contested only—
— in Belgium, Greece, Spain, France, Italy, Luxembourg and in the Netherlands, by an appeal on cassation.
— in Denmark, by an appeal to the højesteret, with the leave of the Minister of Justice,
— in the Federal Republic of Germany, by a Rechtsbeschwerde,
— in Ireland, by an appeal on a point of law to the Supreme Court,
— in Portugal, by an appeal on a point of law,
— in the United Kingdom, by a single further appeal on a point of law.]

Note. The text of art 41 reads as in square brackets above; see the note to art 1 (p 2912).

ARTICLE 42

Where a foreign judgment has been given in respect of several matters and enforcement cannot be authorized for all of them, the court shall authorize enforcement for one or more of them.

An applicant may request partial enforcement of a judgment.

ARTICLE 43

A foreign judgment which orders a periodic payment by way of a penalty shall be enforceable in the State in which enforcement is sought only if the amount of the payment has been finally determined by the courts of the State in which the judgment was given.

[A foreign judgment which orders a periodic payment by way of a penalty shall be enforceable in the State in which enforcement is sought only if the amount of the payment has been finally determined by the courts of the State of origin.]

Note. The text of art 43 reads as in square brackets above, see the note to art 1 (p 2912).

ARTICLE 44

An applicant who, in the State of origin has benefited from complete or partial legal aid or exemption from costs or expenses, shall be entitled, in the procedures provided for in Articles 32 to 35, to benefit from the most favourable legal aid or the most extensive exemption from costs or expenses provided for by the law of the State addressed.

However, an applicant who requests the enforcement of a decision given by an administrative authority in Denmark in respect of a maintenance order may, in the State addressed, claim the benefits referred to in the first paragraph if he presents a statement from the Danish Ministry of Justice to the effect that he fulfils the economic requirements to qualify for the grant of complete or partial legal aid or exemption from costs or expenses.

ARTICLE 45

No security, bond or deposit, however described, shall be required of a party who in one Contracting State applies for enforcement of a judgment given in another Contracting State on the ground that he is a foreign national or that he is not domiciled or resident in the State in which enforcement is sought.

Section 3

Common provisions

ARTICLE 46

A party seeking recognition or applying for enforcement of a judgment shall produce—

  (1) a copy of the judgment which satisfies the conditions necessary to establish its authenticity;

  (2) in the case of a judgment given in default, the original or a certified true copy of the document which establishes that the party in default was served with the document instituting the proceedings or with an equivalent document.

ARTICLE 47

A party applying for enforcement shall also produce:

  (1) documents which establish that, according to the law of the State in which it has been given, the judgment is enforceable and has been served;

  (2) where appropriate, a document showing that the applicant is in receipt of legal aid in the State in which the judgment was given.

[A party applying for enforcement shall also produce—

1. documents which establish that, according to the law of the State of origin the judgment is enforceable and has been served;

2. where appropriate, a document showing that the applicant is in receipt of legal aid in the State of origin.]

Note. The text of art 47 reads as in square brackets above; see the note to art 1 (p 2912).

ARTICLE 48

If the documents specified in point 2 of Articles 46 and 47 are not produced, the court may specify a time for their production, accept equivalent documents or, if it considers that it has sufficient information before it, dispense with their production.

If the court so requires, a translation of the documents shall be produced; the translation shall be certified by a person qualified to do so in one of the Contracting States.

ARTICLE 49

No legalization or other similar formality shall be required in respect of the documents referred to in Articles 46 or 47 or the second paragraph of Article 48, or in respect of a document appointing a representative ad litem.]

TITLE IV

AUTHENTIC INSTRUMENTS AND COURT SETTLEMENTS

ARTICLE 50

A document which has been formally drawn up or registered as an authentic instrument and is enforceable in one Contracting State shall, in another Contracting State, have an order for its enforcement issued there, on application made in accordance with the procedures provided for in Article 31 et seq. The application may be refused only if enforcement of the instrument is contrary to public policy in the State in which enforcement is sought.

The instrument produced must satisfy the conditions necessary to establish its authenticity in the State of origin.

The provisions of Section 3 of Title III shall apply as appropriate.

ARTICLE 51

A settlement which has been approved by a court in the course of proceedings and is enforceable in the State in which it was concluded shall be enforceable in the State in which enforcement is sought under the same conditions as authentic instruments.

[TITLE IV

AUTHENTIC INSTRUMENTS AND COURT SETTLEMENTS

ARTICLE 50

A document which has been formally drawn up or registered as an authentic instrument and is enforceable in one Contracting State shall, in another Contracting State, have an order for its enforcement issued there, on application made in accordance with the procedures provided for in Article 31 et seq. The application may be refused only if enforcement of the instrument is contrary to public policy in the State in which enforcement is sought.

The instrument produced must satisfy the conditions necessary to establish its authenticity in the State of origin.

The provisions of Section 3 of Title III shall apply as appropriate.

[A document which has been formally drawn up or registered as an authentic instrument and is enforceable in one Contracting State shall, in another Contracting State, be declared enforceable there, on application made in accordance with the procedures provided for in Article 31 et seq. The application may be refused only if enforcement of the instument is contrary to public policy in the State addressed.

The instrument produced must satisfy the conditions necessary to establish its authenticity in the State of origin.

The provisions of Section 3 of Title III shall apply as appropriate.]

Note. The text of art 50 reads as in square brackets above; see the note to art 1 (p 2912).

ARTICLE 51

A settlement which has been approved by a court in the course of proceedings and is enforceable in the State in which it was concluded shall be enforceable in the State in which enforcement is sought under the same conditions as authentic instruments.

[A settlement which has been approved by a court in the course of proceedings and is enforceable in the State in which it was concluded shall be enforceable in the State addressed under the same conditions as authentic instruments.]]

Note. The text of art 51 reads as in square brackets above; see the note to art 1 (p 2912).

TITLE V

GENERAL PROVISIONS

ARTICLE 52

In order to determine whether a party is domiciled in the Contracting State whose courts are seised of the matter, the court shall apply its internal law.

If a party is not domiciled in the State whose courts are seised of the matter, then, in order to determine whether the party is domiciled in another Contracting State, the court shall apply the law of that State.

The domicile of a party shall, however, be determined in accordance with his national law if, by that law, his domicile depends on that of another person or on the seat of an authority.

[In order to determine whether a party is domiciled in the Contracting State whose courts are seised of a matter, the Court shall apply its internal law.

If a party is not domiciled in the State whose courts are seised of the matter, then, in order to determine whether the party is domiciled in another Contracting State, the court shall apply the law of that State.]

Note. The text of art 52 reads as in square brackets above; see the note to art 1 (p 2912).

* * * * *

TITLE VI

TRANSITIONAL PROVISIONS

ARTICLE 54

The provisions of this Convention shall apply only to legal proceedings instituted and to documents formally drawn up or registered as authentic instruments after its entry into force.

However, judgments given after the date of entry into force of this Convention in proceedings instituted before that date shall be recognised and enforced in accordance with the provisions of Title III if jurisdiction was founded upon rules which accorded with those provided for either in Title II of this Convention or in a convention concluded between the State of origin and the State addressed which was in force when the proceedings were instituted.

[TITLE VI

TRANSITIONAL PROVISIONS

ARTICLE 54

The provisions of this Convention shall apply only to legal proceedings instituted and to documents formally drawn up or registered as authentic instruments after its entry into force.

However, judgments given after the date of entry into force of this Convention in proceedings instituted before that date shall be recognised and enforced in accordance with the provisions of Title III if jurisdiction was founded upon rules which accorded with those provided for either in Title II of this Convention or in a convention concluded between the State of origin and the the State addressed which was in force when the proceedings were instituted.

[The provisions of the Convention shall apply only to legal proceedings instituted and to documents formally drawn up or registered as authentic instruments after its entry into force in the State of origin and, where recognition or enforcement of a judgment or authentic instruments is sought, in the State addressed.

However, judgments given after the date of entry into force of this Convention between the State of origin and the State addressed in proceedings instituted before that date shall be recognized and enforced in accordance with the provisions of Title III if jurisdiction was founded upon rules which accorded with those provided for either in Title II of this Convention or in a convention concluded between the State of origin and the State addressed which was in force when the proceedings were instituted.

If the parties to a dispute concerning a contract had agreed in writing before 1st June 1988 for Ireland or before 1st January 1987 for the United Kingdom that the contract was to be governed by the law of Ireland or of a part of the United Kingdom, the courts of Ireland or of that part of the United Kingdom shall retain the right to exercise jurisdiction in the dispute.]

Note. The text of art 54 reads as in square brackets above; see the note to art 1 (p 2912).

ARTICLE 54A

[For a period of three years from 1st November 1986 for Denmark and from 1st June 1988 for Ireland, jurisdiction in maritime matters shall be determined in these States not only in accordance with the provisions of Title II, but also in accordance with the provisions of paragraphs 1 to 6 following. However, upon the entry into force of the International Convention relating to the arrest of sea-going ships, signed at Brussels on 10th May 1952, for one of these States, these provisions shall cease to have effect for that State.

1. A person who is domiciled in a Contracting State may be sued in the Courts of one of the States mentioned above in respect of a maritime claim if the ship to which the claim relates or any other ship owned by him has been arrested by judicial process within the territory of the latter State to secure the claim, or could have been so arrested there but bail or other security has been given, and either—

(a) the claimant is domiciled in the latter State, or

(b) the claim arose in the latter State, or

(c) the claim concerns the voyage during which the arrest was made or could have been made, or

(d) the claim arises out of a collision or out of damage caused by a ship to another ship or to goods or persons on board either ship, either by the execution or non-execution of a manoeuvre or by the non-observance of regulations, or

(e) the claim is for salvage, or

(f) the claim is in respect of a mortgage or hypothecation of the ship arrested.

2. A claimant may arrest either the particular ship to which the maritime claim relates, or any other ship which is owned by the person who was, at the time when the maritime claim arose, the owner of the particular ship. However, only the particular ship to which the maritime claim relates may be arrested in respect of the maritime claims set out in (5)(o), (p) or (q) of this Article.

3. Ships shall be deemed to be in the same ownership when all the shares therein are owned by the same person or persons.

4. When in the case of a charter by demise of a ship the charterer alone is liable in respect of a maritime claim relating to that ship, the claimant may arrest that ship or any other ship owned by the charterer, but no other ship owned by the owner may be arrested in respect of such claim. The same shall apply to any case in which a person other than the owner of a ship is liable in respect of a maritime claim relating to that ship.

5. The expression 'maritime claim' means a claim arising out of one or more of the following—

(a) damage caused by any ship either in collision or otherwise;

(b) loss of life or personal injury caused by any ship or occurring in connection with the operation on any ship;

(c) salvage;

(d) agreement relating to the use of hire of any ship whether by charterparty or otherwise;

(e) agreement relating to the carriage of goods in any ship whether by charterparty or otherwise;

(f) loss of or damage to goods including baggage carried in any ship;

(g) general average;

(h) bottomry;

(i) towage;

(j) pilotage;

(k) goods or materials wherever supplied to a ship for her operation or maintenance;

(l) construction, repair or equipment of any ship or dock charges and dues;

(m) wages of master, officers or crew;

(n) master's disbursements, including disbursements made by shippers, charterers or agents on behalf of a ship or her owner;

(o) dispute as to the title to or ownership of any ship;

(p) disputes between co-owners of any ship as to the ownership, possession, employment or earnings of that ship;

(q) the mortgage or hypothecation of any ship.

6. In Denmark, the expression 'arrest' shall be deemed as regards the maritime claims referred to in 5(o) and (p) of this Article, to include a 'forbud', where that is the only procedure allowed in respect of such a claim under Articles 646 to 653 of the law on civil procedure (lov om rettens pleje).]]

Note. This article is inserted on the substitution of the whole Schedule, as noted to art 1 (p 2912).

TITLE VII

RELATIONSHIP TO OTHER CONVENTIONS

ARTICLE 55

Subject to the provisions of the second paragraph of Article 54, and of Article 56, this Convention shall, for the States which are parties to it, supersede the following conventions concluded between two or more of them:

— *the Convention between Belgium and France on Jurisdiction and the Validity and Enforcement of Judgments, Arbitration Awards and Authentic Instruments, signed at Paris on 8 July 1899;*

— *the Convention between Belgium and the Netherlands on Jurisdiction, Bankruptcy, and the Validity and Enforcement of Judgments, Arbitration Awards and Authentic Instruments, signed at Brussels on 28 March 1925;*

— *the Convention between France and Italy on the Enforcement of Judgments in Civil and Commercial Matters, signed at Rome on 3 June 1930;*

— *the Convention between the United Kingdom and the French Republic providing for the Reciprocal Enforcement of Judgments in Civil and Commercial Matters, with Protocol, signed at Paris on 18 January 1934;*

— *the Convention between the United Kingdom and the Kingdom of Belgium providing*

for the Reciprocal Enforcement of Judgments in Civil and Commercial Matters, with Protocol, signed at Brussels on 2 May 1934;
— *the Convention between Germany and Italy on the Recognition and Enforcement of Judgments in Civil and Commercial matters, signed at Rome on 9 March 1936;*
— *the Convention between the Federal Republic of Germany and the Kingdom of Belgium on the Mutual Recognition and Enforcement of Judgments, Arbitration Awards and Authentic Instruments in Civil and Commercial Matters, signed at Bonn on 30 June 1958;*
— *the Convention between the Kingdom of the Netherlands and the Italian Republic on the Recognition and Enforcement of Judgments in Civil and Commercial Matters, signed at Rome on 17 April 1959;*
— *the Convention between the United Kingdom and the Federal Republic of Germany for the Reciprocal Recognition and Enforcement of Judgments in Civil and Commercial Matters, signed at Bonn on 14 July 1960;*
— *the Convention between the Kingdom of Belgium and the Italian Republic on the Recognition and Enforcement of Judgments and other Enforceable Instruments in Civil and Commercial Matters, signed at Rome on 6 April 1962;*
— *the Convention between the Kingdom of the Netherlands and the Federal Republic of Germany on the Mutual Recognition and Enforcement of Judgments and other Enforceable Instruments in Civil and Commercial Matters, signed at The Hague on 30 August 1962;*
— *the Convention between the United Kingdom and the Republic of Italy for the Reciprocal Recognition and Enforcement of Judgments in Civil and Commercial Matters, signed at Rome on 7 February 1964, with amending Protocol signed at Rome on 14 July 1970;*
— *the Convention between the United Kingdom and the Kingdom of the Netherlands providing for the Reciprocal Recognition and Enforcement of Judgments in Civil Matters, signed at The Hague on 17 November 1967,*
and, in so far as it is in force:
— *the Treaty between Belgium, the Netherlands and Luxembourg on Jurisdiction, Bankruptcy, and the Validity and Enforcement of Judgments, Arbitration Awards and Authentic Instruments, signed at Brussels on 24 November 1961.*

ARTICLE 56

The Treaty and the conventions referred to in Article 55 shall continue to have effect in relation to matters to which this Convention does not apply.

They shall continue to have effect in respect of judgments given and documents formally drawn up or registered as authentic instruments before the entry into force of this Convention.

ARTICLE 57

This Convention shall not affect any conventions to which the Contracting States are or will be parties and which, in relation to particular matters, govern jurisdiction or the recognition or enforcement of judgments.

This Convention shall not affect the application of provisions which, in relation to particuar matters, govern jurisdiction or the recognition or enforcement of judgments and which are or will be contained in acts of the Institutions of the European Communities or in national laws harmonised in implementation of such acts.

(Article 25(2) of the Accession Convention provides:

'With a view to its uniform interpretation, paragraph 1 of Article 57 shall be applied in the following manner—

(a) *The 1968 Convention as amended shall not prevent a court of a Contracting State which is a party to a convention on a particular matter from assuming jurisdiction in accordance with that convention, even where the defendant is domiciled in another Contracting State which is not a party to that convention. The court shall, in any event, apply Artcle 20 of the 1968 Convention as amended.*

(b) *A judgment given in a Contracting State in the exercise of jurisdiction provided for in a convention on a particular matter shall be recognized and enforced in the other Contracting State in accordance with the 1968 Convention as amended.*

Where a convention on a particular matter to which both the State of origin and the State addressed are parties lays down conditions for the recognition or enforcement of judgments, those conditions shall apply. In any event, the provisions of the 1968 Convention as amended which concern the procedure for recognition and enforcement of judgments may be applied.)

ARTICLE 58

This Convention shall not affect the rights granted to Swiss nationals by the Convention concluded on 15th June 1869 between France and the Swiss Confederation on Jurisdiction and the Enforcement of Judgments in Civil Matters.

ARTICLE 59

This Convention shall not prevent a Contracting State from assuming, in a convention on the recognition and enforcement of judgments, an obligation towards a third State not to recognise judgments given in other Contracting States against defendants domiciled or habitually resident in the third State where, in cases provided for in Article 4, the judgment could only be founded on a ground of jurisdiction specified in the second paragraph of Article 3.

However, a Contracting State may not assume an obligation towards a third State not to recognise a judgment given in another Contracting State by a court basing its jurisdiction on the presence within that State of property belonging to the defendant, or the seizure by the plaintiff of property situated there:

(*1*) *if the action is brought to assert or declare proprietary or possessory rights in that property, seeks to obtain authority to dispose of it, or arises from another issue relating to such property, or*

(*2*) *if the property constitutes the security for a debt which is the subject-matter of the action.*

[TITLE VII

RELATIONSHIP TO OTHER CONVENTIONS

ARTICLE 55

Subject to the provisions of the second paragraph of Article 54, and of Article 56, this Convention shall, for the States which are parties to it, supersede the following conventions concluded between two or more of them:

— the Convention between Belgium and France on jurisdiction and the validity and enforcement of judgments, arbitration awards and authentic instruments, signed at Paris on 8 July 1899;

— the Convention between Belgium and the Netherlands on jurisdiction, bankruptcy, and the validity and enforcement of judgments, arbitration awards and authentic instruments, signed at Brussels on 28 March 1925;

— the Convention between France and Italy on the enforcement of judgments in civil and commercial matters, signed at Rome on 3 June 1930;

— the Convention between the United Kingdom and the French Republic providing for the reciprocal enforcement of judgments in civil and commercial matters, with Protocol, signed at Paris on 18 January 1934;

— the Convention between the United Kingdom and the Kingdom of Belgium providing for the reciprocal enforcement of judgments in civil and commercial matters, with Protocol, signed at Brussels on 2 May 1934;

— the Convention between Germany and Italy on the recognition and enforcement of judgments in civil and commercial matters, signed at Rome on 9 March 1936;

— the Convention between the Federal Republic of Germany and the Kingdom of Belgium on the mutual recognition and enforcement of judgments, arbitration awards and authentic instruments in civil and commercial matters, signed at Bonn on 30 June 1958;

— the Convention between the Kingdom of the Netherlands and the Italian Republic on the recognition and enforcement of judgments in civil and commercial matters, signed at Rome on 17 April 1959;

— the Convention between the United Kingdom and the Federal Republic of Germany for the reciprocal recognition and enforcement of judgments in civil and commercial matters, signed at Bonn on 14 July 1960;

— the Convention between the Kingdom of Greece and the Federal Republic of Germany for the reciprocal recognition and enforcement of judgments, settlements and authentic instruments in civil and commercial matters, signed in Athens on 4th November 1961,

— the Convention between the Kingdom of Belgium and the Italian Republic on the recognition and enforcement of judgments and other enforceable instruments in civil and commercial matters, signed at Rome on 6 April 1962;

— the Convention between the Kingdom of the Netherlands and the Federal Republic of Germany on the mutual recognition and enforcement of judgments and other enforceable instruments in civil and commercial matters, signed at The Hague on 30 August 1962;

— the Convention between the United Kingdom and the Republic of Italy for the reciprocal recognition and enforcement of judgments in civil and commercial matters, signed at Rome on 7 February 1964, with amending Protocol signed at Rome on 14 July 1970;

— the Convention between the United Kingdom and the Kingdom of the Netherlands providing for the reciprocal recognition and enforcement of judgments in civil matters, signed at The Hague on 17 November 1967,

[— the Convention between Spain and France on the recognition and enforcement of judgment arbitration awards in civil and commercial matters, signed at Paris on 28th May 1969,

— the Convention between Spain and Italy regarding legal aid and the recognition and enforcement of judgments in civil and commercial matters, signed at Madrid on 22nd May 1973.

— the Convention between Spain and the Federal Republic of Germany on the recognition and enforcement of judgments, settlements and enforceable authentic instrments in civil and commercial matters, signed at Bonn on 14th November 1983.]

and, in so far as it is in force—

— the Treaty between Belgium, the Netherlands and Luxembourg on jurisdiction, bankruptcy, and the validity and enforcement of judgments, arbitration awards and authentic instruments, signed at Brussels on 24 November 1961.

Note. The text of art 55 remains unchanged, except for the entries added in square brackets; see the note to art 1 (p 2912).

ARTICLE 56

The Treaty and the conventions referred to in Article 55 shall continue to have effect in relation to matters to which this Convention does not apply.

They shall continue to have effect in respect of judgments given and documents formally drawn up or registered as authentic instruments before the entry into force of this Convention.

ARTICLE 57

This Convention shall not affect any conventions to which the Contracting States are or will be parties and which, in relation to particular matters, govern jurisdiction or the recognition or enforcement of judgments.

This Convention shall not affect the application of provisions which, in relation to particuar matters, govern jurisdiction or the recognition or enforcement of judgments and which are or will be contained in acts of the Institutions of the European Communities or in national laws harmonised in implementation of such acts.

[**1.** This Convention shall not affect any conventions to which the Contracting States are or will be parties and which in relation to particular matters, govern jurisdiction or the recognition or enforcement of judgments.

2. With a view to its uniform interpretation, paragraph 1 shall be applied in the following manner—

(a) This Convention shall not prevent a court of a Contracting State which is a party to a convention on a particular matter from assuming jurisdiction in accordance with that Convention, even where the defendant is domiciled in another Contracting State which is not a party to that Convention. The court hearing the action shall, in any event, apply Article 20 of this Convention;

(b) judgments given in a Contracting State by a court in the exercise of jurisdiction provided for in a convention on a particular matter shall be recognized and enforced in the other Contracting State in accordance with this Convention.

Where a convention on a particular matter to which both the State of origin and the State addressed are parties lays down conditions for the recognition or enforcement of judgments, those conditions shall apply. In any event, the provisions of this Convention which concern the procedure for recognition and enforcement of judgments may be applied.

3. This Convention shall not affect the application of provisions which, in relation to particular matters, govern jurisdiction or the recognition or enforcement of judgments and which are or will be contained in acts of the institutions of the European Communities or in national laws harmonized in implementation of such acts.]

Note. The text of art 57 reads as in square brackets; see the note to art 1 (p 2912).

ARTICLE 58

This Convention shall not affect the rights granted to Swiss nationals by the Convention concluded on 15th June 1869 between France and the Swiss Confederation on Jurisdiction and the Enforcement of Judgments in Civil Matters.

[Until such time as the Convention on jurisdiction and the enforcement of judgments in civil and commercial matters, signed at Lugano on 16th September 1988, takes effect with regard to France and the Swiss Confederation, this Convention shall not affect the rights granted to Swiss nationals by the Convention between France and the Swiss Confederation on jurisdiction and enforcement of judgments in civil matters, signed at Paris on 15th June 1869.]

Note. The text of art 58 reads as in square brackets; see the note to art 1 (p 2912).

ARTICLE 59

This Convention shall not prevent a Contracting State from assuming, in a convention on the recognition and enforcement of judgments, an obligation towards a third State not to recognise judgments given in other Contracting States against defendants domiciled or habitually resident in the third State where, in cases provided for in Article 4, the judgment could only be founded on a ground of jurisdiction specified in the second paragraph of Article 3.

However, a Contracting State may not assume an obligation towards a third State not to recognise a judgment given in another Contracting State by a court basing its jurisdiction on the presence within that State of property belonging to the defendant, or the seizure by the plaintiff of property situated there:

    (*1*) *if the action is brought to assert or declare proprietary or possessory rights in that property, seeks to obtain authority to dispose of it, or arises from another issue relating to such property, or*

    (*2*) *if the property constitutes the security for a debt which is the subject-matter of the action.*

[This Convention shall not prevent a Contracting State from assuming, in a convention on the recognition and enforcement of judgments, an obligation towards a third State not to recognize judgments given in other Contracting States against defendants domiciled or habitually resident in the third State where, in cases provided for in Article 4, the judgment could only be founded on a ground of jurisdiction specified in the second paragraph of Article 3.

However, a Contracting State may not assume an obligation towards a third State not to recognize a judgment given in another Contracting State by a court basing its jurisdiction on the presence within that State of property belonging to the defendant, or the seizure by the plaintiff of property situated there—

1. if the action is brought to assert or declare proprietary or possessory rights in that property, seeks to obtain authority to dispose of it, or arises from another issue relating to such property, or

2. if the property constitutes the security for a debt which is the subject-matter of the action.]]

Note. The text of art 59 reads as in square brackets; see the note to art 1 (p 2912).

*   *   *   *   *

ANNEXED PROTOCOL

ARTICLE I

Any person domiciled in Luxembourg who is sued in a court of another Contracting State pursuant to Article 5(1) may refuse to submit to the jurisdiction of that court. If the defendant does not enter an appearance the court shall declare of its own motion that it has no jurisdiction.

An agreement conferring jurisdiction, within the meaning of Article 17, shall be valid with respect to a person domiciled in Luxembourg only if that person has expressly and specifically so agreed.

ARTICLE II

Without prejudice to any more favourable provisions of national laws, persons domiciled in a Contracting State who are being prosecuted in the criminal courts of another Contracting State of which they are not nationals for an offence which was not intentionally committed may be defended by persons qualified to do so, even if they do not appear in person.

However, the court seised of the matter may order appearance in person; in the case of failure to appear, a judgment given in the civil action without the person concerned having had the opportunity to arrange for his defence need not be recognised or enforced in the other Contracting States.

ARTICLE III

In proceedings for the issue of an order for enforcement, no charge, duty or fee calculated by reference to the value of the matter in issue may be levied in the State in which enforcement is sought.

ARTICLE IV

Judicial and extrajudicial documents drawn up in one Contracting State which have to be served on persons in another Contracting State shall be transmitted in accordance with the procedures laid down in the conventions and agreements concluded between the Contracting States.

Unless the State in which service is to take place objects by declaration to the Secretary-General of the Council of the European Communities, such documents may also be sent by the appropriate public officers of the State in which the document has been drawn up directly to the appropriate public officers of the State in which the addressee is to be found. In this case the officer of the State of origin shall send a copy of the document to the officer of the State addressed who is competent to forward it to the addressee. The document shall be forwarded in the manner specified by the law of the State addressed. The forwarding shall be recorded by a certificate sent directly to the officer of the State of origin.

*   *   *   *   *

ARTICLE VA

In matters relating to maintenance, the expression 'court' includes the Danish administrative authorities.

*   *   *   *   *

ARTICLE VI

The Contracting States shall communicate to the Secretary-General of the Council of the European Communities the text of any provisions of their laws which amend either those articles of their laws mentioned in the Convention or the lists of courts specified in Section 2 of Title III of the Convention.

[ANNEXED PROTOCOL

[The High Contracting Parties have agreed upon the following provisions, which shall be annexed to the Convention.]

ARTICLE I

Any person domiciled in Luxembourg who is sued in a court of another Contracting State pursuant to Article 5(1) may refuse to submit to the jurisdiction of that court. If the defendant does not enter an appearance the court shall declare of its own motion that it has no jurisdiction.

An agreement conferring jurisdiction, within the meaning of Article 17, shall be valid with respect to a person domiciled in Luxembourg only if that person has expressly and specifically so agreed.

ARTICLE II

Without prejudice to any more favourable provisions of national laws, persons domiciled in a Contracting State who are being prosecuted in the criminal courts of another Contracting State of which they are not nationals for an offence which was not intentionally committed may be defended by persons qualified to do so, even if they do not appear in person.

However, the court seised of the matter may order appearance in person; in the case of failure to appear, a judgment given in the civil action without the person concerned having had the opportunity to arrange for his defence need not be recognized or enforced in the other Contracting States.

ARTICLE III

In proceedings for the issue of an order for enforcement, no charge, duty or fee calculated by reference to the value of the matter in issue may be levied in the State in which enforcement is sought.

ARTICLE IV

Judicial and extrajudicial documents drawn up in one Contracting State which have to be served on persons in another Contracting State shall be transmitted in accordance with the procedures laid down in the conventions and agreements concluded between the Contracting States.

Unless the State in which service is to take place objects by declaration to the Secretary-General of the Council of the European Communities, such documents may also be sent by the appropriate public officers of the State in which the document has been drawn up directly to the appropriate public officers of the State in which the addressee is to be found. In this case the officer of the State of origin shall send a copy of the document to the officer of the State applied to who is competent to forward it to the addressee. The document shall be forwarded in the manner specified by the law of the State applied to. The forwarding shall be recorded by a certificate sent directly to the officer of the State of origin.

ARTICLE V

The jurisdiction specified in Articles 6(2) and 10 in actions on a warranty or guarantee or in any other third party proceedings may not be resorted to in the Federal Republic of Germany. In that State, any person domiciled in another Contracting State may be sued in the courts in pursuance of Articles 68, 72, 73 and 74 of the code of civil procedure (Zivilprozeßordnung) concerning third-party notices.

Judgments given in the other Contracting State by virtue of point 2 of Article 6 or Article 10 shall be recognized and enforced in the Federal Republic of Germany in accordance with Title III. Any effects which judgments given in that State may have on third parties by application of Articles 68, 72, 73 and 74 of the code of civil procedure (Zivilprozeßordnung) shall also be recognized in the other Contracting States.

ARTICLE VA

In matters relating to maintenance, the expression 'court' includes the Danish administrative authorities.

ARTICLE VB

In proceedings involving a dispute between the master and a member of the crew of a sea-going ship registered in Denmark, in Greece [, in Ireland or in Portugal], concerning remuneration or other conditions of service, a court in a Contracting State shall establish whether the diplomatic or consular officer responsible for the ship has been notified of the dispute. It shall stay the proceedings so long as he has not been notified. It shall of its own motion decline jurisdiction if the officer, having been duly notified, has exercised the powers accorded to him in the matter by a consular convention, or in the absence of such a convention, has, within the time allowed, raised any objection to the exercise of such jurisdiction.

ARTICLE VC

Articles 52 and 53 of this Convention shall, when applied by Article 69(5) of the Convention for the European patent for the common market, signed at Luxembourg on 15th December 1975, to the provisions relating to 'residence' in the English text of that Convention, operate as if 'residence' in that text were the same as 'domicile' in Articles 52 and 53.

ARTICLE VD

Without prejudice to the jurisdiction of the European Patent Office under the Convention on the grant of European patents, signed at Munich on 5th October 1973, the courts of each Contracting State shall have exclusive jurisdiction, regardless of domicile, in proceedings concerned with the registration or validity of any European patent granted for that State which is not a Community patent by virtue of the provisions of Article 86 of the Convention for the European Patent for the common market, signed at Luxembourg on 15th December 1975.

ARTICLE VI

The Contracting States shall communicate to the Secretary-General of the Council of the European Communities the text of any provisions of their laws which amend either those articles of their laws mentioned in the Convention or the lists of courts specified in Section 2 of Title III of the Convention.

[(*Signatures of Plenipotentiaries of the original six Contracting States*)]]

Note. As to the substitution of this Schedule, see the note to art 1 (p 2912). The text of the Schedule remains unchanged, except for the words in square brackets which are inserted or substituted as noted to the above mentioned art 1.

SCHEDULE 2

TEXT OF 1971 PROTOCOL, AS AMENDED   Section 2(2)

ARTICLE 1

The Court of Justice of the European Communities shall have jurisdiction to give rulings on the interpretation of the Convention on Jurisdiction and the Enforcement of Judgments in Civil and Commercial Matters and of the Protocol annexed to that Convention, signed at Brussels on 27th September 1968, and also on the interpretation of the present Protocol.

The Court of Justice of the European Communities shall also have jurisdiction to give rulings on the interpretation of the Convention on the Accession of the Kingdom of Denmark, Ireland and the United Kingdom of Great Britain and Northern Ireland to the Convention of 27th September 1968 and to this Protocol.

ARTICLE 2

The following courts may request the Court of Justice to give preliminary rulings on questions of interpretation:
  (*1*) — *in Belgium: la Cour de Cassation—het Hof van Cassatie and le Conseil d'État— de Raad van State,*
     — *in Denmark: højesteret,*
     — *in the Federal Republic of Germany: die obersten Gerichtshöfe des Bundes,*
     — *in France: la Cour de Cassation and le Conseil d'État,*
     — *in Ireland, the Supreme Court,*
     — *in Italy: la Corte Suprema di Cassazione,*
     — *in Luxembourg: la Cour supérieure de Justice when sitting as Cour de Cassation,*
     — *in the Netherlands: de Hoge Raad,*
     — *in the United Kingdom: the House of Lords and courts to which application has been made under the second paragraph of Article 37 or under Article 41 of the Convention.*
  (*2*) *the courts of the Contracting States when they are sitting in an appellate capacity;*
  (*3*) *in the cases provided for in Article 37 of the Convention, the courts referred to in that Article.*

ARTICLE 3

(*1*) Where a question of interpretation of the Convention or of one of the other instruments referred to in Article 1 is raised in a case pending before one of the courts listed in Article 2(*1*), that court shall, if it considers that a decision on the question is necessary to enable it to give judgment, request the Court of Justice to give a ruling thereon.

(*2*) Where such a question is raised before any court referred to in Article 2(*2*) or (*3*), that court may, under the conditions laid down in paragraph (*1*), request the Court of Justice to give a ruling thereon.

ARTICLE 4

(*1*) The competent authority of a Contracting State may request the Court of Justice to give a ruling on a question of interpretation of the Convention or of one of the other instruments referred to in Article 1 if judgments given by courts of that State conflict with the interpretation given either by the Court of Justice or in a judgment of one of the courts of another Contracting State referred to in Article 2(*1*) or (*2*). The provisions of this paragraph shall apply only to judgments which have become res judicata.

(*2*) The interpretation given by the Court of Justice in response to such a request shall not affect the judgments which give rise to the request for interpretation.

(*3*) The Procurators-General of the Courts of Cassation of the Contracting States, or any other authority designated by a Contracting State, shall be entitled to request the Court of Justice for a ruling on interpretation in accordance with paragraph (*1*).

(*4*) The Registrar of the Court of Justice shall give notice of the request to the Contracting States, to the Commission and to the Council of the European Communities; they shall then be entitled within two months of the notification to submit statements of case or written observations to the Court.

(*5*) No fees shall be levied or any costs or expenses awarded in respect of the proceedings provided for in this Article.

ARTICLE 5

(*1*) Except where this Protocol otherwise provides, the provisions of the Treaty establishing the European Economic Community and those of the Protocol on the Statute of the Court of Justice annexed thereto, which are applicable when the Court is requested to give a preliminary ruling, shall also apply to any proceedings for the interpretation of the Convention and the other instruments referred to in Article 1.

(*2*) The Rules of Procedure of the Court of Justice shall, if necessary, be adjusted and supplemented in accordance with Article 188 of the Treaty establishing the European Economic Community.

ARTICLE 6

This Protocol shall apply to the European territories of the Contracting States, including Greenland, to the French overseas departments and territories and to Mayotte.

The Kingdom of the Netherlands may declare at the time of signing or ratifying this Protocol or at any later time, by notifying the Secretary-General of the Council of the European Communities, that this Protocol shall be applicable to the Netherlands Antilles.

Notwithstanding the first paragraph, this Protocol shall not apply to:

(*1*) the Faroe Islands, unless the Kingdom of Denmark makes a declaration to the contrary,

(*2*) any European territory situated outside the United Kingdom for the international relations of which the United Kingdom is responsible, unless the United Kingdom makes a declaration to the contrary in respect of any such territory.

Such declarations may be made at any time by notifying the Secretary-General of the Council of the European Communities.

*   *   *   *   *

[SCHEDULE 2

ARTICLE 1

The Court of Justice of the European Communities shall have jurisdiction to give rulings on the interpretation of the Convention on jurisdiction and the enforcement of judgments in civil and commercial matters and of the Protocol annexed to that Convention, signed at Brussels on 27th September 1968, and also on the interpretation of the present Protocol.

The Court of Justice of the European Communities shall also have jurisdiction to give rulings on the interpretation of the Convention on the accession of the Kingdom of Denmark, Ireland and the United Kingdom of Great Britain and Northern Ireland to the Convention of 27th September 1968 and to this Protocol.

The Court of Justice of the European Communities shall also have jurisdiction to give rulings on the interpretation of the Convention on the accession of the Hellenic Republic to the Convention of 27th September 1968 and to this Protocol, as adjusted by the 1978 Convention.

[The Court of Justice of the European Communities shall also have jurisdiction to give rulings on the interpretation of the Convention on the accession of the Hellenic Republic to the Convention of 27th September 1968 and to this Protocol, as adjusted by the 1978 Convention.

The Court of Justice of the European Communities shall also have jurisdiction to give rulings on the interpretation of the Convention on the accession of the Kingdom of Spain and the Portuguese Republic to the Convention of 27th September 1968 and to this Protocol, as adjusted by the 1978 Convention and the 1982 Convention.]

ARTICLE 2

The following courts may request the Court of Justice to give preliminary rulings on questions of interpretation—
1. — in Belgium: la Cour de Cassation—het Hof van Cassatie and le Conseil d'État—de Raad van State,
— in Denmark: højesteret,
— in the Federal Republic of Germany: die obersten Gerichtshöfe des Bundes,
— in Greece: the αμωτατα δικαστηπια
[— in Spain: el Tribunal Supremo,]
— in France: la Cour de Cassation and le Conseil d'État,
— in Ireland: the Supreme Court,
— in Italy: la Corte Suprema di Cassazione,
— in Luxembourg: la Cour supérieure de Justice when sitting as Cour de Cassation,
— in the Netherlands: de Hoge Raad,
[— in Portugal: o Supremo Tribunal de Justiça and o Supremo Tribunal Adminstrativo,]
— in the United Kingdom: the House of Lords and courts to which application has been made under the second paragraph of Article 37 or under Article 41 of the Convention.
2. The courts of the Contracting States when they are sitting in an appellate capacity.
3. In the cases provided for in Article 37 of the Convention, the courts referred to in that Article.

ARTICLE 3

1. Where a question of interpretation of the Convention or of one of the other instruments referred to in Article 1 is raised in a case pending before one of the courts listed in point 1 of Article 2, that court shall, if it considers that a decision on the question is necessary to enable it to give judgment, request the Court of Justice to give a ruling thereon.

2. Where such a question is raised before any court referred to in point 2 or 3 of Article 2, that court may, under the conditions laid down in paragraph 1, request the Court of Justice to give a ruling thereon.

ARTICLE 4

1. The competent authority of a Contracting State may request the Court of Justice to give a ruling on a question of interpretation of the Convention or of one of the other instruments referred to in Article 1 if judgments given by courts of that State conflict with the interpretation given either by the Court of Justice or in a judgment of one of the courts of another Contracting State referred to in point 1 or 2 of Article 12. The provisions of this paragraph shall apply only to judgments which have become res judicata.

2. The interpretation given by the Court of Justice in response to such a request shall not affect the judgments which gave rise to the request for interpretation.

3. The Procurators-General of the Courts of Cassation of the Contracting States, or any other authority designated by a Contracting State, shall be entitled to request the Court of Justice for a ruling on interpretation in accordance with paragraph 1.

4. The Registrar of the Court of Justice shall give notice of the request to the Contracting States, to the Commission and to the Council of the European Communities; they shall then be entitled within two months of the notification to submit statements of case or written observations to the Court.

5. No fees shall be levied or any costs or expenses awarded in respect of the proceedings provided for in this Article.

ARTICLE 5

1. Except where this Protocol otherwise provides, the provisions of the Treaty establishing the European Economic Community and those of the Protocol on the Statute of the Court of Justice annexed thereto, which are applicable when the Court is requested to give a preliminary ruling, shall also apply to any proceedings for the interpretation of the Convention and the other instruments referred to in Article 1.

2. The Rules of Procedure of the Court of Justice shall, if necessary, be adjusted and supplemented in accordance with Article 188 of the Treaty establishing the European Economic Community.

ARTICLE 6

This Protocol shall apply to the European territories of the Contracting States, including Greenland, to the French overseas departments and territories, and to Mayotte.

The Kingdom of the Netherlands may declare at the time of signing or ratifying this Protocol or at any later time, by notifying the Secretary-General of the Council of the European Communities, that this Protocol shall be applicable to the Netherlands Antilles.

Notwithstanding the first paragraph, this Protocol shall not apply to:

(1) the Faroe Islands, unless the Kingdom of Denmark makes a declaration to the contrary,

(2) any European territory situated outside the United Kingdom for the international relations of which the United Kingdom is responsible, unless the United Kingdom makes a declaration to the contrary in respect of any such territory.

Such declarations may be made at any time by notifying the Secretary-General of the Council of the European Communities [deleted].

ARTICLE 7

This Protocol shall be ratified by the signatory States. The instruments of ratification shall be deposited with the Secretary-General of the Council of the European Communities.

ARTICLE 8

This Protocol shall enter into force on the first day of the third month following the deposit of the instrument of ratification by the last signatory State to take this step; provided that it shall at the earliest enter into force at the same time as the Convention of 27 September 1968 on jurisdiction and the enforcement of judgments in civil and commercial matters.

ARTICLE 9

The Contracting States recognize that any State which becomes a member of the European Economic Community, and to which Article 63 of the Convention on jurisdiction and the enforcement of judgments in civil and commercial matters applies, must accept the provisions of this Protocol, subject to such adjustments as may be required.

ARTICLE 10

The Secretary-General of the Council of the European Communities shall notify the signatory States of:
(a) the deposit of each instrument of ratification;
(b) the date of entry into force of this Protocol;
(c) any designation received pursuant to Article 4;
(d) any declaration received pursuant to Article 6.
[The Secretary-General of the Council of the European Communities shall notify the signatory States of—
(a) the deposit of each instrument of ratification;
(b) the date of entry into force of this Protocol;
(c) any designation received pursuant to Article 4(3);
(d) [Deleted].]

ARTICLE 11

The Contracting States shall communicate to the Secretary-General of the Council of the European Communities the texts of any provisions of their laws which necessitate an amendment to the list of courts in point 1 of Article 2.

ARTICLE 12

This Protocol is concluded for an unlimited period.

ARTICLE 13

Any Contracting State may request the revision of this Protocol. In this event, a revision conference shall be convened by the President of the Council of the European Communities.

ARTICLE 14

This Protocol, drawn up in a single original in the Dutch, French, German and Italian languages, all four texts being equally authentic, shall be deposited in the archives of the Secretariat of the Council of the European Communities. The Secretary-General shall transmit a certified copy to the Government of each signatory State.]

Note. This Schedule substituted by Civil Jurisdiction and Judgments Act 1982 (Amendment) Order 1989, SI 1989 No 1346, art 9(2), Sch 2.

This Schedule was again substituted by Civil Jurisdiction and Judgments Act 1982

(Amendment) Order 1990, SI 1990 No 2591, art 12(2), Sch 2, as from 1 December 1991. The text of the new Schedule is the text set out above with any amendments taken in as shown in square brackets. Further substituted by SI 2000 No 1824, art 8(2), Sch 2.

*   *   *   *   *

SCHEDULE 3

TEXT OF TITLES V AND VI OF ACCESSION CONVENTION

TITLE V   Section 2(2)

TRANSITIONAL PROVISIONS

ARTICLE 34

[(1) The 1968 Convention and the 1971 Protocol, with the amendments made by this Convention, shall apply only to legal proceedings instituted and to authentic instruments formally drawn up or registered after the entry into force of this Convention in the State of origin and, where recognition or enforcement of a judgment or authentic instrument is sought, in the State addressed.

(2) However, as between the six Contracting States to the 1968 Convention, judgments given after the date of entry into force of this Convention in proceedings instituted before that date shall be recognised and enforced in accordance with the provisions of Title III of the 1968 Convention as amended.

(3) Moreover, as between the six Contracting States to the 1968 Convention and the three States mentioned in Article 1 of this Convention, and as between those three States, judgments given after the date of entry into force of this Convention between the State of origin and the State addressed in proceedings instituted before that date shall also be recognised and enforced in accordance with the provisions of Title III of the 1968 Convention as amended if jurisdiction was founded upon rules which accorded with the provisions of Title II, as amended, or with provisions of a convention concluded between the State of origin and the State addressed which was in force when the proceedings were instituted.]

*   *   *   *   *

Note. The whole of this Schedule substituted by Civil Jurisdiction and Judgments Act 1982 (Amendment) Order 1990, SI 1990 No 2591, art 12(3), Sch 3, as from 1 December 1991. The text of art 34 is that set out above.

[SCHEDULE 3A

TEXT OF TITLES V AND VI OF 1982 ACCESSION CONVENTION   Section 2(2)

TITLE V

TRANSITIONAL PROVISIONS

ARTICLE 12

(1) The 1968 Convention and the 1971 Protocol, as amended by the 1978 Convention and this Convention, shall apply only to legal proceedings instituted and to authentic instruments formally drawn up or registered after the entry into force of this Convention in the State of origin and, where recognition or enforcement of a judgment or authentic instrument is sought, in the State addressed.

(2) However, judgments given after the date of entry into force of this Convention between the State of origin and the State addressed in proceedings instituted before that date shall be recognized and enforced in accordance with the provisions of Title III of the 1968 Convention, as amended by the 1978 Convention and this Convention, if jurisdiction was founded upon rules which accorded with the provisions of Title II of the 1968 Convention, as amended, or with the provisions of a

convention which was in force between the State of origin and the State addressed when the proceedings were instituted.

TITLE VI

FINAL PROVISIONS

ARTICLE 13

The Secretary-General of the Council of the European Communities shall transmit a certified copy of the 1968 Convention, of the 1971 Protocol and of the 1978 Convention in the Danish, Dutch, English, French, German, Irish and Italian languages to the Government of the Hellenic Republic.

The texts of the 1968 Convention, of the 1971 Protocol and of the 1978 Convention, drawn up in the Greek language, shall be annexed to this Convention. The texts drawn up in the Greek language shall be authentic under the same conditions as the other texts of the 1968 Convention, the 1971 Protocol and the 1978 Convention.

ARTICLE 14

This Convention shall be ratified by the signatory States. The instruments of ratification shall be deposited with the Secretary-General of the Council of the European Communities.

ARTICLE 15

This Convention shall enter into force, as between the States which have ratified it, on the first day of the third month following the deposit of the last instrument of ratification by the Hellenic Republic and those States which have put into force the 1978 Convention in accordance with Article 39 of that Convention.

It shall enter into force for each Member State which subsequently ratifies it on the first day of the third month following the deposit of its instrument of ratification.

ARTICLE 16

The Secretarty-General of the Council of the European Communities shall notify the signatory States of:

    (a) the deposit of each instrument of ratification;

    (b) the dates of entry into force of this Convention for the Contracting States.

ARTICLE 17

This Convention, drawn up in a single original in the Danish, Dutch, English, French, German, Greek, Irish and Italian languages, all eight texts being equally authentic, shall be deposited in the archives of the General Secretariat of the Council of the European Communities. The Secretary-General shall transmit a certified copy to the Government of each signatory State.]

Note. This Schedule inserted by Civil Jurisdiction and Judgments Act 1982 (Amendment) Order 1989, SI 1989 No 1346, art 9(3), Sch 3, as from 1 October 1989.

[SCHEDULE 3B

TEXT OF TITLES VI AND VII OF 1989 ACCESSION CONVENTION   Section 2(2)

TITLE VI

TRANSITIONAL PROVISIONS

ARTICLE 29

(1) The 1968 Convention and the 1971 Protocol, as amended by the 1978 Convention, the 1982 Convention and this Convention, shall apply only to legal proceedings instituted and to authentic instruments formally drawn up or

registered after the entry into force of this Convention in the State of origin and, where recognition or enforcement of a judgment or authentic instrument is sought, in the State addressed.

(2) However, judgments given after the date of entry into force of this Convention between the State of origin and the State addressed in proceedings instituted before that date shall be recognized and enforced in accordance with the provisions of Title III of the 1968 Convention, as amended by the 1978 Convention, the 1982 Convention and this Convention, if jurisdiction was founded upon rules which accorded with the provisions of Title II of the 1968 Convention, as amended, or with the provisions of a convention which was in force between the State of origin and the State addressed when the proceedings were instituted.

TITLE VII

FINAL PROVISIONS

ARTICLE 30

(1) The Secretary-General of the Council of the European Communities shall transmit a certified copy of the 1968 Convention, of the 1971 Protocol, or the 1978 Convention and of the 1982 Convention in the Danish, Dutch, English, French, German, Irish and Italian languages to the Governments of the Kingdom of Spain and of the Portuguese Republic.

(2) The texts of the 1968 Convention, of the 1971 Protocol, of the 1978 Convention and of the 1982 Convention, drawn up in the Portuguese and Spanish languages, are set out in Annexes II, III, IV and V to this Convention. The texts drawn up in the Portuguese and Spanish languages shall be authentic under the same conditions as the other texts of the 1968 Convention, the 1971 Protocol, the 1978 Convention and the 1982 Convention.

ARTICLE 31

This Convention shall be ratified by the signatory States. The instruments of ratification shall be deposited with the Secretary-General of the Council of the European Communities.

ARTICLE 32

(1) This Convention shall enter into force on the first day of the third month following the date on which two signatory States, of which one is the Kingdom of Spain or the Portuguese Republic, deposit their instruments of ratification.

(2) This Convention shall take effect in relation to any other signatory State on the first day of the third month following the deposit of its instrument of ratification.

ARTICLE 33

The Secretary-General of the Council of the European Communities shall notify the signatory States of:
   (a) the deposit of each instrument of ratification;
   (b) the dates of entry into force of this Convention for the Contracting States.

ARTICLE 34

This Convention, drawn up in a single original in the Danish, Dutch, English, French, German, Greek, Irish, Italian, Portuguese and Spanish languages, all 10 texts being equally authentic, shall be deposited in the archives of the General Secretariat of the Council of the European Communities. The Secretary-General shall transmit a certified copy to the Government of each signatory State.]

Note. This Schedule inserted by Civil Jurisdiction and Judgments Act 1982 (Amendment) Order 1990, SI 1990 No 2591, art 12(4), Sch 4, as from 1 December 1991.

[SCHEDULE 3BB   Section 2(2)]

TEXT OF TITLES V AND VI OF 1996 ACCESSION CONVENTION]

TITLE V

TRANSITIONAL PROVISIONS

ARTICLE 13

(1) The 1968 Convention and the 1971 Protocol, as amended by the 1978 Convention, the 1982 Convention, the 1989 Convention and by this Convention, shall apply only to legal proceedings instituted and to authentic instruments formally drawn up or registered after the entry into force of this Convention in the State of origin and, where recognition or enforcement of a judgment or authentic instrument is sought, in the Sate addressed.

(2) However, judgments given after the date of entry into force of this Convention between the State of origin and the State addressed in proceedings instituted before that date shall be recognised and enforced in accordance with the provisions of Title III of the 1968 Convention, as amended by the 1978 Convention, the 1982 Convention, the 1989 Convention and this Convention, if jurisdiction was founded upon rules which accorded with the provision of Title II, as amended, of the 1968 Convention, or with the provisions of a convention which was in force between the State of origin and the State addressed when the proceedings were instituted.

TITLE VI

FINAL PROVISIONS

ARTICLE 14

(1) the Secretary-General of the Council of the European Union shall transmit a certified copy of the 1968 Convention, of the 1971 Protocol, of the 1978 Convention, of the 1982 Convention of the 1989 Convention in the Danish, Dutch, English, German, Greek, Irish, Italian, Spanish and Portuguese languages to the Governments of the Republic of Austria, the Republic of Finland and the Kingdom of Sweden.

(2) The texts of the 1968 Convention, of the 1971 Protocol, of the 1978 Convention, of the 1982 Convention and of the 1989 Convention, drawn up in the Finnish and Swedish languages, shall be authentic under the same conditions as the other texts of the 1968 Convention, the 1971 Protocol, and 1978 Convention, the 1982 Convention and the 1989 Convention.

ARTICLE 15

This Convention shall be ratified by the signatory States. The instruments of ratification shall be deposited with the Secretary-General of the Council of the European Union.

ARTICLE 16

(1) This Convention shall enter into force on the first day of the third month following the date on which two signatory States, one of which is the Republic of Austria, the Republic of Finland or the Kingdom of Sweden, deposit their instruments of ratification.

(2) This Convention shall produce its effects for any other signatory State on the first day of the third month following the deposit of its instrument of ratification.

ARTICLE 17

The Secretary-General of the Council of the European Union shall notify the signatory States of:
  (a) the deposit of each instrument of ratification;
  (b) the dates of entry into force of this Convention for the Contracting States.

ARTICLE 18

This Convention, drawn up in a single original in the Danish, Dutch, English, Finnish, French, German, Greek, Irish, Italian, Portuguese, Spanish and Swedish languages, all twelve texts being equally authentic, shall be deposited in the archives of the General Secretariat of the Council of the European Union. The Secretary-General shall transmit a certified copy to the Government of each signatory State.]

Note. This Schedule inserted by SI 2000 No 1824, art 8(3), Sch 3.

[SCHEDULE 3C   Section 3A(2)

TEXT OF THE LUGANO CONVENTION

ARRANGEMENT OF PROVISIONS

CONVENTION ON JURISDICTION AND THE ENFORCEMENT OF
JUDGMENTS IN CIVIL AND COMMERCIAL MATTERS

Preamble

The High Contracting Parties to this Convention,

Anxious to strengthen in their territories the legal protection of persons therein established,

Considering that it is necessary for this purpose to determine the international jurisdition of their courts, to facilitate recognition and to introduce an expeditious procedure for securing the enforcement of judgments, authentic instruments and court settlements,

Aware of the links between them, which have been sanctioned in the economic field by the free trade agreements concluded between the European Economic Community and the States members of the European Free Trade Association,

Taking into account the Brussels Convention of 27 September 1968 on jurisdiction and the enforcement of judgments in civil and commercial matters, as amended by the Accession Conventions under the successive enlargements of the European Communities,

Persuaded that the extension of the principles of that Convention to the States parties to this instrument will strengthen legal and economic co-operation in Europe,

Desiring to ensure as uniform an interpretation as possible of this instrument,

Have in this spirit decided to conclude this Convention and

Have agreed as follows:

TITLE I

SCOPE

ARTICLE 1

This Convention shall apply in civil and commercial matters whatever the nature of the court or tribunal. It shall not extend, in particular, to revenue, customs or administrative matters.

The Convention shall not apply to:
1. the status or legal capacity of natural persons, rights in property arising out of a matrimonial relationship, wills and succession;
2. bankruptcy, proceedings relating to the winding-up of insolvent companies or other legal persons, judicial arrangements, compositions and analogous proceedings;
3. social security;
4. arbitration.

TITLE II

JURISDICTION

Section 1

General Provisions

ARTICLE 2

Subject to the provisions of this Convention, persons domiciled in a Contracting State shall, whatever their nationality, be sued in the courts of that State.

Persons who are not nationals of the State in which they are domiciled shall be governed by the rules of jurisdiction applicable to nationals of that State.

ARTICLE 3

Persons domiciled in a Contracting State may be sued in the courts of another Contracting State only by virtue of the rules set out in Sections 2 to 6 of this Title.

In particular the following provisions shall not be applicable as against them:
— in Belgium: Article 15 of the civil code (Code civil—Burgerlijk Wetboek) and Article 638 of the judicial code (Code judiciaire—Gerechtelijk Wetboek),
— in Denmark: Article 246(2) and (3) of the law on civil procedure (Lov om rettens pleje),
— in the Federal Republic of Germany: Article 23 of the code of civil procedure (Zivilprozeßordnung),
— in Greece: Article 40 of the code of civil procedure (Κῶδικαζ πολιτικῆζ δικονομίαζ),
— in France: Articles 14 and 15 of the civil code (Code civil),
— in Ireland: the rules which enable jurisdiction to be founded on the document instituting the proceedings having been served on the defendant during his temporary presence in Ireland,
— in Iceland: Article 77 of the Civil Proceedings Act (lög um meðferð einkamála í héraði),
— in Italy: Articles 2 and 4, Nos 1 and 2 of the code of civil procedure (Codice di procedura civile),
— in Luxembourg: Articles 14 and 15 of the civil code (Code civil),
— in the Netherlands: Articles 126(3) and 127 of the code of civil procedure (Wetboek van Bergherlijke Rechtsvordering),
— in Norway: Section 32 of the Civil Proceedings Act (tvistemålsloven),
— in Austria: Article 99 of the Law on Court Jurisdiction (Jurisdiktionsnorm),
— in Portugal: Articles 65(1)(c), 65(2) and 65A(c) of the code of civil procedure (Código de Processo Civil) and Article 11 of the code of labour procedure (Código de Processo de Trabalho),
— in Switzerland: le for du lieu du séquestre/Gerichtsstand des Arrestortes/foro del luogo del sequestro within the meaning of Article 4 of the loi fédérale sur le droit international privé/Bundesgesetz über das internationale Privatrecht/legge federale sul diritto internazionale privato,
— in Finland: the second, third and fourth sentences of Section 1 of Chapter 10 of the Code of Judicial Procedure (oikeudenkäymiskaari/rättegångsbalken),
— in Sweden: the first sentence of Section 3 of Chapter 10 of the Code of Judicial Procedure (Rättegångsbalken),
— in the United Kingdom: the rules which enable jurisdiction to be founded on:
   (a) the document instituting the proceedings having been served on the defendant during his temporary presence in the United Kingdom; or
   (b) the presence within the United Kingdom of property belonging to the defendant; or
   (c) the seizure by the plaintiff of property situated in the United Kingdom.

ARTICLE 4

If the defendant is not domiciled in a Contracting State, the jurisdiction of the courts of each Contracting State shall, subject to the provisions of Article 16, be determined by the law of that State.

As against such a defendant, any person domiciled in a Contracting State may, whatever his nationality, avail himself in that State of the rules of jurisdiction there in force, and in particular those specified in the second paragraph of Article 3, in the same way as the nationals of that State.

Section 2

Special Jurisdiction

ARTICLE 5

A person domiciled in a Contracting State may, in another Contracting State, be sued:

1. in matters relating to a contract, in the courts for the place of performance of the obligation in question; in matters relating to individual contracts of employment, this place is that where the employee habitually carries out his work, or if the employee does not habitually carry out his work in any one country, this place shall be the place of business through which he was engaged;

2. in matters relating to maintenance, in the courts for the place where the maintenance creditor is domiciled or habitually resident or, if the matter is ancillary to proceedings concerning the status of a person, in the court which, according to its own law, has jurisdiction to entertain those proceedings, unless that jurisdiction is based solely on the nationality of one of the parties;

3. in matters relating to tort, delict or quasi-delict, in the courts for the place where the harmful event occurred;

4. as regards a civil claim for damages or restitution which is based on an act giving rise to criminal proceedings, in the court seised of those proceedings, to the extent that that court has jurisdiction under its own law to entertain civil proceedings;

5. as regards a dispute arising out of the operations of a branch, agency or other establishment, in the courts for the place in which the branch, agency or other establishment is situated;

6. in his capacity as settlor, trustee or beneficiary of a trust created by the operation of a statute, or by a written instrument, or created orally and evidenced in writing, in the courts of the Contracting State in which the trust is domiciled;

7. as regards a dispute concerning the payment of remuneration claimed in respect of the salvage of a cargo or freight, in the court under the authority of which the cargo or freight in question:

    (a) has been arrested to secure such payment,

    or

    (b) could have been so arrested, but bail or other security has been given; provided that this provision shall apply only if it is claimed that the defendant has an interest in the cargo or freight or had such an interest at the time of salvage.

ARTICLE 6

A person domiciled in a Contracting State may also be sued:

1. where he is one of a number of defendants, in the courts for the place where any one of them is domiciled;

2. as a third party in an action on a warranty or guarantee or in any other third party procededings, in the court seised of the original proceedings, unless these were instituted solely with the object of removing him from the jurisdiction of the court which would be competent in his case;

3. on a counterclaim arising from the same contract or facts on which the original claim was based, in the court in which the original claim is pending;

4. in matters relating to a contract, if the action may be combined with an action against the same defendant in matters relating to rights *in rem* in

immovable property, in the court of the Contracting State in which the property is situated.

ARTICLE 6A

Where by virtue of this Convention a court of a Contracting State has jurisdiction in actions relating to liability arising from the use of operation of a ship, that court, or any other court substituted for this purpose by the internal law of that State, shall also have jurisdiction over claims for limitation of such liability.

Section 3

Jurisdiction in Matters Relating to Insurance

ARTICLE 7

In matters relating to insurance, jurisdiction shall be determined by this Section, without prejudice to the provisions of Articles 4 and 5(5).

ARTICLE 8

An insurer domiciled in a Contracting State may be sued:
1. in the courts of the State where he is domiciled; or
2. in another Contracting State, in the courts for the place where the policy-holder is domiciled; or
3. if he is a co-insurer, in the courts of a Contracting State in which proceedings are brought against the leading insurer.

An insurer who is not domiciled in a Contracting State but has a branch, agency or other establishment in one of the Contracting States shall, in disputes arising out of the operations of the branch, agency or establishment, be deemed to be domiciled in that State.

ARTICLE 9

In respect of liability insurance or insurance of immovable property, the insurer may in addition be sued in the courts for the place where the harmful event occurred. The same applies if movable and immovable property are covered by the same insurance policy and both are adversely affected by the same contingency.

ARTICLE 10

In respect of liability insurance, the insurer may also, if the law of the court permits it, be joined in proceedings which the injured party has brought against the insured.

The provisions of Articles 7, 8 and 9 shall apply to actions brought by the injured party directly against the insurer, where such direct actions are permitted.

If the law governing such direct actions provides that the policy-holder or the insured may be joined as a party to the action, the same court shall have jurisdiction over them.

ARTICLE 11

Without prejudice to the provisions of the third paragraph of Article 10, an insurer may bring proceedings only in the courts of the Contracting State in which the defendant is domiciled, irrespective of whether he is the policy-holder, the insured or a beneficiary.

The provisions of this Section shall not affect the right to bring a counterclaim in the court in which, in accordance with this Section, the original claim is pending.

ARTICLE 12

The provisions of this Section may be departed from only by an agreement on jurisdiction:

1. which is entered into after the dispute has arisen; or
2. which allows the policy-holder, the insured or a beneficiary to bring proceedings in courts other than those indicated in this Section; or
3. which is concluded between a policy-holder and an insurer, both of whom are at the time of conclusion of the contract domiciled or habitually resident in the same Contracting State, and which has the effect of conferring jurisdiction on the courts of that State even if the harmful event were to occur abroad, provided that such an agreement is not contrary to the law of the State; or
4. which is concluded with a policy-holder who is not domiciled in a Contracting State, except insofar as the insurance is compulsory or relates to immovable property in a Contracting State; or
5. which relates to a contract of insurance insofar as it covers one or more of the risks set out in Article 12A.

ARTICLE 12A

The following are the risks referred to in Article 12(5):
1. any loss of or damage to:
(a) sea-going ships, installations situated offshore or on the high seas, or aircraft, arising from perils which relate to their use for commercial purposes;
(b) goods in transit other than passengers' baggage where the transit consists of or includes carriage by such ships or aircraft;
2. any liability, other than for bodily injury to passengers or loss of or damage to their baggage;
(a) arising out of the use or operation of ships, installations or aircraft as referred to in (1)(a) above in so far as the law of the Contracting State in which such aircraft was registered does not prohibit agreements on jurisdiction regarding insurance of such risks;
(b) for loss or damage caused by goods in transit as described in (1)(b) above;
3. any financial loss connected with the use or operation of ships, installations or aircraft as referred to in (2)(a) above, in particular loss of freight or charter-hire;
4. any risk or interest connected with any of those referred to in (1) to (3) above.

Section 4

Jurisdiction Over Consumer Contracts

ARTICLE 13

In proceedings concerning a contract concluded by a person for a purpose which can be regarded as being outside his trade or profession, hereinafter called 'the consumer', jurisdiction shall be determined by this Section, without prejudice to the provisions of Articles 4 and 5(5), if it is:

1. a contract for the sale of goods on instalment credit terms; or
2. a contract for a loan repayable by instalments, or for any other form of credit, made to finance the sale of goods; or
3. any other contract for the supply of goods or a contract for the supply of services, and
(a) in the State of the consumer's domicile the conclusion of the contract was preceded by a specific invitation addressed to him or by advertising, and
(b) the consumer took in that State the steps necessary for the conclusion of the contract.

Where a consumer enters into a contract with a party who is not domiciled in a Contracting State but has a branch, agency or other establishment in one of the Contracting States, that party shall, in disputes arising out of the operations of the branch, agency or establishment, be deemed to be domiciled in that State.

This Section shall not apply to contracts of transport.

ARTICLE 14

A consumer may bring proceedings against the other party to a contract either in the courts of the Contracting State in which that party is domiciled or in the courts of the Contracting State in which he is himself domiciled.

Proceedings may be brought against a consumer by the other party to the contract only in the courts of the Contracting State in which the consumer is domiciled.

These provisions shall not affect the right to bring a counterclaim in the court in which, in accordance with this Section, the original claim is pending.

ARTICLE 15

This provisions of this Section may be departed from only by an agreement:
1. which is entered into after the dispute has arisen; or
2. which allows the consumer to bring proceedings in courts other than those indicated in this Section; or
3. which is entered into by the consumer and the other party to the contract, both of whom are at the time of conclusion of the contract domiciled or habitually resident in the same Contracting State, and which confers jurisdiction on the courts of that State, provided that such an agreement is not contrary to the law of that State.

Section 5

Exclusive Jurisdiction

ARTICLE 16

The following courts shall have exclusive jurisdiction, regardless of domicile:
1. (a) in proceedings which have as their object rights *in rem* in immovable property or tenancies of immovable property, the courts of the Contracting State in which the property is situated;
   (b) however, in proceedings which have as their object tenancies of immovable property concluded for temporary private use for a maximum period of six consecutive months, the courts of the Contracting State in which the defendant is domiciled shall also have jurisdiction, provided that the tenant is a natural person and neither party is domiciled in the Contracting State in which the property is situated;
2. in proceedings which have as their object the validity of the constitution, the nullity or the dissolution of companies or other legal persons or associations of natural or legal persons, or the decisions of their organs, the courts of the Contracting State in which the company, legal person or association has its seat;
3. in proceedings which have as their object the validity of entries in public registers, the courts of the Contracting State in which the register is kept;
4. in proceedings concerned with the registration or validity of patents, trade marks, designs, or other similar rights required to be deposited or registered, the courts of the Contracting State in which the deposit or registration has been applied for, has taken place or is under the terms of an international convention deemed to have taken place;

5. in proceedings concerned with the enforcement of judgments, the courts of the Contracting State in which the judgment has been or is to be enforced.

Section 6

Prorogation of Jurisdiction

ARTICLE 17

1. If the parties, one or more of whom is domiciled in a Contracting State, have agreed that a court or the courts of a Contracting State are to have jurisdition to settle any disputes which have arisen or which may arise in connection with a particular legal relationship, that court or those courts shall have exclusive jurisdiction. Such an agreement conferring jurisdiction shall be either:

    (a) in writing or evidenced in writing, or

    (b) in a form which accords with practices which the parties have established between themselves, or

    (c) in international trade or commerce, in a form which accords with a usage of which the parties are or ought to have been aware and which in such trade or commerce is widely known to, and regularly observed by, parties to contracts of the type involved in the particular trade or commerce concerned.

Where such an agreement is concluded by parties, none of whom is domiciled in a Contracting State, the courts of other Contracting States shall have no jurisdiction over their disputes unless the court or courts chosen have declined jurisdiction.

2. The court or courts of a Contracting State on which a trust instrument has conferred jurisdiction shall have exclusive jurisdiction in any proceedings brought against a settlor, trustee or beneficiary, if relations between these persons or their rights or obligations under the trust are involved.

3. Agreements or provisions of a trust instrument conferring jurisdiction shall have no legal force if they are contrary to the provisions of Article 12 or 15, or if the courts whose jurisdiction they purport to exclude have exclusive jurisdiction by virtue of Article 16.

4. If an agreement conferring jurisdiction was concluded for the benefit of only one of the parties, that party shall retain the right to bring proceedings in any other court which has jurisdiction by virtue of this Convention.

5. In matters relating to individual contracts of employment an agreement conferring jurisdiction shall have legal force only if it is entered into after the dispute has arisen.

ARTICLE 18

Apart from jurisdiction derived from other provisions of this Convention, a court of a Contracting State before whom a defendant enters an appearance shall have jurisdiction. This rule shall not apply where appearance was entered solely to contest the jurisdiction, or where another court has exclusive jurisdiction by virtue of Article 16.

Section 7

Examination as to Jurisdiction and Admissibility

ARTICLE 19

Where a court of a Contracting State is seised of a claim which is principally concerned with a matter over which the courts of another Contracting State have exclusive jurisdiction by virtue of Article 16, it shall declare of its own motion that it has no jurisdiction.

ARTICLE 20

Where a defendant domiciled in one Contracting State is sued in a court of another Contracting State and does not enter an appearance, the court shall declare of its own motion that it has no jurisdiction unless its jurisdiction is derived from the provisions of this Convention.

The court shall stay the proceedings so long as it is not shown that the defendant has been able to receive the document instituting the proceedings or an equivalent document in sufficient time to enable him to arrange for his defence, or that all necessary steps have been taken to this end.

The provisions of the foregoing paragraph shall be replaced by those of Article 15 of the Hague Convention of 15 November 1965 on the service abroad of judicial and extrajudicial documents in civil or commercial matters, if the document instituting the proceedings or notice thereof had to be transmitted abroad in accordance with that Convention.

Section 8

Lis pendens—**Related Actions**

ARTICLE 21

Where proceedings involving the same cause of action and between the same parties are brought in the courts of different Contracting States, any court other than the court first seised shall of its own motion stay its proceedings until such time as the jurisdiction of the court first seised is established.

Where the jurisdiction of the court first seised is established, any court other than the court first seised shall decline jurisdiction in favour of that court.

ARTICLE 22

Where related actions are brought in the courts of different Contracting States, any court other than the court first seised may, while the actions are pending at first instance, stay its proceedings.

A court other than the court first seised may also, on the application of one of the parties, decline jurisdiction if the law of that court permits the consolidation of related actions and the court first seised has jurisdiction over both actions.

For the purposes of this Article, actions are deemed to be related where they are so closely connected that it is expedient to hear and determine them together to avoid the risk of irreconcilable judgments resulting from separate proceedings.

ARTICLE 23

Where actions come within the exclusive jurisdiction of several courts, any court other than the court first seised shall decline jurisdiction in favour of that court.

Section 9

Provisional, Including Protective, Measures

ARTICLE 24

Application may be made to the courts of a Contracting State for such provisional, including protective, measures as may be available under the law of that State, even if, under this Convention, the courts of another Contracting State have jurisdiction as to the substance of the matter.

TITLE III

RECOGNITION AND ENFORCEMENT

ARTICLE 25

For the purposes of this Convention, 'judgment' means any judgment given by a court or tribunal of a Contracting State, whatever the judgment may be called, including a decree, order, decision or writ of execution, as well as the determination of costs or expenses by an officer of the court.

Section 1

Recognition

ARTICLE 26

A judgment given in a Contracting State shall be recognised in the other Contracting States without any special procedure being required.

Any interested party who raises the recognition of a judgment as the principal issue in a dispute may, in accordance with the procedures provided for in Sections 2 and 3 of this Title, apply for a decision that the judgment be recognised.

If the outcome of proceedings in a court of a Contracting State depends on the determination of an incidental question of recognition that court shall have jurisdiction over that question.

ARTICLE 27

A judgment shall not be recognised:
1.   if such recognition is contrary to public policy in the State in which recognition is sought;
2.   where it was given in default of appearance, if the defendant was not duly served with the document which instituted the proceedings or with an equivalent document in sufficient time to enable him to arrange for his defence;
3.   if the judgment is irreconcilable with a judgment given in a dispute between the same parties in the State in which recognition is sought;
4.   if the court of the State of origin, in order to arrive at its judgment, has decided a preliminary question concerning the status or legal capacity of natural persons, rights in property arising out of a matrimonial relationship, wills or succession in a way that conflicts with a rule of the private international law of the State in which the recognition is sought, unless the same result would have been reached by the application of the rules of private international law of that State.
5.   if the judgment is irreconcilable with an earlier judgment given in a non-contracting State involving the same cause of action and between the same parties, provided that this latter judgment fulfils the conditions necessary for its recognition in the State addressed.

ARTICLE 28

Moreover, a judgment shall not be recognised if it conflicts with the provisions of Section 3, 4 or 5 of Title II or in a case provided for in Article 59.

A judgment may furthermore be refused recognition in any case provided for in Article 54B(3) or 57(4).

In its examination of the grounds of jurisdiction referred to in the foregoing paragraphs, the court or authority applied to shall be bound by the findings of fact on which the court of the State of origin based its jurisdiction.

Subject to the provisions of the first and second paragraphs, the jurisdiction of the court of the State of origin may not be reviewed; the test of public policy referred to in Article 27(1) may not be applied to the rules relating to jurisdiction.

ARTICLE 29

Under no circumstances may a foreign judgment be reviewed as to its substance.

ARTICLE 30

A court of a Contracting State in which recognition is sought of a judgment given in another Contracting State may stay the proceedings if an ordinary appeal against the judgment has been lodged.

A court of a Contracting State in which recognition is sought of a judgment given in Ireland or the United Kingdom may stay the proceedings if enforcement is suspended in the State of origin by reason of an appeal.

Section 2

Enforcement

ARTICLE 31

A judgment given in a Contracting State and enforceable in that State shall be enforced in another Contracting State when, on the application of any interested party, it has been declared enforceable there.

However, in the United Kingdom, such a judgment shall be enforced in England and Wales, in Scotland, or in Northern Ireland when, on the application of any interested party, it has been registered for enforcement in that part of the United Kingdom.

ARTICLE 32

1. The application shall be submitted:
   — in Belgium, to the tribunal de première instance or rechtbank van eerste aanleg,
   — in Denmark, to the byret,
   — in the Federal Republic of Germany, to the presiding judge of a chamber of the Landgericht,
   — in Greece, to the μονομελεζ πρωτοδικείο,
   — in Spain, to the Juzgado de Primera Instancia,
   — in France, to the presiding judge of the tribunal de grande instance,
   — in Ireland, to the High Court,
   — in Iceland, to the héraðsdómari,
   — in Italy, to the corte d'appello,
   — in Luxembourg, to the presiding judge of the tribunal d'arrondissement,
   — in the Netherlands, to the presiding judge of the arrondissementsrechtbank,
   — in Norway, to the herredsrett or byrett as namsrett,
   — in Austria, to the Landesgericht or the Kreisgericht,
   — in Portugal, to the Tribunal Judicial de Círculo,
   — in Switzerland:
      (a) in respect of judgments ordering the payment of a sum of money, to the juge de la mainlevée/Rechtsöffnungsrichter/giudice competente a pronunciare sul rigetto dell'opposizione, within the framework of the procedure governed by Articles 80 and 81 of the loi fédérale sur la poursuite pour dettes et al faillite/Bundesgesetz über Schuldbetreibung und Konkurs/legge federale sulla esecuzione e sul fallimento;

(b) in respect of judgments ordering a performance other than the payment of a sum of money, to the juge cantonal d'exequatur compétent/zuständiger kantonaler Vollstreckungsrichter/giudice cantonale competente a pronunciare l'exequatur,

— in Finland, to the ulosotonhaltija/överexekutor,
— in Sweden, to the Svea hovrätt,
— in the United Kingdom:
   (a) in England and Wales, to the High Court of Justice, or in the case of a maintenance judgment to the Magistrates' Court on transmission by the Secretary of State;
   (b) in Scotland, to the Court of Session, or in the case of a maintenance judgment to the Sheriff Court on transmission by the Secretary of State;
   (c) in Northern Ireland, to the High Court of Justice, or in the case of a maintenance judgment to the Magistrates' Court on transmission by the Secretary of State.

2. The jurisdiction of local courts shall be determined by reference to the place of domicile of the party against whom enforcement is sought. If he is not domiciled in the State in which enforcement is sought, it shall be determined by reference to the place of enforcement.

ARTICLE 33

The procedure for making the application shall be governed by the law of the State in which enforcement is sought.

The applicant must give an address for service of process within the area of jurisdiction of the court applied to. However, if the law of the State in which enforcement is sought does not provide for the furnishing of such an address, the applicant shall appoint a representative *ad litem.*

The documents referred to in Articles 46 and 47 shall be attached to the application.

ARTICLE 34

The court applied to shall give its decision without delay; the party against whom enforcement is sought shall not at this stage of the proceedings be entitled to make any submissions on the application.

The application may be refused only for one of the reasons specified in Articles 27 and 28.

Under no circumstances may the foreign judgment be reviewed as to its substance.

ARTICLE 35

The appropriate officer of the court shall without delay bring the decisions given on the application to the notice of the applicant in accordance with the procedure laid down by the law of the State in which enforcement is sought.

ARTICLE 36

If enforcement is authorised, the party against whom enforcement is sought may appeal against the decision within one month of service thereof.

If that party is domiciled in a Contracting State other than that in which the decision authorising enforcement was given, the time for appealing shall be two months and shall run from the date of service, either on him in person or at his residence. No extension of time may be granted on account of distance.

ARTICLE 37

1. An appeal against the decision authorising enforcement shall be lodged in accordance with the rules governing procedure in contentious matters:
— in Belgium, with the tribunal de première instance or rechtbank van eerste aanleg,
— in Denmark, with the landsret,
— in the Federal Republic of Germany, with the Oberlandesgericht,
— in Greece, with the ἐφετεῖπ,
— in Spain, with the Audiencia Provincial,
— in France, with the cour d'appel,
— in Ireland, with the High Court,
— in Iceland, with the héraðsdómari,
— in Italy, with the corte d'appello,
— in Luxembourg, with Cour supérieure de justice sitting as a court of civil appeal,
— in the Netherlands, with the arrondissementsrechtbank,
— in Norway, with the lagmannsrett,
— in Austria, with the Landesgericht or the Kreisgericht,
— in Portugal, with the Tribunal de Relação,
— in Switzerland, with the tribunal cantonal/Kantonsgericht/tribunale cantonale,
— in Finland, with the hovioikeus/hovrätt,
— in Sweden, with the Svea hovrätt,
— in the United Kingdom:
  (a) in England and Wales, with the High Court of Justice, or in the case of a maintenance judgment with the Magistrates' Court;
  (b) in Scotland, with the Court of Session, or in the case of a maintenance judgment with the Sheriff Court;
  (c) in Northern Ireland, with the High Court of Justice, or in the case of a maintenance judgment with the Magistrates' Court.
2. The judgment given on the appeal may be contested only:
— in Belgium, Greece, Spain, France, Italy, Luxembourg and in the Netherlands, by an appeal in cassation,
— in Denmark, by an appeal to the højesteret, with the leave of the Minister of Justice,
— in the Federal Republic of Germany, by a Rechtsbeschwerde,
— in Ireland, by an appeal on a point of law to the Supreme Court,
— in Iceland, by an appeal to the Hæstiréttur,
— in Norway, by an appeal (kjæremål or anke) to the Hoyesteretts Kjæremålsutvalg or Hoyesterett,
— in Austria, in the case of an appeal, by a Revisionsrekurs and, in the case of opposition proceedings, by a Berufung with the possibility of a Revision,
— in Portugal, by an appeal on a point of law,
— in Switzerland, by a recours de droit public devant le tribunal fédéral/ staatsrechtliche Beschwerde beim Bundesgericht/ricorso di diritto pubblico davanti al tribunale federale,
— in Finland, by an appeal to the korkein oikeus/högsta domstolen,
— in Sweden, by an appeal to the högsta domstolen,
— in the United Kingdom, by a single further appeal on a point of law.

ARTICLE 38

The court with which the appeal under the first paragraph of Article 37 is lodged may, on the application of the appellant, stay the proceedings if an ordinary appeal has been lodged against the judgment in the State of origin or if the time for such an appeal has not yet expired; in the latter case, the court may specify the time within which such an appeal is to be lodged.

Where the judgment was given in Ireland or the United Kingdom, any form of appeal available in the State of origin shall be treated as an ordinary appeal for the purposes of the first paragraph.

The court may also make enforcement conditional on the provision of such security as it shall determine.

ARTICLE 39

During the time specified for an appeal pursuant to Article 36 and until any such appeal has been determined, no measures of enforcement may be taken other than protective measures taken against the property of the party against whom enforcement is sought.

The decision authorising enforcement shall carry with it the power to proceed to any such protective measures.

ARTICLE 40

1. If the application for enforcement is refused, the applicant may appeal:
— in Belgium, to the cour d'appel or hof van beroep,
— in Denmark, to the landsret,
— in the Federal Republic of Germany, to the Oberlandesgericht,
— in Greece, to the ἐφετείπ,
— in Spain, to the Audiencia Provincial,
— in France, to the cour d'appel,
— in Ireland, to the High Court,
— in Iceland, to the héraðsdómari,
— in Italy, to the corte d'appello,
— in Luxembourg, to the Cour supérieure de justice sitting as a court of civil appeal,
— in the Netherlands, to the gerechtshof,
— in Norway, to the lagmannsrett,
— in Austria, to the Landesgericht or the Kreisgericht,
— in Portugal, to the Tribunal de Relação,
— in Switzerland, to the tribunal cantonal/Kantonsgericht/tribunale cantonale,
— in Finland, to the hovioikeus/hovrätt,
— in Sweden, to the Svea hovrätt,
— in the United Kingdom:
  (a) in England and Wales, to the High Court of Justice, or in the case of a maintenance judgment to the Magistrates' Court;
  (b) in Scotland, to the Court of Session, or in the case of a maintenance judgment to the Sheriff Court;
  (c) in Northern Ireland, to the High Court of Justice, or in the case of a maintenance judgment to the Magistrates' Court.

2. The party against whom enforcement is sought shall be summoned to appear before the appellate court. If he fails to appear, the provisions of the second and third paragraphs of Article 20 shall apply even where he is not domiciled in any of the Contracting States.

ARTICLE 41

A judgment given on an appeal provided for in Article 40 may be contested only:
— in Belgium, Greece, Spain, France, Italy, Luxembourg and in the Netherlands, by an appeal in cassation,
— in Denmark, by an appeal to the højesteret, with the leave of the Minister of Justice,
— in the Federal Republic of Germany, by a Rechtsbeschwerde,
— in Ireland, by an appeal on a point of law to the Supreme Court,

— in Iceland, by an appeal to the Hæstiréttur,
— in Norway, by an appeal (kjæremål or anke) to the Hoyesteretts kjæremålsutvalg or Hoyesterett,
— in Austria, by a Revisionsrekurs,
— in Portugal, by an appeal on a point of law,
— in Switzerland, by a recours de droit public devant le tribunal fédéral/ staatsrechtliche Beschwerde beim Bundesgericht/ricorso di diritto pubblico davanti al tribunale federale,
— in Finland, by an appeal to the korkein oikeus/högsta domstolen,
— in Sweden, by an appeal to the högsta domstolen,
— in the United Kingdom, by a single further appeal on a point of law.

ARTICLE 42

Where a foreign judgment has been given in respect of several matters and enforcement cannot be authorised for all of them, the court shall authorise enforcement for one or more of them.

An applicant may request partial enforcement of a judgment.

ARTICLE 43

A foreign judgment which orders a periodic payment by way of a penalty shall be enforceable in the State in which enforcement is sought only if the amount of the payment has been finally determined by the courts of the State of origin.

ARTICLE 44

An applicant who, in the State of origin, has benefited from complete or partial legal aid or exemption from costs or expenses, shall be entitled, in the procedures provided for in Articles 32 to 35, to benefit from the most favourable legal aid or the most extensive exemption from costs or expenses provided for by the law of the State addressed.

However, an applicant who requests the enforcement of a decision given by an administrative authority in Denmark or in Iceland in respect of a maintenance order may, in the State addressed, claim the benefits referred to in the first paragraph if he presents a statement from, respectively, the Danish Ministry of Justice or the Icelandic Ministry of Justice to the effect that he fulfils the economic requirements to qualify for the grant of complete or partial legal aid or exemption from costs or expenses.

ARTICLE 45

No security, bond or deposit, however described, shall be required of a party who in one Contracting State applies for enforcement of a judgment given in another Contracting State on the ground that he is a foreign national or that he is not domiciled or resident in the State in which enforcement is sought.

Section 3

Common Provisions

ARTICLE 46

A party seeking recognition or applying for enforcement of a judgment shall produce:
  1. a copy of the judgment which satisfies the conditions necessary to establish its authenticity;
  2. in the case of a judgment given in default, the original or a certified true copy of the document which establishes that the party in default was served with the document instituting the proceedings or with an equivalent document.

ARTICLE 47

A party applying for enforcement shall also produce:
1. documents which establish that, according to the law of the State of origin, the judgment is enforceable and has been served;
2. where appropriate, a document showing that the applicant is in receipt of legal aid in the State of origin.

ARTICLE 48

If the documents specified in Article 46(2) and Article 47(2) are not produced, the court may specify a time for their production, accept equivalent documents or, if it considers that it has sufficient information before it, dispense with their production.

If the court so requires, a translation of the documents shall be produced; the translation shall be certified by a person qualified to do so in one of the Contracting States.

ARTICLE 49

No legalisation or other similar formality shall be required in respect of the documents referred to in Article 46 or 47 or the second paragraph of Article 48, or in respect of a document appointing a representative *ad litem.*

TITLE IV

AUTHENTIC INSTRUMENTS AND COURT SETTLEMENTS

ARTICLE 50

A document which has been formally drawn up or registered as an authentic instrument and is enforceable in one Contracting State shall, in another Contracting State, be declared enforceable there, on application made in accordance with the procedures provided for in Articles 31 *et seq.* The application may be refused only if enforcement of the instrument is contrary to public policy in the State addressed.

The instrument produced must satisfy the conditions necessary to establish its authenticity in the State of origin.

The provisions of Section 3 of Title III shall apply as appropriate.

ARTICLE 51

A settlement which has been approved by a court in the course of proceedings and is enforceable in the State in which it was concluded shall be enforceable in the State addressed under the same conditions as authentic instruments.

TITLE V

GENERAL PROVISIONS

ARTICLE 52

In order to determine whether a party is domiciled in the Contracting State whose courts are seised of a matter, the court shall apply its internal law.

If a party is not domiciled in the State whose courts are seised of the matter, then, in order to determine whether the pary is domiciled in another Contracting State, the court shall apply the law of that State.

ARTICLE 53

For the purposes of this Convention, the seat of a company or other legal person or association of natural or legal persons shall be treated as its domicile. However, in order to determine that seat, the court shall apply its rules of private international law.

In order to determine whether a trust is domiciled in the Contracting State whose courts are seised of the matter, the court shall apply its rules of private international law.

TITLE VI

TRANSITIONAL PROVISIONS

ARTICLE 54

The provisions of this Convention shall apply only to legal proceedings instituted and to documents formally drawn up or registered as authentic instruments after its entry into force in the State of origin and, where recognition or enforcement of a judgment or authentic instrument is sought, in the State addressed.

However, judgments given after the date of entry into force of this Convention between the State of origin and the State addressed in proceedings instituted before that date shall be recognised and enforced in accordance with the provisions of Title III if jurisdiction was founded upon rules which accorded with those provided for either in Title II of this Convention or in a convention concluded between the State of origin and the State addressed which was in force when the proceedings were instituted.

If the parties to a dispute concerning a contract had agreed in writing before the entry into force of this Convention that the contract was to be governed by the law of Ireland or of a part of the United Kingdom, the courts of Ireland or of that part of the United Kingdom shall retain the right to exercise jurisdiction in the dispute.

ARTICLE 54A

For a period of three years from the entry into force of this Convention for Denmark, Greece, Ireland, Iceland, Norway, Finland and Sweden, respectively, jurisdiction in maritime matters shall be determined in these States not only in accordance with the provisions of Title II, but also in accordance with the provisions of paragraphs 1 to 7 following. However, upon the entry into force of the International Convention relating to the arrest of sea-going ships, signed at Brussels on 10 May 1952, for one of these States, these provisions shall cease to have effect for that State.

1. A person who is domiciled in a Contracting State may be sued in the courts of one of the States mentioned above in respect of a maritime claim if the ship to which the claim relates or any other ship owned by him has been arrested by judicial process within the territory of the latter State to secure the claim, or could have been so arrested there but bail or other security has been given, and either:

    (a) the claimant is domiciled in the latter State; or

    (b) the claim arose in the latter State; or

    (c) the claim concerns the voyage during which the arrest was made or could have been made; or

    (d) the claim arises out of a collision or out of damage caused by a ship to another ship or to goods or persons on board either ship, either by the execution or non-execution of a manoeuvre or by the non-observance of regulations; or

    (e) the claim is for salvage; or

    (f) the claim is in respect of a mortgage or hypothecation of the ship arrested.

2. A claimant may arrest either the particular ship to which the maritime claim relates, or any other ship which is owned by the person who was, at the time when

the maritime claim arose, the owner of the particular ship. However, only the particular ship to which the maritime claim relates may be arrested in respect of the maritime claims set out in 5(o), (p) or (q) of this Article.

3. Ships shall be deemed to be in the same ownership when all the shares therein are owned by the same person or persons.

4. When in the case of a charter by demise of a ship the charterer alone is liable in respect of a maritime claim relating to that ship, the claimant may arrest that ship or any other ship owned by the charterer, but no other ship owned by the owner may be arrested in respect of such claim. The same shall apply to any case in which a person other than the owner of a ship is liable in respect of a maritime claim relating to that ship.

5. The expression 'maritime claim' means a claim arising out of one or more of the following:

(a) damage caused by any ship either in collision or otherwise;

(b) loss of life or personal injury caused by any ship or occurring in connection with the operation of any ship;

(c) salvage;

(d) agreement relating to the use or hire of any ship whether by charterparty or otherwise;

(e) agreement relating to the carriage of goods in any ship whether by charterparty or otherwise;

(f) loss of or damage to goods including baggage carried in any ship;

(g) general average;

(h) bottomry;

(i) towage;

(j) pilotage;

(k) goods or materials wherever supplied to a ship for her operation or maintenance;

(l) construction, repair or equipment of any ship or dock charges and dues;

(m) wages of masters, officers or crew;

(n) master's disbursements, including disbursements made by shippers, charterers or agents on behalf of a ship or her owner;

(o) dispute as to the title to or ownership of any ship;

(p) disputes between co-owners of any ship as to the ownership, possession, employment or earnings of that ship;

(q) the mortgage or hypothecation of any ship.

6. In Denmark, the expression 'arrest' shall be deemed, as regards the maritime claims referred to in 5(o) and (p) of this Article, to include a 'forbud', where that is the only procedure allowed in respect of such a claim under Articles 646 to 653 of the law on civil procedure (lov om rettens pleje).

7. In Iceland, the expression 'arrest' shall be deemed, as regards the maritime claims referred to in 5(o) and (p) of this Article, to include a 'lögbann', where that is the only procedure allowed in respect of such a claim under Chapter III of the law on arrest and injunction (lög um kyrrsetningu og lögbann).

TITLE VII

RELATIONSHIP TO THE BRUSSELS CONVENTION AND TO OTHER CONVENTIONS

ARTICLE 54B

1. This Convention shall not prejudice the application by the Member States of the European Communities of the Convention on Jurisdiction and the Enforcement of Judgments in Civil and Commercial Matters, signed at Brussels on 27 September 1968 and the Protocol on interpretation of that Convention by the Court of Justice, signed at Luxembourg on 3 June 1971, as amended by the Conventions of Accession

to the said Convention and the said Protocol by the States acceding to the European Communities, all of these Conventions and the Protocol being hereinafter referred to as the 'Brussels Convention'.

2. However, this Convention shall in any event be applied:

(a) in matters of jurisdiction, where the defendant is domiciled in the territory of a Contracting State which is not a member of the European Communities, or where Article 16 or 17 of this Convention confers a jurisdiction on the courts of such a Contracting State;

(b) in relation to a *lis pendens* or to related actions as provided for in Articles 21 and 22, when proceedings are instituted in a Contracting State which is not a member of the European Communities and in a Contracting State which is a member of the European Communities;

(c) in matters of recognition and enforcement, where either the State of origin or the State addressed is not a member of the European Communities.

3. In addition to the grounds provided for in Title III recognition or enforcement may be refused if the ground of jurisdiction on which the judgment has been based differs from that resulting from this Convention and recognition or enforcement is sought against a party who is domiciled in a Contracting State which is not a member of the European Communities, unless the judgment may otherwise be recognised or enforced under any rule of law in the State addressed.

ARTICLE 55

Subject to the provisions of the second paragraph of Article 54 and of Article 56, this Convention shall, for the States which are parties to it, supersede the following conventions concluded between two or more of them:

— the Convention between the Swiss Confederation and France on jurisdiction and enforcement of judgments in civil matters, signed at Paris on 15 June 1869.

— the Treaty between the Swiss Confederation and Spain on the mutual enforcement of judgments in civil or commercial matters, signed at Madrid on 19 November 1896,

— the Convention between the Swiss Confederation and the German Reich on the recognition and enforcement of judgments and arbitration awards, signed at Berne on 2 November 1929,

— the Convention between Denmark, Finland, Iceland, Norway and Sweden on the recognition and enforcement of judgments, signed at Copenhagen on 16 March 1932,

— the Convention between the Swiss Confederation and Italy on the recognition and enforcement of judgments, signed at Rome on 3 January 1933,

— the Convention between Sweden and the Swiss Confederation on the recognition and enforcement of judgments and arbitral awards, signed at Stockholm on 15 January 1936,

— the Convention between the Kingdom of Belgium and Austria on the reciprocal recognition and enforcement of judgments and authentic instruments relating to maintenance obligations, signed at Vienna on 25 October 1957,

— the Convention between the Swiss Confederation and Belgium on the recognition and enforcement of judgments and arbitration awards, signed at Berne on 29 April 1959,

— the Convention between the Federal Republic of Germany and Austria on the reciprocal recognition and enforcement of judgments, settlements and authentic instruments in civil and commercial matters, signed at Vienna on 6 June 1959,

— the Convention between the Kingdom of Belgium and Austria on the reciprocal recognition and enforcement of judgments, arbitral awards and authentic instruments in civil and commercial matters, signed at Vienna on 16 June 1959,

— the Convention between Austria and the Swiss Confederation on the recognition and enforcement of judgments, signed at Berne on 16 December 1960,

— the Convention between Norway and the United Kingdom providing for the reciprocal recognition and enforcement of judgments in civil matters, signed at London on 12 June 1961,

— the Convention between the United Kingdom and Austria providing for the reciprocal recognition and enforcement of judgments in civil and commercial matters, signed at Vienna on 14 July 1961, with amending Protocol signed at London on 6 March 1970,

— the Convention between the Kingdom of the Netherlands and Austria on the reciprocal recognition and enforcement of judgments and authentic instruments in civil and commercial matters, signed at The Hague on 6 February 1963,

— the Convention between France and Austria on the recognition and enforcement of judgments and authentic instruments in civil and commercial matters, signed at Vienna on 15 July 1966,

— the Convention between Luxembourg and Austria on the recognition and enforcement of judgments and authentic instruments in civil and commercial matters, signed at Luxembourg on 29 July 1971,

— the Convention between Italy and Austria on the recognition and enforcement of judgments in civil and commercial matters, of judicial settlements and of authentic instruments, signed at Rome on 16 November 1971,

— the Convention between Norway and the Federal Republic of Germany on the recognition and enforcement of judgments and enforceable documents, in civil and commercial matters, signed at Oslo on 17 June 1977,

— the Convention between Denmark, Finland, Iceland, Norway and Sweden on the recognition and enforcement of judgments in civil matters, signed at Copenhagen on 11 October 1977,

— the Convention between Austria and Sweden on the recognition and enforcement of judgments in civil matters, signed at Stockholm on 16 September 1982,

— the Convention between Austria and Spain on the recognition and enforcement of judgments, settlements and enforceable authentic instruments in civil and commercial matters, signed at Vienna on 17 February 1984,

— the Convention between Norway and Austria on the recognition and enforcement of judgments in civil matters, signed at Vienna on 21 May 1984, and

— the Convention between Finland and Austria on the recognition and enforcement of judgments in civil matters, signed at Vienna on 17 November 1986.

ARTICLE 56

The Treaty and the conventions referred to in Article 55 shall continue to have effect in relation to matters to which this Convention does not apply.

They shall continue to have effect in respect of judgments given and documents formally drawn up or registered as authentic instruments before the entry into force of this Convention.

ARTICLE 57

1. This Convention shall not affect any conventions to which the Contracting States are or will be parties and which, in relation to particular matters, govern jurisdiction or the recognition or enforcement of judgments.

2. This Convention shall not prevent a court of a Contracting State which is

party to a convention referred to in the first paragraph from assuming jurisdiction in accordance with that convention, even where the defendant is domiciled in a Contracting State which is not a party to that convention. The court hearing the action shall, in any event, apply Article 20 of this Convention.

3. Judgments given in a Contracting State by a court in the exercise of jurisdiction provided for in a convention referred to in the first paragraph shall be recognised and enforced in the other Contracting States in accordance with Title III of this Convention.

4. In addition to the grounds provided for in Title III, recognition or enforcement may be refused if the State addressed is not a contracting party to a convention referred to in the first paragraph and the person against whom recognition or enforcement is sought is domiciled in that State, unless the judgment may otherwise be recognised or enforced under any rule of law in the State addressed.

5. Where a convention referred to in the first paragraph to which both the State of origin and the State addressed are parties lays down conditions for the recognition or enforcement of judgments, those conditions shall apply. In any event, the provisions of this Convention which concern the procedures for recognition and enforcement of judgments may be applied.

ARTICLE 58

(None)

ARTICLE 59

This Convention shall not prevent a Contracting State from assuming, in a convention on the recognition and enforcement of judgments, an obligation towards a third State not to recognise judgments given in other Contracting States against defendants domiciled or habitually resident in the third State where, in cases provided for in Article 4, the judgment could only be founded on a ground of jurisdiction specified in the second paragraph of Article 3.

However, a Contracting State may not assume an obligation towards a third State not to recognise a judgment given in another Contracting State by a court basing its jurisdiction on the presence within that State of property belonging to the defendant, or the seizure by the plaintiff of property situated there:

1. if the action is brought to assert or declare proprietary or possessory rights in that property, seeks to obtain authority to dispose of it, or rises from another issue relating to such property, or
2. if the property constitutes the security for a debt which is the subject-matter of the action.

TITLE VIII

FINAL PROVISIONS

ARTICLE 60

The following may be parties to this Convention:

(a) States which, at the time of the opening of this Convention for signature, are members of the European Communities or of the European Free Trade Association;
(b) States which, after the opening of this Convention for signature, become members of the European Communities or of the European Free Trade Association;
(c) States invited to accede in accordance with Article 62(1)(b).

ARTICLE 61

1. This Convention shall be opened for signature by the States members of the European Communities or of the European Free Trade Association.

2. The Convention shall be submitted for ratification by the signatory States. The instruments of ratification shall be deposited with the Swiss Federal Council.

3. The Convention shall enter into force on the first day of the third month following the date on which two States, of which one is a member of the European Communities and the other a member of the European Free Trade Association, deposit their instruments of ratification.

4. The Convention shall take effect in relation to any other signatory State on the first day of the third month following the deposit of its instrument of ratification.

ARTICLE 62

1. After entering into force this Convention shall be open to accession by:
   (a) the States referred to in Article 60(b);
   (b) other States which have been invited to accede upon a request made by one of the Contracting States to the depositary State. The depositary State shall invite the State concerned to accede only if, after having communicated the contents of the communications that this State intends to make in accordance with Article 63, it has obtained the unanimous agreement of the signatory States and the Contracting States referred to in Article 60(a) and (b).

2. If an acceding State wishes to furnish details for the purposes of Protocol No 1, negotiations shall be entered into to that end. A negotiating conference shall be convened by the Swiss Federal Council.

3. In respect of an acceding State, the Convention shall take effect on the first day of the third month following the deposit of its instrument of accession.

4. However, in respect of an acceding State referred to in paragraph 1(a) or (b), the Convention shall take effect only in relations between the acceding State and the Contracting States which have not made any objections to the accession before the first day of the third month following the deposit of the instrument of accession.

ARTICLE 63

Each acceding State shall, when depositing its instrument of accession, communicate the information required for the application of Articles 3, 32, 37, 40, 41 and 55 of this Convention and furnish, if need be, the details prescribed during the negotiations for the purposes of Protocol No 1.

ARTICLE 64

1. This Convention is concluded for an initial period of five years from the date of its entry into force in accordance with Article 61(3), even in the case of States which ratify it or accede to it after that date.

2. At the end of the initial five-year period, the Convention shall be automatically renewed from year to year.

3. Upon the expiry of the initial five-year period, any Contracting State may, at any time, denounce the Convention by sending a notification to the Swiss Federal Council.

4. The denunciation shall take effect at the end of the calendar year following the expiry of a period of six months from the date of receipt by the Swiss Federal Council of the notification of denunciation.

ARTICLE 65

The following are annexed to this Convention:
— a Protocol No 1, on certain questions of jurisdiction, procedure and enforcement,

— a Protocol No 2, on the uniform interpretation of the Convention,
— a Protocol No 3, on the application of Article 57.
These Protocols shall form an integral part of the Convention.

ARTICLE 66

Any Contracting State may request the revision of this Convention. To that end, the Swiss Federal Council shall issue invitations to a revision conference within a period of six months from the date of the request for revision.

ARTICLE 67

The Swiss Federal Council shall notify the States represented at the Diplomatic Conference of Lugano and the States who have later acceded to the Convention of:
  (a) the deposit of each instrument of ratification or accession;
  (b) the dates of entry into force of this Convention in respect of the Contracting States;
  (c) any denunciation received pursuant to Article 64;
  (d) any declaration received pursuant to Article IA of Protocol No 1;
  (e) any declaration received pursuant to Article IB of Protocol No 1;
  (f) any declaration received pursuant to Article IV of Protocol No 1;
  (g) any communication made pursuant to Article IV of Protocol No 1.

ARTICLE 68

This Convention, drawn up in a single original in the Danish, Dutch, English, Finnish, French, German, Greek, Icelandic, Irish, Italian, Norwegian, Portuguese, Spanish and Swedish languages, all fourteen texts being equally authentic, shall be deposited in the archives of the Swiss Federal Council. The Swiss Federal Council shall transmit a certified copy to the Government of each State represented at the Diplomatic Conference of Lugano and to the Government of each acceding State.

Protocol No 1

On Certain Questions of Jurisdiction, Procedure and Enforcement

The High Contracting Parties have agreed upon the following provisions, which shall be annexed to the Convention:

ARTICLE I

Any person domiciled in Luxembourg who is sued in a court of another Contracting State pursuant to Article 5(1) may refuse to submit to the jurisdiction of that court. If the defendant does not enter an appearance the court shall declare of its own motion that it has no jurisdiction.

An agreement conferring jurisdiction, within the meaning of Article 17, shall be valid with respect to a person domiciled in Luxembourg only if that person has expressly and specifically so agreed.

ARTICLE IA

1. Switzerland reserves the right to declare, at the time of depositing its instrument of ratification, that a judgment given in another Contracting State shall be neither recognised nor enforced in Switzerland if the following conditions are met:
  (a) the jurisdiction of the court which has given the judgment is based only on Article 5(1) of this Convention; and

(b) the defendant was domiciled in Switzerland at the time of the introduction of the proceedings; for the purposes of this Article, a company or other legal person is considered to be domiciled in Switzerland if it has its registered seat and the effective centre of activities in Switzerland; and

(c) the defendant raises an objection to the recognition or enforcement of the judgment in Switzerland, provided that he has not waived the benefit of the declaration foreseen under this paragraph.

2. This reservation shall not apply to the extent that at the time recognition or enforcement is sought a derogation has been granted from Article 59 of the Swiss Federal Constitution. The Swiss Government shall communicate such derogations to the signatory States and the acceding States.

3. This reservation shall cease to have effect on 31 December 1999. It may be withdrawn at any time.

ARTICLE IB

Any Contracting State may, by declaration made at the time of signing or of deposit of its instrument of ratification or of accession, reserved the right, notwithstanding the provisions of Article 28, not to recognise and enforce judgments given in the other Contracting States if the jurisdiction of the court of the State of origin is based, pursuant to Article 16(1)(b), exclusively on the domicile of the defendant in the State of origin, and the property is situated in the territory of the State which entered the reservation.

ARTICLE II

Without prejudice to any more favourable provisions of national laws, persons domiciled in a Contracting State who are being prosecuted in the criminal courts of another Contracting State of which they are not nationals for an offence which was not intentionally committed may be defended by persons qualified to do so, even if they do not appear in person.

However, the court seised of the matter may order appearance in person; in the case of failure to appear, a judgment given in the civil action without the person concerned having had the opportunity to arrange for his defence need not be recognised or enforced in the other Contracting States.

ARTICLE III

In proceedings for the issue of an order for enforcement, no charge, duty or fee calculated by reference to the value of the matter in issue may be levied in the State in which enforcement is sought.

ARTICLE IV

Judicial and extrajudicial documents drawn up in one Contracting State which have to be served on persons in another Contracting State shall be transmitted in accordance with the procedures laid down in the conventions and agreements concluded between the Contracting States.

Unless the State in which service is to take place objects by declaration to the Swiss Federal Council, such documents may also be sent by the appropriate public officers of the State in which the document has been drawn up directly to the appropriate public officers of the State in which the addressee is to be found. In this case the officer of the State of origin shall send a copy of the document to the officer of the State applied to who is competent to forward it to the addressee. The document shall be forwarded in the manner specified by the law of the State applied to. The forwarding shall be recorded by a certificate sent directly to the officer of the State of origin.

ARTICLE V

The jurisdiction specified in Articles 6(2) and 10 in actions on a warranty or guarantee or in any other third party proceedings may not be resorted to in the Federal Republic of Germany, in Spain, in Austria and in Switzerland. Any person domiciled in another Contracting State may be sued in the courts:

— of the Federal Republic of Germany, pursuant to Articles 68, 72, 73 and 74 of the code of civil procedure (Zivilprozeßordnung) concerning third-party notices,
— of Spain, pursuant to Article 1482 of the civil code,
— of Austria, pursuant to Article 21 of the code of civil procedure (Zivilprozeßordnung) concerning third-party notices,
— of Switzerland, pursuant to the appropriate provisions concerning third-party notices of the cantonal codes of civil procedure.

Judgments given in the other Contracting States by virtue of Article 6(2) or Article 10 shall be recognised and enforced in the Federal Republic of Germany, in Spain, in Austria and in Switzerland in accordance with Title III. Any effects which judgments given in these States may have on third parties by application of the provisions in the preceding paragraph shall also be recognised in the other Contracting States.

ARTICLE VA

In matters relating to maintenance, the expression 'court' includes the Danish, Icelandic and Norwegian administrative authorities.

In civil and commercial matters, the expression 'court' includes the Finnish ulosotonhaltija/överexekutor.

ARTICLE VB

In proceedings involving a dispute between the master and a member of the crew of a sea-going ship registered in Denmark, in Greece, in Ireland, in Iceland, in Norway, in Portugal or in Sweden concerning remuneration or other conditions of service, a court in a Contracting State shall establish whether the diplomatic or consular officer responsible for the ship has been notified of the dispute. It shall stay the proceedings so long as he has not been notified. It shall of its own motion decline jurisdiction if the officer, having been duly notified, has exercised the powers accorded to him in the matter by a consular convention, or in the absence of such a convention has, within the time allowed, raised any objection to the exercise of such jurisdiction.

ARTICLE VC

(None)

ARTICLE VD

Without prejudice to the jurisdiction of the European Patent Office under the Convention on the grant of European patents, signed at Munich on 5 October 1973, the courts of each Contracting State shall have exclusive jurisdiction, regardless of domicile, in proceedings concerned with the registration or validity of any European patent granted for that State which is not a Community patent by virtue of the provision of Article 86 of the Convention for the European patent for the common market, signed at Luxembourg on 15 December 1975.

ARTICLE VI

The Contracting States shall communicate to the Swiss Federal Council the text of any provisions of their laws which amend either those provisions of their laws mentioned in the Convention or the lists of courts specified in Section 2 of Title III.

Protocol No 2
On the Uniform Interpretation of the Convention

PREAMBLE

The High Contracting Parties,
Having regard to Article 65 of this Convention,
Considering the substantial link between this Convention and the Brussels Convention,
Considering that the Court of Justice of the European Communities by virtue of the Protocol of 3 June 1971 has jurisdiction to give rulings on the interpretation of the provisions of the Brussels Convention,
Being aware of the rulings delivered by the Court of Justice of the European Communities on the interpretation of the Brussels Convention up to the time of signature of this Convention,
Considering that the negotiations which led to the conclusion of the Convention were based on the Brussels Convention in the light of these rulings,
Desiring to prevent, in full deference to the independence of the courts, divergent interpretations and to arrive at as uniform an interpretation as possible of the provisions of the Convention, and of these provisions and those of the Brussels Convention which are substantially reproduced in this Convention,
Have agreed as follows:

ARTICLE 1

The courts of each Contracting State shall, when applying and interpreting the provisions of the Convention, pay due account to the principles laid down by any relevant decision delivered by courts of the other Contracting States concerning provisions of this Convention.

ARTICLE 2

1. The Contracting Parties agree to set up a system of exchange of information concerning judgments delivered pursuant to this Convention as well as relevant judgments under the Brussels Convention. This system shall comprise:
— transmission to a central body by the competent authorities of judgments delivered by courts of last instance and the Court of Justice of the European Communities as well as judgments of particular importance which have become final and have been delivered pursuant to this Convention or the Brussels Convention,
— classification of these judgments by the central body including, as far as necessary, the drawing-up and publication of translations and abstracts,
— communication by the central body of the relevant documents to the competent national authorities of all signatories and acceding States to the Convention and to the Commission of the European Communities.
2. The central body is the Registrar of the Court of Justice of the European Communities.

ARTICLE 3

1. A Standing Committee shall be set up for the purposes of this Protocol.

2. The Committee shall be composed of representatives appointed by each signatory and acceding State.

3. The European Communities (Commission, Court of Justice and General Secretariat of the Council) and the European Free Trade Association may attend the meetings as observers.

ARTICLE 4

1. At the request of a Contracting party, the depositary of the Convention shall convene meetings of the Committee for the purpose of exchanging views on the functioning of the Convention and in particular on:
    — the development of the case-law as communicated under the first paragraph first indent of Article 2,
    — the application of Article 57 of the Convention.

2. The Committee, in the light of these exchanges, may also examine the appropriateness of starting on particular topics a revision of the Convention and make recommendations.

Protocol No 3

On the Application of Article 57

The High Contracting Parties have agreed as follows:
1. For the purposes of the Convention, provisions which, in relation to particular matters, govern jurisdiction or the recognition or enforcement of judgments and which are, or will be, contained in acts of the institutions of the European Communities shall be treated in the same way as the conventions referred to in paragraph 1 of Article 57.
2. If one Contracting State is of the opinion that a provision contained in an act of the institutions of the European Communities is incompatible with the Convention, the Contracting States shall promptly consider amending the Convention pursuant to Article 66, without prejudice to the procedure established by Protocol No 2.]

Note. This Schedule inserted by Civil Jurisdiction and Judgments Act 1991, s 1(3), Sch 1, as from 1 May 1992.

This Schedule further amended by SI 2000 No 1824, art 12. Please see art 12 for the amendments.

SCHEDULE 4

TITLE II OF 1968 CONVENTION AS MODIFIED FOR ALLOCATION OF JURISDICTION WITHIN UK

Section 16

TITLE II

JURISDICTION

Section 1

General Provisions

ARTICLE 2

Subject to the provisions of this **Title,** *persons domiciled in a* **part of the United Kingdom** *shall ... be sued in the courts of that* **part.**

*   *   *   *   *

ARTICLE 3

Persons domiciled in a **part of the United Kingdom** may be sued in the courts of another **part of the United Kingdom** only by virtue of the rules set out in Sections 2, **4, 5 and** 6 of this Title.

* * * * *

Section 2

Special jurisdiction

ARTICLE 5

A person domiciled in a **part of the United Kingdom** may, in another **part of the United Kingdom,** be sued:

* * * * *

(2) in matters relating to maintenance, in the courts for the place where the maintenance creditor is domiciled or habitually resident or, if the matter is ancillary to proceedings concerning the status of a person, in the court which, according to its own law, has jurisdiction to entertain those proceedings, unless that jurisdiction is based solely on the nationality of one of the parties;

* * * * *

Section 5

Exclusive jurisdiction

ARTICLE 16

The following courts shall have exclusive jurisdiction, regardless of domicile:

* * * * *

(5) in proceedings concerned with the enforcement of judgments, the courts of the **part of the United Kingdom** in which the judgment has been or is to be enforced.

Section 6

Prorogation of jurisdiction

* * * * *

ARTICLE 18

Apart from jurisdiction derived from other provisions of this **Title,** a court of a **part of the United Kingdom** before whom a defendant enters an appearance shall have jurisdiction. This rule shall not apply where appearance was entered solely to contest the jurisdiction, or where another court has exclusive jurisdiction by virtue of Article 16.

Section 7

Examination as to jurisdiction and admissibility

ARTICLE 19

Where a court of a **part of the United Kingdom** is seised of a claim which is principally concerned with a matter over which the courts of another **part of the United Kingdom** have exclusive jurisdiction by virtue of Article 16, it shall declare of its own motion that it has no jurisdiction.

ARTICLE 20

Where a defendant domiciled in one **part of the United Kingdom** is sued in a court of another **part of the United Kingdom** and does not enter an appearance, the court shall *declare of its own motion that it has no jurisdiction unless its jurisdiction is derived from the provisions of this* **Title.**

The court shall stay the proceedings so long as it is not shown that the defendant has been able to receive the document instituting the proceedings or an equivalent document in sufficient time to enable him to arrange for his defence, or that all necessary steps have been taken to this end.

*   *   *   *   *

Section 9

Provisional, including protective, measures

ARTICLE 24

Application may be made to the courts of a **part of the United Kingdom** *for such provisional, including protective, measures as may be available under the law of that* **part,** *even if, under this* **Title,** *the courts of another* **part of the United Kingdom** *have jurisdiction as to the substance of the matter.*

[SCHEDULE 4

CHAPTER II OF THE REGULATION AS MODIFIED: RULES FOR ALLOCATION OF
JURISDICTION WITHIN UK]   Section 16

[General
1. Subject to the rules of this Schedule, persons domiciled in a part of the United Kingdom shall be sued in the courts of that part.
2. Persons domiciled in a part of the United Kingdom may be sued in the courts of another part of the United Kingdom only by virtue of rules 3 to 13 of this Schedule.

Special jurisdiction
3. A person domiciled in a part of the United Kingdom may, in another part of the United Kingdom, be sued—
   (a) in matters relating to a contract, in the courts for the place of performance of the obligation in question;
   (b) in matters relating to maintenance, in the courts for the place where the maintenance creditor is domiciled or habitually resident or, if the matter is ancillary to proceedings concerning the status of a person, in the court which, according to its own law, has jurisdiction to entertain those proceedings, unless that jurisdiction is based solely on the nationality of one of the parties;
   (c) in matters relating to tort, delict or quasi-delict, in the courts for the place where the harmful event occurred or may occur;
   (d) as regards a civil claim for damages or restitution which is based on an act giving rise to criminal proceedings, in the court seised of those proceedings, to the extent that that court has jurisdiction under its own law to entertain civil proceedings;
   (e) as regards a dispute arising out of the operations of a branch, agency or other establishment, in the courts for the place in which the branch, agency or other establishment is situated;
   (f) as settlor, trustee or beneficiary of a trust created by the operation of a statute, or by a written instrument, or created orally and evidenced in writing, in the courts of the part of the United Kingdom in which the trust is domiciled;
   (g) as regards a dispute concerning the payment of remuneration claimed in respect of the salvage of a cargo or freight, in the court under the authority of which the cargo or freight in question—

    (i) has been arrested to secure such payment; or

    (ii) could have been so arrested, but bail or other security has been given;
provided that this provision shall apply only if it is claimed that the
defendant has an interest in the cargo or freight or had such an interest at
the time of salvage;

  (h) in proceedings—

    (i) concerning a debt secured on immovable property; or

    (ii) which are brought to assert, declare or determine proprietary or
possessory rights, or rights of security, in or over movable property, or
to obtain authority to dispose of movable property,

in the courts of the part of the United Kingdom in which the property is
situated.

4. Proceedings which have as their object a decision of an organ of a company
or other legal person or of an association of natural or legal persons may, without
prejudice to the other provisions of this Schedule, be brought in the courts of the
part of the United Kingdom in which that company, legal person or association has
its seat.

5. A person domiciled in a part of the United Kingdom may, in another part of
the United Kingdom, also be sued—

  (a) where he is one of a number of defendants, in the courts for the place
where anyone of them is domiciled, provided the claims are so closely
connected that it is expedient to hear and determine them together to
avoid the risk of irreconcilable judgments resulting from separate
proceedings;

  (b) as a third party in an action on a warranty or guarantee or in any other third
party proceedings, in the court seised of the original proceedings, unless
these were instituted solely with the object of removing him from the
jurisdiction of the court which would be competent in his case;

  (c) on a counter-claim arising from the same contract or facts on which the
original claim was based, in the court in which the original claim is
pending;

  (d) in matters relating to a contract, if the action may be combined with an
action against the same defendant in matters relating to rights in rem in
immovable property, in the court of the part of the United Kingdom in
which the property is situated.

6. Where by virtue of this Schedule a court of a part of the United Kingdom has
jurisdiction in actions relating to liability arising from the use or operation of a
ship, that court, or any other court substituted for this purpose by the internal law
of that part, shall also have jurisdiction over claims for limitation of such liability.

Jurisdiction over consumer contracts

7. (1) In matters relating to a contract concluded by a person, the consumer, for
a purpose which can be regarded as being outside his trade or profession,
jurisdiction shall be determined by this rule and rules 8 and 9, without prejudice
to rule 3(e) and (h)(ii), if—

  (a) it is a contract for the sale of goods on instalment credit terms; or

  (b) it is a contract for a loan repayable by instalments, or for any other form of
credit, made to finance the sale of goods; or

  (c) in all other cases, the contract has been concluded with a person who
pursues commercial or professional activities in the part of the United
Kingdom in which the consumer is domiciled or, by any means, directs such
activities to that part or to other parts of the United Kingdom including that
part, and the contract falls within the scope of such activities.

(2) This rule shall not apply to a contract of transport other than a contract which,
for an inclusive price, provides for a combination of travel and accommodation, or
to a contract of insurance.

8. (1) A consumer may bring proceedings against the other party to a contract either in the courts of the part of the United Kingdom in which that party is domiciled or in the courts of the part of the United Kingdom in which the consumer is domiciled.

(2) Proceedings may be brought against a consumer by the other party to the contract only in the courts of the part of the United Kingdom in which the consumer is domiciled.

(3) The provisions of this rule shall not affect the right to bring a counter-claim in the court in which, in accordance with this rule and rules 7 and 9, the original claim is pending.

9. The provisions of rules 7 and 8 may be departed from only by an agreement—

(a) which is entered into after the dispute has arisen; or
(b) which allows the consumer to bring proceedings in courts other than those indicated in those rules; or
(c) which is entered into by the consumer and the other party to the contract, both of whom are at the time of conclusion of the contract domiciled or habitually resident in the same part of the United Kingdom, and which confers jurisdiction on the courts of that part, provided that such an agreement is not contrary to the law of that part.

Jurisdiction over individual contracts of employment

10. (1) In matters relating to individual contracts of employment, jurisdiction shall be determined by this rule, without prejudice to rule 3(e).

(2) An employer may be sued—

(a) in the courts of the part of the United Kingdom in which he is domiciled; or
(b) in the courts of the part of the United Kingdom where the employee habitually carries out his work or in the courts of that part where he last did so; or
(c) if the employee does not or did not habitually carry out his work in any one place, in the courts of the part of the United Kingdom where the business which engaged the employee is or was situated.

(3) An employer may bring proceedings only in the courts of the part of the United Kingdom in which the employee is domiciled.

(4) The provisions of this rule shall not affect the right to bring a counter-claim in the court in which, in accordance with this rule, the original claim is pending.

(5) The provisions of this rule may be departed from only by an agreement on jurisdiction—

(a) which is entered into after the dispute has arisen; or
(b) which allows the employee to bring proceedings in courts other than those indicated in this rule.

Exclusive jurisdiction

11. The following courts shall have exclusive jurisdiction, regardless of domicile:—

(a) (i) in proceedings which have as their object rights *in rem* in immovable property or tenancies of immovable property, the courts of the part of the United Kingdom in which the property is situated;
     (ii) however, in proceedings which have as their object tenancies of immovable property concluded for temporary private use for a maximum period of six consecutive months, the courts of the part of the United Kingdom in which the defendant is domiciled shall also have jurisdiction, provided that the tenant is a natural person and that the landlord and the tenant are domiciled in the same part of the United Kingdom;

(b) in proceedings which have as their object the validity of the constitution, the nullity or the dissolution of companies or other legal persons or associations of natural or legal persons, the courts of the part of the United Kingdom in which the company, legal person or association has its seat;

(c) in proceedings which have as their object the validity of entries in public registers, the courts of the part of the United Kingdom in which the register is kept;

(d) in proceedings concerned with the enforcement of judgments, the courts of the part of the United Kingdom in which the judgment has been or is to be enforced.

Prorogation of jurisdiction

12. (1) If the parties have agreed that a court or the courts of a part of the United Kingdom are to have jurisdiction to settle any disputes which have arisen or which may arise in connection with a particular legal relationship, and, apart from this Schedule, the agreement would be effective to confer jurisdiction under the law of that part, that court or those courts shall have jurisdiction.

(2) The court or courts of a part of the United Kingdom on which a trust instrument has conferred jurisdiction shall have jurisdiction in any proceedings brought against a settlor, trustee or beneficiary, if relations between these persons or their rights or obligations under the trust are involved.

(3) Agreements or provisions of a trust instrument conferring jurisdiction shall have no legal force if they are contrary to the provisions of rule 9, or if the courts whose jurisdiction they purport to exclude have exclusive jurisdiction by virtue of rule 11.

13. (1) Apart from jurisdiction derived from other provisions of this Schedule, a court of a part of the United Kingdom before which a defendant enters an appearance shall have jurisdiction.

(2) This rule shall not apply where appearance was entered to contest the jurisdiction, or where another court has exclusive jurisdiction by virtue of rule 11.

Examination as to jurisdiction and admissibility

14. Where a court of a part of the United Kingdom is seised of a claim which is principally concerned with a matter over which the courts of another part of the United Kingdom have exclusive jurisdiction by virtue of rule 11, it shall declare of its own motion that it has no jurisdiction.

15. (1) Where a defendant domiciled in one part of the United Kingdom is sued in a court of another part of the United Kingdom and does not enter an appearance, the court shall declare of its own motion that it has no jurisdiction unless its jurisdiction is derived from the provisions of this Schedule.

(2) The court shall stay the proceedings so long as it is not shown that the defendant has been able to receive the document instituting the proceedings or an equivalent document in sufficient time to enable him to arrange for his defence, or that all necessary steps have been taken to this end.

Provisional, including protective, measures

16. Application may be made to the courts of a part of the United Kingdom for such provisional, including protective, measures as may be available under the law of that part, even if, under this Schedule, the courts of another part of the United Kingdom have jurisdiction as to the substance of the matter.]

Note. Schedule 4 substituted by SI 2001 No 3929, art 4, Sch 2, Pt II, para 4, as from 1 March 2002.

SCHEDULE 5

PROCEEDINGS EXCLUDED FROM SCHEDULE 4   Section 17

*   *   *   *   *

Appeals etc from tribunals

4. Proceedings on appeal from, or for review of, decisions of tribunals.

Maintenance and similar payments to local and other public authorities

5. Proceedings for, or otherwise relating to, an order under any of the following provisions—

(a) *section 47 or 51 of the Child Care Act 1980* [paragraph 23 of Schedule 2 to the Children Act 1989], section 80 of the Social Work (Scotland) Act 1968 *or section 156 of the Children and Young Persons Act (Northern Ireland) 1968* [section 156 of the Children and Young Persons Act (Northern Ireland) 1968 or Article 41 of the Children (Northern Ireland) Order 1995] (contributions in respect of children in care, etc);

(b) section 49 or 50 of the Child Care Act 1980, section 81 of the Social Work (Scotland) Act 1968 or section 159 of the Children and Young Persons Act (Northern Ireland) 1968 (applications for, or for variation of, affiliation orders in respect of children in care, etc);

(c) section 43 of the National Assistance Act 1948, section 18 of the Supplementary Benefits Act 1976, [section 24 of the Social Security Act 1986, *or any enactment applying in Northern Ireland and corresponding to it,* [section 106 of the Social Security Administration 1992 or any enactment applying in Northern Ireland and corresponding to either of them,]] Article 101 of the Health and Personal Social Services (Northern Ireland) Order 1972 or Article 23 of the Supplementary Benefits (Northern Ireland) Order 1977 (recovery of cost of assistance or benefit from person liable to maintain the assisted person);

(d) section 44 of the National Assistance Act 1948, section 19 of the Supplementary Benefits Act 1976, [section 25 of the Social Security Act 1986, or any enactment applying in Northern Ireland and corresponding to it,] Article 102 of the Health and Personal Social Services (Northern Ireland) Order 1972 or Article 24 of the Supplementary Benefits (Northern Ireland) Order 1977 (applications for, or for variation of, affiliation orders in respect of children for whom assistance or benefit provided).

Note. Words 'paragraph 23 ... 1989' in square brackets in sub-para (a) substituted for words in italics by Children Act 1989, s 108(5), Sch 13, para 47, as from 14 October 1991. Words 'section 156 of the ... 1995' in square brackets in sub-para (a) substituted for words in italics by Children (Northern Ireland Consequential Amendments) Order 1995, SI 1995 No 756, art 10, as from 4 November 1996. Words 'section 24 of the ... to it,' in sub-para (c) and words 'section 25 of the ... to it,' in sub-para (d) inserted by Social Security Act 1986, s 86(1), Sch 10, Part II, para 55, as from 11 April 1988. Words 'section 106 ... of them,' in square brackets in sub-para (c) substituted for words 'or any enactment ... to it,' in italics by Social Security (Consequential Provisions) Act 1992, s 4, Sch 2, para 62, as from 1 July 1992.

Proceedings under certain conventions, etc

6. Proceedings brought in any court in pursuance of—

(a) any statutory provision which, in the case of any convention to which Article 57 applies (conventions relating to specific matters which override the general rules *in the 1968 Convention* [, or Article 71 of the Regulaton,]), implements the convention or makes provision with respect to jurisdiction in any field to which the convention relates; and

(b) any rule of law so far as it has the effect of implementing any such convention.

Note. Amended and repealed in part by SI 2001/3929, art 4, Sch 2, Pt II, as from 1 March 2002.

*   *   *   *   *

Schs. 8–12. (*Schs 8, 9 apply to Scotland only; Sch 10, para 1 amends Foreign Judgments (Reciprocal Enforcement) Act 1933, s 1* (p 2084); *para 2 amends s 9(1) of that Act* (p 2090); *para 3 substitutes s 10 of that Act* (p 2090); *para 4 inserts s 10A of that Act* (p 2090); *para 5 amends s 11(1) of that Act* (p 2091); *Schs 11, 12 make minor amendments relating to maintenance orders and consequential amendments respectively, which insofar as they amend legislation printed in this work have been incorporated.*)

SCHEDULE 13   Section 53

COMMENCEMENT, TRANSITIONAL PROVISIONS AND SAVINGS

PART I

COMMENCEMENT

Provisions coming into force on Royal Assent

1. The following provisions come into force on Royal Assent:

Provision	Subject-matter
section 53(1) and Part I of this Schedule.	Commencement.
section 55	Short title.

Provisions coming into force six weeks after Royal Assent

2. The following provisions come into force at the end of the period of six weeks beginning with the day on which this Act is passed:

Provision	Subject-matter
section 24(1)(a), (2)(a) and (3).	Interim relief and protective measures in cases of doubtful jurisdiction.
section 29	Service of county court process outside Northern Ireland.
section 30	Proceedings in England and Wales or Northern Ireland for torts to immovable property.
section 31	Overseas judgments given against states.
section 32	Overseas judgments given in breach of agreement for settlement of disputes.
section 33	Certain steps not to amount to submission to jurisdiction of overseas court.
section 34	Certain judgments a bar to further proceedings on the same cause of action.

Provision	Subject-matter
section 35(3)	Consolidation of Orders in Council under section 14 of the Administration of Justice Act 1920.
section 38	Overseas judgments counteracting an award of multiple damages.

section 40	Power to modify enactments relating to legal aid, etc.
section 49	Saving for powers to stay, sist, strike out or dismiss proceedings.
section 50	Interpretation: general.
section 51	Application to Crown.
section 52	Extent.
paragraphs 7 to 10 of Part II of this Schedule and section 53(2) so far as relates to those paragraphs.	Transitional provisions and savings.
section 54 and Schedule 14 so far as relating to the repeal of provisions in section 4 of the Foreign Judgments (Reciprocal Enforcement) Act 1933.	Repeals consequential on sections 32 and 33.

Provisions coming into force on a day to be appointed

3. (1) The other provisions of this Act come into force on such day as the Lord Chancellor and the Lord Advocate may appoint by order made by statutory instrument.

(2) Different days may be appointed under this paragraph for different purposes.

Note. This Act is now all in force: see SI 1984 No 1553, SI 1986 No 1781, SI 1986 No 2044.

PART II

TRANSITIONAL PROVISIONS AND SAVINGS

Section 16 and Schedule 4

1. (1) Section 16 and Schedule 4 shall not apply to any proceedings begun before the commencement of that section.

(2) Nothing in section 16 or Schedule 4 shall preclude the bringing of proceedings in any part of the United Kingdom in connection with a dispute concerning a contract if the parties to the dispute had agreed before the commencement of that section that the contract was to be governed by the law of that part of the United Kingdom.

Section 18 and Schedule 6 and associated repeals

2. (1) In relation to a judgment a certificate whereof has been registered under the 1868 Act or the 1882 Act before the repeal of that Act by this Act, the 1868 Act or, as the case may be, the 1882 Act shall continue to have effect notwithstanding its repeal.

(2) Where by virtue of sub-paragraph (1) the 1882 Act continues to have effect in relation to an order to which section 47 of the Fair Employment (Northern Ireland) Act 1976 (damages etc for unfair discrimination) applies, that section shall continue to have effect in relation to that order notwithstanding the repeal of that section by this Act.

(3) A certificate issued under Schedule 6 shall not be registered under that Schedule in a part of the United Kingdom if the judgment to which that certificate relates is the subject of a certificate registered in that part under the 1868 Act or the 1882 Act.

(4) In this paragraph—
'the 1868 Act' means the Judgments Extension Act 1868;
'the 1882 Act' means the Inferior Courts Judgments Extension Act 1882;
'judgment' has the same meaning as in section 18.

Section 18 and Schedule 7

3. Schedule 7 and, so far as it relates to that Schedule, section 18 shall not apply to judgments given before the coming into force of that section.

Section 19

4. Section 19 shall not apply to judgments given before the commencement of that section.

5. (*Applies to Scotland only.*)

Section 26

6. The power conferred by section 26 shall not be exercisable in relation to property arrested before the commencement of that section or in relation to bail or other security given—
  (a) before the commencement of that section to prevent the arrest of property; or
  (b) to obtain the release of property arrested before the commencement of that section; or
  (c) in substitution (whether directly or indirectly) for security given as mentioned in sub-paragraph (a) or (b).

Section 31

7. Section 31 shall not apply to any judgment—
  (a) which has been registered under Part II of the Administration of Justice Act 1920 or Part I of the Foreign Judgments (Reciprocal Enforcement) Act 1933 before the time when that section comes into force; or
  (b) in respect of which proceedings at common law for its enforcement have been finally determined before that time.

Section 32 and associated repeal

8. (1) Section 32 shall not apply to any judgment—
  (a) which has been registered under Part II of the Administration of Justice Act 1920, Part I of the Foreign Judgments (Reciprocal Enforcement) Act 1933 or Part I of the Maintenance Orders (Reciprocal Enforcement) Act 1972 before the time when that section comes into force; or
  (b) in respect of which proceedings at common law for its enforcement have been finally determined before that time.

(2) Section 4(3)(b) of the Foreign Judgments (Reciprocal Enforcement) Act 1933 shall continue to have effect, notwithstanding its repeal by this Act, in relation to a judgment registered under Part I of that Act before the commencement of section 32.

Section 33 and associated repeal

9. (1) Section 33 shall not apply to any judgment—
  (a) which has been registered under Part II of the Administration of Justice Act 1920 or Part I of the Foreign Judgments (Reciprocal Enforcement) Act 1933 before the time when that section comes into force; or
  (b) in respect of which proceedings at common law for its enforcement have been finally determined before that time.

(2) The repeal by this Act of words in section 4(2)(a)(i) of the Foreign Judgments (Reciprocal Enforcement) Act 1933 shall not affect the operation of that provision in relation to a judgment registered under Part I of that Act before the commencement of section 33.

Section 34

10. Section 34 shall not apply to judgments given before the commencement of that section.

SCHEDULE 14

REPEALS

Chapter	Short Title	Extent of Repeal
41 Geo 3 c 90.	Crown Debts Act 1801.	The preamble. Sections 1 to 8.
5 Geo 4 c 111.	Crown Debts Act 1824.	The whole Act.
22 & 23 Vict c 21	Queen's Remembrancer Act 1859.	Section 24.
31 & 32 Vict c 54.	Judgments Extension Act 1868.	The whole Act.
31 & 32 Vict c 96.	Ecclesiastical Buildings and Glebes (Scotland) Act 1868.	In section 4, the words 'of the county in which the parish concerned is situated' and the words from 'provided' to the end.
45 & 46 Vict c 31.	Inferior Courts Judgments Extension Act 1882.	The whole Act.
7 Edw 7 c 51.	Sheriff Courts (Scotland) Act 1907.	In section 5, the words from *the first 'Provided'* ['Provided that actions'] to 'that jurisdiction'.
14 & 15 Geo 5 c 27.	Conveyancing (Scotland) Act 1924.	In section 23(6) the words from 'of the county' to 'is situated'.
23 & 24 Geo 5 c 13.	Foreign Judgments (Reciprocal Enforcement) Act 1933.	In section 4(2)(a)(i), the words from 'otherwise' to 'that court'. Section 4(3)(b). In section 9(1), the word 'superior' in both places where it occurs. In section 11(1), the definition of 'Judgments given in the superior courts of the United Kingdom'. In section 12, in paragraph (a) the words from '(except' to 'this Act)', and paragraph (d). In section 13(b), the words 'and section two hundred and thirteen', 'respectively' and 'and 116'.
14 Geo 6 c 37.	Maintenance Orders Act 1950.	Section 6. Section 8.

Chapter	Short Title	Extent of Repeal
14 Geo 6 c 37.	Maintenance Orders Act 1950.	Section 9(1)(a). In section 16(2)(b)(v), the words from the beginning to 'or'.
4 & 5 Eliz 2 c 46.	Administration of Justice Act 1956.	Section 51(a).
1963 c 22.	Sheriff Courts (Civil Jurisdiction and Procedure) (Scotland) Act 1963.	Section 3(2).
1965 c 2.	Administration of Justice Act 1965.1976 c 25.	In Schedule 1, the entry relating to the Crown Debts Act 1801.
1971 c 55.	Law Reform (Jurisdiction in Delict) (Scotland) Act 1971.	The whole Act.
1972 c 18.	Maintenance Orders (Reciprocal Enforcement) Act 1972.	In section 40— (a) in paragraph (a), the words 'against persons in that country or territory'; and (b) in paragraph (b), the words 'against persons in the United Kingdom'. In section 47(3), the words 'or having ceased to reside'. In the Schedule, paragraph 4.
1976 c 25.	Fair Employment (Northern Ireland) Act 1976.	Section 47.
1978 c 23.	Judicature (Northern Ireland) Act 1978.	In Part II of Schedule 5— (a) the entry relating to the Crown Debts Act 1801; and (b) in the entry relating to the Foreign Judgments (Reciprocal Enforcement) Act 1933, the word 'respectively', where last occurring, and the words 'and 116'.
1981 c 54.	Supreme Court Act 1981.	In Schedule 5, paragraph 2 of the entry relating to the Foreign Judgments (Reciprocal Enforcement) Act 1933.

Note. Entry relating to Sheriff Courts (Scotland) Act 1907 amended by Divorce Jurisdiction, Court Fees and Legal Aid (Scotland) Act 1983, s 6(1), Sch 1, para 24.

FORFEITURE ACT 1982

(1982 c 34)

An Act to provide for relief for persons guilty of unlawful killing from forfeiture of
inheritance and other rights; to enable such persons to apply for financial
provision out of the deceased's estate; to provide for the question whether pension
and social security benefits have been forfeited to be determined by the Social
Security Commissioners; and for connected purposes.   [13 July 1982]

1. The 'forfeiture rule'—(1) In this Act, the 'forfeiture rule' means the rule of
public policy which in certain circumstances precludes a person who has
unlawfully killed another from acquiring a benefit in consequence of the killing.

(2) References in this Act to a person who has unlawfully killed another include
a reference to a person who has unlawfully aided, abetted, counselled or procured
the death of that other and references in this Act to unlawful killing shall be
interpreted accordingly.

*   *   *   *   *

2. Power to modify the rule—(1) Where a court determines that the forfeiture
rule has precluded a person (in this section referred to as 'the offender') who has
unlawfully killed another from acquiring any interest in property mentioned in
subsection (4) below, the court may make an order under this section modifying
the effect of that rule.

(2) The court shall not make any order under this section modifying the effect
of the forfeiture rule in any case unless it is satisfied that, having regard to the
conduct of the offender and of the deceased and to such other circumstances as
appear to the court to be material, the justice of the case requires the effect of the
rule to be so modified in that case.

(3) In any case where a person stands convicted of an offence of which unlawful
killing is an element, the court shall not make an order under this section
modifying the effect of the forfeiture rule in that case unless proceedings for the
purpose are brought before the expiry of the period of three months beginning
with his conviction.

(4) The interests in property referred to in subsection (1) above are—
(a) any beneficial interest in property which (apart from the forfeiture rule)
    the offender would have acquired—
    (i) under the deceased's will (including, as respects Scotland, any writing
        having testamentary effect) or the law relating to intestacy or by way
        of ius relicti, ius relictae or legitim;
    (ii) on the nomination of the deceased in accordance with the provisions
        of any enactment;
    (iii) as a donatio mortis causa made by the deceased; or
    (iv) under a special destination (whether relating to heritable or moveable
        property); or
(b) any beneficial interest in property which (apart from the forfeiture rule) the
    offender would have acquired in consequence of the death of the deceased,
    being property which, before the death, was held on trust for any person.

(5) An order under this section may modify the effect of the forfeiture rule in
respect of any interest in property to which the determination referred to in
subsection (1) above relates and may do so in either or both of the following ways,
that is—
(a) where there is more than one such interest, by excluding the application of
    the rule in respect of any (but not all) of those interests; and
(b) in the case of any such interest in property, by excluding the application of
    the rule in respect of part of the property.

(6) On the making of an order under this section, the forfeiture rule shall have effect for all purposes (including purposes relating to anything done before the order is made) subject to the modifications made by the order.

(7) The court shall not make an order under this section modifying the effect of the forfeiture rule in respect of any interest in property which, in consequence of the rule, has been acquired before the coming into force of this section by a person other than the offender or a person claiming through him.

(8) In this section—
'property' includes any chose in action or incorporeal moveable property; and
'will' includes codicil.

3. Application for financial provisions not affected by the rule—(1) The forfeiture rule shall not be taken to preclude any person from making any application under a provision mentioned in subsection (2) below or the making of any order on the application.

(2) The provisions referred to in subsection (1) above are—
(a) any provision of the Inheritance (Provision for Family and Dependants) Act 1975; and
(b) sections 31(6) (variation etc of periodical payments orders) and 36(1) (variation of maintenance agreements) of the Matrimonial Causes Act 1973 and section 5(4) of the Divorce (Scotland) Act 1976 (variation etc of periodical allowances).

*   *   *   *   *

5. Exclusion of murderers. Nothing in this Act or in any order made under section 2 or referred to in section 3(1) of this Act [or in any decision made under section 4(1A) of this Act] shall affect the application of the forfeiture rule in the case of a person who stands convicted of murder.

Note. Words in square brackets inserted by Social Security Act 1986, s 76(1), (4), as from 25 July 1986.

*   *   *   *   *

7. Short title, etc—(1) This Act may be cited as the Forfeiture Act 1982.

(2) Section 4 of this Act shall come into force on such day as the Secretary of State may appoint by order made by statutory instrument; and sections 1 to 3 and 5 of this Act shall come into force on the expiry of the period of three months beginning with the day on which it is passed.

(3) This Act, except section 6, does not extend to Northern Ireland.

(4) Subject to section 2(7) of this Act, an order under section 2 of this Act or an order referred to in section 3(1) of this Act and made in respect of a person who has unlawfully killed another may be made whether the unlawful killing occurred before or after the coming into force of those sections.

CRIMINAL JUSTICE ACT 1982

(1982 c 48)

An Act to make further provision as to the sentencing and treatment of offenders (including provision as to the enforcement of fines and the standardisation of fines and of certain other sums specified in enactments relating to the powers of criminal courts) . . .   [28 October 1982]

PART III

FINES ETC

*   *   *   *   *

Introduction of standard scale of fines

37. The standard scale of fines for summary offences—(1) There shall be a standard scale of fines for summary offences, which shall be known as 'the standard scale'.

(2) *The scale at the commencement of this section is shown below.*

Level on the scale	Amount of fine
1	*£25 [£50]*
2	*£50 [£100]*
3	*£200 [£400]*
4	*£500 [£1,000]*
5	*£1,000 [£2,000]*

[(2) The standard scale is shown below—

Level on the scale	Amount of fine
1	£200
2	£500
3	£1,000
4	£2,500
5	£5,000]

(3) Where any enactment (whether contained in an Act passed before or after this Act) provides—

(a) that a person convicted of a summary offence shall be liable on conviction to a fine or a maximum fine by reference to a specified level on the standard scale; or

(b) confers power by subordinate instrument to make a person liable on conviction of a summary offence (whether or not created by the instrument) to a fine or maximum fine by reference to a specified level on the standard scale,

it is to be construed as referring to the standard scale for which this section provides as that standard scale has effect from time to time by virtue either of this section or of an order under section 143 of the Magistrates' Courts Act 1980.

Note. By the Criminal Penalties etc (Increase) Order 1984, SI 1984 No 447, art 2(4), Sch 4, the amounts of the fines on the standard scale are doubled as indicated by square brackets as from 1 May 1984. Sub-s (2) substituted by Criminal Justice Act 1991, s 17(1), as from 1 October 1992.

The Criminal Justice Act 1988, s 59 provides for the making of orders amending enactments or subordinate instruments which specify a maximum fine which may be imposed on conviction of a summary offence and which is higher than level 5 on the standard scale set out in sub-s (2) of this section, or a maximum fine which may be imposed on summary conviction for an either way offence and which is higher than the statutory maximum. At the time of going to press, no such orders had been made.

Increase of fines

38. General increase of fines for summary offences under Acts of Parliament—(1) Subject to subsection (5) below and to section 39(1) below, this section applies to any enactment contained in an Act passed before this Act (however framed or worded) which, as regards any summary offence created not later than 29th July 1977 (the date of the passing of the Criminal Law Act 1977), makes a person liable on conviction to a fine or maximum fine which—

(a) is less than £1000; and

(b) was not altered by section 30 or 31 of the Criminal Law Act 1977; and

(c) has not been altered since 29th July 1977 or has only been altered since that date by section 35 above.

(2) Subject to subsection (7) below, where an enactment to which this section applies provides on conviction of a summary offence for a fine or maximum fine in respect of a specified quantity or a specified number of things, that fine or maximum

fine shall be treated for the purposes of this section as being the fine or maximum fine for the offence.

(3) Where an enactment to which this section applies provides for different fines or maximum fines in relation to different circumstances or persons of different descriptions, they are to be treated separately for the purposes of this section.

(4) An enactment in which section 31(6) and (7) of the Criminal Law Act 1977 (pre-1949 enactments) produced the same fine or maximum fine for different convictions shall be treated for the purposes of this section as if there were omitted from it so much of it as before 29th July 1977 had the effect that a person guilty of an offence under it was liable on summary conviction to a fine or maximum fine less than the highest fine or maximum fine to which he would have been liable if his conviction had satisfied the conditions required for the imposition of the highest fine or maximum fine.

(5) This section shall not affect so much of any enactment as (in whatever words) makes a person liable on summary conviction to a fine or maximum fine for each period of a specified length during which a continuing offence is continued.

(6) The fine or maximum fine for an offence under an enactment to which this section applies shall be increased to the amount at the appropriate level on the standard scale unless it is an enactment in relation to which section 39(2) below provides for some other increase.

(7) Where an enactment to which this section applies provides on conviction of a summary offence for a fine or maximum fine in respect of a specified quantity or a specified number of things but also specifies an alternative fine or maximum fine, subsection (6) above shall have effect to increase—

(a) the alternative fine; and
(b) any amount that the enactment specifies as the maximum which a fine under it may not exceed,

as well as the fine or maximum fine which it has effect to increase by virtue of subsection (2) above.

(8) Subject to subsection (9) below, the appropriate level on the standard scale for the purposes of subsections (6) and (7) above is the level on that scale next above the amount of the fine or maximum fine that falls to be increased.

(9) If the amount of the fine or maximum fine that falls to be increased is £400 or more but less than £500, the appropriate level is £1,000.

(10) Where section 35 above applies, the amount of the fine or maximum fine that falls to be increased is to be taken to be the fine or maximum fine to which a person is liable by virtue of that section.

* * * * * *

Application of standard scale to existing enactments

46. Conversion of references to amounts to references to levels on scale—
(1) Where—
(a) either—
   (i) a relevant enactment makes a person liable to a fine or maximum fine on conviction of a summary offence; or
   (ii) a relevant enactment confers power by subordinate instrument to make a person liable to a fine or maximum fine on conviction of a summary offence (whether or not created by the instrument); and
(b) the amount of the fine or maximum fine for the offence is, whether by virtue of this Part of this Act or not, an amount shown in the second column of the standard scale,

a reference to the level in the first column of the standard scale corresponding to that amount shall be substituted for the reference in the enactment to the amount of the fine or maximum fine.

(2) Where a relevant enactment confers a power such as is mentioned in subsection (1)(a)(ii) above, the power shall be construed as a power to make a person liable to a fine or, as the case may be, a maximum fine not exceeding the amount corresponding to the level on the standard scale to which the enactment refers by virtue of subsection (1) above or not exceeding a lesser amount.

(3) If an order under section 143 of the Magistrates' Courts Act 1980 alters the sums specified in section 37(2) above, the second reference to the standard scale in subsection (1) above is to be construed as a reference to that scale as it has effect by virtue of the order.

(4) In this section 'relevant enactment' means—

(a) any enactment contained in an Act passed before this Act *except*—

   (*i*) *an enactment mentioned in Schedule 2 to the Companies Act 1980;*

   (*ii*) *an enactment contained in the Companies Act 1981;*

(b) any enactment contained in this Act;

(c) any enactment contained in an Act passed on the same day as this Act;

(d) any enactment contained in an Act passed after this Act but in the same Session as this Act.

(5) This section shall not affect so much of any enactment as (in whatever words) makes a person liable on summary conviction to a maximum fine not exceeding a specified amount for each period of a specified length during which a continuing offence is continued.

Note. Words in italics repealed by Companies Consolidation (Consequential Provisions) Act 1985, s 29, Sch 1, as from 11 March 1985.

47. Provisions supplementary to sections 35 to 46—(1) In sections 35 to 40 and 46 above 'fine' includes a pecuniary penalty but does not include a pecuniary forfeiture or pecuniary compensation.

(2) Nothing in any provision contained in sections 35 to 46 above shall affect the punishment for an offence committed before that provision comes into force.

PART V

MISCELLANEOUS

*   *   *   *   *

75. Construction of references to 'the standard scale'. *In any enactment (whether contained in an Act passed before or after this Act) 'the standard scale'*—

(*a*) *in relation to England and Wales, has the meaning given by section 37 of this Act;*

(*b*) *(applies to Scotland);*

[(*c*) *in relation to Northern Ireland, means the standard scale provided by Article 5 of the Fines and Penalties (Northern Ireland) Order 1984 (the scale set out in Article 5(2) of that Order or as fixed by or under Article 17 of that Order to take account of changes in the value of money)*].

Note. Para (c) added by Fines and Penalties (Northern Ireland) Order 1984, SI 1984 No 703 (NI 3), art 19(1), Sch 6, para 28.

Repealed, except in relation to the Channel Islands and the Isle of Man, by Criminal Justice Act 1988, s 170(2), Sch 16. See now, for the definition of the 'standard scale', Interpretation Act 1978, Sch 1, as amended by s 170(1) of, and Sch 15, para 58(a) to, the 1988 Act (p 2689).

*   *   *   *   *

80. Commencement—(1) The following provisions of this Act shall come into force on the day this Act is passed, namely—

section 75;

*   *   *   *   *

this section; and section 81.

(2) Subject to subsection (1) above, this Act shall come into operation on such day as the Secretary of State may by order made by statutory instrument appoint, and different days may be so appointed for different provisions and for different purposes.

Commencement. Sections 37, 38, 46, 47 were brought into force on 11 April 1983 (SI 1982 No 1857).

Note. Words in italics repealed by Criminal Justice Act 1988, s 170(2), Sch 16, as from 12 October 1988.

81. Citation and extent—(1) This Act may be cited as the Criminal Justice Act 1982.

* * * * *

ADMINISTRATION OF JUSTICE ACT 1982†

(1982 c 53)

†The amendments made by this Act insofar as they affect provisions printed in this work have been incorporated.

An Act to make further provision with respect to the administration of justice and matters connected therewith; to amend the law relating to actions for damages for personal injuries, including injuries resulting in death, and to abolish certain actions for loss of services; to amend the law relating to wills; to make further provision with respect to funds in court, statutory deposits and schemes for the common investment of such funds and deposits and certain other funds; to amend the law relating to deductions by employers under attachment of earnings orders; to make further provision with regard to penalties that may be awarded by the Solicitors' Disciplinary Tribunal under section 47 of the Solicitors Act 1974; to make further provision for the appointment of justices of the peace in England and Wales and in relation to temporary vacancies in the membership of the Law Commission; to enable the title register kept by the Chief Land Registrar to be kept otherwise than in documentary form; and to authorise the payment of travelling, subsistence and financial loss allowances for justices of the peace in Northern Ireland. [28 October 1982]

* * * * *

2. Abolition of actions for loss of services etc. No person shall be liable in tort under the law of England and Wales or the law of Northern Ireland—
   (a) to a husband on the ground only of his having deprived him of the services or society of his wife;
   (b) to a parent (or person standing in the place of a parent) on the ground only of his having deprived him of the services of a child; or
   (c) on the ground only—
       (i) of having deprived another of his menial servant;
       (ii) of having deprived another of the services of his female servant by raping or seducing her; or
       (iii) of enticement of a servant or harbouring a servant.

* * * * *

PART IX

GENERAL AND SUPPLEMENTARY

* * * * *

75. Repeals and revocations—(1) The enactments specified in Part I of Schedule 9 to this Act (which include enactments already obsolete or unnecessary) are repealed to the extent specified in the third column of that Part of that Schedule.

* * * * *

Note. For commencement see note to Sch 9, Part I.

76. Commencement—(1) The provisions of this Act specified in subsection (2) below shall come into operation on such day as the Lord Chancellor may by order appoint.

(2) The provisions of this Act mentioned in subsection (1) above are—

*   *   *   *   *

(b) Part III:
(c) sections 34 and 35;

*   *   *   *   *

(e) section 54;

*   *   *   *   *

(j) section 75, so far as it relates—

*   *   *   *   *

   (iv) to sections 99(3), 168 to 174A and 176 of the County Courts Act 1959;

*   *   *   *   *

(7) Any order under this section shall be made by statutory instrument.

(8) Any such order may appoint different days for different provisions and for different purposes.

(9) The provisions of this Act specified in subsection (10) below shall come into operation on the day this Act is passed.

(10) The provisions of this Act mentioned in subsection (9) above are—

*   *   *   *   *

(c) section 52;

*   *   *   *   *

(g) this section;

*   *   *   *   *

(i) section 78.

(11) Subject to the foregoing provisions of this section, this Act shall come into operation on 1 January 1983.

*   *   *   *   *

78. Short title.   This Act may be cited as the Administration of Justice Act 1982.

*   *   *   *   *

SCHEDULE 9

REPEALS AND REVOCATIONS   Section 75

PART I

REPEALS

Chapter	Short Title	Extent of Repeal
* * * * *		
7 & 8 Eliz 2 c 22	County Courts Act 1959.	...
		Section 99(3).
		Sections 174, 174A.

Chapter	Short Title	Extent of Repeal
	* * * * *	
1969 c 46.	Family Law Reform Act 1969.	Section 16.
	* * * * *	
1974 c 4.	Legal Aid Act 1974.	In Part II of Schedule 1, paragraph 2.
1975 c 63.	Inheritance (Provision for Family and Dependants) Act 1975.	Section 22.

Note. Apart from the repeals in County Courts Act 1959 which came into force on 2 January 1987, the above repeals came into force on 1 January 1983 (s 76(11)).

MATRIMONIAL HOMES ACT 1983*

(1983 c 19)

Note. For table of derivation and destination see p 2937, in relation to statutory provisions printed in this Work.

This Act came into force 9 August 1983 (see s 13(2)).

* Whole Act repealed by Family Law Act 1996, s 66(3), Sch 10, as from 1 October 1997, subject to savings in s 66(2) of, and Sch 9, para 5 to, the 1996 Act.

ARRANGEMENT OF SECTIONS

An Act to consolidate certain enactments relating to the rights of a husband or wife to occupy a dwelling house that has been a matrimonial home.   [*9 May 1983*]

1. Rights concerning matrimonial home where one spouse has no estate, etc—(*1*) *Where one spouse is entitled to occupy a dwelling house by virtue of a beneficial estate or interest or contract or by virtue of any enactment giving him or her the right to remain in occupation, and the other spouse is not so entitled, then, subject to the provisions of this Act, the spouse not so entitled shall have the following rights (in this Act referred to as 'rights of occupation')—*

   (*a*) *if in occupation, a right not to be evicted or excluded from the dwelling house or any part thereof by the other spouse except with the leave of the court given by an order under this section;*

(*b*) if not in occupation, a right with the leave of the court so given to enter into and occupy the dwelling house.

(*2*) So long as one spouse has rights of occupation, either of the spouses may apply to the court for an order—

(*a*) declaring, enforcing, restricting or terminating those rights, or

(*b*) prohibiting, suspending or restricting the exercise by either spouse of the right to occupy the dwelling house, or

(*c*) requiring either spouse to permit the exercise by the other of that right.

(*3*) On an application for an order under this section, the court may make such order as it thinks just and reasonable having regard to the conduct of the spouses in relation to each other and otherwise, to their respective needs and financial resources, to the needs of any children and to all the circumstances of the case, and, without prejudice to the generality of the foregoing provision—

(*a*) may except part of the dwelling house from a spouse's rights of occupation (and in particular a part used wholly or mainly for or in connection with the trade, business or profession of the other spouse),

(*b*) may order a spouse occupying the dwelling house or any part thereof by virtue of this section to make periodical payments to the other in respect of the occupation,

(*c*) may impose on either spouse obligations as to the repair and maintenance of the dwelling house or the discharge of any liabilities in respect of the dwelling house.

(*4*) Orders under this section may, in so far as they have a continuing effect, be limited so as to have effect for a period specified in the order or until further order.

(*5*) Where a spouse is entitled under this section to occupy a dwelling house or any part thereof, any payment or tender made or other thing done by that spouse in or towards satisfaction of any liability of the other spouse in respect of rent, rates, mortgage payments or other outgoings affecting the dwelling house shall, whether or not it is made or done in pursuance of an order under this section, be as good as if made or done by the other spouse.

(*6*) A spouse's occupation by virtue of this section shall, for the purposes of the Rent (Agriculture) Act 1976, and of the Rent Act 1977 (other than Part V and sections 103 to 106), be treated as possession by the other spouse and for purposes of Chapter II of Part I of the Housing Act 1980 [*for purposes of Part IV of the Housing Act 1985 (secure tenancies)*] [*and Chapter I of Part V of the Housing Act 1996 (introductory tenancies)*] [*and Part I of the Housing Act 1988*] be treated as occupation by the other spouse.

(*7*) Where a spouse is entitled under this section to occupy a dwelling house or any part thereof and makes any payment in or towards satisfaction of any liability of the other spouse in respect of mortgage payments affecting the dwelling house, the person to whom the payment is made may treat it as having been made by that other spouse, but the fact that that person has treated any such payment as having been so made shall not affect any claim of the first-mentioned spouse against the other to an interest in the dwelling house by virtue of the payment.

(*8*) Where a spouse is entitled under this section to occupy a dwelling house or part thereof by reason of an interest of the other spouse under a trust, all the provisions of subsections (*5*) to (*7*) above shall apply in relation to the trustees as they apply in relation to the other spouse.

(*9*) The jurisdiction conferred on the court by this section shall be exercisable by the High Court or by a county court, and shall be exercisable by a county court notwithstanding that by reason of the amount of the net annual value for rating of the dwelling house or otherwise the jurisdiction would not but for this subsection be exercisable by a county court.

(*10*) This Act shall not apply to a dwelling house which has at no time been a matrimonial home of the spouses in question: and a spouse's rights of occupation shall continue only so long as the marriage subsists and the other spouse is entitled as mentioned in subsection (*1*) above to occupy the dwelling house, except where provision is made by section 2 of this Act for those rights to be a charge on an estate or interest in the dwelling house.

(*11*) It is hereby declared that a spouse who has an equitable interest in a dwelling house or in the proceedings of sale thereof, not being a spouse in whom is vested (whether solely or as a joint tenant) a legal estate in fee simple or a legal term of years absolute in the dwelling house, is to be treated for the purpose only of determining whether he or she has rights of occupation under this section as not being entitled to occupy the dwelling house by virtue of that interest.

Note. Sub-s (1) contains provisions formerly in Matrimonial Homes Act 1967, s 1(1) as amended by Matrimonial Homes and Property Act 1981, s 1(1). Sub-s (2) contains provisions formerly in s 1(2) of the Act of 1967 as amended by Domestic Violence and Matrimonial Proceedings Act 1976, s 3. Sub-ss (3), (4) contain provisions formerly in s 1(3), (4) of the Act of 1967. Sub-ss (5)–(7) contain provisions formerly in s 1(5) of the Act of 1967 as amended by Rent Act 1977, s 155, Sch 23, para 40, by Housing Act 1980, s 152, Sch 25, para 14; and by s 5(1) of the Act of 1981. Sub-s (8) contains provisions formerly in s 1(5A) of the Act of 1967, as inserted by s 1(2) of the Act of 1981. Sub-ss (9), (10) contain provisions formerly in s 1(6), (8) of the Act of 1967 respectively. Sub-s (11) contains provisions formerly in s 1(9) of the Act of 1967, as inserted by Matrimonial Proceedings and Property Act 1970, s 38.

Words 'for purposes of … tenancies' in square brackets substituted for words 'for purposes of … Housing Act 1980' by Housing (Consequential Provisions) Act 1985, s 4, Sch 2, para 56, as from 1 April 1986; words in second pair of square brackets inserted by Housing Act 1996 (Consequential Amendments) Order 1997, SI 1997 No 74, art 2, Schedule, para 2(a), as from 12 February 1997; words in third pair of square brackets inserted by Housing Act 1988, s 140, Sch 17, para 33, as from 15 January 1989.

2. Effect of rights of occupation as charge on dwelling house—(*1*) *Where, at any time during the subsistence of a marriage, one spouse is entitled to occupy a dwelling house by virtue of a beneficial estate or interest, then the other spouse's rights of occupation shall be a charge on that estate or interest, having the like priority as if it were an equitable interest created at whichever is the latest of the following dates, that is to say—*

(*a*) *the date when the spouse so entitled acquires the estate or interest,*

(*b*) *the date of the marriage, and*

(*c*) *1 January 1968 (which is the date of commencement of the Act of 1967).*

(*2*) *If, at any time when a spouse's rights of occupation are a charge on an interest of the other spouse under a trust, there are, apart from either of the spouses, no persons, living or unborn, who are or could become beneficiaries under the trust, then those rights shall be a charge also on the estate or interest of the trustees for the other spouse, having the like priority as if it were an equitable interest created (under powers overriding the trusts) on the date when it arises.*

(*3*) *In determining for purposes of subsection (2) above whether there are any persons who are not, but could become, beneficiaries under the trust, there shall be disregarded any potential exercise of a general power of appointment exercisable by either or both of the spouses alone (whether or not the exercise of it requires the consent of another person).*

(*4*) *Notwithstanding that a spouse's rights of occupation are a charge on an estate or interest in the dwelling house, those rights shall be brought to an end by—*

(*a*) *the death of the other spouse, or*

(*b*) *the termination (otherwise than by death) of the marriage,*

unless in the event of a matrimonial dispute or estrangement the court sees fit to direct otherwise by an order made under section 1 above during the subsistence of the marriage.

(*5*) *Where a spouse's rights of occupation are a charge on the estate or interest of the other spouse or of trustees for the other spouse—*

(*a*) *any order under section 1 above against the other spouse shall, except in so far as the contrary intention appears, have the like effect against persons deriving title under the other spouse or under the trustees and affected by the charge, and*

(*b*) *subsections (2) to (8) of section 1 above shall apply in relation to any person deriving title under the other spouse or under the trustees and affected by the charge as they apply in relation to the other spouse.*

(*6*) *Where—*

(*a*) *a spouse's rights of occupation are a charge on an estate or interest in the dwelling house, and*

(*b*) *that estate or interest is surrendered so as to merge in some other estate or interest expectant thereon in such circumstances that, but for the merger, the person taking the estate or interest surrendered would be bound by the charge,*

the surrender shall have effect subject to the charge and the persons thereafter entitled to the other estate or interest shall, for so long as the estate or interest surrendered would have endured if not so surrendered, be treated for all purposes of this Act as deriving title to the other estate or interest under the other spouse or, as the case may be, under the trustees for the other spouse, by virtue of the surrender.

(7) *Where a spouse's rights of occupation are a charge on the estate or interest of the other spouse or of trustees for the other spouse, and the other spouse—*

    (a) *is adjudged bankrupt or makes a conveyance or assignment of his or her property (including that estate or interest) to trustees for the benefit of his or her creditors generally, or*

    (b) *dies and his or her estate is insolvent,*

then, notwithstanding that it is registered under section 2 of the Land Charges Act 1972 or subsection (8) below, the charge shall be void against the trustee in bankruptcy, the trustees under the conveyance or assignment or the personal representatives of the deceased spouse, as the case may be.

Note. Sub-s (7) repealed by Insolvency Act 1985, s 235(3), Sch 10, Part III, as from 29 December 1986. See now Insolvency Act 1986, s 336(2), p 3143.

(8) *Where the title to the legal estate by virtue of which a spouse is entitled to occupy a dwelling house (including any legal estate held by the trustees for that spouse) is registered under the Land Registration Act 1925 or any enactment replaced by that Act—*

    (a) *registration of a land charge affecting the dwelling house by virtue of this Act shall be effected by registering a notice under that Act, and*

    (b) *a spouse's right of occupation shall not be an overriding interest within the meaning of that Act affecting the dwelling house notwithstanding that the spouse is in actual occupation of the dwelling house.*

(9) *A spouse's rights of occupation (whether or not constituting a charge) shall not entitle that spouse to lodge a caution under section 54 of the Land Registration Act 1925.*

(10) *Where—*

    (a) *a spouse's rights of occupation are a charge on the estate of the other spouse or of trustees for the other spouse, and*

    (b) *that estate is the subject of a mortgage within the meaning of the Law of Property Act 1925,*

then, if, after the date of creation of the mortgage, the charge is registered under section 2 of the Land Charges Act 1972, the charge shall, for the purposes of section 94 of that Act of 1925 (which regulates the rights of mortgagees to make further advances ranking in priority to subsequent mortgages), be deemed to be a mortgage subsequent in date to the first-mentioned mortgage.

(11) *It is hereby declared that a charge under subsection (1) or (2) above is not registrable under section 2 of the Land Charges Act 1972 or subsection (8) above unless it is a charge on a legal estate.*

Note. Sub-s (1) contains provisions formerly in Matrimonial Homes Act 1967, s 2(1) as amended by Matrimonial Homes and Property Act 1981, s 1(1). Sub-ss (2), (3) contain provisions formerly in s 2(1A) of the Act of 1967, as inserted by s 1(4) of the Act of 1981. Sub-ss (4)–(6) contain provisions formerly in s 2(2)–(4) of the Act of 1967 as amended by Act of 1981, s 1(3), (5), Sch 1, para 1(a), (b). Sub-s (7) contains provisions formerly in s 2(5) of the Act of 1967 as amended by Land Charges Act 1972, s 18(1), Sch 3, para 8(1), and by Act of 1981, s 1(5), Sch 1, para 1(c). Sub-s (8) contains provisions formerly in s 2(7) of the Act of 1967, as amended by Act of 1981, s 1(5), Sch 1, para 1(d) and as repealed in part by ibid, s 10(2), Sch 3. Sub-s (9) contains provisions formerly in s 2(7A) of the Act of 1967, as inserted by s 4(2) of the Act of 1981. Sub-s (10) contains provisions formerly in s 2(8) of the Act of 1967 as amended by Act of 1972, s 18(1), Sch 3, para 8(2) and by Act of 1981, ss 1(5), 5(2), Sch 1, para 1(e), and as repealed in part by Act of 1981, s 10(2), Sch 3. Sub-s (11) contains provisions formerly in s 2(9) of the Act of 1967, as inserted by s 4(3) of the Act of 1981.

3. Restriction on registration where spouse entitled to more than one charge.
Where one spouse is entitled by virtue of section 2 above to a registrable charge in respect of each of two or more dwelling houses, only one of the charges to which that spouse is so entitled shall be registered under section 2 of the Land Charges Act 1972 or section 2(8) above at any one time, and if any of those charges is registered under either of those provisions the Chief Land Registrar, on being satisfied that any other of them is so registered, shall cancel the registration of the charge first registered.

Note. This section contains provisions formerly in Matrimonial Homes Act 1967, s 3 as amended by Land Charges Act 1972, s 18(1), Sch 3, para 9, and by Matrimonial Homes and Property Act 1981, s 1(5), Sch 1, para 2.

4. Contract for sale of house affected by registered charge to include term requiring cancellation of registration before completion—(*1*) *Where one spouse is entitled by virtue of section 2 above to a charge on an estate in a dwelling house and the charge is registered under section 2 of the Land Charges Act 1972 or section 2(8) above, it shall be a term of any contract for the sale of that estate whereby the vendor agrees to give vacant possession of the dwelling house on completion of the contract that the vendor will before such completion procure the cancellation of the registration of the charge at his expense.*

(*2*) *Subsection (1) above shall not apply to any such contract made by a vendor who is entitled to sell the estate in the dwelling house freed from any such charge.*

(*3*) *If, on the completion of such a contract as is referred to in subsection (1) above, there is delivered to the purchaser or his solicitor an application by the spouse entitled to the charge for the cancellation of the registration of that charge, the term of the contract for which subsection (1) above provides shall be deemed to have been performed.*

(*4*) *This section applies only if and so far as a contrary intention is not expressed in the contract.*

(*5*) *This section shall apply to a contract for exchange as it applies to a contract for sale.*

(*6*) *This section shall, with the necessary modifications, apply to a contract for the grant of a lease or underlease of a dwelling house as it applies to a contract for the sale of an estate in a dwelling house.*

Note. Sub-ss (1), (2) contain provisions formerly in Matrimonial Homes Act 1967, s 4(1), as amended by Land Charges Act 1972, s 18(1), Sch 3, para 10, and as repealed in part by Matrimonial Homes and Property Act 1981, s 10(2), Sch 3. Sub-ss (3)–(6) contain provisions formerly in s 4(2)–(5) of the Act of 1967, as repealed in part in the case of s 4(5) by Act of 1981, s 10(2), Sch 3.

5. Cancellation of registration after termination of marriage, etc—(*1*) *Where a spouse's rights of occupation are a charge on an estate in a dwelling house and the charge is registered under section 2 of the Land Charges Act 1972 or section 2(8) above, the Chief Land Registrar shall, subject to subsection (2) below, cancel the registration of the charge if he is satisfied*—

(*a*) *by the production of a certificate or other sufficient evidence, that either spouse is dead, or*

(*b*) *by the production of an official copy of a decree of a court, that the marriage in question has been terminated otherwise than by death, or*

(*c*) *by the production of an order of the court, that the spouse's rights of occupation constituting the charge have been terminated by the order.*

(*2*) *Where*—

(*a*) *the marriage in question has been terminated by the death of the spouse entitled to an estate in the dwelling house or otherwise than by death, and*

(*b*) *an order affecting the charge of the spouse not so entitled had been made by virtue of section 2(4) above,*

then if, after the making of the order, registration of the charge was renewed or the charge registered in pursuance of subsection (3) below, the Chief Land Registrar shall not cancel the registration of the charge in accordance with subsection (1) above unless he is also satisfied that the order has ceased to have effect.

(*3*) *Where such an order has been made, then, for the purposes of subsection (2) above, the spouse entitled to the charge affected by the order may*—

(*a*) *before the date of the order the charge was registered under section 2 of the Land Charges Act 1972 or section 2(8) above, renew the registration of the charge, and*

(*b*) *if before the said date the charge was not so registered, register the charge under section 2 of the Land Charges Act 1972 or section 2(8) above.*

(*4*) *Renewal of the registration of a charge in pursuance of subsection (3) above shall be effected in such manner as may be prescribed, and an application for such renewal or for registration of a charge in pursuance of that subsection shall contain such particulars of any order affecting the charge made by virtue of section 2(4) above as may be prescribed.*

(5) *The renewal in pursuance of subsection (3) above of the registration of a charge shall not affect the priority of the charge.*

(6) *In this section 'prescribed' means prescribed by rules made under section 16 of the Land Charges Act 1972 or section 144 of the Land Registration Act 1925, as the circumstances of the case require.*

Note. Sub-s (1) contains provisions formerly in Matrimonial Homes Act 1967, s 5(1), as amended by Land Charges Act 1972, s 18(1), Sch 3, para 11, and by Matrimonial Homes and Property Act 1981, s 1(5), Sch 1, para 3. Sub-s (2) contains provisions formerly in s 5(2) of the Act of 1967, as repealed in part by Act of 1981, s 10(2), Sch 3. Sub-ss (3)–(6) contain provisions formerly in s 5(3)–(6) of the Act of 1967, as amended in the case of s 5(3) and (6) by Land Charges Act 1972, s 18(1), Sch 3, para 11.

6. Release of rights of occupation and postponement of priority of charge—
(1) *A spouse entitled to rights of occupation may by a release in writing release those rights or release them as respects part only of the dwelling house affected by them.*

(2) *Where a contract is made for the sale of an estate or interest in a dwelling house, or for the grant of a lease or underlease of a dwelling house, being (in either case) a dwelling house affected by a charge registered under section 2 of the Land Charges Act 1972 or section 2(8) above, then, without prejudice to subsection (1) above, the rights of occupation constituting the charge shall be deemed to have been released on the happening of whichever of the following events first occurs—*

(a) *the delivery to the purchaser or lessee, as the case may be, or his solicitor on completion of the contract of an application by the spouse entitled to the charge for the cancellation of the registration of the charge, or*

(b) *the lodging of such an application at Her Majesty's Land Registry.*

(3) *A spouse entitled by virtue of section 2 above to a charge on an estate or interest may agree in writing that any other charge on, or interest in, that estate or interest shall rank in priority to the charge to which that spouse is so entitled.*

Note. This section contains provisions formerly in Matrimonial Homes Act 1967, s 6, as amended in the case of s 6(2) by Land Charges Act 1972, s 18(1), Sch 3, para 12, and as repealed in part in the case of s 6(3) by Matrimonial Homes and Property Act 1981, s 1(5), Sch 1, para 4.

7. Transfer of certain tenancies on divorce, etc. *Schedule 1 to this Act shall have effect.*
Note. This section contains provisions formerly in Matrimonial Homes Act 1967, s 7, as substituted by Matrimonial Homes and Property Act 1981, s 6(2).

8. Dwelling house subject to mortgage—(1) *In determining for the purposes of the foregoing provisions of this Act (including Schedule 1) whether a spouse or former spouse is entitled to occupy a dwelling house by virtue of an estate or interest, there shall be disregarded any right to possession of the dwelling house conferred on a mortgagee of the dwelling house under or by virtue of his mortgage, whether the mortgagee is in possession or not; but the other spouse shall not by virtue of the rights of occupation conferred by this Act have any larger right against the mortgagee to occupy the dwelling house than the one first mentioned has by virtue of his or her estate or interest and of any contract with the mortgagee, unless under section 2 above those rights of occupation are a charge, affecting the mortgagee, on the estate or interest mortgaged.*

(2) *Where a mortgagee of land which consists of or includes a dwelling house brings an action in any court for the enforcement of his security, a spouse who is not a party to the action and who is enabled by section 1(5) or (8) above to meet the mortgagor's liabilities under the mortgage, on applying to the court at any time before the action is finally disposed of in that court, shall be entitled to be made a party to the action if the court—*

(a) *does not see special reason against it, and*

(b) *is satisfied that the applicant may be expected to make such payments or do such things in or towards satisfaction of the mortgagor's liabilities or obligations as might affect the outcome of the proceedings or that the expectation of it should be considered under section 36 of the Administration of Justice Act 1970.*

(*3*)   *Where a mortgagee of land which consists or substantially consists of a dwelling house brings an action for the enforcement of his security, and at the relevant time there is—*

   (*a*)   *in the case of unregistered land, a land charge of Class F registered against the person who is the estate owner at the relevant time or any person who, where the estate owner is a trustee, preceded him as trustee during the subsistence of the mortgage, or*

   (*b*)   *in the case of registered land, a subsisting registration of a notice under section 2(8) above or a notice or caution under section 2(7) of the Act of 1967,*

notice of the action shall be served by the mortgagee on the person on whose behalf the land charge is registered or the notice or caution entered, if that person is not a party to the action.

(*4*)   *For the purposes of subsection (3) above, if there has been issued a certificate of the result of an official search made on behalf of the mortgagee which would disclose any land charge of Class F, notice or caution within subsection 3(a) or (b) above, and the action is commenced within the priority period, the relevant time is the date of that certificate; and in any other case the relevant time is the time when the action is commenced.*

(*5*)   *In subsection (4) above, 'priority period' means, for both registered and unregistered land, the period for which, in accordance with section 11(5) and (6) of the Land Charges Act 1972, a certificate on an official search operates in favour of a purchaser.*

Note. Sub-ss (1)–(3) contain provisions formerly in Matrimonial Homes Act 1967, s 7A(1)–(3)(a), as inserted by Matrimonial Homes and Property Act 1981, s 2. Sub-ss (4), (5) contain provisions formerly in s 7A(3)(b) of the Act of 1967, as inserted by s 2 of the Act of 1981.

9. Rights concerning matrimonial home where both spouses have estate, etc—(*1*)   *Where each of two spouses is entitled, by virtue of a legal estate vested in them jointly, to occupy a dwelling house in which they have or at any time have had a matrimonial home, either of them may apply to the court, with respect to the exercise during the subsistence of the marriage of the right to occupy the dwelling house, for an order prohibiting, suspending or restricting its exercise by the other or requiring the other to permit its exercise by the applicant.*

(*2*)   *In relation to orders under this section, section 1(3), (4) and (9) above shall apply as they apply in relation to orders under that section.*

(*3*)   *Where each of two spouses is entitled to occupy a dwelling house by virtue of a contract, or by virtue of any enactment giving them the right to remain in occupation, this section shall apply as it applies where they are entitled by virtue of a legal estate vested in them jointly.*

(*4*)   *In determining for the purposes of this section whether two spouses are entitled to occupy a dwelling house, there shall be disregarded any right to possession of the dwelling house conferred on a mortgagee of the dwelling house under or by virtue of his mortgage, whether the mortgagee is in possession or not.*

Note. Sub-ss (1)–(3) contain provisions formerly in Domestic Violence and Matrimonial Proceedings Act 1976, s 4(1)–(3). Sub-s (4) contains provisions formerly in s 4(4) of the Act of 1976, as inserted by Matrimonial Homes and Property Act 1981, s 5(3).

10. Interpretation—(*1*)   *In this Act—*

'*Act of 1967*' *means the Matrimonial Homes Act 1967;*

'*Act of 1981*' *means the Matrimonial Homes and Property Act 1981;*

'*dwelling house*' *includes any building or part thereof which is occupied as a dwelling, and any yard, garden, garage or outhouse belonging to the dwelling house and occupied therewith;*

'*mortgage*' *includes a charge and 'mortgagor' and 'mortgagee' shall be construed accordingly;*

'*mortgagor*' *and 'mortgagee' includes any person deriving title under the original mortgagor or mortgagee;*

'*rights of occupation*' *has the meaning assigned to it in section 1(1) above.*

(*2*)   *It is hereby declared that this Act applies as between a husband and a wife notwithstanding that the marriage in question was entered into under a law which permits polygamy (whether or not either party to the marriage in question has for the time being any spouse additional to the other party).*

[(*2*)   *It is hereby declared that this Act applies as between the parties to a marriage notwithstanding that either of them is, or has at any time during the marriage's subsistence been, married to more than one person.*]

Note. Sub-s (2) substituted by Private International Law (Miscellaneous Provisions) Act 1995, s 8(2), Schedule, para 3, as from 8 January 1996.

(*3*) *References in this Act to registration under section 2(8) above include (as well as references to registration by notice under section 2(7) of the Act of 1967) references to registration by caution duly lodged under the said section 2(7) before the 14th February 1983 (the date of commencement of section 4(2) of the Act of 1981).*

Note. Sub-s (1) contains provisions formerly in Matrimonial Homes Act 1967, s 1(7) and s 7A(4), as inserted by Matrimonial Homes and Property Act 1981, s 2; and in Domestic Violence and Matrimonial Proceedings Act 1976, s 4(4), as inserted by s 5(3) of the Act of 1981. Sub-s (2) contains provisions formerly in s 1(10) of the Act of 1967, as inserted by s 3 of the Act of 1981.

11. Transitional provision. *Neither section 2(9) above, nor the repeal by section 4(2) of the Act of 1981 of the words 'or caution' in section 2(7) of the Act of 1967, affects a caution duly lodged as respects any estate of interest before the said 14th February 1983.*

Note. This section derives from Matrimonial Homes and Property Act 1981, s 4(2).

12. Consequential amendments and repeals—(*1*) *The Acts specified in Schedule 2 to this Act shall have effect to the amendments specified in that Schedule.*

(*2*) *The Acts specified in Schedule 3 to this Act are repealed to the extent specified in the third column of that Schedule.*

13. Short title, commencement and extent—(*1*) *This Act may be cited as the Matrimonial Homes Act 1983.*

(*2*) *This Act shall come into force at the end of the period of three months beginning with the day on which it is passed.*

(*3*) *This Act does not extend to Scotland or Northern Ireland.*

SCHEDULES

SCHEDULE 1   Section 7

TRANSFER OF CERTAIN TENANCIES ON DIVORCE, ETC

PART I

General

1. (*1*) *Where one spouse is entitled, either in his or her own right or jointly with the other spouse, to occupy a dwelling house by virtue of—*

(*a*) *a protected tenancy or statutory tenancy within the meaning of the Rent Act 1977, or*

(*b*) *a statutory tenancy within the meaning of the Rent (Agriculture) Act 1976, or*

(*c*) *a secure tenancy within the meaning of section 28 of the Housing Act 1980 [within the meaning of the Housing Act 1985], [or*

(*d*) *an assured tenancy or assured agricultural occupancy within the meaning of Part I of the Housing Act 1988] [; or*

(*e*) *an introductory tenancy within the meaning of Chapter I of Part V of the Housing Act 1996,]*

then, on granting a decree of divorce, a decree of nullity of marriage or a decree of judicial separation, or at any time thereafter (whether, in the case of a decree of divorce or nullity of marriage, before or after the decree is made absolute), the court by which the decree is granted may make an order under Part II below.

(*2*) *References in this Schedule to a spouse being entitled to occupy a dwelling house by virtue of a protected, statutory or secure tenancy [or an assured tenancy or assured agricultural occupancy] [or an introductory tenancy] apply whether that entitlement is in his or her own right, or jointly with the other spouse.*

Note. Words in first pair of square brackets substituted for words 'within the meaning of section 28 of the Housing Act 1980' by Housing (Consequential Provisions) Act 1985, s 4, Sch 2, para 56, as from 1 April 1986. Words in second and fourth pairs of square brackets inserted by Housing Act 1988, s 140, Sch 17, para 34, as from 15 January 1989. Words in third and fifth pairs of square brackets inserted by Housing Act 1996 (Consequential Amendments) Order 1997, SI 1997 No 74, art 2, Schedule, para 2(b), as from 12 February 1997.

PART II

Protected or secure tenancy

2. (*1*) *Where a spouse is entitled to occupy the dwelling house by virtue of a protected tenancy within the meaning of the Rent Act 1977, or a secure tenancy within the meaning of the Housing Act 1980* [*within the meaning of the Housing Act 1985*] [*or an assured tenancy or assured agricultural occupancy within the meaning of Part I of the Housing Act 1988*] [*or an introductory tenancy within the meaning of Chapter I of Part V of the Housing Act 1996*], *the court may by order direct that, as from such date as may be specified in the order, there shall, by virtue of the order and without further assurance, be transferred to, and vested in, the other spouse—*

   (*a*) *the estate or interest which the spouse so entitled had in the dwelling house immediately before that date by virtue of the lease or agreement creating the tenancy and any assignment of that lease or agreement, with all rights, privileges and appurtenances attaching to that estate or interest but subject to all covenants, obligations, liabilities and incumbrances to which it is subject; and*

   (*b*) *where the spouse so entitled is an assignee of such lease or agreement, the liability of that spouse under any covenant of indemnity by the assignee expressed or implied in the assignment of the lease or agreement to that spouse.*

  (*2*) *Where an order is made under this paragraph, any liability or obligation to which the spouse so entitled is subject under any covenant having reference to the dwelling house in the lease or agreement, being a liability or obligation falling due to be discharged or performed on or after the date so specified, shall not be enforceable against that spouse.*

  (*3*) *Where the spouse so entitled is a successor within the meaning of Chapter II of Part I of the Housing Act 1980* [*within the meaning of Part IV of the Housing Act 1985*], *his or her former spouse (or, in the case of judicial separation, his or her spouse) shall be deemed also to be a successor within the meaning of that Chapter.*

  [(*3A*) *Where the spouse so entitled is a successor within the meaning of section 132 of the Housing Act 1996, his or her former spouse (or, in the case of judicial separation, his or her spouse) shall be deemed also to be a successor within the meaning of that section.*]

  [(*4*) *Where the spouse so entitled is for the purposes of section 17 of the Housing Act 1988 a successor in relation to the tenancy or occupancy, his or her former spouse (or, in the case of judicial separation, his or her spouse) shall be deemed to be a successor in relation to the tenancy or occupancy for the purposes of that section.*]

  (*5*) *If the transfer under sub-paragraph (1) above is of an assured agricultural occupancy, then, for the purposes of Chapter III of Part I of the Housing Act 1988,—*

   (*a*) *the agricultural worker condition shall be fulfilled with respect to the dwelling-house while the spouse to whom the assured agricultural occupancy is transferred continues to be the occupier under that occupancy; and*

   (*b*) *that condition shall be treated as so fulfilled by virtue of the same paragraph of Schedule 3 to the Housing Act 1988 as was applicable before the transfer.*]

Note. First words in square brackets in sub-para (1) and words in square brackets in sub-para 3 substituted for words 'within the meaning ... Housing Act 1980' by Housing (Consequential Provisions) Act 1985, s 4, Sch 2, para 56, as from 1 April 1986. Second words in square brackets in sub-para (1) and sub-paras (4), (5) added by Housing Act 1988, s 140, Sch 17, para 33, as from 15 January 1989. Third words in square brackets in sub-para (1) and sub-para (3A) inserted by Housing Act 1996 (Consequential Amendments) Order 1997, SI 1997 No 74, art 2, Schedule, para 2(b), as from 12 February 1997.

Statutory tenancy within the meaning of the Rent Act 1977

3. (*1*) *Where the spouse is entitled to occupy the dwelling house by virtue of a statutory tenancy within the meaning of the Rent Act 1977, the court may by order direct that, as from such date as may be specified in the order, that spouse shall cease to be entitled to occupy the dwelling house and that the other spouse shall be deemed to be the tenant or, as the case may be, the sole tenant under that statutory tenancy.*

  (*2*) *The question whether the provisions of paragraphs 1 to 3 or, as the case may be, paragraphs 5 to 7 of Schedule 1 to the Rent Act 1977 as to the succession by the surviving spouse of a deceased tenant, or by a member of the deceased tenant's family, to the right to retain possession are capable of having effect in the event of the death of the person deemed by an order under this paragraph to be the tenant or sole tenant under the statutory tenancy shall be determined according as those provisions have or have not already had effect in relation to the statutory tenancy.*

Statutory tenancy within the meaning of the Rent (Agriculture) Act 1976

4. *Where the spouse is entitled to occupy the dwelling house by virtue of a statutory tenancy within the meaning of the Rent (Agriculture) Act 1976, the court may by order direct that, as from such date as may be specified in the order, that spouse shall cease to be entitled to occupy the dwelling house and that the other spouse shall be deemed to be the tenant or, as the case may be, the sole tenant under that statutory tenancy; and a spouse who is deemed as aforesaid to be the tenant under a statutory tenancy shall be (within the meaning of that Act) a statutory tenant in his own right, or a statutory tenant by succession, according as the other spouse was a statutory tenant in his own right or a statutory tenant by succession.*

PART III

Ancillary jurisdiction

5. *Where the court makes an order under Part II of this Schedule, it may by the order direct that both spouses shall be jointly and severally liable to discharge or perform any or all of the liabilities and obligations in respect of the dwelling house (whether arising under the tenancy or otherwise) which have at the date of the order fallen due to be discharged or performed by one only of the spouses or which, but for the direction, would before the date specified as the date on which the order is to take effect fall due to be discharged or performed by one only of them; and where the court gives such a direction it may further direct that either spouse shall be liable to indemnify the other in whole or in part against any payment made or expenses incurred by the other in discharging or performing any such liability or obligation.*

Date when order is to take effect

6. *In the case of a decree of divorce or nullity of marriage, the date specified in an order under Part II of this Schedule as the date on which the order is to take effect shall not be earlier than the date on which the decree is made absolute.*

Remarriage of either spouse

7. *If after the grant of a decree dissolving or annulling a marriage either spouse remarries, that spouse shall not be entitled to apply, by reference to the grant of that decree, for an order under Part II of this Schedule.*

Rules of court

8. (*1*) *Rules of court shall be made requiring the court before it makes an order under this Schedule to give the landlord of the dwelling house to which the order will relate an opportunity of being heard.*

(*2*) *Rules of court may provide that an application for an order under this Schedule shall not, without the leave of the court by which the decree of divorce, nullity of marriage or judicial separation was granted, be made after the expiration of such period from the grant of the decree as may be prescribed by the rules.*

(*3*) *Rules of court may provide for the transfer of proceedings pending by virtue of this Schedule in the court which granted the decree of divorce, nullity of marriage or judicial separation as follows—*

(*a*) *if the proceedings are pending in the High Court, for the transfer of the proceedings to a divorce county court;*

(*b*) *if the proceedings are pending in a divorce county court, for the transfer of the proceedings to the High Court or to some other divorce county court;*

and a court shall have jurisdiction to entertain any proceedings transferred to the court by virtue of rules made in pursuance of this sub-paragraph.

(*4*) *For the purposes of sub-paragraph (3) above—*

(*a*) *any proceedings in the divorce registry shall be treated as pending in a divorce county court; and*

(*b*) *the power to provide for the transfer of proceedings to a divorce county court shall include power to provide for the transfer of proceedings to the divorce registry.*

Note. Sch 1, paras 8(3), (4) repealed as from 28 April 1986: Matrimonial and Family Proceedings Act 1984, Sch 3: see now, ibid, Part V.

Savings for sections 1 and 2 of this Act

9. *Where a spouse is entitled to occupy a dwelling house by virtue of a tenancy, this Schedule shall not affect the operation of sections 1 and 2 of this Act in relation to the other spouse's rights of occupation, and the court's power to make orders under this Schedule shall be in addition to the powers conferred by those sections.*

Interpretation

10.   (*1*) *In this Schedule—*
   'divorce county court' means a county court designated under section 1 of the Matrimonial Causes Act 1967;
   'divorce registry' means the principal registry of the Family Division of the High Court;
   'landlord' includes any person from time to time deriving title under the original landlord and also includes, in relation to any dwelling house, any person other than the tenant who is, or but for Part VII of the Rent Act 1977 or Part II of the Rent (Agriculture) Act 1976 would be, entitled to possession of the dwelling house;
   'tenancy' includes sub-tenancy.
   (*2*) *For the avoidance of doubt it is hereby declared that the reference in paragraph 7 above to remarriage includes a reference to a marriage which is by law void or voidable.*

Note. This Schedule contains provisions formerly in Matrimonial Homes Act 1967, Sch 2, as inserted by Matrimonial Homes and Property Act 1981, s 6(3), Sch 2.
   Definitions of 'divorce county court' and 'divorce registry' in para 10 repealed by Matrimonial and Family Proceedings Act 1984, s 46(3), Sch 3, as from 28 April 1986.

SCHEDULE 2   Section 12

CONSEQUENTIAL AMENDMENTS

   (*Sch 2 makes consequential amendments; insofar as it amends provisions printed in this work, those amendments are incorporated.*)

SCHEDULE 3   Section 12

REPEALS

Chapter	Short Title	Extent of Repeal
1967 c 75	*Matrimonial Homes Act 1967*	*The whole Act except section 2(6) so far as it relates to paragraph 4 of the Schedule, and except that paragraph.*
1970 c 45	*Matrimonial Proceedings and Property Act 1970*	*Section 38.*
1972 c 61	*Land Charges Act 1972*	*In Schedule 3, paragraphs 8 to 12.*
1976 c 50	*Domestic Violence and Matrimonial Proceedings Act 1976*	*Sections 3 and 4.*
1977 c 42	*Rent Act 1977*	*In Schedule 23, paragraph 40.*
1980 c 51	*Housing Act 1980*	*In Schedule 25, paragraph 14.*
1981 c 24	*Matrimonial Homes and Property Act 1981*	*Sections 1 to 3. In section 4, subsections (2) and (3). Sections 5 and 6. Schedules 1 and 2.*

DESTINATION TABLE

This table shows in column (1) the enactments repealed by Matrimonial Homes Act 1983, and in column (2) the provisions of that Act corresponding to the repealed provisions. The table is restricted to sections of earlier legislation printed in this Volume.

(1)	(2)	(1)	(2)
Matrimonial Homes Act 1967 (c 75)	Matrimonial Homes Act 1983 (c 19)	Domestic Violence and Matrimonial Proceedings Act 1976 (c 50)	Matrimonial Homes Act 1983 (c 19)
s 1(1)–(4)	s 1(1)–(4)	s 3	s 1(2)
(5)	(5)–(7)	4(1)–(3)	9(1)–(3)
(5A)	(8)	(4)	9(4), 10(1)
(6)	(9)		
(7)	10(1)	Matrimonial Homes and Property Act 1981 (c 24)	
(8), (9)	1(10), (11)		
(10)	10(2)		
2(1)	2(1)		
(1A)	(2), (3)	s 1(1)	1(1), 2(1)
(2)–(4)	(4)–(6)	(2)	1(8)
(5)	(7)	(3)	2(5)
(6)†		(4)	2(2), (3)
(7)	2(8)	(5)	2, 3, 5, 6
(7A)	(9)	2	8, 10(1)
(8), (9)	(10), (11)	3	10(2)
3	3	4(2)	2(9), (11)
4(1)	4(1), (2)	(3)	2(11)
(2)–(5)	(3)–(6)	5(1)	1(6)
5	5	(2)	2(10)
6	6	(3)	9(4), 10(1)
7	7	6(1)	
7A(1)–(3)(a)	8(1)–(3)	(2)	7
(3)(b)	(4), (5)	(3)	Sch 1
(4)	10(1)	(4)	
8(1)		Sch 1, para 1	s 2(5)–(8), (10)(a)
(2)	13(3)		
(3)		para 2	3
Sch 1, para 1	Rep, 1969 c 59, s 17, Sch 2, Part 11	para 3	5(1)
		para 4	6(3)
paras 2, 3	Rep, 1972 c 61, s 18 (3), Sch 5	2	Sch 1
2	Sch 1		

(1)	(2)
Matrimonial Proceedings and Property Act 1970 (c 45)	
s 38	s 1(11)

† Repealed in part.

MENTAL HEALTH ACT 1983

(1983 c 20)

An Act to consolidate the law relating to mentally disordered persons. [9 May 1983]
Note. For table of derivation and destination see p 2952.

PART I

APPLICATION OF ACT

1. Application of Act: 'mental disorder'—(1) The provisions of this Act shall
have effect with respect to the reception, care and treatment of mentally disordered
patients, the management of their property and other related matters.

(2) In this Act—

'mental disorder' means mental illness, arrested or incomplete development of
mind, psychopathic disorder and any other disorder or disability of mind and
'mentally disordered' shall be construed accordingly;

'severe mental impairment' means a state of arrested or incomplete development
of mind which includes severe impairment of intelligence and social functioning
and is associated with abnormally aggressive or seriously irresponsible conduct
on the part of the person concerned and 'severely mentally impaired' shall be
construed accordingly;

'mental impairment' means a state of arrested or incomplete development of
mind (not amounting to severe mental impairment) which includes significant
impairment of intelligence and social functioning and is associated with
abnormally aggressive or seriously irresponsible conduct on the part of the
person concerned and 'mentally impaired' shall be construed accordingly;

'psychopathic disorder' means a persistent disorder or disability of mind (whether
or not including significant impairment of intelligence) which results in
abnormally aggressive or seriously irresponsible conduct on the part of the
person concerned;

and other expressions shall have the meanings assigned to them in section 145 below.

(3) Nothing in subsection (2) above shall be construed as implying that a person
may be dealt with under this Act as suffering from mental disorder, or from any form
of mental disorder described in this section, by reason only of promiscuity or other
immoral conduct, sexual deviancy or dependence on alcohol or drugs.

Note. Sub-s (1) contains provisions formerly in Mental Health Act 1959, s 1. Sub-s (2) contains
provisions formerly in s 4(1)–(4) of that Act as substituted in the case of sub-ss (2)–(4) by
Mental Health (Amendment) Act 1982, ss 1(2), 2(1). Sub-s (3) contains provisions formerly in
Mental Health Act 1959, s 4(5) as amended by Mental Health (Amendment) Act 1982, s 2(2).

PART II

COMPULSORY ADMISSION TO HOSPITAL AND GUARDIANSHIP

Procedure for hospital admission

2. Admission for assessment—(1) A patient may be admitted to a hospital and
detained there for the period allowed by subsection (4) below in pursuance of an
application (in this Act referred to as 'an application for admission for assessment')
made in accordance with subsections (2) and (3) below.

(2) An application for admission for assessment may be made in respect of a
patient on the grounds that—

(a) he is suffering from mental disorder of a nature or degree which warrants
the detention of the patient in a hospital for assessment (or for assessment
followed by medical treatment) for at least a limited period; and

(b) he ought to be so detained in the interests of his own health or safety or
with a view to the protection of other persons.

(3) An application for admission for assessment shall be founded on the written recommendations in the prescribed form of two registered medical practitioners, including in each case a statement that in the opinion of the practitioner the conditions set out in subsection (2) above are complied with.

(4) Subject to the provisions of section 29(4) below, a patient admitted to hospital in pursuance of an application for admission for assessment may be detained for a period not exceeding 28 days beginning with the day on which he is admitted, but shall not be detained after the expiration of that period unless before it has expired he has become liable to be detained by virtue of a subsequent application, order or direction under the following provisions of this Act.

Note. This section contains provisions formerly in Mental Health Act 1959, s 25 as amended by Mental Health (Amendment) Act 1982, s 3(1).

3. Admission for treatment—(1) A patient may be admitted to a hospital and detained there for the period allowed by the following provisions of this Act in pursuance of an application (in this Act referred to as 'an application for admission for treatment') made in accordance with this section.

(2) An application for admission for treatment may be made in respect of a patient on the grounds that—

   (a) he is suffering from mental illness, severe mental impairment, psychopathic disorder or mental impairment and his mental disorder is of a nature or degree which makes it appropriate for him to receive medical treatment in a hospital; and

   (b) in the case of psychopathic disorder or mental impairment, such treatment is likely to alleviate or prevent a deterioration of his condition; and

   (c) it is necessary for the health or safety of the patient or for the protection of other persons that he should receive such treatment and it cannot be provided unless he is detained under this section.

(3) An application for admission for treatment shall be founded on the written recommendations in the prescribed form of two registered medical practitioners, including in each case a statement that in the opinion of the practitioner the conditions set out in subsection (2) above are complied with; and each such recommendation shall include—

   (a) such particulars as may be prescribed of the grounds for that opinion so far as it relates to the conditions set out in paragraphs (a) and (b) of that subsection; and

   (b) a statement of the reasons for that opinion so far as it relates to the conditions set out in paragraph (c) of that subsection, specifying whether other methods of dealing with the patient are available and, if so, why they are not appropriate.

Note. This section contains provisions formerly in Mental Health Act 1959, s 26(1)–(3) as amended in the case of sub-ss (2), (3) by Mental Health (Amendment) Act 1982, s 4(2), (3).

*   *   *   *   *

Guardianship

7. Application for guardianship—(1) A patient who has attained the age of 16 years may be received into guardianship, for the period allowed by the following provisions of this Act, in pursuance of an application (in this Act referred to as 'a guardianship application') made in accordance with this section.

(2) A guardianship application may be made in respect of a patient on the grounds that—

   (a) he is suffering from mental disorder, being mental illness, severe mental impairment, psychopathic disorder or mental impairment and his mental disorder is of a nature or degree which warrants his reception into guardianship under this section; and

(b) it is necessary in the interests of the welfare of the patient or for the protection of other persons that the patient should be so received.

(3) A guardianship application shall be founded on the written recommendations in the prescribed form of two registered medical practitioners, including in each case a statement that in the opinion of the practitioner the conditions set out in subsection (2) above are complied with; and each such recommendation shall include—

(a) such particulars as may be prescribed of the grounds for that opinion so far as it relates to the conditions set out in paragraph (a) of that subsection; and

(b) a statement of the reasons for that opinion so far as it relates to the conditions set out in paragraph (b) of that subsection.

(4) A guardianship application shall state the age of the patient or, if his exact age is not known to the applicant, shall state (if it be the fact) that the patient is believed to have attained the age of 16 years.

(5) The person named as guardian in a guardianship application may be either a local social services authority or any other person (including the applicant himself); but a guardianship application in which a person other than a local social services authority is named as guardian shall be of no effect unless it is accepted on behalf of that person by the local social services authority for the area in which he resides and shall be accompanied by a statement in writing by that person that he is willing to act as guardian.

Note. Sub-ss (1), (2) contain provisions formerly in Mental Health Act 1959, s 33(1), (2) as amended by Mental Health (Amendment) Act 1982, s 7(2)–(4). Sub-ss (3), (4) contain provisions formerly in s 33(2A), (2B) of the Act of 1959, as inserted by Act of 1982, s 65(1), Sch 3, Part I, para 2(a). Sub-s (5) contains provisions formerly in s 33(3), (4) of the Act of 1959 as amended in the case of sub-s (3) by Local Government Act 1972, s 195, Sch 23, para 9(2).

8. Effect of guardianship application, etc—(1) Where a guardianship application, duly made under the provisions of this Part of this Act and forwarded to the local social services authority within the period allowed by subsection (2) below is accepted by that authority, the application shall, subject to regulations made by the Secretary of State, confer on the authority or person named in the application as guardian, to the exclusion of any other person—

(a) the power to require the patient to reside at a place specified by the authority or person named as guardian;

(b) the power to require the patient to attend at places and times so specified for the purpose of medical treatment, occupation, education or training;

(c) the power to require access to the patient to be given, at any place where the patient is residing, to any registered medical practitioner, *approved social worker* [mental welfare officer] or other person so specified.

(2) The period within which a guardianship application is required for the purposes of this section to be forwarded to the local social services authority is the period of 14 days beginning with the date on which the patient was last examined by a registered medical practitioner before giving a medical recommendation for the purposes of the application.

(3) A guardianship application which appears to be duly made and to be founded on the necessary medical recommendations may be acted upon without further proof of the signature or qualification of the person by whom the application or any such medical recommendation is made or given, or of any matter of fact or opinion stated in the application.

(4) If within the period of 14 days beginning with the day on which a guardianship application has been accepted by the local social services authority the application, or any medical recommendation given for the purposes of the application, is found to be in any respect incorrect or defective, the application or recommendation may, within that period and with the consent of that authority, be amended by the person by whom it was signed; and upon such amendment being

made the application or recommendation shall have effect and shall be deemed to have had effect as if it had been originally made as so amended.

(5) Where a patient is received into guardianship in pursuance of a guardianship application, any previous application under this Part of this Act by virtue of which he was subject to guardianship or liable to be detained in a hospital shall cease to have effect.

Note. Sub-s (1) contains provisions formerly in Mental Health Act 1959, s 34(1) as amended by Mental Health (Amendment) Act 1982, s 8, and, as from 24 October 1984, by s 65(1), Sch 3, Part II, para 66. Sub-ss (2), (4) contain provisions formerly in s 34(2), (4) of the Act of 1959 as amended by Local Government Act 1972, s 195(6), Sch 23, para 9(2). Sub-ss (3), (5) contain provisions formerly in s 34(3), (6) of the Act of 1959.

Until 28 October 1984 sub-s (1)(c) had effect as if the words in italics were omitted and the words in square brackets inserted (see Sch 5, para 4(1)(e) (p 2951)).

*   *   *   *   *

Position of patients subject to detention or guardianship

*   *   *   *   *

17. Leave of absence from hospital—(1) The responsible medical officer may grant to any patient who is for the time being liable to be detained in a hospital under this Part of this Act leave to be absent from the hospital subject to such conditions (if any) as that officer considers necessary in the interests of the patient or for the protection of other persons.

(2) Leave of absence may be granted to a patient under this section either indefinitely or on specified occasions or for any specified period; and where leave is so granted for a specified period, that period may be extended by further leave granted in the absence of the patient.

(3) Where it appears to the responsible medical officer that it is necessary so to do in the interests of the patient or for the protection of other persons, he may, upon granting leave of absence under this section, direct that the patient remain in custody during his absence; and where leave of absence is so granted the patient may be kept in the custody of any officer on the staff of the hospital, or if any other person authorised in writing by the managers of the hospital or, if the patient is required in accordance with conditions imposed on the grant of leave of absence to reside in another hospital, of any officer on the staff of that other hospital.

(4) In any case where a patient is absent from a hospital in pursuance of leave of absence granted under this section, and it appears to the responsible medical officer that it is necessary so to do in the interests of the patient's health or safety or for the protection of other persons, that officer may, subject to subsection (5) below, by notice in writing given to the patient or to the person for the time being in charge of the patient, revoke the leave of absence and recall the patient to the hospital.

(5) A patient to whom leave of absence is granted under this section shall not be recalled under subsection (4) above after he has ceased to be liable to be detained under this Part of this Act; *and without prejudice to any other provision of this Part of this Act any such patient shall cease to be so liable at the expiration of the period of six months beginning with the first day of his absence on leave unless either*—

(a) *he has returned to the hospital, or has been transferred to another hospital under the following provisions of this Act, before the expiration of that period; or*

(b) *he is absent without leave at the expiration of that period.*

Note. This section contains provisions formerly in Mental Health Act 1959, s 39 as amended in the case of sub-s (3) thereof by Mental Health (Amendment) Act 1982, s 11(2). Words in italics repealed by Mental Health (Patients in the Community) Act 1995, s 3(1), as from 1 April 1996.

*   *   *   *   *

Functions of relatives of patients

26. Definition of 'relative' and 'nearest relative'—(1) In this Part of this Act
'relative' means any of the following persons—

    (a) husband or wife;

    (b) son or daughter;

    (c) father or mother;

    (d) brother or sister;

    (e) grandparent;

    (f) grandchild;

    (g) uncle or aunt;

    (h) nephew or niece.

(2) In deducing relationships for the purposes of this section, any relationship
of the half-blood shall be treated as a relationship of the whole blood, and an
illegitimate person shall be treated as the legitimate child of *his mother*

    [(a) his mother, and

    (b) if his father has parental responsibility for him within the meaning of
        section 3 of the Children Act 1989, his father].

Note. Words in square brackets substituted by Children Act 1989 (Consequential
Amendment of Enactments) Order 1991, SI 1991 No 1881, art 3, as from 14 October 1991.

(3) In this Part of this Act, subject to the provisions of this section and to the
following provisions of this Part of this Act, the 'nearest relative' means the person
first described in subsection (1) above who is for the time being surviving, relatives of
the whole blood being preferred to relatives of the same description of the half-blood
and the elder or eldest of two or more relatives described in any paragraph of that
subsection being preferred to the other or others of those relatives, regardless of sex.

(4) Subject to the provisions of this section and to the following provisions of
this Part of this Act, where the patient ordinarily resides with or is cared for by one
or more of his relatives (or, if he is for the time being an in-patient in a hospital, he
last ordinarily resided with or was cared for by one or more of his relatives) his
nearest relative shall be determined—

    (a) by giving preference to that relative or those relatives over the other or
        others; and

    (b) as between two or more such relatives, in accordance with subsection (3)
        above.

(5) Where the person who, under subsection (3) or (4) above, would be the
nearest relative of a patient—

    (a) in the case of a patient ordinarily resident in the United Kingdom, the
        Channel Islands or the Isle of Man, is not so resident; or

    (b) is the husband or wife of the patient, but is permanently separated from the
        patient, either by agreement or under an order of a court, or has deserted or
        has been deserted by the patient for a period which has not come to an end; or

    (c) is a person other than the husband, wife, father or mother of the patient,
        and is for the time being under 18 years of age; *or*

    (*d*) *is a person against whom an order divesting him of authority over the patient has*
        been made under section 38 of the Sexual Offences Act 1956 (which relates to incest
        with a person under eighteen) and has not been rescinded,

the nearest relative of the patient shall be ascertained as if that person were dead.

(6) In this section 'husband' and 'wife' include a person who is living with the
patient as the patient's husband or wife, as the case may be (or, if the patient is for
the time being an in-patient in a hospital, was so living until the patient was
admitted), and has been or had been so living for a period of not less than six
months; but a person shall not be treated by virtue of this subsection as the nearest
relative of a married patient unless the husband or wife of the patient is disregarded
by virtue of paragraph (b) of subsection (5) above.

(7) A person, other than a relative, with whom the patient ordinarily resides (or, if the patient is for the time being an in-patient in a hospital, last ordinarily resided before he was admitted), and with whom he has or had been ordinarily residing for a period of not less than five years, shall be treated for the purposes of this Part of this Act as if he were a relative but—

(a) shall be treated for the purposes of subsection (3) above as if mentioned last in subsection (1) above; and

(b) shall not be treated by virtue of this subsection as the nearest relative of a married patient unless the husband or wife of the patient is disregarded by virtue of paragraph (b) of subsection (5) above.

Note. Sub-s (1) contains provisions formerly in Mental Health Act 1959, s 49(1) as amended by Mental Health (Amendment) Act 1982, s 14(2). Sub-ss (2), (3), (6) contain provisions formerly in s 49(2), (3), (6) of the Act of 1959 as partly repealed in the case of sub-s (2) by Children Act 1975, s 108(1)(b), Sch 4, Part I. Sub-ss (4), (7) contain provisions formerly in s 49(3A), (7) of the Act of 1959, as inserted by s 14(3), (5) of the Act of 1982. Sub-s (5) contains provisions formerly in s 49(4) of the Act of 1959 as amended by Family Law Reform Act 1969, s 1(3), Sch 1, Part I, Guardianship Act 1973, ss 1(8), 14(4) of the Act of 1982.

Sub-s (5)(d), and word 'or' preceding it repealed by Children Act 1989, s 108(7), Sch 15, as from 14 October 1991.

27. Children and young persons in care of local authority. *In any case where the rights and powers of a parent of a patient, being a child or young person, are vested in a local authority or other person by virtue of—*

(*a*) *section 3 of the Child Care Act 1980 (which relates to the assumption by a local authority of parental rights and duties in relation to a child in their care);*

(*b*) *section 10 of that Act (which relates to the powers and duties of local authorities with respect to persons committed to their care under the Children and Young Persons Act 1969); or*

(*c*) *section 17 of the Social Work (Scotland) Act 1968 (which makes corresponding provision for Scotland),*

that authority or person shall be deemed to be the nearest relative of the patient in preference to any person except the patient's husband or wife (if any) and except, in a case where the said rights and powers are vested in a local authority by virtue of subsection (1) of the said section 3, any parent of the patient not being the person on whose account the resolution mentioned in that subsection was passed.

Note. This section contains provisions formerly in Mental Health Act 1959, s 50 as amended and partly repealed by Social Work (Scotland) Act 1968, ss 95(1), (2), 97(1), Sch 8, para 49, Sch 9, Part II, and as amended by Child Care Act 1980, s 89, Sch 5, para 14.

[**27. Children and young persons in care.** Where—

(a) a patient who is a child or young person is in the care of a local authority by virtue of a care order within the meaning of the Children Act 1989; or

(b) the rights and powers of a parent of a patient who is a child or young person are vested in a local authority by virtue of section 16 of the Social Work (Scotland) Act 1968,

the authority shall be deemed to be the nearest relative of the patient in preference to any person except the patient's husband or wife (if any).]

Note. This section substituted by Children Act 1989, s 108(5), Sch 13, para 48(1), as from 14 October 1991.

28. Nearest relative of minor under guardianship, etc—(*1*) *Where a patient who has not attained the age of 18 years—*

(*a*) *is, by virtue of an order made by a court in the exercise of jurisdiction (whether under any enactment or otherwise) in respect of the guardianship of minors (including an order under section 38 of the Sexual Offences Act 1956), or by virtue of a deed or will executed by his father or mother, under the guardianship of a person who is not his nearest relative under the foregoing provisions of this Act, or is under the joint guardianship of two persons of whom one is such a person; or* (*b*)   is, by virtue of an order made by a court in the exercise of such jurisdiction or in matrimonial proceedings, or by virtue of a separation agreement between his father and mother, in the custody of any such person,

the person or persons having the guardianship or custody of the patient shall, to the exclusion of any other person, be deemed to be his nearest relative.

[(1)   Where—

(a)   a guardian has been appointed for a person who has not attained the age of eighteen years; or

(b)   a residence order (as defined by section 8 of the Children Act 1989) is in force with respect to such a person,

the guardian (or guardians, where there is more than one) or the person named in the residence order shall, to the exclusion of any other person, be deemed to be his nearest relative.]

(2)   Subsection (5) of section 26 above shall apply in relation to a person who is, or who is one of the persons, deemed to be the nearest relative of a patient by virtue of this section as it applies in relation to a person who would be the nearest relative under subsection (3) of that section.

(*3*)   *A patient shall be treated for the purposes of this section as being in the custody of another person if he would be in that other person's custody apart from section 8 above.*

[(3)   In this section 'guardian' [includes a special guardian (within the meaning of the Children Act 1989), but] does not include a guardian under this Part of this Act.]

(4)   In this section 'court' includes a court in Scotland or Northern Ireland, and 'enactment' includes an enactment of the Parliament of Northern Ireland, a Measure of the Northern Ireland Assembly and an Order in Council under Schedule 1 of the Northern Ireland Act 1974.

Note. Sub-ss (1)–(3) contain provisions formerly in Mental Health Act 1959, s 51(1)–(3) as amended in the case of sub-s (1) by Family Law Reform Act 1969, s 1(3), Sch 1, Part I. Sub-s (4) contains provisions formerly in s 51(4) of the Act of 1959 as affected by Northern Ireland Act 1974, s 1(3), Sch 1, para 1.

Sub-ss (1), (3) in square brackets substituted for sub-ss (1), (3) in italics by Children Act 1989, s 108(5), Sch 13, para 48(2)–(4), as from 14 October 1991. Note also that the words '(including an Order under section 38 of the Sexual Offences Act 1956)' were repealed by s 108(7) of, and Sch 15 to, the 1989 Act, as from that date. Amended by the Adoption and Children Act 2002, s 139(1), Sch 3, para 41, as from a day to be appointed.

29.   Appointment by court of acting nearest relative—(1) The county court may, upon application made in accordance with the provisions of this section in respect of a patient, by order direct that the functions of the nearest relative of the patient under this Part of this Act and sections 66 and 69 below shall, during the continuance in force of the order, be exercisable by the applicant, or by any other person specified in the application, being a person who, in the opinion of the court, is a proper person to act as the patient's nearest relative and is willing to do so.

(2)   An order under this section may be made on the application of—

(a)   any relative of the patient;

(b)   any other person with whom the patient is residing (or, if the patient is then an in-patient in a hospital, was last residing before he was admitted); or

(c)   an *approved social worker* [mental welfare officer];

but in relation to an application made by such a *social worker* [welfare officer], subsection (1) above shall have effect as if for the words 'the applicant' there were substituted the words 'the local social services authority'.

(3)   An application for an order under this section may be made upon any of the following grounds, that is to say—

(a)   that the patient has no nearest relative within the meaning of this Act, or that it is not reasonably practicable to ascertain whether he has such a relative, or who that relative is;

(b) that the nearest relative of the patient is incapable of acting as such by reason of mental disorder or other illness;

(c) that the nearest relative of the patient unreasonably objects to the making of an application for admission for treatment or a guardianship application in respect of the patient; or

(d) that the nearest relative of the patient has exercised without due regard to the welfare of the patient or the interests of the public his power to discharge the patient from hospital or guardianship under this Part of this Act, or is likely to do so.

(4) If, immediately before the expiration of the period for which a patient is liable to be detained by virtue of an application for admission for assessment, an application under this section, which is an application made on the ground specified in subsection (3)(c) or (d) above, is pending in respect of the patient, that period shall be extended—

(a) in any case, until the application under this section has been finally disposed of; and

(b) if an order is made in pursuance of the application under this section, for a further period of seven days;

and for the purposes of this subsection an application under this section shall be deemed to have been finally disposed of at the expiration of the time allowed for appealing from the decision of the court or, if notice of appeal has been given within that time, when the appeal has been heard or withdrawn, and 'pending' shall be construed accordingly.

(5) An order made on the ground specified in subsection (3)(a) or (b) above may specify a period for which it is to continue in force unless previously discharged under section 30 below.

(6) While an order made under this section is in force, the provisions of this Part of this Act (other than this section and section 30 below) and sections 66, 69, 132(4) and 133 below shall apply in relation to the patient as if for any reference to the nearest relative of the patient there were substituted a reference to the person having the functions of that relative and (without prejudice to section 30 below) shall so apply notwithstanding that the person who was the patient's nearest relative when the order was made is no longer his nearest relative; but this subsection shall not apply to section 66 below in the case mentioned in paragraph (h) of subsection (1) of that section.

Note. Sub-s (1) contains provisions formerly in Mental Health Act 1959, s 52(1) as amended by Mental Health (Amendment) Act 1982, s 20(4). Sub-s (2) contains provisions formerly in s 52(2) of the Act of 1959 as amended by Local Government Act 1972, s 195(6), Sch 23, para 9(2), and by Act of 1982, s 65(1), Sch 3, Part II, para 69, as from 24 October 1984. Sub-ss (3)–(5) contain provisions formerly in s 52(3)–(4A) of the Act of 1959 as amended in the case of sub-s (4) by Act of 1982, s 65(1), Sch 3, Part I, para 5, and as inserted in the case of sub-s (4A) by s 15(2) of that Act. Sub-s (6) contains provisions formerly in s 52(5) of the Act of 1959 as amended by ss 57(5), 58(3) of the Act of 1982.

Until 28 October 1984 sub-s (2) had effect as if the words in italics were omitted and the words in square brackets were inserted (see Sch 5, para 4(1)(e)).

30. Discharge and variation of orders under s 29—(1) An order made under section 29 above in respect of a patient may be discharged by the county court upon application made—

(a) in any case, by the person having the functions of the nearest relative of the patient by virtue of the order;

(b) where the order was made on the ground specified in paragraph (a) or paragraph (b) of section 29(3) above, or where the person who was the nearest relative of the patient when the order was made has ceased to be his nearest relative, on the application of the nearest relative of the patient.

(2) An order made under section 29 above in respect of a patient may be varied by the county court, on the application of the person having the functions of the nearest relative by virtue of the order or on the application of an *approved social worker* [mental welfare officer] by substituting for the first-mentioned person a local services authority or any other person who in the opinion of the court is a proper person to exercise those functions, being an authority or person who is willing to do so.

(3) If the person having the functions of the nearest relative of a patient by virtue of an order under section 29 above dies—

(a) subsections (1) and (2) above shall apply as if for any reference to that person there were substituted a reference to any relative of the patient, and

(b) until the order is discharged or varied under those provisions the functions of the nearest relative under this Part of this Act and sections 66 and 69 below shall not be exercisable by any person.

(4) An order under section 29 above shall, unless previously discharged under subsection (1) above, cease to have effect at the expiration of the period, if any, specified under subsection (5) of that section or, where no such period is specified—

(a) if the patient was on the date of the order liable to be detained in pursuance of an application for admission for treatment or by virtue of an order or direction under Part III of this Act (otherwise than under section 35, 36 or 38) or was subject to guardianship under this Part of this Act or by virtue of such an order or direction, or becomes so liable or subject within the period of three months beginning with that date, when he ceases to be so liable or subject (otherwise than on being transferred in pursuance of regulations under section 19 above);

(b) if the patient was not on the date of the order, and has not within the said period become, so liable or subject, at the expiration of that period.

(5) The discharge or variation under this section of an order made under section 29 above shall not affect the validity of anything previously done in pursuance of the order.

Note. Sub-ss (1), (2) contain provisions formerly in Mental Health Act 1959, s 53(1), (2) as amended in the case of sub-s (2) by Local Government Act 1972, s 195(6), Sch 23, para 9(2), and Mental Health (Amendment) Act 1982, s 65(1), Sch 3, Part II, para 70, as from 28 October 1984. Sub-s (3) contains provisions formerly in s 53(3) of the Act of 1959, as amended by s 20(4) of the Act of 1982. Sub-ss (4), (5) contain provisions formerly in s 53(4), (5) of the Act of 1959 as amended in the case of sub-s (4) by ss 15(3), 20(4) of the Act of 1982.

Until 28 October 1984 sub-s (2) had effect as if the words in italics were omitted and the words in square brackets were inserted (see Sch 5, para 4(1)(e)).

* * * * *

33. Special provisions as to wards of court—(1) An application for the admission to hospital of a minor who is a ward of court may be made under this Part of this Act with the leave of the court; and section 11(4) above shall not apply in relation to an application so made.

(2) Where a minor who is a ward of court is liable to be detained in a hospital by virtue of an application for admission under this Part of this Act, any power exercisable under this Part of this Act or under section 66 below in relation to the patient by his nearest relative shall be exercisable by or with the leave of the court.

(3) Nothing in this Part of this Act shall be construed as authorising the making of a guardianship application in respect of a minor who is a ward of court, or the transfer into guardianship of any such minor.

[(4) Where a supervision application has been made in respect of a minor who is a ward of court, the provisions of this Part of this Act relating to after-care under supervision have effect in relation to the minor subject to any order which the court may make in the exercise of its wardship jurisdiction.]

Note. Sub-s (4) added by Mental Health (Patients in the Community) Act 1995, s 1(2), Sch 1, para 3, as from 1 April 1996.

* * * * *

PART IV

CONSENT TO TREATMENT

58. Treatment requiring consent or a second opinion—(1) This section applies to the following forms of medical treatment for mental disorder—
(a) such forms of treatment as may be specified for the purposes of this section by regulations made by the Secretary of State;
(b) the administration of medicine to a patient by any means (not being a form of treatment specified under paragraph (a) above or section 57 above) at any time during a period for which he is liable to be detained as a patient to whom this Part of this Act applies if three months or more have elapsed since the first occasion in that period when medicine was administered to him by any means for his mental disorder.
(2) The Secretary of State may by order vary the length of the period mentioned in subsection (1)(b) above.
(3) Subject to section 62 below, a patient shall not be given any form of treatment to which this section applies unless—
(a) he has consented to that treatment and either the responsible medical officer or a registered medical practitioner appointed for the purposes of this Part of this Act by the Secretary of State has certified in writing that the patient is capable of understanding its nature, purpose and likely effects and has consented to it; or
(b) a registered medical practitioner appointed as aforesaid (not being the responsible medical officer) has certified in writing that the patient is not capable of understanding the nature, purpose and likely effects of that treatment or has not consented to it but that, having regard to the likelihood of its alleviating or preventing a deterioration of his condition, the treatment should be given.
(4) Before giving a certificate under subsection (3)(b) above the registered medical practitioner concerned shall consult two other persons who have been professionally concerned with the patient's medical treatment, and of those persons one shall be a nurse and the other shall be neither a nurse nor a registered medical practitioner.
(5) Before making any regulations for the purposes of this section that Secretary of State shall consult such bodies as appear to him to be concerned.

59. Plans of treatment. Any consent or certificate under section 57 or 58 above may relate to a plan of treatment under which the patient is to be given (whether within a specified period or otherwise) one or more of the forms of treatment to which that section applies.

60. Withdrawal of consent—(1) Where the consent of a patient to any treatment has been given for the purposes of section 57 or 58 above, the patient may, subject to section 62 below, at any time before the completion of the treatment withdraw his consent, and those sections shall then apply as if the remainder of the treatment were a separate form of treatment.
(2) Without prejudice to the application of subsection (1) above to any treatment given under the plan of treatment to which a patient has consented, a patient who has consented to such a plan may, subject to section 62 below, at any time withdraw his consent to further treatment, or to further treatment of any description, under the plan.

61. Review of treatment—(1) Where a patient is given treatment in accordance with section 57(2) or 58(3)(b) above a report on the treatment and the patient's condition shall be given by the responsible medical officer to the Secretary of State—

    (a) on the next occasion on which the responsible medical officer furnishes a report [under section 20(3) or 21B(2) above renewing the authority for the detention of the patient]; and

    (b) at any other time if so required by the Secretary of State.

Note. Words in square brackets in sub-s (1)(a) substituted by Mental Health (Patients in the Community) Act 1995, s 2(5), as from 1 April 1996.

(2) In relation to a patient who is subject to a restriction order [, limitation direction] or restriction direction subsection (1) above shall have effect as if paragraph (a) required the report to be made—

    (a) in the case of treatment in the period of six months beginning with the date of the order or direction, at the end of that period;

    (b) in the case of treatment at any subsequent time, on the next occasion on which the responsible medical officer makes a report in respect of the patient under section 41(6) [, 45B(3)] or 49(3) above.

(3) The Secretary of State may at any time give notice to the responsible medical officer directing that, subject to section 62 below, a certificate given in respect of a patient under section 57(2) or 58(3)(b) above shall not apply to treatment given to him after a date specified in the notice and sections 57 and 58 above shall then apply to any such treatment as if that certificate had not been given.

Note. Words in square brackets in sub-s (2) inserted by Crime (Sentences) Act 1997, s 55, Sch 4, para 12(1), (7), as from 1 October 1997 (SI 1997 No 2200).

62 Urgent treatment—(1) Sections 57 and 58 above shall not apply to any treatment—

    (a) which is immediately necessary to save the patient's life; or

    (b) which (not being irreversible) is immediately necessary to prevent a serious deterioration of his condition; or

    (c) which (not being irreversible or hazardous) is immediately necessary to alleviate serious suffering by the patient; or

    (d) which (not being irreversible or hazardous) is immediately necessary and represents the minimum interference necessary to prevent the patient from behaving violently or being a danger to himself or to others.

(2) Sections 60 and 61(3) above shall not preclude the continuation of any treatment or of treatment under any plan pending compliance with section 57 or 58 above if the responsible medical officer considers that the discontinuance of the treatment or of treatment under the plan would cause serious suffering to the patient.

(3) For the purposes of this section treatment is irreversible if it has unfavourable irreversible physical or psychological consequences and hazardous if it entails significant physical hazard.

63. Treatment not requiring consent. The consent of a patient shall not be required for any medical treatment given to him for the mental disorder from which he is suffering, not being treatment falling within section 57 or 58 above, if the treatment is given by or under the direction of the responsible medical officer.

64. Supplementary provisions for Part IV—(1) In this Part of this Act 'the responsible medical officer' means the registered medical practitioner in charge of the treatment of the patient in question and 'hospital' includes a *mental nursing home* [registered establishment].

(2) Any certificate for the purposes of this Part of this Act shall be in such form as may be prescribed by regulations made by the Secretary of State.

Note. Amended by the Care Standards Act 2000, s 116, Sch 4, para 9(1), (2), as from 1 April 2002 (SI 2001 No 4150, SI 2002 No 920)

*   *   *   *   *

PART X

MISCELLANEOUS AND SUPPLEMENTARY

Miscellaneous provisions

131. Informal admission of patients—(1) Nothing in this Act shall be construed as preventing a patient who requires treatment for mental disorder from being admitted to any hospital or *mental nursing home* [registered establishment] in pursuance of arrangements made in that behalf and without any application, order or direction rendering him liable to be detained under this Act, or from remaining in any hospital or *mental nursing home* [registered establishment] in pursuance of such arrangements after he has ceased to be so liable to be detained.

(2) In the case of a minor who has attained the age of 16 years and is capable of expressing his own wishes, any such arrangements as are mentioned in subsection (1) above may be made, carried out and determined *notwithstanding any right of custody or control vested by law in his parent or guardian* [even though there are one or more persons who have parental responsibility for him (within the meaning of the Children Act 1989)].

Note. This section contains provisions formerly in Mental Health Act 1959, s 5 as affected by Family Law Reform Act 1969, s 12.

Words in square brackets substituted for words in italics by Children Act 1989, s 108(5), Sch 13, para 48(5), as from 14 October 1991.

Further amended by the Care Standards Act 2000, s 116, Sch 4, para 9(1),(2) as from 1 April 2002 (SI 2001 No 4150, SI 2002 No 920).

*   *   *   *   *

Supplemental

*   *   *   *   *

145. Interpretation—(1) In this Act, unless the context otherwise requires—

'absent without leave' has the meaning given to it by section 18 above and related expressions shall be construed accordingly;

'application for admission for assessment' has the meaning given in section 2 above;

'application for admission for treatment' has the meaning given in section 3 above;

'approved social worker' means an officer of a local social services authority appointed to act as an approved social worker for the purposes of this Act;

['care home' has the same meaning as in the Care Standards Act 2000;]

['Health Authority' means a Health Authority established under section 8 of the National Health Service Act 1977;]

['high security psychiatric services' has the same meaning as in the National Health Service Act 1977,]

'hospital' means—

(a) any health service hospital within the meaning of the National Health Service Act 1977; and

(b) any accommodation provided by a local authority and used as a hospital by or on behalf of the Secretary of State under that Act;

and 'hospital within the meaning of Part II of this Act' has the meaning given in section 34 above;

['hospital direction' has the meaning given in section 45A(3)(a) above;]

'hospital order' and 'guardianship order' have the meanings respectively given in section 37 above;

['independent hospital' has the same meaning as in the Care Standards Act 2000;]

'interim hospital order' has the meaning given in section 38 above;

['limitation direction' has the meaning given in section 45A(3)(b) above;]

'local social services authority' means a council which is a local authority for the purpose of the Local Authority Social Services Act 1970;

'the managers' means—

   (a)   in relation to a hospital vested in the Secretary of State for the purposes of his functions under the National Health Service Act 1977, and in relation to any accommodation provided by a local authority and used as a hospital by or on behalf of the Secretary of State under that Act, the *District Health Authority or special health authority* [Primary Care Trust,] [Strategic Health Authority] [Health Authority or Special Health Authority] responsible for the administration of the hospital;

   (b)   in relation to a special hospital, the Secretary of State;

   [(bb)   in relation to a hospital vested in [a Primary Care Trust or] a National Health Service trust, *the directors of* the trust;]

   [(bc)   in relation to a hospital vested in an NHS foundation trust, the trust;]

   (c)   in relation to a mental nursing home registered in pursuance of the Nursing Homes Act 1975 [the Registered Homes Act 1984], the person or persons registered in respect of the home;

   [(c)   in relation to a registered establishment, the person or persons registered in respect of the establishment;]

   and in this definition 'hospital' means a hospital within the meaning of Part II of this Act;

'medical treatment' includes nursing, and also includes care, habilitation and rehabilitation under medical supervision;

'mental disorder', 'severe mental impairment', 'mental impairment' and 'psychopathic disorder' have the meanings given in section 1 above;

'mental nursing home' has the same meaning as in the Nursing Homes Act 1975 [the Registered Homes Act 1984];

'nearest relative', in relation to a patient, has the meaning given in Part II of this Act;

'patient' (except in Part VII of this Act) means a person suffering or appearing to be suffering from mental disorder;

['Primary Care Trust' means a Primary Care Trust established under section 16A of the National Health Service Act 1977;]

['registered establishment' has the meaning given in section 34 above;]

['the responsible after-care bodies' has the meaning given in section 25D above;]

'restriction direction' has the meaning given to it by section 49 above;

'restriction order' has the meaning given to it by section 41 above;

['Special Health Authority' means a Special Health Authority established under section 11 of the National Health Service Act 1977;]

'special hospital' has the same meaning as in the National Health Service Act 1977;

'standard scale' has the meaning given in section 75 of the Criminal Justice Act 1982;

['Strategic Health Authority' means a Strategic Health Authority established under section 8 of the National Health Service Act 1977;]

['supervision application' has the meaning given in section 25A above;]

'transfer direction' has the meaning given to it by section 47 above.

*   *   *   *   *

(2)   *'Statutory maximum' has the meaning given in section 74 of the Criminal Justice Act 1982 and for the purposes of section 128(4)(a) above—*

   (a)   *subsection (1) of section 74 shall have effect as if after the words 'England and Wales' there were inserted the words 'or Northern Ireland'; and*

   (b)   *section 32 of the Magistrates' Courts Act 1980 shall extend to Northern Ireland.*

Note. Definitions 'Health Authority' and 'Special Health Authority' inserted, and words in square brackets in para (a) of definition 'the managers' substituted for words in italics by Health Authorities Act 1995, s 2(1), Sch 1, Part III, para 107, as from 1 April 1996. Definitions 'hospital direction' and 'limitation direction' inserted by Crime (Sentences) Act 1997, s 55, Sch 4, para 12(1), (19), as from 1 October 1997 (SI 1997/2200). References to 'Registered Homes Act 1984' substituted for references to 'Nursing Homes Act 1975' by s 57(1) of and Sch 1, para 11 to the 1984 Act. Para (bb) in definition 'the managers' inserted by National Health Service and Community Care Act 1990, s 66(1), Sch 9, para 24(9), as from 5 July 1990. In definition 'the managers' words in italics repealed by Mental Health (Amendment) Act 1994, s 1, as from 15 April 1994. Words from 'and for the purposes' to the end of sub-s (2) repealed by Fines and Penalties (Northern Ireland) Act 1984. Definitions 'the responsible after-care bodies' and 'supervision application' inserted by Mental Health (Patients in the Community) Act 1995, s 1(2), Sch 1, para 20, as from 1 April 1996. Definition 'standard scale' and sub-s (2) repealed by Statute Law (Repeals) Act 1993, s 1(1), Sch 1, Part XIV, as from 5 November 1993. Further amended by the Care Standards Act 2000, Sch 4, para 9(1), (10), as from 1 April 2002, (SI 2001 No 4150, SI 2002 No 920); the Health Act 1999, ss 41, 65, Sch 4, paras 65, 69(1),(2)(a), Sch 5 as from 1 April 2000 (SI 1999–2793); the National Health Service Reform and Health Care Professions Act 2002, s 2(5), Sch 2, Pt 2, paras 41, 49, as from 1 October (SI 2002 No 2478); SI 2002 No 2469, as from 1 October 2002; SI 2000 No 90, art 3, Sch 1, para 16, as from 8 February 2000; the Health and Social Care (Community Health and Standards) Act 2003, s 34, Sch 4, paras 50, 57, as from 1 April 2004 (SI 2004 No 759); the Care Standards Act 2000, s 117, Sch 6, as from 1 April 2002 (SI 2001 No 4150, SI 2002, No 920).

* * * * *

148. Consequential and transitional provisions and repeals—(1) Schedule 4 (consequential amendments) and Schedule 5 (transitional and saving provisions) to this Act shall have effect but without prejudice to the operation of sections 15 to 17 of the Interpretation Act 1978 (which relate to the effect of repeals).

(2) Where any amendment in Schedule 4 to this Act affects an enactment amended by the Mental Health (Amendment) Act 1982 the amendment in Schedule 4 shall come into force immediately after the provision of the Act of 1982 amending that enactment.

(3) The enactments specified in Schedule 6 to this Act are hereby repealed to the extent mentioned in the third column of that Schedule.

149. Short title, commencement and application to Scilly Isles—(1) This Act may be cited as the Mental Health Act 1983.

(2) Subject to subsection (3) below and Schedule 5 to this Act, this Act shall come into force on 30th September 1983.

* * * * *

SCHEDULE 4   Section 148

CONSEQUENTIAL AMENDMENTS

(*Sch 4 makes consequential amendments: insofar as they are relevant to legislation printed in this work, they have been incorporated.*)

SCHEDULE 5   Section 148

TRANSITIONAL AND SAVING PROVISIONS

1. Where any period of time specified in an enactment repealed by this Act is current at the commencement of this Act, this Act shall have effect as if the corresponding provision of this Act had been in force when that period began to run.

2. Nothing in this Act shall affect the interpretation of any provision of the Mental Health Act 1959 which is not repealed by this Act and accordingly sections 1 and 145(1) of this Act shall apply to those provisions as if they were contained in this Act.

3. Where, apart from this paragraph, anything done under or for the purposes of any enactment which is repealed by this Act would cease to have effect by virtue of that repeal it shall have effect as if it had been done under or for the purposes of the corresponding provision of this Act.

4.   (1) Until the expiration of the period of two years beginning with the day on which the Mental Health (Amendment) Act 1982 is passed this Act shall have effect as if—

*   *   *   *   *

   (b) in section 145(1) the definition of an approved social worker were omitted and there were inserted in the appropriate place the following definition— ' "mental welfare officer" means an officer of a local social services authority appointed to act as mental welfare officer for the purposes of the Mental Health Act 1959 or this Act';

*   *   *   *   *

   (e) for any reference to an approved social worker there were substituted a reference to a mental welfare officer.

   (2) Any appointment of a person as a mental welfare officer for the purposes of the Mental Health Act 1959 or this Act shall terminate at the expiration of the period mentioned in sub-paragraph (1) above but without prejudice to anything previously done by that person or to the continuation by an approved social worker of anything which is then in process of being done by that person.

*   *   *   *   *

6. This Act shall apply in relation to any authority for the detention or guardianship of a person who was liable to be detained or subject to guardianship under the Mental Health Act 1959 immediately before 30th September 1983 as if the provisions of this Act which derive from provisions amended by sections 1 or 2 of the Mental Health (Amendment) Act 1982 and the amendments in Schedule 3 to that Act which are consequential on those sections were included in this Act in the form the provisions from which they derive would take if those amendments were disregarded but this provision shall not apply to any renewal of that authority on or after that date.

*   *   *   *   *

8.   (1) Where on 30 September 1983 a person who has not attained the age of sixteen years is subject to guardianship by virtue of a guardianship application the authority for his guardianship shall terminate on that day.

   (2) Section 8(1) of this Act has effect (instead of section 34(1) of the Mental Health Act 1959) in relation to a guardianship application made before the coming into force of this Act as well as in relation to one made later.

*   *   *   *   *

SCHEDULE 6   Section 134

REPEALS

Chapter	Short Title	Extent of Repeal
7 & 8 Eliz 2 72	The Mental Health Act 1959	Sections 1 to 5. Sections 25 to 35. Sections 37 to 43. Sections 45 to 60. Section 153.
1969 c 46	The Family Law Reform Act 1969	In Schedule 1 the entries relating to the Mental Health Act 1959.
1973 c 29	The Guardianship Act 1973	In section 1(8), the words from 'and' to the end of the subsection.
1980 c 5	The Child Care Act 1980	In Schedule 5, paragraphs 13 and 14.

Commencement. This Act came into force 30 September 1983 (see s 149(2)).

DESTINATION TABLE

This table shows in column (1) the enactments repealed by the Mental Health Act 1983, and in column (2) the provisions of that Act corresponding to the repealed provisions.

The table is restricted to provisions of earlier legislation printed in Volume 2.

(1)	(2)	(1)	(2)
Mental Health Act 1959 (c 72)	Mental Health Act 1983 (c 20)	Mental Health Act 1959 (c 72)	Mental Health Act 1983 (c 20)
s 4(1)–(4)	s 1(2)	s 49(1)–(3)	s 26(1)–(3)
(5)	(3)	(3A), (4)	(4),(5)
5	131	(5)	Rep 1975 c 72, s 108, Sch 4, Part I
25	2	(6)	s 26(6)
26(1)–(3)	3		
(4)	11(6)	50	27
(5)	Rep 1982 c 51 s 65(2), Sch 4, Part I	51	28
		52(1)–(4)	29(1)–(4)
33(1), (2)	s 7(1), (2)	(4A), (5)	(5), (6)
(2A), (2B)	(3), (4)	(6)	66(1)(h)
33(3), (4)	7(5)		(2)(g)
(5)	12(7)	53	30
34(1)–(4)	8(1)–(4)		
(5)	66(1)(c), (2)(c)		
(6)	8(5)		
39	17		

MARRIAGE ACT 1983

(1983 c 32)

An Act to enable marriages of house-bound and detained persons to be solemnised at the place where they reside; and for connected purposes.   [13 May 1983]

Marriages in England and Wales

1. Marriages of house-bound and detained persons in England and Wales—
(1) Subject to the provisions of this Act and the Marriage Act 1949, the marriage of a person who is house-bound or is a detained person may be solemnised in England and Wales, on the authority of *a superintendent registrar's certificate* [certificates of a superintendent registrar] issued under Part III of the Marriage Act 1949, at the place where that person usually resides.

Note. Words in square brackets substituted for words in italics by the Immigration and Asylum Act 1999, s 169(1), (Sch 14, para 77, as from 1 January 2001 (SI 2000 No 2698).

(2) For the purposes of this section a person is house-bound if—
(a) *the notice* [each notice] of his or her marriage given in accordance with section 27 of the Marriage Act 1949 is accompanied by a statement, made in a form prescribed under that Act by a registered medical practitioner not more than fourteen days before that notice is given, that, in his opinion—
  (i) by reason of illness or disability, he or she ought not to move or be moved from his or her home or the other place where he or she is at that time, and

      (ii) it is likely that it will be the case for at least the three months following the date on which the statement is made that by reason of the illness or disability he or she ought not to move or be moved from that place; and

  (b) he or she is not a detained person.

Note. Words in square brackets substituted for words in italics by the Immigration and Asylum Act 1999, s 169(1), Sch 14, para 77, as from 1 January 2001 (SI 2000 No 2698).

(3) For the purposes of this section, a person is a detained person if he or she is for the time being detained—

  (a) otherwise than by virtue of section 2, 4, 5, 35, 36 or 136 of the Mental Health Act 1983 (short term detentions), as a patient in a hospital; or

  (b) in a prison or other place to which the Prison Act 1952 applies.

(4) In subsection (3) above 'hospital' and 'patient' have the same meanings as in Part II of the Mental Health Act 1983.

(5) For the purposes of this section, a person who is house-bound or is a detained person shall be taken, if he or she would not otherwise be, to be usually resident at the place where he or she is for the time being.

(6) Nothing in the preceding provisions of this section shall be taken to relate or have any reference to any marriage according to the usages of the Society of Friends or any marriage between two persons professing the Jewish religion according to the usages of the Jews.

(7) Schedule I to this Act (amendment of the Marriage Act 1949 in consequence of this section) shall have effect.

*   *   *   *   *

General

12. Citation, commencement, etc—(1) This Act may be cited as the Marriage Act 1983 and this Act as it extends to England and Wales and the Marriages Acts 1949 to 1970 may be cited as the Marriage Acts 1949 to 1983.

*   *   *   *   *

(3) Nothing in this Act shall affect any law or custom relating to the marriage of members of the Royal Family.

(4) Nothing in this Act shall affect the right of the Archbishop of Canterbury or any other person by virtue of the Ecclesiastical Licences Act 1533 to grant special licences to marry at any convenient time or place or affect the validity of any marriage solemnised on the authority of such a licence.

(5) This Act shall come into force on such day as the Secretary of State may by order made by statutory instrument appoint, and different days may be appointed for different purposes.

(6) This Act shall not extend to Scotland.

(7) Sections 1 and 2 above and Schedule 1 to this Act, except paragraph 9, shall not extend to Northern Ireland and sections 3 to 11 above and Schedule 2 to this Act, except paragraph 11, shall not extend to England and Wales.

Commencement. This Act came into force 1 May 1984 (SI 1984 No 413).

*   *   *   *   *

COUNTY COURTS (PENALTIES FOR CONTEMPT) ACT 1983

(1983 c 45)

An Act to provide for county courts to be treated as superior courts for the purposes of section 14 of the Contempt of Court Act 1981   [13 May 1983]

Commencement. This Act came into force 13 May 1983.

1. (*Amends Contempt of Court Act 1981, s 14, p 2758.*)

2. Citation, saving and extent—(1) This Act may be cited as the County Courts (Penalties for Contempt) Act 1983.

(2) *This Act does not affect the powers of a county court in relation to a contempt of court committed before the commencement of this Act.*

Note. Repealed by the Statute Law (Repeals) Act 2004, as from 22 July 2004.

(3) This Act extends to Northern Ireland, and accordingly the reference in section 1 to section 14 of the Contempt of Court Act 1981 includes a reference to that section as set out in Schedule 4 to that Act.

MATRIMONIAL AND FAMILY PROCEEDINGS ACT 1984

(1984 c 42)

ARRANGEMENT OF SECTIONS

An Act to amend the Matrimonial Causes Act 1973, so far as it restricts the time within which proceedings for divorce or nullity of marriage can be instituted; to amend that Act, the Domestic Proceedings and Magistrates' Courts Act 1978 and the Magistrates' Courts Act 1980 so far as they relate to the exercise of the jurisdiction of courts in England and Wales to make provision for financial relief or to exercise related powers in matrimonial and certain other family proceedings; to make provision for financial relief to be available where a marriage has been dissolved or annulled, or the parties to a marriage have been legally separated, in a country overseas; to make related amendments in the Maintenance Orders (Reciprocal Enforcement) Act 1972 and the Inheritance (Provision for Family and Dependants) Act 1975; to make provision for the distribution and transfer between the High Court and county courts of, and the exercise in those courts of jurisdiction in, family business and family proceedings and to repeal and re-enact with amendments certain provisions conferring on designated county courts jurisdiction in matrimonial proceedings; to impose a duty to notify changes of address on persons liable to make payments under maintenance orders enforceable under Part II of the Maintenance Orders Act 1950 or Part I of the Maintenance Orders Act 1958; and for connected purposes.   [12 July 1984]

PART I

TIME RESTRICTIONS ON PRESENTATION OF PETITIONS FOR DIVORCE OR NULLITY OF MARRIAGE

1, 2. (*Section 1 substitutes Matrimonial Causes Act 1973, s 3, p 2499, repealed by Family Law Act 1996, s 66(3), Sch 10, as from a day to be appointed, subject to savings in s 66(2) of, and para 5 of Sch 9 to, the 1996 Act; s 2 amends ibid, s 13, p 2504.*)

PART II

FINANCIAL RELIEF IN MATRIMONIAL PROCEEDINGS

3–11. (*Sections 3–7 make amendments to Matrimonial Causes Act 1973 as follows: s 3 substitutes ss 25, 25A, pp 2519, 2521; s 4 substitutes s 27(3), p 2529; s 5 amends ss 28, 29(2), pp 2532, 2534; s 6 amends s 31, p 2536; s 7 inserts s 33A, p 2543; ss 9–11 make amendments to Domestic Proceedings and Magistrates' Courts Act 1978, as follows: s 9 substitutes s 3, p 2693 and amends ss 5(2), 20(11), pp 2695, 2713; s 10 substitutes s 6, p 2651; s 11 substitutes s 20(2), p 2711.*)

PART III*

FINANCIAL RELIEF IN ENGLAND AND WALES AFTER OVERSEAS DIVORCE ETC

* Any proceedings under Part III are 'family proceedings' for the purposes of the Children Act 1989; see ibid, s 8(3)(b), (4)(g), p 3297.

Applications for financial relief

12. Applications for financial relief after overseas divorce etc—(1) Where—
   (a) a marriage has been dissolved or annulled, or the parties to a marriage have been legally separated, by means of judicial or other proceedings in an overseas country, and
   (b) the divorce, annulment or legal separation is entitled to be recognised as valid in England and Wales,
either party to the marriage may apply to the court in the manner prescribed by rules of court for an order for financial relief under this Part of this Act.
   (2) If after a marriage has been dissolved or annulled in an overseas country one of the parties to the marriage remarries that party shall not be entitled to make an application in relation to that marriage.
   (3) For the avoidance of doubt it is hereby declared that the reference in subsection (2) above to remarriage includes a reference to a marriage which is by law void or voidable.
   (4) In this Part of this Act except sections 19, 23 and 24 'order for financial relief' means an order under section 17 or 22 below of a description referred to in that section.

13. Leave of the court required for applications for financial relief—(1) No application for an order for financial relief shall be made under this Part of this Act unless the leave of the court has been obtained in accordance with rules of court; and the court shall not grant leave unless it considers that there is substantial ground for the making of an application for such an order.
   (2) The court may grant leave under this section notwithstanding that an order has been made by a court in a country outside England and Wales requiring the other party to the marriage to make any payment or transfer any property to the applicant or a child of the family.
   (3) Leave under this section may be granted subject to such conditions as the court thinks fit.

14. Interim orders for maintenance—(1) Where leave is granted under section 13 above for the making of an application for an order for financial relief and it appears to the court that the applicant or any child of the family is in immediate need of financial assistance, the court may make an interim order for maintenance, that is to say, an order requiring the other party to the marriage to make to the applicant or to the child such periodical payments, and for such term, being a term beginning not earlier than the date of the grant of leave and ending with the date of the determination of the application for an order for financial relief, as the court thinks reasonable.

(2) If it appears to the court that the court has jurisdiction to entertain the application for an order for financial relief by reason only of paragraph (c) of section 15(1) below the court shall not make an interim order under this section.

(3) An interim order under subsection (1) above may be made subject to such conditions as the court thinks fit.

15. Jurisdiction of the court—(1) Subject to subsection (2) below, the court shall have jurisdiction to entertain an application for an order for financial relief if any of the following jurisdictional requirements are satisfied, that is to say—

(a) either of the parties to the marriage was domiciled in England and Wales on the date of the application for leave under section 13 above or was so domiciled on the date on which the divorce, annulment or legal separation obtained in the overseas country took effect in that country; or

(b) either of the parties to the marriage was habitually resident in England and Wales throughout the period of one year ending with the date of the application for leave or was so resident throughout the period of one year ending with the date on which the divorce, annulment or legal separation obtained in the overseas country took effect in that country; or

(c) either or both of the parties to the marriage had at the date of the application for leave a beneficial interest in possession in a dwelling-house situated in England or Wales which was at some time during the marriage a matrimonial home of the parties to the marriage.

(2) Where the jurisdiction of the court to entertain proceedings under this Part of this Act would fall to be determined by reference to the jurisdictional requirements imposed by virtue of Part I of the Civil Jurisdiction and Judgments Act 1982 (implementation of certain European conventions) [or by virtue of Council Regulation (EC) No 44/2001 of 22nd December 2000 on jurisdiction and the recognition and enforcement of judgments in civil and commercial matters or] then—

(a) satisfaction of the requirements of subsection (1) above shall not obviate the need to satisfy the requirements imposed by virtue of [that Regulation or] Part I of that Act; and

(b) satisfaction of the requirements imposed by virtue of [that Regulation or] Part I of that Act shall obviate the need to satisfy the requirements of subsection (1) above;

and the court shall entertain or not entertain the proceedings accordingly.

Note. Words in square brackets inserted by the Civil Jurisdiction and Judgments Order 2001 (SI 2001/3929), as from 1 March 2002.

16. Duty of the court to consider whether England and Wales is appropriate venue for application—(1) Before making an order for financial relief the court shall consider whether in all the circumstances of the case it would be appropriate for such an order to be made by a court in England and Wales, and if the court is not satisfied that it would be appropriate, the court shall dismiss the application.

(2) The court shall in particular have regard to the following matters—

(a) the connection which the parties to the marriage have with England and Wales;

(b) the connection which those parties have with the country in which the marriage was dissolved or annulled or in which they were legally separated;

(c) the connection which those parties have with any other country outside England and Wales;

(d) any financial benefit which the applicant or a child of the family has received, or is likely to receive, in consequence of the divorce, annulment or legal separation, by virtue of any agreement or the operation of the law of a country outside England and Wales;

(e) in a case where an order has been made by a court in a country outside England and Wales requiring the other party to the marriage to make any payment or transfer any property for the benefit of the applicant or a child of the family, the financial relief given by the order and the extent to which the order has been complied with or is likely to be complied with;

(f) any right which the applicant has, or has had, to apply for financial relief from the other party to the marriage under the law of any country outside England and Wales and if the applicant has omitted to exercise that right the reason for that omission;

(g) the availability in England and Wales of any property in respect of which an order under this Part of this Act in favour of the applicant could be made;

(h) the extent to which any order made under this Part of this Act is likely to be enforceable;

(i) the length of time which has elapsed since the date of the divorce, annulment or legal separation.

Orders for financial provision and property adjustment

17. Orders for financial provision and property adjustment—*(1) Subject to section 20 below, the court on an application by a party to a marriage for an order for financial relief under this section, may make any one or more of the orders which it could make under Part II of the 1973 Act if a decree of divorce, a decree of nullity of marriage or a decree of judicial separation in respect of the marriage had been granted in England and Wales, that is to say—*

(a) any order mentioned in section 23(1) of the 1973 Act (financial provision orders);

(b) any order mentioned in section 24(1) of that Act (property adjustment orders).

[(1) Subject to section 20 below, on an application by a party to a marriage for an order for financial relief under this section, the court may—

(a) make any one or more of the orders which it could make under Part II of the 1973 Act if a decree of divorce, a decree of nullity of marriage or a decree of judicial separation in respect of the marriage had been granted in England and Wales, that is to say—

(i) any order mentioned in section 23(1) of the 1973 Act (financial provision orders); and

(ii) any order mentioned in section 24(1) of that Act (properly adjustment orders); and

(b) if the marriage has been dissolved or annulled, make one or more orders each of which would, within the meaning of that Part of that Act, be a pension sharing order in relation to the marriage.]

Note. Words in square brackets substituted for words in italics by the Welfare Reform and Pensions Act 1999, S 84(1), Sch 12, paras 2, 3, as from 1 December 2000 (SI 2000/1116).

(2) Subject to section 20 below, where the court makes a secured periodical payments order, an order for the payment of a lump sum or a property adjustment

order under subsection (1) above, then, on making that order or at *any time thereafter, the court may make any order mentioned in section 24A(1) of the 1973 Act (orders for sale of property) which the court would have power to make if the order under subsection (1) above had been made under Part II of the 1973 Act* [one or more orders each of which would, within the meaning of Part II of the 1973 Act, be a financial provision order in favour of a party to the marriage or child of the family or a property adjustment order in relation to the marriage.]

Note. Words in square brackets substituted for words in italics by Family Law Act 1996, s 66(1), Sch 8, Part I, para 32(2), as from a day to be appointed, subject to savings in s 66(2) of, and para 5 of Sch 9 to, the 1996 Act.

18. Matters to which the court is to have regard in exercising its powers under s 17—(1) In deciding whether to exercise its powers under section 17 above and, if so, in what manner, the court shall act in accordance with this section.

(2) The court shall have regard to all the circumstances of the case, first consideration being given to the welfare while a minor of any child of the family who has not attained the age of eighteen.

(3) As regards the exercise of those powers in relation to a party to the marriage, the court shall in particular have regard to the matters mentioned in section 25(2)(a) to (h) of the 1973 Act and shall be under duties corresponding with those imposed by section 25A(1) and (2) of the 1973 Act where it decides to exercise under section 17 above powers corresponding with the powers referred to in those subsections.

[(3A) The matters to which the court is to have regard under subsection (3) above—

(a) so far as relating to paragraph (a) of section 25(2) of the 1983 Act, include any benefits under a pension arrangement which a party to the marriage has or is likely to have (whether or not in the foreseeable future), and

(b) so far as relating to paragraph (h) of that provision, include any benefits under a pension arrangement which, by reason of the dissolution or annulment of the marriage, a party to the marriage will lose the chance of acquiring.]

Note. Sub-s (3A) in square brackets inserted by the Welfare Reform and Pensions Act 1999, s 22(1)–(3), as from 1 December 2000 (SI 2000/1116).

(4) As regards the exercise of those powers in relation to a child of the family, the court shall in particular have regard to the matters mentioned in section 25(3)(a) to (e) of the 1973 Act.

(5) As regards the exercise of those powers against a party to the marriage in favour of a child of the family who is not the child of that party, the court shall also have regard to the matters mentioned in section 25(4)(a) to (c) of the 1973 Act.

(6) Where an order has been made by a court outside England and Wales for the making of payments or the transfer of property by a party to the marriage, the court in considering in accordance with this section the financial resources of the other party to the marriage or a child of the family shall have regard to the extent to which that order has been complied with or is likely to be complied with.

[(7) In this section—

(a) 'pension arrangement' has the meaning given by section 25D(3) of the 1973 Act, and

(b) references to benefits under a pension arrangement include any benefits by way of pension, whether under a pension arrangement or not.]

Note. Sub-s (7) in square brackets inserted by the Welfare Reform and Pensions Act 1999, s 22(1)–(3), as from 1 December 2000 (SI 2000/1116).

19. Consent orders for financial provision or property adjustment—(1) Notwithstanding anything in section 18 above, on an application for a consent order for financial relief the court may, unless it has reason to think that there are other circumstances into which it ought to inquire, make an order in the terms agreed on the basis only of the prescribed information furnished with the application.

(2) Subsection (1) above applies to an application for a consent order varying or discharging an order for financial relief as it applies to an application for an order for financial relief.

(3) In this section—

'consent order', in relation to an application for an order, means an order in the terms applied for to which the respondent agrees;

'order for financial relief' means an order under section 17 above; and

'prescribed' means prescribed by rules of court.

20. Restriction of powers of court where jurisdiction depends on matrimonial home in England or Wales—(1) Where the court has jurisdiction to entertain an application for an order for financial relief by reason only of the situation in England or Wales of a dwelling-house which was a matrimonial home of the parties, the court may make under section 17 above any one or more of the following orders (but no other)—

(a) an order that either party to the marriage shall pay to the other such lump sum as may be specified in the order;

(b) an order that a party to the marriage shall pay to such person as may be so specified for the benefit of a child of the family, or to such a child, such lump sum as may be so specified;

(c) an order that a party to the marriage shall transfer to the other party, to any child of the family or to such person as may be so specified for the benefit of such a child, the interest of the first-mentioned party in the dwelling-house, or such part of that interest as may be so specified;

(d) an order that a settlement of the interest of a party to the marriage in the dwelling-house, or such part of that interest as may be so specified, be made to the satisfaction of the court for the benefit of the other party to the marriage and of the children of the family or either or any of them;

(e) an order varying for the benefit of the parties to the marriage and of the children of the family or either or any of them any ante-nuptial or post-nuptial settlement (including such a settlement made by will or codicil) made on the parties to the marriage so far as that settlement relates to an interest in the dwelling-house;

(f) an order extinguishing or reducing the interest of either of the parties to the marriage under any such settlement so far as that interest is an interest in the dwelling house;

(g) an order for the sale of the interest of a party to the marriage in the dwelling-house.

(2) Where, in the circumstances mentioned in subsection (1) above, the court makes an order for the payment of a lump sum by a party to the marriage, the amount of the lump sum shall not exceed, or where more than one such order is made the total amount of the lump sums shall not exceed in aggregate, the following amount, that is to say—

(a) if the interest of that party in the dwelling-house is sold in pursuance of an order made under subsection (1)(g) above, the amount of the proceeds of the sale of that interest after deducting therefrom any costs incurred in the sale thereof;

(b) if the interest of that party is not so sold, the amount which in the opinion of the court represents the value of that interest.

(3) Where the interest of a party to the marriage in the dwelling-house is held jointly or in common with any other person or persons—

(a) the reference in subsection (1)(g) above to the interest of a party to the marriage shall be construed as including a reference to the interest of that other person, or the interest of those other persons, in the dwelling-house, and

(b) the reference in subsection (2)(a) above to the amount of the proceeds of a sale ordered under subsection (1)(g) above shall be construed as a reference to that part of those proceeds which is attributable to the interest of that party to the marriage in the dwelling-house.

21. Application to orders under ss 14 and 17 of certain provisions of Part II of Matrimonial Causes Act 1973.   (1) The following provisions of Part II of the 1973 Act (financial relief for parties to marriage and children of family) shall apply in relation to an order *made* under section 14 or 17 above as they apply in relation to a like order *made* under that Part of that Act, that is to say—

(*a*)   section 23(3) (*provisions as to lump sums*);

[(a)   section 22A(5) (provisions about lump sums in relation to divorce or separation);

(aa)   section 23(4), (5) and (6) (provisions about lump sums in relation to annulment);]

(b)   section 24A(2), (4), (5) and (6) (provisions as to orders for sale);

[(ba)   section 24B(3) to (5) (provisions about pension sharing orders in relation to divorce and nullity);

(bb)   section 24C (duty to stay pension sharing orders);

(bc)   section 24D (apportionment of pension sharing charges);

(bd)   section 25B(3) to (7B) (power, by financial provision order, to attach payments under a pension arrangement, or to require the exercise of a right of commutation under such an arrangement);

(be)   section 25C (extension of lump sum powers in relation to death benefits under a pension arrangement);]

(c)   section 28(1) and (2) (duration of continuing financial provision orders in favour of party to marriage);

(d)   section 29 (duration of continuing financial provision orders in favour of children, and age limit on making certain orders in their favour);

(e)   section 30 (direction for settlement of instrument for securing payments or effecting property adjustment), except paragraph (b);

(f)   section 31 (variation, discharge etc of certain orders for financial relief), *except subsection (2)(e) and subsection (4)*;

(g)   section 32 (payment of certain arrears unenforceable without the leave of the court);

(h)   section 33 (orders for repayment of sums paid under certain orders);

(i)   section 38 (orders for repayment of sums paid after cessation of order by reason of remarriage);

(j)   section 39 (settlements etc made in compliance with a property adjustment order may be avoided on bankruptcy of settlor); and

(k)   section 40 (payments etc under order made in favour of person suffering from mental disorder).

[(l)   section 40A (appeals relating to pension sharing orders which have taken effect)]

[(2) Subsection (1)(bd) and (be) above shall not apply where the court has jurisdiction to entertain an application for an order for financial relief by reason only of the situation in England or Wales of a dwelling-house which was a matrimonial home of the parties.

(3) Section 25D(1) of the 1973 Act (effect of transfers on orders relating to rights under a pension arrangement) shall apply in relation to an order made under section 17 above by virtue of subsection (1)(bd) or (be) above as it applies in relation to an order made under section 23 of that Act by virtue of section 25B or 25C of the 1973 Act.

(4) The Lord Chancellor may by regulations make for the purposes of this Part of this Act provision corresponding to any provision which may be made by him under subsection (2) to (2B) of section 25D of the 1973 Act.

(5) Power to make regulations under this section shall be exercisable by statutory instrument which shall be subject to annulment in pursuance of a resolution of either House of Parliament.]

Note. (a), (aa) in square brackets substituted for (a) in italics and words [words] in italics in (f) repealed by Family Law Act 1996, s 66, Sch 8, Part I, para 32(3), Sch 10, as from a day to be appointed, subject to savings in s 66(2) of, and para 5 of Sch 9 to, the 1996 Act.

Para (1) renumbered as such, first words in italics repealed, paras (ba)–(be) inserted, sub-s (1)(l) inserted and sub-ss (2)–(5) inserted by the Welfare Reform and Pensions Act 1999, ss 22(1), (4), 84(1), 88, Sch 12, paras 2, 4, Sch 13, Pt II, as from 1 December 2000 (SI 2000/1116),

Orders for transfer of tenancies

22. Powers of the court in relation to certain tenancies of dwelling-houses.

Where an application is made by a party to a marriage for an order for financial relief then, if—

  (*a*) *one of the parties to the marriage is entitled, either in his or her own right or jointly with the other party, to occupy a dwelling-house situated in England or Wales by virtue of such a tenancy [or assured agricultural occupancy] as is mentioned in paragraph 1(1) of Schedule 1 to the Matrimonial Homes Act 1983 (certain statutory tenancies), and*

  (*b*) *the dwelling-house has at some time during the marriage been a matrimonial home of the parties to the marriage,*

the court may make in relation to that dwelling-house any order which it could make under Part II of that Schedule if a decree of divorce, a decree of nullity of marriage or a decree of judicial separation in respect of the marriage had been granted in England and Wales; and the provisions of paragraphs 5 and 8(1) in Part III of that Schedule shall apply in relation to any order made under this section as they apply in relation to an order made under Part II of that Schedule.

Note. Words in square brackets inserted by Housing Act 1988, s 140(1), Sch 17, Part I, para 36, as from 15 January 1989.

[**22. Powers of court in relation to certain tenancies of dwelling-houses**—(1) This section applies if—

  (a) an application is made by a party to a marriage for an order for financial relief; and

  (b) one of the parties is entitled, either in his own right or jointly with the other party, to occupy a dwelling-house situated in England or Wales by virtue of a tenancy which is a relevant tenancy within the meaning of Schedule 7 to the Family Law Act 1996 (certain statutory tenancies).

(2) The court may make in relation to that dwelling-house any order which it could make under Part II of that Schedule *if—*

  (*a*) *a divorce order,*

  (*b*) *a separation order, or*

  (*c*) *a decree of nullity of marriage,*

had been made or granted in England and Wales in respect of the marriage.

(3) The provisions of paragraphs 10, 11 and 14(1) in Part III of that Schedule apply in relation to any order under this section as they apply to any order under Part II of that Schedule.]

Note. Section 22 in square brackets substituted for s 22 in italics by Family Law Act 1996, s 66(1), Sch 8, Part III, para 52, as from 1 October 1997. Until such time as the Family Law Act 1996, Part II is brought into force, the words in italics are substituted by the words "if a decree of divorce, a decree of nullity of marriage or a decree of judicial separation has been granted" by SI 1997/1892, art 3(2).

Avoidance of transactions intended to prevent or reduce financial relief

23. Avoidance of transactions intended to defeat applications for financial relief—(1) For the purposes of this section 'financial relief' means relief under

section 14 or 17 above and any reference to defeating a claim by a party to a marriage for financial relief is a reference to preventing financial relief from being granted or reducing the amount of relief which might be granted, or frustrating or impeding the enforcement of any order which might be or has been made under either of those provisions at the instance of that party.

(2) Where leave is granted under section 13 above for the making by a party to a marriage of an application for an order for financial relief under section 17 above, the court may, on an application by that party—

   (a) if it is satisfied that the other party to the marriage is, with the intention of defeating the claim for financial relief, about to make any disposition or to transfer out of the jurisdiction or otherwise deal with any property, make such order as it thinks fit for restraining the other party from so doing or otherwise for protecting the claim;

   (b) if it is satisfied that the other party has, with that intention, made a reviewable disposition and that if the disposition were set aside financial relief or different financial relief would be granted to the applicant, make an order setting aside the disposition.

(3) Where an order for financial relief under section 14 or 17 above has been made by the court at the instance of a party to a marriage, then, on an application made by that party, the court may, if it is satisfied that the other party to the marriage has, with the intention of defeating the claim for financial relief, made a reviewable disposition, make an order setting aside the disposition.

(4) Where the court has jurisdiction to entertain the application for an order for financial relief by reason only of paragraph (c) of section 15(1) above, it shall not make any order under subsection (2) or (3) above in respect of any property other than the dwelling-house concerned.

(5) Where the court makes an order under subsection (2)(b) or (3) above setting aside a disposition it shall give such consequential directions as it thinks fit for giving effect to the order (including directions requiring the making of any payments or the disposal of any property).

(6) Any disposition made by the other party to the marriage (whether before or after the commencement of the application) is a reviewable disposition for the purposes of subsection (2)(b) and (3) above unless it was made for valuable consideration (other than marriage) to a person who, at the time of the disposition, acted in relation to it in good faith and without notice of any intention on the part of the other party to defeat the applicant's claim for financial relief.

(7) Where an application is made under subsection (2) or (3) above with respect to a disposition which took place less than three years before the date of the application or with respect to a disposition or other dealing with property which is about to take place and the court is satisfied—

   (a) in a case falling within subsection (2)(a) or (b) above, that the disposition or other dealing would (apart from this section) have the consequence, or

   (b) in a case falling within subsection (3) above, that the disposition has had the consequence,

of defeating a claim by the applicant for financial relief, it shall be presumed, unless the contrary is shown, that the person who disposed of or is about to dispose of or deal with the property did so or, as the case may be, is about to do so, with the intention of defeating the applicant's claim for financial relief.

(8) In this section 'disposition' does not include any provision contained in a will or codicil but, with that exception, includes any conveyance, assurance or gift of property of any description, whether made by an instrument or otherwise.

(9) The preceding provisions of this section are without prejudice to any power of the High Court to grant injunctions under section 37 of the Supreme Court Act 1981.

24. Prevention of transactions intended to defeat prospective applications for financial relief—(1) Where, on an application by a party to a marriage, it appears to the court—

    (a) that the marriage has been dissolved or annulled, or that the parties to the marriage have been legally separated, by means of judicial or other proceedings in an overseas country; and

    (b) that the applicant intends to apply for leave to make an application for an order for financial relief under section 17 above as soon as he or she has been habitually resident in England and Wales for a period of one year; and

    (c) that the other party to the marriage is, with the intention of defeating a claim for financial relief, about to make any disposition or to transfer out of the jurisdiction or otherwise deal with any property,

the court may make such order as it thinks fit for restraining the other party from taking such action as is mentioned in paragraph (c) above.

    (2) For the purposes of an application under subsection (1) above—

    (a) the reference to defeating a claim for financial relief shall be construed in accordance with subsection (1) of section 23 above (omitting the reference to any order which has been made); and

    (b) subsections (7) and (8) of section 23 above shall apply as they apply for the purposes of an application under that section.

    (3) The preceding provisions of this section are without prejudice to any power of the High Court to grant injunctions under section 37 of the Supreme Court Act 1981.

25, 26 (*Section 25 amends Inheritance (Provision for Family and Dependants) Act 1975, s 25(1), p 2575, and inserts s 15A, p 2571, in that Act; s 26 substitutes Maintenance Order (Reciprocal Enforcement) Act 1972, s 28A(1), (4), p 2432, and repeals s 28(5) of that Act and is repealed by Maintenance Orders (Reciprocal Enforcement) Act 1992, s 2(2), Sch 3, as from 5 April 1993.*)

Interpretation

27. Interpretation of Part III. In this Part of this Act—

    'the 1973 Act' means the Matrimonial Causes Act 1973:

    'child of the family' has the same meaning as in section 52(1) of the 1973 Act;

    'the court' means the High Court or, where a county court has jurisdiction by virtue of Part V of this Act, a county court;

    'dwelling-house' includes any building or part thereof which is occupied as a dwelling, and any yard, garden, garage or outhouse belonging to the dwelling-house and occupied therewith;

    'order for financial relief' has the meaning given by section 12(4) above;

    'overseas country' means a country or territory outside the British Islands;

    'possession' includes receipt of, or the right to receive, rents and profits;

    'property adjustment order' means such an order as is specified in section 24(1)(a), (b), (c) or (d) of the 1973 Act;

    ['property adjustment order' and 'secured periodical payments order' mean any order which would be a property adjustment order or, as the case may be, secured periodical payments order within the meaning of Part II of the 1973 Act;]

    'rent' does not include mortgage interest;

    'secured periodical payments order' means such an order as is specified in section 23(1)(b) or (e) of the 1973 Act.

Note. Definition 'property adjustment order' and 'secured periodical payments order' in square brackets substituted for definition 'property adjustment order' in italics and definition 'secured periodical payments order' repealed by Family Law Act 1996, s 66, Sch 8, Part I, para 32(4), Sch 10, as from a day to be appointed, subject to savings in s 66(2) of, and para 5 of Sch 9 to, the 1996 Act.

PART IV

FINANCIAL PROVISION IN SCOTLAND AFTER OVERSEAS DIVORCE ETC

28–31.   (*Apply to Scotland only*).

PART V

FAMILY BUSINESS: DISTRIBUTION AND TRANSFER

Preliminary

32. What is family business.   In this Part of this Act—
'family business' means business of any description which in the High Court is
for the time being assigned to the Family Division and to no other Division by
or under section 61 of (and Schedule 1 to) the Supreme Court Act 1981;
'family proceedings' means proceedings which are family business;
'*matrimonial cause' means an action for divorce, nullity of marriage, judicial separation
or jactitation of marriage [or judicial separation]*;
['matrimonial cause' means an action for nullity of marriage or any marital
proceedings under the Family Law Act 1996;]
and 'the 1973 Act' means the Matrimonial Causes Act 1973.

Note.   Definition 'matrimonial cause' substituted by Family Law Act 1996, s 66(1), Sch 8, Part
I, para 32(5), as from a day to be appointed, subject to savings in s 66(2) of, and para 5 of Sch
9 to, the 1996 Act. Words 'or judicial separation' in square brackets substituted for words
'judicial separation or jactitation of marriage' by Family Law Act 1986, s 68(1), Sch 1, para 27,
as from 4 April 1988.

Jurisdiction of county courts in matrimonial causes and matters

33. Jurisdiction of county courts in matrimonial causes—(1) The Lord
Chancellor may by order designate any county court as a divorce county court and
any court so designated shall have jurisdiction to hear and determine any
matrimonial cause, except that it shall have jurisdiction to try such a cause only if it
is also designated in the order as a court of trial.
   In this Part of this Act 'divorce county court' means a county court so designated.
   (2) The jurisdiction conferred by this section on a divorce county court shall be
exercisable throughout England and Wales, but rules of court may provide for a
matrimonial cause pending in one such court to be heard and determined in
another or partly in that and partly in another.
   (3) Every matrimonial cause shall be commenced in a divorce county court and
shall be heard and determined in that or another such court unless or except to the
extent it is transferred to the High Court under section 39 below or section 41 of the
County Courts Act 1984 (transfer to High Court by order of the High Court).
   (4) The Lord Chancellor may by order designate a divorce county court as a court
for the exercise of jurisdiction in matrimonial matters arising under Part III of this Act.
   (5) The power to make an order under subsection (1) or (4) above shall be
exercisable by statutory instrument.

**34. Jurisdiction of divorce county courts as respects financial relief and
protection of children**—(1) Subject to subsections (2) and (3) below, a divorce
county court shall have the following jurisdiction, namely—
   (a) jurisdiction to exercise any power exercisable under Part II or Part III of the
       1973 Act in connection with any petition, decree or order pending in or
       made by such a court and to exercise any power under section 27 or 35 of
       that Act;
   (b) if designated by an order under section 33(4) above, jurisdiction to exercise
       any power under Part III of this Act.

(2) Any proceedings for the exercise of a power which a divorce county court has jurisdiction to exercise by virtue of subsection (1)(a) or (b) above shall be commenced in such divorce county court as may be prescribed by rules of court.

(3) A divorce county court shall not by virtue of subsection (1)(a) above have jurisdiction to exercise any power under section 32, 33, 36 or 38 of the 1973 Act; nothing in this section shall prejudice the exercise by a county court of any jurisdiction conferred on county courts by any of those sections.

(4) Nothing in this section shall affect the jurisdiction of a magistrates' court under section 35 of the 1973 Act.

35. Consideration of agreements or arrangements.   Any provision to be made by rules of court for the purposes of section 7 of the 1973 Act with respect to any power exercisable by the court on an application made before the presentation of a petition shall confer jurisdiction to exercise the power on divorce county courts.

36. Assignment of Circuit judges to matrimonial proceedings.   The jurisdiction conferred by the preceding provisions of this Part of this Act on divorce county courts, so far as it is exercisable by judges of such courts, shall be exercised by such Circuit judges as the Lord Chancellor may direct.

Distribution and transfer of family business and proceedings

37. Directions as to distribution and transfer of family business and proceedings.   The President of the Family Division may, with the concurrence of the Lord Chancellor, give directions with respect to the distribution and transfer between the High Court and county courts of family business and family proceedings

38. Transfer of family proceedings from High Court to county court—(1) At any stage in any family proceedings in the High Court the High Court may, if the proceedings are transferable under this section, either of its own motion or on the application of any party to the proceedings, order the transfer of the whole or any part of the proceedings to a county court.

(2) The following family proceedings are transferable to a county court under this section, namely—

(a) all family proceedings commenced in the High Court which are within the jurisdiction of a county court or divorce county court;

(b) wardship proceedings, except applications for an order that a minor be made, or cease to be, a ward of court [or any other proceedings which relate to the exercise of the inherent jurisdiction of the High Court with respect to minors]; and

(c) all family proceedings transferred from a county court to the High Court under section 39 below or section 41 of the County Courts Act 1984 (transfer to High Court by order of the High Court) [and

(d) all matrimonial causes and matters transferred from a county court otherwise than as mentioned in paragraph (c) above].

(3) Proceedings transferred under this section shall be transferred to such county court or, in the case of a matrimonial cause or matter within the jurisdiction of a divorce county court only, such divorce county court as the High Court directs.

(4) The transfer shall not affect any right of appeal from the order directing the transfer, or the right to enforce in the High Court any judgment signed, or order made, in that Court before the transfer.

(5) Where proceedings are transferred to a county court under this section, the county court—

(a) if it has no jurisdiction apart from this paragraph, shall have jurisdiction to hear and determine those proceedings;

(b) shall have jurisdiction to award any relief which could have been awarded by the High Court.

Note. Words in square brackets in sub-s (2)(b) inserted by Children Act 1989, s 108(5), Sch 13, para 51, as from 14 October 1991. Sub-s (2)(d) and word 'and' preceding it added by Matrimonial Proceedings (Transfer) Act 1988, s 1(1), as from 19 May 1988.

39. Transfer of family proceedings to High Court from county court—(1) At any stage in any family proceedings in a county court, the county court may, if the proceedings are transferable under this section, either of its own motion or on the application of any party to the proceedings, order the transfer of the whole or any part of the proceedings to the High Court.

(2) The following family proceedings are transferable to the High Court under this section, namely—

(a) all family proceedings commenced in a county court or divorce county court; and

(b) all family proceedings transferred from the High Court to a county court or divorce county court under section 38 above.

Rules of court and fees

40. Family proceedings rules—*(1) Subject to subsection (2) below, the power to make rules of court for the purposes of family proceedings in the High Court or county courts shall be exercisable by the Lord Chancellor together with any four or more of the following persons, namely—*

(a) the President of the Family Division,

(b) one puisne judge attached to that Division,

(c) one registrar of the principal registry of that Division,

(d) two Circuit Judges,

(e) one registrar appointed under the County Courts Act 1984,

(f) two practising barristers, and

(g) two practising solicitors, of whom one shall be a member of the Council of the Law Society and the other a member of the Law Society and also of a local law society.

[(c) one district judge of the principal registry of that Division,

(d) two Circuit Judges,

(e) one district judge appointed under the County Courts Act 1984,

(f) two persons who have a Supreme Court qualification (within the meaning of section 71 of the Courts and Legal Services Act 1990), and

(g) two persons who have been granted by an authorised body, under Part II of that Act, the right to conduct litigation in relation to all proceedings in the Supreme Court.]

Note. Sub-s (1)(c)–(g) in square brackets substituted for sub-s (1)(c)–(g) in italics by Courts and Legal Services Act 1990, s 125(3), Sch 18, para 50, as from 1 January 1991.

(2) Subsection (1) above is without prejudice to the powers of the following authorities to make rules in respect of the matters referred to below and rules in respect of those matters shall continue to be made by those authorities and shall not be made by the authority constituted by subsection (1) above.

The rules and rule-making authorities are—

(a) adoption rules made by the Lord Chancellor under section 9(3) of the Adoption Act 1958, section 12(1) of the Adoption Act 1968 or section 66(1) of the Adoption Act 1976 [or section 141(1) of the Adoption and Children Act 2002];

(b) probate rules made by the President of the Family Division with the concurrence of the Lord Chancellor under section 127 of the Supreme Court Act 1981.

Note. Sub-s (2)(a) word 'or' in italics repealed, words in square brackets inserted by the Adoption and Children Act 2002 as from a date to be appointed.

(3) The persons to act in pursuance of subsection (1) above with the Lord Chancellor, other than the President of the Family Division, shall be appointed by the Lord Chancellor for such time as he may think fit.

[(3A) Rules made under this section may make different provision for different cases or different areas, including different provision—

    (a) for a specific court, or
    (b) for specific proceedings, or a specific jurisdiction,
specified in the rules.]
    (4) Rules made under this section may, in relation to county court rules, do anything which, as special rules, they are authorised by section 84 of the Supreme Court Act 1981 to do in relation to Supreme Court Rules and may—
    (a) modify or exclude the application of any provision of the County Courts Act 1984; and
    (b) provide for the enforcement in the High Court of orders made in a divorce county court.

Note. Sub-s (3A) inserted as from 14 March 1997, and in sub-s (4) words in italics repealed by Civil Procedure Act 1997, s 10, Sch 2, para 3 [as from 26 April 1999 (SI 1999/1009)].

    (5) Rules of court under this section shall be made by statutory instrument subject to annulment in pursuance of a resolution of either House of Parliament; and the Statutory Instruments Act 1946 shall apply to a statutory instrument containing such rules as if the rules had been made by a Minister of the Crown.

Note. Repealed by the Courts Act 2003, s 109 (1), (3), Sch 8, para 278(a), Sch 10, as from a date to be appointed.

41. Fees in family proceedings.   *The fees to be taken in any family proceedings in the High Court or any county court shall be such as the Lord Chancellor with the concurrence of the Treasury may prescribe from time to time by order made by statutory instrument.*

Note. Repealed by the Courts Act 2003, s 109(1), (3), Sch 8, para 278(b), Sch 10, as from a date to be appointed.

County court proceedings in principal registry

42. County court proceedings in principal registry of Family Division—(1) Sections 33 to 35 above shall not prevent the commencement of any proceedings in the principal registry except where rules of court under section 34(2) above otherwise provide; and the following provisions of this section shall have effect for the purposes of enabling proceedings to be dealt with in that registry as in a divorce county court.

    (2) The jurisdiction in matrimonial causes or matters conferred by sections 33, 34 and 35 above on divorce county courts shall be exercised in the principal registry—
    (a) so far as it is exercisable by judges of such courts, at such sittings and in such places as the Lord Chancellor may direct; and
    (b) so far as it is exercisable by registrars of such courts, by such registrars or by registrars and other officers of the principal registry according as rules of court may provide;
and rules of court may make provision for treating, for any purposes specified in the rules, matrimonial causes and matters pending in the registry with respect to which that jurisdiction is exercisable as pending in a divorce county court and for the application of section 74(3) of the Solicitors Act 1974 (costs) with respect to proceedings so treated.

    (3) Where, by virtue of rules under subsection (2) above, a matrimonial cause is pending in the registry as in a divorce county court, any ancillary or related proceedings which could be taken in a divorce county court and which are not of a description excluded by the rules from the operation of this subsection may be taken and dealt with in the registry as in a divorce county court.

    (4) The principal registry shall be treated as a divorce county court—
    (a) for the purposes of any provision to be made by rules of court under section 33(2) above;
    (b) for the purpose of any provision to be made under section 34(2) above prescribing the county court in which any proceedings are to be commenced; and

(c) for the purpose of any transfer of family proceedings under section 38 or 39 above between the High Court and a divorce county court.

[(4A) Where a district judge of the principal registry is exercising jurisdiction in any matrimonial cause or matter which could be exercised by a district judge of a county court, he shall have the same powers in relation to those proceedings as if he were a district judge of a county court and the proceedings were in a county court.]

Note. Sub-s (4A) inserted by Courts and Legal Services Act 1990, s 74(7), as from 1 July 1991.

(5) Rules of court shall make provision for securing, with respect to family proceedings dealt with under this section, that, as nearly as may be, the same consequences shall follow—

(a) as regards service of process, as if proceedings commenced in the principal registry had been commenced in a divorce county court; and

(b) as regards enforcement of orders, as if orders made in that registry in the exercise of the family jurisdiction conferred by sections 33, 34 and 35 above on divorce county courts were orders made by such a court.

(6) In this section 'the principal registry' means the principal registry of the Family Division of the High Court and, for the purposes of subsection (3) above, proceedings are 'ancillary' to a matrimonial cause if they are connected with the cause and are 'related' to a matrimonial cause if they are for protecting or otherwise relate to any rights, or the exercise of any rights, of the parties to the marriage as husband and wife or any children of the family.

43, 44. (*Section 43 amends Married Women's Property Act 1882, s 17, p 2031; s 44 inserts sub-s (1)(ee) in Magistrates' Courts Act 1980, s 65, p 2725.*)

PART VI

MISCELLANEOUS AND GENERAL

45. (*Amends Maintenance Orders (Reciprocal Enforcement) Act 1972, s 29A, p 2438, as from a day to be appointed; repealed by Children (Northern Ireland) Order 1995, SI 1995 No 755, art 185(2), Sch 10, as from 4 November 1996.*)

46. Amendments, transitional provisions and repeals—(1) The enactments specified in Schedule 1 to this Act shall have effect subject to the amendments specified in that Schedule, being amendments consequential on the provisions of this Act or minor amendments relating to the enforcement of maintenance orders, the area of jurisdiction of magistrates' courts for purposes of altering maintenance agreements and the variation by magistrates' courts of certain existing maintenance, affiliation and other orders.

(2) The transitional provisions contained in Schedule 2 to this Act shall have effect.

(3) The enactments specified in Schedule 3 to this Act are hereby repealed to the extent specified in the third column of that Schedule.

47. Commencement—(1) The provisions of this Act other than this section and section 48 below shall come into force as follows—

(a) With the exception of section 10, Parts I and II and paragraphs 1 and 2 of Schedule 2 shall come into force at the expiry of the period of three months beginning with the day on which this Act is passed and that section shall come into force on such day as the Lord Chancellor appoints;

(b) Part III shall come into force on such day as the Lord Chancellor appoints;

(c) Schedule 1, except paragraphs 1(b), 6, 7 and 28 shall come into force on such day or days as the Lord Chancellor appoints;

(d) Part IV and paragraphs 1(b), 6, 7 and 28 of Schedule 1 shall come into force on such day as the Lord Advocate appoints; and

(e) Part V, section 45 above and paragraph 3 of Schedule 2 and the repeals specified in Schedule 3 shall come into force on such day or days as the Lord Chancellor appoints.

(2) The power to appoint days for the coming into force of provisions of this Act shall be exercised by order made by statutory instrument.

Commencement. Section 10 and Part III (ss 12–27) were brought into force on 16 September 1985 (SI 1985 No 1316). Sections 32–39, 42 and 46(3), for the purpose of certain repeals in Sch 3 were brought into force on 28 April 1986 (SI 1986 No 635). Section 46(3) for the purpose of certain repeals in Sch 3 was brought into force on 12 October 1984 (SI 1984 No 1589). Sections 40, 41 and 46(3) for the purpose of remaining repeals in Sch 3 were brought into force on 14 October 1991 (SI 1991 No 1211). Schedule 2, para 3 is not yet in force.

48. Short title and extent—(1) This Act may be cited as the Matrimonial and Family Proceedings Act 1984.

(2) Parts I to III and V and Schedules 2 and 3 extend to England and Wales only, Part IV extends to Scotland only *and section 45 above extends to Northern Ireland only.*

Note. Words in italics repealed by Family Law (Northern Ireland) Order 1995, SI 1995 No 755, art 185(2), Sch 10, as from 4 November 1996.

(3) Where any enactment amended by Schedule 1 extends to any part of the United Kingdom, the amendment extends to that part.

SCHEDULES

SCHEDULE 1   Section 46(1)

MINOR AND CONSEQUENTIAL AMENDMENTS

(*The amendments made by this Schedule, insofar as they amend legislation printed in this work, have been incorporated.*)

SCHEDULE 2   Section 46(2)

TRANSITIONAL PROVISIONS

Time restrictions on petitions for divorce

1. (1) Where at the coming into force of section 1 of this Act—
   (a) leave has been granted under section 3 of the Matrimonial Causes Act 1973 for the presentation of a petition for divorce or proceedings on an application for leave under that section are pending, and
   (b) the period of one year from the date of the marriage has not expired,
nothing in section 1 of this Act shall prohibit the presentation of a petition for divorce before the expiration of that period; and in relation to such a case sections 1(4) and 3 of that Act of 1973 as in force immediately before the coming into force of section 1 of this Act shall continue to apply.
   (2) Where at the coming into force of section 1 of this Act—
   (a) proceedings on an application for leave under section 3 of the Matrimonial Causes Act 1973 are pending, and
   (b) the period of one year from the date of the marriage has expired,
the proceedings shall abate but without prejudice to the powers of the court as to costs.

Time restrictions on petitions for nullity

2. An application for leave under section 13(4) of the Matrimonial Causes Act 1973 to institute proceedings after the expiration of the period of three years from the date of the marriage may be made where that period expired before as well as where it expires after the coming into force of section 2 of this Act.

Scope of 'matrimonial cause' for Part V purposes

3. For the purposes of Part V of this Act 'matrimonial cause' shall, until the expiration of one year from the coming into force of section 1 of this Act, include an application under section 3 of the Matrimonial Causes Act 1973.

SCHEDULE 3   Section 46(3)

REPEALS

Chapter	Short Title	Extent of Repeal
1967 c 56.	Matrimonial Causes Act 1967.	The whole Act.
1971 c 3.	Guardianship of Minors Act 1971.	Section 16(1).
1971 c 23.	Courts Acts 1971.	Section 45.
1973 c 18.	Matrimonial Causes Act 1973.	Section 43(9) Section 44(6) Section 45(3). Sections 50 and 51. In Schedule 2, paragraphs 6 and 12.
1973 c 45.	Domicile and Matrimonial Proceedings Act 1973.	Section 6(4)(a).
1975 c 72.	Children Act 1975.	Section 101(1).
1976 c 36.	Adoption Act 1976.	Section 63(1).
1983 c 19.	Matrimonial Homes Act 1983.	In Schedule 1, paragraph 8(3) and (4), and in paragraph 10(1), the definitions of 'divorce county court' and 'divorce registry'.
1984 c 28.	County Courts Act 1984.	In section 147(1), the definition of 'matrimonial cause'.

FOREIGN LIMITATION PERIODS ACT 1984

(1984 c 16)

ARRANGEMENT OF SECTIONS

An Act to provide for any law relating to the limitation of actions to be treated, for the purposes of cases in which effect is given to foreign law or to determinations by foreign courts, as a matter of substance rather than as a matter of procedure.
[24 May 1984]

1. Application of foreign limitation law—(1) Subject to the following provisions of this Act, where in any action or proceedings in a court in England and Wales the law of any other country falls (in accordance with rules of private international law applicable by any such court) to be taken into account in the determination of any matter—

    (a) the law of that other country relating to limitation shall apply in respect of that matter for the purposes of the action or proceedings; and

    (b) except where that matter falls within subsection (2) below, the law of England and Wales relating to limitation shall not so apply.

(2) A matter falls within this subsection if it is a matter in the determination of which both the law of England and Wales and the law of some other country fall to be taken into account.

(3) The law of England and Wales shall determine for the purposes of any law applicable by virtue of subsection (1)(a) above whether, and the time at which, proceedings have been commenced in respect of any matter; and, accordingly, section 35 of the Limitation Act 1980 (new claims in pending proceedings) shall apply in relation to time limits applicable by virtue of subsection (1)(a) above as it applies in relation to time limits under that Act.

(4) A court in England and Wales, in exercising in pursuance of subsection (1)(a) above any discretion conferred by the law of any other country, shall so far as practicable exercise that discretion in the manner in which it is exercised in comparable cases by the courts of that other country.

(5) In this section 'law', in relation to any country, shall not include rules of private international law applicable by the courts of that country or, in the case of England and Wales, this Act.

2. Exceptions to s 1—(1) In any case in which the application of section 1 above would to any extent conflict (whether under subsection (2) below or otherwise) with public policy, that section shall not apply to the extent that its application would so conflict.

(2) The application of section 1 above in relation to any action or proceedings shall conflict with public policy to the extent that its application would cause undue hardship to a person who is, or might be made, a party to the action or proceedings.

(3) Where, under a law applicable by virtue of section 1(1)(a) above for the purposes of any action or proceedings, a limitation period is or may be extended or interrupted in respect of the absence of a party to the action or proceedings from any specified jurisdiction or country, so much of that law as provides for the extension or interruption shall be disregarded for those purposes.

(4) (*Amends Limitation (Enemies and War Prisoners) Act 1945, s 2(1)* (*not printed in this work.*)

3. Foreign judgments on limitation points.   Where a court in any country outside England and Wales has determined any matter wholly or partly by reference to the law of that or any other country (including England and Wales) relating to limitation, then, for the purposes of the law relating to the effect to be given in England and Wales to that determination, that court shall, to the extent that it has so determined the matter, be deemed to have determined it on its merits.

4. Meaning of law relating to limitation—(1) Subject to subsection (3) below, references in this Act to the law of any country (including England and Wales) relating to limitation shall, in relation to any matter, be construed as references to so much of the relevant law of that country as (in any manner) makes provision with respect to a limitation period applicable to the bringing of proceedings in respect of that matter in the courts of that country and shall include—

(a) references to so much of that law as relates to, and to the effect of, the application, extension, reduction or interruption of that period; and

(b) a reference, where under that law there is no limitation period which is so applicable, to the rule that such proceedings may be brought within an indefinite period.

(2) In subsection (1) above 'relevant law', in relation to any country, means the procedural and substantive law applicable, apart from any rules of private international law, by the courts of that country.

(3) References in this Act to the law of England and Wales relating to limitation shall not include the rules by virtue of which a court may, in the exercise of any discretion, refuse equitable relief on the grounds of acquiescence or otherwise; but, in applying those rules to a case in relation to which the law of any country outside England and Wales is applicable by virtue of section 1(1)(a) above (not being a law that provides for a limitation period that has expired), a court in England and Wales shall have regard, in particular, to the provisions of the law that is so applicable.

5. Application of Act to arbitrations.   *The references to any other limitation enactment in section 34 of the Limitation Act 1980 (application of limitation enactments to arbitration) include references to sections 1, 2 and 4 of this Act; and, accordingly, in subsection (5) of the said section 34, the reference to the time prescribed by a limitation enactment has effect for the purposes of any case to which section 1 above applies as a reference to the limitation period (if any) applicable by virtue of section 1 above.*

Note. This section repealed by Arbitration Act 1996, s 107(2), Sch 4, as from 31 January 1997.

6. Application to Crown—(1) This Act applies in relation to any action or proceedings by or against the Crown as it applies in relation to actions and proceedings to which the Crown is not a party.

(2) For the purposes of this section references to an action or proceedings by or against the Crown include references to—

(a) any action or proceedings by or against Her Majesty in right of the Duchy of Lancaster;

(b) any action or proceedings by or against any Government department or any officer of the Crown as such or any person acting on behalf of the Crown;

(c) any action or proceedings by or against the Duke of Cornwall.

7. Short title, commencement, transitional provision and extent—(1) This Act may be cited as the Foreign Limitation Periods Act 1984.

(2) This Act shall come into force on such day as the Lord Chancellor may by order made by statutory instrument appoint.

(3) Nothing in this Act shall—

(a) affect any action, proceedings or arbitration commenced in England and Wales before the day appointed under subsection (2) above; or

(b) apply in relation to any matter if the limitation period which, apart from this Act, would have been applied in respect of that matter in England and Wales expired before that day.

(4) This Act extends to England and Wales only.

Commencement. This Act came into force on 1 October 1985 (SI 1985 No 1276).

COUNTY COURTS ACT 1984

(1984 c 28)

An Act to consolidate certain enactments relating to County Courts. [26 June 1984]

* * * * *

PART I

CONSTITUTION AND ADMINISTRATION

Judges

5. Judges of county courts—(1) Every Circuit judge shall, by virtue of his office, be capable of sitting as a judge for any county court district in England and Wales, and the Lord Chancellor shall assign one or more Circuit judges to each district and may from time to time vary the assignment of Circuit judges among the districts.

(2) Subject to any directions given by or on behalf of the Lord Chancellor, in any case where more than one Circuit judge is assigned to a district under subsection (1), any function conferred by or under this Act on the judge for a district may be exercised by any of the Circuit judges for the time being assigned to that district.

(3) The following, that is—

every judge of the Court of Appeal,

every judge of the High Court,

every Recorder,

shall, by virtue of his office, be capable of sitting as a judge for any county court district in England and Wales and, if he consents to do so, shall sit as such a judge at such times and on such occasions as the Lord Chancellor considers desirable.

(4) Notwithstanding that he is not for the time being assigned to a particular district, a Circuit judge—

(a) shall sit as a judge of that district at such times and on such occasions as the Lord Chancellor may direct; and

(b) may sit as a judge of that district in any case where it appears to him that the judge of that district is not, or none of the judges of that district is, available to deal with the case.

Note. This section contains provisions formerly in Courts Act 1971, s 20(1)–(4).

District judge. By virtue of the Courts and Legal Services Act 1990, s 74 post, both county court registrars and High Court district registrars are to become offices of district judge, with corresponding titles for assistant, and deputy registrars. By virtue of sub-s (3) of that section, any reference in any enactment to any of those offices is to be construed accordingly.

* * * * *

Miscellaneous provisions as to officers

* * * * *

14. Penalty for assaulting officers—(1) If any person assaults an officer of a court while in the execution of his duty, he shall be liable—

(a) on summary conviction, to imprisonment for a term not exceeding 3 months or to a fine of an amount not exceeding level 5 on the standard scale, or both; or

(b) on an order made by the judge in that behalf, to be committed for a specified period not exceeding *3 months* [51 weeks] to *any* prison *to which the judge has power to commit* or to such a fine as aforesaid, or to be so committed and to such a fine, and a bailiff of the court may take the offender into custody, with or without warrant, and bring him before the judge.

(2) The judge may at any time revoke an order committing a person to prison under this section and, if he is already in custody, order his discharge.

Note. This section contains provisions formerly in County Courts Act 1959, s 30, as amended by Contempt of Court Act 1981, s 14, Sch 2, Part III, para 2. Words in italics in sub-s (1)(b) repealed by Statute Law (Repeals) Act 1986, Sch 1, Part I. In sub-s (1)(a) words in square brackets substituted for words in italics by Criminal Justice Act 2003, s 280(2), (3), Sch 26, para 33(1), (2), as from a day to be appointed.

[(3) A district judge, assistant district judge or deputy district judge shall have the same powers under this section as a judge.]

Note. Sub-s (3) added by Courts and Legal Services Act 1990, s 74(4), as from 1 July 1991.

* * * * *

25. Jurisdiction under Inheritance (Provision for Family and Dependants) Act 1975. A county court shall have jurisdiction to hear and determine any application for an order under section 2 of the Inheritance (Provision for Family and Dependants) Act 1975 (including any application for permission to apply for such an order and any application made, in the proceedings on an application for such an order, for an order under any other provision of that Act) *where it is shown to the satisfaction of the court that the value at the date of the death of the deceased of all property included in his net estate for the purposes of that Act by virtue of paragraph (a) of the definition of 'net estate' in section 25(1) of that Act does not exceed the county court limit.*

Note. This section contains provisions formerly in County Courts Act 1959, s 52A, as inserted by Administration of Justice Act 1982, s 37, Sch 3, Part II, para 5(1). See Family Law Reform Act 1987, s 16(3). Words in italics repealed by High Court and County Courts Jurisdiction Order 1991, SI 1991 No 724, art 2(8), Schedule, as from 1 July 1991.

* * * * *

32. Amendments relating to jurisdiction of county courts and district probate registrars in probate proceedings
Note. See Administration of Justice Act 1985, s 51. As to s 33, see ibid, Sch 7, para 7, Sch 8, Part III.

PART II

JURISDICTION AND TRANSFER OF PROCEEDINGS

Exercise of jurisdiction and ancillary jurisdiction

37. Persons who may exercise jurisdiction of court—(1) Any jurisdiction and powers conferred by this or any other Act—
  (a) on a county court; or
  (b) on the judge of a county court,
may be exercised by any judge of the court.

(2) Subsection (1) applies to jurisdiction and powers conferred on all county courts or judges of county courts or on any particular county court or the judge of any particular county court.

Note. This section contains provisions formerly in County Courts Act 1959, s 73, as substituted by Supreme Court Act 1981, s 149(1), Sch 3, para 6.

38. General ancillary jurisdiction—(*1*) *Every county court, as regards any cause of action for the time being within its jurisdiction,*—
  (*a*) *shall grant such relief, redress or remedy or combination of remedies, either absolute or conditional; and*
  (*b*) *shall give such and the like effect to every ground of defence or counterclaim equitable or legal,*
as ought to be granted or given in the like case by the High Court and in as full and ample a manner.

(2) For the purposes of this section it shall be assumed (notwithstanding any enactment to the contrary) that any proceedings which can be commenced in a county court could be commenced in the High Court.

Note. This section contains provisions formerly in County Courts Act 1959, s 74, as amended by Administration of Justice Act 1969, ss 6, 35(2), Sch 2.

[**38. Remedies available in county courts**—(1) Subject to what follows, in any proceedings in a county court the court may make any order which could be made by the High Court if the proceedings were in the High Court.

(2) Any order made by a county court may be—

(a) absolute or conditional;

(b) final or interlocutory.

(3) A county court shall not have power—

(a) to order mandamus, certiorari or prohibition; or

(b) to make any order of a prescribed kind.

(4) Regulations under subsection (3)—

(a) may provide for any of their provisions not to apply in such circumstances or descriptions of case as may be specified in the regulations;

(b) may provide for the transfer of the proceedings to the High Court for the purpose of enabling an order of a kind prescribed under subsection (3) to be made;

(c) may make such provision with respect to matters of procedure as the Lord Chancellor considers expedient; and

(d) may make provision amending or repealing any provision made by or under any enactment, so far as may be necessary or expedient in consequence of the regulations.

(5) In this section 'prescribed' means prescribed by regulations made by the Lord Chancellor under this section.

(6) The power to make regulations under this section shall be exercised by statutory instrument.

(7) No such statutory instrument shall be made unless a draft of the instrument has been approved by both Houses of Parliament.]

Note. Section 38 in square brackets substituted for ss 38, 39 in italics by Courts and Legal Services Act 1990, s 3, as from 1 July 1991.

39. Ancillary powers of judge. *A judge shall have jurisdiction in any pending proceedings to make any order or exercise any authority or jurisdiction which, if it related to an action or proceeding pending in the High Court, might be made or exercised by a judge of the High Court in chambers.*

Note. This section contains provisions formerly in County Courts Act 1959, s 75, as substituted by Supreme Court Act 1981, s 149(1), Sch 3, para 7. See the note to s 38.

Transfer of proceedings

40. Transfer of proceedings to county court—(1) *At any stage in any proceedings to which this section applies, the High Court, may, in accordance with rules of the Supreme Court, either of its own motion or on the application of any party to the proceedings, order the transfer of the whole or any part of the proceedings to a county court if—*

(a) *the parties consent to the transfer; or*

(b) *the High Court is satisfied—*

(i) *that, after allowance has been made for any payment, set-off or other amount admitted to be due, the amount remaining in dispute in respect of the claim is within the monetary limit of the jurisdiction of the county court; or*

(ii) *that the amount recoverable in respect of the claim is likely to be within the monetary limit of the jurisdiction of the county court; or* (*iii*)   *in the case of proceedings not involving an unliquidated claim, that the subject matter of the proceedings is or is likely to be within the limits of the jurisdiction of the county court; or*

(*c*)   *where only a counterclaim remains in dispute, the High Court considers that the amount recoverable in respect of the counterclaim is likely to be within the monetary limit of the jurisdiction of the county court; or*

(*d*)   *the High Court considers that the proceedings are not likely to raise any important question of law or fact and are suitable for determination by a county court.*

(2)   *Subject to subsection (3), this section applies to all proceedings commenced in the High Court which a county court would, apart from any limitation by reason of amount or value or annual value, have jurisdiction to hear and determine if commenced in that court.*

(3)   *This section does not apply to the following proceedings, namely—*

(*a*)   *matrimonial causes;*

(*b*)   *applications relating to the adoption or custody of, or access to, minors (including applications relating to guardianship or custodianship).*

[(*3*)   *This section does not apply to proceedings which are family proceedings within the meaning of Part V of the Matrimonial and Family Proceedings Act 1984.*]

(4)   *This section applies to all proceedings transferred to the High Court under section 41 or 42.*

(5)   *An order for the transfer to a county court of any proceedings by or against the Crown in the High Court shall not be made without the consent of the Crown.*

(6)   *Proceedings transferred under this section shall be transferred to such county court as the High Court considers to be convenient to the parties.*

(7)   *Where proceedings are ordered to be transferred from the High Court to a county court—*

(*a*)   *any party may lodge with the registrar of the county court named in the order, or cause to be lodged with him, the order and the writ, or copies of them, and such other documents (if any) as the High Court may direct; and*

(*b*)   *the proper officer of the Supreme Court shall, on the application of that party and on the production of the order and the filing of a copy of it, send by post to the registrar of the county court all pleadings, affidavits and other documents filed in the High Court relating to the proceedings.*

(8)   *Subject to subsection (9), on the documents mentioned in subsection (7) being so lodged or sent, the proceedings shall be transferred to the county court.*

(9)   *The transfer shall not affect any right of appeal from the order directing the transfer, or the right to enforce in the High Court any judgment signed, or order made, in that court before the transfer.*

(10)   *Where proceedings are transferred to a county court under this section, the county court shall have jurisdiction—*

(*a*)   *to hear and determine those proceedings; and*

(*b*)   *to award any relief, including any amount of damages, which could have been awarded by the High Court.*

Note. This section contains provisions formerly in County Courts Act 1959, s 75A, as inserted by Supreme Court Act 1981, s 149(1), Sch 3, para 8.

Sub-s (3) in square brackets substituted for original sub-s (3) by Matrimonial and Family Proceedings Act 1984, s 46(1), Sch 1, para 29, as from 28 April 1986.

[**40. Transfer of proceedings to county court**—(1) Where the High Court is satisfied that any proceedings before it are required by any provision of a kind mentioned in subsection (8) to be in a county court it shall—

(a)   order the transfer of the proceedings to a county court; or

(b)   if the court is satisfied that the person bringing the proceedings knew, or ought to have known, of that requirement, order that they be struck out.

(2)   Subject to any such provision, the High Court may order the transfer of any proceedings before it to a county court.

(3)   An order under this section may be made either on the motion of the High Court itself or on the application of any party to the proceedings.

(4) Proceedings transferred under this section shall be transferred to such county court as the High Court considers appropriate, having taken into account the convenience of the parties and that of any other persons likely to be affected and the state of business in the courts concerned.

(5) The transfer of any proceedings under this section shall not affect any right of appeal from the order directing the transfer.

(6) Where proceedings for the enforcement of any judgment or order of the High Court are transferred under this section—

(a) the judgment or order may be enforced as if it were a judgment or order of a county court; and

(b) subject to subsection (7), it shall be treated as a judgment or order of that court for all purposes.

(7) Where proceedings for the enforcement of any judgment or order of the High Court are transferred under this section—

(a) the powers of any court to set aside, correct, vary or quash a judgment or order of the High Court, and the enactments relating to appeals from such a judgment or order, shall continue to apply; and

(b) the powers of any court to set aside, correct, vary or quash a judgment or order of a county court, and the enactments relating to appeals from such a judgment or order, shall not apply.

(8) The provisions referred to in subsection (1) are any made—

(a) under section 1 of the Courts and Legal Services Act 1990; or

(b) by or under any other enactment.

(9) This section does not apply to family proceedings within the meaning of Part V of the Matrimonial and Family Proceedings Act 1984.]

Note. Section 40 in square brackets substituted for s 40 in italics by Courts and Legal Services Act 1990, s 2(1), as from 1 July 1991.

41. Transfer to High Court by order of High Court—(1) If at any stage in proceedings commenced in a county court or transferred to a county court under section 40, the High Court thinks it desirable that the proceedings, or any part of them, should be heard and determined in the High Court, it may order the transfer to the High Court of the proceedings or, as the case may be, of that part of them.

(2) The power conferred by subsection (1) is without prejudice to section 29 of the Supreme Court Act 1981 (power of High Court to issue prerogative orders) [but shall be exercised in relation to family proceedings (within the meaning of Part V of the Matrimonial and Family Proceedings Act 1984) in accordance with any directions given under section 37 of that Act (directions as to distribution and transfer of family business and proceedings).]

[(3) The power conferred by subsection (1) shall be exercised subject to any provision made—

(a) under section 1 of the Courts Legal Services Act 1990, or

(b) by or under any other enactment.]

Note. This section contains provisions formerly in County Courts Act 1959, s 75B, as inserted by Supreme Court Act 1981, s 149(1), Sch 3, para 8.

Words in square brackets in sub-s (2) added by Matrimonial and Family Proceedings Act 1984, s 46(1), Sch 1, para 30, as from 28 April 1986. Sub-s (3) added by Courts and Legal Services Act 1990, s 2(2), as from 1 July 1991.

42. Transfer to High Court by order of county court—(*1*) *At any stage in any proceedings to which this section applies, the county court may, either of its own motion or on the application of any party to the proceedings, order the transfer of the whole or any part of the proceedings to the High Court if—*

(*a*) *the court considers that some important question of law or fact is likely to arise; or*

(*b*) *the court considers that one or other of the parties is likely to be entitled in respect of a claim or counterclaim to an amount exceeding the amount recoverable in the county court; or*

(c) *any counterclaim or set-off and counterclaim of a defendant involves matters beyond the jurisdiction of the county court.*

(2) *Where—*

(a) *the county court has ordered that the proceedings on a counterclaim or set-off and counterclaim be transferred to the High Court, but the proceedings on the plaintiff's claim and the defence other than any set-off are heard and determined in the county court; and*

(b) *judgment on the claim is given for the plaintiff,*

execution of the judgment shall, unless the High Court at any time otherwise orders, be stayed until the proceedings transferred to the High Court have been concluded.

(3) *This section applies to all proceedings commenced in a county court which the High Court would have jurisdiction to hear and determine if they were commenced in it, other than—*

(a) *matrimonial causes;*

(b) *applications relating to the adoption or custody of, or access to, minors (including applications relating to guardianship or custodianship).*

[*proceedings which are family proceedings within the meaning of Part V of the Matrimonial and Family Proceedings Act 1984.*]

(4) *This section applies to all proceedings transferred to a county court under section 40.*

Note. This section contains provisions formerly in County Courts Act 1959, s 75C, as inserted by Supreme Court Act 1981, s 149(1), Sch 3, para 8.

Words in square brackets substituted for the words after 'other than' in sub-s (3) by Matrimonial and Family Proceedings Act 1984, s 46(1), Sch 1, para 31, as from 28 April 1986.

[**42. Transfer to High Court by order of a county court**—(1) Where a county court is satisfied that any proceedings before it are required by any provision of a kind mentioned in subsection (7) to be in the High Court, it shall—

(a) order the transfer of the proceedings to the High Court; or

(b) if the court is satisfied that the person bringing the proceedings knew, or ought to have known, of that requirement, order that they be struck out.

(2) Subject to any such provision, a county court may order the transfer of any proceedings before it to the High Court.

(3) An order under this section may be made either on the motion of the court itself or on the application of any party to the proceedings.

(4) The transfer of any proceedings under this section shall not affect any right of appeal from the order directing the transfer.

(5) Where proceedings for the enforcement of any judgment or order of a county court are transferred under this section—

(a) the judgment or order may be enforced as if it were a judgment or order of the High Court; and

(b) subject to subsection (6), it shall be treated as a judgment or order of that court for all purposes.

(6) Where proceedings for the enforcement of any judgment or order of a county court are transferred under this section—

(a) the powers of any court to set aside, correct, vary or quash a judgment or order of a county court, and the enactments relating to appeals from such a judgment or order, shall continue to apply; and

(b) the powers of any court to set aside, correct, vary or quash a judgment or order of the High Court, and the enactments relating to appeals from such a judgment or order, shall not apply.

(7) The provisions referred to in subsection (1) are any made—

(a) under section 1 of the Courts and Legal Services Act 1990; or

(b) by or under any other enactment.

(8) This section does not apply to family proceedings within the meaning of Part V of the Matrimonial and Family Proceedings Act 1984.]

Note. Section 42 in square brackets substituted for s 42 in italics by Courts and Legal Services Act 1990, s 2(3), as from 1 July 1991.

* * * * *

44. Transfer of interpleader proceedings from High Court to county court.
If it appears to the High Court that any proceedings in the High Court by way of interpleader, in which the amount or value of the matter in dispute does not exceed the county court limit, may be more conveniently heard and determined in a county court, the High Court may at any time order that the proceedings be transferred to any county court in which proceedings might have been brought by any party to the interpleader against any other party to it if there had been a trust to be executed concerning the matter in question.

Note. This section contains provisions formerly in County Courts Act 1959, s 68, as amended by Administration of Justice Act 1982, s 37, Sch 3, Part II, paras 2, 3.

This section repealed by Courts and Legal Services Act 1990, s 125(7), Sch 20, as from 1 July 1991.

* * * * *

PART III

PROCEDURE

Witnesses and evidence

55. Penalty for neglecting or refusing to give evidence—(1) Subject to
subsections (2) and (3), any person who—
  (a) having been summoned in pursuance of *county court rules* [rules of court] as a witness in a county court refuses or neglects, without sufficient cause, to appear or to produce any documents required by the summons to be produced; or
  (b) having been so summoned or being present in court and being required to give evidence, refuses to be sworn or give evidence,
shall forfeit such fine as the judge may direct.

(2) A judge shall not have power under subsection (1) to direct that a person shall forfeit a fine of an amount exceeding *£400* [£1,000].

Note. Sum '£1,000' substituted for sum '£400' by Criminal Justice Act 1991, s 17(3), Sch 4, Part I, as from 1 October 1992. Words 'rules of court' in square brackets substituted for words 'county court rules' in italics by Civil Court Procedure Act 1997, s 10, Sch 2, para 2(1)–(3) as from 26 April 1999 (SI 1999 No 1009).

(3) No person summoned in pursuance of *county court rules* [rules of court] as a witness in a county court shall forfeit a fine under this section unless there has been paid or tendered to him at the time of the service of the summons such sum in respect of his expenses (including, in such cases as may be prescribed, compensation for loss of time) as may be prescribed for the purposes of this section.

Note. Words 'rules of court' in square brackets substituted for words 'county court rules' in italics by Civil Court Procedure Act 1997, s 10, Sch 2, para 2(1)–(3) as from 26 April 1999 (SI 1999 No 1009).

(4) The judge may at his discretion direct that the whole or any part of any such fine, after deducting the costs, shall be applicable towards indemnifying the party injured by the refusal or neglect.

[(4A) A district judge, assistant district judge or deputy district judge shall have the same powers under this section as a judge.]

(5) This section does not apply to a debtor summoned to attend by a judgment summons.

Note. This section contains provisions formerly in County Courts Act 1959, s 84.

Sub-s (4A) inserted by Courts and Legal Services Act 1990, s 74(5), as from 1 July 1991.

56. Examination of witnesses abroad. The High Court shall have the same
power to issue a commission, request or order to examine witnesses abroad for the purpose of proceedings in a county court as it has for the purpose of an action or matter in the High Court.

Note. This section contains provisions formerly in County Courts Act 1959, s 85. For amendments to s 58 (persons who may take affidavits for use in county courts), see Administration of Justice Act 1985, Sch 7, para 8, Sch 8, Part II.

* * * * *

Right of audience

60. Right of audience—(*1*) *In any proceedings in a county court any of the following persons may address the court*—

(*a*) *any party to the proceedings;*

(*b*) *a barrister retained by or on behalf of any party;*

(*c*) *a solicitor acting generally in the proceedings for a party to them (in this subsection referred to as a 'solicitor on the record');*

(*d*) *any solicitor employed by a solicitor on the record;*

(*e*) *any solicitor engaged as an agent by a solicitor on the record;*

(*f*) *any solicitor employed by a solicitor so engaged; and*

(*g*) *any other person allowed by leave of the court to appear instead of any party;*

but a court may refuse to hear a person claiming to address the court as a solicitor unless that person has signed and delivered to the court a statement of his name and place of business and the name of the firm (if any) of which he is a member.

(2) Where an action is brought in a county court by a local authority for either or both of the following—

(a) the recovery of possession of a house belonging to the authority;

(b) the recovery of any rent, mesne profits, damages or other sum claimed by the authority in respect of the occupation by any person of such a house,

then, in so far as the proceedings in the action are heard by the registrar, any officer of the authority authorised by the authority in that behalf, *not being a person entitled to address the court by virtue of subsection (1)*, may address the registrar *as if he were a person so entitled.*

(3) In this section—

'local authority' means a county council, *the Greater London Council*, a district council [the Broads Authority], [any National Park authority] a London borough council[, a police authority established under *section 3 of the Police Act 1964* [section 3 of the Police Act 1996]] [the Metropolitan Police Authority] [, *the Service Authority for the National Criminal Intelligence Service, the Service Authority for the National Crime Squad*] [*the Inner London Education Authority*, a joint authority established by Part IV of the Local Government Act 1985] [, the London Fire and Emergency Planning Authority] or the Common Council of the City of London; and

'house' includes a part of a house, a flat or any other dwelling and also includes any yard, garden, outhouse or appurtenance occupied with a house or part of a house or with a flat or other dwelling,

and any reference to the occupation of a house by a person includes a reference to anything done by that person, or caused or permitted by him to be done, in relation to the house as occupier of the house, whether under a tenancy or licence or otherwise.

Note. This section contains provisions formerly in County Courts Act 1959, s 89.

Sub-s (1) and words in italics in sub-s (2) repealed by Courts and Legal Services Act 1990, s 125(7), Sch 20, as from 1 January 1991.

Words in italics in the first place in sub-s (3) repealed by Local Government Act 1985, s 102(2), Sch 17; words in first pair of square brackets in sub-s (3) inserted by Norfolk and Suffolk Broads Act 1988, s 21, Sch 6, para 24; words in second pair of square brackets in that subsection inserted by Environment Act 1995, s 78, Sch 10, para 23, as from 23 November 1995. Words ', a police authority ... Police Act 1964' inserted by Police and Magistrates' Courts Act 1994, s 43, Sch 4, Part II, para 57, as from 1 October 1994 for certain purposes, and as from 1 April 1995 otherwise; for purposes see SI 1994 No 2025. Words 'section 3 of the Police Act 1996' substituted for words 'section 3 of the Police Act 1964' by Police Act 1996, s 103(1), Sch 7, Part I, para 1, as from 22 August 1996. Words ', the Metropolitan Police Authority' inserted by Greater London

Authority Act 1999, s 325, Sch 27, para 49 as from 3 July 2000. Words ', the Service Authority ... National Crime Squad' inserted by Police Act 1997, s 134(1), Sch 9, para 45, as from 1 April 1998 (SI 1998 No 354); repealed by Criminal Justice and Police Act 2001, ss 128(1), 137, Sch 6, Pt 3, para 66, Sch 7, Pt 5(1), as from 1 April 2001 (SI 2002 No 344). Words 'the Inner London Education Authority ... 1985' inserted by Local Government Act 1985, s 84, Sch 14, Part II, para 63; and words 'the Inner London Education Authority' in italics repealed by Education Reform Act 1988, s 237(2), Sch 13, Part I, as from 1 April 1990. Words ', the London Fire and Emergency Planning Authority' inserted by Greater London Authority Act 1999, s 328, Sch 29, Pt I, para 38 as from 3 July 2000.

61. Right of Audience by direction of Lord Chancellor—(1) The Lord Chancellor may at any time direct that such categories of persons in relevant legal employment as may be specified in the direction may address the court in any proceedings in a county court, or in proceedings in a county court of such description as may be so specified.

(2) In subsection (1), 'relevant legal employment' means employment which consists of or includes giving assistance in the conduct of litigation to a *solicitor* [legal representative] whether in private practice or not.

(3) A direction under this section may be given subject to such conditions and restrictions as appear to the Lord Chancellor to be necessary or expedient, and may be expressed to have effect as respects every county court or as respects a specified county court or as respects one or more specified places where a county court sits.

(4) The power to give directions conferred by this section includes a power to vary or rescind any direction given under this section.

Note. This section contains provisions formerly in the County Courts Act 1959, s 89A, as inserted by Administration of Justice Act 1977, s 16.

Words in square brackets substituted for word in italics by Courts and Legal Services Act 1990, s 125(3), Sch 18, para 49(2), as from 1 April 1991.

*   *   *   *   *

Mode of trial

*   *   *   *   *

63. Assessors—(*1*) *In any proceedings the judge may, if he thinks fit on the application of any party, summon to his assistance, in such manner as may be prescribed, one or more persons of skill and experience in the matter to which the proceedings relate who may be willing to sit with the judge and act as assessors.*

(*2*) *For the purpose of assisting the judge in reviewing the taxation by the registrar of the costs of any proceedings, the power conferred by subsection (1) shall be exercisable by the judge without any application being made by any party to the proceedings.*

[(1) In any proceedings a judge may, on the application of a party to the proceedings, summon to his assistance one or more persons—

(a)   of skill and experience in the matter to which the proceedings relate; and

(b)   who may be willing to sit with him and act as assessors.

(2) In any proceedings prescribed for the purposes of this subsection a judge may summon to his assistance one or more such persons even though no application has been made for him to do so.

(2A) In any proceedings prescribed for the purposes of this subsection a district judge may, on the application of a party to the proceedings, summon to his assistance one or more such persons.

(2B) In any proceedings prescribed for the purposes of this subsection a district judge may summon to his assistance one or more such persons even though no application has been made for him to do so.

(2C) The summons shall be made in such manner as may be prescribed.]

Note. Sub-ss (1)–(2C) substituted for sub-ss (1), (2) by Courts and Legal Services Act 1990, s 14, as from a day to be appointed. Words 'on the application of any party' in original sub-s (1) and original sub-s (2) repealed by SI 1998 No 2940, art 6(d)(i), (ii), as from 26 April 1999.

(3) Subject to subsection (4), the remuneration of assessors for sitting under this section shall be *at such rate as may be prescribed* [determined by the judge] and shall be costs in the proceedings unless otherwise ordered by the judge.

Note. Words in square brackets substituted for words in italics by SI 1998 No 2940, art 6(d)(iii), as from 26 April 1999.

(*4*) *Where one or more assessors are summoned for the purposes of subsection (2) (otherwise than on the application of a party to the proceedings)* [assisting the judge in reviewing the taxation by the district judge of the costs of any proceedings] *the remuneration of any such assessor—*

(*a*) *shall be at such rate as may be determined by the Lord Chancellor with the approval of the Treasury; and*

(*b*) *shall be payable out of moneys provided by Parliament.*

[(4) In such cases as may be specified by order made by the Lord Chancellor with the consent of the Treasury, the remuneration of any assessor summoned under this section shall be paid, at such rate as may be so specified, out of money provided by Parliament.

(4A) Any power to make an order under subsection (4) shall be exercisable by statutory instrument subject to annulment by resolution of either House of Parliament.]

Note. Sub-ss (4), (4A) substituted for sub-s (4) in italics by Courts and Legal Services Act 1990, s 14, as from a day to be appointed. Words 'for the purposes of subsection (2)' in original sub-s (4) repealed by s 125(7) of, and Sch 20 to, the 1990 Act, as from a day to be appointed. Words 'subsection (2) ... the proceeding)' in original sub-s (4) substituted by words 'assisting the ... any proceedings' by SI 1998 No 2940, art 6(d)(iv), as from 26 April 1999.

(5) Where any person is proposed to be summoned as an assessor, objection to him, either personally or in respect of his qualification, may be taken by any party in the prescribed manner.

Note. This section contains provisions formerly in County Courts Act 1959, s 91.

*   *   *   *   *

Judgments and orders

70. Finality of judgments and orders. Every judgment and order of a county court shall, except as provided by this or any other Act or as may be prescribed, be final and conclusive between the parties.

Note. This section contains provisions formerly in County Courts Act 1959, s 98.

71. Satisfaction of judgments and orders for payment of money—(1) Where a judgment is given or an order is made by a county court under which a sum of money of any amount is payable, whether by way of satisfaction of the claim or counterclaim in the proceedings or by way of costs or otherwise, the court may, as it thinks fit, order the money to be paid either—

(a) in one sum, whether forthwith or within such period as the court may fix; or

(b) by such instalments payable at such times as the court may fix.

(2) If at any time it appears to the satisfaction of the court that any party to any proceedings is unable from any cause to pay any sum recovered against him (whether by way of satisfaction of the claim or counterclaim in the proceedings or by way of costs or otherwise) or any instalment of such a sum, the court may, in its discretion, suspend or stay any judgment or order given or made in the proceedings for such time and on such terms as the court thinks fit, and so from time to time until it appears that the cause of inability has ceased.

Note. This section contains provisions formerly in County Courts Act 1959, s 99(1), (2).

*   *   *   *   *

74. Interest on judgment debts etc—(1) The Lord Chancellor may by order made with the concurrence of the Treasury provide that any sums to which this subsection applies shall carry interest at such rate and between such times as may be prescribed by the order.

(2) The sums to which subsection (1) applies are—

(a) sums payable under judgments or orders given or made in a county court, including sums payable by instalments; and

(b) sums which by virtue of any enactment are, if the county court so orders, recoverable as if payable under an order of that court, and in respect of which the county court has so ordered.

(3) The payment of interest due under subsection (1) shall be enforceable as a sum payable under the judgment or order.

(4) The power conferred by subsection (1) includes power—

(a) to specify the descriptions of judgment or order in respect of which interest shall be payable;

(b) to provide that interest shall be payable only on sums exceeding a specified amount;

(c) to make provision for the manner in which and the periods by reference to which the interest is to be calculated and paid;

(d) to provide that any enactment shall or shall not apply in relation to interest payable under subsection (1) or shall apply to it with such modifications as may be specified in the order; and

(e) to make such incidental or supplementary provisions as the Lord Chancellor considers appropriate.

(5) Without prejudice to the generality of subsection (4), an order under subsection (1) may provide that the rate of interest shall be the rate specified in section 17 of the Judgments Act 1838 as that enactment has effect from time to time.

[(5A) The power conferred by subsection (1) includes power to make provision enabling a county court to order that the rate of interest applicable to a sum expressed in a currency other than sterling shall be such rate as the court thinks fit (instead of the rate otherwise applicable).]

Note. Sub-s (5A) inserted by Private International Law (Miscellaneous Provisions) Act 1995, s 2, as from 1 November 1996.

(6) The power to make an order under subsection (1) shall be exercisable by statutory instrument subject to annulment in pursuance of a resolution of either House of Parliament.

Note. This section contains provisions formerly in County Courts Act 1959, s 101A, as inserted by Supreme Court Act 1981, s 149(1), Sch 3, para 11.

*   *   *   *   *

General rules of procedure

*   *   *   *   *

76. Application of practice of High Court.   In any case not expressly provided for by or in pursuance of this Act, the general principles of practice in the High Court may be adopted and applied to proceedings in a county court.

Note. This section contains provisions formerly in County Courts Act 1959, s 103.

Appeals

77. Appeals: general provisions—(1) Subject to the provisions of this section and the following provisions of this Part of this Act [and to any order made by the Lord Chancellor under section 56(1) of that Access to Justice Act 1999], if any party to any proceedings in a county court is dissatisfied with the determination of the judge or jury, he may appeal from it to the Court of Appeal in such manner and subject to such conditions as may be provided by *the rules of the Supreme Court* [Civil Procedure Rules].

Note. Words 'Civil Court Procedures' in square brackets substituted for words 'the rules of the Supreme Court' in italics by Civil Court Procedure Act 1997, s 10, Sch 2, para 2(1), (7) as from 26 April 1999 (SI 1999 No 1009). Words 'and to any order made by the Lord Chancellor under section 56(1) of that Access to Justice Act 1999' in square brackets inserted by Access to Justice Act 1999 (Destination of Appeals) Order 2000, SI 2000 No 1071, art 8, as from 2 May 2000.

[(1A) Without prejudice to the generality of the power to make *county court rules* [rules of court] under section 75, such rules may make provision for any appeal from the exercise by a district judge, assistant district judge or deputy district judge of any power given to him by virtue of any enactment to be to a judge of a county court.]

Note. Sub-s (1A) inserted by Courts and Legal Services Act 1990, s 125(2), Sch 17, para 15, as from 1 January 1991. Words 'rules of court' in square brackets substituted for words 'county court rules' in italics by Civil Court Procedure Act 1997, s 10, Sch 2, para 2(1)–(3) as from 26 April 1999 (SI 1999 No 1009).

(2) The Lord Chancellor may by order prescribe classes of proceedings in which there is to be no right of appeal under this section without the leave either of the judge of the county court or of the Court of Appeal.

(3) An order under subsection (2)—

(a) may classify proceedings according to the nature of those proceedings;

(b) may classify proceedings according to the amount or value or annual value of the money or other property which is the subject of those proceedings or according to whether that amount or value or annual value exceeds a specified fraction of the relevant county court limit;

(c) may provide that the order shall not apply to determinations made before such date as may be specified in the order; and

(d) may make different provision for different classes of proceedings.

(4) The power to make an order under subsection (2) shall be exercisable by statutory instrument subject to annulment in pursuance of a resolution of either House of Parliament.

Note. Sub-s (2)–(4) repealed by Access to Justice Act 1999, s 106, Sch 15, Pt III, as from 27 September 1999.

(5) Subject to the provisions of this section and the following provisions of this Part of this Act, where an appeal is brought under subsection (1) in any action, an appeal may be brought under that subsection in respect of any claim or counterclaim in the action notwithstanding that there could have been no such appeal if that claim had been the subject of a separate action.

(6) In proceedings in which either the plaintiff or the defendant is claiming possession of any premises this section shall not confer any right of appeal on any question of fact if by virtue of—

(a) section 13(4) of the Landlord and Tenant Act 1954; or

(b) Cases III to IX in Schedule 4 to the Rent (Agriculture) Act 1976; or

(c) section 98 of the Rent Act 1977, as it applies to Cases 1 to 6 and 8 and 9 in Schedule 15 to that Act, or that section as extended or applied by any other enactment; or

(d) section 99 of the Rent Act 1977, as it applies to Cases 1 to 6 and 9 in Schedule 15 to that Act; or

(e) *section 34(3)(a) of the Housing Act 1980* [section 84(2)(a) of the Housing Act 1985]; or

[(ee) section 7 of the Housing Act 1988, as it applies to the grounds in Part II of Schedule 2 to that Act or;]

[(ef) paragraph 13(4) of Schedule 10 to the Local Government and Housing Act 1989; or]

(f) any other enactment,

the court can only grant possession on being satisfied that it is reasonable to do so.

(7) This section shall not—

(a) confer any right of appeal from any judgment or order where a right of appeal is conferred by some other enactment; or

(b) take away any right of appeal from any judgment or order where a right of appeal is so conferred,

and shall have effect subject to any enactment other than this Act.

(8) In this section—

'enactment' means an enactment whenever passed; and

'the relevant county court limit' means, in relation to proceedings of any description, the sum by reference to which the question whether a county court has jurisdiction to hear and determine the proceedings falls to be decided.

Note. This section contains provisions formerly in County Courts Act 1959, s 108, as substituted by Supreme Court Act 1981, s 149(1), Sch 3, para 14. Words in square brackets in sub-s (6)(e) substituted for words in italics by Housing (Consequential Provisions) Act 1985, s 4, Sch 2, para 57(3). Sub-s (6)(ee) inserted by Housing Act 1988, s 140(1), Sch 17, Part I, para 35(2); sub-s (6)(ef) inserted by Local Government and Housing Act 1989, s 194(1), Sch 11, para 60, as from a day to be appointed. Definition 'the relevant county court limit' and preceding word 'and' in sub-s (8) repealed by Access to Justice Act 1999, s 106, sch 15, Pt III, as from 27 September 1999.

* * * * *

80. Judge's note on appeal—(1) At the hearing of any proceedings in a county court in which there is a right of appeal or from which an appeal may be brought with leave, the judge shall, at the request of any party, make a note—

(a) of any question of law raised at the hearing; and

(b) of the facts in evidence in relation to any such question; and

(c) of his decision on any such question and of his determination of the proceedings.

(2) Where such a note has been taken, the judge shall (whether notice of appeal has been served or not), on the application of any party to the proceedings, and on payment by that party of such fee as may be prescribed by *the fees orders* [an order under section 92 of the Courts Act 2003 (fees)], furnish him with a copy of the note, and shall sign the copy, and the copy so signed shall be used at the hearing of the appeal.

Note. This section contains provisions formerly in County Courts Act 1959, s 112, as amended by Supreme Court Act 1981, s 149(1), Sch 3, para 16. Words in square brackets substituted for words in italics by Courts Act 2003, s 109(1), Sch 8, para 271(b), as from a day to be appointed.

81. Powers of Court of Appeal on appeal from county court—(1) On the hearing of an appeal, the Court of Appeal may draw any inference of fact and either—

(a) order a new trial on such terms as the court thinks just; or

(b) order judgment to be entered for any party; or

(c) make a final or other order on such terms as the court thinks proper to ensure the determination on the merits of the real question in controversy between the parties.

(2) Subject to *any rules of the Supreme Court* [Civil Procedure Rules], on any appeal from a county court the Court of Appeal may reverse or vary, in favour of a party seeking to support the judgment or order of the county court in whole or in part, any determinations made in the county court on questions of fact, notwithstanding that the appeal is an appeal on a point of law only, or any such determinations on points of law, notwithstanding that the appeal is an appeal on a question of fact only.

Note. Words in square brackets in sub-s (2) substituted for words in italics by Civil Procedure Act 1997, s 10, Sch 2, para 2(1), (8), as from 26 April 1999 (SI 1999 No 1009).

(3) Subsection (2) shall not enable the Court of Appeal to reverse or vary any determination, unless the party dissatisfied with the determination would have been entitled to appeal in respect of it if aggrieved by the judgment or order.

Note. This section contains provisions formerly in County Courts Act 1959, s 113.

*　　*　　*　　*　　*

PART V

ENFORCEMENT OF JUDGMENTS AND ORDERS

Execution against goods

85. Execution of judgments or orders for payment of money—(1) [Subject to article 8 of the High Court and County Courts Jurisdiction Order 1991,] any sum of money payable under a judgment or order of a county court may be recovered, in case of default or failure of payment, forthwith or at the time or times and in the manner thereby directed, by execution against the goods of the party against whom the judgment or order was obtained.

(2) The registrar, on the application of the party prosecuting any such judgment or order, shall issue a warrant of execution in the nature of a writ of fieri facias whereby the registrar shall be empowered to levy or cause to be levied by distress and sale of the goods, wherever they may be found within the district of the court, the money payable under the judgment or order and the costs of the execution.

*　　*　　*　　*　　*

(4) It shall be the duty of every constable within his jurisdiction to assist in the execution of every such warrant.

Note. This section contains provisions formerly in County Courts Act 1959, s 120.

Words in square brackets inserted by High Court and County Courts Jurisdiction Order 1991, SI 1991 No 724, art 8(2), as from 1 July 1991.

86. Execution of orders for payment by instalments—(1) Where the court has made an order for payment of any sum of money by instalments, execution on the order shall not be issued until after default in payment of some instalment according to the order.

(2) *County court rules* [rules of court] may prescribe the cases in which execution is to issue if there is any such default and limit the amounts for which and the times at which execution may issue.

Note. Words 'rules of court' in square brackets substituted for words 'county court rules' in italics by Civil Court Procedure Act 1997, s 10, Sch 2, para 2(1)–(3) as from 26 April 1999 (SI 1999 No 1009).

(3) Except so far as may be otherwise provided by *county court rules* [rules of court] made for those purposes, execution or successive executions may issue if there is any such default for the whole of the said sum of money and costs then remaining unpaid or for such part as the court may order either at the time of the original order or at any subsequent time; but except so far as may be otherwise provided by such rules, no execution shall issue unless at the time when it issues the whole or some part of an instalment which has already become due remains unpaid.

Note. This section contains provisions formerly in County Courts Act 1959, s 121. Words 'rules of court' in square brackets substituted for words 'county court rules' in italics by Civil Court Procedure Act 1997, s 10, Sch2, para 2(1)–(3) as from 26 April 1999 (SI 1999 No 1009).

87. Execution to be superseded on payment—(1) In or upon every warrant of execution issued from a county court against the goods of any person, the registrar shall cause to be inserted or indorsed the total amount to be levied, inclusive of the fee for issuing the warrant but exclusive of the fees for its execution.

(2) If the person against whom the execution is issued, before the actual sale of the goods, pays or causes to be paid or tendered to the registrar of the court from which the warrant is issued, or to the bailiff holding the warrant, the amount inserted in, or indorsed upon, the warrant under subsection (1), or such part as the person entitled agrees to accept in full satisfaction, together with the amount stated by the officer of the court to whom the payment or tender is made to be the amount of the fees for the execution of the warrant, the execution shall be superseded, and the goods shall be discharged and set at liberty.

Note. This section contains provisions formerly in County Courts Act 1959, s 122.

88. Power to stay execution.   If at any time it appears to the satisfaction of the court that any party to any proceedings is unable from any cause to pay any sum recovered against him (whether by way of satisfaction of the claim or counterclaim in the proceedings or by way of costs or otherwise), or any instalment of such a sum, the court may, in its discretion, stay any execution issued in the proceedings for such time and on such terms as the court thinks fit, and so from time to time until it appears that the cause of inability has ceased.

Note. This section contains provisions formerly in County Courts Act 1959, s 123.

Seizure and custody of goods etc

89. Goods which may be seized—(1) Every bailiff or officer executing any warrant of execution issued from a county court against the goods of any person may by virtue of it seize—

(a) *any of the goods of that person, except the wearing apparel and bedding of that person or his family, and the tools and implements of his trade, to the prescribed value, which shall to that extent be protected from seizure; and*

[(a) any of that person's goods except—

  (i) such tools, books, vehicles and other items of equipment as are necessary to that person for use personally by him in his employment, business or vocation;

  (ii) such clothing, bedding, furniture, household equipment and provisions as are necessary for satisfying the basic domestic needs of that person and his family;]

Note. Sub-s (1)(a) in square brackets substituted for sub-s (1)(a) in italics by Courts and Legal Services Act 1990, s 15(2), as from 1 July 1991.

(b) any money, banknotes, bills of exchange, promissory notes, bonds, specialities or securities for money belonging to that person.

(2) Any reference to the goods of an execution debtor in this Part of this Act includes a reference to anything else of his that may lawfully be seized in execution.

(3) *The prescribed value for the purposes of subsection (1) shall be the same as that prescribed for the purposes of section 8 of the Small Debts Act 1845, by order of the Lord Chancellor under section 37(2) of the Administration of Justice Act 1956.*

Note. This section contains provisions formerly in County Courts Act 1959, s 124, as amended by Supreme Court Act 1981, s 149(1), Sch 3, para 17.

Sub-s (3) repealed by Courts and Legal Services Act 1990, s 125(7), Sch 20, as from 1 July 1991.

90. Custody of goods seized.   Goods seized in execution under process of a county court shall, until sale,—
  (a) be deposited by the bailiff in some fit place; or
  (b) remain in the custody of a fit person approved by the registrar to be put in possession by the bailiff; or
  (c) be safeguarded in such other manner as the registrar directs.
Note. This section contains provisions formerly in County Courts Act 1959, s 125.

*   *   *   *   *

Execution out of jurisdiction of court

103. Execution out of jurisdiction of court—(1) Where a warrant of execution has been issued from a county court (hereafter in this section referred to as a 'home court') against the goods of any person and the goods are out of the jurisdiction of that court, the registrar of that court may send the warrant of execution to the registrar of any other county court within the jurisdiction of which the goods are or are believed to be, with a warrant endorsed on it or annexed to it requiring execution of the original warrant.

(2) The original warrant shall bind the property in goods of the execution debtor which are within the jurisdiction of the court to which it is sent as from the time when it is received by the registrar of that court.

(3) It shall be the duty of the registrar of the court to which the warrant is sent (without fee) on receipt of the warrant to endorse on its back the hour, day, month and year when he received it.

(4) On receipt of the warrant, the registrar of the other county court shall act in all respects as if the original warrant of execution had been issued by the court of which he is registrar and shall within the prescribed time—
  (a) report to the registrar of the home court what he has done in the execution of the warrant; and
  (b) pay over all moneys received in pursuance of the warrant.

(5) Where a warrant of execution is sent by the registrar of a home court to the registrar of another court for execution under this section, that other court shall have the same power as the home court of staying the execution under section 88 as respects any goods within the jurisdiction of that other court.

[(6) *County court rules* [rules of court] may make provision for the suspension of any judgment or order, or terms in connection with any warrant issued with respect to any instalment payable under the judgment or order.]

Note. This section contains provisions formerly in County Courts Act 1959, s 138, as amended by Supreme Court Act 1981, s 149(1), Sch 3, para 20. Sub-s (6) added by Courts and Legal Services Act 1990, s 125(2), Sch 17, para 16, as from 1 January 1991. Words 'rules of court' in square brackets substituted for words 'county court rule' in italics by Civil Court Procedure Act 1997, s 10, Sch 2, para 2(1)–(3) as from 26 April 1999 (SI 1999 No 1009).

104. Information as to writs and warrants of execution—*(1) A sheriff shall on demand inform the registrar of a county court, by writing signed by any clerk in the office of the under-sheriff, of the precise time of the delivery to him of a writ against the goods of any person issued from the High Court, and a bailiff of a county court shall on demand show his warrant to any sheriff's officer.*

(2) Any writing purporting to be signed as mentioned in subsection (1) and the endorsement on any such warrant shall respectively be sufficient justification to any registrar or sheriff acting on it.

Note. This section contains provisions formerly in County Courts Act 1959, s 138A as inserted by Supreme Court Act 1981, s 149(1), Sch 3, para 21.

[104. Information as to writs and warrants of execution—(1) Where a writ against the goods of any person issued from the High Court is delivered to an enforcement officer who is under a duty to execute the writ or to a sheriff, then on demand from the district judge of a county court that person shall—

  (a) in the case of an enforcement officer, by writing signed by that officer or a person acting under his authority, and

  (b) in the case of a sheriff, by writing signed by any clerk in the office of the under-sheriff,

inform the district judge of the precise time the writ was delivered to him.

  (2) A bailiff of a county court shall on demand show his warrant to any enforcement officer, any person acting under the authority of an enforcement officer and any sheriff's officer.

  (3) Any writing purporting to be signed as mentioned in subsection (1) and the endorsement on any warrant issued from a county court shall respectively be sufficient justification to any district judge, or enforcement officer or sheriff, acting on it.

  (4) In this section 'enforcement officer' means an individual who is authorised to act as an enforcement officer under the Courts Act 2003.]

Note. Section 104 in square brackets substituted for s 104 in italics by Courts Act 2003, s 109(1), Sch 8, para 275, as from 15 March 2004 (SI 2004 No 401) (see also SI 2004 No 401, art 3).

Execution in county court of judgments and orders of, or enforceable as judgments and orders of, High Court

105. Execution in county court of judgments and orders of High Court—(*1*) *A judgment or order of the High Court for the payment of money to a person, and any judgment, order, decree or award (however called) of any court or arbitrator (including any foreign court or foreign arbitrator) being a judgment, order, decree or award for the payment of money to a person which is or has become enforceable (whether wholly or to a limited extent) as if it were a judgment or order of the High Court shall be enforceable in the county court as if it were a judgment of that court.*

  (*2*) *Where an application is made to the High Court—*

  (*a*) *for the attachment of a debt not exceeding the county court limit to answer a judgment or order; or*

  (*b*) *for leave to issue execution for a debt not exceeding the county court limit against a person as being a member of a firm against which a judgment or order has been obtained,*

the High Court may make an order either—

  (*i*) *transferring the matter to; or*

  (*ii*) *directing that any issue necessary for determining the matter shall be tried in,*

such county court to be named in the order as the court may deem the most convenient to the parties.

  (*3*) *Where an order is made under subsection (2) directing an issue to be tried in a county court, the order shall define the issue to be tried, and any party may lodge or cause to be lodged the order, together with the affidavits (if any) filed in the matter, and such other documents (if any) as the High Court may direct, with the registrar of the county court named in the order.*

  (*4*) *On the documents being lodged the issue shall, subject to county court rules, be tried in the county court so named, and after the issue has been tried the judge shall certify the result of the trial and send the certificate to the High Court together with the documents and any report which he may think fit to make as to costs or otherwise.*

Note. This section contains provisions formerly in County Courts Act 1959, ss 139, 146, as amended by Administration of Justice Act 1982, s 34(1). For a transitional provision see Sch 3, para 3. Whole section repealed by Courts and Legal Services Act 1990, s 125(7), Sch 20, as from 1 July 1991.

*   *   *   *   *

Receivers and attachment of debts

107. Receivers—(1) The power of the county court to appoint a receiver by way of equitable execution shall operate in relation to all legal estates and interests in land.

(2) The said power may be exercised in relation to an estate or interest in land whether or not a charge has been imposed on that land under section 1 of the Charging Orders Act 1979 for the purpose of enforcing the judgment, decree, order or award in question, and the said power shall be in addition to and not in derogation of any power of any court to appoint a receiver in proceedings for enforcing such a charge.

(3) Where an order under section 1 of the Charging Orders Act 1979 imposing a charge for the purpose of enforcing a judgment, decree, order or award has been registered under section 6 of the Land Charges Act 1972, subsection (4) of that section (which provides that, amongst other things, an order appointing a receiver and any proceedings pursuant to the order or in obedience to it, shall be void against a purchaser unless the order is for the time being registered under that section) shall not apply to an order appointing a receiver made either in proceedings for enforcing the charge or by way of equitable execution of the judgment, decree, order or award or, as the case may be, of so much of it as requires payment of moneys secured by the charge.

Note. This section contains provisions formerly in County Courts Act 1959, s 142.

108. Attachment of debts—(1) Subject to any order for the time being in force under subsection (4), this section applies to [any deposit account, and any withdrawable share account, with a deposit-taker].

(2) In determining whether, for the purposes of the jurisdiction of the county court to attach debts for the purpose of satisfying judgments or orders for the payment of money, a sum standing to the credit of a person in an account to which this section applies is a sum due or accruing to that person and, as such, attachable in accordance with *county court rules* [rules of court], any condition mentioned in subsection (3) which applies to the account shall be disregarded.

(3) Those conditions are—

(a) any condition that notice is required before any money or share is withdrawn;

(b) any condition that a personal application must be made before any money or share is withdrawn;

(c) any condition that a deposit book or share-account book must be produced before any money or share is withdrawn; or

(d) any other prescribed condition.

(4) The Lord Chancellor may by order make such provision as he thinks fit, by way of amendment of this section or otherwise, for all or any of the following purposes, namely—

(a) including in, or excluding from, the accounts to which this section applies accounts of any description specified in the order;

(b) excluding from the accounts to which this section applies all accounts with any particular *deposit-taking institution* [deposit-taker] so specified or with any *deposit-taking institution* [deposit-taker] of a description so specified.

(5) An order under subsection (4) shall be made by statutory instrument subject to annulment in pursuance of a resolution of either House of Parliament.

Note. This section contains provisions formerly in County Courts Act 1959, s 143, as substituted by Supreme Court Act 1981, s 149(1), Sch 3, para 22. In sub-s (1) for words from 'the following' to the end in italics there is substituted words 'any deposit account, and any withdrawable share account, with a deposit-taker' in square brackets by SI 2001 No 3649, art 294(1), (2), as from 1 December 2001. In sub-s (2) for words 'county court rules' in italics there is substituted words 'rules of court' in square brackets by Civil Court Procedure Act 1997, s 10, Sch 2, para 2(1)–(3) as from 26 april 1999 (SI 1999 No 1009). In sub-s (4)(b) for words 'deposit-taking institution' in italics in both places they occur there is substituted words' deposit-taker' in square brackets by SI 2001 No 3649, art 294(1), (3), as from 1 December 2001.

* * * * *

109. Administrative and clerical expenses of garnishees—(*1*) *A sum may be prescribed which, before complying with an order made in the exercise of the jurisdiction mentioned in section 108(2)*—

(*a*) *any deposit-taking institution; or*

(*b*) *any such institution of a prescribed description,*

may deduct, subject to subsection (2), towards the clerical and administrative expenses of complying with the order, from any money which, but for the deduction, would be attached by the order.

[(1) Where an *order nisi* [interim third party debt order] made in the exercise of the jurisdiction mentioned in subsection (2) of the preceding section is served on *any deposit-taking institution* [a deposit-taker, it], the institution may, subject to the provisions of this section, deduct from the relevant debt or debts an amount not exceeding the prescribed sum towards *the administrative and clerical expenses of the institution* [its administrative and clerical expenses] in complying with the order; and the right *of an institution* to make a deduction under this subsection shall be exercisable as from the time the *order nisi* [interim third party debt order] is served on it.

(1A) In subsection (1) 'the relevant debt or debts', in relation to an *order nisi* [interim third party debt order] served on *any such institution as is mentioned in that subsection* [a deposit-taker], means the amount, as at the time the order is served on *the institution* [it], of the debt or debts of which the whole or a part is expressed to be attached by the order.

(1B) A deduction may be made under subsection (1) in a case where the amount referred to in subsection (1A) is insufficient to cover both the amount of the deduction and the amount of the judgment debt and costs in respect of which the attachment was made, notwithstanding that the benefit of the attachment to the creditor is reduced as a result of the deduction.]

Note. Sub-ss (1)–(1B) in square brackets substituted for original sub-s (1) in italics by Administration of Justice Act 1985, s 52, as from 30 December 1985. In sub-s (1) words 'a deposit-taker, it' substituted for words 'any deposit-taking institution, the institution' by SI 2001 No 3649, art 295(1), (2), as from 1 December 2001. In sub-s (1) words 'its administrative and clerical expenses' substituted for words 'the administrative and clerical expenses of the institution' by SI 2001 No 3649, art 295(1), (2), as from 1 December 2001. In sub-s (1) words 'of an institution' in italics repealed by SI No 3649, art 295(1), (2), as from 1 December 2001. In sub-s (1A) words 'a deposit-taker' substituted for words 'any such institution as is mentioned in that subsection' by SI 2001 No 3649, art 295(1), (3), as from 1 December 2001. In sub-s (1A) words 'it' substituted for words 'the institution' by SI 2001 No 3649, art 295(1), (3), as from 1 December 2001. In sub-ss (1)–(1B) words 'interim third party debt order' in each place they occur substituted for words 'order nisi' by SI 2002 No 439, art 7, as from 25 March 2002.

(2) *The prescribed sum may not* [An amount may not in pursuance of subsection (1)] be deducted or, as the case may be, retained in a case where by virtue of *section 40 of the Bankruptcy Act 1914* [section *179 of the Insolvency Act 1985* [346 of the Insolvency Act 1986]] or section 325 of the Companies Act 1948 or otherwise, the creditor is not entitled to retain the benefit of the attachment.

Note. Words in first square brackets substituted for words in italics by Administration of Justice Act 1985, s 52(3). Words in second square brackets substituted for second words in italics by Insolvency Act 1985, Sch 8, para 38(4). Further substitution effected by Insolvency Act 1986, s 439(2), Sch 14.

Companies Act 1948, s 325, has been replaced by Companies Act 1985, s 621.

(3) In this section 'prescribed' means prescribed by an order made by the Lord Chancellor.

(4) An order under this section—

(a) may make different provision for different cases; *and*

(b) without prejudice to the generality of paragraph (a) may prescribe sums differing according to the amount due under the judgment or order to be satisfied;

[(c)   may provide for this section not to apply to *deposit-taking institutions* [deposit-takers] of any prescribed description.]

Note. Sub-s (4)(c) inserted by Administration of Justice Act 1985, s 52(4), Sch 8, Part II. In sub-s (4)(c) words 'a deposit-taker' substituted for words 'deposit-taking institution' by SI 2001 No 3649, art 295(1), (4), as from 1 December 2001.

(5) Any such order shall be made by statutory instrument subject to annulment in pursuance of a resolution of either House of Parliament.

Note. This section contains provisions formerly in County Courts Act 1959, s 143A, as inserted by Administration of Justice Act 1982, s 55(2), Sch 4, Part II.

*   *   *   *   *

Miscellaneous provisions as to enforcement of judgments and orders

110. Penalty for non-attendance on judgment summons—(1) If a debtor summoned to attend a county court by a judgment summons fails to attend on the day and at the time fixed for any hearing of the summons, the judge may adjourn or further adjourn the summons to a specified time on a specified day and order the debtor to attend at that time on that day.

(2) If—

(a) a debtor, having been ordered under subsection (1) to attend at a specified time on a specified day fails to do so; *or*

(b) *a debtor who attends for the hearing of a judgment summons refuses to be sworn or to give evidence;*

the judge may make an order committing him to prison for a period not exceeding 14 days in respect of the failure or refusal.

(3) In any case where the judge has power to make an order of committal under subsection (2) for failure to attend, he may in lieu of or in addition to making that order, order the debtor to be arrested and brought before the court either forthwith or at such time as the judge may direct.

(4) A debtor shall not be committed to prison under subsection (2) for having failed to attend as required by an order under subsection (1) unless there was paid to him at the time of the service of the judgment summons, or paid or tendered to him at the time of the service of the order, such sum in respect of his expenses as may be prescribed for the purposes of this section.

(5) The judge may at any time revoke an order committing a person to prison under this section and, if he is already in custody, order his discharge.

Note. This section contains provisions formerly in County Courts Act 1959, s 144, as amended by Contempt of Court Act 1981, s 14, Sch 2, Part III, para 4. Sub-s (2)(b) and word immediately preceding it repealed by SI 2001 No 439, arts 2, 8, as from 25 March 2002.

*   *   *   *   *

PART VII

COMMITTALS

118. Power to commit for contempt—(1) If any person—

(a) wilfully insults the judge of a county court, or any juror or witness, or any officer of the court during his sitting or attendance in court, or in going to or returning from the court; or

(b) wilfully interrupts the proceedings of a county court or otherwise misbehaves in court;

any officer of the court, with or without the assistance of any other person, may, by order of the judge, take the offender into custody and detain him until the rising of the court, and the judge may, if he thinks fit,—

(i) make an order committing the offender for a specified period not exceeding one month to *any* prison *to which the judge has power to commit;* or

(ii) impose upon the offender, for every offence, a fine of an amount not exceeding *£1,000* [£2,500], or may both make such an order and impose such a fine.

(2) The judge may at any time revoke an order committing a person to prison under this section and, if he is already in custody, order his discharge.

[(3) A district judge, assistant district judge or deputy district judge shall have the same powers under this section in relation to proceedings before him as a judge.]

Note. This section contains provisions formerly in County Courts Act 1959, s 157, as amended by Contempt of Court Act 1981, s 14, Sch 2, Part III, para 5.

Words in italics in sub-s (1)(i) repealed by Statute Law (Repeals) Act 1986. Sum '£2,500' in square brackets substituted for sum '£1,000' in italics by Criminal Justice Act 1991, s 17(3), Sch 4, Part I, as from 1 October 1992.

Sub-s (3) added by Courts and Legal Services Act 1990, s 74(6), as from 1 July 1991.

* * * * *

119. Issue and execution of orders of committal—(1) Whenever any order or warrant for the committal of any person to prison is made or issued by a county court (whether in pursuance of this or any other Act or of *county court rules* [rules of court]), the order or warrant shall be directed to the registrar of the court, who shall thereby be empowered to take the body of the person against whom the order is made or warrant issued.

(2) It shall be the duty of every constable within his jurisdiction to assist in the execution of every such order or warrant.

(3) The governor of the prison mentioned in any such order or warrant shall be bound to receive and keep the person mentioned in it until he is lawfully discharged.

Note. This section contains provisions formerly in County Courts Act 1959, s 158. Words 'rules of court' in square brackets substituted for words 'county court rules' in italics by Civil Court Procedure Act 1997, s 10, Sch 2, para 2(1)–(3) as from 26 April 1999 (SI 1999 No 1009).

* * * * *

120. Prisons to which committals may be made. Any person committed to prison by the judge of any county court, in pursuance of this or any other Act or of *county court rules* [rules of court], shall be committed to such prison as may from time to time be directed in the case of that court by order of the Secretary of State.

Note. This section contains provisions formerly in County Courts Act 1959, s 159. Words 'rules of court' in square brackets substituted for words 'county court rules' in italics by Civil Court Procedure Act 1997, s 10, Sch 2, para 2(1)–(3) as from 26 April 1999 (SI 1999 No 1009).

* * * * *

121. Power of judge to order discharge. If at any time it appears to the satisfaction of a judge of a county court that any debtor arrested or confined in prison by order of the court is unable from any cause to pay any sum recovered against him (whether by way of satisfaction of a claim or counterclaim or by way of costs or otherwise), or any instalment thereof, and ought to be discharged, the judge may order his discharge upon such terms (including liability to re-arrest if the terms are not complied with) as the judge thinks fit.

Note. This section contains provisions formerly in County Courts Act 1959, s 160.

* * * * *

122. Execution of committal orders out of jurisdiction of court—(1) Where any order or warrant for the committal of any person to prison has been made or issued (whether in pursuance of this or any other Act or of *county court rules* [rules of court]) by a county court (hereafter in this section referred to as a 'home court') and that person is out of the jurisdiction of that court, the registrar may send the order or warrant to the registrar of any other county court within the jurisdiction of which that person is or is believed to be, with a warrant endorsed on it or annexed to it requiring execution of the original order or warrant.

(2) On receipt of the warrant, the registrar of the other county court shall act in all respects as if the original order or warrant had been issued by the court of which he is registrar and shall within the prescribed time—

(a) report to the registrar of the home court what he has done in the execution of the order or warrant; and

(b) pay over all moneys received in pursuance of the order or warrant.

(3) Where a person is apprehended under the order or warrant, he shall be forthwith conveyed, in custody of the officer apprehending him, to the prison of the court within the jurisdiction of which he was apprehended and kept there, unless sooner discharged by law, until the expiration of the period mentioned in the order or warrant.

(4) It shall be the duty of every constable within his jurisdiction to assist in the execution of every such order or warrant.

(5) Where an order of committal—

(a) under the Debtors Act 1869; or

(b) under section 110,

is sent by the registrar of a home court to the registrar of another court for execution under this section, the judge of that other court shall have the same powers to order the debtor's discharge as the judge of the home court would have under section 110 or 121.

Note. This section contains provisions formerly in County Courts Act 1959, s 161. Words 'rules of court' in square brackets substituted for words 'county court rules' in italics by Civil Court Procedure Act 1997, s 10, Sch 2, para 2(1)–(3) as from 26 April 1999 (SI 1999 No 1009).

* * * * *

PART IX

MISCELLANEOUS AND GENERAL

Summonses and other documents

133. Proof of service of summonses etc—(1) Where any summons or other process issued from a county court is served by an officer of a court, the service may be proved by a certificate in a prescribed form *under the hand of that officer* showing the fact and mode of the service.

(2) Any officer of a court wilfully and corruptly giving a false certificate under subsection (1) in respect of the service of a summons or other process shall be guilty of an offence and, on conviction thereof, shall be removed from office and shall be liable—

(a) on conviction on indictment, to imprisonment for any term not exceeding 2 years; or

(b) on summary conviction, to imprisonment for any term not exceeding 6 months or to a fine not exceeding the statutory maximum or to both such imprisonment and fine.

Note. This section contains provisions formerly in County Courts Act 1959, s 186, as amended by Administration of Justice Act 1977, s 20. In sub-s (1) words in italics repealed by SI 1998 No 2940, art 6(e), as from 26 April 1999.

* * * * *

134. ...

Note. This section repealed by SI 1998 No 2940, art 6(f), as from 26 April 1999.

* * * * *

Power to raise limits of jurisdiction

145. Power to raise county court limit—(1) If it appears to Her Majesty in Council that the county court limit for the purposes of any enactment referring to that limit should be increased, Her Majesty may by Order in Council direct that the county court limit for the purposes of that enactment shall be such sum as may be specified in the Order.

(2) An Order under subsection (1) may contain such incidental or transitional provisions as Her Majesty considers appropriate.

(3) No recommendation shall be made to Her Majesty in Council to make an Order under this section unless a draft of the Order has been laid before Parliament and approved by resolution of each House of Parliament.

Note. This section contains provisions formerly in County Courts Act 1959, s 192, as substituted by Administration of Justice Act 1982, s 37, Sch 3, para 7.

*   *   *   *   *

147. Interpretation—(1) In this Act, unless the context otherwise requires—

'action' means any proceedings in a county court which may be commenced as prescribed by plaint;

'Admiralty county court' means a county court appointed to have Admiralty jurisdiction by order under this Act;

'Admiralty proceedings' means proceedings in which the claim would not be within the jurisdiction of a county court but for sections 26 and 27;

'bailiff' includes a registrar;

'the county court limit' means—

(a) in relation to any enactment contained in this Act for which a limit is for the time being specified by an Order under section 145, that limit,

(b) (*subject to paragraph (a)*), *in sections 21(1), 21(2)(a) and (b) and 139(2), £1000, and*

(c) in relation to any enactment contained in this Act and not within paragraph (a) *or (b)*, the county court limit for the time being specified by any other Order in Council or order defining the limit of county court jurisdiction for the purposes of that enactment;

'county court rules' means rules made under section 75;

'court' and 'county court' mean a court held for a district under this Act;

'deposit-taking institution' means any person carrying on a business which is a deposit-taking business for the purposes of the Banking Act 1979 [the Banking Act 1987];

['deposit-taking institution' means a person who may, in the course of his business, lawfully accept deposits in the United Kingdom;]

'district' and 'county court district' mean a district for which a court is to be held under section 2;

'fees orders' means orders made under section 128;

'hearing' includes trial, and 'hear' and 'heard' shall be construed accordingly;

'hereditament' includes both a corporeal and an incorporeal hereditament;

'judge', in relation to a county court, means a judge assigned to the district of that court under subsection (1) of section 5 and any person sitting as a judge for that district under subsection (3) or (4) of that section;

'judgment summons' means a summons issued on the application of a person entitled to enforce a judgment or order under section 5 of the Debtors Act 1869 requiring a person, or where two or more persons are liable under the judgment or order, requiring any one or more of them, *to appear and be examined on oath as to his or their means* [to attend court];

'landlord', in relation to any land, means the person entitled to the immediate reversion or, if the property therein is held in joint tenancy, any of the persons entitled to the immediate reversion;

['legal representative' means an authorised advocate or authorised litigator, as
  defined by section 119(1) of the Courts and Legal Services Act 1990;]
'*matrimonial cause*' *has the meaning assigned to it by section 10(1) of the Matrimonial
  Causes Act 1967;*
'matter' means every proceeding in a county court which may be commenced as
  prescribed otherwise than by plaint;
'officer', in relation to a court, means any registrar, deputy registrar, or assistant
  registrar of that court, and any clerk, bailiff, usher or messenger in the service
  of that court;
'part-time registrar' and 'part-time assistant registrar' have the meaning assigned
  to them by section 10(3);
'party' includes every person served with notice of, or attending, any proceeding,
  whether named as a party to that proceeding or not;
'prescribed' means prescribed by county court rules;
'probate proceedings' means proceedings brought in a county court by virtue of
  section 32 or transferred to that court under section 40;
'proceedings' includes both actions and matters;
'registrar' and 'registrar of a county court' mean a registrar appointed for a
  district under this Act, or in a case where two or more registrars are appointed
  jointly, either or any of those registrars;
'return day' means the day appointed in any summons or proceeding for the
  appearance of the defendant or any other day fixed for the hearing of any
  proceedings;
'*the rule committee*' *means the committee constituted under section 75;*
'ship' includes any description of vessel used in navigation;
'solicitor' means solicitor of the Supreme Court;
'*standard scale*' *has the meaning given by section 75 of the Criminal Justice Act 1982;
  and*
'*statutory maximum*' *has the meaning given by section 74 of that Act.*
    [(1A) the definition of deposit-taking institution' in subsection (1) must be read
with—
    (a)   section 22 of the Financial Services and Markets Act 2000;
    (b)   any relevant order under that section; and
    (c)   Schedule 2 to that Act.]
    (*2*) *For the purposes of this Act, the net annual value for rating of any property shall be
determined as at the time when the relevant proceedings are commenced, except in a case
where it is otherwise expressly provided, and, subject to subsection (3), by reference to the
valuation list in force at the time in question.*
    (*3*) *Where the property of which the value is in question does not consist of one or more
hereditaments having at the time in question a separate net annual value for rating, the
property or such part of it as does not so consist—*
    (*a*)   *shall, for the purpose of entitling a county court to exercise jurisdiction (but not
        for any other purpose), be taken to have a net annual value for rating not
        exceeding that of any such hereditament of which at the time in question it forms
        part; and*
    (*b*)   *subject to paragraph (a), shall be taken to have a net annual value for rating equal
        to its value by the year.*
    (4)   Until the coming into force of the first Order under section 145 which
specifies the county court limit for the purposes of any enactment the definition of
'the county court limit' in subsection (1) shall have effect in relation to that
enactment as if the reference to an Order under section 145 were a reference to
any Order in Council or order defining the limit of county court jurisdiction for
the purposes of that enactment.

Note. This section contains provisions formerly in County Courts Act 1959, s 201, as amended
by Supreme Court Act 1981, Sch 3, para 29.

Para (b) and words in italics in para (c) in definition 'the county court limit' repealed by High Court and County Courts Jurisdiction Order 1991, SI 1991 No 724, art 2(8), Schedule, as from 1 July 1991.

Definitions 'county court rules' and 'the rule committee' repealed by Civil Procedure Act 1997, s 10, Sch 2, para 2(1), (9), as from 26 April 1999 (SI 1999 No 1009).

Definition 'deposit-taking institution' substituted by SI 2001 No 3649, art 296(1), (2), as from 1 December 2001.

Definition 'fees orders' repealed by Courts Act 2003, s 109(1), (3), Sch 8, para 227, Sch 10, as from a date to be appointed.

Definition 'judgment summons' amended by SI 2002 No 439, art 9, as from 25 March 2002.

Definition 'matrimonial cause' repealed by Matrimonial and Family Proceedings Act 1984, s 46(3), Sch 3, as from 28 April 1986. As from that date see s 32 of that Act.

Definition 'legal representatives' inserted by Courts and Legal Services Act 1990, s 125(3), Sch 18, para 49(1), as from 1 April 1991. Definitions 'standard scale' and 'statutory maximum' repealed by Statute Law (Repeals) Act 1993, as from 5 November 1993. Sub-ss (2), (3) repealed by Local Government Finance (Repeals, Savings and Consequential Amendments) Order 1990, SI 1990 No 776, art 3(1), Sch 1.

Sub-s (1A) inserted by SI 2001 No 3649, art 296(1), (3), as from 1 December 2001.

* * * * *

148. Amendments of other Acts, transitional provisions, savings and repeals— (1) The enactments specified in Schedule 2 shall have effect subject to the amendments there specified.

(2) This Act shall have effect subject to the transitory provisions and transitional provisions and savings contained in Schedule 3.

(3) The enactments specified in Schedule 4 are hereby repealed to the extent specified in the third column of that Schedule.

* * * * *

149. Extent—(1) Section 148(1) and Schedule 2 extend to Scotland so far as they amend enactments extending to Scotland.

(2) Section 148(1) and Schedule 2 extend to Northern Ireland so far as they amend enactments extending to Northern Ireland.

(3) Subject to subsections (1) and (2), this Act extends to England and Wales only.

150. Commencement. This Act shall come into force on 1st August 1984.

151. Short title. This Act may be cited as the County Courts Act 1984.

SCHEDULE 2

AMENDMENTS OF OTHER ENACTMENTS

(*The amendments made by this Schedule insofar as they effect provisions printed in this work have been incorporated.*)

SCHEDULE 3

TRANSITORY AND TRANSITIONAL PROVISIONS AND SAVINGS

* * * * *

Sections 105(1) and 106 of this Act

3. (*1*) *Until the day appointed under section 76 of the Administration of Justice Act 1982 for the coming into force of section 34(1) of that Act, for section 105(1) of this Act there shall be substituted the following—*

'(*1*) *A judgment or order of the High Court for the payment of money to a person, and any judgment, order, decree or award (however called) of any court or arbitrator (including any foreign court or foreign arbitrator) being a judgment, order, decree or award for the payment of money to a person which is or has become enforceable (whether wholly or to a limited extent) as if it were a judgment or order of the High Court shall, on an application's being made to the county court by the party prosecuting the judgment, be enforceable under section 85 as if it were a judgment of that court, and the remainder of the foregoing provisions of this Part of this Act (including the provisions relating to the staying of execution) shall have effect accordingly in relation to the enforcement under the said section 85.*'

Note. Repealed by Statute Law (Repeals) Act 1989.

*   *   *   *   *

Saving for certain provisions of the County Courts Act 1959

10. *The repeal by this Act of sections 199A, 201, 205(1), (2) and 208(1), (2) of the County Courts Act 1959 shall not have effect until the day appointed under section 76(1) of the Administration of Justice Act 1982 for the coming into force of section 75 of that Act in relation to sections 99(3), 168 to 174A and 176 of the County Courts Act 1959.*

Note. Repealed by Statute Law (Repeals) Act 1989.

*   *   *   *   *

SCHEDULE 4

REPEALS

Chapter	Short Title	Extent of Repeal
7 & 8 Eliz 2 c 22.	County Courts Act 1959.	The whole Act, except section 99(3), sections 168 to 174, 174A and 176.
10 & 11 Eliz 2 c 48.	Law Reform (Husband and Wife) Act 1962.	In section 1(3) the words from 'and' to the end.
	* * * * *	
1969 c 46.	Family Law Reform Act 1969.	In Schedule 1 the entry relating to the County Courts Act 1959.
1969 c 58.	Administration of Justice Act 1969.	Sections 1 to 9. Section 11. Section 20(1) to (4), (6). In section 34(3) the words from the beginning to '1947 and', in their application to section 20 as regards county court rules under section 102 of the County Courts Act 1959.
1970 c 31.	Administration of Justice Act 1970.	Section 29(5)(a). Sections 37 to 38. Section 45(2). In Schedule 2, paragraphs 21 to 24.
1971 c 23.	Courts Act 1971.	Section 20(1) to (4).

*   *   *   *   *

Chapter	Short Title	Extent of Repeal
1977 c 38.	Administration of Justice Act 1977.	Sections 13 to 16. Section 17(1). Section 18. Sections 19(1), (3) and (4). Section 20.
	* * * * *	
1979 c 53.	Charging Orders Act 1979.	Section 7(1) and (2) so far as that subsection relates to the County Courts Act 1959.
1980 c 43.	Magistrates' Courts Act 1980.	In Schedule 6A the entries relating to the County Courts Act 1959. In Schedule 7, paragraph 28.
1981 c 49.	Contempt of Court Act 1981.	In Schedule 2 Part III, paragraphs 2 to 5.
1981 c 54.	Supreme Court Act 1981.	Sections 33 to 35 so far as they relate to county courts. Section 149. Schedule 3. In Schedule 5 the entry relating to the Administration of Justice Act 1970. In Schedule 7 the entries relating to the County Courts Act 1959.
	* * * * *	
1982 c 53.	Administration of Justice Act 1982.	Section 15(2). Part V except sections 34, 35 and 37. Section 55(2). In Schedule 1 Part II. In Schedule 3, paragraphs 1, 1, 3(a) and 5. In Schedule 4 Part II.

CHILD ABDUCTION ACT 1984

(1984 c 37)

An Act to amend the criminal law relating to the abduction of children.

[12 July 1984]

PART I

OFFENCES UNDER LAW OF ENGLAND AND WALES

1. Offence of abduction of child by parent, etc—(1) Subject to subsections (5) and (8) below, a person connected with a child under the age of sixteen commits an offence if he takes or sends the child out of the United Kingdom without the appropriate consent.

(2) *A person is connected with a child for the purposes of this section if—*

(a) *he is a parent or guardian of the child; or*

(b) *there is in force an order of a court in England and Wales [a court in the United Kingdom] awarding custody of the child to him, whether solely or jointly with any other person; or*

(c) *in the case of an illegitimate child, there are reasonable grounds for believing that he is the father of the child.*

Note. Words in square brackets substituted for words 'a court in England and Wales' by Family Law Act 1986, s 65, as from 7 January 1987.

(3) *In this section 'the appropriate consent', in relation to a child, means—*

(a) *the consent of each person—*

(i) *who is a parent or guardian of the child; or*

(ii) *to whom custody of the child has been awarded (whether solely or jointly with any other person) by an order of a court in England or Wales [a court in the United Kingdom]; or*

(b) *if the child is the subject of such a custody order, the leave of the court which made the order; or*

(c) *the leave of the court granted on an application for a direction under section 7 of the Guardianship of Minors Act 1971 or section 1(3) of the Guardianship Act 1973.*

Note. Words in square brackets substituted for words 'a court in England and Wales' by Family Law Act 1986, s 65, as from 7 January 1987.

(4) *In the case of a custody order made by a magistrates' court, subsection (3)(b) above shall be construed as if the reference to the court which made the order included a reference to any magistrates' court acting for the same petty sessions area as that court.*

[(2) A person is connected with a child for the purposes of this section if—

(a) he is a parent of the child; or

(b) in the case of a child whose parents were not married to each other at the time of his birth, there are reasonable grounds for believing that he is the father of the child; or

(c) he is a guardian of the child; or

[(ca) he is special guardian of the child; or]

(d) he is a person in whose favour a residence order is in force with respect to the child; or

(e) he has custody of the child.

(3) In this section 'the appropriate consent', in relation to a child, means—

(a) the consent of each of the following—

(i) the child's mother;

(ii) the child's father, if he has parental responsibility for him;

(iii) any guardian of the child;

[(iiia) any special guardian of the child;]

(iv) any person in whose favour a residence order is in force with respect to the child;

(v) any person who has custody of the child; or

(b) the leave of the court granted under or by virtue of any provision of Part II of the Children Act 1989; or

(c) if any person has custody of the child, the leave of the court which awarded custody to him.

(4) A person does not commit an offence under this section by taking or sending a child out of the United Kingdom without obtaining the appropriate consent if—

(a) *he is a person in whose favour there is a residence order in force with respect to the child, and*

(b) *he takes or sends him out of the United Kingdom for a period of less than one month.*

[(a) he is a person in whose favour there is a residence order in force with respect to the child, and he takes or sends the child out of the United Kingdom for a period of less than one month; or

(b) he is a special guardian of the child and he takes or sends the child out of the United Kingdom for a period of less than three months].

(4A) Subsection (4) above does not apply if the person taking or sending the child out of the United Kingdom does so in breach of an order under Part II of the Children Act 1989.]

Note. Sub-ss (2)–(4A) in square brackets substituted for original sub-ss (2)–(4) in italics by Children Act 1989, s 108(4), Sch 12, para 37(1), (2), as from 14 October 1991. Sub-s (2)(ca) in square brackets inserted by Adoption and Children Act 2002, s 139(1), Sch 3, para 42, as from a day to be appointed. Sub-s (3)(a)(iiia) in square brackets inserted by Adoption and Children Act 2002, s 139(1), Sch 3, para 42, as from a day to be appointed. Sub-s (4)(a), (b) in square brackets substituted for sub-s 4(a), (b) in italics by Adoption and Children Act 2002, s 139(1), Sch 3, para 42, as from a date to be appointed.

(5) A person does not commit an offence under this section by doing anything without the consent of another person whose consent is required under the foregoing provisions if—
  (a) he does it in the belief that the other person—
    (i) has consented; or
    (ii) would consent if he was aware of all the relevant circumstances; or
  (b) he has taken all reasonable steps to communicate with the other person but has been unable to communicate with him; or
  (c) the other person has unreasonably refused to consent;
but paragraph (c) of this subsection does not apply where what is done relates to a child who is the subject of a custody order made by a court in England and Wales [*a court in the United Kingdom*], *or where the person who does it acts in breach of any direction under section 7 of the Guardianship of Minors Act 1971 or section 1(3) of the Guardianship Act 1973.*
  [(5A) Subsection (5)(c) above does not apply if—
  (a) the person who refused to consent is a person—
    (i) in whose favour there is a residence order in force with respect to the child; *or*
    [(ia) who is a special guardian of the child; or]
    (ii) who has custody of the child; or
  (b) the person taking or sending the child out of the United Kingdom is, by so acting, in breach of an order made by a court in the United Kingdom.]

Note. Words in square brackets substituted for words 'a court in England and Wales' by Family Law Act 1986, s 65, as from 7 January 1987. Sub-s (5A) in square brackets substituted for the words 'but' to the end in italics in sub-s (5) by Children Act 1989, s 108(4), Sch 12, para 37(1), (3), as from 14 October 1991. In sub-s (5A)(a)(i) word 'or' in italics repealed by Adoption and Children Act 2002, s 139(1), (3), Sch 3, para 42, as from a date to be appointed. Sub-s (5A)(a)(ia) inserted by Adoption and Children Act 2002, s 139(1), Sch 3, para 42, as from a date to be appointed.

(6) Where, in proceedings for an offence under this section, there is sufficient evidence to raise an issue as to the application of subsection (5) above, it shall be for the prosecution to prove that that subsection does not apply.
  (*7*) *In this section—*
  (*a*) *'guardian' means a person appointed by deed or will or by order of a court of competent jurisdiction to be the guardian of a child; and*
  (*b*) *a reference to a custody order or an order awarding custody includes a reference to an order awarding legal custody and a reference to an order awarding care and control.*
  [(7) For the purposes of this section—
  (a) 'guardian of a child', ['special guardian',] 'residence order' and 'parental responsibility' have the same meaning as in the Children Act 1989; and
  (b) a person shall be treated as having custody of a child if there is in force an order of a court in the United Kingdom awarding him (whether solely or jointly with another person) custody, legal custody or care and control of the child.]

Note. Sub-s (7) in square brackets substituted for sub-s (7) in italics by Children Act 1989, s 108(4), Sch 12, para 37(1), (4), as from 14 October 1991.

(8) This section shall have effect subject to the provisions of the Schedule to this Act in relation to a child who is in the care of a local authority *or voluntary organisation or who is committed to a place of safety or who is the subject of custodianship proceedings or* [detained in a place of safety, remanded to a local authority accommodation or the subject of] proceedings or an order relating to adoption.

Note. Words in square brackets substituted for words in italics by Children Act 1989, s 108(4), Sch 12, para 37(1), (5), as from 14 October 1991. In sub-s (7)(a) word "special guardian"," in square brackets inserted by Adoption and Children Act 2002, s 139(1), Sch 3, para 42, as from a date to be appointed.

2. Offence of abduction of child by other persons—(1) *Subject to subsection (2) below, a person not falling within section 1(2)(a) or (b) above* [Subject to subsection (3) below, a person, other than one mentioned in subsection (2) below] commits an offence if, without lawful authority or reasonable excuse, he takes or detains a child under the age of sixteen—

    (a) so as to remove him from the lawful control of any person having lawful control of the child; or

    (b) so as to keep him out of the lawful control of any person entitled to lawful control of the child.

(2) In proceedings against any person for an offence under this section, it shall be a defence for that person to show that at the time of the alleged offence—

    (a) he believed that the child had attained the age of sixteen; or

    (b) in the case of an illegitimate child, he had reasonable grounds for believing himself to be the child's father.

[(2) The persons are—

    (a) where the father and mother of the child in question were married to each other at the time of his birth, the child's father and mother;

    (b) where the father and mother of the child in question were not married to each other at the time of his birth, the child's mother; and

    (c) any other person mentioned in section 1(2)(c) to (e) above.

(3) In proceedings against any person for an offence under this section, it shall be a defence for that person to prove—

    (a) where the father and mother of the child in question were not married to each other at the time of his birth—

        (i) that he is the child's father; or

        (ii) that, at the time of the alleged offence, he believed, on reasonable grounds that he was the child's father; or

    (b) that, at the time of the alleged offence, he believed that the child had attained the age of sixteen.

Note. Words in square brackets in sub-s (1) substituted for words in italics by Children Act 1989, s 108(4), Sch 12, para 38(1), as from 14 October 1991. Sub-ss (2), (3) in square brackets substituted for original sub-s (2) in italics by s 108(4) of, and Sch 12, para 38(2) to the 1989 Act, as from the same date.

3. Construction of references to taking, sending and detaining. For the purposes of this Part of this Act—

    (a) a person shall be regarded as taking a child if he causes or induces the child to accompany him or any other person or causes the child to be taken;

    (b) a person shall be regarded as sending a child if he causes the child to be sent; *and*

Note. Word 'and' immediately preceding para (c) in italics repealed by Children Act 1989, s 108(7), Sch 15, as from 14 October 1991.

(c) a person shall be regarded as detaining a child if he causes the child to be detained or induces the child to remain with him or any other person.]

[and

(d) references to a child's parents and to a child whose parents were (or were not) married to each other at the time of his birth shall be construed in accordance with section 1 of the Family Law Reform Act 1987 (which extends their meaning).]

Note. Word 'and' and para (d) added by Children Act 1989, s 108(4), Sch 12, para 39, as from 14 October 1991.

4. Penalties and prosecutions—(1) A person guilty of an offence under this Part of this Act shall be liable—

(a) on summary conviction, to imprisonment for a term not exceeding six months or to a fine not exceeding the statutory maximum, *as defined in section 74 of the Criminal Justice Act 1982*, or to both such imprisonment and fine;

(b) on conviction on indictment, to imprisonment for a term not exceeding seven years.

(2) No prosecution for an offence under section 1 above shall be instituted except by or with the consent of the Director of Public Prosecutions.

Note. Words in italics repealed by Statute Law (Repeals) Act 1993, s 1(1), Sch 1, Part XIV, as from 5 November 1993.

5. Restriction on prosecutions for offence of kidnapping. Except by or with the consent of the Director of Public Prosecutions no prosecution shall be instituted for an offence of kidnapping if it was committed—

(a) against a child under the age of sixteen; and

(b) by a person connected with the child, within the meaning of section 1 above.

6–10. (*Apply to Scotland.*)

PART III

SUPPLEMENTARY

11. Consequential amendments and repeals—(1), (2) (*Sub-s (1) amends Visiting Forces Act 1952, Schedule, para 1(b); sub-s (2) inserts para 2A in Firearms Act 1968, Sch 1.*)

(3) The reference to abduction in section 1(1) of the Internationally Protected Persons Act 1978 [and sections 63B(2) and 63C(2) of the Terrorism Act 2000] shall be construed as not including an offence under section 1 above or any corresponding provisions in force in Northern Ireland or Part II of this Act.

Note. Words 'and sections 63B(2) and 63C(2) of the Terrorism Act 2000" in square brackets inserted by Crime (International Co-operation) Act 2003, s 91(1), Sch 5, paras 9, 10, as from 26 April 2004.

(4), (5) (*Sub-s (4) amends Suppression of Terrorism Act 1978, s 4(1)(a), and inserts para 11B in Sch 1 to that Act; sub-s (5) repeals Offences Against the Person Act 1861, s 56, and also repeals in part Extradition Act 1870, Sch 1, and in part Firearms Act 1968, Sch 1.*)

12. Enactment of corresponding provision for Northern Ireland. An Order in Council under paragraph 1(1)(b) of Schedule 1 to the Northern Ireland Act 1974 (legislation for Northern Ireland in the interim period) which contains a statement that it operates only so as to make for Northern Ireland provision corresponding to Part I of this Act—

(a) shall not be subject to paragraph 1(4) and (5) of that Schedule (affirmative resolution of both Houses of Parliament); but

(b) shall be subject to annulment in pursuance of a resolution of either House.

13. Short title, commencement and extent—(1) This Act may be cited as the Child Abduction Act 1984.

(2) This Act shall come into force at the end of the period of three months beginning with the day on which it is passed.

(3) Part I of this Act extends to England and Wales only, Part II extends to Scotland only and in Part III section 11(1) and (5)(a) and section 12 do not extend to Scotland and section 11(1), (2) and (5)(a) and (c) does not extend to Northern Ireland.

SCHEDULE   Section 1(8)

MODIFICATIONS OF SECTION 1 FOR CHILDREN IN CERTAIN CASES

Children in care of local authorities and voluntary organisations

1.   (1) This paragraph applies in the case of a child who is in the care of a local authority *or voluntary organisation* [within the meaning of the Children Act 1989] in England or Wales.

(2) Where this paragraph applies, section 1 of this Act shall have effect as if—

(a) the reference in subsection (1) to the appropriate consent were a reference to the consent of the local authority *or voluntary organisation* in whose care the child is; and

(b) subsections (3) to (6) were omitted.

Note. Words in square brackets substituted for words in italics and words in italics in para 1(2)(a) repealed by Children Act 1989, s 108(4), (7), Sch 12, para 40(1), (2), Sch 15, as from 14 October 1991.

Children in places of safety

2.   *(1) This paragraph applies in the case of a child who is committed to a place of safety in England or Wales in pursuance of—*

(a)   section 40 of the Children and Young Persons Act 1933; or

(b)   section 43 of the Adoption Act 1958; or

(c)   section 2(5) or (10), 16(3) or 28(1) or (4) of the Children and Young Persons Act 1969; or

(d)   section 12 of the Foster Children Act 1980.

(2)   Where this paragraph applies, section 1 of this Act shall have effect as if—

(a)   the reference in subsection (1) to the appropriate consent were a reference to the leave of any magistrates' court acting for the area in which the place of safety is; and

(b)   subsections (3) to (6) were omitted.

[(1)   This paragraph applies in the case of a child who is—

(a)   detained in a place of safety under *section 16(3) of the Children and Young Persons Act 1969* [paragraph 7(4) of Schedule 7 to the Powers of Criminal Courts (Sentencing) Act 2000]; or

(b)   remanded to local authority accommodation under section 23 of *that Act* [the Children and Young Persons Act 1969].]

Note. Para 2(1) in square brackets substituted for para 2(1) in italics by Children Act 1989, s 108(4), Sch 12, para 40(1), (3), as from 14 October 1991. Words in square brackets in sub-paras (1)(a), (b) substituted for words in italics by Powers of Criminal Courts (Sentencing) Act 2000, s 165(1), Sch 9, para 93, as from 25 August 2000.

Adoption and custodianship

3.   *(1) This paragraph applies in the case of a child—*

(a)   who is the subject of an order under section 14 of the Children Act 1975 [section 18 of the Adoption Act 1976] freeing him for adoption; or

(b)   who is the subject of a pending application for such an order; or

(c)   *who is the subject of a pending application for an adoption order; or*

(d)   *who is the subject of an order under section 25 of the Children Act 1975 or section 53 of the Adoption Act 1958 [section 55 of the Adoption Act 1976] relating to adoption abroad or of a pending application for such an order; or*

(e)   *who is the subject of a pending application for a custodianship order.*

(2)   *Where this paragraph applies, section 1 of this Act shall have effect as if—*

(a)   *the reference in subsection (1) to the appropriate consent were a reference—*

     (i)   *in a case within sub-paragraph (1)(a) above, to the consent of the adoption agency which made the application for the order or, if the parental rights and duties in respect of the child have been transferred from that agency to another agency by an order under section 23 of the Children Act 1975 [section 18 order or, if the section 18 order has been varied under section 21 of that Act so as to give parental responsibility to another agency], to the consent of that other agency;*

     (ii)   *in a case within sub-paragraph (1)(b), (c) or (e) [or (c)] above, to the leave of the court to which the application was made; and*

     (iii)   *in a case within sub-paragraph (1)(d) above, to the leave of the court which made the order or, as the case may be, to which the application was made; and*

(b)   *subsections (3) to (6) were omitted.*

[(1)   This paragraph applies where—

(a)   a child is placed for adoption by an adoption agency under section 19 of the Adoption and Children Act 2002, or an adoption agency is authorised to place the child for adoption under that section; or

(b)   a placement order is in force in respect of the child; or

(c)   an application for such an order has been made in respect of the child and has not been disposed of; or

(d)   an application for an adoption order has been made in respect of the child and has not been disposed of; or

(e)   an order under section 84 of the Adoption and Children Act 2002 (giving parental responsibility prior to adoption abroad) has been made in respect of the child, or an application for such an order in respect of him has been made and has not been disposed of.

(2)   Where this paragraph applies, section 1 of this Act shall have effect as if—

(a)   the reference in subsection (1) to the appropriate consent were—

     (i)   in a case within sub-paragraph (1)(a) above, a reference to the consent of each person who has parental responsibility for the child or to the leave of the High Court;

     (ii)   in a case within sub-paragraph (1)(b) above, a reference to the leave of the court which made the placement order;

     (iii)   in a case within sub-paragraph (1)(c) or (d) above, a reference to the leave of the court to which the application was made;

     (iv)   in a case within sub-paragraph (1)(e) above, a reference to the leave of the court which made the order or, as the case may be, to which the application was made;

(b)   subsection (3) were omitted;

(c)   in subsection (4), in paragraph (a), for the words from 'in whose favour' to the first mention of 'child' there were substituted 'who provides the child's home in a case falling within sub-paragraph (1)(a) or (b) of paragraph 3 of the Schedule to this Act'; and

(d)   subsections (4A), (5), (5A) and (6) were omitted.]

[(3)   Sub-paragraph (2) above shall be construed as if the references to the court included, in any case where the court is a magistrates' court, a reference to any magistrates' court acting for the same area as that court.]

Note. Words in square brackets in sub-paras (1)(a), (d), (2)(a)(i), (ii) substituted for words 'section 14 of the Children Act 1975', 'section 25 of the Children Act 1975 or section 53 of the Adoption Act 1958', 'order or, if the ... section 23 of the Children Act 1975' and '(c) or (e)' respectively by Children Act 1989, s 108(4), Sch 12, para 40(1), (4), (5), as from 14 October 1991. Sub-para (1)(e) repealed by s 108(7) of, and Sch 15 to, the 1989 Act, as from the same date. Sub-para (3) added by s 108(4) of, and Sch 12, para 40(1), (6) to, the 1989 Act, as from the same date. Sub-paras (1), (2) substituted by Adoption and Children Act 2002, Sch 3, para 43, as from a day to be appointed

Cases within paragraphs 1 and 3

4. In the case of a child falling within both paragraph 1 and paragraph 3 above, the provisions of paragraph 3 shall apply to the exclusion of those in paragraph 1.

Interpretation

5.   (*1*)   *In this Schedule—*
  (*a*)   *subject to sub-paragraph (2) below, 'adoption agency' has the same meaning as in section 1 of the Children Act 1975;*
  (*b*)   *'adoption order' means as an order under section 8(1) of that Act;*
  (*c*)   *'custodianship order' has the same meaning as in Part II of that Act; and*
  (*d*)   *'local authority' and 'voluntary organisation' have the same meanings as in section 87 of the Child Care Act 1980.*
  (*2*)   *Until the coming into force of section 1 of the Children Act 1975, for the words 'adoption agency' in this Schedule there shall be substituted 'approved adoption society or local authority'; and in this Schedule 'approved adoption society' means an adoption society approved under Part I of that Act.*
  (*3*)   *In paragraph 3(1) above references to an order or to an application for an order are references to an order made by, or to an application to, a court in England or Wales.*
  (*4*)   *Paragraph 3(2) above shall be construed as if the references to the court included, in any case where the court is a magistrates' court, a reference to any magistrates' court acting for the same petty sessions area as that court.*
[**5.** In this Schedule—
  (a)   'adoption agency' *and 'adoption order' have the same meaning as in the Adoption Act 1976; and* [, 'adoption order', 'placed for adoption by an adoption agency' and 'placement order' have the same meaning as in the Adoption and Children Act 2002; and]
  (b)   'area', in relation to a magistrates' court, means the petty sessions area (within the meaning of *the Justices of the Peace Act 1979* [the Justices of the Peace Act 1997]) for which the court is appointed.]

Note. Para 5 in square brackets substituted for para 5 in italics by Children Act 1989, s 108(4), Sch 12, para 40(1), (7), as from 14 October 1991. In sub-para 5(b) words in square brackets substituted for words in italics by Justices of the Peace Act 1997, s 73(2), Sch 5, para 20, as from 19 June 1997. In sub-para 5(a) word in square brackets substituted for words in italics by Adoption and Children Act 2002, Sch 3 para 42, as from a day to be appointed.

Commencement. In force 12 October 1984.

CAPITAL TRANSFER TAX ACT 1984 [INHERITANCE TAX ACT 1984]

(1984 c 51)

Note. Short title substituted by virtue of Finance Act 1986, s 100. References to capital transfer tax in this Act to have effect as references to inheritance tax in relation to liabilities arising after 25 July 1986 by virtue of Finance Act 1986, s 100.

An Act to consolidate provisions of Part III of the Finance Act 1975 and other enactments relating to capital transfer tax.   [31 July 1984]

PART I

GENERAL

Main charges and definitions

1. Charge on transfers. Capital transfer tax shall be charged on the value transferred by a chargeable transfer.

Note. See the Finance Act 1986, s 100(1), (2) (the reference to capital transfer tax must be read as a reference to inheritance tax in respect of a liability to tax arising on or after 25 July 1986).

2. Chargeable transfers and exempt transfers—(1) A chargeable transfer is a transfer of value which is made by an individual but is not (by virtue of Part II of this Act or any other enactment) an exempt transfer.

(2) A transfer of value made by an individual and exempt only to a limited extent—

(a) is, if all the value transferred by it is within the limit, an exempt transfer, and

(b) is, if that value is partly within and partly outside the limit, a chargeable transfer of so much of that value as is outside the limit as well as an exempt transfer of so much of that value as is within the limit.

(3) Except where the context otherwise requires, references in this Act to chargeable transfers, to their making or to the values transferred by them shall be construed as including references to occasions on which tax is chargeable under Chapter III of Part III of this Act (apart from section 79), to their occurrence or to the amounts on which tax is then chargeable.

3. Transfers of value—(1) Subject to the following provisions of this Part of this Act, a transfer of value is a disposition made by a person (the transferor) as a result of which the value of his estate immediately after the disposition is less than it would be but for the disposition; and the amount by which it is less is the value transferred by the transfer.

(2) For the purposes of subsection (1) above no account shall be taken of the value of excluded property which ceases to form part of a person's estate as a result of a disposition.

(3) Where the value of a person's estate is diminished and that of another person's estate, or of settled property in which no interest in possession subsists, is increased by the first-mentioned person's omission to exercise a right, he shall be treated for the purposes of this section as having made a disposition at the time (or latest time) when he could have exercised the right, unless it is shown that the omission was not deliberate.

(4) Except as otherwise provided, references in this Act to a transfer of value made, or made by any person, include references to events on the happening of which tax is chargeable as if a transfer of value had been made, or, as the case may be, had been made by that person; and 'transferor' shall be construed accordingly.

*   *   *   *   *

5. Meaning of estate—(1) For the purposes of this Act a person's estate is the aggregate of all the property to which he is beneficially entitled, except that the estate of a person immediately before his death does not include excluded property.

(2) A person who has a general power which enables him, or would if he were sui juris enable him, to dispose of any property other than settled property, or to charge money on any property other than settled property, shall be treated as beneficially entitled to the property or money; and for this purpose 'general power' means a power or authority enabling the person by whom it is exercisable to appoint or dispose of property as he thinks fit.

(3) In determining the value of a person's estate at any time his liabilities at that time shall be taken into account, except as otherwise provided by this Act.

(4) The liabilities to be taken into account in determining the value of a transferor's estate immediately after a transfer of value include his liability for capital transfer tax on the value transferred but not his liability (if any) for any other tax or duty resulting from the transfer.

(5) Except in the case of a liability imposed by law, a liability incurred by a transferor shall be taken into account only to the extent that it was incurred for a consideration in money or money's worth.

Note. See the Finance Act 1986, s 100(1), (2) (the reference to capital transfer tax must be read as a reference to inheritance tax in respect of a liability to tax arising on or after 25 July 1986).

6. Excluded property—(1) Property situated outside the United Kingdom is excluded property if the person beneficially entitled to it is an individual domiciled outside the United Kingdom.

(2) Where securities have been issued by the Treasury subject to a condition authorised by section 22 of the Finance (No 2) Act 1931 (or section 47 of the Finance (No 2) Act 1915) for exemption from taxation so long as the securities are in the beneficial ownership of persons *neither domiciled nor ordinarily resident in the United Kingdom* [of a description specified in the condition], the securities are excluded property if they are in the beneficial ownership of such a person.

(3) Where the person beneficially entitled to the rights conferred by any of the following, namely—

(a) war savings certificates;

(b) national savings certificates (including Ulster savings certificates);

(c) premium savings bonds;

(d) deposits with the National Savings Bank or with a trustee savings bank;

(e) a certified contractual savings scheme within the meaning of section *415 of the Taxes Act* [326 of the Taxes Act 1988];

is domiciled in the Channel Islands or the Isle of Man, the rights are excluded property.

(4) Property to which this subsection applies by virtue of section 155(1) below is excluded property.

Note. Sub-s (2): words in square brackets substituted for words in italics by the Finance Act 1996, s 154, Sch 28, para 7, as from 31 March 1996.

Sub-s (3): in para (e) words in square brackets substituted for words in italics by Income and Corporation Taxes Act 1988, s 844(1), Sch 29, para 32, as from 6 April 1988.

*   *   *   *   *

Dispositions that are not transfers of value

10. Dispositions not intended to confer gratuitous benefit—(1) A disposition is not a transfer of value if it is shown that it was not intended, and was not made in a transaction intended, to confer any gratuitous benefit on any person and either—

(a) that it was made in a transaction at arm's length between persons not connected with each other, or

(b) that it was such as might be expected to be made in a transaction at arm's length between persons not connected with each other.

(2) Subsection (1) above shall not apply to a sale of *shares or debentures not quoted on a recognised stock exchange* [unquoted shares or unquoted debentures] unless it is shown that the sale was at a price freely negotiated at the time of the sale or at a price such as might be expected to have been freely negotiated at the time of the sale.

(3) In this section—

'disposition' includes anything treated as a disposition by virtue of section 3(3) above;

'transaction' includes a series of transactions and any associated operations.

Note. Words in square brackets substituted for words in italics by Finance Act 1987, s 58, Sch 8, para 1, in relation to transfers of value or other events occurring after 17 March 1987.

11. Dispositions for maintenance of family—(1) A disposition is not a transfer of value if it is made by one party to a marriage in favour of the other party or of a child of either party and is—

(a) for the maintenance of the other party, or

(b) for the maintenance, education or training of the child for a period ending not later than the year in which he attains the age of eighteen or, after attaining that age, ceases to undergo full-time education or training.

(2) A disposition is not a transfer of value if it is made in favour of a child who is not in the care of a parent of his and is for his maintenance, education or training for a period ending not later than the year in which—

(a) he attains the age of eighteen, or

(b) after attaining that age he ceases to undergo full-time education or training; but paragraph (b) above applies only if before attaining that age the child has for substantial periods been in the care of the person making the disposition.

(3) A disposition is not a transfer of value if it is made in favour of a dependent relative of the person making the disposition and is a reasonable provision for his care or maintenance.

(4) A disposition is not a transfer of value if it is made in favour of an illegitimate child of the person making the disposition and is for the maintenance, education or training of the child for a period ending not later than the year in which he attains the age of eighteen or, after attaining that age, ceases to undergo full-time education or training.

(5) Where a disposition satisfies the conditions of the preceding provisions of this section to a limited extent only, so much of it as satisfies them and so much of it as does not satisfy them shall be treated as separate dispositions.

(6) In this section—

'child' includes a step-child and an adopted child and 'parent' shall be construed accordingly;

'dependent relative' means in relation to any person—

(a) a relative of his, or of his spouse, who is incapacitated by old age or infirmity from maintaining himself, or

(b) his mother or his spouse's mother, if she is widowed, or living apart from her husband, or a single woman in consequence of dissolution or annulment of marriage;

'marriage', in relation to a disposition made on the occasion of the dissolution or annulment of a marriage, and in relation to a disposition varying a disposition so made, includes a former marriage;

'year' means period of twelve months ending with 5th April.

Note. This section contains provisions formerly in Finance Act 1975, s 46. A person attains a given age expressed in years at the commencement of the relevant anniversary of the date of his birth; Family Law Reform Act 1969. As to months, see the Interpretation Act 1978, s 5, Sch 1.

* * * * *

PART II

EXEMPT TRANSFERS

CHAPTER I

GENERAL

18. Transfers between spouses—(1) A transfer of value is an exempt transfer to the extent that the value transferred is attributable to property which becomes comprised in the estate of the transferor's spouse or, so far as the value transferred is not so attributable, to the extent that that estate is increased.

(2) If, immediately before the transfer, the transferor but not the transferor's spouse is domiciled in the United Kingdom the value in respect of which the transfer is exempt (calculated as a value on which no tax is chargeable) shall not exceed £55,000 less any amount previously taken into account for the purposes of the exemption conferred by this section.

(3) Subsection (1) above shall not apply in relation to property if the testamentary or other disposition by which it is given—

(a) takes effect on the termination after the transfer of value of any interest or period, or

(b) depends on a condition which is not satisfied within twelve months after the transfer;

but paragraph (a) above shall not have effect by reason only that the property is given to a spouse only if he survives the other spouse for a specified period.

(4) For the purposes of this section, property is given to a person if it becomes his property or is held on trust for him.

Note. Formerly Finance Act 1975, Sch 6, para 1(1), as amended by Finance Act 1976, s 94(2). See also Finance Act 1975, s 1(2).

* * * * *

19. Annual exemption—(1) Transfers of value made by a transferor in any one year are exempt to the extent that the values transferred by them (calculated as values on which no tax is chargeable) do not exceed £3,000.

(2) Where those values fall short of £3,000, the amount by which they fall short shall, in relation to the next following year, be added to the £3,000 mentioned in subsection (1) above.

(3) Where those values exceed £3,000, the excess—

(a) shall, as between transfers made on different days, be attributed so far as possible to a later rather than an earlier transfer, and

(b) shall, as between transfers made on the same day, be attributed to them in proportion to the values transferred by them.

[(3A) A transfer or value which is a potentially exempt transfer—

(a) shall in the first instance be left out of account for the purposes of subsections (1) to (3) above; and

(b) if it proves to be a chargeable transfer, shall for the purposes of those subsections be taken into account as if, in the year in which it was made, it was made later than any transfer of value which was not a potentially exempt transfer.]

Note. Sub-s (3A) inserted by Finance Act 1986, s 101(1), Sch 19, Part I, para 5.

(4) In this section 'year' means period of twelve months ending with 5th April.

(5) Section 3(4) above shall not apply for the purposes of this section (but without prejudice to sections 57 and 94(5) below).

20. Small gifts—(1) Transfers of value made by a transferor in any one year by outright gifts to any one person are exempt if the values transferred by them (calculated as values on which no tax is chargeable) do not exceed £250.

* * * * *

21. Normal expenditure out of income—(1) A transfer of value is an exempt transfer if, or to the extent that, it is shown—

(a) that it was made as part of the normal expenditure of the transferor, and

(b) that (taking one year with another) it was made out of his income, and

(c) that, after allowing for all transfers of value forming part of his normal expenditure, the transferor was left with sufficient income to maintain his usual standard of living.

(2) A payment of a premium on a policy of insurance on the transferor's life, or a gift of money or money's worth applied, directly or indirectly, in payment of such a premium, shall not for the purposes of this section be regarded as part of his normal expenditure if, when the insurance was made or at any earlier or later time, an annuity was purchased on his life, unless it is shown that—

(a) the purchase of the annuity, and

(b) the making or any variation of the insurance or of any prior insurance for which the first-mentioned insurance was directly or indirectly substituted,

were not associated operations.

(3) So much of a purchased life annuity (within the meaning of section *230 of the Taxes Act* [657 of the Taxes Act 1988]) as is, for the purposes of the provisions of the Tax Acts relating to income tax on annuities and other annual payments, treated as the capital element contained in the annuity, shall not be regarded as part of the transferor's income for the purposes of this section.

Note. Words in square brackets substituted for words in italics by Income and Corporation Taxes Act 1988, s 844, Sch 29, para 32, as from 6 April 1988.

(4) Subsection (3) above shall not apply to annuities purchased before 13th November 1974.

(5) Section 3(4) above shall not apply for the purposes of this section.

* * * * *

48. Excluded property—(1) A reversionary interest is excluded property unless—

(a) it has at any time been acquired (whether by the person entitled to it or by a person previously entitled to it) for a consideration in money or money's worth, or

(b) it is one to which either the settlor or his spouse is or has been beneficially entitled, or

(c) it is the interest expectant on the determination of a lease treated as a settlement by virtue of section 43(3) above.

(2) In relation to a reversionary interest under a settlement made before 16th April 1976, subsection (1) above shall have effect with the omission of paragraph (b); and, if the person entitled to a reversionary interest under a settlement made on or after 16th April 1976 acquired the interest before 10th March 1981, that subsection shall have effect with the omission of the words 'or has been' in paragraph (b).

(3) Where property comprised in a settlement is situated outside the United Kingdom—

(a) the property (but not a reversionary interest in the property) is excluded property unless the settlor was domiciled in the United Kingdom at the time the settlement was made, and

(b) section 6(1) above applies to a reversionary interest in the property but does not otherwise apply in relation to the property.

(4) Where securities issued by the Treasury subject to a condition of the kind mentioned in subsection (2) of section 6 above are comprised in a settlement, that subsection shall not apply to them; but the securities are excluded property if—

(a) a person *neither domiciled nor ordinarily resident in the United Kingdom* [of a description specified in the condition in question] is entitled to a qualifying interest in possession in them, or

(b) no qualifying interest in possession subsists in them but it is shown that all known persons for whose benefit the settled property or income from it has been or might be applied, or who are or might become beneficially entitled to an interest in possession in it, are persons *neither domiciled nor ordinarily resident in the United Kingdom* [of a description specified in the condition in question].

(5) Where—

(a) property ceased to be comprised in one settlement before 10th December 1981 and after 19th April 1978 and, by the same disposition, became comprised in another settlement, or

(b) property ceased to be comprised in one settlement after 9th December 1981 and became comprised in another without any person having in the meantime become beneficially entitled to the property (and not merely to an interest in possession in the property),

subsection (4)(b) above shall, in its application to the second settlement, be construed as requiring the matters there stated to be shown both in relation to the property comprised in that settlement and in relation to the property that was comprised in the first settlement.

(6) Subsection (5) above shall not apply where a reversionary interest in the property expectant on the termination of a qualifying interest in possession subsisting under the first settlement was settled on the trusts of the second settlement before 10th December 1981.

(7) In this section 'qualifying interest in possession' has the same meaning as in Chapter III of this Part of this Act.

Note. Sub-s (4): in paras (a), (b) words in square brackets substituted for words in italics by the Finance Act 1996, s 154, Sch 28, para 8 in relation to income tax as respects the year 1996–97 and subsequent years of assessment, and in relation to corporation tax as respects accounting periods ending in or after 31 March 1996.

*   *   *   *   *

51. Disposal of interest in possession—(1) Where a person beneficially entitled to an interest in possession in settled property disposes of his interest the disposal—

(a) is not a transfer of value, but

(b) shall be treated for the purposes of this Chapter as the coming to an end of his interest;

and tax shall be charged accordingly under section 52 below.

(2) Where a disposition satisfying the conditions of section 11 above is a disposal of an interest in possession in settled property, the interest shall not by virtue of subsection (1) above be treated as coming to an end.

(3) References in this section to any property or to an interest in any property include references to part of any property or interest.

*   *   *   *   *

56. Exclusion of certain exemptions—(1) Sections 18 and 23 to 27 above shall not apply to relation to property which is given in consideration of the transfer of a reversionary interest if, by virtue of section 55(1) above, that interest does not form part of the estate of the person acquiring it.

(2) Where a person acquires a reversionary interest in any settled property for a consideration in money or money's worth, section 18 above shall not apply in relation to the property when it becomes the property of that person on the termination of the interest on which the reversionary interest is expectant.

(3) Sections 23 to 27 above shall not apply in relation to any property if—

(a) the property is an interest in possession in settled property and the settlement does not come to an end in relation to that settled property on the making of the transfer of value, or

(b) immediately before the time when it becomes the property of the exempt body it is comprised in a settlement and, at or before that time, an interest under the settlement is or has been acquired for a consideration in money or money's worth by that or another exempt body.

(4) In subsection (3)(b) above 'exempt body' means a charity, political party or other body within sections 23 *to 26* [to 25] above or the trustees of a settlement in relation to which a direction under paragraph 1 of Schedule 4 to this Act has effect; and for the purposes of subsection (3)(b) there shall be disregarded any acquisition from a charity, political party or body within sections 23 to 25.

(5) For the purposes of subsections (2) and (3) above, a person shall be treated as acquiring an interest for a consideration in money or money's worth if he becomes entitled to it as a result of transactions which include a disposition [for such consideration] (whether to him or another) of that interest or of other property.

Note. Words in square brackets inserted by Finance (No 2) Act 1987, s 96(1), (6), Sch 7, para 2, in relation to transfers of value or other events occurring after 17 March 1987.

(6) Nothing in this section shall apply to a transfer of value if or to the extent that it is a disposition whereby the use of money or other property is allowed by one person to another.

(7) Subsection (2) above shall not apply where the acquisition of the reversionary interest was before 16th April 1976; and where the acquisition was on or after that date but before 12th April 1978 that subsection shall have effect—

    (a) with the substitution for the words 'section 18 above' of the words 'sections 18 and 23 *to 26* [to 25] above', and

    (b) with the insertion after the word 'person' in both places where it occurs of the words 'or body'.

(8) Subsection (3)(b) above shall not apply where the acquisition of the interest was before 12th April 1978; and subsection (5) above shall not apply where the person concerned became entitled to the interest before that date.

Note. Sub-ss (4), (7): words in square brackets substituted for words in italics by the Finance Act 1998, s 143(3), in relation to any property becoming the property of any person on or after 17 March 1998.

*   *   *   *   *

Rates of principal charge

66. Rate of ten-yearly charge—(1) Subject to subsection (2) below, the rate at which tax is charged under section 64 above at any time shall be three tenths of the effective rate (that is to say the rate found by expressing the tax chargeable as a percentage of the amount on which it is charged) at which tax would be charged on the value transferred by a chargeable transfer of the description specified in subsection (3) below.

(2) Where the whole or part of the value mentioned in section 64 above is attributable to property which was not relevant property, or was not comprised in the settlement, throughout the period of ten years ending immediately before the ten-year anniversary concerned, the rate at which tax is charged on that value or part shall be reduced by one-fortieth for each of the successive quarters in that period which expired before the property became, or last became, relevant property comprised in the settlement.

(3) The chargeable transfer postulated in subsection (1) above is one—

    (a) the value transferred by which is equal to an amount determined in accordance with subsection (4) below;

    (b) which is made immediately before the ten-year anniversary concerned by a transferor who has in the *preceding ten years* [preceding seven years] made chargeable transfers having an aggregate value determined in accordance with subsection (5) below; and (*c*) *for which the appropriate Table of rates is the second Table in Schedule 1 to this Act*

[(c) on which tax is charged in accordance with section 7(2) of this Act.]

   (4) The amount referred to in subsection (3)(a) above is equal to the aggregate of—

   (a) the value on which tax is charged under section 64 above;
   (b) the value immediately after it became comprised in the settlement of any property which was not then relevant property and has not subsequently become relevant property while remaining comprised in the settlement; and
   (c) the value, immediately after a related settlement commenced, of the property then comprised in it;

but subject to subsection (6) below.

   (5) The aggregate value referred to in subsection (3)(b) above is equal to the aggregate of—

   (a) the values transferred by any chargeable transfers made by the settlor in the period of *ten* [seven] years ending with the day on which the settlement commenced, disregarding transfers made on that day or before 27th March 1974, and
   (b) the amounts on which any charges to tax were imposed under section 65 above in respect of the settlement in the ten years before the anniversary concerned;

but subject to subsection (6) and section 67 below.

   (6) In relation to a settlement which commenced before 27th March 1974—
   (a) subsection (4) above shall have effect with the omission of paragraphs (b) and (c); and
   (b) subsection (5) above shall have effect with the omission of paragraph (a);

and where tax is chargeable under section 64 above by reference to the first ten-year anniversary of a settlement which commenced before 9th March 1982, the aggregate mentioned in subsection (5) above shall be increased by the amounts of any distribution payments (determined in accordance with the rules applicable under paragraph 11 of Schedule 5 to the Finance Act 1975) made out of the settled property before 9th March 1982 (or, where paragraph 6, 7 or 8 of Schedule 15 to the Finance Act 1982 applied, 1st April 1983, or, as the case may be, 1st April 1984) and within the period of ten years before the anniversary concerned.

Note. Words in square brackets substituted for words in italics by Finance Act 1986, s 101(1), (3), Sch 19, Part I, para 16, with respect to transfer of value made or events occurring after 17 March 1986.

67. Added property, etc—(1) This subsection applies where, after the settlement commenced and after 8th March 1982, but before the anniversary concerned, the settlor made a chargeable transfer as a result of which the value of the property comprised in the settlement was increased.

   (2) For the purposes of subsection (1) above, it is immaterial whether the amount of the property so comprised was increased as a result of the transfer, but a transfer as a result of which the value increased but the amount did not shall be disregarded if it is shown that the transfer—
   (a) was not primarily intended to increase the value, and
   (b) did not result in the value being greater immediately after the transfer by an amount exceeding five per cent of the value immediately before the transfer.

   (3) Where subsection (1) above applies in relation to a settlement which commenced after 26th March 1974, section 66(5)(a) above shall have effect as if it referred to the greater of—
   (a) the aggregate of the values there specified, and

(b) the aggregate of the values transferred by any chargeable transfers made by the settlor in the period of *ten* [seven] years ending with the day on which the chargeable transfer falling within subsection (1) above was made—

    (i) disregarding transfers made on that day or before 27th March 1974, and

    (ii) excluding the values mentioned in subsection (5) below;

and where the settlor made two or more chargeable transfers falling within subsection (1) above, paragraph (b) above shall be taken to refer to the transfer in relation to which the aggregate there mentioned is the greatest.

(4) Where subsection (1) above applies in relation to a settlement which commenced before 27th March 1974, the aggregate mentioned in section 66(5) above shall be increased (or further increased) by the aggregate of the values transferred by any chargeable transfers made by the settlor in the period of *ten* [seven] years ending with the day on which the chargeable transfer falling within subsection (1) above was made—

(a) disregarding transfers made on that day or before 27th March 1974, and

(b) excluding the values mentioned in subsection (5) below;

and where the settlor made two or more chargeable transfers falling within subsection (1) above, this subsection shall be taken to refer to the transfer in relation to which the aggregate to be added is the greatest.

(5) The values excluded by subsections (3)(b)(ii) and (4)(b) above are—

(a) any value attributable to property whose value is taken into account in determining the amount mentioned in section 66(4) above; and

(b) any value attributable to property in respect of which a charge to tax has been made under section 65 above and by reference to which an amount mentioned in section 66(5)(b) above is determined.

(6) Where the property comprised in a settlement immediately before the ten-year anniversary concerned, or any part of that property, had on any occasion within the preceding ten years ceased to be relevant property then, if on that occasion tax was charged in respect of the settlement under section 65 above, the aggregate mentioned in section 66(5) above shall be reduced by an amount equal to the lesser of—

(a) the amount on which tax was charged under section 65 (or so much of that amount as is attributable to the part in question), and

(b) the value on which tax is charged under section 64 above (or so much of that value as is attributable to the part in question);

and if there were two or more such occasions relating to the property or the same part of it, this subsection shall have effect in relation to each of them.

(7) References in subsection (6) above to the property comprised in a settlement immediately before an anniversary shall, if part only of the settled property was then relevant property, be construed as references to that part.

Note. 'Seven' substituted for 'ten' in sub-ss (3)(b), (4) by Finance Act 1986, s 101(1), (3), Sch 19, Part I, para 17, with respect to a settlement to which property is added after 17 March 1986.

68. Rate before first ten-year anniversary—(1) The rate at which tax is charged under section 65 above on an occasion preceding the first ten-year anniversary after the settlement's commencement shall be the appropriate fraction of the effective rate at which tax would be charged on the value transferred by a chargeable transfer of the description specified in subsection (4) below (but subject to subsection (6) below).

(2) For the purposes of this section the appropriate fraction is three tenths multiplied by so many fortieths as there are complete successive quarters in the period beginning with the day on which the settlement commenced and ending with the day before the occasion of the charge, but subject to subsection (3) below.

(3) Where the whole or part of the amount on which tax is charged is attributable to property which was not relevant property, or was not comprised in the settlement, throughout the period referred to in subsection (2) above, then in determining the appropriate fraction in relation to that amount or part—

(a) no quarter which expired before the day on which the property became, or last became, relevant property comprised in the settlement shall be counted, but

(b) if that day fell in the same quarter as that in which the period ends, that quarter shall be counted whether complete or not.

(4) The chargeable transfer postulated in subsection (1) above is one—

(a) the value transferred by which is equal to an amount determined in accordance with subsection (5) below;

(b) which is made at the time of the charge to tax under section 65 by a transferor who has in the period of *ten* [seven] years ending with the day of the occasion of the charge made chargeable transfers having an aggregate value equal to that of any chargeable transfers made by the settlor in the period of *ten* [seven] years ending with the day on which the settlement commenced, disregarding transfers made on that day or before 27th March 1974; and

(*c*) *for which the appropriate Table of rates is the second Table in Schedule 1 to this Act*

[(c) on which tax is charged in accordance with section 7(2) of this Act.].

(5) The amount referred to in subsection (4)(a) above is equal to the aggregate of—

(a) the value, immediately after the settlement commenced, of the property then comprised in it;

(b) the value, immediately after a related settlement commenced, of the property then comprised in it; and

(c) the value, immediately after it became comprised in the settlement, of any property which became so comprised after the settlement commenced and before the occasion of the charge under section 65 (whether or not it has remained so comprised).

(6) Where the settlement commenced before 27th March 1974, subsection (1) above shall have effect with the substitution of a reference to three tenths for the reference to the appropriate fraction; and in relation to such a settlement the chargeable transfer postulated in that subsection is one—

(a) the value transferred by which is equal to the amount on which tax is charged under section 65 above;

(b) which is made at the time of that charge to tax by a transferor who has in the period of *ten* [seven] years ending with the day of the occasion of the charge made chargeable transfers having an aggregate value equal to the aggregate of—

(i) any amounts on which any charges to tax have been imposed under section 65 above in respect of the settlement in *that period of ten years* [the period of ten years ending with that day]; and

(ii) the amounts of any distribution payments (determined in accordance with the rules applicable under paragraph 11 of Schedule 5 to the Finance Act 1975) made out of the settled property before 9th March 1982 (or, where paragraph 6, 7, or 8 of Schedule 15 to the Finance Act 1982 applied, 1st April 1983, or, as the case may be, 1st April 1984) and within the said period of ten years; and

(*c*) *for which the appropriate Table of rates is the second Table in Schedule 1 to this Act*

[(c) on which tax is charged in accordance with section 7(2) of this Act.]

Note. Words in square brackets substituted for words in italics by Finance Act 1986, s 101(1), (3), Sch 19, Part I, para 18, with respect to transfer of value made after 17 March 1986.

* * * * *

CHILD ABDUCTION AND CUSTODY ACT 1985

(1985 c 60)

ARRANGEMENT OF SECTIONS

PART I

INTERNATIONAL CHILD ABDUCTION

An Act to enable the United Kingdom to ratify two international Conventions relating respectively to the civil aspects of international child abduction and to the recognition and enforcement of custody decisions.   [25th July 1985]

PART I

INTERNATIONAL CHILD ABDUCTION

1. The Hague Convention—(1) In this Part of this Act 'the Convention' means the Convention on the Civil Aspects of International Child Abduction which was signed at The Hague on 25th October 1980.

(2) Subject to the provisions of this Part of this Act, the provisions of that Convention set out in Schedule 1 to this Act shall have the force of law in the United Kingdom.

2. Contracting States—(1) For the purposes of the Convention as it has effect under this Part of this Act the Contracting States other than the United Kingdom shall be those for the time being specified by an Order in Council under this section.

(2) An Order in Council under this section shall specify the date of the coming into force of the Convention as between the United Kingdom and any State specified in the Order; and, except where the Order otherwise provides, the Convention shall apply as between the United Kingdom and that State only in relation to wrongful removals or retentions occurring on or after that date.

(3) Where the Convention applies, or applies only, to a particular territory or particular territories specified in a declaration made by a Contracting State under Article 39 or 40 of the Convention references to that State in subsections (1) and (2) above shall be construed as references to that territory or those territories.

3. Central Authorities—(1) Subject to subsection (2) below, the functions under the Convention of a Central Authority shall be discharged—
   (a) in England and Wales and in Northern Ireland by the Lord Chancellor; and
   (b) in Scotland by the Secretary of State.

(2) Any application made under the Convention by or on behalf of a person outside the United Kingdom may be addressed to the Lord Chancellor as the Central Authority in the United Kingdom.

(3) Where any such application relates to a function to be discharged under subsection (1) above by the Secretary of State it shall be transmitted by the Lord Chancellor to the Secretary of State and where such an application is addressed to the Secretary of State but relates to a function to be discharged under subsection (1) above by the Lord Chancellor the Secretary of State shall transmit it to the Lord Chancellor.

4. Judicial authorities.   The courts having jurisdiction to entertain applications under the Convention shall be—
   (a) in England and Wales or in Northern Ireland the High Court; and
   (b) in Scotland the Court of Session.

5. Interim powers.   Where an application has been made to a court in the United Kingdom under the Convention, the court may, at any time before the application is determined, give such interim directions as it thinks fit for the purpose of securing the welfare of the child concerned or of preventing changes in the circumstances relevant to the determination of the application.

6. Reports.   Where the Lord Chancellor or the Secretary of State is requested to provide information relating to a child under Article 7(d) of the Convention he may—
   (a) request a local authority or *a probation officer* [an officer of the Service]to make a report to him in writing with respect to any matter which appears to him to be relevant;
   (b) request the Department of Health and Social Services for Northern Ireland to arrange for a suitably qualified person to make such a report to him;
   (c) request any court to which a written report relating to the child has been made to send him a copy of the report;
and such a request shall be duly complied with.

Note. In para (a) words in square brackets substituted for words in italics by the Criminal Justice and Court Services Act 2000, s 74, Sch 7, Pt II, paras 79, 80, as from 1 April 2001.

7. Proof of documents and evidence—(1) For the purposes of Article 14 of the Convention a decision or determination of a judicial or administrative authority outside the United Kingdom may be proved by a duly authenticated copy of the decision or determination; and any document purporting to be such a copy shall be deemed to be a true copy unless the contrary is shown.

(2) For the purposes of subsection (1) above a copy is duly authenticated if it bears the seal, or is signed by a judge or officer, of the authority in question.

(3) For the purposes of Articles 14 and 30 of the Convention any such document as is mentioned in Article 8 of the Convention, or a certified copy of any such document, shall be sufficient evidence of anything stated in it.

8. Declarations by United Kingdom courts. The High Court or Court of Session may, on an application made for the purposes of Article 15 of the Convention by any person appearing to the court to have an interest in the matter, make a declaration or declarator that the removal of any child from, or his retention outside the United Kingdom was wrongful within the meaning of Article 3 of the Convention.

9. Suspension of court's powers in cases of wrongful removal. The reference in Article 16 of the Convention to deciding on the merits of rights of custody shall be construed as a reference to—

(a) making, varying or revoking a custody order, or *any other order under section 1(2) of the Children and Young Persons Act 1969* [a supervision order under section 31 of the Children Act 1989] or *section 95(1), 97(2), 143(6) or 144 of the Children and Young Persons Act (Northern Ireland) 1968 (not being a custody order)* [Article 50 of the Children (Northern Ireland) Order 1995];

[(aa) enforcing under section 29 of the Family Law Act 1986 a custody order within the meaning of Chapter V of Part I of that Act;]

(b) registering or enforcing a decision under Part II of this Act;

(c) *determining a complaint under section 3(5) or 5(4) of the Child Care Act 1980 or an appeal under section 6 or 67(2) or (3) of that Act;*

(d) *determining a summary application under section 16(8), 16A(3) or 18(3) of the Social Work (Scotland) Act 1968;*

[(d) making, varying or discharging an order under section 86 of the Children (Scotland) Act 1995;]

(e) *making a parental rights order under section 104 of the Children and Young Persons Act (Northern Ireland) 1968 or discharging such an order, or giving directions in lieu of the discharge of such an order, under section 106(2) of that Act.*

Note. Words in first pair of square brackets substituted for words in italics in para (a) by Children Act 1989, s 108(5), Sch 13, para 57(1), and para (c) repealed by s 108(7) of, and Sch 15 to, that Act, as from 14 October 1991. Words in second pair of square brackets in para (a) substituted for words in italics and para (e) repealed by Children (Northern Ireland Consequential Amendments) Order 1995, SI 1995 No 756, arts 11, 15, Schedule, as from 4 November 1996. Para (aa) inserted by Family Law Act 1986, s 68(1), Sch 1, para 28, as from 4 April 1988. Para (d) substituted by Children (Scotland) Act 1995, s 105(4), Sch 4, para 37(2), as from 1 April 1997.

10. Rules of court—(1) An authority having power to make rules of court may make such provision for giving effect to this Part of this Act as appears to that authority to be necessary or expedient.

(2) Without prejudice to the generality of subsection (1) above, rules of court may make provision—

(a) with respect to the procedure on applications for the return of a child and with respect to the documents and information to be furnished and the notices to be given in connection with any such application;

(b) for the transfer of any such application between the appropriate courts in the different parts of the United Kingdom;

(c) for the giving of notices by or to a court for the purposes of the provisions of Article 16 of the Convention and section 9 above and generally as respects proceedings to which those provisions apply;

(d) for enabling a person who wishes to make an application under the Convention in a Contracting State other than the United Kingdom to obtain from any court in the United Kingdom an authenticated copy of any decision of that court relating to the child to whom the application is to relate.

11. Cost of applications. The United Kingdom having made such a reservation as is mentioned in the third paragraph of Article 26 of the Convention, the costs mentioned in that paragraph shall not be borne by any Minister or other authority in the United Kingdom except so far as they fall to be so borne *by virtue of the grant of legal aid or legal advice and assistance under Part I of the Legal Aid Act 1974* [*Part III or IV of the Legal Aid Act 1988*] [by virtue of—

(a) the provision of any service funded by the Legal Services Commission as part of the Community Legal Service, or

(b) the grant of legal aid or legal advice and assistance under],

the Legal Aid (Scotland) Act 1967, Part I of the Legal Advice and Assistance Act 1972 or the Legal Aid Advice and Assistance (Northern Ireland) Order 1981.

Note. First words in square brackets substituted for words in italics by Legal Aid Act 1988, s 45(1), (3), Sch 5, para 16, as from 1 April 1989.

Second words in square brackets substituted for words in italics by the Access to Justice Act 1999, s 24, Sch 4, para 31, as from 1 April 2000.

PART II

RECOGNITION AND ENFORCEMENT OF CUSTODY DECISIONS

12. The European Convention—(1) In this Part of this Act 'the Convention' means the European Convention on Recognition and Enforcement of Decisions concerning Custody of Children and on the Restoration of Custody of Children which was signed in Luxembourg on 20th May 1980.

(2) Subject to the provisions of this Part of this Act, the provisions of that Convention set out in Schedule 2 to this Act (which include Articles 9 and 10 as they have effect in consequence of a reservation made by the United Kingdom under Article 17) shall have the force of law in the United Kingdom.

[(3) But those provisions of the convention are subject to Article 37 of Council Regulation (EC) No 1347/2000 of 29th May 2000 on jurisdiction and the recognition and enforcement of judgments in matrimonial matters and in matters of parental responsibility for children of both spouses (under which the Regulation takes precedence over the convention), and the provisions of this Part of this Act, any rules of court made pursuant to section 24 of this Act, shall be construed accordingly.]

Note. Sub-s (3) inserted by the European Communities (Matrimonial Jurisdiction and Judgments) Regulations 2001, SI 2001/310, reg 5, as from 1 March 2001.

13. Contracting States—(1) For the purposes of the Convention as it has effect under this Part of this Act the Contracting States other than the United Kingdom shall be those for the time being specified by an Order in Council under this section.

(2) An Order in Council under this section shall specify the date of the coming into force of the Convention as between the United Kingdom and any State specified in the Order.

(3) Where the Convention applies, or applies only, to a particular territory or particular territories specified by a Contracting State under Article 24 or 25 of the Convention references to that State in subsections (1) and (2) above shall be construed as references to that territory or those territories.

14. Central Authorities—(1) Subject to subsection (2) below, the functions under the Convention of a Central Authority shall be discharged—

(a) in England and Wales and in Northern Ireland by the Lord Chancellor; and

(b) in Scotland by the Secretary of State.

(2) Any application made under the Convention by or on behalf of a person outside the United Kingdom may be addressed to the Lord Chancellor as the Central Authority in the United Kingdom.

(3) Where any such application relates to a function to be discharged under subsection (1) above by the Secretary of State it shall be transmitted by the Lord Chancellor to the Secretary of State and where such an application is addressed to the Secretary of State but relates to a function to be discharged under subsection (1) above by the Lord Chancellor the Secretary of State shall transmit it to the Lord Chancellor.

15. Recognition of decisions—(1) Articles 7 and 12 of the Convention shall have effect in accordance with this section.

(2) A decision to which either of those Articles applies which was made in a Contracting State other than the United Kingdom shall be recognised in each part of the United Kingdom as if made by a court having jurisdiction to make it in that part but—

(a) the appropriate court in any part of the United Kingdom may, on the application of any person appearing to it to have an interest in the matter, declare on any of the grounds specified in Article 9 or 10 of the Convention that the decision is not to be recognised in any part of the United Kingdom; and

(b) the decision shall not be enforceable in any part of the United Kingdom unless registered in the appropriate court under section 16 below.

(3) The references in Article 9(1)(c) of the Convention to the removal of the child are to his improper removal within the meaning of the Convention.

16. Registrations of decisions—(1) A person on whom any rights are conferred by a decision relating to custody made by an authority in a Contracting State other than the United Kingdom may make an application for the registration of the decision in an appropriate court in the United Kingdom.

(2) The Central Authority in the United Kingdom shall assist such a person in making such an application if a request for such assistance is made by him or on his behalf by the Central Authority of the Contracting State in question.

(3) An application under subsection (1) above or a request under subsection (2) above shall be treated as a request for enforcement for the purposes of Articles 10 and 13 of the Convention.

(4) The High Court or Court of Session shall refuse to register a decision if—

(a) the court is of the opinion that on any of the grounds specified in Article 9 or 10 of the Convention the decision should not be recognised in any part of the United Kingdom;

(b) the court is of the opinion that the decision is not enforceable in the Contracting State where it was made and is not a decision to which Article 12 of the Convention applies; or

(c) an application in respect of the child under Part I of this Act is pending.

(5) Where the Lord Chancellor is requested to assist in making an application under this section to the Court of Session he shall transmit the request to the Secretary of State and the Secretary of State shall transmit to the Lord Chancellor any such request to assist in making an application to the High Court.

(6) In this section 'decision relating to custody' has the same meaning as in the Convention.

17. Variation and revocation of registered decisions—(1) Where a decision which has been registered under section 16 above is varied or revoked by an authority in the Contracting State in which it was made, the person on whose behalf the application for registration of the decision was made shall notify the court in which the decision is registered of the variation or revocation.

(2) Where a court is notified under subsection (1) above of the revocation of a decision, it shall—

(a) cancel the registration, and
(b) notify such persons as may be prescribed by rules of court of the cancellation.

(3) Where a court is notified under subsection (1) above of the variation of a decision, it shall—

(a) notify such persons as may be prescribed by rules of court of the variation; and
(b) subject to any conditions which may be so prescribed, vary the registration.

(4) The court in which a decision is registered under section 16 above may also, on the application of any person appearing to the court to have an interest in the matter, cancel or vary the registration if it is satisfied that the decision has been revoked or, as the case may be, varied by an authority in the Contracting State in which it was made.

18. Enforcement of decisions.   Where a decision relating to custody has been registered under section 16 above, the court in which it is registered shall have the same powers for the purpose of enforcing the decision as if it had been made by that court; and proceedings for or with respect to enforcement may be taken accordingly.

19. Interim powers.   Where an application has been made to a court for the registration of a decision under section 16 above or for the enforcement of such a decision, the court may, at any time before the application is determined, give such interim directions as it thinks fit for the purpose of securing the welfare of the child concerned or of preventing changes in the circumstances relevant to the determination of the application or, in the case of an application for registration, to the determination of any subsequent application for the enforcement of the decision.

20. Suspension of court's powers—(1) Where it appears to any court in which such proceedings as are mentioned in subsection (2) below are pending in respect of a child that—

(a) an application has been made for the registration of a decision in respect of the child under section 16 above (other than a decision mentioned in subsection (3) below) or that such a decision is registered; and
(b) the decision was made in proceedings commenced before the proceedings which are pending,

the powers of the court with respect to the child in those proceedings shall be restricted as mentioned in subsection (2) below unless, in the case of an application for registration, the application is refused.

(2) Where subsection (1) above applies the court shall not—

(a)   in the case of custody proceedings, make, vary or revoke any custody order, or *any other order under section 1(2) of the Children and Young Persons Act 1969* [a supervision order under section 31 of the Children Act 1989] or *section 95(1), 97(2), 143(6) or 144 of the Children and Young Persons Act (Northern Ireland) 1968 (not being a custody order)* [Article 50 of the Children (Northern Ireland) Order 1995];

[(aa) in the case of proceedings under section 29 of the Family Law Act 1986 for the enforcement of a custody order within the meaning of Chapter V of Part I of that Act, enforce that order;] [or]

(*b*)   *in the case of proceedings on a complaint under section 3(5) or 5(4) of the Child Care Act 1980 determine, that complaint;*

(*c*)   *in the case of proceedings on an appeal under section 6 or 67(2) or (3) of that Act, determine that appeal;*

[(d)   in the case of proceedings for, or for the variation or discharge of, a parental responsibilities order under section 86 of the Children (Scotland) Act 1995, make, vary or discharge any such order;] *or*

(*e*)   *in the case of proceedings on a complaint under section 104(1) of the Children and Young Persons Act (Northern Ireland) 1968 or on an application under section 106(2) of that Act, make a parental rights order under section 104 or, as the case may be, discharge or give directions in lieu of the discharge of such an order under section 106(2) of that Act.*

[(2A) Where it appears to the Secretary of State—

(a)   that an application has been made for the registration of a decision in respect of a child under section 16 above (other than a decision mentioned in subsection (3) below); or

(b)   that such a decision is registered,

the Secretary of State shall not make, vary or revoke any custody order in respect of the child unless, in the case of an application for registration, the application is refused.]

(3) The decision referred to in subsection (1) [or (2A)] above is a decision which is only a decision relating to custody within the meaning of section 16 of this Act by virtue of being a decision relating to rights of access.

(4) Paragraph (b) of Article 10(2) of the Convention shall be construed as referring to custody proceedings within the meaning of this Act.

(5) This section shall apply to a children's hearing *within the meaning of Part III of the Social Work (Scotland) Act 1968* [(as defined in section 93(1) of the Children (Scotland) Act 1995)] as it does to a court.

Note. Words in first pair of square brackets substituted for words in italics in sub-s (2)(a) by Children Act 1989, s 108(5), Sch 13, para 57(1), and sub-s (2)(b), (c) repealed by s 108(7) of, and Sch 15 to, that Act, as from 14 October 1991. Words in second pair of square brackets substituted for words in italics in sub-s (2)(a), word 'or' at end of sub-s (2)(aa) added, word 'or' at end of sub-s (2)(d) and sub-s (2)(e) repealed, by Children (Northern Ireland Consequential Amendments) Order 1995, SI 1995 No 756, arts 11, 15, Schedule, as from 4 November 1996. Sub-s (2)(aa) inserted by Family Law Act 1986, s 68(1), Sch 1, para 29, as from 4 April 1988, and sub-s (2A) and words in square brackets in sub-s (3) inserted by s 67(1), (2) of that Act, as from 7 January 1987. Sub-s (2)(d) substituted by Children (Scotland) Act 1995, s 105(4), Sch 4, para 37(3)(a), as from 1 April 1997. Words in square brackets in sub-s (5) substituted for words in italics by Children (Scotland) Act 1995, s 105(4), Sch 4, para 37(3)(b), as from 1 April 1997.

21. Reports.   Where the Lord Chancellor or the Secretary of State is requested to make enquiries about a child under Article 15(1)(b) of the Convention he may—

(a)   request a local authority or *a probation officer* [an officer of the Service] to make a report to him in writing with respect to any matter relating to the child concerned which appears to him to be relevant;

(b)   request the Department of Health and Social Services for Northern Ireland to arrange for a suitably qualified person to make such a report to him;

(c)   request any court to which a written report relating to the child has been made to send him a copy of the report;

and any such request shall be duly complied with.

Note. In para (a) words ion square brackets substituted for words in italics by the Criminal Justice and Court Services Act 2000, s 74, Sch 7, Pt II, paras 79, 80, as from 1 April 2001.

22. Proof of documents and evidence—(1) In any proceedings under this Part of this Act a decision of an authority outside the United Kingdom may be proved by a duly authenticated copy of the decision; and any document purporting to be such a copy shall be deemed to be a true copy unless the contrary is shown.

(2) For the purposes of subsection (1) above a copy is duly authenticated if it bears the seal, or is signed by a judge or officer, of the authority in question.

(3) In any proceedings under this Part of this Act any such document as is mentioned in Article 13 of the Convention, or a certified copy of any such document, shall be sufficient evidence of anything stated in it.

23. Decisions of United Kingdom courts—(1) Where a person on whom any rights are conferred by a decision relating to custody made by a court in the United Kingdom makes an application to the Lord Chancellor or the Secretary of State under Article 4 of the Convention with a view to securing its recognition or enforcement in another Contracting State, the Lord Chancellor or the Secretary of State may require the court which made the decision to furnish him with all or any of the documents referred to in Article 13(1)(b), (c) and (d) of the Convention.

(2) Where in any custody proceedings a court in the United Kingdom makes a decision relating to a child who has been removed from the United Kingdom, the court may also, on an application made by any person for the purposes of Article 12 of the Convention, declare the removal to have been unlawful if it is satisfied that the applicant has an interest in the matter and that the child has been taken from or sent or kept out of the United Kingdom without the consent of the person (or, if more than one, all the persons) having the right to determine the child's place of residence under the law of the part of the United Kingdom in which the child was habitually resident.

(3) In this section 'decision relating to custody' has the same meaning as in the Convention.

24. Rules of court—(1) An authority having power to make rules of court may make such provision for giving effect to this Part of this Act as appears to that authority to be necessary or expedient.

(2) Without prejudice to the generality of subsection (1) above, rules of court may make provision—
   (a) with respect to the procedure on applications to a court under any provision of this Part of this Act and with respect to the documents and information to be furnished and the notices to be given in connection with any such application;
   (b) for the transfer of any such application between the appropriate courts in the different parts of the United Kingdom;
   (c) for the giving of directions requiring the disclosure of information about any child who is the subject of proceedings under this Part of this Act and for safeguarding its welfare.

PART III

SUPPLEMENTARY

[24A. Power to order disclosure of child's whereabouts—(1) Where—
   (a) in proceedings for the return of a child under Part I of this Act; or
   (b) on application for the recognition, registration or enforcement of a decision in respect of a child under Part II of this Act,
there is not available to the court adequate information as to where the child is, the court may order any person who it has reason to believe may have relevant information to disclose it to the court.

(2) A person shall not be excused from complying with an order under subsection (1) above by reason that to do so may incriminate him or his spouse of an offence; but a statement or admission made in compliance with such an order shall not be admissible in evidence against either of them in proceedings for any offence other than perjury.]

Note. This section inserted by Family Law Act 1986, s 67(4), as from 7 January 1987.

25. Termination of existing custody orders, etc—(1) Where—
  (a) an order is made for the return of a child under Part I of this Act; or
  (b) a decision with respect to a child (other than a decision mentioned in subsection (2) below) is registered under section 16 of this Act,
any custody order relating to him shall cease to have effect.

  (2) The decision referred to in subsection (1)(b) above is a decision which is only a decision relating to custody within the meaning of section 16 of this Act by virtue of being a decision relating to rights of access.

  (3) *In section 17 of the Children and Young Persons Act 1969 (termination of supervision orders) at the end there shall be added—*
  '(c) *in the case of an order made by virtue of section 1 of this Act, if an event mentioned in paragraph (a) or (b) of section 25(1) of the Child Abduction and Custody Act 1985 occurs with respect to the child.'.*

  (4) *In Schedule 3 to the Children and Young Persons Act (Northern Ireland) 1968 after paragraph 2 there shall be inserted—*
  '2A. *A supervision order made by virtue of section 95(1)(d) or, in the case of a child or young person committed to the care of a fit person under Part V, sections 143(6)(d) or 144 shall cease to have effect if an event mentioned in paragraph (a) or (b) of section 25(1) of the Child Abduction and Custody Act 1985 occurs with respect to the child'.*

  (5) *In section 5(2) of the Child Care Act 1980 (circumstances in which resolutions under section 3 vesting parental rights and duties in a local authority cease to have effect)—*
  (a) *the word 'or' at the end of paragraph (b) shall be omitted; and*
  (b) *at the end there shall be inserted the words 'or*
      (d) *an event mentioned in paragraph (a) or (b) of section 25(1) of the Child Abduction and Custody Act 1985 occurs with respect to the child'.*

  (6) *In section 16 of the Social Work (Scotland) Act 1968 (assumption of parental rights and powers by local authority) in subsection (11) after paragraph (d) there shall be inserted the words '; or*
  (e) *an event mentioned in paragraph (a) or (b) of section 25(1) of the Child Abduction and Custody Act 1985 occurs with respect to the child.'*

  (7) *At the end of section 106 of the Children and Young Persons Act (Northern Ireland) 1968 there shall be inserted—*
  '(3) *A parental rights order shall cease to have effect if an event mentioned in paragraph (a) or (b) of section 25(1) of the Child Abduction and Custody Act 1985 occurs with respect to the child.'*

Note. Sub-ss (3), (5) repealed by Children Act 1989, s 108(7), Sch 15, as from 14 October 1991. Sub-ss (4), (7) repealed by Children (Northern Ireland Consequential Amendments) Order 1995, SI 1995 No 756, art 15, Schedule, as from 4 November 1996. Sub-s (6) repealed by Children (Scotland) Act 1995, s 105, Sch 4, para 37(4), Sch 5, as from 1 April 1997.

26. Expenses.   There shall be paid out of money provided by Parliament—
  (a) any expenses incurred by the Lord Chancellor or the Secretary of State by virtue of this Act; and
  (b) any increase attributable to this Act in the sums so payable under any other Act.

27. Interpretation—(1) In this Act 'custody order' means [(unless the contrary intention appears)] any such order or authorisation as is mentioned in Schedule 3 to this Act and 'custody proceedings' means proceedings in which an order within paragraphs 1, 2, 5, 6, 8 or 9 of that Schedule may be *made or in which any custody order may be varied or revoked* [made, varied or revoked].

Note. Words in first pair of square brackets inserted by Family Law Act 1986, s 68(1), Sch 1, para 30, as from 4 April 1988. Words in second pair of square brackets substituted for words in italics by ibid, s 67(5), as from 7 January 1987.

(2) For the purposes of this Act 'part of the United Kingdom' means England and Wales, Scotland or Northern Ireland and 'the appropriate court', in relation to England and Wales or Northern Ireland means the High Court and, in relation to Scotland, the Court of Session.

(3) In this Act 'local authority' means—

(a) in relation to England and Wales, the council of a non-metropolitan county, a metropolitan district, a London borough or the Common Council of the City of London; and

(b) in relation to Scotland, a *regional or islands council* [council constituted under section 2 of the Local Government etc (Scotland) Act 1994].

Note. Words in square brackets substituted for words in italics by Local Government etc (Scotland) Act 1994, s 180(1), Sch 13, para 139, as from 1 April 1996.

[(4) In this Act a decision relating to rights of access in England and Wales [or Scotland] [or Northern Ireland] means a decision as to the contact which a child may, or may not, have with any person.]

Note. Sub-s (4) added by Children Act 1989, s 108(5), Sch 13, para 57(2), as from 14 October 1991. Words 'or Scotland' inserted by Children (Scotland) Act 1995, s 105(4), Sch 4, para 37(5), as from 1 November 1996. Words 'or Northern Ireland' inserted by Children (Northern Ireland Consequential Amendments) Order 1995, SI 1995 No 756, art 11(4), as from 4 November 1996.

[(5) In this Act 'officer of the Service' has the same meaning as in the Criminal Justice and Court Services Act 2000.

Note. Sub-s (5) added by the Criminal Justice and Court Services Act 2000, s 74, Sch 7, Pt II, paras 79, 81, as from 1 April 2001.

28. Application as respects British Islands and colonies—(1) Her Majesty may by Order in Council direct that any of the provisions of this Act specified in the Order shall extend, subject to such modifications as may be specified in the Order, to—

(a) the Isle of Man,

(b) any of the Channel Islands, and

(c) any colony.

(2) Her Majesty may by Order in Council direct that this Act shall have effect in the United Kingdom as if any reference in this Act, or in any amendment made by this Act, to any order which may be made, or any proceedings which may be brought or any other thing which may be done in, or in any part of, the United Kingdom included a reference to any corresponding order which may be made or, as the case may be, proceedings which may be brought or other thing which may be done in any of the territories mentioned in subsection (1) above.

(3) An Order in Council under this section may make such consequential, incidental and supplementary provision as Her Majesty considers appropriate.

(4) An Order in Council under this section shall be subject to annulment in pursuance of a resolution of either House of Parliament.

29. Short title, commencement and extent—(1) This Act may be cited as the Child Abduction and Custody Act 1985.

(2) This Act shall come into force on such day as may be appointed by an order made by statutory instrument by the Lord Chancellor and the Lord Advocate; and different days may be so appointed for different provisions.

(3) This Act extends to Northern Ireland.

Commencement. This Act was brought into force on 1 August 1986 (SI 1986 No 1048).

SCHEDULES

SCHEDULE 1

See also Articles 1 and 20, which are in the following terms:

Article 1

The objects of the present Convention are—(a) to secure the prompt return of children wrongfully removed to or retained in any Contracting State; and (b) to ensure that rights of custody and of access under the law of one Contracting State are effectively respected in the other Contracting States.

Article 20

The return of the child under the provisions of Article 12 may be refused if this would not be permitted by the fundamental principles of the requested State relating to the protection of human rights and fundamental freedoms.

CONVENTION ON THE CIVIL ASPECTS OF INTERNATIONAL CHILD ABDUCTION

CHAPTER I—SCOPE OF THE CONVENTION

Article 3

The removal or the retention of a child is to be considered wrongful where—
  (a) it is in breach of rights of custody attributed to a person, an institution or any other body, either jointly or alone, under the law of the State in which the child was habitually resident immediately before the removal or retention; and
  (b) at the time of removal or retention those rights were actually exercised, either jointly or alone, or would have been so exercised but for the removal or retention.

The rights of custody mentioned in sub-paragraph (a) above may arise in particular by operation of law or by reason of a judicial or administrative decision, or by reason of an agreement having legal effect under the law of that State.

Article 4

The Convention shall apply to any child who was habitually resident in a Contracting State immediately before any breach of custody or access rights. The Convention shall cease to apply when the child attains the age of sixteen years.

Article 5

For the purposes of this Convention—
  (a) 'rights of custody' shall include rights relating to the care of the person of the child and, in particular, the right to determine the child's place of residence;
  (b) 'rights of access' shall include the right to take a child for a limited period of time to a place other than the child's habitual residence.

CHAPTER II—CENTRAL AUTHORITIES

Article 7

Central Authorities shall co-operate with each other and promote co-operation amongst the competent authorities in their respective States to secure the prompt return of children and to achieve the other objects of this Convention.

In particular, either directly or through any intermediary, they shall take all appropriate measures—
  (a) to discover the whereabouts of a child who has been wrongfully removed or retained;
  (b) to prevent further harm to the child or prejudice to interested parties by taking or causing to be taken provisional measures;

(c) to secure the voluntary return of the child or to bring about an amicable resolution of the issues;
(d) to exchange, where desirable, information relating to the social background of the child;
(e) to provide information of a general character as to the law of their State in connection with the application of the Convention;
(f) to initiate or facilitate the institution of judicial or administrative proceedings with a view to obtaining the return of the child and, in a proper case, to make arrangements for organising or securing the effective exercise of rights of access;
(g) where the circumstances so require, to provide or facilitate the provision of legal aid and advice, including the participation of legal counsel and advisers;
(h) to provide such administrative arrangements as may be necessary and appropriate to secure the safe return of the child;
(i) to keep each other informed with respect to the operation of this Convention and, as far as possible, to eliminate any obstacles to its application.

CHAPTER III—RETURN OF CHILDREN

Article 8

Any person, institution or other body claiming that a child has been removed or retained in breach of custody rights may apply either to the Central Authority of the child's habitual residence or to the Central Authority of any other Contracting State for assistance in securing the return of the child.
The application shall contain—
(a) information concerning the identity of the applicant, of the child and of the person alleged to have removed or retained the child;
(b) where available, the date of birth of the child;
(c) the grounds on which the applicant's claim for return of the child is based;
(d) all available information relating to the whereabouts of the child and the identity of the person with whom the child is presumed to be.
The application may be accompanied or supplemented by—
(e) an authenticated copy of any relevant decision or agreement;
(f) a certificate or an affidavit emanating from a Central Authority, or other competent authority of the State of the child's habitual residence, or from a qualified person, concerning the relevant law of that State;
(g) any other relevant document.

Article 9

If the Central Authority which receives an application referred to in Article 8 has reason to believe that the child is in another Contracting State, it shall directly and without delay transmit the application to the Central Authority of that Contracting State and inform the requesting Central Authority, or the applicant, as the case may be.

Article 10

The Central Authority of the State where the child is shall take or cause to be taken all appropriate measures in order to obtain the voluntary return of the child.

Article 11

The judicial or administrative authorities of Contracting States shall act expeditiously in proceedings for the return of children.
If the judicial or administrative authority concerned has not reached a decision within six weeks from the date of commencement of the proceedings, the applicant or the Central Authority of the requested State on its own initiative or if asked by the Central Authority of the requesting State, shall have the right to

request a statement of the reasons for the delay. If a reply is received by the Central Authority of the requested State, that Authority shall transmit the reply to the Central Authority of the requesting State, or to the applicant, as the case may be.

Article 12

Where a child has been wrongfully removed or retained in terms of Article 3 and, at the date of the commencement of the proceedings before the judicial or administrative authority of the Contracting State where the child is, a period of less than one year has elapsed from the date of the wrongful removal or retention, the authority concerned shall order the return of the child forthwith.

The judicial or administrative authority, even where the proceedings have been commenced after the expiration of the period of one year referred to in the preceding paragraph, shall also order the return of the child, unless it is demonstrated that the child is now settled in its new environment.

Where the judicial or administrative authority in the requested State has reason to believe that the child has been taken to another State, it may stay the proceedings or dismiss the application for the return of the child.

Article 13

Notwithstanding the provisions of the preceding Article, the judicial or administrative authority of the requested State is not bound to order the return of the child if the person, institution or other body which opposes its return establishes that—

(a) the person, institution or other body having the care of the person of the child was not actually exercising the custody rights at the time of removal or retention, or had consented to or subsequently acquiesced in the removal or retention; or

(b) there is a grave risk that his or her return would expose the child to physical or psychological harm or otherwise place the child in an intolerable situation.

The judicial or administrative authority may also refuse to order the return of the child if it finds that the child objects to being returned and has attained an age and degree of maturity at which it is appropriate to take account of its views.

In considering the circumstances referred to in this Article, the judicial and administrative authorities shall take into account the information relating to the social background of the child provided by the Central Authority or other competent authority of the child's habitual residence.

Article 14

In ascertaining whether there has been a wrongful removal or retention within the meaning of Article 3, the judicial or administrative authorities of the requested State may take notice directly of the law of, and of judicial or administrative decisions, formally recognised or not in the State of the habitual residence of the child, without recourse to the specific procedures for the proof of that law or for the recognition of foreign decisions which would otherwise be applicable.

Article 15

The judicial or administrative authorities of a Contracting State may, prior to the making of an order for the return of the child, request that the applicant obtain from the authorities of the State of the habitual residence of the child a decision or other determination that the removal or retention was wrongful within the meaning of Article 3 of the Convention, where such a decision or determination may be obtained in that State. The Central Authorities of the Contracting States shall so far as practicable assist applicants to obtain such a decision or determination.

Article 16

After receiving notice of a wrongful removal or retention of a child in the sense of Article 3, the judicial or administrative authorities of the Contracting State to which the child has been removed or in which it has been retained shall not decide on the merits of rights of custody until it has been determined that the child is not to be returned under this Convention or unless an application under this Convention is not lodged within a reasonable time following receipt of the notice.

Article 17

The sole fact that a decision relating to custody has been given in or is entitled to recognition in the requested State shall not be a ground for refusing to return a child under this Convention, but the judicial or administrative authorities of the requested State may take account of the reasons for that decision in applying this Convention.

Article 18

The provisions of this Chapter do not limit the power of a judicial or administrative authority to order the return of the child at any time.

Article 19

A decision under this Convention concerning the return of the child shall not be taken to be a determination on the merits of any custody issue.

CHAPTER IV—RIGHTS OF ACCESS

Article 21

An application to make arrangements for organising or securing the effective exercise of rights of access may be presented to the Central Authorities of the Contracting States in the same way as an application for the return of a child.

The Central Authorities are bound by the obligations of co-operation which are set forth in Article 7 to promote the peaceful enjoyment of access rights and the fulfilment of any conditions to which the exercise of those rights may be subject. The Central Authorities shall take steps to remove, as far as possible, all obstacles to the exercise of such rights. The Central Authorities, either directly or through intermediaries, may initiate or assist in the institution of proceedings with a view to organising or protecting these rights and securing respect for the conditions to which the exercise of these rights may be subject.

CHAPTER V—GENERAL PROVISIONS

Article 22

No security, bond or deposit, however described, shall be required to guarantee the payment of costs and expenses in the judicial or administrative proceedings falling within the scope of this Convention.

Article 24

Any application, communication or other document sent to the Central Authority of the requested State shall be in the original language, and shall be accompanied by a translation into the official language or one of the official languages of the requested State or, where that is not feasible, a translation into French or English.

Article 26

Each Central Authority shall bear its own costs in applying this Convention.

Central Authorities and other public services of Contracting States shall not impose any charges in relation to applications submitted under this Convention. In particular, they may not require any payment from the applicant towards the costs and expenses of the proceedings or, where applicable, those arising from the participation of legal counsel or advisers. However, they may require the payment of the expenses incurred or to be incurred in implementing the return of the child.

However, a Contracting State may, by making a reservation in accordance with Article 42, declare that it shall not be bound to assume any costs referred to in the preceding paragraph resulting from the participation of legal counsel or advisers or from court proceedings, except insofar as those costs may be covered by its system of legal aid and advice.

Upon ordering the return of a child or issuing an order concerning rights of access under this Convention, the judicial or administrative authorities may, where appropriate, direct the person who removed or retained the child, or who prevented the exercise of rights of access, to pay necessary expenses incurred by or on behalf of the applicant, including travel expenses, any costs incurred or payments made for locating the child, the costs of legal representation of the applicant, and those of returning the child.

Article 27

When it is manifest that the requirements of this Convention are not fulfilled or that the application is otherwise not well founded, a Central Authority is not bound to accept the application. In that case, the Central Authority shall forthwith inform the applicant or the Central Authority through which the application was submitted, as the case may be, of its reasons.

Article 28

A Central Authority may require that the application be accompanied by a written authorisation empowering it to act on behalf of the applicant, or to designate a representative so to act.

Article 29

This Convention shall not preclude any person, institution or body who claims that there has been a breach of custody or access rights within the meaning of Article 3 or 21 from applying directly to the judicial or administrative authorities of a Contracting State, whether or not under the provisions of this Convention.

Article 30

Any application submitted to the Central Authorities or directly to the judicial or administrative authorities of a Contracting State in accordance with the terms of this Convention, together with documents and any other information appended thereto or provided by a Central Authority, shall be admissible in the courts or administrative authorities of the Contracting States.

Article 31

In relation to a State which in matters of custody of children has two or more systems of law applicable in different territorial units—
   (a) any reference to habitual residence in that State shall be construed as referring to habitual residence in a territorial unit of that State;
   (b) any reference to the law of the State of habitual residence shall be construed as referring to the law of the territorial unit in that State where the child habitually resides.

Article 32

In relation to a State which in matters of custody of children has two or more systems of law applicable to different categories of persons, any reference to the law of that State shall be construed as referring to the legal system specified by the law of that State.

SCHEDULE 2

EUROPEAN CONVENTION ON RECOGNITION AND ENFORCEMENT OF DECISIONS CONCERNING CUSTODY OF CHILDREN

Article 1

For the purposes of this Convention:
 (a) 'child' means a person of any nationality, so long as he is under 16 years of age and has not the right to decide on his own place of residence under the law of his habitual residence, the law of his nationality or the internal law of the State addressed;
 (b) 'authority' means a judicial or administrative authority;
 (c) 'decision relating to custody' means a decision of an authority in so far as it relates to the care of the person of the child, including the right to decide on the place of his residence, or to the right of access to him.
 (d) 'improper removal' means the removal of a child across an international frontier in breach of a decision relating to his custody which has been given in a Contracting State and which is enforceable in such a State; 'improper removal' also includes:
  (i) the failure to return a child across an international frontier at the end of a period of the exercise of the right of access to this child or at the end of any other temporary stay in a territory other than that where the custody is exercised;
  (ii) a removal which is subsequently declared unlawful within the meaning of Article 12.

Article 4

(1) Any person who has obtained in a Contracting State a decision relating to the custody of a child and who wishes to have that decision recognised or enforced in another Contracting State may submit an application for this purpose to the central authority in any Contracting State.

(2) The application shall be accompanied by the documents mentioned in Article 13.

(3) The central authority receiving the application, if it is not the central authority in the State addressed, shall send the documents directly and without delay to that central authority.

(4) The central authority receiving the application may refuse to intervene where it is manifestly clear that the conditions laid down by this Convention are not satisfied.

(5) The central authority receiving the application shall keep the applicant informed without delay of the progress of his application.

Article 5

(1) The central authority in the State addressed shall take or cause to be taken without delay all steps which it considers to be appropriate, if necessary by instituting proceedings before its competent authorities, in order:
 (a) to discover the whereabouts of the child;

    (b) to avoid, in particular by any necessary provisional measures, prejudice to the interests of the child or of the applicant;

    (c) to secure the recognition or enforcement of the decision;

    (d) to secure the delivery of the child to the applicant where enforcement is granted;

    (e) to inform the requesting authority of the measures taken and their results.

    (2) Where the central authority in the State addressed has reason to believe that the child is in the territory of another Contracting State it shall send the documents directly and without delay to the central authority of that State.

    (3) With the exception of the cost of repatriation, each Contracting State undertakes not to claim any payment from an applicant in respect of any measures taken under paragraph (1) of this Article by the central authority of that State on the applicant's behalf, including the costs of proceedings and, where applicable, the costs incurred by the assistance of a lawyer.

    (4) If recognition or enforcement is refused, and if the central authority of the State addressed considers that it should comply with a request by the applicant to bring in that State proceedings concerning the substance of the case, that authority shall use its best endeavours to secure the representation of the applicant in the proceedings under conditions no less favourable than those available to a person who is resident in and a national of that State and for this purpose it may, in particular, institute proceedings before its competent authorities.

Article 7

    A decision relating to custody given in a Contracting State shall be recognised and, where it is enforceable in the State of origin, made enforceable in every other Contracting State.

Article 9

    (1) [*Recognition and enforcement may be refused*] if:

    (a) in the case of a decision given in the absence of the defendant or his legal representative, the defendant was not duly served with the document which instituted the proceedings or an equivalent document in sufficient time to enable him to arrange his defence; but such a failure to effect service cannot constitute a ground for refusing recognition or enforcement where service was not effected because the defendant had concealed his whereabouts from the person who instituted the proceedings in the State of origin;

    (b) in the case of a decision given in the absence of the defendant or his legal representative, the competence of the authority giving the decision was not founded:

        (i) on the habitual residence of the defendant; or

        (ii) on the last common habitual residence of the child's parents, at least one parent being still habitually resident there, or

        (iii) on the habitual residence of the child;

    (c) the decision is incompatible with a decision relating to custody which became enforceable in the State addressed before the removal of the child, unless the child has had his habitual residence in the territory of the requesting State for one year before his removal.

    (3) In no circumstances may the foreign decision be reviewed as to its substance.

Article 10

    (1) [*Recognition and enforcement may also be refused*] on any of the following grounds:

    (a) if it is found that the effects of the decision are manifestly incompatible with the fundamental principles of the law relating to the family and children in the State addressed;

(b) if it is found that by reason of a change in the circumstances including the passage of time but not including a mere change in the residence of the child after an improper removal, the effects of the original decision are manifestly no longer in accordance with the welfare of the child;

(c) if at the time when the proceedings were instituted in the State of origin:
  (i) the child was a national of the State addressed or was habitually resident there and no such connection existed with the State of origin;
  (ii) the child was a national both of the State of origin and of the State addressed and was habitually resident in the State addressed;

(d) if the decision is incompatible with a decision given in the State addressed or enforceable in that State after being given in a third State, pursuant to proceedings begun before the submission of the request for recognition or enforcement, and if the refusal is in accordance with the welfare of the child.

(2) Proceedings for recognition or enforcement may be adjourned on any of the following grounds:

(a) if an ordinary form of review of the original decision has been commenced;

(b) if proceedings relating to the custody of the child, commenced before the proceedings in the State of origin were instituted, are pending in the State addressed;

(c) if another decision concerning the custody of the child is the subject of proceedings for enforcement or of any other proceedings concerning the recognition of the decision.

Article 11

(1) Decisions on rights of access and provisions of decisions relating to custody which deal with the rights of access shall be recognised and enforced subject to the same conditions as other decisions relating to custody.

(2) However, the competent authority of the State addressed may fix the conditions for the implementation and exercise of the right of access taking into account, in particular, undertakings given by the parties on this matter.

(3) Where no decision on the right of access has been taken or where recognition or enforcement of the decision relating to custody is refused, the central authority of the State addressed may apply to its competent authorities for a decision on the right of access if the person claiming a right of access so requests.

Article 12

Where, at the time of the removal of a child across an international frontier, there is no enforceable decision given in a Contracting State relating to his custody, the provisions of this Convention shall apply to any subsequent decision, relating to the custody of that child and declaring the removal to be unlawful, given in a Contracting State at the request of any interested person.

Article 13

(1) A request for recognition or enforcement in another Contracting State of a decision relating to custody shall be accompanied by:

(a) a document authorising the central authority of the State addressed to act on behalf of the applicant or to designate another representative for that purpose;

(b) a copy of the decision which satisfies the necessary conditions of authenticity;

(c) in the case of a decision given in the absence of the defendant or his legal representative, a document which establishes that the defendant was duly served with the document which instituted the proceedings or an equivalent document;

(d) if applicable, any document which establishes that, in accordance with the law of the State of origin, the decision is enforceable;

(e) if possible, a statement indicating the whereabouts or likely whereabouts of the child in the State addressed;

(f) proposals as to how the custody of the child should be restored.

Article 15

(1) Before reaching a decision under paragraph (1)(b) of Article 10, the authority concerned in the State addressed:

(a) shall ascertain the child's views unless this is impracticable having regard in particular to his age and understanding; and

(b) may request that any appropriate enquiries be carried out.

(2) The cost of enquiries in any Contracting State shall be met by the authorities of the State where they are carried out.

Requests for enquiries and the results of enquiries may be sent to the authority concerned through the central authorities.

Article 26

(1) In relation to a State which has in matters of custody two or more systems of law of territorial application:

(a) reference to the law of a person's habitual residence or to the law of a person's nationality shall be construed as referring to the system of law determined by the rules in force in that State or, if there are no such rules, to the system of law with which the person concerned is most closely connected;

(b) reference to the State of origin or to the State addressed shall be construed as referring, as the case may be, to the territorial unit where the decision was given or to the territorial unit where recognition or enforcement of the decision or restoration of custody is requested.

(2) Paragraph (1)(a) of this Article also applies *mutatis mutandis* to States which have in matters of custody two or more systems of law of personal application.

SCHEDULE 3

CUSTODY ORDERS

PART I

ENGLAND AND WALES

1. *(1) An order made by a court in England and Wales under any of the following enactments—*

(a) section 7(2) of the Family Law Reform Act 1969;

(b) subsection (2) of section 1 of the Children and Young Persons Act 1969 (being an order made in pursuance of subsection (3)(c) of that section otherwise than in a case where the condition mentioned in subsection (2)(f) is satisfied with respect to the child);

(c) section 15(1) of the Children and Young Persons Act 1969 (being a care order made on the discharge of a supervision order other than a supervision order made in a case where the condition mentioned in section 1(2)(f) of that Act was satisfied with respect to the child);

(d) section 9(1), 10(1)(a) or 11(a) [section 9 or 10] of the Guardianship of Minors Act 1971;

(e) section 42(1) or (2) or 43(1) of the Matrimonial Causes Act 1973;

(f) section 2(2)(b), (4)(b) or (5) [(4) or (5)(b)] of the Guardianship Act 1973;

(g) section 17(1)(b), 33(1), 36(2) or 36(3)(a) of the Children Act 1975 or section 2(2)(b) or (4)(b) of the Guardianship Act 1973 as applied by section 34(5) of the Children Act 1975;

(h) section 8(2)(a), 10(1) or 19(1)(ii) of the Domestic Proceedings and Magistrates' Courts Act 1978;

(i) section 26(1)(b) of the Adoption Act 1976.

(*2*) *After the commencement of section 26(1)(b) of the Adoption Act 1976 paragraph (g)*
of sub-paragraph (1) above shall have effect with the omission of the reference to section
17(1)(b) of the Children Act 1975.

[**1.** The following are the orders referred to in section 27(1) of this Act—
  (a) a care order under the Children Act 1989 (as defined by section 31(11) of
      that Act, read with section 105(1) and Schedule 14);
  (b) a residence order (as defined by section 8 of the Act of 1989); *and*
[(bb) a special guardianship order (within the meaning of the Act of 1989);
      and]
  (c) any order made by a court in England and Wales under any of the following
      enactments—
        (i) section 9(1), 10(1)(a) or 11(a) of the Guardianship of Minors Act 1971;
       (ii) section 42(1) or (2) or 43(1) of the Matrimonial Causes Act 1973;
      (iii) section 2(2)(b), (4)(b) or (5) of the Guardianship Act 1973 as applied
            by section 34(5) of the Children Act 1975;
       (iv) section 8(2)(a), 10(1) or 19(1)(ii) of the Domestic Proceedings and
            Magistrates' Courts Act 1978;
        (v) *section 26(1)(b) of the Adoption Act 1976.*]

Note. Para 1 in square brackets substituted for para 1 in italics by Children Act 1989, s 108(5),
Sch 13, para 57(3), as from 14 October 1991. In addition para 1(2) is repealed by s 108(7) of, and
Sch 15 to, that Act, as from 14 October 1991. In para 1(b) word in italics revoked and sub-para
(bb) added by the Adoption and Children Act 2002, Sch 3, para 45, as from a day to be
appointed. Para 1(c)(v) is omitted by the Adoption and Children Act 2002, Sch 3, para 45, as
from a day to be appointed. Within para 1 in italics, the following amendments have been
made: words 'section 9 or 10' in square brackets in para 1(1)(d) substituted for words 'section
9(1), 10(1)(a) or 11(a)', and words '(4) or (5)(b)' substituted for words '(4)(b) or (5)', by Family
Law Reform Act 1987, s 33(1), Sch 2, para 90, as from 1 April 1989.

2. An order made by the High Court in the exercise of its jurisdiction relating to
wardship so far as it gives the care and control of a child to any person.

3. *An order made by the Secretary of State under section 25(1) of the Children and Young*
Persons Act 1969 (except where the order superseded was made under section 74(1)(a) or (b)
or 78(1) of the Children and Young Persons Act (Northern Ireland) 1968 or was made
under section 97(2)(a) of that Act on a complaint by a person under whose supervision the
child had been placed by an order under section 74(1)(c) of that Act).

Note. Para 3 repealed by Children (Northern Ireland Consequential Amendments) Order
1995, SI 1995 No 756, art 15, Schedule, as from 4 November 1996.

4. An authorisation given by the Secretary of State under section 26(2) of the
Children and Young Persons Act 1969 (except where the relevant order, within the
meaning of that section, was made by virtue of the court which made it being
satisfied that the child was guilty of an offence).

PART II

SCOTLAND

5. An order made by a court of civil jurisdiction in Scotland under any enactment
or rule of law with respect to the *custody, care or control of a child or* [residence,
custody, care or control of a child or contact with, or] access to a child, excluding—
   (i) an order placing a child under the supervision of a local authority;
  (ii) an adoption order under section 12(1) of the Adoption (Scotland) Act
       1978;
[(iia) an order freeing a child for adoption made under section 18 of the Adoption
       (Scotland) Act 1978;]
 (iii) an order relating to the *tutory or curatory* [guardianship] of a child;
  (iv) an order made under section *16(8), 16A(3) or 18(3) of the Social Work*
       (*Scotland) Act 1968* [86 of the Children (Scotland) Act 1995];

(v) *an order made in the exercise of any power under Part III of the Social Work (Scotland) Act 1968 to authorise any person to take a child to a place of safety, to issue, renew or recall a warrant for the apprehension or detention of a child, or to order the detention of a child in secure accommodation;*

[(v) an order made, or warrant or authorisation granted, under or by virtue of Chapter 2 or 3 of Part II of the Children (Scotland) Act 1995 to remove the child to a place of safety or secure accommodation, to keep him at such a place or in such accommodation, or to prevent his removal from a place where he is being accommodated (or an order varying or discharging any order, warrant or authorisation so made or granted);]

(vi) an order made in proceedings under this Act.

Note. Para 5(iia) inserted by Family Law Act 1986, s 68(1), Sch 1, para 31, as from 4 April 1988. Words in first and third pairs of square brackets substituted for words in italics by Children (Scotland) Act 1995, s 105(4), Sch 4, para 37(6)(a), as from 1 November 1996. Other words in square brackets substituted for words in italics by ibid, as from 1 April 1997.

6. *A supervision requirement or other order made by a children's hearing in Scotland under section 44(1), 47, 48, 72(1) or 74(1) of the Social Work (Scotland) Act 1968.*

[**6.** A supervision requirement made by a children's hearing under section 70 of the Children (Scotland) Act 1995 (whether or not continued under section 73 of that Act) or made by the sheriff under section 51(5)(c)(iii) of that Act and any order made by a court in England and Wales or in Northern Ireland if it is an order which, by virtue of section 33(1) of that Act, has effect as if it were such a supervision requirement.]

Note. Para 6 substituted by Children (Scotland) Act 1995, s 105(4), Sch 4, para 37(6)(b), as from 1 April 1997.

7. *An order made by the Secretary of State under section 74(3) of the said Act of 1968.*

Note. Para 7 repealed by Children (Scotland) Act 1995, s 105(4), Sch 4, para 37(6)(c), as from 1 April 1997.

PART III

NORTHERN IRELAND

8. *An order made by a court in Northern Ireland under any of the following enactments—*
(a) *section 5 of the Guardianship of Infants Act 1886 (except so far as it relates to costs);*
(b) *section 49 of the Mental Health Act (Northern Ireland) 1961;*
(c) *any of the following provisions of the Children and Young Persons Act (Northern Ireland) 1968—*
  (i) *section 95(1)(a) or (b);*
  (ii) *in the case of a child or young person with respect to whom a supervision order under section 95(1)(d) has been made, section 97(2)(a);*
  (iii) *section 108;*
  (iv) *in the case of a child or young person committed to the care of a fit person under Part V of that Act, section 143(6)(a) or (b) or 144 (being, in the case of an order under section 144, an order corresponding to an order under section 95(1)(a) or (b) of that Act);*
(d) *paragraph 7 of Schedule 9 to the Education and Libraries (Northern Ireland) Order 1972 (being an order corresponding to an order under section 95(1)(a) or (b) of the said Act of 1968);*
(e) *Article 45(1) or (2) or 46 of the Matrimonial Causes (Northern Ireland) Order 1978;*
(f) *Article 10(2)(a), 12(1) or 20(1)(ii) of the Domestic Proceedings (Northern Ireland) Order 1980.*

[**8.** The following orders—
(a) a care order under the Children (Northern Ireland) Order 1995 (as defined by Article 49(1) of that Order read with Article 2(2) and Schedule 8);
(b) a residence order (as defined by Article 8 of that Order);

(c) any order made by a court in Northern Ireland under any of the following
    enactments—
    (i) section 5 of the Guardianship of Infants Act 1886 (except so far as it
        relates to costs);
    (ii) section 49 of the Mental Health Act (Northern Ireland) 1961;
    (iii) Article 45(1) or (2) or 46 of the Matrimonial Causes (Northern Ireland)
        Order 1978;
    (iv) Article 10(2)(a), 12(1) or 20(1)(ii) of the Domestic Proceedings
        (Northern Ireland) Order 1980;
    (v) Article 27(1)(b) of the Adoption (Northern Ireland) Order 1987.]

Note. Para 8 substituted by Children (Northern Ireland Consequential Amendments) Order
1995, SI 1995 No 756, art 11(5), as from 4 November 1996.

9. An order made by the High Court in the exercise of its jurisdiction relating to
wardship so far as it gives the care and control of a child to any person.

10. *An order made by the Secretary of State under section 25(2) of the Children and Young
Persons Act 1969 superseding an order within paragraph 1(1)(b) or (c) of this Schedule.*

Note. Para 10 repealed by Children (Northern Ireland Consequential Amendments) Order
1995, SI 1995 No 756, art 15, Schedule, as from 4 November 1996.

ENDURING POWERS OF ATTORNEY ACT 1985

(1985 c 29)

ARRANGEMENT OF SECTIONS

An Act to enable powers of attorney to be created which will survive any subsequent
mental incapacity of the donor and to make provision in connection with such
powers.   [26 June 1985]

Note. As to prescribed forms, see SI 1990 No 1376, and as to rules, see SI 1956 No 127, as amended by SI 1990 No 864.

Enduring powers of attorney

1. Enduring power of attorney to survive mental incapacity of donor—
(1) Where an individual creates a power of attorney which is an enduring power within the meaning of this Act then—

(a) the power shall not be revoked by any subsequent mental incapacity of his; but

(b) upon such incapacity supervening the donee of the power may not do anything under the authority of the power except as provided by subsection (2) below or as directed or authorised by the court under section 5 unless or, as the case may be, until the instrument creating the power is registered by the court under section 6; and

(c) section 5 of the Powers of Attorney Act 1971 (protection of donee and third persons) so far as applicable shall apply if and so long as paragraph (b) above operates to suspend the donee's authority to act under the power as if the power had been revoked by the donor's mental incapacity.

(2) Notwithstanding subsection (1)(b) above, where the attorney has made an application for registration of the instrument then, until the application has been initially determined, the attorney may take action under the power—

(a) to maintain the donor or prevent loss to his estate; or

(b) to maintain himself or other persons in so far as section 3(4) permits him to do so.

(3) Where the attorney purports to act as provided by subsection (2) above then, in favour of a person who deals with him without knowledge that the attorney is acting otherwise than in accordance with paragraph (a) or (b) of that subsection, the transaction between them shall be as valid as if the attorney were acting in accordance with paragraph (a) or (b).

2. Characteristics of an enduring power—(1) Subject to subsections (7) to (9) below and section 11, a power of attorney is an enduring power within the meaning of this Act if the instrument which creates the power—

(a) is in the prescribed form; and

(b) was executed in the prescribed manner by the donor and the attorney; and

(c) incorporated at the time of execution by the donor the prescribed explanatory information.

(2) The Lord Chancellor shall make regulations as to the form and execution of instruments creating enduring powers and the regulations shall contain such provisions as appear to him to be appropriate for securing—

(a) that no document is used to create an enduring power which does not incorporate such information explaining the general effect of creating or accepting the power as may be prescribed; and

(b) that such instruments include statements to the following effect—

(i) by the donor, that he intends the power to continue in spite of any supervening mental incapacity of his;

(ii) by the donor, that he read or had read to him the information explaining the effect of creating the power;

(iii) by the attorney, that he understands the duty of registration imposed by this Act.

(3) Regulations under subsection (2) above—

(a) may include different provision for cases where more than one attorney is to be appointed by the instrument than for cases where only one attorney is to be appointed; and

(b) may, if they amend or revoke any regulations previously made under that subsection, include saving and transitional provisions.

(4) Regulations under subsection (2) above shall be made by statutory instrument which shall be subject to annulment in pursuance of a resolution of either House of Parliament.

(5) An instrument in the prescribed form purporting to have been executed in the prescribed manner shall be taken, in the absence of evidence to the contrary, to be a document which incorporated at the time of execution by the donor the prescribed explanatory information.

(6) Where an instrument differs in an immaterial respect in form or mode of expression from the prescribed form the instrument shall be treated as sufficient in point of form and expression.

(7) A power of attorney cannot be an enduring power unless, when he executes the instrument creating it, the attorney is—

    (a) an individual who has attained eighteen years and is not bankrupt; or

    (b) a trust corporation.

(8) A power of attorney under section 25 of the Trustee Act 1925 (power to delegate trusts etc by power of attorney) cannot be an enduring power.

(9) A power of attorney which gives the attorney a right to appoint a substitute or successor cannot be an enduring power.

(10) An enduring power shall be revoked by the bankruptcy of the attorney whatever the circumstances of the bankruptcy.

(11) An enduring power shall be revoked on the exercise by the court of any of its powers under Part VII of the Mental Health Act 1983 if, but only if, the court so directs.

(12) No disclaimer of an enduring power, whether by deed or otherwise, shall be valid unless and until the attorney gives notice of it to the donor or, where section 4(6) or 7(1) applies, to the court.

(13) In this section 'prescribed' means prescribed under subsection (2) above.

3. Scope of authority etc of attorney under enduring power—(1) An enduring power may confer general authority (as defined in subsection (2) below) on the attorney to act on the donor's behalf in relation to all or a specified part of the property and affairs of the donor or may confer on him authority to do specified things on the donor's behalf and the authority may, in either case, be conferred subject to conditions and restrictions.

(2) Where an instrument is expressed to confer general authority on the attorney it operates to confer, subject to the restriction imposed by subsection (5) below and to any conditions or restrictions contained in the instrument, authority to do on behalf of the donor anything which the donor can lawfully do by an attorney.

(3) Subject to any conditions or restrictions contained in the instrument, an attorney under an enduring power, whether general or limited, may (without obtaining any consent) execute or exercise all or any of the trusts, powers or discretions vested in the donor as trustee and may (without the concurrence of any other person) give a valid receipt for capital or other money paid.

(4) Subject to any conditions or restrictions contained in the instrument, an attorney under an enduring power, whether general or limited, may (without obtaining any consent) act under the power so as to benefit himself or other persons than the donor to the following extent but no further, that is to say—

    (a) he may so act in relation to himself or in relation to any other person if the donor might be expected to provide for his or that person's needs respectively; and

    (b) he may do whatever the donor might be expected to do to meet those needs.

(5) Without prejudice to subsection (4) above but subject to any conditions or restrictions contained in the instrument, an attorney under an enduring power, whether general or limited, may (without obtaining any consent) dispose of the property of the donor by way of gift to the following extent but no further, that is to say—

(a) he may make gifts of a seasonal nature or at a time, or on an anniversary, of a birth or marriage, to persons (including himself) who are related to or connected with the donor, and

(b) he may make gifts to any charity to whom the donor made or might be expected to make gifts,

provided that the value of each such gift is not unreasonable having regard to all the circumstances and in particular the size of the donor's estate.

Action on actual or impending incapacity of donor

4. Duties of attorney in event of actual or impending incapacity of donor—
(1) If the attorney under an enduring power has reason to believe that the donor is or is becoming mentally incapable subsections (2) to (6) below shall apply.

(2) The attorney shall, as soon as practicable, make an application to the court for the registration of the instrument creating the power.

(3) Before making an application for registration the attorney shall comply with the provisions as to notice set out in Schedule 1.

(4) An application for registration shall be made in the prescribed form and shall contain such statements as may be prescribed.

(5) The attorney may, before making an application for the registration of the instrument, refer to the court for its determination any question as to the validity of the power and he shall comply with any direction given to him by the court on that determination.

(6) No disclaimer of the power shall be valid unless and until the attorney gives notice of it to the court.

(7) Any person who, in an application for registration, makes a statement which he knows to be false in a material particular shall be liable—

(a) on conviction on indictment, to imprisonment for a term not exceeding two years or to a fine, or both; and

(b) on summary conviction, to imprisonment for a term not exceeding six months or to a fine not exceeding the statutory maximum, or both.

(8) In this section and Schedule 1 'prescribed' means prescribed by rules of the court.

5. Functions of court prior to registration. Where the court has reason to believe that the donor of an enduring power may be, or may be becoming, mentally incapable and the court is of the opinion that it is necessary, before the instrument creating the power is registered, to exercise any power with respect to the power of attorney or the attorney appointed to act under it which would become exercisable under section 8(2) on its registration, the court may exercise that power under this section and may do so whether the attorney has or has not made an application to the court for the registration of the instrument.

6. Functions of court on application for registration—(1) In any case where—

(a) an application for registration is made in accordance with section 4(3) and (4), and

(b) neither subsection (2) nor subsection (4) below applies,

the court shall register the instrument to which the application relates.

(2) Where it appears to the court that there is in force under Part VII of the Mental Health Act 1983 an order appointing a receiver for the donor but the power has not also been revoked then, unless it directs otherwise, the court shall not exercise or further exercise its functions under this section but shall refuse the application for registration.

(3) Where it appears from an application for registration that notice of it has not been given under Schedule 1 to some person entitled to receive it (other than a person in respect of whom the attorney has been dispensed or is otherwise exempt

from the requirement to give notice) the court shall direct that the application be treated for the purposes of this Act as having been made in accordance with section 4(3), if the court is satisfied that, as regards each such person—

    (a) it was undesirable or impracticable for the attorney to give him notice; or

    (b) no useful purpose is likely to be served by giving him notice.

    (4) If, in the case of an application for registration—

    (a) a valid notice of objection to the registration is received by the court before the expiry of the period of five weeks beginning with the date or, as the case may be, the latest date on which the attorney gave notice to any person under Schedule 1, or

    (b) it appears from the application that there is no one to whom notice has been given under paragraph 1 of that Schedule, or

    (c) the court has reason to believe that appropriate inquiries might bring to light evidence on which the court could be satisfied that one of the grounds of objection set out in subsection (5) below was established,

the court shall neither register the instrument nor refuse the application until it has made or caused to be made such inquiries (if any) as it thinks appropriate in the circumstances of the case.

    (5) For the purposes of this Act a notice of objection to the registration of an instrument is valid if the objection is made on one or more of the following grounds, namely—

    (a) that the power purported to have been created by the instrument was not valid as an enduring power of attorney;

    (b) that the power created by the instrument no longer subsists;

    (c) that the application is premature because the donor is not yet becoming mentally incapable;

    (d) that fraud or undue pressure was used to induce the donor to create the power;

    (e) that, having regard to all the circumstances and in particular the attorney's relationship to or connection with the donor, the attorney is unsuitable to be the donor's attorney.

    (6) If, in a case where subsection (4) above applies, any of the grounds of objection in subsection (5) above is established to the satisfaction of the court, the court shall refuse the application but if, in such a case, it is not so satisfied, the court shall register the instrument to which the application relates.

    (7) Where the court refuses an application for registration on ground (d) or (e) in subsection (5) above it shall by order revoke the power created by the instrument.

    (8) Where the court refuses an application for registration on any ground other than that specified in subsection (5)(c) above the instrument shall be delivered up to be cancelled, unless the court otherwise directs.

Legal position after registration

7. Effect and proof of registration, etc—(1) The effect of the registration of an instrument under section 6 is that—

    (a) no revocation of the power by the donor shall be valid unless and until the court confirms the revocation under section 8(3);

    (b) no disclaimer of the power shall be valid unless and until the attorney gives notice of it to the court;

    (c) the donor may not extend or restrict the scope of the authority conferred by the instrument and no instruction or consent given by him after registration shall, in the case of a consent, confer any right and, in the case of an instruction, impose or confer any obligation or right on or create any liability of the attorney or other persons having notice of the instruction or consent.

    (2) Subsection (1) above applies for so long as the instrument is registered under section 6 whether or not the donor is for the time being mentally incapable.

(3) A document purporting to be an office copy of an instrument registered under this Act [or under the Enduring Powers of Attorney (Northern Ireland) Order 1987] shall, in any part of the United Kingdom, be evidence of the contents of the instrument and of the fact that it has been so registered.

(4) Subsection (3) above is without prejudice to section 3 of the Powers of Attorney Act 1971 (proof by certified copies) and to any other method of proof authorised by law.

Note. Words in square brackets in sub-s (3) inserted by Enduring Powers of Attorney (Northern Ireland Consequential Amendment) Order 1987, SI 1987 No 1628, art 2.

8. Functions of court with respect to registered power—(1) Where an instrument has been registered under section 6, the court shall have the following functions with respect to the power and the donor of and the attorney appointed to act under the power.

(2) The court may—

(a) determine any question as to the meaning or effect of the instrument;

(b) give directions with respect to—

   (i) the management or disposal by the attorney of the property and affairs of the donor;

  (ii) the rendering of accounts by the attorney and the production of the records kept by him for the purpose;

 (iii) the remuneration or expenses of the attorney, whether or not in default of or in accordance with any provision made by the instrument, including directions for the repayment of excessive or the payment of additional remuneration;

(c) require the attorney to furnish information or produce documents or things in his possession as attorney;

(d) give any consent or authorisation to act which the attorney would have to obtain from a mentally capable donor;

(e) authorise the attorney to act so as to benefit himself or other persons than the donor otherwise than in accordance with section 3(4) and (5) (but subject to any conditions or restrictions contained in the instrument);

(f) relieve the attorney wholly or partly from any liability which he has or may have incurred on account of a breach of his duties as attorney.

(3) On application made for the purpose by or on behalf of the donor, the court shall confirm the revocation of the power if satisfied that the donor has done whatever is necessary in law to effect an express revocation of the power and was mentally capable of revoking a power of attorney when he did so (whether or not he is so when the court considers the application).

(4) The court shall cancel the registration of an instrument registered under section 6 in any of the following circumstances, that is to say—

(a) on confirming the revocation of the powers under subsection (3) above or receiving notice of disclaimer under section 7(1)(b);

(b) on giving a direction revoking the power on exercising any of its powers under Part VII of the Mental Health Act 1983;

(c) on being satisfied that the donor is and is likely to remain mentally capable;

(d) on being satisfied that the power has expired or has been revoked by the death or bankruptcy of the donor or the death, mental incapacity or bankruptcy of the attorney or, if the attorney is a body corporate, its winding up or dissolution;

(e) on being satisfied that the power was not a valid and subsisting enduring power when registration was effected;

(f) on being satisfied that fraud or undue pressure was used to induce the donor to create the power; or

(g) on being satisfied that, having regard to all the circumstances and in particular the attorney's relationship to or connection with the donor, the attorney is unsuitable to be the donor's attorney.

(5) Where the court cancels the registration of an instrument on being satisfied of the matters specified in paragraph (f) or (g) of subsection (4) above it shall by order revoke the power created by the instrument.

(6) On the cancellation of the registration of an instrument under subsection (4) above except paragraph (c) the instrument shall be delivered up to be cancelled, unless the court otherwise directs.

Protection of attorney and third parties

9. Protection of attorney and third persons where power invalid or revoked—
(1) Subsections (2) and (3) below apply where an instrument which did not create a valid power of attorney has been registered under section 6 (whether or not the registration has been cancelled at the time of the act or transaction in question).

(2) An attorney who acts in pursuance of the power shall not incur any liability (either to the donor or to any other person) by reason of the non-existence of the power unless at the time of acting he knows—

(a) that the instrument did not create a valid enduring power; or

(b) that an event has occurred which, if the instrument had created a valid enduring power, would have had the effect of revoking the power; or

(c) that, if the instrument had created a valid enduring power, the power would have expired before that time.

(3) Any transaction between the attorney and another person shall, in favour of that person, be as valid as if the power had then been in existence, unless at the time of the transaction that person has knowledge of any of the matters mentioned in subsection (2) above.

(4) Where the interest of a purchaser depends on whether a transaction between the attorney and another person was valid by virtue of subsection (3) above, it shall be conclusively presumed in favour of the purchaser that the transaction was valid if—

(a) the transaction between that person and the attorney was completed within twelve months of the date on which the instrument was registered; or

(b) that person makes a statutory declaration, before or within three months after the completion of the purchase, that he had no reason at the time of the transaction to doubt that the attorney had authority to dispose of the property which was the subject of the transaction.

(5) For the purposes of section 5 of the Powers of Attorney Act 1971 (protection of attorney and third persons where action is taken under the power of attorney in ignorance of its having been revoked) in its application to an enduring power the revocation of which by the donor is by virtue of section 7(1)(a) above invalid unless and until confirmed by the court under section 8(3) above, knowledge of the confirmation of the revocation is, but knowledge of the unconfirmed revocation is not, knowledge of the revocation of the power.

(6) Schedule 2 shall have effect to confer protection in cases where the instrument failed to create a valid enduring power and the power has been revoked by the donor's mental incapacity.

(7) In this section 'purchaser' and 'purchase' have the meanings specified in section 205(1) of the Law of Property Act 1925.

Supplementary

10. Application of Mental Health Act provisions relating to the court—(1) The provisions of Part VII of the Mental Health Act 1983 (relating to the Court of Protection) specified below shall apply to persons within and proceedings under this Act in accordance with the following paragraphs of this subsection and subsection (2) below, that is to say—

(a) section 103 (functions of Visitors) shall apply to persons within this Act as it applies to the persons mentioned in that section;

(b) section 104 (powers of judge) shall apply to proceedings under this Act with respect to persons within this Act as it applies to the proceedings mentioned in subsection (1) of that section:

(c) section 105(1) (appeals to nominated judge) shall apply to any decision of the Master of the Court of Protection or any nominated officer in proceedings under this Act as it applies to any decision to which that subsection applies and an appeal shall lie to the Court of Appeal from any decision of a nominated judge whether given in the exercise of his original jurisdiction or on the hearing of an appeal under section 105(1) as extended by this paragraph;

(d) section 106 except subsection (4) (rules of procedure) shall apply to proceedings under this Act and persons within this Act as it applies to the proceedings and persons mentioned in that section.

(2) Any functions conferred or imposed by the provisions of the said Part VII applied by subsection (1) above shall be exercisable also for the purposes of this Act and the persons who are 'within this Act' are the donors of and attorneys under enduring powers of attorney whether or not they would be patients for the purposes of the said Part VII.

(3) In this section 'nominated judge' and 'nominated officer' have the same meanings as in Part VII of the Mental Health Act 1983.

11. Application to joint and joint and several attorneys—(1) An instrument which appoints more than one person to be an attorney cannot create an enduring power unless the attorneys are appointed to act jointly or jointly and severally.

(2) This Act, in its application to joint attorneys, applies to them collectively as it applies to a single attorney but subject to the modifications specified in Part I of Schedule 3.

(3) This Act, in its application to joint and several attorneys, applies with the modifications specified in subsections (4) to (7) below and in Part II of Schedule 3.

(4) A failure, as respects any one attorney, to comply with the requirements for the creation of enduring powers, shall prevent the instrument from creating such a power in his case without however affecting its efficacy for that purpose as respects the other or others or its efficacy in his case for the purpose of creating a power of attorney which is not an enduring power.

(5) Where one or more but not both or all the attorneys makes or joins in making an application for registration of the instrument then—

(a) an attorney who is not an applicant as well as one who is may act pending the initial determination of the application as provided in section 1(2) (or under section 5);

(b) notice of the application shall also be given under Schedule 1 to the other attorney or attorneys; and

(c) objection may validly be taken to the registration on a ground relating to an attorney or to the power of an attorney who is not an applicant as well as to one or the power of one who is an applicant.

(6) The court shall not refuse under section 6(6) to register an instrument because a ground of objection to an attorney or power is established if an enduring power subsists as respects some attorney who is not affected thereby but shall give effect to it by the prescribed qualification of the registration.

(7) The court shall not cancel the registration of an instrument under section 8(4) for any of the causes vitiating registration specified in that subsection if an enduring power subsists as respects some attorney who is not affected thereby but shall give effect to it by the prescribed qualification of the registration.

(8) In this section—

'prescribed' means prescribed by rules of the court; and

'the requirements for the creation of enduring powers' means the provisions of
section 2 other than subsections (10) to (12) and of regulations under
subsection (2) of that section.

**12. Power of Lord Chancellor to modify pre-registration requirements in
certain cases**—(1) The Lord Chancellor may by order exempt attorneys of such
descriptions as he thinks fit from the requirements of this Act to give notice to
relatives prior to registration.

(2) Subject to subsection (3) below, where an order is made under this section
with respect to attorneys of a specified description then, during the currency of the
order, this Act shall have effect in relation to any attorney of that description with
the omission of so much of section 4(3) and Schedule 1 as requires notice of an
application for registration to be given to relatives.

(3) Notwithstanding that an attorney under a joint or joint and several power is
of a description specified in a current order under this section, subsection (2)
above shall not apply in relation to him if any of the other attorneys under the
power is not of a description specified in that or another current order under this
section.

(4) The power to make an order under this section shall be exercisable by
statutory instrument which shall be subject to annulment in pursuance of a
resolution of either House of Parliament.

13. Interpretation—(1) In this Act—
'the court', in relation to any functions under this Act, means the authority
having jurisdiction under Part VII of the Mental Health Act 1983;
'enduring power' is to be construed in accordance with section 2;
'mentally incapable' or 'mental incapacity', except where it refers to revocation
at common law, means, in relation to any person, that he is incapable by
reason of mental disorder of managing and administering his property and
affairs and 'mentally capable' and 'mental capacity' shall be construed
accordingly;
'mental disorder' has the same meaning as it has in the Mental Health Act 1983;
'notice' means notice in writing;
'rules of the court' means rules under Part VII of the Mental Health Act 1983 as
applied by section 10;
*'statutory maximum' has the meaning given by section 74(1) of the Criminal Justice Act
1982;*
'trust corporation' means the Public Trustee or a corporation either appointed by
the High Court or a county court (according to their respective jurisdictions) in
any particular case to be a trustee or entitled by rules under section 4(3) of the
Public Trustee Act 1906 to act as custodian trustee.

Note. Definition 'statutory maximum' repealed by Statute Law (Repeals) Act 1993, s 1(1),
Sch 1, Part XIV, as from 5 November 1993.

(2) Any question arising under or for the purposes of this Act as to what the
donor of the power might at any time be expected to do shall be determined by
assuming that he had full mental capacity at the time but otherwise by reference to
the circumstances existing at that time.

14. Short title, commencement and extent—(1) This Act may be cited as the
Enduring Powers of Attorney Act 1985.

(2) This Act shall come into force on such day as the Lord Chancellor appoints
by order made by statutory instrument.

(3) This Act extends to England and Wales only except that section 7(3) and
section 10(1)(b) so far as it applies section 104(4) of the Mental Health Act 1983
extend also to Scotland and Northern Ireland.

Commencement. This Act was brought into force on 10 March 1986 (SI 1986 No 125).

SCHEDULES

SCHEDULE 1 Section 4(3)

NOTIFICATION PRIOR TO REGISTRATION

PART I

DUTY TO GIVE NOTICE TO RELATIVES AND DONOR

Duty to give notice to relatives

1. Subject to paragraph 3 below, before making an application for registration the attorney shall give notice of his intention to do so to all those persons (if any) who are entitled to receive notice by virtue of paragraph 2 below.

2. (1) Subject to the limitations contained in sub-paragraphs (2) to (4) below, persons of the following classes (referred to in this Act as 'relatives') are entitled to receive notice under paragraph 1 above—

  (a) the donor's husband or wife;

  (b) the donor's children;

  (c) the donor's parents;

  (d) the donor's brothers and sisters, whether of the whole or half blood;

  (e) the widow or widower of a child of the donor;

  (f) the donor's grandchildren;

  (g) the children of the donor's brothers and sisters of the whole blood;

  (h) the children of the donor's brothers and sisters of the half blood;

  (i) the donor's uncles and aunts of the whole blood; and

  (j) the children of the donor's uncles and aunts of the whole blood.

  (2) A person is not entitled to receive notice under paragraph 1 above if—

  (a) his name or address is not known to the attorney and cannot be reasonably ascertained by him; or

  (b) the attorney has reason to believe that he has not attained eighteen years or is mentally incapable.

  (3) Except where sub-paragraph (4) below applies, no more than three persons are entitled to receive notice under paragraph 1 above and, in determining the persons who are so entitled, persons falling within class (a) of sub-paragraph (1) above are to be preferred to persons falling within class (b) of that sub-paragraph, persons falling within class (b) are to be preferred to persons falling within class (c) of that sub-paragraph; and so on.

  (4) Notwithstanding the limit of three specified in sub-paragraph (3) above, where—

  (a) there is more than one person falling within any of classes (a) to (j) of sub-paragraph (1) above, and

  (b) at least one of those persons would be entitled to receive notice under paragraph 1 above,

then, subject to sub-paragraph (2) above, all the persons falling within that class are entitled to receive notice under paragraph 1 above.

3. (1) An attorney shall not be required to give notice under paragraph 1 above to himself or to any other attorney under the power who is joining in making the application, notwithstanding that he or, as the case may be, the other attorney is entitled to receive notice by virtue of paragraph 2 above.

  (2) In the case of any person who is entitled to receive notice under paragraph 1 above, the attorney, before applying for registration, may make an application to the court to be dispensed from the requirement to give him notice; and the court shall grant the application if it is satisfied—

  (a) that it would be undesirable or impracticable for the attorney to give him notice; or

  (b) that no useful purpose is likely to be served by giving him notice.

Duty to give notice to donor

4. (1) Subject to sub-paragraph (2) below, before making an application for registration the attorney shall give notice of his intention to do so to the donor.

(2) Paragraph 3(2) above shall apply in relation to the donor as it applies in relation to a person who is entitled to receive notice under paragraph 1 above.

PART II

CONTENTS OF NOTICES

5. A notice to relatives under this Schedule—
  (a) shall be in the prescribed form;
  (b) shall state that the attorney proposes to make an application to the Court of Protection for the registration of the instrument creating the enduring power in question;
  (c) shall inform the person to whom it is given that he may object to the proposed registration by notice in writing to the Court of Protection before the expiry of the period of four weeks beginning with the day on which the notice under this Schedule was given to him;
  (d) shall specify, as the grounds on which an objection to registration may be made, the grounds set out in section 6(5).
6. A notice to the donor under this Schedule—
  (a) shall be in the prescribed form;
  (b) shall contain the statement mentioned in paragraph 5(b) above; and
  (c) shall inform the donor that, whilst the instrument remains registered, any revocation of the power by him will be ineffective unless and until the revocation is confirmed by the Court of Protection.

PART III

DUTY TO GIVE NOTICE TO OTHER ATTORNEYS

7. (1) Subject to sub-paragraph (2) below, before making an application for registration an attorney under a joint and several power shall give notice of his intention to do so to any other attorney under the power who is not joining in making the application; and paragraphs 3(2) and 5 above shall apply in relation to attorneys entitled to receive notice by virtue of this paragraph as they apply in relation to persons entitled to receive notice by virtue of paragraph 2 above.

(2) An attorney is not entitled to receive notice by virtue of this paragraph if—
  (a) his address is not known to the applying attorney and cannot reasonably be ascertained by him; or
  (b) the applying attorney has reason to believe that he has not attained eighteen years or is mentally incapable.

PART IV

SUPPLEMENTARY

8. (1) For the purposes of this Schedule an illegitimate child shall be treated as if he were the legitimate child of his mother and father.

(2) Notwithstanding anything in section 7 of the Interpretation Act 1978 (construction of references to service by post), for the purposes of this Schedule a notice given by post shall be regarded as given on the date on which it was posted.

SCHEDULE 2   Section 9(6)

FURTHER PROTECTION OF ATTORNEY AND THIRD PERSONS

1. Where—

(a) an instrument in a form prescribed under section 2(2) creates a power which is not a valid enduring power; and

(b) the power is revoked by the mental incapacity of the donor,

paragraphs 2 and 3 below shall apply, whether or not the instrument has been registered.

2. An attorney who acts in pursuance of the power shall not, by reason of the revocation, incur any liability (either to the donor or to any other person) unless at the time of acting he knows—

(a) that the instrument did not create a valid enduring power; and

(b) that the donor has become mentally incapable.

3. Any transaction between the attorney and another person shall, in favour of that person, be as valid as if the power had then been in existence, unless at the time of the transaction that person knows—

(a) that the instrument did not create a valid enduring power; and

(b) that the donor has become mentally incapable.

4. Section 9(4) shall apply for the purpose of determining whether a transaction was valid by virtue of paragraph 3 above as it applies for the purpose of determining whether a transaction was valid by virtue of section 9(3).

SCHEDULE 3　　　　　　　　　　　　　　　　　　　　　　　　　Section 11(2), (3)

JOINT AND JOINT AND SEVERAL ATTORNEYS

PART I

JOINT ATTORNEYS

1. In section 2(7), the reference to the time when the attorney executes the instrument shall be read as a reference to the time when the second or last attorney executes the instrument.

2. In section 2(9) and (10), the reference to the attorney shall be read as a reference to any attorney under the power.

3. In section 5, references to the attorney shall be read as including references to any attorney under the power.

4. Section 6 shall have effect as if the ground of objection to the registration of the instrument specified in subsection (5)(e) applied to any attorney under the power.

5. In section 8(2), references to the attorney shall be read as including references to any attorney under the power.

6. In section 8(4), references to the attorney shall be read as including references to any attorney under the power.

PART II

JOINT AND SEVERAL ATTORNEYS

7. In section 2(10), the reference to the bankruptcy of the attorney shall be construed as a reference to the bankruptcy of the last remaining attorney under the power; and the bankruptcy of any other attorney under the power shall cause that person to cease to be attorney, whatever the circumstances of the bankruptcy.

8. The restriction upon disclaimer imposed by section 4(6) applies only to those attorneys who have reason to believe that the donor is or is becoming mentally incapable.

SURROGACY ARRANGEMENTS ACT 1985

(1985 c 49)　　　　　　　　　　　　　　　　　　　　　　　　　　[16 July 1985]

1. Meaning of 'surrogate mother', 'surrogacy arrangement' and other terms—

(1) The following provisions shall have effect for the interpretation of this Act.

(2) 'Surrogate mother' means a woman who carries a child in pursuance of an arrangement—

(a) made before she began to carry the child, and

(b) made with a view to any child carried in pursuance of it being handed over to, and *the parental rights being exercised* [parental responsibility being met] (so far as practicable) by, another person or other persons.

(3) An arrangement is a surrogacy arrangement if, were a woman to whom the arrangement relates to carry a child in pursuance of it, she would be a surrogate mother.

(4) In determining whether an arrangement is made with such a view as is mentioned in subsection (2) above regard may be had to the circumstances as a whole (and, in particular, where there is a promise or understanding that any payment will or may be made to the woman or for her benefit in respect of the carrying of any child in pursuance of the arrangement, to that promise or understanding).

(5) An arrangement may be regarded as made with such a view though subject to conditions relating to the handing over of any child.

(6) A woman who carries a child is to be treated for the purposes of subsection (2)(a) above as beginning to carry it at the time of the insemination *or, as the case may be, embryo insertion* [or of the placing in her of an embryo, of an egg in the process of fertilisation or of sperm and eggs, as the case may be,] that results in her carrying the child.

(7) 'Body of persons' means a body of persons corporate or unincorporate.

(8) 'Payment' means payment in money or money's worth.

(9) This Act applies to arrangements whether or not they are lawful *and whether or not they are enforceable by or against any of the persons making them.*

Note. Words in square brackets in sub-s (2)(b) substituted for words in italics by Children Act 1989, s 108(5), Sch 13, para 56, as from 14 October 1991, and, in relation to Northern Ireland, by Children (Northern Ireland) Order 1995, SI 1995 No 755, art 185(1), Sch 9, para 119, as from 4 November 1996. For the meaning of 'parental responsibility', see s 3 of the 1989 Act (p 3292). Words in square brackets in sub-s (6) substituted for words in italics and words in italics in sub-s (9) repealed by Human Fertilisation and Embryology Act 1990, s 36(2)(b), as from 7 November 1990.

[**1A. Surrogacy arrangements unenforceable.** No surrogacy arrangement is enforceable by or against any of the persons making it.]

Note. This section inserted by Human Fertilisation and Embryology Act 1990, s 36(1), as from 7 November 1990.

2. Negotiating surrogacy arrangements on a commercial basis, etc—(1) No person shall on a commercial basis do any of the following acts in the United Kingdom, that is—

(a) initiate or take part in any negotiations with a view to the making of a surrogacy arrangement,

(b) offer or agree to negotiate the making of a surrogacy arrangement, or

(c) compile any information with a view to its use in making, or negotiating the making of, surrogacy arrangements;

and no person shall in the United Kingdom knowingly cause another to do any of those acts on a commercial basis.

(2) A person who contravenes subsection (1) above is guilty of an offence; but it is not a contravention of that subsection—

(a) for a woman, with a view to becoming a surrogate mother herself, to do any act mentioned in that subsection or to cause such an act to be done, or

(b) for any person, with a view to a surrogate mother carrying a child for him, to do such an act or to cause such an act to be done.

(3) For the purposes of this section, a person does an act on a commercial basis (subject to subsection (4) below) if—

(a) any payment is at any time received by himself or another in respect of it, or

(b) he does it with a view to any payment being received by himself or another in respect of making, or negotiating or facilitating the making of, any surrogacy arrangement.

In this subsection 'payment' does not include payment to or for the benefit of a surrogate mother or prospective surrogate mother.

(4) In proceedings against a person for an offence under subsection (1) above, he is not to be treated as doing an act on a commercial basis by reason of any payment received by another in respect of the act if it is proved that—

(a) in a case where the payment was received before he did the act, he did not do the act knowing or having reasonable cause to suspect that any payment had been received in respect of the act; and

(b) in any other case, he did not do the act with a view to any payment being received in respect of it.

(5) Where—

(a) a person acting on behalf of a body of persons takes any part in negotiating or facilitating the making of a surrogacy arrangement in the United Kingdom, and

(b) negotiating or facilitating the making of surrogacy arrangements is an activity of the body,

then, if the body at any time receives any payment made by or on behalf of—

(i) a woman who carries a child in pursuance of the arrangement,

(ii) the person or persons for whom she carries it, or

(iii) any person connected with the woman or with that person or those persons,

the body is guilty of an offence.

For the purposes of this subsection, a payment received by a person connected with a body is to be treated as received by the body.

(6) In proceedings against a body for an offence under subsection (5) above, it is a defence to prove that the payment concerned was not made in respect of the arrangement mentioned in paragraph (a) of that subsection.

(7) A person who in the United Kingdom takes part in the management or control—

(a) of any body of persons, or

(b) of any of the activities of any body of persons,

is guilty of an offence if the activity described in subsection (8) below is an activity of the body concerned.

(8) The activity referred to in subsection (7) above is negotiating or facilitating the making of surrogacy arrangements in the United Kingdom, being—

(a) arrangements the making of which is negotiated or facilitated on a commercial basis, or

(b) arrangements in the case of which payments are received (or treated for the purposes of subsection (5) above as received) by the body concerned in contravention of subsection (5) above.

(9) In proceedings against a person for an offence under subsection (7) above, it is a defence to prove that he neither knew nor had reasonable cause to suspect that the activity described in subsection (8) above was an activity of the body concerned; and for the purposes of such proceedings any arrangement falling within subsection (8)(b) above shall be disregarded if it is proved that the payment concerned was not made in respect of the arrangement.

3. Advertisements about surrogacy—(1) This section applies to any advertisement containing an indication (however expressed)—

(a) that any person is or may be willing to enter into a surrogacy arrangement or to negotiate or facilitate the making of a surrogacy arrangement, or

(b) that any person is looking for a woman willing to become a surrogate mother or for persons wanting a woman to carry a child as a surrogate mother.

(2) Where a newspaper or periodical containing an advertisement to which this section applies is published in the United Kingdom, any proprietor, editor or publisher of the newspaper or periodical is guilty of an offence.

(3) Where an advertisement to which this section applies is conveyed by means of *a telecommunications system* [an electronic communications network] so as to be seen or heard (or both) in the United Kingdom, any person who in the United Kingdom causes it to be so conveyed knowing it to contain such an indication as is mentioned in subsection (1) above is guilty of an offence.

(4) A person who publishes or causes to be published in the United Kingdom an advertisement to which this section applies (not being an advertisement contained in a newspaper or periodical or conveyed by means of *a telecommunication system* [an electronic communications network]) is guilty of an offence.

(5) A person who distributes or causes to be distributed in the United Kingdom an advertisement to which this section applies (not being an advertisement contained in a newspaper or periodical published outside the United Kingdom or an advertisement conveyed by means of *a telecommunication system* [an electronic communications network]) knowing it to contain such an indication as it mentioned in subsection (1) above is guilty of an offence.

(6) In this section 'telecommunication system' has the same meaning as in the Telecommunications Act 1984.

Note. In sub-ss (3)–(5) words in square brackets substituted for words in italics by The Communications Act 2003, s 406(1), Sch 17, para 77, as from 29 December 2003. Sub-s (6) is omitted by the Communications Act 2003, s 406(7), Sch 19(1), as from 29 December 2003.

4. Offences—(1) A person guilty of an offence under this Act shall be liable on summary conviction—

  (a) *in the case of an offence under section 2 to a fine not exceeding level 5 on the standard scale or to imprisonment for a term not exceeding 3 months or both,*
  (b) *in the case of an offence under section 3* to a fine not exceeding level 5 on the standard scale.

In this subsection 'the standard scale' has the meaning given by section 75 of the Criminal Justice Act 1982.

Note. Para (a) omitted by the Criminal Justice Act 2003, s 332, Sch 37, Pt 9, as from a day to be appointed. In para (b) words in italics omitted by the Criminal Justice Act 2003, s 332, Sch 37, Pt 9, as from a day to be appointed. Words in italics repealed by Statute Law (Repeals) Act 1993, s 1(1), Sch 1, Part XIV, as from 5 November 1993.

(2) No proceedings for an offence under this Act shall be instituted—
  (a) in England and Wales, except by or with the consent of the Director of Public Prosecutions; and
  (b) in Northern Ireland, except by or with the consent of the Director of Public Prosecutions for Northern Ireland.

(3) Where an offence under this Act committed by a body corporate is proved to have been committed with the consent or connivance of, or to be attributable to any neglect on the part of, any director, manager, secretary or other similar officer of the body corporate or any person who was purporting to act in any such capacity, he as well as the body corporate is guilty of the offence and is liable to be proceeded against and punished accordingly.

(4) Where the affairs of a body corporate are managed by its members, subsection (3) above shall apply in relation to the acts and defaults of a member in connection with his functions of management as if he were a director of the body corporate.

(5) In any proceedings for an offence under section 2 of this Act, proof of things done or of words written, spoken or published (whether or not in the presence of any party to proceedings) by any person taking part in the management or control of a body of persons or of any of the activities of the body, or by any person doing

any of the acts mentioned in subsection (1)(a) to (c) of that section on behalf of the body, shall be admissible as evidence of the activities of the body.

(6) In relation to an offence under this Act, section 127(1) of the Magistrates' Courts Act 1980 (information must be laid within six months of commission of offence), *section 331(1) of the Criminal Procedure (Scotland) Act 1975* [section 136(1) of the Criminal Procedure (Scotland) Act 1995] (proceedings must be commenced within that time) and article 19(1) of the Magistrates' Courts (Northern Ireland) Order 1981 (complaint must be made within that time) shall have effect as if for the reference to six months there were substituted a reference to two years.

Note. Words in square brackets substituted for words in italics by Criminal Procedure (Consequential Provisions) (Scotland) Act 1995, s 5, Sch 4, para 57, as from 1 April 1996.

5. Short title and extent—(1) This Act may be cited as the Surrogacy Arrangements Act 1985.

(2) This Act extends to Northern Ireland.

ADMINISTRATION OF JUSTICE ACT 1985

(1985 c 61)

An Act to make further provision with respect to the administration of justice and matters connected therewith; ... to make further provision with respect to complaints relating to the provision of legal aid services ... [30 October 1985]

* * * * *

PART III

LEGAL AID

Legal aid complaints

40. Legal aid complaints: preliminary—(1) For the purposes of this Part of this Act a legal aid complaint is a complaint relating to the conduct of a barrister or solicitor in connection with [the provision for any person of services *under the Legal Aid Act 1988* [funded by the Legal Services Commission as part of the Community Legal Service or Criminal Defence Service] including in the case of a solicitor, provision for any person of such services in the capacity of agent for that person's solicitor].

(*a*) *the giving of advice or assistance under Part I of the Legal Aid Act 1974;*

(*b*) *the provision of services for any person receiving legal aid under that Part of that Act;*

(*c*) *the provision of services for any legally assisted person in pursuance of Part II of that Act; or*

(*d*) *in the case of a solicitor, the provision of advice and representation pursuant to section 1 of the Legal Aid Act 1982 (duty solicitors);*

and the reference in each of paragraphs (b) and (c) to the provision of services for any such person as is there mentioned includes, in the case of a solicitor, the provision of services for any such person in the capacity of agent for that person's solicitor.

(2) In this Part—

'legally assisted person' means a person to whom aid is ordered to be given under section 28 of the Legal Aid Act 1974;

'the Senate' means the Senate of the Inns of Court and the Bar; and

'Senate Disciplinary Tribunal' means any committee of the Senate which in accordance with the regulations of the Senate is to be known as a Disciplinary Tribunal.

(3) In the Legal Aid Act 1974, sections 12(3) to (5) and 38(2) to (6) (which are superseded by this Part) shall cease to have effect.

Note. First words in square brackets substituted for words in italics by Legal Aid Act 1988, s 45(1), (3), Sch 5, para 17, as from 1 April 1989. Second words in square brackets substituted for words in italics by the Access to Justice Act 1999, s 24, Sch 4, paras 32, 33, as from 1 April 2000.

41. Jurisdiction and powers of Senate Disciplinary Tribunals in relation to complaints against barristers—(*1*) *The jurisdiction of a Senate Disciplinary Tribunal to hear and determine charges of professional misconduct against barristers shall include jurisdiction to hear and determine, as a charge of professional misconduct, any legal aid complaint relating to the conduct of a barrister and referred to the tribunal under this section in accordance with the regulations of the Senate.*

(*2*) *Such a tribunal may on the hearing of any such complaint, if it thinks fit and whether or not it makes any other order on the hearing, order that any fees—*

    (*a*) *otherwise payable under or in accordance with Part I or Part II of the Legal Aid Act 1974, or*

    (*b*) *otherwise chargeable as mentioned in section 5(1) of that Act (payment for advice and assistance otherwise than through client's contribution),*

in connection with services provided by the barrister shall be reduced or cancelled.

(*3*) *Accordingly, in so far as any of sections 4, 5, 10(1) and 37(2) of the Legal Aid Act 1974 (which relate to remuneration for legal aid work) has effect in relation to any fees reduced or cancelled by an order under subsection (2), it shall so have effect subject to the provisions of that order.*

(*4*) *An appeal shall lie in the case of an order of a Senate Disciplinary Tribunal under subsection (2) in the same manner as an appeal would lie in the case of any other order of such a tribunal.*

[**41. Application to legal aid complaints against barristers of disciplinary provisions**—(1) The disciplinary provisions applicable to barristers shall apply to legal aid complaints relating to the conduct of barristers as they apply to other complaints about their conduct.

(2) Subject to any exclusion or restriction made by those provisions, any disciplinary tribunal which hears a legal aid complaint relating to the conduct of a barrister may, if it thinks fit and whether or not it makes any other order, order that any fees—

    (*a*) *otherwise payable in connection with his services under or in accordance with the Legal Aid Act 1988, or*

    (*b*) *otherwise chargeable in connection with his services in respect of advice or assistance made available under Part III of that Act,* [otherwise payable by the Legal Services Commission in connection with services provided by kind as part of the Community Legal Service or Criminal Defence Service]

shall be reduced or cancelled.

(3) Accordingly, in so far as any of sections 9, 11 15(6) and (7) and 25(2) of the Legal Aid Act 1988 (which relate to remuneration for legal aid work) has effect in relation to any fees reduced or cancelled by an order under subsection (2) above, it shall so have effect subject to the provisions of that order.

(4) An appeal shall lie in the case of an order under subsection (2) above in the same manner as an appeal would lie in the case of any other order of such a tribunal.

(5) The reference in subsection (2) above to a disciplinary tribunal is a reference to a tribunal acting under the disciplinary provisions applicable to barristers and it includes a reference to a member exercising any functions of the tribunal delegated to him.]

Note. Section 41 in square brackets substituted for s 41 in italics by Legal Aid Act 1988, s 33, as from 1 April 1989. Sub-s (2) words in square brackets substituted for paras (a), (b), as from 1 April 2000.

42. Exclusion of barrister from legal aid work—(*1*) *Where on the hearing of a charge of professional misconduct against a barrister (whether pursuant to section 41(1) or otherwise) a Senate Disciplinary Tribunal determines that there is good reason for so ordering arising out of—*

    (*a*) *the barrister's conduct in connection with any such matters as are mentioned in paragraphs (a) to (c) of section 40(1); or*

(*b*) his professional conduct generally,
the tribunal may order that the barrister shall be excluded from legal aid work (either permanently or for a specified period).

(*2*) Subsection (*4*) of section 41 shall apply to an order under subsection (*1*) as it applies to an order under subsection (*2*) of that section.

(*3*) A barrister who has been excluded from legal aid work by an order under subsection (*1*) may, in accordance with the regulations of the Senate, make an application to a Senate Disciplinary Tribunal for an order terminating his exclusion from such work.

(*4*) In this section references to a person being excluded from legal aid work are references to his being excluded from those who may be selected under section 12 of the Legal Aid Act 1974 and from those who may be assigned to act for legally assisted persons.

[**42. Exclusion of barristers from legal aid work**—(1) Subject to any exclusion or restriction made by the disciplinary provisions applicable to barristers, where a disciplinary tribunal hears a charge of professional misconduct or breach of professional standards against a barrister, it may order that he shall be excluded from *legal aid work* [providing representation funded by the Legal Services Commission as part of the Criminal Defence Service], either temporarily or for a specified period, if it determines that there is good reason for the exclusion arising out of—

(a) his conduct in connection with any such services as are mentioned in section 40(1), or

(b) his professional conduct generally.

(2) Subsection (4) of section 41 shall apply to an order under subsection (1) as it applies to an order under subsection (2) of that section.

(3) The disciplinary provisions applicable to barristers shall include provision enabling a barrister who has been excluded from *legal aid work* [providing representation funded by the Legal Services Commission as part of the Criminal Defence Service] under this section to apply for an order terminating his exclusion *from such work.*

(4) In this section—

(a) the reference to a disciplinary tribunal shall be construed in accordance with section 41(5); *and*

(b) *references to a person being excluded from legal aid work are references to his being excluded from those who may be selected or assigned under section 32 of the Legal Aid Act 1988.*]

Note. Section 42 in square brackets substituted for s 42 in italics by Legal Aid Act 1988, s 33, as from 1 April 1989. In section 42 in square brackets in sub-ss (1), (3) words in square brackets substituted for words in italics and words in italics in sub-ss (3), (4), omitted by the Access to Justice Act 1999, ss 24, 106, Sch 4, paras 32, 35, Sch 15, Pt 1, as from 2 April 2001.

43. Jurisdiction and powers of Solicitors Disciplinary Tribunal in relation to complaints against solicitors—(1) The Solicitors Disciplinary Tribunal shall have jurisdiction to hear and determine any legal aid complaint relating to the conduct of a solicitor and made to the Tribunal under this section by or on behalf of the Law Society.

(2) In the following provisions of the Solicitors Act 1974, namely—

(a) subsections (7) to (11) of section 46 (procedure of Tribunal); and

(b) section 47(2) (powers of Tribunal),

any reference to a complaint or to a complaint made to the Tribunal under that Act shall be construed as including a reference to a legal aid complaint or to a legal aid complaint made to the Tribunal under this section.

(3) On the hearing of a legal aid complaint against a solicitor the Tribunal may, if it thinks fit and whether or not it makes any other order on the hearing, order that *any costs—*

(*a*)   *otherwise payable under or in accordance with Part I or Part II of the Legal Aid Act 1974; or*

(*b*)   *otherwise chargeable as mentioned in section 5(1) of that Act; or*

(*c*)   *otherwise payable under regulations made by virtue of section 1(6) of the Legal Aid Act 1982,*

[(*a*)   *otherwise payable under or in accordance with the Legal Aid Act 1988, or*

(*b*)   *otherwise chargeable in respect of advice or assistance made available under Part III of that Act;*]

in connection with services provided by the solicitor [any costs otherwise payable by the Legal Service Commission in connection with services provided by the solicitor as part of the Community Legal Service on Criminal Defence Service] shall be reduced or cancelled.

(4) Accordingly, in so far as—

(*a*)   *any of sections 4, 5, 10(1) and 37(2) of the Legal Aid Act 1974; or*

(*b*)   *any provision made by virtue of section 1(1)(b) of the Legal Aid Act 1982,*

[*any of sections 9, 11, 15(6) and (7) and 25(2) of, or any provision made under, the Legal Aid Act 1988*] *has effect in relation to any costs reduced or cancelled by an order under subsection (3), it shall so have effect subject to the provision of that order.*

Note. Words in square brackets in sub-ss (3), (4) substituted for words in italics by Legal Aid Act 1988, s 45(1), (3), Sch 5, para 18, as from 1 April 1989. Words from 'any costs—' to 'by the solicitor' in square brackets in sub-s (3) substituted for words in italics, and sub-s (4) repealed by the Access to Justice Act 1999, ss 24, 106, Sch 4, paras 32, 36, Sch 15, Pt 1, as from 27 September 1999.

(5)   Without prejudice to the generality of subsection (1)(b) of section 49 of the Solicitors Act 1974, an appeal shall lie to the High Court under that section against an order of the Tribunal under subsection (3), but such an appeal shall lie only at the instance of the solicitor with respect to whom the legal aid complaint was made.

(6)   In this section 'costs' includes fees, charges, disbursements, expenses and remuneration.

*   *   *   *   *

Advice and assistance

45, 46.   (*Repealed by the Legal Aid Act 1988, s 45(4), Sch 6*).

PART IV

THE SUPREME COURT AND COUNTY COURTS

Proceedings relating to estates of deceased persons and trusts

47.   Power of High Court to make judgments binding on persons who are not parties—(1) This section applies to actions in the High Court relating to the estates of deceased persons or to trusts and falling within any description specified in rules of court.

(2)   Rules of court may make provision for enabling any judgment given in an action to which this section applies to be made binding on persons who—

(a)   are or may be affected by the judgment and would not otherwise be bound by it; but

(b)   have in accordance with the rules been given notice of the action and of such matters connected with it as the rules may require.

(3)   Different provision may be made under this section in relation to actions of different descriptions.

*   *   *   *   *

49. Powers of High Court on compromise of probate action—(1) Where on a compromise of a probate action in the High Court—

 (a) the court is invited to pronounce for the validity of one or more wills, or against the validity of one or more wills, or for the validity of one or more wills and against the validity of one or more other wills; and

 (b) the court is satisfied that consent to the making of the pronouncement or, as the case may be, each of the pronouncements in question has been given by or on behalf of every relevant beneficiary,

the court may without more pronounce accordingly.

 (2) In this section—

'probate action' means an action for the grant of probate of the will, or letters of administration of the estate, of a deceased person or for the revocation of such a grant or for a decree pronouncing for or against the validity of an alleged will, not being an action which is non-contentious or common form probate business; and

'relevant beneficiary', in relation to a pronouncement relating to any will or wills of a deceased person, means—

 (a) a person who under any such will is beneficially interested in the deceased's estate; and

 (b) where the effect of the pronouncement would be to cause the estate to devolve as on an intestacy (or partial intestacy), or to prevent it from so devolving, a person who under the law relating to intestacy is beneficially interested in the estate.

* * * * *

51, 52. (*Section 51 substitutes County Courts Act 1984, s 32, and amends Supreme Court Act 1981, s 106; section 52 amends Supreme Court Act 1981, s 40A and County Courts Act 1984, s 109*)

Reimbursement of costs

53. Reimbursement of additional costs resulting from death or incapacity of presiding judge etc—(1) Where—

 (a) the judge, or (as the case may be) any of the judges, presiding at any proceedings to which this section applies becomes temporarily or permanently incapacitated from presiding at the proceedings, or dies, at any time prior to the conclusion of the proceedings; and

 (b) any party represented at the proceedings incurs any additional costs in consequence of the judge's incapacity or death,

the *Lord Chancellor* [Secretary of State] may, if he thinks fit, reimburse that party in respect of any such additional costs, or in respect of such part thereof as he may determine; but the amount of any such reimbursement shall not exceed such sum as the *Lord Chancellor* [Secretary of State] may by order prescribe for the purposes of this section.

Note. The amount of £8,000 is prescribed for the purposes of sub-s (1) by the Reimbursement of Costs (Monetary Limits) Order 1988, SI 1988 No 1342.

 (2) Subject to subsection (3), this section applies to—

 (a) proceedings in the civil division of the Court of Appeal;

 (b) civil proceedings in the High Court; and

 (c) proceedings in a county court;

and, in the case of any interlocutory proceedings falling within paragraphs (a) to (c), applies separately to any such proceedings and to any other proceedings in the cause or matter in question.

 (3) *This section does not apply to proceedings in the civil division of the Court of Appeal if the incapacity or death of one or more of the presiding judges does not reduce the number of the remaining judges to less than two.*

(4) For the purposes of this section the amount of any additional costs incurred by any person as mentioned in subsection (1)(b) shall be such amount as may be agreed between the *Lord Chancellor* [Secretary of State] and that person or, in default of agreement, as may be ascertained by taxation.

(5) Where any proceedings to which this section applies—

(a) are due to be begun before a judge at a particular time; but

(b) are not begun at that time by reason of the judge becoming temporarily or permanently incapacitated from presiding at the proceedings or by reason of his death,

subsection (1) shall have effect in relation to the incapacity or death of the judge as it has effect in relation to any such incapacity or death of a presiding judge as is mentioned in paragraph (a) of that subsection, but as if any reference to any party represented at the proceedings were a reference to any party who would have been so represented but for the judge's incapacity or death.

(6) In this section *(except subsection (3))* 'judge' in relation to any proceedings, includes—

(a) a master, registrar or other person acting in a judicial capacity in the proceedings; or

(b) a person assisting at the proceedings as an assessor or as an adviser appointed by virtue of section 70(3) of the Supreme Court Act 1981;

and, in relation to any such person as is mentioned in paragraph (b), any reference to presiding at any proceedings shall be construed as including a reference to assisting at the proceedings.

(7) Any order made by the *Lord Chancellor* [Secretary of State] under this section shall be made with the concurrence of the Treasury, and shall be so made by statutory instrument subject to annulment in pursuance of a resolution of either House of Parliament.

(8) Any sums required by the *Lord Chancellor* [Secretary of State] for making payments under this section shall be paid out of money provided by Parliament.

Note. In sub-s (1) (in both places where they occur) and sub-ss (4), (7), (8) words 'Secretary of State' in square brackets substituted for words in italics by SI 2003/1887, as from 19 August 2003. Whole of sub-s (3) and words in italics in sub-s (6) repealed by the Access to Justice Act 1999, s 106, Sch 15, Pt III, as from 27 September 1999.

Register of county court judgments

54, 55. (*Section 54 amends County Courts Act 1984, s 73, and inserts s 73A in that Act; section 55 amends County Courts Act 1984, ss 138, 139.*)

Interpretation

56. Interpretation of Part IV.   In this Part—

'action' means any civil proceedings commenced by writ or in any other manner prescribed by rules of court;

'judgment' includes an order;

'will' includes a nuncupative will and any testamentary document of which probate may be granted.

PART IV

MISCELLANEOUS AND SUPPLEMENTARY

*   *   *   *   *

61. (*Amends Children and Young Persons Act 1963, Sch 2, Part II, para 15A.*)

*   *   *   *   *

65. Administration of oaths and taking of affidavits by public notaries in London—(1) Subject to the provisions of this section, every member of the Incorporated Company of Scriveners ('the Company') who has been admitted to practise as a public notary within the jurisdiction of the Company shall have the powers conferred on a commissioner for oaths by the Commissioners for Oaths Acts 1889 and 1891; and any reference to such a commissioner in an enactment or instrument (including an enactment passed or instrument made after the commencement of this section) shall include a reference to such a member of the Company unless the context otherwise requires.

(2) A member of the Company shall not exercise the powers conferred by this section in a proceeding in which he is interested.

(3) A member of the Company before whom any oath or affidavit is taken or made in pursuance of this section shall state in the jurat or attestation the place at which and the date on which the oath or affidavit is taken or made.

(4) A document containing such a statement and purporting to be sealed or signed by a member of the Company shall be admitted in evidence without proof of the seal or signature, and without proof that he is a member of the Company or that he has been admitted to practise as mentioned in subsection (1).

(5) Nothing in this section affects the power to appoint commissioners under the Commissioners for Oaths Act 1889.

Note. Repealed by the Access to Justice Act 1999, s 106, Sch 15, Pt III, as from 1 January 2000.

* * * * *

69. Short title, commencement, transitional provisions and savings—(1) This Act may be cited as the Administration of Justice Act 1985.

(2) Subject to subsections (3) and (4), this Act shall come into force on such day as the *Lord Chancellor* [Secretary of State] may by order made by statutory instrument appoint; and an order under this subsection may appoint different days for different provisions and for different purposes.

(3) The following provisions of this Act shall come into force on the day this Act is passed—

(a) section 63;

(b) Part I of Schedule 8 and section 67(2) so far as relating thereto;

(c) section 68;

(d) this section and Schedule 9.

(4) The following provisions of this Act shall come into force at the end of the period of two months beginning with the day on which this Act is passed—

(a) sections 45, 49, 52, 54, 56 to 62 and 64 and 65;

(b) paragraph 8 of Schedule 7 and section 67(1) so far as relating thereto;

(c) Part II of Schedule 8 and section 67(2) so far as relating thereto.

(5) The transitional provisions and savings contained in Schedule 9 shall have effect; but nothing in that Schedule shall be taken as prejudicing the operation of sections 16 and 17 of the Interpretation Act 1978 (which relate to repeals).

Note. Words 'Secretary of State' in square brackets in sub-s (2) substituted for words in italics by SI 2003/1887, as from 19 August 2003.

Commencement. Sections 40, 43 were brought into force on 1 April 1989 (SI 1989 No 287). Section 47 was brought into force on 1 October 1986 (SI 1986 No 1503). Section 53 was brought into force on 1 October 1988 (SI 1988 No 1341).

SCHEDULES

* * * * *

(*Sch 7 makes consequential amendments which, insofar as they are still in force and are within the scope of this work, have been incorporated.*)

SCHEDULE 8

REPEALS

PART I

REPEAL COMING INTO FORCE ON ROYAL ASSENT

Chapter	Short Title	Extent of Repeal
12 & 13 Vict c 16	Justices Protection (Ireland) Act 1849	The whole Act so far as unrepealed.

PART II

REPEALS COMING INTO FORCE TWO MONTHS AFTER ROYAL ASSENT

Chapter	Short Title	Extent of Repeal
1978 c 23	Judicature (Northern Ireland) Act 1978	In section 70(2)(a), the words 'and is in practice as such'.
1981 c 54	Supreme Court Act 1981	In section 40A(4), the word 'and'.
1982 c 53	Administration of Justice Act 1982	Section 71.
1984 c 28	County Courts Act 1984	In section 58(1), the words from 'or a solicitor' onwards. In section 109(4), the word 'and'. Section 113(a)(i).

PART III

REPEALS COMING INTO FORCE ON AN APPOINTED DAY

Chapter	Short Title	Extent of Repeal
1974 c 4	Legal Aid Act 1974	Section 12(3) to (5). Section 38(2) to (6).
1974 c 47	Solicitors Act 1974	In sections 7 and 8(2), the words 'not exceeding £15'. Section 43(6). In Schedule 2, in paragraph 2(1)(b) the words 'not exceeding £50'.
1981 c 54	Supreme Court Act 1981	Section 106(2) to (4).
1984 c 28	County Courts Act 1984	In section 33, the words 'a judge of'. In section 138(5), the words 'Subject to subsection (6),'.

Note. Part I came into force on 30 October 1985; Part II, on 30 December 1985; in Part III, the repeals in the Solicitor Act 1974 came into force on 12 March 1986 (SI 1980 No 364), those in the County Courts Act 1984 and the Supreme Court Act 1981 on 1 October 1986 (SI 1986 No 1503), and those relating to the Legal Aid Act 1974 had not been brought into force before the whole of that Act was repealed by the Legal Aid Act 1988.

SCHEDULE 9

TRANSITIONAL PROVISIONS AND SAVINGS

Imposition of disciplinary sanctions by Council of Law Society

1. Section 1 applies in relation to services provided by a solicitor whether they were provided before or after the commencement of that section.

Examination of solicitors' files in connection with complaints

2. Section 2 applies in relation to a complaint whether it was made before or after the commencement of that section.

Powers of lay observers and Tribunal in relation to inadequate professional services

3. In section 3—
  (a) subsection (1) applies in relation to a complaint whether it was made before or after the commencement of that section; and
  (b) subsection (2) applies in relation to services provided by a solicitor whether they were provided before or after that commencement.

Practising certificates

4. In section 4—
  (a) subsections (2) and (4) apply to applications for practising certificates made after the commencement of that section; and
  (b) subsection (3) applies in relation to practising certificates issued after that commencement.

Restriction on preparation of contracts of sale etc

5. In section 6—
  (a) subsection (3) applies to acts done before or after the commencement of that section; but
  (b) subsection (4) does not apply to acts done before that commencement.

Restriction on preparation of papers for probate etc

6. Where a person has committed an offence under section 23 of the Solicitors Act 1974 before the commencement of section 7 of this Act, he shall not be liable after that commencement to be proceeded against in respect of that offence unless the act constituting that offence would have constituted an offence under section 23, as substituted by section 7 of this Act, if it had been in force at the time when the act was done.

Orders modifying provisions so as to apply to incorporated practices

7. Any provision made by an order under subsection (7) of section 9 after the commencement of that section may be made with retrospective effect as from that commencement or any later date.

Legal aid complaints

8. The repeal by this Act of the provisions referred to in subsection (3) of section 40 shall not affect—
  (a) the hearing and determination by any tribunal established pursuant to any of those provisions of any complaint or other matter where a reference or application was made to the tribunal in respect of the complaint or matter before the commencement of that subsection; or

(b) any repeal against the decision of such a tribunal with respect to any such complaint or matter.

9. Each of sections 41 to 44 applies in relation to conduct of a barrister or solicitor (as the case may be) whether it occurred before or after the commencement of that section.

Substitution or removal of personal representatives

10. Subsection (6) of section 50 applies to an application under section 1 of the Judicial Trustees Act 1896 whether it was made before or after the commencement of section 50.

Administrative and clerical expenses of garnishees

11. (1) Any order of the Lord Chancellor made, or having effect as if made, under section 40A of the Supreme Court Act 1981 or section 109 of the County Courts Act 1984 which is in force immediately before the commencement of section 52 of this Act shall have effect as if made under and for the purposes of that section as amended by section 52, and any reference in any such order to the sum which may be deducted by any deposit-taking institution shall be construed as a reference to the maximum sum which may be so deducted.

(2) The provisions of section 52 shall not apply in relation to any order of the kind mentioned in subsection (1) of either of the said sections 40A and 109 which was made before the commencement of section 52.

Register of county court judgments

12. (1) Where immediately before the commencement of section 54 there is in force any entry in the register relating to—

(a) any judgment of a county court, not being a judgment falling within section 73(1) of the County Courts Act 1984 as substituted by subsection (2) of section 54; or

(b) any order of a county court,

nothing in subsection (2) of section 54 shall affect the continuation in force of that entry; but regulations under the said section 73 may make provision as to the cancellation of any such entry.

(2) In sub-paragraph (1) 'the register' means the register kept under the said section 73.

Relief from forfeiture in county court

13. The provisions inserted by subsections (4) and (5) of section 55 shall not have effect in connection with any recovery of possession of land by a lessor which occurred before the commencement of that section.

Time limits for actions for libel or slander

14. Nothing in section 57 shall apply in relation to an action if the cause of action accrued before the commencement of that section.

Appointment of arbitrator by court

15. *Section 58 applies to an arbitration agreement whether it was entered into before or after the commencement of that section.*

Note. Para 15 repealed by Arbitration Act 1996, s 107(2), Sch 4, as from 31 January 1997.

Limitation of damages against resident magistrates etc in Northern Ireland

16. Nothing in section 63 shall apply in relation to an action if the sentence or order in respect of which the action is brought was passed or made before the passing of this Act.

Increase of penalties under Solicitors Act 1974

17. Nothing in paragraph 6 or 7 of Schedule 1 shall affect the punishment for an offence committed before the commencement of that paragraph.

MARRIAGE (WALES) ACT 1986

(1986 c 7)

An Act to extend section 23 of the Marriage Act 1949 to Wales.   [18 March 1986]

1. Benefices held in plurality.   Section 23 of the Marriage Act 1949 (benefices held in plurality) shall extend to Wales with the omission of the words 'under the Pastoral Reorganisation Measure, 1949,' and accordingly Schedule 6 to that Act (which specifies provisions of the Act which do not extend to Wales) shall be amended by the omission of the reference to that section.

2. Short title and citation—(1) This Act may be cited as the Marriage (Wales) Act 1986.

(2) This Act and the Marriage Acts 1949 to 1983 may be cited together as the Marriage Acts 1949 to 1986.

MARRIAGE (PROHIBITED DEGREES OF RELATIONSHIP) ACT 1986

(1986 c 16)

An Act to make further provision with regard to the marriage of persons related by affinity.   [20 May 1986]

1. Marriage between certain persons related by affinity not be void—(1) A marriage solemnized after the commencement of this Act between a man and a woman who is the daughter or grand-daughter of a former spouse of his (whether the former spouse is living or not) or who is the former spouse of his father or grandfather (whether his father or grandfather is living or not) shall not be void by reason only of that relationship if both the parties have attained the age of twenty-one at the time of the marriage and the younger party has not at any time before attaining the age of eighteen been a child of the family in relation to the other party.

(2) A marriage solemnized after the commencement of this Act between a man and a woman who is the grandmother of a former spouse of his (whether the former spouse is living or not) or is a former spouse of his grandson (whether his grandson is living or not) shall not be void by reason only of that relationship.

(3) A marriage solemnized after the commencement of this Act between a man and a woman who is the mother of a former spouse of his shall not be void by reason only of that relationship if the marriage is solemnized after the death of both that spouse and the father of that spouse and after both the parties to the marriage have attained the age of twenty-one.

(4) A marriage solemnized after the commencement of this Act between a man and a woman who is a former spouse of his son shall not be void by reason only of that relationship if the marriage is solemnized after the death of both his son and the mother of his son and after both the parties to the marriage have attained the age of twenty-one.

(5) In this section 'child of the family' in relation to any person means a child who has lived in the same household as that person and been treated by that person as a child of his family.

(6) The Marriage Act 1949 shall have effect subject to the amendments specified in the Schedule to this Act, being amendments consequential on the preceding provisions of this section.

(7) Where, apart from this Act, any matter affecting the validity of a marriage would fall to be determined (in accordance with the rules of private international law) by reference to the law of a country outside England and Wales nothing in this Act shall preclude the determination of that matter in accordance with that law.

(8) Nothing in this section shall affect any marriage solemnized before the commencement of this Act.

2–5. (*Section 2 applies to Scotland; section 3 inserts s 5A in Marriage Act 1949 (p 2111); section 4 amends Perjury Act 1911, s 3; section 5 amends Supreme Court Act 1981, Sch 1, para 3(c) (p 2867).*)

6. Short title, citation, commencement and extent—(1) This Act may be cited as the Marriage (Prohibited Degrees of Relationship) Act 1986.

(2) This Act so far as it extends to England and Wales may be cited with the Marriage Acts 1949 to 1983 and the Marriage (Wales) Act 1986 as the Marriage Acts 1949 to 1986.

(3) This Act so far as it relates to the Marriage (Scotland) Act 1977 may be cited with that Act as the Marriage (Scotland) Acts 1977 and 1986.

(4) (*Amends Matrimonial Causes Act 1973, s 11(a), p 2503.*)

(5) This Act shall come into force on such day as the Secretary of State may by order made by statutory instrument appoint and different days may be so appointed for different provisions.

(6) Section 2 and Schedule 2 shall extend to Scotland only, but save as aforesaid this Act shall not extend to Scotland or to Northern Ireland.

Commencement. This Act was brought into force on 1 November 1986 (SI 1986 No 1343).

SCHEDULES

SCHEDULE 1

AMENDMENTS OF MARRIAGE ACT 1949

(*Sch 1 makes amendments to the Marriage Act 1949, which have been incorporated into this work; Sch 2 applies to Scotland.*)

INSOLVENCY ACT 1986

(1986 c 45)   [25 July 1986]

*   *   *   *

PART IX

BANKRUPTCY

CHAPTER 1

BANKRUPTCY PETITIONS; BANKRUPTCY ORDERS

Commencement and duration of bankruptcy; discharge

282. Court's power to annul bankruptcy order—(1) The court may annul a bankruptcy order if it at any time appears to the court—

(a) that, on the grounds existing at the time the order was made, the order ought not to have been made, or

(b) that, to the extent required by the rules, the bankruptcy debts and the expenses of the bankruptcy have all, since the making of the order, been either paid or secured for to the satisfaction of the court.

(2) The court may annul a bankruptcy order made against an individual on a petition under paragraph (a), (b) or (c) of section 264(1) if it at any time appears to the court, on an application by the Official Receiver—
  (a)   that the petition was pending at a time when a criminal bankruptcy order was made against the individual or was presented after such an order was so made, and
  (b)   no appeal is pending (within the meaning of section 277) against the individual's conviction of any offence by virtue of which the criminal bankruptcy order was made;
and the court shall annul a bankruptcy order made on a petition under section 264(1)(d) if it at any time appears to the court that the criminal bankruptcy order on which the petition was based has been rescinded in consequence of an appeal.

(3) The court may annul a bankruptcy order whether or not the bankrupt has been discharged from the bankruptcy.

(4) Where the court annuls a bankruptcy order (whether under this section or under section 261 [or 263D] in Part VIII—
  (a)   any sale or other disposition of property, payment may be made or other thing duly done, under any provision in this Group of Parts, by or under the authority of the official receiver or a trustee of the bankrupt's estate or by the court is valid, but
  (b)   if any of the bankrupt's estate is then vested, under any such provision, in such a trustee, it shall vest in such person as the court may appoint or, in default of any such appointment, revert to the bankrupt on such terms (if any) as the court may direct;
and the court may include in its order such supplemental provisions as may be authorised by the rules.

(5) In determining for the purposes of section 279 whether a person was an undischarged bankrupt at any time, any time when he was a bankrupt by virtue of an order that was subsequently annulled is to be disregarded.

Note. Sub-s (2) is prospectively repealed by the Criminal Justice Act 1988, s 107(2), Sch 16, as from a day to be appointed. Sub-s (4): words 'or 263D' prospectively inserted by the Enterprise Act 2002, s 269, Sch 23, paras 1, 4(a) as from 1 April 2004: see SI 2003 No 2093, art 2(2), Sch 2. Sub-s (5): repealed by the Enterprise Act 2002, ss 269, 278(2), Sch 23, paras 1, 4(b), Sch 26 as from 1 April 2004: see SI 2003 No 2093, art 2(2), Sch 2; for transitional provisions see the Enterprise Act 2002, s 256(2), Sch 19 (as amended by SI 2003 No 2096, art 3).

*   *   *   *   *

284. Restrictions on dispositions of property—(1) Where a person is adjudged bankrupt, any disposition of property made by that person in the period to which this section applies is void except to the extent that it is or was made with the consent of the court, or is or was subsequently ratified by the court.

(2) Subsection (1) applies to a payment (whether in cash or otherwise) as it applies to a disposition of property and, accordingly, where any payment is void by virtue of that subsection, the person paid shall hold the sum paid for the bankrupt as part of his estate.

(3) This section applies to the period beginning with the day of the presentation of the petition for the bankruptcy order and ending with the vesting, under Chapter IV of this Part, of the bankrupt's estate in a trustee.

(4) The preceding provisions of this section do not give a remedy against any person—
  (a)   in respect of any property or payment which he received before the commencement of the bankruptcy in good faith, for value and without notice that the petition had been presented, or
  (b)   in respect of any interest in property which derives from an interest in respect of which there is, by virtue of this subsection, no remedy.

(5) Where after the commencement of his bankruptcy the bankrupt has incurred a debt to a banker or other person by reason of the making of a payment

which is void under this section, that debt is deemed for the purposes of any of this Group of Parts to have been incurred before the commencement of the bankruptcy unless—

(a) that banker or person had notice of the bankruptcy before the debt was incurred, or

(b) it is not reasonably practicable for the amount of the payment to be recovered from the person to whom it was made.

(6) A disposition of property is void under this section notwithstanding that the property is not or, as the case may be, would not be comprised in the bankrupt's estate; but nothing in this section affects any disposition made by a person of property held by him on trust for any other person.

CHAPTER 2

PROTECTION OF BANKRUPT'S ESTATE AND INVESTIGATION OF HIS AFFAIRS.

285. Restriction on proceedings and remedies—(1) At any time when proceedings on a bankruptcy petition are pending or an individual has been adjudged bankrupt the court may stay any action, execution or other legal process against the property or person of the debtor or, as the case may be, of the bankrupt.

(2) Any court in which proceedings are pending against any individual may, on proof that a bankruptcy petition has been presented in respect of that individual or that he is an undischarged bankrupt, either stay the proceedings or allow them to continue on such terms as it thinks fit.

(3) After the making of a bankruptcy order no person who is a creditor of the bankrupt in respect of a debt provable in the bankruptcy shall—

(a) have any remedy against the property or person of the bankrupt in respect of that debt, or

(b) before the discharge of the bankrupt, commence any action or other legal proceedings against the bankrupt except with the leave of the court and on such terms as the court may impose.

This is subject to sections 346 (enforcement procedures) and 347 (limited right to distress).

(4) Subject as follows, subsection (3) does not affect the right of a secured creditor of the bankrupt to enforce his security.

(5) Where any goods of an undischarged bankrupt are held by any person by way of pledge, pawn or other security, the official receiver may, after giving notice in writing of his intention to do so, inspect the goods.

Where such a notice has been given to any person, that person is not entitled, without leave of the court, to realise his security unless he has given the trustee of the bankrupt's estate a reasonable opportunity of inspecting the goods and of exercising the bankrupt's right of redemption.

(6) References in this section to the property or goods of the bankrupt are to any of his property or goods, whether or not comprised in his estate.

*   *   *   *   *

313. Charge on bankrupt's home—(1) Where any property consisting of an interest in a dwelling house which is occupied by the bankrupt or by his spouse or former spouse is comprised in the bankrupt's estate and the trustee is, for any reason, unable for the time being to realise that property, the trustee may apply to the court for an order imposing a charge on the property for the benefit of the bankrupt's estate.

(2) If on an application under this section the court imposes a charge on any property, the benefit of that charge shall be comprised in the bankrupt's estate and is enforceable, *up to the value from time to time of the property secured,* [, up to the charged value from time to time,] for the payment of any amount which is payable

otherwise than to the bankrupt out of the estate and of interest on that amount at the prescribed rate.

Note. Words in square brackets substituted for words in italics by the Enterprise Act 2002, s 261(2)(a), as from 1 April 2004.

[(2A) In subsection (2) the charged value means—
(a) the amount specified in the charging order as the value of the bankrupt's interest in the property at the date of the order, plus
(b) interest on that amount from the date of the charging order at the prescribed rate.

(2B) In determining the value of an interest for the purposes of this section the court shall disregard any matter which it is required to disregard by the rules.]

Note. Sub-ss (2A), (2B) inserted by the Enterprise Act 2002, s 261(2)(b), as from 1 April 2004.

(3) An order under this section made in respect of property vested in the trustee shall provide, in accordance with the rules, for the property to cease to be comprised in the bankrupt's estate and, subject to the charge (and any prior charge), to vest in the bankrupt.

(4) Subsections (1) and (2) and (4) to (6) of section 3 of the Charging Orders Act 1979 (supplemental provisions with respect to charging orders) have effect in relation to orders under this section as in relation to charging orders under that act.

[(5) But an order under section 3(5) of that Act may not vary a charged value.]

Note. Sub-s (5) inserted by the Enterprise Act 2002, s 261(2)(c), as from 1 April 2004.

* * * * *

Disclaimer of onerous property

315. Disclaimer (general power)—(1) Subject as follows, the trustee may by the giving of the prescribed notice, disclaim any onerous property and may do so notwithstanding that he has taken possession of it, endeavoured to sell it or otherwise exercised rights of ownership in relation to it.

(2) The following is onerous property for the purposes of this section, that is to say—
(a) any unprofitable contract, and
(b) any other property comprised in the bankrupt's estate which is unsaleable or not readily saleable, or is such that it may give rise to a liability to pay money or perform any other onerous act.

(3) A disclaimer under this section—
(a) operates so as to determine, as from the date of the disclaimer, the rights, interests and liabilities of the bankrupt and his estate in or in respect of the property disclaimed, and
(b) discharges the trustee from all personal liability in respect of that property as from the commencement of his trusteeship,

but does not, except so far as is necessary for the purpose of releasing the bankrupt, the bankrupt's estate and the trustee from any liability, affect the rights or liabilities of any other persons.

(4) A notice of disclaimer shall not be given under this section in respect of any property that has been claimed for the estate under section 307 (after-acquired property) or 308 (personal property of bankrupt exceeding reasonable replacement value), [or 308A] except with the leave of the court.

(5) Any person sustaining loss or damage in consequence of the operation of a dis- claimer under this section is deemed to be a creditor of the bankrupt to the extent of the loss or damage and accordingly may prove for the loss or damage as a bankruptcy debt.

Note. Words in square brackets inserted by Housing Act 1988, s 117(4), as from 15 January 1989.

316. Notice requiring trustee's decision—(1) Notice of disclaimer shall not be given under section 315 in respect of any property if—

   (a) a person interested in the property has applied in writing to the trustee or one of his predecessors as trustee requiring the trustee or that predecessor to decide whether he will disclaim or not, and

   (b) the period of 28 days beginning with the day on which that application was made has expired without a notice of disclaimer having been given under section 315 in respect of that property.

(2) The trustee is deemed to have adopted any contract which by virtue of this section he is not entitled to disclaim.

317. Disclaimer of leasehold—(1) The disclaimer of any property of a leasehold nature does not take effect unless a copy of the disclaimer has been served (so far as the trustee is aware of their addresses) on every person claiming under the bankrupt as underlessee or mortgagee and either—

   (a) no application under section 320 below is made with respect to the property before the end of the period of 14 days beginning with the day on which the last notice served under this subsection was served, or

   (b) where such an application has been made, the court directs that the disclaimer is to take effect.

(2) Where the court gives a direction under subsection (1)(b) it may also, instead of or in addition to any order it makes under section 320, make such orders with respect to fixtures, tenant's improvements and other matters arising out of the lease as it thinks fit.

318. Disclaimer of dwelling house.   Without prejudice to section 317, the disclaimer of any property in a dwelling house does not take effect unless a copy of the disclaimer has been served (so far as the trustee is aware of their addresses) on every person in occupation of or claiming a right to occupy the dwelling house and either—

   (a) no application under section 320 is made with respect to the property before the end of the period of 14 days beginning with the day on which the last notice served under this section was served, or

   (b) where such an application has been made, the court directs that the disclaimer is to take effect.

319. Disclaimer of land subject to rentcharge—(1) The following applies where, in consequence of the disclaimer under section 315 of any land subject to a rentcharge, that land vests by operation of law in the Crown or any other person (referred to in the next subsection as 'the proprietor').

(2) The proprietor, and the successors in title of the proprietor, are not subject to any personal liability in respect of any sums becoming due under the rentcharge, except sums becoming due after the proprietor, or some person claiming under or through the proprietor, has taken possession or control of the land or has entered into occupation of it.

320. Court order vesting disclaimed property—(1) This section and the next apply where the trustee has disclaimed property under section 315.

(2) An application may be made to the court under this section by—

   (a) any person who claims an interest in the disclaimed property,

   (b) any person who is under any liability in respect of the disclaimed property, not being a liability discharged by the disclaimer, or

   (c) where the disclaimed property is property in a dwelling house, any person who at the time when the bankruptcy petition was presented was in occupation of or entitled to occupy the dwelling house.

(3) Subject as follows in this section and the next, the court may, on an application under this section, make an order on such terms as it thinks fit for the vesting of the disclaimed property in, or for its delivery to—

    (a) a person entitled to it or a trustee for such a person,

    (b) a person subject to such a liability as is mentioned in subsection (2)(b) or a trustee for such a person, or

    (c) where the disclaimed property is property in a dwelling house, any person who at the time when the bankruptcy petition was presented was in occupation of or entitled to occupy the dwelling house.

(4) The court shall not make an order by virtue of subsection (3)(b) except where it appears to the court that it would be just to do so for the purpose of compensating the person subject to the liability in respect of the disclaimer.

(5) The effect of any order under this section shall be taken into account in assessing for the purposes of section 315(5) the extent of any loss or damage sustained by any person in consequence of the disclaimer.

(6) An order under this section vesting property in any person need not be completed by any conveyance, assignment or transfer.

321. Order under section 320 in respect of leaseholds—(1) The court shall not make an order under section 320 vesting property of a leasehold nature in any person, except on terms making that person—

    (a) subject to the same liabilities and obligations as the bankrupt was subject to under the lease on the day the bankruptcy petition was presented, or

    (b) if the court thinks fit, subject to the same liabilities and obligations as that person would be subject to if the lease had been assigned to him on that day.

(2) For the purposes of an order under section 320 relating to only part of any property comprised in a lease, the requirements of subsection (1) apply as if the lease comprised only the property to which the order relates.

(3) Where subsection (1) applies and no person is willing to accept an order under section 320 on the terms required by that subsection, the court may (by order under section 320) vest the estate or interest of the bankrupt in the property in any person who is liable (whether personally or in a representative capacity and whether alone or jointly with the bankrupt) to perform the lessee's covenants in the lease.

The court may by virtue of this subsection vest that estate and interest in such a person freed and discharge from all estates, incumbrances and interests created by the bankrupt.

(4) Where subsection (1) applies and a person declines to accept any order under section 320, that person shall be excluded from all interest in the property.

          *   *   *   *   *

328. Priority of debts—(1) In the distribution of the bankrupt's estate, his preferential debts (within the meaning given by section 386 in Part XII) shall be paid in priority to other debts.

(2) Preferential debts rank equally between themselves after the expenses of the bankruptcy and shall be paid in full unless the bankrupt's estate is insufficient for meeting them, in which case they abate in equal proportions between themselves.

(3) Debts which are neither preferential debts nor debts to which the next section applies also rank equally between themselves and, after the preferential debts, shall be paid in full unless the bankrupt's estate is insufficient for meeting them, in which case they abate in equal proportions between themselves.

(4) Any surplus remaining after the payment of the debts that are preferential or rank equally under subsection (3) shall be applied in paying interest on those

debts in respect of the periods during which they have been outstanding since the commencement of the bankruptcy; and interest on preferential debts ranks equally with interest on debts other than preferential debts.

(5) The rate of interest payable under subsection (4) in respect of any debt is whichever is the greater of the following—

(a) the rate specified in section 17 of the Judgments Act 1838 at the commencement of the bankruptcy, and

(b) the rate applicable to that debt apart from the bankruptcy.

(6) This section and the next are without prejudice to any provision of this Act or any other Act under which the payment of any debt or the making of any other payment is, in the event of bankruptcy, to have a particular priority or to be postponed.

329. Debts to spouse—(1) This section applies to bankruptcy debts owed in respect of credit provided by a person who (whether or not the bankrupt's spouse at the time the credit was provided) was the bankrupt's spouse at the commencement of the bankruptcy.

(2) Such debts—

(a) rank in priority after the debts and interest required to be paid in pursuance of section 328(3) and (4), and

(b) are payable with interest at the rate specified in section 328(5) in respect of the period during which they have been outstanding since the commencement of the bankruptcy;

and the interest payable under paragraph (b) has the same priority as the debts on which it is payable.

*   *   *   *   *

332. Saving for bankrupt's home—(1) This section applies where—

(a) there is comprised in the bankrupt's estate property consisting of an interest in a dwelling house which is occupied by the bankrupt or by his spouse or former spouse, and

(b) the trustee has been unable for any reason to realise that property.

(2) The trustee shall not summon a meeting under section 331 unless either—

(a) the court has made an order under section 313 imposing a charge on that property for the benefit of the bankrupt's estate, or

(b) the court has declined, on an application under that section, to make such an order, or

(c) the Secretary of State has issued a certificate to the trustee stating that it would be inappropriate or inexpedient for such an application to be made in the case in question.

*   *   *   *   *

Rights under trusts of land

[335A. Rights under trusts of land—(1) Any application by a trustee of a bankrupt's estate under section 14 of the Trusts of Land and Appointment of Trustees Act 1996 (powers of court in relation to trusts of land) for an order under that section for the sale of land shall be made to the court having jurisdiction in relation to the bankruptcy.

(2) On such an application the court shall make such order as it thinks just and reasonable having regard to—

(a) the interests of the bankrupt's creditors;

(b) where the application is made in respect of land which includes a dwelling house which is or has been the home of the bankrupt or the bankrupt's spouse or former spouse—

(i) the conduct of the spouse or former spouse, so far as contributing to the bankruptcy,

(ii) the needs and financial resources of the spouse or former spouse, and

(iii) the needs of any children; and

(c) all the circumstances of the case other than the needs of the bankrupt.

(3) Where such an application is made after the end of the period of one year beginning with the first vesting under Chapter IV of this Part of the bankrupt's estate in a trustee, the court shall assume, unless the circumstances of the case are exceptional, that the interests of the bankrupt's creditors outweigh all other considerations.

(4) The powers conferred on the court by this section are exercisable on an application whether it is made before or after the commencement of this section.]

Note. This section inserted by Trusts of Land and Appointment of Trustees Act 1996, s 25(1), Sch 3, para 23, as from 1 January 1997.

Rights of occupation

336. Rights of occupation etc of bankrupt's spouse—(1) Nothing occurring in the initial period of the bankruptcy (that is to say, the period beginning with the day of the presentation of the petition for the bankruptcy order and ending with the vesting of the bankrupt's estate in a trustee) is to be taken as having given rise to any *rights of occupation under the Matrimonial Homes Act 1983* [matrimonial home rights under Part IV of the Family Law Act 1996] in relation to a dwelling house comprised in the bankrupt's estate.

(2) Where a spouse's *rights of occupation under the Act of 1983* [matrimonial home rights under the Act of 1996] are a charge on the estate or interest of the other spouse, or of trustees for the other spouse, and the other spouse is adjudged bankrupt—

(a) the charge continues to subsist notwithstanding the bankruptcy and, subject to the provisions of that Act, binds the trustee of the bankrupt's estate and persons deriving title under that trustee, and

(b) any application for an order *under section 1 of that Act* [under section 33 of that Act] shall be made to the court, having jurisdiction in relation to the bankruptcy.

Note. Words in square brackets in sub-ss (1), (2) substituted for words in italics by Family Law Act 1996, s 66(1), Sch 8, Part III, para 57, as from 1 October 1997.

(3) Where a person and his spouse or former spouse are trustees for sale of a dwelling house and that person is adjudged bankrupt, any application by the trustee of the bankrupt's estate for an order under section 30 of the Law of Property Act 1925 (powers of court where trustees for sale refuse to act) shall be made to the court having jurisdiction in relation to the bankruptcy.

Note. Sub-s (3) repealed by Trusts of Land and Appointment of Trustees Act 1996, s 25(2), Sch 4, as from 1 January 1997.

(4) On such an application as is mentioned in subsection (2) or *(3)* the court shall make such order under *section 1 of the Act of 1983* [section 33 of the Act of 1996] *or section 30 of the Act of 1925* as it thinks just and reasonable having regard to—

(a) the interests of the bankrupt's creditors,

(b) the conduct of the spouse or former spouse, so far as contributing to the bankruptcy,

(c) the needs and financial resources of the spouse or former spouse,

(d) the needs of any children, and

(e) all the circumstances of the case other than the needs of the bankrupt.

Note. Words 'or 3' and 'or section 30 of the Act of 1925' in italics repealed by Trusts of Land and Appointment of Trustees Act 1996, s 25(2), Sch 4, as from 1 January 1997. Words in square brackets substituted for words in italics by Family Law Act 1996, s 66(1), Sch 8, Part III, para 57, as from 1 October 1997.

(5) Where such an application is made after the end of the period of one year beginning with the first vesting under Chapter IV of this Part of the bankrupt's estate in a trustee, the court shall assume, unless the circumstances of the case are exceptional that the interests of the bankrupt's creditors outweigh all other considerations.

Note. For the Matrimonial Homes Act 1983, see p 2934. For the Law of Property Act 1925, s 30, see p 2054.

337. Rights of occupation of bankrupt—(1) This section applies where—
   (a) a person who is entitled to occupy a dwelling house by virtue of a beneficial estate or interest is adjudged bankrupt, and
   (b) any persons under the age of 18 with whom that person had at some time occupied that dwelling house had their home with that person at the time when the bankruptcy petition was presented and at the commencement of the bankruptcy.

(2) Whether or not the bankrupt's spouse (if any) has *rights of occupation under the Matrimonial Homes Act 1983* [matrimonial home rights under Part IV of the Family Law Act 1996]—
   (a) the bankrupt has the following rights as against the trustee of his estate—
      (i) if in occupation, a right not to be evicted or excluded from the dwelling house or any part of it, except with the leave of the court,
      (ii) if not in occupation, a right with the leave of the court to enter into and occupy the dwelling house, and
   (b) the bankrupt's rights are a charge, having the like priority as an equitable interest created immediately before the commencement of the bankruptcy, on so much of his estate or interest in the dwelling house as vests in the trustee.

(3) *The Act of 1983 has effect, with the necessary modifications, as if—*
   (a) *the rights conferred by paragraph (a) of subsection (2) were rights of occupation under that Act,*
   (b) *any application for leave such as is mentioned in that paragraph were an application for an order under section 1 of that Act, and*
   (c) *any charge under paragraph (b) of that subsection on the estate or interest of the trustee were a charge under that Act on the estate or interest of a spouse.*

[(3) The Act of 1996 has effect with the necessary modifications, as if—
   (a) the rights conferred by paragraph (a) of subsection (2) were matrimonial home rights under the Act,
   (b) any application for such leave as is mentioned in that paragraph were an application for an order under section 33 of that Act, and
   (c) any charge under paragraph (b) of that subsection on the estate or interest of the trustee were a charge under that Act on the estate or interest of a spouse.]

(4) Any application for leave such as is mentioned in subsection (2)(a) or otherwise by virtue of this section for an order under *section 1 of the Act of 1983* [section 33 of the Act of 1996] shall be made to the court having jurisdiction in relation to the bankruptcy.

(5) On such an application the court shall make such order under *section 1 of the Act of 1983* [section 33 of the Act of 1996] as it thinks just and reasonable having regard to the interests of the creditors, to the bankrupt's financial resources, to the needs of the children and to all the circumstances of the case other than the needs of the bankrupt.

Note. Words in square brackets in sub-ss (2), (4), (5) substituted for words in italics, and sub-s (3) substituted, by Family Law Act 1996, s 66(1), Sch 8, Part III, para 58, as from 1 October 1997.

(6) Where such an application is made after the end of the period of one year beginning with the first vesting (under Chapter IV of this Part) of the bankrupt's

estate in a trustee, the court shall assume, unless the circumstances of the case are exceptional, that the interests of the bankrupt's creditors outweigh all other considerations.

Note. For Matrimonial Homes Act 1983, s 1, see p 2934.

338. Payments in respect of premises occupied by bankrupt—Where any premises comprised in a bankrupt's estate are occupied by him (whether by virtue of the preceding section or otherwise) on condition that he makes payments towards satisfying any liability arising under a mortgage of the premises or otherwise towards the outgoings of the premises, the bankrupt does not, by virtue of those payments, acquire any interest in the premises.

*   *   *   *   *

385. Miscellaneous definitions—(1) The following definitions have effect—
   'the court', in relation to any matter, means the court to which, in accordance with section 373 in Part X and the rules, proceedings with respect to that matter are allocated or transferred

*   *   *   *   *

'dwelling house' includes any building or part of a building which is occupied as a dwelling and any yard, garden, garage or outhouse belonging to the dwelling house and occupied with it;

*   *   *   *   *

'family', in relation to a bankrupt, means the persons (if any) who are living with him and are dependent on him.

*   *   *   *   *

443. Commencement. This Act comes into force on the day appointed under section 236 (2) of the Insolvency Act 1985 for the coming into force of Part III of that Act (individual insolvency and bankruptcy), immediately after that Part of that Act comes into force for England and Wales.

Commencement. This Act was brought into force on 29 December 1986 (SI 1986 No 1924).

*   *   *   *   *

FAMILY LAW ACT 1986
(1986 c 55)

ARRANGEMENT OF SECTIONS

PART I

CHILD CUSTODY

CHAPTER I

PRELIMINARY

An Act to amend the law relating to the jurisdiction of courts in the United
Kingdom to make orders with regard to the custody of children; to make
provision as to the recognition and enforcement of such orders throughout the
United Kingdom; to make further provision as to the imposition, effect and
enforcement of restrictions on the removal of children from the United
Kingdom or from any part of the United Kingdom; to amend the law relating to
the jurisdiction of courts in Scotland as to tutory and curatory; to amend the law
relating to the recognition of divorces, annulments and legal separations; to
make further provision with respect to the effect of divorces and annulments on
wills; to amend the law relating to the powers of courts to make declarations

relating to the status of a person; to abolish the right to petition for jactitation of marriage; to repeal the Greek Marriages Act 1884; to make further provision with respect to family proceedings rules; to amend the Child Abduction Act 1984, the Child Abduction (Northern Ireland) Order 1985 and the Child Abduction and Custody Act 1985; and for connected purposes.

[7 November 1986]

PART I

CHILD CUSTODY

CHAPTER I

PRELIMINARY

1. Orders to which Part I applies—(1) Subject to the following provisions of this section, in this Part '*custody order*' ['Part I order'] means—

(*a*) *an order made by a court in England and Wales under any of the following enactments*—

   (*i*) *section 9(1), 10(1)(a), 11(a) [section 9, 10] or 14A(2) of the Guardianship of Minors Act 1971 or section 2(4)(b) or 2(5) [section 2(4) or (5)(a)] of the Guardianship Act 1973;*

 (*ii*) *section 42(1) of the Matrimonial Causes Act 1973;*

(*iii*) *section 42(2) of the Matrimonial Causes Act 1973;*

(*iv*) *section 33(1) of the Children Act 1975 or section 2(4)(b) [section 2(4)] of the Guardianship Act 1973 as applied by section 34 (5) of the Children Act 1975;*

   (v) *section 8(2) or 19(1)(ii) of the Domestic Proceedings and Magistrates' Courts Act 1978;*

[(a) a section 8 order made by a court in England and Wales under the Children Act 1989, other than an order varying or discharging such an order;]

[(aa) a special guardianship order made by a court in England and Wales under the children Act 1989;

(ab) an order made under section 26 of the Adoption and Children Act 2002 (contact) other than an order varying or revoking such an order;]

(b) an order made by a court of civil jurisdiction in Scotland under any enactment or rule of law with respect to the *custody, care or control of a child,* [residence, custody, care or control of a child, contact with or] access to a child or the education or upbringing of a child, excluding—

  (i) an order committing the care of a child to a local authority or placing a child under the supervision of a local authority;

 (ii) an adoption order as defined in section 12(1) of the Adoption (Scotland) Act 1978;

(iii) an order freeing a child for adoption made under section 18 of the said Act of 1978;

(iv) an order *for the custody of* [giving parental responsibilities and parental rights in relation to] a child made in the course of proceedings for the adoption of the child (other than an order made following the making of a direction under section 53(1) of the Children Act 1975);

 (v) an order made under the Education (Scotland) Act 1980;

(vi) an order made under Part II or III of the Social Work (Scotland) Act 1968;

(vii) an order made under the Child Abduction and Custody Act 1985;

(viii) an order for the delivery of a child or other order for the enforcement of a *custody order* [Part I order];

(ix) an order relating to the *tutory or curatory* [guardianship] of a child;

(*c*) *an order made by a court in Northern Ireland under any of the following enactments*—

    (*i*)   *section 5 of the Guardianship of Infants Act 1886 (except so far as it relates to costs);*

    (*ii*)   *Article 45(1) of the Matrimonial Causes (Northern Ireland) Order 1978;*

    (*iii*)   *Article 45(2) of the Matrimonial Causes (Northern Ireland) Order 1978;*

    (*iv*)   *Article 10(2) or 20(1)(ii) of the Domestic Proceedings (Northern Ireland) Order 1980;*

[(c) an Article 8 order made by a court in Northern Ireland under the Children (Northern Ireland) Order 1995, other than an order varying or discharging such an order;]

(*d*)   *an order made by the High Court in the exercise of its jurisdiction relating to wardship so far as it gives the care and control of a child to any person or provides for the education of, or for access to, a child, excluding an order relating to a child of whom care or care and control is (immediately after the making of the order) vested in a local authority or in the Northern Ireland Department of Health and Social Services.*

[(d)an order made by a court in England and Wales in the exercise of the inherent jurisdiction of the High Court with respect to children—

    (i)   so far as it gives care of a child to any person or provides for contact with, or the education of, a child; but

    (ii)   excluding an order varying or revoking such an order;

[(*e*)   *an order made by the High Court in Northern Ireland in the exercise of its jurisdiction relating to wardship—*

    (*i*)   *so far as it gives care and control of a child to any person or provides for the education of or access to a child; but*

    (*ii*)   *excluding an order relating to a child of whom care or care and control is (immediately after the making of the order) vested in the Department of Health and Social Services or a Health and Social Services Board.*]

[(e) an order made by the High Court in Northern Ireland in the exercise of its inherent jurisdiction with respect to children—

    (i)   so far as it gives care of a child to any person or provides for contact with, or the education of, a child; but

    (ii)   excluding an order varying or discharging such an order;

Note. In sub-s (1)(a) in italics, references in square brackets substituted for references to 'section 9(1), 10(1)(a), 11(a)', 'section 2(4)(b) or 2(5)' and 'section 2(4)(b)' by Family Law Reform Act 1987, s 33(1), Sch 2, para 94, as from 1 April 1989. Sub-s (1)(a) in square brackets substituted for sub-s (1)(a) in italics and references to 'Part I order' substituted by Children Act 1989, s 108(5), Sch 13, para 63, as from 14 October 1991. Subs (1)(aa), (ab) inserted by the Adoption and Children Act 2002, Sch 3, para 47 as from a day to be appointed. In sub-s (1)(b) words in first and second pairs of square brackets substituted for words in italics by Children (Scotland) Act 1995, s 105(4), Sch 4, para 41(2), as from 1 November 1996. Words in square brackets in sub-s (1)(b)(viii), (ix) substituted for words in italics by Age of Legal Capacity (Scotland) Act 1991, s 10(1), Sch 10, para 44, as from 25 September 1991. Sub-s (1)(c), (e) in square brackets substituted for sub-s (1)(c), (e) in italics by Children (Northern Ireland Consequential Amendments) Order 1995, SI 1995 No 756, art 12(2)(a), as from 4 November 1996. Sub-s (1)(d), (e) in square brackets substituted for sub-s (1)(d) in italics by Children Act 1989, s 108(5), Sch 13, para 63, as from 14 October 1991.

Note also the modification of this subsection by the Family Law Act 1986 (Dependent Territories) Order 1991, SI 1991 No 1723, art 3(2), Sch 2, para 1(2).

(2)   In this Part '*custody order*' ['Part I order'] does not include—

(a)   an order within subsection (1)(a) *or* (c) above which varies or revokes a previous order made under the same enactment;

(*b*)   *an order under section 14A(2) of the Guardianship of Minors Act 1971 which varies a previous custody order; or*

(*c*)   *an order within paragraph (d)* [(*e*)] *of subsection (1) above which varies or revokes a previous order within that paragraph.*

Note. References to 'Part I order' substituted, words '(a) or' in sub-s (2)(a) and sub-s (2)(b) repealed, and '(e)' in square brackets in sub-s (2)(c) substituted for '(d)' in italics by Children Act 1989, s 108(5), (7), Sch 13, para 63, Sch 15, as from 14 October 1991. Sub-s (2)(a), (c) repealed by Children (Northern Ireland Consequential Amendments) Order 1995, SI 1995 No 756, art 15, Schedule, as from 4 November 1996.

(3) Subject to sections 32 and 40 of this Act, in this Part 'custody order' does not include any order which—

   (a) was made before the date of the commencement of this Part;

   (b) in the case of an order within subsection (1)(b) or (d) above or an order under any of the enactments mentioned in subsection (4) below, is made on or after that date on an application made before that date; or

   (c) in any other case, is made on or after that date in proceedings commenced before that date.

(4) The said enactments are—

   (a) sections 9(1) [sections 9] and 14A(2) of the Guardianship of Minors Act 1971 and section 33(1) of the Children Act 1975; and

   (b) section 5 of the Guardianship of Infants Act 1886.

Note. Words in square brackets substituted for 'sections 9(1)' by Family Law Reform Act 1987, s 33(1), Sch 2, para 94, as from 1 April 1989.

(5) For the purposes of subsection (3) above an order made on two or more applications which are determined together shall be regarded as made on the first of those applications.

  [(3) In this Part, 'Part I order'—

  (a) includes any order which would have been a custody order by virtue of this section in any form in which it was in force at any time before its amendment by the Children Act 1989 [or the Children (Northern Ireland) Order 1995, as the case may be]; and

  (b) (subject to sections 32 and 40 of this Act) excluding any order which would have been excluded from being a custody order by virtue of this section in any such form.]

Note. Sub-s (3) in square brackets substituted for sub-ss (3)–(5) in italics by Children Act 1989, s 108(5), Sch 13, para 63, as from 14 October 1991. Words in square brackets inserted by Children (Northern Ireland Consequential Amendments) Order 1995, SI 1995 No 756, art 12, as from 4 November 1996.

Note also the modification of this subsection by the Family Law Act 1986 (Dependent Territories) Order 1991, SI 1991 No 1723, art 3(2), Sch 2, para 1(3).

(6) Provision may be made by act of sederunt prescribing, in relation to orders within subsection (1)(b) above, what constitutes an application for the purposes of this Part.

CHAPTER II

JURISDICTION OF COURTS IN ENGLAND AND WALES

2. Jurisdiction in cases other than divorce, etc—*(1) A court in England and Wales shall not have jurisdiction to make a custody order within section 1(1)(a) of this Act, other than one under section 42(1) of the Matrimonial Causes Act 1973, unless the condition in section 3 of this Act is satisfied.*

(2) The High Court in England and Wales shall have jurisdiction to make a custody order within section 1(1)(d) of this Act if, and only if,—

   (a) the condition in section 3 of this Act is satisfied, or

   (b) the ward is present in England and Wales on the relevant date (within the meaning of section 3(6) of this Act) and the court considers that the immediate exercise of its powers is necessary for his protection.

[2. Jurisdiction: general—(*1*) *A court in England and Wales shall not have jurisdiction to make a section 1(1)(a) order with respect to a child in or in connection with matrimonial proceedings in England and Wales unless* [—
  (a) the child concerned is a child of both parties to the matrimonial proceedings and the court has jurisdiction to entertain those proceedings by virtue of the Council Regulation, or
  (b)]
the condition in section 2A of this Act is satisfied.
  (2) *A court in England and Wales shall not have jurisdiction to make a section 1(1)(a) order in a non-matrimonial case (that is to say, where the condition in section 2A of this Act is not satisfied) unless the condition in section 3 of this Act is satisfied.*
  [(2A) A court in England and Wales shall not have jurisdiction to make a special guardianship order under the Children Act 1989 unless the condition in section 3 of this Act is satisfied.
  (2B) A court in England and Wales shall not have jurisdiction to make an order under section 26 of the Adoption and Children Act 2002 unless the condition in section 3 of this Act is satisfied.]
Note. Sub-ss (2A), (2B) inserted by the Adoption and Children Act 2002, Sch 2, para 48 as from a day to be appointed.

  [(1) A court in England and Wales shall not have jurisdiction to make a section 1(1)(a) order with respect to a child unless—
  (a) the case falls within section 2A below; or
  (b) in any other case, the condition in section 3 below is satisfied.]
Note. Sub-s (1) in square brackets substituted for sub-ss (1), (2) in italics by Family Law Act 1996, s 66(1), Sch 8, Part I, para 37(2), as from a day to be appointed, subject to savings in s 66(2) of, and para 5 of Sch 9 to, the 1996 Act. In sub-s (1) in italics paras (a), (b) inserted by SI 2001/310, reg 6 as from 1 March 2001.

  (3) A court in England and Wales shall not have jurisdiction to make a section 1(1)(d) order unless—
  (a) the condition in section 3 of this Act is satisfied, or
  (b) the child concerned is present in England and Wales on the relevant date and the court considers that the immediate exercise of its powers is necessary for his protection.]

[2A. Jurisdiction in or in connection with matrimonial proceedings—(*1*) *The condition referred to in section 2(1) of this Act is that the matrimonial proceedings are proceedings in respect of the marriage of the parents of the child concerned and—*
  (*a*) *the proceedings—*
    (*i*) *are proceedings for divorce or nullity of marriage, and*
    (*ii*) *are continuing;*
  (*b*) *the proceedings—*
    (*i*) *are proceedings for judicial separation,*
    (*ii*) *are continuing,*
      and the jurisdiction of the court is not excluded by subsection (2) below; or
  (*c*) *the proceedings have been dismissed after the beginning of the trial but—*
    (*i*) *the section 1(1)(a) order is being made forthwith, or*
    (*ii*) *the application for the order was made on or before the dismissal.*
  [(1) Subject to subsections (2) to (4) below, a case falls within this section for the purposes of the making of a section 1(1)(a) order if that order is made—
  (a) at a time when—
      (i) a statement of marital breakdown under section 5 of the Family Law Act 1996 with respect to the marriage of the parents of the child concerned has been received by the court; and

(ii) it is or may become possible for an application for a divorce order or for a separation order to be made by reference to that statement; or

(b) at a time when an application in relation to that marriage for a divorce order, or for a separation order under the Act of 1996, has been made and not withdrawn.

(1A) A case also falls within this section for the purposes of the making of a section 1(1)(a) order if that order is made in or in connection with any proceedings for the nullity of the marriage of the parents of the child concerned and—

(a) those proceedings are continuing; or

(b) the order is made—

(i) immediately on the dismissal, after the beginning of the trial, of the proceedings; and

(ii) on an application made before the dismissal.]

Note. Sub-ss (1), (1A) in square brackets substituted for sub-s (1) in italics by Family Law Act 1996, s 66(1), Sch 8, Part I, para 37(3), as from a day to be appointed, subject to savings in s 66(2) of, and para 5 of Sch 9 to, the 1996 Act.

(2) *For the purposes of subsection (1)(b) above, the jurisdiction of the court is excluded if, after the grant of a decree of judicial separation,* [A case does not fall within this section if a separation order under the Family Law Act 1996 is in force in relation to the marriage of the parents of the child concerned if,] on the relevant date, proceedings for divorce or nullity in respect of the marriage are continuing in Scotland or Northern Ireland.

Note. Words in square brackets substituted for words in italics by Family Law Act 1996, s 66(1), Sch 8, Part I, para 37(4), as from a day to be appointed, subject to savings in s 66(2) of, and para 5 of Sch 9 to, the 1996 Act.

(3) Subsection (2) above shall not apply if the court *in which the other proceedings there referred to* [in Scotland, Northern Ireland or a specified dependent territory in which the proceedings for divorce or nullity] are continuing has made—

(a) an order under section 13(6) or *21(5)* [19A(4)] of this Act (not being an order made by virtue of section 13(6)(a)(i)), or

(b) an order under section 14(2) or 22(2) of this Act which is recorded as being made for the purpose of enabling Part I proceedings to be taken in England and Wales with respect to the child concerned.

Note. Words in first pair of square brackets substituted for words in italics by Family Law Act 1996, s 66(1), Sch 8, Part I, para 37(5), as from a day to be appointed, subject to savings in s 66(2) of, and para 5 of Sch 9 to, the 1996 Act. Reference to '19A(4)' in square brackets substituted for reference to '21(5)' in italics by Children (Northern Ireland Consequential Amendments) Order 1995, SI 1995 No 756, art 12(5), as from 4 November 1996.

(4) Where a court—

(a) has jurisdiction to make a section 1(1)(a) order *in or in connection with matrimonial proceedings* [by virtue of the case falling within this section], but

(b) considers that it would be more appropriate for Part I matters relating to the child to be determined outside England and Wales,

the court may by order direct that, while the order under this subsection is in force, no section 1(1)(a) order shall be made by any court *in or in connection with those proceedings* [by virtue of section 2(1)(a) of this Act].]

Note. Sections 2, 2A substituted for original s 2 in italics by Children Act 1989, s 108(5), Sch 13, para 64, as from 14 October 1991. Words in square brackets in sub-s (4) substituted for words in italics by Family Law Act 1996, s 66(1), Sch 8, Part I, para 37(6), as from a day to be appointed, subject to savings in s 66(2) of, and para 5 of Sch 9 to, the 1996 Act.

Note also the modification of section 2A by the Family Law Act 1986 (Dependent Territories) Order 1991, SI 1991 No 1723, art 3(2), Sch 2, para 2.

3. Habitual residence or presence of child—(1) The condition referred to in *section 2 [section 2(2)]* [section 2(1)(b)] of this Act is that on the relevant date the child concerned—

(a) is habitually resident in England and Wales, or

(b) is present in England and Wales and is not habitually resident in any part of the United Kingdom,

and, in either case, the jurisdiction of the court is not excluded by subsection (2) below.

Note. Words 'section 2(2)' in square brackets substituted for words 'section 2' in italics by Children Act 1989, s 108(5), Sch 13, para 62, as from 14 October 1991. Words 'section 2(1)(b)' in square brackets substituted for words 'section 2(2)' in italics by Family Law Act 1996, s 66(1), Sch 8, Part I, para 37(7), as from a day to be appointed, subject to savings in s 66(2) of, and para 5 of Sch 9 to, the 1996 Act.

(2) For the purposes of subsection (1) above, the jurisdiction of the court is excluded if, on the relevant date, *proceedings for divorce, nullity or judicial separation* [matrimonial proceedings] are continuing in a court in Scotland or Northern Ireland in respect of the marriage of the parents of the child concerned.

Note. Words in square brackets substituted for words in italics by Children Act 1989, s 108(5), Sch 13, para 62, as from 14 October 1991.

(3) Subsection (2) above shall not apply if the court in which the other proceedings there referred to are continuing has made—

(a) an order under section 13(6) or *21(5)* [19A(4)] of this Act (not being an order made by virtue of section 13(6)(a)(i)), or

(b) an order under section 14(2) or 22(2) of this Act which is recorded as made for the purpose of enabling *proceedings with respect to the custody of* [Part I proceedings with respect to] the child concerned to be taken in England and Wales.

and that order is in force.

Note. Reference to '19A(4)' in square brackets substituted for reference to '21(5)' in italics by Children (Northern Ireland Consequential Amendments) Order 1995, SI 1995 No 756, art 12(5), as from 4 November 1996. Words in square brackets in sub-s (3)(b) substituted for words in italics by Children Act 1989, s 108(5), Sch 13, para 65, as from 14 October 1991.

(4) Subject to subsections (5) and (6) below, in this section 'the relevant date' means the date of the commencement of the proceedings in which the custody order falls to be made.

(5) In a case where an application is made for a custody order under section 9(1) [section 9] or 14A(2) of the Guardianship of Minors Act 1971 or section 33(1) of the Children Act 1975, 'the relevant date' means the date of the application (or first application, if two or more are determined together).

(6) In the case of a custody order within section 1(1)(d) of this Act 'the relevant date' means—

(a) where an application is made for an order, the date of the application (or first application, if two or more are determined together), and

(b) where no such application is made, the date of the order.

Note. Sub-ss (4)–(6) repealed by Children Act 1989, s 108(7), Sch 15, as from 14 October 1991. Words in square brackets in sub-s (5) substituted for words 'section 9(1)' by Family Law Reform Act 1987, s 33(1), Sch 2, para 95, as from 1 April 1989.

Note also the modification of this section by the Family Law Act 1986 (Dependent Territories) Order 1991, SI 1991 No 1723, art 3(2), Sch 2, para 3.

4. Jurisdiction in divorce proceedings, etc—*(1) The enactments relating to the jurisdiction of courts in England and Wales to make orders under section 42(1) of the Matrimonial Causes Act 1973 shall have effect subject to the modifications provided for by this section.*

(*2*) In section 42(*1*)(*b*) of that Act (*which enables orders as to custody and education to be made immediately, or within a reasonable period, after the dismissal of proceedings for divorce, etc*) for the words 'within a reasonable period' there shall be substituted the words '(*if an application for the order is made on or before the dismissal*)'.

(*3*) A court shall not have jurisdiction to make a custody order under section 42(*1*)(*a*) of that Act after the grant of a degree of judicial separation if, on the relevant date, proceedings for divorce or nullity in respect of the marriage concerned are continuing in Scotland or Northern Ireland.

(*4*) Subsection (*3*) above shall not apply if the court in which the other proceedings there referred to are continuing has made—

(*a*)   an order under section 13(*6*) or 21(*5*) of this Act (*not being an order made by virtue of section 13(6)(a)(i)*), or

(*b*)   an order under section 14(*2*) or 22(*2*) of this Act which is recorded as made for the purpose of enabling proceedings with respect to the custody of the child concerned to be taken in England and Wales,

and that order is in force.

(*5*) Where a court—

(*a*)   has jurisdiction to make a custody order under section 42(*1*) of the Matrimonial Causes Act 1973 in or in connection with proceedings for divorce, nullity of marriage or judicial separation, but

(*b*)   considers that it would be more appropriate for matters relating to the custody of the child to be determined outside England and Wales,

the court may by order direct that, while the order under this subsection is in force, no custody order under section 42(*1*) with respect to the child shall be made by any court in or in connection with those proceedings.

(*6*) In this section 'the relevant date' means—

(*a*)   where an application is made for a custody order under section 42(*1*)(*a*), the date of the application (*or first application, if two or more are determined together*), and

(*b*)   where no such application is made, the date of the order.

Note. This section repealed by Children Act 1989, s 108(7), Sch 15, as from 14 October 1991.

5. Power of court to refuse application or stay proceedings—(1) A court in England and Wales which has jurisdiction to make a *custody order* [Part I order] may refuse an application for the order in any case where the matter in question has already been determined in proceedings outside England and Wales.

(2) Where, at any stage of the proceedings on an application made to a court in England and Wales for a *custody order* [Part I order], or for the variation of a *custody order* [Part I order] [other than proceedings governed by the Council Regulation], it appears to the court—

(a)   that proceedings with respect to the matters to which the application relates are continuing outside England and Wales, or

(b)   that it would be more appropriate for those matters to be determined in proceedings to be taken outside England and Wales,

the court may stay the proceedings on the application.

(3) The court may remove a stay granted in accordance with subsection (2) above if it appears to the court that there has been unreasonable delay in the taking or prosecution of the other proceedings referred to in that subsection, or that those proceedings are stayed, sisted or concluded.

(4) Nothing in this section shall affect any power exercisable apart from this section to refuse an application or to grant or remove a stay.

Note. Words [Part I order] in square brackets in sub-ss (1), (2) substituted for words in italics by Children Act 1989, s 108(5), Sch 13, para 62(1), (2)(a), as from 14 October 1991. In sub-s (2) words in square brackets inserted by SI 2001/310, reg 7, as from 1 March 2001.

6. Duration and variation of custody orders—(1) If a *custody order* [Part I order] made by a court in Scotland or Northern Ireland (or a variation of such an order) comes into force with respect to a child at a time when a *custody order* [Part I order] made by a court in England and Wales has effect with respect to him, the latter order shall cease to have effect so far as it makes provision for any matter for which the same or different provision is made by (or by the variation of) the order made by the court in Scotland or Northern Ireland.

(2) Where by virtue of subsection (1) above a *custody order* [Part I order] has ceased to have effect so far as it makes provision for any matter, a court in England or Wales shall not have jurisdiction to vary that order so as to make provision for that matter.

Note. Words in square brackets in sub-ss (1), (2) substituted for words in italics by Children Act 1989, s 108(5), Sch 13, para 66, as from 14 October 1991.

(*3*) *A court in England and Wales shall not have jurisdiction—*
(*a*) *to vary a custody order, other than one made under section 42(1)(a) of the Matrimonial Causes Act 1973, or*
(*b*) *after the grant of a decree of judicial separation, to vary a custody order made under section 42(1)(a) of that Act,*
if, on the relevant date, proceedings for divorce, nullity or judicial separation are continuing in Scotland or Northern Ireland in respect of the marriage of the parents of the child concerned.

[(3) A court in England and Wales shall not have jurisdiction to vary a Part I order if, on the relevant date, matrimonial proceedings are continuing in Scotland or Northern Ireland in respect of the marriage of the parents of the child concerned.

(*3A*) *Subsection (3) above shall not apply if—*
(*a*) *the Part I order was made in or in connection with proceedings for divorce or nullity in England and Wales in respect of the marriage of the parents of the child concerned; and*
(*b*) *those proceedings are continuing.*
(*3B*) *Subsection (3) above shall not apply if—*
(*a*) *the Part I order was made in or in connection with proceedings for judicial separation in England and Wales;*
(*b*) *those proceedings are continuing; and*
(*c*) *the decree of judicial separation has not yet been granted.*]

[(3A) Subsection (3) above does not apply if the Part I order was made in a case falling within section 2A of this Act.]

Note. Sub-ss (3)–(3B) in square brackets substituted for sub-s (3) in italics by Children Act 1989, s 108(5), Sch 13, para 66, as from 14 October 1991. Sub-s (3A) in square brackets substituted for sub-ss (3A), (3B) in italics by Family Law Act 1996, s 66(1), Sch 8, Part I, para 37(8), as from a day to be appointed, subject to savings in s 66(2) of, and para 5 of Sch 9 to, the 1996 Act.

(4) Subsection (3) above shall not apply if the court in which the proceedings there referred to are continuing has made—
(a) an order under section 13(6) or *21(5)* [19A(4)] of this Act (not being an order made by virtue of section 13(6)(a)(i)), or
(b) an order under section 14(2) or 22(2) of this Act which is recorded as made for the purpose of enabling *proceedings with respect to the custody of* [Part I proceedings with respect to] the child concerned to be taken in England and Wales,
and that order is in force.

Note. Reference to '19A(4)' in square brackets substituted for reference to '21(5)' in italics by Children (Northern Ireland Consequential Amendments) Order 1995, SI 195 No 756, art 12(5), as from 4 November 1996. Words in square brackets in sub-s (4)(b) substituted for words in italics by Children Act 1989, s 108(5), Sch 13, para 66, as from 14 October 1991.

(5) Subsection (3) above shall not apply in the case of a *variation of a custody order within section 1(1)(d) of this Act if the ward* [variation of section 1(1)(d) order of the child concerned] is present in England and Wales on the relevant date and the court considers that the immediate exercise of its powers is necessary for his protection.

(6) *Where any person who is entitled to the actual possession of a child under a custody order made by a court in England and Wales ceases to be so entitled by virtue of subsection (1) above, then, if there is in force an order for the supervision of that child made under—*

    (a) *section 7(4) of the Family Law Reform Act 1969,*

    (b) *section 44 of the Matrimonial Causes Act 1973,*

    (c) *section 2(2)(a) of the Guardianship Act 1973,*

    (d) *section 34(5) or 36(3)(b) of the Children Act 1975, or*

    (e) *section 9 of the Domestic Proceedings and Magistrates' Courts Act 1978,*

that order shall cease to have effect.

(7) *In this section 'the relevant date' means—*

    (a) *where an application is made for a variation, the date of the application (or first application, if two or more are determined together), and*

    (b) *where no such application is made, the date of the variation.*

[(6) Subsection (7) below applies where a Part I order which is—

    (a) a residence order (within the meaning of the Children Act 1989) in favour of a person with respect to a child,

    (b) an order made in the exercise of the High Court's inherent jurisdiction with respect to children by virtue of which a person has care of a child, or

    (c) an order—

        (i) of a kind mentioned in section 1(3)(a) of this Act,

        (ii) under which a person is entitled to the actual possession of a child,

ceases to have effect in relation to that person by virtue of subsection (1) above.

(7) Where this subsection applies, any family assistance order made under section 16 of the Children Act 1989 with respect to the child shall also cease to have effect.

(8) For the purposes of subsection (7) above the reference to a family assistance order under section 16 of the Children Act 1989 shall be deemed to include a reference to an order for the supervision of a child made under—

    (a) section 7(4) of the Family Law Reform Act 1969,

    (b) section 44 of the Matrimonial Causes Act 1973,

    (c) section 2(2)(a) of the Guardianship Act 1973,

    (d) section 34(5) or 36(3)(b) of the Children Act 1975, or

    (e) section 9 of the Domestic Proceedings and Magistrates' Courts Act 1978;

but this subsection shall cease to have effect once all such orders for the supervision of children have ceased to have effect in accordance with Schedule 14 to the Children Act 1989.]

Note. Words in square brackets in sub-s (5) substituted for words in italics and sub-ss (6)–(8) in square brackets substituted for sub-ss (6), (7) in italics by Children Act 1989, s 108(5), Sch 13, paras 62(1), (2)(a), 66, as from 14 October 1991.

    Note also the modification of this section by the Family Law Act 1986 (Dependent Territories) Order 1991, SI 1991 No 1723, art 3(2), Sch 2, para 4.

7. Interpretation of Chapter II. *In this Chapter 'child' means a person who has not attained the age of eighteen.*

[**7. Interpretation of Chapter II.** In this Chapter—

    (a) 'child' means a person who has not attained the age of eighteen;

    (b) 'matrimonial proceedings' means proceedings for divorce, nullity of marriage or judicial separation;

    (c) 'the relevant date' means in relation to the making or variation of an order—

(i) where an application is made for an order to be made or varied, the date of the application (or first application, if two or more are determined together), and

(ii) where no such application is made, the date on which the court is considering whether to make or, as the case may be, vary the order; and

(d) 'section 1(1)(a) order' and 'section 1(1)(d) order' mean orders falling within section 1(1)(a) and (d) of this Act respectively.]

Note. Section 7 in square brackets substituted for s 7 in italics by Children Act 1989, s 108(5), Sch 13, para 67, as from 14 October 1991.

CHAPTER III

JURISDICTION OF COURTS IN SCOTLAND

8. Jurisdiction in independent proceedings. A court in Scotland may entertain an application for a [Part I order] otherwise than in matrimonial proceedings only if it has jurisdiction under section 9, 10, 12 or 15(2) of this Act.

Note. Words in square brackets substituted by Children Act 1989, s 108(5), Sch 13, para 62, as from 14 October 1991.

9. Habitual residence. Subject to section 11 of this Act, an application for a [Part I order] otherwise than in matrimonial proceedings may be entertained by—

(a) The Court of Session if, on the date of the application, the child concerned is habitually resident in Scotland;

(b) the sheriff if, on the date of the application, the child concerned is habitually resident in the sheriffdom.

Note. Words in square brackets substituted by Children Act 1989, s 108(5), Sch 13, para 62, as from 14 October 1991.

10. Presence of child. Subject to section 11 of this Act, an application for a [Part I order] otherwise than in matrimonial proceedings may be entertained by—

(a) the Court of Session if, on the date of the application, the child concerned—

(i) is present in Scotland; and

(ii) is not habitually resident in any part of the United Kingdom;

(b) the sheriff if, on the date of the application,—

(i) the child is present in Scotland;

(ii) the child is not habitually resident in any part of the United Kingdom; and

(iii) either the pursuer or the defender in the application is habitually resident in the sheriffdom.

Note. Words in square brackets substituted by Children Act 1989, s 108(5), Sch 13, para 62, as from 14 October 1991.

11. Provisions supplementary to sections 9 and 10—(1) Subject to subsection (2) below, the jurisdiction of the court to entertain an application for a [Part I order] with respect to a child by virtue of section 9, 10 or 15(2) of this Act is excluded if, on the date of the application, matrimonial proceedings are continuing in a court in any part of the United Kingdom in respect of the marriage of the parents of the child.

Note. Words in square brackets substituted by Children Act 1989, s 108(5), Sch 13, paras 62, 68, as from 14 October 1991.

(2) Subsection (1) above shall not apply in relation to an application for a [Part I order] if the court in which the matrimonial proceedings are continuing has made one of the following orders, that is to say—

(a) an order under section [2A(4)], 13(6) or [19A(4)] of this Act (not being an order made by virtue of section 13(6)(a)(ii); or

(b) an order under section 5(2), 14(2) or 22(2) of this Act which is recorded as made for the purpose of enabling [Part I proceedings with respect to] the child concerned to be taken in Scotland or, as the case may be, in another court in Scotland,

and that order is in force.

Note. First number in square brackets, and words in square brackets substituted by Children Act 1989, s 108(5), Sch 13, paras 62, 68, as from 14 October 1991. Number '19A(4)' in square brackets substituted by Children (Northern Ireland Consequential Amendments) Order 1995, SI 1995 No 756, art 12(5)(d), as from 4 November 1996.

12. Emergency jurisdiction.   Notwithstanding that any other court, whether within or outside Scotland, has jurisdiction to entertain an application for a [Part I order], the Court of Session or the sheriff shall have jurisdiction to entertain such an application if—

(a) the child concerned is present in Scotland or, as the case may be, in the sheriffdom on the date of the application; and

(b) the Court of Session or sheriff considers that, for the protection of the child, it is necessary to make such an order immediately.

Note. Words in square brackets substituted by Children Act 1989, s 108(5), Sch 13, para 62, as from 14 October 1991.

13. Jurisdiction ancillary to matrimonial proceedings—(1) The jurisdiction of a court in Scotland to entertain an application for a [Part I order] in matrimonial proceedings shall be modified by the following provisions of this section.

Note. Words in square brackets substituted by Children Act 1989, s 108(5), Sch 13, paras 62, 68, as from 14 October 1991.

(2) A court in Scotland shall not have jurisdiction, after the dismissal of matrimonial proceedings or after decree of absolvitor is granted therein, to entertain an application for a [Part I order] [in those proceedings] unless the application therefor was made on or before such dismissal or the granting of the decree of absolvitor.

Note. First words in square brackets substituted by Children Act 1989, s 108(5), Sch 13, paras 62, 68, as from 14 October 1991. Second words in square brackets substituted by Children (Scotland) Act 1995, s 105(4), Sch 4, para 41(3), as from 1 November 1996.

(3) Where, after a decree of separation has been granted, an application is made in the separation process for a [Part I order], the court in Scotland shall not have jurisdiction to entertain that application if, on the date of the application, proceedings for divorce or nullity of marriage in respect of the marriage concerned are continuing in another court in the United Kingdom.

Note. Words in square brackets substituted by Children Act 1989, s 108(5), Sch 13, paras 62, 68, as from 14 October 1991.

(4) A court in Scotland shall not have jurisdiction to entertain an application for the variation of a [Part I order] made [in matrimonial proceedings where the court has refused to grant the principal remedy sought in the proceedings] if, on the date of the application, matrimonial proceedings in respect of the marriage concerned are continuing in another court in the United Kingdom.

Note. First words in square brackets substituted by Children Act 1989, s 108(5), Sch 13, paras 62, 68, as from 14 October 1991. Second words in square brackets substituted by Children (Scotland) Act 1995, s 105(4), Sch 4, para 41(3), as from 1 November 1996.

(5) Subsections (3) and (4) above shall not apply if the court in which the other proceedings there referred to are continuing has made—

(a) an order under section [2A(4)] or [19A(4)] of this Act or under subsection (6) below (not being an order made by virtue of paragraph (a)(ii) of that subsection), or

  (b) an order under section 5(2), 14(2) or 22(2) of this Act which is recorded as made for the purpose of enabling [Part I proceedings with respect to] the child concerned to be taken in Scotland or, as the case may be, in another court in Scotland,
and that order is in force.

Note. First number in square brackets, and words in square brackets substituted by Children Act 1989, s 108(5), Sch 13, paras 62, 68, as from 14 October 1991. Number '19A(4)' in square brackets substituted by Children (Northern Ireland Consequential Amendments) Order 1995, SI 1995 No 756, art 12(5)(e), as from 4 November 1996.

  (6) A court in Scotland which has jurisdiction in matrimonial proceedings to entertain an application for a [Part I order] with respect to a child may make an order declining such jurisdiction if—
  (a) it appears to the court with respect to that child that—
   (i) but for section 11(1) of this Act, another court in Scotland would have jurisdiction to entertain an application for a [Part I order], or
   (ii) but for section 3(2), 6(3), 20(2) or 23(3) of this Act, a court in another part of the United Kingdom would have jurisdiction to make a [Part I order] or an order varying a [Part I order]; and
  (b) the court considers that it would be more appropriate for [Part I matters relating to] that child to be determined in that other court or part.

Note. Words in square brackets substituted by Children Act 1989, s 108(5), Sch 13, paras 62, 68, as from 14 October 1991.

  (7) The court may recall an order made under subsection (6) above.

14. Power of court to refuse application or sist proceedings—(1) A court in Scotland which has jurisdiction to entertain an application for a [Part I order] may refuse the application in any case where the matter in question has already been determined in other proceedings.
  (2) Where, at any stage of the proceedings on an application made to a court in Scotland for a [Part I order], it appears to the court—
  (a) that proceedings with respect to the matter to which the application relates are continuing outside Scotland or in another court in Scotland; or
  (b) that it would be more appropriate for those matters to be determined in proceedings outside Scotland or in another court in Scotland and that such proceedings are likely to be taken there,
the court may sist the proceedings on that application.

Note. Words in square brackets substituted by Children Act 1989, s 108(5), Sch 13, para 62, as from 14 October 1991.

15. Duration, variation and recall of orders—(1) Where, after the making by a court in Scotland of a [Part I order] ('the existing order') with respect to a child,—
  (a) a [Part I order], or an order varying a [Part I order], competently made by another court in any part of the United Kingdom with respect to that child; or
  (b) an order [relating to the parental responsibilities or parental rights in relation to] that child which is made outside the United Kingdom and recognised in Scotland by virtue of section 26 of this Act,
comes into force, the existing order shall cease to have effect so far as it makes provision for any matter for which the same or different provision is made by the order of the other court in the United Kingdom or, as the case may be, the order so recognised.

Note. First, second and third words in square brackets substituted by Children Act 1989, s 108(5), Sch 13, para 62, as from 14 October 1991. Fourth words in square brackets substituted by Children (Scotland) Act 1995, s 105(4), Sch 4, para 41(4)(a), as from 1 November 1996.

(2) Subject to sections 11(1) and 13(3) and (4) of this Act, a court in Scotland which has made a [Part I order] ('the original order') may, notwithstanding that it would no longer have jurisdiction to make the original order, make an order varying or recalling the original order; but if the original order has by virtue of subsection (1) above ceased to have effect so far as it makes provision for any matter, the court shall not have power to vary that order under this subsection so as to make provision for that matter.

(3) In subsection (2) above, an order varying an original order means any [Part I order] made with respect to the same child as the original order was made.

Note. Words in square brackets in sub-ss (2), (3) substituted by Children Act 1989, s 108(5), Sch 13, para 62, as from 14 October 1991.

(4) [Where, by virtue of subsection (1) above, a child is to live with a different person], then, if there is in force an order made by a court in Scotland … providing for the supervision of that child by a local authority, that order shall cease to have effect.

Note. Sub-s (4): words in square brackets substituted, and words omitted repealed, by Children (Scotland) Act 1995, s 105(4), (5), Sch 4, para 41(4)(b), Sch 5, as from 1 November 1996.

16. Tutory and curatory—(1) Subject to subsections (2) and (3) below, an application made after the commencement of this Part for an order relating to the [guardianship] of a [child] may be entertained by—

   (a) the Court of Session if, on the date of the application, the pupil or minor is habitually resident in Scotland,

   (b) the sheriff if, on the date of the application, the pupil or minor is habitually resident in the sheriffdom.

(2) Subsection (1) above shall not apply to an application for the appointment or removal of a [judicial factor] or of a curator bonis or any application made by such factor or curator.

(3) Subsection (1) above is without prejudice to any other ground of jurisdiction on which the Court of Session or the sheriff may entertain an application mentioned therein.

(4) Provision may be made by act of sederunt prescribing, in relation to orders relating to the [guardianship] of a [child], what constitutes an application for the purposes of this Chapter.

Note. Words in square brackets in sub-ss (1), (2), (4) substituted by Age of Legal Capacity (Scotland) Act 1991, s 10, Sch 1, para 45, as from 25 September 1991.

17. Orders for delivery of child—(1) … an application by one parent of a child for an order for the delivery of the child from the other parent, where the order is not sought to implement a [Part I order], may be entertained by the Court of Session or a sheriff if, but only if, the Court of Session or, as the case may be, the sheriff would have jurisdiction under this Chapter to make a [Part I order] with respect to the child concerned.

Note. Words omitted repealed by Children (Scotland) Act 1995, s 105(5), Sch 5, as from 1 November 1996. Words in square brackets substituted by Children Act 1989, s 108(5), Sch 13, para 62, as from 14 October 1991.

(2) …

Note. Sub-s (2) repealed by Children (Scotland) Act 1995, s 105(5), Sch 5, as from 1 November 1996.

(3) Subsection (1) above shall apply to an application by one party to a marriage for an order for the delivery of the child concerned from the other party where the child [, although not a child of both parties to the marriage, is a child of the family of those parties] as it applies to an application by one parent of a child for an order for the delivery of the child from the other parent.

Note. Sub-s (3): words in square brackets substituted by Children (Scotland) Act 1995, s 105(4), Sch 4, para 41(5)(a), as from 1 November 1996.

[(4) In subsection (3) above, 'child of the family' means any child who has been treated by both parties as a child of their family, except a child who has been placed with those parties as foster parents by a local authority or a voluntary organisation.]

18. Interpretation of Chapter III—(1) In this Chapter—
    'child' means a person who has not attained the age of sixteen;
    'matrimonial proceedings' means proceedings for divorce, nullity of marriage or judicial separation.

(2) In this Chapter, 'the date of the application' means, where two or more applications are pending, the date of the first of those applications; and, for the purposes of this subsection, an application is pending until a [Part I order] or, in the case of an application mentioned in section 16(1) of this Act, an order relating to the [guardianship of a child], has been granted in pursuance of the application or the court has refused to grant such an order.

Note. Sub-s (2): First words in square brackets substituted by Children Act 1989, s 108(5), Sch 13, para 62, as from 14 October 1991. Second words in square brackets substituted by Age of Legal Capacity (Scotland) Act 1991, s 10, Sch 1, para 46, as from 25 September 1991.

CHAPTER IV

JURISDICTION OF COURTS IN NORTHERN IRELAND

19. Jurisdiction in cases other than divorce, etc—(*1*) *A court in Northern Ireland shall not have jurisdiction to make a custody order [Part I order] within section 1(1)(c) of this Act, other than one under Article 45(1) of the Matrimonial Causes (Northern Ireland) Order 1978, unless the condition in section 20 of this Act is satisfied.*

(*2*) *The High Court in Northern Ireland shall have jurisdiction to make a custody order [Part I order] within section 1(1)(d) [1(1)(e)] of this Act if, and only if,—*
    (*a*) *the condition in section 20 of this Act is satisfied, or*
    (*b*) *the ward is present in Northern Ireland on the relevant date (within the meaning of section 20(6) of this Act) and the court considers that the immediate exercise of its powers is necessary for his protection.*

Note. Words in square brackets substituted for words 'custody order' and '1(1)(d)' by Children Act 1989, s 108(5), Sch 13, paras 62(1), (2)(a), 69(a), as from 14 October 1991.

[**19. Jurisdiction: general—**(1) A court in Northern Ireland shall not have jurisdiction to make a section 1(1)(c) order with respect to a child in or in connection with matrimonial proceedings in Northern Ireland unless the condition in section 19A of this Act is satisfied.

(2) A court in Northern Ireland shall not have jurisdiction to make a section 1(1)(c) order in a non-matrimonial case (that is to say, where the condition in section 19A is not satisfied) unless the condition in section 20 of this Act is satisfied.

(3) A court in Northern Ireland shall not have jurisdiction to make a section 1(1)(e) order unless—
    (a) the condition in section 20 of this Act is satisfied, or
    (c) the child concerned is present in Northern Ireland on the relevant date and the court considers that the immediate exercise of its powers is necessary for his protection.

19A. Jurisdiction in or in connection with matrimonial proceedings—(1) The condition referred to in section 19(1) of this Act is that the matrimonial proceedings are proceedings in respect of the marriage of the parents of the child concerned and—

    (a) the proceedings—
       (i) are proceedings for divorce or nullity of marriage, and
      (ii) are continuing;
    (b) the proceedings—
       (i) are proceedings for judicial separation,
      (ii) are continuing,
and the jurisdiction of the court is not excluded by subsection (2) below; or
    (c) the proceedings have been dismissed after the beginning of the trial but—
       (i) the section 1(1)(c) order is being made forthwith, or
      (ii) the application for the order was made on or before the dismissal.
    (2) For the purposes of subsection (1)(b) above, the jurisdiction of the court is excluded if, after the grant of a decree of judicial separation, on the relevant date, proceedings for divorce or nullity in respect of the marriage are continuing in England and Wales or Scotland.
    (3) Subsection (2) above shall not apply if the court in which the other proceedings there referred to are continuing has made—
    (a) an order under section 2A(4) or 13(6) of this Act (not being an order made by virtue of section 13(6)(a)(i), or
    (b) an order under section 5(2) or 14(2) of this Act which is recorded as being made for the purpose of enabling Part I proceedings to be taken in Northern Ireland with respect to the child concerned.
    (4) Where a court—
    (a) has jurisdiction to make a section 1(1)(c) order in or in connection with matrimonial proceedings, but
    (b) considers that it would be more appropriate for Part I matters relating to the child to be determined outside Northern Ireland,
the court may by order direct that, while the order under this subsection is in force, no section 1(1)(c) order shall be made by any court in or in connection with those proceedings.]

Note. Sections 19, 19A in square brackets substituted for s 19 in italics by Children (Northern Ireland) Order 1995, SI 1995 No 755, art 185(1), Sch 9, para 124, as from 4 November 1996.

20. Habitual residence or presence of child—(1) The condition referred to in *section 19* [section 19(2)] of this Act is that on the relevant date the child concerned—
    (a) is habitually resident in Northern Ireland, or
    (b) is present in Northern Ireland and is not habitually resident in any part of the United Kingdom,
and, in either case, the jurisdiction of the court is not excluded by subsection (2) below.
    (2) For the purposes of subsection (1) above, the jurisdiction of the court is excluded if, on the relevant date, *proceedings for divorce, nullity or judicial separation* [matrimonial proceedings] are continuing in a court in England and Wales or Scotland in respect of the marriage of the parents of the child concerned.

Note. Words in square brackets in sub-ss (1), (2) substituted for words in italics by Children (Northern Ireland) Order 1995, SI 1995 No 755, art 185, Sch 9, para 125, as from 4 November 1996.

    (3) Subsection (2) above shall not apply if the court in which the other proceedings there referred to are continuing has made—
    (a) an order under section *4(5)* [2A(4)] or 13(6) of this Act (not being an order made by virtue of section 13(6)(a)(i)), or
    (b) an order under section 5(2) or 14(2) of this Act which is recorded as made for the purpose of enabling proceedings with respect to the custody of the child concerned to be taken in Northern Ireland,
and that order is in force.

Note. Words in square brackets substituted for words in italics by Children Act 1989, s 108(5), Sch 13, para 68, as from 14 October 1991.

(*4*) *Subject to subsections* (*5*) *and* (*6*) *below, in this section 'the relevant date' means the date of the commencement of the proceedings in which the custody order* [*Part I order*] *falls to be made.*

(*5*) *In the case of a custody order* [*Part I order*] *under section 5 of the Guardianship of Infants Act 1886 'the relevant date' means the date of the application for the order* (*or first application, if two or more are determined together*).

(*6*) *In the case of a custody order* [*Part I order*] *within section 1(1)(d)* [*1(1)(e)*] *of this Act 'the relevant date' means—*

(*a*) *where an application is made for an order, the date of the application* (*or first application, if two or more are determined together*), *and*

(*b*) *where no such application is made, the date of the order.*

Note. Words in square brackets in sub-ss (4)–(6) substituted for words 'custody order' and '1(1)(d)' by Children Act 1989, s 108(5), Sch 13, paras 62(1), (2)(a), 69(b), as from 14 October 1991.

Note also the modification of this section by the Family Law Act 1986 (Dependent Territories) Order 1991, SI 1991 No 1723, art 3(2), Sch 2, para 9.

21. Jurisdiction in divorce proceedings, etc—(*1*) *The enactments relating to the jurisdiction of courts in Northern Ireland to make orders under Article 45(1) of the Matrimonial Causes* (*Northern Ireland*) *Order 1978 shall have effect subject to the modifications provided for by this section.*

(*2*) *In Article 45(1)(b) of that order* (*which enables orders as to custody and education to be made immediately, or within a reasonable period, after the dismissal of proceedings for divorce, etc*), *for the words 'within a reasonable period' there shall be substituted the words '*(*if an application for the order is made on or before the dismissal*)*'.*

(*3*) *A court shall not have jurisdiction to make a custody order* [*Part I order*] *under Article 45(1)(a) of that Order after the grant of a decree of judicial separation if, on the relevant date, proceedings for divorce or nullity in respect of the marriage concerned are continuing in England and Wales or Scotland.*

(*4*) *Subsection* (*3*) *above shall not apply if the court in which the other proceedings there referred to are continuing has made—*

(*a*) *an order under section 4(5)* [*2A(4)*] *or 13(6) of this Act* (*not being an order made by virtue of section 13(6)(a)(i)*), *or*

(*b*) *an order under section 5(2) or 14(2) of this Act which is recorded as made for the purpose of enabling proceedings with respect to the custody of* [*Part I proceedings with respect to*] *the child concerned to be taken in Northern Ireland,*

and that order is in force.

(*5*) *Where a court—*

(*a*) *has jurisdiction to make a custody order* [*Part I order*] *under Article 45(1) of the Matrimonial Causes* (*Northern Ireland*) *Order 1978 in or in connection with proceedings for divorce, nullity of marriage or judicial separation, but*

(*b*) *considers that it would be more appropriate for matters relating to the custody of* [*Part I matters relating to*] *the child to be determined outside Northern Ireland,*

the court may by order direct that, while the order under this subsection is in force, no custody order under Article 45(1) with respect to the child shall be made by any court in or in connection with those proceedings.

(*6*) *In this section 'the relevant date' means—*

(*a*) *where an application is made for a custody order* [*Part I order*] *under Article 45(1)(a), the date of the application* (*or first application, if two or more are determined together*), *and*

(*b*) *where no such application is made, the date of the order.*

Note. Words in square brackets substituted for words 'custody order', '4(5)', 'proceedings with respect to the custody of' and 'matters relating to the custody of' by Children Act 1989, s 108(5), Sch 13, paras 62(1), (2)(a), (b), (c), 68(d), as from 14 October 1991. This section repealed by Children (Northern Ireland) Order 1995, SI 1995 No 755, art 185, Sch 10, as from 4 November 1996.

Note also the modification of this section by the Family Law Act 1986 (Dependent Territories) Order 1991, SI 1991 No 1723, art 3(2), Sch 2, para 10.

22. Power of court to refuse application or stay proceedings—(1) A court in Northern Ireland which has jurisdiction to make a *custody order* [Part I order] may refuse an application for the order in any case where the matter in question has already been determined in proceedings outside Northern Ireland.

(2) Where, at any stage of the proceedings on an application made to a court in Northern Ireland for a *custody order* [Part I order], or for the variation of a *custody order* [Part I order], it appears to the court—

(a) that proceedings with respect to the matters to which the application relates are continuing outside Northern Ireland, or

(b) that it would be more appropriate for those matters to be determined in proceedings to be taken outside Northern Ireland,

the court may stay the proceedings on the application.

(3) The court may remove a stay granted in accordance with subsection (2) above if it appears to the court that there has been unreasonable delay in the taking or prosecution of the other proceedings referred to in that subsection, or that those proceedings are stayed, sisted or concluded.

(4) Nothing in this section shall affect any power exercisable apart from this section to refuse an application or to grant or remove a stay.

Note. Words in square brackets substituted for words in italics in sub-ss (1), (2) by Children Act 1989, s 108(5), Sch 13, para 62(1), (2)(a), as from 14 October 1991.

23. Duration and variation of custody orders—(1) If a *custody order* [Part I order] made by a court in England and Wales or Scotland (or a variation of such an order) comes into force with respect to a child at a time when a *custody order* [Part I order] made by a court in Northern Ireland has effect with respect to him, the latter order shall cease to have effect so far as it makes provision for any matter for which the same or different provision is made by (or by the variation of) the order made by the court in England and Wales or Scotland.

(2) Where by virtue of subsection (1) above a *custody order* [Part I order] has ceased to have effect so far as it makes provision for any matter, a court in Northern Ireland shall not have jurisdiction to vary that order so as to make provision for that matter.

Note. Words in square brackets in sub-ss (1), (2) substituted for words in italics by Children Act 1989, s 108(5), Sch 13, para 62, as from 14 October 1991.

(3) A court in Northern Ireland shall not have jurisdiction—

(a) to vary a custody order [Part I order], other than one made under Article 45(1)(a) of the Matrimonial Causes (Northern Ireland) Order 1978, or

(b) after the grant of a decree of judicial separation, to vary a custody order [Part I order] made under Article 45(1)(a) of that Order,

if, on the relevant date, proceedings for divorce, nullity or judicial separation are continuing in England and Wales or Scotland in respect of the marriage of the parents of the child concerned.

Note. Words in square brackets substituted for words 'custody order' by Children Act 1989, s 108(5), Sch 13, para 62, as from 14 October 1991.

[(3) A court in Northern Ireland shall not have jurisdiction to vary a Part I order if, on the relevant date, matrimonial proceedings are continuing in England and Wales or Scotland in respect of the marriage of the parents of the child concerned.

(3A) Subsection (3) above shall not apply if—

(a) the Part I order was made in or in connection with proceedings for divorce or nullity in Northern Ireland in respect of the marriage of the parents of the child concerned; and

(b) those proceedings are continuing.

(3B) Subsection (3) above shall not apply if—

(a) the Part I order was made in or in connection with proceedings for judicial separation in Northern Ireland;

(b) those proceedings are continuing; and

(c) the decree of judicial separation has not yet been granted.]

Note. Sub-ss (3)–(3B) in square brackets substituted for sub-s (3) in italics by Children (Northern Ireland) Order 1995, SI 1995 No 755, art 185(2), Sch 9, para 126, as from 4 November 1996.

(4) Subsection (3) above shall not apply if the court in which the proceedings there referred to are continuing has made—

(a) an order under section 4(5) [2A(4)] or 13(6) of this Act (not being an order made by virtue of section 13(6)(a)(i)), or

(b) an order under section 5(2) or 14(2) of this Act which is recorded as made for the purpose of enabling *proceedings with respect to the custody of* [Part I proceedings with respect to] the child concerned to be taken in Northern Ireland,

and that order is in force.

Note. Words in square brackets substituted for words in italics by Children Act 1989, s 108(5), Sch 13, paras 62, 68, as from 14 October 1991.

(5) Subsection (3) above shall not apply in the case of a *variation of a custody order* [*Part I order*] *within section 1(1)(d)* [*1(1)(e)*] *of this Act if the ward* [variation of a section 1(1)(e) order if the child concerned] is present in Northern Ireland on the relevant date and the court considers that the immediate exercise of its powers is necessary for his protection.

Note. Words in first and second pairs of square brackets substituted for words 'custody order' and '1(1)(d)' by Children Act 1989, s 108(5), Sch 13, paras 62, 68, as from 14 October 1991. Words in third pair of square brackets substituted for words in italics by Children (Northern Ireland) Order 1995, SI 1995 No 755, art 185(1), Sch 9, para 126, as from 4 November 1996.

(6) *Where any person who is entitled to the actual possession of a child under a custody order* [*Part I order*] *made by a court in Northern Ireland ceases to be so entitled by virtue of subsection (1) above, then, if there is in force an order for the supervision of that child made under—*

(a) *Article 47 of the Matrimonial Causes (Northern Ireland) Order 1978, or*

(b) *Article 11 of the Domestic Proceedings (Northern Ireland) Order 1980,*

that order shall also cease to have effect.

(7) *In this section 'the relevant date' means—*

(a) *where an application is made for a variation, the date of the application (or first application, if two or more are determined together), and*

(b) *where no such application is made, the date of the variation.*

[(6) Subsection (7) below applies where a Part I order which is—

(a) a residence order (within the meaning of the Children (Northern Ireland) Order 1995) in favour of a person with respect to a child,

(b) an order made in the exercise of the High Court's inherent jurisdiction with respect to children by virtue of which a person has care of a child, or

(c) an order—

    (i) of a kind mentioned in section 1(3)(a) of this Act,

    (ii) under which a person is entitled to the actual possession of a child,

ceases to have effect in relation to that person by virtue of subsection (1) above.

(7) Where this subsection applies, any family assistance order made under Article 16 of the Children (Northern Ireland) Order 1995 with respect to the child shall also cease to have effect.

(8) For the purposes of subsection (7) above the reference to a family assistance order under Article 16 of the Children (Northern Ireland) Order 1995 shall be deemed to include a reference to an order for the supervision of a child made under—

(a) Article 47 of the Matrimonial Causes (Northern Ireland) Order 1978, or

(b) Article 11 of the Domestic Proceedings (Northern Ireland) Order 1980;

but this supervision shall cease to have effect once all such orders for the supervision of children have ceased to have effect in accordance with Schedule 8 to the Children (Northern Ireland) Order 1995.]

Note. Words in square brackets substituted for words 'custody order' in sub-s (6) by Children Act 1989, s 108(5), Sch 13, para 62, as from 14 October 1991. Sub-ss (6)–(8) in square brackets substituted for sub-ss (6), (7) in italics by Children (Northern Ireland) Order 1995, SI 1995 No 755, art 185(1), Sch 9, para 126, as from 4 November 1996.

24. Interpretation of Chapter IV. *In this Chapter 'child' means a person who has not attained the age of eighteen.*

[24. Interpretation of Chapter IV. In this Chapter—

(a) 'child means a person who has not attained the age of eighteen;

(b) 'matrimonial proceedings' means proceedings for divorce, nullity of marriage or judicial separation;

(c) 'the relevant date' means, in relation to the making or variation of an order—

  (i) where an application is made for an order to be made or varied, the date of the application (or first application, if two or more are determined together), and

 (ii) where no such application is made, the date on which the court is considering whether to make or, as the case may be, vary the order; and

(d) 'section 1(1)(c) order' and 'section 1(1)(e) order' mean orders falling within section 1(1)(c) and (e) of this Act respectively].

Note. Section 24 in square brackets substituted for s 24 in italics by Children (Northern Ireland) Order 1995, SI 1995 No 755, art 185(1), Sch 9, para 127, as from 4 November 1996.

CHAPTER V

RECOGNITION AND ENFORCEMENT

25. Recognition of custody orders: general—(1) Where a *custody order* [Part I order] made by a court in any part of the United Kingdom is in force with respect to a child who has not attained the age of sixteen, then, subject to subsection (2) below, the order shall be recognised in any other part of the United Kingdom as having the same effect in that other part as if it had been made by the appropriate court in that other part and as if that court had had jurisdiction to make it.

(2) Where a *custody order* [Part I order] includes provision as to the means by which rights conferred by the order are to be enforced, subsection (1) above shall not apply to that provision.

(3) A court in a part of the United Kingdom in which a *custody order* [Part I order] is recognised in accordance with subsection (1) above shall not enforce the order unless it has been registered in that part of the United Kingdom under section 27 of this Act and proceedings for enforcement are taken in accordance with section 29 of this Act.

Note. Words in square brackets substituted for words in italics by Children Act 1989, s 108(5), Sch 13, para 62(1), (2)(a), as from 14 October 1991.

Note also the modification of this section by the Family Law Act 1986 (Dependent Territories) Order 1991, SI 1991 No 1723, art 3(2), Sch 2, para 12.

[26. Recognition: special Scottish rule. An order relating to parental responsibilities or parental rights in relation to a child which is made outside the United Kingdom shall be recognised in Scotland if the order was made in the country where the child was habitually resident.]

Note. This section substituted by Children (Scotland) Act 1995, s 105(4), Sch 4, para 41(6), as from 1 November 1996.

27. Registration—(1) Any person on whom any rights are conferred by a *custody order* [Part I order] may apply to the court which made it for the order to be registered in another part of the United Kingdom under this section.

(2) An application under this section shall be made in the prescribed manner and shall contain the prescribed information and be accompanied by such documents as may be prescribed.

(3) On receiving an application under this section the court which made the *custody order* [Part I order] shall, unless it appears to the court that the order is no longer in force, cause the following documents to be sent to the appropriate court in the part of the United Kingdom specified in the application, namely—

(a) a certified copy of the order, and

(b) where the order has been varied, prescribed particulars of any variation which is in force, and

(c) a copy of the application and of any accompanying documents.

(4) Where the prescribed officer of the appropriate court receives a certified copy of a *custody order* [Part I order] under subsection (3) above, he shall forthwith cause the order, together with particulars of any variation, to be registered in that court in the prescribed manner.

(5) An order shall not be registered under this section in respect of a child who has attained the age of sixteen, and the registration of an order in respect of a child who has not attained the age of sixteen shall cease to have effect on the attainment by the child of that age.

Note. Words in square brackets substituted for words in italics by Children Act 1989, s 108(5), Sch 13, para 62(1), (2)(a), as from 14 October 1991.

Note also the modification of this section by the Family Law Act 1986 (Dependent Territories) Order 1991, SI 1991 No 1723, art 3(2), Sch 2, para 14.

28. Cancellation and variation of registration—(1) A court which revokes, recalls or varies an order registered under section 27 if this Act shall cause notice of the revocation, recall or variation to be given in the prescribed manner to the prescribed officer of the court in which it is registered and, on receiving the notice, the prescribed officer—

(a) in the case of the revocation or recall of the order, shall cancel the registration, and

(b) in the case of the variation of the order, shall cause particulars of the variation to be registered in the prescribed manner.

(2) Where—

(a) an order registered under section 27 of this Act ceases (in whole or in part) to have effect in the part of the United Kingdom in which it was made, otherwise than because of its revocation, recall or variation, or

(b) an order registered under section 27 of this Act in Scotland ceases (in whole or in part) to have effect there as a result of the making of an order in proceedings outside the United Kingdom,

the court in which the order is registered may, of its own motion or on the application of any person who appears to the court to have an interest in the matter, cancel the registration (or, if the order has ceased to have effect in part, cancel the registration so far as it relates to the provisions which have ceased to have effect).

Note. Note the modification of this section by the Family Law Act 1986 (Dependent Territories) Order 1991, SI 1991 No 1723, art 3(2), Sch 2, para 15.

29. Enforcement—(1) Where a *custody order* [Part I order] has been registered under section 27 of this Act, the court in which it is registered shall have the same powers for the purpose of enforcing the order as it would have if it had itself made the order and had jurisdiction to make it; and proceedings for or with respect to enforcement may be taken accordingly.

(2) Where an application has been made to any court for the enforcement of an order registered in that court under section 27 of this Act, the court may, at any time before the application is determined, give such interim directions as it thinks fit for the purpose of securing the welfare of the child concerned or of preventing changes in the circumstances relevant to the determination of the application.

(3) The references in subsection (1) above to a *custody order* [Part I order] do not include references to any provision of the order as to the means by which rights conferred by the order are to be enforced.

Note. Words in square brackets substituted for words in italics by Children Act 1989, s 108(5), Sch 13, para 62(1), (2)(a), as from 14 October 1991.

30. Staying or sisting of enforcement proceedings—(1) Where in accordance with section 29 of this Act proceedings are taken in any court for the enforcement of an order registered in that court, any person who appears to the court to have an interest in the matter may apply for the proceedings to be stayed or sisted on the ground that he has taken or intends to take other proceedings (in the United Kingdom or elsewhere) as a result of which the order may cease to have effect, or may have a different effect, in the part of the United Kingdom in which it is registered.

(2) If after considering an application under subsection (1) above the court considers that the proceedings for enforcement should be stayed or sisted in order that other proceedings may be taken or concluded, it shall stay or sist the proceedings for enforcement accordingly.

(3) The court may remove a stay or recall a sist granted in accordance with subsection (2) above if it appears to the court—

(a) that there has been unreasonable delay in the taking or prosecution of the other proceedings referred to in that subsection, or

(b) that those other proceedings are concluded and that the registered order, or a relevant part of it, is still in force.

(4) Nothing in this section shall affect any power exercisable apart from this section to grant, remove or recall a stay or sist.

31. Dismissal of enforcement proceedings—(1) Where in accordance with section 29 of this Act proceedings are taken in any court for the enforcement of an order registered in that court, any person who appears to the court to have an interest in the matter may apply for those proceedings to be dismissed on the ground that the order has (in whole or in part) ceased to have effect in the part of the United Kingdom in which it was made.

(2) Where in accordance with section 29 of this Act proceedings are taken in the Court of Session for the enforcement of an order registered in that court, any person who appears to the court to have an interest in the matter may apply for those proceedings to be dismissed on the ground that the order has (in whole or in part) ceased to have effect in Scotland as a result of the making of an order in proceedings outside the United Kingdom.

(3) If, after considering an application under subsection (1) or (2) above, the court is satisfied that the registered order has ceased to have effect, it shall dismiss the proceedings for enforcement (or, if it is satisfied that the order has ceased to have effect in part, it shall dismiss the proceedings so far as they relate to the enforcement of provisions which have ceased to have effect).

Note. Note the modification of this section by the Family Law Act 1986 (Dependent Territories) Order 1991, SI 1991 No 1723, art 3(2), Sch 2, para 16.

32. Interpretation of Chapter V—(1) In this Chapter—

'the appropriate court', in relation to England and Wales or Northern Ireland, means the High Court and, in relation to Scotland, means the Court of Session;

'*custody order*' ['Part I order'] includes (except where the context otherwise requires) any order within section 1(3) of this Act which, on the assumptions mentioned in subsection (3) below—

(a) could have been made notwithstanding the provisions of this Part;

(b) would have been a *custody order* [Part I order] for the purposes of this Part; and

(c) would not have ceased to have effect by virtue of section 6, 15 or 23 of this Act.

(2) In the application of this Chapter to Scotland, '*custody order*' [Part I order] also includes (except where the context otherwise requires) any order within section 1(3) of this Act which, on the assumptions mentioned in subsection (3) below—

(a) would have been a *custody order* [Part I order] for the purposes of this Part; and

(b) would not have ceased to have effect by virtue of section 6 or 23 of this Act,

and which, but for the provisions of this Part, would be recognised in Scotland under any rule of law.

(3) The said assumptions are—

(a) that this Part had been in force at all material times; and

(b) that any reference in section 1 of this Act to any enactment included a reference to any corresponding enactment previously in force.

Note. Words in square brackets substituted for words in italics by Children Act 1989, s 108(5), Sch 13, para 62(1), (2)(a), as from 14 October 1991.

Note also the modification of this section by the Family Law Act 1986 (Dependent Territories) Order 1991, SI 1991 No 1723, art 3(2), Sch 2, para 17.

CHAPTER VI

MISCELLANEOUS AND SUPPLEMENTAL

33. Power to order disclosure of child's whereabouts—(1) Where in proceedings for or relating to a *custody order* [Part I order] in respect of a child there is not available to the court adequate information as to where the child is, the court may order any person who it has reason to believe may have relevant information to disclose it to the court.

Note. Words in square brackets substituted for words in italics by Children Act 1989, s 108(5), Sch 13, para 62(1), (2)(a), as from 14 October 1991.

(2) A person shall not be excused from complying with an order under subsection (1) above by reason that to do so may incriminate him or his spouse of an offence; but a statement or admission made in compliance with such an order shall not be admissible in evidence against either of them in proceedings for any offence other than perjury.

(3) A court in Scotland before which proceedings are pending for the enforcement of an order *for the custody of* [relating to parental responsibilities or parental rights in relation to] a child made outside the United Kingdom which is recognised in Scotland shall have the same powers as it would have under subsection (1) above if the order were its own.

Note. Words in square brackets substituted for words in italics by Children (Scotland) Act 1995, s 105(4), Sch 4, para 41(7), as from 1 November 1996.

Note also the modification of this section by the Family Law Act 1986 (Dependent Territories) Order 1991, SI 1991 No 1723, art 3(2), Sch 2, para 18.

34. Power to order recovery of child—(1) Where—

(a) a person is required by a *custody order* [Part I order], or an order for the enforcement of a *custody order* [Part I order], to give up a child to another person ('the person concerned'), and

(b) the court which made the order imposing the requirement is satisfied that the child has not been given up in accordance with the order,

the court may make an order authorising an officer of the court or a constable to take charge of the child and deliver him to the person concerned.

(2) The authority conferred by subsection (1) above includes authority—

(a) to enter and search any premises where the person acting in pursuance of the order has reason to believe the child may be found, and

(b) to use such force as may be necessary to give effect to the purpose of the order.

(3) Where by virtue of—

(*a*) *section 13(1) of the Guardianship of Minors Act 1971, section 43(1) of the Children Act 1975 or section 33 of the Domestic Proceedings and Magistrates' Courts Act 1978, or*

[(a) section 14 of the Children Act 1989]

(*b*) *Article 37 of the Domestic Proceedings (Northern Ireland) Order 1980,*

[(b) Article 14 (enforcement of residence orders) of the Children (Northern Ireland) Order 1995,]

a *custody order* [Part I order] (or a provision of a *custody order* [Part I order]) may be enforced as if it were an order requiring a person to give up a child to another person, subsection (1) above shall apply as if the *custody order* [Part I order] had included such a requirement.

(4) This section is without prejudice to any power conferred on a court by or under any other enactment or rule of law.

Note. References to 'Part I order' substituted for references to 'custody order', and sub-s (3)(a) in square brackets substituted for sub-s (3)(a) in italics by Children Act 1989, s 108(5), Sch 13, paras 62, 70, as from 14 October 1991. Sub-s (3)(b) in square brackets substituted for sub-s (3)(b) in italics by Children (Northern Ireland Consequential Amendments) Order 1995, SI 1995 No 756, art 12, as from 4 November 1996.

35. Powers to restrict removal of child from jurisdiction—(*1*) *In each of the following enactments (which enable courts to restrict the removal of a child from England and Wales)—*

(*a*) *section 13A(1) of the Guardianship of Minors Act 1971,*

(*b*) *section 43A(1) of the Children Act 1975, and*

(*c*) *section 34(1) of the Domestic Proceedings and Magistrates' Courts Act 1978,*

for the words 'England and Wales' there shall be substituted the words 'the United Kingdom, or out of any part of the United Kingdom specified in the order'.

Note. Sub-s (1) repealed by Children Act 1989, s 108(7), Sch 15, as from 14 October 1991.

(*2*) *In Article 38(1) of the Domestic Proceedings (Northern Ireland) Order 1980 (which enables courts to restrict the removal of a child from Northern Ireland) for the words 'Northern Ireland' there shall be substituted the words 'the United Kingdom, or out of any part of the United Kingdom specified in the order'.*

Note. The modification of sub-s (2) by the Family Law Act 1986 (Dependent Territories) Order 1991, SI 1991 No 1723, art 3(2), Sch 2, para 19(1) is amended by SI 1994 No 2800.

Sub-s (2) repealed by Children (Northern Ireland) Order 1995, SI 1995 No 755, art 185(2), Sch 10, as from 4 November 1996.

(3) A court in Scotland—

(a) at any time after the commencement of proceedings in connection with which the court would have jurisdiction to make a *custody order* [Part I order], or

(b) in any proceedings in which it would be competent for the court to grant an interdict prohibiting the removal of a child from its jurisdiction.

may, on an application by any of the persons mentioned in subsection (4) below, grant interdict or interim interdict prohibiting the removal of the child from the United Kingdom or any part of the United Kingdom, or out of the control of the person in *whose custody* [whose care] the child is.

Note. Words 'Part I Order' in square brackets substituted for words 'custody order' in italics by Children Act 1989, s 108(5), Sch 13, para 62, as from 14 October 1991. Words 'whose care' in square brackets substituted for words 'whose custody' in italics by Children (Scotland) Act 1995, s 105(4), Sch 4, para 41(8), as from 1 November 1996.

    (4) The said persons are—

    (a) any party to the proceedings,

    (b) the *tutor or curator* [guardian] of the child concerned, and

    (c) any other person who has or wishes to obtain the *custody or* care of the child.

Note. Word in square brackets substituted for words in italics by Age of Legal Capacity (Scotland) Act 1991, s 10(1), Sch 10, para 47, as from 25 September 1991. Words 'custody or' in sub-s (4)(c) repealed, in relation to Scotland, by Children (Scotland) Act 1995, s 105(5), Sch 5, as from 1 November 1996.

    (5) In subsection (3) above 'the court' means the Court of Session or the sheriff; and for the purposes of subsection (3)(a) above, proceedings shall be held to commence—

    (a) in the Court of Session, when a summons is signeted or a petition is presented;

    (b) in the sheriff court, when the warrant of citation is signed.

36. Effect of orders restricting removal—(1) This section applies to any order made by a court in the United Kingdom prohibiting the removal of a child from the United Kingdom or from any specified part of it.

    (2) An order to which this section applies shall have effect in each part of the United Kingdom other than the part in which it was made—

    (a) as if it had been made by the appropriate court in the other part, and

    (b) in the case of an order which has the effect of prohibiting the child's removal to that other part, as if it had included a prohibition on his further removal to any place except one to which he could be removed consistently with the order.

    (3) The references in subsections (1) and (2) above to prohibitions on a child's removal include references to prohibitions subject to exceptions; and in a case where removal is prohibited except with the consent of the court, nothing in subsection (2) above shall be construed as affecting the identity of the court whose consent is required.

    (4) In this section 'child' means a person who has not attained the age of sixteen; and this section shall cease to apply to an order relating to a child when he attains the age of sixteen.

Note. Note the modification of this section by the Family Law Act 1986 (Dependent Territories) Order 1991, SI 1991 No 1723, art 3(2), Sch 2, para 20.

37. Surrender of passports—(1) Where there is in force an order prohibiting or otherwise restricting the removal of a child from the United Kingdom or from any specified part of it, the court by which the order was in fact made, or by which it is treated under section 36 of this Act as having been made, may require any person to surrender any United Kingdom passport which has been issued to, or contains particulars of, the child.

    (2) In this section 'United Kingdom passport' means a current passport issued by the Government of the United Kingdom.

Note. Note the modification of this section by the Family Law Act 1986 (Dependent Territories) Order 1991, SI 1991 No 1723, art 3(2), Sch 2, para 21.

38. Automatic restriction on removal of wards of court—(1) The rule of law which (without any order of the court) restricts the removal of a ward of court from the jurisdiction of the court shall, in a case to which this section applies, have effect subject to the modifications in subsection (3) below.

(2) This section applies in relation to a ward of court if—

(a) proceedings for divorce, nullity or judicial separation in respect of the marriage of his parents are continuing in a court in another part of the United Kingdom (that is to say, in a part of the United Kingdom outside the jurisdiction of the court of which he is a ward), or

(b) he is habitually resident in another part of the United Kingdom,

except where that other part is Scotland and he has attained the age of sixteen.

(3) Where this section applies, the rule referred to in subsection (1) above shall not prevent—

(a) the removal of the ward of court, without the consent of any court, to the other part of the United Kingdom mentioned in subsection (2) above, or

(b) his removal to any other place with the consent of either the appropriate court in that other part of the United Kingdom or the court mentioned in subsection (2)(a) above.

[(4) The reference in subsection (2) above to a time when proceedings for divorce or judicial separation are continuing in respect of a marriage in another part of the United Kingdom includes, in relation to any case in which England and Wales would be another part of the United Kingdom, any time when—

(a) a statement of marital breakdown under section 5 of the Family Law Act 1996 with respect to that marriage has been received by the court and it is or may become possible for an application for a divorce order or for a separation order to be made by reference to that statement; or

(b) an application in relation to that marriage for a divorce order, or for a separation order under the Act of 1996, has been made and not withdrawn.]

Note. Sub-s (4) added by Family Law Act 1996, s 66(1), Sch 8, Part I, para 37(9), as from a day to be appointed, subject to savings in s 66(2) of, and para 5 of Sch 9 to, the 1996 Act.

Note also the modification of this section by the Family Law Act 1986 (Dependent Territories) Order 1991, SI 1991 No 1723, art 3(2), Sch 2, para 22.

39. Duty to furnish particulars of other proceedings—Parties to proceedings for or relating to a *custody order* [Part I order] shall, to such extent and in such manner as may be prescribed, give particulars of other proceedings known to them which relate to the child concerned (including proceedings instituted abroad and proceedings which are no longer continuing).

Note. Words in square brackets substituted for words in italics by Children Act 1989, s 108(5), Sch 13, para 62(1), (2)(a), as from 14 October 1991.

40. Interpretation of Chapter VI—(1) In this Chapter—

'the appropriate court' has the same meaning as in Chapter V;

'*custody order*' ['Part I order'] includes (except where the context otherwise requires) any such order as is mentioned in section 32(1) of this Act.

(2) In the application of this Chapter to Scotland, '*custody order*' [Part I order] also includes (except where the context otherwise requires) any such order as is mentioned in section 32(2) of this Act.

Note. Words in square brackets substituted for words in italics by Children Act 1989, s 108(5), Sch 13, para 62(1), (2)(a), as from 14 October 1991.

41. Habitual residence after removal without consent, etc—(1) Where a child who—

(a) has not attained the age of sixteen, and

(b) is habitually resident in a part of the United Kingdom,

becomes habitually resident outside that part of the United Kingdom in consequence of circumstances of the kind specified in subsection (2) below, he shall be treated for the purposes of this Part as continuing to be habitually resident in that part of the United Kingdom for the period of one year beginning with the date on which those circumstances arise.

(2) The circumstances referred to in subsection (1) above exist where the child is removed from or retained outside, or himself leaves or remains outside, the part of the United Kingdom in which he was habitually resident before his change of residence—

(a) without the agreement of the person or all the persons having, under the law of that part of the United Kingdom, the right to determine where he is to reside, or

(b) in contravention of an order made by a court in any part of the United Kingdom.

(3) A child shall cease to be treated by virtue of subsection (1) above as habitually resident in a part of the United Kingdom if, during the period there mentioned—

(a) he attains the age of sixteen, or

(b) he becomes habitually resident outside that part of the United Kingdom with the agreement of the person or persons mentioned in subsection (2)(a) above and not in contravention of an order made by a court in any part of the United Kingdom.

Note. Note the modification of this section by the Family Law Act 1986 (Dependent Territories) Order 1991, SI 1991 No 1723, art 3(2), Sch 2, para 23.

42. General interpretation of Part I—(1) In this Part—

'certified copy', in relation to an order of any court, means a copy certified by the prescribed officer of the court to be a true copy of the order or of the official record of the order;

['parental responsibilities' and 'parental rights' have the meanings respectively given by sections 1(3) and 2(4) of the Children (Scotland) Act 1995;]

'part of the United Kingdom' means England and Wales, Scotland or Northern Ireland;

'prescribed' means prescribed by rules of court or act of sederunt;

['the Council Regulation' means Council Regulation (EC) No 1347/2000 of 29th May 2000 on jurisdiction and the recognition and enforcement of judgments in matrimonial matters and in matters of parental responsibility for children of both spouses.]

Note. Definition 'parental responsibilities and parental rights' in square brackets inserted by Children (Scotland) Act 1995, s 105(4), Sch 4, para 41(9), as from 1 November 1996. Definition 'the Council Regulation' inserted by SI 2001/310, reg 8, as from 1 March 2001.

(2) For the purposes of this Part proceedings in England and Wales or in Northern Ireland for divorce, nullity or judicial separation in respect of the marriage of the parents of a child shall, *unless they have been dismissed, be treated as continuing until the child concerned attains the age of eighteen (whether or not a decree has been granted and whether or not, in the case of a decree of divorce or nullity of marriage, that decree has been made absolute)* [be treated as continuing (irrespective of whether a divorce order, separation order or decree of nullity has been made)—

(a) from the time when a statement of marital breakdown under section 5 of the Family Law Act 1996 with respect to the marriage is received by the court in England and Wales until such time as the court may designate or, if earlier, until the time when—

(i) the child concerned attains the age of eighteen; or

(ii) it ceases, by virtue of section 5(3) or 7(9) of that Act (lapse of divorce or separation process) to be possible for an application for a divorce order, or for a separation order, to be made by reference to that statement; and

(b) from the time when a petition for nullity is presented in relation to the marriage in England and Wales or a petition for divorce, judicial separation or nullity is presented in relation to the marriage in Northern Ireland or a specified dependent territory, until the time when—

(i) the child concerned attains the age of eighteen; or

(ii) if earlier, proceedings on the petition are dismissed.]

Note. Words in square brackets substituted for words in italics by Family Law Act 1996, s 66(1), Sch 8, Part I, para 37(10), as from a day to be appointed, subject to savings in s 66(2) of, and para 5 of Sch 9 to, the 1996 Act.

(3) For the purposes of this Part, matrimonial proceedings in a court in Scotland which has jurisdiction in those proceedings to make a *custody order* [Part I order] with respect to a child shall, unless they have been dismissed or decree of absolvitor has been granted therein, be treated as continuing until the child concerned attains the age of sixteen.

Note. Words in square brackets substituted for words in italics by Children Act 1989, s 108(5), Sch 13, para 62, as from 14 October 1991.

(4) Any reference in this Part to proceedings in respect of the marriage of the parents of a child shall, in relation to a child who, although not a child of both parties to the marriage, is a child of the family of those parties, be construed as a reference to proceedings in respect of that marriage; and for this purpose 'child of the family'—

(a) if the proceedings are in England and Wales, means any child who has been treated by both parties as a child of their family, except a child who *has been boarded out with those parties* [is placed with those parties as foster parents] by a local authority or a voluntary organisation;

(b) if the proceedings are in Scotland, means any child *of one of the parties who has been accepted as one of the family by the other party;* [who has been treated by both parties as a child of their family, except a child who has been placed with those parties as foster parents by a local authority or a voluntary organisation;]

(c) if the proceedings are in Northern Ireland, means any child who has been treated by both parties as a child of their family, except a child who *has been boarded out with those parties by or on behalf of the Department of Health and Social Services* [is placed with those parties as foster parents by an authority within the meaning of the Children (Northern Ireland) Order 1995] or a voluntary organisation.

Note. Words in square brackets in sub-s (4)(a) substituted for words in italics by Children Act 1989, s 108(5), Sch 13, para 71, as from 14 October 1991. Words in square brackets in sub-s (4)(b) substituted for words in italics by Children (Scotland) Act 1995, s 105(4), Sch 4, para 41(9), as from 1 November 1996. Words in square brackets in sub-s (4)(c) substituted for words in italics by Children (Northern Ireland Consequential Amendments) Order 1995, SI 1995 No 756, art 12, as from 4 November 1996.

(5) References in this Part to *custody orders* [Part I order] include (except where the context otherwise requires) references to *custody orders* [Part I order] as varied.

(6) For the purposes of this Part each of the following orders shall be treated as varying the *custody order* [Part I order] to which it relates—

(a) an order which provides for a person [to be allowed contact with or] to be given access to a child who is the subject of a *custody order* [Part I order], or which makes provision for the education of such a child,

(b) *an order under section 42(6) of the Matrimonial Causes Act 1973 or Article 45 (6) of the Matrimonial Causes (Northern Ireland) Order 1978,*

(c) *an order under section 42(7) of that Act or Article 45(7) of that Order, and*

(d) *an order under section 19(6) of the Domestic Proceedings and Magistrates' Courts Act 1978 or Article 20(6) of the Domestic Proceedings (Northern Ireland) Order 1980;*

and for the purposes of Chapter V of this Part and this Chapter, this subsection shall have effect as if any reference to any enactment included a reference to any corresponding enactment previously in force.

Note. References to 'Part I order' in sub-ss (5), (6) substituted for references to 'custody order', words 'to be allowed contact with or' in sub-s (6)(a) inserted, and words 'section 42(6) of the Matrimonial Causes Act or', 'section 42(7) of that Act' and 'section 19(6) of the Domestic Proceedings and Magistrates' Courts Act 1978', in sub-s (6)(b), (c), (d) respectively, repealed, by Children Act 1989, s 108(5), (7), Sch 13, paras 62, 71, Sch 15, as from 14 October 1991. Words from '(b)' to the end repealed by Children (Northern Ireland Consequential Amendments) Order 1995, SI 1995 No 756, art 12, as from 4 November 1996.

(7) *References in this Part to proceedings in respect of the custody of a child include, in relation to proceedings outside the United Kingdom, references to proceedings before a tribunal or other authority having power under the law having effect there to determine questions relating to the custody of children.*

[(7) In this Part—

(a) references to Part I proceedings in respect of a child are references to any proceedings for a Part I order or an order corresponding to a Part I order and include, in relation to proceedings outside the United Kingdom, references to proceedings before a tribunal or other authority having power under the law having effect there to determine Part I matters; and

(b) references to Part I matters are references to matters that might be determined by a Part I order or an order corresponding to a Part I order.]

Note. Sub-s (7) in square brackets substituted for sub-s (7) in italics by Children Act 1989, s 108(5), Sch 13, para 62(1), (3), as from 14 October 1991.

Note also the modification of this section by the Family Law Act 1986 (Dependent Territories) Order 1991, SI 1991 No 1723, art 3(2), Sch 2, para 24.

43. Application of Part I to dependent territories—(1) Her Majesty may by Order in Council make provision corresponding to or applying any of the foregoing provisions of this Part, with such modifications as appear to Her Majesty to be appropriate, for the purpose of regulating—

(a) in any dependent territory;

(b) as between any dependent territory and any part of the United Kingdom; or

(c) as between any dependent territory and any other such territory,

the jurisdiction of courts to make *custody orders* [Part I orders], or orders corresponding to *custody orders* [Part I orders], and the recognition and enforcement of such orders.

(2) In subsection (1) above 'dependent territory' means any of the following territories—

(a) the Isle of Man,

(b) any of the Channel Islands, and

(c) any colony.

(3) An Order in Council under subsection (1) above may contain such consequential, incidental and supplementary provisions as appear to Her Majesty to be necessary or expedient.

(4) An Order in Council under subsection (1)(b) above which makes provision affecting the law of any part of the United Kingdom shall be subject to annulment in pursuance of a resolution of either House of Parliament.

Note. Words in square brackets substituted for words in italics by Children Act 1989, s 108(5), Sch 13, para 62(1), (2)(a), as from 14 October 1991.

PART II

RECOGNITION OF DIVORCES, ANNULMENTS AND LEGAL SEPARATIONS

Divorces, annulments and judicial separations granted in the British Islands

44. Recognition in United Kingdom of divorces, annulments and judicial separations granted in the British Islands—(1) Subject to section 52(4) and (5)(a) of this Act, no divorce or annulment obtained in any part of the British Islands shall be regarded as effective in any part of the United Kingdom unless granted by a court of civil jurisdiction.

(2) Subject to section 51 of this Act, the validity of any divorce, annulment or judicial separation granted by a court of civil jurisdiction in any part of the British Islands shall be recognised throughout the United Kingdom.

Overseas divorces, annulments and legal separations

45. Recognition in the United Kingdom of overseas divorces, annulments and legal separations.   *Subject* [(1) Subject to subsection (2) of this section and] to sections 51 and 52 of this Act, the validity of a divorce, annulment or legal separation obtained in a country outside the British Islands (in this part referred to as an overseas divorce, annulment or legal separation) shall be recognised in the United Kingdom if, and only if, it is entitled to recognition—

   (a) by virtue of *sections 40 to 49 of this Act* [Sections 46 to 49 of this Act], or

   (b) by virtue of any enactment other than this Part.

   [(2) Subsection (1) and the following provisions of this Part do not apply to an overseas divorce, annulment or legal separations as regards which provision as to recognition is made by Articles 14 to 20 of the Council Regulation.]

Note. Sub-s (1) numbered as such, words in square brackets substituted for words in italics and sub-s (2) inserted by SI 2001/310, reg 9 as from 1 March 2001.

46. Grounds for recognition—(1) The validity of an overseas divorce, annulment or legal separation obtained by means of proceedings shall be recognised if—

   (a) the divorce, annulment or legal separation is effective under the law of the country in which it was obtained; and

   (b) at the relevant date either party to the marriage—

      (i) was habitually resident in the country in which the divorce, annulment or legal separation was obtained; or

      (ii) was domiciled in that country; or

      (iii) was a national of that country.

   (2) The validity of an overseas divorce, annulment or legal separation obtained otherwise than by means of proceedings shall be recognised if—

   (a) the divorce, annulment or legal separation is effective under the law of the country in which it was obtained;

   (b) at the relevant date—

      (i) each party to the marriage was domiciled in that country; or

      (ii) either party to the marriage was domiciled in that country and the other party was domiciled in a country under whose law the divorce, annulment or legal separation is recognised as valid; and

   (c) neither party to the marriage was habitually resident in the United Kingdom throughout the period of one year immediately preceding that date.

   (3) In this section 'the relevant date' means—

   (a) in the case of an overseas divorce, annulment or legal separation obtained by means of proceedings, the date of the commencement of the proceedings;

   (b) in the case of an overseas divorce, annulment or legal separation obtained otherwise than by means of proceedings, the date on which it was obtained.

   (4) Where in the case of an overseas annulment, the relevant date fell after the death of either party to the marriage, any reference in subsection (1) or (2) above to that date shall be construed in relation to that party as a reference to the date of death.

   (5) For the purpose of this section, a party to a marriage shall be treated as domiciled in a country if he was domiciled in that country either according to the law of that country in family matters or according to the law of the part of the United Kingdom in which the question of recognition arises.

47. Cross-proceedings and divorces following legal separations—(1) Where there have been cross-proceedings, the validity of an overseas divorce, annulment or legal separation obtained either in the original proceedings or in the cross-proceedings shall be recognised if—

(a) the requirements of section 46(1)(b)(i), (ii) or (iii) of this Act are satisfied in relation to the date of the commencement either of the original proceedings or of the cross-proceedings, and

(b) the validity of the divorce, annulment or legal separation is otherwise entitled to recognition by virtue of the provisions of this Part.

(2) Where a legal separation, the validity of which is entitled to recognition by virtue of the provisions of section 46 of this Act or of subsection (1) above is converted, in the country in which it was obtained, into a divorce which is effective under the law of that country, the validity of the divorce shall be recognised whether or not it would itself be entitled to recognition by virtue of those provisions.

48. Proof of facts relevant to recognition—(1) For the purpose of deciding whether an overseas divorce, annulment or legal separation obtained by means of proceedings is entitled to recognition by virtue of section 46 and 47 of this Act, any finding of fact made (whether expressly or by implication) in the proceedings and on the basis of which jurisdiction was assumed in the proceedings shall—

(a) if both parties to the marriage took part in the proceedings, be conclusive evidence of the fact found; and

(b) in any other case, be sufficient proof of that fact unless the contrary is shown.

(2) In this section 'finding of fact' includes a finding that either party to the marriage—

(a) was habitually resident in the country in which the divorce, annulment or legal separation was obtained; or

(b) was under the law of that country domiciled there; or

(c) was a national of that country.

(3) For the purposes of subsection (1)(a) above, a party to the marriage who has appeared in judicial proceedings shall be treated as having taken part in them.

Supplemental

49. Modifications of Part II in relation to countries comprising territories having different systems of law—(1) In relation to a country comprising territories in which different systems of law are in force in matters of divorce, annulment or legal separation, the provisions of this Part mentioned in subsections (2) to (5) below shall have effect subject to the modifications there specified.

(2) In the case of a divorce, annulment or legal separation the recognition of the validity of which depends on whether the requirements of subsection (1)(b)(i) or (ii) of section 46 of this Act are satisfied, that section and, in the case of a legal separation, section 47(2) of this Act shall have effect as if each territory were a separate country.

(3) In the case of a divorce, annulment or legal separation the recognition of the validity of which depends on whether the requirements of subsection (1)(b)(iii) of section 46 of this Act are satisfied—

(a) that section shall have effect as if for paragraph (a) of subsection (1) there were substituted the following paragraph

'(a) the divorce, annulment or legal separation is effective throughout the country in which it was obtained;'; and

(b) in the case of a legal separation, section 47(2) of this Act shall have effect as if for the words 'is effective under the law of that country' there were substituted the words 'is effective throughout that country'.

(4) In the case of a divorce, annulment or legal separation the recognition of the validity of which depends on whether the requirements of subsection (2)(b) of section 46 of this Act are satisfied, that section and section 51(3) and (4) of this Act and, in the case of a legal separation, section 47(2) of this Act shall have effect as if each territory were a separate country.

(5) Paragraphs (a) and (b) of section 48(2) of this Act shall each have effect as if each territory were a separate country.

50. Non-recognition of divorce or annulment in another jurisdiction no bar to remarriage. Where, in any part of the United Kingdom—

(a) a divorce or annulment has been granted by a court of civil jurisdiction, or

(b) the validity of a divorce or annulment is recognised by virtue of this Part,

the fact that the divorce or annulment would not be recognised elsewhere shall not preclude either party to the marriage from remarrying in that part of the United Kingdom or cause the remarriage of either party (wherever the remarriage takes place) to be treated as invalid in that part.

51. Refusal of recognition—(1) Subject to section 52 of this Act, recognition of the validity of—

(a) a divorce, annulment or judicial separation granted by a court of civil jurisdiction in any part of the British Islands, or

(b) an overseas divorce, annulment or legal separation,

may be refused in any part of the United Kingdom if the divorce, annulment or separation was granted or obtained at a time when it was irreconcilable with a decision determining the question of the subsistence or validity of the marriage of the parties previously given (whether before or after the commencement of this Part) by a court of civil jurisdiction in that part of the United Kingdom or by a court elsewhere and recognised or entitled to be recognised in that part of the United Kingdom.

(2) Subject to section 52 of this Act, recognition of the validity of—

(a) a divorce or judicial separation granted by a court of civil jurisdiction in any part of the British Islands, or

(b) an overseas divorce or legal separation,

may be refused in any of the United Kingdom if the divorce or separation was granted or obtained at a time when, according to the law of that part of the United Kingdom (including its rules of private international law and the provisions of this Part), there was no subsisting marriage between the parties.

(3) Subject to section 52 of this Act, recognition by virtue of section 45 of this Act of the validity of an overseas divorce, annulment or legal separation may be refused if—

(a) in the case of a divorce, annulment or legal separation obtained by means of proceedings, it was obtained—

(i) without such steps having been taken for giving notice of the proceedings to a party to the marriage as, having regard to the nature of the proceedings and all the circumstances, should reasonably have been taken; or

(ii) without a party to the marriage having been given (for any reason other than lack of notice) such opportunity to take part in the proceedings as, having regard to those matters, he should reasonably have been given; or

(b) in the case of a divorce, annulment or legal separation obtained otherwise than by means of proceedings—

(i) there is no official document certifying that the divorce, annulment or legal separation is effective under the law of the country in which it was obtained; or

(ii) where either party to the marriage was domiciled in another country at the relevant date, there is no official document certifying that the divorce, annulment or legal separation is recognised as valid under the law of that other country; or

(c) in either case, recognition of the divorce, annulment or legal separation would be manifestly contrary to public policy.

(4) In this section—

'official', in relation to a document certifying that a divorce, annulment or legal separation is effective, or is recognised as valid, under the law of any country, means issued by a person or body appointed or recognised for the purpose under that law;

'the relevant date' has the same meaning as in section 46 of this Act;

['judicial separation' includes a separation order under the Family Law Act 1996;]

and subsection (5) of that section shall apply for the purposes of this section as it applies for the purposes of that section.

Note. Definition in square brackets inserted by Family Law Act 1996, s 66(1), Sch 8, Part I, para 37(11), as from a day to be appointed, subject to savings in s 66(2) of, and para 5 of Sch 9 to, the 1996 Act.

(5) Nothing in this Part shall be construed as requiring the recognition of any finding of fault made in any proceedings for divorce, annulment or separation or of any maintenance, custody or other ancillary order made in any such proceedings.

52. Provisions as to divorces, annulments etc obtained before commencement of Part II—(1) The provisions of this Part shall apply—

(a) to a divorce, annulment or judicial separation granted by a court of civil jurisdiction in the British Islands before the date of the commencement of this Part, and

(b) to an overseas divorce, annulment or legal separation obtained before that date,

as well as to one granted or obtained on or after that date.

(2) In the case of such a divorce, annulment or separation as is mentioned in subsection (1)(a) or (b) above, the provisions of this Part shall require or, as the case may be, preclude the recognition of its validity in relation to any time before that date as well as in relation to any subsequent time, but those provisions shall not—

(a) affect any property to which any person became entitled before that date, or

(b) affect the recognition of the validity of the divorce, annulment or separation if that matter has been decided by any competent court in the British Islands before that date.

(3) Subsections (1) and (2) above shall apply in relation to any divorce or judicial separation granted by a court of civil jurisdiction in the British Islands before the date of the commencement of this Part whether granted before or after the commencement of section 1 of the Recognition of Divorces and Legal Separations Act 1971.

(4) The validity of any divorce, annulment or legal separation mentioned in subsection (5) below shall be recognised in the United Kingdom whether or not it is entitled to recognition by virtue of any of the foregoing provisions of this Part.

(5) The divorces, annulments and legal separations referred to in subsection (4) above are—

(a) a divorce which was obtained in the British Islands before 1 January 1974 and was recognised as valid under rules of law applicable before that date;

(b) an overseas divorce which was recognised as valid under the Recognition of Divorces and Legal Separations Act 1971 and was not affected by section 16(2) of the Domicile and Matrimonial Proceedings Act 1973 (proceedings otherwise than in a court of law where both parties resident in the United Kingdom);

(c) a divorce of which the decree was registered under section 1 of the Indian and Colonial Divorce Jurisdiction Act 1926;

(d) a divorce or annulment which was recognised as valid under section 4 of the Matrimonial Causes (War Marriages) Act 1944; and

(e) an overseas legal separation which was recognised as valid under the Recognition of Divorces and Legal Separations Act 1971.

53. Effect of divorces and annulments on wills. In subsection (1) of section 18A of the Wills Act 1837 (effect of a decree of divorce or nullity of marriage on wills)—

(a) after the word 'court' there shall be inserted the words 'of civil jurisdiction in England and Wales'; and

(b) for the words 'or declares it void' there shall be substituted the words 'or his marriage is dissolved or annulled and the divorce or annulment is entitled to recognition in England and Wales by virtue of Part II of the Family Law Act 1986'.

54. Interpretation of Part II—(1) In this Part—

'annulment' includes any decree or declarator of nullity of marriage, however expressed;

['the Council Regulation' means Council Regulation (EC) No 1347/2000 of 29th May 2000 on jurisdiction and the recognition and enforcement of judgments in matrimonial matters and in matters of parental responsibility for children of both spouses;]

'part of the United Kingdom' means England and Wales, Scotland or Northern Ireland;

'proceedings' means judicial or other proceedings.

(2) In this Part 'country' includes a colony or other dependent territory of the United Kingdom but for the purposes of this Part a person shall be treated as a national of such a territory only if it has a law of citizenship or nationality separate from that of the United Kingdom and he is a citizen or national of that territory under that law.

Note. Definition 'the Council Regulation' inserted by SI 2001/310, reg 10 as from 1 March 2001.

PART III

DECLARATIONS OF STATUS

55. Declarations as to marital status—(1) Subject to the following provisions of this section, any person may apply to the court for one or more of the following declarations in relation to a marriage specified in the application, that is to say—

(a) a declaration that the marriage was at its inception a valid marriage;

(b) a declaration that the marriage subsisted on a date specified in the application;

(c) a declaration that the marriage did not subsist on a date so specified;

(d) a declaration that the validity of a divorce, annulment or legal separation obtained in any country outside England and Wales in respect of the marriage is entitled to recognition in England and Wales;

(e) a declaration that the validity of a divorce, annulment or legal separation so obtained in respect of the marriage is not entitled to recognition in England and Wales.

(2) A court shall have jurisdiction to entertain an application under subsection (1) above if, and only if, either of the parties to the marriage to which the application relates—
   (a) is domiciled in England and Wales on the date of the application, or
   (b) has been habitually resident in England and Wales throughout the period of one year ending with that date, or
   (c) died before that date and either—
      (i) was at death domiciled in England and Wales, or
      (ii) had been habitually resident in England and Wales throughout the period of one year ending with the date of death.

(3) Where an application under section (1) above is made by any person other than a party to the marriage to which the application relates, the court shall refuse to hear the application if it considers that the applicant does not have a sufficient interest in the determination of that application.

[55A Declarations of parentage]
   [(1) Subject to the following provisions of this section, any person may apply to the High Court, a county court or a magistrates' court for a declaration as to whether or not a person named in the application is or was the parent of another person so named.

(2) A court shall have jurisdiction to entertain an application under subsection (1) above if, and only if, either of the persons named in it for the purposes of that subsection—
   (a) is domiciled in England and Wales on the date of the application, or
   (b) has been habitually resident in England and Wales throughout the period of one year ending with that date, or
   (c) died before that date and either—
      (i) was at death domiciled in England and Wales, or
      (ii) had been habitually resident in England and Wales throughout the period of
one year ending with the date of death.

(3) Except in a case falling within subsection (4) below, the court shall refuse to hear an application under subsection (1) above unless it considers that the applicant has a sufficient personal interest in the determination of the application (but this is subject to section 27 of the Child Support Act 1991).

(4) The excepted cases are where the declaration sought is as to whether or not—
   (a) the applicant is the parent of a named person;
   (b) a named person is the parent of the applicant; or
   (c) a named person is the other parent of a named child of the applicant.

(5) Where an application under subsection (1) above is made and one of the persons named in it for the purposes of that subsection is a child, the court may refuse to hear the application if it considers that the determination of the application would not be in the best interests of the child.

(6) Where a court refuses to hear an application under subsection (1) above it may order that the applicant may not apply again for the same declaration without leave of the court.

(7) Where a declaration is made by a court on an application under subsection (1) above, the prescribed officer of the court shall notify the Registrar General, in such a manner and within such period as may be prescribed, of the making of that declaration.]

Note. Inserted by the Child Support, Pensions and Social Security Act 2000, s 83(1), (2) as from 1 April 2001 (SI 2001/774).

56. Declarations as to legitimacy or legitimation—*(1) Any person may apply to the court for a declaration that he is the legitimate child of his parents.*

(*2*) *Any person may apply to the court for one* (*or for one or, in the alternative, the other*) *of the following declarations, that is to say—*
   (*a*)   *a declaration that he has become a legitimated person;*
   (*b*)   *a declaration that he has not become a legitimated person.*
   (*3*)   *A court shall have jurisdiction to entertain an application under subsection* (*1*) *or* (*2*) *above if, and only if, the applicant—*
   (*a*)   *is domiciled in England and Wales on the date of the application, or*
   (*b*)   *has been habitually resident in England and Wales throughout the period of one year ending with that date.*
   (*4*)   *In this section 'legitimated person' means a person legitimated or recognised as legitimated—*
   (*a*)   *under section 2 or 3 of the Legitimacy Act 1976; or*
   (*b*)   *under section 1 or 8 of the Legitimacy Act 1926; or*
   (*c*)   *by a legitimation* (*whether or not by virtue of the subsequent marriage of his parents*) *recognised by the law of England and Wales and effected under the law of any other country.*

[56.   Declarations of parentage, legitimacy or legitimation—(1) Any person may apply to *the court* [the High Court or a county court] for a declaration—
   (a)   or
   (b)   that he is the legitimate child of his parents.
   (2)   Any person may apply to *the court* [the High Court or a county court] for one (or for one, or, in the alternative, the other) of the following declarations, that is to say—
   (a)   a declaration that he has become a legitimated person;
   (b)   a declaration that he has not become a legitimated person.
   (3)   A court shall have jurisdiction to entertain an application under this section if, and only if, the applicant—
   (a)   is domiciled in England and Wales on the date of the application; or
   (b)   has been habitually resident in England and Wales throughout the period of one year ending with that date.
   (4)   Where a declaration is made [by a court] on an application under subsection (1) above, the prescribed officer of the court shall notify the Registrar General, in such a manner and within such period as may be prescribed, of the making of that declaration.
   (5)   In this section 'legitimated person' means a person legitimated or recognised as legitimated—
   (a)   under section 2 or 3 of the Legitimacy Act 1976;
   (b)   under section 1 or 8 of the Legitimacy Act 1926; or
   (c)   by a legitimation (whether or not by virtue of the subsequent marriage of his parents) recognised by the law of England and Wales and effected under the law of another country.]

Note. Section 56 in square brackets substituted for s 56 in italics by Family Law Reform Act 1987, s 22, as from 4 April 1988. Sub-s (1)(a) repealed by the Child Support, Pensions and Social Security Act 2000, s 85, Sch 9, Pt IX as from 1 April 2001.
   In sub-ss (1), (2) words in square brackets substituted for words in italics and in sub-s (4) words in square brackets inserted by the Child Support, Pensions and Social Security Act 2000, s 83(5), Sch 8, paras 3, 5, as from 1 April 2001.

57.   Declarations as to adoptions effected overseas—(1) Any person whose status as an adopted child of any person depends on whether he has been adopted by that person by either—
   (a)   *an overseas adoption as defined by section 72(2) of the Adoption Act 1976, or*
   [(a)   a Convention adoption as defined by subsection (1) of section 72 of the Adoption Act 1976 or an overseas adoption as defined by subsection (2) of that section, or]

(b) an adoption recognised by the law of England and Wales and effected under the law of any country outside the British Islands,

may apply to *the court* [the High Court or a county court] for one (or for one or, in the alternative, the other) of the declarations mentioned in subsection (2) below.

(2) The said declarations are—

(a) a declaration that the applicant is for the purposes of section 39 of the Adoption Act 1976 [or section 67 of the Adoption and Children Act 2002] the adopted child of that person;

[(a) a Convention adoption, or an overseas adoption within the meaning of the Adoption and Children Act 2002, or]

(b) a declaration that the applicant is not for the purposes of that section the adopted child of that person.

(3) A court shall have jurisdiction to entertain an application under subsection (1) above if, and only if, the applicant—

(a) is domiciled in England and Wales on the date of the application, or

(b) has been habitually resident in England and Wales throughout the period of one year ending with that date.

(*4*) *Until the Adoption Act 1976 comes into force—*

(*a*) *subsection (1) above shall have effect as if for the reference to section 72(2) of that Act there were substituted a reference to section 4(3) of the Adoption Act 1968; and*

(*b*) *subsection (2) above shall have effect as if for the reference to section 39 of that Act there were substituted a reference to Part II of Schedule I to the Children Act 1975.*

Note. Sub-s (1) para (a) substituted by the Adoption (Intercountry Aspects) Act 1999, Sch 2, as from 1 June 2003 and further substituted by the Adoption and Children Act 2002, Sch 3, para 49, as from a day to be appointed. In sub-s (1) words in square brackets substituted for words in italics by the Child Support, Pensions and Social Security Act 2000, s 83(5), Sch 8, paras 3, 6, as from 1 April 2001. In sub-s (2)(a) words in square brackets inserted by the Adoption and Children Act 2002, Sch 3, para 49, as from a day to be appointed. Sub-s (4) spent.

58. General provisions as to the making and effect of declarations—(1) Where on an application [to a court] for a declaration under this Part the truth of the proposition to be declared is proved to the satisfaction of the court, the court shall make that declaration unless to do so would manifestly be contrary to public policy.

(2) Any declaration made under this Part shall be binding on Her Majesty and all other persons.

(3) *The* [A] court, on the dismissal of an application for a declaration under this Part, shall not have power to make any declaration for which an application has not been made.

(4) No declaration which may be applied for under this Part may be made otherwise than under this Part by any court.

(5) No declaration may be made by any court, whether under this Part or otherwise—

(a) that a marriage was at its inception void;

(b)

(6) Nothing in this section shall affect the powers of any court to grant a decree of nullity of marriage.

Note. In sub-s (1) words in square brackets inserted and in sub-s (3) word in square brackets substituted for word in italics by the Child Support, Pensions and Social Security Act 2000, s 83(5), Sch 8, paras 3, 7, as from 1 April 2001. Sub-s (5)(b) repealed by the Child Support, Pensions and Social Security Act 2000, ss 83(1), (3), 85, Sch 9, Pt IX, as from 1 April 2001.

59. Provisions relating to the Attorney-General—(1) On an application [to a court] for a declaration under this Part the court may at any stage of the proceedings, of its own motion or on the application of any party to the proceedings, direct that all necessary papers in the matter be sent to the Attorney-General.

(2) The Attorney-General, whether or not he is sent papers in relation to an application [to a court] for a declaration under this Part, may—

(a) intervene in the proceedings on that application in such manner as he thinks necessary or expedient, and

(b) argue before the court any question in relation to the application which the court considers it necessary to have fully argued.

(3) Where any costs are incurred by the Attorney-General in connection with any application [to a court] for a declaration under this part, the court may make such order as it considers just as to the payment of those costs by parties to the proceedings.

Note. Words in square brackets inserted by the Child Support, Pensions and Social Security Act 2000, s 83(5), Sch 8, paras 3, 8, as from 1 April 2001.

60. Supplementary provisions as to declarations—(1) Any declaration made under this Part, and any application for such a declaration, shall be in the form prescribed by rules of court.

(2) Rules of court may make provision—

(a) as to the information required to be given by any applicant for a declaration under this Part;

(b) as to the persons who are to be parties to proceedings on an application under this Part;

(c) requiring notice of an application under this Part to be served on the Attorney-General [and on persons who may be affected by any declarations applied for].

(3) No proceedings under this Part shall affect any final judgment or decree already pronounced or made by any court of competent jurisdiction.

(4) The court hearing an application under this Part may direct that the whole or any part of the proceedings shall be heard in camera, and an application for a direction under this subsection shall be heard in camera unless the court otherwise directs.

[(5) An appeal shall lie to the High Court against—

(a) the making by a magistrates' court of a declaration under section 55A above,

(b) any refusal by a magistrates' court to make such a declaration, or

(c) any order under subsection (6) of that section made on such a refusal.]

Note. Words in square brackets added by Family Law Reform Act 1987, s 33(1), Sch 2, para 96, as from 4 April 1988. Sub-s (5) inserted by the Child Support, Pensions and Social Security Act 2000, s 83(1), (4) as from 1 April 2001.

61. Abolition of right to petition for jactitation of marriage.   No person shall after the commencement of this Part be entitled to petition the High Court or a county court for jactitation of marriage.

62. Repeal of Greek Marriages Act 1884—(1) The Greek Marriages Act 1884 shall cease to have effect.

(2) Any marriage in respect of which a declaration that it was a valid marriage could before the commencement of this Part have been made under the Greek Marriages Act 1884 is hereby declared to have been a valid marriage; but nothing in this subsection shall affect any status or right which would not have been affected by a declaration under that Act.

Note. Repealed by the Child Support, Pensions and Social Security Act 2000, s 85, Sch 9, Pt IX, as from 1 April 2001.

PART IV

MISCELLANEOUS AND GENERAL

64. Family proceedings rules—(*1*) *Rules of court made by the rule-making authority constituted by section 40 of the Matrimonial and Family Proceedings Act 1984 (family proceedings rules) which relate to the costs of proceedings—*

(*a*) *may amend or repeal any statutory provision relating to the practice and procedure of the Supreme Court or county courts so far as may be necessary in consequence of provision made by the rules; and*

(*b*) *may make different provision for different cases or descriptions of cases, for different circumstances or for different areas.*

(*2*) *Notwithstanding anything in the Legal Aid Act 1974, the power conferred by subsection (1)(b) above includes power to make different provision according to whether each or any of the parties is entitled to legal aid in connection with the proceedings.*

(*3*) *In this section—*

'legal aid' means legal aid under Part I of the Legal Aid Act 1974;

'statutory provision' means any enactment, whenever passed, or any provision contained in subordinate legislation (as defined in section 21(1) of the Interpretation Act 1978), whenever made.

(*4*) *In relation to any time before the coming into force of section 40 of the Matrimonial and Family Proceedings Act 1984, this section shall have effect as if the reference in subsection (1) above to that section were a reference to section 50 of the Matrimonial Causes Act 1973 (matrimonial causes rules).*

Note. This section repealed by Legal Aid Act 1988, s 45(1)–(3), Sch 5, para 21, Sch 6, as from 1 April 1989.

65. Amendments of Child Abduction Act 1984—In section 1(2)(b), (3)(a) and (5) of the Child Abduction Act 1984 (offence of abduction of child by parent etc), for the words 'a court in England and Wales' there shall be substituted the words 'a court in the United Kingdom'.

66. (*Amends Child Abduction (Northern Ireland) Order 1985, SI 1985 No 1638 (NI 17); repealed by Children (Northern Ireland) Order 1995, SI 1995 No 755, art 185(2), Sch 10, as from 4 November 1996.*)

67. (*Amends Child Abduction and Custody Act 1985, ss 20, 27(1), pp 3017, 3020, and inserts s 24A in that Act, p 3019.*).

68. Minor and consequential amendments, repeals and savings—(1) The enactments and orders mentioned in Schedule 1 to this Act shall have effect subject to the amendments specified in that Schedule, being minor amendments and amendments consequential on the provisions of this Act.

(2) The enactments mentioned in Schedule 2 to this Act (which include some that are spent or no longer of practical utility) are hereby repealed to the extent specified in the third column of that Schedule.

(3) Nothing in this Act shall affect—

(a) any proceedings under section 45 of the Matrimonial Causes Act 1973 begun before the date of the commencement of Part III of this Act;

(b) any proceedings for jactitation of marriage begun before that date; or

(c) any proceedings for a declaration begun in the High Court before that date by virtue of rules of court relating to declaratory judgments.

(4) The repeal of section 2 of the Legitimacy Declaration Act (Ireland) 1868 shall not affect any proceedings under that section begun before the commencement of that repeal.

69. Short title, commencement and extent—(1) This Act may be cited as the Family Law Act 1986.

(2) Sections 64 to 67 of this Act shall come into force at the end of the period of two months beginning with the day on which this Act is passed.

(3) Subject to subsection (2) above, this Act shall come into force on such day as the relevant Minister or Ministers may by order made by statutory instrument appoint; and different days may be so appointed for different provisions or for different purposes.

(4) In subsection (3) above 'the relevant Minister or Ministers' means—

(a) in the case of an order which appoints a day only for Part III of this Act and its associated amendments and repeals, the Lord Chancellor;

(b) in any other case, the Lord Chancellor and the Lord Advocate.

(5) The following provisions of this Act, namely—

Chapter II of Part I;

section 53;

Part III;

sections 64 and 65;

section 68(3); and

paragraphs 9 to 17, 19 and 23 to 27 of Schedule 1 and section 68(1) so far as relating to those paragraphs,

extend to England and Wales only.

(6) The following provisions of this Act, namely—

Chapter III of Part I;

sections 26; and

paragraphs 1, 3 to 8, 18, 21 and 22 of Schedule 1 and section 68(1) so far as relating to those paragraphs,

extend to Scotland only; and sections 34 and 38 of this Act do not extend to Scotland.

(7) The following provisions of this Act, namely—

Chapter IV of Part I;

section 66;

section 68(4); and

paragraphs 2 and 32 to 34 of Schedule 1 and section 68(1) so far as relating to those paragraphs,

extend to Northern Ireland only; and paragraph 20 of Schedule 1 to this Act and section 68(1) of this Act so far as relating to that paragraph do not extend to Northern Ireland.

Commencement. Sections 1–63, 68, 69, Sch 1, paras 1–9, 10(1), (2), (4), 11–34, Sch 2, were brought into force on 4 April 1988 (SI 1988 No 375). Sch 1, para 10(3), which was never brought into force, repealed by Children Act 1989, s 108(7), Sch 15.

Note. Words in italics repealed by Children (Northern Ireland) Order 1995, SI 1995 No 755, art 185(2), Sch 10, as from 4 November 1996.

SCHEDULES

(Sch 1 makes minor and consequential amendments: insofar as they are still in force and amend provisions printed in this work, their effect has been incorporated.)

SCHEDULE 2   Section 68(2)

REPEALS

Chapter	Short Title	Extent of Repeal
31 & 32 Vict c 20	The Legitimacy Declaration Act (Ireland) 1868	Section 2.
47 & 48 Vict c 20	The Greek Marriages Act 1884	The Whole Act.

Chapter	Short Title	Extent of Repeal
49 & 50 Vict c 27	The Guardianship of Infants Act 1886	In section 9, the words from 'court within' to 'reside'.
16 &17 Geo 5 c 40	Indian and Colonial Jurisdiction Act 1926	The Whole Act.
3 & 4 Geo 6 c 35	Indian and Colonial Divorce Jurisdiction Act 1940	The Whole Act.
7 & 8 Geo 6 c 43	Matrimonial Causes (War Marriages) Act 1944	The Whole Act.
10 & 11 Geo 6 c 30	Indian Independence Act 1947	Section 17.
11 & 12 Geo 6 c 3	Burma Independence Act 1947	Section 4(3).
11 & 12 Geo 6 c 7	Ceylon Independence Act 1947	Section 3. In Schedule 2, paragraph 9.
14 Geo 6 c 20	Colonial and Other Territories (Divorce Jurisdiction) Act 1950	The Whole Act.
14 Geo 6 c 37	The Maintenance Orders Act 1950	Section 7.
6 & 7 Eliz 2 c 40	The Matrimonial Proceedings (Children) Act 1958	Section 13.
8 & 9 Eliz 2 c 52	Cyprus Act 1960	In the Schedule, paragraph 14.
8 & 9 Eliz 2 c 55	Nigeria Independence Act 1960	In Schedule 2, paragraph 14.
9 & 10 Eliz 2 c 16	Sierra Leone Independence Act 1961	In Schedule 3, paragraph 15.
10 & 11 Eliz 2 c 1	Tanganyika Independence Act 1961	In Schedule 2, paragraph 15.
10 & 11 Eliz 2 c 23	South Africa Act 1962	In Schedule 3, paragraph 9.
10 & 11 Eliz 2 c 40	Jamaica Independence Act 1962	In Schedule 2, paragraph 14.
10 & 11 Eliz 2 c 54	Trinidad and Tobago Independence Act 1962	In Schedule 2, paragraph 14.
10 & 11 Eliz 2 c 57	Uganda Independence Act 1962	In Schedule 3, paragraph 13.
1963 c 54	Kenya Independence Act 1963	Section 7.
1964 c 46	Malawi Independence Act 1964	Section 6.
1964 c 65	Zambia Independence Act 1964	Section 7.
1966 c 9	The Law Reform (Miscellaneous Provisions) (Scotland) Act 1966	In section 8(2), the words 'made in a consistorial action'.
1966 c 29	Singapore Act 1966	Section 2.
1968 c 63	The Domestic and Appellate Proceedings (Restriction of Publicity) Act 1968	Section 2(1)(a).

Chapter	Short Title	Extent of Repeal
1969 c 29	Tanzania Act 1969	Section 2. In section 4(3), the words 'or the Divorce Jurisdiction Acts'. Section 7(1).
1971 c 3	The Guardianship of Minors Act 1971	Section 15(3) to (6). Section 17(2).
1971 c 53	Recognition of Divorces and Legal Separation Act 1971	The whole Act.
1973 c 18	The Matrimonial Causes Act 1973	Section 45. In section 50(2), in paragraph (b), the words 'proceedings in a county court under section 45 above or to' and, in paragraph (c), the words 'or to any aspect of section 47 above which is excepted by paragraph (b) above'.
1973 c 29	The Guardianship Act 1973	In section 1(6) the words from 'except that' to the end. In section 2(1), the words '15', 'and section 15(3) to (6)' and 'they are'. Sections 5(3). In Schedule 2, in Part I, paragraph 3, and in Part II, the text of section 15(3) to (6) of the Guardianship of Minors Act 1971.
1973 c 45	Domicile and Matrimonial Proceedings Act 1973	Section 2. Sections 15 and 16.
1973 c 48	The Pakistan Act 1973	In section 4(5), the words from the beginning to '1940, and'.
1975 c 72	The Children Act 1975	In section 33(1), the words from 'if' to the end. In section 53(1), the words from 'but where' to the end. Section 54. In section 100(8), the words 'or 42'.
1981 c 54	The Supreme Court Act 1981	In section 26(b), the words 'or jactitation of marriage'.
1984 c 42	The Matrimonial and Family Proceedings Act 1984	In Schedule 1, paragraph 14.
1985 c 73	The Law Reform (Miscellaneous Provisions) (Scotland) Act 1985	Section 16.

ACCESS TO PERSONAL FILES ACT 1987
(1987 c 37)

An Act to provide access for individuals to information relating to themselves maintained by certain authorities and to allow individuals to obtain copies of, and require amendment of, such information.   [15th May 1987]

Note. Repealed, subject to transitional provisions and savings, by the Data Protection Act 1998, ss 73, 74(2), Sch 14, para 19, Sch 16, Pt 1, as from 1 March 2000.

FAMILY LAW REFORM ACT 1987
(1987 c 42)

ARRANGEMENT OF SECTIONS

PART I

GENERAL PRINCIPLE

PART II

RIGHTS AND DUTIES OF PARENTS ETC

Parental rights and duties: general

PART III

PROPERTY RIGHTS

PART VI

MISCELLANEOUS AND SUPPLEMENTAL

Miscellaneous

Supplemental

An Act to reform the law relating to the consequences of birth outside marriage; to make further provision with respect to the rights and duties of parents and the determination of parentage; and for connected purposes.   [15 May 1987]

PART I

GENERAL PRINCIPLE

1. General principle—(1) In this Act and enactments passed and instruments made after the coming into force of this section, references (however expressed) to any relationship between two persons shall, unless the contrary intention appears, be construed without regard to whether or not the father and mother of either of them, or the father and mother of any person through whom the relationship is deduced, have or had been married to each other at any time.

(2) In this Act and enactments passed after the coming into force of this section, unless the contrary intention appears—

(a) references to a person whose father and mother were married to each other at the time of his birth include; and

(b) references to a person whose father and mother were not married to each other at the time of his birth do not include,

references to any person to whom subsection (3) below applies, and cognate references shall be construed accordingly.

(3) This subsection applies to any person who—

(a) is treated as legitimate by virtue of section 1 of the Legitimacy Act 1976;

(b) is a legitimated person within the meaning of section 10 of that Act;

(c) *is an adopted child within the meaning of Part IV of the Adoption Act 1976;*

[(c) is an adopted person within the meaning of Chapter 4 of Part 1 of the Adoption and Children Act 2002]; or

(d) is otherwise treated in law as legitimate.

(4) For the purpose of construing references falling within subsection (2) above, the time of a person's birth shall be taken to include any time during the period beginning with—

(a) the insemination resulting in his birth; or

(b) where there was no such insemination, his conception,

and (in either case) ending with his birth.

Note. Sub-s (3)(c) substituted by the Adoption and Children Act 2002, Sch 3, para 51 as from a day to be appointed.

PART II

RIGHTS AND DUTIES OF PARENTS ETC

Parental rights and duties: general

2. Construction of enactments relating to parental rights and duties—(1) In the following enactments, namely—

(a) section 42(1) of the National Assistance Act 1948;

(b) section 6 of the Family Law Reform Act 1969;

(c) the Guardianship of Minors Act 1971 (in this Act referred to as 'the 1971 Act');

(d) Part I of the Guardianship Act 1973 (in this Act referred to as 'the 1973 Act');

(e) Part II of the Children Act 1975;

(f) the Child Care Act 1980 except Part I and sections 13, 24, 64 and 65;

(g) *section 26(3) of the Social Security Act 1986,*

references (however expressed) to any relationship between two persons shall be construed in accordance with section 1 above.

Note. Sub-s (1)(g) repealed by Social Security (Consequential Provisions) Act 1992, s 3, Sch 1, as from 1 July 1992.

(2) In subsection (7) of section 1 of the 1973 Act (equality of parental rights) for the words from 'or be taken' to the end there shall be substituted the words 'and nothing in subsection (1) above shall be taken as applying in relation to a child whose father and mother were not married to each other at the time of his birth'.

3–17. (*Sections 3–7, 9–16 (ss 3, 5 of which amended Guardianship Act 1973, s 1, ss 6, 10–14 of which amended Guardianship of Minors Act 1971, s 7 of which amended Adoption Act 1976, ss 18, 72, s 9 of which amended Marriage Act 1949, Sch 2) were all repealed by Children Act 1989, s 108(7), Sch 15, as from 14 October 1991; transitional provisions and savings applying to custody orders, etc, made under the 1971 Act, as amended by ss 10–14, and in force immediately before 14 October 1991, see Sch 14, paras*

5–11 of the 1989 Act, p 3490; s 8 amended Children and Young Persons Act 1969, s 70, p 2335; and s 17 repealed Affiliation Proceedings Act 1957.).

PART III

PROPERTY RIGHTS

18. Succession on intestacy—(1) In Part IV of the Administration of Estates Act 1925 (which deals with the distribution of the estate of an intestate), references (however expressed) to any relationship between two persons shall be construed in accordance with section 1 above.

(2) For the purposes of subsection (1) above and that Part of that Act, a person whose father and mother were not married to each other at the time of his birth shall be presumed not to have been survived by his father, or by any person related to him only through his father, unless the contrary is shown.

(3) In section 50(1) of that Act (which relates to the construction of documents), the reference to Part IV of that Act, or to the foregoing provisions of that Part, shall in relation to an instrument inter vivos made, or a will or codicil coming into operation, after the coming into force of this section (but not in relation to instruments inter vivos made or wills or codicils coming into operation earlier) be construed as including references to this section.

(4) This section does not affect any rights under the intestacy of a person dying before the coming into force of this section.

19. Dispositions of property—(1) In the following dispositions, namely—
  (a) dispositions inter vivos made on or after the date on which this section comes into force; and
  (b) dispositions by will or codicil where the will or codicil is made out on or after that date,
references (whether express or implied) to any relationship between two persons shall be construed in accordance with section 1 above.

(2) It is hereby declared that the use, without more, of the word 'heir' or 'heirs' or any expression *which is used to create* [purporting to create] an entailed interest in real or personal property does not show a contrary intention for the purposes of section 1 as applied by subsection (1) above.

Note. Words in square brackets substituted for words in italics by Trusts of Land and Appointment of Trustees Act 1996, s 25(1), Sch 3, para 25, as from 1 January 1997.

(3) In relation to the dispositions mentioned in subsection (1) above, section 33 of the Trustee Act 1925 (which specifies the trust implied by a direction that income is to be held on protective trusts for the benefit of any person) shall have effect as if any reference (however expressed) to any relationship between two persons were construed in accordance with section 1 above.

(4) Where under any disposition of real or personal property, any interest in such property is limited (whether subject to any preceding limitation or charge or not) in such a way that it would, apart from this section, devolve (as nearly as the law permits) along with a dignity or title of honour, then—
  (a) whether or not the disposition contains an express reference to the dignity or title of honour; and
  (b) whether or not the property or some interest in the property may in some event become severed from it,
nothing in this section shall operate to sever the property or any interest in it from the dignity or title, but the property or interest shall devolve in all respects as if this section had not been enacted.

(5) This section is without prejudice to section 42 of the Adoption Act 1976 [or section 69 of the Adoption and Children Act 2002] (construction of dispositions in cases of adoption).

(6) In this section 'disposition' means a disposition, including an oral disposition, of real or personal property whether inter vivos or by will or codicil.

(7) Notwithstanding any rule of law, a disposition made by will or codicil executed before the date on which this section comes into force shall not be treated for the purposes of this section as made on or after that date by reason only that the will or codicil is confirmed by a codicil executed on or after that date.

Note. In sub-s (5) words in square brackets inserted by the Adoption and Children Act 2002, Sch 3, para 52, as from a day to be appointed.

20. No special protection for trustees and personal representatives. Section 17 of the Family Law Reform Act 1969 (which enables trustees and personal representatives to distribute property without having ascertained that no person whose parents were not married to each other at the time of his birth, or who claims through such a person, is or may be entitled to an interest in the property) shall cease to have effect.

21. Entitlement to grant of probate etc—(1) For the purpose of determining the person or persons who would in accordance with probate rules be entitled to a grant of probate or administration in respect of the estate of a deceased person, the deceased shall be presumed, unless the contrary is shown, not to have been survived—

(a) by any person related to him whose father and mother were not married to each other at the time of his birth; or

(b) by any person whose relationship with him is deduced through such a person as is mentioned in paragraph (a) above.

(2) In this section 'probate rules' means rules of court made under section 127 of the Supreme Court Act 1981.

(3) This section does not apply in relation to the estate of a person dying before the coming into force of this section.

PART IV

DETERMINATION OF RELATIONSHIPS

22, 23. (*Section 22 substitutes Family Law Act 1986, s 56, p 3120; s 23(1) substitutes Family Law Reform Act 1969, s 20(1), (2), (2A) (p 2311, 2312) and s 23(2) amends s 25 (p 2315) of that Act, as from a day to be appointed .*)

PART V

REGISTRATION OF BIRTHS

24-26. (*Section 24 substitutes Births and Deaths Registration Act 1953, s 10, p 2166; s 25 substitutes s 10A of that Act, p 2168; and s 26 inserts s 14A in that Act (not printed in this work).*)

PART VI

MISCELLANEOUS AND SUPPLEMENTAL

Miscellaneous

27. Artificial insemination—(1) Where after the coming into force of this section a child is born in England and Wales as the result of the artificial insemination of a woman who—

(a) was at the time of the insemination a party to a marriage (being a marriage which had not at that time been dissolved or annulled); and

(b) was artificially inseminated with the semen of some person other than the other party to that marriage, then, unless it is proved to the satisfaction of any court by which the matter has to be determined that the other party to that marriage did not consent to the insemination, the child shall be treated in law as the child of the parties to that marriage and shall not be treated as the child of any person other than the parties to that marriage.

(2) Any reference in this section to a marriage includes a reference to a void marriage if at the time of the insemination resulting in the birth of the child both or either of the parties reasonably believed that the marriage was valid; and for the purposes of this section it shall be presumed, unless the contrary is shown, that one of the parties so believed at that time that the marriage was valid.

(3) Nothing in this section shall affect the succession to any dignity or title of honour or render any person capable of succeeding to or transmitting a right to succeed to any such dignity or title.

28, 29. (*Section 28 amends Legitimacy Act 1976, s 1, p 2614; s 29 amends Civil Evidence Act 1968, s 12, p 2292.*)

Supplemental

30. Orders applying section 1 to other enactments—(1) The Lord Chancellor may by order make provision for the construction in accordance with section 1 above of such enactments passed before the coming into force of that section as may be specified in the order.

(2) An order under this section shall so amend the enactments to which it relates as to secure that (so far as practicable) they continue to have the same effect notwithstanding the making of the order.

(3) An order under this section shall be made by statutory instrument which shall be subject to annulment in pursuance of a resolution of either House of Parliament.

31. Interpretation.   In this Act—
'the 1953 Act' means the Births and Deaths Registration Act 1953;
'the 1971 Act' means the Guardianship of Minors Act 1971;
'the 1973 Act' means the Guardianship Act 1973.

32. Text of 1971 Act as amended.   The 1971 Act (excluding consequential amendments of other enactments and savings) is set out in Schedule 1 to this Act as it will have effect, subject to sections 33(2) and 34(3) below, when all the amendments and repeals made in it by this Act come into force.

33. Amendments, transitional provisions, savings and repeals—(1) The enactments mentioned in Schedule 2 to this Act shall have effect subject to the amendments there specified, being minor amendments and amendments consequential on the provisions of this Act.

(2) The transitional provisions and savings in Schedule 3 to this Act shall have effect.

(3) The inclusion in this Act of any express saving or amendment shall not be taken as prejudicing the operation of sections 16 and 17 of the Interpretation Act 1978 (which relate to the effect of repeals).

(4) The enactments mentioned in Schedule 4 to this Act are hereby repealed to the extent specified in the third column of that Schedule.

34. Short title, commencement and extent—(1) This Act may be cited as the Family Law Reform Act 1987.

(2) This Act shall come into force on such day as the Lord Chancellor may by order made by statutory instrument appoint; and different days may be so appointed for different provisions or different purposes.

(3) Without prejudice to the transitional provisions contained in Schedule 3 to this Act, an order under subsection (2) above may make such further transitional provisions as appear to the Lord Chancellor to be necessary or expedient in connection with the provision brought into force by the order, including—

(a) such adaptations of the provisions so brought into force; and

(b) such adaptations of any provisions of this Act then in force,

as appear to him necessary or expedient in consequence of the partial operation of this Act.

(4) The following provisions of this Act extend to Scotland and Northern Ireland, namely—

(a) section 33(1) and paragraphs 12, 13 and 74 of Schedule 2;

(b) section 33(2) and paragraph 7 of Schedule 3 so far as relating to the operation of the Maintenance Orders Act 1950;

(c) section 33(4) and Schedule 4 so far as relating to that Act and the Interpretation Act 1978; and

(d) this section.

(5) Subject to subsection (4) above, this Act extends to England and Wales only.

Commencement. Sections 1, 18–22, 26–29, 31, 34, Sch 2, paras 2–4, 9–11, 16(c), 19, 59, 73, 74, 96, Sch 3, paras 1, 8–10, Sch 4 (in part) came into force on 4 April 1988 (SI 1988 No 425); ss 2–8, 10–17, 24, 25, 30, Sch 2, paras 1, 5–8, 12–15, 16(a), (b), 17, 18, 20, 26–58, 60–73, 75–95, Sch 3, paras 2–7, 11, 12, Sch 4 (remainder) came into force on 1 April 1989 (SI 1989 No 382). Section 23, Sch 2, paras 21–25 have not been brought into force. Section 9 was repealed by the Children Act 1989, s 108(6), (7), Sch 14, paras 1, 27. Section 32 is not in force consequent on errors in Sch 1; Sch 1 is spent.

SCHEDULES

SCHEDULE 1
Section 32

TEXT OF 1971 ACT AS AMENDED

(*Sch 1 sets out the text of the Guardianship of Minors Act 1971; that Act was repealed by Children Act 1989, s 108(7), Sch 15.*)

SCHEDULE 2
Section 33 (1)

MINOR AND CONSEQUENTIAL AMENDMENTS

(*The minor and consequential amendments made by Sch 2 insofar as they are still in force and affect provisions printed in this work have been incorporated.*)

SCHEDULE 3
Section 33 (2)

TRANSITIONAL PROVISIONS AND SAVINGS

Applications pending under amended or repealed enactments

1. This Act (including the repeals and amendments made by it) shall not have effect in relation to any application made under any enactment repealed or amended by this Act if that application is pending at the time when the provision of this Act which repeals or amends that enactment comes into force.

References to provisions of Adoption Act 1976

2. In relation to any time before the coming into force of section 38 of the Adoption Act 1976, the reference in section 1(2) of this Act to Part IV of that Act shall be construed as a reference to Schedule 1 to the Children Act 1975.

3. In relation to any time before the coming into force of section 18 of the Adoption Act 1976, any reference—

    (a) in section 7(1) of or paragraph 61 of Schedule 2 to this Act; or
    (b) in section 9(2) or 10(3) of the 1971 Act as substituted by this Act.
to or to subsection (7) of the said section 18 shall be construed as a reference to or
to subsection (8) of section 14 of the Children Act 1975.
4. In relation to any time before the coming into force of section 72(1) of the
Adoption Act 1976, any reference in section 7(2) of or paragraph 62 of Schedule 2
to this Act to the said section 72(1) shall be construed as a reference to section
107(1) of the Children Act 1975.
5. In relation to any time before the coming into force of section 42 of the Adoption
Act 1976, the reference in section 19 of this Act to the said section 42 shall
be construed as a reference to paragraph 6 of Schedule 1 to the Children Act
1975.

Affiliation orders

6. (1) Neither section 17 of this Act nor any associated amendment or repeal
shall affect, or affect the operation of any enactment in relation to—
    (a) any affiliation order made under the Affiliation Proceedings Act 1957 which
        is in force immediately before the coming into force of that section; or
    (b) any affiliation order made under that Act by virtue of paragraph 1 above.
    (2) Any reference in this paragraph or paragraph 7 below to an affiliation order
made under the Affiliation Proceedings Act 1957 includes a reference to—
    (a) an affiliation order made, by virtue of section 44 of the National Assistance
        Act 1948, section 19 of the Supplementary Benefits Act 1976, section 49 or
        50 of the Child Care Act 1980 or section 25 of the Social Security Act 1986;
        and
    (b) any order made in relation to such an order.
7. Where—
    (a) an application is made to the High Court or a county court for an order
        under section 11B of the 1971 Act in respect of a child whose parents were
        not married to each other at the time of his birth, and
    (b) an affiliation order made under the Affiliation Proceedings Act 1957 and
        providing for periodical payments is in force in respect of the child by virtue
        of this Schedule,
the court may, if it thinks fit, direct that the affiliation order shall cease to have
effect on such date as may be specified in the direction.

Property rights

8. The repeal by this Act of section 14 of the Family Law Reform Act 1969 shall
not affect any rights arising under the intestacy of a person dying before the
coming into force of the repeal.
9. The repeal by this Act of section 15 of the Family Law Reform Act 1969 shall
not affect, or affect the operation of section 33 of the Trustee Act 1925 in relation
to—
    (a) any disposition inter vivos made before the date on which the repeal comes
        into force; or
    (b) any disposition by will or codicil executed before that date.

                *   *   *   *   *

Registration of births

11. *Where—*
    (a) a child whose parents were not married to each other at the time of his birth has been born
        in England and Wales before the date on which section 24 of this Act comes into force;
    (b) the birth has not been registered under the 1953 Act before that date; and
    (c) an order has been made under section 4 of the Affiliation Proceedings Act 1957
        naming any person as the putative father of the child,

the mother of the child, on production of a certified copy of the order, may request the registrar to enter the name of that person as the father of the child under section 10 of the 1953 Act as if the order made under the said section 4 were an order under section 11B of the 1971 Act.

12. Where—

(a) the birth of a child whose parents were not married to each other at the time of his birth has been registered under the 1953 Act before the date on which section 25 of this Act comes into force;

(b) no person has been registered as the father of the child; and

(c) an order has been made under section 4 of the Affiliation Proceedings Act 1957 naming any person as the father of the child,

the mother of the child, on production of a certified copy of the order, may request the registrar to re-register the birth so as to show as the father of the child the person named in the order.

Note. Paras 11, 12 repealed by Children Act 1989, s 108(7), Sch 15, as from 14 October 1991.

SCHEDULE 4   Section 33 (4)

REPEALS

Chapter	Short Title	Extent of Repeal
11 & 12 Geo 6 c 29	The National Assistance Act	Section 42(2) Section 44.
14 Geo 6 c 37	The Maintenance Orders Act 1950	Section 3. In section 16(2)(a)— (a) sub-paragraph (iv); (b) the sub-paragraph (vi) inserted by the Children Act 1975; (c) in the sub-paragraph (vi) inserted by the Supplementary Benefits Act 1976 the words from 'or section 4 of the Affiliation Proceedings Act 1957' to the end; (d) in sub-paragraph (viii) the words from 'or section 4 of the Affiliation Proceedings Act 1957' to the end.
3 & 4 Eliz 2 c 18	The Army Act 1955	In section 150(5), the words from 'references to a sum ordered to be paid' to the end.
3 & 4 Eliz 2 c 19	The Air Force Act 1955	In section 150(5), the words from 'references to a sum ordered to be paid' to the end.
5 & 6 Eliz 2 c 53	The Naval Discipline Act 1957	In section 101(5), the words 'and includes an affiliation order within the meaning of the Affiliation Orders Act 1914'.
5 & 6 Eliz 2 c 55	The Affiliation Proceedings Act 1957	The whole Act.

Chapter	Short Title	Extent of Repeal
6 & 7 Eliz c 39	The Maintenance Orders Act 1958	In section 21(1), the words 'affiliation order'.
7 & 8 Eliz c 73	The Legitimacy Act 1959	The whole Act.
1968 c 63	The Domestic and Appellate Proceedings (Restriction of Publicity) Act 1968	In section 2(1), the word 'and' following paragraph (c).
1969 c 46	The Family Law Reform Act 1969	Sections 14 and 15. Section 17. Section 27.
1970 c 31	The Administration of Justice Act 1970	In Schedule 8, paragraph 5.
1971 c 3	The Guardianship of Minors Act 1971	In section 12B, in sub-section (1), the words 'in maintaining the minor' and, in subsection (3), the words 'of a minor'. Section 14 and the heading preceding that section.
1971 c 32	The Attachment of Earnings Act 1971	In Schedule 1, paragraph 6.
1972 c 18	The Maintenance Orders (Reciprocal Enforcement) Act 1972	Section 3(3). In section 27(9), the words 'section 5(5) of the Affiliation Proceedings Act 1957'. In section 30— (a) in subsection (3), the words 'the Affiliation Proceedings Act 1957 or', the words 'paragraph (b) of section 2(1) of the said Act of 1957 (time for making complaint) or', the words '(provision to the like effect), as the case may be', the words 'three years (or' and the words' in the case of a complaint under the said Act of 1924)'; (b) in subsection (5), the words 'the said Act of 1957' and the words 'as the case may be'; (c) in subsection (6), the words 'or an affiliation order under the said Act of 1957'.

Chapter	Short Title	Extent of Repeal
		In section 41— (a) subsection (1); (b) in subsection (2A), paragraph (a); (c) in subsection (2B), paragraph (a).
1972 c 49	The Affiliation Proceedings (Amendment) Act 1972	The whole Act.
1973 c 29	The Guardianship Act 1973	Section 2(6). Section 4(3D).
1974 c 4	The Legal Aid Act 1974	In Schedule 1, in Part I, paragraph 2.
1975 c72	The Children Act 1975	In section 34, subsections (3) and (4). Section 36(5A). Section 45. In section 85(2), the words '(which relate to separation agreements between husband and wife)'. In section 93, subsections (1) and (2). In Schedule 3, paragraphs 14 and 75(1).
1976 c 36	The Adoption Act 1976	In Schedule 3, paragraph 16.
1978 c 22	The Domestic Proceedings and Magistrates' Courts Act 1978	In section 20, subsections (10) and (13). In section 36(1), paragraph (c).
1978 c 30	The Interpretation Act 1978	Section 38(2). Section 41.
1980 c 5	The Child Care Act 1980	In section 45, subsections (2) and (3). In Schedule 2, paragraphs 30 and 44. In Schedule 2, in paragraph 4, the words 'earlier than the commencement of this Act'. Sections 49 and 50. In section 52(1), paragraph (b). In section 54, in subsections (1) and (2), the words '49, 50'. In section 55, subsection (3) and, in subsection (5), the words from 'and any jurisdiction conferred by this section in affiliation proceedings' to the end.

Chapter	Short Title	Extent of Repeal
		In section 87(1), in the definition of 'relative', the words from 'and includes' to the end.
		In Schedule 2, paragraphs 4 and 5 and, in paragraph 7, the words '49, 50'.
		In Schedule 5, paragraphs 6 to 8.
1980 c 43	The Magistrates Courts Act 1980	In section 59(2). the words 'an affiliation order'.
		In section 65(1)—
		(a) in paragraph (b) the words 'or section 44';
		(b) paragraph (d);
		(c) in paragraph (i), the words 'or section 19';
		(d) in paragraph (k), the words '49 or 50'.
		Section 92(3).
		In section 150(1), the definition of 'affiliation order'.
1981 c 54	The Supreme Court Act 1981	In Schedule 1, in paragraph 3(b)(iii), the words 'affiliation or'.
1982 c 24	The Social Security and Housing Benefits Act 1982	In Schedule 4, paragraph 1.
1986 c 50	The Social Security Act 1986	In section 24, subsections (2) and (3).
		Section 25.

INCOME AND CORPORATION TAXES ACT 1988

(1988 c 1)

ARRANGEMENT OF SECTIONS

*   *   *   *   *

PART V

PROVISIONS RELATING TO THE SCHEDULE E CHARGE

*   *   *   *   *

CHAPTER II

SUPPLEMENTARY CHARGING PROVISIONS APPLICABLE TO EMPLOYEES EARNING £8,500 OR MORE AND DIRECTORS

*   *   *   *   *

Benefits in kind

*   *   *   *   *

*   *   *   *   *

PART XV

SETTLEMENTS

*   *   *   *   *

CHAPTER IA

LIABILITY OF SETTLOR

Main Provisions

Supplementary provisions

CHAPTER II

SETTLEMENTS ON CHILDREN

*   *   *   *   *

[155A. Care for children—*(1) Where a benefit consists in the provision for the employee of care for a child, section 154 does not apply to the benefit to the extent that it is provided in qualifying circumstances.*

(2) For the purposes of subsection (1) above the benefit is provided in qualifying circumstances if—

(a)   the child falls within subsection (3) below,

(b)   the care is provided on premises which are not domestic premises,

(c)   the condition set out in subsection (4) below or the condition set out in subsection (5) below (or each of them) is fulfilled, and

(d)   in a case where the registration requirement applies, it is met.

(3) The child falls within this subsection if—

(a)   he is a child for whom the employee has parental responsibility,

(b)   he is resident with the employee, or

(c)   he is a child of the employee and maintained at his expense.

(4) The condition is that the care is provided on premises which are made available by the employer alone.

(5) The condition is that—

(a)   the care is provided under arrangements made by persons who include the employer,

(b)   the care is provided on premises which are made available by one or more of those persons, and

(c)   under the arrangements the employer is wholly or partly responsible for financing and managing the provision of the care.

(6)   The registration requirement applies where—

(a)   the premises on which the care is provided are required to be registered under section 1 of the Nurseries and Child-Minders Regulation Act 1948 or section 11 of the Children and Young Persons Act (Northern Ireland) 1968, or

(b)   any person providing the care is required to be registered under section 71 [or Part XA] of the Children Act 1989 with respect to the premises on which it is provided;

and the requirement is met if the premises are so registered or (as the case may be) the person is so registered.

(7)   In subsection (3)(c) above the reference to a child of the employee includes a reference to a stepchild of his.

(8)   In this section—

'care' means any form of care or supervised activity, whether or not provided on a regular basis, but excluding supervised activity provided primarily for educational purposes;

'child' means a person under the age of eighteen;

'domestic premises' means any premises wholly or mainly used as a private dwelling;

'parental responsibility' has the meaning given in section 3(1) of the Children Act 1989.]

Note. This section inserted by Finance Act 1990, s 21(1), for the year 1990–91 and subsequent years of assessment.

Words 'or Part XA' inserted by the Care Standards Act 2000, s 116, Sch 4, para 13, (in relation to England) as from 2 July 2001 (SI 2001 No 2041); in relation to Wales) as from 1 April 2002 (SI 2002 No 920)

Repealed by the Income Tax (Earnings and Pensions) Act 2003, ss 722, 724(1), Sch 6, Pt 1, paras 1, 24, Sch 8, Pt 1 for the purposes of income tax for the year 2003–2004 and subsequent years of assessment, and for the purposes of corporation tax for accounting periods ending after 5 April 2003: s 723(1).

*   *   *   *   *

PART VII

GENERAL PROVISIONS RELATING TO TAXATION OF INCOME OF INDIVIDUALS

CHAPTER I

PERSONAL RELIEFS

The reliefs

*   *   *   *   *

[257. Personal allowances—(1) The claimant shall be entitled to a deduction from his total income of £2,605 [*£3,445*] [*£3,765*] [*£3,845*] [*£4,045*] [*£4,195*], [*£4,335*], [*£4,615*], [£4,745].

Note. Sum '£3,445' substituted for sum '£2,605' by SI 1992 No 622, art 2(3), for the year 1992–1993, and the same sum applies for the year 1993–94 by virtue of Finance Act 1993, s 52, and for the year 1994–95 by virtue of Finance Act 1994, s 76. Sum '£3,765' substituted by virtue of Finance Act 1996, s 74, for the year 1996–97. Sum '£3,845' substituted for sum '£3,765' by virtue of SI 1996 No 2952, art 2(3)(a). Sum '£4,045' substituted for sum '£3,845' by virtue of Finance Act 1997, s 55, for the year 1997–98. Sum '£4,195' substituted for sum '£4,045' by virtue of the Income Tax (Indexation) Order 1998, SI 1998 No 755, art 2 (3), for the year 1998–99. Sum '£4,335' substituted for sum '£4,195' by virtue of the Income Tax (Indexation) (No 2) Order 1998, SI 1998 No 2704, art 2, for the year 1999–2000. Sum '£4,615' substituted for sum '£4,335' by virtue of the Income Tax (Indexation) (No 2) Order 2002, SI 2002 No 3773, art 2(1), for the year 2002–2003. Sum '£4,615' further specifies for the year 2003–04 by the virtue of the Finance Act 2002, s 28(1). Sum '£4,745' substituted for sum '£4,615' by virtue of the Income Tax (Indexation) (No 2) Order 2003, SI 2003 No 3215, art 2(1), for the year 2004–05.

(2)   If the claimant *proves that he* is at any time within the year of assessment of the age of 65 or upwards, he shall be entitled to a deduction from his total income

of £3,180 [£4,200] [£4,630] [£4,910] [£5,020] [£5,220] [£5,410], [£5,720], [£5.990], [£6,100], [£6,610], [£6,800], [£6,830] (instead of the deduction provided for by subsection (1) above).

Note. Words in italics repealed by Finance Act 1996, s 134, Sch 20, para 13(a), Sch 41, Part V(10), for the year 1996–97 and subsequent years of assessment. Sum '£4,200' substituted for sum '£3,180' by SI 1992 No 622, art 2(3), for the year 1992–1993, and the same sum applies for the year 1993–94 by virtue of Finance Act 1993, s 52, and for the year 1994–95 by virtue of Finance Act 1994, s 76. Sum '£4,630' substituted for sum '£4,200' by virtue of Finance Act 1995, s 36, for the year 1995–96. Sum '£4,910' substituted for sum '£4,360' by virtue of Finance Act 1996, s 74, for the year 1996–97. Sum '£5,020' substituted for sum '£4,910' by virtue of SI 1996 No 2952, art 2(3)(b). Sum '£5,220' substituted for sum '£5,020' by virtue of Finance Act 1997, s 55, for the year 1997–98. Sum '£5,410' substitutes for sum '£5,220' by virtue of the Income Tax (Indexation) Order 1988, SI 1988 No 755, art 2(3), for the year 1998–99. Sum '£5,720' substitutes for sum '£5,410' by virtue of the Finance Act 1999, s 24(1), for the year 1999–2000. Sum '£5,990' substitutes for sum '£5,720' by virtue of the Income Tax (Indexation) (No 2) Order 2000, SI 2000 No 2996, art 2(1), (2), for the year2001–02. Sum '£6,100' substitutes for sum '£5,990' by virtue of the Income Tax (Indexation) (No 2) Order 2001, SI 2001 No 3773, art 2(1), (2), for the year 2002–03. Sum '£6,610' substitutes for sum '£6,100' by virtue of the Finance Act 2002, s 29(1), for the year 2003–04. Sum '£6,800' substitutes for sum '£6,610' by virtue of the Income Tax (Indexation) (No 2) Order 2003, SI 2003 No 3215, art 2(1), (2), and sum '£6,830' subsequently substitutes for sum £6800 by virtue of the Finance Act 2004, s 24(1), for the year 2004–05.

(3) If the claimant *proves that he* is at any time within the year of assessment of the age of *80* [75] or upwards, he shall be entitled to a deduction from his total income of £3,310 [£4,379] [£4,800] [£5,090] [£5,200] [£5,400] [£5,600], [£5,980], [£6,260], [£6,370], [£6,910], [£6,910], [£6,950] (instead of the deduction provided for by subsection (1) or (2) above).

Note. Words in italics repealed by Finance Act 1996, ss 134, 205, Sch 20, para 13(b), Sch 41, Part V(10), for the year 1996–97 and subsequent years of assessment. Number '75' substituted for '80' by Finance Act 1989, s 33(4). Sum '£4,379' substituted for sum '£3,310' by SI 1992 No 622, art 2(3), for the year 1992–93, and the same sum applies for the year 1993–94 by virtue of Finance Act 1993, s 52, and for the year 1994–95 by virtue of Finance Act 1994, s 76. Sum '£4,800' substituted for sum '£4,379' by virtue of Finance Act 1995, s 36, for the year 1995–96. Sum '£5,090' substituted for sum '£4,800' by virtue of Finance Act 1996, s 74, for the year 1996–97. Sum '£5,200' substituted for sum '£5,090' by virtue of SI 1996 No 2952, art 2(3)(c). Sum '£5,400' substituted for sum '£5,200' by virtue of Finance Act 1997, s 55, for the year 1997–98. Sum '£5,600' substitutes for sum '£5,400 by virtue of the Income Tax (Indexation) (No 2) Order 1988, SI 1998 No 755, art 2(3), for the year 1998–99. Sum '£5,980' substitutes for sum '£5,600' by virtue of the Finance Act 1999, s 24(1), for the year 1999–2000. Sum '£6,260' substitutes for sum '£5,980' by the Income Tax (Indexation) (No 2) Order 2000, SI 200 No 2996, art 2(1), (2), for the year 2001–02. Sum '£6,370' substitutes for sum '£6,260' by virtue of Income Tax (Indexation) (No 2) Order 2001, SI 2001 No 3773, art 2(1), (2), for the year 2002–03. Sum '£6,910' substitutes for sum '£6,370' by virtue of the Income Tax (Indexation) (No 2) Order 2003, SI 2003 No 3215, art 2(1), (2), and sum '£6,950' subsequently substitutes by virtue of the Finance Act 2004, S 24(1), for the year 2004–05.

(4) For the purposes of subsections (2) and (3) above a person who would have been of or over a specified age within the year of assessment if he had not died in the course of it shall be treated as having been of that age within that year.

(5) In relation to a claimant whose total income for the year of assessment exceeds £10,600 [£14,200] [£14,600] [£15,200] [£15,600] [£16,200], [£16,800], [£17,600], [£17,900], [£18,300], [£18,900], subsections (2) and (3) above shall apply as if the amounts specified in them were reduced by *two-thirds* [one-half] of the excess (but not so as to reduce those amounts below that specified in subsection (1) above).]

Note. This section substituted, together with ss 257A–257F, for original s 257 by Finance Act 1988, s 33, for the year 1990–91 and subsequent years of assessment.

Sum '£14,200' substituted for sum '£10,600' by SI 1992 No 622, art 2(3), for the year 1992–93, and the same sum applies for the year 1993–94 by virtue of Finance Act 1993, s 52, and for the year 1994–95 by virtue of Finance Act 1994, s 76. Sum '£14,600' substituted for sum '£14,200' by Income Tax Indexation Order 1994, SI 1994 No 3012, art 2(3), for the year 1995–96. Sum '£15,200' substituted for sum '£14,600' by virtue of Income Tax (Indexation) Order 1995, S1 1995 No 3031, art 2(3)(d), for the year 1996–97. Sum '£15,600' substituted for sum '£15,200' by virtue of Income Tax (Indexation) Order 1996, SI 1996 No 2952, art 2(3)(d), for the year 1997–98. Sum '£16,200' substitutes for sum '£15,600' by virtue of the Income Tax (Indexation) (No 2) Order 1998, SI 1998 No 755, art 2(3), for the year 1998–99. Sum '£16,800' substitutes for sum '£16,200' by Income Tax (Indexation) (No 2) Order 1999, SI 1999 No 597, art 2(1), for the year 1999–2000. Sum '£17,600' substitutes for sum '£16,800' by virtue of the Income Tax (Indexation) (No 2) Order 2000, SI 2000 No 2996, art 2(1), (2), for the year 2001–02. Sum '£17,900' substitutes for the sum '£17,600' by virtue of the Income Tax (Indexation) (No 2) Order 2001, SI 2001 No 3773, art 2(1), (2), for the year 2002–03. Sum '£18,300' substitutes for sum '£17,900' by virtue of the Income Tax (Indexation) (No 2) Order 2002, SI 2002 No 2930, art 2(1), (2), for the year 2003–04. Sum '£18,900' substitutes for sum '£18,300' by virtue of the Income Tax (Indexation) (No 2) Order 2003, SI 2003 No 3215, art 2(1), (2), for the year 2004–05. Words 'one-half' substituted for words 'two-thirds' by Finance Act 1989, s 33(5).

[257AA Children's tax credit—*(1) If a qualifying child (or more than one) is resident with the claimant during the whole or part of the year of assessment, the claimant shall be entitled to an income tax reduction, to be known as a children's tax credit.*

(2) The reduction shall be calculated by reference to £5,290.

(2A) For a year of assessment during the whole or part of which a qualifying baby (or more than one) is resident with the claimant, subsection (2) above has effect as if the amount specified there were increased by £5,200.

(3) Where any part of the claimant's income for the year of assessment falls within section 1(2)(b), his children's tax credit for the year shall be calculated as if the amount specified in subsection (2) above were reduced by £2 for every £3 of that part of his income.

(3A) Where subsection (2A) above applies, the reference in subsection (3) above to the amount specified in subsection (2) above is to the higher amount applicable by virtue of subsection (2A) above.

(4) In this section 'qualifying child' means, in relation to a person—

(a) a child of his who has not attained the age of 16, or

(b) a child who has not attained the age of 16 and who is maintained by, and at the expense of, the person for any part of the year of assessment;

and 'child' includes illegitimate child and stepchild.

(4A) In this section 'qualifying baby', in relation to a year of assessment, means a qualifying child born in that year.'

(5) Schedule 13B (which modifies this section where a child lives with more than one adult during a year of assessment) shall have effect.]

Note. This section repealed by the Tax Credits Act 2002, s 60, Sch 6, with effect from 6 April 2003.

This section inserted by the Finance Act 1999, s 30(1) with effect for the year 2001–02 and subsequent years of assessment. Sub-s (2); sum £5,290' substituted by virtue of SI 2002 No 707, art 2(1), (3) for the year 2002–03. Sub-s (2A) (3A) and (4A): inserted by the Finance Act 2001, s 53(1)–(3) for the year 2002–03 and subsequent years of assessment.

[257A. Married couple's allowance—*(1) If the claimant proves that for the whole or any part of the year of assessment he is [If the claimant is, for the whole or any part of the year of assessment,] a married man whose wife is living with him, he shall be entitled to a deduction from his total income of £1,490 [£1,720] [for that year to an income tax reduction calculated by reference to £1,720 [£1,790] [£1,830] [£1,900]].*

Note. Sub-s (1) repealed by the Finance Act 1999, ss 31(1), (2), 139, Sch 20, Pt III (3), with effect for the year 2000–01 and subsequent years of assessment. Words in first pair of square brackets substituted for words in italics by Finance Act 1996, s 134, Sch 20, para 14(2), for the year 1996–97 and subsequent years of assessment. Sum '£1,720' substituted for sum '£1,490' by virtue of Finance Act 1991, s 22(2), for the year 1991–92, and the same sum applies for the year 1992–93 by virtue of Finance Act 1992, s 10(3) and for the year 1993–94 by virtue of Finance Act 1993, s 52. Words 'for that year ... £1,720' in square brackets substituted for words in italics by Finance Act 1994, s 77(2), (7), for the year 1994–95 and subsequent years of assessment, and the same sum applies for the year 1995–96 by virtue of 77(9) thereof. Sum '£1,790' substituted for sum '£1,720' by Income Tax (Indexation) Order 1995, SI 1995 No 3031, art 2(4)(a), for the year 1996–97. Sum '£1,830' substituted for sum '£1,790' by Income Tax (Indexation) Order 1996, SI 1996 No 2952, art 2(4)(a), for the year 1997–98. Sum '£1,900' substitutes for sum '£1,830' by virtue of the Income Tax (Indexation) (No 2) Order 1998, SI 1998 No 755, art 2(4), for the year 1998–99.

(2) *If the claimant proves that for the whole or any part of the year of assessment he is a married man whose wife is living with him, and that* [If the claimant is, for the whole or any part of the year of assessment, a married man whose wife is living with him, and] either of them *is at any time within the year of the age of 65 or upwards* [was born before 6th April 1935], he shall be entitled *to a deduction from his total income of £1,885* [£2,465] (*instead of the deduction* [for that year to an income tax reduction calculated by reference to £2,665 [£2,995] [£3,115] [£3,185] , [£3,305], [£5,565], [£5,725] (instead of to the reduction] provided for by subsection (1) above).

Note. Words in first pair of square brackets substituted for words in italics by Finance Act 1996, s 134, Sch 20, para 14(3)(a), for the year 1996–97 and subsequent years of assessment. Words in second pair of square brackets substituted for words in italics by the Finance Act 1999, s 31(1), (3)(a), for the year 2000–01 and subsequent years of assessment. Sum '£2,465' substituted for sum '£1,885' by SI 1992 No 622, art 2(4), for the year 1992–93, and the same sum applies for the year 1993–94 by virtue of Finance Act 1993, s 52. Words 'for that year ... reduction' in square brackets substituted for words in italics by Finance Act 1994, s 77(2), (7), for the year 1994–95 and subsequent years of assessment. Sum '£2,995' substituted for sum '£2,665' by Finance Act 1994, s 77(9), for the year 1995–96. Sum '£3,115' substituted for sum '£2,995' by Income Tax (Indexation) Order 1995, SI 1995 No 3031, art 2(4)(b), for the year 1996–97. Sum '£3,185' substituted for sum '£3,115' by Income Tax (Indexation) Order 1996, SI 1996 No 2952, art 2(4)(b), for the year 1997–98. Sum '£3,305' substituted for sum '£3,185' by virtue of the Income Tax (Indexation) (No 2) Order 1998, SI 1998 No 755, art 2(4), for the year 1998–99. Sum '£5,565' substituted for sum '£3,305' by virtue of the Income Tax (Indexation) (No 2) Order 2002, SI 2002 No 2930, art 2, for the year 2003–04. Sum '£5,725' substituted for sum '£5,565' by virtue of the Income Tax (Indexation) (No 2) Order 2003, SI 2003 No 3215, art 2(1), (3), for the year 2004–05.

(3) *If the claimant proves that for the whole or any part of the year of assessment he is a married man whose wife is living with him, and that* [If the claimant is, for the whole or any part of the year of assessment, a married man whose wife is living with him, and] either of them
[(a)] is at any time within that year of the age of 80[75] or upwards, and
(b) was born before 6th April 1935,]
he shall be entitled *to a deduction from his total income of £1,895, [£2,505] (instead of the deduction* [for that year to an income tax reduction calculated by reference to £2,705, [£3,035], [£3,155], [£3,225], [£3,345], [£5,635], [£5,795] (instead of to the reduction] provided for by subsection (1) or (2) above).

Note. Words in first pair of square brackets substituted for words in italics by Finance Act 1996, s 134, Sch 20, para 14(3)(b), for the year 1996–97 and subsequent years of assessment.
    Para (a) numbered as such by the Finance Act 1995, s 31(1), (4)(a), for the year 2000–01 and subsequent years of assessment.
    Para (b) and the word 'and' immediately preceding it inserted by the Finance Act 1999, s 31(1), (4)(b), for the year 2000–01 and subsequent years of assessment. Number '75' in square brackets substituted for '80' in italics by Finance Act 1989, s 33(8), (9). Sum '£2,505' substituted for sum '£1,895' by SI 1992 No 622, art 2(4), for the year 1992–93, and the same sum applies for the year 1993–94 by virtue of Finance Act 1993, s 52. Words 'for that year ...

reduction' in square brackets substituted for words in italics by Finance Act 1994, s 77(2), (7), for the year 1994–95 and subsequent years of assessment. Sum '£3,035' substituted for sum '£2,705' by Finance Act 1994, s 77(9), for the year 1995–96 and subsequent years of assessment. Sum '£3,155' substituted for sum '£3,035' by Income Tax (Indexation) Order 1995, SI 1995 No 3031, art 2(4)(c), for the year 1996–97. Sum '£3,225' substituted for sum '£3,155' by Income Tax (Indexation) Order 1996, SI 1996 No 2952, art 2(4)(b), for the year 1997–98. Sum '£3,345' substituted for sum '£3,225' by virtue of the Income Tax (Indexation) (No 2) Order 1998, SI 1998 No 755, art 2(4), for the year 1998–99. Sum '£5,635' substituted for sum '£3,345' by virtue of the Income Tax (Indexation) (No 2) Order 2002, SI 2002 No 2930, art 2, for the year 2003–04. Sum '£5,795' substituted for sum '£5,635' by virtue of the Income Tax (Indexation) (No 2) Order 2003, SI 2003 No 3215, art 2(1), (3), for the year 2004–05.

(4) For the purposes of *subsections (2) and (3)* [subsection (3)] above a person who would have been of or over *a specified age* [the age of 75] within the year of assessment if he had not died in the course of it shall be treated as having been of that age within that year.

Note. Words in square brackets substituted for words in italics by the Finance Act 1999, s 31(1), (5), for the year 2000–01 and subsequent years of assessment.

(5) In relation to a claimant whose total income for the year of assessment exceeds *£10,600* [*£14,200*] [*£14,600*] [*£15,200*] [*£15,600*] [*£16,200*], [*£18,300*], [£18,900], subsections (2) and (3) above shall apply as if the amounts specified in them were reduced by—

    (a) *two-thirds* [one half] of the excess, less

    (b) any reduction made in his allowance under section 257 by virtue of sub-section (5) of that section,

(but not so as to reduce the amounts so specified below the amount specified in subsection (1) above).

Note. Sum '£14,200' substituted for sum '£10,600' by SI 1992 No 622, art 2(4), for the year 1992–93, and the same sum applies for the year 1993–94 by virtue of Finance Act 1993, s 52, and for the year 1994–95 by virtue of Finance Act 1994, s 78. Sum '£14,600' substituted for sum '£14,200' by Income Tax (Indexation) Order 1994, SI 1994 No 3012, art 2(4), for the year 1995–96. Sum '£15,200' substituted for sum '£14,600' by Income Tax (Indexation) Order 1995, SI 1995 No 3031, art 2(4)(d) for the year 1996–97. Sum '£15,600' substituted for sum '£15,200' by Income Tax (Indexation) Order 1996, SI 1996 No 2952, art 2(4)(d), for the year 1997–98. Sum '£16,200' substituted for sum '£15,600' by virtue of Income Tax (Indexation) (No 2) Order 1998, SI 1998 No 755, art 2(4), for the year 1998–99. Sum '£18,300' substituted for the sum '£16,200' by virtue of Income Tax (Indexation) (No 2) Order 2002, SI 2002 No 2930, art 2, for the year 2003–04. Sum '£18,900' substituted for sum '£18,300' by virtue of the Income Tax (Indexation) (No 2) Order 2003, SI 2003 No 3215, art 2(1), (3), for the year 2004–05. Words 'one-half' in square brackets substituted for words 'two-thirds' in italics by Finance Act 1989, s 33(8), (9). Words in italics repealed by the Finance Act 1999, ss 31(1), (6), 139, Sch 20, Pt III(3), for the year 1999–2000 and subsequent years of assessment.

[(5A) The amounts specified in subsections (2) and (3) above shall not by virtue of subsection (5) above be treated as reduced below [*£2,150*], [£2,210].

Note. Sub-s inserted by the Finance Act 1999, s 31(1), (7), for the year 1999–2000 and subsequent years of assessment. Sum '£2,210' substituted for sum '£2,150' by virtue of Income Tax (Indexation) (No 2) Order 2003, SI 2003 No 3215, art 2(1), (3), for the year 2004–05.

(6) A man shall not be entitled by virtue of this section to more than one *deduction* [income tax reduction] for any year of assessment; and in relation to a claim by a man who becomes married in the year of assessment and has not previously in the year been entitled to relief under this section, this section shall have effect as if the amounts specified in subsections *(1) to (3)* [(2) and (3)] above were reduced by one twelfth for each month of the year ending before the date of the marriage.

In this subsection 'month' means a month beginning with the 6th day of a month of the calendar year.]

Note. See the note to s 257.

Words in first pair of square brackets substituted for words in italics by Finance Act 1994, s 77(7), Sch 8, para 1, for the year 1994–95 and subsequent years of assessment.Words in second pair of square brackets substituted by the Finance Act 1999, s 31(1), (8), for the year 2000–01 and subsequent years of assessment.

[(7) A man who is entitled for any year of assessment to an income tax reduction under this section, or to make a claim for such a reduction, shall not be entitled for that year to any income tax reduction under section 257AA.

(8) Where—

(a) a woman is married to and living with a man for the whole or any part of a year of assessment, and

(b) that man is entitled for that year to an income tax reduction under this section, or to make a claim for such a reduction.

No child shall be regarded for any of the purposes of section 257AA or Schedule 13B as resident with that woman at any time in that year when she is married to and living with that man.

(9) A person may, by notice to an officer of the Board, elect to give up his entitlement for any year of assessment to an income tax reduction under this section; and where he does so and the election is not subsequently revoked, that person shall be taken for the purposes of this section to have no entitlement for that year to a reduction under this section, or to make a claim for such a reduction.]

Note. Sub-ss (7)–(9) repealed by the Tax Credits Act 2002, s 60, Sch 6, as from 6 April 2003. Sub-ss (7)–(9) added by the Finance Act 1999, s 31(1), (9), for the year 2001–02 and subsequent years of assessment.

[257B. Transfer of relief under section 257A—*(1) Where*—

(*a*) *a man is entitled to relief under section 257A, but*

(*b*) *the amount which he is entitled to deduct from his total income by virtue of that section exceeds what is left of his total income after all other deductions have been made from it,*

his wife shall be entitled to a deduction from her total income of an amount equal to the excess.

(*2*) *In determining for the purposes of subsection (1)(b) above the amount that is left of a person's total income for a year of assessment after other deductions have been made from it, there shall be disregarded any deduction made—*

(*a*) *on account of any payments of relevant loan interest which become due in that year and to which section 369 applies, or*

(*b*) *under section 289 [or*

(*c*) *on account of any payments to which section 593(2) or 639(3) applies,] [or,*

(*d*) *on account of any payments to which section 54(5) of Finance Act 1989 applies] [, or*

(*e*) *on account of any payments to which section 32(4) of Finance Act 1991 applies.]*

(*3*) *This section shall not apply for a year of assessment unless the claimant's husband has given to the inspector written notice that it is to apply; and any such notice—*

(*a*) *shall be given not later than six years after the end of the year of assessment to which it relates,*

(*b*) *shall be in such form as the Board may determine, and*

(*c*) *shall be irrevocable.]*

Note. See the note to s 257.

Sub-s (2)(c), (d) added by Finance Act 1989, ss 33(10), 57(4). Sub-s (2)(e) added by Finance Act 1991, s 33(4).

[257BA. Elections as to transfer of relief under section 257A—(1) A woman may elect that for any year of assessment for which her husband is entitled to relief under section 257A—

    (a) she shall be entitled (on making a claim) [to an income tax reduction calculated by reference to] one half of the amount specified in *section 257A(1)* [section 257A(5A)] for that year, and

    (b) the amount [by reference to which the calculation of the income tax reduction to which he is entitled under section 257A is to be made] shall be reduced accordingly.

  (2) A husband and wife may jointly elect that for any year of assessment for which the husband is entitled to relief under section 257A—

    (a) she shall be entitled (on making a claim) [to an income tax reduction calculated by reference to] the amount specified in *section 257A(1)* [section 257A(5A)] for that year, and

    (b) the amount [by reference to which the calculation of the income tax reduction to which he is entitled under section 257A is to be made] shall be reduced accordingly *(to nil, unless section 257A(2) or (3) applies to him)*.

  (3) A man may elect that for any year of assessment for which his wife is entitled to relief by virtue of an election under subsection (2) above—

    (a) he shall be entitled (on making a claim) [to an income tax reduction calculated by reference to] one half of the amount specified in *section 257A(1)* [section 257A(5A)] for that year (in addition to [any income tax reduction to which he is already entitled] under section 257A), and

    (b) the amount [by reference to which the calculation of the income tax reduction to which she is entitled by virtue of that election is to be made] shall be reduced accordingly.

Note. Words in square brackets in sub-ss (1)–(3) substituted by Finance Act 1994, s 77, Sch 8, para 2, for the year 1994–95 and subsequent years of assessment. Words 'section 257A(5A)' in sub-ss (1)–(3) substituted by the Finance Act 1999, s 32(1)(a), for the year 1999–2000 and subsequent years of assessment.

  (4) An election under this section shall be made by giving notice to the inspector in such form as the Board may determine and—

    (a) subject to subsections (5) and (7) below, shall be made before the first year of assessment for which it is to have effect, and

    (b) shall have effect for that and each succeeding year of assessment for which the husband is entitled to relief under section 257A, subject to its withdrawal under subsection (8) below or a subsequent election under this section.

  (5) An election may be made during the first year of assessment for which it is to have effect if that is the year of assessment in which the marriage takes place.

  (6) Where subsection (5) above applies, the references in subsections (1)(a), (2)(a) and (3)(a) above to the amount specified for the year of assessment in *section 257A(1)* [section 257A(5A)] shall be read as references to that amount reduced in accordance with section 257A(6).

Note. Words 'section 257A(5A)' in square brackets substituted by the Finance Act 1999, s 32(1)(a), for the year 1999–2000 and subsequent years of assessment.

  (7) An election may be made within the first thirty days of the first year of assessment for which it is to have effect if before that year the inspector has been given written notification that it is intended to make the election.

  (8) The person or persons by whom an election was made may withdraw it by giving notice to the inspector in such form as the Board may determine; but the withdrawal shall not have effect until the year of assessment after the one in which the notice is given.

  (9) A woman shall not be entitled by virtue of an election under this section to more than one *deduction* [income tax reduction] for any year of assessment.]

Note. Section 257BA in square brackets substituted, together with s 257BB, for s 257B in italics by Finance (No 2) Act 1992, s 20, Sch 5, para 2, in relation to tax for the year 1993–94 and subsequent years of assessment. Words 'income tax reduction' in square brackets substituted by the Finance Act 1999, s 32(1)(c), for the year 1999–2000 and subsequent years of assessment.

[257BB. Transfer of relief under section 257A where relief exceeds income—
(1) Where—
- (a) a man is entitled to relief under section 257A, but
- [(b) the amount of the reduction to which he is entitled is determined in accordance with section 256(2)(b) [(read with section 25(6)(c) of the Finance Act 1990 where applicable)] or, by virtue of his having no income tax liability to which that reduction is applicable, is nil,

his wife shall be entitled (in addition to any reduction to which she is entitled by virtue of an election under section 257BA) to an income tax reduction calculated by reference to an amount equal to the unused part of the amount by reference to which her husband's income tax reduction fell to be calculated in pursuance of section 257A and any election under section 257BA.]

(2) Subsection (1) above shall not apply for a year of assessment unless the claimant's husband gives notice to the inspector that it is to apply.
(3) Where—
- (a) a woman is entitled to relief by virtue of an election under section 257BA, but
- [(b) the amount of the reduction to which she is entitled is determined in accordance with section 256(2)(b) [(read with section 25(6)(c) of the Finance Act 1990 where applicable)] or, by virtue of her having no income tax liability to which that reduction is applicable, is nil,

her husband shall be entitled (in addition to any other reduction to which he is entitled by virtue of section 257A) to an income tax reduction calculated by reference to an amount equal to the unused part of the amount by reference to which his wife's income tax reduction fell to be calculated in pursuance of that election.]

Note. Words in square brackets in sub-ss (1), (3) substituted by Finance Act 1994, s 77, Sch 8, para 3(1), (2), for the year 1994–95 and subsequent years of assessment. Words '(read with section 25(6)(c) of the Finance Act 1990 where applicable)' in square brackets in sub-ss (1), (3), added by the Finance Act 2000, s 39(1), (8) with effect in relation to gifts made on or after 6 April 2000 which are not covenanted payments and covenanted payments falling to be made on or after that date.

[(3A) In this section references, in relation to such an amount as is mentioned in subsection (1)(b) or (3)(b), to the unused part of an amount by reference to which any income tax reduction fell to be calculated are references to so much of it (including, where the amount so mentioned is nil, all of it) as has no practical effect on the determination of the amount so mentioned.]

Note. Sub-s (3A) inserted by Finance Act 1994, s 77, Sch 8, para 3(3), for the year 1994–95 and subsequent years of assessment.

(4) Subsection (3) above shall not apply for a year of assessment unless the claimant's wife gives notice to the inspector that it is to apply.
(5) Any notice under subsection (2) or (4) above—
- (a) shall be given *not later than six years after* [on or before the fifth anniversary of the 31st January next following] the end of the year of assessment to which it relates,
- (b) shall be in such form as the Board may determine, and
- (c) shall be irrevocable.

Note. Words in square brackets substituted for words in italics by Finance Act 1996, s 135, Sch 21, para 4, for the year 1996–97 and subsequent years of assessment.

(6) . . .]

Note. See the note to s 257BA.

Sub-s (6) repealed by Finance Act 1994, ss 77, 258, Sch 8, para 3(4), Sch 26, Part V, for the year 1994–95 and subsequent years of assessment.

[257C. Indexation of amounts in sections 257 and 257A—(1) If the retail prices index for the month of *December* [September] preceding a year of assessment is higher than it was for the previous *December* [September], then, unless Parliament otherwise determines, *sections 257 and 257A* [sections 257, *257AA(2)*, *[257AA(2) and (2A)]* and 257A] shall apply for that year as if for each amount specified in them as they applied for the previous year (whether by virtue of this section or otherwise) there were substituted an amount arrived at by increasing the amount for the previous year by the same percentage as the percentage increase in the retail prices index, and—

(a) if in the case of an amount specified its sections 257(5) and 257A(5) the result is not a multiple of £100, rounding it up to the nearest amount which is such a multiple;

(b) if in the case of any other amount the increase is not a multiple of £10, rounding the increase up to the nearest amount which is such a multiple.

Note. Sub-s (1) does not apply for the year 1992–93, so far as relating to s 257A(1), by virtue of Finance Act 1992, s 10(3), nor for the year 199–94, by virtue of Finance Act 1993, s 52, nor for the year 1994–95, so far as relating to ss 257, 257AA(5), by virtue of Finance Act 1994, ss 76, 78, nor for the year 1995–96, so far as relating to s 257(2), (3), by virtue of Finance Act 1995, s 36, nor for the year 1996–97, so far as relating to s 257(1)–(3), by virtue of Finance Act 1996, s 74. Word 'September' in square brackets substituted for words in italics by Finance Act 1993, s 107(3)(a), (8), for the year 1994–95 and subsequent years of assessment. Words from 'sections 257' to 'and 257A' in square brackets substituted by the Finance Act 1999, s 30(3), with effect for the purposes of the application of s 257AA of the Taxes Act 1988 for the year 2002-03 and subsequent years of assessment. Words '257AA(2) and (2A)' in italics repealed by the Tax Credits Act 2002, s 60, Sch 6, as from 6 April 2003. Words '257AA(2) in italics repealed and subsequent words in square brackets substituted by the Finance Act 2001, s 53(4) with effect for the purposes of the application of s 257AA of this Act for the year 2003–04 and subsequent years of assessment.

(2) *Subsection (1) above shall not require any change to be made in the amounts deductible or repayable under section 203 between the beginning of a year of assessment and 5th May in that year* [during the period beginning with 6th April and ending with 17th May in the year of assessment].

Note. Words in square brackets substituted for words from 'between' to the end by Finance Act 1990, s 17. Sub-s (2) repealed by Finance Act 1993, ss 107(3)(b), (8), 213, Sch 23, Part III(10), for the year 1994–95 and subsequent years of assessment

[(2A) Subsection (1) above shall not require any change to be made in the amounts deductible or repayable under section 203 during the period beginning with 6th April and ending with 17th May [17th June] in the year of assessment.]

Note. Sub-s (2A) added by the Finance Act 1999, s 25(1), (3), for the year 1999–2000 and subsequent years of assessment. Words '17th June' substituted for words '17th May' by the Finance Act 2002, s 27(b), with effect for the application of ss 257AA(2), 265 of this Act for the year 2002–03.

(3) The Treasury shall in each year of assessment make an order specifying the amounts which by virtue of subsection (1) above will be treated as specified for the following year of assessment in *sections 257 and 257A* [sections 257, 257AA(2), *[257AA(2) and (2A)]* and 257A].

Note. Words from 'sections 257' to 'and 257A' in square brackets substituted by the Finance Act 1999, s 30(3), with effect for the purposes of the application of 257AA of the Taxes Act 1988 for the year 2002–03 and subsequent years of assessment. Words '257AA(2) and (2A)' in italics repealed by the Tax Credits Act 2002, s 60, Sch 6, as from 6 April 2003. Words '257AA(2)' in italics repealed and subsequent words in square brackets substituted by the

Finance Act 2001, s 53(4), with effect for the purposes of the application of s 257AA of this Act for the year 2003–04 and subsequent years of assessment.

(4) This section shall have effect in relation to reliefs for the year 1990–91 (as well as for later years); and for that purpose it shall be assumed that sections 257 and 257A applied for the year 1989–90 as they apply, apart from this section, for the year 1990–91.]

Note. See the note to s 257.

Sub-s (4) repealed by Finance Act 1990, s 132, Sch 19, Part IV.

[257D. Transitional relief: husband with excess allowances—*(1) Where—*

(a)   *a husband and wife are living together for the whole or any part of the year 1990–91 and section 279 (but not section 287) applied in relation to them for the whole or any part of the year 1989–90, and*

(b)   *the deductions which the husband was entitled to make from his total income for the year 1989–90 under this Chapter exceed the aggregate mentioned in subsection (2) below,*

the wife shall be entitled to a deduction from her total income for the year 1990–91 of an amount equal to the excess.

(2) The aggregate referred to in subsection (1) above is the aggregate of—

(a)   *the husband's total income for the year 1990–91, and*

(b)   *the deductions which the wife is entitled to make from her total income for that year under this Chapter (apart from this section).*

(3) Where—

(a)   *a husband and wife are living together for the whole or any part of the year 1990–91 and for part of the year 1989–90 but section 279 did not apply in relation to them for any part of the year 1989–90, and*

(b)   *the deductions which the husband was entitled to make from his total income for the year 1989–90 under this Chapter, apart from section 257(6), exceed his total income for the year 1990–91,*

then, subject to subsection (4) below, the wife shall be entitled to a deduction from her total income for the year 1990–91 of an amount equal to the excess.

(4) If the deductions which the wife is entitled to make from her total income for the year 1990–91 under this Chapter (apart from this section) exceed the lesser of—

(a)   *her total income for the year 1989–90, and*

(b)   *the deductions which she was entitled to make from her total income for that year under this Chapter, apart from section 259, section 262 and section 280,*

the deduction provided for by subsection (3) above shall be reduced by an amount equal to the excess.

(5) Where—

(a)   *a husband and wife are living together for the whole or any part of the year 1991–92 or any subsequent year of assessment ('the year in question'), and*

(b)   *they were also living together throughout the immediately preceding year of assessment and the wife made a deduction from her total income for that year under this section, and*

(c)   *the deductions which the wife is entitled to make from her total income under this Chapter (apart from this section) are either no greater for the year in question than for the immediately preceding year, or greater by a margin which does not exceed the deduction referred to in paragraph (b) above, and*

(d)   *the deductions which the husband is entitled to make from his total income for the year in question under this Chapter, apart from section 257A and section 265, exceed his total income for that year,*

the wife shall be entitled to a deduction from her total income for that year.

Note. Words in italics repealed by Finance Act 1994, ss 77, 258, Sch 8, para 4(2), Sch 26, Part V, for the year 1994–95 and subsequent years of assessment.

(6) The amount of that deduction shall be equal to—

(a)   the deduction referred to in subsection (5)(b) above, reduced where applicable by an amount equal to the margin referred to in subsection (5)(c), or
(b)   the excess referred to in subsection (5)(d),
whichever is less.

(7) In determining for the purposes of subsection (5)(b) above whether the wife made a deduction from her total income for the immediately preceding year of assessment under this section, and the amount of any such deduction, it shall be assumed that a deduction under this section is made after all other deductions (except any deduction under section 289).

(8) In determining for the purposes of this section a person's total income for a year of assessment there shall be disregarded any deduction made—

(a)   on account of any payments of relevant loan interest which become due in that year and to which section 369 applies, or
(b)   under this Chapter or under section 289; [or
(c)   on account of any payments to which section 593(2) or 639(3) applies] [, or
(d)   on account of any payments to which section 54(5) of the Finance Act 1989 applies] [, or
(e)   on account of any payments to which section 32(4) of Finance Act 1991 applies]
and in determining for the purposes of subsection (1)(b) above the deductions which a man was entitled to make under this Chapter for the year 1989–90, any application under section 283 shall be disregarded.

Note. Sub-s (8)(a) repealed, in relation to payments of interest made on or after 6 April 1994, and so far as it relates to relevant loan interest, in relation to any payments of interest becoming due on or after 6 April 1994 which have been made at any time before that date but on or after 30 November 1993, by Finance Act 1994, s 258, Sch 26, Part V(2), in accordance with s 81(6) thereof. Words in italics in sub-s (8)(b) repealed by Finance Act 1994, s 258, Sch 26, Part V(17), in relation to shares issued on or after 1 January 1994. Sub-s (8)(c) added by Finance Act 1989, s 33(10), as from 27 July 1989. Sub-s (8)(d) added by Finance Act 1989, s 57(4), repealed by Finance Act 1994, ss 83, 258, Sch 10, para 3, Sch 26, Part V(3), in relation to private medical insurance premiums paid on or after 6 April 1994. Sub-s (8)(e) added by Finance Act 1991, s 33(4), as from 25 July 1991.

(9) This section shall not apply for a year of assessment unless the claimant's husband has given to the inspector written notice that it is to apply; and any such notice—

(a)   shall be given not later than six years after [on or before the fifth anniversary of the 31st January next following] the end of the year of assessment to which it relates,
(b)   shall be in such form as the Board may determine, and
(c)   shall be irrevocable.

Note. Words in square brackets substituted for words in italics by Finance Act 1996, s 135, Sch 21, para 5, for the year 1996–97 and subsequent years of assessment.

(10) A notice given under subsection (9) above in relation to a year of assessment shall have effect also as a notice under section 257B(3) [section 257BB(2)] (and, where it is relevant, under section 265(5)).]

Note. See the note to s 257.
This section repealed by the Finance Act 1999, ss 32(2), 139, Sch 20, Pt III(3), for the year 2000–01 and subsequent years of assessment.
Sub-s (10): words in square brackets substituted by Finance (No 2) Act 1992, s 20, Sch 5, para 3, in relation to tax for the year 1993–94 and subsequent years of assessment.

[257E. Transitional relief: the elderly—(1) This section shall apply in relation to a claimant for any year of assessment for the whole or any part of which he has his wife living with him if he proves—

(a)   that for the year 1989–90 he was entitled to relief by virtue of section 257(2)(a) of this Act (as it had effect for that year) and that his entitlement was due to her age and not to his (he being under the age of 65 throughout that year), or

(b)   *that for the year 1989–90 he was entitled to relief by virtue of section 257(3)(a) of this Act (as it had effect for that year) and that his entitlement was due to her age and not to his (he being under the age of 80 [75] throughout that year),*

and, in either case, that the amount of that relief exceeded the aggregate amount of any relief to which he would be entitled for the year 1990–91 under sections 257 and 257A (apart from this section).

Note. Words in italics repealed by Finance Act 1996, ss 134, 205, Sch 20, para 15, Sch 41, Part V(10), as from 29 April 1996, for the year 1996–97 and subsequent years of assessment. Number '75' in square brackets substituted for number '80' in italics by Finance Act 1989, s 33(11).

(2)   *Where this section applies, section 257 shall have effect—*
(a)   *in a case within subsection (1)(a) above, as if for the amount specified in subsection (1) of that section there were substituted £3,180 [£3,400], and*
(b)   *in in case within subsection (1)(b) above, as if for the amounts specified in subsections (1) and (2) of that section there were substituted £3,310 [£3,540].*

Note. Sums in square brackets substituted for sums in italics by Finance Act 1989, s 33(12), (13), as from 27 July 1989.

(3)   *Section 257(5) shall have effect in relation to section 257(1) as modified by this section as it has effect in relation to section 257(2) and (3); and in all cases the reference in section 257(5) to the amount specified in section 257(1) is a reference to the amount specified apart from this section.*

(4)   *The references in section 257C to the amounts specified in section 257 are references to the amounts specified apart from this section.*

(5)   *In determining for the purposes of this section the amount of any reliefs to which a person was entitled for the year 1989–90, any application under section 283 shall be disregarded.*]

Note. See the note to s 257.

This section repealed by the Finance Act 1999, ss 32(2), 139, Sch 20, Pt III(3), for the year 2000–01 and subsequent years of assessment.

[257F.   Transitional relief: separated couples. *If the claimant proves—*
(a)   *that he [the claimant] and his wife ceased to live together before 6th April 1990 but that ever since they ceased to live together they have continued to be married to one another and she has been wholly maintained by him, and*
(b)   *that he is not entitled to make any deduction in respect of the sums paid for her maintenance in computing for income tax purposes the amount of his income for the year to which the claim relates, and*
(c)   *that he was entitled to a deduction for the year 1989–90 by virtue of section 257(1)(a) of this Act (as it had effect for that year) and, if the claim relates to a year later than 1990–91, that he has been entitled by virtue of this section to a deduction under section 257A [or, as the case may be, an income tax reduction under that section] for each intervening year,*

sections 257A and 257E (but not section 257B [section 257BA, section 257BB] or section 257D) shall have effect for the year to which the claim relates as if his wife were living with him.]

Note. See the note to s 257.

This section repealed by the Finance Act 1999, ss 32(2), 139, Sch 20, Pt III(3), for the year 2000–01 and subsequent years of assessment.

First, third, fourth, fifth and sixth words in italics repealed, and words in first pair of square brackets substituted for preceding words in italics by Finance Act 1996, as from 29 April 1996, ss 134, 205, Sch 20, para 16(2)–(5), Sch 41, Part V(10), for the year 1996–97 and subsequent years of assessment. Words in second pair of square brackets inserted by Finance Act 1994, s 77, Sch 8, para 5, for the year 1994–95 and subsequent years of assessment. Words in third pair of square brackets substituted for preceding words in italics by Finance (No 2) Act 1992, s 20, Sch 5, para 4, in relation to tax for the year 1993–94 and subsequent years of assessment.

CHAPTER II

TAXATION OF INCOME OF SPOUSES

General rules

279. Aggregation of wife's income with husband's—(*1*) *Subject to the provisions of this Chapter, a woman's income chargeable to income tax shall, so far as it is income for—*
   (*a*)   *a year of assessment; or*
   (*b*)   *any part of a year of assessment, being a part beginning with 6th April,*
during which she is a married woman living with her husband, be deemed for income tax purposes to be his income and not to be her income.
   (*2*)   *The question whether there is any income of hers chargeable to income tax for any year of assessment and, if so, what is to be taken to be the amount thereof for income tax purposes shall not be affected by the provisions of subsection (1) above.*
   (*3*)   *Any tax falling to be assessed in respect of any income which, under subsection (1) above, is to be deemed to be the income of a woman's husband shall, instead of being assessed on her, or on her trustee, guardian, curator, receiver or committee, or on her executors or administrators, be assessable on him or, in the appropriate cases, on his trustee, guardian, curator, receiver or committee, or on his executors or administrators.*
   (*4*)   *Nothing in subsection (3) above shall affect the operation of section 111.*
   (*5*)   *Any deduction from a man's total income made under section 257(6) and (7) shall be treated as reducing the earned income of his wife.*
   (*6*)   *References in this section to a woman's income include references to any sum which, apart from the provisions of this section, would fall to be included in computing her total income, and this subsection has effect in relation to any such sum notwithstanding that some enactment (including, except so far as the contrary is expressly provided, an enactment passed after the passing of this Act) requires that that sum should not be treated as income of any person other than her.*
   (*7*)   *For the purposes of sections 380 and 381 of this Act and section 71 of the 1968 Act (set off of capital allowances against general income), subsection (1)(b) above shall have effect as if the words 'being a part beginning with 6th April' were omitted.*
Note. This section repealed by Finance Act 1988, ss 32, 148, Sch 14, Part VIII, with effect from the year 1990–91.

280. Transfer of reliefs—(*1*) *Where during any part of a year of assessment a husband and wife are living together but his income for that year does not or, if there were any, would not include any of hers, then if either of them—*
   (*a*)   *would, if he or she had sufficient income for that year, be entitled to have any amount deducted from or set off against it under a provision to which this subsection applies, and*
   (*b*)   *makes a claim in that behalf,*
that amount or, as the case may be, so much of it as cannot be deducted from or set off against his or her own income for that year shall instead be deducted from and set off against the income for that year of the other spouse.
   (*2*)   *Subsection (1) above applies—*
   (*a*)   *in the case of the husband, to any provision of Chapter I of this Part and sections 289 and 353;*
   (*b*)   *in the case of the wife, to—*
      (*i*)   *any provision of that Chapter except sections 257(1)(b), (2)(b) and (3)(b), 258, 259 and 262;*
      (*ii*)   *section 289 but only in respect of amounts subscribed by her for shares issued in the part of the year of assessment mentioned in subsection (1) above; and]*
      (*iii*)   *section 353 so far as applicable to interest paid in the part of the year mentioned in subsection (1) above.*
Note. This section repealed by Finance Act 1988, s 148, Sch 14, Part VIII, with effect from the year 1990–91.

281. Tax repayments to wives—(*1*) *Where in any year of assessment tax has been deducted under section 203 from the earned income of a wife and, apart from this section, a repayment of tax for that year would fall to be made to her husband in consequence of an assessment under Schedule E, so much of the repayment as is attributable to the tax so deducted shall be made to her and not to him.*

(*2*) *The amount of a repayment attributable to tax deducted as mentioned in subsection (1) above is the excess (if any) of the total net tax so deducted in the year of assessment over the tax chargeable on the wife's relevant earned income included in her husband's total income for that year after allowing*—

(*a*) *any relief for that year under section 266 in respect of any payment made by her of the kind mentioned in paragraph 5 of Schedule 14; and*

(*b*) *any relief for that year to which her husband is entitled under any other provision of the Income Tax Acts to the extent to which it cannot be allowed because his income, exclusive of her earned income, is insufficient;*

but that amount shall not exceed the aggregate of the amounts repayable for that year in respect of the total net tax deducted in that year under section 203 from the income of the wife and the income of her husband.

(*3*) *Where in consequence of an assessment under Schedule E any amount is repayable under this section to the wife of the person on whom the assessment is made the inspector shall notify both of them of his determination of that amount and, subject to subsection (4) below, an appeal shall lie against the determination as if it were a decision on a claim.*

(*4*) *Any appeal under subsection (3) above shall be to the General Commissioners for the division in which the spouses reside or, if they reside in different divisions, for the division in which one of them resides, as the Board may direct, or, if neither of them resides in Great Britain, to the Special Commissioners; and on any such appeal by one of the spouses the other shall have the same rights as an appellant, including any right to require the statement of a case for the opinion of the court.*

(*5*) *The Board may make regulations*—

(*a*) *modifying subsection (2) above in relation to such cases as may be specified in the regulations;*

(*b*) *modifying section 824 in relation to cases in which a repayment falls to be made under this section.*

(*6*) *This section does not apply to any repayment for a year of assessment*—

(*a*) *for which the husband is chargeable to income tax at a rate or rates higher than the basic rate; or*

(*b*) *for which any earned income of the wife has been assessed otherwise than under Schedule E.*

(*7*) *For the purposes of this section earned income of a wife has the same meaning as for the purposes of subsection (6) of section 257 and relevant earned income of a wife means so much of her earned income as exceeds the relief available in respect of it under that subsection.*

(*8*) *References in this section to the total net tax deducted in any year under section 203 are references to the total income tax deducted during that year by virtue of regulations made under that section less any income tax repaid by virtue of any such regulations.*

Note. This section repealed by Finance Act 1988, s 148, Sch 14, Part VIII, with effect from the year 1990–91.

282. Construction of references to married women living with their husbands—(*1*) *A married woman shall be treated for income tax purposes as living with her husband unless*—

(*a*) *they are separated under an order of a court of competent jurisdiction, or by deed of separation, or*

(*b*) *they are in fact separated in such circumstances that the separation is likely to be permanent.*

(*2*) *Where a married woman is living with her husband and either*—

(*a*) *one of them is, and the other is not, resident in the United Kingdom for a year of assessment, or* (*b*)   both of them are resident in the United Kingdom for a year of assessment, but one of them is, and the other is not, absent from the United Kingdom throughout that year,

the same consequences shall follow for income tax purposes as would have followed if, throughout that year of assessment, they had been in fact separated in such circumstances that the separation was likely to be permanent.

(*3*) Where subsection (*2*) above applies and the net aggregate amount of income tax falling to be borne by the husband and the wife for the year is greater than it would have been but for that subsection, the Board shall cause such relief to be given (by the reduction of such assessments on the husband or the wife or the repayment of such tax paid, by deduction or otherwise, by the husband or the wife, as the Board may direct) as will reduce that net aggregate amount by the amount of the excess.

[282. Construction of references to husband and wife living together.   A husband and wife shall be treated for income tax purposes as living together unless—

(a) they are separated under an order of a court of competent jurisdiction, or by deed of separation, or

(b) they are in fact separated in such circumstances that the separation is likely to be permanent.]

Note. Section 282 in square brackets substituted for s 282 in italics, by Finance Act 1988, s 35, Sch 3, paras 1, 11, with effect from the year 1990–91.

[282A. Jointly held property—(1) Subject to the following provisions of this section, income arising from property held in the names of a husband and his wife shall for the purposes of income tax be regarded as income to which they are beneficially entitled in equal shares.

(2) Subsection (1) above shall not apply to income to which neither the husband nor the wife is beneficially entitled.

(3) Subsection (1) above shall not apply to income—

(a) to which either the husband or the wife is beneficially entitled to the exclusion of the other, or

(b) to which they are beneficially entitled in unequal shares, if a declaration relating to it has effect under section 282B.

(4) Subsection (1) above shall not apply to—

(a) earned income, or

(b) income which is not earned income but to which section 11 applies.

[(4A) Subsection (1) above shall not apply to income consisting of a distribution arising from property consisting of —

(a) close company shares to which either the husband or the wife is beneficially entitled to the exclusion of the other, or

(b) close company shares to which they are beneficially entitled in equal or unequal shares.

In this subsection 'close company shares' means shares in or securities of a close company; and for this purpose 'shares' and 'securities' have the same meaning as in Part 6 (see section 254).]

(5) Subsection (1) above shall not apply to income to which the husband or the wife is beneficially entitled if or to the extent that it is treated by virtue of any other provision of the Income Tax Acts as the income of the other of them or of a third party.

(6) References in this section to a husband and his wife are references to a husband and wife living together.]

Note. This section inserted by Finance Act 1988, s 34, for the year 1990–91 and subsequent years of assessment. Sub-s (4A) inserted by the Finance Act 2004, s 91(1), (2), for the year 2004–05 and subsequent years of assessment.

[282B. Jointly held property: declarations—(1) The declaration referred to in section 282A(3) is a declaration by both the husband and the wife of their beneficial interests in—

(a) the income to which the declaration relates, and

(b) the property from which that income arises.

(2) Subject to the following subsections, a declaration shall have effect under this section in relation to income arising on or after the date of the declaration; but a declaration made before 6th June 1990 shall also have effect in relation to income arising before that date.

(3) A declaration shall not have effect under this section unless notice of it is given to the inspector, in such form and manner as the Board may prescribe, within the period of 60 days beginning with the date of the declaration.

(4) A declaration shall not have effect under this section in relation to income from property if the beneficial interests of the husband and the wife in the property itself do not correspond to their beneficial interests in the income.

(5) A declaration having effect under this section shall continue to have effect unless and until the beneficial interests of the husband and wife in either the income to which it relates, or the property from which the income arises, cease to accord with the declaration.]

Note. This section inserted by Finance Act 1988, s 34, for the year 1990–91 and subsequent years of assessment.

Separate assessments

283. Option for separate assessment—(*1*) *If, within six months before the 6th July in any year of assessment for which his income would include any of hers, a husband or a wife makes an application for the purpose in such manner and form as the Board may prescribe, income tax for that year shall be assessed, charged and recovered on the income of the husband and on the income of the wife as if they were not married, and all the provisions of the Income Tax Acts with respect to the assessment, charge and recovery of income tax shall, save as otherwise provided by those Acts, apply as if they were not married.*

(*2*) *Notwithstanding an application under subsection (1) above the income of the husband and the wife shall be treated as one in estimating total income; and the amount of tax payable by each of them shall be ascertained by first dividing between them, in proportion to the amounts of their respective incomes, the amount that would be payable by them if no reliefs were given under Chapter I or III of this Part and then applying section 284 to give effect to those reliefs.*

(*3*) *Subject to subsection (4) below, an application duly made by a husband or wife under subsection (1) above shall have effect, not only as respects the year of assessment for which it is made, but also for any subsequent year of assessment.*

(*4*) *A person who has made any such application for any year of assessment may give, for any subsequent year of assessment, a notice to withdraw that application, and where such a notice is given, the application shall not have effect with respect to the year for which the notice is given or any subsequent year.*

(*5*) *A notice of withdrawal under subsection (4) above shall be in such form, and be given in such manner, as may be prescribed by the Board, and shall not be valid unless it is given within the period allowed by law for making, for the year for which the notice is given, applications similar to that to which the notice relates.*

Note. This section repealed by Finance Act 1988, s 148, Sch 14, Part VIII, with effect from the year 1990–91.

284. Effect of separate assessment on personal reliefs—(*1*) *Where, by virtue of an application under section 283(1), income tax for any year of assessment is to be assessable and chargeable on the incomes of a husband and wife as if they were not married, the total relief given to the husband and the wife by way of personal reliefs shall be the same as if the application had not had effect with respect to the year and, subject to subsections (2) and (3)* *below, the reduction of tax flowing from the personal reliefs shall be allocated to the husband and the wife—*

   (*a*)   *so far as it flows from relief under section 273 or Chapter III of this Part, to the husband or the wife according as he or she made the payment giving rise to the relief;*

   (*b*)   *so far as it flows from relief in respect of a dependent relative under section 263 or relief in respect of a son or daughter under section 264, to the husband or the wife according as he or she maintains the relative or son or daughter; and*

   (*c*)   *as to the balance, in proportion to the amounts of tax which would have been payable by them respectively if no personal reliefs had been allowable.*

   (*2*)   *Subject to subsection (3) below, the amount of reduction of tax allocated to the wife by virtue of subsection (1) above shall not be less than the reduction resulting from section 279(5) in the tax chargeable in respect of her earned income, and the amount of reduction of tax allocated to the husband shall be correspondingly reduced.*

   (*3*)   *Where the amount of reduction of tax allocated to the husband under subsection (1) above exceeds the tax chargeable on the income of the husband for the year of assessment, the balance shall be applied to reduce the tax chargeable on the income of the wife for that year; and where the amount of reduction of tax allocated to the wife under that subsection exceeds the tax chargeable on her income for the year of assessment, the balance shall be applied to reduce the tax chargeable on the income of the husband for that year.*

   (*4*)   *Returns of the total incomes of the husband and the wife may be made for the purposes of this section either by the husband or by the wife, but, if the Board are not satisfied with any such return, they may obtain a return from the wife or the husband, as the case may be.*

   (*5*)   *In this section 'personal reliefs' means the reliefs provided for by Chapters I and III of this Part.*

Note. This section repealed by Finance Act 1988, s 148, Sch 14, Part VIII, with effect from the year 1990–91.

285.   Collection from wife of tax assessed on husband but attributable to her income—(*1*)   *Where—*

   (*a*)   *an assessment to income tax ('the original assessment') is made on a man, or on a man's trustee, guardian, curator, receiver or committee, or on a man's executors or administrators; and*

   (*b*)   *the Board are of opinion that, if an application for separate assessment under section 283(1) had been in force with respect to the year for which the assessment is made, an assessment ('the potential assessment') in respect of, or of part of, the same income would have fallen to be made on, or on the trustee, guardian, curator, receiver or committee of, or on the executors or administrators of, a woman who is that man's wife, or was his wife in that year of assessment; and*

   (*c*)   *the whole or part of the amount payable under the original assessment has remained unpaid at the expiration of 38 days from the time when it became due;*

the Board may serve on her, or, if she is dead, on her executors or administrators, or, if the potential assessment could in the event referred to in paragraph (b) above have been made on her trustee, guardian, curator, receiver or committee, on her or on her trustee, guardian, curator, receiver or committee, a notice—

      (*i*)   *giving particulars of the original assessment, and of the amount remaining unpaid thereunder, and*

      (*ii*)   *giving particulars, to the best of their judgment, of the potential assessment,*

and requiring the person on whom the notice is served to pay the amount which would have been payable under the potential assessment if it conformed with those particulars, or the amount remaining unpaid under the original assessment, whichever is the less.

   (*2*)   *The same consequences as respects—*

   (*a*)   *the imposition of a liability to pay, and the recovery of, the tax, with or without interest; and*

   (*b*)   *priority for the tax in bankruptcy, or in the administration of the estate of a deceased person; and*

(c) appeals to the General or Special Commissioners, and the stating of cases for the opinion of the High Court; and

(d) the ultimate incidence of the liability imposed,

shall follow on the service of a notice under subsection (1) above on a woman, or on her trustee, guardian, curator, receiver or committee, or on her executors or administrators, as would have followed on the making on her, or on her trustee, guardian, curator, receiver or committee, or on her executors or administrators, as the case may be, of the potential assessment, being an assessment which—

    (i) was made on the day of the service of the notice, and]

    (ii) charged the same amount of income tax as is required to be paid by the notice, and]

    (iii) fell to be made, and was made, by the authority who made the original assessment, and]

    (iv) was made by that authority to the best of their judgment,

and the provisions of the Income Tax Acts relating to the matters specified in paragraphs (a) to (d) above shall, with the necessary adaptations, have effect accordingly.

(3) Where an appeal against the original assessment has been heard in whole or in part by the Special Commissioners, any appeal from the notice under subsection (1) above shall be an appeal to the Special Commissioners, and where an appeal against the original assessment has been heard in whole or in part by the General Commissioners for any division, any appeal from the notice shall be an appeal to the General Commissioners for that division.

(4) Where a notice is given under subsection (1) above—

(a) income tax up to the amount required to be paid by the notice shall cease to be recoverable under the original assessment, and

(b) where the tax charged by the original assessment carried interest under section 86 of the Management Act, such adjustment shall be made of the amount payable under that section in relation to that assessment, and such repayment shall be made of any amounts previously paid under that section in relation thereto, as are necessary to secure that the total sum, if any, paid or payable under that section in relation to that assessment is the same as it would have been if the amount which ceases to be recoverable had never been charged.

(5) Where the amount payable under a notice given under subsection (1) above is reduced as the result of an appeal, or of the stating of a case for the opinion of the High Court—

(a) the Board shall, if in the light of that result they are satisfied that the original assessment was excessive, cause such relief to be given by way of repayment or otherwise as appears to them to be just, but

(b) subject to any relief so given, a sum equal to the reduction in the amount payable under the notice shall again become recoverable under the original assessment.

(6) The Board and the inspector shall have the like powers of obtaining information with a view to the giving of, and otherwise in connection with, a notice under subsection (1) above as they would have had with a view to the making of, and otherwise in connection with, the potential assessment if the necessary conditions had been fulfilled for the making of such an assessment.

Note. This section repealed by Finance Act 1988, s 148, Sch 14, Part VIII, with effect from the year 1990–91.

286. Right of husband to disclaim liability for tax on deceased wife's income—(1) Where a woman dies who at any time before her death was a married woman living with her husband, he or, if he is dead, his executors or administrators, may, not later than two months from the date of the grant of probate or letters of administration in respect of her estate or, with the consent of her executors or administrators, at any later date, serve on her executors or administrators and on the inspector a notice declaring that, to the extent permitted by this section, he disclaims or they disclaim responsibility for unpaid income tax in respect of all income of hers for any year of assessment or part of a year of assessment during which he was her husband and she was living with him.

(*2*) *A notice under subsection (1) above shall not be deemed to be validly served on the inspector unless it specifies the names and addresses of the woman's executors or administrators.*

(*3*) *Where a notice under subsection (1) above has been duly served on a woman's executors or administrators and on the inspector—*

(*a*) *it shall be the duty of the Board to exercise such powers as they may then or thereafter be entitled to exercise under section 285 in connection with any assessment made on or before the date when the service of the notice is completed, being an assessment in respect of any of the income to which the notice relates; and*

(*b*) *the assessments (if any) which may be made after that date shall in all respects, and in particular as respects the persons assessable and the tax payable, be the assessments which would have fallen to be made if—*

(*i*) *an application for separate assessment under section 283(1) had been in force in respect of the year of assessment in question; and*

(*ii*) *all assessments previously made had been made accordingly.*

(*4*) *In the application of this section to Scotland, the reference to the date of the grant of probate or letters of administration shall be construed as a reference to the date of confirmation.*

Note. This section repealed by Finance Act 1988, s 148, Sch 14, Part VIII, with effect from the year 1990–91.

Separate taxation

287. Separate taxation of wife's earnings—(*1*) *Where a man and his wife living with him jointly so elect or have elected for any year of assessment, the wife's earnings and their other income shall be chargeable to income tax as provided in the following provisions of this section.*

(*2*) *References in this section to the wife's earnings are references to any earned income of hers other than—*

(*a*) *income arising in respect of any pension, superannuation or other allowance, deferred pay or compensation for loss of office given in respect of the husband's past services in any office or employment; or*

(*b*) *any payment of benefit under the Social Security Acts except a Category A retirement pension (exclusive of any increase under section 10 of the Social Security Pensions Act 1975 or Article 12 of the Social Security Pensions (Northern Ireland) Order 1975), unemployment benefit or invalid care allowance.*

In this subsection 'the Social Security Acts' means the Social Security Acts 1975 and the Social Security (Northern Ireland) Acts 1975.

(*3*) *In charging the income of the husband and wife in accordance with section 279—*

(*a*) *the wife's earnings shall be charged to income tax as if she were a single woman with no other income; and*

(*b*) *the husband's other income shall be charged to income tax as if the wife's earnings were nil.*

(*4*) *Subject to subsections (5) and (6) below, the reliefs to be given under Chapter I of this Part shall be determined as if the husband and the wife were not married and—*

(*a*) *the wife's earnings were her only income; and*

(*b*) *the husband's income included all income of the wife, other than her earnings;*

and accordingly the reliefs to be given under that Chapter in respect of the income chargeable under either paragraph (a) or paragraph (b) of subsection (3) above shall not reduce the tax or the income chargeable under the other of those paragraphs.

(*5*) *No relief shall be given to either the husband or the wife under section 257(2) or (3) or 259.*

(*6*) *References in Chapter I of this Part to the claimant shall be construed as including the wife.*

(*7*) *Notwithstanding anything to the contrary in the Income Tax Acts, where any amount is under any provision of those Acts to be deducted from or set off against income in respect of any payments, loss or capital allowance, then—*

(*a*) if under that provision it is (*or is in the first instance*) to reduce the wife's earned income, or is to be deducted or set off in respect of payments made by her or, in the case of relief under Chapter III of this Part, in respect of a payment made by her as a subscription for shares, it shall be treated as reducing her earnings and as not reducing any other income; and

(*b*) in any other case, it shall be treated as not reducing the wife's earnings.

(8) Subsection (7) above shall not affect the giving of any relief under section 388 for a year of assessment for which no election under this section was in force.

(9) Income tax charged on the wife's earnings under subsection (3)(*a*) above shall, whether or not an application under section 283 is in force, be assessed and recovered as if she were a single woman, and any repayment of tax assessed in pursuance of this subsection shall be made to her.

(10) Where subsection (4) of section 284 applies for the purposes of subsections (1) to (3) of that section, it shall apply also for the purposes of this section; but, subject to that, nothing in this section shall be taken to affect the provisions of the Management Act as to returns.

Note. This section repealed by Finance Act 1988, s 148, Sch 14, Part VIII, with effect from the year 1990–91.

288. Elections under section 287—(1) An election under section 287 ('an election') must be made in such form and manner as the Board may prescribe and must be made not earlier than six months before the beginning of the year of assessment for which it is made nor later than 12 months after the end of that year or such later time as the Board may in any particular case allow.

(2) An election for any year of assessment shall, unless revoked, have effect for any subsequent year of assessment.

(3) An election in force for any year may be revoked by notice in such form and manner as the Board may prescribe and any such notice must be given jointly by the husband and the wife not later than 12 months after the end of that year or such later time as the Board may in any particular case allow.

(4) An election or revocation of an election under this section that could have been made jointly with a person who has died may, within the time permitted by this section, be made jointly with his personal representatives.

Note. This section repealed by Finance Act 1988, s 148, Sch 14, Part VIII, with effect from the year 1990–91.

* * * * *

CHAPTER IV

SPECIAL PROVISIONS

* * * * *

331. Scholarship income—(1) Income arising from a scholarship held by a person receiving full-time instruction at a university, college, school or other educational establishment shall be exempt from income tax, and no account shall be taken of any such income in computing the amount of income for income tax purposes.

(2) In this section 'scholarship' includes an exhibition, bursary or any other similar educational endowment.

* * * * *

PART IX

ANNUAL PAYMENTS AND INTEREST

Annual payments

[347A. General rule—(1) A payment to which this section applies shall not be a charge on the income of the person liable to make it, and accordingly—

(a) his income shall be computed without any deduction being made on account of the payment, and

(b) the payment shall not form part of the income of the person to whom it is made or of any other person.

(2) This section applies to any annual payment made by an individual which would otherwise be within the charge to tax under Case III of Schedule D except—

(a) a payment of interest;

(b) *a covenanted payment to charity (within the meaning given by section 660(3))*;

(c) a payment made for bona fide commercial reasons in connection with the individual's trade, profession or vocation; and

(d) a payment to which section 125(1) applies.

Note. Sub-s (2)(b) repealed by the Finance Act 2000, s 41(2), 156, Sch 40, Pt II(1), with effect in relation to covenanted payments made by companies on or after 1 April 2000.

(3) This section applies to a payment made by personal representatives (within the meaning given in section 701(4)) where—

(a) the deceased would have been liable to make the payment if he had not died, and

(b) this section would have applied to the payment if he had made it.

(4) A maintenance payment arising outside the United Kingdom shall not be within the charge to tax under Case V of Schedule D if, because of this section, it would not have been within the charge to tax under Case III had it arisen in the United Kingdom; and for this purpose 'maintenance payment' means a periodical payment (not being an instalment of a lump sum) which satisfies the conditions set out in paragraphs (a) and (b) of section 347B(5).

(5) No deduction shall be made under section 65(1)(b) [, *68(1)(b) or 192(3)*] [or 68(1)(b) of this Act or section 355 of ITEPA 2003 (deductions for certain payments by non-domiciled employees with foreign employers)] on account of an annuity or other annual payment which would not have been within the charge to tax under Case III of Schedule D if it had arisen in the United Kingdom.

Note. Words ', 68(1)(b) or 192(3)' in square brackets inserted by Finance (No 2) Act 1992, s 60, for the year 1992–93 and subsequent years of assessment. Words 'or 68(1)(b)' to 'with foreign employers)' in square brackets substituted for words ', 68(1)(b) or 192(3)' by the Income Tax (Earnings and Pensions) Act 2003, s 722, Sch 6, Pt 1, paras 1, 49 with effect, for the purposes of income tax for the year 2003–04 and subsequent years of assessment, and for the purposes of corporation tax for accounting periods ending after 5 April 2003.

(6) References in subsection (2) above to an individual include references to a Scottish partnership in which at least one partner is an individual.

[*(7) In subsection (2)(b) above 'a covenanted payment to charity' means a payment made under a covenant made otherwise than for consideration in money or money's worth in favour of a body of persons or trust established for charitable purposes only whereby the like annual payments (of which the payment in question is one) become payable for a period which may exceed three years and is not capable of earlier termination under any power exercisable without the consent of the persons for the time being entitled to the payments.*

(8) For the purposes of subsection (7) above the bodies mentioned in section 507 shall each be treated as a body of persons established for charitable purposes only.]

Note. Sub-ss (7), (8) repealed by the Finance Act 2000, s 41(2), 156, Sch 40, Pt II(1) with effect in relation to covenanted payments made by companies on or after 1 April 2000: see s 41(9)(b) and in relation to covenanted payments failing to be made by individuals on or after 6 April 2000: see s 41(9)(a). This section inserted by Finance Act 1988, s 36, in relation to any payment falling due on or after 15 March 1988, unless made in pursuance of an existing obligation. Sub-ss (7), (8) added by Finance Act 1995, s 74, Sch 17, para 4(2), for the year 1995–96 and subsequent years of assessment, and applying to every settlement, wherever and whenever it was made or entered into.

[347B. Qualifying maintenance payments—(1) [Subject to subsection (1A) below] in this section 'qualifying maintenance payment' means a periodical payment which—

(a) is made under an order made by a court *in the United Kingdom* [in a member State], or under a written agreement the *proper law of* [law applicable to] which is the law of *a part of the United Kingdom* [a member State or of a part of a member State],

(b) is made by one of the parties to a marriage (including a marriage which has been dissolved or annulled) either—

  (i) to or for the benefit of the other party and for the maintenance of the other party, or

  (ii) to the other party for the maintenance by the other party of any child of the family,

(c) is due at a time when—

  (i) the two parties are not a married couple living together, and

  (ii) the party to whom or for whose benefit the payment is made has not remarried, and

(d) is not a payment in respect of which relief from tax is available to the person making the payment under any provision of the Income Tax Acts other than this section.

Note. Words 'subject to subsection (1A) below 'inserted by the Finance Act 1999, s 36(1), with effect in relation to any payment falling due on or after 6 April 2000. Sub-s (1)(a) words in first and third pairs of square brackets substituted for words in italics by Finance (No 2) Act 1992, s 61, for the year 1992–93 and subsequent years of assessment. Words in second pair of square brackets substituted for words in italics by Contracts (Applicable Law) Act 1990, s 5, Sch 4, as from 1 April 1991.

[(1A) A periodical payment is not a qualifying maintenance payment unless either of the parties to the marriage mentioned in subsection (1)(b) above was born before 6th April 1935.]

Note. Sub-s (1A) inserted by the Finance Act 1999, s 36(2), with effect in relation to any payment falling due on or after 6 April 2000.

(2) *Notwithstanding section 347A(1)(a) but* subject to *subsections (3) and (4) [sub-section (3)]* below, a person making a claim for the purpose shall be entitled, *in computing his total income for a year of assessment, to deduct* [for a year of assessment to an income tax reduction calculated by reference to] an amount equal to the aggregate amount of any qualifying maintenance payments made by him which fall due in that year.

Note. First words in italics repealed, and second words in square brackets substituted for preceding words in italics, in relation to maintenance payments becoming due on or after 6 April 1994, by Finance Act 1994, ss 79(1), (3), 258, Sch 26, Part V(1). First words in square brackets substituted for preceding words in italics by the Finance Act 1999,s 36(3) with effect in relation to any payment falling due on or after 6 April 2000.

(3) *The amount which may be deducted under this section by a person in computing his total income for a year of assessment shall not exceed* [The amount by reference to which any income tax reduction is to be calculated under this section shall be limited to] the amount *of the difference between the higher (married person's) relief and the lower (single person's) relief under subsection (1) of section 257 as it applies for the year to a person not falling within subsection (2) or (3) of that section* [specified in *section 257A(1)* [section 257A(5A)] for the year].

Note. Words in first pair of square brackets substituted for words in italics by Finance Act 1994, s 79(1), (4), in relation to maintenance payments becoming due on or after 6 April 1994. Words in second pair of square brackets substituted for words in italics by Finance Act 1988, s 35, Sch 3, Part I, para 13, as from 29 July 1988, for the year 1990–91 and subsequent years of assessment. Words 'section 257A(5A)' substituted for words 'section 257A(1)' by the Finance Act 1999, s 36(4) with effect in relation to any payment falling due on or after 6 April 2000.

(4) *Where qualifying maintenance payments falling due in a year of assessment are made by a person who also makes other maintenance payments attracting relief for that year, subsection (3) above shall apply as if the limit imposed by it were reduced by an amount equal to the aggregate amount of those other payments.*

(5) *The reference in subsection (4) above to other maintenance payments attracting relief for a year is a reference to periodical payments which—*

    (a) *are made under an order made by a court (whether in the United Kingdom or elsewhere) or under a written or oral agreement, and*

    (b) *are made by a person—*

      (i) *as one of the parties to a marriage (including a marriage which has been dissolved or annulled) to or for the benefit of the other party to the marriage and for the maintenance of the other party, or*

     (ii) *to any person under 21 years of age for his own benefit, maintenance or education, or*

    (iii) *to any person for the benefit, maintenance or education of a person under 21 years of age,*

and in respect of which the person making them is entitled otherwise than under this section [by virtue of section 36(3) of Finance Act 1988 but otherwise than in accordance with section 38(2)(a) of that Act] to make a deduction in computing his income for the year.

Note. Sub-ss (4), (5) repealed by the Finance Act 1999, s 139, Sch 20, Pt III(6) with effect in relation to any payment falling due on or after 6 April 2000. Words in square brackets substituted for words in italics by Finance Act 1994, s 79(1), (5), in relation to maintenance payments becoming due on or after 6 April 1994.

[(5A) Where any person is entitled under this section for any year of assessment to an income tax reduction calculated by reference to the amount determined in accordance with *subsections (2) to (5)* [subsections (2) and (3)] above ('the relevant amount'), the amount of that person's liability for that year to income tax on his total income shall be the amount to which he would have been liable apart from this section less whichever is the smaller of—

    (a) the amount equal to *the appropriate percentage* [10 per cent] of the relevant amount; and

    (b) the amount which reduces his liability to nil;

and in this subsection 'the appropriate percentage' means 20 per cent for the year 1994–95 and 15 per cent for the year 1995–96 and subsequent years of assessment.

(5B) In determining for the purposes of subsection (5A) above the amount of income tax to which a person would be liable apart from any income tax reduction under this section, no account shall be taken of—

    (a) any income tax reduction under Chapter I of Part VII;

    (b) any relief by way of a reduction of liability to tax which is given in accordance with any arrangements having effect by virtue of section 788 or by way of a credit under section 790(1); or

    (c) any tax at the basic rate on so much of that person's income as is income the income tax on which he is entitled to charge against any other person or to deduct, retain or satisfy out of any payment.]

Note. Sub-ss (5A), (5B) inserted by Finance Act 1994, s 79(1), (6), as from 3 May 1994, in relation to maintenance payments becoming due on or after 6 April 1994. Sub-s (5A) words 'subsections (2) and (3)' substituted for words in italics by the Finance Act 1999, s36(5), with effect in relation to any payment falling due on or after 6 April 2000. Sub-s (5A)(a) words '10 per cent' substituted for words in italics by the Finance Act 1998, s 27(1)(b) with effect for the year 1999–2000 and subsequent years of assessment. Sub-s (5A) final words in italics repealed by the Finance Act 1998, s 165, Sch 27, Pt III(1) with effect for the year 1999–2000 and subsequent years of assessment.

(6) *The reference in subsection (1) above to a married couple living together shall be construed in accordance with section 282(1), but section 282(2) shall not apply for the purposes of this section.*

Note. Sub-s (6) repealed by Finance Act 1988, s 148, Sch 14, Part VIII, as from 29 July 1988, for the year 1990–91 and subsequent years of assessment.

(7) In this section—

'child of the family', in relation to the parties to a marriage, means a person under 21 years of age—

    (a) who is a child of both those parties, or

    (b) who (not being a person who has been boarded out with them by a public authority or voluntary organisation) has been treated by both of them as a child of their family;

'periodical payment' does not include an instalment of a lump sum.

(8) In *subsections (1)(a) and (5)(a)* [subsection (1)(a)] above, the reference to an order made by a court in the United Kingdom includes a reference to a *maintenance assessment* [maintenance calculation].

(9) Where—

    (a) any periodical payment is made under a *maintenance assessment* [maintenance calculation] by one of the parties to a marriage (including a marriage which has been dissolved or annulled),

    (b) the other party to the marriage is, for the purposes of the Child Support Act 1991 or (as the case may be) the Child Support (Northern Ireland) Order 1991, a parent of the child or children with respect to whom *the assessment* [the calculation] has effect,

    (c) *the assessment* [the calculation] was not made under section 7 of the Child Support Act 1991 (right of child in Scotland to apply for *maintenance assessment* [maintenance calculation]), and

    (d) any of the conditions mentioned in subsection (10) below is satisfied,

this section shall have effect as if the payment had been made to the other party for the maintenance by that other party of that child or (as the case may be) those children.

(10) The conditions are that—

    (a) the payment is made to the Secretary of State in accordance with regulations made under section 29 of the Child Support Act 1991, by virtue of subsection (3)(a)(ii) of that section;

    (b) the payment is made to the Department of Health and Social Services for Northern Ireland in accordance with regulations made under Article 29 of the Child Support (Northern Ireland) Order 1991, by virtue of paragraph (3)(a)(ii) of that Article;

    (c) the payment is retained by the Secretary of State in accordance with regulations made under section 41 of that Act;

    (d) the payment is retained by the Department of Health and Social Services for Northern Ireland in accordance with regulations made under Article 38 of that Order.

(11) In this section 'maintenance assessment' means a maintenance assessment made under the Child Support Act 1991 or the Child Support (Northern Ireland) Order 1991.

[(11) In this section 'maintenance calculation' means a maintenance calculation made under the Child Support Act 1991 or a maintenance assessment made under the Child Support (Northern Ireland) Order 1991.]

(12) Where any periodical payment is made to the Secretary of State or to the Department of Health and Social Services for Northern Ireland—

    (a) by one of the parties to a marriage (including a marriage which has been dissolved or annulled), and

    (*b*) *under an order made under section 106 of the Social Security Administration Act 1992 or section 101 of the Social Security Administration (Northern Ireland) Act 1992 (recovery of expenditure on benefit from person liable for maintenance) in respect of income support claimed by the other party to the marriage,*

[(b) under an order—
  (i) made under section 106 of the Social Security Administration Act 1992 or section 101 of the Social Security Administration (Northern Ireland) Act 1992 (recovery of expenditure on benefit from person liable for maintenance) in respect of income support claimed by the other party to the marriage; or
  (ii) made by virtue of section 23 of the Jobseekers Act 1995 (recovery of sums in respect of maintenance), or any corresponding enactment in Northern Ireland, in respect of an income-based jobseeker's allowance claimed by the other party to the marriage,]

this section shall have effect as if the payment had been made to the other party to the marriage to or for the benefit, and for the maintenance, of that other party or (as the case may be) to that other party for the maintenance of the child or children concerned.]

Note. Sub-ss (8)–(12) added by Finance (No 2) Act 1992, s 62(1), (4), (6), as from 6 April 1993, and in relation to payments falling due after 6 April 1993, so far as it concerns orders under sub-s (12)(b). Sub-s (12)(b) in square brackets substituted for sub-s (12)(b) in italics by Jobseekers Act 1995, s 41(4), Sch 2, para 15(2), as from 7 October 1996. Sub-s (8) words 'subsection (1)(a)' substituted for words in italics by the Finance Act 1999, s 36(6), with effect in relation to any payment falling due on or after 6 April 2000. Sub-s (8) words 'maintenance calculation' substituted for words in italics by the Child Support, Pensions and Social Security Act 2000, s 26, Sch 3, para 8(1), (2)(a) for certain cases with effect from 3 March 2003: see SI 2003/192, arts 3, 8, Sch. Sub-s (9) words 'maintenance calculation' substituted for words in italics by the Child Support, Pensions and Social Security Act 2000, s 26, Sch 3, para 8(1), (2)(a) for certain cases with effect from 3 March 2003: see SI 2003/192, arts 3, 8, Sch. Sub-s (9) words 'the calculation' substituted for words in italics by the Child Support, Pensions and Social Security Act 2000, s 26, Sch 3, para 8(1), (2)(b) for certain cases with effect from 3 March 2003: see SI 2003/192, arts 3, 8, Sch. Sub-s (11) substituted by the Child Support, Pensions and Social Security Act 2000, S26, Sch 3, para 8(1), (2)(c) for certain cases with effect from 3 March 2003: see SI 2003/192, arts 3, 8, Sch.

[(13) In subsection (12) above, 'income-based jobseeker's allowance' has the same meaning as in the Jobseekers Act 1995 or, for Northern Ireland, the same meaning as in any corresponding enactment in Northern Ireland.]]

Note. This section inserted by Finance Act 1988, s 36, in relation to any payment falling due on or after 15 March 1988, unless made in pursuance of an existing obligation. Sub-s (13) added by Jobseekers Act 1995, s 41(4), Sch 2, para 15(3), as from 7 October 1996.

*   *   *   *   *

351. Small maintenance payments—(*1*) *In this section 'small maintenance payments' means payments under an order made by a court in the United Kingdom—*
  (*a*) *by one of the parties to a marriage (including a marriage which has been dissolved or annulled) to or for the benefit of the other party to that marriage for that other party's maintenance,*
  (*b*) *to any person under 21 years of age for his own benefit, maintenance or education, or*
  (*c*)   *to any person for the benefit, maintenance or education of a person under 21 years of age,*
in respect of which the two conditions mentioned in subsection (2) below are satisfied; and 'small maintenance order' means an order providing for the making of small maintenance payments.
  (*2*) *The first of the conditions referred to in subsection (1) above is—*
  (*a*) *in the case of payments falling within paragraph (a) of that subsection, that the order for the time being requires them to be made—*
     (*i*)   *weekly at a rate not exceeding £48 per week, or*
     (*ii*) *monthly at a rate not exceeding £208 per month;*
  (*b*) *in the case of payments falling within paragraph (b) (but not within paragraph (a)) of that subsection, that the order for the time being requires them to be made—*

       (i) *weekly at a rate not exceeding £48 per week, or*

      (ii) *monthly at a rate not exceeding £208 per month;*

  (c) *in the case of payments falling within paragraph (c) (but not within paragraph (a) or (b)) of that subsection, that the order for the time being requires them to be made—*

       (i) *weekly at a rate not exceeding £25 per week, or*

      (ii) *monthly at a rate not exceeding £108 per month;*

and the second of those conditions is that the payments would fall within section 348 or 349(1), apart from subsections (3) of each of those sections and subsection (3) below.

   (3) Small maintenance payments shall be made without deduction of income tax.

   (4) Any sums paid in or towards the discharge of a small maintenance payment shall be chargeable under Case III of Schedule D, but the tax shall (notwithstanding anything in sections 64 to 67) be computed in all cases on the payments falling due in the year of assessment, so far as paid in that or any other year.

   (5) A person making a claim in that behalf shall be entitled, in computing his total income for any year of assessment for any of the purposes of the Income Tax Acts, to deduct sums paid by him in or towards the discharge of any small maintenance payments which fall due in that year; and, for the purposes of section 276, any amount which can be deducted under this subsection in computing the total income of a person shall be treated as if it were income the tax on which that person is entitled to charge against another person.

   (6) The Treasury may from time to time by order increase any, or all, of the amounts for the time being specified in subsection (2) above.

   (7) An order under subsection (6) above which increases the amount for the time being specified in sub-paragraph (i) of paragraph (a), (b) or (c) of subsection (2) above shall increase the amount for the time being specified in sub-paragraph (ii) of that paragraph so that it is 52 twelfths of the amount specified in sub-paragraph (i) by virtue of the order or, if that does not give a convenient round sum, such other amount as appears to the Treasury to be the nearest convenient round sum; and an order under that subsection may contain provision whereby it—

  (a) *does not in general affect payments falling due in the year of assessment in which it comes into force under small maintenance orders made before its coming into force, but*

  (b) *in the case of a small maintenance order which was made before that time but is varied or revived after that time, does apply in relation to payments falling due under that order at any time after the variation or revival.*

   (8) Where a court—

  (a) *makes or revives a small maintenance order, or*

  (b) *varies or revives an order so that it becomes, or ceases to be, a small maintenance order, or*

  (c) *changes the persons who are entitled to small maintenance payments,*

the court shall furnish to the Board, in such form as the Board may prescribe, particulars of the order or variation, as the case may be, the names of the persons affected by the order, and, so far as is known to the court, the addresses of those persons.

In this subsection—

       (i) *'the persons affected', in relation to a small maintenance order, means the person liable to make the payments under the order and any person for the time being entitled to the payments, and*

      (ii) *references to the variation of an order include references to the making of an order changing the persons entitled to the payments under it.*

Note. This section repealed by Finance Act 1988, s 148, Sch 14, Part IV, in relation to payments made after 5 April 1989 and in relation to orders and variations made after 5 April 1989.

352. Certificates of deduction of tax—(1) A person making any payment which is subject to deduction of income tax by virtue of section 339, 348, 349 *or 687* [, 480A or 687 or by virtue of regulations under section 477A(1)] shall, if the recipient so requests in writing, furnish him with a statement in writing showing the gross amount of the payment, the amount of tax deducted, and the actual amount paid.

Note. Words in square brackets substituted for words in italics by Finance Act 1990, s 30, Sch 5, para 11, in relation to payments made on or after 6 April 1991.

(2) The duty imposed by subsection (1) above shall be enforceable at the suit or instance of the person requesting the statement.

*   *   *   *   *

PART XV

SETTLEMENTS

CHAPTER 1A

LIABILITY OF SETTLOR

Main provisions

[660A. Income arising under settlement where settlor retains an interest—
(1) Income arising under a settlement during the life of the settlor shall be treated for all purposes of the Income Tax Acts as the income of the settlor and not as the income of any other person unless the income arises from property in which the settlor has no interest.

(2) Subject to the following provisions of this section, a settlor shall be regarded as having an interest in property if that property or any derived property is, or will or may become, payable to or applicable for the benefit of the settlor or his spouse in any circumstances whatsoever.

(3) The reference in subsection (2) above to the spouse of the settlor does not include—

(a) a person to whom the settlor is not for the time being married but may later marry, or

(b) a spouse from whom the settlor is separated under an order of a court, or under a separation agreement or in such circumstances that the separation is likely to be permanent, or

(c) the widow or widower of the settlor.

(4) A settlor shall not be regarded as having an interest in property by virtue of subsection (2) above if and so long as none of that property, and no derived property, can become payable or applicable as mentioned in that subsection except in the event of—

(a) the bankruptcy of some person who is or may become beneficially entitled to the property or any derived property, or

(b) an assignment of or charge on the property or any derived property being made or given by some such person, or

(c) in the case of a marriage settlement, the death of both parties to the marriage and of all or any of the children of the marriage, or

(d) the death of a child of the settlor who had become beneficially entitled to the property or any derived property at an age not exceeding 25.

(5) A settlor shall not be regarded as having an interest in property by virtue of subsection (2) above if and so long as some person is alive and under the age of 25 during whose life that property, or any derived property, cannot become payable or applicable as mentioned in that subsection except in the event of that person becoming bankrupt or assigning or charging his interest in the property or any derived property.

(6) The reference in subsection (1) above to a settlement does not include an outright gift by one spouse to the other of property from which income arises, unless—

(a) the gift does not carry a right to the whole of that income, or

(b) the property given is wholly or substantially a right to income.

For this purpose a gift is not an outright gift if it is subject to conditions, or if the property given or any derived property is or will or may become, in any circumstances whatsoever, payable to or applicable for the benefit of the donor.

(7) The reference in subsection (1) above to a settlement does not include an irrevocable allocation of pension rights by one spouse to the other in accordance with the terms of a relevant statutory scheme (within the meaning of Chapter I of Part XIV).

(8) Subsection (1) above does not apply to income arising under a settlement made by one party to a marriage by way of provision for the other—

(a) after the dissolution or annulment of the marriage, or

(b) while they are separated under an order of a court, or under a separation agreement or in such circumstances that the separation is likely to be permanent,

being income payable to or applicable for the benefit of that other party.

(9) Subsection (1) above does not apply to income consisting of—

(a) annual payments made by an individual for bona fide commercial reasons in connection with his trade, profession or vocation; or

(b) covenanted payments to charity (as defined by section 347A(7)).

[(b) qualifying donations for the purposes of section 25 of the Finance Act 1990]

[; or

(c) a benefit under an approved pension arrangement] [; or

(c) a benefit under a relevant pension scheme].

(10) In this section 'derived property', in relation to any property, means income from that property or any other property directly or indirectly representing proceeds of, or of income from, that property or income therefrom.

[(11) In this section 'approved pension arrangement' means—

(a) an approved scheme or exempt approved scheme;

(b) a relevant statutory scheme;

(c) a retirement benefits scheme set up by a government outside the United Kingdom for the benefit, or primarily for the benefit, of its employees;

(d) a contract or scheme which is approved under chapter III of Part XIV (retirement annuities);

(e) a personal pension scheme which is approved under chapter IV of that Part;

(f) an annuity purchased for the purpose of giving effect to rights under a scheme falling within any of paragraphs (a) to (c) and (e) above;

(g) any pension arrangements of any description which may be prescribed by regulations made by the Secretary of State.

(12) In subsection (11) above 'approved scheme', 'exempt approved scheme', 'relevant statutory scheme' and 'retirement benefits scheme' have the same meaning as in Chapter I of Part XIV.]]

[(11) In this section 'relevant pension scheme' means—

(a) a registered pension scheme;

(b) a pension scheme established by a government outside the United kingdom for the benefit, or primarily for the benefit, of its employees (or an annuity acquired using finds held for the purposes of such a pension scheme); or

(c) a pension scheme of any description which may be prescribed by regulations made by the Secretary of State.]

Note. Sub-s 7 repealed by the Finance Act 2000, s 61, 156, Sch 13, Pt I, paras 1, 26(1), (2) Sch 40, Pt II(4) with effect for the year 2001–02 and subsequent years of assessment. Sub-s(9)(b) substituted by the Finance Act 2000, s 41(6) with effect in relation to covenanted payments made by companies on or after 1 April 2000: see the Finance Act 2000, s 41(9)(b) and with effect in relation to covenanted payments falling to be made by individuals on or after 6 April 2000: see the Finance Act 2000, s 41(9)(a). Sub-s (9)(c) and word '; or' immediately preceding it inserted by the Finance Act 2000, s 61, Sch 13, Pt I, paras 1, 26(1), (3) with effect for the year 2001–02 and subsequent years of assessment. Sub-s (9)(c) and word '; or' immediately preceding it substituted by the Finance Act 2004, s 281(1), Sch 35, paras 2, 28(1), (2) with effect from 6 April 2006. Sub-ss (11), (12) inserted by the Finance Act

2000, s 61, Sch 13, Pt I, paras 1, 26(1), (4) with effect for the year 2001–02 and subsequent years of assessment. Sub-ss (11), (12) substituted by subsequent sub-s (11), by the Finance Act 2004, s 281(1), Sch 35, paras 2, 28(1), (3), with effect from 6 April 2006.

660B. Payments to unmarried minor children of settlor—(1) Income arising under a settlement which does not fall to be treated as income of the settlor under section 660A but which during the life of the settlor *is paid to or for the benefit of an unmarried minor child of the settlor in any year of assessment shall be treated for all the purposes of the Income Tax Acts as the income of the settlor for that year and not as the income of any other person.*

[(a) is paid to or for the benefit of an unmarried minor child of the settlor, or
   (b) would otherwise be treated (apart from this section) as income of an unmarried minor child of the settlor,]

in any year of assessment shall be treated for all the purposes of the Income Tax Acts as the income of the settlor for that year and not as the income of any other person.

(2) Where income arising under a settlement is retained or accumulated by the trustees, any payment whatsoever made thereafter by virtue or in consequence of the settlement, or any enactment relating thereto, to or for the benefit of an unmarried minor child of the settlor shall be deemed for the purposes of subsection (1) above to be a payment of income if or to the extent that there is available retained or accumulated income.

(3) There shall be taken to be available retained or accumulated income at any time when the aggregate amount of the income which has arisen under the settlement since it was made or entered into exceeds the aggregate amount of income so arising which has been—

(a) *treated as income of the settlor or a beneficiary, or*
(b) *paid (whether as income or capital) to or for the benefit of a beneficiary other than an unmarried minor child of the settlor, or*

[(a) treated as income of the settlor, or
   (b) paid (whether as income or capital) to or for the benefit of, or otherwise treated as the income of, a beneficiary other than an unmarried minor child of the settlor, or
(bb) treated as the income of an unmarried minor child of the settlor, and subject to tax, in any of the years 1995–96, 1996–97 or 1997–98, or]
   (c) applied in defraying expenses of the trustees which were properly chargeable to income (or would have been so chargeable but for any express provisions of the trust).

[(3A) For the purposes of subsection (3)(bb) above—
(a) the amount of a child's income that is subject to tax in a year of assessment is the amount ('the taxable amount') by which the child's total income for income tax purposes exceeds the aggregate amount of allowances that may be set against it; and
(b) income arising under the settlement that is treated as income of the child is subject to tax to the extent that it does not exceed the taxable amount.
In this subsection 'allowance' includes any deduction allowed against total income.]

(4) Where an offshore income gain (within the meaning of Chapter V of Part XVII) accrues in respect of a disposal of assets made by a trustee holding them for a person who would be absolutely entitled as against the trustee but for being a minor, the income which by virtue of section 761(1) is treated as arising by reference to that gain shall for the purposes of this section be deemed to be paid to that person.

(5) *Income paid to or for the benefit of a child of a settlor shall not be treated as provided in subsection (1) above for a year of assessment in which the aggregate amount paid to or for the benefit of that child which but for this subsection would be so treated does not exceed £100.*

[(5) If in any year of assessment the aggregate amount of a child's relevant settlement income does not exceed £100, subsection (1) does not apply in relation to that income.

A child's 'relevant settlement income' means income paid to or for the benefit of, or otherwise treated as income of, that child which apart from this subsection would be treated as income of the settlor under subsection (1).]

(6) In this section—

(a) 'child' includes a stepchild and an illegitimate child;

(b) 'minor' means a person under the age of 18 years, and 'minor child' shall be construed accordingly; and

(c) references to payments include payments in money or money's worth.

Note. Sub-s (1) para (a) numbered as such and para (b) and the word 'or' immediately preceding it inserted by the Finance Act 1999, s 64(1), with effect in relation to income arising under a settlement made or entered into on or after 9 March 1999 and income arising under a settlement made or entered into before that date so far as it arises directly or indirectly from funds provided on or after that date.

Sub-s (3) paras (a)–(b) substituted for paras (a) and (b) in italics by the Finance Act 1999, s 64(2), with effect in relation to any payment within sub-s (2) above made on or after 9 March 1999 (whenever the facts mentioned in sub-s (3) above occurred). Sub-s (3A) inserted by the Finance Act 1999, 64(3), with effect in relation to any payment within sub-s (2) above made on or after 9 March 1999 (whenever the facts mentioned in sub-s (3) above occurred).

Sub-s (5) substituted for sub-s (5) in italics by the Finance Act 1999, s 64(4), with effect in relation to income arising under a settlement made or entered into on or after 9 March 1999 and income arising under a settlement made or entered into before that date so far as it arises directly or indirectly from funds provided on or after that date.

660C. Nature of charge on settlor—(1) Tax chargeable by virtue of this Chapter shall be charged *under Case VI of Schedule D.*

[(a) in the case of incoming falling within subsection (1A) below, as if it were income to which section 1A applies by virtue of subsection (2)(b) of that section; and

(b) in the case of any other income, under Case VI of Schedule D].

[(1A) Income falls within this subsection if it is—

(a) income chargeable under Schedule F;

(b) income to which section 1A applies by virtue of its being equivalent foreign income falling within subsection (3)(b) of that section and chargeable under Case V of Schedule D;

(c) a distribution in relation to which section 233(1) applies;

(d) a qualifying distribution whose amount or value is determined in accordance with section 233(1A);

(e) a non-qualifying distribution, within the meaning of section 233(1B);

(f) income treated as arising by virtue of section 249;

(g) income treated as received by virtue of section 421(1)(a).]

(2) In computing the liability to income tax of a settlor chargeable by virtue of this Chapter the same deductions and reliefs shall be allowed as would have been allowed if the income treated as his by virtue of this Chapter had been received by him.

(3) Subject to section 833(3), income which is treated by virtue of this Chapter as income of a settlor shall be deemed for the purposes of this section to be the highest part of his income.

Note. Sub-s (1) paras (a), (b) substituted for words in italics by the Finance (No 2) Act 1997 s 34, Sch 4, para 14(2), with effect in relation to the year 1999-00 and subsequent years of assessment. Sub-s (1A) inserted by the Finance (Nos 2) Act 1997, s 34, Sch 4, para 14(3), with effect in relation to the year 1999–00 and subsequent years of assessment.

660D. Adjustments between settlor and trustees, etc—(1) Where by virtue of this Chapter income tax becomes chargeable on and is paid by a settlor, he is entitled—

(a) to recover from any trustee, or any other person to whom the income is payable by virtue or in consequence of the settlement, the amount of the tax so paid; and

(b) for that purpose to require an officer of the Board to furnish to him a certificate specifying the amount of income in respect of which he has so paid tax and the amount of tax so paid.

A certificate so furnished is conclusive evidence of the facts stated therein.

(2) Where a person obtains, in respect of an allowance or relief, a repayment of income tax in excess of the amount of the repayment to which he would, but for this Chapter, have been entitled, an amount equal to the excess shall be paid by him to the trustee, or other person to whom the income is payable by virtue or in consequence of the settlement, or, where there are two or more such persons, shall be apportioned among those persons as the case may require.

If any question arises as to the amount of a payment or as to an apportionment to be made under this subsection, that question shall be decided by the General Commissioners whose decision shall be final.

(3) Nothing in this Chapter shall be construed as excluding a charge to tax on the trustees as persons by whom any income is received.

Supplementary provisions

660E. Application to settlements by two or more settlors—(1) In the case of a settlement where there is more than one settlor, this Chapter shall have effect in relation to each settlor as if he were the only settlor, as follows.

(2) In this Chapter, in relation to a settlor—

(a) references to the property comprised in a settlement include only property originating from that settlor, and

(b) references to income arising under the settlement include only income originating from that settlor.

(3) For the purposes of section 660B there shall be taken into account, *in relation to a settlor, as income paid to or for the benefit of a child of the settlor* [in relation to a child of the settlor] only—

(a) income originating from that settlor, and

(b) in a case in which section 660B(2) applies, payments which are under that provision (as adapted by subsection (4) below) to be deemed to be payments of income.

(4) In applying section 660B(2) to a settlor—

(a) the reference to income arising under the settlement includes only income originating from that settlor; and

(b) the reference to any payment made by virtue or in consequence of the settlement or any enactment relating thereto includes only a payment made out of property originating from that settlor or income originating from that settlor.

(5) References in this section to property originating from a settlor are references to—

(a) property which that settlor has provided directly or indirectly for the purposes of the settlement; and

(b) property representing that property; and

(c) so much of any property which represents both property so provided and other property as, on a just apportionment, represents the property so provided.

(6) References in this section to income originating from a settlor are references to—

(a) income from property originating from that settlor; and

(b) income provided directly or indirectly by that settlor.

(7) In subsections (5) and (6) above—

(a) references to property or income which a settlor has provided directly or indirectly include references to property or income which has been provided directly or indirectly by another person in pursuance of reciprocal arrangements with that settlor, but do not include references to property or income which that settlor has provided directly or indirectly in pursuance of reciprocal arrangements with another person; and

(b) references to property which represents other property include references to property which represents accumulated income from that other property.

Note. Sub-s (3) words 'in relation to a child of the settlor' substituted for words in italics by the Finance Act 1999, s 64(7), with effect from 27 July 1999 in the absence of any specific commencement provision.

660F. Power to obtain information. An officer of the Board may by notice require any party to a settlement to furnish him within such time as he may direct (not being less than 28 days) with such particulars as he thinks necessary for the purposes of this Chapter.

660G. Meaning of 'settlement' and related expressions—(1) In this Chapter—

'settlement' includes any disposition, trust, covenant, agreement, arrangement or transfer of assets, and

'settlor', in relation to a settlement, means any person by whom the settlement was made.

(2) A person shall be deemed for the purposes of this Chapter to have made a settlement if he has made or entered into the settlement directly or indirectly, and, in particular, but without prejudice to the generality of the preceding words, if he has provided or undertaken to provide funds directly or indirectly for the purpose of the settlement, or has made with any other person a reciprocal arrangement for that other person to make or enter into the settlement.

(3) References in this Chapter to income arising under a settlement include, subject to subsection (4) below, any income chargeable to income tax by deduction or otherwise, and any income which would have been so chargeable if it had been received in the United Kingdom by a person domiciled, resident and ordinarily resident in the United Kingdom.

(4) Where the settlor is not domiciled, or not resident, or not ordinarily resident, in the United Kingdom in a year of assessment, references in this Chapter to income arising under a settlement do not include income arising under the settlement in that year in respect of which the settlor, if he were actually entitled thereto, would not be chargeable to income tax by deduction or otherwise by reason of his not being so domiciled, resident or ordinarily resident.

But where such income is remitted to the United Kingdom in circumstances such that, if the settlor were actually entitled to that income when remitted, he would be chargeable to income tax by reason of his residence in the United Kingdom, it shall be treated for the purposes of this Chapter as arising under the settlement in the year in which it is remitted.]

Note. Chapter 1A, (ss 660A–660G) inserted (in place of ss 660–676, 683–685) by Finance Act 1995, s 74, Sch 17, Part I, para 1, for the year 1995–96 and subsequent years of assessment and applying to every settlement, wherever and whenever it was made or entered into.

CHAPTER *II*

SETTLEMENTS ON CHILDREN

*　*　*　*　*

663. The general rule—(*1*) *Where, by virtue or in consequence of any settlement to which this Chapter applies and during the life of the settlor, any income is paid to or for the benefit of the settlor in any year of assessment, the income shall, if at the time of the payment the child was unmarried and below the age of 18, be treated for all the purposes of the Income Tax Acts as the income of the settlor for that year and not as the income of any other person.*

(*2*) *Where an offshore income gain (within the meaning of Chapter V of Part XVII) accrues in respect of a disposal of assets made by a person holding them as trustee for a person who would be absolutely entitled as against the trustee but for being an infant, the income which by virtue of section 761(1) is treated as arising by reference to that gain shall for the purposes of this Chapter be deemed to be paid to the infant; and in this subsection, in relation to Scotland, 'infant' means pupil or minor [person under the age of 18 years].*

Note. Words in square brackets substituted for words 'pupil or minor' by Age of Legal Capacity (Scotland) Act 1991, s 10, Sch 1, para 4, as from 25 September 1991.

(*3*) *This Chapter applies to every settlement, wheresoever it was made or entered into, and whether it was made or entered into before or after the passing of this Act, except a settlement made or entered into before 22nd April 1936 which immediately before that date was irrevocable.*

Paragraph 10 of Schedule 30 shall have effect as respects certain earlier settlements on children.

(*4*) *Income paid to or for the benefit of a child of a settlor shall not be treated as provided in subsection (1) above for any year of assessment in which the aggregate amount of the income paid to or for the benefit of that child, which, but for this subsection, would be so treated by virtue of subsection (1) above, does not exceed £5 [£100].*

Note. Sum '£100' substituted for sum '£5' by Finance Act 1990, s 82, for the year 1991–92 and subsequent years of assessment.

(*5*) *This Chapter shall not apply in relation to any income arising under a settlement in any year of assessment for which the settlor is not chargeable to income tax as a resident in the United Kingdom, and references in this Chapter to income shall be construed accordingly.*

Note. Chapter II (ss 663–670) repealed by Finance Act 1995, s 162, Sch 29, Part VIII(8), for the year 1995–96 and subsequent years of assessment and applying to every settlement, wherever and whenever it was made or entered into.

664. Accumulation settlements—(*1*) *Subject to the provisions of this section, for the purposes of this Chapter—*

(*a*) *income which, by virtue or in consequence of a settlement to which this Chapter applies, is so dealt with that it, or assets representing it, will or may become payable or applicable to or for the benefit of a child of the settlor in the future (whether on fulfilment of a condition, or the happening of a contingency, or as the result of the exercise of a power or discretion conferred on any person, or otherwise) shall be deemed to be paid to or for the benefit of that child; and*

(*b*) *any income so dealt with which is not required by the settlement to be allocated, at the time when it is so dealt with, to any particular child or children of the settlor shall be deemed to be paid in equal shares to or for the benefit of each of the children to or for the benefit of whom or any of whom the income or assets representing it will or may become payable or applicable.*

(*2*) *Where any income is dealt with as mentioned in subsection (1) above by virtue or in consequence of a settlement to which this Chapter applies, being a settlement which, at the time when the income is so dealt with, is an irrevocable settlement—*

(*a*) *subsection (1) above shall not apply to that income unless and except to the extent that that income consists of, or represents directly or indirectly, sums paid by the settlor which are allowable as deductions in computing his total income; and*

(*b*) *subject to subsection (3) below, any sum whatsoever paid thereafter by virtue or in consequence of the settlement, or any enactment relating thereto, to or for the benefit of a child of the settlor, being a child who at the time of the payment is unmarried and below the age of 18, shall be deemed for the purposes of section 663 to be paid as income.*

(3) *Subsection (2)(b) above shall not apply if and to the extent that the sum paid as mentioned in that paragraph together with any other sums previously so paid (whether to that child or to any other child who, at the time of the payment, was unmarried and below the age of 18) exceeds the aggregate amount of the income which, by virtue or in consequence of the settlement, has been paid to or for the benefit of a child of the settlor, or dealt with as mentioned in subsection (1) above, since the date when the settlement took effect or the date when it became irrevocable, whichever is the later.*

Note. See note to s 663.

665. Meaning of 'irrevocable'—(1) *For the purposes of this Chapter, a settlement shall not be deemed to be irrevocable if its terms provide—*

(a) *for the payment to the settlor or, during the life of the settlor, to the wife or husband of the settlor for his or her benefit, or for the application for the benefit of the settlor or, during the life of the settlor, of the wife or husband of the settlor, of any income or assets in any circumstances whatsoever during the life of the settlor's child; or*

(b) *for the determination of the settlement by the act or on the default of any person, or*

(c) *for the payment of any penalty by the settlor in the event of his failing to comply with the provisions of the settlement.*

In this section 'the settlor's child', in relation to any settlement, means any child of the settlor to or for the benefit of whom any income, or assets representing it, is or are or may be payable or applicable by virtue or in consequence of the settlement.

(2) *For the purposes of this Chapter, a settlement shall not be deemed to be revocable by reason only—*

(a) *that it contains a provision under which any income or assets will or may become payable to or applicable for the benefit of the settlor, or the wife or husband of the settlor, on the bankruptcy of the settlor's child or in the event of an assignment of or charge on that income or those assets being executed by the settlor's child; or*

(b) *that it provides for the determination of the settlement by the act or on the default of any person in such a manner that the determination will not, during the lifetime of the settlor's child, benefit the settlor or the wife or husband of the settlor; or*

(c) *in the case of a settlement to which section 33 of the Trustee Act 1925 applies, that it directs income to be held for the benefit of the settlor's child on protective trusts, unless the trust period is a period less than the life of the child or the settlement specifies some event on the happening of which the child would, if the income were payable during the trust period to him absolutely during that period, be deprived of the right to receive all or part of the income.*

Note. See note to s 663.

666. Interest paid by trustees—(1) *Where interest is paid by the trustees of a settlement to which this Chapter applies there shall be deemed for the purposes of this Chapter to be paid to or for the benefit of a child of the settlor who at the time of the payment is unmarried and below the age of 18 (in addition to any other amount deemed to be so paid) an amount equal to a fraction—*

$$\frac{B}{A}$$

of the interest, where—

A   *is the whole of the income arising under the settlement in the year of assessment, less any expenses of the trustees of the settlement paid in that year which, in the absence of any express provision of the settlement, would be properly chargeable to income, and*

B   *is such part of A as is paid to or for the benefit of any child of the settlor who is unmarried and below the age of 18.*

(2) *This section shall not apply to interest in respect of which relief from tax is allowable under any provision of the Income Tax Acts or to interest payable to the settlor or the wife of the settlor (if living with the settlor).*

(3) Nothing in this section shall be construed as affecting the liability to tax of the person receiving or entitled to the interest.

(4) For the purpose of this section 'income arising under the settlement' has the meaning given by section 681, which for that purpose shall be deemed to apply in relation to settlements to which this Chapter applies as it applies in relation to settlements to which Chapter III of this Part applies.

(5) In this section the reference to the trustees' expenses exclude sums mentioned in section 682(1)(a).

Note. See note to s 663.

667. Adjustments between disponor and trustees—(1) Where, by virtue of this Chapter, any income tax becomes chargeable on and is paid by the person by whom a settlement was made or entered into, that person shall be entitled—

  (a) to recover from any trustee or other person to whom the income is payable by virtue or in consequence of the settlement the amount of the tax so paid; and

  (b) for that purpose to require an inspector to furnish to him a certificate specifying the amount of income in respect of which he has so paid tax and the amount of the tax so paid,

and any certificate so furnished shall be conclusive evidence of the facts appearing thereby.

(2) Where any person obtains in respect of any allowance or relief a repayment of income tax in excess of the amount of the repayment to which he would but for the provisions of this Chapter have been entitled, an amount equal to the excess shall be paid by him to the trustee or other person to whom the income is payable by virtue or in consequence of the settlement, or, where there are two or more such persons, shall be apportioned among those persons as the case may require.

If any question arises as to the amount of any payment or as to any apportionment to be made under this subsection, that question shall be decided by the General Commissioners whose decision thereon shall be final.

(3) Subject to section 833(3), any income which is deemed by virtue of this Chapter to be the income of any person shall be deemed to be the highest part of his income.

Note. See note to s 663.

668. Application of Chapter II to settlements by two or more settlors—(1) In the case of any settlement where there is more than one settlor, this Chapter shall, subject to the provisions of this section, have effect in relation to each settlor as if he were the only settlor.

(2) In the case of any such settlement, only the following can, for the purposes of this Chapter, be taken into account, in relation to any settlor, as income paid by virtue or in consequence of the settlement to or for the benefit of a child of the settlor, that is to say—

  (a) income originating from that settlor; and

  (b) in a case in which section 664(2)(b) applies, any sums which are under that paragraph to be deemed to be paid as income.

(3) In applying section 664(2)(b) to any settlor—

  (a) the references to sums paid by virtue or in consequence of the settlement or any enactment relating thereto include only sums paid out of property originating from that settlor or income originating from that settlor; and

  (b) the reference to income which by virtue or in consequence of the settlement has been paid to or for the benefits of a child of the settlor or dealt with as mentioned in section 664(1) includes only income originating from that settlor.

(4) References in this section to property originating from a settlor are references to—

  (a) property which that settlor has provided directly or indirectly for the purposes of the settlement; and

  (b) property representing that property; and

  (c) so much of any property which represents both property provided as mentioned in paragraph (a) above and other property as, on a just apportionment, represents the property so provided.

(5) *References in this section to income originating from a settlor are references to—*

(a) *income from property originating from that settlor; and*

(b) *income provided directly or indirectly by that settlor.*

(6) *In subsections (4) and (5) above—*

(a) *references to property or income which a settlor has provided directly or indirectly include references to property or income which has been provided directly or indirectly by another person in pursuance of reciprocal arrangements with that settlor but do not include references to property or income which that settlor has provided directly or indirectly in pursuance of reciprocal arrangements with another person; and*

(b) *references to property which represents other property include references to property which represents accumulated income from that other property.*

Note. See note to s 663.

669. Power to obtain information under Chapter II.   *An inspector may by notice require any party to a settlement to furnish him within such time as he may direct (not being less than 28 days) with such particulars as he thinks necessary for the purposes of this Chapter.*

Note. See note to s 663.

670. Interpretation of Chapter II.   *In this chapter—*

'child' *includes a stepchild and an illegitimate child;*

'settlement' *includes any disposition, trust, covenant, agreement, arrangement or transfer of assets;*

'settlor', *in relation to a settlement, includes any person by whom the settlement was made or entered into directly or indirectly, and in particular (but without prejudice to the generality of the preceding words of this definition) includes any person who has provided or undertaken to provide funds directly or indirectly for the purpose of the settlement, or has made with any other person a reciprocal arrangement for that other person to make or enter into the settlement;*

'income', *except in the phrase (occurring in section 663(1)) 'be treated for all the purposes of the Income Tax Acts as the income of the settlor for that year and not as the income of any other person', includes any income chargeable to income tax by deduction or otherwise and any income which would have been so chargeable if it had been received in the United Kingdom by a person resident and ordinarily resident in the United Kingdom.*

Note. See note to s 663.

MATRIMONIAL PROCEEDINGS (TRANSFERS) ACT 1988

(1988 c 18)

An Act to empower the High Court to transfer to county courts certain matrimonial proceedings and to validate certain High Court orders purporting to transfer such proceedings to county courts; and for connected purposes.   [19 May 1988]

1. Transfer to county courts of proceedings transferred to the High Court before 28 April 1986—(1) (*Amends Matrimonial and Family Proceedings Act 1984, s 38(2) (p 2965)*)

(2) Where before the passing of this Act the High Court has made an order purporting to transfer to a county court the whole or any part of any such proceedings as are mentioned in subsection (3) below, the order shall be deemed not to be, and never to have been, invalid by reason of the fact that the proceedings were not transferable under section 38 of the Matrimonial and Family Proceedings Act 1984.

(3) The proceedings referred to above are any matrimonial cause or matter which at the time of the order was pending in the High Court by virtue of its having been transferred from a county court before 28 April 1986, otherwise than under section 41 of the County Courts Act 1984.

(4) Where before the passing of this Act the High Court has continued to exercise jurisdiction in a transferred cause because of the invalidity of the order purporting to transfer the proceedings to a county court and, in so exercising jurisdiction, has granted a decree which has been made absolute, subsection (2) above shall not have effect—

(a) to invalidate an order made in the proceedings by the High Court; or

(b) to validate an order made in the proceedings by the county court;

and if, immediately before the passing of this Act, the proceedings were still pending in the High Court, that court shall continue to have jurisdiction in them notwithstanding the validation of the purported transfer to the county court.

(5) The reference in subsection (4) above to a transferred cause is to a matrimonial cause which the High Court has purported to transfer to a county court by means of an order validated by this Act.

2. Short title. This Act may be cited as the Matrimonial Proceedings (Transfers) Act 1988.

Commencement. Act in force 19 May 1988 (ie the date of Royal Assent).

FINANCE ACT 1988

(1988 c 39)

An Act to grant certain duties, to alter other duties, and to amend the law relating to the National Debt and the Public Revenue, and to make further provision in connection with Finance. [29 July 1988]

*   *   *   *   *

PART III

INCOME TAX, CORPORATION TAX AND CAPITAL GAINS TAX

CHAPTER I

GENERAL

Tax rates and personal reliefs.

37. Maintenance payments under existing obligations: 1988-89—(1) This section applies to any annual payment due in the year 1988–89 which—

(a) is made in pursuance of an existing obligation under an order made by a court (whether in the United Kingdom or elsewhere) or under a written or oral agreement,

(b) is made by one of the parties to a marriage (including a marriage which has been dissolved or annulled) either—

    (i) to or for the benefit of the other party and for the maintenance of the other party, or

    (ii) to the other party for the maintenance by the other party of any child of the family,

(c) is due at a time when—

    (i) the two parties are not a married couple living together, and

    (ii) the party to whom or for whose benefit the payments are made has not remarried, and

(d) is within the charge to tax under Case III or Case V of Schedule D, and is not by virtue of Part XV of the Taxes Act 1988 treated for any purpose as the income of the person making it.

(2) On making a claim for the purpose a person chargeable to tax in respect of payments to which this section applies shall be entitled, in computing his total income for the year 1988–89, to deduct an amount equal to the aggregate amount of the payments, or £1,490, whichever is less.

38. Maintenance payments under existing obligations: 1989⁻90 onwards—
(1) This section applies to any annual payment due in the year 1989–90 or any subsequent year of assessment which—

    (a) is made in pursuance of an existing obligation under an order made by a court (whether in the United Kingdom or elsewhere) or under a written or oral agreement,

    (b) is made by an individual—

        (i) as one of the parties to a marriage (including a marriage which has been dissolved or annulled) to or for the benefit of the other party to the marriage and for the maintenance of the other party, or

        (ii) to any person under 21 years of age for his own benefit, maintenance or education, or

        (iii) to any person for the benefit, maintenance or education of a person under 21 years of age, and

    (c) is (apart from this section) within the charge to tax under Case III or Case V of Schedule D, and is not by virtue of Part XV of the Taxes Act 1988 treated for any purpose as the income of the person making it.

(2) A payment to which this section applies shall not be a charge on the income of the person liable to make it, *but—*

    (a) that person shall be entitled, on making a claim for the purpose, to make a deduction of an amount determined in accordance with subsection (3) below in computing his total income for the year of assessment in which the payment falls due, and

    (b) the payment shall form part of the income of the recipient, but subject to subsections (4) and (5) below.

(3) The amount which a person may deduct under subsection (2)(a) above in computing his total income for a year of assessment shall be equal to the aggregate amount of the payments made by him which fall due in that year and to which this section applies, except that it shall not in any event exceed [amount (if any) by which the relevant aggregate exceeds the amount specified in section 257A(1) of the Taxes Act 1988 for the year; and in this subsection and subsection (3A) below 'the relevant aggregate' means whichever is the smaller of the following, that is to say, the aggregate amount of the payments made by him which fall due in that year and to which this section applies and] the aggregate amount of any payments due in the year 1988–89—

    (a) which satisfy the conditions in paragraphs (a), (b) and (c) of subsection (1) above, and

    (b) in respect of which he was entitled to make a deduction in computing his income for that year.

Note. Words in italics repealed by the Finance Act 1999, s 139, Sch 20, Pt III(6), with effect in relation to any payment falling due on or after 6 April 2000. Words in square brackets substituted in relation to maintenance payments becoming due on or after 6 April 1994, by Finance Act 1994, s 79, as from 3 May 1994.

[(3A) Sections 347A and 347B of the Taxes Act 1988 (except, in the case of section 347A, so far as it restricts the extent to which any payment is to be treated as forming part of the income of the person to whom it is made or any other person) shall have effect as if so much of the relevant aggregate for any year of assessment as does not exceed the amount specified for that year in section 257A(1) of that Act were a qualifying maintenance payment made otherwise than in pursuance of an existing obligation.]

Note. Sub-s (3) repealed by the Finance act 1999, s 139, Sch 20, Pt III(6) with effect in relation to any payment falling due on or after 6 April 2000. Sub-s (3A) inserted in relation to maintenance payments becoming due on or after 6 April 1994, by Finance Act 1994, s 79, as from 3 May 1994.

(4) The amount which, by virtue of subsection (2)(b) above, is treated as forming part of a person's income for a year of assessment by reason of payments made by another person ('the payer') shall not exceed the aggregate amount of any payments made by the payer which—

(a) formed part of the same recipient's income for the year 1988–89, and

(b) satisfy the conditions in paragraphs (a), (b) and (c) of subsection (1) above.

(5) The amount which, by virtue of subsection (2)(b) above, would apart from this subsection be treated as forming part of a person's income for a year of assessment by reason of payments within subsection (6) below shall, if he makes a claim for the purpose, be reduced by the amount of the difference between the higher (married person's) relief and the lower (single person's) relief under subsection (1) of section 257 of the Taxes Act 1988 as it applies for that year to a person not falling within subsection (2) or (3) of that section [specified in section 257A(1) of the Taxes Act 1988 for the year].

Note. Sub-ss (4), (5) repealed by the Finance Act 1999, s 139, Sch 20, Pt III(6) with effect in relation to any payment falling due on or after 6 April 2000. Words in square brackets substituted by Finance Act 1988, s 35, Sch 3, Part II, for the year 1990–91 and subsequent years of assessment, as from 29 July 1988.

(6) The payments referred to in subsection (5) above are payments which—

(a) are made by one of the parties to a marriage (including a marriage which has been dissolved or annulled) either—

(i) to or for the benefit of the other party and for the maintenance of the other party, or

(ii) to the other party for the maintenance by the other party of any child of the family, and

(b) are due at a time when—

(i) the two parties are not a married couple living together, and

(ii) the party to whom or for whose benefit the payments are made has not remarried.

Note. Sub-s (6) repealed by the Finance Act 1999, s 139, Sch 20, Pt III(6) with effect in relation to any payment falling due on or after 6 April 2000.

(7) A payment to which this section applies shall be made without deduction of income tax.

(8) A payment to which this section applies shall be within the charge to tax under Case III or (if it arises outside the United Kingdom) Case V of Schedule D; and tax chargeable under Case III shall, notwithstanding anything in sections 64 to 67 of the Taxes Act 1988, be computed on the payments falling due in the year of assessment, so far as paid in that or any other year.

Note. Sub-s (8) repealed by the Finance Act 1999, s 139, Sch 20, Pt III(6) with effect in relation to any payment falling due on or after 6 April 2000.

[(8A) The reference in subsection (1)(a) above to an order made by a court includes a reference to a *maintenance assessment made* [maintenance calculation or maintenance assessment made respectively] under the Child Support Act 1991 or under the Child Support (Northern Ireland) Order 1991.]

Note. Sub-s (8A) inserted by Finance (No 2) Act 1992, s 62, as from 6 April 1993. Words 'maintenance calculation' or 'maintenance assessment made respectively' substituted for words in italics by the Child Support, Pensions and Social Security Act 2000, s 26, Sch 3, para 9, with effect from 3 March 2003 for certain cases.

(9) No deduction shall be made under section 65(1)(b) [, *68(1)(b) or 192(3)*] [or 68(1)(b)] of the Taxes Act 1988 [or section 355 of the Income Tax (Earnings and Pensions) Act 2003] on account of a payment to which this section applies.

Note. Words '68(1)(b) 192(3)' in square brackets inserted by Finance (No 2) Act 1992, s 60, as from 6 April 1993, for the year 1992–93 and subsequent years of assessment. Words '68(1)(b)' substituted for words in italics and words 'or section 355 of the Income Tax (Earnings and Pensions) Act 2003' inserted by the Finance Act 2004, s 92, Sch 17, para 10(3) with effect from 22 July 2004, the date of the Royal Assent of the Finance Act 2004, in the absence of any specific commencement provision.

39. Maintenance payments under existing obligations: election for new rules—*(1) If an election is duly made for the purpose by any person, section 36 above shall have effect in relation to all payments made by him—*

(a)   to which section 37 or section 38 above would apply apart from the election, and

(b)   which fall due in a year of assessment for which the election has effect;

and accordingly sections 37 and 38 shall not apply to the payments.

(2) An election under subsection (1) above—

(a)   shall be made in such form and manner as the Board may prescribe,

(b)   shall be made not later than twelve months after the end of [on or before the first anniversary of the 31st January next following] the first year of assessment for which it is to have effect,

(c)   shall have effect for any subsequent year of assessment, and

(d)   shall be irrevocable.

Note. Words in square brackets in sub-s (2)(b) substituted by Finance Act 1996, s 135(1), (2), Sch 21, para 25, for the year 1996–97 and subsequent years of assessment.

(3) A person making an election under subsection (1) above shall, before the end of the period of 30 days beginning with the day on which it is made, give notice of it to every recipient of a payment affected by the election.

Note. Repealed by the Finance Act 1999, s 139, Sch 20, Pt III(6) with effect in relation to any payment falling due on or after 6 April 2000.

40. Provisions supplementary to sections 37 to 39—(1) In sections 37 to 39 above—

'child of the family', in relation to the parties to a marriage, means a person under 21 years of age—

(a)   who is a child of both those parties, or

(b)   who (not being a person who has been boarded out with them by a public authority or voluntary organisation) has been treated by both of them as a child of their family;

'existing obligation' has the same meaning as in section 36(3) above.

(2) The references in sections 38(2)(b) and (4) and 39(3) above to the recipient of a payment are, in a case of the kind described in sections 37(1)(b)(i) and 38(1)(b)(i), references to the other party there mentioned.

(3) The references in sections 37 and 38 above to a married couple living together shall be construed in accordance with section 282(1) of the Taxes Act 1988, but section 282(2) shall not apply for the purposes of those sections.

Note. Sub-s (1) words in italics repealed by the Finance Act 1999, s 139, Sch 20, Pt III(6) with effect in relation to any payment falling due on or after 6 April 2000. Sub-s(2) repealed by the Finance Act 1999, s 139, Sch 20, Pt III(6) with effect in relation to any payment falling due on or after 6 April 2000. Sub-s (3) repealed by Finance Act 1988, s 148, Sch 14, Part VIII, with effect from the year 1990–91.

*   *   *   *   *

CHAPTER IV

CAPITAL GAINS

Unification of rates of tax on income and capital gains

*   *   *   *   *

98. Rates of capital gains tax—*(1) Subject to the provisions of this section and sections 99 and 100 below, the rate of capital gains tax in respect of gains accruing to a person in a year of assessment shall be equivalent to the basic rate of income tax for the year.*

(2) If income tax is chargeable at the higher rate in respect of any part of the income of an individual for a year of assessment, the rate of capital gains tax in respect of gains accruing to him in the year shall be equivalent to the higher rate.

(3) If no income tax is chargeable at the higher rate in respect of the income of an individual for a year of assessment, but the amount on which he is chargeable to capital gains tax exceeds the unused part of his basic rate band, the rate of capital gains tax on the excess shall be equivalent to the higher rate of income tax for the year.

(4) The reference in subsection (3) above to the unused part of an individual's basic rate band is a reference to the amount by which the basic rate limit exceeds his total income (as reduced by any deductions made in accordance with the Income Tax Acts).

Note. This section repealed by Taxation of Chargeable Gains Act 1992, s 290(3), Sch 12, and replaced by s 4 of that Act, as from 6 April 1992.

99. Husband and wife—*(1) Where*—

  (a) *gains accrue to a woman in a year of assessment during which she is a married woman living with her husband, and*

  (b) *if her chargeable amount were added to, and constituted the highest part of, her husband's chargeable amount for the year, capital gains tax would be chargeable on it or any part of it at a rate equivalent to the higher rate of income tax for the year,*

the rate of capital gains tax on her chargeable amount or that part of it shall be equivalent to the higher rate.

(2) For the purposes of this section a person's chargeable amount for a year of assessment is the amount on which he is (or would apart from section 45 of the Capital Gains Tax Act 1979 be) chargeable to capital gains tax for the year.

(3) In relation to a year of assessment for which an application under section 45(2) of the Capital Gains Tax Act 1979 (separate assessment) has effect, the amounts of tax payable by the husband and by the wife shall be determined by—

  (a) *aggregating the amounts that would be payable by each of them apart from this subsection, and*

  (b) *dividing that aggregate between them in proportion to their chargeable amounts for the year.*

(4) This section shall apply in relation to a part of a year of assessment, being a part beginning with 6th April, as it applies in relation to a whole year (except that references to a husband's chargeable amount are references to his chargeable amount for the whole year).

(5) This section shall have effect for the years 1988–89 and 1989–90 only.

Note. This section repealed by Taxation of Chargeable Gains Act 1992, s 290(3), Sch 12, as from 6 April 1992.

100. Accumulation and discretionary settlements—*(1) The rate of capital gains tax in respect of gains accruing to trustees of an accumulation or discretionary settlement in a year of assessment shall be equivalent to the sum of the basic and additional rates of income tax for the year.*

(2) For the purposes of subsection (1) above a trust is an accumulation or discretionary settlement where—

  (a) *all or any part of the income arising to the trustees in the year of assessment is income to which section 686 of the Taxes Act 1988 (liability to income tax at the additional rate) applies, or*

  (b) *all the income arising to the trustees in the year of assessment is treated as the income of the settlor, but that section would apply to it if it were not so treated, or*

  (c) *all the incoming arising to the trustees in the year of assessment is applied in defraying expenses of the trustees in that year, but that section would apply to it if it were not so applied, or*

  (d) *no income arises to the trustees in the year of assessment, but that section would apply if there were income arising to the trustees and none of it were treated as the income of the settlor or applied as mentioned in paragraph (c) above.*

Note. This section repealed by Taxation of Chargeable Gains Act 1992, s 290(3), Sch 12, and replaced by s 5 of that Act, as from 6 April 1992.

*   *   *   *   *

LEGAL AID ACT 1988

(1988 c 34)

ARRANGEMENT OF SECTIONS

An Act to make new provision for the administration of, and to revise the law relating to, legal aid, advice and assistance. [29 July 1988]

Note. The Access to Justice Act 1999, Pt I (ss 1–26, and Schs 1–4), replaces the existing legal aid system in England and Wales with two new schemes and establishes the Legal Services Commission to run the two schemes, replacing the existing Legal Aid Board.
—Note: ss 1–11, 19–23, 24 (so far as relates to Sch 4 as noted below) of, and Schs 1–3, Sch 4, paras 1, 2, 10(1), (3)(b), 11–15, 19, 20, 26, 31–34, 36, 37, 41–46, 48, 50–52, 56, to the 1999 Act were brought into force on 1 April 2000 by SI 2000 No 774.
Sections 1–32, 34–43, 45, 46 of, and Schs 1–3, 6, 7 to this Act, are repealed by the Access to Justice Act 1999, s 106, Sch 15, Pt I, as from the 1 April 2000 subject to transitional provisions and savings in s 105 of, Sch 14, Pts I, para 1, Pt II, paras 2–9, Pt V, paras 26, 37 to the 1999 Act, the Access to Justice Act 1999 (Commencement No 3, Transition Provisions and Savings) Order 2000, SI 2000 No 774, arts 3–11 and the Access to Justice Act 1999 (Commencement No 7, Transitional Provisions and Savings) Order 2001 (SI 2001 No 916), art 3.

PART I

PRELIMINARY

1. Purpose of this Act. *The purpose of this Act is to establish a framework for the provision under Parts II, III, [IIIA], IV, V and VI of advice, assistance[, mediation] and representation which is publicly funded with a view to helping persons who might otherwise be unable to obtain advice, assistance[, mediation] or representation on account of their means.*

Note. Words in square brackets inserted by Family Law Act 1996, s 66(1), Sch 8, Part II, para 44, as from 21 March 1997.

2. Interpretation—*(1) This section has effect for the interpretation of this Act.*

(2) 'Advice' means oral or written advice on the application of English law to any particular circumstances that have arisen in relation to the person seeking the advice and as to the steps which that person might appropriately take having regard to the application of English law to those circumstances.

(3) 'Assistance' means assistance in taking any of the steps which a person might take, including steps with respect to proceedings, having regard to the application of English law to any particular circumstances that have arisen in relation to him, whether by taking such steps on his behalf (including assistance by way of representation) or by assisting him in taking them on his own behalf.

[(3A) 'Mediation' means mediation to which Part IIIA of this Act applies; and includes steps taken by a mediator in any case—

(a)   in determining whether to embark on mediation;

(b)   in preparing for mediation; and

(c)   in making any assessment under that Part.]

Note. Sub-s (3A) inserted by Family Law Act 1996, s 26(2), as from 21 March 1997.

(4) 'Representation' means representation for the purposes of proceedings and it includes—

(a)   all such assistance as is usually given by a solicitor or counsel [legal representative] in the steps preliminary or incidental to any proceedings;

(b)   all such assistance as is usually so given in civil proceedings in arriving at or giving effect to a compromise to avoid or bring to an end any proceedings; and

(c)   in the case of criminal proceedings, advice and assistance as to any appeal;

and related expressions have corresponding meanings.

(5) Regulations may specify what is, or is not, to be included in advice or assistance of any description, or representation for the purposes of proceedings of any description, to which any Part or provision of a Part of this Act applies and the regulations may provide for the inclusion, in prescribed circumstances, of advice or assistance given otherwise than under this Act.

(6) Advice, assistance and representation under this Act, except when made available under Part II, is only by persons who are solicitors or barristers [shall only be by legal representative], but in the case of Part II, may be by other persons.

(7) In any particular case, advice, assistance and representation under this Act, except when made available under Part II, shall be by solicitor and, so far as necessary counsel; but regulations may prescribe the circumstances in which representation is to be by counsel only or by solicitor only and regulate representation by more than one counsel.

[(7) Subject to section 59 of the Courts and Legal Services Act 1990, regulations—

(a)   may prescribe the circumstances in which representation shall be only by one legal representative and may require him to be from a prescribed category;

(b)   may regulate representation by more than one legal representative from any one or more prescribed categories.]

(7A) If it is satisfied that the circumstances of a particular case in the Supreme Court or the House of Lords warrant a direction under this subsection, the Board or, in the case of criminal proceedings the competent authority, may direct that representation in that case shall be by one legal representative.

(7B)   In subsection (7A), 'competent authority' shall be construed in accordance with section 20.]

(8)   The Lord Chancellor may, if it appears to him to be necessary to do so for the purpose of fulfilling any obligation imposed on the United Kingdom or Her Majesty's Government in the United Kingdom by any international agreement, by order direct that such advice or assistance relating to the application of other laws than English law as is specified in the order shall be advice or assistance for any of the purposes of this Act.

(9)   For the purposes of the application of subsection (8) above in the case of an obligation to provide for the transmission to other countries of applications for legal aid under their laws, the reference to advice or assistance relating to the application of other laws includes a reference to advice or assistance for the purposes of making and transmitting such an application.

(10)   In this Act 'person' does not include a body of persons corporate or unincorporate which is not concerned in a representative, fiduciary or official capacity so as to authorise advice, assistance or representation to be granted to such a body.

(11)   In this Act 'legally assisted person' means any person who receives, under this Act, advice, assistance[, mediation] or representation and, in relation to proceedings, any reference to an assisted party or an unassisted party is to be construed accordingly.

Note. Words in square brackets in sub-ss (4)(a), (6) substituted and sub-ss (7), (7A), (7B) in square brackets substituted for sub-s (7) by Courts and Legal Services Act 1990, s 125(3), Sch 18, paras 61(1), (2), 63(3)(a), as from 1 April 1991. Word in square brackets in sub-s (11) inserted by Family Law Act 1996, s 66(1), Sch 8, Part II, para 44, as from 21 March 1997.

PART II

LEGAL AID BOARD AND LEGAL AID

3. The Legal Aid Board—*(1)   There shall be established a body to be known as the Legal Aid Board (in this Act referred to as 'the Board').*

(2)   Subject to subsections (3) and (4) below, the Board shall have the general function of securing that advice, assistance[, mediation] and representation are available in accordance with this Act and of administering this Act.

Note. Word in square brackets inserted by Family Law Act 1996, s 66(1), Sch 8, Part II, para 44, as from 21 March 1997.

(3)   Subsection (2) above does not confer on the Board any functions with respect to the grant of representation under Part VI for the purposes of proceedings for contempt.

(4)   Subsection (2) above does not confer on the Board any of the following functions unless the Lord Chancellor so directs by order and then only to the extent specified in the order. The functions referred to are—

(a)   determination of the costs of representation under Part IV;

(b)   functions as respects representation under Part V other than determination of the costs of representation for the purposes of proceedings in magistrates' courts;

(c)   functions as respects representation under Part VI for the purposes of care proceedings other than proceedings on an appeal from the decision of a juvenile court to the High Court;

(d)   determination of the financial resources of persons for the purposes of this Act.

Note. Sub-s (4)(c) repealed by Children Act 1989, s 108(7), Sch 15, as from 14 October 1991.

(5)   Subject to subsection (6) below, the board shall consist of no fewer than 11 and no more than 17 members appointed by the Lord Chancellor; and the Lord Chancellor shall appoint one of the members to be chairman.

(6)   The Lord Chancellor may, by order, substitute, for the number for the time being specified in subsection (5) above as the maximum or minimum membership of the Board, such other number as he thinks appropriate.

(7)   The Board shall include at least two solicitors appointed after consultation with the Law Society.

(8) The Lord Chancellor shall consult the General Council of the Bar with a view to the inclusion on the Board of at least two barristers.

(9) In appointing persons to be members of the Board the Lord Chancellor shall have regard to the desirability of securing that the Board includes persons having expertise in or knowledge of—

(a)   *the provision of legal services;*

[(aa)   *the provision of mediation;]*

(b)   *the work of the courts and social conditions; and*

(c)   *management.*

Note. Sub-s 9(aa) inserted by Family Law Act 1996, s 66(1), Sch 8, Part II, para 44, as from 21 March 1997.

(10) Schedule 1 to this Act shall have effect with respect to the Board.

4. Powers of the Board—*(1) Subject to the provisions of this Act, the Board may do anything—*

(a)   *which it considers necessary or desirable to provide or secure the provision of advice, assistance[, mediation] and representation under this Act; or*

(b)   *which is calculated to facilitate or is incidental or conducive to the discharge of its functions;*

and advice, assistance[, mediation] and representation may be provided in different ways in different areas in England and Wales and in different ways in different fields of law.

(2) Without prejudice to the generality of subsection (1) above, the Board shall have power—

(a)   *to enter into any contract including, subject to subsection (7) below, any contract to acquire or dispose of land;*

(b)   *to make grants (with or without conditions, including conditions as to repayment);*

(c)   *to make loans;*

(d)   *to invest money;*

(e)   *to promote or assist in the promotion of publicity relating to the functions of the Board;*

(f)   *to undertake any inquiry or investigation which the Board considers necessary or expedient in relation to the discharge of its functions; and*

(g)   *to give the Lord Chancellor such advice as it may consider appropriate in relation to the provision of advice, assistance[, mediation] and representation under this Act.*

(3) Subsection (1) above does not confer on the Board power to borrow money or to acquire and hold shares in bodies corporate or take part in forming bodies corporate.

(4) The powers to provide advice, assistance[, mediation] or representation under this Part and to secure its provision under this Part by means of contracts with, or grants or loans to, other persons or bodies—

(a)   *shall not be exercisable unless the Lord Chancellor so directs and then only to the extent specified in the direction; and*

(b)   *if exercisable, shall be exercised in accordance with any directions given by him.*

(5) The power to secure the provision of representation under Part IV by means of contracts with other persons shall only be exercisable in the classes of case prescribed in regulations.

(6) Advice, assistance and representation provided by the Board under this Part may be granted with or without limitations and may be amended, withdrawn or revoked.

(7) The power under subsection (2) above to enter into contracts to acquire or dispose of land shall not be exercised without the approval in writing of the Lord Chancellor.

(8) The Board may, from time to time, prepare and submit to the Lord Chancellor proposals for the assumption by it of any functions in relation to the provision of advice, assistance or representation under this Act.

Note. Word in square brackets in sub-ss (1), (2), (4) inserted by Family Law Act 1996, s 66(1), Sch 8, Part II, para 44, as from 21 March 1997.

5. Duties of the Board—*(1) The Board shall, from time to time, publish information as to the discharge of its functions in relation to advice, assistance [, mediation] and representation including the forms and procedures and other matters connected therewith.*

(2) The Board shall, from time to time, furnish to the Lord Chancellor such information as he may require relating to its property and to the discharge or proposed discharge of its functions.

(3) It shall be the duty of the Board to provide to the Lord Chancellor, as soon as possible after 31st March in each year, a report on the discharge of its functions during the preceding twelve months.

(4) The Board shall deal in any report under subsection (3) above with such matters as the Lord Chancellor may from time to time direct.

(5) The Board shall have regard, in discharging its functions, to such guidance as may from time to time be given by the Lord Chancellor.

(6) Guidance under subsection (5) above shall not relate to the consideration or disposal, in particular cases, of—

   (a)   applications for advice, assistance[, mediation] or representation;
   (b)   supplementary or incidental applications or requests to the Board in connection with any case where advice, assistance[, mediation] or representation has been made available.

(7) For the purposes of subsection (2) above the Board shall permit any person authorised by the Lord Chancellor for the purpose to inspect and make copies of any accounts or documents of the Board and shall furnish such explanations of them as that person or the Lord Chancellor may require.

Note. Words in square brackets in sub-ss (1), (6) inserted by Family Law Act 1996, s 66(1), Sch 8, Part II, para 44, as from 21 March 1997.

6. Board to have separate legal aid fund—*(1) The Board shall establish and maintain a separate legal aid fund.*

(2) Subject to regulations, there shall be paid out of the fund—

   (a)   such sums as are, by virtue of any provision of or made under this Act, due from the Board in respect of remuneration and expenses properly incurred in connection with the provision, under this Act, of advice, assistance[, mediation] or representation;
   (b)   costs awarded to any unassisted party under section 13 or 18;
   (c)   any part of a contribution repayable by the Board under section 16(4) or 23(7); and
   (d)   such other payments for the purposes of this Act as the Lord Chancellor may, with the concurrence of the Treasury, determine.

(3) Subject to regulations, there shall be paid into the fund—

   (a)   any contributions payable to the Board by any person in respect of advice, assistance[, mediation] or representation under this Act;
   (b)   any sum awarded under an order of a court or agreement as to costs in any proceedings in favour of any legally assisted party which is payable to the Board;
   (c)   any sum which is to be paid out of property recovered or preserved for any legally assisted party to any proceedings;
   [(ca)   any sum which is to be paid out of property on which it is charged under regulations under section 13C(5) below].
   (d)   any sum in respect of the costs of an unassisted party awarded under section 13 or 18 which is repaid to the Board under that section;
   (e)   the sums to be paid by the Lord Chancellor in pursuance of section 42(1)(a); and
   (f)   such other receipts of the Board as the Lord Chancellor may, with the concurrence of the Treasury, determine.

Note. Words in square brackets inserted by Family Law Act 1996, s 66(1), Sch 8, Part II, para 44, as from 21 March 1997.

7. Accounts and audit—*(1) The Board shall keep separate accounts with respect to—*

   (a)   its legal aid fund; and
   (b)   the receipts and expenditure of the Board which do not relate to that fund;
and shall prepare in respect of each financial year a statement of accounts.

(2) The accounts shall be kept and the statement of accounts shall be prepared in such form as the Lord Chancellor may, with the approval of the Treasury, direct.

(3) The accounts shall be audited by persons to be appointed in respect of each financial year by the Lord Chancellor in accordance with a scheme of audit approved by him, and the auditors shall be furnished by the Board with copies of the statement and shall prepare a report to the Lord Chancellor on the accounts and statement.

(4) No person shall be qualified to be appointed auditor under subsection *(3)* above unless he is—

    (a) a member of a body of accountants established in the United Kingdom and for the time being recognised for the purposes of section *389(1)(a)* of the Companies Act 1985;

    (b) authorised by the Secretary of State under section *389(1)(b)* of that Act to be appointed auditor of a company; or

    (c) a member of the Chartered Institute of Public Finance and Accountancy;

but a firm may be so appointed if each of its members is qualified to be so appointed.

[(4) No person shall be appointed auditor under subsection *(3)* above unless he is—

    (a) eligible for appointment as a company auditor under section 25 of the Companies Act 1989; or

    (b) a member of the Chartered Institute of Public Finance and Accountancy.]*

Note. Sub-s (4) in square brackets substituted for sub-s (4) by Companies Act 1989 (Eligibility for Appointment as Company Auditors) (Consequential Amendments) Regulations 1991, SI 1991 No 1997, reg 2, Schedule, para 69, as from 1 October 1991.

(5) Upon completion of the audit of the accounts, the auditors shall send to the Lord Chancellor a copy of the statement of accounts and of their report, and the Lord Chancellor shall send a copy of the statement and of the report to the Comptroller and Auditor General.

(6) The Lord Chancellor and the Comptroller and Auditor General may inspect the accounts and any records relating to them.

(7) The Lord Chancellor shall lay before each House of Parliament a copy of every statement of accounts and report of the auditors sent to him under subsection *(5)* above.

(8) In this section 'financial year' means the period beginning with the day on which the Board is established and ending with 31st March next following and each subsequent period of 12 months ending with 31st March in each year.

PART *III*

ADVICE AND ASSISTANCE

8. Scope of this Part—*(1)* Subject to the provisions of this section, this Part applies to any advice or assistance and advice and assistance under this Part shall be available to any person subject to and in accordance with the provisions of this section and sections 9, 10 and 11.

(2) This Part only applies to assistance by way of representation if, and to the extent that, regulations so provide; and regulations may make such provision in relation to representation for the purposes of any proceedings before a court or tribunal or at a statutory inquiry.

(3) Advice or assistance of all descriptions or advice or assistance of any prescribed description is excluded from this Part, or is so excluded as regards any area, if regulations so provide; and if regulations provide for all descriptions to be excluded as regards all areas then, so long as the regulations so provide, this Part (other than this subsection) shall not have effect.

(4) Advice or assistance of any prescribed description is restricted to its provision to prescribed descriptions of persons if regulations so provide.

(5) This Part does not apply to advice or assistance given to a person in connection with proceedings before a court or tribunal or at a statutory inquiry at a time when he is being represented in those proceedings under any other Part of this Act.

9. Availability of, and payment for, advice and assistance—*(1) Advice and assistance to which this Part applies shall be available to any person whose financial resources are such as, under regulations, make him eligible for advice or assistance under this Part.*

(2) If regulations so provide, advice or assistance to which this Part applies shall be available, in prescribed circumstances and subject to any prescribed conditions, to persons without reference to their financial resources.

(3) Subject to any prescribed exceptions, assistance by way of representation under this Part shall not be given without the approval of the Board.

(4) Approval under subsection (3) above may be given with or without limitations and may be amended, withdrawn or revoked.

(5) Except as provided by subsection (6) or (7) below, the legally assisted person shall not be required to pay to his solicitor [legal representative] any charge or fee.

(6) Except as provided by subsection (7) below, a legally assisted person shall, if his financial resources are such as, under regulations, make him liable to make a contribution, be liable to pay to his solicitor [legal representative], in respect of the advice or assistance, charges or fees of such amount as is determined or fixed by or under the regulations.

(7) A legally assisted person to whom advice or assistance is made available by virtue of regulations under subsection (2) above shall, in circumstances prescribed by the regulations and, if the regulations apply only to persons of a prescribed description, he is a person of that description, be liable to pay to his solicitor [legal representative], in respect of the advice or assistance, a fee of such amount as is fixed by or under the regulations (in lieu of a contribution under subsection (6) above).

Note. References to 'legal representative' substituted for references to 'solicitor' by Courts and Legal Services Act 1990, s 125(3), Sch 18, para 63(4), as from 1 April 1991.

10. Financial limit on prospective cost of advice or assistance—*(1) Where at any time (whether before or after the advice or assistance has begun to be given) it appears to a solicitor [legal representative] that the cost of giving advice or assistance to a person under this Part is likely to exceed the prescribed limit—*

    (a) *the solicitor shall determine to what extent that advice or assistance can be given without exceeding that limit; and*

    (b) *shall not give it (nor, as the case may be, instruct counsel [an additional legal representative] to give it) so as to exceed that limit except with the approval of the Board.*

(2) Approval under subsection (1)(b) above may be given with or without limitations and may be amended, withdrawn or revoked.

(3) For the purposes of this section the cost of giving advice or assistance shall be taken to consist of such of the following as are applicable in the circumstances, namely—

    (a) *any disbursements, that is to say, expenses (including fees payable to counsel [an additional legal representative]) which may be incurred by the solicitor or his firm in, or in connection with, the giving of the advice or assistance; and*

    (b) *any charges or fees (other than charges for disbursements) which would be properly chargeable by the solicitor or his firm [legal representative] in respect of the advice or assistance.*

Note. Words in square brackets substituted by Courts and Legal Services Act 1990, s 125(3), Sch 18, para 61(3), 63(3)(d), (4), as from 1 April 1991.

11. Payment for advice or assistance otherwise than through legally assisted person's contribution—*(1) This section applies to any charges or fees which, apart from section 9, would be properly chargeable in respect of advice or assistance given under this Part, in so far as those charges or fees are not payable by the legally assisted person in accordance with that section.*

(2) Except in so far as regulations otherwise provide, charges or fees to which this section applies shall constitute a first charge for the benefit of the solicitor [legal representative]—

(a) on any costs which are payable to the legally assisted person by any other person in respect of the matter in connection with which the advice or assistance is given, and

(b) on any property which is recovered or preserved for the legally assisted person in connection with that matter.

(3) *In so far as the charge created by subsection (2) above in respect of any charges or fees to which this section applies is insufficient to meet them, the deficiency shall, subject to subsection (5) below, be payable to the solicitor [legal representative] by the Board.*

(4) *For the purposes of subsection (2) above, it is immaterial, in the case of costs, whether the costs are payable by virtue of a judgment, order of a court or otherwise and, in the case of property, what its nature is and where it is situated and the property within the charge includes the legally assisted person's rights under any compromise or settlement arrived at to avoid proceedings or bring them to an end.*

(5) *For the purpose of determining what charges or fees would be properly chargeable, and whether there is a deficiency to be paid by the Board, charges or fees in respect of advice or assistance under this Part shall, in prescribed circumstances, be determined in such manner as may be prescribed.*

Note. References to 'legal representative' substituted for reference to 'solicitor' by Courts and Legal Services Act 1990, s 125(3), Sch 18, para 63(4), as from 1 April 1991.

12. Limit on costs against person receiving assistance by way of representation—*(1) Where a person receives any assistance by way of representation in any proceedings before a court or tribunal or at a statutory inquiry, then, except in so far as regulations otherwise provide, his liability by virtue of an order for costs made against him with respect to the proceedings shall not exceed the amount (if any) which is a reasonable one for him to pay having regard to all the circumstances, including the financial resources of all the parties and their conduct in connection with the dispute.*

(2) *Regulations shall make provision as to the court, tribunal or person by whom that amount is to be determined and the extent to which any determination of that amount is to be final.*

(3) *None of the following, namely, a legally assisted person's dwelling house, clothes, household furniture and the tools and implements of his trade shall—*

(a) *be taken into account in assessing his financial resources for the purposes of this section, or*

(b) *be subject to execution or any corresponding process in any part of the United Kingdom to enforce the order,*

except so far as regulations may prescribe.

13. Costs of successful unassisted parties—*(1) This section applies to proceedings in which a person who receives assistance by way of representation is a party and which are finally decided in favour of an unassisted party.*

(2) *In any proceedings to which this section applies the court by which the proceedings are so decided may, subject to subsections (3) and (4) below, make an order for the payment by the Board to the unassisted party of the whole or any part of the costs incurred by him in the proceedings.*

(3) *Before making an order under this section, the court shall consider what order for costs should be made against the assisted party and for determining his liability in respect of such costs.*

(4) *An order under this section in respect of any costs may only be made if—*

(a) *an order for costs would be made in the proceedings apart from this Act;*

(b) *as respects the costs incurred in a court of first instance, those proceedings were instituted by the assisted party and the court is satisfied that the unassisted party will suffer severe financial hardship unless the order is made; and*

(c) *in any case, the court is satisfied that it is just and equitable in all the circumstances of the case that provision for the costs should be made out of public funds.*

(5) Without prejudice to any other provision restricting appeals from any court, no appeal shall lie against an order under this section, or against a refusal to make such an order, except on a point of law.

(6) In this section 'costs' means costs as between party and party, and includes the costs of applying for an order under this section; and where a party begins to receive the assistance after the proceedings have been instituted, or ceases to receive the assistance before they are finally decided or otherwise receives the assistance in connection with part only of the proceedings, the reference in subsection (2) above to the costs incurred by the unassisted party in the proceedings shall be construed as a reference to so much of those costs as is attributable to that part.

(7) For the purposes of this section proceedings shall be treated as finally decided in favour of the unassisted party—

   (a) if no appeal lies against the decision in his favour;

   (b) if an appeal lies against the decision with leave, and the time limited for applications for leave expires without leave being granted; or

   (c) if leave to appeal against the decision is granted or is not required, and no appeal is brought within the time limited for appeal;

and where an appeal against the decision is brought out of time the court by which the appeal (or any further appeal in those proceedings) is determined may make an order for the repayment by the unassisted party to the Board of the whole or any part of any sum previously paid to him under this section in respect of those proceedings.

(8) Where a court decides any proceedings in favour of the unassisted party and an appeal lies (with or without leave) against that decision, the court may, if it thinks fit, make or refuse to make an order under this section forthwith, but if an order is made forthwith it shall not take effect—

   (a) where leave to appeal is required, unless the time limited for applications for leave to appeal expires without leave being granted;

   (b) where leave to appeal is granted or is not required, unless the time limited for appeal expires without an appeal being brought.

(9) For the purposes of this section 'court' includes a tribunal.

[PART IIIA

MEDIATION

13A. Scope of this Part—*(1) This Part applies to mediation in disputes relating to family matters.*

(2) 'Family matters' means matters which are governed by English law and in relation to which any question has arisen, or may arise—

   (a) under any provision of—

      (i) the 1973 Act;

      (ii) the Domestic Proceedings and Magistrates' Courts Act 1978;

      (iii) Parts I to V of the Children Act 1989;

      (iv) Parts II and IV of the Family Law Act 1996; or

      (v) any other enactment prescribed;

   (b) under any prescribed jurisdiction of a prescribed court or tribunal; or

   (c) under any prescribed rule of law.

(3) Regulations may restrict this Part to mediation in disputes of any prescribed description.

(4) The power to—

   (a) make regulations under subsection (2), or

   (b) revoke any regulations made under subsection (3),

is exercisable only with the consent of the Treasury.]

Note. Section 13A and preceding Part heading inserted by Family Law Act 1996, s 26(1), as from 21 March 1997.

[13B. Provision and availability of mediation—*(1) The Board may secure the provision of mediation under this Part.*

(2) If mediation is provided under this Part, it is to be available to any person whose financial resources are such as, under regulations, make him eligible for mediation.

(3) A person is not to be granted mediation in relation to any dispute unless mediation appears to the mediator suitable to the dispute and the parties and all the circumstances.

(4) A grant of mediation under this Part may be amended, withdrawn or revoked.

(5) The power conferred by subsection (1) shall be exercised in accordance with any directions given by the Lord Chancellor.

(6) Any contract entered into by the Board for the provision of mediation under this Part must require the mediator to comply with a code of practice.

(7) The code must require the mediator to have arrangements designed to ensure—

(a) that parties participate in mediation only if willing and not influenced by fear of violence or other harm;

(b) that cases where either party may be influenced by fear of violence or other harm are identified as soon as possible;

(c) that the possibility of reconciliation is kept under review throughout mediation; and

(d) that each party is informed about the availability of independent legal advice.

(8) Where there are one or more children of the family, the code must also require the mediator to have arrangements designed to ensure that the parties are encouraged to consider—

(a) the welfare, wishes and feelings of each child; and

(b) whether and to what extent each child should be given the opportunity to express his or her wishes and feelings in the mediation.

(9) A contract entered into by the Board for the provision of mediation under this Part must also include such other provision as the Lord Chancellor may direct the Board to include.

(10) Directions under this section may apply generally to contracts, or to contracts of any description, entered into by the Board, but shall not be made with respect to any particular contract.]

Note. Section 13B inserted by Family Law Act 1996, s 27, as from 21 March 1997.

[13C. Payment for mediation under this Part—*(1) Except as provided by this section, the legally assisted person is not to be required to pay for mediation provided under this Part.*

(2) Subsection (3) applies if the financial resources of a legally assisted person are such as, under regulations, make him liable to make a contribution.

(3) The legally assisted person is to pay to the Board in respect of the costs of providing the mediation, a contribution of such amount as is determined or fixed by or under the regulations.

(4) If the total contribution made by a person in respect of any mediation exceeds the Board's liability on his account, the excess shall be repaid to him.

(5) Regulations may provide that, where—

(a) mediation under this Part is made available to a legally assisted person, and

(b) property is recovered or preserved for the legally assisted person as a result of the mediation,

a sum equal to the Board's liability on the legally assisted person's account is, except so far as the regulations otherwise provide, to be a first charge on the property in favour of the Board.

(6) Regulations under subsection (5) may, in particular, make provision—

(a) as to circumstances in which property is to be taken to have been, or not to have been, recovered or preserved; and

(b) as to circumstances in which the recovery or preservation of property is to be taken to be, or not to be, the result of any mediation.

(7) For the purposes of subsection (5), the nature of the property and where it is situated is immaterial.

(8) The power to make regulations under section 34(2)(f) and (8) is exercisable in relation to any charge created under subsection (5) as it is exercisable in relation to the charge created by section 16.

(9) For the purposes of subsections (4) and (5), the Board's liability on any person's account in relation to any mediation is the aggregate amount of—
* (a)   the sums paid or payable by the Board on his account for the mediation, determined in accordance with subsection (10);*
* (b)   any sums paid or payable in respect of its net liability on his account, determined in accordance with subsection (11) and the regulations—*
* (i)   in respect of any proceedings, and*
* (ii) for any advice or assistance under Part III in connection with the proceedings or any matter to which the proceedings relate,*
* so far as the proceedings relate to any matter to which the mediation relates; and*
* (c)   any sums paid or payable in respect of its net liability on his account, determined in accordance with the regulations, for any other advice or assistance under Part III in connection with the mediation or any matter to which the mediation relates.*

(10) For the purposes of subsection (9)(a), the sums paid or payable by the Board on any person's account for any mediation are—
* (a)   sums determined under the contract between the Board and the mediator as payable by the Board on that person's account for the mediation; or*
* (b)   if the contract does not differentiate between such sums and sums payable on any other person's account or for any other mediation, such part of the remuneration payable under the contract as may be specified in writing by the Board.*

(11) For the purposes of subsection (9)(b), the Board's net liability on any person's account in relation to any proceedings is its net liability on his account under section 16(9)(a) and (b) in relation to the proceedings.]

Note. Section 13C inserted by Family Law Act 1996, s 28(1), as from 21 March 1997.

PART IV

CIVIL LEGAL AID

14. Scope of this Part—*(1) This Part applies to such proceedings before courts or tribunals or at statutory inquiries in England and Wales as—*
* (a)   are proceedings of a description for the time being specified in Part I of Schedule 2 to this Act, except proceedings for the time being specified in Part II of that Schedule, and*
* (b)   are not proceedings for which representation may be granted under Part V,*
and representation under this Part shall be available to any person subject to and in accordance with sections 15 and 16.

(2) Subject to subsection (3) below, Schedule 2 may be varied by regulations so as to extend or restrict the categories of proceedings for the purposes of which representation is available under this Part, by reference to the court, tribunal or statutory inquiry, to the issues involved, to the capacity in which the person seeking representation is concerned or otherwise.

(3) Regulations under subsection (2) above may not have the effect of adding any proceedings before any court or tribunal or at any statutory inquiry before or at which persons have no right, and are not normally allowed, to be represented by counsel or a solicitor [a legal representative].

(4) Regulations under subsection (2) above which extend the categories of proceedings for the purposes of which representation is available under this Part shall not be made without the consent of the Treasury.

Note. Sub-s (3) words in square brackets substituted by Courts and Legal Services Act 1990, s 125(3), Sch 18, para 63(1)(a), as from 1 April 1991.

15. Availability of, and payment for, representation under this Part—*(1) Subject to subsections (2) and (3) [to (3B)] [(3D)] [and (3F)] below, representation under this Part* for the purposes of proceedings to which this Part applies shall be available to any person whose financial resources are such as, under regulations, make him eligible for representation under this Part.

(2) A person shall not be granted representation for the purposes of any proceedings unless he satisfies the Board that he has reasonable grounds for taking, defending or being a party to the proceedings.

(3) A person may be refused representation for the purposes of any proceedings if, in the particular circumstances of the case it appears to the Board—

    (a)   unreasonable that he should be granted representation under this Part, or

    (b)   more appropriate that he should be given assistance by way of representation under Part III;

and regulations may prescribe the criteria for determining any questions arising under paragraph (b) above.

[(3A) Representation under this Part shall not be available—

    (a)   to any local authority; or

    (b)   to any other body which falls within a prescribed description, [or

    (c)   to a guardian ad litem,]

for the purposes of any proceedings under the Children Act 1989.

(3B) Regardless of subsection (2) or (3), representation under this Part must be granted where a child who is brought before a court under section 25 of the 1989 Act (use of accommodation for restricting liberty) is not, but wishes to be, legally represented before the court.]

[(3C) Subject to subsection (3A) but regardless of subsections (2) or (3), representation under this Part must be granted to the child in respect of whom the application is made, to any parent of such a child and to any person with parental responsibility for him within the meaning of the 1989 Act to cover proceedings relating to an application for the following orders under that Act—

    (a)   an order under section 31 (a care or supervision order);

    (b)   an order under section 43 (a child assessment order);

    (c)   an order under section 44 (an emergency protection order); or

    (d)   an order under section 45 (extension or discharge of an emergency protection order).

(3D) Subject to subsections (2) and (3) [and (3F)] , representation must be granted to cover proceedings relating to an appeal against an order made under section 31 of the 1989 Act to a person who has been granted representation by virtue of subsection (3C).

(3E) Subject to subsections (1) and (3A) but regardless of subsections (2) or (3), representation under this Part must be granted where a person applies to be or has been joined as a party to any of the proceedings mentioned in subsection (3C).]

[(3F) A person shall not be granted representation for the purposes of proceedings relating to family matters, unless he has attended a meeting with a mediator—

    (a)   to determine—

        (i)   whether mediation appears suitable to the dispute and the parties and all the circumstances, and

        (ii)   in particular, whether mediation could take place without either party being influenced by fear of violence or other harm; and

    (b)   if mediation does appear suitable, to help the person applying for representation to decide whether instead to apply for mediation.

(3G) Subsection (3F) does not apply—

    (a)   in relation to proceedings under—

        (i)   Part IV of the Family Law Act 1996;

        (ii)   section 37 of the Matrimonial Causes Act 1973;

        (iii)   Part IV or V of the Children Act 1989;

    (b)   in relation to proceedings of any other description that may be prescribed; or

    (c)   in such circumstances as may be prescribed.

(3H) So far as proceedings relate to family matters, the Board, in determining under subsection (3)(a) whether, in relation to the proceedings, it is reasonable that a person should be granted representation under this Part—

(a) must have regard to whether and to what extent recourse to mediation would be a suitable alternative to taking the proceedings; and

(b) must for that purpose have regard to the outcome of the meeting held under subsection (3F) and to any assessment made for the purposes of section 13B(3).]

[(3I) A person may be refused representation for the purposes of any proceedings if—

(a) the proceedings are marital proceedings within the meaning of Part II of the Family Law Act 1996; and

(b) he is being provided with marriage counselling under section 23 of that Act in relation to the marriage.]

(4) Representation under this Part may be granted by the Board with or without limitations and may be amended, withdrawn or revoked.

[(4A) A person may not be refused representation for the purposes of any proceedings on the ground (however expressed) that it would be more appropriate for him and a legal representative of his to enter into a conditional fee agreement (as defined by section 58 of the Courts and Legal Services Act 1990).]

(5) Where the case is one in which the Board has power to secure the provision of representation under this Part by means of contracts with other persons, the grant of representation under this Part may be limited under subsection (4) above as regards the persons who may represent the legally assisted person to representation only in pursuance of a contract made with the Board.

(6) Except in so far as he is required under section 16 to make a contribution, a legally assisted person shall not be required to make any payment in respect of representation under this Part and it shall be for the Board to pay his solicitor for acting for him and to pay any fees of counsel for so acting [legal representative].

(7) The Board's obligation under subsection (6) above is—

(a) in the case of representation provided in pursuance of a contract between the Board and the legally assisted person's solicitor [legal representative], to make such payments as are due under the contract; and

(b) in the case of representation provided otherwise than in pursuance of such a contract, to make such payments as are authorised by regulations.

(8) Nothing in subsection (6) above affects the duty of the solicitor [legal representative] to pay in the first instance expenses incurred in connection with the proceedings that would ordinarily be paid in the first instance by a person's solicitor.

Note. Words 'to (3B)' in square brackets in sub-s (1) substituted and sub-ss (3A), (3B) inserted by Children Act 1989, s 99(1), (2), as from 14 October 1991. Sub-s (4A) inserted by Courts and Legal Services Act 1990, s 125(2), Sch 17, para 19, as from 1 April 1991 and words in square brackets substituted in sub-ss (6), (7), (8), by ibid, s 125(3), Sch 18, paras 61(4), 63(4), as from the same date. Word '(3D)' in square brackets in sub-s (1) substituted for word '(3B)' and sub-ss (3C)–(3E) inserted by Legal Aid Act 1988 (Children Act 1989) Order 1991, SI 1991 No 1924, art 2(a), as from 14 October 1991. Words 'and (3F)' in square brackets in sub-ss (1), (3D), and sub-ss (3F)–(3I), inserted by Family Law Act 1996, ss 23(9), 29, 66(1), Sch 8, Part II, para 44, as from 21 March 1997. Words in square brackets in sub-s (3A) added by Civil Legal Aid (General) (Amendment) (No 2) Regulations 1991, SI 1991 No 2036, reg 3, as from 14 October 1991.

16. Reimbursement of Board by contributions and out of costs or property recovered—(1) A legally assisted person shall, if his financial resources are such as, under regulations, make him liable to make such a contribution, pay to the Board a contribution in respect of the costs of his being represented under this Part.

(2) The contribution to be required of him by the Board shall be determined by the Board in accordance with the regulations and may take the form of periodical payments or one or more capital sums or both.

(3) The contribution required of a person may, in the case of periodical payments, be made payable by reference to the period during which he is represented under this Part or any shorter period and, in the case of a capital sum, be made payable by instalments.

(4) *If the total contribution made by a person in respect of any proceedings exceeds the net liability of the Board on his account, the excess shall be repaid to him.*

(5) *Any sums recovered by virtue of an order or agreement for costs made in favour of a legally assisted person with respect to the proceedings shall be paid to the Board.*

(6) *Except so far as regulations otherwise provide—*

(a) *any sums remaining unpaid on account of a person's contribution in respect of the sums payable by the Board in respect of any proceedings, and*

(b) *a sum equal to any deficiency by reason of his total contributions being less than the net liability of the Board on his account,*

shall be a first charge for the benefit of the Board on any property which is recovered or preserved for him in the proceedings.

(7) *For the purposes of subsection (6) above it is immaterial what the nature of the property is and where it is situated and the property within the charge includes the rights of a person under any compromise or settlement arrived at to avoid the proceedings or bring them to an end and any sums recovered by virtue of an order for costs made in his favour in the proceedings (not being sums payable to the Board under subsection (5) above).*

(8) *The charge created by subsection (6) above on any damages or costs shall not prevent a court allowing them to be set off against other damages or costs in any case where a solicitor's [legal representative's] lien for costs would not prevent it.*

Note. Words in square brackets substituted by Courts and Legal Services Act 1990, s 125(3), Sch 18, para 63, as from 1 April 1991.

(9) *In this section references to the net liability of the Board on a legally assisted person's account in relation to any proceedings are references to the aggregate amount of—*

(a) *the sums paid or payable by the Board on his account in respect of those proceedings to any solicitor or counsel [legal representative], and*

(b) *any sums so paid or payable for any advice or assistance under Part III in connection with those proceedings or any matter to which those proceedings relate, [and*

(c) *if and to the extent that regulations so provide, any sums paid or payable in respect of the Board's liability on the legally assisted person's account in relation to any mediation in connection with any matter to which these proceedings relate,]*

being sums not recouped by the Board by sums which are recoverable by virtue of an order or agreement for costs made in his favour with respect to those proceedings or by virtue of any right of his to be indemnified against expenses incurred by him in connection with those proceedings.

Note. Words 'legal representative' in square brackets substituted by Courts and Legal Services Act 1990, s 125(3), Sch 18, para 63, as from 1 April 1991. Word 'and' and sub-s (9)(c) in square brackets inserted, by Family Law Act 1996, ss 28(2), 66, Sch 8, Part II, para 44, Sch 10, as from 21 March 1997.

(10) *Where a legally assisted person has been represented in any proceedings in pursuance of a contract made with the Board on terms which do not differentiate between the remuneration for his and other cases, the reference in subsection (9)(a) above to the sums paid or payable by the Board on his account in respect of the proceedings shall be construed as a reference to such part of the remuneration payable under the contract as may be specified in writing by the Board.*

[(11) *For the purposes of subsection (9)(c) above, the Board's liability on any person's account in relation to any mediation is its liability on his account under section 13C(9)(a) and (c) above in relation to the mediation.]*

Note. Sub-s (11) added by Family Law Act 1996, s 28(3), as from 21 March 1997.

17. Limit on costs against assisted party—(1) *The liability of a legally assisted party under an order for costs made against him with respect to any proceedings shall not exceed the amount (if any) which is a reasonable one for him to pay having regard to all the circumstances, including the financial resources of all the parties and their conduct in connection with the dispute.*

(2) *Regulations shall make provision as to the court, tribunal or person by whom that amount is to be determined and the extent to which any determination of that amount is to be final.*

(3) *None of the following, namely, a legally assisted person's dwelling house, clothes, household furniture and the tools and implements of his trade shall—*

(a) *be taken into account in assessing his financial resources for the purposes of this section, or*

(b) *be subject to execution or any corresponding process in any part of the United Kingdom to enforce the order,*

except so far as regulations may prescribe.

18. Costs of successful unassisted parties—*(1) This section applies to proceedings to which a legally assisted person is a party and which are finally decided in favour of an unassisted party.*

(2) *In any proceedings to which this section applies the court by which the proceedings were so decided may, subject to subsections (3) and (4) below, make an order for the payment by the Board to the unassisted party of the whole or any part of the costs incurred by him in the proceedings.*

(3) *Before making an order under this section, the court shall consider what order for costs should be made against the assisted party and for determining his liability in respect of such costs.*

(4) *An order under this section in respect of any costs may only be made if—*

(a) *an order for costs would be made in the proceedings apart from this Act;*

(b) *as respects the costs incurred in a court of first instance, those proceedings were instituted by the assisted party and the court is satisfied that the unassisted party will suffer severe financial hardship unless the order is made; and*

(c) *in any case, the court is satisfied that it is just and equitable in all the circumstances of the case that provision for the costs should be made out of public funds.*

(5) *Without prejudice to any other provision restricting appeals from any court, no appeal shall lie against an order under this section, or against a refusal to make such an order, except on a point of law.*

(6) *In this section 'costs' means costs as between party and party, and includes the costs of applying for an order under this section; and where a party begins to receive representation after the proceedings have been instituted, or ceases to receive representation before they are finally decided or otherwise receives representation in connection with part only of the proceedings, the reference in subsection (2) above to the costs incurred by the unassisted party in the proceedings shall be construed as a reference to so much of those costs as is attributable to that part.*

(7) *For the purposes of this section proceedings shall be treated as finally decided in favour of the unassisted party—*

(a) *if no appeal lies against the decision in his favour;*

(b) *if an appeal lies against the decision with leave, and the time limited for applications for leave expires without leave being granted; or*

(c) *if leave to appeal against the decision is granted or is not required, and no appeal is brought within the time limited for appeal;*

and where an appeal against the decision is brought out of time the court by which the appeal (or any further appeal in those proceedings) is determined may make an order for the repayment by the unassisted party to the Board of the whole or any part of any sum previously paid to him under this section in respect of those proceedings.

(8) *Where a court decides any proceedings in favour of the unassisted party and an appeal lies (with or without leave) against that decision, the court may, if it thinks fit, make or refuse to make an order under this section forthwith, but if an order is made forthwith it shall not take effect—*

(a) *where leave to appeal is required, unless the time limited for applications for leave to appeal expires without leave being granted;*

(b) where leave to appeal is granted or is not required, unless the time limited for appeal expires without an appeal being brought.

(9) For the purposes of this section 'court' includes a tribunal.

PART V

CRIMINAL LEGAL AID

19. Scope of this Part—(1) This Part applies to criminal proceedings before any of the following—

(a) a magistrates' court;

(b) the Crown Court;

(c) the criminal division of the Court of Appeal or the Courts-Martial Appeal Court; and

(d) the House of Lords in the exercise of its jurisdiction in relation to appeals from either of those courts;

and representation under this Part shall be available to any person subject to and in accordance with sections 21, 22, 23, 24 and 25.

(2) Representation under this Part for the purposes of the proceedings before any court extends to any proceedings preliminary or incidental to the proceedings, including bail proceedings, whether before that or another court.

(3) Representation under this Part for the purposes of the proceedings before a magistrates' court extends to any proceedings before a juvenile court [youth court] or other magistrates' court to which the case is remitted.

Note. Words in square brackets substituted by Criminal Justice Act 1991, s 100, Sch 11, para 40, as from 1 October 1992.

(4) In subsection (2) above in its application to bail proceedings, 'court' has the same meaning as in the Bail Act 1976, but that subsection does not extend representation to bail proceedings before a judge of the High Court exercising the jurisdiction of that Court.

(5) In this Part—

'competent authority' is to be construed in accordance with section 20;

'Court of Appeal' means the criminal division of that Court;

'criminal proceedings' includes proceedings for dealing with an offender for an offence or in respect of a sentence or as a fugitive offender and also includes proceedings instituted under section 115 of the Magistrates' Courts Act 1980 (binding over) in respect of an actual or apprehended breach of the peace or other misbehaviour and proceedings for dealing with a person for a failure to comply with a condition of a recognizance to keep the peace or be of good behaviour [and also includes proceedings under section 15 of the Children and Young Persons Act 1969 (variation and discharge of supervision orders) and section 16(8) of that Act (appeals in such proceedings)];

'proceedings for dealing with an offender as a fugitive offender' means proceedings before a metropolitan stipendiary magistrate under section 9 of the Extradition Act 1870, section 7 of the Fugitive Offenders Act 1967 or section 6 of the Criminal Justice Act 1988; and

'remitted', in relation to a juvenile court [youth court], means remitted under section 56(1) of the Children and Young Persons Act 1933;

and any reference, in relation to representation for the purposes of any proceedings, to the proceedings before a court includes a reference to any proceedings to which representation under this Part extends by virtue of subsection (2) or (3) above.

Note. Words in square brackets in definition 'criminal proceedings' added by Children Act 1989, s 99(1), (3), as from 14 October 1991. Words in square brackets in definition 'remitted' substituted by Criminal Justice Act 1991, s 100, Sch 11, para 40, as from 1 October 1992.

20. Competent authorities to grant representation under this Part—(1) Subject to any provision made by virtue of subsection (10) below, the following courts are competent to grant representation under this Part for the purposes of the following proceedings, on an application made for the purpose.

(2) The court before which any proceedings take place, or are to take place, is always competent as respects those proceedings, except that this does not apply to the House of Lords; and, in the case of the Court of Appeal and the Courts-Martial Appeal Court, the reference to proceedings which are to take place includes proceedings which may take place if notice of appeal is given or an application for leave to appeal is made.

(3) The Court of Appeal or, as the case may be, the Courts-Martial Appeal Court is also competent as respects proceedings on appeal from decisions of theirs to the House of Lords.

(4) The magistrates' court—

(a) which commits a person for trial or sentence or to be dealt with in respect of a sentence,

(b) which has been given a notice of transfer under section 4 of the Criminal Justice Act 1987 (transfer of serious fraud cases) [or section 53 of the Criminal Justice Act 1991 (transfer of certain cases involving children)], or [or]

[(bb) which has been given a notice of transfer under Part I of the Schedule to the War Crimes Act 1991, or]

(c) from which a person appeals against his conviction or sentence,
is also competent as respects the proceedings before the Crown Court.

Note. Words in first pair of square brackets in sub-s (4)(b) inserted by Criminal Justice Act 1991, s 53(5), Sch 6, para 9, as from 1 October 1992. Word 'or' repealed, and sub-s (4)(bb) inserted by War Crimes Act 1991, s 3(2), as from 9 May 1991. Word 'or' in square brackets inserted, and sub-s (4)(bb) repealed by Criminal Procedure and Investigations Act 1996, ss 46(2), 80, Sch 5(2), as from 4 July 1996.

(5) The magistrates' courts inquiring into an offence as examining justices is also competent, before it decides whether or not to commit the person for trial, as respects any proceedings before the Crown Court on his trial.

(6) The Crown Court is also competent as respects applications for leave to appeal and proceedings on any appeal to the Court of Appeal under section 9(11) of the Criminal Justice Act 1987 (appeals against orders or rulings at preparatory hearings).

(7) On ordering a retrial under section 7 of the Criminal Appeal Act 1968 (new trials ordered by Court of Appeal or House of Lords on fresh evidence) the court ordering the retrial is also competent as respects the proceedings before the Crown Court.

(8) Any magistrates' court to which, in accordance with regulations, a person applies for representation when he has been arrested for an offence but has not appeared or been brought before a court is competent as respects the proceedings in relation to the offence in any magistrates' court.

(9) In the event of the Lord Chancellor making an order under section 3(4) as respects the function of granting representation under this Part for the purposes of proceedings before any court, the Board shall be competent as respects those proceedings, on an application made for the purpose.

(10) An order under section 3(4) may make provision restricting or excluding the competence of any court mentioned in any of subsections (2) to (8) above and may contain such transitional provisions as appear to the Lord Chancellor necessary or expedient.

21. Availability of representation under this Part—*(1) Representation under this Part for the purposes of any criminal proceedings shall be available in accordance with this section to the accused or convicted person but shall not be available to the prosecution except in the case of an appeal to the Crown Court against conviction or sentence, for the purpose of enabling an individual who is not acting in an official capacity to resist the appeal.*

(2) Subject to subsection (5) below, representation may be granted where it appears to the competent authority to be desirable to do so in the interests of justice; and section 22 applies for the interpretation of this subsection in relation to the proceedings to which that section applies.

(3) Subject to subsection (5) below, representation must be granted—

(a) where a person is committed for trial on a charge of murder, for his trial;

(b) where the prosecutor appeals or applies for leave to appeal to the House of Lords, for the proceedings on the appeal;

   (c) *where a person charged with an offence before a magistrates' court—*
        (i) *is brought before the court in pursuance of a remand in custody when he may be again remanded or committed in custody, and*
       (ii) *is not, but wishes to be, legally represented before the court (not having been legally represented when he was so remanded),]*
     for so much of the proceedings as relates to the grant of bail; and
   (d) *where a person—*
        (i) *is to be sentenced or otherwise dealt with for an offence by a magistrates' court or the Crown Court, and*
       (ii) *is to be kept in custody to enable enquiries or a report to be made to assist the court,]*
     for the proceedings on sentencing or otherwise dealing with him.

(4) Subject to any provision made under section 3(4) by virtue of section 20(10), in a case falling within subsection (3)(a) above, it shall be for the magistrates' court which commits the person for trial, and not for the Crown Court, to make the grant of representation for his trial.

(5) Representation shall not be granted to any person unless it appears to the competent authority that his financial resources are such as, under regulations, make him eligible for representation under this Part.

(6) Before making a determination for the purposes of subsection (5) above in the case of any person, the competent authority shall, except in prescribed cases, require a statement of his financial resources in the prescribed form to be furnished to the authority.

(7) Where a doubt arises whether representation under this Part should be granted to any person, the doubt shall be resolved in that person's favour.

(8) Where an application for representation for the purposes of an appeal to the Court of Appeal or the Courts-Martial Appeal Court is made to a competent authority before the giving of notice of appeal or the making of an application for leave to appeal, the authority may, in the first instance, exercise its power to grant representation by making a grant consisting of advice on the question whether there appear to be reasonable grounds of appeal and assistance in the preparation of an application for leave to appeal or in the giving of a notice of appeal.

(9) Representation granted by a competent authority may be amended or withdrawn, whether by that or another authority competent to grant representation under this Part.

(10) Regulations may provide for an appeal to lie to a specified court or body against any refusal by a magistrates' court to grant representation under this Part and for that other court or body to make any grant of representation that could have been made by the magistrates' court.

[(10A) Where section 44A of the Criminal Appeal Act 1968 (death of convicted person) applies, the reference in subsection (1) above to the convicted person shall be construed as a reference to the person approved under that section.]

Note. Sub-s (10A) inserted by Criminal Appeal Act 1995, s 29(1), Sch 2, para 17, as from 1 January 1996.

(11) Subsection (3) above shall have effect in its application to a person who has not attained the age of eighteen as if the references in paragraphs (c) and (d) to remand in custody and to being remanded or kept in custody included references to being committed under section 23 of the Children and Young Persons Act 1969 to the care of a local authority or a remand centre.

22. Criteria for grant of representation for trial proceedings—*(1) This section applies to proceedings by way of a trial by or before a magistrates' court or the Crown Court or on an appeal to the Crown Court against a person's conviction.*

(2) The factors to be taken into account by a competent authority in determining whether it is in the interests of justice that representation be granted for the purposes of proceedings to which this section applies to an accused shall include the following—
   (a) *the offence is such that if proved it is likely that the court would impose a sentence which would deprive the accused of his liberty or lead to loss of his livelihood or serious damage to his reputation;*

(b)   the determination of the case may involve consideration of a substantial question of law;

(c)   the accused may be unable to understand the proceedings or to state his own case because of his inadequate knowledge of English, mental illness or other mental or physical disability;

(d)   the nature of the defence is such as to involve the tracing and interviewing of witnesses or expert cross-examination of a witness for the prosecution;

(e)   it is in the interests of someone other than the accused that the accused be represented.

(3)   The Lord Chancellor may, by order, vary the factors listed in subsection (2) above by amending factors in the list or by adding new factors to the list.

23. Reimbursement of public funds by contributions—(1) Where representation under this Part is granted to any person whose financial resources are such as, under regulations, make him liable to make a contribution, the competent authority shall order him to pay a contribution in respect of the costs of his being represented under this Part.

(2)   Where the legally assisted person has not attained the age of sixteen, the competent authority may, instead of or in addition to ordering him to make a contribution, order any person—

(a)   who is an appropriate contributor in relation to him, and

(b)   whose financial resources are such as, under regulations, make him liable to make a contribution,

to pay a contribution in respect of the costs of the representation granted to the legally assisted person.

(3)   Regulations may authorise the making of a contribution order under subsection (1) or (2) above after the grant of representation in prescribed circumstances.

(4)   The amount of the contribution to be required under subsection (1) or (2) above by the competent authority shall be such as is determined in accordance with the regulations.

(5)   A legally assisted person or appropriate contributor may be required to make his contribution in one sum or by instalments as may be prescribed.

(6)   Regulations may provide that no contribution order shall be made in connection with a grant of representation under this Part for the purposes of proceedings in the Crown Court, the Court of Appeal or the House of Lords in a case where a contribution order was made in connection with a grant of such representation to the person in question in respect of proceedings in a lower court.

(7)   Subject to subsection (8) below, if the total contribution made in respects of the costs of representing any person under this Part exceeds those costs, the excess shall be repaid—

(a)   where the contribution was made by one person only, to him; and

(b)   where the contribution was made by two or more persons, to them in proportion to the amounts contributed by them.

(8)   Where a contribution has been made in respect of the costs of representing any person under this Part in any proceedings and an order for costs is made in favour of that person in respect of those proceedings, then, where sums due under the order for costs are paid to the Board or the Lord Chancellor under section 20(2) of the Prosecution of Offences Act 1985 (recovery regulations)—

(a)   if the costs of the representation do not exceed the sums so paid, subsection (7) above shall not apply and the contribution shall be repaid;

(b)   if the costs of the representation do exceed the sums so paid, subsection (7) above shall apply as if the costs of the representation were equal to the excess.

(9)   References in subsection (8) above to the costs of representation include any charge or fee treated as part of those costs by section 26(2).

(10) In this Part—

'appropriate contributor', means a person of a description prescribed under section 34(2)(c); and

'contribution order' means an order under subsection (1) or (2) above.

24. Contribution orders: supplementary—*(1) Where a competent authority grants representation under this Part and in connection with the grant makes a contribution order under which any sum is required to be paid on the making of the order, it may direct that the grant of representation shall not take effect until that sum is paid.*

(2) Where a legally assisted person fails to pay any relevant contribution when it is due, the court in which the proceedings for the purposes of which he has been granted representation are being heard may, subject to subsection (3) below, revoke the grant.

(3) A court shall not exercise the power conferred by subsection (2) above unless, after affording the legally assisted person an opportunity of making representations in such manner as may be prescribed, it is satisfied—

(a) that he was able to pay the relevant contribution when it was due; and

(b) that he is able to pay the whole or part of it but has failed or refused to do so.

(4) In subsection (2) above 'relevant contribution', in relation to a legally assisted person, means any sum—

(a) which he is required to pay by a contribution order made in connection with the grant to him of representation under this Part, and

(b) which falls due after the making of the order and before the conclusion of the proceedings for the purposes of which he has been granted such representation.

(5) Regulations with respect to contribution orders may—

(a) provide for their variation or revocation in prescribed circumstances;

(b) provide for their making in default of the prescribed evidence of a person's financial resources;

(c) regulate their making after the grant of representation;

(d) authorise the remission or authorise or require the repayment in prescribed circumstances of sums due or paid under such orders; and

(e) prescribe the court or body by which any function under the regulations is to be exercisable.

(6) Schedule 3 to this Act shall have effect with respect to the enforcement of contribution orders.

25. Payment of costs of representation under this Part—*(1) Where representation under this Part has been granted to any person the costs of representing him shall be paid—*

(a) by the Lord Chancellor, or

(b) by the Board,

as the Lord Chancellor may direct.

(2) Subject to regulations, the costs of representing any person under this Part shall include sums on account of the fees payable to his counsel or solicitor [legal representative] and disbursements reasonably incurred by his solicitor [legal representative] for or in connection with his representation.

(3) The costs required by this section to be paid in respect of representing him shall not include any sum in respect of allowances to witnesses attending to give evidence in the proceedings for the purposes of which he is represented in any case where such allowances are payable under any other enactment.

Note. Words in square brackets substituted in sub-s (2) by Courts and Legal Services Act 1990, s 125(3), Sch 18, para 63(3)(b), (4), as from 1 April 1991.

26. Payment for advice or assistance where representation under this Part is subsequently granted—*(1) This section has effect where—*

(a) advice or assistance under Part III is given to a person in respect of any matter which is or becomes the subject of criminal proceedings against him; and

(b) he is subsequently granted representation under this Part for the purposes of those proceedings.

(2) If the solicitor [legal representative] acting for the person under the grant of representation is the same as the solicitor [one] who gave him the advice or assistance, any charge

or fee in respect of the advice or assistance which, apart from this section, would fall to be secured, recovered or paid as provided by section 11 shall instead be paid under section 25 as if it were part of the costs of the representation.

(3) If a contribution order is made in connection with the grant of representation under this Part to him—

  (a) any sum which he is required by virtue of section 9(6) or (7) to pay in respect of the advice or assistance (whether or not already paid) shall be credited against the contribution to be made by him under the contribution order; and

  (b) section 25 shall have effect in a case to which subsection (2) above applies as if the charges and fees properly chargeable in respect of the advice or assistance were part of the costs of the representation under this Part and as if any such sum as is mentioned in paragraph (a) above which he has paid were part of the contribution made under the contribution order.

Note. Words in square brackets substituted in sub-s (2) by Courts and Legal Services Act 1990, s 125(3), Sch 18, paras 61(5), 63(4), as from 1 April 1991.

PART VI

LEGAL AID IN SPECIAL CASES

Care proceedings

27. Representation in care proceedings: scope and competent authorities—

(1) This section and section 28 apply, subject to subsection (2) below, to the following proceedings (referred to as 'care proceedings'), that is to say—

  (a) proceedings under section 1 of the 1969 Act or under section 21A of the 1980 Act (care proceedings);

  (b) proceedings under section 15 or 21 of the 1969 Act (variation and discharge of supervision or care orders);

  (c)   proceedings under section 2(12), 3(8), 16(8) or 21(4) of the 1969 Act or section 21A of the 1980 Act (appeals in such proceedings);

  (d) proceedings under section 3 of the Children and Young Persons Act 1963 (application by parent or guardian for an order directing a local authority to take proceedings under section 1 of the 1969 Act);

  (e) proceedings under section 3, 5 or 67(2) of the 1980 Act (proceedings in connection with resolutions by local authorities with respect to the assumption of parental rights and duties); and

  (f) proceedings under Part 1A of the 1980 Act (access orders);

and representation for the purposes of care proceedings to which this section applies shall be available to any person subject to and in accordance with section 28.

(2) Subsection (1) above may be varied by regulations so as to restrict the categories of proceedings for the purposes of which representation is available under this section and section 28.

(3) Representation for the purposes of care proceedings before a juvenile court extends to the proceedings before any juvenile court to which the case is remitted.

(4) Subject to any provision made by virtue of subsection (6) below, the authorities competent, on an application made for the purpose, to grant representation for the purposes of care proceedings are—

  (a) as respects proceedings before a juvenile court, the court;

  (b) as respects appeals from decisions of juvenile courts to the Crown Court, the Crown Court or the juvenile court from which the appeal is brought;

  (c) as respects appeals from decisions of juvenile courts to the High Court, the Board;

  (d) as respects proceedings before a justice of the peace under section 12E of the 1980 Act (applications for emergency orders), the justice of the peace.

(5) In the event of the Lord Chancellor making an order under section 3(4) as respects the function of granting representation for the purposes of any care proceedings, the Board shall be competent as respects those proceedings, on an application made for the purpose.

(6) An order under section 3(4) may make provision restricting or excluding the competence of any authority mentioned in subsection (4) above and may contain such transitional provisions as appear to the Lord Chancellor necessary or expedient.

(7) in this section and section 28—

'the 1969 Act' means the Children and Young Persons Act 1969;

'the 1980 Act' means the Child Care Act 1980; and

'remitted' in relation to a juvenile court, means remitted under section 2(11) of the 1969 Act.

Note. This section repealed by Children Act 1989, ss 99(1), (4), 108(7), Sch 15, as from 14 October 1991.

28. Care proceedings: availability—(1) Representation for the purposes of care proceedings to which this section applies shall be available to any person, other than a local authority, who is a party to the proceedings.

(2) Subject to subsection (4) below, representation may be granted where it appears to the competent authority to be desirable to do so in the interests of justice.

(3) Subject to subsection (4) below, representation must be granted where a child—

(a) is brought before a juvenile court under section 21A of the 1980 Act, and

(b) is not legally represented before the court but wishes to be.

(4) Representation shall not be granted to any person unless it appears to the competent authority that his financial resources are such as, under regulations, make him eligible for representation.

(5) Where a doubt arises whether representation should be granted to any person, the doubt shall be resolved in that person's favour.

(6) Representation granted by a competent authority may be amended or withdrawn, whether by that or another authority competent to grant representation.

(7) Regulations may provide for an appeal to lie to a specified court or body against any refusal by a juvenile court to grant representation for the purposes of care proceedings and for that other court or body to make any grant of representation that could have been made by the juvenile court.

Note. This section 28 repealed by Children Act 1989, ss 99(1), (4), 108(7), Sch 15, as from 14 October 1991.

Contempt proceedings

29. Representation in contempt proceedings—(1) This section applies to any proceedings where a person is liable to be committed or fined—

(a) by a magistrates' court under section 12 of the Contempt of Court Act 1981;

(b) by a county court under section 14, 92 or 118 of the County Courts Act 1984;

(c) by any superior court for contempt in the face of that or any other court;

and in this Act 'proceedings for contempt' means so much of any proceedings as relates to dealing with a person as mentioned in paragraph (a), (b) or (c) above.

(2) In any proceedings for contempt against a person the court may order that he be granted representation under this section for the purposes of the proceedings if it appears to the court to be desirable to do so in the interests of justice.

(3) In this section, 'superior court' means the Court of Appeal, the High Court, the Crown Court, the Courts-Martial Appeal Court, the Restrictive Practices Court, the Employment Appeal Tribunal and any other court exercising in relation to its proceedings powers equivalent to those of the High Court, and includes the House of Lords in the exercise of its jurisdiction in relation to appeals from courts in England and Wales.

Supplementary

30. Supplementary—(1) In Part V, the following provisions—

(a) sections 23 and 24 together with Schedule 3, and

(b) section 25,

shall apply for the purposes of representation in care proceedings to which sections 27 and 28 apply as they apply for the purposes of representation under that Part in criminal proceedings with the modification mentioned below.

(2) The modification referred to above is the substitution for paragraphs 9(b) and 10(2)(b) of Schedule 3 of the following sub-paragraph—

'(b) references to the proceedings for the purposes of which a grant of representation has been made include, where the proceedings result in the giving of a direction under section 2(11) of the Children and Young Persons Act 1969 (duty in care proceedings to direct that the infant be brought before a juvenile court acting for the area in which he resides), the proceedings before the court before which the legally assisted person is brought in pursuance of the direction.'

(3) In Part V, section 25 shall apply for the purposes of representation in proceedings for contempt as it applies for the purposes of representation under that Part in criminal proceedings.

Note. Sub-ss (1), (2) repealed by Children Act 1989, ss 99(1), (4), 108(7), Sch 15, as from 14 October 1991.

PART VII

GENERAL AND SUPPLEMENTARY

31. Act not generally to affect position of legal representatives or other parties—(1) Except as expressly provided by this Act or regulations under it—

(a) the fact that the services of counsel or a solicitor [a legal representative] are given under this Act shall not affect the relationship between or rights of counsel, solicitor [the legal representative] and client or any privilege arising out of such relationship; and

(b) the rights conferred by this Act on a person receiving advice, assistance or representation under it shall not affect the rights or liabilities of other parties to the proceedings or the principles on which the discretion of any court or tribunal is normally exercised.

(2) Without prejudice to the generality of subsection (1)(b) above, for the purpose of determining the costs of a legally assisted person in pursuance of an order for costs or an agreement for costs in his favour (other than an order under Part II of the Prosecution of Offences Act 1985) the services of his solicitor and counsel [legal representative] shall be treated as having been provided otherwise than under this Act and his solicitor shall be treated as having paid counsel's fees [legal representative shall be treated as having paid the fees of any additional legal representative instructed by him.]

(3) A person who provides advice, assistance or representation under this Act shall not take any payment in respect of the advice, assistance or representation except such payment as is made by the Board or authorised by, or by regulations under, this Act.

(4) The revocation under this Act of a grant (or, in the case of Part III, of approval for a grant) of advice, assistance or representation to a legally assisted person shall not affect the right of any legal representative of his, arising otherwise than under a contract, to remuneration for work done before the date of the revocation.

Note. Words in square brackets substituted in sub-ss (1)(a), (2) by Courts and Legal Services Act 1990, s 125(3), Sch 18, paras 62(1), 63(1)(a), (3)(c), as from 1 April 1991.

32. Selection and assignment of legal representatives—(1) Subject to the provisions of this section, a person entitled to receive advice or assistance or representation may select—

(a) the solicitor to advise or assist or act for him, and

(b) if the case requires counsel, his counsel,

from among the solicitors and counsel willing [select the legal representative to advise, assist or act for him from among the legal representatives willing] to provide advice, assistance or representation under this Act.

(2) Where the Board limits a grant of representation under Part IV to representation in pursuance of a contract made by the Board, it may, as it thinks fit, *assign to the legally assisted person a solicitor or a solicitor and counsel or direct that he may only select a solicitor from among those with whom such a contract subsists [one or more legal representatives or direct that he may only select a legal representative from among those with whom such a contract subsists].*

(3) A person's right to select his solicitor or counsel [legal representative] is subject, in the case of representation under Part V, to regulations under subsection (8) below.

(4) Subsection (1) above does not confer any right of selection in relation to proceedings under section 29 for the purposes of proceedings for contempt.

(5) Where a court grants representation to a person for the purposes of proceedings for contempt, it may assign to him for the purposes of the proceedings any counsel or solicitor [legal representative] who is within the precincts of the court at the time.

(6) The selection by or assignment to a person of solicitor or counsel [a legal representative] shall not prejudice the law and practice relating to the conduct or proceedings by a solicitor or counsel or the circumstances in which a solicitor or counsel [legal representative] may refuse or give up a case or entrust it to another.

(7) Regulations may provide that the right conferred by subsection (1) above shall be exercisable only in relation to solicitors [legal representatives] who are for the time being members of a prescribed panel.

(8) Regulations may provide as respects representation under Part V that subsection (1) above shall not apply in cases of any prescribed description and that in any such case a prescribed authority shall assign solicitor or counsel or solicitor and counsel [one or more legal representatives] in accordance with regulations under section 2(7) to the person entitled to receive such representation.

(9) No solicitor or counsel who is for the time being excluded from legal aid work under section 47(2) of the Solicitors Act 1974 (powers of Solicitors Disciplinary Tribunal) or section 42 of the Administration of Justice Act 1985 (exclusion of barristers from legal aid work) may be selected or assigned under this section.

[(9) None of the following persons may be selected or assigned under this section—

(a)   a solicitor who is for the time being excluded from legal aid work under section 47(2) of the Solicitors Act 1974 (powers of Solicitors Disciplinary Tribunal);

(b)   a barrister excluded from such work under section 42 of the Administration of Justice Act 1985 (exclusion of barristers from legal aid work);

(c)   any other legal representative excluded from such work for disciplinary reasons by an authorised body.]

(10) Notwithstanding subsection (1) above, a solicitor [legal representative] who has been selected to act for a person under that subsection may himself select to act for that person, as the solicitor's [legal representative's] agent, any other solicitor [legal representative] who is not for the time being excluded from selection.

Note. Words in square brackets substituted and sub-s (9) in square brackets substituted for sub-s (9) by Courts and Legal Services Act 1990, s 125(3), Sch 18, paras 62(2), 63(1)(b), (2), (3)(a),(b), (4), (5)(a), as from 1 April 1991.

33. (*Substitutes Administration of Justice Act 1985, ss 41, 42, p 3048.*)

34. Regulations—*(1) The Lord Chancellor may make such regulations as appear to him necessary or desirable for giving effect to this Act or for preventing abuses of it.*

(2) Without prejudice to the generality of subsection (1) above, any such regulations may—

(a)   make provision as to the matters which are or are not to be treated as distinct matters for the purposes of advice or assistance under Part III, as to the proceedings which are or are not to be treated as distinct proceedings for the purposes of representation under Part IV, and as to the apportionment of sums recoverable or recovered by virtue of any order for costs made generally with respect to matters or proceedings treated as distinct;

(b) *regulate the procedure of any court or tribunal in relation to advice, assistance or representation under this Act or orders for costs made thereunder and authorise the delegation (subject to appeal) or the exercise of their functions by members, officers or other courts or the judges or members of other courts;*

(c) *regulate the availability of advice, assistance[, mediation] or representation (other than for the purposes of proceedings for contempt) and the making of contributions towards its provision by reference to the financial resources or, in prescribed cases, the aggregate financial resources, of persons and provide for the courts, persons or bodies who are to determine the financial resources of persons and the persons who are to be required or permitted to furnish information for those purposes;*

(d) *provide for the cases in which a person may be refused advice, assistance[, mediation] or representation or have the grant of it withdrawn or revoked by reason of his conduct when seeking or receiving advice, assistance[, mediation] or representation (whether in the same or a different matter);*

(e) *make provision for the remuneration and payment of the expenses of solicitors and counsel [legal representatives] and for the courts, persons or bodies by whom, and the manner in which, any determinations which may be required for those purposes are to be made, reviewed or appealed;*

(f) *make provision for the recovery of sums due to the Board and for making effective the charge created by this Act on property recovered or preserved for a legally assisted person and regulating the release or postponement of the enforcement of any charge (however created) in favour of the Board.*

Note. Words in square brackets in sub-s (2)(c), (d) inserted by Family Law Act 1996, s 66(1), Sch 8, Part II, para 44, as from 21 March 1997. Words in square brackets in sub-s (2)(e) substituted by Courts and Legal Services Act 1990, s 125(3), Sch 18, para 63, as from 1 April 1991.

(3) *Regulations may also modify this Act for the purposes of its application to prescribed descriptions of persons or in prescribed circumstances.*

(4) *Without prejudice to subsection (3) above, regulations may also modify this Act for the purposes of its application—*

(a) *in cases where its modification appears to the Lord Chancellor necessary for the purpose of fulfilling any obligation imposed on the United Kingdom or Her Majesty's Government in the United Kingdom by any international agreement; or*

(b) *in relation to proceedings for securing the recognition or enforcement in England and Wales of judgments given outside the United Kingdom for whose recognition or enforcement in the United Kingdom provision is made by any international agreement.*

(5) *Regulations made for the purposes mentioned in subsection (2)(b) above may include provisions—*

(a) *as to the determination of costs incurred in connection with proceedings not actually begun; and*

(b) *as to the cases in which and extent to which a person receiving advice, assistance or representation may be required to give security for costs, and the manner in which it may be so given.*

(6) *Regulations made for the purposes mentioned in subsection (2)(c) above may provide that the income or capital of a person in receipt of prescribed social security benefits [benefits under Part VII of the Social Security Contributions and Benefits Act 1992 (income-related benefits)] is to be taken as not exceeding a prescribed amount.*

Note. Words in square brackets substituted by Social Security (Consequential Provisions) Act 1992, s 4, Sch 2, para 97, as from 1 July 1992.

(7) *Regulations made for the purposes mentioned in subsection (2)(e) above may include provisions—*

(a) *imposing conditions for the allowance of remuneration and expenses;*

(b) *attaching financial penalties in the event of appeals or reviews of determinations being unsuccessful;*

    (c)   *authorising the making of interim payments of remuneration or in respect of expenses.*

    (8) *Regulations made for the purposes mentioned in subsection (2)(f) above may include provisions—*

    (a)   *for the enforcement for the benefit of the Board of an order or agreement for costs made in favour of a legally assisted person;*

    (b)   *for making a solicitor's [legal representative's] right to payment by the Board wholly or partly dependent on his performance of the duties imposed on him by regulations made for the purposes of that paragraph; and*

    (c)   *requiring interest to be charged at a prescribed rate in circumstances where enforcement of a charge in favour of the Board is postponed.*

    (9) *The Lord Chancellor, in making regulations for the purposes mentioned in subsection (2)(e) above as respects any description of legal aid work, shall have regard, among the matters which are relevant, to—*

    (a)   *the time and skill which it requires;*

    (b)   *the general level of fee income arising from it;*

    (c)   *the general level of expenses of barristers and solicitors [legal representatives] which is attributable to it;*

    (d)   *the number and general level of competence of barristers and solicitors [legal representatives] undertaking it;*

    (e)   *the effect of the regulations on the handling of the work; and*

    (f)   *the cost to public funds of any provision made by the regulations.*

Note. Words in square brackets in sub-ss (8)(b), (9)(c), (d) substituted by Courts and Legal Services Act 1990, s 125(3), Sch 18, para 63(2), (5)(b), (c), as from 1 April 1991.

    (10) *Before making regulations for the purposes mentioned in subsection (2)(e) above, the Lord Chancellor shall consult the General Council of the Bar and the Law Society.*

    (11) *Regulations under this Act may make different provision for different descriptions of advice, assistance[, mediation] or representation, for different cases or classes of case, for different areas or for other different circumstances and for different descriptions of persons.*

Note. Word in square brackets inserted by Family Law Act 1996, s 66(1), Sch 8, Part II, para 44, as from 21 March 1997.

    (12) *Before making regulations as to the procedure of any court or tribunal, the Lord Chancellor shall so far as practicable consult any rule committee or similar body by whom or on whose advice rules of procedure for the court or tribunal may be made apart from this provision or whose consent or concurrence is required to any such rules so made.*

    (13) *No regulations shall be made under this section which include provision for the purposes mentioned in subsection (2)(c) or (e) above except with the consent of the Treasury.*

    (14) *In subsection (6) above 'social security benefits' means any benefit provided under section 20 (1) of the Social Security Act 1986 (income-related benefits).*

Note. Sub-s (14) repealed by Social Security (Consequential Provisions) Act 1992, s 3, Sch 1, as from 1 July 1992.

35. Advisory Committee—(*1*) *The existing advisory committee shall continue in being to advise the Lord Chancellor on such questions relating to the provision of advice, assistance or representation under this Act as he may from time to time refer to them and to make recommendations or furnish comments to him on such matters as they consider appropriate.*

    (2) *Appointments to the committee by the Lord Chancellor, whether by way of replacing existing members or making additional appointments, shall be made so as to secure that the committee is constituted of persons having knowledge of the work of the courts and social conditions.*

    (3) *The Lord Chancellor may pay to the members of the advisory committee such travelling and other allowances as he may, with the consent of the Treasury, determine; and any expenses of the Lord Chancellor under this subsection shall be defrayed out of money provided by Parliament.*

(4) It shall be the duty of the advisory committee to provide to the Lord Chancellor, as soon as possible after 31st March in each year, a report containing any advice, recommendations or comments of theirs on questions or matters arising during the preceding twelve months.

(5) The Lord Chancellor shall lay before each House of Parliament a copy of the annual report of the committee made to him under subsection (4) above.

(6) The Lord Chancellor may, by order dissolve the advisory committee on such day as is specified in the order and on that day this section shall cease to have effect as regards the defrayal out of money provided by Parliament of the allowances falling to be paid thereafter under subsection (3) above.

(7) In this section 'the existing advisory committee' means the advisory committee in existence under section 21 of the Legal Aid Act 1974 at the passing of this Act.

Note. This section repealed by virtue of Legal Aid Advisory Committee (Dissolution) Order 1995, SI 1995 No 162, as from 26 January 1995, as specified in sub-s (6).

36. Orders and regulations: general—(1) Any power under this Act to make an order or regulations shall be exercisable by statutory instrument.

(2) As respects orders under this Act other than orders under section 47—

(a) except in the case of an order under section 3(4) and 35(6), any instrument containing the order shall be subject to annulment in pursuance of a resolution of either House of Parliament;

(b) in the case of an order under section 3(4) or 35(6), no such order shall be made unless a draft of it has been laid before and approved by resolution of each House of Parliament.

(3) As respects regulations under this Act—

(a) except in the case of regulations under section 8, 14(2) and 32(7), any instrument containing the regulations shall be subject to annulment in pursuance of a resolution of either House of Parliament;

(b) in the case of regulations under section 8, 14(2) or 32(7), no such regulations shall be made unless a draft of them has been laid before and approved by resolution of each House of Parliament.

37. Laying of Board's annual reports before Parliament.   The Lord Chancellor shall lay before each House of Parliament a copy of the annual report of the Board made to him under section 5(3).

38. Restriction of disclosure of information—(1) Subject to the following provisions of this section, no information furnished for the purposes of this Act to the Board or any court or other person or body of persons upon whom functions are imposed or conferred by regulations and so furnished in connection with the case of a person seeking or receiving advice, assistance[, mediation] or representation shall be disclosed otherwise than—

(a) for the purpose of enabling or assisting the Lord Chancellor to perform his functions under or in relation to this Act,

(b) for the purpose of enabling the Board to discharge its functions under this Act,

(c) for the purpose of facilitating the proper performance by any court, tribunal or other person or body of persons of functions under this Act,

(d) with a view to the institution of, or otherwise for the purposes of, any criminal proceedings for an offence under this Act,

(e) in connection with any other proceedings under this Act, or

(f) for the purpose of facilitating the proper performance by any tribunal of disciplinary functions as regards barristers or solicitors [legal representatives] [or mediators].

Note. Words in first and third pairs of square brackets inserted by Family Law Act 1996, s 66, Sch 8, Part II, para 44, as from 21 March 1997. Words in second pair of square brackets substituted by Courts and Legal Services Act 1990, s 125(3), Sch 18, para 63, as from 1 April 1991.

(2) This section does not apply to information in the form of a summary or collection of information so framed as not to enable information relating to any particular person to be ascertained from it.

(3) Subsection (1) above shall not prevent the disclosure of information for any purpose with the consent of the person in connection with whose case it was furnished and, where he did not furnish it himself, with that of the person or body of persons who did.

(4) A person who, in contravention of this section, discloses any information furnished to the Board or any court or other person or body of persons for the purposes of this Act shall be liable on summary conviction to a fine not exceeding level 4 on the standard scale.

(5) Proceedings for an offence under this section shall not be brought without the written consent of the Attorney General.

(6) For the avoidance of doubt it is hereby declared that information furnished to counsel or a solicitor [a legal representative] [or mediator] as such by or on behalf of a person seeking or receiving advice, assistance[, mediation] or representation under this Act is not information furnished to the board or a person upon whom functions are imposed or conferred as mentioned in subsection (1) above.

Note. Words in first pair of square brackets substituted by Courts and Legal Services Act 1990, s 125(3), Sch 18, para 63(1)(a), (5)(d), as from 1 April 1991. Words in second and third pairs of square brackets inserted by Family Law Act 1996, s 66(1), Sch 8, Part II, para 44, as from 21 March 1997.

39. Proceedings for misrepresentation etc—*(1) If any person seeking or receiving advice, assistance[, mediation] or representation under this Act—*

    (a) intentionally fails to comply with regulations as to the information to be furnished by him, or

    (b) in furnishing any information required by regulations knowingly makes any false statement or false representation,

he shall be liable on summary conviction to a fine not exceeding level 4 on the standard scale or to imprisonment for a term not exceeding three months or to both.

Note. Words in square brackets inserted by Family Law Act 1996, s 66(1), Sch 8, Part II, para 44, as from 21 March 1997.

(2) Notwithstanding anything in the Magistrates' Courts Act 1980, proceedings in respect of an offence under subsection (1) above may be brought at any time within the period of six months beginning with the date on which evidence sufficient in the opinion of the prosecutor to justify a prosecution comes to his knowledge.

(3) Nothing in subsection (2) above shall authorise the commencement of proceedings for an offence at a time more than two years after the date on which the offence was committed.

(4) A county court shall have jurisdiction to hear and determine any action brought by the Board to recover the loss sustained by it on account of its legal aid fund by reason of—

    (a) the failure of a person seeking or receiving advice, assistance[, mediation] or representation to comply with regulations as to the information to be furnished by him, or

    (b) a false statement or false representation made by such a person in furnishing information for the purposes of this Act,

notwithstanding that the claim in the action is for a greater amount than that which for the time being is the county court limit for the purposes of section 15 of the County Courts Act 1984.

Note. Word in square brackets in sub-s (4)(a) inserted by Family Law Act 1996, s 66(1), Sch 8, Part II, para 44, as from 21 March 1997. Words 'notwithstanding' to 'County Courts Act 1984' repealed by High Court and County Courts Jurisdiction Order 1991, SI 1991 No 724, art 2(8), Schedule, Part I, as from 1 July 1991.

40. Adaptation of rights of indemnity in cases of advice, assistance or representation in civil proceedings—*(1) This section shall have effect for the purpose of adapting in relation to Parts III and IV any right (however and whenever created or arising) which a person may have to be indemnified against expenses incurred by him.*

(2) In determining for the purposes of any such right the reasonableness of any expenses, the possibility of avoiding them or part of them by taking advantage of Part III or Part IV shall be disregarded.

(3) Where a person having any such right to be indemnified against expenses incurred in connection with any proceedings receives in connection with those proceedings advice, assistance or representation then (without prejudice to the effect of the indemnity in relation to his contribution, if any, under section 9 or 16) the right shall enure also for the benefit of the Board as if any expenses incurred by the Board on his account in connection with the advice, assistance or representation had been incurred by him.

(4) Where a person's right to be indemnified enures for the benefit of the Board under subsection (3) above in a case where he has been represented in pursuance of a contract made with the Board on terms which do not differentiate between the remuneration for his and other cases, the reference in that subsection to any expenses incurred by the Board on his account shall be construed as a reference to such part of the remuneration payable under the contract as may be specified in writing by the Board.

(5) Where—

(a) a person's right to be indemnified against expenses incurred in connection with any proceedings arises by virtue of an agreement and is subject to any express condition conferring on those liable under it any right with respect to the bringing or conduct of the proceedings, and

(b) those liable have been given a reasonable opportunity of exercising the right so conferred and have not availed themselves of the opportunity,

the right to be indemnified shall be treated for the purpose of subsection (3) above as not being subject to that condition.

(6) Nothing in subsections (3) and (5) above shall be taken as depriving any person or body of persons of the protection of any enactment or, except as provided in subsection (5), as conferring any larger right to recover money in respect of any expenses than the person receiving advice, assistance or representation would have had if the expenses had been incurred by him.

41. Application to Crown.   *This Act binds the Crown.*

42. Finance—(1) The Lord Chancellor shall pay to the Board out of money provided by Parliament—

(a) such sums as are required (after allowing for payments by the Board into its legal aid fund under paragraphs (a), (b), (c), (d) and (f) of section 6(3)) to meet the payments which, under subsection (2) of that section, are to be paid by the Board out of that fund; and

(b) such sums as he may, with the approval of the Treasury, determine are required for the other expenditure of the Board.

(2) The Lord Chancellor may, with the approval of the Treasury—

(a) determine the manner in which and times at which the sums referred to in subsection (1)(a) above shall be paid to the Board; and

(b) impose conditions on the payment of the sums referred to in subsection (1)(b) above.

43. Definitions.   *In this Act—*

'advice', 'assistance'[, 'mediation'] and 'representation' have the meanings assigned to them by section 2(2), (3)[, (3A)] and (4) respectively subject, however, to the other provisions of that section;

['authorised body' has the meaning assigned by section 119(1) of the Courts and Legal Services Act 1990;]

'the Board' has the meaning assigned to it by section 3(1);

'determination', in relation to the costs of advice or assistance or representation for the purposes of proceedings, includes taxation and assessment;

'*financial resources*', *in relation to any person, includes any valuable facility which is available to him;*

[*'family matters' has the meaning assigned by section 13A(2);*]

[*'legal representative' means an authorised advocate or authorised litigator, as defined by section 119(1) of the Courts and Legal Services Act 1990;*]

[*'mediator' means a person with whom the Board contracts for the provision of mediation by any person;*]

'*order for costs' includes any judgment, order, decree, award or direction for the payment of the costs of one party to any proceedings by another party, whether given or made in those proceedings or not;*

'*prescribed' means prescribed by regulations made by the Lord Chancellor under this Act;*

'*proceedings for contempt' has the meaning assigned to it by section 29(1);*

'*regulations' means regulations by the Lord Chancellor under this Act;*

'*sentence', in relation to a person, includes any order made on his conviction of an offence;*

'*solicitor' means solicitor of the Supreme Court;*

'*statutory inquiry' has the meaning assigned to it by section 19(1) of the Tribunals and Inquiries Act 1971 [section 16(1) of the Tribunals and Inquiries Act 1992]; and*

'*tribunal' includes an arbitrator or umpire, however appointed, and whether the arbitration takes place under a reference by consent or otherwise.*

Note. In first definition words in square brackets inserted, and definitions 'family matters' and 'mediator' inserted by Family Law Act 1996, ss 26(3), 66(1), Sch 8, Part II, para 44, as from 21 March 1997. Definitions 'authorised body' and 'legal representative' in square brackets inserted by Courts and Legal Services Act 1990, s 125(3), Sch 18, para 60, as from 1 April 1991. In definition 'statutory inquiry' words in square brackets substituted by Tribunals and Inquiries Act 1992, s 18(1), Sch 3, para 21, as from 1 October 1992.

* * * * *

Supplementary

45. Amendments, repeals and transitional provisions—(*1*) *The enactments specified in Schedule 5 to this Act shall have effect subject to the amendments there specified.*

(*2*) *Subject to subsection (4) below, the enactments specified in Schedule 6 to this Act are repealed to the extent specified in the third column of that Schedule.*

(*3*) *Where any enactment amended or repealed by subsection (1) or (2) above extends to the United Kingdom or any part of it, the amendment or repeal has a corresponding extent.*

(*4*) *Schedule 7 to this Act shall have effect for the purpose of making the transitional and saving provisions set out there.*

46. (*Introduced Sch 8 (transitory amendments of Legal Aid Act 1974).*)

47. Short title, commencement and extent—(1) This Act may be cited as the Legal Aid Act 1988.

(2) Subject to subsections (3) and (4) below, this Act shall come into force on such day as the Lord Chancellor appoints by order and different days may be appointed for different provisions.

(3) Section 44 and Schedule 4 shall come into force on such day as the Secretary of State appoints by order and different days may be appointed for different provisions.

(4) Sections 35 (together with the repeal of section 21 of the Legal Aid Act 1974) and 46 shall come into force on the date on which this Act is passed.

(5) An order under subsection (2) or (3) above may contain such transitional and saving provisions as appear to the Lord Chancellor or, as the case may be, the Secretary of State necessary or expedient.

(6) This Act, with the exception of sections 12(3) and 17(3), section 44 and Schedule 4 and the amendments or repeals of the enactments referred to in section 45(3), extends to England and Wales only and section 44 and Schedule 4 extend to Scotland only.

Commencement. Sections 1, 2, 3(2)–(4), 4–28, 30(1), (2), 31–34, 36–43, Schs 2, 3, 5, 6 (in part), Sch 7, paras 1–5, 9–11 came into force on 1 April 1989 (SI 1989 No 288); ss 3(1), (5)–(10), Sch 1, paras 6–8 came into force on 20 August 1988 (SI 1988 No 1361); ss 35, 46, 47, Sch 4, paras 1, 2, 4, 6–9, Sch 6 (in part), Sch 8 came into force on 29 July 1988 (s 47(4)); ss 29, 30(3) came into force on 1 May 1991 (SI 1991 No 790); Sch 4, paras 3, 5 have not yet been brought into force.

SCHEDULES

SCHEDULE 1   *Section 3*

THE LEGAL AID BOARD

Incorporation and Status

1. *The Board shall be a body corporate.*

2. *The Board shall not be regarded as the servant or agent of the Crown or as enjoying any status, immunity or privilege of the Crown; and the Board's property shall not be regarded as property of, or held on behalf of, the Crown.*

Tenure of Members

3. *Subject to paragraphs 4 and 5 any member of the Board shall hold and vacate office in accordance with the terms of his appointment, but a person shall not be appointed a member of the Board for a period of more than 5 years.*

4. *(1) The chairman or a member may resign office by giving notice in writing to the Lord Chancellor, and if the chairman ceases to be a member he shall cease to be the chairman.*

(2) A person who ceases to be the chairman or a member shall be eligible for reappointment.

5. *The Lord Chancellor may terminate the appointment of a member of the Board if satisfied that—*

(a) *he has become bankrupt or made an arrangement with his creditors;*
(b) *he is unable to carry out his duties as a Board member by reason of physical or mental illness;*
(c) *he has been absent from meetings of the Board for a period longer than six consecutive months without the permission of the Board; or*
(d) *he is otherwise unable or unfit to discharge the functions of a member of the Board.*

Members' interests

6. *(1) Before appointing a person to be a member of the Board, the Lord Chancellor shall satisfy himself that that person will have no such financial or other interest as is likely to affect prejudicially the exercise or performance by him of his functions as a member of the Board.*

(2) The Lord Chancellor shall from time to time satisfy himself with respect to every member of the Board that he has no such interest as is referred to in sub-paragraph (1) above.

(3) Any person whom the Lord Chancellor proposes to appoint as, and who has consented to be, a member of the Board, and any member of the Board, shall, whenever requested by the Lord Chancellor to do so, supply him with such information as the Lord Chancellor considers necessary for the performance by the Lord Chancellor of his duties under this paragraph.

7. *(1) A member of the Board who is in any way directly or indirectly interested in a contract made or proposed to be made by the Board shall disclose the nature of his interest at a meeting of the Board; and the disclosure shall be recorded in the minutes of the Board, and the member shall not take any part in any deliberation or decision of the Board with respect to that contract.*

(2) For the purposes of sub-paragraph (1) above, a general notice given at a meeting of the Board by a member of the Board to the effect that he is a member of a specified company or firm and is to be regarded as interested in any contract which may, after the date of the notice, be made with the company or firm shall be regarded as a sufficient disclosure of his interest in relation to any contract so made.

(3) A member of the Board need not attend in person at a meeting of the Board in order to make any disclosure which he is required to make under this paragraph if he takes reasonable steps to secure that the disclosure is made by a notice which is brought up and read out at the meeting.

Remuneration of Members

8. (1) The Board may—

(a) pay to its members such remuneration; and

(b) make provision for the payment of such pensions, allowances or gratuities to or in respect of its members,

as the Lord Chancellor may, with the approval of the Treasury, determine.

(2) Where a person ceases to be a member of the Board otherwise than on the expiry of his term of office, and it appears to the Lord Chancellor that there are special circumstances which make it right for that person to receive compensation, the Lord Chancellor may, with the consent of the Treasury, direct the Board to make that person a payment of such amount as the Lord Chancellor may, with the consent of the Treasury, determine.

Staff

9. (1) The Board shall appoint a person to be the chief executive of the Board who shall be responsible to the Board for the exercise of its functions.

(2) The Board may appoint such other employees as it thinks fit.

(3) The Board may only appoint a person to be its chief executive or the holder of any other employment of a specified description after consultation with, and subject to the approval of, the Lord Chancellor.

(4) The reference in sub-paragraph (3) above to employment of a specified description is a reference to any employment for the time being specified by the Lord Chancellor in a direction given for the purposes of that sub-paragraph.

(5) An appointment under this paragraph may be made on such terms and conditions as the Board, with the approval of the Lord Chancellor and consent of the Treasury, may determine.

10. (1) The Board shall make, in respect of such of its employees as, with the approval of the Lord Chancellor and the consent of the Treasury, it may determine such arrangements for providing pensions, allowances or gratuities, including pensions, allowances or gratuities by way of compensation for loss of employment, as it may determine.

(2) Arrangements under sub-paragraph (1) above may include the establishment and administration, by the Board or otherwise, of one or more pension schemes.

(3) If an employee of the Board—

(a) becomes a member of the Board; and

(b) was by reference to his employment by the Board a participant in a pension scheme established and administered by it for the benefit of its employees,

the Board may determine that his service as a member shall be treated for the purposes of the scheme as service as an employee of the Board whether or not any benefits are to be payable to or in respect of him by virtue of paragraph 8.

(4) Where the Board exercises the power conferred by sub-paragraph (3) above, any discretion as to the benefits payable to or in respect of the member concerned which the scheme confers on the Board shall be exercised only with the approval of the Lord Chancellor and consent of the Treasury.

Proceedings

11. (1) Subject to anything in regulations, the Board may regulate its own proceedings.

(2) The Board may make such arrangements as it considers appropriate for the discharge of its functions, including the delegation of specified functions and shall make such arrangements for the delegation of functions to committees and persons as may be prescribed.

(3) Subject to anything in regulations, committees may be appointed and may be dissolved by the Board, and may include, or consist entirely of, persons who are not members of the Board.

(4) A committee shall act in accordance with such directions as the Board may from time to time give, and the Board may provide for anything done by a committee to have effect as if it had been done by the Board.

(5) The validity of any proceedings of the Board or of any committee appointed by the Board shall not be affected by any vacancy among its members or by any defect in the appointment of any member.

Instruments

12. (1) The fixing of the seal of the Board shall be authenticated by the chairman or another member of the Board and by some other person authorised either generally or specially by the Board to act for that purpose.

(2) A document purporting to be duly executed under the seal of the Board, or to be signed on the board's behalf, shall be received in evidence and, unless the contrary is proved, be deemed to be so executed or signed.

Allowances

13. The Board may pay to the members of any committee such fees and allowances as the Lord Chancellor may, with the consent of the Treasury, determine.

SCHEDULE 2   Section 14

CIVIL PROCEEDINGS: SCOPE OF PART IV REPRESENTATION

PART *I*

DESCRIPTION OF PROCEEDINGS

1. Proceedings in, or before any person to whom a case is referred in whole or in part by, any of the following courts, namely—
   (a) the House of Lords in the exercise of its jurisdiction in relation to appeals from courts in England and Wales;
   (b) the Court of Appeal;
   (c) the High Court;
   (d) any county court.
2. The following proceedings in a magistrates' court, namely—
   (a) proceedings under the Guardianship of Minors Acts 1971 and 1973;
   (b) proceedings under section 43 of the National Assistance Act 1948, section 22 of the Maintenance Orders Act 1950, section 4 of the Maintenance Orders Act 1958, or section 18 of the Supplementary Benefits Act 1976;
   (c) proceedings in relation to an application for leave of the court to remove a child from a person's custody under section 27 or 28 of the Adoption Act 1976 or proceedings in which the making of an order under Part II or section 29 or 55 of the Adoption Act 1976 is opposed by any party to the proceedings;
   (d) proceedings under Part I of the Maintenance Orders (Reciprocal Enforcement) Act 1972 relating to a maintenance order made by a court of a country outside the United Kingdom;
   (e) proceedings under Part II of the Children Act 1975;
   (f) proceedings for or in relation to an order under Part I of the Domestic Proceedings and Magistrates' Courts Act 1978.
   [(g) proceedings under the Children Act 1989.]

[(h) appeals under section 20, where they are to be made to a magistrates' court, and proceedings under section 27 of the Child Support Act 1991;]

[(i) proceedings under section 30 of the Human Fertilisation and Embryology Act 1990.]

3. *Proceedings in the Employment Appeal Tribunal.*

4. *Proceedings in the Lands Tribunal.*

5. *Proceedings before a Commons Commissioner appointed under section 17(1) of the Commons Registration Act 1965.*

6. *Proceedings in the Restrictive Practices Court under Part III of the Fair Trading Act 1973, and any proceedings in that court in consequence of an order made, or undertaking given to the court, under that Part of that Act.*

Note. Para 2(a), (e) repealed by Children Act 1989, s 108(7), Sch 15, and para 2(g) added by s 108(4) of, and Sch 12, para 45 to, that Act, as from 14 October 1991. Para 2(h) added by Civil Legal Aid (Scope) Regulations 1993, SI 1993 No 1354, reg 2, as from 27 May 1993. Para 2(i) added by Legal Aid (Scope) Regulations 1994, SI 1994 No 2768, reg 2, as from 1 November 1994.

PART II

EXCEPTED PROCEEDINGS

1. *Proceedings wholly or partly in respect of defamation, but so that the making of a counterclaim for defamation in proceedings for which representation may be granted shall not of itself affect any right of the defendant to the counterclaim to representation for the purposes of the proceedings and so that representation may be granted to enable him to defend the counterclaim.*

2. *Relator actions.*

3. *Proceedings for the recovery of a penalty where the proceedings may be taken by any person and the whole or part of the penalty is payable to the person taking the proceedings.*

4. *Election petitions under the Representation of the People Act 1983.*

5. *In a county court, proceedings for or consequent on the issue of a judgment summons and, in the case of a defendant, proceedings where the only question to be brought before the court is as to the time and mode of payment by him of a debt (including liquidated damages) and costs.*

[5A. Proceedings for a decree of divorce or judicial separation [a divorce order or a separation order] unless the cause is defended, or the petition is directed to be heard in open court, or it is not practicable by reason of physical or mental incapacity for the applicant to proceed without representation; except that representation shall be available for the purpose of making or opposing an application—

(a) for an injunction;

(b) for ancillary relief, excluding representation for the purpose only of inserting a prayer for ancillary relief in the petition [application];

(c) for an order relating to the custody of (or access to) a child, or the education or care or supervision of a child, excluding representation for the purpose only of making such an application where there is no reason to believe that the application will be opposed;

(d) for an order declaring that the court is satisfied as to arrangements for the welfare of the children of the family, excluding representation for the purpose only of making such an application where there is no reason to believe that the application will be opposed; or

(e) for the purpose of making or opposing any other application, or satisfying the court on any other matter which raise a substantial question for determination by the court.]

Note. Para 5A inserted by Civil Legal Aid (Matrimonial Proceedings) Regulations 1989, SI 1989 No 549, reg 2, as from 1 April 1989. Words in square brackets substituted for words in italics by Family Law Act 1996, s 66(1), Sch 8, Part I, para 39, as from a day to be appointed, subject to savings in s 66(2) of, and para 5 of Sch 9 to, the 1996 Act.

[**5B.** *Proceedings to the extent that they consist in, or arise out of, an application to the court under section 235A of the Trade Union and Labour Relations (Consolidation) Act 1992.*]

Note. Para 5B inserted by Trade Union Reform and Employment Rights Act 1993, s 49(2), Sch 8, para 39, as from 30 August 1993.

6. *Proceedings incidental to any proceedings excepted by this Part of this Schedule.*

SCHEDULE 3   *Sections 24 and 30*

CRIMINAL PROCEEDINGS: ENFORCEMENT OF CONTRIBUTION ORDERS

PART I

ORDERS MADE BY A COURT

Collecting court

1. *In this Part 'collecting court', in relation to a contribution order, means a magistrates' court specified in the order; and the court so specified shall be—*
  (a) in a case where the court making the order is itself a magistrates' court, that court;
  (b) in a case where the order is made on an appeal from a magistrates' court, or in respect of a person who was committed (whether for trial or otherwise by a magistrates' court) to the Crown Court, the court from which the appeal is brought or, as the case may be, which committed him; and
  (c) in any other case, a magistrates' court nominated by the court making the order.

Enforcement proceedings

2. *(1) Any sum required to be paid by a contribution order shall be recoverable as if it had been adjudged to be paid by an order of the collecting court, subject to and in accordance with the provisions of this paragraph.*
(2) Sections 17 (not more than one committal for same arrears) and 18 (power to review committal) of the Maintenance Orders Act 1958 shall apply as if a contribution order were a maintenance order.
(3) The collecting court may exercise, in relation to a contribution order, the power conferred by section 75 of the Magistrates' Courts Act 1980 (power to dispense with immediate payment); and for the purposes of that section any provisions made by the authority which made the order as to time for payment, or payment by instalments, shall be treated as made by the collecting court.
(4) The following provisions of the Magistrates' Courts Act 1980 shall apply as if a contribution order were enforceable as an affiliation order—
    section 80 (application of money found on defaulter to satisfy sum adjudged);
    section 93 (complaint for arrears);
    section 94 (effect of committal on arrears); and
    section 95 (power to remit arrears).
(5) Any costs awarded under section 64 of the Magistrates' Courts Act 1980 on the hearing of a complaint for the enforcement of a contribution order shall be enforceable as a sum required to be paid by that order.
3. *(1) Without prejudice to paragraph 2, any sum required to be paid by a contribution order shall be enforceable by the High Court or a county court as if the sum were due to the clerk of the collecting court in pursuance of a judgment or order of the High Court or county court, as the case may be.*
  (2) The clerk of the collecting court shall not take proceedings by virtue of this paragraph unless authorised to do so by the court.
  (3) This paragraph shall not authorise—
  (a) the enforcement of a sum required to be paid by a contribution order by issue of a writ of fieri facias or other process against goods or by imprisonment or attachment of earnings; or

(*b*)   the enforcement by a county court of payment of any sum exceeding the amount which for the time being is the county court limit for the purposes of section 15 of the County Courts Act 1984.

Note. Sub-s 3(1)(b) repealed by High Court and County Courts Jurisdiction Order 1991, SI 1991 No 724, art 2(8), Schedule, as from 1 July 1991.

4. (*1*) Any expenses incurred by the clerk of a magistrates' court in recovering any sum required to be paid by a contribution order shall be treated for the purposes of Part VI of the Justices of the Peace Act 1979 [the Justices of the Peace Act 1997] as expenses of the magistrates' courts committee.

(*2*) Any sum paid to a clerk of a magistrates' court in or towards satisfaction of a liability imposed by a contribution order shall be paid by him to the Lord Chancellor and section 61(4) of the Justices of the Peace Act 1979 [section 60(4) of the Justices of the Peace Act 1997] (regulations as to accounts of justices' clerks) shall apply in relation to sums payable to the Lord Chancellor under this sub-paragraph as it applies in relation to sums payable to the Secretary of State under that section.

Note. Words in square brackets substituted for by Justices of the Peace Act 1997, s 73(2), Sch 5, para 24, as from 19 June 1997.

Transfer of enforcement proceedings to different court

5. (*1*) Where in relation to any contribution order it appears to the collecting court that the person subject to it is residing in a petty sessions area other than that for which the court acts, the court may make an order under this paragraph ('a transfer order') with respect to the contribution order specifying the other petty sessions area.

(*2*) Where a court makes a transfer order in relation to any contribution order—

(*a*)   payment under the contribution order shall be enforceable in the petty sessions area specified in the transfer order; and

(*b*)   as from the date of the transfer order, a magistrates' court for that petty sessions area shall be substituted for the court which made the transfer order as the collecting court in relation to the contribution order.

Limitations on enforcement by proceedings

6. Any sum due under a contribution order shall not be recoverable, and payment of any such sum shall not be enforced, under paragraph 2 or 3 until—

(*a*)   the conclusion of the proceedings for the purposes of which the relevant grant of representation was made; or

(*b*)   if earlier, the revocation or withdrawal of the relevant grant of representation.

7. Where a contribution order has been made in respect of a member of Her Majesty's armed forces and the Secretary of State notifies the collecting court that any sum payable under the order will be recovered by deductions from the person's pay, the collecting court shall not enforce payment of any sum unless and until the Secretary of State subsequently notifies it that the person is no longer a member of those forces and that sum has not been fully recovered.

Power to defer enforcement proceedings

8. The collecting court may defer recovering any sum due under a contribution order if—

(*a*)   an appeal is pending in respect of the proceedings for the purposes of which the relevant grant of representation was made; or

(*b*)   the person granted representation has been ordered to be retried.

Interpretation

9. In this Part—

(*a*)   'relevant grant of representation', in relation to a contribution order, means the grant of representation in connection with which the order was made; and

(*b*)   references to the proceedings for the purposes of which a grant of representation has been made include, where the proceedings are proceedings before a magistrates' court which result—

> (i)   in the legally assisted person being committed to the Crown Court for trial or
>   sentence, or
> (ii)   in his case being remitted to a juvenile court [youth court] in pursuance of
>   section 56(1) of the Children and Young Persons Act 1933,
> the proceedings before the Crown Court or that juvenile court [youth court].

Note. Words in square brackets substituted by Criminal Justice Act 1991, s 100, Sch 11, para
40, as from 1 October 1992.

PART *II*

ORDERS MADE BY THE BOARD

Limitations on enforcement by proceedings

10. *(1) Any sum due under a contribution order shall not be recoverable, and payment of
any such sum shall not be enforced until—*
- *(a)   the conclusion of the proceedings for the purposes of which the relevant grant of
        representation was made; or*
- *(b)   if earlier, the revocation or withdrawal of the relevant grant of representation.*

(2) In this paragraph—
- *(a)   'relevant grant of representation', in relation to a contribution order, means the grant
        of representation in connection with which the order was made; and*
- *(b)   the reference to the proceedings for the purposes of which the relevant grant of
        representation was made includes, where the proceedings are proceedings before a
        magistrates' court which result—*
  - *(i)   in the legally assisted person being committed to the Crown Court for trial or
           sentence, or*
  - *(ii) in his case being remitted to a juvenile court [youth court] in pursuance of
           section 56(1) of the Children and Young Persons Act 1933,*
  - *the proceedings before the Crown Court or that juvenile court [youth court]*

Note. Words in square brackets substituted by Criminal Justice Act 1991, s 100, Sch 11,
para 40, as from 1 October 1992.

11. *Where a contribution order has been made in respect of a member of Her Majesty's
armed forces and the Secretary of State notifies the Board that any sum payable under
the order will be recovered by deductions from the person's pay, the Board shall not
enforce payment of any sum unless and until the Secretary of State subsequently notifies it
that the person is no longer a member of those forces and that sum has not been fully
recovered.*

*(Sch 4 applies to Scotland only; Sch 5 makes minor and consequential amendments;
insofar as those amendments affect provisions printed in this work, they have been
incorporated.)*

SCHEDULE 6

REPEALS   Section 45

Chapter	Short Title	Extent of Repeal
1967 c 80.	The Criminal Justice Act 1967.	Section 90.
1974 c 4.	The Legal Aid Act 1974.	The whole Act.
1974 c 47.	The Solicitors Act 1974.	Section 75(d).
		In Schedule 3, paragraph 10.
1975 c 72.	The Children Act 1975.	Section 65.
		In Schedule 3, paragraph 82.
1976 c 36.	The Adoption Act 1976.	In Schedule 3, paragraph 18.
1976 c 63.	The Bail Act 1976.	Section 11.

Chapter	Short Title	Extent of Repeal
1976 c 71.	The Supplementary Benefits Act 1976.	In Schedule 7, paragraphs 33 and 35.
1977 c 38.	The Administration of Justice Act 1977.	In Schedule 1, Part I.
1977 c 45.	The Criminal Law Act 1977.	In Schedule 12, the entry relating to the Legal Aid Act 1974.
1978 c 22.	The Domestic Proceedings and Magistrates' Courts Act 1978.	In Schedule 2, paragraphs 45 and 52.
1979 c 26.	The Legal Aid Act 1979.	The whole Act.
1979 c 55.	The Justices of the Peace Act 1979.	In Schedule 2, paragraph 27.
1980 c 5.	The Child Care Act 1980.	In Schedule 5, paragraph 36.
1980 c 30.	The Social Security Act 1980.	In Schedule 4, paragraph 9.
1980 c 43.	The Magistrates' Courts Act 1980.	In Schedule 7, paragraphs 126 to 129.
1981 c 49.	The Contempt of Court Act 1981.	Section 13. In Schedule 2, Part I.
1982 c 27.	The Civil Jurisdiction and Judgments Act 1982.	Section 40(1).
1982 c 44.	The Legal Aid Act 1982.	The whole Act.
1982 c 48.	The Criminal Justice Act 1982.	Section 25(2). Section 29(3). Section 60(4).
1983 c 41.	The Health and Social Services and Social Security Adjudications Act 1983.	In Schedule 1, paragraph 3.
1984 c 42.	The Matrimonial and Family Proceedings Act 1984.	In Schedule 1, paragraph 18.
1984 c 60.	The Police and Criminal Evidence Act 1984.	Section 59.
1985 c 23.	The Prosecution of Offences Act 1985.	Section 16(8). In section 19(2)(b), the words '(including any legal aid order)'. In section 21(1), the definition of 'legal aid order'.
1985 c 61.	The Administration of Justice Act 1985.	Sections 45 and 46. In Schedule 7, paragraphs 1 to 3.
1986 c 28.	The Children and Young Persons (Amendment) Act 1986.	Section 3(3).
1986 c 47.	The Legal Aid (Scotland) Act 1986.	In section 4(2)(c) the words 'for the purposes of this Act'. In section 16, subsection (1) and, in subsection (2), the words 'in this section and'. In section 17, subsections (3) to (8). Section 18(1). In section 32(a), the words 'out of the Fund'. In Schedule 1 paragraph 2(4).

Chapter	Short Title	Extent of Repeal
1986 c 50.	*The Social Security Act 1986.*	In Schedule 10, paragraphs 46, 47 and 56.
1986 c 55.	*The Family Law Act 1986.*	Section 64.
1987 c 38	*The Criminal Justice Act 1987.*	In Schedule 2, paragraphs 7 and 8.

SCHEDULE 7

TRANSITION   Section 45

Preliminary

1. *In this Schedule—*
'the 1974 Act' means the Legal Aid Act 1974; and
'the appointed day' means the day appointed by the Lord Chancellor under section 47(2) of this Act for the coming into force of section 3(2) thereof.

The Legal Aid Fund

2. *(1) On the appointed day the legal aid fund ('the Old Fund') maintained by the Law Society under section 17 of the 1974 Act shall be wound up.*

(2) If, as at the appointed day, after taking account of all receipts and expenses of the Law Society attributable to their functions under the 1974 Act and the Legal Aid Act 1982 ('the 1982 Act'), there is in relation to the Old Fund any surplus or deficit—
  (a) *such surplus shall be paid by the Law Society to the Lord Chancellor; and*
  (b) *such deficit shall be made up by payment to the Law Society by the Lord Chancellor of the amount of the deficit.*

(3) Notwithstanding their repeal by this Act—
  (a) *sections 15(9) and 18 of the 1974 Act shall continue to have effect for the purposes of requiring the Law Society to account for the Old Fund and to report on the discharge of its functions under that Act up to the appointed day; and*
  (b) *section 17(5) of that Act shall continue to have effect for the purposes of any determination as to the expenses or receipts of the Law Society;*

and, if the appointed day falls on a day which is not the last day of the financial year (for the purposes of the said section 18), references in those sections to the financial year shall be construed as references to the period commencing on the day immediately following the end of the last complete financial year and ending with the appointed day.

(4) The Lord Chancellor shall pay to the Law Society such expenses incurred after the appointed day in connection with their functions under sections 15(9) and 18 of the 1974 Act as appear to him to be reasonable.

(5) Any payments received by the Lord Chancellor under sub-paragraph (2)(a) above shall be paid by him into the legal aid fund established by the Board under section 6.

(6) Any amount required to be paid by the Lord Chancellor under sub-paragraph (2)(b) or (4) above shall be defrayed out of money provided by Parliament.

Rights, obligations and property

3. *(1) Subject to paragraph 2, on the appointed day all rights, obligations and property of the Law Society which are referable to its functions under the 1974 Act and the 1982 Act shall become rights, obligations and property of the Board.*

(2) Any payments which are required to be made into or out of the Old Fund in connection with legal aid or advice or assistance under the 1974 Act shall, on and after the appointed day, be paid to or by the Board.

Transfer of functions

4. (1) Any grant of legal aid under Part I of the 1974 Act which is in force immediately before the appointed day shall, on and after the appointed day, have effect as a grant by the Board of representation under Part IV of this Act.

(2) Any approval given in connection with the grant of legal aid or advice or assistance under Part I of the 1974 Act which is in force immediately before the appointed day shall, on and after the appointed day, have effect as an approval by the Board in connection with the corresponding advice, assistance or representation under Part III or IV of this Act.

(3) Anything which, immediately before the appointed day, is in the process of being done by or in relation to the Law Society in connection with any function which it has relating to legal aid or advice or assistance under Part I of the 1974 Act, may be continued, on and after the appointed day, by or in relation to the Board.

Legal aid contribution orders

5. Notwithstanding their repeal by this Act, the provisions of the 1974 Act and the 1982 Act with respect to legal aid contribution orders shall continue to have effect in relation to any such order made in connection with a legal aid order made by virtue of section 28(11A) of the 1974 Act (legal aid for proceedings for contempt).

[The Board: transfers of employment

6. (1) The Board shall make, not later than such date as the Lord Chancellor may determine, an offer of employment by the Board to such of the persons employed immediately before that date by the Law Society for the purpose of their functions under the 1974 Act as fall within such descriptions as the Lord Chancellor designates for the purposes of this paragraph or are persons whom the Board wishes to employ.

(2) The terms of the offer shall be such that they are, taken as a whole, not less favourable to the person to whom the offer is made than the terms on which he is employed on the date on which the offer is made.

(3) An offer made in pursuance of this paragraph shall not be revocable during the period of 3 months commencing with the date on which it is made.

7. (1) Where a person becomes an employee of the Board on acceptance of an offer made under paragraph 6, then, for the purposes of the Employment Protection (Consolidation) Act 1978 [the Employment Rights Act 1996], his period of employment with the Law Society shall count as a period of employment by the Board, and the change of employment shall not break the continuity of the period of employment.

(2) Where an offer is made under paragraph 6 to any person, none of the agreed redundancy procedures applicable to employees of the Law Society shall apply to him.

(3) Where a person employed by the Law Society ceases to be so employed—

(a)   on becoming a member of the staff of the Board on accepting an offer under paragraph 6, or

(b)   having unreasonably refused such an offer,

Part VI of the Employment Protection (Consolidated) Act 1978 shall not apply to him and he shall not be related for the purposes of any scheme in force under section 19 of the 1974 Act as having been retired on redundancy.

(4) Where a person to whom an offer under paragraph 6 has been made continues in employment in the Law Society after having not unreasonably refused that offer he shall be treated for all purposes as if no offer under paragraph 6 had been made to him.

Note. Words in square brackets in para 7(1) substituted for, and words 'Part VI of' to 'shall not apply to him and' in para 7(3) repealed by Employment Rights Act 1996, ss 240, 242, Sch 1, para 36, Sch 3, Part I, as from 22 August 1996.

8. (1) Any dispute as to whether an offer purporting to be made under paragraph 6 complies with that paragraph shall be referred to and be determined by an industrial tribunal.

(2) An industrial tribunal shall not consider a complaint referred to it under sub-paragraph (1) above unless the complaint is presented to the tribunal before the end of

the period of 3 months beginning with the date of the offer of employment or within such further period as the tribunal considers reasonable in a case where it is satisfied that it was not reasonably practicable for the complaint to be presented before the end of the period of 3 months.

(3) An appeal shall lie to the Employment Appeal Tribunal on a question of law arising from the decision of, or in proceedings before, an industrial tribunal under this paragraph.

(4) Except as mentioned in sub-paragraph (3) above, no appeal shall lie from the decision of an industrial tribunal under this paragraph.

9. (1) In the event of the Board assuming under section 3(4) any of the functions specified in that subsection the Lord Chancellor shall by regulations make such provision corresponding to paragraphs 6, 7 and 8 in respect of employees to whom this paragraph applies as appears to him to be appropriate.

(2) This paragraph applies to persons employed—

(a) in the civil service of the State, or

(b) by a magistrates' courts committee,

and so employed wholly or mainly in connection with the functions referred to in sub-paragraph (1) above.

Pensions

10. Any arrangements made by the Law Society under section 19 of the 1974 Act in respect of any pension shall be treated on and after the appointed day (so far as may be necessary to preserve their effect) as having been made under paragraph 10(2) of Schedule 1 to this Act, and any pension scheme administered by the Law Society immediately before the appointed day shall be deemed to be a pension scheme established and administered by the Board under that paragraph and shall continue to be administered accordingly.

Representation in affiliation proceedings: transitory provisions

11. Until the repeal of the Affiliation Proceedings Act 1957 by the Family Law Reform Act 1987 takes effect, Schedule 2 to this Act shall be taken to include proceedings in the Crown Court or a magistrates' court for or in relation to an affiliation order within the meaning of the Affiliation Proceedings Act 1957.

(Sch 8 contained transitory amendments of Legal Aid Act 1974.)

FOREIGN MARRIAGE (AMENDMENT) ACT 1988

(1988 c 44)

An Act to amend the Foreign Marriage Act 1892 and to repeal certain enactments which are spent relating to the validation of marriages of British subjects solemnised outside the United Kingdom.   [2 November 1988]

1-6. (*Section 1 amends Foreign Marriage Act 1892, ss 1, 18(1), 21(1)(a), 24; s 2 substitutes s 4 of that Act, and amends s 7 of that Act; s 3 amends s 5 of that Act; s 4 amends s 8 of that Act; s 5 amends ss 9, 10, 17 of that Act; s 6 amends s 22 of that Act.*)

7. Short title, repeals, commencement and extent—(1) This Act may be cited as the Foreign Marriage (Amendment) Act 1988.

(2) The enactments mentioned in the Schedule to this Act (which include some which are spent or no longer of practical utility) are hereby repealed to the extent specified in column 3 of that Schedule.

(3) This Act shall come into force on such a day as the Lord Chancellor and the Lord Advocate may by order made by statutory instrument appoint.

(4) This Act extends to Northern Ireland.

Commencement. Act in force 12 April 1990 (SI 1990 No 522).

SCHEDULE

ENACTMENTS REPEALED   Section 7(2)

Chapter	Short Title	Extent of Repeal
3 & 4 Will 4 c 45	An Act to declare valid marriage solemnised at Hamburgh since the abolition of the British Factory there.	The whole Act.
17 & 18 Vict c 88.	An Act to render valid certain marriages of British subjects in Mexico.	The whole Act.
21 & 22 Vict c 46.	An Act to remove doubts as to the validity of certain marriages of British subjects abroad.	The whole Act.
22 & 23 Vict c 64.	An Act to remove doubts as to the validity of certain marriages of British subjects in Lisbon.	The whole Act.
27 & 28 Vict c 77.	An Act to repeal and in part re-enact certain Acts of Parliament relating to the Ionian States, and to establish the validity of certain things done in the said States.	The whole Act.
30 & 31 Vict c 2.	The Odessa Marriage Act 1867.	The whole Act.
30 & 31 Vict c 93.	The Morro Velho Marriage Act 1867.	The whole Act.
41 & 42 Vict 61.	The Fiji Marriage Act 1878.	The whole Act.
42 & 43 Vict c 29.	The Confirmation of Marriages on Her Majesty's Ships Act 1879.	The whole Act.
52 & 53 Vict c 38.	The Basutoland and British Bechuanaland Marriage Act 1889.	The whole Act.
55 & 56 Vict c 23.	The Foreign Marriage Act 1892.	Sections 14 and 15. In section 21(3), the words from 'including' to 'or oath'. In section 22(4), the words from 'and for the application' onwards. In section 24, the definitions of the expressions 'Registrar-General', 'Attorney General' and 'the Marriage Registration Acts'. Section 26(2).
2 & 3 Geo 5 c 15.	The Marriages in Japan (Validity) Act 1912.	The whole Act.
24 & 25 Geo 5 c 13.	The Marriage (Extension of Hours) Act 1934.	The whole Act.

Chapter	Short Title	Extent of Repeal
10 & 11 Geo 6 c 33.	The Foreign Marriage Act 1947.	Sections 1 and 5.
1969 c 46.	The Family Law Reform Act 1969.	Section 2(1)(a). In section 28(4)(b), the words 'the Foreign Marriage Act 1892 or'.
1977 c 15.	The Marriage (Scotland) Act 1977.	In Schedule 2, paragraph 1.

CHILDREN ACT 1989
(1989 c 41)

ARRANGEMENT OF SECTIONS

PART I

INTRODUCTORY

PART II

ORDERS WITH RESPECT TO CHILDREN IN FAMILY PROCEEDINGS

General

Special guardianship

Financial relief

Family assistance orders

PART III

LOCAL AUTHORITY SUPPORT FOR CHILDREN AND FAMILIES

PART IV

CARE AND SUPERVISION

PART XII

MISCELLANEOUS AND GENERAL

An Act to reform the law relating to children; to provide for local authority services for children in need and others; to amend the law with respect to children's homes, community homes, voluntary homes and voluntary organisations; to make provision with respect to fostering, child minding and day care for young children and adoption; and for connected purposes.   [16 November 1989]

PART I

INTRODUCTORY

1. Welfare of the child—(1) When a court determines any question with respect to—
   (a) the upbringing of a child; or
   (b) the administration of a child's property or the application of any Income arising from it,
the child's welfare shall be the court's paramount consideration.

   (2) In any proceedings in which any question with respect to the upbringing of a child arises, the court shall have regard to the general principle that any delay in determining the question is likely to prejudice the welfare of the child.

   (3) In the circumstances mentioned in subsection (4), a court shall have regard in particular to—
   (a) the ascertainable wishes and feelings of the child concerned (considered in the light of his age and understanding);
   (b) his physical, emotional and educational needs;
   (c) the likely effect on him of any change in his circumstances
   (d) his age, sex. background and any characteristics of his which the court considers relevant;
   (e) any harm which he has suffered or is at risk of suffering;
   (f) how capable each of his parents, and any other person in relation to whom the court considers the question to be relevant, is of meeting his needs;
   (g) the range of powers available to the court under this Act in the proceedings in question.
   (4) The circumstances are that—
   (a) the court is considering whether to make, vary or discharge a section 8 order, and the making, van ation or discharge of the order by opposed to any party to the proceedings; or
   (b) the court is considering whether to make, vary or discharge [a special guardianship order or] an order under Part IV.
Note. In sub-s (4)(b) words 'a special guardianship order or' in square brackets inserted by the Adoption and Children Act 2002, s 115(2), as from a day to be appointed.

   (5) Where a court is considering whether or not to make one or more orders under this Act with respect to a child, it shall not make the order or any of the orders unless it considers that doing so would be better for the child than making no order at all.

2. Parental responsibility for children—(1) Where a child's father and mother were married to each other at the time of his birth, they shall each have parental responsibility for the child.
   (2) Where a child's father and mother were not married to each other at the time of his birth—
   (a) the mother shall have parental responsibility for the child.
   (b) the father *shall not have parental responsibility for the child, unless he acquires it* [shall have parental responsibility for the child if he has acquired it (and has not ceased to have it)] in accordance with the provisions of this Act.
Note. In sub-s (2)(b) words 'shall have…have it)' in square brackets substituted for words in italics by the Adoption and Children Act 2002, s 111(5), as from 1 December 2003 (SI 2003 No 3079).

(3) References in this Act to a child whose father and mother were. or (as the case may be) were not. married to each other at the time of his birth must be read with section 1 of the Family Law Reform Act 1987 (which extends their meaning).

(4) The rule of law that a father is the natural guardian of his legitimate child is abolished.

(5) More than one person may have parental responsibility for the same child at the same time.

(6) A person who has parental responsibility for a child at any time shall not cease to have that responsibility solely because some other person subsequently acquires parental responsibility for the child.

(7) Where more than one person has parental responsibility for a child, each of them may act alone and without the other (or others) in meeting that responsibility; but nothing in this Part shall be taken to affect the operation of any enactment which requires the consent of more than one person in a matter affecting the child.

(8) The fact that a person has parental responsibility for a child shall not entitle him to act in any way which would be incompatible with any order made with respect to the child under this Act.

(9) A person who has parental responsibility for a child may not surrender or transfer any part of that responsibility to another but may arrange for some or all of it to be met by one or more persons acting on his behalf.

(10) The person with whom any such arrangement is made may himself be a person who already has parental responsibility for the child concerned

(11) The making of any such arrangement shall not affect any liability of the person making it which may arise from any failure to meet any part of his parental responsibility for the child concerned.

3. Meaning of 'parental responsibility'—(1) In this Act 'parental responsibility' means all the rights, duties, powers, responsibilities and authority which by law a parent of a child has in relation to the child and his property.

(2) It also includes the rights, powers and duties which a guardian of the child's estate (appointed, before the commencement of section 5, to act generally) would have had in relation to the child and his property.

(3) The rights referred to in subsection (2) include, in particular, the right of the guardian to receive or recover in his own name, for the benefit of the child, property of whatever description and wherever situated which the child is entitled to receive or recover.

(4) The fact that a person has, or does not have, parental responsibility for a child shall not affect—

    (a) any obligation which he may have in relation to the child (such as a statutory duty to maintain the child); or

    (b) any rights which, in the event of the child's death, he (or any other person) may have in relation to the child's property.

(5) A person who—

    (a) does not have parental responsibility for a particular child; but

    (b) has care of the child,

may (subject to the provisions of this Act) do what is reasonable in all the circumstances of the case for the purpose of safeguarding or promoting the child's welfare.

4. Acquisition of parental responsibility by father—(1) Where a child's father and mother were not married to each other at the time of his birth—

    (a) the court may, on the application of the father, order that he shall have parental responsibility for the child; or

    (b) the father and mother may by agreement (a parental responsibility agreement') provide for the father to have parental responsibility for the child [, the father shall acquire parental responsibility for the child if—

(a) he becomes registered as the child's father under any of the enactments specified in subsection (1A);
(b) he and the child's mother make an agreement (a 'parental responsibility agreement') providing for him to have parental responsibility for the child; or
(c) the court, on his application, orders that he shall have parental responsibility for the child.]

Note. Words ', the father...for the child' in square brackets substituted for words in italics by the Adoption and Children Act 2002, s 111(1), (2), (7), as from 1 December 2003 (SI 2003 No 3079).

[(1A) The enactments referred to in subsection (1)(a) are—
(a) paragraphs (a), (b) and (c) of section 10(1) and of section 10A(1) of the Births and Deaths Registration Act 1953;
(b) paragraphs (a), (b)(i) and (c) of section 18(1), and sections 18(2)(b) and 20(1)(a) of the Registration of Births, Deaths and Marriages (Scotland) Act 1965; and
(c) sub-paragraphs (a), (b) and (c) of Article 14(3) of the Births and Deaths Registration (Northern Ireland) Order 1976.

(1B) *The Lord Chancellor* [Secretary of State] may by order amend subsection (1A) so as to add further enactments to the list in that subsection.]

Note. Sub-ss (1A), (1B) inserted by the Adoption and Children Act 2002, s 111(1), (3), as from 1 December 2003 (SI 2003 No 3079). In sub-s (1B) words 'Secretary of State' in square brackets substituted for words in italics by the Transfer of Functions (Children, Young People and Family) Order 2003, SI 2003 No 3191, as from 12 January 2004.

(2) No parental responsibility agreement shall have effect for the purposes of this Act unless—
(a) it is made in the form prescribed by regulations made by the Lord Chancellor; and
(b) where regulations are made by the Lord Chancellor prescribing the manner in which such agreements must be recorded. it is recorded in the prescribed manner.

(3) Subject to section 12(4), an order under subsection (1)(a), or a parental responsibility agreement, may only be brought to an end by an order of the court made on the application—
(a) of any person who has parental responsibility for the child; or
(b) with leave of the court, of the child himself.

[(2A) A person who has acquired parental responsibility under subsection (1) shall cease to have that responsibility only if the court so orders.

(3) The court may make an order under subsection (2A) on the application—
(a) of any person who has parental responsibility for the child; or
(b) with the leave of the court, of the child himself,
subject, in the case of parental responsibility acquired under subsection (1)(c), to section 12(4).]

Note. Sub-ss (2A), (3) substituted for sub-s (3) in italics by the Adoption and Children Act 2002, s 111(1), (4), as from 1 December 2003 (SI 2003 No 3079).

(4) The court may only grant leave under subsection (3)(b) if it is satisfied that the child has sufficient understanding to make the proposed application.

[4A. Acquisition of parental responsibility by step-parent—(1) Where a child's parent ('parent A') who has parental responsibility for the child is married to a person who is not the child's parent ('the step-parent')—
(a) parent A or, if the other parent of the child also has parental responsibility for the child, both parents may by agreement with the step-parent provide for the step-parent to have parental responsibility for the child; or
(b) the court may, on the application of the step-parent, order that the step-parent shall have parental responsibility for the child.

(2) An agreement under subsection (1)(a) is also a 'parental responsibility agreement', and section 4(2) applies in relation to such agreements as it applies in relation to parental responsibility agreements under section 4.

(3) A parental responsibility agreement under subsection (1)(a), or an order under subsection (1)(b), may only be brought to an end by an order of the court made on the application—

(a) of any person who has parental responsibility for the child; or

(b) with the leave of the court, of the child himself.

(4) The court may only grant leave under subsection (3)(b) if it is satisfied that the child has sufficient understanding to make the proposed application.]

Note. This section inserted by the Adoption and Children Act 2002, s 112, as from a day to be appointed.

5. Appointment of guardians—(1) Where an application with respect to a child is made to the court by any individual, the court may by order appoint that individual to be the child's guardian if—

(a) the child has no parent with parental responsibility for him; or

(b) a residence order has been made with respect to the child in favour of a parent *or guardian* [, guardian or special guardian] of his who has died while the order was in force [; or

(c) paragraph (b) does not apply, and the child's only or last surviving special guardian dies].

Note. In para (b) words 'guardian or special guardian' in square brackets substituted for words in italics and para (c) and word '; or' immediately preceding it inserted, by the Adoption and Children Act 2002, s 115(4), as from a day to be appointed.

(2) The power conferred by subsection (i) may also be exercised in any family proceedings if the court considers that the order should be made even though no application has been made for it.

(3) A parent who has parental responsibility for his child may appoint another individual to be the child's guardian in the event of his death.

(4) A guardian of a child may appoint another individual to take his place as the child's guardian in the event of his death [; and a special guardian of a child may appoint another individual to be the child's guardian in the event of his death].

Note. In sub-s (4) words '; and a special...of his death' in square brackets inserted by the Adoption and Children Act 2002, s 115(4), as from a day to be appointed.

(5) An appointment under subsection (3) or (4) shall not have effect unless it is made in writing, is dated and is signed by the person making the appointment or—

(a) in the case of an appointment made by a will which is not signed by the testator. is signed at the direction of the testator in accordance with the requirements of section 9 of the Wills Act 1837; or

(b) in any other case, is signed at the direction of the person making the appointment, in his presence and in the presence of two witnesses who each attest the signature.

(6) A person appointed as a child's guardian under this section shall have parental responsibility for the child concerned.

(7) Where—

(a) on the death of any person making an appointment under subsection (3) or (4), the child concerned has no parent with parental responsibility for him; or

(b) immediately before the death of any person making such an appointment, a residence order in his favour was in force with respect to the child [or he was the child's only (or last surviving) special guardian],

the appointment shall take effect on the death of that person.

Note. In sub-s (7) words 'or he was...special guardian' in square brackets inserted by the Adoption and Children Act 2002, s 115(4), as from a day to be appointed.

(8) Where, on the death of any person making an appointment under subsection (3) or (4)—

  (a) the child concerned has a parent with parental responsibility for him; and

  (b) subsection (7)(b) does not apply,

the appointment shall take effect when the child no longer has a parent who has parental responsibility for him.

(9) Subsections (1) and (7) do not apply if the residence order referred to in paragraph (b) of those subsections was also made in favour of a surviving parent of the child.

(10) Nothing in this section shall be taken to prevent an appointment under subsection (3) or (4) being made by two or more persons acting jointly.

(11) Subject to any provision made by rules of court, no court shall exercise the High Courts inherent jurisdiction to appoint a guardian of the estate of any child.

(12) Where rules of court are made under subsection (11) they may prescribe the circumstances in which, and conditions subject to which, an appointment of such a guardian may be made.

(13) A guardian of a child may only be appointed in accordance with the provisions of this section.

6. Guardians revocation and disclaimer—(1) An appointment under section 5(3) or (4) revokes an earlier such appointment (including one made in an unrevoked will or codicil) made by the same person in respect of the same child, unless it is clear (whether as the result of an express provision in the later appointment or by any necessary implication) that the purpose of the later appointment is to appoint an additional guardian.

(2) An appointment under section 5(3) or (4) (including one made in an unrevoked will or codicil) is revoked if the person who made the appointment revokes it by a written and dated instrument which is signed—

  (a) by him; or

  (b) at his direction, in his presence and in the presence of two witnesses who each attest the signature.

(3) An appointment under section 5(3) or (4) (other than one made in a will or codicil) is revoked if, with the intention of revoking the appointment, the person who made it—

  (a) destroys the instrument by which it was made; or

  (b) has some other person destroy that instrument in his presence.

[(3A) An appointment under section 5(3) or (4) (including one made in an unrevoked will or codicil) is revoked if the person appointed is the spouse of the person who made the appointment and either—

  (a) *a decree of a court of civil jurisdiction in England and Wales dissolves or annuls the marriage, or*

  [(a) a court of civil jurisdiction in England and Wales by order dissolves, or by decree annuls, a marriage, or]

  (b) the marriage is dissolved or annulled and the divorce or annulment is entitled to recognition in England and Wales by virtue of Part II of the Family Law 1986,

unless a contrary intention appears by the appointment.]

Note. Sub-s (3A) inserted by Law Reform (Succession) Act 1995, s 4, as from 8 November 1995, as respects an appointment made by a person dying on or after 1 January 1996. Sub-s (3A)(a) in square brackets substituted for sub-s (3A)(a) in italics by Family Law Act 1996, s 66(1), Sch 8, Part I, para 41(2), as from a day to be appointed, subject to savings in s 66(2) of, and para 5 of Sch 9 to, the 1996 Act.

(4) For the avoidance of doubt, an appointment under section 5(3) or (4) made in a will or codicil is revoked if the will or codicil is revoked.

(5) A person who is appointed as a guardian under section 5(3) or (4) may disclaim his appointment by an instrument in writing signed by him and made within a reasonable time of his first knowing that the appointment has taken effect.

(6) Where regulations are made by the Lord Chancellor prescribing the manner in which such disclaimers must be recorded, no such disclaimer shall have effect unless it ss recorded in the prescribed manner.

(7) Any appointment of a guardian under section 5 may be brought to an end at any time by order of the court—

(a) on the application of any person who has parental responsibility for the child;

(b) on the application of the child concerned, with leave of the court; or

(c) in any family proceedings, if the court considers that it should be brought to an end even though no application has been made.

7. Welfare reports—(1) A court considering any question with respect to a child under this Act may—

(a) ask *a probation officer* [an officer of the service]; or

(b) ask a local authority to arrange for—

  (i) an officer of the authority; or

  (ii) such other person (other than *a probation officer* [an officer of the service]) as the authority considers appropriate,

Note. Words 'an officer of the service' in square brackets substituted for words in italics by the Criminal Justice and Court Services Act 2000, s 74, sch 7, Pt II, paras 87, 88, as from 1 April 2001 (SI 2001 No 919).

to report to the court on such matters relating to the welfare of that child as are required to be dealt with in the report.

(2) The Lord Chancellor may make regulations specifying matters which, unless the court orders otherwise, must be dealt with in any report under this section.

(3) The report may be made in writing, or orally, as the court requires.

(4) Regardless of any enactment or rule of law which would otherwise prevent it from doing so, the court may take account of—

(a) any statement contained in the report; and

(b) any evidence given in respect of the matters referred to in the report,

in so far as the statement or evidence is, in the opinion of the court, relevant to the question which it is considering.

(5) It shall be the duty of the authority or probation officer to comply with any request for a report under this section.

PART II

ORDERS WITH RESPECT TO CHILDREN IN FAMILY PROCEEDINGS

General

8. Residence, contact and other orders with respect to children—(1) In this Act—

'a contact order' means an order requiring the person with whom a child lives, or is to live, to allow the child to visit or stay with the person named in the order, or for that person and the child otherwise to have contact with each other;

'a prohibited steps order' means an order that no step which could be taken by a parent in meeting his parental responsibility for a child, and which is of a kind specified in the order, shall be taken by any person without the consent of the court;

'a residence order' means an order settling the arrangements to be made as to the person with whom a child is to live; and 'a specific issue order' means an order giving directions for the purpose of determining a specific question which has arisen, or which may arise, in connection with any aspect of parental responsibility for a child.

(2) In this Act a section 8 order' means any of the orders mentioned in subsection (s) and any order varying or discharging such an order.

(3) For the purposes of this Act 'family proceedings' means [(subject to subsection (5))] any proceedings—

(a) under the inherent jurisdiction of the High Court in relation to children; and

(b) under the enactments mentioned in subsection (4),

but does not include proceedings on an application for leave under section 100(3).

Note. Words in square brackets added by Family Law Act 1996, s 66(1), Sch 8, Part I, para 41(3), as from a day to be appointed, subject to savings in s 66(2) of, and para 5 of Sch 9 to, the 1996 Act.

(4) The enactments are—

(a) Parts I, II and IV of this Act;

(b) the Matrimonial Causes Act 1973;

(c) *the Domestic Violence and Matrimonial Proceeding Act 1976;*

(d) *the Adoption Act 1976;*

[(d) the Adoption and Children Act 2002;]

(e) the Domestic Proceedings and Magistrates' Courts Act 1978;

(f) *sections 1 and 9 of the Matrimonial Homes Act 1983;*

(g) Part III of the Matrimonial and Family Proceedings Act I984.

[(h) the Family Law Act 1996];

[(i) sections 11 and 12 of the Crime and Disorder Act 1998].

Note. Sub-s (4)(c), (f) repealed, and sub-s (4)(h) added by Family Law Act 1996, s 66, Sch 8, Part III, para 60(1), Sch 10, as from 1 October 1997, subject to savings in s 66(2) of, and para 5 of Sch 9 to, the 1996 Act. Sub-s (4)(d) substituted for sub-s (4)(d) in italics by the Adoption and Children Act 2002, Sch 3, para 55, as from a day to be appointed. Sub-s (4)(i) inserted by the Crime and Disorder Act 1998, s 119, Sch 8, para 68 as from 30 September 1998 (SI 1998 No 2327).

[(5) For the purposes of any reference in this Act to family proceedings powers which under this Act are exercisable in family proceedings shall also be exercisable in relation to a child, without any such proceedings having been commenced or any application having been made to the court under this Act, if—

(a) a statement of marital breakdown under section 5 of the Family Law Act 1996 with respect to the marriage in relation to which that child is a child of the family has been received by the court; and

(b) it may, in due course, become possible for an application for a divorce order or for a separation order to be made by reference to that statement.]

Note. Sub-s (5) added by Family Law Act 1996, s 66(1), Sch 8, Part I, para 41(4), as from a day to be appointed, subject to savings in s 66(2) of, and para 5 of Sch 9 to, the 1996 Act.

9. Restrictions on making section 8 orders—(1) No court shall make any section 8 order, other than a residence order, with respect to a child who is in the care of a local authority.

(2) No application may be made by a local authority for a residence order or contact order and no court shall make such an order in favour of a local authority.

(3) A person who is, or was at any time within the last six months, a local authority foster parent of a child may not apply for leave to apply for a section 8 order with respect to the child unless—

(a) he has the consent of the authority;

(b) he is a relative of the child; or

(c) the child has lived with him for at least *three years* [one year] preceding the application.

Note. In sub-s (3)(c) words 'one year' in square brackets substituted for words in italics by the Adoption and Children Act 2002, s 113(a), as from a day to be appointed.

(4) The period of three years mentioned in subsection (3)(c) need not be continuous but must have begun not more than five years before the making of the application.

Note. Sub-s (4) repealed by the Adoption and Children Act 2002, ss 113(b), 139(3), Sch 5, as from a day to be appointed.

(5) No court shall exercise its powers to make a specific issue order or prohibited steps order—

(a) with a view to achieving a result which could be achieved by making a residence or contact order; or

(b) in any way which is denied to the High Court (by section 100(2)) in the exercise of its inherent jurisdiction with respect to children.

(6) [Subject to section 12(5)] no court shall make any section 8 order which is to have effect for a period which will end after the child has reached the age of sixteen unless it is satisfied that the circumstances of the case are exceptional.

Note. In sub-s (6)(b) words 'Subject to section 12(5)' in square brackets inserted by the Adoption and Children Act 2002, s 114(2), as from a day to be appointed.

(7) No court shall make any section 8 order, other than one varying or discharging such an order, with respect to a child who has reached the age of sixteen unless it is satisfied that the circumstances of the case are exceptional.

10. Power of court to make section 8 orders—(1) In any family proceedings in which a question arises with respect to the welfare of any child, the court may make a section 8 order with respect to the child if—

(a) an application for the order has been made by a person who—

(i) is entitled to apply for a section 8 order with respect to the child; or

(ii) has obtained the leave of the court to make the application; or

(b) the court considers that the order should be made even though no such application has been made.

(2) The court may also make a section 8 order with respect to any child on the application of a person who—

(a) is entitled to apply for a section 8 order with respect to the child; or

(b) has obtained the leave of the court to make the application.

(3) This section is subject to the restrictions imposed by section 9.

(4) The following persons are entitled to apply to the court for any section 8 order with respect to a child—

(a) any parent *or guardian* [, guardian or special guardian] of the child;

[(aa) any person who by virtue of section 4A has parental responsibility for the child;]

Note. In sub-s (4)(a) words ', guardian or special guardian' in square brackets substituted for words in italics by the Adoption and Children Act 2002, s 139(1), Sch 3, paras 54, 56(a), as from a day to be appointed. Sub-s (4)(aa) inserted by the Adoption and Children Act 2002, s 139(1), Sch 3, paras 54, 56(b), as from a day to be appointed.

(b) any person in whose favour a residence order is in force with respect to the child.

(5) The following persons are entitled to apply for a residence or contact order with respect to a child—

(a) any party to a marriage (whether or not subsisting) in relation to whom the child is a child of the family;

(b) any person with whom the child has lived for a period of at least three years;

(c) any person who—

> (i) in any case where a residence order is in force with respect to the child, has the consent of each of the persons in whose favour the order was made;
> (ii) in any case where the child is in the care of a local authority, has the consent of that authority; or
> (iii) in any other case, has the consent of each of those (if any) who have parental responsibility for the child.

[(5A) A local authority foster parent is entitled to apply for a residence order with respect to a child if the child has lived with him for a period of at least one year immediately preceding the application.]

Note. Sub-s (5A) inserted by the Adoption and Children Act 2002, s 139(1), Sch 3, paras 54, 56(c), as from a day to be appointed.

(6) A person who would not otherwise be entitled (under the previous provisions of this section) to apply for the variation or discharge of a section 8 order shall be entitled to do so if—
(a) the order was made on his application or
(b) in the case of a contact order, he is named in the order.

(7) Any person who falls within a category' of person prescribed by rules of court is entitled to apply for any such section 8 order as may be prescribed in relation to that category of person.

[(7A) If a special guardianship order is in force with respect to a child, an application for a residence order may only be made with respect to him, if apart from this subsection the leave of the court is not required, with such leave.]

Note. Sub-s (7A) inserted by the Adoption and Children Act 2002, s 139(1), Sch 3, paras 54, 56(d).

(8) Where the person applying for leave to make an application for a section 8 order is the child concerned, the court may only grant leave if it is satisfied that he has sufficient understanding to make the proposed application for the section 8 order.

(9) Where the person applying for leave to make an application for a section 8 order is not the child concerned, the court shall. in deciding whether or not to grant leave, have particular regard to—
(a) the nature of the proposed application for the section 8 order;
(b) the applicant's connection with the child;
(c) any risk there might be of that proposed application disrupting the child's life to such an extent that he would be harmed by it; and
(d) where the child is being looked after by a local authority—
> (i) the authority's plans for the child's future; and
> (ii) the wishes and feelings of the child's parents.

(10) The period of three years mentioned in subsection (5)(b) need not be continuous but must not have begun more than five years before, or ended more than three months before, the making of the application.

11. General principles and supplementary provisions—(1) In proceedings in which any question of making a section 8 order, or any other' question with respect to such an order, arises, the court shall (in the light of any rules made by virtue of subsection (2))—
(a) draw up a timetable with a view to determining the question without delay; and
(b) give such directions as it considers appropriate for the purpose of ensuring, so far as is reasonably practicable, that that timetable is adhered to.

(2) Rules of court may—
(a) specify periods within which specified steps must be taken in relation to proceedings in which such questions arise; and

(b) make other provision with respect to such proceedings for the purpose of ensuring, so far as is reasonably practicable, that such questions are determined without delay.

(3) Where a court has power to make a section 8 order, it may do so at any time during the course of the proceedings in question even though it is not in a position to dispose finally of those proceedings.

(4) Where a residence order is made in favour of two or more persons who do not themselves all live together. the order may specify the periods during which the child is to live in the different households concerned.

(5) Where—

(a) a residence order has been made with respect to a child; and
(b) as a result of the order the child lives, or is to live, with one of two parents who each have parental responsibility for him,

the residence order shall cease to have effect if the parents live together for a continuous period of more than six months.

(6) A contact order which requires the parent with whom a child lives to allow the child to visit, or otherwise have contact with, his other parent shall cease to have effect if the parents live together for a continuous period of more than six months.

(7) A section 8 order may—

(a) contain directions about how it is to be carried into effect;
(b) impose conditions which must be complied with by any person—
    (i) in whose favour the order is made;
    (ii) who is a parent of the child concerned;
    (iii) who is not a parent of his but who has parental responsibility for him; or
    (iv) with whom the child is living,
    and to whom the conditions are expressed to apply;
(c) be made to have effect for a specified period, or contain provisions which are to have effect for a specified period;
(d) make such incidental, supplemental or consequential provision as the court thinks fit.

12. Residence orders and parental responsibility—(1) Where the court makes a residence order in favour of the father of a child it shall, if the father would not otherwise have parental responsibility for the child, also make an order under section 4 giving him that responsibility.

(2) Where the court makes a residence order in favour of any person who is not the parent or guardian of the child concerned that person shall have parental responsibility for the child while the residence order remains in force.

(3) Where a person has parental responsibility for a child as a result of subsection (2), he shall not have the right—

(a) *to consent, or refuse to consent, to the making of an application with respect to the child under section 18 of the Adoption Act 1976;*
(b) to agree, or refuse to agree, to the making of an adoption order, or an order under *section 55 of the Act of 1976* [section 84 of The Adoption and Children Act 2002], with respect to the child; or
(c) to appoint a guardian for the child.

Note. Sub-s (3)(a) repealed by the Adoption and Children Act 2002, s 139(1), (3), Sch 3, paras 54, 57(a), Sch 5.

(4) Where subsection (1) requires the court to make an order under section 4 in respect of the father of a child, the court shall not bring that order to an end at any time while the residence order concerned remains in force.

[(5) The power of a court to make a residence order in favour of any person who is not the parent or guardian of the child concerned includes power to direct, at the request of that person, that the order continue in force until the child reaches the age of eighteen (unless the order is brought to an end earlier); and any power to vary a residence order is exercisable accordingly.

(6) Where a residence order includes such a direction, an application to vary or discharge the order may only be made, if apart from this subsection the leave of the court is not required, with such leave.]

Note. Sub-ss (5), (6) inserted by the Adoption and Children Act 2002, s 114(1), as from a day to be appointed.

13. Change of child's name or removal from jurisdiction—(1) Where a residence order is in force with respect to a child, no person may—

(a) cause the child to be known by a new surname; or

(b) remove him from the United Kingdom;

without either the written consent of every person who has parental responsibility for the child or the leave of the court.

(2) Subsection (1)(b) does not prevent the removal of a child, for a period of less than one month, by the person in whose favour the residence order is made.

(3) In making a residence order with respect to a child the court may grant the leave required by subsection (1)(b), either generally or for specified purposes.

14. Enforcement of residence orders—(1) Where—

(a) a residence order is in force with respect to a child in favour of any person; and

(b) any other person (including one in whose favour the order is also in force) is in breach of the arrangements settled by that order,

the person mentioned in paragraph (a) may, as soon as the requirement in subsection (2) is complied with, enforce the order under section 63(3) of the Magistrates' Courts Act 1980 as if it were an order requiring the other person to produce the child to him.

(2) The requirement is that a copy of the residence order has been served on the other person.

(3) Subsection (1) is without prejudice to any other remedy open to the person in whose favour the residence order is in force.

[Special guardianship

14A. Special guardianship orders—(1) A 'special guardianship order' is an order appointing one or more individuals to be a child's 'special guardian' (or special guardians).

(2) A special guardian—

(a) must be aged eighteen or over; and

(b) must not be a parent of the child in question,

and subsections (3) to (6) are to be read in that light.

(3) The court may make a special guardianship order with respect to any child on the application of an individual who—

(a) is entitled to make such an application with respect to the child; or

(b) has obtained the leave of the court to make the application,

or on the joint application of more than one such individual.

(4) Section 9(3) applies in relation to an application for leave to apply for a special guardianship order as it applies in relation to an application for leave to apply for a section 8 order.

(5) The individuals who are entitled to apply for a special guardianship order with respect to a child are—

(a) any guardian of the child;

(b) any individual in whose favour a residence order is in force with respect to the child;

(c) any individual listed in subsection (5)(b) or (c) of section 10 (as read with subsection (10) of that section);

(d) a local authority foster parent with whom the child has lived for a period of at least one year immediately preceding the application.]

(6) The court may also make a special guardianship order with respect to a child in any family proceedings in which a question arises with respect to the welfare of the child if—

(a) an application for the order has been made by an individual who falls within subsection (3)(a) or (b) (or more than one such individual jointly); or

(b) the court considers that a special guardianship order should be made even though no such application has been made.

(7) No individual may make an application under subsection (3) or (6)(a) unless, before the beginning of the period of three months ending with the date of the application, he has given written notice of his intention to make the application—

(a) if the child in question is being looked after by a local authority, to that local authority, or

(b) otherwise, to the local authority in whose area the individual is ordinarily resident.

(8) On receipt of such a notice, the local authority must investigate the matter and prepare a report for the court dealing with—

(a) the suitability of the applicant to be a special guardian;

(b) such matters (if any) as may be prescribed by the Secretary of State; and

(c) any other matter which the local authority consider to be relevant.

(9) The court may itself ask a local authority to conduct such an investigation and prepare such a report, and the local authority must do so.

(10) The local authority may make such arrangements as they see fit for any person to act on their behalf in connection with conducting an investigation or preparing a report referred to in subsection (8) or (9).

(11) The court may not make a special guardianship order unless it has received a report dealing with the matters referred to in subsection (8).

(12) Subsections (8) and (9) of section 10 apply in relation to special guardianship orders as they apply in relation to section 8 orders.

(13) This section is subject to section 29(5) and (6) of the Adoption and Children Act 2002.

14B. Special guardianship orders: making—(1) Before making a special guardianship order, the court must consider whether, if the order were made—

(a) a contact order should also be made with respect to the child, and

(b) any section 8 order in force with respect to the child should be varied or discharged.

(2) On making a special guardianship order, the court may also—

(a) give leave for the child to be known by a new surname;

(b) grant the leave required by section 14C(3)(b), either generally or for specified purposes.

14C. Special guardianship orders: effect—(1) The effect of a special guardianship order is that while the order remains in force—

(a) a special guardian appointed by the order has parental responsibility for the child in respect of whom it is made; and

(b) subject to any other order in force with respect to the child under this Act, a special guardian is entitled to exercise parental responsibility to the exclusion of any other person with parental responsibility for the child (apart from another special guardian).

(2) Subsection (1) does not affect—

(a) the operation of any enactment or rule of law which requires the consent of more than one person with parental responsibility in a matter affecting the child; or

(b) any rights which a parent of the child has in relation to the child's adoption or placement for adoption.

(3) While a special guardianship order is in force with respect to a child, no person may—

(a) cause the child to be known by a new surname; or

(b) remove him from the United Kingdom,

without either the written consent of every person who has parental responsibility for the child or the leave of the court.

(4) Subsection (3)(b) does not prevent the removal of a child, for a period of less than three months, by a special guardian of his.

(5) If the child with respect to whom a special guardianship order is in force dies, his special guardian must take reasonable steps to give notice of that fact to—

(a) each parent of the child with parental responsibility; and

(b) each guardian of the child,

but if the child has more than one special guardian, and one of them has taken such steps in relation to a particular parent or guardian, any other special guardian need not do so as respects that parent or guardian.

(6) This section is subject to section 29(7) of the Adoption and Children Act 2002.

14D. Special guardianship orders: variation and discharge—(1) The court may vary or discharge a special guardianship order on the application of—

(a) the special guardian (or any of them, if there are more than one);

(b) any parent or guardian of the child concerned;

(c) any individual in whose favour a residence order is in force with respect to the child;

(d) any individual not falling within any of paragraphs (a) to (c) who has, or immediately before the making of the special guardianship order had, parental responsibility for the child;

(e) the child himself; or

(f) a local authority designated in a care order with respect to the child.

(2) In any family proceedings in which a question arises with respect to the welfare of a child with respect to whom a special guardianship order is in force, the court may also vary or discharge the special guardianship order if it considers that the order should be varied or discharged, even though no application has been made under subsection (1).

(3) The following must obtain the leave of the court before making an application under subsection (1)—

(a) the child;

(b) any parent or guardian of his;

(c) any step-parent of his who has acquired, and has not lost, parental responsibility for him by virtue of section 4A;

(d) any individual falling within subsection (1)(d) who immediately before the making of the special guardianship order had, but no longer has, parental responsibility for him.

(4) Where the person applying for leave to make an application under subsection (1) is the child, the court may only grant leave if it is satisfied that he has sufficient understanding to make the proposed application under subsection (1).

(5) The court may not grant leave to a person falling within subsection (3)(b)(c) or (d) unless it is satisfied that there has been a significant change in circumstances since the making of the special guardianship order.

14E. Special guardianship orders: supplementary—(1) In proceedings in which any question of making, varying or discharging a special guardianship order arises, the court shall (in the light of any rules made by virtue of subsection (3))—

    (a) draw up a timetable with a view to determining the question without delay; and

    (b) give such directions as it considers appropriate for the purpose of ensuring, so far as is reasonably practicable, that the timetable is adhered to.

    (2) Subsection (1) applies also in relation to proceedings in which any other question with respect to a special guardianship order arises.

    (3) The power to make rules in subsection (2) of section 11 applies for the purposes of this section as it applies for the purposes of that.

    (4) A special guardianship order, or an order varying one, may contain provisions which are to have effect for a specified period.

    (5) Section 11(7) (apart from paragraph (c)) applies in relation to special guardianship orders and orders varying them as it applies in relation to section 8 orders.

14F. Special guardianship support services—(1) Each local authority must make arrangements for the provision within their area of special guardianship support services, which means—

    (a) counselling, advice and information; and

    (b) such other services as are prescribed,

in relation to special guardianship.

    (2) The power to make regulations under subsection (1)(b) is to be exercised so as to secure that local authorities provide financial support.

    (3) At the request of any of the following persons—

    (a) a child with respect to whom a special guardianship order is in force;

    (b) a special guardian;

    (c) a parent;

    (d) any other person who falls within a prescribed description,

a local authority may carry out an assessment of that person's needs for special guardianship support services (but, if the Secretary of State so provides in regulations, they must do so if he is a person of a prescribed description, or if his case falls within a prescribed description, or if both he and his case fall within prescribed descriptions).

    (4) A local authority may, at the request of any other person, carry out an assessment of that person's needs for special guardianship support services.

    (5) Where, as a result of an assessment, a local authority decide that a person has needs for special guardianship support services, they must then decide whether to provide any such services to that person.

    (6) If—

    (a) a local authority decide to provide any special guardianship support services to a person, and

    (b) the circumstances fall within a prescribed description,

the local authority must prepare a plan in accordance with which special guardianship support services are to be provided to him, and keep the plan under review.

    (7) The Secretary of State may by regulations make provision about assessments, preparing and reviewing plans, the provision of special guardianship support services in accordance with plans and reviewing the provision of special guardianship support services.

    (8) The regulations may in particular make provision—

    (a) about the type of assessment which is to be carried out, or the way in which an assessment is to be carried out;

    (b) about the way in which a plan is to be prepared;

(c) about the way in which, and the time at which, a plan or the provision of special guardianship support services is to be reviewed;

(d) about the considerations to which a local authority are to have regard in carrying out an assessment or review or preparing a plan;

(e) as to the circumstances in which a local authority may provide special guardianship support services subject to conditions (including conditions as to payment for the support or the repayment of financial support);

(f) as to the consequences of conditions imposed by virtue of paragraph (e) not being met (including the recovery of any financial support provided);

(g) as to the circumstances in which this section may apply to a local authority in respect of persons who are outside that local authority's area;

(h) as to the circumstances in which a local authority may recover from another local authority the expenses of providing special guardianship support services to any person.

(9) A local authority may provide special guardianship support services (or any part of them) by securing their provision by—

(a) another local authority; or

(b) a person within a description prescribed in regulations of persons who may provide special guardianship support services,

and may also arrange with any such authority or person for that other authority or that person to carry out the local authority's functions in relation to assessments under this section.

(10) A local authority may carry out an assessment of the needs of any person for the purposes of this section at the same time as an assessment of his needs is made under any other provision of this Act or under any other enactment.

(11) Section 27 (co-operation between authorities) applies in relation to the exercise of functions of a local authority under this section as it applies in relation to the exercise of functions of a local authority under Part 3.

14G. Special guardianship support services: representations—*(1) Every local authority shall establish a procedure for considering representations (including complaints) made to them by any person to whom they may provide special guardianship support services about the discharge of their functions under section 14F in relation to him.*

(2) Regulations may be made by the Secretary of State imposing time limits on the making of representations under subsection (1).

(3) In considering representations under subsection (1), a local authority shall comply with regulations (if any) made by the Secretary of State for the purposes of this subsection.]

Note. Sections 14A–14G inserted by the Adoption and Children Act 2002, s 115(1), as from a day to be appointed. Section 14G repealed by the Health and Social Care (Community Health and Standards) Act 2003, ss 117(2), 196, Sch 14, Pt 2, as from a day to be appointed.

Financial relief

15. Orders for financial relief with respect to children—(1) Schedule 1 (which consists primarily of the re-enactment, with consequential amendments and minor modifications, of provisions of [section 6 of the Family Law Reform Act 1969] the Guardianship of Minors Acts 1971 and 1973, the Children Act 1975 and of sections 15 and 16 of the Family Law Reform Act 1987) makes provision in relation to financial relief for children.

(2) The powers of a magistrates' court under section 60 of the Magistrates' Courts Act 1980 to revoke, revive or vary an order for the periodical payment of money [and the power of the clerk of a magistrates' court to vary such an order] shall not apply in relation to an order made under Schedule 1.

Note. Words in square brackets in sub-s (1) inserted by Courts and Legal Services Act 1990, s 116, Sch 16, para 10(1), as from 14 October 1991. Words in square brackets in sub-s (2) inserted by Maintenance Enforcement Act 1991, s 11(1), Sch 2, para 10, as from 1 April 1992.

Family assistance orders

16. Family assistance orders—(1) Where, in any family proceedings the court has power to make an order under this Part with respect to any child, it may (whether or not it makes such an order) make an order requiring—

    (a) *a probation officer* [an officer of the service] to be made available; or

    (b) a local authority to make an officer of the authority available,

to advise, assist and (where appropriate) befriend any person named in the order.

Note. In para (a) words 'an officer of the service' in square brackets substituted for words in italics by the Criminal Justice and Court Services Act 2000, s 74, Sch 7, Pt 2, paras 87, 89(a), as from 1 April 2001 (SI 2001 No 919).

(2) The persons who may be named in an order under this section ('a family assistance order') are—

    (a) any parent *or guardian* [, guardian or special guardian] of the child.

    (b) any person with whom the child is living or in whose favour a contact order is in force with respect to the child;

    (c) the child himself.

Note. In para (a) words ', guardian or special guardian' in square brackets substituted for words in italics by the Adoption and Children Act 2002, s 139(1), Sch 3, paras 54, 58, as from a day to be appointed.

(3) No court may make a family assistance order unless—

    (a) it is satisfied that the circumstances of the case are exceptional; and

    (b) it has obtained the consent of every person to be named in the order other than the child.

(4) A family assistance order may direct—

    (a) the person named in the order; or

    (b) such of the persons named in the order as may be specified in the order,

to take such steps as may be so specified with a view to enabling the officer concerned to be kept informed of the address of any person named in the order and to be allowed to visit any such person.

(5) Unless it specifies a shorter period, a family assistance order shall have effect for a period of six months beginning with the day on which it is made.

(6) Where—

    (a) a family assistance order is in force with respect to a child; and

    (b) a section 8 order is also in force with respect to the child,

the officer concerned may refer to the court the question whether the section 8 order should be varied or discharged.

(7) A family assistance order shall not be made so as to require a local authority to make an officer of theirs available unless—

    (a) the authority agree; or

    (b) the child concerned lives or will live within their area.

(8) ...

(9) ...

Note. Sub-ss (8), (9) repealed by the Criminal Justice and Court Services Act 2000, ss 74, 75, Sch 7, Pt 2, pars 87, 89(b), Sch 8, as from 1 April 2001 (SI 2001 No 919).

PART III

LOCAL AUTHORITY SUPPORT FOR CHILDREN AND FAMILIES

Provision of services for children and their families

17. Provision of services for children in need, their families and others—(1) It shall be the general duty of every local authority (in addition to the other duties imposed on them by this Part)—

(a) to safeguard and promote the welfare of children within their area who are in need; and

(b) so far as is consistent with that duty. to promote the upbringing of such children by their families,

by providing a range and level of services appropriate to those children's needs.

(2) For the purpose principally of facilitating the discharge of their general duty under this section. every local authority shall have the specific duties and powers set out in Part I of Schedule 2.

(3) Any service provided by an authority in the exercise of functions conferred on them by this section may be provided for the family of a particular child in need or for any member of his family, if it is provided with a view to safeguarding or promoting the child's welfare.

(4) The Secretary of State may by order amend any provision of Part I of Schedule 2 or add any further duty or power to those for the time being mentioned there.

(5) Every local authority—

(a) shall facilitate the provision by others including in particular voluntary organisations; of services which the authority have power to provide by virtue of this section or sections 18, 20, *23 or 24* [23, 23B to 23D, 24A or 24B]; and

(b) may make such arrangements as they see fit for any person to act on their behalf in the provision of any such service.

Note. In sub-s (5)(a) words '23, 23B to 23D, 24A or 24B' in square brackets substituted for words in italics by the Children (Leaving Care) Act 2000, s 7(1), (2), as from 1 October 2001 (SI 2001 No 2878, SI 2001 No 2191).

(6) The services provided by a local authority in the exercise of functions conferred on them by this section may include [providing accommodation and] giving assistance in kind or, in exceptional circumstances, in cash.

Note. Words 'providing accommodation and' in square brackets inserted by the Adoption and Children Act 2002, s 116(1), as from 7 November 2002 (date of Royal Assent, in the absence of any specific commencement provision.

(7) Assistance may be unconditional or subject to conditions as to the repayment of the assistance or of its value (in whole or in part).

(8) Before giving any assistance or imposing any conditions, a local authority shall have regard to the means of the child concerned and of each of his parents.

(9) No person shall be liable to make any repayment of assistance or of its value at any time when he is in receipt of income support or *family credit* or [working families' tax credit] or *disability working allowance* [or disabled person's tax credit] under [under] *the Social Security Act 1986* [Part VII of the Social Security Contributions and Benefits Act 1992] [or any element of child tax credit other than the family element, of working tax credit] [or of an income-based jobseeker's allowance].

Note. In sub-s (9) words 'family credit or disability working allowance' in square brackets substituted for words 'or family credit' by the Disability Living Allowance and Disability Working Allowance Act 1991, s 7(2), Sch 3, Pt 2, para 13, as from 19 November 1991 for certain purposes and as from 10 March 1992 for remaining purposes. Words 'Part VII...Act 1992' in square brackets substituted for words 'the Social Security Act 1986' by the Social Security (Consequential Provisions) Act 1992, s 4, Sch 2, para 108, as from 1 July 1992. Words 'or of an...allowance' in square brackets inserted by the Jobseekers Act 1995, s 41(4), Sch 2, para 19, as from 7 October 1996. Words 'working families' tax credit' and 'or disabled person's tax credit' in square brackets substituted for words 'family credit' and 'disability working allowance' respectively by the Tax Credits Act 1999, s 1(2), Sch 1, paras 1, 6(d)(i), as from 5 October 1999. Word 'under' in square brackets substituted for words 'working families' ... under' and words ', or any...tax credit' in square brackets inserted by the Tax Credits Act 2002, s 47, Sch 3, paras 15, 16(1), (2), as from 6 April 2003 (SI 2003 No 962); for savings see arts 3–5 thereof.

(10) For the purposes of this Part a child shall be taken to be in need if—

(a) he is unlikely to achieve or maintains, or to have the opportunity of achieving or maintaining, a reasonable standard of health or development without the provision for him of services by a local authority under this Part;

(b) his health or development is likely to be significantly impaired, or further impaired, without the provision for him of such services; or

(c) he is disabled,

and family', in relation to such a child. includes any person who has parental responsibility for the child and any other person with whom he has been living.

(11) For the purposes of this Part a child is disabled if he is blind, deaf or dumb or suffers from mental disorder of any kind or is substantially and permanently handicapped by illness, injury or congenital deformity or such other disability as may be prescribed; and in this Part—

'development' means physical, intellectual, emotional social or behavioural development; and

'health' means physical or mental health.

[(12) The Treasury may by regulations prescribe circumstances in which a person is to be treated for the purposes of this Part (or for such of those purposes as are prescribed) as in receipt of any element of child tax credit other than the family element or of working tax credit.]

Note. Sub-s (12) inserted by the Tax Credits Act 2002, s 47, Sch 3, paras 15, 16(1), (3), as from 6 April 2003 (SI 2003 No 962); for savings see arts 3–5 thereof.

[17A. Direct payments—(1) The Secretary of State may by regulations make provision for and in connection with requiring or authorising the responsible authority in the case of a person of a prescribed description who falls within subsection (2) to make, with that person's consent, such payments to him as they may determine in accordance with the regulations in respect of his securing the provision of the service mentioned in that subsection.

(2) A person falls within this subsection if he is—

(a) a person with parental responsibility for a disabled child,

(b) a disabled person with parental responsibility for a child, or

(c) a disabled child aged 16 or 17,

and a local authority ('the responsible authority') have decided for the purposes of section 17 that the child's needs (or, if he is such a disabled child, his needs) call for the provision by them of a service in exercise of functions conferred on them under that section.

(3) Subsections (3) to (5) and (7) of section 57 of the 2001 Act shall apply, with any necessary modifications, in relation to regulations under this section as they apply in relation to regulations under that section.

(4) Regulations under this section shall provide that, where payments are made under the regulations to a person falling within subsection (5)—

(a) the payments shall be made at the rate mentioned in subsection (4)(a) of section 57 of the 2001 Act (as applied by subsection (3)); and

(b) subsection (4)(b) of that section shall not apply.

(5) A person falls within this subsection if he is—

(a) a person falling within subsection (2)(a) or (b) and the child in question is aged 16 or 17, or

(b) a person who is in receipt of income support . . . under Part 7 of the Social Security Contributions and Benefits Act 1992 (c 4)[, of any element of child tax credit other than the family element, of working tax credit] or of an income-based jobseeker's allowance.

(6) In this section—

'the 2001 Act' means the Health and Social Care Act 2001;

'disabled' in relation to an adult has the same meaning as that given by section 17(11) in relation to a child;

'prescribed' means specified in or determined in accordance with regulations under this section (and has the same meaning in the provisions of the 2001 Act mentioned in subsection (3) as they apply by virtue of that subsection).]

Note. This section inserted by the Carers and Disabled Children Act 2000, s 7(1), as from (in relation to England): 1 April 2001 (SI 2001 No 510); (in relation to Wales): 1 July 2001 (SI 2001 No 2196). Substituted by the Health and Social Care Act 2001, s 58, as from (in relation to England for certain purposes): 16 March 2003 (SI 2003 No 850); (in relation to England for remaining purposes): 8 April 2003 (SI 2003 No 850); (in relation to Wales for certain purposes): 8 July 2004 (SI 2004 No 1754); (in relation to Wales for remaining purposes): 1 November 2004 (SI 2004 No 1754). In sub-s (5)(b) words omitted repealed by the Tax Credits Act 2002, s 60, Sch 6, as from 6 April 2003 (SI 2003 No 692); for savings see arts 3–5 thereof. Words ', of any element...working tax credit' in square brackets inserted by the Tax Credits Act 2002, s 47, Sch 3, paras 15, 17, as from 6 April 2003 (SI 2003/692); for savings see arts 3–5.

[17B. Vouchers for persons with parental responsibility for disabled children—
(1)   The Secretary of State may by regulations make provision for the issue by a local authority of vouchers to a person with parental responsibility for a disabled child.

(2)   'Voucher' means a document whereby, if the local authority agrees with the person with parental responsibility that it would help him care for the child if the person with parental responsibility had a break from caring, that person may secure the temporary provision of services for the child under section 17.

(3)   The regulations may, in particular, provide—
(a)   for the value of a voucher to be expressed in terms of money, or of the delivery of a service for a period of time, or both;
(b)   for the person who supplies a service against a voucher, or for the arrangement under which it is supplied, to be approved by the local authority;
(c)   for a maximum period during which a service (or a service of a prescribed description) can be provided against a voucher.]

Note. This section inserted by the Carers and Disabled Children Act 2000, s 7(1), as from a day to be appointed.

18. Day care for pre-school and other children—(1) Every local authority shall provide such day care for children in need within their area who are—
(a)   aged five or under; and
(b)   not yet attending schools,
as is appropriate.

(2)   A local authority may provide day care for children within their area who satisfy the conditions mentioned in subsection (1)(a) and (b) even though they are not in need.

(3)   A local authority may provide facilities including training. advice, guidance and counselling for those—
(a)   caring for children in day care; or
(b)   who at any time accompany such children while they are in day care.

(4)   In this section 'day care' means any form of care or supervised activity provided for children during the day (whether or not it is provided on a regular basis).

(5)   Every local authority shall provide for children in need within their area who are attending any school such care or supervised activities as is appropriate—
(a)   outside school hours; or
(b)   during school holidays.

(6)   A local authority may provide such care or supervised activities for children within their area who are attending any school even though those children are not in need.

(7) In this section supervised activity means an activity supervised by a responsible person.

19. ...

Note. This section repealed in relation to Scotland by the Regulation of Care (Scotland) Act 2001, s 80, Sch 4 and in relation to England and Wales by virtue of the Education Act 2002, s 149(2), as from (in relation to Scotland): 1 April 2002 (SSI 2002 No 162); for transitional provisions see arts 3, 4(6), (9), (10), 7, 8(c), 12, 13 thereof; (in relation to England): 1 October 2002 (SI 2002 No 2439); (in relation to Wales): 31 March 2003 (SI 2002 No 3185).

Provision of accommodation for children

20. Provision of accommodation for children: general—(1) Every local authority shall provide accommodation for any child in need within their area who appears to them to require accommodation as a result of—

    (a) there being no person who has parental responsibility for him;

    (b) his being lost or having been abandoned; or

    (c) the person who has been caring for him being prevented (whether or not permanently. and for whatever reason) from providing him with suitable accommodation or care.

(2) Where a local authority provide accommodation under subsection (1) for a child who is ordinarily resident in the area of another local authority, that other local authority may take over the provision of accommodation for the child within—

    (a) three months of being notified in writing that the child is being provided with accommodation; or

    (b) such other longer period as may he prescribed.

(3) Every local authority shall provide accommodation for any child in need within their area who has reached the age of sixteen and whose welfare the authority consider is likely to be seriously produced if they do not provide him with accommodation.

(4) A local authority may provide accommodation for any child within their area (even though a person who has parental responsibility for him is able to provide him with accommodation) if they consider that to do so would safeguard or promote the child's welfare.

(5) A local authority may provide accommodation for any person who has reached the age of sixteen but is under twenty-one in any community home which takes children who have reached the age of sixteen if they consider that to do so would safeguard or promote his welfare.

(6) Before providing accommodation under this section, a local authority shall, so far as is reasonably practicable and consistent with the child's welfare—

    (a) ascertain the child's wishes regarding the provision of accommodation; and

    (b) give due consideration (having regard to his age and understanding) to such wishes of the child as they have been able to ascertain.

(7) A local authority may not provide accommodation under this section for any child if any person who—

    (a) has parental responsibility for him; and

    (b) is willing and able to—

        (i) provide accommodation for him; or

        (ii) arrange for accommodation to be provided for him, objects.

(8) Any person who has parental responsibility for a child may at any time remove the child from accommodation provided by or on behalf of the local authority under this section.

(9) Subsections (7) and (8) do not apply while any person—

    (a) in whose favour a residence order is in force with respect to the child; ...

[(aa) who is a special guardian of the child; or]

(b) who has care of the child by virtue of an order made in the exercise of the High Court's inherent jurisdiction with respect to children,

agrees to the child being looked after in accommodation provided by or on behalf of the local authority.

Note. In sub-s (9)(a) word omitted repealed and para (aa) inserted by the Adoption and Children Act 2002, s 139(1), (3), Sch 3, paras 54, 59, Sch 5, as from a day to be appointed.

(10) Where there is more than one such person as is mentioned in subsection (9), all of them must agree.

(11) Subsections (7) and (8) do not apply where a child who has reached the age of sixteen agrees to being provided with accommodation under this section.

21. Provision of accommodation for children in police protection or detention or on remand, etc—(1) Every local authority shall make provision for the reception and accommodation of children who are removed or kept away from home under Part V.

(2) Every local authority shall receive, and provide accommodation for, children—

(a) in police protection whom they are requested to receive under section 46(3)(f);

(b) whom they are requested to receive under section 38(6) of the Police and Criminal Evidence Act 1984;

(c) who are—

    (i) on remand [(within the meaning of the section)] under section *[16(3A) or]* [paragraph 7(5) of Schedule 7 to the Powers of Criminal Courts (Sentencing) Act 2000 or section] 23(1) of the Children and Young Persons Act 1969; or

    (ii) the subject of a suspension order imposing a *residence requirement under section 12AA of that Act* [local authority residence requirement under paragraph 5 of Schedule 6 to that Act of 2000] [or a foster parent residence requirement under paragraph 5A of that Schedule],

and with respect to whom they are the designated authority.

Note. In sub-s (2)(c)(i) words '(within the meaning of the section)' in square brackets inserted by the Criminal Justice and Public Order Act 1994, s 168(1), Sch 9, para 38, as from a day to be appointed. Words '16(3A) or' in square brackets inserted by the Courts and Legal Services Act 1990, s 116, Sch 16, para 11, as from 14 October 1991. Words 'paragraph 7(5)...or section' in square brackets substituted for words in italics and in para (c)(ii) words 'local authority...of 2000' in square brackets substituted for words in italics by the Powers of Criminal Courts (Sentencing) Act 2000, s 165(1), Sch 9, para 126, as from 25 August 2000. In para (c)(ii) words 'or a foster...of that Schedule' in square brackets inserted by the Anti-Social Behaviour Act 2003, s 88, Sch 2, para 5, as from 30 September 2004 (SI 2004 No 2168).

(3) Where a child has been—

(a) removed under Part V. or

(b) detained under section 38 of the Police and Criminal Evidence Act 1984, and he is not being provided with accommodation by a local authority or in a hospital vested in the Secretary of State [or a Primary Care Trust] [or otherwise made available pursuant to arrangements made by a *District Health Authority* [Health Authority]] [or a Primary Care Trust], any reasonable expenses of accommodating him shall be recoverable from the local authority in whose area he is ordinarily resident.

Note. Words 'or a Primary Care Trust' in square brackets in both places they occur inserted by the Health Act 1999 (Supplementary, Consequential etc Provisions) Order 2000, SI 2000 No 90, art 3(1), Sch 1, para 24(1), (3), as from 8 February 2000. Words in second pair of square brackets inserted by National Health Service and Community Care Act 1990, s 66(1), Sch 9, para 36(1), as from 5 July 1990. Words 'Health Authority' in square brackets substituted for words in italics by Health Authorities Act 1995, s 2(1), Sch 1, Part III, para 118, as from 28 June 1995, in so far as is necessary for enabling the making of any regulations, orders, directions, schemes or appointments, and as from 1 April 1996 otherwise.

Duties of local authorities in relation to children looked after by them

22. General duty of local authority in relation to children looked after by them—(1) In this Act, any reference to a child who is looked after by a local authority is a reference to a child who is—

(a) in their care; or

(b) provided with accommodation by the authority in the exercise of any functions (in particular those under this Act) which *stand referred to their social services committee under* [are social service functions within the meaning of] the Local Authority Social Services Act 1970 [, apart from functions under sections [17], 23B and 24B].

Note. In para (b) words 'are social services...meaning of' in square brackets substituted for words in italics by the Local Government Act 2000, s 107, Sch 5, para 19, as from (in relation to England): 26 October 2000; (in relation to Wales): 28 July 2001. Words 'apart from...and 24B' in square brackets inserted by the Children (Leaving Care) Act 2000, s 2(1), (2), as from 1 October 2001 (SI 2001 No 2878, SI 2001 No 2191). Reference to '17' in square brackets inserted by the Adoption and Children Act 2002, s 116(1), as from a day to be appointed.

(2) In subsection (1) accommodation' means accommodation which is provided for a continuous period of more than 24 hours.

(3) It shall be the duty of a local authority looking after any child—

(a) to safeguard and promote his welfare; and

(b) to make such use of services available for children cared for by their own parents as appears to the authority reasonable in his case.

(4) Before making any decision with respect to a child whom they are looking after, or proposing to look after, a local authority shall, so far as is reasonably practicable, ascertain the wishes and feelings of—

(a) the child;

(b) his parents;

(c) any person who is not a parent of his but who has parental responsibility for him; and

(d) any other person whose wishes and feelings the authority consider to be relevant, regarding the matter to be decided.

(5) In making any such decision a local authority shall give due consideration—

(a) having regard to his age and understanding, to such wishes and feelings of the child as they have been able to ascertain;

(b) to such wishes and feelings of any person mentioned in subsection (4)(b) to (d) as they have been able to ascertain; and

(c) to the child's religious persuasion, racial origin and cultural and linguistic background.

(6) If it appears to a local authority that it is necessary, for the purpose of protecting members of the public from serious injury, to exercise their powers with respect to a child whom they are looking after in a manner which may not be consistent with their duties under this section, they may do so.

(7) If the Secretary of State considers it necessary, for the purpose of protecting members of the public from serious injury, to give directions to a local authority with respect to the exercise of their powers with respect to a child whom they are looking after. he may give such directions to the authority.

(8) Where any' such directions are given to an authority they shall comply with them even though doing so is inconsistent with their duties under this section.

23. Provision of accommodation and maintenance by local authority for children whom they are looking after—(1) It shall he the duty of any local authority looking after a child—

(a) when he is in their care, to provide accommodation for him; and
(b) to maintain him in other respects apart from providing accommodation for him.
(2) A local authority shall provide accommodation and maintenance for any child whom they are looking after by—
(a) placing him subject to subsection (5) and any regulations made by the Secretary of State with—
  (i) a family;
  (ii) a relative of his; or
  (iii) any other suitable person,
  on such terms as to payment by the authority and otherwise as the authority may determine;
(b) maintaining him in a community home;
(c) maintaining him in a voluntary home;
(d) maintaining him in a registered children's home;
(e) maintaining him in a home provided [in accordance with arrangements made] by the Secretary of State under section 82(5) on such terms as the Secretary of State may from time to time determine; or
[(aa) maintaining him in an appropriate children's home;]
(f) making such other arrangements as—
  (i) seem appropriate to them; and
  (ii) comply with any regulations made by the Secretary of State.
Note. In sub-s (2)(e) words 'in accordance with arrangements made' in square brackets inserted by the Courts and Legal Services Act 1990, s 116, Sch 16, para 12, as from 14 October 1991. In sub-s (2) para (aa) substituted for paras (b)–(e) in italics by the Care Standards Act 2000, s 116, Sch 4, para 14(1), (3)(a), as from 1 April 2002 (SI 2002 No 4150, SI 2002 No 920).

[(2A) Where under subsection (2)(aa) a local authority maintains a child in a home provided, equipped and maintained by the Secretary of State under section 82(5), it shall do so on such terms as the Secretary of State may from time to time determine.]
Note. Sub-s (2A) inserted by the Care Standards Act 2000, s 116, Sch 4, para 14(1), (3)(b), as from 1 April 2002 (SI 2002 No 4150, SI 2002 No 920).

(3) Any person with whom a child has been placed under subsection (2)(a) is referred to in this Act as a local authority foster parent unless he falls within subsection (4).
(4) A person falls within this subsection if he is—
(a) a parent of the child;
(b) a person who is not a parent of the child but who has parental responsibility for him; or
(c) where the child is in care and there was a residence order in force with respect to him immediately before the care order was made, a person in whose favour the residence order was made.
(5) Where a child is in the care of a local authority, the authority may only allow him to live with a person who falls within subsection (4) in accordance with regulations made by the Secretary of State.
[(5A) For the purposes of subsection (5) a child shall be regarded as living with a person if he stays with that person for a continuous period of more than 24 hours.]
Note. Sub-s (5A) inserted by the Courts and Legal Services Act 1990, s 116, Sch 16, para 12, as from 14 October 1991.

(6) Subject to any regulations made by the Secretary of State for the purposes of this subsection, any local authority looking after a child shall make arrangements to enable him to live with—

(a) a person falling within subsection (4); or

(b) a relative, friend or other person connected with him,

unless that would not be reasonably practicable or consistent with his welfare.

(7) Where a local authority provide accommodation for a child whom they are looking after, they shall, subject to the provisions of this Part and so far as is reasonably practicable and consistent with his welfare, secure that—

(a) the accommodation is near his home; and

(b) where the authority are also providing accommodation for a sibling of his, they are accommodated together.

(8) Where a local authority provide accommodation for a child whom they are looking after and who is disabled, they shall, so far as is reasonably practicable. secure that the accommodation is not unsuitable to his particular needs.

(9) Part II of Schedule 2 shall have effect for the purposes of making further provision as to children looked after by local authorities and in particular as to the regulations that may be made under subsections (2)(a) and (f) and (5).

[(10) In this Act—

'appropriate children's home' means a children's home in respect of which a person is registered under Part II of the Care Standards Act 2000; and

'children's home' has the same meaning as in that Act.]

Note. Sub-s (10) inserted by the Care Standards Act 2000, s 116, Sch 4, para 14(1), (3)(c), as from 1 April 2002 (SI 2002 No 4150, SI 2002 No 920).

Advice and assistance for certain children [and young persons]

[23A. The responsible authority and relevant children—(1) The responsible local authority shall have the functions set out in section 23B in respect of a relevant child.

(2) In subsection (1) 'relevant child' means (subject to subsection (3)) a child who—

(a) is not being looked after by any local authority;

(b) was, before last ceasing to be looked after, an eligible child for the purposes of paragraph 19B of Schedule 2; and

(c) is aged sixteen or seventeen.

(3) The Secretary of State may prescribe—

(a) additional categories of relevant children; and

(b) categories of children who are not to be relevant children despite falling within subsection (2).

(4) In subsection (1) the 'responsible local authority' is the one which last looked after the child.

(5) If under subsection (3)(a) the Secretary of State prescribes a category of relevant children which includes children who do not fall within subsection (2)(b) (for example, because they were being looked after by a local authority in Scotland), he may in the regulations also provide for which local authority is to be the responsible local authority for those children.

23B. Additional functions of the responsible authority in respect of relevant children—[(1) It is the duty of each local authority to take reasonable steps to keep in touch with a relevant child for whom they are the responsible authority, whether he is within their area or not.

(2) It is the duty of each local authority to appoint a personal adviser for each relevant child (if they have not already done so under paragraph 19C of Schedule 2).

(3) It is the duty of each local authority, in relation to any relevant child who does not already have a pathway plan prepared for the purposes of paragraph 19B of Schedule 2—

(a) to carry out an assessment of his needs with a view to determining what advice, assistance and support it would be appropriate for them to provide him under this Part; and

(b)   to prepare a pathway plan for him.

(4) The local authority may carry out such an assessment at the same time as any assessment of his needs is made under any enactment referred to in sub-paragraphs (a) to (c) of paragraph 3 of Schedule 2, or under any other enactment.

(5) The Secretary of State may by regulations make provision as to assessments for the purposes of subsection (3).

(6) The regulations may in particular make provision about—

(a) who is to be consulted in relation to an assessment;

(b) the way in which an assessment is to be carried out, by whom and when;

(c) the recording of the results of an assessment;

(d) the considerations to which the local authority are to have regard in carrying out an assessment.

(7) The authority shall keep the pathway plan under regular review.

(8) The responsible local authority shall safeguard and promote the child's welfare and, unless they are satisfied that his welfare does not require it, support him by—

(a) maintaining him;

(b) providing him with or maintaining him in suitable accommodation; and

(c) providing support of such other descriptions as may be prescribed.

(9) Support under subsection (8) may be in cash.

(10) The Secretary of State may by regulations make provision about the meaning of 'suitable accommodation' and in particular about the suitability of landlords or other providers of accommodation.

(11) If the local authority have lost touch with a relevant child, despite taking reasonable steps to keep in touch, they must without delay—

(a) consider how to re-establish contact; and

(b) take reasonable steps to do so,

and while the child is still a relevant child must continue to take such steps until they succeed.

(12) Subsections (7) to (9) of section 17 apply in relation to support given under this section as they apply in relation to assistance given under that section.

(13) Subsections (4) and (5) of section 22 apply in relation to any decision by a local authority for the purposes of this section as they apply in relation to the decisions referred to in that section.

23C. Continuing functions in respect of former relevant children—[(1) Each local authority shall have the duties provided for in this section towards—

(a) a person who has been a relevant child for the purposes of section 23A (and would be one if he were under eighteen), and in relation to whom they were the last responsible authority; and

(b) a person who was being looked after by them when he attained the age of eighteen, and immediately before ceasing to be looked after was an eligible child,

and in this section such a person is referred to as a 'former relevant child'.

(2) It is the duty of the local authority to take reasonable steps—

(a) to keep in touch with a former relevant child whether he is within their area or not; and

(b) if they lose touch with him, to re-establish contact.

(3) It is the duty of the local authority—

(a) to continue the appointment of a personal adviser for a former relevant child; and

(b) to continue to keep his pathway plan under regular review.

(4) It is the duty of the local authority to give a former relevant child—

(a) assistance of the kind referred to in section 24B(1), to the extent that his welfare requires it;

(b) assistance of the kind referred to in section 24B(2), to the extent that his welfare and his educational or training needs require it;

(c) other assistance, to the extent that his welfare requires it.

(5) The assistance given under subsection (4)(c) may be in kind or, in exceptional circumstances, in cash.

(6) Subject to subsection (7), the duties set out in subsections (2), (3) and (4) subsist until the former relevant child reaches the age of twenty-one.

(7) If the former relevant child's pathway plan sets out a programme of education or training which extends beyond his twenty-first birthday—

(a) the duty set out in subsection (4)(b) continues to subsist for so long as the former relevant child continues to pursue that programme; and

(b) the duties set out in subsections (2) and (3) continue to subsist concurrently with that duty.

(8) For the purposes of subsection (7)(a) there shall be disregarded any interruption in a former relevant child's pursuance of a programme of education or training if the local authority are satisfied that he will resume it as soon as is reasonably practicable.

(9) Section 24B(5) applies in relation to a person being given assistance under subsection (4)(b) as it applies in relation to a person to whom section 24B(3) applies.

(10) Subsections (7) to (9) of section 17 apply in relation to assistance given under this section as they apply in relation to assistance given under that section.]

Note. In cross-heading words 'and young persons' in square brackets inserted and sections 23A–23C inserted by the Children (Leaving Care) Act 2000, s 2(1), (3), (4), as from 1 October 2001 (SI 2001 No 2878, SI 2001 No 2191).

[*Personal advisers and pathway plans*

23D. Personal advisers—(1) The Secretary of State may by regulations require local authorities to appoint a personal adviser for children or young persons of a prescribed description who have reached the age of sixteen but not the age of twenty-one who are not—

(a) children who are relevant children for the purposes of section 23A;

(b) the young persons referred to in section 23C; or

(c) the children referred to in paragraph 19C of Schedule 2.

(2) Personal advisers appointed under or by virtue of this Part shall (in addition to any other functions) have such functions as the Secretary of State prescribes.

23E. Pathway plans—(1) In this Part, a reference to a 'pathway plan' is to a plan setting out—

(a) in the case of a plan prepared under paragraph 19B of Schedule 2—

(i) the advice, assistance and support which the local authority intend to provide a child under this Part, both while they are looking after him and later; and

(ii) when they might cease to look after him; and

(b) in the case of a plan prepared under section 23B, the advice, assistance and support which the local authority intend to provide under this Part,

and dealing with such other matters (if any) as may be prescribed.

(2) The Secretary of State may by regulations make provision about pathway plans and their review.]

Note. Sections 23D, 23E inserted by the Children (Leaving Care) Act 2000, s 3, as from 1 October 2001 (SI 2001 No 2878, SI 2001 No 2191).

24. Advice and assistance for certain children—*(1) Where a child is being looked after by a local authority, it shall be the duty of the authority to advise, assist and befriend him with a view to promoting his welfare when he ceases to be looked after by them.*

(2) In this Part a person qualifying for advice and assistance' means a person within the area of the authority who is under twenty-one and who was, at any time after reaching the age of sixteen but while still a child—

(a)   *looked after by a local authority;*

(b)   *accommodated by or on behalf of a voluntary Organisation;*

(c)   *accommodated in a registered [private] children's home;*

(d)   *accommodated—*

    (i)   *by any health authority [Health Authority, Special Health Authority] [, Primary Care Trust] or local education authority; or*

    (ii)   *in any residential care home, nursing home or mental nursing home [care home or independent hospital] [or in any accommodation provided by a National Health Service trust],*

    for a consecutive period of at least three months; or

(e)   *privately fostered,*

but who is no longer so looked after, accommodated or fostered.

Note. In sub-s (2)(c) word 'private' in square brackets substituted for word 'registered' and in para (d)(ii) words 'care home or independent hospital' in square brackets substituted for words 'residential care...nursing home' by the Care Standards Act 2000, s 116, Sch 4, para 14(1), (4), (5), as from a day to be appointed. In para (d)(i) words 'Health Authority, Special Health Authority' in square brackets substituted for words 'health authority' by the Health Authorities Act 1995, s 2(1), Sch 1, Pt 3, para 118, as from 28 June 1995, in so far as is necessary for enabling the making of any regulations, orders, directions, schemes or appointments, and as from 1 April 1996 otherwise. Words ', Primary Care Trust' in square brackets inserted by the Health Act 1999 (Supplementary Consequential etc Provisions) Order 2000, SI 2000 No 90, art 3(1), Sch 1, para 24(1), (4), as from 8 February 2000. In para (d)(ii) words 'or in any...trust' in square brackets inserted by the National Health Service and Community Care Act 1990, s 66(1), Sch 9, para 36(2), as from 5 July 1990.

(3) Subsection (2)(d) applies even if the period of three months mentioned there began before the child reached the age of sixteen.

(4) Where—

(a)   *a local authority know that there is within their area a person qualifying for advice and assistance;*

(b)   *the conditions in subsection (5) are satisfied; and*

(c)   *that person has asked them for help of a kind which they can give under this section,*

they shall (if he was being looked after by a local authority or was accommodated by or on behalf of a voluntary organisation) and may (in any other case) advise and befriend him.

(5) The conditions are that—

(a)   *it appears to the authority that the person concerned is in need of advice and being befriended;*

(b)   *where that person was not being looked after by the authority, they are satisfied that the person by whom he was being looked after does not have the necessary facilities for advising or befriending him.*

(6) Where as a result of this section a local authority are under a duty, or are empowered, to advise and befriend a person, they may also give him assistance.

(7) Assistance given under subsections (1) to (6) may be in kind or, in exceptional circumstances, in cash.

(8) A local authority may. give assistance to any person who qualifies for advice and assistance by virtue of subsection (2)(a) by—

(a)   *contributing to expenses incurred by him in living near the place where he is, or will be—*

    (i)   *employed or seeking employment; or*

    (ii)   *receiving education or training; or*

(b)   *making a grant to enable him to meet expenses connected with his education or training.*

(9) Where a local authority are assisting the person under subsection (8) by making a contribution or grant with respect to a course of education or training, they may—

(a)   continue to do so even though he reaches the age of twenty-one before completing the course; and

(b)   disregard any interruption in his attendance on the course if he resumes it as soon as is reasonably practicable.

(10) Subsections (7) to (9) of section 17 shall apply in relation to assistance given under this section (otherwise than under subsection (8)) as they apply in relation to assistance given under that section.

(11) Where it appears to a local authority that a person whom they have been advising and befriending under this section, as a person qualifying for advice and assistance, proposes to live, or is living, in the area of another local authority, they shall inform that other local authority.

(12) Where a child who is accommodated—

(a)   by a voluntary organisation or in a registered [private] children's home;

(b)   by any health authority [Health Authority, Special Health Authority] [, Primary Care Trust] or local education authority; or

(c)   in any residential care home, nursing home or mental nursing home [care home or independent hospital] [or any accommodation provided by a National Health Service trust],

ceases to be so accommodated, after reaching the age of sixteen, the organisation, authority or (as the case may be) person carrying on the home shall inform the local authority within whose area the child proposes to live.

Note. In sub-s 12(a) word 'private' in square brackets substituted for word 'registered' and in para (c) words 'care home or independent hospital' in square brackets substituted for words 'residential care...nursing home' by the Care Standards Act 2000, s 116, Sch 4, para 14(1), (4),(5), as from a day to be appointed. In para (b) words 'Health Authority, Special Health Authority' in square brackets substituted for words 'health authority' by the Health Authorities Act 1995, s 2(1), Sch 1, Pt 3, para 118, as from 28 June 1995, in so far as is necessary for enabling the making of any regulations, orders, directions, schemes or appointments, and as from 1 April 1996 otherwise. Words ', Primary Care Trust' in square brackets inserted by the Health Act 1999 (Supplementary, Consequential etc Provisions) Order 2000, SI 2000 No 90, art 3(1), Sch 1, para 24(1), (4), as from 8 February 2000. In para (c) words 'or any...trust' in square brackets inserted by the National Health Service and Community Care Act 1990, s 66(1), Sch 9, paras 36(2), as from 5 July 1990.

(13) Subsection (12) only applies, by virtue of paragraph (b) or (c), if the accommodation has been provided for a consecutive period of at least three months.

[(14) Every local authority shall establish a procedure for considering any representations (including any complaint) made to them by a person qualifying for advice and assistance about the discharge of their functions under this Part in relation to him.

(15) To carrying out any consideration of representations under subsection (14), a local authority shall comply with any regulations made by the secretary of State for the purposes of this subsection.]

Note. Sub-ss (14), (15) inserted by the Courts and Legal Services Act 1990, s 116, Sch 16, para 13, as from 14 October 1991.

[24. Persons qualifying for advice and assistance—*(1) In this Part 'a person qualifying for advice and assistance' means a person who—*

(a)   *is under twenty-one; and*

(b)   *at any time after reaching the age of sixteen but while still a child was, but is no longer, looked after, accommodated or fostered.*

[(1) In this Part 'a person qualifying for advice and assistance' means a person to whom subsection (1A) or (1B) applies.

(1A) This subsection applies to a person—

(a)   who has reached the age of sixteen but not the age of twenty-one;

(b)   with respect to whom a special guardianship order is in force (or, if he has reached the age of eighteen, was in force when he reached that age); and

(c) who was, immediately before the making of that order, looked after by a local authority.

(1B) This subsection applies to a person to whom subsection (1A) does not apply, and who—
(a) is under twenty-one; and
(b) at any time after reaching the age of sixteen but while still a child was, but is no longer, looked after, accommodated or fostered.]

(2) In subsection (1)(b) [subsection (1B)(b)], 'looked after, accommodated or fostered' means—
(a) looked after by a local authority;
(b) accommodated by or on behalf of a voluntary organisation;
(c) accommodated in a private children's home;
(d) accommodated for a consecutive period of at least three months—
    (i) by any Health Authority, Special Health Authority, Primary Care Trust or local education authority, or
    (ii) in any care home or independent hospital or in any accommodation provided by a National Health Service trust [or an NHS foundation trust]; or
(e) privately fostered.

(3) Subsection (2)(d) applies even if the period of three months mentioned there began before the child reached the age of sixteen.

(4) In the case of a person qualifying for advice and assistance by virtue of subsection (2)(a), it is the duty of the local authority which last looked after him to take such steps as they think appropriate to contact him at such times as they think appropriate with a view to discharging their functions under sections 24A and 24B.

(5) In each of sections 24A and 24B, the local authority under the duty or having the power mentioned there ('the relevant authority') is—
[(za) in the case of a person to whom subsection (1A) applies, a local authority determined in accordance with regulations made by the Secretary of State;]
(a) in the case of a person qualifying for advice and assistance by virtue of subsection (2)(a), the local authority which last looked after him; or
(b) in the case of any other person qualifying for advice and assistance, the local authority within whose area the person is (if he has asked for help of a kind which can be given under section 24A or 24B).

24A. Advice and assistance—(1) The relevant authority shall consider whether the conditions in subsection (2) are satisfied in relation to a person qualifying for advice and assistance.

(2) The conditions are that—
(a) he needs help of a kind which they can give under this section or section 24B; and
(b) in the case of a person [to whom section 24(1A) applies, or to whom section 24(1B) applies and] who was not being looked after by any local authority, they are satisfied that the person by whom he was being looked after does not have the necessary facilities for advising or befriending him.

(3) If the conditions are satisfied—
(a) they shall advise and befriend him if [he is a person to whom section 24(1A) applies, or he is a person to whom section 24(1B) applies and] he was being looked after by a local authority or was accommodated by or on behalf of a voluntary organisation; and
(b) in any other case they may do so.

(4) Where as a result of this section a local authority are under a duty, or are empowered, to advise and befriend a person, they may also give him assistance.

(5) The assistance may be in kind *or, in exceptional circumstances, in cash* [and, in exceptional circumstances, assistance may be given—

(a) by providing accommodation, if in the circumstances assistance may not be given in respect of the accommodation under section 24B, or

(b) in cash].

(6) Subsections (7) to (9) of section 17 apply in relation to assistance given under this section or section 24B as they apply in relation to assistance given under that section.

24B. Employment, education and training—(1) The relevant local authority may give assistance to any person who qualifies for advice and assistance by virtue of [section 24(1A) or] section 24(2)(a) by contributing to expenses incurred by him in living near the place where he is, or will be, employed or seeking employment.

(2) The relevant local authority may give assistance to a person to whom subsection (3) applies by—

(a) contributing to expenses incurred by the person in question in living near the place where he is, or will be, receiving education or training; or

(b) making a grant to enable him to meet expenses connected with his education or training.

(3) This subsection applies to any person who—

(a) is under twenty-four; and

(b) qualifies for advice and assistance by virtue of [section 24(1A) or] section 24(2)(a), or would have done so if he were under twenty-one.

(4) Where a local authority are assisting a person under subsection (2) they may disregard any interruption in his attendance on the course if he resumes it as soon as is reasonably practicable.

(5) Where the local authority are satisfied that a person to whom subsection (3) applies who is in full-time further or higher education needs accommodation during a vacation because his term-time accommodation is not available to him then, they shall give him assistance by—

(a) providing him with suitable accommodation during the vacation; or

(b) paying him enough to enable him to secure such accommodation himself.

(6) The Secretary of State may prescribe the meaning of 'full-time', 'further education', 'higher education' and 'vacation' for the purposes of subsection (5).

24C. Information—(1) Where it appears to a local authority that a person—

(a) with whom they are under a duty to keep in touch under section 23B, 23C or 24; or

(b) whom they have been advising and befriending under section 24A; or

(c) to whom they have been giving assistance under section 24B,

proposes to live, or is living, in the area of another local authority, they must inform that other authority.

(2) Where a child who is accommodated—

(a) by a voluntary organisation or in a private children's home;

(b) by any Health Authority, Special Health Authority, Primary Care Trust or local education authority; or

(c) in any care home or independent hospital or any accommodation provided by a National Health Service trust [or an NHS foundation trust],

ceases to be so accommodated, after reaching the age of sixteen, the organisation, authority or (as the case may be) person carrying on the home shall inform the local authority within whose area the child proposes to live.

(3) Subsection (2) only applies, by virtue of paragraph (b) or (c), if the accommodation has been provided for a consecutive period of at least three months.]

Note. Sections 24, 24A–24D substituted, for s 24 as originally enacted, by the Children (Leaving Care) Act 2000, s 4(1), as from 1 October 2001 (SI 2001 No 2878, SI 2001 No 2191) (s 24C in relation to Wales in so far as sub-s (2) relates to Primary Care Trusts to be appointed). Temporary amendments were made to new s 24(2) by virtue of the Children (Leaving Care) Act 2000, s 4(2), as from 1 October 2001 (SI 2001 No 2191) until the Care Standards Act 2000, s 11 came into force (1 April 2002: SI 2001 No 2852; SI 2002 No 920). In s 24 sub-s (1) substituted, by subsequent sub-ss (1), (1A), (1B), and in sub-s (2) words 'subsection (1B)(b)' in square brackets substituted for words in italics by the Adoption and Children Act 2002, s 139(1), Sch 3, paras 54, 60(a), (b), as from a day to be appointed. In sub-s (2)(d)(ii) words 'or an NHS foundation trust' in square brackets inserted by the Health and Social Care (Community Health and Standards) Act 2003, s 34, Sch 4, paras 75, 76, as from 1 April 2004 (SI 2004 No 759). Sub-s (5)(za) inserted by the Adoption and Children Act 2002, s 139(1), Sch 3, paras 54, 60(c), as from a day to be appointed. In s 24A(2)(b) words 'to whom...applies and' in square brackets inserted and in sub-s (3)(a) words 'he is a...applies and' in square brackets inserted by the Adoption and Children Act 2002, s 139(1), Sch 3, paras 54, 61(a), (b), as from a day to be appointed. In sub-s (5) words 'and, in exceptional...in cash' in square brackets substituted for words in italics by the Adoption and Children Act 2002, s 116(3), as from 7 November 2002 (date of Royal Assent in the absence of any specific commencement provision). In s 24B(1), (3)(b) words 'section 24(1A) or' in square brackets inserted by the Adoption and Children Act 2002, s 139(1), Sch 3, paras 54, 62, as from a day to be appointed. In s 24C(2) words 'or an NHS foundation trust' in square brackets inserted by the Health and Social Care (Community Health and Standards) Act 2003, s 34, Sch 4, paras 75, 77, as from 1 April 2004 (SI 2004 No 759).

[24D. Representations: sections 24A to 24B—(1) Every local authority shall establish a procedure for considering representations (including complaints) made to them by—

(a) a relevant child for the purposes of section 23A or a young person falling within section 23C;

(b) a person qualifying for advice and assistance; or

(c) a person falling within section 24B(2),

about the discharge of their functions under this Part in relation to him.

[(1A) Regulations may be made by the Secretary of State imposing time limits on the making of representations under subsection (1).]

(2) In considering representations under subsection (1), a local authority shall comply with regulations (if any) made by the Secretary of State for the purposes of this subsection.]

Note. This section inserted by the Children (Leaving Care) Act 2000, s 5, as from 1 October 2001 (SI 2001 No 2878, SI 2001 No 2191). Sub-s (1A) inserted by the Adoption and Children Act 2002, s 117(1), as from a day to be appointed.

Secure accommodation

25. Use of accommodation for restricting liberty—(1) Subject to the following provisions of this section, a child who is being looked after by a local authority may not be placed, and, if placed, may not be kept, in accommodation provided for the purpose of restricting liberty ('secure accommodation') unless it appears—

(a) that—

(i) he has a history of absconding and is likely to abscond from any other description of accommodation; and

(ii) if he absconds, he is likely to suffer significant harm; or

(b) that if he is kept in any other description of accommodation he is likely to injure himself or other persons.

(2) The Secretary of State may by regulations—

(a) specify a maximum period—

(i) beyond which a child may not be kept in secure accommodation without the authority of the court; and

(ii) for which the court may authorise a child to be kept in secure accommodation;

(b) empower the court from time to time to authorise a child to be kept in secure accommodation for such further period as the regulations may specify; and

(c) provide that applications to the court under this section shall be made only by local authorities.

(3) It shall be the duty of a court hearing an application under this section to determine whether any relevant criteria for keeping a child in secure accommodation are satisfied in his case.

(4) If a court determines that any such criteria are satisfied, it shall make an order authorising the child to be kept in secure accommodation and specifying the maximum period for which he may be so kept.

(5) On any adjournment of the hearing of an application under this section, a court may make an interim order permitting the child to be kept during the period of the adjournment in secure accommodation.

(6) No court shall exercise the powers conferred by this section in respect of a child who is not legally represented in that court unless. having been informed of his right to apply for *legal aid* [representation funded by the Legal Services Commission as part of the Community Legal Service or Criminal Defence Service] and having had the opportunity to do so, he refused or failed to apply.

Note. In sub-s (6) words 'representation...Defence Service' in square brackets substituted for words in italics by the Access to Justice Act 1999, s 24, Sch 4, para 45, as from 1 April 2000 (SI 2000 No 774).

(7) The Secretary of State may by regulations provide that—

(a) this section shall or shall not apply to any description of children specified in the regulations.

(b) this section shall have effect in relation to children of a description specified in the regulations subject to such modifications as may be so specified;

(c) such other provisions as may be so specified shall have effect for the purpose of determining whether a child of a description specified in the regulations may be placed or kept in secure accommodation.

(8) The giving of an authorisation under this section shall not prejudice any power of any court in England and Wales or Scotland to give directions relating to the child to whom the authorisation relates.

(9) This section is subject to section 20(8).

Supplemental

26. Review of cases and enquiries into representations—(1) The Secretary of State may make regulations requiring the case of each child who is being looked after by a local authority to be reviewed in accordance with the provisions of the regulations.

(2) The regulations may, in particular, make provision—

(a) as to the manner in which each case is to be reviewed;

(b) as to the considerations to which the local authority are to have regard in reviewing each case;

(c) as to the time when each case is first to be reviewed and the frequency of subsequent reviews;

(d) requiring the authority, before conducting any review, to seek the views of—

    (i) the child;

    (ii) his parents;

    (ii) any person who is not a parent of his but who has parental responsibility for him; and

    (iv) any other person whose views the authority consider to be relevant,

including, in particular, the views of those persons in relation to any particular matter which is to be considered in the course of the review;

(e) requiring the authority ..., in the case of a child who is in their care—

      [(i) to keep the section 31A plan for the child under review and, if they are of the opinion that some change is required, to revise the plan, or make a new plan, accordingly,

      (ii) to consider], whether an application should be made to discharge the care order;

  (f) requiring the authority ..., in the case of a child in accommodation provided by the authority—

      [(i) if there is no plan for the future care of the child, to prepare one,

      (ii) if there is such a plan for the child, to keep it under review and, if they are of the opinion that some change is required, to revise the plan or make a new plan, accordingly,

      (iii) to consider], whether the accommodation accords with the requirements of this Part;

  (g) requiring the authority to inform the child, so far as is reasonably practicable, of any steps he may take under this Act;

  (h) requiring the authority to make arrangements, including arrangements with such other bodies providing services as it considers appropriate, to implement any decision which they propose to make in the course, or as a result, of the review;

  (i) requiring the authority to notify details of the result of the review and of any decision taken by them in consequence of the review to—

      (i) the child;

      (ii) his parents;

      (iii) any person who is not a parent of his but who has parental responsibility for him; and

      (iv) any other person whom they consider ought to be notified;

  (j) requiring the authority to monitor the arrangements which they have made with a view to ensuring that they comply with the regulations.

  [(k) for the authority to appoint a person in respect of each case to carry out in the prescribed manner the functions mentioned in subsection (2A) and any prescribed function].

Note. In sub-s (2)(e), (f) words omitted, words in square brackets substituted for words in italics, and para (k) inserted, by the Adoption and Children Act 2002, s 118(1), as from 21 May 2004 (SI 2004 No 1403).

  [(2A) The functions referred to in subsection (2)(k) are—

  (a) participating in the review of the case in question,

  (b) monitoring the performance of the authority's functions in respect of the review,

  (c) referring the case to an officer of the Children and Family Court Advisory and Support Service, if the person appointed under subsection (2)(k) considers it appropriate to do so.

  (2B) A person appointed under subsection (2)(k) must be a person of a prescribed description.

  (2C) In relation to children whose cases are referred to officers under subsection (2A)(c), the Lord Chancellor may by regulations—

  (a) extend any functions of the officers in respect of family proceedings (within the meaning of section 12 of the Criminal Justice and Court Services Act 2000) to other proceedings,

  (b) require any functions of the officers to be performed in the manner prescribed by the regulations.]

Note. Sub-ss (2A)–(2C) inserted by the Adoption and Children Act 2002, s 118(2), as from 21 May 2004 (SI 2004 No 1403).

  (3) Every local authority shall establish a procedure for considering any representations (including any complaint) made to them by—

    (a) any child who is being looked after by them or who is not being looked after
        by them but is in need;

    (b) a parent of his;

    (c) any person who is not a parent of his but who has parental responsibility for
        him;

    (d) any local authority foster parent;

    (e) such other person as the authority consider has a sufficient interest in the
        child's welfare to warrant his representations being considered by them,

about the discharge by the authority of any of their *functions under this Part*
[qualifying functions] in relation to the child.

Note. In sub-s (3)(e) words 'qualifying functions' in square brackets substituted for words in
italics by the Adoption and Children Act 2002, s 117(3), as from a day to be appointed.

    [(3A) The following are qualifying functions for the purposes of subsection
(3)—

    (a) functions under this Part,

    (b) such functions under Part 4 or 5 as are specified by the Secretary of State in
        regulations.

    (3B) The duty under subsection (3) extends to representations (including
complaints) made to the authority by—

    (a) any person mentioned in section 3(1) of the Adoption and Children Act
        2002 (persons for whose needs provision is made by the Adoption Service)
        and any other person to whom arrangements for the provision of adoption
        support services (within the meaning of that Act) extend,

    (b) such other person as the authority consider has sufficient interest in a child
        who is or may be adopted to warrant his representations being considered
        by them,

about the discharge by the authority of such functions under the Adoption and
Children Act 2002 as are specified by the Secretary of State in regulations.]

Note. Sub-ss (3A), (3B) inserted by the Adoption and Children Act 2002, s 117(2), (4), as
from a day to be appointed.

    [(3C) The duty under subsection (3) extends to any representations (including
complaints) which are made to the authority by—

    (a) a child with respect to whom a special guardianship order is in force,

    (b) a special guardian or a parent of such a child,

    (c) any other person the authority consider has a sufficient interest in the
        welfare of such a child to warrant his representations being considered by
        them, or

    (d) any person who has applied for an assessment under section 14F(3) or (4),

about the discharge by the authority of such functions under section 14F as may be
specified by the Secretary of State in regulations.]

Note. Sub-s (3C) inserted by the Health and Social Care (Community Health and Standards)
Act 2003, s 117(1), as from a day to be appointed.

    (4) The procedure shall ensure that at least one person who is not a member or
officer of the authority takes part in—

    (a) the consideration; and

    (b) any discussions which are held by the authority about the action (if any) to
        be taken in relation to the child in the light of the consideration.

[but this subsection is subject to subsection (5A)].

Note. Words in square brackets inserted by the Adoption and Children Act 2002, s 117(5), as
from a day to be appointed.

    [(4A) Regulations may be made by the Secretary of State imposing time limits
on the making of representations under this section.]

Note. Sub-s (4A) inserted by the Adoption and Children Act 2002, s 148(1), (2), as from a day to be appointed.

(5) In carrying out any consideration of representations under this section a local authority shall comply with any regulations made by the Secretary of State for the purposes of regulating the procedure to be followed.

[(5A) Regulations under subsection (5) may provide that subsection (4) does not apply in relation to any consideration or discussion which takes place as part of a procedure for which provision is made by the regulations for the purpose of resolving informally the matters raised in the representations.]

Note. Sub-s (5A) inserted by the Adoption and Children Act 2002, s 148(1), (2), as from a day to be appointed.

(6) The Secretary of State may make regulations requiring local authorities to monitor the arrangements that they have made with a view to ensuring that they comply with any regulations made for the purposes of subsection (5).

(7) Where any representation has been considered under the procedure established by a local authority under this section, the authority shall—

(a) have due regard to the findings of those considering the representation; and

(b) take such steps as are reasonably practicable to notify (in writing)—

  (i) the person making the representation;

  (ii) the child (if the authority consider that he has sufficient understanding); and

  (iii) such other persons (if any) as appear to the authority to be likely to be affected,

of the authority's decision in the matter and their reasons for taking that decision and of any action which they have taken, or propose to take.

(8) Every local authority shall give such publicity to their procedure for considering representations under this section as they consider appropriate.

[26ZA. Representations: further considerations—[(1) The Secretary of State may by regulations make provision for the further consideration of representations which have been considered by a local authority in England under section 24D or section 26.

(2) The regulations may in particular make provision—

(a) for the further consideration of a representation by the Commission for Social Care Inspection ('the CSCI');

(b) for a representation to be referred by the CSCI for further consideration by an independent panel established under the regulations;

(c) about the procedure to be followed on the further consideration of a representation;

(d) for the making of recommendations about the action to be taken as the result of a representation;

(e) about the making of reports about a representation;

(f) about the action to be taken by the local authority concerned as a result of the further consideration of a representation;

(g) for a representation to be referred by the CSCI back to the local authority concerned for reconsideration by the authority;

(h) for a representation or any matter raised by the representation to be referred by the CSCI—

  (i) to a Local Commissioner in England for him to consider whether to investigate the representation or matter under Part 3 of the Local Government Act 1974 as if it were a complaint duly made under section 26 of that Act; or

  (ii) to any other person or body for him or it to consider whether to take any action otherwise than under the regulations.

(3) The regulations may require—
(a) the making of a payment, in relation to the further consideration of a representation under this section, by any local authority in respect of whose functions the representation is made;
(b) any such payment to be—
    (i) made to such person or body as may be specified in the regulations;
    (ii) of such amount as may be specified in, or calculated or determined under, the regulations;
(c) an independent panel to review the amount chargeable under paragraph (a) in any particular case and, if the panel thinks fit, to substitute a lesser amount.
(4) The regulations may also—
(a) provide for different parts or aspects of a representation to be treated differently;
(b) require the production of information or documents in order to enable a representation to be properly considered;
(c) authorise the disclosure of information or documents relevant to a representation—
    (i) to a person or body who is further considering a representation under the regulations; or
    (ii) to a Local Commissioner in England (when a representation is referred to him under the regulations);
and any such disclosure may be authorised notwithstanding any rule of common law that would otherwise prohibit or restrict the disclosure.
(5) In this section, 'Local Commissioner in England' means a Local Commissioner under Part 3 of the Local Government Act 1974 (c 7), who is a member of the Commission for Local Administration in England.

26ZB. Representations: further consideration (Wales)—(1) The Secretary of State may by regulations make provision for the further consideration of representations which have been considered by a local authority in Wales under section 24D or section 26.
(2) The regulations may in particular make provision—
(a) for the further consideration of a representation by an independent panel established under the regulations;
(b) about the procedure to be followed on the further consideration of a representation;
(c) for the making of recommendations about the action to be taken as the result of a representation;
(d) about the making of reports about a representation;
(e) about the action to be taken by the local authority concerned as a result of the further consideration of a representation;
(f) for a representation to be referred back to the local authority concerned for reconsideration by the authority.
(3) The regulations may require—
(a) the making of a payment, in relation to the further consideration of a representation under this section, by any local authority in respect of whose functions the representation is made;
(b) any such payment to be—
    (i) made to such person or body as may be specified in the regulations;
    (ii) of such amount as may be specified in, or calculated or determined under, the regulations; and
(c) for an independent panel to review the amount chargeable under paragraph (a) in any particular case and, if the panel thinks fit, to substitute a lesser amount.

(4) The regulations may also—
(a) provide for different parts or aspects of a representation to be treated differently;
(b) require the production of information or documents in order to enable a representation to be properly considered;
(c) authorise the disclosure of information or documents relevant to a representation to a person or body who is further considering a representation under the regulations;
and any such disclosure may be authorised notwithstanding any rule of common law that would otherwise prohibit or restrict the disclosure.]

Note. Sections 26ZA, 26ZB inserted by the Health and Social Care (Community Health and Standards) Act 2003, s 116(2), as from a day to be appointed.

[26A. Advocacy services—(1) Every local authority shall make arrangements for the provision of assistance to—
(a) persons who make or intend to make representations under section 24D; and
(b) children who make or intend to make representations under section 26.

(2) The assistance provided under the arrangements shall include assistance by way of representation.

[(2A) The duty under subsection (1) includes a duty to make arrangements for the provision of assistance where representations under section 24D or 26 are further considered under section 26ZA or 26ZB.]

(3) The arrangements—
(a) shall secure that a person may not provide assistance if he is a person who is prevented from doing so by regulations made by the Secretary of State; and
(b) shall comply with any other provision made by the regulations in relation to the arrangements.

(4) The Secretary of State may make regulations requiring local authorities to monitor the steps that they have taken with a view to ensuring that they comply with regulations made for the purposes of subsection (3).

(5) Every local authority shall give such publicity to their arrangements for the provision of assistance under this section as they consider appropriate.]

Note. This section inserted by the Adoption and Children Act 2002, s 119, as from (for the purpose of making regulations): 30 January 2004; (for remaining purposes): 1 April 2004 (SI 2003 No 3079). Sub-s (2A) inserted by the Health and Social Care (Community Health and Standards) Act 2003, s 116(3), as from a day to be appointed.

27. Co-operation between authorities—(1) Where it appears to a local authority that any authority *or other person* mentioned in subsection (3) could, by taking any specified action, help in the exercise of any of their functions under this Part, they may request the help of that other authority *or person*, specifying the action in question.

(2) An authority whose help is so requested shall comply with the request if it is compatible with their own statutory or other duties and obligations and does not unduly prejudice the discharge of any of their functions.

(3) The *persons* [authorities] are—
(a) any local authority;
(b) any local education authority;
(c) any local housing authority;
(d) any *health authority* [Health Authority, Special Health Authority] [, Primary Care Trust] [*or National Health Service trust*] [National Health Service Trust or NHS foundation trust]; and
(e) any person authorised by the Secretary of State for the purposes of this section.

(*4*) *Every local authority shall assist any local education authority with the provision of services for any child within the local authority's area who has special educational needs.*

Note. Words in italics in sub-s (1) repealed, first word in square brackets in sub-s (3) substituted for word in italics immediately preceding it, and words 'or National Health Service trust' in sub-s (3)(d) inserted by Courts and Legal Services Act 1990, s 116, Sch 16, para 14, as from 14 October 1991. Words 'Health Authority, Special Health Authority' in sub-s (3)(d) substituted for words in italics by Health Authorities Act 1995, s 2(1), Sch 1, para 118, as from 28 June 1995, in so far as is necessary for enabling the making of any regulations, orders, directions, schemes or appointments, and as from 1 April 1996 otherwise. Words ', Primary Care Trust' in square brackets inserted by the Health Act 1999 (Supplementary, Consequential etc Provisions) Order 2000, SI 2000 No 90, art 3(1), Sch 1, para 24(1), (5), as from 8 February 2000. Words 'National Health Service Trust or NHS foundation trust' in square brackets substituted for words 'or National Health Service Trust' by the Health and Social Care (Community Health and Standards) Act 2003, s 34, Sch 4, paras 75, 78, as from 1 April 2004 (SI 2004 No 759). Sub-s (4) repealed by Education Act 1993, s 307, Sch 19, para 147, Sch 21, Part II, as from 1 September 1994.

28. Consultation with local education authorities—(1) Where—
   (a) a child is being looked after by a local authority; and
   (b) the authority propose to provide accommodation for him in an establishment at which education is provided for children who are accommodated there,
they shall, so far as is reasonably practicable, consult the appropriate local education authority before doing so.

(2) Where any such proposal is carried out, the local authority shall, as soon as is reasonably practicable, inform the appropriate local education authority of the arrangements that have been made for the child's accommodation.

(3) Where the child ceases to be accommodated as mentioned in subsection (1)(b), the local authority shall inform and appropriate local education authority.

(4) In this section 'the appropriate local education authority' means—
   (a) the local education authority within whose area the local authority's area falls; or,
   (b) where the child has special educational needs and a statement of his needs is maintained under *the Education Act 1981* [*Part III of the Education Act 1993*] [Part IV of the Education Act 1996] the local education authority who maintain the statement.

Note. Words 'Part III of the Education Act 1993' substituted for words 'the Education Act 1981' by Education Act 1993, s 307, Sch 19, para 148, as from 1 September 1994. Words 'Part IV of the Education Act 1996' substituted for words 'Part III of the Education Act 1993' by Education Act 1996, s 582(1), Sch 37, Part 5, para 84, as from 1 November 1996.

29. Recoupment of cost of providing services etc—(1) Where a local authority provide any service under section 17 or 18, other than advice, guidance or counselling, they may recover from a person specified in subsection (4) such charge for the service as they consider reasonable.

(2) Where the authority are satisfied that the person's means are insufficient for it to be reasonably practicable for him to pay the charge, they shall not require him to pay more than he can reasonably be expected to pay.

(3) No person shall be liable to pay any charge under subsection (1) [for a service provided under section 17 or 18(1) or (5)] at any time when he is in receipt of income support *or family credit under* [family credit [, *working families' tax credit*] or disability working allowance [*or disabled person's tax credit*]] under [under] *the Social Security Act 1986* [Part VII of the Social Security Contributions and Benefits Act 1992] [, of any element of child tax credit other than the family element, of working tax credit] [or of an income-based jobseeker's allowance].

Note. Words 'for a service...or (5)' in square brackets inserted by the Local Government Act 2000, s 103(1), as from (in relation to England): 25 August 2000 (SI 2000 No 2420); (in relation to Wales): 28 July 2001.Words 'family credit or disability working allowance' in square brackets substituted for words 'or family credit under' by the Disability Living Allowance and Disability Working Allowance Act 1991, s 7(2), Sch 3, Pt 2, para 14, as from 19 November 1991 for certain purposes, and as from 10 March 1992 for remaining purposes. Words 'or working families' tax credit' in square brackets substituted for words ', family credit' and words 'or disabled person's tax credit' in square brackets substituted for words 'or disability working allowance' by virtue of the Tax Credits Act 1999, s 1(2), Sch 1, paras 1(a), 6(d)(ii), as from 5 October 1999. Word 'under' in square brackets substituted for words ', working families'...under' by the Tax Credits Act 2002, s 47, Sch 3, paras 15, 18(a), as from 6 April 2003 (SI 2003 No 692); for savings see arts 3–5 thereof. Words 'Part VII...1992' in square brackets substituted for words 'the Social Security Act 1986' by the the Social Security (Consquential Provisions) Act 1992, s 4, Sch 2, para 108, as form 1 July 1992. Words ', of any element...tax credit' in square brackets inserted by the Tax Credits Act 2002, s 47, Sch 3, paras 15, 18(b), as from 6 April 2003 (SI 2003 No 692); for savings see arts 3–5 thereof. Words 'or of an...allowance' in square brackets inserted by the Jobseekers Act 1995, s 41(4), Sch 2, para 19, as from 7 October 1996.

[(3A) No person shall be liable to pay any charge under subsection (1) for a service provided under section 18(2) or (6) at any time when he is in receipt of income support under Part VII of the Social Security Contributions and Benefits Act 1992 or of an income-based jobseeker's allowance.]

Note. Sub-s (3A): inserted by the Local Government Act 2000, s 103(2), as from (in relation to England): 25 August 2000; (in relation to Wales): 28 July 2001.

[(3B) No person shall be liable to pay any charge under subsection (1) for a service provided under section 18(2) or (6) at any time when—

(a) he is in receipt of guarantee state pension credit under section 1(3)(a) of the State Pension Credit Act 2002, or

(b) he is a member of a married or unmarried couple (within the meaning of that Act) the other member of which is in receipt of guarantee state pension credit.]

Note. Sub-s (3B) inserted by the State Pension Credit Act 2002, s 14, Sch 2, Pt 3, para 30, as from (for the purpose only of exercising any power to make orders or regulations): 2 July 2002 (SI 2002 No 1691); for remaining purposes: 6 October 2003 (SI 2003 No 1766).

(4) The persons are—

(a) where the service is provided for a child under sixteen, each of his parents;

(b) where it is provided for a child who has reached the age of sixteen, the child himself; and

(c) where it is provided for a member of the child's family, that member.

(5) Any charge under subsection (1) may, without prejudice to any other method of recovery, be recovered summarily as a civil debt.

(6) Part III of Schedule 2 makes provision in connection with contributions towards the maintenance of children who are being looked after by local authorities and consists of the re-enactment with modifications of provisions in Part V of the Child Care Act 1980.

(7) Where a local authority provide any accommodation under section 20(1) for a child who was (immediately before they began to look after him) ordinarily resident within the area of another local authority, they may recover from that other authority any reasonable expenses incurred by them in providing the accommodation and maintaining him.

(8) Where a local authority provide accommodation under section 21(1) or (2)(a) or (b) for a child who is ordinarily resident within the area of another local authority and they are not maintaining him in—

(a) a community home provided by them;

(b) a controlled community home; or

(c) a hospital vested in the Secretary of State [or a Primary Care Trust] [or any other hospital made available pursuant to arrangements made by [a

Strategic Health Authority] a *District Health Authority* [Health Authority] [or a Primary Care Trust,],

they may recover from that other authority any reasonable expenses incurred by them in providing the accommodation and maintaining him.

Note. In sub-s (8)(c) words 'or a Primary Care Trust' and 'or a Primary Care Trust,' in square brackets inserted by the Health Act 1999 (Supplementary, Consequential etc Provisions) Order 2000, SI 2000 No 90, art 3(1), Sch 1, para 24(1), (6), as from 8 February 2000. Words in square brackets beginning with the words 'or any other' inserted by the National Health Service and Community Care Act 1990, s 66(1), Sch 9, para 36(3), as from 5 July 1990. Words 'a Strategic Health Authority' in square brackets inserted by the National Health Service Reform and Healthcare Professions Act 2002 (Supplementary, Consequential etc Provisions) Regulations 2002, SI 2002 No 2469, reg 4, Sch 1, Pt 1, para 16(1), (2), as from 1 October 2002. Words 'Health Authority' in square brackets substituted for words in italics by the Health Authorities Act 1995, s 2(1), Sch 1, para 118(6), as from 28 June 1995.

(9) [Except where subsection (10) applies,] where a local authority comply with any request under section 27(2) in relation to a child or other person who is not ordinarily resident within their area, they may recover from the local authority in whose area the child or person is ordinarily resident any *expenses reasonably* [reasonable expenses] incurred by them in respect of that person.

Note. Words 'Except where subsection (10) applies,' in square brackets inserted by the Children (Leaving Care) Act 2000, s 7(1), (3), as from 1 October 2001 (SI 2001 No 2878, SI 2001 No 2191). Words 'reasonable expenses' in square brackets substituted for words in italics by the Courts and Legal Services Act 1990, s 116, Sch 16, para 15, as from 14 October 1991.

[(10) Where a local authority ('authority A') comply with any request under section 27(2) from another local authority ('authority B') in relation to a child or other person—

(a) whose responsible authority is authority B for the purposes of section 23B or 23C; or

(b) whom authority B are advising or befriending or to whom they are giving assistance by virtue of section 24(5)(a),

authority A may recover from authority B any reasonable expenses incurred by them in respect of that person.]

Note. Sub-s (10) inserted by the Children (Leaving Care) Act 2000, s 7(1), (3), as from 1 October 2001 (SI 2001 No 2878, SI 2001 No 2191).

30. Miscellaneous—(1) Nothing in this Part shall affect any duty imposed on a local authority by or under any other enactment.

(2) Any question arising under section 20(2), 21(3) or 29(7) to (9) as to the ordinary residence of a child shall be determined by agreement between the local authorities concerned or, in default of agreement, by the Secretary of State.

(3) Where the functions conferred on a local authority by this Part and the functions of a local education authority are concurrent, the Secretary of State may by regulations provide by which authority the functions are to be exercised.

(4) The Secretary of State may make regulations for determining, as respects any local education authority functions specified in the regulations, whether a child who is being looked after by a local authority is to be treated, for purposes so specified, as a child of parents of sufficient resources or as a child of parents without resources.

PART IV

CARE AND SUPERVISION

General

31. Care and supervision orders—(1) On the application of any local authority or authorised person, the court may make an order—

(a) placing the child with respect to whom the application is made in the care of a designated local authority; or

(b) putting him under the supervision of a designated local authority ...

(2) A court may only make a care order or supervision order if it is satisfied—

(a) that the child concerned is suffering, or is likely to suffer, significant harm; and

(b) that the harm, or likelihood of harm, is attributable to—

    (i) the care given to the child, or likely to be given to him if the order were not made, not being what it would be reasonable to expect a parent to give to him; or

    (ii) the child's being beyond parental control.

(3) No care order or supervision order may be made with respect to a child who has reached the age of seventeen (or sixteen, in the case of a child who is married).

[(3A) No care order may be made with respect to a child until the court has considered a section 31A plan.]

Note. Sub-s (3A) inserted by the Adoption and Children Act 2002, s 121(1), as from a day to be appointed.

(4) An application under this section may be made on its own or in any other family proceedings.

(5) The court may—

(a) on an application for a care order, make a supervision order;

(b) on an application for a supervision order, make a care order.

(6) Where an authorised person proposes to make an application under this section he shall—

(a) if it is reasonably practicable to do so; and

(b) before making the application,

consult the local authority appearing to him to be the authority in whose area the child concerned is ordinarily resident.

(7) An application made by an authorised person shall not be entertained by the court if, at the time when it is made, the child concerned is—

(a) the subject of an earlier application for a care order, or supervision order, which has not been disposed of; or

(b) subject to—

    (i) a care order or supervision order;

    (ii) an order under *section 7(7)(b) of the Children and Young Persons Act 1969* [section 63(1) of the Powers of Criminal Courts (Sentencing) Act 2000]; or

    (iii) a supervision requirement within the meaning of *the Social Work (Scotland) Act 1968* [Part II of the Children (Scotland) Act 1995].

Note. Words in square brackets in sub-s (7)(b)(ii) substituted for words in italics by the Powers of Criminal Courts Sentencing Act 2000, s 165(1), Sch 9, para 127, as from 25 August 2000. Words in square brackets in sub-s (7)(b)(iii) substituted for words in italics by Children (Scotland) Act 1995, s 105(4), para 48(2), as from 1 April 1997.

(8) The local authority designated in a care order must be—

(a) the authority within whose area the child is ordinarily resident; or

(b) where the child does not reside in the area of a local authority, the authority within whose area any circumstances arose in consequence of which the order is being made.

(9) In this section—

'authorised person' means—

    (a) the National Society for the Prevention of Cruelty to Children and any of its officers; and

    (b) any person authorised by order of the Secretary of State to bring proceedings under this section and any officer of a body which is so authorised;

'harm' means ill-treatment or the impairment of health or development [including, for example, impairment suffered from seeing or hearing the ill-treatment of another];

'development' means physical, intellectual, emotional, social or behavioural development;

'health' means physical or mental health; and

'ill-treatment' includes sexual abuse and forms of ill-treatment which are not physical.

Note. In definition 'harm' words 'including, for...of another' in square brackets inserted by the Adoption and Children Act 2002, s 120, as from a day to be appointed.

(10) Where the question of whether harm suffered by a child is significant turns on the child's health or development, his health or development shall be compared with that which could reasonably be expected of a similar child.

(11) In this Act—

'a care order' means (subject to section 105(1)) an order under subsection (1)(a) and (except where express provision to the contrary is made) includes an interim care order made under section 38; and

'a supervision order' means an order under subsection (1)(b) and (except where express provision to the contrary is made) includes an interim supervision order made under section 38.

32. Period within which application for order under this Part must be disposed of—(1) A court hearing an application for an order under this Part shall (in the light of any rules made by virtue of subsection (2))—

(a) draw up a timetable with a view to disposing of the application without delay; and

(b) give such directions as it considers appropriate for the purpose of ensuring, so far as is reasonably practicable, that that timetable is adhered to.

(2) Rules of court may—

(a) specify periods within which specified steps must be taken in relation to such proceedings; and

(b) make other provision with respect to such proceedings for the purpose of ensuring, so far as is reasonably practicable, that they are disposed of without delay.

Care orders

33. Effect of care order—(1) Where a care order is made with respect to a child it shall be the duty of the local authority designated by the order to receive the child into their care and to keep him in their care while the order remains in force.

(2) Where—

(a) a care order has been made with respect to a child on the application of an authorised person; but

(b) the local authority designated by the order was not informed that that person proposed to make the application,

the child may be kept in the care of that person until received into the care of the authority.

(3) While a care order is in force with respect to a child, the local authority designated by the order shall—

(a) have parental responsibility for the child; and

(b) have the power (subject to the following provisions of this section) to determine the extent to which *a parent or guardian of the child* [—

    (i) a parent, guardian or special guardian of the child; or

    (ii) a person who by virtue of section 4A has parental responsibility for the child,]

may meet his parental responsibility for him.

Note. In sub-s (3)(b) words in square brackets substituted for words in italics by the Adoption and Children Act 2002, s 139(1), Sch 3, para 63, as from a day to be appointed.

(4) The authority may not exercise the power in subsection (3)(b) unless they are satisfied that it is necessary to do so in order to safeguard or promote the child's welfare.

(5) Nothing in subsection (3)(b) shall prevent *a parent or guardian of the child who has care of him* [a person mentioned in that provision who has care of the child] from doing what is reasonable in all the circumstances of the case for the purpose of safeguarding or promoting his welfare.

Note. In sub-s (5) words 'a person...the child' in square brackets substituted for words in italics by the Adoption and Children Act 2002, s 139(1), Sch 3, paras 54, 63(b), as from a day to be appointed.

(6) While a care order is in force with respect to a child, the local authority designated by the order shall not—

(a) cause the child to be brought up in any religious persuasion other than that in which he would have been brought up if the order had not been made; or

(b) have the right—

  (i) *to consent or refuse to consent to the making of an application with respect to the child under section 18 of the Adoption Act 1976;*

  (ii) to agree or refuse to agree to the making of an adoption order, or an order under *section 55 of the Act of 1976* [section 84 of the Adoption and Children Act 2002], with respect to the child; or

  (iii) to appoint a guardian for the child.

Note. Sub-s (6)(b)(i) in italics repealed and in para (b)(ii) words 'section 84...Act 2002' in square brackets substituted for words in italics by the Adoption and Children Act 2002, s 139(1), (3), Sch 3, paras 54, 63(c)(i), (ii), Sch 5.

(7) While a care order is in force with respect to a child, no person may—

(a) cause the child to be known by a new surname; or

(b) remove him from the United Kingdom,

without either the written consent of every person who has parental responsibility for the child or the leave of the court.

(8) Subsection (7)(b) does not—

(a) prevent the removal of such a child, for a period of less than one month, by the authority in whose care he is; or

(b) apply to arrangements for such a child to live outside England and Wales (which are governed by paragraph 19 of Schedule 2).

(9) The power in subsection (3)(b) is subject (in addition to being subject to the provisions of this section) to any right, duty, power, responsibility or authority which *a parent or guardian of the child* [a person mentioned in that provision] has in relation to the child and his property by virtue of any other enactment.

Note. In sub-s (9) words 'a person mentioned...provision' in square brackets substituted for words in italics by the Adoption and Children Act 2002, s 139(1), Sch 3, paras 54, 63(d).

34. Parental contact etc with children in care—(1) Where a child is in the care of a local authority, the authority shall (subject to the provisions of this section) allow the child reasonable contact with—

(a) his parents;

(b) any guardian [or special guardian] of his;

[(ba) any person who by virtue of section 4A has parental responsibility for him;]

(c) where there was a residence order in force with respect to the child immediately before the care order was made, the person in whose favour the order was made; and

(d) where, immediately before the care order was made, a person had care of the child by virtue of an order made in the exercise of the High Court's inherent jurisdiction with respect to children, that person.

Note. In para (b) words 'or special guardian' in square brackets inserted and para (ba) inserted by the Adoption and Children Act 2002, s 139(1), Sch 3, paras 54, 64, as from a day to be appointed.

(2) On an application made by the authority or the child, the court may make such order as it considers appropriate with respect to the contact which is to be allowed between the child and any named person.

(3) On an application made by—

(a) any person mentioned in paragraphs (a) to (d) of subsection (1); or

(b) any person who has obtained the leave of the court to make the application, the court may make such order as it considers appropriate with respect to the contact which is to be allowed between the child and that person.

(4) On an application made by the authority or the child, the court may make an order authorising the authority to refuse to allow contact between the child and any person who is mentioned in paragraphs (a) to (d) of subsection (1) and named in the order.

(5) When making a care order with respect to a child, or in any family proceedings in connection with a child who is in the care of a local authority, the court may make an order under this section, even though no application for such an order has been made with respect to the child, if it considers that the order should be made.

(6) An authority may refuse to allow the contact that would otherwise be required by virtue of subsection (1) or an order under this section if—

(a) they are satisfied that it is necessary to do so in order to safeguard or promote the child's welfare; and

(b) the refusal—

(i) is decided upon as a matter of urgency; and

(ii) does not last for more than seven days.

(7) An order under this section may impose such conditions as the court considers appropriate.

(8) The Secretary of State may by regulations make provision as to—

(a) the steps to be taken by a local authority who have exercised their powers under subsection (6);

(b) the circumstances in which, and conditions subject to which, the terms of any order under this section may be departed from by agreement between the local authority and the person in relation to whom the order is made;

(c) notification by a local authority of any variation or suspension of arrangements made (otherwise than under an order under this section) with a view to affording any person contact with a child to whom this section applies.

(9) The court may vary or discharge any order made under this section on the application of the authority, the child concerned or the person named in the order.

(10) An order under this section may be made either at the same time as the care order itself or later.

(11) Before making a care order with respect to any child the court shall—

(a) consider the arrangements which the authority have made, or propose to make, for affording any person contact with a child to whom this section applies; and

(b) invite the parties to the proceedings to comment on those arrangements.

Supervision orders

35. Supervision orders—(1) While a supervision order is in force it shall be the duty of the supervisor—

(a) to advise, assist and befriend the supervised child;

(b) to take such steps as are reasonably necessary to give effect to the order; and

(c) where—

    (i) the order is not wholly complied with; or

    (ii) the supervisor considers that the order may no longer be necessary,]
to consider whether or not to apply to the court for its variation or discharge.

(2) Parts I and II of Schedule 3 make further provision with respect to supervision orders.

36. Education supervision orders—(1) On the application of any local education authority, the court may make an order putting the child with respect to whom the application is made under the supervision of a designated local education authority.

(2) In this Act 'an education supervision order' means an order under subsection (1).

(3) A court may only make an education supervision order if it is satisfied that the child concerned is of compulsory school age and is not being properly educated.

(4) For the purposes of this section, a child is being properly educated only if he is receiving efficient full-time education suitable to his age, ability and aptitude and any special educational needs he may have.

(5) Where a child is—

(a) the subject of a school attendance order which is in force under *section 37 of the Education Act 1944* [section 437 of the Education Act 1996] and which has not been complied with; or

(b) a registered pupil at a school which he is not attending regularly within the meaning of *section 39* [section 444] of that Act,

then, unless it is proved that he is being properly educated, it shall be assumed that he is not.

Note. Words in square brackets substituted for words in italics by Education Act 1996, s 582(1), Sch 37, para 85, as from 1 November 1996.

(6) An education supervision order may not be made with respect to a child who is in the care of a local authority.

(7) The local education authority designated in an education supervision order must be—

(a) the authority within whose area the child concerned is living or will live; or

(b) where—

    (i) the child is a registered pupil at a school; and

    (ii) the authority mentioned in paragraph (a) and the authority within whose area the school is situated agree,
the latter authority.

(8) Where a local education authority propose to make an application for an education supervision order they shall, before making the application, consult the *social services committee (within the meaning of the Local Authority Social Services Act 1970) of the* appropriate local authority.

Note. Words in italics repealed by Education Act 1993, s 307, Sch 19, para 149, Sch 21, Part II, as from 1 October 1993.

(9) The appropriate local authority is—

(a) in the case of a child who is being provided with accommodation by, or on behalf of, a local authority, that authority; and

(b) in any other case, the local authority within whose area the child concerned lives, or will live.

(10) Part III of Schedule 3 makes further provision with respect to education supervision orders.

Powers of court

37. Powers of court in certain family proceedings—(1) Where, in any family proceedings in which a question arises with respect to the welfare of any child, it appears to the court that it may be appropriate for a care or supervision order to be made with respect to him, the court may direct the appropriate authority to undertake an investigation of the child's circumstances.

(2) Where the court gives a direction under this section the local authority concerned shall, when undertaking the investigation, consider whether they should—

(a)   apply for a care order or for a supervision order with respect to the child;

(b)   provide services or assistance for the child or his family; or

(c)   take any other action with respect to the child.

(3) Where a local authority undertake an investigation under this section, and decide not to apply for a care order or supervision order with respect to the child concerned, they shall inform the court of—

(a)   their reasons for so deciding;

(b)   any service or assistance which they have provided, or intend to provide, for the child and his family; and

(c)   any other action which they have taken, or propose to take, with respect to the child.

(4) The information shall be given to the court before the end of the period of eight weeks beginning with the date of the direction, unless the court otherwise directs.

(5) The local authority named in a direction under subsection (1) must be—

(a)   the authority in whose area the child is ordinarily resident; or

(b)   where the child *does not reside* [is not ordinarily resident] in the area of a local authority, the authority within whose area any circumstances arose in consequence of which the direction is being given.

(6) If, on the conclusion of any investigation or review under this section, the authority decide not to apply for a care order or supervision order with respect to the child—

(a)   they shall consider whether it would be appropriate to review the case at a later date; and

(b)   if they decide that it would be, they shall determine the date on which that review is to begin.

Note. Words in square brackets in sub-s (5)(b) substituted for words in italics by Courts and Legal Services Act 1990, s 116, Sch 16, para 16, as from 14 October 1991.

38. Interim orders—(1) Where—

(a)   in any proceedings on an application for a care order or supervision order, the proceedings are adjourned; or

(b)   the court gives a direction under section 37(1),

the court may make an interim care order or an interim supervision order with respect to the child concerned.

(2) A court shall not make an interim care order or interim supervision order under this section unless it is satisfied that there are reasonable grounds for believing that the circumstances with respect to the child are as mentioned in section 31(2).

(3) Where, in any proceedings on an application for a care order or supervision order, a court makes a residence order with respect to the child concerned, it shall also make an interim supervision order with respect to him unless satisfied that his welfare will be satisfactorily safeguarded without an interim order being made.

(4) An interim order made under or by virtue of this section shall have effect for such period as may be specified in the order, but shall in any event cease to have effect on whichever of the following events first occurs—

(a) the expiry of the period of eight weeks beginning with the date on which the order is made;
(b) if the order is the second or subsequent such order made with respect to the same child in the same proceedings, the expiry of the relevant period;
(c) in a case which falls within subsection (1)(a), the disposal of the application;
(d) in a case which falls within subsection (1)(b), the disposal of an application for a care order or supervision order made by the authority with respect to the child;
(e) in a case which falls within subsection (1)(b) and in which—
　(i) the court has given a direction under section 37(4), but
　(ii) no application for a care order or supervision order has been made with respect to the child,
the expiry of the period fixed by that direction.
(5) In subsection (4)(b) 'the relevant period' means—
(a) the period of four weeks beginning with the date on which the order in question is made; or
(b) the period of eight weeks beginning with the date on which the first order was made if that period ends later than the period mentioned in paragraph (a).

(6) Where the court makes an interim care order, or interim supervision order, it may give such directions (if any) as it considers appropriate with regard to the medical or psychiatric examination or other assessment of the child; but if the child is of sufficient understanding to make an informed decision he may refuse to submit to the examination or other assessment.
(7) A direction under subsection (6) may be to the effect that there is to be—
(a) no such examination or assessment; or
(b) no such examination or assessment unless the court directs otherwise.
(8) A direction under subsection (6) may be—
(a) given when the interim order is made or at any time while it is in force; and
(b) varied at any time on the application of any person falling within any class of person prescribed by rules of court for the purposes of this subsection.
(9) Paragraphs 4 and 5 of Schedule 3 shall not apply in relation to an interim supervision order.
(10) Where a court makes an order under or by virtue of this section it shall, in determining the period for which the order is to be in force, consider whether any party who was, or might have been, opposed to the making of the order was in a position to argue his case against the order in full.

[38A. Power to include exclusion requirement in interim care order—(1) Where—
(a) on being satisfied that there are reasonable grounds for believing that the circumstances with respect to a child are as mentioned in section 31(2)(a) and (b)(i), the court makes an interim care order with respect to a child, and
(b) the conditions mentioned in subsection (2) are satisfied,
the court may include an exclusion requirement in the interim care order.
(2) The conditions are—
(a) that there is reasonable cause to believe that, if a person ('the relevant person') is excluded from a dwelling-house in which the child lives, the child will cease to suffer, or cease to be likely to suffer, significant harm, and
(b) that another person living in the dwelling-house (whether a parent of the child or some other person)—
　(i) is able and willing to give to the child the care which it would be reasonable to expect a parent to give him, and
　(ii) consents to the inclusion of the exclusion requirement.

(3) For the purposes of this section an exclusion requirement is any one or more of the following—

 (a) a provision requiring the relevant person to leave a dwelling-house in which he is living with the child,

 (b) a provision prohibiting the relevant person from entering a dwelling-house in which the child lives, and

 (c) a provision excluding the relevant person from a defined area in which a dwelling-house in which the child lives is situated.

(4) The court may provide that the exclusion requirement is to have effect for a shorter period than the other provisions of the interim care order.

(5) Where the court makes an interim care order containing an exclusion requirement, the court may attach a power of arrest to the exclusion requirement.

(6) Where the court attaches a power of arrest to an exclusion requirement of an interim care order, it may provide that the power of arrest is to have effect for a shorter period than the exclusion requirement.

(7) Any period specified for the purposes of subsection (4) or (6) may be extended by the court (on one or more occasions) on an application to vary or discharge the interim care order.

(8) Where a power of arrest is attached to an exclusion requirement of an interim care order by virtue of subsection (5), a constable may arrest without warrant any person whom he has reasonable cause to believe to be in breach of the requirement.

(9) Sections 47(7), (11) and (12) and 48 of, and Schedule 5 to, the Family Law Act 1996 shall have effect in relation to a person arrested under subsection (8) of this section as they have effect in relation to a person arrested under section 47(6) of that Act.

(10) If, while an interim care order containing an exclusion requirement is in force, the local authority have removed the child from the dwelling-house from which the relevant person is excluded to other accommodation for a continuous period of more than 24 hours, the interim care order shall cease to have effect in so far as it imposes the exclusion requirement.

38B. Undertakings relating to interim care orders—(1) In any case where the court has power to include an exclusion requirement in an interim care order, the court may accept an undertaking from the relevant person.

(2) No power of arrest may be attached to any undertaking given under subsection (1).

(3) An undertaking given to a court under subsection (1)—

 (a) shall be enforceable as if it were an order of the court, and

 (b) shall cease to have effect if, while it is in force, the local authority have removed the child from the dwelling-house from which the relevant person is excluded to other accommodation for a continuous period of more than 24 hours.

(4) This section has effect without prejudice to the powers of the High Court and county court apart from this section.

(5) In this section 'exclusion requirement' and 'relevant person' have the same meaning as in section 38A.]

Note. Sections 38A, 38B inserted by Family Law Act 1996, s 52, Sch 6, para 1, as from 1 October 1997.

39. Discharge and variation etc of care orders and supervision orders—(1) A care order may be discharged by the court on the application of—

 (a) any person who has parental responsibility for the child;

 (b) the child himself; or

 (c) the local authority designated by the order.

(2) A supervision order may be varied or discharged by the court on the application of—

(a) any person who has parental responsibility for the child;

(b) the child himself; or

(c) the supervisor.

(3) On the application of a person who is not entitled to apply for the order to be discharged, but who is a person with whom the child is living, a supervision order may be varied by the court in so far as it imposes a requirement which affects that person.

[(3A) On the application of a person who is not entitled to apply for the order to be discharged, but who is a person to whom an exclusion requirement contained in the order applies, an interim care order may be varied or discharged by the court in so far as it imposes the exclusion requirement.

(3B) Where a power of arrest has been attached to an exclusion requirement of an interim care order, the court may, on the application of any person entitled to apply for the discharge of the order so far as it imposes the exclusion requirement, vary or discharge the order in so far as it confers a power of arrest (whether or not any application has been made to vary or discharge any other provision of the order).]

Note. Sub-ss (3A), (3B) inserted by Family Law Act 1996, s 52, Sch 6, para 2, as from 1 October 1997.

(4) Where a care order is in force with respect to a child the court may, on the application of any person entitled to apply for the order to be discharged, substitute a supervision order for the care order.

(5) When a court is considering whether to substitute one order for another under subsection (4) any provision of this Act which would otherwise require section 31(2) to be satisfied at the time when the proposed order is substituted or made shall be disregarded.

40. Orders pending appeals in cases about care or supervision orders—(1) Where—

(a) a court dismisses an application for a care order; and

(b) at the time when the court dismisses the application, the child concerned is the subject of an interim care order,

the court may make a care order with respect to the child to have effect subject to such directions (if any) as the court may see fit to include in the order.

(2) Where—

(a) a court dismisses an application for a care order, or an application for a supervision order; and

(b) at the time when the court dismisses the application, the child concerned is the subject of an interim supervision order,

the court may make a supervision order with respect to the child to have effect subject to such directions (if any) as the court may see fit to include in the order.

(3) Where a court grants an application to discharge a care order or supervision order, it may order that—

(a) its decision is not to have effect; or

(b) the care order, or supervision order, is to continue to have effect but subject to such directions as the court sees fit to include in the order.

(4) An order made under this section shall only have effect for such period, not exceeding the appeal period, as may be specified in the order.

(5) Where—

(a) an appeal is made against any decision of a court under this section; or

(b) any application is made to the appellate court in connection with a proposed appeal against that decision,

the appellate court may extend the period for which the order in question is to have effect, but not so as to extend it beyond the end of the appeal period.

(6) In this section 'the appeal period' means—
(a) where an appeal is made against the decision in question, the period between the making of that decision and the determination of the appeal; and
(b) otherwise, the period during which an appeal may be made against the decision.

Guardians ad litem [Representation of child]

41. Representation of child and of his interests in certain proceedings—(1) For the purpose of any specified proceedings, the court shall appoint a *guardian ad litem* [an officer of the service] for the child concerned unless satisfied that it is not necessary to do so in order to safeguard his interests.
Note. Cross-heading substituted by the Criminal Justice and Court Services Act 2000, s 74, Sch 7, Pt 2, paras 87, 91(e), as from 1 April 2001 (SI 2001 No 919). In sub-s (1) words 'an officer of the service' in square brackets substituted for words in italics by the Criminal Justice and Court Services Act 2000, ss 74, 75, Sch 7, Pt 2, paras 87, 91(a), as from a day to be appointed.

(2) The *guardian ad litem* [officer of the service] shall—
(a) be appointed in accordance with rules of court; and
(b) be under a duty to safeguard the interests of the child in the manner prescribed by such rules.
(3) Where—
(a) the child concerned is not represented by a solicitor; and
(b) any of the conditions mentioned in subsection (4) is satisfied,
the court may appoint a solicitor to represent him.
(4) The conditions are that—
(a) no *guardian ad litem* [officer of the service] has been appointed for the child;
(b) the child has sufficient understanding to instruct a solicitor and wishes to do so;
(c) it appears to the court that it would be in the child's best interests for him to be represented by a solicitor.
Note. In sub-ss (2), (4)(a) words 'officer of the service' in square brackets substituted for words in italics by the Criminal Justice and Court Services Act 2000, s 74, Sch 7, Pt 2, paras 87, 91(b), as from 1 April 2001 (SI 2001 No 919).

(5) Any solicitor appointed under or by virtue of this section shall be appointed, and shall represent the child, in accordance with rules of court.
(6) In this section 'specified proceedings' means any proceedings—
(a) on an application for a care order or supervision order;
(b) in which the court has given a direction under section 37(1) and has made, or is considering whether to make, an interim care order;
(c) on an application for the discharge of a care order or the variation or discharge of a supervision order;
(d) on an application under section 39(4);
(e) in which the court is considering whether to make a residence order with respect to a child who is the subject of a care order;
(f) with respect to contact between a child who is the subject of a care order and any other person;
(g) under Part V;
(h) on an appeal against—
(i) the making of, or refusal to make, a care order, supervision order or any order under section 34;
(ii) the making of, or refusal to make, a residence order with respect to a child who is the subject of a care order; or
(iii) the variation or discharge, or refusal of an application to vary or discharge, an order of a kind mentioned in sub-paragraph (i) or (ii);

(iv) the refusal of an application under section 39(4);

(v) the making of, or refusal to make, an order under Part V; or

[(hh) on an application for the making or revocation of a placement order (within the meaning of section 21 of the Adoption and Children Act 2002);]

(i) which are specified for the time being, for the purposes of this section, by rules of court.

Note. Sub-s (6)(hh) inserted by the Adoption and Children Act 2002, s 122(1), as from a day to be appointed.

[(6A) The proceedings which may be specified under subsection (6)(i) include (for example) proceedings for the making, varying or discharging of a section 8 order.]

Note. Sub-s (6A) inserted by the Adoption and Children Act 2002, s 122(1), as from a day to be appointed.

(7) ...

(8) ...

(9) ...

Note. Sub-ss (7)–(9) repealed by the Criminal Justice and Court Services Act 2000, ss 74, 75, Sch 7, Pt 2, paras 87, 91(d), Sch 8, as from 1 April 2001 (SI 2001 No 919).

(10) Rules of court may make provision as to—

(a) the assistance which any *guardian ad litem* [officer of the service] may be required by the court to give to it;

(b) the consideration to be given by any *guardian ad litem* [officer of the service], where an order of a specified kind has been made in the proceedings in question, as to whether to apply for the variation or discharge of the order;

(c) the participation of *guardian ad litem* [officer of the service] in reviews, of a kind specified in the rules, which are conducted by the court.

Note. In sub-s (10) words 'officer of the service' in square brackets in both places they occur and words 'officers of the service' in square brackets substituted for words in italics by the Criminal Justice and Court Services Act 2000, s 74, Sch 7, Pt 2, paras 87, 91(b), (c), as from 1 April 2001 (SI 2001 No 919).

(11) Regardless of any enactment or rule of law which would otherwise prevent it from doing so, the court may take account of—

(a) any statement contained in a report made by a *guardian ad litem* [an officer of the service] who is appointed under this section for the purpose of the proceedings in question; and

(b) any evidence given in respect of the matters referred to in the report,

in so far as the statement or evidence is, in the opinion of the court, relevant to the question which the court is considering.

Note. In sub-s (11)(a) words 'an officer of the service' in square brackets substituted for words in italics by the Criminal Justice and Court Services Act 2000, s 74, Sch 7, Pt 2, paras 87, 91(a), as from 1 April 2001 (SI 2001 No 919).

[(12) ...

Note. Sub-s (12) added by Courts and Legal Services Act 1990, s 116, Sch 16, para 17, as from 14 October 1991. Repealed by the Criminal Justice and Court Services Act 2000, s 74, Sch 7, Pt 2, paras 87, 91(d), Sch 8, as from 1 April 2001 (SI 2001 No 919).

42. *Right of guardian ad litem to have access to local authority records* [42. Right of officer of the Service to have access to local authority records]—(1) Where *a person* [an officer of the service] has been appointed *as a guardian ad litem under this Act* [under section 41] he shall have the right at all reasonable times to examine and take copies of—

(a) any records of, or held by, a local authority [or an authorised person] which were compiled in connection with the making, or proposed making, by any person of any application under this Act with respect to the child concerned; *or*

(b) any *other* records of, or held by, a local authority which were compiled in connection with any functions which *stand referred to their social services committee under* [are social services functions within the meaning of] the Local Authority Social Services Act 1970, so far as those records relate to that child[; or

(c) any records of, or held by, an authorised person which were compiled in connection with the activities of that person, so far as those records relate to that child].

Note. Section heading substituted by the Criminal Justice and Court Services Act 2000, s 74, Sch 7, Pt 2, paras 87, 92(c), as from 1 April 2001 (SI 2001 No 919). In sub-s (1) words 'an officer of the service' and 'under section 41' in square brackets substituted for words in italics by the Criminal Justice and Court Services Act 2000, s 74, Sch 7, Pt 2, paras 87, 92(a), as from 1 April 2001 (SI 2001 No 919). In para (b) words 'are social...meaning of' in square brackets substituted for words in italics by the Local Government Act 2000, s 107, Sch 5, para 20, as from (in relation to England): 26 October 2000; (in relation to Wales): 28 July 2001.

(2) Where a *guardian ad litem* [officer of the service] takes a copy of any record which he is entitled to examine under this section, that copy or any part of it shall be admissible as evidence of any matter referred to in any—

(a) report which he makes to the court in the proceedings in question; or

(b) evidence which he gives in those proceedings.

Note. Words 'an officer of the service' in square brackets substituted for words in italics by the Criminal Justice and Court Services Act 2000, s 74, Sch 7, Pt 2, paras 87, 92(b), as from 1 April 2001 (SI 2001 No 919).

(3) Subsection (2) has effect regardless of any enactment or rule of law which would otherwise prevent the record in question being admissible in evidence.

[(4) In this section, 'authorised person' has the same meaning as in section 31.]

Note. Words in square brackets in sub-s (1)(a), and sub-ss (1)(c), (4) added by Courts and Legal Services Act 1990, s 116, Sch 16, para 18. Words in italics in sub-ss (1)(a), (b) repealed by s 125(7) of, and Sch 20 to, that Act.

PART V

PROTECTION OF CHILDREN

43. Child assessment orders—(1) On the application of a local authority or authorised person for an order to be made under this section with respect to a child, the court may make the order if, but only if, it is satisfied that—

(a) the applicant has reasonable cause to suspect that the child is suffering, or is likely to suffer, significant harm;

(b) an assessment of the state of the child's health or development, or of the way in which he has been treated, is required to enable the applicant to determine whether or not the child is suffering, or is likely to suffer, significant harm; and

(c) it is unlikely that such an assessment will be made, or be satisfactory, in the absence of an order under this section.

(2) In this Act 'a child assessment order' means an order under this section.

(3) A court may treat an application under this section as an application for an emergency protection order.

(4) No court shall make a child assessment order if it is satisfied—

(a) that there are grounds for making an emergency protection order with respect to the child; and

(b) that it ought to make such an order rather than a child assessment order.

(5) A child assessment order shall—

(a) specify the date by which the assessment is to begin; and

(b) have effect for such period, not exceeding 7 days beginning with that date, as may be specified in the order.

(6) Where a child assessment order is in force with respect to a child it shall be the duty of any person who is in a position to produce the child—

(a) to produce him to such person as may be named in the order; and

(b) to comply with such directions relating to the assessment of the child as the court thinks fit to specify in the order.

(7) A child assessment order authorises any person carrying out the assessment, or any part of the assessment, to do so in accordance with the terms of the order.

(8) Regardless of subsection (7), if the child is of sufficient understanding to make an informed decision he may refuse to submit to a medical or psychiatric examination or other assessment.

(9) The child may only be kept away from home—

(a) in accordance with directions specified in the order;

(b) if it is necessary for the purposes of the assessment; and

(c) for such period or periods as may be specified in the order.

(10) Where the child is to be kept away from home, the order shall contain such directions as the court thinks fit with regard to the contact that he must be allowed to have with other persons while away from home.

(11) Any person making an application for a child assessment order shall take such steps as are reasonably practicable to ensure that notice of the application is given to—

(a) the child's parents;

(b) any person who is not a parent of his but who has parental responsibility for him;

(c) any other person caring for the child;

(d) any person in whose favour a contact order is in force with respect to the child;

(e) any person who is allowed to have contact with the child by virtue of an order under section 34; and

(f) the child,

before the hearing of the application.

(12) Rules of court may make provision as to the circumstances in which—

(a) any of the persons mentioned in subsection (11); or

(b) such other person as may be specified in the rules,

may apply to the court for a child assessment order to be varied or discharged.

(13) In this section 'authorised person' means a person who is an authorised person for the purposes of section 31.

44. Orders for emergency protection of children—(1) Where any person ('the applicant') applies to the court for an order to be made under this section with respect to a child, the court may make the order if, but only if it is satisfied that—

(a) there is reasonable cause to believe that the child is likely to suffer significant harm if—

(i) he is not removed to accommodation provided by or on behalf of the applicant; or

(ii) he does not remain in the place in which he is then being accommodated;

(b) in the case of an application made by a local authority—

(i) enquiries are being made with respect to the child under section 47(1)(b); and

(ii) those enquiries are being frustrated by access to the child being unreasonably refused to a person authorised to seek access and that the applicant has reasonable cause to believe that access to the child is required as a matter of urgency; or

(c) in the case of an application made by an authorised person—

    (i) the applicant has reasonable cause to suspect that a child is suffering, or is likely to suffer, significant harm;

    (ii) the applicant is making enquiries with respect to the child's welfare; and

    (iii) those enquiries are being frustrated by access to the child being unreasonably refused to a person authorised to seek access and the applicant has reasonable cause to believe that access to the child is required as a matter of urgency.

(2) In this section—

(a) 'authorised person' means a person who is an authorised person for the purposes of section 31; and

(b) 'a person authorised to seek access' means—

    (i) in the case of an application by a local authority, an officer of the local authority or a person authorised by the authority to act on their behalf in connection with the enquiries; or

    (ii) in the case of an application by an authorised person, that person.

(3) Any person—

(a) seeking access to a child in connection with enquiries of a kind mentioned in subsection (1); and

(b) purporting to be a person authorised to do so,

shall, on being asked to do so, produce some duly authenticated document as evidence that he is such a person.

(4) While an order under this section ('an emergency protection order') is in force it—

(a) operates as a direction to any person who is in a position to do so to comply with any request to produce the child to the applicant;

(b) authorises—

    (i) the removal of the child at any time to accommodation provided by or on behalf of the applicant and his being kept there; or

    (ii) the prevention of the child's removal from any hospital, or other place, in which he was being accommodated immediately before the making of the order; and

(c) gives the applicant parental responsibility for the child.

(5) Where an emergency protection order is in force with respect to a child, the applicant—

(a) shall only exercise the power given by virtue of subsection (4)(b) in order to safeguard the welfare of the child;

(b) shall take and shall only take, such action in meeting his parental responsibility for the child as is reasonably required to safeguard or promote the welfare of the child, (having regard in particular to the duration of the order); and

(c) shall comply with the requirements of any regulations made by the Secretary of State for the purposes of this subsection.

(6) Where the court makes an emergency protection order, it may give such directions (if any) as it considers appropriate with respect to—

(a) the contact which is, or is not, to be allowed between the child and any named person;

(b) the medical or psychiatric examination or other assessment of the child.

(7) Where any direction is given under subsection (6)(b), the child may, if he is of sufficient understanding to make an informed decision, refuse to submit to the examination or other assessment.

(8) A direction under subsection (6)(a) may impose conditions and one under subsection (6)(b) may be to the effect that there is to be—

(a) no such examination or assessment; or

(b) no such examination or assessment unless the court directs otherwise.

(9) A direction under subsection (6) may be—

(a) given when the emergency protection order is made or at any time while it is in force; and

(b) varied at any time on the application of any person falling within any class of person prescribed by rules of court for the purposes of this subsection.

(10) Where an emergency protection order is in force with respect to a child and—

(a) the applicant has exercised the power given by subsection (4)(b)(i) but it appears to him that it is safe for the child to be returned; or

(b) the applicant has exercised the power given by subsection (4)(b)(ii) but it appears to him that it is safe for the child to be allowed to be removed from the place in question,

he shall return the child or (as the case may be) allow him to be removed.

(11) Where he is required by subsection (10) to return the child the applicant shall—

(a) return him to the care of the person from whose care he was removed; or

(b) if that is not reasonably practicable, return him to the care of—

    (i) a parent of his;

    (ii) any person who is not a parent of his but who has parental responsibility for him; or

    (iii) such other person as the applicant (with the agreement of the court) considers appropriate.

(12) Where the applicant has been required by subsection (10) to return the child, or to allow him to be removed, he may again exercise his powers with respect to the child (at any time while the emergency protection order remains in force) if it appears to him that a change in the circumstances of the case makes it necessary for him to do so.

(13) Where an emergency protection order has been made with respect to a child, the applicant shall, subject to any direction given under subsection (6), allow the child reasonable contact with—

(a) his parents;

(b) any person who is not a parent of his but who has parental responsibility for him;

(c) any person with whom he was living immediately before the making of the order;

(d) any person in whose favour a contact order is in force with respect to him;

(e) any person who is allowed to have contact with the child by virtue of an order under section 34; and

(f) any person acting on behalf of any of those persons.

(14) Wherever it is reasonably practicable to do so, an emergency protection order shall name the child; and where it does not name him it shall describe him as clearly as possible.

(15) A person shall be guilty of an offence if he intentionally obstructs any person exercising the power under subsection (4)(b) to remove, or prevent the removal of, a child.

(16) A person guilty of an offence under subsection (15) shall be liable on summary conviction to a fine not exceeding level 3 on the standard scale.

[44A. Power to include exclusion requirement in emergency protection order—
(1) Where—

(a) on being satisfied as mentioned in section 44(1)(a), (b) or (c), the court makes an emergency protection order with respect to a child, and

(b) the conditions mentioned in subsection (2) are satisfied, the court may include an exclusion requirement in the emergency protection order.

(2) The conditions are—

(a) that there is reasonable cause to believe that, if a person ('the relevant person') is excluded from a dwelling-house in which the child lives, then—

    (i) in the case of an order made on the ground mentioned in section 44(1)(a), the child will not be likely to suffer significant harm, even though the child is not removed as mentioned in section 44(1)(a)(i) or does not remain as mentioned in section 44(1)(a)(ii), or

    (ii) in the case of an order made on the ground mentioned in paragraph (b) or (c) of section 44(1), the enquiries referred to in that paragraph will cease to be frustrated, and

(b) that another person living in the dwelling-house (whether a parent of the child or some other person)—

    (i) is able and willing to give to the child the care which it would be reasonable to expect a parent to give him, and

    (ii) consents to the inclusion of the exclusion requirement.

(3) For the purposes of this section an exclusion requirement is any one or more of the following—

(a) a provision requiring the relevant person to leave a dwelling-house in which he is living with the child,

(b) a provision prohibiting the relevant person from entering a dwelling-house in which the child lives, and

(c) a provision excluding the relevant person from a defined area in which a dwelling-house in which the child lives is situated.

(4) The court may provide that the exclusion requirement is to have effect for a shorter period than the other provisions of the order.

(5) Where the court makes an emergency protection order containing an exclusion requirement, the court may attach a power of arrest to the exclusion requirement.

(6) Where the court attaches a power of arrest to an exclusion requirement of an emergency protection order, it may provide that the power of arrest is to have effect for a shorter period than the exclusion requirement.

(7) Any period specified for the purposes of subsection (4) or (6) may be extended by the court (on one or more occasions) on an application to vary or discharge the emergency protection order.

(8) Where a power of arrest is attached to an exclusion requirement of an emergency protection order by virtue of subsection (5), a constable may arrest without warrant any person whom he has reasonable cause to believe to be in breach of the requirement.

(9) Sections 47(7), (11) and (12) and 48 of, and Schedule 5 to, the Family Law Act 1996 shall have effect in relation to a person arrested under subsection (8) of this section as they have effect in relation to a person arrested under section 47(6) of that Act.

(10) If, while an emergency protection order containing an exclusion requirement is in force, the applicant has removed the child from the dwelling-house from which the relevant person is excluded to other accommodation for a continuous period of more than 24 hours, the order shall cease to have effect in so far as it imposes the exclusion requirement.

44B. Undertakings relating to emergency protection orders—(1) In any case where the court has power to include an exclusion requirement in an emergency protection order, the court may accept an undertaking from the relevant person.

(2) No power of arrest may be attached to any undertaking given under subsection (1).

(3) An undertaking given to a court under subsection (1)—
(a) shall be enforceable as if it were an order of the court, and
(b) shall cease to have effect if, while it is in force, the applicant has removed the child from the dwelling-house from which the relevant person is excluded to other accommodation for a continuous period of more than 24 hours.

(4) This section has effect without prejudice to the powers of the High Court and county court apart from this section.

(5) In this section 'exclusion requirement' and 'relevant person' have the same meaning as in section 44A.]

Note. Sections 44A, 44B inserted by Family Law Act 1996, s 52, Sch 6, para 3, as from 1 October 1997.

45. Duration of emergency protection orders and other supplemental provisions—(1) An emergency protection order shall have effect for such period, not exceeding eight days, as may be specified in the order.

(2) Where—
(a) the court making an emergency protection order would, but for this subsection, specify a period of eight days as the period for which the order is to have effect; but
(b) the last of those eight days is a public holiday (that is to say, Christmas Day, Good Friday, a bank holiday or a Sunday),
the court may specify a period which ends at noon on the first later day which is not such a holiday.

(3) Where an emergency protection order is made on an application under section 46(7), the period of eight days mentioned in subsection (1) shall begin with the first day on which the child was taken into police protection under section 46.

(4) Any person who—
(a) has parental responsibility for a child as the result of an emergency protection order; and
(b) is entitled to apply for a care order with respect to the child,
may apply to the court for the period during which the emergency protection order is to have effect to be extended.

(5) On an application under subsection (4) the court may extend the period during which the order is to have effect by such period, not exceeding seven days, as it thinks fit, but may do so only if it has reasonable cause to believe that the child concerned is likely to suffer significant harm if the order is not extended.

(6) An emergency protection order may only be extended once.

(7) Regardless of any enactment or rule of law which would otherwise prevent it from doing so, a court hearing an application for, or with respect to, an emergency protection order may take account of—
(a) any statement contained in any report made to the court in the course of, or in connection with, the hearing; or
(b) any evidence given during the hearing,
which is, in the opinion of the court, relevant to the application.

(8) Any of the following may apply to the court for an emergency protection order to be discharged—
(a) the child;
(b) a parent of his;
(c) any person who is not a parent of his but who has parental responsibility for him; or
(d) any person with whom he was living immediately before the making of the order.

[(8A) On the application of a person who is not entitled to apply for the order to be discharged, but who is a person to whom an exclusion requirement contained in the order applies, an emergency protection order may be varied or discharged by the court in so far as it imposes the exclusion requirement.

(8B) Where a power of arrest has been attached to an exclusion requirement of an emergency protection order, the court may, on the application of any person entitled to apply for the discharge of the order so far as it imposes the exclusion requirement, vary or discharge the order in so far as it confers a power of arrest (whether or not any application has been made to vary or discharge any other provision of the order).]

Note. Sub-ss (8A), (8B) inserted by Family Law Act 1996, s 52, Sch 6, para 4, as from 1 October 1997.

(9) No application for the discharge of an emergency protection order shall be heard by the court before the expiry of the period of 72 hours beginning with the making of the order.

(*10*) *No appeal may be made against the making of, or refusal to make, an emergency protection order or against any direction given by the court in connection with such an order.*

[(10) No appeal may be made against—
  (a) the making of, or refusal to make, an emergency protection order;
  (b) the extension of, or refusal to extend, the period during which such an order is to have effect;
  (c) the discharge of, or refusal to discharge, such an order; or
  (d) the giving of, or refusal to give, any direction in connection with such an order.]

Note. Sub-s (10) in square brackets substituted for sub-s (10) in italics by Courts and Legal Services Act 1990, s 116, Sch 16, para 19, as from 14 October 1991.

(11) Subsection (8) does not apply—
  (a) where the person who would otherwise be entitled to apply for the emergency protection order to be discharged—
      (i) was given notice (in accordance with rules of court) of the hearing at which the order was made; and
      (ii) was present at that hearing; or
  (b) to any emergency protection order the effective period of which has been extended under subsection (5).

(12) A court making an emergency protection order may direct that the applicant may, in exercising any powers which he has by virtue of the order, be accompanied by a registered medical practitioner, registered nurse or *registered health visitor* [registered midwife], if he so chooses.

Note. In sub-s (12) words 'registered midwife' in square brackets substituted for words in italics by the Nursing and Midwifery Order 2001, SI 2002 No 253, art 54(3), Sch 5, para 10(a), as from 1 August 2004 (the London Gazette, 21 July 2004); for transitional provisions see SI 2002 No 253, Sch 2.

[(13) The reference in subsection (12) to a registered midwife is to such a midwife who is also registered in the Specialist Community Public Health Nurses' Part of the register maintained under article 5 of the Nursing and Midwifery Order 2001.]

Note. Sub-s (13) inserted by the Health Act 1999 (Consequential Amendments) (Nursing and Midwifery) Order 2004, SI 2004 No 1771, art 3, Schedule, Pt 1, para 4(a), as from 1 August 2004.

46. Removal and accommodation of children by police in cases of emergency—
(1) Where a constable has reasonable cause to believe that a child would otherwise be likely to suffer significant harm, he may—
  (a) remove the child to suitable accommodation and keep him there; or
  (b) take such steps as are reasonable to ensure the the child's removal from any hospital, or other place, in which he is then being accommodated is prevented.

(2) For the purposes of this Act, a child with respect to whom a constable has exercised his powers under this section is referred to as having been taken into police protection.

(3) As soon as is reasonably practicable after taking a child into police protection, the constable concerned shall—

(a) inform the local authority within whose area the child was found of the steps that have been, and are proposed to be, taken with respect to the child under this section and the reasons for taking them;

(b) give details to the authority within whose area the child is ordinarily resident ('the appropriate authority') of the place at which the child is being accommodated;

(c) inform the child (if he appears capable of understanding)—

(i) of the steps that have been taken with respect to him under this section and of the reasons for taking them; and

(ii) of the further steps that may be taken with respect to him under this section;

(d) take such steps as are reasonably practicable to discover the wishes and feelings of the child;

(e) secure that the case is enquired into by an officer designated for the purposes of this section by the chief officer of the police area concerned; and

(f) where the child was taken into police protection by being removed to accommodation which is not provided—

(i) by or on behalf of a local authority; or

(ii) as a refuge, in compliance with the requirements of section 51, secure that he is moved to accommodation which is so provided.

(4) As soon as is reasonably practicable after taking a child into police protection, the constable concerned shall take such steps as are reasonably practicable to inform—

(a) the child's parents;

(b) every person who is not a parent of his but who has parental responsibility for him; and

(c) any other person with whom the child was living immediately before being taken into police protection,

of the steps that he has taken under this section with respect to the child, the reasons for taking them and the further steps that may be taken with respect to him under this section.

(5) On completing any enquiry under subsection (3)(e), the officer conducting it shall release the child from police protection unless he considers that there is still reasonable cause for believing that the child would be likely to suffer significant harm if released.

(6) No child may be kept in police protection for more than 72 hours.

(7) While a child is being kept in police protection, the designated officer may apply on behalf of the appropriate authority for an emergency protection order to be made under section 44 with respect to the child.

(8) An application may be made under subsection (7) whether or not the authority know of it or agree to its being made.

(9) While a child is being kept in police protection—

(a) neither the constable concerned nor the designated officer shall have parental responsibility for him; but

(b) the designated officer shall do what is reasonable in all the circumstances of the case for the purpose of safeguarding or promoting the child's welfare (having regard in particular to the length of the period during which the child will be so protected).

(10) Where a child has been taken into police protection, the designated officer shall allow—

   (a) the child's parents;
   (b) any person who is not a parent of the child but who has parental responsibility for him;
   (c) any person with whom the child was living immediately before he was taken into police protection;
   (d) any person in whose favour a contact order is in force with respect to the child;
   (e) any person who is allowed to have contact with the child by virtue of an order under section 34; and
   (f) any person acting on behalf of any of those persons,
to have such contact (if any) with the child as, in the opinion of the designated officer, is both reasonable and in the child's best interests.

(11) Where a child who has been taken into police protection is in accommodation provided by, or on behalf of, the appropriate authority, subsection (10) shall have effect as if it referred to the authority rather than to the designated officer.

47. Local authority's duty to investigate—(1) Where a local authority—
   (a) are informed that a child who lives, or is found, in their area—
      (i) is the subject of an emergency protection order; or
      (ii) is in police protection; or
   [(iii) has contravened a ban imposed by a curfew notice within the meaning of Chapter I of Part I of the Crime and Disorder Act 1998; or]
   (b) have reasonable cause to suspect that a child who lives, or is found, in their area is suffering, or is likely to suffer, significant harm,
the authority shall make, or cause to be made, such enquiries as they consider necessary to enable them to decide whether they should take any action to safeguard or promote the child's welfare.
[In the case of a child falling within paragraph (a)(iii) above, the enquiries shall be commenced as soon as practicable and, in any event, within 48 hours of the authority receiving the information.]

Note. Sub-s (1)(a)(iii) inserted and in sub-s (1) words 'In the case...the information' in square brackets inserted by the Crime and Disorder Act 1998, s 15(4)(a), (b), as from 30 September 1998 (SI 1998 No 2327).

(2) Where a local authority have obtained an emergency protection order with respect to a child, they shall make, or cause to be made, such enquiries as they consider necessary to enable them to decide what action they should take to safeguard or promote the child's welfare.

(3) The enquiries shall, in particular, be directed towards establishing—
   (a) whether the authority should make any application to the court, or exercise any of their other powers under this Act [or section 11 of the Crime and Disorder Act 1998 (child safety orders)], with respect to the child;
   (b) whether, in the case of a child—
      (i) with respect to whom an emergency protection order has been made; and
      (ii) who is not in accommodation provided by or on behalf of the authority,
      it would be in the child's best interests (while an emergency protection order remains in force) for him to be in such accommodation; and
   (c) whether, in the case of a child who has been taken into police protection, it would be in the child's best interests for the authority to ask for an application to be made under section 46(7).

Note. In sub-s (3)(a) words 'or section...orders)' in square brackets inserted by the Crime and Disorder Act 1998, s 119, Sch 8, para 69, as from 30 September 1998 (SI 1998 No 2327).

(4) Where enquiries are being made under subsection (1) with respect to a child, the local authority concerned shall (with a view to enabling them to determine what action, if any, to take with respect to him) take such steps as are reasonably practicable—

(a) to obtain access to him; or

(b) to ensure that access to him is obtained, on their behalf, by a person authorised by them for the purpose,

unless they are satisfied that they already have sufficient information with respect to him.

(5) Where, as a result of any such enquiries, it appears to the authority that there are matters connected with the child's education which should be investigated, they shall consult the relevant local education authority.

(6) Where, in the course of enquiries made under this section—

(a) any officer of the local authority concerned; or

(b) any person authorised by the authority to act on their behalf in connection with those enquiries—

(i) is refused access to the child concerned; or

(ii) is denied information as to his whereabouts,

the authority shall apply for an emergency protection order, a child assessment order, a care order or a supervision order with respect to the child unless they are satisfied that his welfare can be satisfactorily safeguarded without their doing so.

(7) If, on the conclusion of any enquiries or review made under this section, the authority decide not to apply for an emergency protection order, a child assessment order, a care order or a supervision order they shall—

(a) consider whether it would be appropriate to review the case at a later date; and

(b) if they decide that it would be, determine the date on which that review is to begin.

(8) Where, as a result of complying with this section, a local authority conclude that they should take action to safeguard or promote the child's welfare they shall take that action (so far as it is both within their power and reasonably practicable for them to do so).

(9) Where a local authority are conducting enquiries under this section, it shall be the duty of any person mentioned in subsection (11) to assist them with those enquiries (in particular by providing relevant information and advice) if called upon by the authority to do so.

(10) Subsection (9) does not oblige any person to assist a local authority where doing so would be unreasonable in all the circumstances of the case.

(11) The persons are—

(a) any local authority;

(b) any local education authority;

(c) any local housing authority;

(d) any *health authority* [Health Authority, Special Health Authority] [Primary Care Trust] [*or National Health Service trust*] [, National Health service trust or NHS foundation trust]; and

(e) any person authorised by the Secretary of State for the purposes of this section.

(12) Where a local authority are making enquiries under this section with respect to a child who appears to them to be ordinarily resident within the area of another authority, they shall consult that other authority, who may undertake the necessary enquiries in their place.

Note. Words in first pair of square brackets in sub-s (11)(d) substituted for words 'health authority' by Health Authorities Act 1995, s 2(1), Sch 1, Part III, para 118, as from 28 June 1995, in so far as is necessary for enabling the making of any regulations, orders, directions, schemes or appointments, and as from 1 April 1996 otherwise. Words in second pair of square brackets inserted by the Health Act 1999 (Supplementary, Consequential etc Provisions) Order 2000, SI 2000 No 90, art 3(1), Sch 1, para 24(1), (7) as from 8 February 2000. Words in third pair of square brackets in sub-s (11)(d) inserted by Courts and Legal Services Act 1990, s 116, Sch 16, para 20, as from 14 October 1991. Words in final pair of square brackets substituted for words 'or the National Health Service Trust' by the Health and Social Care (Community Health and Standards) Act 2003, s 34, Sch 4, paras 75, 79, as from 1 April 2004 (SI 2004 No 759).

48. Powers to assist in discovery of children who may be in need of emergency protection—(1) Where it appears to a court making an emergency protection order that adequate information as to the child's whereabouts—

(a) is not available to the applicant for the order; but

(b) is available to another person,

it may include in the order a provision requiring that other person to disclose, if asked to do so by the applicant, any information that he may have as to the child's whereabouts.

(2) No person shall be excused from complying with such a requirement on the ground that complying might incriminate him or his spouse of an offence; but a statement or admission made in complying shall not be admissible in evidence against either of them in proceedings for any offence other than perjury.

(3) An emergency protection order may authorise the applicant to enter premises specified by the order and search for the child with respect to whom the order is made.

(4) Where the court is satisfied that there is reasonable cause to believe that there may be another child on those premises with respect to whom an emergency protection order ought to be made, it may make an order authorising the applicant to search for that other child on those premises.

(5) Where—

(a) an order has been made under subsection (4);

(b) the child concerned has been found on the premises; and

(c) the applicant is satisfied that the grounds for making an emergency protection order exist with respect to him,

the order shall have effect as if it were an emergency protection order.

(6) Where an order has been made under subsection (4), the applicant shall notify the court of its effect.

(7) A person shall be guilty of an offence if he intentionally obstructs any person exercising the power of entry and search under subsection (3) or (4).

(8) A person guilty of an offence under subsection (7) shall be liable on summary conviction to a fine not exceeding level 3 on the standard scale.

(9) Where, on an application made by any person for a warrant under this section, it appears to the court—

(a) that a person attempting to exercise powers under an emergency protection order has been prevented from doing so by being refused entry to the premises concerned or access to the child concerned; or

(b) that any such person is likely to be so prevented from exercising any such powers,

it may issue a warrant authorising any constable to assist the person mentioned in paragraph (a) or (b) in the exercise of those powers, using reasonable force if necessary.

(10) Every warrant issued under this section shall be addressed to, and executed by, a constable who shall be accompanied by the person applying for the warrant if—

(a) that person so desires; and

(b) the court by whom the warrant is issued does not direct otherwise.

(11) A court granting an application for a warrant under this section may direct that the constable concerned may, in executing the warrant, be accompanied by a

registered medical practitioner, *registered nurse* [registered midwife] or registered health visitor if he so chooses.

Note. In sub-s (11) words 'registered midwife' in square brackets substituted for words in italics by the Nursing and Midwifery Order 2001, SI 2002 No 253, art 54(3), Sch 5, para 10(b), as from 1 August 2004 (the London Gazette, 21 July 2004); for transitional provisions see SI 2002 No 253, Sch 2.

[(11A) The reference in subsection (11) to a registered midwife is to such a midwife who is also registered in the Specialist Community Public Health Nurses' Part of the register maintained under article 5 of the Nursing and Midwifery Order 2001.]

Note. Sub-s (11A) inserted by the Health Act 1999 (Consequential Amendments) (Nursing and Midwifery) Order 2004, SI 2004 No 1771, art 3, Schedule, Pt 1, para 4(b), as from 1 August 2004.

(12) An application for a warrant under this section shall be made in the manner and form prescribed by rules of court.

(13) Wherever it is reasonably practicable to do so, an order under subsection (4), an application for a warrant under this section and any such warrant shall name the child; and where it does not name him it shall describe him as clearly as possible.

49. Abduction of children in care etc—(1) A person shall be guilty of an offence if, knowingly and without lawful authority or reasonable excuse, he—

    (a) takes a child to whom this section applies away from the responsible person;

    (b) keeps such a child away from the responsible person; or

    (c) induces, assists or incites such a child to run away or stay away from the responsible person.

(2) This section applies in relation to a child who is—

    (a) in care;

    (b) the subject of an emergency protection order; or

    (c) in police protection,

and in this section 'the responsible person' means any person who for the time being has care of him by virtue of the care order, the emergency protection order, or section 46, as the case may be.

(3) A person guilty of an offence under this section shall be liable on summary conviction to imprisonment for a term not exceeding six months, or to a fine not exceeding level 5 on the standard scale, or to both.

50. Recovery of abducted children etc—(1) Where it appears to the court that there is reason to believe that a child to whom this section applies—

    (a) has been unlawfully taken away or is being unlawfully kept away from the responsible person;

    (b) has run away or is staying away from the responsible person; or

    (c) is missing,

the court may make an order under this section ('a recovery order').

(2) This section applies to the same children to whom section 49 applies and in this section 'the responsible person' has the same meaning as in section 49.

(3) A recovery order—

    (a) operates as a direction to any person who is in a position to do so to produce the child on request to any authorised person;

    (b) authorises the removal of the child by any authorised person;

    (c) requires any person who has information as to the child's whereabouts to disclose that information, if asked to do so, to a constable or an officer of the court;

    (d) authorises a constable to enter any premises specified in the order and search for the child, using reasonable force if necessary.

(4) The court may make a recovery order only on the application of—

(a) any person who has parental responsibility for the child by virtue of a care order or emergency protection order; or

(b) where the child is in police protection, the designated officer.

(5) A recovery order shall name the child and—

(a) any person who has parental responsibility for the child by virtue of a care order or emergency protection order; or

(b) where the child is in police protection, the designated officer.

(6) Premises may only be specified under subsection (3)(d) if it appears to the court that there are reasonable grounds for believing the child to be on them.

(7) In this section—

'an authorised person' means—

(a) any person specified by the court;

(b) any constable;

(c) any person who is authorised—

(i) after the recovery order is made; and

(ii) by a person who has parental responsibility for the child by virtue of a care order or an emergency protection order,

to exercise any power under a recovery order; and

'the designated officer' means the officer designated for the purposes of section 46.

(8) Where a person is authorised as mentioned in subsection (7)(c)—

(a) the authorisation shall identify the recovery order; and

(b) any person claiming to be so authorised shall, if asked to do so, produce some duly authenticated document showing that he is so authorised.

(9) A person shall be guilty of an offence if he intentionally obstructs an authorised person exercising the power under subsection (3)(b) to remove a child.

(10) A person guilty of an offence under this section shall be liable on summary conviction to a fine not exceeding level 3 on the standard scale.

(11) No person shall be excused from complying with any request made under subsection (3)(c) on the ground that complying with it might incriminate him or his spouse of an offence; but a statement or admission made in complying shall not be admissible in evidence against either of them in proceedings for an offence other than perjury.

(12) Where a child is made the subject of a recovery order whilst being looked after by a local authority, any reasonable expenses incurred by an authorised person in giving effect to the order shall be recoverable from the authority.

(13) A recovery order shall have effect in Scotland as if it had been made by the Court of Session and as if that court had had jurisdiction to make it.

(14) In this section 'the court', in relation to Northern Ireland, means a magistrates' court within the meaning of the Magistrates' Courts (Northern Ireland) Order 1981.

51. Refuges for children at risk—(1) Where it is proposed to use a voluntary home or *registered* [private] children's home to provide a refuge for children who appear to be at risk of harm, the Secretary of State may issue a certificate under this section with respect to that home.

Note. Word 'private' in square brackets substituted for word 'registered' by the Care Standards Act 2000, s 116, Sch 4, para 14(1), (7), as from 1 April 2002 (SI 2001 No 4150, SI 2002 No 920).

(2) Where a local authority or voluntary organisation arrange for a foster parent to provide such a refuge, the Secretary of State may issue a certificate under this section with respect to that foster parent.

(3) In subsection (2) 'foster parent' means a person who is, or who from time to time is, a local authority foster parent or a foster parent with whom children are placed by a voluntary organisation.

(4) The Secretary of State may by regulations—

(a) make provision as to the manner in which certificates may be issued;

(b) impose requirements which must be complied with while any certificate is in force; and

(c) provide for the withdrawal of certificates in prescribed circumstances.

(5) Where a certificate is in force with respect to a home, none of the provisions mentioned in subsection (7) shall apply in relation to any person providing a refuge for any child in that home.

(6) Where a certificate is in force with respect to a foster parent, none of those provisions shall apply in relation to the provision by him of a refuge for any child in accordance with arrangements made by the local authority or voluntary organisation.

(7) The provisions are—

(a) section 49;

(b) *section 71 of the Social Work (Scotland) Act 1968 (harbouring children who have absconded from residential establishments etc), so far as it applies in relation to anything done in England and Wales;*

[(b) sections 82 (recovery of certain fugitive children) and 83 (harbouring) of the Children (Scotland) Act 1995, so far as they apply in relation to anything done in England and Wales;]

(c) section 32(3) of the Children and Young Persons Act 1969 (compelling, persuading, inciting or assisting any person to be absent from detention, etc), so far as it applies in relation to anything done in England and Wales;

(d) section 2 of the Child Abduction Act 1984.

Note. Sub-s (7)(b) in square brackets substituted for sub-s (7)(b) in italics by Children (Scotland) Act 1995, s 105(4), Sch 4, para 48(3), as from 1 April 1997.

52. Rules and regulations—(1) Without prejudice to section 93 or any other power to make such rules, rules of court may be made with respect to the procedure to be followed in connection with proceedings under this Part.

(2) The rules may, in particular make provision—

(a) as to the form in which any application is to be made or direction is to be given;

(b) prescribing the persons who are to be notified of—

(i) the making, or extension, of an emergency protection order; or

(ii) the making of an application under section 45(4) or (8) or 46(7); and

(c) as to the content of any such notification and the manner in which, and person by whom, it is to be given.

(3) The Secretary of State may by regulations provide that, where—

(a) an emergency protection order has been made with respect to a child;

(b) the applicant for the order was not the local authority within whose area the child is ordinarily resident; and

(c) that local authority are of the opinion that it would be in the child's best interests for the applicant's responsibilities under the order to be transferred to them,

that authority shall (subject to their having complied with any requirements imposed by the regulations) be treated, for the purposes of this Act, as though they and not the original applicant had applied for, and been granted, the order.

(4) Regulations made under subsection (3) may, in particular, make provision as to—

(a) the considerations to which the local authority shall have regard in forming an opinion as mentioned in subsection (3)(c); and

(b) the time at which responsibility under any emergency protection order is to be treated as having been transferred to a local authority.

PART VI

COMMUNITY HOMES

53. Provision of community homes by local authorities—(1) Every local authority shall make such arrangements as they consider appropriate for securing that homes ('community homes') are available—

(a) for the care and accommodation of children looked after by them; and

(b) for purposes connected with the welfare of children (whether or not looked after by them),

and may do so jointly with one or more other local authorities.

(2) In making such arrangements, a local authority shall have regard to the need for ensuring the availability of accommodation—

(a) of different descriptions; and

(b) which is suitable for different purposes and the requirements of different descriptions of children.

(3) A community home may be a home—

(a) provided, *managed, equipped and maintained* [equipped, maintained and (subject to subsection (3A)) managed] by a local authority; or

(b) provided by a voluntary organisation but in respect of which a local authority and the organisation—

(i) propose that, in accordance with an instrument of management, the *management, equipment and maintenance* [equipment, maintenance and (subject to subsection (3B)) management] of the home shall be the responsibility of the local authority; or

(ii) so propose that the management, equipment and maintenance of the home shall be the responsibility of the voluntary organisation.

Note. Words in square brackets substituted for words in italics by Criminal Justice and Public Order Act 1994, s 22(2), as from 8 March 1996.

[(3A) A local authority may make arrangements for the management by another person of accommodation provided by the local authority for the purpose of restricting the liberty of children.

(3B) Where a local authority are to be responsible for the management of a community home provided by a voluntary organisation, the local authority may, with the consent of the body of managers constituted by the instrument of management for the home, make arrangements for the management by another person of accommodation provided for the purpose of restricting the liberty of children.]

Note. Sub-ss (3A), (3B) inserted by Criminal Justice and Public Order Act 1994, s 22(2), as from 8 March 1996.

(4) Where a local authority are to be responsible for the management of a community home provided by a voluntary organisation, the authority shall designate the home as a controlled community home.

(5) Where a voluntary organisation are to be responsible for the management of a community home provided by the organisation, the local authority shall designate the home as an assisted community home.

(6) Schedule 4 shall have effect for the purpose of supplementing the provisions of this Part.

54. ...

Note. This section repealed by the Care Standards Act 2000, s 117(2), Sch 6, as from 1 April 2002 (SI 2001 No 4150, SI 2002 No 920).

55. Determination of disputes relating to controlled and assisted community homes—(1) Where any dispute relating to a controlled community home arises between the local authority specified in the home's instrument of management and—

(a) the voluntary organisation by which the home is provided; or

(b) any other local authority who have placed, or desire or are required to place, in the home a child who is looked after by them,

the dispute may be referred by either party to the Secretary of State for his determination.

(2) Where any dispute relating to an assisted community home arises between the voluntary organisation by which the home is provided and any local authority who have placed, or desire to place, in the home a child who is looked after by them, the dispute may be referred by either party to the Secretary of State for his determination.

(3) Where a dispute is referred to the Secretary of State under this section he may, in order to give effect to his determination of the dispute, give such directions as he thinks fit to the local authority or voluntary organisation concerned.

(4) This section applies even though the matter in dispute may be one which, under or by virtue of Part II of Schedule 4, is reserved for the decision, or is the responsibility, of—

(a) the local authority specified in the home's instrument of management; or

(b) (as the case may be) the voluntary organisation by which the home is provided.

(5) Where any trust deed relating to a controlled or assisted community home contains provision whereby a bishop or any other ecclesiastical or denominational authority has power to decide questions relating to religious instruction given in the home, no dispute which is capable of being dealt with in accordance with that provision shall be referred to the Secretary of State under this section.

(6) In this Part 'trust deed', in relation to a voluntary home, means any instrument (other than an instrument of management) regulating—

(a) the maintenance, management or conduct of the home; or

(b) the constitution of a body of managers or trustees of the home.

56. Discontinuance by voluntary organisation of controlled or assisted community home—(1) The voluntary organisation by which a controlled or assisted community home is provided shall not cease to provide the home except after giving to the Secretary of State and the local authority specified in the home's instrument of management not less than two years' notice in writing of their intention to do so.

(2) A notice under subsection (1) shall specify the date from which the voluntary organisation intend to cease to provide the home as a community home.

(3) Where such a notice is given and is not withdrawn before the date specified in it, the home's instrument of management shall cease to have effect on that date and the home shall then cease to be a controlled or assisted community home.

(4) Where a notice is given under subsection (1) and the home's managers give notice in writing to the Secretary of State that they are unable or unwilling to continue as its managers until the date specified in the subsection (1) notice, the Secretary of State may by order—

(a) revoke the home's instrument of management; and

(b) require the local authority who were specified in that instrument to conduct the home until—

(i) the date specified in the subsection (1) notice; or

(ii) such earlier date (if any) as may be specified for the purposes of this paragraph in the order,

as if it were a community home provided by the local authority.

(5) Where the Secretary of State imposes a requirement under subsection (4)(b)—

(a) nothing in the trust deed for the home shall affect the conduct of the home by the local authority;

(b) the Secretary of State may by order direct that for the purposes of any provision specified in the direction and made by or under any enactment relating to community homes (other than this section) the home shall, until the date or earlier date specified as mentioned in subsection (4)(b), be treated as a controlled or assisted community home;

(c) except in so far as the Secretary of State so directs, the home shall until that date be treated for the purposes of any such enactment as a community home provided by the local authority; and

(d) on the date or earlier date specified as mentioned in subsection (4)(b) the home shall cease to be a community home.

57. Closure by local authority of controlled or assisted community home—(1) The local authority specified in the instrument of management for a controlled or assisted community home may give—

(a) the Secretary of State; and

(b) the voluntary organisation by which the home is provided,

not less than two years' notice in writing of their intention to withdraw their designation of the home as a controlled or assisted community home.

(2) A notice under subsection (1) shall specify the date ('the specified date') on which the designation is to be withdrawn.

(3) Where—

(a) a notice is given under subsection (1) in respect of a controlled or assisted community home;

(b) the home's managers give notice in writing to the Secretary of State that they are unable or unwilling to continue as managers until the specified date; and

(c) the managers' notice is not withdrawn,

the Secretary of State may by order revoke the home's instrument of management from such date earlier than the specified date as may be specified in the order.

(4) Before making an order under subsection (3), the Secretary of State shall consult the local authority and the voluntary organisation.

(5) Where a notice has been given under subsection (1) and is not withdrawn, the home's instrument of management shall cease to have effect on—

(a) the specified date; or

(b) where an earlier date has been specified under subsection (3), that earlier date,

and the home shall then cease to be a community home.

58. Financial provisions applicable on cessation of controlled or assisted community home or disposal etc of premises—(1) Where—

(a) the instrument of management for a controlled or assisted community home is revoked or otherwise ceases to have effect under section ..., 56(3) or (4)(a) or 57(3) or (5); or

(b) any premises used for the purposes of such a home are (at any time after 13th January 1987) disposed of, or put to use otherwise than for those purposes,

the proprietor shall become liable to pay compensation ('the appropriate compensation') in accordance with this section.

Note. In para (a) reference omitted repealed by the Care Standards Act 2000, s 117(2), Sch 6, as from 1 April 2002 (SI 2001 No 4150, SI 2002 No 920).

(2) Where the instrument of management in force at the relevant time relates—

(a) to a controlled community home; or

(b) to an assisted community home which, at any time before the instrument came into force, was a controlled community home,

the appropriate compensation is a sum equal to that part of the value of any premises which is attributable to expenditure incurred in relation to the premises, while the home was a controlled community home, by the authority who were then the responsible authority.

(3) Where the instrument of management in force at the relevant time relates—

(a) to an assisted community home; or
(b) to a controlled community home which, at any time before the instrument came into force, was an assisted community home,

the appropriate compensation is a sum equal to that part of the value of the premises which is attributable to the expenditure of money provided by way of grant under section 82, section 65 of the Children and Young Persons Act 1969 or section 82 of the Child Care Act 1980.

(4) Where the home is, at the relevant time, conducted in premises which formerly were used as an approved school or were an approved probation hostel or home, the appropriate compensation is a sum equal to that part of the value of the premises which is attributable to the expenditure—

(a) of sums paid towards the expenses of the managers of an approved school under section 104 of the Children and Young Persons Act 1933; ...
(b) of sums paid under section 51(3)(c) of the Powers of Criminal Courts Act 1973 [or section 20(1)(c) of the Probation Service Act 1993] in relation to expenditure on approved probation hostels or homes; [; or
(c) of sums paid under section 3, 5 or 9 of the Criminal Justice and Court Services Act 2000 in relation to expenditure on approved premises (within the meaning of Part I of that Act)].

Note. In sub-s (4)(a) word omitted repealed and para (c) and word 'or' immediately preceding it inserted by the Criminal Justice and Court Services Act 2000, ss 74, 75, Sch 7, Pt 2, paras 87, 93(a), (b), as from 1 April 2001 (SI 2001 No 919). In para (b) words 'or section...1993' in square brackets inserted by the Probation Service Act 1993, s 32, Sch 3, para 9(2), as from 5 February 1994.

(5) The appropriate compensation shall be paid—
(a) in the case of compensation payable under subsection (2), to the authority who were the responsible authority at the relevant time; and
(b) in any other case, to the Secretary of State.
(6) In this section—

'disposal' includes the grant of a tenancy and any other conveyance, assignment, transfer, grant, variation or extinguishment of an interest in or right over land, whether made by instrument or otherwise;

'premises' means any premises or part of premises (including land) used for the purposes of the home and belonging to the proprietor;

'the proprietor' means—
(a) the voluntary organisation by which the home is, at the relevant time, provided; or
(b) if the premises are not, at the relevant time, vested in that organisation, the persons in whom they are vested;

'the relevant time' means the time immediately before the liability to pay arises under subsection (1); and

'the responsible authority' means the local authority specified in the instrument of management in question.

(7) For the purposes of this section an event of a kind mentioned in subsection (1)(b) shall be taken to have occurred—
(a) in the case of a disposal, on the date on which the disposal was completed or, in the case of a disposal which is effected by a series of transactions, the date on which the last of those transactions was completed;
(b) in the case of premises which are put to different use, on the date on which they first begin to be put to their new use.

(8) The amount of any sum payable under this section shall be determined in accordance with such arrangements—
(a) as may be agreed between the voluntary organisation by which the home is, at the relevant time, provided and the responsible authority or (as the case may be) the Secretary of State; or
(b) in default of agreement, as may be determined by the Secretary of State.

(9) With the agreement of the responsible authority or (as the case may be) the Secretary of State, the liability to pay any sum under this section may be discharged, in whole or in part, by the transfer of any premises.

(10) This section has effect regardless of—

(a) anything in any trust deed for a controlled or assisted community home;

(b) the provisions of any enactment or instrument governing the disposition of the property of a voluntary organisation.

PART VII

VOLUNTARY HOMES AND VOLUNTARY ORGANISATIONS

59. Provision of accommodation by voluntary organisations—(1) Where a voluntary organisation provide accommodation for a child, they shall do so by—

(a) placing him (subject to subsection (2)) with—

(i) a family;

(ii) a relative of his; or

(iii) any other suitable person,

on such terms as to payment by the organisation and otherwise as the organisation may determine;

(b) *maintaining him in a voluntary home;*

(c) *maintaining him in a community home;*

(d) *maintaining him in a registered children's home;*

(e) *maintaining him in a home provided by the Secretary of State under section 82(5) on such terms as the Secretary of State may from time to time determine; or*

[(aa) maintaining him in an appropriate children's home;]

(f) making such other arrangements (subject to subsection (3)) as seem appropriate to them.

Note. Sub-s (1)(aa) substituted, for sub-s (1)(b)–(e) as originally enacted, by the Care Standards Act 2000, s 116, Sch 4, para 14(1), (8)(a), as from 1 April 2002 (SI 2002 No 4150, SI 2002 No 920).

[(1A) Where under subsection (1)(aa) a local authority maintains a child in a home provided, equipped and maintained by the Secretary of State under section 82(5), it shall do so on such terms as the Secretary of State may from time to time determine.]

Note. Sub-s (1A) inserted by the Care Standards Act 2000, s 116, Sch 4, para 14(1), (8)(b), as from 1 April 2002 (SI 2001 No 4150, SI 2002 No 920).

(2) The Secretary of State may make regulations as to the placing of children with foster parents by voluntary organisations and the regulations may, in particular, make provision which (with any necessary modifications) is similar to the provision that may be made under section 23(2)(a).

(3) The Secretary of State may make regulations as to the arrangements which may be made under subsection (1)(f) and the regulations may in particular make provision which (with any necessary modifications) is similar to the provision that may be made under section 23(2)(f).

(4) The Secretary of State may make regulations requiring any voluntary organisation who are providing accommodation for a child—

(a) to review his case; and

(b) to consider any representations (including any complaint) made to them by any person falling within a prescribed class of person,

in accordance with the provisions of the regulations.

(5) Regulations under subsection (4) may in particular make provision which (with any necessary modifications) is similar to the provision that may be made under section 26.

(6) Regulations under subsections (2) to (4) may provide that any person who, without reasonable excuse, contravenes or fails to comply with a regulation shall be guilty of an offence and liable on summary conviction to a fine not exceeding level 4 on the standard scale.

60. Registration and regulation of voluntary homes [60. Voluntary homes]—

(1) ...

(2) ...

Note. Section heading substituted and sub-ss (1), (2) repealed by the Care Standards Act 2000, ss 116, 117(2), Sch 4, para 14(1), (9)(a), Sch 6, as from 1 April 2002 (SI 2001 No 4150, SI 2002 No 920).

(3) *In this Act 'voluntary home' means any home or other institution providing care and accommodation for children which is carried on by a voluntary organisation but does not include—*

(a) *a nursing home, mental nursing home or residential care home [(other than a small home)];*

(b) *a school;*

(c) *any health service hospital;*

(d) *any community home;*

(e) *any home or other institution provided, equipped and maintained by the Secretary of State; or*

(f) *any home which is exempted by regulations made for the purposes of this section by the Secretary of State.*

[(3) In this Act 'voluntary home' means a children's home which is carried on by a voluntary organisation but does not include a community home.]

Note. In sub-s (3)(a) words omitted inserted by the Registered Homes (Amendment) Act 1991, s 2(6), as from 1 April 1993. Words omitted repealed by the Care Standards Act 2000, s 117(2), Sch 6, as from 1 April 2002 (SI 2001 No 4150, SI 2002 No 920). Sub-s (3) substituted by the Care Standards Act 2000, s 116, Sch 4, para 14(1), (9)(b), as from 1 April 2002 (SI 2001 No 4150, SI 2002 No 920).

(4) Schedule 5 shall have effect for the purpose of supplementing the provisions of this Part.

61. Duties of voluntary organisations—(1) Where a child is accommodated by or on behalf of a voluntary organisation, it shall be the duty of the organisation—

(a) to safeguard and promote his welfare;

(b) to make such use of the services and facilities available for children cared for by their own parents as appears to the organisation reasonable in his case; and

(c) to advise, assist and befriend him with a view to promoting his welfare when he ceases to be so accommodated.

(2) Before making any decision with respect to any such child the organisation shall, so far as is reasonably practicable, ascertain the wishes and feelings of—

(a) the child;

(b) his parents;

(c) any person who is not a parent of his but who has parental responsibility for him; and

(d) any other person whose wishes and feelings the organisation consider to be relevant,

regarding the matter to be decided.

(3) In making any such decision the organisation shall give due consideration—

(a) having regard to the child's age and understanding, to such wishes and feelings of his as they have been able to ascertain;

(b) to such other wishes and feelings mentioned in subsection (2) as they have been able to ascertain; and

(c) to the child's religious persuasion, racial origin and cultural and linguistic background.

62. Duties of local authorities—(1) Every local authority shall satisfy themselves that any voluntary organisation providing accommodation—

(a) within the authority's area for any child; or

(b) outside that area for any child on behalf of the authority,

are satisfactorily safeguarding and promoting the welfare of the children so provided with accommodation.

(2) Every local authority shall arrange for children who are accommodated within their area by or on behalf of voluntary organisations to be visited, from time to time, in the interests of their welfare.

(3) The Secretary of State may make regulations—

(a) requiring every child who is accommodated within a local authority's area, by or on behalf of a voluntary organisation, to be visited by an officer of the authority—

(i) in prescribed circumstances; and

(ii) on specified occasions or within specified periods; and

(b) imposing requirements which must be met by any local authority, or officer of a local authority, carrying out functions under this section.

(4) Subsection (2) does not apply in relation to community homes.

(5) Where a local authority are not satisfied that the welfare of any child who is accommodated by or on behalf of a voluntary organisation is being satisfactorily safeguarded or promoted they shall—

(a) unless they consider that it would not be in the best interests of the child, take such steps as are reasonably practicable to secure that the care and accommodation of the child is undertaken by—

(i) a parent of his;

(ii) any person who is not a parent of his but who has parental responsibility for him; or

(iii) a relative of his; and

(b) consider the extent to which (if at all) they should exercise any of their functions with respect to the child.

(6) Any person authorised by a local authority may, for the purpose of enabling the authority to discharge their duties under this section—

(a) enter, at any reasonable time, and inspect any premises in which children are being accommodated as mentioned in subsection (1) or (2);

(b) inspect any children there;

(c) require any person to furnish him with such records of a kind required to be kept by regulations made under *paragraph 7 of Schedule 5* [section 22 of the Care Standards Act 2000] (in whatever form they are held), or allow him to inspect such records, as he may at any time direct.

Note. In sub-s (6)(c) words 'section 22 of the Care Standards Act 2000' in square brackets substituted for words in italics by the Care Standards Act 2000, s 116, Sch 4 para 14(1), (10)(a), as from 1 April 2002 (SI 2001 No 4150, SI 2002 No 920).

(7) Any person exercising the power conferred by subsection (6) shall, if asked to do so, produce some duly authenticated document showing his authority to do so.

(8) Any person authorised to exercise the power to inspect records conferred by subsection (6)—

(a) shall be entitled at any reasonable time to have access to, and inspect and check the operation of, any computer and any associated apparatus or material which is or has been in use in connection with the records in question; and

(b) may require—

(i) the person by whom or on whose behalf the computer is or has been so used; or

(ii) any person having charge of, or otherwise concerned with the operation of, the computer, apparatus or material,

to afford him such assistance as he may reasonably require.

(9) Any person who intentionally obstructs another in the exercise of any power conferred by subsections (6) or (8) shall be guilty of an offence and liable on summary conviction to a fine not exceeding level 3 on the standard scale.

[(10) This section does not apply in relation to any voluntary organisation which is an institution within the further education sector, as defined in section 91 of the Further and Higher Education Act 1992, or a school.]

Note. Sub-s (10) inserted by the Care Standards Act 2000, s 105(5), as from (in relation to England): 1 April 2002 (SI 2001 No 3852); (in relation to Wales): 1 February 2003 (SI 2003 No 152).

PART VIII

REGISTERED CHILDREN'S HOMES

63. *Children not to be cared for and accommodated in unregistered children's homes* [63. **Private children's homes etc**]—(1)–(10) ...

Note. Section heading substituted and sub-ss (1)–(10) repealed by the Care Standards Act 2000, ss 116, 117(2), Sch 4, para 14(1), (11)(a), Sch 6, as from 1 April 2002 (SI 2001 No 4150, SI 2002 No 920).

(11) Schedule 6 shall have effect with respect to [private] children's homes.

(12) Schedule 7 shall have effect for the purpose of setting out the circumstances in which a person may foster more than three children without being treated [, for the purposes of this Act and the Care Standards Act 2000] as carrying on a children's home.

Note. In sub-s (11) word 'private' in square brackets inserted and in sub-s (12) words ', for the...Act 2000' in square brackets inserted by the Care Standards Act 2000, s 116, Sch 4, para 14(1), (11)(c), as from 1 April 2002 (SI 2001 No 4150, SI 2002 No 920).

64. **Welfare of children in children's homes**—(1) Where a child is accommodated in a [private] children's home, it shall be the duty of the person carrying on the home to—

(a) safeguard and promote the child's welfare;

(b) make such use of the services and facilities available for children cared for by their own parents as appears to that person reasonable in the case of the child; and

(c) advise, assist and befriend him with a view to promoting his welfare when he ceases to be so accommodated.

Note. Word 'private' in square brackets inserted by the Care Standards Act 2000, s 116, Sch 4, para 14(1), (12), as from 1 April 2002 (SI 2001 No 4150, SI 2002 No 920).

(2) Before making any decision with respect to any such child the person carrying on the home shall, so far as is reasonably practicable, ascertain the wishes and feelings of—

(a) the child;

(b) his parents;

(c) any other person who is not a parent of his but who has parental responsibility for him; and

(d) any person whose wishes and feelings the person carrying on the home considers to be relevant,

regarding the matter to be decided.

(3) In making any such decision the person concerned shall give due consideration—

(a) having regard to the child's age and understanding, to such wishes and feelings of his as he has been able to ascertain;

(b) to such other wishes and feelings mentioned in subsection (2) as he has been able to ascertain; and

(c) to the child's religious persuasion, racial origin and cultural and linguistic background.

(4) Section 62, except subsection (4), shall apply in relation to any person who is carrying on a [private] children's home as it applies in relation to any voluntary organisation.

Note. In sub-s (4) word 'private' in square brackets inserted by the Care Standards Act 2000, s 116, Sch 4, para 14(1), (12), as from 1 April 2002 (SI 2001 No 4150, SI 2002 No 920).

65. Persons disqualified from carrying on, or being employed in, children's homes—(1) A person who is disqualified (under section 68) from fostering a child privately shall not carry on, or be otherwise concerned in the management of, or have any financial interest in, a children's home unless he has—

(a) disclosed to *the responsible authority* [the appropriate authority] the fact that he is so disqualified; and

(b) obtained *their* [its] written consent.

(2) No person shall employ a person who is so disqualified in a children's home unless he has—

(a) disclosed to *the responsible authority* [the appropriate authority] the fact that that person is so disqualified; and

(b) obtained *their* [its] written consent.

Note. In sub-ss (1), (2) words 'the appropriate authority' and 'its' substituted for words in italics by the Care Standards Act 2000, s 116, Sch 4, para 14(1), (13)(a), as from 1 April 2002 (SI 2001 No 4150, SI 2002 No 920).

(3) Where *an authority refuse to give their consent under this section, they* [the appropriate authority refuses to give its consent under this section, it] shall inform the applicant by a written notice which states—

(a) the reason for the refusal;

(b) *the applicant's right to appeal against the refusal to a Registered Homes Tribunal under paragraph 8 of Schedule 6;*

[(b) the applicant's right to appeal under section 65A against the refusal to the Tribunal established under section 9 of the Protection of Children Act 1999]; and

(c) the time within which he may do so.

Note. In sub-s (3) words 'the appropriate...section, it' in square brackets substituted for words in italics and para (b) substituted by the Care Standards Act 2000, s 116, Sch 4, para 14(1), (13)(b), (c), as from 1 April 2002 (SI 2001 No 4150, 2002 No 920).

(4) Any person who contravenes subsection (1) or (2) shall be guilty of an offence and liable on summary conviction to imprisonment for a term not exceeding six months or to a fine not exceeding level 5 on the standard scale or to both.

(5) Where a person contravenes subsection (2) he shall not be guilty of an offence if he proves that he did not know, and had no reasonable grounds for believing, that the person whom he was employing was disqualified under section 68.

[(6) In this section and section 65A 'appropriate authority' means—

(a) in relation to England, the *National Care Standards Commission* [the Commission for Social Care Inspection]; and

(b) in relation to Wales, the National Assembly for Wales.]

Note. Sub-s (6) inserted by the Care Standards Act 2000, s 116, Sch 4, para 14(1), (13)(d), as from 1 April 2002 (SI 2001 No 4150, SI 2002 No 920). In para (a) words 'the Commission for Social Care and Inspection' in square brackets substituted for words in italics by the Health and Social Care (Community Health and Standards) Act 2003, s 147, Sch 9, para 10(1), (2), as from 1 April 2004 (SI 2004 No 759).

[65A. Appeal against refusal of authority to give consent under section 65—
(1) An appeal against a decision of an appropriate authority under section 65 shall lie to the Tribunal established under section 9 of the Protection of Children Act 1999.

(2) On an appeal the Tribunal may confirm the authority's decision or direct it to give the consent in question.]

Note. This section inserted by the Care Standards Act 2000, s 116, Sch 4, para 14(1), (14), as from (in relation to England): 1 April 2002: see the 2000 Act, s 122 and SI 2002 No 1493, art 3(2)(b); for transitional provisions see arts 3(1), 4 thereof; as from (in relation to Wales): 1 April 2002 No 920, art 3(3)(d); for transitional provisions see arts 2, 3(2), (4), (6)–(10), Schs 1–3 thereto.

PART IX

PRIVATE ARRANGEMENTS FOR FOSTERING CHILDREN

66. Privately fostered children—(1) In this Part—
    (a) 'a privately fostered child' means a child who is under the age of sixteen and who is cared for, and provided with accommodation [in their own home] by, someone other than—
        (i) a parent of his;
        (ii) a person who is not a parent of his but who has parental responsibility for him; or
        (iii) a relative of his; and
    (b) 'to foster a child privately' means to look after the child in circumstances in which he is a privately fostered child as defined by this section.

Note. In para (a) words 'in their own home' in square brackets inserted by the Care Standards Act 2000, s 116, Sch 4, para 14(1), (15)(a), as from 1 January 2001 (in relation to England) and 28 February 2001 (in relation to Wales).

(2) A child is not a privately fostered child if the person caring for and accommodating him—
    (a) has done so for a period of less than 28 days; and
    (b) does not intend to do so for any longer period.

(3) Subsection (1) is subject to—
    (a) the provisions of section 63; and
    (b) the exceptions made by paragraphs 1 to 5 of Schedule 8.

(4) In the case of a child who is disabled, subsection (1)(a) shall have effect as if for 'sixteen' there were substituted 'eighteen'.

[(4A) The Secretary of State may by regulations make provision as to the circumstances in which a person who provides accommodation to a child is, or is not, to be treated as providing him with accommodation in the person's own home.]

Note. Sub-s (4A) inserted by the Care Standards Act 2000, s 116, Sch 4, para 14(1), 15(b), as from 1 January 2001 (in relation to England) and 28 February 2001 (in relation to Wales).

(5) Schedule 8 shall have effect for the purposes of supplementing the provision made by this Part.

67. Welfare of privately fostered children—(1) It shall be the duty of every local authority to satisfy themselves that the welfare of children who are privately fostered within their area is being satisfactorily safeguarded and promoted and to secure that such advice is given to those caring for them as appears to the authority to be needed.

(2) The Secretary of State may make regulations—
    (a) requiring every child who is privately fostered within a local authority's area to be visited by an officer of the authority—

      (i) in prescribed circumstances; and

      (ii) on specified occasions or within specified periods; and

  (b) imposing requirements which are to be met by any local authority, or officer of a local authority, in carrying out functions under this section.

(3) Where any person who is authorised by a local authority to visit privately fostered children has reasonable cause to believe that—

  (a) any privately fostered child is being accommodated in premises within the authority's area; or

  (b) it is proposed to accommodate any such child in any such premises,

he may at any reasonable time inspect those premises and any children there.

(4) Any person exercising the power under subsection (3) shall, if so required, produce some duly authenticated document showing his authority to do so.

(5) Where a local authority are not satisfied that the welfare of any child who is privately fostered within their area is being satisfactorily safeguarded or promoted they shall—

  (a) unless they consider that it would not be in the best interests of the child, take such steps as are reasonably practicable to secure that the care and accommodation of the child is undertaken by—

      (i) a parent of his;

      (ii) any person who is not a parent of his but who has parental responsibility for him; or

      (iii) a relative of his; and

  (b) consider the extent to which (if at all) they should exercise any of their functions under this Act with respect to the child.

68. Persons disqualified from being private foster parents—(1) Unless he has disclosed the fact to the appropriate local authority and obtained their written consent, a person shall not foster a child privately if he is disqualified from doing so by regulations made by the Secretary of State for the purposes of this section.

(2) The regulations may, in particular, provide for a person to be so disqualified where—

  (a) an order of a kind specified in the regulations has been made at any time with respect to him;

  (b) an order of a kind so specified has been made at any time with respect to any child who has been in his care;

  (c) a requirement of a kind so specified has been imposed at any time with respect to any such child, under or by virtue of any enactment;

  (d) he has been convicted of any offence of a kind so specified, or *has been placed on probation or [a probation order has been made in respect of him or he has been]* discharged absolutely or conditionally for any such offence;

  (e) a prohibition has been imposed on him at any time under section 69 or under any other specified enactment;

  (f) his rights and powers with respect to a child have at any time been vested in a specified authority under a specified enactment.

Note. In sub-s (2)(d) words 'a probation...has been' in square brackets substituted for words 'has been placed on probation or' by the Criminal Justice and Court Services Act 2000, s 74, Sch 7, Pt 2, paras 87, 94, as from 1 April 2001 (SI 2001 No 919). Words 'a probation...has been' in italics repealed by the Criminal Justice Act 2003, ss 304, 332, Sch 32, Pt 1, paras 59, 60(1), (2), Sch 37, Pt 7, as from a day to be appointed.

[(2A) A conviction in respect of which a probation order was made before 1st October 1992 (which would not otherwise be treated as a conviction) is to be treated as a conviction for the purposes of subsection (2)(d).]

Note. Sub-s (2A) inserted by the Criminal Justice Act 2003, s 304, Sch 32, Pt 1, paras 59, 60(1), (3), as from a day to be appointed.

(3) Unless he has disclosed the fact to the appropriate local authority and obtained their written consent, a person shall not foster a child privately if—
  (a) he lives in the same household as a person who is himself prevented from fostering a child by subsection (1); or
  (b) he lives in a household at which any such person is employed.
(4) Where an authority refuse to give their consent under this section, they shall inform the applicant by a written notice which states—
  (a) the reason for the refusal;
  (b) the applicant's right under paragraph 8 of Schedule 8 to appeal against the refusal; and
  (c) the time within which he may do so.
(5) In this section—
'the appropriate authority' means the local authority within whose area it is proposed to foster the child in question; and
'enactment' means any enactment having effect, at any time, in any part of the United Kingdom.

69. Power to prohibit private fostering—(1) This section applies where a person—
  (a) proposes to foster a child privately; or
  (b) is fostering a child privately.
(2) Where the local authority for the area within which the child is proposed to be, or is being, fostered are of the opinion that—
  (a) he is not a suitable person to foster a child;
  (b) the premises in which the child will be, or is being, accommodated are not suitable; or
  (c) it would be prejudicial to the welfare of the child for him to be, or continue to be, accommodated by that person in those premises,
the authority may impose a prohibition on him under subsection (3).
(3) A prohibition imposed on any person under this subsection may prohibit him from fostering privately—
  (a) any child in any premises within the area of the local authority; or
  (b) any child in premises specified in the prohibition;
  (c) a child identified in the prohibition, in premises specified in the prohibition.
(4) A local authority who have imposed a prohibition on any person under subsection (3) may, if they think fit, cancel the prohibition—
  (a) of their own motion; or
  (b) on an application made by that person,
if they are satisfied that the prohibition is no longer justified.
(5) Where a local authority impose a requirement of any person under paragraph 6 of Schedule 8, they may also impose a prohibition on him under subsection (3).
(6) Any prohibition imposed by virtue of subsection (5) shall not have effect unless—
  (a) the time specified for compliance with the requirement has expired; and
  (b) the requirement has not been complied with.
(7) A prohibition imposed under this section shall be imposed by notice in writing addressed to the person on whom it is imposed and informing him of—
  (a) the reason for imposing the prohibition;
  (b) his right under paragraph 8 of Schedule 8 to appeal against the prohibition; and
  (c) the time within which he may do so.

70. Offences—(1) A person shall be guilty of an offence if—
  (a) being required, under any provision made by or under this Part, to give any notice or information—
    (i) he fails without reasonable excuse to give the notice within the time specified in that provision; or

(ii)   he fails without reasonable excuse to give the information within a reasonable time; or

(iii)   he makes, or causes or procures another person to make, any statement in the notice or information which he knows to be false or misleading in a material particular;

(b)   he refuses to allow a privately fostered child to be visited by a duly authorised officer of a local authority;

(c)   he intentionally obstructs another in the exercise of the power conferred by section 67(3);

(d)   he contravenes section 68;

(e)   he fails without reasonable excuse to comply with any requirement imposed by a local authority under this Part;

(f)   he accommodates a privately fostered child in any premises in contravention of a prohibition imposed by a local authority under this Part;

(g)   he knowingly causes to be published, or publishes, an advertisement which he knows contravenes paragraph 10 of Schedule 8.

(2)   Where a person contravenes section 68(3), he shall not be guilty of an offence under this section if he proves that he did not know, and had no reasonable ground for believing, that any person to whom section 68(1) applied was living or employed in the premises in question.

(3)   A person guilty of an offence under subsection (1)(a) shall be liable on summary conviction to a fine not exceeding level 5 on the standard scale.

(4)   A person guilty of an offence under subsection (1)(b), (c) or (g) shall be liable on summary conviction to a fine not exceeding level 3 on the standard scale.

(5)   A person guilty of an offence under subsection (1)(d) or (f) shall be liable on summary conviction to imprisonment for a term not exceeding six months, or to a fine not exceeding level 5 on the standard scale, or to both.

(6)   A person guilty of an offence under subsection (1)(e) shall be liable on summary conviction to a fine not exceeding level 4 on the standard scale.

(7)   If any person who is required, under any provision of this Part, to give a notice fails to give the notice within the time specified in that provision, proceedings for the offence may be brought at any time within six months from the date when evidence of the offence came to the knowledge of the local authority.

(8)   Subsection (7) is not affected by anything in section 127(1) of the Magistrates' Courts Act 1980 (time limit for proceedings).

PART X

71.–79. ...

Note. Sections 71–78 repealed in relation to England and Wales by the Care Standards Act 2000, s 79(5), and in relation to Scotland by the Regulation of Care (Scotland) Act 2001, s 80(1), Sch 4, as from (in relation to England): 2 July 2001 (SI 2001 No 2041); (in relation to Wales): 1 April 2002 (SI 2002 No 920); (in relation to Scotland): 1 April 2002 (SSI 2002 No 162). Section 79 repealed by the Regulation of Care (Scotland) Act 2001, s 80(1), Sch 4, as from 1 April 2002 (SSI 2002 No 162).

[PART XA

CHILD MINDING AND DAY CARE FOR CHILDREN IN ENGLAND AND WALES

Introductory

79A. Child minders and day care providers—(1) This section and section 79B apply for the purposes of this Part.

(2)   'Act as a child minder' means (subject to the following subsections) look after one or more children under the age of eight on domestic premises for reward; and 'child minding' shall be interpreted accordingly.

(3)   A person who—

(a) is the parent, or a relative, of a child;
(b) has parental responsibility for a child;
(c) is a local authority foster parent in relation to a child;
(d) is a foster parent with whom a child has been placed by a voluntary organisation; or
(e) fosters a child privately,

does not act as a child minder when looking after that child.

(4) Where a person—
(a) looks after a child for the parents ('P1'), or
(b) in addition to that work, looks after another child for different parents ('P2'),

and the work consists (in a case within paragraph (a)) of looking after the child wholly or mainly in P1's home or (in a case within paragraph (b)) of looking after the children wholly or mainly in P1's home or P2's home or both, the work is not to be treated as child minding.

(5) In subsection (4), 'parent', in relation to a child, includes—
(a) a person who is not a parent of the child but who has parental responsibility for the child;
(b) a person who is a relative of the child.

(6) 'Day care' means care provided at any time for children under the age of eight on premises other than domestic premises.

(7) This Part does not apply in relation to a person who acts as a child minder, or provides day care on any premises, unless the period, or the total of the periods, in any day which he spends looking after children or (as the case may be) during which the children are looked after on the premises exceeds two hours.

(8) In determining whether a person is required to register under this Part for child minding, any day on which he does not act as a child minder at any time between 2am and 6pm is to be disregarded.

Note. This section inserted by the Care Standards Act 2000, s 79(1), as from (in relation to England): 2 July 2001 (SI 2001 No 2041); for transitional, transitory and savings provisions see art 3, Schedule thereto; (in relation to Wales): 1 April 2002 (SI 2002 No 920); for transitional provisions see arts 2, 3(2), Sch 2 thereto.

79B. Other definitions, etc—(1) The registration authority in relation to England is Her Majesty's Chief Inspector of Schools in England (referred to in this Part as the Chief Inspector) and references to the Chief Inspector's area are references to England.

(2) The registration authority in relation to Wales is the National Assembly for Wales (referred to in this Act as 'the Assembly').

(3) A person is qualified for registration for child minding if—
(a) he, and every other person looking after children on any premises on which he is or is likely to be child minding, is suitable to look after children under the age of eight;
(b) every person living or employed on the premises in question is suitable to be in regular contact with children under the age of eight;
(c) the premises in question are suitable to be used for looking after children under the age of eight, having regard to their condition and the condition and appropriateness of any equipment on the premises and to any other factor connected with the situation, construction or size of the premises; and
(d) he is complying with regulations under section 79C and with any conditions imposed by the registration authority.

(4) A person is qualified for registration for providing day care on particular premises if—

(a) every person looking after children on the premises is suitable to look after children under the age of eight;

(b) every person living or working on the premises is suitable to be in regular contact with children under the age of eight;

(c) the premises are suitable to be used for looking after children under the age of eight, having regard to their condition and the condition and appropriateness of any equipment on the premises and to any other factor connected with the situation, construction or size of the premises; and

(d) he is complying with regulations under section 79C and with any conditions imposed by the registration authority.

(5) For the purposes of subsection (4)(b) a person is not treated as working on the premises in question if—

(a) none of his work is done in the part of the premises in which children are looked after; or

(b) he does not work on the premises at times when children are looked after there.

[(5A) Where, for the purposes of determining a person's qualification for registration under this Part—

(a) the registration authority requests any person ('A') to consent to the disclosure to the authority by another person ('B') of any information relating to A which is held by B and is of a prescribed description, and

(b) A does not give his consent (or withdraws it after having given it),

the registration authority may, if regulations so provide and it thinks it appropriate to do so, regard A as not suitable to look after children under the age of eight, or not suitable to be in regular contact with such children.]

(6) 'Domestic premises' means any premises which are wholly or mainly used as a private dwelling and 'premises' includes any area and any vehicle.

(7) 'Regulations' means—

(a) in relation to England, regulations made by the Secretary of State;

(b) in relation to Wales, regulations made by the Assembly.

(8) 'Tribunal' means the Tribunal established by section 9 of the Protection of Children Act 1999.

(9) Schedule 9A (which supplements the provisions of this Part) shall have effect.

Note. This section inserted by the Care Standards Act 2000, s 79(1), as from (in relation to Wales for certain purposes): 1 July 2001 (SI 2001 No 2190); (in relation to England for certain purposes): 2 July 2001 (SI 2001 No 2041); for transitional transitory and savings provisions see art 3, Schedule thereto; (in relation to Wales for remaining purposes): 1 April 2002 (SI 2002 No 920); for transitional provisions see arts 2, 3(2), Sch 2 thereto; (in relation to England for remaining purposes): 1 April 2002 (SI 2002 No 839). Sub-s (5A) inserted by the Education Act 2002, s 152, Sch 13, para 1, as from (in relation to England): 1 October 2002 (SI 2002 No 2439); (in relation to Wales): 19 December 2002 (SI 2002 No 3185).

Regulations

79C. Regulations etc governing child minders and day care providers—
(1) The Secretary of State may, after consulting the Chief Inspector and any other person he considers appropriate, make regulations governing the activities of registered persons who act as child minders, or provide day care, on premises in England.

(2) The Assembly may make regulations governing the activities of registered persons who act as child minders, or provide day care, on premises in Wales.

(3) The regulations under this section may deal with the following matters (among others)—

(a) the welfare and development of the children concerned;
(b) suitability to look after, or be in regular contact with, children under the age of eight;
(c) qualifications and training;
(d) the maximum number of children who may be looked after and the number of persons required to assist in looking after them;
(e) the maintenance, safety and suitability of premises and equipment;
(f) the keeping of records;
(g) the provision of information.

(4) In relation to activities on premises in England, the power to make regulations under this section may be exercised so as to confer powers or impose duties on the Chief Inspector in the exercise of his functions under this Part.

(5) In particular they may be exercised so as to require or authorise the Chief Inspector, in exercising those functions, to have regard to or meet factors, standards and other matters prescribed by or referred to in the regulations.

(6) If the regulations require any person (other than the registration authority) to have regard to or meet factors, standards and other matters prescribed by or referred to in the regulations, they may also provide for any allegation that the person has failed to do so to be taken into account—
(a) by the registration authority in the exercise of its functions under this Part, or
(b) in any proceedings under this Part.

(7) Regulations may provide—
(a) that a registered person who without reasonable excuse contravenes, or otherwise fails to comply with, any requirement of the regulations shall be guilty of an offence; and
(b) that a person guilty of the offence shall be liable on summary conviction to a fine not exceeding level 5 on the standard scale.

Note. This section inserted by the Care Standards Act 2000, s 79(1), as from (in relation to England for certain purposes): 16 March 2001 (SI 2001 No 1210); (in relation to England for remaining purposes): 2 July 2001 (SI 2001 No 2041); for transitional transitory and savings provisions see art 3, Schedule thereto; (in relation to Wales): 1 April 2002 (SI 2002 No 920); for transitional provisions see arts 2, 3(2), Sch 2 thereto.

Registration

79D. Requirement to register—(1) No person shall—
(a) act as a child minder in England unless he is registered under this Part for child minding by the Chief Inspector; or
(b) act as a child minder in Wales unless he is registered under this Part for child minding by the Assembly.

(2) Where it appears to the registration authority that a person has contravened subsection (1), the authority may serve a notice ('an enforcement notice') on him.

(3) An enforcement notice shall have effect for a period of one year beginning with the date on which it is served.

(4) If a person in respect of whom an enforcement notice has effect contravenes subsection (1) without reasonable excuse (whether the contravention occurs in England or Wales), he shall be guilty of an offence.

(5) No person shall provide day care on any premises unless he is registered under this Part for providing day care on those premises by the registration authority.

(6) If any person contravenes subsection (5) without reasonable excuse, he shall be guilty of an offence.

(7) A person guilty of an offence under this section shall be liable on summary conviction to a fine not exceeding level 5 on the standard scale.

Note. This section inserted by the Care Standards Act 2000, s 79(1), as from (in relation to England): 2 July 2001 (SI 2001 No 2041); for transitional, transitory and savings provisions see art 3, Schedule thereto; (in relation to Wales): 1 April 2002 (SI 2002 No 920); for transitional provisions see arts 2, 3(2), Sch 2 thereto.

79E. Applications for registration—(1) A person who wishes to be registered under this Part shall make an application to the registration authority.

(2) The application shall—

(a) give prescribed information about prescribed matters;

(b) give any other information which the registration authority reasonably requires the applicant to give.

(3) Where a person provides, or proposes to provide, day care on different premises, he shall make a separate application in respect of each of them.

(4) Where the registration authority has sent the applicant notice under section 79L(1) of its intention to refuse an application under this section, the application may not be withdrawn without the consent of the authority.

(5) A person who, in an application under this section, knowingly makes a statement which is false or misleading in a material particular shall be guilty of an offence and liable, on summary conviction, to a fine not exceeding level 5 on the standard scale.

Note. This section inserted by the Care Standards Act 2000, s 79(1), as from (in relation to England for certain purposes): 16 March 2001 (SI 2001 No 1210); (in relation to England for remaining purposes): 2 July 2001 (SI 2001 No 2041); for transitional transitory and savings provisions see art 3, Schedule thereto; (in relation to Wales): 1 April 2002 (SI 2002 No 920); for transitional provisions see arts 2, 3(2), Sch 2 thereto.

79F. Grant or refusal of registration—(1) If, on an application by a person for registration for child minding—

(a) the registration authority is of the opinion that the applicant is, and will continue to be, qualified for registration for child minding (so far as the conditions of section 79B(3) are applicable); and

(b) the applicant pays the prescribed fee,

the authority shall grant the application; otherwise, it shall refuse it.

(2) If, on an application by any person for registration for providing day care on any premises—

(a) the registration authority is of the opinion that the applicant is, and will continue to be, qualified for registration for providing day care on those premises (so far as the conditions of section 79B(4) are applicable); and

(b) the applicant pays the prescribed fee,

the authority shall grant the application; otherwise, it shall refuse it.

(3) An application may, as well as being granted subject to any conditions the authority thinks necessary or expedient for the purpose of giving effect to regulations under section 79C, be granted subject to any other conditions the authority thinks fit to impose.

(4) The registration authority may as it thinks fit vary or remove any condition to which the registration is subject or impose a new condition.

(5) Any register kept by a registration authority of persons who act as child minders or provide day care shall be open to inspection by any person at all reasonable times.

(6) A registered person who without reasonable excuse contravenes, or otherwise fails to comply with, any condition imposed on his registration shall be guilty of an offence.

(7) A person guilty of an offence under subsection (6) shall be liable on summary conviction to a fine not exceeding level 5 on the standard scale.

Note. This section inserted by the Care Standards Act 2000, s 79(1), as from (in relation to England for certain purposes): 16 March 2001 (SI 2001 No 1210); (in relation to England for remaining purposes): 2 July 2001 (SI 2001 No 2041); for transitional transitory and savings provisions see art 3, Schedule thereto; (in relation to Wales): 1 April 2002 (SI 2002 No 920); for transitional provisions see arts 2, 3(2), Sch 2 thereto.

79G. Cancellation of Registration—(1) The registration authority may cancel the registration of any person if—

(a) in the case of a person registered for child minding, the authority is of the opinion that the person has ceased or will cease to be qualified for registration for child minding;

(b) in the case of a person registered for providing day care on any premises, the authority is of the opinion that the person has ceased or will cease to be qualified for registration for providing day care on those premises,

or if an annual fee which is due from the person has not been paid.

(2) Where a requirement to make any changes or additions to any services, equipment or premises has been imposed on a registered person under section 79F(3), his registration shall not be cancelled on the ground of any defect or insufficiency in the services, equipment or premises if—

(a) the time set for complying with the requirements has not expired; and

(b) it is shown that the defect or insufficiency is due to the changes or additions not having been made.

(3) Any cancellation under this section must be in writing.

Note. This section inserted by the Care Standards Act 2000, s 79(1), as from (in relation to England): 2 July 2001 (SI 2001 No 2041); for transitional, transitory and savings provisions see art 3, Schedule thereto; (in relation to Wales): 1 April 2002 (SI 2002 No 920); for transitional provisions see arts 2, 3(2), Sch 2 thereto.

79H. Suspension of registration—(1) Regulations may provide for the registration of any person for acting as a child minder or providing day care to be suspended for a prescribed period by the registration authority in prescribed circumstances.

(2) Any regulations made under this section shall include provision conferring on the person concerned a right of appeal to the Tribunal against suspension.

[(3) A person registered under this Part for child minding by the Chief Inspector shall not act as a child minder in England at a time when that registration is suspended in accordance with regulations under this section.

(4) A person registered under this Part for child minding by the Assembly shall not act as a child minder in Wales at a time when that registration is so suspended.

(5) A person registered under this Part for providing day care on any premises shall not provide day care on those premises at any time when that registration is so suspended.

(6) If any person contravenes subsection (3), (4) or (5) without reasonable excuse, he shall be guilty of an offence and liable on summary conviction to a fine not exceeding level 5 on the standard scale.]

Note. This section inserted by the Care Standards Act 2000, s 79(1), as from (in relation to England for certain purposes): 16 March 2001 (SI 2001 No 1210); (in relation to England for remaining purposes): 2 July 2001 (SI 2001 No 2041); for transitional transitory and savings provisions see art 3, Schedule thereto; (in relation to Wales): 1 April 2002 (SI 2002 No 920); for transitional provisions see arts 2, 3(2), Sch 2 thereto. Sub-ss (3)–(6) inserted by the Education Act 2002, s 152, Sch 13, para 2, as from (in relation to England): 1 October 2002: (SI 2002/2439); (in relation to Wales): 19 December 2002: (SI 2002/3185).

79J. Resignation of registration—(1) A person who is registered for acting as a child minder or providing day care may by notice in writing to the registration authority resign his registration.

(2) But a person may not give a notice under subsection (1)—

(a) if the registration authority has sent him a notice under section 79L(1) of its intention to cancel the registration, unless the authority has decided not to take that step; or

(b) if the registration authority has sent him a notice under section 79L(5) of its decision to cancel the registration and the time within which an appeal may be brought has not expired or, if an appeal has been brought, it has not been determined.

Note. This section inserted by the Care Standards Act 2000, s 79(1), as from (in relation to England): 2 July 2001 (SI 2001 No 2041); for transitional, transitory and savings provisions see art 3, Schedule thereto; (in relation to Wales): 1 April 2002 (SI 2002 No 920); for transitional provisions see arts 2, 3(2), Sch 2 thereto.

79K. Protection of children in an emergency—(1) If, in the case of any person registered for acting as a child minder or providing day care—

(a) the registration authority applies to a justice of the peace for an order—
   (i) cancelling the registration;
   (ii) varying or removing any condition to which the registration is subject; or
   (iii) imposing a new condition; and

(b) it appears to the justice that a child who is being, or may be, looked after by that person, or (as the case may be) in accordance with the provision for day care made by that person, is suffering, or is likely to suffer, significant harm,

the justice may make the order.

(2) The cancellation, variation, removal or imposition shall have effect from the time when the order is made.

(3) An application under subsection (1) may be made without notice.

(4) An order under subsection (1) shall be made in writing.

(5) Where an order is made under this section, the registration authority shall serve on the registered person, as soon as is reasonably practicable after the making of the order—

(a) a copy of the order;

(b) a copy of any written statement of the authority's reasons for making the application for the order which supported that application; and

(c) notice of any right of appeal conferred by section 79M.

(6) Where an order has been so made, the registration authority shall, as soon as is reasonably practicable after the making of the order, notify the local authority in whose area the person concerned acts or acted as a child minder, or provides or provided day care, of the making of the order.

Note. This section inserted by the Care Standards Act 2000, s 79(1), as from (in relation to England for certain purposes): 2 July 2001 (SI 2001 No 2041); for transitional transitory and savings provisions see art 3, Schedule thereto; (in relation to Wales): 1 April 2002 (SI 2002 No 920); for transitional provisions see arts 2, 3(2), Sch 2 thereto; (in relation to England for remaining purposes): 1 April 2002 (SI 2002 No 839).

79L. Notice of intention to take steps—(1) Not less than 14 days before—

(a) refusing an application for registration;

(b) cancelling a registration;

(c) removing or varying any condition to which a registration is subject or imposing a new condition; or

(d) refusing to grant an application for the removal or variation of any condition to which a registration is subject,

the registration authority shall send to the applicant, or (as the case may be) registered person, notice in writing of its intention to take the step in question.

(2) Every such notice shall—

(a) give the authority's reasons for proposing to take the step; and

(b) inform the person concerned of his rights under this section.

(3) Where the recipient of such a notice informs the authority in writing of his desire to object to the step being taken, the authority shall afford him an opportunity to do so.

(4) Any objection made under subsection (3) may be made orally or in writing, by the recipient of the notice or a representative.

(5) If the authority, after giving the person concerned an opportunity to object to the step being taken, decides nevertheless to take it, it shall send him written notice of its decision.

(6) A step of a kind mentioned in subsection (1)(b) or (c) shall not take effect until the expiry of the time within which an appeal may be brought under section 79M or, where such an appeal is brought, before its determination.

(7) Subsection (6) does not prevent a step from taking effect before the expiry of the time within which an appeal may be brought under section 79M if the person concerned notifies the registration authority in writing that he does not intend to appeal.

Note. This section inserted by the Care Standards Act 2000, s 79(1), as from (in relation to England for certain purposes): 2 July 2001 (SI 2001 No 2041); for transitional transitory and savings provisions see art 3, Schedule thereto; (in relation to Wales): 1 April 2002 (SI 2002 No 920); for transitional provisions see arts 2, 3(2), Sch 2 thereto; (in relation to England for remaining purposes): 1 April 2002 (SI 2002 No 839).

79M. Appeals—(1) An appeal against—

(a) the taking of any step mentioned in section 79L(1); ...

(b) an order under section 79K, [or

(c) a determination made by the registration authority under this Part (other than one falling within paragraph (a) or (b)) which is of a prescribed description,]

shall lie to the Tribunal.

(2) On an appeal, the Tribunal may—

(a) confirm the taking of the step or the making of the order [or determination] or direct that it shall not have, or shall cease to have, effect; and

(b) impose, vary or cancel any condition.

Note. This section inserted by the Care Standards Act 2000, s 79(1), as from (in relation to Wales): 1 April 2002 (SI 2002 No 920); for transitional provisions see arts 2, 3(2), Sch 2 thereto; (in relation to England): 1 April 2002 (SI 2002 No 839). In sub-s (1)(a) word omitted repealed, para (c) and word 'or' immediately preceding it inserted and in sub-s (2)(a) words 'or determination' in square brackets inserted by the Education Act 2002, ss 148, 215(2), Sch 13, para 3(1)–(3), Sch 22, Pt 3, as from (in relation to England): 1 October 2002 (SI 2002/2439); (in relation to Wales): 19 December 2002 (SI 2002/3185).

Inspection: England

79N. General functions of the Chief Inspector—(1) The Chief Inspector has the general duty of keeping the Secretary of State informed about the quality and standards of child minding and day care provided by registered persons in England.

(2) When asked to do so by the Secretary of State, the Chief Inspector shall give advice or information to the Secretary of State about such matters relating to the provision of child minding or day care by registered persons in England as may be specified in the Secretary of State's request.

(3) The Chief Inspector may at any time give advice to the Secretary of State, either generally or in relation to provision by particular persons or on particular premises, on any matter connected with the provision of child minding or day care by registered persons in England.

(4) The Chief Inspector may secure the provision of training for persons who provide or assist in providing child minding or day care, or intend to do so.

(5) Regulations may confer further functions on the Chief Inspector relating to child minding and day care provided in England.

(6) The annual reports of the Chief Inspector required by subsection (7)(a) of section 2 of the School Inspections Act 1996 to be made to the Secretary of State shall include an account of the exercise of the Chief Inspector's functions under this Part, and the power conferred by subsection (7)(b) of that section to make other reports to the Secretary of State includes a power to make reports with respect to matters which fall within the scope of his functions by virtue of this Part.

Note. This section inserted by the Care Standards Act 2000, s 79(1), as from (for certain purposes): 16 March 2001 (SI 2001 No 1210); (for remaining purposes): 2 July 2001 (SI 2001 No 2041); for transitional transitory and savings provisions see art 3, Schedule thereto.

79P. Early years child care inspectorate—(1) The Chief Inspector shall establish and maintain a register of early years child care inspectors for England.

(2) The register may be combined with the register maintained for England under paragraph 8(1) of Schedule 26 to the School Standards and Framework Act 1998 (register of nursery education inspectors).

(3) Paragraphs 8(2) *to (9)* [to (8)], 9(1) to (4), 10 and 11 of that Schedule shall apply in relation to the register of early years child care inspectors as they apply in relation to the register maintained for England under paragraph 8(1) of that Schedule, but with the modifications set out in subsection (4).

(4) In the provisions concerned—

(a) references to registered nursery education inspectors shall be read as references to registered early years child care inspectors;

(b) references to inspections under paragraph 6 of that Schedule shall be read as references to inspections under section 79Q (and references to the functions of a registered nursery education inspector under paragraph 6 shall be interpreted accordingly);

(c) references to the registration of a person under paragraph 6 of that Schedule shall be read as references to the registration of a person under subsection (1) (and references to applications made under paragraph 6 shall be interpreted accordingly); *and*

(d) *in paragraph 10(2), for the words from 'to a tribunal' to the end there shall be substituted 'to the Tribunal established under section 9 of the Protection of Children Act 1999'.*

(5) Registered early years child care inspectors are referred to below in this Part as registered inspectors.

Note. This section inserted by the Care Standards Act 2000, s 79(1), as from (for certain purposes): 2 July 2001 (SI 2001 No 2041); for transitional transitory and savings provisions see art 3, Schedule thereto; (for certain purposes): 2 September 2002 (SI 2001 No 2041); for transitional transitory and savings provisions see art 3, Schedule thereto; (for certain purposes): 2 September 2002 (SI 2002 No 2215); (for remaining purposes): to be appointed. In sub-s (3) words 'to (8)' in square brackets substituted for words in italics by the Education Act 2002, s 155, Sch 14, para 4, as from 2 September 2002 (SI 2002/2002). Sub-s (4)(d) and word 'and' immediately preceding it repealed by the Education Act 2002, s 215(2), Sch 22, Pt 3, as from (in relation to Wales): 1 September 2004 (SI 2004/1728); (in relation to England): to be appointed.

79Q. Inspection of provision of child minding and day care in England—(1) The Chief Inspector may at any time require any registered person to provide him with any information connected with the person's activities as a child minder, or provision of day care, which the Chief Inspector considers it necessary to have for the purposes of his functions under this Part.

(2) The Chief Inspector shall *secure that any child minding provided in England by a registered person is inspected by a registered inspector at prescribed intervals* [at prescribed intervals inspect, or secure the inspection by a registered inspector of, any child minding provided in England by a registered person].

(3) The Chief Inspector shall *secure that any day care provided by a registered person on any premises in England is inspected by a registered inspector at prescribed intervals* [at prescribed intervals inspect, or secure the inspection by a registered inspector of, any day care provided by a registered person on any premises in England].

(4) The Chief Inspector may comply with subsection (2) or (3) either by organising inspections or by making arrangements with others for them to organise inspections.

(5) In prescribing the intervals mentioned in subsection (2) or (3) the Secretary of State may make provision as to the period within which the first inspection of child minding or day care provided by any person or at any premises is to take place.

(6) A person conducting an inspection under this section shall report on the quality and standards of the child minding or day care provided.

(7) The Chief Inspector may arrange for an inspection conducted by a registered inspector under this section to be monitored by another registered inspector.

Note. This section inserted by the Care Standards Act 2000, s 79(1), as from (for certain purposes): 16 March 2001 (SI 2001 No 1210); (for certain purposes): 2 July 2001 (SI 2001 No 2041); for transitional transitory and savings provisions see art 3, Schedule thereto; (for remaining purposes): 2 September 2002 (SI 2001 No 2041); for transitional transitory and savings provisions see art 3, Schedule thereto. In sub-ss (2), (3) words in square brackets substituted for words in italics by the Education Act 2002, s 148, Sch 13, para 4(1), (2), as from 2 September 2002 (SI 2002/2002).

79R. Reports of inspections—(1) A person who has conducted an inspection under section 79Q shall report in writing on the matters inspected to the Chief Inspector within the prescribed period.

(2) The period mentioned in subsection (1) may, if the Chief Inspector considers it necessary, be extended by up to three months.

(3) Once the report of an inspection has been made to the Chief Inspector under subsection (1) he—

(a) may send a copy of it to the Secretary of State, and shall do so without delay if the Secretary of State requests a copy;

(b) shall send a copy of it, or of such parts of it as he considers appropriate, to any prescribed authorities or persons; and

(c) may arrange for the report (or parts of it) to be further published in any manner he considers appropriate.

(4) Subsections (2) to (4) of section 42A of the School Inspections Act 1996 shall apply in relation to the publication of any report under subsection (3) as they apply in relation to the publication of a report under any of the provisions mentioned in subsection (2) of section 42A.

Note. This section inserted by the Care Standards Act 2000, s 79(1), as from (for certain purposes): 16 March 2001 (SI 2001 No 1210); (for remaining purposes): 2 July 2001 (SI 2001 No 2041); for transitional transitory and savings provisions see art 3, Schedule thereto.

Inspection: Wales

79S. General functions of the Assembly—(1) The Assembly may secure the provision of training for persons who provide or assist in providing child minding or day care, or intend to do so.

(2) In relation to child minding and day care provided in Wales, the Assembly shall have any additional function specified in regulations made by the Assembly; but the regulations may only specify a function corresponding to a function which, by virtue of section 79N(5), is exercisable by the Chief Inspector in relation to child minding and day care provided in England.

Note. This section inserted by the Care Standards Act 2000, s 79(1), as from 1 April 2002 (SI 2002 No 920); for transitional transitory and savings provisions see art 3, Schedule thereto.

79T. Inspection: Wales—(1) The Assembly may at any time require any registered person to provide it with any information connected with the person's activities as a child minder or provision of day care which the Assembly considers it necessary to have for the purposes of its functions under this Part.

(2) The Assembly may by regulations make provision—

(a) for the inspection of the quality and standards of child minding provided in Wales by registered persons and of day care provided by registered persons on premises in Wales;

(b) for the publication of reports of the inspections in such manner as the Assembly considers appropriate.

(3) The regulations may provide for the inspections to be organised by—

(a) the Assembly; or

(b) Her Majesty's Chief Inspector of Education and Training in Wales, or any other person, under arrangements made with the Assembly.

(4) The regulations may provide for subsections (2) to (4) of section 42A of the School Inspections Act 1996 to apply with modifications in relation to the publication of reports under the regulations.

Note. This section inserted by the Care Standards Act 2000, s 79(1), as from 1 April 2002 (SI 2002 No 920); for transitional transitory and savings provisions see art 3, Schedule thereto.

Supplementary

79U. Rights of entry etc—(1) *An authorised inspector* [Any person authorised for the purposes of this subsection by the registration authority] may at any reasonable time enter any premises in England or Wales on which child minding or day care is at any time provided.

(2) Where *an authorised inspector* [a person who is authorised for the purposes of this subsection by the registration authority] has reasonable cause to believe that a child is being looked after on any premises in contravention of this Part, he may enter those premises at any reasonable time.

[(2A) Authorisation under subsection (1) or (2)—

(a) may be given for a particular occasion or period;

(b) may be given subject to conditions.]

(3) *An inspector entering premises under this section may*— [A person entering premises under this section may (subject to any conditions imposed under subsection (2A)(b))—]

(a) inspect the premises;

(b) inspect, and take copies of—

(i) any records kept by the person providing the child minding or day care; and

(ii) any other documents containing information relating to its provision;

(c) seize and remove any document or other material or thing found there which he has reasonable grounds to believe may be evidence of a failure to comply with any condition or requirement imposed by or under this Part;

(d) require any person to afford him such facilities and assistance with respect to matters within the person's control as are necessary to enable him to exercise his powers under this section;

(e) take measurements and photographs or make recordings;
(f) inspect any children being looked after there, and the arrangements made for their welfare;
(g) interview in private the person providing the child minding or day care; and
(h) interview in private any person looking after children, or living or working, there who consents to be interviewed.

(4) Section 42 of the School Inspections Act 1996 (inspection of computer records for purposes of Part I of that Act) shall apply for the purposes of subsection (3) as it applies for the purposes of Part I of that Act.

(5) ...

(6) A person exercising any power conferred by this section shall, if so required, produce some duly authenticated document showing his authority to do so.

(7) It shall be an offence wilfully to obstruct a person exercising any such power.

(8) Any person guilty of an offence under subsection (7) shall be liable on summary conviction to a fine not exceeding level 4 on the standard scale.

(9) In this section—

...

'documents' and 'records' each include information recorded in any form.

Note. This section inserted by the Care Standards Act 2000, s 79(1), as from (in relation to England): 2 July 2001 (SI 2001 No 2041); for transitional transitory and savings provisions see art 3, Schedule thereto; (in relation to Wales): 1 April 2002 (SI 2002 No 920); for transitional provisions see arts 2, 3(2), Sch 2 thereto. In sub-ss (1)–(3) words in square brackets substituted for words in italics by the Education Act 2002, s 152, Sch 13, para 5(1)–(3), (5), as from (in relation to England): 2 September 2002 (SI 2002/2002); (in relation to Wales) 19 December 2002 (SI 2002/3185). Sub-s (2A) inserted by the Education Act 2002, s 152, Sch 13, para 5(1), (4), as from (in relation to England): 2 September 2002 (SI 2002/2002); (in relation to Wales): 19 December 2002 (SI 2002/3185). Sub-s (5) and in sub-s (9) definition 'authorised inspector' (omitted) repealed by the Education Act 2002, ss 152, 215(2), Sch 13, para 5(1), (6), (7), Sch 22, Pt 3, as from (in relation to England): 2 September 2002 (SI 2002/2002); (in relation to Wales): 19 December 2002 (SI 2002/3185).

79V. Function of local authorities—Each local authority shall, in accordance with regulations, secure the provision—
(a) of information and advice about child minding and day care; and
(b) of training for persons who provide or assist in providing child minding or day care.

Note. This section inserted by the Care Standards Act 2000, s 79(1), as from (in relation to England for certain purposes): 16 March 2001 (SI 2001 No 1210); (in relation to England for remaining purposes): 2 July 2001 (SI 2001 No 2041); for transitional transitory and savings provisions see art 3, Schedule thereto; (in relation to Wales): 1 April 2002 (SI 2002 No 920); for transitional provisions see arts 2, 3(2), Sch 2 thereto.

Checks on suitability of persons working with children over the age of seven

79W. Requirement for certificate of suitability—(1) This section applies to any person not required to register under this Part who looks after, or provides care for, children and meets the following conditions.

References in this section to children are to those under the age of 15 or (in the case of disabled children) 17.

(2) The first condition is that the period, or the total of the periods, in any week which he spends looking after children or (as the case may be) during which the children are looked after exceeds five hours.

(3) The second condition is that he would be required to register under this Part (or, as the case may be, this Part if it were subject to prescribed modifications) if the children were under the age of eight.

(4) Regulations may require a person to whom this section applies to hold a certificate issued by the registration authority as to his suitability, and the suitability of each prescribed person, to look after children.

(5) The regulations may make provision about—

(a) applications for certificates;

(b) the matters to be taken into account by the registration authority in determining whether to issue certificates;

(c) the information to be contained in certificates;

(d) the period of their validity.

(6) The regulations may provide that a person to whom this section applies shall be guilty of an offence—

(a) if he does not hold a certificate as required by the regulations; or

(b) if, being a person who holds such a certificate, he fails to produce it when reasonably required to do so by a prescribed person.

(7) The regulations may provide that a person who, for the purpose of obtaining such a certificate, knowingly makes a statement which is false or misleading in a material particular shall be guilty of an offence.

(8) The regulations may provide that a person guilty of an offence under the regulations shall be liable on summary conviction to a fine not exceeding level 5 on the standard scale.

Note. This section inserted by the Care Standards Act 2000, s 79(1), as from (in relation to England for certain purposes): 16 March 2001 (SI 2001 No 1210); (in relation to England for remaining purposes): 2 July 2001 (SI 2001 No 2041); for transitional transitory and savings provisions see art 3, Schedule thereto; (in relation to Wales): 1 April 2002 (SI 2002 No 920); for transitional provisions see arts 2, 3(2), Sch 2 thereto.

Time limit for proceedings

79X. Time limit for proceedings—Proceedings for an offence under this Part or regulations made under it may be brought within a period of six months from the date on which evidence sufficient in the opinion of the prosecutor to warrant the proceedings came to his knowledge; but no such proceedings shall be brought by virtue of this section more than three years after the commission of the offence.

Note. This section inserted by the Care Standards Act 2000, s 79(1), as from (in relation to England): 2 July 2001 (SI 2001 No 2041); for transitional transitory and savings provisions see art 3, Schedule thereto; (in relation to Wales): 1 April 2002 (SI 2002 No 920); for transitional provisions see arts 2, 3(2), Sch 2 thereto.

PART XI

SECRETARY OF STATE'S SUPERVISORY FUNCTIONS AND RESPONSIBILITIES

80. Inspection of children's homes etc by persons authorised by Secretary of State—(1) The Secretary of State may cause to be inspected from time to time any—

(a) [private] children's home;

(b) premises in which a child who is being looked after by a local authority is living;

(c) premises in which a child who is being accommodated by or on behalf of a local education authority or voluntary organisation is living;

(d) premises in which a child who is being accommodated by or on behalf of a *health authority* [Health Authority, Special Health Authority] [, Primary Care Trust] [*or National Health Service trust*] [, National Health service trust or NHS foundation trust] is living;

(e) *premises in which a child is living with a person with whom he has been placed by an adoption agency;*

(f) *premises in which a child who is a protected child is, or will be, living;*

(g) premises in which a privately fostered child, or child who is treated as a foster child by virtue of paragraph 9 of Schedule 8, is living or in which it is proposed that he will live;

(h)   premises on which any person is acting as a child minder;

(i)   premises with respect to which a person is registered under section 71(1)(b) [or with respect to which a person is registered for providing day care under Part XA];

(j)   *residential care home, nursing home or mental nursing home required to be registered under the Registered Homes Act 1984 and used to accommodate children;*

[(j)   care home or independent hospital used to accommodate children;]

(k)   premises which are provided by a local authority and in which any service is provided by that authority under Part III;

(l)   *independent school* [school or college] providing accommodation for any child.

Note. In para (a) word 'private' and in para (i) words 'or with...Part XA' in square brackets inserted by the Care Standards Act 2000, s 116, Sch 4, para 14(1), (16)(a), (b), as from 1 April 2002 (SI 2002 No 920, SI 2001 No 2041). In para (d) words 'Health Authority, Special Health Authority' in square brackets substituted for words in italics by the Health Authorities Act 1995, s 2(1), Sch 1, Pt 3, para 118, as from 28 June 1995, in so far as is necessary for enabling the making of any regulations, orders, directions, schemes or appointments, and as from 1 April 1996 otherwise. Words ', Primary Care Trust' in square brackets inserted by the Health Act 1999 (Supplementary, Consequential etc Provisions) Order 2000, SI 2000 No 90, art 3(1), Sch 1, para 24(1), (8)(a), as from 8 February 2000. Words 'or National Health Service trust' in square brackets inserted by the National Health Service and Community Care Act 1990, s 66(1), Sch 9, para 36(4), as from 5 July 1990. Words ', National Health Service Trust or NHS foundation trust' in square brackets substituted for words in italics by the Health and Social Care (Community Health and Standards) Act 2003, s 34, Sch 4, paras 75, 80(a), as from 1 April 2004. Paras (e), (f) repealed by the Adoption and Children Act 2002, s 139(1), (3), Sch 3, paras 54, 65, Sch 5, as from a day to be appointed. Para (j) substituted by the Care Standards Act 2000, s 109(1), (2), as from 1 April 2002 (SI 2001 No 4150, SI 2002 No 920). In para (l) words 'school or college' in square brackets substituted for words in italics by the Care Standards Act 2000, s 109(1), (2), as from (in relation to England): 1 April 2002 (SI 2002 No 4150); (in relation to Wales): to be appointed.

(2) An inspection under this section shall be conducted by a person authorised to do so by the Secretary of State.

(3) An officer of a local authority shall not be so authorised except with the consent of that authority.

(4) The Secretary of State may require any person of a kind mentioned in subsection (5) to furnish him with such information, or allow him to inspect such records (in whatever form they are held), relating to—

(a)   any premises to which subsection (1) or, in relation to Scotland, subsection (1)(h) or (i) applies;

(b)   any child who is living in any such premises;

(c)   the discharge by the Secretary of State of any of his functions under this Act;
...

(d)   the discharge by any local authority of any of their functions under this Act, as the Secretary of State may at any time direct.

Note. In sub-s (4)(c) word omitted repealed by the Care Standards Act 2000, s 117(2), Sch 6, as from 1 April 2002 (SI 2001 No 4150, SI 2002 No 920).

(5) The persons are any—

(a)   local authority;

(b)   voluntary organisation;

(c)   person carrying on a [private] children's home;

(d)   proprietor of an independent school [or governing body of any other school];

[(da)   governing body of an institution designated under section 28 of the Further and Higher Education Act 1992;

(db)   further education corporation;]

(e)   person fostering any privately fostered child or providing accommodation for a child on behalf of a local authority, local education authority, *health authority* [Health Authority, Special Health Authority] [, Primalry Care Trust][, *National Health Service trust*] [, NHS foundation trust] or voluntary organisation;

(f) local education authority providing accommodation for any child;

(g) person employed in a teaching or administrative capacity at any educational establishment (whether or not maintained by a local education authority) at which a child is accommodated on behalf of a local authority or local education authority;

(h) person who is the occupier of any premises in which any person acts as a child minder (within the meaning of Part X) or provides day care for young children (within the meaning of that Part);

[(hh) person who is the occupier of any premises—

    (i) in which any person required to be registered for child minding under Part XA acts as a child minder (within the meaning of that Part); or

    (ii) with respect to which a person is required to be registered under that Part for providing day care;]

(i) person carrying on any home of a kind mentioned in subsection (1)(j).

[(j) person carrying on a fostering agency].

Note. In para (c) word 'private' in square brackets inserted by the Care Standards Act 2000, s 116, Sch 4, para 14(1), (16)(a), as from 1 April 2002 (SI 2001 No 4150, SI 2002 No 920). In para (d) words 'or governing body of any other school' in square brackets inserted and paras (da), (db), (hh), (j) inserted by the Care Standards Act 2000, ss 109(1), (3), 116, Sch 4, para 14(1), (16)(d), as from (in relation to England): 1 April 2002 (SI 2001 No 3852); (in relation to Wales): to be appointed. In para (e) words 'Health Authority' in square brackets substituted for words in italics by the Health Authorities Act 1995, s 2(1), Sch 1, Pt 3, para 118, as from 28 June 1995, in so far as is necessary for enabling the making of any regulations, orders, directions, schemes or appointments, and as from 1 April 1996 otherwise. Words ', Primary Care Trust' in square brackets inserted by the Health Act 1999 (Supplementary, Consequential etc Provisions) Order 2000, SI 2000 No 90, art 3(1), Sch 1, para 24(1), (8)(b), as from 8 February 2000. Words 'National Health Service trust' in square brackets inserted by the National Health Service and Community Care Act 1990, s 66(1), Sch 9, para 36(4), as from 5 July 1990. Words ', NHS foundation trust' in square brackets inserted by the Health and Social Care (Community Health and Standards) Act 2003, s 34, Sch 4, paras 75, 80(b), as from 1 April 2004 (SI 2004 No 759).

(6) Any person inspecting any home or other premises under this section may—

(a) inspect the children there; and

(b) make such examination into the state and management of the home or premises and the treatment of the children there as he thinks fit.

(7) Any person authorised by the Secretary of State to exercise the power to inspect records conferred by subsection (4)—

(a) shall be entitled at any reasonable time to have access to, and inspect and check the operation of, any computer and any associated apparatus or material which is or has been in use in connection with the records in question; and

(b) may require—

    (i) the person by whom or on whose behalf the computer is or has been so used; or

    (ii) any person having charge of, or otherwise concerned with the operation of, the computer, apparatus or material,

to afford him such reasonable assistance as he may require.

(8) A person authorised to inspect any premises under this section shall have a right to enter the premises for that purpose, and for any purpose specified in subsection (4), at any reasonable time.

(9) Any person exercising that power shall, if so required, produce some duly authenticated document showing his authority to do so.

(10) Any person who intentionally obstructs another in the exercise of that power shall be guilty of an offence and liable on summary conviction to a fine not exceeding level 3 on the standard scale.

(11) The Secretary of State may by order provide for subsections (1), (4) and (6) not to apply in relation to such homes, or other premises, as may be specified in the order.

(12) Without prejudice to section 104, any such order may make different provision with respect to each of those subsections.

[(13) In this section—

'college' means an institution within the further education sector as defined in section 91 of the Further and Higher Education Act 1992;

'fostering agency' has the same meaning as in the Care Standards Act 2000;

'further education corporation' has the same meaning as in the Further and Higher Education Act 1992.]

Note. Sub-s (13) inserted by the Care Standards Act 2000, s 109(1), (4), as from (in relation to England): 1 April 2002; (in relation to Wales): to be appointed.

This section repealed, in relation to Scotland, by the Regulation of Care (Scotland) Act 2001, s 80(1), Sch 4, as from 1 April 2002 (SSI 2002 No 162).

81. Inquiries—(1) The Secretary of State may cause an inquiry to be held into any matter connected with—

(a) the functions of *the social services committee of a local authority* [a local authority which are social services functions within the meaning of the Local Authority Social Services Act 1970], in so far as those functions relate to children;

(b) *the functions of an adoption agency;*

(c) the functions of a voluntary organisation, in so far as those functions relate to children;

(d) a [private] ... children's home or voluntary home;

(e) *a residential care home, nursing home or mental nursing home* [a care home or independent hospital], so far as it provides accommodation for children;

(f) a home provided [in accordance with arrangements made] by the Secretary of State under section 82(5);

(g) the detention of a child under *section 53 of the Children and Young Persons Act 1933* [section 92 of the Powers of Criminal Courts (Sentencing) Act 2000].

Note. In para(a) words in square brackets substituted for words in italics by the Local Government Act 2000, s 107, Sch 5, para 21, as from (in relation to England): 26 October 2000; (in relation to Wales): 28 July 2001. Para (b) repealed by the Adoption and Children Act 2002, Sch 3, para 66, as from a day to be appointed. In para (d) word 'private' in square brackets inserted and in para (e) words 'a care home or independent hospital' in square brackets substituted for words in italics by the Care Standards Act 2000, s 116, Sch 4, para 14(1), (17)(b), as from 1 April 2002 (SI 2001 No 4150, SI 2002 No 920). In para (d) word omitted repealed and in para (f) words in square brackets inserted by the Courts and Legal Services Act 1990, ss 116, 125(7), Sch 16, para 21, Sch 20, as from 14 October 1991. In para (g) words in square brackets substituted for words in italics by the Powers of Criminal Courts (Sentencing) Act 2000, s 165(1), Sch 9, para 128, as from 25 August 2000.

(2) Before an inquiry is begun, the Secretary of State may direct that it shall be held in private.

(3) Where no direction has been given, the person holding the inquiry may if he thinks fit hold it, or any part of it, in private.

(4) Subsections (2) to (5) of section 250 of the Local Government Act 1972 (powers in relation to local inquiries) shall apply in relation to an inquiry under this section as they apply in relation to a local inquiry under that section.

(5) In this section 'functions' includes powers and duties which a person has otherwise than by virtue of any enactment.

82. Financial support by Secretary of State—(1) The Secretary of State may (with the consent of the Treasury) defray or contribute towards—
  (a) any fees or expenses incurred by any person undergoing approved child care training;
  (b) any fees charged, or expenses incurred, by any person providing approved child care training or preparing material for use in connection with such training; or
  (c) the cost of maintaining any person undergoing such training.
  (2) The Secretary of State may make grants to local authorities in respect of expenditure incurred by them in providing secure accommodation in community homes other than assisted community homes.
  (3) Where—
  (a) a grant has been made under subsection (2) with respect to any secure accommodation; but
  (b) the grant is not used for the purpose for which it was made or the accommodation is not used as, or ceases to be used as, secure accommodation,
the Secretary of State may (with the consent of the Treasury) require the authority concerned to repay the grant, in whole or in part.
  (4) The Secretary of State may make grants to voluntary organisations towards—
  (a) expenditure incurred by them in connection with the establishment, maintenance or improvement of voluntary homes which, at the time when the expenditure was incurred—
     (i) were assisted community homes; or
     (ii) were designated as such; or
  (b) expenses incurred in respect of the borrowing of money to defray any such expenditure.
  (5) The Secretary of State may arrange for the provision, equipment and maintenance of homes for the accommodation of children who are in need of particular facilities and services which—
  (a) are or will be provided in those homes; and
  (b) in the opinion of the Secretary of State, are unlikely to be readily available in community homes.
  (6) In this Part—
'child care training' means training undergone by any person with a view to, or in the course of—
  (a) his employment for the purposes of any of the functions mentioned in section 83(9) or in connection with the adoption of children or with the accommodation of children in a *residential care home, nursing home or mental nursing home* [care home or independent hospital]; or
  (b) his employment by a voluntary organisation for similar purposes;
'approved child care training' means child care training which is approved by the Secretary of State; and
'secure accommodation' means accommodation provided for the purpose of restricting the liberty of children.

Note. In sub-s (6)(a) words in square brackets substituted for words in italics by the Care Standards Act 2000, s 116, Sch 4, (18), as from 1 April 2002 (SI 2001 No 4150, SI 2002 No 920).

  (7) Any grant made under this section shall be of such amount, and shall be subject to such conditions, as the Secretary of State may (with the consent of the Treasury) determine.

83. Research and returns of information—(1) The Secretary of State may conduct, or assist other persons in conducting, research into any matter connected with—
  (a) his functions, or the functions of local authorities, under the enactments mentioned in subsection (9);

(b) the adoption of children; or

(c) the accommodation of children in a *residential care home, nursing home or mental nursing home* [care home or independent hospital].

(2) Any local authority may conduct, or assist other persons in conducting, research into any matter connected with—

(a) their functions under the enactments mentioned in subsection (9);

(b) the adoption of children; or

(c) the accommodation of children in a *residential care home, nursing home or mental nursing home* [care home or independent hospital].

(3) Every local authority shall, at such times and in such form as the Secretary of State may direct, transmit to him such particulars as he may require with respect to—

(a) the performance by the local authority of all or any of their functions—

  (i) under the enactments mentioned in subsection (9); or

  (ii) in connection with the accommodation of children in a *residential care home, nursing home or mental nursing home* [care home or independent hospital]; and

(b) the children in relation to whom the authority have exercised those functions.

Note. In sub-ss (1)(c), (2)(c), (3)(a)(ii) words in square brackets substituted for words in italics by the Care Standards Act 2000, s 116, Sch 4, para 14(1), (19), as from 1 April 2002 (SI 2001 No 4150, SI 2002 No 920).

(4) Every voluntary organisation shall, at such times and in such form as the Secretary of State may direct, transmit to him such particulars as he may require with respect to children accommodated by them or on their behalf.

(5) The Secretary of State may direct the *clerk of* [*justices' chief executive for*] [designated officer for] each magistrates' court to which the direction is expressed to relate to transmit—

(a) to such person as may be specified in the direction; and

(b) at such times and in such form as he may direct,

such particulars as he may require with respect to proceedings of the court which relate to children.

Note. In sub-s (5) words 'justices' chief executive for' in square brackets substituted for words 'clerk of' by the Access to Justice Act 1999, s 90, Sch 13, paras 159, 160, as from 1 April 2001 (SI 2001 No 916). Words 'designated officer for' in square brackets substituted for words 'justices' chief executive for' by the Courts Act 2003, s 109(1), Sch 8, para 336, as from a day to be appointed.

(6) The Secretary of State shall in each year lay before Parliament a consolidated and classified abstract of the information transmitted to him under subsections (3) to (5).

(7) The Secretary of State may institute research designed to provide information on which requests for information under this section may be based.

(8) The Secretary of State shall keep under review the adequacy of the provision of child care training and for that purpose shall receive and consider any information from or representations made by—

(a) the Central Council for Education and Training in Social Work;

(b) such representatives of local authorities as appear to him to be appropriate; or

(c) such other persons or organisations as appear to him to be appropriate,

concerning the provision of such training.

(9) The enactments are—

(a) this Act;

(b) the Children and Young Persons Acts 1933 to 1969;

(c) section 116 of the Mental Health Act 1983 (so far as it relates to children looked after by local authorities);

(d) section 10 of the Mental Health (Scotland) Act 1984 (so far as it relates to children for whom local authorities have responsibility).

84. Local authority failure to comply with statutory duty: default power of Secretary of State—(1) If the Secretary of State is satisfied that any local authority has failed, without reasonable excuse, to comply with any of the duties imposed on them by or under this Act he may make an order declaring that authority to be in default with respect to that duty.

(2) An order under subsection (1) shall give the Secretary of State's reasons for making it.

(3) An order under subsection (1) may contain such directions for the purpose of ensuring that the duty is complied with, within such period as may be specified in the order, as appear to the Secretary of State to be necessary.

(4) Any such directions shall, on the application of the Secretary of State, be enforceable by mandamus.

PART XII

MISCELLANEOUS AND GENERAL

Notification of children accommodated in certain establishments

85. Children accommodated by health authorities and local education authorities—(1) Where a child is provided with accommodation by any *health authority* [Health Authority, Special Health Authority,] [Primary Care Trust] [, National Health Service trust] [NHS foundation trust] or local education authority ('the accommodating authority')—

(a) for a consecutive period of at least three months; or

(b) with the intention, on the part of that authority, of accommodating him for such a period,

the accommodating authority shall notify the responsible authority.

(2) Where subsection (1) applies with respect to a child, the accommodating authority shall also notify the responsible authority when they cease to accommodate the child.

(3) In this section 'the responsible authority' means—

(a) the local authority appearing to the accommodating authority to be the authority within whose area the child was ordinarily resident immediately before being accommodated; or

(b) where it appears to the accommodating authority that a child was not ordinarily resident within the area of any local authority, the local authority within whose area the accommodation is situated.

(4) Where a local authority have been notified under this section, they shall—

(a) take such steps as are reasonably practicable to enable them to determine whether the child's welfare is adequately safeguarded and promoted while he is accommodated by the accommodating authority; and

(b) consider the extent to which (if at all) they should exercise any of their functions under this Act with respect to the child.

Note. Words in first pair of square brackets in sub-s (1) substituted for words in italics by Health Authorities Act 1995, s 2(1), Sch 1, para 118, as from 28 June 1995 in so far as is necessary for enabling the making of any regulations, orders, directions, schemes or appointments, and as from 1 April 1996 otherwise. Words in second pair of square brackets inserted by the Health Act 1999 (Supplementary, Consequential etc Provisions) Order 2000 SI 2000 No 90, art 3(1), Sch 1, para 24(1), (9), as from 8 February 2000. Words in third pair of square brackets in sub-s (1) inserted by National Health Service and Community Care Act 1990, s 66(1), Sch 9, para 36(5), as from 5 July 1990. Words in final pair of square brackets inserted by the Health and Social Care (Community Health and Standards) Act 2003, s 34, Sch 4, paras 75, 81, as from 1 April 2004 (SI 2004 No 759).

86. Children accommodated in residential care, nursing or mental nursing homes [86. Children accommodated in care homes or independent hospitals]— (1) Where a child is provided with accommodation in any *residential care home, nursing home or mental nursing home* [care home or independent hospital]—

(a) for a consecutive period of at least three months; or

(b) with the intention, on the part of the person taking the decision to accommodate him, of accommodating him for such period,

the person carrying on the home shall notify the local authority within whose area the home is carried on.

(2) Where subsection (1) applies with respect to a child, the person carrying on the home shall also notify that authority when he ceases to accommodate the child in the home.

(3) Where a local authority have been notified under this section, they shall—

(a) take such steps as are reasonably practicable to enable them to determine whether the child's welfare is adequately safeguarded and promoted while he is accommodated in the home; and

(b) consider the extent to which (if at all) they should exercise any of their functions under this Act with respect to the child.

(4) If the person carrying on any home fails, without reasonable excuse, to comply with this section he shall be guilty of an offence.

(5) A person authorised by a local authority may enter any *residential care home, nursing home or mental nursing home* [care home or independent hospital] within the authority's area for the purpose of establishing whether the requirements of this section have been complied with.

Note. Section heading substituted and in sub-ss (1), (5) words in square brackets substituted for words in italics by the Care Standards Act 2000, s 116, Sch 4, para 14(1), (2)(a), (b), as from 1 April 2002 (SI 2001/4150, SI 2002/920).

(6) Any person who intentionally obstructs another in the exercise of the power of entry shall be guilty of an offence.

(7) Any person exercising the power of entry shall, if so required, produce some duly authenticated document showing his authority to do so.

(8) Any person committing an offence under this section shall be liable on summary conviction to a fine not exceeding level 3 on the standard scale.

87. *Welfare of children accommodated in independent schools* [87. Welfare of children in boarding schools and colleges]—*(1) It shall be the duty of—*

(a) the proprietor of any independent school which provides accommodation for any child; and

(b) any person who is not the proprietor of such a school but who is responsible for conducting it,

to safeguard and promote the child's welfare.

(2) Subsection (1) does not apply in relation to a school which is a children's home or a residential care home [(other than a small home)].

(3) Where accommodation is provided for a child by an independent school within the area of a local authority, the authority shall take such steps as are reasonably practicable to enable them to determine whether the child's welfare is adequately safeguarded and promoted while he is accommodated by the school.

(4) Where a local authority are of the opinion that there has been a failure to comply with subsection (1) in relation to a child provided with accommodation by a school within their area, they shall notify the Secretary of State.

(5) Any person authorised by a local authority may, for the purpose of enabling the authority to discharge their duty under this section, enter at any reasonable time any independent school within their area which provides accommodation for any child.

[(1) Where a school or college provides accommodation for any child, it shall be the duty of the relevant person to safeguard and promote the child's welfare.

(2) Subsection (1) does not apply in relation to a school or college which is a children's home or care home.

(3) Where accommodation is provided for a child by any school or college the appropriate authority shall take such steps as are reasonably practicable to enable

them to determine whether the child's welfare is adequately safeguarded and promoted while he is accommodated by the school or college.

(4) Where the Commission are of the opinion that there has been a failure to comply with subsection (1) in relation to a child provided with accommodation by a school or college, they shall—

(a) in the case of a school other than an independent school or a special school, notify the local education authority for the area in which the school is situated;

(b) in the case of a special school which is maintained by a local education authority, notify that authority;

(c) in any other case, notify the Secretary of State.

(4A) Where the National Assembly for Wales are of the opinion that there has been a failure to comply with subsection (1) in relation to a child provided with accommodation by a school or college, they shall—

(a) in the case of a school other than an independent school or a special school, notify the local education authority for the area in which the school is situated;

(b) in the case of a special school which is maintained by a local education authority, notify that authority.

(5) Where accommodation is, or is to be, provided for a child by any school or college, a person authorised by the appropriate authority may, for the purpose of enabling that authority to discharge its duty under this section, enter at any time premises which are, or are to be, premises of the school or college.]

Note. Section heading substituted by the Care Standards Act 2000, s 116, Sch 4, para 14(1), (21), as from (in relation to England): 1 April 2002; (in relation to Wales): to be appointed. Sub-ss (1)–(4), (4A), (5) substituted, for sub-ss (1)–(5) as originally enacted, by the Care Standards Act 2000, s 105(1), (2), as from (in relation to England for certain purposes): 20 November 2001 (SI 2001 No 3852); (in relation to England for remaining purposes): 1 April 2002 (SI 2001 No 3852); (in relation to Wales): 1 February 2003 (SI 2003 No 152). In original sub-s (2) words in square brackets inserted by the Registered Homes (Amendment) Act 1991, s 2(6), as from 1 April 1993. In original sub-s (10) words in square brackets substituted for words in italics by the Education Act 1996, s 582(1), Sch 37, para 87, as from 1 November 1996.

(6) Any person *entering an independent school in exercise of* [exercising] the power conferred by subsection (5) may carry out such inspection of premises, children and records as is prescribed by regulations made by the Secretary of State for the purposes of this section.

Note. In sub-s (6) word 'exercising' in square brackets substituted for words in italics by the Care Standards Act 2000, s 105(1), (3), as from (in relation to England for certain purposes): 20 November 2001 (SI 2001 No 3852); (in relation to England for remaining purposes): 1 April 2002 (SI 2001 No 3852); (in relation to Wales): 1 February 2003 (SI 2003 No 152).

(7) Any person exercising that power shall, if asked to do so, produce some duly authenticated document showing his authority to do so.

(8) Any person authorised by the regulations to inspect records—

(a) shall be entitled at any reasonable time to have access to, and inspect and check the operation of, any computer and any associated apparatus or material which is or has been in use in connection with the records in question; and

(b) may require—

(i) the person by whom or on whose behalf the computer is or has been so used; or

(ii) any person having charge of, or otherwise concerned with the operation of, the computer, apparatus or material,

to afford him such assistance as he may reasonably require.

(9) Any person who intentionally obstructs another in the exercise of any power

conferred by this section or the regulations shall be guilty of an offence and liable on summary conviction to a fine not exceeding level 3 on the standard scale.

[(9A) Where the Commission or the National Assembly for Wales exercises the power conferred by subsection (5) in relation to a child, it must publish a report on whether the child's welfare is adequately safeguarded and promoted while he is accommodated by the school or college.

(9B) Where the Commission or the National Assembly for Wales publishes a report under this section, it must—

(a) send a copy of the report to the school or college concerned; and
(b) make copies of the report available for inspection at its offices by any person at any reasonable time.

(9C) Any person who requests a copy of a report published under this section is entitled to have one on payment of such reasonable fee (if any) as the Commission or the National Assembly for Wales (as the case may be) considers appropriate.]

Note. Sub-ss (9A)–(9C) inserted by the Health and Social Care (Community Health and Standards) Act 2003, s 111, as from (in relation to England): 1 April 2004 (SI 2004 No 759); (in relation to Wales): 1 April 2004 (SI 2004 No 873).

(10) In this section 'proprietor' has the same meaning as in the Education Act 1944 [the Education Act 1996].

[(10) In this section and sections 87A to 87D—
'the 1992 Act' means the Further and Higher Education Act 1992;
'appropriate authority' means—

(a) in relation to England, the *National Care Standards Commission* [the Commission for Social Care Inspection];
(b) in relation to Wales, the National Assembly for Wales;

college' means an institution within the further education sector as defined in section 91 of the 1992 Act;
'the Commission' means the *National Care Standards Commission* [the Commission for Social Care Inspection];
'further education corporation' has the same meaning as in the 1992 Act;
'local education authority' and 'proprietor' have the same meanings as in the Education Act 1996.

(11) In this section and sections 87A and 87D 'relevant person' means—

(a) in relation to an independent school, the proprietor of the school;
(b) in relation to any other school, or an institution designated under section 28 of the 1992 Act, the governing body of the school or institution;
(c) in relation to an institution conducted by a further education corporation, the corporation.

(12) Where a person other than the proprietor of an independent school is responsible for conducting the school, references in this section to the relevant person include references to the person so responsible.]

Note. Sub-ss (10)–(12) substituted, for sub-s (10) as originally enacted, by the Care Standards Act 2000, s 105(1), (4), as from (in relation to England, for the purpose of making regulations): 20 November 2001 (SI 2001 No 3852); (in relation to England for remaining puropses): 1 April 2002 (SI 2001 No 3852); (in relation to Wales): 1 February 2003 (SI 2003 No 152). In new sub-s (10) words 'the Commission for Social Care Inspection' in square brackets in both places they occur substituted for words in italics by the Health and Social Care (Community Health and Standards) Act 2003, s 147, Sch 9, para 10(1), (3)(a), as from 1 April 2004 (SI 2004 No 759). See also s 110 of the 2003 Act.

[87A. Suspension of duty under section 87(3)—*(1) The Secretary of State may appoint a person to be an inspector for the purposes of this section if—*

(a) that person already acts as an inspector for other purposes in relation to independent schools to which section 87(1) applies, and

   (b)   *the Secretary of State is satisfied that the person is an appropriate person to determine whether the welfare of children provided with accommodation by such schools is adequately safeguarded and promoted while they are accommodated by them.*

  (2) *Where—*

   (a)   *the proprietor of an independent school to which section 87(1) applies enters into an agreement in writing with a person appointed under subsection (1),*

   (b)   *the agreement provides for the person so appointed to have in relation to the school the function of determining whether section 87(1) is being complied with, and*

   (c)   *the local authority in whose area the school is situated receive from the person with whom the proprietor of the school has entered into the agreement notice in writing that the agreement has come into effect,*

the authority's duty under section 87(3) in relation to the school shall be suspended.

  (3) *Where a local authority's duty under section 87(3) in relation to any school is suspended under this section, it shall cease to be so suspended if the authority receive—*

   (a)   *a notice under subsection (4) relating to the person with whom the proprietor of the school entered into the relevant agreement, or*

   (b)   *a notice under subsection (5) relating to that agreement.*

  (4) *The Secretary of State shall terminate a person's appointment under subsection (1) if—*

   (a)   *that person so requests, or*

   (b)   *the Secretary of State ceases, in relation to that person, to be satisfied that he is such a person as is mentioned in paragraph (b) of that subsection,*

and shall give notice of the termination of that person's appointment to every local authority.

  (5) *Where—*

   (a)   *a local authority's duty under section 87(3) in relation to any school is suspended under this section, and*

   (b)   *the relevant agreement ceases to have effect,*

the person with whom the proprietor of the school entered into that agreement shall give to the authority notice in writing of the fact that it has ceased to have effect.

  (6) *In this section—*

   (a)   *'proprietor' has the same meaning as in the Education Act 1944 [the Education Act 1996], and*

   (b)   *references to the relevant agreement, in relation to the suspension of a local authority's duty under section 87(3) as regards any school, are to the agreement by virtue of which the authority's duty under that provision as regards that school is suspended.*

Note. Words in square brackets in sub-s (6)(a) substituted for words 'the Education Act 1944' by Education Act 1996, s 582(1), Sch 37, Part I, para 88, as from 1 November 1996.

[87A. Suspension of duty under section 87(3)—(1) The Secretary of State may appoint a person to be an inspector for the purposes of this section if—

  (a) that person already acts as an inspector for other purposes in relation to schools or colleges to which section 87(1) applies, and

  (b) the Secretary of State is satisfied that the person is an appropriate person to determine whether the welfare of children provided with accommodation by such schools or colleges is adequately safeguarded and promoted while they are accommodated by them.

  (2) Where—

  (a) the relevant person enters into an agreement in writing with a person appointed under subsection (1),

  (b) the agreement provides for the person so appointed to have in relation to the school or college the function of determining whether section 87(1) is being complied with, and

  (c) the appropriate authority receive from the person mentioned in paragraph (b) ('the inspector') notice in writing that the agreement has come into effect, the appropriate authority's duty under section 87(3) in relation to the school or college shall be suspended.

(3) Where the appropriate authority's duty under section 87(3) in relation to any school or college is suspended under this section, it shall cease to be so suspended if the appropriate authority receive—

(a) a notice under subsection (4) relating to the inspector, or

b) a notice under subsection (5) relating to the relevant agreement.

(4) The Secretary of State shall terminate a person's appointment under subsection (1) if—

(a) that person so requests, or

(b) the Secretary of State ceases, in relation to that person, to be satisfied that he is such a person as is mentioned in paragraph (b) of that subsection,

and shall give notice of the termination of that person's appointment to the appropriate authority.

(5) Where—

(a) the appropriate authority's duty under section 87(3) in relation to any school or college is suspended under this section, and

(b) the relevant agreement ceases to have effect,

the inspector shall give to the appropriate authority notice in writing of the fact that it has ceased to have effect.

(6) In this section references to the relevant agreement, in relation to the suspension of the appropriate authority's duty under section 87(3) as regards any school or college, are to the agreement by virtue of which the appropriate authority's duty under that provision as regards that school or college is suspended.]

Note. This section substituted for s 87A in italics by the Care Standards Act 2000, s 106(1), as from (in relation to England): 1 April 2002 (SI 2001 No 3852); (in relation to Wales): 1 February 2003 (SI 2003 No 152).

87B. Duties of inspectors under section 87A—(1) The Secretary of State may impose on a person appointed under section 87A(1) ('an authorised inspector') such requirements relating to, or in connection with, the carrying out under substitution agreements of the function mentioned in section 87A(2)(b) as the Secretary of State thinks fit.

(2) Where, in the course of carrying out under a substitution agreement the function mentioned in section 87A(2)(b), it appears to an authorised inspector that there has been a failure to comply with section 87(1) in the case of a child provided with accommodation by the school [or college] to which the agreement relates, the inspector shall give notice of that fact *to the Secretary of State*

[(a) in the case of a school other than an independent school or a special school, to the local education authority for the area in which the school is situated;

(b) in the case of a special school which is maintained by a local education authority, to that authority;

(c) in any other case, to the Secretary of State].

Note. In sub-s (2) words 'or college' in square brackets inserted by the Care Standards Act 2000, s 106(2)(a), as from (in relation to England): 1 April 2002 (SI 2001 No 3852); (in relation to Wales): 1 February 2003 (SI 2003 No 152). Paras (a)–(c) substituted for words 'the Secretary of State' by the Care Standards Act 2000, s 106(2)(b), as from (in relation to England): 1 April 2002 (SI 2001 No 3852); (in relation to Wales): 1 February 2003 (SI 2003 No 152).

(3) Where, in the course of carrying out under a substitution agreement the function mentioned in section 87A(2)(b), it appears to an authorised inspector that a child provided with accommodation by the school [or college] to which the agreement relates is suffering, or is likely to suffer, significant harm, the inspector shall—

(a) give notice of that fact to the local authority in whose area the school is situated, and

(b) where the inspector is required to make inspection reports to the Secretary of State, supply that local authority with a copy of the latest inspection report to have been made by the inspector to the Secretary of State in relation to the school [or college].

Note. Words 'or college' in square brackets in both places they occur inserted by the Care Standards Act 2000, s 106(2), (b), as from (in relation to England): 1 April 2002 (SI 2001 No 3852); (in relation to Wales): 1 February 2003 (SI 2003 No 152).

(4) In this section—

(a) 'proprietor' has the same meaning as in the Education Act 1944 [the Education Act 1996], and

(b) references to substitution agreement are to an agreement between an authorised inspector and the proprietor of an independent school by virtue of which the local authority's duty in relation to the school under section 87(3) is suspended.]

[(4) In this section 'substitution agreement' means an agreement by virtue of which the duty of the appropriate authority under section 87(3) in relation to a school or college is suspended.]

Note. Sections 87A, 87B inserted in relation to England and Wales only, by Deregulation and Contracting Out Act 1994, s 38, as from 1 January 1996. Words in square brackets in sub-s (4)(a) substituted for words 'the Education Act 1944' by Education Act 1996, s 582(1), Sch 37, Part I, para 89, as from 1 November 1996. Sub-s (4) substituted for sub-s (4) in italics by the Care Standards Act 2000, s 106(2)(c), a form (in relation to England): 1 April 2002 (SI 2001 No 3852); (in relation to Wales): 1 February 2003 (Si 2003 No 152).

[87C. Boarding Schools: national minimum standards—(1) The Secretary of State may prepare and publish statements of national minimum standards for safeguarding and promoting the welfare of children for whom accommodation is provided in a school or college.

(2) The Secretary of State shall keep the standards set out in the statements under review and may publish amended statements whenever he considers it appropriate to do so.

(3) Before issuing a statement, or an amended statement which in the opinion of the Secretary of State effects a substantial change in the standards, the Secretary of State shall consult any persons he considers appropriate.

(4) The standards shall be taken into account—

(a) in the making by the appropriate authority of any determination under section 87(4) or (4A);

(b) in the making by a person appointed under section 87A(1) of any determination under section 87B(2); and

(c) in any proceedings under any other enactment in which it is alleged that the person has failed to comply with section 87(1).]

Note. This section inserted by the Care Standards Act 2000, s 107, as from (in relation to Wales): 1 July 2001 (SI 2001 No 2190); (in relation to England for certain purposes): 20 November 2001 (SI 2001 No 3852); (in relation to England for remaining purposes): 1 April 2002 (SI 2002 No 3852).

[87D. Annual fee for boarding school inspections—(1) Regulations under subsection (2) may be made in relation to any school or college in respect of which the appropriate authority is required to take steps under section 87(3).

(2) The Secretary of State may by regulations require the relevant person to pay the appropriate authority an annual fee of such amount, and within such time, as the regulations may specify.

(3) A fee payable by virtue of this section may, without prejudice to any other method of recovery, be recovered summarily as a civil debt.]

Note. This section inserted by the Care Standards Act 2000, s 108, as from (in relation to Wales): 1 July 2001 (SI 2001 No 2190); (in relation to England for certain purposes): 20 November 2001 (SI 2001 No 3852); (in relation to England for remaining purposes): 1 April 2002 (SI 2002 No 3852).

Adoption

88. Amendments of adoption legislation—*(1) The Adoption Act 1976 shall have effect subject to the amendments made by Part I of Schedule 10.*

(2) The Adoption (Scotland) Act 1978 shall have effect subject to the amendments made by Part II of Schedule 10.

Note. Sub-s (1) repealed by the Adoption and Children Act 2002, s 139(1), (3), Sch 3, paras 54, 67, Sch 5.

...

89. ...

Note. This section repealed by the Child Support, Pensions and Social Security Act 2000, s 85, Sch 9, Pt IX, as from 1 April 2001 (SI 2001 No 774).

Criminal care and supervision orders

90. Care and supervision orders in criminal proceedings—(1) The power of a court to make an order under subsection (2) of section 1 of the Children and Young Persons Act 1969 (care proceedings in *juvenile courts* [youth courts]) where it is of the opinion that the condition mentioned in paragraph (f) of that subsection ('the offence condition') is satisfied is hereby abolished.

(2) The powers of the court to make care orders—

(a) under section 7(7)(a) of the Children and Young Persons Act 1969 (alteration in treatment of young offenders etc); and

(b) under section 15(1) of that Act, on discharging a supervision order made under section 7(7)(b) of that Act,

are hereby abolished.

(3) The powers given by that Act to include requirements in supervision orders shall have effect subject to amendments made by Schedule 12.

Note. Words in square brackets substituted for words in italics by Criminal Justice Act 1991, s 100, Sch 11, para 40(1), (2)(v), as from 1 October 1992.

Effect and duration of orders etc

91. Effect and duration of orders etc—(1) The making of a residence order with respect to a child who is the subject of a care order discharges the care order.

(2) The making of a care order with respect to a child who is the subject of any section 8 order discharges that order.

(3) The making of a care order with respect to a child who is the subject of a supervision order discharges that other order.

(4) The making of a care order with respect to a child who is a ward of court brings that wardship to an end.

(5) The making of a care order with respect to a child who is the subject of a school attendance order made under *section 37 of the Education Act 1944* [section 437 of the Education Act 1996] discharges the school attendance order.

Note. Words in square brackets substituted for words in italics by Education Act 1996, s 582(1), Sch 37, Part I, para 90, as from 1 November 1996.

[(5A) The making of a special guardianship order with respect to a child who is the subject of—

(a) a care order; or

(b) an order under section 34,

discharges that order.]

Note. Sub-s (5A) inserted by the Adoption and Children Act 2002, s 139(1), Sch 3, paras 54, 68, as from a day to be appointed.

(6) Where an emergency protection order is made with respect to a child who is in care, the care order shall have effect subject to the emergency protection order.

(7) Any order made under section 4(1), [4A(1)] or 5(1) shall continue in force until the child reaches the age of eighteen, unless it is brought to an end earlier.

Note. In sub-s (7) reference to '4A(1)' in square brackets inserted by the Adoption and Children Act 2002, s 139(1), Sch 3, paras 54, 68, as from a day to be appointed.

(8) Any—

(a) agreement under section 4 [or 4A]; or

(b) appointment under section 5(3) or (4),

shall continue in force until the child reaches the age of eighteen, unless it is brought to an end earlier.

Note. In sub-s (8)(a) words 'or 4A' in square brackets inserted by the Adoption and Children Act 2002, s 139(1), Sch 3, paras 54, 68, as from a day to be appointed.

(9) An order under Schedule 1 has effect as specified in that Schedule.

(10) A section 8 order shall, if it would otherwise still be in force, cease to have effect when the child reaches the age of sixteen, unless it is to have effect beyond that age by virtue of section 9(6) [or 12(5)].

Note. In sub-s (10) words 'or 12(5)' in square brackets inserted by the Adoption and Children Act 2002, s 114(3), as from a day to be appointed.

(11) Where a section 8 order has effect with respect to a child who has reached the age of sixteen, it shall, if it would otherwise still be in force, cease to have effect when he reaches the age of eighteen.

(12) Any care order, other than an interim care order, shall continue in force until the child reaches the age of eighteen, unless it is brought to an end earlier.

(13) Any order made under any other provision of this Act in relation to a child shall, if it would otherwise still be in force, cease to have effect when he reaches the age of eighteen.

(14) On disposing of any application for an order under this Act, the court may (whether or not it makes any other order in response to the application) order that no application for an order under this Act of any specified kind may be made with respect to the child concerned by any person named in the order without leave of the court.

(15) Where an application ('the previous application') has been made for—

(a) the discharge of a care order;

(b) the discharge of a supervision order;

(c) the discharge of an education supervision order;

(d) the substitution of a supervision order for a care order; or

(e) a child assessment order,

no further application of a kind mentioned in paragraphs (a) to (e) may be made with respect to the child concerned, without leave of the court, unless the period between the disposal of the previous application and the making of the further application exceeds six months.

(16) Subsection (15) does not apply to applications made in relation to interim orders.

(17) Where—

(a) a person has made an application for an order under section 34;

(b) the application has been refused; and

(c) a period of less than six months has elapsed since the refusal, that person may not make a further application for such an order with respect to the same child, unless he has obtained the leave of the court.

Jurisdiction and procedure etc

92. Jurisdiction of courts—(1) The name 'domestic proceedings', given to certain proceedings in magistrates' courts, is hereby changed to 'family proceedings' and the names 'domestic court' and 'domestic court panel' are hereby changed to 'family proceedings court' and 'family panel', respectively.

(2) Proceedings under this Act shall be treated as family proceedings in relation to magistrates' courts.

(3) Subsection (2) is subject to the provisions of section 65(1) and (2) of the Magistrates' Courts Act 1980 (proceedings which may be treated as not being family proceedings), as amended by this Act.

(4) A magistrates' court shall not be competent to entertain any application, or make any order, involving the administration or application of—

(a) any property belonging to or held in trust for a child; or

(b) the income of any such property.

(5) The powers of a magistrates' court under section 63(2) of the Act of 1980 to suspend or rescind orders shall not apply in relation to any order made under this Act.

(6) Part I of Schedule 11 makes provision, including provision for the Lord Chancellor to make orders, with respect to the jurisdiction of courts and justices of the peace in relation to—

(a) proceedings under this Act; and

(b) proceedings under certain other enactments.

(7) For the purposes of this Act 'the court' means the High Court, a county court or a magistrates' court.

(8) Subsection (7) is subject to the provision made by or under Part I of Schedule 11 and to any express provision as to the jurisdiction of any court made by any other provision of this Act.

(9) The Lord Chancellor may by order make provision for the principal registry of the Family Division of the High Court to be treated as if it were a county court for such purposes of this Act, or of any provision made under this Act, as may be specified in the order.

(10) Any order under subsection (9) may make such provision as the Lord Chancellor thinks expedient for the purpose of applying (with or without modifications) provisions which apply in relation to the procedure in county courts to the principal registry when it acts as if it were a county court.

(11) Part II of Schedule 11 makes amendments consequential on this section.

93. Rules of court—(1) An authority having power to make rules of court may make such provision for giving effect to—

(a) this Act;

(b) the provisions of any statutory instrument made under this Act; or

[(bb) for children to be separately represented in relevant proceedings,]

(c) any amendment made by this Act in any other enactment,

as appears to that authority to be necessary or expedient.

Note. Para (bb) inserted by the Adoption and Children Act 2002, s 122(2), as from a day to be appointed.

(2) The rules may, in particular, make provision—

(a) with respect to the procedure to be followed in any relevant proceedings (including the manner in which any application is to be made or other proceedings commenced);

(b) as to the persons entitled to participate in any relevant proceedings, whether as parties to the proceedings or by being given the opportunity to make representations to the court;

(c) with respect to the documents and information to be furnished, and notices to be given, in connection with any relevant proceedings;

(d) applying (with or without modification) enactments which govern the procedure to be followed with respect to proceedings brought on a complaint made to a magistrates' court to relevant proceedings in such a court brought otherwise than on a complaint;

(e) with respect to preliminary hearings;

(f) for the service outside *the United Kingdom* [England and Wales], in such circumstances and in such manner as may be prescribed, of any notice of proceedings in a magistrates' court;

(g) for the exercise by magistrates' courts, in such circumstances as may be prescribed, of such powers as may be prescribed (even though a party to the proceedings in question is [or resides] outside England and Wales);

(h) enabling the court, in such circumstances as may be prescribed, to proceed on any application even though the respondent has not been given notice of the proceedings;

(i) authorising a single justice to discharge the functions of a magistrates' court with respect to such relevant proceedings as may be prescribed;

(j) authorising a magistrates' court to order any of the parties to such relevant proceedings as may be prescribed, in such circumstances as may be prescribed, to pay the whole or part of the costs of all or any of the other parties.

(3) In subsection (2)—

'notice of proceedings' means a summons or such other notice of proceedings as is required; and 'given', in relation to a summons, means 'served';

'prescribed' means prescribed by the rules; and

'relevant proceedings' means any application made, or proceedings brought, under any of the provisions mentioned in paragraphs (a) to (c) of subsection (1) and any part of such proceedings.

(4) This section and any other power in this Act to make rules of court are not to be taken as in any way limiting any other power of the authority in question to make rules of court.

(5) When making any rules under this section an authority shall be subject to the same requirements as to consultation (if any) as apply when the authority makes rules under its general rule making power.

Note. Words in square brackets in sub-s (1)(f) substituted for words in italics and words in square brackets in sub-s (1)(g) inserted by Courts and Legal Services Act 1990, s 116, Sch 16, para 22, as from 14 October 1991.

94. Appeals—(1) *An* [Subject to any express provisions to the contrary made by or under this Act, an] appeal shall lie to the High Court against—

(a) the making by a magistrates' court of any order under this Act; or

(b) any refusal by a magistrates' court to make such an order.

(2) Where a magistrates' court has power, in relation to any proceedings under this Act, to decline jurisdiction because it considers that the case can more conveniently be dealt with by another court, no appeal shall lie against any exercise by that magistrates' court of that power.

(3) Subsection (1) does not apply in relation to an interim order for periodical payments made under Schedule 1.

(4) On an appeal under this section, the High Court may make such orders as may be necessary to give effect to its determination of the appeal.

(5) Where an order is made under subsection (4) the High Court may also make such incidental or consequential orders as appear to it to be just.

(6) Where an appeal from a magistrates' court relates to an order for the making of periodical payments, the High Court may order that its determination of the appeal shall have effect from such date as it thinks fit to specify in the order.

(7) The date so specified must not be earlier than the earliest date allowed in accordance with rules of court made for the purposes of this section.

(8) Where, on an appeal under this section in respect of an order requiring a person to make periodical payments, the High Court reduces the amount of those payments or discharges the order—

(a) it may order the person entitled to the payments to pay to the person making them such sum in respect of payments already made as the High Courts thinks fit; and

(b) if any arrears are due under the order for periodical payments, it may remit payment of the whole, or part, of those arrears.

(9) Any order of the High Court made on an appeal under this section (other than one directing that an application be re-heard by a magistrates' court) shall, for the purposes—

(a) of the enforcement of the order; and

(b) of any power to vary, revive or discharge orders,

be treated as if it were an order of the magistrates' court from which the appeal was brought and not an order of the High Court.

(10) The Lord Chancellor may by order make provision as to the circumstances in which appeals may be made against decisions taken by courts on questions arising in connection with the transfer, or proposed transfer, of proceedings by virtue of any order under paragraph 2 of Schedule 11.

(11) Except to the extent provided for in any order made under subsection (10), no appeal may be made against any decision of a kind mentioned in that subsection.

Note. Words in square brackets substituted for word in italics by Courts and Legal Services Act 1990, s 116, Sch 16, para 23, as from 14 October 1991.

95. Attendance of child at hearing under Part IV or V—(1) In any proceedings in which a court is hearing an application for an order under Part IV or V, or is considering whether to make any such order, the court may order the child concerned to attend such stage or stages of the proceedings as may be specified in the order.

(2) The power conferred by subsection (1) shall be exercised in accordance with rules of court.

(3) Subsections (4) to (6) apply where—

(a) an order under subsection (1) has not been not complied with; or

(b) the court has reasonable cause to believe that it will not be complied with.

(4) The court may make an order authorising a constable, or such person as may be specified in the order—

(a) to take charge of the child and to bring him to the court; and

(b) to enter and search any premises specified in the order if he has reasonable cause to believe that the child may be found on the premises.

(5) The court may order any person who is in a position to do so to bring the child to the court.

(6) Where the court has reason to believe that a person has information about the whereabouts of the child it may order him to disclose it to the court.

96. Evidence given by, or with respect to, children—(1) Subsection (2) applies where a child who is called as a witness in any civil proceedings does not, in the opinion of the court, understand the nature of an oath.

(2) The child's evidence may be heard by the court if, in its opinion—

(a) he understands that it is his duty to speak the truth; and

(b) he has sufficient understanding to justify his evidence being heard.

(3) The Lord Chancellor may by order make provision for the admissibility of evidence which would otherwise be inadmissible under any rule of law relating to hearsay.

(4) An order under subsection (3) may only be made with respect to—

(a) civil proceedings in general or such civil proceedings, or class of civil proceedings, as may be prescribed; and

(b) evidence in connection with the upbringing, maintenance or welfare of a child.

(5) An order under subsection (3)—

(a) may, in particular, provide for the admissibility of statements which are made orally or in a prescribed form or which are recorded by any prescribed method of recording;

(b) may make different provision for different purposes and in relation to different descriptions of court; and

(c) may make such amendments and repeals in any enactment relating to evidence (other than in this Act) as the Lord Chancellor considers necessary or expedient in consequence of the provision made by the order.

(6) Subsection (5)(b) is without prejudice to section 104(4).

(7) In this section—

'civil proceedings' and 'court' have the same meaning as they have in the Civil Evidence Act 1968 by virtue of section 18 of that Act;

['civil proceedings' means civil proceedings, before any tribunal, in relation to which the strict rules of evidence apply, whether as a matter of law or by agreement of the parties, and references to 'the court' shall be construed accordingly;] and

'prescribed' means prescribed by an order under subsection (3).

Note. Definition in square brackets substituted for definition in italics by Civil Evidence Act 1995, s 15(1), Sch 1, para 16, as from 31 January 1997.

97. Privacy for children involved in certain proceedings—(1) *Rules made under section 144 of the Magistrates' Courts Act 1980* [Family Procedure Rules] may make provision for a magistrates' court to sit in private in proceedings in which any powers under this Act may be exercised by the court with respect to any child.

Note. Words in square brackets substituted for words in italics by the Courts Act 2003, s 109(1), Sch 8, para 337(1), (2), as from a day to be appointed.

(2) No person shall publish any material which is intended, or likely, to identify—

(a) any child as being involved in any proceedings before [the High Court, a county court or] a magistrates' court in which any power under this Act [or the Adoption and Children Act 2002], may be exercised by the court with respect to that or any other child; or

(b) an address or school as being that of a child involved in any such proceedings.

Note. In para (a) words 'the High Court, a county court or' in square brackets inserted by the Access to Justice Act 1999, s 72, as from 27 September 1999, subject to a transitional provision in s 105 of, Sch 14, Pt IV, para 18 to that Act. Words 'or the Adoption and Children Act 2002' in square brackets inserted by the Adoption and Children Act 2002, s 101(3), as from a day to be appointed.

(3) In any proceedings for an offence under this section it shall be a defence for the accused to prove that he did not know, and had no reason to suspect, that the published material was intended, or likely, to identify the child.

(4) The court or the *Secretary of State* [Lord Chancellor] may, if satisfied that the welfare of the child requires it, by order dispense with the requirements of subsection (2) to such extent as may be specified in the order.

Note. Words in square brackets substituted for words in italics by Transfer of Functions (Magistrates' Courts and Family Law) Order 1992, SI 1992 No 709, art 3(2), Sch 2, as from 1 April 1992.

(5) For the purposes of this section—
'publish' includes—
(*a*) *broadcast by radio, television or cable television;*
[(a) include in a programme service (within the meaning of the Broadcasting Act 1990;] or
(b) cause to be published; and
'material' includes any picture or representation.

Note. In definition 'publish' para (a) in square brackets substituted for para (a) in italics by Broadcasting Act 1990, s 203(1), Sch 20, para 53, as from 1 January 1991.

(6) Any person who contravenes this section shall be guilty of an offence and liable, on summary conviction, to a fine not exceeding level 4 on the standard scale.
(7) Subsection (1) is without prejudice to—
(*a*) *the generality of the rule making power in section 144 of the Act of 1980; or*
(b) any other power of a magistrates' court to sit in private.

Note. Sub-s (7)(a) repealed by the Courts Act 2003, s 109(1), (3), Sch 8, para 337(1), (3), Sch 10, as from a day to be appointed.

(8) *Section 71 of the Act of 1980 (newspaper reports of certain proceedings)* [Sections 69 (sittings of magistrates' courts for family proceedings) and 71 (newspaper reports of certain proceedings) of the Act of 1980] shall apply in relation to any proceedings [before a magistrates' court] to which this section applies subject to the provisions of this section.

Note. Words 'sections ... of 1980' in square brackets substituted for words in italics by Courts and Legal Services Act 1990, s 116, Sch 16, para 24, as from 14 October 1991. Words 'before a magistrates' court' in square brackets inserted by the Access to Justice Act 1999, s 72, as from 27 September 1999, subject to a transitional provision in s 105 of, Sch 14, Pt IV, para 18 to that Act.

98. Self-incrimination—(1) In any proceedings in which a court is hearing an application for an order under Part IV or V, no person shall be excused from—
(a) giving evidence on any matter; or
(b) answering any question put to him in the course of his giving evidence,
on the ground that doing so might incriminate him or his spouse of an offence.
(2) A statement or admission made in such proceedings shall not be admissible in evidence against the person making it or his spouse in proceedings for an offence other than perjury.

99. ...

Note. This section repealed by the Access to Justice Act 1999, s 106, Sch 15, Pt 1, as from (repeal of sub-ss (1), (2), (4), (5)): 1 April 2000; (repeal of sub-s (3)): 2 April 2001.

100. Restrictions on use of wardship jurisdiction—(1) Section 7 of the Family Law Reform Act 1969 (which gives the High Court power to place a ward of court in the care, or under the supervision, of a local authority) shall cease to have effect.
(2) No court shall exercise the High Court's inherent jurisdiction with respect to children—
(a) so as to require a child to be placed in the care, or put under the supervision, of a local authority;
(b) so as to require a child to be accommodated by or on behalf of a local authority;
(c) so as to make a child who is the subject of a care order a ward of court; or
(d) for the purpose of conferring on any local authority power to determine any question which has arisen, or which may arise, in connection with any aspect of parental responsibility for a child.
(3) No application for any exercise of the court's inherent jurisdiction with

respect to children may be made by a local authority unless the authority have obtained the leave of the court.

(4) The court may only grant leave if it is satisfied that—

(a) the result which the authority wish to achieve could not be achieved through the making of any order of a kind to which subsection (5) applies; and

(b) there is reasonable cause to believe that if the court's inherent jurisdiction is not exercised with respect to the child he is likely to suffer significant harm.

(5) This subsection applies to any order—

(a) made otherwise than in the exercise of the court's inherent jurisdiction; and

(b) which the local authority is entitled to apply for (assuming, in the case of any application which may only be made with leave, that leave is granted).

101. Effect of orders as between England and Wales and Northern Ireland, the Channel Islands or the Isle of Man—(1) The Secretary of State may make regulations providing—

(a) for prescribed orders which—

   (i) are made by a court in Northern Ireland; and

   (ii) appear to the Secretary of State to correspond in their effect to orders which may be made under any provision of this Act,

   to have effect in prescribed circumstances, for prescribed purposes of this Act, as if they were orders of a prescribed kind made under this Act;

(b) for prescribed orders which—

   (i) are made by a court in England and Wales; and

   (ii) appear to the Secretary of State to correspond in their effect to orders which may be made under any provision in force in Northern Ireland,

   to have effect in prescribed circumstances, for prescribed purposes of the law of Northern Ireland, as if they were orders of a prescribed kind made in Northern Ireland.

(2) Regulations under subsection (1) may provide for the order concerned to cease to have effect for the purposes of the law of Northern Ireland, or (as the case may be) the law of England and Wales, if prescribed conditions are satisfied.

(3) The Secretary of State may make regulations providing for prescribed orders which—

(a) are made by a court in the Isle of Man or in any of the Channel Islands; and

(b) appear to the Secretary of State to correspond in their effect to orders which may be made under this Act,

to have effect in prescribed circumstances for prescribed purposes of this Act, as if they were orders of a prescribed kind made under this Act.

(4) Where a child who is in the care of a local authority is lawfully taken to live in Northern Ireland, the Isle of Man or any of the Channel Islands, the care order in question shall cease to have effect if the conditions prescribed in regulations made by the Secretary of State are satisfied.

(5) Any regulations made under this section may—

(a) make such consequential amendments (including repeals) in—

   (i) section 25 of the Children and Young Persons Act 1969 (transfers between England and Wales and Northern Ireland); or

   (ii) section 26 (transfers between England and Wales and Channel Islands or Isle of Man) of that Act,

   as the Secretary of State considers necessary or expedient; and

(b) modify any provision of this Act, in its application (by virtue of the regulations) in relation to an order made otherwise than in England and Wales.

Search warrants

102. Power of constable to assist in exercise of certain powers to search for children or inspect premises—(1) Where, on an application made by any person for a warrant under this section, it appears to the court—

(a) that a person attempting to exercise powers under any enactment mentioned in subsection (6) has been prevented from doing so by being refused entry to the premises concerned or refused access to the child concerned; or

(b) that any such person is likely to be so prevented from exercising any such powers,

it may issue a warrant authorising any constable to assist that person in the exercise of those powers using reasonable force if necessary.

(2) Every warrant issued under this section shall be addressed to, and executed by, a constable who shall be accompanied by the person applying for the warrant if—

(a) that person so desires; and

(b) the court by whom the warrant is issued does not direct otherwise.

(3) A court granting an application for a warrant under this section may direct that the constable concerned may, in executing the warrant, be accompanied by a registered medical practitioner, registered nurse or *registered health visitor* [registered midwife] if he so chooses.

Note. In sub-s (3) words in square brackets substituted for words in italics by the Nursing and Midwifery Order 2001, SI 2002 No 253, art 54(3), Sch 5, para 10(c), as from 1 August 2004 (the London Gazette, 21 July 2004); for transitional provisions see SI 2002 No 253, Sch 2.

[(3A) The reference in subsection (3) to a registered midwife is to such a midwife who is also registered in the Specialist Community Public Health Nurses' Part of the register maintained under article 5 of the Nursing and Midwifery Order 2001.]

Note. Sub-s (3A) inserted by the Health Act 1999 (Consequential Amendments) (Nursing and Midwifery) Order 2004, SI 2004 No 1771, art 3, Schedule, Pt 1, para 4(c), as from 1 August 2004.

(4) An application for a warrant under this section shall be made in the manner and form prescribed by rules of court.

(5) Where—

(a) an application for a warrant under this section relates to a particular child; and

(b) it is reasonably practicable to do so,

the application and any warrant granted on the application shall name the child; and where it does not name him it shall describe him as clearly as possible.

(6) The enactments are—

(a) sections 62, 64, 67, 76, [79U,] 80, 86 and 87;

(b) paragraph 8(1)(b) and (2)(b) of Schedule 3;

(c) *section 33 of the Adoption Act 1976 (duty of local authority to secure that protected children are visited from time to time).*

Note. In sub-s (6)(a) reference to '79U,' in square brackets inserted by the Care Standards Act 2000, s 116, Sch 4, para 14(1), (22), as from (in relation to Wales): 1 April 2002 (SI 2002 No 920); (in relation to England): to be appointed. Para (c) repealed by the Adoption Act 2002, s 139(1), (3), Sch 3, paras 54, 69, Sch 5, as from a day to be appointed.

General

103. Offences by bodies corporate—(1) This section applies where any offence under this Act is committed by a body corporate.

(2) If the offence is proved to have been committed with the consent or connivance of or to be attributable to any neglect on the part of any director, manager, secretary or other similar officer of the body corporate, or any person who was purporting to act in any such capacity, he (as well as the body corporate)

shall be guilty of the offence and shall be liable to be proceeded against and punished accordingly.

104. Regulations and orders—(1) Any power of the Lord Chancellor [, the Treasury] or the Secretary of State under this Act to make an order, regulations, or rules, except an order under section ... 56(4)(a), 57(3), 84 or 97 or paragraph 1(1) of Schedule 4, shall be exercisable by statutory instrument.

Note. Words ', the Treasury' in square brackets inserted by the Tax Credits Act 2002, s 47, Sch 3, paras 15–19, as from 6 April 2003 (SI 2003 No 962); for savings see arts 3–5 thereof. Reference omitted repealed by the Care Standards Act 2000, s 117(2), Sch 6, as from 1 April 2002 (SI 2001 No 4150, SI 2002 No 920).

(2) Any such statutory instrument, except one made under section [4(1B),] 17(4), 107 or 108(2), shall be subject to annulment in pursuance of a resolution of either House of Parliament.

(3) An order under section [4(1B) or] 17(4), shall not be made unless a draft of it has been laid before, and approved by a resolution of, each House of Parliament.

Note. In sub-ss (2), (3) words in square brackets inserted by the Adoption and Children Act 2002, s 111(6)(a), (b), as from 1 December 2003 (SI 2003 No 3079).

(4) Any statutory instrument made under this Act may—
(a) make different provision for different cases;
(b) provide for exemptions from any of its provisions; and
(c) contain such incidental, supplemental and transitional provisions as the person making it considers expedient.

105. Interpretation—(1) In this Act—
'adoption agency' means a body which may be referred to as an adoption agency by virtue of *section 1 of the Adoption Act 1976* [section 2 of the Adoption and Children Act 2002];

Note. Words in square brackets substituted for words in italics by the Adoption and Children Act 2002, s 139(1), Sch 3, para 70 as from a day to be appointed.

['appropriate children's home' has the meaning given by section 23;]

Note. Above definition inserted by the Care Standards Act 2000, s 116, Sch 4, para 14(1), (23)(a)(i), as from (in relation to England): 1 April 2002 (SI 2001 No 4150); for transitional provisions see arts 3(2), 4(1), (3), (4) thereof; (in relation to Wales): 1 April 2002 (SI 2002 No 920); for transitional provisions see arts 2, 3(2), (4), (6)–(10), Sch 1 thereto.

'bank holiday' means a day which is a bank holiday under the Banking and Financial Dealings Act 1971;
['care home' has the same meaning as in the Care Standards Act 2000;]

Note. Above definition inserted by the Care Standards Act 2000, s 116, Sch 4, para 14(1), (23)(a)(ii), as from (in relation to England): 1 April 2002 (SI 2001 No 4150); for transitional provisions see arts 3(2), 4(1), (3), (4) thereof; (in relation to Wales): 1 April 2002 (SI 2002 No 920); for transitional provisions see arts 2, 3(2), (4), (6)–(10), Sch 1 thereto.

'care order' has the meaning given by section 31(11) and also includes any order which by or under any enactment has the effect of, or is deemed to be, a care order for the purposes of this Act; and any reference to a child who is in the care of an authority is a reference to a child who is in their care by virtue of a care order;
'child' means, subject to paragraph 16 of Schedule 1, a person under the age of eighteen;
'child assessment order' has the meaning given by section 43(2);
'child minder' has the meaning given by section 71;

Note. Above definition repealed by the Care Standards Act 2000, s 117(2), Sch 6, as (in relation to Wales): 1 April 2002 (SI 2002 No 920); for transitional provisions see arts 2, 3(2), (4), (5)–(10), Sch 1 thereto; (in relation to England): to be appointed.

'child of the family', in relation to the parties to a marriage, means—
    (a) a child of both of those parties;
    (b) any other child, not being a child who is placed with those parties as foster parents by a local authority or voluntary organisation, who has been treated by both of those parties as a child of their family;
'children's home' has the same meaning as in section 63;]
['children's home' has the meaning given by section 23;]

Note. Above definition substituted by the Care Standards Act 2000, s 116, Sch 4, para 14(1), (23)(a)(iii), as from (in relation to England): 1 April 2002 (SI 2001 No 4150); for transitional provisions see arts 3(2), 4(1), (3), (4) thereof; (in relation to Wales): 1 April 2002 (SI 2002 No 920); for transitional provisions see arts 2, 3(2), (4), (6)–(10), Sch 1 thereto.

'community home' has the meaning given by section 53;
'contact order' has the meaning given by section 8(1);
'day care' [(except in Part XA)] has the same meaning as in section 18;

Note. In definition 'day care' words in square brackets inserted by the Care Standards Act 2000, s 116, Sch 4, para 14(1), (23)(a)(iv), as from (in relation to England): 2 July 2001 (SI 2001 No 2041); (in relation to Wales): 1 April 2002 (SI 2002 No 920); for transitional provisions see arts 2, 3(2), (4), (6)–(10), Schs 1, 2 thereto.

'disabled', in relation to a child, has the same meaning as in section 17(11);
...

Note. Definition 'district health authority' (omitted) repealed by the Health Authorities Act 1995, ss 2(1), 5(1), Sch 1, para 118(10)(a), Sch 3, as from 28 June 1995 in so far as is necessary for enabling the making of any regulations, orders, directions, schemes or appointments, and as from 1 April 1996 otherwise.

'domestic premises' has the meaning given by section 71(12);
[dwelling-house' includes—
    (a) any building or part of a building which is occupied as a dwelling;
    (b) any caravan, house-boat or structure which is occupied as a dwelling;
    and any yard, garden, garage or outhouse belonging to it and occupied with it;]

Note. Above definition inserted by the Family Law Act 1996, s 52, Sch 6, para 5, as from 1 October 1997 (SI 1997 No 1892).

'education supervision order' has the meaning given in section 36;
'emergency protection order' means an order under section 44;
'family assistance order' has the meaning given in section 16(2);
'family proceedings' has the meaning given by section 8(3);
'functions' includes powers and duties;
'guardian of a child' means a guardian (other than a guardian of the estate of a child) appointed in accordance with the provisions of section 5;
'harm' has the same meaning as in section 31(9) and the question of whether harm is significant shall be determined in accordance with section 31(10);
'health authority' means any district health authority and any special health authority established under the National Health Service Act 1977;
['Health Authority' means a Health Authority established under section 8 of the National Health Service Act 1977;]

Note. Above definition substituted by the Health Authorities Act 1995, ss 2(1), 5(1), Sch 1, para 118(10)(b), as from 28 June 1995 in so far as is necessary for enabling the making of any regulations, orders, directions, schemes or appointments, and as from 1 April 1996 otherwise.

'health service hospital' has the same meaning as in the National Health Service Act 1977;

'hospital' [(except in Schedule 9A)] has the same meaning as in the Mental
Health Act 1983, except that it does not include a *special hospital within the
meaning of that Act* [hospital at which high security psychiatric services within
the meaning of that Act are provided];

Note. In definition 'hospital' words '(except in Schedule 9A)' in square brackets inserted by
the Care Standards Act 2000, s 116, Sch 4, para 14(1), (23)(a)(v), as from (in relation to
England): 2 July 2001 (SI 2001 No 4150); (in relation to Wales): 1 April 2002 (SI 2002 No
920); for transitional provisions see arts 2, 3(2), (4), (6)–(10), Schs 1, 2 thereto. Words
'hospital at...are provided' in square brackets substituted for words in italics by the Health Act
1999 (Supplementary , Consequential etc Provisions) Order 2000, SI 2000 No 90, arts 2(1),
3(2), Sch 2, para 5, as from 1 April 2000.

'ill-treatment' has the same meaning as in section 31(9);
['income-based jobseeker's allowance' has the same meaning as in the
Jobseekers Act 1995;]

Note. Above definition inserted by the Jobseekers Act 1995, s 41(4), Sch 2, para 19(4), as
from 7 October 1996.

['independent hospital' has the same meaning as in the Care Standards Act
2000;]

Note. Above definition inserted by the Care Standards Act 2000, s 116, Sch 4, para 14(1),
(23)(a)(iv), as from (in relation to England): 1 April 2002 (SI 2001 No 4150); for transitional
provisions see arts 3(2) (as amended by SI 2002/1493, art 6), 4(1), (3), (4) thereof and SI
2002 No 1493, art 4; (in relation to Wales): 1 April 2002 (SI 2002 No 920); for transitional
provisions see arts 2, 3(2), (4), (6)–(10), Sch 1 thereto.

'independent school' has the same meaning as in *the Education Act 1944* [the
Education Act 1996];

Note. In above definition words in square brackets substituted for words in italics by the
Education Act 1996, s 582(1), Sch 37, para 91, as from 1 November 1996.

'local authority' means, in relation to England ... , the council of a county, a
metropolitan district, a London Borough or the Common Council of the
City of London[, in relation to Wales, the council of a county or a county
borough] and, in relation to Scotland, a local authority within the meaning
of section 1(2) of the Social Work (Scotland) Act 1968;

Note. In above definition words omitted repealed and words in square brackets inserted by
the Local Government (Wales) Act 1994, ss 22(4), 66(8), Sch 10, para 13, Sch 18, as from
1 April 1996.

'local authority foster parent' has the same meaning as in section 23(3);
'local education authority' has the same meaning as in *the Education Act 1944*
[the Education Act 1996];

Note. In above definition words in square brackets substituted for words in italics by the
Education Act 1996, s 582(1), Sch 37, para 91, as from 1 November 1996.

'local housing authority' has the same meaning as in the Housing Act 1985;
...
...

Note. Definitions 'mental nursing home' and 'nursing home' (omitted) repealed by the
Care Standards Act 2000, s 117(2), Sch 6, as from (in relation to England): 1 April 2002 (SI
2001 No 4150); for transitional provisions see arts 3(2)(as amended by SI 2002 No 1493, art
6), 4(1)–(3), (5) thereof and SI 2002 No 1493, art 4; (in relation to Wales): 1 April 2002 (SI
2002 No 920); for transitional provisions see arts 2, 3(2), (5)–(10), Sch 1 thereto.

['officer of the Service' has the same meaning as in the Criminal Justice and
Court Services Act 2000;]

Note. Above definition inserted by the Criminal Justice and Court Services Act 2000, s 74,
Sch 7, Pt 2, paras 87, 95, as from 1 April 2001 (SI 2001 No 919).

'parental responsibility' has the meaning given in section 3;
'parental responsibility agreement' has the meaning given in *section 4(1)*
[sections 4(1) and 4A(2)];

Note. In definition 'parental responsibility agreement' words in square brackets substituted for words in italics by the Adoption and Children Act 2002, s 139(1), Sch 3, paras 54, 70(c), as from a day to be appointed.

'prescribed' means prescribed by regulations made under this Act;
['private children's home' means a children's home in respect of which a person
is registered under Part II of the Care Standards Act 2000 which is not a
community home or a voluntary home;]

Note. Above definition inserted by the Care Standards Act 2000, s 116, Sch 4, para 14(1), (23)(a)(iv), as from (in relation to England): 1 April 2002 (SI 2001 No 4150); for transitional provisions see arts 3(2) (as amended by SI 2002 No 1493, art 6), 4(1), (3), (4) and SI 2002 No 1493, art 4; (in relation to Wales): 1 April 2002 (SI 2002 No 920); for transitional provisions see arts 2, 3(2), (5)–(10), Sch 1 thereto.

['Primary Care Trust' means a Primary Care Trust established under section
16A of the National Health Service Act 1977;]

Note. Above definition inserted by the Health Act 1999 (Supplementary, Consequential etc Provisions) Order 2000, SI 2000 No 90, arts 2(1), 3(1), Sch 1, para 24(1), (10), as from 8 February 2000.

'privately fostered child' and 'to foster a child privately' have the same meaning
as in section 66;
'prohibited steps order' has the meaning given by section 8(1);
'protected child' has the same meaning as in Part III of the Adoption Act 1976;

Note. Above definition repealed by the Adoption and Children Act 2002, s 139(1), (3), Sch 3, paras 54, 70(d), Sch 5, as from a day to be appointed.

...

Note. Definition 'registered children's home' (omitted) repealed by the Care Standards Act 2000, s 117(2), Sch 6, as from (in relation to England): 1 April 2002 (SI 2001 No 4150); for transitional provisions see arts 3(2) (as amended by SI 2002 No 1493, art 6), 4(1), (3)–(5) and SI 2002 No 1493, art 4; (in relation to Wales): 1 April 2002 (SI 2002 No 920); for transitional provisions see arts 2, 3(2), (5)–(10), Schs 1, 3 thereto.

'registered pupil' has the same meaning as in *the Education Act 1944* [the
Education Act 1996];

Note. In above definition words in square brackets substituted for words in italics by the Education Act 1996, s 582(1), Sch 37, para 91, as from 1 November 1996.

'relative', in relation to a child, means a grandparent, brother, sister, uncle or
aunt (whether of the full blood or half blood or by affinity) or step-parent;
'residence order' has the meaning given by section 8(1);
...

Note. Definition 'residential care home' (omitted) repealed by the Care Standards Act 2000, s 117(2), Sch 6, as from as from (in relation to England): 1 April 2002 (SI 2001 No 4150); for transitional provisions see arts 3(2) (as amended by SI 2002 No 1493, art 6), 4(1), (3)–(5) and SI 2002 No 1493, art 4; (in relation to Wales): 1 April 2002 (SI 2002 No 920); for transitional provisions see arts 2, 3(2), (5)–(10), Sch 1 thereto.

'responsible person', in relation to a child who is the subject of a supervision
order, has the meaning given in paragraph 1 of Schedule 3;
'school' has the same meaning as in *the Education Act 1944* [the Education Act
1996] or, in relation to Scotland, in the Education (Scotland) Act 1980;

Note. In above definition words in square brackets substituted for words in italics by the Education Act 1996, s 582(1), Sch 37, para 91, as from 1 November 1996.

['section 31A plan' has the meaning given by section 31A(6);]

3406   Children Act 1989, s 105

Note. Above definition inserted by the Adoption and Children Act 2002, s 139(1), Sch 3, paras 54, 70(b), as from a day to be appointed.

'service', in relation to any provision made under Part III, includes any facility;

'signed', in relation to any person, includes the making by that person of his mark;

'special educational needs' has the same meaning as in *the Education Act 1981 [1993]* [the Education Act 1996];

Note. In above definition reference to '1993' in square brackets substituted for '1981' by the Education Act 1993, s 307, Sch 19, para 150, as from 1 January 1994. Words 'the Education Act 1996' in square brackets substituted for words in italics by the Education Act 1996, s 582(1), Sch 37, para 91, as from 1 November 1996.

['special guardian' and 'special guardianship order' have the meaning given by section 14A;]

Note. Above definition inserted by the Adoption and Children Act 2002, s 139(1), Sch 3, paras 54, 70(e), as from a day to be appointed.

'special health authority' has the same meaning as in the National Health Service Act 1977;

['Special Health Authority' means a Special Health Authority established under section 11 of the National Health Service Act 1977;]

Note. Above definition substituted by the Health Authorities Act 1995, ss 2(1), 5(1), Sch 1, para 118, Sch 3, as from 28 June 1995 in so far as is necessary for enabling the making of any regulations, orders, directions, schemes or appointments, and as from 1 April 1996 otherwise.

'specific issue order' has the meaning given by section 8(1);

['Strategic Health Authority' means a Strategic Health Authority established under section 8 of the National Health Service Act 1977;]

Note. Above definition inserted by the National Health Service Reform and Health Care Professions Act 2002 (Supplementary, Consequential etc, Provisions) Regulations 2002, SI 2002 No 2469, reg 4, Sch 1, Pt 1, para 16(1), (3), as from 1 October 2002.

'supervision order' has the meaning given by section 31(11);

'supervised child' and 'supervisor', in relation to a supervision order or an education supervision order, mean respectively the child who is (or is to be) under supervision and the person under whose supervision he is (or is to be) by virtue of the order;

'upbringing', in relation to any child, includes the care of the child but not his maintenance;

'voluntary home' has the meaning given by section 60;

'voluntary organisation' means a body (other than a public or local authority) whose activities are not carried on for profit.

(2) References in this Act to a child whose father and mother were, or (as the case may be) were not, married to each other at the time of his birth must be read with section 1 of the Family Law Reform Act 1987 (which extends the meaning of such references).

(3) References in this Act to—

(a) a person with whom a child lives, or is to live, as the result of a residence order; or

(b) a person in whose favour a residence order is in force,

shall be construed as references to the person named in the order as the person with whom the child is to live.

(4) References in this Act to a child who is looked after by a local authority have the same meaning as they have (by virtue of section 22) in Part III.

(5) References in this Act to accommodation provided by or on behalf of a local authority are references to accommodation so provided in the exercise of functions

which stand referred to the social services committee of that or any other local authority under [of that or any other local authority which are social services functions within the meaning of] the Local Authority Social Services Act 1970.

Note. In sub-s (5) words in square brackets substituted for words in italics by the Local Government Act 2000, s 107, Sch 5, para 22, as from 26 October 2000, as from (in relation to England): 26 October 2000; (in relation to Wales): 28 July 2001.

[(5A) References in this Act to a child minder shall be construed—

(a) ...;

(b) in relation to England and Wales, in accordance with section 79A.]

Note. Sub-s (5A) inserted by the Care Standards Act 2000, s 116, Sch 4, para 14(1), (23)(b), as from (in relation to England): 2 July 2001 (SI 2001 No 2041); (in relation to Wales): 1 April 2002 (SI 2002 No 920). Para (b) repealed by the Regulation of Care (Scotland) Act 2001, s 79, Sch 3, para 15(1), (2)(a), as from 1 April 2002 (SSI 2002 No 162); for transitional provisions arts 3, 4(6), (9), (10), 7, 8(c), 12, 13 thereof.

(6) In determining the 'ordinary residence' of a child for any purpose of this Act, there shall be disregarded any period in which he lives in any place—

(a) which is a school or other institution;

(b) in accordance with the requirements of a supervision order under this Act or an order under *section 7(7)(b) of the Children and Young Persons Act 1969;* [section 63(1) of the Powers of Criminal Courts (Sentencing) Act 2000] or

(c) while he is being provided with accommodation by or on behalf of a local authority.

Note. In para (b) words in square brackets substituted for words in italics by the Powers of Criminal Courts (Sentencing) Act 2000, s 165(1), Sch 9, para 129, as from 25 August 2000.

(7) References in this Act to children who are in need shall be construed in accordance with section 17.

(8) Any notice or other document required under this Act to be served on any person may be served on him by being delivered personally to him, or being sent by post to him in a registered letter or by the recorded delivery service at his proper address.

(9) Any such notice or other document required to be served on a body corporate or a firm shall be duly served if it is served on the secretary or clerk of that body or a partner of that firm.

(10) For the purposes of this section, and of section 7 of the Interpretation Act 1978 in its application to this section, the proper address of a person—

(a) in the case of a secretary or clerk of a body corporate, shall be that of the registered or principal office of that body;

(b) in the case of a partner of a firm, shall be that of the principal office of the firm; and

(c) in any other case, shall be the last known address of the person to be served.

106. Financial provisions—(1) Any—

(a) grants made by the Secretary of State under this Act; and

(b) any other expenses incurred by the Secretary of State under this Act, shall be payable out of money provided by Parliament.

(2) Any sums received by the Secretary of State under section 58, or by way of the repayment of any grant made under section 82(2) or (4) shall be paid into the Consolidated Fund.

107. Application to Channel Islands. Her Majesty may by Order in Council direct that any of the provisions of this Act shall extend to any of the Channel Islands with such exceptions and modifications as may be specified in the Order.

108. Short title, commencement, extent etc—(1) This Act may be cited as the Children Act 1989.

(2) Sections 89 and 96(3) to (7), and paragraph 35 of Schedule 12, shall come into force on the passing of this Act and paragraph 36 of Schedule 12 shall come into force at the end of the period of two months beginning with the day on which this Act is passed but otherwise this Act shall come into force on such date as may be appointed by order made by the Lord Chancellor or the Secretary of State, or by both acting jointly.

(3) Different dates may be appointed for different provisions of this Act and in relation to different cases.

(4) The minor amendments set out in Schedule 12 shall have effect.

(5) The consequential amendments set out in Schedule 13 shall have effect.

(6) The transitional provisions and savings set out in Schedule 14 shall have effect.

(7) The repeals set out in Schedule 15 shall have effect.

(8) An order under subsection (2) may make such transitional provisions or savings as appear to the person making the order to be necessary or expedient in connection with the provisions brought into force by the order, including—

(a) provisions adding to or modifying the provisions of Schedule 14; and

(b) such adaptations—

(i) of the provisions brought into force by the order; and

(ii) of any provisions of this Act then in force,

as appear to him necessary or expedient in consequence of the partial operation of this Act.

(9) The Lord Chancellor may by order make such amendments or repeals, in such enactments as may be specified in the order, as appear to him to be necessary or expedient in consequence of any provision of this Act.

(10) This Act shall, in its application to the Isles of Scilly, have effect subject to such exceptions, adaptations and modifications as the Secretary of State may by order prescribe.

(11) The following provisions of this Act extend to Scotland—

section 19;

section 25(8);

section 50(13);

Part X;

section 80(1)(h) and (i), (2) to (4), (5)(a), (b) and (h) and (6) to (12);

section 88;

section 104 (so far as necessary);

section 105 (so far as necessary);

subsections (1) to (3), (8) and (9) and this subsection;

in Schedule 2, paragraph 24;

in Schedule 12, paragraphs 1, 7 to 10, 18, 27, 30(a) and 41 to 44;

in Schedule 13, paragraphs 18 to 23, 32, 46, 47, 50, 57, 62, 63, 68(a) and (b) and 71;

in Schedule 14, paragraphs 1, 33 and 34;

in Schedule 15, the entries relating to—

(a) the Custody of Children Act 1891;

(b) the Nurseries and Child Minders Regulation Act 1948;

(c) section 53(3) of the Children and Young Persons Act 1963;

(d) section 60 of the Health Services and Public Health Act 1968;

(e) the Social Work (Scotland) Act 1968;

(f) the Adoption (Scotland) Act 1978;

(g) the Child Care Act 1980;

(h) the Foster Children (Scotland) Act 1984;

(i) the Child Abduction and Custody Act 1985; and

(j) the Family Law Act 1986.

(12) The following provisions of this Act extend to Northern Ireland—

section 50;

section 101(1)(b), (2) and (5)(a)(i);

subsections (1) to (3), (8) and (9) and this subsection;
in Schedule 2, paragraph 24;
in Schedule 12, paragraphs 7 to 10, 18 and 27;
in Schedule 13, paragraphs 21, 22, 46, 47, 57, 62, 63, 68(c) to (e), and 69 to 71;
in Schedule 14, paragraphs *18*, 28 to 30 and 38(a); and
in Schedule 15, the entries relating to the Guardianship of Minors Act 1971, the Children Act 1975, the Child Care Act 1980 and the Family Law Act 1986.

Commencement. With the exception of ss 89, 96(3)–(7), 108, Sch 12, para 35, which came into force on 16 November 1989 (s 108(2)) and Sch 12, para 36, which came into force on 16 January 1990 (s 108(2)), the whole of this Act was brought into force on 14 October 1991 (SI 1991 No 828).

Note. Reference to '18' in sub-s (12) repealed by Courts and Legal Services Act 1990, ss 116, 125(7), Sch 16, para 25, Sch 20, as from 14 October 1991.

SCHEDULES

SCHEDULE 1   Section 15(1)

FINANCIAL PROVISION FOR CHILDREN

Orders for financial relief against parents

1.—(1) On an application made by a parent *or guardian* [, guardian or special guardian] of a child, or by any person in whose favour a residence order is in force with respect to a child, the court may—
  (a) in the case of an application to the High Court or a county court, make one or more of the orders mentioned in sub-paragraph (2);
  (b) in the case of an application to a magistrates' court, make one or both of the orders mentioned in paragraphs (a) and (c) of that sub-paragraph.
  (2) The orders referred to in sub-paragraph (1) are—
  (a) an order requiring either or both parents of a child—
      (i) to make to the applicant for the benefit of the child; or
      (ii) to make to the child himself,
    such periodical payments, for such term, as may be specified in the order;
  (b) an order requiring either or both parents of a child—
      (i) to secure to the applicant for the benefit of the child; or
      (ii) to secure to the child himself,
    such periodical payments, for such term, as may be so specified;
  (c) an order requiring either or both parents of a child—
      (i) to pay to the applicant for the benefit of the child; or
      (ii) to pay to the child himself,
    such lump sum as may be so specified;
  (d) an order requiring a settlement to be made for the benefit of the child, and to the satisfaction of the court, of property—
      (i) to which either parent is entitled (either in possession or in reversion); and
      (ii) which is specified in the order;
  (e) an order requiring either or both parents of a child—
      (i) to transfer to the applicant, for the benefit of the child; or
      (ii) to transfer to the child himself,
    such property to which the parent is, or the parents are, entitled (either in possession or in reversion) as may be specified in the order.
  (3) The powers conferred by this paragraph may be exercised at any time.
  (4) An order under sub-paragraph (2)(a) or (b) may be varied or discharged by a subsequent order made on the application of any person by or to whom payments were required to be made under the previous order.
  (5) Where a court makes an order under this paragraph—

    (a) it may at any time make a further such order under sub-paragraph (2)(a), (b) or (c) with respect to the child concerned if he has not reached the age of eighteen;

    (b) it may not make more than one order under sub-paragraph (2)(d) or (e) against the same person in respect of the same child.

    (6) On making, varying or discharging a residence order [special guardianship order] the court may exercise any of its powers under this Schedule even though no application has been made to it under this Schedule.

    [(7) Where a child is a ward of court, the court may exercise any of its powers under this Schedule even though no application has been made to it.]

Note. Words in square brackets in sub-para (1) substituted for words in italics and words in square brackets in sub-para (6) inserted by the Adoption and Children Act 2002, s 139(1), Sch 3, paras 54, 71, as from a day to be appointed. Sub-para (7) added by Courts and Legal Services Act 1990, s 116, Sch 16, para 10(2), as from 14 October 1991.

Orders for financial relief for persons over eighteen

2.—(1) If, on an application by a person who has reached the age of eighteen, it appears to the court—

    (a) that the applicant is, will be or (if an order were made under this paragraph) would be receiving instruction at an educational establishment or undergoing training for a trade, profession or vocation, whether or not while in gainful employment; or

    (b) that there are special circumstances which justify the making of an order under this paragraph,

the court may make one or both of the orders mentioned in sub-paragraph (2).

    (2) The orders are—

    (a) an order requiring either or both of the applicant's parents to pay to the applicant such periodical payments, for such term, as may be specified in the order;

    (b) an order requiring either or both of the applicant's parents to pay to the applicant such lump sum as may be so specified.

    (3) An application may not be made under this paragraph by any person if, immediately before he reached the age of sixteen, a periodical payments order was in force with respect to him.

    (4) No order shall be made under this paragraph at a time when the parents of the applicant are living with each other in the same household.

    (5) An order under sub-paragraph (2)(a) may be varied or discharged by a subsequent order made on the application of any person by or to whom payments were required to be made under the previous order.

    (6) In sub-paragraph (3) 'periodical payments order' means an order made under—

    (a) this Schedule;

    (*b*) *section 6(3) of the Family Law Reform Act 1969;*

    (c) section 23 or 27 of the Matrimonial Causes Act 1973;

    (d) Part I of the Domestic Proceedings and Magistrates' Courts Act 1978,

for the making or securing of periodical payments.

    (7) The powers conferred by this paragraph shall be exercisable at any time.

    (8) Where the court makes an order under this paragraph it may from time to time while that order remains in force make a further such order.

Note. Sub-para (6)(b) repealed by Child Support Act 1991, s 58(14), as from 25 July 1991.

Duration of orders for financial relief

3.—(1) The term to be specified in an order for periodical payments made under paragraph 1(2)(a) or (b) in favour of a child may begin with the date of the making of an application for the order in question or any later date [or a date ascertained in accordance with sub-paragraph (5) or (6)] but—

  (a) shall not in the first instance extend beyond the child's seventeenth birthday unless the court thinks it right in the circumstances of the case to specify a later date; and

  (b) shall not in any event extend beyond the child's eighteenth birthday.

(2) Paragraph (b) of sub-paragraph (1) shall not apply in the case of a child if it appears to the court that—

  (a) the child is, or will be or (if an order were made without complying with that paragraph) would be receiving instruction at an educational establishment or undergoing training for a trade, profession or vocation, whether or not while in gainful employment; or

  (b) there are special circumstances which justify the making of an order without complying with that paragraph.

(3) An order for periodical payments made under paragraph 1(2)(a) or 2(2)(a) shall, notwithstanding anything in the order, cease to have effect on the death of the person liable to make payments under the order.

(4) Where an order is made under paragraph 1(2)(a) or (b) requiring periodical payments to be made or secured to the parent of a child, the order shall cease to have effect if—

  (a) any parent making or securing the payments; and

  (b) any parent to whom the payments are made or secured,

live together for a period of more than six months.

  [(5) Where—

  (a) a *maintenance assessment* [maintenance calculation] ('the *current assessment*' [current calculation]) is in force with respect to a child; and

  (b) an application is made for an order under paragraph 1(2)(a) or (b) of this Schedule for periodical payments in favour of that child—

    (i) in accordance with section 8 of the Child Support Act 1991; and

    (ii) before the end of the period of 6 months beginning with the making of the *current assessment* [current calculation],

the term to be specified in any such order made on that application may be expressed to begin on, or at any time after, the earliest permitted date.

(6) For the purposes of subsection (5) above, 'the earliest permitted date' is whichever is the later of—

  (a) the date 6 months before the application is made; or

  (b) the date on which the *current assessment* [current calculation] took effect or, where successive *maintenance assessments* [maintenance calculations] have been continuously in force with respect to a child, on which the first of *those assessments* [those calculations] took effect.

(7) Where—

  (a) a *maintenance assessment* [maintenance calculation] ceases to have effect *or is cancelled* by or under any provision of the Child Support Act 1991, and

  (b) an application is made, before the end of the period of 6 months beginning with the relevant date, for an order for periodical payments under paragraph 1(2)(a) or (b) in favour of a child with respect to whom that *maintenance assessment* [maintenance calculation] was in force immediately before it ceased to have effect *or was cancelled,*

the term to be specified in any such order, or in any interim order under paragraph 9, made on that application may begin with the date on which that maintenance assessment ceased to have effect *or, as the case may be, the date with effect from which it was cancelled,* or any later date.

(8) In subsection (7)(b)—

  (a) where the *maintenance assessment* [maintenance calculation] ceased to have effect, the relevant date is the date on which it so ceased; *and*

   (b)   where the maintenance assessment was cancelled, the relevant date is the later of—
      (i)   the date on which the person who cancelled it did so, and
      (ii)   the date from which the cancellation first had effect.]

Note. Words 'or a date ... or (6)' in square brackets in sub-para (1), and sub-paras (5)–(8) added by Maintenance Orders (Backdating) Order 1993, SI 1993 No 623, art 2, Sch 1, paras 10, 11, as from 5 April 1993. Words 'maintenance calculation' in square brackets in sub-paras (5)(a), (7), (8)(a), words 'current calculation' in square brackets in sub-paras (5)(a), (b)(ii), (6)(b) and words 'maintenance calculations' and 'those calculations' in square brackets in sub-para (6)(b) substituted for words in italics by the Child Support, Pensions and Social Security Act 2000, s 26, Sch 3, para 10(1), (2), as from (in relation to certain cases): 3 March 2003 (SI 2003 No 192); (for remaining purposes): to be appointed. In sub-paras (7), (8)(a) words in italics repealed and sub-para (8)(b) repealed by the Child Support, Pensions and Social Security Act 2000, s 85, Sch 9, Pt 1, as from (in relation to certain cases): 3 March 2003 (SI 2003 No 192): (for remaining purposes): to be appointed.

Matters to which court is to have regard in making orders for financial relief

4.—(1) In deciding whether to exercise its powers under paragraph 1 or 2, and if so in what manner, the court shall have regard to all the circumstances including—
   (a)   the income, earning capacity, property and other financial resources which each person mentioned in sub-paragraph (4) has or is likely to have in the foreseeable future;
   (b)   the financial needs, obligations and responsibilities which each person mentioned in sub-paragraph (4) has or is likely to have in the foreseeable future;
   (c)   the financial needs of the child;
   (d)   the income, earning capacity (if any), property and other financial resources of the child;
   (e)   any physical or mental disability of the child;
   (f)   the manner in which the child was being, or was expected to be, educated or trained.
   (2) In deciding whether to exercise its powers under paragraph 1 against a person who is not the mother or father of the child, and if so in what manner, the court shall in addition have regard to—
   (a)   whether that person had assumed responsibility for the maintenance of the child and, if so, the extent to which and basis on which he assumed that responsibility and the length of the period during which he met that responsibility;
   (b)   whether he did so knowing that the child was not his child;
   (c)   the liability of any other person to maintain the child.
   (3) Where the court makes an order under paragraph 1 against a person who is not the father of the child, it shall record in the order that the order is made on the basis that the person against whom the order is made is not the child's father.
   (4) The persons mentioned in sub-paragraph (1) are—
   (a)   in relation to a decision whether to exercise its powers under paragraph 1, any parent of the child;
   (b)   in relation to a decision whether to exercise its powers under paragraph 2, the mother and father of the child;
   (c)   the applicant for the order;
   (d)   any other person in whose favour the court proposes to make the order.

Provisions relating to lump sums

5.—(1) Without prejudice to the generality of paragraph 1, an order under that paragraph for the payment of a lump sum may be made for the purpose of enabling any liabilities or expenses—

(a) incurred in connection with the birth of the child or in maintaining the child; and

(b) reasonably incurred before the making of the order,

to be met.

(2) The amount of any lump sum required to be paid by an order made by a magistrates' court under paragraph 1 or 2 shall not exceed £1000 or such larger amount as the *Secretary of State* [Lord Chancellor] may from time to time by order fix for the purposes of this sub-paragraph.

(3) The power of the court under paragraph 1 or 2 to vary or discharge an order for the making or securing of periodical payments by a parent shall include power to make an order under that provision for the payment of a lump sum by that parent.

(4) The amount of any lump sum which a parent may be required to pay by virtue of sub-paragraph (3) shall not, in the case of an order made by a magistrates' court, exceed the maximum amount that may at the time of the making of the order be required to be paid under sub-paragraph (2), but a magistrates' court may make an order for the payment of a lump sum not exceeding that amount even though the parent was required to pay a lump sum by a previous order under this Act.

(5) An order made under paragraph 1 or 2 for the payment of a lump sum may provide for the payment of that sum by instalments.

(6) Where the court provides for the payment of a lump sum by instalments the court, on an application made either by the person liable to pay or the person entitled to receive that sum, shall have power to vary that order by varying—

(a) the number of instalments payable;

(b) the amount of any instalment payable;

(c) the date on which any instalment becomes payable.

Note. Words in square brackets in sub-para (2) substituted for words in italics by Transfer of Functions (Magistrates' Courts and Family Law) Order 1992, SI 1992 No 709, art 3(2), Sch 2, as from 1 April 1992.

Variation etc of orders for periodical payments

6.—(1) In exercising its powers under paragraph 1 or 2 to vary or discharge an order for the making or securing of periodical payments the court shall have regard to all the circumstances of the case, including any change in any of the matters to which the court was required to have regard when making the order.

(2) The power of the court under paragraph 1 or 2 to vary an order for the making or securing of periodical payments shall include power to suspend any provision of the order temporarily and to revive any provision so suspended.

(3) Where on an application under paragraph 1 or 2 for the variation or discharge of an order for the making or securing of periodical payments the court varies the payments required to be made under that order, the court may provide that the payments as so varied shall be made from such date as the court may specify, *not being* [except that, subject so sub-paragraph (9), the date shall not be] earlier than the date of the making of the application.

(4) An application for the variation of an order made under paragraph 1 for the making or securing of periodical payments to or for the benefit of a child may, if the child has reached the age of sixteen, be made by the child himself.

(5) Where an order for the making or securing of periodical payments made under paragraph 1 ceases to have effect on the date on which the child reaches the age of sixteen, or at any time after that date but before or on the date on which he reaches the age of eighteen, the child may apply to the court which made the order for an order for its revival.

(6) If on such an application it appears to the court that—

(a) the child is, will be or (if an order were made under this sub-paragraph) would be receiving instruction at an educational establishment or undergoing training for a trade, profession or vocation, whether or not while in gainful employment; or

(b) there are special circumstances which justify the making of an order under this paragraph,

the court shall have power by order to revive the order from such date as the court may specify, not being earlier than the date of the making of the application.

(7) Any order which is revived by an order under sub-paragraph (5) may be varied or discharged under that provision, on the application of any person by whom or to whom payments are required to be made under the revived order.

(8) An order for the making or securing of periodical payments made under paragraph 1 may be varied or discharged, after the death of either parent, on the application of a guardian [or special guardian] of the child concerned.

[(9) Where—

(a) an order under paragraph 1(2)(a) or (b) for the making or securing of periodical payments in favour of more than one child ('the order') is in force;

(b) the order requires payments specified in it to be made to or for the benefit of more than one child without apportioning those payments between them;

(c) a *maintenance assessment* [maintenance calculation] ('*the assessment* [the calculation]') is made with respect to one or more, but not all, of the children with respect to whom those payments are to be made; and

(d) an application is made, before the end of the period of 6 months beginning with the date on which the assessment was made, for the variation or discharge of the order,

the court may, in exercise of its powers under paragraph 1 to vary or discharge the order, direct that the variation or discharge shall take effect from the date on which the assessment took effect or any later date.]

Note. Words in square brackets in sub-para (9) substituted for words in italics, and sub-para (9) added by Maintenance Orders (Backdating) Order 1993, SI 1993 No 623, art 2, Sch 1, paras 12, 13, as from 5 April 1993. Words in square brackets in sub-para (8) inserted by the Adoption and Children Act 2002, s 139(1), Sch 3, paras 54, 71, as from a day to be appointed. Words in square brackets in sub-para (9) substituted for words in italics by the Child Support, Pensions and Social Security Act 2000, s 26, Sch 3, para 10(1), (3), as from (in relation to certain cases): 3 March 2003 (SI 2001 No 192); (for remaining purposes): to be appointed.

[*Variation of orders for periodical payments etc made by magistrates' courts*

6A.—(1) Subject to sub-paragraphs (7) and (8), the power of a magistrates' court—

(a) under paragraph 1 or 2 to vary an order for the making of periodical payments, or

(b) under paragraph 5(6) to vary an order for the payment of a lump sum by instalments,

shall include power, if the court is satisfied that payment has not been made in accordance with the order, to exercise one of its powers under paragraphs (a) to (d) of section 59(3) of the Magistrates' Courts Act 1980.

(2) In any case where—

(a) a magistrates' court has made an order under this Schedule for the making of periodical payments or for the payment of a lump sum by instalments, and

(b) payments under the order are required to be made by any method of payment falling within section 59(6) of the Magistrates' Courts Act 1980 (standing order, etc),

any person entitled to make an application under this Schedule for the variation of the order (in this paragraph referred to as 'the applicant') may apply to *the clerk to the justices for the petty sessions area for which the court is acting* [a magistrates' court acting in the same local justice area as the court which made the order] for the order to be varied as mentioned in sub-paragraph (3).

(3) Subject to sub-paragraph (5), where an application is made under sub-

paragraph (2), *the clerk* [a justices' chief clerk], after giving written notice (by post or otherwise) of the application to any interested party and allowing that party, within the period of 14 days beginning with the date of the giving of that notice, an opportunity to make written representations, may vary the order to provide that payments under the order shall be made *to the clerk* [*to the justices' chief executive for the court*] [to the designated officer for the court].

(4) The clerk may proceed with an application under sub-paragraph (2) notwithstanding that any such interested party as is referred to in sub-paragraph (3) has not received written notice of the application.

(5) Where an application has been made under sub-paragraph (2), the clerk may, if he considers it inappropriate to exercise his power under sub-paragraph (3), refer the matter to the court which, subject to sub-paragraphs (7) and (8), may vary the order by exercising one of its powers under paragraphs (a) to (d) of section 59(3) of the Magistrates' Courts Act 1980.

(6) Subsection (4) of section 59 of the Magistrates' Courts Act 1980 (power of court to order that account be opened) shall apply for the purposes of sub-paragraphs (1) and (5) as it applies for the purposes of that section.

(7) Before varying the order by exercising one of its powers under paragraphs (a) to (d) of section 59(3) of the Magistrates' Courts Act 1980, the court shall have regard to any representations made by the parties to the application.

(8) If the court does not propose to exercise its power *under paragraph (c) or (d)* [under paragraph (c), (cc) or (d)] of subsection (3) of section 59 of the Magistrates' Courts Act 1980, the court shall, unless upon representations expressly made in that behalf by the applicant for the order it is satisfied that it is undesirable to do so, exercise its power under paragraph (b) of that subsection.

(9) None of the powers of the court, or of *the clerk to the justices* [a justices' clerk], conferred by this paragraph shall be exercisable in relation to an order under this Schedule for the making of periodical payments, or for the payment of a lump sum by instalments, which is not a qualifying maintenance order (within the meaning of section 59 of the Magistrates' Courts Act 1980).

(10) In sub-paragraphs (3) and (4) 'interested party', in relation to an application made by the applicant under sub-paragraph (2), means a person who would be entitled to be a party to an application for the variation of the order made by the applicant under any other provision of this Schedule if such an application were made.]

Note. Para 6A inserted by Maintenance Enforcement Act 1991, s 6, (p 3477) as from 1 April 1992. Words in square brackets in sub-para (8) substituted for words in italics by Child Support Act 1991 (Consequential Amendments) Order 1994, SI 1994 No 731, art 4, as from 11 April 1994. Words in square brackets in sub-para (2), first and third words in square brackets in sub-para (3) and words in square brackets in sub-para (9) substituted for words in italics by the Courts Act 2003, s 109(1), Sch 8, para 338(1)–(4), as from a day to be appointed. Second words in square brackets in sub-para (3) substituted by the Access to Justice Act 1999, s 90(1), Sch 13, paras 159, 161, as from 1 April 2001 (SI 2001 No 916).

Variation of orders for secured periodical payments after death of parent

7.—(1) Where the parent liable to make payments under a secured periodical payments order has died, the persons who may apply for the variation or discharge of the order shall include the personal representatives of the deceased parent.

(2) No application for the variation of the order shall, except with the permission of the court, be made after the end of the period of six months from the date on which representation in regard to the estate of that parent is first taken out.

(3) The personal representatives of a deceased person against whom a secured periodical payments order was made shall not be liable for having distributed any part of the estate of the deceased after the end of the period of six months

referred to in sub-paragraph (2) on the ground that they ought to have taken into account the possibility that the court might permit an application for variation to be made after that period by the person entitled to payments under the order.

(4) Sub-paragraph (3) shall not prejudice any power to recover any part of the estate so distributed arising by virtue of the variation of an order in accordance with this paragraph.

(5) Where an application to vary a secured periodical payments order is made after the death of the parent liable to make payments under the order, the circumstances to which the court is required to have regard under paragraph 6(1) shall include the changed circumstances resulting from the death of the parent.

(6) In considering for the purposes of sub-paragraph (2) the question when representation was first taken out, a grant limited to settled land or to trust property shall be left out of account and a grant limited to real estate or to personal estate shall be left out of account unless a grant limited to the remainder of the estate has previously been made or is made at the same time.

(7) In this paragraph 'secured periodical payments order' means an order for secured periodical payments under paragraph 1(2)(b).

Financial relief under other enactments

8.—(1) This paragraph applies where a residence order [or a special guardianship order] is made with respect to a child at a time when there is in force an order ('the financial relief order') made under any enactment other than this Act and requiring a person to contribute to the child's maintenance.

(2) Where this paragraph applies, the court may, on the application of—

(a) any person required by the financial relief order to contribute to the child's maintenance; or

(b) any person in whose favour a residence order [or a special guardianship order] with respect to the child is in force,

make an order revoking the financial relief order, or varying it by altering the amount of any sum payable under that order or by substituting the applicant for the person to whom any such sum is otherwise payable under that order.

Note. Words in square brackets inserted by the Adoption and Children Act 2002, s 139(1), Sch 3, paras 54, 71, as from a day to be appointed.

Interim orders

9.—(1) Where an application is made under paragraph 1 or 2 the court may, at any time before it disposes of the application, make an interim order—

(a) requiring either or both parents to make such periodical payments, at such times and for such term as the court thinks fit; and

(b) giving any direction which the court thinks fit.

(2) An interim order made under this paragraph may provide for payments to be made from such date as the court may specify, *not being* [except that, subject to paragraph 3(5) and (6), the date shall not be] earlier than the date of the making of the application under paragraph 1 or 2.

(3) An interim order made under this paragraph shall cease to have effect when the application is disposed of or, if earlier, on the date specified for the purposes of this paragraph in the interim order.

(4) An interim order in which a date has been specified for the purposes of sub-paragraph (3) may be varied by substituting a later date.

Note. Words in square brackets in sub-para (2) substituted for words in italics by Maintenance Orders (Backdating) Order 1993, SI 1993 No 623, art 2, Sch 1, para 14, as from 5 April 1993.

Alteration of maintenance agreements

10.—(1) In this paragraph and in paragraph 11 'maintenance agreement' means any agreement in writing made with respect to a child, whether before or after the commencement of this paragraph, which—

(a) is or was made between the father and mother of the child; and

(b) contains provision with respect to the making or securing of payments, or the disposition or use of any property, for the maintenance or education of the child,

and any such provisions are in this paragraph, and paragraph 11, referred to as 'financial arrangements'.

(2) Where a maintenance agreement is for the time being subsisting and each of the parties to the agreement is for the time being either domiciled or resident in England and Wales, then, either party may apply to the court for an order under this paragraph.

(3) If the court to which the application is made is satisfied either—

(a) that, by reason of a change in the circumstances in the light of which any financial arrangements contained in the agreement were made (including a change foreseen by the parties when making the agreement), the agreement should be altered so as to make different financial arrangements; or

(b) that the agreement does not contain proper financial arrangements with respect to the child,

then that court may by order make such alterations in the agreement by varying or revoking any financial arrangements contained in it as may appear to it to be just having regard to all the circumstances.

(4) If the maintenance agreement is altered by an order under this paragraph, the agreement shall have effect thereafter as if the alteration had been made by agreement between the parties and for valuable consideration.

(5) Where a court decides to make an order under this paragraph altering the maintenance agreement—

(a) by inserting provision for the making or securing by one of the parties to the agreement of periodical payments for the maintenance of the child; or

(b) by increasing the rate of periodical payments required to be made or secured by one of the parties for the maintenance of the child,

then, in deciding the term for which under the agreement as altered by the order the payments or (as the case may be) the additional payments attributable to the increase are to be made or secured for the benefit of the child, the court shall apply the provisions of sub-paragraphs (1) and (2) of paragraph 3 as if the order were an order under paragraph 1(2)(a) or (b).

(6) A magistrates' court shall not entertain an application under sub-paragraph (2) unless both the parties to the agreement are resident in England and Wales *and at least one of the parties is resident in the commission area ... for which the court is appointed* [the courts act in, or is authorised by the Lord Chancellor to act for, a local justice area in which at least one of the parties is resident], and shall not have power to make any order on such an application except—

(a) in a case where the agreement contains no provision for periodical payments by either of the parties, an order inserting provision for the making by one of the parties of periodical payments for the maintenance of the child;

(b) in a case where the agreement includes provision for the making by one of the parties of periodical payments, an order increasing or reducing the rate of, or terminating, any of those payments.

Note. Words omitted in sub-para (6) repealed by the Access to Justice Act 1999, s 106, Sch 15, pt V(I), as from 27 September 1999. Words in square brackets substituted for words in italics by the Courts Act 2003, s 109(1), Sch 8, para 339, as from a day to be appointed.

(7) For the avoidance of doubt it is hereby declared that nothing in this paragraph affects any power of a court before which any proceedings between the

parties to a maintenance agreement are brought under any other enactment to make an order containing financial arrangements or any right of either party to apply for such an order in such proceedings.

11.—(1) Where a maintenance agreement provides for the continuation, after the death of one of the parties, of payments for the maintenance of a child and that party dies domiciled in England and Wales, the surviving party or the personal representatives of the deceased party may apply to the High Court or a county court for an order under paragraph 10.

(2) If a maintenance agreement is altered by a court on an application under this paragraph, the agreement shall have effect thereafter as if the alteration had been made, immediately before the death, by agreement between the parties and for valuable consideration.

(3) An application under this paragraph shall not, except with leave of the High Court or a county court, be made after the end of the period of six months beginning with the day on which representation in regard to the estate of the deceased is first taken out.

(4) In considering for the purposes of sub-paragraph (3) the question when representation was first taken out, a grant limited to settled land or to trust property shall be left out of account and a grant limited to real estate or to personal estate shall be left out of account unless a grant limited to the remainder of the estate has previously been made or is made at the same time.

(5) A county court shall not entertain an application under this paragraph, or an application for leave to make an application under this paragraph, unless it would have jurisdiction to hear and determine proceedings for an order under section 2 of the Inheritance (Provision for Family and Dependants) Act 1975 in relation to the deceased's estate by virtue of section 25 of the County Courts Act 1984 (jurisdiction under the Act of 1975).

(6) The provisions of this paragraph shall not render the personal representatives of the deceased liable for having distributed any part of the estate of the deceased after the expiry of the period of six months referred to in sub-paragraph (3) on the ground that they ought to have taken into account the possibility that a court might grant leave for an application by virtue of this paragraph to be made by the surviving party after that period.

(7) Sub-paragraph (6) shall not prejudice any power to recover any part of the estate so distributed arising by virtue of the making of an order in pursuance of this paragraph.

Enforcement of orders for maintenance

12.—(1) Any person for the time being under an obligation to make payments in pursuance of any order for the payment of money made by a magistrates' court under this Act shall give notice of any change of address to such person (if any) as may be specified in the order.

(2) Any person failing without reasonable excuse to give such a notice shall be guilty of an offence and liable on summary conviction to a fine not exceeding level 2 on the standard scale.

(3) An order for the payment of money made by a magistrates' court under this Act shall be enforceable as a magistrates' court maintenance order within the meaning of section 150(1) of the Magistrates' Courts Act 1980.

Direction for settlement of instrument by conveyancing counsel

13. Where the High Court or a county court decides to make an order under this Act for the securing of periodical payments or for the transfer or settlement of property, it may direct that the matter be referred to one of the conveyancing counsel of the court to settle a proper instrument to be executed by all necessary parties.

Financial provision for child resident in country outside England and Wales

14.—(1) Where one parent of a child lives in England and Wales and the child lives outside England and Wales with—

(a) another parent of his;

(b) a guardian [or special guardian] of his; or

(c) a person in whose favour a residence order is in force with respect to the child,

the court shall have power, on an application made by any of the persons mentioned in paragraphs (a) to (c), to make one or both of the orders mentioned in paragraph 1(2)(a) and (b) against the parent living in England and Wales.

(2) Any reference in this Act to the powers of the court under paragraph 1(2) or to an order made under paragraph 1(2) shall include a reference to the powers which the court has by virtue of sub-paragraph (1) or (as the case may be) to an order made by virtue of sub-paragraph (1).

Note. Words in square brackets in sub-para (1)(b) inserted by the Adoption and Children Act 2002, s 139(1), Sch 3, paras 54, 71, as from a day to be appointed.

Local authority contribution to child's maintenance

15.—(1) Where a child lives, or is to live, with a person as the result of a residence order, a local authority may make contributions to that person towards the cost of the accommodation and maintenance of the child.

(2) Sub-paragraph (1) does not apply where the person with whom the child lives, or is to live, is a parent of the child or the husband or wife of a parent of the child.

Interpretation

16.—(1) In this Schedule 'child' includes, in any case where an application is made under paragraph 2 or 6 in relation to a person who has reached the age of eighteen, that person.

(2) In this Schedule, except paragraphs 2 and 15, 'parent' includes any party to a marriage (whether or not subsisting) in relation to whom the child concerned is a child of the family; and for this purpose any reference to either parent or both parents shall be construed as references to any parent of his and to all of his parents.

[(3) In this Schedule, '*maintenance assessment* [maintenance calculation]' has the same meaning as it has in the Child Support Act 1991 by virtue of section 54 of that Act as read with any regulations in force under that section.]

Note. Sub-para (3) added by Maintenance Orders (Backdating) Order 1993, SI 1993 No 623, art 2, Sch 1, para 15, as from 5 April 1993. Words in square brackets substituted for words in italics by the Child Support, Pensions and Social Security Act 2000, s 26, Sch 3, para 10(1), (4), as from (in relation to certain cases): 3 March 2003 (SI 2003 No 192); (for remaining purposes): to be appointed.

SCHEDULE 2   Sections 17, 23 and 29

LOCAL AUTHORITY SUPPORT FOR CHILDREN AND FAMILIES

PART I

PROVISION OF SERVICES FOR FAMILIES

Identification of children in need and provision of information

1.—(1) Every local authority shall take reasonable steps to identify the extent to which there are children in need within their area.

(2) Every local authority shall—

(a) publish information—

(i) about services provided by them under sections 17, 18, *20 and 24* [20, 23B to 23D, 24A and 24B]; and

(ii) where they consider it appropriate, about the provision by others (including, in particular, voluntary organisations) of services which the authority have power to provide under those sections; and

(b) take such steps as are reasonably practicable to ensure that those who might benefit from the services receive the information relevant to them.

Note. Words in square brackets in sub-para (2)(a)(i) substituted for words in italics by the Children (Leaving Care) Act 2000, s 7(1), (4), as from 1 October 2001 (SI 2001 No 2878, SI 2001 No 2191).

[*Children's services plans*

1A.—(1) Every local authority shall, on or before 31st March 1997—
   (a) review their provision of services under sections 17, 20, 21, 23 and 24; and
   (b) having regard to that review and to their most recent review under section 19, prepare and publish a plan for the provision of services under Part III.
   (2) Every local authority—
   (a) shall, from time to time review the plan prepared by them under sub-paragraph (1)(b) (as modified or last substituted under this sub-paragraph), and
   (b) may, having regard to that review and to their most recent review under section 19, prepare and publish—
      (i) modifications (or, as the case may be, further modifications) to the plan reviewed; or
      (ii) a plan in substitution for that plan.
   (3) In carrying out any review under this paragraph and in preparing any plan or modifications to a plan, a local authority shall consult—
   (a) every *health authority* [Health Authority and Primary Care Trust] the whole or any part of whose area lies within the area of the local authority;
   (b) every National Health Service trust which manages a hospital, establishment or facility (within the meaning of the National Health Service and Community Care Act 1990) in the authority's area;
[(ba) every NHS foundation trust which manages a hospital (within the meaning of the Health and Social Care (Community Health and Standards) Act 2003) in the authority's area;]
   (c) if the local authority is not itself a local education authority, every local education authority the whole or any part of whose area lies within the area of the local authority;
   (d) any organisation which represents schools in the authority's area which are grant-maintained schools or grant-maintained special schools (within the meaning of the Education Act 1993);
   (e) the governing body of every such school in the authority's area which is not so represented;
   (f) such voluntary organisations as appear to the local authority—
      (i) to represent the interests of persons who use or are likely to use services provided by the local authority under Part III; or
      (ii) to provide services in the area of the local authority which, were they to be provided by the local authority, might be categorised as services provided under that Part.
   (g) the chief constable of the police force for the area;
   (h) the probation committee for the area;
   (i) such other persons as appear to the local authority to be appropriate; and
   (j) such other persons as the Secretary of State may direct.
   (4) Every local authority shall, within 28 days of receiving a written request from the Secretary of State, submit to him a copy of—

(a) the plan prepared by them under sub-paragraph (1); or

(b) where that plan has been modified or substituted, the plan as modified or last substituted.]

Note. Para 1A inserted by Children Act 1989 (Amendment) (Children's Services Planning) Order 1996, SI 1996 No 785, art 2, as from 1 April 1996. In sub-para (3)(a) words in square brackets substituted for words in italics by the Health Act 1999 (Supplementary, Consequential etc Provisions) Order 2000, SI 2000 No 90, art 3(1), Sch 1, para 24(1), (11), as from 8 February 2000. Sub-para (3)(ba) inserted by the Health and Social Care (Community Health and Standards) Act 2003, s 34, Sch 4, paras 75, 82.

Maintenance of a register of disabled children

2.—(1) Every local authority shall open and maintain a register of disabled children within their area.

(2) The register may be kept by means of a computer.

Assessment of children's needs

3. Where it appears to a local authority that a child within their area is in need, the authority may assess his needs for the purposes of this Act at the same time as any assessment of his needs is made under—

(a) the Chronically Sick and Disabled Persons Act 1970;

(b) *the Education Act 1981* [*Part III of the Education Act 1993*] [Part IV of the Education Act 1996];

(c) the Disabled Persons (Services, Consultation and Representation) Act 1986; or

(d) any other enactment.

Note. Reference to Education Act 1993 substituted for reference to Education Act 1981 by Education Act 1993, s 307, Sch 19, para 151, as from 1 September 1994. Reference to Education Act 1996 substituted for reference to Education Act 1993 by Education Act 1996, s 582(1), Sch 37, Part I, para 92, as from 1 November 1996.

Prevention of neglect and abuse

4.—(1) Every local authority shall take reasonable steps, through the provision of services under Part III of this Act, to prevent children within their area suffering ill-treatment or neglect.

(2) Where a local authority believe that a child who is at any time within their area—

(a) is likely to suffer harm; but

(b) lives or proposes to live in the area of another local authority,

they shall inform that other local authority.

(3) When informing that other local authority they shall specify—

(a) the harm that they believe he is likely to suffer; and

(b) (if they can) where the child lives or proposes to live.

Provision of accommodation in order to protect child

5.—(1) Where—

(a) it appears to a local authority that a child who is living on particular premises is suffering, or is likely to suffer, ill-treatment at the hands of another person who is living on those premises; and

(b) that other person proposes to move from the premises,

the authority may assist that other person to obtain alternative accommodation.

(2) Assistance given under this paragraph may be in cash.

(3) Subsections (7) to (9) of section 17 shall apply in relation to assistance given under this paragraph as they apply in relation to assistance given under that section.

Provision for disabled children

6. Every local authority shall provide services designed—
- (a) to minimise the effect on disabled children within their area of their disabilities; and
- (b) to give such children the opportunity to lead lives which are as normal as possible.

Provision to reduce need for care proceedings etc

7. Every local authority shall take reasonable steps designed—
- (a) to reduce the need to bring—
  - (i) proceedings for care or supervision orders with respect to children within their area;
  - (ii) criminal proceedings against such children;
  - (iii) any family or other proceedings with respect to such children which might lead to them being placed in the authority's care; or
  - (iv) proceedings under the inherent jurisdiction of the High Court with respect to children;
- (b) to encourage children within their area not to commit criminal offences; and
- (c) to avoid the need for children within their area to be placed in secure accommodation.

Provision for children living with their families

8. Every local authority shall make such provision as they consider appropriate for the following services to be available with respect to children in need within their area while they are living with their families—
- (a) advice, guidance and counselling;
- (b) occupational, social, cultural or recreational activities;
- (c) home help (which may include laundry facilities);
- (d) facilities for, or assistance with, travelling to and from home for the purpose of taking advantage of any other service provided under this Act or of any similar service;
- (e) assistance to enable the child concerned and his family to have a holiday.

Family centres

9.—(1) Every local authority shall provide such family centres as they consider appropriate in relation to children within their area.

(2) 'Family centre' means a centre at which any of the persons mentioned in sub-paragraph (3) may—
- (a) attend for occupational, social, cultural or recreational activities;
- (b) attend for advice, guidance or counselling; or
- (c) be provided with accommodation while he is receiving advice, guidance or counselling.

(3) The persons are—
- (a) a child;
- (b) his parents;
- (c) any person who is not a parent of his but who has parental responsibility for him;
- (d) any other person who is looking after him.

Maintenance of the family home

10. Every local authority shall take such steps as are reasonably practicable, where any child within their area who is in need and whom they are not looking after is living apart from his family—

(a) to enable him to live with his family; or

(b) to promote contact between him and his family,

if, in their opinion, it is necessary to do so in order to safeguard or promote his welfare.

Duty to consider racial groups to which children in need belong

11. Every local authority shall, in making any arrangements—

(a) for the provision of day care within their area; or

(b) designed to encourage persons to act as local authority foster parents,

have regard to the different racial groups to which children within their area who are in need belong.

PART II

CHILDREN LOOKED AFTER BY LOCAL AUTHORITIES

Regulations as to placing of children with local authority foster parents

12. Regulations under section 23(2)(a) may, in particular, make provision—

(a) with regard to the welfare of children placed with local authority foster parents;

(b) as to the arrangements to be made by local authorities in connection with the health and education of such children;

(c) as to the records to be kept by local authorities;

(d) for securing that a child is not placed with a local authority foster parent unless that person is for the time being approved as a local authority foster parent by such local authority as may be prescribed;

(e) for securing that where possible the local authority foster parent with whom a child is to be placed is—

(i) of the same religious persuasion as the child; or

(ii) gives an undertaking that the child will be brought up in that religious persuasion;

(f) for securing that children placed with local authority foster parents, and the premises in which they are accommodated, will be supervised and inspected by a local authority and that the children will be removed from those premises if their welfare appears to require it;

(g) as to the circumstances in which local authorities may make arrangements for duties imposed on them by the regulations to be discharged, on their behalf.

Regulations as to arrangements under section 23(2)(f)

13. Regulations under section 23(2)(f) may, in particular, make provision as to—

(a) the persons to be notified of any proposed arrangements;

(b) the opportunities such persons are to have to make representations in relation to the arrangements proposed;

(c) the persons to be notified of any proposed changes in arrangements;

(d) the records to be kept by local authorities;

(e) the supervision by local authorities of any arrangements made.

Regulations as to conditions under which child in care is allowed to live with parent, etc

14. Regulations under section 23(5) may, in particular, impose requirements on a local authority as to—

(a) the making of any decision by a local authority to allow a child to live with any person falling within section 23(4) (including requirements as to those who must be consulted before the decision is made, and those who must be notified when it has been made);

    (b)   the supervision or medical examination of the child concerned;

    (c)   the removal of the child, in such circumstances as may be prescribed, from the care of the person with whom he has been allowed to live;

    [(d) the records to be kept by local authorities.]

Note. Sub-para (d) added by Courts and Legal Services Act 1990, s 116, Sch 16, para 26, as from 14 October 1991.

Promotion and maintenance of contact between child and family

15.—(1) Where a child is being looked after by a local authority, the authority shall, unless it is not reasonably practicable or consistent with his welfare, endeavour to promote contact between the child and—

    (a)   his parents;

    (b)   any person who is not a parent of his but who has parental responsibility for him; and

    (c)   any relative, friend or other person connected with him.

    (2) Where a child is being looked after by a local authority—

    (a)   the authority shall take such steps as are reasonably practicable to secure that—

        (i)   his parents; and

        (ii) any person who is not a parent of his but who has parental responsibility for him,

    are kept informed of where he is being accommodated; and

    (b)   every such person shall secure that the authority are kept informed of his or her address.

    (3) Where a local authority ('the receiving authority') take over the provision of accommodation for a child from another local authority ('the transferring authority') under section 20(2)—

    (a)   the receiving authority shall (where reasonably practicable) inform—

        (i)   the child's parents; and

        (ii) any person who is not a parent of his but who has parental responsibility for him;

    (b)   sub-paragraph (2)(a) shall apply to the transferring authority, as well as the receiving authority, until at least one such person has been informed of the change; and

    (c)   sub-paragraph (2)(b) shall not require any person to inform the receiving authority of his address until he has been so informed.

    (4) Nothing in this paragraph requires a local authority to inform any person of the whereabouts of a child if—

    (a)   the child is in the care of the authority; and

    (b)   the authority has reasonable cause to believe that informing the person would prejudice the child's welfare.

    (5) Any person who fails (without reasonable excuse) to comply with sub-paragraph (2)(b) shall be guilty of an offence and liable on summary conviction to a fine not exceeding level 2 on the standard scale.

    (6) It shall be a defence in any proceedings under sub-paragraph (5) to prove that the defendant was residing at the same address as another person who was the child's parent or had parental responsibility for the child and had reasonable cause to believe that the other person had informed the appropriate authority that both of them were residing at that address.

Visits to or by children: expenses

16.—(1) This paragraph applies where—

    (a)   a child is being looked after by a local authority; and

    (b)   the conditions mentioned in sub-paragraph (3) are satisfied.

(2) The authority may—
(a) make payments to—
 (i) a parent of the child;
 (ii) any person who is not a parent of his but who has parental responsibility for him; or
 (iii) any relative, friend or other person connected with him,
 in respect of travelling, subsistence or other expenses incurred by that person in visiting the child; or
(b) make payments to the child, or to any person on his behalf, in respect of travelling, subsistence or other expenses incurred by or on behalf of the child in his visiting—
 (i) a parent of his;
 (ii) any person who is not a parent of his but who has parental responsibility for him; or
 (iii) any relative, friend or other person connected with him.
(3) The conditions are that—
(a) it appears to the authority that the visit in question could not otherwise be made without undue financial hardship; and
(b) the circumstances warrant the making of the payments.

Appointment of visitor for child who is not being visited

17.—(1) Where it appears to a local authority in relation to any child that they are looking after that—
(a) communication between the child and—
 (i) a parent of his, or
 (ii) any person who is not a parent of his but who has parental responsibility for him,
 has been infrequent; or
(b) he has not visited or been visited by (or lived with) any such person during the preceding twelve months,
and that it would be in the child's best interests for an independent person to be appointed to be his visitor for the purposes of this paragraph, they shall appoint such a visitor.
(2) A person so appointed shall—
(a) have the duty of visiting, advising and befriending the child; and
(b) be entitled to recover from the authority who appointed him any reasonable expenses incurred by him for the purposes of his functions under this paragraph.
(3) A person's appointment as a visitor in pursuance of this paragraph shall be determined if—
(a) he gives notice in writing to the authority who appointed him that he resigns the appointment; or
(b) the authority give him notice in writing that they have terminated it.
(4) The determination of such an appointment shall not prejudice any duty under this paragraph to make a further appointment.
(5) Where a local authority propose to appoint a visitor for a child under this paragraph, the appointment shall not be made if—
(a) the child objects to it; and
(b) the authority are satisfied that he has sufficient understanding to make an informed decision.
(6) Where a visitor has been appointed for a child under this paragraph, the local authority shall determine the appointment if—
(a) the child objects to its continuing; and
(b) the authority are satisfied that he has sufficient understanding to make an informed decision.

(7) The Secretary of State may make regulations as to the circumstances in which a person appointed as a visitor under this paragraph is to be regarded as independent of the local authority appointing him.

Power to guarantee apprenticeship deeds etc

18.—(1) While a child is being looked after by a local authority, or is a person qualifying for advice and assistance, the authority may undertake any obligation by way of guarantee under any deed of apprenticeship or articles of clerkship which he enters into.

(2) Where a local authority have undertaken any such obligation under any deed or articles they may at any time (whether or not they are still looking after the person concerned) undertake the like obligation under any supplemental deed or articles.

Arrangements to assist children to live abroad

19.—(1) A local authority may only arrange for, or assist in arranging for, any child in their care to live outside England and Wales with the approval of the court.

(2) A local authority may, with the approval of every person who has parental responsibility for the child arrange for, or assist in arranging for, any other child looked after by them to live outside England and Wales.

(3) The court shall not give its approval under sub-paragraph (1) unless it is satisfied that—

(a) living outside England and Wales would be in the child's best interests;

(b) suitable arrangements have been, or will be, made for his reception and welfare in the country in which he will live;

(c) the child has consented to living in that country; and

(d) every person who has parental responsibility for the child has consented to his living in that country.

(4) Where the court is satisfied that the child does not have sufficient understanding to give or withhold his consent, it may disregard sub-paragraph (3)(c) and give its approval if the child is to live in the country concerned with a parent, guardian [special guardian], or other suitable person.

(5) Where a person whose consent is required by sub-paragraph (3)(d) fails to give his consent, the court may disregard that provision and give its approval if it is satisfied that that person—

(a) cannot be found;

(b) is incapable of consenting; or

(c) is withholding his consent unreasonably.

(6) *Section 56 of the Adoption Act 1976 (which requires authority for the taking or sending abroad for adoption of a child who is a British subject)* [Section 85 of the Adoption and Children Act 2002 (which imposes restrictions on taking children out of the United Kingdom)] shall not apply in the case of any child who is to live outside England and Wales with the approval of the court given under this paragraph.

(7) Where a court decides to give its approval under this paragraph it may order that its decision is not to have effect during the appeal period.

(8) In sub-paragraph (7) 'the appeal period' means—

(a) where an appeal is made against the decision, the period between the making of the decision and the determination of the appeal; and

(b) otherwise, the period during which an appeal may be made against the decision.

[(9) This paragraph does not apply to a local authority placing a child for adoption with prospective adopters.]

Note. In sub-para (4) words in square brackets inserted, in sub-para (6) words in square brackets substituted for words in italics, and sub-para (9) inserted by the Adoption and Children Act 2002, s 139(1), Sch 3, paras 54, 72, as from a day to be appointed.

[Preparation for ceasing to be looked after

19A.—It is the duty of the local authority looking after a child to advise, assist and befriend him with a view to promoting his welfare when they have ceased to look after him.

19B.—(1) A local authority shall have the following additional functions in relation to an eligible child whom they are looking after.

(2) In sub-paragraph (1) 'eligible child' means, subject to sub-paragraph (3), a child who—

(a) is aged sixteen or seventeen; and
(b) has been looked after by a local authority for a prescribed period, or periods amounting in all to a prescribed period, which began after he reached a prescribed age and ended after he reached the age of sixteen.

(3) The Secretary of State may prescribe—

(a) additional categories of eligible children; and
(b) categories of children who are not to be eligible children despite falling within sub-paragraph (2).

(4) For each eligible child, the local authority shall carry out an assessment of his needs with a view to determining what advice, assistance and support it would be appropriate for them to provide him under this Act—

(a) while they are still looking after him; and
(b) after they cease to look after him,

and shall then prepare a pathway plan for him.

(5) The local authority shall keep the pathway plan under regular review.

(6) Any such review may be carried out at the same time as a review of the child's case carried out by virtue of section 26.

(7) The Secretary of State may by regulations make provision as to assessments for the purposes of sub-paragraph (4).

(8) The regulations may in particular provide for the matters set out in section 23B(6).

Personal advisers

19C.—A local authority shall arrange for each child whom they are looking after who is an eligible child for the purposes of paragraph 19B to have a personal adviser.]

Note. Paras 19A–19C inserted by the Children (Leaving Care) Act 2000, s 1, as from 1 October 2001 (SI 2001 No 2878, SI 2001 No 2191).

Death of children being looked after by local authorities

20.—(1) If a child who is being looked after by a local authority dies, the authority—

(a) shall notify the Secretary of State [and the Commission for Social Care Inspection];
(b) shall, so far as is reasonably practicable, notify the child's parents and every person who is not a parent of his but who has parental responsibility for him;
(c) may, with the consent (so far as it is reasonably practicable to obtain it) of every person who has parental responsibility for the child, arrange for the child's body to be buried or cremated; and
(d) may, if the conditions mentioned in sub-paragraph (2) are satisfied, make payments to any person who has parental responsibility for the child, or any

relative, friend or other person connected with the child, in respect of
travelling, subsistence or other expenses incurred by that person in attending
the child's funeral.

(2) The conditions are that—

(a) it appears to the authority that the person concerned could not otherwise
attend the child's funeral without undue financial hardship; and

(b) that the circumstances warrant the making of the payments.

(3) Sub-paragraph (1) does not authorise cremation where it does not accord
with the practice of the child's religious persuasion.

(4) Where a local authority have exercised their power under sub-paragraph
(1)(c) with respect to a child who was under sixteen when he died, they may
recover from any parent of the child any expenses incurred by them.

(5) Any sums so recoverable shall, without prejudice to any other method of
recovery, be recoverable summarily as a civil debt.

(6) Nothing in this paragraph affects any enactment regulating or authorising
the burial, cremation or anatomical examination of the body of a deceased person.

Note. In sub-para (1)(a) words in square brackets inserted by the Health and Social Care
(Community Health and Standards) Act 2003, s 147, Sch 9, para 10(1), (4).

PART III

CONTRIBUTIONS TOWARDS MAINTENANCE OF CHILDREN LOOKED AFTER BY LOCAL
AUTHORITIES

Liability to contribute

21.—(1) Where a local authority are looking after a child (other than in the cases
mentioned in sub-paragraph (7)) they shall consider whether they should recover
contributions towards the child's maintenance from any person liable to contribute
('a contributor').

(2) An authority may only recover contributions from a contributor if they
consider it reasonable to do so.

(3) The persons liable to contribute are—

(a) where the child is under sixteen, each of his parents;

(b) where he has reached the age of sixteen, the child himself.

(4) A parent is not liable to contribute during any period when he is in receipt
of income support *or family credit* [family credit [working families' tax credit] *or
disability working allowance* [disabled person's tax credit] *under* [under] *the Social Security
Act 1986* [Part VI of the Social Security Contributions and Benefits Act 1992] [, of
any element of child tax credit other than the family element, of working tax
credit] [or of an income-based jobseeker's allowance].

(5) A person is not liable to contribute towards the maintenance of a child in
the care of a local authority in respect of any period during which the child is
allowed by the authority (under section 23(5)) to live with a parent of his.

(6) A contributor is not obliged to make any contribution towards a child's
maintenance except as agreed or determined in accordance with this Part of this
Schedule.

(7) The cases are where the child is looked after by a local authority under—

(a) section 21;

(b) an interim care order;

(c) *section 53 of the Children and Young Persons Act 1933* [section 92 of the Powers
of Criminal Courts (Sentencing) Act 2000].

Note. Words in square brackets beginning with the words 'family credit' in sub-para (4)
substituted for words in italics by Disability Living Allowance and Disability Working
Allowance Act 1991, s 7(2), Sch 3, Part II, para 15, as from 19 November 1991 for certain
purposes and as from 10 March 1992 for remaining purposes. Words 'working families' tax
credit' and 'disabled person's tax credit' in square brackets substituted for words 'family

credit' and 'disability working allowance' respectively by the Tax Credits Act 1999, s 1(2), Sch 1, paras 1, 6(d)(iii), as from 5 October 1999. Word 'under' in square brackets substituted for words ', working families' tax credit or disabled person's tax credit under' by the Tax Credits Act 2002, s 47, Sch 3, paras 15, 20(a), as from 6 April 2003 (SI 2003 No 962); for savings and transitional provisions see arts 3–5 thereof. Words 'Part VI ... 1992' in square brackets substituted for words in italics by Social Security (Consequential Provisions) Act 1992, s 4, Sch 2, para 108(c), as from 1 July 1992. Words ', of any...tax credit' in square brackets inserted by the Tax Credits Act 2002, s 47, Sch 3, paras 15, 20(b), as from 6 April 2003 (SI 2003 No 962); for savings and transitional provisions see arts 3–5 thereof. Words 'or of ... allowance' in square brackets added by Jobseekers Act 1995, s 41(4), Sch 2, para 19, as from 7 October 1996. In sub-para (7) words 'section 92...Act 2000' in square brackets substituted for words in italics by the Powers of Criminal Courts (Sentencing) Act 2000, s 165(1), Sch 9, para 130, as from 25 August 2000.

Agreed contributions

22.—(1) Contributions towards a child's maintenance may only be recovered if the local authority have served a notice ('a contribution notice') on the contributor specifying—
  (a) the weekly sum which they consider that he should contribute; and
  (b) arrangements for payment.
  (2) The contribution notice must be in writing and dated.
  (3) Arrangements for payment shall, in particular, include—
  (a) the date on which liability to contribute begins (which must not be earlier than the date of the notice).
  (b) the date on which liability under the notice will end (if the child has not before that date ceased to be looked after by the authority); and
  (c) the date on which the first payment is to be made.
  (4) The authority may specify in a contribution notice a weekly sum which is a standard contribution determined by them for all children looked after by them.
  (5) The authority may not specify in a contribution notice a weekly sum greater than that which they consider—
  (a) they would normally be prepared to pay if they had placed a similar child with local authority foster parents; and
  (b) it is reasonably practicable for the contributor to pay (having regard to his means).
  (6) An authority may at any time withdraw a contribution notice (without prejudice to their power to serve another).
  (7) Where the authority and the contributor agree—
  (a) the sum which the contributor is to contribute; and
  (b) arrangements for payment,
(whether as specified in the contribution notice or otherwise) and the contributor notifies the authority in writing that he so agrees, the authority may recover summarily as a civil debt any contribution which is overdue and unpaid.
  (8) A contributor may, by serving a notice in writing on the authority, withdraw his agreement in relation to any period of liability falling after the date of service of the notice.
  (9) Sub-paragraph (7) is without prejudice to any other method of recovery.

Contribution orders

23.—(1) Where a contributor has been served with a contribution notice and has—
  (a) failed to reach any agreement with the local authority as mentioned in paragraph 22(7) within the period of one month beginning with the day on which the contribution notice was served; or
  (b) served a notice under paragraph 22(8) withdrawing his agreement,
the authority may apply to the court for an order under this paragraph.

(2) On such an application the court may make an order ('a contribution order') requiring the contributor to contribute a weekly sum towards the child's maintenance in accordance with arrangements for payment specified by the court.

(3) A contribution order—

(a) shall not specify a weekly sum greater than that specified in the contribution notice; and

(b) shall be made with due regard to the contributor's means.

(4) A contribution order shall not—

(a) take effect before the date specified in the contribution notice; or

(b) have effect while the contributor is not liable to contribute (by virtue of paragraph 21); or

(c) remain in force after the child has ceased to be looked after by the authority who obtained the order.

(5) An authority may not apply to the court under sub-paragraph (1) in relation to a contribution notice which they have withdrawn.

(6) Where—

(a) a contribution order is in force;

(b) the authority serve another contribution notice; and

(c) the contributor and the authority reach an agreement under paragraph 22(7) in respect of that other contribution notice,

the effect of the agreement shall be to discharge the order from the date on which it s agreed that the agreement shall take effect.

(7) Where an agreement is reached under sub-paragraph (6) the authority shall notify the court—

(a) of the agreement; and

(b) of the date on which it took effect.

(8) A contribution order may be varied or revoked on the application of the contributor or the authority.

(9) In proceedings for the variation of a contribution order, the authority shall specify—

(a) the weekly sum which, having regard to paragraph 22, they propose that the contributor should contribute under the order as varied; and

(b) the proposed arrangements for payment.

(10) Where a contribution order is varied, the order—

(a) shall not specify a weekly sum greater than that specified by the authority in the proceedings for variation; and

(b) shall be made with due regard to the contributor's means.

(11) An appeal shall lie in accordance with rules of court from any order made under this paragraph.

Enforcement of contribution orders etc

24.—(1) A contribution order made by a magistrates' court shall be enforceable as a magistrates' court maintenance order (within the meaning of section 150(1) of the Magistrates' Courts Act 1980).

(2) Where a contributor has agreed, or has been ordered, to make contributions to a local authority, any other local authority within whose area the contributor is for the time being living may—

(a) at the request of the local authority who served the contribution notice; and

(b) subject to agreement as to any sum to be deducted in respect of services rendered,

collect from the contributor any contributions due on behalf of the authority who served the notice.

(3) In sub-paragraph (2) the reference to any other local authority includes a reference to—

(a) a local authority within the meaning of section 1(2) of the Social Work (Scotland) Act 1968; and

(b) a Health and Social Services Board established under Article 16 of the Health and Personal Social Services (Northern Ireland) Order 1972.

(4) The power to collect sums under sub-paragraph (2) includes the power to—

(a) receive and give a discharge for any contributions due; and

(b) (if necessary) enforce payment of any contributions,

even though those contributions may have fallen due at a time when the contributor was living elsewhere.

(5) Any contribution collected under sub-paragraph (2) shall be paid (subject to any agreed deduction) to the local authority who served the contribution notice.

(6) In any proceedings under this paragraph, a document which purports to be—

(a) a copy of an order made by a court under or by virtue of paragraph 23; and

(b) certified as a true copy by the *clerk of* [*justices' chief executive for*] [designated officer for] the court,

shall be evidence of the order.

(7) In any proceedings under this paragraph, a certificate which—

(a) purports to be signed by the clerk or some other duly authorised officer of the local authority who obtained the contribution order; and

(b) states that any sum due to the authority under the order is overdue and unpaid,

shall be evidence that the sum is overdue and unpaid.

Note. In sub-para (6)(b) words 'justices' chief executive for' in square brackets substituted for words 'clerk of' by the Access to Justice Act 1999, s 90, Sch 13, paras 159, 162, as from 1 April 2001 (SI 2001 No 916). Words 'designated officer for' in square brackets substituted for words 'justices' chief executive for' by the Courts Act 2003, s 109(1), Sch 8, para 340.

Regulations

25. The Secretary of State may make regulations—

(a) as to the considerations which a local authority must take into account in deciding—

    (i) whether it is reasonable to recover contributions; and

    (ii) what the arrangements for payment should be;

(b) as to the procedures they must follow in reaching agreements with—

    (i) contributors (under paragraphs 22 and 23); and

    (ii) any other local authority (under paragraph 23).

SCHEDULE 3   Sections 35 and 36

SUPERVISION ORDERS

PART I

GENERAL

Meaning of 'responsible person'

1. In this Schedule, 'the responsible person', in relation to a supervised child, means—

(a) any person who has parental responsibility for the child; and

(b) any other person with whom the child is living

Power of supervisor to give directions to supervised child

2.—(1) A supervision order may require the supervised child to comply with any directions given from time to time by the supervisor which require him to do all or any of the following things—

(a) to live at a place or places specified in the directions for a period or periods so specified;

(b) to present himself to a person or persons specified in the directions at a place or places and on a day or days so specified;

(c) to participate in activities specified in the directions on a day or days so specified.

(2) It shall be for the supervisor to decide whether, and to what extent, he exercises his power to give directions and to decide the form of any directions which he gives.

(3) Sub-paragraph (1) does not confer on a supervisor power to give directions in respect of any medical or psychiatric examination or treatment (which are matters dealt with in paragraphs 4 and 5).

Imposition of obligations on responsible person

3.—(1) With the consent of any responsible person, a supervision order may include a requirement—

(a) that he take all reasonable steps to ensure that the supervised child complies with any direction given by the supervisor under paragraph 2;

(b) that he take all reasonable steps to ensure that the supervised child complies with any requirement included in the order under paragraph 4 or 5;

(c) that he comply with any directions given by the supervisor requiring him to attend at a place specified in the directions for the purpose of taking part in activities so specified.

(2) A direction given under sub-paragraph (1)(c) may specify the time at which the responsible person is to attend and whether or not the supervised child is required to attend with him.

(3) A supervision order may require any person who is a responsible person in relation to the supervised child to keep the supervisor informed of his address, if it differs from the child's.

Psychiatric and medical examinations

4.—(1) A supervision order may require the supervised child—

(a) to submit to a medical or psychiatric examination; or

(b) to submit to any such examination from time to time as directed by the supervisor.

(2) Any such examination shall be required to be conducted—

(a) by, or under the direction of, such registered medical practitioner as may be specified in the order;

(b) at a place specified in the order and at which the supervised child is to attend as a non-resident patient; or

(c) at—

    (i) a health service hospital; or

    (ii) in the case of a psychiatric examination, a hospital *or mental nursing home* [, independent hospital or care home],

at which the supervised child is, or is to attend as, a resident patient.

(3) A requirement of a kind mentioned in sub-paragraph (2)(c) shall not be included unless the court is satisfied, on the evidence of a registered medical practitioner, that—

(a) the child may be suffering from a physical or mental condition that requires, and may be susceptible to, treatment; and

(b) a period as a resident patient is necessary if the examination is to be carried out properly.

(4) No court shall include a requirement under this paragraph in a supervision order unless it is satisfied that—

(a) where the child has sufficient understanding to make an informed decision, he consents to its inclusion; and

(b) satisfactory arrangements have been, or can be, made for the examination.

Note. In sub-para (2)(c)(ii) words in square brackets substituted for words in italics by the Care Standards Act 2000, s 116, Sch 4, para 14(1), (24), as from 1 April 2002 (SI 2001 No 4150, SI 2002 No 920).

Psychiatric and medical treatment

5.—(1) Where a court which proposes to make or vary a supervision order is satisfied, on the evidence of a registered medical practitioner approved for the purposes of section 12 of the Mental Health Act 1983, that the mental condition of the supervised child—

(a) is such as requires, and may be susceptible to, treatment; but

(b) is not such as to warrant his detention in pursuance of a hospital order under Part III of that Act,

the court may include in the order a requirement that the supervised child shall, for a period specified in the order, submit to such treatment as is so specified.

(2) The treatment specified in accordance with sub-paragraph (1) must be—

(a) by, or under the direction of, such registered medical practitioner as may be specified in the order;

(b) as a non-resident patient at such a place as may be so specified; or

(c) as a resident patient in a hospital *or mental nursing home* [independent hospital or care home].

(3) Where a court which proposes to make or vary a supervision order is satisfied, on the evidence of a registered medical practitioner, that the physical condition of the supervised child is such as requires, and may be susceptible to, treatment, the court may include in the order a requirement that the supervised child shall, for a period specified in the order, submit to such treatment as is so specified.

(4) The treatment specified in accordance with sub-paragraph (3) must be—

(a) by, or under the direction of, such registered medical practitioner as may be specified in the order;

(b) as a non-resident patient at such place as may be so specified; or

(c) as a resident patient in a health service hospital.

(5) No court shall include a requirement under this paragraph in a supervision order unless it is satisfied—

(a) where the child has sufficient understanding to make an informed decision, that he consents to its inclusion; and

(b) that satisfactory arrangements have been, or can be, made for the treatment.

(6) If a medical practitioner by whom or under whose direction a supervised person is being treated in pursuance of a requirement included in a supervision order by virtue of this paragraph is unwilling to continue to treat or direct the treatment of the supervised child or is of the opinion that—

(a) the treatment should be continued beyond the period specified in the order;

(b) the supervised child needs different treatment;

(c) he is not susceptible to treatment; or

(d) he does not require further treatment,

the practitioner shall make a report in writing to that effect to the supervisor.

(7) On receiving a report under this paragraph the supervisor shall refer it to the court, and on such a reference the court may make an order cancelling or varying the requirement.

Note. In sub-para (5)(c) words in square brackets substituted for words in italics by the Care Standards Act 2000, s 116, Sch 4, para 14(1), (24), as from 1 April 2002 (SI 2001 No 4150, SI 2002 No 920).

PART II

MISCELLANEOUS

Life of supervision order

6.—(1) Subject to sub-paragraph (2) and section 91, a supervision order shall cease to have effect at the end of the period of one year beginning with the date on which it was made.

(2) A supervision order shall also cease to have effect if an event mentioned in section 25(1)(a) or (b) of the Child Abduction and Custody Act 1985 (termination of existing orders) occurs with respect to the child.

(3) Where the supervisor applies to the court to extend, or further extend, a supervision order the court may extend the order for such period as it may specify.

(4) A supervision order may not be extended so as to run beyond the end of the period of three years beginning with the date on which it was made.

Limited life of directions

7.—(*1*) *The total number of days in respect of which a supervised child or (as the case may be) responsible person may be required to comply with directions given under paragraph 2 or 3 shall not exceed 90 or such lesser number (if any) as the supervision order may specify.*

(*2*) *For the purpose of calculating that total number of days, the supervisor may disregard any day in respect of which directions previously given in pursuance of the order were not complied with.*

Note. Para 7 repealed by Courts and Legal Services Act 1990, ss 116, 125(7), Sch 16, para 27, Sch 20, as from 14 October 1991.

Information to be given to supervisor etc

8.—(1) A supervision order may require the supervised child—

    (a) to keep the supervisor informed of any change in his address; and

    (b) to allow the supervisor to visit him at the place where he is living.

(2) The responsible person in relation to any child with respect to whom a supervision order is made shall—

    (a) if asked by the supervisor, inform him of the child's address (if it is known to him); and

    (b) if he is living with the child, allow the supervisor reasonable contact with the child.

Selection of supervisor

9.—(1) A supervision order shall not designate a local authority as the supervisor unless—

    (a) the authority agree; or

    (b) the supervised child lives or will live within their area.

(2) ...

(3) ...

(4) ...

(5) ...

Note. Sub-paras (2)–(5) repealed by the Criminal Justice and Court Services Act 2000, ss 74, 75, Sch 7, Pt 2, paras 87, 96, Sch 8, as from 1 April 2001 (SI 2001 No 919).

Effect of supervision order on earlier orders

10. The making of a supervision order with respect to any child brings to an end any earlier care or supervision order which—

    (a) was made with respect to that child; and

    (b) would otherwise continue in force.

Local authority functions and expenditure

11.—(1) The Secretary of State may make regulations with respect to the exercise by a local authority of their functions where a child has been placed under their supervision by a supervision order.

(2) Where a supervision order requires compliance with directions given by virtue of this section, any expenditure incurred by the supervisor for the purposes of the directions shall be defrayed by the local authority designated in the order.

PART III

EDUCATION SUPERVISION ORDERS

Effect of orders

12.—(1) Where an education supervision order is in force with respect to a child, it shall be the duty of the supervisor—

    (a) to advise, assist and befriend, and give directions to—
        (i) the supervised child; and
        (ii) his parents;
    in such a way as will, in the opinion of the supervisor. secure that he is properly educated;

    (b) where any such directions given to—
        (i) the supervised child; or
        (ii) a parent of his.
    have not been complied with, to consider what further steps to take in the exercise of the supervisor's powers under this Act.

(2) Before giving any directions under sub-paragraph (1) the supervisor shall, so far as is reasonably practicable, ascertain the wishes and feelings of—

    (a) the child; and
    (b) his parents;

including, in particular, their wishes as to the place at which the child should be educated.

(3) When settling the terms of any such directions, the supervisor shall give due consideration—

    (a) having regard to the child's age and understanding, to such wishes and feelings of his as the supervisor has been able to ascertain; and
    (b) to such wishes and feelings of the child's parents as he has been able to ascertain.

(4) Directions may be given under this paragraph at any time while the education supervision order is in force.

13.—(1) Where an education supervision order is in force with respect to a child, the duties of the child's parents under *sections 36 and 39 of the Education Act 1944 (duty to secure education of children and [section 36 of the Education Act 1944 (duty to secure education of children) and section 199 of the Education Act 1993 (duty]* [sections 7 and 444 of the Education Act 1996 (duties to secure education of children and] to secure regular attendance of registered pupils) shall be superseded by their duty to comply with any directions in force under the education supervision order.

(2) Where an education supervision order is made with respect to a child—

    (a) any school attendance order—
        (i) made under section *37 of the Act of 1944 [192 of that Act]* [section 437 of the Education Act 1996] with respect to the child; and
        (ii) in force immediately before the making of the education supervision order,
    shall cease to have effect; and

    (b) while the education supervision order remains in force, the following provisions shall not apply with respect to the child—
        (i) *section 37 [192]* [section 437] of that Act (school attendance orders);

    (ii) *section 76 of that Act* [*the Education Act 1944*] [section 9 of that Act] (pupils to be educated in accordance with wishes of their parents);

    (iii) *sections 6 and 7 of the Education Act 1980* [sections 411 and 423 of that Act] (parental preference and appeals against admission decisions);

  (c) a supervision order made with respect to the child in criminal proceedings, while the education supervision order is in force, may not include an education requirement of the kind which could otherwise be included under *section 12C of the Children and Young Persons Act 1969* [paragraph 7 of Schedule 6 to the Powers of Criminal Courts (Sentencing) Act 2000];

  (d) any education requirement of a kind mentioned in paragraph (c), which was in force with respect to the child immediately before the making of the education supervision order, shall cease to have effect.

Note. Words 'the Education Act 1944' in square brackets in sub-para (2)(b)(ii) substituted for words in italics by Education Act 1993, s 307, Sch 19, para 152, as from 1 October 1993. Words 'section 9 of that Act' and 'sections 411 and 423' in square brackets in sub-para (2)(b)(ii), (iii) substituted for words in italics by Education Act 1996, s 582(1), Sch 37, para 93, as from 1 November 1996. In sub-para (2)(c) words 'paragraph 7...Act 2000' in square brackets substituted for words in italics by the Powers of Criminal Courts (Sentencing) Act 2000, s 165(1), Sch 9, para 131(1), (2), as from 25 August 2000.

Effect where child also subject to supervision order

14.—(1) This paragraph applies where an education supervision order and a supervision order, or order under *section 7(7)(b) of the Children and Young Persons Act 1969* [section 63(1) of the Powers of Criminal Courts (Sentencing) Act 2000], are in force at the same time with respect to the same child.

    (2) Any failure to comply with a direction given by the supervisor under the education supervision order shall be disregarded if it would not have been reasonably practicable to comply with it without failing to comply with a direction given under the other order.

Note. In sub-s (1) words in square brackets substituted for words in italics by the Powers of Criminal Courts (Sentencing) Act 2000, s 165(1), Sch 9, para 131(1), (3), as from 25 August 2000.

Duration of orders

15.—(1) An education supervision order shall have effect for a period of one year, beginning with the date on which it is made.

    (2) An education supervision order shall not expire if, before it would otherwise have expired, the court has (on the application of the authority in whose favour the order was made) extended the period during which it is in force.

    (3) Such an application may not be made earlier than three months before the date on which the order would otherwise expire.

    (4) The period during which an education supervision order is in force may be extended under sub-paragraph 2 on more than one occasion.

    (5) No one extension may be for a period of more than three years.

    (6) An education supervision order shall cease to have effect on—

  (a) the child's ceasing to be of compulsory school age; or

  (b) the making of a care order with respect to the child;

and sub-paragraphs (1) to (4) are subject to this sub-paragraph.

Information to be given to supervisor etc

16.—(1) An education supervision order may require the child—

  (a) to keep the supervisor informed of any change in his address; and

  (b) to allow the supervisor to visit him at the place where he is living.

    (2) A person who is the parent of a child with respect to whom an education supervision order has been made shall—

(a) if asked by the supervisor, inform him of the child's address (if it is known to him); and

(b) if he is living with the child, allow the supervisor reasonable contact with the child.

Discharge of orders

17.—(1) The court may discharge any education supervision order on the application of—

(a) the child concerned;

(b) a parent of his; or

(c) the local education authority concerned.

(2) On discharging an education supervision order, the court may direct the local authority within whose area the child lives, or will live, to investigate the circumstances of the child.

Offences

18.—(1) If a parent of a child with respect to whom an education supervision order is in force persistently fails to comply with a direction given under the order he shall be guilty of an offence.

(2) It shall be a defence for any person charged with such an offence to prove that—

(a) he took all reasonable steps to ensure that the direction was complied with;

(b) the direction was unreasonable; or

(c) he had complied with—

    (i) a requirement included in a supervision order made with respect to the child; or

    (ii) directions given under such a requirement,

and that it was not reasonably practicable to comply both with the direction and with the requirement or directions mentioned in this paragraph.

(3) A person guilty of an offence under this paragraph shall be liable on summary conviction to a fine not exceeding level 3 on the standard scale.

Persistent failure of child to comply with directions

19.—(1) Where a child with respect to whom an education supervision order is in force persistently fails to comply with any direction given under the order, the local education authority concerned shall notify the appropriate local authority.

(2) Where a local authority have been notified under sub-paragraph (1) they shall investigate the circumstances of the child.

(3) In this paragraph 'the appropriate local authority' has the same meaning as in section 36.

Miscellaneous

20. The Secretary of State may by regulations make provision modifying, or displacing, the provisions of any enactment about education in relation to any child with respect to whom an education supervision order is in force to such extent as appears to the Secretary of State to be necessary or expedient in consequence of the provision made by this Act with respect to such orders.

Interpretation

21. In this Part of this Schedule 'parent' has the same meaning as in *the Education Act 1944 (as amended by Schedule 13)* [the Education Act 1996].

Note. Words in square brackets substituted for words in italics by Education Act 1996, s 582(1), Sch 37, para 93, as from 1 November 1996.

SCHEDULE 4 Section 53(6)

MANAGEMENT AND CONDUCT OF COMMUNITY HOMES

PART I

INSTRUMENTS OF MANAGEMENT

Instruments of management for controlled and assisted community homes

1.—(1) The Secretary of State may by order make an instrument of management providing for the constitution of a body of managers for any *voluntary* home which is designated as a controlled or assisted community home.

(2) Sub-paragraph (3) applies where two or more *voluntary* homes are designated as controlled community homes or as assisted community homes.

(3) If—

(a) those homes are, or are to be, provided by the same voluntary organisation; and

(b) the same local authority is to be represented on the body of managers for those homes,

a single instrument of management may be made by the Secretary of State under this paragraph constituting one body of managers for those homes or for any two or more of them.

(4) The number of persons who, in accordance with an instrument of management, constitute the body of managers for a *voluntary* home shall be such number (which must be a multiple of three) as may be specified in the instrument.

(5) The instrument shall provide that the local authority specified in the instrument shall appoint—

(a) in the case of a *voluntary* home which is designated as a controlled community home, two-thirds of the managers; and

(b) in the case of a *voluntary* home which is designated as an assisted community home, one-third of them.

(6) An instrument of management shall provide that the foundation managers shall be appointed, in such manner and by such persons as may be specified in the instrument—

(a) so as to represent the interests of the voluntary organisation by which the home is, or is to be, provided; and

(b) for the purpose of securing that—

(i) so far as is practicable, the character of the home *as a voluntary home* will be preserved; and

(ii) subject to paragraph 2(3), the terms of any trust deed relating to the home are observed.

(7) An instrument of management shall come into force on such date as it may specify.

(8) If an instrument of management is in force in relation to a *voluntary* home the home shall be (and be known as) a controlled community home or an assisted community home, according to its designation.

(9) In this paragraph—

'foundation managers', in relation to a *voluntary* home, means those of the managers of the home who are not appointed by a local authority in accordance with sub-paragraph (5); and

'designated' means designated in accordance with section 53.

Note. Words in italics repealed by Courts and Legal Services Act 1990, ss 116, 125(7), Sch 16, para 28, Sch 20, as from 14 October 1991.

2.—(1) An instrument of management shall contain such provisions as the Secretary of State considers appropriate.

(2) Nothing in the instrument of management shall affect the purposes for which the premises comprising the home are held.

(3) Without prejudice to the generality of sub-paragraph (1), an instrument of management may contain provisions—

(a) specifying the nature and purpose of the home (or each of the homes) to which it relates;

(b) requiring a specified number or proportion of the places in that home (or those homes) to be made available to local authorities and to any other body specified in the instrument; and

(c) relating to the management of that home (or those homes) and the charging of fees with respect to—

(i) children placed there; or

(ii) places made available to any local authority or other body.

(4) Subject to sub-paragraphs (1) and (2), in the event of any inconsistency between the provisions of any trust deed and an instrument of management, the instrument of management shall prevail over the provisions of the trust deed in so far as they relate to the home concerned.

(5) After consultation with the voluntary organisation concerned and with the local authority specified in its instrument of management, the Secretary of State may by order vary or revoke any provisions of the instrument.

PART II

MANAGEMENT OF CONTROLLED AND ASSISTED COMMUNITY HOMES

3.—(1) The management, equipment and maintenance of a controlled community home shall be the responsibility of the local authority specified in its instrument of management.

(2) The management, equipment and maintenance of an assisted community home shall be the responsibility of the voluntary organisation by which the home is provided.

(3) In this paragraph—

'home' means a controlled community home or (as the case may be) assisted community home; and

'the managers', in relation to a home, means the managers constituted by its instrument of management; and

'the responsible body', in relation to a home, means the local authority or (as the case may be) voluntary organisation responsible for its management, equipment and maintenance.

(4) The functions of a home's responsible body shall be exercised through the managers[, except in so far as, under section 53(3B), any of the accommodation is to be managed by another person].

(5) Anything done, liability incurred or property acquired by a home's managers shall be done, incurred or acquired by them as agents of the responsible body[; and similarly, to the extent that a contract so provides, as respects anything done, liability incurred or property acquired by a person by whom, under section 53(3B), any of the accommodation is to be managed].

(6) In so far as any matter is reserved for the decision of a home's responsible body by—

(a) sub-paragraph (8);

(b) the instrument of management;

(c) the service by the body on the managers, or any of them, of a notice reserving any matter,

that matter shall be dealt with by the body and not by the managers.

(7) In dealing with any matter so reserved, the responsible body shall have regard to any representations made to the body by the managers.

(8) The employment of persons at a home shall be a matter reserved for the decision of the responsible body.

(9) Where the instrument of management of a controlled community home so provides, the responsible body may enter into arrangements with the voluntary organisation by which that home is provided whereby, in accordance with such terms as may be agreed between them and the voluntary organisation, persons who are not in the employment of the responsible body shall undertake duties at that home.

(10) Subject to sub-paragraph (11)—

(a) where the responsible body for an assisted community home proposes to engage any person to work at that home or to terminate without notice the employment of any person at that home, it shall consult the local authority specified in the instrument of management and, if that authority so direct, the responsible body shall not carry out its proposal without their consent; and

(b) that local authority may, after consultation with the responsible body, require that body to terminate the employment of any person at that home.

(11) Paragraphs (a) and (b) of sub-paragraph (10) shall not apply—

(a) in such cases or circumstances as may be specified by notice in writing given by the local authority to the responsible body; and

(b) in relation to the employment of any persons or class of persons specified in the home's instrument of management.

(12) The accounting year of the managers of a home shall be such as may be specified by the responsible body.

(13) Before such date in each accounting year as may be so specified, the managers of a home shall submit to the responsible body estimates, in such form as the body may require, of expenditure and receipts in respect of the next accounting year.

(14) Any expenses incurred by the managers of a home with the approval of the responsible body shall be defrayed by that body.

(15) The managers of a home shall keep—

(a) proper accounts with respect to the home; and

(b) proper records in relation to the accounts.

(16) Where an instrument of management relates to more than one home, one set of accounts and records may be kept in respect of all the homes to which it relates.

Note. Words in square brackets in sub-paras (4), (5) added by Criminal Justice and Public Order Act 1994, s 22, as from 8 March 1996.

PART III

REGULATIONS

4.—(1) The Secretary of State may make regulations—

(a) as to the placing of children in community homes;

(b) ...

(c) ...

(2) ...

(3) ...

Note. Sub-paras (1)(b), (c), (2), (3) repealed by the Care Standards Act 2000, s 117(2), Sch 6, as from 1 April 2002 (SI 2001 No 4150, SI 2002 No 920).

SCHEDULE 5   Section 60(4)

VOLUNTARY HOMES AND VOLUNTARY ORGANISATIONS

PART I

REGISTRATION OF VOLUNTARY HOMES

...

1.—...

Note. Repealed by the Care Standards Act 2000, s 117(2), Sch 6, as from 1 April 2002 (SI 2001 No 3582, SI 2002 No 920).

...

2.—...

Note. Repealed by the Care Standards Act 2000, s 117(2), Sch 6, as from 1 April 2002 (SI 2001 No 3582, SI 2002 No 920).

...

3.—...

4.—...

Note. Repealed by the Care Standards Act 2000, s 117(2), Sch 6, as from 1 April 2002 (SI 2001 No 3582, SI 2002 No 920).

...

5.—...

Note. Repealed by the Care Standards Act 2000, s 117(2), Sch 6, as from 1 April 2002 (SI 2001 No 3582, SI 2002 No 920).

Notification of particulars with respect to voluntary homes

6.—...

Note. Repealed by the Care Standards Act 2000, s 117(2), Sch 6, as from 1 April 2002 (SI 2001 No 3582, SI 2002 No 920).

PART II

REGULATIONS AS TO VOLUNTARY HOMES

Regulations as to conduct of voluntary homes

7.—(1) The Secretary of State may make regulations—
 (a) as to the placing of children in voluntary homes;
 (b) ...
 (c) ...
 (2) ...
 (3) ...
 (4) ...

Note. Sub-paras (1)(b), (c), (2)–(4) repealed by the Care Standards Act 2000, s 117(2), Sch 6, as from 1 April 2002 (SI 2001 No 3582, SI 2002 No 920).

...

8. ...

Note. Repealed by the Care Standards Act 2000, s 117(2), Sch 6, as from 1 April 2002 (SI 2001 No 3582, SI 2002 No 920).

SCHEDULE 6   Section 63(11)

REGISTERED CHILDREN'S HOMES

PART I

...

Note. Repealed by the Care Standards Act 2000, s 117(2), Sch 6, as from 1 April 2002 (SI 2001 No 3582, SI 2002 No 920).

PART II

REGULATIONS

10.—(1) The Secretary of State may make regulations—
  (a) as to the placing of children in *registered* [private] children's homes;
  (b) ...
  (c) ...
  (2) The regulations may in particular—
  (a) ...
  (b) ...
  (c) ...
  (d) ...
  (e) ...
      ...
  (f) ...
  (g) ...
  (h) ...
  (i) ...
  (j) ...
  [(jj) ...
  (k) ...
  (l) make provision similar to that made by regulations under section 26.
  (3) ...
  (4) ...

Note. Sub-para (2)(j) repealed, and sub-para (2)(jj) inserted, by Criminal Justice and Public Order Act 1994, ss 19(2)(b), 168(3), Sch 11, as from 30 May 1995. In sub-para (1)(a) word 'private' in square brackets substituted for word in italics by the Care Standards Act 2000, s 116, Sch 4, para 14(1), (25)(b), as from 1 April 2002 (SI 2001 No 4150, SI 2002 No 920). Sub-paras (1)(b), (c), (2)(a)–(k), (3), (4) repealed by the Care Standards Act 2000, s 117(2), Sch 6, as from 1 April 2002 (SI 2001 No 3582, SI 2002 No 920).

SCHEDULE 7   Section 63(12)

FOSTER PARENTS: LIMITS ON NUMBER OF FOSTER CHILDREN

Interpretation

1. For the purposes of this Schedule, a person fosters a child if—
  (a) he is a local authority foster parent in relation to the child;
  (b) he is a foster parent with whom the child has been placed by a voluntary organisation; or
  (c) he fosters the child privately.

The usual fostering limit

2. Subject to what follows, a person may not foster more than three children ('the usual fostering limit').

Siblings

3. A person may exceed the usual fostering limit if the children concerned are all siblings with respect to each other.

Exemption by local authority

4.—(1) A person may exceed the usual fostering limit if he is exempted from it by the local authority within whose area he lives.

(2) In considering whether to exempt a person, a local authority shall have regard, in particular, to—

(a) the number of children whom the person proposes to foster;

(b) the arrangements which the person proposes for the care and accommodation of the fostered children;

(c) the intended and likely relationship between the person and the fostered children;

(d) the period of time for which he proposes to foster the children; and

(e) whether the welfare of the fostered children (and of any other children who are or will be living in the accommodation) will be safeguarded and promoted.

(3) Where a local authority exempt a person, they shall inform him by notice in writing—

(a) that he is so exempted;

(b) of the children, described by name, whom he may foster; and

(c) of any condition to which the exemption is subject.

(4) A local authority may at any time by notice in writing—

(a) vary or cancel an exemption; or

(b) impose, vary or cancel a condition to which the exemption is subject,

and, in considering whether to do so, they shall have regard in particular to the considerations mentioned in sub-paragraph (2).

(5) The Secretary of State may make regulations amplifying or modifying the provisions of this paragraph in order to provide for cases where children need to be placed with foster parents as a matter of urgency.

Effect of exceeding fostering limit

5.—(1) A person shall cease to be treated [, for the purposes of this Act and the Care Standards Act] as fostering and shall be treated as carrying on a children's home if—

(a) he exceeds the usual fostering limit; or

(b) where he is exempted under paragraph 4,—

(i) he fosters any child not named in the exemption; and

(ii) in so doing, he exceeds the usual fostering limit.

(2) Sub-paragraph (1) does not apply if the children concerned are all siblings in respect of each other.

Note. In sub-para (1) words in square brackets inserted by the Care Standards Act 2000, s 116, Sch 4, para 14(1), (26), as from 1 April 2002 (SI 2001 No 4150, SI 2002 No 920).

Complaints etc

6.—(1) Every local authority shall establish a procedure for considering any representations (including any complaint) made to them about the discharge of their functions under paragraph 4 by a person exempted or seeking to be exempted under that paragraph.

(2) In carrying out any consideration or representations under sub-paragraph (1), a local authority shall comply with any regulations made by the Secretary of State for the purposes of this paragraph.

SCHEDULE 8   Section 66(5)

PRIVATELY FOSTERED CHILDREN

Exemptions

1. A child is not a privately fostered child while he is being looked after by a local authority.

2.—(1) A child is not a privately fostered child while he is in the care of any person—

    (a) in premises in which any—

        (i) parent of his;

        (ii) person who is not a parent of his but who has parental responsibility for him; or

        (iii) person who is a relative of his and who has assumed responsibility for his care,

    is for the time being living;

    (b) ...

    (c) in accommodation provided by or on behalf of any voluntary organisation;

    (d) in any school in which he is receiving full-time education;

    (e) in any health service hospital;

    (f) in any residential care home [(other than a small home)], nursing home or mental nursing home; or

    [(f) in any care home or independent hospital;]

    (g) in any home or institution not specified in this paragraph but provided, equipped and maintained by the Secretary of State.

Note. Sub-para (1)(b) repealed by the Care Standards Act 2000, ss 116, 117(2), Sch 4, para 14(1), (27)(a), Sch 6, as from 1 April 2002 (SI 2001 No 4150, SI 2002 No 920). Words in square brackets in first sub-para (1)(f) inserted by Registered Homes (Amendment) Act 1991, s 2(6), as from 1 April 1993. Sub-para (f) in square brackets substituted for sub-para (f) in italics by the Care Standards Act 2000, s 116, Sch 4, para 14(1), (28), as from 1 April 2002 (SI 2001 No 4150, SI 2002 No 920).

(2) Sub-paragraph *(1)(b)* [(1)(c)] to (g) does not apply where the person caring for the child is doing so in his personal capacity and not in the course of carrying out his duties in relation to the establishment mentioned in the paragraph in question.

Note. Reference to '(1)(c)' substituted for reference in italics by the Care Standards Act 2000, ss 116, 117(2), Sch 4, para 14(1), (27)(a), Sch 6, as from 1 April 2002 (SI 2001 No 4150, SI 2002 No 920).

3. A child is not a privately fostered child while he is in the care of any person in compliance with—

    (a) an order under *section 7(7)(b) of the Children and Young Persons Act 1969* [section 63(1) of the Powers of Criminal Courts (Sentencing) Act 2000]; or

    (b) a supervision requirement within the meaning of *the Social Work (Scotland) Act 1968* [Part II of the Children (Scotland) Act 1995].

Note. In para (a) words in square brackets substituted for words in italics by the Powers of Criminal Courts (Sentencing) Act 2000, s 165(1), Sch 9, para 132, as from 25 August 2000. In para (b) words in square brackets substituted for words in italics by Children (Scotland) Act 1995, s 105(4), Sch 4, para 48(5), as from 1 April 1997.

4. A child is not a privately fostered child while he is liable to be detained, or subject to guardianship, under the Mental Health Act 1983.

5. A child is not a privately fostered child while—

    (a) he is placed in the care of a person who proposes to adopt him under arrangements made by an adoption agency within the meaning of—

        (i) section 1 of the Adoption Act 1976;

        (ii) section 1 of the Adoption (Scotland) Act 1978; or

        (iii) Article 3 of the Adoption (Northern Ireland) Order 1987; or

(b) *is a protected child* [he is placed in the care of a person who proposes to adopt him under arrangements made by an adoption agency within the meaning of—
  (a) section 2 of the Adoption and Children Act 2002;
  (b) section 1 of the Adoption (Scotland) Act 1978; or
  (c) Article 3 of the Adoption (Northern Ireland) Order 1987.]

Note. Words in square brackets substituted for words in italics by the Adoption and Children Act 2002, s 139(1), Sch 3, para 73, as from a day to be appointed.

Power of local authority to impose requirements

6.—(1) Where a person is fostering any child privately, or proposes to foster any child privately, the appropriate local authority may impose on him requirements as to—
  (a) the number, age and sex of the children who may be privately fostered by him;
  (b) the standard of the accommodation and equipment to be provided for them;
  (c) the arrangements to be made with respect to their health and safety; and
  (d) particular arrangements which must be made with respect to the provision of care for them,
and it shall be his duty to comply with any such requirement before the end of such period as the authority may specify unless, in the case of a proposal, the proposal is not carried out.

(2) A requirement may be limited to a particular child, or class of child.

(3) A requirement (other than one imposed under sub-paragraph (1)(a)) may be limited by the authority so as to apply only when the number of children fostered by the person exceeds a specified number.

(4) A requirement shall be imposed by notice in writing addressed to the person on whom it is imposed and informing him of—
  (a) the reason for imposing the requirement;
  (b) his right under paragraph 8 to appeal against it; and
  (c) the time within which he may do so.

(5) A local authority may at any time vary any requirement, impose any additional requirement or remove any requirement.

(6) In this Schedule—
  (a) 'the appropriate local authority' means—
      (i) the local authority within whose area the child is being fostered; or
      (ii) in the case of a proposal to foster a child, the local authority within whose area it is proposed that he will be fostered; and
  (b) 'requirement', in relation to any person, means a requirement imposed on him under this paragraph.

Regulations requiring notification of fostering etc

7.—(1) The Secretary of State may by regulations make provision as to—
  (a) the circumstances in which notification is required to be given in connection with children who are, have been or are proposed to be fostered privately; and
  (b) the manner and form in which such notification is to be given.

(2) The regulations may, in particular—
  (a) require any person who is, or proposes to be, involved (whether or not directly) in arranging for a child to be fostered privately to notify the appropriate authority;
  (b) require any person who is—
      (i) a parent of a child; or
      (ii) a person who is not a parent of his but who has parental responsibility for a child,
    and who knows that it is proposed that the child should be fostered privately, to notify the appropriate authority;

   (c) require any parent of a privately fostered child, or person who is not a parent of such a child but who has parental responsibility for him, to notify the appropriate authority of any change in his address;

   (d) require any person who proposes to foster a child privately, to notify the appropriate authority of his proposal;

   (e) require any person who is fostering a child privately, or proposes to do so, to notify the appropriate authority of—
     (i) any offence of which he has been convicted;
     (ii) any disqualification imposed on him under section 68; or
     (iii) any prohibition imposed on him under section 69;

   (f) require any person who is fostering a child privately, to notify the appropriate authority of any change in his address;

   (g) require any person who is fostering a child privately to notify the appropriate authority in writing of any person who begins, or ceases, to be part of his household;

   (h) require any person who has been fostering a child privately, but has ceased to do so, to notify the appropriate authority (indicating, where the child has died, that that is the reason).

Appeals

8.—(1) A person aggrieved by—
   (a) a requirement imposed under paragraph 6;
   (b) a refusal of consent under section 68;
   (c) a prohibition imposed under section 69;
   (d) a refusal to cancel such a prohibition;
   (e) a refusal to make an exemption under paragraph 4 of Schedule 7;
   (f) a condition imposed in such an exemption; or
   (g) a variation or cancellation of such an exemption,
may appeal to the court.

   (2) The appeal must be made within fourteen days from the date on which the person appealing is notified of the requirement, refusal, prohibition, condition, variation or cancellation.

   (3) Where the appeal is against—
   (a) a requirement imposed under paragraph 6;
   (b) a condition of an exemption imposed under paragraph 4 of Schedule 7; or
   (c) a variation or cancellation of such an exemption,
the requirement, condition, variation or cancellation shall not have effect while the appeal is pending.

   (4) Where it allows an appeal against a requirement or prohibition, the court may, instead of cancelling the requirement or prohibition—
   (a) vary the requirement, or allow more time for compliance with it; or
   (b) if an absolute prohibition has been imposed, substitute for it a prohibition on using the premises after such time as the court may specify unless such specified requirements as the local authority had power to impose under paragraph 6 are complied with.

   (5) Any requirement or prohibition specified or substituted by a court under this paragraph shall be deemed for the purposes of Part IX (other than this paragraph) to have been imposed by the local authority under paragraph 6 or (as the case may be) section 69.

   (6) Where it allows an appeal against a refusal to make an exemption, a condition imposed in such an exemption or a variation or cancellation of such an exemption, the court may—
   (a) make an exemption;
   (b) impose a condition; or

(c) vary the exemption.

(7) Any exemption made or varied under sub-paragraph (6), or any condition imposed under that sub-paragraph, shall be deemed for the purposes of Schedule 7 (but not for the purposes of this paragraph) to have been made, varied or imposed under that Schedule.

(8) Nothing in sub-paragraph (1)(e) to (g) confers any right of appeal on—

(a) a person who is, or would be if exempted under Schedule 7, a local authority foster parent; or

(b) a person who is, or would be if so exempted, a person with whom a child is placed by a voluntary organisation.

Extension of Part IX to certain school children during holidays

9.—(1) Where a child under sixteen who is a pupil at a school … lives at the school during school holidays for a period of more than two weeks, Part IX shall apply in relation to the child as if—

(a) while living at the school, he were a privately fostered child; and

(b) paragraphs *2(1)(d)* [2(1)(c) and (d)] and 6 were omitted.
[But this sub-paragraph does not apply to a school which is an appropriate children's home.]

(2) Sub-paragraph (3) applies to any person who proposes to care for and accommodate one or more children at a school in circumstances in which some or all of them will be treated as private foster children by virtue of this paragraph.

(3) That person shall, not less than two weeks before the first of those children is treated as a private foster child by virtue of this paragraph during the holiday in question, give written notice of his proposal to the local authority within whose area the child is ordinarily resident ('the appropriate authority'), stating the estimated number of the children.

(4) A local authority may exempt any person from the duty of giving notice under sub-paragraph (3).

(5) Any such exemption may be granted for a special period or indefinitely and may be revoked at any time by notice in writing given to the person exempted.

(6) Where a child who is treated as a private foster child by virtue of this paragraph dies, the person caring for him at the school shall, not later than 48 hours after the death, give written notice of it—

(a) to the appropriate local authority; and

(b) where reasonably practicable, to each parent of the child and to every person who is not a parent of his but who has parental responsibility for him.

(7) Where a child who is treated as a foster child by virtue of this paragraph ceases for any other reason to be such a child, the person caring for him at the school shall give written notice of the fact to the appropriate local authority.

Note. In sub-para (1) words omitted repealed by the Care Standards Act 2000, ss 110, 117(2), Sch 6, as from 1 April 2002 (SI 2001 No 4150, SI 2002 No 920). In sub-para (1)(b) reference to '2(1)(c)' in square brackets substituted for reference in italics and words 'But this...children's home' in square brackets inserted by the Care Standards Act 2000, s 116, Sch 4, para 14(1), (27)(b), as from 1 April 2002 (SI 2001 No 4150, SI 2002 No 920).

Prohibition of advertisements relating to fostering

10. No advertisement indicating that a person will undertake, or will arrange for, a child to be privately fostered shall be published, unless it states that person's name and address.

Avoidance of insurances on lives of privately fostered children

11. A person who fosters a child privately and for reward shall be deemed for the purposes of the Life Assurance Act 1774 to have no interest in the life of the child.

SCHEDULE 9

...

Note. This Schedule repealed in relation to England and Wales by the Care Standards Act 2000, s 79(5), and in relation to Scotland by the Regulation of Care (Scotland) Act 2001, s 80(1), Sch 4, as from (in relation to England): 2 July 2001 (SI 2001 No 2041); for transitional, transitory and savings provisions see art 3, Schedule thereto; (in relation to Wales): 1 April 2002 (2002 No 920); for transitional provisions see arts 2, 3(2), Sch 2 thereto; (in relation to Scotland): 1 April 2002 (SI 2002 No 162); for transitional provisions see arts 3, 4(6), (9), (10), 7, 8(c), 12, 13 thereof.

[SCHEDULE 9A   Section 79B(9)

CHILD MINDING AND DAY CARE FOR YOUNG CHILDREN

[Exemption of certain schools

1.—(1) Except in prescribed circumstances, Part XA does not apply to provision of day care within sub-paragraph (2) for any child looked after in—
  (a) a maintained school;
  (b) a school assisted by a local education authority;
  (c) a school in respect of which payments are made by the Secretary of State or the Assembly under section 485 of the Education Act 1996;
  (d) an independent school.
  (2) The provision mentioned in sub-paragraph (1) is provision of day care made by—
  (a) the person carrying on the establishment in question as part of the establishment's activities; or
  (b) a person employed to work at that establishment and authorised to make that provision as part of the establishment's activities.
  (3) In sub-paragraph (1)—
  'assisted' has the same meaning as in the Education Act 1996;
  'maintained school' has the meaning given by section 20(7) of the School Standards and Framework Act 1998.

Exemption for other establishments

2.—(1) Part XA does not apply to provision of day care within sub-paragraph (2) for any child looked after—
  (a) in an appropriate children's home;
  (b) in a care home;
  (c) as a patient in a hospital (within the meaning of the Care Standards Act 2000);
  (d) in a residential family centre.
  (2) The provision mentioned in sub-paragraph (1) is provision of day care made by—
  (a) the department, authority or other person carrying on the establishment in question as part of the establishment's activities; or
  (b) a person employed to work at that establishment and authorised to make that provision as part of the establishment's activities.

Exemption for occasional facilities

3.—(1) Where day care is provided on particular premises on less than six days in any year, that provision shall be disregarded for the purposes of Part XA if the person making it has notified the registration authority in writing before the first occasion on which the premises concerned are so used in that year.

(2) In sub-paragraph (1) 'year' means the year beginning with the day (after the commencement of paragraph 5 of Schedule 9) on which the day care in question was or is first provided on the premises concerned and any subsequent year.

Disqualification for registration

4.—(1) Regulations may provide for a person to be disqualified for registration for child minding or providing day care.

(2) The regulations may, in particular, provide for a person to be disqualified where—

(a) he is included in the list kept under section 1 of the Protection of Children Act 1999;

(b) *he is included on the grounds mentioned in subsection (6ZA)(c) of section 218 of the Education Reform Act 1988 in the list kept for the purposes of regulations made under subsection (6) of that section;*

[(b) he is subject to a direction under section 142 of the Education Act 2002, given on the grounds that he is unsuitable to work with children;]

(c) an order of a prescribed kind has been made at any time with respect to him;

(d) an order of a prescribed kind has been made at any time with respect to any child who has been in his care;

(e) a requirement of a prescribed kind has been imposed at any time with respect to such a child, under or by virtue of any enactment;

(f) he has at any time been refused registration under Part X or Part XA or any prescribed enactment or had any such registration cancelled;

(g) he has been convicted of any offence of a prescribed kind, or has been *placed on probation or* discharged absolutely or conditionally for any such offence;

(h) he has at any time been disqualified from fostering a child privately;

(j) a prohibition has been imposed on him at any time under section 69, section 10 of the Foster Children (Scotland) Act 1984 or any prescribed enactment;

(k) his rights and powers with respect to a child have at any time been vested in a prescribed authority under a prescribed enactment.

(3) Regulations may provide for a person who lives—

(a) in the same household as a person who is himself disqualified for registration for child minding or providing day care; or

(b) in a household at which any such person is employed,

to be disqualified for registration for child minding or providing day care.

[(3A) Regulations under this paragraph may provide for a person not to be disqualified for registration by reason of any fact which would otherwise cause him to be disqualified if—

(a) he has disclosed the fact to the registration authority, and

(b) the registration authority has consented in writing to his registration and has not withdrawn that consent.]

(4) A person who is disqualified for registration for providing day care shall not provide day care, or be concerned in the management of, or have any financial interest in, any provision of day care.

(5) No person shall employ, in connection with the provision of day care, a person who is disqualified for registration for providing day care.

(6) In this paragraph 'enactment' means any enactment having effect, at any time, in any part of the United Kingdom.

[(7) A conviction in respect of which a probation order was made before 1st October 1992 (which would not otherwise be treated as a conviction) is to be treated as a conviction for the purposes of this paragraph.]

5.—(1) If any person—
   (a) acts as a child minder at any time when he is disqualified for registration for child minding; or
   (b) contravenes any of sub-paragraphs (3) to (5) of paragraph 4,
he shall be guilty of an offence.

(2) Where a person contravenes sub-paragraph (3) of paragraph 4, he shall not be guilty of an offence under this paragraph if he proves that he did not know, and had no reasonable grounds for believing, that the person in question was living or employed in the household.

(3) Where a person contravenes sub-paragraph (5) of paragraph 4, he shall not be guilty of an offence under this paragraph if he proves that he did not know, and had no reasonable grounds for believing, that the person whom he was employing was disqualified.

(4) A person guilty of an offence under this paragraph shall be liable on summary conviction to imprisonment for a term not exceeding six months, or to a fine not exceeding level 5 on the standard scale, or to both.

Certificates of registration

6.—(1) If an application for registration is granted, the registration authority shall give the applicant a certificate of registration.

(2) A certificate of registration shall give prescribed information about prescribed matters.

(3) Where, due to a change of circumstances, any part of the certificate requires to be amended, the registration authority shall issue an amended certificate.

(4) Where the registration authority is satisfied that the certificate has been lost or destroyed, the authority shall issue a copy, on payment by the registered person of any prescribed fee.

(5) For the purposes of Part XA, a person is—
   (a) registered for providing child minding (in England or in Wales); or
   (b) registered for providing day care on any premises,
if a certificate of registration to that effect is in force in respect of him.

Annual fees

7. Regulations may require registered persons to pay to the registration authority at prescribed times an annual fee of a prescribed amount.

Co-operation between authorities

8.—(1) Where it appears to the Chief Inspector that any local authority in England could, by taking any specified action, help in the exercise of any of his functions under Part XA, he may request the help of that authority specifying the action in question.

(2) Where it appears to the Assembly that any local authority in Wales could, by taking any specified action, help in the exercise of any of its functions under Part XA, the Assembly may request the help of that authority specifying the action in question.

(3) An authority whose help is so requested shall comply with the request if it is compatible with their own statutory or other duties and obligations and does not unduly prejudice the discharge of any of their functions.]

Note. Inserted by the Care Standards Act 2000, s 79, Sch 3, as from (in relation to England, for the purpose of exercising powers to make regulations under paras 1(1), 4(1), (3), 6(2), (4), 7): 16 March 2001: (SI 2001 No 1210); (in relation to Wales, for the purposes of enabling subordinate legislation to be made): 1 July 2001 (SI 2001 No 2190); (in relation to England for remaining purposes): 2 July 2001 (SI 2001 No 2041); for transitional, transitory and savings provisions see art 3, Schedule thereto; (in relation to Wales for remaining purposes): 1 April 2002 (SI 2002 No 920); for transitional provisions see arts 2, 3(2), Sch 2 thereto. Para 4(2)(b) substituted by the Education Act 2002, s 215(1), Sch 21, para 9, as from (in relation to Wales): 31 March 2003 (SI 2002 No 3185); (in relation to England): 1 June 2003 (SI 2003 No 1115). In para 4(2)(g) words 'placed on probation or' in italics repealed by the Criminal Justice Act 2003, ss 304, 332, Sch 32, Pt 1, paras 59, 61(1), (2), Sch 37, Pt 7, as from a day to be appointed. Para 4(3A) inserted by the Education Act 2002, s 152, Sch 13, para 6, as from (in relation to England): 1 October 2002 (SI 2002 No 2439); (in relation to Wales): 19 December 2002 (SI 2002 No 3185). Para 4(7) inserted by the Criminal Justice Act 2003, s 304, Sch 32, Pt 1, paras 59, 61(1), (3), as from a day to be appointed.

SCHEDULE 10   Section 88

AMENDMENTS OF ADOPTION LEGISLATION

PART I

AMENDMENTS OF ADOPTION ACT (1976 c 36)

1. *In section 2 (local authorities' social services) for the words from 'relating to' to the end there shall be substituted—*

    '(a) under the Children Act 1989, relating to family assistance orders, local authority support for children and families, care and supervision and emergency protection of children, community homes, voluntary homes and organisations, registered children's homes, private arrangements for fostering children, child minding and day care for young children and children accommodated by health authorities and local education authorities or in residential care, nursing or mental nursing homes or in independent schools; and

    (b) under the National Health Service Act 1977, relating to the provision of care for expectant and nursing mothers.'

2. *In section 11 (restrictions on arranging adoptions and placing of children) for subsection (2) there shall be substituted—*

    '(2) An adoption society which is—

    (a) approved as respects Scotland under section 3 of the Adoption (Scotland) Act 1978; or

    (b) registered as respects Northern Ireland under Article 4 of the Adoption (Northern Ireland) Order 1987,

but which is not approved under section 3 of this Act, shall not act as an adoption society in England and Wales except to the extent that the society considers it necessary to do so in the interests of a person mentioned in section 1 of the Act of 1978 or Article 3 of the Order of 1987.'

3.—*(1) In section 12 (adoption orders), in subsection (1) for the words 'vesting the parental rights and duties relating to a child in' there shall be substituted 'giving parental responsibility for a child to'.*

    (2) In subsection (2) of that section for the words 'the parental rights and duties so far as they relate' there shall be substituted 'parental responsibility so far as it relates'.

    (3) In subsection (3) of that section for paragraph (a) there shall be substituted—

    '(a) the parental responsibility which any person has for the child immediately before the making of the order;

    (aa) any order under the Children Act 1989';

and in paragraph (b) for the words from 'for any period' to the end there shall be substituted 'or upbringing for any period after the making of the order.'

4. *For section 14(1) (adoption by married couple) there shall be substituted—*

    '(1) An adoption order shall not be made on the application of more than one person except in the circumstances specified in subsections (1A) and (1B).

    (1A) An adoption order may be made on the application of a married couple where both the husband and the wife have attained the age of 21 years.

(1B) An adoption order may be made on the application of a married couple where—
   (a) the husband or the wife—
       (i) is the father or mother of the child; and
      (ii) has attained the age of 18 years:
     and
   (b) his or her spouse has attained the age of 21 years.'

5.—*(1) In section 16 (parental agreement), in subsection (1) for the words from 'in England' to 'Scotland)' there shall be substituted—*
       '(i) in England and Wales, under section 18;
      (ii) in Scotland, under section 18 of the Adoption (Scotland) Act 1978; or
     (iii) in Northern Ireland, under Article 17(1) or 18(1) of the Adoption (Northern Ireland) Order 1987.'

(2) In subsection (2)(c) of that section for the words 'the parental duties in relation to' there shall be substituted 'his parental responsibility for'.

6.—*(1) In section 18 (freeing child for adoption), after subsection (2) there shall be inserted—*
   '(2A) For the purposes of subsection (2) a child is in the care of an adoption agency if the adoption agency is a local authority and he is in their care.'

(2) In subsection (5) of that section, for the words from 'the parental rights' to 'vest in' there shall be substituted 'parental responsibility for the child is given to', and for the words 'and (3)' there shall be substituted 'to (4)'.

(3) For subsections (7) and (8) of that section there shall be substituted—
   '(7) Before making an order under this section in the case of a child whose father does not have parental responsibility for him, the court shall satisfy itself in relation to any person claiming to be the father that—
   (a) he has no intention of applying for—
      (i) an order under section 4(1) of the Children Act 1989, or
      (ii) a residence order under section 10 of that Act, or
   (b) if he did make any such application, it would be likely to be refused.
   (8) Subsections (5) and (7) of section 12 apply in relation to the making of an order under this section as they apply in relation to the making of an order under that section.'

7. *In section 19(2) (progress reports to former parents) for the words 'in which the parental rights and duties were vested' there shall be substituted 'to which parental responsibility was given'.*

8.—*(1) In section 20 (revocation of section 18 order), in subsections (1) and (2) for the words 'the parental rights and duties', in both places where they occur, there shall be substituted 'parental responsibility'.*

(2) For subsection (3) of that section there shall be substituted—
   '(3) The revocation of an order under section 18 ("a section 18 order") operates—
   (a) to extinguish the parental responsibility given to the adoption agency under the section 18 order;
   (b) to give parental responsibility for the child to—
      (i) the child's mother; and
      (ii) where the child's father and mother were married to each other at the time of his birth, the father; and
   (c) to revive—
      (i) any parental responsibility agreement,
      (ii) any order under section 4(1) of the Children Act 1989, and
      (iii) any appointment of a guardian in respect of the child (whether made by a court or otherwise),
     extinguished by the making of the section 18 order.
   (3A) Subject to subsection (3)(c), the revocation does not—
   (a) operate to revive—
      (i) any order under the Children Act 1989, or
      (ii) any duty referred to in section 12(3)(b),
     extinguished by the making of the section 18 order; or

(b) *affect any person's parental responsibility so far as it relates to the period between the making of the section 18 order and the date of revocation of that order.'*

9. *For section 21 (transfer of parental rights and duties between adoption agencies) there shall be substituted—*

'21. Variation of section 18 order so as to substitute one adoption agency for another—*(1) On an application to which this section applies, an authorised court may vary an order under section 18 so as to give parental responsibility for the child to another adoption agency ("the substitute agency") in place of the agency for the time being having parental responbility for the child under the order ("the existing agency").*

(2) This section applies to any application made jointly by—

(a) *the existing agency; and*

(b) *the would-be substitute agency.*

(3) Where an order under section 18 is varied under this section, section 19 shall apply as if the substitute agency had been given responsibility for the child on the making of the order.'

10.—*(1) In section 22 (notification to local authority of adoption application), after subsection (1) there shall be inserted the following subsections—*

'(1A) An application for such an adoption order shall not be made unless the person wishing to make the application has, within the period of two years preceding the making of the application, given notice as mentioned in subsection (1).

(1B) In subsections (1) and (1A) the references to the area in which the applicant or person has his home are references to the area in which he has his home at the time of giving the notice.'

(2) In subsection (4) of that section for the word 'receives' there shall be substituted 'receive' and for the words 'in the care of' there shall be substituted 'looked after by'.

11. *In section 25(1) (interim orders) for the words 'vesting the legal custody of the child in' there shall be substituted 'giving parental responsibility for the child to'.*

12. *In—*

(a) *section 27(1) and (2) (restrictions on removal where adoption agreed or application made under section 18); and*

(b) *section 28(1) and (2) (restrictions on removal where applicant has provided home for 5 years),*

for the words 'actual custody', in each place where they occur, there shall be substituted 'home'.

13. *After section 27(2) there shall be inserted—*

'(2A) For the purposes of subsection (2) a child is in the care of an adoption agency if the adoption agency is a local authority and he is in their care.'

14.—*(1) After section 28(2) there shall be inserted—*

'(2A) The reference in subsections (1) and (2) to any enactment does not include a reference to section 20(8) of the Children Act 1989'.

(2) For subsection (3) of that section there shall be substituted—

'(3) In any case where subsection (1) or (2) applies and—

(a) *the child was being looked after by a local authority before he began to have his home with the applicant or, as the case may be, the prospective adopter, and*

(b) *the child is still being looked after by a local authority,*

the authority which are looking after the child shall not remove him from the home of the applicant or the prospective adopter except in accordance with section 30 or 31 or with the leave of a court.'

(3) In subsection (5) of that section—

(a) *for the word 'receives' there shall be substituted 'receive'; and*

(b) *for the words 'in the care of another local authority or of a voluntary organisation' there shall be substituted 'looked after by another local authority'.*

15. *In section 29 (return of child taken away in breach of section 27 or 28) for subsections (1) and (2) there shall be substituted—*

'(1) An authorised court may, on the application of a person from whose home a child has been removed in breach of—

(a) section 27 or 28,

(b) section 27 or 28 of the Adoption (Scotland) Act 1978, or

(c) Article 28 or 29 of the Adoption (Northern Ireland) Order 1987,

order the person who has so removed the child to return the child to the applicant.

(2) An authorised court may, on the application of a person who has reasonable grounds for believing that another person is intending to remove a child from his home in breach of—

(a) section 27 or 28,

(b) section 27 or 28 of the Adoption (Scotland) Act 1978, or

(c) Article 28 or 29 of the Adoption (Northern Ireland) Order 1987,

by order direct that other person not to remove the child from the applicant's home in breach of any of those provisions.'

16.—(1) In section 30 (return of children placed for adoption by adoption agencies), in subsection (1) there shall be substituted—

(a) for the words 'delivered into the actual custody of' the words 'placed with';

(b) in paragraph (a) for the words 'retain the actual custody of the child' the words 'give the child a home'; and

(c) in paragraph (b) for the words 'actual custody' the word 'home'.

(2) In subsection (3) of that section for the words 'in his actual custody' there shall be substituted 'with him'.

17.—(1) In section 31 (application of section 30 where child not placed for adoption), in subsection (1) for the words from 'child', where it first occurs, to 'except' there shall be substituted 'child—

(a) who is (when the notice is given) being looked after by a local authority; but

(b) who was placed with that person otherwise than in pursuance of such arrangements as are mentioned in section 30(1),

that section shall apply as if the child had been placed in pursuance of such arrangements'.

(2) In subsection 2) of that section for the words 'for the time being in the care of' there shall be substituted '(when the notice is given) being looked after by'.

(3) In subsection (3) of that section—

(a) for the words 'remains in the actual custody of' there shall be substituted 'has his home with'; and

(b) for the words 'section 45 of the Child Care Act 1980' there shall be substituted 'Part III of Schedule 2 to the Children Act 1989'.

(4) At the end of that section there shall be added—

'(4) Nothing in this section affects the right of any person who has parental responsibility for a child to remove him under section 20(8) of the Children Act 1989'.

18.—(1) In section 32 (meaning of 'protected child'), in subsection (2) for the words 'section 37 of the Adoption Act 1958' there shall be substituted—

'(a) section 32 of the Adoption (Scotland) Act 1978; or

(b) Article 33 of the Adoption (Northern Ireland) Order 1987.'

(2) In subsection (3) of that section for paragraph (a) there shall be substituted—

'(a) he is in the care of any person—

(i) in any community home, voluntary home or registered children's home;

(ii) in any school in which he is receiving full-time education;

(iii) in any health service hospital';

and at the end of that subsection there shall be added—

'(d) he is in the care of any person in any home or institution not specified in this subsection but provided, equipped and maintained by the Secretary of State,'

(3) After that subsection there shall be inserted—

'(3A) In subsection (3) "community home", "voluntary home", "registered children's home", "school" and "health service hospital" have the same meaning as in the Children Act 1989.'

(4) For subsection (4) of that section there shall be substituted—

'(4) A protected child ceases to be a protected child—

(a) on the grant or refusal of the application for an adoption order;

(b) on the notification to the local authority for the area where the child has his home that the application for an adoption order has been withdrawn;

(c) in a case where no application is made for an adoption order, on the expiry of the period of two years from the giving of the notice;

(d) on the making of a residence order, a care order or a suspension order under the Children Act 1989 in respect of the child;

(e) on the appointment of a guardian for him under that Act;

(f) on his attaining the age of 18 years; or

(g) on his marriage,

whichever first occurs.

(5) In subsection (4)(d) the references to a care order and a supervision order do not include references to an interim care order or interim supervision order.' **19.**—(1) In section 35 (notices and information to be given to local authorities), in subsection (1) for the words 'who has a protected child in his actual custody' there shall be substituted 'with whom a protected child has his home'.

(2) In subsection (2) of that section for the words 'in whose actual custody he was' there shall be substituted 'with whom he had his home'.

20.—(1) In section 51 (disclosure of birth records of adopted children), in subsection (1) for the words 'subsections (4) and (6)' there shall be substituted 'what follows'.

(2) For subsections (3) to (7) of that section there shall be substituted—

'(3) Before supplying any information to an applicant under subsection (1), the Registrar General shall inform the applicant that counselling services are available to him—

(a) if he is in England and Wales—

    (i) at the General Register Office;

    (ii) from the local authority in whose area he is living;

    (iii) where the adoption order relating to him was made in England and Wales, from the local authority in whose area the court which made the order sat; or

    (iv) from any other local authority;

(b) if he is in Scotland—

    (i) from the regional or islands council in whose area he is living;

    (ii) where the adoption order relating to him was made in Scotland, from the council in whose area the court which made the order sat; or

    (iii) from any other regional or islands council;

(c) if he is in Northern Ireland—

    (i) from the Board in whose area he is living;

    (ii) where the adoption order relating to him was made in Northern Ireland, from the Board in whose area the court which made the order sat; or

    (iii) from any other Board;

(d) if he is in the United Kingdom and his adoption was arranged by an adoption society—

    (i) approved under section 3,

    (ii) approved under section 3 of the Adoption (Scotland) Act 1978,

    (iii) registered under Article 4 of the Adoption (Northern Ireland) Order 1987, from that society.

(4) Where an adopted person who is in England and Wales—

(a) applies for information under—

    (i) subsection (1), or

    (ii) Article 54 of the Adoption (Northern Ireland) Order 1987, or

(b) is supplied with information under section 45 of the Adoption (Scotland) Act 1978, it shall be the duty of the persons and bodies mentioned in subsection (5) to provide counselling for him if asked by him to do so.

(5) The persons and bodies are—

(a) the Registrar General;

(b) any local authority falling within subsection (3)(a)(ii) to (iv);

(c)   any adoption society falling within subsection (3)(d) in so far as it is acting as an adoption society in England and Wales.

(6) If the applicant chooses to receive counselling from a person or body falling within subsection (3), the Registrar General shall send to the person or body the information to which the applicant is entitled under subsection (1).

(7) Where a person—

(a)   was adopted before 12th November 1975, and

(b)   applies for information under subsection (1),

the Registrar General shall not supply the information to him unless he has attended an interview with a counsellor arranged by a person or body from whom counselling services are available as mentioned in subsection (3).

(8) Where the Registrar General is prevented by subsection (7) from supplying information to a person who is not living in the United Kingdom, he may supply the information to any body which—

(a)   the Registrar General is satisfied is suitable to provide counselling to that person, and

(b)   has notified the Registrar General that it is prepared to provide such counselling.

(9) In this section—

"a Board" means a Health and Social Services Board established under Article 16 of the Health and Personal Social Services (Northern Ireland) Order 1972; and

"prescribed" means prescribed by regulations made by the Registrar General.'

21.   After section 51 there shall be inserted—

'51A. Adoption Contact Register—(1) The Registrar General shall maintain at the General Register Office a register to be called the Adoption Contact Register.

(2) The register shall be in two parts—

(a)   Part I: Adopted Persons; and

(b)   Part II: Relatives.

(3) The Registrar General shall, on payment of such fee as may be prescribed, enter in Part I of the register the name and address of any adopted person who fulfils the conditions in subsection (4) and who gives notice that he wishes to contact any relative of his.

(4) The conditions are that—

(a)   a record of the adopted person's birth is kept by the Registrar General; and

(b)   the adopted person has attained the age of 18 years and—

(i)   has been supplied by the Registrar General with information under section 51; or

(ii)   has satisfied the Registrar General that he has such information as is necessary to enable him to obtain a certified copy of the record of his birth.

(5) The Registrar General shall, on payment of such fee as may be prescribed, enter in Part II of the register the name and address of any person who fulfils the conditions in subsection (6) and who gives notice that he wishes to contact an adopted person.

(6) The conditions are that—

(a)   a record of the adopted person's birth is kept by the Registrar General; and

(b)   the person giving notice under subsection (5) has attained the age of 18 years and has satisfied the Registrar General that—

(i)   he is a relative of the adopted person; and

(ii)   he has such information as is necessary to enable him to obtain a certified copy of the record of the adopted person's birth.

(7) The Registrar General shall, on receiving notice from any person named in an entry in the register that he wishes the entry to be cancelled, cancel the entry.

(8) Any notice given under this section must be in such form as may be determined by the Registrar General.

(9) The Registrar General shall transmit to an adopted person whose name is entered in Part I of the register the name and address of any relative in respect of whom there is an entry in Part II of the register.

(10) *Any entry cancelled under subsection (7) ceases from the time of cancellation to be an entry for the purposes of subsection (9).*

(11) *The register shall not be open to public inspection or search and the Registrar General shall not supply any person with information entered in the register (whether in an uncancelled or a cancelled entry) except in accordance with this section.*

(12) *The register may be kept by means of a computer.*

(13) *In this section—*

(a) *"relative" means any person (other than an adoptive relative) who is related to the adopted person by blood (including half-blood) or marriage;*

(b) *"address" includes any address at or through which the person concerned may be contacted; and*

(c) *"prescribed" means prescribed by the Secretary of State.'*

22.—(1) *In section 55 (adoption of children abroad), in subsection (1) after the word 'Scotland' there shall be inserted 'or Northern Ireland' and for the words 'vesting in him the parental rights and duties relating to the child' there shall be substituted 'giving him parental responsibility for the child'.*

(2) *In subsection (3) of that section for the words 'word "(Scotland)"' there shall be substituted 'words "(Scotland)" or "(Northern Ireland)".'*

23.—(1) *In section 56 (restriction on removal of children for adoption outside Great Britain),—*

(a) *in subsections (1) and (3) for the words 'transferring the actual custody of a child to', in both places where they occur, there shall be substituted 'placing a child with'; and*

(b) *in subsection (3)(a) for the words 'in the actual custody of' there shall be substituted 'with'.*

(2) *In subsection (1) of that section—*

(a) *for the words from 'or under' to 'abroad)' there shall be substituted 'section 49 of the Adoption (Scotland) Act 1978 or Article 57 of the Adoption (Northern Ireland) Order 1987'; and*

(b) *for the words 'British Islands' there shall be substituted 'United Kingdom, the Channel Islands and the Isle of Man'.*

24.—(1) *In section 57 (prohibited on certain payments) in subsection (1)(c), for the words 'transfer by that person of the actual custody of a child' there shall be substituted 'handing over of a child by that person'.*

(2) *In subsection (3A)(b) of that section, for the words 'in the actual custody of' there shall be substituted 'with'.*

25. *After section 57 there shall be inserted—*

'57A. Permitted allowances—(1) *The Secretary of State may make regulations for the purpose of enabling adoption agencies to pay allowances to persons who have adopted, or intend to adopt, children in pursuance of arrangements made by the agencies.*

(2) *Section 57(1) shall not apply to any payment made by an adoption agency in accordance with the regulations.*

(3) *The regulations may, in particular, make provision as to—*

(a) *the procedure to be followed by any agency in determining whether a person should be paid an allowance;*

(b) *the circumstances in which an allowance may be paid;*

(c) *the factors to be taken into account in determining the amount of an allowance;*

(d) *the procedure for review, variation and termination of allowances; and*

(e) *the information about allowances to be supplied by any agency to any person who is intending to adopt a child.*

(4) *Any scheme approved under section 57(4) shall be revoked as from the coming into force of this section.*

(5) *Section 57(1) shall not apply in relation to any payment made—*

(a) *in accordance with a scheme revoked under subsection (4) or section 57(5)(b); and*

(b) *to a person to whom such payments were made before the revocation of the scheme.*

(6) *Subsection (5) shall not apply where any person to whom any payments may lawfully be made by virtue of subsection (5) agrees to receive (instead of such payments) payments complying with regulations made under this section.'*

26.—(1) *In section 59 (effect of determination and orders made in Scotland and overseas in adoption proceedings), in subsection (1) for the words 'Great Britain' there shall be substituted 'the United Kingdom'.*

(2) *For subsection (2) of that section there shall be substituted—*

'(2) *Subsections (2) to (4) of section 12 shall apply in relation to an order freeing a child for adoption (other than an order under section 18) as if it were an adoption order; and, on the revocation in Scotland or Northern Ireland of an order freeing a child for adoption, subsections (3) and (3A) of section 20 shall apply as if the order had been revoked under that section.'*

27. *In section 60 (evidence of adoption in Scotland and Northern Ireland), in paragraph (a) for the words 'section 22(2) of the Adoption Act 1958' there shall be substituted 'section 45(2) of the Adoption (Scotland) Act 1978' and in paragraph (b) for the words from 'section 23(4)' to 'in force' there shall be substituted 'Article 63(1) of the Adoption (Northern Ireland) Order 1987'.*

28. *In section 62(5)(b) (courts), for the words from 'section 8' to 'child)' there shall be substituted—*

'(i)   *section 12 or 18 of the Adoption (Scotland) Act 1978; or*

(ii)   *Article 12, 17 or 18 of the Adoption (Northern Ireland) Order 1987'.*

29. ...

30.—(1) Section 72(1) (interpretation) shall be amended as follows.

(2) In the definition of 'adoption agency' for the words from 'section 1' to the end there shall be substituted '—

(a)   section 1 of the Adoption (Scotland) Act 1978; and

(b)   Article 3 of the Adoption (Northern Ireland) Order 1987.'

(3) For the definition of 'adoption order' there shall be substituted—

' "adoption order"—

(a)   means an order under section 12(1); and

(b)   in sections 12(3) and (4), 18 to 20, 27, 28 and 30 to 32 and in the definition of "British adoption order" in this subsection includes an order under section 12 of the Adoption (Scotland) Act 1978 and Article 12 of the Adoption (Northern Ireland) Order 1987 (adoption orders in Scotland and Northern Ireland respectively); and

(c)   in sections 27, 28 and 30 to 32 includes an order under section 55, section 49 of the Adoption (Scotland) Act 1978 and Article 57 of the Adoption (Northern Ireland) Order 1987 (orders in relation to children being adopted abroad).'

(4) For the definition of 'British adoption order' there shall be substituted—

' "British adoption order" means—

(a)   an adoption order as defined in this subsection, and

(b)   an order under any provision for the adoption of a child effected under the law of any British territory outside the United Kingdom.'

(5) For the definition of 'guardian' there shall be substituted—

' "guardian" has the same meaning as in the Children Act 1989.'

(6) In the definition of 'order freeing a child for adoption' for the words from 'section 27(2)' to the end there shall be substituted 'sections 27(2) and 59 includes an order under—

(a)   section 18 of the Adoption (Scotland) Act 1978; and

(b)   Article 17 or 18 of the Adoption (Northern Ireland) Order 1987'.

(7) After the definition of 'overseas adoption' there shall be inserted—

' "parent" means, in relation to a child, any parent who has parental responsibility for the child under the Children Act 1989;

"parental responsibility" and "parental responsibility agreement" have the same meaning as in the Children Act 1989.'

(8) After the definition of 'United Kingdom national' there shall be inserted—
' "upbringing" has the same meaning as in the Children Act 1989.'

(9) For section 72(1A) there shall be substituted the following subsections—

'(1A) In this Act, in determining with what person, or where, a child has his home, any absence of the child at a hospital or boarding school and any other temporary absence shall be disregarded.

(1B) In this Act, references to a child who is in the care of or lo*oked after by a local authority have the same meaning as in the Children Act 1989.*'

31. *For section 74(3) and (4) (extent) there shall be substituted—*
'*(3) This Act extends to England and Wales only.*'

Note. Repealed by the Adoption And Children Act 2002, s 139(1), (3), Sch 3, para 74, Sch 5, as from a day to be appointed.

(*Part II amends Adoption (Scotland) Act 1978 (not printed in this work*).)

SCHEDULE 11   Section 92

JURISDICTION

PART I

GENERAL

Commencement of proceedings

1.—(1) The Lord Chancellor may by order specify proceedings under this Act or *the Adoption Act 1976* [the Adoption and Children Act 2002] which may only be commenced in—

(a) a specified level of court;

(b) a court which falls within a specified class of court; or

(c) a particular court determined in accordance with, or specified in, the order.

(2) The Lord Chancellor may by order specify circumstances in which specified proceedings under this Act or *the Adoption Act 1976* [the Adoption and Children Act 2002] (which might otherwise be commenced elsewhere) may only be commenced in—

(a) a specified level of court;

(b) a court which falls within a specified class of court; or

(c) a particular court determined in accordance with, or specified in, the order.

[(2A) Sub-paragraphs (1) and (2) shall also apply in relation to proceedings—

(a) *under section 27 of the Child Support Act 1991 (reference to court for declaration of parentage); or*

[(a) under section 55A of the Family Law Act 1986 (declarations of parentage); or]

(b) which are to be dealt with in accordance with an order made under section 45 *of that Act* [of the Child Support Act 1991] (jurisdiction of courts in certain proceedings under that Act).]

(3) The Lord Chancellor may by order make provision by virtue of which, where specified proceedings with respect to a child under—

(a)   this Act;

(b)   *the Adoption Act 1976* [the Adoption and Children Act 2002];

[(bb) section 20 (appeals) ... of the Child Support Act 1991,] or

(c)   the High Court's inherent jurisdiction with respect to children,

have been commenced in or transferred to any court (whether or not by virtue of an order under this Schedule), any other specified family proceedings which may affect, or are otherwise connected with, the child may, in specified circumstances, only be commenced in that court.

(4) A class of court specified in an order under this Schedule may be described by reference to a description of proceedings and may include different levels of court.

Note. Sub-paras (2A), (3)(bb) inserted by Child Support Act 1991, s 45, as from 17 June 1992. Words in square brackets substituted for wods in italics, by the Adoption and Children Act 2002, Sch 3, para 75, as from a date to be appointed. Sub-para (2A)(a) substituted, and in sub-para (2A)(b), words in italics substituted for square brackets, by the Child Support, Pensions and Social Security Act 2000, s 83(5), Sch 8, para 10, as from 1 April 2001 (SI 2001 No 774). Words in sub-para (3)(bb) repealed by the Child Support, Pensions and Social Security Act 2000, s 85, Sch 9, Pt IX, as from 1 April 2001 (SI 2001 No 774).

Transfer of proceedings

2.—(1) The Lord Chancellor may by order provide that in specified circumstances the whole, or any specified part of, specified proceedings to which this paragraph applies shall be transferred to—
  (a) a specified level of court;
  (b) a court which falls within a specified class of court; or
  (c) a particular court determined in accordance with, or specified in, the order.
  (2) Any order under this paragraph may provide for the transfer to be made at any stage, or specified stage, of the proceedings and whether or not the proceedings, or any part of them, have already been transferred.
  (3) The proceedings to which this paragraph applies are—
  (a)   any proceedings under this Act;
  (b)   any proceedings under *the Adoption Act 1976* [the Adoption and Children Act 2002];
  [(ba) any proceedings under section 55A of the Family Law Act 1986;]
  [(bb) [any proceedings under] section 20 (appeals) ... of the Child Support Act 1991;]
  (c)   any other proceedings which—
        (i) are family proceedings for the purposes of this Act, other than proceedings under the inherent jurisdiction of the High Court; and
        (ii) may affect, or are otherwise connected with, the child concerned.
  (4) Proceedings to which this paragraph applies by virtue of sub-paragraph (3)(c) may only be transferred in accordance with the provisions of an order made under this paragraph for the purpose of consolidating them with proceedings under—
  (a) this Act;
  (b) *the Adoption Act 1976* [the Adoption and Children Act 2002]; or
  (c) the High Court's inherent jurisdiction with respect to children.
  (5) An order under this paragraph may make such provision as the Lord Chancellor thinks appropriate for excluding proceedings to which this paragraph applies from the operation of any enactment which would otherwise govern the transfer of those proceedings, or any part of them.
Note. Sub-para (3)(bb) inserted by Child Support Act 1991, s 45, as from 17 June 1992. Words in square brackets substituted for words in italics, by the Adoption and Children Act 2002, Sch 3, para 75, as from a date to be appointed. Sub-para (3)(ba) inserted by the Child Support, Pensions and Social Security Act 2000, s 83(5), Sch 8, para 10, as from 1 April 2001 (SI 2001 No 774). Words in sub-para (3)(bb) inserted, and words repealed by the Child Support, Pensions and Social Security Act 2000, ss 83(5), 85, Sch 8, para 10, Sch 9, Pt IX, as from 1 April 2001 (SI 2001 No 774).

Hearings by single justice

3.—(1) In such circumstances as the Lord Chancellor may by order specify—
  (a) the jurisdiction of a magistrates' court to make an emergency protection order;
  (b) any specified question with respect to the transfer of specified proceedings to or from a magistrates' court in accordance with the provisions of an order under paragraph 2,
may be exercised by a single justice.
  (2) Any provision made under this paragraph shall be without prejudice to any

other enactment or rule of law relating to the functions which may be performed by a single justice of the peace.

General

4.—(1) For the purposes of this Schedule—

    (a) the commencement of proceedings under this Act includes the making of any application under this Act in the course of proceedings (whether or not those proceedings are proceedings under this Act); and

    (b) there are three levels of court, that is to say the High Court, any county court and any magistrates' court.

(2) In this Schedule 'specified' means specified by an order made under this Schedule.

(3) Any order under paragraph 1 may make provision as to the effect of commencing proceedings in contravention of any of the provisions of the order.

(4) An order under paragraph 2 may make provision as to the effect of a failure to comply with any of the provisions of the order.

(5) An order under this Schedule may—

    (a) make such consequential, incidental or transitional provision as the Lord Chancellor considers expedient, including provision amending any other enactment so far as it concerns the jurisdiction of any court or justice of the peace;

    (b) make provision for treating proceedings which are—

        (i) in part proceedings of a kind mentioned in paragraph (a) or (b) of paragraph 2(3); and

        (ii) in part proceedings of a kind mentioned in paragraph (c) of paragraph 2(3),

    as consisting entirely of proceedings of one or other of those kinds, for the purposes of the application of any order made under paragraph 2.

PART II

CONSEQUENTIAL AMENDMENTS

Administration of Justice Act 1964 (c 42)

5. In section 38 of the Administration of Justice Act 1964 (interpretation), the definition of 'domestic court', which is spent, shall be omitted.

Domestic Proceedings and Magistrates' Courts Act 1978 (c 22)

6. In the Domestic Proceedings and Magistrates' Courts Act 1978—

    (a) for the words 'domestic proceedings', wherever they occur in *sections 16(5)(c) and* [section] 88(1), there shall be substituted 'family proceedings';

    (b) for the words 'domestic court panel', wherever they occur in section 16(5)(b), there shall be substituted 'family panel'.

Note. Words in square brackets substituted for words in italics, and sub-para (b) repealed by Family Law Act 1996, s 66, Sch 8, para 60(2), Sch 10, as from 1 October 1997, subject to savings in s 66(2) of, and para 5 of Sch 9 to, the 1996 Act.

Justices of the Peace Act 1979 (c 55)

7. *In the Justices of the Peace Act 1979—*

    (a) for the words 'domestic proceedings', wherever they occur in section 16(5), there shall be substituted 'family proceedings';

    (b) for the words 'domestic court', wherever they occur in section 17(3), there shall be substituted 'family proceedings court';

    (c) for the words 'domestic courts', wherever they occur in sections 38(2) and 58(1) and (5), there shall be substituted 'family proceedings courts'.

Note. Para 7 repealed by Justices of the Peace Act 1997, s 73(3), Sch 6, Part I, as from a day to be appointed so far as the repeal relates to sub-para (1), and as from 19 June 1997 otherwise.

Magistrates' Courts Act 1980 (c 43)

8. In the Magistrates' Courts Act 1980—
- (a) in section 65(1) (meaning of family proceedings), the following paragraph shall be inserted after paragraph (m)—
  '(n) the Children Act 1989';
- (b) in section 65(2)(a) for the words 'and (m)' there shall be substituted '(m) and (n)';
- (c) for the words 'domestic proceedings', wherever they occur in sections 65(1), (2) and (3), ..., 67(1) and (2), and (7), 69(1), (2), (3) and (4), 70(2) and (3), 71(1) and (2), 72(1), 73, 74(1), 121(8) and 150(1), there shall be substituted 'family proceedings';
- (d) *for the words 'domestic court panel', wherever they occur in sections ..., 67(2), (4), (5), (7) and (8) and 68(1), (2) and (3), there shall be substituted 'family panel';*
- (e) *for the words 'domestic court panels', wherever they occur in section 67(3) and (4), (5) and (6), there shall be substituted 'family panels';*
- (f) *for the words 'domestic courts', wherever they occur in sections 67(1) and (3) and 68(1), there shall be substituted 'family proceedings courts';*
- (g) *for the words 'domestic court', wherever they occur in section 67(2) and (5), there shall be substituted 'family proceedings court'.*

Note. In sub-para (c), words repealed, and in sub-para (d), reference "66(2)" repealed by the Access to Justice Act 1999, s 106, Sch 15, Pt V(3), as from 31 August 2000 (SI 2000 No 1920). In sub-para (d), words "and 8" repealed by the Access to Justice Act 1999, s 106, Sch 15, Pt V(1), as from a day to be appointed. Sub-paras (d)–(g) repealed by the Courts Act 2003, s 109(3), Sch 10, as from a date to be appointed.

Supreme Court Act 1981 (c 54)

9. In paragraph 3 of Schedule 1 to the Supreme Court Act 1981 (distribution of business to the Family Division of the High Court), the following sub-paragraph shall be added at the end—
'(e) proceedings under the Children Act 1989'.

Matrimonial and Family Proceedings Act 1984 (c 42)

10. In section 44 of the Matrimonial and Family Proceedings Act 1984 (domestic proceedings in magistrates' courts to include applications to alter maintenance agreements) for the words 'domestic proceedings', wherever they occur, there shall be substituted 'family proceedings'.

Insolvency Act 1986 (c 45)

11.—(1) In section 281(5)(b) of the Insolvency Act 1986 (discharge not to release bankrupt from bankruptcy debt arising under any order make in family proceedings or in domestic proceedings), the words 'or in domestic proceedings' shall be omitted.

(2) In section 281(8) of that Act (interpretation), for the definitions of 'domestic proceedings' and 'family proceedings' there shall be substituted—
' "family proceedings" means—
- (a) family proceedings within the meaning of the Magistrates' Courts Act 1980 and any proceedings which would be such proceedings but for section 65(1)(ii) of that Act (proceedings for variation of order for periodical payments); and
- (b) family proceedings within the meaning of Part V of the Matrimonial and Family Proceedings Act 1984.'.

SCHEDULE 12   Section 108(4)

MINOR AMENDMENTS

Custody of Children Act 1891 (c 3)

1. The Custody of Children Act 1891 (which contains miscellaneous obsolete provisions with respect to the custody of children) shall cease to have effect.

Children and Young Persons Act 1933 (c 12)

2. In section 1(2)(a) of the Children and Young Persons Act 1933 (cruelty to persons under sixteen), after the words 'young person' there shall be inserted ', or the legal guardian of a child or young person,'.
3. Section 40 of that Act shall cease to have effect.

Education Act 1944 (c 31)

4. *In section 40(1) of the Education Act 1944 (enforcement of school attendance), the words from 'or to imprisonment' to the end shall cease to have effect.*
Note. Para 4 repealed by Education Act 1993, s 307, Sch 19, para 154, Sch 21, Part I, as from 1 October 1993.

Marriage Act 1949 (c 76)

5.—(1) In section 3 of the Marriage Act 1949 (consent required to the marriage of a child by common licence or superintendent registrar's certificate), in subsection (1) for the words 'the Second Schedule to this Act' there shall be substituted 'subsection (1A) of this section'.
   (2) After that subsection there shall be inserted—
   '(1A) The consents are—
   (a) subject to paragraphs (b) to (d) of this subsection, the consent of—
        (i) each parent (if any) of the child who has parental responsibility for him; and
        (ii) each guardian (if any) of the child;
   (b) where a residence order is in force with respect to the child, the consent of the person or persons with whom he lives, or is to live, as a result of the order (in substitution for the consents mentioned in paragraph (a) of this subsection);
   (c) where a care order is in force with respect to the child, the consent of the local authority designated in the order (in addition to the consents mentioned in paragraph (a) of this subsection);
   (d) where neither paragraph (b) nor (c) of this subsection applies but a residence order was in force with respect to the child immediately before he reached the age of sixteen, the consent of the person or persons with whom he lived, or was to live, as a result of the order (in substitution for the consents mentioned in paragraph (a) of this subsection).
   (1B) In this section 'guardian of a child', 'parental responsibility', 'residence order' and 'care order' have the same meaning as in the Children Act 1989.'

Births and Deaths Registration Act 1953 (c 20)

6.—(1) Sections 10 and 10A of the Births and Deaths Registration Act 1953 (registration of father, and re-registration, where parents not married) shall be amended as follows.
   (2) In sections 10(1) and 10A(1) for paragraph (d) there shall be substituted—
   '(d) at the request of the mother or that person on production of—
        (i) a copy of a parental responsibility agreement made between them in relation to the child; and

 (ii) a declaration in the prescribed form by the person making the request stating that the agreement was made in compliance with section 4 of the Children Act 1989 and has not been brought to an end by an order of a court; or

(e) at the request of the mother or that person on production of—

 (i) a certified copy of an order under section 4 of the Children Act 1989 giving that person parental responsibility for the child; and

 (ii) a declaration in the prescribed form by the person making the request stating that the order has not been brought to an end by an order of a court; or

(f) at the request of the mother or that person on production of—

 (i) a certified copy of an order under paragraph 1 of Schedule 1 to the Children Act 1989 which requires that person to make any financial provision for the child and which is not an order falling within paragraph 4(3) of that Schedule; and

 (ii) a declaration in the prescribed form by the person making the request stating that the order has not been discharged by an order of a court; or

(g) at the request of the mother or that person on production of—

 (i) a certified copy of any of the orders which are mentioned in subsection (1A) of this section which has been made in relation to the child; and

 (ii) a declaration in the prescribed form by the person making the request stating that the order has not been brought to an end or discharged by an order of a court.'

(3) After sections 10(1) and 10A(1) there shall be inserted—

'(1A) The orders are—

(a) an order under section 4 of the Family Law Reform Act 1987 that that person shall have all the parental rights and duties with respect to the child;

(b) an order that that person shall have custody or care and control or legal custody of the child made under section 9 of the Guardianship of Minors Act 1971 at a time when such an order could only be made in favour of a parent;

(c) an order under section 9 or 11B of that Act which requires that person to make any financial provision in relation to the child;

(d) an order under section 4 of the Affiliation Proceedings Act 1957 naming that person as putative father of the child.'

(4) In section 10(2) for the words 'or (d)' there shall be substituted 'to (g)'.

(5) In section 10(3) for the words from ' "relevant order" ' to the end there shall be substituted ' "parental responsibility agreement" has the same meaning as in the Children Act 1989'.

(6) In section 10A(2), in paragraphs (b) and (c) for the words 'paragraph (d)' in both places where they occur there shall be substituted 'any of paragraphs (d) to (g)'.

Army Act 1955 (c 18)

7. In section 151 of the Army Act 1955 (deductions from pay for maintenance of wife or child), in subsection (1A)(a) for the words 'in the care of a local authority in England or Wales' there shall be substituted 'being looked after by a local authority in England or Wales (within the meaning of the Children Act 1989)'.

8.—(1) *Schedule 5A to that Act (powers of court on trial of civilian) shall be amended as follows.*

(2) *For paragraphs 7(3) and (4) there shall be substituted—*

'(3) *While an authorisation under a reception order is in force the order shall (subject to sub-paragraph (4) below) be deemed to be a care order for the purposes of the Children Act 1989, and the authorised authority shall be deemed to be the authority designated in that deemed care order.*

(3A) *In sub-paragraph (3) above "care order" means a care order which is not an interim care order under section 38 of the Children Act 1989.*

(4) The Children Act 1989 shall apply to a reception order which is deemed to be a care order by virtue of sub-paragraph (3) above as if sections 31(8) (designated local authority), 91 (duration of care order etc) and 101 (effect of orders as between different jurisdictions) were omitted.'

(3) In sub-paragraph (5)(c) for the words from 'attains' to the end there shall be substituted 'attains 18years of age'.

(4) In paragraph 8(1) for the words 'Children and Young Persons Act 1969' there shall be substituted 'Children Act 1989'.

Note. Para 8 repealed by Armed Forces Act 1991, s 26(2), Sch 3, as from 1 January 1992.

Air Force Act 1955 (c 19)

9. Section 151(1A) of the Air Force Act 1955 (deductions from pay for maintenance of wife or child) shall have effect subject to the amendment that is set out in paragraph 7 in relation to section 151(1A) of the Army Act 1955.

10. *Schedule 5A to that Act (powers of court on trial of civilian) shall have effect subject to the amendments that are set out in paragraph 8(2) to (4) in relation to Schedule 5A to the Army Act 1955.*

Note. Para 10 repealed by Armed Forces Act 1991, s 26(2), Sch 3, as from 1 January 1992.

Sexual Offences Act 1956 (c 69)

11. *In section 19(3) of the Sexual Offences Act 1956 (abduction of unmarried girl under eighteen from parent or guardian) for the words 'the lawful care or charge of' there shall be substituted 'parental responsibility for or care of'.*

Note. Para 11 repealed by the Sexual Offences Act 2003, s 140, Sch 7, as from 1 May 2004 (SI 2004 No 874).

12. *In section 20(2) of that Act (abduction of unmarried girl under sixteen from parent or guardian) for the words 'the lawful care or charge of' there shall be substituted 'parental responsibility for or care of'.*

Note. Para 12 repealed by the Sexual Offences Act 2003, s 140, Sch 7, as from 1 May 2004 (SI 2004 No 874).

13. *In section 21(3) of that Act (abduction of defective from parent or guardian) for the words 'the lawful care or charge of' there shall be substituted 'parental responsibility for or care of'.*

Note. Para 13 repealed by the Sexual Offences Act 2003, s 140, Sch 7, as from 1 May 2004 (SI 2004 No 874).

14. *In section 28 of that Act (causing or encouraging prostitution of, intercourse with, or indecent assault on, girl under sixteen) for subsections (3) and (4) there shall be substituted—*

'(3) The persons who are to be treated for the purposes of this section as responsible for a girl are (subject to subsection (4) of this section)—

(a) her parents;

(b) any person who is not a parent of hers but who has parental responsibility for her; and

(c) any person who has care of her.

(4) An individual falling within subsection (3)(a) or (b) of this section is not to be treated as responsible for a girl if—

(a) a residence order under the Children Act 1989 is in force with respect to her and he is not named in the order as the person with whom she is to live; or

(b) a care order under that Act is in force with respect to her.'

Note. Para 14 repealed by the Sexual Offences Act 2003, s 140, Sch 7, as from 1 May 2004 (SI 2004 No 874).

15. Section 38 of that Act (power of court to divest person of authority over girl or boy in case of incest) shall cease to have effect.

16.—(1) *In section 43 of that Act (power to search for and recover woman detained for immoral purposes), in subsection (5) for the words 'the lawful care or charge of' there shall be substituted 'parental responsibility for or care of'.*

(2) *In subsection (6) of that section, for the words 'section forty of the Children and Young Persons Act 1933' there shall be substituted 'Part V of the Children Act 1989'.*

Note. Para 16 repealed by the Sexual Offences Act 2003, s 140, Sch 7, as from 1 May 2004 (SI 2004 No 874).

17. After section 46 of that Act there shall be inserted—

'**46A. Meaning of "parental responsibility"**—In this Act "parental responsibility" has the same meaning as in the Children Act 1989.'

Naval Discipline Act 1957 (c 53)

18. *Schedule 4A to the Naval Discipline Act 1957 (powers of court on trial of civilian) shall have effect subject to the amendments that are set out in paragraph 8(2) to (4) in relation to Schedule 5A to the Army Act 1955.*

Note. Para 18 repealed by Armed Forces Act 1991, s 26(2), Sch 3, as from 1 January 1992.

Children and Young Persons Act 1963 (c 37)

19. Section 3 of the Children and Young Persons Act 1963 (children and young persons beyond control) shall cease to have effect.

Children and Young Persons Act 1969 (c 54)

20. In section 5 of the Children and Young Persons Act 1969 (restrictions on criminal proceedings for offences by young persons), in subsection (2), for the words 'section 1 of this Act' there shall be substituted 'Part IV of the Children Act 1989'.

21. *After section 7(7) of that Act (alteration in treatment of young offenders, etc) there shall be inserted—*

'(7B) *An order under subsection (7)(c) of this section shall not require a person to enter into a recognisance—*

(a) *for an amount exceeding £1,000; or*

(b) *for a period exceeding—*

(i) *three years; or*

(ii) *where the young person concerned will attain the age of eighteen in a period shorter than three years, that shorter period.*

(7C) *Section 120 of the Magistrates' Courts Act 1980 shall apply to a recognisance entered into in pursuance of an order under subsection (7)(c) of this section as it applies to a recognisance to keep the peace.'*

Note. Para 21 repealed by Criminal Justice Act 1991, s 101(2), Sch 13, as from 1 October 1992.

22. *In section 12A of that Act (young offenders) for subsections (1) and (2) there be substituted—*

'(1) *This subsection applies to any supervision order made under section 7(7) of this Act unless it requires the supervised person to comply with directions given by the supervisor under section 12(2) of this Act.'*

Note. Para 22 repealed by the Powers of Criminal Courts (Sentencing) Act 2000, s 165(4), Sch 12, Pt I, as from 25 August 2000.

23. *After that section there shall be inserted—*

'**12AA. Requirement for young offender to live in local authority accommodation**—(1) *Where the conditions mentioned in subsection (6) of this section are* *satisfied, a supervision order may impose a requirement ("a residence requirement") that a child or young person shall live for a specified period in local authority accommodation.*

(2) A residence requirement shall designate the local authority who are to receive the child or young person and that authority shall be the authority in whose area the child or young person resides.

(3) The court shall not impose a residence requirement without first consulting the designated authority.

(4) A residence requirement may stipulate that the child or young person shall not live with a named person.

(5) The maximum period which may be specified in a residence requirement is six months.

(6) The conditions are that—

(a) a supervision order has previously been made in respect of the child or young person;

(b) that order imposed—

    (i) a requirement under section 12A(3) of this Act; or

    (ii) a residence requirement;

(c) he is found guilty of an offence which—

    (i) was committed while that order was in force;

    (ii) if it had been committed by a person over the age of twenty-one, would have been punishable with imprisonment; and

    (iii) in the opinion of the court is serious; and

(d) the court is satisfied that the behaviour which constituted the offence was due, to a significant extent, to the circumstances in which he was living,

except that the condition in paragraph (d) of this subsection does not apply where the condition in paragraph (b)(ii) is satisfied.

(7) For the purposes of satisfying itself as mentioned in subsection (6)(d) of this section, the court shall obtain a social inquiry report which makes particular reference to the circumstances in which the child or young person was living.

(8) Subsection (7) of this section does not apply if the court already has before it a social inquiry report which contains sufficient information about the circumstances in which the child or young person was living.

(9) A court shall not include a residence requirement in respect of a child or young person who is not legally represented at the relevant time in that court unless—

(a) he has applied for legal aid for the purposes of the proceedings and the application was refused on the ground that it did not appear that his resources were such that he required assistance; or

(b) he has been informed of his right to apply for legal aid for the purposes of the proceedings and has had the opportunity to do so, but nevertheless refused or failed to apply.

(10) In subsection (9) of this section—

(a) "the relevant time" means the time when the court is considering whether or not to impose the requirement; and

(b) "the proceedings" means—

    (i) the whole proceedings; or

    (ii) the part of the proceedings relating to the imposition of the requirement.

(11) A supervision order imposing a residence requirement may also impose any of the requirements mentioned in sections 12, 12A, 12B or 12C of this Act.

(12) In this section "social inquiry report" has the same meaning as in section 2 of the Criminal Justice Act 1982.'

Note. Para 23 repealed by the Powers of Criminal Courts (Sentencing) Act 2000, s 165(4), Sch 12, Pt I, as from 25 August 2000.

24.—*(1) In section 15 of that Act (variation and discharge of supervision orders), in subsections (1)(a), (2A), (3)(e) and (4) after the word '12A', in each place where it occurs, there shall be inserted '12AA'.*

(2) In subsection (4) of that section for the words '(not being a juvenile court)' there shall be substituted 'other than a juvenile court'.

Note. Para 24 repealed by Criminal Justice Act 1991, s 101(2), Sch 13, as from 1 October 1992.

25.—(*1*) *In section 16 of that Act (provisions supplementary to section 15), in subsection* (*3*) *for the words 'either direct' to the end there shall be substituted—*

    '(*i*) *direct that he be released forthwith; or*

    (*ii*) *remand him.'*

  (*2*) *In subsection (4) of that section—*

  (*a*) *in paragraph (a) for the words 'an interim order made by virtue of' there shall be substituted 'a remand under';*

  (*b*) *in paragraph (b) for the words 'makes an interim order in respect of' there shall be substituted 'remands', and*

  (*c*) *for the words 'make an interim order in respect of' there shall be substituted 'remand'.*

  (*3*) *In subsections (5)(b) and (c) and (6)(a) after the word '12A', in each place where it occurs, there shall be inserted '12AA'.*

Note. Para 25 repealed by Courts and Legal Services Act 1990, ss 116, 125(7), Sch 16, para 37, Sch 20, as from 14 October 1991.

26. For section 23 of that Act (remand to care of local authorities etc) there shall be substituted—

'**23. Remand to local authority accommodation, committal of young persons of unruly character, etc**—(1) Where a court—

  (a) remands or commits for trial a child charged with homicide or remands a child convicted of homicide; or

  (b) remands a young person charged with or convicted of one or more offences or commits him for trial or sentence,

and he is not released on bail, then, unless he is a young person who is certified by the court to be of unruly character, the court shall remand him to local authority accommodation.

  (2) A court remanding a person to local authority accommodation shall designate the authority who are to receive him and that authority shall be the authority in whose area it appears to the court that—

  (a) he resides; or

  (b) the offence or one of the offences was committed.

  (3) Where a person is remanded to local authority accommodation, it shall be lawful for any person acting on behalf of the designated authority to detain him.

  (4) The court shall not certify a young person as being of unruly character unless—

  (a) he cannot safely be remanded to local authority accommodation; and

  (b) the conditions prescribed by order made by the Secretary of State under this subsection are satisfied in relation to him.

  (5) Where the court certifies that a young person is of unruly character, it shall commit him—

  (a) to a remand centre, if it has been notified that such a centre is available for the reception from the court of such persons; and

  (b) to a prison, if it has not been so notified.

  (6) Where a young person is remanded to local authority accommodation, a court may, on the application of the designated authority, certify him to be of unruly character in accordance with subsection (4) of this section (and on so doing he shall cease to be remanded to local authority accommodation and subsection (5) of this section shall apply).

  (7) For the purposes of subsection (6) of this section, "a court" means—

  (a) the court which remanded the young person; or

  (b) any magistrates' court having jurisdiction in the place where that person is for the time being,

and in this section "court" and "magistrates' court" include a justice.

(8) This section has effect subject to—

(a) section 37 of the Magistrates' Courts Act 1980 (committal to the Crown Court with a view to a sentence of detention in a young offender institution); and

(b) section 128(7) of that Act (remands to the custody of a constable for periods of not more than three days),

but section 128(7) shall have effect in relation to a child or young person as if for the reference to three clear days there were substituted a reference to twenty-four hours.'

27.—(1) In section 32 of that Act (detention of absentees), for subsection (1A) there shall be substituted the following subsections—

'(1A) If a child or young person is absent, without the consent of the responsible person—

(a) from a place of safety to which he has been taken under section 16(3) of this Act; or

(b) from local authority accommodation—

(i) in which he is required to live under section 12AA of this Act; or

(ii) to which he has been remanded under section 23(1) of this Act,

he may be arrested by a constable anywhere in the United Kingdom or Channel Islands without a warrant.

(1B) A person so arrested shall be conducted to—

(a) the place of safety;

(b) the local authority accommodation; or

(c) such other place as the responsible person may direct,

at the responsible person's expense.

(1C) In this section "the responsible person" means the person who made the arrangements under section 16(3) of this Act or, as the case may be, the authority designated under section 12AA or 23 of this Act.'

(2) In subsection (2B) of that section for the words 'person referred to in subsection (1A)(a) or (b) (as the case may be) of this section' there shall be substituted 'responsible person'.

28. In section 34(1) of that Act (transitional modifications of Part I for persons of specified ages)—

(a) in paragraph (a), for the words '13(2) or 28(4) or (5)' there shall be substituted 'or 13(2)'; and

(b) in paragraph (e), for the words 'section 23(2) or (3)' there shall be substituted 'section 23(4) to (6)'.

29. In section 70(1) of that Act (interpretation)—

(a) after the definition of 'local authority' there shall be inserted—

' "local authority accommodation" means accommodation provided by or on behalf of a local authority (within the meaning of the Children Act 1989)'; ...

(b) ...

Note. Sub-para (b) and word preceding it repealed by the Powers of Criminal Courts (Sentencing) Act 2000, s 165(4), Sch 12, Pt I, as from 25 August 2000.

30. In section 73 of that Act (extent, etc)—

(a) in subsection (4)(a) for '32(1), (3) and (4)' there shall be substituted '32(1) to (1C) and (2A) to (4)'; and

(b) in subsection (6) for '32(1), (1A)' there shall be substituted '32(1) to (1C)'.

Matrimonial Causes Act 1973 (c 18)

31. For section 41 of the Matrimonial Causes Act 1973 (restrictions on decrees for dissolution, annulment or separation affecting children) there shall be substituted—

'41. Restrictions on decrees for dissolution, annulment or separation affecting children—(1) In any proceedings for a decree of divorce or nullity of marriage, or a decree of judicial separation, the court shall consider—

(a) whether there are any children of the family to whom this section applies; and

(b) where there are any such children, whether (in the light of the arrangements which have been, or are proposed to be, made for their upbringing and welfare) it should exercise any of its powers under the Children Act 1989 with respect to any of them.

(2) Where, in any case to which this section applies, it appears to the court that—

(a) the circumstances of the case require it, or are likely to require it, to exercise any of its powers under the Act of 1989 with respect to any such child;

(b) it is not in a position to exercise that power or (as the case may be) those powers without giving further consideration to the case; and

(c) there are exceptional circumstances which make it desirable in the interests of the child that the court should give a direction under this section,

it may direct that the decree of divorce or nullity is not to be made absolute, or that the decree of judicial separation is not to be granted, until the court orders otherwise.

(3) This section applies to—

(a) any child of the family who has not reached the age of sixteen at the date when the court considers the case in accordance with the requirements of this section; and

(b) any child of the family who has reached that age at that date and in relation to whom the court directs that this section shall apply.'

32. In section 42 of that Act, subsection (3) (declaration by court that party to marriage unfit to have custody of children of family) shall cease to have effect.

33. In section 52(1) of that Act (interpretation), in the definition of 'child of the family', for the words 'has been boarded-out with those parties' there shall be substituted 'is placed with those parties as foster parents'.

National Health Service Act 1977 (c 49)

34. In Schedule 8 to the National Health Service Act 1977 (functions of local social services authorities), the following sub-paragraph shall be added at the end of paragraph 2—

'(4A) This paragraph does not apply in relation to persons under the age of 18.'

Child Care Act 1980 (c 5)

35. Until the repeal of the Child Care Act 1980 by this Act takes effect, the definition of 'parent' in section 87 of that Act shall have effect as if it applied only in relation to Part I and sections 13, 24, 64 and 65 of that Act (provisions excluded by section 2(1)(f) of the Family Law Reform Act 1987 from the application of the general rule in that Act governing the meaning of references to relationships between persons).

Education Act 1981 (c 60)

36. *The following section shall be inserted in the Education Act 1981, after section 3—*

'3A. Provision outside England and Wales for certain children—(*1*) *A local authority may make such arrangements as they think fit to enable any child in respect of whom they maintain a statement under section 7 to attend an establishment outside England and Wales which specialises in providing for children with special needs.*

(2) In subsection (1) above "children with special needs" means children who have particular needs which would be special educational needs if those children were in England and Wales.

(3) Where an authority make arrangements under this section with respect to a child, those arrangements may, in particular, include contributing to or paying—

(*a*) *fees charged by the establishment;*
(*b*) *expenses reasonably incurred in maintaining him while he is at the establishment or travelling to or from it;*
(*c*) *those travelling expenses;*
(*d*) *expenses reasonably incurred by any person accompanying him while he is travelling or staying at the establishment.*
(*4*) *This section is not to be taken as in any way limiting any other powers of a local education authority.'*

Note. Para 36 repealed by Education Act 1993, s 307, Sch 19, para 154, Sch 21, Part I, as from 1 September 1994.

Child Abduction Act 1984 (c 37)

37.—(1) Section 1 of the Child Abduction Act 1984 (offence of abduction by parent, etc) shall be amended as follows.

(2) For subsections (2) to (4) there shall be substituted—

'(2) A person is connected with a child for the purposes of this section if—
(a) he is a parent of the child; or
(b) in the case of a child whose parents were not married to each other at the time of his birth, there are reasonable grounds for believing that he is the father of the child; or
(c) he is a guardian of the child; or
(d) he is a person in whose favour a residence order is in force with respect to the child; or
(e) he has custody of the child.
(3) In this section "the appropriate consent", in relation to a child, means—
(a) the consent of each of the following—
   (i) the child's mother;
   (ii) the child's father, if he has parental responsibility for him;
   (iii) any guardian of the child;
   (iv) any person in whose favour a residence order is in force with respect to the child;
   (v) any person who has custody of the child; or
(b) the leave of the court granted under or by virtue of any provision of Part II of the Children Act 1989; or
(c) if any person has custody of the child, the leave of the court which awarded custody to him.
(4) A person does not commit an offence under this section by taking or sending a child out of the United Kingdom without obtaining the appropriate consent if—
(a) he is a person in whose favour there is a residence order in force with respect to the child, and
(b) he takes or sends him out of the United Kingdom for a period of less than one month.
(4A) Subsection (4) above does not apply if the person taking or sending the child out of the United Kingdom does so in breach of an order under Part II of the Children Act 1989.'

(3) In subsection (5) for the words from 'but' to the end there shall be substituted—

'(5A) Subsection (5)(c) above does not apply if—
(a) the person who refused to consent is a person—
   (i) in whose favour there is a residence order in force with respect to the child; or
   (ii) who has custody of the child; or
(b) the person taking or sending the child out of the United Kingdom is, by so acting, in breach of an order made by a court in the United Kingdom.'

(4) For subsection (7) there shall be substituted—

'(7) For the purposes of this section—

(a) "guardian of a child", "residence order" and "parental responsibility" have the same meaning as in the Children Act 1989; and

(b) a person shall be treated as having custody of a child if there is in force an order of a court in the United Kingdom awarding him (whether solely or jointly with another person) custody, legal custody or care and control of the child.'

(5) In subsection (8) for the words from 'or voluntary organisation' to 'custodianship proceedings or' there shall be substituted 'detained in a place of safety, remanded to a local authority accommodation or the subject of'.

38.—(1) In section 2 of that Act (offence of abduction of child by other persons), in subsection (1) for the words from 'Subject' to 'above' there shall be substituted 'Subject to subsection (3) below, a person, other than one mentioned in subsection (2) below.'

(2) For subsection (2) of that section there shall be substituted—

'(2) The persons are—

(a) where the father and mother of the child in question were married to each other at the time of his birth, the child's father and mother;

(b) where the father and mother of the child in question were not married to each other at the time of his birth, the child's mother; and

(c) any other person mentioned in section 1(2)(c) to (e) above.

(3) In proceedings against any person for an offence under this section, it shall be a defence for that person to prove—

(a) where the father and mother of the child in question were not married to each other at the time of his birth—

(i) that he is the child's father; or

(ii) that, at the time of the alleged offence, he believed, on reasonable grounds, that he was the child's father; or

(b) that, at the time of the alleged offence, he believed that the child had attained the age of sixteen.'

39. At the end of section 3 of that Act (construction of references to taking, sending and detaining) there shall be added 'and

(d) references to a child's parents and to a child whose parents were (or were not) married to each other at the time of his birth shall be construed in accordance with section 1 of the Family Law Reform Act 1987 (which extends their meaning).'

40.—(1) The Schedule to that Act (modifications of section 1 for children in certain cases) shall be amended as follows.

(2) In paragraph 1(1) for the words 'or voluntary organisation' there shall be substituted 'within the meaning of the Children Act 1989'.

(3) For paragraph 2(1) there shall be substituted—

'(1) This paragraph applies in the case of a child who is—

(a) detained in a place of safety under section 16(3) of the Children and Young Persons Act 1969; or

(b) remanded to a local authority accommodation under section 23 of that Act.'

(4) In paragraph 3(1)—

(a) in paragraph (a) for the words 'section 14 of the Children Act 1975' there shall be substituted 'section 18 of the Adoption Act 1976'; and

(b) in paragraph (d) for the words 'section 25 of the Children Act 1975 or section 53 of the Adoption Act 1958' there shall be substituted 'section 55 of the Adoption Act 1976'.

(5) In paragraph 3(2)(a)—

(a) in sub-paragraph (i), for the words from 'order or', to 'Children Act 1975' there shall be substituted 'section 18 order or, if the section 18 order has been varied under section 21 of that Act so as to give parental responsibility to another agency', and

(b) in sub-paragraph (ii), for the words '(c) or (e)' there shall be substituted 'or (c)'.

(6) At the end of paragraph 3 there shall be added—

'(3) Sub-paragraph (2) above shall be construed as if the references to the court included, in any case where the court is a magistrates' court, a reference to any magistrates' court acting for the same area as that court'.

(7) For paragraph 5 there shall be substituted—

'**5.** In this Schedule—

(a) "adoption agency" and "adoption order" have the same meaning as in the Adoption Act 1976; and

(b) "area", in relation to a magistrates' court, means the petty sessions area (within the meaning of the Justices of the Peace Act 1979) for which the court is appointed.'.

Foster Children (Scotland) Act 1984 (c 56)

41. In section 1 of the Foster Children (Scotland) Act 1984 (definition of foster child)—

(a) for the words 'he is— (a)' there shall be substituted '(a) he is'; and

(b) the words 'for a period of more than 6 days' and the words from 'The period' to the end shall cease to have effect.

42. In section 2(2) of that Act (exceptions to section 1), for paragraph (f) there shall be substituted—

'(f) if he has been in that person's care for a period of less than 28 days and that person does not intend to undertake his care for any longer period.'

43. In section 7(1) of that Act (persons disqualified from keeping foster children)—

(a) the word 'or' at the end of paragraph (e) shall be omitted; and

(b) after paragraph (f) there shall be inserted 'or

(g) he is disqualified from fostering a child privately (within the meaning of the Children Act 1989) by regulations made under section 68 of that Act,'.

Disabled Persons (Services, Consultation and Representation) Act 1986 (c 33)

44. In section 2(5) of the Disabled Persons (Services, Consultation and Representation Act 1986 (circumstances in which authorised representative has right to visit etc disabled person), after paragraph (d) there shall be inserted—

'(dd) in accommodation provided by any educational establishment'.

Legal Aid Act 1988 (c 34)

45. *In paragraph 2 of Part I of Schedule 2 to the Legal Aid Act 1988 (proceedings in magistrates' courts to which the civil legal aid provisions of Part IV of the Act apply), the following sub-paragraph shall be added at the end—*

'(g) *proceedings under the Children Act 1989'.*

Note. Para 45 repealed by the Access to Justice Act 1999, s 106, Sch 15, Pt I, as from 1 April 2000.

SCHEDULE 13 Section 108(5)

CONSEQUENTIAL AMENDMENTS

Wills Act 1837 (c 26)

1. In section 1 of the Wills Act 1837 (interpretation), in the definition of 'will', for the words 'and also to a disposition by will and testament or devise of the custody and tuition of any child' there shall be substituted 'and also to an appointment by will of a guardian of a child'.

Children and Young Persons Act 1933 (c 12)

2. In section 1(1) of the Children and Young Persons Act 1933 (cruelty to persons under sixteen) for the words 'has the custody, charge or care of' there shall be substituted 'has responsibility for'.

3. In the following sections of that Act—

(a) 3(1) (allowing persons under sixteen to be in brothels);

(b) 4(1) and (2) (causing or allowing persons under sixteen to be used for begging);

(c) 11 (exposing children under twelve to risk of burning); and

(d) 25(1) (restrictions on persons under eighteen going abroad for the purpose of performing for profit),

for the words 'the custody, charge or care of' there shall, in each case, be substituted 'responsibility for'.

4. *In section 10(1A) of that Act (vagrants preventing children from receiving education), for the words from 'to bring the child' to the end there shall be substituted 'to make an application in respect of the child or young person for an education supervision order under section 36 of the Children Act 1989'.*

Note. Para 4 repealed by Education Act 1993, s 307, Sch 19, para 155, Sch 21, Part I, as from 1 October 1993.

5. For section 17 of that Act (interpretation of Part I) there shall be substituted the following section—

'**17. Interpretation of Part I**—(1) For the purposes of this Part of this Act, the following shall be presumed to have responsibility for a child or young person—

(a) any person who—

(i) has parental responsibility for him (within the meaning of the Children Act 1989); or

(ii) is otherwise legally liable to maintain him; and

(b) any person who has care of him.

(2) A person who is presumed to be responsible for a child or young person by virtue of subsection (1)(a) shall not be taken to have ceased to be responsible for him by reason only that he does not have care of him.'

6.—(1) In section 34 of that Act (attendance at court of parent of child or young person charged with an offence etc), in subsection (1) after the word 'offence' there shall be inserted 'is the subject of an application for a care or supervision order under Part IV of the Children Act 1989'.

(2) In subsection (7) of that section after the words 'Children and Young Persons Act 1969' there shall be inserted 'or Part IV of the Children Act 1989'.

(3) After subsection (7) of that section there shall be inserted—

'(7A) If it appears that at the time of his arrest the child or young person is being provided with accommodation by or on behalf of a local authority under section 20 of the Children Act 1989, the local authority shall also be informed as described in subsection (3) above as soon as it is reasonably practicable to do so.'

7. In section 107(1) of that Act (interpretation)—

(a) in the definition of 'guardian', for the words 'charge of or control over' there shall be substituted 'care of';

(b) for the definition of legal guardian there shall be substituted—

' "legal guardian", in relation to a child or young person, means a guardian of a child as defined in the Children Act 1989'.

Education Act 1944 (c 31)

8.—(*1*) *Section 40 of the Education Act 1944 (enforcement of school attendance) shall be amended as follows.*

(*2*) *For subsection (2) there shall be substituted—*

'(*2*) *Proceedings for such offences shall not be instituted except by a local education authority.*

(*2A*) Before instituting such proceedings the local education authority shall consider whether it would be appropriate, instead of or as well as instituting the proceedings, to apply for an education supervision order with respect to the child.'

(*3*) For subsections (*3*) and (*4*) there shall be substituted—

'(*3*) The court—

(*a*) by which a person is convicted of an offence against section 37 of this Act; or

(*b*) before which a person is charged with an offence under section 39 of this Act, may direct the local education authority instituting the proceedings to apply for an education supervision order with respect to the child unless the authority, having consulted the appropriate local authority, decide that the child's welfare will be satisfactorily safeguarded even though no education supervision order is made.

(*3A*) Where, following such a direction, a local education authority decide not to apply for an education supervision order they shall inform the court of the reasons for their decision.

(*3B*) Unless the court has directed otherwise, the information required under subsection (*3A*) shall be given to the court before the end of the period of eight weeks beginning with the date on which the direction was given.

(*4*) Where—

(*a*) a local education authority apply for an education supervision order with respect to a child who is the subject of a school attendance order; and

(*b*) the court decides that section 36(*3*) of the Children Act 1989 prevents it from making the order;

the court may direct that the school attendance order shall cease to be in force.'

(*4*) After subsection (*4*) there shall be inserted—

'(*5*) In this section—

"appropriate local authority" has the same meaning as in section 36(*9*) of the Children Act 1989; and

"education supervision order" means an education supervision order under that Act.'

Note. Para 8 repealed by Education Act 1993, s 307, Sch 19, para 155, Sch 21, Part I, as from 1 October 1993.

9. In section 71 of that Act (*complaints with respect to independent schools*), the following paragraph shall be added after paragraph (*d*), in subsection (*1*)—

'(*e*) there has been a failure, in relation to a child provided with accommodation by the school, to comply with the duty imposed by section 87 of the Children Act 1989 (*welfare of children accommodated in independent schools*);'.

10. After section 114(*1C*) of that Act (*interpretation*) there shall be inserted the following subsections—

'(*1D*) In this Act, unless the context otherwise requires, "parent", in relation to a child or young person, includes any person—

(*a*) who is not a parent of his but who has parental responsibility for him, or

(*b*) who has care of him,

except for the purposes of the enactments mentioned in subsection (*1E*) of this section, where it only includes such a person if he is an individual.

(*1E*) The enactments are—

(*a*) sections 5(*4*), 15(*2*) and (*6*), 31 and 65(*1*), and paragraph 7(*6*) of Schedule 2 to, the Education (No 2) Act 1986; and

(*b*) sections 53(*8*), 54(*2*), 58(*5*)(*k*), 60 and 61 of the Education Reform Act 1988.

(*1F*) For the purposes of subsection (*1D*) of this section—

(*a*) "parental responsibility" has the same meaning as in the Children Act 1989; and

(*b*) in determining whether an individual has care of a child or young person any absence of the child or young person at a hospital or boarding school and any other temporary absence shall be disregarded.'

Note. Paras 9, 10 repealed by Education Act 1996, s 582(2), Sch 38, Part I, as from 1 November 1996.

National Assistance Act 1948 (c 29)

11.—(1) In section 21(1)(a) of the National Assistance Act 1948 (persons for whom local authority is to provide residential accommodation) after the word 'persons' there shall be inserted 'aged eighteen or over'.

(2) In section 29(1) of that Act (welfare arrangements for blind, deaf, dumb and crippled persons) after the words 'that is to say persons' and after the words 'and other persons' there shall, in each case, be inserted 'aged eighteen or over'.

Reserve and Auxiliary Forces (Protection of Civil Interests) Act 1951 (c 65)

12. For section 2(1)(d) of the Reserve and Auxiliary Forces (Protection of Civil Interests) Act 1951 (cases in which leave of an appropriate court is required before enforcing certain orders for the payment of money), there shall be substituted—

'(d) an order for alimony, maintenance or other payment made under sections 21 to 33 of the Matrimonial Causes Act 1973 or made, or having effect as if made, under Schedule 1 to the Children Act 1989'.

Mines and Quarries Act 1954 (c 70)

13. *In section 182(1) of the Mines and Quarries Act 1954 (interpretation), in the definition of 'parent', for the words from 'or guardian' to first 'young person' there shall be substituted 'of a young person or any person who is not a parent of his but who has parental responsibility for him (within the meaning of the Children Act 1989)'.*

Note. Para 13 repealed by Children (Scotland) Act 1995, s 105(5), Sch 5, as from 1 November 1996.

Administration of Justice Act 1960 (c 65)

14. In section 12 of the Administration of Justice Act 1960 (publication of information relating to proceedings in private), in subsection (1) for paragraph (a) there shall be substituted—

'(a) where the proceedings—
  (i)   relate to the exercise of the inherent jurisdiction of the High Court with respect to minors;
  (ii) are brought under the Children Act 1989; or
  (iii) otherwise relate wholly or mainly to the maintenance or upbringing of a minor;'.

Factories Act 1961 (c 34)

15. In section 176(1) of the Factories Act 1961 (interpretation), in the definition of 'parent', for the words from 'or guardian' to first 'young person' there shall be substituted 'of a child or young person or any person who is not a parent of his but who has parental responsibility for him (within the meaning of the Children Act 1989)'.

Criminal Justice Act 1967 (c 80)

16. In section 67(1A)(c) of the Criminal Justice Act 1967 (computation of sentences of imprisonment passed in England and Wales) for the words 'in the care of a local authority' there shall be substituted 'remanded to local authority accommodation'.

Health Services and Public Health Act 1968 (c 46)

17.—(1) In section 64(3)(a) of the Health Services and Public Health Act 1968 (meaning of 'relevant enactments' in relation to power of Minister of Health or Secretary of State to provide financial assistance), for sub-paragraph (xix) inserted by paragraph 19 of Schedule 5 to the Child Care Act 1980 there shall be substituted—

'(xx) the Children Act 1989.'

(2) In section 65(3)(b) of that Act (meaning of 'relevant enactments' in relation to power of local authority to provide financial and other assistance), for sub-paragraph (xx) inserted by paragraph 20 of Schedule 5 to the Child Care Act 1980 there shall be substituted—

'(xxi) the Children Act 1989.'

Social Work (Scotland) Act 1968 (c 49)

18. In section 2(2) of the Social Work (Scotland) Act 1968 (matters referred to social work committee) after paragraph (j) there shall be inserted—

'(k) section 19 and Part X of the Children Act 1989,'.

19. In section 5(2)(c) of the Act (power of Secretary of State to make regulations) for the words 'and (j)' there shall be substituted 'to (k)'.

20. In section 21(3) of that Act (mode of provision of accommodation and maintenance) for the words 'section 21 of the Child Care Act 1980' there shall be substituted 'section 23 of the Children Act 1989'.

21. In section 74(6) of that Act (parent of child in residential establishment moving to England or Wales) for the words from 'Children and Young Persons Act 1969' to the end there shall be substituted 'Children Act 1989, but as if section 31(8) were omitted'.

22. In section 75(2) of that Act (parent of child subject to care order etc moving to Scotland), for the words 'Children and Young Persons Act 1969' there shall be substituted 'Children Act 1989'.

23. In section 86(3) of that Act (meaning of ordinary residence for purpose of adjustments between authority providing accommodation and authority of area of residence), the words 'the Child Care Act 1980 or' shall be omitted and after the words 'education authority' there shall be inserted 'or placed with local authority foster parents under the Children Act 1989'.

Civil Evidence Act 1968 (c 64)

24. *In section 12(5)(b) of the Civil Evidence Act 1968 (findings of paternity etc as evidence in civil proceedings—meaning of 'relevant proceedings') for sub-paragraph (iv) there shall be substituted—*

'(iv) paragraph 23 of Schedule 2 to the Children Act 1989.'

Administration of Justice Act 1970 (c 31)

25. *In Schedule 8 to the Administration of Justice Act 1970 (maintenance orders for purposes of Maintenance Orders Act 1958 and the 1970 Act), in paragraph 6 for the words 'section 47 or 51 of the Child Care Act 1980' there shall be substituted 'paragraph 23 of Schedule 2 to the Children Act 1989'.*

Note. Paras 24, 25 repealed by Courts and Legal Services Act 1990, ss 116, 125(7), Sch 16, paras 2(2), 6(2), Sch 20.

Local Authority Social Services Act 1970 (c 42)

26.—(1) In Schedule 1 to the Local Authority Social Services Act 1970 (enactments conferring functions assigned to social service committee)—

(a) in the entry relating to the Mental Health Act 1959, for the words 'sections 8 and 9' there shall be substituted 'section 8'; and

(b) in the entry relating to the Children and Young Persons Act 1969, for the words 'sections 1, 2 and 9' there shall be substituted 'section 9'.

(2) At the end of that Schedule there shall be added—

'Children Act 1989

The whole Act, in so far as it confers functions on a local authority within the meaning of that Act.

Welfare reports.

Consent to application for residence order in respect of child in care.

Family assistance orders.

Functions under Part III of the Act (local authority support for children and families).

Care and supervision.

Protection of children.

Functions in relation to community homes, voluntary homes and voluntary organisations, registered children's homes, private arrangements for fostering children, child minding and day care for young children.

Inspection of children's homes on behalf of Secretary of State.

Research and returns of information.

Functions in relation to children accommodated by health authorities and local education authorities or in residential care, nursing or mental nursing homes or in independent schools.'

Chronically Sick and Disabled Persons Act 1970 (c 44)

27. After section 28 of the Chronically Sick and Disabled Persons Act 1970 there shall be inserted—

'**28A. Application of Act to authorities having functions under the Children Act 1989.** This Act applies with respect to disabled children it relation to whom a local authority have functions under Part III of the Children Act 1989 as it applies in relation to persons to whom section 29 of the National Assistance Act 1948 applies.'

Courts Act 1971 (c 23)

28. In Part I of Schedule 9 to the Courts Act Act 1971 (substitution of references to Crown Court), in the entry relating to the Children and Young Persons Act 1969, for the words 'Sections 2(12), 3(8), 16(8), 21(4)(5)' there shall be substituted 'Section 16(8).'.

Attachment of Earnings Act 1971 (c 32)

29. In Schedule 1 to the Attachment of Earnings Act 1971 (maintenance orders to which that Act applies), in paragraph 7, for the words 'section 47 or 51 of the Child Care Act 1980' there shall be substituted 'paragraph 23 of Schedule 2 to the Children Act 1989'.

Tribunals and Inquiries Act 1971 (c 62)

30. *In Schedule 1 to the Tribunals and Inquiries Act 1971 (tribunals under direct supervision of the Council on Tribunals), for paragraph 4 there shall be substituted—*

'*Registration of voluntary homes and children's homes under the Children Act 1989.*

4. *Registered Homes Tribunals constituted under Part III of the Registered Homes Act 1984.*'

Note. Para 30 repealed by Tribunals and Inquiries Act 1992, s 18(2), Sch 4, Part I, as from 1 October 1992.

Local Government Act 1972 (c 70)

31.—(1) In section 102(1) of the Local Government Act 1972 (appointment of committees) for the words 'section 31 of the Child Care Act 1980' there shall be substituted 'section 53 of the Children Act 1989'.

(2) In Schedule 12A to that Act (access to information: exempt information), in Part III (interpretation), in paragraph 1(1)(b) for the words 'section 20 of the Children and Young Persons Act 1969' there shall be substituted 'section 31 of the Children Act 1989'.

Employment of Children Act 1973 (c 24)

32.—(1) In section 2 of the Employment of Children Act 1973 (supervision by education authorities), in subsection (2)(a) for the words 'guardian or a person who has actual custody of' there shall be substituted 'any person responsible for'.

(2) After that subsection there shall be inserted—

'(2A) For the purposes of subsection (2)(a) above a person is responsible for a child—

(a) in England and Wales, if he has parental responsibility for the child or care of him; and

(b) in Scotland, if he is his guardian or has actual custody of him.'.

Domicile and Matrimonial Proceedings Act 1973 (c 45)

33.—(*1*) *In Schedule 1 to the Domicile and Matrimonial Proceedings Act 1973 (proceedings in divorce etc stayed by reference to proceedings in other jurisdiction), paragraph 11(1) shall be amended as follows—*

(*a*) *at the end of the definition of 'lump sum' there shall be added 'or an order made in equivalent circumstances under Schedule 1 to the Children Act 1989 and of a kind mentioned in paragraph 1(2)(c) of that Schedule';*

(*b*) *in the definition of 'relevant order', at the end of paragraph (b), there shall be added 'or an order made in equivalent circumstances under Schedule 1 to the Children Act 1989 and of a kind mentioned in paragraph 1(2)(a) or (b) of that Schedule';*

(*c*) *in paragraph (c) of that definition, after the word 'children)' there shall be inserted 'or a section 8 order under the Children Act 1989'; and*

(*d*) *in paragraph (d) of that definition for the words 'the custody, care or control' there shall be substituted 'care'.*

(2) In paragraph 11(3) of that Schedule—

(a) the words 'four' shall be omitted; and

(b) for the words 'the custody of a child and the education of a child' there shall be substituted 'or any provision which could be made by a section 8 order under the Children Act 1989'.

Note. Para 33(1) repealed by Family Law Act 1996, s 66(3), Sch 10, as from a day to be appointed, subject to savings in s 66(2) of, and para 5 of Sch 9 to, the 1996 Act.

Powers of Criminal Courts Act 1973 (c 62)

34. *In Schedule 3 to the Powers of Criminal Courts Act 1973 (the probation and after-care service and its functions), in paragraph 3(2A) after paragraph (b) there shall be inserted—*

'and

(*c*) *directions given under paragraph 2 or 3 of Schedule 3 to the Children Act 1989'.*

Note. Para 34 repealed by Probation Service Act 1993, s 32(3), Sch 4, as from 5 February 1994.

Rehabilitation of Offenders Act 1974 (c 53)

35.—(1) Section 7(2) of the Rehabilitation of Offenders Act 1974 (limitations on rehabilitation under the Act) shall be amended as follows.

(2) For paragraph (c) there shall be substituted—

'(c) in any proceedings relating to adoption, the marriage of any minor, the exercise of the inherent jurisdiction of the High Court with respect to minors or the provision by any person of accommodation, care or schooling for minors;

(cc) in any proceedings brought under the Children Act 1989;'

(3) For paragraph (d) there shall be substituted—

'(d) in any proceedings relating to the variation or discharge of a supervision order under the Children and Young Persons Act 1969, or on appeal from any such proceedings'.

Domestic Proceedings and Magistrates' Courts Act 1978 (c 22)

36. For section 8 of the Domestic Proceedings and Magistrates' Courts Act 1978 (orders for the custody of children) there shall be substituted—

'**8. Restrictions on making of orders under this Act: welfare of children.** Where an application is made by a party to a marriage for an order under section 2, 6 or 7 of this Act, then, if there is a child of the family who is under the age of eighteen, the court shall not dismiss it or make a final order on the application until it has decided whether to exercise any of its powers under the Children Act 1989 with respect to the child.'

37. In section 19(3A)(b) (interim orders) for the words 'subsections (2) and' there shall be substituted 'subsection'.

38. For section 20(12) of that Act (variation and revocation of orders for periodical payments) there shall be substituted—

'(12) An application under this section may be made—

(a) where it is for the variation or revocation of an order under section 2, 6, 7 or 19 of this Act for periodical payments, by either party to the marriage in question; and

(b) where it is for the variation of an order under section 2(1)(c), 6, or 7 of this Act for periodical payments to or in respect of a child, also by the child himself, if he has attained the age of sixteen.'

39.—(1) For section 20A of that Act (revival of orders for periodical payments) there shall be substituted—

'**20A. Revival of orders for periodical payments**—(1) Where an order made by a magistrates' court under this Part of this Act for the making of periodical payments to or in respect of a child (other than an interim maintenance order) ceases to have effect—

(a) on the date on which the child attains the age of sixteen, or

(b) at any time after that date but before or on the date on which he attains the age of eighteen,

the child may apply to the court which made the order for an order for its revival.

(2) If on such an application it appears to the court that—

(a) the child is, will be or (if an order were made under this subsection) would be receiving instruction at an educational establishment or undergoing training for a trade, profession or vocation, whether or not while in gainful employment, or

(b) there are special circumstances which justify the making of an order under this subsection,

the court shall have power by order to revive the order from such date as the court may specify, not being earlier than the date of the making of the application.

(3) Any order revived under this section may be varied or revoked under section 20 in the same way as it could have been varied or revoked had it continued in being.'

40. *In section 23(1) of that Act (supplementary provisions with respect to the variation and revocation of orders) for the words '14(3), 20 or 21' there shall be substituted '20' and for the words 'section 20 of this Act' there shall be substituted 'that section'.*

Note. Para 40 repealed by Courts and Legal Services Act 1990, s 116, 125(7), Sch 16, para 32, Sch 20.

41.—(1) In section 25 of that Act (effect on certain orders of parties living together), in subsection (1)(a) for the words '6 or 11(2)' there shall be substituted 'or 6'.

(2) In subsection (2) of that section—

(a) in paragraph (a) for the words '6 or 11(2)' there shall be substituted 'or 6'; and

(b) after paragraph (a) there shall be inserted 'or'.

42. In section 29(5) of that Act (appeals) for the words 'sections 14(3), 20 and 21' there shall be substituted 'section 20'.

43. In section 88(1) of that Act (interpretation)—

(a) in the definition of 'child', for the words from 'an illegitimate' to the end there shall be substituted 'a child whose father and mother were not married to each other at the time of his birth'; and

(b) in the definition of 'child of the family', for the words 'being boarded-out with those parties' there shall be substituted 'placed with those parties as foster parents'.

Magistrates' Courts Act 1980 (c 43)

44.—(*1*) *In section 59(2) of the Magistrates' Courts Act 1980 (periodical payments through justices' clerk) for the words 'the Guardianship of Minors Acts 1971 and 1973' there shall be substituted '(or having effect as if made under) Schedule 1 to the Children Act 1989'.*

Note. Para 44(1) repealed by Maintenance Enforcement Act 1991, s 11(2), Sch 3, as from 1 April 1992.

(2) For section 62(5) of that Act (payments to children) there shall be substituted—

'(5) In this section references to the person with whom a child has his home—

(a) in the case of any child who is being looked after by a local authority (within the meaning of section 22 of the Children Act 1989), are references to that local authority; and

(b) in any other case, are references to the person who, disregarding any absence of the child at a hospital or boarding school and any other temporary absence, has care of the child.'.

Supreme Court Act 1981 (c 54)

45.—(1) In section 18 of the Supreme Court Act 1981 (restrictions on appeals to Court of Appeal)—

(a) in subsection (1)(h)(i), for the word 'custody' there shall be substituted 'residence'; and

(b) in subsection (1)(h)(ii) for the words 'access to', in both places, there shall be substituted 'contact with'.

(2) In section 41 of that Act (wards of court), the following subsection shall be inserted after subsection (2)—

'(2A) Subsection (2) does not apply with respect to a child who is the subject of a care order (as defined by section 105 of the Children Act 1989).'

(3) In Schedule 1 to that Act (distribution of business in High Court), for paragraph 3(b)(ii) there shall be substituted—

'(ii) the exercise of the inherent jurisdiction of the High Court with respect to minors, the maintenance of minors and any proceedings under the Children Act 1989, except proceedings solely for the appointment of a guardian of a minor's estate;'.

Armed Forces Act 1981 (c 55)

46. In section 14 of the Armed Forces Act 1981 (temporary removal to, and detention in, place of safety abroad or in the United Kingdom of service children in need of care and control), in subsection (9A) for the words 'the Children and Young Persons Act 1933, the Children and Young Persons Act 1969' there shall be substituted 'the Children Act 1989'.

Civil Jurisdiction and Judgments Act 1982 (c 27)

47. In paragraph 5(a) of Schedule 5 to the Civil Jurisdiction and Judgments Act 1982 (maintenance and similar payments excluded from Schedule 4 to that Act) for the words 'section 47 or 51 of the Child Care Act 1980' there shall be substituted 'paragraph 23 of Schedule 2 to the Children Act 1989'.

Mental Health Act 1983 (c 20)

48.—(1) For section 27 of the Mental Health Act 1983 (children and young persons in care of local authority) there shall be substituted the following section—

'27. Children and young persons in care.   Where—
   (a) a patient who is a child or young person is in the care of a local authority by virtue of a care order within the meaning of the Children Act 1989; or
   (b) the rights and powers of a parent of a patient who is a child or young person are vested in a local authority by virtue of section 16 of the Social Work (Scotland) Act 1968,
the authority shall be deemed to be the nearest relative of the patient in preference to any person except the patient's husband or wife (if any).'

(2) Section 28 of that Act (nearest relative of minor under guardianship, etc) is amended as mentioned in sub-paragraphs (3) and (4).

(3) For subsection (1) there shall be substituted—
'(1) Where—
   (a) a guardian has been appointed for a person who has not attained the age eighteen years; or
   (b) a residence order (as defined by section 8 of the Children Act 1989) is in force with respect to such a person,
the guardian (or guardians, where there is more than one) or the person named in the residence order shall, to the exclusion of any other person, be deemed to be his nearest relative.'

(4) For subsection (3) there shall be substituted—
'(3) In this section "guardian" does not include a guardian under this Part of this Act.'

(5) In section 131(2) of that Act (informal admission of patients aged sixteen or over) for the words from 'notwithstanding' to the end there shall be substituted 'even though there are one or more persons who have parental responsibility for him (within the meaning of the Children Act 1989)'.

Registered Homes Act 1984 (c 23)

49.—*(1) In section 1(5) of the Registered Homes Act 1984 (requirement of registration) for paragraphs (d) and (e) there shall be substituted—*
   '(d) any community home, voluntary home or children's home within the meaning of the Children Act 1989.'

(2) In section 39 of that Act (preliminary) for paragraphs (a) and (b) there shall be substituted—
   '(a) the Children Act 1989.'

Note. Para 49 repealed by the Care Standards Act 2000, s 117(2), Sch 6, as from 1 April 2002 (SI 2001 No 4150, SI 2002 No 920).

Mental Health (Scotland) Act 1984 (c 36)

50. For section 54 of the Mental Health (Scotland) Act 1984 (children and young persons in care of local authority) there shall be substituted the following section—

'**54. Children and young persons in care of local authority.**   Where—
  (a) the rights and powers of a parent of a patient who is a child or young person
      are vested in a local authority by virtue of section 16 of the Social Work
      (Scotland) Act 1968; or
  (b) a patient who is a child or young person is in the care of a local authority by
      virtue of a care order made under the Children Act 1989,
the authority shall be deemed to be the nearest relative of the patient in preference
to any person except the patient's husband or wife (if any).'.

Matrimonial and Family Proceedings Act 1984 (c 42)

51. In section 38(2)(b) of the Matrimonial and Family Proceedings Act 1984
(transfer of family proceedings from High Court to county court) after the words
'a ward of court' there shall be inserted 'or any other proceedings which relate to
the exercise of the inherent jurisdiction of the High Court with respect to minors'.

Police and Criminal Evidence Act 1984 (c 60)

52. In section 37(14) of the Police and Criminal Evidence Act 1984 (duties of
custody officer before charge) after the words 'Children and Young Persons Act
1969' there shall be inserted 'or in Part IV of the Children Act 1989'.
53.—(*1*) *In section 38 of that Act (duties of custody officer after charge), in subsection (6)
for the words from 'make arrangements' to the end there shall be substituted 'secure that the
arrested juvenile is moved to local authority accommodation'.*
  (2) After that subsection there shall be inserted—
  '(6A) In this section "local authority accommodation" means accommodation
provided by or on behalf of a local authority (within the meaning of the Children
Act 1989).
  (6B) Where an arrested juvenile is moved to local authority accommodation
under subsection (6) above, it shall be lawful for any person acting on behalf of the
authority to detain him.'.
  (3) In subsection (8) of that section for the words 'Children and Young Persons
Act 1969' there shall be substituted 'Children Act 1989'.
Note. Sub-para (1) repealed by Criminal Justice Act 1991, s 101(2), Sch 13, as from 1 October
1992.
54. In section 39(4) of that Act (responsibilities in relation to persons detained)
for the words 'transferred to the care of a local authority in pursuance of
arrangements made' there shall be substituted 'moved to local authority
accommodation'.
55. In Schedule 2 to that Act (preserved powers of arrest) in the entry relating to
the Children and Young Persons Act 1969 for the words 'Sections 28(2) and' there
shall be substituted 'Section'.

Surrogacy Arrangements Act 1985 (c 49)

56. In section 1(2)(b) of the Surrogacy Arrangements Act 1985 (meaning of
'surrogate mother', etc) for the words 'the parental rights being exercised' there
shall be substituted 'parental responsibility being met'.

Child Abduction and Custody Act 1985 (c 60)

57.—(1) In sections 9(a) and 20(2)(a) of the Child Abduction and Custody Act
1985 (orders with respect to which court's powers suspended), for the words 'any
other order under section 1(2) of the Children and Young Persons Act 1969' there
shall be substituted 'a supervision order under section 31 of the Children Act 1989'.
  (2) At the end of section 27 of that Act (interpretation), there shall be added—

'(4) In this Act a decision relating to rights of access in England and Wales means a decision as to the contact which a child may, or may not, have with any person.

(3) In Part I of Schedule 3 to that Act (orders in England and Wales which are custody orders for the purposes of the Act), for paragraph 1 there shall be substituted—

'**1.** The following are the orders referred to in section 27(1) of this Act—

(a) a care order under the Children Act 1989 (as defined by section 31(11) of that Act, read with section 105(1) and Schedule 14);

(b) a residence order (as defined by section 8 of the Act of 1989); and

(c) any order made by a court in England and Wales under any of the following enactments—

    (i) section 9(1), 10(1)(a) or 11(a) of the Guardianship of Minors Act 1971;

    (ii) section 42(1) or (2) or 43(1) of the Matrimonial Causes Act 1973;

    (iii) section 2(2)(b), (4)(b) or (5) of the Guardianship Act 1973 as applied by section 34(5) of the Children Act 1975;

    (iv) section 8(2)(a), 10(1) or 19(1)(ii) of the Domestic Proceedings and Magistrates Courts Act 1978;

    (v) section 26(1)(b) of the Adoption Act 1976.'

Disabled Persons (Services, Consultation and Representation) Act 1986 (c 33)

58. In section 1(3) of the Disabled Persons (Services, Consultation and Representation) Act 1986 (circumstances in which regulations may provide for the appointment of authorised representatives of disabled persons)—

(a) in paragraph (a), for the words 'parent or guardian of a disabled person under the age of sixteen' there shall be substituted—

    '(i) the parent of a disabled person under the age of sixteen, or

    (ii) any other person who is not a parent of his but who has parental responsibility for him'; and

(b) in paragraph (b), for the words 'in the care of' there shall be substituted 'looked after by'.

59.—(1) Section 2 of that Act (circumstances in which authorised representative has right to visit etc disabled person) shall be amended as follows.

(2) In subsection 3(a) for the words from second 'the' to 'by' there shall be substituted 'for the words "if so requested by the disabled person" there shall be substituted "if so requested by any person mentioned in section 1(3)(a)(i) or (ii)".'

(3) In subsection (5) after paragraph (b) there shall be inserted—

'(bb) in accommodation provided by or on behalf of a local authority under Part III of the Children Act 1989, or'.

(4) After paragraph (c) of subsection (5) there shall be inserted—

'(cc) in accommodation provided by a voluntary organisation in accordance with arrangements made by a local authority under section 17 of the Children Act 1989, or'.

60. In section 5(7)(b) of that Act (disabled persons leaving special education) for the word 'guardian' there shall be substituted 'other person who is not a parent of his but who has parental responsibility for him'.

61.—(1) In section 16 of that Act (interpretation) in the definition of 'disabled person', in paragraph (a) for the words from 'means' to 'applies' there shall be substituted 'means—

    (i) in the case of a person aged eighteen or over, a person to whom section 29 of the 1948 Act applies, and

    (ii) in the case of a person under the age of eighteen, a person who is disabled within the meaning of Part III of the Children Act 1989'.

(2) After the definition of 'parent' in that section there shall be inserted—

' "parental responsibility" has the same meaning as in the Children Act 1989.'

(3) In the definition of 'the welfare enactments' in that section, in paragraph (a) after the words 'the 1977 Act' there shall be inserted 'and Part III of the Children Act 1989'.

(4) At the end of that section there shall be added—

'(2) In this Act any reference to a child who is looked after by a local authority has the same meaning as in the Children Act 1989.'

Family Law Act 1986 (c 55)

62.—(1) The Family Law Act 1986 shall be amended as follows.

(2) Subject to paragraphs 63 to 71, in Part I—

(a) for the words 'custody order', in each place where they occur, there shall be substituted 'Part I order';

(b) for the words 'proceedings with respect to the custody of', in each place where they occur, there shall be substituted 'Part I proceedings with respect to'; and

(c) for the words 'matters relating to the custody of', in each place where they occur, there shall be substituted 'Part I matters relating to'.

(3) For section 42(7) (general interpretation of Part I) there shall be substituted—

'(7) In this Part—

(a) references to Part I proceedings in respect of a child are references to any proceedings for a Part I order or an order corresponding to a Part I order and include, in relation to proceedings outside the United Kingdom, references to proceedings before a tribunal or other authority having power under the law having effect there to determine Part I matters; and

(b) references to Part I matters are references to matters that might be determined by a Part I order or an order corresponding to a Part I order.'

63.—(1) In section 1 (orders to which Part I of the Act of 1986 applies), in subsection (1)—

(a) for paragraph (a) there shall be substituted—

'(a) a section 8 order made by a court in England and Wales under the Children Act 1989, other than an order varying or discharging such an order'; and

(b) for paragraph (d) there shall be substituted the following paragraphs—

'(d) an order made by a court in England and Wales in the exercise of the inherent jurisdiction of the High Court with respect to children—

(i) so far as it gives care of a child to any person or provides for contact with, or the education of, a child; but

(ii) excluding an order varying or revoking such an order;

(e) an order made by the High Court in Northern Ireland in the exercise of its jurisdiction relating to wardship—

(i) so far as it gives care and control of a child to any person or provides for the education of or access to a child; but

(ii) excluding an order relating to a child of whom care or care and control is (immediately after the making of the order) vested in the Department of Health and Social Services or a Health and Social Services Board.'

(2) *In subsection (2) of that section, in paragraph (c) for '(d)' there shall be substituted '(e)'.*

(3) For subsections (3) to (5) of that section there shall be substituted—

'(3) In this Part, "Part I order"—

(a) includes any order which would have been a custody order by virtue of this section in any form in which it was in force at any time before its amendment by the Children Act 1989; and

(b) (subject to sections 32 and 40 of this Act) excludes any order which would have been excluded from being a custody order by virtue of this section in any such form.'

Note. Sub-para (2) repealed by Children (Northern Ireland Consequential Amendments) Order 1995, SI 1995 No 756, art 15, Schedule, as from 4 November 1996.

64. For section 2 there shall be substituted the following sections—

'**2. Jurisdiction: general**—(1) A court in England and Wales shall not have jurisdiction to make a section 1(1)(a) order with respect to a child in or in connection with matrimonial proceedings in England and Wales unless the condition in section 2A of this Act is satisfied.

(2) A court in England and Wales shall not have jurisdiction to make a section 1(1)(a) order in a non-matrimonial case (that is to say, where the condition in section 2A of this Act is not satisfied) unless the condition in section 3 of this Act is satisfied.

(3) A court in England and Wales shall not have jurisdiction to make a section 1(1)(d) order unless—

(a) the condition in section 3 of this Act is satisfied, or

(b) the child concerned is present in England and Wales on the relevant date and the court considers that the immediate exercise of its powers is necessary for his protection.

2A. Jurisdiction in or in connection with matrimonial proceedings—(1) The condition referred to in section 2(1) of this Act is that the matrimonial proceedings are proceedings in respect of the marriage of the parents of the child concerned and—

(a) the proceedings—
  (i) are proceedings for divorce or nullity of marriage, and
  (ii) are continuing;

(b) the proceedings—
  (i) are proceedings for judicial separation,
  (ii) are continuing,
  and the jurisdiction of the court is not excluded by subsection (2) below; or

(c) the proceedings have been dismissed after the beginning of the trial but—
  (i) the section 1(1)(a) order is being made forthwith, or
  (ii) the application for the order was made on or before the dismissal.

(2) For the purposes of subsection (1)(b) above, the jurisdiction of the court is excluded if, after the grant of a decree of judicial separation, on the relevant date, proceedings for divorce or nullity in respect of the marriage are continuing in Scotland or Northern Ireland.

(3) Subsection (2) above shall not apply if the court in which the other proceedings there referred to are continuing has made—

(a) an order under section 13(6) or 21(5) of this Act (not being an order made by virtue of section 13(6)(a)(i)), or

(b) an order under section 14(2) or 22(2) of this Act which is recorded as being made for the purpose of enabling Part I proceedings to be taken in England and Wales with respect to the child concerned.

(4) Where a court—

(a) has jurisdiction to make a section 1(1)(a) order in or in connection with matrimonial proceedings, but

(b) considers that it would be more appropriate for Part I matters relating to the child to be determined outside England and Wales,

the court may by order direct that, while the order under this subsection is in force, no section 1(1)(a) order shall be made by any court in or in connection with those proceedings.

65.—(*1*) *In section 3 (habitual residence or presence of child concerned) in subsection (1) for 'section 2' there shall be substituted 'section 2(2)'.*

(2) In subsection (2) of that section for the words 'proceedings for divorce, nullity or judicial separation' there shall be substituted 'matrimonial proceedings'.

Note. Sub-para (1) repealed by Family Law Act 1996, s 66(3), Sch 10, as from a day to be appointed, subject to savings in s 66(2) of, and para 5 of Sch 9 to, the 1996 Act.

66.—(1) In section 6 (duration and variation of Part I orders), for subsection (3) there shall be substituted the following subsections—

'(3) A court in England and Wales shall not have jurisdiction to vary a Part I order if, on the relevant date, matrimonial proceedings are continuing in Scotland or Northern Ireland in respect of the marriage of the parents of the child concerned.

(3A) Subsection (3) above shall not apply if—

(a) the Part I order was made in or in connection with proceedings for divorce or nullity in England and Wales in respect of the marriage of the parents of the child concerned; and

(b) those proceedings are continuing.

(3B) Subsection (3) above shall not apply if—

(a) the Part I order was made in or in connection with proceedings for judicial separation in England and Wales;

(b) those proceedings are continuing; and

(c) the decree of judicial separation has not yet been granted.'

(2) In subsection (5) of that section for the words from 'variation of' to 'if the ward' there shall be substituted 'variation of a section 1(1)(d) order if the child concerned'.

(3) For subsections (6) and (7) of that section there shall be substituted the following subsections—

'(6) Subsection (7) below applies where a Part I order which is—

(a) a residence order (within the meaning of the Children Act 1989) in favour of a person with respect to a child,

(b) an order made in the exercise of the High Court's inherent jurisdiction with respect to children by virtue of which a person has care of a child, or

(c) an order—

(i) of a kind mentioned in section 1(3)(a) of this Act,

(ii) under which a person is entitled to the actual possession of a child,

ceases to have effect in relation to that person by virtue of subsection (1) above.

(7) Where this subsection applies, any family assistance order made under section 16 of the Children Act 1989 with respect to the child shall also cease to have effect.

(8) For the purposes of subsection (7) above the reference to a family assistance order under section 16 of the Children Act 1989 shall be deemed to include a reference to an order for the supervision of a child made under—

(a) section 7(4) of the Family Law Reform Act 1969,

(b) section 44 of the Matrimonial Causes Act 1973,

(c) section 2(2)(a) of the Guardianship Act 1973,

(d) section 34(5) or 36(3)(b) of the Children Act 1975, or

(e) section 9 of the Domestic Proceedings and Magistrates' Courts Act 1978;

but this subsection shall cease to have effect once all such orders for the supervision of children have ceased to have effect in accordance with Schedule 14 to the Children Act 1989.'

67. For section 7 (interpretation of Chapter II) there shall be substituted—

'**7. Interpretation of Chapter II.** In this Chapter—

(a) "child" means a person who has not attained the age of eighteen;

(b) "matrimonial proceedings" means proceedings for divorce, nullity of marriage or judicial separation;

(c) "the relevant date" means in relation to the making or variation of an order—
   (i) where an application is made for an order to be made or varied, the date of the application (or first application, if two or more are determined together), and
   (ii) where no such application is made, the date on which the court is considering whether to make or, as the case may be, vary the order; and
(d) "section 1(1)(a) order" and "section 1(1)(d) order" mean orders falling within section 1(1)(a) and (d) of this Act respectively.'

68. In each of the following sections—
   (a) section 11(2)(a) (provisions supplementary to sections 9 and 10).
   (b) section 13(5)(a) (jurisdiction ancillary to matrimonial proceedings),
   (c) section 20(3)(a) (habitual residence or presence of child),
   (d) section 21(4)(a) (jurisdiction in divorce proceedings, etc), and
   (e) section 23(4)(a) (duration and variation of custody orders),
for '4(5)' there shall be substituted '2A(4)'.

69. In each of the following sections—
   (*a*) *section 19(2) (jurisdiction in cases other than divorce, etc)*,
   (b) section 20(6) (habitual residence or presence of child), and
   (c) section 23(5) (duration and variation of custody orders),
for 'section 1(1)(d)' there shall be substituted 'section 1(1)(e)'.

Note. Sub-para (a) repealed by Children (Northern Ireland) Order 1995, SI 1995 No 755, art 185(2), Sch 10, as from 4 November 1996.

70. In section 34(3) (power to order recovery of child) for paragraph (a) there shall be substituted—
   '(a) section 14 of the Children Act 1989'.

71.—(1) In section 42 (general interpretation of Part I), in subsection (4)(a) for the words 'has been boarded out with those parties' there shall be substituted 'is placed with those parties as foster parents'.

(2) In subsection (6) of that section, in paragraph (a) after the word 'person' there shall be inserted 'to be allowed contact with or'.

Local Government Act 1988 (c 9)

72. In Schedule 1 to the Local Government Act 1988 (competition) at the end of paragraph 2(4) (cleaning of buildings: buildings to which competition provisions do not apply) for paragraph (c) there shall be substituted—
   '(c) section 53 of the Children Act 1989.'

Amendments of local Acts

73.—(1) Section 16 of the Greater London Council (General Powers) Act 1981 (exemption from provisions of Part IV of the Act of certain premises) shall be amended as follows.
   (2) After paragraph (g) there shall be inserted—
   '(gg) used as a children's home as defined in section 63 of the Children Act 1989'.
   (3) In paragraph (h)—
   (a) for the words 'section 56 of the Child Care Act 1980' there shall be substituted 'section 60 of the Children Act 1989';
   (b) for the words 'section 57' there shall be substituted 'section 60'; and
   (c) for the words 'section 32' there shall be substituted 'section 53'.

Note. Sub-paras (2), (3) repealed by the Care Standards Act 2000, s 117(2), Sch 6, as from 1 April 2002 (SI 2001 No 4150, SI 2002 No 920).

   (4) In paragraph (i), for the words 'section 8 of the Foster Children Act 1980' there shall be substituted 'section 67 of the Children Act 1989'.

74.—(1) Section 10(2) of the Greater London Council (General Powers) Act 1984 (exemption from provisions of Part IV of the Act of certain premises) shall be amended as follows.

(2) In paragraph (d)—

(a) for the words 'section 56 of the Child Care Act 1980' there shall be substituted 'section 60 of the Children Act 1989';

(b) for the words 'section 57' there shall be substituted 'section 60'; and

(c) for the words 'section 31' there shall be substituted 'section 53'.

(3) In paragraph (e), for the words 'section 8 of the Foster Children Act 1980' there shall be substituted 'section 67 of the Children Act 1989'.

(4) In paragraph (1) for the words 'section 1 of the Children's Homes Act 1982' there shall be substituted 'section 63 of the Children Act 1989'.

Note. Sub-paras (2), (4) repealed by the Care Standards Act 2000, s 117(2), Sch 6, as from 1 April 2002 (SI 2001 No 4150, SI 2002 No 920).

SCHEDULE 14   Section 108(6)

TRANSITIONALS AND SAVINGS

Note. For the words 'juvenile court' or 'juvenile courts', in each place where they occur throughout this Schedule, there are substituted for the words 'youth court' or, as the case may require 'youth courts', by the Criminal Justice Act 1991, s 100, Sch 11, para 40(1), (2)(r), as from 1 October 1992.

Pending proceedings, etc

1.—(1) *Subject to sub-paragraph (4)* [Subject to sub-paragraphs (1A) and (4)], nothing in any provision of this Act (other than the repeals mentioned in sub-paragraph (2)) shall affect any proceedings which are pending immediately before the commencement of that provision.

[(1A) Proceedings pursuant to section 7(2) of the Family Law Reform Act 1969 (committal of wards of court to care of local authority) or in the exercise of the High Court's inherent jurisdiction with respect to children which are pending in relation to a child who has been placed or allowed to remain in the care of a local authority shall not be treated as pending proceedings after 13th October 1992 for the purposes of this Schedule if no final order has been made by that date pursuant to section 7(2) of the 1969 Act or in the exercise of the High Court's inherent jurisdiction in respect of the child's care.]

(2) The repeals are those of—

(a) section 42(3) of the Matrimonial Causes Act 1973 (declaration by court that party to marriage unfit to have custody of children of family); and

(b) section 38 of the Sexual Offences Act 1956 (power of court to divest person of authority over girl or boy in cases of incest).

(3) For the purposes of the following provisions of this Schedule, any reference to an order in force immediately before the commencement of a provision of this Act shall be construed as including a reference to an order made after that commencement in proceedings pending before that commencement.

(4) Sub-paragraph (3) is not to be read as making the order in question have effect from a date earlier than that on which it was made.

(5) An order under section 96(3) may make such provision with respect to the application of the order in relation to proceedings which are pending when the order comes into force as the Lord Chancellor considers appropriate.

Note. Words in square brackets in sub-para (1) substituted for words in italics, and sub-para (1A) inserted by Children Act 1989 (Commencement and Transitional Provisions) Order 1991, SI 1991 No 828, art 4, Schedule, para 1A (as inserted by Children Act 1989 (Commencement No 2—Amendment and Transitional Provisions) Order 1991, SI 1991 No 1990, art 2(c), Schedule, para 1), as from 14 October 1991.

2. Where, immediately before the date on which Part IV comes into force, there was in force an order under section 3(1) of the Children and Young Persons Act 1963 (order directing a local authority to bring a child or young person before a juvenile court under section 1 of the Children and Young Persons Act 1969), the order shall cease to have effect on that day.

CUSTODY ORDERS, ETC

Cessation of declarations at unfitness, etc

3. Where, immediately before the day on which Parts I and II come into force, there was in force—

    (a) a declaration under section 42(3) of the Matrimonial Causes Act 1973 (declaration by court that party to marriage unfit to have custody of children of family); or

    (b) an order under section 38(1) of the Sexual Offences Act 1956 divesting a person of authority over a girl or boy in a case of incest;

the declaration or, as the case may be, the order shall cease to have effect on that day.

FAMILY LAW REFORM ACT 1987 (c 42)

Conversion of orders under section 4

4. Where, immediately before the day on which Parts I and II come into force, there was in force an order under section 4(1) of the Family Law Reform Act 1987 (order giving father parental rights and duties in relation to a child), then, on and after that day, the order shall be deemed to be an order under section 4 of this Act giving the father parental responsibility for the child.

Orders to which paragraphs 6 to 11 apply

5.—(1) In paragraphs 6 to 11 'an existing order' means any order which—

    (a) was in force immediately before the commencement of Parts I and II;

    (b) was made under any enactment mentioned in sub-paragraph (2);

    (c) determines all or any of the following—

        (i) who is to have custody of a child;

        (ii) who is to have care and control of a child;

        (iii) who is to have access to a child;

        (iv) any matter with respect to a child's education or upbringing; and

    (d) is not an order of a kind mentioned in paragraph 15(1).

    (2) The enactments are—

    (a) the Domestic Proceedings and Magistrates' Courts Act 1978;

    (b) the Children Act 1975;

    (c) the Matrimonial Causes Act 1973;

    (d) the Guardianship of Minors Acts 1971 and 1973;

    (e) the Matrimonial Causes Act 1965;

    (f) the Matrimonial Proceedings (Magistrates' Courts) Act 1960.

    (3) For the purposes of this paragraph and paragraphs 6 to 11 'custody' includes legal custody and joint as well as sole custody but does not include access.

Parental responsibility of parents

6.—(1) Where—

    (a) a child's father and mother were married to each other at the time of his birth; and

    (b) there is an existing order with respect to the child,

each parent shall have parental responsibility for the child in accordance with section 2 as modified by sub-paragraph (3).

    (2) Where—

    (a) a child's father and mother were not married to each other at the time of his birth; and

    (b) there is an existing order with respect to the child,

section 2 shall apply as modified by sub-paragraphs (3) and (4).

(3) The modification is that for section 2(8) there shall be substituted—

'(8) The fact that a person has parental responsibility for a child does not entitle him to act in a way which would be incompatible with any existing order or any order made under this Act with respect to the child',

(4) The modifications are that—

(a) for the purposes of section 2(2), where the father has custody or care and control of the child by virtue of any existing order, the court shall be deemed to have made (at the commencement of that section) an order under section 4(1) giving him parental responsibility for the child; and

(b) where by virtue of paragraph (a) a court is deemed to have made an order under section 4(1) in favour of a father who has care and control of a child by virtue of an existing order, the court shall not bring the order under section 4(1) to an end at any time while he has care and control of the child by virtue of the order.

Persons who are not parents but who have custody or care and control

7.—(1) Where a person who is not the parent or guardian of a child has custody or care and control of him by virtue of an existing order, that person shall have parental responsibility for him so long as he continues to have that custody or care and control by virtue of the order.

(2) Where sub-paragraph (1) applies, *Parts I and II* [Parts I and II and paragraph 15 of Schedule 1] shall have effect as modified by this paragraph.

(3) The modifications are that—

(a) for section 2(8) there shall be substituted—

'(8) The fact that a person has parental responsibility for a child does not entitle him to act in a way which would be incompatible with any existing order or with any order made under this Act with respect to the child';

(b) at the end of section 10(4) there shall be inserted—

'(c) any person who has custody or care and control of a child by virtue of any existing order'; and

(c) at the end of section 34(1)(c) there shall be inserted—

'(cc) where immediately before the care order was made there was an existing order by virtue of which a person had custody or care and control of the child, that person.'

[(d) for paragraph 15 of Schedule 1 there shall be substituted—

15. Where a child lives with a person as the result of a custodianship order within the meaning of section 33 of the Children Act 1975, a local authority may make contributions to that person towards the cost of accommodation and maintenance of the child so long as that person continues to have legal custody of that child by virtue of the order.]

Note. Words in square brackets in sub-para (2) substituted for words in italics, and sub-para (3)(d) inserted by Children Act 1989 (Commencement and Transitional Provisions) Order 1991, SI 1991 No 828, art 4, Schedule, para 1B (as inserted by Children Act 1989 (Commencement No 2—Amendment and Transitional Provisions) Order 1991, SI 1991 No 1990, art 2(c), Schedule), as from 14 October 1991.

Persons who have care and control

8.—(1) Sub-paragraphs (2) to (6) apply where a person has care and control of a child by virtue of an existing order, but they shall cease to apply when that order ceases to have effect.

(2) Section 5 shall have effect as if—

(a) for any reference to a residence order in favour of a parent or guardian there were substituted a reference to any existing order by virtue of which the parent or guardian has care and control of the child; and

(b) for subsection (9) there were substituted—

'(9) Subsections (1) and (7) do not apply if the existing order referred to in paragraph (b) of those subsections was one by virtue of which a surviving parent of the child also had care and control of him.'

(3) Section 10 shall have effect as if for subsection (5)(c)(i) there were substituted—

'(i)   in any case where by virtue of an existing order any person or persons has or have care and control of the child, has the consent of that person or each of those persons'.

(4) Section 20 shall have effect as if for subsection (9)(a) there were substituted 'who has care and control of the child by virtue of an existing order.'

(5) Section 23 shall have effect as if for subsection (4)(c) there were substituted—

'(c)   where the child is in care and immediately before the care order was made there was an existing order by virtue of which a person had care and control of the child, that person.'

(6) In Schedule 1, paragraphs 1(1) and 14(1) shall have effect as if for the words 'in whose favour a residence order is in force with respect to the child' there were substituted 'who has been given care and control of the child by virtue of an existing order'.

Persons who have access

9.—(1) Sub-paragraphs (2) to (4) apply where a person has access by virtue of an existing order.

(2) Section 10 shall have effect as if after subsection (5) there were inserted—

'(5A) Any person who has access to a child by virtue of an existing order is entitled to apply for a contact order.'

(3) Section 16(2) shall have effect as if after paragraph (b) there were inserted—

'(bb)   any person who has access to the child by virtue of an existing order.'

(4) Sections 43(11), 44(13) and 46(10), shall have effect as if in each case after paragraph (d) there were inserted—

'(dd)   any person who has been given access to him by virtue of an existing order.'

Enforcement of certain existing orders

10.—(1) Sub-paragraph (2) applies in relation to any existing order which, but for the repeal by this Act of—

(a)   section 13(1) of the Guardianship of Minors Act 1971;

(b)   section 43(1) of the Children Act 1975; or

(c)   section 33 of the Domestic Proceedings and Magistrates' Courts Act 1978,

(provisions concerning the enforcement of custody orders) might have been enforced as if it were an order requiring a person to give up a child to another person.

(2) Where this sub-paragraph applies, the existing order may, after the repeal of the enactments mentioned in sub-paragraph (1)(a) to (c), be enforced under section 14 as if—

(a)   any reference to a residence order were a reference to the existing order; and

(b)   any reference to a person in whose favour the residence order is in force were a reference to a person to whom actual custody of the child is given by an existing order which is in force.

(3) In sub-paragraph (2) 'actual custody' in relation to a child, means the actual possession of his person.

Discharge of existing orders

11.—(1) The making of a residence order or a care order with respect to a child who is the subject of an existing order discharges the existing order.

(2) Where the court makes any section 8 order (other than a residence order) with respect to a child with respect to whom any existing order is in force, the existing order shall have effect subject to the section 8 order.

(3) The court may discharge an existing order which is in force with respect to a child—

(a) in any family proceedings relating to the child or in which any question arises with respect to the child's welfare; or

(b) on the application of—

(i) any parent or guardian of the child;

(ii) the child himself; or

(iii) any person named in the order.

(4) A child may not apply for the discharge of an existing order except with the leave of the court.

(5) The power in sub-paragraph (3) to discharge an existing order includes the power to discharge any part of the order.

(6) In considering whether to discharge an order under the power conferred by sub-paragraph (3) the court shall, if the discharge of the order is opposed by any party to the proceedings, have regard in particular to the matters mentioned in section 1(3).

GUARDIANS

Existing guardians to be guardians under this Act

12.—(1) Any appointment of a person as guardian of a child which—

(a) was made—

(i) under sections 3 to 5 of the Guardianship of Minors Act 1971;

(ii) under section 38(3) of the Sexual Offences Act 1956; or

(iii) under the High Court's inherent jurisdiction with respect to children; and

(b) has taken effect before the commencement of section 5,

shall (subject to sub-paragraph (2)) be deemed, on and after the commencement of section 5, to be an appointment made and having effect under that section.

(2) Where an appointment of a person as guardian of a child has effect under section 5 by virtue of sub-paragraph (1)(a)(ii), the appointment shall not have effect for a period which is longer than any period specified in the order.

Note. References in paras 12, 13 and 14 to the commencement of section 5 shall be construed as references to the commencement of sub-ss (11) and (12) of that section, by virtue of Children Act 1989 (Commencement No 2—Amendment and Transitional Provisions) Order 1991, SI 1991 No 1990, art 2(c), Schedule, as from 14 October 1991.

Appointment of guardian not yet in effect

13. Any appointment of a person to be a guardian of a child—

(a) which was made as mentioned in paragraph 12(1)(a)(i); but

(b) which, immediately before the commencement of section 5, had not taken effect,

shall take effect in accordance with section 5 (as modified, where it applies, by paragraph 8(2)).

Note. See the note to para 12 above.

Persons deemed to be appointed as guardians under existing wills

14. For the purposes of the Wills Act 1837 and of this Act any disposition by will and testament or devise of the custody and tuition of any child, made before the commencement of section 5 and paragraph 1 of Schedule 13, shall be deemed to be an appointment by will of a guardian of the child.

Note. See the note to para 12 above.

CHILDREN IN CARE

Children in compulsory care

15.—(1) Sub-paragraph (2) applies where, immediately before the day on which Part IV comes into force, a person was—

    (a) in care by virtue of—
        (i) a care order under section 1 of the Children and Young Persons Act 1969;
        (ii) a care order under section 15 of that Act, on discharging a supervision order made under section 1 of that Act; or
        (iii) an order or authorisation under section 25 or 26 of that Act;
    (*b*) *deemed, by virtue of—*
        (*i*) *paragraph 7(3) of Schedule 5A to the Army Act 1955;*
        (*ii*) *paragraph 7(3) of Schedule 5A to the Air Force Act 1955; or*
        (*iii*) *paragraph 7(3) of Schedule 4A to the Naval Discipline Act 1957,*
    to be the subject of a care order under the Children and Young Persons Act 1969;

Note. Sub-para (b) repealed by Armed Forces Act 1991, s 26(2), Sch 3, as from 1 January 1992.

    (c) in care—
        (i) under section 2 of the Child Care Act 1980; or
        (ii) by virtue of paragraph 1 of Schedule 4 to that Act (which extends the meaning of a child in care under section 2 to include children in care under section 1 of the Children Act 1948),
    and a child in respect of whom a resolution under section 3 of the Act of 1980 or section 2 of the Act of 1948 was in force;
    (d) a child in respect of whom a resolution had been passed under section 65 of the Child Care Act 1980;
    (e) in care by virtue of an order under—
        (i) section 2(1)(e) of the Matrimonial Proceedings (Magistrates' Courts) Act 1960;
        (ii) section 7(2) of the Family Law Reform Act 1969;
        (iii) section 43(1) of the Matrimonial Causes Act 1973; or
        (iv) section 2(2)(b) of the Guardianship Act 1973;
        (v) section 10 of the Domestic Proceedings and Magistrates' Courts Act 1978,
    (orders having effect for certain purposes as if the child had been received into care under section 2 of the Child Care Act 1980);
    (f) in care by virtue of an order made, on the revocation of a custodianship order, under section 36 of the Children Act 1975;
    (g) in care by virtue of an order made, on the refusal of an adoption order, under section 26 of the Adoption Act 1976 or any order having effect (by virtue of paragraph 1 of Schedule 2 to that Act) as if made under that section[; or
    (h) in care by virtue of an order of the court made in the exercise of the High Court's inherent jurisdiction with respect to children].

(2) Where this sub-paragraph applies, then, on and after the day on which Part IV commences—

    (a) the order or resolution in question shall be deemed to be a care order;
    (b) the authority in whose care the person was immediately before that commencement shall be deemed to be the authority designated in that deemed care order; and
    (c) any reference to a child in the care of a local authority shall include a reference to a person who is the subject of such a deemed care order,

and the provisions of this Act shall apply accordingly, subject to paragraph 16.

Note. Sub-para (h) added by Courts and Legal Services Act 1990, s 116, Sch 16, para 33(2), as from 14 October 1991.

Modifications

16.—(1) Sub-paragraph (2) only applies where a person who is the subject of a care order by virtue of paragraph 15(2) is a person falling within sub-paragraph (1)(a) *or* (*b*) of that paragraph.

(2) Where the person would otherwise have remained in care until reaching the age of nineteen, by virtue of—

    (a) section 20(3)(a) or 21(1) of the Children and Young Persons Act 1969; or

    (*b*) *paragraph 7(5)(c)(i) of—*

        (*i*) *Schedule 5A to the Army Act 1955;*

        (*ii*) *Schedule 5A to the Air Force Act 1955; or*

        (*iii*) *Schedule 4A to the Naval Discipline Act 1957,*

this Act applies as if in section 91(12) for the word 'eighteen' there were substituted 'nineteen'.

(3) Where a person who is the subject of a care order by virtue of paragraph 15(2) is a person falling within sub-paragraph (1)(b) of that paragraph, this Act applies as if section 101 were omitted.

[(3A) Where in respect of a child who has been placed or allowed to remain in the care of a local authority pursuant to section 7(2) of the Family Law Reform Act 1969 or in the exercise of the High Court's inherent jurisdiction and the child is still in the care of a local authority, proceedings have ceased by virtue of paragraph 1(1A) to be treated as pending, paragraph 15(2) shall apply on 14th October as if the child was in care pursuant to an order as specified in paragraph 15(1)(e)(iii) or (h) as the case may be.]

(4) *Sub-paragraph (5) only applies* [Sub-paragraphs (5) and (6) only apply] where a child who is the subject of a care order by virtue of paragraph 15(2) is a person falling within sub-paragraph (1)(e) to (*g*) [(h)] of that paragraph.

(5) [Subject to sub-paragraph (6)] Where a court, on making the order, or at any time thereafter, gave directions under—

    (*a*) *section 4(4)(a) of the Guardianship Act 1973; or*

    (*b*) *section 43(5)(a) of the Matrimonial Causes Act 1973,*

[—

    (a) under section 4(4)(a) of the Guardianship Act 1973;

    (b) under section 43(5)(a) of the Matrimonial Causes Act 1973; or

    (c) in the exercise of the High Court's inherent jurisdiction with respect to children,]

as to the exercise by the authority of any powers, those directions shall[, subject to the provisions of section 25 of this Act and of any regulations made under that section,] continue to have effect (regardless of any conflicting provision in this Act [other than section 25]) until varied or discharged by a court under this sub-paragraph.

[(6) Where directions referred to in sub-paragraph (5) are to the effect that a child be placed in accommodation provided for the purpose of restricting liberty then the directions shall cease to have effect upon the expiry of the maximum period specified by regulations under section 25(2)(a) in relation to children of his description, calculated from 14th October 1991.]

Note. Words in italics in sub-para (1), the whole of sub-paras (2)(b), (3) and the word 'or' immediately preceding sub-para (3) repealed by Armed Forces Act 1991, s 26(2), Sch 3, as from 1 January 1992. Sub-para (3A) inserted by Children (Commencement and Transitional Provisions) Order 1991, SI 1991 No 828, art 4, Schedule, para 1D (as inserted by Children Act 1989 (Commencement No 2—Amendment and Transitional Provisions) Order 1991, SI 1991 No 1990, art 2(c), Schedule), as from 14 October 1991. Words in square brackets in sub-para (4) substituted for words in italics by Children Act 1989 (Commencement and Transitional Provisions) Order 1991, SI 1991 No 828, art 4, Schedule. Reference to '(h)' substituted for reference to '(g)' in that sub-paragraph, and words in second pair of square brackets in sub-para (5) substituted for words in italics by Courts and Legal Services Act 1990, s 116, Sch 16, para 33(1), (3), as from 14 October 1991. Words in first, third and fourth pairs of square brackets in sub-para (5), and the whole of sub-para (6) inserted by Children Act 1989 (Commencement and Transitional Provisions) Order 1991, SI 1991 No 828, art 4, Schedule, paras 2, 3.

[Cessation of wardship where ward in care

16A.[—(1)] Where a child who is a ward of court is in care by virtue of—
  (a) an order under section 7(2) of the Family Law Reform Act 1969; or
  (b) an order made in the exercise of the High Court's inherent jurisdiction with respect to children,
he shall, on the day on which Part IV commences, cease to be a ward of court.
  [(2) Where immediately before the day on which Part IV commences a child was in the care of a local authority and as the result of an order—
  (a) pursuant to section 7(2) of the Family Law Reform Act 1969; or
  (b) made in the exercise of the High Court's inherent jurisdiction with respect to children,
continued to be in the care of a local authority and was made a ward of court, he shall on the day on which Part IV commences, cease to be a ward of court.
  (3) Sub-paragraphs (1) and (2) do not apply in proceedings which are pending.]

Note. Para 16A added by Courts and Legal Services Act 1990, s 116, Sch 16, para 33(4). Words at the beginning of para 16A in square brackets and sub-paras (2), (3) in square brackets inserted by Children Act 1989 (Commencement and Transitional Provisions) Order 1991, SI 1991 No 828, art 4, Schedule, para 4 (as substituted by Children (Commencement No 2—Amendment and Transitional Provisions) Order 1991, SI 1991 No 1990, art 2(c), Schedule, para 2).

Children placed with parent etc while in compulsory care

17.—(1) This paragraph applies where a child is deemed by paragraph 15 to be in the care of a local authority under an order or resolution which is deemed by that paragraph to be a care order.
  (2) If, immediately before the day on which Part III comes into force, the child was allowed to be under the charge and control of—
  (a) a parent or guardian under section 21(2) of the Child Care Act 1980; or
  (b) a person who, before the child was in the authority's care, had care and control of the child by virtue of an order falling within paragraph 5,
on and after that day the provision made by and under section 23(5) shall apply as if the child had been placed with the person in question in accordance with that provision.

Orders for access to children in compulsory care

18.—(1) This paragraph applies to any access order—
  (a) made under section 12C of the Child Care Act 1980 (access orders with respect to children in care of local authorities); and
  (b) in force immediately before the commencement of Part IV.
  (2) On and after the commencement of Part IV, the access order shall have effect as an order made under section 34 in favour of the person named in the order.

[**18A.**—(1) This paragraph applies to any decision of a local authority to terminate arrangements for access or to refuse to make such arrangements—
  (a) of which notice has been given under, and in accordance with, section 12B of the Child Care Act 1980 (termination of access); and
  (b) which is in force immediately before the commencement of Part IV.
  (2) On and after the commencement of Part IV, a decision to which this paragraph applies shall have effect as a court order made under section 34(4) authorising the local authority to refuse to allow contact between the child and the person to whom notice was given under section 12B of the Child Care Act 1980.]

Note. Para 18A inserted by Children Act 1989 (Commencement and Transitional Provisions) Order 1991, SI 1991 No 828, art 4, Schedule, para 5, as from 14 October 1991.

19.—(1) This paragraph applies where, immediately before the commencement of Part IV, an access order made under section 12C of the Act of 1980 was suspended by virtue of an order made under section 12E of that Act (suspension of access orders in emergencies).

(2) The suspending order shall continue to have effect as if this Act had not been passed.

(3) If—

(a) before the commencement of Part IV; and

(b) during the period for which the operation of the access order is suspended, the local authority concerned made an application for its variation or discharge to an appropriate *juvenile court* [youth court], its operation shall be suspended until the date on which the application to vary or discharge it is determined or abandoned.

Children in voluntary care

20.—(1) This paragraph applies where, immediately before the day on which Part III comes into force—

(a) a child was in the care of a local authority—

   (i) under section 2(1) of the Child Care Act 1980; or

   (ii) by virtue of paragraph 1 of Schedule 4 to that Act (which extends the meaning of references to children in care under section 2 to include references to children in care under section 1 of the Children Act 1948); and

(b) he was not a person in respect of whom a resolution under section 3 of the Act of 1980 or section 2 of the Act of 1948 was in force.

(2) Where this paragraph applies, the child shall, on and after the day mentioned in sub-paragraph (1), be treated for the purposes of this Act as a child who is provided with accommodation by the local authority under Part III, but he shall cease to be so treated once he ceases to be so accommodated in accordance with the provisions of Part III.

(3) Where—

(a) this paragraph applies; and

(b) the child, immediately before the day mentioned in sub-paragraph (1), was (by virtue of section 21(2) of the Act of 1980) under the charge and control of a person falling within paragraph 17(2)(a) or (b),

the child shall not be treated for the purposes of this Act as if he were being looked after by the authority concerned.

Boarded out children

21.—(1) Where, immediately before the day on which Part III comes into force, a child in the care of a local authority—

(a) was—

   (i) boarded out with a person under section 21(1)(a) of the Child Care Act 1980; or

   (ii) placed under the charge and control of a person, under section 21(2) of that Act; and

(b) the person with whom he was boarded out, or (as the case may be) placed, was not a person falling within paragraph 17(2)(a) or (b),

on and after that day, he shall be treated (subject to sub-paragraph (2)) as having been placed with a local authority foster parent and shall cease to be so treated when he ceases to be placed with that person in accordance with the provisions of this Act.

(2) Regulations made under section 23(2)(a) shall not apply in relation to a person who is a local authority foster parent by virtue of sub-paragraph (1) before the end of the period of twelve months beginning with the day on which Part III comes into force and accordingly that person shall for that period be subject—

(a) in a case falling within sub-paragraph (1)(a)(i), to terms and regulations mentioned in section 21(1)(a) of the Act of 1980; and
(b) in a case falling within sub-paragraph (1)(a)(ii), to terms fixed under section 21(2) of that Act and regulations made under section 22A of that Act, as if that Act had not been repealed by this Act.

Children in care to qualify for advice and assistance

22. Any reference in Part III to a person qualifying for advice and assistance shall be construed as including a reference to a person within the area of the local authority in question who is under twenty-one and who was, at any time after reaching the age of sixteen but while still a child—
(a) a person falling within—
  (i) any of paragraphs (a) to (*g*) [(h)] of paragraph 15(1); or
  (ii) paragraph 20(1); or
(b) the subject of a criminal care order (within the meaning of paragraph 34).
Note. Reference to '(h)' substituted for reference to '(g)' by Courts and Legal Services Act 1990, s 116, Sch 16, para 33(5), as from 14 October 1991.

Emigration of children in care

23. Where—
(a) the Secretary of State has received a request in writing from a local authority that he give his consent under section 24 of the Child Care Act 1980 to the emigration of a child in their care; but
(b) immediately before the repeal of the Act of 1980 by this Act, he has not determined whether or not to give his consent,
section 24 of the Act of 1980 shall continue to apply (regardless of that repeal) until the Secretary of State has determined whether or not to give his consent to the request.

Contributions for maintenance of children in care

24.—(1) Where, immediately before the day on which Part III of Schedule 2 comes into force, there was in force an order made (or having effect as if made) under any of the enactments mentioned in sub-paragraph (2), then, on and after that day—
(a) the order shall have effect as if made under paragraph 23(2) of Schedule 2 against a person liable to contribute; and
(b) Part III of Schedule 2 shall apply to the order, subject to the modifications in sub-paragraph (3).
(2) The enactments are—
(a) section 11(4) of the Domestic Proceedings and Magistrates' Courts Act 1978;
(b) section 26(2) of the Adoption Act 1976;
(c) section 36(5) of the Children Act 1975;
(d) section 2(3) of the Guardianship Act 1973;
(e) section 2(1)(h) of the Matrimonial Proceedings (Magistrates' Courts) Act 1960,
(provisions empowering the court to make an order requiring a person to make periodical payments to a local authority in respect of a child in care).
(3) The modifications are that, in paragraph 23 of Schedule 2—
(a) in sub-paragraph (4), paragraph (a) shall be omitted;
(b) for sub-paragraph (6) there shall be substituted—
'(6) Where—
(a) a contribution order is in force;
(b) the authority serve a contribution notice under paragraph 22; and
(c) the contributor and the authority reach an agreement under paragraph 22(7) in respect of the contribution notice,

the effect of the agreement shall be to discharge the order from the date on which it is agreed that the agreement shall take effect'; and
   (c) at the end of sub-paragraph (10) there shall be inserted—
'and
   (c) where the order is against a person who is not a parent of the child, shall be made with due regard to—
      (i) whether that person had assumed responsibility for the maintenance of the child, and, if so, the extent to which and basis on which he assumed that responsibility and the length of the period during which he met that responsibility;
      (ii) whether he did so knowing that the child was not his child;
      (iii) the liability of any other person to maintain the child.

SUPERVISION ORDERS

Orders under section 1(3)(b) or 21(2) of the 1969 Act

25.—(1) This paragraph applies to any supervision order—
   (a) made—
      (i) under section 1(3)(b) of the Children and Young Persons Act 1969; or
      (ii) under section 21(2) of that Act on the discharge of a care order made under section 1(3)(c) of that Act; and
   (b) in force immediately before the commencement of Part IV.
(2) On and after the commencement of Part IV, the order shall be deemed to be a supervision order made under section 31 and—
   (a) any requirement of the order that the child reside with a named individual shall continue to have effect while the order remains in force, unless the court otherwise directs;
   (b) any other requirement imposed by the court, or directions given by the supervisor, shall be deemed to have been imposed or given under the appropriate provisions of Schedule 3.
(3) Where, immediately before the commencement of Part IV, the order had been in force for a period of *more than six months* [six months or more], it shall cease to have effect at the end of the period of six months beginning with the day on which Part IV comes into force unless—
   (a) the court directs that it shall cease to have effect at the end of a different period (which shall not exceed three years);
   (b) it ceases to have effect earlier in accordance with section 91; or
   (c) it would have ceased to have had effect earlier had this Act not been passed.
(4) Where sub-paragraph (3) applies, paragraph 6 of Schedule 3 shall not apply.
(5) Where, immediately before the commencement of Part IV, the order had been in force for less than six months it shall cease to have effect in accordance with section 91 and paragraph 6 of Schedule 3 unless—
   (a) the court directs that it shall cease to have effect at the end of a different period (which shall not exceed three years); or
   (b) it would have ceased to have had effect earlier had this Act not been passed.
Note. Words in square brackets in sub-para (3) substituted for words in italics by Children Act 1989 (Commencement and Transitional Provisions) Order 1991, SI 1991 No 828, art 4, Schedule, para 6, as from 14 October 1991.

Other supervision orders

26.—(1) This paragraph applies to any order for the supervision of a child which was in force immediately before the commencement of Part IV and was made under—
   (a) section 2(1)(f) of the Matrimonial Proceedings (Magistrates' Courts) Act 1960;

   (b) section 7(4) of the Family Law Reform Act 1969;
   (c) section 44 of the Matrimonial Causes Act 1973;
   (d) section 2(2)(a) of the Guardianship Act 1973;
   (e) section 34(5) or 36(3)(b) of the Children Act 1975;
   (f) section 26(1)(a) of the Adoption Act 1976; or
   (g) section 9 of the Domestic Proceedings and Magistrates' Courts Act 1978.
   (2) The order shall not be deemed to be a supervision order made under any provision of this Act but shall nevertheless continue in force for a period of one year beginning with the day on which Part IV comes into force unless—
   (a) the court directs that it shall cease to have effect at the end of a lesser period; or
   (b) it would have ceased to have had effect earlier had this Act not been passed.

Places of safety orders

27.—(1) This paragraph applies to—
   (a) any order or warrant authorising the removal of a child to a place of safety which—
      (i) was made, or issued, under any of the enactments mentioned in sub-paragraph (2); and
      (ii) was in force immediately before the commencement of Part IV; and
   (b) any interim order made under section 23(5) of the Children and Young Persons Act 1963 or section 28(6) of the Children and Young Persons Act 1969.
   (2) The enactments are—
   (a) section 40 of the Children and Young Persons Act 1933 (warrant to search for or remove child);
   (b) section 28(1) of the Children and Young Persons Act 1969 (detention of child in place of safety);
   (c) section 34(1) of the Adoption Act 1976 (removal of protected children from unsuitable surroundings);
   (d) section 12(1) of the Foster Children Act 1980 (removal of foster children kept in unsuitable surroundings).
   (3) The order or warrant shall continue to have effect as if this Act had not been passed.
   (4) Any enactment repealed by this Act shall continue to have effect in relation to the order or warrant so far as is necessary for the purposes of securing that the effect of the order is what it would have been had this Act not been passed.
   (5) Sub-paragraph (4) does not apply to the power to make an interim order or further interim order given by section 23(5) of the Children and Young Persons Act 1963 or section 28(6) of the Children and Young Persons Act 1969.
   (6) Where, immediately before section 28 of the Children and Young Persons Act 1969 is repealed by this Act, a child is being detained under the powers granted by that section, he may continue to be detained in accordance with that section but subsection (6) shall not apply.

Recovery of children

28. The repeal by this Act of subsection (1) of section 16 of the Child Care Act 1980 (arrest of child absent from compulsory care) shall not affect the operation of that section in relation to any child arrested before the coming into force of the repeal.
29.—(1) This paragraph applies where—
   (a) a summons has been issued under section 15 or 16 of the Child Care Act 1980 (recovery of children in voluntary or compulsory care); and
   (b) the child concerned is not produced in accordance with the summons before the repeal of that section by this Act comes into force.

(2) The summons, any warrant issued in connection with it and section 15 or (as the case may be) section 16, shall continue to have effect as if this Act had not been passed.

30. The amendment by paragraph 27 of Schedule 12 of section 32 of the Children and Young Persons Act 1969 (detention of absentees) shall not affect the operation of that section in relation to—

(a) any child arrested; or

(b) any summons or warrant issued,

under that section before the coming into force of that paragraph.

Voluntary organisations: Parental rights resolutions

31.—(1) This paragraph applies to a resolution—

(a) made under section 64 of the Child Care Act 1980 (transfer of parental rights and duties to voluntary organisations); and

(b) in force immediately before the commencement of Part IV.

(2) The resolution shall continue to have effect until the end of the period of six months beginning with the day on which Part IV comes into force unless it is brought to an end earlier in accordance with the provisions of the Act of 1980 preserved by this paragraph.

(3) While the resolution remains in force, any relevant provisions of, or made under, the Act of 1980 shall continue to have effect with respect to it.

(4) Sub-paragraph (3) does not apply to—

(a) section 62 of the Act of 1980 and any regulations made under that section (arrangements by voluntary organisations for emigration of children); or

(b) section 65 of the Act of 1980 (duty of local authority to assume parental rights and duties).

(5) Section 5(2) of the Act of 1980 (which is applied to resolutions under Part VI of that Act by section 64(7) of that Act) shall have effect with respect to the resolution as if the reference in paragraph (c) to an appointment of a guardian under section 5 of the Guardianship of Minors Act 1971 were a reference to an appointment of a guardian under section 5 of this Act.

Foster children

32.—(1) This paragraph applies where—

(a) immediately before the commencement of Part VIII, a child was a foster child within the meaning of the Foster Children Act 1980; and

(b) the circumstances of the case are such that, had Parts VIII and IX then been in force, he would have been treated for the purposes of this Act as a child who was being provided with accommodation in a children's home and not as a child who was being privately fostered.

(2) If the child continues to be cared for and provided with accommodation as before, section 63(1) and (10) shall not apply in relation to him if—

(a) an application for registration of the home in question is made under section 63 before the end of the period of three months beginning with the day on which Part VIII comes into force; and

(b) the application has not been refused or, if it has been refused—

(i) the period for an appeal against the decision has not expired; or

(ii) an appeal against the refusal has been made but has not been determined or abandoned.

(3) While section 63(1) and (10) does not apply, the child shall be treated as a privately fostered child for the purposes of Part IX.

Nurseries and child minding

33.—(1) Sub-paragraph (2) applies where, immediately before the commencement of Part X, any premises are registered under section 1(1)(a) of the Nurseries and

Child-Minders Regulation Act 1948 (registration of premises, other than premises wholly or mainly used as private dwellings, where children are received to be looked after).

(2) During the transitional period, the provisions of the Act of 1948 shall continue to have effect with respect to those premises to the exclusion of Part X.

(3) Nothing in sub-paragraph (2) shall prevent the local authority concerned from registering any person under section 71(1)(b) with respect to the premises.

(4) In this paragraph 'the transitional period' means the period ending with—

(a) the first anniversary of the commencement of Part X; or

(b) if earlier, the date on which the local authority concerned registers any person under section 71(1)(b) with respect to the premises.

34.—(1) Sub-paragraph (2) applies where, immediately before the commencement of Part X—

(a) a person is registered under section 1(1)(b) of the Act of 1948 (registration of persons who for reward receive into their homes children under the age of five to be looked after); and

(b) all the children looked after by him as mentioned in section 1(1)(b) of that Act are under the age of five.

(2) During the transitional period, the provisions of the Act of 1948 shall continue to have effect with respect to that person to the exclusion of Part X.

(3) Nothing in sub-paragraph (2) shall prevent the local authority concerned from registering that person under section 71(1)(a).

(4) In this paragraph 'the transitional period' means the period ending with—

(a) the first anniversary of the commencement of Part X; or

(b) if earlier, the date on which the local authority concerned registers that person under section 71(1)(a).

Children accommodated in certain establishments

35. In calculating, for the purposes of section 85(1)(a) or 86(1)(a), the period of time for which a child has been accommodated any part of that period which fell before the day on which that section came into force shall be disregarded.

Criminal care orders

36.—(1) This paragraph applies where, immediately before the commencement of section 90(2) there was in force an order ('a criminal care order') made—

(a) under section 7(7)(a) of the Children and Young Persons Act 1969 (alteration in treatment of young offenders etc); or

(b) under section 15(1) of that Act, on discharging a supervision order made under section 7(7)(b) of that Act.

(2) The criminal care order shall continue to have effect until the end of the period of six months beginning with the day on which section 90(2) comes into force unless it is brought to an end earlier in accordance with—

(a) the provisions of the Act of 1969 preserved by sub-paragraph (3)(a); or

(b) this paragraph.

(3) While the criminal care order remains in force, any relevant provisions—

(a) of the Act of 1969; and

(b) of the Child Care Act 1980,

shall continue to have effect with respect to it.

(4) While the criminal care order remains in force, a court may, on the application of the appropriate person, make—

(a) a residence order;

(b) a care order or a supervision order under section 31;

(c) an education supervision order under section 36 (regardless of subsection (6) of that section); or

(d) an order falling within sub-paragraph (5),

and shall, on making any of those orders, discharge the criminal care order.

(5) The order mentioned in sub-paragraph (4)(d) is an order having effect as if it were a supervision order of a kind mentioned in section 12AA of the Act of 1969 (as inserted by paragraph 23 of Schedule 12), that is to say, a supervision order—

(a) imposing a requirement that the child shall live for a specified period in local authority accommodation; but

(b) in relation to which the conditions mentioned *in subsection (4)* [subsection (6)] of section 12AA are not required to be satisfied.

(6) The maximum period which may be specified in an order made under sub-paragraph (4)(d) is six months and such an order may stipulate that the child shall not live with a named person.

(7) Where this paragraph applies, section 5 of the Rehabilitation of Offenders Act 1974 (rehabilitation periods for particular sentences) shall have effect regardless of the repeals in it made by this Act.

(8) In sub-paragraph (4) 'appropriate person' means—

(a) in the case of an application for a residence order, any person (other than a local authority) who has the leave of the court;

(b) in the case of an application for an education supervision order, a local education authority; and

(c) in any other case, the local authority to whose care the child was committed by the order.

Note. Reference in sub-para (5)(b) to 'subsection (6)' substituted for reference to 'subsection (4)' by Courts and Legal Services Act 1990, s 116, Sch 16, para 33(6), as from 14 October 1991.

Miscellaneous

Consents under the Marriage Act 1949 (c 76)

37.—(1) In the circumstances mentioned in sub-paragraph (2), section 3 of and Schedule 2 to the Marriage Act 1949 (consents to marry) shall continue to have effect regardless of the amendment of that Act by paragraph 5 of Schedule 12.

(2) The circumstances are that—

(a) immediately before the day on which paragraph 5 of Schedule 12 comes into force, there is in force—

(i) an existing order, as defined in paragraph 5(1); or

(ii) an order of a kind mentioned in paragraph 16(1); and

(b) section 3 of and Schedule 2 to the Act of 1949 would, but for this Act, have applied to the marriage of the child who is the subject of the order.

Children Act 1975 (c 72)

38. The amendments of other enactments made by the following provisions of the Children Act 1975 shall continue to have effect regardless of the repeal of the Act of 1975 by this Act—

(a) section 68(4), (5) and (7) (amendments of section 32 of the Children and Young Persons Act 1969); and

(b) in Schedule 3—

(i) paragraph 13 (amendments of Births and Deaths Registration Act 1953);

(ii) paragraph 43 (amendment of Perpetuities and Accumulations Act 1964);

(iii) paragraphs 46 and 47 (amendments of Health Services and Public Health Act 1968); and

(iv) paragraph 77 (amendment of Parliamentary and Other Pensions Act 1972).

Child Care Act 1980 (c 5)

39. The amendment made to section 106(2)(a) of the Children and Young Persons Act 1963 by paragraph 26 of Schedule 5 to the Child Care Act 1980 shall continue to have effect regardless of the repeal of the Act of 1980 by this Act.

Legal aid

40. *The Lord Chancellor may by order make such transitional and saving provisions as appear to him to be necessary or expedient, in consequence of any provision made by or under this Act, in connection with the operation of any provisions of the Legal Aid Act 1988 (including any provision of that Act which is amended or repealed by this Act).*

Note. Para 40 repealed by the Access to Justice Act 1999, s 106, Sch 15, Pt I, as from 1 April 2000.

SCHEDULE 15   Section 108(7)

REPEALS

Chapter	Short Title	Extent of Repeal
1891 c 3	The Custody of Children Act 1891	The whole Act.
1933 c 12	The Children and Young Persons Act 1933	In section 14(2), the words from 'may also' to 'together, and'. In section 34(8), '(a)' and the words from 'and (b)' to the end. Section 40. In section 107(1), the definitions of 'care order' and 'interim order'.
1944 c 31	The Education Act 1944	In section 40(1), the words from 'or to imprisonment' to the end. In section 114(1), the definition of 'parent'.
1948 c 53	The Nurseries and Child-Minders Regulation Act 1948	The whole Act.
1949 c 76	The Marriage Act 1949	In section 3(1), the words 'unless the child is subject to a custodianship order, when the consent of the custodian and, where the custodian is the husband or wife of a parent of the child of that parent shall be required'. Section 78(1A). Schedule 2.
1956 c 69	The Sexual Offences Act 1956	Section 38.
1959 c 72	The Mental Health Act 1959	Section 9.
1963 c 37	The Children and Young Persons Act 1963	Section 3. Section 23. In section 29(1), the words 'under section 1 of the Children and Young Persons Act 1969 or'. Section 53(3). In Schedule 3, paragraph 11.
1964 c 42	The Administration of Justice Act 1964	In section 38, the definition of 'domestic court'.

Chapter	Short Title	Extent of Repeal
1968 c 46	The Health Services and Public Health Act 1968	Section 60. In section 64(3)(a), sub-paragraphs (vi), (vii), (ix) and (xv). In section 65(3)(b), paragraphs (vii), (viii) and (x).
1968 c 49	The Social Work (Scotland) Act 1968	Section 1(4)(a). Section 5(2)(d). In section 86(3), the words 'the Child Care Act 1980 or'. In Schedule 8, paragraph 20.
1969 c 46	The Family Law Reform Act 1969	Section 7.
1969 c 54	The Children and Young Persons Act 1969	Sections 1 to 3. In section 7, in subsection (7) the words 'to subsection (7A) of this section and', paragraph (a) and the words from 'and subsection (13) of section 2 of this Act' to the end; and subsection (7A). Section 7A. In section 8(3), the words from 'and as if the reference to acquittal' to the end. In section 9(1), the words 'proceedings under section 1 of this Act or'. Section 11A. Section 14A. In section 15, in subsection (1) the words 'and may on discharging the supervision order make a care order (other than an interim order) in respect of the supervised person'; in subsection (2) the words 'and the supervision order was not made by virtue of section 1 of this Act or on the occasion of the discharge of a care order'; in subsection (2A), the words 'or made by a court on discharging a care order made under that sub-

Chapter	Short Title	Extent of Repeal
		section'; and in subsection (4), the words 'or made by a court on discharging a care order made under that section'.
		In section 16, in subsection (6)(a), the words 'a care order or'; and in subsection (8) the words 'or, in a case where a parent or guardian of his was a party to the proceedings on an application under the preceding section by virtue of an order under section 32A of this Act, the parent or guardian'.
		In section 17, paragraphs (b) and (c).
		Sections 20 to 22.
		Section 27(4).
		Section 28.
		Sections 32A to 32C.
		In section 34(2) the words 'under section 1 of this Act or', the words '2(3) or' and the words 'and accordingly in the case of such a person the reference in section 1(1) of this Act to the said section 2(3) shall be construed as including a reference to this subsection'.
		In section 70, in subsection (1), the definitions of 'care order' and 'interim order'; and in subsection (2), the words '21(2), 22(4) or (6) or 28(5)' and the words 'care order or warrant'.
		In Schedule 5, paragraphs 12(1), 37, 47 and 48.
1970 c 34	The Marriage (Registrar General's Licence) Act 1970	In section 3(b), the words from 'as amended' to '1969'.
1970 c 42	The Local Authority Social Services Act 1970	In Schedule 1, in the entry relating to the Children and Young Persons Act 1969, the words 'welfare, etc of foster children';

Chapter	Short Title	Extent of Repeal
		the entries relating to the Matrimonial Causes Act 1973, section 44, the Domestic Proceedings and Magistrates' Courts Act 1978, section 9, the Child Care Act 1980 and the Foster Children Act 1980.
1971 c 3	The Guardianship of Minors Act 1971	The whole Act.
1971 c 23	The Courts Act 1971	In Schedule 8, paragraph 59(1).
1972 c 18	The Maintenance Orders Reciprocal Enforcement Act 1972	Section 41.
1972 c 70	The Local Government Act 1972	In Schedule 23, paragraphs 4 and 9(3).
1972 c 71	The Criminal Justice Act 1972	Section 51(1).
1973 c 18	The Matrimonial Causes Act 1973	Sections 42 to 44. In section 52(1), the definition of 'custody'. In Schedule 2, paragraph 11.
1973 c 29	The Guardianship Act 1973	The whole Act.
1973 c 45	The Domicile and Matrimonial Proceedings Act 1973	In Schedule 1, in paragraph 11(1) the definitions of 'custody' and 'education' and in paragraph 11(3) the word 'four'.
1973 c 62	The Powers of Criminal Courts Act 1973	In section 13(1), the words 'and the purposes of section 1(2)(bb) of the Children and Young Persons Act 1969'. In Schedule 3, in paragraph 3(2A), the word 'and' immediately preceding paragraph (b).
1974 c 53	The Rehabilitation of Offenders Act 1974	In section 1(4)(b) the words 'or in care proceedings under section 1 of the Children and Young Persons Act 1969'. In section 5, in subsection 5(e), the words 'a care order or'; and in subsection (10), the words 'care order or'.
1975 c 72	The Children Act 1975	The whole Act.
1976 c 36	The Adoption Act 1976	Section 11(5). Section 14(3). In section 15, in subsection (1), the words from

Chapter	Short Title	Extent of Repeal
		'subject' to 'cases)' and subsection (4).
		Section 26.
		In section 28(5), the words 'or the organisation'.
		Section 34
		Section 36(1)(c).
		Section 37(1), (3) and (4).
		Section 55(4).
		In section 57, in subsection (2), the words from 'and the court' to the end and subsections (4) to (10).
		In section 72(1), the definition of 'place of safety', in the definition of 'local authority' the words from 'and' to the end and, in the definition of 'specified order', the words 'Northern Ireland or'.
		In Schedule 3, paragraphs 8, 11, 19, 21 and 22.
1977 c 45	The Criminal Law Act 1977	Section 58(3).
1977 c 49	The National Health Service Act 1977	In section 21, in subsection (1)(a) the words 'and young children'.
		In Schedule 8, in paragraph 1(1), the words from 'and of children' to the end; in paragraph 2(2) the words from 'or (b) to persons who' to 'arrangements'; and in paragraph 3(1) '(a)' and the w ords from 'or (b) a child' to 'school age'.
		In Schedule 15, paragraphs 10 and 25.
1978 c 22	The Domestic Proceedings and Magistrates' Courts Act 1978	Sections 9 to 15.
		In section 19, in subsection (1) the words 'following powers, that is to say' and sub-paragraph (ii), subsections (2) and (4), in subsection (7) the words 'and one interim custody order' and in subsection (9) the words 'or 21'.
		In section 20, subsection (4) and in subsection (9) the words 'subject to

Chapter	Short Title	Extent of Repeal
		the provisions of section 11(8) of this Act'.
		Section 21.
		In section 24, the words 'or 21' in both places where they occur.
		In section 25, in subsection (1) paragraph (b) and the word 'or' immediately preceding it and in subsection (2) paragraphs (c) and (d).
		Section 29(4).
		Sections 33 and 34.
		Sections 36 to 53.
		Sections 64 to 72.
		Sections 73(1) and 74(1) and (3).
		In section 88(1), the definition of 'actual custody'.
		In Schedule 2, paragraphs 22, 23, 27, 29, 31, 36, 41 to 43, 46 to 50.
1978 c 28	The Adoption (Scotland) Act 1978	In section 20(3)(c), the words 'section 12(3)(b) of the Adoption Act 1976 or of'.
		In section 45(5), the word 'approved'.
		Section 49(4).
		In section 65(1), in the definition of 'local authority', the words from 'and' to the end and, in the definition of 'specified order', the words 'Northern Ireland or'.
1978 c 30	The Interpretation Act 1978	In Schedule 1, the entry with respect to the construction of certain expressions relating to children.
1980 c 5	The Child Care Act 1980	The whole Act.
1980 c 6	The Foster Children Act 1980	The whole Act.
1980 c 43	The Magistrates' Courts Act 1980	In section 65(1), paragraphs (e) and (g) and the paragraph (m) inserted in section 65 by paragraph 82 of Schedule 2 to the Family Law Reform Act 1987.
		In section 81(8), in the definition of 'guardian'

Chapter	Short Title	Extent of Repeal
		the words 'by deed or will' and in the definition of 'sums adjudged to be paid by a conviction' the words from 'as applied' to the end.
		In section 143(2), paragraph (i).
		In Schedule 7, paragraphs 78, 83, 91, 92, 110, 116, 117, 138, 157, 158, 165, 166 and 199 to 201.
1981 c 60	The Education Act 1981	In Schedule 3, paragraph 9.
1982 c 20	The Children's Homes Act 1982	The whole Act.
1982 c 48	The Criminal Justice Act 1982	Sections 22 to 25.
		Section 27.
		In Schedule 14, paragraphs 45 and 46.
1983 c 20	The Mental Health Act 1983	In section 26(5), paragraph (d) and the word 'or' immediately preceding it.
		In section 28(1), the words '(including an order under section 38 of the Sexual Offences Act 1956)'.
		In Schedule 4, paragraphs 12, 26(a), (b) and (c), 35, 44, 50 and 51.
1983 c 41	The Health and Social Services and Social Security Adjudications Act 1983	Section 4(1).
		Sections 5 and 6.
		In section 11, in subsection (2) the words 'the Child Care Act 1980 and the Children's Homes Act 1982'.
		In section 19, subsections (1) to (5).
		Schedule 1.
		In Schedule 2, paragraphs 3, 9 to 14, 20 to 24, 27, 28, 34, 37 and 46 to 62.
		In Schedule 4, paragraphs 38 to 48.
		In Schedule 9, paragraphs 5, 16 and 17.
1984 c 23	The Registered Homes Act 1984	In Schedule 1, in paragraph 5, sub-paragraph (a) and paragraphs 6, 7 and 8.
1984 c 28	The County Courts Act 1984	In Schedule 2, paragraph 56.

Chapter	Short Title	Extent of Repeal
1984 c 37	The Child Abduction Act 1984	In section 3, the word 'and' immediately preceding paragraph (c). In the Schedule, in paragraph 1(2) the words 'or voluntary organisation' and paragraph 3(1)(e).
1984 c 42	The Matrimonial and Family Proceedings Act 1984	In Schedule 1, paragraphs 19 and 23.
1984 c 56	The Foster Children (Scotland) Act 1984	In section 1, the words 'for a period of more than 6 days' and the words from 'The period' to the end. In section 7(1), the word 'or' at the end of paragraph (e). In Schedule 2, paragraphs 1 to 3 and 8.
1984 c 60	The Police and Criminal Evidence Act 1984	In section 37(15), the words 'and is not excluded from this Part of this Act by section 52 below'. Section 39(5). Section 52. In section 118(1), in the definition of parent or guardian, paragraph (b) and the word 'and' immediately preceding it. In Schedule 2, the entry relating to section 16 of the Child Care Act 1980. In Schedule 6, paragraphs 19(a) and 22.
1985 c 23	The Prosecution of Offences Act 1985	Section 27.
1985 c 60	The Child Abduction and Custody Act 1985	Section 9(c). Section 20(2)(b) and (c). Section 25(3) and (5). In Schedule 3, paragraph 1(2).
1986 c 28	The Children and Young Persons (Amendment Act) 1986	The whole Act.
1986 c 33	The Disabled Persons (Services, Consultation and Representation) Act 1986	In section 16, in the definition of 'guardian', paragraph (a).
1986 c 45	The Insolvency Act 1986	In section 281(5)(b), the words 'in domestic proceedings'.
1986 c 50	The Social Security Act 1986	In Schedule 10, paragraph 51.

Chapter	Short Title	Extent of Repeal
1986 c 55	The Family Law Act 1986	In section 1(2), in paragraph (a) the words '(a) or' and paragraph (b). Section 3(4) to (6). Section 4. Section 35(1). In section 42(6), in paragraph (b) the words 'section 42(6) of the Matrimonial Causes Act 1973 or', in paragraph (c) the words 'section 42(7) of that Act or' and in paragraph (d) the words 'section 19(6) of the Domestic Proceedings and Magistrates' Courts Act 1978 or'. In Schedule 1, paragraphs 10, 11, 13 to 17, 20 and 23.
1987 c 42	The Family Law Reform Act 1987	Section 3. Sections 4 to 7. Sections 9 to 16. In Schedule 2, paragraphs 11, 14, 51, 67, 68, 94 and 95. In Schedule 3, paragraphs 11 and 12.
1988 c 34	The Legal Aid Act 1988	Section 3(4)(c). Section 27. Section 28. In section 30, subsections (1) and (2). In Part I of Schedule 2, paragraph 2(a) and (e).

HUMAN FERTILISATION AND EMBRYOLOGY ACT 1990

(1990 c 37)

ARRANGEMENT OF SECTIONS

An Act to make provision in connection with human embryos and any subsequent development of such embryos; to prohibit certain practices in connection with embryos and gametes; to establish a Human Fertilisation and Embryology Authority; to make provision about the persons who in certain circumstances are to be treated in law as the parents of a child; and to amend the Surrogacy Arrangements Act 1985.   [1 November 1990]

Principal terms used

1. Meaning of 'embryo', 'gamete' and associated expressions—(1) In this Act, except where otherwise stated—
   (a) embryo means a live human embryo where fertilisation is complete, and
   (b) references to an embryo include an egg in the process of fertilisation,
and, for this purpose, fertilisation is not complete until the appearance of a two cell zygote.
   (2) This Act, so far as it governs bringing about the creation of an embryo, applies only to bringing about the creation of an embryo outside the human body; and in this Act—

(a) references to embryos the creation of which was brought about *in vitro* (in their application to those where fertilisation is complete) are to those where fertilisation began outside the human body whether or not it was completed there, and

(b) references to embryos taken from a woman do not include embryos whose creation was brought about *in vitro*.

(3) This Act, so far as it governs the keeping or use of an embryo, applies only to keeping or using an embryo outside the human body.

(4) References in this Act to gametes, eggs or sperm, except where otherwise stated, are to live human gametes, eggs or sperm but references below in this Act to gametes or eggs do not include eggs in the process of fertilisation.

2. Other terms—(1) In this Act—

'the Authority' means the Human Fertilisation and Embryology Authority established under section 5 of this Act,

'directions' means directions under section 23 of this Act,

'licence' means a licence under Schedule 2 to this Act and, in relation to a licence, 'the person responsible' has the meaning given by section 17 of this Act, and

'treatment services' means medical, surgical or obstetric services provided to the public or a section of the public for the purpose of assisting women to carry children.

(2) References in this Act to keeping, in relation to embryos or gametes, include keeping while preserved, whether preserved by cryopreservation or in any other way; and embryos or gametes so kept are referred to in this Act as 'stored' (and 'store' and 'storage' are to be interpreted accordingly).

(3) For the purposes of this Act, a woman is not to be treated as carrying a child until the embryo has become implanted.

Activities governed by the Act

3. Prohibitions in connection with embryos—(1) No person shall—

(a) bring about the creation of an embryo, or

(b) keep or use an embryo,

except in pursuance of a licence.

(2) No person shall place in a woman—

(a) a live embryo other than a human embryo, or

(b) any live gametes other than human gametes.

(3) A licence cannot authorise—

(a) keeping or using an embryo after the appearance of the primitive streak,

(b) placing an embryo in any animal,

(c) keeping or using an embryo in any circumstances in which regulations prohibit its keeping or use, or

(d) replacing a nucleus of a cell of an embryo with a nucleus taken from a cell of any person, embryo or subsequent development of an embryo.

(4) For the purposes of subsection (3)(a) above, the primitive streak is to be taken to have appeared in an embryo not later than the end of the period of 14 days beginning with the day when the gametes are mixed, not counting any time during which the embryo is stored.

[3A. Prohibition in connection with germ cells—(1) No person shall, for the purpose of providing fertility services for any woman, use female germ cells taken or derived from an embryo or a foetus or use embryos created by using such cells.

(2) In this section—

'female germ cells' means cells of the female germ line and includes such cells at any stage of maturity and accordingly includes eggs, and 'fertility services' means medical, surgical or obstetric services provided for the purpose of assisting women to carry children.]

Note. This section inserted by Criminal Justice and Public Order Act 1994, s 156, as from 10 April 1995.

4. Prohibitions in connection with gametes—(1) No person shall—
  (a) store any gametes, or
  (b) in the course of providing treatment services for any woman, use the sperm of any man unless the services are being provided for the woman and the man together or use the eggs of any other woman, or
  (c)   mix gametes with the live gametes of any animal,
except in pursuance of a licence.

(2) A licence cannot authorise storing or using gametes in any circumstances in which regulations prohibit their storage or use.

(3) No person shall place sperm and eggs in a woman in any circumstances specified in regulations except in pursuance of a licence.

(4) Regulations made by virtue of subsection (3) above may provide that, in relation to licences only to place sperm and eggs in a woman in such circumstances, sections 12 to 22 of this Act shall have effect with such modifications as may be specified in the regulations.

(5) Activities regulated by this section or section 3 of this Act are referred to in this Act as 'activities governed by this Act'.

The Human Fertilisation and Embryology Authority, its functions and procedure

5. The Human Fertilisation and Embryology Authority—(1) There shall be a body corporate called the Human Fertilisation and Embryology Authority.

(2) The Authority shall consist of—
  (a) a chairman and deputy chairman, and
  (b) such number of other members as the Secretary of State appoints.

(3) Schedule 1 to this Act (which deals with the membership of the Authority, etc) shall have effect.

6. Accounts and audit—(1) The Authority shall keep proper accounts and proper records in relation to the accounts and shall prepare for each accounting year a statement of accounts.

(2) The annual statement of accounts shall comply with any direction given by the Secretary of State, with the approval of the Treasury, as to the information to be contained in the statement, the way in which the information is to be presented or the methods and principles according to which the statement is to be prepared.

(3) Not later than five months after the end of an accounting year, the Authority shall send a copy of the statement of accounts for that year to the Secretary of State and to the Comptroller and Auditor General.

(4) The Comptroller and Auditor General shall examine, certify and report on every statement of accounts received by him under subsection (3) above and shall lay a copy of the statement and of his report before each House of Parliament.

(5) The Secretary of State and the Comptroller and Auditor General may inspect any records relating to the accounts.

(6) In this section 'accounting year' means the period beginning with the day when the Authority is established and ending with the following 31st March, or any later period of twelve months ending with the 31st March.

7. Reports to Secretary of State—(1) The Authority shall prepare a report for the first twelve months of its existence, and a report for each succeeding period of twelve months, and shall send each report to the Secretary of State as soon as practicable after the end of the period for which it is prepared.

(2) A report prepared under this section for any period shall deal with the activities of the Authority in the period and the activities the Authority proposes to undertake in the succeeding period of twelve months.

(3) The Secretary of State shall lay before each House of Parliament a copy of every report received by him under this section.

8. General functions of the Authority.   The Authority shall—

(a) keep under review information about embryos and any subsequent development of embryos and about the provision of treatment services and activities governed by this Act, and advise the Secretary of State, if he asks it to do so, about those matters,

(b) publicise the services provided to the public by the Authority or provided in pursuance of licences,

(c) provide, to such extent as it considers appropriate, advice and information for persons to whom licences apply or who are receiving treatment services or providing gametes or embryos for use for the purposes of activities governed by this Act, or may wish to do so, and

(d) perform such other functions as may be specified in regulations.

9. Licence committees and other committees—(1) The Authority shall maintain one or more committees to discharge the Authority's functions relating to the grant, variation, suspension and revocation of licences, and a committee discharging those functions is referred to in this Act as a 'licence committee'.

(2) The Authority may provide for the discharge of any of its other functions by committees or by members or employees of the Authority.

(3) A committee (other than a licence committee) may appoint sub-committees.

(4) Persons, committees or sub-committees discharging functions of the Authority shall do so in accordance with any general directions of the Authority.

(5) A licence committee shall consist of such number of persons as may be specified in or determined in accordance with regulations, all being members of the Authority, and shall include at least one person who is not authorised to carry on or participate in any activity under the authority of a licence and would not be so authorised if outstanding applications were granted.

(6) A committee (other than a licence committee) or a sub-committee may include a minority of persons who are not members of the Authority.

(7) Subject to subsection (10) below, a licence committee, before considering an application for authority—

(a) for a person to carry on an activity governed by this Act which he is not then authorised to carry on, or

(b) for a person to carry on any such activity on premises where he is not then authorised to carry it on,

shall arrange for the premises where the activity is to be carried on to be inspected on its behalf, and for a report on the inspection to be made to it.

(8) Subject to subsection (9) below, a licence committee shall arrange for any premises to which a licence relates to be inspected on its behalf once in each calendar year, and for a report on the inspection to be made to it.

(9) Any particular premises need not be inspected in any particular year if the licence committee considers an inspection in that year unnecessary.

(10) A licence committee need not comply with subsection (7) above where the premises in question have been inspected in pursuance of that subsection or subsection (8) above at some time during the period of one year ending with the date of the application, and the licence committee considers that a further inspection is not necessary.

(11) An inspection in pursuance of subsection (7) or (8) above may be carried out by a person who is not a member of a licence committee.

10. Licensing procedure—(1) Regulations may make such provision as appears to the Secretary of State to be necessary or desirable about the proceedings of licence committees and of the Authority on any appeal from such a committee.

(2) The regulations may in particular include provision—
(a) for requiring persons to give evidence or to produce documents, and
(b) about the admissibility of evidence.

Scope of licences

11. Licences for treatment, storage and research—(1) The Authority may grant the following and no other licences—
(a) licences under paragraph 1 of Schedule 2 to this Act authorising activities in the course of providing treatment services,
(b) licences under that Schedule authorising the storage of gametes and embryos, and
(c) licences under paragraph 3 of that Schedule authorising activities for the purposes of a project of research.
(2) Paragraph 4 of that Schedule has effect in the case of all licences.

Licence conditions

12. General conditions. The following shall be conditions of every licence granted under this Act—
(a) that the activities authorised by the licence shall be carried on only on the premises to which the licence relates and under the supervision of the person responsible,
(b) that any member or employee of the Authority, on production, if so required, of a document identifying the person as such, shall at all reasonable times be permitted to enter those premises and inspect them (which includes inspecting any equipment or records and observing any activity),
(c) that the provisions of Schedule 3 to this Act shall be complied with,
(d) that proper records shall be maintained in such form as the Authority may specify in directions,
(e) that no money or other benefit shall be given or received in respect of any supply of gametes or embryos unless authorised by directions,
(f) that, where gametes or embryos are supplied to a person to whom another licence applies, that person shall also be provided with such information as the Authority may specify in directions, and
(g) that the Authority shall be provided, in such form and at such intervals as it may specify in directions, with such copies of or extracts from the records, or such other information, as the directions may specify.

13. Conditions of licences for treatment—(1) The following shall be conditions of every licence under paragraph 1 of Schedule 2 to this Act.
(2) Such information shall be recorded as the Authority may specify in directions about the following—
(a) the persons for whom services are provided in pursuance of the licence,
(b) the services provided for them,
(c) the persons whose gametes are kept or used for the purposes of services provided in pursuance of the licence or whose gametes have been used in bringing about the creation of embryos so kept or used,
(d) any child appearing to the person responsible to have been born as a result of treatment in pursuance of the licence,
(e) any mixing of egg and sperm and any taking of an embryo from a woman or other acquisition of an embryo, and
(f) such other matters as the Authority may specify in directions.
(3) The records maintained in pursuance of the licence shall include any information recorded in pursuance of subsection (2) above and any consent of a person whose consent is required under Schedule 3 to this Act.

(4) No information shall be removed from any records maintained in pursuance of the licence before the expiry of such period as may be specified in directions for records of the class in question.

(5) A woman shall not be provided with treatment services unless account has been taken of the welfare of any child who may be born as a result of the treatment (including the need of that child for a father), and of any other child who may be affected by the birth.

(6) A woman shall not be provided with any treatment services involving—

(a) the use of any gametes of any person, if that person's consent is required under paragraph 5 of Schedule 3 to this Act for the use in question,

(b) the use of any embryo the creation of which was brought about *in vitro*, or

(c) the use of any embryo taken from a woman, if the consent of the woman from whom it was taken is required under paragraph 7 of that Schedule for the use in question,

unless the woman being treated and, where she is being treated together with a man, the man have been given a suitable opportunity to receive proper counselling about the implications of taking the proposed steps, and have been provided with such relevant information as is proper.

(7) Suitable procedures shall be maintained—

(a) for determining the persons providing gametes or from whom embryos are taken for use in pursuance of the licence, and

(b) for the purpose of securing that consideration is given to the use of practices not requiring the authority of a licence as well as those requiring such authority.

14. Conditions of storage licences—(1) The following shall be conditions of every licence authorising the storage of gametes or embryos—

(a) that gametes of a person or an embryo taken from a woman shall be placed in storage only if received from that person or woman or acquired from a person to whom a licence applies and that an embryo the creation of which has been brought about *in vitro* otherwise than in pursuance of that licence shall be placed in storage only if acquired from a person to whom a licence applies,

(b) that gametes or embryos which are or have been stored shall not be supplied to a person otherwise than in the course of providing treatment services unless that person is a person to whom a licence applies,

(c) that no gametes or embryos shall be kept in storage for longer than the statutory storage period and, if stored at the end of the period, shall be allowed to perish, and

(d) that such information as the Authority may specify in directions as to the persons whose consent is required under Schedule 3 to this Act, the terms of their consent and the circumstances of the storage and as to such other matters as the Authority may specify in directions shall be included in the records maintained in pursuance of the licence.

(2) No information shall be removed from any records maintained in pursuance of such a licence before the expiry of such period as may be specified in directions for records of the class in question.

(3) The statutory storage period in respect of gametes is such period not exceeding ten years as the licence may specify.

(4) The statutory storage period in respect of embryos is such period not exceeding five years as the licence may specify.

(5) Regulations may provide that subsection (3) or (4) above shall have effect as if for ten years or, as the case may be, five years there were substituted—

(a) such shorter period, or

(b) in such circumstances as may be specified in the regulations, such longer period,

as may be specified in the regulations.

15. Conditions of research licences—(1) The following shall be conditions of every licence under paragraph 3 of Schedule 2 to this Act.

(2) The records maintained in pursuance of the licence shall include such information as the Authority may specify in directions about such matters as the Authority may so specify.

(3) No information shall be removed from any records maintained in pursuance of the licence before the expiry of such period as may be specified in directions for records of the class in question.

(4) No embryo appropriated for the purposes of any project of research shall be kept or used otherwise than for the purposes of such a project.

Grant, revocation and suspension of licences

16. Grant of licence—(1) Where application is made to the Authority in a form approved for the purpose by it accompanied by the initial fee, a licence may be granted to any person by a licence committee if the requirements of subsection (2) below are met and any additional fee is paid.

(2) The requirements mentioned in subsection (1) above are—

(a) that the application is for a licence designating an individual as the person under whose supervision the activities to be authorised by the licence are to be carried on,

(b) that either that individual is the applicant or—
  (i) the application is made with the consent of that individual, and
  (ii) the licence committee is satisfied that the applicant is a suitable person to hold a licence,

(c) that the licence committee is satisfied that the character, qualifications and experience of that individual are such as are required for the supervision of the activities and that the individual will discharge the duty under section 17 of this Act,

(d) that the licence committee is satisfied that the premises in respect of which the licence is to be granted are suitable for the activities, and

(e) that all the other requirements of this Act in relation to the granting of the licence are satisfied.

(3) The grant of a licence to any person may be by way of renewal of a licence granted to that person, whether on the same or different terms.

(4) Where the licence committee is of the opinion that the information provided in the application is insufficient to enable it to determine the application, it need not consider the application until the applicant has provided it with such further information as it may require him to provide.

(5) The licence committee shall not grant a licence unless a copy of the conditions to be imposed by the licence has been shown to, and acknowledged in writing by, the applicant and (where different) the person under whose supervision the activities are to be carried on.

(6) In subsection (1) above 'initial fee' and 'additional fee' mean a fee of such amount as may be fixed from time to time by the Authority with the approval of the Secretary of State and the Treasury, and in determining any such amount, the Authority may have regard to the costs of performing all its functions.

(7) Different fees may be fixed for different circumstances and fees paid under this section are not repayable.

17. The person responsible—(1) It shall be the duty of the individual under whose supervision the activities authorised by a licence are carried on (referred to in this Act as the 'person responsible') to secure—

(a) that the other persons to whom the licence applies are of such character, and are so qualified by training and experience, as to be suitable persons to participate in the activities authorised by the licence,

   (b) that proper equipment is used,

   (c) that proper arrangements are made for the keeping of gametes and embryos and for the disposal of gametes or embryos that have been allowed to perish,

   (d) that suitable practices are used in the course of the activities, and

   (e) that the conditions of the licence are complied with.

   (2) References in this Act to the persons to whom a licence applies are to—

   (a) the person responsible,

   (b) any person designated in the licence, or in a notice given to the Authority by the person who holds the licence or the person responsible, as a person to whom the licence applies, and

   (c) any person acting under the direction of the person responsible or of any person so designated.

   (3) References below in this Act to the nominal licensee are to a person who holds a licence under which a different person is the person responsible.

18. Revocation and variation of licence—(1) A licence committee may revoke a licence if it is satisfied—

   (a) that any information given for the purposes of the application for the grant of the licence was in any material respect false or misleading,

   (b) that the premises to which the licence relates are no longer suitable for the activities authorised by the licence,

   (c) that the person responsible has failed to discharge, or is unable because of incapacity to discharge, the duty under section 17 of this Act or has failed to comply with directions given in connection with any licence, or

   (d) that there has been any other material change of circumstances since the licence was granted.

   (2) A licence committee may also revoke a licence if—

   (a) it ceases to be satisfied that the character of the person responsible is such as is required for the supervision of those activities or that the nominal licensee is a suitable person to hold a licence, or

   (b) the person responsible dies or is convicted of an offence under this Act.

   (3) Where a licence committee has power to revoke a licence under subsection (1) above it may instead vary any terms of the licence.

   (4) A licence committee may, on an application by the person responsible or the nominal licensee, vary or revoke a licence.

   (5) A licence committee may, on an application by the nominal licensee, vary the licence so as to designate another individual in place of the person responsible if—

   (a) the committee is satisfied that the character, qualifications and experience of the other individual are such as are required for the supervision of the activities authorised by the licence and that the individual will discharge the duty under section 17 of this Act, and

   (b) the application is made with the consent of the other individual.

   (6) Except on an application under subsection (5) above, a licence can only be varied under this section—

   (a) so far as it relates to the activities authorised by the licence, the manner in which they are conducted or the conditions of the licence, or

   (b) so as to extend or restrict the premises to which the licence relates.

19. Procedure for refusal, variation or revocation of licence—(1) Where a licence committee proposes to refuse a licence or to refuse to vary a licence so as to designate another individual in place of the person responsible, the committee shall give notice of the proposal, the reasons for it and the effect of subsection (3) below to the applicant.

   (2) Where a licence committee proposes to vary or revoke a licence, the committee shall give notice of the proposal, the reasons for it and the effect of subsection (3) below to the person responsible and the nominal licensee (but not to any person who has applied for the variation or revocation).

3522 Human Fertilisation and Embryology Act 1990, s 19

(3) If, within the period of twenty-eight days beginning with the day on which notice of the proposal is given, any person to whom notice was given under subsection (1) or (2) above gives notice to the committee of a wish to make to the committee representations about the proposal in any way mentioned in subsection (4) below, the committee shall, before making its determination, give the person an opportunity to make representations in that way.

(4) The representations may be—

(a) oral representations made by the person, or another acting on behalf of the person, at a meeting of the committee, and

(b) written representations made by the person.

(5) A licence committee shall—

(a) in the case of a determination to grant a licence, give notice of the determination to the person responsible and the nominal licensee,

(b) in the case of a determination to refuse a licence, or to refuse to vary a licence so as to designate another individual in place of the person responsible, give such notice to the applicant, and

(c) in the case of a determination to vary or revoke a licence, give such notice to the person responsible and the nominal licensee.

(6) A licence committee giving notice of a determination to refuse a licence or to refuse to vary a licence so as to designate another individual in place of the person responsible, or of a determination to vary or revoke a licence otherwise than on an application by the person responsible or the nominal licensee, shall give in the notice the reasons for its decision.

20. Appeal to Authority against determinations of licence committee—(1) Where a licence committee determines to refuse a licence or to refuse to vary a licence so as to designate another individual in place of the person responsible, the applicant may appeal to the Authority if notice has been given to the committee and to the Authority before the end of the period of twenty-eight days beginning with the date on which notice of the committee's determination was served on the applicant.

(2) Where a licence committee determines to vary or revoke a licence, any person on whom notice of the determination was served (other than a person who applied for the variation or revocation) may appeal to the Authority if notice has been given to the committee and to the Authority before the end of the period of twenty-eight days beginning with the date on which notice of the committee's determination was served.

(3) An appeal under this section shall be by way of rehearing by the Authority and no member of the Authority who took any part in the proceedings resulting in the determination appealed against shall take any part in the proceedings on appeal.

(4) On the appeal—

(a) the appellant shall be entitled to appear or be represented,

(b) the members of the licence committee shall be entitled to appear, or the committee shall be entitled to be represented, and

(c) the Authority shall consider any written representations received from the appellant or any member of the committee and may take into account any matter that could be taken into account by a licence committee,

and the Authority may make such determination on the appeal as it thinks fit.

(5) The Authority shall give notice of its determination to the appellant and, if it is a determination to refuse a licence or to refuse to vary a licence so as to designate another individual in place of the person responsible or a determination to vary or revoke a licence, shall include in the notice the reasons for the decision.

(6) The functions of the Authority on an appeal under this section cannot be discharged by any committee, member or employee of the Authority and, for the purposes of the appeal, the quorum shall not be less than five.

21. Appeals to High Court or Court of Session.   Where the Authority determines under section 20 of this Act—

(a) to refuse a licence or to refuse to vary a licence so as to designate another individual in place of the person responsible, or

(b) to vary or revoke a licence,

any person on whom notice of the determination was served may appeal to the High Court or, in Scotland, the Court of Session on a point of law.

22. Temporary suspension of licence—(1) Where a licence committee—

(a) has reasonable grounds to suspect that there are grounds for revoking the licence under section 18 of this Act, and

(b) is of the opinion that the licence should immediately be suspended,

it may by notice suspend the licence for such period not exceeding three months as may be specified in the notice.

(2) Notice under subsection (1) above shall be given to the person responsible or, where the person responsible has died or appears to the licence committee to be unable because of incapacity to discharge the duty under section 17 of this Act, to some other person to whom the licence applies or the nominal licensee and a licence committee may, by a further notice to that person, renew or further renew the notice under subsection (1) above for such further period not exceeding three months as may be specified in the renewal notice.

(3) While suspended under this section a licence shall be of no effect, but application may be made under section 18(5) of this Act by the nominal licensee to designate another individual as the person responsible.

Directions and guidance

23. Directions: general—(1) The Authority may from time to time give directions for any purpose for which directions may be given under this Act or directions varying or revoking such directions.

(2) A person to whom any requirement contained in directions is applicable shall comply with the requirement.

(3) Anything done by a person in pursuance of directions is to be treated for the purposes of this Act as done in pursuance of a licence.

(4) Where directions are to be given to a particular person, they shall be given by serving notice of the directions on the person.

(5) In any other case, directions may be given—

(a) in respect of any licence (including a licence which has ceased to have effect), by serving notice of the directions on the person who is or was the person responsible or the nominal licensee, or

(b) if the directions appear to the Authority to be general directions or it appears to the Authority that it is not practicable to give notice in pursuance of paragraph (a) above, by publishing the directions in such way as, in the opinion of the Authority, is likely to bring the directions to the attention of the persons to whom they are applicable.

(6) This section does not apply to directions under section 9(4) of this Act.

24. Directions as to particular matters—(1) If, in the case of any information about persons for whom treatment services were provided, the person responsible does not know that any child was born following the treatment, the period specified in directions by virtue of section 13(4) of this Act shall not expire less than 50 years after the information was first recorded.

(2) In the case of every licence under paragraph 1 of Schedule 2 to this Act, directions shall require information to be recorded and given to the Authority about each of the matters referred to in section 13(2)(a) to (e) of this Act.

(3) Directions may authorise, in such circumstances and subject to such conditions as may be specified in the directions, the keeping, by or on behalf of a person to whom a licence applies, of gametes or embryos in the course of their carriage to or from any premises.

(4) Directions may authorise any person to whom a licence applies to receive gametes or embryos from outside the United Kingdom or to send gametes or embryos outside the United Kingdom in such circumstances and subject to such conditions as may be specified in the directions, and directions made by virtue of this subsection may provide for sections 12 to 14 of this Act to have effect with such modifications as may be specified in the directions.

(5) A licence committee may from time to time give such directions as are mentioned in subsection (7) below where a licence has been varied or has ceased to have effect (whether by expiry, suspension, revocation or otherwise).

(6) A licence committee proposing to suspend, revoke or vary a licence may give such directions as are mentioned in subsection (7) below.

(7) The directions referred to in subsections (5) and (6) above are directions given for the purpose of securing the continued discharge of the duties of the person responsible under the licence concerned ('the old licence'), and such directions may, in particular—

(a) require anything kept or information held in pursuance of the old licence to be transferred to the Authority or any other person, or

(b) provide for the discharge of the duties in question by any individual, being an individual whose character, qualifications and experience are, in the opinion of the committee, such as are required for the supervision of the activities authorised by the old licence, and authorise those activities to be carried on under the supervision of that individual,

but cannot require any individual to discharge any of those duties unless the individual has consented in writing to do so.

(8) Directions for the purpose referred to in subsection (7)(a) above shall be given to the person responsible under the old licence or, where that person has died or appears to the licence committee to have become unable because of incapacity to discharge the duties in question, to some other person to whom the old licence applies or applied or to the nominal licensee.

(9) Directions for the purpose referred to in subsection (7)(b) above shall be given to the individual who under the directions is to discharge the duty.

(10) Where a person who holds a licence dies, anything done subsequently by an individual which that individual would have been authorised to do if the licence had continued in force shall, until directions are given by virtue of this section, be treated as authorised by a licence.

(11) Where the Authority proposes to give directions specifying any animal for the purposes of paragraph 1(1)(f) or 3(5) of Schedule 2 to this Act, it shall report the proposal to the Secretary of State; and the directions shall not be given until the Secretary of State has laid a copy of the report before each House of Parliament.

25. Code of practice—(1) The Authority shall maintain a code of practice giving guidance about the proper conduct of activities carried on in pursuance of a licence under this Act and the proper discharge of the functions of the person responsible and other persons to whom the licence applies.

(2) The guidance given by the code shall include guidance for those providing treatment services about the account to be taken of the welfare of children who may be born as a result of treatment services (including a child's need for a father), and of other children who may be affected by such births.

(3) The code may also give guidance about the use of any technique involving the placing of sperm and eggs in a woman.

(4) The Authority may from time to time revise the whole or any part of the code.

(5) The Authority shall publish the code as for the time being in force.

(6) A failure on the part of any person to observe any provision of the code shall not of itself render the person liable to any proceedings, but—

(a) a licence committee shall, in considering whether there has been any failure to comply with any conditions of a licence and, in particular, conditions requiring anything to be 'proper' or 'suitable', take account of any relevant provision of the code, and

(b) a licence committee may, in considering, where it has power to do so, whether or not to vary or revoke a licence, take into account any observance of or failure to observe the provisions of the code.

26. Procedure for approval of code—(1) The Authority shall send a draft of the proposed first code of practice under section 25 of this Act to the Secretary of State within twelve months of the commencement of section 5 of this Act.

(2) If the Authority proposes to revise the code or, if the Secretary of State does not approve a draft of the proposed first code, to submit a further draft, the Authority shall send a draft of the revised code or, as the case may be, a further draft of the proposed first code to the Secretary of State.

(3) Before preparing any draft, the Authority shall consult such persons as the Secretary of State may require it to consult and such other persons (if any) as it considers appropriate.

(4) If the Secretary of State approves a draft, he shall lay it before Parliament and, if he does not approve it, he shall give reasons to the Authority.

(5) A draft approved by the Secretary of State shall come into force in accordance with directions.

Status

27. Meaning of 'mother'—(1) The woman who is carrying or has carried a child as a result of the placing in her of an embryo or of sperm and eggs, and no other woman, is to be treated as the mother of the child.

(2) Subsection (1) above does not apply to any child to the extent that the child is treated by virtue of adoption as not being the *child of any person other than the adopter or adopters* [woman's child].

Note. Words in square brackets substituted for words in italics by the Adoption and Children Act 2002, s 139 (1), Sch 3, paras 76, 77, as from a day to be appointed.

(3) Subsection (1) above applies whether the woman was in the United Kingdom or elsewhere at the time of the placing in her of the embryo or the sperm and eggs.

28. Meaning of 'father'—(1) [Subject to subsections (5A) to (5I) below,] this section applies in the case of a child who is being or has been carried by a woman as the result of the placing in her of an embryo or of sperm and eggs or her artificial insemination.

Note. Words in square brackets inserted by the Human Fertilisation and Embryology (Deceased Fathers) Act 2003, s 2(1), Schedule, para 13, as from 1 December 2003 (SI 2003 No 3095). For retrospective, transitional and transitory provision see s 3(1) of the 2003 Act.

(2) If—

(a) at the time of the placing in her of the embryo or the sperm and eggs or of her insemination, the woman was a party to a marriage, and

(b) the creation of the embryo carried by her was not brought about with the sperm of the other party to the marriage,

then, subject to subsection (5) below, the other party to the marriage shall be treated as the father of the child unless it is shown that he did not consent to the placing in her of the embryo or the sperm and eggs or to her insemination (as the case may be).

(3) If no man is treated, by virtue of subsection (2) above, as the father of the child but—

(a) the embryo or the sperm and eggs were placed in the woman, or she was artificially inseminated, in the course of treatment services provided for her and a man together by a person to whom a licence applies, and

(b) the creation of the embryo carried by her was not brought about with the sperm of that man, then, subject to subsection (5) below, that man shall be treated as the father of the child.

(4) Where a person is treated as the father of the child by virtue of subsection (2) or (3) above, no other person is to be treated as the father of the child.

(5) Subsections (2) and (3) above do not apply—

(a) in relation to England and Wales and Northern Ireland, to any child who, by virtue of the rules of common law, is treated as the legitimate child of the parties to a marriage,

(b) (*applies to Scotland only*), or

(c) to any child to the extent that the child is treated by virtue of adoption as not being the *child of any person other than the adopter or adopters* [man's child].

Note. Sub-s (5)(c) modified, in relation to parental orders, by the Parental Orders (Human Fertilisation and Embryology) Regulations 1994, SI 1994 No 2767 and the Parental Orders (Human Fertilisation and Embryology) (Scotland) Regulations 1994, SI 1994 No 2804. Words in square brackets in sub-s (5)(c) substituted by the Adoption and Children Act 2002, s 139(1), Sch 3, paras 76, 78, as from a day to be appointed.

[(5A) If—

(a) a child has been carried by a woman as the result of the placing in her of an embryo or of sperm and eggs or her artificial insemination,

(b) the creation of the embryo carried by her was brought about by using the sperm of a man after his death, or the creation of the embryo was brought about using the sperm of a man before his death but the embryo was placed in the woman after his death,

(c) the woman was a party to a marriage with the man immediately before his death,

(d) the man consented in writing (and did not withdraw the consent)—

(i) to the use of his sperm after his death which brought about the creation of the embryo carried by the woman or (as the case may be) to the placing in the woman after his death of the embryo which was brought about using his sperm before his death, and

(ii) to being treated for the purpose mentioned in subsection (5I) below as the father of any resulting child,

(e) the woman has elected in writing not later than the end of the period of 42 days from the day on which the child was born for the man to be treated for the purpose mentioned in subsection (5I) below as the father of the child, and

(f) no-one else is to be treated as the father of the child by virtue of subsection (2) or (3) above or by virtue of adoption or the child being treated as mentioned in paragraph (a) or (b) of subsection (5) above,

then the man shall be treated for the purpose mentioned in subsection (5I) below as the father of the child.

(5B) If—

(a) a child has been carried by a woman as the result of the placing in her of an embryo or of sperm and eggs or her artificial insemination,

(b) the creation of the embryo carried by her was brought about by using the sperm of a man after his death, or the creation of the embryo was brought about using the sperm of a man before his death but the embryo was placed in the woman after his death,

(c) the woman was not a party to a marriage with the man immediately before his death but treatment services were being provided for the woman and the man together before his death either by a person to whom a licence applies or outside the United Kingdom,

(d) the man consented in writing (and did not withdraw the consent)-

(i) to the use of his sperm after his death which brought about the creation of the embryo carried by the woman or (as the case may be) to the placing in the woman after his death of the embryo which was brought about using his sperm before his death, and

    (ii) to being treated for the purpose mentioned in subsection (5I) below as the father of any resulting child,

(e) the woman has elected in writing not later than the end of the period of 42 days from the day on which the child was born for the man to be treated for the purpose mentioned in subsection (5I) below as the father of the child, and

(f) no-one else is to be treated as the father of the child by virtue of subsection (2) or (3) above or by virtue of adoption or the child being treated as mentioned in paragraph (a) or (b) of subsection (5) above,

then the man shall be treated for the purpose mentioned in subsection (5I) below as the father of the child.

(5C) If—

(a) a child has been carried by a woman as the result of the placing in her of an embryo,

(b) the embryo was created at a time when the woman was a party to a marriage,

(c) the creation of the embryo was not brought about with the sperm of the other party to the marriage,

(d) the other party to the marriage died before the placing of the embryo in the woman,

(e) the other party to the marriage consented in writing (and did not withdraw the consent)—

    (i) to the placing of the embryo in the woman after his death, and

    (ii) to being treated for the purpose mentioned in subsection (5I) below as the father of any resulting child,

(f) the woman has elected in writing not later than the end of the period of 42 days from the day on which the child was born for the other party to the marriage to be treated for the purpose mentioned in subsection (5I) below as the father of the child, and

(g) no-one else is to be treated as the father of the child by virtue of subsection (2) or (3) above or by virtue of adoption or the child being treated as mentioned in paragraph (a) or (b) of subsection (5) above,

then the other party to the marriage shall be treated for the purpose mentioned in subsection (5I) below as the father of the child.

(5D) If—

(a) a child has been carried by a woman as the result of the placing in her of an embryo,

(b) the embryo was not created at a time when the woman was a party to a marriage but was created in the course of treatment services provided for the woman and a man together either by a person to whom a licence applies or outside the United Kingdom,

(c) the creation of the embryo was not brought about with the sperm of that man,

(d) the man died before the placing of the embryo in the woman,

(e) the man consented in writing (and did not withdraw the consent)—

    (i) to the placing of the embryo in the woman after his death, and

    (ii) to being treated for the purpose mentioned in subsection (5I) below as the father of any resulting child,

(f) the woman has elected in writing not later than the end of the period of 42 days from the day on which the child was born for the man to be treated for the purpose mentioned in subsection (5I) below as the father of the child, and

(g) no-one else is to be treated as the father of the child by virtue of subsection
(2) or (3) above or by virtue of adoption or the child being treated as
mentioned in paragraph (a) or (b) of subsection (5) above,

then the man shall be treated for the purpose mentioned in subsection (5I) below
as the father of the child.

(5E) In the application of subsections (5A) to (5D) above to Scotland, for any
reference to a period of 42 days there shall be substituted a reference to a period
of 21 days.

(5F) The requirement under subsection (5A), (5B), (5C) or (5D) above as to
the making of an election (which requires an election to be made either on or
before the day on which the child was born or within the period of 42 or, as the
case may be, 21 days from that day) shall nevertheless be treated as satisfied if the
required election is made after the end of that period but with the consent of the
Registrar General under subsection (5G) below.

(5G) The Registrar General may at any time consent to the making of an
election after the end of the period mentioned in subsection (5F) above if, on an
application made to him in accordance with such requirements as he may specify,
he is satisfied that there is a compelling reason for giving his consent to the making
of such an election.

(5H) In subsections (5F) and (5G) above 'the Registrar General' means the
Registrar General for England and Wales, the Registrar General of Births, Deaths
and Marriages for Scotland or (as the case may be) the Registrar General for
Northern Ireland.

(5I) The purpose referred to in subsections (5A) to (5D) above is the purpose
of enabling the man's particulars to be entered as the particulars of the child's
father in (as the case may be) a register of live-births or still-births kept under the
Births and Deaths Registration Act 1953 or the Births and Deaths Registration
(Northern Ireland) Order 1976 or a register of births or still-births kept under the
Registration of Births, Deaths and Marriages (Scotland) Act 1965.]

Note. Sub-ss (5A)–(5I) inserted by the Human Fertilisation and Embryology (Deceased
Fathers) Act 2003, s 1(1), as from 1 December 2003 (SI 2003 No 3095). For retrospective,
transitional and transitory provision and for further effect see s 3(1)–(6) of the 2003 Act.

(6) Where—
(a) the sperm of a man who had given such consent as is required by paragraph
5 of Schedule 3 to this Act was used for a purpose for which such consent
was required, or
(b) the sperm of a man, or any embryo the creation of which was brought about
with his sperm, was used after his death,

he is not [, subject to subsections (5A) and (5B) above,] to be treated as the father
of the child.

(7) The references in subsection (2) above [and subsections (5A) to (5D)
above] to the parties to a marriage at the time there referred to—
(a) are to the parties to a marriage subsisting at that time, unless a judicial
separation was then in force, but
(b) include the parties to a void marriage if either or both of them reasonably
believed at that time that the marriage was valid; and for the purposes of
this subsection it shall be presumed, unless the contrary is shown, that one
of them reasonably believed at that time that the marriage was valid.

Note. Words in square brackets inserted by the Human Fertilisation and Embryology
(Deceased Fathers) Act 2003, s 2(1), Schedule, para 15, as from 1 December 2003 (SI 2003
No 3095). For retrospective, transitional and transitory provision see s 3(1) of the 2003 Act.

(8) This section applies whether the woman was in the United Kingdom or
elsewhere at the time of the placing in her of the embryo or the sperm and eggs or
her artificial insemination.

(9) In subsection (7)(a) above, 'judicial separation' includes a legal separation obtained in a country outside the British Islands and recognised in the United Kingdom.

29. Effect of sections 27 and 28—(1) Where by virtue of section 27 or 28 of this Act a person is to be treated as the mother or father of a child, that person is to be treated in law as the mother or, as the case may be, father of the child for all purposes.

(2) Where by virtue of section 27 or 28 of this Act a person is not to be treated as the mother or father of a child, that person is to be treated in law as not being the mother or, as the case may be, father of the child for any purpose.

(3) Where subsection (1) or (2) above has effect, references to any relationship between two people in any enactment, deed or other instrument or document (whenever passed or made) are to be read accordingly.

[(3A) Subsections (1) to (3) above do not apply in relation to the treatment in law of a deceased man in a case to which section 28(5A), (5B), (5C) or (5D) of this Act applies.

(3B) Where subsection (5A), (5B), (5C) or (5D) of section 28 of this Act applies, the deceased man—

(a) is to be treated in law as the father of the child for the purpose referred to in that subsection, but

(b) is to be treated in law as not being the father of the child for any other purpose.

(3C) Where subsection (3B) above has effect, references to any relationship between two people in any enactment, deed or other instrument or document (whenever passed or made) are to be read accordingly.

(3D) In subsection (3C) above 'enactment' includes an enactment comprised in, or in an instrument made under, an Act of the Scottish Parliament or Northern Ireland legislation.]

Note. Sub-ss (3A)–(3D) inserted by the Human Fertilisation and Embryology (Deceased Fathers) Act 2003, s 1(2), as from 1 October 2003 (SI 2003 No 3095). For retrospective, transitional and transitory provision see s 3(1) of the 2003 Act.

(4) In relation to England and Wales and Northern Ireland, nothing in the provisions of section 27(1) or 28(2) to (4) [or (5A) to 5I)], read with this section, affects—

(a) the succession to any dignity or title of honour or renders any person capable of succeeding to or transmitting a right to succeed to any such dignity or title, or

(b) the devolution of any property limited (expressly or not) to devolve (as nearly as the law permits) along with any dignity or title of honour.

(5) (*Applies to Scotland only.*)

Note. In sub-s (4) words in square brackets inserted by the Human Fertilisation and Embryology (Decreased Fathers) Act 2003, s 2(1), Schedule, para 16, as from 1 December 2003 (SI 2003 No 3095). For retrospective, transitional and transitory provision see s 3(1) of the 2003 Act.

30. Parental orders in favour of gamete donors—(1) The court may make an order providing for a child to be treated in law as the child of the parties to a marriage (referred to in this section as 'the husband' and 'the wife') if—

(a) the child has been carried by a woman other than the wife as the result of the placing in her of an embryo or sperm and eggs or her artificial insemination,

(b) the gametes of the husband or the wife, or both, were used to bring about the creation of the embryo, and

(c) the conditions in subsections (2) to (7) below are satisfied.

(2) The husband and the wife must apply for the order within six months of the birth of the child or, in the case of a child born before the coming into force of this Act, within six months of such coming into force.

(3) At the time of the application and of the making of the order—
(a) the child's home must be with the husband and the wife, and
(b) the husband or the wife, or both of them, must be domiciled in a part of the United Kingdom or in the Channel Islands or the Isle of Man.

(4) At the time of the making of the order both the husband and the wife must have attained the age of eighteen.

(5) The court must be satisfied that both the father of the child (including a person who is the father by virtue of section 28 of this Act), where he is not the husband, and the woman who carried the child have freely, and with full understanding of what is involved, agreed unconditionally to the making of the order.

(6) Subsection (5) above does not require the agreement of a person who cannot be found or is incapable of giving agreement and the agreement of the woman who carried the child is ineffective for the purposes of that subsection if given by her less than six weeks after the child's birth.

(7) The court must be satisfied that no money or other benefit (other than for expenses reasonably incurred) has been given or received by the husband or the wife for or in consideration of—
(a) the making of the order,
(b) any agreement required by subsection (5) above,
(c) the handing over of the child to the husband and the wife, or
(d) the making of any arrangements with a view to the making of the order, unless authorised by the court.

(8) For the purposes of an application under this section—
(a) in relation to England and Wales, section 92(7) to (10) of, and Part I of Schedule 11 to, the Children Act 1989 (jurisdiction of courts) shall apply for the purposes of this section to determine the meaning of 'the court' as they apply for the purposes of that Act and proceedings on the application shall be 'family proceedings' for the purposes of that Act,
(b) (*applies to Scotland only*), and
(c) in relation to Northern Ireland, 'the court' means the High Court or any county court within whose division the child is.

(9) Regulations may provide—
(a) for any provision of the enactments about adoption to have effect, with such modifications (if any) as may be specified in the regulations, in relation to orders under this section, and applications for such orders, as it has effect in relation to adoption, and applications for adoption orders, and
(b) for references in any enactment to adoption, an adopted child or an adoptive relationship to be read (respectively) as references to the effect of an order under this section, a child to whom such an order applies and a relationship arising by virtue of the enactments about adoption, as applied by the regulations, and for similar expressions in connection with adoption to be read accordingly,
and the regulations may include such incidental or supplemental provision as appears to the Secretary of State necessary or desirable in consequence of any provision made by virtue of paragraph (a) or (b) above.

Note. The reference to 'any enactment' in sub-s (9)(b) above shall be read as including a reference to any enactment contained in s 28(5A)-(5I) hereof: see the Human Fertilisation and Embryology (Decreased Fathers) Act 2003, ss 2(1), 3, Schedule, para 17.

(10) In this section 'the enactments about adoption' means the *Adoption Act 1976*, [Adoption and Children Act 2002] he Adoption (Scotland) Act 1978 and the Adoption (Northern Ireland) Order 1987.

Note. Words in square brackets substituted for words in italics by the Adoption and Children Act 2002, s 139(1), Sch 3, paras 76, 79, as from a day to be appointed.

(11) Subsection (1)(a) above applies whether the woman was in the United Kingdom or elsewhere at the time of the placing in her of the embryo or the sperm and eggs or her artificial insemination.

Information

31. The Authority's register of information—(1) The Authority shall keep a register which shall contain any information obtained by the Authority which falls within subsection (2) below.

(2) Information falls within this subsection if it relates to—

(a) the provision of treatment services for any identifiable individual, or

(b) the keeping or use of the gametes of any identifiable individual or of an embryo taken from any identifiable woman,

or if it shows that any identifiable individual was, or may have been, born in consequence of treatment services.

(3) A person who has attained the age of eighteen ('the applicant') may by notice to the Authority require the Authority to comply with a request under subsection (4) below, and the Authority shall do so if—

(a) the information contained in the register shows that the applicant was, or may have been, born in consequence of treatment services, and

(b) the applicant has been given a suitable opportunity to receive proper counselling about the implications of compliance with the request.

(4) The applicant may request the Authority to give the applicant notice stating whether or not the information contained in the register shows that a person other than a parent of the applicant would or might, but for sections 27 to 29 of this Act, be a parent of the applicant and, if it does show that—

(a) giving the applicant so much of that information as relates to the person concerned as the Authority is required by regulations to give (but no other information), or

(b) stating whether or not that information shows that, but for sections 27 to 29 of this Act, the applicant, and a person specified in the request as a person whom the applicant proposes to marry, would or might be related.

(5) Regulations cannot require the Authority to give any information as to the identity of a person whose gametes have been used or from whom an embryo has been taken if a person to whom a licence applied was provided with the information at a time when the Authority could not have been required to give information of the kind in question.

(6) A person who has not attained the age of eighteen ('the minor') may by notice to the Authority specifying another person ('the intended spouse') as a person whom the minor proposes to marry require the Authority to comply with a request under subsection (7) below, and the Authority shall do so if—

(a) the information contained in the register shows that the minor was, or may have been, born in consequence of treatment services, and

(b) the minor has been given a suitable opportunity to receive proper counselling about the implications of compliance with the request.

(7) The minor may request the Authority to give the minor notice stating whether or not the information contained in the register shows that, but for sections 27 to 29 of this Act, the minor and the intended spouse would or might be related.

32. Information to be provided to Registrar General—(1) This section applies where a claim is made before the Registrar General that a man is or is not the father of a child and it is necessary or desirable for the purpose of any function of the Registrar General to determine whether the claim is or may be well-founded.

(2) The Authority shall comply with any request made by the Registrar General by notice to the Authority to disclose whether any information on the register kept in pursuance of section 31 of this Act tends to show that the man may be the father of the child by virtue of section 28 of this Act and, if it does, disclose that information.

(3) In this section and section 33 of this Act, 'the Registrar General' means the Registrar General for England and Wales, the Registrar General of Births, Deaths and Marriages for Scotland or the Registrar General for Northern Ireland, as the case may be.

33. Restrictions on disclosure of information—(1) No person who is or has been a member or employee of the Authority shall disclose any information mentioned in subsection (2) below which he holds or has held as such a member or employee.

(2) The information referred to in subsection (1) above is—

(a) any information contained or required to be contained in the register kept in pursuance of section 31 of this Act, and

(b) any other information obtained by any member or employee of the Authority on terms or in circumstances requiring it to be held in confidence.

(3) Subsection (1) above does not apply to any disclosure of information mentioned in subsection (2)(a) above made—

(a) to a person as a member or employee of the Authority,

(b) to a person to whom a licence applies for the purposes of his functions as such,

(c) so that no individual to whom the information relates can be identified,

(d) in pursuance of an order of a court under section 34 or 35 of this Act,

(e) to the Registrar General in pursuance of a request under section 32 of this Act, or

(f) in accordance with section 31 of this Act.

(4) Subsection (1) above does not apply to any disclosure of information mentioned in subsection (2)(b) above—

(a) made to a person as a member or employee of the Authority,

(b) made with the consent of the person or persons whose confidence would otherwise be protected, or

(c) which has been lawfully made available to the public before the disclosure is made.

(5) No person who is or has been a person to whom a licence applies and no person to whom directions have been given shall disclose any information falling within section 31(2) of this Act which he holds or has held as such a person.

(6) Subsection (5) above does not apply to any disclosure of information made—

(a) to a person as a member or employee of the Authority,

(b) to a person to whom a licence applies for the purposes of his functions as such,

(c) so far as it identifies a person who, but for sections 27 to 29 of this Act, would or might be a parent of a person who instituted proceedings under section 1A of the Congenital Disabilities (Civil Liability) Act 1976, but only for the purpose of defending such proceedings, or instituting connected proceedings for compensation against that parent,

(d) so that no individual to whom the information relates can be identified, *or*

(e) in pursuance of directions given by virtue of section 24(5) or (6) of this Act

[(f) necessarily—

(i) for any purpose preliminary to proceedings, or

(ii) for the purposes of, or in connection with, any proceedings,

(g) for the purpose of establishing, in any proceedings relating to an application for an order under subsection (1) of section 30 of this Act, whether the condition specified in paragraph (a) or (b) of that subsection is met, *or*

(h) under section 3 of the Access to Health Records Act 1990 (right of access to health records) [or]]

[(i) under Article 5 of the Access to Health Records (Northern Ireland) Order 1993 (right of access to health records).]

Note. Word in italics in sub-s (6)(d) repealed, and sub-s (6)(f)–(h) added, by Human Fertilisation and Embryology (Disclosure of Information) Act 1992, s 1(2), as from 16 July 1992. Word in italics in sub-s (6)(g) repealed, word in square brackets in sub-s (6)(h) added, and sub-s (6)(i) added, by Access to Health Records (Northern Ireland) Order 1993, SI 1993 No 1250, art 13, as from 30 May 1994.

[(6A) Paragraph (f) of subsection (6) above, so far as relating to disclosure for the purposes of, or in connection with, any proceedings, does not apply—

(a) to disclosure of information enabling a person to be identified as a person whose gametes were used, in accordance with consent given under paragraph 5 of Schedule 3 to this Act, for the purposes of treatment services in consequence of which an identifiable individual was, or may have been, born, or

(b) to disclosure, in circumstances in which subsection (1) of section 34 of this Act applies, of information relevant to the determination of the question mentioned in that subsection.

(6B) In the case of information relating to the provision of treatment services for any identifiable individual—

(a) where one individual is identifiable, subsection (5) above does not apply to disclosure with the consent of that individual;

(b) where both a woman and a man treated together with her are identifiable, subsection (5) above does not apply—

   (i) to disclosure with the consent of them both, or

   (ii) if disclosure is made for the purpose of disclosing information about the provision of treatment services for one of them, to disclosure with the consent of that individual.

(6C) For the purposes of subsection (6B) above, consent must be to disclosure to a specific person, except where disclosure is to a person who needs to know—

(a) in connection with the provision of treatment services, or any other description of medical, surgical or obstetric services, for the individual giving the consent,

(b) in connection with the carrying out of an audit of clinical practice, or

(c) in connection with the auditing of accounts.

(6D) For the purpoes of subsection (6B) above, consent to disclosure given at the request of another shall be disregarded unless, before it is given, the person requesting it takes reasonable steps to explain to the idividual from whom it is requested the implications of compliance with the request.

(6E) In the case of information which relates to the provision of treatment services for any identifiable individual, subsection (5) above does not apply to disclosure in an emergency, that is to say, to disclosure made—

(a) by a person who is satisfied that it is necessary to make the disclosure to avert an imminent danger to the health of an individual with whose consent the information could be disclosed under subsection (6B) above, and

(b) in circumstances where it is not reasonably practicable to obtain that individual's consent.

(6F) In the case of information which shows that any identifiable individual was, or may have been, born in consequence of treatment services, subsection (5) above does not apply to any disclosure which is necessarily incidental to disclosure under subsection (6B) or (6E) above.

(6G) Regulations may provide for additional exceptions from subsection (5) above, but no exception may be made under this subsection—

(a) for disclosure of a kind mentioned in paragraph (a) or (b) of subsection (6A) above, or

(b) for disclosure, in circumstances in which section 32 of this Act applies, of information having the tendency mentioned in subsection (2) of that section.]

Note. Sub-ss (6A)–(6G) inserted by Human Fertilisation and Embryology (Disclosure of Information) Act 1992, s 1(3), as from 16 July 1992.

(7) This section does not apply to the disclosure to any individual of information which—

(a) falls within section 31(2) of this Act by virtue of paragraph (a) or (b) of that subsection, and

(b) relates only to that individual or, in the case of an individual treated together with another, only to that individual and that other.

(8) *At the end of Part IV of the Data Protection Act 1984 (Exemptions) there is inserted—*

'35A. Information about human embryos, etc. *Personal data consisting of information showing that an identifiable individual was, or may have been, born in consequence of treatment services (within the meaning of the Human Fertilisation and Embryology Act 1990) are exempt from the subject access provisions except so far as their disclosure under those provisions is made in accordance with section 31 of that Act (the Authority's register of information).'*

Note. Sub-s (8) repealed by the Data Protection Act 1998, s 74(2), Sch 16, Pt 1, as from 1 March 2000.

[(9) In subsection (6)(f) above, references to proceedings include any formal procedure for dealing with a complaint.]

Note. Sub-s (9) added by Human Fertilisation and Embryology (Disclosure of Information) Act 1992, s 1(4), as from 16 July 1992.

34. Disclosure in interests of justice—(1) Where in any proceedings before a court the question whether a person is or is not the parent of a child by virtue of sections 27 to 29 of this Act falls to be determined, the court may on the application of any party to the proceedings make an order requiring the Authority—
- (a) to disclose whether or not any information relevant to that question is contained in the register kept in pursuance of section 31 of this Act, and
- (b) if it is, to disclose so much of it as is specified in the order,

but such an order may not require the Authority to disclose any information falling within section 31(2)(b) of this Act.

(2) The court must not make an order under subsection (1) above unless it is satisfied that the interests of justice require it to do so, taking into account—
- (a) any representations made by any individual who may be affected by the disclosure, and
- (b) the welfare of the child, if under 18 years old, and of any other person under that age who may be affected by the disclosure.

(3) If the proceedings before the court are civil proceedings, it—
- (a) may direct that the whole or any part of the proceedings on the application for an order under subsection (2) above shall be heard in camera, and
- (b) if it makes such an order, may then or later direct that the whole or any part of any later stage of the proceedings shall be heard in camera.

(4) An application for a direction under subsection (3) above shall be heard in camera unless the court otherwise directs.

35. Disclosure in interests of justice: congenital disabilities, etc—(1) Where for the purpose of instituting proceedings under section 1 of the Congenital Disabilities (Civil Liability) Act 1976 (civil liability to child born disabled) it is necessary to identify a person who would or might be the parent of a child but for sections 27 to 29 of this Act, the court may, on the application of the child, make an order requiring the Authority to disclose any information contained in the register kept in pursuance of section 31 of this Act identifying that person.

(2) *(Applies to Scotland only.)*

(3) Subsections (2) to (4) of section 34 of this Act apply for the purposes of this section as they apply for the purposes of that.

(4) After section 4(4) of the Congenital Disabilities (Civil Liability) Act 1976 there is inserted—

'(4A) In any case where a child carried by a woman as the result of the placing in her of an embryo or of sperm and eggs or her artificial insemination is born disabled, any reference in section 1 of this Act to a parent includes a reference to a person who would be a parent but for sections 27 to 29 of the Human Fertilisation and Embryology Act 1990.'.

Surrogacy

36. Amendment of Surrogacy Arrangements Act 1985—(1) After section 1 of the Surrogacy Arrangements Act 1985 there is inserted—

'**1A. Surrogacy arrangements unenforceable.** No surrogacy arrangement is enforceable by or against any of the persons making it.'
  (2) In section 1 of that Act (meaning of 'surrogate mother', etc)—
  (a) in subsection (6), for 'or, as the case may be, embryo insertion' there is substituted 'or of the placing in her of an embryo, of an egg in the process of fertilisation or of sperm and eggs, as the case may be,', and
  (b) in subsection (9), the words from 'and whether' to the end are repealed.

Abortion

37. Amendment of law relating to termination of pregnancy—(1) For paragraphs (a) and (b) of section 1(1) of the Abortion Act 1967 (grounds for medical termination of pregnancy) there is substituted—
  '(a) that the pregnancy has not exceeded its twenty-fourth week and that the continuance of the pregnancy would involve risk, greater than if the pregnancy were terminated, of injury to the physical or mental health of the pregnant woman or any existing children of her family; or
  (b) that the termination is necessary to prevent grave permanent injury to the physical or mental health of the pregnant woman; or
  (c) that the continuance of the pregnancy would involve risk to the life of the pregnant woman, greater than if the pregnancy were terminated; or
  (d) that there is a substantial risk that if the child were born it would suffer from such physical or mental abnormalities as to be seriously handicapped.'
  (2) In section 1(2) of that Act, after '(a)' there is inserted 'or (b)'.
  (3) After section 1(3) of that Act there is inserted—
  '(3A) The power under subsection (3) of this section to approve a place includes power, in relation to treatment consisting primarily in the use of such medicines as may be specified in the approval and carried out in such manner as may be so specified, to approve a class of places.'
  (4) For section 5(1) of that Act (effect on Infant Life (Preservation) Act 1929) there is substituted—
  '(1) No offence under the Infant Life (Preservation) Act 1929 shall be committed by a registered medical practitioner who terminates a pregnancy in accordance with the provisions of this Act.'
  (5) In section 5(2) of that Act, for the words from 'the miscarriage' to the end there is substituted 'a woman's miscarriage (or, in the case of a woman carrying more than one foetus, her miscarriage of any foetus) is unlawfully done unless authorised by section 1 of this Act and, in the case of a woman carrying more than one foetus, anything done with intent to procure her miscarriage of any foetus is authorised by that section if—
  (a) the ground for termination of the pregnancy specified in subsection (1)(d) of that section applies in relation to any foetus and the thing is done for the purpose of procuring the miscarriage of that foetus, or
  (b) any of the other grounds for termination of the pregnancy specified in that section applies'.

Conscientious objection

38. Conscientious objection—(1) No person who has a conscientious objection to participating in any activity governed by this Act shall be under any duty, however arising, to do so.
  (2) In any legal proceedings the burden of proof of conscientious objection shall rest on the person claiming to rely on it.
  (3) (*Applies to Scotland only.*)

Enforcement

39. Powers of members and employees of Authority—(1) Any member or employee of the Authority entering and inspecting premises to which a licence relates may—

    (a) take possession of anything which he has reasonable grounds to believe may be required—

        (i) for the purpose of the functions of the Authority relating to the grant, variation, suspension and revocation of licences, or

        (ii) for the purpose of being used in evidence in any proceedings for an offence under this Act,

    and retain it for so long as it may be required for the purpose in question, and

    (b) for the purpose in question, take such steps as appear to be necessary for preserving any such thing or preventing interference with it, including requiring any person having the power to do so to give such assistance as may reasonably be required.

    (2) In subsection (1) above—

    (a) the references to things include information recorded in any form, and

    (b) the reference to taking possession of anything includes, in the case of information recorded otherwise than in legible form, requiring any person having the power to do so to produce a copy of the information in legible form and taking possession of the copy.

    (3) Nothing in this Act makes it unlawful for a member or employee of the Authority to keep any embryo or gametes in pursuance of that person's functions as such.

40. Power to enter premises—(1) A justice of the peace (including, in Scotland, a sheriff) may issue a warrant under this section if satisfied by the evidence on oath of a member or employee of the Authority that there are reasonable grounds for suspecting that an offence under this Act is being, or has been, committed on any premises.

    (2) A warrant under this section shall authorise any named member or employee of the Authority (who must, if so required, produce a document identifying himself), together with any constables—

    (a) to enter the premises specified in the warrant, using such force as is reasonably necessary for the purpose, and

    (b) to search the premises and—

        (i) take possession of anything which he has reasonable grounds to believe may be required to be used in evidence in any proceedings for an offence under this Act, or

        (ii) take such steps as appear to be necessary for preserving any such thing or preventing interference with it, including requiring any person having the power to do so to give such assistance as may reasonably be required.

    (3) A warrant under this section shall continue in force until the end of the period of one month beginning with the day on which it is issued.

    (4) Anything of which possession is taken under this section may be retained—

    (a) for a period of six months, or

    (b) if within that period proceedings to which the thing is relevant are commenced against any person for an offence under this Act, until the conclusion of those proceedings.

    (5) In this section—

    (a) the references to things include information recorded in any form, and

    (b) the reference in subsection (2)(b)(i) above to taking possession of anything includes, in the case of information recorded otherwise than in legible form [, or in a form from which it can readily be produced in visible and legible form], requiring any person having the power to do so to produce a copy of the information in legible form and taking possession of the copy.

Note. In sub-s (4)(b) words in square brackets inserted by the Criminal Justice and Police Act 2001, s 70, Sch 2, Pt 2, para 16(1), (2)(e), as from 1 April 2003 (SI 2003 No 708).

Offences

41. Offences—(1) A person who—

    (a) contravenes section 3(2)[, 3A] or 4(1)(c) of this Act, or

    (b) does anything which, by virtue of section 3(3) of this Act, cannot be authorised by a licence,

is guilty of an offence and liable on conviction on indictment to imprisonment for a term not exceeding ten years or a fine or both.

Note. Number in square brackets inserted by Criminal Justice and Public Order Act 1994, s 156, as from 10 April 1995.

    (2) A person who—

    (a) contravenes section 3(1) of this Act, otherwise than by doing something which, by virtue of section 3(3) of this Act, cannot be authorised by a licence,

    (b) keeps or uses any gametes in contravention of section 4(1)(a) or (b) of this Act,

    (c) contravenes section 4(3) of this Act, or

    (d) fails to comply with any directions given by virtue of section 24(7)(a) of this Act,

is guilty of an offence.

    (3) If a person—

    (a) provides any information for the purposes of the grant of a licence, being information which is false or misleading in a material particular, and

    (b) either he knows the information to be false or misleading in a material particular or he provides the information recklessly,

he is guilty of an offence.

    (4) A person guilty of an offence under subsection (2) or (3) above is liable—

    (a) on conviction on indictment, to imprisonment for a term not exceeding two years or a fine or both, and

    (b) on summary conviction, to imprisonment for a term not exceeding six months or a fine not exceeding the statutory maximum or both.

    (5) A person who discloses any information in contravention of section 33 of this Act is guilty of an offence and liable—

    (a) on conviction on indictment, to imprisonment for a term not exceeding two years or a fine or both, and

    (b) on summary conviction, to imprisonment for a term not exceeding six months or a fine not exceeding the statutory maximum or both.

    (6) A person who—

    (a) fails to comply with a requirement made by virtue of section 39(1)(b) or (2)(b) or 40(2)(b)(ii) or (5)(b) of this Act, or

    (b) intentionally obstructs the exercise of any rights conferred by a warrant issued under section 40 of this Act,

is guilty of an offence.

    (7) A person who without reasonable excuse fails to comply with a requirement imposed by regulations made by virtue of section 10(2)(a) of this Act is guilty of an offence.

    (8) Where a person to whom a licence applies or the nominal licensee gives or receives any money or other benefit, not authorised by directions, in respect of any supply of gametes or embryos, he is guilty of an offence.

    (9) A person guilty of an offence under subsection (6), (7) or (8) above is liable on summary conviction to imprisonment for a term not exceeding six months or a fine not exceeding level five on the standard scale or both.

(10) It is a defence for a person ('the defendant') charged with an offence of doing anything which, under section 3(1) or 4(1) of this Act, cannot be done except in pursuance of a licence to prove—

    (a) that the defendant was acting under the direction of another, and

    (b) that the defendant believed on reasonable grounds—

        (i) that the other person was at the material time the person responsible under a licence, a person designated by virtue of section 17(2)(b) of this Act as a person to whom a licence applied, or a person to whom directions had been given by virtue of section 24(9) of this Act, and

        (ii) that the defendant was authorised by virtue of the licence or directions to do the thing in question.

(11) It is a defence for a person charged with an offence under this Act to prove—

    (a) that at the material time he was a person to whom a licence applied or to whom directions had been given, and

    (b) that he took all such steps as were reasonable and exercised all due diligence to avoid committing the offence.

42. Consent to prosecution. No proceedings for an offence under this Act shall be instituted—

    (a) in England and Wales, except by or with the consent of the Director of Public Prosecutions, and

    (b) in Nothern Ireland, except by or with the consent of the Director of Public Prosecutions for Northern Ireland.

Miscellaneous and general

43. Keeping and examining gametes and embryos in connection with crime, etc—(1) Regulations may provide—

    (a) for the keeping and examination of gametes or embryos, in such manner and on such conditions (if any) as may be specified in regulations, in connection with the investigation of, or proceedings for, an offence (wherever committed), or

    (b) for the storage of gametes, in such manner and on such conditions (if any) as may be specified in regulations, where they are to be used only for such purposes, other than treatment services, as may be specified in regulations.

(2) Nothing in this Act makes unlawful the keeping or examination of any gametes or embryos in pursuance of regulations made by virtue of this section.

(3) In this section 'examination' includes use for the purposes of any test.

44. Civil liability to child with disability—(1) After section 1 of the Congenital Disabilities (Civil Liability) Act 1976 (civil liability to child born disabled) there is inserted—

'1A. Extension of section 1 to cover infertility treatments—(1) In any case where—

    (a) a child carried by a woman as the result of the placing in her of an embryo or of sperm and eggs or her artificial insemination is born disabled,

    (b) the disability results from an act or omission in the course of the selection, or the keeping or use outside the body, of the embryo carried by her or of the gametes used to bring about the creation of the embryo, and

    (c) a person is under this section answerable to the child in respect of the act or omission,

the child's disabilities are to be regarded as damage resulting from the wrongful act of that person and actionable accordingly at the suit of the child.

(2) Subject to subsection (3) below and the applied provisions of section 1 of this Act, a person (here referred to as "the defendant") is answerable to the child if he was liable in tort to one or both of the parents (here referred to as "the parent or parents concerned") or would, if sued in due time, have been so; and it is no

answer that there could not have been such liability because the parent or parents concerned suffered no actionable injury, if there was a breach of legal duty which, accompanied by injury, would have given rise to the liability.

(3) The defendant is not under this section answerable to the child if at the time the embryo, or the sperm and eggs, are placed in the woman or the time of her insemination (as the case may be) either or both of the parents knew the risk of their child being born disabled (that is to say, the particular risk created by the act or omission).

(4) Subsections (5) to (7) of section 1 of this Act apply for the purposes of this section as they apply for the purposes of that but as if references to the parent or the parent affected were references to the parent or parents concerned.'

(2) In section 4 of that Act (interpretation, etc)—

(a) at the end of subsection (2) there is inserted—

'and references to embryos shall be construed in accordance with section 1 of the Human Fertilisation and Embryology Act 1990',

(b) in subsection (3), after 'section 1' there is inserted '1A', and

(c) in subsection (4), for 'either' there is substituted 'any'.

45. Regulations—(1) The Secretary of State may make regulations for any purpose for which regulations may be made under this Act.

(2) The power to make regulations shall be exercisable by statutory instrument.

(3) Regulations may make different provision for different cases.

(4) The Secretary of State shall not make regulations by virtue of section 3(3)(c), 4(2) or (3), 30, 31(4)(a), [33(6G),] or 43 of this Act or paragraph 1(1)(g) or 3 of Schedule 2 to this Act unless a draft has been laid before and approved by resolution of each House of Parliament.

(5) A statutory instrument containing regulations shall, if made without a draft having been approved by resolution of each House of Parliament, be subject to annulment in pursuance of a resolution of either House of Parliament.

(6) In this Act 'regulations' means regulations under this section.

Note. Number in square brackets in sub-s (4) inserted by Human Fertilisation and Embryology (Disclosure of Information) Act 1992, s 2(2), as from 16 July 1992.

46. Notices—(1) This section has effect in relation to any notice required or authorised by this Act to be given to or served on any person.

(2) The notice may be given to or served on the person—

(a) by delivering it to the person,

(b) by leaving it at the person's proper address, or

(c) by sending it by post to the person at that address.

(3) The notice may—

(a) in the case of a body corporate, be given to or served on the secretary or clerk of the body,

(b) in the case of a partnership, be given to or served on any partner, and

(c) in the case of an unincorporated association other than a partnership, be given to or served on any member of the governing body of the association.

(4) For the purposes of this section and section 7 of the Interpretation Act 1978 (service of documents by post) in its application to this section, the proper address of any person is the person's last known address and also—

(a) in the case of a body corporate, its secretary or its clerk, the address of its registered or principal office, and

(b) in the case of an unincorporated association or a member of its governing body, its principal office.

(5) Where a person has notified the Authority of an address or a new address at which notices may be given to or served on him under this Act, that address shall also be his proper address for the purposes mentioned in subsection (4) above or, as the case may be, his proper address for those purposes in substitution for that previously notified.

47. Index.   The expressions listed in the left-hand column below are respectively defined or (as the case may be) are to be interpreted in accordance with the provisions of this Act listed in the right-hand column in relation to those expressions.

Expression	Relevant provision
Activities governed by this Act	Section 4(5)
Authority	Section 2(1)
Carry, in relation to a child	Section 2(3)
Directions	Section 2(1)
Embryo	Section 1
Gametes, eggs or sperm	Section 1
Keeping, in relation to embryos or gametes	Section 2(2)
Licence	Section 2(1)
Licence committee	Section 9(1)
Nominal licensee	Section 17(3)
Person responsible	Section 17(1)
Person to whom a licence applies	Section 17(2)
Statutory storage period	Section 14(3) to (5)
Store, and similar expressions, in relation to embryos or gametes	Section 2(2)
Treatment services	Section 2(1)

48. Northern Ireland—(1) This Act (except *section* [sections 33(6)(h) and] 37) extends to Northern Ireland.

(2) *Subject to any Order made after the passing of this Act by virtue of subsection (1)(a) of section 3 of the Northern Ireland Constitution Act 1973, the activities governed by this Act shall not be transferred matters for the purposes of that Act, but shall for the purposes of subsection (2) of that section be treated as specified in Schedule 3 to that Act.*

Note. Words in square brackets in sub-s (1) substituted for word in italics by Human Fertilisation and Embryology (Disclosure of Information) Act 1992, s 2(4), as from 16 July 1992. Sub-s (2) repealed by the Northern Ireland Act 1998, s 100(2), Sch 15, as from 2 December 1999 (SI 1999 No 3209).

49. Short title, commencement, etc—(1) This Act may be cited as the Human Fertilisation and Embryology Act 1990.

(2) This Act shall come into force on such day as the Secretary of State may by order made by statutory instrument appoint and different days may be appointed for different provisions and for different purposes.

(3) Sections 27 to 29 of this Act shall have effect only in relation to children carried by women as a result of the placing in them of embryos or of sperm and eggs, or of their artificial insemination (as the case may be), after the commencement of those sections.

(4) Section 27 of the Family Law Reform Act 1987 (artificial insemination) does not have effect in relation to children carried by women as the result of their artificial insemination after the commencement of sections 27 to 29 of this Act.

(5) Schedule 4 to this Act (which makes minor and consequential amendments) shall have effect.

(6) An order under this section may make such transitional provision as the Secretary of State considers necessary or desirable and, in particular, may provide that where activities are carried on under the supervision of a particular individual, being activities which are carried on under the supervision of that individual at the commencement of sections 3 and 4 of this Act, those activities are to be treated, during such period as may be specified in or determined in accordance with the order, as authorised by a licence (having, in addition to the conditions required by

this Act, such conditions as may be so specified or determined) under which that individual is the person responsible.

(7) Her Majesty may by Order in Council direct that any of the provisions of this Act shall extend, with such exceptions, adaptations and modifications (if any) as may be specified in the Order, to any of the Channel Islands.

Commencement. For the commencement provisions of this Act, see the Human Fertilisation and Embryology Act 1990 (Commencement No 1) Order 1990, SI 1990 No 2165; the Human Fertilisation and Embryology Act 1990 (Commencement No 2 and Transitional Provision) Order 1991, SI 1991 No 480; the Human Fertilisation and Embryology Act 1990 (Commencement No 3 and Transitional Provisions) Order 1991, SI 1991 No 1400 (as amended by the Human Fertilisation and Embryology Act 1990 (Commencement No 4—Amendment of Transitional Provisions) Order 1991, SI 1991 No 1781) and the Human Fertilisation and Embryology Act 1990 (Commencement No 5) Order 1994, SI 1994 No 1776.

SCHEDULES

SCHEDULE 1 Section 5

THE AUTHORITY: SUPPLEMENTARY PROVISIONS

Status and capacity

1. The Authority shall not be regarded as the servant or agent of the Crown, or as enjoying any status, privilege or immunity of the Crown; and its property shall not be regarded as property of, or property held on behalf of, the Crown.

2. The Authority shall have power to do anything which is calculated to facilitate the discharge of its functions, or is incidental or conducive to their discharge, except the power to borrow money.

Expenses

3. The Secretary of State may, with the consent of the Treasury, pay the Authority out of money provided by Parliament such sums as he thinks fit towards its expenses.

Appointment of members

4.—(1) All the members of the Authority (including the chairman and deputy chairman who shall be appointed as such) shall be appointed by the Secretary of State.

(2) In making appointments the Secretary of State shall have regard to the desirability of ensuring that the proceedings of the Authority, and the discharge of its functions, are informed by the views of both men and women.

(3) The following persons are disqualified for being appointed as chairman or deputy chairman of the Authority—

(a) any person who is, or has been, a medical practitioner registered under the Medical Act 1983 (whether fully, provisionally or with limited registration), or under any repealed enactment from which a provision of that Act is derived,

(b) any person who is, or has been, concerned with keeping or using gametes or embryos outside the body, and

(c) any person who is, or has been, directly concerned with commissioning or funding any research involving such keeping or use, or who has actively participated in any decision to do so.

(4) The Secretary of State shall secure that at least one-third but fewer than half of the other members of the Authority fall within sub-paragraph (3)(a), (b) or (c) above, and that at least one member falls within each of paragraphs (a) and (b).

Tenure of office

5.—(1) Subject to the following provisions of this paragraph, a person shall hold and vacate office as a member of the Authority in accordance with the terms of his appointment.

(2) A person shall not be appointed as a member of the Authority for more than three years at a time.

(3) A member may at any time resign his office by giving notice to the Secretary of State.

(4) A person who ceases to be a member of the Authority shall be eligible for re-appointment (whether or not in the same capacity).

(5) If the Secretary of State is satisfied that a member of the Authority—

(a) has been absent from meetings of the Authority for six consecutive months or longer without the permission of the Authority, or

(b) has become bankrupt or made an arrangement with his creditors, or, in Scotland, has had his estate sequestrated or has granted a trust deed for or entered into an arrangement with his creditors, or

(c) is unable or unfit to discharge the functions of a member,

the Secretary of State may declare his office as a member of the Authority vacant, and notify the declaration in such manner as he thinks fit; and thereupon the office shall become vacant.

Disqualification of members of Authority for House of Commons and Northern Ireland Assembly

6. In Part II of Schedule 1 to the House of Commons Disqualification Act 1975 and in Part II of Schedule 1 to the Northern Ireland Assembly Disqualification Act 1975 (bodies of which all members are disqualified) the following entry shall be inserted at the appropriate place in alphabetical order—

'The Human Fertilisation and Embryology Authority'.

Remuneration and pensions of members

7.—(1) The Authority may—

(a) pay to the chairman such remuneration, and

(b) pay or make provision for paying to or in respect of the chairman or any other member such pensions, allowances, fees, expenses or gratuities,

as the Secretary of State may, with the approval of the Treasury, determine.

(2) Where a person ceases to be a member of the Authority otherwise than on the expiry of his term of office and it appears to the Secretary of State that there are special circumstances which make it right for him to receive compensation, the Authority may make to him a payment of such amount as the Secretary of State may, with the consent of the Treasury, determine.

Staff

8.—(1) The Authority may appoint such employees as it thinks fit, upon such terms and conditions as the Authority, with the approval of the Secretary of State and the consent of the Treasury, may determine.

(2) The Authority shall secure that any employee whose function is, or whose functions include, the inspection of premises is of such character, and is so qualified by training and experience, as to be a suitable person to perform that function.

(3) The Authority shall, as regards such of its employees as with the approval of the Secretary of State it may determine, pay to or in respect of them such pensions, allowances or gratuities (including pensions, allowances or gratuities by way of compensation for loss of employment), or provide and maintain for them such pension schemes (whether contributory or not), as may be so determined.

(4) If an employee of the Authority—

(a) is a participant in any pension scheme applicable to that employment, and

(b) becomes a member of the Authority,

he may, if the Secretary of State so determines, be treated for the purposes of the pension scheme as if his service as a member of the Authority were service as employee of the Authority, whether or not any benefits are to be payable to or in respect of him by virtue of paragraph 7 above.

Proceedings

9.—(1) The Authority may regulate its own proceedings, and make such arrangements as it thinks appropriate for the discharge of its functions.

(2) The Authority may pay to the members of any committee or sub-committee such fees and allowances as the Secretary of State may, with the consent of the Treasury, determine.

10.—(1) A member of the Authority who is in any way directly or indirectly interested in a licence granted or proposed to be granted by the Authority shall, as soon as possible after the relevant circumstances have come to his knowledge, disclose the nature of his interest to the Authority.

(2) Any disclosure under sub-paragraph (1) above shall be recorded by the Authority.

(3) Except in such circumstances (if any) as may be determined by the Authority under paragraph 9(1) above, the member shall not participate after the disclosure in any deliberation or decision of the Authority or any licence committee with respect to the licence, and if he does so the deliberation or decision shall be of no effect.

11. The validity of any proceedings of the Authority, or of any committee or sub-committee, shall not be affected by any vacancy among the members or by any defect in the appointment of a member.

Instruments

12. The fixing of the seal of the Authority shall be authenticated by the signature of the chairman or deputy chairman of the Authority or some other member of the Authority authorised by the Authority to act for that purpose.

13. A document purporting to be duly executed under the seal of the Authority, or to be signed on the Authority's behalf, shall be received in evidence and shall be deemed to be so executed or signed unless the contrary is proved.

Investigation by Parliamentary Commissioner

14. The Authority shall be subject to investigation by the Parliamentary Commissioner and accordingly, in Schedule 2 to the Parliamentary Commissioner Act 1967 (which lists the authorities subject to investigation under that Act), the following entry shall be inserted at the appropriate place in alphabetical order—

'Human Fertilisation and Embryology Authority'.

SCHEDULE 2   Section 11 etc

ACTIVITIES FOR WHICH LICENCES MAY BE GRANTED

Licences for treatment

1.—(1) A licence under this paragraph may authorise any of the following in the course of providing treatment services—

    (a) bringing about the creation of embryos *in vitro*,

    (b) keeping embryos,

    (c) using gametes,

    (d) practices designed to secure that embryos are in a suitable condition to be placed in a woman or to determine whether embryos are suitable for that purpose,

    (e) placing any embryo in a woman,

    (f) mixing sperm with the egg of a hamster, or other animal specified in directions, for the purpose of testing the fertility or normality of the sperm, but only where anything which forms is destroyed when the test is complete and, in any event, not later than the two cell stage, and

(g) such other practices as may be specified in, or determined in accordance with, regulations.

(2) Subject to the provisions of this Act, a licence under this paragraph may be granted subject to such conditions as may be specified in the licence and may authorise the performance of any of the activities referred to in sub-paragraph (1) above in such manner as may be so specified.

(3) A licence under this paragraph cannot authorise any activity unless it appears to the Authority to be necessary or desirable for the purpose of providing treatment services.

(4) A licence under this paragraph cannot authorise altering the genetic structure of any cell while it forms part of an embryo.

(5) A licence under this paragraph shall be granted for such period not exceeding five years as may be specified in the licence.

Licences for storage

2.—(1) A licence under this paragraph or paragraph 1 or 3 of this Schedule may authorise the storage of gametes or embryos or both.

(2) Subject to the provisions of this Act, a licence authorising such storage may be granted subject to such conditions as may be specified in the licence and may authorise storage in such manner as may be so specified.

(3) A licence under this paragraph shall be granted for such period not exceeding five years as may be specified in the licence.

Licences for research

3.—(1) A licence under this paragraph may authorise any of the following—
(a) bringing about the creation of embryos *in vitro*, and
(b) keeping or using embryos,
for the purposes of a project of research specified in the licence.

(2) A licence under this paragraph cannot authorise any activity unless it appears to the Authority to be necessary or desirable for the purpose of—
(a) promoting advances in the treatment of infertility,
(b) increasing knowledge about the causes of congenital disease,
(c) increasing knowledge about the causes of miscarriages,
(d) developing more effective techniques of contraception, or
(e) developing methods for detecting the presence of gene or chromosome abnormalities in embryos before implantation,
or for such other purposes as may be specified in regulations.

(3) Purposes may only be so specified with a view to the authorisation of projects of research which increase knowledge about the creation and development of embryos, or about disease, or enable such knowledge to be applied.

(4) A licence under this paragraph cannot authorise altering the genetic structure of any cell while it forms part of an embryo, except in such circumstances (if any) as may be specified in or determined in pursuance of regulations.

(5) A licence under this paragraph may authorise mixing sperm with the egg of a hamster, or other animal specified in directions, for the purpose of developing more effective techniques for determining the fertility or normality of sperm, but only where anything which forms is destroyed when the research is complete and, in any event, not later than the two cell stage.

(6) No licence under this paragraph shall be granted unless the Authority is satisfied that any proposed use of embryos is necessary for the purposes of the research.

(7) Subject to the provisions of this Act, a licence under this paragraph may be granted subject to such conditions as may be specified in the licence.

(8) A licence under this paragraph may authorise the performance of any of the activities referred to in sub-paragraph (1) or (5) above in such manner as may be so specified.

(9) A licence under this paragraph shall be granted for such period not exceeding three years as may be specified in the licence.

General

4.—(1) A licence under this Schedule can only authorise activities to be carried on on premises specified in the licence and under the supervision of an individual designated in the licence.

(2) A licence cannot—

(a) authorise activities falling within both paragraph 1 and paragraph 3 above,

(b) apply to more than one project of research,

(c) authorise activities to be carried on under the supervision of more than one individual, or

(d) apply to premises in different places.

SCHEDULE 3   Section 12 etc

CONSENTS TO USE OF GAMETES OR EMBRYOS

Consent

1. A consent under this Schedule must be given in writing and, in this Schedule, 'effective consent' means a consent under this Schedule which has not been withdrawn.

2.—(1) A consent to the use of any embryo must specify one or more of the following purposes—

(a) use in providing treatment services to the person giving consent, or that person and another specified person together,

(b) use in providing treatment services to persons not including the person giving consent, or

(c) use for the purposes of any project of research,

and may specify conditions subject to which the embryo may be so used.

(2) A consent to the storage of any gametes or any embryo must—

(a) specify the maximum period of storage (if less than the statutory storage period), and

(b) state what is to be done with the gametes or embryo if the person who gave the consent dies or is unable because of incapacity to vary the terms of the consent or to revoke it,

and may specify conditions subject to which the gametes or embryo may remain in storage.

(3) A consent under this Schedule must provide for such other matters as the Authority may specify in directions.

(4) A consent under this Schedule may apply—

(a) to the use or storage of a particular embryo, or

(b) in the case of a person providing gametes, to the use or storage of any embryo whose creation may be brought about using those gametes,

and in the paragraph (b) case the terms of the consent may be varied, or the consent may be withdrawn, in accordance with this Schedule either generally or in relation to a particular embryo or particular embryos.

Procedure for giving consent

3.—(1) Before a person gives consent under this Schedule—

(a) he must be given a suitable opportunity to receive proper counselling about the implications of taking the proposed steps, and

(b) he must be provided with such relevant information as is proper.

(2) Before a person gives consent under this Schedule he must be informed of the effect of paragraph 4 below.

Variation and withdrawal of consent

4.—(1) The terms of any consent under this Schedule may from time to time be varied, and the consent may be withdrawn, by notice given by the person who gave the consent to the person keeping the gametes or embryo to which the consent is relevant.

(2) The terms of any consent to the use of any embryo cannot be varied, and such consent cannot be withdrawn, once the embryo has been used—

(a) in providing treatment services, or

(b) for the purposes of any project of research.

Use of gametes for treatment of others

5.—(1) A person's gametes must not be used for the purposes of treatment services unless there is an effective consent by that person to their being so used and they are used in accordance with the terms of the consent.

(2) A person's gametes must not be received for use for those purposes unless there is an effective consent by that person to their being so used.

(3) This paragraph does not apply to the use of a person's gametes for the purpose of that person, or that person and another together, receiving treatment services.

In vitro fertilisation and subsequent use of embryo

6.—(1) A person's gametes must not be used to bring about the creation of any embryo *in vitro* unless there is an effective consent by that person to any embryo the creation of which may be brought about with the use of those gametes being used for one or more of the purposes mentioned in paragraph 2(1) above.

(2) An embryo the creation of which was brought about *in vitro* must not be received by any person unless there is an effective consent by each person whose gametes were used to bring about the creation of the embryo to the use for one or more of the purposes mentioned in paragraph 2(1) above of the embryo.

(3) An embryo the creation of which was brought about *in vitro* must not be used for any purpose unless there is an effective consent by each person whose gametes were used to bring about the creation of the embryo to the use for that purpose of the embryo and the embryo is used in accordance with those consents.

(4) Any consent required by this paragraph is in addition to any consent that may be required by paragraph 5 above.

Embryos obtained by lavage, etc

7.—(1) An embryo taken from a woman must not be used for any purpose unless there is an effective consent by her to the use of the embryo for that purpose and it is used in accordance with the consent.

(2) An embryo taken from a woman must not be received by any person for use for any purpose unless there is an effective consent by her to the use of the embryo for that purpose.

(3) This paragraph does not apply to the use, for the purpose of providing a woman with treatment services, of an embryo taken from her.

Storage of gametes and embryos

8.—(1) A person's gametes must not be kept in storage unless there is an effective consent by that person to their storage and they are stored in accordance with the consent.

(2) An embryo the creation of which was brought about *in vitro* must not be kept in storage unless there is an effective consent, by each person whose gametes were used to bring about the creation of the embryo, to the storage of the embryo and the embryo is stored in accordance with those consents.

(3) An embryo taken from a woman must not be kept in storage unless there is an effective consent by her to its storage and it is stored in accordance with the consent.

SCHEDULE 4

(*The amendments made by this Schedule, insofar as they amend legislation printed in this work have been incorporated.*)

COURTS AND LEGAL SERVICES ACT 1990

(1990 c 41)

ARRANGEMENT OF SECTIONS

PART VI

MISCELLANEOUS AND SUPPLEMENTAL

* * * * *

Miscellaneous

* * * * *

* * * * *

* * * * *

An Act to make provision with respect to the procedure in, and allocation of business between, the High Court and other courts; to make provision with respect to legal services; to establish a body to be known as the Lord Chancellor's Advisory Committee on Legal Education and Conduct and a body to be known as the Authorised Conveyancing Practitioners Board; to provide for the appointment of a Legal Services Ombudsman; to make provision for the establishment of a Conveyancing Ombudsman Scheme; to provide for the establishment of Conveyancing Appeal Tribunals; to amend the law relating to judicial and related pensions and judicial and other appointments; to make provision with respect to certain officers of the Supreme Court; to amend the Solicitors Act 1974; to amend the Arbitration Act 1950; to make provision with respect to certain loans in respect of residential property; to make provision with respect to the jurisdiction of the Parliamentary Commissioner for Administration in connection with the functions of court staff; to amend the Children Act 1989 and make further provision in connection with that Act; and for connected purposes. [1 November 1990]

PART I

PROCEDURE ETC IN CIVIL COURTS

Allocation and transfer of business

1. Allocation of business between High Court and county courts—(1) The Lord Chancellor may by order make provision—
(a) conferring jurisdiction on the High Court in relation to proceedings in which county courts have jurisdiction;
(b) conferring jurisdiction on county courts in relation to proceedings in which the High Court has jurisdiction;
(c) allocating proceedings to the High Court or to county courts;
(d) specifying proceedings which may be commenced only in the High Court;
(e) specifying proceedings which may be commenced only in a county court;
(f) specifying proceedings which may be taken only in the High Court;
(g) specifying proceedings which may be taken only in a county court.

(2) Without prejudice to the generality of section 120(2), any such order may differentiate between categories of proceedings by reference to such criteria as the Lord Chancellor sees fit to specify in the order.

(3) The criteria so specified may, in particular, relate to—

(a) the value of an action (as defined by the order);

(b) the nature of the proceedings;

(c) the parties to the proceedings;

(d) the degree of complexity likely to be involved in any aspect of the proceedings; and

(e) the importance of any question likely to be raised by, or in the course of, the proceedings.

(4) An order under subsection (1)(b), (e) or (g) may specify one or more particular county courts in relation to the proceedings so specified.

(5) Any jurisdiction exercisable by a county court, under any provision made by virtue of subsection (4), shall be exercisable throughout England and Wales.

(6) Rules of court may provide for a matter—

(a) which is pending in one county court; and

(b) over which that court has jurisdiction under any provision made by virtue of subsection (4),

to be heard and determined wholly or partly in another county court which also has jurisdiction in that matter under any such provision.

(7) Any such order may—

(a) amend or repeal any provision falling within subsection (8) and relating to—

> (i) the jurisdiction, practice or procedure of the Supreme Court; or
> (ii) the jurisdiction, practice or procedure of any county court,

so far as the Lord Chancellor considers it to be necessary, or expedient, in consequence of any provision made by the order; or

(b) make such incidental or transitional provision as the Lord Chancellor considers necessary, or expedient, in consequence of any provision made by the order.

(8) A provision falls within this subsection if it is made by any enactment other than this Act or made under any enactment.

(9) Before making any such order the Lord Chancellor shall consult the Lord Chief Justice, the Master of the Rolls, the President of the Family Division, the Vice-Chancellor and the Senior Presiding Judge (appointed under section 72).

(10) No such order shall be made so as to confer jurisdiction on any county court to hear any application for judicial review.

(11) For the purposes of this section the commencement of proceedings may include the making of any application in anticipation of any proceedings or in the course of any proceedings.

(12) The Lord Chancellor shall, within one year of the coming into force of the first order made under this section, and annually thereafter, prepare and lay before both Houses of Parliament a report as to the business of the Supreme Court and county courts.

Note. Sub-s (12) repealed by the Courts Act 2003, s 109(1), (3), Sch 8, para 348, Sch 10, as from a day to be appointed.

2, 3. *(Section 2 substitutes County Courts Act 1984, ss 40, 42 (pp 3048, 3050), and amends ss 41, 75 of that Act (p 3049); s 3 substitutes s 38 of that Act for original ss 38, 39 (p 3047).)*

Costs

4. Costs—(1) The following section shall be substituted for section 51 of the Supreme Court Act 1981 (costs in civil division of Court of Appeal and High Court)—

'51. Costs in civil division of Court of Appeal, High Court and county courts—(1) Subject to the provisions of this or any other enactment and to rules of court, the costs of and incidental to all proceedings in—

(a) the civil division of the Court of Appeal;

(b) the High Court; and

(c) any county court,

shall be in the discretion of the court.

(2) Without prejudice to any general power to make rules of court, such rules may make provision for regulating matters relating to the costs of those proceedings including, in particular, prescribing scales of costs to be paid to legal or other representatives.

(3) The court shall have full power to determine by whom and to what extent the costs are to be paid.

(4) In subsections (1) and (2) "proceedings" includes the administration of estates and trusts.

(5) Nothing in subsection (1) shall alter the practice in any criminal cause, or in bankruptcy.

(6) In any proceedings mentioned in subsection (1), the court may disallow, or (as the case may be) order the legal or other representative concerned to meet, the whole of any wasted costs or such part of them as may be determined in accordance with rules of court.

(7) In subsection (6), "wasted costs" means any costs incurred by a party—

(a) as a result of any improper, unreasonable or negligent act or omission on the part of any legal or other representative or any employee of such a representative; or

(b) which, in the light of any such act or omission occurring after they were incurred, the court considers it is unreasonable to expect that party to pay.

(8) Where—

(a) a person has commenced proceedings in the High Court; but

(b) those proceedings should, in the opinion of the court, have been commenced in a county court in accordance with any provision made under section 1 of the Courts and Legal Services Act 1990 or by or under any other enactment,

the person responsible for determining the amount which is to be awarded to that person by way of costs shall have regard to those circumstances.

(9) Where, in complying with subsection (8), the responsible person reduces the amount which would otherwise be awarded to the person in question—

(a) the amount of that reduction shall not exceed 25 per cent; and

(b) on any taxation of the costs payable by that person to his legal representative, regard shall be had to the amount of the reduction.

(10) The Lord Chancellor may by order amend subsection (9)(a) by substituting, for the percentage for the time being mentioned there, a different percentage.

(11) Any such order shall be made by statutory instrument and may make such transitional or incidental provision as the Lord Chancellor considers expedient.

(12) No such statutory instrument shall be made unless a draft of the instrument has been approved by both Houses of Parliament.

(13) In this section "legal or other representative", in relation to a party to proceedings, means any person exercising a right of audience or right to conduct litigation on his behalf.'

(2) In section 52 of that Act (costs in Crown Court) the following subsection shall be inserted after subsection (2)—

'(2A) Subsection (6) of section 51 applies in relation to any civil proceedings in the Crown Court as it applies in relation to any proceedings mentioned in subsection (1) of that section'.

Evidence

5. Witness statements—(1) Rules of court may make provision—
  (a) requiring, in specified circumstances, any party to civil proceedings to serve on the other parties a written statement of the oral evidence which he intends to adduce on any issue of fact to be decided at the trial;
  (b) enabling the court to direct any party to civil proceedings to serve such a statement on the other party; and
  (c) prohibiting a party who fails to comply with such a requirement or direction from adducing oral evidence on the issue of fact to which it relates.
  (2) Where a party to proceedings has refused to comply with such a requirement or direction, the fact that his refusal was on the ground that the required statement would have been a document which was privileged from disclosure shall not affect any prohibition imposed by virtue of subsection (1)(c).
  (3) This section is not to be read as prejudicing in any way any other power to make rules of court.

6. (*Amends County Courts Act 1984, s 64.*)

Appeals

7. Appeals to Court of Appeal—(1) Section 18 of the Supreme Court Act 1981 (restrictions on appeals to Court of Appeal) shall be amended as follows.
  (2) In subsection (1), paragraphs (e), (f) and (h) (which deal with cases in which leave is required for an appeal) shall be omitted.
  (3) After subsection (1) there shall be inserted the following subsections—
  '(1A) In any such class of case as may be prescribed by Rules of the Supreme Court, an appeal shall lie to the Court of Appeal only with the leave of the Court of Appeal or such court or tribunal as may be specified by the rules in relation to that class.
  (1B) Any enactment which authorises leave to appeal to the Court of Appeal being given by a single judge, or by a court consisting of two judges, shall have effect subject to any provision which—
  (a) is made by Rules of the Supreme Court; and
  (b) in such classes of case as may be prescribed by the rules, requires leave to be given by such greater number of judges (not exceeding three) as may be so specified.'
  (4) In section 54(4) of the Act of 1981 (cases in which court is duly constituted when consisting of two judges), the following paragraph shall be inserted after paragraph (a)—
  '(aa) hearing and determining any application for leave to appeal;'.

Note. Sub-ss (3), (1) repealed by the Access to Justice Act 1999, s 106, Sch 15, Pt III, as from 27 September 1999.

8. Powers of Court of Appeal to award damages—(1) In this section 'case' means any case where the Court of Appeal has power to order a new trial on the ground that damages awarded by a jury are excessive or inadequate.
  (2) Rules of court may provide for the Court of Appeal, in such classes of case as may be specified in the rules, to have power, in place of ordering a new trial, to substitute for the sum awarded by the jury such sum as appears to the court to be proper.
  (3) This section is not to be read as prejudicing in any way any other power to make rules of court.

Family proceedings

9. Allocation of family proceedings which are within the jurisdiction of county courts—(1) The Lord Chancellor may, with the concurrence of the President of the Family Division, give directions that, in such circumstances as may be specified—

(a)   any family proceedings which are within the jurisdiction of county courts; or

(b)   any specified description of such proceedings,

shall be allocated to specified judges or to specified descriptions of judge.

(2)   Any such direction shall have effect regardless of any rules of court.

(3)   Where any directions have been given under this section allocating any proceedings to specified judges, the validity of anything done by a judge in, or in relation to, the proceedings shall not be called into question by reason only of the fact that he was not a specified judge.

(4)   For the purposes of subsection (1) 'county court' includes the principal registry of the Family Division of the High Court in so far as it is treated as a county court.

(5)   In this section—

'family proceedings' has the same meaning as in the Matrimonial and Family Proceedings Act 1984 and also includes any other proceedings which are family proceedings for the purposes of the Children Act 1989;

'judge' means any person who—

(a)   is capable of sitting as a judge for a county court district;

(b)   is a district judge, an assistant district judge or a deputy district judge; or

(c)   is a district judge of the principal registry of the Family Division of the High Court; and

'specified' means specified in the directions.

10.   Family proceedings in magistrates' courts and related matters—(*1*)   *In this section 'family proceedings' has the meaning given by section 65(1) of the Magistrates' Courts Act 1980.*

[(1)   In subsection (2) 'family proceedings' means proceedings under Part I of the Domestic Proceedings and Magistrates' Courts Act 1978.]

Note. Sub-s (1) in square brackets substituted for sub-s (1) in italics by Maintenance Enforcement Act 1991, s 11(1), Sch 2, para 11, as from 14 October 1991.

(2)   *For the purpose of giving effect to any enactment mentioned in that section, rules made under section 144 of that Act* [Rules made under section 144 of the Magistrates' Courts Act 1980] [Family Procedure Rules] may make, in relation to any family proceedings, any provision which—

(a)   falls within subsection (2) of section 93 of the Children Act 1989 (rules of court); and

(b)   may be made in relation to relevant proceedings under section 93 of the Act of 1989.

Note. Words 'Rules made under section 144 of the Magistrates' Courts Act 1980' in square brackets substituted for words 'For the purpose ... of that Act' by Maintenance Enforcement Act 1991, s 11(1), Sch 2, para 11, as from 14 October 1991. Words 'Family Procedure Rules' in square brackets substituted for words 'Rules made under section 144 of the Magistrates' Courts Act 1980' by the Courts Act 2003, s 109(1), Sch 8, para 349, as from a day to be appointed.

(3)   *In section 35 of the Justices of the Peace Act 1979 (composition of committee of magistrates for inner London area), in subsection (3)—*

(a)   *in paragraph (b) for the words 'three members of the juvenile court panel' there shall be substituted 'one member of the juvenile court panel'; and*

(b)   *after that paragraph there shall be inserted the following paragraph—*

'(bb)   *two members chosen, in such manner as may be prescribed by rules made for the purposes of this subsection, from any family panel or combined family panel for the inner London area'.*

(4)   *At the end of that section there shall be added the following subsection—*

'(7)   *No rules shall be made under subsection (3)(bb) above except on the advice of, or after consultation with, the rule committee established under section 144 of the Magistrates' Courts Act 1980.'*

(5) *In section 37(1)(a) of that Act (justices' clerks) after the words 'juvenile courts' there shall be inserted 'and family proceedings courts'.*

Note. Sub-ss (3)–(5) repealed by Police and Magistrates' Courts Act 1994, s 93, Sch 9, Part II, as from 1 April 1995.

Miscellaneous

11. Representation in certain county court cases—(1) The Lord Chancellor may by order provide that there shall be no restriction on the persons who may exercise rights of audience, or rights to conduct litigation, in relation to proceedings in a county court of such a kind as may be specified in the order.

(2) The power to make an order may only be exercised in relation to proceedings—

   (a) for the recovery of amounts due under contracts for the supply of goods or services;

   (b) for the enforcement of any judgment or order of any court or the recovery of any sum due under any such judgment or order;

   (c) on any application under the Consumer Credit Act 1974;

   (d) in relation to domestic premises; or

   (e) *referred to arbitration in accordance with county court rules made under section 64 of the County Courts Act 1984 (small claims),*

or any category (determined by reference to such criteria as the Lord Chancellor considers appropriate) of such proceedings.

[(e) dealt with as a small claim in accordance with rules of court,]

Note. In sub-s (2) para (e) substituted by the Civil Procedure (Modification) of Enactments) Order 1999, SI 1999 No 1217, art 3, as from 26 April 1999.

(3) Where an order is made under this section, section 20 of the Solicitors Act 1974 (unqualified person not to act as solicitor) shall cease to apply in relation to proceedings of the kind specified in the order.

(4) Where a county court is of the opinion that a person who would otherwise have a right of audience by virtue of an order under this section is behaving in an unruly manner in any proceedings, it may refuse to hear him in those proceedings.

(5) Where a court exercises its power under subsection (4), it shall specify the conduct which warranted its refusal.

(6) Where, in any proceedings in a county court—

   (a) a person is exercising a right of audience or a right to conduct litigation;

   (b) he would not be entitled to do so were it not for an order under this section; and

   (c) the judge has reason to believe that (in those or any other proceedings in which he has exercised a right of audience or a right to conduct litigation) that person has intentionally misled the court, or otherwise demonstrated that he is unsuitable to exercise that right,

the judge may order that person's disqualification from exercising any right of audience or any right to conduct litigation in proceedings in any county court.

(7) Where a judge makes an order under subsection (6) he shall give his reasons for so doing.

(8) Any person against whom such an order is made may appeal to the Court of Appeal.

(9) Any such order may be revoked at any time by any judge of a county court.

(10) Before making any order under this section the Lord Chancellor shall consult the Senior Presiding Judge.

(11) In this section 'domestic premises' means any premises which are wholly or mainly used as a private dwelling.

12. Penalty for failure to warn that hearing will not be attended—*(1) This section applies where an appointment has been fixed for any hearing in the High Court or in any county court, but a party to the proceedings—*

    (a)   has failed to appear; or

    (b)   has failed to give the court due notice of his desire to cancel the hearing or of his inability to appear at it.

    (2)   The court may summon the party concerned, or the person conducting the proceedings on his behalf, to explain his failure.

    (3)   Where a court—

    (a)   has summoned a person under subsection (2); and

    (b)   is not satisfied that he took reasonable steps to give due notice to the court of his desire to cancel the hearing or (as the case may be) of his inability to appear at it,

the court may declare that person to be in contravention of this section.

    (4)   On declaring a person to be in contravention of this section a court may impose on him a penalty equivalent to a fine not exceeding level 3 on the standard scale.

    (5)   Before deciding whether or not to impose any such penalty, the court shall consider the extent to which (if any) the person concerned will, or is likely to—

    (a)   suffer any financial loss (by way of a reduction of costs or otherwise); or

    (b)   be subject to any disciplinary action,

as a result of his failure.

    (6)   Sections 129 and 130 of the County Courts Act 1984 (enforcement, payment and application of fines) shall apply with respect to any penalty imposed by a county court under this section as they apply with respect to any fine imposed by any county court under that Act.

    (7)   In subsection (1) 'due notice' means—

    (a)   such notice as is required by rules of court; or

    (b)   where there is no such requirement applicable to the circumstances of the case, such notice as the court considers reasonable.

Note. This section repealed by the Statute Law (Repeals) Act 2004, as from 22 July 2004.

13. Administration orders—(1) For subsection (1) of section 112 of the County Courts Act 1984 (power to make administration orders) there shall be substituted—

    '(1) Where a debtor is unable to pay forthwith the amount of any debt owed by him, a county court may make an order providing for the administration of his estate.

    (1A) The order may be made—

    (a) on the application of the debtor (whether or not a judgment debt has been obtained against the debtor in respect of his debt, or any of his debts);

    (b) on the application of any creditor under a judgment obtained against the debtor; or

    (c) of the court's own motion during the course of, or on the determination of, any enforcement or other proceedings.'

    (2) In that section the following subsection shall be inserted after subsection (4)—

    '(4A) Subsection (4) is subject to section 112A.'

    (3) Subsection (5) of that section shall be omitted.

    (4) The following subsection shall be added at the end of that section—

    '(9) An administration order shall cease to have effect—

    (a) at the end of the period of three years beginning with the date on which it is made; or

    (b) on such earlier date as may be specified in the order.'

    (5) After that section there shall be inserted the following sections—

'112A. Further powers of the court—(1) Where the court is satisfied—

    (a) that it has power to make an administration order with respect to the debtor concerned; but

    (b) that an order restricting enforcement would be a more satisfactory way of dealing with the case, it may make such an order instead of making an administration order.

(2) Where an order restricting enforcement is made, no creditor specified in the order shall have any remedy against the person or property of the debtor in respect of any debt so specified, without the leave of the court.

(3) Subsection (4) applies to any creditor—

(a) who is named in the schedule to an administration order or in an order restricting enforcement; and

(b) who provides the debtor with mains gas, electricity or water for the debtor's own domestic purposes.

(4) While the order has effect, the creditor may not stop providing the debtor with—

(a) mains gas, electricity or (as the case may be) water for the debtor's own domestic purposes; or

(b) any associated service which it provides for its customers,

without leave of the court unless the reason for doing so relates to the non-payment of charges incurred by the debtor after the making of the order or is unconnected with non-payment by him of any charges.

(5) In this section 'mains gas' means a supply of gas by a public gas supplier within the meaning of Part I of the Gas Act 1986.

(6) Rules of court may make provision with respect to the period for which any order restricting enforcement is to have effect and for the circumstances in which any such order may be revoked.

112B. Administration orders with composition provisions—(1) Where the court is satisfied—

(a) that it has power to make an administration order with respect to the debtor concerned; and

(b) that the addition of a composition provision would be a more satisfactory way of dealing with the case,

it may make an administration order subject to such a provision.

(2) Where, at any time while an administration order is in force—

(a) the debtor has not discharged the debts to which that order relates; and

(b) the court considers that he is unlikely to be able to discharge them,

the court may add a composition provision to that order.

(3) A composition provision shall specify an amount to which the debtor's total indebtedness in respect of debts owed to creditors scheduled to the administration order is to be reduced.

(4) The amount of the debt owed to each of the creditors so scheduled shall be reduced in proportion to the reduction in his total indebtedness specified by the composition provision.

(5) Where a composition provision is added to an administration order after the order is made, section 113(a) shall apply as if the addition of the composition provision amounted to the making of a new administration order.'

14. Assessors—*(1) Section 63 of the County Courts Act 1984 (assessors) shall be amended as follows.*

(2) The following subsections shall be substituted for subsections (1) and (2)—

'(1) In any proceedings a judge may, on the application of a party to the proceedings, summon to his assistance one or more persons—

(a) of skill and experience in the matter to which the proceedings relate; and

(b) who may be willing to sit with him and act as assessors.

(2) In any proceedings prescribed for the purposes of this subsection a judge may summon to his assistance one or more such persons even though no application has been made for him to do so.

(2A) In any proceedings prescribed for the purposes of this subsection a district judge

may, on the application of a party to the proceedings, summon to his assistance one or more such persons.

(2B) In any proceedings prescribed for the purposes of this subsection a district judge may summon to his assistance one or more such persons even though no application has been made for him to do so.

(2C) The summons shall be made in such manner as may be prescribed.'

(3) For subsection (4) there shall be substituted—

'(4) In such cases as may be specified by order made by the Lord Chancellor with the consent of the Treasury, the remuneration of any assessor summoned under this section shall be paid, at such rate as may be so specified, out of money provided by Parliament.

(4A) Any power to make an order under subsection (4) shall be exercisable by statutory instrument subject to annulment by resolution of either House of Parliament.'

Note. This section repealed by the Statute Law (Repeals) Act 2004, as from 22 July 2004.

15. Enforcement—(1), (2) (*Sub-s (1) inserts Supreme Court Act 1981, s 138(3A) (p 2864); sub-s (2) substitutes s 89(1)(a) of that Act.*)

Note. Sub-s (1) repealed by the Courts Act 2003, s 109(3), Sch 10, as from a day to be appointed.

(3) Where a person takes steps to enforce a judgment or order of the High Court or a county court for the payment of any sum due, the costs of any previous attempt to enforce that judgment shall be recoverable to the same extent as if they had been incurred in the taking of those steps.

(4) Subsection (3) shall not apply in respect of any costs which the court considers were unreasonably incurred (whether because the earlier attempt was unreasonable in all the circumstances of the case or for any other reason).

16.   (*Amends County Courts Act 1984, s 75.*)

*   *   *   *   *

PART III

JUDICIAL AND OTHER OFFICES AND JUDICIAL PENSIONS

Judicial appointments

*   *   *   *   *

Judges

*   *   *   *   *

74. District judges—(1) The offices of—
   (a) registrar, assistant registrar and deputy registrar for each county court district; and
   (b) district registrar, assistant district registrar and deputy district registrar for each district registry of the High Court,
shall become the offices of district judge, assistant district judge and deputy district judge respectively.

(2) The office of registrar of the principal registry of the Family Division of the High Court shall become the office of district judge of the principal registry of the Family Division.

(3) Any reference in any enactment, instrument or other document to an office which is, or includes, one to which this section applies shall be construed as a reference to, or (as the case may be) as including a reference to, that office by its new name.

(4)–(7) (*Sub-ss (4)–(6) amend County Courts Act 1984, ss 14, 55, 118 (pp 3045, 3051, 3064); Sub-s (7) amends Matrimonial and Family Proceedings Act 1984, s 42 (p 3050)*.)

* * * * *

PART VI

MISCELLANEOUS AND SUPPLEMENTAL

* * * * *

Miscellaneous

* * * * *

116. Provision with respect to the Children Act 1989—(1) The provisions of Part I of Schedule 16 shall have effect for the purpose of making amendments to the Children Act 1989 or to provisions of other enactments amended by that Act.

(2) Part II of Schedule 16 shall have effect for the purpose of making further provision consequential on the Act of 1989.

(3) The general rule making power of any authority having power to make rules of court for Northern Ireland shall include power to make any provision which may be made under section 93 of the Act of 1989 (rules of court) subject to the modifications that in subsection (2)—

(a) paragraphs (e) and (i) shall be omitted; and

(b) in paragraphs (f) and (g) the references to England and Wales shall be read as references to Northern Ireland.

* * * * *

Supplemental

119. Interpretation—(1) In this Act—

* * * *

['Consultative Panel' means the Legal Services Consultative Panel;]

Note. Above definition inserted by the Access to Justice Act 1999, s 35(3), as from 1 January 2000 (SI 1999 No 3344).

'court' includes—

(a) any tribunal which the Council on Tribunals is under a duty to keep under review;

(b) any court-martial; and

(c) a statutory inquiry within the meaning of *section 19(1) of the Tribunals and Inquiries Act 1971* [section 16(1) of the Tribunals and Inquiries Act 1992];

Note. In above definition words in square brackets in para (c) substituted for words in italics by Tribunals and Inquiries Act 1992, s 18(1), Sch 3, para 35, as from 1 October 1992.

'designated judge' means the Lord Chief Justice, the Master of the Rolls, the President of the Family Division or the Vice-Chancellor;

* * * * *

['officer', in relation to a limited partnership, means a member of the limited liability partnership;]

Note. Above definition inserted by the Limited Liability Partnership Regulations 2001, SI 2001 No 1090, reg 9(1), Sch 5, para 17, as from 6 April 2001.

['the OFT' means the Office of Fair Trading;]

Note. Above definition inserted by the Enterprise Act 2002, s 278(1), Sch 25, para 23(1), (9)(b), as from 1 April 2003 (SI 2003 No 766). For transitional and Transitory provision see Sch 24, paras 2–6 of the 2002 Act.

'prescribed' means prescribed by regulations under this Act;
'proceedings' means proceedings in any court;

*   *   *   *   *

'qualification regulations' and 'rules of conduct'

*   *   *   *   *

    (b) in relation to any right to conduct litigation or proposed right to conduct litigation, have the meanings given in section 28;

*   *   *   *   *

(3) In this Act any reference (including those in sections 27(9) and 28(5)) to rules of conduct includes a reference to rules of practice.

Note. See also the European Communities (Lawyer's Practice) Regulations 2000, SI 2000 No 1119, reg 14.

120. Regulations and orders—(1) Any power to make orders or regulations conferred by this Act shall be exercisable by statutory instrument.

(2) Any such regulations or order may make different provision for different cases or classes of case.

(3) Any such regulations or order may contain such incidental, supplemental or transitional provisions or savings as the person making the regulations or order considers expedient.

(4) No instrument shall be made under section *1(1)*, 26(1), 37(10), 40(1), *58* [58(4)], 60, 89(5) or (7), 125(4) *or paragraph 4* [, paragraph 24 of Schedule 4, paragraph 4] or 6 of Schedule 9 or paragraph 9(c) of Schedule 14 unless a draft of the instrument has been approved by both Houses of Parliament.

Note. In sub-s (4) '1(1)' in italics repealed by Civil Procedure Act 1997, s 10, Sch 2, para 4, as from 27 April 1997. Reference to '58(4)' in square brackets substituted for reference to '58' by the Access to Justice Act 1999, s 27(2), as from 1 April 2000 (with savings in relation to existing cases) (SI 2000 No 774 and SI 2000 No 900). Words 'paragraph 24 of Schedule 4, paragraph 4' in square brackets substituted for words 'or paragraph 4' by the Access to Justice Act 1999, s 43, Sch 6, paras 4, 11(1), (2), as from 1 January 2000 (SI 1999 No 3344).

(5) An Order in Council shall not be made in pursuance of a recommendation made under section 29(2) or 30(1) unless a draft of the Order has been approved by both Houses of Parliament.

(6) Any other statutory instrument made under this Act other than one under section 124(3) shall be subject to annulment in pursuance of a resolution of either House of Parliament.

121. Financial provisions.   Any expenses incurred by the Lord Chancellor under this Act shall be payable out of money provided by Parliament.

122. Power to make corresponding provision for Northern Ireland.   An Order in Council made under paragraph 1(1)(b) of Schedule 1 to the Northern Ireland Act 1974 which contains a statement—

    (a) that it amends the law in Northern Ireland with respect to—
        (i) the pensions of county court judges and resident magistrates, and
       (ii) pensions in relation to which provisions of the Judicial Pensions Act (Northern Ireland) 1951 apply; and
    (b) that it is made only for purposes corresponding to those of—

   (i)   sections 79 to 83 and Schedules 12 and 13 and such other provisions
         of this Act as are consequential on those sections and those Schedules;
   (ii) section 118,
shall not be subject to sub-paragraphs (4) and (5) of paragraph 1 of that Schedule
(affirmative resolution of both Houses of Parliament) but shall be subject to
annulment in pursuance of a resolution of either House of Parliament.

123.   (*Specifies provisions which apply to Scotland only.*)

124. Commencement—(1) The following provisions come into force on the
passing of this Act—
   (a)   sections 1, 5, 119 to 123, this section and section 125(1); and
   (b)   paragraphs 2 and 3 of Schedule 17.
   (2)   The following provisions come into force at the end of the period of two
months beginning on the day on which this Act is passed—
   (a)   sections 6, 8, 11, 16, 64, 65, 72, 73, 85, 87 and 88, 90 to 92, 94 to 97, 98 and
         108 to 110;
   (b)   paragraphs 1, 11, 12, 16 and 20 of Schedule 17;
   (c)   paragraphs 7, 8, 14 to 16, 55 and 57 of Schedule 18; and
   (d)   paragraph 1 of Schedule 19.
   (3)   The other provisions of this Act shall come into force on such date as may
be appointed by order made by the Lord Chancellor or by the Secretary of State or
by both, acting jointly.
   (4)   Different dates may be appointed for different provisions of this Act and for
different purposes.

Commencement.   Sections 4, 116 (so far as it applies to remainder of Sch 16) were brought
into force on 1 October 1991 (SI 1991 No 1883). Section 7(1), (except so far as it relates to
s 7(2)), (3), (4) was brought into force on 23 July 1993 and s 7(1) (so far as not already in
force), (2) was brought into force on 1 October 1993 (SI 1993 No 2132). Sections 9,
74(1)–(3), 116 (so far as it applies to Sch 16, para 8) were brought into force on 1 January
1991 (SI 1990 No 2484). Sections 12–14 have not been brought into force.

**125. Short title, minor and consequential amendments, transitionals and
repeals**—(1) This Act may be cited as the Courts and Legal Services Act 1990.
   (2)   The minor amendments set out in Schedule 17 shall have effect.
   (3)   The consequential amendments set out in Schedule 18 shall have effect.
   (4)   The *Lord Chancellor* [Secretary of State] may by order make such
amendments or repeals in relevant enactments as appear to him to be necessary or
expedient in consequence of any provision made by Part II with respect to
advocacy, litigation, conveyancing or probate services.

Note.   In sub-s (4) words 'Secretary of State' in square brackets substituted for words in italics
by the Secretary of State for Constitutional Affairs Order 2003, SI 2003 No 1887, as from
19 August 2003.

   (5)   In subsection (4) 'relevant enactments' means such enactments or instruments
passed or made before or in the same Session as this Act as may be specified in the
order.
   (6)   The transitional provisions and savings set out in Schedule 19 shall have
effect.
   (7)   The repeals set out in Schedule 20 (which include repeals of certain
enactments that are spent or of no further practical utility) shall have effect.

SCHEDULES

   (*Only Schedule 16 (which makes amendments to the Children Act 1989 and other related
enactments which have been incorporated where relevant) is within the scope of this work.*)

CIVIL JURISDICTION AND JUDGMENTS ACT 1991

(1991 c 12)

ARRANGEMENT OF SECTIONS

An Act to give effect to the Convention on jurisdiction and the enforcement of judgments in civil and commercial matters, including the Protocols annexed thereto, opened for signature at Lugano on 16th September 1988; and for purposes connected therewith. [9 May 1991]

1. Implementation and interpretation of the Lugano Convention—(1) The Civil Jurisdiction and Judgments Act 1982 (in this Act referred to as 'the 1982 Act') shall have effect with the insertion of the following after section 3—

'**3A. The Lugano Convention to have the force of law**—(1) The Lugano Convention shall have the force of law in the United Kingdom, and judicial notice shall be taken of it.

(2) For convenience of reference there is set out in Schedule 3C the English text of the Lugano Convention.

3B. Interpretation of the Lugano Convention—(1) In determining any question as to the meaning or effect of a provision of the Lugano Convention, a court in the United Kingdom shall, in accordance with Protocol No 2 to that Convention, take account of any principles laid down in any relevant decision delivered by a court of any other Lugano Contracting State concerning provisions of the Convention.

(2) Without prejudice to any practice of the courts as to the matters which may be considered apart from this section, the report on the Lugano Convention by Mr P Jenard and Mr G Möller (which is reproduced in the Official Journal of the Communities of 28th July 1990) may be considered in ascertaining the meaning or effect of any provision of the Convention and shall be given such weight as is appropriate in the circumstances.'

(2) In section 9 of that Act, after subsection (1) (which, as amended, will govern the relationship between other conventions and the 1968 and Lugano Conventions) there shall be inserted—

'(1A) Any question arising as to whether it is the Lugano Convention or any of the Brussels Conventions which applies in the circumstances of a particular case falls to be determined in accordance with the provisions of Article 54B of the Lugano Convention.'

(3) After Schedule 3B to that Act there shall be inserted the Schedule 3C set out in Schedule 1 to this Act.

2. Interpretation of the 1982 Act—(1) Section 1 of the 1982 Act (interpretation of references to the Conventions and Contracting States) shall be amended in accordance with the following provisions of this section.

(2) In subsection (1), in the definition of 'the Conventions', for the words 'the Conventions' there shall be substituted the words 'the Brussels Conventions'.

(3) At the end of that subsection there shall be added—

' "the Lugano Convention" means the Convention on jurisdiction and the enforcement of judgments in civil and commercial matters (including the Protocols annexed to that Convention) opened for signature at Lugano on 16th September 1988 and signed by the United Kingdom on 18th September 1989.'

(4) In subsection (2), for paragraph (b) (citation of Articles) there shall be substituted—

'(b) any reference in any provision to a numbered Article without more is a reference—

    (i) to the Article so numbered of the 1968 Convention, in so far as the provision applies in relation to that Convention, and

    (ii) to the Article so numbered of the Lugano Convention, in so far as the provision applies in relation to that Convention,

and any reference to a sub-division of a numbered Article shall be construed accordingly.'

(5) In subsection (3) (definition of 'Contracting State') for the words 'In this Act "Contracting State" means—' there shall be substituted the words—

'In this Act—

"Contracting State", without more, in any provision means—

(a) in the application of the provision in relation to the Brussels Conventions, a Brussels Contracting State; and

(b) in the application of the provision in relation to the Lugano Convention, a Lugano Contracting State;

"Brussels Contracting State" means—'.

(6) At the end of that subsection there shall be added—

' "Lugano Contracting State" means one of the original parties to the Lugano Convention, that is to say—

Austria, Belgium, Denmark, Finland, France, the Federal Republic of Germany, the Hellenic Republic, Iceland, the Republic of Ireland, Italy, Luxembourg, the Netherlands, Norway, Portugal, Spain, Sweden, Switzerland and the United Kingdom,

being a State in relation to which that Convention has taken effect in accordance with paragraph 3 or 4 of Article 61.'

3. Other amendments of the 1982 Act.   The 1982 Act shall have effect with the amendments specified in Schedule 2 to this Act, which are either consequential on the amendments made by sections 1 and 2 above or otherwise for the purpose of implementing the Lugano Convention.

4. Application to the Crown.   The amendments of the 1982 Act made by this Act bind the Crown in accordance with the provisions of section 51 of that Act.

5. Short title, interpretation, commencement and extent—(1) This Act may be cited as the Civil Jurisdiction and Judgments Act 1991.

(2) In this Act—

'the 1982 Act' means the Civil Jurisdiction and Judgments Act 1982;

'the Lugano Convention' has the same meaning as it has in the 1982 Act by virtue of section 2(3) above.

(3) This Act shall come into force on such day as the Lord Chancellor and the Lord Advocate may appoint in an order made by statutory instrument.

(4) This Act extends to Northern Ireland.

Commencement. This Act was brought into force on 1 May 1992 (SI 1992 No 745).

SCHEDULES

SCHEDULE 1   Section 1(3)

SCHEDULE TO BE INSERTED AS SCHEDULE TO THE 1982 ACT

'SCHEDULE 3C   Section 3A(2)

TEXT OF THE LUGANO CONVENTION

ARRANGEMENT OF PROVISIONS

Convention On Jurisdiction and the Enforcement of Judgments in Civil and Commercial Matters

Preamble

The High Contracting Parties to this Convention,

Anxious to strengthen in their territories the legal protection of persons therein established,

Considering that it is necessary for this purpose to determine the international jurisdiction of their courts, to facilitate recognition and to introduce an expeditious procedure for securing the enforcement of judgments, authentic instruments and court settlements,

Aware of the links between them, which have been sanctioned in the economic field by the free trade agreements concluded between the European Economic Community and the States members of the European Free Trade Association,

Taking into account the Brussels Convention of 27 September 1968 on jurisdiction and the enforcement of judgments in civil and commercial matters, as amended by the Accession Conventions under the successive enlargements of the European Communities,

Persuaded that the extension of the principles of that Convention to the States parties to this instrument will strengthen legal and economic co-operation in Europe,

Desiring to ensure as uniform an interpretation as possible of this instrument,
Have in this spirit decided to conclude this Convention and
Have agreed as follows:

TITLE I

SCOPE

ARTICLE 1

This Convention shall apply in civil and commercial matters whatever the nature of the court or tribunal. It shall not extend, in particular, to revenue, customs or administrative matters.

The Convention shall not apply to:

(1) the status or legal capacity of natural persons, rights in property arising out of a matrimonial relationship, wills and succession;
(2) bankruptcy, proceedings relating to the winding-up of insolvent companies or other legal persons, judicial arrangements, compositions and analogous proceedings;
(3) social security;
(4) arbitration.

TITLE II

JURISDICTION

Section 1

General provisions

ARTICLE 2

Subject to the provisions of this Convention, persons domiciled in a Contracting State shall, whatever their nationality, be sued in the courts of that State.

Persons who are not nationals of the State in which they are domiciled shall be governed by the rules of jurisdiction applicable to nationals of that State.

ARTICLE 3

Persons domiciled in a Contracting State may be sued in the courts of another Contracting State only by virtue of the rules set out in Sections 2 to 6 of this Title.

In particular the following provisions shall not be applicable as against them:

—in Belgium:	Article 15 of the civil code (*Code civil—Burgerlijk Wetboek*) and Article 638 of the judicial code (*Code judiciaire—Gerechtelijk Wetboek*);
—in Denmark:	Article 246(2) and (3) of the law on civil procedure (*Lov om rettens pleje*);
—in the Federal Republic of Germany:	Article 23 of the code of civil procedure (*Zivilprozeßordnung*);
—in Greece:	Article 40 of the code of civil procedure (*Κῶδιτικαζ πολιτικῇζ δικομιαζ*);
—in France:	Articles 14 and 15 of the civil code (*Code civil*);
—in Ireland:	the rules which enable jurisdiction to be founded on the document instituting the proceedings having been served on the defendant during his temporary presence in Ireland;

—in Iceland:	Article 77 of the Civil Proceedings Act (*lög um meðferð einkamála í héraði*);
—in Italy:	Articles 2 and 4, Nos 1 and 2 of the code of civil procedure (*Codice di procedura civile*);
—in Luxembourg:	Articles 14 and 15 of the civil code (*Code civil*);
—in the Netherlands:	Articles 126(3) and 127 of the code of civil procedure (*Wetboek van Burgerlijke Rechtsvordering*);
—in Norway:	Section 32 of the Civil Proceedings Act (*tvistemålsloven*);
—in Austria:	Article 99 of the Law on Court Jurisdiction (*Jurisdiktionsnorm*);
—in Portugal:	Articles 65(1)(c), 65(2) and 65A(c) of the code of civil procedure (*Código de Processo Civil*) and Article 11 of the code of labour procedure (*Código de Processo de Trabalho*);
—in Switzerland:	le for du lieu du sé questre/ Gerichtsstand des Arrestortes/foro del luogo del sequestro within the meaning of Article 4 of the loi fédérale sur le droit international privé/Bundesgesetz über das internationale Privatrecht/ legge federale sul diritto internazionale privato;
—in Finland:	the second, third and fourth sentences of Section 1 of Chapter 10 of the Code of Judicial Procedure (*oikeudenkäymiskaari/ rättegångsbalken*);
—in Sweden:	the first sentence of Section 3 of Chapter 10 of the Code of Judicial Procedure (*Rättegångsbalken*);
—in the United Kingdom:	the rules which enable jurisdiction to be founded on:

(a) the document instituting the proceedings having been served on the defendant during his temporary presence in the United Kingdom; or

(b) the presence within the United Kingdom of property belonging to the defendant; or

(c) the seizure by the plaintiff of property situated in the United Kingdom.

ARTICLE 4

If the defendant is not domiciled in a Contracting State, the jurisdiction of the courts of each Contracting State shall, subject to the provisions of Article 16, be determined by the law of that State.

As against such a defendant, any person domiciled in a Contracting State may, whatever his nationality, avail himself in that State of the rules of jurisdiction there in force, and in particular those specified in the second paragraph of Article 3, in the same way as the nationals of that State.

Section 2

Special jurisdiction

ARTICLE 5

A person domiciled in a Contracting State may, in another Contracting State, be sued:

(1) in matters relating to a contract, in the courts for the place of performance of the obligation in question; in matters relating to individual contracts of employment, this place is that where the employee habitually carries out his work, or if the employee does not habitually carry out his work in any one country, this place shall be the place of business through which he was engaged;

(2) in matters relating to maintenance, in the courts for the place where the maintenance creditor is domiciled or habitually resident or, if the matter is ancillary to proceedings concerning the status of a person, in the court which, according to its own law, has jurisdiction to entertain those proceedings, unless that jurisdiction is based solely on the nationality of one of the parties;

(3) in matters relating to tort, delict or quasi-delict, in the courts for the place where the harmful event occurred;

(4) as regards a civil claim for damages or restitution which is based on an act giving rise to criminal proceedings, in the court seised of those proceedings, to the extent that that court has jurisdiction under its own law to entertain civil proceedings;

(5) as regards a dispute arising out of the operations of a branch, agency or other establishment, in the courts for the place in which the branch, agency or other establishment is situated;

(6) in his capacity as settlor, trustee or beneficiary of a trust created by the operation of a statute, or by a written instrument, or created orally and evidenced in writing, in the courts of the Contracting State in which the trust is domiciled;

(7) as regards a dispute concerning the payment of remuneration claimed in respect of the salvage of a cargo or freight, in the court under the authority of which the cargo or freight in question:

(a)   has been arrested to secure such payment, or

(b)   could have been so arrested, but bail or other security has been given;

provided that this provision shall apply only if it is claimed that the defendant has an interest in the cargo or freight or had such an interest at the time of salvage.

ARTICLE 6

A person domiciled in a Contracting State may also be sued:

(1) where he is one of a number of defendants, in the courts for the place where any one of them is domiciled;

(2) as a third party in an action on a warranty or guarantee or in any other third party proceedings, in the court seised of the original proceedings, unless these were instituted solely with the object of removing him from the jurisdiction of the court which would be competent in his case;

(3) on a counterclaim arising from the same contract or facts on which the original claim was based, in the court in which the original claim is pending;

(4) in matters relating to a contract, if the action may be combined with an action against the same defendant in matters relating to rights *in rem* in immovable property, in the court of the Contracting State in which the property is situated.

ARTICLE 6A

Where by virtue of this Convention a court of a Contracting State has jurisdiction in actions relating to liability arising from the use or operation of a ship, that court, or any other court substituted for this purpose by the internal law of that State, shall also have jurisdiction over claims for limitation of such liability.

Section 3

Jurisdiction in matters relating to insurance

ARTICLE 7

In matters relating to insurance, jurisdiction shall be determined by this Section, without prejudice to the provisions of Articles 4 and 5(5).

ARTICLE 8

An insurer domiciled in a Contracting State may be sued:
(1) in the courts of the State where he is domiciled; or
(2) in another Contracting State, in the courts for the place where the policy-holder is domiciled; or
(3) if he is a co-insurer, in the courts of a Contracting State in which proceedings are brought against the leading insurer.

An insurer who is not domiciled in a Contracting State but has a branch, agency or other establishment in one of the Contracting States shall, in disputes arising out of the operations of the branch, agency or establishment, be deemed to be domiciled in that State.

ARTICLE 9

In respect of liability insurance or insurance of immovable property, the insurer may in addition be sued in the courts for the place where the harmful event occurred. The same applies if movable and immovable property are covered by the same insurance policy and both are adversely affected by the same contingency.

ARTICLE 10

In respect of liability insurance, the insurer may also, if the law of the court permits it, be joined in proceedings which the injured party has brought against the insured.

The provisions of Articles 7, 8 and 9 shall apply to actions brought by the injured party directly against the insurer, where such direct actions are permitted.

If the law governing such direct actions provides that the policy-holder or the insured may be joined as a party to the action, the same court shall have jurisdiction over them.

ARTICLE 11

Without prejudice to the provisions of the third paragraph of Article 10, an insurer may bring proceedings only in the courts of the Contracting State in which the defendant is domiciled, irrespective of whether he is the policy-holder, the insured or a beneficiary.

The provisions of this Section shall not affect the right to bring a counterclaim in the court in which, in accordance with this Section, the original claim is pending.

ARTICLE 12

The provisions of this Section may be departed from only by an agreement on jurisdiction:

(1) which is entered into after the dispute has arisen; or
(2) which allows the policy-holder, the insured or a beneficiary to bring proceedings in courts other than those indicated in this Section; or
(3) which is concluded between a policy-holder and an insurer, both of whom are at the time of conclusion of the contract domiciled or habitually resident in the same Contracting State, and which has the effect of conferring jurisdiction on the courts of that State even if the harmful event were to occur abroad, provided that such an agreement is not contrary to the law of the State; or
(4) which is concluded with a policy-holder who is not domiciled in a Contracting State, except in so far as the insurance is compulsory or relates to immovable property in a Contracting State; or
(5) which relates to a contract of insurance in so far as it covers one or more of the risks set out in Article 12A.

ARTICLE 12A

The following are the risks referred to in Article 12(5):
(1) any loss of or damage to:
    (a) sea-going ships, installations situated offshore or on the high seas, or aircraft, arising from perils which relate to their use for commercial purposes;
    (b) goods in transit other than passengers' baggage where the transit consists of or includes carriage by such ships or aircraft;
(2) any liability, other than for bodily injury to passengers or loss of or damage to their baggage;
    (a) arising out of the use or operation of ships, installations or aircraft as referred to in (1)(a) above in so far as the law of the Contracting State in which such aircraft are registered does not prohibit agreements on jurisdiction regarding insurance of such risks;
    (b) for loss or damage caused by goods in transit as described in (1)(b) above;
(3) any financial loss connected with the use or operation of ships, installations or aircraft as referred to in (1)(a) above, in particular loss of freight or charter-hire:
(4) any risk or interest connected with any of those referred to in (1) to (3) above.

Section 4

Jurisdiction over consumer contracts

ARTICLE 13

In proceedings concerning a contract concluded by a person for a purpose which can be regarded as being outside his trade or profession, hereinafter called 'the consumer', jurisdiction shall be determined by this Section, without prejudice to the provisions of Articles 4 and 5(5), if it is:
(1) a contract for the sale of goods on instalment credit terms; or
(2) a contract for a loan repayable by instalments, or for any other form of credit, made to finance the sale of goods; or
(3) any other contract for the supply of goods or a contract for the supply of services, and
    (a) in the State of the consumer's domicile the conclusion of the contract was preceded by a specific invitation addressed to him or by advertising, and
    (b) the consumer took in that State the steps necessary for the conclusion of the contract.

Where a consumer enters into a contract with a party who is not domiciled in a Contracting State but has a branch, agency or other establishment in one of the Contracting States, that party shall, in disputes arising out of the operations of the branch, agency or establishment, be deemed to be domiciled in that State.

This Section shall not apply to contracts of transport.

ARTICLE 14

A consumer may bring proceedings against the other party to a contract either in the courts of the Contracting State in which that party is domiciled or in the courts of the Contracting State in which he is himself domiciled.

Proceedings may be brought against a consumer by the other party to the contract only in the courts of the Contracting State in which the consumer is domiciled.

These provisions shall not affect the right to bring a counterclaim in the court in which, in accordance with this Section, the original claim is pending.

ARTICLE 15

The provisions of this Section may be departed from only by an agreement:
(1) which is entered into after the dispute has arisen; or
(2) which allows the consumer to bring proceedings in courts other than those indicated in this Section; or
(3) which is entered into by the consumer and the other party to the contract, both of whom are at the time of conclusion of the contract domiciled or habitually resident in the same Contracting State, and which confers jurisdiction on the courts of that State, provided that such an agreement is not contrary to the law of that State.

Section 5

Exclusive jurisdiction

ARTICLE 16

The following courts shall have exclusive jurisdiction, regardless of domicile:
(1) (a) in proceedings which have as their object rights *in rem* in immovable property or tenancies of immovable property, the courts of the Contracting State in which the property is situated;
    (b) however, in proceedings which have as their object tenancies of immovable property concluded for temporary private use for a maximum period of six consecutive months, the courts of the Contracting State in which the defendant is domiciled shall also have jurisdiction, provided that the tenant is a natural person and neither party is domiciled in the Contracting State in which the property is situated;
(2) in proceedings which have as their object the validity of the constitution, the nullity or the dissolution of companies or other legal persons or associations of natural or legal persons, or the decisions of their organs, the courts of the Contracting State in which the company, legal person or association has its seat,
(3) in proceedings which have as their object the validity of entries in public registers, the courts of the Contracting State in which the register is kept;
(4) in proceedings concerned with the registration or validity of patents, trade marks, designs, or other similar rights required to be deposited or registered, the courts of the Contracting State in which the deposit or registration has been applied for, has taken place or is under the terms of an international convention deemed to have taken place;
(5) in proceedings concerned with the enforcement of judgments, the courts of the Contracting State in which the judgment has been or is to be enforced.

Section 6

Prorogation of jurisdiction

ARTICLE 17

(1) If the parties, one or more of whom is domiciled in a Contracting State, have agreed that a court or the courts of a Contracting State are to have jurisdiction to settle any disputes which have arisen or which may arise in connection with a particular legal relationship, that court or those courts shall have exclusive jurisdiction. Such an agreement conferring jurisdiction shall be either:

(a) in writing or evidenced in writing, or

(b) in a form which accords with practices which the parties have established between themselves, or

(c) in international trade or commerce, in a form which accords with a usage of which the parties are or ought to have been aware and which in such trade or commerce is widely known to, and regularly observed by, parties to contracts of the type involved in the particular trade or commerce concerned.

Where such an agreement is concluded by parties, none of whom is domiciled in a Contracting State, the courts of other Contracting States shall have no jurisdiction over their disputes unless the court or courts chosen have declined jurisdiction.

(2) The court or courts of a Contracting State on which a trust instrument has conferred jurisdiction shall have exclusive jurisdiction in any proceedings brought against a settlor, trustee or beneficiary, if relations between these persons or their rights or obligations under the trust are involved.

(3) Agreements or provisions of a trust instrument conferring jurisdiction shall have no legal force if they are contrary to the provisions of Article 12 or 15, or if the courts whose jurisdiction they purport to exclude have exclusive jurisdiction by virtue of Article 16.

(4) If an agreement conferring jurisdiction was concluded for the benefit of only one of the parties, that party shall retain the right to bring proceedings in any other court which has jurisdiction by virtue of this Convention.

(5) In matters relating to individual contracts of employment an agreement conferring jurisdiction shall have legal force only if it is entered into after the dispute has arisen.

ARTICLE 18

Apart from jurisdiction derived from other provisions of this Convention, a court of a Contracting State before whom a defendant enters an appearance shall have jurisdiction. This rule shall not apply where appearance was entered solely to contest the jurisdiction, or where another court has exclusive jurisdiction by virtue of Article 16.

Section 7

Examination as to jurisdiction and admissibility

ARTICLE 19

Where a court of a Contracting State is seised of a claim which is principally concerned with a matter over which the courts of another Contracting State have exclusive jurisdiction by virtue of Article 16, it shall declare of its own motion that it has no jurisdiction.

ARTICLE 20

Where a defendant domiciled in one Contracting State is sued in a court of another Contracting State and does not enter an appearance, the court shall declare of its own motion that it has no jurisdiction unless its jurisdiction is derived from the provisions of this Convention.

The court shall stay the proceedings so long as it is not shown that the defendant has been able to receive the document instituting the proceedings or an equivalent document in sufficient time to enable him to arrange for his defence, or that all necessary steps have been taken to this end.

The provisions of the foregoing paragraph shall be replaced by those of Article 15 of the Hague Convention of 15 November 1965 on the service abroad of judicial and extrajudicial documents in civil or commercial matters, if the document instituting the proceedings or notice thereof had to be transmitted abroad in accordance with that Convention.

Section 8

Lis pendens—related actions

ARTICLE 21

Where proceedings involving the same cause of action and between the same parties are brought in the courts of different Contracting States, any court other than the court first seised shall of its own motion stay its proceedings until such time as the jurisdiction of the court first seised is established.

Where the jurisdiction of the court first seised is established, any court other than the court first seised shall decline jurisdiction in favour of that court.

ARTICLE 22

Where related actions are brought in the courts of different Contracting States, any court other than the court first seised may, while the actions are pending at first instance, stay its proceedings.

A court other than the court first seised may also, on the application of one of the parties, decline jurisdiction if the law of that court permits the consolidation of related actions and the court first seised has jurisdiction over both actions.

For the purposes of this Article, actions are deemed to be related where they are so closely connected that it is expedient to hear and determine them together to avoid the risk of irreconcilable judgments resulting from separate proceedings.

ARTICLE 23

Where actions come within the exclusive jurisdiction of several courts, any court other than the court first seised shall decline jurisdiction in favour of that court.

Section 9

Provisional, including protective, measures

ARTICLE 24

Application may be made to the courts of a Contracting State for such provisional, including protective, measures as may be available under the law of that State, even if, under this Convention, the courts of another Contracting State have jurisdiction as to the substance of the matter.

TITLE III

RECOGNITION AND ENFORCEMENT

ARTICLE 25

For the purposes of this Convention, 'judgment' means any judgment given by a court or tribunal of a Contracting State, whatever the judgment may be called, including a decree, order, decision or writ of execution, as well as the determination of costs or expenses by an officer of the court.

Section 1

Recognition

ARTICLE 26

A judgment given in a Contracting State shall be recognised in the other Contracting States without any special procedure being required.

Any interested party who raises the recognition of a judgment as the principal issue in a dispute may, in accordance with the procedures provided for in Sections 2 and 3 of this Title, apply for a decision that the judgment be recognised.

If the outcome of proceedings in a court of a Contracting State depends on the determination of an incidental question of recognition that court shall have jurisdiction over that question.

ARTICLE 27

A judgment shall not be recognised:
(1) if such recognition is contrary to public policy in the State in which recognition is sought;
(2) where it was given in default of appearance, if the defendant was not duly served with the document which instituted the proceedings or with an equivalent document in sufficient time to enable him to arrange for his defence;
(3) if the judgment is irreconcilable with a judgment given in a dispute between the same parties in the State in which recognition is sought;
(4) if the court of the State of origin, in order to arrive at its judgment, has decided a preliminary question concerning the status or legal capacity of natural persons, rights in property arising out of a matrimonial relationship, wills or succession in a way that conflicts with a rule of the private international law of the State in which the recognition is sought, unless the same result would have been reached by the application of the rules of private international law of that State;
(5) if the judgment is irreconcilable with an earlier judgment given in a non-contracting State involving the same cause of action and between the same parties, provided that this latter judgment fulfils the conditions necessary for its recognition in the State addressed.

ARTICLE 28

Moreover, a judgment shall not be recognised if it conflicts with the provisions of Section 3, 4 or 5 of Title II or in a case provided for in Article 59.

A judgment may furthermore be refused recognition in any case provided for in Article 54B(3) or 57(4).

In its examination of the grounds of jurisdiction referred to in the foregoing paragraphs, the court or authority applied to shall be bound by the findings of fact on which the court of the State of origin based its jurisdiction.

Subject to the provisions of the first and second paragraphs, the jurisdiction of the court of the State of origin may not be reviewed; the test of public policy referred to in Article 27(1) may not be applied to the rules relating to jurisdiction.

ARTICLE 29

Under no circumstances may a foreign judgment be reviewed as to its substance.

ARTICLE 30

A court of a Contracting State in which recognition is sought of a judgment given in another Contracting State may stay the proceedings if an ordinary appeal against the judgment has been lodged.

A court of a Contracting State in which recognition is sought of a judgment given in Ireland or the United Kingdom may stay the proceedings if enforcement is suspended in the State of origin by reason of an appeal.

Section 2

Enforcement

ARTICLE 31

A judgment given in a Contracting State and enforceable in that State shall be enforced in another Contracting State when, on the application of any interested party, it has been declared enforceable there.

However, in the United Kingdom, such a judgment shall be enforced in England and Wales, in Scotland, or in Northern Ireland when, on the application of any interested party, it has been registered for enforcement in that part of the United Kingdom.

ARTICLE 32

(1) The application shall be submitted:
—in Belgium, to the tribunal de première instance or rechtbank van eerste aanleg;
—in Denmark, to the byret;
—in the Federal Republic of Germany, to the presiding judge of a chamber of the Landgericht;
—in Greece, to the μονομεκεζ πρϖτοδικειο;
—in Spain, to the Juzgado de Primera Instancia:
—in France, to the presiding judge of the tribunal de grande instance;
—in Ireland, to the High Court;
—in Iceland, to the héraðsdómari;
—in Italy, to the corte d'appello;
—in Luxembourg, to the presiding judge of the tribunal d'arrondissement;
—in the Netherlands, to the presiding judge of the arrondissementsrechtbank;
—in Norway, to the herredsrett or byrett as namsrett;
—in Austria, to the Landesgericht or the Kreisgericht;
—in Portugal, to the Tribunal Judicial de Círculo;
—in Switzerland:
(a) in respect of judgments ordering the payment of a sum of money, to the juge de la mainlevée/Rechtsöffnungsrichter/giudice competente a pronunciare sul rigetto dell'opposizione, within the framework of the procedure governed by Articles 80 and 81 of the loi fédérale sur la poursuite pour dettes et la faillite/Bundesgesetz über Schuldbetreibung und Konkurs/legge federale sulla esecuzione e sul fallimento;
(b) in respect of judgments ordering a performance other than the payment of a sum of money, to the juge cantonal d'exequatur compétent/zuständiger kantonaler Vollstreckungsrichter/giudice cantonale competente a pronunciare l'exequatur;
—in Finland, to the ulosotonhaltija/överexekutor;
—in Sweden, to the Svea hovrätt;
—in the United Kingdom:
(a) in England and Wales, to the High Court of Justice, or in the case of a maintenance judgment to the Magistrates' Court on transmission by the Secretary of State;
(b) in Scotland, to the Court of Session or in the case of a maintenance judgment to the Sheriff Court on transmission by the Secretary of State;
(c) in Northern Ireland, to the High Court of Justice, or in the case of a maintenance judgment to the Magistrates' Court on transmission by the Secretary of State.

(2) The jurisdiction of local courts shall be determined by reference to the place of domicile of the party against whom enforcement is sought. If he is not domiciled in the State in which enforcement is sought, it shall be determined by reference to the place of enforcement.

ARTICLE 33

The procedure for making the application shall be governed by the law of the State in which enforcement is sought.

The applicant must give an address for service of process within the area of jurisdiction of the court applied to. However, if the law of the State in which enforcement is sought does not provide for the furnishing of such an address, the applicant shall appoint a representative *ad litem*.

The documents referred to in Articles 46 and 47 shall be attached to the application.

ARTICLE 34

The court applied to shall give its decision without delay; the party against whom enforcement is sought shall not at this stage of the proceedings be entitled to make any submissions on the application.

The application may be refused only for one of the reasons specified in Articles 27 and 28.

Under no circumstances may the foreign judgment be reviewed as to its substance.

ARTICLE 35

The appropriate officer of the court shall without delay bring the decision given on the application to the notice of the applicant in accordance with the procedure laid down by the law of the State in which enforcement is sought.

ARTICLE 36

If enforcement is authorised, the party against whom enforcement is sought may appeal against the decision within one month of service thereof.

If that party is domiciled in a Contracting State other than that in which the decision authorising enforcement was given, the time for appealing shall be two months and shall run from the date of service, either on him in person or at his residence. No extension of time may be granted on account of distance.

ARTICLE 37

(1) An appeal against the decision authorising enforcement shall be lodged in accordance with the rules governing procedure in contentious matters:
  —in Belgium, with the tribunal de première instance or rechtbank van eerste aanleg;
  —in Denmark, with the landsret;
  —in the Federal Republic of Germany, with the Oberlandesgericht;
  —in Greece, with the εφετείο;
  —in Spain, with the Audiencia Provincial;
  —in France, with the cour d'appel;
  —in Ireland, with the High Court;
  —in Iceland, with the héraðsdómari;
  —in Italy, with the corte d'appello;
  —in Luxembourg, with the Cour supérieure de justice sitting as a court of civil appeal;
  —in the Netherlands, with the arrondissementsrechtbank;

—in Norway, with the lagmannsrett;
—in Austria, with the Landesgericht or the Kreisgericht;
—in Portugal, with the Tribunal da Relação;
—in Switzerland, with the tribunal cantonal/Kantonsgericht/tribunale cantonale;
—in Finland, with the hovioikeus/hovrätt;
—in Sweden, with the Svea hovrätt;
—in the United Kingdom:
  (a) in England and Wales, with the High Court of Justice, or in the case of a maintenance judgment with the Magistrates' Court;
  (b) in Scotland, with the Court of Session, or in the case of a maintenance judgment with the Sheriff Court;
  (c) in Northern Ireland, with the High Court of Justice, or in the case of a maintenance judgment with the Magistrates' Court.
(2) The judgment given on the appeal may be contested only:
—in Belgium, Greece, Spain, France, Italy, Luxembourg and in the Netherlands, by an appeal in cassation;
—in Denmark, by an appeal to the højesteret, with the leave of the Minister of Justice;
—in the Federal Republic of Germany, by a Rechtsbeschwerde;
—in Ireland, by an appeal on a point of law to the Supreme Court;
—in Iceland, by an appeal to the Hæstiréttur;
—in Norway, by an appeal (kjæremål or anke) to the Hoyesteretts Kjæremålsutvalg or Hoyesterett;
—in Austria, in the case of an appeal, by a Revisionsrekurs and, in the case of opposition proceedings, by a Berufung with the possibility of a Revision;
—in Portugal, by an appeal on a point of law;
—in Switzerland, by a recours de droit public devant le tribunal fédéral/staats-rechtliche Beschwerde beim Bundesgericht/ricorso di diritto pubblico davanti al tribunale federale;
—in Finland, by an appeal to the korkein oikeus/högsta domstolen;
—in Sweden, by an appeal to the högsta domstolen;
—in the United Kingdom, by a single further appeal on a point of law.

ARTICLE 38

The court with which the appeal under the first paragraph of Article 37 is lodged may, on the application of the appellant, stay the proceedings if an ordinary appeal has been lodged against the judgment in the State of origin or if the time for such an appeal has not yet expired; in the latter case, the court may specify the time within which such an appeal is to be lodged.

Where the judgment was given in Ireland or the United Kingdom, any form of appeal available in the State of origin shall be treated as an ordinary appeal for the purposes of the first paragraph.

The court may also make enforcement conditional on the provision of such security as it shall determine.

ARTICLE 39

During the time specified for an appeal pursuant to Article 36 and until any such appeal has been determined, no measures of enforcement may be taken other than protective measures taken against the property of the party against whom enforcement is sought.

The decision authorising enforcement shall carry with it the power to proceed to any such protective measures.

ARTICLE 40

(1) If the application for enforcement is refused, the applicant may appeal:

—in Belgium, to the cour d'appel or hof van beroep;
—in Denmark, to the landsret;
—in the Federal Republic of Germany, to the Oberlandesgericht;
—in Greece, to the ἐφετεῖο;
—in Spain, to the Audiencia Provincial;
—in France, to the cour d'appel;
—in Ireland, to the High Court;
—in Iceland, to the héraðsdómari;
—in Italy, to the corte d'appello;
—in Luxembourg, to the Cour supérieure de justice sitting as a court of civil appeal;
—in the Netherlands, to the gerechtshof;
—in Norway, to the lagmannsrett;
—in Austria, to the Landesgericht or the Kreisgericht;
—in Portugal, to the Tribunal da Relação;
—in Switzerland, to the tribunal cantonal/Kantonsgericht/tribunale cantonale;
—in Finland, to the hovioikeus/hovrätt;
—in Sweden, to the Svea hovrätt;
—in the United Kingdom:
  (a) in England and Wales, to the High Court of Justice, or in the case of a maintenance judgment to the Magistrates' Court;
  (b) in Scotland, to the Court of Session, or in the case of a maintenance judgment to the Sheriff Court;
  (c) in Northern Ireland, to the High Court of Justice, or in the case of a maintenance judgment to the Magistrates' Court.

(2) The party against whom enforcement is sought shall be summoned to appear before the appellate court. If he fails to appear, the provisions of the second and third paragraphs of Article 20 shall apply even where he is not domiciled in any of the Contracting States.

ARTICLE 41

A judgment given on an appeal provided for in Article 40 may be contested only:
—in Belgium, Greece, Spain, France, Italy, Luxembourg and in the Netherlands, by an appeal in cassation,
—in Denmark, by an appeal to the højesteret, with the leave of the Minister of Justice,
—in the Federal Republic of Germany, by a Rechtsbeschwerde,
—in Ireland, by an appeal on a point of law to the Supreme Court,
—in Iceland, by an appeal to the Hæstiréttur,
—in Norway, by an appeal (kjæremål or anke) to the Hoyesteretts kjæremålsutvalg or Hoyesterett,
—in Austria, by a Revisionsrekurs,
—in Portugal, by an appeal on a point of law,
—in Switzerland, by a recours de droit public devant le tribunal fédéral/staats-rechtliche Beschwerde beim Bundesgericht/ricorso di diritto pubblico davanti al tribunale federale,
—in Finland, by an appeal to the korkein oikeus/högsta domstolen,
—in Sweden, by an appeal to the högsta domstolen,
—in the United Kingdom, by a single further appeal on a point of law.

ARTICLE 42

Where a foreign judgment has been given in respect of several matters and enforcement cannot be authorised for all of them, the court shall authorise enforcement for one or more of them.

An applicant may request partial enforcement of a judgment.

ARTICLE 43

A foreign judgment which orders a periodic payment by way of a penalty shall be enforceable in the State in which enforcement is sought only if the amount of the payment has been finally determined by the courts of the State of origin.

ARTICLE 44

An applicant who, in the State of origin, has benefited from complete or partial legal aid or exemption from costs or expenses, shall be entitled, in the procedures provided for in Articles 32 to 35, to benefit from the most favourable legal aid or the most extensive exemption from costs or expenses provided for by the law of the State addressed.

However, an applicant who requests the enforcement of a decision given by an administrative authority in Denmark or in Iceland in respect of a maintenance order may, in the State addressed, claim the benefits referred to in the first paragraph if he presents a statement from, respectively, the Danish Ministry of Justice or the Icelandic Ministry of Justice to the effect that he fulfils the economic requirements to qualify for the grant of complete or partial legal aid or exemption from costs or expenses.

ARTICLE 45

No security, bond or deposit, however described, shall be required of a party who in one Contracting State applies for enforcement of a judgment given in another Contracting State on the ground that he is a foreign national or that he is not domiciled or resident in the State in which enforcement is sought.

Section 3

Common provisions

ARTICLE 46

A party seeking recognition or applying for enforcement of a judgment shall produce:
(1) a copy of the judgment which satisfies the conditions necessary to establish its authenticity;
(2) in the case of a judgment given in default, the original or a certified true copy of the document which establishes that the party in default was served with the document instituting the proceedings or with an equivalent document.

ARTICLE 47

A party applying for enforcement shall also produce:
(1) documents which establish that, according to the law of the State of origin, the judgment is enforceable and has been served;
(2) where appropriate, a document showing that the applicant is in receipt of legal aid in the State of origin.

ARTICLE 48

If the documents specified in Article 46(2) and Article 47(2) are not produced, the court may specify a time for their production, accept equivalent documents or, if it considers that it has sufficient information before it, dispense with their production.

If the court so requires, a translation of the documents shall be produced; the translation shall be certified by a person qualified to do so in one of the Contracting States.

ARTICLE 49

No legalisation or other similar formality shall be required in respect of the documents referred to in Article 46 or 47 or the second paragraph of Article 48, or in respect of a document appointing a representative *ad litem.*

TITLE IV

AUTHENTIC INSTRUMENTS AND COURT SETTLEMENTS

ARTICLE 50

A document which has been formally drawn up or registered as an authentic instrument and is enforceable in one Contracting State shall, in another Contracting State, be declared enforceable there, on application made in accordance with the procedures provided for in Articles 31 *et seq.* The application may be refused only if enforcement of the instrument is contrary to public policy in the State addressed.

The instrument produced must satisfy the conditions necessary to establish its authenticity in the State of origin.

The provisions of Section 3 of Title III shall apply as appropriate.

ARTICLE 51

A settlement which has been approved by a court in the course of proceedings and is enforceable in the State in which it was concluded shall be enforceable in the State addressed under the same conditions as authentic instruments.

TITLE V

GENERAL PROVISIONS

ARTICLE 52

In order to determine whether a party is domiciled in the Contracting State whose courts are seised of a matter, the court shall apply its internal law.

If a party is not domiciled in the State whose courts are seised of the matter, then, in order to determine whether the party is domiciled in another Contracting State, the court shall apply the law of that State.

ARTICLE 53

For the purposes of this Convention, the seat of a company or other legal person or association of natural or legal persons shall be treated as its domicile. However, in order to determine that seat, the court shall apply its rules of private international law.

In order to determine whether a trust is domiciled in the Contracting State whose courts are seised of the matter, the court shall apply its rules of private international law.

TITLE VI

TRANSITIONAL PROVISIONS

ARTICLE 54

The provisions of this Convention shall apply only to legal proceedings instituted and to documents formally drawn up or registered as authentic instruments after its entry into force in the State of origin and, where recognition or enforcement of a judgment or authentic instrument is sought, in the State addressed.

However, judgments given after the date of entry into force of this Convention between the State of origin and the State addressed in proceedings instituted before that date shall be recognised and enforced in accordance with the provisions of Title III if jurisdiction was founded upon rules which accorded with those provided for either in Title II of this Convention or in a convention concluded between the State of origin and the State addressed which was in force when the proceedings were instituted.

If the parties to a dispute concerning a contract had agreed in writing before the entry into force of this Convention that the contract was to be governed by the law of Ireland or of a part of the United Kingdom, the courts of Ireland or of that part of the United Kingdom shall retain the right to exercise jurisdiction in the dispute.

ARTICLE 54A

For a period of three years from the entry into force of this Convention for Denmark, Greece, Ireland, Iceland, Norway, Finland and Sweden, respectively, jurisdiction in maritime matters shall be determined in these States not only in accordance with the provisions of Title II, but also in accordance with the provisions of paragraphs 1 to 7 following. However, upon the entry into force of the International Convention relating to the arrest of sea-going ships, signed at Brussels on 10 May 1952, for one of these States, these provisions shall cease to have effect for that State.

(1) A person who is domiciled in a Contracting State may be sued in the courts of one of the States mentioned above in respect of a maritime claim if the ship to which the claim relates or any other ship owned by him has been arrested by judicial process within the territory of the latter State to secure the claim, or could have been so arrested there but bail or other security has been given, and either:
   (a) the claimant is domiciled in the latter State; or
   (b) the claim arose in the latter State; or
   (c) the claim concerns the voyage during which the arrest was made or could have been made; or
   (d) the claim arises out of a collision or out of damage caused by a ship to another ship or to goods or persons on board either ship, either by the execution or non-execution of a manoeuvre or by the non-observance of regulations; or
   (e) the claim is for salvage; or
   (f) the claim is in respect of a mortgage or hypothecation of the ship arrested.
(2) A claimant may arrest either the particular ship to which the maritime claim relates, or any other ship which is owned by the person who was, at the time when the maritime claim arose, the owner of the particular ship. However, only the particular ship to which the maritime claim relates may be arrested in respect of the maritime claims set out in 5(o), (p) or (q) of this Article.
(3) Ships shall be deemed to be in the same ownership when all the shares therein are owned by the same person or persons.
(4) When in the case of a charter by demise of a ship the charterer alone is liable in respect of a maritime claim relating to that ship, the claimant may arrest that ship or any other ship owned by the charterer, but no other ship owned by the owner may be arrested in respect of such claim. The same shall apply to any case in which a person other than the owner of a ship is liable in respect of a maritime claim relating to that ship.
(5) The expression 'maritime claim' means a claim arising out of one or more of the following:
   (a) damage caused by any ship either in collision or otherwise;
   (b) loss of life or personal injury caused by any ship or occurring in connection with the operation of any ship;
   (c) salvage;

- (d) agreement relating to the use or hire of any ship whether by charterparty or otherwise;
- (e) agreement relating to the carriage of goods in any ship whether by charterparty or otherwise;
- (f) loss of or damage to goods including baggage carried in any ship;
- (g) general average;
- (h) bottomry;
- (i) towage;
- (j) pilotage;
- (k) goods or materials wherever supplied to a ship for her operation or maintenance;
- (l) construction, repair or equipment of any ship or dock charges and dues;
- (m) wages of masters, officers or crew;
- (n) master's disbursements, including disbursements made by shippers, charterers or agents on behalf of a ship or her owner;
- (o) dispute as to the title to or ownership of any ship;
- (p) disputes between co-owners of any ship as to the ownership, possession, employment or earnings of that ship;
- (q) the mortgage or hypothecation of any ship.
- (6) In Denmark, the expression 'arrest' shall be deemed, as regards the maritime claims referred to in 5(o) and (p) of this Article, to include a 'forbud', where that is the only procedure allowed in respect of such a claim under Articles 646 to 653 of the law on civil procedure (lov om rettens pleje).
- (7) In Iceland, the expression 'arrest' shall be deemed, as regards the maritime claims referred to in 5(o) and (p) of this Article, to include a 'lögbann', where that is the only procedure allowed in respect of such a claim under Chapter III of the law on arrest and injunction (lög um kyrrsetningu og lögbann).

TITLE VII

RELATIONSHIP TO THE BRUSSELS CONVENTION AND TO OTHER CONVENTIONS

ARTICLE 54B

(1) This Convention shall not prejudice the application by the Member States of the European Communities of the Convention on Jurisdiction and the Enforcement of Judgments in Civil and Commercial Matters, signed at Brussels on 27 September 1968 and of the Protocol on interpretation of that Convention by the Court of Justice, signed at Luxembourg on 3 June 1971, as amended by the Conventions of Accession to the said Convention and the said Protocol by the States acceding to the European Communities, all of these Conventions and the Protocol being hereinafter referred to as the 'Brussels Convention'.

(2) However, this Convention shall in any event be applied:

- (a) in matters of jurisdiction, where the defendant is domiciled in the territory of a Contracting State which is not a member of the European Communities, or where Article 16 or 17 of this Convention confers a jurisdiction on the courts of such a Contracting State;
- (b) in relation to a *lis pendens* or to related actions as provided for in Articles 21 and 22, when proceedings are instituted in a Contracting State which is not a member of the European Communities and in a Contracting State which is a member of the European Communities;
- (c) in matters of recognition and enforcement, where either the State of origin or the State addressed is not a member of the European Communities.

(3) In addition to the grounds provided for in Title III recognition or enforcement may be refused if the ground of jurisdiction on which the judgment has been based differs from that resulting from this Convention and recognition or enforcement is

sought against a party who is domiciled in a Contracting State which is not a member of the European Communities, unless the judgment may otherwise be recognised or enforced under any rule of law in the State addressed.

ARTICLE 55

Subject to the provisions of the second paragraph of Article 54 and of Article 56, this Convention shall, for the States which are parties to it, supersede the following conventions concluded between two or more of them:

—the Convention between the Swiss Confederation and France on jurisdiction and enforcement of judgments in civil matters, signed at Paris on 15 June 1869,

—the Treaty between the Swiss Confederation and Spain on the mutual enforcement of judgments in civil or commercial matters, signed at Madrid on 19 November 1896,

—the Convention between the Swiss Confederation and the German Reich on the recognition and enforcement of judgments and arbitration awards, signed at Berne on 2 November 1929,

—the Convention between Denmark, Finland, Iceland, Norway and Sweden on the recognition and enforcement of judgments, signed at Copenhagen on 16 March 1932,

—the Convention between the Swiss Confederation and Italy on the recognition and enforcement of judgments, signed at Rome on 3 January 1933,

—the Convention between Sweden and the Swiss Confederation on the recognition and enforcement of judgments and arbitral awards, signed at Stockholm on 15 January 1936,

—the Convention between the Kingdom of Belgium and Austria on the reciprocal recognition and enforcement of judgments and authentic instruments relating to maintenance obligations, signed at Vienna on 25 October 1957.

—the Convention between the Swiss Confederation and Belgium on the recognition and enforcement of judgments and arbitration awards, signed at Berne on 29 April 1959,

—the Convention between the Federal Republic of Germany and Austria on the reciprocal recognition and enforcement of judgments, settlements and authentic instruments in civil and commercial matters, signed at Vienna on 6 June 1959,

—the Convention between the Kingdom of Belgium and Austria on the reciprocal recognition and enforcement of judgments, arbitral awards and authentic instruments in civil and commercial matters, signed at Vienna on 16 June 1959,

—the Convention between Austria and the Swiss Confederation on the recognition and enforcement of judgments, signed at Berne on 16 December 1960,

—the Convention between Norway and the United Kingdom providing for the reciprocal recognition and enforcement of judgments in civil matters, signed at London on 12 June 1961,

—the Convention between the United Kingdom and Austria providing for the reciprocal recognition and enforcement of judgments in civil and commercial matters, signed at Vienna on 14 July 1961, with amending Protocol signed at London on 6 March 1970,

—the Convention between the Kingdom of the Netherlands and Austria on the reciprocal recognition and enforcement of judgments and authentic instruments in civil and commercial matters, signed at The Hague on 6 February 1963,

—the Convention between France and Austria on the recognition and enforcement of judgments and authentic instruments in civil and commercial matters, signed at Vienna on 15 July 1966,

—the Convention between Luxembourg and Austria on the recognition and enforcement of judgments and authentic instruments in civil and commercial matters, signed at Luxembourg on 29 July 1971,

—the Convention between Italy and Austria on the recognition and enforcement of judgments in civil and commercial matters, of judicial settlements and of authentic instruments, signed at Rome on 16 November 1971,

—the Convention between Norway and the Federal Republic of Germany on the recognition and enforcement of judgments and enforceable documents, in civil and commercial matters, signed at Oslo on 17 June 1977,

—the Convention between Denmark, Finland, Iceland, Norway and Sweden on the recognition and enforcement of judgments in civil matters, signed at Copenhagen on 11 October 1977,

—the Convention between Austria and Sweden on the recognition and enforcement of judgments in civil matters, signed at Stockholm on 16 September 1982,

—the Convention between Austria and Spain on the recognition and enforcement of judgments, settlements and enforceable authentic instruments in civil and commercial matters, signed at Vienna on 17 February 1984,

—the Convention between Norway and Austria on the recognition and enforcement of judgments in civil matters, signed at Vienna on 21 May 1984, and

—the Convention between Finland and Austria on the recognition and enforcement of judgments in civil matters, signed at Vienna on 17 November 1986.

ARTICLE 56

The Treaty and the conventions referred to in Article 55 shall continue to have effect in relation to matters to which this Convention does not apply.

They shall continue to have effect in respect of judgments given and documents formally drawn up or registered as authentic instruments before the entry into force of this Convention.

ARTICLE 57

(1) This Convention shall not affect any conventions to which the Contracting States are or will be parties and which, in relation to particular matters, govern jurisdiction or the recognition or enforcement of judgments.

(2) This Convention shall not prevent a court of a Contracting State which is party to a convention referred to in the first paragraph from assuming jurisdiction in accordance with that convention, even where the defendant is domiciled in a Contracting State which is not a party to that convention. The court hearing the action shall, in any event, apply Article 20 of this Convention.

(3) Judgments given in a Contracting State by a court in the exercise of jurisdiction provided for in a convention referred to in the first paragraph shall be recognised and enforced in the other Contracting States in accordance with Title III of this Convention.

(4) In addition to the grounds provided for in Title III, recognition or enforcement may be refused if the State addressed is not a contracting party to a convention referred to in the first paragraph and the person against whom recognition or enforcement is sought is domiciled in that State, unless the judgment may otherwise be recognised or enforced under any rule of law in the State addressed.

(5) Where a convention referred to in the first paragraph to which both the State of origin and the State addressed are parties lays down conditions for the recognition or enforcement of judgments, those conditions shall apply. In any event, the provisions of this Convention which concern the procedures for recognition and enforcement of judgments may be applied.

ARTICLE 58

(None)

ARTICLE 59

This Convention shall not prevent a Contracting State from assuming, in a convention on the recognition and enforcement of judgments, an obligation towards a third State not to recognise judgments given in other Contracting States against defendants domiciled or habitually resident in the third State where, in cases provided for in Article 4, the judgment could only be founded on a ground of jurisdiction specified in the second paragraph of Article 3.

However, a Contracting State may not assume an obligation towards a third State not to recognise a judgment given in another Contracting State by a court basing its jurisdiction on the presence within that State of property belonging to the defendant, or the seizure by the plaintiff of property situated there:

(1) if the action is brought to assert or declare proprietary or possessory rights in that property, seeks to obtain authority to dispose of it, or arises from another issue relating to such property, or

(2) if the property constitutes the security for a debt which is the subject-matter of the action.

TITLE VIII

FINAL PROVISIONS

ARTICLE 60

The following may be parties to this Convention:

(a) States which, at the time of the opening of this Convention for signature, are members of the European Communities or of the European Free Trade Association;

(b) States which, after the opening of this Convention for signature, become members of the European Communities or of the European Free Trade Association;

(c) States invited to accede in accordance with Article 62(1)(b).

ARTICLE 61

(1) This Convention shall be opened for signature by the States members of the European Communities or of the European Free Trade Association.

(2) The Convention shall be submitted for ratification by the signatory States. The instruments of ratification shall be deposited with the Swiss Federal Council.

(3) The Convention shall enter into force on the first day of the third month following the date on which two States, of which one is a member of the European Communities and the other a member of the European Free Trade Association, deposit their instruments of ratification.

(4) The Convention shall take effect in relation to any other signatory State on the first day of the third month following the deposit of its instrument of ratification.

ARTICLE 62

(1) After entering into force this Convention shall be open to accession by:

(a) the States referred to in Article 60(b);

(b) other States which have been invited to accede upon a request made by one of the Contracting States to the depositary State. The depositary State shall invite the State concerned to accede only if, after having communicated the contents of the communications that this State intends to make in accordance with Article 63, it has obtained the unanimous agreement of the signatory States and the Contracting States referred to in Article 60(a) and (b).

(2) If an acceding State wishes to furnish details for the purposes of Protocol No 1, negotiations shall be entered into to that end. A negotiating conference shall be convened by the Swiss Federal Council.

(3) In respect of an acceding State, the Convention shall take effect on the first day of the third month following the deposit of its instrument of accession.

(4) However, in respect of an acceding State referred to in paragraph 1(a) or (b), the Convention shall take effect only in relations between the acceding State and the Contracting States which have not made any objections to the accession before the first day of the third month following the deposit of the instrument of accession.

ARTICLE 63

Each acceding State shall, when depositing its instrument of accession, communicate the information required for the application of Articles 3, 32, 37, 40, 41 and 55 of this Convention and furnish, if need be, the details prescribed during the negotiations for the purposes of Protocol No 1.

ARTICLE 64

(1) This Convention is concluded for an initial period of five years from the date of its entry into force in accordance with Article 61(3), even in the case of States which ratify it or accede to it after that date.

(2) At the end of the initial five-year period, the Convention shall be automatically renewed from year to year.

(3) Upon the expiry of the initial five-year period, any Contracting State may, at any time, denounce the Convention by sending a notification to the Swiss Federal Council.

(4) The denunciation shall take effect at the end of the calendar year following the expiry of a period of six months from the date of receipt by the Swiss Federal Council of the notification of denunciation.

ARTICLE 65

The following are annexed to this Convention:
—a Protocol No 1, on certain questions of jurisdiction, procedure and enforcement,
—a Protocol No 2, on the uniform interpretation of the Convention,
—a Protocol No 3, on the application of Article 57.
These Protocols shall form an integral part of the Convention.

ARTICLE 66

Any Contracting State may request the revision of this Convention. To that end, the Swiss Federal Council shall issue invitations to a revision conference within a period of six months from the date of the request for revision.

ARTICLE 67

The Swiss Federal Council shall notify the States represented at the Diplomatic Conference of Lugano and the States who have later acceded to the Convention of:
   (a) the deposit of each instrument of ratification or accession;
   (b) the dates of entry into force of this Convention in respect of the Contracting States;
   (c) any denunciation received pursuant to Article 64;
   (d) any declaration received pursuant to Article IA of Protocol No 1;
   (e) any declaration received pursuant to Article IB of Protocol No 1;
   (f) any declaration received pursuant to Article IV of Protocol No 1;
   (g) any communication made pursuant to Article VI of Protocol No 1.

ARTICLE 68

This Convention, drawn up in a single original in the Danish, Dutch, English, Finnish, French, German, Greek, Icelandic, Irish, Italian, Norwegian, Portuguese,

Spanish and Swedish languages, all fourteen texts being equally authentic, shall be deposited in the archives of the Swiss Federal Council. The Swiss Federal Council shall transmit a certified copy to the Government of each State represented at the Diplomatic Conference of Lugano and to the Government of each acceding State.

Protocol No 1

On Certain Questions of Jurisdiction, Procedure and Enforcement

The High Contracting Parties have agreed upon the following provisions, which shall be annexed to the Convention:

ARTICLE I

Any person domiciled in Luxembourg who is sued in a court of another Contracting State pursuant to Article 5(1) may refuse to submit to the jurisdiction of that court. If the defendant does not enter an appearance the court shall declare of its own motion that it has no jurisdiction.

An agreement conferring jurisdiction, within the meaning of Article 17, shall be valid with respect to a person domiciled in Luxembourg only if that person has expressly and specifically so agreed.

ARTICLE IA

(1) Switzerland reserves the right to declare, at the time of depositing its instrument of ratification, that a judgment given in another Contracting State shall be neither recognised nor enforced in Switzerland if the following conditions are met:
  (a) the jurisdiction of the court which has given the judgment is based only on Article 5(1) of this Convention; and
  (b) the defendant was domiciled in Switzerland at the time of the introduction of the proceedings; for the purposes of this Article, a company or other legal person is considered to be domiciled in Switzerland if it has its registered seat and the effective centre of activities in Switzerland; and
  (c) the defendant raises an objection to the recognition or enforcement of the judgment in Switzerland, provided that he has not waived the benefit of the declaration foreseen under this paragraph.

(2) This reservation shall not apply to the extent that at the time recognition or enforcement is sought a derogation has been granted from Article 59 of the Swiss Federal Constitution. The Swiss Government shall communicate such derogations to the signatory States and the acceding States.

(3) This reservation shall cease to have effect on 31 December 1999. It may be withdrawn at any time.

ARTICLE IB

Any Contracting State may, by declaration made at the time of signing or of deposit of its instrument of ratification or of accession, reserve the right, notwithstanding the provisions of Article 28, not to recognise and enforce judgments given in the other Contracting States if the jurisdiction of the court of the State of origin is based, pursuant to Article 16(1)(b), exclusively on the domicile of the defendant in the State of origin, and the property is situated in the territory of the State which entered the reservation.

ARTICLE II

Without prejudice to any more favourable provisions of national laws, persons domiciled in a Contracting State who are being prosecuted in the criminal courts of another Contracting State of which they are not nationals for an offence which was not intentionally committed may be defended by persons qualified to do so, even if they do not appear in person.

However, the court seised of the matter may order appearance in person; in the case of failure to appear, a judgment given in the civil action without the person concerned having had the opportunity to arrange for his defence need not be recognised or enforced in the other Contracting States.

ARTICLE III

In proceedings for the issue of an order for enforcement, no charge, duty or fee calculated by reference to the value of the matter in issue may be levied in the State in which enforcement is sought.

ARTICLE IV

Judicial and extrajudicial documents drawn up in one Contracting State which have to be served on persons in another Contracting State shall be transmitted in accordance with the procedures laid down in the conventions and agreements concluded between the Contracting States.

Unless the State in which service is to take place objects by declaration to the Swiss Federal Council, such documents may also be sent by the appropriate public officers of the State in which the document has been drawn up directly to the appropriate public officers of the State in which the addressee is to be found. In this case the officer of the State of origin shall send a copy of the document to the officer of the State applied to who is competent to forward it to the addressee. The document shall be forwarded in the manner specified by the law of the State applied to. The forwarding shall be recorded by a certificate sent directly to the officer of the State of origin.

ARTICLE V

The jurisdiction specified in Articles 6(2) and 10 in actions on a warranty or guarantee or in any other third party proceedings may not be resorted to in the Federal Republic of Germany, in Spain, in Austria and in Switzerland. Any person domiciled in another Contracting State may be sued in the courts:
— of the Federal Republic of Germany, pursuant to Articles 68, 72, 73 and 74 of the code of civil procedure (Zivilprozeßordnung) concerning third-party notices,
— of Spain, pursuant to Article 1482 of the civil code,
— of Austria, pursuant to Article 21 of the code of civil procedure (Zivil-prozeßordnung) concerning third-party notices,
— of Switzerland, pursuant to the appropriate provisions concerning third-party notices of the cantonal codes of civil procedure.

Judgments given in the other Contracting States by virtue of Article 6(2) or Article 10 shall be recognised and enforced in the Federal Republic of Germany, in Spain, in Austria and in Switzerland in accordance with Title III. Any effects which judgments given in these States may have on third parties by application of the provisions in the preceding paragraph shall also be recognised in the other Contracting States.

ARTICLE VA

In matters relating to maintenance, the expression 'court' includes the Danish, Icelandic and Norwegian administrative authorities.

In civil and commercial matters, the expression 'court' includes the Finnish ulosotonhaltija/överexekutor.

ARTICLE VB

In proceedings involving a dispute between the master and a member of the crew of a sea-going ship registered in Denmark, in Greece, in Ireland, in Iceland, in

Norway, in Portugal or in Sweden concerning remuneration or other conditions of service, a court in a Contracting State shall establish whether the diplomatic or consular officer responsible for the ship has been notified of the dispute. It shall stay the proceedings so long as he has not been notified. It shall of its own motion decline jurisdiction if the officer, having been duly notified, has exercised the powers accorded to him in the matter by a consular convention, or in the absence of such a convention has, within the time allowed, raised any objection to the exercise of such jurisdiction.

ARTICLE VC

(None)

ARTICLE VD

Without prejudice to the jurisdiction of the European Patent Office under the Convention on the grant of European patents, signed at Munich on 5 October 1973, the courts of each Contracting State shall have exclusive jurisdiction, regardless of domicile, in proceedings concerned with the registration or validity of any European patent granted for that State which is not a Community patent by virtue of the provision of Article 86 of the Convention for the European patent for the common market, signed at Luxembourg on 15 December 1975.

ARTICLE VI

The Contracting States shall communicate to the Swiss Federal Council the text of any provisions of their laws which amend either those provisions of their laws mentioned in the Convention or the lists of courts specified in Section 2 of Title III.

Protocol No 2
On the Uniform Interpretation of the Convention

PREAMBLE

The High Contracting Parties,
Having regard to Article 65 of this Convention,
Considering the substantial link between this Convention and the Brussels Convention,
Considering that the Court of Justice of the European Communities by virtue of the Protocol of 3 June 1971 has jurisdiction to give rulings on the interpretation of the provisions of the Brussels Convention,
Being aware of the rulings delivered by the Court of Justice of the European Communities on the interpretation of the Brussels Convention up to the time of signature of this Convention,
Considering that the negotiations which led to the conclusion of the Convention were based on the Brussels Convention in the light of these rulings,
Desiring to prevent, in full deference to the independence of the courts, divergent interpretations and to arrive at as uniform an interpretation as possible of the provisions of the Convention, and of these provisions and those of the Brussels Convention which are substantially reproduced in this Convention,
Have agreed as follows:

ARTICLE 1

The courts of each Contracting State shall, when applying and interpreting the provisions of the Convention, pay due account to the principles laid down by any relevant decision delivered by courts of the other Contracting States concerning provisions of this Convention.

ARTICLE 2

(1) The Contracting Parties agree to set up a system of exchange of information concerning judgments delivered pursuant to this Convention as well as relevant judgments under the Brussels Convention. This system shall comprise:
—transmission to a central body by the competent authorities of judgments delivered by courts of last instance and the Court of Justice of the European Communities as well as judgments of particular importance which have become final and have been delivered pursuant to this Convention or the Brussels Convention,
—classification of these judgments by the central body including, as far as necessary, the drawing-up and publication of translations and abstracts,
—communication by the central body of the relevant documents to the competent national authorities of all signatories and acceding States to the Convention and to the Commission of the European Communities.
(2) The central body is the Registrar of the Court of Justice of the European Communities.

ARTICLE 3

(1) A Standing Committee shall be set up for the purposes of this Protocol.
(2) The Committee shall be composed of representatives appointed by each signatory and acceding State.
(3) The European Communities (Commission, Court of Justice and General Secretariat of the Council) and the European Free Trade Association may attend the meetings as observers.

ARTICLE 4

(1) At the request of a Contracting party, the depositary of the Convention shall convene meetings of the Committee for the purpose of exchanging views on the functioning of the Convention and in particular on:
—the development of the case-law as communicated under the first paragraph first indent of Article 2,
—the application of Article 57 of the Convention.
(2) The Committee, in the light of these exchanges, may also examine the appropriateness of starting on particular topics a revision of the Convention and make recommendations.

Protocol No 3

On the Application of Article 57

The High Contracting Parties have agreed as follows:
(1) For the purposes of the Convention, provisions which, in relation to particular matters, govern jurisdiction or the recognition or enforcement of judgments and which are, or will be, contained in acts of the institutions of the European Communities shall be treated in the same way as the conventions referred to in paragraph 1 of Article 57.
(2) If one Contracting State is of the opinion that a provision contained in an act of the institutions of the European Communities is incompatible with the Convention, the Contracting States shall promptly consider amending the Convention pursuant to Article 66, without prejudice to the procedure established by Protocol No 2.'

SCHEDULE 2   Section 3

OTHER AMENDMENTS OF THE 1982 ACT

(1) The words 'Brussels Conventions' shall be substituted for the word 'Conventions' wherever occurring in section 2 (the Conventions to have the force of law) and section 3 (interpretation of the Conventions).

(2) In section 4(1) (enforcement of judgments other than maintenance orders) and section 5(1) (recognition and enforcement of maintenance orders) after the words 'an application under Article 31' there shall be inserted the words 'of the 1968 Convention or of the Lugano Convention'.

(3) In section 6 (appeals under Article 37, second paragraph and Article 41)—

(a) in subsection (1), after the words 'referred to' there shall be inserted the words 'in the 1968 Convention and the Lugano Convention'; and

(b) in subsection (3), after the words 'referred to' there shall be inserted the words 'in each of those Conventions'.

(4) In section 9 (provisions supplementary to Title VII of the 1968 Convention) in subsection (1)—

(a) after the words 'Title VII of the 1968 Convention' there shall be inserted the words 'and, apart from Article 54B, of Title VII of the Lugano Convention'; and

(b) for the words 'that convention' there shall be substituted the words 'the Convention in question'.

(5) In section 10 (allocation within UK of jurisdiction in proceedings with respect to trusts and consumer contracts in respect of which the 1968 Convention confers jurisdiction on UK courts generally) in subsection (1), after the words 'the 1968 Convention' there shall be inserted the words 'or the Lugano Convention'.

(6) In section 11 (proof and admissibility of certain judgments and related documents for the purposes of the 1968 Convention) in subsection (1), after the words 'For the purposes of the 1968 Convention' there shall be inserted the words 'and the Lugano Convention'.

(7) In section 12 (provision for issue of copies of, and certificates in connection with, UK judgments for purposes of the 1968 Convention) after the words 'the 1968 Convention' there shall be inserted the words 'or the Lugano Convention'.

(8) In section 13 (modifications to cover authentic instruments and court settlements) in subsection (1)—

(a) after the words 'the 1968 Convention' in paragraph (a) there shall be inserted the words 'or the Lugano Convention';

(b) after the words 'Title IV of the 1968 Convention' there shall be inserted the words 'or, as the case may be, Title IV of the Lugano Convention'; and

(c) for the words 'that Convention' there shall be substituted the words 'the Convention in question'.

(9) In section 14 (modifications consequential on revision of the Conventions)—

(a) for the words 'any of the Conventions', wherever occurring in subsections (1) and (3), there shall be substituted the words 'the Lugano Convention or any of the Brussels Conventions'; and

(b) in subsection (1), after the words 'any revision connected with the accession to' there shall be inserted the words 'the Lugano Convention or'.

(10) In section 15 (interpretation of Part I)—

(a) in subsection (1), in the definition of 'maintenance order', after the words 'maintenance judgment within the meaning of the 1968 Convention' there shall be inserted the words 'or, as the case may be, the Lugano Convention'; and

(b) in subsection (3), after the words 'authorised or required by the 1968 Convention' there shall be inserted the words 'the Lugano Convention'.

(11) In section 16 (allocation within UK of jurisdiction in certain civil proceedings)—

(a) in paragraph (a) of subsection (1), for the words 'the Convention' there shall be substituted the words 'that or any other Convention';

(b) in paragraph (b) of that subsection, after the words 'Article 16' there shall be inserted the words 'of the 1968 Convention'; and

(c) in subsection (4), after the words 'subject to the 1968 Convention' there shall be inserted the words 'and the Lugano Convention'.

(12) The words 'Brussels or Lugano Contracting State' shall be substituted for the words 'Contracting State' wherever occurring in each of the following provisions, that is to say—

(a) in subsections (1)(a) and (3)(a) of section 25 (interim relief in England and Wales or Northern Ireland in the absence of substantive proceedings);

(b) in subsections (2)(a) and (3)(a) and (d) of section 27 (which makes for Scotland similar provision to that made by section 25 for England and Wales); and

(c) in section 28 (application of section 1 of the Administration of Justice (Scotland) Act 1972);

and, in section 25(1)(b), for the words 'the Convention' there shall be substituted the words 'that or any other Convention'.

(13) In section 30 (proceedings in England and Wales or Northern Ireland for torts to immovable property) in subsection (2), after the words 'subject to the 1968 Convention' there shall be inserted the words 'and the Lugano Convention'.

(14) In section 32 (overseas judgments given in proceedings brought in breach of agreement for settlement of disputes) in subsection (4) (saving for judgments required to be recognised or enforced in UK under the 1968 Convention etc) in paragraph (a), after the words 'under the 1968 Convention' there shall be inserted the words 'or the Lugano Convention'.

(15) In section 33 (certain steps not to amount to submission to the jurisdiction of an overseas court) in subsection (2) (saving for judgments required to be recognised or enforced in England and Wales or Northern Ireland under the 1968 Convention) after the words 'under the 1968 Convention' there shall be inserted the words 'or the Lugano Convention'.

(16) In section 41 (determination of domicile of individuals for the purposes of the 1968 Convention etc) in subsection (1), after the words 'for the purposes of the 1968 Convention' there shall be inserted the words 'the Lugano Convention'.

(17) In section 42 (domicile and seat of corporation or association) in subsection (2)(a), after the words 'for the purposes of the 1968 Convention' there shall be inserted the words 'or, as the case may be, the Lugano Convention'.

(18) In section 43 (seat of corporation or association for purposes of Article 16(2) and related provisions) in subsection (1)(a), after the words 'Article 16(2)' there shall be inserted the words 'of the 1968 Convention or of the Lugano Convention'.

(19)—(1) In section 44 (persons deemed to be domiciled in UK for certain purposes) in subsection (1)—

(a) in paragraph (a) (which provides that the section applies to proceedings within Section 3 of Title II of the 1968 Convention) after the words 'the 1968 Convention' there shall be inserted the words 'or Section 3 of Title II of the Lugano Convention'; and

(b) in paragraph (b) (proceedings within Section 2 of that Title) for the words 'that Title' there shall be substituted the words 'Title II of either of those Conventions'.

(2) In subsection (2) of that section, after the words 'is deemed for the purposes of the 1968 Convention' there shall be inserted the words 'or, as the case may be, of the Lugano Convention'.

(20) In section 45 (domicile of trusts) in subsection (1), after the words 'for the purposes of the 1968 Convention' there shall be inserted the words 'the Lugano Convention'.

(21)—(1) In section 46 (domicile and seat of the Crown) in subsection (2)(a), after the words 'for the purposes of the 1968 Convention' there shall be inserted the words 'and the Lugano Convention' and for the words '(in which' there shall be substituted the words '(in each of which'.

(2) In subsection (4) of that section (Order in Council with respect to seat of the Crown) after the words 'for the purposes of the 1968 Convention' there shall be inserted the words 'the Lugano Convention'.

(22) In section 47 (modifications occasioned by decisions of the European Court as to meaning or effect of the Conventions) for the word 'Conventions', wherever occurring, there shall be substituted the words 'Brussels Conventions'.

(23) In section 48 (matters for which rules of court may provide)—

(a) in subsection (1), for the words 'or the Conventions' there shall be substituted the words 'the Lugano Convention or the Brussels Conventions'; and

(b) in subsection (3), for the words 'the Conventions' there shall be substituted the words 'the Lugano Convention, the Brussels Conventions'.

(24) In section 49 (saving for powers to stay, sist, strike out or dismiss proceedings where to do so is not inconsistent with the 1968 Convention) after the words 'the 1968 Convention' there shall be inserted the words 'or, as the case may be, the Lugano Convention'.

(25) In section 50 (general interpretation) the following definitions shall be inserted at the appropriate places—

' "Brussels Contracting State" has the meaning given by section 1(3)';
' "the Brussels Conventions" has the meaning given by section 1(1)';
' "Lugano Contracting State" has the meaning, given by section 1(3)';
' "the Lugano Convention" has the meaning given by section 1(1)';
and the entry relating to 'the Conventions' is hereby repealed.

MAINTENANCE ENFORCEMENT ACT 1991

(1991 c 17)

ARRANGEMENT OF SECTIONS

The High Court and county courts

An Act to make provision as to the methods of payment, and the variation of the methods of payment, under maintenance orders made by the High Court and county courts; to re-enact with modifications certain provisions relating to the making and variation of orders requiring money to be paid periodically; to make further provision as to the making, variation and enforcement by magistrates' courts of maintenance orders; to make further provision about proceedings by clerks of magistrates' courts in relation to arrears under certain orders requiring money to be paid periodically; to make further provision as to maintenance orders registered in, or confirmed by, magistrates' courts or registered in the High Court, to extend the power to make attachment of earnings orders in the case of maintenance orders; to amend section 10 of the Courts and Legal Services Act 1990; and for connected purposes. [27 June 1991]

The High Court and county courts

1. Maintenance orders in the High Court and county courts: means of payment, attachment of earnings and revocation, variation, etc—(1) Where the High Court or a county court makes a qualifying periodical maintenance order, it may at the same time exercise either of its powers under subsection (4) below in relation to the order, whether of its own motion or on an application made under this subsection by an interested party.

(2) For the purposes of this section, a periodical maintenance order is an order—

(a) which requires money to be paid periodically by one person ('the debtor') to another ('the creditor'); and

(b) which is a maintenance order;

and such an order is a 'qualifying periodical maintenance order' if, at the time it is made, the debtor is ordinarily resident in England and Wales.

(3) Where the High Court or a county court has made a qualifying periodical maintenance order, it may at any later time—

(a) on an application made under this subsection by an interested party, or

(b) of its own motion, in the course of any proceedings concerning the order,

exercise either of its powers under subsection (4) below in relation to the order.

(4) The powers mentioned in subsections (1) and (3) above are—

(a) the power to order that payments required to be made by the debtor to the creditor under the qualifying periodical maintenance order in question shall be so made by such a method of payment falling within subsection (5) below as the court may specify in the particular case; or

(b) the power, by virtue of this section, to make an attachment of earnings order under the Attachment of Earnings Act 1971 to secure payments under the qualifying periodical maintenance order in question.

(5) The methods of payment mentioned in subsection (4)(a) above are—

(a) payment by standing order; or

(b) payment by any other method which requires the debtor to give his authority for payments of a specific amount to be made from an account of his to an account of the creditor's on specific dates during the period for which the authority is in force and without the need for any further authority from the debtor.

(6) In any case where—

(a) the court proposes to exercise its power under paragraph (a) of subsection (4) above, and

(b) having given the debtor an opportunity of opening an account from which payments under the order may be made in accordance with the method of payment proposed to be ordered under that paragraph, the court is satisfied that the debtor has failed, without reasonable excuse, to open such an account,

the court in exercising its power under that paragraph may order that the debtor open such an account.

(7) Where in the exercise of its powers under subsection (1) or (3) above, the High Court or a county court has made in relation to a qualifying periodical maintenance order such an order as is mentioned in subsection (4)(a) above (a 'means of payment order'), it may at any later time—

(a) on an application made under this subsection by an interested party, or

(b) of its own motion, in the course of any proceedings concerning the qualifying periodical maintenance order,

revoke, suspend, revive or vary the means of payment order.

(8) In deciding whether to exercise any of its powers under this section the court in question having (if practicable) given every interested party an opportunity to make representations shall have regard to any representations made by any such party.

(9) Nothing in this section shall be taken to prejudice—

(a) any power under the Attachment of Earnings Act 1971 which would, apart from this section, be exercisable by the High Court or a county court; or

(b) any right of any person to make any application under that Act;

and subsection (7) above is without prejudice to any other power of the High Court or a county court to revoke, suspend, revive or vary an order.

(10) For the purposes of this section—

'debtor' and 'creditor' shall be construed in accordance with subsection (2) above;

'interested party' means any of the following, that is to say—

(a) the debtor;

(b) the creditor; and

(c) in a case where the person who applied for the qualifying periodical maintenance order in question is a person other than the creditor, that other person;

'maintenance order' means any order specified in Schedule 8 to the Administration of Justice Act 1970 and includes any such order which has been discharged, if any arrears are recoverable under it;

'qualifying periodical maintenance order' shall be construed in accordance with subsection (2) above, and the references to such an order in subsections (3) and (7) above are references to any such order, whether made before or after the coming into force of this section;

and the reference in subsection (2) above to an order requiring money to be paid periodically by one person to another includes a reference to an order requiring a lump sum to be paid by instalments by one person to another.

Magistrates' courts

2. Orders for periodical payment in magistrates' courts: means of payment.
For section 59 of the Magistrates' Courts Act 1980 (periodical payments through justices' clerk) there shall be substituted the following section—

'**59. Orders for periodical payment: means of payment**—(1) In any case where a magistrates' court orders money to be paid periodically by one person (in this section referred to as "the debtor") to another (in this section referred to as "the creditor"), then—

(a) if the order is a qualifying maintenance order, the court shall at the same time exercise one of its powers under paragraphs (a) to (d) of subsection (3) below;

(b) if the order is not a maintenance order, the court shall at the same time exercise one of its powers under paragraphs (a) and (b) of that subsection.

(2) For the purposes of this section a maintenance order is a "qualifying maintenance order" if, at the time it is made, the debtor is ordinarily resident in England and Wales.

(3) The powers of the court are—

(a) the power to order that payments under the order be made directly by the debtor to the creditor;

(b) the power to order that payments under the order be made to the clerk of the court or to the clerk of any other magistrates' court;

(c) the power to order that payments under the order be made by the debtor to the creditor by such method of payment falling within subsection (6) below as may be specified;

(d) the power to make an attachment of earnings order under the Attachment of Earnings Act 1971 to secure payments under the order.

(4) In any case where—

(a) the court proposes to exercise its power under paragraph (c) of subsection (3) above, and

(b) having given the debtor an opportunity of opening an account from which payments under the order may be made in accordance with the method of payment proposed to be ordered under that paragraph, the court is satisfied that the debtor has failed, without reasonable excuse, to open such an account,

the court in exercising its power under that paragraph may order that the debtor open such an account.

(5) In deciding, in the case of a maintenance order, which of the powers under paragraphs (a) to (d) of subsection (3) above it is to exercise, the court having (if practicable) given them an opportunity to make representations shall have regard to any representations made—

(a) by the debtor,

(b) by the creditor, and

(c) if the person who applied for the maintenance order is a person other than the creditor, by that other person.

(6) The methods of payment referred to in subsection (3)(c) above are the following, that is to say—

(a) payment by standing order; or

(b) payment by any other method which requires one person to give his authority for payments of a specific amount to be made from an account of his to an account of another's on specific dates during the period for which the authority is in force and without the need for any further authority from him.

(7) Where the maintenance order is an order—

(a) under the Guardianship of Minors Acts 1971 and 1973,

(b) under Part I of the Domestic Proceedings and Magistrates' Courts Act 1978, or

(c) under, or having effect as if made under, Schedule 1 to the Children Act 1989,

and the court does not propose to exercise its power under paragraph (c) or (d) of subsection (3) above, the court shall, unless upon representations expressly made in that behalf by the person who applied for the maintenance order it is satisfied that it is undesirable to do so, exercise its power under paragraph (b) of that subsection.

(8) The Secretary of State may by regulations confer on magistrates' courts, in addition to their powers under paragraphs (a) to (d) of subsection (3) above, the power (the "additional power") to order that payments under a qualifying maintenance order be made by the debtor to the creditor or the clerk of a magistrates' court (as the regulations may provide) by such method of payment as may be specified in the regulations.

(9) Any reference in any enactment to paragraphs (a) to (d) of subsection (3) above (but not a reference to any specific paragraph of that subsection) shall be taken to include a reference to the additional power, and the reference in subsection (10) below to the additional power shall be construed accordingly.

(10) Regulations under subsection (8) above may make provision for any enactment concerning, or connected with, payments under maintenance orders to apply, with or without modifications, in relation to the additional power.

(11) The power of the Secretary of State to make regulations under subsection (8) above shall be exercisable by statutory instrument and any such statutory instrument shall be subject to annulment in pursuance of a resolution of either House of Parliament.

(12) For the purposes of this section the reference in subsection (1) above to money paid periodically by one person to another includes, in the case of a maintenance order, a reference to a lump sum paid by instalments by one person to another.'

3. Orders for periodical payment in magistrates' courts: proceedings by clerk and penalty for breach. After section 59 of the Magistrates' Courts Act 1980 (orders for periodical payment: means of payment), as substituted by section 2 above, there shall be inserted the following sections—

'**59A. Orders for periodical payment: proceedings by clerk**—(1) Where payments under a relevant UK order are required to be made periodically—

(a) to or through the clerk of a magistrates' court, or

(b) by any method of payment falling within section 59(6) above,

and any sums payable under the order are in arrear, the clerk of the relevant court shall, if the person for whose benefit the payments are required to be made so requests in writing, and unless it appears to the clerk that it is unreasonable in the circumstances to do so, proceed in his own name for the recovery of those sums.

(2) Where payments under a relevant UK order are required to be made periodically to or through the clerk of a magistrates' court, the person for whose benefit the payments are required to be made may, at any time during the period in which the payments are required to be so made, give authority in writing to the clerk of the relevant court for the clerk to proceed as mentioned in subsection (3) below.

(3) Where authority under subsection (2) above is given to the clerk of the relevant court, the clerk shall, unless it appears to him that it is unreasonable in the circumstances to do so, proceed in his own name for the recovery of any sums payable to or through him under the order in question which, on or after the date of the giving of the authority, fall into arrear.

(4) In any case where—

(a) authority under subsection (2) above has been given to the clerk of a relevant court, and

(b) the person for whose benefit the payments are required to be made gives notice in writing to the clerk cancelling the authority,

the authority shall cease to have effect and, accordingly, the clerk shall not continue any proceedings already commenced by virtue of the authority.

(5) The person for whose benefit the payments are required to be made shall have the same liability for all the costs properly incurred in or about proceedings taken under subsection (1) above at his request or under subsection (3) above by virtue of his authority (including any costs incurred as a result of any proceedings commenced not being continued) as if the proceedings had been taken by him.

(6) Nothing in subsection (1) or (3) above shall affect any right of a person to proceed in his own name for the recovery of sums payable on his behalf under an order of any court.

(7) In this section—

"the relevant court", in relation to an order, means—

(a) in a case where payments under the order are required to be made to or through the clerk of a magistrates' court, that magistrates' court; and

(b) in a case where such payments are required to be made by any method of payment falling within section 59(6) above, the magistrates' court which made the order or, if the order was not made by a magistrates' court, the magistrates' court in which the order is registered;

"relevant UK order" means—

(a) an order made by a magistrates' court, other than an order made by virtue of Part II of the Maintenance Orders (Reciprocal Enforcement) Act 1972;

(b) an order made by the High Court or a county court (including an order deemed to be made by the High Court by virtue of section 1(2) of the Maintenance Orders Act 1958) and registered under Part I of that Act of 1958 in a magistrates' court; or

(c) an order made by a court in Scotland or Northern Ireland and registered under Part II of the Maintenance Orders Act 1950 in a magistrates' court;

and any reference to payments required to be made periodically includes, in the case of a maintenance order, a reference to instalments required to be paid in respect of a lump sum payable by instalments.

59B. Maintenance orders: penalty for breach—(1) In any case where—

(a) payments under a relevant English maintenance order are required to be made periodically in the manner mentioned in paragraph (a) or (b) of section 59A(1) above, and

(b) the debtor fails, on or after the date of commencement of this section, to comply with the order in so far as the order relates to the manner of payment concerned,

the person for whose benefit the payments are required to be made may make a complaint to a relevant justice giving details of the failure to comply.

(2) If the relevant justice is satisfied that the nature of the alleged failure to comply may be such as to justify the relevant court in exercising its power under subsection (3) below, he shall issue a summons directed to the debtor requiring him to appear before the relevant court to answer the complaint.

(3) On the hearing of the complaint, the relevant court may order the debtor to pay a sum not exceeding £1,000.

(4) Any sum ordered to be paid under subsection (3) above shall for the purposes of this Act be treated as adjudged to be paid by a conviction of a magistrates' court.

(5) In this section—

"debtor" has the same meaning as it has in section 59 above;

"the relevant court" has the same meaning as it has in section 59A above;

"relevant English maintenance order" means—

(a) a maintenance order made by a magistrates' court, other than an order made by virtue of Part II of the Maintenance Orders (Reciprocal Enforcement) Act 1972; or

(b) an order made by the High Court or a county court (other than an order deemed to be made by the High Court by virtue of section 1(2) of the Maintenance Orders Act 1958) and registered under Part I of that Act of 1958 in a magistrates' court;

"relevant justice", in relation to a relevant court, means a justice of the peace for the petty sessions area for which the relevant court is acting;

and any reference to payments required to be made periodically includes a reference to instalments required to be paid in respect of a lump sum payable by instalments.'

4. Revocation, variation, etc of orders for periodical payment in magistrates' courts: general.   For section 60 of the Magistrates' Courts Act 1980 (revocation, variation etc, of orders for periodical payment) there shall be substituted the following section—

'**60. Revocation, variation, etc of orders for periodical payment**—(1) Where a magistrates' court has made an order for money to be paid periodically by one person to another, the court may, by order on complaint, revoke, revive or vary the order.

(2) The power under subsection (1) above to vary an order shall include power to suspend the operation of any provision of the order temporarily and to revive the operation of any provision so suspended.

(3) Where the order mentioned in subsection (1) above is a maintenance order, the power under that subsection to vary the order shall include power, if the court is satisfied that payment has not been made in accordance with the order, to exercise one of its powers under paragraphs (a) to (d) of section 59(3) above.

(4) In any case where—

(a) a magistrates' court has made a maintenance order, and

(b) payments under the order are required to be made by any method of payment falling within section 59(6) above,

an interested party may apply in writing to the clerk of the court for the order to be varied as mentioned in subsection (5) below.

(5) Subject to subsection (8) below, where an application has been made under subsection (4) above, the clerk, after giving written notice (by post or otherwise) of the application to any other interested party and allowing that party, within the period of 14 days beginning with the date of the giving of that notice, an opportunity to make written representations, may vary the order to provide that payments under the order shall be made to the clerk.

(6) The clerk may proceed with an application under subsection (4) above notwithstanding that any such interested party as is referred to in subsection (5) above has not received written notice of the application.

(7) In subsections (4) to (6) above "interested party", in relation to a maintenance order, means—

(a) the debtor;

(b) the creditor; and

(c) if the person who applied for the maintenance order is a person other than the creditor, that other person.

(8) Where an application has been made under subsection (4) above, the clerk may, if he considers it inappropriate to exercise his power under subsection (5) above, refer the matter to the court which may vary the order by exercising one of its powers under paragraphs (a) to (d) of section 59(3) above.

(9) Subsections (4), (5) and (7) of section 59 above shall apply for the purposes of subsections (3) and (8) above as they apply for the purposes of that section.

(10) None of the powers of the court, or of the clerk of the court, conferred by subsections (3) to (9) above shall be exercisable in relation to a maintenance order which is not a qualifying maintenance order (within the meaning of section 59 above).

(11) For the purposes of this section—

(a) "creditor" and "debtor" have the same meaning as they have in section 59 above; and

(b) the reference in subsection (1) above to money paid periodically by one person to another includes, in the case of a maintenance order, a reference to a lump sum paid by instalments by one person to another.'

5. Variation of orders for periodical payment made under Part I of the Domestic Proceedings and Magistrates' Courts Act 1978.   After section 20 of the Domestic Proceedings and Magistrates' Courts Act 1978 (variation, revival and revocation of orders for periodical payments) there shall be inserted the following section—

'**20ZA. Variation of orders for periodical payments: further provisions—**
(1) Subject to subsections (7) and (8) below, the power of the court under section 20 of this Act to vary an order for the making of periodical payments shall include power, if the court is satisfied that payment has not been made in accordance with the order, to exercise one of its powers under paragraphs (a) to (d) of section 59(3) of the Magistrates' Courts Act 1980.
(2) In any case where—
(a) a magistrates' court has made an order under this Part of this Act for the making of periodical payments, and
(b) payments under the order are required to be made by any method of payment falling within section 59(6) of the Magistrates' Courts Act 1980 (standing order, etc),
an application may be made under this subsection to the clerk to the justices for the petty sessions area for which the court is acting for the order to be varied as mentioned in subsection (3) below.
(3) Subject to subsection (5) below, where an application is made under subsection (2) above, the clerk, after giving written notice (by post or otherwise) of the application to the respondent and allowing the respondent, within the period of 14 days beginning with the date of the giving of that notice, an opportunity to make written representations, may vary the order to provide that payments under the order shall be made to the clerk.
(4) The clerk may proceed with an application under subsection (2) above notwithstanding that the respondent has not received written notice of the application.
(5) Where an application has been made under subsection (2) above, the clerk may, if he considers it inappropriate to exercise his power under subsection (3) above, refer the matter to the court which, subject to subsections (7) and (8) below, may vary the order by exercising one of its powers under paragraphs (a) to (d) of section 59(3) of the Magistrates' Courts Act 1980.
(6) Subsection (4) of section 59 of the Magistrates' Courts Act 1980 (power of court to order that account be opened) shall apply for the purposes of subsections (1) and (5) above as it applies for the purposes of that section.
(7) Before varying the order by exercising one of its powers under paragraphs (a) to (d) of section 59(3) of the Magistrates' Courts Act 1980, the court shall have regard to any representations made by the parties to the application.
(8) If the court does not propose to exercise its power under paragraph (c) or (d) of subsection (3) of section 59 of the Magistrates' Courts Act 1980, the court shall, unless upon representations expressly made in that behalf by the person to whom payments under the order are required to be made it is satisfied that it is undesirable to do so, exercise its power under paragraph (b) of that subsection.
(9) Subsection (12) of section 20 of this Act shall have effect for the purposes of applications under subsection (2) above as it has effect for the purposes of applications under that section.
(10) None of the powers of the court, or of the clerk to the justices, conferred by this section shall be exercisable in relation to an order under this Part of this Act for the making of periodical payments which is not a qualifying maintenance order (within the meaning of section 59 of the Magistrates' Courts Act 1980).'

6. Variation of orders for periodical payment made in magistrates' courts under Schedule 1 to the Children Act 1989.   In Schedule 1 to the Children Act

1989 (financial provision for children), after paragraph 6 (variation etc of orders for periodical payments) there shall be inserted the following paragraph—

'Variation of orders for periodical payments etc made by magistrates' courts

6A.—(1) Subject to sub-paragraphs (7) and (8), the power of a magistrates' court—

(a) under paragraph 1 or 2 to vary an order for the making of periodical payments, or

(b) under paragraph 5(6) to vary an order for the payment of a lump sum by instalments,

shall include power, if the court is satisfied that payment has not been made in accordance with the order, to exercise one of its powers under paragraphs (a) to (d) of section 59(3) of the Magistrates' Courts Act 1980.

(2) In any case where—

(a) a magistrates' court has made an order under this Schedule for the making of a periodical payments or for the payment of a lump sum by instalments, and

(b) payments under the order are required to be made by any method of payment falling within section 59(6) of the Magistrates' Courts Act 1980 (standing order, etc),

any person entitled to make an application under this Schedule for the variation of the order (in this paragraph referred to as "the applicant") may apply to the clerk to the justices for the petty sessions area for which the court is acting for the order to be varied as mentioned in sub-paragraph (3).

(3) Subject to sub-paragraph (5), where an application is made under sub-paragraph (2), the clerk, after giving written notice (by post or otherwise) of the application to any interested party and allowing that party, within the period of 14 days beginning with the date of the giving of that notice, an opportunity to make written representations, may vary the order to provide that payments under the order shall be made to the clerk.

(4) The clerk may proceed with an application under sub-paragraph (2) notwithstanding that any such interested party as is referred to in sub-paragraph (3) has not received written notice of the application.

(5) Where an application has been made under sub-paragraph (2), the clerk may, if he considers it inappropriate to exercise his power under sub-paragraph (3), refer the matter to the court which, subject to sub-paragraphs (7) and (8), may vary the order by exercising one of its powers under paragraphs (a) to (d) of section 59(3) of the Magistrates' Courts Act 1980.

(6) Subsection (4) of section 59 of the Magistrates' Courts Act 1980 (power of court to order that account be opened) shall apply for the purposes of sub-paragraphs (1) and (5) as it applies for the purposes of that section.

(7) Before varying the order by exercising one of its powers under paragraphs (a) to (d) of section 59(3) of the Magistrates' Courts Act 1980, the court shall have regard to any representations made by the parties to the application.

(8) If the court does not propose to exercise its power *under paragraph (c) or (d)* [under paragraph (c), (cc) or (d)] of subsection (3) of section 59 of the Magistrates' Courts Act 1980, the court shall, unless upon representations expressly made in that behalf by the applicant for the order it is satisfied that it is undesirable to do so, exercise its power under paragraph (b) of that subsection.

Note. Words in square brackets substituted for words in italics by Child Support Act 1991 (Consequential Amendments) Order 1994, SI 1994 No 731, art 4, as from 11 April 1994.

(9) None of the powers of the court, or of the clerk to the justices, conferred by this paragraph shall be exercisable in relation to an order under this Schedule for the making of periodical payments, or for the payment of a lump sum by instalments, which is not a qualifying maintenance order (within the meaning of section 59 of the Magistrates' Courts Act 1980).

(10) In sub-paragraphs (3) and (4) "interested party", in relation to an application made by the applicant under sub-paragraph (2), means a person who would be entitled to be a party to an application for the variation of the order made by the applicant under any other provision of this Schedule if such an application were made.'

7. Maintenance orders in magistrates' courts: enforcement. In section 76 of the Magistrates' Courts Act 1980 (enforcement of sums adjudged to be paid), after subsection (3) there shall be inserted the following subsections—

'(4) Where proceedings are brought for the enforcement of a magistrates' court maintenance order under this section, the court may vary the order by exercising one of its powers under paragraphs (a) to (d) of section 59(3) above.

(5) Subsections (4), (5) and (7) of section 59 above shall apply for the purposes of subsection (4) above as they apply for the purposes of that section.

(6) Subsections (4) and (5) above shall not have effect in relation to a maintenance order which is not a qualifying maintenance order (within the meaning of section 59 above).'

8. Interest on arrears. After section 94 of the Magistrates' Courts Act 1980 (effect of committal on arrears) there shall be inserted the following section—

'**94A. Interest on arrears**—(1) The Secretary of State may by order provide that a magistrates' court, on the hearing of a complaint for the enforcement, revocation, revival, variation or discharge of an English maintenance order, may order that interest of an amount calculated at the prescribed rate shall be paid on so much of the sum due under the order as they may determine.

(2) In subsection (1) above "the prescribed rate" means such rate of interest as the Secretary of State may by order prescribe.

(3) An order under this section may make provision for the manner in which and the periods by reference to which interest is to be calculated.

(4) Where, by virtue of subsection (1) above, a magistrates' court orders the payment of interest on any sum due under a maintenance order—

(a) then if it orders that the whole or any part of the interest be paid by instalments that order shall be regarded as an instalments order for the purposes of section 95 below and that section shall accordingly apply in relation to it; and

(b) the whole of the interest shall be enforceable as a sum adjudged to be paid by the maintenance order.

(5) In this section—

"English maintenance order" means—

(a) a qualifying maintenance order made by a magistrates' court, other than an order made by virtue of Part II of the Maintenance Orders (Reciprocal Enforcement) Act 1972; or

(b) an order made by the High Court or a county court (other than an order deemed to be made by the High Court by virtue of section 1(2) of the Maintenance Orders Act 1958) and registered under Part I of that Act of 1958 in a magistrates' court;

"qualifying maintenance order" has the same meaning as it has in section 59 above.

(6) The power of the Secretary of State to make an order under this section shall be exercisable by statutory instrument made with the concurrence of the Treasury and any such statutory instrument shall be subject to annulment in pursuance of a resolution of either House of Parliament.'

9. Amendment of orders transferred under s 24A of the Social Security Act 1986—(1) *In section 24A of the Social Security Act 1986 (recovery of expenditure on income support: additional amounts and transfer of orders under s 24), after subsection (4) (transfer* *of right to receive payments under the order to the dependent parent) there shall be inserted the following subsection—*

'*(4A)   In any case where—*

(*a*)   *notice is given to a magistrates' court under subsection (3) above,*

(*b*)   *payments under the order are required to be made by any method of payment falling within section 59(6) of the Magistrates' Courts Act 1980 (standing order, etc), and*

(*c*)   *the clerk to the justices for the petty sessions area for which the court is acting decides that payment by that method is no longer possible,*

the clerk shall amend the order to provide that payments under the order shall be made by the liable parent to the clerk.'

(2)   *After subsection (7) of that section (transfer back of right to receive payments under the order to the Secretary of State) there shall be inserted the following subsections—*

'*(7A)   Subject to subsections (7B) and (7C) below, in any case where—*

(*a*)   *notice is given to a magistrates' court under subsection (7) above, and*

(*b*)   *the method of payment under the order which subsists immediately before the day on which the transfer under subsection (7) above takes effect differs from the method of payment which subsisted immediately before the day on which the transfer under subsection (3) above (or, if there has been more than one such transfer, the last such transfer) took effect,*

the clerk to the justices for the petty sessions area for which the court is acting shall amend the order by reinstating the method of payment under the order which subsisted immediately before the day on which the transfer under subsection (3) above (or, as the case may be, the last such transfer) took effect.

(7B)   The clerk shall not amend the order under subsection (7A) above if the Secretary of State gives notice in writing to the clerk, on or before the day on which the notice under subsection (7) above is given, that the method of payment under the order which subsists immediately before the day on which the transfer under subsection (7) above takes effect is to continue.

(7C)   In any case where—

(*a*)   *notice is given to a magistrates' court under subsection (7) above,*

(*b*)   *the method of payment under the order which subsisted immediately before the day on which the transfer under subsection (3) above (or, if there has been more than one such transfer, the last such transfer) took effect was any method of payment falling within section 59(6) of the Magistrates' Courts Act 1980 (standing order, etc), and*

(*c*)   *the clerk decides that payment by that method is no longer possible,*

the clerk shall amend the order to provide that payments under the order shall be made by the liable parent to the clerk.'

Note. This section repealed by Social Security (Consequential Provisions) Act 1992, s 3, Sch 1, as from 1 July 1992.

Registered maintenance orders

10. Amendment of certain enactments relating to registered or confirmed maintenance orders. Schedule 1 to this Act, which by amending certain enactments applies some of the preceding provisions of this Act with modifications to maintenance orders registered in or confirmed by magistrates' courts or registered in the High Court, shall have effect.

General

11. Minor and consequential amendments and repeals—(1) Schedule 2 to this Act, which contains minor amendments and amendments consequential on the provisions of this Act, shall have effect.

(2) The enactments specified in Schedule 1 to this Act are hereby repealed to the extent specified in the third column of that Schedule.

12. Short title, commencement, application and extent—(1) This Act may be cited as the Maintenance Enforcement Act 1991.

(2) The provisions of this Act, other than this section (which comes into force on the passing of this Act), shall come into force on such day as the Secretary of State may by order made by statutory instrument appoint, and different days may be so appointed for different provisions or for different purposes of the same provision.

(3) In the application of any amendment made by this Act which has effect in relation to orders made, confirmed or registered by a court, it is immaterial whether the making, confirmation or registration occurred before or after the coming into force of the amendment.

(4) Except for paragraphs 3 to 6 of Schedule 1, section 10 (in so far as it relates to those paragraphs) and this section, which extend to Scotland and Northern Ireland, this Act extends to England and Wales only.

Commencement. Section 11(1) (to the extent necessary to bring into force Sch 2, para 11), and Sch 2, para 11, were brought into force on 14 October 1991 (SI 1991 No 2042). The remainder of the Act was brought into force on 1 April 1992 (SI 1992 No 455).

SCHEDULES

SCHEDULE 1   Section 10

AMENDMENT OF CERTAIN ENACTMENTS RELATING TO MAINTENANCE ORDERS REGISTERED IN OR CONFIRMED BY MAGISTRATES' COURTS OR REGISTERED IN THE HIGH COURT

Maintenance Orders (Facilities for Enforcement) Act 1920 (c 33)

1.—(1) In section 4 of the Maintenance Orders (Facilities for Enforcement) Act 1920 (power of court of summary jurisdiction to confirm maintenance order made out of UK), after subsection (5) there shall be inserted the following subsections—

'(5A) Where a magistrates' court confirms a provisional order under this section, it shall at the same time exercise one of its powers under subsection (5B).

(5B) The powers of the court are—

(a) the power to order that payments under the order be made directly to the clerk of the court or the clerk of any other magistrates' court;

(b) the power to order that payments under the order be made to the clerk of the court, or to the clerk of any other magistrates' court, by such method of payment falling within section 59(6) of the Magistrates' Courts Act 1980 (standing order, etc) as may be specified;

(c) the power to make an attachment of earnings order under the Attachment of Earnings Act 1971 to secure payments under the order.

(5C) In deciding which of the powers under subsection (5B) it is to exercise, the court shall have regard to any representations made by the person liable to make payments under the order.

(5D) Subsection (4) of section 59 of the Magistrates' Courts Act 1980 (power of court to require debtor to open account) shall apply for the purposes of subsection (5B) as it applies for the purposes of that section but as if for paragraph (a) there were substituted—

"(a) the court proposes to exercise its power under paragraph (b) of section 4(5B) of the Maintenance Orders (Facilities for Enforcement) Act 1920, and".'

(2) For subsection (6) of that section (which provides that where a provisional order is confirmed it may be varied or rescinded as if it had been made by the confirming court and includes power to remit the order to the court which made it) there shall be substituted the following subsections—

'(6) Subject to subsection (6A), where a provisional order has been confirmed under this section, it may be varied or revoked in like manner as if it had originally been made by the confirming court.

(6A) Where the confirming court is a magistrates' court, section 60 of the Magistrates' Courts Act 1980 (revocation, variation etc of orders for periodical payment) shall have effect in relation to a provisional order confirmed under this section—

(a) as if in subsection (3) for the words "paragraphs (a) to (d) of section 59(3) above" there were substituted "section 4(5B) of the Maintenance Orders (Facilities for Enforcement) Act 1920";

(b) as if in subsection (4) for paragraph (b) there were substituted—

"(b) payments under the order are required to be made to the clerk of the court, or to the clerk of any other magistrates' court, by any method of payment falling within section 59(6) above (standing order, etc)";

and as if after the words "the court" there were inserted "which made the order";

(c) as if in subsection (5) for the words "to the clerk" there were substituted "in accordance with paragraph (a) of section 4(5B) of the Maintenance Orders (Facilities for Enforcement) Act 1920";

(d) as if in subsection (7), paragraph (c) and the word "and" immediately preceding it were omitted;

(e) as if in subsection (8) for the words "paragraphs (a) to (d) of section 59(3) above" there were substituted "section 4(5B) of the Maintenance Orders (Facilities for Enforcement) Act 1920";

(f) as if for subsections (9) and (10) there were substituted the following subsections—

"(9) In deciding, for the purposes of subsections (3) and (8) above, which of the powers under section 4(5B) of the Maintenance Orders (Facilities for Enforcement) Act 1920 it is to exercise, the court shall have regard to any representations made by the debtor.

(10) Subsection (4) of section 59 above (power of court to require debtor to open account) shall apply for the purposes of subsections (3) and (8) above as it applies for the purposes of that section but as if for paragraph (a) there were substituted—

'(a) the court proposes to exercise its power under paragraph (b) of section 4(5B) of the Maintenance Orders (Facilities for Enforcement) Act 1920, and'.".

(6B) Where on an application for variation or revocation the confirming court is satisfied that it is necessary to remit the case to the court which made the order for the purpose of taking any further evidence, the court may so remit the case and adjourn the proceedings for the purpose.'

2. In section 6 of that Act (mode of enforcing orders registered in or confirmed by courts under Act), in subsection (2) (which provides that if the order is of such a nature that if made by the court it would be enforceable as a magistrates' court maintenance order it shall be so enforceable), for the words 'the order shall be so enforceable' there shall be substituted 'the order shall, subject to the modifications of sections 76 and 93 of the Magistrates' Courts Act 1980 (enforcement of sums adjudged to be paid and complaint for arrears) specified in subsections (2ZA) and (2ZB) of section 18 of the Maintenance Orders Act 1950 (enforcement of registered orders), be so enforceable'.

Maintenance Orders Act 1950 (c 37)

3.—(1) In section 18 of the Maintenance Orders Act 1950 (enforcement of registered orders), in subsection (2) (orders registered in magistrates' courts to be enforceable as magistrates' courts maintenance orders) for the words 'shall be enforceable' there shall be substituted 'shall, subject to the modifications of sections 76 and 93 of the Magistrates' Courts Act 1980 specified in subsections (2ZA) and (2ZB) of this section, be enforceable'.

(2) After that subsection there shall be inserted the following subsections—

'(2ZA) Section 76 (enforcement of sums adjudged to be paid) shall have effect as if for subsections (4) to (6) there were substituted the following subsections—

"(4) Where proceedings are brought for the enforcement of a magistrates' court maintenance order under this section, the court may vary the order by exercising one of its powers under subsection (5) below.

(5) The powers of the court are—

(a) the power to order that payments under the order be made directly to the clerk of the court or the clerk of any other magistrates' court;

(b) the power to order that payments under the order be made to the clerk of the court, or to the clerk of any other magistrates' court, by such method of payment falling within section 59(6) above (standing order, etc) as may be specified;

(c) the power to make an attachment of earnings order under the Attachment of Earnings Act 1971 to secure payments under the order.

(6) In deciding which of the powers under subsection (5) above it is to exercise, the court shall have regard to any representations made by the debtor (within the meaning of section 59 above).

(7) Subsection (4) of section 59 above (power of court to require debtor to open account) shall apply for the purposes of subsection (5) above as it applies for the purposes of that section but as if for paragraph (a) there were substituted—

'(a) the court proposes to exercise its power under paragraph (b) of section 76(5) below, and'."

(2ZB) In section 93 (complaint for arrears), subsection (6) (court not to impose imprisonment in certain circumstances) shall have effect as if for paragraph (b) there were substituted—

"(b) if the court is of the opinion that it is appropriate—

(i) to make an attachment of earnings order; or

(ii) to exercise its power under paragraph (b) of section 76(5) above.".'

4.—(1) In section 19 of that Act (functions of collecting officers, etc), in subsection (2) (court to order that payments under maintenance order registered in court of summary jurisdiction in England or Northern Ireland be made to collecting officer, unless court satisfied it is undesirable to do so) for the words 'unless it is satisfied that it is undesirable to do so' there shall be substituted 'unless, in the case of a court of summary jurisdiction in Northern Ireland, it is satisfied that it is undesirable to do so'.

(2) For subsection (3) of that section (order under subsection (2) may be varied or revoked) there shall be substituted the following subsection—

'(3) An order made under subsection (2) of this section—

(a) by a court of summary jurisdiction in England may be varied or revoked by an exercise of the powers conferred by virtue of section 18(2ZA) or section 22(1A) or (1E) of this Act;

(b) by a court of summary jurisdiction in Northern Ireland may be varied or revoked by a subsequent order.'

5. In section 22 of that Act (discharge and variation of maintenance orders registered in summary or sheriff courts), after subsection (1) (power of registering court to vary rate of payments under order) there shall be inserted the following subsections—

'(1A) The power of a magistrates' court in England and Wales to vary a maintenance order under subsection (1) of this section shall include power, if the court is satisfied that payment has not been made in accordance with the order, to vary the order by exercising one of its powers under subsection (1B) of this section.

(1B) The powers of the court are—

(a) the power to order that payments under the order be made directly to the clerk of the court or the clerk of any other magistrates' court in England and Wales;

(b) the power to order that payments under the order be made to the clerk of the court, or to the clerk of any other magistrates' court in England and Wales, by such method of payment falling within section 59(6) of the Magistrates' Courts Act 1980 (standing order, etc) as may be specified;

(c) the power to make an attachment of earnings order under the Attachment of Earnings Act 1971 to secure payments under the order.

(1C) In deciding which of the powers under subsection (1B) of this section it is to exercise, the court shall have regard to any representations made by the person liable to make payments under the order.

(1D) Subsection (4) of section 59 of the Magistrates' Courts Act 1980 (power of court to require debtor to open account) shall apply for the purposes of subsection (1B) of this section as it applies for the purposes of that section but as if for paragraph (a) there were substituted—

"(a) the court proposes to exercise its power under paragraph (b) of section 22(1B) of the Maintenance Orders Act 1950, and".

(1E) Subsections (4) to (11) of section 60 of the Magistrates' Courts Act 1980 (power of clerk and court to vary maintenance order) shall apply in relation to a maintenance order for the time being registered under this Part of this Act in a magistrates' court in England and Wales as they apply in relation to a maintenance order made by a magistrates' court in England and Wales but—

(a) as if in subsection (4) for paragraph (b) there were substituted—

"(b) payments under the order are required to be made to the clerk of the court, or to the clerk of any other magistrates' court, by any method of payment falling within section 59(6) above (standing order, etc)";

and as if after the words "the court" there were inserted "which made the order";

(b) as if in subsection (5) for the words "to the clerk" there were substituted "in accordance with paragraph (a) of section 22(1B) of the Maintenance Orders Act 1950";

(c) as if in subsection (7), paragraph (c) and the word "and" immediately preceding it were omitted;

(d) as if in subsection (8) for the words "paragraphs (a) to (d) of section 59(3) above" there were substituted "section 22(1B) of the Maintenance Orders Act 1950";

(e) as if for subsections (9) and (10) there were substituted the following subsections—

"(9) In deciding which of the powers under section 22(1B) of the Maintenance Orders Act 1950 it is to exercise, the court shall have regard to any representations made by the debtor.

(10) Subsection (4) of section 59 above (power of court to require debtor to open account) shall apply for the purposes of subsection (8) above as it applies for the purposes of that section but as if for paragraph (a) there were substituted—

'(a) the court proposes to exercise its power under paragraph (b) of section 22(1B) of the Maintenance Orders Act 1950, and'.".'

6. In section 24 of that Act (cancellation of registration), after subsection (5) (effect of cancellation of order registered in court of summary jurisdiction) there shall be inserted the following subsection—

'(5A) On the cancellation of the registration of a maintenance order registered in a magistrates' court in England and Wales, any order—

(a) made in relation thereto by virtue of the powers conferred by section 18(2ZA) or section 22(1A) or (1E) of this Act, and

(b) requiring payment to the clerk of a magistrates' court in England and Wales (whether or not by any method of payment falling within section 59(6) of the Magistrates' Courts Act 1980), shall cease to have effect; but until the person liable to make payments under the maintenance order receives the prescribed notice of the cancellation, he shall be deemed to comply with the maintenance order if he makes payments in accordance with any such order which was in force immediately before the cancellation.'

Maintenance Orders Act 1958 (c 39)

7. In section 2 of the Maintenance Orders Act 1958 (registration of orders), for subsection (6) (section 19(1) to (4) of Maintenance Orders Act 1950 to have effect for the purposes of Part I) there shall be substituted the following subsections—

'(6) Where a magistrates' court order is registered under this Part of this Act in the High Court, then—

    (a) if payments under the magistrates' court order are required to be made (otherwise than to the clerk of a magistrates' court) by any method of payment falling within section 59(6) of the Magistrates' Courts Act 1980 (standing order, etc) any order requiring payment by that method shall continue to have effect after registration;

    (b) any order by virtue of which sums payable under the magistrates' court order are required to be paid to the clerk of a magistrates' court (whether or not by any method of payment falling within section 59(6) of that Act) on behalf of the person entitled thereto shall cease to have effect.

(6ZA) Where a High Court or county court order is registered under this Part of this Act in a magistrates' court, then—

    (a) if a means of payment order (within the meaning of section 1(7) of the Maintenance Enforcement Act 1991) has effect in relation to the order in question, it shall continue to have effect after registration; and

    (b) in any other case, the magistrates' court shall order that all payments to be made under the order in question (including any arrears accrued before registration) shall be made to the clerk of the court or the clerk of any other magistrates' court.

(6ZB) Any such order as to payment—

    (a) as if referred to in paragraph (a) of subsection (6) of this section may be revoked, suspended, revived or varied by an exercise of the powers conferred by section 4A of this Act; and

    (b) as is referred to in paragraph (a) or (b) of subsection (6ZA) of this section may be varied or revoked by an exercise of the powers conferred by section 3(2A) or (2B) or section 4(2A), (5A) or (5B) of this Act.

(6ZC) Where by virtue of the provisions of this section or any order under subsection (6ZA)(b) of this section payments under an order cease to be or become payable to the clerk of a magistrates' court, the person liable to make the payments shall, until he is given the prescribed notice to that effect, be deemed to comply with the order if he makes payments in accordance with the order and any order under subsection (6ZA)(b) of this section of which he has received such notice.'

8.—(1) In section 3 of that Act (enforcement of registered orders), in subsection (2) (order registered in magistrates' court to be enforceable as magistrates' court maintenance order) for the words 'Subject to the provisions of the next following subsection' there shall be substituted 'Subject to the provisions of subsections (2A) to (3) of this section'.

(2) After that subsection there shall be inserted the following subsections—

'(2A) Where an order registered in a magistrates' court is an order other than one deemed to be made by the High Court by virtue of section 1(2) of this Act, section 76 of the Magistrates' Courts Act 1980 (enforcement of sums adjudged to be paid) shall have effect as if for subsections (4) to (6) there were substituted the following subsections—

"(4) Where proceedings are brought for the enforcement of a magistrates' court maintenance order under this section, the court may vary the order by exercising one of its powers under paragraphs (a) to (d) of section 59(3) above.

(5) In deciding which of the powers under paragraphs (a) to (d) of section 59(3) above it is to exercise, the court shall have regard to any representations made by the debtor and the creditor (which expressions shall have the same meaning as they have in section 59 above).

(6) Subsection (4) of section 59 above shall apply for the purposes of subsection (4) above as it applies for the purposes of that section."

(2B) Where an order registered in a magistrates' court is an order deemed to be made by the High Court by virtue of section 1(2) of this Act, sections 76 and 93 of the Magistrates' Courts Act 1980 (enforcement of sums adjudged to be paid and complaint for arrears) shall have effect subject to the modifications specified in subsections (2ZA) and (2ZB) of section 18 of the Maintenance Orders Act 1950 (enforcement of registered orders).'

9.—(1) In section 4 of that Act (variation of orders registered in magistrates' courts), after subsection (2) (power of court to vary rate of payments under order) there shall be inserted the following subsections—

'(2A) The power of a magistrates' court to vary a registered order under subsection (2) of this section shall include power, if the court is satisfied that payment has not been made in accordance with the order, to vary the order by exercising one of its powers under paragraphs (a) to (d) of section 59(3) of the Magistrates' Courts Act 1980.

(2B) Subsection (4) of section 59 of that Act shall apply for the purposes of subsection (2A) of this section as it applies for the purposes of that section.

(2C) In deciding which of the powers under paragraphs (a) to (d) of section 59(3) of that Act it is to exercise, the court shall have regard to any representations made by the debtor and the creditor (which expressions have the same meaning as they have in section 59 of that Act).'

(2) After subsection (5) of that section there shall be inserted the following subsections—

'(5A) Subject to the following provisions of this section, subsections (4) to (11) of section 60 of the Magistrates' Courts Act 1980 (power of clerk and court to vary maintenance orders) shall apply in relation to a registered order (other than one deemed to be made by the High Court by virtue of section 1(2) of this Act) as they apply in relation to a maintenance order made by a magistrates' court (disregarding section 23(2) of the Domestic Proceedings and Magistrates' Courts Act 1978 and section 15(2) of the Children Act 1989) but—

(a) as if in subsection (8) after the words "the court which may" there were inserted "subject to subsection (10) below"; and

(b) as if for subsections (9) and (10) there were substituted the following subsections—

"(9) Subsection (4) of section 59 above shall apply for the purposes of subsection (8) above as it applies for the purposes of that section.

(10) In deciding which of the powers under paragraphs (a) to (d) of section 59(3) above it is to exercise, the court shall have regard to any representations made by the debtor and the creditor."

(5B) Subject to the following provisions of this section, subsections (4) to (11) of section 60 of the Magistrates' Courts Act 1980 (power of clerk and court to vary maintenance orders) shall apply in relation to a registered order deemed to be made by the High Court by virtue of section 1(2) of this Act as they apply in relation to a maintenance order made by a magistrates' court (disregarding section 23(2) of the Domestic Proceedings and Magistrates' Courts Act 1978 and section 15(2) of the Children Act 1989) but—

(a) as if in subsection (4) for paragraph (b) there were substituted—

"(b) payments under the order are required to be made to the clerk of the court, or to the clerk of any other magistrates' court, by any method of payment falling within section 59(6) above (standing order, etc)";
and as if after the words "the court" there were inserted "which made the order";'

(b) as if in subsection (5) for the words "to the clerk" there were substituted "in accordance with paragraph (a) of subsection (9) below";

(c) as if in subsection (7), paragraph (c) and the word "and" immediately preceding it were omitted;

(d) as if in subsection (8) for the words "paragraphs (a) to (d) of section 59(3) above" there were substituted "subsection (9) below";

(e) as if for subsections (9) and (10) there were substituted the following subsections—

"(9) The powers of the court are—

(a) the power to order that payments under the order be made directly to the clerk of the court or the clerk of any other magistrates' court;

(b) the power to order that payments under the order be made to the clerk of the court, or to the clerk of any other magistrates' court, by such method of payment falling within section 59(6) above (standing order, etc) as may be specified;

(c) the power to make an attachment of earnings order under the Attachment of Earnings Act 1971 to secure payments under the order.

(10) In deciding which of the powers under subsection (9) above it is to exercise, the court shall have regard to any representations made by the debtor.

(10A) Subsection (4) of section 59 above (power of court to require debtor to open account) shall apply for the purposes of subsection (9) above as it applies for the purposes of that section but as if for paragraph (a) there were substituted—

'(a) the court proposes to exercise its power under paragraph (b) of section 60(9) below'.".'

(3) At the beginning of subsection (6A) of that section (no application for variation in respect of order deemed to be made by High Court by virtue of section 1(2) of Act) there shall be inserted the words 'Except as provided by subsection (5B) of this section'.

10. After section 4 of that Act (variation of orders registered in magistrates' courts) there shall be inserted the following section—

'**4A. Variation etc of orders registered in the High Court**—(1) The provisions of this section shall have effect with respect to orders registered in the High Court other than maintenance orders deemed to be made by a magistrates' court by virtue of section 1(4) of this Act, and the reference in subsection (2) of this section to a registered order shall be construed accordingly.

(2) The High Court may exercise the same powers in relation to a registered order as are exercisable by the High Court under section 1 of the Maintenance Enforcement Act 1991 in relation to a qualifying periodical maintenance order (within the meaning of that section) which has been made by the High Court, including the power under subsection (7) of that section to revoke, suspend, revive or vary—

(a) any such order as is referred to in paragraph (a) of section 2(6) of this Act which continues to have effect by virtue of that paragraph; and

(b) any means of payment order (within the meaning of section 1(7) of that Act of 1991) made by virtue of the provisions of this section.'

11. In section 5 of that Act (cancellation of registration), for subsection (5) (effect of cancellation on order registered in magistrates' court), there shall be substituted the following subsections—

'(5) On the cancellation of the registration of a High Court or county court order—

(a) any order which requires payments under the order in question to be made (otherwise than to the clerk of a magistrates' court) by any method of payment falling within section 59(6) of the Magistrates' Courts Act 1980 or section 1(5) of the Maintenance Enforcement Act 1991 (standing order, etc) shall continue to have effect; and

(b) any order made under section 2(6ZA)(b) of this Act or by virtue of the powers conferred by section 3(2A) or (2B) or section 4(2A), (5A) or (5B) of this Act and which requires payments under the order in question to be made to the clerk of a magistrates' court (whether or not by any method of payment falling within section 59(6) of the Magistrates' Courts Act 1980) shall cease to have effect;

but, in a case falling within paragraph (b) of this subsection, until the defendant receives the prescribed notice of the cancellation he shall be deemed to comply with the High Court or county court order if he makes payment in accordance with any such order as is referred to in paragraph (b) of this subsection which was in force immediately before the cancellation and of which he has notice.

(6) On the cancellation of the registration of a magistrates' court order—

(a) any order which requires payments under the magistrates' court order to be made by any method of payment falling within section 59(6) of the Magistrates' Courts Act 1980 or section 1(5) of the Maintenance Enforcement Act 1991 (standing order, etc) shall continue to have effect; and

(b) in any other case, payments shall become payable to the clerk of the original court;

but, in a case falling within paragraph (b) of this subsection, until the defendant receives the prescribed notice of the cancellation he shall be deemed to comply with the magistrates' court order if he makes payments in accordance with any order which was in force immediately before the cancellation and of which he has notice.

(7) In subsections (5) and (6) of this section "High Court order" and "magistrates' court order" shall be construed in accordance with section 2(6A) of this Act.'

Maintenance Orders (Reciprocal Enforcement) Act 1972 (c 18)

12. In section 7 of the Maintenance Orders (Reciprocal Enforcement) Act 1972 (confirmation by UK court of provisional maintenance order made in reciprocating country), after subsection (5) (registration etc of order) there shall be inserted the following subsections—

'(5A) Where a magistrates' court in England and Wales confirms a provisional order under this section, it shall at the same time exercise one of its powers under subsection (5B) below.

(5B) The powers of the court are—

(a) the power to order that payments under the order be made directly to the clerk of the court or the clerk of any other magistrates' court in England and Wales;

(b) the power to order that payments under the order be made to the clerk of the court, or to the clerk of any other magistrates' court in England and Wales, by such method of payment falling within section 59(6) of the Magistrates' Courts Act 1980 (standing order, etc) as may be specified;

(c) the power to make an attachment of earnings order under the Attachment of Earnings Act 1971 to secure payments under the order.

(5C) In deciding which of the powers under subsection (5B) above it is to exercise, the court shall have regard to any representations made by the payer under the order.

(5D) Subsection (4) of section 59 of the Magistrates' Courts Act 1980 (power of court to require debtor to open account) shall apply for the purposes of subsection (5B) above as it applies for the purposes of that section but as if for paragraph (a) there were substituted—

"(a) the court proposes to exercise its power under paragraph (b) of section 7(5B) of the Maintenance Orders (Reciprocal Enforcement) Act 1972, and".'

13.—(1) In section 8 of that Act (enforcement of maintenance order registered in UK court), in subsection (4) (orders enforceable as magistrates' court maintenance orders) after the words 'An order which by virtue of this section is enforceable by a magistrates' court shall' there shall be inserted 'subject to the modifications of sections 76 and 93 of the Magistrates' Courts Act 1980 specified in subsections (4A) and (4B) below'.

(2) After that subsection there shall be inserted the following subsections—

'(4A) Section 76 (enforcement of sums adjudged to be paid) shall have effect as if for subsections (4) to (6) there were substituted the following subsections—

"(4) Where proceedings are brought for the enforcement of a magistrates' court maintenance order under this section, the court may vary the order by exercising one of its powers under subsection (5) below.

(5) The powers of the court are—

(a) the power to order that payments under the order be made directly to the clerk of the court or the clerk of any other magistrates' court;

(b) the power to order that payments under the order be made to the clerk of the court, or to the clerk of any other magistrates' court, by such method of payment falling within section 59(6) above (standing order, etc) as may be specified;

(c) the power to make an attachment of earnings order under the Attachment of Earnings Act 1971 to secure payments under the order.

(6) In deciding which of the powers under subsection (5) above it is to exercise, the court shall have regard to any representations made by the debtor (within the meaning of section 59 above).

(7) Subsection (4) of section 59 above (power of court to require debtor to open account) shall apply for the purposes of subsection (5) above as it applies for the purposes of that section but as if for paragraph (a) there were substituted—

'(a) the court proposes to exercise its power under paragraph (b) of section 76(5) below, and'."

(4B) In section 93 (complaint for arrears), subsection (6) (court not to impose imprisonment in certain circumstances) shall have effect as if for paragraph (b) there were substituted—

"(b) if the court is of the opinion that it is appropriate—

(i) to make an attachment of earnings order; or

(ii) to exercise its power under paragraph (b) of section 76(5) above.".'

14. In section 9 of that Act (variation and revocation of maintenance order registered in UK court), after subsection (1) (registering court to have same power to revoke or vary order as if order had been made by court, including power to revoke or vary order by way of provisional order) there shall be inserted the following subsection—

'(1ZA) Where the registering court is a magistrates' court in England and Wales, section 60 of the Magistrates' Courts Act 1980 (revocation, variation etc of orders for periodical payment) shall have effect in relation to the registered order—

(a) as if in subsection (3) for the words "paragraphs (a) to (d) of section 59(3) above" there were substituted "subsection (3A) below" and after that subsection there were inserted—

"(3A) The powers of the court are—

(a) the power to order that payments under the order by made directly to the clerk of the court or the clerk of any other magistrates' court;

  (b) the power to order that payments under the order be made to the clerk of the court, or to the clerk of any other magistrates' court, by such method of payment falling within section 59(6) above (standing order, etc) as may be specified;

  (c) the power to make an attachment of earnings order under the Attachment of Earnings Act 1971 to secure payments under the order.";

(b) as if in subsection (4) for paragraph (b) there were substituted—

  "(b) payments under the order are required to be made to the clerk of the court, or to the clerk of any other magistrates' court, by any method of payment falling within section 59(6) above (standing order, etc)";

  and as if after the words "the court" there were inserted "which made the order";

(c) as if in subsection (5) for the words "to the clerk" there were substituted "in accordance with paragraph (a) of subsection (3A) above";

(d) as if in subsection (7), paragraph (c) and the word "and" immediately preceding it were omitted;

(e) as if in subsection (8) for the words "paragraphs (a) to (d) of section 59(3) above" there were substituted "subsection (3A) above";

(f) as if for subsections (9) and (10) there were substituted the following subsections—

  "(9) In deciding, for the purposes of subsections (3) and (8) above, which of the powers under subsection (3A) above it is to exercise, the court shall have regard to any representations made by the debtor.

  (10) Subsection 4 of section 59 above (power of court to require debtor to open account) shall apply for the purposes of subsection (3A) above as it applies for the purposes of that section but as if for paragraph (a) there were substituted—

   '(a) the court proposes to exercise its power under paragraph (b) of section 60(3A) below, and'.".'

15.—(*1*) *In section 27 of that Act (general provisions relating to application for recovery of maintenance in England, etc), after subsection (7) there shall be inserted the following subsections—*

 '(7A) Where a magistrates' court in England and Wales makes an order on the complaint, section 59 of the Magistrates' Courts Act 1980 (orders for periodical payment: means of payment) and subsection (2) of section 32 of the Domestic Proceedings and Magistrates' Courts Act 1978 (extension of section 59) shall not apply, but the court shall, at the same time that it makes the order, exercise one of its powers under subsection (7B) below.

 (7B) The powers of the court are—

  (*a*) *the power to order that payments under the order be made directly to the clerk of the court or the clerk of any other magistrates' court in England and Wales;*

  (*b*) *the power to order that payments under the order be made to the clerk of the court, or to the clerk of any other magistrates' court in England and Wales, by such method of payment falling within section 59(6) of the Magistrates' Courts Act 1980 (standing order, etc) as may be specified;*

  (*c*) *the power to make an attachment of earnings order under the Attachment of Earnings Act 1971 to secure payments under the order.*

 (7C) In deciding which of the powers under subsection (7B) above it is to exercise, the court shall have regard to any representations made by the person liable to make payments under the order.

 (7D) Subsection (4) of section 59 of the Magistrates' Courts Act 1980 (power of court to require debtor to open account) shall apply for the purposes of subsection (7B) above as it applies for the purposes of that section but as if for paragraph (a) there were substituted—

  "(a) the court proposes to exercise its power under paragraph (b) of section 27(7B) of the Maintenance Orders (Reciprocal Enforcement) Act 1972, and".'

(*2*) Subsection (*9*) of that section (*payment to be in such manner and to such person as may be prescribed and certain enactments not to apply*) shall cease to have effect.

16. In section 28 of that Act (*complaint by spouse in convention country for recovery in England and Wales of maintenance from other spouse*), after the word '*18*' there shall be inserted '*20ZA*'.

17. In section 28A of that Act (*complaint by former spouse in convention country for recovery in England and Wales of maintenance from other spouse*), in subsection (*3*) (*modifications of 1978 Act*), in paragraph (*e*) after the word '*18*' there shall be inserted '*20ZA*'.

Note. Paras 15–17 repealed by Maintenance Orders (Reciprocal Enforcement) Act 1992, s 2(2), Sch 3, as from 5 April 1993.

18.—(1) In section 33 of that Act (enforcement of orders), in subsection (3) (order registered in magistrates' court other than court by which order made enforceable as magistrates' court maintenance order), for the words 'shall be enforceable' there shall be substituted 'shall, subject to the modifications of sections 76 and 93 of the Magistrates' Courts Act 1980 (enforcement of sums adjudged to be paid and complaint for arrears) specified in subsections (4A) and (4B) of section 8 of this Act, be enforceable'.

(2) After that subsection there shall be inserted the following subsection—

'(3A) Where, by virtue of being registered in the magistrates' court in which it was made, a registered order is enforceable as a magistrates' court maintenance order, sections 76 and 93 of the Magistrates' Courts Act 1980 shall have effect subject to the modifications specified in subsections (4A) and (4B) of section 8 of this Act.'

19.—(1) In section 34 of that Act (variation and enforcement of orders), at the beginning of subsection (1) (order registered in court other than court which made it variable as if made by registering court) there shall be inserted the words 'Subject to section 34A of this Act'.

(2) After that section there shall be inserted the following section—

'**34A. Variation of orders by magistrates' courts in England and Wales**—(1) The provisions of this section shall have effect in relation to a registered order which is registered in a magistrates' court in England and Wales (whether or not the court made the order) in place of the following enactments, that is to say—

(a) subsections (3) to (11) of section 60 of the Magistrates' Courts Act 1980;

(b) section 20ZA of the Domestic Proceedings and Magistrates' Courts Act 1978; and

(c) paragraph 6A of Schedule 1 to the Children Act 1989.

(2) The power of a magistrates' court in England and Wales to vary a registered order shall include power, if the court is satisfied that payment has not been made in accordance with the order, to exercise one of its powers under subsection (3) below.

(3) The powers of the court are—

(a) the power to order that payments under the order be made directly to the clerk of the court or the clerk of any other magistrates' court in England and Wales;

(b) the power to order that payments under the order be made to the clerk of the court, or to the clerk of any other magistrates' court in England and Wales, by such method of payment falling within section 59(6) of the Magistrates' Courts Act 1980 (standing order, etc) as may be specified;

(c) the power to make an attachment of earnings order under the Attachment of Earnings Act 1971 to secure payments under the order.

(4) In any case where—

(a) a registered order is registered in a magistrates' court in England and Wales, and

(b) payments under the order are required to be made to the clerk of the court, or to the clerk of any other magistrates' court in England and

Wales, by any method of payment falling within section 59(6) of the Magistrates' Courts Act 1980 (standing order, etc),

an interested party may apply in writing to the clerk of the court in which the order is registered for the order to be varied as mentioned in subsection (5) below.

(5) Subject to subsection (8) below, where an application has been made under subsection (4) above, the clerk, after giving written notice (by post or otherwise) of the application to any other interested party and allowing that party, within the period of 14 days beginning with the date of the giving of that notice, an opportunity to make written representations, may vary the order to provide that payments under the order shall be made in accordance with paragraph (a) of subsection (3) above.

(6) The clerk may proceed with an application under subsection (4) above notwithstanding that any such interested party as is referred to in subsection (5) above has not received written notice of the application.

(7) In subsections (4) to (6) above "interested party", in relation to an order, means the debtor or the creditor.

(8) Where an application has been made under subsection (4) above, the clerk may, if he considers it inappropriate to exercise his power under subsection (5) above, refer the matter to the court which may vary the order by exercising one of its powers under subsection (3) above.

(9) In deciding, for the purposes of subsections (2) and (8) above, which of the powers under subsection (3) above it is to exercise, the court shall have regard to any representations made by the debtor.

(10) Subsection (4) of section 59 of the Magistrates' Courts Act 1980 (power of court to require debtor to open account) shall apply for the purposes of subsection (3) above as it applies for the purposes of that section but as if for paragraph (a) there were substituted—

"(a) the court proposes to exercise its power under paragraph (b) of section 34A(3) of the Maintenance Orders (Reciprocal Enforcement) Act 1972, and".

(11) In this section "creditor" and "debtor" have the same meaning as they have in section 59 of the Magistrates' Courts Act 1980.'

20. *In section 35 of that Act (further provisions with respect to variation etc of orders by magistrates' courts), at the end of subsection (1) (court to have jurisdiction to hear application for variation or revocation notwithstanding one of the parties is outside England and Wales) there shall be inserted the words 'but none of the powers of the court, or of the clerk of the court, conferred by section 34A of this Act shall be exercisable in relation to such an application'.*

Note. Para 20 repealed by Maintenance Orders (Reciprocal Enforcement) Act 1992, s 2(2), Sch 3, as from 5 April 1993.

Civil Jurisdiction and Judgments Act 1982 (c 27)

21.—(1) In section 5 of the Civil Jurisdiction and Judgments Act 1982 (recognition and enforcement of maintenance orders), in subsection (5A) (registered order enforceable as magistrates' court maintenance order), for the words 'shall be enforceable' there shall be substituted 'shall, subject to the modifications of sections 76 and 93 of the Magistrates' Courts Act 1980 specified in subsections (5B) and (5C) below, be enforceable'.

(2) After that subsection there shall be inserted the following subsections—

'(5B) Section 76 (enforcement of sums adjudged to be paid) shall have effect as if for subsections (4) to (6) there were substituted the following subsections—

"(4) Where proceedings are brought for the enforcement of a magistrates' court maintenance order under this section, the court may vary the order by exercising one of its powers under subsection (5) below.

(5) The powers of the court are—

    (a) the power to order that payments under the order be made directly to the clerk of the court or the clerk of any other magistrates' court;

    (b) the power to order that payments under the order be made to the clerk of the court, or to the clerk of any other magistrates' court, by such method of payment falling within section 59(6) above (standing order, etc) as may be specified;

    (c) the power to make an attachment of earnings order under the Attachment of Earnings Act 1971 to secure payments under the order.

(6) In deciding which of the powers under subsection (5) above it is to exercise, the court shall have regard to any representations made by the debtor (within the meaning of section 59 above).

(7) Subsection (4) of section 59 above (power of court to require debtor to open account) shall apply for the purposes of subsection (5) above as it applies for the purposes of that section but as if for paragraph (a) there were substituted—

    '(a) the court proposes to exercise its power under paragraph (b) of section 76(5) below, and'."

(5C) In section 93 (complaint for arrears), subsection (6) (court not to impose imprisonment in certain circumstances) shall have effect as if for paragraph (b) there were substituted—

    "(b) if the court is of the opinion that it is appropriate—

        (i) to make an attachment of earnings order; or

        (ii) to exercise its power under paragraph (b) of section 76(5) above."'

SCHEDULE 2   Section 11(1)

MINOR AND CONSEQUENTIAL AMENDMENTS

Attachment of Earnings Act 1971 (c 32)

1.—(1) In section 3 of the Attachment of Earnings Act 1971 (application for attachment of earnings order and conditions of court's power to make it), in subsection (1) (persons who may apply for order), in paragraph (c) for the words 'section 59(1)' there shall be substituted 'section 59'.

(2) Subsection (2) of that section (application, other than by debtor, for attachment of earnings order to secure maintenance payments not to be made unless at least 15 days have elapsed since maintenance order made) shall cease to have effect.

(3) At the beginning of subsection (3) of that section (attachment of earnings order not to be made, other than on application of debtor, unless one or more payments have not been made) there shall be inserted the words 'Subject to subsection (3A) below'.

(4) After that subsection there shall be inserted the following subsection—

    '(3A) Subsection (3) above shall not apply where the relevant adjudication is a maintenance order.'

(5) In subsection (4) of that section (power of court to make attachment of earnings order where certain enforcement proceedings brought), the words 'subject to subsection (5) below' shall cease to have effect.

(6) Subsection (5) of that section (attachment of earnings order not to be made, other than on application of debtor, if debtor's failure to make payments is not due to his wilful refusal or culpable neglect) shall cease to have effect.

Domestic Proceedings and Magistrates' Courts Act 1978 (c 22)

2. In section 23 of the Domestic Proceedings and Magistrates' Courts Act 1978 (supplementary provisions with respect to variation and revocation of orders), in subsection (2) (power of magistrates' court under section 60 of 1980 Act to vary etc order not to apply to order under Part I of Act)—

    (a) after the word 'money' there shall be inserted 'and the power of the clerk of a magistrates' court to vary such an order'; and

    (b) after the word 'and' there shall be inserted 'the power of a magistrates' court'.

3. In section 32 of that Act (enforcement etc of orders for payment of money), in subsection (2) (which applies section 59 of 1980 Act with modifications to orders under Part I of Act)—

    (a) for the words 'subsection (2)' there shall be substituted 'subsection (7)'; and

    (b) for the words 'the applicant for the order' there shall be substituted 'the person who applied for the maintenance order'.

Justices of the Peace Act 1979 (c 55)

4. *In section 29 of the Justices of the Peace Act 1979 (functions of justices' clerk as collecting officer), in subsection (3) (powers under section without prejudice to provisions of section 59 of 1980 Act)—*

    (a) for the words 'section 59' there shall be substituted 'sections 59 and 59A'; and

    (b) after the words 'justices' clerk' there shall be inserted 'and proceedings by the clerk, etc'.

Note. Para 4 repealed by Justices of the Peace Act 1997, s 73(3), Sch 6, Part I, as from 19 June 1997.

Magistrates' Courts Act 1980 (c 43)

5. In section 62 of the Magistrates' Courts Act 1980 (provisions as to payments required to be made to a child, etc), in subsection (1) (which permits payments to be made to person with whom child has his home and permits that person to request clerk of court, under section 59(3) of 1980 Act, to proceed for recovery of arrears), in sub-paragraph (ii) for the words 'request the clerk to the magistrates' court, under subsection (3) of section 59 above' there shall be substituted 'request or authorise the clerk of the magistrates' court under subsection (1) or subsection (2) respectively of section 59A above'.

6. In section 75 of that Act (power to dispense with immediate payment), after subsection (2) (power to order payment by instalments) there shall be inserted the following subsections—

    '(2A) An order under this section that a lump sum required to be paid under a maintenance order shall be paid by instalments (a "maintenance instalments order") shall be treated for the purposes of sections 59, 59B and 60 above as a maintenance order.

    (2B) Subsections (5) and (7) of section 59 above (including those subsections as they apply for the purposes of section 60 above) shall have effect in relation to a maintenance instalments order—

        (a) as if in subsection (5), paragraph (c) and the word "and" immediately preceding it were omitted; and

        (b) as if in subsection (7)—

            (i) the reference to the maintenance order were a reference to the maintenance order in respect of which the maintenance instalments order in question is made;

           (ii) for the words "the person who applied for the maintenance order" there were substituted "the debtor".

    (2C) Section 60 above shall have effect in relation to a maintenance instalments order as if in subsection (7), paragraph (c) and the word "and" immediately preceding it were omitted.'

7. In section 93 of that Act (complaint for arrears), in subsection (6) (court not to impose imprisonment in certain circumstances) for paragraphs (a) and (b) there shall be substituted—

    '(a) in the absence of the defendant; or

    (b) in a case where the court has power to do so, if it is of the opinion that it is appropriate—

      (i) to make an attachment of earnings order; or

     (ii) to order that payments under the order be made by any method of payment falling within section 59(6) above; or

  (c) where the sum to which the default relates comprises only interest which the defendant has been ordered to pay by virtue of section 94A(1) below.'

8. For section 95 of that Act (power to remit arrears) there shall be substituted the following section—

'**95. Remission of arrears and manner in which arrears to be paid**—(1) On the hearing of a complaint for the enforcement, revocation, revival, variation or discharge of a magistrates' court maintenance order, a magistrates' court may remit the whole or any part of the sum due under the order.

(2) If, on the hearing of a complaint for the enforcement, revocation, revival, variation or discharge of a magistrates' court maintenance order, a magistrates' court orders that the whole or any part of the sum due under the order be paid by instalments (an "instalments order"), then—

  (a) if the maintenance order is an English maintenance order, the court shall at the same time exercise one of its powers under paragraphs (a) to (d) of section 59(3) above in relation to the instalments order;

  (b) if the maintenance order is a non-English maintenance order, the court shall at the same time exercise one of its powers under subsection (3) below in relation to the instalments order.

(3) The powers of the court referred to in subsection (2)(b) above are—

  (a) the power to order that payments under the order be made directly to the clerk of the court or the clerk of any other magistrates' court;

  (b) the power to order that payments under the order be made to the clerk of the court, or to the clerk of any other magistrates' court, by such method of payment falling within section 59(6) above as may be specified;

  (c) the power to make an attachment of earnings order under the Attachment of Earnings Act 1971 to secure payments under the order.

(4) The court may in the course of any proceedings concerning an instalments order or the magistrates' court maintenance order to which it relates vary the instalments order by exercising—

  (a) in respect of an English maintenance order, one of the powers referred to in subsection (2)(a) above;

  (b) in respect of a non-English maintenance order, one of its powers under subsection (3) above.

(5) In respect of an English maintenance order, subsections (4), (5) and (7) of section 59 above shall apply for the purposes of subsections (2)(a) and (4)(a) above as they apply for the purposes of that section.

(6) In respect of a non-English maintenance order—

  (a) subsection (4) of section 59 above shall apply for the purposes of subsections (2)(b) and (4)(b) above as it applies for the purposes of that section but as if for paragraph (a) there were substituted—

     "(a) the court proposes to exercise its power under paragraph (b) of section 95(3) below;"; and

  (b) in deciding which of the powers under subsection (3) above it is to exercise the court shall have regard to any representations made by the debtor (within the meaning of section 59 above).

(7) In this section—

"English maintenance order" has the same meaning as it has in section 94A above;

    "non-English maintenance order" means—

  (a) a maintenance order registered in, or confirmed by, a magistrates' court—

     (i) under the Maintenance Orders (Facilities for Enforcement) Act 1920;

    (ii) under Part II of the Maintenance Orders Act 1950;

      (iii) under Part I of the Maintenance Orders (Reciprocal Enforcement) Act 1972; or

      (iv) under Part I of the Civil Jurisdiction and Judgments Act 1982;

  (b) an order deemed to be made by the High Court by virtue of section 1(2) of the Maintenance Orders Act 1958 and registered under Part I of that Act in a magistrates' court; or

  (c) a maintenance order made by a magistrates' court by virtue of Part II of the Maintenance Orders (Reciprocal Enforcement) Act 1972.'

9. In section 143 of that Act (power to alter sums specified in certain provisions), in subsection (2) (which lists those provisions) after paragraph (d) there shall be inserted the following paragraph—

'(dd) section 59B(3) above;'.

Children Act 1989 (c 41)

10. In section 15 of the Children Act 1989 (orders for financial relief with respect to children), in subsection (2) (power of magistrates' court under section 60 of 1980 Act to vary etc order not to apply to order under Schedule 1) after the word 'money' there shall be inserted 'and the power of the clerk of a magistrates' court to vary such an order'.

Courts and Legal Services Act 1990 (c 41)

11.—(1) In section 10 of the Courts and Legal Services Act 1990 (family proceedings in magistrates' courts and related matters), for subsection (1) (meaning of 'family proceedings') there shall be substituted the following subsection—

'(1) In subsection (2) "family proceedings" means proceedings under Part I of the Domestic Proceedings and Magistrates' Courts Act 1978.'

(2) In subsection (2) of that section (which allows the same provision to be made by rules under section 144 of the 1980 Act in relation to family proceedings as may be made under section 93 of the Children Act 1989 in relation to relevant proceedings under that section) for the words from the beginning to 'section 144 of that Act' there shall be substituted 'Rules made under section 144 of the Magistrates' Courts Act 1980'.

Note. Sub-para (2) repealed by the Courts Act 2003, s 109(3), Sch 10, as from a day to be appointed.

SCHEDULE 3   Section 11(2)

ENACTMENTS REPEALED

Chapter	Short title	Extent of repeal
1971 c 32	The Attachment of Earnings Act 1971	In section 3, subsection (2), in subsection (4) the words 'subject to subsection (5) below', and subsection (5).
1972 c 18	The Maintenance Orders (Reciprocal Enforcement) Act 1972	Section 27(9).
1980 c 43	The Magistrates' Courts Act 1980	In Schedule 7, paragraph 97(b).
1989 c 41	The Children Act 1989	In Schedule 13, paragraph 44(1).

CHILD SUPPORT ACT 1991

(1991 c 48)

ARRANGEMENT OF SECTIONS

An Act to make provision for the *assessment* [calculation], collection and
enforcement of periodical maintenance payable by certain parents with respect
to children of theirs who are not in their care; for the collection and
enforcement of certain other kinds of maintenance; and for connected
purposes.   [25 July 1991]

Note. Word 'calculation' in square brackets substituted for word 'assessment' by the Child
Support, Pensions and Social Security Act 2000, s 1(2)(b), as from (in relation to certain
cases): 3 March 2003 (SI 2003 No 192); for remaining purposes: to be appointed.

The basic principles

1. The duty to maintain—(1) For the purposes of this Act, each parent of a
qualifying child is responsible for maintaining him.

(2) For the purposes of this Act, *an absent parent* [a non-resident parent] shall be
taken to have met his responsibility to maintain any qualifying child of his by
making periodical payments of maintenance with respect to the child of such
amount, and at such intervals, as may be determined in accordance with the
provisions of this Act.

(3) Where a *maintenance assessment* [maintenance calculation] made under this
Act requires the making of periodical payments, it shall be the duty of the *absent
parent* [non-resident parent] with respect to whom the *assessment* [calculation] was
made to make those payments.

Note. Words 'a non resident parent' and 'non-resident parent' in square brackets
substituted for words in italics by The Child Support, Pensions and Social Security Act 2000,
s 26, Sch 3, para 11(1), (2), as from (in relation to certain cases; 3 March 2003 (SI 2003
No 192); for remaining purposes: to be appointed. Words 'maintenance calculation' and
'calculation' in square brackets substituted for words in italics by The Child Support,
Pensions and social Security Act 2000, s 1(2), as from (in relation to certain cases): 3 March
2003 (SI 2003 No 192); for remaining purposes: to be appointed.

2. Welfare of children: the general principle. Where, in any case which falls
to be dealt with under this Act, the Secretary of State *or any child support officer* is
considering the exercise of any discretionary power conferred by this Act, he shall
have regard to the welfare of any child likely to be affected by his decision.

Note. Words 'or any child support officer' in italics repealed by the Social Security Act 1998,
s 86(1), (2), Sch 7, para 18, Sch 8, as from 1 June 1999 (SI 1999 No 1510).

3. Meaning of certain terms used in this Act—(1) A child is a 'qualifying child'
if—

(a) one of his parents is, in relation to him, *an absent parent* [a non-resident
    parent]; or
(b) both of his parents are, in relation to him, *absent parents* [non-resident
    parents].

(2) The parent of any child is an *'absent parent'* ['non-resident parent'], in relation to him, if—

(a) that parent is not living in the same household with the child; and

(b) the child has his home with a person who is, in relation to him, a person with care,

Note. In sub-ss (1), (2) words 'a non-resident parent', 'non-resident parents' and 'non-resident parent' in square brackets substituted for words in italics by the Child support, Pensions and Social Security Act 2000, s 26, Sch 3, para 11(1), (2), as from (in relation to certain cases): 3 March 2003 (SI 2003 No 192); for remaining purposes to be appointed.

(3) A person is a 'person with care', in relation to any child, if he is a person—

(a) with whom the child has his home;

(b) who usually provides day to day care for the child (whether exclusively or in conjunction with any other person); and

(c) who does not fall within a prescribed category of person.

(4) The Secretary of State shall not, under subsection (3)(c), prescribe as a category—

(a) parents;

(b) guardians;

(c) persons in whose favour residence orders under section 8 of the Children Act 1989 are in force;

(d) in Scotland, persons *having the right to custody of a child* [with whom a child is to live by virtue of a residence order under section 11 of the Children (Scotland) Act 1995.]

Note. In sub-s (4) words in square brackets substituted for words in italics by Children (Scotland) Act 1995, s 105(4), Sch 4, para 52(2), as from 1 November 1996.

(5) For the purposes of this Act there may be more than one person with care in relation to the same qualifying child.

(6) Periodical payments which are required to be paid in accordance with a *maintenance assessment* [maintenance calculation] are referred to in this Act as 'child support maintenance'.

Note. In sub-s (6) words 'maintenance calculation' in square brackets substituted for words 'maintenance assessment by the Child Support, Pensions and Social Security Act 2000, s 1(2)(a), as from (in relation to certain cases): 3 March 2003 (SI 2003 No 192); for remaining purposes: to be appointed.

(7) Expressions are defined in this section only for the purposes of this Act.

4. Child support maintenance—(1) A person who is, in relation to any qualifying child or any qualifying children, either the person with care or the *absent parent* [non-resident parent] may apply to the Secretary of State for a *maintenance assessment* [maintenance calculation] to be made under this Act with respect to that child, or any of those children.

(2) Where a *maintenance assessment* [maintenance calculation] has been made in response to an application under this section the Secretary of State may, if the person with care or *absent parent* [non-resident parent] with respect to whom the *assessment* [calculation] was made applies to him under this subsection, arrange for—

(a) the collection of the child support maintenance payable in accordance with the *assessment* [calculation];

(b) the enforcement of the obligation to pay child support maintenance in accordance with the *assessment* [calculation].

Note. In sub-ss (1), (2) words 'maintenance calculation' in square brackets in both places they occur and word 'calculation' in square brackets in each place it occurs substituted for words 'maintenance assessment' and 'assessment' respectively by the Child Support, Pensions and Social Security Act 2000, s 1(2), as from (in relation to certain cases): 3 March 2003 (SI 2003 No 192); for remaining purposes: to be appointed. Words 'non-resident parent' in square brackets in both places they occur substituted for words 'absent parent' by the Child

Support, Pensions and Social Security Act 2000, s 26, Sch 3, para 11(1), (2), as from (in relation to certain cases): 3 March 2003 (SI 2003 No 192); for remaining purposes: to be appointed.

(3) Where an application under subsection (2) for the enforcement of the obligation mentioned in subsection (2)(b) authorises the Secretary of State to take steps to enforce that obligation whenever he considers it necessary to do so, the Secretary of State may act accordingly.

(4) A person who applies to the Secretary of State under this section shall, so far as that person reasonably can, comply with such regulations as may be made by the Secretary of State with a view to the Secretary of State *or the child support officer* being provided with the information which is required to enable—

(a) the *absent parent* [non-resident parent] to be [identified or] traced (where that is necessary);

(b) the amount of child support maintenance payable by the *absent parent* [non-resident parent] to be *assessed* [calculated]; and

(c) that amount to be recovered from the *absent parent* [non-resident parent].

Note. In sub-s (4) words 'or the child support officer' in italics repealed by the Social Security Act 1998, s 86, Sch 7, para 19, Sch 8, as from 1 June 1999 (SI 1999 No 1510). Words 'non-resident parent' in square brackets in each place they occur and word 'calculated' in square brackets substituted for words 'absent parent' and 'assessed' respectively by the Child Support, Pensions and Social Security Act 2000, ss 1(2), 26, Sch 3, para 11(1), (2), as from (in relation to certain cases): 3 March 2003 (SI 2003 No 192); for remaining purposes: to be appointed. Words 'identified or' in square brackets in para (a) inserted by the Child Support, Pensions and Social Security Act 2000, s 26, Sch 3, para 11(1), 3(a), as from (in relation to certain cases): 3 March 2003 (SI 2003 No 192); for remaining purposes: to be appointed.

(5) Any person who has applied to the Secretary of State under this section may at any time request him to cease acting under this section.

(6) It shall be the duty of the Secretary of State to comply with any request made under subsection (5) (but subject to any regulations made under subsection (8)).

(7) The obligation to provide information which is imposed by subsection (4)—

(a) shall not apply in such circumstances as may be prescribed; and

(b) may, in such circumstances as may be prescribed, be waived by the Secretary of State.

(8) The Secretary of State may by regulations make such incidental, supplemental or transitional provision as he thinks appropriate with respect to cases in which he is requested to cease to act under this section.

(9) No application [treated as made] may be made under this section if there is in force with respect to the person with care and *absent parent* [non-resident parent] in question a *maintenance assessment* [maintenance calculation] made in response to an application under section 6.

Note. In sub-s (9) words 'treated as made' in square brackets inserted and words 'non-resident parent' and 'maintenance calculation' in square brackets substituted for words in italics by the Child Support, Pensions and Social Security Act 2000, s 26, Sch 3, para 11(1), (2), (3)(b), as from (in relation to certain cases): 3 March 2003 (SI 2003 No 192); for remaining purposes: to be appointed.

[(10) No application may be made at any time under the section with respect to a qualifying child or any qualifying children if—

(a) there is in force a written maintenance agreement made before 5th April 1993, or a maintenance order [made before a prescribed date], in respect of that child or those children and the person who is, at that time, the *absent parent* [non-resident parent]; or

[(aa) a maintenance order made on or after the date prescribed for the purposes of paragraph (a) is in force in respect of them, but has been so for less than the period of one year beginning with the date on which it was made; or]

(b) benefit is being paid to, or in respect of, a parent with care of that child or those children.

(11) In subsection (10) 'benefit' means any benefit which is mentioned in, or prescribed by regulations under, section 6(1).]

Note. Sub-ss (10), (11) inserted by Child Support Act 1995, s 18(1), as from 4 September 1995. In sub-s (10)(a) words 'made before a prescribed date' in square brackets and para (aa) inserted by the Child support, Pensions and Social Security Act 2000, s 2, as from (in relation to certain cases): 3 March 2003 (SI 2003 No 192); for remaining purposes: to be appointed. In para (a) words 'non-resident parent' in square brackets substituted for words in italics by the Child support, Pensions and Social Security Act 2000, s 26, Sch 3, para 11(1), (2), as from (in relation to certain cases 3 March 2003 (SI 2003 No 192); for remaining purposes: to be appointed.

5. Child support maintenance: supplemental provisions—(1) Where—
(a) there is more than one person with care of a qualifying child; and
(b) one or more, but not all, of them have parental responsibility for (*or, in Scotland, parental rights over*) the child;
no application may be made for a *maintenance assessment* [maintenance calculation] with respect to the child by any of those persons who do not have parental responsibility for (*or, in Scotland, parental rights over*) the child.

Note. First and third words in italics repealed by Children (Scotland) Act 1995, s 105(4), (5), Sch 4, para 52(3), Sch 5, as from 1 November 1996. Words 'maintenance calculation' in square brackets substituted for second words in italics by the Child Support, Pensions and Social Security Act 2000, s 26, Sch 3, para 11(1), (2), as from (in relation to certain cases): 3 March 2003 (SI 2003 No 192); for remaining purposes: to be appointed.

(2) Where more than one application for a *maintenance assessment* [maintenance calculation] is made with respect to the child concerned, only one of them may be proceeded with.

(3) The Secretary of State may by regulations make provision as to which of two or more applications for a *maintenance assessment* [maintenance calculation] with respect to the same child is to be proceeded with,

Note. In sub-ss (2), (3) words 'maintenance calculaltion' in square brackets substituted for words in italics by the Child Support, Pensions and Social Security Act 2000, s 1(2)(a), as from (in relation to certain cases): 3 March 2003 (or SI 2003 No 192); for remaining purposes: to be appointed.

6. Applications by those receiving benefit—*(1) Where income support, [an income-based jobseeker's allowance,] family credit or any other benefit of a prescribed kind is claimed by or in respect of, or paid to or in respect of, the parent of a qualifying child she shall, if—*
(a)   she is a person with care of the child; and
(b)   she is required to do so by the Secretary of State,
authorise the Secretary of State to take action under this Act to recover child support maintenance from the absent parent [non-resident parent].

Note. Words 'an income-based jobseeker's allowance' in square brackets inserted by Jobseekers Act 1995, s 41(4), Sch 2, para 20(1), (2), as from 7 October 1996. Words ', family credit' repealed by the Tax Credits Act 1999, s 2, Sch 2, Pt IV, para 17(a), Sch 6, as from 5 October 1999. Words 'non-resident parent' in square brackets substituted for words 'absent parent' by the Child Support, Pensions and Social Security Act 2000, s 26, Sch 3, para 11(1), (2), as from (in relation to certain cases): 3 March 2003 (SI 2003 No 192); for remaining purposes: to be appointed.

(2) The Secretary of State shall not require a person ('the parent') to give him the authorisation mentioned in subsection (1) if he considers that there are reasonable grounds for believing that—
(a)   if the parent were to be required to give that authorisation; or
(b)   if she were to give it,
there would be a risk of her, or of any child living with her, suffering harm or undue distress as a result,

(3) Subsection (2) shall not apply if the parent requests the Secretary of State to disregard it.

(4) The authorisation mentioned in subsection (1) shall extend to all children of the absent parent [non-resident parent] in relation to whom the parent first mentioned in subsection (1) is a person with care.

(5) That authorisation shall be given, without unreasonable delay, by completing and returning to the Secretary of State an application—

  (a) for the making of a maintenance assessment [maintenance calculation] with respect to the qualifying child or qualifying children; and
  (b) for the Secretary of State to take action under this Act to recover, on her behalf, the amount of child support maintenance so assessed [calculated].

Note. In sub-ss (4), (5) words in square brackets substituted for words 'absent paent', 'maintenance assessment' and 'assessed' by the Child Support, Pensions and social Security Act 2000, ss 1(2), 26, Sch 3, para 11(1) (2), as from (in relation to certain cases): 3 March 2003 (SI 2003 No 192); for remaining purposes: to be appointed.

(6) Such an application shall be made on a form ('a maintenance application form') provided by the Secretary of State.

(7) A maintenance application form shall indicate in general terms the effect of completing and returning it.

(8) Subsection (1) has effect regardless of whether any of the benefits mentioned there is payable with respect to any qualifying child.

(9) A person who is under the duty imposed by subsection (1) shall, so far as she reasonably can, comply with such regulations as may be made by the Secretary of State with a view to the Secretary of State or the child support officer being provided with the information which is required to enable—

  (a) the absent parent [non-resident parent] to be traced;
  (b) the amount of child support maintenance payable by the absent parent [non-resident parent] to be assessed [calculated]; and
  (c) that amount to be recovered from the absent parent [non-resident parent].

(10) The obligation to provide information which is imposed by subsection (9)—

  (a) shall not apply in such circumstances as may be prescribed; and
  (b) may, in such circumstances as may be prescribed, be waived by the Secretary of State.

(11) A person with care who has authorised the Secretary of State under subsection (1) but who subsequently ceases to fall within that subsection may request the Secretary of State to cease acting under this section.

(12) It shall be the duty of the Secretary of State to comply with any request made under subsection (11) (but subject to any regulations made under subsection (13)).

(13) The Secretary of State may by regulations make such incidental or transitional provision as he thinks appropriate with respect to cases in which he is requested under subsection (11) to cease to act under this section.

(14) The fact that a maintenance assessment [maintenance calculation] is in force with respect to a person with care shall not prevent the making of a new maintenance assessment [maintenance calculation] with respect to her in response to an application under this section.

Note. In sub-s (9) words 'or the child support officer' repealed by the Social Security Act 1998, s 86, Sch 7, para 20, Sch 8, as from 1 June 1999 (SI 1999 No 15100. In sub-ss (9), (14) words in square brackets substituted for words 'absent parent', 'assessed' and 'maintenance assessment' in each place they occur by the Child Support, Pensions and Social Security Act 2000, ss 1(2), 26, Sch 3, para 11(1), (2), as from (in relation to certain cases): 3 March 2003 (SI 2003 No 192); for remaining purposes: to be appointed.

[6. Applications by those claiming or receiving benefit—(1) This section applies where income support, an income-based jobseeker's allowance or any other benefit of a prescribed kind is claimed by or in respect of, or paid to or in respect of, the parent of a qualifying child who is also a person with care of the child.

(2) In this section, that person is referred to as "the parent". (3) The Secretary of State may—

    (a) treat the parent as having applied for a maintenance calculation with respect to the qualifying child and all other children of the non-resident parent in relation to whom the parent is also a person with care; and

    (b) take action under this Act to recover from the non-resident parent, on the parent's behalf, the child support maintenance so determined.

    (4) Before doing what is mentioned in subsection (3), the Secretary of State must notify the parent in writing of the effect of subsections (3) and (5) and section 46.

    (5) The Secretary of State may not act under subsection (3) if the parent asks him not to (a request which need not be in writing).

    (6) Subsection (1) has effect regardless of whether any of the benefits mentioned there is payable with respect to any qualifying child.

    (7) Unless she has made a request under subsection (5), the parent shall, so far as she reasonably can, comply with such regulations as may be made by the Secretary of State with a view to the Secretary of State's being provided with the information which is required to enable-

    (a) the non-resident parent to be identified or traced;

    (b) the amount of child support maintenance payable by him to be calculated; and

    (c) that amount to be recovered from him.

    (8) The obligation to provide information which is imposed by subsection (7)-

    (a) does not apply in such circumstances as may be prescribed; and

    (b) may, in such circumstances as may be prescribed, be waived by the Secretary of State.

    (9) If the parent ceases to fall within subsection (1), she may ask the Secretary of State to cease acting

under this section, but until then he may continue to do so.

    (10) The Secretary of State must comply with any request under subsection (9) (but subject to any regulations made under subsection (11)).

    (11) The Secretary of State may by regulations make such incidental or transitional provision as .he thinks appropriate with respect to cases in which he is asked under subsection (9) to cease to act under this section.

    (12) The fact that a maintenance calculation is in force with respect to a person with care does not prevent the making of a new maintenance calculation with respect to her as a result of the Secretary of State's acting under subsection (3).]

Note. Section 6 above substituted for s 6 in italics by the Child Support, Pensions and Social Security Act 2000, s 3, as from for certain purposes: 10 November 2000 (SI 2000 No 2994); for certain cases: 3 March 2003 (SI 2003 No 192); for remaining purposes: to be appointed.

7. (*Applies to Scotland only.*)

8. Role of the courts with respect to maintenance for children—(1) This subsection applies in any case where a *child support officer* [the Secretary of State] would have jurisdiction to make a *maintenance assessment* [maintenance calculation] with respect to a qualifying child and an *absent parent* [non-resident parent] of his on an application duly made [(or treated as made)] by a person entitled to apply for such an *assessment* [a calculation] with respect to that child.

Note. Words 'the Secretary of State' in square brackets substituted for words 'a child support officer' by the Social Security Act 1998, s 86(1), Sch 7, para 22, as from 1 June 1999 (SI 1999 No 1510). Words 'maintenance calculation', 'non-resident parent' and 'a calculation' in square brackets substituted for words in italics by the Child Support, Pensions and Social Security Act 2000, ss 1(2), 26, Sch 3, para 11(1), (2), as from (in relation to certain cases): 3 March 2003 (SI 2003 No 192); for remaining purposes: to be appointed. Words '(or treated as made)' in square brackets inserted by the Child Support, Pensions and Social Security Act 2000, s 26, Sch 3, para 11(1), (5)(a), as from (in relation to certain cases): 3 March 2003 (SI 2003 No 192); for remaining purposes: to be appointed.

(2) Subsection (1) applies even though the circumstances of the case are such that *a child support officer* [the Secretary of State] would not make *an assessment* [a calculation] if it were applied for.

(3) [Except as provided in subsection (3A),] in any case where subsection (1) applies, no court shall exercise any power which it would otherwise have to make, vary or revive any maintenance order in relation to the child and *absent parent* [non-resident parent] concerned.

Note. In sub-s (2) words 'the Secretary of State' in square brackets substituted for words 'a child support officer' by the Social Security Act 1998, s 86(1), Sch 7, para 22, as from 1 June 1999 (SI 1999 No 1510). In sub-ss (2), (3) words 'a calculation' and 'non-resident parent' in square brackets substituted for words in italics and words 'Except as provided in subsection (3A),' in square brackets in sub-s (3) inserted by the Child Support, Pensions and Social Security Act 2000, ss 1(2), 26, Sch 3, para 11(1), (2), (5)(b), as from (in relation to certain cases): 3 March 2003 (SI 2003 No 192); for remaining purposes: to be appointed.

[(3A) In any case in which section 4(10) or 7(10) prevents the making of an application for a maintenance assessment [maintenance calculation], and—
(a) no application has been made for a maintenance assessment [maintenance calculation] under section 6, or
(b) such an application has been made but no maintenance assessment [maintenance calculation] has been made in response to it,
subsection (3) shall have effect with the omission of the word 'vary'.]

Note. Sub-s (3A) inserted by Child Support Act 1995, s 18(3), as from 4 September 1995. Words 'maintenance calculation' in square brackets in each place they occur substituted for words 'maintenance assessment' by the Child Support, Pensions and Social Security Act 2000, s 1(2)(a), as from (in relation to certain cases): 3 March 2003 (SI 2003 No 192); for remaining purposes: to be appointed.

[(3A) Unless a maintenance calculation has been made with respect to the child concerned, subsection (3) does not prevent a court from varying a maintenance order in relation to that child and the non-resident parent concerned—
(a) if the maintenance order was made on or after the date prescribed for the purposes of section 4(10)(a) or 7(10)(a); or
(b) where the order was made before then, in any case in which section 4(10) or 7(10) prevents the making of an application for a maintenance calculation with respect to or by that child.]

Note. Sub-s (3A) substituted for sub-s (3A) in italics by the Child Support, Pensions and Social Security Act 2000, s 26, Sch 3, para 11(1), (5)(c), as from (in relation to certain cases): 3 March 2003 (SI 2003 No 192); for remaining purposes: to be appointed.

(4) Subsection (3) does not prevent a court from revoking a maintenance order.

(5) The Lord Chancellor or in relation to Scotland the Lord Advocate may by order provide that, in such circumstances as may be specified by the order, this section shall not prevent a court from exercising any power which it has to make a maintenance order in relation to a child if—
(a) a written agreement (whether or not enforceable) provides for the making, or securing, by an *absent parent* [a non-resident parent] of the child of periodical payments to or for the benefit of the child; and
(b) the maintenance order which the court makes is, in all material respects, in the same terms as that agreement.

(6) This section shall not prevent a court from exercising any power which it has to make a maintenance order in relation to a child if—
(a) a *maintenance assessment* [maintenance calculation] is in force with respect to the child;
(b) *the amount of the child support maintenance payable in accordance with the assessment [calculation] was determined by reference to the alternative formula mentioned in paragraph 4(3) of Schedule 1; and*

[(b) the non-resident parent's net weekly income exceeds the figure referred to in paragraph 10(3) of Schedule 1 (as it has effect from time to time pursuant to regulations made under paragraph 10A(1)(b)); and]

    (c) the court is satisfied that the circumstances of the case make it appropriate for the *absent parent* [non-resident parent] to make or secure the making of periodical payments under a maintenance order in addition to the child support maintenance payable by him in accordance with the *maintenance assessment* [maintenance calculation].

Note. In sub-ss (5), (6) words in square brackets substituted for words 'an absent parent', 'maintenance assessment', 'assessment' and 'absent parent' in each place they occur, and sub-s (6)(b) substituted, by the Child Support, Pensions and Social Security Act 2000, ss 1(2), 26, Sch 3, para 11(1), (2), (5)(d), as from (in relation to certain cases): 3 March 2003 (SI 2003 No 192); for remaining purposes: to be appointed.

(7) This section shall not prevent a court from exercising any power which it has to make a maintenance order in relation to a child if—

    (a) the child is, will be or (if the order were to be made) would be receiving instruction at an educational establishment or undergoing training for a trade, profession or vocation (whether or not while in gainful employment); and

    (b) the order is made solely for the purposes of requiring the person making or securing the making of periodical payments fixed by the order to meet some or all of the expenses incurred in connection with the provision of the instruction or training.

(8) This section shall not prevent a court from exercising any power which it has to make a maintenance order in relation to a child if—

    (a) a disability living allowance is paid to or in respect of him; or

    (b) no such allowance is paid but he is disabled,

and the order is made solely for the purpose of requiring the person making or securing the making of periodical payments fixed by the order to meet some or all of any expenses attributable to the child's disability.

(9) For the purposes of subsection (8), a child is disabled if he is blind, deaf or dumb or is substantially and permanently handicapped by illness, injury, mental disorder or congenital deformity or such other disability as may be prescribed.

(10) This section shall not prevent a court from exercising any power which it has to make a maintenance order in relation to a child if the order is made against a person with care of the child.

(11) In this Act 'maintenance order', in relation to any child, means an order which requires the making or securing of periodical payments to or for the benefit of the child and which is made under—

    (a) Part II of the Matrimonial Causes Act 1973;

    (b) the Domestic Proceedings and Magistrates' Courts Act 1978;

    (c) Part III of the Matrimonial and Family Proceedings Act 1984;

    (d) the Family Law (Scotland) Act 1985;

    (e) Schedule 1 to the Children Act 1989; or

    (f) any other prescribed enactment,

and includes any order varying or reviving such an order.

9. Agreements about maintenance—(1) In this section 'maintenance agreement' means any agreement for the making, or for securing the making, of periodical payments by way of maintenance, or in Scotland aliment, to or for the benefit of any child.

(2) Nothing in this Act shall be taken to prevent any person from entering into a maintenance agreement.

(3) [Subject to section 4(10)(a) and section 7(10),] the existence of a maintenance agreement shall not prevent any party to the agreement, or any other person, from

applying for a *maintenance assessment* [maintenance calculation] with respect to any child to or for whose benefit periodical payments are to be made or secured under the agreement.

Note. Words 'Subject to ... 7(10),' in square brackets inserted by Child Support Act 1995, s 18(4), as from 4 September 1995. Words 'maintenance calculation' in square brackets substituted for words in italics by the Child Support, Pensions and Social Security Act 2000, s 1(2)(a), as from (in relation to certain cases): 3 March 2003 (SI 2003 No 192); for remaining purposes: to be appointed.

(4) Where any agreement contains a provision which purports to restrict the right of any person to apply for a *maintenance assessment* [maintenance calculation], that provision shall be void.

(5) Where section 8 would prevent any court from making a maintenance order in relation to a child and *an absent parent* [a non-resident parent] of his, no court shall exercise any power that it has to vary any agreement so as—

(a) to insert a provision requiring that *absent parent* [a non-resident parent] to make or secure the making of periodical payments by way of maintenance, or in Scotland aliment, to or for the benefit of that child; or

(b) to increase the amount payable under such a provision.

[(6) In any case in which section 4(10) or 7(10) prevents the making of an application for a *maintenance assessment* [maintenance calculation], and—

(a) no application has been made for a maintenance assessment [maintenance calculation] under section 6, or

(b) such an application has been made but no maintenance assessment [maintenance calculation] has been made in response to it,

[(a) no parent has been treated under section 6(3) as having applied for a maintenance calculation with respect to the child; or

(b) a parent has been so treated but no maintenance calculation has been made,]

subsection (5) shall have effect with the omission of paragraph (b).]

Note. Sub-s (6) added by Child Support Act 1995, s 18(4), as from 4 September 1995. In sub-ss (4)–(6) words in square brackets substituted for words 'maintenance assessment', 'an absent parent' and 'absent parent' in each place they occur and sub-s (6)(a),(b) substituted by the Child Support, Pensions and Social Security Act 2000, ss 1(2)(a), 26, Sch 3, para 11(1), (2), (6), as from (in relation to certain cases): 3 March 2003 (SI 2003 No 192); for remaining purposes: to be appointed.

10. Relationship between *maintenance assessments* [maintenance calculations] and certain court orders and related matters—(1) Where an order of a kind prescribed for the purposes of this subsection is in force with respect to any qualifying child with respect to whom a *maintenance assessment* [maintenance calculation] is made, the order—

(a) shall, so far as it relates to the making or securing of periodical payments, cease to have effect to such extent as may be determined in accordance with regulations made by the Secretary of State; or

(b) where the regulations so provide, shall, so far as it so relates, have effect subject to such modifications as may be so determined.

(2) Where an agreement of a kind prescribed for the purposes of this subsection is in force with respect to any qualifying child with respect to whom a *maintenance assessment* [maintenance calculation] is made, the agreement—

(a) shall, so far as it relates to the making or securing of periodical payments, be unenforceable to such extent as may be determined in accordance with regulations made by the Secretary of State; or

(b) where the regulations so provide, shall, so far as it so relates, have effect subject to such modifications as may be so determined.

(3) Any regulations under this section may, in particular, make such provision with respect to—

(a) any case where any person with respect to whom an order or agreement of a kind prescribed for the purposes of subsection (1) or (2) has effect applies to the prescribed court, before the end of the prescribed period, for the order or agreement to be varied in the light of the *maintenance assessment* [maintenance calculation] and of the provisions of this Act;

(b) the recovery of any arrears under the order or agreement which fell due before the coming into force of the *maintenance assessment* [maintenance calculation],

as the Secretary of State considers appropriate and may provide that, in prescribed circumstances, an application to any court which is made with respect to an order of a prescribed kind relating to the making or securing of periodical payments to or for the benefit of a child shall be treated by the court as an application for the order to be revoked.

Note. In section heading words 'maintenance calculations' in square brackets and in sub-ss (1)–(3) words 'maintenance calculation' in square brackets in each place they occur substituted for words in italics by the Child Support, Pensions and Social Security Act 2000, s 1(2)(a), as from (in relation to certain cases): 3 March 2003 (SI 2003 No 192); for remaining purposes: to be appointed.

(4) The Secretary of State may by regulations make provision for—

(a) notification to be given by *the child support officer* [the Secretary of State] concerned to the prescribed person in any case where *that officer* [he] considers that the making of a *maintenance assessment* [maintenance calculation] has affected, or is likely to affect, any order of a kind prescribed for the purposes of this subsection;

(b) notification to be given by the prescribed person to the Secretary of State in any case where a court makes an order which it considers has affected, or is likely to affect, a *maintenance assessment* [maintenance calculation].

(5) Rules may be made under section 144 of the Magistrates' Courts Act 1980 (rules of procedure) requiring any person who, in prescribed circumstances, makes an application to a magistrates' court for a maintenance order to furnish the court with a statement in a prescribed form, and signed by *a child support officer* [an officer of the Secretary of State], as to whether or not, at the time when the statement is made, there is a *maintenance assessment* [maintenance calculation] in force with respect to that person or the child concerned.

In this subsection—

'maintenance order' means an order of a prescribed kind for the making or securing of periodical payments to or for the benefit of a child; and

'prescribed' means prescribed by the rules.

Note. In sub-ss (4), (5) words 'the Secretary of State', 'he' and 'an officer of the Secretary of State' in square brackets substituted for words in italics by the Social Security Act 1998, s 86(1), Sch 7, para 23(2), as from 1 June 1999 (SI 1999 No 1510). Words 'maintenance calculation' in square brackets in each place they occur substituted for words in italics by the Child Support, Pensions and Social Security Act 2000, s 1(2)(a), as from (in relation to certain cases): 3 March 2003 (SI 2003 No 192); for remaining purposes: to be appointed.

Maintenance assessments [maintenance calculations]

11. Maintenance assessments [maintenance calculation]—*(1) Any application for a maintenance assessment made to the Secretary of State shall be referred by him to a child support officer whose duty it shall be to deal with the application [dealt with by him] in accordance with the provision made by or under this Act.*

[(1A) Where—

(a) *an application for a maintenance assessment [maintenance calculation] is made under section 6, but*

(b) *the Secretary of State becomes aware, before referring the application to a child support officer [before determing the application], that the claim mentioned in subsection (1) of that section has been disallowed or withdrawn,*

he shall, subject to subsection (1B), treat the application as if it had not been made.

(1B) If it appears to the Secretary of State that subsection (10) of section 4 would not have prevented the parent with care concerned from making an application for a maintenance assessment [maintenance calculation] under that section he shall—

(a) *notify her of the effect of this subsection, and*

(b) *if, before the end of the period of 28 days beginning with the day on which notice was sent to her, she asks him to do so, treat the application as having been made not under section 6 but under section 4.*

(1C) Where the application is not preserved under subsection (1B) (and so is treated as not having been made) the Secretary of State shall notify—

(a) *the parent with care concerned; and*

(b) *the absent parent [non-resident parent] (or alleged absent parent [non-resident parent]), where it appears to him that that person is aware of the application.]*

Note. Sub-ss (1A)–(1C) inserted by Child Support Act 1995, s 19, as from 4 September 1995. In cross-heading, in section heading and in sub-ss (1A)–(1C) words 'maintenance calculations', 'maintenance calculation' and 'non-resident parent' in square brackets in each place they occur substituted for words 'maintenance assessments', 'maintenance assessment' and 'absent parent' respectively by the Child Support, Pensions and Social Security Act 2000, ss 1(2)(a), 26, Sch 3, para 11(1), (2), as from (in relation to certain cases): 3 March 2003 (SI 2003 No 192); for remaining purposes: to be appointed. In sub-ss (1), (1A) words 'dealt with by him' and 'before determining the application' in square brackets substituted for words 'referred by ... application' and 'before referring ... officer' by the Social Security Act 1998, s 86(1), Sch 7, para 24(1), as from 1 June 1999 (SI 1999 No 1510).

(2) The amount of child support maintenance to be fixed by any maintenance assessment [maintenance calculation] shall be determined in accordance with the provisions of Part I of Schedule 1.

(3) Part II of Schedule 1 makes further provision with respect to maintenance assessments [maintenance calculations].

Note. In sub-ss (2), (3) words 'maintenance calculation' in square brackets substituted for words 'maintenance assessment' by the Child Support, Pensions and Social Security Act 2000, s 1(2)(a), as from (in relation to certain cases): 3 March 2003 (SI 2003 No 192); for remaining purposes: to be appointed.

[11. Maintenance calculations—*(1) An application for a maintenance calculation made to the Secretary of State shall be dealt with by him in accordance with the provision made by or under this Act.*

(2) The Secretary of State shall (unless he decides not to make a maintenance calculation in response to the application, or makes a decision under section 12) determine the application by making a decision under this section about whether any child support maintenance is payable and, if so, how much.

(3) Where-

(a) *a parent is treated under section 6(3) as having applied for a maintenance calculation; but*

(b) *the Secretary of State becomes aware before determining the application that the parent has ceased to fall within section 6(1),*

he shall, subject to subsection (4), cease to treat that parent as having applied for a maintenance calculation.

(4) If it appears to the Secretary of State that subsection (10) of section 4 would not have prevented the parent with care concerned from making an application for a maintenance calculation under that section he shall-

(a) *notify her of the effect of this subsection; and*

(b) *if, before the end of the period of one month beginning with the day on which notice was sent to her, she asks him to do so, treat her as having applied not under section 6 but under section 4.*

(5) Where subsection (3) applies but subsection (4) does not, the Secretary of State shall notify-
(a)   the parent with care concerned; and
(b)   the non-resident parent (or alleged non-resident parent), where it appears to him that that person
is aware that the parent with care has been treated as having applied for a maintenance calculation.

(6) The amount of child support maintenance to be fixed by a maintenance calculation shall be I determined in accordance with Part I of Schedule 1 unless an application for a variation has been made and agreed.

(7) If the Secretary of State has agreed to a variation, the amount of child support maintenance to be fixed shall be determined on the basis he determines under section 28F(4).

(8) Part II of Schedule 1 makes further provision with respect to maintenance calculations.]

Note. Section 11 above substituted for s 11 in italics by the Child Support, Pensions and Social Security Act 2000, s 1(1), as from (in relation to certain cases): 3 March 2003 (SI 2003 No 192); for remaining purposes to be appointed.

12. Interim *maintenance assessments*—*(1) Where it appears to a child support officer who is required to make a maintenance assessment that he does not have sufficient information to enable him to make an assessment in accordance with the provision made by or under this Act, he may make an interim maintenance assessment.*

[(1)   This section applies where a child support officer—
(a)   is required to make a maintenance assessment [maintenance calculation];
(b)   is proposing to conduct a review under section 16, 17, 18 or 19; or
(c)   is conducting such a review.

(1A)   If it appears to the child support officer that he does not have sufficient information to enable him—
(a)   in a case falling within subsection (1)(a), to make the assessment,
(b)   in a case falling within subsection (1)(b), to conduct the proposed review, or
(c)   in a case falling within subsection (1)(c), to complete the review,
he may make an interim maintenance assessment [maintenance calculation].]

[(1)   Where the Secretary of State—
(a)   is required to make a maintenance assessment [maintenance calculation]; or
(b)   is proposing to make a decision under section 16 or 17,
and (in either case) it appears to him that he does not have sufficient information to enable him to do so, he may make an interim maintenance assessment [maintenance calculation].]

Note. Sub-ss (1), (1A) in square brackets substituted for original sub-s (1) by Child Support Act 1995, s 11, as from 22 January 1996. In sub-ss (1), (1A) words 'maintenance calculation' in square brackets substituted for words 'maintenance assessment' by the Child Support, Pensions and Social Security Act 2000, s 1(2)(a), as from (in relation to certain cases): 3 March 2003 (SI 2003 No 912); for remaining purposes: to be appointed. New sub-s (1) substituted for sub-ss (1), (1A), by the Social Security Act 1998, s 86(1), Sch 7, para 25(1), as from 1 June 1999 (SI 1999 No 1510).

(2) The Secretary of State may by regulations make provision as to interim maintenance assessments [maintenance calculations].

(3) The regulations may, in particular, make provision as to—
(a)   the procedure to be followed in making an interim maintenance assessment [maintenance calcuation]; and
(b)   the basis on which the amount of child support maintenance fixed by an interim assessment [calculation] is to be calculated.

(4) Before making any interim assessment [calculation] a child support officer [the Secretary of State] shall, if it is reasonably practicable to do so, give written notice of his intention to make such an assessment [a calculation] to—
(a)   the absent parent [non-resident parent] concerned;
(b)   the person with care concerned; and

(c) *where the application for a maintenance assessment [maintenance calculation] was made under section 7, the child concerned.*

(5) *Where a child support officer [the Secretary of State] serves notice under subsection (4), he shall not make the proposed interim assessment [calculation] before the end of such period as may be prescribed.*

Note. In sub-ss (2)–(5) words 'in square brackets (except as mentioned below) substituted for words 'maintenance assessments', 'maintenance assessment', 'assessment', 'an assessment' and 'absent parent' in each place they occur by the Child Support, Pensions and Social Security Act 2000, ss 1(2), 26, Sch 3, para 11(1), (2), as from (in relation to certain cases): 3 March 2003 (SI 2003 No 192); for remaining purposes: to be appointed. In sub-ss (4), (5) words 'the Secretary of State' in square brackets substituted for words 'a child support officer; by the Social Security Act 1998, s 86(1), Sch 7, para 25(2), as from 1 June 1999 (SI 1999 No 1510).

[12. Default and interim maintenance decisions—*(1) Where the Secretary of State-*

(a) *is required to make a maintenance calculation; or*

(b) *is proposing to make a decision under section 16 or 17,*

and it appears to him that he does not have sufficient information to enable him to do so, he may make a default maintenance decision.

(2) *Where an application for a variation has been made under section 28A(1) in connection with an application for a maintenance calculation (or in connection with such an application which is treated as having been made), the Secretary of State may make an interim maintenance decision.*

(3) *The amount of child support maintenance fixed by an interim maintenance decision shall be determined in accordance with Part I of Schedule 1.*

(4) *The Secretary of State may by regulations make provision as to default and interim maintenance decisions.*

(5) *The regulations may, in particular, make provision as to-*

(a) *the procedure to be followed in making a default or an interim maintenance decision; and*

(b) *a default rate of child support maintenance to apply where a default maintenance decision is made.]*

Note. Section 12 above substituted for s 12 in italics by the Child Support, Pensions and Social Security Act 2000, s 4, as from (for certain purposes): 10 November 2000 (SI 2000 No 2994); (in relation to certain cases): 3 March 2003 (SI 2003 No 192); (for remaining purposes): to be appointed.

Child support officers

13. Child support officers—*(1) The Secretary of State shall appoint persons (to be known as child support officers) for the purpose of exercising functions—*

(a) *conferred on them by this Act, or by any other enactment,; or*

(b) *assigned to them by the Secretary of State.*

(2) *A child support officer may be appointed to perform only such functions as may be specified in his instrument of appointment.*

(3) *The Secretary of State shall appoint a Chief Child Support Officer.*

(4) *It shall be the duty of the Chief Child Support Officer to—*

(a) *advise child support officers on the discharge of their functions in relation to making, reviewing or cancelling maintenance assessments;*

(b) *keep under review the operation of the provision made by or under this Act with respect to making, reviewing or cancelling maintenance assessments; and*

(c) *report to the Secretary of State annually, in writing, on the matters with which the Chief Child Support Officer is concerned.*

(5) *The Secretary of State shall publish, in such manner as he considers appropriate, any report which he receives under subsection (4)(c).*

(6) *Any proceedings (other than for an offence) in respect of any act or omission of a child support officer which, apart from this subsection, would fall to be brought against a child support officer resident in Northern Ireland may instead be brought against the Chief Child Support Officer.*

(7) For the purposes of any proceedings brought by virtue of subsection (6), the acts or omissions of the child support officer shall be treated as the acts or omissions of the Chief Child Support Officer.

Note. Section 13 repealed by the Social Security Act 1998, s 86(1), (2), Sch 7, para 26, Sch 8, as from 1 June 1999 (SI 1999 No 1510).

Information

14. Information required by Secretary of State—(1) The Secretary of State may make regulations requiring any information or evidence needed for the determination of any application [made or treated as made] under this Act, or any question arising in connection with such an application[(or application treated as made), or needed for the making of any decision or in connection with the imposition of any condition or requirement under this Act,], or needed in connection with the collection or enforcement of child support or other maintenance under this Act, to be furnished—

(a) by such persons as may be determined in accordance with regulations made by the Secretary of State; and

(b) in accordance with the regulations.

Note. Words in square brackets inserted by the Child Support, Pensions and Social Security Act 2000, ss 12, 26, Sch 3, para 11(1), (7), as from (in relation to certain cases): 3 March 2003 (SI 2003 No 192); for remaining purposes: to be appointed.

[(1A) Regulations under subsection (1) may make provision for notifying any person who is required to furnish any information or evidence under the regulations of the possible consequences of failing to do so.]

Note. Sub-s (1A) inserted by Child Support Act 1995, s 30(5), Sch 3, para 3, as from 1 October 1995.

(2) Where the Secretary of State has in his possession any information acquired by him in connection with his functions under any of the benefit Acts [or the Jobseekers Act 1995], he may—

(a) make use of that information for purposes of this Act; or

(b) disclose it to the Department of Health and Social Services for Northern Ireland for purposes of any enactment corresponding to this Act and having effect with respect to Northern Ireland.

Note. Sub-s (2) repealed by the Social Security Act 1998, s 86, Sch 7, para 27(a), (b), Sch 8, as from 8 September 1998 (SI 1998 No 2209). Words in square brackets inserted by Jobseekers Act 1995, s 41(4), Sch 2, para 20(1), (3), as from 7 October 1996.

[(2A) Where the Secretary of State has in his possession any information acquired by him in connection with his functions under this Act, he may—

(a) make use of that information for purposes of any of the benefit Acts or of the Jobseekers Act 1995; or

(b) disclose it to the Department of Health and Social Services for Northern Ireland for purposes of any enactment corresponding to any of those Acts and having effect with respect to Northern Ireland.]

Note. Sub-s (2A) inserted by Child Support Act 1995, s 30(5), Sch 3, para 3, as from 4 September 1995. Repealed by the Social Security Act 1998, s 86, Sch 7, para 27(a), (b), Sch 8, as from 8 September 1998 (SI 1998 No 2209).

(3) The Secretary of State may by regulations make provision authorising the disclosure by him *or by child support officers*, in such circumstances as may be prescribed, of such information held by *them* [him] for purposes of this Act as may be prescribed.

Note. Words 'or by child support officers' in italics repealed and word in square brackets substituted for word 'them' in italics by the Social Security Act 1998, s 86, Sch 7, para 27(a), (b), Sch 8, as from 8 September 1998 (SI 1998 No 2209).

(4) The provisions of Schedule 2 (which relate to information which is held for purposes other than those of this Act but which is required by the Secretary of State) shall have effect.

[14A. Information—offence—(1) This section applies to-

(a) persons who are required to comply with regulations under section 4(4) or 7(5); and

(b) persons specified in regulations under section 14(1)(a).

(2) Such a person is guilty of an offence if, pursuant to a request for information under or by virtue of those regulations-

(a) he makes a statement or representation which he knows to be false; or

(b) he provides, or knowingly causes or knowingly allows to be provided, a document or other information which he knows to be false in a material particular.

(3) Such a person is guilty of an offence if, following such a request, he fails to comply with it.

(4) It is a defence for a person charged with an offence under subsection (3) to prove that he had a reasonable excuse for failing to comply.

(5) A person guilty of an offence under this section is liable on summary conviction to a fine not exceeding level 3 on the standard scale.]

Note. This section inserted by the Child Support, Pensions and Social Security Act 2000, s 13, as from 31 January 2001 (SI 2000 No 3354).

15. Powers of inspectors—*(1) Where, in a particular case, the Secretary of State considers it appropriate to do so for the purpose of acquiring information which he or any child support officer requires for purposes of this Act, he may appoint a person to act as an inspector under this section.*

Words 'or any child support officer' repealed by the Social Security Act 1998, s 86, Sch 7, para 28, Sch 8, as from 1 June 1999 (SI 1999 No 1510).

(2) Every inspector shall be furnished with a certificate of his appointment.

(3) Without prejudice to his being appointed to act in relation to any other case, or being appointed to act for a further period in relation to the case in question, an inspector's appointment shall cease at the end of such period as may be specified.

(4) An inspector shall have power—

(a) to enter at all reasonable times—

(i) any specified premises, other than premises used solely as a dwelling-house; and

(ii) any premises which are not specified but which are used by any specified person for the purpose of carrying on any trade, profession, vocation or business; and

(b) to make such examination and enquiry there as he considers appropriate.

[(1) The Secretary of State may appoint, on such terms as he thinks fit, persons to act as inspectors under this section.

(2) The function of inspectors is to acquire information which the Secretary of State needs for any of the purposes of this Act.

(3) Every inspector is to be given a certificate of his appointment.

(4) An inspector has power, at any reasonable time and either alone or accompanied by such other persons as he thinks fit, to enter any premises which-

(a) are liable to inspection under this section; and

(b) are premises to which it is reasonable for him to require entry in order that he may exercise his functions under this section,

and may there make such examination and inquiry as he considers appropriate.

(4A) Premises liable to inspection under this section are those which are not used wholly as a dwelling house and which the inspector has reasonable grounds for suspecting are-

(a) premises at which a non-resident parent is or has been employed;

(b) premises at which a non-resident parent carries out, or has carried out, a trade, profession, vocation or business;

(c) premises at which there is information held by a person ('A') whom the inspector has reasonable grounds for suspecting has information about a non-resident parent acquired in the course of A's own trade, profession, vocation or business.]

Note. Sub-ss (1)–(4), (4A) in square brackets substituted for sub-ss (1)–(4) in italics by the Child Support, Pensions and Social Security Act 2000, s 14(1), (2), as from 31 January 2001 (SI 2000 No 3354).

(5) An inspector exercising his powers may question any person aged 18 or over whom he finds on the premises.

(6) If required to do so by an inspector exercising his powers, *any person who is or has been—*

(a) *an occupier of the premises in question;*
(b) *an employer or an employee working at or from those premises;*
(c) *carrying on at or from those premises any trade, profession, vocation or business;*
(d) *an employee or agent of any person mentioned in paragraphs (a) to (c),* [any such person]

shall furnish to the inspector all such information and documents as the inspector may reasonably require.

Note. In sub-s (6) words in square brackets substituted for words in italics by the Child Support, Pensions and Social Security Act 2000, s 14(1), (3), as from 31 January 2001 (SI 2000 No 3354).

(7) No person shall be required under this section to answer any question or to give any evidence tending to incriminate himself or, in the case of a person who is married, his or her spouse.

(8) On applying for admission to any premises in the exercise of his powers, an inspector shall, if so required, produce his certificate.

(9) If any person—

(a) intentionally delays or obstructs any inspector exercising his powers; or
(b) without reasonable excuse, refuses or neglects to answer any question or furnish any information or to produce any document when required to do so under this section,

he shall be guilty of an offence and liable on summary conviction to a fine not exceeding level 3 on the standard scale.

(10) In this section—

'certificate' means a certificate of appointment issued under this section;
'inspector' means an inspector appointed under this section;
'powers' means powers conferred by this section; *and*
'specified' means specified in the certificate in question.

Note. Definition 'specified' above and word 'and' immediately preceding it repealed by the Child Support, Pensions and Social Security Act 2000, s 85, Sch 9, Pt 1, as from 2 April 2001 (SI 2001 No 12520.

[(11) In this section, "premises" includes-

(a) moveable structures and vehicles, vessels, aircraft and hovercraft;
(b) installations that are offshore installations for the purposes of the Mineral Workings (Offshore Installations) Act 1971; and
(c) places of all other descriptions whether or not occupied as land or otherwise,

and references in this section to the occupier of premises are to be construed, in relation to premises that are not occupied as land, as references to any person for the time being present at the place in question.]

Note. Sub-s (11) inserted by the Child Support, Pensions and Social Security Act 2000, s 14(1), (4), as from 31 January 2001 (SI 2001 No 3354).

Reviews and appeals

16. Periodical reviews—*(1) The Secretary of State shall make such arrangements as he considers necessary to secure that, where any maintenance assessment has been in force for a* *prescribed period, the amount of child support maintenance fixed by that assessment ('the original assessment') is reviewed by a child support officer under this section as soon as is reasonably practicable after the end of that prescribed period.*

(2) Before conducting any review under this section, the child support officer concerned shall give, to such persons as may be prescribed, such notice of the proposed review as may be prescribed.

(3) A review shall be conducted under this section as if a fresh application for a maintenance assessment had been made by the person in whose favour the original assessment was made.

(4) On completing any review under this section, the child support officer concerned shall make a fresh maintenance assessment unless he is satisfied that the original assessment has ceased to have effect or should be brought to an end.

(5) Where a fresh maintenance assessment is made under subsection (4), it shall take effect—

(a) on the day immediately after the end of the prescribed period mentioned in subsection (1); or

(b) in such circumstances as may be prescribed, or such later date as may be determined in accordance with regulations made by the Secretary of State.

(6) The Secretary of State may by regulations prescribe circumstances (for example, where the maintenance assessment is about to terminate) in which a child support officer may decide not to conduct a review under this Section.

[16. Revision of decisions—(1) Any decision of the *Secretary State under section 11, 12 or 17* [to which subsection (1A) applies] may be revised by the Secretary of State—

(a) either within the prescribed period or in prescribed cases or circumstances; and

(b) either on an application made for the purpose or on his own initiative;

and regulations may prescribe the procedure by which a decision of the Secretary of State may be so revised.

[(1A) This subsection applies to—

(a) a decision of the Secretary of State under section 11, 12 or 17;

(b) a reduced benefit decision under section 46;

(c) a decision of an appeal tribunal on a referral under section 28D(1)(b).

(1B) Where the Secretary of State revises a decision under section 12(1)—

(a) he may (if appropriate) do so as if he were revising a decision under section 11; and

(b) if he does that, his decision as revised is to be treated as one under section 11 instead of section

(2) In making a decision under subsection (1), the Secretary of State need not consider any issue that is not raised by the application or, as the case may be, did not cause him to act on his own initiative.

(3) Subject to subsections (4) and (5) and section 28ZC, a revision under this section shall take effect as from the date on which the original decision took (or was to take) effect.

(4) Regulations may provide that, in prescribed cases or circumstances, a revision under this section shall take effect as from such other date as may be prescribed.

(5) Where a decision is revised under this section, for the purpose of any rule as to the time allowed for bringing an appeal, the decision shall be regarded as made on the date on which it is so revised.

(6) Except in prescribed circumstances, an appeal against a decision of the Secretary of State shall lapse if the decision is revised under this section before the appeal is determined.]

Note. Section 16 substituted for s 16 in italics by the Social Security Act 1998, s 40, as from (for certain purposes with a saving): 16 November 1998; for remaining purposes: 7 December

1998 (SI 1998 No 2780). In sub-s (1) words in square brackets substituted for words in italics and sub-ss (1A), (1B) inserted by the Child Support, Pensions and Social Security Act 2000, s 8(1), (3), as from (in relation to certain cases): 3 March 2003 (SI 2003 No 192); for remaining purposes: to be appointed.

17. Reviews on change of circumstances—*(1) Where a maintenance assessment is in force—*

    (a)   the absent parent or person with care with respect to whom it was made; or

    (b)   where the application for the assessment was made under section 7, either of them or the child concerned,

may apply to the Secretary of State for the amount of child support maintenance fixed by that assessment ('the original assessment') to be reviewed under this section.

(2) An application under this section may be made only on the ground that, by reason of a change of circumstance since the original assessment was made, the amount of child support maintenance payable by the absent parent would be significantly different if it were to be fixed by a maintenance assessment made by reference to the circumstances of the case as at the date of the application.

[(2A) The Secretary of State shall refer to a child support officer any application under this section which is duly made.]

Note. Sub-s (2A) inserted by Child Support Act 1995, s 12(2), as from 22 January 1996.

(3) The child support officer to whom an application under this section has been referred shall not proceed unless, on the information before him, he considers that it is likely that he will be required by subsection (6)[, or by virtue of subsection (7),] to make a fresh maintenance assessment if he conducts the review applied for [a review].

Note. Words in first pair of square brackets inserted, and words in second pair of square brackets substituted for words 'the review applied for' by Child Support Act 1995, s 12(3), as from 22 January 1996.

(4) Before conducting any review under this section, the child support officer concerned shall give to such persons as may be prescribed, such notice of the proposed review as may be prescribed.

[(4A) Where a child support officer is conducting a review under this section, and the original assessment has ceased to have effect, he may continue the review as if the application for a review related to the original assessment and any subsequent assessment.]

Note. Sub-s (4A) inserted by Child Support Act 1995, s 12(4), as from 22 January 1996.

(5) A review shall be conducted under this section as if a fresh application for a maintenance assessment had been made by the person in whose favour the original assessment was made.

[(5) In conducting a review under this section, the child support officer shall take into account a change of circumstance only if—

    (a)   he has been notified of it in such manner, and by such person, as may be prescribed; or

    (b)   it is one which he knows has taken place.]

Note. Sub-s (5) in square brackets substituted for sub-s (5) as originally enacted by Child Support Act 1995, s 12(5), as from 22 January 1996.

(6) On completing any review [a review of the original assessment] under this section, the child support officer concerned shall make a fresh maintenance assessment [by reference to the circumstances of the case as at the date of the application under this section], unless—

    (a)   he is satisfied that the original assessment has ceased to have effect or should be brought to an end; or

    (b)   the difference between the amount of child support maintenance fixed by the original assessment and the amount that would be fixed if a fresh assessment were to be made as a result of the review is less than such amount as may prescribed.

Note. Words in first pair of square brackets substituted for words 'any review' and words in second pair of square brackets inserted by Child Support Act 1995, s 12(6), as from 22 January 1996.

[(7) On completing a review of any subsequent assessment under this section, the child support officer concerned shall make a fresh maintenance assessment except in such circumstances as may be prescribed.

(8) In this section 'subsequent assessment' means a maintenance assessment made after the original assessment with respect to the same persons as the original assessment.]

Note. Sub-ss (7), (8) added by Child Support Act 1995, s 12(7), as from 22 January 1996.

18. Reviews of decisions of child support officers—*(1) Where—*

(a) an application for a maintenance assessment is refused; or

(b) an application, under section 17, for the review of a maintenance assessment which is in force is refused,

the person who made that application may apply to the Secretary of State for the refusal to be reviewed.

(2) Where a maintenance assessment is in force—

(a) the absent parent or person with care with respect to whom it was made; or

(b) where the application for the assessment was made under section 7, either of them or the child concerned,

may apply to the Secretary of State for the assessment to be reviewed.

(3) Where a maintenance assessment is cancelled the appropriate person may apply to the Secretary of State for the cancellation to be reviewed.

(4) Where an application for the cancellation of a maintenance assessment is refused, the appropriate person may apply to the Secretary of State for the refusal to be reviewed.

(5) An application under this section shall give the applicant's reasons (in writing) for making it.

(6) The Secretary of State shall refer to a child support officer any application under this section which is duly made; and the child support officer shall conduct the review applied for unless in his opinion there are no reasonable grounds for supposing that the refusal, assessment or cancellation in question—

(a) was made in ignorance of a material fact;

(b) was based on a mistake as to a material fact; [or]

(c) was wrong in law.

Note. Word in square brackets inserted by Child Support Act 1995, s 30(5), Sch 3, para 4, as from 4 September 1995.

[(6A) Where a child support officer is conducting a review under this section and the maintenance assessment in question ('the original assessment') is no longer in force, he may continue the review as if the application for a review related to the original assessment and any maintenance assessment made after the original assessment with respect to the same persons as the original assessment.]

Note. Sub-s (6A) inserted by Child Support Act 1995, s 13, as from 22 January 1996.

(7) The Secretary of State shall arrange for a review under this section to be conducted by a child support officer who played no part in taking the decision which is to be reviewed.

(8) Before conducting any review under this section, the child support officer concerned shall give to such persons as may be prescribed, such notice of the proposed review as may be prescribed.

(9) If a child support officer conducting a review under this section is satisfied that a maintenance assessment or (as the case may be) a fresh maintenance assessment should be made, he shall proceed accordingly.

(10) In making a maintenance assessment by virtue of subsection (9), a child support officer shall, if he is aware of any material change of circumstance since the decision being reviewed was taken, take account of that change of circumstance in making the assessment.

[(10A) If a child support officer conducting a review under this section is satisfied that the maintenance assessment in question was not validly made he may cancel it with effect from the date on which it took effect.]

Note. Sub-s (10A) inserted by Child Support Act 1995, s 14(1), as from 22 January 1996.

(11)   The Secretary of State may make regulations—

(a)   as to the manner in which applications under this section are to be made;

(b)   as to the procedure to be followed with respect to such applications; and

(c)   with respect to reviews conducted under this section.

(12)   In this section 'appropriate person' means—

(a)   the absent parent or person with care with respect to whom the maintenance assessment in question was, or remains, in force; or

(b)   where the application for that assessment was made under section 7, either of those persons or the child concerned.

19.   Reviews at instigation of child support officers—*(1)   Where a child support officer is not conducting a review under section 16, 17 or 18 but is nevertheless satisfied that a maintenance assessment which is in force is defective by reason of—*

(a)   having been made in ignorance of a material fact;

(b)   having been based on a mistake as to a material fact; or

(c)   being wrong in law,

he may make a fresh maintenance assessment on the assumption that the person in whose favour the original assessment was made has made a fresh application for a maintenance assessment.

(2)   Where a child support officer is not conducting such a review but is nevertheless satisfied that if an application were to be made under section 17 or 18 it would be appropriate to make a fresh maintenance assessment, he may do so.

(3)   Before making a fresh maintenance assessment under this section, a child support officer shall give to such persons as may be prescribed such notice of his proposal to make a fresh assessment as may be prescribed.

[**19.   Reviews at instigation of child support officers**—*(1)   Where a child support officer is not conducting a review under section 16, 17 or 18, he may nevertheless review—*

(a)   a refusal to make a maintenance assessment,

(b)   a refusal to review a maintenance assessment under section 17,

(c)   a maintenance assessment (whether or not in force),

(d)   a cancellation of a maintenance assessment, or

(e)   a refusal to cancel a maintenance assessment,

if he suspects that it may be defective for one or more of the reasons set out in subsection (2).

(2)   The reasons are that the refusal, assessment or cancellation—

(a)   was made in ignorance of a material fact;

(b)   was based on a mistake as to a material fact; or

(c)   was wrong in law.

(3)   If, on completing such a review, the child support officer is satisfied that the refusal, assessment or cancellation is defective for one or more of those reasons, he may—

(a)   take no further action;

(b)   in the case of a maintenance assessment which has been cancelled, set aside the cancellation;

(c)   make a maintenance assessment;

(d)   make a fresh maintenance assessment;

(e)   cancel the maintenance assessment in question.

(4)   Where a child support officer sets a cancellation aside under subsection (3), the maintenance assessment in question shall have effect as if it had never been cancelled.

(5)   Any cancellation of a maintenance assessment under this section shall have effect from such date as may be determined by the child support officer.

(6)   Where a child support officer suspects that if an application for a review of a maintenance assessment were to be made under section 17 it would be appropriate to make one or more fresh maintenance assessments, he may review the maintenance assessment even though no application for its review has been made under that section.

(7)   If, on completing a review by virtue of subsection (6), the child support officer is satisfied that it would be appropriate to make one or more fresh maintenance assessments, he may do so.]

Note. Section 19 in square brackets substituted for s 19 as originally enacted by Child Support Act 1995, s 15, as from 22 January 1996.

[17. Decisions superseding earlier decisions]

[(1) Subject to subsection (2), the following, namely-

(a) any decision of the Secretary of State under section 11 or 12 or this section, whether as originally made or as revised under section 16;

(b) any decision of an appeal tribunal under section 20; and

(c) any decision of a Child Support Commissioner on an appeal from such a decision as is mentioned in paragraph (b)

[(c) any reduced benefit decision under section 46;

(d) any decision of an appeal tribunal on a referral under section 28D(1)(b);

(e) any decision of a Child Support Commissioner on an appeal from such a decision as is mentioned in paragraph (b) or (d)],

may be superseded by a decision made by the Secretary of State, either on an application made for the purpose or on his own initiative.

(2) In making a decision under subsection (1), the Secretary of State need not consider any issue that is not raised by the application or, as the case may be, did not cause him to act on his own initiative.

(3) Regulations may prescribe the cases and circumstances in which, and the procedure by which, a decision may be made under this section.

(4) Subject to subsection (5) and section 28ZC, a decision under this section shall take effect as from the date on which it is made or, where applicable, the date on which the application was made.

[(4) Subject to subsection (5) and section 28ZC, a decision under this section shall take effect as from the beginning of the maintenance period in which it is made or, where applicable, the beginning of the maintenance period in which the application was made.

(4A) In subsection (4), a "maintenance period" is (except where a different meaning is prescribed for

prescribed cases) a period of seven days, the first one beginning on the effective date of the first decision made by the Secretary of State under section 11 or (if earlier) his first default or interim maintenance decision (under section 12) in relation to the non-resident parent in question, and each subsequent one beginning on the day after the last day of the previous one.]

(5) Regulations may provide that, in prescribed cases or circumstances, a decision under this section shall take effect as from such other date as may be prescribed.]

Note. New s 17 above substituted, for ss 17–19, by the Social Security Act 1998, s 41, as from 1 June 1999 (SI 1999 No 1510). In sub-s (1)(b) word 'and' in italics repealed by the Child Support, Pensions and social Security Act 2000, s 85, Sch 9, Pt 1, as from (in relation to certain cases): 3 March 2003 (SI 2003 No 192); for remaining purposes; to be appointed. In sub-s (1) para (c) substituted, by subsequent paras (c)–(e), and sub-s (4) substituted, by subsequent sub-ss (4), (4A), by the Child Support, Pensions and Social Security Act 2000, s 9(1)–(3), as from (for certain purposes): 10 November 2000 (SI 2000 No 2994); (in relation to certain cases): 3 March 2003 (SI 2003 No 192); for remaining purposes: to be appointed.

20. Appeals—*(1) Any person who is aggrieved by the decision of a child support officer—*

(a) on a review under section 18;

(b) to refuse an application for such a review,

may appeal to a child support appeal tribunal against that decision.

(2) Except with leave of the chairman of a child support appeal tribunal, no appeal under this section shall be brought after the end of the period of 28 days beginning with the date on which notification was given of the decision in question.

[(2A) A tribunal hearing an appeal under this section may, at the request of any party to the appeal, take into account—
(a)   any later maintenance assessment made with respect to the same parties;
(b)   any change in the circumstances of the case.]

Note. Sub-s (2A) inserted by Child Support Act 1995, s 30(5), Sch 3, para 5, as from a day to be appointed.

(3) Where an appeal under this section is allowed, the tribunal shall remit the case to the Secretary of State, who shall arrange for it to be dealt with by a child support officer.
(4) The tribunal may, in remitting any case under this section, give such directions as it considers appropriate.

[20A. Lapse of appeals—*(1) This section applies where—*
(a)   a person has brought an appeal under section 20; and
(b)   before the appeal is heard, the decision appealed against is reviewed under section 19.
(2) If the child support officer conducting the review considers that the decision which he has made on the review is the same as that which would have been made on the appeal had every ground of the appeal succeeded, the appeal shall lapse.
(3) In any other case, the review shall be of no effect and the appeal shall proceed accordingly.]

Note. This section inserted by Child Support Act 1995, s 16, as from 18 December 1995.

21. Child support appeal tribunals—*(1) There shall be tribunals to be known as child support appeal tribunals which shall, subject to any order made under section 45, hear and determine appeals under section 20 [and have such other functions as are conferred by this Act].*

Note. Words in square brackets added by Child Support Act 1995, s 30(5), Sch 3, para 6, as from 2 December 1996.

(2) The Secretary of State may make such regulations with respect to proceedings before child support appeal tribunals as he considers appropriate.
(3) The regulations may in particular make provision—
(a)   as to procedure;
(b)   for the striking out of appeals for want of prosecution;
(c)   as to the persons entitled to appear and be heard or behalf of any of the parties;
(d)   requiring persons to attend and give evidence or to produce documents;
(e)   about evidence;
(f)   for authorising the administration of oaths;
(g)   as to confidentiality;
(h)   for notification of the result of an appeal to be given to such persons as may be prescribed.
(4) Schedule 3 shall have effect with respect to child support appeal tribunals.

[20. Appeals to appeals tribunals—*(1) Where an application for a maintenance assessment [maintenance calculation] is refused, the person who made that application shall have a right of appeal to an appeal tribunal against the refusal.*
(2) Where a maintenance assessment [maintenance calculation] is in force—
(a)   the absent parent or person with care with respect to whom it was made; or
(b)   where the application for the assessment [calculation] was made under section 7, either of them or the child concerned,
shall have a right of appeal to an appeal tribunal against the amount of the assessment [calculation] or the date from which the assessment [calculation] takes effect.*
(3) Where a maintenance assessment [maintenance calculation] is cancelled, or an application for the cancellation of a maintenance assessment [maintenance calculation] is refused—
(a)   the absent parent or person with care with respect to whom the maintenance assessment [maintenance[calculation] in question was, or remains, in force; or
(b)   where the application for that assessment [calculation] was made under section 7, either of them or the child concerned,

shall have a right of appeal to an appeal tribunal against the cancellation or refusal.

(4) A person with a right of appeal under this section shall be given such notice of that right and, in the case of a right conferred by subsection (1) or (3), such notice of the decision as may be prescribed.

(5) Regulations may make—

(a) *provision as to the manner in which, and the time within which, appeals are to be brought; and*

(b) *such provision with respect to proceedings before appeal tribunals as the Secretary of State considers appropriate.*

(6) The regulations may in particular make any provision of a kind mentioned in Schedule 5 to the Social Security Act 1998.

(7) In deciding an appeal under this section, an appeal tribunal—

(a) *need not consider any issue that is not raised by the appeal; and*

(b) *shall not take into account any circumstances not obtaining at the time when the decision or assessment [calculation] appealed against was made.]*

Note. Section 20 above substituted for ss 20, 20A, 21 in italics by the Social Security Act 1998, s 42, as from 1 June 1999 (SI 1999 No 1510). (For transitory amendments see the Social Security Act 1998, s 83, Sch 6, para 9.) In sun-ss (1)–(3), (7) words 'maintenance calculation' and 'calculation' in square brackets in each place they occur substituted for words 'maintenance assessment' and 'assessment' respectively by the Child Support, Pensions and Social Security Act 2000, s 1(2), as from (in relation to certain cases): 3 March 2003 (SI 2003 No 192); for remaining purposes: to be appointed.

[20. Appeals to appeal tribunals—(1) A qualifying person has a right of appeal to an appeal tribunal against—

(a) a decision of the Secretary of State under section 11, 12 or 17 (whether as originally made or as revised under section 16);

(b) a decision of the Secretary of State not to make a maintenance calculation under section 11 or not to supersede a decision under section 17;

(c) a reduced benefit decision under section 46;

(d) the imposition (by virtue of section 41A) of a requirement to make penalty payments, or their amount;

(e) the imposition (by virtue of section 47) of a requirement to pay fees.

(2) In subsection (1), "qualifying person" means-

(a) in relation to paragraphs (a) and (b)-

(i) the person with care, or non-resident parent, with respect to whom the Secretary of State made the decision, or

(ii) in a case relating to a maintenance calculation which was applied for under section 7, either of those persons or the child concerned;

(b) in relation to paragraph (c), the person in respect of whom the benefits are payable;

(c) in relation to paragraph (d), the parent who has been required to make penalty payments; and

(d) in relation to paragraph (e), the person required to pay fees.

(3) A person with a right of appeal under this section shall be given such notice as may be prescribed of—

(a) that right; and

(b) the relevant decision, or the imposition of the requirement.

(4) Regulations may make—

(a) provision as to the manner in which, and the time within which, appeals are to be brought; and

(b) such provision with respect to proceedings before appeal tribunals as the Secretary of State considers appropriate.

(5) The regulations may in particular make any provision of a kind mentioned in Schedule 5 to the Social Security Act 1998.

(6) No appeal lies by virtue of subsection (1)(c) unless the amount of the person's benefit is reduced in accordance with the reduced benefit decision; and

the time within which such an appeal may be brought runs from the date of notification of the reduction.

(7) In deciding an appeal under this section, an appeal tribunal—

(a) need not consider any issue that is not raised by the appeal; and

(b) shall not take into account any circumstances not obtaining at the time when the Secretary of State made the decision or imposed the requirement.

(8) If an appeal under this section is allowed, the appeal tribunal may—

(a) itself make such decision as it considers appropriate; or

(b) remit the case to the Secretary of State, together with such directions (if any) as it considers appropriate.]

Note. New s 20 above substituted for second s 20 in italics by the Child Support, Pensions and Social Security Act 2000, s 10, as from (for certain purposes): 10 November 2000 (SI 2000 No 2994); (in relation to certain cases): 3 March 2003 (SI 2003 No 192); for remaining purposes: to be appointed.

22. Child Support Commissioners—(1) Her Majesty may from time to time appoint a Chief Child Support Commissioner and such number of other Child Support Commissioners as she may think fit.

(2) The Chief Child Support Commissioner and the other Child Support Commissioners shall be appointed from among persons who—

(a) have a 10 year general qualification; or

(b) are advocates or solicitors in Scotland of 10 years' standing.

(3) The Lord Chancellor, after consulting the *Lord Advocate* [Secretary of State], may make such regulations with respect to proceedings before Child Support Commissioners as he considers appropriate.

Note. Words 'Secretary of State' in square brackets substituted for words in italics by virtue of the Transfer of Functions (Lord Advocate and Secretary of State) Order 1999, SI 1999/678, art 2(1), Schedule, as from 19 May 1999.

(4) The regulations—

(a) may, in particular, make any provision of a kind mentioned in *section 21(3)* [Schedule 5 to the Social Security Act 1998]; and

(b) shall provide that any hearing before a Child Support Commissioner shall be in public except in so far as the Commissioner for special reasons directs otherwise.

Note. In sub-s (4)(a) words in square brackets substituted for words in italics by the Social Security Act 1998, s 86(1), Sch 7, para 29, as from 1 June 1999 (SI 1999 No 1510).

(5) Schedule 4 shall have effect with respect to Child Support Commissioners.

23. Child Support Commissioners for Northern Ireland—(1) Her Majesty may from time to time appoint a Chief Child Support Commissioner for Northern Ireland and such number of other Child Support Commissioners for Northern Ireland as she may think fit.

(2) The Chief Child Support Commissioner for Northern Ireland and the other Child Support Commissioners for Northern Ireland shall be appointed from among persons who are barristers or solicitors of not less than 10 years' standing.

(3) Schedule 4 shall have effect with respect to Child Support Commissioners for Northern Ireland, subject to the modifications set out in paragraph 8.

(4) Subject to any Order made after the passing of this Act by virtue of subsection (1)(a) of section 3 of the Northern Ireland Constitution Act 1973, the matters to which this subsection applies shall not be transferred matters for the purposes of that Act but shall for the purposes of subsection (2) of that section be treated as specified in Schedule 3 to that Act.

(5) Subsection (4) applies to all matters relating to Child Support Commissioners, including procedure and appeals, other than those specified in paragraph 9 of Schedule 2 to the Northern Ireland Constitution Act 1973.

Note. Sub-ss (4), (5) repealed by the Northern Ireland Act 1998, s 100(2), Sch 15, as from 2 December 1999 (SI 1999 No 3209).

[23A. Redetermination of appeals—(1) This section applies where an application is made to a person under section 24(6)(a) for leave to I appeal from a decision of an appeal tribunal.

(2) If the person who constituted, or was the chairman of, the appeal tribunal considers that the decision was erroneous in law, he may set aside the decision and refer the case either for redetermination by the tribunal or for determination by a differently constituted tribunal.

(3) If each of the principal parties to the case expresses the view that the decision was erroneous in point of law, the person shall set aside the decision and refer the case for determination by a differently constituted tribunal.

(4) The "principal parties" are-

(a) the Secretary of State; and

(b) those who are qualifying persons for the purposes of section 20(2) in relation to the decision in question.]

Note. This section inserted by the Child Support, Pensions and Social Security Act 2000, s 11, as from 15 February 2001 (SI 2000 No 3354). See also the Child Support (Consequential Amendments and Transitional Provisions) Regulations 2001 (SI 2001 No 158), reg 11.

24. Appeal to Child Support Commissioner—(1) Any person who is aggrieved by a decision of *a child support appeal tribunal, and any child support officer* [an appeal tribunal, and the Secretary of State], may appeal to a Child Support Commissioner on a question of law.

[(1A) The Secretary of State may appeal to a Child Support Commissioner on a question of law in relation to any decision of a child support appeal tribunal made in connection with an application for a departure direction.]

Note. Sub-s (1A) inserted by Child Support Act 1995, s 30(5), Sch 3, para 7(2), as from 2 December 1996. In sub-s (1) words in square brackets substituted for words in italics, and sub-s (1A) repealed, by the Social Security Act 1998, s 86(1), Sch 7, para 30(4), as from 1 June 1999 (SI 1999 No 1510).

(2) Where, on an appeal under this section, a Child Support Commissioner holds that the decision appealed against was wrong in law he shall set it aside.

(3) Where a decision is set aside under subsection (2), the Child Support Commissioner may—

(a) if he can do so without making fresh or further findings of fact, give the decision which he considers should have been given by *the child support* [a child support appeal tribunal] *appeal tribunal.*;

(b) if he considers it expedient, make such findings and give such decision as he considers appropriate in the light of those findings; or

(c) *refer the case, with directions for its determination, to a child support officer or, if he considers it appropriate, to a child support appeal tribunal.*

[(c) on an appeal by the Secretary of State, refer the case to *a child support appeal tribunal* [an appeal tribunal] with directions for its determination; or

(d) on any other appeal, refer the case to *a child support officer* [the Secretary of State] or, if he considers it appropriate, to *a child support appeal tribunal* [an appeal tribunal] with directions for its determination.]

Note. Sub-s (3)(c), (d) in square brackets substituted for sub-s (3)(c) in italics by Child Support Act 1995, s 30(5), Sch 3, para 7(3), as from 2 December 1996. In sub-s (3)(a), (c), (d) words in square brackets substituted for words in italics by the Social Security Act 1998, s 86(1), Sch 7, para 30(3), as from 1 June 1999 (SI 1999 No 1510).

(4) Any reference under subsection (3) to a child support officer shall, subject to any direction of the Child Support Commissioner, be to a child support officer who has taken no part in the decision originally appealed against.

[(4) The reference under subsection (3) to the Secretary of State shall, subject to any direction of the Child Support Commissioner, be to an officer of his, or a person providing him with services, who has taken no part in the decision originally appealed against.]

Note. Sub-s (4) in square brackets substituted for sub-s (4) in italics by the Social Security Act 1998, s 86(1), Sch 7, para 30(4), as from 1 June 1999 (SI 1999 No 1510).

(5) On a reference under subsection (3) to *a child support appeal tribunal* [an appeal tribunal], the tribunal shall, subject to any direction of the Child Support Commissioner, consist of persons who were not members of the tribunal which gave the decision which has been appealed against.

Note. Words in square brackets substituted for words in italics by the Social Security Act 1998, s 86(1), Sch 7, para 30(7), as from 1 June 1999 (SI 1999 No 1510).

(6) No appeal lies under this section without the leave—
(a) of the person *who was the chairman of the child support appeal tribunal* [who constituted, or was the chairman of, the appeal tribunal] when the decision appealed against was given or of *such other chairman of a child support appeal tribunal* [such other person] as may be determined in accordance with regulations made by the Lord Chancellor; or
(b) subject to and in accordance with regulations so made, of a Child Support Commissioner.

Note. In para (a) words in square brackets substituted for words in italics by the Social Security Act 1998, s 86(1), Sch 7, para 30(7), as from 1 June 1999 (SI 1999 No 1010).

(7) The Lord Chancellor may by regulations make provision as to the manner in which, and the time within which, appeals under this section are to be brought and applications for leave under this section are to be made.

(8) Where a question which would otherwise fall to be determined by *a child support officer* [the Secretary of State] first arises in the course of an appeal to a Child Support Commissioner, he may, if he thinks fit, determine it even though it has not been considered by *a child support officer* [the Secretary of State].

Note. Words in square brackets substituted for words in italics by the Social Security Act 1998, s 86(1), Sch 7, para 30(7), as from 1 June 1999 (SI 1999 No 1510).

(9) Before making any regulations under subsection (6) or (7), the Lord Chancellor shall consult the *Lord Advocate* [Secretary of State].

Note. Words in square brackets substituted for words in italics by virtue of the Transfer of Functions (Lord Advocate and Secretary of State) Order 1999 (SI 1999 No 678), art 2(1), Schedule, as from 19 May 1999.

25. Appeal from Child Support Commissioner on question of law—(1) An appeal on a question of law shall lie to the appropriate court from any decision of a Child Support Commissioner.

(2) No such appeal may be brought except—
(a) with leave of the Child Support Commissioner who gave the decision or, where regulations made by the Lord Chancellor so provide, of a Child Support Commissioner selected in accordance with the regulations; or
(b) if the Child Support Commissioner refuses leave, with the leave of the appropriate court.

(3) An application for leave to appeal under this section against a decision of a Child Support Commissioner ('the appeal decision') may only be made by—
(a) a person who was a party to the proceedings in which the original decision, or appeal decision, was given;
(b) the Secretary of State; or
(c) any other person who is authorised to do so by regulations made by the Lord Chancellor.

[(3A) The Child Support Commissioner to whom an application for leave to appeal under this section is made shall specify as the appropriate court either the Court of Appeal or the Court of Session.

(3B) In determining the appropriate court, the Child Support Commissioner shall have regard to the circumstances of the case, in particular the convenience of the persons who may be parties to the appeal.]

Note. Sub-ss (3A), (3B) inserted by Child Support Act 1995, s 30(5), Sch 3, para 8(1), as from 4 September 1995.

(4) In this section—

'appropriate court' *means the Court of Appeal unless in a particular case the Child Support Commissioner to whom the application for leave is made directs that, having regard to the circumstances of the case, and in particular the convenience of the persons who may be parties to the appeal, the appropriate court is the Court of Session*[, except in subsections (3A) and (3B), means the court specified in accordance with those subsections]; and

'original decision' means the decision to which the appeal decision in question relates.

Note. Words in square brackets substituted for words in italics by Child Support Act 1995, s 30(5), Sch 3, para 8(2), as from 4 September 1995.

(5) The Lord Chancellor may by regulations make provision with respect to—
(a) the manner in which and the time within which applications must be made to a Child Support Commissioner for leave under this section; and
(b) the procedure for dealing with such applications.

(6) Before making any regulations under subsection (2), (3) or (5), the Lord Chancellor shall consult the *Lord Advocate* [Secretary of State].

Note. In sub-s (6) words in square brackets substituted for words in italics by virtue of the Transfer of Functions (Lord Advocate and Secretary of State) Order 1999, SI 1999 No 678, art 2(1), Schedule, as from 19 May 1999.

26. Disputes about parentage—(1) Where a person who is alleged to be a parent of the child with respect to whom an application for a *maintenance assessment* [maintenance calculation] has been made [or treated as made] ('the alleged parent') denies that he is one of the child's parents, the *child support officer concerned* [the Secretary of State] shall not make a *maintenance assessment* [maintenance calculation] on the assumption that the alleged parent is one of the child's parents unless the case falls within one of those set out in subsection (2).

Note. Words 'maintenance calculation' in square brackets in both places they occur substituted for words in italics and words 'treated as made' in square brackets inserted by the Child Support, Pensions and Social Security Act 2000, ss 1(2)(a), 26, Sch 3, para 1191), (8), as from (in relation to certain cases): 3 March 2003 (SI 2003 No 192); for remaining purposes: to be appointed. Words 'the Secretary of State' in square brackets substituted for words in italics by the Social Security Act 1998, s 86(1), Sch 7, para 31(1), as from 1 June 1999 (SI 1999 No 1510).

(2) The cases are—

[CASE A1

Where—
(a) the child is habitually resident in England and Wales;
(b) the Secretary of State is satisfied that the alleged parent was married to the child's mother at some time in the period beginning with the conception and ending with the birth of the child; and
(c) the child has not been adopted.

CASE A2

Where—
(a) the child is habitually resident in England and Wales;
(b) the alleged parent has been registered as father of the child under section 10 or 10A of the Births and Deaths Registration Act 1953, or in any register kept under section 13 (register of births and still-births) or section 44

(Register of Corrections Etc) of the Registration of Births, Deaths and Marriages (Scotland) Act 1965, or under Article 14 or 18(1)(b)(ii) of the Births and Deaths Registration (Northern Ireland) Order 1976; and

(c) the child has not subsequently been adopted.

CASE A3

Where the result of a scientific test (within the meaning of section 27A) taken by the alleged parent would be relevant to determining the child's parentage, and the alleged parent-

(a) refuses to take such a test; or

(b) has submitted to such a test, and it shows that there is no reasonable doubt that the alleged parent is a parent of the child.]

Note. In sub-s (6) words in square brackets substituted for words in italics by virtue of the Transfer of Functions (Lord Advocate and Secretary of State) Order 1999, SI 1999 No 678, art 2(1), Schedule, as from 19 May 1999.

CASE A

Where the alleged parent is a parent of the child in question by virtue of having adopted him.

CASE B1

Where the Secretary of State is satisfied that the alleged parent is a parent of the child in question by virtue of section 27 or 28 of that Act (meaning of 'mother' and of 'father' respectively).]

CASE B

Where the alleged parent is a parent of the child in question by virtue of an order under section 30 of the Human Fertilisation and Embryology Act 1990 (parental orders in favour of gamete donors).

CASE C

Where—

(a) either—

(i) a declaration that the alleged parent is a parent of the child in question (or a declaration which has that effect) is in force under section [55A or] 56 of the Family Law Act 1986 [or Article 43 of the Matrimonial and Family Proceedings (Northern Ireland) Order 1989] (declarations of parentage); or

(ii) (*applies to Scotland only*); and

(b) the child has not subsequently been adopted.

CASE D

Where—

(a) a declaration to the effect that the alleged parent is one of the parents of the child in question has been made under section 27; and

(b) the child has not subsequently been adopted.

CASE E

(*Applies to Scotland only.*)

CASE F

Where—

(a) the alleged parent has been found, or adjudged, to be the father of the child in question—

(i) in proceedings before any court in England and Wales which are relevant proceedings for the purposes of section 12 of the Civil Evidence Act 1968 [or in proceedings before any court in Northern Ireland which are relevant proceedings for the purposes of section 8 of the Civil Evidence Act (Northern Ireland) 1971]; or

(ii) in affiliation proceedings before any court in the United Kingdom, (whether or not he offered any defence to the allegation of paternity) and that finding or adjudication still subsists; and

(b) the child has not subsequently been adopted.

Note. Cases A1–A3, B1 inserted by the Child Support, Pensions and Social Security Act 2000, s 15(1), as from 31 January 2001 (SI 2000 No 3354). In Case C words '55A or' in square brackets inserted by the Child Support, Pensions and Social Security Act 2000, s 85(5), Sch 8, paras 11, 12 as from 1 April 2001 (SI 2001 No 774). Words 'or Article 43 ... 1989' and 'or in proceedings ... 1971' in square brackets in Cases C and F inserted by Children (Northern Ireland Consequential Amendments) Order 1995, SI 1995 No 756, art 13, as from 4 November 1996. Case D in italics repealed by the Child Support, Pensions and Social Security Act 2000, s 85, Sch 9, Pt 1X as from 1 April 2001 (SI 2001 No 774).

(3) In this section—

'adopted' means adopted within the meaning of Part IV of the Adoption Act 1976 [or Chapter 4 of Part 1 of the Adoption and Children Act 2002] or, in relation to Scotland, Part IV of the Adoption (Scotland) Act 1978; and

'affiliation proceedings', in relation to Scotland, means any action of affiliation and aliment.

Note. In definition 'adopted' words in square brackets inserted by the Adoption and Children Act 2002, s 139(1), Sch 3, para 81, as from a day to be appointed.

27. Reference to court for declaration of parentage—(*1*) *Where*—

(*a*) *a child support officer is considering whether to make a maintenance assessment with respect to a person who is alleged to be a parent of the child, or one of the children, in question ('the alleged parent');*

(*b*) *the alleged parent denies that he is one of the child's parents; and*

(*c*) *the child support officer is not satisfied that the case falls within one of those set out in section 26(2).*

the Secretary of State or the person with care may apply to the court for a declaration as to whether or not the alleged parent is one of the child's parents.

[*(1) Subsection (1A) applies in any case where—*

(*a*) *an application for a maintenance assessment [maintenance calculation] has been made, or a maintenance assessment [maintenance calculation] is in force, with respect to a person ('the alleged parent') who denies that he is a parent of a child with respect to whom the application or assessment [calculation] was made; and*

(*b*) *a child support officer to whom the case is referred [the Secretary of State] is not satisfied that the case falls within one of those set out in section 26(2).*

(1A) In any case where this subsection applies, the Secretary of State or the person with care may apply to the court for a declaration as to whether or not the alleged parent is one of the child's parents.]

Note. Sub-ss (1), (1A) in square brackets substituted for sub-s (1) as originally enacted by Child Support Act 1995, s 20(2), as from 4 September 1995. In new sub-s (1)(a) words 'maintenance calculation' in square brackets in both places they occur substituted for words 'maintenance assessment', and word 'calculation' in square brackets substituted for word 'assessed' by the Child Support, Pensions and Social Security Act 2000, s 1(2), as from (in relation to certain cases): 3 March 2003; (SI 2003 No 192); for remaining purposes: to be appointed. In new sub-s (1)(b) words 'the Secretary of State' substituted for words 'a child ... referred' by the Social Security Act 1998, s 86(1), Sch 7, para 32, as from 1 June 1999 (SI 1999 No 1510).

(2) If, on hearing any application under subsection (1) [(1A)], the court is satisfied that the alleged parent is, or is not, a parent of the child in question it shall make a declaration to that effect.

Note. Reference to '(1A)' substituted for reference to '(1)' by Child Support Act 1995, s 20(3), as from 4 September 1995.

    (3) A declaration under this section shall have effect only for the purposes of this Act.

    [(3) A declaration under this section shall have effect only for the purposes of—

    (a)   this Act; and

    (b)   proceedings in which a court is considering whether to make a maintenance order in the circumstances mentioned in subsection (6), (7) or (8) of section 8.]

Note. Sub-s (3) in square brackets substituted for sub-s (3) as originally enacted by Child Support Act 1995, s 20(4), as from 4 September 1995.

    (4) In this section 'court' means, subject to any provision made under Schedule 11 to the Children Act 1989 (jurisdiction of courts with respect to certain proceedings relating to children) the High Court, a county court or a magistrates' court.

    (5) In the definition of 'relevant proceedings' in section 12(5) of the Civil Evidence Act 1968 (findings of paternity etc as evidence in civil proceedings) the following paragraph shall be added at the end—

    '(d)   section 27 of the Child Support Act 1991.'

    (6) This section does not apply to Scotland.

[27. Applications for declaration of parentage under Family Law Act 1986—
(1) This section applies where—

    (a)   an application for a maintenance calculation has been made (or is treated as having been made), or a maintenance calculation is in force, with respect to a person ("the alleged parent") who denies that he is a parent of a child with respect to whom the application or calculation was made or treated as made;

    (b)   the Secretary of State is not satisfied that the case falls within one of those set out in section 26(2); and

    (c)   the Secretary of State or the person with care makes an application for a declaration under section 55A of the Family Law Act 1986 as to whether or not the alleged parent is one of the child's parents.

(2) Where this section applies-

    (a)   if it is the person with care who makes the application, she shall be treated as having a sufficient personal interest for the purposes of subsection (3) of that section; and

    (b)   if it is the Secretary of State who makes the application, that subsection shall not apply.

(3) This section does not apply to Scotland.]

Note. Section 27 above substituted for s 27 in italics by the Child Support, Pensions and Social Security Act 2000, s 83(5), (6)(b) paras 11, 13, as from 1 April 2001 (SI 2001 No 774).

[27A. Recovery of fees for scientific tests—(1) This section applies in any case where—

    (a)   an application for a *maintenance assessment* [maintenance calculation] has been made [treated as made] or a *maintenance assessment* [maintenance calculation] is in force;

    (b)   scientific tests have been carried out (otherwise than under a direction or in response to a request) in relation to bodily samples obtained from a person who is alleged to be a parent of a child with respect to whom the application or *assessment* [calculation] is made [or as the case may be treated as made];

    (c)   the results of the tests do not exclude the alleged parent from being one of the child's parents; and

    (d)   one of the conditions set out in subsection (2) is satisfied.

(2) The conditions are that—

    (a)   the alleged parent does not deny that he is one of the child's parents;

    (b)   in proceedings under *section 27* [section 55A of the Family Law Act 1986], a court has made a declaration that the alleged parent is a parent of the child in question; or

(c) in an action under section 7 of the Law Reform (Parent and Child) (Scotland) Act 1986, brought by the Secretary of State by virtue of section 28, a court has granted a decree of declarator of parentage to the effect that the alleged parent is a parent of the child in question.

(3) In any case to which this section applies, any fee paid by the Secretary of State in connection with scientific tests may be recovered by him from the alleged parent as a debt due to the Crown.

(4) In this section—

'bodily sample' means a sample of bodily fluid or bodily tissue taken for the purpose of scientific tests;

'direction' means a direction given by a court under section 20 of the Family Law Reform Act 1969 (tests to determine paternity);

'request' means a request made by a court under section 70 of the Law Reform (Miscellaneous Provisions) (Scotland) Act 1990 (blood and other samples in civil proceedings); and

'scientific tests' means scientific tests made with the object of ascertaining the inheritable characteristics of bodily fluids or bodily tissue.

(5) Any sum recovered by the Secretary of State under this section shall be paid by him into the Consolidated Fund.]

Note. This section inserted by Child Support Act 1995, s 21, as from 4 September 1995. In sub-s (1) words 'maintenance assessment' in square brackets in both places they occur and word 'calculation' in square brackets substituted for words in italics, and words 'treated as made' and 'as the case may be treated as made' in square brackets inserted, by the Child Support, Pensions and Social Security Act 2000, ss 1(2), 26, Sch 3, para 11(1), (0) as from (in relation to certain cases): 3 March 2003 (SI 2003 No 192); for remaining purposes: to be appointed. In sub-s (2)(b) words 'section 55A of the Family Law Act 1986' in square brackets substituted for words in italics by the Child Support, Pensions and Social Security Act 2000, s 83(5), Sch 8, paras 11, 14, ass from 1 April 2001 (SI 2001 No 774).

28. (*Applies to Scotland only.*)

[Decisions and appeals dependent on other cases

28ZA. Decisions involving issues that arise on appeal in other cases—(1) This section applies where—

(a) a decision by the Secretary of State falls to be made under section 11, 12, 16 or 17 in relation to a maintenance assessment [or with respect to a reduced benefit decision under section 46]; and

(b) *an appeal is pending against a decision given in relation to a different maintenance assessment [maintenance calculation] by a Child Support Commissioner or a court*

[(b) an appeal is pending against a decision given in relation to a different matter by a Child Support Commissioner or a court].

(2) If the Secretary of State considers it possible that the result of the appeal will be such that, if it were already determined, it would affect the decision in some way—

(a) he need not, except in such cases or circumstances as may be prescribed, make the decision while the appeal is pending;

(b) he may, in such cases or circumstances as may be prescribed, make the decision on such basis as may be prescribed.

(3) Where the Secretary of State acts in accordance with subsection (2)(b), following the determination of the appeal he shall if appropriate revise his decision (under section 16) in accordance with that determination.

(4) For the purposes of this section, an appeal against a.decision is pending if—

(a) an appeal against the decision has been brought but not determined;

(b) an application for leave to appeal against the decision has been made but not determined; or

   (c) in such circumstances as may be prescribed, an appeal against the decision has not been brought (or, as the case may be, an application for leave to appeal against the decision has not been made) but the time for doing so has not yet expired.

   (5) In paragraphs (a), (b) and (c) of subsection (4), any reference to an appeal, or an application for leave to appeal, against a decision includes a reference to—

   (a) an application for, or for leave to apply for, judicial review of the decision under section 31 of the Supreme Court Act 1981; or

   (b) an application to the supervisory jurisdiction of the Court of Session in respect of the decision.

Note. In sub-s (1)(a) words in square brackets substituted for words in italics and sub-s (1)(b) substituted by the Child support, Pensions and Social Security Act 2000, s 26, Sch 3, para 11(1), (11)(a), (b), as from (in relation to certain cases): 3 March 2003 (SI 2003 No 192); for remaining purposes: to be appointed.

28ZB. Appeals involving issues that arise on appeal in other cases—(1) This section applies where—

   (a) an appeal ('appeal A') in relation to a decision falling within section 20(1) or (3), or an assessment [a calculation] falling within section 20(2), is made to an appeal tribunal, or from an appeal tribunal to a Child Support Commissioner; and

   [(a) an appeal ('appeal A') in relation to a decision or the imposition of a requirement falling within section 20(1) is made to an appeal tribunal, or from an appeal tribunal to a Child Support Commissioner;]

   (b) an appeal ('appeal B') is pending against a decision given in a different case by a Child Support Commissioner or a court.

   (2) If the Secretary of State considers it possible that the result of appeal B will be such that, if it were already determined, it would affect the determination of appeal A, he may serve notice requiring the tribunal or Child Support Commissioner—

   (a) not to determine appeal A but to refer it to him; or

   (b) to deal with the appeal in accordance with subsection (4).

   (3) Where appeal A is referred to the Secretary of State under subsection (2)(a), following the determination of appeal B and in accordance with that determination, he shall if appropriate—

   (a) in a case where appeal A has not been determined by the tribunal, revise (under section 16) his decision which gave rise to that appeal; or

   (b) in a case where appeal A has been determined by the tribunal, make a decision (under section 17) superseding the tribunal's decision.

   (4) Where appeal A is to be dealt with in accordance with this subsection, the appeal tribunal or Child Support Commissioner shall either—

   (a) stay appeal A until appeal B is determined; or

   (b) if the tribunal or Child Support Commissioner considers it to be in the interests of the appellant to do so, determine appeal A as if—

      (i) appeal B had already been determined; and

      (ii) the issues arising on appeal B had been decided in the way that was most unfavourable to the appellant.

In this subsection 'the appellant' means the person who appealed or, as the case may be, first appealed against the decision or *assessment* [or the imposition of the requirement] mentioned in subsection (1)(a).

   (5) Where the appeal tribunal or Child Support Commissioner acts in accordance with subsection (4)(b), following the determination of appeal B the Secretary of State shall, if appropriate, make a decision (under section 17) superseding the decision of the tribunal or Child Support Commissioner in accordance with that determination.

   (6) For the purposes of this section, an appeal against a decision is pending if—

   (a) an appeal against the decision has been brought but not determined;

(b) an application for leave to appeal against the decision has been made but not determined; or

(c) in such circumstances as may be prescribed, an appeal against the decision has not been brought (or, as the case may be, an application for leave to appeal against the decision has not been made) but the time for doing so has not yet expired.

(7) In this section—

(a) the reference in subsection (1)(a) to an appeal to a Child Support Commissioner includes a reference to an application for leave to appeal to a Child Support Commissioner; and

(b any reference in paragraph (a), (b) or (c) of subsection (6) to an appeal, or to an application for leave to appeal, against a decision includes a reference to—

 (i) an application for, or for leave to apply for, judicial review of the decision under section 31 of the Supreme Court Act 1981; or

 (ii) an application to the supervisory jurisdiction of the Court of Session in respect of the decision.

(8) Regulations may make provision supplementing that made by this section.

Note. In sub-ss (1)(a), (4) words in square brackets substituted for words an assessment and or assessment respectively, and sub-s (1)(a) as a whole substituted, by the Child Support, Pensions and Social Security Act 2000, ss 1(2)(b), 26, Sch 3, para 11(1), (12)(a), (b), as from (in relation to certain cases): 3 March 2003 (SI 2003 No 192); for remaining purposes: to be appointed.

Cases of errors

28ZC. Restrictions on liability in certain cases of error—(1) Subject to subsection (2), this section applies where—

(a) the effect of the determination, whenever made, of an appeal to a Child Support Commissioner or the court ('the relevant determination') is that the adjudicating authority's decision out of which the appeal arose was erroneous in point of law; and

(b) after the date of the relevant determination a decision falls to be made by the Secretary of State in accordance with that determination (or would, apart from this section, fall to be so made)—

 (i) with respect to an application for a *maintenance assessment* [maintenance calculation] (made after the commencement date) [or one treated as having been so made, or under section 46 as to the reduction of benefit];

 (ii) as to whether to revise, under section 16, *a decision (made after the commencement date) with respect to such an assessment; or* [any decision (made after the commencement date) referred to in section 16(1A);]

 (iii) on an application under section 17 (made after the commencement date) for *a decision with respect to such an assessment to be superseded* [any decision (made after the commencement date) referred to in section 17(1)].

(2) This section does not apply where the decision of the Secretary of State mentioned in subsection (1)(b)—

(a) is one which, but for section 28ZA(2)(a), would have been made before the date of the relevant determination; or

(b) is one made in pursuance of section 28ZB(3) or (5).

(3) In so far as the decision relates to a person's liability [or the reduction of a person's benefit] in respect of a period before the date of the relevant determination, it shall be made as if the adjudicating authority's decision had been found by the Commissioner or court not to have been erroneous in point of law.

(4) Subsection (1)(a) shall be read as including a case where—

(a) the effect of the relevant determination is that part or all of a purported regulation or order is invalid; and

(b) the error of law made by the adjudicating authority was to act on the basis that the purported regulation or order (or the part held to be invalid) was valid. .

(5) It is immaterial for the purposes of subsection (1)—

(a) where such a decision as is mentioned in paragraph (b)(i) falls to be made; or

(b) where such a decision as is mentioned in paragraph (b)(ii) or (iii) falls to be made on an application under section 16 or (as the case may be) section 17,

whether the application was made before or after the date of the relevant determination.

(6) In this section—

'adjudicating authority' means the Secretary of State, or a child support officer [or, in the case of a decision made on a referral under section 2BO(1)(b), an appeal tribunal];

'the commencement date' means the date of the coming into force of section 44 of the Social Security Act 199B; and

'the court' means the High Court, the Court of Appeal, the Court of Session, the High Court or Court of Appeal in Northern Ireland, the House of Lords or the Court of Justice of the European Community.

(7) The date of the relevant determination shall, in prescribed cases, be determined for the purposes of this section in accordance with any regulations made for that purpose.

(8) Regulations made under subsection (7) may include provision—

(a) for a determination of a higher court to be treated as if it had been made on the date of a determination of a lower court or a Child Support Commissioner; or

(b) for a determination of a lower court or a Child Support Commissioner to be treated as if it had been made on the date of a determination of a higher court.

Note. In sub-s (1) words in square brackets substituted for words in italics, and in sub-ss (3), (6) words in square brackets inserted by the Child Support, Pensions and Social Security Act 2000, ss 1(2)(a), 26, Sch 3, para 11(1), (13)(a)-(e), as from (in relation to certain cases): 3 March 2003 (SI 2003 No 192); for remaining purposes: to be appointed.

28ZD. Correction of errors and setting aside of decisions—(1) Regulations may make provision with respect to—

(a) the correction of accidental errors in any decision or record of a decision given under this Act; and

(b) the setting aside of any such decision in a case where it appears just to set the decision aside on the ground that-

(i) a document relating to the proceedings in which the decision was given was not sent to, or was not received at an appropriate time by, a party to the proceedings or a party's representative or was not received at an appropriate time by the body or person who gave the decision; or

(ii) a party to the proceedings or a party's representative was not present at a hearing related to the proceedings.

(2) Nothing in subsection (1) shall be construed as derogating from any power to correct errors or set aside decisions which is exercisable apart from regulations made by virtue of that subsection.]

Note. Sections 28ZA-28ZD inserted by the Social Security Act 1998, s 44, as from 1 June 1999 (SI1999 No 1510).

[*Departure from usual rules for determining maintenance assessments* [maintenance calculations]

28A. Application for a departure direction—*(1) Where a maintenance assessment [maintenance calculation] ('the current assessment' [calculation]) is in force—*

(a) *the person with care, or absent parent [non-resident parent], with respect to whom it was made, or*

(b) *where the application for the current assessment [calculation] was made under section 7, either of those persons or the child concerned,*

may apply to the Secretary of State for a direction under section 28F (a 'departure direction').

(2) An application for a departure direction shall state in writing the grounds on which it is made and shall, in particular, state whether it is based on—

(a) *the effect of the current assessment [calculation]; or*

(b) *a material change in the circumstances of the case since the current assessment [calculation] was made.*

(3) In other respects, an application for a departure direction shall be made in such manner as may be prescribed.

(4) An application may be made under this section even though—

(a) *an application for a review has been made under section 17 or 18 with respect to the current assessment [calculation]; or*

(b) *a child support officer is conducting a review of the current assessment [calculation] under section 16 or 19.*

[(4) An application may be made under this section even though an application has been made under section 16(1) or 17(1) with respect to the current assessment.]

(5) If the Secretary of State considers it appropriate to do so, he may by regulations provide for the question whether a change of circumstances is material to be determined in accordance with the regulations.

(6) Schedule 4A has effect in relation to departure directions.]

Note. This section and preceding cross-heading inserted by Child Support Act 1995, s 1(1), as from 14 October 1996 for the purpose of making regulations hereunder, and as from 2 December 1996 otherwise. In cross-heading and sub-ss (1)–(4) words 'maintenance calculations', 'maintenance calculation', 'non-resident parent' and 'calculation' in square brackets substituted for words 'maintenance assessments', 'maintenance assessment', 'absent parent' and 'assessment' respectively in each place they occur by the Child Support, Pensions and Social Security Act 2000, ss 1(2), 26, Sch 3, para 11(1), (2). Sub-s (4) substituted by the Social Security Act 1998, s 86(1). Sch 7, para 34, as from 1 June 1999 (SI 1999 No 1510).

[28B. Preliminary consideration of applications—*(1) Where an application for a departure direction has been duly made to the Secretary of State, he may give the application a preliminary consideration.*

(2) Where the Secretary of State does so he may, on completing the preliminary consideration, reject the application if it appears to him—

(a) *that there are no grounds on which a departure direction could be given in response to the application; or*

(b) *that the difference between the current amount and the revised amount is less than an amount to be calculated in accordance with regulations made by the Secretary of State for the purposes of this subsection and section 28F(4).*

(3) In subsection (2)—

'the current amount' means the amount of the child support maintenance fixed by the current assessment [calculation]; and

'the revised amount' means the amount of child support maintenance which, but for subsection (2)(b), would be fixed if a fresh maintenance assessment [maintenance calculation] were to be made as a result of a departure direction allowing the departure applied for.

(4) Before completing any preliminary consideration, the Secretary of State may refer the current assessment to a child support officer for it to be reviewed as if an application for a review had been made under section 17 or 18.

(5) A review initiated by a reference under subsection (4) shall be conducted as if subsection (4) of section 17, or (as the case may be) subsection (8) of section 18, were omitted.

(6) Where, as a result of a review of the current assessment [calculation] under section 16, 17, 18 or 19 (including a review initiated by a reference under subsection (4)), a fresh maintenance assessment is made, the Secretary of State—

    (a) shall notify the applicant and such other persons as may be prescribed that the fresh maintenance assessment has been made; and

    (b) may direct that the application is to lapse unless, before the end of such period as may be prescribed, the applicant notifies the Secretary of State that he wishes it to stand.]

Note. This section inserted by Child Support Act 1995, s 2, as from 14 October 1996 in respect of sub-ss (2), (3) for the purpose of making regulations under sub-s (2), as from 14 December 1996 in respect of sub-ss (1), (4), (5) and sub-ss (2), (3) so far as not already in force. In sub-s (3), (6) words 'calculation' and 'maintenance assessment' in square brackets substituted for words 'assessment' and 'maintenance assessment' by the Child Support, Pensions and Social Security Act 2000, s 1(2), as from (in relation to certain cases): 3 March 2003 (SI 2003 No 192); for remaining purposes: to be appointed.

[28C. Imposition of a regular payments condition—*(1) Where an application for a departure direction is made by an absent parent [a non-resident parent], the Secretary of State may impose on him one of the conditions mentioned in subsection (2) ('a regular payments condition').*

(2) The conditions are that—

    (a) the applicant must make the payments of child support maintenance fixed by the current assessment [calculation];

    (b) the applicant must make such reduced payments of child support maintenance as may be determined in accordance with regulations made by the Secretary of State.

(3) Where the Secretary of State imposes a regular payments condition, he shall give written notice to the absent parent [non-resident parent] and person with care concerned of the imposition of the condition and of the effect of failure to comply with it.

(4) A regular payments condition shall cease to have effect on the failure or determination of the application.

(5) For the purposes of subsection (4), an application for a departure direction fails if—

    (a) it lapses or is withdrawn; or

    (b) the Secretary of State rejects it on completing a preliminary consideration under section 28B.

(6) Where an absent parent [a non-resident parent] has failed to comply with a regular payments condition—

    (a) the Secretary of State may refuse to consider the application; and

    (b) in prescribed circumstances the application shall lapse.

[(6) Where a decision as to a maintenance assessment is revised or superseded under section 16 or 17, the Secretary of State—

    (a) shall notify the applicant and such other persons as may be prescribed that the decision has been revised or superseded; and

    (b) may direct that the application is to lapse unless, before the end of such period as may be prescribed, the applicant notifies the Secretary of State that he wishes it to stand.]

(7) The question whether an absent parent [a non-resident parent] has failed to comply with a regular payments condition shall be determined by the Secretary of State.

(8) Where the Secretary of State determines that an absent parent [a non-resident parent] has failed to comply with a regular payments condition he shall give that parent, and the person with care concerned, written notice of his decision.]

Note. This section inserted by Child Support Act 1995, s 3, as from 14 October 1996 for the purpose of making regulations hereunder, and as from 2 December 1996 otherwise. In sub-ss (1), (3), (6)–(8) words 'a non-resident parent' and 'non resident parent' in square brackets substituted for words 'an absent parent' and 'absent parent' in each place they occur, and word 'calculation' in square brackets in sub-s (2)(a) substituted for word 'assessment' by the Child Support, Pensions and Social Security Act 2000, s 1(2), as from (in relation to certain cases): 3 March 2003 (SI 2003 No 192); for remaining purposes: to be appointed. Sub-s (6) substituted by the Social Security Act 1998, s 86(1), Sch 7, para 35(2), as from 1 June 1999 (SI 1999 No 1510).

[Variations

28A. Application for variation of usual rules for calculating maintenance—
(1) Where an application for a maintenance calculation is made under section 4 or 7, or treated as made under section 6, the person with care or the non-resident parent or (in the case of an application under section 7) either of them or the child concerned may apply to the Secretary of State for the rules by which the calculation is made to be varied in accordance with this Act.

(2) Such an application is referred to in this Act as an 'application for a variation'.

(3) An application for a variation may be made at any time before the Secretary of State has reached a decision (under section 11 or 12(1)) on the application for a maintenance calculation (or the application treated as having been made under section 6).

(4) A person who applies for a variation—
(a) need not make the application in writing unless the Secretary of State directs in any case that he must; and
(b) must say upon what grounds the application is made.

(5) In other respects an application for a variation is to be made in such manner as may be prescribed.

(6) Schedule 4A has effect in relation to applications for a variation.

28B. Preliminary consideration of applications—(1) Where an application for a variation has been duly made to the Secretary of State, he may give it a preliminary consideration.

(2) Where he does so he may, on completing the preliminary consideration, reject the application (and proceed to make his decision on the application for a maintenance calculation without any variation) if it appears to him-
(a) that there are no grounds on which he could agree to a variation;
(b) that he has insufficient information to make a decision on the application for the maintenance calculation under section 11 (apart from any information needed in relation to the application for a variation), and therefore that his decision would be made under section 12(1); or
(c) that other prescribed circumstances apply.

28C. Imposition of regular payment condition—(1) Where—
(a) an application for a variation is made by the non-resident parent; and
(b) the Secretary of State makes an interim maintenance decision,
the Secretary of State may also, if he has completed his preliminary consideration (under section 28B) of the application for a variation and has not rejected it under that section, impose on the non-resident parent one of the conditions mentioned in subsection (2) (a 'regular payments condition').

(2) The conditions are that—
(a) the non-resident parent must make the payments of child support maintenance specified in the interim maintenance decision;
(b) the non-resident parent must make such lesser payments of child support maintenance as may be determined in accordance with regulations made by the Secretary of State.

(3) Where the Secretary of State imposes a regular payments condition, he shall give written notice of the imposition of the condition and of the effect of failure to comply with it to—
(a) the non-resident parent;
(b) all the persons with care concerned; and
(c) if the application for the maintenance calculation was made under section 7, the child who made the application.

(4) A regular payments condition shall cease to have effect—

(a) when the Secretary of State has made a decision on the application for a maintenance calculation under section 11 (whether he agrees to a variation or not);

(b) on the withdrawal of the application for a variation.

(5) Where a non-resident parent has failed to comply with a regular payments condition, the Secretary of State may in prescribed circumstances refuse to consider the application for a variation, and instead reach his decision under section 11 as if no such application had been made.

(6) The question whether a non-resident parent has failed to comply with a regular payments condition is to be determined by the Secretary of State.

(7) Where the Secretary of State determines that a non-resident parent has failed to comply with a regular payments condition he shall give written notice of his determination to—

(a) that parent;

(b) all the persons with care concerned; and

(c) if the application for the maintenance calculation was made under section 7, the child who made the application.]

Note. Sections 28A-28C above substituted for ss 28A-28C in italics by the Child Support, Pensions and Social Security Act 2000, s 5(1), (2), as from (for certain purposes): 10 November 2000 (SI 2000 No 2994); (in relation to certain cases): 3 March 2003 (SI 2003 No 192); for remaining purposes: to be appointed.

[28D. Determination of applications—(1) Where an application for a departure direction has not failed, the Secretary of State shall—

(a) determine the application in accordance with the relevant provisions of or made under, this Act; or

(b) refer the application to *a child support appeal tribunal* [an appeal tribunal] for the tribunal to determine it in accordance with those provisions.

[(1) Where an application for a variation has not failed, the Secretary of State shall, in accordance with the relevant provisions of, or made under, this Act—

(a) either agree or not to a variation, and make a decision under section 11 or 12(1); or

(b) refer the application to an appeal tribunal for the tribunal to determine what variation, if any, is to be made.]

(2) For the purposes of subsection (1), *an application for a departure direction* [an application for a variation] has failed if—

(a) it has *lapsed* or been withdrawn; *or*

(b) the Secretary of State has rejected it on completing a preliminary consideration under section 28B [; or (c) the Secretary of State has refused to consider it under section 28C(5)].

[(3) In dealing with *an application for a departure direction* [an application for a variation] which has been referred to it under subsection (1)(b), *a child support appeal tribunal* [an appeal tribunal] shall have the same powers, and be subject to the same duties, as would the Secretary of State if he were dealing with the application.]

Note. This section inserted by Child Support Act 1995, s 4, as from 2 December 1996. In sub-ss (1)(b), (3) words 'an appeal tribunal' in square brackets substituted for words 'a child support appeal tribunal' by the Social Security Act 1998, s 86(1), Sch 7, para 36, as from 1 June 1999 (SI 1999 No 1510). Sub-s (1) substituted and in sub-ss (2), (3) words. 'an application for a variation' substituted for words in Italics by the Child Support Pensions and Social Security Act 2000, s 5(1),(3)(a), (b), as from (In relation to certain cases): 3 March I2003 (SI 2003 No 192); for remaining purposes: to be appointed. In sub-s (2)(a) word or in italics repealed and sub-s (2)(c) inserted by the Child Support Pensions and Social Security Act 2000, s 5(1), (3)(c), as from (in relation to certain cases): 3 March 2003 (SI 2003 No 192); for remaining purposes: to be appointed.

[28E. Matters to be taken into account—(1) In determining *any application for a departure direction* [whether to agree to a variation], the Secretary of State shall have regard both to the general principles set out in subsection (2) and to such other considerations as may be prescribed.

(2) The general principles are that—

(a) parents should be responsible for maintaining their children whenever they can afford to do so;

(b) where a parent has more than one child, his obligation to maintain any one of them should be no less of an obligation than his obligation to maintain any other of them.

(3) In determining *any application for a departure direction* [whether to agree to a variation], the Secretary of State shall take into account any representations made to him—

(a) by the person with care or *absent parent* [non-resident parent] concerned; or

(b) where the application for the current *assessment* [calculation] was made under section 7, by either of them or the child concerned.

(4) In determining *any application for a departure direction* [whether to agree to a variation], no account shall be taken of the fact that—

(a) any part of the income of the person with care concerned is, or would be if *a departure direction were made* [the Secretary of State agreed to a variation], derived from any benefit; or

(b) some or all of any child support maintenance might be taken into account in any manner in relation to any entitlement to benefit.

(5) In this section 'benefit' has such meaning as may be prescribed.]

Note. This section inserted by Child Support Act 1995, s 5, as from 14 October 1996 for the purpose of making regulations hereunder, and as from 2 December 1996 otherwise. In sub-ss (1), (3), (4) words 'whether to agree to a variation' in square brackets substituted for words in italics and in sub-s (4)(a) words 'the Secretary of State agreed to a variation' in square brackets substituted for words in italics by the Child Support, Pensions and Social Security Act 2000, s 5(1), (4), as from (for certain purposes): 10 November 2000 (SI 2000 No 2994); (in relation to certain cases): 3 March 2003 (SI 2003 No 192); for remaining purposes: to be appointed. In sub-ss (3)(a) words 'non-resident parent' and 'calculation' in square brackets substituted for words in italics by the Child Support, Pensions and Social Security Act 2000, ss 1(2), 26, Sch 3, para 11(1), (2), as from (in relation to certain cases): 3 March 2003 (SI 2003 No 192); for remaining purposes: to be appointed.

[28F. Departure directions—*(1) The Secretary of State may give a departure direction if—*

(a) *he is satisfied that the case is one which falls within one or more of the cases set out in Part I of Schedule 4B or in regulations made under that Part; and*

(b) *it is his opinion that, in all the circumstances of the case, it would be just and equitable to give a departure direction.*

(2) In considering whether it would be just and equitable in any case to give a departure direction, the Secretary of State shall have regard, in particular, to—

(a) *the financial circumstances of the absent parent* [non-resident parent] *concerned,*

(b) *the financial circumstances of the person with care concerned, and*

(c) *the welfare of any child likely to be affected by the direction.*

(3) The Secretary of State may by regulations make provision—

(a) *for factors which are to be taken into account in determining whether it would be just and equitable to give a departure direction in any case;*

(b) *for factors which are not to be taken into account in determining such a question.*

(4) The Secretary of State shall not give a departure direction if he is satisfied that the difference between the current amount and the revised amount is less than an amount to be calculated in accordance with regulations made by the Secretary of State for the purposes of this subsection and section 28B(2).

(5) In subsection (4)—

'the current amount' means the amount of the child support maintenance fixed by the current assessment [calculation]*, and*

'*the revised amount*' means the amount of child support maintenance which would be fixed if a fresh maintenance assessment [maintenance calculation] were to be made as a result of the departure direction which the Secretary of State would give in response to the application but for subsection (4).

(6) A departure direction shall—

(a) require a child support officer to make [the making of] one or more fresh maintenance assessments [maintenance calculations]; and

(b) specify the basis on which the amount of child support maintenance is to be fixed by any assessment [calculation] made in consequence of the direction.

(7) In giving a departure direction, the Secretary of State shall comply with the provisions of regulations made under Part II of Schedule 4B.

(8) Before the end of such period as may be prescribed, the Secretary of State shall notify the applicant for a departure direction, and such other persons as may be prescribed—

(a) of his decision in relation to the application, and

(b) of the reasons for his decision.]

Note. This section inserted by Child Support Act 1995, s 6(1), as from 14 October 1996 for the purpose of making regulations hereunder, and as from 2 December 1996 otherwise. In sub-s (2)(a) words 'non-resident parent' in square brackets substituted for words 'absent parent' by the Child Support, Pensions and Social Security Act 2000, s 26, Sch 3, para 11(1), (2), as from (in relation to certain cases): 3 March 2003 (SI 2003 No 192); for remaining purposes: to be appointed. In sub-ss (5), (6) words 'calculation', 'maintenance calculation' and 'maintenance calculations' in square brackets substituted for words 'assessment', 'maintenance assessment' and 'maintenance assessments' respectively by the Child Support, Pensions and Social Security Act 2000, s 1(2), as from (in relation to certain cases): 3 March 2003 (SI 2003 No 192); for remaining purposes: to be appointed. In sub-s (6)(a) words' the making of' in square brackets substituted for words 'a child support offer to make' by the Social Security Act 1998, s 86(1), Sch 7, para 37, as from 1 June 1999 (SI 1999 No 1510).

[28F. Agreement to a variation—(1) The Secretary of State may agree to a variation if—

(a) he is satisfied that the case is one which falls within one or more of the cases set out in Part I of Schedule 4B or in regulations made under that Part; and

(b) it is his opinion that, in all the circumstances of the case, it would be just and equitable to agree to a variation.

(2) In considering whether it would be just and equitable in any case to agree to a variation, the Secretary of State—

(a) must have regard, in particular, to the welfare of any child likely to be affected if he did agree to a variation; and

(b) must, or as the case may be must not, take any prescribed factors into account, or must take them into account (or not) in prescribed circumstances.

(3) The Secretary of State shall not agree to a variation (and shall proceed to make his decision on the application for a maintenance calculation without any variation) if he is satisfied that—

(a) he has insufficient information to make a decision on the application for the maintenance calculation under section 11, and therefore that his decision would be made under section 12(1); or

(b) other prescribed circumstances apply.

(4) Where the Secretary of State agrees to a variation, he shall—

(a) determine the basis on which the amount of child support maintenance is to be calculated in response to the application for a maintenance calculation (including an application treated as having been made); and

(b) make a decision under section 11 on that basis.

(5) If the Secretary of State has made an interim maintenance decision, it is to be treated as having been replaced by his decision under section 11, and except in prescribed circumstances any appeal connected with it (under section 20) shall lapse.

(6) In determining whether or not to agree to a variation, the Secretary of State shall comply with regulations made under Part II of Schedule 48.]

Note. Section 28F above substituted for s 28F in italics by the Child Support, pension and Social Security Act 2000, s 5(1), (5), as from (for certain purposes): 10 November 2000 (SI 2000 No 2994); (in relation to certain cases): 3 March 2003 (SI 2003 No 192); for remaining purposes: to be appointed.

[28G. Effect and duration of departure directions—*(1) Where a departure direction is given, it shall be the duty of the child support officer to whom the case is referred to comply with the direction as soon as is reasonably practicable.*

(2) A departure direction may be given so as to have effect—

(a) for a specified period; or

(b) until the occurrence of a specified event.

(3) The Secretary of State may by regulations make provision for the cancellation of a departure direction in prescribed circumstances.

(4) The Secretary of State may by regulations make provision as to when a departure direction is to take effect.

(5) Regulations under subsection (4) may provide for a departure direction to have effect from a date earlier than that on which the direction is given.]

Note. This section inserted by Child Support Act 1995, s 7, as from 14 October 1996 for the purpose of making regulations hereunder, and as from 2 December 1996 otherwise. Sub-s (1) repealed by the Social Security Act 1998, s 86, Sch 7, para 38, Sch 8, as from 1 June 1999 (SI 1999 No 1510).

[28G. Variations: revision and supersession—(1) An application for a variation may' also be made when a maintenance calculation is in force.

(2) The Secretary of State may by regulations provide for—

(a) sections 16, 17 and 20; and

(b) sections 28A to 28F and Schedules 4A and 48,

to apply with prescribed modifications in relation to such applications.

(3) The Secretary of State may by regulations provide that, in prescribed cases (or except in prescribed cases), a decision under section 17 made otherwise than pursuant to an application for a variation may be made on the basis of a variation agreed to for the purposes of an earlier decision without a new application for a variation having to be made.]

Note. Section 28G above substituted for s 28G in italics by the Child Support, Pensions and Social Security Act 2000, s 7, as from (for certain purposes): 10 November 2000 (SI 2000 No 2994); (in relation to certain cases): 3 March 2003 (SI 2003 No 192); for remaining purposes: to be appointed.

[28H. Appeals in relation to applications for departure directions—*(1) Any qualifying person who is aggrieved by any decision of the Secretary of State on an application for a departure direction may appeal to a child support appeal tribunal against that decision.*

(2) In subsection (1), 'qualifying person' means—

(a) the person with care, or absent parent, with respect to whom the current assessment was made, or

(b) where the application for the current assessment was made under section 7, either of those persons or the child concerned.

(3) Except with leave of the chairman of a child support appeal tribunal, no appeal under this section shall be brought after the end of the period of 28 days beginning with the date on which notification was given of the decision in question.

(4) On an appeal under this section, the tribunal shall—

(a) consider the matter—

(i) as if it were exercising the powers of the Secretary of State in relation to the application in question; and

(ii) as if it were subject to the duties imposed on him in relation to that application;

(b) have regard to any representations made to it by the Secretary of State; and

(c) confirm the decision or replace it with such decision as the tribunal considers appropriate.]

[28H. Departure directions: decisions and appeals—*[Schedule 4C shall have effect for applying sections 16, 17, 20 and 28ZA to 28ZG to decisions with respect to departure directions.]*

Note. Section 28H above substituted for s 28H in italics by the Social Security Act 1998, s 86(1), Sch 7, para 39, as from 1 June 1999 (SI 1999 No 1510). Repealed by the Child Support, Pensions and Social Security Act 2000, ss 26, 85, Sch 3, para 11(1), (4), Sch 9, Pt 1, as from (in relation to certain cases): 3 March 2003 (SI 2003 No 192); for remaining purposes: to be appointed.

Note. This section inserted by Child Support Act 1995, s 8, as from 2 December 1996.

[28I. Transitional provisions—*(1) In the case of an application for a departure direction relating to a maintenance assessment [maintenance calculation] which was made before the coming into force of section 28A, the period within which the application must be made shall be such period as may be prescribed.*

(2) The Secretary of State may by regulations make provision for applications for departure directions to be dealt with according to an order determined in accordance with the regulations.

(3) The regulations may, for example, provide for—

(a) applications relating to prescribed descriptions of maintenance assessment [maintenance calculation], or

(b) prescribed descriptions of application,

to be dealt with before applications relating to other prescribed descriptions of assessment [calculation] or (as the case may be) other prescribed descriptions of application.

(4) The Secretary of State may by regulations make provision—

(a) enabling applications for departure directions made before the coming into force of section 28A to be considered even though that section is not in force;

(b) for the determination of any such application as if section 28A and the other provisions of this Act relating to departure directions were in force; and

(c) as to the effect of any departure direction given before the coming into force of section 28A.

(5) Regulations under section 28G(4) may not provide for a departure direction to have effect from a date earlier than that on which that section came into force.]

Note. This section inserted by Child Support Act 1995, s 9, as from 22 January 1996 as respects sub-s (4), as from 14 October 1996 as respects sub-s (5), and as from a day to be appointed otherwise. In sub-s (1), (3) words 'maintenance calculation' and 'calculation' in square brackets substituted for words 'maintenance assessment' and 'assessment' respectively by the Child Support, Pensions and Social Security Act 2000, s 1(2), as from (in relation to certain cases): 3 March 2003 (SI 2003 No 192); for remaining purposes: to be appointed. Whole section repealed by the Child Support, Pensions and Social Security Act 2000, s 26, 85, Sch 3, para 11(1), (14), Sch 9, Pt 1, as from (in relation to certain cases): 3 March 2003 (SI 2003 No 192); for remaining purposes: to be appointed.

[Voluntary payments

[28J. Voluntary payments—(1) This section applies where-

(a) a person has applied for a maintenance calculation under section 4(1) or 7(1), or is treated as having applied for one by virtue of section 6;

(b) the Secretary of State has neither made a decision under section 11 or 12 on the application, nor decided not to make a maintenance calculation; and

(c) the non-resident parent makes a voluntary payment.

(2) A 'voluntary payment' is a payment—

(a) on account of child support maintenance which the non-resident parent expects to become liable to pay following the determination of the application (whether or not the amount of the payment is based on any estimate of his potential liability which the Secretary of State has agreed to give); and

(b) made before the maintenance calculation has been notified to the non-resident parent or (as the case may be) before the Secretary of State has notified the non-resident parent that he has decided not to make a maintenance calculation.

(3) In such circumstances and to such extent as may be prescribed—

(a) the voluntary payment may be set off against arrears of child support maintenance which accrued by virtue of the maintenance calculation taking effect on a date earlier than that on which it was notified to the non-resident parent;

(b) the amount payable under a maintenance calculation may be adjusted to take account of the voluntary payment.

(4) A voluntary payment shall be made to the Secretary of State unless he agrees, on such conditions as he may specify, that it may be made to the person with care, or to or through another person.

(5) The Secretary of State may by regulations make provision as to voluntary payments, and the regulations may in particular—

(a) prescribe what payments or descriptions of payment are, or are not, to count as 'voluntary payments';

(b) prescribe the extent to which and circumstances in which a payment, or a payment of a prescribed description, counts.]

Note. This section inserted by the Child Support, Pensions and Social Security Act 2000, s 20(1), as from (for certain purposes): 10 November 2000 (SI 2000 No 2994); (in relation to certain cases): 3 March 2003 (SI 2003 No 192); for remaining purposes: to be appointed.

Collection and enforcement

29. Collection of child support maintenance—(1) The Secretary of State may arrange for the collection of any child support maintenance payable in accordance with a *maintenance assessment* [maintenance calculation] where—

(a) the *assessment* [calculation] is made by virtue of section 6; or

(b) an application has been made to the Secretary of State under section 4(2) or 7(3) for him to arrange for its collection.

(2) Where a *maintenance assessment* [maintenance calculation] is made under this Act, payments of child support maintenance under the *assessment* [calculation] shall be made in accordance with regulations made by the Secretary of State.

(3) The regulations may, in particular, make provision—

(a) for payments of child support maintenance to be made—
  (i) to the person caring for the child or children in question;
  (ii) to, or through, the Secretary of State; or
  (iii) to, or through, such other person as the Secretary of State may, from time to time, specify;

(b) as to the method by which payments of child support maintenance are to be made;

(c) as to the intervals at which such payments are to be made;

(d) as to the method and timing of the transmission of payments which are made, to or through the Secretary of State or any other person, in accordance with the regulations;

(e) empowering the Secretary of State to direct any person liable to make payments in accordance with the *assessment* [calculation]—
  (i) to make them by standing order or by any other method which requires one person to give his authority for payments to be made from an account of his to an account of another's on specific dates during the period for which the authority is in force and without the need for any further authority from him;

(ii) to open an account from which payments under the *assessment* [calculation] may be made in accordance with the method of payment which that person is obliged to adopt;

(f) providing for the making of representations with respect to matters with which the regulations are concerned.

Note. In sub-ss (1)–(3) words in square brackets substituted for words in italics by the Child Support, Pensions and Social Security Act 2000, s 1(2), as from (in relation to certain cases): 3 March 2003 (SI 2003 No 192); for remaining purposes: to be appointed.

30. Collection and enforcement of other forms of maintenance—(1) Where the Secretary of State is arranging for the collection of any payments under section 29 or subsection (2), he may also arrange for the collection of any periodical payments, or secured periodical payments, of a prescribed kind which are payable to or for the benefit of any person who falls within a prescribed category.

(2) The Secretary of State may arrange for the collection of any periodical payments or secured periodical payments of a prescribed kind which are payable for the benefit of a child even though he is not arranging for the collection of child support maintenance with respect to that child.

[(2) The Secretary of State may, except in prescribed cases, arrange for the collection of any periodical payments, or secured periodical payments, of a prescribed kind which are payable for the benefit of a child even though he is not arranging for the collection of child support maintenance with respect to that child.]

Note. Sub-s (2) above substituted for sub-s (2) in italics by the Child Support, Pensions and Social Security Act 2000, s 26, Sch 3, para 11 (1), (15), as from 3 March 2003 (SI 2003 No 192).

(3) Where—

(a) the Secretary of State is arranging, under this Act, for the collection of different payments ('the payments') from the same *absent parent* [non-resident parent];

(b) an amount is collected by the Secretary of State from the *absent parent* [non-resident parent] which is less than the total amount due in respect of the payments; and

(c) the *absent parent* [non-resident parent] has not stipulated how that amount is to be allocated by the Secretary of State as between the payments,

the Secretary of State may allocate that amount as he sees fit.

Note. Words in square brackets substituted for words in italics by the Child Support, Pensions and Social Security Act 2000, s 26, Sch 3, para 11(1), (2).

(4) In relation to England and Wales, the Secretary of State may by regulations make provision for sections 29 and 31 to 40 to apply, with such modifications (if any) as he considers necessary or expedient, for the purpose of enabling him to enforce any obligation to pay any amount which he is authorised to collect under this section.

(5) *(Applies to Scotland only.)*

[(5A) Regulations made under subsection (1) or (2) prescribing payments which may be collected by the Secretary of State may make provision for the payment to him by such person or persons as may be prescribed of such fees as may be prescribed.]

Note. Sub-s (5A) inserted by Child Support Act 1995, s 30(5), Sch 3, para 9, as from a day to be appointed.

31. Deduction from earnings orders—(1) This section applies where any person ('the liable person') is liable to make payments of child support maintenance.

(2) The Secretary of State may make an order ('a deduction from earnings order') against a liable person to secure the payment of any amount due under the *maintenance assessment* [maintenance calculation] in question.

(3) A deduction from earnings order may be made so as to secure the payment of—

(a) arrears of child support maintenance payable under the *assessment* [calculation];

(b) amounts of child support maintenance which will become due under the *assessment* [calculation]; or

(c) both such arrears and such future amounts.

Note. In sub-ss (2), (3) words in square brackets substituted for words in italics by the Child Support, Pensions and Social Security Act 2000, s 1(2), as from (in relation to certain cases): 3 March 2003 (SI 2003 No 192); for remaining purposes: to be appointed.

(4) A deduction from earnings order—

(a) shall be expressed to be directed at a person ('the employer') who has the liable person in his employment; and

(b) shall have effect from such date as may be specified in the order.

(5) A deduction from earnings order shall operate as an instruction to the employer to—

(a) make deductions from the liable person's earnings; and

(b) pay the amounts deducted to the Secretary of State.

(6) The Secretary of State shall serve a copy of any deduction from earnings order which he makes under this section on—

(a) the person who appears to the Secretary of State to have the liable person in question in his employment; and

(b) the liable person.

(7) Where—

(a) a deduction from earnings order has been made; and

(b) a copy of the order has been served on the liable person's employer,

it shall be the duty of that employer to comply with the order; but he shall not be under any liability for non-compliance before the end of the period of 7 days beginning with the date on which the copy was served on him.

(8) In this section and in section 32 'earnings' has such meaning as may be prescribed.

32. Regulations about deduction from earnings orders—(1) The Secretary of State may by regulations make provision with respect to deduction from earnings orders.

(2) The regulations may, in particular, make provision—

(a) as to the circumstances in which one person is to be treated as employed by another;

(b) requiring any deduction from earnings under an order to be made in the prescribed manner;

[(bb) for the amount or amounts which are to be deducted from the liable person's earnings not to exceed a prescribed proportion of his earnings (as determined by the employer);]

(c) requiring an order to specify the amount or amounts to which the order relates and the amount or amounts which are to be deducted from the liable person's earnings in order to meet his liabilities under the *maintenance assessment* [maintenance calculation] in question;

(d) requiring the intervals between deductions to be made under an order to be specified in the order;

(e) as to the payment of sums deducted under an order to the Secretary of State;

(f) allowing the person who deducts and pays any amount under an order to deduct from the liable person's earnings a prescribed sum towards his administrative costs;

(g) with respect to the notification to be given to the liable person of amounts deducted, and amounts paid, under the order;

(h) requiring any person on whom a copy of an order is served to notify the Secretary of State in the prescribed manner and within a prescribed period if he does not have the liable person in his employment or if the liable person ceases to be in his employment;

(i) as to the operation of an order where the liable person is in the employment of the Crown;

(j) for the variation of orders;

(k) similar to that made by Section 31(7), in relation to any variation of an order;

(l) for an order to lapse when the employer concerned ceases to have the liable person in his employment;

(m) as to the revival of an order in such circumstances as may be prescribed;

(n) allowing or requiring an order to be discharged;

(o) as to the giving of notice by the Secretary of State to the employer concerned that an order has lapsed or has ceased to have effect.

Note. Sub-s (2)(bb) inserted by the Child Support, Pensions and Social Security Act 2000, s 26, Sch 3, para 11(1), (15), as from 3 March 2003 (SI 2003 No 192). In sub-s (2)(c) words in square brackets substituted for words in italics by the Child Support, Pensions and Social Security Act 2000, s 1(2)(a), as from (in relation to certain cases): 3 March 2003 (SI 2003 No 192); for remaining purposes: to be appointed.

(3) The regulations may include provision that while a deduction from earnings order is in force—

(a) the liable person shall from time to time notify the Secretary of State, in the prescribed manner and within a prescribed period, of each occasion on which he leaves any employment or becomes employed, or re-employed, and shall include in such a notification a statement of his earnings and expected earnings from the employment concerned and of such other matters as may be prescribed;

(b) any person who becomes the liable person's employer and knows that the order is in force shall notify the Secretary of State, in the prescribed manner and within a prescribed period, that he is the liable person's employer, and shall include in such a notification a statement of the liable person's earnings and expected earnings from the employment concerned and of such other matters as may be prescribed.

(4) The regulations may include provision with respect to the priority as between a deduction from earnings order and—

(a) any other deduction from earnings order;

(b) any order under any other enactment relating to England and Wales which provides for deductions from the liable person's earnings;

(c) any diligence against earnings.

(5) The regulations may include a provision that a liable person may appeal to a magistrates' court (or in Scotland to the sheriff) if he is aggrieved by the making of a deduction from earnings order against him, or by the terms of any such order, or there is a dispute as to whether payments constitute earnings or as to any other prescribed matter relating to the order.

(6) On an appeal under subsection (5) the court or (as the case may be) the sheriff shall not question the *maintenance assessment* [maintenance calculation] by reference to which the deduction from earnings order was made.

Note. In sub-s (6) words in square brackets substituted for words in italics by the Child Support, Pensions and Social Security Act 2000, s 1(2)(a), as from (in relation to certain cases): 3 March 2003 (SI 2003 No 192); for remaining purposes: to be appointed.

(7) Regulations made by virtue of subsection (5) may include provision as to the powers of a magistrates' court, or in Scotland of the sheriff, in relation to an appeal (which may include provision as to the quashing of a deduction from earnings order or the variation of the terms of such an order).

(8) If any person fails to comply with the requirements of a deduction from earnings order, or with any regulation under this section which is designated for the purposes of this subsection, he shall be guilty of an offence.

(9) In subsection (8) 'designated' means designated by the regulations.

(10) It shall be a defence for a person charged with an offence under subsection (8) to prove that he took all reasonable steps to comply with the requirements in question.

(11) Any person guilty of an offence under subsection (8) shall be liable on summary conviction to a fine not exceeding level two on the standard scale.

33. Liability orders—(1) This section applies where—
- (a) a person who is liable to make payments of child support maintenance ('the liable person') fails to make one or more of those payments; and
- (b) it appears to the Secretary of State that—
  - (i) it is inappropriate to make a deduction from earnings order against him (because, for example, he is not employed); or
  - (ii) although such an order has been made against him, it has proved ineffective as a means of securing that payments are made in accordance with the *maintenance assessment* [maintenance calculation] in question.

Note. In sub-s (6) words in square brackets substituted for words in italics by the Child Support, Pensions and Social Security Act 2000, s 1(2)(a), as from (in relation to certain cases): 3 March 2003 (SI 2003 No 192); for remaining purposes: to be appointed.

(2) The Secretary of State may apply to a magistrates' court or, in Scotland, to the sheriff for an order ('a liability order') against the liable person.

(3) Where the Secretary of State applies for a liability order, the magistrates' court or (as the case may be) sheriff shall make the order if satisfied that the payments in question have become payable by the liable person and have not been paid.

(4) On an application under subsection (2), the court or (as the case may be) the sheriff shall not question the *maintenance assessment* [maintenance calculation] under which the payments of child support maintenance fell to be made.

Note. In sub-s (4) words in square brackets substituted for words in italics by the Child Support, Pensions and Social Security Act 2000, s 1(2)(a), as from (in relation to certain cases): 3 March 2003 (SI 2003 No 192); for remaining purposes: to be appointed.

[(5) If the Secretary of State designates a liability order for the purposes of this subsection it shall be treated as a judgment entered in a county court for the purposes of section 73 of the County Courts Act 1984 (register of judgments and orders).]

Note. Sub-s (5) added by Child Support Act 1995, s 30(5), Sch 3, para 10, as from 4 September 1995.

[(6) Where regulations have been made under section 29(3)(a)-
- (a) the liable person fails to make a payment (for the purposes of subsection (1)(a) of this section); and
- (b) a payment is not paid (for the purposes of subsection (3)),
unless the payment is made to, or through, the person specified in or by virtue of those regulations for the case of the liable person in question.]

Note. Sub-s (6) inserted by the Child Support, Pensions and Social Security Act 2000, s 26, Sch 3, para 11(1), (17), as from 1 January 2001 (SI 2000 No 2994).

34. Regulations about liability orders—(1) The Secretary of State may make regulations in relation to England and Wales—
- (a) prescribing the procedure to be followed in dealing with an application by the Secretary of State for a liability order;
- (b) prescribing the form and contents of a liability order; and

(c) providing that where a magistrates' court has made a liability order, the person against whom it is made shall, during such time as the amount in respect of which the order was made remains wholly or partly unpaid, be under a duty to supply relevant information to the Secretary of State.

(2) In subsection (1) 'relevant information' means any information of a prescribed description which is in the possession of the liable person and which the Secretary of State has asked him to supply.

35. Enforcement of liability orders by distress—(1) Where a liability order has been made against a person ('the liable person'), the Secretary of State may levy the appropriate amount by distress and sale of the liable person's goods.

(2) In subsection (1), 'the appropriate amount' means the aggregate of—

(a) the amount in respect of which the order was made, to the extent that it remains unpaid; and

(b) an amount, determined in such manner as may be prescribed, in respect of the charges connected with the distress.

(3) The Secretary of State may, in exercising his powers under subsection (1) against the liable person's goods, seize—

(a) any of the liable person's goods except—

   (i) such tools, books, vehicles and other items of equipment as are necessary to him for use personally by him in his employment, business or vocation;

   (ii) such clothing, bedding, furniture, household equipment and provisions as are necessary for satisfying his basic domestic needs; and

(b) any money, banknotes, bills of exchange, promissory notes, bonds, specialties or securities for money belonging to the liable person.

(4) For the purposes of subsection (3), the liable person's domestic needs shall be taken to include those of any member of his family with whom he resides.

(5) No person levying a distress under this section shall be taken to be a trespasser—

(a) on that account; or

(b) from the beginning, on account of any subsequent irregularity in levying the distress.

(6) A person sustaining special damage by reason of any irregularity in levying a distress under this section may recover full satisfaction for the damage (and no more) by proceedings in trespass or otherwise.

(7) The Secretary of State may make regulations supplementing the provisions of this section.

(8) The regulations may, in particular—

(a) provide that a distress under this section may be levied anywhere in England and Wales;

(b) provide that such a distress shall not be deemed unlawful on account of any defect or want of form in the liability order;

(c) provide for an appeal to a magistrates' court by any person aggrieved by the levying of, or an attempt to levy, a distress under this section;

(d) make provision as to the powers of the court on an appeal (which may include provision as to the discharge of goods distrained or the payment of compensation in respect of goods distrained and sold).

36. Enforcement in county courts—(1) Where liability order has been made against a person, the amount in respect of which the order was made, to the extent that it remains unpaid, shall, if a county court so orders, be recoverable by means of garnishee proceedings or a charging order, as if it were payable under a county court order.

(2) In subsection (1) 'charging order' has the same meaning as in section 1 of the Charging Orders Act 1979.

37, 38.   (*Apply to Scotland only.*)

39. Liability orders: enforcement throughout United Kingdom—(1) The Secretary of State may by regulations provide for—

(a)   any liability order made by a court in England and Wales; or

(b)   any corresponding order made by a court in Northern Ireland,

to be enforced in Scotland as if it had been made by the sheriff.

(2)   (*Applies to Scotland only.*)

(3)   The Secretary of State may by regulations make provision for, or in connection with, the enforcement in England and Wales of—

(a)   any liability order made by the sheriff in Scotland; or

(b)   any corresponding order made by a court in Northern Ireland,

as if it had been made by a magistrates' court in England and Wales.

(4)   Regulations under subsection (3) may, in particular, make provision for the registration of any such order as is referred to in that subsection in connection with its enforcement in England and Wales.

[39A Commitment to prison and disqualification from driving—(1) Where the Secretary of State has sought—

(a)   in England and Wales to levy an amount by distress under this Act; or

(b)   to recover an amount by virtue of section 36 or 38,

and that amount, or any portion of it, remains unpaid he may apply to the court under this section.

(2)   An application under this section is for whichever the court considers appropriate in all the circumstances of—

(a)   the issue of a warrant committing the liable person to prison; or

(b)   an order for him to be disqualified from holding or obtaining a driving licence.

(3)   On any such application the court shall (in the presence of the liable person) inquire as to—

(a)   whether he needs a driving licence to earn his living;

(b)   his means; and

(c)   whether there has been wilful refusal or culpable neglect on his part.

(4)   The Secretary of State may make representations to the court as to whether he thinks it more appropriate to commit the liable person to prison or to disqualify him from holding or obtaining a driving licence; and the liable person may reply to those representations.

(5)   In this section and section 408, 'driving licence' means a licence to drive a motor vehicle granted under Part III of the Road Traffic Act 1988.

(6)   In this section 'the court' means—

(a)   in England and Wales, a magistrates' court;

(b)   in Scotland, the sheriff.]

Note. This section inserted by the Child Support, Pensions and Social Security Act 2000, s 16(1), as from 2 April 2001 (SI 2000 No 3354).

40. Commitment to prison—*(1) Where the Secretary of State has sought—*

(a)   to levy an amount by distress under this Act; or

(b)   to recover an amount by virtue of section 36,

and that amount, or any portion of it, remains unpaid he may apply to a magistrates' court for the issue of a warrant committing the liable person to prison.

(2)   On any such application the court shall (in the presence of the liable person) inquire as to—

(a)   the liable person's means; and

(b)   whether there has been wilful refusal or culpable neglect on his part.

Note. Sub-ss (1), (2) repealed by the Child Support, Pensions and Social Security Act 2000, s 16(2), 85, Sch 9, Pt 1, as from 2 April 2001 (SI 2001 No 1252).

(3) If, but only if, the court is of the opinion that there has been wilful refusal or culpable neglect on the part of the liable person it may—

(a) issue a warrant of commitment against him; or

(b) fix a term of imprisonment and postpone the issue of the warrant until such time and on such conditions (if any) as it thinks just.

(4) Any such warrant—

(a) shall be made in respect of an amount equal to the aggregate of—

    (i) the amount mentioned in section 35(1) or so much of it as remains outstanding; and

    (ii) an amount (determined in accordance with regulations made by the Secretary of State) in respect of the costs of commitment; and

(b) shall state that amount.

(5) No warrant may be issued under this section against a person who is under the age of 18.

(6) A warrant issued under this section shall order the liable person—

(a) to be imprisoned for a specified period; but

(b) to be released (unless he is in custody for some other reason) on payment of the amount stated in the warrant.

(7) The maximum period of imprisonment which may be imposed by virtue of subsection (6) shall be calculated in accordance with Schedule 4 to the Magistrates' Courts Act 1980 (maximum periods of imprisonment in default of payment) but shall not exceed six weeks.

(8) The Secretary of State may by regulations make provision for the period of imprisonment specified in any warrant issued under this section to be reduced where there is part payment of the amount in respect of which the warrant was issued.

(9) A warrant issued under this section may be directed to such person or persons as the court issuing it thinks fit.

(10) Section 80 of the Magistrates' Courts Act 1980 (application of money found on defaulter) shall apply in relation to a warrant issued under this section against a liable person as it applies in relation to the enforcement of a sum mentioned in subsection (1) of that section.

(11) The Secretary of State may by regulations make provision—

(a) as to the form of any warrant issued under this section;

(b) allowing an application under this section to be renewed where no warrant is issued or term of imprisonment is fixed;

(c) that a statement in writing to the effect that wages of any amount have been paid to the liable person during any period, purporting to be signed by or on behalf of his employer, shall be evidence of the facts stated;

(d) that, for the purposes of enabling an inquiry to be made as to the liable person's conduct and means, a justice of the peace may issue a summons to him to appear before a magistrates' court and (if he does not obey) may issue a warrant for his arrest;

(e) that for the purpose of enabling such an inquiry, a justice of the peace may issue a warrant for the liable person's arrest without issuing a summons;

(f) as to the execution of a warrant for arrest.

(12) Subsections (1) to (11) do not apply to Scotland.

(13), (14) (Apply to Scotland only.)

[(12 This section does not apply to Scotland.]

Note. Sub-s (12) above substituted for sub-ss (12)–(14) in italics by the Child Support, Pensions and Social Security Act 2000, s 17(1), as from 10 November 2000, for certain purposes (SI 2000 No 2994), 2 April 2001, for remaining purposes (SI 2000 No 3354).

[40A.] *(Applies to Scotland only.)*

Note. This section inserted by the Child Support, Pensions and Social Security Act 2000, s 17(2), as from 10 November 2000, for certain purposes (SI 2000 No 2994), 2 April 2001, for remaining purposes (SI 2000 No 3354).

[40B. Disqualification from driving: further provision—(1) If, but only if, the court is of the opinion that there has been wilful refusal or culpable neglect on the part of the liable person, it may—
   (a) order him to be disqualified, for such period specified in the order but not exceeding two years as it thinks fit, from holding or obtaining a driving licence (a 'disqualification order'); or
   (b) make a disqualification order but suspend its operation until such time and on :1 such conditions (if any) as it thinks just.
  (2 The court may not take action under both section 40 and this section.
  (3) A disqualification order must state the amount in respect of which it is made, which is to be the aggregate of—
   (a) the amount mentioned in section 35(1), or so much of it as remains outstanding; and
   (b) an amount (determined in accordance with regulations made by the Secretary of State) in respect of the costs of the application under section 39A.
  (4) A court which makes a disqualification order shall require the person to whom it relates to produce any driving licence held by him, and its counterpart (within the meaning of section 108(1) of the Road Traffic Act 1988).
  (5) On an application by the Secretary of State or the liable person, the court—
   (a) may make an order substituting a shorter period of disqualification, or make an order revoking the disqualification order, if part of the amount referred to in subsection (3) (the 'amount due') is paid to any person authorised to receive it; and
   (b) must make an order revoking the disqualification order if all of the amount due is so paid.
  (6) The Secretary of State may make representations to the court as to the amount which should be paid before it would be appropriate to make an order revoking the disqualification order under subsection (5)(a), and the person liable may reply to those representations.
  (7) The Secretary of State may make a further application under section 39A if the amount due has not been paid in full when the period of disqualification specified in the disqualification order expires.
  (8) Where a court—
   (a) makes a disqualification order;
   (b) makes an order under subsection (5); or
   (c) allows an appeal against a disqualification order, it shall send notice of that fact to the Secretary of State; and the notice shall contain such particulars and be sent in such manner and to such address as the Secretary of State may determine.
  (9) Where a court makes a disqualification order, it shall also send the driving licence and its counterpart, on their being produced to the court, to the Secretary of State at such address as he may determine.
  (10) Section 80 of the Magistrates' Courts Act 1980 (application of money found on defaulter) shall apply in relation to a disqualification order under this section in relation to a liable person as it applies in relation to the enforcement of a sum mentioned in subsection (1) of that section.
  (11) The Secretary of State may by regulations make provision in relation to disqualification orders corresponding to the provision he may make under section 40(11).
  (12) In the application to Scotland of this section—
   (a) in subsection (2) for 'section 40' substitute 'section 40A';
   (b) in subsection (3) for paragraph (a) substitute—
'(a) the appropriate amount under section 38;';
   (c) subsection (10) is omitted; and
   (d) for subsection (11) substitute—

'(11) The power of the Court of Session by Act of Sederunt to regulate the procedure and t practice in civil proceedings in the sheriff court shall include power to make, in relation to disqualification orders, provision corresponding to that which may be made by virtue of f section 40A(8).'.]

Note. This section inserted by the Child Support, Pensions and Social Security Act 2000, s 16(3), as from 10 November 2000, for certain purposes (SI 2000 No 2994), 2 April 2001, for remaining purposes (SI 2000 No 3354).

41. Arrears of child support maintenance—(1) This section applies where—

  (a) the Secretary of State is authorised under section 4, 6 or 7 to recover child support maintenance payable by *an absent parent* [a non-resident parent] in accordance with a *maintenance assessment* [maintenance calculation]; and

  (b) the *absent parent* [non-resident parent] has failed to make one or more payments of child support maintenance due from him in accordance with that *assessment* [calculation].

  (2) Where the Secretary of State recovers any such arrears he may, in such circumstances as may be prescribed and to such extent as may be prescribed, retain them if he is satisfied that the amount of any benefit paid to the person with care of the child or children in question would have been less had the absent parent not been in arrears with his payments of child support maintenance.

Note. Words in square brackets substituted for words in italics by the Child Support, Pensions and Social Security Act 2000, ss 1(2), 26, Sch 3, para 11(1), (2) as from (in relation to certain cases): 3 March 2003 (SI 2003 No 192); for remaining purposes: to be appointed.

[(2) Where the Secretary of State recovers any such arrears he may, in such circumstances as may be prescribed and to such extent as may be prescribed, retain them if he is satisfied that the amount of any benefit paid to or in respect of the person with care of the child or children in question would have been less had the *absent parent* [non-resident parent] made the payment or payments of child support maintenance in question.

(2A) In determining for the purposes of subsection (2) whether the amount of any benefit paid would have been less at any time than the amount which was paid at that time, in a case where the *maintenance assessment* [maintenance calculation] had effect from a date earlier than that on which it was made, the *assessment* [calculation[shall be taken to have been in force at that time.]

Note. Sub-ss (2), (2A) in square brackets substituted for sub-s (2) in italics by Child Support Act 1995, s 30(5), Sch 3, para 11, as from 1 October 1995. In new sub-s (2) and sub-s (2A) words in square brackets substituted for words in italics by the Child Support, Pensions and Social Security Act 2000, ss 1(2), 26, Sch 3, para 11(1, (2) as from (in relation to certain cases): 3 March 2003 (SI 2003 No 192); for remaining purposes: to be appointed.

  (3) In such circumstances as may be prescribed, the absent parent shall be liable to make such payments of interest with respect to the arrears of child support maintenance as may be prescribed.

  (4) The Secretary of State may by regulations make provision—

  (a) as to the rate of interest payable by virtue of subsection (3);

  (b) as to the time at which, and person to whom, any such interest shall be payable;

  (c) as to the circumstances in which, in a case where the Secretary of State has been acting under section 6, any such interest may be retained by him;

  (d) for the Secretary of State, in a case where he has been acting under section 6 and in such circumstances as may be prescribed to waive any such interest (or part of any such interest).

  (5) The provisions of this Act with respect to—

  (a) the collection of child support maintenance;

  (b) the enforcement of any obligation to pay child support maintenance,

shall apply equally to interest payable by virtue of this section.

Note. Sub-ss (3)–(5) repealed by the Child Support, Pensions and Social Security Act 2000, ss 18(1), 85, Sch 9, Pt 1, as from (in relation to certain cases): 3 March 2003 (SI 2003 No 192); for remaining purposes: to be appointed.

(6) Any sums retained by the Secretary of State by virtue of this section shall be paid by him into the Consolidated Fund.

[**41A. Arrears: alternative to interest payments**—*(1) The Secretary of State may by regulations make provision for the payment by absent parents [non-resident parents] who are in arrears with payments of child support maintenance of sums determined in accordance with the regulations.*

(2) A sum payable under any such regulations is referred to in this section as an 'additional sum'.

(3) Any liability of an absent parent [non-resident parent] to pay an additional sum shall not affect any liability of his to pay the arrears of child support maintenance concerned.

(4) The Secretary of State shall exercise his powers under this section and those under section 41(3) in such a way as to ensure that no absent parent is liable to pay both interest and an additional sum in respect of the same period (except by reference to different maintenance assessments [maintenance calculations]).

(5) Regulations under subsection (1) may, in particular, make provision—

(a) as to the calculation of any additional sum;

(b) as to the time at which, and person to whom, any additional sum shall be payable;

(c) as to the circumstances in which, in a case where the Secretary of State has been acting under section 6, any additional sum may be retained by him;

(d) for the Secretary of State, in a case where he has been acting under section 6 and in such circumstances as may be prescribed, to waive any additional sum (or part of any additional sum).

(6) The provisions of this Act with respect to—

(a) the collection of child support maintenance;

(b) the enforcement of any obligation to pay child support maintenance,

shall apply equally to additional sums payable by virtue of regulations made under this section.

(7) Any sum retained by the Secretary of State by virtue of this section shall be paid by him into the Consolidated Fund.]

Note. This section inserted by Child Support Act 1995, s 22, as from a day to be appointed. In sub-ss (1), (3), (4) words 'non-resident parents', 'a non-resident parent' and 'maintenance calculations' in square brackets substituted for words 'absent parents', 'an absent parent' and 'maintenance assessments' respectively by the Child Support, Pensions and Social Security Act 2000, ss 1(2)(a), 26, Sch 3, para 11(1), (2), as from (in relation to certain cases): 3 March 2003 (SI 2003 No 192); for remaining purposes: to be appointed.

[**41A. Penalty payments**—(1) The Secretary of State may by regulations make provision for the payment to him by non-resident parents who are in arrears with payments of child support maintenance of penalty payments determined in accordance with the regulations.

(2) The amount of a penalty payment in respect of any week may not exceed 25% of the amount of child support maintenance payable for that week, but otherwise is to be determined by the Secretary of State.

(3) The liability of a non-resident parent to make a penalty payment does not affect his liability to pay the arrears of child support maintenance concerned.

(4) Regulations under subsection (1) may, in particular, make provision—

(a) to the time at which a penalty payment is to be payable;

(b) for the Secretary of State to waive a penalty payment, or part of it.

(5) The provisions of this Act with respect to—

(a) the collection of child support maintenance;,

(b) the enforcement of an obligation to pay child support maintenance,

apply equally (with any necessary modifications) to penalty payments payable by virtue of regulations under this section.

(6) The Secretary of State shall pay penalty payments received by him into the Consolidated Fund.

Note. Section 41A above substituted for s 41A in italics by the Child Support, Pensions and Social Security Act 2000, s 18(2), as from (for certain purposes): 10 November 2000 (SI 2000 No 2994); (in relation to certain cases): 3 March 2003 (SI 2003 No 192); for remaining purposes: to be appointed.

[41B. Repayment of overpaid child support maintenance—(1) This section applies where it appears to the Secretary of State that an absent parent has made a payment by way of child support maintenance which amounts to an overpayment by him of that maintenance and that—

(a) it would not be possible for the *absent parent* [non-resident parent] to recover the amount of the overpayment by way of an adjustment of the amount payable under a *maintenance assessment* [maintenance calculation]; or

(b) it would be inappropriate to rely on an adjustment of the amount payable under a *maintenance assessment* [maintenance calculation] as the means of enabling the *absent parent* [non-resident parent] to recover the amount of the overpayment.

[(1A) This section also applies where the non-resident parent has made a voluntary payment and it appears to the Secretary of State—

(a) that he is not liable to pay child support maintenance; or

(b) that he is liable, but some or all of the payment amounts to an overpayment, and, in a case falling within paragraph (b), it also appears to him that subsection (1)(a) or (b) applies.]

(2) The Secretary of State may make such payment to the absent parent by way of reimbursement, or partial reimbursement, of the overpayment as the Secretary of State considers appropriate.

(3) Where the Secretary of State has made a payment under this section he may, in such circumstances as may be prescribed, require the relevant person to pay to him the whole, or a specified proportion, of the amount of that payment.

(4) Any such requirement shall be imposed by giving the relevant person a written demand for the amount which the Secretary of State wishes to recover from him.

(5) Any sum which a person is required to pay to the Secretary of State under this section shall be recoverable from him by the Secretary of State as a debt due to the Crown.

(6) The Secretary of State may by regulations make provision in relation to any case in which—

(a) one or more overpayments of child support maintenance are being reimbursed to the Secretary of State by the relevant person; and

(b) child support maintenance has continued to be payable by the absent parent concerned to the person with care concerned, or again becomes so payable.

(7) *For the purposes of this section any payments made by a person under a maintenance assessment [maintenance calculation] which was not validly made shall be treated as overpayments of child support maintenance made by an absent parent [a non-resident parent].*

[(7) For the purposes of this section—

(a) a payment made by a person under a maintenance calculation which was not validly made; and

(b) a voluntary payment made in the circumstances set out in subsection (1A)(a), shall be treated as an overpayment of child support maintenance made by a non-resident parent.]

(8) In this section 'relevant person', in relation to an overpayment, means the person with care to whom the overpayment was made.

(9) Any sum recovered by the Secretary of State under this section shall be paid by him into the Consolidated Fund.]

Note. This section inserted by Child Support Act 1995, s 23, as from 4 September 1995 in relation to sub-ss (1), (2), (7), and as from 1 October 1995 otherwise. In sub-ss (1), (2), (7) words 'non-resident parent' 'a non resident parent' and 'maintenance calculation' in square brackets substituted for words 'absent parent' 'an absent parent' and 'maintenance assessment' in each place they occur by the Child Support, Pensions and Social Security Act 2000, ss 1(2)(a), 26, Sch 3, para 11(1), (2) as from (in relation to certain cases): 3 March 2003 (SI 2003 No 192); for remaining purposes: to be appointed. Sub-s (1A) inserted and sub-s (7) substituted for sub-s (7) in italics by the Child Support, Pensions and Social Security Act 2000, s 20(2)-(4) as from (in relation to certain cases): 3 March 2003 (SI 2003 No 192); for remaining purposes: to be appointed.

Special cases

42. Special cases—(1) The Secretary of State may by regulations provide that in prescribed circumstanccs a case is to be treated as a special case for the purposes of this Act.

(2) Those regulations may, for example, provide for the following to be special cases—

(a) each parent of a child is *an absent parent* [a non-resident parent] in relation to the child;

(b) there is more than one person who is a person with care in relation to the same child;

(c) there is more than one qualifying child in relation to the same *absent parent* [non-resident parent] but the person who is the person with care in relation to one of those children is not the person who is the person with care in relation to all of them;

(d) a person is *an absent parent* [a non-resident parent] in relation to more than one child and the other parent of each of those children is not the same person;

(e) the person with care has care of more than one qualifying child and there is more than one *absent parent* [non-resident parent] in relation to those children;

(f) a qualifying child has his home in two or more separate households.

Note. Words 'a non-resident parent' and 'non-resident parent' in square brackets in each place they occur substituted for words in italics by the Child Support, Pensions and Social Security Act 2000, s 26, Sch 3, para 11(1), (2), as from (in relation to certain cases): 3 March 2003 (SI 2003 No 192); for remaining purposes: to be appointed.

(3) The Secretary of State may by regulations make provision with respect to special cases.

(4) Regulations made under subsection (3) may, in particular—

(a) modify any provision made by or under this Act, in its application to any special case or any special case falling within a prescribed category;

(b) make new provision for any such case; or

(c) provide for any prescribed provision made by or under this Act not to apply to any such case.

43. Contribution to maintenance by deduction from benefit—*(1) This section applies where—*

(a) by virtue of paragraph 5(4) of Schedule 1, an absent parent [a non-resident parent] is taken for the purposes of that Schedule to have no assessable income; and

(b) such conditions as may be prescribed for the purposes of this section are satisfied.

(2) The power of the Secretary of State to make regulations under section 51 of the Social Security Act 1986 by virtue of subsection (1)(r) [section 5 of the Social Security Administration Act 1992 by virtue of subsection (1)(t)], (deductions from benefits) may be exercised in relation to cases to which this section applies with a view to securing that—

(a) payments of prescribed amounts are made with respect to qualifying children in place of payments of child support maintenance; and

(b)   arrears of child support maintenance are recovered.

[(3)   Schedule 4C shall have effect for applying sections 16, 17, 20 and 28ZA to 28ZC to any decision with respect to a person's liability under this section, that is to say, his liability to make payments under regulations made by virtue of this section.]

Note. In sub-s (1)(a) words 'a non-resident' parent in square brackets substituted for words 'an absent parent' by the Child Support, Pensions and Social Security Act 2000, s 26, Sch 3, para 11(1), (2), as from (in relation to certain cases): 3 March 2003 (SI 2003 No 192); for remaining purposes: to be appointed. In sub-s (2) words in square brackets substituted for words 'section 51 of … (1)(r)' by Social Security (Consequential Provisions) Act 1992, s 4, Sch 2, para 113, as from 1 July 1992. Sub-s (3) inserted by the Social Security Act 1998, s 86(1). Sch 7 para 40 as from 1 June 1999 (SI 1999 No 1510).

[43. Recovery of child support maintenance by deduction from benefit—(1) This section applies where—

(a)   a non-resident parent is liable to pay a flat rate of child support maintenance would be so liable but for a variation having been agreed to), and that rate applies (or would have applied) because he falls within paragraph 4(1)(b) or (c) or 4(2) of Schedule 1; and

(b)   such conditions as may be prescribed for the purposes of this section are satisfied.

(2)   The power of the Secretary of State to make regulations under section 5 of the Social Security Administration Act 1992 by virtue of subsection (1)(p) (deductions from benefits) may be exercised in relation to cases to which this section applies with a view to securing that payments in respect of child support maintenance are made or that arrears of child support maintenance are recovered.

(3)   For the purposes of this section. the benefits to which section 5 of the 1992 Act applies are to be taken as including war disablement pensions and war widows' pensions (within the meaning of section 150 of the Social Security Contributions and Benefits Act 1992 (interpretation)).]

Note. Section 43 above substituted for s 43 in italics by the Child Support, Pensions and Social Security Act 2000, s 21, as from (for certain purposes): 10 November 2000 (SI 200 No 2994); (in relation to certain cases): 3 March 2003 (SI 2003 No 192); for remaining purposes: to be appointed.

Jurisdiction

44. Jurisdiction—(1) *A child support officer* [The Secretary of State} shall have jurisdiction to make a *maintenance assessment* [maintenance calculation] with respect to a person who is—

(a)   a person with care;

(b)   *an absent parent* [a non-resident parent]; or

(c)   a qualifying child,

only if that person is habitually resident in the United Kingdom [, except in the case of a non-resident parent who falls within subsection (2A)].

Note. Words 'The Secretary of State' substituted for words in italics by the Social Security Act '1998, s 86(1), Sch 7, para 41, as from 1 June 1999 (SI 1999 No 1510). Words 'maintenance calculation' and 'a non-resident parent' in square brackets substituted for words in italics by the Child Support, Pensions and Social Security Act 2000, ss 1 (2)(a), 26, Sch 3, para 11(1), (2), as from (in relation to certain cases): 3 March 2003 (SI 2003 No 192); for remaining purposes: to be appointed. Words ', except in … subsection (2A)' in square brackets inserted by the Child Support, Pensions and Social Security Act 2000, s 22(1}, (2), as from 31 January 2001 (SI 2000 No 3554).

(2)   Where the person with care is not an individual, subsection (1) shall have effect as if paragraph (a) were omitted.

[(2A) A non-resident parent falls within this subsection if he is not habitually resident in the United Kingdom, but is—

(a) employed in the civil service of the Crown, including Her Majesty's Diplomatic Service and Her Majesty's Overseas Civil Service;

(b) a member of the naval, military or air forces of the Crown, including any person employed by an association established for the purposes of Part XI of the Reserve Forces Act 1996;

(c) employed by a company of a prescribed description registered under the Companies Act 1985 in England and Wales or in Scotland, or under the Companies (Northern Ireland) Order 1986; or

(d) employed by a body of a prescribed description.]

Note. Sub-s (2A) inserted by the Child Support, Pensions and Social Security Act 2000, s 22(1), (3), as from (for certain purposes): 10 November 2000 (SI 2000 No 2994); (for remaining purposes): 31 January 2001 (SI 2001 No 3354).

(3) The Secretary of State may by regulations make provision for the cancellation of any maintenance assessment [maintenance calculation] where—

(a) the person with care, absent parent [non-resident parent] or qualifying child with respect to whom it was made ceases to be habitually resident in the United Kingdom;

(b) in a case falling within subsection (2), the absent parent [non-resident parent] or qualifying child with respect to whom it was made ceases to be habitually resident in the United Kingdom; or

(c) in such circumstances as may be prescribed, a maintenance order of a prescribed kind is made with respect to any qualifying child with respect to whom the maintenance assessment [maintenance calculation] was made.

Note. Words 'maintenance calculation' and 'non-resident .parent' in square brackets substituted for words 'maintenance assessment' and 'absent parent' by the Child Support, Pensions and Social Security Act 2000, ss 1 (2)(a), 26, Sch 3, para 11(1), (2). Sub-s (3) repealed by the Child Support, Pensions and Social Security Act 2000, ss 22(1), (4), 85, Sch 9, Pt 1, as from (in relation to certain cases): March 2003 (SI 2003 No 192); for remaining purposes: to be appointed.

45. Jurisdiction of courts in certain proceedings under this Act—(1) The Lord Chancellor or, in relation to Scotland, the *Lord Advocate* [Secretary of State] may by order made such provision as he considers necessary to secure that appeals, or such class of appeals as may be specified in the order—

(a) shall be made to a court instead of being made to *a child support appeal tribunal* [an appeal tribunal]; or

(b) shall be so made in such circumstances as may be so specified.

Note. Words 'the Secretary of State' in square brackets substituted for words in italics by virtue of the Transfer of Functions (Lord Advocate and Secretary of State) Order 1998, SI 1998 No 678, art 2(1), Schedule as from 18 May 1999. In para (a) words 'on appeal tribunal' in square brackets substituted for words in italics by the Social Security At 1998, s 86(1), Sch 7, para 42(1), (2), as from 1 June 1999 (SI 1999 No 1510).

(2) In subsection (1), 'court' means—

(a) in relation to England and Wales and subject to any provision made under Schedule 11 to the Children Act 1989 (jurisdiction of courts with respect to certain proceedings relating to children) the High Court, a county court or a magistrates' court; and

(b) *(applies to Scotland only)*.

(3) Schedule 11 to the Act of 1989 shall be amended in accordance with subsections (4) and (5).

(4) The following sub-paragraph shall be inserted in paragraph 1, after sub-paragraph (2)—

'(2A) Sub-paragraphs (1) and (2) shall also apply in relation to proceedings—

(a) under section 27 of the Child Support Act 1991 (reference to court for declaration of parentage); or

(b) which are to be dealt with in accordance with an order made under section 45 of that Act (jurisdiction of courts in certain proceedings under that Act)'.

(5) In paragraphs 1(3) and 2(3), the following shall be inserted after 'Act 1976'—
'(bb) section 20 (appeals) or 27 (reference to court for declaration of parentage) of the Child Support Act 1991;'.

(6) Where the effect of any order under subsection (1) is that there are no longer any appeals which fall to be dealt with by *child support appeal tribunals* [appeal tribunals], the Lord Chancellor after consultation with the Lord Advocate [Secretart if Sate] may by order provide for the abolition of those tribunals.

Note. In sub-s (6) words 'appeal tribunals' in square brackets substituted for words in italics by the Social Security Act 1998, s 86(1), Sch 7, para 42(1), (2), as from 1 June 1999 (SI 1999 No 1510). Words 'Secretary of State' in square brackets substituted for words in italics by virtue of the Transfer of Functions (Lord Advocate and Secretary of State) Order 1999, SI 1999 No 678, art 2(1), Schedule, as from 19 May 1999.

(7) Any order under subsection (1) or (6) may make—
(a) such modifications of any provision of this Act or of any other enactment; and
(b) such transitional provision,
as the Minister making the order considers appropriate in consequence of any provision made by the order.

Miscellaneous and supplemental

46. Failure to comply with obligations imposed by section 6—*(1) This section applies where any person ('the parent')—*
(a) fails to comply with a requirement imposed on her by the Secretary of State under section 6(1); or
(b) fails to comply with any regulation made under section 6(9).
(2) A child support officer [The Secretary of State] may serve written notice on the parent requiring her, before the end of the specified period, either to comply or to give him her reasons for failing to do so.

Note. In sub-s (2) words 'The Secretary of State' in square brackets substituted for words 'A child support officer' by the Social Security Act 1998, s 86(1), Sch 7, para 43(1), (2), as from 1 June 1999 (SI 1999 No 1510).

(3) When the specified period has expired, the child support officer [the Secretary of Sate] shall consider whether, having regard to any reasons given by the parent, there are reasonable grounds for believing that, if she were to be required to comply, there would be a risk of her or of any children living with her suffering harm or undue distress as a result of complying.
(4) If the child support officer [the Secretary of Sate] considers that there are such reasonable grounds, he shall—
(a) take no further action under this section in relation to the failure in question; and
(b) notify the parent, in writing, accordingly.

Note. In sub-ss (3), (4) words 'the Secretary of State' in square brackets substituted for words 'a child support officer' by the Social Security Act 1998, s 86(1), Sch 7, para 43(1), (2), as from 1 June 1999 (SI 1999 No 1510).

(5) If the child support officer [the Secretary of Sate] considers that there are no such reasonable grounds, he may[, except in prescribed circumstances,] give a reduced benefit direction with respect to the parent.

Note. Words 'the Secretary of State' in square brackets substituted for words 'a child support officer' by the Social Security Act 1998, s 86(1), Sch 7, para 43(1), (2), as from 1 June 1999 (SI 1999 No 1510). Words [, except in prescribed circumstances] in square brackets inserted by Child Support Act 1995, s 30(5), Sch 3, para 12, as from 1 October 1995.

(6) Where the child support officer [the Secretary of State] gives a reduced benefit direction he shall send a copy of it to the parent.

Note. Words 'the Secretary of State' in square brackets substituted for words 'a child support officer' by the Social Security Act 1998, s 86(1), Sch 7, para 43(1), (2), as from 1 June 1999 (SI 1999 No 1510).

(7) Any person who is aggrieved by a decision of a child support officer to give a reduced benefit direction may appeal to a child support appeal tribunal against that decision.

(8) Sections 20(2) to (4) and 21 shall apply in relation to appeals under subsection (7) as they apply in relation to appeals under section 20.

[(7) Schedule 4C shall have effect for applying sections 16, 17, 20 and 28ZA to 28ZA to decisions with respect to reduced benefit directions.]

Note. Sub-s (7) substituted for sub-ss (7), (8) as originally enacted by the Social Security Act 1998, s 86(1), Sch 7, para 43(3), as from 1 June 1999 (SI 1999 No 1510).

(9) A reduced benefit direction shall take effect on such date as may be specified in the direction.

(10) Reasons given in response to a notice under subsection (2) may be given either in writing or orally.

(11) In this section—

'comply' means to comply with the requirement or with the regulation in question; and 'complied' and 'complying' shall be construed accordingly;

'reduced benefit direction' means a direction, binding on the adjudication officer, that the amount payable by way of any relevant benefit to, or in respect of, the parent concerned be reduced by such amount, and for such period, as may be prescribed;

'relevant benefit' means income support, [an income-based jobseeker's allowance,] family credit or any other benefit of a kind prescribed for the purposes of section 6; and

'specified', in relation to any notice served under this section, means specified in the notice; and the period to be specified shall be determined in accordance with regulations made by the Secretary of State.

Note. In definition 'reduced benefit direction' words 'binding on the adjudication officer' repealed by the Social Security Act 1998, s 86(1), (2), Sch 7, para 43(4), Sch 8, as from 1 June 1999 (SI 1999 No 1510). Words in square brackets in definition 'relevant benefit' inserted by Jobseekers Act 1995, s 41(4), Sch 2, para 20, as from 7 October 1996. In definition 'relevant benefit' words 'family credit' repealed by the Tax Credits Act 1999, s 19(4), Sch 6, as from 5 October 1999.

[46. Reduced benefit decision—(1) This section applies where any person ('the parent')—

  (a) has made a request under section 6(5);
  (b) fails to comply with any regulation made under section 6(7); or
  (c) having been treated as having applied for a maintenance calculation under section 6, refuses to take a scientific test (within the meaning of section 27A).

(2) The Secretary of State may serve written notice on the parent requiring her, before the end of a specified period—

  (a) in a subsection (1)(a) case, to give him her reasons for making the request;
  (b) in a subsection (1)(b) case, to give him her reasons for failing to do so; or
  (c) in a subsection (1)(c) case, to give him her reasons for her refusal.

(3) When the specified period has expired, the Secretary of State shall consider whether, having regard to any reasons given by the parent, there are reasonable grounds for believing that—

  (a) in a subsection (1)(a) case, if the Secretary of State were to do what is mentioned in section 6(3);
  (b) in a subsection (1)(b) case, if she were to be required to comply; or
  (c) in a subsection (1)(c) case, if she took the scientific test,

there would be a risk of her, or of any children living with her, suffering harm or undue distress as a result of his taking such action, or her complying or taking the test.

(4) If the Secretary of State considers that there are such reasonable grounds, he shall—

  (a) take no further action under this section in relation to the request, the failure or the refusal in question; and

(b) notify the parent, in writing, accordingly.

(5) If the Secretary of State considers that there are no such reasonable grounds, he may, except in prescribed circumstances, make a reduced benefit decision with respect to the parent.

(6) In a subsection (1)(a) case, the Secretary of State may from time to time serve written notice on the parent requiring her, before the end of a specified period—

(a) to state whether her request under section 6(5) still stands; and

(b) if so, to give him her reasons for maintaining her request,

and subsections (3) to (5) have effect in relation to such a notice and any response to it as they have effect in relation to a notice under subsection (2)(a) and any response to it.

(7) Where the Secretary of State makes a reduced benefit decision he must send a copy of it to the parent

(8) A reduced benefit decision is to take effect on such date as may be specified in the decision.

(9) Reasons given in response to a notice under subsection (2) or (6) need not be given in writing unless the Secretary of State directs in any case that they must.

(10) In this section—

(a) 'comply' means to comply with the requirement or with the regulation in question; and 'complied' and 'complying' are to be construed accordingly;

(b) 'reduced benefit decision' means a decision that the amount payable by way of any relevant benefit to, or in respect of, the parent concerned be reduced by such amount, and for such period, as may be prescribed;

(c) 'relevant benefit' means income support or an income-based jobseeker's allowance or any other benefit of a kind prescribed for the purposes of section 6; and

(d) 'specified', in relation to a notice served under this section, means specified in the notice; and the period to be specified is to be determined in accordance with regulations made by the Secretary of State.]

Note. Section 46 above substituted for s 46 in italics by the Child Support, Pensions and Social Security Act 2000, s 19, as from (for certain purposes): 10 November 2000 (SI 2000 No 2994); for remaining purposes: to be appointed.

[46A. Finality of decisions—(1) Subject to the provisions of this Act, any decision of the Secretary of State or an appeal tribunal made in accordance with the foregoing provisions of this Act shall be final.

(2) If and to the extent that regulations so provide, any finding of fact or other determination embodied in or necessary to such a decision, or on which such a decision is based, shall be conclusive for the purposes of—

(a) further such decisions;

(b) decisions made in accordance with sections 8 to 16 of the Social Security Act 1998, or with regulations under section 11 of that Act; and

(c) decisions made under the Vaccine Damage Payments Act 1979.

46B. Matters arising as respects decisions—(1) Regulations may make provision as respects matters arising pending—

(a) any decision of the Secretary of State under section 11, 12 or 17;

(b) any decision of an appeal tribunal under section 20; or

(c) any decision of a Child Support Commissioner under section 24.

(2) Regulations may also make provision as respects matters arising out of the revision under section 16, or on appeal, of any such decision as is mentioned in subsection (1).

(3) *Any reference in this section to section 16, 17 or 20 includes a reference to that section as extended by Schedule 4C.]*

Note. Sections 46A, 46B above inserted by the Social Security Act 1998, s 86(1), Sch 7, para 44, as from 1 June 1999 (SI 1999 No 1510). In s 46B sub-s (3) repealed by the Child Support, Pensions and Social Security Act 2000, s 85, Sch 9, Pt 1, as from (in relation to certain cases): 3 March 2003 (SI 2003 No 192); for remaining purposes: to be appointed.

47. Fees—(1) The Secretary of State may by regulations provide for the payment, by the *absent parent* [non-resident parent] or the person with care (or by both), of such fees as may be prescribed in cases where the Secretary of State takes[, or proposes to take] any action under section 4 or 6.

(2) The Secretary of State may by regulations provide for the payment, by the *absent parent* [non-resident parent], the person with care or the child concerned (or by any or all of them), of such fees as may be prescribed in cases where the Secretary of State takes[, or proposes to take] any action under section 7.

Note. Words 'or proposes to take' in square brackets in sub-ss (1), (2) inserted by Child Support Act 1995, s 30(5), Sch 3, para 13, as from a day to be appointed. Words 'non-resident parent' in square brackets in sub-ss (1), (2) substituted for words 'absent parent' by the Child Support, Pensions and Social Security Act 2000, s 26, Sch 3, para 11 (1), (2), as from (in relation to certain cases): 3 March 2003 (SI 2003 No 192); for remaining purposes: to be appointed.

(3) Regulations made under this section—

(a) may require any information which is needed for the purpose of determining the amount of any such fee to be furnished, in accordance with the regulations, by such person as may be prescribed;

(b) shall provide that no such fees shall be payable by any person to or in respect of whom income support, [an income-based jobseeker's allowance,] family credit [*working families' tax credit*] [any element of child tax credit other than the family element, working tax credit] or any other benefit of a prescribed kind is paid; and

(c) may, in principle, make provision with respect to the recovery by the Secretary of State of any fees payable under the regulations.

Note. Words 'on income-based jobseeker's allowance' in square brackets in sub-s (3)(b) inserted by Jobseekers Act 1995, s 41(4), Sch 2, para 20(5), as from 7 October 1996. Words 'working families' tax credit' in square brackets substituted for words 'family credit' by the Tax Credits Act 1999, s 1(2), Sch 1, paras 1, 6(f)(i), as from 5 October 1999. Words 'any element...working tax credit' in square brackets substituted for words 'working families' tax credit' by the Tax Credits Act 2002, s 47, Sch 3, para 22, as from 6 April 2003 (SI 2003 No 962); for savings and transitional provisions see arts 3–5 thereof.

[(4) The provisions of this Act with respect to—

(a) the collection of child support maintenance;

(b) the enforcement of any obligation to pay child support maintenance,

shall apply equally (with any necessary modifications) to fees payable by virtue of regulations made under this section.]

Note. Sub-s (4) inserted by the Child Support, Pensions and Social Security Act 2000, s 26, Sch 3, para 11 (1), (18), as from (in relation to certain cases): 3 March 2003 (SI 2003 No 192); for remaining purposes: to be appointed.

48. Right of audience—(1) Any *person authorised* [officer of the Secretary of State who is authorised] by the Secretary of State for the purposes of this section shall have, in relation to any proceedings under this Act before a magistrates' court, a right of audience and the right to conduct litigation.

Note. Words in square brackets substituted for words in italics by Child Support Act 1995, s 30(5), Sch 3, para 14, as from 4 September 1995.

(2) In this section 'right of audience' and 'right to conduct litigation' have the same meaning as in section 119 of the Courts and Legal Services Act 1990.

49. (*Applies to Scotland only.*)

50. Unauthorised disclosure of information—(1) Any person who is, or has been, employed in employment to which this section applies is guilty of an offence if, without lawful authority, he discloses any information which—

(a) was acquired by him in the course of that employment; and

(b) relates to a particular person.

(2) It is not an offence under this section—

(a) to disclose information in the form of a summary or collection of information so framed as not to enable information relating to any particular person to be ascertained from it; or

(b) to disclose information which has previously been disclosed to the public with lawful authority.

(3) It is a defence for a person charged with an offence under this section to prove that at the time of the alleged offence—

(a) he believed that he was making the disclosure in question with lawful authority and had no reasonable cause to believe otherwise; or

(b) he believed that the information in question had previously been disclosed to the public with lawful authority and had no reasonable cause to believe otherwise.

(4) A person guilty of an offence under this section shall be liable—

(a) on conviction on indictment, to imprisonment for a term not exceeding two years or a fine or both; or

(b) on summary conviction, to imprisonment for a term not exceeding six months or a fine not exceeding the statutory maximum or both.

(5) This section applies to employment as—

(a) the Chief Child Support Officer;

(b) any other child support officer;

(c) any clerk to, or other officer of, [on appeal tribunal or] a child support appeal tribunal;

(d) any member of the staff of such a tribunal;

(e) a civil servant in connection with the carrying out of any functions under this Act,

and to employment of any other kind which is prescribed for the purposes of this section.

Note. In sub-s (5)(c) words 'an appeal tribunal or' in square brackets inserted by the Social Security Act 1998, s 86(1), Sch 7, para 45, as from 1 June 1999 (SI 1999 No 1510).

(6) For the purposes of this section a disclosure is to be regarded as made with lawful authority if, and only if, it is made—

(a) by a civil servant in accordance with his official duty; or

(b) by any other person either—

(i) for the purposes of the function in the exercise of which he holds the information and without contravening any restriction duly imposed by the responsible person; or

(ii) to, or in accordance with an authorisation duly given by, the responsible person;

(c) in accordance with any enactment or order of a court;

(d) for the purpose of instituting, or otherwise for the purposes of, any proceedings before a court or before any tribunal or other body or person mentioned in this Act; or

(e) with the consent of the appropriate person.

(7) 'The responsible person' means—

(a) the Lord Chancellor;

(b) the Secretary of State;

(c) any person authorised by the Lord Chancellor, or Secretary of State, for the purposes of this subsection; or

(d) any other prescribed person, or person falling within a prescribed category.

(8) 'The appropriate person' means the person to whom the information in question relates, except that if the affairs of that person are being dealt with—

(a) under a power of attorney;

(b) by a receiver appointed under section 99 of the Mental Health Act 1983;

(c) (*applies to Scotland only*); or

(d) by a mental health appointee, that is to say—

    (i) a person directed or authorised as mentioned in sub-paragraph (a) of rule 41(1) of the Court of Protection Rules 1984; or

    (ii) a receiver ad interim appointed under sub-paragraph (b) of that rule;

the appropriate person is the attorney, receiver, custodian or appointee (as the case may be) or, in a case falling within paragraph (a), the person to whom the information relates.

51. Supplementary powers to make regulations—(1) The Secretary of State may by regulations make such incidental, supplemental and transitional provision as he considers appropriate in connection with any provision made by or under this Act.

(2) The regulations may, in particular, make provision—

(a) as to the procedure to be followed with respect to—

    (i) the making of applications for *maintenance assessments* [maintenance calculations];

    (*ii*) *the making, cancellation or refusal to make maintenance assessments* [maintenance calculations];

    (*iii*) *reviews under sections 16 to 19;*

    [(iii) the making of decisions under section 16 or 17;]

    [(ii) the making of decisions under section 11;

    (iii) the making of decisions under section 16 or 17;]

(b) *extending the categories of case to which section 18 or 19* [Schedule 4C] *applies;*

[(b) extending the categories of case to which section 16, 7 or 20 applies;]

(c) as to the date on which an application for a *maintenance assessment* [maintenance calculations] is to be treated as having been made;

(d) for attributing payments made under *maintenance assessments* [maintenance calculations] to the payment of arrears;

(e) for the adjustment, for the purpose of taking account of the retrospective effect of a *maintenance assessment* [maintenance calculations], of amounts payable under the *assessment* [calculation];

(f) for the adjustment, for the purpose of taking account of over-payments or under-payments of child support maintenance, of amounts payable under a *maintenance assessment* [maintenance calculation];

(g) as to the evidence which is to be required in connection with such matters as may be prescribed;

(h) as to the circumstances in which any official record or certificate is to be conclusive (or in Scotland, sufficient) evidence;

(i) with respect to the giving of notices or other documents;

(j) for the rounding up or down of any amounts calculated, estimated or otherwise arrived at in applying any provision made by or under this Act.

Note. In sub-s (2)(a), (c)–(f) words 'maintenance calculations', 'maintenance calculation' and 'calculation' In square brackets substituted for words 'maintenance assessments', 'maintenance assessment' and 'assessment' respectively by the Child Support, Pensions and Social Security Act 2000, s 1 (2), as from (in relation to certain cases): 3 March 2003 (SI 2003 No 192); for remaining purposes: to be appointed. Second para (a)(iii) substituted, with a saving, for first para (a)(iii) in italics by the Social Security Act 1998, s 86(1), Sch 7, para : 46(a), as from 16 November 1998 (SI 1998 No 2780). New para (a)(ii), (iii) substituted for para (a)(ii), and second para (a)(iii) in italics by the Child Support, Pensions and Social ; Security Act 2000, s 26, Sch 3, para 11(1), (19)(a), as from (in relation to certain cases): 3

March 2003 (SI 2003 No 192); for remaining purposes: to be appointed. In para (b) words 'Schedule 4C' in square brackets substituted for words 'section 18 or 19' by the Social Security Act 1998, s 86(1), Sch 7, para 46(b), as from 1 June 1999 (SI 1999 No 1510). Para (b) in square brackets substituted for para (b) in italics by the Child Support, Pensions and Social Security Act 2000, s 26, Sch 3, para 11(1), (19)(b), as from (in relation to certain cases): 3 March 2003 (SI 2003 No 192); for remaining purposes: to be appointed.

(3) No power to make regulations conferred by any other provision of this Act shall be taken to limit the powers given to the Secretary of State by this section.

52. Regulations and orders—(1) Any power conferred on the Lord Chancellor, the Lord Advocate or the Secretary of State by this Act to make regulations or orders (other than a deduction from earnings order) shall be exercisable by statutory instrment.

(2) No statutory instrument containing (whether alone or with other provisions) regulations made under section 4(7), 5(3), 6(1), (9) or (10), 7(8), 12(2), [28C(2)(b), 28F(3), 30(5A)] 41(2), (3) or (4), [41A, 41B(6)] 42, 43(1), 46 or 47 or under Part I of Schedule 1 [or under Schedule 4B], or an order made under section 45(1) or (6), shall be made unless a draft of the instrument has been laid before Parliament and approved by a resolution of each House of Parliament.

Note. Words in square brackets inserted by Child Support Act 1995, s 30(5), Sch 3, para 15, as from 4 September 1995.

(3) Any other statutory instrument made under this Act (except an order made under section 58(2)) shall be subject to annulment in pursuance of a resolution of either House of Parliament.

(4) Any power of a kind mentioned in subsection (1) may be exercised—
(a) in relation to all cases to which it extends, in relation to those cases but subject to specified exceptions or in relation to any specified cases or classes of case;
(b) so as to make, as respects the cases in relation to which it is exercised—
  (i) the full provision to which it extends or any lesser provision (whether by way of exception or otherwise);
  (ii) the same provision for all cases, different provision for different cases or classes of case or different provision as respects the same case or class of case but for different purposes of this Act;
  (iii) provision which is either unconditional or is subject to any specified condition;
(c) so to provide for a person to exercise a discretion in dealing with any matter.

53. Financial provisions.   Any expenses of the Lord Chancellor or the Secretary of State under this Act shall be payable out of money provided by Parliament.

54. Interpretation.   In this Act—
'*absent parent* [non-resident parent]', has the meaning given in section 3(2);
'*adjudication officer' has the same meaning as in the benefit Acts;*
['application for a *departure direction* [variation]' means an application under section 28A [or 28G];]
['appeal tribunal' means an appeal tribunal constituted under Chapter I of Part I of the Social Security Act 1998;]
'*assessable income' has the meaning given in paragraph 5 of Schedule 1;*
'benefit Acts' means the *Social Security Acts 1975 to 1991* [Social Security Contributions and Benefits Act 1992 and the Social Security Administration Act 1992];
'*Chief Adjudication Officer' has the same meaning as in the benefit Acts;*
'*Chief Child Support Officer' has the meaning given in section 13;*
'child benefit' has the same meaning as in the Child Benefit Act 1975;
'*child support appeal tribunal' means a tribunal appointed under section 21;*
'child support maintenance' has the meaning given in section 3(6);

'child support officer' has the meaning given in section 13;

['current assessment [calculation]', in relation to an application for a departure direction, means (subject to any regulations made under paragraph 10 of Schedule 4A) the maintenance assessment [maintenance calculation] with respect to which the application is made;]

'deduction from earnings order' has the meaning given in section 31(2);

['default maintenance decision' has the meaning given in section 12;]

['departure direction' has the meaning given in section 28A;]

'disability living allowance' has the same meaning as in the *Social Security Act 1975* [benefit Acts];

'family credit [working families' tax credit]' has the same meaning as in the benefit Acts;

'general qualification' shall be construed in accordance with section 71 of the Courts and Legal Services Act 1990 (qualification for judicial appointments);

'income support' has the same meaning as in the benefit Acts;

['income-based jobseeker's allowance' has the same meaning as in the Jobseekers Act 1995;]

'interim maintenance *assessment* [decision]' has the meaning given in section 12;

'liability order' has the meaning given in section 33(2);

'maintenance agreement' has the meaning given in section 9(1);

'maintenance assessment [maintenance calculation]' means an assessment [calculation] of maintenance made under this Act and, except in prescribed circumstances, includes an interim maintenance assessment [maintenance calculation];

['maintenance calculation' means a calculation of maintenance made under this Act and, except in prescribed circumstances, includes a default maintenance decision and an interim maintenance decision;]

'maintenance order' has the meaning given in section 8(11);

'maintenance requirement' means the amount calculated in accordance with paragraph 1 of Schedule 1;

'parent', in relation to any child, means any person who is in law the mother or father of the child;

['parent with care' means a person who is, in relation to a child, both a parent and a person with care;]

'parental responsibility' has the same meaning as in the Children Act 1989;

['parental responsibility', in the application of this Act—

   (a) to England and Wales, has the same meaning as in the Children Act 1989; and

   (b) to Scotland, shall be construed as a reference to 'parental responsibilities' within the meaning given by section 1(3) of the Children (Scotland) Act 1995;]

'parental rights' has the same meaning as in the Law Reform (Parent and Child) (Scotland) Act 1986;

'person with care' has the meaning given in section 3(3);

'prescribed' means prescribed by regulations made by the Secretary of State;

'qualifying child' has the meaning given in section 3(1);

['voluntary payment' has the meaning given in section 28J].

Note. In definition 'absent parent' words 'non-resident parent' in square brackets substituted for words 'absent parent' by the Child Support, Pensions and Social Security Act 2000, s 26, Sch 3, para 11(1), (2), as from (in relation to certain cases): 3 March 2003 (SI 2003 No 192); for remaining purposes: to be appointed. Definition 'appeal tribunal' inserted and definitions 'adjudication officer', 'Chief Adjudication Officer', 'Chief Child Support Officer', 'child support appeal tribunal' and 'child support officer' repealed by the Social Security Act 1998, s 86, Sch 7, para 47, Sch 8, as from 1 June 1999 (SI 1999 No 1510). Definitions 'application for a departure direction', 'current assessment', 'departure direction' and 'parent with care' inserted by the Child Support Act 1995, s 30(5), Sch 3, para 16, as from 4 September 1995. In definition 'application for a departure direction' word 'variation' in square brackets substituted for words 'departure direction' and words 'or 28G' in square brackets inserted by the Child Support,

Pensions and Social Security Act 2000, s 26, Sch 3, para 11(1), (20)(a), as from (in relation to certain cases): 3 March 2003 (SI 2003 No 192); for remaining purposes: to be appointed. Definitions 'assessable income', 'current assessment', 'departure direction' and 'maintenance requirement' repealed by the Child Support, Pensions and Social Security Act 2000, ss 26, 85, Sch 3, para 11(1), (20)(e), Sch 9, Pt 1, as from (in relation to certain cases): 3 March 2003 (SI 2003 No 192); for remaining purposes: to be appointed. In definitions 'benefits Acts' and 'disability living allowance' words in square brackets substituted for words in italics by the Social Security (Consequential Provisions) Act 1992, s 4, Sch 2, para 114, as from 1 July 1992. In definitions 'current assessment' and 'maintenance assessment' words 'calculation' and 'maintenance calculation' in square brackets substituted for words 'assessment' and 'maintenance assessment' respectively by the Child Support, Pensions and Social Security Act 2000, s 1 (2), as from (in relation to certain cases): 3 March 2003 (SI 2003 No 192); for remaining purposes: to be appointed. Definition 'default maintenance decision' inserted by the Child Support, Pensions and Social Security Act 2000, s 26, Sch 3, para 11(1), (20)(b), as from (in relation to certain cases): 3 March 2003 (SI 2003 No 192); for remaining purposes: to be appointed. In definition 'family credit' words 'working families' tax credit' in square brackets substituted for words 'family credit' by the Tax Credits Act 1999, s 1 (2), Sch 1, paras 1, 6(f)(ii), as from 5 October 1999. Definition 'working families' tax credit' repealed by the Tax Credits Act 2002, s 60, Sch 6, as from 6 April 2003 (SI 2003 No 692); for savings and transitional provisions see arts 3-5 thereof. Definition 'income-based jobseeker's allowance' inserted by the Jobseekers Act 1995, s 41 (4), Sch 2, para 20(6), as from 7 October 1996. In definition 'interim maintenance' word in square brackets substituted for word in italics by the Child Support, Pensions and Social Security Act 2000, s 26, Sch 3, para 11(1), 20(c), as from a day to be appointed. Definition 'maintenance calculation' substituted for definition 'maintenance assessment' by the Child Support, Pensions and Social Security Act 2000, s 26, Sch 3, para 11(1), (20)(d), as from (in relation to certain cases): 3 March 2003 (SI 2003 No 192); for remaining purposes: to be appointed. Definition 'parental responsibility' in square brackets substituted for definition 'parental responsibility' in italics, and definition 'parental rights' repealed by the Children (Scotland) Act 1995, s 105(4), (5), Sch 4, para 52(4), Sch 5, as from 1 November 1996. Definition 'voluntary payment' inserted by the Child Support, Pensions and Social Security Act 2000, s 26, Sch 3, para 11(1), (20)(f), as from (in relation to certain cases): 3 March 2003 (SI 2003 No 192); for remaining purposes: to be appointed.

55. Meaning of 'child'—(1) For the purposes of this Act a person is a child if—

(a) he is under the age of 16;

(b) he is under the age of 19 and receiving full-time education (which is not advanced education)—

(i) by attendance at a recognised educational establishment; or

(ii) elsewhere, if the education is recognised by the Secretary of State; or

(c) he does not fall within paragraph (a) or (b) but—

(i) he is under the age of 18, and

(ii) prescribed conditions are satisfied with respect to him.

(2) A person is not a child for the purposes of this Act if he—

(a) is or has been married;

(b) has celebrated a marriage which is void; or

(c) has celebrated a marriage in respect of which a decree of nullity has been granted.

(3) In this section—

'advanced education' means education of a prescribed description; and

'recognised educational establishment' means an establishment recognised by the Secretary of State for the purposes of this section as being, or as comparable to, a university, college or school.

(4) Where a person has reached the age of 16, the Secretary of State may recognise education provided for him otherwise than at a recognised educational establishment only if the Secretary of State is satisfied that education was being so provided for him immediately before he reached the age of 16.

(5) The Secretary of State may provide that in prescribed circumstances education is or is not to be treated for the purposes of this section as being full-time.

(6) In determining whether a person falls within subsection (1)(b), no account shall be taken of such interruptions in his education as may be prescribed.

(7) The Secretary of State may by regulations provide that a person who ceases to fall within subsection (1) shall be treated as continuing to fall within that subsection for a prescribed period.

(8) No person shall be treated as continuing to fall within subsection (1) by virtue of regulations made under subsection (7) after the end of the week in which he reaches the age of 19.

56. Corresponding provision for and co-ordination with Northern Ireland—
(1) An Order in Council made under paragraph 1(1)(b) of Schedule 1 to the Northern Ireland Act 1974 which contains a statement that it is made only for purposes corresponding to those of the provisions of this Act, other than provisions which relate to the appointment of Child Support Commissioners for Northern Ireland—

(a) shall not be subject to sub-paragraphs (4) and (5) of paragraph 1 of that Schedule (affirmative resolution of both Houses of Parliament); but

(b) shall be subject to annulment in pursuance of a resolution of either House of Parliament.

(2) *The Secretary of State may make arrangements with the Department of Health and Social Services for Northern Ireland with a view to securing, to the extent allowed for in the arrangements, that—*

(a) *the provision made by or under this Act ('the provision made for Great Britain'); and*

(b) *the provision made by or under any corresponding enactment having effect with respect to Northern Ireland ('the provision made for Northern Ireland'),*

provide for a single system within the United Kingdom.

(3) *The Secretary of State may make regulations for giving effect to any such arrangements.*

(4) *The regulations may, in particular—*

(a) *adapt legislation (including subordinate legislation) for the time being in force in Great Britain so as to secure its reciprocal operation with the provision made for Northern Ireland; and*

(b) *make provision to secure that acts, omissions and events which have any effect for the purposes of the provision made for Northern Ireland have a corresponding effect for the purposes of the provision made for Great Britain.*

Note. Sub-ss (2)–(4) repealed by the Northern Ireland Act 1998, s 100(2), Sch 15, as from 2 December 1999 (SI 1999 No 3209).

57. Application to Crown—(1) The power of the Secretary of State to make regulations under section 14 requiring prescribed persons to furnish information may be exercised so as to require information to be furnished by persons employed in the service of the Crown or otherwise in the discharge of Crown functions.

(2) In such circumstances, and subject to such conditions, as may be prescribed, an inspector appointed under section 15 may enter any Crown premises for the purpose of exercising any powers conferred on him by that section.

(3) Where such an inspector duly enters any Crown premises for those purposes, section 15 shall apply in relation to persons employed in the service of the Crown or otherwise in the discharge of Crown functions as it applies in relation to other persons.

(4) Where a liable person is in the employment of the Crown, a deduction from earnings order may be made under section 31 in relation to that person; but in such a case subsection (8) of section 32 shall apply only in relation to the failure of that person to comply with any requirement imposed on him by regulations made under section 32.

58. Short title, commencement and extent, etc—(1) This Act may be cited as the Child Support Act 1991.

(2) Section 56(1) and subsections (1) to (11) and (14) of this section shall come into force on the passing of this Act but otherwise this Act shall come into

force on such date as may be appointed by order made by the Lord Chancellor, the Secretary of State or Lord Advocate, or by any of them acting jointly.

(3) Different dates may be appointed for different provisions of this Act and for different purposes (including, in particular, for different cases or categories of case).

(4) An order under subsection (2) may make such supplemental, incidental or transitional provisions as appears to the person making the order to be necessary or expedient in connection with the provisions brought into force by the order, including such adaptations or modifications of—

    (a) the provisions so brought into force;

    (b) any provisions of this Act then in force; or

    (c) any provision of any other enactment,

as appear to him to be necessary or expedient.

(5) Different provision may be made by virtue of subsection (4) with respect to different periods.

(6) Any provision made by virtue of subsection (4) may, in particular, include provision for—

    (a) the enforcement of a *maintenance assessment* [maintenance calculation] (including the collection of sums payable under the *assessment* [calculation]) as if the *assessment* [calculation]were a court order of a prescribed kind;

    (b) the registration of *maintenance assessments* [maintenance calculations]with the appropriate court in connection with any provision of a kind mentioned in paragraph (a);

    (c) the variation, on application made to a court, of the provisions of a *maintenance assessment* [maintenance calculation] relating to the method of making payments fixed by the *assessment* [calculation] or the intervals at which such payments are to be made;

    (d) a *maintenance assessment* [maintenance calculation], or an order of a prescribed kind relating to one or more children, to be deemed, in prescribed circumstances, to have been validly made for all purposes or for such purposes as may be prescribed.

In paragraph (c) 'court' includes a single justice.

Note. In sub-s 96) words in square brackets substituted for words in italics by the Child Support, Pensions and Social Security Act 2000, s 1(2), as from (in relation to certain cases): 3 March 2003 (SI 2003 No 192); for remaining purposes: to be appointed.

(7) The Lord Chancellor, the Secretary of State or the Lord Advocate may by order make such amendments or repeals in, or such modifications of, such enactments as may be specified in the order, as appear to him to be necessary or expedient in consequence of any provision made by or under this Act (including any provision made by virtue of subsection (4)).

(8) This Act shall, in its application to the Isles of Scilly, have effect subject to such exceptions, adaptations and modifications as the Secretary of State may by order prescribe.

(9) Sections 27, 35[40] and 48 and paragraph 7 of Schedule 5 do not extend to Scotland.

(10) Sections 7, 28[, 40A] and 49 extend only to Scotland.

Note. In sub-ss (9), (10) words in square brackets substituted for words in italics by the Child Support, Pensions and Social Security Act 2000, s 26, Sch 3, para 11(1), 21(a), (b), as from (in relation to certain cases): 3 March 2003 (SI 2003 No 192); for remaining purposes: to be appointed.

(11) With the exception of sections 23 and 56(1), subsections (1) to (3) of this section and Schedules 2 and 4, and (in so far as it amends any enactment extending to Northern Ireland) Schedule 5, this Act does not extend to Northern Ireland.

(12) Until Schedule 1 to the Disability Living Allowance and Disability Working Allowance Act 1991 comes into force, paragraph 1(1) of Schedule 3 shall have effect with the omission of the words 'and disability appeal tribunals' and the insertion, after 'social security appeal tribunals', of the word 'and'.

(13) The consequential amendments set out in Schedule 5 shall have effect.

(14) In Schedule 1 to the Children Act 1989 (financial provision for children), paragraph 2(6)(b) (which is spent) is hereby repealed.

Commencement. Sections 3(3)(c), 4(4), (7), (8), 5(3), 6(1) (in so far as it confers power to prescribe kinds of benefit for the purposes of that subsection), (9), (10), (13), 7(5), (8), (9), 8(5), (9), (11)(f), 10, 12(2), (3), (5), 14(1), (3), 16(1), (2), (5), (6), 17(4), (6)(b), 18(8), (11), 21(2), (3), 22(3), (4), 24(6), (7), 25(2)(a), (3)(c), (5), (6), 29(2), (3), 30(1), (4), (5), 31(8), 32(1)–(5), (7)–(9), 34(1), 35(2)(b), (7), (8), 39, 40(4)(a)(ii), (8), (11), 41(2)–(4), 42, 43(1)(b), (2)(a), 44(3), 45, 46(11), 47, 49, 50(5), (7)(d), 51, 52, 54, 55, 56(2)–(4), 57, Sch 1, paras 1(3), (5), 2(1), 4(1), (3), 5(1), (2), (4), 6(2)–(6), 7–9, 11, 14, 16(5), 10, 11 (and s 11 so far as it relates to those paragraphs), Sch 2, para 2(4) (and s 14(4) so far as it relates to that sub-paragraph), Sch 3, para 3(3) (and s 21(4) so far as it relates to that sub-paragraph) were brought into force on 17 June 1992 (SI 1992 No 1431). Sections 13, 21(1), (4) (so far as not already in force), 22(1), (2), (5), 23, 24(9), Sch 3 (so far as not already in force), Sch 4, Sch 5, paras 1–4 (and s 58(13) so far as it relates to those paragraphs) were brought into force on 1 September 1992 (SI 1992 No 1938). The remainder of the Act, except ss 19(3) (now substituted), 30(2), 34(2), 37(2), (3), 58(12) was brought into force on 5 April 1993 (SI 1992 No 2644 as amended by SI 1993 No 966).

SCHEDULES

SCHEDULE 1   Section 11

MAINTENANCE *ASSESSMENTS* [CALCULATIONS]

Note. Word in square brackets in Schedule heading substituted for word in italics by the Child Support, Pensions and Social Security Act 2000, s 1(2), as from (in relation to certain cases): 3 March 2003 (SI 2003 No 192); for remaining purposes: to be appointed.

PART *I*

CALCULATION OF CHILD SUPPORT MAINTENANCE

The maintenance requirement

1.—*(1) In this Schedule 'the maintenance requirement' means the amount, calculated in accordance with the formula set out in sub-paragraph (2), which is to be taken as the minimum amount necessary for the maintenance of the qualifying child or, where there is more than one qualifying child, all of them.*

(2) The formula is—

$$MR = AG - CB$$

where—

MR is the amount of the maintenance requirement;

AG is the aggregate of the amounts to be taken into account under sub-paragraph (3); and

CB is the amount payable by way of child benefit (or which would be so payable if the person with care of the qualifying child were an individual) or, where there is more than one qualifying child, the aggregate of the amounts so payable with respect to each of them.

(3) The amounts to be taken into account for the purpose of calculating AG are—

(a) such amount or amounts (if any), with respect to each qualifying child, as may be prescribed;

(b) such amount or amounts (if any), with respect to the person with care of the qualifying child or qualifying children, as may be prescribed; and

(c) such further amount or amounts (if any) as may be prescribed.

(4) For the purposes of calculating CB it shall be assumed that child benefit is payable with respect to any qualifying child at the basic rate.

(5) In sub-paragraph (4) 'basic rate' has the meaning for the time being prescribed.

The general rule

2.—*(1) In order to determine the amount of any maintenance assessment [maintenance calculation] , first calculate—*

$$(A + C) \times P$$

where—

   A   *is the absent parent's [non-resident parent's] assessable [calculable] income;*

   C   *is the assessable [calculable] income of the other parent, where that parent is the person with care, and otherwise has such value (if any) as may be prescribed; and*

   P   *is such number greater than zero but less than 1 as may be prescribed.*

(2) Where the result of the calculation made under sub-paragraph (1) is an amount which is equal to, or less than, the amount of the maintenance requirement for the qualifying child or qualifying children, the amount of maintenance payable by the absent parent [non-resident parent] for that child or those children shall be an amount equal to—

$$A \times P$$

where A and P have the same values as in the calculation made under sub-paragraph (1).

(3) Where the result of the calculation made under sub-paragraph (1) is an amount which exceeds the amount of the maintenance requirement for the qualifying child or qualifying children, the amount of maintenance payable by the absent parent [non-resident parent] for that child or those children shall consist of—

   (a)   a basic element calculated in accordance with the provisions of paragraph 3; and

   (b)   an additional element calculated in accordance with the provisions of paragraph 4.

Note. In para 2 words 'maintenance calculation and 'non-resident parent' in square brackets in each place they occur substituted for words 'maintenance assessment' and 'absent parent' respectively by the Child Support, Pensions and Social Security Act 2000, ss 1(2)(a), 26, Sch 3, para 11(1), (2), as from (in relation to certain cases): 3 March 2003 (SI 2003 No 192); for remaining purposes: to be appointed.

The basic element

3.—*(1) The basic element shall be calculated by applying the formula—*

$$BE = A \times G \times P$$

where—

   BE is the amount of the basic element;

   A and P have the same values as in the calculation made under paragraph 2(1); and

   G has the value determined under sub-paragraph (2).

   (2) The value of G shall be determined by applying the formula—

$$G = \frac{MR}{(A + C)\ 3\ P}$$

where—

   MR is the amount of the maintenance requirement for the qualifying child or qualifying children; and

   A, C and P have the same values as in the calculation made under paragraph 2(1).

The additional element

4.—*(1) Subject to sub-paragraph (2), the additional element shall be calculated by applying the formula—*

$$AE = (1 - G) \times A \times R$$

where—

AE *is the amount of the additional element;*

A *has the same value as in the calculation made under paragraph 2(1);*

G *has the value determined under paragraph 3(2); and*

R *is such number greater than zero but less than 1 as may be prescribed.*

(2) *Where applying the alternative formula set out in sub-paragraph (3) would result in a lower amount for the additional element, that formula shall be applied in place of the formula set out in sub-paragraph (1).*

(3) *The alternative formula is—*

$$AE = Z \times Q \times \left(\frac{A}{A + C} \right)$$

where—

A *and* C *have the same values as in the calculation made under paragraph 2(1);*

Z *is such number as may be prescribed; and*

Q *is the aggregate of—*

(a) *any amount taken into account by virtue of paragraph 1(3)(a) in calculating the maintenance requirement; and*

(b) *any amount which is both taken into account by virtue of paragraph 1(3)(c) in making that calculation and is an amount prescribed for the purposes of this paragraph.*

Assessable income

5.—(1) *The assessable income of an absent parent [non-resident parent] shall be calculated by applying the formula—*

$$A = N - E$$

where—

A *is the amount of that parent's assessable income;*

N *is the amount of that parent's net income, calculated or estimated in accordance with regulations made by the Secretary of State for the purposes of this sub-paragraph; and*

E *is the amount of that parent's exempt income, calculated or estimated in accordance with regulations made by the Secretary of State for those purposes.*

(2) *The assessable income of a parent who is a person with care of the qualifying child or children shall be calculated by applying the formula—*

$$C = M - F$$

where—

C *is the amount of that parent's assessable income;*

M *is the amount of that parent's net income, calculated or estimated in accordance with regulations made by the Secretary of State for the purposes of this sub-paragraph; and*

F *is the amount of that parent's exempt income, calculated or estimated in accordance with regulations made by the Secretary of State for those purposes.*

(3) *Where the preceding provisions of this paragraph would otherwise result in a person's assessable income being taken to be a negative amount his assessable income shall be taken to be nil.*

(4) *Where income support[, an income-based jobseeker's allowance] or any other benefit of a prescribed kind is paid to or in respect of a parent who is an absent parent [a non-resident parent] or a person with care that parent shall, for the purposes of this Schedule, be taken to have no assessable income.*

Note. *In para 5(1), (4) words 'a non-resident parent' in square brackets substituted for words 'an absent parent' by the Child Support, Pensions and Social Security Act 2000, s 26, Sch 3, para 11(1), (2), as from (in relation to certain cases): 3 March 2003 (SI 2003 No 192); for remaining purposes: to be appointed. In para 5(4) words [, an income based jobseeker's allowance] in square brackets inserted by Jobseekers Act 1995, s 41(4), Sch 2, para 20(7), as from 7 October 1996.*

Protected income

6.—*(1) This paragraph applies where—*
   (a)   one or more maintenance assessments [maintenance calculations] have been made with respect to an absent parent [a non-resident parent]; and
   (b)   payment by him of the amount, or the aggregate of the amounts, so assessed [calculated] would otherwise reduce his disposable income below his protected income level.

   (2)   The amount of the assessment [calculation], or (as the case may be) of each assessment [calculation], shall be adjusted in accordance with such provisions as may be prescribed with a view to securing so far as is reasonably practicable that payment by the absent parent [non-resident parent] of the amount, or (as the case may be) aggregate of the amounts, so assessed [calculated] will not reduce his disposable income below his protected income level.

   (3)   Regulations made under sub-paragraph (2) shall secure that, where the prescribed minimum amount fixed by regulations made under paragraph 7 applies, no maintenance assessment [maintenance calculation] is adjusted so as to provide for the amount payable by an absent parent [non-resident parent] in accordance with that assessment [calculation] to be less than that amount.

   (4)   The amount which is to be taken for the purposes of this paragraph as an absent parent's [a non-resident parent's] disposable income shall be calculated, or estimated, in accordance with regulations made by the Secretary of State.

   (5)   Regulations made under sub-paragraph (4) may, in particular, provide that, in such circumstances and to such extent as may be prescribed—
   (a)   income of any child who is living in the same household with the absent parent [non-resident parent]; and
   (b)   where the absent parent [non-resident parent] is living together in the same household with another adult of the opposite sex (regardless of whether or not they are married), income of that other adult,
is to be treated as the absent parent's [non-resident parent's] income for the purposes of calculating his disposable income.

   (6)   In this paragraph the 'protected income level' of a particular absent parent [non-resident parent] means an amount of income calculated, by reference to the circumstances of that parent, in accordance with regulations made by the Secretary of State.

Note. Words 'maintenance calculations', 'a non-resident parent', 'calculated', 'calculation', 'maintenance calculation' and 'non-resident parent's' in square brackets in each place they occur substituted for words 'maintenance assessments', 'an absent parent', 'assessed', 'assessment', 'absent parent', 'maintenance assessment' and 'absent parent's' respectively by the Child Support, Pensions and Social Security Act 2000, ss 1(2), 26, Sch 3, para 11(1), (2), as from (in relation to certain cases): 3 March 2003 (SI 2003 No 192); for remaining purposes: to be appointed.

The minimum amount of child support maintenance

7.—*(1) The Secretary of State may prescribe a minimum amount for the purposes of this paragraph.*

   (2)   Where the amount of child support maintenance which would be fixed by a maintenance assessment [maintenance calculation] but for this paragraph is nil, or less than the prescribed minimum amount, the amount to be fixed by the assessment [calculation] shall be the prescribed minimum amount.

   (3)   In any case to which section 43 applies, and in such other cases (if any) as may be prescribed, sub-paragraph (2) shall not apply.

Note. In sub-para (2) words 'maintenance calculation' and 'calculation' in square brackets substituted for words 'maintenance assessment' and 'assessment' respectively by the Child Support, Pensions and Social Security Act 2000, s 1(2), as from (in relation to certain cases): 3 March 2003 (SI 2003 No 192); for remaining purposes: to be appointed.

Housing costs

8. *Where regulations under this Schedule require a child support officer [the Secretary of State] to take account of the housing costs of any person in calculating, or estimating, his assessable income or disposable income, those regulations may make provision—*

(a) *as to the costs which are to be treated as housing costs for the purpose of the regulations;*

(b) *for the apportionment of housing costs; and*

(c) *for the amount of housing costs to be taken into account for prescribed purposes not to exceed such amount (if any) as may be prescribed by, or determined in accordance with, the regulations.*

Note. Words 'the Secretary of State' in square brackets substituted for words ' a child support officer' by the Social Security Act 1998, s 86(1), Sch 7, para 48(1), as from 1 June 1999 (SI 1999 No 1510).

Regulations about income and capital

9. *The Secretary of State may by regulations provide that, in such circumstances and to such extent as may be prescribed—*

(a) *income of a child shall be treated as income of a parent of his;*

(b) *where the child support officer concerned [the Secretary of State] is satisfied that a person has intentionally deprived himself of a source of income with a view to reducing the amount of his assessable income, his net income shall be taken to include income from that source of an amount estimated by the child support officer [the Secretary of State];*

(c) *a person is to be treated as possessing capital or income which he does not possess;*

(d) *capital or income which a person does possess is to be disregarded;*

(e) *income is to be treated as capital;*

(f) *capital is to be treated as income.*

Note. Words 'the Secretary of State' in square brackets in both places they occur substituted for words 'the child support officer concerned' and 'the child support officer' by the Social Security Act 1998, s 86(1), Sch 7, para 48(2), as from 1 June 1999 (SI 1999 No 1510).

References to qualifying children

10. *References in this Part of this Schedule to 'qualifying children' are to those qualifying children with respect to whom the maintenance assessment [maintenance calculation] falls to be made.*

[PART I

CALCULATION OF WEEKLY AMOUNT OF CHILD SUPPORT MAINTENANCE

General rule

1.—(1) The weekly rate of child support maintenance is the basic rate unless a reduced rate, a flat rate or the nil rate applies.

(2) Unless the nil rate applies, the amount payable weekly to a person with care is—

(a) the applicable rate, if paragraph 6 does not apply; or

(b) if paragraph 6 does apply, that rate as apportioned between the persons with care in accordance with paragraph 6,

as adjusted, in either case, by applying the rules about shared care in paragraph 7 or 8.

Basic rate

2.—(1) The basic rate is the following percentage of the non-resident parent's net weekly income—

15% where he has one qualifying child;

20% where he has two qualifying children;

25% where he has three or more qualifying children.

(2) If the non-resident parent also has one or more relevant other children, the appropriate percentage referred to in sub-paragraph (1) is to be applied instead to his net weekly income less—
15% where he has one relevant other child;
20% where he has two relevant other children;
25% where he has three or more relevant other children.

Reduced rate

3.—(1) A reduced rate is payable if—
  (a) neither a flat rate nor the nil rate applies; and
  (b) the non-resident parent's net weekly income is less than £200 but more than £100.
(2) The reduced rate payable shall be prescribed in, or determined in accordance with, regulations.
(3) The regulations may not prescribe, or result in, a rate of less than £5.

Flat rate

4.—(1) Except in a case falling within sub-paragraph (2), a flat rate of £5 is payable if the nil rate does not apply and—
  (a) the non-resident parent's net weekly income is £100 or less; or
  (b) he receives any benefit, pension or allowance prescribed for the purposes of this paragraph of this sub-paragraph; or
  (c) he or his partner (if any) receives any benefit prescribed for the purposes of this paragraph of this sub-paragraph.
(2) A flat rate of a prescribed amount is payable if the nil rate does not apply and—
  (a) the non-resident parent has a partner who is also a non-resident parent;
  (b) the partner is a person with respect to whom a maintenance calculation is in force; and
  (c) the non-resident parent or his partner receives any benefit prescribed under sub-paragraph (1)(c).
(3) The benefits, pensions and allowances which may be prescribed for the purposes of sub-paragraph (1)(b) include ones paid to the non-resident parent under the law of a place outside the United Kingdom.

Nil rate

5. The rate payable is nil if the non-resident parent—
  (a) is of a prescribed description; or
  (b) has a net weekly income of below £5.

Apportionment

6.—(1) If the non-resident parent has more than one qualifying child and in relation to them there is more than one person with care, the amount of child support maintenance payable is (subject to paragraph 7 or 8) to be determined by apportioning the rate between the persons with care.
(2) The rate of maintenance liability is to be divided by the number of qualifying children, and shared among the persons with care according to the number of qualifying children in relation to whom each is a person with care.

Shared care—basic and reduced rate

7.—(1) This paragraph applies only if the rate of child support maintenance payable is the basic rate or a reduced rate.

(2) If the care of a qualifying child is shared between the non-resident parent and the person with care, so that the non-resident parent from time to time has care of the child overnight, the amount of child support maintenance which he would otherwise have been liable to pay the person with care, as calculated in accordance with the preceding paragraphs of this Part of this Schedule, is to be decreased in accordance with this paragraph.

(3) First, there is to be a decrease according to the number of such nights which the Secretary of State determines there to have been, or expects there to be, or both during a prescribed twelve-month period.

(4) The amount of that decrease for one child is set out in the following Table—

Number of nights	Fraction to subtract
52 to 103	One-seventh
104 to 155	Two-sevenths
156 to 174	three-sevenths
175 or more	One-half

(5) If the person with care is caring for more than one qualifying child of the non-resident parent, the applicable decrease is the sum of the appropriate fractions in the Table divided by the number of such qualifying children.

(6) If the applicable fraction is one-half in relation to any qualifying child in the care of the person with care, the total amount payable to the person with care is then to be further decreased by £7 for each such child.

(7) If the application of the preceding provisions of this paragraph would decrease the weekly amount of child support maintenance (or the aggregate of all such amounts) payable by the non-resident parent to the person with care (or all of them) to less than £5, he is instead liable to pay child support maintenance at the rate of £5 a week, apportioned (if appropriate) in accordance with paragraph 6.

Shared care—flat rate

8.—(1) This paragraph applies only if—
  (a) the rate of child support maintenance payable is a flat rate; and
  (b) that rate applies because the non-resident parent falls within paragraph 4(1)(b) or (c) or 4(2).

(2) If the care of a qualifying child is shared as mentioned in paragraph 7(2) for at least 52 nights during a prescribed 12-month period, the amount of child support maintenance payable by the non-resident parent to the person with care of that child is nil.

Regulations about shared care

9.—The Secretary of State may by regulations provide—
  (a) for which nights are to count for the purposes of shared care under paragraphs 7 and 8, or for how it is to be determined whether a night counts;
  (b) for what counts, or does not count, as 'care' for those purposes; and
  (c) for paragraph 7(3) or 8(2) to have effect, in prescribed circumstances, as if the period mentioned there were other than 12 months, and in such circumstances for the Table in paragraph 7(4) (or that Table as modified pursuant to regulations made under paragraph 10A(2)(a)), or the period mentioned in paragraph 8(2), to have effect with prescribed adjustments.

Net weekly income

10.—(1) For the purposes of this Schedule, net weekly income is to be determined in such manner as is provided for in regulations.

(2) The regulations may, in particular, provide for the Secretary of State to estimate any income or make an assumption as to any fact where, in his view, the information at his disposal is unreliable, insufficient, or relates to an atypical period in the life of the non-resident parent.

(3) Any amount of net weekly income (calculated as above) over £2,000 is to be ignored for the purposes of this Schedule.

Regulations about rates, figures, etc

10A.—(1) The Secretary of State may by regulations provide that—
  (a) paragraph 2 is to have effect as if different percentages were substituted for those set out there;
  (b) paragraph 3(1) or (3), 4(1), 5, 7(7) or 10(3) is to have effect as if different amounts were substituted for those set out there.
(2) The Secretary of State may by regulations provide that—
  (a) the Table in paragraph 7(4) is to have effect as if different numbers of nights were set out in the first column and different fractions were substituted for those set out in the second column;
  (b) paragraph 7(6) is to have effect as if a different amount were substituted for that mentioned there, or as if the amount were an aggregate amount and not an amount for each qualifying child, or both.

Regulations about income

10B. The Secretary of State may by regulations provide that, in such circumstances and to such extent as may be prescribed—
  (a) where the Secretary of State is satisfied that a person has intentionally deprived himself of a source of income with a view to reducing the amount of his net weekly income, his net weekly income shall be taken to include income from that source of an amount estimated by the Secretary of State;
  (b) a person is to be treated as possessing income which he does not possess;
  (c) income which a person does possess is to be disregarded.

References to various terms

10C.—(1) References in this Part of this Schedule to 'qualifying children' are to those qualifying children with respect to whom the maintenance calculation falls to be made.
(2) References in this Part of this Schedule to 'relevant other children' are to—
  (a) children other than qualifying children in respect of whom the non-resident parent or his partner receives child benefit under Part IX of the Social Security Contributions and Benefits Act 1992; and
  (b) such other description of children as may be prescribed.
(3) In this Part of this Schedule, a person 'receives' a benefit, pension, or allowance for any week if it is paid or due to be paid to him in respect of that week.
(4) In this Part of this Schedule, a person's 'partner' is—
  (a) if they are a couple, the other member of that couple;
  (b) if the person is a husband or wife by virtue of a marriage entered into under a law which permits polygamy, another party to the marriage who is of the opposite sex and is a member of the same household.
(5) In sub-paragraph (4)(a), 'couple' means a man and a woman who are—
  (a) married to each other and are members of the same household; or
  (b) not married to each other but are living together as husband and wife.]

Note. Sch 1, Part I above substituted for Sch 1, Part I in italics by the Child Support, Pensions and Social Security Act 2000, s 1(3), Sch 1, as from (for certain purposes): 10 November 2000 (SI 2000 No 2994); (in relation to certain cases): 3 March 2003 (SI 2003 No 192); for remaining purposes: to be appointed.

PART II

GENERAL PROVISIONS ABOUT *MAINTENANCE ASSESSMENTS* [MAINTENANCE CALCULATIONS]

Effective date of assessment [calculation]

11.—(1) A *maintenance assessment* [maintenance calculation] shall take effect on such date as may be determined in accordance with regulations made by the Secretary of State.

(2) That date may be earlier than the date on which the *assessment* [calculation] is made.

Note. In Part heading and cross heading words 'maintenance calculations' and 'calculation' in square brackets substituted for words 'maintenance assessments' and 'assessment' respectively and in para 11 words in square brackets substituted for words in italics by the Child Support, Pensions and Social Security Act 2000, s 1(2), as from (in relation to certain cases): 3 March 2003 (SI 2003 No 192); for remaining purposes: to be appointed.

Form of assessment [calculation]

12. Every *maintenance assessment* [maintenance calculation] shall be made in such form and contain such information as the Secretary of State may direct.

Note. In cross heading word 'calculation' in square brackets substituted for word 'assessment' and in para 13 words in square brackets substituted for words in italics by the Child Support, Pensions and Social Security Act 2000, s 1(2), as from (in relation to certain cases): 3 March 2003 (SI 2003 No 192); for remaining purposes: to be appointed.

Assessments where amount of child support is nil

13. *A child support officer* [the Secretary of State] *shall not decline to make a maintenance assessment [maintenance calculation] only on the ground that the amount of the assessment [calculation] is nil.*

Note. Words 'the Secretary of State' in square brackets substituted for words 'A child support officer' by the Social Security Act 1998, s 86(1), Sch 7, para 48(3), as from 1 June 1999 (SI 1999 No 1510). Word 'calculation' in square brackets substituted for word 'assessment' by the Child Support, Pensions and Social Security Act 2000, s 1(2), as from (in relation to certain cases): 3 March 2003 (SI 2003 No 192); for remaining purposes: to be appointed. Para 13 repealed by the Child Support, Pensions and Social Security Act 2000, ss 26, 85, Sch 3, para 11(1), 22(a), Sch 9, Pt 1, as from a day to be appointed.

Consolidated applications and assessments [calculations]

14. The Secretary of State may by regulations provide—(1)—

(a) for two or more applications for *maintenance assessments* [maintenance calculations] to be treated, in prescribed circumstances, as a single application; and

(b) for the replacement, in prescribed circumstances, of a *maintenance assessment* [maintenance calculation] made on the application of one person by a later *maintenance assessment* [maintenance calculation] made on the application of that or any other person.

[(2) In sub-paragraph (1), the references (however expressed) to applications for maintenance calculations include references to applications treated as made.]

Note. Sub-para (1) numbered as such and sub-para (2) inserted by the Child Support, Pensions and Social Security Act 2000, s 26, Sch 3, para 11(1), 22(b), as from (in relation to certain cases): 3 March 2003 (SI 2003 No 192); for remaining purposes: to be appointed. In sub-para (1) words in square brackets substituted for words in italics by the Child Support, Pensions and Social Security Act 2000, s 1(2), as from (in relation to certain cases): 3 March 2003 (SI 2003 No 192); for remaining purposes: to be appointed.

Separate assessments [calculations] for different periods

15. Where *a child support officer* [the Secretary of State] is satisfied that the circumstances of a case require different amounts of child support maintenance to be *assessed* [calculated] in respect of different periods, he may make separate *maintenance assessments* [maintenance calculations] each expressed to have effect in relation to a different specified period.

Note. In cross-heading word 'calculations' in square brackets substituted for word 'assessments' and in para 15 words 'calculated' and 'maintenance calculations' in square brackets substituted for words 'assessed' and 'maintenance assessments' respectively by the Child Support, Pensions and Social Security Act 2000, s 1(2), as from (in relation to certain cases): 3 March 2003 (SI 2003 No 192); for remaining purposes: to be appointed. Words 'the Secretary of State' in square brackets substituted for words 'a child support officer' by the Social Security Act 1998, s 86(1), Sch 7, para 48(4), as from 1 June 1999 (SI 1999 No 1510).

Termination of assessments [calculations]

16.—(1) A *maintenance assessment* [maintenance calculation] shall cease to have effect—

   (a)   on the death of the *absent parent* [non-resident parent], or of the person with care, with respect to whom it was made;

   (b)   on there no longer being any qualifying child with respect to whom it would have effect;

   (c)   on the *absent parent* [non-resident parent] with respect to whom it was made ceasing to be a parent of—

      (i)   the qualifying child with respect to whom it was made; or

      (ii)   where it was made with respect to more than one qualifying child, all of the qualifying children with respect to whom it was made;

   (d)   *where the absent parent [non-resident parent] and the person with care with respect to whom it was made have been living together for a continuous period of six months;*

   (e)   *where a new maintenance assessment [maintenance calculation] is made with respect to any qualifying child with respect to whom the assessment [calculation] in question was in force immediately before the making of the new assessment [calculation].*

   (2)   *A maintenance assessment made in response to an application under section 4 to 7 shall be cancelled by a child support officer [the Secretary of State] if the person on whose application the assessment [calculation] was made asks him to do so.*

   (3)   *A maintenance assessment [maintenance calcualtion] made in response to an application under section 6 shall be cancelled by a child support officer [the Secretary of State] if—*

   (a)   *the person on whose application the assessment [calculation] was made ('the applicant') asks him to do so; and*

   (b)   *he is satisfied that the applicant has ceased to fall within subsection (1) of that section.*

   (4)   *Where a child support officer [the Secretary of State] is satisfied that the person with care with respect to whom a maintenance assessment [maintenance calculation] was made has ceased to be a person with care in relation to the qualifying child, or any of the qualifying children, with respect to whom the assessment [calculation] was made, he may cancel the assessment [calculation] with effect from the date on which, in his opinion, the change of circumstances took place.*

   [(4A)   *A maintenance assessment [maintenace calculation] may be cancelled by a child support officer [the Secretary of State] if he is conducting a review under section 16, 17, 18 or 19 [proposing to make a decision under section 16 or 17] and it appears to him—*

   (a)   *that the person with care with respect to whom the maintenance assessment [maintenance calculation] in question was made has failed to provide him with sufficient information to enable him to complete the review [make the decision]; and*

   (b)   *where the maintenance assessment [maintenance calculation] in question was made in response to an application under section 6, that the person with care with respect to whom the assessment [calculation] was made has ceased to fall within subsection (1) of that section.]*

(5) *Where—*

(a) *at any time a maintenance assessment [maintenance calculation] is in force but a child support officer [the Secretary of State] would no longer have jurisdiction to make it if it were to be applied for at that time; and*

(b) *the assessment [calculation] has not been cancelled, or has not ceased to have effect, under or by virtue of any other provision made by or under this Act,*

it shall be taken to have continuing effect unless cancelled by a child support officer in accordance with such prescribed provision (including provision as to the effective date of cancellation) as the Secretary of State considers it appropriate to make.

(6) *Where both the absent parent [non-resident parent] and the person with care with respect to whom a maintenance assessment [maintenance calculation] was made request a child support officer [the Secretary of State] to cancel the assessment [calculation], he may do so if he is satisfied that they are living together.*

(7) *Any cancellation of a maintenance assessment [maintenance calculation] under sub-paragraph [(4A),] (5) or (6) shall have effect from such date as may be determined by the child support officer [the Secretary of State].*

(8) *Where a child support officer [the Secretary of State] cancels a maintenance assessment [maintenance calculation], he shall immediately notify the absent parent [non-resident parent] and person with care, so far as that is reasonably practicable.*

(9) *Any notice under sub-paragraph (8) shall specify the date with effect from which the cancellation took effect.*

(10) A person with care with respect to whom a *maintenance assessment* [maintenance calculation] is in force shall provide the Secretary of State with such information, in such circumstances, as may be prescribed, with a view to assisting the Secretary of State *or a child support officer* in determining whether the *assessment* [calculation] has ceased to have effect, *or should be cancelled.*

(11) The Secretary of State may by regulations make such supplemental, incidental or transitional provision as he thinks necessary or expedient in consequence of the provisions of this paragraph.

Note. In cross-heading word 'calculations' in square brackets substituted for word 'assessments' and in para 16 words 'maintenance calculation', 'non-resident parent', and 'calculation' in square brackets in each place they occur substituted for words 'maintenance assessment', 'absent parent' and 'assessment' respectively by the Child Support, Pensions and Social Security Act 2000, ss 1(2), 26, Sch 3, para 11(1), (2), as from (in relation to certain cases): 3 March 2003 (SI 2003 No 192); for remaining purposes: to be appointed. Sub-para (4A) inserted, and number in square brackets in sub-para (7) inserted, by the Child Support Act 1995, s 14(2), (3), as from 22 January 1996. In sub-paras (2)–(6), (8) words 'the Secretary of State' in square brackets in each place they occur substituted for words 'a child support officer'" in sub-para (4A) words 'proposing...16 or 17' in square brackets substituted for words 'conducting...or 19', in sub-para (7) words 'the Secretary of State' in square brackets substituted for words 'the child support officer', and in sub-para (10) words 'or a child support officer' in italics repealed, by the Social Security Act 1998, s 86, Sch 7, para 48(5), Sch 8, as from 1 June 1999 (SI 1999 No 1510). Sub-paras (1)(d), (e), (2)–(9), and in sub-para (10) words 'or should be cancelled' repealed by the Child Support, Pensions and Social Security Act 2000, ss 26, 85, Sch 3, para 11 (1), (22)(c), Sch 9, Pt 1, as from (in relation to certain cases): 3 March 2003 (SI 2003 No 192); for remaining purposes: to be appointed.

SCHEDULE 2   Section 14(4)

PROVISION OF INFORMATION TO SECRETARY OF STATE

Inland Revenue records

1.—(1) This paragraph applies where the Secretary of State or the Department of Health and Social Services for Northern Ireland requires information for the purpose of tracing—

(a) the current address of *an absent parent* [a non-resident parent]; or

(b) the current employer of *an absent parent* [a non-resident parent].

(2) In such a case, no obligation as to secrecy imposed by statute or otherwise on a person employed in relation to the Inland Revenue shall prevent any information obtained or held in connection with the *assessment* [calculation] or collection of income tax from being disclosed to—

   (a)   the Secretary of State;
   (b)   the Department of Health and Social Services for Northern Ireland; or
   (c)   an officer of either of them authorised to receive such information in connection with the operation of this Act or of any corresponding Northern Ireland legislation.

(3) This paragraph extends only to disclosure by or under the authority of the Commissioners of Inland Revenue.

(4) Information which is the subject of disclosure to any person by virtue of this paragraph shall not be further disclosed to any person except where the further disclosure is made—

   (a)   to a person to whom disclosure could be made by virtue of sub-paragraph (2); or
   (b)   for the purposes of any proceedings (civil or criminal) in connection with the operation of this Act or of any corresponding Northern Ireland legislation.

Note. Words 'a non-resident parent' in square brackets in both places they occur and word 'calculation' in square brackets substituted for words in italics by the Child Support, Pensions and Social Security Act 2000, ss 1(2), 26, Sch 3, para 11(1), (2), as from (in relation to certain cases): 3 March 2003 (SI 2003 No 192); for remaining purposes: to be appointed.

[1A—(1) This paragraph applies to any information which—

   (a)   relates to any earnings or other income of an *absent parent* [a non-resident parent] in respect of a tax year in which he is or was a self-employed earner, and
   (b)   is required by the Secretary of State or the Department of Health and Social Services for Northern Ireland for any purposes of this Act.

(2) No obligation as to secrecy imposed by statute or otherwise on a person employed in relation to the Inland Revenue shall prevent any such information obtained or held in connection with the *assessment* [calculation] or collection of income tax from being disclosed to—

   (a)   the Secretary of State;
   (b)   the Department of Health and Social Services for Northern Ireland; or
   (c)   an officer of either of them authorised to receive such information in connection with the operation of this Act.

(3) This paragraph extends only to disclosure by or under the authority of the Commissioners of Inland Revenue.

(4) Information which is the subject of disclosure to any person by virtue of this paragraph shall not be further disclosed to any person except where the further disclosure is made—

   (a)   to a person to whom disclosure could be made by virtue of sub-paragraph (2); or
   (b)   for the purposes of any proceedings (civil or criminal) in connection with the operation of this Act.

(5) For the purposes of this paragraph 'self-employed earner' and 'tax year' have the same meaning as in Parts I to VI of the Social Security Contributions and Benefits Act 1992.]

Note. This para inserted by the Welfare Reform and Pensions Act 1999, s 80, as from 11 November 1999. Words in square brackets in sub-paras (1)(a), (2) substituted for words in italics by the Child Support, Pensions and Social Security Act 2000, ss 1(2)(a), 26, Sch 3, para 11(1), (2), as from (in relation to certain cases): 3 March 2003 (SI 2003 No 192); for remaining purposes: to be appointed.

Local authority records

2.—(*1*) This paragraph applies where—
   (a)   the Secretary of State requires relevant information in connection with the discharge by him, or by any child support officer, of functions under this Act; or
   (b)   the Department of Health and Social Services for Northern Ireland requires relevant information in connection with the discharge of any functions under any corresponding Northern Ireland legislation.

(2) The Secretary of State may give a direction to the appropriate authority requiring them to give him such relevant information in connection with any housing benefit or community charge benefit [council tax benefit] to which an absent parent or person with care is entitled as the Secretary of State considers necessary in connection with his determination of—
   (a)   that person's income of any kind;
   (b)   the amount of housing costs to be taken into account in determining that person's income of any kind; or
   (c)   the amount of that person's protected income.

(3) The Secretary of State may give a similar direction for the purposes of enabling the Department of Health and Social Services for Northern Ireland to obtain such information for the purposes of any corresponding Northern Ireland legislation.

(4) In this paragraph—
'appropriate authority' means—
   (a)   in relation to housing benefit, the housing or local authority concerned; and
   (b)   in relation to community charge benefit, the charging authority [council tax benefit, the billing authority] or, in Scotland, the levying authority; and
'relevant information' means information of such a description as may be prescribed.

Note. Words in square brackets substituted for words 'community charge benefit and 'community charge ... authority' by Local Government Finance Act 1992, s 117(1), Sch 13, para 94, as from 1 April 1993. This para repealed by the Social Security Act 1998, s 86(1), (2), Sch 7, para 49, Sch 8, as from 8 September 1998 (SI 1998 No 2209).

SCHEDULE 3   Section 21(4)

CHILD SUPPORT APPEAL TRIBUNALS

The President

1.—(*1*) The person appointed under Schedule 10 to the Social Security Act 1975 as President of the social security appeal tribunals, medical appeal tribunals and disability appeal tribunals shall, by virtue of that appointment, also be President of the child support appeal tribunals.

(2) It shall be the duty of the President to arrange such meetings of the chairmen and members of child support appeal tribunals, and such training for them, as he considers appropriate.

(3) The President may, with the consent of the Secretary of State as to numbers, remuneration and other terms and conditions of service, appoint such officers and staff as he thinks fit for the child support appeal tribunals and their full-time chairmen.

Note. Words in 'under Schedule 10 to the Social Security Act 1975' repealed by Social Security (Consequential Provisions) Act 1992, s 3, Sch 1, as from 1 July 1992.

Membership of child support appeal tribunals

2.—(*1*) A child support appeal tribunal shall consist of a chairman and two other persons.

(2) The chairman and the other members of the tribunal must not all be of the same sex.

(3) Sub-paragraph (2) shall not apply to any proceedings before a child support appeal tribunal if the chairman of the tribunal rules that it is not reasonably practicable to comply with that sub-paragraph in those proceedings.

[(4) This paragraph is subject to the provisions of any regulations made under paragraph 9 of Schedule 4A.]

Note. Sub-para (4) added by Child Support Act 1995, s 30(5), Sch 3, para 17, as from 2 December 1996.

The chairmen

3.—(1) The chairman of a child support appeal tribunal shall be nominated by the President.

(2) The President may nominate himself or a person drawn—

(a) from the appropriate panel appointed by the Lord Chancellor, or (as the case may be) the Lord President of the Court of Session, under section 7 of the Tribunals and Inquiries Act 1971;

(b) from among those appointed under paragraph 4; or

(c) from among those appointed under paragraph 1A of Schedule 10 to the Social Security Act 1975 to act as full-time chairmen of social security appeal tribunals.

(3) Subject to any regulations made by the Lord Chancellor, no person shall be nominated as a chairman of a child support appeal tribunal by virtue of sub-paragraph (2)(a) unless he has a 5 year general qualification or is an advocate or solicitor in Scotland of 5 years' standing.

Note. Words 'under paragraph ... 1975' repealed by Social Security (Consequential Provisions) Act 1992, s 3, Sch 1, as from 1 July 1992.

4.—(1) The Lord Chancellor may appoint regional and other full-time chairmen for child support appeal tribunals.

(2) A person is qualified to be appointed as a full-time chairman if he has a 7 year general qualification or is an advocate or solicitor in Scotland of 7 years' standing.

(3) A person appointed to act as a full-time chairman shall hold and vacate office in accordance with the terms of his appointment, except that he must vacate his office at the end of the completed year of service in which he reaches the age of 72 unless his appointment is continued under sub-paragraph (4) [on the date on which he reaches the age of 70; but this sub-paragraph is subject to section 26(4) to (6) of the Judicial Pensions and Retirement Act 1993 (power to authorise continuance in office up to the age of 75)].

(4) Where the Lord Chancellor considers it desirable in the public interest to retain a full-time chairman in office after the end of the completed year of service in which he reaches the age of 72, he may from time to time authorise the continuance of that person in office until any date not later than that on which that person reaches the age of 75.

(5) A person appointed as a full-time chairman may be removed from office by the Lord Chancellor, on the ground of misbehaviour or incapacity.

(6) Section 75 of the Courts and Legal Services Act 1990 (judges etc barred from legal practice) shall apply to any person appointed as a full-time chairman under this Schedule as it applies to any person holding as a full-time appointment any of the offices listed in Schedule 11 to that Act.

(7) The Secretary of State may pay, or make such payments towards the provision of, such remuneration, pensions, allowances or gratuities to or in respect of persons appointed as full-time chairmen under this paragraph as, with the consent of the Treasury, he may determine.

[(8) Sub-paragraph (7), so far as relating to pensions, allowances or gratuities, shall not have effect in relation to any person to whom Part I of the Judicial Pensions and Retirement Act 1993 applies, except to the extent provided by or under that Act.]

Note. Words in square brackets in sub-para (3) substituted for words 'at the ... sub-paragraph (4)', sub-para (4) repealed and sub-para (8) added by Judicial Pensions and Retirement Act 1993, ss 26(10), 31(3), (4), Sch 6, para 23(1), Sch 8, para 21(1), Sch 9, as from 31 March 1995.

Other members of child support appeal tribunals

5.—(1) The members of a child support appeal tribunal other than the chairman shall be drawn from the appropriate panel constituted under this paragraph.

(2) The panels shall be constituted by the President for the whole of Great Britain, and shall—

(a) act for such areas; and

(b) be composed of such persons,

as the President thinks fit.

(3) *The panel for an area shall be composed of persons appearing to the President to have knowledge or experience of conditions in the area and to be representative of persons living or working in the area.*

(4) *Before appointing members of a panel, the President shall take into consideration any recommendations from such organisations or persons as he considers appropriate.*

(5) *The members of the panels shall hold office for such period as the President may direct.*

(6) *The President may at any time terminate the appointment of any member of a panel.*

Clerks of tribunals

6.—(1) *Each child support appeal tribunal shall be serviced by a clerk appointed by the President.*

(2) *The duty of summoning members of a panel to serve on a child support appeal tribunal shall be performed by the clerk to the tribunal.*

Expenses of tribunal members and others

7.—(1) *The Secretary of State may pay—*

    (a) *to any member of a child support appeal tribunal, such remuneration and travelling and other allowances as the Secretary of State may determine with the consent of the Treasury;*

    (b) *to any person required to attend at any proceedings before a child support appeal tribunal, such travelling and other allowances as may be so determined; and*

    (c) *such other expenses in connection with the work of any child support appeal tribunal as may be so determined.*

(2) *In sub-paragraph (1), references to travelling and other allowances include references to compensation for loss of remunerative time.*

(3) *No compensation for loss of remunerative time shall be paid to any person under this paragraph in respect of any time during which he is in receipt of other remuneration so paid.*

Consultation with Lord Advocate

8. *Before exercising any of his powers under paragraph 3(3) or 4(1), (4) or (5), the Lord Chancellor shall consult the Lord Advocate.*

Note. Number '(4)' repealed by Judicial Pensions and Retirement Act 1993, s 31(4), Sch 9, as from 31 March 1995.

Schedule 3 repealed by the Social Security Act 1998, s 86(1), (2), Sch 7, para 50, Sch 8, as from 1 June 1999 (SI 1999 No 1510).

SCHEDULE 4   Section 22(5)

CHILD SUPPORT COMMISSIONERS

Tenure of office

1.—(1) Every Child Support Commissioner shall vacate his office *at the end of the completed year of service in which he reaches the age of 72* [on the date on which he reaches the age of 70; but this sub-paragraph is subject to section 26(4) to (6) of the Judicial Pensions and Retirement Act 1993 (power to authorise continuance in office up to the age of 75)].

(2) *Where the Lord Chancellor considers it desirable in the public interest to retain a Child Support Commissioner in office after the end of the completed year of service in which he reaches the age of 72, he may from time to time authorise the continuance of that Commissioner in office until any date not later than that on which he reaches the age of 75.*

(3) A Child Support Commissioner may be removed from office by the Lord Chancellor on the ground of misbehaviour or incapacity.

Note. Words in square brackets in sub-para (1) substituted for words in italics and sub-para (2) repealed by Judicial Pensions and Retirement Act 1993, ss 26(10), 31(4), Sch 6, para 23(2), Sch 9, as from 31 March 1995.

Commissioners' remuneration and their pensions

2.—(1) The Lord Chancellor may pay, or make such payments towards the provision of such remuneration, pensions, allowances or gratuities to or in respect of persons appointed as Child Support Commissioners as, with the consent of the Treasury, he may determine.

[(1) The Lord Chancellor or, in Scotland, the Secretary of State may pay to any person who attends any proceedings before a Child Support commissioner such travelling and other allowances as he may determine.]

(2) The Lord Chancellor shall pay to a Child Support Commissioner such expenses incurred in connection with his work as such a Commissioner as may be determined by the Treasury.

[(3) Sub-paragraph (1), so far as relating to pensions, allowances or gratuities, shall not have effect in relation to any person to whom Part I of the Judicial Pensions and Retirement Act 1993 applies, except to the extent provided by or under that Act.]

Note. Sub-para (3) added by Judicial Pensions and Retirement Act 1993, s 31(3), Sch 8, para 21(2), as from 31 March 1995.

[Expenses of other persons

2A.—*(1) The Secretary of State may pay to any person required to attend at any proceedings before a Child Support Commissioner such travelling and other allowances as, with the consent of the Treasury, the Secretary of State may determine.]*

[(1) The Lord Chancellor or, in Scotland, the Secretary of State may pay to any person who attends any proceedings before a Child Support Commissioner such travelling and other allowances as he may determine.

(2) In sub-paragraph (1), references to travelling and other allowances include references to compensation for loss of remunerative time.

(3) No compensation for loss of remunerative time shall be paid to any person under this paragraph in respect of any time during which he is in receipt of other remuneration so paid.]

Note. Para 2A and preceding cross-heading inserted by Child Support Act 1995, s 30(5), Sch 3, para 18(1), as from 18 December 1995. Sub-para (1) substituted by the Social Security Act 1998, s 86(1), Sch 7, para 51, as from 1 June 1999 (SI 1999 No 1510).

Commissioners barred from legal practice

3. Section 75 of the Courts and Legal Services Act 1990 (judges etc barred from legal practice) shall apply to any person appointed as a Child Support Commissioner as it applies to any person holding as a full-time appointment any of the offices listed in Schedule 11 to that Act.

Deputy Child Support Commissioners

4.—(1) The Lord Chancellor may appoint persons to act as Child Support Commissioners (but to be known as deputy Child Support Commissioners) in order to facilitate the disposal of the business of Child Support Commissioners.

(2) A deputy Child Support Commissioner shall be appointed—

(a) from among persons who have a 10 year general qualification or are advocates or solicitors in Scotland of 10 years' standing; and

(b) [subject to sub-paragraph (2A)] for such period or on such occasions as the Lord Chancellor thinks fit.

[(2A) No appointment of a person to be a deputy Child Support Commissioner shall be such as to extend beyond the date on which he reaches the age of 70; but this sub-paragraph is subject to section 26(4) to (6) of the Judicial Pensions and Retirement Act 1993 (power to authorise continuance in office up to the age of 75).]

(3) Paragraph 2 applies to deputy Child Support Commissioners as if the reference to pensions were omitted and paragraph 3 does not apply to them.

Note. Words in square brackets in sub-para (2) added and sub-para (2A) added by Judicial Pensions and Retirement Act 1993, s 26(10), Sch 6, para 23(3), as from 31 March 1995.

[*Determination of questions by other officers*

4A.—(1) The Lord Chancellor may by regulations provide—
  (a) for officers authorised—
      (i) by the Lord Chancellor; or
      (ii) in Scotland, by the Secretary of State,
      to determine any question which is determinable by a Child Support Commissioner and which does not involve the determination of any appeal, application for leave to appeal or reference;
  (b) for the procedure to be followed by any such officer in determining any such question;
  (c) for the manner in which determinations of such questions by such officers may be called in question.

(2) A determination which would have the effect of preventing an appeal, application for leave to appeal or reference being determined by a Child Support Commissioner is not a determination of the appeal, application or reference for the purposes of sub-paragraph (1).]

Note. Para 4A and preceding cross-heading inserted by Child Support Act 1995, s 17(1), as from 18 December 1995.

Tribunals of Commissioners

5.—(1) If it appears to the Chief Child Support Commissioner (or, in the case of his inability to act, to such other of the Child Support Commissioners as he may have nominated to act for the purpose) *that an appeal* [that—
  (a) an application for leave under section 24(6)(b); or
  (b) an appeal,]
falling to be heard by one of the Child Support Commissioners involves a question of law of special difficulty, he may direct that the *appeal* [that application or appeal] be dealt with by a tribunal consisting of any three [or more] of the Child Support Commissioners.

(2) If the decision of such a tribunal is not unanimous, the decision of the majority shall be the decision of the tribunal [; and the presiding Child Support Commissioner shall have a casting vote if the votes are equally divided].

[(3) Where a direction is given under sub-paragraph (1)(a), section 24(6)(b) shall have effect as if the reference to a Child Support Commissioner were a reference to such a tribunal as is mentioned in subparagraph (1).]

Note. In sub-para (1) words 'that—... an appeal,' and 'that the application or appeal' in square brackets substituted for words 'that an appeal' and 'the appeal' respectively and words 'or more' in square brackets inserted by the Social Security Act 1998, s 86(1), Sch 7, para 52(2), as from 1 June 1999 (SI 1999 No 1510). In sub-para (2) words '; and the ... equally divided' in square brackets inserted and sub-para (3) inserted, by the Social Security Act 1998, s 86(1), Sch 7, para 52(2), (3) as from 1 June 1999 (SI1999 No 1510).

Finality of decisions

6.—(1) Subject to section 25, the decision of any Child Support Commissioner shall be final.

(2) Sub-paragraph (1) shall not be taken to make any finding of fact or other determination embodied in, or necessary to, a decision, or on which it is based, conclusive for the purposes of any further decision.

[(2) If and to the extent that regulations so provide, any finding of fact or other determination which is embodied in or necessary to a decision, or on which a decision is based, shall be conclusive for the purposes of any further decision.]

Note. Sub-para (2) substituted by the Social Security Act 1998, s 86(1), Sch 7, para 52(4), as from 1 June 1999 (SI 1999 No 1510).

Consultation with Lord Advocate [Secretary of State]

7. Before exercising any of his powers under *paragraph 1(2) or (3)* [paragraph 1(3)], *or 4(1) or (2)(b)* [4(1) or (2)(b) or 4A(1)], the Lord Chancellor shall consult the *Lord Advocate* [Secretary of State].

Note. Words in first pair of square brackets substituted for words in italics by Judicial Pensions and Retirement Act 1993, s 26(10), Sch 6, para 23(4), as from 31 March 1995. Words in second pair of square brackets substituted for words in italics by Child Support Act 1995, s 17(2), as from 18 December 1995.

Northern Ireland

8. In its application to Northern Ireland this Schedule shall have effect as if—
  (a)   for any reference to a Child Support Commissioner (however expressed) there were substituted a corresponding reference to a Child Support Commissioner for Northern Ireland.
  (b)   in paragraph 2(1), the word 'pensions' were omitted;
  [(bb) paragraph 2A were omitted;]
  (c)   for paragraph 3, there were substituted—
        '3. A Child Support Commissioner for Northern Ireland, so long as he holds office as such, shall not practise as a barrister or act for any remuneration to himself as arbitrator or referee or be directly or indirectly concerned in any matter as a conveyancer, notary public or solicitor.';
  (d)   in paragraph 4—
        (i) for paragraph (a) of sub-paragraph (2) there were substituted—
              '(a) from among persons who are barristers or solicitors of not less than 10 years' standing; and';
        (ii) for sub-paragraph (3) there shall be substituted—
              '(3) Paragraph 2 applies to deputy Child Support Commissioners for Northern Ireland, but paragraph 3 does not apply to them.'; and
  (e)   *paragraphs 5* [paragraphs 4A] to 7 were omitted.

Note. Sub-para (bb) inserted and words in square brackets in sub-para (e) substituted for words in italics by Child Support Act 1995, ss 17(3), 30(5), Sch 3, para 18(2), as from 18 December 1995.

[SCHEDULE 4A   Section 1(2)

DEPARTURE DIRECTIONS

Interpretation

1. *In this Schedule—*
    'departure direction' means an application for a departure direction;
    'regulations' means regulations made by the Secretary of State;
    'review' means a review under section 16, 17, 18 or 19.

Applications for departure directions

2. *Regulations may make provision—*

(a) as to the procedure to be followed in considering a departure application;
(b) as to the procedure to be followed when a departure application is referred to a child support appeal tribunal [an appeal tribunal] under section 28D(1)(b);
(c) for the giving of a direction by the Secretary of State as to the order in which, in a particular case, a departure application and a review are to be dealt with [a decision on a departure application and a decision under section 16 or 17 are to be made];
(d) for the reconsideration of a departure application in a case where further information becomes available to the Secretary of State after the application has been determined.

Completion of preliminary consideration

3. Regulations may provide for determining when the preliminary consideration of a departure application is to be taken to have been completed.

Information

4.—(1) Regulations may make provision for the use for any purpose of this Act of—
(a) information acquired by the Secretary of State in connection with an application for, or the making of, a departure direction;
(b) information acquired by a child support officer or the Secretary of State in connection with an application for, or the making of, a maintenance assessment [maintenance calculation].

(2) If any information which is required (by regulations under this Act) to be furnished to the Secretary of State in connection with a departure application has not been furnished within such period as may be prescribed, the Secretary of State may nevertheless proceed to determine the application.

Anticipation of change of circumstances

5.—(1) A departure direction may be given so as to provide that if the circumstances of the case change in such manner as may be specified in the direction a fresh maintenance assessment [maintenance calculation] is to be made.

(2) Where any such provision is made, the departure direction may provide for the basis on which the amount of child support maintenance is to be fixed by the fresh maintenance assessment [maintenance calculation] to differ from the basis on which the amount of child support maintenance was fixed by any earlier maintenance assessment [maintenance calculation] made as a result of the direction.

Reviews and departure directions

6. Regulations may make provision—
(a) with respect to cases in which a child support officer is conducting a review of a maintenance assessment [maintenance calculation] which was made as a result of a departure direction;
(b) with respect to cases in which a departure direction is made at a time when a child support officer is conducting a review.

Subsequent departure directions

7.—(1) Regulations may make provision with respect to any departure application made with respect to a maintenance assessment [maintenance calculation] which was made as a result of a departure direction.

(2) The regulations may, in particular, provide for the application to be considered by reference to the maintenance assessment [maintenance calculation] which would have been made had the departure direction not been given.

Joint consideration of departure applications and appeals

8.—(1) *Regulations may provide for two or more departure applications with respect to the same current assessment [calculation] to be considered together.*

(2) *A child support appeal tribunal [an appeal tribunal] considering—*

(a) *a departure application referred to it under section 28D(1)(b), or*

(b) *an appeal under section 28H,*

may consider it at the same time as hearing an appeal under section 20 in respect of the current assessment [calculation], if it considers that to be appropriate.

Child support appeal tribunals [appeals tribunal]

9.—(1) *Regulations may provide that, in prescribed circumstances, where—*

(a) *a departure application is referred to a child support appeal tribunal [an appeal tribunal] under section 28D(1)(b), or*

(b) *an appeal is brought under section 28H,*

the application or appeal may be dealt with by a tribunal constituted by the chairman sitting alone.

(2) *Sub-paragraph (1) does not apply in relation to any appeal which is being heard together with an appeal under section 20.*

Current assessments [calculations] which are replaced by fresh assessments [calculations]

10. *Regulations may make provision as to the circumstances in which prescribed references in this Act to a current assessment [calculation] are to have effect as if they were references to any later maintenance assessment [maintenance calculation] made with respect to the same persons as the current assessment [calculation].]*

Note. This Schedule inserted by Child Support Act 1995, s 1(2), Sch 1, as from 14 October 1996 for the purpose of making regulations hereunder, and as from 2 December 1996 otherwise. In paras 4–8, 10 words 'maintenance calculation', 'calculation' and 'calculations' in square brackets in each place they occur substituted for words 'maintenance assessment', 'assessment' and 'assessments' respectively by the Child Support, Pensions and Social Security Act 2000, s 1(2), as from (in relation to certain cases): 3 March 2003 (SI 2003 No 192); for remaining purposes: to be appointed. In para 1 definition 'review' repealed by the Social Security Act 1998, s 86, Sch 7, para 53(1), Sch 8, as from 1 June 1999 (SI 1999 No 1510). In para 2(b) words 'an appeal tribunal' in square brackets substituted for words 'a child support appeal tribunal', and in para 2(c) words 'a decision ... be made' in square brackets substituted for words 'a departure ... dealt with', by the Social Security Act 1998, s 86(1), Sch 7, para 53(2), as from 1 June 1999 (SI 1999 No 1510). In para 4(1) words 'a child support officer' repealed and para 6 repealed, by the Social Security Act 1998, s 86, Sch 7, para 53(3), (4), Sch 8, as from 1 June 1999 (SI 1999 No 1510). In para 8 words 'An appeal tribunal' in square brackets substituted for words 'A child support appeal tribunal', in para 9 heading words 'Appeal tribunals' substituted for words 'Child Support appeal tribunal' and in para 9(1) words 'an appeal tribunal' in square brackets substituted for words 'a child support appeal tribunal', by the Social Security Act 1998, s 86(1), Sch 7, para 53(6), as from 1 June 1999 (SI 1999 No 1510).

[SCHEDULE 4A   Section 28A

APPLICATIONS FOR A VARIATION

Interpretation

1. In this Schedule, 'regulations' means regulations made by the Secretary of State.

Applications for a variation

2. Regulations may make provision—

(a) as to the procedure to be followed in considering an application for a variation;

(b) as to the procedure to be followed when an application for a variation is referred

to an appeal tribunal under section 28D(1)(b).

Completion of preliminary consideration

3. Regulations may provide for determining when the preliminary consideration of an application for a variation is to be taken to have been completed.

Information

4. If any information which is required (by regulations under this Act) to be furnished to the Secretary of State in connection with an application for a variation has not been furnished within such period as may be prescribed, the Secretary of State may nevertheless proceed to consider the application.

Joint consideration of applications for a variation and appeals

5.—(1) Regulations may provide for two or more applications for a variation with respect to the same application for a maintenance calculation to be considered together.

(2) In sub-paragraph (1), the reference to an application for a maintenance calculation includes an application treated as having been made under section 6.

(3) An appeal tribunal considering an application for a variation under section 28D(1)(b) may consider it at the same time as an appeal under section 20 in connection with an interim maintenance decision, if it considers that to be appropriate.]

Note. Schedule 4A above substituted for Sch 4A in italics by the Child Support, Pensions and Social Security Act 2000, s 6(1), Sch 2, Pt 1, (for certain purposes): 10 November 2000 (SI 2000 No 2994); as from (in relation to certain cases): 3 March 2003 (SI 2003 No 192); for remaining purposes: to be appointed.

[SCHEDULE 4B   Section 6(2)

DEPARTURE DIRECTIONS: THE CASES AND CONTROLS

PART I   THE CASES

General

1.—*(1) The cases in which a departure direction may be given are those set out in this Part of this Schedule or in regulations made under this Part.*

(2) In this Schedule 'applicant' means the person whose application for a departure direction is being considered.

Special expenses

2.—*(1) A departure direction may be given with respect to special expenses of the applicant which were not, and could not have been, taken into account in determining the current assessment [calculation] in accordance with the provisions of, or made under, Part I of Schedule 1.*

(2) In this paragraph 'special expenses' means the whole, or any prescribed part, of expenses which fall within a prescribed description of expenses.

(3) In prescribing descriptions of expenses for the purposes of this paragraph, the Secretary of State may, in particular, make provision with respect to—

(a) costs incurred in travelling to work;

(b) costs incurred by an absent parent [a non-resident parent] in maintaining contact with the child, or with any of the children, with respect to whom he is liable to pay child support maintenance under the current assessment [calculation];

(c) costs attributable to a long-term illness or disability of the applicant or of a dependant of the applicant;

(d) debts incurred, before the absent parent [non-resident parent] became an absent
parent [a non-resident parent] in relation to a child with respect to whom the current
assessment [calculation] was made—
    (i) for the joint benefit of both parents;
    (ii) for the benefit of any child with respect to whom the current assessment
    [calculation] was made; or
    (iii) for the benefit of any other child falling within a prescribed category;
(e) pre-1993 financial commitments from which it is impossible for the parent concerned
to withdraw or from which it would be unreasonable to expect that parent to have to
withdraw;
(f) costs incurred by a parent in supporting a child who is not his child but who is part
of his family.
(4) For the purposes of sub-paragraph (3)(c)—
(a) the question whether one person is a dependant of another shall be determined in
accordance with regulations made by the Secretary of State;
(b) 'disability' and 'illness' have such meaning as may be prescribed; and
(c) the question whether an illness or disability is long-term shall be determined in
accordance with regulations made by the Secretary of State.
(5) For the purposes of sub-paragraph (3)(e), 'pre-1993 financial commitments' means
financial commitments of a prescribed kind entered into before 5th April 1993 in any case
where—
(a) a court order of a prescribed kind was in force with respect to the absent parent [non-
resident parent] and the person with care concerned at the time when they were entered
into; or
(b) an agreement between them of a prescribed kind was in force at that time.
(6) For the purposes of sub-paragraph (3)(f), a child who is not the child of a particular
person is a part of that person's family in such circumstances as may be prescribed.

Property or capital transfers

3.—(1) A departure direction may be given if—
(a) before 5th April 1993—
    (i) a court order of a prescribed kind was in force with respect to the absent parent
    [non-resident parent] and either the person with care with respect to whom the
    current assessment [calculation] was made or the child, or any of the children,
    with respect to whom that assessment [calculation] was made, or
    (ii) an agreement of a prescribed kind between the absent parent [non-resident
    parent] and any of those persons was in force;
(b) in consequence of one or more transfers of property of a prescribed kind—
    (i) the amount payable by the absent parent [non-resident parent] by way of
    maintenance was less than would have been the case had that transfer or those
    transfers not been made; or
    (ii) no amount was payable by the absent parent [non-resident parent] by way of
    maintenance; and
(c) the effect of that transfer, or those transfers, is not properly reflected in the current
assessment [calculation].
(2) For the purposes of sub-paragraph (1)(b), 'maintenance' means periodical payments of
maintenance made (otherwise than under this Act) with respect to the child, or any of the
children, with respect to whom the current assessment [calculation] was made.
(3) For the purposes of sub-paragraph (1)(c), the question whether the effect of one or more
transfers of property is properly reflected in the current assessment [calculation] shall be
determined in accordance with regulations made by the Secretary of State.
4.—(1) A departure direction may be given if—
(a) before 5th April 1993—
    (i) a court order of a prescribed kind was in force with respect to the absent parent

[non-resident parent] and either the person with care with respect to whom the current assessment [calculation] was made or the child, or any of the children, with respect to whom that assessment [calculation] was made, or

   (ii) an agreement of a prescribed kind between the absent parent [non-resident parent] and any of those persons was in force;

(b) in pursuance of the court order or agreement, the absent parent has made one or more transfers of property of a prescribed kind;

(c) the amount payable by the absent parent [non-resident parent] by way of maintenance was not reduced as a result of that transfer or those transfers;

(d) the amount payable by the absent parent [non-resident parent] by way of child support maintenance under the current assessment [calculation] has been reduced as a result of that transfer or those transfers, in accordance with provisions of or made under this Act; and

(e) it is nevertheless inappropriate, having regard to the purposes for which the transfer or transfers was or were made, for that reduction to have been made.

(2) For the purposes of sub-paragraph (1)(c), 'maintenance' means periodical payments of maintenance made (otherwise than under this Act) with respect to the child, or any of the children, with respect to whom the current assessment [calculation] was made.

Additional cases

5.—(1) The Secretary of State may by regulations prescribe other cases in which a departure direction may be given.

(2) Regulations under this paragraph may, for example, make provision with respect to cases where—

(a) assets which do not produce income are capable of producing income;

(b) a person's life-style is inconsistent with the level of his income;

(c) housing costs are unreasonably high;

(d) housing costs are in part attributable to housing persons whose circumstances are such as to justify disregarding a part of those costs;

(e) travel costs are unreasonably high; or

(f) travel costs should be disregarded.

PART II   REGULATORY CONTROLS

6.—(1) The Secretary of State may by regulations make provision with respect to the directions which may be given in a departure direction.

(2) No directions may be given other than those which are permitted by the regulations.

(3) Regulations under this paragraph may, in particular, make provision for a departure direction to require—

(a) the substitution, for any formula set out in Part I of Schedule 1, of such other formula as may be prescribed;

(b) any prescribed amount by reference to which any calculation is to be made in fixing the amount of child support maintenance to be increased or reduced in accordance with the regulations;

(c) the substitution, for any provision in accordance with which any such calculation is to be made, of such other provision as may be prescribed.

(4) Regulations may limit the extent to which the amount of the child support maintenance fixed by a maintenance assessment [maintenance calculation] made as a result of a departure direction may differ from the amount of the child support maintenance which would be fixed by a maintenance assessment [maintenance calcualtion] made otherwise than as a result of the direction.

(5) Regulations may provide for the amount of any special expenses to be taken into account in a case falling within paragraph 2, for the purposes of a departure direction, not to exceed such amount as may be prescribed or as may be determined in accordance with the regulations.

(6) No departure direction may be given so as to have the effect of denying to an absent parent [non-resident parent] the protection of paragraph 6 of Schedule 1.

(7) Sub-paragraph (6) does not prevent the modification of the provisions of, or made under, paragraph 6 of Schedule 1 to the extent permitted by regulations under this paragraph.

(8) Any regulations under this paragraph may make different provision with respect to different levels of income.]

Note. This Schedule inserted by Child Support Act 1995, s 6(2), Sch 2, as from 14 October 1996 for the purpose of making regulations hereunder, and as from 2 December 1996 otherwise. In paras 2–4, 6 words 'calculation', 'a non-resident parent', 'non-resident parent' and 'maintenance calculation' in square brackets substituted for words 'assessment', 'an absent parent', 'absent parent' and 'maintenance assessment' respectively by the Child Support, Pensions and Social Security Act 2000, ss 1(2), 26, Sch 3, para 11(1), (2).

[SCHEDULE 4B   Section 28F

APPLICATION FOR A VARIATION: THE CASES AND CONTROLS

PART I

THE CASES

[General

1.—(1) The cases in which a variation may be agreed are those set out in this Part of this Schedule or in regulations made under this Part.

(2) In this Schedule 'applicant' means the person whose application for a variation is being considered.

Special expenses

2.—(1) A variation applied for by a non-resident parent may be agreed with respect to his special expenses.

(2) In this paragraph 'special expenses' means the whole, or any amount above a prescribed amount, or any prescribed part, of expenses which fall within a prescribed description of expenses.

(3) In prescribing descriptions of expenses for the purposes of this paragraph, the Secretary of State may, in particular, make provision with respect to—

(a) costs incurred by a non-resident parent in maintaining contact with the child, or with any of the children, with respect to whom the application for a maintenance calculation has been made (or treated as made);

(b) costs attributable to a long-term illness or disability of a relevant other child (within the meaning of paragraph 10C(2) of Schedule 1);

(c) debts of a prescribed description incurred, before the non-resident parent became a non-resident parent in relation to a child with respect to whom the maintenance calculation has been applied for (or treated as having been applied for)—

(i) for the joint benefit of both parents;

(ii) for the benefit of any such child; or

(iii) for the benefit of any other child falling within a prescribed category;

(d) boarding school fees for a child in relation to whom the application for a maintenance calculation has been made (or treated as made);

(e) the cost to the non-resident parent of making payments in relation to a mortgage on the home he and the person with care shared, if he no longer has an interest in it, and she and a child in relation to whom the application for a maintenance calculation has been made (or treated as made) still live there.

(4) For the purposes of sub-paragraph (3)(b)—

(a) 'disability' and 'illness' have such meaning as may be prescribed; and

(b) the question whether an illness or disability is long-term shall be determined in accordance with regulations made by the Secretary of State.

(5) For the purposes of sub-paragraph (3)(d), the Secretary of State may prescribe—

(a) the meaning of 'boarding school fees'; and
(b) components of such fees (whether or not itemised as such) which are, or are not, to be taken into account,

and may provide for estimating any such component.

Property or capital transfers

3.—(1) A variation may be agreed in the circumstances set out in sub-paragraph (2) if before 5th April 1993—

(a) a court order of a prescribed kind was in force with respect to the non-resident parent and either the person with care with respect to the application for the maintenance calculation or the child, or any of the children, with respect to whom that application was made; or
(b) an agreement of a prescribed kind between the non-resident parent and any of those persons was in force.

(2) The circumstances are that in consequence of one or more transfers of property of a prescribed kind and exceeding (singly or in aggregate) a prescribed minimum value—

(a) the amount payable by the non-resident parent by way of maintenance was less than would have been the case had that transfer or those transfers not been made; or
(b) no amount was payable by the non-resident parent by way of maintenance.

(3) For the purposes of sub-paragraph (2), 'maintenance' means periodical payments of maintenance made (otherwise than under this Act) with respect to the child, or any of the children, with respect to whom the application for a maintenance calculation has been made.

Additional cases

4.—(1) The Secretary of State may by regulations prescribe other cases in which a variation may be agreed.

(2) Regulations under this paragraph may, for example, make provision with respect to cases where—

(a) the non-resident parent has assets which exceed a prescribed value;
(b) a person's lifestyle is inconsistent with his income for the purposes of a calculation made under Part I of Schedule 1;
(c) a person has income which is not taken into account in such a calculation;
(d) a person has unreasonably reduced the income which is taken into account in such a calculation.

PART II

REGULATORY CONTROLS

5.—(1) The Secretary of State may by regulations make provision with respect to the variations from the usual rules for calculating maintenance which may be allowed when a variation is agreed.

(2) No variations may be made other than those which are permitted by the regulations.

(3) Regulations under this paragraph may, in particular, make provision for a variation to result in—

(a) a person's being treated as having more, or less, income than would be taken into account without the variation in a calculation under Part I of Schedule 1;

(b) a person's being treated as liable to pay a higher, or a lower, amount of child support maintenance than would result without the variation from a calculation under that Part.

(4) Regulations may provide for the amount of any special expenses to be taken into account in a case falling within paragraph 2, for the purposes of a variation, not to exceed such amount as may be prescribed or as may be determined in accordance with the regulations.

(5) Any regulations under this paragraph may in particular make different provision with respect to different levels of income.

6.—The Secretary of State may by regulations provide for the application, in connection with child support maintenance payable following a variation, of paragraph 7(2) to (7) of Schedule 1 (subject to any prescribed modifications).]

Note. Schedule 4B above substituted for Sch 4B in italics by the Child Support, Pensions and Social Security Act 2000, s 6(2), Sch 2, Pt II, as from (for certain purposes): 10 November 2000 (SI 2000 No 2994); (in relation to certain cases): 3 March 2003 (SI 2003 No 192); for remaining purposes: to be appointed.

[SCHEDULE 4C   Section 28H

DECISIONS AND APPEALS: DEPARTURE DIRECTIONS AND REDUCED BENEFIT DIRECTIONS ETC

Revision of decisions

1. Section 16 shall apply in relation to—
 (a) any decision of the Secretary of State with respect to a departure direction, a reduced benefit direction or a person's liability under section 43;
 (b) any decision of the Secretary of State under section 17 as extended by paragraph 2; and
 (c) any decision of an appeal tribunal on a referral under section 28D(1)(b),
as it applies in relation to any decision of the Secretary of State under section 11, 12 or 17.

Decisions superseding earlier decisions

2.—(1) Section 17 shall apply in relation to—
 (a) any decision of the Secretary of State with respect to a departure direction, a reduced benefit direction or a person's liability under section 43;
 (b) any decision of the Secretary of State under section 17 as extended by this sub-paragraph; and
 (c) any decision of an appeal tribunal on a referral under section 28D(1)(b),
whether as originally made or as revised under section 16 as extended by paragraph 1, as it applies in relation to any decision of the Secretary of State under section 11, 12 or 17, whether as originally made or as revised under section 16.

(2) Section 17 shall apply in relation to any decision of an appeal tribunal under section 20 as extended by paragraph 3 as it applies in relation to any decision of an appeal tribunal under section 20.

Appeals to appeal tribunals

3.—(1) Subject to sub-paragraphs (2) and (3), section 20 shall apply—
 (a) in relation to a qualifying person who is aggrieved by any decision of the Secretary of State with respect to a departure direction; and
 (b) in relation to any person who is aggrieved by a decision of the Secretary of State—
  (i) with respect to a reduced benefit direction; or
  (ii) with respect to a person's liability under section 43,
as it applies in relation to a person whose application for a maintenance assessment [maintenance calculation] is refused or to such a person as is mentioned in subsection (2) of section 20.

(2) On an appeal under section 20 as extended by sub-paragraph (1)(a), the appeal tribunal shall—

(a) consider the matter—
    (i) as if it were exercising the powers of the Secretary of State in relation to the application in question; and
    (ii) as if it were subject to the duties imposed on him in relation to that application;

(b) have regard to any representations made to it by the Secretary of State; and

(c) confirm the decision or replace it with such decision as the tribunal considers appropriate.

(3) No appeal shall lie under section 20 as extended by sub-paragraph (1)(b)(i) unless the amount of the person's benefit is reduced in accordance with the reduced benefit direction; and the time within which such an appeal may be brought shall run from the date of the notification of the reduction.

(4) In sub-paragraph (1) 'qualifying person' means—

(a) the person with care, or absent parent [non-resident parent], with respect to whom the current assessment [calculation] was made; or

(b) where the application for the current assessment [calculation] was made under section 7, either of those persons or the child concerned.

Decisions and appeals dependent on other cases

4.—(1) Section 28ZA shall also apply where—

(a) a decision falls to be made—
    (i) with respect to a departure direction, a reduced benefit direction or a person's liability under section 43, by the Secretary of State; or .
    (ii) with respect to a departure direction, by an appeal tribunal on a referral under section 28D(1)(b); and

(b) an appeal is pending against a decision given with respect to a different direction by a Child Support Commissioner or a court.

(2) Section 28ZA as it applies by virtue of sub-paragraph (1) shall have effect as if the reference in subsection (3) to section 16 were a reference to that section as extended by paragraph 1.

(3) Section 28ZA as it applies by virtue of sub-paragraph (1)(a)(ii) shall have effect as if—

(a) in subsection (2)—
    (i) for the words 'the Secretary of State' there were substituted the words 'the appeal tribunal'; and
    (ii) for the word 'he', in both places where it occurs, there were substituted the word 'it'; and

(b) in subsection (3)—
    (i) for the words 'the Secretary of State' there were substituted the words 'the appeal tribunal';
    (ii) for the word 'he' there were substituted the words 'the Secretary of State'; and
    (iii) for the word 'his' there were substituted the words 'the tribunal's'.

5.—(1) Section 28ZB shall also apply where—

(a) an appeal is made to an appeal tribunal under section 20 as extended by paragraph 3; and

(b) an appeal is pending against a decision given in a different case by a Child Support Commissioner or a court.

(2) Section 28ZB as it applies by virtue of sub-paragraph (1) shall have effect as if any reference to section 16 or section 17 were a reference to that section as extended by paragraph 1 or, as the case may be, paragraph 2.

Cases of error

6.—(1) Subject to sub-paragraph (2) below, section 28ZC shall also apply where—

    (a) the effect of the determination, whenever made, of an appeal to a Child Support Commissioner or the court ('the relevant determination') is that the adjudicating authority's decision out of which the appeal arose was erroneous in point of law; and

    (b) after the date of the relevant determination a decision falls to be made by the Secretary of State in accordance with that determination (or would, apart from this paragraph, fall to be so made)—

        (i) in relation to an application for a departure direction (made after the commencement date);

        (ii) as to whether to revise, under section 16 as extended by paragraph 1, a decision (made after the commencement date) in relation to a departure direction, a reduced benefit direction or a person's liability under section 43; or

        (iii) on an application made under section 17 as extended by paragraph 2 before the date of the relevant determination (but after the commencement date) for a decision in relation to a departure direction, a reduced benefit direction or a person's liability under section 43 to be superseded.

    (2) Section 28ZC shall not apply where the decision of the Secretary of State mentioned in sub-paragraph (1)(b) above—

    (a) is one which, but for section 28ZA(2)(a) as it applies by virtue of paragraph 4(1), would have been made before the date of the relevant determination; or

    (b) is one made in pursuance of section 28ZB(3) or (5) as it applies by virtue of paragraph 5(1).

    (3) Section 28ZC as it applies by virtue of sub-paragraph (1) shall have effect as if in subsection (4), in the definition of 'adjudicating authority', at the end there were inserted the words 'or, in the case of a decision made on a referral under section 28D(1)(b), an appeal tribunal'.

    (4) In this paragraph 'adjudicating authority', 'the commencement date' and 'the court' have the same meanings as in section 28ZC.]

Note. This Schedule inserted by the Social Security Act 1998, s 86(1), Sch 7, para 54, as from 1 June 1999 (SI 1999 No 1510). In para 3 words 'maintenance calculation', 'non-resident parent' and 'calculation' in square brackets substituted for words 'maintenance assessment', 'absent parent' and 'assessment' respectively by the Child Support, Pensions and Social Security Act 2000, ss 1 (2), 26, Sch 3, para 11(1), (2), as from (in relation to certain cases): 3 March 2003 (SI 2003 No 192); for remaining purposes: to be appointed.

SCHEDULE 5   Section 58(13)

CONSEQUENTIAL AMENDMENTS

Tribunals and Inquiries Act 1971 (c 62)

1.—(1) In section 7(3) of the Tribunals and Inquiries Act 1971 (chairmen of certain tribunals to be drawn from panels) after 'paragraph' there shall be inserted '4A'.

    (2) In Schedule 1 to that Act (tribunals under the general supervision of the Council on Tribunals) the following entry shall be inserted at the appropriate place—

'Child support maintenance

    4A.—(a) The child support appeal tribunals established under section 21 of the Child Support Act 1991.

    (b) A Child Support Commissioner appointed under section 22 of the Child Support Act 1991 and any tribunal presided over by such a Commissioner.'

Note. Para 1 repealed by Tribunals and Inquiries Act 1992, s 18(2), Sch 4, Part I, as from 1 October 1992.

Northern Ireland Constitution Act 1973 (c 36)

2. *In paragraph 9 of Schedule 2 to the Northern Ireland Constitution Act 1973 (certain judicial appointments to be an excepted matter), after the words 'for Northern Ireland', where they first occur, there shall be inserted 'the Chief and other Child Support Commissioners for Northern Ireland'.*

Note. Para 2 repealed by the Northern Ireland Act 1998, s 100(2), Sch 15, as from 2 December 1999 (SI 1999 No 3209).

House of Commons Disqualification Act 1975 (c 24)

3.—(1) The House of Commons Disqualification Act 1975 shall be amended as follows.

(2) In Part I [of Schedule 1] (disqualifying judicial offices), the following entries shall be inserted at the appropriate places—

'Chief or other Chid Support Commissioner (excluding a person appointed under paragraph 4 of Schedule 4 to the Child Support Act 1991).'

'Chief or other Child Support Commissioner for Northern Ireland (excluding a person appointed under paragraph 4 of Schedule 4 to the Child Support Act 1991).'

(3) In Part III [of Schedule 1] (other disqualifying offices), the following entry shall be inserted at the appropriate place—

'Regional or other full-time chairman of a child support appeal tribunal established under section 21 of the Child Support Act 1991'.

Note. Words in square brackets inserted by Child Support Act 1995, s 30(5), Sch 3, para 19(1), (2), as from 4 September 1995. Sub-para (3) repealed by the Social Security Act 1998, s 86(2), Sch 8, as from 1 June 1999 (SI 1999 No 1510).

Northern Ireland Assembly Disqualification Act 1975 (c 25)

4.—(1) In Part I of [Schedule 1 to] the Northern Ireland Assembly Disqualification Act 1975 (disqualifying judicial offices), the following entries shall be inserted at the appropriate places—

'Chief or other Child Support Commissioner (excluding a person appointed under paragraph 4 of Schedule 4 to the Child Support Act 1991).'

'Chief or other Child Support Commissioner for Northern Ireland (excluding a person appointed under paragraph 4 of Schedule 4 to the Child Support Act 1991).'

Note. Words in square brackets inserted by Child Support Act 1995, s 30(5), Sch 3, para 19(3), as from 4 September 1995.

5, 6. *(Apply to Scotland only.)*

Insolvency Act 1986 (c 45)

7. In section 281(5)(b) of the Insolvency Act 1986 (effect of discharge of bankrupt), after 'family proceedings' there shall be inserted 'or under a maintenance assessment made under the Child Support Act 1991'.

8. *(Applies to Scotland only.)*

SOCIAL SECURITY CONTRIBUTIONS AND BENEFITS ACT 1992

(1992 c 4)

An Act to consolidate certain enactments relating to social security contributions and benefits with amendments to give effect to recommendations of the Law Commission and the Scottish Law Commission.   [13 February 1992]

*   *   *   *   *

PART IX

CHILD BENEFIT

141. Child benefit.   A person who is responsible for one or more children in any week shall be entitled, subject to the provisions of this Part of this Act, to a benefit (to be known as 'child benefit') for that week in respect of the child or each of the children for whom he is responsible.

142. Meaning of 'child'—(1) For the purposes of this Part of this Act a person shall be treated as a child for any week in which—

(a) he is under the age of 16; or

(b) he is under the age of 18 and not receiving full-time education and prescribed conditions are satisfied in relation to him; or

(c) he is under the age of 19 and receiving full-time education either by attendance at a recognised educational establishment or, if the education is recognised by the Secretary of State, elsewhere.

(2) The Secretary of State may recognise education provided otherwise than at a recognised educational establishment for a person who, in the opinion of the Secretary of State, could reasonably be expected to attend such an establishment only if the Secretary of State is satisfied that education was being so provided for that person immediately before he attained the age of 16.

(3) Regulations may prescribe the circumstances in which education is or is not to be treated for the purposes of this Part of this Act as full-time.

(4) In determining for the purposes of paragraph (c) of subsection (1) above whether a person is receiving full-time education as mentioned in that paragraph, no account shall be taken of such interruptions as may be prescribed.

(5) Regulations may provide that a person who in any week ceases to fall within subsection (1) above shall be treated as continuing to do so for a prescribed period; but no person shall by virtue of any such regulations be treated as continuing to fall within that subsection for any week after that in which he attains the age of 19.

143. Meaning of 'person responsible for child'—(1) For the purposes of this Part of this Act a person shall be treated as responsible for a child in any week if—

(a) he has the child living with him in that week; or

(b) he is contributing to the cost of providing for the child at a weekly rate which is not less than the weekly rate of child benefit payable in respect of the child for that week.

(2) Where a person has had a child living with him at some time before a particular week he shall be treated for the purposes of this section as having the child living with him in that week notwithstanding their absence from one another unless, in the 16 weeks preceding that week, they were absent from one another for more than 56 days not counting any day which is to be disregarded under subsection (3) below.

(3) Subject to subsection (4) below, a day of absence shall be disregarded for the purposes of subsection (2) above if it is due solely to the child's—

(a) receiving full-time education by attendance at a recognised educational establishment;

(b) undergoing medical or other treatment as an in-patient in a hospital, or similar institution; or

(c) being, in such circumstances as may be prescribed, in residential accommodation pursuant to arrangements made under—

(i)   section 21 of the National Assistance Act 1948;

(ii) the Children Act 1989; or

(iii) the Social Work (Scotland) Act 1968.

Note. By virtue of the Social Security (Consequential Provisions) Act 1992, s 6, Sch 4, Part I, paras 1, 5, since no date has been appointed as the date on which the National Health

Service and Community Care Act 1990, s 66(1), Sch 9, para 15 is to come into force, until the appointed day, sub-paras (c)(i)–(iii) are substituted as follows, as from 1 July 1992:

'(i)   paragraph 2 of Schedule 8 to the National Health Service Act 1977;

(ii)   the Children act 1989; or

(iii)   section 37 of the National Health Service (Scotland) Act 1978.'.

Sub-para (c)(iii) is further substituted by sub-paras (iii)–(vii) by the Child Support, Pensions and Social Security Act 2000, s 72, as from 9 October 2000, as follows:

'(iii)   the Social Work (Scotland) Act 1968;

(iv)   the National Health Service (Scotland) Act 1978;

(v)   the Education (Scotland) Act 1980;

(vi)   the Mental Health (Scotland) Act 1984; or

(vii)   the Children (Scotland) Act 1995.'

(4)   The number of days that may be disregarded by virtue of subsection (3)(b) or (c) above in the case of any child shall not exceed such number as may be prescribed unless the person claiming to be responsible for the child regularly incurs expenditure in respect of the child.

(5)   Regulations may prescribe the circumstances in which a person is or is not to be treated—

(a)   as contributing to the cost of providing for a child as required by subsection (1)(b) above; or

(b)   as regularly incurring expenditure in respect of a child as required by subsection (4) above;

and such regulations may in particular make provision whereby a contribution made or expenditure incurred by two or more persons is to be treated as made or incurred by one of them or whereby a contribution made or expenditure incurred by one of two spouses residing together is to be treated as made or incurred by the other.

144. Exclusions and priority—(1) Regulations may provide that child benefit shall not be payable by virtue—

(a)   of paragraph (b) of section 142(1) above and regulations made under that paragraph; or

(b)   of paragraph (c) of that subsection,

in such cases as may be prescribed.

(2)   Schedule 9 to this Act shall have effect for excluding entitlement to child benefit in other cases.

(3)   Where, apart from this subsection, two or more persons would be entitled to child benefit in respect of the same child for the same week, one of them only shall be entitled; and the question which of them is entitled shall be determined in accordance with Schedule 10 to this Act.

145. Rate of child benefit—(1) Child benefit shall be payable at such weekly rate as may be prescribed.

(2)   Different rates may be prescribed in relation to different cases, whether by reference to the age of the child in respect of whom the benefit is payable or otherwise.

(3)   The power to prescribe different rates under subsection (2) above shall be exercised so as to bring different rates into force on such day as the Secretary of State may by order specify.

(4)   No rate prescribed in place of a rate previously in force shall be lower than the rate that it replaces.

(5)   *Regulations under this section shall be made by the Secretary of State in conjunction with the Treasury.*

(6)   An order under subsection (3) above may be varied or revoked at any time before the date specified thereby.

(7)   An order under that subsection shall be laid before Parliament after being made.

Note. Sub-s (5) repealed by the Tax Credits Act 2002, s 60, Sch 6, as from 1 April 2003 (SI 2003 No 392).

[145A. Entitlement after death of child—(1) If a child dies and a person is entitled to child benefit in respect of him for the week in which his death occurs, that person shall be entitled to child benefit in respect of the child for a prescribed period following that week.

(2) If the person entitled to child benefit under subsection (1) dies before the end of that prescribed period and, at the time of his death, was—

(a) a member of a married couple and living with the person to whom he was married, or

(b) a member of an unmarried couple,

that other member of the married couple or unmarried couple shall be entitled to child benefit for the period for which the dead person would have been entitled to child benefit under subsection (1) above but for his death.

(3) If a child dies before the end of the week in which he is born, subsections (1) and (2) apply in his case as if references to the person entitled to child benefit in respect of a child for the week in which his death occurs were to the person who would have been so entitled if the child had been alive at the beginning of that week (and if any conditions which were satisfied, and any facts which existed, at the time of his death were satisfied or existed then).

(4) Where a person is entitled to child benefit in respect of a child under this section, section 77 applies with the omission of subsections (4) to (6).

(5) In this section—

'married couple' means a man and a woman who are married to each other and are neither—

(a) separated under a court order, nor

(b) separated in circumstances in which the separation is likely to be permanent, and

'unmarried couple' means a man and a woman who are not a married couple but are living together as husband and wife.]

Note. Inserted by the Tax Credits Act 2002, s 55(1)(a), (2), as from 26 February 2003 (SI 2003 No 392), 1 April 2003 (SI 2003 No 392) and 7 April 2003 (SI 2003 No 392).

146. Persons outside Great Britain—*(1) Regulations may modify the provisions of this Part of this Act in their application to persons who are or have been outside Great Britain at any prescribed time or in any prescribed circumstances.*

(2) Subject to any regulations under subsection (1) above, no child benefit shall be payable in respect of a child for any week unless—

(a) he is in Great Britain in that week; and

(b) either he or at least one of his parents has been in Great Britain for more than 182 days in the 52 weeks preceding that week.

(3) Subject to any regulations under subsection (1) above, no person shall be entitled to child benefit for any week unless—

(a) he is in Great Britain in that week; and

(b) he has been in Great Britain for more than 182 days in the 52 weeks preceding that week.

[146. Presence in Great Britain—(1) No child benefit shall be payable in respect of a child for a week unless he is in Great Britain in that week.

(2) No person shall be entitled to child benefit for a week unless he is in Great Britain in that week.

(3) Circumstances may be prescribed in which a child or other person is to be treated for the purposes of this section as being, or as not being, in Great Britain.]

Note. This section substituted by the Tax Credits Act 2002, s 56(1), as from 26 February 2003 (SI 2003 No 392), 1 April 2003 (SI 2003 No 392) and 7 April 2003 (SI 2003 No 392).

[146A. Persons subject to immigration control. *No person subject to immigration control within the meaning of the Asylum and Immigration Act 1996 shall be entitled to child benefit for any week unless he satisfies certain conditions.]*

Note. This section inserted by Asylum and Immigration Act 1996, s 10, as from 19 August 1996 for the purpose of prescribing conditions, and as from 7 October 1996 otherwise. Repealed by the Immigration and Asylum Act 1999, s 169(1), (3), Sch 14, para 92, Sch 16, as from 3 April 2000 (SI 2000 No 464).

147. Interpretation of Part IX and supplementary provisions—(1) In this Part of this Act—

'prescribed' means prescribed by regulations;

'recognised educational establishment' means an establishment recognised by the Secretary of State as being, or as comparable to, a university, college or school;

'voluntary organisation' means a body, other than a public or local authority, the activities of which are carried on otherwise than for profit; and

'week' means a period of 7 days beginning with a Monday.

(2) Subject to any provision made by regulations, references in this Part of this Act to any condition being satisfied or any facts existing in a week shall be construed as references to the condition being satisfied or the facts existing at the beginning of that week.

(3) References in this Part of this Act to a parent, father or mother of a child shall be construed as including references to a step-parent, step-father or step-mother.

(4) Regulations may prescribe the circumstances in which persons are or are not to be treated for the purposes of this Part of this Act as residing together.

(5) Regulations may make provision as to the circumstances in which—

(*a*) *a marriage celebrated under a law which permits polygamy; or*

(*b*) *a marriage during the subsistence of which a party to it is at any time married to more than one person,*

is to be treated for the purposes of this Part of this Act as having, or not having, the consequences of a marriage celebrated under a law which does not permit polygamy.

[a marriage during the subsistence of which a party to it is at any time married to more than one person is to be treated for the purposes of this Part of this Act as having, or not having, the same consequences as any other marriage.]

(6) Nothing in this Part of this Act shall be construed as conferring a right to child benefit on any body corporate; but regulations may confer such a right on voluntary organisations and for that purpose may make such modifications as the Secretary of State thinks fit—

(a) of any provision of this Part of this Act; or

(b) of any provision of the Administration Act relating to child benefit.

Note. Words in square brackets in sub-s (5) substituted for words in italics by Private International Law (Miscellaneous Provisions) Act 1995, s 8(2), Schedule, para 4(1), (3), as from 8 January 1996.

*   *   *   *   *

177. Short title, commencement and extent—(1) This Act may be cited as the Social Security Contributions and Benefits Act 1992.

(2) This Act is to be read, where appropriate, with the Administration Act and the Consequential Provisions Act.

(3) The enactments consolidated by this Act are repealed, in consequence of the consolidation, by the Consequential Provisions Act.

(4) Except as provided in Schedule 4 to the Consequential Provisions Act, this Act shall come into force on 1st July 1992.

(5) The following provisions extend to Northern Ireland—

section 16 and Schedule 2;

section 116(2); and

this section.

(6) Except as provided by this section, this Act does not extend to Northern Ireland.

SOCIAL SECURITY ADMINISTRATION ACT 1992

(1992 c 5)

An Act to consolidate certain enactments relating to the administration of social security and related matters with amendments to give effect to recommendations of the Law Commission and the Scottish Law Commission. [13 February 1992]

* * * * *

PART I

CLAIMS FOR AND PAYMENTS AND GENERAL ADMINISTRATION OF BENEFIT

* * * * *

Child benefit

13. Necessity of application for child benefit—(1) Subject to the provisions of this Act, no person shall be entitled to child benefit unless he claims it in the manner, and within the time, prescribed in relation to child benefit by regulations under section 5 above.

[(1A) No person shall be entitled to child benefit unless sub-section (1B) below is satisfied in relation to him.

(1B) This subsection is satisfied in relation to a person if—

(a) his claim for child benefit is accompanied by—
  (i) a statement of his national insurance number and information or evidence establishing that that number has been allocated to him; or
  (ii) information or evidence enabling the national insurance number that has been allocated to him to be ascertained; or

(b) he makes an application for a national insurance number to be allocated to him which is accompanied by information or evidence enabling such a number to be so allocated.

(1C) Regulations may make provision disapplying subsection (1A) above in the case of—

(a) prescribed descriptions of persons making claims, or

(b) prescribed descriptions of children in respect of whom child benefit is claimed,

or in other prescribed circumstances.]

Note. Sub-ss (1A)–(1C) inserted by the Welfare Reform and Pensions Act 1999, s 69, as from 17 April 2000 for the purpose of making regulations and as from 15 May 2000 for remaining purposes (SI 2000 No 464).

(2) Except where regulations otherwise provide, no person shall be entitled to child benefit for any week on a claim made by him after that week if child benefit in respect of the same child has already been paid for that week to another person, whether or not that other person was entitled to it.

* * * * *

PART III

OVERPAYMENTS AND ADJUSTMENTS OF BENEFIT

* * * * *

Adjustment of child benefit

80. Child benefit—overlap with benefits under legislation of other member states. Regulations may provide for adjusting child benefit payable in respect of any child in respect of whom any benefit is payable under the legislation of any member State other than the United Kingdom.

* * * * *

PART XII

FINANCE

*   *   *   *   *

163. General financial arrangements—(1) There shall be paid out of the National Insurance Fund—
  (a) benefit under Part II of the Contributions and Benefits Act;
  (b) guardian's allowance;
  (c) Christmas bonus if the relevant qualifying benefit is payable out of that Fund;
  (d) any sum falling to be paid by or on behalf of the *Secretary of State* [Inland Revenue] under regulations relating to statutory sick pay or maternity pay; and
  (e) any expenses of the Secretary of State in making payments under section 85, 97 or 99 above to the extent that he estimates that those payments relate to sums paid into the National Insurance Fund.

Note. In sub-s (1)(d) words in square brackets substituted by the Social Security Contributions (Transfer of Functions, etc) Act 1999, s 1(1), Sch 1, para 29(a) as from 1 April 1999. Sub-s (1)(e) repealed by Social Security (Recovery of Benefits) Act 1997, s 33(1), Sch 3, para 6, Sch 4, as from 6 October 1997 (SI 1997 No 2085).

  (2) There shall be paid out of money provided by Parliament—
  (a) any administrative expenses of the Secretary of State or other government department in carrying into effect the Contributions and Benefits Act or this Act;
  [(aa) any administrative expenses of the Secretary of State in supplying information about benefits under Part II of that Act in accordance with regulations under section 23 of the Welfare Reform and Pensions Act 1999;]
  (b) benefit under Part III of *that Act* [the Contributions and Benefits Act], other than guardian's allowance;
  (c) benefit under Part V of that Act;
  (d) any sums payable by way of the following—
      (i) income support;
      (ii) *family credit* [*working families' tax credit*];
      (iii) *disability working allowance* [*disabled person's tax credit*];
      (iv) rate rebate subsidy;
      (v) rent rebate subsidy;
      (vi) rent allowance subsidy;
      (vii) *community charge benefit subsidy* [council tax benefit subsidy];
  (e) payments by the Secretary of State into the social fund under section 167(3) below;
  (f) child benefit;
  (g) Christmas bonus if the relevant qualifying benefit is payable out of such money;
  (h) any sums falling to be paid by the Secretary of State under or by virtue of this Act by way of travelling expenses;
  (i) any expenses of the Secretary of State in making payments under section 85, 97 or 99 above to the extent that he estimates that those payments relate to sums paid into the Consolidated Fund;
except in so far as they may be required by any enactment to be paid or borne in some other way.

Note. Sub-s (2)(aa) inserted and in sub-s (2)(b) words in square brackets substituted by the Welfare Reform and Pensions Act 1999, s 84(1), Sch 12, paras 23, 26, as from 1 December 2000 (SI 2000 No 1047). Sub-s (2)(d)(ii), (iii) substituted by the Tax Credits Act 1999, s 1, Sch 1, paras 1(a), (b), 3(f), as from 5 October 1999, and repealed by the Tax Credits Act 2002, s 60, Sch 6, as from 8 April 2003 (SI 2003 No 962). Words in square brackets in sub-s (2)(d)(vii) substituted for words in italics by Local Government Finance Act 1992, s 103,

Sch 9, para 22, as from 6 March 1992. Sub-s (2)(i) repealed by Social Security (Recovery of Benefits) Act 1997, s 33(1), Sch 3, para 6, Sch 4, as from 6 October 1997 (SI 1997 No 1085).

(3) The administrative expenses referred to in subsection (2)(a) above include those in connection with any inquiry *undertaken on behalf of the Secretary of State with a view to obtaining statistics relating to the operation of Parts I to VI and XI of the Contributions and Benefits Act* [undertaken—

(a)   on behalf of the Inland Revenue with a view to obtaining statistics relating to the operation of Part I of the Contributions and Benefits Act, and

(b)   on behalf of the Secretary of State with a view to obtaining statistics relating to the operation of Parts II to VI and XI of that Act.]

(4) Any sums required by a *secondary contributor* [any person] for the purpose of paying any secondary Class I contributions [, or any Class 1A [or 1B] contributions] which are payable by him in respect of an earner in consequence of the earner's employment in any office of which the emoluments are payable out of the Consolidated Fund shall be paid out of that Fund.

(5) Any expenditure in respect of the payment of interest or repayment supplements under or by virtue of paragraph 6 [or 7B] of Schedule 1 to the Contributions and Benefits Act or paragraph 6 of Schedule 2 to that Act shall be defrayed out of the National Insurance Fund in accordance with any directions given by the Treasury.

Note. In sub-s (3) words in square brackets substituted by the Social Securities (Transfer of Functions, etc) Act 1999, s 2, Sch 3, para 53, as from 1 April 1999. In sub-s (4) first words in square brackets substituted and second words in square brackets inserted by the Social Security Act 1998, s 66(1), with retrospective effect. In sub-s (4) words 'or 1B' and in sub-s (5) words 'or 7B' inserted by the Social Security Act 1998, s 86(1), Sch 7, para 100(1), as from 6 April 1999 (SI 1998 No 2209, SI 1999 No 526).

*   *   *   *   *

PART XVI

192. Short title, commencement and extent—(1) This Act may be cited as the Social Security Administration Act 1992.

(2) This Act is to be read, where appropriate, with the Contributions and Benefits Act and the Consequential Provisions Act.

(3) The enactments consolidated by this Act are repealed, in consequence of the consolidation, by the Consequential Provisions Act.

(4) Except as provided in Schedule 4 to the Consequential Provisions Act, this Act shall come into force on 1st July 1992.

(5) The following provisions extend to Northern Ireland—
section 24;
section 101;
section 170 (with Schedule 5);
[section 171 (with Schedule 6);]
section 177 (with Schedule 8); and
this section.

Note. First words in italics repealed by the Social Security Act 1998, s 86, Sch 7, para 112, Sch 8, as from 2 December 1999 (SI 1999 No 3209). Second words in italics repealed by Social Security (Recovery of Benefits) Act 1997, s 33(1), Sch 3, para 13, Sch 4, as from 6 October 1997 (SI 1997 No 1085). Words in square brackets inserted by the Northern Ireland Act 1998, s 89(a), as from 2 December 1999 (SI 1999 No 3209).

(6) Except as provided by this section, this Act does not extend to Northern Ireland.

TAXATION OF CHARGEABLE GAINS ACT 1992

(1992 c 12)

An Act to consolidate certain enactments relating to the taxation of chargeable gains.   [6 March 1992]

PART I

CAPITAL GAINS TAX AND CORPORATION TAX ON CHARGEABLE GAINS

General

1. The charge to tax—(1) Tax shall be charged in accordance with this Act in respect of capital gains, that is to say chargeable gains computed in accordance with this Act and accruing to a person on the disposal of assets.

(2) Companies shall be chargeable to corporation tax in respect of chargeable gains accruing to them in accordance with section 6 of the Taxes Act and the other provisions of the Corporation Tax Acts.

(3) Without prejudice to subsection (2), capital gains tax shall be charged for all years of assessment in accordance with the following provisions of this Act.

Capital gains tax

2. Persons and gains chargeable to capital gains tax, and allowable losses— (1) Subject to any exceptions provided by this Act, and without prejudice to sections 10 and 276, a person shall be chargeable to capital gains tax in respect of chargeable gains accruing to him in a year of assessment during any part of which he is resident in the United Kingdom, or during which he is ordinarily resident in the United Kingdom.

(2) Capital gains tax shall be charged on the total amount of chargeable gains accruing to the person chargeable in the year of assessment, after deducting—

  (a) any allowable losses accruing to that person in that year of assessment, and

  (b) so far as they have not been allowed as a deduction from chargeable gains accruing in any previous year of assessment, any allowable losses accruing to that person in any previous year of assessment (not earlier than the year 1965–66).

(3) Except as provided by section 62, an allowable loss accruing in a year of assessment shall not be allowable as a deduction from chargeable gains accruing in any earlier year of assessment, and relief shall not be given under this Act more than once in respect of any loss or part of a loss, and shall not be given under this Act if and so far as relief has been or may be given in respect of it under the Income Tax Acts.

[(4) Where any amount is treated by virtue of any of sections 77, 86, 87 and 89(2) (read, where applicable, with section 10A) as an amount of chargeable gains accruing to any person in any year of assessment—

  (a) that amount shall be disregarded for the purposes of subsection (2) above; and

  (b) the amount on which that person shall be charged to capital gains tax for that year (instead of being the amount given by that subsection) shall be the sum of the amounts specified in subsection (5) below.

(5) Those amounts are—

  (a) the amount which after—

      (i) making any deductions for which subsection (2) provides, and

      (ii) applying any reduction in respect of taper relief under section 2A,

     is the amount given for the year of assessment by the application of that subsection in accordance with subsection (4)(a) above; and

  (b) every amount which is treated by virtue of sections 77, 86, 87 and 89(2) (read, where applicable, with section 10A) as an amount of chargeable gains accruing to the person in question in that year.]

Note. Sub-ss (4), (5) inserted by the Finance At 1998, s 121(3), (4), Sch 21, paras 1, 2, with effect for the year 1998–99 and subsequent years of assessment.

[2A. Taper relief—(1) This section applies where, for any year of assessment—

  (a) there is, in any person's case, an excess of the total amount referred to in subsection (2) of section 2 over the amounts falling to be deducted from that amount in accordance with that subsection; and

(b) the excess is or includes an amount representing the whole or part of any chargeable gain that is eligible for taper relief.

(2) The amount on which capital gains tax is taken to be charged by virtue of section 2(2) shall be reduced to the amount computed by—

(a) applying taper relief to so much of every chargeable gain eligible for that relief as is represented in the excess;

(b) aggregating the results; and

(c) adding to the aggregate of the results so much of every chargeable gain not eligible for taper relief as is represented in the excess.

(3) Subject to the following provisions of this Act, a chargeable gain is eligible for taper relief if—

(a) it is a gain on the disposal of a business asset with a qualifying holding period of at least one year; or

(b) it is a gain on the disposal of a non-business asset with a qualifying holding period of at least three years.

(4) Where taper relief falls to be applied to the whole or any part of a gain on the disposal of a business or non-business asset, that relief shall be applied by multiplying the amount of that gain or part of a gain by the percentage given by the table it in subsection (5) below for the number of whole years in the qualifying holding period of that asset.

(5) That table is as follows—

Gains on disposals of business assets		Gains on disposals of non-business assets	
Number of whole years in qualifying holding period	Percentage of gain chargeable	Number of whole years in qualifying holding period	Percentage of gain chargeable
[1	87.5	–	–
2	75	–	–
3	50	3	95
4 or more	25]	4	90
		5	85
		6	80
		7	75
		8	70
		9	65
		10 or more	60

Note. Figures in square brackets substituted by the Finance Act 2000, s 66(1), (2), in relation to disposals on or after 6 April 2000.

(6) The extent to which the whole or any part of a gain on the disposal of a business or non-business asset is to be treated as represented in the excess mentioned in subsection (1) above shall be determined by treating deductions made in accordance with section 2(2)(a) and (b) as set against chargeable gains in such order as results in the largest reduction under this section of the amount charged to capital gains tax under section 2.

(7) Schedule A1 shall have effect for the purposes of this section.

(8) *Subject to paragraph 2(4) of that Schedule, references in this section to the qualifying holding period of an asset are references—*

(a) *except in the case of an asset falling within subsection (9) below, to the period after 5th April 1998 for which that asset had been held at the time of its disposal; and*

(b) *in the case of an asset falling within that subsection, to the period mentioned in paragraph (a) above plus one year.*

(9) An asset falls within this subsection if—

(a) *the time which, for the purpose of paragraph 2 of Schedule A1, is the time when the asset is taken to have been acquired by the person making the disposal is a time before 17th March 1998; and*

(b) *there is no period which in the case of that asset is a period which by virtue of paragraph 11 or 12 of Schedule does not count for the purposes of taper relief.*

[(8) The qualifying holding period of an asset for the purposes of this section is—

(a) in the case of a business asset, the period after 5th April 1998 for which the asset had been held at the time of its disposal;

(b) in the case of a non-business asset where—

    (i) the time which, for the purposes of paragraph 2 of Schedule A1, is the time when the asset is taken to have been acquired by the person making the disposal is a time before 17th March 1998, and

    (ii) there is no period which by virtue of paragraph 11 or 12 of that Schedule does not count for the purposes of taper relief,

the period mentioned in paragraph (a) plus one year;

(c) in the case of any other non-business asset, the period mentioned in paragraph (a).

This subsection is subject to paragraph 2(4) of Schedule Al and paragraph 3 of Schedule 5BA.]]

Note. Inserted by the Finance Act 1998, s 121(1), (4), with effect for the year 1998–99 and subsequent years of assessment. Sub-s (8) substituted for original sub-ss (8), (9), by the Finance Act 2000, s 66(1), (3), in relation to disposals on or after 6 April 2000.

3. Annual exempt amount—(1) An individual shall not be chargeable to capital gains tax in respect of so much of his taxable amount for any year of assessment as does not exceed the exempt amount for the year.

(2) Subject to subsection (3) below, the exempt amount for any year of assessment shall be [*£6,300*] [*£6,500*] [*£6,800*] [*£7,100*] [*£7,200*] [*£7,500*] [*£7,700*] [*£7,900*] [*£8,200*].

(3) If the retail prices index for the month of December preceding a year of assessment is higher than it was for the previous December, then, unless Parliament otherwise determines, subsection (2) above shall have effect for that year as if for the amount specified in that subsection as it applied for the previous year (whether by virtue of this subsection or otherwise) there were substituted an amount arrived at by increasing the amount for the previous year by the same percentage as the percentage increase in the retail price index and, if the result is not a multiple of £100, rounding it up to the nearest amount which is such a multiple.

(4) The Treasury shall, before each year of assessment, make an order specifying the amount which by virtue of this section is the exempt amount for that year.

(5) For the purposes of this section an individual's taxable amount for a year of assessment is the amount on which he is chargeable under section 2(2) for that year but—

(a) *where the amount of chargeable gains less allowable losses accruing to an individual in any year of assessment does not exceed the exempt amount for the year, no deduction from that amount shall be made for that year in respect of allowable losses carried forward from a previous year or carried back from a subsequent year in which the individual dies, and*

(b) *where the amount of chargeable gains less allowable losses accruing to an individual in any year of assessment exceeds the exempt amount for the year, the deduction from that amount for that year in respect of allowable losses carried forward from a previous year or carried back from a subsequent year in which the individual dies shall not be greater than the excess.*

[(5) For the purposes of this section an individual's taxable amount for any year of assessment is the amount which, after—

(a) making every deduction for which section 2(2) provides,

(b) applying any reduction in respect of taper relief under section 2A, and

(c)   adding any amounts falling to be added by virtue of section 2(5)(b).
is (apart from this section) the amount of that year on which that individual is chargeable to capital gains tax in accordance with section 2.

(5A) Where, in the case of any individual, the amount of the adjusted net gains for any year of assessment is equal to or less than the exempt amount for that year, no deduction shall be made for that year in respect of—

(a) any allowable losses carried forward from a previous year; or
(b) any allowable losses carried back from a subsequent year in which the individual dies.

(5B) Where, in the case of any individual, the amount of the adjusted net gains for any year of assessment exceeds the exempt amount for the year, the deductions made for that year in respect of allowable losses falling within subsection (5A)(a) or (b) above shall not be greater than the excess.

(5C) In subsections (5A) and (5B) above the references, in relation to any individual's case, to the adjusted net gains for any year are references to the amount given in his case by—

(a) taking the amount for that year from which the deductions for which section 2(2)(a) and (b) provides are to be made;
(b) deducting only the amounts falling to be deducted in accordance with section 2(2)(a); and
(c) in a year in which any amount falls to be brought into account by virtue of section 2(5)(b), adding whichever is the smaller of the exempt amount for that year and the amount falling to be so brought into account.]

(6) Where in a year of assessment—

(a) the amount of chargeable gains accruing to an individual does not exceed the exempt amount for the year, and
(b) the aggregate amount or value of the consideration for all the disposals of assets made by him (other than disposals gains accruing on which are not chargeable gains) does not exceed an amount equal to twice the exempt amount for the year,

a statement to the effect of paragraphs (a) and (b) above shall, unless the inspector otherwise requires, be sufficient compliance with any notice under section 8 of the Management Act requiring the individual to make a return of the chargeable gains accruing to him in that year.

(7) For the year of assessment in which an individual dies and for the next 2 following years, subsections (1) to (6) above shall apply to his personal representatives as they apply to an individual.

(8) Schedule 1 shall have effect as respects the application of this section to trustees.

Note. Sum '£6,300' in square brackets in sub-s (2) substituted, in relation to the year 1996–97, by virtue of Capital Gains (Annual Exempt Amount) Order 1995, SI 1995 No 3033, art 2, further substituted by subsequent sum '£6,500' in square brackets, in relation to the year 1997–98, by virtue of SI 1996 No 2957, art 2, further substituted by subsequent sum '£6,800' in square brackets, in relation to the year 1998–99, by virtue of SI 1998 No 757, art 2, further substituted by subsequent sum '£7,100' in square brackets, in relation to the year 1999–00, by virtue of SI 1999 No 591, art 2, further substituted by subsequent sum '£7,200' in square brackets, in relation to the year 2000–01, by virtue of SI 2000 No 808, art 2, further substituted by subsequent sum '£7,500' in square brackets, in relation to the year 2001–02, by virtue of SI 2001 No 636, art 2, further substituted by subsequent sum £7,700' in square brackets, in relation to the year 2002–03, by virtue of SI 2002 No 702, art 2, further substituted by subsequent sum '£7,900' in square brackets, in relation to the year 2003–04, by virtue of SI 2003 No 842, art 2, further substituted by subsequent sum '£8,200' in square brackets, in relation to the year 2004–05, by virtue of SI 2004 No 774, art 2. Sub-s (3) does not apply in relation to the year 1993–94, by virtue of Finance Act 1992, s 82 nor for the year 1994–95, by virtue of Finance Act 1994, s 90. In sub-s (3) the word 'December' (in each place where it occurs) is substituted by the word 'September', by Finance Act 1993, s 83, with effect for the year 1994–95 and subsequent years of assessment. Sub-ss (5), (5A)–(5C) substituted, for sub-s (5) as originally enacted, by the Finance Act 1998, s 121(3), (4), Sch 21, paras 1, 3, with effect for the year 1998–99 and subsequent years of assessment.

[3A. Reporting limits—(1) Where in the case of an individual—
 (a) the amount of chargeable gains accruing to him in any year of assessment does not exceed the exempt amount for that year, and
 (b) the aggregate amount or value of the consideration for all chargeable disposals of assets made by him in that year does not exceed four times the exempt amount for that year,
a statement to that effect is sufficient compliance with so much of any notice under section 8 of the Management Act as requires information for the purposes of establishing the amount in which he is chargeable to capital gains tax for that year.

(2) For the purposes of subsection (1)(a) above—
 (a) the amount of chargeable gains accruing to an individual in a year of assessment for which no deduction falls to be made in respect of allowable losses is the amount after any reduction for taper relief;
 (b) the amount of chargeable gains accruing to an individual in a year of assessment for which such a deduction does fall to be made is the amount before deduction of losses or any reduction for taper relief.

(3) For the purposes of subsection (1)(b) above a 'chargeable disposal' is any disposal other than—
 (a) a disposal on which any gain accruing is not a chargeable gain, or
 (b) a disposal the consideration for which is treated by virtue of section 58 (husband and wife) as being such that neither a gain nor a loss would accrue.

(4) Subsection (1) above applies to personal representatives (for the year of assessment in which the individual in question dies and for the next 2 following years) as it applies to an individual.

(5) Subsection (1) above applies to the trustees of a settlement in accordance with Schedule 1.

(6) In this section 'exempt amount' has the meaning given by section 3 (read, where appropriate, with Schedule 1).]

Note. Inserted by the Finance Act 2003, s 159(1), Sch 28, Pt I, para 1, in relation to the year 2003–04 and subsequent years of assessment.

4. Rates of capital gains tax—(1) Subject to the provisions of this section *and section 5*, the rate of capital gains tax in respect of gains accruing to a person in a year of assessment shall be equivalent to the *basic rate* [lower rate] of income tax for the year.

Note. In sub-s (1) words 'and section 5' repealed by the Finance Act 1998, s 165, Sch 27, Pt III(29), with effect for the year 1998–99 and subsequent years of assessment, and words 'lower rate' in square brackets substituted by the Finance Act 1999, s 26(1), (2) for the year 1999–00 and subsequent years of assessment.

 [*(1A) If (after allowing for any deductions in accordance with the Income Tax Acts) an individual has no income for a year of assessment or his total income for the year is less than the lower rate limit, then—*
 (a) if the amount on which he is chargeable to capital gains tax does not exceed the relevant amount, the rate of capital gains tax in respect of gains accruing to him in the year shall be equivalent to the lower rate;
 (b) if the amount on which he is chargeable to capital gains tax exceeds the relevant amount, the rate of capital gains tax in respect of such gains accruing to him in the year as correspond to the relevant amount shall be equivalent to the lower rate.

 (1B) For the purposes of subsection (1A) above the relevant amount is—
 (a) an amount equal to the lower rate limit, where the individual has no income;
 (b) an amount equal to the difference between his total income and that limit, in any other case.]

Note. Sub-ss (1A), (1B) inserted, in relation to the year 1992–93 and subsequent years of assessment, by the Finance (No 2) Act 1992, s 23(1), (3); repealed by the Finance Act 1999, ss 26(1), (4), 139, Sch 20, Pt III(1), with effect for the year 1999–00 and subsequent years of assessment.

[1AA) The rate of capital gains tax in respect of gains accruing to—
(a) the trustees of a settlement, or
(b) the personal representatives of a deceased person,
in a year of assessment shall be equivalent to the rate which for that year is *applicable to trusts under section 686(1) of the Taxes Act* [the rate applicable to trusts under section 686 of the Taxes Act].

Note. Sub-s (1AA) inserted by the Finance Act 1998, s 120, with effect for the year 1998–99 and subsequent years of assessment. Words in square brackets substitued for the words in italics by the Finance Act 1999, s 26(1), (3), with effect for the year 1999–2000 and subsequent years of assessment.

[1AB) If (after allowing for any deductions in accordance with the Income Tax Acts) an individual has no income for a year of assessment or his total income for the year is less than the starting rate limit, then—
(a) if the amount on which he is chargeable to capital gains tax does not exceed the unused part of his starting rate band, the rate of capital gains tax in respect of gains accruing to him in the year shall be equivalent to the starting rate;
(b) if the amount on which he is chargeable to capital gains tax exceeds the unused part of his starting rate band, the rate of capital gains tax in respect of such gains accruing to him in the year as correspond to the unused part shall be equivalent to the starting rate.
(1AC) The references in subsection (1AB) above to the unused part of an individual's starting rate band are to the amount by which the starting rate limit exceeds his total income (as reduced by any deductions made in accordance with the Income Tax Acts).]

Note. Sub-ss (1AB), (1AC) inserted by the Finance Act 2000, s 37(1), with effect for the year 2000–01 and subsequent years of assessment.

(2) If income tax is chargeable at the higher rate [or the Schedule F upper rate] in respect of any part of the income of an individual for a year of assessment, the rate of capital gains tax in respect of gains accruing to him in the year shall be equivalent to the higher rate.
(3) If no income tax is chargeable at the higher rate [or the Schedule F upper rate] in respect of the income of an individual for a year of assessment, but the amount on which he is chargeable to capital gains tax exceeds the unused part of his basic rate band, the rate of capital gains tax on the excess shall be equivalent to the higher rate of income tax for the year.

Note. In sub-ss (2), (3) words in square brackets inserted by the Finance (No 2) Act 1997, s 34, Sch 4, para 24, with effect for the year 1999–00 and subsequent years of assessment.

[*(3A) Income chargeable to income tax at the lower rate [or the Schedule F ordinary rate] in accordance with section 207A [section 1A] of the Taxes Act, and any income which would be chargeable at the higher rate [or the Schedule F upper rate], shall be disregarded in determining for the purposes of subsections (1A) and (1B) above—*
(a) whether any individual has income for any year of assessment; or
(b) an individual's total income for any year of assessment.
(3B) Where any amount on which an individual is chargeable for a year of assessment to capital gains tax at a rate equivalent to the lower rate is or includes an amount ('the amount of the lower rate gains') on which he is also chargeable by virtue only of subsection (3A) above then—
(a) for the purposes of the Income Tax Acts and this section, the amount (if any) of income comprised in the individual's total income which is chargeable to income tax at the higher rate [or the Schedule F upper rate] shall be determined as if the basic rate limit for that year were reduced in relation to that individual by the amount of the lower rate gains; and
(b) the amount (if any) on which, but for this paragraph, the individual would be chargeable under subsection (2) above to capital gains tax at a rate equivalent to the higher rate shall be treated as reduced by the amount of the lower rate gains or, if the amount to be reduced is not more than the amount of those gains, to nil.]

(4) The reference in subsection (3) above to the unused part of an individual's basic rate band is a reference to the amount by which [(*disregarding subsection (3B)(a) above*)] the basic rate limit exceeds his total income (as reduced by any deductions made in accordance with the Income Tax Acts).

Note. Sub-ss (3A), (3B) and the words in square brackets in sub-s (4) are inserted by Finance Act 1993, s 79(1), Sch 6, paras 22, 25(1), with effect for the year 1993–94 and subsequent years of assessment; repealed by the Finance Act 1999, ss 26(1), (4), (5), Sch 20, Pt III(1), with effect for the year 1999–00 and subsequent years of assessment. In sub-s (3A) words 'section 1A' in square brackets substituted by the Finance Act 1996, s 73, Sch 6, paras 27, 28, with effect for the year 1996–97 and subsequent years of assessment. Other words in square brackets in sub-ss (3A), (3B) inserted by the Finance (No 2) Act 1997, s 34, Sch 4, para 24, with effect for the year 1999–00 and subsequent years of assessment.

5. Accumulation and discretionary settlements—(*1*) *The rate of capital gains tax in respect of gains accruing to trustees of an accumulation or discretionary settlement in a year of assessment shall be equivalent to [the rate which for that year is applicable to trusts under section 686(1) of the Taxes Act.]*

(*2*) *For the purposes of subsection (1) above a trust is an accumulation or discretionary settlement where—*

(a) *all or any part of the income arising to the trustees in the year of assessment is income to which section 686 of the Taxes Act … applies, or*

(b) *all the income arising to the trustees in the year of assessment is treated as the income of the settlor, but that section would apply to it if it were not so treated, or*

(c) *all the income arising to the trustees in the year of assessment is applied in defraying expenses of the trustees in that year, but that section would apply to it if it were not so applied, or*

(d) *no income arises to the trustees in the year of assessment, but that section would apply if there were income arising to the trustees and none of it were treated as the income of the settlor or applied as mentioned in paragraph (c) above.*

Note. This section repealed by the Finance Act 1998, s 165, Sch 27, Pt III(29), with effect for the year 1998–99 and subsequent years of assessment. Words in square brackets in sub-s (1) substituted, and words omitted from sub-s (2)(a) repealed, by Finance Act 1993, ss 79(1), 213, Sch 6, paras 23, 25(1), Sch 23, Part III, with effect for the year 1993–94 and subsequent years of assessment. Sub-s (2)(c) repealed, and in sub-s (2)(d) words 'or applied as mentioned in paragraph (c) above' repealed, by Finance Act 1997, s 113, Sch 18, Part VI(7), with effect for the year 1997–98 and subsequent years of assessment and deemed to have effect for the year 1996–97.

*   *   *   *   *

Residence etc

9. Residence, including temporary residence—(1) In this Act 'resident' and 'ordinarily resident' have the same meanings as in the Income Tax Acts.

(2) Section 207 of the Taxes Act (disputes as to domicile or ordinary residence) shall apply in relation to capital gains tax as it applies for the purposes mentioned in that section.

(3) Subject to *section 10(1)* [section 10(1) and 10A], an individual who is in the United Kingdom for some temporary purpose only and not with any view or intent to establish his residence in the United Kingdom shall be charged to capital gains tax on chargeable gains accruing in any year of assessment if and only if the period (or the sum of the periods) for which he is resident in the United Kingdom in that year of assessment exceeds 6 months.

[(4) The question whether for the purposes of subsection (3) above an individual is in the United Kingdom for some temporary purposes only and not with any view or intent to establish his residence there shall be decided without regard to any living accommodation available in the United Kingdom for his use.]

Note. In sub-s (3) words 'section 10(1) and 10A' substituted by the Finance Act 1998, s 127(1), (2), (4), with effect in any case in which the year of departure is the year 1998–99 or a subsequent year of assessment, and in any case in which the year of departure is the year

1997–98 and the taxpayer was resident in the United Kingdom at a time in that year on or after 17 March 1998. Sub-s (4) added by Finance Act 1993, s 208(2), (4), with effect for the year 1993–94 and subsequent years of assessment.

10. Non-resident with United Kingdom branch or agency—(1) Subject to any exceptions provided by this Act, a person shall be chargeable to capital gains tax in respect of chargeable gains accruing to him in a year of assessment in which he is not resident and not ordinarily resident in the United Kingdom but is carrying on a trade in the United Kingdom through a branch or agency, and shall be so chargeable on chargeable gains accruing on the disposal—

    (a) of assets situated in the United Kingdom and used in or for the purposes of the trade at or before the time when the capital gain accrued, or

    (b) of assets situated in the United Kingdom and used or held for the purposes of the branch or agency at or before that time, or assets acquired for use by or for the purposes of the branch or agency.

(2) Subsection (1) above does not apply unless the disposal is made at a time when the person is carrying on the trade in the United Kingdom through a branch or agency.

(3) For the purposes of corporation tax the chargeable profits of a company not resident in the United Kingdom but carrying on a trade or vocation there through a branch or agency shall be, or include, such chargeable gains accruing on the disposal of assets situated in the United Kingdom as are by this section made chargeable to capital gains tax in the case of an individual not resident or ordinarily resident in the United Kingdom.

(4) This section shall not apply to a person who, by virtue of Part XVIII of the Taxes Act (double taxation relief agreements), is exempt from income tax or corporation tax chargeable for the chargeable period in respect of the profits or gains of the branch or agency.

(5) This section shall apply as if references in subsections (1) and (2) above to a trade included references to a profession or vocation, but subsection (1) shall not apply in respect of chargeable gains accruing on the disposal of assets only used in or for the purposes of the profession or vocation before 14th March 1989 or only used or held for the purposes of the branch or agency before that date.

(6) In this Act, unless the context otherwise requires, 'branch or agency' means any factorship, agency, receivership, branch or management, but does not include any person within the exemptions in section 82 of the Management Act (general agents and brokers).

[10A. Temporary non-residents—(1) This section applies in the case of any individual ('the taxpayer') if—

    (a) he satisfies the residence requirements for any year of assessment ('the year of return');

    (b) he did not satisfy those requirements for one or more years of assessment immediately preceding the year of return but there are years of assessment before that year for which he did satisfy those requirements;

    (c) there are fewer than five years of assessment falling between the year of departure and the year of return; and

    (d) four out of the seven years of assessment immediately preceding the year of departure are also years of assessment for each of which he satisfied those requirements.

(2) Subject to the following provisions of this section and section 86A, the taxpayer shall be chargeable to capital gains tax as if—

    (a) all the chargeable gains and losses which (apart from this subsection) would have accrued to him in an intervening year,

    (b) all the chargeable gains which under section 13 or 86 would be treated as having accrued to him in an intervening year if he had been resident in the United Kingdom throughout that intervening year; and

    (c) any losses which by virtue of section 13(8) would have been allowable in his case in any intervening year if he had been resident in the United Kingdom throughout that intervening year,

were gains or, as the case may be, losses accruing to the taxpayer in the year of return.

    (3) Subject to subsection (4) below, the gains and losses which by virtue of subsection (2) above are to be treated as accruing to the taxpayer in the year of return shall not include any gain or loss accruing on the disposal by the taxpayer of any asset if—

    (a) that asset was acquired by the taxpayer at a time in the year of departure or any intervening year when he was neither resident nor ordinarily resident in the United Kingdom;

    (b) that asset was so acquired otherwise than by means of a relevant disposal which by virtue of section 58, 73 or 258(4) is treated as having been a disposal on which neither a gain nor a loss accrued;

    (c) that asset is not an interest created by or arising under a settlement; and

    (d) the amount or value of the consideration for the acquisition of that asset by the taxpayer does not fall by reference to any relevant disposal, to be treated as reduced under section 23(4)(b) or (5)(b), 152(1)(b), 162(3)(b) or 247(2)(b) or (3)(b).

    (4) Where—

    (a) any chargeable gain that has accrued or would have accrued on the disposal of any asset ('the first asset') is a gain falling (apart from this section) to be treated by virtue of section 116(10) or (11), 134 or 154(2) or (4) as accruing on tile disposal of the whole or any part of another asset, and

    (b) the other asset is an asset falling within paragraphs (a) to (d) of subsection (3) above but the first asset is not,

subsection (3) above shall not exclude that gain from the gains which by virtue of subsection (2) above are to be treated as accruing to the taxpayer in the year of return.

    (5) The gains and losses which by virtue of subsection (2) above are to be treated as accruing to the taxpayer in the year of return shall not include any chargeable gain or allowable loss accruing to the taxpayer in an intervening year which, in the taxpayer's case, has fallen to be brought into account for that year by virtue of section 10 or 16(3).

    (6) The reference in subsection (2)(c) above to losses allowable in an individual's case in an intervening year is a reference to only so much of the aggregate of the losses that would have been available in accordance with subsection (8) of section 13 for reducing gains accruing by virtue of that section to that individual in that year as does not exceed the amount of the gains that would have accrued to him in that year if it had been a year throughout which he was resident in the United Kingdom.

    (7) Where this section applies in the case of any individual, nothing in any enactment imposing any limit on the time within which an assessment to capital gains tax may be made shall prevent any such assessment for the year of departure from being made in the taxpayer's case at any time before the end of two years after the 31st January next following the year of return.

    (8) In this section—

'intervening year' means any year of assessment which, in a case where the conditions in paragraphs (a) to (d) of subsection (1) above are satisfied, falls between the year of departure and the year of return;

'relevant disposal', means a disposal of an asset acquired by the person making the disposal at a time when that person was resident or ordinarily resident in the United Kingdom; and

'the year of departure' means the last year of assessment before the year of return for which the taxpayer satisfied the residence requirements.

(9) For the purposes of this section an individual satisfies the residence requirements for a year of assessment if that year of assessment is one during any part of which he is resident in the United Kingdom or during which he is ordinarily resident in the United Kingdom.

(10) This section is without prejudice to any right to claim relief in accordance with any double taxation relief arrangements.]

Note. Inserted by the Finance Act 1998, s 127(1), (4), with effect in any case in which the year of departure is the year 1998–99 or a subsequent year of assessment, and in any case in which the year of departure is the year 1997–98 and the taxpayer was resident or ordinarily resident in the United Kingdom at a time in that year on or after 17 March 1998.

11. Visiting forces, Agents-General etc—(1) A period during which a member of a visiting force to whom section 323(1) of the Taxes Act applies is in the United Kingdom by reason solely of his being a member of that force shall not be treated for the purposes of capital gains tax either as a period of residence in the United Kingdom or as creating a change in his residence or domicile.

This subsection shall be construed as one with subsection (2) of section 323 and subsections (4) to (8) of that section shall apply accordingly.

(2) An Agent-General who is resident in the United Kingdom shall be entitled to the same immunity from capital gains tax as that to which the head of a mission so resident is entitled under the Diplomatic Privileges Act 1964.

(3) Any person having or exercising any employment to which section 320(2) of the Taxes Act (staff of Agents-General etc) applies (not being a person employed in any trade, business or other undertaking carried on for the purposes of profit) shall be entitled to the same immunity from capital gains tax as that to which a member of the staff of a mission is entitled under the Diplomatic Privileges Act 1964.

(4) Subsections (2) and (3) above shall be construed as one with section 320 of the Taxes Act.

*   *   *   *   *

PART II

GENERAL PROVISIONS RELATING TO COMPUTATION OF GAINS AND ACQUISITIONS AND DISPOSALS OF ASSETS

CHAPTER I

INTRODUCTORY

*   *   *   *   *

18. Transactions between connected persons—(1) This section shall apply where a person acquires an asset and the person making the disposal is connected with him.

(2) Without prejudice to the generality of section 17(1) the person acquiring the asset and the person making the disposal shall be treated as parties to a transaction otherwise than by way of a bargain made at arm's length.

(3) Subject to subsection (4) below, if on the disposal a loss accrues to the person making the disposal, it shall not be deductible except from a chargeable gain accruing to him on some other disposal of an asset to the person acquiring the asset mentioned in subsection (1) above, being a disposal made at a time when they are connected persons.

(4) Subsection (3) above shall not apply to a disposal by way of gift in settlement if the gift and the income from it is wholly or primarily applicable for educational, cultural or recreational purposes, and the persons benefiting from the application for those purposes are confined to members of an association of persons for whose benefit the gift was made, not being persons all or most of whom are connected persons.

(5) Where the asset mentioned in subsection (1) above is an option to enter into a sale or other transaction given by the person making the disposal a loss accruing to the person acquiring the asset shall not be an allowable loss unless it accrues on a disposal of the option at arm's length to a person who is not connected with him.

(6) Subject to subsection (7) below, in a case where the asset mentioned in subsection (1) above is subject to any right or restriction enforceable by the person making the disposal, or by a person connected with him, then (where the amount of the consideration for the acquisition is, in accordance with subsection (2) above, deemed to be equal to the market value of the asset) that market value shall be—

(a) what its market value would be if not subject to the right of restriction, minus—

(b) the market value of the right or restriction or the amount by which its extinction would enhance the value of the asset to its owner, whichever is the less.

(7) If the right or restriction is of such a nature that its enforcement would or might effectively destroy or substantially impair the value of the asset without bringing any countervailing advantage either to the person making the disposal or a person connected with him or is an option or other right to acquire the asset or, in the case of incorporeal property, is a right to extinguish the asset in the hands of the person giving the consideration by forfeiture or merger or otherwise, the market value of the asset shall be determined, and the amount of the gain accruing on the disposal shall be computed, as if the right or restriction did not exist.

(8) Subsections (6) and (7) above shall not apply to a right of forfeiture or other right exercisable on breach of a covenant contained in a lease of land or other property, and shall not apply to any right or restriction under a mortgage or other charge.

* * * * *

PART III

INDIVIDUALS, PARTNERSHIPS, TRUSTS AND COLLECTIVE INVESTMENT SCHEMES

CHAPTER I

MISCELLANEOUS PROVISIONS

58. Husband and wife—(1) If, in any year of assessment, and in the case of a woman who in that year of assessment is a married woman living with her husband, the man disposes of an asset to the wife, or the wife disposes of an asset to the man, both shall be treated as if the asset was acquired from the one making the disposal for a consideration of such amount as would secure that on the disposal neither a gain nor a loss would accrue to the one making the disposal.

(2) This section shall not apply—

(a) if until the disposal the asset formed part of trading stock of a trade carried on by the one making the disposal, or if the assets is acquired as trading stock for the purposes of a trade carried on by the one acquiring the asset, or

(b) if the disposal is by way of donatio mortis causa,

but this section shall have effect notwithstanding the provisions of section 18 or 161, or of any othe provisions of this Act fixing the amount of the consideration deemed to be given on a disposal or acquisition.

* * * * *

PART VI

COMPANIES, OIL, INSURANCE, ETC

* * * * *

CHAPTER III

INSURANCE

* * * * *

210. Life assurance and deferred annuities—*(1) This section has effect as respects any policy of assurance or contract for a deferred annuity on the life of any person.*

(2) No chargeable gain shall accrue on the disposal of, or of an interest in, the rights under any such policy of assurance or contract except where the person making the disposal is not the original beneficial owner and acquired the rights or interest for a consideration in money or money's worth.

(3) Subject to subsection (2) above, the occasion of—

(a) the payment of the sum or sums assured by a policy of assurance, or

(b) the transfer of investments or other assets to the owner of a policy of assurance in accordance with the policy,

and the occasion of the surrender of a policy of assurance, shall be the occasion of a disposal of the rights under the policy of assurance.

(4) Subject to subsection (2) above, the occasion of the payment of the first instalment of a deferred annuity, and the occasion of the surrender of the rights under a contract for a deferred annuity, shall be the occasion of a disposal of the rights under the contract for a deferred annuity and the amount of the consideration for the disposal of a contract for a deferred annuity shall be the market value at that time of the right to that and further instalments of the annuity.

[**210. Life insurance and deferred annuities**—(1) This section has effect in relation to any policy of insurance or contract for a deferred annuity on the life of any person.

(2) A gain accruing on a disposal of, or of an interest in, the rights conferred by the policy of insurance or contract for a deferred annuity is not a chargeable gain unless subsection (3) below applies.

(3) This subsection applies if—

(a) (in the case of a disposal of the rights) the rights or any interest in the rights, or

(b) (in the case of a disposal of an interest in the rights) the rights, the interest or any interest from which the interest directly or indirectly derives (in whole or in part),

have or has at any time been acquired by any person for actual consideration (as opposed to consideration deemed to be given by any enactment relating to the taxation of chargeable gains).

(4) For the purposes of subsection (3) above—

(a) (in the case of a policy of insurance) amounts paid under the policy by way of premiums, and

(b) (in the case of a contract for a deferred annuity) amounts paid under the contract, whether by way of premiums or as lump sum consideration,

do not constitute actual consideration.

(5) And for those purposes actual consideration for—

(a) a disposal which is made by one spouse to the other or is an approved post-marriage disposal, or

(b) a disposal to which section 171(1) applies,

is to be treated as not constituting actual consideration.

(6) For the purposes of subsection (5)(a) above a disposal is an approved post-marriage disposal if—

(a) it is made in consequence of the dissolution or annulment of a marriage by one person who was a party to the marriage to the other,

(b) it is made with the approval, agreement or authority of a court (or other person or body) having jurisdiction under the law of any country or territory or pursuant to an order of such a court (or other person or body), and

(c) the rights disposed of were, or the interest disposed of was, held by the person by whom the disposal is made immediately before the marriage was dissolved or annulled.

(7) Subsection (8) below applies for the purposes of tax on chargeable gains where—

(a) (if that subsection did not apply) a loss would accrue on a disposal of, or of an interest in, the rights conferred by the policy of insurance or contract for a deferred annuity, but

(b) if sections 37 and 39 were disregarded, there would accrue on the disposal a loss of a smaller amount, a gain or neither a loss nor a gain.

(8) If (disregarding those sections) a loss of a smaller amount would accrue, that smaller amount is to be taken to be the amount of the loss accruing on the disposal; and in any other case, neither a loss nor a gain is to be taken to accrue on the disposal.

(9) But subsection (8) above does not affect the treatment for the purposes of tax on chargeable gains of the person who acquired rights, or an interest in rights, on the disposal.

(10) The occasion of—

(a) the receipt of the sum or sums assured by the policy of insurance,

(b) the transfer of investments or other assets to the owner of the policy of insurance in accordance with the policy, or

(c) the surrender of the policy of insurance,

is for the purposes of tax on chargeable gains an occasion of a disposal of the rights (or of all of the interests in the rights) conferred by the policy of insurance.

(11) The occasion of—

(a) the receipt of the first instalment of the annuity under the contract for a deferred annuity, or

(b) the surrender of the rights conferred by the contract for a deferred annuity,

is for the purposes of tax on chargeable gains an occasion of a disposal of the rights (or of all of the interests in the rights) conferred by the contract for a deferred annuity.

(12) Where there is a disposal on the occasion of the receipt of the first instalment of the annuity under the contract for a deferred annuity—

(a) in the case of a disposal of the rights conferred by the contract, the consideration for the disposal is the aggregate of the amount or value of the first instalment and the market value at the time of the disposal of the right to receive the further instalments of the annuity, and

(b) in the case of a disposal of an interest in the rights, the consideration for the disposal is such proportion of that aggregate as is just and reasonable;

and no gain accruing on any subsequent disposal of, or of any interest in, the rights is a chargeable gain (even if subsection (3) above applies).

(13) In this section 'interest', in relation to rights conferred by a policy of insurance or contract for a deferred annuity, means an interest as a co-owner of the rights (whether the rights are owned jointly or in common and whether or not the interests of the co-owners are equal).]

Note. Substituted by the Finance Act 2003, s 157(1), in relation to disposals on or after 9 April 2003.

*   *   *   *   *

PART VII

OTHER PROPERTY, BUSINESSES, INVESTMENTS ETC

Private residences

222. Relief on disposal of private residence—(1) This section applies to a gain accruing to an individual so far as attributable to the disposal of, or of an interest in—

(a) a dwelling-house or part of a dwelling-house which is, or has at any time in his period of ownership been, his only or main residence, or

(b) land which he has for his own occupation and enjoyment with that residence as its garden or grounds up to the permitted area.

(2) In this section 'the permitted area' means, subject to subsections (3) and (4) below, an area (inclusive of the site of the dwelling-house) of 0.5 of a hectare.

(3) In any particular case the permitted area shall be such area, larger than 0.5 of a hectare, as the Commissioners concerned may determine if satisfied that, regard being had to the size and character of the dwelling-house, that larger area is required for the reasonable enjoyment of it (or of the part in question) as a residence.

[(3) Where the area required for the reasonable enjoyment of the dwelling-house (or of the part in question) as a residence, having regard to the size and character of the dwelling-house, is larger than 0.5 of a hectare, that larger area shall be the permitted area.]

(4) Where part of the land occupied with a residence is and part is not within subsection (1) above, then (up to the permitted area) that part shall be taken to be within subsection (1) above which, if the remainder were separately occupied, would be the most suitable for occupation and enjoyment with the residence.

(5) So far as it is necessary for the purposes of this section to determine which of 2 or more residences is an individual's main residence for any period—

(a) the individual may conclude that question by notice to *the inspector* [an officer of the Board] given within 2 years from the beginning of that period but subject to a right to vary that notice by a further notice to *the inspector* [an officer of the Board] as respects any period beginning not earlier than 2 years before the giving of the further notice,

(b) *subject to paragraph (a) above, the question shall be concluded by the determination of the inspector, which may be as respects the whole or specified parts of the period of ownership in question,*

and notice of any determination of the inspector under paragraph (b) above shall be given to the individual who may appeal to the General Commissioners or the Special Commissioners against that determination within 30 days of service of the notice.

(6) In the case of a man and his wife living with him—

(a) there can only be one residence or main residence for both, so long as living together and, where a notice under subsection (5)(a) above affects both the husband and the wife, it must be given by both, *and*

(b) *any notice under subsection (5)(b) above which affects a residence owned by the husband and a residence owned by the wife shall be given to each and either may appeal under that subsection.*

(7) In this section and sections 223 to 226, 'the period of ownership' where the individual has had different interests at different times shall be taken to begin from the first acquisition taken into account in arriving at the expenditure which under Chapter III of Part II is allowable as a deduction in the computation of the gain to which this section applies, and in the case of a man and his wife living with him—

(a) if the one disposes of, or of his or her interest in, the dwelling-house or part of a dwelling-house which is their only or main residence to the other, and in particular if it passes on death to the other as legatee, the other's period of ownership shall begin with the beginning of the period of ownership of the one making the disposal, and

(b) if paragraph (a) above applies, but the dwelling-house or part of a dwelling-house was not the only or main residence of both throughout the period of ownership of the one making the disposal, account shall be taken of any part of that period during which it was his only or main residence as if it was also that of the other.

(8) If at any time during an individual's period of ownership of a dwelling-house or part of a dwelling-house he—

(a) resides in living accommodation which is for him job-related *within the meaning of section 356 of the Taxes Act*, and

(b) intends in due course to occupy the dwelling-house or part of a dwelling-house as his only or main residence,

this section and sections 223 to 226 shall apply as if the dwelling-house or part of a dwelling-house were at that time occupied by him as a residence.

[(8A) Subject to subsections (8B), (8C) and (9) below, for the purposes of subsection (8) above living accommodation is job-related for a person if—

(a) it is provided for him by reason of his employment, or for his spouse by reason of her employment, in any of the following cases—

   (i) where it is necessary for the proper performance of the duties of the employment that the employee should reside in that accommodation;

   (ii) where the accommodation is provided for the better performance of the duties of the employment, and it is one of the kinds of employment in the case of which it is customary for employers to provide living accommodation for employees;

   (iii) where, there being a special threat to the employee's security, special security arrangements are in force and the employee resides in the accommodation as part of those arrangements;

   or

(b) under a contract entered into at arm's length and requiring him or his spouse to carry on a particular trade, profession or vocation, he or his spouse is bound—

   (i) to carry on that trade, profession or vocation on premises or other land provided by another person (whether under a tenancy or otherwise); and

   (ii) to live either on those premises or on other premises provided by that other person.

(8B) If the living accommodation is provided by a company and the employee is a director of that or an associated company, subsection (8A)(a)(i) or (ii) above shall not apply unless—

(a) the company of which the employee is a director is one in which he or she has no material interest; and

(b) either—

   (i) the employment is as a full-time working director, or

   (ii) the company is non-profit making, that is to say, it does not carry on a trade nor do its functions consist wholly or mainly in the holding of investments or other property, or

   (iii) the company is established for charitable purposes only.

(8C) Subsection (8A)(b) above does not apply if the living accommodation concerned is in whole or in part provided by—

(a) a company in which the borrower or his spouse has a material interest; or

(b) any person or persons together with whom the borrower or his spouse carries on a trade or business in partnership.

(8D) For the purposes of this section—

(a) a company is an associated company of another if one of them has control of the other or both are under the control of the same person; and

(b) 'employment', 'director', 'full-time working director', 'material interest' and 'control', in relation to a body corporate, have the same meanings as they have for the purposes of Chapter II of Part V of the Taxes Act.]

(9) *Section 356(3)(b) and (5) of the Taxes Act* [Subsections (8A)(b) and (8C) above] shall apply for the purposes of subsection (8) above only in relation to residence on or after 6th April 1983 in living accommodation which is job-related *within the meaning of that section* [for the purposes of that subsection].

(10) Apportionments of consideration shall be made wherever required by this section or sections 223 to 226 and, in particular, where a person disposes of a dwelling-house only part of which is his only or main residence.

Note. Sub-s (3) substituted by the Finance Act 1996, s 205, in relation to capital gains tax for the year 1996–97 and subsequent years of assessment. In sub-s (5) words 'an officer of the Board' in square brackets in both places they occur substituted by the Finance Act 2004, s 117, Sch 22, para 7(1). Sub-s (5)(b) and words from 'and notice' to 'service of the notice' in italics, and sub-s (6)(b), repealed by the Finance Act 1996, s 205, Sch 41, Pt V, in relation to capital gains tax for the year 1996–97 and subsequent years of assessment. In sub-s (8) words 'within the meaning of section 356 of the Taxes Act' in italics repealed, and in sub-s (9) words in square brackets substituted, by the Finance Act 1999, ss 38(8),139, Sch 4, para 17(1), (2), (4), Sch 20, Pt III(7), with effect for the year 2000–01 and subsequent years of assessment.

223. Amount of relief—(1) No part of a gain to which section 222 applies shall be a chargeable gain if the dwelling-house or part of a dwelling-house has been the individual's only or main residence throughout the period of ownership, or throughout the period of ownership except for all or any part of the last 36 months of that period.

(2) Where subsection (1) above does not apply, a fraction of the gain shall not be a chargeable gain, and that fraction shall be—

    (a) the length of the part or parts of the period of ownership during which the dwelling-house or the part of the dwelling-house was the individual's only or main residence, but inclusive of the last 36 months of the period of ownership in any event, divided by

    (b) the length of the period of ownership.

(3) For the purposes of subsections (1) and (2) above—

    (a) a period of absence not exceeding 3 years (or periods of absence which together did not exceed 3 years), and in addition

    (b) any period of absence throughout which the individual worked in an employment or office all the duties of which were performed outside the United Kingdom, and in addition

    (c) any period of absence not exceeding 4 years (or periods of absence which together did not exceed 4 years) throughout which the individual was prevented from residing in the dwelling-house or part of the dwelling-house in consequence of the situation of his place of work or in consequence of any condition imposed by his employer requiring him to reside elsewhere, being a condition reasonably imposed to secure the effective performance by the employee of his duties,

shall be treated as if in that period of absence the dwelling-house or the part of the dwelling-house was the individual's only or main residence if both before and after the period there was a time when the dwelling-house was the individual's only or main residence.

(4) Where a gain to which section 222 applies accrues to any individual and the dwelling-house in question or any part of it is or has at any time in his period of ownership been wholly or partly let by him as residential accommodation, the part of the gain, if any, which (apart from this subsection) would be a chargeable gain by reason of the letting, shall be such a gain only to the extent, if any, to which it exceeds whichever is the lesser of—

    (a) the part of the gain which is not a chargeable gain by virtue of the provisions of subsection (1) to (3) above *or those provisions as applied by section 225*; and

    (b) £40,000.

(5) Where at any time the number of months specified in subsections (1) and (2)(a) above is 36, the Treasury may by order amend those subsections by substituting references to 24 for the references to 36 in relation to disposals on or after such date as is specified in the order.

(6) Subsection (5) above shall also have effect as if 36 (in both places) read 24 and as if 24 read 36.

(7) In this section—

'period of absence' means a period during which the dwelling-house or the part of the dwelling-house was not the individual's only or main residence and throughout which he had no residence or main residence eligible for relief under this section; and

'period of ownership' does not include any period before 31st March 1982.

[(8) This section is subject to—

(a) section 224 (amount of relief: further provisions), and

(b) section 226A (private residence relief: cases where relief obtained under section 260).]

Note. In sub-s (4)(a) words in italics repealed, in relation to disposals made on or after 10 December 2003, and sub-s (8) inserted (with transitional provisions), in relation to gains or parts of gains accruing on later disposals (within the meaning of section 226A hereof) made on or after 10 December 2003 (whenever any relevant earlier disposal was made), by the Finance Act 2004, ss 117, 326, Sch 22, paras 2(1)–(3), 8, Sch 42, Pt 2(15).

224. Amount of relief: further provisions—(1) If the gain *accrues from* [accrues on] the disposal of a dwelling-house or part of a dwelling-house part of which is used exclusively for the purpose of a trade or business, or of a profession or vocation, the gain shall be apportioned and section 223 shall apply in relation to the part of the gain apportioned to the part which is not exclusively used for those purposes.

(2) If at any time in the period of ownership there is a change in what is occupied as the individual's residence, whether on account of a reconstruction or conversion of a building or for any other reason, or there have been changes as regards the use of part of the dwelling-house for the purpose of a trade or business, or of a profession or vocation, or for any other purpose, the relief given by section 223 *may be adjusted in such manner as the Commissioners concerned may consider to be just and reasonable* [may be adjusted in a manner which is just and reasonable].

(3) Section 223 shall not apply in relation to a gain if the acquisition of, or of the interest in, the dwelling-house or the part of a dwelling-house was made wholly or partly for the purpose of realising a gain from the disposal of it, and shall not apply in relation to a gain so far as attributable to any expenditure which was incurred after the beginning of the period of ownership and was incurred wholly or partly for the purpose of realising a gain from the disposal.

Note. In sub-s (1) words in square brackets substituted by the Finance Act 2004, s 117, Sch 22, para 3, in relation to disposals made on or after 10 December 2003. Words in square brackets in sub-s (2) substituted for words in italics by Finance Act 1996, s 134(1), (2), Sch 20, para 60, in relation to capital gains tax for the year 1996–97 and subsequent years of assessment.

225. Private residence occupied under terms of settlement. Sections 222 to 224 shall also apply in relation to a gain accruing to *a trustee* [the trustees of a settlement] on a disposal of settled properly being an asset within section 222(1) where, during the period of ownership of *the trustee* [the trustees], the dwelling-house or part of the dwelling-house mentioned in that subsection has been the only or main residence of a person entitled to occupy it under the terms of the settlement, and in those sections as so applied—

(a) references to the individual shall be taken as references to *the trustee* [the trustees] except in relation to the occupation of the dwelling-house or part of the dwelling-house, and

(b) the notice which may be given to *the inspector* [an officer of the Board] under section 222(5)(a) shall be a joint notice by *the trustee* [the trustees] and the person entitled to occupy the dwelling-house or part of the dwelling-house [; but section 223 (as so applied) shall apply only on the making of a claim by the trustees].

Note. Final words in square brackets inserted, and other words in square brackets substituted, by the Finance Act 2004, s 117, Sch 22, paras 4, 7(2).

[225A. Private residence held by personal representatives—(1) Sections 222 to 224 shall also apply in relation to a gain accruing to the personal representatives of a deceased person on a disposal of an asset within section 222(1) if the following conditions are satisfied.

(2) The first condition is that, immediately before and immediately after the death of the deceased person, the dwelling-house or part of the dwelling-house mentioned in section 222(1) was the only or main residence of one or more individuals.

(3) The second condition is that—

(a) that individual or one of those individuals has a relevant entitlement, or two or more of those individuals have relevant entitlements, and

(b) the relevant entitlement accounts for, or the relevant entitlements together account for, 75% or more of the net proceeds of disposal;

and for this purpose 'relevant entitlement' means an entitlement as legatee of the deceased person to, or to an interest in possession in, the whole or any part of the net proceeds of disposal.

(4) In subsection (3) above 'net proceeds of disposal' means—

(a) the proceeds of the disposal of the asset realised by the personal representatives, less

(b) any incidental costs allowable as a deduction in accordance with section 38(1)(c) in computing the gain accruing to the personal representatives on that disposal,

but on the assumption that none of the proceeds is required to meet the liabilities of the deceased person's estate (including any liability to inheritance tax).

(5) In sections 222 to 224 as applied by this section—

(a) references to the individual shall be taken as references to the personal representatives except in relation to the occupation of the dwelling-house or part of the dwelling-house, and

(b) the notice which may be given to an officer of the Board under section 222(5)(a) shall be a joint notice by the personal representatives and the individual or individuals entitled to occupy the dwelling-house or part of the dwelling-house.

(6) But section 223 (as so applied) shall apply only on the making of a claim by the personal representatives.]

Note. Inserted by the Finance Act 2004, s 117, Sch 22, paras 5, 7(2), in relation to disposals made on or after 10 December 2003.

226. Private residence occupied by dependent relative before 6th April 1988—(1) Subject to subsection (3) below, this section applies to a gain accruing to an individual so far as attributable to the disposal of, or of an interest in, a dwelling-house or part of a dwelling-house which, on 5th April 1988 or at any earlier time in his period of ownership, was the sole residence of a dependent relative of the individual, provided rent-free and without any other consideration.

(2) If the individual so claims, such relief shall be given in respect of it and its garden or grounds as he would be given under sections 222 to 224 if the dwelling-house (or part of the dwelling-house) had been the individual's only or main residence in the period of residence by the dependent relative, and shall be so given in addition to any relief available under those sections apart from this section.

(3) If in a case within subsection (1) above the dwelling-house or part ceases, whether before 6th April 1988 or later, to be the sole residence (provided as mentioned above) of the dependent relative, any subsequent period of residence beginning on or after that date by that or any other dependent relative shall be disregarded for the purposes of subsection (2) above.

(4) Not more than one dwelling-house (or part of a dwelling-house) may qualify for relief as being the residence of a dependent relative of the claimant at any one time nor, in the case of a man and his wife living with him, as being the residence of a dependent relative of the claimant or of the claimant's husband or wife at any one time.

(5) *The inspector, before allowing a claim, may require the claimant to show that the giving of the relief claimed will not under subsection (4) above preclude the giving of relief to the claimant's wife or husband or that a claim to any such relief has been relinquished.*

(6) In this section 'dependent relative' means, in relation to an individual—

(a) any relative of his or of his wife who is incapacitated by old age or infirmity from maintaining himself, or

(b) his of his wife's mother who, whether or not incapacitated, is either widowed, or living apart from her husband, or a single woman in consequence of dissolution or annulment of marriage.

(7) If the individual mentioned in subsection (6) above is a woman the references in that subsection to the individual's wife shall be construed as references to the individual's husband.

Note. Sub-s (5) repealed by Finance Act 1996, s 205, Sch 41, Part V, in relation to capital gains tax for the year 1996–97 and subsequent years of assessment.

* * * * *

Superannuation funds, profit sharing schemes, employee trusts etc

237. Superannuation funds, annuities and annual payments. No chargeable gain shall accrue to any person on the disposal of a right to, or to any part of—

(a) any allowance, annuity or capital sum payable out of any superannuation fund, or under any superannuation scheme, established solely or mainly for persons employed in a profession, trade, undertaking or employment, and their dependants,

(b) an annuity granted otherwise than under a contract for a deferred annuity by a company as part of its business of granting annuities on human life, whether or not including instalments of capital, or an annuity granted or deemed to be granted under the Government Annuities Act 1929, or

(c) annual payments which are due under a covenant made by any person and which are not secured on any property.

* * * * *

Miscellaneous gifts and exemptions

262. Chattel exemption—(1) Subject to this section a gain accruing on a disposal of an asset which is tangible movable property shall not be a chargeable gain if the amount or value of the consideration for the disposal does not exceed £6,000.

(2) Where the amount or value of the consideration for the disposal of an asset which is tangible movable property exceeds £6,000, there shall be excluded from any chargeable gain accruing on the disposal so much of it as exceeds five-thirds of the difference between—

(a) the amount or value of the consideration, and

(b) £6,000.

(3) Subsections (1) and (2) above shall not affect the amount of an allowable loss accruing on the disposal of an asset, but for the purposes of computing under this Act the amount of a loss accruing on the disposal of tangible movable property the consideration for the disposal shall, if less than £6,000, be deemed to be £6,000 and the losses which are allowable losses shall be restricted accordingly.

(4) If 2 or more assets which have formed part of a set of articles of any description all owned at one time by one person are disposed of by that person, and—

   (a) to the same person, or

   (b) to persons who are acting in concert or who are connected persons,

whether on the same or different occasions, the 2 or more transactions shall be treated as a single transaction disposing of a single asset, but with any necessary apportionments of the reductions in chargeable gains, and in allowable losses, under subsections (2) and (3) above.

  (5) If the disposal is of a right or interest in or over tangible movable property—

   (a) in the first instance subsections (1), (2) and (3) above shall be applied in relation to the asset as a whole, taking the consideration as including the market value of what remains undisposed of, in addition to the actual consideration,

   (b) where the sum of the actual consideration and that market value exceeds £6,000, the part of any chargeable gain that is excluded from it under subsection (2) above shall be so much of the gain as exceeds five-thirds of the difference between that sum and £6,000 multiplied by the fraction equal to the actual consideration divided by the said sum, and

   (c) where that sum is less than £6,000 any loss shall be restricted under subsection (3) above by deeming the consideration to be the actual consideration plus the said fraction of the difference between the said sum and £6,000.

  (6) This section shall not apply—

   (a) in relation to a disposal of commodities of any description by a person dealing on a terminal market or dealing with or through a person ordinarily engaged in dealing on a terminal market, or

   (b) in relation to a disposal of currency of any description.

*   *   *   *   *

PART VIII

SUPPLEMENTAL

*   *   *   *   *

273. Unquoted shares and securities—(1) The provisions of subsection (3) below shall have effect in any case where, in relation to an asset to which this section applies, there falls to be determined by virtue of section 272(1) the price which the asset might reasonably be expected to fetch on a sale in the open market.

  (2) The assets to which this section applies are shares and securities which are not quoted on a recognised stock exchange at the time as at which their market value for the purposes of tax on chargeable gains falls to be determined.

  (3) For the purposes of a determination falling within subsection (1) above, it shall be assumed that, in the open market which is postulated for the purposes of that determination, there is available to any prospective purchaser of the asset in question all the information which a prudent prospective purchaser of the asset might reasonably require if he were proposing to purchase it from a willing vendor by private treaty and at arm's length.

*   *   *   *   *

275. Location of assets. For the purposes of this Act—

   (a) the situation of rights or interests (otherwise than by way of security) in or over immovable property is that of the immovable property,

   (b) subject to the following provisions of this subsection, the situation of rights or interests (otherwise than by way of security) in or over tangible movable property is that of the tangible movable property,

   (c) subject to the following provisions of this subsection, a debt secured or unsecured, is situated in the United Kingdom if and only if the creditor is resident in the United Kingdom,

(d) shares or securities issued by any municipal or governmental authority, or by any body created by such an authority, are situated in the country of that authority,

(e) subject to paragraph (d) above, registered shares or securities are situated where they are registered and, if registered in more than one register, where the principal register is situated,

(f) a ship or aircraft is situated in the United Kingdom if and only if the owner is then resident in the United Kingdom, and an interest or right in or over a ship or aircraft is situated in the United Kingdom if and only if the person entitled to the interest or right is resident in the United Kingdom,

(g) the situation of good-will as a trade, business or professional asset is at the place where the trade, business or profession is carried on,

(h) patents, trade marks, ... and registered designs are situated where they are registered, and if registered in more than one register, where each register is situated, and rights or licences to use a patent, tade mark, ... or registered design are situated in the United Kingdom if they or any right derived from them are exercisable in the United Kingdom,

(j) copyright, design right and franchises, and rights or licences to use any copyright work or design in which design rights subsists, are situated in the United Kingdom if they or any right derived from them are exercisable in the United Kingdom,

(k) a judgment debt is situated where the judgment is recorded,

(l) a debt which—
 (i) is owed by a bank, and
 (ii) is not in sterling, and
 (iii) is represented by a sum standing to the credit of an account in the bank of an individual who is not domiciled in the United Kingdom,
 is situated in the United Kingdom if and only if that individual is resident in the United Kingdom and the branch or other place of business of the bank at which the account is maintained is itself situated in the United Kingdom.

* * * * *

Note. Words omitted from para (h) repealed by Trade Marks Act 1994, s 106(2), Sch 5, as from 31 October 1994.

286. Connected persons: interpretation—(1) Any question whether a person is connected with another shall for the purposes of this Act be determined in accordance with the following subsections of this section (any provision that one person is connected with another being taken to mean that they are connected with one another).

(2) A person is connected with an individual if that person is the individual's husband or wife, or is a relative, or the husband or wife of a relative, of the individual or of the individual's husband or wife.

[(3) A person, in his capacity as trustee of a settlement, is connected with—

(a) any individual who in relation to the settlement is a settlor,

(b) any person who is connected with such an individual, and

(c) any body corporate which is connected with that settlement.

In this subsection 'settlement' and 'settlor' have the same meaning as in Chapter IA of Part XV of the Taxes Act (see section 660G(1) and (2) of that Act).

(3A) For the purpose of subsection (3) above a body corporate is connected with a settlement if—

(a) it is a close company (or only not a close company because it is not resident in the United Kingdom) and the participators include the trustees of the settlement; or

(b) it is controlled (within the meaning of section 840 of the Taxes Act) by a company falling within paragraph (a) above.]

(4) Except in relation to acquisitions or disposals of partnership assets pursuant to bona fide commercial arrangements, a person is connected with any person with whom he is in partnership, and with the husband or wife or a relative of any individual with whom he is in partnership.

(5) A company is connected with another company—

(a) if the same person has control of both, or a person has control of one and persons connected with him, or he and persons connected with him, have control of the other, or

(b) if a group of 2 or more persons has control of each company, and the groups either consist of the same persons or could be regarded as consisting of the same persons by treating (in one or more cases) a member of either group as replaced by a person with whom he is connected.

(6) A company is connected with another person, if that person has control of it or if that person and persons connected with him together have control of it.

(7) Any 2 or more persons acting together to secure or exercise control of a company shall be treated in relation to that company as connected with one another and with any person acting on the directions of any of them to secure or exercise control of the company.

(8) In this section 'relative' means brother, sister, ancestor or lineal descendant.

Note. Sub-ss (3), (3A) substituted for sub-s (3) as originally enacted by Finance Act 1995, s 74, Sch 17, Part III, para 31, with effect for the year 1995–96 and subsequent years of assessment and applying to every settlement, wherever and whenever it was made or entered into.

287. Orders and regulations made by the Treasury or the Board—(1) Subject to subsection (2) below, any power of the Treasury or the Board to make any order or regulations under this Act or any other enactment relating to the taxation of chargeable gains passed after this Act shall be exercisable by statutory instrument.

(2) Subsection (1) above shall not apply in relation to any power conferred by section 288(6).

(3) Subject to subsection (4) below and to any other provision to the contrary, any statutory instrument to which subsection (1) above applies shall be subject to annulment in pursuance of a resolution of the House of Commons.

(4) Subsection (3) above shall not apply in relation to an order or regulations made under section 3(4) or 265 or paragraph 1 of Schedule 9, or—

(a) if any other Parliamentary procedure is expressly provided; or

(b) if the order in question is an order appointing a day for the purposes of any provision, being a day as from which the provision will have effect, with or without amendments, or will cease to have effect.

288. Interpretation—(1) In this Act, unless the context otherwise requires—

'the 1979 Act' means the Capital Gains Tax Act 1979;

'the 1990 Act' means the Capital Allowances Act 1990;

'allowable loss' shall be construed in accordance with sections 8(2) and 16;

'the Board' means the Commissioners of Inland Revenue;

'building society' has the same meaning as in the Building Societies Act 1986;

['the Capital Allowances Act' means the Capital Allowances Act 2001;]

'chargeable period' means a year of assessment or an accounting period of a company for purposes of corporation tax;

'class', in relation to shares or securities, means a class of shares or securities of any one company;

'close company' has the meaning given by sections 414 and 415 of the Taxes Act;

'collective investment scheme' has the *same meaning as in the Financial Services Act 1986* [meaning given by section 235 of the Financial Services and Markets Act 2000] [subject to section 99A];

'company' includes any body corporate or unincorporated association but does not include a partnership, and shall be construed in accordance with section 99;

'control' shall be construed in accordance with section 416 of the Taxes Act;

'double taxation relief arrangements' means, in relation to a company, arrangements having effect by virtue of section 788 of the Taxes Act and, in relation to any other person, means arrangements having effect by virtue of that section as extended to capital gains tax by section 277;

'dual resident investing company' has the meaning given by section 404 of the Taxes Act;

'inspector' means any inspector of taxes;

'investment trust' has the meaning given by section 842 of the Taxes Act;

'land' includes messuages, tenements, and hereditaments, houses and buildings of any tenure;

'local authority' has the meaning given by section 842A of the Taxes Act;

'the Management Act' means the Taxes Management Act 1970;

'notice' means notice in writing;

'personal representatives' has the meaning given by section 701(4) of the Taxes Act;

['property investment LLP' has the meaning given by section 842B of the Taxes Act;]

'recognised stock exchange' has the meaning given by section 841 of the Taxes Act;

['registered pension scheme' has the meaning given by section 150(2) of the Finance Act 2004;]

['Registrar of government Stock' means the person or persons appointed in accordance with regulations under section 47(1)(b) of the Finance Act 1942 (see regulation 3 of the Government Stock Regulations 2004;]

'shares' includes stock;

'the Taxes Act' means the Income and Corporation Taxes Act 1988;

'trade' has the same meaning as in the Income Tax Acts;

'trading stock' has the meaning given by section 100(2) of the Taxes Act;

['venture capital trust' has the meaning given by section 842AA of the Taxes Act;]

'wasting asset' has the meaning given by section 44 and paragraph 1 of Schedule 8;

'year of assessment' means, in relation to capital gains tax, a year beginning on 6th April and ending on 5th April in the following calendar year, and '1992–93' and so on indicate years of assessment as in the Income Tax Acts;

and any reference to a particular section, Part or Schedule is a reference to that section or Part of, or that Schedule to, this Act.

[(1A) If any employment-related securities option would not otherwise be regarded as an option for the purposes of this Act, it shall be so regarded; and the acquisition of securities by an associated person pursuant to an employment-related securities option is to be treated for the purposes of this Act as the exercise of the option.

Expressions used in this subsection and Chapter 5 of Part 7 of ITEPA 2003 have the same meaning in this subsection as in that Chapter.]

(2) In this Act 'retail prices index' has the same meaning as in the Income Tax Acts and, accordingly, any reference in this Act to the retail prices index shall be construed in accordance with section 833(2) of the Taxes Act.

(3) References in this Act to a married woman living with her husband shall be construed in accordance with section 282 of the Taxes Act.

(4) *References in this Act to quotation on a stock exchange in the United Kingdom or a recognised stock exchange in the United Kingdom shall be construed as references to listing in the Official List of The Stock Exchange.*

(5) For the purposes of this Act, shares or debentures comprised in any letter of allotment or similar instrument shall be treated as issued unless the right to the shares or debentures thereby conferred remains provisional until accepted and there has been no acceptance.

(6) In this Act 'recognised futures exchange' means the London International Financial Futures Exchange and any other futures exchange which is for the time being designated for the purposes of this Act by order made by the Board.

(7) An order made by the Board under subsection (6) above—

(a) may designate a futures exchange by name or by reference to any class or description of futures exchanges, including, in the case of futures exchanges in a country outside the United Kingdom, a class or description framed by reference to any authority or approval given in that country; and

(b) may contain such transitional and other supplemental provisions as appear to the Board to be necessary or expedient.

(8) The Table below indexes other general definitions in this Act.

Expressed defined	*Reference*
'Absolutely entitled as against the trustee'	s 60(2)
'Authorised unit trust'	s 99
'Branch or agency'	s 10(6)
'Chargeable gain'	s 15(2)
'Connected', in references to persons being connected with one another	s 286
'Court invested fund'	s 100
'Gilt-edged securities'	Sch 9
'Indexation allowance'	s 53
'Lease' and cognate expressions	Sch 8, para 10(1)
'Legatee'	s 64(2), (3)
'Market value'	ss 272 to 274 and Sch 11
'Part disposal'	s 21(2)
'Qualifying corporate bond'	s 117
'Relevant allowable expenditure'	s 53
'Resident' and 'ordinarily resident'	s 9(1)
'Settled property'	s 68
'Unit trust scheme' [and 'unit holder']	*s 99* [ss 99 and 99A]

Note. In sub-s (1) definition 'the 1990 Act' repealed and definition 'the Capital Allowances Act' inserted, by the Capital Allowances Act 2001, ss 578, 580, Sch 2, para 80, Sch 4, in relation to corporation tax as respects allowances and charges falling to be made for chargeable periods ending on or after 1 April 2001, and in relation to income tax as respects allowances and charges falling to be made for chargeable periods ending on or after 6 April 2001. In sub-s (1) in definition 'collective investment scheme' words in square brackets substituted by SI 2001 No 3629, arts 61, 70. In sub-s (1) definition 'property investment LLP' inserted by the Finance Act 2001, s 76(1), Sch 25, para 1(3). In sub-s (1) in definition 'collective investement scheme' words '(subject to section 99A)' in square brackets inserted, and in the table in sub-s (8) words 'and "unit holder"' and 'ss 99 and 99A' in square brackets substituted, by the Finance Act 2004, s 118(1), (4), in relation to years of assessment and accounting periods begining on or after 1 April 2004. In sub-s (1) definition 'registered pension scheme' inserted, with transitional provisions, by the Finance Act 2004, ss 281(1), 283(1), Sch 35, paras 38, 41, Sch 36. In sub-s (1) definition 'Registrar of Government Stock' inserted, with transitional provisions, by SI 2004 No 2744, arts 2, 3, Schedule, paras 3(1), (3). In sub-s (1) definition 'venture capital trust' inserted by the Finance Act 1995, s 72(1), (7), (8), with effect for the year 1995–96 and subsequent years of assessment. Sub-s (IA) inserted by the Finance Act 2003, s 140, Sch 22, paras 10(2), 49, 54; this amendment has effect on or after 16 April 2003 in relation to employment-related securities options which are not share options, but does not apply to employment-related securities options which are share options until 1 September 2003 (see also SI 2003 No 1997, art 2). Sub-s (4) repealed by the Finance Act 1996, s 205, Sch 41, Pt VIII(3).

289. Commencement—(1) Except where the context otherwise requires, this Act has effect in relation to tax for the year 1992–93 and subsequent years of assessment, and tax for other chargeable periods beginning on or after 6th April 1992, and references to the coming into force of this Act or any provision in this Act shall be construed accordingly.

(2) The following provisions of this Act, that is—

(a) so much of any provision of this Act as authorises the making of any order or other instrument, and

(b) except where the tax concerned is all tax for chargeable periods to which this Act does not apply, so much of any provision of this Act as confers any power or imposes any duty the exercise or performance of which operates or may operate in relation to tax for more than one chargeable period,

shall come into force for all purposes on 6th April 1992 to the exclusion of the corresponding enactments repealed by this Act.

290. Savings, transitionals, consequential amendments and repeals—(1) Schedules 10 (consequential amendments) and 11 (transitory provisions and savings) shall have effect.

(2) No letters patent granted or to be granted by the Crown to any person, city, borough or town corporate of any liberty, privilege, or exemption from subsidies, tolls, taxes, assessments or aids, and no statute which grants any salary, annuity or pension to any person free of any taxes, deductions or assessments, shall be construed or taken to exempt any person, city, borough or town corporate, or any inhabitant of the same, from tax chargeable in pursuance of this Act.

(3) Subject to Schedule 11, the enactments and instruments mentioned in Schedule 12 to this Act are hereby repealed to the extent specified in the third column of that Schedule (but Schedule 12 shall not have effect in relation to any enactment in so far as it has previously been repealed subject to a saving which still has effect on the coming into force of this section).

(4) The provisions of this Part of this Act are without prejudice to the provisions of the Interpretation Act 1978 as respects the effect of repeals.

291. Short title.   This Act may be cited as the Taxation of Chargeable Gains Act 1992.

SCHEDULES

SCHEDULE A1   Section 2A

APPLICATION OF TAPER RELIEF

[Introductory

1.—(1) Section 2A shall be construed subject to and in accordance with this Schedule.

(2) The different provisions of this Schedule have effect for construing the other provisions of this Schedule, as well as for construing section 2A.

Period for which an asset is held and relevant period of ownership

2.—(1) In relation to any gain on the disposal of a business or non-business asset, the period after 5th April 1998 for which the asset had been held at the time of its disposal is the period which—

(a) begins with whichever is the later of 6th April 1998 and the time when the asset disposed of was acquired by the person making the disposal; and

(b) ends with the time of the disposal on which the gain accrued.

(2) Where an asset is disposed of, its relevant period of ownership is whichever is the shorter of—

(a) the period after 5th April 1998 for which the asset had been held at the time of its disposal; and

(b) the period of ten years ending with that time.

(3) The following shall be disregarded for determining when a person is to be treated for the purposes of this paragraph as having acquired an asset, that is to say—

(a) so much of section 73(1)(b) as treats the asset as acquired at a date before 6th April 1965; and

(b) sections 239(2)(b), 257(2)(b) and 259(2)(b).

(4) Where the period after 5th April 1998 for which an asset had been held at the time of its disposal includes any period which, in accordance with any of paragraphs 10 to 12 below [or paragraph 4 of Schedule 5BA], is a period that does not count for the purposes of taper relief—

(a) the qualifying holding period of the asset shall be treated for the purposes of section 2A as reduced by the length of the period that does not count or, as the case may be, of the aggregate of the periods that do not count; and

(b) the period that does not count or, as the case may be, every such period—

(i) shall be left out of account in computing for the purposes of sub-paragraph (2) above the period of ten years ending with the time of the asset's disposal; and

(ii) shall be assumed not to be comprised in the asset's relevant period of ownership.

(5) Sub-paragraphs (1) to (3) above have effect subject to the provisions of paragraphs 13 to 19 below.

Rules for determining whether a gain is a gain on the disposal of a business asset or non-business asset

3.—(1) Subject to the following provisions of this Schedule, a chargeable gain accruing to any person on the disposal of any asset is a gain on the disposal of a business asset if that asset was a business asset throughout its relevant period of ownership.

(2) Where—

(a) a chargeable gain accrues to any person on the disposal of any asset,

(b) that gain does not accrue on the disposal of an asset that was a business asset throughout its relevant period of ownership, and

(c) that asset has been a business asset throughout one or more periods comprising part of its relevant period of ownership,

a part of that gain shall be taken to be a gain on the disposal of a business asset and, in accordance with sub-paragraph (4) below, the remainder shall be taken to be a gain on the disposal of a non-business asset.

(3) Subject to the following provisions of this Schedule, where sub-paragraph (2) above applies, the part of the chargeable gain accruing on the disposal of the asset that shall be taken to be a gain on the disposal of a business asset is the part of it that bears the same proportion to the whole of the gain as is borne to the whole of its relevant period of ownership by the aggregate of the periods which—

(a) are comprised in its relevant period of ownership, and

(b) are periods throughout which the asset is to be taken (after applying paragraphs 8 and 9 below) to have been a business asset.

(4) So much of any chargeable gain accruing to any person on the disposal of any asset as is not a gain on the disposal of a business asset shall be taken to be a gain on the disposal of a non-business asset.

(5) Where, by virtue of sub-paragraphs (2) to (4) above, a gain on the disposal of a business asset accrues on the same disposal as a gain on the disposal of a non-business asset—

(a) the two gains shall be treated for the purposes of taper relief as separate gains accruing on separate disposals of separate assets; but

(b) the periods after 5th April 1998 for which each of the assets shall be taken to have been held at the time of their disposal shall be the same and shall be determined without reference to the length of the periods mentioned in sub-paragraph (3)(a) and (b) above.

Conditions for shares to qualify as business assets

4.—(1) This paragraph applies, in the case of the disposal of any asset, for determining (subject to the following provisions of this Schedule) whether the asset was a business asset at a time before its disposal when it consisted of, or of an interest in, any shares in a company ('the relevant company').

(2) Where the disposal is made by an individual, the asset was a business asset at that time if at that time the relevant company was a qualifying company by reference to that individual.

(3) Where the disposal is made by the trustees of a settlement, the asset was a business asset at that time if at that time the relevant company was a qualifying company by reference to the trustees of that settlement.

(4) Where the disposal is made by an individual's personal representatives, the asset was a business asset at that time if at that time—

(a) *the relevant company was a trading company or the holding company of a trading group; and*

(b) *the voting rights in that company were exercisable, as to not less than 25 per cent, by the deceased's personal representatives*

[the relevant company was a qualifying company by reference to the personal representatives].

(5) Where the disposal is made by an individual who acquired the asset as legatee (as defined in section 64) and that time is not a time when the asset was a business asset by virtue of sub-paragraph (2) above, the asset shall be taken to have been a business asset at that time if at that time—

(a) it was held by the personal representatives of the deceased; and

(b) *the conditions in sub-paragraph (4)(a) and (b) above were satisfied*

[(b) the relevant company was a qualifying company by reference to the personal representatives].

Conditions for other assets to qualify as business assets

5.—(1) This paragraph applies, in the case of the disposal of any asset [by an individual, the trustees of a settlement or an individual's personal representatives], for determining (subject to the following provisions of this Schedule) whether the asset was a business asset at a time before its disposal when it was neither shares in a company nor an interest in shares in a company.

(2) *Where the disposal is made by an individual, the asset was a business asset at that time if at that time it was being used, wholly or partly, for purposes falling within one or more of the following paragraphs—*

(a) *the purposes of a trade carried on at that time by that individual or by a partnership of which that individual was at that time a member;*

(b) *the purposes of any trade carried on by a company which at that time was a qualifying company by reference to that individual;*

(c) *the purposes of any trade carried on by a company which at that time was a member of a trading group the holding company of which was at that time a qualifying company by reference to that individual;*

(d) *the purposes of any qualifying office or employment to which that individual was at that time required to devote substantially the whole of his time;*

[(d) *the purposes of any office or employment held by that individual with a person carrying on a trade].*

(3) *Where the disposal is made by the trustees of a settlement, the asset was a business asset at that time if at that time it was being used, wholly or partly, for purposes falling within one or more of the following paragraphs—*

(a)   *the purposes of a trade carried on by the trustees of the settlement [or by a partnership whose members at that time included—*

    (i)   *the trustees of the settlement; or*

    (ii) *any one or more of the persons who at that time were the trustees of the settlement (so far as acting in their capacity as such trustees)];*

(b)   *the purposes of a trade carried on at that time by an eligible beneficiary or by a partnership of which an eligible beneficiary was at that time a member;*

(c)   *the purposes of any trade carried on by a company which at that time was a qualifying company by reference to the trustees of the settlement or an eligible beneficiary;*

(d)   *the purposes of any trade carried on by a company which at that time was a member of a trading group the holding company of which was at that time a qualifying company by reference to the trustees of the settlement or an eligible beneficiary;*

(e)   *the purposes of any qualifying office or employment to which an eligible beneficiary was at that time required to devote substantially the whole of his time;*

(f)   *the purposes of any office or employment that does not fall within paragraph (e) above but was an office or employment with a trading company in relation to which an eligible beneficiary falls to be treated as having, at that time, been a full-time working officer or employee*

[(e) *the purposes of any office or employment held by an eligible beneficiary with a person carrying on a trade].*

(4) *Where the disposal is made by an individual's personal representatives, the asset was a business asset at that time if at that time it was being used, wholly or partly, for purposes falling within one or more of the following paragraphs—*

(a)   *the purposes of a trade carried on by the deceased's personal representatives;*

(b)   *the purposes of any trade carried on by a company which at that time was a qualifying company by reference to the deceased's personal representatives;*

(c)   *the purposes of any trade carried on by a company which at that time was a member of a trading group the holding company of which was at that time a qualifying company by reference to the deceased's personal representatives.*

(5) *Where the disposal is made by an individual who acquired the asset as legatee (as defined in section 64) and that time is not a time when the asset was a business asset by virtue of sub-paragraph (2) above, the asset shall be taken to have been a business asset at that time if at that time it was—*

(a)   *being held by the personal representatives of the deceased, and*

(b)   *being used, wholly or partly, for purposes falling within one or more of paragraphs (a) to (c) of sub-paragraph (4) above.*

[(1A) The asset was a business asset at that time if at that time it was being used, wholly or partly, for the purposes of a trade carried on by—

(a)   an individual or a partnership of which an individual was at that time a member, or

(b)   the trustees of a settlement or a partnership whose members at that time included—

    (i)   the trustees of a settlement, or

    (ii) any one or more of the persons who at that time were the trustees of a settlement (so far as acting in their capacity as trustees), or

(c)   the personal representatives of a deceased person or a partnership whose members at that time included—

    (i)   the personal representatives of a deceased person, or

    (ii) any one or more of the persons who at that time were the personal representatives of a deceased person (so far as acting in their capacity as personal representatives).

(2) Where the disposal is made by an individual, the asset was a business asset at that time if at that time it was being used, wholly or partly, for the purposes of a trade carried on by—

(a) a company which at that time was a qualifying company by reference to that individual,

(b) a company which at that time was a member of a trading group the holding company of which was at that time a qualifying company by reference to that individual, or

(c) a partnership whose members at that time included a company within paragraph (a) or (b),

or for the purposes of any office or employment held by that individual with a person carrying on a trade.

(3) Where the disposal is made by the trustees of a settlement, the asset was a business asset at that time if at that time it was being used, wholly or partly, for the purposes of a trade carried on by—

(a) a company which at that time was a qualifying company by reference to the trustees of the settlement or an eligible beneficiary,

(b) a company which at that time was a member of a trading group the holding company of which was at that time a qualifying company by reference to the trustees of the settlement or an eligible beneficiary, or

(c) a partnership whose members at that time included a company within paragraph (a) or (b),

or for the purposes of any office or employment held by an eligible beneficiary with a person carrying on a trade.

(4) Where the disposal is made by an individual's personal representatives, the asset was a business asset at that time if at that time it was being used, wholly or partly, for the purposes of a trade carried on by—

(a) a company which at that time was a qualifying company by reference to the deceased's personal representatives,

(b) a company which at that time was a member of a trading group the holding company of which was at that time a qualifying company by reference to the deceased's personal representatives, or

(c) a partnership whose members at that time included a company within paragraph (a) or (b).

(5) Where the disposal is made by an individual who acquired the asset as legatee (as defined in section 64), the asset shall be taken to have been a business asset at that time if at that time it was—

(a) being held by the personal representatives of the deceased, and

(b) being used, wholly or partly, for the purposes of a trade carried on by—

(i) a company which at that time was a qualifying company by reference to the deceased's personal representatives,

(ii) a company which at that time was a member of a trading group the holding company of which was at that time a qualifying company by reference to the deceased's personal representatives, or

(iii) a partnership whose members at that time included a company within sub-paragraph (i) or (ii).]

Companies which are qualifying companies

6.—*(1) The times when a company shall be taken to have been a qualifying company by reference to an individual, the trustees of a settlement or an individual's personal representatives are—*

(a) in the case of an individual, those set out in sub-paragraphs (2) and (3) below; and

(b) in the case of the trustees of a settlement, those set out in sub-paragraphs (2) and (4) below; and

(c)   in the case of personal representatives, those set out in sub-paragraph (2) below.

(2) A company was a qualifying company by reference to an individual, the trustees of a settlement or personal representatives at any time when both the following conditions were satisfied, that is to say—

(a)   the company was a trading company or the holding company of a trading group; and

(b)   the voting rights in that company were exercisable, as to not less than 25 per cent, by that individual or, as the case may be, the trustees of the settlement or the personal representatives.

(3) A company was also a qualifying company by reference to an individual at any time when all of the following conditions were satisfied, that is to say—

(a)   the company was a trading company or the holding company of a trading group;

(b)   the voting rights in that company were exercisable, as to not less than 5 per cent, by that individual; and

(c)   that individual was a full-time working officer or employee of that company or of a company which at the time had a relevant connection with that company.

(4) A company was also a qualifying company by reference to the trustees of a settlement at any time when all the following conditions were satisfied, that is to say—

(a)   the company was a trading company or the holding company of a trading group;

(b)   the voting rights in that company were exercisable, as to not less than 5 per cent, by the trustees of that settlement; and

(c)   an eligible beneficiary was a full-time working officer or employee of that company or of a company which at the time had a relevant connection with that company.

Companies which are qualifying companies

[**6.**—(1) A company shall be taken to have been a qualifying company by reference to an individual at any time when—

(a)   the company was a trading company or the holding company of a trading group, and

(b)   one or more of the following conditions was met—

   (i)   the company was unlisted,

  (ii)   the individual was an officer or employee of the company, or of a company having a relevant connection with it, or

 (iii)   the voting rights in the company were exercisable, as to not less than 5%, by the individual.

[(1A) A company shall also be taken to have been a qualifying company by reference to an individual at any time when—

(a)   the company was a non-trading company or the holding company of a non-trading group,

(b)   the individual was an officer or employee of the company, or of a company having a relevant connection with it, and

(c)   the individual did not have a material interest in the company or in any company which at that time had control of the company.]

(2) A company shall be taken to have been a qualifying company by reference to the trustees of a settlement at any time when—

(a)   the company was a trading company or the holding company of a trading group, and

(b)   one or more of the following conditions was met—

   (i)   the company was unlisted,

  (ii)   an eligible beneficiary was an officer or employee of the company, or of a company having a relevant connection with it, or

 (iii)   the voting rights in the company were exercisable, as to not less than 5%, by the trustees.

[(2A) A company shall also be taken to have been a qualifying company by reference to the trustees of a settlement at any time when—

(a) the company was a non-trading company or the holding company of a non-trading group,

(b) an eligible beneficiary was an officer or employee of the company, or of a company having a relevant connection with it, and

(c) the trustees of the settlement did not have a material interest in the company or in any company which at that time had control of the company.]

(3) A company shall be taken to have been a qualifying company by reference to an individual's personal representatives at any time when—

(a) the company was a trading company or the holding company of a trading group, and

(b) one or more of the following conditions was met—

   (i) the company was unlisted, or

   (ii) the voting rights in the company were exercisable, as to not less than 5%, by the personal representatives.

[(4) For the purposes of this paragraph an individual shall be regarded as having a material interest in a company if—

(a) the individual,

(b) the individual together with one or more persons connected with him, or

(c) any person connected with the individual, with or without any other such persons,

has a material interest in the company.

(5) For the purposes of this paragraph the trustees of a settlement shall be regarded as having a material interest in a company if—

(a) the trustees of the settlement,

(b) the trustees of the settlement together with one or more persons connected with them, or

(c) any person connected with the trustees of the settlement, with or without any other such persons,

has a material interest in the company.

(6) In this paragraph 'company' does not include a unit trust scheme, notwithstanding anything in section 99.

(7) This paragraph is supplemented by paragraph 6A below (meaning of 'material interest').]]

[Meaning of "material interest"

6A.—(1) For the purposes of paragraph 6 above, a material interest in a company means possession of, or the ability to control (directly or through the medium of other companies or by any other indirect means),—

(a) more than 10% of the issued shares in the company of any particular class,

(b) more than 10% of the voting rights in the company,

(c) such rights as would, if the whole of the income of the company were distributed among the participators (without regard to any rights of any person as a loan creditor) give an entitlement to receive more than 10% of the amount distributed, or

(d) such rights as would, in the event of the winding up of the company or in any other circumstances, give an entitlement to receive more than 10% of the assets of the company which would then be available for distribution among the participators.

(2) For the purposes of sub-paragraph (1) above a right to acquire shares or rights (however arising) shall be treated as a right to control them.

(3) A person shall be treated for the purposes of this paragraph as having a right to acquire any shares or rights—

(a) which he is entitled to acquire at a future date, or

(b) which he will at a future date be entitled to acquire.

(4) Where—

(a) in the case of any shares or rights, an entitlement falling within sub-paragraph (3)(a) or (b) above is conferred on a person by a contract, but

(b) the contract is conditional,

the person shall be treated for the purposes of this paragraph as having a right to acquire the shares or rights as from the time at which the contract is made.

(5) In any case where—

(a) the shares of any particular class attributed to a person consist of or include shares which he or another person has a right to acquire, and

(b) the circumstances are such that if that right were to be exercised the shares acquired would be shares which were previously unissued and which the company is contractually bound to issue in the event of the exercise of the right,

then in determining at any time prior to the exercise of the right whether the number of shares of that class attributed to the person exceeds a particular percentage of the issued shares of that class, the number of issued shares of that class shall be taken to be increased by the number of unissued shares referred to in paragraph (b) above.

(6) The references in sub-paragraph (5) above to the shares of any particular class attributed to a person are to the shares which in accordance with sub-paragraph (1)(a) above fall to be brought into account in his case to determine whether their number exceeds a particular percentage of the issued shares of the company of that class.

(7) Sub-paragraphs (5) and (6) above shall apply, with the necessary modifications, in relation to—

(a) voting rights in the company (and attribution of such rights to a person in accordance with sub-paragraph (1)(b) above),

(b) rights which would, if the whole of the income of the company were distributed among the participators (without regard to any rights of any person as a loan creditor) give an entitlement to receive any of the amount distributed (and attribution of such rights to a person in accordance with sub-paragraph (1)(c) above), and

(c) rights which would, in the event of the winding up of the company or in any other circumstances, give an entitlement to receive any of the assets of the company which would then be available for distribution among the participators (and attribution of such rights to a person in accordance with sub-paragraph (1)(d) above),

as they apply in relation to shares of any particular class (and their attribution to a person in accordance with sub-paragraph (1)(a) above).

(8) For the purposes of this paragraph "participator" and "loan creditor" have the meaning given by section 417 of the Taxes Act.]

Persons who are eligible beneficiaries

7.—(1) An eligible beneficiary, in relation to an asset comprised in a settlement and a time, is any individual having at that time a relevant interest in possession under the settlement in either—

(a) the whole of the settled property; or

(b) a part of the settled property that is or includes that asset.

(2) In this paragraph 'relevant interest in possession', in relation to property comprised in a settlement, means any interest in possession under that settlement other than—

(a) a right under that settlement to receive an annuity; or

(b) a fixed-term entitlement.

(3) In sub-paragraph (2) above 'fixed-term entitlement', in relation to property comprised in a settlement, means any interest under that settlement which is limited to a term that is fixed and is not a term at the end of which the person with that interest will become entitled to the property.

Cases where there are non-qualifying beneficiaries

8.—(1) This paragraph applies in the case of a disposal of an asset by the trustees of a settlement where the asset's relevant period of ownership is or includes a period ('a sharing period') throughout which—
- (a) the asset was a business asset by reference to one or more eligible beneficiaries;
- (b) the asset would not otherwise have been a business asset; and
- (c) there is a non-qualifying part of the relevant income, or there would be if there were any relevant income for that period.

(2) The period throughout which the asset disposed of is to be taken to have been a business asset shall be determined as if the relevant fraction of every sharing period were a period throughout which the asset was not a business asset.

(3) In sub-paragraph (2) above 'the relevant fraction', in relation to any sharing period, means the fraction which represents the proportion of relevant income for that period which is, or (if there were such income) would be, a non-qualifying part of that income.

(4) Where a sharing period is a period in which the proportion mentioned in sub-paragraph (3) above has been different at different times, this paragraph shall require a separate relevant fraction to be determined for, and applied to, each part of that period for which there is a different proportion.

(5) For the purposes of this paragraph the non-qualifying part of any relevant income for any period is so much of that income for that period as is or, as the case may be, would be—
- (a) income to which no eligible beneficiary has any entitlement; or
- (b) income to which a non-qualifying eligible beneficiary has an entitlement.

(6) In sub-paragraph (5) above 'non-qualifying eligible beneficiary', in relation to a period, means an eligible beneficiary who is not a beneficiary by reference to whom (if he were the only beneficiary) the asset disposed of would be a business asset throughout that period.

(7) In this paragraph 'relevant income' means income from the part of the settled property comprising the asset disposed of.

Cases where an asset is used at the same time for different purposes

9.—(1) This paragraph applies in the case of a disposal by any person of an asset where the asset's relevant period of ownership is or includes a period ("a mixed-use period") throughout which the asset—
- (a) was a business asset by reference to its use for purposes mentioned in *paragraph 5(2) to (5)* [any provision of paragraph 5] above; but
- (b) was, at the same time, being put to a non-qualifying use.

(2) The period throughout which the asset disposed of is to be taken to have been a business asset shall be determined as if the relevant fraction of every mixed-use period were a period throughout which the asset was not a business asset.

(3) In sub-paragraph (2) above 'the relevant fraction', in relation to any mixed-use period, means the fraction which represents the proportion of the use of the asset during that period that was a non-qualifying use.

(4) Where both this paragraph and paragraph 8 above apply in relation to the whole or any part of a period—
- (a) effect shall be given to that paragraph first; and
- (b) further reductions by virtue of this paragraph in the period for which the

asset disposed of is taken to have been a business asset shall be made in respect of only the relevant part of any non-qualifying use.

(5) In sub-paragraph (4) above the reference to the relevant part of any non-qualifying use is a reference to the proportion of that use which is not a use to which a non-qualifying part of any relevant income is attributable.

(6) Where a mixed-use period is a period in which—

(a) the proportion mentioned in sub-paragraph (3) above has been different at different times, or

(b) different attributions have to be made for the purposes of sub-paragraphs (4) and (5) above for different parts of the period,

this paragraph shall require a separate relevant fraction to be determined for, and applied to, each part of the period for which there is a different proportion or attribution.

(7) In this paragraph—

'non-qualifying use', in relation to an asset, means any use of the asset for purposes which are not purposes in respect of which the asset would fall to be treated as a business asset at the time of its use; and

'non-qualifying part' and 'relevant income' have the same meanings as in paragraph 8 above.

Periods of limited exposure to fluctuations in value not to count

10.—(1) Where, in the case of any asset disposed of ('the relevant asset'), the period after 5th April 1998 for which that asset had been held at the time of its disposal is or includes a period during which—

(a) the person making the disposal, or

(b) a relevant predecessor of his,

had limited exposure to fluctuations in the value of the asset, the period during which that person or predecessor had that limited exposure shall not count for the purposes of taper relief.

(2) The times when a person shall be taken for the purposes of this paragraph to have had such limited exposure in the case of the relevant asset shall be all the times while he held that asset when a transaction entered into at any time by him, or by a relevant predecessor of his, had the effect that he—

(a) was not exposed, or not exposed to any substantial extent, to the risk of loss from fluctuations in the value of the relevant asset; and

(b) was not able to enjoy, or to enjoy to any substantial extent, any opportunities to benefit from such fluctuations.

(3) The transactions referred to in sub-paragraph (2) above do not include—

(a) any insurance policy which the person in question might reasonably have been expected to enter into and which is insurance against the loss of the relevant asset or against damage to it, or against both; or

(b) any transaction having effect in relation to fluctuations in the value of the relevant asset so far only as they are fluctuations resulting from fluctuations in the value of foreign currencies.

(4) In this paragraph 'relevant predecessor'—

(a) in relation to a person disposing of an asset, means any person other than the person disposing of it who held that asset at a time falling in the period which is taken to be the whole period for which it had been held at the time of its disposal; and

(b) in relation to a relevant predecessor of a person disposing of an asset, means any other relevant predecessor of that person.

(5) In sub-paragraph (4) above, the reference, in relation to an asset, to the whole period for which it had been held at the time of its disposal is a reference to the period that would be given for that asset by paragraph 2(1) above if, in paragraph (a), the words "whichever is the later of 6th April 1998 and" were omitted.

11.— ...

[Periods of share ownership not to count if company is not active

11A.—(1) Where there is a disposal of an asset consisting of shares in a company, any period after 5th April 1998 during which the asset consisted of shares in a company that—
    (a) was a close company, and
    (b) was not active,
shall not count for the purposes of taper relief.

(2) Subject to the following provisions of this paragraph, a company is regarded as active at any time when—
    (a) it is carrying on a business of any description,
    (b) it is preparing to carry on a business of any description, or
    (c) it or another person is winding up the affairs of a business of any description that it has ceased to carry on.

(3) In sub-paragraph (2) above—
    (a) references to a business include a business that is not conducted on a commercial basis or with a view to the realisation of a profit, and
    (b) references to carrying on a business include holding assets and managing them.

(4) For the purposes of this paragraph a company is not regarded as active by reason only of its doing all or any of the following—
    (a) holding money (in any currency) in cash or on deposit;
    (b) holding other assets whose total value is insignificant;
    (c) holding shares in or debentures of a company that is not active;
    (d) making loans to an associated company or to a participator or an associate of a participator;
    (e) carrying out administrative functions in order to comply with requirements of the Companies Act 1985 or the Companies (Northern Ireland) Order 1986 or other regulatory requirements.

(5) Notwithstanding anything in sub-paragraphs (2) to (4) above a company shall be treated as active for the purposes of this paragraph if—
    (a) it is the holding company of a group of companies that contains at least one active company, or
    (b) it has a qualifying shareholding in a joint venture company or is the holding company of a group of companies any member of which has a qualifying shareholding in a joint venture company.

(6) In this paragraph 'associated company' has the meaning given by section 416 of the Taxes Act and 'participator' and 'associate' have the meaning given by section 417 of that Act.

(7) Any reference in this paragraph to shares in or debentures of a company includes an interest in, or option in respect of, shares in or debentures of a company.]

Periods of share ownership not to count in a case of value shifting

12.—(1) This paragraph applies (subject to sub-paragraph (4) below) where—
    (a) there is a disposal of an asset consisting of shares in a close company, and
    (b) at least one relevant shift of value involving that asset has occurred between the relevant time and the time of the disposal.

(2) So much of the period after 5th April 1998 for which the asset had been held at the time of its disposal as falls before the time, or latest time, in that period at which there was a relevant shift of value involving that asset shall not count for the purposes of taper relief.

(3) For the purposes of this paragraph a relevant shift of value involving any asset shall be taken to have occurred whenever—

(a) a person having control of a close company exercised his control of that company so that value passed into that asset out of a relevant holding; or

(b) effect was given to any other transaction by virtue of which value passed into that asset out of a relevant holding.

(4) A relevant shift of value involving an asset shall be disregarded for the purposes of this paragraph if—

(a) that shift of value is one in which the value passing into that asset out of the relevant holding is insignificant; or

(b) that shift of value took place at a time when the qualifying holding period of the relevant holding was at least as long as the qualifying holding period of that asset.

(5) In sub-paragraphs (3) and (4) above the references to a relevant holding shall be construed, in relation to any case in which value has passed out of one asset into another asset consisting of shares in a company, as a reference to any holding by—

(a) the person who, following the exercise of control or other transaction by virtue of which the value has passed, held the other asset, or

(b) a person connected with him, of any shares in that company or in a company under the control of the same person or persons as that company.

(6) For the purposes of sub-paragraph (4)(b) above the reference to the qualifying holding period of a holding or other asset at the time when a shift of value takes place shall be taken to be what, in relation to a disposal at that time of that holding or other asset by the person then entitled to dispose of it, would be taken to have been its qualifying holding period for the purposes of section 2A.

(7) In this paragraph references to shares in a company include references to rights over a company.

(8) In this paragraph "the relevant time", in relation to the disposal of an asset consisting of shares in a company, means the beginning of the period after 5th April 1998 for which that asset had been held at the time of its disposal.

Rules for options

13.—(1) This paragraph applies where by virtue of section 144—

(a) the grant of an option and the transaction entered into by the grantor in fulfilment of his obligations under the option, or

(b) the acquisition of an option and the transaction entered into by the person exercising the option,

fall to be treated as one transaction.

(2) The time of the disposal of any asset disposed of in pursuance of the transaction shall be the time of the following disposal—

(a) if the option binds the grantor to sell, the disposal made in fulfilment of the grantor's obligations under the option;

(b) if the option binds the grantor to buy, the disposal made to the grantor in consequence of the exercise of the option.

(3) The time of the acquisition of any asset acquired in pursuance of the option, or in consequence of its exercise, shall be the time of the exercise of the option.

(4) Any question whether the asset disposed of or acquired was a business asset at any time shall be determined by reference to the asset to which the option related, and not the option.

Further rules for assets derived from other assets

14.—(1) This paragraph applies if, in a case where—

(a) assets have merged,

(b) an asset has divided or otherwise changed its nature, or

(c) different rights or interests in or over any asset have been created or extinguished at different times,

the value of any asset disposed of is derived (through one or more successive events falling within paragraphs (a) to (c) above but not otherwise) from one or more other assets acquired into the same ownership at a time before the acquisition of the asset disposed of.

(2) The asset disposed of shall be deemed for the purposes of this Schedule to have been acquired at the earliest time at which any asset from which its value is derived was acquired into the same ownership.

(3) Any determination of whether the asset disposed of was a business asset at a time when another asset from which its value is derived was in the ownership of the person making the disposal shall be made as if that other asset were the asset disposed of or, as the case may be, were comprised in it.

Special rules for assets transferred between spouses

15.—(1) This paragraph applies where a person ('the transferring spouse') has disposed of any asset to another ('the transferee spouse') by a disposal falling within section 58(1).

(2) Paragraph 2 above shall have effect in relation to any subsequent disposal of the asset as if the time when the transferee spouse acquired the asset were the time when the transferring spouse acquired it.

(3) Where for the purposes of paragraph 2 above the transferring spouse would be treated—

(a) in a case where there has been one or more previous disposals falling within section 58(1), by virtue of sub-paragraph (2) above, or by virtue of that sub-paragraph together with any other provision of this Schedule, or

(b) in a case where there has not been such a previous disposal, by virtue of such another provision,

as having acquired the asset at a time other than the time when the transferring spouse did acquire it, the reference in that sub-paragraph to the time when the transferring spouse acquired it shall be read as a reference to the time when for the purposes of that paragraph the transferring spouse is treated as having acquired it.

(4) Where there is a disposal by the transferee spouse, any question whether the asset was a business asset at a time before that disposal shall be determined as if—

(a) in relation to times when the asset was held by the transferring spouse, references in *paragraph 5(2)* [paragraph 5(1) and (2)] above to the individual by whom the disposal is made included references to the transferring spouse; and

(b) the reference in paragraph 5(5) above to the acquisition of the asset as a legatee by the individual by whom the disposal is made included a reference to its acquisition as a legatee by the transferring spouse.

(5) Where, in the case of any asset, there has been more than one transfer falling within section 58(1) during the period after 5th April 1998 for which the transferee spouse has held it at the time of that spouse's disposal of that asset, sub-paragraph (4) above shall have effect as if a reference, in relation to any time, to the transferring spouse were a reference to the individual who was the transferring spouse in relation to the next disposal falling within section 58(1) to have been made after that time.

Special rules for postponed gains

16.—(1) Sub-paragraph (3) below applies where the whole or any part of any gain which—

(a) would (but for any provision of this Act) have accrued on the disposal of any asset, or

    (b) would have accrued on any disposal assumed under any enactment to have been made at any time,

falls by virtue of an enactment mentioned in sub-paragraph (2) below to be treated as accruing on or after 6th April 1998 at a time (whether or not the time of a subsequent disposal) which falls after the time of the actual or assumed disposal mentioned in paragraph (a) or (b) above ("the charged disposal").

    (2) Those enactments are—

    (a) section 10A,

    (b) section 116(10),

    (c) section 134,

    (d) section 154(2) or (4),

  [(da) section 169C(7),]

    (e) Schedule 5B or 5C, or

    (f) paragraph 27 of Schedule 15 to the Finance Act 1996 (qualifying indexed securities).

    (3) In relation to the gain or part of a gain that is treated as accruing after the time of the charged disposal—

    (a) references in this Schedule (except this sub-paragraph) to the disposal on which the gain or part accrues are references to the charged disposal; and

    (b) references in this Schedule to the asset disposed of by that disposal are references to the asset that was or would have been disposed of by the charged disposal;

and, accordingly, the end of the period after 5th April 1998 for which that asset had been held at the time of the disposal on which that gain or part accrues shall be deemed to have been the time of the charged disposal.

    (4) In relation to any gain that is treated by virtue of—

    (a) subsection (1) of section 12, or

    (b) subsection (2) of section 279,

as accruing after the time of the disposal from which it accrues, references in this Schedule to the disposal on which the gain accrues, to the asset disposed of on that disposal and to the time of that disposal shall be construed disregarding that subsection.

    (5) It shall be immaterial for the purposes of this paragraph—

    (a) that the time of the charged disposal or, as the case may be, the time of the actual disposal from which the gain accrues was before 6th April 1998; and

    (b) that the time at which the charged disposal is treated as accruing is postponed on more than one occasion under an enactment specified in sub-paragraph (2) above.

Special rule for property settled by a company

17.—(1) No part of any chargeable gain accruing to the trustees of a settlement on the disposal of any asset shall be treated as a gain on the disposal of a business asset if—

    (a) the settlor is a company, and

    (b) that company has an interest in the settlement at the time of the disposal.

    (2) Subject to the following provisions of this paragraph, a company which is a settlor in relation to any settlement shall be regarded as having an interest in a settlement if—

    (a) any property which may at any time be comprised in the settlement, or any derived property is, or will or may become, payable to or applicable for the benefit of that company or an associated company; or

    (b) that company or an associated company enjoys a benefit deriving directly or indirectly from any property which is comprised in the settlement or any derived property.

(3) This paragraph does not apply unless the settlor or an associated company is within the charge to corporation tax in respect of chargeable gains for the accounting period in which the chargeable gain accrues.

(4) In this paragraph 'derived property', in relation to any property, means income from that property or any other property directly or indirectly representing proceeds of, or of income from, that property or income therefrom.

(5) For the purposes of this paragraph a company is to be treated as another's associated company at any time if at that time, or at another time within one year previously—

(a) one of them has had control of the other; or

(b) both have been under the control of the same person or persons.

(6) In this paragraph 'settlor' has the meaning given by section 660G(1) and (2) of the Taxes Act.

(7) This paragraph has effect subject to paragraph 20 below.

Special rules for assets acquired in the reconstruction of mutual businesses etc

18.—(1) Where—

(a) shares in a company have been issued under any arrangements for the issue of shares in that company in respect of the interests of the members of a mutual company; and

(b) a person to whom shares were issued under those arrangements falls by virtue of *subsection (3)* [subsection (2)(a)] of section 136 to be treated as having exchanged interests of his as a member of the mutual company for shares issued under those arrangements,

paragraph 2 above shall have effect (notwithstanding that section) as if the time of that person's acquisition of the shares were the time when they were issued to him.

(2) Where—

(a) a registered friendly society has been incorporated under the Friendly Societies Act 1992, and

(b) there has been a change under Schedule 4 to that Act as a result of which a member of the registered society, or of a branch of the registered society, has become a member of the incorporated society or of a branch of the incorporated society,

paragraph 2 above shall have effect (notwithstanding anything in section 217B) in relation to the interests and rights in the incorporated society, or the branch of the incorporated society, which that person had immediately after the change, as if the time of their acquisition by him were the time of the change.

(3) In this paragraph—

'the incorporated society', in relation to the incorporation of a registered friendly society, means the society after incorporation;

'insurance company' has the meaning given by section 96(1) of the Insurance Companies Act 1982;

['insurance company' means an undertaking carrying on the business of effecting or carrying out contracts of insurance and, for the purposes of this definition, 'contract of insurance' has the meaning given by Article 3(1) of the Financial Services and Markets Act 2000 (Regulated Activities) Order 2001;]

'mutual company' means—

(a) a mutual insurance company; or

(b) a company of another description carrying on a business on a mutual basis;

'mutual insurance company' means any insurance company carrying on a business without having a share capital;

'the registered society', in relation to the incorporation of a registered friendly society, means the society before incorporation.

Special rule for ancillary trust funds

19.—(1) Use of an asset as part of an ancillary trust fund of a member of Lloyd's—

(a) shall not be regarded as a use in respect of which the asset is to be treated as a business asset at any time; but

(b) shall be disregarded in any determination for the purposes of paragraph 9 above of whether it was being put to a non-qualifying use at the same time as it was being used for purposes mentioned in *paragraph 5(2) to (5)* [any provision of paragraph 5] above.

(2) In this section 'ancillary trust fund' has the same meaning as in Chapter III of Part II of the Finance Act 1993.

General rules for settlements

20.—(1) Where, in the case of any settlement, the settled property originates from more than one settlor, this Schedule shall have effect as if there were a separate and distinct settlement for the property originating from each settlor, and references in this Schedule to an eligible beneficiary shall be construed accordingly.

(2) Subsections (1) to (5) of section 79 apply for the purposes of this paragraph as they apply for the purposes of that section.

General rule for apportionments under this Schedule

21. Where any apportionment falls to be made for the purposes of this Schedule it shall be made—

(a) on a just and reasonable basis; and

(b) on the assumption that an amount falling to be apportioned by reference to any period arose or accrued at the same rate throughout the period over which it falls to be treated as having arisen or accrued.

Interpretation of Schedule

22.—(1) In this Schedule—

'51 per cent subsidiary' . . . has the meaning given by section 838 of the Taxes Act;

'commercial association of companies' means a company together with such of its associated companies (within the meaning of section 416 of the Taxes Act) as carry on businesses which are of such a nature that the businesses of the company and the associated companies, taken together, may be reasonably considered to make up a single composite undertaking;

'eligible beneficiary' shall be construed in accordance with paragraphs 7 and 20 above;

...

'group of companies' means a company which has one or more 51 per cent subsidiaries, together with those subsidiaries;

'holding company' means a company whose business (disregarding any trade carried on by it) consists wholly or mainly of the holding of shares in one or more companies which are its 51 per cent subsidiaries;

['holding company' means a company that has one or more 51% subsidiaries;]

['interest in shares' means an interest as a co-owner (whether the shares are owned jointly or in common, and whether or not the interests of the co-owners are equal), and 'interest in debentures', in relation to any debentures, has a corresponding meaning;]

['joint venture company' has the meaning given by paragraph 23(2) below;]

['non-trading company' means a company which is not a trading company;

'non-trading group' means a group of companies which is not a trading group;]
'office' and 'employment' have the same meanings as in the Income Tax Acts;
['ordinary share capital' has the meaning given by section 832(1) of the Taxes
   Act;]
   ...
'qualifying company' shall be construed in accordance with paragraph 6 above;
['qualifying shareholding', in relation to a joint venture company, has the
   meaning given by paragraph 23(3) below;]
'relevant period of ownership' shall be construed in accordance with paragraph
   2 above;
'shares', in relation to a company, *includes any securities of that company*
   [includes—
      (a) any securities of that company, and
      (b) any debentures of that company that are deemed, by virtue of section
         251(6), to be securities for the purposes of that section];
'trade' means (subject to section 241(3)) anything which—
      (a) is a trade, profession or vocation, within the meaning of the Income
         Tax Acts; and
      (b) is conducted on a commercial basis and with a view to the realisation
         of profits;
'trading company' means a company which is either—
      (a) a company existing wholly for the purpose of carrying on one or more trades; or
      (b) a company that would fall within paragraph (a) above apart from any
         purposes capable of having no substantial effect on the extent of the company's
         activities;
['trading company' has the meaning given by paragraph 22A below;]
'trading group' means a group of companies the activities of which (if all the activities of
   the companies in the group are taken together) do not, or not to any substantial extent,
   include activities carried on otherwise than in the course of, or for the purposes of, a
   trade;
['trading group' has the meaning given by paragraph 22B below;]
'transaction' includes any agreement, arrangement or understanding, whether
   or not legally enforceable, and a series of transactions.
['unlisted company' means a company—
      (a) none of whose shares is listed on a recognised stock exchange, and
      (b) which is not a 51 per cent subsidiary of a company whose shares, or
         any class of whose shares, is so listed.]

(2) For the purposes of this Schedule one company has a relevant connection
with another company at any time when they are both members of the same group
of companies or of the same commercial association of companies.

(3) References in this Schedule to the acquisition of an asset that was provided,
rather than acquired, by the person disposing of it are references to its provision.

(4) References in this Schedule, in relation to a part disposal, to the asset
disposed of are references to the asset of which there is a part disposal.

[Meaning of 'trading company'

22A.—(1) In this Schedule 'trading company' means a company carrying on
trading activities whose activities do not include to a substantial extent activities
other than trading activities.

(2) For the purposes of sub-paragraph (1) above 'trading activities' means
activities carried on by the company—
      (a) in the course of, or for the purposes of, a trade being carried on by it,
      (b) for the purposes of a trade that it is preparing to carry on,
      (c) with a view to its acquiring or starting to carry on a trade, or

(d) with a view to its acquiring a significant interest in the share capital of another company that—
    (i) is a trading company or the holding company of a trading group, and
    (ii) if the acquiring company is a member of a group of companies, is not a member of that group.

(3) Activities do not qualify as trading activities under sub-paragraph (2)(c) or (d) above unless the acquisition is made, or (as the case may be) the company starts to carry on the trade, as soon as is reasonably practicable in the circumstances.

(4) The reference in sub-paragraph (2)(d) above to the acquisition of a significant interest in the share capital of another company is to an acquisition of ordinary share capital in the other company—
    (a) such as would make that company a 51% subsidiary of the acquiring company, or
    (b) such as would give the acquiring company a qualifying shareholding in a joint venture company without making the two companies members of the same group of companies.]

[Meaning of 'trading group'

22B.—(1) In this Schedule 'trading group' means a group of companies—
    (a) one or more of whose members carry on trading activities, and
    (b) the activities of whose members, taken together, do not include to a substantial extent activities other than trading activities.

(2) For the purposes of sub-paragraph (1) above 'trading activities' means activities carried on by a member of the group—
    (a) in the course of, or for the purposes of, a trade being carried on by any member of the group,
    (b) for the purposes of a trade that any member of the group is preparing to carry on,
    (c) with a view to any member of the group acquiring or starting to carry on a trade, or
    (d) with a view to any member of the group acquiring a significant interest in the share capital of another company that—
        (i) is a trading company or the holding company of a trading group, and
        (ii) is not a member of the same group of companies as the acquiring company.

(3) Activities do not qualify as trading activities under sub-paragraph (2)(c) or (d) above unless the acquisition is made, or (as the case may be) the group member in question starts to carry on the trade, as soon as is reasonably practicable in the circumstances.

(4) The reference in sub-paragraph (2)(d) above to the acquisition of a significant interest in the share capital of another company is to an acquisition of ordinary share capital in the other company—
    (a) such as would make that company a member of the same group of companies as the acquiring company, or
    (b) such as would give the acquiring company a qualifying shareholding in a joint venture company without making the joint venture companies a member of the same group of companies as the acquiring company.

(5) For the purposes of this paragraph the activities of the members of the group shall be treated as one business (with the result that activities are disregarded to the extent that they are intra-group activities).]

[Qualifying shareholdings in joint venture companies

23.—(1) This Schedule has effect subject to the following provisions where a company ('the investing company') has a qualifying shareholding in a joint venture company.

(2) For the purposes of *this paragraph* [this Schedule] a company is a 'joint venture company' if, and only if—

(a) it is a trading company or the holding company of a trading group, and

(b) 75% or more of its ordinary share capital (in aggregate) is held by not more than five *companies* [persons].

For the purposes of paragraph (b) above the shareholdings of members of a group of companies shall be treated as held by a single company.

(3) For the purposes of *this paragraph* [this Schedule] a company has a 'qualifying shareholding' in a joint venture company if—

(a) it holds *more than 30%* [10% or more] of the ordinary share capital of the joint venture company, or

(b) it is a member of a group of companies, it holds ordinary share capital of the joint venture company and the members of the group between them hold more than 30% [10% or more] of that share capital.

(4) For the purpose of determining whether the investing company is a trading company—

(a) any holding by it of shares in the joint venture company shall be disregarded, and

(b) it shall be treated as carrying on an appropriate proportion—

    (i) of the activities of the joint venture company, or

    (ii) where the joint venture company is the holding company of a trading group, of the activities of that group.

...

(5) ...

(6) For the purpose of determining whether a group of companies is a trading group—

(a) every holding of shares in the joint venture company by a member of the group having a qualifying shareholding in that company shall be disregarded, and

(b) each member of the group having such a qualifying shareholding shall be treated as carrying on an appropriate proportion of the activities—

    (i) of the joint venture company, or

    (ii) where the joint venture company is the holding company of a trading group, of that group.

This sub-paragraph does not apply if the joint venture company is a member of the group.

(7) In sub-paragraphs (4)(b) ... and (6)(b) above 'an appropriate proportion' means a proportion corresponding to the percentage of the ordinary share capital of the joint venture company held by the investing company or, as the case may be, by the group member concerned.

[(7A) For the purposes of this paragraph the activities of a joint venture company that is a holding company and its 51% subsidiaries shall be treated as a single business (so that activities are disregarded to the extent that they are intra-group activities).]

(8) ...

(9) ...

(10) ...]

[Joint enterprise companies: relevant connection

24.—(1) This Schedule has effect subject to sub-paragraph (5) below in any case where a company ('the investing company') has a qualifying shareholding in a joint enterprise company.

(2) For the purposes of this paragraph, a company is a 'joint enterprise company' if, and only if, 75% or more of its ordinary share capital (in aggregate) is held by not more than five *companies* [persons].

(3) For the purposes of sub-paragraph (2) above the shareholdings of members of a group of companies shall be treated as held by a single company.

(4) For the purposes of this paragraph a company has a 'qualifying shareholding' in a joint enterprise company if—

(a) it holds *more than 30%* [10% or more] of the ordinary share capital of the joint enterprise company, or

(b) it is a member of a group of companies, it holds ordinary share capital of the joint enterprise company and the members of the group between them hold more than 30% [10% or more] of that share capital.

(5) The following shall be treated as having a relevant connection with each other—

(a) the investing company;

(b) the joint enterprise company;

(c) any company having a relevant connection with the investing company;

(d) any company having a relevant connection with the joint enterprise company by virtue of being—

(i) a 51 per cent subsidiary of that company, or

(ii) a member of the same commercial association of companies.

(6) . . .]]

Note. This Schedule was inserted by the Finance Act 1998, s 121(2), (4), Sch 20 and has effect for the year 1998–99 and subsequent years of assessment. In para 2(4) words 'or paragraph 4 of Schedule 5BA' in square brackets inserted by the Finance Act 1999, s 72(3)(b) as from 27 July 1999.

In para 4, sub-para (4)(a), (b) substituted by words 'the relevant company was a qualifying company by reference to the personal representatives' in square brackets, and sub-para (5)(b) substituted by the Finance Act 2000, s 67(1), (2)(a), (7) and has effect for determining whether an asset is a business asset at any time on or after 6 April 2000, but it does not affect the determination on or after that date whether an asset was a business asset at a time before that date.

In para 5(1) words from 'by an individual' to 'individual's personal representatives' in square brackets inserted by the Finance Act 2003, s 160(1), (2), (5) and applies to disposals on or after 6 April 2004 and as it so applies has effect in relation to periods of ownership on or after that date. Para 5(2)–(5) substituted by sub-paras (1A), (2)–(5) by the Finance Act 2003, s 160(1), (3), (5) and this amendment applies to disposals on or after 6 April 2004 and as it so applies has effect in relation to periods of ownership on or after that date. In original para 5, sub-para (2)(d), (e) substituted by sub-para (2)(d) by the Finance Act 2000, s 67(1), (3)(a), (7) and this amendment has effect for determining whether an asset is a business asset at any time on or after 6 April 2000, but it does not affect the determination on or after that date whether an asset was a business asset at a time before that date. In original para 5(3)(a) words in square brackets from 'or by a partnership' to the end of para (a) inserted by the Finance Act 2001, s 78(1), Sch 26, para 1, 2 and this amendment has effect, and is deemed always to have had effect, as if it had been included among the amendments made by the Finance Act 2000, s 67. In original para 5, sub-para (3)(e), (f) substituted, by sub-para (e) by the Finance Act 2000, s 67(1), (3)(b), (7) and this amendment has effect for determining whether an asset is a business asset at any time on or after 6 April 2000, but it does not affect the determination on or after that date whether an asset was a business asset at a time before that date.

Para 6 substituted by the Finance Act 2000, s 67(1), (4), (7) and this amendment has effect for determining whether an asset is a business asset at any time on or after 6 April 2000, but it does not affect the determination on or after that date whether an asset was a business asset at a time before that date. Para 6(1A), (2A), (4)–(7) inserted by the Finance Act 2001, s 78(1), (2), Sch 26, paras 1, 3(1), (2) and this amendment has effect, and is deemed always to have had effect, as if it had been included among the amendments made by the Finance Act 2000, s 67.

Para 6A inserted by the Finance Act 2001, s 78(1), (2), Sch 26, paras 1, 4 and this amendment has effect, and is deemed always to have had effect, as if it had been included among the amendments made by the Finance Act 2000, s 67.

In para 9(1)(a) words 'paragraph 5(2) to (5)' substituted by words 'any provision of paragraph 5' in square brackets substituted by the Finance Act 2003, s 160(1), (4)(a), (5) and this amendment applies to disposals on or after 6 April 2004 and as it so applies has effect in relation to periods of ownership on or after that date.

Para 11 repealed by the Finance Act 2002, ss 47, 141, Sch 10, paras 1, 2, Sch 40, Pt 3(3) and this repeal has effect in relation to disposals on or after 17 April 2002.

Para 11A inserted by the Finance Act 2002, s 47, Sch 10, paras 1, 3(1), (2) and this amendment has effect in relation to disposals on or after 17 April 2002.

In para 15(4)(a) words 'paragraph 5(2)' substituted by words 'paragraph 5(1) and (2)' in square brackets by the Finance Act 2003, s 160(1), (4)(b), (5) and this amendment applies to disposals on or after 6 April 2004 and as it so applies has effect in relation to periods of ownership on or after that date.

Para 16(2)(da) inserted by the Finance Act 2004, s 116, Sch 21, paras 8, 10(4) and this amendment has effect in relation to disposals on or after 10th December 2003 (whenever any earlier disposal as mentioned in s 169B(3)(b) or 169C(3)(b) hereof was made).

In para 18(1)(b) words 'subsection (3)' substituted by words 'subsection (2)(a)' in square brackets by the Finance Act 2002, s 45(1), Sch 9, Pt 2, para 5(1), (13), Sch 9, Pt 3, para 7 and this amendment has effect in relation to shares or debentures issued on or after 17 April 2002. In para 18(3) definition 'insurance company' substituted by SI 2001/3629, arts 61, 71(1) as from 1 December 2001 (with effect for the purposes of determining whether a company is a mutual company within the meaning of para 18 above on or after that date, being the date on which the Financial Services and Markets Act 2000, ss 411, 432(1), Sch 20 came fully into force): see SI 2001/3538, art 2(1) and SI 2001/3629, arts 1(2)(a), 71(2).

In para 19(1)(b) words 'paragraph 5(2) to (5)' substituted by words 'any provision of paragraph 5' in square brackets by the Finance Act 2003, s 160(1), (4)(a), (5) and this amendment applies to disposals on or after 6 April 2004 and as it so applies has effect in relation to periods of ownership on or after that date.

In para 22(1) in definition '51 per cent subsidiary' words omitted repealed by the Finance Act 2002, s 141, Sch 40, Pt 3(3) and this repeal has effect in relation to disposals on or after 17 April 2002: see the Finance Act 2002, s 47, Sch 10, para 2, Sch 40, Pt 3(3).

In para 22(1) definitions 'full-time working officer or employee' and 'qualifying office or employment' (omitted) repealed by the Finance Act 2000, ss 67(1), (5), (7), 156, Sch 40, Pt II(6) and these repeals have effect for determining whether an asset is a business asset at any time on or after 6 April 2000, but it does not affect the determination on or after that date whether an asset was a business asset at a time before that date. In para 22(1) definition 'holding company' substituted, and definitions 'interest in shares', 'joint venture company' inserted by the Finance Act 2002, s 47, Sch 10, paras 1, 4(1), (3), 5(1), 6(1), (3) and applies to disposals on or after 17 April 2002 and has effect in relation to periods of ownership on or after that date. In para 22(1) definitions 'non-trading company' and 'non-trading group' inserted by the Finance Act 2001, s 78(1), (2), Sch 26, paras 1, 5 and this amendment shall have effect, and is deemed always to have had effect, as if it had been included among the amendments made by the Finance Act 2000, s 67. In para 22(1) definitions 'ordinary share capital' and 'qualifying shareholding' inserted by the Finance Act 2002, s 47, Sch 10, paras 1, 6(1), (3), 7(1), (3) and applies to disposals on or after 17 April 2002. In para 22(1) in definition 'shares' words 'includes any securities of that company' substituted by words from 'includes— (a) any' to 'of that section' in square brackets by the Finance Act 2002, s 47, Sch 10, paras 1, 8(1); this amendment applies in relation to disposals on or after 6 April 2001 (so that assets disposed of on or after that date are treated as shares by virtue of this amendment and shall be treated as having been shares in relation to all times relevant for the purposes of this Schedule): see the Finance Act 2002, Sch 10, para 8(2); for further application in relation to the references to shares, mentioned in paras 5, 6A, 11, 11A, 12, 18(1), 22 above, to any time before 17 April 2002 see the Finance Act 2002, Sch 10, para 8(3), (4) thereof. In para 22(1) definition 'trading company' and 'trading group' substituted by the Finance Act 2002, s 47, Sch 10, paras 1, 9(1) (3), 10(1), (3) and this amendment applies in relation to disposals on or after 17 April 2002 and has effect in relation to periods of ownership on or after that date. In para 22(1) definition 'unlisted company' inserted by the Finance Act 2000, s 67(1), (5), (7) and this amendment has effect for determining whether an asset is a business asset at any time on or after 6 April 2000, but it does not affect the determination on or after that date whether an asset was a business asset at a time before that date.

Paras 22A, 22B inserted by the Finance Act 2002, s 47, Sch 10, paras 1, 9(2), (3), 10(2) (3) and this amendment has effect in relation to disposals on or after 17 April 2002 and has effect in relation to periods of ownership on or after that date.

Para 23 inserted by the Finance Act 2000, s 67(1), (6) (7)and this amendment has effect for determining whether an asset is a business asset at any time on or after 6 April 2000, but it does not affect the determination on or after that date whether an asset was a business asset at a time before that date. In para 23(2), (3) words 'this paragraph' substituted by words 'this Schedule' in square brackets by the Finance Act 2002, s 47, Sch 10, paras 1, 6(2), (3) and this amendment has effect in relation to disposals on or after 17 April 2002. In para 23(2)(b) word 'companies' substituted by word 'persons' in square brackets by the Finance Act 2002, s 47, Sch 10, paras 1, 11(1), (2), (5) and this amendment applies to disposals on or after 17 April 2002 and has effect in relation to periods of ownership on or after that date.In para 23(3) words 'more than 30%' in both places substituted by words '10% or more' in square brackets by the Finance Act 2002, s 47, Sch 10, paras 1, 11(1), (3), (5) and this amendment applies to disposals on or after 17 April 2002 and has effect in relation to periods of ownership on or after that date. In para 23, in sub-para (4) words omitted, sub-para (5) repealed and in sub-para (7) reference omitted by the Finance Act 2002, ss 47, 141, Sch 10, paras 1, 4(2), (3), Sch 40, Pt 3(3) and these repeals apply to disposals on or after 17 April 2002 and has effect in relation to periods of ownership on or after that date. Para 23(7A) inserted by the Finance Act 2002, s 47, Sch 10, paras 1, 11(1), (4), (5) and this amendment applies to disposals on or after 17 April 2002 and has effect in relation to periods of ownership on or after that date. Para 23(8) repealed by the Finance Act 2001, ss 78, 110, Sch 26, paras 1, 6, Sch 33, Pt 2(7) and this repeal has effect, and is deemed always to have had effect, as if it had been included among the amendments made by the Finance Act 2000, s 67. Para 23(9), (10) repealed by the Finance Act 2002, ss 47, 141, Sch 10, para 2, Sch 40, Pt 3(3) and this repeal has effect in relation to disposals on or after 17 April 2002.

Para 24 inserted by the Finance Act 2001, s 78, Sch 26, paras 1, 7 and this amendment has effect, and is deemed always to have had effect, as if it had been included among the amendments made by the Finance Act 2000, s 67. In para 24(2) word 'companies' substituted by word 'persons' in square brackets by the Finance Act 2002, s 47, Sch 10, paras 1, 12(1), (2), (4) and this amendment applies to disposals on or after 17 April 2002 and has effect in relation to periods of ownership on or after that date. In para 24(4) words 'more than 30%' in both places substituted by words '10% or more' in square brackets by the Finance Act 2002, s 47, Sch 10, paras 1, 12(1), (3), (4) and this amendment applies to disposals on or after 17 April 2002 and has effect in relation to periods of ownership on or after that date. Para 24(6) repealed by the Finance Act 2002, ss 47, 141, Sch 10, paras 1, 7(2), Sch 40, Pt 3(3) and this repeal applies in relation to disposals on or after 17 April 2002.

SCHEDULE 1   Section 3

APPLICATION OF EXEMPT AMOUNT IN CASES INVOLVING SETTLED PROPERTY

1.—(1) For any year of assessment during the whole or part of which settled property is held on trusts which secure that, during the lifetime of a mentally disabled person or a person in receipt of attendance allowance or of a disability living allowance by virtue of entitlement to the care component at the highest or middle rate—

    (a) no less than half of the property which is applied is applied for the benefit of that person, and

    (b) that person is entitled to not less than half of the income arising from the property, or no such income may be applied for the benefit of any other person,

section 3(1) to (6) [sections 3(1) to (5C) and 3A] shall apply to the trustees of the settlement as they apply to an individual, but with the modifications specified in this paragraph).

(2) The trusts on which settled property is held shall not be treated as falling outside sub-paragraph (1) above by reason only of the powers conferred on the trustees by section 32 of the Trustee Act 1925 or section 33 of the Trustee Act (Northern Ireland) 1958 (powers of advancement); and the reference in that sub-paragraph to the lifetime of a person shall, where the income from the settled property is held for his benefit on trusts of the kind described in section 33 of the Trustee Act 1925 (protective trusts), be construed as a reference to the period during which the income is held on trust for him.

  [(2A) As they apply by virtue of sub-paragraph (1) above—

    (a) section 3(5A) has effect with the omission of paragraph (b), and

(b) section 3(5B) has effect with the omission of the words 'or (b)'.]

(3) In relation to a settlement which is one of 2 or more qualifying settlements comprised in a group, this paragraph shall have effect as if for the references in *section 3* [sections 3 and 3A(1)(a)]to the exempt amount for the year [(except the one in section 3(2))] there were substituted references to one-tenth of that exempt amount or, if it is more, to such amount as results from dividing the exempt amount for the year by the number of settlements in the group.

(4) For the purposes of sub-paragraph (3) above—

(a) a qualifying settlement is any settlement (other than an excluded settlement) which is made on or after 10th March 1981 and to the trustees of which this paragraph applies for the year of assessment; and

(b) all qualifying settlements in relation to which the same person is the settlor constitute a group.

(5) If, in consequence of 2 or more persons being settlors in relation to it, a settlement is comprised in 2 or more groups comprising different numbers of settlements, sub-paragraph (3) above shall apply to it as if the number by which the exempt amount for the year is to be divided were the number of settlements in the largest group.

[(5A) In its application to the trustees of a settlement, section 3A(1) has effect with the substitution for the reference to section 8 of the Management Act of a reference to section 8A of that Act.]

(6) In this paragraph—

'mentally disabled person' means a person who by reason of mental disorder within the meaning of the Mental Health Act 1983 is incapable of administering his property or managing his affairs;

'attendance allowance' means an allowance under section 64 of the Social Security Contributions and Benefits Act 1992 or section 64 of the Social Security Contributions and Benefits (Northern Ireland) Act 1992;

'disability living allowance' means a disability living allowance under section 71 of the Social Security Contributions and Benefits Act 1992 or section 71 of the Social Security Contributions and Benefits (Northern Ireland) Act 1992; and

'settlor' and 'excluded settlement' have the same meanings as in paragraph 2 below.

(7) *An inspector* [An Officer of the Board] may by notice require any person, being a party to a settlement, to furnish him within such time as he may direct (not being less than 28 days) with such particulars as he thinks necessary for the purposes of this paragraph.

2.—(1) For any year of assessment during the whole or part of which any property is settled property, not being a year of assessment for which paragraph 1(1) above applies, *section 3(1) to (6)* [sections 3(1) to (5C) and 3A] shall apply to the trustees of a settlement as they apply to an individual but with the following modifications.

(2) In *subsections (1) and (5)* [section 3(1), 5(A), (5B) and (5C)] [and section 3A(1)(a)] for 'the exempt amount for the year' there shall be substituted 'one-half of the exempt amount for the year'.

[(2A) As they apply by virtue of sub-paragraph (1) above—

(a) section 3(5A) has effect with the omission of paragraph (b), and

(b) section 3(5B) has effect with the omission of the words 'or (b)'.]

(3) *Section 3(6) shall apply only to the trustees of a settlement made before 7th June 1978 and, in relation to such trustees, shall have effect with the substitution for 'the exempt amount for the year' and 'twice the exempt amount for the year' of 'one-half of the exempt amount for the year' and 'the exempt amount for the year' respectively.*

(4) In relation to a settlement which is one of 2 or more qualifying settlements comprised in a group, sub-paragraph (2) above shall have effect as if for the reference to one-half of the exempt amount for the year there were substituted a reference to one-tenth of that exempt amount or, if it is more, to such amount as

results from dividing one-half of the exempt amount for the year by the number of settlements in the group.

(5) For the purposes of sub-paragraph (4) above—

(a) a qualifying settlement is any settlement (other than an excluded settlement) which is made after 6th June 1978 and to the trustees of which this paragraph applies for the year of assessment; and

(b) all qualifying settlements in relation to which the same person is the settlor constitute a group.

(6) If, in consequence of 2 or more persons being settlors in relation to it, a settlement is comprised in 2 or more groups comprising different numbers of settlements, sub-paragraph (4) above shall apply to it as if the number by which one-half of the exempt amount for the year is to be divided were the number of settlements in the largest group.

[(6A) In its application to the trustees of a settlement, section 3A(1) has effect with the substitution for the reference to section 8 of the Management Act of reference to section 8A of that Act.]

(7) In this paragraph 'settlor' has the meaning given by [section 660G(1) and (2)] of the Taxes Act and includes, in the case of a settlement arising under a will or intestacy, the testator or intestate, and 'excluded settlement' means—

(a) any settlement the trustees of which are not for the whole or any part of the year of assessment treated under section 69(1) as resident and ordinarily resident in the United Kingdom; and

(b) any settlement the property comprised in which—

(i) is held for charitable purposes only and cannot become applicable for other purposes; or

(ii) is held for the purposes of *any such scheme or fund as is mentioned in sub-paragraph (8) below* [a registered pension scheme, a superannuation fund to which section 615(3) of the Taxes Act applies or an occupational pension scheme (within the meaning of section 150(5) of the Finance Act 2004) that is not a registered pension scheme].

(8) *The schemes and funds referred to in sub-paragraph (7)(b)(ii) above are funds to which section 615(3) of the Taxes Act applies, schemes and funds approved under section 620 or 621 of that Act, sponsored superannuation schemes as defined in section 624 of that Act and exempt approved schemes and statutory schemes as defined in Chapter I of Part XIV of that Act.*

(9) *An inspector may* [An officer of the Board] by notice require any person, being a party to a settlement, to furnish him within such time as he may direct (not being less than 28 days) with such particulars as he thinks necessary for the purposes of this paragraph.

Note. In paras 1 (1), 2(1) words 'sections 3(1) to (5C) and 3A' in square brackets substituted, in para 1(3) words 'sections 3 and 3A(1)(a)' in square brackets substituted, paras 1(5A), 2(6A) inserted, in paras 1(7), 2(9) words 'An officer of the Board' in square brackets substituted, in para 2(2) words 'and section 3A(1)(a)' in square brackets inserted, and para 2(3) repealed, by the Finance Act 2003, ss 159(1), 216, Sch 28, Pt 1, para 2(2); (3), Pt 2, paras 4(1), (2)(a), (4)(a), (5), 5(1), (2), (3)(b), (5), (6), Pt 3, paras 7, 9, Sch 43, Pt 3(7), in relation to any notice under the Taxes Management Act 1970, s 8A given in relation to the year 2003-04 or any subsequent year of assessment: In para 1(1) words ', but with the modifications specified in this paragraph' in square brackets inserted, paras 1(2A), 2(2A) inserted, in para 1 (3) words '(except the one in section 3(2))' in square brackets inserted, and in para 2(2) words 'section 3(1), (5A), (5B) and (5C)' in square brackets substituted, with retrospective effect, by the Finance Act 2003, s 159(1), Sch 28, Pt 2, paras 4(1), (2)(b), (3), (4)(b), 5(1), (3)(a), (4), Pt 3, para 8. In para 2(7) words 'section 660G(1) and (2)' in square brackets substituted, in relation to the year 1995–96 and subsequent years of assessment, by the Finance Act 1995, s 74, Sch 17, para 32. In para 2(7)(b)(ii) words 'any such scheme or fund as is mentioned in sub-paragraph (8) below' in italics repealed and subsequent words in square brackets substituted, and para 2(8) repealed, by the Finance Act 2004, ss 281(1), 284, 326, Sch 35, paras 38, 42(1)–(3), Sch 42, Pt 3, as from 6 April 2006; for transitional provisions and savings see s 283(1), Sch 36 thereto.

*   *   *   *   *

SCHEDULE 11

TRANSITIONAL PROVISIONS AND SAVINGS

PART I

VALUATION

Preliminary

1.—(1) This Part of this Schedule has effect in cases where the market value of an asset at a time before the commencement of this Act is material to the computation of a gain under this Act; and in this Part any reference to an asset includes a reference to any part of an asset.

(2) Where sub-paragraph (1) above applies, the market value of an asset (or part of an asset) at any time before the commencement of this Act shall be determined in accordance with sections 272 to 274 but subject to the following provisions of this Part.

(3) In any case where section 274 applies in accordance with sub-paragraph (2) above the reference in that section to inheritance tax shall be construed as a reference to capital transfer tax.

Gifts and transactions between connected persons before 20th March 1985

2.—(1) Where sub-paragraph (1) above applies for the purpose of determining the market value of any asset at any time before 20th March 1985 (the date when section 71 of the Finance Act 1985, now section 19, replaced section 151 of the 1979 Act, which is reproduced below) sub-paragraphs (2) to (4) below shall apply.

(2) Except as provided by sub-paragraph (4) below section 19 shall not apply in relation to transactions occurring before 20th March 1985.

(3) If a person is given, or acquires from one or more persons with whom he is connected, by way of 2 or more gifts or other transactions, assets of which the aggregate market value, when considered separately, in relation to the separate gifts or other transactions, is less than their aggregate market value when considered together, then for the purposes of this Act their market value shall be taken to be the larger market value, to be apportioned rateably to the respective disposals.

(4) Where—

(a) one or more transactions occurred on or before 19th March 1985 and one or more after that date, and

(b) had all the transactions occurred before that date sub-paragraph (3) above would apply, and had all the transactions occurred after that date section 19 would have applied,

then those transactions which occurred on or before that date and not more than 2 years before the first of those which occurred after that date shall be treated as material transactions for the purposes of section 19.

Valuation of assets before 6th July 1973

3. Section 273 shall apply for the purposes of determining the market value of any asset at any time before 6th July 1973 (the date when the provisions of section 51(1) to (3) of the Finance Act 1973, which are now contained in section 273, came into force) notwithstanding that the asset was acquired before that date or that the market value of the asset may have been fixed for the purposes of a contemporaneous disposal, and in paragraphs 4 and 5 below a 'section 273 asset' is an asset to which section 273 applies.

4.—(1) This paragraph applies if, in a case where the market value of a section 273 asset at the time of its acquisition is material to the computation of any chargeable gain under this Act—

(a) the acquisition took place on the occasion of a death occurring after 30th March 1971 and before 6th July 1973, and

(b) by virtue of paragraph 9 below, the principal value of the asset for the purposes of estate duty on that death would, apart from this paragraph, be taken to be the market value of the asset at the date of the death for the purposes of this Act.

(2) If the principal value referred to in sub-paragraph (1)(b) above falls to be determined as mentioned in section 55 of the Finance Act 1940 or section 15 of the Finance (No 2) Act (Northern Ireland) 1946 (certain controlling shareholdings to be valued on a assets basis), nothing in section 273 shall affect the operation of paragraph 9 below for the purpose of determining the market value of the asset at the date of the death.

(3) If sub-paragraph (2) above does not apply, paragraph 9 below shall not apply as mentioned in sub-paragraph (1)(b) above and the market value of the asset on its acquisition at the date of the death shall be determined in accordance with sections 272 (but with the same modifications as are made by paragraphs 7 and 8 below) and 273.

5.—(1) In any case where—

(a) before 6th July 1973 there has been a part disposal of a section 273 asset ('the earlier disposal'), and

(b) by virtue of any enactment, the acquisition of the asset or any part of it was deemed to be for a consideration equal to its market value, and

(c) on or after 6th July 1973 there is a disposal (including a part disposal) of the property which remained undisposed of immediately before that date ('the later disposal'),

sub-paragraph (2) below shall apply in computing any chargeable gain accruing on the later disposal.

(2) Where this sub-paragraph applies, the apportionment made by virtue of paragraph 7 of Schedule 6 to the Finance Act 1965 (corresponding to section 42 of this Act) on the occasion of the earlier disposal shall be recalculated on the basis that section 273(3) of this Act was in force at the time, and applied for the purposes, of the determination of—

(a) the market value referred to in sub-paragraph (1)(b) above, and

(b) the market value of the property which remained undisposed of after the earlier disposal, and

(c) if the consideration for the earlier disposal was, by virtue of any enactment, deemed to be equal to the market value of the property disposed of, that market value.

Valuation of assets on 6th April 1965

6.—(1) For the purpose of ascertaining the market value of any shares or securities in accordance with paragraph 1(2) of Schedule 2, section 272 shall have effect subject to the provisions of this paragraph.

(2) Subsection (3)(a) shall have effect as if for the words 'one-quarter' there were substituted the words 'one-half', and as between the amount under paragraph (a) and the amount under paragraph (b) of that subsection the higher, and not the lower, amount shall be chosen.

(3) Subsection (5) shall have effect as if for the reference to an amount equal to the buying price there were substituted a reference to an amount halfway between the buying and selling prices.

(4) Where the market value of any shares or securities not within section 272(3) falls to be ascertained by reference to a pair of prices quoted on a stock exchange, an adjustment shall be made so as to increase the market value by an amount corresponding to that by which any market value is increased under sub-paragraph (2) above.

References to the London Stock Exchange before 25th March 1973 and Exchange Control restrictions before 13th December 1979

7.—(1) For the purposes of ascertaining the market value of an asset before 25th March 1973 section 272(3) and (4) shall have effect subject to the following modifications—

(a) for '*listed* [quoted] in The Stock Exchange Daily Official List' and 'quoted in that List' there shall be substituted respectively 'quoted on the London Stock Exchange' and 'so quoted';

(b) for 'The Stock Exchange Daily Official List' there shall be substituted 'the Stock Exchange Official Daily List';

(c) for 'The Stock Exchange provides a more active market elsewhere than on the London trading floor' there shall be substituted 'some other stock exchange in the United Kingdom affords a more active market'; and

(d) for 'if the London trading floor is closed' there shall be substituted 'if the London Stock Exchange is closed'.

(2) For the purposes of ascertaining the market value of an asset before 13th December 1979 section 272 shall have effect as if the following subsection were inserted after subsection (5)—

'(5A) In any case where the market value of an asset is to be determined at a time before 13th December 1979 and the asset is of a kind the sale of which was (at the time the market value is to be determined) subject to restrictions imposed under the Exchange Control Act 1947 such that part of what was paid by the purchaser was not retainable by the seller, the market value, as arrived at under subsection (1), (3), (4) or (5) above, shall be subject to such adjustment as is appropriate having regard to the difference between the amount payable by a purchaser and the amount receivable by a seller.'

Note. Word in square brackets in sub-para (1)(a) substituted for word in italics by Finance Act 1996, s 199, Sch 38, para 12(2), (3), with effect where the relevant date falls on or after 1 April 1996.

Depreciated valuations referable to deaths before 31st March 1973

8. In any case where this Part applies, section 272(2) shall have effect as if the following proviso were inserted at the end—

'Provided that where capital gains tax is chargeable, or an allowable loss accrues, in consequence of a death before 31st March 1973 and the market value of any property on the date of death taken into account for the purposes of that tax or loss has been depreciated by reason of the death, the estimate of the market value shall take that depreciation into account.'

Estate duty

9.—(1) Where estate duty (including estate duty leviable under the law of Northern Ireland) is chargeable in respect of any property passing on a death after 30th March 1971 and the principal value of an asset forming part of that property has been ascertained (whether in any proceedings or otherwise) for the purposes of that duty, the principal value so ascertained shall, subject to paragraph 4(3) above, be taken for the purposes of this Act to be the market value of that asset at the date of the death.

(2) Where the principal value has been reduced under section 35 of the Finance Act 1968 or section 1 of the Finance Act (Northern Ireland) 1968 (tapering relief for gifts inter vivos etc), the reference in sub-paragraph (1) above to the principal value as ascertained for the purposes of estate duty is a reference to that value as so ascertained before the reduction.

PART II

OTHER TRANSITORY PROVISIONS

Value-shifting

10.—(1) Section 30 applies only where the reduction in value mentioned in subsection (1) of that section (or, in a case within subsection (9) of that section, the reduction or increase in value) is after 29th March 1977.

(2) No account shall be taken by virtue of section 31 of any reduction in the value of an asset attributable to the payment of a dividend before 14th March 1989.

(3) No account shall be taken by virtue of section 32 of any reduction in the value of an asset attributable to the disposal of another asset before 14th March 1989.

(4) Section 34 shall not apply where the reduction in value, by reason of which the amount referred to in subsection (1)(b) of that section falls to be calculated, occurred before 14th March 1989.

Assets acquired on disposal chargeable under Case VII of Schedule D

11.—(1) In this paragraph references to a disposal chargeable under Case VII are references to cases where the acquisition and disposal was in circumstances that the gain accruing on it was chargeable under Case VII of Schedule D, or where it would have been so chargeable if there were a gain so accruing.

(2) The amount or value of the consideration for the acquisition of an asset by the person acquiring it on a disposal chargeable under Case VII shall not under any provision of this Act be deemed to be an amount greater than the amount taken into account as consideration on that disposal for the purposes of Case VII.

(3) Any apportionment of consideration or expenditure falling to be made in relation to a disposal chargeable under Case VII in accordance with section 164(4) of the Income and Corporation Taxes Act 1970, and in particular in a case where section 164(6) of that Act (enhancement of value of land by acquisition of adjoining land) applied, shall be followed for the purposes of this Act both in relation to a disposal of the assets acquired on the disposal chargeable under Case VII and, where the disposal chargeable under Case VII was a part disposal in relation to a disposal of what remains undisposed of.

(4) Sub-paragraph (3) above has effect notwithstanding section 52(4).

Unrelieved Case VII losses

12. Where no relief from income tax (for a year earlier than 1971–72) has been given in respect of a loss or part of a loss allowable under Case VII of Schedule D, the loss or part shall, notwithstanding that the loss accrued before that year be an allowable loss for the purposes of capital gains tax, but subject to any restrictions imposed by section 18.

Devaluation of sterling: securities acquired with borrowed foreign currency

13.—(1) This paragraph applies where, in pursuance of permission granted under the Exchange Control Act 1947, currency other than sterling was borrowed before 19th November 1967 for the purpose of investing in foreign securities (and had not been repaid before that date), and it was a condition of the permission—

(a) that repayment of the borrowed currency should be made from the proceeds of the sale in foreign currency of the foreign securities so acquired or out of investment currency, and

(b) that the foreign securities so acquired should be kept in separate accounts to distinguish them from others in the same ownership,

and securities held in such a separate account on 19th November 1967 are in this paragraph referred to as 'designated securities'.

(2) In computing the gain accruing to the borrower on the disposal of any designated securities or on the disposal of any currency or amount standing in a

bank account on 19th November 1967 and representing the loan, the sums allowable as a deduction under section 38(1)(a) shall, subject to sub-paragraph (3) below, be increased by multiplying them by seven-sixths.

(3) The total amount of the increases so made in computing all gains (and losses) which are referable to any one loan (made before 19th November 1967) shall not exceed one-sixth of the sterling parity value of that loan at the time it was made.

(4) Designated securities which on the commencement of this paragraph constitute a separate 1982 holding (within the meaning of section 109), shall continue to constitute a separate 1982 holding until such time as a disposal takes place on the occurrence of which sub-paragraph (3) above operates to limit the increases which would otherwise be made under sub-paragraph (2) in allowable deductions.

(5) In this paragraph and paragraph 14 below, 'foreign securities' means securities expressed in a currency other than sterling, or shares having a nominal value expressed in a currency other than sterling, or the dividends on which are payable in a currency other than sterling.

Devaluation of sterling: foreign insurance funds

14.—(1) The sums allowable as a deduction under section 38(1)(a) in computing any gains to which this paragraph applies shall be increased by multiplying by seven-sixths.

(2) This paragraph applies to gains accruing—

(a) to any underwriting member of Lloyd's, or

(b) to any company engaged in the business of marine protection and indemnity insurance on a mutal basis,

on the disposal by that person after 18th November 1967 of any foreign securities which on that date formed part of a trust fund—

 (i) established by that person in any country or territory outside the United Kingdom, and

 (ii) representing premiums received in the course of that person's business; and

 (iii) wholly or mainly used for the purpose of meeting liabilities arising in that country or territory in respect of that business.

Gilt-edged securities past redemption date

15. So far as material for the purposes of this or any other Act, the definition of 'gilt-edged securities' in Schedule 9 to this Act shall include any securities which were gilt-edged securities for the purposes of the 1979 Act, and the redemption date of which fell before 1st January 1992.

Qualifying corporate bonds, company reorganisations, share conversions etc

16.—(1) Part IV of this Act has effect subject to the provisions of this paragraph.

(2) The substitution of Chapter II of that Part for the enactments repealed by this Act shall not alter the law applicable to any reorganisation or reduction of share capital, conversion of securities or company amalgamation taking place before the coming into force of this Act.

(3) Sub-paragraph (2) above applies in particular to the law determining whether or not any assets arising on an event mentioned in that sub-paragraph are to be treated as the same asset as the original holding of shares, securities or other assets.

(4) In relation to a disposal or exchange on or after 6th April 1992, the following amendments shall be regarded as always having had effect, that is to say, the amendments to section 64 of, or Schedule 13 to, the Finance Act 1984 made by section 139 of, or paragraph 6 of Schedule 14 to, the Finance Act 1989, paragraph 28 of Schedule 10 to the Finance Act 1990 or section 98 of, or paragraph 1 of Schedule 10 to, the Finance Act 1991, or by virtue of the amendments to paragraph 1 of Schedule 18 to the Taxes Act made by section 77 of the Finance Act 1991.

Land: allowance for betterment levy

17.—(1) Where betterment levy charged in the case of any land in respect of an
act or event which fell within Case B or Case C or, if it was the renewal, extension
or variation of a tenancy, Case F—

(a) has been paid, and

(b) has not been allowed as a deduction in computing the profits or gains or
losses of a trade for the purposes of Case I of Schedule D;

then, if the person by whom the levy was paid disposes of the land or any part of it
and so claims, the following provisions of this paragraph shall have effect.

(2) Paragraph 9 of Schedule 2 shall apply where the condition stated in sub-
paragraph (1)(a) of that paragraph is satisfied, notwithstanding that the condition
in sub-paragraph (1)(b) of that paragraph is not satisfied.

(3) Subject to the following provisions of this paragraph, there shall be
ascertained the excess, if any, of—

(a) the net development value ascertained for the purposes of the levy, over

(b) the increment specified in sub-paragraph (6) below; and the amount of the
excess shall be treated as an amount allowable under section 38(1)(b).

(4) Where the act or event in respect of which the levy was charged was a part
disposal of the land, section 38 shall apply as if the part disposal had not taken
place and sub-paragraph (5) below shall apply in lieu of sub-paragraph (3) above.

(5) The amount or value of the consideration for the disposal shall be treated as
increased by the amount of any premium or like sum paid in respect of the part
disposal, and there shall be ascertained the excess, if any, of—

(a) the aggregate specified in sub-paragraph (7) below, over

(b) the increment specified in sub-paragraph (6) below;

and the amount of the excess shall be treated as an amount allowable under
section 38(1)(b).

(6) The increment referred to in sub-paragraphs (3)(b) and (5)(b) above is the
excess, if any, of—

(a) the amount or value of the consideration brought into account under
section 38(1)(a), over

(b) the base value ascertained for the purposes of the levy.

(7) The aggregate referred to in sub-paragraph (5)(a) above is the aggregate of—

(a) the net development value ascertained for the purposes of the levy, and

(b) the amount of any premium or like sum paid in respect of the part disposal,
in so far as charged to tax under Schedule A (or, as the case may be, Case
VIII of Schedule D), and

(c) the chargeable gain accruing on the part disposal.

(8) Where betterment levy in respect of more than one act or event has been
charged and paid as mentioned in sub-paragraph (1) above, sub-paragraphs (2) to
(7) above shall apply without modifications in relation to the betterment levy in
respect of the first of them; but in relation to the other or others sub-paragraph (3)
or, as the case may be, (5) above shall have effect as if the amounts to be treated
thereunder as allowable under section 38(1)(b) were the net development value
specified in sub-paragraph (3)(a) or, as the case may be, the aggregate referred to
in sub-paragraph (5)(a) of this paragraph.

(9) Where the disposal is of part only of the land sub-paragraphs (2) to (8)
above shall have effect subject to the appropriate apportionments.

(10) References in this paragraph to a premium include any sum payable as
mentioned in section 34(4) or (5) of the Taxes Act (sums payable in lieu of rent or
as consideration for the surrender of lease or for variation or waiver of term) and,
in relation to Scotland, a grassum.

Non-resident trusts

18. Without prejudice to section 289 or Part III of this Schedule—

(a) any tax chargeable on a person which is postponed under subsection (4)(b) of section 17 of the 1979 Act, shall continue to be postponed until that person becomes absolutely entitled to the part of the settled property concerned or disposes of the whole or part of his interest, as mentioned in that subsection; and

(b) section 70 of and Schedule 14 to the Finance Act 1984 shall continue to have effect in relation to amounts of tax which are postponed under that Schedule, and accordingly in paragraph 12 of that Schedule the references to section 80 of the Finance Act 1981 and to subsections (3) and (4) of that section include references to section 87 of this Act and subsections (4) and (5) of that section respectively.

Private residences

19. The reference in section 222(5)(a) to a notice given by any person within 2 years from the beginning of the period mentioned in section 222(5) includes a notice given before the end of the year 1966–67, if that was later.

Works of art etc

20. The repeals made by this Act do not affect the continued operation of sections 31 and 32 of the Finance Act 1965, in the form in which they were before 13th March 1975, in relation to estate duty in respect of deaths occurring before that date.

Disposal before acquisition

21. The substitution of this Act for the corresponding enactments repealed by this Act shall not alter the effect of any provision enacted before this Act (whether or not there is a corresponding provision in this Act) so far as it relates to an asset which—

(a) was disposed of before being acquired, and

(b) was disposed of before the commencement of this Act.

Estate duty

22. Nothing in the repeals made by this Act shall affect any enactment as it applies to the determination of any principal value for the purposes of estate duty.

Validity of subordinate legislation

23. So far as this Act re-enacts any provision contained in a statutory instrument made in exercise of powers conferred by any Act, it shall be without prejudice to the validity of that provision, and any question as to its validity shall be determined as if the re-enacted provision were contained in a statutory instrument made under those powers.

Amendments in other Acts

24.—(1) The repeal by this Act of the Income and Corporation Taxes Act 1970 does not affect—

(a) the amendment made by paragraph 3 of Schedule 15 of that Act to section 26 of the Finance Act 1956, or

(b) paragraph 10 of that Schedule so far as it applies in relation to the Management Act.

(2) The repeal by this Act of Schedule 7 to the 1979 Act does not affect the amendments made by that Schedule to any enactment not repealed by this Act.

Savings for Part III of this Schedule

25. The provisions of this Part of this Schedule are without prejudice to the generality of Part III of this Schedule.

PART III

ASSETS ACQUIRED BEFORE COMMENCEMENT

26.—(1) The substitution of this Act for the enactments repealed by this Act shall not alter the effect of any provision enacted before this Act (whether or not there is a corresponding provision in this Act) so far as it determines—

(a) what amount the consideration is to be taken to be for the purpose of the computation under this Act of any chargeable gain; or

(b) whether and to what extent events in, or expenditure incurred in, or other amounts referable to, a period earlier than the chargeable periods to which this Act applies may be taken into account for any tax purposes in a chargeable period to which this Act applies.

(2) Without prejudice to sub-paragraph (1) above, the repeals made by this Act shall not affect—

(a) the enactments specified in Part V of Schedule 14 to the Finance Act 1971 (charge on death) so far as their operation before repeal falls to be taken into account in chargeable periods to which this Act applies,

(b) the application of the enactments repealed by the 1979 Act to events before 6th April 1965 in accordance with paragraph 31 of Schedule 6 to the Finance Act 1965.

(3) This paragraph has no application to the law relating to the determination of the market value of assets.

27. Where the acquisition or provision of any asset by one person was, immediately before the commencement of this paragraph and by virtue of any enactment, to be taken for the purposes of Schedule 5 to the 1979 Act to be the acquisition or disposal of it by another person, then, notwithstanding the repeal by this Act of that enactment, Schedule 2 to this Act shall also have effect as if the acquisition or provision of the asset by the first-mentioned person had been the acquisition or provision of it by that other person.

PART IV

OTHER GENERAL SAVINGS

28. Where under any Act passed before this Act and relating to a country or territory outside the United Kingdom there is a power to affect Acts passed or in force before a particular time, or instruments made or having effect under such Acts, and the power would, but for the passing of this Act, have included power to change the law which is reproduced in, or is made or has effect under, this Act, then that power shall include power to make such provision as will secure the like change in the law reproduced in, or made or having effect under, this Act notwithstanding that this Act is not an Act passed or in force before that time.

29.—(1) The continuity of the law relating to the taxation of chargeable gains shall not be affected by the substitution of this Act for the enactments repealed by this Act and earlier enactments repealed by and corresponding to any of those enactments ('the repealed enactments').

(2) Any reference, whether express or implied, in any enactment, instrument or document (including this Act or any Act amended by this Act) to, or to things done or falling to be done under or for the purposes of, any provision of this Act shall, if and so far as the nature of the reference permits, be construed as including, in relation to the times, years or periods, circumstances or purposes in relation to which the corresponding provision in the repealed enactments has or had effect, a reference to, or as the case may be, to things done or falling to be done under or for the purposes of, that corresponding provision.

(3) Any reference, whether express or implied, in any enactment, instrument or document (including the repealed enactments and enactments, instruments and

documents passed or made after the passing of this Act) to, or to things done or falling to be done under or for the purposes of, any of the repealed enactments shall, if and so far as the nature of the reference permits, be construed as including, in relation to the times, years or periods, circumstances or purposes in relation to which the corresponding provision of this Act has effect, a reference to, or as the case may be to things done or falling to be done under or for the purposes of, that corresponding provision.

HUMAN FERTILISATION AND EMBRYOLOGY (DISCLOSURE OF INFORMATION) ACT 1992

(1992 c 54)

An Act to relax the restrictions on the disclosure of information imposed by section 33(5) of the Human Fertilisation and Embryology Act 1990.

[16 July 1992]

1. Relaxation of section 33(5) of the Human Fertilisation and Embryology Act 1990—(1) Section 33 of the Human Fertilisation and Embryology Act 1990 (subsection (5) of which prohibits disclosure of information falling within section 31(2) of that Act by a person to whom a licence under Schedule 2 to that Act applies or to whom directions under section 23 of that Act have been given) shall be amended as mentioned in subsections (2) to (4) below.

(2) In subsection (6) (general exceptions from subsection (5)) the word 'or' at the end of paragraph (d) is hereby repealed and at the end there shall be inserted—

'(f) necessarily—
    (i) for any purpose preliminary to proceedings, or
    (ii) for the purposes of, or in connection with, any proceedings,
(g) for the purpose of establishing, in any proceedings relating to an application for an order under subsection (1) of section 30 of this Act, whether the condition specified in paragraph (a) or (b) of that subsection is met, or
(h) under section 3 of the Access to Health Records Act 1990 (right of access to health records).'

(3) After subsection (6) there shall be inserted—

'(6A) Paragraph (f) of subsection (6) above, so far as relating to disclosure for the purposes of, or in connection with, any proceedings, does not apply—
(a) to disclosure of information enabling a person to be identified as a person whose gametes were used, in accordance with consent given under paragraph 5 of Schedule 3 to this Act, for the purposes of treatment services in consequence of which an identifiable individual was or may have been, born, or
(b) to disclosure, in circumstances in which subsection (1) of section 34 of this Act applies, of information relevant to the determination of the question mentioned in that subsection.

(6B) In the case of information relating to the provision of treatment services for any identifiable individual—
(a) where one individual is identifiable, subsection (5) above does not apply to disclosure with the consent of that individual;
(b) where both a woman and a man treated together with her are identifiable, subsection (5) above does not apply—
    (i) to disclosure with the consent of them both, or
    (ii) if disclosure is made for the purpose of disclosing information about the provision of treatment services for one of them, to disclosure with the consent of that individual.

(6C) For the purposes of subsection (6B) above, consent must be to disclosure to a specific person, except where disclosure is to a person who needs to know—
  (a) in connection with the provision of treatment services, or any other description of medical, surgical or obstetric services, for the individual giving the consent,
  (b) in connection with the carrying out of an audit of clinical practice, or
  (c) in connection with the auditing of accounts.

(6D) For the purposes of subsection (6B) above, consent to disclosure given at the request of another shall be disregarded unless, before it is given, the person requesting it takes reasonable steps to explain to the individual from whom it is requested the implications of compliance with the request.

(6E) In the case of information which relates to the provision of treatment services for any identifiable individual, subsection (5) above does not apply to disclosure in an emergency, that is to say, to disclosure made—
  (a) by a person who is satisfied that it is necessary to make the disclosure to avert an imminent danger to the health of an individual with whose consent the information could be disclosed under subsection (6B) above, and
  (b) in circumstances where it is not reasonably practicable to obtain that individual's consent.

(6F) In the case of information which shows that any identifiable individual was, or may have been, born in consequence of treatment services, subsection (5) above does not apply to any disclosure which is necessarily incidental to disclosure under subsection (6B) or (6E) above.

(6G) Regulations may provide for additional exceptions from subsection (5) above, but no exception may be made under this subsection—
  (a) for disclosure of a kind mentioned in paragraph (a) or (b) of subsection (6A) above, or
  (b) for disclosure, in circumstances in which section 32 of this Act applies, of information having the tendency mentioned in subsection (2) of that section.'

(4) At the end there shall be inserted—
'(9) In subsection (6)(f) above, references to proceedings include any formal procedure for dealing with a complaint.'

(5) This section applies in relation to information obtained before, as well as in relation to information obtained after, the passing of this Act.

2. Short title, etc—(1) This Act may be cited as the Human Fertilisation and Embryology (Disclosure of Information) Act 1992.

(2) In section 45(4) of the Human Fertilisation and Embryology Act 1990, after '31(4)(a),' there shall be inserted '33(6G),'.

(3) This Act (except section 1(2), so far as relating to the inserted section 33(6)(h)) extends to Northern Ireland.

(4) In section 48(1) of the Human Fertilisation and Embryology Act 1990 (extent to Northern Ireland) for 'section' there shall be substituted 'sections 33(6)(h) and'.

(5) Her Majesty may by Order in Council direct that any of the provisions of this Act shall extend, with such exceptions, adaptations and modifications (if any) as may be specified in the Order, to any of the Channel Islands.

MAINTENANCE ORDERS (RECIPROCAL ENFORCEMENT) ACT 1992

(1992 c 56)

An Act to amend the Maintenance Orders (Facilities for Enforcement) Act 1920 and the Maintenance Orders (Reciprocal Enforcement) Act 1972; and for connected purposes.   [12 November 1992]

1. Amendment of the 1920 and 1972 Acts—(1) The Maintenance Orders (Facilities for Enforcement) Act 1920 shall have effect (until its repeal by the Maintenance Orders (Reciprocal Enforcement) Act 1972 comes into force) with the amendments set out in Part I of Schedule 1 to this Act.

(2) The Maintenance Orders (Reciprocal Enforcement) Act 1972 shall have effect with the amendments set out in Part II of Schedule 1 to this Act.

2. Consequential amendments and repeals—(1) The amendments set out in Schedule 2 to this Act shall have effect.

(2) The enactments and subordinate legislation mentioned in Schedule 3 to this Act are repealed or revoked to the extent specified in the third column of that Schedule.

3. Commencement. This Act shall come into force on such day as the Lord Chancellor may by order made by statutory instrument appoint; and different days may be appointed for different provisions or different purposes.

Commencement. This Act was brought into force on 5 April 1993 (SI 1993 No 618).

4. Short title. This Act may be cited as the Maintenance Orders (Reciprocal Enforcement) Act 1992.

SCHEDULES

SCHEDULE 1   Section 1

AMENDMENT OF THE 1920 AND 1972 ACTS

PART I

AMENDMENT OF THE MAINTENANCE ORDERS (FACILITIES FOR ENFORCEMENT) ACT 1920 (C 33)

1.—(1) Section 3 (power to make provisional orders of maintenance against persons resident in certain Commonwealth countries) shall be amended as follows.

(2) In subsection (1), for the words 'a summons had been duly served on that person and he' there shall be substituted 'that person had been resident in England and Wales, had received reasonable notice of the date of the hearing of the application and'.

(3) In subsection (3), for the words 'duly served with a summons' there shall be substituted 'resident in England and Wales, had received reasonable notice of the date of the hearing'.

(4) In subsection (4), for the word 'rescind' there shall be substituted 'revoke'.

(5) In subsection (5), for the words 'rescind' and 'rescinding' there shall be substituted 'revoke' and 'revoking' respectively.

(6) In subsection (6), for the words from 'a summons' to the end there shall be substituted 'the person against whom the order is sought to be made been resident in England and Wales and received reasonable notice of the date of the hearing of the application'.

(7) After subsection (6), there shall be added—

'(7) Where subsection (1) of section 60 of the Magistrates' Courts Act 1980 (revocation, variation etc of orders for periodical payment) applies in relation to an order made under this section which has been confirmed, that subsection shall have effect as if for the words "by order on complaint," there were substituted "on an application being made, by order".

(8) In this section "revoke" includes discharge.'

2.—(1) Section 4 (power of court of summary jurisdiction to confirm maintenance order made out of the United Kingdom) shall be amended as follows.

(2) In subsection (1)—

(a) for the words 'summons be issued calling upon the person' there shall be substituted 'notice be served on the person informing him that he may attend a hearing at the time and place specified in the notice', and

(b) for the words 'issue such a summons and cause it' there shall be substituted 'cause such a notice'.

(3) For subsection (2) there shall be substituted—

'(2) A notice required to be served under this section may be served by post.'

(4) In subsection (3)—

(a) for the word 'summons' there shall be substituted 'notice', and

(b) for the words from 'raise any defence' to 'no other defence' there shall be substituted 'oppose the confirmation of the order on any grounds on which he might have opposed the making of the order in the original proceedings had he been a party to them, but on no other grounds'.

(5) In subsection (4), for the word 'summons' there shall be substituted 'notice'.

(6) In subsection (5)—

(a) for the words 'against whom the summons was issued' there shall be substituted 'served with the notice', and

(b) for the words 'any defence' there shall be substituted 'establishing any grounds on which he opposes the confirmation of the order'.

(7) In subsection (6A), before paragraph (a) there shall be inserted—

'(za) as if in subsection (1) for the words "by order on complaint" there were substituted "on an application being made, by order".'

3. After section 4, there shall be inserted—

'**4A. Variation and revocation of maintenance orders**—(1) This section applies to—

(a) any maintenance order made by virtue of section 3 of this Act which has been confirmed as mentioned in that section; and

(b) any maintenance order which has been confirmed under section 4 of this Act.

(2) Where the respondent to an application for the variation or revocation of a maintenance order to which this section applies is residing in a part of Her Majesty's dominions outside the United Kingdom to which this Act extends, a magistrates' court in England and Wales shall have jurisdiction to hear the application (where it would not have such jurisdiction apart from this subsection) if that court would have had jurisdiction to hear it had the respondent been residing in England and Wales.

(3) Where the defendant to a complaint for the variation or revocation of a maintenance order to which this section applies is residing in a part of Her Majesty's dominions outside the United Kingdom to which this Act extends, a court of summary jurisdiction in Northern Ireland shall have jurisdiction to hear the complaint if that court would have had jurisdiction to hear it had the defendant been residing in Northern Ireland.

(4) Where—

(a) the respondent to an application for the variation or revocation of a maintenance order to which this section applies does not appear at the time and place appointed for the hearing of the application by a magistrates' court in England and Wales, and

(b) the court is satisfied that the respondent is residing in a part of Her Majesty's dominions outside the United Kingdom to which this Act extends, the court may proceed to hear and determine the application at the time and place appointed for the hearing or for any adjourned hearing in like manner as if the respondent had appeared at that time and place.

(5) Subsection (4) shall apply to Northern Ireland with the following modifications—

(a) for the word "respondent" (in each place where it occurs) there shall be substituted "defendant",

(b) for the words "an application" and "the application" (in each place where they occur) there shall be substituted "a complaint" and "the complaint" respectively, and

(c) for the words "a magistrates' court in England and Wales" there shall be substituted "a court of summary jurisdiction in Northern Ireland".

(6) In this section "revocation" includes discharge.'

4. The provisions of section 7 (application of the Magistrates' Courts Act 1980) shall become subsection (1) of that section and the following subsection shall be added after that subsection—

'(2) Without prejudice to the generality of the power to make rules under section 144 of the Magistrates' Courts Act 1980 (magistrates' courts rules), for the purpose of giving effect to this Act such rules may make, in relation to any proceedings brought under or by virtue of this Act, any provision which—

(a) falls within subsection (2) of section 93 of the Children Act 1989, and

(b) may be made in relation to relevant proceedings under that section.'

5. In section 11 (application to Ireland), after paragraph (c) there shall be inserted—

'(d) the amendments of section 3(1), (3) and (6) and section 4 made by the Maintenance Orders (Reciprocal Enforcement) Act 1992 shall be disregarded.'

PART II

AMENDMENT OF THE MAINTENANCE ORDERS (RECIPROCAL ENFORCEMENT) ACT 1972 (C 18)

6.—(1) Section 3 (power of magistrates' court to make provisional maintenance order against person residing in reciprocating country) shall be amended as follows.

(2) For subsection (1) there shall be substituted—

'(1) Where an application is made to a magistrates' court for a maintenance order against a person residing in a reciprocating country and the court would have jurisdiction to determine the application under the Domestic Proceedings and Magistrates' Courts Act 1978 or the Children Act 1989 if that person—

(a) were residing in England and Wales, and

(b) received reasonable notice of the date of the hearing of the application, the court shall (subject to subsection (2) below) have jurisdiction to determine the application.'

(3) For subsection (4) there shall be substituted—

'(4) No enactment (or provision made under an enactment) requiring or enabling—

(a) a court to transfer proceedings from a magistrates' court to a county court or the High Court, or

(b) a magistrates' court to refuse to make an order on an application on the ground that any matter in question is one that would be more conveniently dealt with by the High Court,

shall apply in relation to an application to which subsection (1) above applies.'

(4) For subsection (7) there shall be substituted—

'(7) In the application of this section to Northern Ireland—

(a) for subsection (1) there shall be substituted—

"(1) Where a complaint is made to a magistrates' court against a person residing in a reciprocating country and the complaint is one on which the court would have jurisdiction by virtue of any enactment to make a maintenance order if—

(a) that person were residing in Northern Ireland, and

(b) a summons to appear before the court to answer the complaint had been duly served on him,

the court shall have jurisdiction to hear the complaint and may (subject to subsection (2) below) make a maintenance order on the complaint.",

and

(b) for subsection (4) there shall be substituted—

"(4) No enactment empowering a magistrates' court to refuse to make an order on a complaint on the ground that any matter in question is one which would be more conveniently dealt with by the High Court of Justice in Northern Ireland shall apply in relation to a complaint to which subsection (1) above applies." '

7. In section 5 (variation and revocation of maintenance order made in United Kingdom), after subsection (3) there shall be inserted—

'(3A) Where subsection (1) of section 60 of the Magistrates' Courts Act 1980 (revocation, variation etc of orders for periodical payment) applies in relation to a maintenance order to which this section applies, that subsection shall have effect as if for the words "by order on complaint," there were substituted "on an application being made, by order".'

8.—(1) Section 7 (confirmation by United Kingdom court of provisional maintenance order made in reciprocating country) shall be amended as follows.

(2) In subsection (2)(i), for the words 'any such defence as he might have raised' there shall be substituted 'any grounds on which he might have opposed the making of the order'.

(3) In subsection (3), for the words from 'raised a defence' to the end there shall be substituted 'opposed the making of the order on any of those grounds.'

(4) In subsection (4), for the words 'the court' there shall be substituted 'a magistrates' court in Northern Ireland'.

(5) In subsection (6), for the words 'a summons to appear in' there shall be substituted 'notice of'.

(6) After subsection (7) there shall be added—

'(8) In the application of this section to Northern Ireland—

(a) in subsection (2)(i), for the words from "any grounds" to "making of the order" there shall be substituted "any such defence as he might have raised",

(b) in subsection (3), for the words from "opposed the making" to the end there shall be substituted "raised a defence on any of those grounds in the proceedings in which the order was made.", and

(c) in subsection (6), for the words "notice of" there shall be substituted "a summons to appear in".'

9. In section 9 (variation and revocation of maintenance order registered in United Kingdom court), in subsection (1ZA) before paragraph (a) there shall be inserted—

'(za) as if in subsection (1) for the words "by order on complaint," there were substituted "on an application being made, by order";'.

10.—(1) Section 17 (proceedings in magistrates' courts) shall be amended as follows.

(2) In subsection (5), after the words 'magistrates' court' there shall be inserted 'in Northern Ireland'.

(3) After subsection (5), there shall be inserted—

'(5A) Where the respondent to an application for the variation or revocation of—

(a) a maintenance order made by a magistrates' court in England and Wales, being an order to which section 5 of this Act applies; or

(b) a registered order which is registered in such a court,

is residing in a reciprocating country, a magistrates' court in England and Wales shall have jurisdiction to hear the application (where it would not have such jurisdiction apart from this subsection) if it would have had jurisdiction to hear it had the respondent been residing in England and Wales.'

(4) In subsection (7)—

(a) for the word 'defendant', in each place where it occurs, there shall be substituted 'respondent', and

(b) for the words 'a complaint' and 'the complaint', in each place where they occur, there shall be substituted 'an application' and 'the application' respectively.

(5) After subsection (7), there shall be added—

'(7A) In the application of this section to Northern Ireland, in subsection (7)—

(a) for the word "respondent", in each place where it occurs, there shall be substituted "defendant"; and

(b) for the words "an application" and "the application", in each place where they occur, there shall be substituted "a complaint" and "the complaint" respectively.'

11. In section 18 (magistrates' courts rules), after subsection (1) there shall be inserted—

'(1A) For the purpose of giving effect to this Part of this Act, rules made under section 144 of the Magistrates' Courts Act 1980 may make, in relation to any proceedings brought under or by virtue of this Part of this Act, any provision not covered by subsection (1) above which—

(a) falls within subsection (2) of section 93 of the Children Act 1989, and

(b) may be made in relation to relevant proceedings under that section.'

12. In section 21 (interpretation of Part I), in subsection (1) at the end there shall be added—

' "revoke" and "revocation" include discharge.'

13. For sections 27, 28 and 28A there shall be substituted—

'**27A. Applications for recovery of maintenance in England and Wales—**

(1) This section applies to any application which—

(a) is received by the Lord Chancellor from the appropriate authority in a convention country, and

(b) is an application by a person in that country for the recovery of maintenance from another person who is for the time being residing in England and Wales.

(2) Subject to sections 27B and 28B of this Act, an application to which this section applies shall be treated for the purposes of any enactment as if it were an application for a maintenance order under the relevant Act, made at the time when the application was received by the Lord Chancellor.

(3) In the case of an application for maintenance for a child (or children) alone, the relevant Act is the Children Act 1989.

(4) In any other case, the relevant Act is the Domestic Proceedings and Magistrates' Courts Act 1978.

(5) In subsection (3) above, "child" means the same as in Schedule 1 to the Children Act 1989.

27B. Sending application to the appropriate magistrates' court—(1) On receipt of an application to which section 27A of this Act applies, the Lord Chancellor shall send it, together with any accompanying documents, to the clerk of a magistrates' court acting for the petty sessions area in which the respondent is residing.

(2) Subject to subsection (4) below, if notice of the hearing of the application by a magistrates' court having jurisdiction to hear it cannot be duly served on the respondent, the clerk of the court shall return the application and the accompanying documents to the Lord Chancellor with a statement giving such information as he possesses as to the whereabouts of the respondent.

(3) If the application is returned to the Lord Chancellor under subsection (2) above, then, unless he is satisfied that the respondent is not residing in the United Kingdom, he shall deal with it in accordance with subsection (1) above or section 28C of this Act or send it to the Secretary of State to be dealt with in accordance with section 31 of this Act (as the circumstances of the case require).

(4) If the clerk of a court to whom the application is sent under this section is satisfied that the respondent is residing within the petty sessions area for which another magistrates' court acts, he shall send the application and accompanying documents to the clerk of that other court and shall inform the Lord Chancellor that he has done so.

(5) If the application is sent to the clerk of a court under subsection (4) above, he shall proceed as if it had been sent to him under subsection (1) above.

27C. Applications to which section 27A applies: general—(1) This section applies where a magistrates' court makes an order on an application to which section 27A of this Act applies.

(2) Section 59 of the Magistrates' Courts Act 1980 (orders for periodical payment: means of payment) shall not apply.

(3) The court shall, at the same time that it makes the order, exercise one of its powers under subsection (4) below.

(4) Those powers are—

(a) the power to order that payments under the order be made directly to the clerk of the court or the clerk of any other magistrates' court in England and Wales;

(b) the power to order that payments under the order be made to the clerk of the court, or to the clerk of any other magistrates' court in England and Wales, by such method of payment falling within section 59(6) of the Magistrates' Courts Act 1980 (standing order, etc) as may be specified;

(c) the power to make an attachment of earnings order under the Attachment of Earnings Act 1971 to secure payments under the order.

(5) In deciding which of the powers under subsection (4) above it is to exercise, the court shall have regard to any representations made by the person liable to make payments under the order.

(6) Subsection (4) of section 59 of the Magistrates' Courts Act 1980 (power of court to require debtor to open account) shall apply for the purposes of subsection (4) above as it applies for the purposes of that section, but as if for paragraph (a) there were substituted—

"(a) the court proposes to exercise its power under paragraph (b) of section 27C(4) of the Maintenance Orders (Reciprocal Enforcement) Act 1972, and".

(7) The clerk of the court shall register the order in the prescribed manner in the court.

28. Applications by spouses under the Domestic Proceedings and Magistrates' Courts Act 1978—(1) The magistrates' court hearing an application which by virtue of section 27A of this Act is to be treated as if it were an application for a maintenance order under the Domestic Proceedings and Magistrates' Courts Act 1978 may make any order on the application which it has power to make under section 2 or 19(1) of that Act.

(2) Part I of that Act shall apply in relation to such an application, and to any order made on such an application, with the following modifications—

(a) sections 6 to 8, 16 to 18, 20ZA, 25 to 27 and 28(2) shall be omitted,

(b) in section 30(1), for the words "either the applicant or the respondent ordinarily resides" there shall be substituted "the respondent resides", and

(c) section 32(2) shall be omitted.

(3) Subsections (1) and (2) above do not apply where section 28A of this Act applies.

28A. Applications by former spouses under the Domestic Proceedings and Magistrates' Courts Act 1978—(1) This section applies where in the case of any application which by virtue of section 27A of this Act is to be treated as if it were an application for a maintenance order under the Domestic Proceedings and Magistrates' Courts Act 1978 ("the 1978 Act")—

   (a) the applicant and respondent were formerly married,

   (b) their marriage was dissolved or annulled in a country or territory outside the United Kingdom by a divorce or annulment which is recognised as valid by the law of England and Wales,

   (c) an order for the payment of maintenance for the benefit of the applicant or a child of the family has, by reason of the divorce or annulment, been made by a court in a convention country, and

   (d) where the order for the payment of maintenance was made by a court of a different country from that in which the divorce or annulment was obtained, either the applicant or the respondent was resident in the convention country whose court made that order at the time that order was applied for.

(2) Any magistrates' court that would have jurisdiction to hear the application under section 30 of the 1978 Act (as modified in accordance with subsection (6) below) if the applicant and the respondent were still married shall have jurisdiction to hear it notwithstanding the dissolution or annulment of the marriage.

(3) If the magistrates' court hearing the application is satisfied that the respondent has failed to comply with the provisions of any order such as is mentioned in subsection (1)(c) above, it may (subject to subsections (4) and (5) below) make any order which it has power to make under section 2 or 19(1) of the 1978 Act.

(4) The court shall not make an order for the making of periodical payments for the benefit of the applicant or any child of the family unless the order made in the convention country provides for the making of periodical payments for the benefit of the applicant or, as the case may be, that child.

(5) The court shall not make an order for the payment of a lump sum for the benefit of the applicant or any child of the family unless the order made in the convention country provides for the payment of a lump sum to the applicant or, as the case may be, to that child.

(6) Part I of the 1978 Act shall apply in relation to the application, and to any order made on the application, with the following modifications—

   (a) section 1 shall be omitted,

   (b) for the reference in section 2(1) to any ground mentioned in section 1 of that Act there shall be substituted a reference to non-compliance with any such order as is mentioned in subsection (1)(c) of this section,

   (c) for the references in section 3(2) and (3) to the occurrence of the conduct which is alleged as the ground of the application there shall be substituted references to the breakdown of the marriage,

   (d) the reference in section 4(2) to the subsequent dissolution or annulment of the marriage of the parties affected by the order shall be omitted,

   (e) sections 6 to 8, 16 to 18, 20ZA and 25 to 28 shall be omitted,

   (f) in section 30(1), for the words "either the applicant or the respondent ordinarily resides" there shall be substituted "the respondent resides", and

   (g) section 32(2) shall be omitted.

(7) A divorce or annulment obtained in a country or territory outside the United Kingdom shall be presumed for the purposes of this section to be one the validity of which is recognised by the law of England and Wales, unless the contrary is proved by the respondent.

(8) In this section, "child of the family" has the meaning given in section 88 of the 1978 Act.

28B. Applications under the Children Act 1989.   No provision of an order made under Schedule 11 to the Children Act 1989 requiring or enabling a court to transfer proceedings from a magistrates' court to a county court or the High Court shall apply in relation to an application which by virtue of section 27A of this Act is to be treated as if it were an application for a maintenance order under that Act.

28C. Applications for recovery of maintenance in Northern Ireland—(1) This section applies where the Lord Chancellor receives from the appropriate authority in a convention country an application by a person in that country for the recovery of maintenance from another person who is for the time being residing in Northern Ireland.

(2) The Lord Chancellor shall send the application, together with any accompanying documents, to the clerk of a magistrates' court acting for the petty sessions district in which that other person is residing.

(3) The application shall be treated for the purposes of any enactment as if it were a complaint made at the time when the application was received by the Lord Chancellor, and references in this section and in sections 29, 29A and 30 of this Act to the complaint, the complainant and the defendant shall be construed accordingly.

(4) Where the complaint is for an affiliation order, a magistrates' court acting for the petty sessions district in which the defendant is residing shall have jurisdiction to hear the complaint.

(5) If a summons to appear before a magistrates' court having jurisdiction to hear the complaint cannot be duly served on the defendant, the clerk of the court shall (subject to subsection (7) below) return the complaint and the accompanying documents to the Lord Chancellor with a statement giving such information as he possesses as to the whereabouts of the defendant.

(6) If the complaint is returned to the Lord Chancellor under subsection (5) above, then, unless he is satisfied that the respondent is not residing in the United Kingdom, he shall deal with it in accordance with subsection (2) above or section 27B of this Act or send it to the Secretary of State to be dealt with in accordance with section 31 of this Act (as the circumstances of the case require).

(7) If the clerk of a court to whom the complaint is sent under this section is satisfied that the defendant is residing within the jurisdiction of another magistrates' court in Northern Ireland, he shall send the complaint and accompanying documents to the clerk of that other court and shall inform the Lord Chancellor that he has done so.

(8) If the complaint is sent to the clerk of a court under subsection (7) above, he shall proceed as if it had been sent to him under subsection (2) above.

(9) When hearing the complaint, a magistrates' court shall proceed as if complainant were before the court.

(10) If a magistrates' court makes an order on the complaint, the clerk of the court shall register the order in the prescribed manner in that court.

(11) Payment of sums due under a registered order shall, while the order is registered in a magistrates' court in Northern Ireland, be made in such manner and to such person as may be prescribed, and neither Article 36(1) of the Domestic Proceedings (Northern Ireland) Order 1980 nor Article 85(1) to (7) of the Magistrates' Courts (Northern Ireland) Order 1981 (which relate to the power of a magistrates' court to direct payments to be made to or through the collecting officer of the court or some other person) shall apply in relation to a registered order.'

14. *In section 29A (complaint by former spouse for recovery of maintenance in Northern Ireland), in subsection (1) for 'section 27(1)' there shall be substituted 'section 28C(1)'.*

15.—(1) Section 34 (variation and revocation of orders) shall be amended as follows.

(2) In subsection (1) after the words 'Subject to' there shall be inserted 'subsection (3A) below and'.

(3) After subsection (3) there shall be inserted—

'(3A) Where subsection (1) of section 60 of the Magistrates' Courts Act 1980 (revocation, variation etc of orders for periodical payment) applies in relation to a registered order, that subsection shall have effect as if for the words "by order on complaint," there were substituted "on an application being made, by order".'

16. For section 35 there shall be substituted—

'**35. Further provisions with respect to variation etc of orders by magistrates' courts in England and Wales**—(1) Notwithstanding anything in section 28(2) or 28A(6)(e) of this Act, a magistrates' court in England and Wales shall have jurisdiction to hear an application—

(a) for the variation or revocation of a registered order registered in that court, and

(b) made by the person against whom or on whose application the order was made,

notwithstanding that the person by or against whom the application is made is residing outside England and Wales.

(2) None of the powers of the court, or of the clerk of the court, under section 34A of this Act shall be exercisable in relation to such an application.

(3) Where the respondent to an application for the variation or revocation of a registered order which is registered in a magistrates' court in England and Wales does not appear at the time and place appointed for the hearing of the application, but the court is satisfied—

(a) that the respondent is residing outside England and Wales, and

(b) that the prescribed notice of the making of the application and of the time and place appointed for the hearing has been given to the respondent in the prescribed manner,

the court may proceed to hear and determine the application at the time and place appointed for the hearing or for any adjourned hearing in like manner as if the respondent had appeared at that time and place.

35A. Further provisions with respect to variation etc of orders by magistrates' courts in Northern Ireland—(1) Notwithstanding anything in section 29 or 29A(3)(e) of this Act, a magistrates' court in Northern Ireland shall have jurisdiction to hear an application for the variation or revocation of a registered order registered in that court, being—

(a) an application being made by the person against whom or on whose application the order was made, or

(b) an application made by some other person in pursuance of section 30(5) of this Act for the variation of an affiliation order,

notwithstanding that the person by or against whom the application is made is residing outside Northern Ireland.

(2) Where an application by a person in a convention country for the variation of a registered order is received from the Lord Chancellor by the clerk of a magistrates' court in Northern Ireland, he shall treat the application as if it were a complaint for the variation of the order to which the application relates, and the court hearing the application shall proceed as if the application were a complaint and the applicant were before the court.

(3) Without prejudice to subsection (2) above, an application to a magistrates' court in Northern Ireland for the variation or revocation of a registered order shall be made by complaint.

(4) Where the defendant to a complaint for the variation or revocation of a registered order which is registered in a magistrates' court in Northern Ireland does not appear at the time and place appointed for the hearing of the complaint, but the court is satisfied—

    (a) that the defendant is residing outside Northern Ireland, and

    (b) that the prescribed notice of the making of the complaint and of the time and place appointed for the hearing has been given to the defendant in the prescribed manner,

the court may proceed to hear and determine the complaint at the time and place appointed for the hearing or for any adjourned hearing in like manner as if the defendant had appeared at that time and place.'

17. In section 36 (admissibility of evidence given in convention country), in subsection (1) for the words from 'received by' to 'or out of' there shall be substituted 'to which section 27A(1) of this Act applies, an application received by the Lord Chancellor as mentioned in section 28C(1) of this Act, an application received by the Secretary of State as mentioned in section 31(1) of this Act or'.

18. After section 38 there shall be inserted—

'**38A. Magistrates' court rules**—(1) Without prejudice to the generality of the power to make rules under section 144 of the Magistrates' Courts Act 1980 (magistrates' courts rules), such rules may make provision with respect to the orders made or other things done by a magistrates' court, or an officer of such a court, by virtue of this Part of this Act, notice of which is to be given to such persons as the rules may provide and the manner in which such notice shall be given.

    (2) For the purpose of giving effect to this Part of this Act, rules made under section 144 of the Magistrates' Courts Act 1980 may make, in relation to any proceedings brought under or by virtue of this Part of this Act, any provision not covered by subsection (1) above which—

    (a) falls within subsection (2) of section 93 of the Children Act 1989, and

    (b) may be made in relation to relevant proceedings under that section.

    (3) In the application of this section to Northern Ireland—

    (a) in subsection (1), for the reference to section 144 of the Magistrates' Courts Act 1980 there shall be substituted a reference to Article 13 of the Magistrates' Courts (Northern Ireland) Order 1981, and

    (b) subsection (2) shall be omitted.'

19. In section 39 (interpretation of Part II), after the definition of 'maintenance' there shall be inserted—

' "maintenance order" has the same meaning as in Part I of this Act,',

and at the end there shall be added—

' "revoke" and "revocation" include discharge.'

Note. Para 14 repealed by Children (Northern Ireland) Order 1995, SI 1995 No 755, art 185(2), Sch 10, as from 4 November 1996.

SCHEDULE 2   Section 2(1)

CONSEQUENTIAL AMENDMENTS

The Domestic Proceedings and Magistrates' Courts Act 1978 (c 22)

1. In section 90(3)(b) of the Domestic Proceedings and Magistrates' Courts Act 1978 (which lists the provisions of Schedule 2 to that Act that extend to Northern Ireland), for 'paragraphs 12, 13, 14, 33 and 34(a)' there shall be substituted 'paragraphs 12, 13, 14 and 33'.

The Magistrates' Courts (Northern Ireland) Order 1981 (SI 1981/1675 (NI 26))

2.—*(1) The Magistrates' Courts (Northern Ireland) Order 1981 shall be amended as follows.*

    (2) In Article 100 (power of court to make attachment of earnings order), in paragraph (2), in the definition of 'prescribed person' for 'section 27(9)' there shall be substituted 'section 28C(11)'.

    (3) In Article 101 (making of attachment of earnings order), in paragraph (3)(b)(ii) for 'section 27(8)' there shall be substituted 'section 28C(10)'.

Note. Para 2 repealed by Children (Northern Ireland) Order 1995, SI 1995 No 755, art 185(2), Sch 10, as from 4 November 1996.

SCHEDULE 3   Section 2(2)

REPEALS

Chapter or number	Short title or title	Extent of repeal or revocation
1978 c 22.	The Domestic Proceedings and Magistrates' Courts Act 1978.	Sections 57 and 58. In Schedule 2, paragraphs 34 and 35.
1980 c 43.	The Magistrates' Courts Act 1980.	In Schedule 7, paragraph 108.
1982 c 27.	The Civil Jurisdiction and Judgments Act 1982.	Section 37(2).
1984 c 42.	The Matrimonial and Family Proceedings Act 1984.	Section 26. In Schedule 1, paragraph 9.
1987 c 42.	The Family Law Reform Act 1987.	In Schedule 2, paragraph 46.
1990 c 41.	The Courts and Legal Services Act 1990.	In Schedule 16, paragraph 39(1) and (2).
1991 c 17.	The Maintenance Enforcement Act 1991.	In Schedule 1, paragraphs 15, 16, 17 and 20.
SI 1980/564.	The Maintenance Orders (Northern Ireland Consequential Amendments) Order 1980.	Article 4(2) and (5).
SI 1981/1675 (NI 26).	The Magistrates' Courts (Northern Ireland) Order 1981.	In Schedule 6, paragraph 24.

PENSIONS ACT 1995

(1995 c 26)

An Act to amend the law about pensions and for connected purposes.

[19 July 1995]

*   *   *   *   *

PART IV

MISCELLANEOUS AND GENERAL

*   *   *   *   *

Pensions on divorce etc

166. Pensions on divorce etc—(1)–(3) (*Amend Matrimonial Causes Act 1973.*)

(4) Nothing in the provisions mentioned in subsection (5) applies to a court exercising its powers under *section 23* [section 22A or 23] of the Matrimonial Causes Act 1973 (financial provision in connection with divorce proceedings, etc) in respect of any benefits under a pension *scheme* [arrangement] (within the meaning of section 25B(1) of the Matrimonial Causes Act 1973) which a party to the marriage has or is likely to have.

Note. First words in square brackets substituted for words in italics by Family Law Act 1996, s 66(1), Sch 8, Part I, para 43, as from a day to be appointed, subject to savings in s 66(2) of, and para 5 of Sch 9 to, the 1996 Act. Word 'arrangement' in square brackets substituted by the Welfare Reform and Pensions Act 1999, s 84(1), Sch 12, paras 43, 62, as from 1 December 2000 (SI 2000 No 1047).

(5) The provisions referred to in subsection (4) are—
(a) section 203(1) and (2) of the Army Act 1955, 203(1) and (2) of the Air Force Act 1955, 128G(1) and (2) of the Naval Discipline Act 1957 or 159(4) and (4A) of the Pension Schemes Act 1993 (which prevent assignment, or orders being made restraining a person from receiving anything which he is prevented from assigning),
(b) section 91 of this Act,
(c) any provision of any enactment (whether passed or made before or after this Act is passed) corresponding to any of the enactments mentioned in paragraphs (a) and (b), and
(d) any provision of the *scheme* [arrangement] in question corresponding to any of those enactments.

Note. Word 'arrangement' in square brackets substituted by the Welfare Reform and Pensions Act 1999, s 84 (1), Sch 12, paras 43, 62, as from 1 December 2000 (SI 2000 No 1047).

(6) Subsections (3) to (7) of section 25B, and section 25C of the Matrimonial Causes Act 1973, as inserted by this section, do not affect the powers of the court under section 31 of that Act (variation, discharge, etc) in relation to any order made before the commencement of this section.

*   *   *   *   *

180. Commencement—(1), (2) (*Not reproduced in this work.*)
(3) Section 166 shall come into force on such day as the Lord Chancellor may by order made by statutory instrument appoint and different days may be appointed for different purposes.
(4) (*Not reproduced in this work.*)

Commencement. Section 166 was brought into force (in relation to the insertion of Matrimonial Causes Act 1973, s 25D(2)–(4)) on 27 June 1996, and on 1 August 1996, otherwise (SI 1996 No 1675).

181. Short title.   This Act may be cited as the Pensions Act 1995.

CHILD SUPPORT ACT 1995

(1995 c 34)

An Act to make provision with respect to child support maintenance and other maintenance; and to provide for a child maintenance bonus.   [19 July 1995]

*   *   *   *   *

The child maintenance bonus

10. The child maintenance bonus—*(1) The Secretary of State may by regulations make provision for the payment, in prescribed circumstances, of sums to persons—*
(a) who are or have been in receipt of child maintenance; and
(b) to or in respect of whom income support or a jobseeker's allowance is or has been paid.
(2) A sum payable under the regulations shall be known as 'a child maintenance bonus'.
(3) A child maintenance bonus shall be treated for all purposes as payable by way of income support or (as the case may be) a jobseeker's allowance.
(4) Subsection (3) is subject to section 617 of the Income and Corporation Taxes Act 1988 (which, as amended by paragraph 1 of Schedule 3, provides for a child maintenance bonus not to be taxable).
(5) The regulations may, in particular, provide for—
(a) a child maintenance bonus to be payable only on the occurrence of a prescribed event;
(b) a bonus not to be payable unless a claim is made before the end of the prescribed period;
(c) the amount of a bonus (subject to any maximum prescribed by virtue of paragraph (f)) to be determined in accordance with the regulations;

(d) enabling amounts to be calculated by reference to periods of entitlement to income support and periods of entitlement to a jobseeker's allowance;

(e) treating a bonus as payable wholly by way of a jobseeker's allowance or wholly by way of income support, in a case where amounts have been calculated in accordance with provision made by virtue of paragraph (d);

(f) the amount of a bonus not to exceed a prescribed maximum;

(g) a bonus not to be payable if the amount of the bonus which would otherwise be payable is less than the prescribed minimum;

(h) prescribed periods to be disregarded for prescribed purposes;

(i) a bonus which has been paid to a person to be treated, in prescribed circumstances and for prescribed purposes, as income or capital of hers or of any other member of her family;

(j) treating the whole or a prescribed part of an amount which has accrued towards a person's bonus—

(i) as not having accrued towards her bonus; but

(ii) as having accrued towards the bonus of another person.

(6) The Secretary of State may by regulations provide—

(a) for the whole or a prescribed part of a child maintenance bonus to be paid in such circumstances as may be prescribed to such person, other than the person who is or had been in receipt of child maintenance, as may be determined in accordance with the regulations;

(b) for any payments of a prescribed kind which have been collected by the Secretary of State, and retained by him, to be treated for the purposes of this section as having been received by the appropriate person as payments of child maintenance.

(7) In this section—

'appropriate person' has such meaning as may be prescribed;

'child' means a person under the age of 16;

'child maintenance' has such meaning as may be prescribed;

'family' means—

(a) a married or unmarried couple;

(b) a married or unmarried couple and a member of the same household for whom one of them is, or both are, responsible and who is a child or a person of a prescribed description;

(c) except in prescribed circumstances, a person who is not a member of a married or unmarried couple and a member of the same household for whom that person is responsible and who is a child or a person of a prescribed description;

'married couple' means a man and woman who are married to each other and are members of the same household; and

'unmarried couple' means a man and woman who are not married to each other but are living together as husband and wife otherwise than in prescribed circumstances.

(8) For the purposes of this section, the Secretary of State may by regulations make provision as to the circumstances in which—

(a) persons are to be treated as being or not being members of the same household;

(b) one person is to be treated as responsible or not responsible for another.

Note. This section repealed by the Child Support, Pensions and Social Security Act 2000, ss 23, 85, Sch 9, Pt I (in relation to certain cases) as from 3 March 2003 (SI 2003 No 192); for remaining purposes, to be appointed. References to 'a child maintenance bonus', 'income support', 'jobseeker's allowance', 'the Secretary of State' modified by the Child Maintenance Bonus (Northern Ireland Reciprocal Arrangements) Regulations 1997, SI 1997 No 645, reg 2(3).

*　　*　　*　　*　　*

Miscellaneous

18. Deferral of right to apply for maintenance assessment—(1)–(4) ...

(5) *The Secretary of State may by order repeal any of the provisions of this section.*

(6) Neither section 4(10) nor section 7(10) of the 1991 Act shall apply in relation to a maintenance order made in the circumstances mentioned in subsection (7) or (8) of section 8 of the 1991 Act.

(7) The Secretary of State may by regulations make provision for section 4(10), or section 7(10), of the 1991 Act not to apply in relation to such other cases as may be prescribed.

(8) ...

(9) At any time before 7th April 1997, neither section 8(3), nor section 9(5)(b), of the 1991 Act shall apply in relation to any case which fell within paragraph 5(2) of the Schedule to the 1992 order (pending cases during the transitional period set by that order).

Note. Sub-ss (1)–(4): add the Child Support Act 1991, ss 4(10), (11), 7(10), 8(3A), 9(6) and amend s 9(3).

Sub-ss (3), (5): repealed by the Child Support, Pensions and Social Security Act 2000, ss 26, 85, Sch 3, para 13(1), (2), Sch 9, Pt I (in relation to certain cases) as from 3 March 2003 (SI 2003 No 192); for remaining purposes, to be appointed.

Sub-s (8): revokes SI 1992 No 2644, Schedule, Part I.

1992 order: Child Support Act 1991 (Commencement No 3 and Transitional Provisions) Order 1992, SI 1992 No 2644.

* * * * *

24. Compensation payments—(1) The Secretary of State may by regulations make provision for the payment by him, in prescribed circumstances and to or in respect of qualifying persons, of sums by way of compensation or partial compensation for any reduction which is attributable to one or more prescribed changes in child support legislation.

(2) For the purposes of this section—

'child support legislation' means—

(a) the provisions of the 1991 Act and this Act;

(b) any provision made under that Act or this Act; and

(c) such other provisions (if any) of primary or subordinate legislation with respect to child support maintenance as may be prescribed;

'compensation payment' means any sum payable under the regulations;

'qualifying person' means a person with care—

(a) with respect to whom a maintenance assessment ('the revised assessment') is in force or was made after the change or changes took effect;

(b) to or in respect of whom *family credit* [working families' tax credit] or *disability working allowance* [disabled person's tax credit] is or has been paid; and

(c) with respect to whom an earlier maintenance assessment was in force at the relevant time;

'reduction' means a reduction in the amount of child support maintenance payable under the revised assessment when compared with the amount payable under the earlier assessment; and

'relevant time' has such meaning as may be prescribed.

(3) The regulations may include provision—

(a) as to the calculation of the amount of any compensation payment;

(b) for any compensation payment to be made in instalments or as a lump sum;

(c) as to the manner in which any compensation payment is to be made;

(d) for a compensation payment which would otherwise be made under the regulations not to be made if the amount of the payment would be less than the prescribed minimum.

(4) The Secretary of State may by order provide that, for the purposes of specified provisions of the Social Security Administration Act 1992, a compensation payment is to be treated as if it were a payment of a benefit (as defined by section 191 of that Act) or of a benefit of a prescribed kind.

Note. In sub-s (2) words in square brackets substituted by the Tax Credits Act 1999, s 1(2), Sch 1, paras 1, 6(i), as from 5 October 1999. This section repealed by the Child Support, Pensions and Social Security Act 2000, ss 26, 85, Sch 3, para 13(1), (3), Sch 9, Pt I, as from 2 April 2001 (SI 2001 No 1252).

* * * * *

Supplemental

26. Regulations and orders—(1) Any power under this Act to make regulations or orders shall be exercisable by statutory instrument.

(2) Any such power may be exercised to make different provision for different cases, including different provision for different areas.

(3) Any such power includes power—

(a) to make such incidental, supplemental, consequential or transitional provision as appears to the Secretary of State to be expedient; and

(b) to provide for a person to exercise a discretion in dealing with any matter.

(4) Subsection (5) applies to—

(a) the first regulations made under section 10;

(b) any order made under section 18(5);

(c) *the first regulations made under section 24.*

(5) No regulations or order to which this subsection applies shall be made unless a draft of the statutory instrument containing the regulations or order has been laid before Parliament and approved by a resolution of each House.

(6) Any other statutory instrument made under this Act, other than one made under section 30(4), shall be subject to annulment in pursuance of a resolution of either House of Parliament.

Note. Sub-s (4)(c) repealed by the Child Support, Pensions and Social Security Act 2000, s 85, Sch 9, Pt I (in relation to certain cases) as from 3 March 2003 (SI 2003 No 192); for remaining purposes, to be appointed.

27. Interpretation—(1) In this Act 'the 1991 Act' means the Child Support Act 1991.

(2) Expressions in this Act which are used in the 1991 Act have the same meaning in this Act as they have in that Act.

28. Financial provisions. There shall be paid out of money provided by Parliament—

(a) any expenditure incurred by the Secretary of State under or by virtue of this Act;

(b) any increase attributable to this Act in the sums payable out of money so provided under or by virtue of any other enactment.

29. Provision for Northern Ireland—(1) An Order in Council under paragraph 1(1)(b) of Schedule 1 to the Northern Ireland Act 1974 (legislation for Northern Ireland in the interim period) which states that it is made only for purposes corresponding to those of this Act—

(a) shall not be subject to paragraph 1(4) and (5) of that Schedule (affirmative resolution of both Houses of Parliament); but

(b) shall be subject to annulment in pursuance of a resolution of either House of Parliament.

(2) The Secretary of State may make arrangements with the Department of Health and Social Services for Northern Ireland with a view to securing, to the extent allowed for in the arrangements, that—

(a) the provision made by or under sections 10 and 24 ('the provision made for Great Britain'); and

(b) the provision made by or under any corresponding enactment having effect with respect to Northern Ireland ('the provision made for Northern Ireland'), provide for a single system within the United Kingdom.

(3) The Secretary of State may make regulations for giving effect to any such arrangements.

(4) The regulations may, in particular—

(a) adapt legislation (including subordinate legislation) for the time being in force in Great Britain so as to secure its reciprocal operation with the provision made for Northern Ireland; and

(b)   make provision to secure that acts, omissions and events which have any effect for the purposes of the provision made for Northern Ireland have a corresponding effect for the purposes of the provision made for Great Britain.

30. Short title, commencement, extent etc—(1) This Act may be cited as the Child Support Act 1995.

(2) This Act and the 1991 Act may be cited together as the Child Support Acts 1991 and 1995.

(3) Section 29 and this section (apart from subsection (5)) come into force on the passing of this Act.

(4) The other provisions of this Act come into force on such day as the Secretary of State may by order appoint and different days may be appointed for different purposes.

(5) Schedule 3 makes minor and consequential amendments.

(6) This Act, except for—

(a)   sections 17, 27 and 29,

(b)   this section, and

(c)   paragraphs 1, 18, 19 and 20 of Schedule 3,

does not extend to Northern Ireland.

Commencement. Sections 18, 26 (in part), 27, 28 came into force on 4 September 1995, and sections 24, 26 (in part) came into force on 1 October 1995; see SI 1995/2302. Sections 10, 26 (in part) came into force on 14 October 1996; see SI 1996/2630.

CIVIL EVIDENCE ACT 1995

(1995 c 38)

An Act to provide for the admissibility of hearsay evidence, the proof of certain documentary evidence and the admissibility and proof of official actuarial tables in civil proceedings; and for connected purposes.   [8 November 1995]

Admissibility of hearsay evidence

1. Admissibility of hearsay evidence—(1) In civil proceedings evidence shall not be excluded on the ground that it is hearsay.

(2) In this Act—

(a)   'hearsay' means a statement made otherwise than by a person while giving oral evidence in the proceedings which is tendered as evidence of the matters stated; and

(b)   references to hearsay include hearsay of whatever degree.

(3) Nothing in this Act affects the admissibility of evidence admissible apart from this section.

(4) The provisions of sections 2 to 6 (safeguards and supplementary provisions relating to hearsay evidence) do not apply in relation to hearsay evidence admissible apart from this section, notwithstanding that it may also be admissible by virtue of this section.

Safeguards in relation to hearsay evidence

2. Notice of proposal to adduce hearsay evidence—(1) A party proposing to adduce hearsay evidence in civil proceedings shall, subject to the following provisions of this section, give to the other party or parties to the proceedings—

(a)   such notice (if any) of that fact, and

(b)   on request, such particulars of or relating to the evidence,

as is reasonable and practical in the circumstances for the purpose of enabling him or them to deal with any matters arising from its being hearsay.

(2) Provision may be made by rules of court—

(a) specifying classes of proceedings or evidence in relation to which subsection (1) does not apply, and

(b) as to the manner in which (including the time within which) the duties imposed by that subsection are to be compiled with in the cases where it does apply.

(3) Subsection (1) may also be excluded by agreement of the parties; and compliance with the duty to give notice may in any case be waived by the person to whom notice is required to be given.

(4) A failure to comply with subsection (1), or with rules under subsection (2)(b), does not affect the admissibility of the evidence but may be taken into account by the court—

(a) in considering the exercise of its powers with respect to the course of proceedings and costs, and

(b) as a matter adversely affecting the weight to be given to the evidence in accordance with section 4.

3. Power to call witness for cross-examination on hearsay statement. Rules of court may provide that where a party to civil proceedings adduces hearsay evidence of a statement made by a person and does not call that person as a witness, any other party to the proceedings may, with the leave of the court, call that person as a witness and cross-examine him on the statement as if he had been called by the first-mentioned party and as if the hearsay statement were his evidence in chief.

4. Considerations relevant to weighing of hearsay evidence—(1) In estimating the weight (if any) to be given to hearsay evidence in civil proceedings the court shall have regard to any circumstances from which any inference can reasonably be drawn as to the reliability or otherwise of the evidence.

(2) Regard may be had, in particular, to the following—

(a) whether it would have been reasonable and practicable for the party by whom the evidence was adduced to have produced the maker of the original statement as a witness;

(b) whether the original statement was made contemporaneously with the occurrence or existence of the matters stated;

(c) whether the evidence involves multiple hearsay;

(d) whether any person involved had any motive to conceal or misrepresent matters;

(e) whether the original statement was an edited account, or was made in collaboration with another or for a particular pupose;

(f) whether the circumstances in which the evidence is adduced as hearsay are such as to suggest an attempt to prevent proper evalution of its weight.

Supplementary provisions as to hearsay evidence

5. Competence and credibility—(1) Hearsay evidence shall not be admitted in civil proceedings if or to the extent that it is shown to consist of, or to be proved by means of, a statement made by a person who at the time he made the statement was not competent as a witness.

For this purpose 'not competent as a witness' means suffering from such mental or physical infirmity, or lack of understanding, as would render a person incompetent as a witness in civil proceedings; but a child shall be treated as competent as a witness if he satisfies the requirements of section 96(2)(a) and (b) of the Children Act 1989 (conditions for reception of unsworn evidence of child).

(2) Where in civil proceedings hearsay evidence is adduced and the maker of the original statement, or of any statement relied upon to prove another statement, is not called as a witness—

(a) evidence which if he had been so called would be admissible for the purpose of attacking or supporting his credibility as a witness is admissible for that purpose in the proceedings; and

(b) evidence tending to prove that, whether before or after he made the statement, he made any other statement inconsistent with it is admissible for the purpose of showing that he had contradicted himself.

Provided that evidence may not be given of any matter of which, if he had been called as a witness and had denied that matter in cross-examination, evidence could not have been adduced by the cross-examining party.

6. Previous statements of witnesses—(1) Subject as follows, the provisions of this Act as to hearsay evidence in civil proceedings apply equally (but with any necessary modifications) in relation to a previous statement made by a person called as a witness in the proceedings.

(2) A party who has called or intends to call a person as a witness in civil proceedings may not in those proceedings adduce evidence of a previous statement made by that person, except—

(a) with the leave of the court, or

(b) for the purpose of rebutting a suggestion that his evidence has been fabricated.

This shall not be construed as preventing a witness statement (that is, a written statement of oral evidence which a party to the proceedings intends to lead) from being adopted by a witness in giving evidence or treated as his evidence.

(3) Where in the case of civil proceedings section 3, 4 or 5 of the Criminal Procedure Act 1865 applies, which make provision as to—

(a) how far a witness may be discredited by the party producing him,

(b) the proof of contradictory statements made by a witness, and

(c) cross-examination as to previous statements in writing,

this Act does not authorise the adducing of evidence of a previous inconsistent or contradictory statement otherwise than in accordance with those sections.

This is without prejudice to any provision made by rules of court under section 3 above (power to call witness for cross-examination on hearsay statement).

(4) Nothing in this Act affects any of the rules of law as to the circumstances in which, where a person called as a witness in civil proceedings is cross-examined on a document used by him to refresh his memory, that document may be made evidence in the proceedings.

(5) Nothing in this section shall be construed as preventing a statement of any description referred to above from being admissible by virtue of section 1 as evidence of the matters stated.

7. Evidence formerly admissible at common law—(1) The common law rule effectively preserved by section 9(1) and (2)(a) of the Civil Evidence Act 1968 (admissibility of admissions adverse to a party) is superseded by the provisions of this Act.

(2) The common law rules effectively preserved by section 9(1) and (2)(b) to (d) of the Civil Evidence Act 1968, that is, any rule of law whereby in civil proceedings—

(a) published works dealing with matters of a public nature (for example, histories, scientific works, dictionaries and maps) are admissible as evidence of facts of a public nature stated in them,

(b) public documents (for example, public registers, and returns made under public authority with respect to matters of public interest) are admissible as evidence of facts stated in them, or

(c) records (for example, the records of certain courts, treaties, Crown grants, pardons and commissions) are admissible as evidence of facts stated in them,

shall continue to have effect.

(3) The common law rules effectively preserved by section 9(3) and (4) of the Civil Evidence Act 1968, that is, any rule of law whereby in civil proceedings—

(a) evidence of a person's reputation is admissible for the purpose of proving his good or bad character, or

(b) evidence of reputation or family tradition is admissible—
 (i) for the purpose of proving or disproving pedigree or the existence of a marriage, or
 (ii) for the purpose of proving or disproving the existence of any public or general right or of identifying any person or thing,

shall continue to have effect in so far as they authorise the court to treat such evidence as proving or disproving that matter.

Where any such rule applies, reputation or family tradition shall be treated for the purposes of this Act as a fact and not as a statement or multiplicity of statements about the matter in question.

(4) The words in which a rule of law mentioned in this section is described are intended only to identify the rule and shall not be construed as altering it in any way.

Other matters

8. Proof of statements contained in documents—(1) Where a statement contained in a document is admissible as evidence in civil proceedings, it may be proved—
 (a) by the production of that document, or
 (b) whether or not that document is still in existence, by the production of a copy of that document or of the material part of it,

authenticated in such manner as the court may approve.

(2) It is immaterial for this purpose how many removes there are between a copy and the original.

9. Proof of records of business or public authority—(1) A document which is shown to form part of the records of a business or public authority may be received in evidence in civil proceedings without further proof.

(2) A document shall be taken to form part of the records of a business or public authority if there is produced to the court a certificate to that effect signed by an officer of the business or authority to which the records belong.

For this purpose—
 (a) a document purporting to be a certificate signed by an officer of a business or public authority shall be deemed to have been duly given by such an officer and signed by him; and
 (b) a certificate shall be treated as signed by a person if it purports to bear a facsimile of his signature.

(3) The absence of an entry in the records of a business or public authority may be proved in civil proceedings by affidavit of an officer of the business or authority to which the records belong.

(4) In this section—

'records' means records in whatever form;

'business' includes any activity regularly carried on over a period of time, whether for profit or not, by any body (whether corporate or not) or by an individual;

'officer' includes any person occupying a responsible position in relation to the relevant activities of the business or public authority or in relation to its records; and

'public authority' includes any public or statutory undertaking, any government department and any person holding office under Her Majesty.

(5) The court may, having regard to the circumstances of the case, direct that all or any of the above provisions of this section do not apply in relation to a particular document or record, or description of documents or records.

10. Admissibility and proof of Ogden Tables—(1) The actuarial tables (together with explanatory notes) for use in personal injury and fatal accident cases issued from time to time by the Government Actuary's Department are admissible in evidence for the purpose of assessing, in an action for personal injury, the sum to be awarded as general damages for future pecuniary loss.

(2) They may be proved by the production of a copy published by Her Majesty's Stationery Office.

(3) For the purposes of this section—

(a) 'personal injury' includes any disease and any impairment of a person's physical or mental condition; and

(b) 'action for personal injury' includes an action brought by virtue of the Law Reform (Miscellaneous Provisions) Act 1934 or the Fatal Accidents Act 1976.

General

11. Meaning of 'civil proceedings'. In this Act 'civil proceedings' means civil proceedings, before any tribunal, in relation to which the strict rules of evidence apply, whether as a matter of law or by agreement of the parties.

References to 'the court' and 'rules of court' shall be construed accordingly.

12. Provisions as to rules of court—(1) Any power to make rules of court regulating the practice or procedure of the court in relation to civil proceedings includes power to make such provision as may be necessary or expedient for carrying into effect the provisions of this Act.

(2) Any rules of court made for the purposes of this Act as it applies in relation to proceedings in the High Court apply, except in so far as their operation is excluded by agreement, to arbitration proceedings to which this Act applies, subject to such modifications as may be appropriate.

Any question arising as to what modifications are appropriate shall be determined, in default of agreement, by the arbitrator or umpire, as the case may be.

13. Interpretation. In this Act—

'civil proceedings' has the meaning given by section 11 and 'court' and 'rule of court' shall be construed in accordance with that section;

'document' means anything in which information of any description is recorded, and 'copy', in relation to a document, means anything onto which information recorded in the document has been copied, by whatever means and whether directly or indirectly;

'hearsay' shall be construed in accordance with section 1(2);

'oral evidence' includes evidence which, by reason of a defect of speech or hearing, a person called as a witness gives in writing or by signs;

'the original statement', in relation to hearsay evidence, means the underlying statement (if any) by—

(a) in the case of evidence of fact, a person having personal knowledge of that fact, or

(b) in the case of evidence of opinion, the person whose opinion it is; and

'statement' means any representation of fact or opinion, however made.

14. Savings—(1) Nothing in this Act affects the exclusion of evidence on grounds other than that it is hearsay.

This applies whether the evidence falls to be excluded in pursuance of any enactment or rule of law, for failure to comply with rules of court or an order of the court, or otherwise.

(2) Nothing in this Act affects the proof of documents by means other than those specified in section 8 or 9.

(3) Nothing in this Act affects the operation of the following enactments—

(a) section 2 of the Documentary Evidence Act 1868 (mode of proving certain official documents);
(b) section 2 of the Documentary Evidence Act 1882 (documents printed under the superintendence of Stationery Office);
(c) section 1 of the Evidence (Colonial Statutes) Act 1907 (proof of statutes of certain legislatures);
(d) section 1 of the Evidence (Foreign, Dominion and Colonial Documents) Act 1933 (proof and effect of registers and official certificates of certain countries);
(e) section 5 of the Oaths and Evidence (Overseas Authorities and Countries) Act 1963 (provision in respect of public registers of other countries).

15. Consequential amendments and repeals—(1) The enactments specified in Schedule 1 are amended in accordance with that Schedule, the amendments being consequential on the provisions of this Act.

(2) The enactments specified in Schedule 2 are repealed to the extent specified.

16. Short title, commencement and extent—(1) This Act may be cited as the Civil Evidence Act 1995.

(2) The provisions of this Act come into force on such day as the Lord Chancellor may appoint by order made by statutory instrument, and different days may be appointed for different provisions and for different purposes.

(3) An order under subsection (2) may contain such transitional provisions as appear to the Lord Chancellor to be appropriate; and subject to any such provision, the provisions of this Act shall not apply in relation to proceedings begun before commencement.

(4) This Act extends to England and Wales.

(5) Section 10 (admissibility and proof of Ogden Tables) also extends to Northern Ireland.

As it extends to Northern Ireland, the following shall be substituted for subsection (3)(b)—

'(b) "action for personal injury" includes an action brought by virtue of the Law Reform (Miscellaneous Provisions) (Northern Ireland) Act 1937 or the Fatal Accidents (Northern Ireland) Order 1977.'

(6) The provisions of Schedules 1 and 2 (consequential amendments and repeals) have the same extent as the enactments respectively amended or repealed.

Commencement. Whole Act brought into force on 31 January 1997 (SI 1996 No 3217), except ss 10, 16(5), which are yet to be brought into force.

SCHEDULE 1 Section 15(1)

CONSEQUENTIAL AMENDMENTS

...

Note. This Schedule contains amendments to Army Act 1955, s 62, Air Force Act 1955, s 62, Naval Discipline Act 1957, s 35, Gaming Act 1968, s 43, Vehicle and Driving Licences Act 1969, s 27, Taxes Management Act 1970, s 20D, Civil Evidence Act 1972, s 5, International Carriage of Perishable Foodstuffs Act 1976, s 15, Police and Criminal Evidence Act 1984, s 60, Companies Act 1985, s 709, Finance Act 1985, s 10, Criminal Justice Act 1988, Sch 2, Finance Act 1988, s 127, Housing Act 1988, s 97, Road Traffic Offenders Act 1988, s 13, Children Act 1989, s 96, Leasehold Reform, Housing and Urban Development Act 1993, s 11, Finance Act 1993, Sch 21, Vehicle Excise and Registration Act 1994, s 52, and Value Added Tax Act 1994, s 96.

This Schedule repealed in part with savings by Housing Act 1996, s 227, Sch 19, Part IX; for savings see Housing Act 1996 (Commencement No 3 and Transitional Provisions) Order 1996, SI 1996 No 2402, Schedule, para 12. Further repealed in part by the Youth Justice and Criminal Evidence Act 1999, s 67(3), Sch 6, as from 14 April 2000 (SI 2000 No 1034), and in part by the Criminal Justice Act 2003, s 332, Sch 37, Pt 6, as from a day to be appointed.

SCHEDULE 2   Section 15(2)

REPEALS

Chapter	Short title	Extent of repeal
1938 c 28	Evidence Act 1938	Sections 1 and 2. Section 6(1) except the words from 'Proceedings' to 'references'. Section 6(2)(b).
1968 c 64	Civil Evidence Act 1968	Part I.
1971 c 33	Armed Forces Act 1971	Section 26.
1972 c 30	Civil Evidence Act 1972	Section 1. Section 2(1) and (2). In section 2(3)(b), the words from 'by virtue of section 2' to 'out-of-court statements)'. In section 3(1), the words 'Part I of the Civil Evidence Act 1968 or'. In section 6(3), the words '1 and', in both places where they occur.
1975 c 63	Inheritance (Provision for Family and Dependants) Act 1975	Section 21.
1979 c 2	Customs and Excise Management Act 1979	Section 75A(6)(a). Section 118A(6)(a).
1980 c 43	Magistrates' Courts Act 1980	In Schedule 7, paragraph 75.
1984 c 28	County Courts Act 1984	In Schedule 2, paragraphs 33 and 34.
1985 c 54	Finance Act 1985	Section 10(7).
1986 c 21	Armed Forces Act 1986	Section 3.
1988 c 39	Finance Act 1988	Section 127(5).
1990 c 26	Gaming (Amendment) Act 1990	In the Schedule, paragraph 2(7).
1994 c 9	Finance Act 1994	Section 22(2)(a). In Schedule 7, paragraph 1(6)(a).

PRIVATE INTERNATIONAL LAW (MISCELLANEOUS PROVISIONS) ACT 1995

(1995 c 42)

An Act to make provision about interest on judgment debts and arbitral awards expressed in a currency other than sterling; to make further provision as to marriages entered into by unmarried persons under a law which permits polygamy; to make provision for choice of law rules in tort and delict; and for connected purposes.   [8 November 1995]

*   *   *   *   *

PART II

VALIDITY OF MARRIAGES UNDER A LAW WHICH PERMITS POLYGAMY

5. Validity in English law of potentially polygamous marriages—(1) A marriage entered into outside England and Wales between parties neither of whom is already married is not void under the law of England and Wales on the ground that it is entered into under a law which permits polygamy and that either party is domiciled in England and Wales.

(2) This section does not affect the determination of the validity of a marriage by reference to the law of another country to the extent that it falls to be so determined in accordance with the rules of private international law.

6. Application of section 5 to prior marriages—(1) Section 5 above shall be deemed to apply, and always to have applied, to any marriage entered into before commencement which is not excluded by subsection (2) or (3) below.

(2) That section does not apply to a marriage a party to which has (before commencement) entered into a later marriage which either—
  (a) is valid apart from this section but would be void if section 5 above applied to the earlier marriage; or
  (b) is valid by virtue of this section.

(3) That section does not apply to a marriage which has been annulled before commencement, whether by a decree granted in England and Wales or by an annulment obtained elsewhere and recognised in England and Wales at commencement.

(4) An annulment of a marriage resulting from legal proceedings begun before commencement shall be treated for the purposes of subsection (3) above as having taken effect before that time.

(5) For the purposes of subsections (3) and (4) above a marriage which has been declared to be invalid by a court of competent jurisdiction in any proceedings concerning either the validity of the marriage or any right dependent on its validity shall be treated as having been annulled.

(6) Nothing in section 5 above, in its application to marriages entered into before commencement—
  (a) gives or affects any entitlement to an interest—
      (i) under the will or codicil of, or on the intestacy of, a person who died before commencement; or
      (ii) under a settlement or other disposition of property made before that time (otherwise than by will or codicil);
  (b) gives or affects any entitlement to a benefit, allowance, pension or other payment—
      (i) payable before, or in respect of a period before, commencement; or
      (ii) payable in respect of the death of a person before that time;
  (c) affects tax in respect of a period or event before commencement; or
  (d) affects the succession to any dignity or title of honour.

(7) (*This section applies to Scotland only.*)

8. Part II: Supplemental—(1) Nothing in this Part affects any law or custom relating to the marriage of members of the Royal Family.

(2) The enactments specified in the Schedule to this Act (which contains consequential amendments and amendments removing unnecessary references to potentially polygamous marriages) are amended in accordance with that Schedule.

(3) Nothing in that Schedule affects either the generality of any enactment empowering the making of subordinate legislation or any such legislation made before the commencement of this Part.

*   *   *   *   *

PART IV

SUPPLEMENTAL

16. Commencement—(1) (*Relates to Part I.*)
   (2) Part II shall come into force at the end of the period of two months beginning with the day on which this Act is passed.
   (3) (*Relates to Part III.*)

FAMILY LAW ACT 1996

(1996 c 27)

ARRANGEMENT OF SECTIONS

An Act to make provision with respect to: divorce and separation; legal aid in connection with mediation in disputes relating to family matters; proceedings in cases where marriages have broken down; rights of occupation of certain domestic premises; prevention of molestation; the inclusion in certain orders under the Children Act 1989 of provisions about the occupation of a dwelling-house; the transfer of tenancies between spouses and persons who have lived together as husband and wife; and for connected purposes.   [4 July 1996]

PART I

PRINCIPLES OF PARTS II AND III

1. The general principles underlying Parts II and III.   The court and any person, in exercising functions under or in consequence of Parts II and III, shall have regard to the following general principles—

   (a) that the institution of marriage is to be supported;
   (b) that the parties to a marriage which may have broken down are to be encouraged to take all practicable steps, whether by marriage counselling or otherwise, to save the marriage;
   (c) that a marriage which has irretrievably broken down and is being brought to an end should be brought to an end—
      (i)   with minimum distress to the parties and to the children affected;
      (ii) with questions dealt with in a manner designed to promote as good a

continuing relationship between the parties and any children affected
as is possible in the circumstances; and
   (iii) without costs being unreasonably incurred in connection with the
      procedures to be followed in bringing the marriage to an end; and
   (d) that any risk to one of the parties to a marriage, and to any children, of
      violence from the other party should, so far as reasonably practicable, be
      removed or diminished.

PART II

DIVORCE AND SEPARATION

Court orders

2. Divorce and separation—(1) The court may—
   (a) by making an order (to be known as a divorce order), dissolve a marriage;
      or
   (b) by making an order (to be known as a separation order), provide for the
      separation of the parties to a marriage.
   (2) Any such order comes into force on being made.
   (3) A separation order remains in force—
   (a) while the marriage continues; or
   (b) until cancelled by the court on the joint application of the parties.

3. Circumstances in which orders are made—(1) If an application for a
divorce order or for a separation order is made to the court under this section by
one or both of the parties to a marriage, the court shall make the order applied for
if (but only if)—
   (a) the marriage has broken down irretrievably;
   (b) the requirements of section 8 about information meetings are satisfied;
   (c) the requirements of section 9 about the parties' arrangements for the
      future are satisfied; and
   (d) the application has not been withdrawn.
   (2) A divorce order may not be made if an order preventing divorce is in force
under section 10.
   (3) If the court is considering an application for a divorce order and an
application for a separation order in respect of the same marriage it shall proceed
as if it were considering only the application for a divorce order unless—
   (a) an order preventing divorce is in force with respect to the marriage;
   (b) the court makes an order preventing divorce; or
   (c) section 7(6) or (13) applies.

4. Conversion of separation order into divorce order—(1) A separation order
which is made before the second anniversary of the marriage may not be
converted into a divorce order under this section until after that anniversary.
   (2) A separation order may not be converted into a divorce order under this
section at any time while—
   (a) an order preventing divorce is in force under section 10; or
   (b) subsection (4) applies.
   (3) Otherwise, if a separation order is in force and an application for a divorce
order—
   (a) is made under this section by either or both of the parties to the marriage,
      and
   (b) is not withdrawn,
the court shall grant the application once the requirements of section 11 have
been satisfied.
   (4) Subject to subsection (5), this subsection applies if—

(a) there is a child of the family who is under the age of sixteen when the application under this section is made; or

(b) the application under this section is made by one party and the other party applies to the court, before the end of such period as may be prescribed by rules of court, for time for further reflection.

(5) Subsection (4)—

(a) does not apply if, at the time when the application under this section is made, there is an occupation order or a non-molestation order in force in favour of the applicant, or of a child of the family, made against the other party;

(b) does not apply if the court is satisfied that delaying the making of a divorce order would be significantly detrimental to the welfare of any child of the family;

(c) ceases to apply—

    (i) at the end of the period of six months beginning with the end of the period for reflection and consideration by reference to which the separation order was made; or

    (ii) if earlier, on there ceasing to be any children of the family to whom subsection (4)(a) applied.

Marital breakdown

5. Marital breakdown—(1) A marriage is to be taken to have broken down irretrievably if (but only if)—

(a) a statement has been made by one (or both) of the parties that the maker of the statement (or each of them) believes that the marriage has broken down;

(b) the statement complies with the requirements of section 6;

(c) the period for reflection and consideration fixed by section 7 has ended; and

(d) the application under section 3 is accompanied by a declaration by the party making the application that—

    (i) having reflected on the breakdown, and

    (ii) having considered the requirements of this Part as to the parties' arrangements for the future,

the applicant believes that the marriage cannot be saved.

(2) The statement and the application under section 3 do not have to be made by the same party.

(3) An application may not be made under section 3 by reference to a particular statement if—

(a) the parties have jointly given notice (in accordance with rules of court) withdrawing the statement; or

(b) a period of one year ('the specified period') has passed since the end of the period for reflection and consideration.

(4) Any period during which an order preventing divorce is in force is not to count towards the specified period mentioned in subsection (3)(b).

(5) Subsection (6) applies if, before the end of the specified period, the parties jointly give notice to the court that they are attempting reconciliation but require additional time.

(6) The specified period—

(a) stops running on the day on which the notice is received by the court; but

(b) resumes running on the day on which either of the parties gives notice to the court that the attempted reconciliation has been unsuccessful.

(7) If the specified period is interrupted by a continuous period of more than 18 months, any application by either of the parties for a divorce order or for a separation order must be by reference to a new statement received by the court at any time after the end of the 18 months.

(8) The Lord Chancellor may by order amend subsection (3)(b) by varying the specified period.

6. Statement of marital breakdown—(1) A statement under section 5(1)(a) is to be known as a statement of marital breakdown; but in this Part it is generally referred to as 'a statement'.

(2) If a statement is made by one party it must also state that that party—

(a) is aware of the purpose of the period for reflection and consideration as described in section 7; and

(b) wishes to make arrangements for the future.

(3) If a statement is made by both parties it must also state that each of them—

(a) is aware of the purpose of the period for reflection and consideration as described in section 7; and

(b) wishes to make arrangements for the future.

(4) A statement must be given to the court in accordance with the requirements of rules made under section 12.

(5) A statement must also satisfy any other requirements imposed by rules made under that section.

(6) A statement made at a time when the circumstances of the case include any of those mentioned in subsection (7) is ineffective for the purposes of this Part.

(7) The circumstances are—

(a) that a statement has previously been made with respect to the marriage and it is, or will become, possible—

(i) for an application for a divorce order, or

(ii) for an application for a separation order,

to be made by reference to the previous statement;

(b) that such an application has been made in relation to the marriage and has not been withdrawn;

(c) that a separation order is in force.

Reflection and consideration

7. Period for reflection and consideration—(1) Where a statement has been made, a period for the parties—

(a) to reflect on whether the marriage can be saved and to have an opportunity to effect a reconciliation, and

(b) to consider what arrangements should be made for the future,

must pass before an application for a divorce order or for a separation order may be made by reference to that statement.

(2) That period is to be known as the period for reflection and consideration.

(3) The period for reflection and consideration is nine months beginning with the fourteenth day after the day on which the statement is received by the court.

(4) Where—

(a) the statement has been made by one party,

(b) rules made under section 12 require the court to serve a copy of the statement on the other party, and

(c) failure to comply with the rules causes inordinate delay in service,

the court may, on the application of that other party, extend the period for reflection and consideration.

(5) An extension under subsection (4) may be for any period not exceeding the time between—

(a) the beginning of the period for reflection and consideration; and

(b) the time when service is effected.

(6) A statement which is made before the first anniversary of the marriage to which it relates is ineffective for the purposes of any application for a divorce order.

(7) Subsection (8) applies if, at any time during the period for reflection and consideration, the parties jointly give notice to the court that they are attempting a reconciliation but require additional time.

(8) The period for reflection and consideration—

(a) stops running on the day on which the notice is received by the court; but

(b) resumes running on the day on which either of the parties gives notice to the court that the attempted reconciliation has been unsuccessful.

(9) If the period for reflection and consideration is interrupted under subsection (8) by a continuous period of more than 18 months, any application by either of the parties for a divorce order or for a separation order must be by reference to a new statement received by the court at any time after the end of the 18 months.

(10) Where an application for a divorce order is made by one party, subsection (13) applies if—

(a) the other party applies to the court, within the prescribed period, for time for further reflection; and

(b) the requirements of section 9 (except any imposed under section 9(3)) are satisfied.

(11) Where any application for a divorce order is made, subsection (13) also applies if there is a child of the family who is under the age of sixteen when the application is made.

(12) Subsection (13) does not apply if—

(a) at the time when the application for a divorce order is made, there is an occupation order or a non-molestation order in force in favour of the applicant, or of a child of the family, made against the other party; or

(b) the court is satisfied that delaying the making of a divorce order would be significantly detrimental to the welfare of any child of the family.

(13) If this subsection applies, the period for reflection and consideration is extended by a period of six months, but—

(a) only in relation to the application for a divorce order in respect of which the application under subsection (10) was made; and

(b) without invalidating that application for a divorce order.

(14) A period for reflection and consideration which is extended under subsection (13), and which has not otherwise come to an end, comes to an end on there ceasing to be any children of the family to whom subsection (11) applied.

8. Attendance at information meetings—(1) The requirements about information meetings are as follows.

(2) A party making a statement must (except in prescribed circumstances) have attended an information meeting not less than three months before making the statement.

(3) Different information meetings must be arranged with respect to different marriages.

(4) In the case of a statement made by both parties, the parties may attend separate meetings or the same meeting.

(5) Where one party has made a statement, the other party must (except in prescribed circumstances) attend an information meeting before—

(a) making any application to the court—

(i) with respect to a child of the family; or

(ii) of a prescribed description relating to property or financial matters; or

(b) contesting any such application.

(6) In this section 'information meeting' means a meeting organised, in accordance with prescribed provisions for the purpose—

(a) of providing, in accordance with prescribed provisions, relevant information to the party or parties attending about matters which may arise in connection with the provisions of, or made under, this Part or Part III; and

(b) of giving the party or parties attending the information meeting the opportunity of having a meeting with a marriage counsellor and of encouraging that party or those parties to attend that meeting.

(7) An information meeting must be conducted by a person who—

  (a) is qualified and appointed in accordance with prescribed provisions; and

  (b) will have no financial or other interest in any marital proceedings between the parties.

(8) Regulations made under this section may, in particular, make provision—

  (a) about the places and times at which information meetings are to be held;

  (b) for written information to be given to persons attending them;

  (c) for the giving of information to parties (otherwise than at information meetings) in cases in which the requirement to attend such meetings does not apply;

  (d) for information of a prescribed kind to be given only with the approval of the Lord Chancellor or only by a person or by persons approved by him; and

  (e) for information to be given, in prescribed circumstances, only with the approval of the Lord Chancellor or only by a person, or by persons, approved by him.

(9) Regulations made under subsection (6) must, in particular, make provision with respect to the giving of information about—

  (a) marriage counselling and other marriage support services;

  (b) the importance to be attached to the welfare, wishes and feelings of children;

  (c) how the parties may acquire a better understanding of the ways in which children can be helped to cope with the breakdown of a marriage;

  (d) the nature of the financial questions that may arise on divorce or separation, and services which are available to help the parties;

  (e) protection available against violence, and how to obtain support and assistance;

  (f) mediation;

  (g) the availability to each of the parties of independent legal advice and representation;

  (h) *the principles of legal aid and where the parties can get advice about obtaining legal aid;*

  [(h) the availability of services funded by the Legal Services Commission as part of the Community Legal Service, and where parties can get advice about obtaining such services;]

  (i) the divorce and separation process.

(10) Before making any regulations under subsection (6), the Lord Chancellor must consult such persons concerned with the provision of relevant information as he considers appropriate.

(11) A meeting with a marriage counsellor arranged under this section—

  (a) must be held in accordance with prescribed provisions; and

  (b) must be with a person qualified and appointed in accordance with prescribed provisions.

(12) A person who would not be required to make any contribution towards mediation *provided for him under Part IIIA of the Legal Aid Act 1988* [funded for him by the Legal Services Commission as part of the Community Legal Service] shall not be required to make any contribution towards the cost of a meeting with a marriage counsellor arranged for him under this section.

(13) In this section 'prescribed' means prescribed by regulations made by the Lord Chancellor.

Note. Sub-s (9)(h) substituted and words in square brackets in sub-s (12) substituted for words in italics, by the Access to Justice Act 1999, s 24, Sch 4, paras 50, 51, as from 1 April 2000 (SI 2000 No 774); for savings in relation to existing cases, see SI 2000 No 774, arts 2(a)(ii), 5.

9. Arrangements for the future—(1) The requirements as to the parties' arrangements for the future are as follows.

(2) One of the following must be produced to the court—

(a) a court order (made by consent or otherwise) dealing with their financial arrangements;

(b) a negotiated agreement as to their financial arrangements;

(c) a declaration by both parties that they have made their financial arrangements;

(d) a declaration by one of the parties (to which no objection has been notified to the court by the other party) that—

    (i) he has no significant assets and does not intend to make an application for financial provision;

    (ii) he believes that the other party has no significant assets and does not intend to make an application for financial provision; and

    (iii) there are therefore no financial arrangements to be made.

(3) ...

(4) ...

(5) The requirements of section 11 must have been satisfied.

(6) Schedule 1 supplements the provisions of this section.

(7) If the court is satisfied, on an application made by one of the parties after the end of the period for reflection and consideration, that the circumstances of the case are—

(a) those set out in paragraph 1 of Schedule 1,

(b) those set out in paragraph 2 of that Schedule,

(c) those set out in paragraph 3 of that Schedule, or

(d) those set out in paragraph 4 of that Schedule,

it may make a divorce order or a separation order even though the requirements of subsection (2) have not been satisfied.

(8) ...

Note. Sub-ss (3), (4): repealed by the Divorce (Religious Marriages) Act 2002, s 1(2), as from 24 February 2003 (SI 2003 No 186). Sub-s (8) is repealed by the Welfare Reform and Pensions Act 1999, s 88, Sch 13, Pt II, as from 1 December 2000 (SI 2000 No 1116).

Orders preventing divorce

10. Hardship: orders preventing divorce—(1) If an application for a divorce order has been made by one of the parties to a marriage, the court may, on the application of the other party, order that the marriage is not to be dissolved.

(2) Such an order (an 'order preventing divorce') may be made only if the court is satisfied—

(a) that dissolution of the marriage would result in substantial financial or other hardship to the other party or to a child of the family; and

(b) that it would be wrong, in all the circumstances (including the conduct of the parties and the interests of any child of the family), for the marriage to be dissolved.

(3) If an application for the cancellation of an order preventing divorce is made by one or both of the parties, the court shall cancel the order unless it is still satisfied—

(a) that dissolution of the marriage would result in substantial financial or other hardship to the party in whose favour the order was made or to a child of the family; and

(b) that it would be wrong, in all the circumstances (including the conduct of the parties and the interests of any child of the family), for the marriage to be dissolved.

(4) If an order preventing a divorce is cancelled, the court may make a divorce order in respect of the marriage only if an application is made under section 3 or 4(3) after the cancellation.

(5) An order preventing divorce may include conditions which must be satisfied before an application for cancellation may be made under subsection (3).

(6) In this section 'hardship' includes the loss of a chance to obtain a future benefit (as well as the loss of an existing benefit).

Welfare of children

11. Welfare of children—(1) In any proceedings for a divorce order or a separation order, the court shall consider—

(a) whether there are any children of the family to whom this section applies; and

(b) where there are any such children, whether (in the light of the arrangements which have been, or are proposed to be, made for their upbringing and welfare) it should exercise any of its powers under the Children Act 1989 with respect to any of them.

(2) Where, in any case to which this section applies, it appears to the court that—

(a) the circumstances of the case require it, or are likely to require it, to exercise any of its powers under the Children Act 1989 with respect to any such child,

(b) it is not in a position to exercise the power, or (as the case may be) those powers, without giving further consideration to the case, and

(c) there are exceptional circumstances which make it desirable in the interests of the child that the court should give a direction under this section,

it may direct that the divorce order or separation order is not to be made until the court orders otherwise.

(3) In deciding whether the circumstances are as mentioned in subsection (2)(a), the court shall treat the welfare of the child as paramount.

(4) In making that decision, the court shall also have particular regard, on the evidence before it, to—

(a) the wishes and feelings of the child considered in the light of his age and understanding and the circumstances in which those wishes were expressed;

(b) the conduct of the parties in relation to the upbringing of the child;

(c) the general principle that, in the absence of evidence to the contrary, the welfare of the child will be best served by—

(i) his having regular contact with those who have parental responsibility for him and with other members of his family; and

(ii) the maintenance of as good a continuing relationship with his parents as is possible; and

(d) any risk to the child attributable to—

(i) where the person with whom the child will reside is living or proposes to live;

(ii) any person with whom that person is living or with whom he proposes to live; or

(iii) any other arrangements for his care and upbringing.

(5) This section applies to—

(a) any child of the family who has not reached the age of sixteen at the date when the court considers the case in accordance with the requirements of this section; and

(b) any child of the family who has reached that age at that date and in relation to whom the court directs that this section shall apply.

Supplementary

12. Lord Chancellor's rules—(1) The Lord Chancellor may make rules—

(a) as to the form in which a statement is to be made and what information must accompany it;

(b) requiring the person making the statement to state whether or not, since satisfying the requirements of section 8, he has made any attempt at reconciliation;

   (c) as to the way in which a statement is to be given to the court;

   (d) requiring a copy of a statement made by one party to be served by the court on the other party;

   (e) as to circumstances in which such service may be dispensed with or may be effected otherwise than by delivery to the party;

   (f) requiring a party who has made a statement to provide the court with information about the arrangements that need to be made in consequence of the breakdown;

   (g) as to the time, manner and (where attendance in person is required) place at which such information is to be given;

   (h) where a statement has been made, requiring either or both of the parties—

      (i) to prepare and produce such other documents, and

      (ii) to attend in person at such places and for such purposes,

   as may be specified;

   (i) as to the information and assistance which is to be given to the parties and the way in which it is to be given;

   (j) requiring the parties to be given, in such manner as may be specified, copies of such statements and other documents as may be specified.

   (2) The Lord Chancellor may make rules requiring a person who is the legal representative of a party to a marriage with respect to which a statement has been, or is proposed to be, made—

   (a) to inform that party, at such time or times as may be specified—

      (i) about the availability to the parties of marriage support services;

      (ii) about the availability to them of mediation; and

      (iii) where there are children of the family, that in relation to the arrangements to be made for any child the parties should consider the child's welfare, wishes and feelings;

   (b) to give that party, at such time or times as may be specified, names and addresses of persons qualified to help—

      (i) to effect a reconciliation; or

      (ii) in connection with mediation; and

   (c) to certify, at such time or times as may be specified—

      (i) whether he has complied with the provision made in the rules by virtue of paragraphs (a) and (b);

      (ii) whether he has discussed with that party any of the matters mentioned in paragraph (a) or the possibility of reconciliation; and

      (iii) which, if any, of those matters they have discussed.

   (3) In subsections (1) and (2) 'specified' means determined under or described in the rules.

   (4) This section does not affect any power to make rules of court for the purposes of this Act.

Resolution of disputes

13. Directions with respect to mediation—(1) After the court has received a statement, it may give a direction requiring each party to attend a meeting arranged in accordance with the direction for the purpose—

   (a) of enabling an explanation to be given of the facilities available to the parties for mediation in relation to disputes between them; and

   (b) of providing an opportunity for each party to agree to take advantage of those facilities.

   (2) A direction may be given at any time, including in the course of proceedings connected with the breakdown of the marriage (as to which see section 25).

   (3) A direction may be given on the application of either of the parties or on the initiative of the court.

(4) The parties are to be required to attend the same meeting unless—

(a) one of them asks, or both of them ask, for separate meetings; or

(b) the court considers separate meetings to be more appropriate.

(5) A direction shall—

(a) specify a person chosen by the court (with that person's agreement) to arrange and conduct the meeting or meetings; and

(b) require such person as may be specified in the direction to produce to the court, at such time as the court may direct, a report stating—

    (i) whether the parties have complied with the direction; and

    (ii) if they have, whether they have agreed to take part in any mediation.

14. Adjournments—(1) The court's power to adjourn any proceedings connected with the breakdown of a marriage includes power to adjourn—

(a) for the purpose of allowing the parties to comply with a direction under section 13; or

(b) for the purpose of enabling disputes to be resolved amicably.

(2) In determining whether to adjourn for either purpose, the court shall have regard in particular to the need to protect the interests of any child of the family.

(3) If the court adjourns any proceedings connected with the breakdown of a marriage for either purpose, the period of the adjournment must not exceed the maximum period prescribed by rules of court.

(4) Unless the only purpose of the adjournment is to allow the parties to comply with a direction under section 13, the court shall order one or both of them to produce to the court a report as to—

(a) whether they have taken part in mediation during the adjournment;

(b) whether, as a result, any agreement has been reached between them;

(c) the extent to which any dispute between them has been resolved as a result of any such agreement;

(d) the need for further mediation; and

(e) how likely it is that further mediation will be successful.

Financial provision

15. Financial arrangements—(1) Schedule 2 amends the 1973 Act.

(2) The main object of Schedule 2 is—

(a) to provide that, in the case of divorce or separation, an order about financial provision may be made under that Act before a divorce order or separation order is made; but

(b) to retain (with minor changes) the position under that Act where marriages are annulled.

(3) Schedule 2 also makes minor and consequential amendments of the 1973 Act connected with the changes mentioned in subsection (1).

16. …

Note. S 16 repealed by the Welfare Reform and Pensions Act 1999, s 88, Sch 13, Pt II, as from 1 December 2000 (SI 2000 No 1116).

17. …

Note. S 17 repealed by the Welfare Reform and Pensions Act 1999, s 88, Sch 13, Pt II, as from 6 April 2002 (SI 2001 No 4049).

18. Grounds for financial provision orders in magistrates' courts—(1) In section 1 of the Domestic Proceedings and Magistrates' Courts Act 1978, omit paragraphs (c) and (d) (which provide for behaviour and desertion to be grounds on which an application for a financial provision order may be made).

(2) In section 7(1) of that Act (powers of magistrates' court where spouses are living apart by agreement), omit 'neither party having deserted the other'.

Jurisdiction and commencement of proceedings

19. Jurisdiction in relation to divorce and separation—(1) In this section 'the court's jurisdiction' means—

    (a) the jurisdiction of the court under this Part to entertain marital proceedings; and

    (b) any other jurisdiction conferred on the court under this Part, or any other enactment, in consequence of the making of a statement.

    (2) The court's jurisdiction is exercisable only if—

    (a) at least one of the parties was domiciled in England and Wales on the statement date;

    (b) at least one of the parties was habitually resident in England and Wales throughout the period of one year ending with the statement date; or

    (c) nullity proceedings are pending in relation to the marriage when the marital proceedings commence.

    (3) Subsection (4) applies if—

    (a) a separation order is in force; or

    (b) an order preventing divorce has been cancelled.

    (4) The court—

    (a) continues to have jurisdiction to entertain an application made by reference to the order referred to in subsection (3); and

    (b) may exercise any other jurisdiction which is conferred on it in consequence of such an application.

    (5) Schedule 3 amends Schedule 1 to the Domicile and Matrimonial Proceedings Act 1973 (orders to stay proceedings where there are proceedings in other jurisdictions).

    (6) The court's jurisdiction is exercisable subject to any order for a stay under Schedule 1 to that Act.

    (7) In this section—

'nullity proceedings' means proceedings in respect of which the court has jurisdiction under section 5(3) of the Domicile and Matrimonial Proceedings Act 1973; and

'statement date' means the date on which the relevant statement was received by the court.

20. Time when proceedings for divorce or separation begin—(1) The receipt by the court of a statement is to be treated as the commencement of proceedings.

    (2) The proceedings are to be known as marital proceedings.

    (3) Marital proceedings are also—

    (a) separation proceedings, if an application for a separation order has been made under section 3 by reference to the statement and not withdrawn;

    (b) divorce proceedings, if an application for a divorce order has been made under section 3 by reference to the statement and not withdrawn.

    (4) Marital proceedings are to be treated as being both divorce proceedings and separation proceedings at any time when no application by reference to the statement, either for a divorce order or for a separation order, is outstanding.

    (5) Proceedings which are commenced by the making of an application under section 4(3) are also marital proceedings and divorce proceedings.

    (6) Marital proceedings come to an end—

    (a) on the making of a separation order;

    (b) on the making of a divorce order;

    (c) on the withdrawal of the statement by a notice in accordance with section 5(3)(a);

    (d) at the end of the specified period mentioned in section 5(3)(b), if no application under section 3 by reference to the statement is outstanding;

    (e) on the withdrawal of all such applications which are outstanding at the end of that period;

    (f) on the withdrawal of an application under section 4(3).

Intestacy

21. Intestacy: effect of separation. Where—
(a) a separation order is in force, and
(b) while the parties to the marriage remain separated, one of them dies intestate as respects any real or personal property,
that property devolves as if the other had died before the intestacy occurred.

Marriage support services

22. Funding for marriage support services—(1) *The Lord Chancellor* [Secretary of State] may, with the approval of the Treasury, make grants in connection with—
(a) the provision of marriage support services;
(b) research into the causes of marital breakdown;
(c) research into ways of preventing marital breakdown.

(2) Any grant under this section may be made subject to such conditions as the *Lord Chancellor* [Secretary of State] considers appropriate.

(3) In exercising his power to make grants in connection with the provision of marriage support services, the *Lord Chancellor* [Secretary of State] is to have regard, in particular, to the desirability of services of that kind being available when they are first needed.

Note. Words 'Secretary of State' in square brackets in each place they occur substituted for words in italics by the Transfer of Functions (Children, Young People and Families) Order 2003, SI 2003 No 3191, arts 3(b), 6, Schedule, para 2, as from 12 January 2004.

23. Provision of marriage counselling—(1) The Lord Chancellor or a person appointed by him may secure the provision, in accordance with regulations made by the Lord Chancellor, of marriage counselling.

(2) Marriage counselling may only be provided under this section at a time when a period for reflection and consideration—
(a) is running in relation to the marriage; or
(b) is interrupted under section 7(8) (but not for a continuous period of more than 18 months).

(3) Marriage counselling may only be provided under this section for persons who would not be required to make any contribution towards the cost of mediation *provided for them under Part IIIA of the Legal Aid Act 1988* [funded for them by the Legal Services Commission as part of the Community Legal Service].

(4) Persons for whom marriage counselling is provided under this section are not to be required to make any contribution towards the cost of the counselling.

(5) Marriage counselling is only to be provided under this section if it appears to the marriage counsellor to be suitable in all the circumstances.

(6) Regulations under subsection (1) may—
(a) make provision about the way in which marriage counselling is to be provided; and
(b) prescribe circumstances in which the provision of marriage counselling is to be subject to the approval of the Lord Chancellor.

(7) A contract entered into for the purposes of subsection (1) by a person appointed under that subsection must include such provision as the Lord Chancellor may direct.

(8) If the person appointed under subsection (1) is *the Legal Aid Board* [the Legal Services Commisson], the powers conferred on *the Board* [the Commission] by or under *the Legal Aid Act 1988* [Part I of the Access to Justice Act 1999] shall be exercisable for the purposes of this section as they are exercisable for the purposes of that Part of that Act.

(9) . . .

Note. In sub-ss (3), (8) words in square brackets substituted for words in italics, and sub-s (9) repealed, by the Access to Justice Act 1999, ss 24, 106, Sch 4, paras 50, 52, Sch 15, Pt I, as from 1 April 2000 (SI 2000 No 774); for savings in relation to existing cases, see SI 2000 No 774, arts 2(a)(ii), (c)(i), 5.

Interpretation

24. Interpretation of Part II etc—(1) In this Part—
'the 1973 Act' means the Matrimonial Causes Act 1973;
'child of the family' and 'the court' have the same meaning as in the 1973 Act;
'divorce order' has the meaning given in section 2(1)(a);
'divorce proceedings' is to be read with section 20;
'marital proceedings' has the meaning given in section 20;
'non-molestation order' has the meaning given by section 42(1);
'occupation order' has the meaning given by section 39;
'order preventing divorce' has the meaning given in section 10(2);
'party', in relation to a marriage, means one of the parties to the marriage;
'period for reflection and consideration' has the meaning given in section 7;
'separation order' has the meaning given in section 2(1)(b);
'separation proceedings' is to be read with section 20;
'statement' means a statement of marital breakdown;
'statement of marital breakdown' has the meaning given in section 6(1).
(2) For the purposes of this Part, references to the withdrawal of an application are references, in relation to an application made jointly by both parties, to its withdrawal by a notice given, in accordance with rules of court—
    (a) jointly by both parties; or
    (b) separately by each of them.
(3) Where only one party gives such a notice of withdrawal, in relation to a joint application, the application shall be treated as if it had been made by the other party alone.

25. Connected proceedings—(1) For the purposes of this Part, proceedings are connected with the breakdown of a marriage if they fall within subsection (2) and, at the time of the proceedings—
    (a) a statement has been received by the court with respect to the marriage and it is or may become possible for an application for a divorce order or separation order to be made by reference to that statement;
    (b) such an application in relation to the marriage has been made and not withdrawn; or
    (c) a divorce order has been made, or a separation order is in force, in relation to the marriage.
(2) The proceedings are any under Parts I to V of the Children Act 1989 with respect to a child of the family or any proceedings resulting from an application—
    (a) for, or for the cancellation of, an order preventing divorce in relation to the marriage;
    (b) by either party to the marriage for an order under Part IV;
    (c) for the exercise, in relation to a party to the marriage or child of the family, of any of the court's powers under Part II of the 1973 Act;
    (d) made otherwise to the court with respect to, or in connection with, any proceedings connected with the breakdown of the marriage.

PART III

LEGAL AID FOR MEDIATION IN FAMILY MATTERS

26. ...

Note. Part III of this Act (ss 26—29) repealed by the Access to Justice Act 1999, s 106, Sch 15, Pt I, as from 1 April 2000 (SI 2000 No 774); for savings in relation to existing cases, see SI 2000 No 774, arts 2(c)(i), 5, Schedule.

27. ...

Note. Repealed as noted to s 26 ante.

28. ...

Note. Repealed as noted to s 26 ante.

29. ...

Note. Repealed as noted to s 26 ante.

PART IV

FAMILY HOMES AND DOMESTIC VIOLENCE

Rights to occupy matrimonial home

30. Rights concerning matrimonial home where one spouse has no estate, etc—(1) This section applies if—

   (a) one spouse is entitled to occupy a dwelling-house by virtue of—

      (i) a beneficial estate or interest or contract; or

      (ii) any enactment giving that spouse the right to remain in occupation; and

   (b) the other spouse is not so entitled.

(2) Subject to the provisions of this Part, the spouse not so entitled has the following rights ('matrimonial home rights')—

   (a) if in occupation, a right not to be evicted or excluded from the dwelling-house or any part of it by the other spouse except with the leave of the court given by an order under section 33;

   (b) if not in occupation, a right with the leave of the court so given to enter into and occupy the dwelling-house.

(3) If a spouse is entitled under this section to occupy a dwelling-house or any part of a dwelling-house, any payment or tender made or other thing done by that spouse in or towards satisfaction of any liability of the other spouse in respect of rent, mortgage payments or other outgoings affecting the dwelling-house is, whether or not it is made or done in pursuance of an order under section 40, as good as if made or done by the other spouse.

(4) A spouse's occupation by virtue of this section—

   (a) is to be treated, for the purposes of the Rent (Agriculture) Act 1976 and the Rent Act 1977 (other than Part V and sections 103 to 106 of that Act), as occupation by the other spouse as the other spouse's residence, and

   (b) if the spouse occupies the dwelling-house as that spouse's only or principal home, is to be treated, for the purposes of the Housing Act 1985 *and Part I of the Housing Act 1988* [, Part I of the Housing Act 1988 and Chapter I of Part V of the Housing Act 1996], as occupation by the other spouse as the other spouse's only or principal home.

Note. In sub-s (4)(b) words in square brackets substituted for words in italics by the Housing Act 1996 (Consequential Amendments) Order 1997, SI 1997 No 74, art 2, Schedule, para 10(a), as from 12 February 1997.

(5) If a spouse ('the first spouse')—

   (a) is entitled under this section to occupy a dwelling-house or any part of a dwelling-house, and

   (b) makes any payment in or towards satisfaction of any liability of the other spouse ('the second spouse') in respect of mortgage payments affecting the dwelling-house,

the person to whom the payment is made may treat it as having been made by the second spouse, but the fact that that person has treated any such payment as having been so made does not affect any claim of the first spouse against the second spouse to an interest in the dwelling-house by virtue of the payment.

(6) If a spouse is entitled under this section to occupy a dwelling-house or part of a dwelling-house by reason of an interest of the other spouse under a trust, all the provisions of subsections (3) to (5) apply in relation to the trustees as they apply in relation to the other spouse.

(7) This section does not apply to a dwelling-house which has at no time been, and which was at no time intended by the spouses to be, a matrimonial home of theirs.

(8) A spouse's matrimonial home rights continue—

(a) only so long as the marriage subsists, except to the extent that an order under section 33(5) otherwise provides; and

(b) only so long as the other spouse is entitled as mentioned in subsection (1) to occupy the dwelling-house, except where provision is made by section 31 for those rights to be a charge on an estate or interest in the dwelling-house.

(9) It is hereby declared that a spouse—

(a) who has an equitable interest in a dwelling-house or in its proceeds of sale, but

(b) is not a spouse in whom there is vested (whether solely or as joint tenant) a legal estate in fee simple or a legal term of years absolute in the dwelling-house,

is to be treated, only for the purpose of determining whether he has matrimonial home rights, as not being entitled to occupy the dwelling-house by virtue of that interest.

31. Effect of matrimonial home rights as charge on dwelling-house—(1) Subsections (2) and (3) apply if, at any time during a marriage, one spouse is entitled to occupy a dwelling-house by virtue of a beneficial estate or interest.

(2) The other spouse's matrimonial home rights are a charge on the estate or interest.

(3) The charge created by subsection (2) has the same priority as if it were an equitable interest created at whichever is the latest of the following dates—

(a) the date on which the spouse so entitled acquires the estate or interest;

(b) the date of the marriage; and

(c) 1st January 1968 (the commencement date of the Matrimonial Homes Act 1967).

(4) Subsections (5) and (6) apply if, at any time when a spouse's matrimonial home rights are a charge on an interest of the other spouse under a trust, there are, apart from either of the spouses, no persons, living or unborn, who are or could become beneficiaries under the trust.

(5) The rights are a charge also on the estate or interest of the trustees for the other spouse.

(6) The charge created by subsection (5) has the same priority as if it were an equitable interest created (under powers overriding the trusts) on the date when it arises.

(7) In determining for the purposes of subsection (4) whether there are any persons who are not, but could become, beneficiaries under the trust, there is to be disregarded any potential exercise of a general power of appointment exercisable by either or both of the spouses alone (whether or not the exercise of it requires the consent of another person).

(8) Even though a spouse's matrimonial home rights are a charge on an estate or interest in the dwelling-house, those rights are brought to an end by—

(a) the death of the other spouse, or

(b) the termination (otherwise than by death) of the marriage,

unless the court directs otherwise by an order made under section 33(5).

(9) If—

(a) a spouse's matrimonial home rights are a charge on an estate or interest in the dwelling-house, and

(b) that estate or interest is surrendered to merge in some other estate or interest expectant on it in such circumstances that, but for the merger, the person taking the estate or interest would be bound by the charge,

the surrender has effect subject to the charge and the persons thereafter entitled to the other estate or interest are, for so long as the estate or interest surrendered would have endured if not so surrendered, to be treated for all purposes of this Part as deriving title to the other estate or interest under the other spouse or, as the case may be, under the trustees for the other spouse, by virtue of the surrender.

(10) If the title to the legal estate by virtue of which a spouse is entitled to occupy a dwelling-house (including any legal estate held by trustees for that spouse) is registered under the *Land Registration Act 1925* [Land Registration Act 2002] or any enactment replaced by that Act—

   (a) registration of a land charge affecting the dwelling-house by virtue of this Part is to be effected by registering a notice under that Act; and

   (b) a spouse's matrimonial home rights are not an overriding interest within the meaning of that Act affecting the dwelling-house even though the spouse is in actual occupation of the dwelling-house.

   [(b) a spouse's matrimonial home rights are not to be capable of falling within paragraph 2 of Schedule 1 or 3 to that Act.]

(11) ...

(12) If—

   (a) a spouse's matrimonial home rights are a charge on the estate of the other spouse or of trustees of the other spouse, and

   (b) that estate is the subject of a mortgage,

then if, after the date of the creation of the mortgage ('the first mortgage'), the charge is registered under section 2 of the Land Charges Act 1972, the charge is, for the purposes of section 94 of the Law of Property Act 1925 (which regulates the rights of mortgagees to make further advances ranking in priority to subsequent mortgages), to be deemed to be a mortgage subsequent in date to the first mortgage.

(13) It is hereby declared that a charge under subsection (2) or (5) is not registrable under subsection (10) or under section 2 of the Land Charges Act 1972 unless it is a charge on a legal estate.

Note. In sub-s (10) words 'Land Registration Act 2002' in square brackets substituted for words in italics, and para (b) substituted, by the Land Registration Act 2002, s 133, Sch 11, para 34(1), (2)(a), (b), as from 13 October 2003 (SI 2003 No 1725). Sub-s (11) repealed by the the 2002 Act, s 135, Sch 13, as from 13 October 2003 (SI 2003 No 1725).

32. Further provisions relating to matrimonial home rights. Schedule 4 re-enacts with consequential amendments and minor modifications provisions of the Matrimonial Homes Act 1983.

Occupation orders

33. Occupation orders where applicant has estate or interest etc or has matrimonial home rights—(1) If—

   (a) a person ('the person entitled')—

      (i) is entitled to occupy a dwelling-house by virtue of a beneficial estate or interest or contract or by virtue of any enactment giving him the right to remain in occupation, or

      (ii) has matrimonial home rights in relation to a dwelling-house, and

   (b) the dwelling-house—

      (i) is or at any time has been the home of the person entitled and of another person with whom he is associated, or

      (ii) was at any time intended by the person entitled and any such other person to be their home,

the person entitled may apply to the court for an order containing any of the provisions specified in subsections (3), (4) and (5).

(2) If an agreement to marry is terminated, no application under this section may be made by virtue of section 62(3)(e) by reference to that agreement after the end of the period of three years beginning with the day on which it is terminated.

(3) An order under this section may—

(a) enforce the applicant's entitlement to remain in occupation as against the other person ('the respondent');
(b) require the respondent to permit the applicant to enter and remain in the dwelling-house or part of the dwelling-house;
(c) regulate the occupation of the dwelling-house by either or both parties;
(d) if the respondent is entitled as mentioned in subsection (1)(a)(i), prohibit, suspend or restrict the exercise by him of his right to occupy the dwelling-house;
(e) if the respondent has matrimonial home rights in relation to the dwelling-house and the applicant is the other spouse, restrict or terminate those rights;
(f) require the respondent to leave the dwelling-house or part of the dwelling-house; or
(g) exclude the respondent from a defined area in which the dwelling-house is included.

(4) An order under this section may declare that the applicant is entitled as mentioned in subsection (1)(a)(i) or has matrimonial home rights.

(5) If the applicant has matrimonial home rights and the respondent is the other spouse, an order under this section made during the marriage may provide that those rights are not brought to an end by—
(a) the death of the other spouse; or
(b) the termination (otherwise than by death) of the marriage.

(6) In deciding whether to exercise its powers under subsection (3) and (if so) in what manner, the court shall have regard to all the circumstances including—
(a) the housing needs and housing resources of each of the parties and of any relevant child;
(b) the financial resources of each of the parties;
(c) the likely effect of any order, or of any decision by the court not to exercise its powers under subsection (3), on the health, safety or well-being of the parties and of any relevant child; and
(d) the conduct of the parties in relation to each other and otherwise.

(7) If it appears to the court that the applicant or any relevant child is likely to suffer significant harm attributable to conduct of the respondent if an order under this section containing one or more of the provisions mentioned in subsection (3) is not made, the court shall make the order unless it appears to it that—
(a) the respondent or any relevant child is likely to suffer significant harm if the order is made; and
(b) the harm likely to be suffered by the respondent or child in that event is as great as, or greater than, the harm attributable to conduct of the respondent which is likely to be suffered by the applicant or child if the order is not made.

(8) The court may exercise its powers under subsection (5) in any case where it considers that in all the circumstances it is just and reasonable to do so.

(9) An order under this section—
(a) may not be made after the death of either of the parties mentioned in subsection (1); and
(b) except in the case of an order made by virtue of subsection (5)(a), ceases to have effect on the death of either party.

(10) An order under this section may, in so far as it has continuing effect, be made for a specified period, until the occurrence of a specified event or until further order.

34. Effect of order under s 33 where rights are charge on dwelling-house—
(1) If a spouse's matrimonial home rights are a charge on the estate or interest of the other spouse or of trustees for the other spouse—
(a) an order under section 33 against the other spouse has, except so far as a

contrary intention appears, the same effect against persons deriving title under the other spouse or under the trustees and affected by the charge, and
(b) sections 33(1), (3), (4) and (10) and 30(3) to (6) apply in relation to any person deriving title under the other spouse or under the trustees and affected by the charge as they apply in relation to the other spouse.
(2) The court may make an order under section 33 by virtue of subsection (1)(b) if it considers that in all the circumstances it is just and reasonable to do so.

35. One former spouse with no existing right to occupy—(1) This section applies if—
(a) one former spouse is entitled to occupy a dwelling-house by virtue of a beneficial estate or interest or contract, or by virtue of any enactment giving him the right to remain in occupation;
(b) the other former spouse is not so entitled; and
(c) the dwelling-house was at any time their matrimonial home or was at any time intended by them to be their matrimonial home.
(2) The former spouse not so entitled may apply to the court for an order under this section against the other former spouse ('the respondent').
(3) If the applicant is in occupation, an order under this section must contain provision—
(a) giving the applicant the right not to be evicted or excluded from the dwelling-house or any part of it by the respondent for the period specified in the order; and
(b) prohibiting the respondent from evicting or excluding the applicant during that period.
(4) If the applicant is not in occupation, an order under this section must contain provision—
(a) giving the applicant the right to enter into and occupy the dwelling-house for the period specified in the order; and
(b) requiring the respondent to permit the exercise of that right.
(5) An order under this section may also—
(a) regulate the occupation of the dwelling-house by either or both of the parties;
(b) prohibit, suspend or restrict the exercise by the respondent of his right to occupy the dwelling-house;
(c) require the respondent to leave the dwelling-house or part of the dwelling-house; or
(d) exclude the respondent from a defined area in which the dwelling-house is included.
(6) In deciding whether to make an order under this section containing provision of the kind mentioned in subsection (3) or (4) and (if so) in what manner, the court shall have regard to all the circumstances including—
(a) the housing needs and housing resources of each of the parties and of any relevant child;
(b) the financial resources of each of the parties;
(c) the likely effect of any order, or of any decision by the court not to exercise its powers under subsection (3) or (4), on the health, safety or well-being of the parties and of any relevant child;
(d) the conduct of the parties in relation to each other and otherwise;
(e) the length of time that has elapsed since the parties ceased to live together;
(f) the length of time that has elapsed since the marriage was dissolved or annulled; and
(g) the existence of any pending proceedings between the parties—
　　(i) for an order under section 23A or 24 of the Matrimonial Causes Act 1973 (property adjustment orders in connection with divorce proceedings etc);

      (ii) for an order under paragraph 1(2)(d) or (e) of Schedule 1 to the Children Act 1989 (orders for financial relief against parents); or

      (iii) relating to the legal or beneficial ownership of the dwelling-house.

(7) In deciding whether to exercise its power to include one or more of the provisions referred to in subsection (5) ('a subsection (5) provision') and (if so) in what manner, the court shall have regard to all the circumstances including the matters mentioned in subsection (6)(a) to (e).

(8) If the court decides to make an order under this section and it appears to it that, if the order does not include a subsection (5) provision, the applicant or any relevant child is likely to suffer significant harm attributable to conduct of the respondent, the court shall include the subsection (5) provision in the order unless it appears to the court that—

    (a) the respondent or any relevant child is likely to suffer significant harm if the provision is included in the order; and

    (b) the harm likely to be suffered by the respondent or child in that event is as great as or greater than the harm attributable to conduct of the respondent which is likely to be suffered by the applicant or child if the provision is not included.

(9) An order under this section—

    (a) may not be made after the death of either of the former spouses; and

    (b) ceases to have effect on the death of either of them.

(10) An order under this section must be limited so as to have effect for a specified period not exceeding six months, but may be extended on one or more occasions for a further specified period not exceeding six months.

(11) A former spouse who has an equitable interest in the dwelling-house or in the proceeds of sale of the dwelling-house but in whom there is not vested (whether solely or as joint tenant) a legal estate in fee simple or a legal term of years absolute in the dwelling-house is to be treated (but only for the purpose of determining whether he is eligible to apply under this section) as not being entitled to occupy the dwelling-house by virtue of that interest.

(12) Subsection (11) does not prejudice any right of such a former spouse to apply for an order under section 33.

(13) So long as an order under this section remains in force, subsections (3) to (6) of section 30 apply in relation to the applicant—

    (a) as if he were the spouse entitled to occupy the dwelling-house by virtue of that section; and

    (b) as if the respondent were the other spouse.

36. One cohabitant or former cohabitant with no existing right to occupy—

(1) This section applies if—

    (a) one cohabitant or former cohabitant is entitled to occupy a dwelling-house by virtue of a beneficial estate or interest or contract or by virtue of any enactment giving him the right to remain in occupation;

    (b) the other cohabitant or former cohabitant is not so entitled; and

    (c) that dwelling-house is the home in which they live together as husband and wife or a home in which they at any time so lived together or intended so to live together.

(2) The cohabitant or former cohabitant not so entitled may apply to the court for an order under this section against the other cohabitant or former cohabitant ('the respondent').

(3) If the applicant is in occupation, an order under this section must contain provision—

    (a) giving the applicant the right not to be evicted or excluded from the dwelling-house or any part of it by the respondent for the period specified in the order; and

(b) prohibiting the respondent from evicting or excluding the applicant during that period.

(4) If the applicant is not in occupation, an order under this section must contain provision—

(a) giving the applicant the right to enter into and occupy the dwelling-house for the period specified in the order; and

(b) requiring the respondent to permit the exercise of that right.

(5) An order under this section may also—

(a) regulate the occupation of the dwelling-house by either or both of the parties;

(b) prohibit, suspend or restrict the exercise by the respondent of his right to occupy the dwelling-house;

(c) require the respondent to leave the dwelling-house or part of the dwelling-house; or

(d) exclude the respondent from a defined area in which the dwelling-house is included.

(6) In deciding whether to make an order under this section containing provision of the kind mentioned in subsection (3) or (4) and (if so) in what manner, the court shall have regard to all the circumstances including—

(a) the housing needs and housing resources of each of the parties and of any relevant child;

(b) the financial resources of each of the parties;

(c) the likely effect of any order, or of any decision by the court not to exercise its powers under subsection (3) or (4), on the health, safety or well-being of the parties and of any relevant child;

(d) the conduct of the parties in relation to each other and otherwise;

(e) the nature of the parties' relationship [and in particular the level of commitment involved in it];

(f) the length of time during which they have lived together as husband and wife;

(g) whether there are or have been any children who are children of both parties or for whom both parties have or have had parental responsibility;

(h) the length of time that has elapsed since the parties ceased to live together; and

(i) the existence of any pending proceedings between the parties—

(i) for an order under paragraph 1(2)(d) or (e) of Schedule to the Children Act 1989 (orders for financial relief against parents); or

(ii) relating to the legal or beneficial ownership of the dwelling-house.

Note. In para (e) words in square brackets inserted by the Domestic Violence, Crime and Victims Act 2004, s 2(2), as from a day to be appointed.

(7) In deciding whether to exercise its powers to include one or more of the provisions referred to in subsection (5) ('a subsection (5) provision') and (if so) in what manner, the court shall have regard to all the circumstances including—

(a) the matters mentioned in subsection (6)(a) to (d); and

(b) the questions mentioned in subsection (8).

(8) The questions are—

(a) whether the applicant or any relevant child is likely to suffer significant harm attributable to conduct of the respondent if the subsection (5) provision is not included in the order; and

(b) whether the harm likely to be suffered by the respondent or child if the provision is included is as great as or greater than the harm attributable to conduct of the respondent which is likely to be suffered by the applicant or child if the provision is not included.

(9) An order under this section—

(a) may not be made after the death of either of the parties; and

(b) ceases to have effect on the death of either of them.

(10) An order under this section must be limited so as to have effect for a specified period not exceeding six months, but may be extended on one occasion for a further specified period not exceeding six months.

(11) A person who has an equitable interest in the dwelling-house or in the proceeds of sale of the dwelling-house but in whom there is not vested (whether solely or as joint tenant) a legal estate in fee simple or a legal term of years absolute in the dwelling-house is to be treated (but only for the purpose of determining whether he is eligible to apply under this section) as not being entitled to occupy the dwelling-house by virtue of that interest.

(12) Subsection (11) does not prejudice any right of such a person to apply for an order under section 33.

(13) So long as the order remains in force, subsections (3) to (6) of section 30 apply in relation to the applicant—
    (a) as if he were a spouse entitled to occupy the dwelling-house by virtue of that section; and
    (b) as if the respondent were the other spouse.

37. Neither spouse entitled to occupy—(1) This section applies if—
    (a) one spouse or former spouse and the other spouse or former spouse occupy a dwelling-house which is or was the matrimonial home; but
    (b) neither of them is entitled to remain in occupation—
        (i) by virtue of a beneficial estate or interest or contract; or
        (ii) by virtue of any enactment giving him the right to remain in occupation.

(2) Either of the parties may apply to the court for an order against the other under this section.

(3) An order under this section may—
    (a) require the respondent to permit the applicant to enter and remain in the dwelling-house or part of the dwelling-house;
    (b) regulate the occupation of the dwelling-house by either or both of the spouses;
    (c) require the respondent to leave the dwelling-house or part of the dwelling-house; or
    (d) exclude the respondent from a defined area in which the dwelling-house is included.

(4) Subsections (6) and (7) of section 33 apply to the exercise by the court of its powers under this section as they apply to the exercise by the court of its powers under subsection (3) of that section.

(5) An order under this section must be limited so as to have effect for a specified period not exceeding six months, but may be extended on one or more occasions for a further specified period not exceeding six months.

38. Neither cohabitant or former cohabitant entitled to occupy—(1) This section applies if—
    (a) one cohabitant or former cohabitant and the other cohabitant or former cohabitant occupy a dwelling-house which is the home in which they live or lived together as husband and wife; but
    (b) neither of them is entitled to remain in occupation—
        (i) by virtue of a beneficial estate or interest or contract; or
        (ii) by virtue of any enactment giving him the right to remain in occupation.

(2) Either of the parties may apply to the court for an order against the other under this section.

(3) An order under this section may—
    (a) require the respondent to permit the applicant to enter and remain in the dwelling-house or part of the dwelling-house;
    (b) regulate the occupation of the dwelling-house by either or both of the parties;

(c) require the respondent to leave the dwelling-house or part of the dwelling-house; or

(d) exclude the respondent from a defined area in which the dwelling-house is included.

(4) In deciding whether to exercise its powers to include one or more of the provisions referred to in subsection (3) ('a subsection (3) provision') and (if so) in what manner, the court shall have regard to all the circumstances including—

(a) the housing needs and housing resources of each of the parties and of any relevant child;

(b) the financial resources of each of the parties;

(c) the likely effect of any order, or of any decision by the court not to exercise its powers under subsection (3), on the health, safety or well-being of the parties and of any relevant child;

(d) the conduct of the parties in relation to each other and otherwise; and

(e) the questions mentioned in subsection (5).

(5) The questions are—

(a) whether the applicant or any relevant child is likely to suffer significant harm attributable to conduct of the respondent if the subsection (3) provision is not included in the order; and

(b) whether the harm likely to be suffered by the respondent or child if the provision is included is as great as or greater than the harm attributable to conduct of the respondent which is likely to be suffered by the applicant or child if the provision is not included.

(6) An order under this section shall be limited so as to have effect for a specified period not exceeding six months, but may be extended on one occasion for a further specified period not exceeding six months.

39. Supplementary provisions—(1) In this Part an 'occupation order' means an order under section 33, 35, 36, 37 or 38.

(2) An application for an occupation order may be made in other family proceedings or without any other family proceedings being instituted.

(3) If—

(a) an application for an occupation order is made under section 33, 35, 36, 37 or 38, and

(b) the court considers that it has no power to make the order under the section concerned, but that it has power to make an order under one of the other sections,

the court may make an order under that other section.

(4) The fact that a person has applied for an occupation order under sections 35 to 38, or that an occupation order has been made, does not affect the right of any person to claim a legal or equitable interest in any property in any subsequent proceedings (including subsequent proceedings under this Part).

40. Additional provisions that may be included in certain occupation orders—(1) The court may on, or at any time after, making an occupation order under section 33, 35 or 36—

(a) impose on either party obligations as to—

(i) the repair and maintenance of the dwelling-house; or

(ii) the discharge of rent, mortgage payments or other outgoings affecting the dwelling-house;

(b) order a party occupying the dwelling-house or any part of it (including a party who is entitled to do so by virtue of a beneficial estate or interest or contract or by virtue of any enactment giving him the right to remain in occupation) to make periodical payments to the other party in respect of the accommodation, if the other party would (but for the order) be entitled to occupy the dwelling-house by virtue of a beneficial estate or interest or contract or by virtue of any such enactment;

(c) grant either party possession or use of furniture or other contents of the dwelling-house;

(d) order either party to take reasonable care of any furniture or other contents of the dwelling-house;

(e) order either party to take reasonable steps to keep the dwelling-house and any furniture or other contents secure.

(2) In deciding whether and, if so, how to exercise its powers under this section, the court shall have regard to all the circumstances of the case including—

(a) the financial needs and financial resources of the parties; and

(b) the financial obligations which they have, or are likely to have in the foreseeable future, including financial obligations to each other and to any relevant child.

(3) An order under this section ceases to have effect when the occupation order to which it relates ceases to have effect.

41. Additional considerations if parties are cohabitants or former cohabitants—*(1) This section applies if the parties are cohabitants or former cohabitants.*

(2) Where the court is required to consider the nature of the parties' relationship, it is to have regard to the fact that they have not given each other the commitment involved in marriage.

Note. S 41 repealed by the Domestic Violence, Crime and Victims Act 2004, s 2(1), as from a day to be appointed.

Non-molestation orders

42. Non-molestation orders—(1) In this Part a 'non-molestation order' means an order containing either or both of the following provisions—

(a) provision prohibiting a person ('the respondent') from molesting another person who is associated with the respondent;

(b) provision prohibiting the respondent from molesting a relevant child.

(2) The court may make a non-molestation order—

(a) if an application for the order has been made (whether in other family proceedings or without any other family proceedings being instituted) by a person who is associated with the respondent; or

(b) if in any family proceedings to which the respondent is a party the court considers that the order should be made for the benefit of any other party to the proceedings or any relevant child even though no such application has been made.

(3) In subsection (2) 'family proceedings' includes proceedings in which the court has made an emergency protection order under section 44 of the Children Act 1989 which includes an exclusion requirement (as defined in section 44A(3) of that Act).

(4) Where an agreement to marry is terminated, no application under subsection (2)(a) may be made by virtue of section 62(3)(e) by reference to that agreement after the end of the period of three years beginning with the day on which it is terminated.

(5) In deciding whether to exercise its powers under this section and, if so, in what manner, the court shall have regard to all the circumstances including the need to secure the health, safety and well-being—

(a) of the applicant or, in a case falling within subsection (2)(b), the person for whose benefit the order would be made; and

(b) of any relevant child.

(6) A non-molestation order may be expressed so as to refer to molestation in general, to particular acts of molestation, or to both.

(7) A non-molestation order may be made for a specified period or until further order.

(8) A non-molestation order which is made in other family proceedings ceases to have effect if those proceedings are withdrawn or dismissed.

Further provisions relating to occupation and non-molestation orders

[42A. Offence of breaching non-molestation order—(1) A person who without reasonable excuse does anything that he is prohibited from doing by a non-molestation order is guilty of an offence.

(2) In the case of a non-molestation order made by virtue of section 45(1), a person can be guilty of an offence under this section only in respect of conduct engaged in at a time when he was aware of the existence of the order.

(3) Where a person is convicted of an offence under this section in respect of any conduct, that conduct is not punishable as a contempt of court.

(4) A person cannot be convicted of an offence under this section in respect of any conduct which has been punished as a contempt of court.

(5) A person guilty of an offence under this section is liable—
(a) on conviction on indictment, to imprisonment for a term not exceeding five years, or a fine, or both;
(b) on summary conviction, to imprisonment for a term not exceeding 12 months, or a fine not exceeding the statutory maximum, or both.

(6) A reference in any enactment to proceedings under this Part, or to an order under this Part, does not include a reference to proceedings for an offence under this section or to an order made in such proceedings.

'Enactment' includes an enactment contained in subordinate legislation within the meaning of the Interpretation Act 1978 (c 30).]

Note. This section inserted by the Domestic Violence, Crime and Victims Act 2004, s 1, as from a day to be appointed.

43. Leave of court required for applications by children under sixteen—(1) A child under the age of sixteen may not apply for an occupation order or a non-molestation order except with the leave of the court.

(2) The court may grant leave for the purposes of subsection (1) only if it is satisfied that the child has sufficient understanding to make the proposed application for the occupation order or non-molestation order.

44. Evidence of agreement to marry—(1) Subject to subsection (2), the court shall not make an order under section 33 or 42 by virtue of section 62(3)(e) unless there is produced to it evidence in writing of the existence of the agreement to marry.

(2) Subsection (1) does not apply if the court is satisfied that the agreement to marry was evidenced by—
(a) the gift of an engagement ring by one party to the agreement to the other in contemplation of their marriage, or
(b) a ceremony entered into by the parties in the presence of one or more other persons assembled for the purpose of witnessing the ceremony.

45. Ex parte orders—(1) The court may, in any case where it considers that it is just and convenient to do so, make an occupation order or a non-molestation order even though the respondent has not been given such notice of the proceedings as would otherwise be required by rules of court.

(2) In determining whether to exercise its powers under subsection (1), the court shall have regard to all the circumstances including—
(a) any risk of significant harm to the applicant or a relevant child, attributable to conduct of the respondent, if the order is not made immediately;
(b) whether it is likely that the applicant will be deterred or prevented from pursuing the application if an order is not made immediately; and

(c)   whether there is reason to believe that the respondent is aware of the proceedings but is deliberately evading service and that the applicant or a relevant child will be seriously prejudiced by the delay involved—
    (i)   where the court is a magistrates' court, in effecting service of proceedings; or
    (ii)   in any other case, in effecting substituted service.

(3)   If the court makes an order by virtue of subsection (1) it must afford the respondent an opportunity to make representations relating to the order as soon as just and convenient at a full hearing.

(4)   If, at a full hearing, the court makes an occupation order ('the full order'), then—
    (a)   for the purposes of calculating the maximum period for which the full order may be made to have effect, the relevant section is to apply as if the period for which the full order will have effect began on the date on which the initial order first had effect; and
    (b)   the provisions of section 36(10) or 38(6) as to the extension of orders are to apply as if the full order and the initial order were a single order.

(5)   In this section—
'full hearing' means a hearing of which notice has been given to all the parties in accordance with rules of court;
'initial order' means an occupation order made by virtue of subsection (1); and
'relevant section' means section 33(10), 35(10), 36(10), 37(5) or 38(6).

46. Undertakings—(1) In any case where the court has power to make an occupation order or non-molestation order, the court may accept an undertaking from any party to the proceedings.

(2)   No power of arrest may be attached to any undertaking given under subsection (1).

(3)   The court shall not accept an undertaking under subsection (1) in any case where apart from this section a power of arrest would be attached to the order.

(4)   An undertaking given to a court under subsection (1) is enforceable as if it were an order of the court.

(5)   This section has effect without prejudice to the powers of the High Court and the county court apart from this section.

47. Arrest for breach of order—(1) In this section 'a relevant order' means an occupation order or a non-molestation order.

(2)   If—
    (a)   the court makes a relevant order; and
    (b)   it appears to the court that the respondent has used or threatened violence against the applicant or a relevant child,
it shall attach a power of arrest to one or more provisions of the order unless satisfied that in all the circumstances of the case the applicant or child will be adequately protected without such a power of arrest.

(3)   Subsection (2) does not apply in any case where the relevant order is made by virtue of section 45(1), but in such a case the court may attach a power of arrest to one or more provisions of the order if it appears to it—
    (a)   that the respondent has used or threatened violence against the applicant or a relevant child; and
    (b)   that there is a risk of significant harm to the applicant or child, attributable to conduct of the respondent, if the power of arrest is not attached to those provisions immediately.

(4)   If, by virtue of subsection (3), the court attaches a power of arrest to any provisions of a relevant order, it may provide that the power of arrest is to have effect for a shorter period than the other provisions of the order.

(5)   Any period specified for the purposes of subsection (4) may be extended by

the court (on one or more occasions) on an application to vary or discharge the relevant order.

(6) If, by virtue of subsection (2) or (3), a power of arrest is attached to certain provisions of an order, a constable may arrest without warrant a person whom he has reasonable cause for suspecting to be in breach of any such provision.

(7) If a power of arrest is attached under subsection (2) or (3) to certain provisions of the order and the respondent is arrested under subsection (6)—

(a) he must be brought before the relevant judicial authority within the period of 24 hours beginning at the time of his arrest; and

(b) if the matter is not then disposed of forthwith, the relevant judicial authority before whom he is brought may remand him.

In reckoning for the purposes of this subsection any period of 24 hours, no account is to be taken of Christmas Day, Good Friday or any Sunday.

(8) If the court has made a relevant order but—

(a) has not attached a power of arrest under subsection (2) or (3) to any provisions of the order, or

(b) has attached that power only to certain provisions of the order,

then, if at any time the applicant considers that the respondent has failed to comply with the order, he may apply to the relevant judicial authority for the issue of a warrant for the arrest of the respondent.

(9) The relevant judicial authority shall not issue a warrant on an application under subsection (8) unless—

(a) the application is substantiated on oath; and

(b) the relevant judicial authority has reasonable grounds for believing that the respondent has failed to comply with the order.

(10) If a person is brought before a court by virtue of a warrant issued under subsection (9) and the court does not dispose of the matter forthwith, the court may remand him.

(11) Schedule 5 (which makes provision corresponding to that applying in magistrates' courts in civil cases under sections 128 and 129 of the Magistrates' Courts Act 1980) has effect in relation to the powers of the High Court and a county court to remand a person by virtue of this section.

(12) If a person remanded under this section is granted bail (whether in the High Court or a county court under Schedule 5 or in a magistrates' court under section 128 or 129 of the Magistrates' Courts Act 1980), he may be required by the relevant judicial authority to comply, before release on bail or later, with such requirements as appear to that authority to be necessary to secure that he does not interfere with witnesses or otherwise obstruct the course of justice.

48. Remand for medical examination and report—(1) If the relevant judicial authority has reason to consider that a medical report will be required, any power to remand a person under section 47(7)(b) or (10) may be exercised for the purpose of enabling a medical examination and report to be made.

(2) If such a power is so exercised, the adjournment must not be for more than 4 weeks at a time unless the relevant judicial authority remands the accused in custody.

(3) If the relevant judicial authority so remands the accused, the adjournment must not be for more than 3 weeks at a time.

(4) If there is reason to suspect that a person who has been arrested—

(a) under section 47(6), or

(b) under a warrant issued on an application made under section 47(8),

is suffering from mental illness or severe mental impairment, the relevant judicial authority has the same power to make an order under section 35 of the Mental Health Act 1983 (remand for report on accused's mental condition) as the Crown Court has under section 35 of the Act of 1983 in the case of an accused person within the meaning of that section.

49. Variation and discharge of orders—(1) An occupation order or non-molestation order may be varied or discharged by the court on an application by—

    (a) the respondent, or

    (b) the person on whose application the order was made.

(2) In the case of a non-molestation order made by virtue of section 42(2)(b), the order may be varied or discharged by the court even though no such application has been made.

(3) If a spouse's matrimonial home rights are a charge on the estate or interest of the other spouse or of trustees for the other spouse, an order under section 33 against the other spouse may also be varied or discharged by the court on an application by any person deriving title under the other spouse or under the trustees and affected by the charge.

(4) If, by virtue of section 47(3), a power of arrest has been attached to certain provisions of an occupation order or non-molestation order, the court may vary or discharge the order under subsection (1) in so far as it confers a power of arrest (whether or not any application has been made to vary or discharge any other provision of the order).

Enforcement powers of magistrates' courts

50. Power of magistrates' court to suspend execution of committal order— (1) If, under section 63(3) of the Magistrates' Courts Act 1980, a magistrates' court has power to commit a person to custody for breach of a relevant requirement, the court may by order direct that the execution of the order of committal is to be suspended for such period or on such terms and conditions as it may specify.

(2) In subsection (1) 'a relevant requirement' means—

    (a) an occupation order or non-molestation order;

    (b) an exclusion requirement included by virtue of section 38A of the Children Act 1989 in an interim care order made under section 38 of that Act; or

    (c) an exclusion requirement included by virtue of section 44A of the Children Act 1989 in an emergency protection order under section 44 of that Act.

51. Power of magistrates' court to order hospital admission or guardianship— (1) A magistrates' court has the same power to make a hospital order or guardianship order under section 37 of the Mental Health Act 1983 or an interim hospital order under section 38 of that Act in the case of a person suffering from mental illness or severe mental impairment who could otherwise be committed to custody for breach of a relevant requirement as a magistrates' court has under those sections in the case of a person convicted of an offence punishable on summary conviction with imprisonment.

(2) In subsection (1) 'a relevant requirement' has the meaning given by section 50(2).

Interim care orders and emergency protection orders

52. Amendments of Children Act 1989. Schedule 6 makes amendments of the provisions of the Children Act 1989 relating to interim care orders and emergency protection orders.

Transfer of tenancies

53. Transfer of certain tenancies. Schedule 7 makes provision in relation to the transfer of certain tenancies on divorce etc or on separation of cohabitants.

Dwelling-house subject to mortgage

54. Dwelling-house subject to mortgage—(1) In determining for the purposes of this Part whether a person is entitled to occupy a dwelling-house by virtue of an estate or interest, any right to possession of the dwelling-house conferred on a mortgagee of the dwelling-house under or by virtue of his mortgage is to be disregarded.

(2) Subsection (1) applies whether or not the mortgagee is in possession.

(3) Where a person ('A') is entitled to occupy a dwelling-house by virtue of an estate or interest, a connected person does not by virtue of—

(a) any matrimonial home rights conferred by section 30, or

(b) any rights conferred by an order under section 35 or 36,

have any larger right against the mortgagee to occupy the dwelling-house than A has by virtue of his estate or interest and of any contract with the mortgagee.

(4) Subsection (3) does not apply, in the case of matrimonial home rights, if under section 31 those rights are a charge, affecting the mortgagee, on the estate or interest mortgaged.

(5) In this section 'connected person', in relation to any person, means that person's spouse, former spouse, cohabitant or former cohabitant.

55. Actions by mortgagees: joining connected persons as parties—(1) This section applies if a mortgagee of land which consists of or includes a dwelling-house brings an action in any court for the enforcement of his security.

(2) A connected person who is not already a party to the action is entitled to be made a party in the circumstances mentioned in subsection (3).

(3) The circumstances are that—

(a) the connected person is enabled by section 30(3) or (6) (or by section 30(3) or (6) as applied by section 35(13) or 36(13)), to meet the mortgagor's liabilities under the mortgage;

(b) he has applied to the court before the action is finally disposed of in that court; and

(c) the court sees no special reason against his being made a party to the action and is satisfied—

(i) that he may be expected to make such payments or do such other things in or towards satisfaction of the mortgagor's liabilities or obligations as might affect the outcome of the proceedings; or

(ii) that the expectation of it should be considered under section 36 of the Administration of Justice Act 1970.

(4) In this section 'connected person' has the same meaning as in section 54.

56. Actions by mortgagees: service of notice on certain persons—(1) This section applies if a mortgagee of land which consists, or substantially consists, of a dwelling-house brings an action for the enforcement of his security, and at the relevant time there is—

(a) in the case of unregistered land, a land charge of Class F registered against the person who is the estate owner at the relevant time or any person who, where the estate owner is a trustee, preceded him as trustee during the subsistence of the mortgage; or

(b) in the case of registered land, a subsisting registration of—

(i) a notice under section 31(10);

(ii) a notice under section 2(8) of the Matrimonial Homes Act 1983; or

(iii) a notice or caution under section 2(7) of the Matrimonial Homes Act 1967.

(2) If the person on whose behalf—

(a) the land charge is registered, or

(b) the notice or caution is entered,

is not a party to the action, the mortgagee must serve notice of the action on him.

(3) If—

(a) an official search has been made on behalf of the mortgagee which would disclose any land charge of Class F, notice or caution within subsection (1)(a) or (b),

(b) a certificate of the result of the search has been issued, and

(c) the action is commenced within the priority period,

the relevant time is the date of the certificate.

(4) In any other case the relevant time is the time when the action is commenced.

(5) The priority period is, for both registered and unregistered land, the period for which, in accordance with section 11(5) and (6) of the Land Charges Act 1972, a certificate on an official search operates in favour of a purchaser.

Jurisdiction and procedure etc

57. Jurisdiction of courts—(1) For the purposes of this Part 'the court' means the High Court, a county court or a magistrates' court.

(2) Subsection (1) is subject to the provision made by or under the following provisions of this section, to section 59 and to any express provision as to the jurisdiction of any court made by any other provision of this Part.

(3) The Lord Chancellor may by order specify proceedings under this Part which may only be commenced in—

(a) a specified level of court;

(b) a court which falls within a specified class of court; or

(c) a particular court determined in accordance with, or specified in, the order.

(4) The Lord Chancellor may by order specify circumstances in which specified proceedings under this Part may only be commenced in—

(a) a specified level of court;

(b) a court which falls within a specified class of court; or

(c) a particular court determined in accordance with, or specified in, the order.

(5) The Lord Chancellor may by order provide that in specified circumstances the whole, or any specified part of any specified proceedings under this Part is to be transferred to—

(a) a specified level of court;

(b) a court which falls within a specified class of court; or

(c) a particular court determined in accordance with, or specified in, the order.

(6) An order under subsection (5) may provide for the transfer to be made at any stage, or specified stage, of the proceedings and whether or not the proceedings, or any part of them, have already been transferred.

(7) An order under subsection (5) may make such provision as the Lord Chancellor thinks appropriate for excluding specified proceedings from the operation of section 38 or 39 of the Matrimonial and Family Proceedings Act 1984 (transfer of family proceedings) or any other enactment which would otherwise govern the transfer of those proceedings, or any part of them.

(8) For the purposes of subsections (3), (4) and (5), there are three levels of court—

(a) the High Court;

(b) any county court; and

(c) any magistrates' court.

(9) The Lord Chancellor may by order make provision for the principal registry of the Family Division of the High Court to be treated as if it were a county court for specified purposes of this Part, or of any provision made under this Part.

(10) Any order under subsection (9) may make such provision as the Lord Chancellor thinks expedient for the purpose of applying (with or without modifications) provisions which apply in relation to the procedure in county courts to the principal registry when it acts as if it were a county court.

(11) In this section 'specified' means specified by an order under this section.

58. Contempt proceedings.   The powers of the court in relation to contempt of court arising out of a person's failure to comply with an order under this Part may be exercised by the relevant judicial authority.

59. Magistrates' courts—(1) A magistrates' court shall not be competent to entertain any application, or make any order, involving any disputed question as to a party's entitlement to occupy any property by virtue of a beneficial estate or interest or contract or by virtue of any enactment giving him the right to remain in occupation, unless it is unnecessary to determine the question in order to deal with the application or make the order.

(2) A magistrates' court may decline jurisdiction in any proceedings under this Part if it considers that the case can more conveniently be dealt with by another court.

(3) The powers of a magistrates' court under section 63(2) of the Magistrates' Courts Act 1980 to suspend or rescind orders shall not apply in relation to any order made under this Part.

60. Provision for third parties to act on behalf of victims of domestic violence—(1) Rules of court may provide for a prescribed person, or any person in a prescribed category, ('a representative') to act on behalf of another in relation to proceedings to which this Part applies.

(2) Rules made under this section may, in particular, authorise a representative to apply for an occupation order or for a non-molestation order for which the person on whose behalf the representative is acting could have applied.

(3) Rules made under this section may prescribe—
  (a) conditions to be satisfied before a representative may make an application to the court on behalf of another; and
  (b) considerations to be taken into account by the court in determining whether, and if so how, to exercise any of its powers under this Part when a representative is acting on behalf of another.

(4) Any rules made under this section may be made so as to have effect for a specified period and may make consequential or transitional provision with respect to the expiry of the specified period.

(5) Any such rules may be replaced by further rules made under this section.

61. Appeals—(1) An appeal shall lie to the High Court against—
  (a) the making by a magistrates' court of any order under this Part, or
  (b) any refusal by a magistrates' court to make such an order,
but no appeal shall lie against any exercise by a magistrates' court of the power conferred by section 59(2).

(2) On an appeal under this section, the High Court may make such orders as may be necessary to give effect to its determination of the appeal.

(3) Where an order is made under subsection (2), the High Court may also make such incidental or consequential orders as appear to it to be just.

(4) Any order of the High Court made on an appeal under this section (other than one directing that an application be re-heard by a magistrates' court) shall, for the purposes—
  (a) of the enforcement of the order, and
  (b) of any power to vary, revive or discharge orders,
be treated as if it were an order of the magistrates' court from which the appeal was brought and not an order of the High Court.

(5) The Lord Chancellor may by order make provision as to the circumstances in which appeals may be made against decisions taken by courts on questions arising in connection with the transfer, or proposed transfer, of proceedings by virtue of any order under section 57(5).

(6) Except to the extent provided for in any order made under subsection (5), no appeal may be made against any decision of a kind mentioned in that subsection.

General

62. Meaning of 'cohabitants', 'relevant child' and 'associated persons'—(1) For the purposes of this Part—

(a) 'cohabitants' are *a man and a woman who, although not married to each other, are living together as husband and wife; and* [two persons who, although not married to each other, are living together as husband and wife or (if of the same sex) in an equivalent relationship; and]

(b) 'former cohabitants' is to be read accordingly, but does not include cohabitants who have subsequently married each other.

Note. In para (a) words in square brackets substituted for words in italics by the Domestic Violence, Crime and Victims Act 2004, s 3, as from a day to be appointed.

(2) In this Part, 'relevant child', in relation to any proceedings under this Part, means—

(a) any child who is living with or might reasonably be expected to live with either party to the proceedings;

(b) any child in relation to whom an order under the Adoption Act 1976 [, the Adoption and Children Act 2002] or the Children Act 1989 is in question in the proceedings; and

(c) any other child whose interests the court considers relevant.

Note. In para (b) words in square brackets inserted by the Adoption and Children Act 2002, s 139(1), Sch 3, paras 85, 86(a), as from a day to be appointed.

(3) For the purposes of this Part, a person is associated with another person if—

(a) they are or have been married to each other;

(b) they are cohabitants or former cohabitants;

(c) they live or have lived in the same household, otherwise than merely by reason of one of them being the other's employee, tenant, lodger or boarder;

(d) they are relatives;

(e) they have agreed to marry one another (whether or not that agreement has been terminated);

[(ea) they have or have had an intimate personal relationship with each other which is or was of significant duration;]

(f) in relation to any child, they are both persons falling within subsection (4); or

(g) they are parties to the same family proceedings (other than proceedings under this Part).

Note. Para (ea) inserted by the Domestic Violence, Crime and Victims Act 2004, s 4, as from a day to be appointed.

(4) A person falls within this subsection in relation to a child if—

(a) he is a parent of the child; or

(b) he has or has had parental responsibility for the child.

(5) If a child has been adopted or *has been freed for adoption by virtue of any of the enactments mentioned in section 16(1) of the Adoption Act 1976* [falls within subsection (7)], two persons are also associated with each other for the purposes of this Part if—

(a) one is a natural parent of the child or a parent of such a natural parent; and

(b) the other is the child or any person—

(i) who has become a parent of the child by virtue of an adoption order or has applied for an adoption order, or

(ii) with whom the child has at any time been placed for adoption.

Note. In sub-s (5) words in square brackets substituted for words in italics by the Adoption and Children Act 2002, s 139(1), Sch 3, paras 85, 86(b), as from a day to be appointed.

(6) A body corporate and another person are not, by virtue of subsection (3)(f) or (g), to be regarded for the purposes of this Part as associated with each other.

[(7) A child falls within this subsection if—

(a) an adoption agency, within the meaning of section 2 of the Adoption and

Children Act 2002, has power to place him for adoption under section 19 of that Act (placing children with parental consent) or he has become the subject of an order under section 21 of that Act (placement orders), or

(b) he is freed for adoption by virtue of an order made—

   (i) in England and Wales, under section 18 of the Adoption Act 1976,

   (ii) in Scotland, under section 18 of the Adoption (Scotland) Act 1978, or

   (iii) in Northern Ireland, under Article 17(1) or 18(1) of the Adoption (Northern Ireland) Order 1987.]

Note. Sub-s (7) inserted by the Adoption and Children Act 2002, s 139(1), Sch 3, paras 85, 87, as from a day to be appointed.

63. Interpretation of Part IV—(1) In this Part—

'adoption order' has the meaning given by section 72(1) of the Adoption Act 1976;

['adoption order' means an adoption order within the meaning of section 72(1) of the Adoption Act 1976 or section 46(1) of the Adoption and Children Act 2002;]

'associated', in relation to a person, is to be read with section 62(3) to (6);

'child' means a person under the age of eighteen years;

'cohabitant' and 'former cohabitant' have the meaning given by section 62(1);

'the court' is to be read with section 57;

'development' means physical, intellectual, emotional, social or behavioural development;

'dwelling-house' includes (subject to subsection (4))—

(a) any building or part of a building which is occupied as a dwelling,

(b) any caravan, house-boat or structure which is occupied as a dwelling,

and any yard, garden, garage or outhouse belonging to it and occupied with it;

'family proceedings' means any proceedings—

(a) under the inherent jurisdiction of the High Court in relation to children; or

(b) under the enactments mentioned in subsection (2);

'harm'—

(a) in relation to a person who has reached the age of eighteen years, means ill-treatment or the impairment of health; and

(b) in relation to a child, means ill-treatment or the impairment of health or development;

'health' includes physical or mental health;

'ill-treatment' includes forms of ill-treatment which are not physical and, in relation to a child, includes sexual abuse;

'matrimonial home rights' has the meaning given by section 30;

'mortgage', 'mortgagor' and 'mortgagee' have the same meaning as in the Law of Property Act 1925;

'mortgage payments' includes any payments which, under the terms of the mortgage, the mortgagor is required to make to any person;

'non-molestation order' has the meaning given by section 42(1);

'occupation order' has the meaning given by section 39;

'parental responsibility' has the same meaning as in the Children Act 1989;

'relative', in relation to a person, means—

(a) the father, mother, stepfather, stepmother, son, daughter, stepson, step-daughter, grandmother, grandfather, grandson or granddaughter of that person or of that person's spouse or former spouse, or

(b) the brother, sister, uncle, aunt, niece or nephew (whether of the full blood or of the half blood or by affinity) of that person or of that person's spouse or former spouse,

and includes, in relation to a person who is living or has lived with another person as husband and wife, any person who would fall within paragraph (a) or (b) if the parties were married to each other;

'relevant child', in relation to any proceedings under this Part, has the meaning given by section 62(2);

'the relevant judicial authority', in relation to any order under this Part, means—

(a) where the order was made by the High Court, a judge of that court;

(b) where the order was made by a county court, a judge or district judge of that or any other county court; or

(c) where the order was made by a magistrates' court, any magistrates' court.

(2) The enactments referred to in the definition of 'family proceedings' are—

(a) Part II;

(b) this Part;

(c) the Matrimonial Causes Act 1973;

(d) the Adoption Act 1976;

(e) the Domestic Proceedings and Magistrates' Courts Act 1978;

(f) Part III of the Matrimonial and Family Proceedings Act 1984;

(g) Parts I, II and IV of the Children Act 1989;

(h) section 30 of the Human Fertilisation and Embryology Act 1990;

[(i) the Adoption and Children Act 2002].

(3) Where the question of whether harm suffered by a child is significant turns on the child's health or development, his health or development shall be compared with that which could reasonably be expected of a similar child.

(4) For the purposes of sections 31, 32, 53 and 54 and such other provisions of this Part (if any) as may be prescribed, this Part is to have effect as if paragraph (b) of the definition of 'dwelling-house' were omitted.

(5) It is hereby declared that this Part applies as between the parties to a marriage even though either of them is, or has at any time during the marriage been, married to more than one person.

Note. In sub-s (1) definition 'adoption order' substituted and sub-s (2)(i) inserted, by the Adoption and Children Act 2002, s 139(1), Sch 3, paras 85, 88, as from a day to be appointed.

PART V

SUPPLEMENTAL

64. Provision for separate representation for children—(1) The Lord Chancellor may by regulations provide for the separate representation of children in proceedings in England and Wales which relate to any matter in respect of which a question has arisen, or may arise, under—

(a) Part II;

(b) Part IV;

(c) the 1973 Act; or

(d) the Domestic Proceedings and Magistrates' Courts Act 1978.

(2) The regulations may provide for such representation only in specified circumstances.

65. Rules, regulations and orders—(1) Any power to make rules, orders or regulations which is conferred by this Act is exercisable by statutory instrument.

(2) Any statutory instrument made under this Act may—

(a) contain such incidental, supplemental, consequential and transitional provision as the Lord Chancellor considers appropriate; and

(b) make different provision for different purposes.

(3) Any statutory instrument containing an order, rules or regulations made under this Act, other than an order made under section 5(8) or 67(3), shall be subject to annulment by a resolution of either House of Parliament.

(4) No order shall be made under section 5(8) unless a draft of the order has been laid before, and approved by a resolution of, each House of Parliament.

(5) This section does not apply to rules of court made, or any power to make rules of court, for the purposes of this Act.

66. Consequential amendments, transitional provisions and repeals—(1) Schedule 8 makes minor and consequential amendments.

(2) Schedule 9 provides for the making of other modifications consequential on provisions of this Act, makes transitional provisions and provides for savings.

(3) Schedule 10 repeals certain enactments.

67. Short title, commencement and extent—(1) This Act may be cited as the Family Law Act 1996.

(2) Section 65 and this section come into force on the passing of this Act.

(3) The other provisions of this Act come into force on such day as the Lord Chancellor may by order appoint; and different days may be appointed for different purposes.

(4) This Act, other than section 17, extends only to England and Wales, except that—

(a) in Schedule 8—

(i) the amendments of section 38 of the Family Law Act 1986 extend also to Northern Ireland;

(ii) the amendments of the Judicial Proceedings (Regulation of Reports) Act 1926 extend also to Scotland; and

(iii) the amendments of the Maintenance Orders Act 1950, the Civil Jurisdiction and Judgments Act 1982, the Finance Act 1985 and sections 42 and 51 of the Family Law Act 1986 extend also to both Northern Ireland and Scotland; and

(b) in Schedule 10, the repeal of section 2(1)(b) of the Domestic and Appellate Proceedings (Restriction of Publicity) Act 1968 extends also to Scotland.

Commencement. Sections 1, 22, 26–29, 66(1) (so far as it relates to Part II of Schedule 8), 66(3) (so far as it relates to the entry in Schedule 10 in respect of the Legal Aid Act 1988) were brought into force on 21 March 1997 (SI 1997 No 1077). Section 57 was brought into force on 28 July 1997, and sections 30–56, 58, 59, 61–63, 66(1) (so far as it relates to Part III of Schedule 8), 66(2) (so far as it relates to paragraphs 7–15 of Schedule 9), 66(3) (so far as it relates to the entries in Schedule 10 in respect of the Domestic Violence and Matrimonial Proceedings Act 1976, the Domestic Proceedings and Magistrates' Courts Act 1978, ss 16–18, 28(2), Sch 2, para 53, the Matrimonial Homes Act 1983, the Administration of Justice Act 1985, s 34(2), Sch 2, para 37, the Housing (Consequential Provisions) Act 1985, Sch 2, para 56, the Housing Act 1988, Sch 17, paras 33, 34, the Children Act 1989, s 8(4), the Courts and Legal Services Act 1990, s 58(10), Sch 18, para 21, the Private International Law (Miscellaneous Provisions) Act 1995, Schedule, para 3) were brought into force on 1 October 1997 (SI 1997 No 1892).

SCHEDULES

SCHEDULE 1   Section 9(6)

ARRANGEMENTS FOR THE FUTURE

The first exemption

1. The circumstances referred to in section 9(7)(a) are that—

(a) the requirements of section 11 have been satisfied;

(b) the applicant has, during the period for reflection and consideration, taken such steps as are reasonably practicable to try to reach agreement about the parties' financial arrangements; and

(c) the applicant has made an application to the court for financial relief and has complied with all requirements of the court in relation to proceedings for financial relief but—

(i) the other party has delayed in complying with requirements of the court or has otherwise been obstructive; or

(ii) for reasons which are beyond the control of the applicant, or of the other party, the court has been prevented from obtaining the information which it requires to determine the financial position of the parties.

The second exemption

2. The circumstances referred to in section 9(7)(b) are that—

   (a) the requirements of section 11 have been satisfied;

   (b) the applicant has, during the period for reflection and consideration, taken such steps as are reasonably practicable to try to reach agreement about the parties' financial arrangements;

   (c) because of—

      (i) the ill health or disability of the applicant, the other party or a child of the family (whether physical or mental), or

     (ii) an injury suffered by the applicant, the other party or a child of the family,

     the applicant has not been able to reach agreement with the other party about those arrangements and is unlikely to be able to do so in the foreseeable future; and

   (d) a delay in making the order applied for under section 3—

      (i) would be significantly detrimental to the welfare of any child of the family; or

     (ii) would be seriously prejudicial to the applicant.

The third exemption

3. The circumstances referred to in section 9(7)(c) are that—

   (a) the requirements of section 11 have been satisfied;

   (b) the applicant has found it impossible to contact the other party; and

   (c) as a result, it has been impossible for the applicant to reach agreement with the other party about their financial arrangements.

The fourth exemption

4. The circumstances referred to in section 9(7)(d) are that—

   (a) the requirements of section 11 have been satisfied;

   (b) an occupation order or a non-molestation order is in force in favour of the applicant or a child of the family, made against the other party;

   (c) the applicant has, during the period for reflection and consideration, taken such steps as are reasonably practicable to try to reach agreement about the parties' financial arrangements;

   (d) the applicant has not been able to reach agreement with the other party about those arrangements and is unlikely to be able to do so in the foreseeable future; and

   (e) a delay in making the order applied for under section 3—

      (i) would be significantly detrimental to the welfare of any child of the family; or

     (ii) would be seriously prejudicial to the applicant.

Court orders and agreements

5.—(1) Section 9 is not to be read as requiring any order or agreement to have been carried into effect at the time when the court is considering whether arrangements for the future have been made by the parties.

   (2) The fact that an appeal is pending against an order of the kind mentioned in section 9(2)(a) is to be disregarded.

Financial arrangements

6. In section 9 and this Schedule 'financial arrangements' has the same meaning as in section 34(2) of the 1973 Act.

Negotiated agreements

7. In section 9(2)(b) 'negotiated agreement' means a written agreement between the parties as to future arrangements—
  (a) which has been reached as the result of mediation or any other form of negotiation involving a third party; and
  (b) which satisfies such requirements as may be imposed by rules of court.

Declarations

8.—(1) Any declaration of a kind mentioned in section 9—
  (a) must be in a prescribed form;
  (b) must, in prescribed cases, be accompanied by such documents as may be prescribed; and
  (c) must, in prescribed cases, satisfy such other requirements as may be prescribed.
  (2) The validity of a divorce order or separation order made by reference to such a declaration is not to be affected by any inaccuracy in the declaration.

Interpretation

9. In this Schedule—
  'financial relief' has such meaning as may be prescribed; and
  'prescribed' means prescribed by rules of court.

SCHEDULE 2   Section 15

FINANCIAL PROVISION

Introductory

1. Part II of the 1973 Act (financial provision and property adjustment orders) is amended as follows.

The orders

2. For *section 21* [sections 21 and 21A] (definitions) substitute—
  '**21. Financial provision and property adjustment orders [Financial provision orders, property adjustment orders and pension sharing orders]**—(1) For the purposes of this Act, a financial provision order is—
    (a) an order that a party must make in favour of another person such periodical payments, for such term, as may be specified (a "periodical payments order");
    (b) an order that a party must, to the satisfaction of the court, secure in favour of another person such periodical payments, for such term, as may be specified (a "secured periodical payments order");
    (c) an order that a party must make a payment in favour of another person of such lump sum or sums as may be specified (an "order for the payment of a lump sum").
  (2) For the purposes of this Act, a property adjustment order is—
    (a) an order that a party must transfer such of his or her property as may be specified in favour of the other party or a child of the family;
    (b) an order that a settlement of such property of a party as may be specified must be made, to the satisfaction of the court, for the benefit of the other party and of the children of the family, or either or any of them;
    (c) an order varying, for the benefit of the parties and of the children of the family, or either or any of them, any marriage settlement [, other than one in the form of a pension arrangement (within the meaning of section 25D below)];

(d) an order extinguishing or reducing the interest of either of the parties under any marriage settlement [, other than one in the form of a pension arrangement (within the meaning of section 25D below)].

[(3) For the purposes of this Act, a pension sharing order is an order which—
(a) provides that one party's—
(i) shareable rights under a specified pension arrangement, or
(ii) shareable state scheme rights,
be subject to pension sharing for the benefit of the other party, and
(b) specifies the percentage value to be transferred.]

(4) Subject to section 40 below, where an order of the court under this Part of this Act requires a party to make or secure a payment in favour of another person or to transfer property in favour of any person, that payment must be made or secured or that property transferred—
(a) if that other person is the other party to the marriage, to that other party; and
(b) if that other person is a child of the family, according to the terms of the order—
(i) to the child; or
(ii) to such other person as may be specified, for the benefit of that child.

(5) References in this section to the property of a party are references to any property to which that party is entitled either in possession or in reversion.

(6) Any power of the court under this Part of this Act to make such an order as is mentioned in subsection (2)(b) to (d) above is exercisable even though there are no children of the family.

[(7) In subsection (3)—
(a) the reference to shareable rights under a pension arrangement is to rights in relation to which pension sharing is available under Chapter I of Part IV of the Welfare Reform and Pensions Act 1999, or under corresponding Northern Ireland legislation, and
(b) the reference to shareable state scheme rights is to rights in relation to which pension sharing is available under Chapter II of Part IV of the Welfare Reform and Pensions Act 1999, or under corresponding Northern Ireland legislation.]

(8) In this section—
"marriage settlement" means an ante-nuptial or post-nuptial settlement made on the parties (including one made by will or codicil);
"party" means a party to a marriage; and
"specified" means specified in the order in question.'

Note. In the sidenote, words in square brackets substituted for words in italics, words in square brackets in sub-s 2(c), (d) and new sub-ss (3) and (7) added, and original sub-ss (3)–(5), (6) renumbered as (4)–(6), (8), by the Welfare Reform and Pensions Act 1999, s 84(1), Sch 12, paras 64, 65(1)–(8), as from 1 December 2000 (SI 2000 No 1116).

Financial provision: divorce and separation

3. Insert, before section 23—

'**22A. Financial provision orders: divorce and separation**—(1) On an application made under this section, the court may at the appropriate time make one or more financial provision orders in favour of—
(a) a party to the marriage to which the application relates; or
(b) any of the children of the family.
(2) The "appropriate time" is any time—
(a) after a statement of marital breakdown has been received by the court and before any application for a divorce order or for a separation order is made to the court by reference to that statement;

(b) when an application for a divorce order or separation order has been made under section 3 of the 1996 Act and has not been withdrawn;

(c) when an application for a divorce order has been made under section 4 of the 1996 Act and has not been withdrawn;

(d) after a divorce order has been made;

(e) when a separation order is in force.

(3) The court may make—

(a) a combined order against the parties on one occasion,

(b) separate orders on different occasions,

(c) different orders in favour of different children,

(d) different orders from time to time in favour of the same child,

but may not make, in favour of the same party, more than one periodical payments order, or more than one order for payment of a lump sum, in relation to any marital proceedings, whether in the course of the proceedings or by reference to a divorce order or separation order made in the proceedings.

(4) If it would not otherwise be in a position to make a financial provision order in favour of a party or child of the family, the court may make an interim periodical payments order, an interim order for the payment of a lump sum or a series of such orders, in favour of that party or child.

(5) Any order for the payment of a lump sum made under this section may—

(a) provide for the payment of the lump sum by instalments of such amounts as may be specified in the order; and

(b) require the payment of the instalments to be secured to the satisfaction of the court.

(6) Nothing in subsection (5) above affects—

(a) the power of the court under this section to make an order for the payment of a lump sum; or

(b) the provisions of this Part of this Act as to the beginning of the term specified in any periodical payments order or secured periodical payments order.

(7) Subsection (8) below applies where the court—

(a) makes an order under this section ("the main order") for the payment of a lump sum; and

(b) directs—

(i) that payment of that sum, or any part of it, is to be deferred; or

(ii) that that sum, or any part of it, is to be paid by instalments.

(8) In such a case, the court may, on or at any time after making the main order, make an order ("the order for interest") for the amount deferred, or the instalments, to carry interest (at such rate as may be specified in the order for interest)—

(a) from such date, not earlier than the date of the main order, as may be so specified;

(b) until the date when the payment is due.

(9) This section is to be read subject to any restrictions imposed by this Act and to section 19 of the 1996 Act.

22B. Restrictions affecting section 22A—(1) No financial provision order, other than an interim order, may be made under section 22A above so as to take effect before the making of a divorce order or separation order in relation to the marriage, unless the court is satisfied—

(a) that the circumstances of the case are exceptional; and

(b) that it would be just and reasonable for the order to be so made.

(2) Except in the case of an interim periodical payments order, the court may not make a financial provision order under section 22A above at any time while the period for reflection and consideration is interrupted under section 7(8) of the 1996 Act.

(3) No financial provision order may be made under section 22A above by reference to the making of a statement of marital breakdown if, by virtue of section 5(3) or 7(9) of the 1996 Act (lapse of divorce or separation process), it has ceased to be possible—

(a) for an application to be made by reference to that statement; or

(b) for an order to be made on such an application.

(4) No financial provision order may be made under section 22A after a divorce order has been made, or while a separation order is in force, except—

(a) in response to an application made before the divorce order or separation order was made; or

(b) on a subsequent application made with the leave of the court.

(5) In this section, "period for reflection and consideration" means the period fixed by section 7 of the 1996 Act.'

Financial provision: nullity of marriage

4. For section 23 substitute—

'**23. Financial provision orders: nullity**—(1) On or after granting a decree of nullity of marriage (whether before or after the decree is made absolute), the court may, on an application made under this section, make one or more financial provision orders in favour of—

(a) either party to the marriage; or

(b) any child of the family.

(2) Before granting a decree in any proceedings for nullity of marriage, the court may make against either or each of the parties to the marriage—

(a) an interim periodical payments order, an interim order for the payment of a lump sum, or a series of such orders, in favour of the other party;

(b) an interim periodical payments order, an interim order for the payment of a lump sum, a series of such orders or any one or more other financial provision orders in favour of each child of the family.

(3) Where any such proceedings are dismissed, the court may (either immediately or within a reasonable period after the dismissal) make any one or more financial provision orders in favour of each child of the family.

(4) An order under this section that a party to a marriage must pay a lump sum to the other party may be made for the purpose of enabling that other party to meet any liabilities or expenses reasonably incurred by him or her in maintaining himself or herself or any child of the family before making an application for an order under this section in his or her favour.

(5) An order under this section for the payment of a lump sum to or for the benefit of a child of the family may be made for the purpose of enabling any liabilities or expenses reasonably incurred by or for the benefit of that child before the making of an application for an order under this section in his favour to be met.

(6) An order under this section for the payment of a lump sum may—

(a) provide for the payment of that sum by instalments of such amount as may be specified in the order; and

(b) require the payment of the instalments to be secured to the satisfaction of the court.

(7) Nothing in subsections (4) to (6) above affects—

(a) the power under subsection (1) above to make an order for the payment of a lump sum; or

(b) the provisions of this Act as to the beginning of the term specified in any periodical payments order or secured periodical payments order.

(8) The powers of the court under this section to make one or more financial provision orders are exercisable against each party to the marriage by the making of—

(a) a combined order on one occasion, or

(b) separate orders on different occasions,

but the court may not make more than one periodical payments order, or more than one order for payment of a lump sum, in favour of the same party.

(9) The powers of the court under this section so far as they consist in power to make one or more orders in favour of the children of the family—

(a) may be exercised differently in favour of different children; and

(b) except in the case of the power conferred by subsection (3) above, may be exercised from time to time in favour of the same child; and

(c) in the case of the power conferred by that subsection, if it is exercised by the making of a financial provision order of any kind in favour of a child, shall include power to make, from time to time, further financial provision orders of that or any other kind in favour of that child.

(10) Where an order is made under subsection (1) above in favour of a party to the marriage on or after the granting of a decree of nullity of marriage, neither the order nor any settlement made in pursuance of the order takes effect unless the decree has been made absolute.

(11) Subsection (10) above does not affect the power to give a direction under section 30 below for the settlement of an instrument by conveyancing counsel.

(12) Where the court—

(a) makes an order under this section ('the main order') for the payment of a lump sum; and

(b) directs—

(i) that payment of that sum or any part of it is to be deferred; or

(ii) that that sum or any part of it is to be paid by instalments,

it may, on or at any time after making the main order, make an order ("the order for interest") for the amount deferred or the instalments to carry interest at such rate as may be specified by the order for interest from such date, not earlier than the date of the main order, as may be so specified, until the date when payment of it is due.

(13) This section is to be read subject to any restrictions imposed by this Act.'

Property adjustment orders: divorce and separation

5. Insert, before section 24—

'**23A. Property adjustment orders: divorce and separation**—(1) On an application made under this section, the court may, at any time mentioned in section 22A(2) above, make one or more property adjustment orders.

(2) If the court makes, in favour of the same party to the marriage, more than one property adjustment order in relation to any marital proceedings, whether in the course of the proceedings or by reference to a divorce order or separation order made in the proceedings, each order must fall within a different paragraph of section 21(2) above.

(3) The court shall exercise its powers under this section, so far as is practicable, by making on one occasion all such provision as can be made by way of one or more property adjustment orders in relation to the marriage as it thinks fit.

(4) Subsection (3) above does not affect section 31 or 31A below.

(5) This section is to be read subject to any restrictions imposed by this Act and to section 19 of the 1996 Act.

23B. Restrictions affecting section 23A—(1) No property adjustment order may be made under section 23A above so as to take effect before the making of a divorce order or separation order in relation to the marriage unless the court is satisfied—

(a) that the circumstances of the case are exceptional; and

(b) that it would be just and reasonable for the order to be so made.

(2) The court may not make a property adjustment order under section 23A above at any time while the period for reflection and consideration is interrupted under section 7(8) of the 1996 Act.

(3) No property adjustment order may be made under section 23A above by virtue of the making of a statement of marital breakdown if, by virtue of section 5(3) or 7(5) of the 1996 Act (lapse of divorce or separation process), it has ceased to be possible—

(a) for an application to be made by reference to that statement; or

(b) for an order to be made on such an application.

(4) No property adjustment order may be made under section 23A above after a divorce order has been made, or while a separation order is in force, except—

(a) in response to an application made before the divorce order or separation order was made; or

(b) on a subsequent application made with the leave of the court.

(5) In this section, "period for reflection and consideration" means the period fixed by section 7 of the 1996 Act.'

Property adjustment orders: nullity

6. For section 24, substitute—

'**24. Property adjustment orders: nullity of marriage**—(1) On or after granting a decree of nullity of marriage (whether before or after the decree is made absolute), the court may, on an application made under this section, make one or more property adjustment orders in relation to the marriage.

(2) The court shall exercise its powers under this section, so far as is practicable, by making on one occasion all such provision as can be made by way of one or more property adjustment orders in relation to the marriage as it thinks fit.

(3) Subsection (2) above does not affect section 31 or 31A below.

(4) Where a property adjustment order is made under this section on or after the granting of a decree of nullity of marriage, neither the order nor any settlement made in pursuance of the order is to take effect unless the decree has been made absolute.

(5) That does not affect the power to give a direction under section 30 below for the settlement of an instrument by conveyancing counsel.

(6) This section is to be read subject to any restrictions imposed by this Act.'

['Pension sharing orders: divorce and nullity

6A. For section 24B substitute—

'**24B. Pension sharing orders: divorce**—(1) On an application made under this section, the court may at the appropriate time make one or more pension sharing orders.

(2) The "appropriate time" is any time—

(a) after a statement of marital breakdown has been received by the court and before any application for a divorce order or for a separation order is made to the court by reference to that statement;

(b) when an application for a divorce order has been made under section 3 of the 1996 Act and has not been withdrawn;

(c) when an application for a divorce order has been made under section 4 of the 1996 Act and has not been withdrawn;

(d) after a divorce order has been made.

(3) The court shall exercise its powers under this section, so far as is practicable, by making on one occasion all such provision as can be made by way of one or more pension sharing orders in relation to the marriage as it thinks fit.

(4) This section is to be read subject to any restrictions imposed by this Act and to section 19 of the 1996 Act.

24BA. Restrictions affecting section 24B—(1) No pension sharing order may be made under section 24B above so as to take effect before the making of a divorce order in relation to the marriage.

(2) The court may not make a pension sharing order under section 24B above at any time while the period for reflection and consideration is interrupted under section 7(8) of the 1996 Act.

(3) No pension sharing order may be made under section 24B above by virtue of a statement of marital breakdown if, by virtue of section 5(3) or 7(9) of the 1996 Act (lapse of divorce process), it has ceased to be possible—

(a) for an application to be made by reference to that statement, or

(b) for an order to be made on such an application.

(4) No pension sharing order may be made under section 24B above after a divorce order has been made, except—

(a) in response to an application made before the divorce order was made, or

(b) on a subsequent application made with the leave of the court.

(5) A pension sharing order under section 24B above may not be made in relation to a pension arrangement which—

(a) is the subject of a pension sharing order in relation to the marriage, or

(b) has been the subject of pension sharing between the parties to the marriage.

(6) A pension sharing order under section 24B above may not be made in relation to shareable state scheme rights if—

(a) such rights are the subject of a pension sharing order in relation to the marriage, or

(b) such rights have been the subject of pension sharing between the parties to the marriage.

(7) A pension sharing order under section 24B above may not be made in relation to the rights of a person under a pension arrangement if there is in force a requirement imposed by virtue of section 25B or 25C below which relates to benefits or future benefits to which he is entitled under the pension arrangement.

(8) In this section, "period for reflection and consideration" means the period fixed by section 7 of the 1996 Act.

24BB. Pension sharing orders: nullity of marriage—(1) On or after granting a decree of nullity of marriage (whether before or after the decree is made absolute), the court may, on an application made under this section, make one or more pension sharing orders in relation to the marriage.

(2) The court shall exercise its powers under this section, so far as is practicable, by making on one occasion all such provision as can be made by way of one or more pension sharing orders in relation to the marriage as it thinks fit.

(3) Where a pension sharing order is made under this section on or after the granting of a decree of nullity of marriage, the order is not to take effect unless the decree has been made absolute.

(4) This section is to be read subject to any restrictions imposed by this Act.

24BC. Restrictions affecting section 24BB—(1) A pension sharing order under section 24BB above may not be made in relation to a pension arrangement which—

(a) is the subject of a pension sharing order in relation to the marriage, or

(b) has been the subject of pension sharing between the parties to the marriage.

(2) A pension sharing order under section 24BB above may not be made in relation to shareable state scheme rights if—

(a) such rights are the subject of a pension sharing order in relation to the marriage, or

(b) such rights have been the subject of pension sharing between the parties to the marriage.

(3) A pension sharing order under section 24BB above may not be made in relation to the rights of a person under a pension arrangement if there is in force a requirement imposed by virtue of section 25B or 25C below which relates to benefits or future benefits to which he is entitled under the pension arrangement."]

Note. Inserted by the Welfare Reform and Pensions Act 1999, s 84(1), Sch 12, paras 64, 65 (1), (9), as from 1 December 2000 (SI 2000 No 1116).

Period of secured and unsecured payments orders

7.—(1) In section 28(1) (duration of a continuing financial provision order in favour of a party to a marriage), for paragraphs (a) and (b) substitute—

'(a) a term specified in the order which is to begin before the making of the order shall begin no earlier—

(i) where the order is made by virtue of section 22A(2)(a) or (b) above, unless sub-paragraph (ii) below applies, than the beginning of the day on which the statement of marital breakdown in question was received by the court;

(ii) where the order is made by virtue of section 22A(2)(b) above and the application for the divorce order was made following cancellation of an order preventing divorce under section 10 of the 1996 Act, than the date of the making of that application;

(iii) where the order is made by virtue of section 22A(2)(c) above, than the date of the making of the application for the divorce order; or

(iv) in any other case, than the date of the making of the application on which the order is made;

(b) a term specified in a periodical payments order or secured periodical payments order shall be so defined as not to extend beyond—

(i) in the case of a periodical payments order, the death of the party by whom the payments are to be made; or

(ii) in either case, the death of the party in whose favour the order was made or the remarriage of that party following the making of a divorce order or decree of nullity.'

(2) In section 29 (duration of continuing financial provision order in favour of a child of the family) insert after subsection (1)—

'(1A) The term specified in a periodical payments order or secured periodical payments order made in favour of a child shall be such term as the court thinks fit.

(1B) If that term is to begin before the making of the order, it may do so no earlier than—

(a) in the case of an order made by virtue of section 22A(2)(a) or (b) above, except where paragraph (b) below applies, the beginning of the day on which the statement of marital breakdown in question was received by the court;

(b) in the case of an order made by virtue of section 22A(2)(b) above where the application for the divorce order was made following cancellation of an order preventing divorce under section 10 of the 1996 Act, the date of the making of that application;

(c) in the case of an order made by virtue of section 22A(2)(c) above, the date of the making of the application for the divorce order; or

(d) in any other case, the date of the making of the application on which the order is made.'

Variations etc following reconciliations

8. Insert after section 31—

'**31A. Variation etc following reconciliations**—(1) Where, at a time before the making of a divorce order—

(a) an order ("a paragraph (a) order") for the payment of a lump sum has been made under section 22A above in favour of a party,

(b) such an order has been made in favour of a child of the family but the payment has not yet been made, or

(c) a property adjustment order ("a paragraph (c) order") has been made under section 23A above,

the court may, on an application made jointly by the parties to the marriage, vary or discharge the order.

(2) Where the court varies or discharges a paragraph (a) order, it may order the repayment of an amount equal to the whole or any part of the lump sum.

(3) Where the court varies or discharges a paragraph (c) order, it may (if the order has taken effect)—

(a) order any person to whom property was transferred in pursuance of the paragraph (c) order to transfer—

(i) the whole or any part of that property, or

(ii) the whole or any part of any property appearing to the court to represent that property,

in favour of a party to the marriage or a child of the family; or

(b) vary any settlement to which the order relates in favour of any person or extinguish or reduce any person's interest under that settlement.

(4) Where the court acts under subsection (3) it may make such supplemental provision (including a further property adjustment order or an order for the payment of a lump sum) as it thinks appropriate in consequence of any transfer, variation, extinguishment or reduction to be made under paragraph (a) or (b) of that subsection.

(5) Sections 24A and 30 above apply for the purposes of this section as they apply where the court makes a property adjustment order under section 23A or 24 above.

(6) The court shall not make an order under subsection (2), (3) or (4) above unless it appears to it that there has been a reconciliation between the parties to the marriage.

(7) The court shall also not make an order under subsection (3) or (4) above unless it appears to it that the order will not prejudice the interests of—

(a) any child of the family; or

(b) any person who has acquired any right or interest in consequence of the paragraph (c) order and is not a party to the marriage or a child of the family.'

SCHEDULE 3   Section 19(5)

STAY OF PROCEEDINGS

Introductory

1. Schedule 1 to the Domicile and Matrimonial Proceedings Act 1973 (which relates to the staying of matrimonial proceedings) is amended as follows.

Interpretation

2. In paragraph 1, for 'The following five paragraphs' substitute 'Paragraphs 2 to 6 below'.

3. For paragraph 2 substitute—

'**2.**—(1) "Matrimonial proceedings" means—

(a) marital proceedings;

(b) proceedings for nullity of marriage;

(c) proceedings for a declaration as to the validity of a marriage of the petitioner; or

(d) proceedings for a declaration as to the subsistence of such a marriage.

(2) "Marital proceedings" has the meaning given by section 20 of the Family Law Act 1996.

(3) "Divorce proceedings" means marital proceedings that are divorce proceedings by virtue of that section.'

4. Insert, after paragraph 4—

'**4A.**—(1) "Statement of marital breakdown" has the same meaning as in the Family Law Act 1996.

(2) "Relevant statement" in relation to any marital proceedings, means—

(a) the statement of marital breakdown with which the proceedings commenced; or

(b) if the proceedings are for the conversion of a separation order into a divorce order under section 4 of the Family Law Act 1996, the statement of marital breakdown by reference to which the separation order was made.'

Duty to furnish particulars of concurrent proceedings

5. For paragraph 7 substitute—

'**7.**—(1) While marital proceedings are pending in the court with respect to a marriage, this paragraph applies—

(a) to the party or parties to the marriage who made the relevant statement; and

(b) in prescribed circumstances where the statement was made by only one party, to the other party.

(2) While matrimonial proceedings of any other kind are pending in the court with respect to a marriage and the trial or first trial in those proceedings has not begun, this paragraph applies—

(a) to the petitioner; and

(b) if the respondent has included a prayer for relief in his answer, to the respondent.

(3) A person to whom this paragraph applies must give prescribed information about any proceedings which—

(a) he knows to be continuing in another jurisdiction; and

(b) are in respect of the marriage or capable of affecting its validity or subsistence.

(4) The information must be given in such manner, to such persons and on such occasions as may be prescribed.'

Obligatory stays in divorce cases

6.—(1) Paragraph 8 is amended as follows.

(2) For the words before paragraph (a) of sub-paragraph (1) substitute—

'(1) This paragraph applies where divorce proceedings are continuing in the court with respect to a marriage.

(2) Where it appears to the court, on the application of a party to the marriage—'.

(3) In sub-paragraph (1), in the words after paragraph (d), for 'proceedings' substitute 'divorce proceedings'.

(4) For sub-paragraph (2) substitute—

'(3) The effect of such an order is that, while it is in force—

(a) no application for a divorce order in relation to the marriage may be made either by reference to the relevant statement or by reference to any subsequent statement of marital breakdown; and

(b) if such an application has been made, no divorce order may be made on that application.'

Discretionary stays

7.—(1) Paragraph 9 is amended as follows.

(2) For sub-paragraph (1), substitute—

'(1) Sub-paragraph (1A) below applies where—

(a) marital proceedings are continuing in the court; or

(b) matrimonial proceedings of any other kind are continuing in the court, if the trial or first trial in the proceedings has not begun.

(1A) The court may make an order staying the proceedings if it appears to the court—

(a) that proceedings in respect of the marriage, or capable of affecting its validity or subsistence, are continuing in another jurisdiction; and

(b) that the balance of fairness (including convenience) as between the parties to the marriage is such that it is appropriate for proceedings in that jurisdiction to be disposed of before further steps are taken in the proceedings to which the order relates.'

(3) For sub-paragraph (3) substitute—

'(3) Where an application for a stay is pending under paragraph 8 above, the court shall not make an order under sub-paragraph (1A) staying marital proceedings in relation to the marriage.'

(4) In sub-paragraph 4, after 'pending in the court,' insert 'other than marital proceedings,'.

(5) After sub-paragraph (4), insert—

'(5) The effect of an order under sub-paragraph (1A) for a stay of marital proceedings is that, while it is in force—

(a) no application for a divorce order or separation order in relation to the marriage may be made either by reference to the relevant statement or by reference to any subsequent statement of marital breakdown; and

(b) if such an application has been made, no divorce order or separation order shall be made on that application.'

Discharge of orders

8. In paragraph 10, for sub-paragraph (2), substitute—

'(1A) Where the court discharges an order staying any proceedings, it may direct that the whole or a specified part of any period while the order has been in force—

(a) is not to count towards any period specified in section 5(3) or 7(9) of the Family Law Act 1996; or

(b) is to count towards any such period only for specified purposes.

(2) Where the court discharges an order under paragraph 8 above, it shall not again make such an order in relation to the marriage except in a case where the obligation to do so arises under that paragraph following receipt by the court of a statement of marital breakdown after the discharge of the order.'

Ancillary matters

9.—(1) Paragraph 11 is amended as follows.

(2) For sub-paragraph (1) substitute—

'(1) Sub-paragraphs (2) and (3) below apply where a stay of marital proceedings or proceedings for nullity of marriage—

(a) has been imposed by reference to proceedings in a related jurisdiction for divorce, separation or nullity of marriage, and

(b) is in force.

(1A) In this paragraph—

"lump sum order", in relation to a stay, means an order—

(a) under section 22A or 23, 31 or 31A of the Matrimonial Causes Act 1973 which is an order for the payment of a lump sum for the purposes of Part II of that Act, or

(b) made in any equivalent circumstances under Schedule 1 to the Children Act 1989 and of a kind mentioned in paragraph 1(2)(a) or (b) of that Schedule,

so far as it satisfies the condition mentioned in sub-paragraph (1C) below;

"the other proceedings", in relation to a stay, means the proceedings in another jurisdiction by reference to which the stay was imposed;

"relevant order", in relation to a stay, means—

(a) any financial provision order (including an interim order), other than a lump sum order;

(b) any order made in equivalent circumstances under Schedule 1 to the Children Act 1989 and of a kind mentioned in paragraph 1(2)(a) or (b) of that Schedule;

(c) any section 8 order under the Act of 1989; and

(d) except for the purposes of sub-paragraph (3) below, any order restraining a person from removing a child out of England and Wales or out of the care of another person,

so far as it satisfies the condition mentioned in sub-paragraph (1C) below.

(1C) The condition is that the order is, or (apart from this paragraph) could be, made in connection with the proceedings to which the stay applies.'

(3) In sub-paragraph (2)—

(a) for 'any proceedings are stayed' substitute 'this paragraph applies in relation to a stay';

(b) in paragraph (a), and in the first place in paragraph (c), omit 'in connection with the stayed proceedings'; and

(c) in paragraphs (b) and (c), for 'made in connection with the stayed proceedings' substitute 'already made'.

(4) In sub-paragraph (3)—

(a) for 'any proceedings are stayed' substitute 'this paragraph applies in relation to a stay';

(b) in paragraph (a), for 'made in connection with the stayed proceedings' substitute 'already made';

(c) in paragraphs (b) and (c), omit 'in connection with the stayed proceedings'.

(5) In sub-paragraph (3A), for the words before 'any order made' substitute—

'Where a secured periodical payments order within the meaning of the Matrimonial Causes Act 1973—

(a) has been made under section 22A(1)(b) or 23(1)(b) or (2)(b) of that Act, but

(b) ceases to have effect by virtue of sub-paragraph (2) or (3) above,'.

(6) For sub-paragraph (4), substitute—

'(4) Nothing in sub-paragraphs (2) and (3) above affects any relevant order or lump sum order or any power to make such an order in so far as—

(a) where the stay applies to matrimonial proceedings other than marital proceedings, the order has been made or the power may be exercised following the receipt by the court of a statement of marital breakdown;

(b) where the stay is of marital proceedings, the order has been made or the power may be exercised in matrimonial proceedings of any other kind; or

(c) where the stay is of divorce proceedings only, the order has been made or the power may be exercised—

    (i) in matrimonial proceedings which are not marital proceedings, or

    (ii) in marital proceedings in which an application has been made for a separation order.'

(7) In sub-paragraph (5)(c), for the words from 'in connection' onwards substitute 'where a stay no longer applies'.

SCHEDULE 4   Section 32

PROVISIONS SUPPLEMENTARY TO SECTIONS 30 AND 31

Interpretation

1.—(1) In this Schedule—

(a) any reference to a solicitor includes a reference to a licensed conveyancer or a recognised body, and

(b) any reference to a person's solicitor includes a reference to a licensed conveyancer or recognised body acting for that person.

(2) In sub-paragraph (1)—

'licensed conveyancer' has the meaning given by section 11(2) of the Administration of Justice Act 1985;

'recognised body' means a body corporate for the time being recognised under section 9 (incorporated practices) or section 32 (provision of conveyancing by recognised bodies) of that Act.

Restriction on registration where spouse entitled to more than one charge

2. Where one spouse is entitled by virtue of section 31 to a registrable charge in respect of each of two or more dwelling-houses, only one of the charges to which that spouse is so entitled shall be registered under section 31(10) or under section 2 of the Land Charges Act 1972 at any one time, and if any of those charges is registered under either of those provisions the Chief Land Registrar, on being satisfied that any other of them is so registered, shall cancel the registration of the charge first registered.

Contract for sale of house affected by registered charge to include term requiring cancellation of registration before completion

3.—(1) Where one spouse is entitled by virtue of section 31 to a charge on an estate in a dwelling-house and the charge is registered under section 31(10) or section 2 of the Land Charges Act 1972, it shall be a term of any contract for the sale of that estate whereby the vendor agrees to give vacant possession of the dwelling-house on completion of the contract that the vendor will before such completion procure the cancellation of the registration of the charge at his expense.

(2) Sub-paragraph (1) shall not apply to any such contract made by a vendor who is entitled to sell the estate in the dwelling-house freed from any such charge.

(3) If, on the completion of such a contract as is referred to in sub-paragraph (1), there is delivered to the purchaser or his solicitor an application by the spouse entitled to the charge for the cancellation of the registration of that charge, the term of the contract for which sub-paragraph (1) provides shall be deemed to have been performed.

(4) This paragraph applies only if and so far as a contrary intention is not expressed in the contract.

(5) This paragraph shall apply to a contract for exchange as it applies to a contract for sale.

(6) This paragraph shall, with the necessary modifications, apply to a contract for the grant of a lease or underlease of a dwelling-house as it applies to a contract for the sale of an estate in a dwelling-house.

Cancellation of registration after termination of marriage, etc

4.—(1) Where a spouse's matrimonial home rights are a charge on an estate in the dwelling-house and the charge is registered under section 31(10) or under section 2 of the Land Charges Act 1972, the Chief Land Registrar shall, subject to sub-paragraph (2), cancel the registration of the charge if he is satisfied—
- (a) by the production of a certificate or other sufficient evidence, that either spouse is dead, or
- (b) by the production of an official copy of a decree or order of a court, that the marriage in question has been terminated otherwise than by death, or
- (c) by the production of an order of the court, that the spouse's matrimonial home rights constituting the charge have been terminated by the order.

(2) Where—
- (a) the marriage in question has been terminated by the death of the spouse entitled to an estate in the dwelling-house or otherwise than by death, and
- (b) an order affecting the charge of the spouse not so entitled had been made under section 33(5),

then if, after the making of the order, registration of the charge was renewed or the charge registered in pursuance of sub-paragraph (3), the Chief Land Registrar shall not cancel the registration of the charge in accordance with sub-paragraph (1) unless he is also satisfied that the order has ceased to have effect.

(3) Where such an order has been made, then, for the purposes of sub-paragraph (2), the spouse entitled to the charge affected by the order may—
- (a) if before the date of the order the charge was registered under section 31(10) or under section 2 of the Land Charges Act 1972, renew the registration of the charge, and
- (b) if before the said date the charge was not so registered, register the charge under section 31(10) or under section 2 of the Land Charges Act 1972.

(4) Renewal of the registration of a charge in pursuance of sub-paragraph (3) shall be effected in such manner as may be prescribed, and an application for such renewal or for registration of a charge in pursuance of that sub-paragraph shall contain such particulars of any order affecting the charge made under section 33(5) as may be prescribed.

(5) The renewal in pursuance of sub-paragraph (3) of the registration of a charge shall not affect the priority of the charge.

(6) In this paragraph 'prescribed' means prescribed by rules made under section 16 of the Land Charges Act 1972 or *section 144 of the Land Registration Act 1925* [by land registration rules under the Land Registration Act 2002], as the circumstances of the case require.

Note. Words in italics substituted by words in square brackets by the Land Registration Act 2002, s 133, Sch 11, para 34(1), (3) as from 13 October 2003: see SI 2003/1725, art 2(1).

Release of matrimonial home rights

5.—(1) A spouse entitled to matrimonial home rights may by a release in writing release those rights or release them as respects part only of the dwelling-house affected by them.

(2) Where a contract is made for the sale of an estate or interest in a dwelling-house, or for the grant of a lease or underlease of a dwelling-house, being (in either case) a dwelling-house affected by a charge registered under section 31(10) or under

section 2 of the Land Charges Act 1972, then, without prejudice to sub-paragraph (1), the matrimonial home rights constituting the charge shall be deemed to have been released on the happening of whichever of the following events first occurs—

(a) the delivery to the purchaser or lessee, as the case may be, or his solicitor on completion of the contract of an application by the spouse entitled to the charge for the cancellation of the registration of the charge; or

(b) the lodging of such an application at Her Majesty's Land Registry.

Postponement of priority of charge

6. A spouse entitled by virtue of section 31 to a charge on an estate or interest may agree in writing that any other charge on, or interest in, that estate or interest shall rank in priority to the charge to which that spouse is so entitled.

SCHEDULE 5   Section 47(11)

POWERS OF HIGH COURT AND COUNTY COURT TO REMAND

Interpretation

1. In this Schedule 'the court' means the High Court or a county court and includes—

(a) in relation to the High Court, a judge of that court, and

(b) in relation to a county court, a judge or district judge of that court.

Remand in custody or on bail

2.—(1) Where a court has power to remand a person under section 47, the court may—

(a) remand him in custody, that is to say, commit him to custody to be brought before the court at the end of the period of remand or at such earlier time as the court may require, or

(b) remand him on bail—

(i) by taking from him a recognizance (with or without sureties) conditioned as provided in sub-paragraph (3), or

(ii) by fixing the amount of the recognizances with a view to their being taken subsequently in accordance with paragraph 4 and in the meantime committing the person to custody in accordance with paragraph (a).

(2) Where a person is brought before the court after remand, the court may further remand him.

(3) Where a person is remanded on bail under sub-paragraph (1), the court may direct that his recognizance be conditioned for his appearance—

(a) before that court at the end of the period of remand, or

(b) at every time and place to which during the course of the proceedings the hearing may from time to time be adjourned.

(4) Where a recognizance is conditioned for a person's appearance in accordance with sub-paragraph (1)(b), the fixing of any time for him next to appear shall be deemed to be a remand; but nothing in this sub-paragraph or sub-paragraph (3) shall deprive the court of power at any subsequent hearing to remand him afresh.

(5) Subject to paragraph 3, the court shall not remand a person under this paragraph for a period exceeding 8 clear days, except that—

(a) if the court remands him on bail, it may remand him for a longer period if he and the other party consent, and

(b) if the court adjourns a case under section 48(1), the court may remand him for the period of the adjournment.

(6) Where the court has power under this paragraph to remand a person in custody it may, if the remand is for a period not exceeding 3 clear days, commit him to the custody of a constable.

Further remand

3.—(1) If the court is satisfied that any person who has been remanded under paragraph 2 is unable by reason of illness or accident to appear or be brought before the court at the expiration of the period for which he was remanded, the court may, in his absence, remand him for a further time; and paragraph 2(5) shall not apply.

(2) Notwithstanding anything in paragraph 2(1), the power of the court under sub-paragraph (1) to remand a person on bail for a further time may be exercised by enlarging his recognizance and those of any sureties for him to a later time.

(3) Where a person remanded on bail under paragraph 2 is bound to appear before the court at any time and the court has no power to remand him under sub-paragraph (1), the court may in his absence enlarge his recognizance and those of any sureties for him to a later time; and the enlargement of his recognizance shall be deemed to be a further remand.

Postponement of taking of recognizance

4. Where under paragraph 2(1)(b)(ii) the court fixes the amount in which the principal and his sureties, if any, are to be bound, the recognizance may thereafter be taken by such person as may be prescribed by rules of court, and the same consequences shall follow as if it had been entered into before the court.

SCHEDULE 6   Section 52

AMENDMENTS OF CHILDREN ACT 1989

1. After section 38 of the Children Act 1989 insert—

'**38A. Power to include exclusion requirement in interim care order**—(1) Where—
   (a) on being satisfied that there are reasonable grounds for believing that the circumstances with respect to a child are as mentioned in section 31(2)(a) and (b)(i), the court makes an interim care order with respect to a child, and
   (b) the conditions mentioned in subsection (2) are satisfied,
the court may include an exclusion requirement in the interim care order.
   (2) The conditions are—
   (a) that there is reasonable cause to believe that, if a person ("the relevant person") is excluded from a dwelling-house in which the child lives, the child will cease to suffer, or cease to be likely to suffer, significant harm, and
   (b) that another person living in the dwelling-house (whether a parent of the child or some other person)—
      (i) is able and willing to give to the child the care which it would be reasonable to expect a parent to give him, and
      (ii) consents to the inclusion of the exclusion requirement.
   (3) For the purposes of this section an exclusion requirement is any one or more of the following—
   (a) a provision requiring the relevant person to leave a dwelling-house in which he is living with the child,
   (b) a provision prohibiting the relevant person from entering a dwelling-house in which the child lives, and
   (c) a provision excluding the relevant person from a defined area in which a dwelling-house in which the child lives is situated.
   (4) The court may provide that the exclusion requirement is to have effect for a shorter period than the other provisions of the interim care order.
   (5) Where the court makes an interim care order containing an exclusion requirement, the court may attach a power of arrest to the exclusion requirement.

(6) Where the court attaches a power of arrest to an exclusion requirement of an interim care order, it may provide that the power of arrest is to have effect for a shorter period than the exclusion requirement.

(7) Any period specified for the purposes of subsection (4) or (6) may be extended by the court (on one or more occasions) on an application to vary or discharge the interim care order.

(8) Where a power of arrest is attached to an exclusion requirement of an interim care order by virtue of subsection (5), a constable may arrest without warrant any person whom he has reasonable cause to believe to be in breach of the requirement.

(9) Sections 47(7), (11) and (12) and 48 of, and Schedule 5 to, the Family Law Act 1996 shall have effect in relation to a person arrested under subsection (8) of this section as they have effect in relation to a person arrested under section 47(6) of that Act.

(10) If, while an interim care order containing an exclusion requirement is in force, the local authority have removed the child from the dwelling-house from which the relevant person is excluded to other accommodation for a continuous period of more than 24 hours, the interim care order shall cease to have effect in so far as it imposes the exclusion requirement.

38B. Undertakings relating to interim care orders—(1) In any case where the court has power to include an exclusion requirement in an interim care order, the court may accept an undertaking from the relevant person.

(2) No power of arrest may be attached to any undertaking given under subsection (1).

(3) An undertaking given to a court under subsection (1)—

(a) shall be enforceable as if it were an order of the court, and

(b) shall cease to have effect if, while it is in force, the local authority have removed the child from the dwelling house from which the relevant person is excluded to other accommodation for a continuous period of more than 24 hours.

(4) This section has effect without prejudice to the powers of the High Court and county court apart from this section.

(5) In this section "exclusion requirement" and "relevant person" have the same meaning as in section 38A.'

2. In section 39 of the Children Act 1989 (discharge and variation etc of care orders and supervision orders) after subsection (3) insert—

'(3A) On the application of a person who is not entitled to apply for the order to be discharged, but who is a person to whom an exclusion requirement contained in the order applies, an interim care order may be varied or discharged by the court in so far as it imposes the exclusion requirement.

(3B) Where a power of arrest has been attached to an exclusion requirement of an interim care order, the court may, on the application of any person entitled to apply for the discharge of the order so far as it imposes the exclusion requirement, vary or discharge the order in so far as it confers a power of arrest (whether or not any application has been made to vary or discharge any other provision of the order).'

3. After section 44 of the Children Act 1989 insert—

'**44A. Power to include exclusion requirement in emergency protection order**—(1) Where—

(a) on being satisfied as mentioned in section 44(1)(a), (b) emergency or (c), the court makes an emergency protection order with respect to a child, and

(b) the conditions mentioned in subsection (2) are satisfied,

the court may include an exclusion requirement in the emergency protection order.

(2) The conditions are—

(a) that there is reasonable cause to believe that, if a person ("the relevant person") is excluded from a dwelling-house in which the child lives, then—

   (i) in the case of an order made on the ground mentioned in section 44(1)(a), the child will not be likely to suffer significant harm, even though the child is not removed as mentioned in section 44(1)(a)(i) or does not remain as mentioned in section 44(1)(a)(ii), or

   (ii) in the case of an order made on the ground mentioned in paragraph (b) or (c) of section 44(1), the enquiries referred to in that paragraph will cease to be frustrated, and

(b) that another person living in the dwelling-house (whether a parent of the child or some other person)—

   (i) is able and willing to give to the child the care which it would be reasonable to expect a parent to give him, and

   (ii) consents to the inclusion of the exclusion requirement.

(3) For the purposes of this section an exclusion requirement is any one or more of the following—

(a) a provision requiring the relevant person to leave a dwelling-house in which he is living with the child,

(b) a provision prohibiting the relevant person from entering a dwelling-house in which the child lives, and

(c) a provision excluding the relevant person from a defined area in which a dwelling-house in which the child lives is situated.

(4) The court may provide that the exclusion requirement is to have effect for a shorter period than the other provisions of the order.

(5) Where the court makes an emergency protection order containing an exclusion requirement, the court may attach a power of arrest to the exclusion requirement.

(6) Where the court attaches a power of arrest to an exclusion requirement of an emergency protection order, it may provide that the power of arrest is to have effect for a shorter period than the exclusion requirement.

(7) Any period specified for the purposes of subsection (4) or (6) may be extended by the court (on one or more occasions) on an application to vary or discharge the emergency protection order.

(8) Where a power of arrest is attached to an exclusion requirement of an emergency protection order by virtue of subsection (5), a constable may arrest without warrant any person whom he has reasonable cause to believe to be in breach of the requirement.

(9) Sections 47(7), (11) and (12) and 48 of, and Schedule 5 to, the Family Law Act 1996 shall have effect in relation to a person arrested under subsection (8) of this section as they have effect in relation to a person arrested under section 47(6) of that Act.

(10) If, while an emergency protection order containing an exclusion requirement is in force, the applicant has removed the child from the dwelling-house from which the relevant person is excluded to other accommodation for a continuous period of more than 24 hours, the order shall cease to have effect in so far as it imposes the exclusion requirement.

44B. Undertakings relating to emergency protection orders—(1) In any case where the court has power to include an exclusion requirement in an emergency protection order, the court may accept an undertaking from the relevant person.

(2) No power of arrest may be attached to any undertaking given under subsection (1).

(3) An undertaking given to a court under subsection (1)—

(a) shall be enforceable as if it were an order of the court, and

(b) shall cease to have effect if, while it is in force, the applicant has removed the child from the dwelling-house from which the relevant person is excluded to other accommodation for a continuous period of more than 24 hours.

(4) This section has effect without prejudice to the powers of the High Court and county court apart from this section.

(5) In this section "exclusion requirement" and "relevant person" have the same meaning as in section 44A.'

4. In section 45 of the Children Act 1989 (duration of emergency protection orders and other supplemental provisions), insert after subsection (8)—

'(8A) On the application of a person who is not entitled to apply for the order to be discharged, but who is a person to whom an exclusion requirement contained in the order applies, an emergency protection order may be varied or discharged by the court in so far as it imposes the exclusion requirement.

(8B) Where a power of arrest has been attached to an exclusion requirement of an emergency protection order, the court may, on the application of any person entitled to apply for the discharge of the order so far as it imposes the exclusion requirement, vary or discharge the order in so far as it confers a power of arrest (whether or not any application has been made to vary or discharge any other provision of the order).'

5. In section 105(1) of the Children Act 1989 (interpretation), after the definition of 'domestic premises', insert—

' "dwelling-house" includes—

(a) any building or part of a building which is occupied as a dwelling;

(b) any caravan, house-boat or structure which is occupied as a dwelling;

and any yard, garden, garage or outhouse belonging to it and occupied with it;'.

SCHEDULE 7   Section 53

TRANSFER OF CERTAIN TENANCIES ON DIVORCE ETC OR ON SEPARATION OF COHABITANTS

PART I

GENERAL

Interpretation

1. In this Schedule—

'cohabitant', except in paragraph 3, includes (where the context requires) former cohabitant;

'the court' does not include a magistrates' court,

'landlord' includes—

(a) any person from time to time deriving title under the original landlord; and

(b) in relation to any dwelling-house, any person other than the tenant who is, or (but for Part VII of the Rent Act 1977 or Part II of the Rent (Agriculture) Act 1976) would be, entitled to possession of the dwelling-house;

'Part II order' means an order under Part II of this Schedule;

'a relevant tenancy' means—

(a) a protected tenancy or statutory tenancy within the meaning of the Rent Act 1977;

(b) a statutory tenancy within the meaning of the Rent (Agriculture) Act 1976;

(c) a secure tenancy within the meaning of section 79 of the Housing Act 1985; *or*

(d) an assured tenancy or assured agricultural occupancy within the meaning of Part I of the Housing Act 1988; [or

(e) an introductory tenancy within the meaning of Chapter I of Part V of the Housing Act 1996;]

'spouse', except in paragraph 2, includes (where the context requires) former spouse; and

'tenancy' includes sub-tenancy.

Note. In definition 'a relevant tenancy' word in italics repealed and words in square brackets added, by Housing Act 1996 (Consequential Amendments) Order 1997, SI 1997 No 74, art 2, Schedule, para 10(b), as from 12 February 1997.

Cases in which the court may make an order

2.—(1) This paragraph applies if one spouse is entitled, either in his own right or jointly with the other spouse, to occupy a dwelling-house by virtue of a relevant tenancy.

(2) *At any time when it has power to make a property adjustment order under section 23A (divorce or separation) or 24 (nullity) of the Matrimonial Causes Act 1973 with respect to the marriage, the court may make a Part II order.*

Note. Until such time as Part II of the Family Law Act 1996 is brought into force, para (2) is substituted, by virtue of SI 1997/1892, as follows—

"(2) On granting a decree of divorce, a decree of nullity of marriage or a decree of judicial separation or at any time thereafter (whether, in the case of a decree of divorce or nullity of marriage, before or after the decree is made absolute), the court may make a Part II order."

3.—(1) This paragraph applies if one cohabitant is entitled, either in his own right or jointly with the other cohabitant, to occupy a dwelling-house by virtue of a relevant tenancy.

(2) If the cohabitants cease to live together as husband and wife, the court may make a Part II order.

4. The court shall not make a Part II order unless the dwelling-house is or was—

   (a) in the case of spouses, a matrimonial home; or
   (b) in the case of cohabitants, a home in which they lived together as husband and wife.

Matters to which the court must have regard

5. In determining whether to exercise its powers under Part II of this Schedule and, if so, in what manner, the court shall have regard to all the circumstances of the case including—

   (a) the circumstances in which the tenancy was granted to either or both of the spouses or cohabitants or, as the case requires, the circumstances in which either or both of them became tenant under the tenancy;
   (b) the matters mentioned in section 33(6)(a), (b) and (c) and, where the parties are cohabitants and only one of them is entitled to occupy the dwelling-house by virtue of the relevant tenancy, the further matters mentioned in section 36(6)(e), (f), (g) and (h); and
   (c) the suitability of the parties as tenants.

PART II

ORDERS THAT MAY BE MADE

References to entitlement to occupy

6. References in this Part of this Schedule to a spouse or a cohabitant being entitled to occupy a dwelling-house by virtue of a relevant tenancy apply whether that entitlement is in his own right or jointly with the other spouse or cohabitant.

Protected, secure or assured tenancy or assured agricultural occupancy

7.—(1) If a spouse or cohabitant is entitled to occupy the dwelling-house by virtue of a protected tenancy within the meaning of the Rent Act 1977, a secure tenancy within the meaning of the Housing Act 1985 *or an assured tenancy* [, an assured tenancy] or assured agricultural occupancy within the meaning of Part I of the Housing Act 1988 [or an introductory tenancy within the meaning of Chapter I of Part V of the Housing Act 1996], the court may by order direct that, as from such date as may be specified in the order, there shall, by virtue of the order and without further assurance, be transferred to, and vested in, the other spouse or cohabitant—

    (a) the estate or interest which the spouse or cohabitant so entitled had in the dwelling-house immediately before that date by virtue of the lease or agreement creating the tenancy and any assignment of that lease or agreement, with all rights, privileges and appurtenances attaching to that estate or interest but subject to all covenants, obligations, liabilities and incumbrances to which it is subject; and

    (b) where the spouse or cohabitant so entitled is an assignee of such lease or agreement, the liability of that spouse or cohabitant under any covenant of indemnity by the assignee express or implied in the assignment of the lease or agreement to that spouse or cohabitant.

    (2) If an order is made under this paragraph, any liability or obligation to which the spouse or cohabitant so entitled is subject under any covenant having reference to the dwelling-house in the lease or agreement, being a liability or obligation falling due to be discharged or performed on or after the date so specified, shall not be enforceable against that spouse or cohabitant.

    (3) If the spouse so entitled is a successor within the meaning of Part IV of the Housing Act 1985, his former spouse or former cohabitant (*or, if a separation order is in force, his spouse*) shall be deemed also to be a successor within the meaning of that Part.

    [(3A) If the Spouse or cohabitant so entitled is a successor within the meaning of section 132 of the Housing Act 1996, his former spouse or former cohabitant (or, if a separation order is in force, his spouse) shall be deemed also to be a successor within the meaning of that section.]

    (4) If the spouse or cohabitant so entitled is for the purpose of section 17 of the Housing Act 1988 a successor in relation to the tenancy or occupancy, his former spouse or former cohabitant (*or, if a separation order is in force, his spouse*) is to be deemed to be a successor in relation to the tenancy or occupancy for the purposes of that section.

    (5) If the transfer under sub-paragraph (1) is of an assured agricultural occupancy, then, for the purposes of Chapter III of Part I of the Housing Act 1988—

    (a) the agricultural worker condition is fulfilled with respect to the dwelling-house while the spouse or cohabitant to whom the assured agricultural occupancy is transferred continues to be the occupier under that occupancy, and

    (b) that condition is to be treated as so fulfilled by virtue of the same paragraph of Schedule 3 to the Housing Act 1988 as was applicable before the transfer.

    (6) *In this paragraph, references to a separation order being in force include references to there being a judicial separation in force.*

Note. First words in square bracket in para (1) substituted for words in italics, and second words in square brackets in para (1) inserted, by Housing Act 1996 (Consequential Amendments) Order 1997, SI 1997 No 74, art 2, Schedule, para 10(b), as from 12 February 1997.

Sub-para (3A) inserted by Housing Act 1996 (Consequential Amendments) Order 1997, SI 1997 No 74, art 2, Schedule, para 10(b), as from 12 February 1997.

Note. Until such time as Part II of the Family Law Act 1996 is brought into force, the words in italics in paras (3) and (4) are substituted by the words "(or, in the case of judicial separation, his spouse)" and para (6) is omitted, by virtue of SI 1997/1892.

Statutory tenancy within the meaning of the Rent Act 1977

8.—(1) This paragraph applies if the spouse or cohabitant is entitled to occupy the dwelling-house by virtue of a statutory tenancy within the meaning of the Rent Act 1977.

    (2) The court may by order direct that, as from the date specified in the order—

    (a) that spouse or cohabitant is to cease to be entitled to occupy the dwelling-house; and

    (b) the other spouse or cohabitant is to be deemed to be the tenant or, as the case may be, the sole tenant under that statutory tenancy.

(3) The question whether the provisions of paragraphs 1 to 3, or (as the case may be) paragraphs 5 to 7 of Schedule 1 to the Rent Act 1977, as to the succession by the surviving spouse of a deceased tenant, or by a member of the deceased tenant's family, to the right to retain possession are capable of having effect in the event of the death of the person deemed by an order under this paragraph to be the tenant or sole tenant under the statutory tenancy is to be determined according as those provisions have or have not already had effect in relation to the statutory tenancy.

Statutory tenancy within the meaning of the Rent (Agriculture) Act 1976

9.—(1) This paragraph applies if the spouse or cohabitant is entitled to occupy the dwelling-house by virtue of a statutory tenancy within the meaning of the Rent (Agriculture) Act 1976.

(2) The court may by order direct that, as from such date as may be specified in the order—

(a)   that spouse or cohabitant is to cease to be entitled to occupy the dwelling-house; and

(b)   the other spouse or cohabitant is to be deemed to be the tenant or, as the case may be, the sole tenant under that statutory tenancy.

(3) A spouse or cohabitant who is deemed under this paragraph to be the tenant under a statutory tenancy is (within the meaning of that Act) a statutory tenant in his own right, or a statutory tenant by succession, according as the other spouse or cohabitant was a statutory tenant in his own right or a statutory tenant by succession.

PART III

SUPPLEMENTARY PROVISIONS

Compensation

10.—(1) If the court makes a Part II order, it may by the order direct the making of a payment by the spouse or cohabitant to whom the tenancy is transferred ('the transferee') to the other spouse or cohabitant ('the transferor').

(2) Without prejudice to that, the court may, on making an order by virtue of sub-paragraph (1) for the payment of a sum—

(a)   direct that payment of that sum or any part of it is to be deferred until a specified date or until the occurrence of a specified event, or

(b)   direct that that sum or any part of it is to be paid by instalments.

(3) Where an order has been made by virtue of sub-paragraph (1), the court may, on the application of the transferee or the transferor—

(a)   exercise its powers under sub-paragraph (2), or

(b)   vary any direction previously given under that sub-paragraph,

at any time before the sum whose payment is required by the order is paid in full.

(4) In deciding whether to exercise its powers under this paragraph and, if so, in what manner, the court shall have regard to all the circumstances including—

(a)   the financial loss that would otherwise be suffered by the transferor as a result of the order;

(b)   the financial needs and financial resources of the parties; and

(c)   the financial obligations which the parties have, or are likely to have in the foreseeable future, including financial obligations to each other and to any relevant child.

(5) The court shall not give any direction under sub-paragraph (2) unless it appears to it that immediate payment of the sum required by the order would cause the transferee financial hardship which is greater than any financial hardship that would be caused to the transferor if the direction were given.

Liabilities and obligations in respect of the dwelling-house

11.—(1) If the court makes a Part II order, it may by the order direct that both spouses or cohabitants are to be jointly and severally liable to discharge or perform any or all of the liabilities and obligations in respect of the dwelling-house (whether arising under the tenancy or otherwise) which—

    (a) have at the date of the order fallen due to be discharged or performed by one only of them; or

    (b) but for the direction, would before the date specified as the date on which the order is to take effect fall due to be discharged or performed by one only of them.

    (2) If the court gives such a direction, it may further direct that either spouse or cohabitant is to be liable to indemnify the other in whole or in part against any payment made or expenses incurred by the other in discharging or performing any such liability or obligation.

Date when order made between spouses is to take effect

12.—(1) In the case of a decree of [divorce or] nullity of marriage, the date specified in a Part II order as the date on which the order is to take effect must not be earlier than the date on which the decree is made absolute.

    (2) In the case of divorce proceedings or separation proceedings, the date specified in a Part II order as the date on which the order is to take effect is to be determined as if the court were making a property adjustment order under section 23A of the Matrimonial Causes Act 1973 (regard being had to the restrictions imposed by section 23B of that Act).

Note. Until such time as Part II of the Family Law Act 1996 is brought into force, the words in square brackets in para (1) are inserted and para (2) is omitted, by virtue of SI 1997/1892.

Remarriage of either spouse

13.—(1) If after *the making of a divorce order or* the grant of a decree [dissolving or] annulling a marriage either spouse remarries, that spouse is not entitled to apply, by reference to *the making of that order or* the grant of that decree, for a Part II order.

    (2) For the avoidance of doubt it is hereby declared that the reference in sub-paragraph (1) to remarriage includes a reference to a marriage which is by law void or voidable.

Note. Until such time as Part II of the Family Law Act 1996 is brought into force, the words in italics in para (1) are omitted and the words in square brackets are inserted, by virtue of SI 1997/1892.

Rules of court

14.—(1) Rules of court shall be made requiring the court, before it makes an order under this Schedule, to give the landlord of the dwelling-house to which the order will relate an opportunity of being heard.

    (2) Rules of court may provide that an application for a Part II order by reference to an order or decree may not, without the leave of the court by which that order was made or decree was granted, be made after the expiration of such period from the order or grant as may be prescribed by the rules.

Saving for other provisions of Act

15.—(1) If a spouse is entitled to occupy a dwelling-house by virtue of a tenancy, this Schedule does not affect the operation of sections 30 and 31 in relation to the other spouse's matrimonial home rights.

    (2) If a spouse or cohabitant is entitled to occupy a dwelling-house by virtue of a tenancy, the court's powers to make orders under this Schedule are additional to those conferred by sections 33, 35 and 36.

SCHEDULE 8   Section 66(1)

MINOR AND CONSEQUENTIAL AMENDMENTS

PART I

AMENDMENTS CONNECTED WITH PART II

Wills Act 1837 (c 26)

1. In section 18A(1) of the Wills Act 1837 (effect of dissolution or annulment of marriage on wills), for 'a decree' substitute 'an order or decree'.

Judicial Proceedings (Regulation of Reports) Act 1926 (c 61)

2. In section 1(1)(b) of the Judicial Proceedings (Regulation of Reports) Act 1926 (restriction on reporting) after 'in relation to' insert 'any proceedings under Part II of the Family Law Act 1996 or otherwise in relation to'.

Maintenance Orders Act 1950 (c 37)

3. In section 16 of the Maintenance Orders Act 1950 (orders to which Part II of that Act applies)—
  (a) in subsection (2)(a)(i), for '23(1), (2) and (4)' substitute '22A, 23'; and
  (b) in subsection (2)(c)(v), after 'Matrimonial Causes Act 1973' insert '(as that Act had effect immediately before the passing of the Family Law Act 1996)'.

Matrimonial Causes Act 1973 (c 18)

4. The 1973 Act is amended as follows.

5. In section 8 (intervention of Queen's Proctor)—
  (a) for 'a petition for divorce' substitute 'proceedings for a divorce order';
  (b) in subsection (1)(b), omit 'or before the decree nisi is made absolute'; and
  (c) in subsection (2), for 'a decree nisi in any proceedings for divorce' substitute 'the making of a divorce order'.

6. For section 15 (application of provisions relating to divorce to nullity proceedings) substitute—

'**15. Decrees of nullity to be decrees nisi.**   Every decree of nullity of marriage shall in the first instance be a decree nisi and shall not be made absolute before the end of six weeks from its grant unless—
  (a) the High Court by general order from time to time fixes a shorter period; or
  (b) in any particular case, the court in which the proceedings are for the time being pending from time to time by special order fixes a shorter period than the period otherwise applicable for the time being by virtue of this section.

15A. Intervention of Queen's Proctor—(1) In the case of a petition for nullity of marriage—
  (a) the court may, if it thinks fit, direct all necessary papers in the matter to be sent to the Queen's Proctor, who shall under the directions of the Attorney-General instruct counsel to argue before the court any question in relation to the matter which the court considers it necessary or expedient to have fully argued;
  (b) any person may at any time during the progress of the proceedings or before the decree nisi is made absolute give information to the Queen's Proctor on any matter material to the due decision of the case, and the Queen's Proctor may thereupon take such steps as the Attorney-General considers necessary or expedient.
  (2) If the Queen's Proctor intervenes or shows cause against a decree nisi in any proceedings for nullity of marriage, the court may make such order as may be just as to the payment by other parties to the proceedings of the costs

incurred by him in so doing or as to the payment by him of any costs incurred by any of those parties by reason of his so doing.

(3) Subsection (3) of section 8 above applies in relation to this section as it applies in relation to that section.

15B. Proceedings after decree nisi: general powers of court—(1) Where a decree of nullity of marriage has been granted under this Act but not made absolute, then, without prejudice to section 15A above, any person (excluding a party to the proceedings other than the Queen's Proctor) may show cause why the decree should not be made absolute by reason of material facts not having been brought before the court; and in such a case the court may—

   (a) notwithstanding anything in section 15 above (but subject to section 41 below) make the decree absolute; or

   (b) rescind the decree; or

   (c) require further inquiry; or

   (d) otherwise deal with the case as it thinks fit.

(2) Where a decree of nullity of marriage has been granted under this Act and no application for it to be made absolute has been made by the party to whom it was granted, then, at any time after the expiration of three months from the earliest date on which that party could have made such an application, the party against whom it was granted may make an application to the court, and on that application the court may exercise any of the powers mentioned in paragraphs (a) to (d) of subsection (1) above.'

7. In section 19(4) (application of provisions relating to divorce to proceedings under section 19)—

   (a) for '1(5), 8 and 9' substitute '15, 15A and 15B'; and

   (b) for 'divorce' in both places substitute 'nullity of marriage'.

8. In section 24A(1) (orders for sale of property), for 'section 23 or 24 of this Act' substitute 'any of sections 22A to 24 above'.

9.—(1) Section 25 (matters to which the court is to have regard) is amended as follows.

(2) In subsection (1), for 'section 23, 24 or *24A* [24A or 24B]' substitute 'any of sections 22A to *24A* [to 24BB]'.

(3) In subsection (2)—

   (a) for 'section 23(1)(a), (b) or (c)' substitute 'section 22A or 23 above to make a financial provision order in favour of a party to a marriage or the exercise of its powers under section 23A,';

   (aa) for "or 24B" substitute ", 24B or 24BB";

   (b) in paragraph (g), after 'parties' insert ', whatever the nature of the conduct and whether it occurred during the marriage or after the separation of the parties or (as the case may be) dissolution or annulment of the marriage,'; and

   (c) in paragraph (h), omit 'in the case of proceedings for divorce or nullity of marriage,'.

(4) In subsection (3), for 'section 23(1)(d), (e) or (f), (2) or (4)' substitute 'section 22A or 23 above to make a financial provision order in favour of a child of the family or the exercise of its powers under section 23A,'.

(5) In subsection (4), for 'section 23(1)(d), (e) or (f), (2) or (4), 24 or 24A' substitute 'any of sections 22A to 24A'.

(6) After subsection (4) insert—

   '(5) In relation to any power of the court to make an interim periodical payments order or an interim order for the payment of a lump sum, the preceding provisions of this section, in imposing any obligation on the court with respect to the matters to which it is to have regard, shall not require the court to do anything which would cause such a delay as would, in the opinion of the court, be inappropriate having regard—

     (a) to any immediate need for an interim order;

     (b) to the matters in relation to which it is practicable for the court to inquire before making an interim order; and

(c) to the ability of the court to have regard to any matter and to make appropriate adjustments when subsequently making a financial provision order which is not interim.'

Note. In sub-para (2) words in square brackets substituted for words in italics, and sub para (3) (aa) inserted by the Welfare Reform and Pensions Act 1999, s 84(1), Sch 12, paras 64, 66 (1), (2), as from 1 December 2000 (SI 2000 No 1116).

10.—(1) Section 25A (requirement to consider need to provide for 'a clean break') is amended as follows.

(2) In subsection (1), for the words from the beginning to 'the marriage' substitute—

'If the court decides to exercise any of its powers under any of sections 22A to **24A** [24BB]above in favour of a party to a marriage (other than its power to make an interim periodical payments order or an interim order for the payment of a lump sum)'.

(3) In subsection (1), for 'the decree' substitute 'a divorce order or decree of nullity'.

(4) For subsection (3) substitute—

'(3) If the court—

(a) would have power under section 22A or 23 above to make a financial provision order in favour of a party to a marriage ("the first party"), but

(b) considers that no continuing obligation should be imposed on the other party to the marriage ("the second party") to make or secure periodical payments in favour of the first party,

it may direct that the first party may not at any time after the direction takes effect, apply to the court for the making against the second party of any periodical payments order or secured periodical payments order and, if the first party has already applied to the court for the making of such an order, it may dismiss the application.

(3A) If the court—

(a) exercises, or has exercised, its power under section 22A at any time before making a divorce order, and

(b) gives a direction under subsection (3) above in respect of a periodical payments order or a secured periodical payments order,

it shall provide for the direction not to take effect until a divorce order is made.'

Note. In sub-para (2), words in square brackets substituted for words in italics by the Welfare Reform and Pensions Act 1999, s 84(1), Sch 12, paras 64, 66 (1), (3), as from 1 December 2000 (SI 2000 No 1116).

11. *In each of sections 25B(2) and (3), 25C(1) and (3) and 25D(1)(a), (2)(a), (c) and (e) (benefits under a pension scheme on divorce, etc) for 'section 23' substitute 'section 22A or 23'.*

[**'11.** In each of sections 25B(3) and 25C(1) and (3), for 'section 23' substitute 'section 22A or 23'.]

Note. New para 11 substituted for old para 11 by the Welfare Reform and Pensions Act 1999, s 84(1), Sch 12, paras 64, 66 (1), (4), as from 1 December 2000 (SI 2000 No 1116).

[**11A.** In section 25D—

(a) in each of subsections (1)(a) and (2)(a) and (ab), for "section 23" substitute "section 22A or 23", and

(b) in subsection (3), in the definition of "shareable state scheme rights", for "section 21A(1)" substitute "section 21(3)".]

Note. Para 11A inserted by the Welfare Reform and Pensions Act 1999, s 84(1), Sch 12, paras 64, 66 (1), (4), as from 1 December 2000 (SI 2000 No 1116).

12. In section 26(1) (commencement of proceedings for ancillary relief), for the words from the beginning to '22 above' substitute—

'(1) If a petition for nullity of marriage has been presented, then, subject to subsection (2) below, proceedings'.

13.—(1) Section 27 (financial provision orders etc in case of failure to provide proper maintenance) is amended as follows.

(2) In subsection (5)—

(a) after 'an order requiring the respondent' insert

'—

(a)'; and

(b) at the end insert ', or

(b) to pay to the applicant such lump sum or sums as the court thinks reasonable.'

(3) For subsection (6) substitute—

'(6) Subject to the restrictions imposed by the following provisions of this Act, if on an application under this section the applicant satisfies the court of any ground mentioned in subsection (1) above, the court may make one or more financial provision orders against the respondent in favour of the applicant or a child of the family.'

(4) In subsection (7), for '(6)(c) or (f)' substitute '(6)'.

14.—(1) Section 28 (duration of continuing financial provision order in favour of a party to a marriage) is amended as follows.

(2) In subsection (1A), for the words from the beginning to 'nullity of marriage' substitute—

'(1A) At any time when—

(a) the court exercises, or has exercised, its power under section 22A or 23 above to make a financial provision order in favour of a party to a marriage,

(b) but for having exercised that power, the court would have power under one of those sections to make such an order, and

(c) an application for a divorce order or a petition for a decree of nullity of marriage is outstanding or has been granted in relation to the marriage,'

(3) Insert, after subsection (1A)—

'(1B) If the court—

(a) exercises, or has exercised, its power under section 22A at any time before making a divorce order, and

(b) gives a direction under subsection (1A) above in respect of a periodical payments order or a secured periodical payments order,

it shall provide for the direction not to take effect until a divorce order is made.'

(4) In subsection (2), for the words from 'on or after' to 'nullity of marriage' substitute 'at such a time as is mentioned in subsection (1A)(c) above'.

(5) In subsection (3)—

(a) for 'a decree' substitute 'an order or decree'; and

(b) for 'that decree' substitute 'that order or decree'.

15. In section 29(1) (duration of a continuing financial provision order in favour of a child of the family), for 'under section 24(1)(a)' substitute 'such as is mentioned in section 21(2)(a)'.

16.—(1) Section 31 (variation etc of orders) is amended as follows.

(2) In subsection (2)—

(a) after 'following orders' insert 'under this Part of this Act';

(b) for paragraph (d) substitute—

'(d) an order for the payment of a lump sum in a case in which the payment is to be by instalments;';

(c) in paragraph (dd), for '23(1)(c)' substitute '21(1)(c)';

(d) after paragraph (dd) insert—

'(de) any other order for the payment of a lump sum, if it is made at a time when no divorce order has been made, and no separation order is in force, in relation to the marriage;';

(e) for paragraph (e) substitute—

'(e) any order under section 23A of a kind referred to in section 21(2)(b), (c) or (d) which is made on or after the making of a separation order;

(ea) any order under section 23A which is made at a time when no divorce order has been made, and no separation order is in force, in relation to the marriage;'.

['(f)   after paragraph (f) there is inserted—
'(fa)   a pension sharing order under section 24B which is made at a time when
no divorce order has been made, and no separation order is in force, in
relation to the marriage;"
(g)   in paragraph (g), for "24B" substitute "24BB".']
(3)   In subsection (4)—
(a)   for the words from 'for a settlement' to '24(1)(c) or (d)', substitute
'referred to in subsection (2)(e)'; and
(b)   for paragraphs (a) and (b) substitute 'on an application for a divorce order
in relation to the marriage'.
['(3A)   In subsection (4A), after "paragraph" insert "(de), (ea), (fa) or".']
(4)   After *subsection (4) insert—*
'*(4A)   In relation to an order which falls within subsection (2)(de) or (ea) above ("the
subsection (2) order")—*
(a)   the powers conferred by this section may be exercised—
*(i)   only on an application made before the subsection (2) order has or, but for
paragraph (b) below, would have taken effect; and*
*(ii)   only if, at the time when the application is made, no divorce order has been
made in relation to the marriage and no separation order has been so made
since the subsection (2) order was made; and*
*(b)   an application made in accordance with paragraph (a) above prevents the
subsection (2) order from taking effect before the application has been dealt with.*
[subsection (4A) insert]
(4AA)   No variation—
(a)   of a financial provision order made under section 22A above, other than
an interim order, or
(b)   of a property adjustment order made under section 23A above,
shall be made so as to take effect before the making of a divorce order or
separation order in relation to the marriage, unless the court is satisfied that the
circumstances of the case are exceptional, and that it would be just and reasonable
for the variation to be so made.'
['(4AB)   No variation of a pension sharing order under section 24B above shall
be made so as to take effect before the making of a divorce order in relation to the
marriage.']
['(4A)   In subsection (4B), after "order" insert "under section 24BB above".']
(5)   In subsection (5)—
(a)   insert, at the beginning, 'Subject to subsections (7A) to (7F) below and
without prejudice to any power exercisable by virtue of subsection (2)(d),
(dd) or (e) above or otherwise than by virtue of this section,'; and
(b)   for 'section 23', in each place, substitute 'section 22A or 23'.
(6)   In subsection (7)(a)—
(a)   for 'on or after' to 'consider' substitute 'in favour of a party to a marriage,
the court shall, if the marriage has been dissolved or annulled, consider';
and
(b)   after 'sufficient' insert '(in the light of any proposed exercise by the court,
where the marriage has been dissolved, of its powers under subsection (7B)
below)'.
(7)   After subsection (7), insert—
'(7A)   Subsection (7B) below applies where, after the dissolution of a marriage,
the court—
(a)   discharges a periodical payments order or secured periodical payments
order made in favour of a party to the marriage; or
(b)   varies such an order so that payments under the order are required to be
made or secured only for such further period as is determined by the court.
(7B)   The court has power, in addition to any power it has apart from this
subsection, to make supplemental provision consisting of any of—

(a) an order for the payment of a lump sum in favour of a party to the marriage;
(b) one or more property adjustment orders in favour of a party to the marriage;
(c) a direction that the party in whose favour the original order discharged or varied was made is not entitled to make any further application for—
   (i) a periodical payments or secured periodical payments order, or
   (ii) an extension of the period to which the original order is limited by any variation made by the court.

(7C) An order for the payment of a lump sum made under subsection (7B) above may—
(a) provide for the payment of that sum by instalments of such amount as may be specified in the order; and
(b) require the payment of the instalments to be secured to the satisfaction of the court.

(7D) Subsections (7) and (8) of section 22A above apply where the court makes an order for the payment of a lump sum under subsection (7B) above as they apply where it makes such an order under section 22A above.

(7E) If under subsection (7B) above the court makes more than one property adjustment order in favour of the same party to the marriage, each of those orders must fall within a different paragraph of section 21(2) above.

(7F) Sections 24A and 30 above apply where the court makes a property adjustment order under subsection (7B) above as they apply where it makes such an order under section 23A above.'

['(8) After subsection (7F) insert—
   "(7FA) Section 24B(3) above applies where the court makes a pension sharing order under subsection (7B) above as it applies where the court makes such an order under section 24B above."

(9) In subsection (7G)—
(a) for "Subsections (3) to (5) of section 24B" substitute "Section 24BA(5) to (7)", and
(b) for "that section" substitute "section 24B above".']

Note. Sub-paras (2)(f) and (g), (3A), (4AB), (4A), (8) and (9) inserted, and words in italics in sub-para (4) substituted by words in square brackets, by the Welfare Reform and Pensions Act 1999, s 84(1), Sch 12, paras 64, 66 (1), (5)-(9), as from 1 December 2000 (SI 2000 No 1116).

['**16A.** After section 31A insert—
   "31B. Discharge of pension sharing orders on making of separation order
   Where, after the making of a pension sharing order under section 24B above in relation to a marriage, a separation order is made in relation to the marriage, the pension sharing order is discharged."']

Note. Para 16A inserted by the Welfare Reform and Pensions Act 1999, s 84(1), Sch 12, paras 64, 66 (1), (10) as from 1 December 2000 (SI 2000 No 1116).

17. In section 32(1) (payment of certain arrears to be unenforceable), for the words from 'an order' to 'financial provision order' substitute 'any financial provision order under this Part of this Act or any interim order for maintenance'.

18. For section 33(2) (repayment of sums paid under certain orders) substitute—
   '(2) This section applies to the following orders under this Part of this Act—
(a) any periodical payments order;
(b) any secured periodical payments order; and
(c) any interim order for maintenance, so far as it requires the making of periodical payments.'

19.—(1) Section 33A (consent orders) is amended as follows.
(2) In subsection (2), after 'applies', in the first place, insert '(subject, in the case of the powers of the court under section 31A above, to subsections (6) and (7) of that section)'.

(3) In subsection (3), in the definition of 'order for financial relief', for 'an order under any of sections 23, 24, 24A [, 24B] or 27 above' substitute 'any of the following orders under this Part of this Act, that is to say, any financial provision order, any property adjustment order, [any pension sharing order] any order for the sale of property or any interim order for maintenance'.

Note. Words ', 24B' and 'any pension sharing order' inserted by the Welfare Reform and Pensions Act 1999, s 84(1), Sch 12, paras 64, 66 (1), (11) as from 1 December 2000 (SI 2000 No 1116).

20. In section 35 (alteration of maintenance agreements), after subsection (6), insert—

'(7) Subject to subsection (5) above, references in this Act to any such order as is mentioned in section 21 above shall not include references to any order under this section.'

21. In section 37(1) (avoidance of transactions intended to prevent or reduce financial relief), for '22, 23, 24, [24B], 27, 31 (except subsection (6))' substitute '22A to [24BB], 27, 31 (except subsection (6)), 31A'.

Note. Words ', 24B' inserted, and second appearance of '24' substituted by '24BB', by the Welfare Reform and Pensions Act 1999, s 84(1), Sch 12, paras 64, 66 (1), (12), as from 1 December 2000 (SI 2000 No 1116).

22. In section 47(2) (relief in cases of polygamous marriages)—
- (a) in paragraph (a), after 'any' insert the words 'divorce order, any separation order under the 1996 Act or any'; and
- (b) in paragraph (d), after 'this Act' insert 'or the 1996 Act' and for 'such decree or order' substitute 'a statement of marital breakdown or any such order or decree'.

23. Omit section 49 (under which a person who is alleged to have committed adultery with a party to a marriage is required to be made a party to certain proceedings).

24.—(1) Section 52(1) (interpretation) is amended as follows.
- (2) After 'In this Act', insert—
' "the 1996 Act" means the Family Law Act 1996;'.
- (3) After the definition of 'maintenance assessment' insert—
' "statement of marital breakdown" has the same meaning as in the Family Law Act 1996.'

25. In section 52(2)(a), for 'with section 21 above' substitute '(subject to section 35(7) above) with section 21 above and—
- (i) in the case of a financial provision order or periodical payments order, as including (except where the context otherwise requires) references to an interim periodical payments order under section 22A or 23 above; and
- (ii) in the case of a financial provision order or order for the payment of a lump sum, as including (except where the context otherwise requires) references to an interim order for the payment of a lump sum under section 22A or 23 above;'.

['25A. In section 52(2)(aa), for "section 21A" substitute "section 21".']

Note. Para 25A inserted by the Welfare Reform and Pensions Act 1999, s 84(1), Sch 12, paras 64, 66 (1), (13) as from 1 December 2000 (SI 2000 No 1116).

Domicile and Matrimonial Proceedings Act 1973 (c 45)

26. For section 5(5) of the Domicile and Matrimonial Proceedings Act 1973 (jurisdiction in cases of change of domicile or habitual residence) substitute—

'(5) The court shall have jurisdiction to entertain proceedings for nullity of marriage (even though it would not otherwise have jurisdiction) at any time when marital proceedings, as defined by section 20 of the Family Law Act 1996, are pending in relation to the marriage.'

Inheritance (Provision for Family and Dependants) Act 1975 (c 63)

27.—(1) The Inheritance (Provision for Family and Dependants) Act 1975 (meaning of reasonable financial provision) is amended as follows.

(2) In section 1(2)(a), for the words from 'the marriage' to 'in force' substitute ', at the date of death, a separation order under the Family Law Act 1996 was in force in relation to the marriage'.

(3) In section 3(2) (matters to which the court is to have regard)—

(a) for 'decree of judicial separation' substitute 'separation order under the Family Law Act 1996'; and

(b) for 'a decree of divorce' substitute 'a divorce order'.

(4) In section 14 (provision where no financial relief was granted on divorce)—

(a) in subsection (1), for the words from 'a decree' to first 'granted' substitute 'a divorce order or separation order has been made under the Family Law Act 1996 in relation to a marriage or a decree of nullity of marriage has been made absolute';

(b) in subsection (1)(a), for 'section 23' and 'section 24' substitute, respectively, 'section 22A or 23' and 'section 23A or 24';

(c) after paragraph (b), for the words from 'the decree of divorce' to the end substitute ', as the case may be, the divorce order or separation order had not been made or the decree of nullity had not been made absolute'; and

(d) in subsection (2), for 'decree of judicial separation' and 'the decree' substitute, respectively, 'separation order' and 'the order'.

(5) In section 15(1) (restriction imposed in divorce proceedings on applications under that Act), for the words from the beginning to 'thereafter' substitute—

'At any time when the court—

(a) has jurisdiction under section 23A or 24 of the Matrimonial Causes Act 1973 to make a property adjustment order in relation to a marriage; or

(b) would have such jurisdiction if either the jurisdiction had not already been exercised or an application for such an order were made with the leave of the court,'.

(6) In section 15, for subsections (2) to (4) substitute—

'(2) An order made under subsection (1) above with respect to any party to a marriage has effect in accordance with subsection (3) below at any time—

(a) after the marriage has been dissolved;

(b) after a decree of nullity has been made absolute in relation to the marriage; and

(c) while a separation order under the Family Law Act 1996 is in force in relation to the marriage and the separation is continuing.

(3) If at any time when an order made under subsection (1) above with respect to any party to a marriage has effect the other party to the marriage dies, the court shall not entertain any application made by the surviving party to the marriage for an order under section 2 of this Act.'

(7) In section 19(2)(b) (effect and duration of certain orders), for the words from 'the marriage' to 'in force' substitute ', at the date of death, a separation order under the Family Law Act 1996 was in force in relation to the marriage with the deceased'.

(8) In section 25 (interpretation), in the definition of 'former wife' and 'former husband', for 'a decree', in the first place, substitute 'an order or decree'.

Domestic Proceedings and Magistrates' Courts Act 1978 (c 22)

28.—(1) Section 28(1) of the Domestic Proceedings and Magistrates' Courts Act 1978 (powers of High Court in respect of orders under Part I) is amended as follows.

(2) After 'this Act' insert—

'(a) a statement of marital breakdown under section 5 of the Family Law Act

1996 with respect to the marriage has been received by the court but no application has been made under that Act by reference to that statement, or

(b)'.

(3) For the words from 'then' to 'lump sum' substitute 'then, except in the case of an order for the payment of a lump sum, any court to which an application may be made under that Act by reference to that statement or, as the case may be,'.

Housing Act 1980 (c 51)

29. In section 54(2) of the Housing Act 1980 (prohibition of assignment of shorthold tenancy under that section) for 'section 24' substitute 'sections 23A or 24'.

Supreme Court Act 1981 (c 54)

30. In section 18 of the Supreme Court Act 1981 (restrictions on appeals to Court of Appeal), in paragraph (d) of subsection (1) omit 'divorce or' and after that paragraph insert—

'(dd) from a divorce order;'.

Civil Jurisdiction and Judgments Act 1982 (c 27)

31. In section 18(6)(a) of the Civil Jurisdiction and Judgments Act 1982 (decrees of judicial separation), for 'a decree' substitute 'an order or decree'.

Matrimonial and Family Proceedings Act 1984 (c 42)

32.—(1) The Matrimonial and Family Proceedings Act 1984 is amended as follows.

(2) In section 17(1) (financial relief in the case of overseas divorces etc), for *the words from 'any' where it first occurs to the end substitute 'one or more orders each of which would, within the meaning of Part II of the 1973 Act, be a financial provision order in favour of a party to the marriage or child of the family or a property adjustment order in relation to the marriage.'.* ["paragraph (a) substitute—

'(a) make one or more orders each of which would, within the meaning of Part II of the 1973 Act, be a financial provision order in favour of a party to the marriage or a child of the family or a property adjustment order in relation to the marriage;".']

(3) For section *21(a)* [21(1)(a)](provisions of the 1973 Act applied for the purposes of the powers to give relief in the case of overseas divorces etc) substitute—

'(a) section 22A(5) (provisions about lump sums in relation to divorce or separation);

(aa) section 23(4), (5) and (6) (provisions about lump sums in relation to annulment);'.

['(3A) For section 21(1)(ba) substitute—

"(ba) sections 24BA(5) to (7) (provisions about pension sharing orders in relation to divorce);

(baa) section 24BC(1) to (3) (provisions about pension sharing orders in relation to nullity);".

(3B) In section 21(3), for "section 23" substitute "section 22A or 23".']

Note. In sub-paras (2) and (3) words in italics substituted by words in square brackets, and sub-paras (3A) and (3A) inserted, by the Welfare Reform and Pensions Act 1999, s 84(1), Sch 12, paras 64, 66 (1), (14)-(16) as from 1 December 2000 (SI 2000 No 1116).

(4) In section 27 (interpretation), for the definition of 'property adjustment order', substitute—

' "property adjustment order" and "secured periodical payments order" mean any order which would be a property adjustment order or, as the case may be, secured periodical payments order within the meaning of Part II of the 1973 Act;'

(5) In section 32 (meaning of 'family business'), for the definition of 'matrimonial cause' substitute—

' "matrimonial cause" means an action for nullity of marriage or any marital proceedings under the Family Law Act 1996;'.

Finance Act 1985 (c 54)

33. In section 83(1) of the Finance Act 1985 (stamp duty for transfers of property in connection with divorce etc)—

(a) after paragraph (b), insert—

'(bb) is executed in pursuance of an order of a court which is made at any time under section 22A, 23A or 24A of the Matrimonial Causes Act 1973, or'; and

(b) in paragraph (c), for 'or their judicial separation' substitute ', their judicial separation or the making of a separation order in respect of them'.

Housing Act 1985 (c 68)

34. In each of sections 39(1)(c), 88(2), 89(3), 90(3)(a), 91(3)(b), 99B(2)(e), 101(3)(c), 160(1)(c), 171B(4)(b)(i) of, and paragraph 1(2)(c) to, Schedule 6A of the Housing Act 1985 (which refers to the 1973 Act), for 'section 24' substitute 'section 23A or 24'.

Housing Associations Act 1985 (c 69)

35. In paragraph 5(1)(c) of Schedule 2 to the Housing Associations Act 1985 (which refers to the 1973 Act), for 'section 24' substitute 'section 23A or 24'.

Agricultural Holdings Act 1986 (c 5)

36. In paragraph 1(3) of Schedule 6 to the Agricultural Holdings Act 1986 (spouse of close relative not to be treated as such when marriage subject to decree nisi etc), for the words from 'when' to the end substitute 'when a separation order or a divorce order under the Family Law Act 1996 is in force in relation to the relative's marriage or that marriage is the subject of a decree nisi of nullity.'.

Family Law Act 1986 (c 55)

37.—(1) The Family Law Act 1986 is amended as follows.

(2) For section 2(1) and (2) (jurisdiction to make orders under section 1) substitute—

'(1) A court in England and Wales shall not have jurisdiction to make a section 1(1)(a) order with respect to a child unless—

(a) the case falls within section 2A below; or

(b) in any other case, the condition in section 3 below is satisfied.'

(3) For section 2A(1) (jurisdiction in or in connection with matrimonial proceedings), substitute—

'(1) Subject to subsections (2) to (4) below, a case falls within this section for the purposes of the making of a section 1(1)(a) order if that order is made—

(a) at a time when—

(i) a statement of marital breakdown under section 5 of the Family Law Act 1996 with respect to the marriage of the parents of the child concerned has been received by the court; and

(ii) it is or may become possible for an application for a divorce order or for a separation order to be made by reference to that statement; or

(b) at a time when an application in relation to that marriage for a divorce
order, or for a separation order under the Act of 1996, has been made
and not withdrawn.

(1A) A case also falls within this section for the purposes of the making of a
section 1(1)(a) order if that order is made in or in connection with any
proceedings for the nullity of the marriage of the parents of the child concerned
and—

(a) those proceedings are continuing; or

(b) the order is made—

  (i) immediately on the dismissal, after the beginning of the trial, of the
  proceedings; and

  (ii) on an application made before the dismissal.'

(4) In section 2A(2), for the words from the beginning to 'judicial separation'
substitute 'A case does not fall within this section if a separation order under the
Family Law Act 1996 is in force in relation to the marriage of the parents of the
child concerned if,'.

(5) In section 2A(3), for 'in which the other proceedings there referred to'
substitute 'in Scotland, Northern Ireland or a specified dependent territory in
which the proceedings for divorce or nullity'.

(6) In section 2A(4)—

(a) for 'in or in connection with matrimonial proceedings' substitute 'by virtue
of the case falling within this section'; and

(b) for 'in or in connection with those proceedings' substitute 'by virtue of
section 2(1)(a) of this Act'.

(7) In section 3 (child habitually resident or present in England and Wales), for
'section 2(2)' substitute 'section 2(1)(b)'.

(8) In section 6 (duration and variation of Part I orders), for subsections (3A)
and (3B) substitute—

'(3A) Subsection (3) above does not apply if the Part I order was made in a
case falling within section 2A of this Act.'

(9) In section 38 (restriction on removal of wards of court from the
jurisdiction), insert after subsection (3)—

'(4) The reference in subsection (2) above to a time when proceedings for
divorce or judicial separation are continuing in respect of a marriage in another
part of the United Kingdom includes, in relation to any case in which England
and Wales would be another part of the United Kingdom, any time when—

(a) a statement of marital breakdown under section 5 of the Family Law Act
1996 with respect to that marriage has been received by the court and it
is or may become possible for an application for a divorce order or for a
separation order to be made by reference to that statement; or

(b) an application in relation to that marriage for a divorce order, or for a
separation order under the Act of 1996, has been made and not withdrawn.'

(10) In section 42(2) (times when divorce etc proceedings are to be treated as
continuing for the purposes of certain restrictions on the removal of children from
the jurisdiction), for the words from 'unless' to the end substitute 'be treated as
continuing (irrespective of whether a divorce order, separation order or decree of
nullity has been made)—

(a) from the time when a statement of marital breakdown under section 5 of
the Family Law Act 1996 with respect to the marriage is received by the
court in England and Wales until such time as the court may designate or, if
earlier, until the time when—

  (i) the child concerned attains the age of eighteen; or

  (ii) it ceases, by virtue of section 5(3) or 7(9) of that Act (lapse of divorce or
  separation process) to be possible for an application for a divorce order,
  or for a separation order, to be made by reference to that statement; and

(b) from the time when a petition for nullity is presented in relation to the marriage in England and Wales or a petition for divorce, judicial separation or nullity is presented in relation to the marriage in Northern Ireland or a specified dependent territory, until the time when—
    (i) the child concerned attains the age of eighteen; or
    (ii) if earlier, proceedings on the petition are dismissed.'.
(11) In section 51(4) (definitions), after the definition of 'the relevant date' insert—
  ' "judicial separation" includes a separation order under the Family Law Act 1996;'.

Landlord and Tenant Act 1987 (c 31)

38. In section 4(2)(c) of the Landlord and Tenant Act 1987 (which refers to the 1973 Act), for 'section 24' substitute 'section 23A, 24'.

Legal Aid Act 1988 (c 34)

39. ... *Repealed by the Access to Justice Act 1999, s 106, Sch 15, Pt I as from 1 April 2000 (SI 2000/774).*

Housing Act 1988 (c 50)

40. In paragraph 4(1)(c) of Schedule 11 (which refers to the 1973 Act), for 'section 24' substitute 'section 23A or 24'.

Children Act 1989 (c 41)

41.—(1) The Children Act 1989 is amended as follows.
(2) In section 6(3A) (revocation or appointment of guardian) for paragraph (a) substitute—
  '(a) a court of civil jurisdiction in England and Wales by order dissolves, or by decree annuls, a marriage, or'.
(3) In section 8(3) after 'means' insert '(subject to subsection (5))'.
(4) In section 8, insert after subsection (4)—
  '(5) For the purposes of any reference in this Act to family proceedings powers which under this Act are exercisable in family proceedings shall also be exercisable in relation to a child, without any such proceedings having been commenced or any application having been made to the court under this Act, if—
    (a) a statement of marital breakdown under section 5 of the Family Law Act 1996 with respect to the marriage in relation to which that child is a child of the family has been received by the court; and
    (b) it may, in due course, become possible for an application for a divorce order or for a separation order to be made by reference to that statement.'

Local Government and Housing Act 1989 (c 42)

42. In section 124(3)(c) of the Local Government and Housing Act 1989 (which refers to the 1973 Act), for 'section 24' substitute 'section 23A or 24'.

Pensions Act 1995 (c 26)

43. In section 166(4) of the Pensions Act 1995 (jurisdiction of the court under the Matrimonial Causes Act 1973 in respect of pensions to which that section applies) for 'section 23' substitute section 22A or 23'.

["The Welfare Reform and Pensions Act 1999

43A. In section 24 of the Welfare Reform and Pensions Act 1999 (charges by pension arrangements in relation to earmarking orders), for "section 23" substitute "section 22A or 23"."]

Note. Para 43A inserted by the Welfare Reform and Pensions Act 1999, s 84(1), Sch 12, paras 64, 66 (1), (17) as from 1 December 2000 (SI 2000 No 1116).

PART II

AMENDMENTS CONNECTED WITH PART III

Legal Aid Act 1988 (c 34)

44. *...Repealed by the Access to Justice Act 1999, s 106, Sch 15, Pt I as from 1 April 2000 (SI 2000/774).*

PART III

AMENDMENTS CONNECTED WITH PART IV

Land Registration Act 1925 (c 21)

45. *...Repealed by the Land Registration Act 2002, s 135, Sch 13, Pt I as from 13 October 2003 (SI 2003/1725, art 2(1).*

Land Charges Act 1972 (c 61)

46. In section 1(6A) of the Land Charges Act 1972 (cases where county court has jurisdiction to vacate registration) in paragraph (d)—
   (a) after 'section 1 of the Matrimonial Homes Act 1983' insert 'or section 33 of the Family Law Act 1996'; and
   (b) for 'that section' substitute 'either of those sections'.

47. In section 2(7) of that Act (Class F land charge) for 'Matrimonial Homes Act 1983' substitute 'Part IV of the Family Law Act 1996'.

Land Compensation Act 1973 (c 26)

48.—(1) Section 29A of the Land Compensation Act 1973 (spouses having statutory rights of occupation) is amended as follows.

   (2) In subsection (1), for 'rights of occupation (within the meaning of the Matrimonial Homes Act 1983)' substitute 'matrimonial home rights (within the meaning of Part IV of the Family Law Act 1996)'.

   (3) In subsection (2)(a), for 'rights of occupation' substitute 'matrimonial home rights'.

Magistrates' Court Act 1980 (c 43)

49. In section 65(1) of the Magistrates' Courts Act 1980 (meaning of family proceedings) after paragraph (o) insert—
   '(p) Part IV of the Family Law Act 1996;'.

Contempt of Court Act 1981 (c 49)

50. In Schedule 3 to the Contempt of Court Act 1981 (application of Magistrates' Courts Act 1980 to civil contempt proceedings), in paragraph 3 for the words from 'or, having been arrested' onwards substitute—
   'or, having been arrested under section 47 of the Family Law Act 1996 in connection with the matter of the complaint, is at large after being remanded under subsection (7)(b) or (10) of that section.'

Supreme Court Act 1981 (c 54)

51. In Schedule 1 to the Supreme Court Act 1981 (distribution of business in High Court), in paragraph 3 (Family Division)—
   (a) in paragraph (d), after 'matrimonial proceedings ' insert 'or proceedings under Part IV of the Family Law Act 1996', and
   (b) in paragraph (f)(i), for 'Domestic Violence and Matrimonial Proceedings Act 1976' substitute 'Part IV of the Family Law Act 1996'.

Matrimonial and Family Proceedings Act 1984 (c 42)

52. For section 22 of the Matrimonial and Family Proceedings Act 1984 substitute—

'**22. Powers of court in relation to certain tenancies of dwelling-houses**—
(1) This section applies if—
  (a) an application is made by a party to a marriage for an order for financial relief; and
  (b) one of the parties is entitled, either in his own right or jointly with the other party, to occupy a dwelling-house situated in England or Wales by virtue of a tenancy which is a relevant tenancy within the meaning of Schedule 7 to the Family Law Act 1996 (certain statutory tenancies).
(2) The court may make in relation to that dwelling-house any order which it could make under Part II of that Schedule if—
  (a) a divorce order,
  (b) a separation order, or
  (c) a decree of nullity of marriage,
had been made or granted in England and Wales in respect of the marriage.
(3) The provisions of paragraphs 10, 11 and 14(1) in Part III of that Schedule apply in relation to any order under this section as they apply to any order under Part II of that Schedule.'

Housing Act 1985 (c 68)

53.—(1) Section 85 of the Housing Act 1985 (extended discretion of court in certain proceedings for possession) is amended as follows.
(2) In subsection (5)—
(a) in paragraph (a), for 'rights of occupation under the Matrimonial Homes Act 1983' substitute 'matrimonial home rights under Part IV of the Family Law Act 1996'; and
(b) for 'those rights of occupation' substitute 'those matrimonial home rights'.
(3) After subsection (5) insert—
  '(5A) If proceedings are brought for possession of a dwelling-house which is let under a secure tenancy and—
    (a) an order is in force under section 35 of the Family Law Act 1996 conferring rights on the former spouse of the tenant or an order is in force under section 36 of that Act conferring rights on a cohabitant or former cohabitant (within the meaning of that Act) of the tenant,
    (b) the former spouse, cohabitant or former cohabitant is then in occupation of the dwelling-house, and
    (c) the tenancy is terminated as a result of those proceedings,
  the former spouse, cohabitant or former cohabitant shall, so long as he or she remains in occupation, have the same rights in relation to, or in connection with, any adjournment, stay, suspension or postponement in pursuance of this section as he or she would have if the rights conferred by the order referred to in paragraph (a) were not affected by the termination of the tenancy.'
54. In section 99B of that Act (persons qualifying for compensation for improvements) in subsection (2) for paragraph (f) substitute—
  '(f) a spouse, former spouse, cohabitant or former cohabitant of the improving tenant to whom the tenancy has been transferred by an order made under Schedule 1 to the Matrimonial Homes Act 1983 or Schedule 7 to the Family Law Act 1996.'
55. In section 101 of that Act (rent not to be increased on account of tenant's improvements) in subsection (3) for paragraph (d) substitute—
  '(d) a spouse, former spouse, cohabitant or former cohabitant of the tenant to whom the tenancy has been transferred by an order made under Schedule

1 to the Matrimonial Homes Act 1983 or Schedule 7 to the Family Law Act 1996.'

56. In section 171B of that Act (extent of preserved right to buy: qualifying persons and dwelling-houses) in subsection (4)(b)(ii) after 'Schedule 1 to the Matrimonial Homes Act 1983' insert 'or Schedule 7 to the Family Law Act 1996'.

Insolvency Act 1986 (c 45)

57.—(1) Section 336 of the Insolvency Act 1986 (rights of occupation etc of bankrupt's spouse) is amended as follows.

(2) In subsection (1), for 'rights of occupation under the Matrimonial Homes Act 1983' substitute 'matrimonial home rights under Part IV of the Family Law Act 1996'.

(3) In subsection (2)—

(a) for 'rights of occupation under the Act of 1983' substitute 'matrimonial home rights under the Act of 1996', and

(b) in paragraph (b), for 'under section 1 of that Act' substitute 'under section 33 of that Act'.

(4) In subsection (4), for 'section 1 of the Act of 1983' substitute 'section 33 of the Act of 1996'.

58.—(1) Section 337 of that Act is amended as follows.

(2) In subsection (2), for 'rights of occupation under the Matrimonial Homes Act 1983' substitute 'matrimonial home rights under Part IV of the Family Law Act 1996'.

(3) For subsection (3) substitute—

'(3) The Act of 1996 has effect, with the necessary modifications, as if—

(a) the rights conferred by paragraph (a) of subsection (2) were matrimonial home rights under that Act,

(b) any application for such leave as is mentioned in that paragraph were an application for an order under section 33 of that Act, and

(c) any charge under paragraph (b) of that subsection on the estate or interest of the trustee were a charge under that Act on the estate or interest of a spouse.'

(4) In subsections (4) and (5) for 'section 1 of the Act of 1983' substitute 'section 33 of the Act of 1996'.

Housing Act 1988 (c 50)

59.—(1) Section 9 of the Housing Act 1988 (extended discretion of court in possession claims) is amended as follows.

(2) In subsection (5)—

(a) in paragraph (a), for 'rights of occupation under the Matrimonial Homes Act 1983' substitute 'matrimonial home rights under Part IV of the Family Law Act 1996', and

(b) for 'those rights of occupation' substitute 'those matrimonial home rights'.

(3) After subsection (5) insert—

'(5A) In any case where—

(a) at a time when proceedings are brought for possession of a dwelling-house let on an assured tenancy—

   (i) an order is in force under section 35 of the Family Law Act 1996 conferring rights on the former spouse of the tenant, or

   (ii) an order is in force under section 36 of that Act conferring rights on a cohabitant or former cohabitant (within the meaning of that Act) of the tenant,

(b) that cohabitant, former cohabitant or former spouse is then in occupation of the dwelling-house, and

(c) the assured tenancy is terminated as a result of those proceedings,
the cohabitant, former cohabitant or former spouse shall have the same rights
in relation to, or in connection with, any such adjournment as is referred to in
subsection (1) above or any such stay, suspension or postponement as is referred
to in subsection (2) above as he or she would have if the rights conferred by the
order referred to in paragraph (a) above were not affected by the termination
of the tenancy.'

Children Act 1989 (c 41)

60.—(1) In section 8(4) of the Children Act 1989 (meaning of 'family proceedings'
for purposes of that Act), omit paragraphs (c) and (f) and after paragraph (g)
insert—
    '(h) the Family Law Act 1996.'
    (2) In Schedule 11 to that Act, in paragraph 6(a) (amendment of the Domestic
Proceedings and Magistrates' Courts Act 1978), for 'sections 16(5)(c) and' substitute
'section'.

Courts and Legal Services Act 1990 (c 41)

61. ...*Repealed by the Access to Justice Act 1999, s 106, Sch 15, Pt II as from 31 July 2000
(SI 2000/1920).*

SCHEDULE 9   Section 66(2)

MODIFICATIONS, SAVING AND TRANSITIONAL

Transitional arrangements for those who have been living apart

1.—(1) The Lord Chancellor may by order provide for the application of Part II
to marital proceedings which—
    (a) are begun during the transitional period, and
    (b) relate to parties to a marriage who immediately before the beginning of
        that period were living apart,
subject to such modifications (which may include omissions) as may be prescribed.
    (2) An order made under this paragraph may, in particular, make provision as
to the evidence which a party who claims to have been living apart from the other
party immediately before the beginning of the transitional period must produce to
the court.
    (3) In this paragraph—
'marital proceedings' has the same meaning as in section 24;
'prescribed' means prescribed by the order; and
'transitional period' means the period of two years beginning with the day on
    which section 3 is brought into force.

Modifications of enactments etc

2.—(1) The Lord Chancellor may by order make such consequential modifications
of any enactment or subordinate legislation as appear to him necessary or expedient
in consequence of Part II in respect of any reference (in whatever terms) to—
    (a) a petition;
    (b) the presentation of a petition;
    (c) the petitioner or respondent in proceedings on a petition;
    (d) proceedings on a petition;
    (e) proceedings in connection with any proceedings on a petition;
    (f) any other matrimonial proceedings;
    (g) a decree; or

(h) findings of adultery in any proceedings.

(2) An order under sub-paragraph (1) may, in particular—

(a) make provision applying generally in relation to enactments and subordinate legislation of a description specified in the order;

(b) modify the effect of sub-paragraph (3) in relation to documents and agreements of a description so specified.

(3) Otherwise a reference (in whatever terms) in any instrument or agreement to the presentation of a petition or to a decree has effect, in relation to any time after the coming into force of this paragraph—

(a) in the case of a reference to the presentation of a petition, as if it included a reference to the making of a statement; and

(b) in the case of a reference to a decree, as if it included a reference to a divorce order or (as the case may be) a separation order.

3. If an Act or subordinate legislation—

(a) refers to an enactment repealed or amended by or under this Act, and

(b) was passed or made before the repeal or amendment came into force,

the Lord Chancellor may by order make such consequential modifications of any provision contained in the Act or subordinate legislation as appears to him necessary or expedient in respect of the reference.

Expressions used in paragraphs 2 and 3

4. In paragraphs 2 and 3—

'decree' means a decree of divorce (whether a decree nisi or a decree which has been made absolute) or a decree of judicial separation;

'instrument' includes any deed, will or other instrument or document;

'petition' means a petition for a decree of divorce or a petition for a decree of judicial separation; and

'subordinate legislation' has the same meaning as in the Interpretation Act 1978.

Proceedings under way

5.—(1) Except for paragraph 6 of this Schedule, nothing in any provision of Part II, Part I of Schedule 8 or Schedule 10—

(a) applies to, or affects—

(i) any decree granted before the coming into force of the provision;

(ii) any proceedings begun, by petition or otherwise, before that time; or

(iii) any decree granted in any such proceedings;

(b) affects the operation of—

(i) the 1973 Act,

(ii) any other enactment, or

(iii) any subordinate legislation,

in relation to any such proceedings or decree or to any proceedings in connection with any such proceedings or decree; or

(c) without prejudice to paragraph (b), affects any transitional provision having effect under Schedule 1 to the 1973 Act.

(2) In this paragraph, 'subordinate legislation' has the same meaning as in the Interpretation Act 1978.

6.—(1) Section 31 of the 1973 Act has effect as amended by this Act in relation to any order under Part II of the 1973 Act made after the coming into force of the amendments.

(2) Subsections (7) to (7F) of that section also have effect as amended by this Act in relation to any order made before the coming into force of the amendments.

Interpretation

7. In paragraphs 8 to 15 'the 1983 Act' means the Matrimonial Homes Act 1983.

Pending applications for orders relating to occupation and molestation

8.—(1) In this paragraph and paragraph 10 'the existing enactments' means—
  (a) the Domestic Violence and Matrimonial Proceedings Act 1976;
  (b) sections 16 to 18 of the Domestic Proceedings and Magistrates' Courts Act 1978; and
  (c) sections 1 and 9 of the 1983 Act.

(2) Nothing in Part IV, Part III of Schedule 8 or Schedule 10 affects any application for an order or injunction under any of the existing enactments which is pending immediately before the commencement of the repeal of that enactment.

Pending applications under Schedule 1 to the Matrimonial Homes Act 1983

9. Nothing in Part IV, Part III of Schedule 8 or Schedule 10 affects any application for an order under Schedule 1 to the 1983 Act which is pending immediately before the commencement of the repeal of that Schedule.

Existing orders relating to occupation and molestation

10.—(1) In this paragraph 'an existing order' means any order or injunction under any of the existing enactments which—
  (a) is in force immediately before the commencement of the repeal of that enactment; or
  (b) was made or granted after that commencement in proceedings brought before that commencement.

(2) Subject to sub-paragraphs (3) and (4), nothing in Part IV, Part III of Schedule 8 or Schedule 10—
  (a) prevents an existing order from remaining in force; or
  (b) affects the enforcement of an existing order.

(3) Nothing in Part IV, Part III of Schedule 8 or Schedule 10 affects any application to extend, vary or discharge an existing order, but the court may, if it thinks it just and reasonable to do so, treat the application as an application for an order under Part IV.

(4) The making of an order under Part IV between parties with respect to whom an existing order is in force discharges the existing order.

Matrimonial home rights

11.—(1) Any reference (however expressed) in any enactment, instrument or document (whether passed or made before or after the passing of this Act) to rights of occupation under, or within the meaning of, the 1983 Act shall be construed, so far as is required for continuing the effect of the instrument or document, as being or as the case requires including a reference to matrimonial home rights under, or within the meaning of, Part IV.

(2) Any reference (however expressed) in this Act or in any other enactment, instrument or document (including any enactment amended by Schedule 8) to matrimonial home rights under, or within the meaning of, Part IV shall be construed as including, in relation to times, circumstances and purposes before the commencement of sections 30 to 32, a reference to rights of occupation under, or within the meaning of, the 1983 Act.

12.—(1) Any reference (however expressed) in any enactment, instrument or document (whether passed or made before or after the passing of this Act) to registration under section 2(8) of the 1983 Act shall, in relation to any time after the commencement of sections 30 to 32, be construed as being or as the case requires including a reference to registration under section 31(10).

(2) Any reference (however expressed) in this Act or in any other enactment, instrument or document (including any enactment amended by Schedule 8) to registration under section 31(10) shall be construed as including a reference to—

    (a) registration under section 2(7) of the Matrimonial Homes Act 1967 or section 2(8) of the 1983 Act, and

    (b) registration by caution duly lodged under section 2(7) of the Matrimonial Homes Act 1967 before 14th February 1983 (the date of the commencement of section 4(2) of the Matrimonial Homes and Property Act 1981).

13. In sections 30 and 31 and Schedule 4—

    (a) any reference to an order made under section 33 shall be construed as including a reference to an order made under section 1 of the 1983 Act, and

    (b) any reference to an order made under section 33(5) shall be construed as including a reference to an order made under section 1 of the 1983 Act by virtue of section 2(4) of that Act.

14. Neither section 31(11) nor the repeal by the Matrimonial Homes and Property Act 1981 of the words 'or caution' in section 2(7) of the Matrimonial Homes Act 1967, affects any caution duly lodged as respects any estate or interest before 14th February 1983.

15. Nothing in this Schedule is to be taken to prejudice the operation of sections 16 and 17 of the Interpretation Act 1978 (which relate to the effect of repeals).

SCHEDULE 10   Section 66(3)

REPEALS

Chapter	Short title	Extent of repeal
1968 c 63	The Domestic and Appellate Proceedings (Restriction of Publicity) Act 1968.	Section 2(1)(b).
1973 c 18	The Matrimonial Causes Act 1973	Sections 1 to 7. In section 8(1)(b), the words 'or before the decree nisi is made absolute'. Sections 9 and 10. Sections 17 and 18. Section 20. Section 22. In section 24A(3), the words 'divorce or'. In section 25(2)(h), the words 'in the case of proceedings for divorce or nullity of marriage,'. In section 28(1), the words from 'in', in the first place where it occurs, to 'nullity of marriage' in the first place where those words occur. In section 29(2), the words from 'may begin' to 'but'. In section 30, the words 'divorce' and 'or judicial separation'. In section 31, in subsection (2)(a), the words 'order for maintenance pending suit and any'.

Chapter	Short title	Extent of repeal
		In section 41, in subsection (1) the words 'divorce or' and 'or a decree of judicial separation' and in subsection (2) the words 'divorce or' and 'or that the decree of judicial separation is not to be granted.'.
		Section 49.
		In section 52(2)(b), the words 'to orders for maintenance pending suit and', 'respectively'and 'section 22 and'
		In Schedule 1, paragraph 8.
1973 c 45	The Domicile and Matrimonial Proceedings Act 1973	In section 5, in subsection (1), the words 'subject to section 6(3) and (4) of this Act' and, in paragraph (a), 'divorce, judicial separation or' and subsection (2).
		Section 6(3) and (4).
		In Schedule 1, in paragraph 11, in sub-paragraph (2)(a), in sub-paragraph (2)(c), in the first place where they occur, and in sub-paragraph (3)(b) and (c), the words 'in connection with the stayed proceedings'.
1976 c 50	The Domestic Violence and Matrimonial Proceedings Act 1976	The whole Act.
1978 c 22	The Domestic Proceedings and Magistrates' Court Act 1978	In section 1, paragraphs (c) and (d) and the word 'or' preceding paragraph (c).
		In section 7(1), the words 'neither party having deserted the other'.
		Sections 16 to 18.
		Section 28(2).
		Section 63(3).
		In Schedule 2, paragraphs 38 and 53.
1980 c 43	The Magistrates' Court Act 1980	In Schedule 7, paragraph 159.
1981 c 54	The Supreme Court Act 1981	In section 18(1)(d), the words 'divorce or'.
1982 c 53	The Administration of Justice Act 1982	Section 16.
1983 c 19	The Matrimonial Homes Act 1983	The whole Act.

Chapter	Short title	Extent of repeal
1984 c 42	The Matrimonial and Family Proceedings Act 1984	Section 1. In section 21(f) the words 'except subsection (2)(e) and subsection (4)'. In section 27, the definition of 'secured periodical payments order'. In Schedule 1, paragraph 10.
1985 c 61	The Administration of Justice Act 1985	In section 34(2), paragraph (f) and the word 'and' immediately preceding it. In Schedule 2, in paragraph 37, paragraph (e) and the word 'and' immediately preceding it.
1985 c 71	The Housing (Consequential Provisions) Act 1985	In Schedule 2, paragraph 56.
1986 c 53	The Building Societies Act 1986	In Schedule 21, paragraph 9(f).
1986 c 55	The Family Law Act 1986	In Schedule 1, paragraph 27.
1988 c 34	The Legal Aid Act 1988	In section 16(9), the word 'and' at the end of paragraph (a).
1988 c 50	The Housing Act 1988	In Schedule 17, paragraphs 33 and 34.
1989 c 41	The Children Act 1989	Section 8(4)(c) and (f). In Schedule 11, paragraph 6(b). In Schedule 13, paragraphs 33(1) and 65(1).
1990 c 41	The Courts and Legal Services Act 1990	Section 58(10)(b) and (e). In Schedule 18, paragraph 21.
1995 c 42	The Private International Law (Miscellaneous Provisions) Act 1995	In the Schedule, paragraph 3.

TRUSTS OF LAND AND APPOINTMENT OF TRUSTEES ACT 1996

(1996 c 47)

ARRANGEMENT OF SECTIONS

PART I

TRUSTS OF LAND

Introductory

An Act to make new provision about trusts of land including provision phasing out
the Settled Land Act 1925, abolishing the doctrine of conversion and otherwise
amending the law about trusts for sale of land; to amend the law about the
appointment and retirement of trustees of any trust; and for connected purposes.

[24 July 1996]

PART I

TRUSTS OF LAND

Introductory

1. Meaning of 'trust of land'—(1) In this Act—
  (a) 'trust of land' means (subject to subsection (3)) any trust of property which
      consists of or includes land, and
  (b) 'trustees of land' means trustees of a trust of land.
  (2) The reference in subsection (1)(a) to a trust—

(a) is to any description of trust (whether express, implied, resulting or constructive), including a trust for sale and a bare trust, and

(b) includes a trust created, or arising, before the commencement of this Act.

(3) The reference to land in subsection (1)(a) does not include land which (despite section 2) is settled land or which is land to which the Universities and College Estates Act 1925 applies.

Settlements and trusts for sale as trusts of land

2. Trusts in place of settlements—(1) No settlement created after the commencement of this Act is a settlement for the purposes of the Settled Land Act 1925; and no settlement shall be deemed to be made under that Act after that commencement.

(2) Subsection (1) does not apply to a settlement created on the occasion of an alteration in any interest in, or of a person becoming entitled under, a settlement which—

(a) is in existence at the commencement of this Act, or

(b) derives from a settlement within paragraph (a) or this paragraph.

(3) But a settlement created as mentioned in subsection (2) is not a settlement for the purposes of the Settled Land Act 1925 if provision to the effect that it is not is made in the instrument, or any of the instruments, by which it is created.

(4) Where at any time after the commencement of this Act there is in the case of any settlement which is a settlement for the purposes of the Settled Land Act 1925 no relevant property which is, or is deemed to be, subject to the settlement, the settlement permanently ceases at that time to be a settlement for the purposes of that Act.

In this subsection 'relevant property' means land and personal chattels to which section 67(1) of the Settled Land Act 1925 (heirlooms) applies.

(5) No land held on charitable, ecclesiastical or public trusts shall be or be deemed to be settled land after the commencement of this Act, even if it was or was deemed to be settled land before that commencement.

(6) Schedule 1 has effect to make provision consequential on this section (including provision to impose a trust in circumstances in which, apart from this section, there would be a settlement for the purposes of the Settled Land Act 1925 (and there would not otherwise be a trust)).

3. Abolition of doctrine of conversion—(1) Where land is held by trustees subject to a trust for sale, the land is not to be regarded as personal property; and where personal property is subject to a trust for sale in order that the trustees may acquire land, the personal property is not to be regarded as land.

(2) Subsection (1) does not apply to a trust created by a will if the testator died before the commencement of this Act.

(3) Subject to that, subsection (1) applies to a trust whether it is created, or arises, before or after that commencement.

4. Express trusts for sale as trusts of land—(1) In the case of every trust for sale of land created by a disposition there is to be implied, despite any provision to the contrary made by the disposition, a power of the trustees to postpone sale of the land; and the trustees are not liable in any way for postponing sale of the land, in the exercise of their discretion, for an indefinite period.

(2) Subsection (1) applies to a trust whether it is created, or arises, before or after the commencement of this Act.

(3) Subsection (1) does not affect any liability incurred by trustees before that commencement.

5. Implied trusts for sale as trusts of land—(1) Schedule 2 has effect in relation to statutory provisions which impose a trust for sale of land in certain circumstances so that in those circumstances there is instead a trust of the land (without a duty to sell).

(2) Section 1 of the Settled Land Act 1925 does not apply to land held on any trust arising by virtue of that Schedule (so that any such land is subject to a trust of land).

Functions of trustees of land

6. General powers of trustees—(1) For the purpose of exercising their functions as trustees, the trustees of land have in relation to the land subject to the trust all the powers of an absolute owner.

(2) Where in the case of any land subject to a trust of land each of the beneficiaries interested in the land is a person of full age and capacity who is absolutely entitled to the land, the powers conferred on the trustees by subsection (1) include the power to convey the land to the beneficiaries even though they have not required the trustees to do so; and where land is conveyed by virtue of this subsection—

   (a) the beneficiaries shall do whatever is necessary to secure that it vests in them, and

   (b) if they fail to do so, the court may make an order requiring them to do so.

(3) The trustees of land have power to *purchase a legal estate in any land in England or Wales* [acquire land under the power conferred by section 8 of the Trustee Act 2000].

Note. Words in square brackets substituted for words in italics by the Trustee Act 2000, s 40(1), Sch 2, Pt II, para 45(1), as from 1 February 2001.

(4) ...*Repealed by the Trustee Act 2000, s 40(1), (3) Sch 2, Pt II, para 45(2), as from 1 February 2001.*

(5) In exercising the powers conferred by this section trustees shall have regard to the rights of the beneficiaries.

(6) The powers conferred by this section shall not be exercised in contravention of, or of any order made in pursuance of, any other enactment or any rule of law or equity.

(7) The reference in subsection (6) to an order includes an order of any court or of the Charity Commissioners.

(8) Where any enactment other than this section confers on trustees authority to act subject to any restriction, limitation or condition, trustees of land may not exercise the powers conferred by this section to do any act which they are prevented from doing under the other enactment by reason of the restriction, limitation or condition.

[(9) The duty of care under section 1 of the Trustee Act 2000 applies to trustees of land when exercising the powers conferred by this section.]

Note. Sub-s (9) inserted by the Trustee Act 2000, s 40(1), Sch 2, Pt II, para 45(3), as from 1 February 2001.

7. Partition by trustees—(1) The trustees of land may, where beneficiaries of full age are absolutely entitled in undivided shares to land subject to the trust, partition the land, or any part of it, and provide (by way of mortgage or otherwise) for the payment of any equality money.

(2) The trustees shall give effect to any such partition by conveying the partitioned land in severalty (whether or not subject to any legal mortgage created for raising equality money), either absolutely or in trust, in accordance with the rights of those beneficiaries.

(3) Before exercising their powers under subsection (2) the trustees shall obtain the consent of each of those beneficiaries.

(4) Where a share in the land is affected by an incumbrance, the trustees may either give effect to it or provide for its discharge from the property allotted to that share as they think fit.

(5) If a share in the land is absolutely vested in a minor, subsections (1) to (4) apply as if he were of full age, except that the trustees may act on his behalf and retain land or other property representing his share in trust for him.

[(6) Subsection (1) is subject to sections 21 (part-unit: interests) and 22 (part-unit: charging) of the Commonhold and Leasehold Reform Act 2002.]

Note. Sub-s (6) inserted by the Commonhold and Leasehold Reform Act 2002, s 68, Sch 5, para 8, as from 27 September 2004 (SI 2004 No 1832, art 2).

8. Exclusion and restriction of powers—(1) Sections 6 and 7 do not apply in the case of a trust of land created by a disposition in so far as provision to the effect that they do not apply is made by the disposition.

(2) If the disposition creating such a trust makes provision requiring any consent to be obtained to the exercise of any power conferred by section 6 or 7, the power may not be exercised without that consent.

(3) Subsection (1) does not apply in the case of charitable, ecclesiastical or public trusts.

(4) Subsections (1) and (2) have effect subject to any enactment which prohibits or restricts the effect of provision of the description mentioned in them.

9. Delegation by trustees—(1) The trustees of land may, by power of attorney, delegate to any beneficiary or beneficiaries of full age and beneficially entitled to an interest in possession in land subject to the trust any of their functions as trustees which relate to the land.

(2) Where trustees purport to delegate to a person by a power of attorney under subsection (1) functions relating to any land and another person in good faith deals with him in relation to the land, he shall be presumed in favour of that other person to have been a person to whom the functions could be delegated unless that other person has knowledge at the time of the transaction that he was not such a person.

And it shall be conclusively presumed in favour of any purchaser whose interest depends on the validity of that transaction that that other person dealt in good faith and did not have such knowledge if that other person makes a statutory declaration to that effect before or within three months after the completion of the purchase.

(3) A power of attorney under subsection (1) shall be given by all the trustees jointly and (unless expressed to be irrevocable and to be given by way of security) may be revoked by any one or more of them; and such a power is revoked by the appointment as a trustee of a person other than those by whom it is given (though not by any of those persons dying or otherwise ceasing to be a trustee).

(4) Where a beneficiary to whom functions are delegated by a power of attorney under subsection (1) ceases to be a person beneficially entitled to an interest in possession in land subject to the trust—

(a) if the functions are delegated to him alone, the power is revoked,

(b) if the functions are delegated to him and to other beneficiaries to be exercised by them jointly (but not separately), the power is revoked if each of the other beneficiaries ceases to be so entitled (but otherwise functions exercisable in accordance with the power are so exercisable by the remaining beneficiary or beneficiaries), and

(c) if the functions are delegated to him and to other beneficiaries to be exercised by them separately (or either separately or jointly), the power is revoked in so far as it relates to him.

(5) A delegation under subsection (1) may be for any period or indefinite.

(6) A power of attorney under subsection (1) cannot be an enduring power within the meaning of the Enduring Powers of Attorney Act 1985.

(7) Beneficiaries to whom functions have been delegated under subsection (1) are, in relation to the exercise of the functions, in the same position as trustees (with the same duties and liabilities); but such beneficiaries shall not be regarded as trustees for any other purposes (including, in particular, the purposes of any enactment permitting the delegation of functions by trustees or imposing requirements relating to the payment of capital money).

(8) ...*Repealed by the Trustee Act 2000, s 40(1), (3), Sch 2, Pt II para 46, Sch 4, Pt II as from 1 February 2001.*

(9) Neither this section nor the repeal by this Act of section 29 of the Law of Property Act 1925 (which is superseded by this section) affects the operation after the commencement of this Act of any delegation effected before that commencement.

[9A. Duties of trustees in connection with delegation etc

(1) The duty of care under section 1 of the Trustee Act 2000 applies to trustees of land in deciding whether to delegate any of their functions under section 9.

(2) Subsection (3) applies if the trustees of land—
  (a) delegate any of their functions under section 9, and
  (b) the delegation is not irrevocable.

(3) While the delegation continues, the trustees—
  (a) must keep the delegation under review,
  (b) if circumstances make it appropriate to do so, must consider whether there is a need to exercise any power of intervention that they have, and
  (c) if they consider that there is a need to exercise such a power, must do so.

(4) "Power of intervention" includes—
  (a) a power to give directions to the beneficiary;
  (b) a power to revoke the delegation.

(5) The duty of care under section 1 of the 2000 Act applies to trustees in carrying out any duty under subsection (3).

(6) A trustee of land is not liable for any act or default of the beneficiary, or beneficiaries, unless the trustee fails to comply with the duty of care in deciding to delegate any of the trustees' functions under section 9 or in carrying out any duty under subsection (3).

(7) Neither this section nor the repeal of section 9(8) by the Trustee Act 2000 affects the operation after the commencement of this section of any delegation effected before that commencement.]

Note. S 9A inserted by the Trustee Act 2000, s 40(1), (3), Sch 2, Pt II para 47 as from 1 February 2001 (SI 2000 No 1116).

Consents and consultation

10. Consents—(1) If a disposition creating a trust of land requires the consent of more than two persons to the exercise by the trustees of any function relating to the land, the consent of any two of them to the exercise of the function is sufficient in favour of a purchaser.

(2) Subsection (1) does not apply to the exercise of a function by trustees of land held on charitable, ecclesiastical or public trusts.

(3) Where at any time a person whose consent is expressed by a disposition creating a trust of land to be required to the exercise by the trustees of any function relating to the land is not of full age—
  (a) his consent is not, in favour of a purchaser, required to the exercise of the function, but
  (b) the trustees shall obtain the consent of a parent who has parental responsibility for him (within the meaning of the Children Act 1989) or of a guardian of his.

11. Consultation with beneficiaries—(1) The trustees of land shall in the exercise of any function relating to land subject to the trust—
  (a) so far as practicable, consult the beneficiaries of full age and beneficially entitled to an interest in possession in the land, and
  (b) so far as consistent with the general interest of the trust, give effect to the wishes of those beneficiaries, or (in case of dispute) of the majority (according to the value of their combined interests).

(2) Subsection (1) does not apply—
  (a) in relation to a trust created by a disposition in so far as provision that it does not apply is made by the disposition,
  (b) in relation to a trust created or arising under a will made before the

commencement of this Act, or

(c) in relation to the exercise of the power mentioned in section 6(2).

(3) Subsection (1) does not apply to a trust created before the commencement of this Act by a disposition, or a trust created after that commencement by reference to such a trust, unless provision to the effect that it is to apply is made by a deed executed—

(a) in a case in which the trust was created by one person and he is of full capacity, by that person, or

(b) in a case in which the trust was created by more than one person, by such of the persons who created the trust as are alive and of full capacity.

(4) A deed executed for the purposes of subsection (3) is irrevocable.

Right of beneficiaries to occupy trust land

12. The right to occupy—(1) A beneficiary who is beneficially entitled to an interest in possession in land subject to a trust of land is entitled by reason of his interest to occupy the land at any time if at that time—

(a) the purposes of the trust include making the land available for his occupation (or for the occupation of beneficiaries of a class of which he is a member or of beneficiaries in general), or

(b) the land is held by the trustees so as to be so available.

(2) Subsection (1) does not confer on a beneficiary a right to occupy land if it is either unavailable or unsuitable for occupation by him.

(3) This section is subject to section 13.

13. Exclusion and restriction of right to occupy—(1) Where two or more beneficiaries are (or apart from this subsection would be) entitled under section 12 to occupy land, the trustees of land may exclude or restrict the entitlement of any one or more (but not all) of them.

(2) Trustees may not under subsection (1)—

(a) unreasonably exclude any beneficiary's entitlement to occupy land, or

(b) restrict any such entitlement to an unreasonable extent.

(3) The trustees of land may from time to time impose reasonable conditions on any beneficiary in relation to his occupation of land by reason of his entitlement under section 12.

(4) The matters to which trustees are to have regard in exercising the powers conferred by this section include—

(a) the intentions of the person or persons (if any) who created the trust,

(b) the purposes for which the land is held, and

(c) the circumstances and wishes of each of the beneficiaries who is (or apart from any previous exercise by the trustees of those powers would be) entitled to occupy the land under section 12.

(5) The conditions which may be imposed on a beneficiary under subsection (3) include, in particular, conditions requiring him—

(a) to pay any outgoings or expenses in respect of the land, or

(b) to assume any other obligation in relation to the land or to any activity which is or is proposed to be conducted there.

(6) Where the entitlement of any beneficiary to occupy land under section 12 has been excluded or restricted, the conditions which may be imposed on any other beneficiary under subsection (3) include, in particular, conditions requiring him to—

(a) make payments by way of compensation to the beneficiary whose entitlement has been excluded or restricted, or

(b) forgo any payment or other benefit to which he would otherwise be entitled under the trust so as to benefit that beneficiary.

(7) The powers conferred on trustees by this section may not be exercised—

(a) so as to prevent any person who is in occupation of land (whether or not by reason of an entitlement under section 12) from continuing to occupy the land, or

(b) in a manner likely to result in any such person ceasing to occupy the land,
unless he consents or the court has given approval.

(8) The matters to which the court is to have regard in determining whether to
give approval under subsection (7) include the matters mentioned in subsection
(4)(a) to (c).

Powers of court

14. Applications for order—(1) Any person who is a trustee of land or has an
interest in a property subject to a trust of land may make an application to the
court for an order under this section.

(2) On an application for an order under this section the court may make any
such order—

(a) relating to the exercise by the trustees of any of their functions (including an
order relieving them of any obligation to obtain the consent of, or to consult,
any person in connection with the exercise of any of their functions), or

(b) declaring the nature or extent of a person's interest in property subject to
the trust,

as the court thinks fit.

(3) The court may not under this section make any order as to the appointment
or removal of trustees.

(4) The powers conferred on the court by this section are exercisable on an
application whether it is made before or after the commencement of this Act.

15. Matters relevant in determining applications—(1) The matters to which
the court is to have regard in determining an application for an order under
section 14 include—

(a) the intentions of the person or persons (if any) who created the trust,

(b) the purposes for which the property subject to the trust is held,

(c) the welfare of any minor who occupies or might reasonably be expected to
occupy any land subject to the trust as his home, and

(d) the interests of any secured creditor of any beneficiary.

(2) In the case of an application relating to the exercise in relation to any land
of the powers conferred on the trustees by section 13, the matters to which the
court is to have regard also include the circumstances and wishes of each of the
beneficiaries who is (or apart from any previous exercise by the trustees of those
powers would be) entitled to occupy the land under section 12.

(3) In the case of any other application, other than one relating to the exercise
of the power mentioned in section 6(2), the matters to which the court is to have
regard also include the circumstances and wishes of any beneficiaries of full age
and entitled to an interest in possession in property subject to the trust or (in case
of dispute) of the majority (according to the value of their combined interests).

(4) This section does not apply to an application if section 335A of the
Insolvency Act 1986 (which is inserted by Schedule 3 and relates to applications by
a trustee of a bankrupt) applies to it.

Purchaser protection

16. Protection of purchasers—(1) A purchaser of land which is or has been
subject to a trust need not be concerned to see that any requirement imposed on
the trustees by section 6(5), 7(3) or 11(1) has been complied with.

(2) Where—

(a) trustees of land who convey land which (immediately before it is conveyed)
is subject to the trust contravene section 6(6) or (8), but

(b) the purchaser of the land from the trustees has no actual notice of the
contravention,

the contravention does not invalidate the conveyance.

(3) Where the powers of trustees of land are limited by virtue of section 8—

(a) the trustees shall take all reasonable steps to bring the limitation to the notice of any purchaser of the land from them, but

(b) the limitation does not invalidate any conveyance by the trustees to a purchaser who has no actual notice of the limitation.

(4) Where trustees of land convey land which (immediately before it is conveyed) is subject to the trust to persons believed by them to be beneficiaries absolutely entitled to the land under the trust and of full age and capacity—

(a) the trustees shall execute a deed declaring that they are discharged from the trust in relation to that land, and

(b) if they fail to do so, the court may make an order requiring them to do so.

(5) A purchaser of land to which a deed under subsection (4) relates is entitled to assume that, as from the date of the deed, the land is not subject to the trust unless he has actual notice that the trustees were mistaken in their belief that the land was conveyed to beneficiaries absolutely entitled to the land under the trust and of full age and capacity.

(6) Subsections (2) and (3) do not apply to land held on charitable, ecclesiastical or public trusts.

(7) This section does not apply to registered land.

17. Application of provisions to trusts of proceeds of sale—(1) ...*Repealed by the Trustee Act 2000, s 40(1), (3), Sch 2, Pt II para 48, Sch 4, Pt II as from 1 February 2001.*

(2) Section 14 applies in relation to a trust of proceeds of sale of land and trustees of such a trust as in relation to a trust of land and trustees of land.

(3) In this section 'trust of proceeds of sale of land' means (subject to subsection (5)) any trust of property (other than a trust of land) which consists of or includes—

(a) any proceeds of a disposition of land held in trust (including settled land), or

(b) any property representing any such proceeds.

(4) The references in subsection (3) to a trust—

(a) are to any description of trust (whether express, implied, resulting or constructive), including a trust for sale and a bare trust, and

(b) include a trust created, or arising, before the commencement of this Act.

(5) A trust which (despite section 2) is a settlement for the purposes of the Settled Land Act 1925 cannot be a trust of proceeds of sale of land.

(6) In subsection (3)—

(a) 'disposition' includes any disposition made, or coming into operation, before the commencement of this Act, and

(b) the reference to settled land includes personal chattels to which section 67(1) of the Settled Land Act 1925 (heirlooms) applies.

18. Application of Part to personal representatives—(1) The provisions of this Part relating to trustees, other than sections 10, 11 and 14, apply to personal representatives, but with appropriate modifications and without prejudice to the functions of personal representatives for the purposes of administration.

(2) The appropriate modifications include—

(a) the substitution of references to persons interested in the due administration of the estate for references to beneficiaries, and

(b) the substitution of references to the will for references to the disposition creating the trust.

(3) Section 3(1) does not apply to personal representatives if the death occurs before the commencement of this Act.

PART II

APPOINTMENT AND RETIREMENT OF TRUSTEES

*   *   *   *   *

PART III

SUPPLEMENTARY

22. Meaning of 'beneficiary'—(1) In this Act 'beneficiary', in relation to a trust, means any person who under the trust has an interest in property subject to the trust (including a person who has such an interest as a trustee or a personal representative).

(2) In this Act references to a beneficiary who is beneficially entitled do not include a beneficiary who has an interest in property subject to the trust only by reason of being a trustee or personal representative.

(3) For the purposes of this Act a person who is a beneficiary only by reason of being an annuitant is not to be regarded as entitled to an interest in possession in land subject to the trust.

23. Other interpretation provisions—(1) In this Act 'purchaser' has the same meaning as in Part I of the Law of Property act 1925.

(2) Subject to that, where an expression used in this Act is given a meaning by the Law of Property Act 1925 it has the same meaning as in that Act unless the context otherwise requires.

(3) In this Act 'the court' means—
(a) the High Court, or
(b) a county court.

24. Application to Crown—(1) Subject to subsection (2), this Act binds the Crown.

(2) This Act (except so far as it relates to undivided shares and joint ownership) does not affect or alter the descent, devolution or nature of the estates and interests of or in—
(a) land for the time being vested in Her Majesty in right of the Crown or of the Duchy of Lancaster, or
(b) land for the time being belonging to the Duchy of Cornwall and held in right or respect of the Duchy.

25. Amendments, repeals etc—(1) The enactments mentioned in Schedule 3 have effect subject to the amendments specified in that Schedule (which are minor or consequential on other provisions of this Act).

(2) The enactments mentioned in Schedule 4 are repealed to the extent specified in the third column of that Schedule.

(3) Neither section 2(5) nor the repeal by this Act of section 29 of the Settled Land Act 1925 applies in relation to the deed of settlement set out in the Schedule to the Chequers Estate Act 1917 or the trust instrument set out in the Schedule to the Chevening Estate Act 1959.

(4) The amendments and repeals made by this Act do not affect any entailed interest created before the commencement of this Act.

(5) The amendments and repeals made by this Act in consequence of section 3—
(a) do not affect a trust created by a will if the testator died before the commencement of this Act, and
(b) do not affect personal representatives of a person who died before that commencement;
and the repeal of section 22 of the Partnership Act 1890 does not apply in any circumstances involving the personal representatives of a partner who died before that commencement.

26. Power to make consequential provision—(1) The Lord Chancellor may by order made by statutory instrument make any such supplementary, transitional or incidental provision as appears to him to be appropriate for any of the purposes of this Act or in consequence of any of the provisions of this Act.

(2) An order under subsection (1) may, in particular, include provision modifying any enactment contained in a public general or local Act which is passed before, or in the same Session as, this Act.

(3) A statutory instrument made in the exercise of the power conferred by this section is subject to annulment in pursuance of a resolution of either House of Parliament.

27. Short title, commencement and extent—(1) This Act may be cited as the Trusts of Land and Appointment of Trustees Act 1996.

(2) This Act comes into force on such day as the Lord Chancellor appoints by order made by statutory instrument.

(3) Subject to subsection (4), the provisions of this Act extend only to England and Wales.

(4) The repeal in section 30(2) of the Agriculture Act 1970 extends only to Northern Ireland.

Commencement. This Act was brought into force on 1 January 1997 (SI 1996 No 2974).

SCHEDULE 1   Section 2

PROVISIONS CONSEQUENTIAL ON SECTION 2

Minors

1.—(1) Where after the commencement of this Act a person purports to convey a legal estate in land to a minor, or two or more minors, alone, the conveyance—
   (a) is not effective to pass the legal estate, but
   (b) operates as a declaration that the land is held in trust for the minor or minors (or if he purports to convey it to the minor or minors in trust for any persons, for those persons).

(2) Where after the commencement of this Act, a person purports to convey a legal estate in land to—
   (a) a minor or two or more minors, and
   (b) another person who is, or other persons who are, of full age,
the conveyance operates to vest the land in the other person or persons in trust for the minor or minors and the other person or persons (or if he purports to convey it to them in trust for any persons, for those persons).

(3) Where immediately before the commencement of this Act a conveyance is operating (by virtue of section 27 of the Settled Land Act 1925) as an agreement to execute a settlement in favour of a minor or minors—
   (a) the agreement ceases to have effect on the commencement of this Act, and
   (b) the conveyance subsequently operates instead as a declaration that the land is held in trust for the minor or minors.

2. Where after the commencement of this Act a legal estate in land would, by reason of intestacy or in any other circumstances not dealt with in paragraph 1, vest in a person who is a minor if he were a person of full age, the land is held in trust for the minor.

Family charges

3. Where, by virtue of an instrument coming into operation after the commencement of this Act, land becomes charged voluntarily (or in consideration of marriage) or by way of family arrangement, whether immediately or after an interval, with the payment of—
   (a) a rentcharge for the life of a person or a shorter period, or
   (b) capital, annual or periodical sums for the benefit of a person,
the instrument operates as a declaration that the land is held in trust for giving effect to the charge.

Charitable, ecclesiastical and public trusts

4.—(1) This paragraph applies in the case of land held on charitable, ecclesiastical or public trusts (other than land to which the Universities and College Estates Act 1925 applies).

(2) Where there is a conveyance of such land—

(a) if neither section 37(1) nor section 39(1) of the Charities Act 1993 applies to the conveyance, it shall state that the land is held on such trusts, and

(b) if neither section 37(2) nor section 39(2) of that Act has been complied with in relation to the conveyance and a purchaser has notice that the land is held on such trusts, he must see that any consents or orders necessary to authorise the transaction have been obtained.

(3) Where any trustees or the majority of any set of trustees have power to transfer or create any legal estate in the land, the estate shall be transferred or created by them in the names and on behalf of the persons in whom it is vested.

Entailed interests

5.—(1) Where a person purports by an instrument coming into operation after the commencement of this Act to grant to another person an entailed interest in real or personal property, the instrument—

(a) is not effective to grant an entailed interest, but

(b) operates instead as a declaration that the property is held in trust absolutely for the person to whom an entailed interest in the property was purportedly granted.

(2) Where a person purports by an instrument coming into operation after the commencement of this Act to declare himself a tenant in tail of real or personal property, the instrument is not effective to create an entailed interest.

Property held on settlement ceasing to exist

6. Where a settlement ceases to be a settlement for the purposes of the Settled Land Act 1925 because no relevant property (within the meaning of section 2(4)) is, or is deemed to be, subject to the settlement, any property which is or later becomes subject to the settlement is held in trust for the persons interested under the settlement.

*   *   *   *   *

CIVIL PROCEDURE ACT 1997

(1997 c 12)

ARRANGEMENT OF SECTIONS

Section

An Act to amend the law about civil procedure in England and Wales; and for connected purposes.   [27th February 1997]

Rules and directions
1. Civil Procedure Rules—(1) There are to be rules of court (to be called 'Civil Procedure Rules') governing the practice and procedure to be followed in—
    (a) the civil division of the Court of Appeal,
    (b) the High Court, and
    (c) county courts.
    (2) Schedule 1 (which makes further provision about the extent of the power to make Civil Procedure Rules) is to have effect.
    (3) *The power to make Civil Procedure Rules is to be exercised with a view to securing that the civil justice system is accessible, fair and efficient.*
    [(3) Any power to make or alter Civil Procedure Rules is to be exercised with a view to securing that—
    (a) the system of civil justice is accessible, fair and efficient, and
    (b) the rules are both simple and simply expressed.]
Note. Sub-s 3 in square brackets substituted for former sub-s (3) in italics by the Courts Act 2003, s 82(1) from a date to be appointed: see the Courts Act 2003, s 110(1).

2. Rule Committee—(1) Civil Procedure Rules are to be made by a committee known as the Civil Procedure Rule Committee, which is to consist of—
    (a) the Master of the Rolls,
    (b) the Vice-Chancellor, and
    ['(aa) the Head of Civil Justice,
    (ab)the Deputy Head of Civil Justice (if there is one),
    (a) the Master of the Rolls (unless he holds an office mentioned in paragraph (aa) or (ab)), and'.]
    (c) the persons currently appointed by the Lord Chancellor under subsection (2).
Note. Paras (aa), (bb) and (a) in square brackets substituted for paras (a) and (b) as originally enacted in italics by the Courts Act 2003, s 83(1) as from 26 January 2004: see SI 2003/3345, art 2(b)(viii).

    (2) The Lord Chancellor must appoint—
    (a) *one judge of the Supreme Court* [either two or three judges of the Supreme Court],
    (b) one Circuit judge,
    (c) one district judge,
    (d) one person who is a Master referred to in Part II of Schedule 2 to the Supreme Court Act 1981,
    (e) three persons who have a Supreme Court qualification (within the meaning of section 71 of the Courts and Legal Services Act 1990), including at least one with particular experience of practice in county courts,
    (f) three persons who have been granted by an authorised body, under Part II of that Act, the right to conduct litigation in relation to all proceedings in the Supreme Court, including at least one with particular experience of practice in county courts, and
    (g) *one person with experience in and knowledge of consumer affairs, and*

(h) one person with experience in and knowledge of the lay advice sector.
["and
(g) two persons with experience in and knowledge of the lay advice sector or consumer affairs."]

Note. Para (a) in square brackets substituted for former para (a) in italics by the Courts Act 2003, s 83(2); para (g) in square brackets and word "and" immediately preceding it substituted for former paras (g) and (h) in italics by the Courts Act 2003, s 83(3): both amendments in force from 26 January 2004: see SI 2003/3345, art 2(b)(viii).

(3) Before appointing a judge of the Supreme Court under subsection (2)(a), the Lord Chancellor must consult the Lord Chief Justice.

(4) Before appointing a person under paragraph (e) or (f) of subsection (2), the Lord Chancellor must consult any body which—

(a) has members who are eligible for appointment under that paragraph, and

(b) is an authorised body for the purposes of section 27 or 28 of the Courts and Legal Services Act 1990.

(5) The Lord Chancellor may reimburse the members of the Civil Procedure Rule Committee their travelling and out-of-pocket expenses.

(6) The Civil Procedure Rule Committee must, before making or amending Civil Procedure Rules—

(a) consult such persons as they consider appropriate, and

(b) meet (unless it is inexpedient to do so).

(7) The Civil Procedure Rule Committee must, when making Civil Procedure Rules, try to make rules which are both simple and simply expressed.

(8) Rules made by the Civil Procedure Rule Committee must be signed by at least eight members of the Committee and be submitted to the Lord Chancellor, who may allow or disallow them.

Note. Sub-ss (6)-(8) repealed by the Courts Act 2003, s 85(1), 109(3), Sch 10 from a date to be appointed: see the Courts Act 2003, s 110(1).

[2A. Power to change certain requirements relating to Committee

(1) The Lord Chancellor may by order—

(a) amend section 2(2) (persons to be appointed to Committee by Lord Chancellor), and

(b) make consequential amendments in any other provision of section 2.

(2) Before making an order under this section the Lord Chancellor must consult—

(a) the Head of Civil Justice,

(b) the Deputy Head of Civil Justice (if there is one), and

(c) the Master of the Rolls (unless he holds an office mentioned in paragraph (a) or (b)).

(3) The power to make an order under this section is exercisable by statutory instrument.

(4) A statutory instrument containing such an order is subject to annulment in pursuance of a resolution of either House of Parliament.]

Note. S 2A inserted by the Courts Act 2003, s 84 as from 26 January 2004: see SI 2003/3345, art 2(b)(ix).

3. Section 2: supplementary—*(1) Rules made and allowed under section 2 are to—*

(a) come into force on such day as the Lord Chancellor may direct, and

(b) be contained in a statutory instrument to which the Statutory Instruments Act 1946 is to apply as if it contained rules made by a Minister of the Crown.

(2) A statutory instrument containing Civil Procedure Rules shall be subject to annulment in pursuance of a resolution of either House of Parliament.

[3. Process for making Civil Procedure Rules—(1) The Civil Procedure Rule Committee must, before making Civil Procedure Rules—

(a) consult such persons as they consider appropriate, and
(b) meet (unless it is inexpedient to do so).
(2) Rules made by the Civil Procedure Rule Committee must be—
(a) signed by a majority of the members of the Committee, and
(b) submitted to the Lord Chancellor.
(3) The Lord Chancellor may allow, disallow or alter rules so made.
(4) Before altering rules so made the Lord Chancellor must consult the Committee.
(5) Rules so made, as allowed or altered by the Lord Chancellor—
(a) come into force on such day as the Lord Chancellor directs, and
(b) are to be contained in a statutory instrument to which the Statutory Instruments Act 1946 applies as if the instrument contained rules made by a Minister of the Crown.
(6) Subject to subsection (7), a statutory instrument containing Civil Procedure Rules is subject to annulment in pursuance of a resolution of either House of Parliament.
(7) A statutory instrument containing rules altered by the Lord Chancellor is of no effect unless approved by a resolution of each House of Parliament before the day referred to in subsection (5)(a).]

Note. S 3 in square brackets substituted for former s 3 in italics by the Courts Act 2003, s 85(2) from a date to be appointed: see the Courts Act 2003, s 110(1).

4. Power to make consequential amendments—(1) The Lord Chancellor may by order amend, repeal or revoke any enactment to the extent he considers necessary or desirable in consequence of—
(a) section 1 or 2, or
(b) Civil Procedure Rules.
(2) The Lord Chancellor may by order amend, repeal or revoke any enactment passed or made before the commencement of this section to the extent he considers necessary or desirable in order to facilitate the making of Civil Procedure Rules.
(3) Any power to make an order under this section is exercisable by statutory instrument.
(4) A statutory instrument containing an order under subsection (1) shall be subject to annulment in pursuance of a resolution of either House of Parliament.
(5) No order may be made under subsection (2) unless a draft of it has been laid before and approved by resolution of each House of Parliament.

5. Practice directions—(1) Practice directions may provide for any matter which, by virtue of paragraph 3 of Schedule 1, may be provided for by Civil Procedure Rules.
(2) After section 74 of the County Courts Act 1984 there is inserted—

'*Practice directions*
74A. Practice directions—(1) Directions as to the practice and procedure of county courts may be made by the Lord Chancellor.
(2) Directions as to the practice and procedure of county courts may not be made by any other person without the approval of the Lord Chancellor.
(3) The power of the Lord Chancellor to make directions under subsection (1) includes power—
(a) to vary or revoke directions made by him or any other person, and
(b) to make different provision for different cases or different areas, including different provision—
(i) for a specific court, or
(ii) for specific proceedings, or a specific jurisdiction, specified in the directions.
(4) References in this section to the Lord Chancellor include any person authorised by him to act on his behalf.'

Civil Justice Council
6. Civil Justice Council—(1) The Lord Chancellor is to establish and maintain an advisory body, to be known as the Civil Justice Council.

(2) The Council must include—

(a) members of the judiciary,

(b) members of the legal professions,

(c) civil servants concerned with the administration of the courts,

(d) persons with experience in and knowledge of consumer affairs,

(e) persons with experience in and knowledge of the lay advice sector, and

(f) persons able to represent the interests of particular kinds of litigants (for example, businesses or employees).

(3) The functions of the Council are to include—

(a) keeping the civil justice system under review,

(b) considering how to make the civil justice system more accessible, fair and efficient,

(c) advising the Lord Chancellor and the judiciary on the development of the civil justice system,

(d) referring proposals for changes in the civil justice system to the Lord Chancellor and the Civil Procedure Rule Committee, and

(e) making proposals for research.

(4) The Lord Chancellor may reimburse the members of the Council their travelling and out-of-pocket expenses.

Court orders
7. Power of courts to make orders for preserving evidence, etc—(1) The court may make an order under this section for the purpose of securing, in the case of any existing or proposed proceedings in the court—

(a) the preservation of evidence which is or may be relevant, or

(b) the preservation of property which is or may be the subject-matter of the proceedings or as to which any question arises or may arise in the proceedings.

(2) A person who is, or appears to the court likely to be, a party to proceedings in the court may make an application for such an order.

(3) Such an order may direct any person to permit any person described in the order, or secure that any person so described is permitted—

(a) to enter premises in England and Wales, and

(b) while on the premises, to take in accordance with the terms of the order any of the following steps.

(4) Those steps are—

(a) to carry out a search for or inspection of anything described in the order, and

(b) to make or obtain a copy, photograph, sample or other record of anything so described.

(5) The order may also direct the person concerned—

(a) to provide any person described in the order, or secure that any person so described is provided, with any information or article described in the order, and

(b) to allow any person described in the order, or secure that any person so described is allowed, to retain for safe keeping anything described in the order.

(6) An order under this section is to have effect subject to such conditions as are specified in the order.

(7) This section does not affect any right of a person to refuse to do anything on the ground that to do so might tend to expose him or his spouse to proceedings for an offence or for the recovery of a penalty.

(8) In this section—

'court' means the High Court, and

'premises' includes any vehicle;

and an order under this section may describe anything generally, whether by reference to a class or otherwise.

8. Disclosure etc of documents before action begun—(1) The Lord Chancellor may by order amend the provisions of section 33(2) of the Supreme Court Act 1981, or section 52(2) of the County Courts Act 1984 (power of court to order disclosure etc of documents where claim may be made in respect of personal injury or death), so as to extend the provisions—

(a) to circumstances where other claims may be made, or

(b) generally.

(2) The power to make an order under this section is exercisable by statutory instrument which shall be subject to annulment in pursuance of a resolution of either House of Parliament.

General

9. Interpretation—(1) A court the practice and procedure of which is governed by Civil Procedure Rules is referred to in this Act as being 'within the scope' of the rules; and references to a court outside the scope of the rules are to be read accordingly.

(2) In this Act—

'enactment' includes an enactment contained in subordinate legislation (within the meaning of the Interpretation Act 1978), and

'practice directions' means directions as to the practice and procedure of any court within the scope of Civil Procedure Rules.

10. Minor and consequential amendments. Schedule 2 (which makes minor and consequential amendments) is to have effect.

11. Short title, commencement and extent—(1) This Act may be cited as the Civil Procedure Act 1997.

(2) Sections 1 to 10 are to come into force on such day as the Lord Chancellor may by order made by statutory instrument appoint, and different days may be appointed for different purposes.

(3) This Act extends to England and Wales only.

Commencement. Sections 1 to 9 and section 10 so far as it relates to Sch 2, paras 1(1), (2), (4)(c), 2(1), (4), (5), 4 brought into force on 27 April 1997, and section 10 so far as it relates to Sch 2, para 3(a) brought into force on 14 March 1997 (SI 1997 No 841).

SCHEDULE 1   Section 1

CIVIL PROCEDURE RULES

Matters dealt with by the former rules

1. Among the matters which Civil Procedure Rules may be made about are any matters which were governed by the former Rules of the Supreme Court or the former county court rules (that is, the Rules of the Supreme Court (Revision) 1965 and the County Court Rules 1981).

Exercise of jurisdiction

2. Civil Procedure Rules may provide for the exercise of the jurisdiction of any court within the scope of the rules by officers or other staff of the court.

Removal of proceedings

3. (1) Civil Procedure Rules may provide for the removal of proceedings at any stage—

(a) within the High Court (for example, between different divisions or different district registries), or

(b) between county courts.

(2) In sub-paragraph (1)—

(a) 'provide for the removal of proceedings' means—
    (i) provide for transfer of proceedings, or
    (ii) provide for any jurisdiction in any proceedings to be exercised (whether concurrently or not) elsewhere within the High Court or, as the case may be, by another county court without the proceedings being transferred, and
(b) 'proceedings' includes any part of proceedings.

Evidence
4. Civil Procedure Rules may modify the rules of evidence as they apply to proceedings in any court within the scope of the rules.

Application of other rules
5. (1) Civil Procedure Rules may apply any rules of court which relate to a court which is outside the scope of Civil Procedure Rules.

(2) Any rules of court, not made by the Civil Procedure Rule Committee, which apply to proceedings of a particular kind in a court within the scope of Civil Procedure Rules may be applied by Civil Procedure Rules to other proceedings in such a court.

(3) In this paragraph 'rules of court' includes any provision governing the practice and procedure of a court which is made by or under an enactment.

(4) Where Civil Procedure Rules may be made by applying other rules, the other rules may be applied—
(a) to any extent,
(b) with or without modification, and
(c) as amended from time to time.

Practice directions
6. Civil Procedure Rules may, instead of providing for any matter, refer to provision made or to be made about that matter by directions.

Different provision for different cases etc
7. The power to make Civil Procedure Rules includes power to make different provision for different cases or different areas, including different provision—
(a) for a specific court or specific division of a court, or
(b) for specific proceedings, or a specific jurisdiction,
specified in the rules.

SCHEDULE 2   Section 10

MINOR AND CONSEQUENTIAL AMENDMENTS

Supreme Court Act 1981 (c 54)
1. (1) The Supreme Court Act 1981 is amended as follows.

(2) *...Repealed by the Access to Justice Act 1999, s 106, Sch 15, Pt III as from 27 September 1999.*

(3) In section 68 (exercise of High Court jurisdiction otherwise than by judges)—
(a) in subsection (1), paragraph (c) and the word 'or' immediately preceding it are omitted,
(b) in subsection (2)—
    (i) paragraph (a) is omitted, and
    (ii) in paragraph (b), for 'any such person' there is substituted 'a special referee',
(c) in subsection (3), for the words from 'any' onwards there is substituted 'a special referee or any officer or other staff of the court', and
(d) in subsection (4)—
    (i) after 'decision of' there is inserted '(a)', and

(ii) after 'subsection (1)' there is inserted—
'or
(b) any officer or other staff of the court'.
(4) In section 84 (power to make rules of court)—
(a) in subsection (1), for 'Supreme Court' there is substituted 'Crown Court and the criminal division of the Court of Appeal',
(b) subsection (4) is omitted,
(c) for subsections (5) and (6) there is substituted—
'(5) Special rules may apply—
(a) any rules made under this section, or
(b) Civil Procedure Rules,
to proceedings to which the special rules apply.
(5A) Rules made under this section may apply—
(a) any special rules, or
(b) Civil Procedure Rules,
to proceedings to which rules made under this section apply.
(6) Where rules may be applied under subsection (5) or (5A), they may be applied—
(a) to any extent,
(b) with or without modification, and
(c) as amended from time to time.', and
(d) in subsection (9), for 'Supreme Court Rule Committee' there is substituted 'Civil Procedure Rule Committee'.
(5) Section 85 (Supreme Court Rule Committee) is omitted.
(6) In section 87 (particular matters for which rules of court may provide)—
(a) subsections (1) and (2) are omitted, and
(b) in subsection (3), for 'Supreme Court' there is substituted 'Crown Court or the criminal division of the Court of Appeal'.
(7) In section 151 (interpretation)—
(a) in subsection (3), after the second 'rules of court' there is inserted 'in relation to the Supreme Court' and for 'Supreme Court Rule Committee' there is substituted 'Civil Procedure Rule Committee', and
(b) in subsection (4), the definition of 'Rules of the Supreme Court' is omitted.

County Courts Act 1984 (c 28)
2. (1) The County Courts Act 1984 is amended as follows.
(2) For 'county court rules', wherever occurring, there is substituted 'rules of court'.
(3) For 'rule committee', wherever occurring, there is substituted 'Civil Procedure Rule Committee'.
(4) In section 1 (county courts to be held for districts), in subsection (1), for the words from 'throughout' to 'the district' there is substituted 'each court'.
(5) In section 3 (places and times of sittings of courts), subsection (3) is omitted.
(6) Section 75 (county court rules) is omitted.
(7) In section 77(1), for 'the rules of the Supreme Court' there is substituted 'Civil Procedure Rules'.
(8) In section 81(2), for 'any rules of the Supreme Court' there is substituted 'Civil Procedure Rules'.
(9) In section 147(1), the definitions of 'county court rules' and 'the rule committee' are omitted.

Matrimonial and Family Proceedings Act 1984 (c 42)
3. In section 40 of the Matrimonial and Family Proceedings Act 1984 (family proceedings rules)—
(a) after subsection (3) there is inserted—

'(3A) Rules made under this section may make different provision for different cases or different areas, including different provision—
  (a)   for a specific court, or
  (b)   for specific proceedings, or a specific jurisdiction,
  specified in the rules.', and
 (b) in subsection (4), the words from the first 'in' to 'and may' are omitted.

Courts and Legal Services Act 1990 (c 41)
4. In section 120 of the Courts and Legal Services Act 1990 (regulations and orders), in subsection (4), '1(1)' is omitted.

PROTECTION FROM HARASSMENT ACT 1997
(1997 c 40)

An Act to make provision for protecting persons from harassment and similar conduct

[21 March 1997]

England and Wales

1. Prohibition of harassment—(1) A person must not pursue a course of conduct—

(a) which amounts to harassment of another, and

(b) which he knows or ought to know amounts to harassment of the other.

(2) For the purposes of this section, the person whose course of conduct is in question ought to know that it amounts to harassment of another if a reasonable person in possession of the same information would think the course of conduct amounted to harassment of the other.

(3) Subsection (1) does not apply to a course of conduct if the person who pursued it shows—

(a) that it was pursued for the purpose of preventing or detecting crime,

(b) that it was pursued under any enactment or rule of law or to comply with any condition or requirement imposed by any person under any enactment, or

(c) that in the particular circumstances the pursuit of the course of conduct was reasonable.

2. Offence of harassment—(1) A person who pursues a course of conduct in breach of section 1 is guilty of an offence.

(2) A person guilty of an offence under this section is liable on summary conviction to imprisonment for a term not exceeding six months, or a fine not exceeding level 5 on the standard scale, or both.

(3) In section 24(2) of the Police and Criminal Evidence Act 1984 (arrestable offences), after paragraph (m) there is inserted—

'(n) an offence under section 2 of the Protection from Harassment Act 1997 (harassment).'.

Note. Sub-s (3) repealed by the Police Reform Act 2002, s 107(2), Sch 8 as from 1 October 2002.

3. Civil remedy (1) An actual or apprehended breach of section 1 may be the subject of a claim in civil proceedings by the person who is or may be the victim of the course of conduct in question.

(2) On such a claim, damages may be awarded for (among other things) any anxiety caused by the harassment and any financial loss resulting from the harassment.

(3) Where—

(a) in such proceedings the High Court or a county court grants an injunction for the purpose of restraining the defendant from pursuing any conduct which amounts to harassment, and

(b) the plaintiff considers that the defendant has done anything which he is prohibited from doing by the injunction,

the plaintiff may apply for the issue of a warrant for the arrest of the defendant.

(4) An application under subsection (3) may be made—

(a) where the injunction was granted by the High Court, to a judge of that court, and

(b) where the injunction was granted by a county court, to a judge or district judge of that or any other county court.

(5) The judge or district judge to whom an application under subsection (3) is made may only issue a warrant if—
(a) the application is substantiated on oath, and
(b) the judge or district judge has reasonable grounds for believing that the defendant has done anything which he is prohibited from doing by the injunction.
(6) Where—
(a) the High Court or a county court grants an injunction for the purpose mentioned in subsection (3)(a), and
(b) without reasonable excuse the defendant does anything which he is prohibited from doing by the injunction,
he is guilty of an offence.
(7) Where a person is convicted of an offence under subsection (6) in respect of any conduct, that conduct is not punishable as a contempt of court.
(8) A person cannot be convicted of an offence under subsection (6) in respect of any conduct which has been punished as a contempt of court.
(9) A person guilty of an offence under subsection (6) is liable—
(a) on conviction on indictment, to imprisonment for a term not exceeding five years, or a fine, or both, or
(b) on summary conviction, to imprisonment for a term not exceeding six months, or a fine not exceeding the statutory maximum, or both.

4. Putting people in fear of violence—(1) A person whose course of conduct causes another to fear, on at least two occasions, that violence will be used against him is guilty of an offence if he knows or ought to know that his course of conduct will cause the other so to fear on each of those occasions.
(2) For the purposes of this section, the person whose course of conduct is in question ought to know that it will cause another to fear that violence will be used against him on any occasion if a reasonable person in possession of the same information would think the course of conduct would cause the other so to fear on that occasion.
(3) It is a defence for a person charged with an offence under this section to show that—
(a) his course of conduct was pursued for the purpose of preventing or detecting crime,
(b) his course of conduct was pursued under any enactment or rule of law or to comply with any condition or requirement imposed by any person under any enactment, or
(c) the pursuit of his course of conduct was reasonable for the protection of himself or another or for the protection of his or another's property.
(4) A person guilty of an offence under this section is liable—
(a) on conviction on indictment, to imprisonment for a term not exceeding five years, or a fine, or both, or
(b) on summary conviction, to imprisonment for a term not exceeding six months, or a fine not exceeding the statutory maximum, or both.
(5) If on the trial on indictment of a person charged with an offence under this section the jury find him not guilty of the offence charged, they may find him guilty of an offence under section 2.
(6) The Crown Court has the same powers and duties in relation to a person who is by virtue of subsection (5) convicted before it of an offence under section 2 as a magistrates' court would have on convicting him of the offence.

5. Restraining orders—(1) A court sentencing or otherwise dealing with a person ('the defendant') convicted of an offence under section 2 or 4 may (as well as sentencing him or dealing with him in any other way) make an order under this section.

3906 Protection from Harassment Act 1997, s 5

(2) The order may, for the purpose of protecting the victim of the offence, or any other person mentioned in the order, from further conduct which—

(a) amounts to harassment, or

(b) will cause a fear of violence,

prohibit the defendant from doing anything described in the order.

(3) The order may have effect for a specified period or until further order.

(4) The prosecutor, the defendant or any other person mentioned in the order may apply to the court which made the order for it to be varied or discharged by a further order.

(5) If without reasonable excuse the defendant does anything which he is prohibited from doing by an order under this section, he is guilty of an offence.

(6) A person guilty of an offence under this section is liable—

(a) on conviction on indictment, to imprisonment for a term not exceeding five years, or a fine, or both, or

(b) on summary conviction, to imprisonment for a term not exceeding six months, or a fine not exceeding the statutory maximum, or both.

6. Limitation In section 11 of the Limitation Act 1980 (special time limit for actions in respect of personal injuries), after subsection (1) there is inserted—

'(1A) This section does not apply to any action brought for damages under section 3 of the Protection from Harassment Act 1997.'

7. Interpretation of this group of sections—(1) This section applies for the interpretation of sections 1 to 5.

(2) References to harassing a person include alarming the person or causing the person distress.

(3) A 'course of conduct' must involve conduct on at least two occasions.

[(3A) A person's conduct on any occasion shall be taken, if aided, abetted, counselled or procured by another—

(a) to be conduct on that occasion of the other (as well as conduct of the person whose conduct it is); and

(b) to be conduct in relation to which the other's knowledge and purpose, and what he ought to have known, are the same as they were in relation to what was contemplated or reasonably foreseeable at the time of the aiding, abetting, counselling or procuring.]

(4) 'Conduct' includes speech.

Note. Sub-s (3A) inserted by the Criminal Justice and Police Act 2001, s 44(1), in relation to any aiding, abetting, counselling or procuring taking place after 1 August 2001.

* * * * *

General

12. National security, etc—(1) If the Secretary of State certifies that in his opinion anything done by a specified person on a specified occasion related to—

(a) national security,

(b) the economic well-being of the United Kingdom, or

(c) the prevention or detection of serious crime,

and was done on behalf of the Crown, the certificate is conclusive evidence that this Act does not apply to any conduct of that person on that occasion.

(2) In subsection (1), 'specified' means specified in the certificate in question.

(3) A document purporting to be a certificate under subsection (1) is to be received in evidence and, unless the contrary is proved, be treated as being such a certificate.

13. Corresponding provision for Northern Ireland—An Order in Council made under paragraph 1(1)(b) of Schedule 1 to the Northern Ireland Act 1974 which contains a statement that it is made only for purposes corresponding to those of sections 1 to 7 and 12 of this Act—

(a) shall not be subject to sub-paragraphs (4) and (5) of paragraph 1 of that Schedule (affirmative resolution of both Houses of Parliament), but
(b) shall be subject to annulment in pursuance of a resolution of either House of Parliament.

14. Extent—(1)   Sections 1 to 7 extend to England and Wales only.
(2)   Sections 8 to 11 extend to Scotland only.
(3)   This Act (except section 13) does not extend to Northern Ireland.

15. Commencement—(1)   Sections 1, 2, 4, 5 and 7 to 12 are to come into force on such day as the Secretary of State may by order made by statutory instrument appoint.
(2)   Sections 3 and 6 are to come into force on such day as the Lord Chancellor may by order made by statutory instrument appoint.
(3)   Different days may be appointed under this section for different purposes.

16. Short title—This Act may be cited as the Protection from Harassment Act 1997.

HUMAN RIGHTS ACT 1998
(1998 c 42)

An Act to give further effect to rights and freedoms guaranteed under the European Convention on Human Rights; to make provision with respect to holders of certain judicial offices who become judges of the European Court of Human Rights; and for connected purposes.

[9 November 1998]

Introduction

1. The Convention Rights—(1)   In this Act 'the Convention rights' means the rights and fundamental freedoms set out in—
(a)   Articles 2 to 12 and 14 of the Convention,
(b)   Articles 1 to 3 of the First Protocol, and
(c)   *Articles 1 and 2 of the Sixth Protocol* [Article 1 of the Thirteenth Protocol], as read with Articles 16 to 18 of the Convention.
(2)   Those Articles are to have effect for the purposes of this Act subject to any designated derogation or reservation (as to which see sections 14 and 15).
(3)   The Articles are set out in Schedule 1.
(4)   The [*Lord Chancellor*] Secretary of State may by order make such amendments to this Act as he considers appropriate to reflect the effect, in relation to the United Kingdom, of a protocol.
(5)   In subsection (4) 'protocol' means a protocol to the Convention—
(a)   which the United Kingdom has ratified; or
(b)   which the United Kingdom has signed with a view to ratification.
(6)   No amendment may be made by an order under subsection (4) so as to come into force before the protocol concerned is in force in relation to the United Kingdom.
Note. Words in square brackets in sub-s (1)(c) substituted by SI 2004 No 1574, art 2(1) as from 22 June 2004.Words in italics in sub-s (4) repealed and words in square brackets substituted by SI 2003 No 1887, art 9, Sch 2, para 10(1) as from 19 August 2003.

2. Interpretation of Convention rights—(1)   A court or tribunal determining a question which has arisen in connection with a Convention right must take into account any—

(a) judgment, decision, declaration or advisory opinion of the European Court of Human Rights,
(b) opinion of the Commission given in a report adopted under Article 31 of the Convention,
(c) decision of the Commission in connection with Article 26 or 27(2) of the Convention, or
(d) decision of the Committee of Ministers taken under Article 46 of the Convention,

whenever made or given, so far as, in the opinion of the court or tribunal, it is relevant to the proceedings in which that question has arisen.

(2) Evidence of any judgment, decision, declaration or opinion of which account may have to be taken under this section is to be given in proceedings before any court or tribunal in such manner as may be provided by rules.

(3) In this section 'rules' means rules of court or, in the case of proceedings before a tribunal, rules made for the purposes of this section—
(a) by the *Lord Chancellor* [Secretary of State] or the Secretary of State, in relation to any proceedings outside Scotland;
(b) by the Secretary of State, in relation to proceedings in Scotland; or
(c) by a Northern Ireland department, in relation to proceedings before a tribunal in Northern Ireland—
    (i)   which deals with transferred matters; and
    (ii) for which no rules made under paragraph (a) are in force.

Note. Words in italics in sub-s (3) repealed and words in square brackets substituted by SI 2003 No 1887, art 9, Sch 2, para 10(2) as from 19 August 2003.

Legislation

3. Interpretation of legislation—(1) So far as it is possible to do so, primary legislation and subordinate legislation must be read and given effect in a way which is compatible with the Convention rights.
(2) This section—
(a) applies to primary legislation and subordinate legislation whenever enacted;
(b) does not affect the validity, continuing operation or enforcement of any incompatible primary legislation; and
(c) does not affect the validity, continuing operation or enforcement of any incompatible subordinate legislation if (disregarding any possibility of revocation) primary legislation prevents removal of the incompatibility.

4. Declaration of incompatibility—(1) Subsection (2) applies in any proceedings in which a court determines whether a provision of primary legislation is compatible with a Convention right.
(2) If the court is satisfied that the provision is incompatible with a Convention right, it may make a declaration of that incompatibility.
(3) Subsection (4) applies in any proceedings in which a court determines whether a provision of subordinate legislation, made in the exercise of a power conferred by primary legislation, is compatible with a Convention right.
(4) If the court is satisfied—
(a) that the provision is incompatible with a Convention right, and
(b) that (disregarding any possibility of revocation) the primary legislation concerned prevents removal of the incompatibility,
it may make a declaration of that incompatibility.
(5) In this section 'court' means—
(a) the House of Lords;
(b) the Judicial Committee of the Privy Council;

(c) the Courts-Martial Appeal Court;

(d) in Scotland, the High Court of Justiciary sitting otherwise than as a trial court or the Court of Session;

(e) in England and Wales or Northern Ireland, the High Court or the Court of Appeal.

(6) A declaration under this section ('a declaration of incompatibility')—

(a) does not affect the validity, continuing operation or enforcement of the provision in respect of which it is given; and

(b) is not binding on the parties to the proceedings in which it is made.

5. Right of Crown to intervene—(1) Where a court is considering whether to make a declaration of incompatibility, the Crown is entitled to notice in accordance with rules of court.

(2) In any case to which subsection (1) applies—

(a) a Minister of the Crown (or a person nominated by him),

(b) a member of the Scottish Executive,

(c) a Northern Ireland Minister,

(d) a Northern Ireland department,

is entitled, on giving notice in accordance with rules of court, to be joined as a party to the proceedings.

(3) Notice under subsection (2) may be given at any time during the proceedings.

(4) A person who has been made a party to criminal proceedings (other than in Scotland) as the result of a notice under subsection (2) may, with leave, appeal to the House of Lords against any declaration of incompatibility made in the proceedings.

(5) In subsection (4)—

'criminal proceedings' includes all proceedings before the Courts-Martial Appeal Court; and

'leave' means leave granted by the court making the declaration of incompatibility or by the House of Lords.

Public authorities

6. Acts of public authorities—(1) It is unlawful for a public authority to act in a way which is incompatible with a Convention right.

(2) Subsection (1) does not apply to an act if—

(a) as the result of one or more provisions of primary legislation, the authority could not have acted differently; or

(b) in the case of one or more provisions of, or made under, primary legislation which cannot be read or given effect in a way which is compatible with the Convention rights, the authority was acting so as to give effect to or enforce those provisions.

(3) In this section 'public authority' includes—

(a) a court or tribunal, and

(b) any person certain of whose functions are functions of a public nature,

but does not include either House of Parliament or a person exercising functions in connection with proceedings in Parliament.

(4) In subsection (3) 'Parliament' does not include the House of Lords in its judicial capacity.

(5) In relation to a particular act, a person is not a public authority by virtue only of subsection (3)(b) if the nature of the act is private.

(6) 'An act' includes a failure to act but does not include a failure to—

(a) introduce in, or lay before, Parliament a proposal for legislation; or

(b) make any primary legislation or remedial order.

7. Proceedings—(1) A person who claims that a public authority has acted (or proposes to act) in a way which is made unlawful by section 6(1) may—
    (a) bring proceedings against the authority under this Act in the appropriate court or tribunal, or
    (b) rely on the Convention right or rights concerned in any legal proceedings,
but only if he is (or would be) a victim of the unlawful act.
    (2) In subsection (1)(a) 'appropriate court or tribunal' means such court or tribunal as may be determined in accordance with rules; and proceedings against an authority include a counterclaim or similar proceeding.
    (3) If the proceedings are brought on an application for judicial review, the applicant is to be taken to have a sufficient interest in relation to the unlawful act only if he is, or would be, a victim of that act.
    (4) If the proceedings are made by way of a petition for judicial review in Scotland, the applicant shall be taken to have title and interest to sue in relation to the unlawful act only if he is, or would be, a victim of that act.
    (5) Proceedings under subsection (1)(a) must be brought before the end of—
    (a) the period of one year beginning with the date on which the act complained of took place; or
    (b) such longer period as the court or tribunal considers equitable having regard to all the circumstances,
but that is subject to any rule imposing a stricter time limit in relation to the procedure in question.
    (6) In subsection (1)(b) 'legal proceedings' includes—
    (a) proceedings brought by or at the instigation of a public authority; and
    (b) an appeal against the decision of a court or tribunal.
    (7) For the purposes of this section, a person is a victim of an unlawful act only if he would be a victim for the purposes of Article 34 of the Convention if proceedings were brought in the European Court of Human Rights in respect of that act.
    (8) Nothing in this Act creates a criminal offence.
    (9) In this section 'rules' means—
    (a) in relation to proceedings before a court or tribunal outside Scotland, rules made by the *Lord Chancellor* [Secretary of State] or the Secretary of State for the purposes of this section or rules of court,
    (b) in relation to proceedings before a court or tribunal in Scotland, rules made by the Secretary of State for those purposes,
    (c) in relation to proceedings before a tribunal in Northern Ireland—
        (i) which deals with transferred matters; and
        (ii) for which no rules made under paragraph (a) are in force,
rules made by a Northern Ireland department for those purposes,
and includes provision made by order under section 1 of the Courts and Legal Services Act 1990.
    (10) In making rules, regard must be had to section 9.
    (11) The Minister who has power to make rules in relation to a particular tribunal may, to the extent he considers it necessary to ensure that the tribunal can provide an appropriate remedy in relation to an act (or proposed act) of a public authority which is (or would be) unlawful as a result of section 6(1), by order add to—
    (a) the relief or remedies which the tribunal may grant; or
    (b) the grounds on which it may grant any of them.
    (12) An order made under subsection (11) may contain such incidental, supplemental, consequential or transitional provision as the Minister making it considers appropriate.
    (13) 'The Minister' includes the Northern Ireland department concerned.

Note. Words in italics in sub-s (9) repealed and words in square brackets substituted by SI 2003 No 1887, art 9, Sch 2, para 10(2) as from 19 August 2003.

8. Judicial remedies—(1) In relation to any act (or proposed act) of a public authority which the court finds is (or would be) unlawful, it may grant such relief or remedy, or make such order, within its powers as it considers just and appropriate.

(2) But damages may be awarded only by a court which has power to award damages, or to order the payment of compensation, in civil proceedings.

(3) No award of damages is to be made unless, taking account of all the circumstances of the case, including—

(a) any other relief or remedy granted, or order made, in relation to the act in question (by that or any other court), and

(b) the consequences of any decision (of that or any other court) in respect of that act,

the court is satisfied that the award is necessary to afford just satisfaction to the person in whose favour it is made.

(4) In determining—

(a) whether to award damages, or

(b) the amount of an award,

the court must take into account the principles applied by the European Court of Human Rights in relation to the award of compensation under Article 41 of the Convention.

(5) A public authority against which damages are awarded is to be treated—

(a) in Scotland, for the purposes of section 3 of the Law Reform (Miscellaneous Provisions) (Scotland) Act 1940 as if the award were made in an action of damages in which the authority has been found liable in respect of loss or damage to the person to whom the award is made;

(b) for the purposes of the Civil Liability (Contribution) Act 1978 as liable in respect of damage suffered by the person to whom the award is made.

(6) In this section—

'court' includes a tribunal;

'damages' means damages for an unlawful act of a public authority; and

'unlawful' means unlawful under section 6(1).

9. Judicial acts—(1) Proceedings under section 7(1)(a) in respect of a judicial act may be brought only—

(a) by exercising a right of appeal;

(b) on an application (in Scotland a petition) for judicial review; or

(c) in such other forum as may be prescribed by rules.

(2) That does not affect any rule of law which prevents a court from being the subject of judicial review.

(3) In proceedings under this Act in respect of a judicial act done in good faith, damages may not be awarded otherwise than to compensate a person to the extent required by Article 5(5) of the Convention.

(4) An award of damages permitted by subsection (3) is to be made against the Crown; but no award may be made unless the appropriate person, if not a party to the proceedings, is joined.

(5) In this section—

'appropriate person' means the Minister responsible for the court concerned, or a person or government department nominated by him;

'court' includes a tribunal;

'judge' includes a member of a tribunal, a justice of the peace [(or, in Northern Ireland, a lay magistrate)] and a clerk or other officer entitled to exercise the jurisdiction of a court;

'judicial act' means a judicial act of a court and includes an act done on the instructions, or on behalf, of a judge; and

'rules' has the same meaning as in section 7(9).

Note. Sub-s (5): Words in square brackets inserted by the Justice (Northern Ireland) Act 2002, s 10(6), Sch 4, para 39 as from a day to be appointed.

Remedial action

10. Power to take remedial action—(1) This section applies if—
   (a) a provision of legislation has been declared under section 4 to be incompatible with a Convention right and, if an appeal lies—
      (i)   all persons who may appeal have stated in writing that they do not intend to do so;
      (ii) the time for bringing an appeal has expired and no appeal has been brought within that time; or
      (iii) an appeal brought within that time has been determined or abandoned; or
   (b) it appears to a Minister of the Crown or Her Majesty in Council that, having regard to a finding of the European Court of Human Rights made after the coming into force of this section in proceedings against the United Kingdom, a provision of legislation is incompatible with an obligation of the United Kingdom arising from the Convention.
   (2) If a Minister of the Crown considers that there are compelling reasons for proceeding under this section, he may by order make such amendments to the legislation as he considers necessary to remove the incompatibility.
   (3) If, in the case of subordinate legislation, a Minister of the Crown considers—
   (a) that it is necessary to amend the primary legislation under which the subordinate legislation in question was made, in order to enable the incompatibility to be removed, and
   (b) that there are compelling reasons for proceeding under this section,
he may by order make such amendments to the primary legislation as he considers necessary.
   (4) This section also applies where the provision in question is in subordinate legislation and has been quashed, or declared invalid, by reason of incompatibility with a Convention right and the Minister proposes to proceed under paragraph 2(b) of Schedule 2.
   (5) If the legislation is an Order in Council, the power conferred by subsection (2) or (3) is exercisable by Her Majesty in Council.
   (6) In this section 'legislation' does not include a Measure of the Church Assembly or of the General Synod of the Church of England.
   (7) Schedule 2 makes further provision about remedial orders.

Other rights and proceedings

11. Safeguard for existing human rights—A person's reliance on a Convention right does not restrict—
   (a) any other right or freedom conferred on him by or under any law having effect in any part of the United Kingdom; or
   (b) his right to make any claim or bring any proceedings which he could make or bring apart from sections 7 to 9.

12. Freedom of expression—(1) This section applies if a court is considering whether to grant any relief which, if granted, might affect the exercise of the Convention right to freedom of expression.
   (2) If the person against whom the application for relief is made ('the respondent') is neither present nor represented, no such relief is to be granted unless the court is satisfied—

(a) that the applicant has taken all practicable steps to notify the respondent; or

(b) that there are compelling reasons why the respondent should not be notified.

(3) No such relief is to be granted so as to restrain publication before trial unless the court is satisfied that the applicant is likely to establish that publication should not be allowed.

(4) The court must have particular regard to the importance of the Convention right to freedom of expression and, where the proceedings relate to material which the respondent claims, or which appears to the court, to be journalistic, literary or artistic material (or to conduct connected with such material), to—

(a) the extent to which—

> (i) the material has, or is about to, become available to the public; or

> (ii) it is, or would be, in the public interest for the material to be published;

(b) any relevant privacy code.

(5) In this section—

'court' includes a tribunal; and

'relief' includes any remedy or order (other than in criminal proceedings).

13. Freedom of thought, conscience and religion—(1) If a court's determination of any question arising under this Act might affect the exercise by a religious organisation (itself or its members collectively) of the Convention right to freedom of thought, conscience and religion, it must have particular regard to the importance of that right.

(2) In this section 'court' includes a tribunal.

Derogations and reservations

14. Derogations—(1) In this Act 'designated derogation' means—

(a) the United Kingdom's derogation from Article 5(3) of the Convention; and

(b) any derogation by the United Kingdom from an Article of the Convention, or of any protocol to the Convention, which is designated for the purposes of this Act in an order made by the *Secretary of State [Lord Chancellor]*[Secretary of State].

(2) The derogation referred to in subsection (1)(a) is set out in Part I of Schedule 3.

(3) If a designated derogation is amended or replaced it ceases to be a designated derogation.

(4) But subsection (3) does not prevent the *Secretary of State [Lord Chancellor]* [Secretary of State] from exercising his power under subsection (1)*(b)* to make a fresh designation order in respect of the Article concerned.

(5) The *Secretary of State [Lord Chancellor]* [Secretary of State]must by order make such amendments to Schedule 3 as he considers appropriate to reflect—

(a) any designation order; or

(b) the effect of subsection (3).

(6) A designation order may be made in anticipation of the making by the United Kingdom of a proposed derogation.

Note. Words in italics in sub-ss (1), (4), and the whole of sub-s (2) repealed by SI 2001 No 1216, art 2(a)-(c), as from 1 April 2001. In sub-ss (1), (4) and (5) words 'Secretary of State' in italics repealed and words in square brackets substituted by SI 2001 No 3500, art 8, Sch 2, Pt I, para 7(b) as from 26 November 2001; sub-ss (1), (4), (5): words further substituted by SI 2003 No 1887, art 9, Sch 2, para 10(1) as from 19 August 2003.

15. Reservations—(1) In this Act 'designated reservation' means—

(a) the United Kingdom's reservation to Article 2 of the First Protocol to the Convention; and

3914 Human Rights Act 1998, s 15

(b) any other reservation by the United Kingdom to an Article of the Convention, or of any protocol to the Convention, which is designated for the purposes of this Act in an order made by the *Secretary of State [Lord Chancellor]* [Secretary of State].

(2) The text of the reservation referred to in subsection (1)(a) is set out in Part II of Schedule 3.

(3) If a designated reservation is withdrawn wholly or in part it ceases to be a designated reservation.

(4) But subsection (3) does not prevent the *Secretary of State [Lord Chancellor]* [Secretary of State] from exercising his power under subsection (1)(b) to make a fresh designation order in respect of the Article concerned.

(5) The *Secretary of State [Lord Chancellor]* [Secretary of State] must by order make such amendments to this Act as he considers appropriate to reflect—

(a) any designation order; or

(b) the effect of subsection (3).

Note. Words in italics in sub-ss (1), (4) and (5) repealed and words in square brackets substituted by SI 2001 No 3500, art 8, Sch 2, Pt I, para 7(c) as from 26 November 2001. Words in sub-ss (1), (4) and (5) 'Secretary of State' substituted by SI 2003 No 1887, art 9, Sch 2, para 10(1) as from 19 August 2003.

16. Period for which designated derogations have effect—(1) If it has not already been withdrawn by the United Kingdom, a designated derogation ceases to have effect for the purposes of this Act—

(a) *in the case of the derogation referred to in section 14(1)(a), at the end of the period of five years beginning with the date on which section 1(2) came into force;*

(b) *in the case of any other derogation,* at the end of the period of five years beginning with the date on which the order designating it was made.

(2) At any time before the period—

(a) fixed by subsection (1)(a) or (b), or

(b) extended by an order under this subsection,

comes to an end, the *Secretary of State [Lord Chancellor]* [Secretary of State] may by order extend it by a further period of five years.

(3) An order under section 14(1)(b) ceases to have effect at the end of the period for consideration, unless a resolution has been passed by each House approving the order.

(4) Subsection (3) does not affect—

(a) anything done in reliance on the order; or

(b) the power to make a fresh order under section 14(1)(b).

(5) In subsection (3) 'period for consideration' means the period of forty days beginning with the day on which the order was made.

(6) In calculating the period for consideration, no account is to be taken of any time during which—

(a) Parliament is dissolved or prorogued; or

(b) both Houses are adjourned for more than four days.

(7) If a designated derogation is withdrawn by the United Kingdom, the *Secretary of State [Lord Chancellor]* [Secretary of State] must by order make such amendments to this Act as he considers are required to reflect that withdrawal.

Note. Words in italics in sub-ss (1)-(4) repealed by SI 2001 No 1216, art 3(a)-(d), as from 1 April 2001. Words in italics in sub-ss (2) and (7) repealed and words in square brackets substituted by SI 2001 No 3500, art 8, Sch 2, Pt I, para 7(d) as from 26 November 2001. Words 'Secretary of State' in square brackets in sub-ss (2) and (7) substituted by SI 2003 No 1887, art 9, Sch 2, para 10(1) as from 19 August 2003.

17. Periodic review of designated reservations—(1) The appropriate Minister must review the designated reservation referred to in section 15(1)(a)—

(a) before the end of the period of five years beginning with the date on which section 1(2) came into force; and

(b) if that designation is still in force, before the end of the period of five years beginning with the date on which the last report relating to it was laid under subsection (3).

(2) The appropriate Minister must review each of the other designated reservations (if any)—

(a) before the end of the period of five years beginning with the date on which the order designating the reservation first came into force; and

(b) if the designation is still in force, before the end of the period of five years beginning with the date on which the last report relating to it was laid under subsection (3).

(3) The Minister conducting a review under this section must prepare a report on the result of the review and lay a copy of it before each House of Parliament.

Judges of the European Court of Human Rights

18. Appointment to European Court of Human Rights—(1) In this section 'judicial office' means the office of—

(a) Lord Justice of Appeal, Justice of the High Court or Circuit judge, in England and Wales;

(b) judge of the Court of Session or sheriff, in Scotland;

(c) Lord Justice of Appeal, judge of the High Court or county court judge, in Northern Ireland.

(2) The holder of a judicial office may become a judge of the European Court of Human Rights ('the Court') without being required to relinquish his office.

(3) But he is not required to perform the duties of his judicial office while he is a judge of the Court.

(4) In respect of any period during which he is a judge of the Court—

(a) a Lord Justice of Appeal or Justice of the High Court is not to count as a judge of the relevant court for the purposes of section 2(1) or 4(1) of the Supreme Court Act 1981 (maximum number of judges) nor as a judge of the Supreme Court for the purposes of section 12(1) to (6) of that Act (salaries etc);

(b) a judge of the Court of Session is not to count as a judge of that court for the purposes of section 1(1) of the Court of Session Act 1988 (maximum number of judges) or of section 9(1)(c) of the Administration of Justice Act 1973 ('the 1973 Act') (salaries etc);

(c) a Lord Justice of Appeal or judge of the High Court in Northern Ireland is not to count as a judge of the relevant court for the purposes of section 2(1) or 3(1) of the Judicature (Northern Ireland) Act 1978 (maximum number of judges) nor as a judge of the Supreme Court of Northern Ireland for the purposes of section 9(1)(d) of the 1973 Act (salaries etc);

(d) a Circuit judge is not to count as such for the purposes of section 18 of the Courts Act 1971 (salaries etc);

(e) a sheriff is not to count as such for the purposes of section 14 of the Sheriff Courts (Scotland) Act 1907 (salaries etc);

(f) a county court judge of Northern Ireland is not to count as such for the purposes of section 106 of the County Courts Act (Northern Ireland) 1959 (salaries etc).

(5) If a sheriff principal is appointed a judge of the Court, section 11(1) of the Sheriff Courts (Scotland) Act 1971 (temporary appointment of sheriff principal) applies, while he holds that appointment, as if his office is vacant.

(6) Schedule 4 makes provision about judicial pensions in relation to the holder of a judicial office who serves as a judge of the Court.

(7) The Lord Chancellor or the Secretary of State may by order make such transitional provision (including, in particular, provision for a temporary increase in the maximum number of judges) as he considers appropriate in relation to any holder of a judicial office who has completed his service as a judge of the Court.

Parliamentary procedure

19. Statements of compatibility—(1) A Minister of the Crown in charge of a Bill in either House of Parliament must, before Second Reading of the Bill—
  (a) make a statement to the effect that in his view the provisions of the Bill are compatible with the Convention rights ('a statement of compatibility'); or
  (b) make a statement to the effect that although he is unable to make a statement of compatibility the government nevertheless wishes the House to proceed with the Bill.
  (2) The statement must be in writing and be published in such manner as the Minister making it considers appropriate.

Supplemental

20. Orders etc under this Act—(1) Any power of a Minister of the Crown to make an order under this Act is exercisable by statutory instrument.
  (2) The power of the *Lord Chancellor [Secretary of State] or* the Secretary of State to make rules (other than rules of court) under section 2(3) or 7(9) is exercisable by statutory instrument.
  (3) Any statutory instrument made under section 14, 15 or 16(7) must be laid before Parliament.
  (4) No order may be made by the *Lord Chancellor [Secretary of State] or* the Secretary of State under section 1(4), 7(11) or 16(2) unless a draft of the order has been laid before, and approved by, each House of Parliament.
  (5) Any statutory instrument made under section 18(7) or Schedule 4, or to which subsection (2) applies, shall be subject to annulment in pursuance of a resolution of either House of Parliament.
  (6) The power of a Northern Ireland department to make—
  (a) rules under section 2(3)(c) or 7(9)(c), or
  (b) an order under section 7(11),
is exercisable by statutory rule for the purposes of the Statutory Rules (Northern Ireland) Order 1979.
  (7) Any rules made under section 2(3)(c) or 7(9)(c) shall be subject to negative resolution; and section 41(6) of the Interpretation Act (Northern Ireland) 1954 (meaning of 'subject to negative resolution') shall apply as if the power to make the rules were conferred by an Act of the Northern Ireland Assembly.
  (8) No order may be made by a Northern Ireland department under section 7(11) unless a draft of the order has been laid before, and approved by, the Northern Ireland Assembly.
Note. Words in italics in sub-ss (2), (4) repealed and words in square brackets substituted by SI 2003 No 1887, art 9, Sch 2, para 10(2) as from 19 August 2003.

21. Interpretation, etc—(1) In this Act—
  'amend' includes repeal and apply (with or without modifications);
  'the appropriate Minister' means the Minister of the Crown having charge of the appropriate authorised government department (within the meaning of the Crown Proceedings Act 1947);
  'the Commission' means the European Commission of Human Rights;
  'the Convention' means the Convention for the Protection of Human Rights and Fundamental Freedoms, agreed by the Council of Europe at Rome on

4th November 1950 as it has effect for the time being in relation to the United Kingdom;

'declaration of incompatibility' means a declaration under section 4;

'Minister of the Crown' has the same meaning as in the Ministers of the Crown Act 1975;

'Northern Ireland Minister' includes the First Minister and the deputy First Minister in Northern Ireland;

'primary legislation' means any—

(a)   public general Act;

(b)   local and personal Act;

(c)   private Act;

(d)   Measure of the Church Assembly;

(e)   Measure of the General Synod of the Church of England;

(f)   Order in Council—

  (i)   made in exercise of Her Majesty's Royal Prerogative;

  (ii)   made under section 38(1)(a) of the Northern Ireland Constitution Act 1973 or the corresponding provision of the Northern Ireland Act 1998; or

  (iii)   amending an Act of a kind mentioned in paragraph (a), (b) or (c);

and includes an order or other instrument made under primary legislation (otherwise than by the National Assembly for Wales, a member of the Scottish Executive, a Northern Ireland Minister or a Northern Ireland department) to the extent to which it operates to bring one or more provisions of that legislation into force or amends any primary legislation;

'the First Protocol' means the protocol to the Convention agreed at Paris on 20th March 1952;

'the Sixth Protocol' means the protocol to the Convention agreed at Strasbourg on 28th April 1983;

'the Eleventh Protocol' means the protocol to the Convention (restructuring the control machinery established by the Convention) agreed at Strasbourg on 11th May 1994;

['the Thirteenth protocol' means the protocol to the Convention (concerning the abolition of the death penalty in all circumstances) agreed at Vilnius on 3rd May 2002;]

'remedial order' means an order under section 10;

'subordinate legislation' means any—

(a)   Order in Council other than one—

  (i)   made in exercise of Her Majesty's Royal Prerogative;

  (ii)   made under section 38(1)(a) of the Northern Ireland Constitution Act 1973 or the corresponding provision of the Northern Ireland Act 1998; or

  (iii)   amending an Act of a kind mentioned in the definition of primary legislation;

(b)   Act of the Scottish Parliament;

(c)   Act of the Parliament of Northern Ireland;

(d)   Measure of the Assembly established under section 1 of the Northern Ireland Assembly Act 1973;

(e)   Act of the Northern Ireland Assembly;

(f)   order, rules, regulations, scheme, warrant, byelaw or other instrument made under primary legislation (except to the extent to which it operates to bring one or more provisions of that legislation into force or amends any primary legislation);

(g)   order, rules, regulations, scheme, warrant, byelaw or other instrument made under legislation mentioned in paragraph (b), (c), (d) or (e) or made under an Order in Council applying only to Northern Ireland;

(h) order, rules, regulations, scheme, warrant, byelaw or other instrument made by a member of the Scottish Executive, a Northern Ireland Minister or a Northern Ireland department in exercise of prerogative or other executive functions of Her Majesty which are exercisable by such a person on behalf of Her Majesty;

'transferred matters' has the same meaning as in the Northern Ireland Act 1998; and

'tribunal' means any tribunal in which legal proceedings may be brought.

(2) The references in paragraphs (b) and (c) of section 2(1) to Articles are to Articles of the Convention as they had effect immediately before the coming into force of the Eleventh Protocol.

(3) The reference in paragraph (d) of section 2(1) to Article 46 includes a reference to Articles 32 and 54 of the Convention as they had effect immediately before the coming into force of the Eleventh Protocol.

(4) The references in section 2(1) to a report or decision of the Commission or a decision of the Committee of Ministers include references to a report or decision made as provided by paragraphs 3, 4 and 6 of Article 5 of the Eleventh Protocol (transitional provisions).

(5) Any liability under the Army Act 1955, the Air Force Act 1955 or the Naval Discipline Act 1957 to suffer death for an offence is replaced by a liability to imprisonment for life or any less punishment authorised by those Acts; and those Acts shall accordingly have effect with the necessary modifications.

Note. Sub-s (1): definition 'the Sixth protocol' (omitted) repealed by SI 2004 No 1574, art 2(2) as from 22 June 2004; definition 'the Thirteenth protocol' inserted by SI 2004 No 1574, art 2(2) as from 22 June 2004.

22. Short title, commencement, application and extent—(1) This Act may be cited as the Human Rights Act 1998.

(2) Sections 18, 20 and 21(5) and this section come into force on the passing of this Act.

(3) The other provisions of this Act come into force on such day as the Secretary of State may by order appoint; and different days may be appointed for different purposes.

(4) Paragraph (b) of subsection (1) of section 7 applies to proceedings brought by or at the instigation of a public authority whenever the act in question took place; but otherwise that subsection does not apply to an act taking place before the coming into force of that section.

(5) This Act binds the Crown.

(6) This Act extends to Northern Ireland.

(7) Section 21(5), so far as it relates to any provision contained in the Army Act 1955, the Air Force Act 1955 or the Naval Discipline Act 1957, extends to any place to which that provision extends.

SCHEDULE 1   Section 1(3)
THE ARTICLES

PART I
THE CONVENTION

RIGHTS AND FREEDOMS

Article 2
Right to life

1. Everyone's right to life shall be protected by law. No one shall be deprived of his life intentionally save in the execution of a sentence of a court following his conviction of a crime for which this penalty is provided by law.

2. Deprivation of life shall not be regarded as inflicted in contravention of this Article when it results from the use of force which is no more than absolutely necessary:

    (a) in defence of any person from unlawful violence;

    (b) in order to effect a lawful arrest or to prevent the escape of a person lawfully detained;

    (c) in action lawfully taken for the purpose of quelling a riot or insurrection.

Article 3
Prohibition of torture

No one shall be subjected to torture or to inhuman or degrading treatment or punishment.

Article 4
Prohibition of slavery and forced labour

1. No one shall be held in slavery or servitude.

2. No one shall be required to perform forced or compulsory labour.

3. For the purpose of this Article the term 'forced or compulsory labour' shall not include:

    (a) any work required to be done in the ordinary course of detention imposed according to the provisions of Article 5 of this Convention or during conditional release from such detention;

    (b) any service of a military character or, in case of conscientious objectors in countries where they are recognised, service exacted instead of compulsory military service;

    (c) any service exacted in case of an emergency or calamity threatening the life or well-being of the community;

    (d) any work or service which forms part of normal civic obligations.

Article 5
Right to liberty and security

1. Everyone has the right to liberty and security of person. No one shall be deprived of his liberty save in the following cases and in accordance with a procedure prescribed by law:

    (a) the lawful detention of a person after conviction by a competent court;

    (b) the lawful arrest or detention of a person for non-compliance with the lawful order of a court or in order to secure the fulfilment of any obligation prescribed by law;

    (c) the lawful arrest or detention of a person effected for the purpose of bringing him before the competent legal authority on reasonable suspicion of having committed an offence or when it is reasonably considered necessary to prevent his committing an offence or fleeing after having done so;

    (d) the detention of a minor by lawful order for the purpose of educational supervision or his lawful detention for the purpose of bringing him before the competent legal authority;

    (e) the lawful detention of persons for the prevention of the spreading of infectious diseases, of persons of unsound mind, alcoholics or drug addicts or vagrants;

    (f) the lawful arrest or detention of a person to prevent his effecting an unauthorised entry into the country or of a person against whom action is being taken with a view to deportation or extradition.

2. Everyone who is arrested shall be informed promptly, in a language which he understands, of the reasons for his arrest and of any charge against him.

3. Everyone arrested or detained in accordance with the provisions of paragraph 1(c) of this Article shall be brought promptly before a judge or other officer authorised by law to exercise judicial power and shall be entitled to trial within a reasonable time or to release pending trial. Release may be conditioned by guarantees to appear for trial.

4. Everyone who is deprived of his liberty by arrest or detention shall be entitled to take proceedings by which the lawfulness of his detention shall be decided speedily by a court and his release ordered if the detention is not lawful.

5. Everyone who has been the victim of arrest or detention in contravention of the provisions of this Article shall have an enforceable right to compensation.

Article 6
Right to a fair trial

1. In the determination of his civil rights and obligations or of any criminal charge against him, everyone is entitled to a fair and public hearing within a reasonable time by an independent and impartial tribunal established by law. Judgment shall be pronounced publicly but the press and public may be excluded from all or part of the trial in the interest of morals, public order or national security in a democratic society, where the interests of juveniles or the protection of the private life of the parties so require, or to the extent strictly necessary in the opinion of the court in special circumstances where publicity would prejudice the interests of justice.

2. Everyone charged with a criminal offence shall be presumed innocent until proved guilty according to law.

3. Everyone charged with a criminal offence has the following minimum rights:
  (a) to be informed promptly, in a language which he understands and in detail, of the nature and cause of the accusation against him;
  (b) to have adequate time and facilities for the preparation of his defence;
  (c) to defend himself in person or through legal assistance of his own choosing or, if he has not sufficient means to pay for legal assistance, to be given it free when the interests of justice so require;
  (d) to examine or have examined witnesses against him and to obtain the attendance and examination of witnesses on his behalf under the same conditions as witnesses against him;
  (e) to have the free assistance of an interpreter if he cannot understand or speak the language used in court.

Article 7
No punishment without law

1. No one shall be held guilty of any criminal offence on account of any act or omission which did not constitute a criminal offence under national or international law at the time when it was committed. Nor shall a heavier penalty be imposed than the one that was applicable at the time the criminal offence was committed.

2. This Article shall not prejudice the trial and punishment of any person for any act or omission which, at the time when it was committed, was criminal according to the general principles of law recognised by civilised nations.

Article 8
Right to respect for private and family life

1. Everyone has the right to respect for his private and family life, his home and his correspondence.

2. There shall be no interference by a public authority with the exercise of this right except such as is in accordance with the law and is necessary in a democratic society in the interests of national security, public safety or the economic well-being of the country, for the prevention of disorder or crime, for the protection of health or morals, or for the protection of the rights and freedoms of others.

Article 9
Freedom of thought, conscience and religion

1. Everyone has the right to freedom of thought, conscience and religion; this right includes freedom to change his religion or belief and freedom, either alone or in community with others and in public or private, to manifest his religion or belief, in worship, teaching, practice and observance.

2. Freedom to manifest one's religion or beliefs shall be subject only to such limitations as are prescribed by law and are necessary in a democratic society in the interests of public safety, for the protection of public order, health or morals, or for the protection of the rights and freedoms of others.

Article 10
Freedom of expression

1. Everyone has the right to freedom of expression. This right shall include freedom to hold opinions and to receive and impart information and ideas without interference by public authority and regardless of frontiers. This Article shall not prevent States from requiring the licensing of broadcasting, television or cinema enterprises.

2. The exercise of these freedoms, since it carries with it duties and responsibilities, may be subject to such formalities, conditions, restrictions or penalties as are prescribed by law and are necessary in a democratic society, in the interests of national security, territorial integrity or public safety, for the prevention of disorder or crime, for the protection of health or morals, for the protection of the reputation or rights of others, for preventing the disclosure of information received in confidence, or for maintaining the authority and impartiality of the judiciary.

Article 11
Freedom of assembly and association

1. Everyone has the right to freedom of peaceful assembly and to freedom of association with others, including the right to form and to join trade unions for the protection of his interests.

2. No restrictions shall be placed on the exercise of these rights other than such as are prescribed by law and are necessary in a democratic society in the interests of national security or public safety, for the prevention of disorder or crime, for the protection of health or morals or for the protection of the rights and freedoms of others. This Article shall not prevent the imposition of lawful restrictions on the exercise of these rights by members of the armed forces, of the police or of the administration of the State.

Article 12
Right to marry

Men and women of marriageable age have the right to marry and to found a family, according to the national laws governing the exercise of this right.

Article 14
Prohibition of discrimination

The enjoyment of the rights and freedoms set forth in this Convention shall be secured without discrimination on any ground such as sex, race, colour, language, religion, political or other opinion, national or social origin, association with a national minority, property, birth or other status.

Article 16
Restrictions on political activity of aliens

Nothing in Articles 10, 11 and 14 shall be regarded as preventing the High Contracting Parties from imposing restrictions on the political activity of aliens.

Article 17
Prohibition of abuse of rights

Nothing in this Convention may be interpreted as implying for any State, group or person any right to engage in any activity or perform any act aimed at the destruction of any of the rights and freedoms set forth herein or at their limitation to a greater extent than is provided for in the Convention.

Article 18
Limitation on use of restrictions on rights

The restrictions permitted under this Convention to the said rights and freedoms shall not be applied for any purpose other than those for which they have been prescribed.

PART II
THE FIRST PROTOCOL

Article 1
Protection of property

Every natural or legal person is entitled to the peaceful enjoyment of his possessions. No one shall be deprived of his possessions except in the public interest and subject to the conditions provided for by law and by the general principles of international law.

The preceding provisions shall not, however, in any way impair the right of a State to enforce such laws as it deems necessary to control the use of property in accordance with the general interest or to secure the payment of taxes or other contributions or penalties.

Article 2
Right to education

No person shall be denied the right to education. In the exercise of any functions which it assumes in relation to education and to teaching, the State shall respect the right of parents to ensure such education and teaching in conformity with their own religious and philosophical convictions.

Article 3
Right to free elections

The High Contracting Parties undertake to hold free elections at reasonable intervals by secret ballot, under conditions which will ensure the free expression of the opinion of the people in the choice of the legislature.

PART III
THE SIXTH PROTOCOL

Article 1
Abolition of the death penalty

The death penalty shall be abolished. No one shall be condemned to such penalty or executed.

Article 2
Death penalty in time of war

A State may make provision in its law for the death penalty in respect of acts committed in time of war or of imminent threat of war; such penalty shall be applied only in the instances laid down in the law and in accordance with its provisions. The State shall communicate to the Secretary General of the Council of Europe the relevant provisions of that law.

[PART III
ARTICLE 1 OF THE THIRTEENTH PROTOCOL

Abolition of the death penalty

The death penalty shall be abolished. No one shall be condemned to such penalty or executed.]

Note. Part III substituted by SI 2004 No 1574, art 2(3) as from 22 June 2004.

SCHEDULE 2   Section 10
REMEDIAL ORDERS

Orders

1.—(1) A remedial order may—
 (a) contain such incidental, supplemental, consequential or transitional provision as the person making it considers appropriate;
 (b) be made so as to have effect from a date earlier than that on which it is made;
 (c) make provision for the delegation of specific functions;
 (d) make different provision for different cases.
 (2) The power conferred by sub-paragraph (1)(a) includes—
 (a) power to amend primary legislation (including primary legislation other than that which contains the incompatible provision); and
 (b) power to amend or revoke subordinate legislation (including subordinate legislation other than that which contains the incompatible provision).
 (3) A remedial order may be made so as to have the same extent as the legislation which it affects.
 (4) No person is to be guilty of an offence solely as a result of the retrospective effect of a remedial order.

Procedure

2. No remedial order may be made unless—
  (a) a draft of the order has been approved by a resolution of each House of Parliament made after the end of the period of 60 days beginning with the day on which the draft was laid; or
  (b) it is declared in the order that it appears to the person making it that, because of the urgency of the matter, it is necessary to make the order without a draft being so approved.

Orders laid in draft

3.—(1) No draft may be laid under paragraph 2(a) unless—
  (a) the person proposing to make the order has laid before Parliament a document which contains a draft of the proposed order and the required information; and
  (b) the period of 60 days, beginning with the day on which the document required by this sub-paragraph was laid, has ended.
  (2) If representations have been made during that period, the draft laid under paragraph 2(a) must be accompanied by a statement containing—
  (a) a summary of the representations; and
  (b) if, as a result of the representations, the proposed order has been changed, details of the changes.

Urgent cases

4.—(1) If a remedial order ('the original order') is made without being approved in draft, the person making it must lay it before Parliament, accompanied by the required information, after it is made.
  (2) If representations have been made during the period of 60 days beginning with the day on which the original order was made, the person making it must (after the end of that period) lay before Parliament a statement containing—
  (a) a summary of the representations; and
  (b) if, as a result of the representations, he considers it appropriate to make changes to the original order, details of the changes.
  (3) If sub-paragraph (2)(b) applies, the person making the statement must—
  (a) make a further remedial order replacing the original order; and
  (b) lay the replacement order before Parliament.
  (4) If, at the end of the period of 120 days beginning with the day on which the original order was made, a resolution has not been passed by each House approving the original or replacement order, the order ceases to have effect (but without that affecting anything previously done under either order or the power to make a fresh remedial order).

Definitions

5. In this Schedule—
  'representations' means representations about a remedial order (or proposed remedial order) made to the person making (or proposing to make) it and includes any relevant Parliamentary report or resolution; and
  'required information' means—
  (a) an explanation of the incompatibility which the order (or proposed order) seeks to remove, including particulars of the relevant declaration, finding or order; and
  (b) a statement of the reasons for proceeding under section 10 and for making an order in those terms.

Calculating periods

6. In calculating any period for the purposes of this Schedule, no account is to be taken of any time during which—

(a) Parliament is dissolved or prorogued; or

(b) both Houses are adjourned for more than four days.

*   *   *   *   *

SCHEDULE 3   Sections 14 and 15
DEROGATION

[PART I
DEROGATION

The 1988 notification

The United Kingdom Permanent Representative to the Council of Europe presents his compliments to the Secretary General of the Council, and has the honour to convey the following information in order to ensure compliance with the obligations of Her Majesty's Government in the United Kingdom under Article 15(3) of the Convention for the Protection of Human Rights and Fundamental Freedoms signed at Rome on 4 November 1950.

There have been in the United Kingdom in recent years campaigns of organised terrorism connected with the affairs of Northern Ireland which have manifested themselves in activities which have included repeated murder, attempted murder, maiming, intimidation and violent civil disturbance and in bombing and fire raising which have resulted in death, injury and widespread destruction of property. As a result, a public emergency within the meaning of Article 15(1) of the Convention exists in the United Kingdom.

The Government found it necessary in 1974 to introduce and since then, in cases concerning persons reasonably suspected of involvement in terrorism connected with the affairs of Northern Ireland, or of certain offences under the legislation, who have been detained for 48 hours, to exercise powers enabling further detention without charge, for periods of up to five days, on the authority of the Secretary of State. These powers are at present to be found in Section 12 of the Prevention of Terrorism (Temporary Provisions) Act 1984, Article 9 of the Prevention of Terrorism (Supplemental Temporary Provisions) Order 1984 and Article 10 of the Prevention of Terrorism (Supplemental Temporary Provisions) (Northern Ireland) Order 1984.

Section 12 of the Prevention of Terrorism (Temporary Provisions) Act 1984 provides for a person whom a constable has arrested on reasonable grounds of suspecting him to be guilty of an offence under Section 1, 9 or 10 of the Act, or to be or to have been involved in terrorism connected with the affairs of Northern Ireland, to be detained in right of the arrest for up to 48 hours and thereafter, where the Secretary of State extends the detention period, for up to a further five days. Section 12 substantially re-enacted Section 12 of the Prevention of Terrorism (Temporary Provisions) Act 1976 which, in turn, substantially re-enacted Section 7 of the Prevention of Terrorism (Temporary Provisions) Act 1974.

Article 10 of the Prevention of Terrorism (Supplemental Temporary Provisions) (Northern Ireland) Order 1984 (SI 1984/417) and Article 9 of the Prevention of Terrorism (Supplemental Temporary Provisions) Order 1984 (SI 1984/418) were both made under Sections 13 and 14 of and Schedule 3 to the 1984 Act and substantially re-enacted powers of detention in Orders made under the 1974 and 1976 Acts. A person who is being examined under Article 4 of either Order on his arrival in, or on seeking to leave, Northern Ireland or Great Britain for the purpose of determining whether he is or has been involved in terrorism connected with the affairs of Northern Ireland, or whether there are grounds for suspecting that he has committed an offence under Section 9 of the 1984 Act, may be detained under Article 9 or 10, as appropriate, pending the conclusion of his examination. The period of this examination may exceed 12 hours if an examining officer has reasonable grounds for suspecting him to be or to have been involved in acts of terrorism connected with the affairs of Northern Ireland.

Where such a person is detained under the said Article 9 or 10 he may be detained for up to 48 hours on the authority of an examining officer and thereafter, where the Secretary of State extends the detention period, for up to a further five days.

In its judgment of 29 November 1988 in the Case of Brogan and Others, the European Court of Human Rights held that there had been a violation of Article 5(3) in respect of each of the applicants, all of whom had been detained under Section 12 of the 1984 Act. The Court held that even the shortest of the four periods of detention concerned, namely four days and six hours, fell outside the constraints as to time permitted by the first part of Article 5(3). In addition, the Court held that there had been a violation of Article 5(5) in the case of each applicant.

Following this judgment, the Secretary of State for the Home Department informed Parliament on 6 December 1988 that, against the background of the terrorist campaign, and the over-riding need to bring terrorists to justice, the Government did not believe that the maximum period of detention should be reduced. He informed Parliament that the Government were examining the matter with a view to responding to the judgment. On 22 December 1988, the Secretary of State further informed Parliament that it remained the Government's wish, if it could be achieved, to find a judicial process under which extended detention might be reviewed and where appropriate authorised by a judge or other judicial officer. But a further period of reflection and consultation was necessary before the Government could bring forward a firm and final view.

Since the judgment of 29 November 1988 as well as previously, the Government have found it necessary to continue to exercise, in relation to terrorism connected with the affairs of Northern Ireland, the powers described above enabling further detention without charge for periods of up to 5 days, on the authority of the Secretary of State, to the extent strictly required by the exigencies of the situation to enable necessary enquiries and investigations properly to be completed in order to decide whether criminal proceedings should be instituted. To the extent that the exercise of these powers may be inconsistent with the obligations imposed by the Convention the Government has availed itself of the right of derogation conferred by Article 15(1) of the Convention and will continue to do so until further notice.

Dated 23 December 1988

The 1989 notification

The United Kingdom Permanent Representative to the Council of Europe presents his compliments to the Secretary General of the Council, and has the honour to convey the following information.

In his communication to the Secretary General of 23 December 1988, reference was made to the introduction and exercise of certain powers under section 12 of the Prevention of Terrorism (Temporary Provisions) Act 1984, Article 9 of the Prevention of Terrorism (Supplemental Temporary Provisions) Order 1984 and Article 10 of the Prevention of Terrorism (Supplemental Temporary Provisions) (Northern Ireland) Order 1984.

These provisions have been replaced by section 14 of and paragraph 6 of Schedule 5 to the Prevention of Terrorism (Temporary Provisions) Act 1989, which make comparable provision. They came into force on 22 March 1989. A copy of these provisions is enclosed.

The United Kingdom Permanent Representative avails himself of this opportunity to renew to the Secretary General the assurance of his highest consideration.

23 March 1989

[United Kingdom's derogation from Article 5(1)

The United Kingdom Permanent Representative to the Council of Europe presents his compliments to the Secretary General of the Council, and has the honour to convey the following information in order to ensure compliance with the obligations of Her Majesty's Government in the United Kingdom under Article

15(3) of the Convention for the Protection of Human Rights and Fundamental Freedoms signed at Rome on 4 November 1950.

Public emergency in the United Kingdom

The terrorist attacks in New York, Washington, DC and Pennsylvania on 11th September 2001 resulted in several thousand deaths, including many British victims and others from 70 different countries. In its resolutions 1368 (2001) and 1373 (2001), the United Nations Security Council recognised the attacks as a threat to international peace and security.

The threat from international terrorism is a continuing one. In its resolution 1373 (2001), the Security Council, acting under Chapter VII of the United Nations Charter, required all States to take measures to prevent the commission of terrorist attacks, including by denying safe haven to those who finance, plan, support or commit terrorist attacks.

There exists a terrorist threat to the United Kingdom from persons suspected of involvement in international terrorism. In particular, there are foreign nationals present in the United Kingdom who are suspected of being concerned in the commission, preparation or instigation of acts of international terrorism, of being members of organisations or groups which are so concerned or of having links with members of such organisations or groups, and who are a threat to the national security of the United Kingdom.

As a result, a public emergency, within the meaning of Article 15(1) of the Convention, exists in the United Kingdom.

The Anti-terrorism, Crime and Security Act 2001

As a result of the public emergency, provision is made in the Anti-terrorism, Crime and Security Act 2001, inter alia, for an extended power to arrest and detain a foreign national which will apply where it is intended to remove or deport the person from the United Kingdom but where removal or deportation is not for the time being possible, with the consequence that the detention would be unlawful under existing domestic law powers. The extended power to arrest and detain will apply where the Secretary of State issues a certificate indicating his belief that the person's presence in the United Kingdom is a risk to national security and that he suspects the person of being an international terrorist. That certificate will be subject to an appeal to the Special Immigration Appeals Commission ('SIAC'), established under the Special Immigration Appeals Commission Act 1997, which will have power to cancel it if it considers that the certificate should not have been issued. There will be an appeal on a point of law from a ruling by SIAC. In addition, the certificate will be reviewed by SIAC at regular intervals. SIAC will also be able to grant bail, where appropriate, subject to conditions. It will be open to a detainee to end his detention at any time by agreeing to leave the United Kingdom.

The extended power of arrest and detention in the Anti-terrorism, Crime and Security Act 2001 is a measure which is strictly required by the exigencies of the situation. It is a temporary provision which comes into force for an initial period of 15 months and then expires unless renewed by Parliament. Thereafter, it is subject to annual renewal by Parliament. If, at any time, in the Government's assessment, the public emergency no longer exists or the extended power is no longer strictly required by the exigencies of the situation, then the Secretary of State will, by Order, repeal the provision.

Domestic law powers of detention (other than under the Anti-terrorism, Crime and Security Act 2001)

The Government has powers under the Immigration Act 1971 ('the 1971 Act') to remove or deport persons on the ground that their presence in the United

Kingdom is not conducive to the public good on national security grounds. Persons can also be arrested and detained under Schedules 2 and 3 to the 1971 Act pending their removal or deportation. The courts in the United Kingdom have ruled that this power of detention can only be exercised during the period necessary, in all the circumstances of the particular case, to effect removal and that, if it becomes clear that removal is not going to be possible within a reasonable time, detention will be unlawful (*R v Governor of Durham Prison, ex parte Singh* [1984] 1 All ER 983).

Article 5(1)(f) of the Convention

It is well established that Article 5(1)(f) permits the detention of a person with a view to deportation only in circumstance where 'action is being taken with a view to deportation' (*Chahal v United Kingdom* (1996) 23 EHRR 413 at paragraph 112). In that case the European Court of Human Rights indicated that detention will cease to be permissible under Article 5(1)(f) if deportation proceedings are not prosecuted with due diligence and that it was necessary in such cases to determine whether the duration of the deportation proceedings was excessive (paragraph 113).

In some cases, where the intention remains to remove or deport a person on national security grounds, continued detention may not be consistent with Article 5(1)(f) as interpreted by the Court in the *Chahal* case. This may be the case, for example, if the person has established that removal to their own country might result in treatment contrary to Article 3 of the Convention. In such circumstances, irrespective of the gravity of the threat to national security posed by the person concerned, it is well established that Article 3 prevents removal or deportation to a place where there is a real risk that the person will suffer treatment contrary to that article. If no alternative destination is immediately available then removal or deportation may not, for the time being, be possible even though the ultimate intention remains to remove or deport the person once satisfactory arrangements can be made. In addition, it may not be possible to prosecute the person for a criminal offence given the strict rules on the admissibility of evidence in the criminal justice system of the United Kingdom and the high standard of proof required.

Derogation under Article 15 of the Convention

The Government has considered whether the exercise of the extended power to detain contained in the Anti-terrorism, Crime and Security Act 2001 may be inconsistent with the obligations under Article 5(1) of the Convention. As indicated above, there may be cases where, notwithstanding a continuing intention to remove or deport a person who is being detained, it is not possible to say that 'action is being taken with a view to deportation' within the meaning of Article 5(1)(f) as interpreted by the Court in the *Chahal* case. To the extent, therefore, that the exercise of the extended power may be inconsistent with the United Kingdom's obligations under Article 5(1), the Government has decided to avail itself of the right of derogation conferred by Article 15(1) of the Convention and will continue to do so until further notice.

Strasbourg, 18 December 2001]

Note: Schedule 3, Pt I in italics repealed by SI 2001 No 1216, art 4, as from 1 April 2001. Sch 3, Pt I in square brackets inserted by SI 2001 No 4032, art 2, Schedule, as from 20 December 2001.

PART II

RESERVATION

At the time of signing the present (First) Protocol, I declare that, in view of certain provisions of the Education Acts in the United Kingdom, the principle affirmed in the second sentence of Article 2 is accepted by the United Kingdom only so far as it is compatible with the provision of efficient instruction and training, and the avoidance of unreasonable public expenditure.

Dated 20 March 1952. Made by the United Kingdom Permanent Representative to the Council of Europe.

SCHEDULE 4   Section 18(6)

JUDICIAL PENSIONS

Duty to make orders about pensions

1. (1) The appropriate Minister must by order make provision with respect to pensions payable to or in respect of any holder of a judicial office who serves as an ECHR judge.

(2) A pensions order must include such provision as the Minister making it considers is necessary to secure that—

(a) an ECHR judge who was, immediately before his appointment as an ECHR judge, a member of a judicial pension scheme is entitled to remain as a member of that scheme;

(b) the terms on which he remains a member of the scheme are those which would have been applicable had he not been appointed as an ECHR judge; and

(c) entitlement to benefits payable in accordance with the scheme continues to be determined as if, while serving as an ECHR judge, his salary was that which would (but for section 18(4)) have been payable to him in respect of his continuing service as the holder of his judicial office.

Contributions

2. A pensions order may, in particular, make provision—

(a) for any contributions which are payable by a person who remains a member of a scheme as a result of the order, and which would otherwise be payable by deduction from his salary, to be made otherwise than by deduction from his salary as an ECHR judge; and

(b) for such contributions to be collected in such manner as may be determined by the administrators of the scheme.

Amendments of other enactments

3. A pensions order may amend any provision of, or made under, a pensions Act in such manner and to such extent as the Minister making the order considers necessary or expedient to ensure the proper administration of any scheme to which it relates.

Definitions

4. In this Schedule—

'appropriate Minister' means—

(a) in relation to any judicial office whose jurisdiction is exercisable exclusively in relation to Scotland, the Secretary of State; and

(b) otherwise, the Lord Chancellor;

'ECHR judge' means the holder of a judicial office who is serving as a judge of
   the Court;
'judicial pension scheme' means a scheme established by and in accordance with
   a pensions Act;
'pensions Act' means—
(a)   the County Courts Act (Northern Ireland) 1959;
(b)   the Sheriffs' Pensions (Scotland) Act 1961;
(c)   the Judicial Pensions Act 1981; or
(d)   the Judicial Pensions and Retirement Act 1993; and
'pensions order' means an order made under paragraph 1.

PROTECTION OF CHILDREN ACT 1999
(1999 c 14)

An Act to require a list to be kept of persons considered unsuitable to work with
   children; to extend the power to make regulations under section 218(6) of the
   Education Reform Act 1988; to make further provision with respect to that list
   and the list kept for the purposes of such regulations; to enable the protection
   afforded to children to be afforded to persons suffering from mental
   impairment; and for connected purposes.

[15 July 1999]

Department of Health list

1 Duty of Secretary of State to keep list—(1) The Secretary of State shall keep a
list of individuals who are considered unsuitable to work with children.
   (2) An individual shall not be included in the list unless—
      (a)   he has been referred to the Secretary of State under section 2 [or 2A]
            [or 2D] below [or Part VII of the Care Standards Act 2000]; *or*
   [(aa)   he has been included in the list under section 2B below;] or
      (b)   he is transferred to the list from the Consultancy Service Index under
            section 3 below.
   (3) The Secretary of State may at any time remove an individual from the list if
he is satisfied that the individual should not have been included in it.
Note. 2 October 2000 (SI 2000 No 2337, art 2(2)).
Sub-s (2)(a): words 'or 2A' inserted by the Care Standards Act 2000, s 95(2) by SI 2002 No
1493, art 3(2)(a) in relation to England (1 April 2002) and by SI 2002 No 920, art 3(3)(c) in
relation to Wales (1 April 2002). Words 'or Part VII of the Care Standards Act 2000' in sub-s
(2)(a) inserted by the Care Standards Act 2000, s 97(2) as from 26 July 2004: see SI 2004 No
1757, art 2(b). Sub-s (2)(aa) inserted by the Care Standards Act 2000, ss 95(2), 97(2), as from
a day to be appointed. Words 'or 2D' inserted by the Care Standards Act 2000, s 98(4) by SI
2001 No 1193, art 2(2) in relation to England (1 April 2001) and by SI 2001 No 2354, art 2(2)
in relation to Wales (1 July 2001).

**2 *Inclusion in list on reference to Secretary of State* [Inclusion in list on
reference following disciplinary action etc]**—(1) A child care organisation
shall, and any other organisation may, refer to the Secretary of State an individual
who is or has been employed in a child care position if there is fulfilled—
      (a)   any of the conditions mentioned in subsection (2) below; or
      (b)   the condition mentioned in subsection (3) below.
   (2) The conditions referred to in subsection (1)(a) above are—
      (a)   that the organisation has dismissed the individual on the grounds of
            misconduct (whether or not in the course of his employment) which
            harmed a child or placed a child at risk of harm;

(b) that the individual has resigned *or retired* [, retired or made redundant] in circumstances such that the organisation would have dismissed him, or would have considered dismissing him, on such grounds if he had not resigned or *retired* [, retired or made redundant];

(c) that the organisation has, on such grounds, transferred the individual to a position within the organisation which is not a child care position;

(d) that the organisation has, on such grounds, suspended the individual or provisionally transferred him to such a position as is mentioned in paragraph (c) above, but has not yet decided whether to dismiss him or to confirm the transfer.

(3) The condition referred to in subsection (1)(b) above is that—

(a) in circumstances not falling within subsection (2) above, the organisation has dismissed the individual, he has resigned or retired or the organisation has transferred him to a position within the organisation which is not a child care position;

(b) information not available to the organisation at the time of the dismissal, resignation, retirement or transfer has since become available; and

(c) the organisation has formed the opinion that, if that information had been available at that time and if (where applicable) the individual had not resigned or retired, the organisation would have dismissed him, or would have considered dismissing him, on such grounds as are mentioned in subsection (2)(a) above.

(4) If it appears from the information submitted with a reference under subsection (1) above that it may be appropriate for the individual to be included in the list kept under section 1 above, the Secretary of State shall—

(a) determine the reference in accordance with subsections (5) to (7) below; and

(b) pending that determination, provisionally include the individual in the list.

(5) The Secretary of State shall—

(a) invite observations from the individual on the information submitted with the reference and, if he thinks fit, on any observations submitted under paragraph (b) below; and

(b) invite observations from the organisation on any observations on the information submitted with the reference and, if he thinks fit, on any other observations under paragraph (a) above.

(6) Where—

(a) the Secretary of State has considered the information submitted with the reference, any observations submitted to him and any other information which he considers relevant; and

(b) in the case of a reference under subsection (2)(d) above, the organisation has dismissed the individual or, as the case may be, has confirmed his transfer on such grounds as are there mentioned,

the Secretary of State shall confirm the individual's inclusion in the list if subsection (7) below applies; otherwise he shall remove him from the list.

(7) This subsection applies if the Secretary of State is of the opinion—

(a) that the organisation reasonably considered the individual to be guilty of misconduct (whether or not in the course of his employment) which harmed a child or placed a child at risk of harm; and

(b) that the individual is unsuitable to work with children.

(8) The reference in subsection (6)(b) above to the organisation dismissing the individual on such grounds as are mentioned in subsection (2)(d) above includes—

(a) a reference to his resigning *or retiring* [, retiring or being made redundant] in circumstances such that the organisation would have dismissed him, or would have considered dismissing him, on such grounds if he had not resigned *or retired* [retired or been made redundant]; and

(b)   a reference to the organisation transferring him, on such grounds, to a position within the organisation which is not a child care position.

(9)   *This section* [Subsections (1) to (8) and (10) of this section] shall have effect in relation to an organisation which carries on an employment agency, *or an agency for the supply of nurses,* as if—

    (a)   in subsection (1), for the words from 'there is' to the end there were substituted the words 'the organisation has refused to do any further business with the individual on the grounds of misconduct (whether or not in the course of his employment) which harmed a child or placed a child at risk of harm'; and

    [(a)   in subsection (1), for the words from 'there is' to the end there were substituted the following paragraphs—

    '(a)   the organisation has decided not to do any further business with the individual on the grounds of misconduct (whether or not in the course of his employment) which harmed a child or placed a child at risk of harm; or

    (b)   the organisation has decided on such grounds not to find the individual further employment, or supply him for further employment, in a child care position'.]

    (b)   subsections (2), (3), (6)(b) and (8) were omitted.

    [(9A)   Subsections (1) to (8) and (10) of this section shall have effect in relation to an organisation which carries on an employment business as if—

    (a)   in subsection (1)—

        (i)   for the words from 'who' to 'position' there were substituted the words 'who has been supplied by the organisation for employment in a child care position'; and

        (ii)   paragraph (b) and the word 'or' preceding it were omitted;

    (b)   for subsection (2)(c) and (d) there were substituted the following paragraph—

    '(c)   that the organisation has, on such grounds, decided not to supply the individual for further employment in a child care position.' and

    (c)   subsections (3), (6)(b) and (8) were omitted.].

(10)   Nothing in this section shall require a child care organisation to refer an individual to the Secretary of State in any case where the dismissal, resignation, retirement, transfer or suspension took place or, as the case may be, the opinion was formed before the commencement of this section.

Note.   To be appointed: see s 14(2).

In the heading, words in square brackets substituted for words in italics by the Care Standards Act 2000, s 95(1), (3) by SI 2002 No 1493, art 3(2)(a) in relation to England (1 April 2002) and by SI 2002 No 920, art 3(3)(c) in relation to Wales (1 April 2002). Sub-ss (2)(b), (8)(a): words in italic substituted by words in square brackets by the Care Standards Act 2000, s 116, Sch 4, para 26 (1), (2) as from 2 October 2000 (SI 2000 No 2544). Sub-s (9): words 'This section' in italics substituted by subsequent words in square brackets by the Care Standards Act 2000, s 94(1)(a), as from 2 October 2000 (SI 2000 No 2544). Sub-s (9)(a) in italics substituted by sub-s (9)(a) in square brackets by the Care Standards Act 2000, s 94(1)(b), as from 2 October 2000 (SI 2000 No 2544). Sub-s (9): words 'or an agency for the supply of nurses' in italics repealed by the Care Standards Act 2000, s 117(2), Sch 6, as from a day to be appointed. Sub-s (9A) is inserted by the Care Standards Act 2000, s 94(2), as from 2 October 2000 (SI 2000 No 2544).

[2A   Power of certain authorities to refer individuals for inclusion in list—(1) A person to whom this section applies may refer to the Secretary of State an individual who is or has been employed in a child care position if—

    (a)   on the basis of evidence obtained by him in the exercise of his functions under Part II of the Care Standards Act 2000 or Part XA of the Children Act 1989, the person considers that the individual has been guilty of misconduct (whether or not in the course of his employment) which harmed a child or placed a child at risk of harm; and

(b)   the individual has not been referred to the Secretary of State under section 1 above in respect of the misconduct.

(2)   The persons to whom this section applies are—

(a)   *the National Care Standards Commission;*

[(a) the Commission for Social Care Inspection;

(aa) the Commission for Healthcare Audit and Inspection;]

(b)   the National Assembly for Wales; and

(c)   Her Majesty's Chief Inspector of Schools in England.

(3)   Section 2(4) to (7) above shall apply in relation to a reference made by a person under subsection (1) above as it applies in relation to a reference made by an organisation under section 2(1) above.

(4)   The reference in subsection (1) above to misconduct is to misconduct which occurred after the commencement of this section.]

Note. Inserted by the Care Standards Act 2000, s 95(1) by SI 2002 No 1493, art 3(2)(a) in relation to England (1 April 2002) and by SI 2002 No 920, art 3(3)(c); in relation to Wales (1 April 2002). Sub-s (2): paras (a), (aa) substituted, for para (a), by the Health and Social Care (Community Health and Standards) Act 2003, s 147, Sch 9, para 14 as from 1 April 2004.

[2B Individuals named in the findings of certain inquiries—(1) Subsection (2) applies where—

(a)   a relevant inquiry has been held;

(b)   the report of the person who held the inquiry names an individual who is or has been employed in a child care position; and

(c)   it appears to the Secretary of State from the report—

(i)   that the person who held the inquiry found that the individual was guilty of relevant misconduct; and

(ii)   that the individual is unsuitable to work with children.

(2)   The Secretary of State—

(a)   may provisionally include the individual in the list kept under section 1 above; and

(b)   if he does so, shall determine in accordance with subsections (3) to (5) below whether the individual's inclusion in the list should be confirmed.

(3)   The Secretary of State shall—

(a)   invite observations from the individual on the report, so far as relating to him, and, if the Secretary of State thinks fit, on any observations submitted under paragraph (b) below; and

(b)   invite observations from the relevant employer on any observations on the report and, if the Secretary of State thinks fit, on any other observations under paragraph (a) above.

(4)   Where the Secretary of State has considered the report, any observations submitted to him and any other information which he considers relevant, he shall confirm that individual's inclusion in the list if subsection (5) below applies; otherwise he shall remove him from the list.

(5)   This subsection applies if the Secretary of State is of the opinion—

(a)   that the person who held the inquiry reasonably considered the individual to be guilty of relevant misconduct; and

(b)   that the individual is unsuitable to work with children.

(6)   In this section—

'relevant employer' means the person who, at the time referred to in the definition of 'relevant misconduct' below, employed the individual in a child care position;

'relevant misconduct' means misconduct which harmed a child or placed a child at risk of harm and was committed (whether or not in the course of his employment) at a time when the individual was employed in a child care position.

(7) In this section 'relevant inquiry' means any of the following—
(a) an inquiry held under—
    (i)   section 10 of the Care Standards Act 2000;
    (ii)   section 35 of the Government of Wales Act 1998;
    (iii)   section 81 of the Children Act 1989;
    (iv)   section 84 of the National Health Service Act 1977;
    (v)   section 7C of the Local Authority Social Services Act 1970;
    [(vi)   section 17 of the Adoption and Children Act 2002;]
(b) an inquiry to which the Tribunals of Inquiry (Evidence) Act 1921 applies;
(c) any other inquiry or hearing designated for the purposes of this section by an order made by the Secretary of State.
(8) An order under subsection (7) above shall be made by statutory instrument which shall be subject to annulment in pursuance of a resolution of either House of Parliament.
(9) Before making an order under subsection (7) above the Secretary of State shall consult the National Assembly for Wales.]

Note. Inserted by the Care Standards Act 2000, s 96(1), as from 15 September 2000 (certain purposes) (SI 2000 No 2544, art 2(1)(a)); 2 October 2000 (remaining purposes) (SI 2000 No 2544, art 2(2)(c)). In sub-s (7), words in square brackets inserted by the Adoption and Children Act 2002, s 139(1), Sch 3, para 94, as from a date to be appointed.

[2C Inclusion in list on reference under Part VII of Care Standards Act 2000—(1) Section 82(4) to (7) of the Care Standards Act 2000 (persons who provide care for vulnerable adults: duty to refer) shall, in the case of any reference under subsection (1) of that section or section 84 of that Act, apply in relation to the list kept under section 1 above as it applies in relation to the list kept under section 81 of that Act, but as if the reference in subsection (7)(b) to vulnerable adults were a reference to children.

(2) Section 83(4) to (7) of that Act (employment agencies and businesses: duty to refer) shall, in the case of any reference under subsection (1) of that section, apply in relation to the list kept under section 1 above as it applies in relation to the list kept under section 81 of that Act, but as if the reference in subsection (7)(b) to vulnerable adults were a reference to children.

(3) Section 85 of that Act (individuals named in the findings of certain inquiries) shall apply in relation to the list kept under section 1 above as it applies in relation to the list kept under section 81 of that Act, but as if the references in subsections (1)(c)(ii) and (5)(b) to vulnerable adults were references to children.

(4) But the Secretary of State may not by virtue of this section provisionally include an individual in the list kept under section 1 above, or confirm his inclusion in that list, unless he provisionally includes him in the list kept under section 81 of that Act or, as the case requires, confirms his inclusion in that list.

(5) Where an individual has by virtue of this section been included in the list kept under section 1 above, section 4 below shall apply to him as if the references in subsections (3)(a) and (4) to a child were references to a vulnerable adult.]

Note. Inserted by the Care Standards Act 2000, s 97(1), as from 26 July 2004.

[2D Local authorities proposing to make direct payments in respect of services—(1) A local authority may refer a relevant individual to the Secretary of State where, as a result of enquiries made, or caused to be made, by it under section 47 of the Children Act 1989, the authority considers that the individual has been guilty of misconduct (whether or not in the course of his employment) which harmed a child or placed a child at risk of harm.

(2) Section 2(4) to (7) above shall apply in relation to a reference made by a local authority under subsection (1) above as it applies in relation to a reference made by an organisation under section 2(1) above.

(3) In this section—

'funded care' means care in respect of a person's securing the provision of which the authority has made a payment under section 17A of the Children Act 1989 (direct payments);

'relevant individual' means an individual who is or has been employed to provide funded care to a child.

(4) The reference in subsection (1) above to misconduct is to misconduct which occurred after the commencement of this section.]

Note. Inserted by the Care Standards Act 2000, s 98(1), as from 1 April 2001, in relation to England (SI 2001 No 1193) and as from 1 July 2001 in relation to Wales (SI 2001 No 2354).

3 Inclusion in list on transfer from Consultancy Service Index—(1) *This section* [Subsections (2) and (3) below] applies where—

(a) an individual is included in the Consultancy Service Index (otherwise than provisionally) immediately before the commencement of *this section* [section 1 above];

(b) he was so included on a reference made to the Secretary of State by an organisation; and

(c) any of the conditions mentioned in section 2(2)(a) to (c) above, or the condition mentioned in section 2(3) above, was fulfilled in relation to that reference.

(2) If it appears from the information submitted with the reference that it may be appropriate for the individual to be included in the list kept by the Secretary of State under section 1 above, the Secretary of State shall—

(a) invite observations from the individual on the information submitted with the reference and, if he thinks fit, on any observations submitted under paragraph (b) below; and

(b) invite observations from the organisation on any observations on the information submitted with the reference and, if he thinks fit, on any other observations under paragraph (a) above.

(3) The Secretary of State shall include the individual in the list kept by him under section 1 above if, after he has considered the information submitted with the reference, any observations submitted to him and any other information which he considers relevant, he is of the opinion—

(a) that the organisation reasonably considered the individual to be guilty of misconduct (whether or not in the course of his employment) which harmed a child or placed a child at risk of harm; and

(b) that the individual is unsuitable to work with children.

[(4) Subsections (5) and (6) below apply where—

(a) a relevant inquiry has been held;

(b) the report of the person who held the inquiry names an individual who is or has been employed in a child care position;

(c) it appears to the Secretary of State from the report—

　　(i) that the person who held the inquiry found that the individual was guilty of relevant misconduct; and

　　(ii) that the individual is unsuitable to work with children; and

(d) the individual is included in the Consultancy Service Index (otherwise than provisionally) immediately before the commencement of section 1 above.

(5) The Secretary of State shall—

(a) invite observations from the individual on the report, so far as relating to him, and, if the Secretary of State thinks fit, on any observations submitted under paragraph (b) below; and

(b) invite observations from the relevant employer on any observations on the report and, if the Secretary of State thinks fit, on any other observations under paragraph (a) above.

(6) The Secretary of State shall include the individual in the list kept by him under section 1 above if, after he has considered the report, any observations submitted to him and any other information which he considers relevant, he is of the opinion—

(a) that the person who held the inquiry reasonably considered the individual to be guilty of relevant misconduct; and

(b) that the individual is unsuitable to work with children.

(7) In this section—

'relevant employer', in relation to an individual named in the report of a relevant inquiry, means the person who, at the time referred to in the definition of 'relevant misconduct' below, employed the individual in a child care position;

'relevant inquiry' has the same meaning as in section 2B above;

'relevant misconduct' means misconduct which harmed a child or placed a child at risk of harm and was committed (whether or not in the course of his employment) at a time when the individual was employed in a child care position.]

Note. Sub-ss (1), (2): 5 June 2000: SI 2000 No 1459, art 2. Sub-s (3): 1 September 2000 (certain purposes); 2 October 2000 (remaining purposes): SI 2000 No 2337, art 2(1)(b), (2). In sub-s (1), words in italics substituted by words in square brackets, and sub-ss (4)-(7) inserted by the Care Standards Act 2000, s 99(1), (3) as from 15 September 2000 (SI 2000 No 2544).

4 Appeals against inclusion in list—(1) An individual who is included (otherwise than provisionally) in the list kept by the Secretary of State under section 1 above may appeal to the Tribunal against—

(a) the decision to include him in the list; or

(b) with the leave of the Tribunal, any decision of the Secretary of State not to remove him from the list under section 1(3) above.

(2) Subject to subsection (5) below, an individual who has been provisionally included for a period of more than nine months in the list kept by the Secretary of State under section 1 above may, with the leave of the Tribunal, have the issue of his inclusion in the list determined by the Tribunal instead of by the Secretary of State.

(3) If on an appeal or determination under this section the Tribunal is not satisfied of either of the following, namely—

(a) that the individual was guilty of misconduct (whether or not in the course of his duties) which harmed a child or placed a child at risk of harm; and

(b) that the individual is unsuitable to work with children,

the Tribunal shall allow the appeal or determine the issue in the individual's favour and (in either case) direct his removal from the list; otherwise it shall dismiss the appeal or direct the individual's inclusion in the list.

(4) Where an individual has been convicted of an offence involving misconduct (whether or not in the course of his employment) which harmed a child or placed a child at risk of harm, no finding of fact on which the conviction must be taken to have been based shall be challenged on an appeal or determination under this section.

(5) Where the misconduct of which the individual is alleged to have been guilty is the subject of any civil or criminal proceedings, an application for leave under subsection (2) above may not be made before the end of the period of six months immediately following the final determination of the proceedings.

(6) For the purposes of subsection (5) above, proceedings are finally determined when—

(a) the proceedings are terminated without a decision being made;

(b) a decision is made against which no appeal lies;

(c) in a case where an appeal lies with leave against a decision, the time limited for applications for leave expires without leave being granted; or

(d) in a case where leave to appeal against a decision is granted or is not required, the time limited for appeal expires without an appeal being brought.

Note. 2 October 2000: SI 2000 No 2337, art 2(2).

[4A Applications for removal from list—(1) Subject to section 4B below, an individual who is included in the list kept by the Secretary of State under section 1 above may make an application to the Tribunal under this section.

(2) On an application under this section the Tribunal shall determine whether or not the individual should continue to be included in the list.

(3) If the Tribunal is satisfied that the individual is no longer unsuitable to work with children it shall direct his removal from the list; otherwise it shall dismiss the application.]

Note. Inserted together with ss 4B, 4C, by the Criminal Justice and Court Services Act 2000, s 74, Sch 7, Pt II, paras 154, 155, as from 11 January 2001 (SI 2000 No 3302).

[4B Conditions for application under section 4A—(1) An individual may only make an application under section 4A above with the leave of the Tribunal.

(2) An application for leave under this section may not be made unless the appropriate conditions are satisfied in the individual's case.

(3) In the case of an individual who was a child when he was included (otherwise than provisionally) in the list, the appropriate conditions are satisfied if—

(a) he has been so included for a continuous period of at least five years; and

(b) in the period of five years ending with the time when he makes the application under this section, he has made no other such application.

(4) In the case of any other individual, the appropriate conditions are satisfied if—

(a) he has been included (otherwise than provisionally) in the list for a continuous period of at least ten years; and

(b) in the period of ten years ending with the time when he makes the application under this section, he has made no other such application.

(5) The Tribunal shall not grant an application under this section unless it considers—

(a) that the individual's circumstances have changed since he was included (otherwise than provisionally) in the list, or, as the case may be, since he last made an application under this section; and

(b) that the change is such that leave should be granted.].

Note. Inserted as noted to s 4A.

[4C Restoration to list—(1) If it appears to a chief officer of police or a director of social services of a local authority that the conditions set out in subsection (2) below are satisfied in the case of an individual, the chief officer or (as the case may be) the director may apply to the High Court for an order under this section to be made in respect of the individual.

(2) The conditions are that—

(a) the individual is no longer included in the list kept by the Secretary of State under section 1 above, and

(b) the individual has acted in such a way (whether before or after he ceased to be included in the list) as to give reasonable cause to believe that an order under this section is necessary to protect children in general, or any children in particular, from serious harm from him.

(3) An application under this section may be made at any time after the individual ceased to be included in the list.

(4) If the High Court is satisfied that the conditions set out in subsection (2) above are satisfied, it must order the restoration of the individual's inclusion in the list; otherwise it must dismiss the application.

(5) Where an order is made under this section, section 4B above has effect with the following modifications—

(a) in subsection (3), the reference to the individual being a child when he was included in the list is to be read as a reference to his being a child when the order under this section was made,

(b) subsections (3)(a) and (4)(a) are to have effect as if at the end there were inserted 'beginning with the making of the order under section 4C below',

(c) in subsection (5)(a), the reference to the individual's circumstances changing since he was included in the list is to be read as a reference to his circumstances changing since the order under this section was made.

(6) For the purposes of this section an individual is no longer included in the list if a direction under section 4A(3) above has been given in respect of him and his inclusion in the list is not restored by virtue of an order under this section.

(7) In this section, 'local authority' has the same meaning as in the Education Act 1996.']

Note. Inserted as noted to s 4A.

Department for Education and Employment list

Headnote repealed by virtue of the Education Act 2002, s 215, Sch 21, para 120, Sch 22, Pt 3 (in relation to England); 1 June 2003 (SI 2003 No 1115); (in relation to Wales): 31 March 2003 (SI 2002 No 3185).

5 Additional grounds for prohibiting or restricting employment—*(1) In subsection (6) of section 218 (provision for prohibiting or restricting employment of teachers etc) of the Education Reform Act 1988 ('the 1988 Act'), for the words from 'on medical grounds' to the end there shall be substituted the words 'on the grounds mentioned in subsection (6ZA) below'.*

(2) After that subsection there shall be inserted the following subsection—

'(6ZA) The grounds are—

(a) medical grounds;

(b) the grounds of misconduct;

(c) the grounds that the persons concerned are not fit and proper persons to be employed as teachers or in such work as is mentioned in subsection (5)(c) above;

(d) the grounds that the persons concerned are included (otherwise than provisionally) in the list kept by the Secretary of State under section 1 of the Protection of Children Act 1999 (list of individuals considered unsuitable to work with children); and

(e) as respects employment or further employment as teachers, educational grounds.'

(3) In subsection (6A) of that section, for the words 'on medical grounds, or in cases of misconduct,' there shall be substituted the words 'on the grounds mentioned in subsection (6ZA)(a) to (d) above'.

(4) In section 15 of the Teaching and Higher Education Act 1998 (supply of information relating to the dismissal or resignation of teachers), after the words 'on the grounds of misconduct or incompetence' there shall be inserted the words ', on the grounds mentioned in section 218(6ZA)(c) of that Act'.

Note. Repealed by the Education Act 2002, s 215, Sch 21, para 120, Sch 22, Pt 3 (in relation to Wales) as from 31 March 2003 (SI 2003 No 3185) and (in relation to England) as from 1 June 2003 (SI 2003 No 1115).

6 Appeals against prohibition or restriction of employment—*(1) The power to make regulations under subsection (6) of section 218 of the 1988 Act includes power to provide that a person may appeal to the Tribunal against—*

(a) a decision to prohibit or restrict the person's employment or further employment on the grounds mentioned in subsection (6ZA)(a) to (d) of that section; or

(b) a decision not to revoke or vary such a decision as is mentioned in paragraph (a) above.

(2) Regulations made by virtue of this section may make provision as to the circumstances in which the Tribunal shall allow an appeal under the regulations and as to the powers available to it on allowing such an appeal.

(3) Such regulations may provide that, where a person has been convicted of an offence involving misconduct, no finding of fact on which the conviction must be taken to have been based shall be challenged on an appeal under the regulations.

Note. 1 September 2000: SI 2000 No 2337, art 2(1)(d).

Section repealed by the Criminal Justice and Court Services Act 2000, ss 74, 75, Sch 7, Pt II, paras 154, 156, Sch 8, as from 11 January 2001 (SI 2000 No 3302).

General

7 Effect of inclusion in either list—(1) Where a child care organisation proposes to offer an individual employment in a child care position, the organisation—

(a) shall ascertain whether the individual is included in the list kept under section 1 above, or the list kept for the purposes of regulations made under section 218(6) of the 1988 Act; and

(b) if he is included in either list, shall not offer him employment in such a position.

[(1) Where a child care organisation proposes to offer an individual employment in a child care position, the organisation—

(a) shall ascertain whether the individual is included in—

(i) the list kept under section 1 above;

(ii) the list kept for the purposes of regulations made under section 218(6) of the 1988 Act ('the 1988 Act list'); or

(iii) any list kept by the Secretary of State or the National Assembly for Wales of persons disqualified under section 470 or 471 of the Education Act 1996 ('the 1996 Act list'); and

(b) if he is included in any of those lists [that list], shall not offer him employment in such a position;]

[(c) shall ascertain whether he is subject to a direction under section 142 of the Education Act 2002, given on the grounds that he is unsuitable to work with children; and

(d) if he is subject to a direction under that section given on those grounds, shall not offer him employment in a child care position.]

[(1A) Where—

(a) a person ('the recipient') employs, or proposes to employ, an individual to provide care for a child; and

(b) a local authority proposes to make a payment to the recipient under section 17A of the Children Act 1989 (direct payments) in respect of his securing the provision of the care,

the authority shall, if the recipient asks it to do so, ascertain whether the individual is included in any of the lists mentioned in subsection (1) above.]

[(1A) Where a child care organisation discovers that an individual employed by it in a child care position is included in any of the lists mentioned in subsection (1) above, it shall cease to employ him in a child care position.

For the purposes of this subsection an individual is not employed in a child care position if he has been suspended or provisionally transferred to a position which is not a child care position.]

(2) Where a child care organisation proposes to offer employment in a child care position to an individual who has been supplied by an organisation which carries on an employment agency [or an employment business], *or an agency for the*

supply of nurses, there is a sufficient compliance with subsection (1) above if the child care organisation—

    (a) satisfies itself that, on a date within the last 12 months, the other organisation ascertained whether the individual was included in *the list kept under section 1 above, or the list kept for the purposes of regulations made under section 218(6) of the 1988 Act* [any of those lists mentioned in sub-s (1) above] [the list kept under section 1 above or subject to a direction under section 142 of the Education Act 2002, given on the grounds that he is unsuitable to work with children];

    (b) obtains written confirmation of the facts as ascertained by that organisation; *and*

    (c) if the individual was included in *either list* [any of those lists] [the list kept under section 1 above] on that date, does not offer him employment in a child care position [; and

    (d) if the individual was subject to a direction under section 142 of the Education Act 2002, given on those grounds that he is unsuitable to work with children, does not offer him employment in a child care position.]

[(2A) Where a local authority is required under subsection (1A) above to ascertain whether an individual who has been supplied as mentioned in subsection (2) above is included in any of the lists there mentioned, there is sufficient compliance with subsection (1A) above if the authority—

    (a) satisfies itself that, on a date within the last 12 months, the organisation which supplied the individual ascertained whether he was included in any of those lists; and

    (b) obtains written confirmation of the facts as ascertained by the organisation.]

(3) It is immaterial for the purposes of subsection (1) or (2) above whether the individual is already employed by the child care organisation.

[(3A) This section does not apply in relation to an offer of relevant NHS employment if each of the following paragraphs applies in respect of the individual to whom the offer is made—

    (a) at the time the offer is made he is employed by an NHS body;

    (b) that NHS body has ascertained that he is not included in the list kept under section 1 above or (during the period that he is employed by that body) another NHS body or an employment agency or employment business has ascertained that he is not included in the list;

    (c) subsection (1A) (inserted by paragraph 26(2) of Schedule 4 to the Care Standards Act 2000) does not apply to him;

    (d) he accepts the offer and for so long as he is employed in the employment to which the offer relates paragraph (c) applies.

(3B) Relevant NHS employment is employment in a child care position with an NHS body.

    (3C) Each of the following is an NHS body—

    (a) a National Health Service trust;

    (b) a Strategic Health Authority;

    (c) an NHS foundation trust;

    (d) a Health Authority;

    (e) a Local Health Board;

    (f) a Special Health Authority;

    (g) a Primary Care Trust.]

    (4) Any reference in this section to inclusion in the list kept for the purposes of regulations made under subsection (6) of section 218 of the 1988 Act is a reference to inclusion in that list on the grounds mentioned in subsection (6ZA)(c) of that section.

    [(4) In this section—

(a) *any reference to inclusion in the 1988 Act list is a reference to inclusion in that list on the grounds mentioned in section 218(6ZA)(c) of the 1988 Act; and*

(b) *any reference to inclusion in the 1996 Act list is a reference to inclusion in that list as a person disqualified on the grounds mentioned in section 469(1)(d)(i) of the Education Act 1996.]*

Note. 2 October 2000: SI 2000 No 2337, art 2(2).

Sub-s (1) in square brackets substituted for sub-s (1) in italics, by the Care Standards Act 2000, s 101(1), (2), as from 2 October 2000 (SI 2000 No 2544). Sub-s (1)(a) (ii), (iii) repealed by the Education Act 2002, s 215, Sch 21, para 121(1), (2)(a), Sch 22, Pt 3 as from 31 March 2003 (SI 2002 No 3185) (in relation to Wales); as from 1 June 2003 (SI 2003 No 1115) (in relation to England). Sub-s (1): in para (b) words 'any of those lists' repealed and words in square brackets substituted by the Education Act 2002, s 215(1), Sch 21, para 121(1), (2)(b) as from 31 March 2003 (SI 2002 No 3185) (in relation to Wales); as from 1 June 2003 (SI 2003 No 1115) (in relation to England). Sub-s (1): paras (c), (d) inserted by the Education Act 2002, s 215(1), Sch 21, para 121(1), (2)(c) as from 31 March 2003 (SI 2002 No 3185) (in relation to Wales); as from 1 June 2003 (SI 2003 No 1115) (in relation to England). Sub-s (1A) is inserted by the Care Standards Act 2000, s 98(2), as from 1 April 2001 (in relation to England); 1 July 2001 (in relation to Wales) SI 2001 No 1193, SI 2001 No 2354. Second sub-s (1A) is inserted by the Care Standards Act 2000, s 116, Sch 4, para 26(1), (2)(a), as from 2 October 2000 (SI 2000 No 2544). Sub-s (2), after 'employment agency' there is inserted 'or an employment business' by the Care Standards Act 2000, s 116, Sch 4, para 26(1), (2)(b), as from 2 October 2000 (SI 2000 No 2544). Sub-s (2), the words 'or an agency for the supply of nurses' are repealed by the Care Standards Act 2000, s 117(2), Sch 6, as from a day to be appointed. Sub-s (2)(a), (c), words in square brackets substituted for words in italics by the Care Standards Act 2000, s 101(1), (3), as from 2 October 2000 (SI 2000 No 2544). Sub-s (2): in para (a) words 'any of the lists mentioned in subsection (1) above' repealed and subsequent words in square brackets substituted by the Education Act 2002, s 215(1), Sch 21, para 121(1), (3)(a) as from 31 March 2003 (SI 2003 No 3185) (in relation to Wales); as from 1 June 2003 (SI 2003 No 1115) (in relation to England). Sub-s (2): in para (b) word 'and' repealed by the Education Act 2002, s 215, Sch 21, para 121(1), (3)(b), Sch 22, Pt 3 as from as from 31 March 2003 (SI 2002 No 3185) (in relation to Wales); as from 1 June 2003 (SI 2003 No 1115) (in relation to England). Sub-s (2): in para (c) words 'any of those lists' repealed and subsequent words in square brackets substituted by the Education Act 2002, s 215(1), Sch 21, para 121(1), (3)(c) as from 31 March 2003 (SI 2002 No 3185) (in relation to Wales); as from 1 June 2003 (SI 2003 No 1115) (in relation to England). Sub-s (2): para (d) and word '; and' immediately preceding it inserted by the Education Act 2002, s 215(1), Sch 21, para 121(1), (3)(d) as from 31 March 2003 (SI 2002 No 3185) (in relation to Wales); as from 1 June 2003 (SI 2003 No 1115) (in relation to England). Sub-s (2A): inserted by the Care Standards Act 2000, s 98(3), as from 1 April 2001 (in relation to England); 1 July 2001 (in relation to Wales) SI 2001 No 1193, SI 2001 No 2354. Sub-ss (3A)-(3C) inserted by the Health and Social Care (Community Health and Standards) Act 2003, s 189(1), (4); for further effect in relation to sub-s (£A), see s 189(3) thereof, as from 1 April 2004. Sub-s (4) substituted by the Care Standards Act 2000, s 101(1), (4), as from 2 October 2000 (SI 2000 No 2544). Sub-s (4) repealed by the Education Act 2002, s 215, Sch 21, para 121(1), (4), Sch 22, Pt 3 as from 31 March 2003 (SI 2002 No 3185) (in relation to Wales); as from 1 June 2003 (SI 2003 No 1115) (in relation to England).

8 Searches of both lists under Part V of Police Act 1997—(1) After subsection (3) of section 113 of the Police Act 1997 (criminal record certificates) there shall be inserted the following subsections—

'(3A) If an application under this section is accompanied by a statement by the registered person that the certificate is required for the purpose of considering the applicant's suitability for a position (whether paid or unpaid) within subsection (3B), the criminal record certificate shall also state—

(a) whether the applicant is included in the list kept under section 1 of the Protection of Children Act 1999, or the list kept for the purposes of regulations made under section 218(6) of the Education Reform Act 1988; and

(b) if he is included in either list, such details of his inclusion as may be prescribed, including (in the case of the latter list) the grounds on which he is so included.

(3B) A position is within this subsection if it is—

(a) a child care position within the meaning of the Protection of Children Act 1999;

(b) a position employment or further employment in which may be prohibited or restricted by regulations made under subsection (6) of section 218 of the Education Reform Act 1988;

(c) a position such that the holder's access to persons aged under 19 may be prohibited or restricted by regulations under subsection (6A) of that section; or

(d) a position of such other description as may be prescribed;

and the reference to employment or further employment in paragraph (b) shall be construed in accordance with subsection (13) of that section.'

(2) After subsection (6) of section 115 of that Act (enhanced criminal record certificates) there shall be inserted the following subsection—

'(6A) If an application under this section is accompanied by a statement by the registered person that the certificate is required for the purpose of considering the applicant's suitability for a position (whether paid or unpaid) falling within subsection (3B) of section 113, the enhanced criminal record certificate shall also state—

(a) whether the applicant is included in the list kept under section 1 of the Protection of Children Act 1999, or the list kept for the purposes of regulations made under section 218(6) of the Education Reform Act 1988; and

(b) if he is included in either list, such details of his inclusion as may be prescribed, including (in the case of the latter list) the grounds on which he is so included.'

Note. 12 March 2002 (SI 2002 No 1436).

9 The Tribunal—(1) There shall be a tribunal ('the Tribunal') which shall exercise the jurisdiction conferred on it by section 4 and regulations made under section 6 above.

(2) The Secretary of State may by regulations make provision about the proceedings of the Tribunal *on an appeal or determination under section 4 or regulations made under section 6 above.*

[(a) on an appeal or determination under section 4[, 4A or 4B] above;

(b) on an appeal under regulations made under section 6 above;

[(b) on an appeal or determination under regulations made under section 218(6) of the 1988 Act;]

[(b) on an appeal, application for leave or review under section 144 of the Education Act 2002;]

(c) on an appeal under section 65A of the Children Act 1989 or under, or by virtue of, Part XA of that Act; *or*

[(ca) on a determination under section 473A or 473B of the Education Act 1996;]

[(ca) on an appeal under paragraph 10(1A) of Schedule 26 to the School Standards and Framework Act 1998;]

(d) on an appeal or determination under section 21, 68, 86, 87 or 88 of the Care Standards Act 2000]; [or

(e) on a determination under section 32 or 33 of the Criminal Justice and Court Services Act 2000]; [or

(f) on an appeal under section 166 of the Education Act 2002].

(3) The regulations may, in particular, include provision—

(a) as to the manner in which appeals are to be instituted or applications for determinations are to be made;

(b) as to the period within which appeals are to be instituted;

(c) as to the circumstances in which applications for leave may be made;

(d) for enabling any functions which relate to applications for leave or other matters preliminary or incidental to an appeal or determination to be performed by the President, or by the chairman;

(e) for the holding of hearings in private in prescribed circumstances;

(f) for imposing reporting restrictions in prescribed circumstances;

(g) as to the persons who may appear on behalf of the parties;

(h) for granting any person such discovery or inspection of documents or right to further particulars as might be granted by a county court;

(i) for obtaining a medical report in a case where the decision appealed against was made on medical grounds;

(j) for requiring persons to attend to give evidence and produce documents;

(k) for authorising the administration of oaths to witnesses;

(l) for the determination of appeals or issues or applications for leave without a hearing in prescribed circumstances;

(m) as to the withdrawal of appeals or applications for determinations;

(n) for the award of costs or expenses;

(o) for taxing or otherwise settling any such costs or expenses (and, in particular, for enabling such costs to be taxed in the county court);

(p) for the recording and proof of decisions and orders of the Tribunal;

(q) for enabling the Tribunal to review its decisions, or revoke or vary its orders, in such circumstances as may be determined in accordance with the regulations; and

(r) for notification of the result of an appeal or determination to be given to such persons as may be prescribed.

[(3A) The regulations may also include provision for enabling the Tribunal to make investigations for the purposes of a determination under section 87 or 88 of the Care Standards Act 2000; and the provision that may be made by virtue of subsection (3)(j) and (k) above includes provision in relation to such investigations.

(3B) Regulations under this section may make different provision for different cases or classes of case.

(3C) Before making in regulations under this section provision such as is mentioned in subsection (2)(c) or (d) above, the Secretary of State shall consult the National Assembly for Wales.]

(4) Part I of the Arbitration Act 1996 shall not apply to any proceedings before the Tribunal but regulations may make provision corresponding to any provision of that Act.

(5) Any person who without reasonable excuse fails to comply with—

(a) any requirement imposed by the regulations by virtue of subsection (3)(f) above;

(b) any requirement in respect of the discovery or inspection of documents imposed by the regulations by virtue of subsection (3)(h) above; or

(c) any requirement imposed by the regulations by virtue of subsection (3)(j) above,

is liable on summary conviction to a fine not exceeding level 3 on the standard scale.

(6) An appeal shall lie to the High Court on a point of law from a decision of the Tribunal.

(7) The Schedule to this Act shall have effect with respect to the Tribunal.

Note. 1 September 2000 (for the purpose of making regulations); 2 October 2000 (otherwise): SI 2000 No 2337, art 2(1)(e), (2).

Sub-s (2): words from 'on an appeal' to 'section 6 above' in italics repealed and substituted by subsequent paras (a)–(d), by the Care Standards Act 2000, s 116, Sch 4, para 26(1), (3)(a) in force in relation to England in so far as it relates to paras (a), (c): 1 April 2002: SI 2001 No 3852, art 3(7)(i); in relation to Wales in so far as it relates to paras (a), (c): 1 April 2002: SI 2002 No 920, art 3(3)(f); for transitional provisions see arts 2, 3(2), 94), (6)-(10), Schs 1, 3 thereto; in relation to Wales in so far as it relates to para (d) for certain purposes: 1 April 2002: see SI 2002 No 920, art 3(3)(f); for transitional provisions see arts 2, 3 (2), (4), (6)-(10), Sch 1 thereto; in relation to Wales in so far as it relates to para (d) for certain purposes: 5 March 2003: see SI 2003 No 501, art 2(1); in relation to England in so far as it relates to para (d) for certain purposes: 7 March 2003: see SI 2003 No 933, art 2(1)(c); and in relation to England and Wales for remaining purposes: to be appointed: see the Care Standards Act 2000, s 122. Sub-s (2)(a): words ', 4A or 4B' in square brackets inserted by the Criminal Justice and Court Services Act 2000, s 74, Sch 7, Pt II, paras 154, 157(a), as from 11 January 2001 (SI 2000 No 3302). Sub-s (2)(b): para (b) in italics substituted by para (b) in square brackets by the Criminal Justice and Court Services Act 2000, s 74, Sch 7, Pt II, paras 154, 157(b), as from 11 January 2001 (SI 2000 No 3302). Sub-s (2): para (b) further substituted by the Education Act 2002, s 215(1), Sch 21, para 122(a) as from 31 March 2003 (in relation to Wales); as from 1 June 2003 (in relation to England): SI 2003 No 1115. Sub-s (2)(ca): para (ca) substituted, for original word 'or' in italics at the end of para (c), by the Criminal Justice and Court Services Act 2000, s 74, Sch 7, Pt II, paras 154, 157(c), as from 11 January 2001 (SI 2000 No 3302). Sub-s (2)(ca) further substituted by the Education Act 2002, s 155, Sch 14, para 6 as from (in relation to England): 1 October 2002 (except in relation to appeals made under the School Standards and Framework Act 1998, Sch 26, para 10(1), before that date: SI 2002 No 2439, art 3 and the Education Act 2002, Sch 14, para 7; as from (in relation to Wales): to be appointed (Education Act 2002, s 216(4)). Sub-s (2): in para (d) word 'or' repealed by the Education Act 2002, s 215(2), Sch 22, Pt 3 as from 31 March 2003 (in relation to Wales) (SI 2002 No 3185); as from 1 June 2003 (in relation to England) (SI 2003 No 1115). Sub-s (2)(e) and word '; or' immediately preceding it: inserted by the Criminal Justice and Court Services Act 2000, s 74, Sch 7, Pt II, paras 154, 157(d), as from 11 January 2001 (SI 2000 No 3302). Sub-s (2): para (f) and word 'or' immediately preceding it inserted by the Education Act 2002, s 215(1), Sch 21, para 122(b) as from (in relation to England): 1 June 2003 (SI 2003 No 1115); as from (in relation to Wales): to be appointed. Sub-ss (3A)–(3C): inserted by the Care Standards Act 2000, s 116, Sch 4, para 26(1), (3)(b) in force in relation to England in so far as it relates to (3B), (3C): 1 April 2002: SI 2001 No 3852, art 3(7)(i); in force (in relation to Wales in so far as it relates to sub-ss (3B), (3C): 1 April 2002: SI 2002 No 920, art 3(3)(f); for transitional provisions see arts 2, 3(2), (4), (6), (10), Sch 1 thereto; in force (in relation to England and Wales for remaining purposes): to be appointed: Care Standards Act 2000, s 122.).

10   Power to extend protection of Act—*(1) The Secretary of State may by order made by statutory instrument provide that this Act shall have effect as if*—

(a)   *the references to children in sections 1(1), 2(7)(b), 3(3)(b) and 4(3)(b) above and section 12(1) below included references to persons aged 18 or over who are suffering from mental impairment; and*

(b)   *the references to a child in sections 2(2)(a), (7)(a) and (9)(a), 3(3)(a) and 4(3)(a) and (4) above included references to a person aged 18 or over who is suffering from such impairment.*

(2) The power to make an order under this section shall include power to make such consequential, supplemental, incidental or transitional provision as the Secretary of State thinks fit.

(3) No order shall be made under this section unless a draft of the order has been laid before and approved by a resolution of each House of Parliament.

Note. Repealed by the Care Standards Act 2000, s 117(2), Sch 6, as from 2 October 2000 (SI 2000 No 2544).

Supplemental

11 Financial provisions   There shall be paid out of money provided by Parliament—

(a)   any expenditure incurred by the Secretary of State under or by virtue of this Act;

(b) any increase attributable to this Act in the sums payable out of money so provided under any other Act.

12 Interpretation—(1) In this Act—

'the 1988 Act' means the Education Reform Act 1988;

'agency for the supply of nurses' has the same meaning as in the Nurses Agencies Act 1957;

'child' means a person aged under 18;

'child care organisation' means an organisation—

    (a) which is concerned with the provision of accommodation, social services or health care services to children or the supervision of children;

    (b) whose activities are regulated by or by virtue of any prescribed enactment; and

    (c) which fulfils such other conditions as may be prescribed;

'child care position' means a position which—

    (a) is concerned with the provision of accommodation, social services or health care services to children or the supervision of children;

    (b) is such as to enable the holder to have regular contact with children in the course of his duties; and

    (c) is not a position within subsection (3) below;

    [(a) is a regulated position for the purposes of Part II of the Criminal Justice and Court Services Act 2000; but

    (b) is not a position within subsection (3) below;]

'the Consultancy Service Index' means the list kept under that name by the Secretary of State;

'employment'—

    (a) means any employment, whether paid or unpaid and whether under a contract of service or apprenticeship, under a contract for services, or otherwise than under a contract; and

    (b) includes an office established by or by virtue of a prescribed enactment,

and references to an individual being employed shall be construed accordingly;

'employment agency' *has the same meaning* [and 'employment business' have the same meanings], as in the Employment Agencies Act 1973;

'harm' has the same meaning as in section 31 of the Children Act 1989;

['local authority' has the same meaning as in the Children Act 1989;]

'mental impairment' means a state of arrested or incomplete development of mind which includes a significant impairment of intelligence and social functioning;

'organisation' means a body corporate or unincorporate or an individual who employs others in the course of a business;

'prescribed' means prescribed by regulations made by the Secretary of State;

'the Tribunal' means the tribunal established under section 9 above.

(2) Where part of an organisation fulfils the condition in paragraph (b) of the above definition of 'child care organisation' and part of it does not, this Act shall have effect as if the two parts were separate organisations.

(3) A position is within this subsection if—

(a) employment or further employment in it may be prohibited or restricted by regulations made under section 218(6) of the 1988 Act; and

[(a) it involves work to which section 142 of the Education Act 2002 applies;] and

(b) it is not a position at *an independent school which is a children's home for the purposes of Part VIII of the Children Act 1989* [a school which is a children's home for the purposes of the Care Standards Act 2000].

[(3A) For the purposes of this Act, an individual is made redundant if—
(a) he is dismissed; and
(b) for the purposes of the Employment Rights Act 1996 the dismissal is by reason of redundancy.]

(4) Regulations under this Act shall be made by statutory instrument which shall be subject to annulment in pursuance of a resolution of either House of Parliament.

Note. Sub-s (1): definition 'the 1988 Act' repealed by the Education Act 2002, s 215, Sch 21, para 123(1), (2), Sch 22, Pt 3 as from 31 March 2003 (SI 2002 No 3185) (in relation to Wales); as from 1 June 2003 (SI 2003 No 1115) (in relation to England). Sub-s (1), the definition 'agency for the supply of nurses' is repealed by the Care Standards Act 2000, s 117(2), Sch 6, as from a date to be appointed. Sub-s (1), in the definition 'child care position', for paras (a) to (c) there are substituted new paras (a), (b), by the Criminal Justice and Court Services Act 2000, s 74, Sch 7, Pt II, paras 154, 158(a), as from 11 January 2001 (SI 2000 No 3302). Sub-s (1), in the definition 'employment agency', words in italics substituted by words in square brackets and the definition 'local authority' is inserted by the Care Standards Act 2000, s 116, Sch 4, para 26(1), (4)(a)(i),(ii), as from 2 October 2000 (SI 2000 No 2544). Sub-s (3): para (a) substituted by the Education Act 2002, s 215(1), Sch 21, para 123(1), (3) as from 31 March 2003 (SI 2002 No 3185) (in relation to Wales); as from 1 June 2003 (SI 2003 No 1115) (in relation to England). Sub-s (3)(b), words in italics substituted by words in square brackets, by the Criminal Justice and Court Services Act 2000, s 74, Sch 7, Pt II, paras 154, 158(b), as from 11 January 2001 (SI 2000 No 3302). Sub-s (3A): inserted by the Care Standards Act 2000, s 116, Sch 4, para 26(1), (4)(b), as from 2 October 2000 (SI 2000 No 2544).

13 Transitional provisions—(1) Where—
(a) an individual who is or has been employed in a child care position has been referred by an organisation to the Secretary of State for inclusion in the Consultancy Service Index;
(b) the reference has not been determined at the commencement of section 2 above; and
(c) any of the conditions mentioned in subsection (2), or the condition mentioned in subsection (3), of that section was fulfilled in relation to the reference,
that section shall apply as if the reference had been a reference made by the organisation under subsection (1) of that section.

(2) For the purposes of subsection (1) above, a reference of an individual for inclusion in that Index is determined only when, following the reference—
(a) the individual is included (otherwise than provisionally) in the Index; or
(b) the Secretary of State determines that he should not be included in it.

(3) In relation to any time before the commencement of section 8 above, any organisation seeking to ascertain whether an individual to whom it proposes to offer a child care position or, in the case of an organisation which carries on an employment agency or an agency for the supply of nurses, with whom it proposes to do business is included in—
(a) the list kept under section 1 above; or
(b) the list kept for the purposes of regulations made under section 218(6) of the 1988 Act,
shall be entitled to that information on making application for the purpose to the Secretary of State.

(4) Subsection (3)(b) above is without prejudice to any right conferred otherwise than by virtue of that provision.

Note. Sub-ss (3), (4) are repealed by the Care Standards Act 2000, s 117(2), Sch 6, as from 2 October 2000 (SI 2000 No 2544).

14 Short title, commencement and extent—(1) This Act may be cited as the Protection of Children Act 1999.

(2) This Act shall come into force on such day as the Secretary of State may by order made by statutory instrument appoint; and different days may be appointed for different purposes.

(3) *This Act, except section 8 and this section* [Subject to subsections (4) and (5) below, this Act], extends to England and Wales only.

(4) Section 8 above and this section extend to Northern Ireland.

[(5) Section 9 above and the Schedule to this Act extend to the whole of the United Kingdom.]

Notes. Sub-s (3): words in square brackets substituted for words in italics by the Criminal Justice and Court Services Act 2000, s 74, Sch 7, Pt II, paras 154, 159(a), as from 11 January 2001 (SI 2000 No 3302). Sub-s (5) is added by the Criminal Justice and Court Services Act 2000, s 74, Sch 7, Pt II, paras 154, 159(b), as from 11 January 2001 (SI 2000 No 3302).

SCHEDULE   Section 9(7)
THE TRIBUNAL

Constitution of Tribunal

1—(1) There shall be appointed—
- (a) a President of the Tribunal ('the President');
- (b) a panel of persons ('the chairmen's panel') who may serve as chairmen of the Tribunal; and
- (c) a panel of persons ('the lay panel') who may serve as the other two members of the Tribunal apart from the chairman.

(2) The Tribunal shall consist of—
- (a) a chairman nominated by the President from the chairmen's panel; and
- (b) two other persons nominated by the President from the lay panel.

Appointment of President and members of the panels

2—(1) The President and the members of the chairmen's panel shall each be appointed by the Lord Chancellor.

(2) No person may be appointed President or member of the chairmen's panel unless he has a seven year general qualification (within the meaning of section 71 of the Courts and Legal Services Act 1990).

(3) The members of the lay panel shall each be appointed by the Lord Chancellor after consultation with the Secretary of State.

(4) No person may be appointed member of the lay panel unless he satisfies such requirements as may be prescribed.

Tenure of office

3—(1) The President and each member of the chairmen's panel or lay panel shall hold and vacate office under the terms of the instrument under which he is appointed.

(2) The President or a member of the chairmen's panel or lay panel—
- (a) may resign office by notice in writing to the Lord Chancellor; and
- (b) is eligible for re-appointment if he ceases to hold office.

Meetings and training

4 The President shall arrange such meetings for the members of the chairmen's and lay panels, and such training for them, as he considers appropriate.

Staff and accommodation

5 The Secretary of State may, with the consent of the Treasury, provide such staff and accommodation as the Tribunal may require.

Remuneration and expenses

6—(1) The Secretary of State may pay to the President, and to any other person in respect of his service as a member of the Tribunal, such remuneration and allowances as the Secretary of State may, with the consent of the Treasury, determine.

(2) The Secretary of State may defray the expenses of the Tribunal to such amount as he may, with the consent of the Treasury, determine.

Attendance allowances

7 The Secretary of State may pay such allowances for the purpose of or in connection with the attendance of persons at the Tribunal as he may, with the consent of the Treasury, determine.

Council on Tribunals

8 In Schedule 1 to the Tribunals and Inquiries Act 1992 (tribunals under the supervision of the Council on Tribunals), after paragraph 36 there shall be inserted—

> **'36A Protection of children**
> The tribunal constituted under section 9 of the Protection of Children Act 1999.'

ADOPTION (INTERCOUNTRY ASPECTS) ACT 1999
(1999 c 18)

An Act to make provision for giving effect to the Convention on Protection of Children and Co-operation in respect of Intercountry Adoption, concluded at the Hague on 29th May 1993; to make further provision in relation to adoptions with an international element; and for connected purposes.

[27 July 1999]

Implementation of Convention

1 Regulations giving effect to Convention—(1) Subject to the provisions of this Act, regulations made by the Secretary of State may make provision for giving effect to the Convention on Protection of Children and Co-operation in respect of Intercountry Adoption, concluded at the Hague on 29th May 1993 ('the Convention').

(2) The text of the Convention (so far as material) is set out in Schedule 1 to this Act.

(3) Regulations under this section may—

(a) apply, with or without modifications, any provision of the enactments relating to adoption;

(b) provide that any person who contravenes or fails to comply with any provision of the regulations is to be guilty of an offence and liable on summary conviction to imprisonment for a term not exceeding three months, or a fine not exceeding level 5 on the standard scale, or both;

(c) make different provision for different purposes or areas; and

(d) make such incidental, supplementary, consequential or transitional provision as appears to the Secretary of State to be expedient.

(4) Regulations under this section shall be made by statutory instrument which shall be subject to annulment in pursuance of a resolution of either House of Parliament.

(5) Subject to subsection (6), any power to make subordinate legislation under or for the purposes of the enactments relating to adoption includes power to do so with a view to giving effect to the provisions of the Convention.

(6) Subsection (5) does not apply in relation to any power which is exercisable by the National Assembly for Wales.

Note. 14 January 2003: SSI 2002 No 562, art 2(a); 23 January 2003: SI 2003 No 189.

2 Central Authorities and accredited bodies (1) The functions under the Convention of the Central Authority are to be discharged—

(a) separately in relation to England and Scotland by the Secretary of State; and

(b) in relation to Wales by the National Assembly for Wales.

(2) A communication may be sent to the Central Authority in relation to any part of Great Britain by sending it (for forwarding if necessary) to the Central Authority in relation to England.

[(2A) A voluntary adoption agency in respect of which a person is registered under Part II of the Care Standards Act 2000 [A registered Adoption Society] is an accredited body for the purposes of the Convention if, in accordance with the conditions of the registration, the *agency* [society] may provide facilities in respect of Convention adoptions and adoptions effected by Convention adoption orders.]

[(2B) A registered adoption service is an accredited body for the purposes of the Convention if, in accordance with the conditions of its registration, the service may provide facilities in respect of Convention adoptions and adoptions effected by Convention adoption orders.]

(3) An approved adoption society is an accredited body for the purposes of the Convention if the approval extends to the provision of facilities in respect of Convention adoptions and adoptions effected by Convention adoption orders.

(4) The functions under Article 9(a) to (c) of the Convention are to be discharged by local authorities and accredited bodies on behalf of the Central Authority.

(5) In this section in its application to England and Wales, 'approved adoption society' has the same meaning as in Part I of the Adoption Act 1976 ('the 1976 Act'); and expressions which are also used in that Act have the same meanings as in that Act.

[(5) In this section in its application to England and Wales, 'voluntary adoption agency' has the same meaning as in the Care Standards Act 2000; and expressions which are also used in the Adoption Act 1976 ('the 1976 Act') have the same meanings as in that Act.]

[(5) In this section, 'registered adoption society' has the same meaning as in section 2 of the Adoption and Children Act 2002 (basic definitions); and expressions used in this section in its application to England and Wales which are also used in that Act have the same meanings as in that Act.]

[(6) In this section in its application to Scotland, 'approved adoption society' has the same meaning as in section 65(1) (interpretation) of the Adoption (Scotland) Act 1978 ('the 1978 Act'); and expressions [used in this section in its application to Scotland] which are also used in that Act have the same meanings as in that Act.]

[(6) In this section in its application to Scotland, 'registered adoption service' means an adoption service provided as mentioned in section 2 (11)(b) of the Regulation of Care (Scotland) Act 2002 (asp 8) and registered under Part 1 of that Act; and ' registration' shall be construed accordingly.]

Note. Sub-ss 2(1), (2), (4): 1 June 2003: SI 2003 No 189.

Sub-s (2): repealed, in relation to Scotland by the Regulation of Care (Scotland) Act 2001, s 79, Sch 3, para 22 as from a date to be appointed. Sub-s (2A) is inserted by the Care Standards Act 2000, s 116, Sch 4, para 27(a), as from 30 April 2003 (SI 2003 No 501) (in relation to Wales); as from 1 June 2003 (SI 2003 No 365) (in relation to England). Sub-s (2A): words from 'A voluntary adoption agency' to 'Care Standards Act 2002' in italics repealed and words in square brackets substituted by the Adoption and Children Act 2002, s 139(1), Sch 3, paras 96, 97(a) as from a date to be appointed. Sub-s (2A): word 'agency' repealed and subsequent word in square brackets substituted by the Adoption and Children Act 2002, s 139(1), Sch 3, paras 96, 97(b) as from a date to be appointed. Sub-s (2B): inserted, in relation to Scotland, by the Regulation of Care (Scotland) Act 2001, s 79, Sch 3, para 22(b) as from a day to be appointed: see the Regulation of Care (Scotland) Act 2001, s 81(2). Sub-s (5) in italics substituted by sub-s (5) in square brackets by the Care Standards Act 2000, s 116, Sch 4, para 27(b), as from 30 April 2003 (SI 2003 No 501); as from 1 June 2003 (SI 2003 No 365) (in relation to England). Sub-s (5) further substituted by the Adoption and Children Act 2002, s 139(1), Sch 3, paras 96, 98 as from a date to be appointed. Sub-s (6): substituted by the Regulation of Care (Scotland) Act 2001, s 79, Sch 3, para 22(c) as from a day to be appointed: see the Regulation of Care (Scotland) Act 2001, s 81(2). Sub-s (6): words in italics omitted and words in square brackets inserted by the Adoption and Children Act 2002, s 139(1), (3), Sch 3, paras 96, 99(a), (b) as from a date to be appointed. Sub-s (6): substituted by the Regulation of Care (Scotland) Act 2002, s 79, Sch 3, para 22(c) as from a date to be appointed.

Convention adoptions

3 Convention adoption orders *For section 17 of the 1976 and 1978 Acts there shall be substituted—*

> **'17 Convention adoption orders**
> *An adoption order shall be made as a Convention adoption order if—*
> > *(a) the application is for a Convention adoption order; and*
> > *(b) such requirements as may be prescribed by regulations made by the Secretary of State are complied with.'*

Note. 23 January 2003: SI 2003 No 189 (for certain purposes); 1 June 2003; SI 2003 No 189 (for all other purposes).

Repealed by the Adoption and Children Act 2002, s 139(1), Sch 3, para 95 as from a date to be appointed.

4 Effect of Convention adoptions in England and Wales—(1) In subsection (1) of section 38 of the 1976 Act (meaning of 'adoption' for purposes of provisions relating to status of adopted children), after paragraph (c) there shall be inserted—

'(cc) which is a Convention adoption;'.

(2) In subsection (2) of section 39 of that Act (status conferred by adoption), for 'subsection (3)' there shall be substituted 'subsections (3) and (3A)'.

(3) After subsection (3) of that section there shall be inserted—

'(3A) Where, in the case of a Convention adoption, the High Court is satisfied, on an application under this subsection—

> (a) that under the law of the country in which the adoption was effected the adoption is not a full adoption;
> (b) that the consents referred to in Article 4(c) and (d) of the Convention have not been given for a full adoption, or that the United Kingdom is not the receiving State (within the meaning of Article 2 of the Convention); and
> (c) that it would be more favourable to the adopted child for a direction to be given under this subsection,

the Court may direct that subsection (2) shall not apply, or shall not apply to such extent as may be specified in the direction.

In this subsection 'full adoption' means an adoption by virtue of which the adopted child falls to be treated in law as if he were not the child of any person other than the adopters or adopter.

(3B) The following provisions of the Family Law Act 1986—

> (a) section 59 (provisions relating to the Attorney General); and
> (b) section 60 (supplementary provision as to declarations), shall apply in relation to, and to an application for, a direction under subsection (3A) as

they apply in relation to, and to an application for, a declaration under Part III of that Act.'

Note. 1 June 2003: SI 2003 No 189.

5 Effect of Convention adoptions in Scotland—(1) In subsection (1) of section 38 of the 1978 Act (meaning of 'adoption order' for purposes of provisions relating to status of adopted children), after paragraph (c) there shall be inserted—

'(cc) a Convention adoption;'.

(2) In subsection (1) of section 39 of that Act (status conferred by adoption), in sub-paragraph (ii) of each of paragraphs (a), (b) and (c), at the beginning there shall be inserted 'subject to subsection (2A)'.

(3) After subsection (2) of that section there shall be inserted—

'(2A) Where, in the case of a child adopted under a Convention adoption, the Court of Session is satisfied, on an application under this subsection—

(a) that under the law of the country in which the adoption was effected the adoption is not a full adoption;

(b) that the consents referred to in Article 4(c) and (d) of the Convention have not been given for a full adoption, or that the United Kingdom is not the receiving State (within the meaning of Article 2 of the Convention); and

(c) that it would be more favourable to the child for a direction to be given under this subsection,

the Court may direct that sub-paragraph (ii) of, as the case may be, paragraph (a), (b) or (c) of subsection (1) shall not apply, or shall not apply to such extent as may be specified in the direction: and in this subsection 'full adoption' means an adoption by virtue of which the child falls to be treated in law as if he were not the child of any person other than the adopters or adopter.'

Note. 1 June 2003 (SSI 2003 No 121).

6 Annulment of Convention adoptions etc—*(1) For subsection (1) of section 53 of the 1976 Act (annulment etc of overseas adoptions) there shall be substituted—*

'(1) The High Court may, on an application under this subsection, by order annul a Convention adoption or a Convention adoption order on the ground that the adoption or order is contrary to public policy.';

and the same amendment shall be made to section 47 of the 1978 Act (corresponding provision for Scotland) except that for 'the High Court' there shall substituted 'the Court of Session'.

(2) In subsection (5) of each of those sections, after 'validity of' there shall be inserted 'a Convention adoption, a Convention adoption order,'.

(3) In subsection (4) of section 54 of the 1976 Act (provisions supplementary to sections 52(3) and 53), and in subsection (4) of section 48 of the 1978 Act (provisions supplementary to sections 46(2) and 47), the definitions of 'notified provision' and 'relevant time' shall cease to have effect.

(4) For subsection (1) of section 59 of the 1976 Act (effect of determinations and orders made in Scotland and overseas in adoption proceedings) there shall be substituted—

'(1) Where—

(a) an authority of a Convention country (other than the United Kingdom) having power under the law of that country—

(i) to authorise, or review the authorisation of, a Convention adoption; or

(ii) to give or review a decision revoking or annulling such an adoption or a Convention adoption order; or

(b) an authority of any of the Channel Islands, the Isle of Man or any colony having power under the law of that territory—

(i) to authorise, or review the authorisation of, a Convention adoption or an adoption effected in that territory; or

(ii) *to give or review a decision revoking or annulling such an adoption or a Convention adoption order,*

makes a determination in the exercise of that power, then, subject to section 53 and any subsequent determination having effect under this subsection, the determination shall have effect in England and Wales for the purpose of effecting, confirming or terminating the adoption in question or confirming its termination as the case may be.';

and the same amendment shall be made to section 53 of the 1978 Act (effect of determinations and orders made in England and Wales and overseas in adoption proceedings) except that for 'section 53' there shall be substituted 'section 47' and for 'England and Wales' there shall be substituted 'Scotland'.

Note. 1 June 2003: SI 2003 No 189 (in relation to England and Wales); 1 June 2003: SSI 2003 No 121 (in relation to Scotland).

Repealed by the Adoption and Children Act 2002, s 139(1), Sch 3, para 95 as from a date to be appointed.

7 Acquisition of British citizenship by Convention adoptions—(1) For subsection (5) of section 1 of the British Nationality Act 1981 (acquisition by birth or adoption) there shall be substituted—

'(5) Where—

(a) any court in the United Kingdom makes an order authorising the adoption of a minor who is not a British citizen; or

(b) a minor who is not a British citizen is adopted under a Convention adoption,

that minor shall, if the requirements of subsection (5A) are met, be a British citizen as from the date on which the order is made or the Convention adoption is effected, as the case may be.

(5A) Those requirements are that on the date on which the order is made or the Convention adoption is effected (as the case may be)—

(a) the adopter or, in the case of a joint adoption, one of the adopters is a British citizen; and

(b) in a case within subsection (5)(b), the adopter or, in the case of a joint adoption, both of the adopters are habitually resident in the United Kingdom.'

(2) In subsection (6) of that section, after 'order' there shall be inserted 'or a Convention adoption'.

(3) At the end of subsection (8) of that section there shall be inserted 'and in this section 'Convention adoption' has the same meaning as in the Adoption Act 1976 and the Adoption (Scotland) Act 1978'.

Note. 1 June 2003 (SI 2003 No 362). Sub-s (3) repealed by the Adoption and Children Act 2002, s 139(3), Sch 5 as from a date to be appointed.

8 Meaning of 'Convention adoption' and related expressions in 1976 and 1978 Acts *In subsection (1) of section 72 of the 1976 Act and section 65 of the 1978 Act (interpretation), for the definitions of 'the Convention', 'Convention adoption order' and 'Convention country' there shall be substituted—*

the Convention' means the Convention on Protection of Children and Co-operation in respect of Intercountry Adoption, concluded at the Hague on 29th May 1993;

'Convention adoption' means an adoption effected under the law of a Convention country outside the British Islands, and certified in pursuance of Article 23(1) of the Convention;

'Convention adoption order' means an adoption order made in accordance with section 17;

'Convention country' means any country or territory in which the Convention is in force.'

Note. 1 June 2003 (SSI 2003 No 121) (in relation to Scotland); 1 June 2003 (SI 2003 No 189) (in relation to England and Wales with respect to definitions 'the Convention' and

'Convention country'. 23 January 2003 (SI 2003 No 189) (in relation to England and Wales with respect to definitions 'Convention adoption' and 'Convention adoption order' for the purposes of making regulations). 1 June 2003 (SI 2003 No 189) (in relation to England and Wales with respect to definitions 'Convention adoption' and 'Convention adoption order' for remaining purposes.

Repealed by the Adoption and Children Act 2002, s 139(1), Sch 3, para 95 as from a date to be appointed.

Intercountry adoptions

9 Adoption Service to include intercountry adoptions etc *After subsection (3) of section 1 of the 1976 and 1978 Acts (establishment of Adoption Service) there shall be inserted—*

'*(3A) In this Part, references to adoption are to the adoption of children, wherever they may be habitually resident, effected under the law of any country or territory, whether within or outside the British Islands.*'

Note. 30 April 2001 (so far as inserts s 1(3A) of the Adoption Act 1976) (SI 2001 No 1279, art 2)); 2 July 2001 (for remaining purposes) (SSI 2001 No 235, art 2).

Repealed by the Adoption and Children Act 2002, s 139(1), Sch 3, para 95 as from a date to be appointed.

10 Approval of adoption societies to provide intercountry adoption services
After subsection (6) of section 3 of the 1976 Act (approval of adoption societies) there shall be inserted—

'*(6A) Approval under this section may be given on terms that the applicant may act as an adoption society either—*
   (a) in relation to facilities provided in respect of adoptions other than those mentioned in subsection (6B); or
   (b) in relation to facilities provided in respect of any adoptions, including those so mentioned.
(6B) The adoptions are—
(a) a Convention adoption;
(b) an adoption effected by a Convention adoption order;
(c) an overseas adoption;
(d) an adoption of a child habitually resident in the British Islands which is not a Convention adoption and is effected under the law of a country or territory outside the British Islands; and
(e) an adoption of a child habitually resident outside the British Islands which is effected by an adoption order other than a Convention adoption order.'

Note. Repealed by the Care Standards Act 2000, s 117(2), Sch 6, as from 30 April 2003 (SI 2003 No 501) (in relation to Wales); as from 1 June 2003 (SI 2003 No 365) (in relation to England).

11 Six months residence required for certain intercountry adoptions *After subsection (3) of section 13 of the 1976 and 1978 Acts (child to live with adopters before order is made) there shall be inserted—*

'*(4) In relation to—*
(a) an adoption proposed to be effected by a Convention adoption order; or
(b) an adoption of a child habitually resident outside the British Islands which is proposed to be effected by an adoption order other than a Convention adoption order, subsection (1) shall have effect as if the reference to the preceding 13 weeks were a reference to the preceding six months.'

Commencement 1 June 2003 (SSI 2003 No 121) (in relation to Scotland).

Repealed by the Adoption and Children Act 2002, s 139(1), Sch 3, para 95 as from a date to be appointed.

12 Registration of certain intercountry adoptions—(*1*) *In subsection (1) of section 50 of the 1976 Act and section 45 of the 1978 Act (Adopted Children Register), for the words from 'shall be made' to the end there shall be substituted—*
'*such entries as may be—*
(a) directed to be made in it by adoption orders, or
(b) required to be made under Schedule 1 to this Act,
and no other entries, shall be made'.
(*2*) *In paragraph 1 of Schedule 1 to the 1976 and 1978 Acts (registration of adoption orders), sub-paragraph (2) shall cease to have effect.*
(*3*) *For paragraph 3 of Schedule 1 to the 1976 Act there shall be substituted—*

'*Registration of foreign adoptions*

3—(1) If the Registrar General is satisfied, on an application under this paragraph, that he has sufficient particulars relating to a child adopted under a registrable foreign adoption to enable an entry to be made in the Adopted Children Register for the child—
(a) he must make the entry accordingly, and
(b) if he is also satisfied that an entry in the Registers of Births relates to the child, he must secure that the entry in those Registers is marked 'Adopted' or 'Re-adopted', as the case may be, followed by the name in brackets of the country in which the adoption was effected.
(2) An entry made in the Adopted Children Register by virtue of this paragraph must be made in the specified form.
(3) An application under this paragraph must be made, in the specified manner, by a specified person and give the specified particulars.
(4) In this paragraph—
'registrable foreign adoption' means a Convention or overseas adoption which satisfies specified requirements;
'specified' means specified by regulations made by the Registrar General.';
and the same amendment shall be made to Schedule 1 to the 1978 Act (corresponding provision for Scotland) except that for 'the Registrar General' (in both places) there shall be substituted 'the Registrar General for Scotland', for 'the Registers of Births' there shall be substituted 'the register of births' and for 'those Registers' there shall be substituted 'that register'.
(*4*) *In paragraph 4(5)(a) of Schedule 1 to the 1976 Act and paragraph 4(4)(a) of Schedule 1 to the 1978 Act, after 'that' there shall be inserted 'a Convention adoption,'.*
Note. 23 January 2003: SI 2003 No 189 (certain purposes); 1 June 2003: SI 2003 No 189 (for remaining purposes); 14 January 2003: see SSI 2002 No 562 (in relation to Scotland).
Repealed by the Adoption and Children Act 2002, s 139(1), Sch 3, para 95 as from a date to be appointed.

13 Construction of certain references in 1976 and 1978 Acts *After subsection (3) of section 72 of the 1976 Act and section 65 of the 1978 Act (interpretation) there shall be inserted—*
'*(3A) In this Act, in relation to the proposed adoption of a child resident outside the British Islands, references to arrangements for the adoption of a child include references to arrangements for an assessment for the purpose of indicating whether a person is suitable to adopt a child or not.*
(3B) In this Act, in relation to—
(a) an adoption proposed to be effected by a Convention adoption order; or
(b) an adoption of a child habitually resident outside the British Islands which is proposed to be effected by an adoption order other than a Convention adoption order,
references to a child placed with any persons by an adoption agency include references to a child who, in pursuance of arrangements made by such an agency, has been

> *adopted by or placed with those persons under the law of a country or territory outside the British Islands.'*

Note. 31 January 2000 (in relation to England and Wales, for the purposes of sub-s (3A)) (SI 2000 No 52, art 2); 10 November 2000 (in relation to Scotland, for the purposes of sub-s (3A)) (SSI 2000 No 390, art 2).

Repealed by the Adoption and Children Act 2002, s 139(1), Sch 3, para 95 as from a date to be appointed.

Miscellaneous and supplemental

14 Restriction on bringing children into the United Kingdom for adoption
The following provision shall be inserted after section 56 of the 1976 Act as section 56A and after section 50 of the 1978 Act as section 50A—

'Restriction on bringing children into the United Kingdom for adoption

(1) A person habitually resident in the British Islands who at any time brings into the United Kingdom for the purpose of adoption a child who is habitually resident outside those Islands shall be guilty of an offence unless such requirements as may be prescribed by regulations made by the Secretary of State are satisfied either—

(a) before that time; or

(b) within such period beginning with that time as may be so prescribed.

(2) Subsection (1) does not apply where the child is brought into the United Kingdom for the purpose of adoption by a parent, guardian or relative.

(3) A person guilty of an offence under this section is liable on summary conviction to imprisonment for a term not exceeding three months, or a fine not exceeding level 5 on the standard scale, or both.

(4) Proceedings for an offence under this section may be brought within a period of six months from the date on which evidence sufficient in the opinion of the prosecutor to warrant the proceedings came to his knowledge; but no such proceedings shall be brought by virtue of this subsection more than three years after the commission of the offence.'

Note. 30 April 2001 (so far as inserts the Adoption Act 1976, s 56A) (SI 2001 No 1279, art 2); 2 July 2001 (for remaining purposes) (SSI 2001 No 235, art 2).

Repealed by the Adoption and Children Act 2002, s 139(1), (3), Sch 3, para 100, Sch 5 as from a date to be appointed.

15 Amendments and repeals—(1) The enactments mentioned in Schedule 2 to this Act shall have effect subject to the amendments specified in that Schedule, being minor amendments and amendments consequential on the provisions of this Act.

(2) The enactments mentioned in Schedule 3 to this Act are repealed to the extent specified in that Schedule.

Note. Sub-s (1): 1 June 2003 (SI 2003 No 189) (in relation to England and Wales for certain purposes); 1 June 2003 (SI 2003 No 362) (in relation to England and Wales for remaining purposes); 1 June 2003 (SI 2003 No 362) (in relation to Scotland for certain purposes); 1 June 2003 (SSI 2003 No 121) (in relation to Scotland for remaining purposes). Sub-s (2): 1 June 2003 (SI 2003 No 189) (in relation to England and Wales); 1 June 2003 (SSI 2003 No 121).

16 Devolution—(1) Any function of the Secretary of State under section 1 or 18(3), *or section 17 or 56A of the 1976 Act,* is exercisable only after consultation with the National Assembly for Wales.

(2) For the purposes of the Scotland Act 1998, any provision of this Act which extends to Scotland is to be taken to be a pre-commencement enactment within the meaning of that Act.

Note. Sub-s (1): 23 January 2003: SI 2003 No 189; sub-s (2): 16 October 2000 (SI 2000 No 2821, art 2).

Sub-s (1): words in italic omitted by the Adoption and Children Act 2002, s 139(1), (3), Sch 3, para 101, Sch 5 as from a date to be appointed.

17 Savings for adoptions etc under 1965 Convention—(1) In relation to—
(a) a 1965 Convention adoption order or an application for such an order; or
(b) a 1965 Convention adoption,
the 1976 and 1978 Acts shall have effect without the amendments made by sections 3 to 6 and 8 and Schedule 2 to this Act and the associated repeals made by Schedule 3 to this Act.
(2) In subsection (1) in its application to the 1976 or 1978 Act—
'1965 Convention adoption order' has the meaning which 'Convention adoption order' has in that Act as it has effect without the amendments and repeals mentioned in that subsection;
'1965 Convention adoption' has the meaning which 'regulated adoption' has in that Act as it so has effect.
Note. 1 June 2003 (SI 2003 No 189) (in relation to England and Wales); 1 June 2003 (SSI 2003 No 121) (in relation to Scotland).

18 Short title, interpretation, commencement and extent—(1) This Act may be cited as the Adoption (Intercountry Aspects) Act 1999.
(2) In this Act—
'the 1976 Act' means the Adoption Act 1976;
'the 1978 Act' means the Adoption (Scotland) Act 1978;
'the Convention' means the Convention on Protection of Children and Co-operation in respect of Intercountry Adoption, concluded at the Hague on 29th May 1993.
(3) This Act, except this section, shall come into force on such day as the Secretary of State may by order made by statutory instrument appoint and different days may be appointed for different purposes.
(4) Subject to subsection (5), this Act extends to Great Britain only.
(5) Any amendment of an enactment which extends to any other part of the British Islands or any colony also extends to that part or colony.
Note. Royal Assent: 27 July 1999: (no specific commencement provision).

SCHEDULE 1   Section 1

CONVENTION ON PROTECTION OF CHILDREN AND CO-OPERATION IN RESPECT OF
INTERCOUNTRY ADOPTION

The States signatory to the present Convention.
Recognizing that the child, for the full and harmonious development of his or her personality, should grow up in a family environment, in an atmosphere of happiness, love and understanding,
Recalling that each State should take, as a matter of priority, appropriate measures to enable the child to remain in the care of his or her family of origin,
Recognizing that intercountry adoption may offer the advantage of a permanent family to a child for whom a suitable family cannot be found in his or her State of origin,
Convinced of the necessity to take measures to ensure that intercountry adoptions are made in the best interests of the child and with respect for his or her fundamental rights, and to prevent the abduction, the sale of, or traffic in children,
Desiring to establish common provisions to this effect, taking into account the principles set forth in international instruments, in particular the United Nations Convention on the Rights of the Child, of 20 November 1989, and the United Nations Declaration on Social and Legal Principles relating to the Protection and Welfare of Children, with Special Reference to Foster Placement and Adoption Nationally and Internationally (General Assembly Resolution 41/85, of 3 December 1986),
Have agreed upon the following provisions—

CHAPTER I
SCOPE OF THE CONVENTION

Article 1

The objects of the present Convention are—
  (a) to establish safeguards to ensure that intercountry adoptions take place in the best interests of the child and with respect for his or her fundamental rights as recognised in international law;
  (b) to establish a system of co-operation amongst Contracting States to ensure that those safeguards are respected and thereby prevent the abduction, the sale of, or traffic in children;
  (c) to secure the recognition in Contracting States of adoptions made in accordance with the Convention.

Article 2

1 The Convention shall apply where a child habitually resident in one Contracting State ('the State of origin') has been, is being, or is to be moved to another Contracting State ('the receiving State') either after his or her adoption in the State of origin by spouses or a person habitually resident in the receiving State, or for the purposes of such an adoption in the receiving State or in the State of origin.

2 The Convention covers only adoptions which create a permanent parent-child relationship.

Article 3

The Convention ceases to apply if the agreements mentioned in Article 17, sub-paragraph (c), have not been given before the child attains the age of eighteen years.

CHAPTER II
REQUIREMENTS FOR INTERCOUNTRY ADOPTIONS

Article 4

An adoption within the scope of the Convention shall take place only if the competent authorities of the State of origin—
  (a) have established that the child is adoptable;
  (b) have determined, after possibilities for placement of the child within the State of origin have been given due consideration, that an intercountry adoption is in the child's best interests;
  (c) have ensured that—
     (i) the persons, institutions and authorities whose consent is necessary for adoption, have been counselled as may be necessary and duly informed of the effects of their consent, in particular whether or not an adoption will result in the termination of the legal relationship between the child and his or her family of origin,
     (ii) such persons, institutions and authorities have given their consent freely, in the required legal form, and expressed or evidenced in writing,
     (iii) the consents have not been induced by payment or compensation of any kind and have not been withdrawn, and
     (iv) the consent of the mother, where required, has been given only after the birth of the child; and

   (d) have ensured, having regard to the age and degree of maturity of the child, that—

      (i) he or she has been counselled and duly informed of the effects of the adoption and of his or her consent to the adoption, where such consent is required,

      (ii) consideration has been given to the child's wishes and opinions,

      (iii) the child's consent to the adoption, where such consent is required, has been given freely, in the required legal form, and expressed or evidenced in writing, and

      (iv) such consent has not been induced by payment or compensation of any kind.

Article 5

An adoption within the scope of the Convention shall take place only if the competent authorities of the receiving State—

   (a) have determined that the prospective adoptive parents are eligible and suited to adopt;

   (b) have ensured that the prospective adoptive parents have been counselled as may be necessary; and

   (c) have determined that the child is or will be authorised to enter and reside permanently in that State.

CHAPTER III
CENTRAL AUTHORITIES AND ACCREDITED BODIES

Article 6

1 A Contracting State shall designate a Central Authority to discharge the duties which are imposed by the Convention upon such authorities.

2 Federal States, States with more than one system of law or States having autonomous territorial units shall be free to appoint more than one Central Authority and to specify the territorial or personal extent of their functions. Where a State has appointed more than one Central Authority, it shall designate the Central Authority to which any communication may be addressed for transmission to the appropriate Central Authority within that State.

Article 7

1 Central Authorities shall co-operate with each other and promote co-operation amongst the competent authorities in their States to protect children and to achieve the other objects of the Convention.

2 They shall take directly all appropriate measures to—

   (a) provide information as to the laws of their States concerning adoption and other general information, such as statistics and standard forms;

   (b) keep one another informed about the operation of the Convention and, as far as possible, eliminate any obstacles to its application.

Article 8

Central Authorities shall take, directly or through public authorities, all appropriate measures to prevent improper financial or other gain in connection with an adoption and to deter all practices contrary to the objects of the Convention.

Article 9

Central Authorities shall take, directly or through public authorities or other bodies duly accredited in their State, all appropriate measures, in particular to—
  (a) collect, preserve and exchange information about the situation of the child and the prospective adoptive parents, so far as is necessary to complete the adoption;
  (b) facilitate, follow and expedite proceedings with a view to obtaining the adoption;
  (c) promote the development of adoption counselling and post-adoption services in their States;
  (d) provide each other with general evaluation reports about experience with intercountry adoption;
  (e) reply, in so far as is permitted by the law of their State, to justified requests from other Central Authorities or public authorities for information about a particular adoption situation.

Article 10

Accreditation shall only be granted to and maintained by bodies demonstrating their competence to carry out properly the tasks with which they may be entrusted.

Article 11

An accredited body shall—
  (a) pursue only non-profit objectives according to such conditions and within such limits as may be established by the competent authorities of the State of accreditation;
  (b) be directed and staffed by persons qualified by their ethical standards and by training or experience to work in the field of intercountry adoption; and
  (c) be subject to supervision by competent authorities of that State as to its composition, operation and financial situation.

Article 12

A body accredited in one Contracting State may act in another Contracting State only if the competent authorities of both States have authorised it to do so.

Article 13

The designation of the Central Authorities and, where appropriate, the extent of their functions, as well as the names and addresses of the accredited bodies shall be communicated by each Contracting State to the Permanent Bureau of the Hague Conference on Private International Law.

CHAPTER IV
PROCEDURAL REQUIREMENTS IN INTERCOUNTRY ADOPTION

Article 14

Persons habitually resident in a Contracting State, who wish to adopt a child habitually resident in another Contracting State, shall apply to the Central Authority in the State of their habitual residence.

Article 15

1 If the Central Authority of the receiving State is satisfied that the applicants are eligible and suited to adopt, it shall prepare a report including information about their identity, eligibility and suitability to adopt, background, family and medical history, social environment, reasons for adoption, ability to undertake an intercountry adoption, as well as the characteristics of the children for whom they would be qualified to care.

2 It shall transmit the report to the Central Authority of the State of origin.

Article 16

1 If the Central Authority of the State of origin is satisfied that the child is adoptable, it shall—
   (a) prepare a report including information about his or her identity, adoptability, background, social environment, family history, medical history including that of the child's family, and any special needs of the child;
   (b) give due consideration to the child's upbringing and to his or her ethnic, religious and cultural background;
   (c) ensure that consents have been obtained in accordance with Article 4; and
   (d) determine, on the basis in particular of the reports relating to the child and the prospective adoptive parents, whether the envisaged placement is in the best interests of the child.

2 It shall transmit to the Central Authority of the receiving State its report on the child, proof that the necessary consents have been obtained and the reasons for its determination on the placement, taking care not to reveal the identity of the mother and the father if, in the State of origin, these identities may not be disclosed.

Article 17

Any decision in the State of origin that a child should be entrusted to prospective adoptive parents may only be made if—
   (a) the Central Authority of that State has ensured that the prospective adoptive parents agree;
   (b) the Central Authority of the receiving State has approved such decision, where such approval is required by the law of that State or by the Central Authority of the State of origin;
   (c) the Central Authorities of both States have agreed that the adoption may proceed; and
   (d) it has been determined, in accordance with Article 5, that the prospective adoptive parents are eligible and suited to adopt and that the child is or will be authorised to enter and reside permanently in the receiving State.

Article 18

The Central Authorities of both States shall take all necessary steps to obtain permission for the child to leave the State of origin and to enter and reside permanently in the receiving State.

Article 19

1 The transfer of the child to the receiving State may only be carried out if the requirements of Article 17 have been satisfied.

2 The Central Authorities of both States shall ensure that this transfer takes place in secure and appropriate circumstances and, if possible, in the company of the adoptive or prospective adoptive parents.

3 If the transfer of the child does not take place, the reports referred to in Articles 15 and 16 are to be sent back to the authorities who forwarded them.

Article 20

The Central Authorities shall keep each other informed about the adoption process and the measures taken to complete it, as well as about the progress of the placement if a probationary period is required.

Article 21

1 Where the adoption is to take place after the transfer of the child to the receiving State and it appears to the Central Authority of that State that the continued placement of the child with the prospective adoptive parents is not in the child's best interests, such Central Authority shall take the measures necessary to protect the child, in particular—

(a) to cause the child to be withdrawn from the prospective adoptive parents and to arrange temporary care;

(b) in consultation with the Central Authority of the State of origin, to arrange without delay a new placement of the child with a view to adoption or, if this is not appropriate, to arrange alternative long-term care; an adoption shall not take place until the Central Authority of the State of origin has been duly informed concerning the new prospective adoptive parents;

(c) as a last resort, to arrange the return of the child, if his or her interests so require.

2 Having regard in particular to the age and degree of maturity of the child, he or she shall be consulted and, where appropriate, his or her consent obtained in relation to measures to be taken under this Article.

Article 22

1 The functions of a Central Authority under this Chapter may be performed by public authorities or by bodies accredited under Chapter III, to the extent permitted by the law of its State.

2 Any Contracting State may declare to the depositary of the Convention that the functions of the Central Authority under Articles 15 to 21 may be performed in that State, to the extent permitted by the law and subject to the supervision of the competent authorities of that State, also by bodies or persons who—

(a) meet the requirements of integrity, professional competence, experience and accountability of that State; and

(b) are qualified by their ethical standards and by training or experience to work in the field of intercountry adoption.

3 A Contracting State which makes the declaration provided for in paragraph 2 shall keep the Permanent Bureau of the Hague Conference on Private International Law informed of the names and addresses of these bodies and persons.

4 Any Contracting State may declare to the depositary of the Convention that adoptions of children habitually resident in its territory may only take place if the functions of the Central Authorities are performed in accordance with paragraph 1.

5 Notwithstanding any declaration made under paragraph 2, the reports provided for in Articles 15 and 16 shall, in every case, be prepared under the responsibility of the Central Authority or other authorities or bodies in accordance with paragraph 1.

CHAPTER V
RECOGNITION AND EFFECTS OF THE ADOPTION

Article 23

1 An adoption certified by the competent authority of the State of the adoption as having been made in accordance with the Convention shall be recognised by operation of law in the other Contracting States. The certificate shall specify when and by whom the agreements under Article 17, sub-paragraph c, were given.

2 Each Contracting State shall, at the time of signature, ratification, acceptance, approval or accession, notify the depositary of the Convention of the identity and the functions of the authority or the authorities which, in that State, are competent to make the certification. It shall also notify the depositary of any modification in the designation of these authorities.

Article 24

The recognition of an adoption may be refused in a contracting State only if the adoption is manifestly contrary to its public policy, taking into account the best interests of the child.

Article 25

Any Contracting State may declare to the depositary of the convention that it will not be bound under this Convention to recognise adoptions made in accordance with an agreement concluded by application of Article 39, paragraph 2.

Article 26

1 The recognition of an adoption includes recognition of—
  (a) the legal parent-child relationship between the child and his or her adoptive parents;
  (b) parental responsibility of the adoptive parents for the child;
  (c) the termination of a pre-existing legal relationship between the child and his or her mother and father, if the adoption has this effect in the Contracting State where it was made.

2 In the case of an adoption having the effect of terminating a pre-existing legal parent-child relationship, the child shall enjoy in the receiving State, and in any other Contracting State where the adoption is recognised, rights equivalent to those resulting from adoptions having this effect in each such State.

3 The preceding paragraphs shall not prejudice the application of any provision more favourable for the child, in force in the Contracting State which recognises the adoption.

Article 27

1 Where an adoption granted in the State of origin does not have the effect of terminating a pre-existing legal parent-child relationship, it may, in the receiving State which recognises the adoption under the Convention, be converted into an adoption having such an effect—

(a) if the law of the receiving State so permits; and

(b) if the consents referred to in Article 4, sub-paragraphs c and d, have been or are given for the purpose of such an adoption.

2 Article 23 applies to the decision converting the adoption.

CHAPTER VI
GENERAL PROVISIONS

Article 28

The Convention does not affect any law of a State of origin which requires that the adoption of a child habitually resident within that State take place in that State or which prohibits the child's placement in, or transfer to, the receiving State prior to adoption.

Article 29

There shall be no contact between the prospective adoptive parents and the child's parents or any other person who has care of the child until the requirements of Article 4, sub-paragraphs a to c, and Article 5, sub-paragraph a, have been met, unless the adoption takes place within a family or unless the contact is in compliance with the conditions established by the competent authority of the State of origin.

Article 30

1 The competent authorities of a Contracting State shall ensure that information held by them concerning the child's origin, in particular information concerning the identity of his or her parents, as well as the medical history, is preserved.

2 They shall ensure that the child or his or her representative has access to such information, under appropriate guidance, in so far as is permitted by the law of that State.

Article 31

Without prejudice to Article 30, personal data gathered or transmitted under the Convention, especially data referred to in Articles 15 and 16, shall be used only for the purposes for which they were gathered or transmitted.

Article 32

1 No one shall derive improper financial or other gain from an activity related to an intercountry adoption.

2 Only costs and expenses, including reasonable professional fees of persons involved in the adoption, may be charged or paid.

3 The directors, administrators and employees of bodies involved in an adoption shall not receive remuneration which is unreasonably high in relation to services rendered.

Article 33

A competent authority which finds that any provision of the Convention has not been respected or that there is a serious risk that it may not be respected, shall immediately inform the Central Authority of its State. This Central Authority shall be responsible for ensuring that appropriate measures are taken.

Article 34

If the competent authority of the State of destination of a document so requests, a translation certified as being in conformity with the original must be furnished. Unless otherwise provided, the costs of such translation are to be borne by the prospective adoptive parents.

Article 35

The competent authorities of the contracting States shall act expeditiously in the process of adoption.

Article 36

In relation to a State which has two or more systems of law with regard to adoption applicable in different territorial units—
  (a) any reference to habitual residence in that State shall be construed as referring to habitual residence in a territorial unit of that State;
  (b) any reference to the law of that State shall be construed as referring to the law in force in the relevant territorial unit;
  (c) any reference to the competent authorities or to the public authorities of that State shall be construed as referring to those authorised to act in the relevant territorial unit;
  (d) any reference to the accredited bodies of that State shall be construed as referring to bodies accredited in the relevant territorial unit.

Article 37

In relation to a State which with regard to adoption has two or more systems of law applicable to different categories of persons, any reference to the law of that State shall be construed as referring to the legal system specified by the law of that State.

Article 38

A State within which different territorial units have their own rules of law in respect of adoption shall not be bound to apply the Convention where a State with a unified system of law would not be bound to do so.

Article 39

1 The convention does not affect any international instrument to which Contracting States are Parties and which contains provisions on matters governed by the Convention, unless a contrary declaration is made by the States parties to such instrument.

2 Any Contracting State may enter into agreements with one or more other Contracting States, with a view to improving the application of the Convention in their mutual relations. These agreements may derogate only from the provisions of Articles 14 to 16 and 18 to 21. The States which have concluded such an agreement shall transmit a copy to the depositary of the Convention.

Article 40

No reservation to the Convention shall be permitted.

Article 41

The Convention shall apply in every case where an application pursuant to Article 14 has been received after the Convention has entered into force in the receiving State and the State of origin.

Article 42

The Secretary General of the Hague Conference on Private International Law shall at regular intervals convene a Special Commission in order to review the practical operation of the Convention.

Notes. 23 January 2003 (SI 2003 No 189) (in relation to England and Wales); 14 January 2003 (SSI 2002 No 562) (in relation to Scotland).

SCHEDULE 2   Section 15(1)
MINOR AND CONSEQUENTIAL AMENDMENTS

Local Authority and Social Services Act 1970 (c 42)

1 In Schedule 1 to the Local Authority and Social Services Act 1970 (enactments conferring functions assigned to social services committee), at the end there shall be inserted—

'Adoption (Intercountry Aspects) Act 1999 (c 18)
Section 2(4)   Functions under Article 9(a) to (c) of the
                                               Convention on Protection of Children
                                               and Co-operation in respect of
                                               Intercountry Adoption, concluded at the
                                               Hague on 29th May 1993.'

Immigration Act 1971 (c 77)

2 In subsection (1) of section 33 of the Immigration Act 1971 (interpretation)—
  (a) after the definition of 'certificate of entitlement' there shall be inserted—
       'Convention adoption' has the same meaning as in the Adoption Act 1976
       and the Adoption (Scotland) Act 1978;'; and
  (b) in the definition of 'legally adopted', after 'Islands' there shall be inserted ',
       under a Convention adoption'.

Adoption Act 1976 (c 36)

3—*(1) In subsection (2) of section 14 of the 1976 Act (adoption by married couple), in paragraph (b), for 'section 17 is' there shall be substituted 'the requirements of regulations under section 17 are'.*

(2) In subsection (2) of section 15 of that Act (adoption by one person), in paragraph (b), for 'section 17 is' there shall be substituted 'the requirements of regulations under section 17 are'.

(3) In section 16 of that Act (parental agreement), subsection (3) shall cease to have effect.

(4) In section 52 of that Act (revocation of adoptions on legitimation), subsection (3) shall cease to have effect.

(5) In subsection (4) of section 62 of that Act (courts), for 'paragraphs (b), (c) and (d) of subsection (2) do not apply' there shall be substituted 'paragraph (d) of subsection (2) does not apply'.

(6) In subsection (6) of section 67 of that Act (orders, rules and regulations), after 'paragraph 1(1)' insert 'or 3'.

(7)   Section 70 of that Act (nationality) shall cease to have effect.

(8)   In subsection (2) of section 72 of that Act (interpretation), for 'Great Britain' there shall be substituted 'the British Islands'.

Adoption (Scotland) Act 1978 (c 28)

4—(1)   In subsection (2) of section 14 of the 1978 Act (adoption by married couple), in paragraph (b), for 'section 17 is' there shall be substituted 'the requirements of regulations under section 17 are'.

(2)   In subsection (2) of section 15 of that Act (adoption by one person), in paragraph (b), for 'section 17 is' there shall be substituted 'the requirements of regulations under section 17 are'.

(3)   In section 16 of that Act (parental agreement), subsection (3) shall cease to have effect.

(4)   In section 46 of that Act (revocation of adoptions on legitimation), subsection (2) shall cease to have effect.

(5)   In section 56 of that Act (courts)—

(a)   in subsection (2), for 'subsections (4) and (5)' there shall substituted 'subsection (5)'; and

(b)   subsection (4) shall cease to have effect.

(6)   In subsection (6) of section 60 of that Act (orders, rules and regulations), after 'paragraph 1(1)' there shall be inserted 'or 3'.

(7)   Section 63 of that Act (nationality) shall cease to have effect.

(8)   In subsection (2) of section 65 of that Act (interpretation), for 'Great Britain' there shall be substituted 'the British Islands'.

Family Law Act 1986 (c 55)

5   In subsection (1) of section 57 of the Family Law Act 1986 (declarations as to adoptions effected overseas), for paragraph (a) there shall be substituted—

'(a)   a Convention adoption as defined by subsection (1) of section 72 of the Adoption Act 1976 or an overseas adoption as defined by subsection (2) of that section, or'.

Note.   Paras 1, 3, 5: 1 June 2003 (SI 2003 No 189). Para 2: 1 June 2003 (SI 2003 No 362). Para 4: 1 June 2003 (SSI 2003 No 121).

Para 3: repealed by the Adoption and Children Act 2002, s 139(1), Sch 3, para 95 as from a date to be appointed.

SCHEDULE 3   Section 15(2)
REPEALS

Chapter	Short title	Extent of repeal
1976 c 36	Adoption Act 1976.	Section 16(3). Section 52(3). In section 53(5), the words 'and section 52(3)'. In section 54, in subsections (1) and (2), the words '52(3) or', and in subsection (4), the definitions of 'notified provision' and 'relevant time'. In section 61(1), the words '(other than an order to which section 17(6) applies)'. Section 70.

Chapter	Short title	Extent of repeal
1978 c 28	Adoption (Scotland) Act 1978.	In section 72(1), the definitions of 'regulated adoption' and 'specified order'. In Schedule 1, paragraph 1(2). Section 16(3). Section 46(2). In section 47(5), the words 'and section 46(2)'. In section 48, in subsections (1) and (2), the words '46(2) or', and in subsection (4), the definitions of 'notified provision' and 'relevant time'. In section 55(1), the words '(other than an order to which section 17(6) applies)'. Section 56(4). Section 63. In section 65(1), the definitions of 'regulated adoption' and 'specified order'. In Schedule 1, paragraph 1(2).

ACCESS TO JUSTICE ACT 1999

(1999 c 22)

An Act to establish the Legal Services Commission, the Community Legal Service and the Criminal Defence Service; to amend the law of legal aid in Scotland; to make further provision about legal services; to make provision about appeals, courts, judges and court proceedings; to amend the law about magistrates and magistrates' courts; and to make provision about immunity from action and costs and indemnities for certain officials exercising judicial functions.

[27 July 1999]

PART I
LEGAL SERVICES COMMISSION

Commission

1 Legal Services Commission—(1) There shall be a body known as the Legal Services Commission (in this Part referred to as 'the Commission').

(2) The Commission shall have the functions relating to—

(a) the Community Legal Service, and

(b) the Criminal Defence Service,

which are conferred or imposed on it by the provisions of this Act or any other enactment.

(3) The Commission shall consist of—

(a) not fewer than seven members, and

(b) not more than twelve members;

but the *Lord Chancellor* [Secretary of State] may by order substitute for either or both of the numbers for the time being specified in paragraphs (a) and (b) such other number or numbers as he thinks appropriate.

(4) The members of the Commission shall be appointed by the *Lord Chancellor* [Secretary of State]; and the *Lord Chancellor* [Secretary of State]shall appoint one of the members to chair the Commission.

(5) In appointing persons to be members of the Commission the *Lord Chancellor* [Secretary of State] shall have regard to the desirability of securing that the Commission includes members who (between them) have experience in or knowledge of—

(a) the provision of services which the Commission can fund as part of the Community Legal Service or Criminal Defence Service,

(b) the work of the courts,

(c) consumer affairs,

(d) social conditions, and

(e) management.

(6) Schedule 1 (which makes further provision about the Commission) has effect.

Note. Sub-ss (3),(4), (5): words 'Secretary of State' substituted by SI 2003 No 1887, art 9, Sch 2, para 11(1)(a) as from 19 August 2003.

2 Power to replace Commission with two bodies (1) The *Lord Chancellor* [Secretary of State]may by order establish in place of the Commission two bodies—

(a) one to have functions relating to the Community Legal Service, and

(b) the other to have functions relating to the Criminal Defence Service.

(2) The order may make any consequential, incidental, supplementary or transitional provisions, and any savings, which appear to the *Lord Chancellor* [Secretary of State] to be appropriate.

(3) The order shall include amendments of—
(a) any provisions of, or amended by, this Part which refer to the Commission, and
(b) any other enactments which so refer,
to replace references to the Commission with references to either or both of the bodies established by the order.

Note. Sub-ss (1),(2): words 'Secretary of State' substituted by SI 2003 No 1887, art 9, Sch 2, para 11(1)(a) as from 19 August 2003.

3 Powers of Commission (1) Subject to the provisions of this Part, the Commission may do anything which it considers—
(a) is necessary or appropriate for, or for facilitating, the discharge of its functions, or
(b) is incidental or conducive to the discharge of its functions.
(2) In particular, the Commission shall have power—
(a) to enter into any contract,
(b) to make grants (with or without conditions),
(c) to make loans,
(d) to invest money,
(e) to promote or assist in the promotion of publicity relating to its functions,
(f) to undertake any inquiry or investigation which it may consider appropriate in relation to the discharge of any of its functions, and
(g) to give the *Lord Chancellor* [Secretary of State] any advice which it may consider appropriate in relation to matters concerning any of its functions.
(3) Subsections (1) and (2) do not confer on the Commission power to borrow money.
(4) The Commission may make such arrangements as it considers appropriate for the discharge of its functions, including the delegation of any of its functions.
(5) The *Lord Chancellor* [Secretary of State] may by order require the Commission—
(a) to delegate any function specified in the order or to delegate any function so specified to a person (or person of a description) so specified,
(b) not to delegate any function so specified or not to delegate any function so specified to a person (or person of a description) so specified, or
(c) to make arrangements such as are specified in the order in relation to the delegation of any function so specified.

Note. Sub-ss (2), (5): words 'Secretary of State' substituted by SI 2003 No 1887, art 9, Sch 2, para 11(1)(a) as from 19 August 2003.

Community Legal Service

4 Community Legal Service (1) The Commission shall establish, maintain and develop a service known as the Community Legal Service for the purpose of promoting the availability to individuals of services of the descriptions specified in subsection (2) and, in particular, for securing (within the resources made available, and priorities set, in accordance with this Part) that individuals have access to services that effectively meet their needs.
(2) The descriptions of services referred to in subsection (1) are—
(a) the provision of general information about the law and legal system and the availability of legal services,
(b) the provision of help by the giving of advice as to how the law applies in particular circumstances,
(c) the provision of help in preventing, or settling or otherwise resolving, disputes about legal rights and duties,
(d) the provision of help in enforcing decisions by which such disputes are resolved, and

(e) the provision of help in relation to legal proceedings not relating to disputes.

(3) Services which the Commission is required to fund as part of the Criminal Defence Service do not fall within subsection (2).

(4) Every person who exercises any function relating to the Community Legal Service shall have regard to the desirability of exercising it, so far as is reasonably practicable, so as to—

(a) promote improvements in the range and quality of services provided as part of the Community Legal Service and in the ways in which they are made accessible to those who need them,

(b) secure that the services provided in relation to any matter are appropriate having regard to its nature and importance, and

(c) achieve the swift and fair resolution of disputes without unnecessary or unduly protracted proceedings in court.

(5) The Commission shall fund services of the descriptions specified in subsection (2) as part of the Community Legal Service in accordance with the following sections.

(6) The Commission shall also inform itself about the need for, and the provision of, services of the descriptions specified in subsection (2) and about the quality of the services provided and, in co-operation with such authorities and other bodies and persons as it considers appropriate—

(a) plan what can be done towards meeting that need by the performance by the Commission of its functions, and

(b) facilitate the planning by other authorities, bodies and persons of what can be done by them to meet that need by the use of any resources available to them;

and the Commission shall notify the *Lord Chancellor* [Secretary of State] of what it has done under this subsection.

(7) The Commission may set and monitor standards in relation to services of the descriptions specified in subsection (2).

(8) In particular, the Commission may accredit, or authorise others to accredit, persons or bodies providing services of the descriptions specified in subsection (2); and any system of accreditation shall include provision for the monitoring of the services provided by accredited persons and bodies and for the withdrawal of accreditation from any providing services of unsatisfactory quality.

(9) The Commission may charge—

(a) for accreditation,

(b) for monitoring the services provided by accredited persons and bodies, and

(c) for authorising accreditation by others;

and persons or bodies authorised to accredit may charge for accreditation, and for such monitoring, in accordance with the terms of their authorisation.

(10) The *Lord Chancellor* [Secretary of State] may by order require the Commission to discharge the functions in subsections (6) to (9) in accordance with the order.

Note. Sub-ss (6), (10): words 'Secretary of State' substituted by SI 2003 No 1887, art 9, Sch 2, para 11 (1)(a) as from 19 August 2003.

5 Funding of services—(1) The Commission shall establish and maintain a fund known as the Community Legal Service Fund from which it shall fund services as part of the Community Legal Service.

(2) The *Lord Chancellor* [Secretary of State]—

(a) shall pay to the Commission the sums which he determines are appropriate for the funding of services by the Commission as part of the Community Legal Service, and

(b) may determine the manner in which and times at which the sums are to be paid to the Commission and may impose conditions on the payment of the sums.

(3) In making any determination under subsection (2) the *Lord Chancellor* [Secretary of State] shall take into account (in addition to such other factors as he considers relevant) the need for services of the descriptions specified in subsection (2) of section 4 as notified to him by the Commission under subsection (6) of that section.

(4) The *Lord Chancellor* [Secretary of State] shall lay before each House of Parliament a copy of every determination under subsection (2) (a).

(5) The Commission shall pay into the Community Legal Service Fund—

(a) sums received from the *Lord Chancellor* [Secretary of State] under subsection (2), and

(b) sums received by the Commission by virtue of regulations under section 10 or 11.

(6) The *Lord Chancellor* [Secretary of State] may by direction impose requirements on the Commission as to the descriptions of services to be funded from any specified amount paid into the Community Legal Service Fund.

(7) In funding services as part of the Community Legal Service the Commission shall aim to obtain the best possible value for money.

Note. Sub-ss (2)-(6): words 'Secretary of State' substituted by SI 2003 No 1887, art 9, Sch 2, para 11(1)(a) as from 19 August 2003.

6 Services which may be funded—(1) The Commission shall set priorities in its funding of services as part of the Community Legal Service and the priorities shall be set—

(a) in accordance with any directions given by the *Lord Chancellor* [Secretary of State], and

(b) after taking into account the need for services of the descriptions specified in section 4(2).

(2) Subject to that (and to subsection (6)), the services which the Commission may fund as part of the Community Legal Service are those which the Commission considers appropriate.

(3) The Commission may fund services as part of the Community Legal Service by—

(a) entering into contracts with persons or bodies for the provision of services by them,

(b) making payments to persons or bodies in respect of the provision of services by them,

(c) making grants or loans to persons or bodies to enable them to provide, or facilitate the provision of, services,

(d) establishing and maintaining bodies to provide, or facilitate the provision of, services,

(e) making grants or loans to individuals to enable them to obtain services,

(f) itself providing services, or

(g) doing anything else which it considers appropriate for funding services.

(4) The *Lord Chancellor* [Secretary of State] may by order require the Commission to discharge the function in subsection (3) in accordance with the order.

(5) The Commission may fund as part of the Community Legal Service different descriptions of services or services provided by different means—

(a) in relation to different areas or communities in England and Wales, and

(b) in relation to descriptions of cases.

(6) The Commission may not fund as part of the Community Legal Service any of the services specified in Schedule 2.

(7) Regulations may amend that Schedule by adding new services or omitting or varying any services.

(8) The *Lord Chancellor* [Secretary of State]—

(a) may by direction require the Commission to fund the provision of any of the services specified in Schedule 2 in circumstances specified in the direction, and

(b) may authorise the Commission to fund the provision of any of those services in specified circumstances or, if the Commission request him to do so, in an individual case.

(9) The *Lord Chancellor* [Secretary of State] shall either—

(a) publish, or

(b) require the Commission to publish,

any authorisation under subsection (8)(b) unless it relates to an individual case (in which case he or the Commission may publish it if appropriate).

Note. Sub-ss (1), (4), (8), (9): words 'Secretary of State' substituted by SI 2003 No 1887, art 9, Sch 2, para 11(1)(a) as from 19 August 2003.

7 Individuals for whom services may be funded—(1) The Commission may only fund services for an individual as part of the Community Legal Service if his financial resources are such that, under regulations, he is an individual for whom they may be so funded.

(2) Regulations may provide that, in prescribed circumstances and subject to any prescribed conditions, services of a prescribed description may be so funded for individuals without reference to their financial resources.

(3) Regulations under this section may include provision requiring the furnishing of information.

8 Code about provision of funded services (1) The Commission shall prepare a code setting out the criteria according to which it is to decide whether to fund (or continue to fund) services as part of the Community Legal Service for an individual for whom they may be so funded and, if so, what services are to be funded for him.

(2) In settling the criteria to be set out in the code the Commission shall consider the extent to which they ought to reflect the following factors—

(a) the likely cost of funding the services and the benefit which may be obtained by their being provided,

(b) the availability of sums in the Community Legal Service Fund for funding the services and (having regard to present and likely future demands on that Fund) the appropriateness of applying them to fund the services,

(c) the importance of the matters in relation to which the services would be provided for the individual,

(d) the availability to the individual of services not funded by the Commission and the likelihood of his being able to avail himself of them,

(e) if the services are sought by the individual in relation to a dispute, the prospects of his success in the dispute,

(f) the conduct of the individual in connection with services funded as part of the Community Legal Service (or an application for funding) or in, or in connection with, any proceedings,

(g) the public interest, and

(h) such other factors as the *Lord Chancellor* [Secretary of State] may by order require the Commission to consider.

(3) The criteria set out in the code shall reflect the principle that in many family disputes mediation will be more appropriate than court proceedings.

(4) The code shall seek to secure that, where more than one description of service is available, the service funded is that which (in all the circumstances) is the most appropriate having regard to the criteria set out in the code.

(5) The code shall also specify procedures for the making of decisions about the funding of services by the Commission as part of the Community Legal Service, including—

(a) provision about the form and content of applications for funding,

(b) provision imposing conditions which must be satisfied by an individual applying for funding,

(c) provision requiring applicants to be informed of the reasons for any decision to refuse an application,

(d) provision for the giving of information to individuals whose applications are refused about alternative ways of obtaining or funding services, and

(e) provision establishing procedures for appeals against decisions about funding and for the giving of information about those procedures.

(6) The code may make different provision for different purposes.

(7) The Commission may from time to time prepare a revised version of the code.

(8) Before preparing the code the Commission shall undertake such consultation as appears to it to be appropriate; and before revising the code the Commission shall undertake such consultation as appears to it to be appropriate unless it considers that it is desirable for the revised version to come into force without delay.

(9) The *Lord Chancellor* [Secretary of State] may by order require the Commission to discharge its functions relating to the code in accordance with the order.

Note. Sub-ss (1)(h), (9): words 'Secretary of State' substituted by SI 2003 No 1887, art 9, Sch 2, para 11(1)(a) as from 19 August 2003.

9 Procedure relating to funding code—(1) After preparing the code or a revised version of the code the Commission shall send a copy to the *Lord Chancellor* [Secretary of State].

(2) If he approves it he shall lay it before each House of Parliament.

(3) The Commission shall publish—

(a) the code as first approved by the *Lord Chancellor* [Secretary of State], and

(b) where he approves a revised version, either the revisions or the revised code as appropriate.

(4) The code as first approved by the *Lord Chancellor* [Secretary of State] shall not come into force until it has been approved by a resolution of each House of Parliament.

(5) A revised version of the code which does not contain changes in the criteria set out in the code shall not come into force until it has been laid before each House of Parliament.

(6) Subject as follows, a revised version of the code which does contain such changes shall not come into force until it has been approved by a resolution of each House of Parliament.

(7) Where the *Lord Chancellor* [Secretary of State] considers that it is desirable for a revised version of the code containing such changes to come into force without delay, he may (when laying the revised version before Parliament) also lay before each House a statement of his reasons for so considering.

(8) In that event the revised version of the code—

(a) shall not come into force until it has been laid before each House of Parliament, and

(b) shall cease to have effect at the end of the period of 120 days beginning with the day on which it comes into force unless a resolution approving it has been made by each House (but without that affecting anything previously done in accordance with it).

Note. Sub-ss (1), (3), (4), (7): words 'Secretary of State' substituted by SI 2003 No 1887, art 9, Sch 2, para 11(1)(a) as from 19 August 2003.

3974 *Access to Justice Act 1999, s 10*

10 Terms of provision of funded services—(1) An individual for whom services are funded by the Commission as part of the Community Legal Service shall not be required to make any payment in respect of the services except where regulations otherwise provide.

(2) Regulations may provide that, in prescribed circumstances, an individual for whom services are so funded shall—

(a) pay a fee of such amount as is fixed by or determined under the regulations,

(b) if his financial resources are, or relevant conduct is, such as to make him liable to do so under the regulations, pay the cost of the services or make a contribution in respect of the cost of the services of such amount as is so fixed or determined, or

(c) if the services relate to a dispute and he has agreed to make a payment (which may exceed the cost of the services) only in specified circumstances, make in those circumstances a payment of the amount agreed, or determined in the manner agreed, by him;

and in paragraph (b) 'relevant conduct' means conduct in connection with the services (or any application for their funding) or in, or in connection with, any proceedings in relation to which they are provided.

(3) The regulations may include provision for any amount payable in accordance with the regulations to be payable by periodical payments or one or more capital sums, or both.

(4) The regulations may also include provision for the payment by an individual of interest (on such terms as may be prescribed) in respect of—

(a) any loan made to him by the Commission as part of the Community Legal Service,

(b) any payment in respect of the cost of services required by the regulations to be made by him later than the time when the services are provided, or

(c) so much of any payment required by the regulations to be made by him which remains unpaid after the time when it is required to be paid.

(5) The regulations shall include provision for the repayment to an individual of any payment made by him in excess of his liability under the regulations.

(6) The regulations may—

(a) include provision requiring the furnishing of information, and

(b) make provision for the determination of the cost of services for the purposes of the regulations.

(7) Except so far as regulations otherwise provide, where services have been funded by the Commission for an individual as part of the Community Legal Service—

(a) sums expended by the Commission in funding the services (except to the extent that they are recovered under section 11), and

(b) other sums payable by the individual by virtue of regulations under this section,

shall constitute a first charge on any property recovered or preserved by him (whether for himself or any other person) in any proceedings or in any compromise or settlement of any dispute in connection with which the services were provided.

(8) Regulations may make provision about the charge, including—

(a) provision as to whether it is in favour of the Commission or the body or person by whom the services were provided, and

(b) provision about its enforcement.

11 Costs in funded cases—(1) Except in prescribed circumstances, costs ordered against an individual in relation to any proceedings or part of proceedings funded for him shall not exceed the amount (if any) which is a reasonable one for him to pay having regard to all the circumstances including—

(a)   the financial resources of all the parties to the proceedings, and

(b)   their conduct in connection with the dispute to which the proceedings relate;

and for this purpose proceedings, or a part of proceedings, are funded for an individual if services relating to the proceedings or part are funded for him by the Commission as part of the Community Legal Service.

(2) In assessing for the purposes of subsection (1) the financial resources of an individual for whom services are funded by the Commission as part of the Community Legal Service, his clothes and household furniture and the tools and implements of his trade shall not be taken into account, except so far as may be prescribed.

(3) Subject to subsections (1) and (2), regulations may make provision about costs in relation to proceedings in which services are funded by the Commission for any of the parties as part of the Community Legal Service.

(4) The regulations may, in particular, make provision—

(a)   specifying the principles to be applied in determining the amount of any costs which may be awarded against a party for whom services are funded by the Commission as part of the Community Legal Service,

(b)   limiting the circumstances in which, or extent to which, an order for costs may be enforced against such a party,

(c)   as to the cases in which, and extent to which, such a party may be required to give security for costs and the manner in which it is to be given,

(d)   requiring the payment by the Commission of the whole or part of any costs incurred by a party for whom services are not funded by the Commission as part of the Community Legal Service,

(e)   specifying the principles to be applied in determining the amount of any costs which may be awarded to a party for whom services are so funded,

(f)   requiring the payment to the Commission, or the person or body by which the services were provided, of the whole or part of any sum awarded by way of costs to such a party, and

(g)   as to the court, tribunal or other person or body by whom the amount of any costs is to be determined and the extent to which any determination of that amount is to be final.

Supplementary

19 Foreign law—(1) The Commission may not fund as part of the Community Legal Service or Criminal Defence Service services relating to any law other than that of England and Wales, unless any such law is relevant for determining any issue relating to the law of England and Wales.

(2) But the *Lord Chancellor* [Secretary of State] may, if it appears to him necessary to do so for the purpose of fulfilling any obligation imposed on the United Kingdom by any international agreement, by order specify that there may be funded as part of the Community Legal Service or Criminal Defence Service (or both) services relating to the application of such other law as may be specified in the order.

Note. Sub-s (2): words 'Secretary of State' substituted by SI 2003 No 1887, art 9, Sch 2, para 11(1)(a) as from 19 August 2003.

20 Restriction of disclosure of information—(1) Subject to the following provisions of this section, information which is furnished—

(a)   to the Commission or any court, tribunal or other person or body on whom functions are imposed or conferred by or under this Part, and

(b)   in connection with the case of an individual seeking or receiving services funded by the Commission as part of the Community Legal Service or Criminal Defence Service,

shall not be disclosed except as permitted by subsection (2).

(2) Such information may be disclosed—

(a) for the purpose of enabling or assisting the Commission to discharge any functions imposed or conferred on it by or under this Part,

(b) for the purpose of enabling or assisting the *Lord Chancellor* [Secretary of State] to discharge any functions imposed or conferred on him by or under this Part,

(c) for the purpose of enabling or assisting any court, tribunal or other person or body to discharge any functions imposed or conferred on it by or under this Part,

(d) except where regulations otherwise provide, for the purpose of the investigation or prosecution of any offence (or suspected offence) under the law of England and Wales or any other jurisdiction,

(e) in connection with any proceedings relating to the Community Legal Service or Criminal Defence Service, or

(f) for the purpose of facilitating the proper performance by any tribunal of disciplinary functions.

(3) Subsection (1) does not limit the disclosure of—

(a) information in the form of a summary or collection of information so framed as not to enable information relating to any individual to be ascertained from it, or

(b) information about the amount of any grant, loan or other payment made to any person or body by the Commission.

(4) Subsection (1) does not prevent the disclosure of information for any purpose with the consent of the individual in connection with whose case it was furnished and, where he did not furnish it himself, with that of the person or body who did.

(5) A person who discloses any information in contravention of this section shall be guilty of an offence and liable on summary conviction to a fine not exceeding level 4 on the standard scale.

(6) Proceedings for an offence under this section shall not be brought without the consent of the Director of Public Prosecutions.

(7) Nothing in this section applies to information furnished to a person providing services funded as part of the Community Legal Service or the Criminal Defence Service by or on behalf of an individual seeking or receiving such services.

Note. Sub-s (2)(b): words 'Secretary of State' substituted by SI 2003 No 1887, art 9, Sch 2, para 11(1)(a) as from 19 August 2003.

21 Misrepresentation etc—(1) Any person who—

(a) intentionally fails to comply with any requirement imposed by virtue of this Part as to the information to be furnished by him, or

(b) in furnishing any information required by virtue of this Part makes any statement or representation which he knows or believes to be false,

shall be guilty of an offence.

(2) A person guilty of an offence under subsection (1) is liable on summary conviction to—

(a) a fine not exceeding level 4 on the standard scale, or

(b) imprisonment for a term not exceeding *three months* [51 weeks],

or to both.

(3) Proceedings in respect of an offence under subsection (1) may (despite anything in the Magistrates' Courts Act 1980) be brought at any time within the period of six months beginning with the date on which evidence sufficient in the opinion of the prosecutor to justify a prosecution comes to his knowledge.

(4) But subsection (3) does not authorise the commencement of proceedings for an offence at a time more than two years after the date on which the offence was committed.

(5) A county court shall have jurisdiction to hear and determine any action brought by the Commission to recover loss sustained by reason of—

(a) the failure of any person to comply with any requirement imposed by virtue of this Part as to the information to be furnished by him, or

(b) a false statement or false representation made by any person in furnishing any information required by virtue of this Part.

Note. Sub-s (2)(b): words '51 weeks' substituted by the Criminal Justice Act 2003, s 280(2), (3), Sch 26, para 51 as from a date to be appointed.

22 Position of service providers and other parties etc—(1) Except as expressly provided by regulations, the fact that services provided for an individual are or could be funded by the Commission as part of the Community Legal Service or Criminal Defence Service shall not affect—

(a) the relationship between that individual and the person by whom they are provided or any privilege arising out of that relationship, or

(b) any right which that individual may have to be indemnified in respect of expenses incurred by him by any other person.

(2) A person who provides services funded by the Commission as part of the Community Legal Service or Criminal Defence Service shall not take any payment in respect of the services apart from—

(a) that made by way of that funding, and

(b) any authorised by the Commission to be taken.

(3) The withdrawal of a right to representation previously granted to an individual shall not affect the right of any person who has provided to him services funded by the Commission as part of the Criminal Defence Service to remuneration for work done before the date of the withdrawal.

(4) Except as expressly provided by regulations, any rights conferred by or by virtue of this Part on an individual for whom services are funded by the Commission as part of the Community Legal Service or Criminal Defence Service in relation to any proceedings shall not affect—

(a) the rights or liabilities of other parties to the proceedings, or

(b) the principles on which the discretion of any court or tribunal is normally exercised.

(5) Regulations may make provision about the procedure of any court or tribunal in relation to services funded by the Commission as part of the Community Legal Service or Criminal Defence Service.

(6) Regulations made under subsection (5) may in particular authorise the exercise of the functions of any court or tribunal by any member or officer of that or any other court or tribunal.

23 Guidance—(1) The *Lord Chancellor* [Secretary of State] may give guidance to the Commission as to the manner in which he considers it should discharge its functions.

(2) The Commission shall take into account any such guidance when considering the manner in which it is to discharge its functions.

(3) Guidance may not be given under this section in relation to individual cases.

(4) The *Lord Chancellor* [Secretary of State] shall either—

(a) publish, or

(b) require the Commission to publish,

any guidance given under this section.

Note. Sub-ss (2), (4): words 'Secretary of State' substituted by SI 2003 No 1887, art 9, Sch 2, para 11(1)(a) as from 19 August 2003.

24 Consequential amendments Schedule 4 (which makes amendments consequential on this Part) has effect.

25 Orders, regulations and directions—(1) Any power of the *Lord Chancellor* [Secretary of State] under this Part to make an order or regulations is exercisable by statutory instrument.

(2) Before making any remuneration order relating to the payment of remuneration to barristers or solicitors the *Lord Chancellor* [Secretary of State] shall consult the General Council of the Bar and the Law Society.

(3) When making any remuneration order the *Lord Chancellor* [Secretary of State] shall have regard to—

  (a) the need to secure the provision of services of the description to which the order relates by a sufficient number of competent persons and bodies,

  (b) the cost to public funds, and

  (c) the need to secure value for money.

(4) In subsections (2) and (3) 'remuneration order' means an order under section 6(4), 13(3) or 14(3) which relates to the payment by the Commission of remuneration—

  (a) for the provision of services by persons or bodies in individual cases, or

  (b) by reference to the provision of services by persons or bodies in specified numbers of cases.

(5) No directions may be given by the *Lord Chancellor* [Secretary of State] to the Commission under this Part in relation to individual cases.

(6) Any directions given by the *Lord Chancellor* [Secretary of State] to the Commission under this Part may be varied or revoked.

(7) The *Lord Chancellor* [Secretary of State] shall either—

  (a) publish, or

  (b) require the Commission to publish,

any directions given by him under this Part.

(8) Orders, regulations and directions of the *Lord Chancellor* [Secretary of State] under this Part may make different provision for different purposes (including different areas).

(9) No order shall be made under section 2 or 8 or paragraph 5(3) of Schedule 3, and no regulations shall be made under section 6(7), 11(1) or (4)(b) or (d) or 15(2)(a) or (5) or paragraph 4 of Schedule 3, unless a draft of the order or regulations has been laid before, and approved by a resolution of, each House of Parliament.

(10) A statutory instrument containing any other order or regulations under this Part shall be subject to annulment in pursuance of a resolution of either House of Parliament.

Note. Sub-ss (1)-(3), (5)-(8): words 'Secretary of State' substituted by SI 2003 No 1887, art 9, Sch 2, para 11(1)(a) as from 19 August 2003.

26 Interpretation In this Part—

  'the Commission' means the Legal Services Commission,

  'the Community Legal Service Fund' has the meaning given by section 5(1),

  'criminal proceedings' has the meaning given in section 12(2),

  'prescribed' means prescribed by regulations and 'prescribe' shall be construed accordingly,

  'regulations' means regulations made by the *Lord Chancellor* [Secretary of State], and

  'representation' means representation for the purposes of proceedings and includes the assistance which is usually given by a representative in the steps preliminary or incidental to any proceedings and, subject to any time limits which may be prescribed, advice and assistance as to any appeal.

Note. Words 'Secretary of State' substituted by SI 2003 No 1887, art 9, Sch 2, para 11(1)(a) as from 19 August 2003.

*   *   *   *   *

PART IV
APPEALS, COURTS, JUDGES AND COURT PROCEEDINGS

Appeals

54 Permission to appeal—(1) Rules of court may provide that any right of appeal to—

    (a) a county court,

    (b) the High Court, or

    (c) the Court of Appeal,

may be exercised only with permission.

    (2) This section does not apply to a right of appeal in a criminal cause or matter.

    (3) For the purposes of subsection (1) rules of court may make provision as to—

    (a) the classes of case in which a right of appeal may be exercised only with permission,

    (b) the court or courts which may give permission for the purposes of this section,

    (c) any considerations to be taken into account in deciding whether permission should be given, and

    (d) any requirements to be satisfied before permission may be given,

and may make different provision for different circumstances.

    (4) No appeal may be made against a decision of a court under this section to give or refuse permission (but this subsection does not affect any right under rules of court to make a further application for permission to the same or another court).

    (5) For the purposes of this section a right to make an application to have a case stated for the opinion of the High Court constitutes a right of appeal.

    (6) For the purposes of this section a right of appeal to the Court of Appeal includes—

    (a) the right to make an application for a new trial, and

    (b) the right to make an application to set aside a verdict, finding or judgment in any cause or matter in the High Court which has been tried, or in which any issue has been tried, by a jury.

55 Second appeals—(1) Where an appeal is made to a county court or the High Court in relation to any matter, and on hearing the appeal the court makes a decision in relation to that matter, no appeal may be made to the Court of Appeal from that decision unless the Court of Appeal considers that—

    (a) the appeal would raise an important point of principle or practice, or

    (b) there is some other compelling reason for the Court of Appeal to hear it.

    (2) This section does not apply in relation to an appeal in a criminal cause or matter.

56 Power to prescribe alternative destination of appeals—(1) The Lord Chancellor may by order provide that appeals which would otherwise lie to—

    (a) a county court,

    (b) the High Court, or

    (c) the Court of Appeal,

shall lie instead to another of those courts, as specified in the order.

    (2) This section does not apply to an appeal in a criminal cause or matter.

    (3) An order under subsection (1)—

    (a) may make different provision for different classes of proceedings or appeals, and

    (b) may contain consequential amendments or repeals of enactments.

(4) Before making an order under subsection (1) the Lord Chancellor shall consult—

(a) the Lord Chief Justice,

(b) the Master of the Rolls,

(c) the President of the Family Division, and

(d) the Vice-Chancellor.

(5) An order under subsection (1) shall be made by statutory instrument.

(6) No such order may be made unless a draft of it has been laid before and approved by resolution of each House of Parliament.

(7) For the purposes of this section an application to have a case stated for the opinion of the High Court constitutes an appeal.

57 Assignment of appeals to Court of Appeal—(1) Where in any proceedings in a county court or the High Court a person appeals, or seeks permission to appeal, to a court other than the Court of Appeal or the House of Lords—

(a) the Master of the Rolls, or

(b) the court from which or to which the appeal is made, or from which permission to appeal is sought,

may direct that the appeal shall be heard instead by the Court of Appeal.

(2) The power conferred by subsection (1)(b) shall be subject to rules of court.

58 Criminal appeals: minor amendments—(1) *In section 40(6) of the Criminal Justice Act 1991 (order returning offender to prison for unserved portion of sentence to be treated for purposes of appeal provisions as sentence passed for original offence), for the words from 'any enactment' to 'made' substitute 'sections 9 and 10 of the Criminal Appeal Act 1968, any order made by the Crown Court under subsection (2) above, or made under subsection (3A) above,'.*

(2) In section 8(1B)(b) of the Criminal Appeal Act 1968 (power of Court to direct entry of judgment and verdict of acquittal on applications relating to order for retrial), after 'to' insert 'set aside the order for retrial and'.

(3) In section 9(2) of that Act (right of appeal against sentence for summary offence), insert at the end 'or sub-paragraph (4) of that paragraph.'

(4) Section 10 of that Act (appeal to Court of Appeal by person dealt with by Crown Court for offence of which he was not convicted on indictment) is amended in accordance with subsections (5) to (7).

(5) *In subsection (2) (proceedings from which an appeal lies), insert at the end—*

'; or

(c) having been released under Part II of the Criminal Justice Act 1991 after serving part of a sentence of imprisonment or detention imposed for the offence, is ordered by the Crown Court to be returned to prison or detention.'

(6) *In subsection (3) (cases where person may appeal), in paragraph (cc) (order under section 40(3A)), for '40(3A)' substitute '40(2) or (3A)'.*

(7) In subsection (4) (calculation of length of term of imprisonment), after 'imprisonment' insert 'or detention'.

Note. Sub-ss (1), (6) repealed by the Powers of Criminal Courts (Sentencing) Act 2000, s 165(4), Sch 12, Pt I as from 25 August 2000. Sub-s (5) repealed by the Criminal Justice Act 2003, s 336(3) as from a date to be appointed.

Civil division of Court of Appeal

59 Composition In section 54 of the Supreme Court Act 1981 (composition of court of civil division of Court of Appeal), for subsections (2) to (4) (number of judges) substitute—

'(2) Subject as follows, a court shall be duly constituted for the purpose of exercising any of its jurisdiction if it consists of one or more judges.

(3) The Master of the Rolls may, with the concurrence of the Lord Chancellor, give (or vary or revoke) directions about the minimum number of judges of which a court must consist if it is to be duly constituted for the purpose of any description of proceedings.

(4) The Master of the Rolls, or any Lord Justice of Appeal designated by him, may (subject to any directions under subsection (3)) determine the number of judges of which a court is to consist for the purpose of any particular proceedings.

(4A) The Master of the Rolls may give directions as to what is to happen in any particular case where one or more members of a court which has partly heard proceedings are unable to continue.'

60 Calling into question of incidental decisions For section 58 of the Supreme Court Act 1981 (exercise of incidental jurisdiction in civil division of Court of Appeal) substitute—

'58 Calling into question of incidental decisions in civil division—(1) Rules of court may provide that decisions of the Court of Appeal which—

(a) are taken by a single judge or any officer or member of staff of that court in proceedings incidental to any cause or matter pending before the civil division of that court; and

(b) do not involve the determination of an appeal or of an application for permission to appeal,

may be called into question in such manner as may be prescribed.

(2) No appeal shall lie to the House of Lords from a decision which may be called into question pursuant to rules under subsection (1).'

High Court

64 Contempt of court—(1) Section 13(2) of the Administration of Justice Act 1960 (appeals in cases of contempt of court) is amended as follows.

(2) In paragraph (a) (appeal from inferior courts from which appeal does not lie to Court of Appeal to lie to a Divisional Court of the High Court), omit 'a Divisional Court of'.

(3) In paragraph (b) (appeal to Court of Appeal from county court or single judge of High Court), for 'decision, of a single' substitute 'decision (other than a decision on an appeal under this section) of a single'.

(4) In paragraph (c) (appeal from Divisional Court or Court of Appeal to House of Lords), insert at the beginning 'from a decision of a single judge of the High Court on an appeal under this section,'.

65 Habeas corpus—(1) In the Administration of Justice Act 1960, omit—

(a) section 14(1) (order for release on criminal application for habeas corpus to be refused only by Divisional Court of Queen's Bench Division), and

(b) section 15(2) (no appeal to House of Lords from order made by single judge on criminal application for habeas corpus).

(2) In section 15 of that Act (appeals in habeas corpus cases)—

(a) in subsection (3) (no restriction on grant of leave to appeal to House of Lords against decision of Divisional Court on a criminal application for habeas corpus), and

(b) in subsection (4) (exceptions to right to be discharged in case of appeal to House of Lords against order of Divisional Court on such an application),

for 'a Divisional Court' substitute 'the High Court'.

Judges etc

68 Judges holding office in European or international courts—(1) A holder of a United Kingdom judicial office may hold office in a relevant international court without being required to relinquish the United Kingdom judicial office.

(2) In this section—

'United Kingdom judicial office' means the office of—

    (a) Lord Justice of Appeal, Justice of the High Court or Circuit judge, in England and Wales,

    (b) judge of the Court of Session or sheriff, in Scotland, or

    (c) Lord Justice of Appeal, judge of the High Court or county court judge, in Northern Ireland, and

'relevant international court' means—

    (a) any court established for any purposes of the European Communities, or

    (b) any international court (apart from the European Court of Human Rights) which is designated for the purposes of this section by the Lord Chancellor or the Secretary of State.

(3) A holder of a United Kingdom judicial office who also holds office in a relevant international court is not required to perform any duties as the holder of the United Kingdom judicial office but does not count as holding the United Kingdom judicial office—

    (a) for the purposes of section 12(1) to (6) of the Supreme Court Act 1981, section 9(1)(c) or (d) of the Administration of Justice Act 1973, section 18 of the Courts Act 1971, section 14 of the Sheriff Courts (Scotland) Act 1907 or section 106 of the County Courts Act (Northern Ireland) 1959 (judicial salaries),

    (b) for the purposes of, or of any scheme established by and in accordance with, the Judicial Pensions and Retirement Act 1993, the Judicial Pensions Act 1981, the Sheriffs' Pensions (Scotland) Act 1961 or the County Courts Act (Northern Ireland) 1959 (judicial pensions), or

    (c) for the purposes of section 2(1) or 4(1) of the Supreme Court Act 1981, section 1(1) of the Court of Session Act 1988 or section 2(1) or 3(1) of the Judicature (Northern Ireland) Act 1978 (judicial numbers).

(4) If the sheriff principal of any sheriffdom also holds office in a relevant international court, section 11(1) of the Sheriff Courts (Scotland) Act 1971 (temporary appointment of sheriff principal) applies as if the office of sheriff principal of that sheriffdom were vacant.

(5) The appropriate Minister may by order made by statutory instrument make in relation to a holder of a United Kingdom judicial office who has ceased to hold office in a relevant international court such transitional provision (including, in particular, provision for a temporary increase in the maximum number of judges) as he considers appropriate.

(6) In subsection (5) 'the appropriate Minister' means—

    (a) in relation to any United Kingdom judicial office specified in paragraph (a) or (c) of the definition in subsection (2), the Lord Chancellor, and

    (b) in relation to any United Kingdom judicial office specified in paragraph (b) of that definition, the Secretary of State.

(7) A statutory instrument containing an order made under subsection (5) shall be subject to annulment in pursuance of a resolution of either House of Parliament.

69 Vice-president of Queen's Bench Division

(1) The Lord Chancellor may appoint one of the ordinary judges of the Court of Appeal as vice-president of the Queen's Bench Division; and any person so appointed shall hold that office in accordance with the terms of his appointment.

(2) In section 4 of the Supreme Court Act 1981 (composition of High Court)—

(a) in subsection (1) (membership), after the words 'the Senior Presiding Judge;' insert—

'(ddd) the vice-president of the Queen's Bench Division;', and

(b) in subsection (6) (vacancy in offices not to affect constitution), at the end insert 'and whether or not an appointment has been made to the office of vice-president of the Queen's Bench Division.'

(3) In section 5 of that Act (divisions of High Court), in subsection (1)(b) (Queen's Bench Division), after 'thereof,' insert 'the vice-president of the Queen's Bench Division'.

70 Registrar of civil appeals *The office of registrar of civil appeals is abolished.*

Note. Repealed by the Statute Law (Repeals) Act 2004 as from 22 July 2004.

Court proceedings

72 Reporting of proceedings relating to children In section 97 of the Children Act 1989 (privacy for children involved proceedings in certain proceedings)—

(a) in subsection (2) (which prohibits the publication of material intended or likely to identify a child as being involved in proceedings before a magistrates' court in which powers under that Act may be exercised), after 'before' insert 'the High Court, a county court or', and

(b) in subsection (8) (which makes provision about the application of certain provisions of the Magistrates' Courts Act 1980 in relation to proceedings to which section 97 applies), after 'any proceedings' insert '(before a magistrates' court)'.

PART VII
SUPPLEMENTARY

105 Transitional provisions and savings Schedule 14 (transitional provisions and savings) has effect.

106 Repeals and revocations Schedule 15 (repeals and revocations) has effect.

107 Crown application This Act binds the Crown.

108 Commencement—(1) Subject to subsections (2) and (3), the preceding provisions of this Act shall come into force on such day as the Lord Chancellor [or Secretary of State] may by order made by statutory instrument appoint; and different days may be appointed for different purposes and, in the case of section 67(2), for different areas.

(2) Section 45 shall come into force on the day on which this Act is passed.

(3) The following provisions shall come into force at the end of the period of two months beginning with the day on which this Act is passed—

(a) in Part II, sections 32 to 34,

(b) Part IV, apart from section 66 and Schedule 9 and sections 67(2) and 71,

(c) in Part V, sections 74 to 76, 81, 82, 84, 86 and 87 and Schedule 10,

(d) in Part VI, section 104,

(e) Schedule 14,

(f) in Schedule 15, Part III and Part V(1) and (5), apart from the provisions specified in subsection (4), and

(g) section 107.

(4) The provisions excepted from subsection (3)(f) are the repeal of section 67(8) of the Magistrates' Courts Act 1980 (and that in Schedule 11 to the Children Act 1989) contained in Part V(1) of Schedule 15.

Note. Sub-s (1): words 'or Secretary of State' inserted by SI 2003 No 1887, art 9, Sch 2, para 11(2) as from 19 August 2003.

109 Extent—(1) Sections 32 to 34 and 73(2) extend to Scotland.

(2) Sections 98(2) and (3) and 104(2) extend to Northern Ireland.

(3) Sections 68, 101, 102 and 103 extend to England and Wales, Scotland and Northern Ireland.

(4) The other provisions of this Act which make amendments or repeals or revocations in other enactments also have the same extent as the enactments which they amend or repeal or revoke.

(5) Subject to subsection (4), the provisions of this Part (including paragraph 1, but not the rest, of Schedule 14) extend to England and Wales, Scotland and Northern Ireland.

(6) Subject to the preceding provisions, this Act extends to England and Wales.

(7) For the purposes of the Scotland Act 1998 this Act, so far as it extends to Scotland, shall be taken to be a pre-commencement enactment within the meaning of that Act.

110 Short title This Act may be cited as the Access to Justice Act 1999.

SCHEDULE 1   Section 1
LEGAL SERVICES COMMISSION

Incorporation and status

1 The Commission shall be a body corporate.

2 The Commission shall not be regarded—
  (a) as the servant or agent of the Crown, or
  (b) as enjoying any status, immunity or privilege of the Crown;
and the Commission's property shall not be regarded as property of, or held on behalf of, the Crown.

Tenure of members

3—(1) Subject to paragraphs 4 and 5, any member of the Commission shall hold and vacate office in accordance with the terms of his appointment.

(2)   But a person shall not be appointed a member of the Commission for a period of more than five years.

4—(1) A member of the Commission, or the person appointed to chair it, may resign office by giving notice in writing to the *Lord Chancellor* [Secretary of State].

(2) If the person appointed to chair the Commission ceases to be a member of it, he shall cease to chair it.

(3) A person who ceases to be a member of the Commission, or to chair it, shall be eligible for reappointment.

5 The *Lord Chancellor* [Secretary of State] may terminate the appointment of a member of the Commission if satisfied that—
  (a) he has become bankrupt or made an arrangement with his creditors,
  (b) he is unable to carry out his duties as a member of the Commission by reason of illness,
  (c) he has been absent from meetings of the Commission for a period longer than six consecutive months without the permission of the Commission, or
  (d) he is otherwise unable or unfit to discharge the functions of a member of the Commission.

Members' interests

6 (1) Before appointing a person to be a member of the Commission, the *Lord Chancellor* [Secretary of State] shall satisfy himself that that person will have no such financial or other interest as is likely to affect prejudicially the exercise or performance by him of his functions as a member of the Commission.

(2) The *Lord Chancellor* [Secretary of State] shall from time to time satisfy himself with respect to every member of the Commission that he has no such interest as is referred to in sub-paragraph (1).

(3) Any person whom the *Lord Chancellor* [Secretary of State] proposes to appoint as, and who has consented to be, a member of the Commission, and any member of the Commission, shall (whenever requested by the *Lord Chancellor* [Secretary of State] to do so) supply him with such information as the Lord Chancellor considers necessary for the performance by the *Lord Chancellor* [Secretary of State] of his duties under this paragraph.

7 (1) A member of the Commission who is in any way directly or indirectly interested in an individual contract entered into or proposed to be entered into, or an individual grant, loan or other payment made or proposed to be made, by the Commission shall disclose the nature of his interest at a meeting of the Commission; and—

    (a) the disclosure shall be recorded in the minutes of the Commission, and

    (b) the member shall not take any part in any deliberation or decision of the Commission with respect to that contract or grant, loan or other payment.

(2) For the purposes of sub-paragraph (1), a general notice given at a meeting of the Commission by a member of the Commission to the effect—

    (a) that he is a person with whom a contract may be entered into, or to whom a grant, loan or other payment may be made, by the Commission, or

    (b) that he is a member of a specified body with which a contract may be entered into, or to which a grant, loan or other payment may be made, by the Commission,

shall be regarded as a sufficient disclosure of his interest in relation to any contract subsequently entered into with, or grant, loan or other payment made to, him or the body.

(3) A member of the Commission need not attend in person at a meeting of the Commission in order to make any disclosure which he is required to make under this paragraph if he takes reasonable steps to secure that the disclosure is made by a notice which is brought up and read out at the meeting.

Remuneration of members

8—(1) The Commission may—

    (a) pay to its members such remuneration, and

    (b) make provision for the payment of such pensions, allowances or gratuities to or in respect of its members,

as the *Lord Chancellor* [Secretary of State] may determine.

(2) Where a person ceases to be a member of the Commission otherwise than on the expiry of his term of office, and it appears to the *Lord Chancellor* [Secretary of State] that there are special circumstances which make it right for that person to receive compensation, the *Lord Chancellor* [Secretary of State] may require the Commission to make that person a payment of such amount as the *Lord Chancellor* [Secretary of State] may determine.

Staff

9—(1) The Commission shall appoint a person to be the chief executive of the Commission who shall be responsible to the Commission for the exercise of its functions.

(2) The Commission may appoint such other employees as it thinks fit.

(3) The Commission may only appoint a person to be—

(a) its chief executive, or

(b) the holder of any other employment of a description specified by the *Lord Chancellor* [Secretary of State] by direction given to the Commission,

after consultation with, and subject to the approval of, the *Lord Chancellor* [Secretary of State] .

(4) An appointment under this paragraph may be made on such terms and conditions as the Commission, with the approval of the *Lord Chancellor* [Secretary of State] , may determine.

10—(1) The Commission shall make, in respect of such of its employees as, with the approval of the *Lord Chancellor* [Secretary of State], it may determine such arrangements for providing pensions, allowances or gratuities, including pensions, allowances or gratuities by way of compensation for loss of employment, as it may determine.

(2) Arrangements under sub-paragraph (1) may include the establishment and administration, by the Commission or otherwise, of one or more pension schemes.

(3) If an employee of the Commission—

(a) becomes a member of the Commission, and

(b) was by reference to his employment by the Commission a participant in a pension scheme established and administered by it for the benefit of its employees,

the Commission may determine that his service as a member shall be treated for the purposes of the scheme as service as an employee of the Commission whether or not any benefits are to be payable to or in respect of him by virtue of paragraph 8.

(4) Where the Commission exercises the power conferred by sub-paragraph (3), any discretion as to the benefits payable to or in respect of the member concerned which the scheme confers on the Commission shall be exercised only with the approval of the *Lord Chancellor* [Secretary of State] .

Funding of costs relating to administration etc

11—(1) The *Lord Chancellor* [Secretary of State] shall pay to the Commission such sums as he may determine as appropriate for—

(a) the exercise by the Commission of functions in relation to the Community Legal Service other than the funding of services, and

(b) the administrative costs of the Commission.

(2) The *Lord Chancellor* [Secretary of State] may—

(a) determine the manner in which and times at which the sums mentioned in sub-paragraph (1) are to be paid to the Commission, and

(b) impose conditions on the payment of those sums.

Proceedings

12—(1) Subject to anything in any instrument made under this Part, the Commission may regulate its own proceedings.

(2) Committees—

(a) may be appointed, and may be dissolved, by the Commission, and

(b) may include, or consist entirely of, persons who are not members of the Commission,

but the *Lord Chancellor* [Secretary of State] may by direction require the Commission to make such provision relating to committees as is specified in the direction.

(3) A committee shall act in accordance with such instructions as the Commission may from time to time give; and the Commission may provide for

anything done by a committee to have effect as if it had been done by the Commission.

(4) The Commission may pay to the members of any committee such fees and allowances as the *Lord Chancellor* [Secretary of State] may determine.

(5) The validity of any proceedings of the Commission or of any committee appointed by the Commission shall not be affected by any vacancy among its members or by any defect in the appointment of any member.

Provision of information

13—(1) The Commission shall provide the *Lord Chancellor* [Secretary of State] with such information as he may require relating to its property and to the discharge or proposed discharge of its functions.

(2) The Commission shall—

(a) permit any person authorised by the *Lord Chancellor* [Secretary of State] to inspect and make copies of any accounts or documents of the Commission, and

(b) provide such explanation of them as any such person, or the *Lord Chancellor* [Secretary of State] , may require.

Annual report

14—(1) The Commission shall provide to the *Lord Chancellor* [Secretary of State] , as soon as possible after the end of each financial year, a report on how it has during that year—

(a) funded services from the Community Legal Service Fund,

(b) funded services as part of the Criminal Defence Service, and

(c) exercised its other functions.

(2) The *Lord Chancellor* [Secretary of State] may by direction require the Commission to deal with the matters specified in the direction in reports, or a particular report, under this paragraph.

(3) The *Lord Chancellor* [Secretary of State] shall lay before each House of Parliament a copy of each report provided to him under this paragraph and the Commission shall publish a report once it has been so laid.

(4) In this paragraph and paragraphs 15 and 16 'financial year' means—

(a) the period beginning with the day on which the Commission is established and ending with the next 31st March, and

(b) each subsequent period of twelve months ending with 31st March.

Annual plan

15—(1) The Commission shall, before the beginning of each financial year (other than that specified in paragraph 14(4)(a)), prepare a plan setting out how it intends in that year—

(a) to fund services from the Community Legal Service Fund,

(b) to fund services as part of the Criminal Defence Service, and

(c) to exercise its other functions,

and the plan shall include a summary of what the Commission has ascertained in the exercise of its functions under section 4(6).

(2) The *Lord Chancellor* [Secretary of State] may by direction require the Commission to deal with the matters specified in the direction in plans, or a particular plan, under sub-paragraph (1).

(3) The Commission shall send a copy of each plan prepared under sub-paragraph (1) to the *Lord Chancellor* [Secretary of State] .

(4) If the *Lord Chancellor* [Secretary of State] approves it, he shall lay a copy before each House of Parliament and the Commission shall publish the plan once it has been so laid.

(5) If he does not approve it, he shall by direction require the Commission to revise it in accordance with the direction; and the direction shall include the *Lord Chancellor's* [Secretary of State's] reasons for not approving the plan.

(6) When the Commission has revised the plan it shall send the *Lord Chancellor* [Secretary of State] a copy of the revised plan and he shall lay a copy before each House of Parliament and the Commission shall publish the revised plan once it has been so laid.

Accounts and audit

16—(1) The Commission shall keep accounts and shall prepare in respect of each financial year a statement of accounts.

(2) The accounts shall be kept, and the statement of accounts shall be prepared, in such form as the *Lord Chancellor* [Secretary of State] may, with the approval of the Treasury, specify by direction given to the Commission.

(3) The Commission shall send a copy of the statement of accounts in respect of each financial year to the *Lord Chancellor* [Secretary of State] and to the Comptroller and Auditor General within such period after the end of the financial year to which it relates as the *Lord Chancellor* [Secretary of State] may specify by direction given to the Commission.

(4) The Comptroller and Auditor General shall—

(a) examine, certify and report on each statement of accounts received by him under sub-paragraph (3), and

(b) lay a copy of each such statement of accounts, and his report on it, before each House of Parliament.

Instruments

17—(1) The fixing of the seal of the Commission shall be authenticated by a member of the Commission or by some other person authorised either generally or specially by the Commission to act for that purpose.

(2) A document purporting to be duly executed under the seal of the Commission or to be signed on the Commission's behalf—

(a) shall be received in evidence, and

(b) unless the contrary is proved, shall be deemed to be so executed or signed.

Note. Para (4)-(6), (8)-(16)words 'Secretary of State' substituted by SI 2003 No 1887, art 9, Sch 2, para 11(1)(f), (3) as from 19 August 2003.

SCHEDULE 2   Section 6
COMMUNITY LEGAL SERVICE: EXCLUDED SERVICES

The services which may not be funded as part of the Community Legal Service are as follows.

1 Services consisting of the provision of help (beyond the provision of general information about the law and the legal system and the availability of legal services) in relation to—

(a) allegations of negligently caused injury, death or damage to property, apart from allegations relating to clinical negligence,

(b) conveyancing,

(c) boundary disputes,

(d) the making of wills,

(e) matters of trust law,

(f) defamation or malicious falsehood,

(g) matters of company or partnership law, or

(h) other matters arising out of the carrying on of a *business* [business, or
(i) attending an interview conducted on behalf of the Secretary of State with a
view to his reaching a decision on a claim for asylum (as defined by section
167(1) of the Immigration and Asylum Act 1999)].

2 Advocacy in any proceedings except—
(1) proceedings in—
(a) the House of Lords in its judicial capacity,
(b) the Judicial Committee of the Privy Council in the exercise of its
jurisdiction under the Government of Wales Act 1998, the Scotland Act
1998 or the Northern Ireland Act 1998,
(c) the Court of Appeal,
(d) the High Court,
(e) any county court,
(f) the Employment Appeal Tribunal, *or*
(g) any Mental Health Review Tribunal,
[(h) the Immigration Appeal Tribunal or before an adjudicator,]
[(h) the Asylum and Immigration Tribunal,]
[(ha) the Special Immigration Appeals Commission,] [or
(i) the Proscribed Organisations Appeal Commission]
(2) proceedings in the Crown Court—
(a) for the variation or discharge of an order under section 5 of the Protection
from Harassment Act 1997,
(b) which relate to an order under section ... 10 of the Crime and Disorder Act
1998, *or*
(c) ... [*or*
(d) which relate to an order under paragraph 6 of Schedule 1 to the Anti-
terrorism, Crime and Security Act 2001,] [or
(e) under the Proceeds of Crime Act 2002 to the extent specified in paragraph
3,]
(3) proceedings in a magistrates' court—
(a) under section 43 or 47 of the National Assistance Act 1948, section 22 of
the Maintenance Orders Act 1950, section 4 of the Maintenance Orders
Act 1958 or section 106 of the Social Security Administration Act 1992,
(b) under Part I of the Maintenance Orders (Reciprocal Enforcement) Act
1972 relating to a maintenance order made by a court of a country outside
the United Kingdom,
(c) in relation to an application for leave of the court to remove a child from a
person's custody under *section 27 or 28 of the Adoption Act 1976* [section 36
of the Adoption and Children Act 2002] or in which the making of *an order
under Part II or section 29 or 55* [a placement order or adoption order
(within the meaning of the Adoption and Children Act 2002) or an order
under section 42 or 84] of that Act is opposed by any party to the
proceedings,
(d) for or in relation to an order under Part I of the Domestic Proceedings
and Magistrates' Courts Act 1978,
[(da) under section 55A of the Family Law Act 1986 (declarations of
parentage),]
(e) under the Children Act 1989,
(f) under section 30 of the Human Fertilisation and Embryology Act 1990,
(g) under section 20 *or 27* of the Child Support Act 1991,
(h) under Part IV of the Family Law Act 1996,
(i) for the variation or discharge of an order under section 5 of the Protection
from Harassment Act 1997, *or*
(j) under [section 8 or 11] of the Crime and Disorder Act 1998, [*or*

   (k)   for an order or direction under paragraph 3, 5, 6, 9 or 10 of Schedule 1 to the Anti-terrorism, Crime and Security Act 2001,]

   [(l)   for an order or direction under section 295, 297, 298, 301 or 302 of the Proceeds of Crime Act 2002,] and

(4) proceedings before any person to whom a case is referred (in whole or in part) in any proceedings within paragraphs (1) to (3).

[**3**—(1) These are the proceedings under the Proceeds of Crime Act 2002—

   (a)   an application under section 42(3) to vary or discharge a restraint order or an order under section 41(7);

   (b)   proceedings which relate to a direction under section 54(3) or 56(3) as to the distribution of funds in the hands of a receiver;

   (c)   an application under section 62 relating to action taken or proposed to be taken by a receiver;

   (d)   an application under section 63 to vary or discharge an order under any of sections 48 to 53 for the appointment of or conferring powers on a receiver;

   (e)   an application under section 72 or 73 for the payment of compensation;

   (f)   proceedings which relate to an order under section 298 for the forfeiture of cash;

   (g)   an application under section 351(3), 362(3), 369(3) or 375(2) to vary or discharge certain orders made under Part 8.

(2) But sub-paragraph (1) does not authorise the funding of the provision of services to a defendant (within the meaning of Part 1 of that Act) in relation to—

   (a)   proceedings mentioned in paragraph (b);

   (b)   an application under section 73 for the payment of compensation if the confiscation order was varied under section 29.]

Note. Para 1 in sub-para (g) word omitted repealed by SI 2004 No 1055, reg 2(a) as from 1 April 2004. Para (1)(h): words 'business, or' in square brackets substituted by SI 2004 No 1055, reg 2 (b). Para (1): sub-para (i) inserted by SI 2004 No 1055, reg 2(c) as from1 April 2004. Para 2: sub-para (1)(f) word omitted repealed by the Terrorism Act 2000, s 125(2), Sch 16, Pt I as from 19 February 2001. Para 2: sub-para (1)(h) inserted by SI 2000 No 822, reg 3(a) as from 1 April 2000. Para 2: sub-para (1)(h) substituted by the Asylum and Immigration (Treatment of Claimants, etc) Act 2004, s 26(7), Sch 2, Pt 1, para 14; for transitional provisions see s 26(7), Sch 2, Pt 2 thereto. as from a date to be appointed: see the Asylum and Immigration (Treatment of Claimants, etc) Act 2004, s 48(3)-(6). Para 2: sub-para (1)(ha) inserted by the Nationality, Immigration and Asylum Act 2002, s 116 as from 1 April 2003 (SI 2003 No 754). Para 2: sub-para (1)(i) and word 'or' immediately preceding it inserted by the Terrorism Act 2000, s 125(1), Sch 15, para 19(1) as from 19 February 2001. Para 2: sub-para (2)(b) first words omitted repealed by SI 2000 No 822, reg 3(b)(i) as from 1 April 2000. Para 2: sub-para (2)(b) final word omitted repealed by the Anti-terrorism, Crime and Security Act 2001, ss 2(1), (2), 125, Sch 8, Pt 1 as from 20 December 2001. Para 2: sub-para (2)(c) repealed by SI 2000 No 822, reg 3(b)(ii) as from 1 April 2000. Para 2: sub-para (2)(c) word omitted repealed by the Proceeds of Crime Act 2002, ss 456, 457, Sch 11, paras 1, 36(1), (2), Sch 12 as from 30 December 2002. Para (2): sub-para (3)(c) words in italics repealed and words in square brackets substituted by the Adoption and Children Act 2002, Sch 3, para 102(a) as from a date to be appointed. Para 2: sub-para (2)(d) and word 'or' immediately preceding it inserted by the Anti-terrorism, Crime and Security Act 2001, s 2(1), (2) as from 20 December 2001. Para 2: sub-para (3)(da) inserted by the Child Support, Pensions and Social Security Act 2000, s 83(5), Sch 8, paras 11, 15 as from 1 April 2001. Para 2: sub-para (3)(g) words omitted repealed by the Child Support, Pensions and Social Security Act 2000, s 85, Sch 9, Pt IX as from 1 April 2001. Para 2: sub-para (3)(i) word omitted repealed by the Anti-terrorism, Crime and Security Act 2001, s 2(1), (3), 125, Sch 8, Pt 1 as from 20 December 2001. Para 2: sub-para (3)(j) words 'section 8 or 11' in square brackets substituted by SI 2000 No 822, reg 3(c) as from 1 April 2000. Para 2: in sub-para (3)(j) word 'or' in italics repealed by the Proceeds of Crime Act 2002, ss 456, 457, Sch 11, paras 1, 36(1), (3), Sch 12 as from 30 December 2002. Para 2: sub-para (3)(k) and word 'or' immediately preceding it inserted by the Anti-terrorism, Crime and Security Act 2001, s 2(1), (3), as from 20 December 2001. Para 2: sub-para (3)(l) inserted by the Proceeds of Crime Act 2002, s 456, Sch 11, paras

1, 36(1), (3) as from 30 December 2002. Para 3: inserted by the Proceeds of Crime Act 2002, s 456, Sch 11, paras 1, 36(1), (4) as from 30 December 2002.

WELFARE REFORM AND PENSIONS ACT 1999
(1999 c 30)

An Act to make provision about pensions and social security; to make provision for reducing under-occupation of dwellings by housing benefit claimants; to authorise certain expenditure by the Secretary of State having responsibility for social security; and for connected purposes.

[11 November 1999]

*   *   *   *   *

PART II
PENSIONS: GENERAL

*   *   *   *   *

Pensions and bankruptcy

11 Effect of bankruptcy on pension rights: approved arrangements—(1) Where a bankruptcy order is made against a person on a petition presented after the coming into force of this section, any rights of his under an approved pension arrangement are excluded from his estate.

(2) In this section 'approved pension arrangement' means—
  (a) an exempt approved scheme;
  (b) a relevant statutory scheme;
  (c) a retirement benefits scheme set up by a government outside the United Kingdom for the benefit, or primarily for the benefit, of its employees;
  (d) a retirement benefits scheme which is being considered for approval under Chapter I of Part XIV of the Taxes Act;
  (e) a contract or scheme which is approved under Chapter III of that Part (retirement annuities);
  (f) a personal pension scheme which is approved under Chapter IV of that Part;
  (g) an annuity purchased for the purpose of giving effect to rights under a scheme falling within any of paragraphs (a) to (c) and (f);
  (h) any pension arrangements of any description which may be prescribed by regulations made by the Secretary of State.

(3) The reference in subsection (1) to rights under an approved pension arrangement does not include rights under a personal pension scheme approved under Chapter IV of Part XIV of the Taxes Act unless those rights arise by virtue of approved personal pension arrangements.

(4) Subsection (5) applies if—
  (a) at the time when a bankruptcy order is made against a person a retirement benefits scheme is being considered for approval under Chapter I of Part XIV of the Taxes Act, and
  (b) the decision of the Commissioners of Inland Revenue is that approval is not to be given to the scheme.

(5) Any rights of that person under the scheme shall (without any conveyance, assignment or transfer) vest in his trustee in bankruptcy, as part of his estate, immediately on—
  (a) the Commissioners' decision being made, or
  (b) (if later) the trustee's appointment taking effect or, in the case of the official receiver, his becoming trustee.

(6) Subsection (7) applies if, at any time after a bankruptcy order is made against a person, the Commissioners of Inland Revenue give notice—

(a) withdrawing their approval under Chapter I of Part XIV of the Taxes Act from a retirement benefits scheme, or

(b) withdrawing their approval under Chapter IV of that Part from a personal pension scheme or from any approved personal pension arrangements,

and the date specified as being that from which the approval is withdrawn ('the withdrawal date') is a date not later than that on which the bankruptcy order is made.

(7) Any rights of that person under the scheme or arising by virtue of the arrangements, and any rights of his under any related annuity, shall (without any conveyance, assignment or transfer) vest in his trustee in bankruptcy, as part of his estate, immediately on—

(a) the giving of the notice, or

(b) (if later) the trustee's appointment taking effect or, in the case of the official receiver, his becoming trustee.

(8) In subsection (7) 'related annuity' means an annuity purchased on or after the withdrawal date for the purpose of giving effect to rights under the scheme or (as the case may be) to rights arising by virtue of the arrangements.

(9) Where under subsection (5) or (7) any rights vest in a person's trustee in bankruptcy, the trustee's title to them has relation back to the commencement of the person's bankruptcy; but where any transaction is entered into by the trustees or managers of the scheme in question—

(a) in good faith, and

(b) without notice of the making of the decision mentioned in subsection (4)(b) or (as the case may be) the giving of the notice mentioned in subsection (6),

the trustee in bankruptcy is not in respect of that transaction entitled by virtue of this subsection to any remedy against them or any person whose title to any property derives from them.

(10) Without prejudice to section 83, regulations under subsection (2)(h) may, in the case of any description of arrangements prescribed by the regulations, make provision corresponding to any provision made by subsections (4) to (9).

(11) In this section—

(a) 'exempt approved scheme', 'relevant statutory scheme' and 'retirement benefits scheme' have the same meaning as in Chapter I of Part XIV of the Taxes Act;

(b) 'approved personal pension arrangements' and 'personal pension scheme' have the same meaning as in Chapter IV of that Part;

(c) 'estate', in relation to a person against whom a bankruptcy order is made, means his estate for the purposes of Parts VIII to XI of the Insolvency Act 1986;

(d) 'the Taxes Act' means the Income and Corporation Taxes Act 1988.

(12) For the purposes of this section a person shall be treated as having a right under an approved pension arrangement where—

(a) he is entitled to a credit under section 29(1)(b) as against the person responsible for the arrangement (within the meaning of Chapter I of Part IV), and

(b) the person so responsible has not discharged his liability in respect of the credit.

Note. 11 November 1999 (for the purpose of the exercise of any power to make regulations; 29 May 2000 (sub-ss (1)-(3), (11) for remaining purposes) (SI 2000 No 1382, art 2(a)); 1 December 2000 (sub-s (12) for remaining purposes) (SI 2000 No 1382, art 2(b)); 6 April 2002 (sub-ss (4)-(10) for remaining purposes) (SI 2002 No 153, art 2(a)).

12 Effect of bankruptcy on pension rights: unapproved arrangements (1) The Secretary of State may by regulations make provision for or in connection with enabling rights of a person under an unapproved pension arrangement to be excluded, in the event of a bankruptcy order being made against that person, from his estate for the purposes of Parts VIII to XI of the Insolvency Act 1986.

(2) Regulations under this section may, in particular, make provision—

(a) for rights under an unapproved pension arrangement to be excluded from a person's estate—

    (i) by an order made on his application by a prescribed court, or

    (ii) in accordance with a qualifying agreement made between him and his trustee in bankruptcy;

(b) for the court's decision whether to make such an order in relation to a person to be made by reference to—

    (i) future likely needs of him and his family, and

    (ii) whether any benefits (by way of a pension or otherwise) are likely to be received by virtue of rights of his under other pension arrangements and (if so) the extent to which they appear likely to be adequate for meeting any such needs;

(c) for the prescribed persons in the case of any pension arrangement to provide a person or his trustee in bankruptcy on request with information reasonably required by that person or trustee for or in connection with the making of such applications and agreements as are mentioned in paragraph (a).

(3) In this section—

'prescribed' means prescribed by regulations under this section;

'qualifying agreement' means an agreement entered into in such circumstances, and satisfying such requirements, as may be prescribed;

'unapproved pension arrangement' means a pension arrangement which—

(a) is not an approved pension arrangement within the meaning of section 11, and

(b) is of a prescribed description.

(4) For the purposes of this section a person shall be treated as having a right under an unapproved pension arrangement where—

(a) he is entitled to a credit under section 29(1)(b) as against the person responsible for the arrangement (within the meaning of Chapter I of Part IV), and

(b) the person so responsible has not discharged his liability in respect of the credit.

Note. 11 November 1999 (for the purpose only of the exercise of any power to make regulations); 6 April 2002 (SI 2002 No 153, art 2(b)) (remaining purposes).

13 Sections 11 and 12: application to Scotland—(1) This section shall have effect for the purposes of the application of sections 11 and 12 to Scotland.

(2) A reference to—

(a) the making of a bankruptcy order against a person is a reference to the award of sequestration on his estate or the making of the appointment on his estate of a judicial factor under section 41 of the Solicitors (Scotland) Act 1980;

(b) the estate of a person is a reference to his estate for the purposes of the Bankruptcy (Scotland) Act 1985 or of the Solicitors (Scotland) Act 1980, as the case may be;

(c) assignment is a reference to assignation;

(d) a person's trustee in bankruptcy is a reference to his permanent trustee or judicial factor, as the case may be;

(e) the commencement of a person's bankruptcy is a reference to the date of sequestration (within the meaning of section 12(4) of the Bankruptcy

(Scotland) Act 1985) or of the judicial factor's appointment taking effect, as the case may be.

(3) For paragraph (b) of each of subsections (5) and (7) of section 11 there shall be substituted—

'(b) if later, the date of sequestration (within the meaning of section 12(4) of the Bankruptcy (Scotland) Act 1985) or of the judicial factor's appointment taking effect, as the case may be.'

Note. 11 November 1999 (for the purpose only of the exercise of any power to make regulations); 29 May 2000 (sub-ss (1), (2)) (SI 2000 No 1382, art 2(a)); 6 April 2002 (sub-s (3)) (SI 2002 No 153, art 2(c)).

14 No forfeiture on bankruptcy of rights under pension schemes—(1) In the Pension Schemes Act 1993, after section 159 there shall be inserted—

'159A No forfeiture on bankruptcy of rights under personal pension schemes—(1) A person's rights under a personal pension scheme cannot be forfeited by reference to his bankruptcy.

(2) For the purposes of this section—

(a) a person shall be treated as having a right under a personal pension scheme where—

　　(i) he is entitled to a credit under section 29(1)(b) of the Welfare Reform and Pensions Act 1999 (sharing of rights on divorce etc),

　　(ii) he is so entitled as against the person responsible for the scheme (within the meaning of Chapter I of Part IV of that Act), and

　　(iii) the person so responsible has not discharged his liability in respect of the credit; and

(b) forfeiture shall be taken to include any manner of deprivation or suspension.'

(2) In section 159(6) of that Act (application of section 159 to Scotland), after 'this section' there shall be inserted 'and section 159A'.

(3) In section 92(2) of the Pensions Act 1995 (exceptions to the rule preventing forfeiture of rights under occupational pension schemes), paragraph (b) (which allows forfeiture of such rights by reference to a scheme member's bankruptcy) shall cease to have effect.

Note. 6 April 2002 (SI 2002 No 153, art 2(d)).

15 Excessive pension contributions made by persons who have become bankrupt For sections 342A to 342C of the Insolvency Act 1986 there shall be substituted—

342A Recovery of excessive pension contributions—(1) Where an individual who is adjudged bankrupt—

(a) has rights under an approved pension arrangement, or

(b) has excluded rights under an unapproved pension arrangement,

the trustee of the bankrupt's estate may apply to the court for an order under this section.

(2) If the court is satisfied—

(a) that the rights under the arrangement are to any extent, and whether directly or indirectly, the fruits of relevant contributions, and

(b) that the making of any of the relevant contributions ('the excessive contributions') has unfairly prejudiced the individual's creditors,

the court may make such order as it thinks fit for restoring the position to what it would have been had the excessive contributions not been made.

(3) Subsection (4) applies where the court is satisfied that the value of the rights under the arrangement is, as a result of rights of the individual under the

arrangement or any other pension arrangement having at any time become subject to a debit under section 29(1)(a) of the Welfare Reform and Pensions Act 1999 (debits giving effect to pension-sharing), less than it would otherwise have been.

(4) Where this subsection applies—

(a) any relevant contributions which were represented by the rights which became subject to the debit shall, for the purposes of subsection (2), be taken to be contributions of which the rights under the arrangement are the fruits, and

(b) where the relevant contributions represented by the rights under the arrangement (including those so represented by virtue of paragraph (a)) are not all excessive contributions, relevant contributions which are represented by the rights under the arrangement otherwise than by virtue of paragraph (a) shall be treated as excessive contributions before any which are so represented by virtue of that paragraph.

(5) In subsections (2) to (4) 'relevant contributions' means contributions to the arrangement or any other pension arrangement—

(a) which the individual has at any time made on his own behalf, or

(b) which have at any time been made on his behalf.

(6) The court shall, in determining whether it is satisfied under subsection (2)(b), consider in particular—

(a) whether any of the contributions were made for the purpose of putting assets beyond the reach of the individual's creditors or any of them, and

(b) whether the total amount of any contributions—

(i) made by or on behalf of the individual to pension arrangements, and

(ii) represented (whether directly or indirectly) by rights under approved pension arrangements or excluded rights under unapproved pension arrangements,

is an amount which is excessive in view of the individual's circumstances when those contributions were made.

(7) For the purposes of this section and sections 342B and 342C ('the recovery provisions'), rights of an individual under an unapproved pension arrangement are excluded rights if they are rights which are excluded from his estate by virtue of regulations under section 12 of the Welfare Reform and Pensions Act 1999.

(8) In the recovery provisions—

'approved pension arrangement' has the same meaning as in section 11 of the Welfare Reform and Pensions Act 1999;

'unapproved pension arrangement' has the same meaning as in section 12 of that Act.

342B Orders under section 342A—(1) Without prejudice to the generality of section 342A(2), an order under section 342A may include provision—

(a) requiring the person responsible for the arrangement to pay an amount to the individual's trustee in bankruptcy,

(b) adjusting the liabilities of the arrangement in respect of the individual,

(c) adjusting any liabilities of the arrangement in respect of any other person that derive, directly or indirectly, from rights of the individual under the arrangement,

(d) for the recovery by the person responsible for the arrangement (whether by deduction from any amount which that person is ordered to pay or otherwise) of costs incurred by that person in complying in the bankrupt's case with any requirement under section 342C(1) or in giving effect to the order.

(2) In subsection (1), references to adjusting the liabilities of the arrangement in respect of a person include (in particular) reducing the amount of any benefit or future benefit to which that person is entitled under the arrangement.

(3) In subsection (1)(c), the reference to liabilities of the arrangement does not include liabilities in respect of a person which result from giving effect to an order or provision falling within section 28(1) of the Welfare Reform and Pensions Act 1999 (pension sharing orders and agreements).

(4) The maximum amount which the person responsible for an arrangement may be required to pay by an order under section 342A is the lesser of—

(a) the amount of the excessive contributions, and

(b) the value of the individual's rights under the arrangement (if the arrangement is an approved pension arrangement) or of his excluded rights under the arrangement (if the arrangement is an unapproved pension arrangement).

(5) An order under section 342A which requires the person responsible for an arrangement to pay an amount ('the restoration amount') to the individual's trustee in bankruptcy must provide for the liabilities of the arrangement to be correspondingly reduced.

(6) For the purposes of subsection (5), liabilities are correspondingly reduced if the difference between—

(a) the amount of the liabilities immediately before the reduction, and

(b) the amount of the liabilities immediately after the reduction,

is equal to the restoration amount.

(7) An order under section 342A in respect of an arrangement—

(a) shall be binding on the person responsible for the arrangement, and

(b) overrides provisions of the arrangement to the extent that they conflict with the provisions of the order.

342C Orders under section 342A: supplementary

(1) The person responsible for—

(a) an approved pension arrangement under which a bankrupt has rights,

(b) an unapproved pension arrangement under which a bankrupt has excluded rights, or

(c) a pension arrangement under which a bankrupt has at any time had rights,

shall, on the bankrupt's trustee in bankruptcy making a written request, provide the trustee with such information about the arrangement and rights as the trustee may reasonably require for, or in connection with, the making of applications under section 342A.

(2) Nothing in—

(a) any provision of section 159 of the Pension Schemes Act 1993 or section 91 of the Pensions Act 1995 (which prevent assignment and the making of orders that restrain a person from receiving anything which he is prevented from assigning),

(b) any provision of any enactment (whether passed or made before or after the passing of the Welfare Reform and Pensions Act 1999) corresponding to any of the provisions mentioned in paragraph (a), or

(c) any provision of the arrangement in question corresponding to any of those provisions,

applies to a court exercising its powers under section 342A.

(3) Where any sum is required by an order under section 342A to be paid to the trustee in bankruptcy, that sum shall be comprised in the bankrupt's estate.

(4) Regulations may, for the purposes of the recovery provisions, make provision about the calculation and verification of—

(a) any such value as is mentioned in section 342B(4)(b);

(b) any such amounts as are mentioned in section 342B(6)(a) and (b).

(5) The power conferred by subsection (4) includes power to provide for calculation or verification—

(a) in such manner as may, in the particular case, be approved by a prescribed person; or

(b) in accordance with guidance—

(i) from time to time prepared by a prescribed person, and

(ii) approved by the Secretary of State.

(6) References in the recovery provisions to the person responsible for a pension arrangement are to—

(a) the trustees, managers or provider of the arrangement, or

(b) the person having functions in relation to the arrangement corresponding to those of a trustee, manager or provider.

(7) In this section and sections 342A and 342B—

'prescribed' means prescribed by regulations;

'the recovery provisions' means this section and sections 342A and 342B;

'regulations' means regulations made by the Secretary of State.

(8) Regulations under the recovery provisions may—

(a) make different provision for different cases;

(b) contain such incidental, supplemental and transitional provisions as appear to the Secretary of State necessary or expedient.

(9) Regulations under the recovery provisions shall be made by statutory instrument subject to annulment in pursuance of a resolution of either House of Parliament.'

Note. Specified date (for the purpose only of the exercise of any power to make regulations): 11 November 1999: see s 89(5)(a); 6 April 2002 (for remaining purposes) (SI 2002 No 153, art 2(e)).

16 Excessive pension contributions made by persons who have become bankrupt: Scotland For sections 36A to 36C of the Bankruptcy (Scotland) Act 1985 there shall be substituted—

'36A Recovery of excessive pension contributions—(1) Where a debtor's estate has been sequestrated and he—

(a) has rights under an approved pension arrangement, or

(b) has excluded rights under an unapproved pension arrangement,

the permanent trustee may apply to the court for an order under this section.

(2) If the court is satisfied—

(a) that the rights under the arrangement are to any extent, and whether directly or indirectly, the fruits of relevant contributions, and

(b) that the making of any of the relevant contributions ('the excessive contributions') has unfairly prejudiced the debtor's creditors,

the court may make such order as it thinks fit for restoring the position to what it would have been had the excessive contributions not been made.

(3) Subsection (4) applies where the court is satisfied that the value of the rights under the arrangement is, as a result of rights of the debtor under the arrangement or any other pension arrangement having at any time become subject to a debit under section 29(1)(a) of the Welfare Reform and Pensions Act 1999 (debits giving effect to pension-sharing), less than it would otherwise have been.

(4) Where this subsection applies—

(a) any relevant contributions which were represented by the rights which became subject to the debit shall, for the purposes of subsection (2), be taken to be contributions of which the rights under the arrangement are the fruits, and

    (b) where the relevant contributions represented by the rights under the arrangement (including those so represented by virtue of paragraph (a)) are not all excessive contributions, relevant contributions which are represented by the rights under the arrangement otherwise than by virtue of paragraph (a) shall be treated as excessive contributions before any which are so represented by virtue of that paragraph.

(5) In subsections (2) to (4) 'relevant contributions' means contributions to the arrangement or any other pension arrangement—

    (a) which the debtor has at any time made on his own behalf, or

    (b) which have at any time been made on his behalf.

(6) The court shall, in determining whether it is satisfied under subsection (2)(b), consider in particular—

    (a) whether any of the contributions were made for the purpose of putting assets beyond the reach of the debtor's creditors or any of them, and

    (b) whether the total amount of any contributions—

        (i)   made by or on behalf of the debtor to pension arrangements, and

        (ii) represented (whether directly or indirectly) by rights under approved pension arrangements or excluded rights under unapproved pensions arrangements,

    is an amount which is excessive in view of the debtor's circumstances when those contributions were made.

(7) For the purposes of this section and sections 36B and 36C ('the recovery provisions'), rights of a debtor under an unapproved pension arrangement are excluded rights if they are rights which are excluded from his estate by virtue of regulations under section 12 of the Welfare Reform and Pensions Act 1999.

(8) In the recovery provisions—

'approved pension arrangement' has the same meaning as in section 11 of the Welfare Reform and Pensions Act 1999;

'unapproved pension arrangement' has the same meaning as in section 12 of that Act.

36B Orders under section 36A—(1) Without prejudice to the generality of section 36A(2) an order under section 36A may include provision—

    (a) requiring the person responsible for the arrangement to pay an amount to the permanent trustee,

    (b) adjusting the liabilities of the arrangement in respect of the debtor,

    (c) adjusting any liabilities of the arrangement in respect of any other person that derive, directly or indirectly, from rights of the debtor under the arrangement,

    (d) for the recovery by the person responsible for the arrangement (whether by deduction from any amount which that person is ordered to pay or otherwise) of costs incurred by that person in complying in the debtor's case with any requirement under section 36C(1) or in giving effect to the order.

(2) In subsection (1), references to adjusting the liabilities of the arrangement in respect of a person include (in particular) reducing the amount of any benefit or future benefit to which that person is entitled under the arrangement.

(3) In subsection (1)(c), the reference to liabilities of the arrangement does not include liabilities in respect of a person which result from giving effect to an order or provision falling within section 28(1) of the Welfare Reform and Pensions Act 1999 (pension sharing orders and agreements).

(4) The maximum amount which the person responsible for an arrangement may be required to pay by an order under section 36A is the lesser of—

(a) the amount of the excessive contributions, and

(b) the value of the debtor's rights under the arrangement (if the arrangement is an approved pension arrangement) or of his excluded rights under the arrangement (if the arrangement is an unapproved pension arrangement).

(5) An order under section 36A which requires the person responsible for an arrangement to pay an amount ('the restoration amount') to the permanent trustee must provide for the liabilities of the arrangement to be correspondingly reduced.

(6) For the purposes of subsection (5), liabilities are correspondingly reduced if the difference between—

(a) the amount of the liabilities immediately before the reduction, and

(b) the amount of the liabilities immediately after the reduction,

is equal to the restoration amount.

(7)   An order under section 36A in respect of an arrangement—

(a) shall be binding on the person responsible for the arrangement; and

(b) overrides provisions of the arrangement to the extent that they conflict with the provisions of the order.

36C Orders under section 36A: supplementary—(1) The person responsible for—

(a) an approved pension arrangement under which a debtor has rights,

(b) an unapproved pension arrangement under which a debtor has excluded rights, or

(c) a pension arrangement under which a debtor has at any time had rights,

shall, on the permanent trustee making a written request, provide the permanent trustee with such information about the arrangement and rights as the permanent trustee may reasonably require for, or in connection with, the making of applications under section 36A.

(2) Nothing in—

(a) any provision of section 159 of the Pensions Schemes Act 1993 or section 91 of the Pensions Act 1995 (which prevent assignation and the making of orders that restrain a person from receiving anything which he is prevented from assigning),

(b) any provision of any enactment (whether passed or made before or after the passing of the Welfare Reform and Pensions Act 1999) corresponding to any of the provisions mentioned in paragraph (a), or

(c) any provision of the arrangement in question corresponding to any of those provisions,

applies to a court exercising its powers under section 36A.

(3) Where any sum is required by an order under section 36A to be paid to the permanent trustee, that sum shall be comprised in the debtor's estate.

(4) Regulations may, for the purposes of the recovery provisions, make provision about the calculation and verification of—

(a) any such value as is mentioned in section 36B(4)(b);

(b) any such amounts as are mentioned in section 36B(6)(a) and (b).

(5) The power conferred by subsection (4) includes power to provide for calculation or verification—

(a) in such manner as may, in the particular case, be approved by a prescribed person; or

(b) in accordance with guidance—

(i)   from time to time prepared by a prescribed person, and

(ii) approved by the Secretary of State.

(6) References in the recovery provisions to the person responsible for a pension arrangement are to—

(a) the trustees, managers or provider of the arrangement, or

(b) the person having functions in relation to the arrangement corresponding to those of a trustee, manager or provider.

(7) In this section and sections 36A and 36B—

'the recovery' provisions means this section and sections 36A and 36B;

'regulations' means regulations made by the Secretary of State.

(8) Regulations under the recovery provisions may contain such incidental, supplemental and transitional provisions as appear to the Secretary of State necessary or expedient.'

Note. Specified date (for the purpose only of the exercise of any power to make regulations): 11 November 1999: see s 89(5)(a); 6 April 2002 (for remaining purposes) (SI 2002 No 153, art 2(f)).

*   *   *   *   *

PART III

PENSIONS ON DIVORCE ETC

Pension sharing orders

19 Orders in England and Wales Schedule 3 (which amends the Matrimonial Causes Act 1973 for the purpose of enabling the court to make pension sharing orders in connection with proceedings in England and Wales for divorce or nullity of marriage, and for supplementary purposes) shall have effect.

Note. 1 December 2000: see SI 2000 No 1116, art 2(a).

20 Orders in Scotland—(1) The Family Law (Scotland) Act 1985 shall be amended as follows.

(2) In section 8(1) (orders for financial provision), after paragraph (b) there shall be inserted—

'(baa) a pension sharing order.'

(3) In section 27 (interpretation), in subsection (1), there shall be inserted at the appropriate place—

'pension sharing order' is an order which—

(a) provides that one party's—

(i)   shareable rights under a specified pension arrangement, or

(ii) shareable state scheme rights,

be subject to pension sharing for the benefit of the other party, and

(b) specifies the percentage value, or the amount, to be transferred;'.

(4) In that section, after subsection (1) there shall be inserted—

'(1A) In subsection (1), in the definition of 'pension sharing order'—

(a) the reference to shareable rights under a pension arrangement is to rights in relation to which pension sharing is available under Chapter I of Part IV of the Welfare Reform and Pensions Act 1999, or under corresponding Northern Ireland legislation, and

(b) the reference to shareable state scheme rights is to rights in relation to which pension sharing is available under Chapter II of Part IV of the Welfare Reform and Pensions Act 1999, or under corresponding Northern Ireland legislation.'

Note. Specified date (for the purpose only of the exercise of any power to make regulations): 11 November 1999: see s 89(5)(a); Appointment (for remaining purposes): 1 December 2000: see SI 2000 No 1047, art 2(2)(d), Schedule, Pt IV.

Sections 25B to 25D of the Matrimonial Causes Act 1973

21 Amendments Schedule 4 (which amends the sections about pensions inserted in the Matrimonial Causes Act 1973 by section 166 of the Pensions Act 1995) shall have effect.

Note. Appointment: 1 December 2000: see SI 2000 No 1116, art 2(a).

22 Extension to overseas divorces etc—(1) Part III of the Matrimonial and Family Proceedings Act 1984 (financial relief in England and Wales after overseas divorce etc) shall be amended as follows.

(2) In section 18 (matters to which the court is to have regard in exercising its powers to make orders for financial relief), after subsection (3) there shall be inserted—

'(3A) The matters to which the court is to have regard under subsection (3) above—

(a) so far as relating to paragraph (a) of section 25(2) of the 1973 Act, include any benefits under a pension arrangement which a party to the marriage has or is likely to have (whether or not in the foreseeable future), and

(b) so far as relating to paragraph (h) of that provision, include any benefits under a pension arrangement which, by reason of the dissolution or annulment of the marriage, a party to the marriage will lose the chance of acquiring.'

(3) In that section, at the end there shall be added—

'(7) In this section—

(a) 'pension arrangement' has the meaning given by section 25D(3) of the 1973 Act, and

(b) references to benefits under a pension arrangement include any benefits by way of pension, whether under a pension arrangement or not.'

(4) In section 21 (application of provisions of Part II of the Matrimonial Causes Act 1973), the existing provision shall become subsection (1) and, in that subsection, after paragraph (b) there shall be inserted—

'(bd) section 25B(3) to (7B) (power, by financial provision order, to attach payments under a pension arrangement, or to require the exercise of a right of commutation under such an arrangement);

(be) section 25C (extension of lump sum powers in relation to death benefits under a pension arrangement);'.

(5) In that section, after subsection (1) there shall be inserted—

'(2) Subsection (1)(bd) and (be) above shall not apply where the court has jurisdiction to entertain an application for an order for financial relief by reason only of the situation in England or Wales of a dwelling-house which was a matrimonial home of the parties.

(3) Section 25D(1) of the 1973 Act (effect of transfers on orders relating to rights under a pension arrangement) shall apply in relation to an order made under section 17 above by virtue of subsection (1)(bd) or (be) above as it applies in relation to an order made under section 23 of that Act by virtue of section 25B or 25C of the 1973 Act.

(4) The Lord Chancellor may by regulations make for the purposes of this Part of this Act provision corresponding to any provision which may be made by him under subsections (2) to (2B) of section 25D of the 1973 Act.

(5) Power to make regulations under this section shall be exercisable by statutory instrument which shall be subject to annulment in pursuance of a resolution of either House of Parliament.'

Note. 1 December 2000: see SI 2000 No 1116, art 2(a).

Miscellaneous

23 Supply of pension information in connection with divorce etc—(1) The
Secretary of State may by regulations—
  (a) make provision imposing on the person responsible for a pension
      arrangement, or on the Secretary of State, requirements with respect to the
      supply of information relevant to any power with respect to—
        (i) financial relief under Part II of the Matrimonial Causes Act 1973 or
            Part III of the Matrimonial and Family Proceedings Act 1984
            (England and Wales powers in relation to domestic and overseas
            divorce etc),
        (ii) financial provision under the Family Law (Scotland) Act 1985 or
            Part IV of the Matrimonial and Family Proceedings Act 1984
            (corresponding Scottish powers), or
        (iii) financial relief under Part III of the Matrimonial Causes (Northern
            Ireland) Order 1978 or Part IV of the Matrimonial and Family
            Proceedings (Northern Ireland) Order 1989 (corresponding
            Northern Ireland powers);
  (b) make provision about calculation and verification in relation to the
      valuation of—
        (i) benefits under a pension arrangement, or
        (ii) shareable state scheme rights,
    for the purposes of regulations under paragraph (a)(i) or (iii);
  (c) make provision about calculation and verification in relation to—
        (i) the valuation of shareable rights under a pension arrangement or
            shareable state scheme rights for the purposes of regulations under
            paragraph (a)(ii), so far as relating to the making of orders for
            financial provision (within the meaning of the Family Law
            (Scotland) Act 1985), or
        (ii) the valuation of benefits under a pension arrangement for the
            purposes of such regulations, so far as relating to the making of
            orders under section 12A of that Act;
  (d) make provision for the purpose of enabling the person responsible for a
      pension arrangement to recover prescribed charges in respect of providing
      information in accordance with regulations under paragraph (a).
  (2) Regulations under subsection (1)(b) or (c) may include provision for
calculation or verification in accordance with guidance from time to time prepared
by a person prescribed by the regulations.
  (3) Regulations under subsection (1)(d) may include provision for the
application in prescribed circumstances, with or without modification, of any
provision made by virtue of section 41(2).
  (4) In subsection (1)—
  (a) the reference in paragraph (c)(i) to shareable rights under a pension
      arrangement is to rights in relation to which pension sharing is available
      under Chapter I of Part IV, or under corresponding Northern Ireland
      legislation, and
  (b) the references to shareable state scheme rights are to rights in relation to
      which pension sharing is available under Chapter II of Part IV, or under
      corresponding Northern Ireland legislation.
Note. Specified date (for the purpose only of the exercise of any power to make
regulations): 11 November 1999: see s 89(5)(a); (for remaining purposes): 1 December 2000:
see SI 2000 No 1047, art 2(2)(d), Schedule, Pt IV.

24 Charges by pension arrangements in relation to earmarking orders The
Secretary of State may by regulations make provision for the purpose of enabling

the person responsible for a pension arrangement to recover prescribed charges in respect of complying with—

    (a) an order under section 23 [section 22A or 23] of the Matrimonial Causes Act 1973 (financial provision orders in connection with divorce etc), so far as it includes provision made by virtue of section 25B or 25C of that Act (powers to include provision about pensions),

    (b) an order under section 12A(2) or (3) of the Family Law (Scotland) Act 1985 (powers in relation to pensions lump sums when making a capital sum order), or

    (c) an order under Article 25 of the Matrimonial Causes (Northern Ireland) Order 1978, so far as it includes provision made by virtue of Article 27B or 27C of that Order (Northern Ireland powers corresponding to those mentioned in paragraph (a)).

Note. Specified date (for the purpose only of the exercise of any power to make regulations): 11 November 1999: see s 89(5)(a); (for remaining purposes): 1 December 2000: see SI 2000 No 1047, art 2(2)(d), Schedule, Pt IV.

In para (a) words 'section 23' repealed with savings and subsequent words in square brackets substituted with savings by the Family Law Act 1996, s 66(1), Sch 8, Pt I, para 43A; for savings see the Family Law Act 1996, s 66(2), Sch 9, para 5.

Supplementary

25 Power to make consequential amendments of Part III—(1) If any amendment by the Family Law Act 1996 of Part II or IV of the Matrimonial Causes Act 1973 comes into force before the day on which any provision of this Part comes into force, the Lord Chancellor may by order make such consequential amendment of that provision as he thinks fit.

    (2) No order under this section may be made unless a draft of the order has been laid before and approved by resolution of each House of Parliament.

Note. Specified date (for the purpose only of the exercise of any power to make regulations): 11 November 1999: see s 89(5)(a); for remaining purposes: see s 89(1).

26 Interpretation of Part III—(1) In this Part—

    'occupational pension scheme' has the same meaning as in the Pension Schemes Act 1993;

    'pension arrangement' means

    (a) an occupational pension scheme,

    (b) a personal pension scheme,

    (c) a retirement annuity contract,

    (d) an annuity or insurance policy purchased, or transferred, for the purpose of giving effect to rights under an occupational pension scheme or a personal pension scheme, and

    (e) an annuity purchased, or entered into, for the purpose of discharging liability in respect of a pension credit under section 29(1)(b) or under corresponding Northern Ireland legislation;

    'personal pension scheme' has the same meaning as in the Pension Schemes Act 1993;

    'prescribed' means prescribed by regulations made by the Secretary of State;

    'retirement annuity contract' means a contract or scheme approved under Chapter III of Part XIV of the Income and Corporation Taxes Act 1988;

    'trustees or managers', in relation to an occupational pension scheme or a personal pension scheme, means—

    (a) in the case of a scheme established under a trust, the trustees of the scheme, and

    (b) in any other case, the managers of the scheme.

    (2) References to the person responsible for a pension arrangement are—

(a) in the case of an occupational pension scheme or a personal pension scheme, to the trustees or managers of the scheme,
(b) in the case of a retirement annuity contract or an annuity falling within paragraph (d) or (e) of the definition of 'pension arrangement' above, the provider of the annuity, and
(c) in the case of an insurance policy falling within paragraph (d) of the definition of that expression, the insurer.

Note. 1 December 2000 (SI 2000 No 1047).

PART IV
PENSION SHARING

CHAPTER I
SHARING OF RIGHTS UNDER PENSION ARRANGEMENTS

Pension sharing mechanism

27 Scope of mechanism—(1) Pension sharing is available under this Chapter in relation to a person's shareable rights under any pension arrangement other than an excepted public service pension scheme.

(2) For the purposes of this Chapter, a person's shareable rights under a pension arrangement are any rights of his under the arrangement, other than rights of a description specified by regulations made by the Secretary of State.

(3) For the purposes of subsection (1), a public service pension scheme is excepted if it is specified by order made by such Minister of the Crown or government department as may be designated by the Treasury as having responsibility for the scheme.

Note. Specified date (for the purpose only of the exercise of any power to make regulations): 11 November 1999: see s 89(5)(a); (for remaining purposes): 1 December 2000: see SI 2000 No 1047, art 2(2)(d), Schedule, Pt IV.

28 Activation of pension sharing—(1) Section 29 applies on the taking effect of any of the following relating to a person's shareable rights under a pension arrangement—
(a) a pension sharing order under the Matrimonial Causes Act 1973,
(b) provision which corresponds to the provision which may be made by such an order and which—
(i) is contained in a qualifying agreement between the parties to a marriage, and
(ii) takes effect on the dissolution of the marriage under the Family Law Act 1996,
(c) provision which corresponds to the provision which may be made by such an order and which—
(i) is contained in a qualifying agreement between the parties to a marriage or former marriage, and
(ii) takes effect after the dissolution of the marriage under the Family Law Act 1996,
(d) an order under Part III of the Matrimonial and Family Proceedings Act 1984 (financial relief in England and Wales in relation to overseas divorce etc) corresponding to such an order as is mentioned in paragraph (a),
(e) a pension sharing order under the Family Law (Scotland) Act 1985,
(f) provision which corresponds to the provision which may be made by such an order and which—
(i) is contained in a qualifying agreement between the parties to a marriage,

(ii)   is in such form as the Secretary of State may prescribe by regulations, and

(iii)   takes effect on the grant, in relation to the marriage, of decree of divorce under the Divorce (Scotland) Act 1976 or of declarator of nullity,

(g)   an order under Part IV of the Matrimonial and Family Proceedings Act 1984 (financial relief in Scotland in relation to overseas divorce etc) corresponding to such an order as is mentioned in paragraph (e),

(h)   a pension sharing order under Northern Ireland legislation, and

(i)   an order under Part IV of the Matrimonial and Family Proceedings (Northern Ireland) Order 1989 (financial relief in Northern Ireland in relation to overseas divorce etc) corresponding to such an order as is mentioned in paragraph (h).

(2) For the purposes of subsection (1)(b) and (c), a qualifying agreement is one which—

(a)   has been entered into in such circumstances as the Lord Chancellor may prescribe by regulations, and

(b)   satisfies such requirements as the Lord Chancellor may so prescribe.

(3) For the purposes of subsection (1)(f), a qualifying agreement is one which—

(a)   has been entered into in such circumstances as the Secretary of State may prescribe by regulations, and

(b)   is registered in the Books of Council and Session.

(4) Subsection (1)(b) does not apply if—

(a)   the pension arrangement to which the provision relates is the subject of a pension sharing order under the Matrimonial Causes Act 1973 in relation to the marriage, or

(b)   there is in force a requirement imposed by virtue of section 25B or 25C of that Act (powers to include in financial provision orders requirements relating to benefits under pension arrangements) which relates to benefits or future benefits to which the party who is the transferor is entitled under the pension arrangement to which the provision relates.

(5) Subsection (1)(c) does not apply if—

(a)   the marriage was dissolved by an order under section 3 of the Family Law Act 1996 (divorce not preceded by separation) and the satisfaction of the requirements of section 9(2) of that Act (settlement of future financial arrangements) was a precondition to the making of the order,

(b)   the pension arrangement to which the provision relates—

(i)   is the subject of a pension sharing order under the Matrimonial Causes Act 1973 in relation to the marriage, or

(ii)   has already been the subject of pension sharing between the parties, or

(c)   there is in force a requirement imposed by virtue of section 25B or 25C of that Act which relates to benefits or future benefits to which the party who is the transferor is entitled under the pension arrangement to which the provision relates.

(6) Subsection (1)(f) does not apply if there is in force an order under section 12A(2) or (3) of the Family Law (Scotland) Act 1985 which relates to benefits or future benefits to which the party who is the transferor is entitled under the pension arrangement to which the provision relates.

(7) For the purposes of this section, an order or provision falling within subsection (1)(e), (f) or (g) shall be deemed never to have taken effect if the person responsible for the arrangement to which the order or provision relates does not receive before the end of the period of 2 months beginning with the relevant date—

(a) copies of the relevant matrimonial documents, and

(b) such information relating to the transferor and transferee as the Secretary of State may prescribe by regulations under section 34(1)(b)(ii).

(8) The relevant date for the purposes of subsection (7) is—

(a) in the case of an order or provision falling within subsection (1)(e) or (f), the date of the extract of the decree or declarator responsible for the divorce or annulment to which the order or provision relates, and

(b) in the case of an order falling within subsection (1)(g), the date of disposal of the application under section 28 of the Matrimonial and Family Proceedings Act 1984.

(9) The reference in subsection (7)(a) to the relevant matrimonial documents is—

(a) in the case of an order falling within subsection (1)(e) or (g), to copies of the order and the order, decree or declarator responsible for the divorce or annulment to which it relates, and

(b) in the case of provision falling within subsection (1)(f), to—

    (i) copies of the provision and the order, decree or declarator responsible for the divorce or annulment to which it relates, and

    (ii) documentary evidence that the agreement containing the provision is one to which subsection (3)(a) applies.

(10) The sheriff may, on the application of any person having an interest, make an order—

(a) extending the period of 2 months referred to in subsection (7), and

(b) if that period has already expired, providing that, if the person responsible for the arrangement receives the documents and information concerned before the end of the period specified in the order, subsection (7) is to be treated as never having applied.

(11) In subsections (4)(b), (5)(c) and (6), the reference to the party who is the transferor is to the party to whose rights the provision relates.

Note. Specified date (for the purpose only of the exercise of any power to make regulations): 11 November 1999: see s 89(5)(a); for remaining purposes: 1 December 2000: see SI 2000 No 1047, art 2(2)(d), Schedule, Pt IV.

Where an action of divorce or an action for declarator of nullity has been brought before 1 December 2000, sub-s (1)(f) above shall not apply in relation to that divorce or declarator: see the Welfare Reform and Pensions Act 1999, s 85(5)(b).

29 Creation of pension debits and credits—(1) On the application of this section—

(a) the transferor's shareable rights under the relevant arrangement become subject to a debit of the appropriate amount, and

(b) the transferee becomes entitled to a credit of that amount as against the person responsible for that arrangement.

(2) Where the relevant order or provision specifies a percentage value to be transferred, the appropriate amount for the purposes of subsection (1) is the specified percentage of the cash equivalent of the relevant benefits on the valuation day.

(3) Where the relevant order or provision specifies an amount to be transferred, the appropriate amount for the purposes of subsection (1) is the lesser of—

(a) the specified amount, and

(b) the cash equivalent of the relevant benefits on the valuation day.

(4) Where the relevant arrangement is an occupational pension scheme and the transferor is in pensionable service under the scheme on the transfer day, the relevant benefits for the purposes of subsections (2) and (3) are the benefits or future benefits to which he would be entitled under the scheme by virtue of his shareable rights under it had his pensionable service terminated immediately before that day.

(5) Otherwise, the relevant benefits for the purposes of subsections (2) and (3) are the benefits or future benefits to which, immediately before the transfer day, the transferor is entitled under the terms of the relevant arrangement by virtue of his shareable rights under it.

(6) The Secretary of State may by regulations provide for any description of benefit to be disregarded for the purposes of subsection (4) or (5).

(7) For the purposes of this section, the valuation day is such day within the implementation period for the credit under subsection (1)(b) as the person responsible for the relevant arrangement may specify by notice in writing to the transferor and transferee.

(8) In this section—

'relevant arrangement' means the arrangement to which the relevant order or provision relates;

'relevant order or provision' means the order or provision by virtue of which this section applies;

'transfer day' means the day on which the relevant order or provision takes effect;

'transferor' means the person to whose rights the relevant order or provision relates;

'transferee' means the person for whose benefit the relevant order or provision is made.

Note. Specified date (for the purpose only of the exercise of any power to make regulations): 11 November 1999: see s 89(5)(a); (for remaining purposes): 1 December 2000: see SI 2000 No1047, art 2(2)(d), Schedule, Pt IV.

30 Cash equivalents—(1) The Secretary of State may by regulations make provision about the calculation and verification of cash equivalents for the purposes of section 29.

(2) The power conferred by subsection (1) includes power to provide for calculation or verification—

(a) in such manner as may, in the particular case, be approved by a person prescribed by the regulations, or

(b) in accordance with guidance from time to time prepared by a person so prescribed.

Note. Specified date (for the purpose only of the exercise of any power to make regulations): 11 November 1999: see s 89(5)(a); Appointment (for remaining purposes): 1 December 2000: see SI 2000 No 1047, art 2(2)(d), Schedule, Pt IV.

Pension debits

31 Reduction of benefit—(1) Subject to subsection (2), where a person's shareable rights under a pension arrangement are subject to a pension debit, each benefit or future benefit—

(a) to which he is entitled under the arrangement by virtue of those rights, and

(b) which is a qualifying benefit,

is reduced by the appropriate percentage.

(2) Where a pension debit relates to the shareable rights under an occupational pension scheme of a person who is in pensionable service under the scheme on the transfer day, each benefit or future benefit—

(a) to which the person is entitled under the scheme by virtue of those rights, and

(b) which corresponds to a qualifying benefit,

is reduced by an amount equal to the appropriate percentage of the corresponding qualifying benefit.

(3) A benefit is a qualifying benefit for the purposes of subsections (1) and (2)

if the cash equivalent by reference to which the amount of the pension debit is determined includes an amount in respect of it.

(4) The provisions of this section override any provision of a pension arrangement to which they apply to the extent that the provision conflicts with them.

(5) In this section—

'appropriate percentage', in relation to a pension debit, means—
  (a) if the relevant order or provision specifies the percentage value to be transferred, that percentage;
  (b) if the relevant order or provision specifies an amount to be transferred, the percentage which the appropriate amount for the purposes of subsection (1) of section 29 represents of the amount mentioned in subsection (3)(b) of that section;
'relevant order or provision', in relation to a pension debit, means the pension sharing order or provision on which the debit depends;
'transfer day', in relation to a pension debit, means the day on which the relevant order or provision takes effect.

Note. 1 December 2000 (SI 2000 No 1047).

32 Effect on contracted-out rights—(1) The Pension Schemes Act 1993 shall be amended as follows.

(2) In section 10 (protected rights), in subsection (1), for 'subsections (2) and (3)' there shall be substituted 'the following provisions of this section', and at the end there shall be added—

'(4) Where, in the case of a scheme which makes such provision as is mentioned in subsection (2) or (3), a member's rights under the scheme become subject to a pension debit, his protected rights shall exclude the appropriate percentage of the rights which were his protected rights immediately before the day on which the pension debit arose.

(5) For the purposes of subsection (4), the appropriate percentage is—
  (a) if the order or provision on which the pension debit depends specifies the percentage value to be transferred, that percentage;
  (b) if the order or provision on which the pension debit depends specifies an amount to be transferred, the percentage which the appropriate amount for the purposes of subsection (1) of section 29 of the Welfare Reform and Pensions Act 1999 (lesser of specified amount and cash equivalent of transferor's benefits) represents of the amount mentioned in subsection (3)(b) of that section (cash equivalent of transferor's benefits).'

(3) After section 15 there shall be inserted—

'15A Reduction of guaranteed minimum in consequence of pension debit—(1) Where—
  (a) an earner has a guaranteed minimum in relation to the pension provided by a scheme, and
  (b) his right to the pension becomes subject to a pension debit,
his guaranteed minimum in relation to the scheme is, subject to subsection (2), reduced by the appropriate percentage.

(2) Where the earner is in pensionable service under the scheme on the day on which the order or provision on which the pension debit depends takes effect, his guaranteed minimum in relation to the scheme is reduced by an amount equal to the appropriate percentage of the corresponding qualifying benefit.

(3) For the purposes of subsection (2), the corresponding qualifying benefit is the guaranteed minimum taken for the purpose of calculating the cash equivalent by reference to which the amount of the pension debit is determined.

(4) For the purposes of this section the appropriate percentage is—

(a) if the order or provision on which the pension debit depends specifies the percentage value to be transferred, that percentage;

(b) if the order or provision on which the pension debit depends specifies an amount to be transferred, the percentage which the appropriate amount for the purposes of subsection (1) of section 29 of the Welfare Reform and Pensions Act 1999 (lesser of specified amount and cash equivalent of transferor's benefits) represents of the amount mentioned in subsection (3)(b) of that section (cash equivalent of transferor's benefits).'

(4) In section 47 (entitlement to guaranteed minimum pensions for the purposes of the relationship with social security benefits), at the end there shall be added—

'(6) For the purposes of section 46, a person shall be treated as entitled to any guaranteed minimum pension to which he would have been entitled but for any reduction under section 15A.'

(5) In section 181(1), there shall be inserted at the appropriate place—

'"pension debit" means a debit under section 29(1)(a) of the Welfare Reform and Pensions Act 1999;'.

Note. 1 December 2000 (SI 2000 No 1047).

Pension credits

33 Time for discharge of liability—(1) A person subject to liability in respect of a pension credit shall discharge his liability before the end of the implementation period for the credit.

(2) Where the trustees or managers of an occupational pension scheme have not done what is required to discharge their liability in respect of a pension credit before the end of the implementation period for the credit—

(a) they shall, except in such cases as the Secretary of State may prescribe by regulations, notify the Regulatory Authority of that fact within such period as the Secretary of State may so prescribe, and

(b) section 10 of the Pensions Act 1995 (power of the Regulatory Authority to impose civil penalties) shall apply to any trustee or manager who has failed to take all such steps as are reasonable to ensure that liability in respect of the credit was discharged before the end of the implementation period for it.

(3) If trustees or managers to whom subsection (2)(a) applies fail to perform the obligation imposed by that provision, section 10 of the Pensions Act 1995 shall apply to any trustee or manager who has failed to take all reasonable steps to ensure that the obligation was performed.

(4) On the application of the trustees or managers of an occupational pension scheme who are subject to liability in respect of a pension credit, the Regulatory Authority may extend the implementation period for the credit for the purposes of this section if it is satisfied that the application is made in such circumstances as the Secretary of State may prescribe by regulations.

(5) In this section 'the Regulatory Authority' means the Occupational Pensions Regulatory Authority.

Note. Specified date (for the purpose only of the exercise of any power to make regulations): 11 November 1999: see s 89(5)(a); (for remaining purposes): 1 December 2000: see SI 2000 No 1047, art 2(2)(d), Schedule, Pt IV.

34 'Implementation period'—(1) For the purposes of this Chapter, the implementation period for a pension credit is the period of 4 months beginning with the later of—

    (a)   the day on which the relevant order or provision takes effect, and

    (b)   the first day on which the person responsible for the pension arrangement to which the relevant order or provision relates is in receipt of—

        (i)   the relevant matrimonial documents, and

        (ii) such information relating to the transferor and transferee as the Secretary of State may prescribe by regulations.

   (2) The reference in subsection (1)(b)(i) to the relevant matrimonial documents is to copies of—

    (a)   the relevant order or provision, and

    (b)   the order, decree or declarator responsible for the divorce or annulment to which it relates,

and, if the pension credit depends on provision falling within subsection (1)(f) of section 28, to documentary evidence that the agreement containing the provision is one to which subsection (3)(a) of that section applies.

   (3) Subsection (1) is subject to any provision made by regulations under section 41(2)(a).

   (4) The Secretary of State may by regulations—

    (a)   make provision requiring a person subject to liability in respect of a pension credit to notify the transferor and transferee of the day on which the implementation period for the credit begins;

    (b)   provide for this section to have effect with modifications where the pension arrangement to which the relevant order or provision relates is being wound up;

    (c)   provide for this section to have effect with modifications where the pension credit depends on a pension sharing order and the order is the subject of an application for leave to appeal out of time.

   (5) In this section—

'relevant order or provision', in relation to a pension credit, means the pension sharing order or provision on which the pension credit depends;

'transferor' means the person to whose rights the relevant order or provision relates;

'transferee' means the person for whose benefit the relevant order or provision is made.

Note. Specified date (for the purpose only of the exercise of any power to make regulations): 11 November 1999: see s 89(5)(a); to be appointed (for remaining purposes): see s 89(1).

35 Mode of discharge of liability—(1) Schedule 5 (which makes provision about how liability in respect of a pension credit may be discharged) shall have effect.

   (2) Where the person entitled to a pension credit dies before liability in respect of the credit has been discharged—

    (a)   Schedule 5 shall cease to have effect in relation to the discharge of liability in respect of the credit, and

    (b)   liability in respect of the credit shall be discharged in accordance with regulations made by the Secretary of State.

Note. Specified date (for the purpose only of the exercise of any power to make regulations): 11 November 1999: see s 89(5)(a); (for remaining purposes): 1 December 2000: see SI 2000 No 1047, art 2(2)(d), Schedule, Pt IV.

Treatment of pension credit rights under schemes

36 Safeguarded rights After section 68 of the Pension Schemes Act 1993 there shall be inserted—

'PART IIIA

SAFEGUARDED RIGHTS

68A Safeguarded rights

(1) Subject to subsection (2), the safeguarded rights of a member of an occupational pension scheme or a personal pension scheme are such of his rights to future benefits under the scheme as are attributable (directly or indirectly) to a pension credit in respect of which the reference rights are, or include, contracted-out rights or safeguarded rights.

(2) If the rules of an occupational pension scheme or a personal pension scheme so provide, a member's safeguarded rights are such of his rights falling within subsection (1) as—

    (a) in the case of rights directly attributable to a pension credit, represent the safeguarded percentage of the rights acquired by virtue of the credit, and

    (b) in the case of rights directly attributable to a transfer payment, represent the safeguarded percentage of the rights acquired by virtue of the payment.

(3) For the purposes of subsection (2)(a), the safeguarded percentage is the percentage of the rights by reference to which the amount of the credit is determined which are contracted-out rights or safeguarded rights.

(4)   For the purposes of subsection (2)(b), the safeguarded percentage is the percentage of the rights in respect of which the transfer payment is made which are contracted-out rights or safeguarded rights.

(5)   In this section—

'contracted-out rights' means such rights under, or derived from—

    (a) an occupational pension scheme contracted-out by virtue of section 9(2) or (3), or

    (b) an appropriate personal pension scheme,

as may be prescribed;

'reference rights', in relation to a pension credit, means the rights by reference to which the amount of the credit is determined.

68B Requirements relating to safeguarded rights Regulations may prescribe requirements to be met in relation to safeguarded rights by an occupational pension scheme or a personal pension scheme.

68C Reserve powers in relation to non-complying schemes—(1) This section applies to—

    (a) any occupational pension scheme, other than a public service pension scheme, and

    (b) any personal pension scheme.

(2) If any scheme to which this section applies does not comply with a requirement prescribed under section 68B and there are any persons who—

    (a) have safeguarded rights under the scheme, or

    (b) are entitled to any benefit giving effect to such rights under the scheme,

the Inland Revenue may direct the trustees or managers of the scheme to take or refrain from taking such steps as they may specify in writing for the purpose of safeguarding the rights of persons falling within paragraph (a) or (b).

(3) A direction under subsection (2) shall be final and binding on the trustees or managers to whom the direction is given and any person claiming under them.

(4) An appeal on a point of law shall lie to the High Court or, in Scotland, the Court of Session from a direction under subsection (2) at the instance of the trustees or managers, or any person claiming under them.

(5) A direction under subsection (2) shall be enforceable—

(a) in England and Wales, in a county court, as if it were an order of that court, and

(b) in Scotland, by the sheriff, as if it were an order of the sheriff and whether or not the sheriff could himself have given such an order.

68D Power to control transfer or discharge of liability Regulations may prohibit or restrict the transfer or discharge of any liability under an occupational pension scheme or a personal pension scheme in respect of safeguarded rights except in prescribed circumstances or on prescribed conditions.'

Note. Specified date (for the purpose only of the exercise of any power to make regulations): 11 November 1999: see s 89(5)(a); to be appointed (for remaining purposes): see s 89(1); for remaining purposes: 1 December 2000: see SI 2000 No 1047, art 2(2)(d), Schedule, Pt IV.

37 Requirements relating to pension credit benefit After section 101 of the Pension Schemes Act 1993 there shall be inserted—

'PART IVA
REQUIREMENTS RELATING TO PENSION CREDIT BENEFIT

CHAPTER I
PENSION CREDIT BENEFIT UNDER OCCUPATIONAL SCHEMES

101A Scope of Chapter I—(1) This Chapter applies to any occupational pension scheme whose resources are derived in whole or part from—

(a) payments to which subsection (2) applies made or to be made by one or more employers of earners to whom the scheme applies, or

(b) such other payments by the earner or his employer, or both, as may be prescribed for different categories of scheme.

(2) This subsection applies to payments—

(a) under an actual or contingent legal obligation, or

(b) in the exercise of a power conferred, or the discharge of a duty imposed, on a Minister of the Crown, government department or any other person, being a power or duty which extends to the disbursement or allocation of public money.

101B Interpretation In this Chapter—

'scheme' means an occupational pension scheme to which this Chapter applies;

'pension credit rights' means rights to future benefits under a scheme which are attributable (directly or indirectly) to a pension credit;

'pension credit benefit', in relation to a scheme, means the benefits payable under the scheme to or in respect of a person by virtue of rights under the scheme attributable (directly or indirectly) to a pension credit;

'normal benefit age', in relation to a scheme, means the earliest age at which a person who has pension credit rights under the scheme is entitled to receive a pension by virtue of those rights (disregarding any scheme rule making special provision as to early payment of pension on grounds of ill-health or otherwise).

101C Basic principle as to pension credit benefit—(1) Normal benefit age under a scheme must be between 60 and 65.

(2) A scheme must not provide for payment of pension credit benefit in the form of a lump sum at any time before normal benefit age, except in such circumstances as may be prescribed.

101D Form of pension credit benefit and its alternatives—(1) Subject to subsection (2) and section 101E, a person's pension credit benefit under a scheme must be—

(a) payable directly out of the resources of the scheme, or

(b) assured to him by such means as may be prescribed.

(2) Subject to subsections (3) and (4), a scheme may, instead of providing a person's pension credit benefit, provide—

(a) for his pension credit rights under the scheme to be transferred to another occupational pension scheme or a personal pension scheme with a view to acquiring rights for him under the rules of the scheme, or

(b) for such alternatives to pension credit benefit as may be prescribed.

(3) The option conferred by subsection (2) (a) is additional to any obligation imposed by Chapter II of this Part.

(4) The alternatives specified in subsection (2) (a) and (b) may only be by way of complete or partial substitute for pension credit benefit—

(a) if the person entitled to the benefit consents, or

(b) in such other cases as may be prescribed.

101E Discharge of liability where pension credit or alternative benefits secured by insurance policies or annuity contracts—(1) A transaction to which section 19 applies discharges the trustees or managers of a scheme from their liability to provide pension credit benefit or any alternative to pension credit benefit for or in respect of a member of the scheme if and to the extent that—

(a) it results in pension credit benefit, or any alternative to pension credit benefit, for or in respect of the member being appropriately secured (within the meaning of that section),

(b) the transaction is entered into with the consent of the member or, if the member has died, of the member's widow or widower, and

(c) such requirements as may be prescribed are met.

(2) Regulations may provide that subsection (1)(b) shall not apply in prescribed circumstances.

CHAPTER II
TRANSFER VALUES

101F Power to give transfer notice—(1) An eligible member of a qualifying scheme may by notice in writing require the trustees or managers of the scheme to use an amount equal to the cash equivalent of his pension credit benefit for such one or more of the authorised purposes as he may specify in the notice.

(2) In the case of a member of an occupational pension scheme, the authorised purposes are—

(a) to acquire rights allowed under the rules of an occupational pension scheme, or personal pension scheme, which is an eligible scheme,

(b) to purchase from one or more insurance companies such as are mentioned in section 19(4)(a), chosen by the member and willing to accept payment on account of the member from the trustees or managers, one or more annuities which satisfy the prescribed requirements, and

(c) in such circumstances as may be prescribed, to subscribe to other pension arrangements which satisfy prescribed requirements.

(3) In the case of a member of a personal pension scheme, the authorised purposes are—

(a) to acquire rights allowed under the rules of an occupational pension scheme, or personal pension scheme, which is an eligible scheme, and

(b)   in such circumstances as may be prescribed, to subscribe to other pension arrangements which satisfy prescribed requirements.

(4)   The cash equivalent for the purposes of subsection (1) shall—

(a)   in the case of a salary related occupational pension scheme, be taken to be the amount shown in the relevant statement under section 101H, and

(b)   in any other case, be determined by reference to the date the notice under that subsection is given.

(5)   The requirements which may be prescribed under subsection (2) or (3) include, in particular, requirements of the Inland Revenue.

(6)   In subsections (2) and (3), references to an eligible scheme are to a scheme—

(a)   the trustees or managers of which are able and willing to accept payment in respect of the member's pension credit rights, and

(b)   which satisfies the prescribed requirements.

(7)   In this Chapter, 'transfer notice' means a notice under subsection (1).

101G Restrictions on power to give transfer notice—(1) In the case of a salary related occupational pension scheme, the power to give a transfer notice may only be exercised if—

(a)   the member has been provided with a statement under section 101H, and

(b)   not more than 3 months have passed since the date by reference to which the amount shown in the statement is determined.

(2)   The power to give a transfer notice may not be exercised in the case of an occupational pension scheme if—

(a)   there is less than a year to go until the member reaches normal benefit age, or

(b)   the pension to which the member is entitled by virtue of his pension credit rights, or benefit in lieu of that pension, or any part of it has become payable.

(3)   Where an eligible member of a qualifying scheme—

(a)   is entitled to make an application under section 95 to the trustees or managers of the scheme, or

(b)   would be entitled to do so, but for the fact that he has not received a statement under section 93A in respect of which the guarantee date is sufficiently recent,

he may not, if the scheme so provides, exercise the power to give them a transfer notice unless he also makes an application to them under section 95.

(4)   The power to give a transfer notice may not be exercised if a previous transfer notice given by the member to the trustees or managers of the scheme is outstanding.

101H Salary related schemes: statements of entitlement—(1) The trustees or managers of a qualifying scheme which is a salary related occupational pension scheme shall, on the application of an eligible member, provide him with a written statement of the amount of the cash equivalent of his pension credit benefit under the scheme.

(2)   For the purposes of subsection (1), the amount of the cash equivalent shall be determined by reference to a date falling within—

(a)   the prescribed period beginning with the date of the application, and

(b)   the prescribed period ending with the date on which the statement under that subsection is provided to the applicant.

(3)   Regulations may make provision in relation to applications under subsection (1) and may, in particular, restrict the making of successive applications.

(4)   If trustees or managers to whom subsection (1) applies fail to perform an obligation under that subsection, section 10 of the Pensions Act 1995 (power of

the Regulatory Authority to impose civil penalties) shall apply to any trustee or manager who has failed to take all such steps as are reasonable to secure that the obligation was performed.

101I Calculation of cash equivalents Cash equivalents for the purposes of this Chapter shall be calculated and verified in the prescribed manner.

101J Time for compliance with transfer notice—(1) Trustees or managers of a qualifying scheme who receive a transfer notice shall comply with the notice—
  (a) in the case of an occupational pension scheme, within 6 months of the valuation date or, if earlier, by the date on which the member to whom the notice relates reaches normal benefit age, and
  (b) in the case of a personal pension scheme, within 6 months of the date on which they receive the notice.
  (2) The Regulatory Authority may, in prescribed circumstances, extend the period for complying with the notice.
  (3) If the Regulatory Authority are satisfied—
  (a) that there has been a relevant change of circumstances since they granted an extension under subsection (2), or
  (b) that they granted an extension under that subsection in ignorance of a material fact or on the basis of a mistake as to a material fact,
they may revoke or reduce the extension.
  (4) Where the trustees or managers of an occupational pension scheme have failed to comply with a transfer notice before the end of the period for compliance—
  (a) they shall, except in prescribed cases, notify the Regulatory Authority of that fact within the prescribed period, and
  (b) section 10 of the Pensions Act 1995 (power of the Regulatory Authority to impose civil penalties) shall apply to any trustee or manager who has failed to take all such steps as are reasonable to ensure that the notice was complied with before the end of the period for compliance.
  (5) If trustees or managers to whom subsection (4)(a) applies fail to perform the obligation imposed by that provision, section 10 of the Pensions Act 1995 shall apply to any trustee or manager who has failed to take all such steps as are reasonable to ensure that the obligation was performed.
  (6) Regulations may—
  (a) make provision in relation to applications under subsection (2), and
  (b) provide that subsection (4) shall not apply in prescribed circumstances.
  (7) In this section, 'valuation date', in relation to a transfer notice given to the trustees or managers of an occupational pension scheme, means—
  (a) in the case of a salary related scheme, the date by reference to which the amount shown in the relevant statement under section 101H is determined, and
  (b) in the case of any other scheme, the date the notice is given.

101K Withdrawal of transfer notice—(1) Subject to subsections (2) and (3), a person who has given a transfer notice may withdraw it by giving the trustees or managers to whom it was given notice in writing that he no longer requires them to comply with it.
  (2) A transfer notice may not be withdrawn if the trustees or managers have already entered into an agreement with a third party to use the whole or part of the amount they are required to use in accordance with the notice.
  (3) If the giving of a transfer notice depended on the making of an application under section 95, the notice may only be withdrawn if the application is also withdrawn.

101L Variation of the amount required to be used—(1) Regulations may make provision for the amount required to be used under section 101F(1) to be increased or reduced in prescribed circumstances.

(2) Without prejudice to the generality of subsection (1), the circumstances which may be prescribed include—

(a) failure by the trustees or managers of a qualifying scheme to comply with a notice under section 101F(1) within 6 months of the date by reference to which the amount of the cash equivalent falls to be determined, and

(b) the state of funding of a qualifying scheme.

(3) Regulations under subsection (1) may have the effect of extinguishing an obligation under section 101F(1).

101M Effect of transfer on trustees' duties Compliance with a transfer notice shall have effect to discharge the trustees or managers of a qualifying scheme from any obligation to provide the pension credit benefit of the eligible member who gave the notice.

101N Matters to be disregarded in calculations In making any calculation for the purposes of this Chapter—

(a) any charge or lien on, and

(b) any set-off against,

the whole or part of a pension shall be disregarded.

101O Service of notices A notice under section 101F(1) or 101K(1) shall be taken to have been given if it is delivered to the trustees or managers personally or sent by post in a registered letter or by recorded delivery service.

101P Interpretation of Chapter II—(1) In this Chapter—

'eligible member', in relation to a qualifying scheme, means a member who has pension credit rights under the scheme;

'normal benefit age', in relation to an eligible member of a qualifying scheme, means the earliest age at which the member is entitled to receive a pension by virtue of his pension credit rights under the scheme (disregarding any scheme rule making special provision as to early payment of pension on grounds of ill-health or otherwise);

'pension credit benefit', in relation to an eligible member of a qualifying scheme, means the benefits payable under the scheme to or in respect of the member by virtue of rights under the scheme attributable (directly or indirectly) to a pension credit;

'pension credit rights', in relation to a qualifying scheme, means rights to future benefits under the scheme which are attributable (directly or indirectly) to a pension credit;

'qualifying scheme' means a funded occupational pension scheme and a personal pension scheme;

'transfer notice' has the meaning given by section 101F(7).

(2) For the purposes of this Chapter, an occupational pension scheme is salary related if—

(a) it is not a money purchase scheme, and

(b) it does not fall within a prescribed class.

(3) In this Chapter, references to the relevant statement under section 101H, in relation to a transfer notice given to the trustees or managers of a salary related occupational pension scheme, are to the statement under that section on which the giving of the notice depended.

(4) For the purposes of this section, an occupational pension scheme is funded if it meets its liabilities out of a fund accumulated for the purpose during the life of the scheme.

101Q Power to modify Chapter II in relation to hybrid schemes
Regulations may apply this Chapter with prescribed modifications to occupational pension schemes—
(a) which are not money purchase schemes, but
(b) where some of the benefits that may be provided are money purchase benefits.'

Note Specified date (for the purpose only of the exercise of any power to make regulations): 11 November 1999: see s 89(5)(a); (for remaining purposes): see s 89(1); (for remaining purposes): 1 December 2000: see SI 2000 No 1047, art 2(2)(d), Schedule, Pt IV.

38 Treatment in winding up—(1) In section 73 of the Pensions Act 1995 (treatment of rights on winding up of an occupational pension scheme to which section 56 of that Act (minimum funding requirement) applies), in subsection (3) (classification of liabilities), in paragraph (c) (accrued rights), at the end of sub-paragraph (i) there shall be inserted—
'(ia) future pensions, or other future benefits, attributable (directly or indirectly) to pension credits (but excluding increases to pensions),'.
(2) In the case of an occupational pension scheme which is not a scheme to which section 56 of the Pensions Act 1995 applies, rights attributable (directly or indirectly) to a pension credit are to be accorded in a winding up the same treatment—
(a) if they have come into payment, as the rights of a pensioner member, and
(b) if they have not come into payment, as the rights of a deferred member.
(3) Subsection (2) overrides the provisions of a scheme to the extent that it conflicts with them, and the scheme has effect with such modifications as may be required in consequence.
(4) In subsection (2)—
(a) 'deferred member' and 'pensioner member' have the same meanings as in Part I of the Pensions Act 1995,
(b) 'pension credit' includes a credit under Northern Ireland legislation corresponding to section 29(1)(b), and
(c) references to rights attributable to a pension credit having come into payment are to the person to whom the rights belong having become entitled by virtue of the rights to the present payment of pension or other benefits.

Note. 1 December 2000 (SI 2000 No 1047, art 2(d), Sch, Pt IV).

Indexation

39 Public service pension schemes—(1) The Pensions (Increase) Act 1971 shall be amended as follows.
(2) In section 3 (qualifying conditions), after subsection (2) there shall be inserted—
'(2A) A pension attributable to the pensioner having become entitled to a pension credit shall not be increased unless the pensioner has attained the age of fifty-five years.'
(3) In section 8, in subsection (1) (definition of 'pension'), in paragraph (a), the words from '(either' to 'person)' shall be omitted.
(4) In that section, in subsection (2) (when pension deemed for purposes of the Act to begin), after 'pension', in the first place, there shall be inserted 'which is not attributable to a pension credit', and after that subsection there shall be inserted—
'(2A) A pension which is attributable to a pension credit shall be deemed for purposes of this Act to begin on the day on which the order or provision on which the credit depends takes effect.'

(5) In section 17(1) (interpretation)—
(a) for the definitions of 'derivative pension' and 'principal pension' there shall be substituted—
    '"derivative pension" means a pension which—
        (a)   is not payable in respect of the pensioner's own services, and
        (b)   is not attributable to the pensioner having become entitled to a pension credit;',
(b) after the definition of 'pension' there shall be inserted—
    '"pension credit" means a credit under section 29(1)(b) of the Welfare Reform and Pensions Act 1999 or under corresponding Northern Ireland legislation;
    "principal pension" means a pension which—
        (a)   is payable in respect of the pensioner's own services, or
        (b)   is attributable to the pensioner having become entitled to a pension credit;', and
(c) for the definition of 'widow's pension' there shall be substituted—
    '"widow's pension" means a pension payable—
        (a)   in respect of the services of the pensioner's deceased husband, or
        (b)   by virtue of the pensioner's deceased husband having become entitled to a pension credit.'

Note. 1 December 2000 (SI 2000 No 1047).

40 Other pension schemes—(1) The Secretary of State may by regulations make provision for a pension to which subsection (2) applies to be increased, as a minimum, by reference to increases in the retail prices index, so far as not exceeding 5% per annum.
(2) This subsection applies to—
(a) a pension provided to give effect to eligible pension credit rights of a member under a qualifying occupational pension scheme, and
(b) a pension provided to give effect to safeguarded rights of a member under a personal pension scheme.
(3) In this section—
'eligible', in relation to pension credit rights, means of a description prescribed by regulations made by the Secretary of State;
'pension credit rights', in relation to an occupational pension scheme, means rights to future benefits under the scheme which are attributable (directly or indirectly) to a credit under section 29(1)(b) or under corresponding Northern Ireland legislation;
'qualifying occupational pension scheme' means an occupational pension scheme which is not a public service pension scheme;
'safeguarded rights' has the meaning given in section 68A of the Pension Schemes Act 1993.

Note. Specified date (for the purpose only of the exercise of any power to make regulations): 11 November 1999: see s 89(5)(a); (for remaining purposes): see s 89(1); (for remaining purposes): 1 December 2000: see SI 2000 No 1047, art 2(2)(d), Schedule, Pt IV.

Charges by pension arrangements

41 Charges in respect of pension sharing costs—(1) The Secretary of State may by regulations make provision for the purpose of enabling the person responsible for a pension arrangement involved in pension sharing to recover from the parties to pension sharing prescribed charges in respect of prescribed descriptions of pension sharing activity.
(2) Regulations under subsection (1) may include—
(a) provision for the start of the implementation period for a pension credit to be postponed in prescribed circumstances;

  (b) provision, in relation to payments in respect of charges recoverable under the regulations, for reimbursement as between the parties to pension sharing;

  (c) provision, in relation to the recovery of charges by deduction from a pension credit, for the modification of Schedule 5;

  (d) provision for the recovery in prescribed circumstances of such additional amounts as may be determined in accordance with the regulations.

  (3) For the purposes of regulations under subsection (1), the question of how much of a charge recoverable under the regulations is attributable to a party to pension sharing is to be determined as follows—

  (a) where the relevant order or provision includes provision about the apportionment of charges under this section, there is attributable to the party so much of the charge as is apportioned to him by that provision;

  (b) where the relevant order or provision does not include such provision, the charge is attributable to the transferor.

  (4) For the purposes of subsection (1), a pension arrangement is involved in pension sharing if section 29 applies by virtue of an order or provision which relates to the arrangement.

  (5) In that subsection, the reference to pension sharing activity is to activity attributable (directly or indirectly) to the involvement in pension sharing.

  (6) In subsection (3)—

  (a) the reference to the relevant order or provision is to the order or provision which gives rise to the pension sharing, and

  (b) the reference to the transferor is to the person to whose rights that order or provision relates.

  (7) In this section 'prescribed' means prescribed in regulations under subsection (1).

Note. Specified date (for the purpose only of the exercise of any power to make regulations): 11 November 1999: see s 89(5)(a); to be appointed (for remaining purposes): see s 89(1); (for remaining purposes): 1 December 2000: see SI 2000 No 1047, art 2(2)(d), Schedule, Pt IV.

Adaptation of statutory schemes

42 Extension of scheme-making powers—(1) Power under an Act to establish a pension scheme shall include power to make provision for the provision, by reference to pension credits which derive from rights under—

  (a) the scheme, or

  (b) a scheme in relation to which the scheme is specified as an alternative for the purposes of paragraph 2 of Schedule 5,

of benefits to or in respect of those entitled to the credits.

  (2) Subsection (1) is without prejudice to any other power.

  (3) Subsection (1) shall apply in relation to Acts whenever passed.

  (4) No obligation to consult shall apply in relation to the making, in exercise of a power under an Act to establish a pension scheme, of provision of a kind authorised by subsection (1).

  (5) Any provision of, or under, an Act which makes benefits under a pension scheme established under an Act a charge on, or payable out of—

  (a) the Consolidated Fund,

  (b) the Scottish Consolidated Fund, or

  (c) the Consolidated Fund of Northern Ireland,

shall be treated as including any benefits under the scheme which are attributable (directly or indirectly) to a pension credit which derives from rights to benefits charged on, or payable out of, that fund.

  (6) In this section—

'pension credit' includes a credit under Northern Ireland legislation
corresponding to section 29(1)(b);
'pension scheme' means a scheme or arrangement providing benefits, in the
form of pensions or otherwise, payable on termination of service, or on
death or retirement, to or in respect of persons to whom the scheme or
arrangement applies.

Note. 1 December 2000 (SI 2000 No 1047).

43 Power to extend judicial pension schemes—(1) The appropriate minister
may by regulations amend the Sheriffs' Pensions (Scotland) Act 1961, the Judicial
Pensions Act 1981 or the Judicial Pensions and Retirement Act 1993 for the
purpose of—

(a) extending a pension scheme under the Act to include the provision, by
reference to pension credits which derive from rights under—
    (i) the scheme, or
    (ii) a scheme in relation to which the scheme is specified as an
alternative for the purposes of paragraph 2 of Schedule 5,
of benefits to or in respect of those entitled to the credits, or
(b) restricting the power of the appropriate minister to accept payments into a
pension scheme under the Act, where the payments represent the cash
equivalent of rights under another pension scheme which are attributable
(directly or indirectly) to a pension credit.

(2) Regulations under subsection (1)—
(a) may make benefits provided by virtue of paragraph (a) of that subsection a
charge on, and payable out of, the Consolidated Fund;
(b) may confer power to make subordinate legislation, including subordinate
legislation which provides for calculation of the value of rights in
accordance with guidance from time to time prepared by a person specified
in the subordinate legislation.

(3) The appropriate minister for the purposes of subsection (1) is—
(a) in relation to a pension scheme whose ordinary members are limited to
those who hold judicial office whose jurisdiction is exercised exclusively in
relation to Scotland, the Secretary of State, and
(b) in relation to any other pension scheme, the Lord Chancellor.

(4) In this section—
'pension credit' includes a credit under Northern Ireland legislation
corresponding to section 29(1)(b);
'pension scheme' means a scheme or arrangement providing benefits, in the
form of pensions or otherwise, payable on termination of service, or on
death or retirement, to or in respect of persons to whom the scheme or
arrangement applies.

Note. Specified date (for the purpose only of the exercise of any power to make
regulations): 11 November 1999: see s 89(5)(a); to be appointed (for remaining purposes):
see s 89(1); (for remaining purposes): 1 December 2000: see SI 2000 No 1047, art 2(2)(d),
Schedule, Pt IV.

Supplementary

44 Disapplication of restrictions on alienation—(1) Nothing in any of the
following provisions (restrictions on alienation of pension rights) applies in
relation to any order or provision falling within section 28(1)—

(a) section 203(1) and (2) of the Army Act 1955, section 203(1) and (2) of the
Air Force Act 1955, section 128G(1) and (2) of the Naval Discipline Act
1957 and section 159(4) and (4A) of the Pension Schemes Act 1993,
(b) section 91 of the Pensions Act 1995,

(c) any provision of any enactment (whether passed or made before or after this Act is passed) corresponding to any of the enactments mentioned in paragraphs (a) and (b), and

(d) any provision of a pension arrangement corresponding to any of those enactments.

(2) In this section, 'enactment' includes an enactment comprised in subordinate legislation (within the meaning of the Interpretation Act 1978).

Note. 1 December 2000 (SI 2000 No 1047).

45 Information—(1) The Secretary of State may by regulations require the person responsible for a pension arrangement involved in pension sharing to supply to such persons as he may specify in the regulations such information relating to anything which follows from the application of section 29 as he may so specify.

(2) Section 168 of the Pension Schemes Act 1993 (breach of regulations) shall apply as if this section were contained in that Act (otherwise than in Chapter II of Part VII).

(3) For the purposes of this section, a pension arrangement is involved pension sharing if section 29 applies by virtue of an order or provision which relates to the arrangement.

Note. Specified date (for the purpose only of the exercise of any power to make regulations): 11 November 1999: see s 89(5)(a); to be appointed (for remaining purposes): see s 89(1); (for remaining purposes): 1 December 2000: see SI 2000 No 1047, art 2(2)(d), Schedule, Pt IV.

46 Interpretation of Chapter I—(1) In this Chapter—

'implementation period', in relation to a pension credit, has the meaning given by section 34;

'occupational pension scheme' has the meaning given by section 1 of the Pension Schemes Act 1993;

'pension arrangement' means—

    (a) an occupational pension scheme,

    (b) a personal pension scheme,

    (c) a retirement annuity contract,

    (d) an annuity or insurance policy purchased, or transferred, for the purpose of giving effect to rights under an occupational pension scheme or a personal pension scheme, and

    (e) an annuity purchased, or entered into, for the purpose of discharging liability in respect of a credit under section 29(1)(b) or under corresponding Northern Ireland legislation;

'pension credit' means a credit under section 29(1)(b);

'pension debit' means a debit under section 29(1)(a);

'pensionable service', in relation to a member of an occupational pension scheme, means service in any description or category of employment to which the scheme relates which qualifies the member (on the assumption that it continues for the appropriate period) for pension or other benefits under the scheme;

'personal pension scheme' has the meaning given by section 1 of the Pension Schemes Act 1993;

'retirement annuity contract' means a contract or scheme approved under Chapter III of Part XIV of the Income and Corporation Taxes Act 1988;

'shareable rights' has the meaning given by section 27(2);

'trustees or managers', in relation to an occupational pension scheme or a personal pension scheme means—

    (a) in the case of a scheme established under a trust, the trustees of the scheme, and

    (b) in any other case, the managers of the scheme.

(2) In this Chapter, references to the person responsible for a pension arrangement are—
  (a) in the case of an occupational pension scheme or a personal pension scheme, to the trustees or managers of the scheme,
  (b) in the case of a retirement annuity contract or an annuity falling within paragraph (d) or (e) of the definition of 'pension arrangement' in subsection (1), to the provider of the annuity, and
  (c) in the case of an insurance policy falling within paragraph (d) of the definition of that expression, to the insurer.

(3) In determining what is 'pensionable service' for the purposes of this Chapter—
  (a) service notionally attributable for any purpose of the scheme is to be disregarded, and
  (b) no account is to be taken of any rules of the scheme by which a period of service can be treated for any purpose as being longer or shorter than it actually is.

Note. 1 December 2000 (SI 2000 No 1047).

CHAPTER II
SHARING OF STATE SCHEME RIGHTS

47 Shareable state scheme rights
(1) Pension sharing is available under this Chapter in relation to a person's shareable state scheme rights.

(2) For the purposes of this Chapter, a person's shareable state scheme rights are—
  (a) his entitlement, or prospective entitlement, to a Category A retirement pension by virtue of section 44(3)(b) of the Contributions and Benefits Act (earnings-related additional pension), and
  (b) his entitlement, or prospective entitlement, to a pension under section 55A of that Act (shared additional pension).

Note. 1 December 2000 (SI 2000 No 1047).

48 Activation of benefit sharing (1) Section 49 applies on the taking effect of any of the following relating to a person's shareable state scheme rights—
  (a) a pension sharing order under the Matrimonial Causes Act 1973,
  (b) provision which corresponds to the provision which may be made by such an order and which—
    (i) is contained in a qualifying agreement between the parties to a marriage, and
    (ii) takes effect on the dissolution of the marriage under the Family Law Act 1996,
  (c) provision which corresponds to the provision which may be made by such an order and which—
    (i) is contained in a qualifying agreement between the parties to a marriage or former marriage, and
    (ii) takes effect after the dissolution of the marriage under the Family Law Act 1996,
  (d) an order under Part III of the Matrimonial and Family Proceedings Act 1984 (financial relief in England and Wales in relation to overseas divorce etc) corresponding to such an order as is mentioned in paragraph (a),
  (e) a pension sharing order under the Family Law (Scotland) Act 1985,
  (f) provision which corresponds to the provision which may be made by such an order and which—
    (i) is contained in a qualifying agreement between the parties to a marriage,

(ii) is in such form as the Secretary of State may prescribe by regulations, and

(iii) takes effect on the grant, in relation to the marriage, of decree of divorce under the Divorce (Scotland) Act 1976 or of declarator of nullity,

(g) an order under Part IV of the Matrimonial and Family Proceedings Act 1984 (financial relief in Scotland in relation to overseas divorce etc) corresponding to such an order as is mentioned in paragraph (e),

(h) a pension sharing order under Northern Ireland legislation, and

(i) an order under Part IV of the Matrimonial and Family Proceedings (Northern Ireland) Order 1989 (financial relief in Northern Ireland in relation to overseas divorce etc) corresponding to such an order as is mentioned in paragraph (h).

(2) For the purposes of subsection (1)(b) and (c), a qualifying agreement is one which—

(a) has been entered into in such circumstances as the Lord Chancellor may prescribe by regulations, and

(b) satisfies such requirements as the Lord Chancellor may so prescribe.

(3) For the purposes of subsection (1)(f), a qualifying agreement is one which—

(a) has been entered into in such circumstances as the Secretary of State may prescribe by regulations, and

(b) is registered in the Books of Council and Session.

(4) Subsection (1)(b) does not apply if the provision relates to rights which are the subject of a pension sharing order under the Matrimonial Causes Act 1973 in relation to the marriage.

(5) Subsection (1)(c) does not apply if—

(a) the marriage was dissolved by an order under section 3 of the Family Law Act 1996 (divorce not preceded by separation) and the satisfaction of the requirements of section 9(2) of that Act (settlement of future financial arrangements) was a precondition to the making of the order,

(b) the provision relates to rights which are the subject of a pension sharing order under the Matrimonial Causes Act 1973 in relation to the marriage, or

(c) shareable state scheme rights have already been the subject of pension sharing between the parties.

(6) For the purposes of this section, an order or provision falling within subsection (1)(e), (f) or (g) shall be deemed never to have taken effect if the Secretary of State does not receive before the end of the period of 2 months beginning with the relevant date—

(a) copies of the relevant matrimonial documents, and

(b) such information relating to the transferor and transferee as the Secretary of State may prescribe by regulations under section 34(1)(b)(ii).

(7) The relevant date for the purposes of subsection (6) is—

(a) in the case of an order or provision falling within subsection (1)(e) or (f), the date of the extract of the decree or declarator responsible for the divorce or annulment to which the order or provision relates, and

(b) in the case of an order falling within subsection (1)(g), the date of disposal of the application under section 28 of the Matrimonial and Family Proceedings Act 1984.

(8) The reference in subsection (6)(a) to the relevant matrimonial documents is—

(a) in the case of an order falling within subsection (1)(e) or (g), to copies of the order and the order, decree or declarator responsible for the divorce or annulment to which it relates, and

(b) in the case of provision falling within subsection (1)(f), to—
   (i) copies of the provision and the order, decree or declarator responsible for the divorce or annulment to which it relates, and
   (ii) documentary evidence that the agreement containing the provision is one to which subsection (3)(a) applies.

(9) The sheriff may, on the application of any person having an interest, make an order—

(a) extending the period of 2 months referred to in subsection (6), and
(b) if that period has already expired, providing that, if the Secretary of State receives the documents and information concerned before the end of the period specified in the order, subsection (6) is to be treated as never having applied.

Note. Specified date (for the purpose only of the exercise of any power to make regulations): 11 November 1999: see s 89(5)(a); to be appointed (for remaining purposes): see s 89(1); (for remaining purposes): 1 December 2000: see SI 2000 No 1047, art 2(2)(d), Schedule, Pt IV.

Where an action of divorce or an action for declarator of nullity has been brought before 1 December 2000, sub-s (1)(f) above shall not apply in relation to that divorce or declarator: see the Welfare Reform and Pensions Act 1999, s 85(5)(b).

49 Creation of state scheme pension debits and credits—(1) On the application of this section—

(a) the transferor becomes subject, for the purposes of Part II of the Contributions and Benefits Act (contributory benefits), to a debit of the appropriate amount, and
(b) the transferee becomes entitled, for those purposes, to a credit of that amount.

(2) Where the relevant order or provision specifies a percentage value to be transferred, the appropriate amount for the purposes of subsection (1) is the specified percentage of the cash equivalent on the transfer day of the transferor's shareable state scheme rights immediately before that day.

(3) Where the relevant order or provision specifies an amount to be transferred, the appropriate amount for the purposes of subsection (1) is the lesser of—

(a) the specified amount, and
(b) the cash equivalent on the transfer day of the transferor's relevant state scheme rights immediately before that day.

[(4) The Secretary of State may by regulations make provision about the calculation and verification of cash equivalents for the purposes of this section.

(4A) The power conferred by subsection (4) above includes power to provide—
(a) for calculation or verification in such manner as may be approved by or on behalf of the Government Actuary, and
(b) for things done under the regulations to be required to be done in accordance with guidance from time to time prepared by a person prescribed by the regulations.]

(5) In determining prospective entitlement to a Category A retirement pension for the purposes of this section, only tax years before that in which the transfer day falls shall be taken into account.

(6) In this section—
'relevant order or provision' means the order or provision by virtue of which this section applies;
'transfer day' means the day on which the relevant order or provision takes effect;
'transferor' means the person to whose rights the relevant order or provision relates;
'transferee' means the person for whose benefit the relevant order or provision is made.

Note. Specified date (for the purpose only of the exercise of any power to make regulations): 11 November 1999: see s 89(5)(a); to be appointed (for remaining purposes): see s 89(1); (for remaining purposes): 1 December 2000: see SI 2000 No 1047, art 2(2)(d), Schedule, Pt IV.

Sub-ss (4), (4A): substituted, for sub-s (4) as originally enacted, by the Child Support, Pensions and Social Security Act 2000, s 41(1) as from 29 September 2000 (SI 2000 No 2666).

50 Effect of state scheme pension debits and credits—(1) Schedule 6 (which amends the Contributions and Benefits Act for the purpose of giving effect to debits and credits under section 49(1)) shall have effect.

(2) Section 55C of that Act (which is inserted by that Schedule) shall have effect, in relation to incremental periods (within the meaning of that section) beginning on or after 6th April 2010, with the following amendments—

(a) in subsection (3), for 'period of enhancement' there is substituted 'period of deferment',

(b) in subsection (4), for '1/7th per cent' there is substituted '1/5th per cent',

(c) in subsection (7), for 'period of enhancement', in both places, there is substituted 'period of deferment', and

(d) in subsection (9), the definition of 'period of enhancement' (and the preceding 'and') are omitted.

Note. Specified date (for the purpose only of the exercise of any power to make regulations): 11 November 1999: see s 89(5)(a); to be appointed (for remaining purposes): see s 89(1); (for remaining purposes): 1 December 2000: see SI 2000 No 1047, art 2(2)(d), Schedule, Pt IV.

51 Interpretation of Chapter II In this Chapter—

'shareable state scheme rights' has the meaning given by section 47(2); and

'tax year' has the meaning given by section 122(1) of the Contributions and Benefits Act.

Note. 1 December 2000 (SI 2000 No 1047).

* * * * *

SCHEDULE 3   Section 19
PENSION SHARING ORDERS: ENGLAND AND WALES

1 The Matrimonial Causes Act 1973 is amended as follows.

2 After section 21 there is inserted—

'**21A Pension sharing orders—**(1) For the purposes of this Act, a pension sharing order is an order which—

(a) provides that one party's—

(i) shareable rights under a specified pension arrangement, or

(ii) shareable state scheme rights,

be subject to pension sharing for the benefit of the other party, and

(b) specifies the percentage value to be transferred.

(2) In subsection (1) above—

(a) the reference to shareable rights under a pension arrangement is to rights in relation to which pension sharing is available under Chapter I of Part IV of the Welfare Reform and Pensions Act 1999, or under corresponding Northern Ireland legislation,

(b) the reference to shareable state scheme rights is to rights in relation to which pension sharing is available under Chapter II of Part IV of the Welfare Reform and Pensions Act 1999, or under corresponding Northern Ireland legislation, and

(c) 'party' means a party to a marriage.'

3 In section 24 (property adjustment orders in connection with divorce proceedings, etc), in paragraphs (c) and (d) of subsection (1), there is inserted at the end ', other than one in the form of a pension arrangement (within the meaning of section 25D below)'.

4 After section 24A there is inserted—

'24B Pension sharing orders in connection with divorce proceedings etc—
(1) On granting a decree of divorce or a decree of nullity of marriage or at any time thereafter (whether before or after the decree is made absolute), the court may, on an application made under this section, make one or more pension sharing orders in relation to the marriage.

(2) A pension sharing order under this section is not to take effect unless the decree on or after which it is made has been made absolute.

(3) A pension sharing order under this section may not be made in relation to a pension arrangement which—
(a) is the subject of a pension sharing order in relation to the marriage, or
(b) has been the subject of pension sharing between the parties to the marriage.

(4) A pension sharing order under this section may not be made in relation to shareable state scheme rights if—
(a) such rights are the subject of a pension sharing order in relation to the marriage, or
(b) such rights have been the subject of pension sharing between the parties to the marriage.

(5) A pension sharing order under this section may not be made in relation to the rights of a person under a pension arrangement if there is in force a requirement imposed by virtue of section 25B or 25C below which relates to benefits or future benefits to which he is entitled under the pension arrangement.

24C Pension sharing orders: duty to stay—(1) No pension sharing order may be made so as to take effect before the end of such period after the making of the order as may be prescribed by regulations made by the Lord Chancellor.

(2) The power to make regulations under this section shall be exercisable by statutory instrument which shall be subject to annulment in pursuance of a resolution of either House of Parliament.

24D Pension sharing orders: apportionment of charges If a pension sharing order relates to rights under a pension arrangement, the court may include in the order provision about the apportionment between the parties of any charge under section 41 of the Welfare Reform and Pensions Act 1999 (charges in respect of pension sharing costs), or under corresponding Northern Ireland legislation.'

5 In section 25 (matters to which the court is to have regard in deciding how to exercise its powers with respect to financial relief)—
(a) in subsection (1), for 'or 24A' there is substituted ', 24A or 24B', and
(b) in subsection (2), for 'or 24A' there is substituted ', 24A or 24B'.

6 In section 25A(1) (court's duty to consider desirability of exercising power to achieve clean break), for 'or 24A' there is substituted ', 24A or 24B'.

7—(1) Section 31 (variation, discharge etc of certain orders for financial relief) is amended as follows.

(2) In subsection (2), at the end there is inserted—

'(g) a pension sharing order under section 24B above which is made at a time before the decree has been made absolute.'

(3) After subsection (4) there is inserted—

'(4A) In relation to an order which falls within paragraph (g) of subsection (2) above ('the subsection (2) order')—

(a) the powers conferred by this section may be exercised—

(i) only on an application made before the subsection (2) order has or, but for paragraph (b) below, would have taken effect; and

(ii) only if, at the time when the application is made, the decree has not been made absolute; and

(b) an application made in accordance with paragraph (a) above prevents the subsection (2) order from taking effect before the application has been dealt with.

(4B) No variation of a pension sharing order shall be made so as to take effect before the decree is made absolute.

(4C) The variation of a pension sharing order prevents the order taking effect before the end of such period after the making of the variation as may be prescribed by regulations made by the Lord Chancellor.'

(4) In subsection (5)—

(a) for '(7F)' there is substituted '(7G)',

(b) for 'or (e)' there is substituted ', (e) or (g)', and

(c) after 'property adjustment order' there is inserted 'or pension sharing order'.

(5) In subsection (7B), after paragraph (b) there is inserted—

'(ba) one or more pension sharing orders;'.

(6) After subsection (7F) there is inserted—

'(7G) Subsections (3) to (5) of section 24B above apply in relation to a pension sharing order under subsection (7B) above as they apply in relation to a pension sharing order under that section.'

(7) After subsection (14) there is inserted—

'(15) The power to make regulations under subsection (4C) above shall be exercisable by statutory instrument which shall be subject to annulment in pursuance of a resolution of either House of Parliament.'

8 In section 33A (consent orders), in subsection (3), in the definition of 'order for financial relief', after '24A' there is inserted ', 24B'.

9 In section 37 (avoidance of transactions intended to prevent or reduce financial relief), in subsection (1), after '24,' there is inserted '24B,'.

10 After section 40 there is inserted—

'40A Appeals relating to pension sharing orders which have taken effect—

(1) Subsections (2) and (3) below apply where an appeal against a pension sharing order is begun on or after the day on which the order takes effect.

(2) If the pension sharing order relates to a person's rights under a pension arrangement, the appeal court may not set aside or vary the order if the person responsible for the pension arrangement has acted to his detriment in reliance on the taking effect of the order.

(3) If the pension sharing order relates to a person's shareable state scheme rights, the appeal court may not set aside or vary the order if the Secretary of State has acted to his detriment in reliance on the taking effect of the order.

(4) In determining for the purposes of subsection (2) or (3) above whether a person has acted to his detriment in reliance on the taking effect of the order, the appeal court may disregard any detriment which in its opinion is insignificant.

(5) Where subsection (2) or (3) above applies, the appeal court may make such further orders (including one or more pension sharing orders) as it thinks fit for the purpose of putting the parties in the position it considers appropriate.

(6) Section 24C above only applies to a pension sharing order under this section if the decision of the appeal court can itself be the subject of an appeal.

(7) In subsection (2) above, the reference to the person responsible for the pension arrangement is to be read in accordance with section 25D(4) above.'

11 In section 52 (interpretation), in subsection (2), for 'and' at the end of paragraph (a) there is substituted—

'(aa) references to pension sharing orders shall be construed in accordance with section 21A above; and'.

Note. 1 December 2000 (SI 2000 No 1116).

SCHEDULE 4 — Section 21

AMENDMENTS OF SECTIONS 25B TO 25D OF THE MATRIMONIAL CAUSES ACT 1973

1—(1) Section 25B of the Matrimonial Causes Act 1973 is amended as follows.

(2) In subsection (1), for 'scheme', wherever occurring, there is substituted 'arrangement'.

(3) Subsection (2) ceases to have effect.

(4) In subsection (3), for 'scheme' there is substituted 'arrangement'.

(5) In subsection (4)—

(a) for 'scheme', wherever occurring, there is substituted 'arrangement', and

(b) for 'trustees or managers of' there is substituted 'person responsible for'.

(6) For subsection (5) there is substituted—

'(5) The order must express the amount of any payment required to be made by virtue of subsection (4) above as a percentage of the payment which becomes due to the party with pension rights.'

(7) In subsection (6)—

(a) for 'trustees or managers', in the first place, there is substituted 'person responsible for the arrangement', and

(b) for 'the trustees or managers', in the second place, there is substituted 'his'.

(8) In subsection (7)—

(a) for the words from 'may require any' to 'those benefits' there is substituted 'has a right of commutation under the arrangement, the order may require him to exercise it to any extent',

(b) for 'the payment of any amount commuted' there is substituted 'any payment due in consequence of commutation', and

(c) for 'scheme' there is substituted 'arrangement'.

(9) After that subsection there is inserted—

'(7A) The power conferred by subsection (7) above may not be exercised for the purpose of commuting a benefit payable to the party with pension rights to a benefit payable to the other party.

(7B) The power conferred by subsection (4) or (7) above may not be exercised in relation to a pension arrangement which—

(a) is the subject of a pension sharing order in relation to the marriage, or

(b) has been the subject of pension sharing between the parties to the marriage.

(7C) In subsection (1) above, references to benefits under a pension arrangement include any benefits by way of pension, whether under a pension arrangement or not.'

2—(1) Section 25C of that Act is amended as follows.

(2) In subsection (1), for 'scheme' there is substituted 'arrangement'.

(3) In subsection (2)—

(a) in paragraph (a)—

    (i) for the words from 'trustees' to 'have' there is substituted 'person responsible for the pension arrangement in question has', and

    (ii) for 'them' there is substituted 'him', and

(b) in paragraph (c), for 'trustees or managers of the pension scheme' there is substituted 'person responsible for the pension arrangement'.

(4) In subsection (3)—

(a) for 'trustees or managers' there is substituted 'person responsible for the arrangement', and

(b) for 'the trustees, or managers,' there is substituted 'his'.

(5) At the end there is inserted—

'(4) The powers conferred by this section may not be exercised in relation to a pension arrangement which—

(a) is the subject of a pension sharing order in relation to the marriage, or

(b) has been the subject of pension sharing between the parties to the marriage.'

3—(1) Section 25D of that Act is amended as follows.

(2) For subsection (1) there is substituted—

'(1) Where—

(a) an order made under section 23 above by virtue of section 25B or 25C above imposes any requirement on the person responsible for a pension arrangement ("the first arrangement") and the party with pension rights acquires rights under another pension arrangement ("the new arrangement") which are derived (directly or indirectly) from the whole of his rights under the first arrangement, and

(b) the person responsible for the new arrangement has been given notice in accordance with regulations made by the Lord Chancellor,

the order shall have effect as if it had been made instead in respect of the person responsible for the new arrangement.'

(3) In subsection (2)—

(a) for 'Regulations may' there is substituted 'The Lord Chancellor may by regulations',

(b) in paragraph (a), for 'trustees or managers of a pension scheme' there is substituted 'person responsible for a pension arrangement',

(c) after that paragraph there is inserted—

'(ab) make, in relation to payment under a mistaken belief as to the continuation in force of a provision included by virtue of section 25B or 25C above in an order under section 23 above, provision about the rights or liabilities of the payer, the payee or the person to whom the payment was due,'

(d) after paragraph (b) there is inserted—

'(ba) make provision for the person responsible for a pension arrangement to be discharged in prescribed circumstances from a requirement imposed by virtue of section 25B or 25C above,'

(e) paragraphs (c) and (d) are omitted,

(f) for paragraph (e) there is substituted—

'(e) make provision about calculation and verification in relation to the valuation of—

    (i) benefits under a pension arrangement, or

    (ii) shareable state scheme rights,

for the purposes of the court's functions in connection with the exercise of any of its powers under this Part of this Act.', and

(g) the words after paragraph (e) are omitted.

(4) After that subsection there is inserted—

'(2A) Regulations under subsection (2)(e) above may include—

(a) provision for calculation or verification in accordance with guidance from time to time prepared by a prescribed person, and

(b) provision by reference to regulations under section 30 or 49(4) of the Welfare Reform and Pensions Act 1999.

(2B) Regulations under subsection (2) above may make different provision for different cases.

(2C) Power to make regulations under this section shall be exercisable by statutory instrument which shall be subject to annulment in pursuance of a resolution of either House of Parliament.'

(5) For subsections (3) and (4) there is substituted—

'(3) In this section and sections 25B and 25C above—

'occupational pension scheme' has the same meaning as in the Pension Schemes Act 1993;

'the party with pension rights' means the party to the marriage who has or is likely to have benefits under a pension arrangement and 'the other party' means the other party to the marriage;

'pension arrangement' means—

(a) an occupational pension scheme,

(b) a personal pension scheme,

(c) a retirement annuity contract,

(d) an annuity or insurance policy purchased, or transferred, for the purpose of giving effect to rights under an occupational pension scheme or a personal pension scheme, and

(e) an annuity purchased, or entered into, for the purpose of discharging liability in respect of a pension credit under section 29(1)(b) of the Welfare Reform and Pensions Act 1999 or under corresponding Northern Ireland legislation;

'personal pension scheme' has the same meaning as in the Pension Schemes Act 1993;

'prescribed' means prescribed by regulations;

'retirement annuity contract' means a contract or scheme approved under Chapter III of Part XIV of the Income and Corporation Taxes Act 1988;

'shareable state scheme rights' has the same meaning as in section 21A(1) above; and

'trustees or managers', in relation to an occupational pension scheme or a personal pension scheme, means—

(a) in the case of a scheme established under a trust, the trustees of the scheme, and

(b) in any other case, the managers of the scheme.

(4) In this section and sections 25B and 25C above, references to the person responsible for a pension arrangement are—

(a) in the case of an occupational pension scheme or a personal pension scheme, to the trustees or managers of the scheme,

(b) in the case of a retirement annuity contract or an annuity falling within paragraph (d) or (e) of the definition of 'pension arrangement' above, the provider of the annuity, and

(c) in the case of an insurance policy falling within paragraph (d) of the definition of that expression, the insurer.'

Note. 1 December 2000 (SI 2000 No 1116).

CARE STANDARDS ACT 2000

(2000 c 14)

An Act to establish a National Care Standards Commission; to make provision for the registration and regulation of children's homes, independent hospitals, independent clinics, care homes, residential family centres, independent medical agencies, domiciliary care agencies, fostering agencies, nurses agencies and voluntary adoption agencies; to make provision for the regulation and inspection of local authority fostering and adoption services; to establish a General Social Care Council and a Care Council for Wales and make provision for the registration, regulation and training of social care workers; to establish a Children's Commissioner for Wales; to make provision for the registration, regulation and training of those providing child minding or day care; to make provision for the protection of children and vulnerable adults; to amend the law about children looked after in schools and colleges; to repeal the Nurses Agencies Act 1957; to amend Schedule 1 to the Local Authority Social Services Act 1970; and for connected purposes.

[20 July 2000]

* * * * *

PART VII
PROTECTION OF CHILDREN AND VULNERABLE ADULTS

* * * * *

Restrictions on working with children in independent schools

100 Additional ground of complaint—(*1*) *In subsection (1) of section 469 (notice of complaint) of the Education Act 1996, for paragraph (d) there shall be substituted—*
    '*(d) the proprietor of the school or any teacher or other employee employed in the school—*
        (*i*) *is unsuitable to work with children; or*
        (*ii*) *is for any other reason not a proper person to be the proprietor of an independent school or (as the case may be) to be a teacher or other employee in any school;*'.
    (*2*) *In subsection (2) of section 470 of that Act (determination of complaint by an Independent Schools Tribunal), for paragraph (f) there shall be substituted—*
    '*(f) if satisfied that any person alleged by the notice of complaint to be a person who—*
        (*i*) *is unsuitable to work with children; or*
        (*ii*) *is for any other reason not a proper person to be the proprietor of an independent school or to be a teacher or other employee in any school,*
    is in fact such a person, by order disqualify that person from being the proprietor of any independent school or (as the case may be) from being a teacher or other employee in any school.'

Note. 2 October 2000 (SI 2000 No 2544).
    Repealed by the Education Act 2002, s 215(2), Sch 22, Pt 3 as from 1 September 2003 (in relation to England): see SI 2003 No 1667, art 4; as from 1 January 2004 (in relation to Wales): see SI 2003 No 2961, art 6, Schedule, Pt III.

102 Searches of 1996 Act list—(1) In subsection (3A) of section 113 of the Police Act 1997 (criminal record certificates), for the words from 'in the list' to the end there shall be substituted—
    'in—
        (i)   the list kept under section 1 of the Protection of Children Act 1999;
        (ii) the list kept for the purposes of regulations made under section 218(6) of the Education Reform Act 1988 ('the 1988 Act list'); or

> > > (iii) any list kept by the Secretary of State or the National Assembly for Wales of persons disqualified under section 470 or 471 of the Education Act 1996 ('the 1996 Act list'); and
> >
> > (b) if he is included in any of those lists, such details of his inclusion as may be prescribed, including—
> > > (i) in the case of the 1988 Act list, the grounds on which he is so included; or
> > > (ii) in the case of the 1996 Act list, the grounds on which he was disqualified under section 470 or 471.'

(2) In subsection (6A) of section 115 of that Act (enhanced criminal record certificates), for the words from 'in the list' to the end there shall be substituted 'in—

> > (i) the list kept under section 1 of the Protection of Children Act 1999;
> > (ii) the list kept for the purposes of regulations made under section 218(6) of the Education Reform Act 1988 ('the 1988 Act list'); or
> > (iii) any list kept by the Secretary of State or the National Assembly for Wales of persons disqualified under section 470 or 471 of the Education Act 1996 ('the 1996 Act list'); and
>
> (b) if he is included in any of those lists, such details of his inclusion as may be prescribed, including—
> > (i) in the case of the 1988 Act list, the grounds on which he is so included; or
> > (ii) in the case of the 1996 Act list, the grounds on which he was disqualified under section 470 or 471.'

Note. 18 March 2002 (SI 2002 No 629, art 2(2)(a)).

General

103 Temporary provision for access to lists—(1) Any person seeking to ascertain whether a relevant individual is included in—

> (a) the list kept under section 1 of the 1999 Act;
> (b) the list kept for the purposes of regulations made under section 218(6) of the Education Reform Act 1988; or
> (c) any list kept by the Secretary of State or the Assembly of persons disqualified under section 470 or 471 of the Education Act 1996,

shall be entitled to that information on making, before the relevant commencement, an application for the purpose to the Secretary of State.

(2) In this section 'relevant individual' means—

> (a) in relation to a person who carries on an employment agency, an individual with whom he proposes to do business or an individual of any other prescribed description;
> (b) in relation to any other person, an individual to whom he proposes to offer, or whom he proposes to supply for employment in, a child care position or an individual of any other prescribed description.

(3) The relevant commencement is—

> (a) for applications relating to the list mentioned in subsection (1)(a) or (b), the commencement of section 8 of the 1999 Act; and
> (b) for applications relating to the list mentioned in subsection (1)(c), the commencement of section 102.

(4) Paragraphs (b) and (c) of subsection (1) are without prejudice to any right conferred otherwise than by virtue of those provisions.

Note. 2 October 2000 (SI 2000 No 2544).

104 Suitability to adopt a child: searches of lists—(1) The Police Act 1997 shall be amended as follows.

(2)   In section 113 (criminal record certificates)—
  (a) in subsection (3A), after '(3B),' there shall be inserted 'or his suitability to
       adopt a child,'; and
  (b) after subsection (3D) (inserted by section 90) there shall be inserted—
  '(3E) The references in subsections (3A) and (3C) to suitability to be employed,
supplied to work, found work or given work in a position falling within
subsection (3B) or (3D) include references to suitability to be registered—
    (a) under Part II of the Care Standards Act 2000 (establishments and
         agencies);
    (b) under Part IV of that Act (social care workers); or
    (c) for child minding or providing day care under Part XA of the Children
         Act 1989, or under section 71 of that Act or Article 118 of the Children
         (Northern Ireland) Order 1995 (child minding and day care).'
  (3) In section 115 (enhanced criminal record certificates)—
    (a) in subsection (5)—
       (i)   after paragraph (e) there shall be inserted—
    *'(ea) registration under Part II of the Care Standards Act 2000 (establishments and
          agencies);*
    (eb) registration under Part IV of that Act (social care workers);'; and
       (ii) after paragraph (g) there shall be inserted—
    *'(h) a decision made by an adoption agency within the meaning of section 11 of the
          Adoption Act 1976 as to a person's suitability to adopt a child.'; and*
  (b) in subsection (6A), after '113,' there shall be inserted 'or his suitability to
       adopt a child,'.

Note. Sub-s (1) (for certain purposes): 18 March 2002 (SI 2002 No 629); (for certain
purposes): 1 April 2002 (SI 2002 No 629) (in relation to Wales for certain purposes): 1 April
2003 (SI 2003 No 501). Sub-s (2)(a), (3)(a)(ii), (b): 18 March 2002 (SI 2002 No 629). Sub-s
2(b) (in so far as it inserts the Police Act 1997, s 113(3E)(a): 1 April 2002 (SI 2002 No 629).
Sub-s (2)(b) (in relation to Wales in so far as it inserts the Police Act 1997, s 113(3E)(b): 1
April 2003 (SI 2003 No 501). Sub-s 2(b) (in so far as it inserts the Police Act 1997, s
113(3E)(c): 18 March 2002 (SI 2002 No 629). Sub-s (3)(a)(i) (in so far as it inserts the Police
Act 1997, s 115(5)(ea): 1 April 2002 (SI 2002 No 629). Sub-s (3)(a)(i) (in relation to Wales in
so far as it inserts the Police Act 1997, s 115(5)(eb): 1 April 2003 (SI 2002 No 501).
   Sub-s (3): para (a) repealed by the Criminal Justice Act 2003, s 332, Sch 37, Pt 11 as from a
date to be appointed.

CRIMINAL JUSTICE AND COURT SERVICES ACT 2000
(2000 c 43)

An Act to establish a National Probation Service for England and Wales and a
   Children and Family Court Advisory and Support Service; to make further
   provision for the protection of children; to make further provision about
   dealing with persons suspected of, charged with or convicted of offences; to
   amend the law relating to access to information held under Part III of the Road
   Traffic Act 1988; and for connected purposes.

[30 November 2000]

*   *   *   *   *

CHAPTER II
CHILDREN AND FAMILY COURT ADVISORY AND SUPPORT SERVICE

11 Establishment of the Service—(1) There shall be a body corporate to be
known as the Children and Family Court Advisory and Support Service (referred
to in this Part as the Service) which is to exercise the functions conferred on it by
virtue of this Act and any other enactment.

(2) Schedule 2 (which makes provision about the constitution of the Service, its powers and other matters relating to it) is to have effect.

(3) References in this Act or any other enactment to an officer of the Service are references to—

(a) any member of the staff of the Service appointed under paragraph 5(1)(a) of that Schedule, and

(b) any other individual exercising functions of an officer of the Service by virtue of section 13(2) or (4).

Note. 1 April 2001 (SI 2001 No 919).

12 Principal functions of the Service—(1) In respect of family proceedings in which the welfare of children is or may be in question, it is a function of the Service to—

(a) safeguard and promote the welfare of the children,

(b) give advice to any court about any application made to it in such proceedings,

(c) make provision for the children to be represented in such proceedings,

(d) provide information, advice and other support for the children and their families.

(2) The Service must also make provision for the performance of any functions conferred on officers of the Service by virtue of this Act or any other enactment (whether or not they are exercisable for the purposes of the functions conferred on the Service by subsection (1)).

(3) Regulations may provide for grants to be paid by the Service to any person for the purpose of furthering the performance of any of the Service's functions.

(4) The regulations may provide for the grants to be paid on conditions, including conditions—

(a) regulating the purposes for which the grant or any part of it may be used,

(b) requiring repayment to the Service in specified circumstances.

(5) In this section, 'family proceedings' has the same meaning as in the Matrimonial and Family Proceedings Act 1984 and also includes any other proceedings which are family proceedings for the purposes of the Children Act 1989, but—

(a) references to family proceedings include (where the context allows) family proceedings which are proposed or have been concluded, [*and*

(b) *for the purposes of paragraph (a), where a supervision order (within the meaning of the Children Act 1989) is made in family proceedings, the proceedings are not to be treated as concluded until the order has ceased to have effect*].

Note. Sub-s (5) para (b) and the preceding word 'and' omitted by the Adoption and Children Act 2002, s 139(1), (3), Sch 3, para 118, Sch 5 as from 28 November 2003 (SI 2003 No 3079).

13 Other powers of the Service—(1) The Service may make arrangements with organisations under which the organisations perform functions of the Service on its behalf.

(2) Arrangements under subsection (1) may provide for the organisations to designate individuals who may perform functions of officers of the Service.

(3) But the Service may only make an arrangement under subsection (1) if it is of the opinion—

(a) that the functions in question will be performed efficiently and to the required standard, and

(b) that the arrangement represents good value for money.

(4) The Service may make arrangements with individuals under which they may perform functions of officers of the Service.

(5) The Service may commission, or assist the conduct of, research by any person into matters concerned with the exercise of its functions.

Note. 1 April 2001 (SI 2001 No 919).

14 Provision of staff or services to other organisations—(1) The Service may make arrangements with an organisation or individual under which staff of the Service may work for the organisation or individual.

(2) The Service may make arrangements with an organisation or individual under which any services provided to the Service by its staff are also made available to the organisation or individual.

(3) The Service may charge for anything done under arrangements under this section.

Note. 1 April 2001 (SI 2001 No 919).

15 Right to conduct litigation and right of audience—(1) The Service may authorise an officer of the Service of a prescribed description—

(a) to conduct litigation in relation to any proceedings in any court,

(b) to exercise a right of audience in any proceedings before any court,

in the exercise of his functions.

(2) An officer of the Service exercising a right to conduct litigation by virtue of subsection (1)(a) who would otherwise have such a right by virtue of section 28(2)(a) of the Courts and Legal Services Act 1990 is to be treated as having acquired that right solely by virtue of this section.

(3) An officer of the Service exercising a right of audience by virtue of subsection (1)(b) who would otherwise have such a right by virtue of section 27(2)(a) of the Courts and Legal Services Act 1990 is to be treated as having acquired that right solely by virtue of this section.

(4) In this section and section 16, 'right to conduct litigation' and 'right of audience' have the same meanings as in section 119 of the Courts and Legal Services Act 1990.

Note. 1 April 2001 (SI 2001 No 919).

16 Cross-examination of officers of the Service—(1) An officer of the Service may, subject to rules of court, be cross-examined in any proceedings to the same extent as any witness.

(2) But an officer of the Service may not be cross-examined merely because he is exercising a right to conduct litigation or a right of audience granted in accordance with section 15.

Note. 1 April 2001 (SI 2001 No 919).

*   *   *   *   *

CHAPTER III
GENERAL

Provision for the protection of children

24 Provision for the protection of children

(1) The Protection of Children Act 1999 ('the 1999 Act') shall have effect as if the Service were a child care organisation within the meaning of that Act.

(2) Arrangements which the Service makes with an organisation under section 13(1) must provide that, before selecting an individual to be employed under the arrangements in a child care position, the organisation—

(a) must ascertain whether the individual is included in any of the lists mentioned in section 7(1) of the 1999 Act, and

(b) if he is included in any of those lists, must not select him for that employment.

(3) Such arrangements must provide that, if at any time the organisation has power to refer a relevant individual to the Secretary of State under section 2 of the 1999 Act (inclusion in list on reference following disciplinary action etc), the organisation must so refer him.

In this subsection, 'relevant individual' means an individual who is or has been employed in a child care position under the arrangements.

(4) In this section, 'child care position' and 'employment' have the same meanings as in the 1999 Act.

Note. 1 April 2001 (SI 2001 No 919).

*   *   *   *   *

LAND REGISTRATION ACT 2002
(2002 c 9)

An Act to make provision about land registration; and for connected purposes.

[26 February 2002]

PART 3
DISPOSITIONS OF REGISTERED LAND

Powers of disposition

23 Owner's powers—(1) Owner's powers in relation to a registered estate consist of—

   (a) power to make a disposition of any kind permitted by the general law in relation to an interest of that description, other than a mortgage by demise or sub-demise, and

   (b) power to charge the estate at law with the payment of money.

(2) Owner's powers in relation to a registered charge consist of—

   (a) power to make a disposition of any kind permitted by the general law in relation to an interest of that description, other than a legal sub-mortgage, and

   (b) power to charge at law with the payment of money indebtedness secured by the registered charge.

(3) In subsection (2)(a), 'legal sub-mortgage' means—

   (a) a transfer by way of mortgage,

   (b) a sub-mortgage by sub-demise, and

   (c) a charge by way of legal mortgage.

Note. Appointment: 13 October 2003: see SI 2003 No 1725, art 2(1).

24 Right to exercise owner's powers A person is entitled to exercise owner's powers in relation to a registered estate or charge if he is—

   (a) the registered proprietor, or

   (b) entitled to be registered as the proprietor.

Note. Appointment: 13 October 2003: see SI 2003 No 1725, art 2(1).

25 Mode of exercise

(1) A registrable disposition of a registered estate or charge only has effect if it complies with such requirements as to form and content as rules may provide.

(2) Rules may apply subsection (1) to any other kind of disposition which depends for its effect on registration.

Note. Appointment: 13 October 2003: see SI 2003 No 1725, art 2(1).

26 Protection of disponees—(1) Subject to subsection (2), a person's right to exercise owner's powers in relation to a registered estate or charge is to be taken to be free from any limitation affecting the validity of a disposition.

(2) Subsection (1) does not apply to a limitation—

(a) reflected by an entry in the register, or

(b) imposed by, or under, this Act.

(3) This section has effect only for the purpose of preventing the title of a disponee being questioned (and so does not affect the lawfulness of a disposition).

Note. Appointment: 13 October 2003: see SI 2003 No 1725, art 2(1).

Registrable dispositions

27 Dispositions required to be registered—(1) If a disposition of a registered estate or registered charge is required to be completed by registration, it does not operate at law until the relevant registration requirements are met.

(2)   In the case of a registered estate, the following are the dispositions which are required to be completed by registration—

(a) a transfer,

(b) where the registered estate is an estate in land, the grant of a term of years absolute—

  (i) for a term of more than seven years from the date of the grant,

  (ii) to take effect in possession after the end of the period of three months beginning with the date of the grant,

  (iii) under which the right to possession is discontinuous,

  (iv) in pursuance of Part 5 of the Housing Act 1985 (c 68) (the right to buy), or

  (v) in circumstances where section 171A of that Act applies (disposal by landlord which leads to a person no longer being a secure tenant),

(c) where the registered estate is a franchise or manor, the grant of a lease,

(d) the express grant or reservation of an interest of a kind falling within section 1(2)(a) of the Law of Property Act 1925 (c 20), other than one which is capable of being registered under the Commons Registration Act 1965 (c 64),

(e) the express grant or reservation of an interest of a kind falling within section 1(2)(b) or (e) of the Law of Property Act 1925, and

(f) the grant of a legal charge.

(3) In the case of a registered charge, the following are the dispositions which are required to be completed by registration—

(a) a transfer, and

(b) the grant of a sub-charge.

(4) Schedule 2 to this Act (which deals with the relevant registration requirements) has effect.

(5) This section applies to dispositions by operation of law as it applies to other dispositions, but with the exception of the following—

(a) a transfer on the death or bankruptcy of an individual proprietor,

(b) a transfer on the dissolution of a corporate proprietor, and

(c) the creation of a legal charge which is a local land charge.

(6) Rules may make provision about applications to the registrar for the purpose of meeting registration requirements under this section.

(7) In subsection (2)(d), the reference to express grant does not include grant as a result of the operation of section 62 of the Law of Property Act 1925 (c 20).

Note. Appointment: 13 October 2003: see SI 2003 No 1725, art 2(1).

Effect of dispositions on priority

28 Basic rule—(1) Except as provided by sections 29 and 30, the priority of an interest affecting a registered estate or charge is not affected by a disposition of the estate or charge.

(2) It makes no difference for the purposes of this section whether the interest or disposition is registered.

Note. Appointment: 13 October 2003: see SI 2003 No 1725, art 2(1).

29 Effect of registered dispositions: estates

(1) If a registrable disposition of a registered estate is made for valuable consideration, completion of the disposition by registration has the effect of postponing to the interest under the disposition any interest affecting the estate immediately before the disposition whose priority is not protected at the time of registration.

(2) For the purposes of subsection (1), the priority of an interest is protected—

(a) in any case, if the interest—

    (i)   is a registered charge or the subject of a notice in the register,

    (ii) falls within any of the paragraphs of Schedule 3, or

    (iii) appears from the register to be excepted from the effect of registration, and

(b) in the case of a disposition of a leasehold estate, if the burden of the interest is incident to the estate.

(3) Subsection (2)(a)(ii) does not apply to an interest which has been the subject of a notice in the register at any time since the coming into force of this section.

(4) Where the grant of a leasehold estate in land out of a registered estate does not involve a registrable disposition, this section has effect as if—

(a) the grant involved such a disposition, and

(b) the disposition were registered at the time of the grant.

Note. Appointment: 13 October 2003: see SI 2003 No 1725, art 2(1).

30 Effect of registered dispositions: charges—(1) If a registrable disposition of a registered charge is made for valuable consideration, completion of the disposition by registration has the effect of postponing to the interest under the disposition any interest affecting the charge immediately before the disposition whose priority is not protected at the time of registration.

(2) For the purposes of subsection (1), the priority of an interest is protected—

(a) in any case, if the interest—

    (i)   is a registered charge or the subject of a notice in the register,

    (ii) falls within any of the paragraphs of Schedule 3, or

    (iii) appears from the register to be excepted from the effect of registration, and

(b) in the case of a disposition of a charge which relates to a leasehold estate, if the burden of the interest is incident to the estate.

(3) Subsection (2)(a)(ii) does not apply to an interest which has been the subject of a notice in the register at any time since the coming into force of this section.

Note. Appointment: 13 October 2003: see SI 2003 No 1725, art 2(1).

31 Inland Revenue charges The effect of a disposition of a registered estate or charge on a charge under section 237 of the Inheritance Tax Act 1984 (c 51) (charge for unpaid tax) is to be determined, not in accordance with sections 28 to 30 above, but in accordance with sections 237(6) and 238 of that Act (under which a purchaser in good faith for money or money's worth takes free from the charge in the absence of registration).

Note. Appointment: 13 October 2003: see SI 2003 No 1725, art 2(1).

PART 4
NOTICES AND RESTRICTIONS

Notices

32 Nature and effect—(1) A notice is an entry in the register in respect of the burden of an interest affecting a registered estate or charge.

(2) The entry of a notice is to be made in relation to the registered estate or charge affected by the interest concerned.

(3) The fact that an interest is the subject of a notice does not necessarily mean that the interest is valid, but does mean that the priority of the interest, if valid, is protected for the purposes of sections 29 and 30.

Note. Appointment: 13 October 2003: see SI 2003 No 1725, art 2(1).

33 Excluded interests No notice may be entered in the register in respect of any of the following—

  (a) an interest under—
    (i) a trust of land, or
    (ii) a settlement under the Settled Land Act 1925 (c 18),
  (b) a leasehold estate in land which—
    (i) is granted for a term of years of three years or less from the date of the grant, and
    (ii) is not required to be registered,
  (c) a restrictive covenant made between a lessor and lessee, so far as relating to the demised premises,
  (d) an interest which is capable of being registered under the Commons Registration Act 1965 (c 64), and
  (e) an interest in any coal or coal mine, the rights attached to any such interest and the rights of any person under section 38, 49 or 51 of the Coal Industry Act 1994 (c 21).

Note. Appointment: 13 October 2003: see SI 2003 No 1725, art 2(1).

34 Entry on application—(1) A person who claims to be entitled to the benefit of an interest affecting a registered estate or charge may, if the interest is not excluded by section 33, apply to the registrar for the entry in the register of a notice in respect of the interest.

(2) Subject to rules, an application under this section may be for—

  (a) an agreed notice, or
  (b) a unilateral notice.

(3) The registrar may only approve an application for an agreed notice if—

  (a) the applicant is the relevant registered proprietor, or a person entitled to be registered as such proprietor,
  (b) the relevant registered proprietor, or a person entitled to be registered as such proprietor, consents to the entry of the notice, or
  (c) the registrar is satisfied as to the validity of the applicant's claim.

(4) In subsection (3), references to the relevant registered proprietor are to the proprietor of the registered estate or charge affected by the interest to which the application relates.

Note. Appointment: 13 October 2003: see SI 2003 No 1725, art 2(1).

35 Unilateral notices—(1) If the registrar enters a notice in the register in pursuance of an application under section 34(2)(b) ('a unilateral notice'), he must give notice of the entry to—

  (a) the proprietor of the registered estate or charge to which it relates, and
  (b) such other persons as rules may provide.

(2) A unilateral notice must—

  (a) indicate that it is such a notice, and
  (b) identify who is the beneficiary of the notice.

(3) The person shown in the register as the beneficiary of a unilateral notice, or such other person as rules may provide, may apply to the registrar for the removal of the notice from the register.

Note. Appointment: 13 October 2003: see SI 2003 No 1725, art 2(1).

36 Cancellation of unilateral notices—(1) A person may apply to the registrar for the cancellation of a unilateral notice if he is—
   (a) the registered proprietor of the estate or charge to which the notice relates, or
   (b) a person entitled to be registered as the proprietor of that estate or charge.
   (2) Where an application is made under subsection (1), the registrar must give the beneficiary of the notice notice of the application and of the effect of subsection (3).
   (3) If the beneficiary of the notice does not exercise his right to object to the application before the end of such period as rules may provide, the registrar must cancel the notice.
   (4) In this section—
'beneficiary', in relation to a unilateral notice, means the person shown in the register as the beneficiary of the notice, or such other person as rules may provide;
'unilateral notice' means a notice entered in the register in pursuance of an application under section 34(2)(b).
Note. Appointment: 13 October 2003: see SI 2003 No 1725, art 2(1).

37 Unregistered interests—(1) If it appears to the registrar that a registered estate is subject to an unregistered interest which—
   (a) falls within any of the paragraphs of Schedule 1, and
   (b) is not excluded by section 33,
he may enter a notice in the register in respect of the interest.
   (2) The registrar must give notice of an entry under this section to such persons as rules may provide.
Note. Appointment: 13 October 2003: see SI 2003 No 1725, art 2(1).

38 Registrable dispositions Where a person is entered in the register as the proprietor of an interest under a disposition falling within section 27(2)(b) to (e), the registrar must also enter a notice in the register in respect of that interest.
Note. Appointment: 13 October 2003: see SI 2003 No 1725, art 2(1).

39 Supplementary Rules may make provision about the form and content of notices in the register.
Note. Appointment: 13 October 2003: see SI 2003 No 1725, art 2(1).

Restrictions
40 Nature—(1) A restriction is an entry in the register regulating the circumstances in which a disposition of a registered estate or charge may be the subject of an entry in the register.
   (2) A restriction may, in particular—
   (a) prohibit the making of an entry in respect of any disposition, or a disposition of a kind specified in the restriction;
   (b) prohibit the making of an entry—
      (i) indefinitely,
      (ii) for a period specified in the restriction, or
      (iii) until the occurrence of an event so specified.
   (3) Without prejudice to the generality of subsection (2)(b)(iii), the events which may be specified include—
   (a) the giving of notice,
   (b) the obtaining of consent, and
   (c) the making of an order by the court or registrar.
   (4) The entry of a restriction is to be made in relation to the registered estate or charge to which it relates.
Note. Appointment: 13 October 2003: see SI 2003 No 1725, art 2(1).

41 Effect—(1) Where a restriction is entered in the register, no entry in respect of a disposition to which the restriction applies may be made in the register otherwise than in accordance with the terms of the restriction, subject to any order under subsection (2).

(2) The registrar may by order—

(a) disapply a restriction in relation to a disposition specified in the order or dispositions of a kind so specified, or

(b) provide that a restriction has effect, in relation to a disposition specified in the order or dispositions of a kind so specified, with modifications so specified.

(3) The power under subsection (2) is exercisable only on the application of a person who appears to the registrar to have a sufficient interest in the restriction.

Note. Appointment: 13 October 2003: see SI 2003 No 1725, art 2(1).

42 Power of registrar to enter—(1) The registrar may enter a restriction in the register if it appears to him that it is necessary or desirable to do so for the purpose of—

(a) preventing invalidity or unlawfulness in relation to dispositions of a registered estate or charge,

(b) securing that interests which are capable of being overreached on a disposition of a registered estate or charge are overreached, or

(c) protecting a right or claim in relation to a registered estate or charge.

(2) No restriction may be entered under subsection (1)(c) for the purpose of protecting the priority of an interest which is, or could be, the subject of a notice.

(3) The registrar must give notice of any entry made under this section to the proprietor of the registered estate or charge concerned, except where the entry is made in pursuance of an application under section 43.

(4) For the purposes of subsection (1)(c), a person entitled to the benefit of a charging order relating to an interest under a trust shall be treated as having a right or claim in relation to the trust property.

Note. Appointment: 13 October 2003: see SI 2003 No 1725, art 2(1).

43 Applications—(1) A person may apply to the registrar for the entry of a restriction under section 42(1) if—

(a) he is the relevant registered proprietor, or a person entitled to be registered as such proprietor,

(b) the relevant registered proprietor, or a person entitled to be registered as such proprietor, consents to the application, or

(c) he otherwise has a sufficient interest in the making of the entry.

(2) Rules may—

(a) require the making of an application under subsection (1) in such circumstances, and by such person, as the rules may provide;

(b) make provision about the form of consent for the purposes of subsection (1)(b);

(c) provide for classes of person to be regarded as included in subsection (1)(c);

(d) specify standard forms of restriction.

(3) If an application under subsection (1) is made for the entry of a restriction which is not in a form specified under subsection (2)(d), the registrar may only approve the application if it appears to him—

(a) that the terms of the proposed restriction are reasonable, and

(b) that applying the proposed restriction would—

(i) be straightforward, and

(ii) not place an unreasonable burden on him.

(4) In subsection (1), references to the relevant registered proprietor are to the

proprietor of the registered estate or charge to which the application relates.

Note. Appointment: 13 October 2003: see SI 2003 No 1725, art 2(1).

44 Obligatory restrictions—(1) If the registrar enters two or more persons in the register as the proprietor of a registered estate in land, he must also enter in the register such restrictions as rules may provide for the purpose of securing that interests which are capable of being overreached on a disposition of the estate are overreached.

(2) Where under any enactment the registrar is required to enter a restriction without application, the form of the restriction shall be such as rules may provide.

Note. Appointment: 13 October 2003: see SI 2003 No 1725, art 2(1).

45 Notifiable applications—(1) Where an application under section 43(1) is notifiable, the registrar must give notice of the application, and of the right to object to it, to—

(a) the proprietor of the registered estate or charge to which it relates, and

(b) such other persons as rules may provide.

(2) The registrar may not determine an application to which subsection (1) applies before the end of such period as rules may provide, unless the person, or each of the persons, notified under that subsection has exercised his right to object to the application or given the registrar notice that he does not intend to do so.

(3) For the purposes of this section, an application under section 43(1) is notifiable unless it is—

(a) made by or with the consent of the proprietor of the registered estate or charge to which the application relates, or a person entitled to be registered as such proprietor,

(b) made in pursuance of rules under section 43(2)(a), or

(c) an application for the entry of a restriction reflecting a limitation under an order of the court or registrar, or an undertaking given in place of such an order.

Note. Appointment: 13 October 2003: see SI 2003 No 1725, art 2(1).

46 Power of court to order entry—(1) If it appears to the court that it is necessary or desirable to do so for the purpose of protecting a right or claim in relation to a registered estate or charge, it may make an order requiring the registrar to enter a restriction in the register.

(2) No order under this section may be made for the purpose of protecting the priority of an interest which is, or could be, the subject of a notice.

(3) The court may include in an order under this section a direction that an entry made in pursuance of the order is to have overriding priority.

(4) If an order under this section includes a direction under subsection (3), the registrar must make such entry in the register as rules may provide.

(5) The court may make the exercise of its power under subsection (3) subject to such terms and conditions as it thinks fit.

Note. Appointment: 13 October 2003: see SI 2003 No 1725, art 2(1).

PART 12
MISCELLANEOUS AND GENERAL

Supplementary

132 General interpretation—(1) In this Act—

'adjudicator' means the Adjudicator to Her Majesty's Land Registry;

'caution against first registration' means a caution lodged under section 15;

'cautions register' means the register kept under section 19(1);

'charge' means any mortgage, charge or lien for securing money or money's worth;

'demesne land' means land belonging to Her Majesty in right of the Crown which is not held for an estate in fee simple absolute in possession;

'land' includes—
  (a) buildings and other structures,
  (b) land covered with water, and
  (c) mines and minerals, whether or not held with the surface;

'land registration rules' means any rules under this Act, other than rules under section 93, Part 11, section 121 or paragraph 1, 2 or 3 of Schedule 5;

'legal estate' has the same meaning as in the Law of Property Act 1925 (c 20);

'legal mortgage' has the same meaning as in the Law of Property Act 1925;

'mines and minerals' includes any strata or seam of minerals or substances in or under any land, and powers of working and getting any such minerals or substances;

'registrar' means the Chief Land Registrar;

'register' means the register of title, except in the context of cautions against first registration;

'registered' means entered in the register;

'registered charge' means a charge the title to which is entered in the register;

'registered estate' means a legal estate the title to which is entered in the register, other than a registered charge;

'registered land' means a registered estate or registered charge;

'registrable disposition' means a disposition which is required to be completed by registration under section 27;

'requirement of registration' means the requirement of registration under section 4;

'sub-charge' means a charge under section 23(2)(b);

'term of years absolute' has the same meaning as in the Law of Property Act 1925 (c 20);

'valuable consideration' does not include marriage consideration or a nominal consideration in money.

(2) In subsection (1), in the definition of 'demesne land', the reference to land belonging to Her Majesty does not include land in relation to which a freehold estate in land has determined, but in relation to which there has been no act of entry or management by the Crown.

(3) In this Act—
  (a) references to the court are to the High Court or a county court,
  (b) references to an interest affecting an estate or charge are to an adverse right affecting the title to the estate or charge, and
  (c) references to the right to object to an application to the registrar are to the right under section 73.

Note Appointment: 4 April 2003: see SI 2003 No 935, art 2.

PROCEEDS OF CRIME ACT 2002
(2002 c 29)

An Act to establish the Assets Recovery Agency and make provision about the appointment of its Director and his functions (including Revenue functions), to provide for confiscation orders in relation to persons who benefit from criminal conduct and for restraint orders to prohibit dealing with property, to allow the recovery of property which is or represents property obtained through unlawful conduct or which is intended to be used in unlawful conduct, to make provision about money laundering, to make provision about investigations relating to benefit from criminal conduct or to property which is or represents property obtained through unlawful conduct or to money laundering, to make provision to give effect to overseas requests and orders made where property is found or believed to be obtained through criminal conduct, and for connected purposes.

[24 July 2002]

*   *   *   *   *

PART 7
MONEY LAUNDERING

Offences

327 Concealing etc—(1) A person commits an offence if he—
(a) conceals criminal property;
(b) disguises criminal property;
(c) converts criminal property;
(d) transfers criminal property;
(e) removes criminal property from England and Wales or from Scotland or from Northern Ireland.
(2) But a person does not commit such an offence if—
(a) he makes an authorised disclosure under section 338 and (if the disclosure is made before he does the act mentioned in subsection (1)) he has the appropriate consent;
(b) he intended to make such a disclosure but had a reasonable excuse for not doing so;
(c) the act he does is done in carrying out a function he has relating to the enforcement of any provision of this Act or of any other enactment relating to criminal conduct or benefit from criminal conduct.
(3) Concealing or disguising criminal property includes concealing or disguising its nature, source, location, disposition, movement or ownership or any rights with respect to it.

Note. 24 February 2003: see SI 2003 No 120, art 2(1), Schedule; for transitional provisions and savings see arts 1(2)(d), (e), 3 thereof (as amended by SI 2003 No 333, art 14).

328 Arrangements—(1) A person commits an offence if he enters into or becomes concerned in an arrangement which he knows or suspects facilitates (by whatever means) the acquisition, retention, use or control of criminal property by or on behalf of another person.
(2) But a person does not commit such an offence if—
(a) he makes an authorised disclosure under section 338 and (if the disclosure is made before he does the act mentioned in subsection (1)) he has the appropriate consent;
(b) he intended to make such a disclosure but had a reasonable excuse for not doing so;

(c) the act he does is done in carrying out a function he has relating to the enforcement of any provision of this Act or of any other enactment relating to criminal conduct or benefit from criminal conduct.

Note. 24 February 2003: see SI 2003 No 120, art 2(1), Schedule; for transitional provisions and savings see arts 1(2)(d), (e), 3 thereof (as amended by SI 2003 No 333, art 14).

329 Acquisition, use and possession—(1) A person commits an offence if he—
(a) acquires criminal property;
(b) uses criminal property;
(c) has possession of criminal property.
(2) But a person does not commit such an offence if—
(a) he makes an authorised disclosure under section 338 and (if the disclosure is made before he does the act mentioned in subsection (1)) he has the appropriate consent;
(b) he intended to make such a disclosure but had a reasonable excuse for not doing so;
(c) he acquired or used or had possession of the property for adequate consideration;
(d) the act he does is done in carrying out a function he has relating to the enforcement of any provision of this Act or of any other enactment relating to criminal conduct or benefit from criminal conduct.
(3) For the purposes of this section—
(a) a person acquires property for inadequate consideration if the value of the consideration is significantly less than the value of the property;
(b) a person uses or has possession of property for inadequate consideration if the value of the consideration is significantly less than the value of the use or possession;
(c) the provision by a person of goods or services which he knows or suspects may help another to carry out criminal conduct is not consideration.

Note. 24 February 2003: see SI 2003 No 120, art 2(1), Schedule; for transitional provisions and savings see arts 1(2)(d), (e), 3 thereof (as amended by SI 2003 No 333, art 14).

330 Failure to disclose: regulated sector—(1) A person commits an offence if each of the following three conditions is satisfied.
(2) The first condition is that he—
(a) knows or suspects, or
(b) has reasonable grounds for knowing or suspecting,
that another person is engaged in money laundering.
(3) The second condition is that the information or other matter—
(a) on which his knowledge or suspicion is based, or
(b) which gives reasonable grounds for such knowledge or suspicion,
came to him in the course of a business in the regulated sector.
(4) The third condition is that he does not make the required disclosure as soon as is practicable after the information or other matter comes to him.
(5) The required disclosure is a disclosure of the information or other matter—
(a) to a nominated officer or a person authorised for the purposes of this Part by the Director General of the National Criminal Intelligence Service;
(b) in the form and manner (if any) prescribed for the purposes of this subsection by order under section 339.
(6) But a person does not commit an offence under this section if—
(a) he has a reasonable excuse for not disclosing the information or other matter;
(b) he is a professional legal adviser and the information or other matter came to him in privileged circumstances;
(c) subsection (7) applies to him.

(7) This subsection applies to a person if—

(a) he does not know or suspect that another person is engaged in money laundering, and

(b) he has not been provided by his employer with such training as is specified by the Secretary of State by order for the purposes of this section.

(8) In deciding whether a person committed an offence under this section the court must consider whether he followed any relevant guidance which was at the time concerned—

(a) issued by a supervisory authority or any other appropriate body,

(b) approved by the Treasury, and

(c) published in a manner it approved as appropriate in its opinion to bring the guidance to the attention of persons likely to be affected by it.

(9) A disclosure to a nominated officer is a disclosure which—

(a) is made to a person nominated by the alleged offender's employer to receive disclosures under this section, and

(b) is made in the course of the alleged offender's employment and in accordance with the procedure established by the employer for the purpose.

(10) Information or other matter comes to a professional legal adviser in privileged circumstances if it is communicated or given to him—

(a) by (or by a representative of) a client of his in connection with the giving by the adviser of legal advice to the client,

(b) by (or by a representative of) a person seeking legal advice from the adviser, or

(c) by a person in connection with legal proceedings or contemplated legal proceedings.

(11) But subsection (10) does not apply to information or other matter which is communicated or given with the intention of furthering a criminal purpose.

(12) Schedule 9 has effect for the purpose of determining what is—

(a) a business in the regulated sector;

(b) a supervisory authority.

(13) An appropriate body is any body which regulates or is representative of any trade, profession, business or employment carried on by the alleged offender.

Note. 24 February 2003: see SI 2003 No 120, art 2(1), Schedule; for transitional provisions and savings see arts 1(2)(b), (c), 4 thereof.

331 Failure to disclose: nominated officers in the regulated sector—(1) A person nominated to receive disclosures under section 330 commits an offence if the conditions in subsections (2) to (4) are satisfied.

(2) The first condition is that he—

(a) knows or suspects, or

(b) has reasonable grounds for knowing or suspecting,

that another person is engaged in money laundering.

(3) The second condition is that the information or other matter—

(a) on which his knowledge or suspicion is based, or

(b) which gives reasonable grounds for such knowledge or suspicion,

came to him in consequence of a disclosure made under section 330.

(4) The third condition is that he does not make the required disclosure as soon as is practicable after the information or other matter comes to him.

(5) The required disclosure is a disclosure of the information or other matter—

(a) to a person authorised for the purposes of this Part by the Director General of the National Criminal Intelligence Service;

(b) in the form and manner (if any) prescribed for the purposes of this subsection by order under section 339.

(6) But a person does not commit an offence under this section if he has a reasonable excuse for not disclosing the information or other matter.

(7) In deciding whether a person committed an offence under this section the court must consider whether he followed any relevant guidance which was at the time concerned—

(a) issued by a supervisory authority or any other appropriate body,

(b) approved by the Treasury, and

(c) published in a manner it approved as appropriate in its opinion to bring the guidance to the attention of persons likely to be affected by it.

(8) Schedule 9 has effect for the purpose of determining what is a supervisory authority.

(9) An appropriate body is a body which regulates or is representative of a trade, profession, business or employment.

Note. 24 February 2003: see SI 2003 No 120, art 2(1), Schedule; for transitional provisions and savings see arts 1(2)(b), (c), 4 thereof.

332 Failure to disclose: other nominated officers—(1) A person nominated to receive disclosures under section 337 or 338 commits an offence if the conditions in subsections (2) to (4) are satisfied.

(2) The first condition is that he knows or suspects that another person is engaged in money laundering.

(3) The second condition is that the information or other matter on which his knowledge or suspicion is based came to him in consequence of a disclosure made under section 337 or 338.

(4) The third condition is that he does not make the required disclosure as soon as is practicable after the information or other matter comes to him.

(5) The required disclosure is a disclosure of the information or other matter—

(a) to a person authorised for the purposes of this Part by the Director General of the National Criminal Intelligence Service;

(b) in the form and manner (if any) prescribed for the purposes of this subsection by order under section 339.

(6) But a person does not commit an offence under this section if he has a reasonable excuse for not disclosing the information or other matter.

Note. 24 February 2003: see SI 2003 No 120, art 2(1), Schedule; for transitional provisions and savings see arts 1(2)(b), (c), 4 thereof.

333 Tipping off—(1) A person commits an offence if—

(a) he knows or suspects that a disclosure falling within section 337 or 338 has been made, and

(b) he makes a disclosure which is likely to prejudice any investigation which might be conducted following the disclosure referred to in paragraph (a).

(2) But a person does not commit an offence under subsection (1) if—

(a) he did not know or suspect that the disclosure was likely to be prejudicial as mentioned in subsection (1);

(b) the disclosure is made in carrying out a function he has relating to the enforcement of any provision of this Act or of any other enactment relating to criminal conduct or benefit from criminal conduct;

(c) he is a professional legal adviser and the disclosure falls within subsection (3).

(3) A disclosure falls within this subsection if it is a disclosure—

(a) to (or to a representative of) a client of the professional legal adviser in connection with the giving by the adviser of legal advice to the client, or

(b) to any person in connection with legal proceedings or contemplated legal proceedings.

(4) But a disclosure does not fall within subsection (3) if it is made with the intention of furthering a criminal purpose.

Note. 24 February 2003: see SI 2003 No 120, art 2(1), Schedule; for transitional provisions and savings see arts 1(2)(b)–(e), 3, 4, thereof (as amended by SI 2003 No 333, art 14).

334 Penalties—(1) A person guilty of an offence under section 327, 328 or 329 is liable—
  (a) on summary conviction, to imprisonment for a term not exceeding six months or to a fine not exceeding the statutory maximum or to both, or
  (b) on conviction on indictment, to imprisonment for a term not exceeding 14 years or to a fine or to both.
  (2) A person guilty of an offence under section 330, 331, 332 or 333 is liable—
  (a) on summary conviction, to imprisonment for a term not exceeding six months or to a fine not exceeding the statutory maximum or to both, or
  (b) on conviction on indictment, to imprisonment for a term not exceeding five years or to a fine or to both.

Note. 24 February 2003: see SI 2003 No 120, art 2(1), Schedule; for transitional provisions and savings see arts 1(2)(b)–(e), 3, 4, thereof (as amended by SI 2003 No 333, art 14).

Consent

335 Appropriate consent—(1) The appropriate consent is—
  (a) the consent of a nominated officer to do a prohibited act if an authorised disclosure is made to the nominated officer;
  (b) the consent of a constable to do a prohibited act if an authorised disclosure is made to a constable;
  (c) the consent of a customs officer to do a prohibited act if an authorised disclosure is made to a customs officer.
  (2) A person must be treated as having the appropriate consent if—
  (a) he makes an authorised disclosure to a constable or a customs officer, and
  (b) the condition in subsection (3) or the condition in subsection (4) is satisfied.
  (3) The condition is that before the end of the notice period he does not receive notice from a constable or customs officer that consent to the doing of the act is refused.
  (4) The condition is that—
  (a) before the end of the notice period he receives notice from a constable or customs officer that consent to the doing of the act is refused, and
  (b) the moratorium period has expired.
  (5) The notice period is the period of seven working days starting with the first working day after the person makes the disclosure.
  (6) The moratorium period is the period of 31 days starting with the day on which the person receives notice that consent to the doing of the act is refused.
  (7) A working day is a day other than a Saturday, a Sunday, Christmas Day, Good Friday or a day which is a bank holiday under the Banking and Financial Dealings Act 1971 (c 80) in the part of the United Kingdom in which the person is when he makes the disclosure.
  (8) References to a prohibited act are to an act mentioned in section 327(1), 328(1) or 329(1) (as the case may be).
  (9) A nominated officer is a person nominated to receive disclosures under section 338.
  (10) Subsections (1) to (4) apply for the purposes of this Part.

Note. 24 February 2003: see SI 2003 No 120, art 2(1), Schedule; for transitional provisions and savings see arts 1(2)(b)–(e), 3, 4, thereof (as amended by SI 2003 No 333, art 14).

336 Nominated officer: consent—(1) A nominated officer must not give the appropriate consent to the doing of a prohibited act unless the condition in subsection (2), the condition in subsection (3) or the condition in subsection (4) is satisfied.

(2) The condition is that—

(a) he makes a disclosure that property is criminal property to a person authorised for the purposes of this Part by the Director General of the National Criminal Intelligence Service, and

(b) such a person gives consent to the doing of the act.

(3) The condition is that—

(a) he makes a disclosure that property is criminal property to a person authorised for the purposes of this Part by the Director General of the National Criminal Intelligence Service, and

(b) before the end of the notice period he does not receive notice from such a person that consent to the doing of the act is refused.

(4) The condition is that—

(a) he makes a disclosure that property is criminal property to a person authorised for the purposes of this Part by the Director General of the National Criminal Intelligence Service,

(b) before the end of the notice period he receives notice from such a person that consent to the doing of the act is refused, and

(c) the moratorium period has expired.

(5) A person who is a nominated officer commits an offence if—

(a) he gives consent to a prohibited act in circumstances where none of the conditions in subsections (2), (3) and (4) is satisfied, and

(b) he knows or suspects that the act is a prohibited act.

(6) A person guilty of such an offence is liable—

(a) on summary conviction, to imprisonment for a term not exceeding six months or to a fine not exceeding the statutory maximum or to both, or

(b) on conviction on indictment, to imprisonment for a term not exceeding five years or to a fine or to both.

(7) The notice period is the period of seven working days starting with the first working day after the nominated officer makes the disclosure.

(8) The moratorium period is the period of 31 days starting with the day on which the nominated officer is given notice that consent to the doing of the act is refused.

(9) A working day is a day other than a Saturday, a Sunday, Christmas Day, Good Friday or a day which is a bank holiday under the Banking and Financial Dealings Act 1971 (c 80) in the part of the United Kingdom in which the nominated officer is when he gives the appropriate consent.

(10) References to a prohibited act are to an act mentioned in section 327(1), 328(1) or 329(1) (as the case may be).

(11) A nominated officer is a person nominated to receive disclosures under section 338.

Note. 24 February 2003: see SI 2003 No 120, art 2(1), Schedule; for transitional provisions and savings see arts 1(2)(b)–(e), 3, 4, thereof (as amended by SI 2003 No 333, art 14).

Disclosures

337 Protected disclosures—(1) A disclosure which satisfies the following three conditions is not to be taken to breach any restriction on the disclosure of information (however imposed).

(2) The first condition is that the information or other matter disclosed came to the person making the disclosure (the discloser) in the course of his trade, profession, business or employment.

(3) The second condition is that the information or other matter—

(a) causes the discloser to know or suspect, or

(b) gives him reasonable grounds for knowing or suspecting,

that another person is engaged in money laundering.

(4) The third condition is that the disclosure is made to a constable, a customs officer or a nominated officer as soon as is practicable after the information or other matter comes to the discloser.

(5) A disclosure to a nominated officer is a disclosure which—

(a) is made to a person nominated by the discloser's employer to receive disclosures under this section, and

(b) is made in the course of the discloser's employment and in accordance with the procedure established by the employer for the purpose.

Note. 24 February 2003: see SI 2003 No 120, art 2(1), Schedule; for transitional provisions and savings see arts 1(2)(b)–(e), 3, 4, thereof (as amended by SI 2003 No 333, art 14).

338 Authorised disclosures—(1) For the purposes of this Part a disclosure is authorised if—

(a) it is a disclosure to a constable, a customs officer or a nominated officer by the alleged offender that property is criminal property,

(b) it is made in the form and manner (if any) prescribed for the purposes of this subsection by order under section 339, and

(c) the first or second condition set out below is satisfied.

(2) The first condition is that the disclosure is made before the alleged offender does the prohibited act.

(3) The second condition is that—

(a) the disclosure is made after the alleged offender does the prohibited act,

(b) there is a good reason for his failure to make the disclosure before he did the act, and

(c) the disclosure is made on his own initiative and as soon as it is practicable for him to make it.

(4) An authorised disclosure is not to be taken to breach any restriction on the disclosure of information (however imposed).

(5) A disclosure to a nominated officer is a disclosure which—

(a) is made to a person nominated by the alleged offender's employer to receive authorised disclosures, and

(b) is made in the course of the alleged offender's employment and in accordance with the procedure established by the employer for the purpose.

(6) References to the prohibited act are to an act mentioned in section 327(1), 328(1) or 329(1) (as the case may be).

Note. 24 February 2003: see SI 2003 No 120, art 2(1), Schedule; for transitional provisions and savings see arts 1(2)(b)–(e), 3, 4, thereof (as amended by SI 2003 No 333, art 14).

339 Form and manner of disclosures—(1) The Secretary of State may by order prescribe the form and manner in which a disclosure under section 330, 331, 332 or 338 must be made.

(2) An order under this section may also provide that the form may include a request to the discloser to provide additional information specified in the form.

(3) The additional information must be information which is necessary to enable the person to whom the disclosure is made to decide whether to start a money laundering investigation.

(4) A disclosure made in pursuance of a request under subsection (2) is not to be taken to breach any restriction on the disclosure of information (however imposed).

(5) The discloser is the person making a disclosure mentioned in subsection (1).

(6) Money laundering investigation must be construed in accordance with section 341(4).

(7) Subsection (2) does not apply to a disclosure made to a nominated officer.

Note. 24 February 2003: see SI 2003 No 120, art 2(1), Schedule; for transitional provisions and savings see arts 1(2)(b)–(e), 3, 4, thereof (as amended by SI 2003 No 333, art 14).

Interpretation

340 Interpretation—(1) This section applies for the purposes of this Part.

(2) Criminal conduct is conduct which—

(a) constitutes an offence in any part of the United Kingdom, or

(b) would constitute an offence in any part of the United Kingdom if it occurred there.

(3) Property is criminal property if—

(a) it constitutes a person's benefit from criminal conduct or it represents such a benefit (in whole or part and whether directly or indirectly), and

(b) the alleged offender knows or suspects that it constitutes or represents such a benefit.

(4) It is immaterial—

(a) who carried out the conduct;

(b) who benefited from it;

(c) whether the conduct occurred before or after the passing of this Act.

(5) A person benefits from conduct if he obtains property as a result of or in connection with the conduct.

(6) If a person obtains a pecuniary advantage as a result of or in connection with conduct, he is to be taken to obtain as a result of or in connection with the conduct a sum of money equal to the value of the pecuniary advantage.

(7) References to property or a pecuniary advantage obtained in connection with conduct include references to property or a pecuniary advantage obtained in both that connection and some other.

(8) If a person benefits from conduct his benefit is the property obtained as a result of or in connection with the conduct.

(9) Property is all property wherever situated and includes—

(a) money;

(b) all forms of property, real or personal, heritable or moveable;

(c) things in action and other intangible or incorporeal property.

(10) The following rules apply in relation to property—

(a) property is obtained by a person if he obtains an interest in it;

(b) references to an interest, in relation to land in England and Wales or Northern Ireland, are to any legal estate or equitable interest or power;

(c) references to an interest, in relation to land in Scotland, are to any estate, interest, servitude or other heritable right in or over land, including a heritable security;

(d) references to an interest, in relation to property other than land, include references to a right (including a right to possession).

(11) Money laundering is an act which—

(a) constitutes an offence under section 327, 328 or 329,

(b) constitutes an attempt, conspiracy or incitement to commit an offence specified in paragraph (a),

(c) constitutes aiding, abetting, counselling or procuring the commission of an offence specified in paragraph (a), or

(d) would constitute an offence specified in paragraph (a), (b) or (c) if done in the United Kingdom.

(12) For the purposes of a disclosure to a nominated officer—

(a) references to a person's employer include any body, association or organisation (including a voluntary organisation) in connection with whose activities the person exercises a function (whether or not for gain or reward), and

(b) references to employment must be construed accordingly.

(13) References to a constable include references to a person authorised for the purposes of this Part by the Director General of the National Criminal Intelligence Service.

Note. 24 February 2003: see SI 2003 No 120, art 2(1), Schedule; for transitional provisions and savings see arts 1(2)(b)–(e), 3, 4, thereof (as amended by SI 2003 No 333, art 14).

ADOPTION AND CHILDREN ACT 2002

(2002 c 38)

An Act to restate and amend the law relating to adoption; to make further amendments of the law relating to children; to amend section 93 of the Local Government Act 2000; and for connected purposes.

[7 November 2002]

PART 1
ADOPTION

CHAPTER 1
INTRODUCTORY

CHAPTER 2
THE ADOPTION SERVICE

The Adoption Service

Regulations

Supplemental

CHAPTER 3
PLACEMENT FOR ADOPTION AND ADOPTION ORDERS

Placement of children by adoption agency for adoption

PART 1
ADOPTION

CHAPTER 1
INTRODUCTORY

1 Considerations applying to the exercise of powers—(1) This section applies whenever a court or adoption agency is coming to a decision relating to the adoption of a child.

(2) The paramount consideration of the court or adoption agency must be the child's welfare, throughout his life.

(3) The court or adoption agency must at all times bear in mind that, in general, any delay in coming to the decision is likely to prejudice the child's welfare.

(4) The court or adoption agency must have regard to the following matters (among others)—

(a) the child's ascertainable wishes and feelings regarding the decision (considered in the light of the child's age and understanding),
(b) the child's particular needs,
(c) the likely effect on the child (throughout his life) of having ceased to be a member of the original family and become an adopted person,
(d) the child's age, sex, background and any of the child's characteristics which the court or agency considers relevant,
(e) any harm (within the meaning of the Children Act 1989 (c 41)) which the child has suffered or is at risk of suffering,

(f) the relationship which the child has with relatives, and with any other person in relation to whom the court or agency considers the relationship to be relevant, including—

    (i) the likelihood of any such relationship continuing and the value to the child of its doing so,

    (ii) the ability and willingness of any of the child's relatives, or of any such person, to provide the child with a secure environment in which the child can develop, and otherwise to meet the child's needs,

    (iii) the wishes and feelings of any of the child's relatives, or of any such person, regarding the child.

(5) In placing the child for adoption, the adoption agency must give due consideration to the child's religious persuasion, racial origin and cultural and linguistic background.

(6) The court or adoption agency must always consider the whole range of powers available to it in the child's case (whether under this Act or the Children Act 1989); and the court must not make any order under this Act unless it considers that making the order would be better for the child than not doing so.

(7) In this section, 'coming to a decision relating to the adoption of a child', in relation to a court, includes—

(a) coming to a decision in any proceedings where the orders that might be made by the court include an adoption order (or the revocation of such an order), a placement order (or the revocation of such an order) or an order under section 26 (or the revocation or variation of such an order),

(b) coming to a decision about granting leave in respect of any action (other than the initiation of proceedings in any court) which may be taken by an adoption agency or individual under this Act,

but does not include coming to a decision about granting leave in any other circumstances.

(8) For the purposes of this section—

(a) references to relationships are not confined to legal relationships,

(b) references to a relative, in relation to a child, include the child's mother and father.

CHAPTER 2
THE ADOPTION SERVICE

The Adoption Service

2 Basic definitions—(1) The services maintained by local authorities under section 3(1) may be collectively referred to as 'the Adoption Service', and a local authority or registered adoption society may be referred to as an adoption agency.

(2) In this Act, 'registered adoption society' means a voluntary organisation which is an adoption society registered under Part 2 of the Care Standards Act 2000 (c 14); but in relation to the provision of any facility of the Adoption Service, references to a registered adoption society or to an adoption agency do not include an adoption society which is not registered in respect of that facility.

(3) A registered adoption society is to be treated as registered in respect of any facility of the Adoption Service unless it is a condition of its registration that it does not provide that facility.

(4) No application for registration under Part 2 of the Care Standards Act 2000 may be made in respect of an adoption society which is an unincorporated body.

(5) In this Act—

'the 1989 Act' means the Children Act 1989 (c 41),

'adoption society' means a body whose functions consist of or include making arrangements for the adoption of children, 'voluntary organisation' means a body other than a public or local authority the activities of which are not carried on for profit.

(6) In this Act, 'adoption support services' means—

(a) counselling, advice and information, and

(b) any other services prescribed by regulations,

in relation to adoption.

(7) The power to make regulations under subsection (6)(b) is to be exercised so as to secure that local authorities provide financial support.

(8) In this Chapter, references to adoption are to the adoption of persons, wherever they may be habitually resident, effected under the law of any country or territory, whether within or outside the British Islands.

3 Maintenance of Adoption Service—(1) Each local authority must continue to maintain within their area a service designed to meet the needs, in relation to adoption, of—

(a) children who may be adopted, their parents and guardians,

(b) persons wishing to adopt a child, and

(c) adopted persons, their parents, natural parents and former guardians;

and for that purpose must provide the requisite facilities.

(2) Those facilities must include making, and participating in, arrangements—

(a) for the adoption of children, and

(b) for the provision of adoption support services.

(3) As part of the service, the arrangements made for the purposes of subsection (2)(b)—

(a) must extend to the provision of adoption support services to persons who are within a description prescribed by regulations,

(b) may extend to the provision of those services to other persons.

(4) A local authority may provide any of the requisite facilities by securing their provision by—

(a) registered adoption societies, or

(b) other persons who are within a description prescribed by regulations of persons who may provide the facilities in question.

(5) The facilities of the service must be provided in conjunction with the local authority's other social services and with registered adoption societies in their area, so that help may be given in a co-ordinated manner without duplication, omission or avoidable delay.

(6) The social services referred to in subsection (5) are the functions of a local authority which are social services functions within the meaning of the Local Authority Social Services Act 1970 (c 42) (which include, in particular, those functions in so far as they relate to children).

4 Assessments etc for adoption support services—(1) A local authority must at the request of—

(a) any of the persons mentioned in paragraphs (a) to (c) of section 3(1), or

(b) any other person who falls within a description prescribed by regulations (subject to subsection (7)(a)),

carry out an assessment of that person's needs for adoption support services.

(2) A local authority may, at the request of any person, carry out an assessment of that person's needs for adoption support services.

(3) A local authority may request the help of the persons mentioned in paragraph (a) or (b) of section 3(4) in carrying out an assessment.

(4) Where, as a result of an assessment, a local authority decide that a person has needs for adoption support services, they must then decide whether to provide any such services to that person.

(5) If—

(a) a local authority decide to provide any adoption support services to a person, and

(b) the circumstances fall within a description prescribed by regulations,

the local authority must prepare a plan in accordance with which adoption support services are to be provided to the person and keep the plan under review.

(6) Regulations may make provision about assessments, preparing and reviewing plans, the provision of adoption support services in accordance with plans and reviewing the provision of adoption support services.

(7) The regulations may in particular make provision—

(a) as to the circumstances in which a person mentioned in paragraph (b) of subsection (1) is to have a right to request an assessment of his needs in accordance with that subsection,

(b) about the type of assessment which, or the way in which an assessment, is to be carried out,

(c) about the way in which a plan is to be prepared,

(d) about the way in which, and time at which, a plan or the provision of adoption support services is to be reviewed,

(e) about the considerations to which a local authority are to have regard in carrying out an assessment or review or preparing a plan,

(f) as to the circumstances in which a local authority may provide adoption support services subject to conditions,

(g) as to the consequences of conditions imposed by virtue of paragraph (f) not being met (including the recovery of any financial support provided by a local authority),

(h) as to the circumstances in which this section may apply to a local authority in respect of persons who are outside that local authority's area,

(i) as to the circumstances in which a local authority may recover from another local authority the expenses of providing adoption support services to any person.

(8) A local authority may carry out an assessment of the needs of any person under this section at the same time as an assessment of his needs is made under any other enactment.

(9) If at any time during the assessment of the needs of any person under this section, it appears to a local authority that—

(a) there may be a need for the provision of services to that person by a Primary Care Trust (in Wales, a Health Authority or Local Health Board), or

(b) there may be a need for the provision to him of any services which fall within the functions of a local education authority (within the meaning of the Education Act 1996 (c 56)),

the local authority must notify that Primary Care Trust, Health Authority, Local Health Board or local education authority.

(10) Where it appears to a local authority that another local authority could, by taking any specified action, help in the exercise of any of their functions under this section, they may request the help of that other local authority, specifying the action in question.

(11) A local authority whose help is so requested must comply with the request if it is consistent with the exercise of their functions.

5 Local authority plans for adoption services—(1) Each local authority must prepare a plan for the provision of the services maintained under section 3(1) and secure that it is published.

(2) The plan must contain information of a description prescribed by regulations (subject to subsection (4)(b)).

(3) The regulations may make provision requiring local authorities—

(a) to review any plan,

(b) in the circumstances prescribed by the regulations, to modify that plan and secure its publication or to prepare a plan in substitution for that plan and secure its publication.

(4) The appropriate Minister may direct—

(a) that a plan is to be included in another document specified in the direction,

(b) that the requirements specified in the direction as to the description of information to be contained in a plan are to have effect in place of the provision made by regulations under subsection (2).

(5) Directions may be given by the appropriate Minister for the purpose of making provision in connection with any duty imposed by virtue of this section including, in particular, provision as to—

(a) the form and manner in which, and the time at which, any plan is to be published,

(b) the description of persons who are to be consulted in the preparation of any plan,

(c) the time at which any plan is to be reviewed.

(6) Subsections (2) to (5) apply in relation to a modified or substituted plan (or further modified or substituted plan) as they apply in relation to a plan prepared under subsection (1).

(7) Directions given under this section may relate—

(a) to a particular local authority,

(b) to any class or description of local authorities, or

(c) except in the case of a direction given under subsection (4)(b), to local authorities generally,

and accordingly different provision may be made in relation to different local authorities or classes or descriptions of local authorities.

6 Arrangements on cancellation of registration Where, by virtue of the cancellation of its registration under Part 2 of the Care Standards Act 2000 (c 14), a body has ceased to be a registered adoption society, the appropriate Minister may direct the body to make such arrangements as to the transfer of its functions relating to children and other transitional matters as seem to him expedient.

7 Inactive or defunct adoption societies etc—(1) This section applies where it appears to the appropriate Minister that—

(a) a body which is or has been a registered adoption society is inactive or defunct, or

(b) a body which has ceased to be a registered adoption society by virtue of the cancellation of its registration under Part 2 of the Care Standards Act 2000 has not made such arrangements for the transfer of its functions relating to children as are specified in a direction given by him.

(2) The appropriate Minister may, in relation to such functions of the society as relate to children, direct what appears to him to be the appropriate local authority to take any such action as might have been taken by the society or by the society jointly with the authority.

(3) A local authority are entitled to take any action which—

(a) apart from this subsection the authority would not be entitled to take, or would not be entitled to take without joining the society in the action, but

(b) they are directed to take under subsection (2).

(4) The appropriate Minister may charge the society for expenses necessarily incurred by him or on his behalf in securing the transfer of its functions relating to children.

(5) Before giving a direction under subsection (2) the appropriate Minister must, if practicable, consult both the society and the authority.

8 Adoption support agencies—(1) In this Act, 'adoption support agency' means an undertaking the purpose of which, or one of the purposes of which, is the provision of adoption support services; but an undertaking is not an adoption support agency—

   (a) merely because it provides information in connection with adoption other than for the purpose mentioned in section 98(1), or

   (b) if it is excepted by virtue of subsection (2).

'Undertaking' has the same meaning as in the Care Standards Act 2000 (c 14).

   (2) The following are excepted—

   (a) a registered adoption society, whether or not the society is registered in respect of the provision of adoption support services,

   (b) a local authority,

   (c) a local education authority (within the meaning of the Education Act 1996 (c 56)),

   (d) a Special Health Authority, Primary Care Trust (in Wales, a Health Authority or Local Health Board) *or NHS trust* [, NHS trust or NHS foundation trust],

   (e) the Registrar General,

   (f) any person, or description of persons, excepted by regulations.

   (3) In section 4 of the Care Standards Act 2000 (basic definitions)—

   (a) after subsection (7) there is inserted—

   '(7A) 'Adoption support agency' has the meaning given by section 8 of the Adoption and Children Act 2002.',

   (b) in subsection (9)(a) (construction of references to descriptions of agencies), for 'or a voluntary adoption agency' there is substituted 'a voluntary adoption agency or an adoption support agency'.

Note Sub-s (2): in para (d) words in square brackets substituted by the Health and Social Care (Community Health and Standards) Act 2003, s 34, Sch 4, paras 125, 126 as from 1 April 2004.

Regulations

9 General power to regulate adoption etc agencies—(1) Regulations may make provision for any purpose relating to—

   (a) the exercise by local authorities or voluntary adoption agencies of their functions in relation to adoption, or

   (b) the exercise by adoption support agencies of their functions in relation to adoption.

   (2) The extent of the power to make regulations under this section is not limited by sections 10 to 12, 45, 54, 56 to 65 and 98 or by any other powers exercisable in respect of local authorities, voluntary adoption agencies or adoption support agencies.

   (3) Regulations may provide that a person who contravenes or fails to comply with any provision of regulations under this section is to be guilty of an offence and liable on summary conviction to a fine not exceeding level 5 on the standard scale.

   (4) In this section and section 10, 'voluntary adoption agency' means a voluntary organisation which is an adoption society.

10 Management etc of agencies—(1) In relation to local authorities, voluntary adoption agencies and adoption support agencies, regulations under section 9 may make provision as to—

   (a) the persons who are fit to work for them for the purposes of the functions mentioned in section 9(1),

   (b) the fitness of premises,

   (c) the management and control of their operations,

   (d) the number of persons, or persons of any particular type, working for the purposes of those functions,

   (e) the management and training of persons working for the purposes of those functions,

   (f) the keeping of information.

   (2) Regulations made by virtue of subsection (1)(a) may, in particular, make provision for prohibiting persons from working in prescribed positions unless they are registered in, or in a particular part of, one of the registers maintained under section 56(1) of the Care Standards Act 2000 (c 14) (registration of social care workers).

   (3) In relation to voluntary adoption agencies and adoption support agencies, regulations under section 9 may—

   (a) make provision as to the persons who are fit to manage an agency, including provision prohibiting persons from doing so unless they are registered in, or in a particular part of, one of the registers referred to in subsection (2),

   (b) impose requirements as to the financial position of an agency,

   (c) make provision requiring the appointment of a manager,

   (d) in the case of a voluntary adoption agency, make provision for securing the welfare of children placed by the agency, including provision as to the promotion and protection of their health,

   (e) in the case of an adoption support agency, make provision as to the persons who are fit to carry on the agency.

   (4) Regulations under section 9 may make provision as to the conduct of voluntary adoption agencies and adoption support agencies, and may in particular make provision—

   (a) as to the facilities and services to be provided by an agency,

   (b) as to the keeping of accounts,

   (c) as to the notification to the registration authority of events occurring in premises used for the purposes of an agency,

   (d) as to the giving of notice to the registration authority of periods during which the manager of an agency proposes to be absent, and specifying the information to be given in such a notice,

   (e) as to the making of adequate arrangements for the running of an agency during a period when its manager is absent,

   (f) as to the giving of notice to the registration authority of any intended change in the identity of the manager,

   (g) as to the giving of notice to the registration authority of changes in the ownership of an agency or the identity of its officers,

   (h) requiring the payment of a prescribed fee to the registration authority in respect of any notification required to be made by virtue of paragraph (g),

   (i) requiring arrangements to be made for dealing with complaints made by or on behalf of those seeking, or receiving, any of the services provided by an agency and requiring the agency or manager to take steps for publicising the arrangements.

11 Fees—(1) Regulations under section 9 may prescribe—

   (a) the fees which may be charged by adoption agencies in respect of the provision of services to persons providing facilities as part of the Adoption Service (including the Adoption Services in Scotland and Northern Ireland),

   (b) the fees which may be paid by adoption agencies to persons providing or assisting in providing such facilities.

   (2) Regulations under section 9 may prescribe the fees which may be charged by local authorities in respect of the provision of prescribed facilities of the Adoption Service where the following conditions are met.

(3) The conditions are that the facilities are provided in connection with—
   (a) the adoption of a child brought into the United Kingdom for the purpose of adoption, or
   (b) a Convention adoption, an overseas adoption or an adoption effected under the law of a country or territory outside the British Islands.

(4) Regulations under section 9 may prescribe the fees which may be charged by adoption agencies in respect of the provision of counselling, where the counselling is provided in connection with the disclosure of information in relation to a person's adoption.

12 Independent review of determinations—(1) Regulations under section 9 may establish a procedure under which any person in respect of whom a qualifying determination has been made by an adoption agency may apply to a panel constituted by the appropriate Minister for a review of that determination.

(2) The regulations must make provision as to the description of determinations which are qualifying determinations for the purposes of subsection (1).

(3) The regulations may include provision as to—
   (a) the duties and powers of a panel (including the power to recover the costs of a review from the adoption agency by which the determination reviewed was made),
   (b) the administration and procedures of a panel,
   (c) the appointment of members of a panel (including the number, or any limit on the number, of members who may be appointed and any conditions for appointment),
   (d) the payment of expenses of members of a panel,
   (e) the duties of adoption agencies in connection with reviews conducted under the regulations,
   (f) the monitoring of any such reviews.

(4) The appropriate Minister may make an arrangement with an organisation under which functions in relation to the panel are performed by the organisation on his behalf.

(5) If the appropriate Minister makes such an arrangement with an organisation, the organisation is to perform its functions under the arrangement in accordance with any general or special directions given by the appropriate Minister.

(6) The arrangement may include provision for payments to be made to the organisation by the appropriate Minister.

(7) Where the appropriate Minister is the Assembly, subsections (4) and (6) also apply as if references to an organisation included references to the Secretary of State.

(8) In this section, 'organisation' includes a public body and a private or voluntary organisation.

Supplemental

13 Information concerning adoption—(1) Each adoption agency must give to the appropriate Minister any statistical or other general information he requires about—
   (a) its performance of all or any of its functions relating to adoption,
   (b) the children and other persons in relation to whom it has exercised those functions.

(2) The following persons—
   (a) the *justices' chief executive* [designated officer] for each magistrates' court,
   (b) the relevant officer of each county court,
   (c) the relevant officer of the High Court,

must give to the appropriate Minister any statistical or other general information he requires about the proceedings under this Act of the court in question.

(3) In subsection (2), 'relevant officer', in relation to a county court or the High Court, means the officer of that court who is designated to act for the purposes of that subsection by a direction given by the Lord Chancellor.

(4) The information required to be given to the appropriate Minister under this section must be given at the times, and in the form, directed by him.

(5) The appropriate Minister may publish from time to time abstracts of the information given to him under this section.

Note. Sub-s (2): words 'justices' chief executive' in italics repealed and subsequent words in square brackets substituted by the Courts Act 2003, s 109(1), Sch 8, para 411 as from a date to be appointed.

14 Default power of appropriate Minister—(1) If the appropriate Minister is satisfied that any local authority have failed, without reasonable excuse, to comply with any of the duties imposed on them by virtue of this Act or of section 1 or 2(4) of the Adoption (Intercountry Aspects) Act 1999 (c 18), he may make an order declaring that authority to be in default in respect of that duty.

(2) An order under subsection (1) must give the appropriate Minister's reasons for making it.

(3) An order under subsection (1) may contain such directions as appear to the appropriate Minister to be necessary for the purpose of ensuring that, within the period specified in the order, the duty is complied with.

(4) Any such directions are enforceable, on the appropriate Minister's application, by a mandatory order.

15 Inspection of premises etc—(1) The appropriate Minister may arrange for any premises in which—

(a) a child is living with a person with whom the child has been placed by an adoption agency, or

(b) a child in respect of whom a notice of intention to adopt has been given under section 44 is, or will be, living,

to be inspected from time to time.

(2) The appropriate Minister may require an adoption agency—

(a) to give him any information, or

(b) to allow him to inspect any records (in whatever form they are held),

relating to the discharge of any of its functions in relation to adoption which the appropriate Minister specifies.

(3) An inspection under this section must be conducted by a person authorised by the appropriate Minister.

(4) An officer of a local authority may only be so authorised with the consent of the authority.

(5) A person inspecting any premises under subsection (1) may—

(a) visit the child there,

(b) make any examination into the state of the premises and the treatment of the child there which he thinks fit.

(6) A person authorised to inspect any records under this section may at any reasonable time have access to, and inspect and check the operation of, any computer (and associated apparatus) which is being or has been used in connection with the records in question.

(7) A person authorised to inspect any premises or records under this section may—

(a) enter the premises for that purpose at any reasonable time,

(b) require any person to give him any reasonable assistance he may require.

(8) A person exercising a power under this section must, if required to do so, produce a duly authenticated document showing his authority.

(9) Any person who intentionally obstructs another in the exercise of a power under this section is guilty of an offence and liable on summary conviction to a fine not exceeding level 3 on the standard scale.

16 Distribution of functions in relation to registered adoption societies
After section 36 of the Care Standards Act 2000 (c 14) there is inserted—

'36A Voluntary adoption agencies: distribution of functions—(1) This section applies to functions relating to voluntary adoption agencies conferred on the registration authority by or under this Part or under Chapter 2 of Part 1 of the Adoption and Children Act 2002.

(2) Subject to the following provisions, functions to which this section applies are exercisable—
    (a) where the principal office of an agency is in England, by the Commission,
    (b) where the principal office of an agency is in Wales, by the Assembly.

(3) So far as those functions relate to the imposition, variation or removal of conditions of registration, they may only be exercised after consultation with the Assembly or (as the case may be) the Commission.

(4) But—
    (a) where such a function as is mentioned in subsection (3) is exercisable by the Commission in relation to an agency which has a branch in Wales, it is exercisable only with the agreement of the Assembly,
    (b) where such a function as is mentioned in subsection (3) is exercisable by the Assembly in relation to an agency which has a branch in England, it is exercisable only with the agreement of the Commission.

(5) The functions conferred on the registration authority by sections 31 and 32 of this Act in respect of any premises of a voluntary adoption agency are exercisable—
    (a) where the premises are in England, by the Commission
    (b) where the premises are in Wales, by the Assembly.

(6) In spite of subsections (2) to (5), regulations may provide for any function to which this section applies to be exercisable by the Commission instead of the Assembly, or by the Assembly instead of the Commission, or by one concurrently with the other, or by both jointly or by either with the agreement of or after consultation with the other.

(7) In this section, 'regulations' means regulations relating to England and Wales.'

17 Inquiries—(1) The appropriate Minister may cause an inquiry to be held into any matter connected with the functions of an adoption agency.

(2) Before an inquiry is begun, the appropriate Minister may direct that it is to be held in private.

(3) Where no direction has been given, the person holding the inquiry may if he thinks fit hold it, or any part of it, in private.

(4) Subsections (2) to (5) of section 250 of the Local Government Act 1972 (c 70) (powers in relation to local inquiries) apply in relation to an inquiry under this section as they apply in relation to a local inquiry under that section.

CHAPTER 3
PLACEMENT FOR ADOPTION AND ADOPTION ORDERS

Placement of children by adoption agency for adoption

18 Placement for adoption by agencies—(1) An adoption agency may—
    (a) place a child for adoption with prospective adopters, or
    (b) where it has placed a child with any persons (whether under this Part or not), leave the child with them as prospective adopters,

but, except in the case of a child who is less than six weeks old, may only do so under section 19 or a placement order.

(2) An adoption agency may only place a child for adoption with prospective adopters if the agency is satisfied that the child ought to be placed for adoption.

(3) A child who is placed or authorised to be placed for adoption with prospective adopters by a local authority is looked after by the authority.

(4) If an application for an adoption order has been made by any persons in respect of a child and has not been disposed of—

(a) an adoption agency which placed the child with those persons may leave the child with them until the application is disposed of, but

(b) apart from that, the child may not be placed for adoption with any prospective adopters.

'Adoption order' includes a Scottish or Northern Irish adoption order.

(5) References in this Act (apart from this section) to an adoption agency placing a child for adoption—

(a) are to its placing a child for adoption with prospective adopters, and

(b) include, where it has placed a child with any persons (whether under this Act or not), leaving the child with them as prospective adopters;

and references in this Act (apart from this section) to a child who is placed for adoption by an adoption agency are to be interpreted accordingly.

(6) References in this Chapter to an adoption agency being, or not being, authorised to place a child for adoption are to the agency being or (as the case may be) not being authorised to do so under section 19 or a placement order.

(7) This section is subject to sections 30 to 35 (removal of children placed by adoption agencies).

19 Placing children with parental consent—(1) Where an adoption agency is satisfied that each parent or guardian of a child has consented to the child—

(a) being placed for adoption with prospective adopters identified in the consent, or

(b) being placed for adoption with any prospective adopters who may be chosen by the agency,

and has not withdrawn the consent, the agency is authorised to place the child for adoption accordingly.

(2) Consent to a child being placed for adoption with prospective adopters identified in the consent may be combined with consent to the child subsequently being placed for adoption with any prospective adopters who may be chosen by the agency in circumstances where the child is removed from or returned by the identified prospective adopters.

(3) Subsection (1) does not apply where—

(a) an application has been made on which a care order might be made and the application has not been disposed of, or

(b) a care order or placement order has been made after the consent was given.

(4) References in this Act to a child placed for adoption under this section include a child who was placed under this section with prospective adopters and continues to be placed with them, whether or not consent to the placement has been withdrawn.

(5) This section is subject to section 52 (parental etc consent).

20 Advance consent to adoption—(1) A parent or guardian of a child who consents to the child being placed for adoption by an adoption agency under section 19 may, at the same or any subsequent time, consent to the making of a future adoption order.

(2) Consent under this section—

(a) where the parent or guardian has consented to the child being placed for adoption with prospective adopters identified in the consent, may be consent to adoption by them, or

   (b) may be consent to adoption by any prospective adopters who may be chosen by the agency.

   (3) A person may withdraw any consent given under this section.

   (4) A person who gives consent under this section may, at the same or any subsequent time, by notice given to the adoption agency—

   (a) state that he does not wish to be informed of any application for an adoption order, or

   (b) withdraw such a statement.

   (5) A notice under subsection (4) has effect from the time when it is received by the adoption agency but has no effect if the person concerned has withdrawn his consent.

   (6) This section is subject to section 52 (parental etc consent).

21 Placement orders—(1) A placement order is an order made by the court authorising a local authority to place a child for adoption with any prospective adopters who may be chosen by the authority.

   (2) The court may not make a placement order in respect of a child unless—

   (a) the child is subject to a care order,

   (b) the court is satisfied that the conditions in section 31(2) of the 1989 Act (conditions for making a care order) are met, or

   (c) the child has no parent or guardian.

   (3) The court may only make a placement order if, in the case of each parent or guardian of the child, the court is satisfied—

   (a) that the parent or guardian has consented to the child being placed for adoption with any prospective adopters who may be chosen by the local authority and has not withdrawn the consent, or

   (b) that the parent's or guardian's consent should be dispensed with.

This subsection is subject to section 52 (parental etc consent).

   (4) A placement order continues in force until—

   (a) it is revoked under section 24,

   (b) an adoption order is made in respect of the child, or

   (c) the child marries or attains the age of 18 years.

'Adoption order' includes a Scottish or Northern Irish adoption order.

22 Applications for placement orders—(1) A local authority must apply to the court for a placement order in respect of a child if—

   (a) the child is placed for adoption by them or is being provided with accommodation by them,

   (b) no adoption agency is authorised to place the child for adoption,

   (c) the child has no parent or guardian or the authority consider that the conditions in section 31(2) of the 1989 Act are met, and

   (d) the authority are satisfied that the child ought to be placed for adoption.

   (2) If—

   (a) an application has been made (and has not been disposed of) on which a care order might be made in respect of a child, or

   (b) a child is subject to a care order and the appropriate local authority are not authorised to place the child for adoption,

the appropriate local authority must apply to the court for a placement order if they are satisfied that the child ought to be placed for adoption.

   (3) If—

   (a) a child is subject to a care order, and

   (b) the appropriate local authority are authorised to place the child for adoption under section 19,

the authority may apply to the court for a placement order.

   (4) If a local authority—

(a) are under a duty to apply to the court for a placement order in respect of a child, or

(b) have applied for a placement order in respect of a child and the application has not been disposed of,

the child is looked after by the authority.

(5) Subsections (1) to (3) do not apply in respect of a child—

(a) if any persons have given notice of intention to adopt, unless the period of four months beginning with the giving of the notice has expired without them applying for an adoption order or their application for such an order has been withdrawn or refused, or

(b) if an application for an adoption order has been made and has not been disposed of.

'Adoption order' includes a Scottish or Northern Irish adoption order.

(6) Where—

(a) an application for a placement order in respect of a child has been made and has not been disposed of, and

(b) no interim care order is in force,

the court may give any directions it considers appropriate for the medical or psychiatric examination or other assessment of the child; but a child who is of sufficient understanding to make an informed decision may refuse to submit to the examination or other assessment.

(7) The appropriate local authority—

(a) in relation to a care order, is the local authority in whose care the child is placed by the order, and

(b) in relation to an application on which a care order might be made, is the local authority which makes the application.

23 Varying placement orders—(1) The court may vary a placement order so as to substitute another local authority for the local authority authorised by the order to place the child for adoption.

(2) The variation may only be made on the joint application of both authorities.

24 Revoking placement orders—(1) The court may revoke a placement order on the application of any person.

(2) But an application may not be made by a person other than the child or the local authority authorised by the order to place the child for adoption unless—

(a) the court has given leave to apply, and

(b) the child is not placed for adoption by the authority.

(3) The court cannot give leave under subsection (2)(a) unless satisfied that there has been a change in circumstances since the order was made.

(4) If the court determines, on an application for an adoption order, not to make the order, it may revoke any placement order in respect of the child.

(5) Where—

(a) an application for the revocation of a placement order has been made and has not been disposed of, and

(b) the child is not placed for adoption by the authority,

the child may not without the court's leave be placed for adoption under the order.

25 Parental responsibility—(1) This section applies while—

(a) a child is placed for adoption under section 19 or an adoption agency is authorised to place a child for adoption under that section, or

(b) a placement order is in force in respect of a child.

(2) Parental responsibility for the child is given to the agency concerned.

(3) While the child is placed with prospective adopters, parental responsibility is given to them.

(4) The agency may determine that the parental responsibility of any parent or guardian, or of prospective adopters, is to be restricted to the extent specified in the determination.

26 Contact—(1) On an adoption agency being authorised to place a child for adoption, or placing a child for adoption who is less than six weeks old, any provision for contact under the 1989 Act ceases to have effect.

(2) While an adoption agency is so authorised or a child is placed for adoption—

(a) no application may be made for any provision for contact under that Act, but

(b) the court may make an order under this section requiring the person with whom the child lives, or is to live, to allow the child to visit or stay with the person named in the order, or for the person named in the order and the child otherwise to have contact with each other.

(3) An application for an order under this section may be made by—

(a) the child or the agency,

(b) any parent, guardian or relative,

(c) any person in whose favour there was provision for contact under the 1989 Act which ceased to have effect by virtue of subsection (1),

(d) if a residence order was in force immediately before the adoption agency was authorised to place the child for adoption or (as the case may be) placed the child for adoption at a time when he was less than six weeks old, the person in whose favour the order was made,

(e) if a person had care of the child immediately before that time by virtue of an order made in the exercise of the High Court's inherent jurisdiction with respect to children, that person,

(f) any person who has obtained the court's leave to make the application.

(4) When making a placement order, the court may on its own initiative make an order under this section.

(5) This section does not prevent an application for a contact order under section 8 of the 1989 Act being made where the application is to be heard together with an application for an adoption order in respect of the child.

(6) In this section, 'provision for contact under the 1989 Act' means a contact order under section 8 of that Act or an order under section 34 of that Act (parental contact with children in care).

27 Contact: supplementary—(1) An order under section 26—

(a) has effect while the adoption agency is authorised to place the child for adoption or the child is placed for adoption, but

(b) may be varied or revoked by the court on an application by the child, the agency or a person named in the order.

(2) The agency may refuse to allow the contact that would otherwise be required by virtue of an order under that section if—

(a) it is satisfied that it is necessary to do so in order to safeguard or promote the child's welfare, and

(b) the refusal is decided upon as a matter of urgency and does not last for more than seven days.

(3) Regulations may make provision as to—

(a) the steps to be taken by an agency which has exercised its power under subsection (2),

(b) the circumstances in which, and conditions subject to which, the terms of any order under section 26 may be departed from by agreement between the agency and any person for whose contact with the child the order provides,

   (c) notification by an agency of any variation or suspension of arrangements made (otherwise than under an order under that section) with a view to allowing any person contact with the child.

   (4) Before making a placement order the court must—

   (a) consider the arrangements which the adoption agency has made, or proposes to make, for allowing any person contact with the child, and

   (b) invite the parties to the proceedings to comment on those arrangements.

   (5) An order under section 26 may provide for contact on any conditions the court considers appropriate.

28 Further consequences of placement—(1) Where a child is placed for adoption under section 19 or an adoption agency is authorised to place a child for adoption under that section—

   (a) a parent or guardian of the child may not apply for a residence order unless an application for an adoption order has been made and the parent or guardian has obtained the court's leave under subsection (3) or (5) of section 47,

   (b) if an application has been made for an adoption order, a guardian of the child may not apply for a special guardianship order unless he has obtained the court's leave under subsection (3) or (5) of that section.

   (2) Where—

   (a) a child is placed for adoption under section 19 or an adoption agency is authorised to place a child for adoption under that section, or

   (b) a placement order is in force in respect of a child,

then (whether or not the child is in England and Wales) a person may not do either of the following things, unless the court gives leave or each parent or guardian of the child gives written consent.

   (3) Those things are—

   (a) causing the child to be known by a new surname, or

   (b) removing the child from the United Kingdom.

   (4) Subsection (3) does not prevent the removal of a child from the United Kingdom for a period of less than one month by a person who provides the child's home.

29 Further consequences of placement orders—(1) Where a placement order is made in respect of a child and either—

   (a) the child is subject to a care order, or

   (b) the court at the same time makes a care order in respect of the child,

the care order does not have effect at any time when the placement order is in force.

   (2) On the making of a placement order in respect of a child, any order mentioned in section 8(1) of the 1989 Act, and any supervision order in respect of the child, ceases to have effect.

   (3) Where a placement order is in force—

   (a) no prohibited steps order, residence order or specific issue order, and

   (b) no supervision order or child assessment order,

may be made in respect of the child.

   (4) Subsection (3)(a) does not apply in respect of a residence order if—

   (a) an application for an adoption order has been made in respect of the child, and

   (b) the residence order is applied for by a parent or guardian who has obtained the court's leave under subsection (3) or (5) of section 47 or by any other person who has obtained the court's leave under this subsection.

   (5) Where a placement order is in force, no special guardianship order may be made in respect of the child unless—

(a) an application has been made for an adoption order, and
(b) the person applying for the special guardianship order has obtained the court's leave under this subsection or, if he is a guardian of the child, has obtained the court's leave under section 47(5).

(6) Section 14A(7) of the 1989 Act applies in respect of an application for a special guardianship order for which leave has been given as mentioned in subsection (5)(b) with the omission of the words 'the beginning of the period of three months ending with'.

(7) Where a placement order is in force—
(a) section 14C(1)(b) of the 1989 Act (special guardianship: parental responsibility) has effect subject to any determination under section 25(4) of this Act,
(b) section 14C(3) and (4) of the 1989 Act (special guardianship: removal of child from UK etc) does not apply.

Removal of children who are or may be placed by adoption agencies

30 General prohibitions on removal—(1) Where—
(a) a child is placed for adoption by an adoption agency under section 19, or
(b) a child is placed for adoption by an adoption agency and either the child is less than six weeks old or the agency has at no time been authorised to place the child for adoption,
a person (other than the agency) must not remove the child from the prospective adopters.

(2) Where—
(a) a child who is not for the time being placed for adoption is being provided with accommodation by a local authority, and
(b) the authority have applied to the court for a placement order and the application has not been disposed of,
only a person who has the court's leave (or the authority) may remove the child from the accommodation.

(3) Where subsection (2) does not apply, but—
(a) a child who is not for the time being placed for adoption is being provided with accommodation by an adoption agency, and
(b) the agency is authorised to place the child for adoption under section 19 or would be so authorised if any consent to placement under that section had not been withdrawn,
a person (other than the agency) must not remove the child from the accommodation.

(4) This section is subject to sections 31 to 33 but those sections do not apply if the child is subject to a care order.

(5) This group of sections (that is, this section and those sections) apply whether or not the child in question is in England and Wales.

(6) This group of sections does not affect the exercise by any local authority or other person of any power conferred by any enactment, other than section 20(8) of the 1989 Act (removal of children from local authority accommodation).

(7) This group of sections does not prevent the removal of a child who is arrested.

(8) A person who removes a child in contravention of this section is guilty of an offence and liable on summary conviction to imprisonment for a term not exceeding three months, or a fine not exceeding level 5 on the standard scale, or both.

31 Recovery by parent etc where child not placed or is a baby—(1) Subsection (2) applies where—

   (a) a child who is not for the time being placed for adoption is being provided
      with accommodation by an adoption agency, and

   (b) the agency would be authorised to place the child for adoption under
      section 19 if consent to placement under that section had not been
      withdrawn.

   (2) If any parent or guardian of the child informs the agency that he wishes the
child to be returned to him, the agency must return the child to him within the
period of seven days beginning with the request unless an application is, or has
been, made for a placement order and the application has not been disposed of.

   (3) Subsection (4) applies where—

   (a) a child is placed for adoption by an adoption agency and either the child is
      less than six weeks old or the agency has at no time been authorised to
      place the child for adoption, and

   (b) any parent or guardian of the child informs the agency that he wishes the
      child to be returned to him,

unless an application is, or has been, made for a placement order and the
application has not been disposed of.

   (4) The agency must give notice of the parent's or guardian's wish to the
prospective adopters who must return the child to the agency within the period of
seven days beginning with the day on which the notice is given.

   (5) A prospective adopter who fails to comply with subsection (4) is guilty of an
offence and liable on summary conviction to imprisonment for a term not
exceeding three months, or a fine not exceeding level 5 on the standard scale, or
both.

   (6) As soon as a child is returned to an adoption agency under subsection (4),
the agency must return the child to the parent or guardian in question.

32 Recovery by parent etc where child placed and consent withdrawn—(1)
This section applies where—

   (a) a child is placed for adoption by an adoption agency under section 19, and

   (b) consent to placement under that section has been withdrawn,

unless an application is, or has been, made for a placement order and the
application has not been disposed of.

   (2) If a parent or guardian of the child informs the agency that he wishes the
child to be returned to him—

   (a) the agency must give notice of the parent's or guardian's wish to the
      prospective adopters, and

   (b) the prospective adopters must return the child to the agency within the
      period of 14 days beginning with the day on which the notice is given.

   (3) A prospective adopter who fails to comply with subsection (2)(b) is guilty of
an offence and liable on summary conviction to imprisonment for a term not exceeding three months, or a fine not exceeding level 5 on the standard scale, or both.

   (4) As soon as a child is returned to an adoption agency under this section, the
agency must return the child to the parent or guardian in question.

   (5) Where a notice under subsection (2) is given, but—

   (a) before the notice was given, an application for an adoption order
      (including a Scottish or Northern Irish adoption order), special
      guardianship order or residence order, or for leave to apply for a special
      guardianship order or residence order, was made in respect of the child,
      and

   (b) the application (and, in a case where leave is given on an application to
      apply for a special guardianship order or residence order, the application
      for the order) has not been disposed of,

the prospective adopters are not required by virtue of the notice to return the
child to the agency unless the court so orders.

33 Recovery by parent etc where child placed and placement order refused
(1) This section applies where—
- (a) a child is placed for adoption by a local authority under section 19,
- (b) the authority have applied for a placement order and the application has been refused, and
- (c) any parent or guardian of the child informs the authority that he wishes the child to be returned to him.

(2) The prospective adopters must return the child to the authority on a date determined by the court.

(3) A prospective adopter who fails to comply with subsection (2) is guilty of an offence and liable on summary conviction to imprisonment for a term not exceeding three months, or a fine not exceeding level 5 on the standard scale, or both.

(4) As soon as a child is returned to the authority, they must return the child to the parent or guardian in question.

34 Placement orders: prohibition on removal—(1) Where a placement order in respect of a child—
- (a) is in force, or
- (b) has been revoked, but the child has not been returned by the prospective adopters or remains in any accommodation provided by the local authority,

a person (other than the local authority) may not remove the child from the prospective adopters or from accommodation provided by the authority.

(2) A person who removes a child in contravention of subsection (1) is guilty of an offence.

(3) Where a court revoking a placement order in respect of a child determines that the child is not to remain with any former prospective adopters with whom the child is placed, they must return the child to the local authority within the period determined by the court for the purpose; and a person who fails to do so is guilty of an offence.

(4) Where a court revoking a placement order in respect of a child determines that the child is to be returned to a parent or guardian, the local authority must return the child to the parent or guardian as soon as the child is returned to the authority or, where the child is in accommodation provided by the authority, at once.

(5) A person guilty of an offence under this section is liable on summary conviction to imprisonment for a term not exceeding three months, or a fine not exceeding level 5 on the standard scale, or both.

(6) This section does not affect the exercise by any local authority or other person of a power conferred by any enactment, other than section 20(8) of the 1989 Act.

(7) This section does not prevent the removal of a child who is arrested.

(8) This section applies whether or not the child in question is in England and Wales.

35 Return of child in other cases—(1) Where a child is placed for adoption by an adoption agency and the prospective adopters give notice to the agency of their wish to return the child, the agency must—
- (a) receive the child from the prospective adopters before the end of the period of seven days beginning with the giving of the notice, and
- (b) give notice to any parent or guardian of the child of the prospective adopters' wish to return the child.

(2) Where a child is placed for adoption by an adoption agency, and the agency—
- (a) is of the opinion that the child should not remain with the prospective adopters, and
- (b) gives notice to them of its opinion,

the prospective adopters must, not later than the end of the period of seven days beginning with the giving of the notice, return the child to the agency.

(3) If the agency gives notice under subsection (2)(b), it must give notice to any parent or guardian of the child of the obligation to return the child to the agency.

(4) A prospective adopter who fails to comply with subsection (2) is guilty of an offence and liable on summary conviction to imprisonment for a term not exceeding three months, or a fine not exceeding level 5 on the standard scale, or both.

(5) Where—

(a) an adoption agency gives notice under subsection (2) in respect of a child,

(b) before the notice was given, an application for an adoption order (including a Scottish or Northern Irish adoption order), special guardianship order or residence order, or for leave to apply for a special guardianship order or residence order, was made in respect of the child, and

(c) the application (and, in a case where leave is given on an application to apply for a special guardianship order or residence order, the application for the order) has not been disposed of,

prospective adopters are not required by virtue of the notice to return the child to the agency unless the court so orders.

(6) This section applies whether or not the child in question is in England and Wales.

Removal of children in non-agency cases

36 Restrictions on removal—(1) At any time when a child's home is with any persons ('the people concerned') with whom the child is not placed by an adoption agency, but the people concerned—

(a) have applied for an adoption order in respect of the child and the application has not been disposed of,

(b) have given notice of intention to adopt, or

(c) have applied for leave to apply for an adoption order under section 42(6) and the application has not been disposed of,

a person may remove the child only in accordance with the provisions of this group of sections (that is, this section and sections 37 to 40).

The reference to a child placed by an adoption agency includes a child placed by a Scottish or Northern Irish adoption agency.

(2) For the purposes of this group of sections, a notice of intention to adopt is to be disregarded if—

(a) the period of four months beginning with the giving of the notice has expired without the people concerned applying for an adoption order, or

(b) the notice is a second or subsequent notice of intention to adopt and was given during the period of five months beginning with the giving of the preceding notice.

(3) For the purposes of this group of sections, if the people concerned apply for leave to apply for an adoption order under section 42(6) and the leave is granted, the application for leave is not to be treated as disposed of until the period of three days beginning with the granting of the leave has expired.

(4) This section does not prevent the removal of a child who is arrested.

(5) Where a parent or guardian may remove a child from the people concerned in accordance with the provisions of this group of sections, the people concerned must at the request of the parent or guardian return the child to the parent or guardian at once.

(6) A person who—

(a) fails to comply with subsection (5), or

(b) removes a child in contravention of this section,

is guilty of an offence and liable on summary conviction to imprisonment for a term not exceeding three months, or a fine not exceeding level 5 on the standard scale, or both.

(7) This group of sections applies whether or not the child in question is in England and Wales.

37 Applicants for adoption If section 36(1)(a) applies, the following persons may remove the child—

(a) a person who has the court's leave,

(b) a local authority or other person in the exercise of a power conferred by any enactment, other than section 20(8) of the 1989 Act.

38 Local authority foster parents

(1) This section applies if the child's home is with local authority foster parents.

(2) If—

(a) the child has had his home with the foster parents at all times during the period of five years ending with the removal and the foster parents have given notice of intention to adopt, or

(b) an application has been made for leave under section 42(6) and has not been disposed of,

the following persons may remove the child.

(3) They are—

(a) a person who has the court's leave,

(b) a local authority or other person in the exercise of a power conferred by any enactment, other than section 20(8) of the 1989 Act.

(4) If subsection (2) does not apply but—

(a) the child has had his home with the foster parents at all times during the period of one year ending with the removal, and

(b) the foster parents have given notice of intention to adopt,

the following persons may remove the child.

(5) They are—

(a) a person with parental responsibility for the child who is exercising the power in section 20(8) of the 1989 Act,

(b) a person who has the court's leave,

(c) a local authority or other person in the exercise of a power conferred by any enactment, other than section 20(8) of the 1989 Act.

39 Partners of parents—(1) This section applies if a child's home is with a partner of a parent and the partner has given notice of intention to adopt.

(2) If the child's home has been with the partner for not less than three years (whether continuous or not) during the period of five years ending with the removal, the following persons may remove the child—

(a) a person who has the court's leave,

(b) a local authority or other person in the exercise of a power conferred by any enactment, other than section 20(8) of the 1989 Act.

(3) If subsection (2) does not apply, the following persons may remove the child—

(a) a parent or guardian,

(b) a person who has the court's leave,

(c) a local authority or other person in the exercise of a power conferred by any enactment, other than section 20(8) of the 1989 Act.

40 Other non-agency cases—(1) In any case where sections 37 to 39 do not apply but—

(a) the people concerned have given notice of intention to adopt, or

(b) the people concerned have applied for leave under section 42(6) and the application has not been disposed of,

the following persons may remove the child.

(2) They are—

(a) a person who has the court's leave,

(b) a local authority or other person in the exercise of a power conferred by any enactment, other than section 20(8) of the 1989 Act.

Breach of restrictions on removal

41 Recovery orders—(1) This section applies where it appears to the court—

(a) that a child has been removed in contravention of any of the preceding provisions of this Chapter or that there are reasonable grounds for believing that a person intends to remove a child in contravention of those provisions, or

(b) that a person has failed to comply with section 31(4), 32(2), 33(2), 34(3) or 35(2).

(2) The court may, on the application of any person, by an order—

(a) direct any person who is in a position to do so to produce the child on request to any person mentioned in subsection (4),

(b) authorise the removal of the child by any person mentioned in that subsection,

(c) require any person who has information as to the child's whereabouts to disclose that information on request to any constable or officer of the court,

(d) authorise a constable to enter any premises specified in the order and search for the child, using reasonable force if necessary.

(3) Premises may only be specified under subsection (2)(d) if it appears to the court that there are reasonable grounds for believing the child to be on them.

(4) The persons referred to in subsection (2) are—

(a) any person named by the court,

(b) any constable,

(c) any person who, after the order is made under that subsection, is authorised to exercise any power under the order by an adoption agency which is authorised to place the child for adoption.

(5) A person who intentionally obstructs a person exercising a power of removal conferred by the order is guilty of an offence and liable on summary conviction to a fine not exceeding level 3 on the standard scale.

(6) A person must comply with a request to disclose information as required by the order even if the information sought might constitute evidence that he had committed an offence.

(7) But in criminal proceedings in which the person is charged with an offence (other than one mentioned in subsection (8))—

(a) no evidence relating to the information provided may be adduced, and

(b) no question relating to the information may be asked,

by or on behalf of the prosecution, unless evidence relating to it is adduced, or a question relating to it is asked, in the proceedings by or on behalf of the person.

(8) The offences excluded from subsection (7) are—

(a) an offence under section 2 or 5 of the Perjury Act 1911 (c 6) (false statements made on oath otherwise than in judicial proceedings or made otherwise than on oath),

(b) an offence under section 44(1) or (2) of the Criminal Law (Consolidation) (Scotland) Act 1995 (c 39) (false statements made on oath or otherwise than on oath).

(9) An order under this section has effect in relation to Scotland as if it were an order made by the Court of Session which that court had jurisdiction to make.

Preliminaries to adoption

42 Child to live with adopters before application—(1) An application for an adoption order may not be made unless—
- (a) if subsection (2) applies, the condition in that subsection is met,
- (b) if that subsection does not apply, the condition in whichever is applicable of subsections (3) to (5) applies.

(2) If—
- (a) the child was placed for adoption with the applicant or applicants by an adoption agency or in pursuance of an order of the High Court, or
- (b) the applicant is a parent of the child,

the condition is that the child must have had his home with the applicant or, in the case of an application by a couple, with one or both of them at all times during the period of ten weeks preceding the application.

(3) If the applicant or one of the applicants is the partner of a parent of the child, the condition is that the child must have had his home with the applicant or, as the case may be, applicants at all times during the period of six months preceding the application.

(4) If the applicants are local authority foster parents, the condition is that the child must have had his home with the applicants at all times during the period of one year preceding the application.

(5) In any other case, the condition is that the child must have had his home with the applicant or, in the case of an application by a couple, with one or both of them for not less than three years (whether continuous or not) during the period of five years preceding the application.

(6) But subsections (4) and (5) do not prevent an application being made if the court gives leave to make it.

(7) An adoption order may not be made unless the court is satisfied that sufficient opportunities to see the child with the applicant or, in the case of an application by a couple, both of them together in the home environment have been given—
- (a) where the child was placed for adoption with the applicant or applicants by an adoption agency, to that agency,
- (b) in any other case, to the local authority within whose area the home is.

(8) In this section and sections 43 and 44(1)—
- (a) references to an adoption agency include a Scottish or Northern Irish adoption agency,
- (b) references to a child placed for adoption by an adoption agency are to be read accordingly.

43 Reports where child placed by agency Where an application for an adoption order relates to a child placed for adoption by an adoption agency, the agency must—
- (a) submit to the court a report on the suitability of the applicants and on any other matters relevant to the operation of section 1, and
- (b) assist the court in any manner the court directs.

44 Notice of intention to adopt—(1) This section applies where persons (referred to in this section as 'proposed adopters') wish to adopt a child who is not placed for adoption with them by an adoption agency.

(2) An adoption order may not be made in respect of the child unless the proposed adopters have given notice to the appropriate local authority of their intention to apply for the adoption order (referred to in this Act as a 'notice of intention to adopt').

(3) The notice must be given not more than two years, or less than three months, before the date on which the application for the adoption order is made.

(4) Where—
(a) if a person were seeking to apply for an adoption order, subsection (4) or (5) of section 42 would apply, but
(b) the condition in the subsection in question is not met,

the person may not give notice of intention to adopt unless he has the court's leave to apply for an adoption order.

(5) On receipt of a notice of intention to adopt, the local authority must arrange for the investigation of the matter and submit to the court a report of the investigation.

(6) In particular, the investigation must, so far as practicable, include the suitability of the proposed adopters and any other matters relevant to the operation of section 1 in relation to the application.

(7) If a local authority receive a notice of intention to adopt in respect of a child whom they know was (immediately before the notice was given) looked after by another local authority, they must, not more than seven days after the receipt of the notice, inform the other local authority in writing that they have received the notice.

(8) Where—
(a) a local authority have placed a child with any persons otherwise than as prospective adopters, and
(b) the persons give notice of intention to adopt,

the authority are not to be treated as leaving the child with them as prospective adopters for the purposes of section 18(1)(b).

(9) In this section, references to the appropriate local authority, in relation to any proposed adopters, are—
(a) in prescribed cases, references to the prescribed local authority,
(b) in any other case, references to the local authority for the area in which, at the time of giving the notice of intention to adopt, they have their home,

and 'prescribed' means prescribed by regulations.

45 Suitability of adopters—(1) Regulations under section 9 may make provision as to the matters to be taken into account by an adoption agency in determining, or making any report in respect of, the suitability of any persons to adopt a child.

(2) In particular, the regulations may make provision for the purpose of securing that, in determining the suitability of a couple to adopt a child, proper regard is had to the need for stability and permanence in their relationship.

The making of adoption orders

46 Adoption orders—(1) An adoption order is an order made by the court on an application under section 50 or 51 giving parental responsibility for a child to the adopters or adopter.

(2) The making of an adoption order operates to extinguish—
(a) the parental responsibility which any person other than the adopters or adopter has for the adopted child immediately before the making of the order,
(b) any order under the 1989 Act or the Children (Northern Ireland) Order 1995 (SI 1995/755 (NI 2)),
(c) any order under the Children (Scotland) Act 1995 (c 36) other than an excepted order, and
(d) any duty arising by virtue of an agreement or an order of a court to make payments, so far as the payments are in respect of the adopted child's maintenance or upbringing for any period after the making of the adoption order.

'Excepted order' means an order under section 9, 11(1)(d) or 13 of the Children (Scotland) Act 1995 or an exclusion order within the meaning of section 76(1) of that Act.

(3) An adoption order—

(a) does not affect parental responsibility so far as it relates to any period before the making of the order, and

(b) in the case of an order made on an application under section 51(2) by the partner of a parent of the adopted child, does not affect the parental responsibility of that parent or any duties of that parent within subsection (2)(d).

(4) Subsection (2)(d) does not apply to a duty arising by virtue of an agreement—

(a) which constitutes a trust, or

(b) which expressly provides that the duty is not to be extinguished by the making of an adoption order.

(5) An adoption order may be made even if the child to be adopted is already an adopted child.

(6) Before making an adoption order, the court must consider whether there should be arrangements for allowing any person contact with the child; and for that purpose the court must consider any existing or proposed arrangements and obtain any views of the parties to the proceedings.

47 Conditions for making adoption orders—(1) An adoption order may not be made if the child has a parent or guardian unless one of the following three conditions is met; but this section is subject to section 52 (parental etc consent).

(2) The first condition is that, in the case of each parent or guardian of the child, the court is satisfied—

(a) that the parent or guardian consents to the making of the adoption order,

(b) that the parent or guardian has consented under section 20 (and has not withdrawn the consent) and does not oppose the making of the adoption order, or

(c) that the parent's or guardian's consent should be dispensed with.

(3) A parent or guardian may not oppose the making of an adoption order under subsection (2)(b) without the court's leave.

(4) The second condition is that—

(a) the child has been placed for adoption by an adoption agency with the prospective adopters in whose favour the order is proposed to be made,

(b) either—

    (i) the child was placed for adoption with the consent of each parent or guardian and the consent of the mother was given when the child was at least six weeks old, or

    (ii) the child was placed for adoption under a placement order, and

(c) no parent or guardian opposes the making of the adoption order.

(5) A parent or guardian may not oppose the making of an adoption order under the second condition without the court's leave.

(6) The third condition is that the child is free for adoption by virtue of an order made—

(a) in Scotland, under section 18 of the Adoption (Scotland) Act 1978 (c 28), or

(b) in Northern Ireland, under Article 17(1) or 18(1) of the Adoption (Northern Ireland) Order 1987 (SI 1987/2203 (NI 22)).

(7) The court cannot give leave under subsection (3) or (5) unless satisfied that there has been a change in circumstances since the consent of the parent or guardian was given or, as the case may be, the placement order was made.

(8) An adoption order may not be made in relation to a person who is or has been married.

(9) An adoption order may not be made in relation to a person who has attained the age of 19 years.

48 Restrictions on making adoption orders—(1) The court may not hear an application for an adoption order in relation to a child, where a previous application to which subsection (2) applies made in relation to the child by the same persons was refused by any court, unless it appears to the court that, because of a change in circumstances or for any other reason, it is proper to hear the application.

(2) This subsection applies to any application—

(a) for an adoption order or a Scottish or Northern Irish adoption order, or

(b) for an order for adoption made in the Isle of Man or any of the Channel Islands.

49 Applications for adoption—(1) An application for an adoption order may be made by—

(a) a couple, or

(b) one person,

but only if it is made under section 50 or 51 and one of the following conditions is met.

(2) The first condition is that at least one of the couple (in the case of an application under section 50) or the applicant (in the case of an application under section 51) is domiciled in a part of the British Islands.

(3) The second condition is that both of the couple (in the case of an application under section 50) or the applicant (in the case of an application under section 51) have been habitually resident in a part of the British Islands for a period of not less than one year ending with the date of the application.

(4) An application for an adoption order may only be made if the person to be adopted has not attained the age of 18 years on the date of the application.

(5) References in this Act to a child, in connection with any proceedings (whether or not concluded) for adoption, (such as 'child to be adopted' or 'adopted child') include a person who has attained the age of 18 years before the proceedings are concluded.

50 Adoption by couple—(1) An adoption order may be made on the application of a couple where both of them have attained the age of 21 years.

(2) An adoption order may be made on the application of a couple where—

(a) one of the couple is the mother or the father of the person to be adopted and has attained the age of 18 years, and

(b) the other has attained the age of 21 years.

51 Adoption by one person—(1) An adoption order may be made on the application of one person who has attained the age of 21 years and is not married.

(2) An adoption order may be made on the application of one person who has attained the age of 21 years if the court is satisfied that the person is the partner of a parent of the person to be adopted.

(3) An adoption order may be made on the application of one person who has attained the age of 21 years and is married if the court is satisfied that—

(a) the person's spouse cannot be found,

(b) the spouses have separated and are living apart, and the separation is likely to be permanent, or

(c) the person's spouse is by reason of ill-health, whether physical or mental, incapable of making an application for an adoption order.

(4) An adoption order may not be made on an application under this section by the mother or the father of the person to be adopted unless the court is satisfied that—

(a) the other natural parent is dead or cannot be found,

(b) by virtue of section 28 of the Human Fertilisation and Embryology Act 1990 (c 37), [(disregarding subsections (5A) to (5I) of that section)], there is no other parent, or

(c) there is some other reason justifying the child's being adopted by the applicant alone,

and, where the court makes an adoption order on such an application, the court must record that it is satisfied as to the fact mentioned in paragraph (a) or (b) or, in the case of paragraph (c), record the reason.

Note Sub-s (4): in para (b) words '(disregarding subsections (5A) to (5I) of that section)' in square brackets inserted by the Human Fertilisation and Embryology (Deceased Fathers) Act 2003, s 2(1), Schedule, para 18 as from 1 December 2003, for retrospective, transitional and transitory provision see the Human Fertilisation and Embryology (Deceased Fathers) Act 2003, s 3(1).

Placement and adoption: general

52 Parental etc consent—(1) The court cannot dispense with the consent of any parent or guardian of a child to the child being placed for adoption or to the making of an adoption order in respect of the child unless the court is satisfied that—

(a) the parent or guardian cannot be found or is incapable of giving consent, or

(b) the welfare of the child requires the consent to be dispensed with.

(2) The following provisions apply to references in this Chapter to any parent or guardian of a child giving or withdrawing—

(a) consent to the placement of a child for adoption, or

(b) consent to the making of an adoption order (including a future adoption order).

(3) Any consent given by the mother to the making of an adoption order is ineffective if it is given less than six weeks after the child's birth.

(4) The withdrawal of any consent to the placement of a child for adoption, or of any consent given under section 20, is ineffective if it is given after an application for an adoption order is made.

(5) 'Consent' means consent given unconditionally and with full understanding of what is involved; but a person may consent to adoption without knowing the identity of the persons in whose favour the order will be made.

(6) 'Parent' (except in subsections (9) and (10) below) means a parent having parental responsibility.

(7) Consent under section 19 or 20 must be given in the form prescribed by rules, and the rules may prescribe forms in which a person giving consent under any other provision of this Part may do so (if he wishes).

(8) Consent given under section 19 or 20 must be withdrawn—

(a) in the form prescribed by rules, or

(b) by notice given to the agency.

(9) Subsection (10) applies if—

(a) an agency has placed a child for adoption under section 19 in pursuance of consent given by a parent of the child, and

(b) at a later time, the other parent of the child acquires parental responsibility for the child.

(10) The other parent is to be treated as having at that time given consent in accordance with this section in the same terms as those in which the first parent gave consent.

53 Modification of 1989 Act in relation to adoption—(1) Where—

(a) a local authority are authorised to place a child for adoption, or

(b) a child who has been placed for adoption by a local authority is less than six weeks old,

regulations may provide for the following provisions of the 1989 Act to apply with modifications, or not to apply, in relation to the child.

(2) The provisions are—

(a) section 22(4)(b), (c) and (d) and (5)(b) (duty to ascertain wishes and feelings of certain persons),

(b) paragraphs 15 and 21 of Schedule 2 (promoting contact with parents and parents' obligation to contribute towards maintenance).

(3) Where a registered adoption society is authorised to place a child for adoption or a child who has been placed for adoption by a registered adoption society is less than six weeks old, regulations may provide—

(a) for section 61 of that Act to have effect in relation to the child whether or not he is accommodated by or on behalf of the society,

(b) for subsections (2)(b) to (d) and (3)(b) of that section (duty to ascertain wishes and feelings of certain persons) to apply with modifications, or not to apply, in relation to the child.

(4) Where a child's home is with persons who have given notice of intention to adopt, no contribution is payable (whether under a contribution order or otherwise) under Part 3 of Schedule 2 to that Act (contributions towards maintenance of children looked after by local authorities) in respect of the period referred to in subsection (5).

(5) That period begins when the notice of intention to adopt is given and ends if—

(a) the period of four months beginning with the giving of the notice expires without the prospective adopters applying for an adoption order, or

(b) an application for such an order is withdrawn or refused.

(6) In this section, 'notice of intention to adopt' includes notice of intention to apply for a Scottish or Northern Irish adoption order.

54 Disclosing information during adoption process Regulations under section 9 may require adoption agencies in prescribed circumstances to disclose in accordance with the regulations prescribed information to prospective adopters.

55 Revocation of adoptions on legitimation—(1) Where any child adopted by one natural parent as sole adoptive parent subsequently becomes a legitimated person on the marriage of the natural parents, the court by which the adoption order was made may, on the application of any of the parties concerned, revoke the order.

(2) In relation to an adoption order made by a magistrates' court, the reference in subsection (1) to the court by which the order was made includes a court acting for the same *petty sessions* [local justice] area.

Note. Sub-s (2): words 'petty sessions' in italics repealed and subsequent words in square brackets substituted by the Courts Act 2003, s 109(1), Sch 8, para 412 as from a date to be appointed.

Disclosure of information in relation to a person's adoption

56 Information to be kept about a person's adoption—(1) In relation to an adopted person, regulations may prescribe—

(a) the information which an adoption agency must keep in relation to his adoption,

(b) the form and manner in which it must keep that information.

(2) Below in this group of sections (that is, this section and sections 57 to 65), any information kept by an adoption agency by virtue of subsection (1)(a) is referred to as section 56 information.

(3) Regulations may provide for the transfer in prescribed circumstances of information held, or previously held, by an adoption agency to another adoption agency.

57 Restrictions on disclosure of protected etc information—(1) Any section 56 information kept by an adoption agency which—

(a) is about an adopted person or any other person, and

(b) is or includes identifying information about the person in question,

may only be disclosed by the agency to a person (other than the person the information is about) in pursuance of this group of sections.

(2) Any information kept by an adoption agency—

(a) which the agency has obtained from the Registrar General on an application under section 79(5) and any other information which would enable the adopted person to obtain a certified copy of the record of his birth, or

(b) which is information about an entry relating to the adopted person in the Adoption Contact Register,

may only be disclosed to a person by the agency in pursuance of this group of sections.

(3) In this group of sections, information the disclosure of which to a person is restricted by virtue of subsection (1) or (2) is referred to (in relation to him) as protected information.

(4) Identifying information about a person means information which, whether taken on its own or together with other information disclosed by an adoption agency, identifies the person or enables the person to be identified.

(5) This section does not prevent the disclosure of protected information in pursuance of a prescribed agreement to which the adoption agency is a party.

(6) Regulations may authorise or require an adoption agency to disclose protected information to a person who is not an adopted person.

58 Disclosure of other information—(1) This section applies to any section 56 information other than protected information.

(2) An adoption agency may for the purposes of its functions disclose to any person in accordance with prescribed arrangements any information to which this section applies.

(3) An adoption agency must, in prescribed circumstances, disclose prescribed information to a prescribed person.

59 Offence Regulations may provide that a registered adoption society which discloses any information in contravention of section 57 is to be guilty of an offence and liable on summary conviction to a fine not exceeding level 5 on the standard scale.

60 Disclosing information to adopted adult—(1) This section applies to an adopted person who has attained the age of 18 years.

(2) The adopted person has the right, at his request, to receive from the appropriate adoption agency—

(a) any information which would enable him to obtain a certified copy of the record of his birth, unless the High Court orders otherwise,

(b) any prescribed information disclosed to the adopters by the agency by virtue of section 54.

(3) The High Court may make an order under subsection (2)(a), on an application by the appropriate adoption agency, if satisfied that the circumstances are exceptional.

(4) The adopted person also has the right, at his request, to receive from the court which made the adoption order a copy of any prescribed document or prescribed order relating to the adoption.

(5) Subsection (4) does not apply to a document or order so far as it contains information which is protected information.

61 Disclosing protected information about adults—(1) This section applies where—

(a) a person applies to the appropriate adoption agency for protected information to be disclosed to him, and

(b) none of the information is about a person who is a child at the time of the application.

(2) The agency is not required to proceed with the application unless it considers it appropriate to do so.

(3) If the agency does proceed with the application it must take all reasonable steps to obtain the views of any person the information is about as to the disclosure of the information about him.

(4) The agency may then disclose the information if it considers it appropriate to do so.

(5) In deciding whether it is appropriate to proceed with the application or disclose the information, the agency must consider—

(a) the welfare of the adopted person,

(b) any views obtained under subsection (3),

(c) any prescribed matters,

and all the other circumstances of the case.

(6) This section does not apply to a request for information under section 60(2) or to a request for information which the agency is authorised or required to disclose in pursuance of regulations made by virtue of section 57(6).

62 Disclosing protected information about children—(1) This section applies where—

(a) a person applies to the appropriate adoption agency for protected information to be disclosed to him, and

(b) any of the information is about a person who is a child at the time of the application.

(2) The agency is not required to proceed with the application unless it considers it appropriate to do so.

(3) If the agency does proceed with the application, then, so far as the information is about a person who is at the time a child, the agency must take all reasonable steps to obtain—

(a) the views of any parent or guardian of the child, and

(b) the views of the child, if the agency considers it appropriate to do so having regard to his age and understanding and to all the other circumstances of the case,

as to the disclosure of the information.

(4) And, so far as the information is about a person who has at the time attained the age of 18 years, the agency must take all reasonable steps to obtain his views as to the disclosure of the information.

(5) The agency may then disclose the information if it considers it appropriate to do so.

(6) In deciding whether it is appropriate to proceed with the application, or disclose the information, where any of the information is about a person who is at the time a child—

(a) if the child is an adopted child, the child's welfare must be the paramount consideration,

(b) in the case of any other child, the agency must have particular regard to the child's welfare.

(7) And, in deciding whether it is appropriate to proceed with the application or disclose the information, the agency must consider—

(a) the welfare of the adopted person (where subsection (6)(a) does not apply),

(b) any views obtained under subsection (3) or (4),

(c) any prescribed matters,

and all the other circumstances of the case.

(8) This section does not apply to a request for information under section 60(2) or to a request for information which the agency is authorised or required to disclose in pursuance of regulations made by virtue of section 57(6).

63 Counselling—(1) Regulations may require adoption agencies to give information about the availability of counselling to persons—

(a) seeking information from them in pursuance of this group of sections,

(b) considering objecting or consenting to the disclosure of information by the agency in pursuance of this group of sections, or

(c) considering entering with the agency into an agreement prescribed for the purposes of section 57(5).

(2) Regulations may require adoption agencies to make arrangements to secure the provision of counselling for persons seeking information from them in prescribed circumstances in pursuance of this group of sections.

(3) The regulations may authorise adoption agencies—

(a) to disclose information which is required for the purposes of such counselling to the persons providing the counselling,

(b) where the person providing the counselling is outside the United Kingdom, to require a prescribed fee to be paid.

(4) The regulations may require any of the following persons to provide counselling for the purposes of arrangements under subsection (2)—

(a) a local authority, a council constituted under section 2 of the Local Government etc (Scotland) Act 1994 (c 39) or a Health and Social Services Board established under Article 16 of the Health and Personal Social Services (Northern Ireland) Order 1972 (SI 1972/1265 (NI 14)),

(b) a registered adoption society, an organisation within section 144(3)(b) or an adoption society which is registered under Article 4 of the Adoption (Northern Ireland) Order 1987 (SI 1987/2203 (NI 22)),

(c) an adoption support agency in respect of which a person is registered under Part 2 of the Care Standards Act 2000 (c 14).

(5) For the purposes of subsection (4), where the functions of a Health and Social Services Board are exercisable by a Health and Social Services Trust, the reference in sub-paragraph (a) to a Board is to be read as a reference to the Health and Social Services Trust.

64 Other provision to be made by regulations—(1) Regulations may make provision for the purposes of this group of sections, including provision as to—

(a) the performance by adoption agencies of their functions,

(b) the manner in which information may be received, and

(c) the matters mentioned below in this section.

(2) Regulations may prescribe—

(a) the manner in which agreements made by virtue of section 57(5) are to be recorded,

(b) the information to be provided by any person on an application for the disclosure of information under this group of sections.

(3) Regulations may require adoption agencies—

(a) to give to prescribed persons prescribed information about the rights or opportunities to obtain information, or to give their views as to its disclosure, given by this group of sections,

(b) to seek prescribed information from, or give prescribed information to, the Registrar General in prescribed circumstances.

(4) Regulations may require the Registrar General—

(a) to disclose to any person (including an adopted person) at his request any information which the person requires to assist him to make contact with the adoption agency which is the appropriate adoption agency in the case of an adopted person specified in the request (or, as the case may be, in the applicant's case),

(b) to disclose to the appropriate adoption agency any information which the agency requires about any entry relating to the adopted person on the Adoption Contact Register.

(5) Regulations may provide for the payment of a prescribed fee in respect of the disclosure in prescribed circumstances of any information in pursuance of section 60, 61 or 62; but an adopted person may not be required to pay any fee in respect of any information disclosed to him in relation to any person who (but for his adoption) would be related to him by blood (including half-blood) or marriage.

(6) Regulations may provide for the payment of a prescribed fee by an adoption agency obtaining information under subsection (4)(b).

65 Sections 56 to 65: interpretation—(1) In this group of sections—
'appropriate adoption agency', in relation to an adopted person or to information relating to his adoption, means—
    (a) if the person was placed for adoption by an adoption agency, that agency or (if different) the agency which keeps the information in relation to his adoption,
    (b) in any other case, the local authority to which notice of intention to adopt was given,
'prescribed' means prescribed by subordinate legislation,
'regulations' means regulations under section 9,
'subordinate legislation' means regulations or, in relation to information to be given by a court, rules.
(2) But—
(a) regulations under section 63(2) imposing any requirement on a council constituted under section 2 of the Local Government etc (Scotland) Act 1994 (c 39), or an organisation within section 144(3)(b), are to be made by the Scottish Ministers,
(b) regulations under section 63(2) imposing any requirement on a Health and Social Services Board established under Article 16 of the Health and Personal Social Services (Northern Ireland) Order 1972 (SI 1972/ 1265 (NI 14)), or an adoption society which is registered under Article 4 of the Adoption (Northern Ireland) Order 1987 (SI 1987/2203 (NI 22)), are to be made by the Department of Health, Social Services and Public Safety.
(3) The power of the Scottish Ministers or of the Department of Health, Social Services and Public Safety to make regulations under section 63(2) includes power to make—
(a) any supplementary, incidental or consequential provision,
(b) any transitory, transitional or saving provision,
which the person making the regulations considers necessary or expedient.
(4) Regulations prescribing any fee by virtue of section 64(6) require the approval of the Chancellor of the Exchequer.
(5) Regulations making any provision as to the manner in which any application is to be made for the disclosure of information by the Registrar General require his approval.

CHAPTER 4
STATUS OF ADOPTED CHILDREN

66 Meaning of adoption in Chapter 4—(1) In this Chapter 'adoption' means—
  (a) adoption by an adoption order or a Scottish or Northern Irish adoption order,
  (b) adoption by an order made in the Isle of Man or any of the Channel Islands,
  (c) an adoption effected under the law of a Convention country outside the British Islands, and certified in pursuance of Article 23(1) of the Convention (referred to in this Act as a 'Convention adoption'),
  (d) an overseas adoption, or
  (e) an adoption recognised by the law of England and Wales and effected under the law of any other country;
and related expressions are to be interpreted accordingly.

(2) But references in this Chapter to adoption do not include an adoption effected before the day on which this Chapter comes into force (referred to in this Chapter as 'the appointed day').

(3) Any reference in an enactment to an adopted person within the meaning of this Chapter includes a reference to an adopted child within the meaning of Part 4 of the Adoption Act 1976 (c 36).

67 Status conferred by adoption—(1) An adopted person is to be treated in law as if born as the child of the adopters or adopter.

(2) An adopted person is the legitimate child of the adopters or adopter and, if adopted by—
  (a) a couple, or
  (b) one of a couple under section 51(2),
is to be treated as the child of the relationship of the couple in question.

(3) An adopted person—
  (a) if adopted by one of a couple under section 51(2), is to be treated in law as not being the child of any person other than the adopter and the other one of the couple, and
  (b) in any other case, is to be treated in law, subject to subsection (4), as not being the child of any person other than the adopters or adopter;
but this subsection does not affect any reference in this Act to a person's natural parent or to any other natural relationship.

(4) In the case of a person adopted by one of the person's natural parents as sole adoptive parent, subsection (3)(b) has no effect as respects entitlement to property depending on relationship to that parent, or as respects anything else depending on that relationship.

(5) This section has effect from the date of the adoption.

(6) Subject to the provisions of this Chapter and Schedule 4, this section—
  (a) applies for the interpretation of enactments or instruments passed or made before as well as after the adoption, and so applies subject to any contrary indication, and
  (b) has effect as respects things done, or events occurring, on or after the adoption.

68 Adoptive relatives—(1) A relationship existing by virtue of section 67 may be referred to as an adoptive relationship, and—
  (a) an adopter may be referred to as an adoptive parent or (as the case may be) as an adoptive father or adoptive mother,
  (b) any other relative of any degree under an adoptive relationship may be referred to as an adoptive relative of that degree.

(2) Subsection (1) does not affect the interpretation of any reference, not qualified by the word 'adoptive', to a relationship.

(3) A reference (however expressed) to the adoptive mother and father of a child adopted by—
  (a) a couple of the same sex, or
  (b) a partner of the child's parent, where the couple are of the same sex,
is to be read as a reference to the child's adoptive parents.

69 Rules of interpretation for instruments concerning property—(1) The rules of interpretation contained in this section apply (subject to any contrary indication and to Schedule 4) to any instrument so far as it contains a disposition of property.

(2) In applying section 67(1) and (2) to a disposition which depends on the date of birth of a child or children of the adoptive parent or parents, the disposition is to be interpreted as if—
  (a) the adopted person had been born on the date of adoption,
  (b) two or more people adopted on the same date had been born on that date in the order of their actual births;
but this does not affect any reference to a person's age.

(3) Examples of phrases in wills on which subsection (2) can operate are—
1 Children of A 'living at my death or born afterwards'.
2 Children of A 'living at my death or born afterwards before any one of such children for the time being in existence attains a vested interest and who attain the age of 21 years'.
3 As in example 1 or 2, but referring to grandchildren of A instead of children of A.
4 A for life 'until he has a child', and then to his child or children.

Note. Subsection (2) will not affect the reference to the age of 21 years in example 2.

(4) Section 67(3) does not prejudice—
  (a) any qualifying interest, or
  (b) any interest expectant (whether immediately or not) upon a qualifying interest.
'Qualifying interest' means an interest vested in possession in the adopted person before the adoption.

(5) Where it is necessary to determine for the purposes of a disposition of property effected by an instrument whether a woman can have a child—
  (a) it must be presumed that once a woman has attained the age of 55 years she will not adopt a person after execution of the instrument, and
  (b) if she does so, then (in spite of section 67) that person is not to be treated as her child or (if she does so as one of a couple) as the child of the other one of the couple for the purposes of the instrument.

(6) In this section, 'instrument' includes a private Act settling property, but not any other enactment.

70 Dispositions depending on date of birth—(1) Where a disposition depends on the date of birth of a person who was born illegitimate and who is adopted by one of the natural parents as sole adoptive parent, section 69(2) does not affect entitlement by virtue of Part 3 of the Family Law Reform Act 1987 (c 42) (dispositions of property).

(2) Subsection (1) applies for example where—
  (a) a testator dies in 2001 bequeathing a legacy to his eldest grandchild living at a specified time,
  (b) his unmarried daughter has a child in 2002 who is the first grandchild,
  (c) his married son has a child in 2003,
  (d) subsequently his unmarried daughter adopts her child as sole adoptive parent.
In that example the status of the daughter's child as the eldest grandchild of the testator is not affected by the events described in paragraphs (c) and (d).

71 Property devolving with peerages etc—(1) An adoption does not affect the descent of any peerage or dignity or title of honour.

(2) An adoption does not affect the devolution of any property limited (expressly or not) to devolve (as nearly as the law permits) along with any peerage or dignity or title of honour.

(3) Subsection (2) applies only if and so far as a contrary intention is not expressed in the instrument, and has effect subject to the terms of the instrument.

72 Protection of trustees and personal representatives—(1) A trustee or personal representative is not under a duty, by virtue of the law relating to trusts or the administration of estates, to enquire, before conveying or distributing any property, whether any adoption has been effected or revoked if that fact could affect entitlement to the property.

(2) A trustee or personal representative is not liable to any person by reason of a conveyance or distribution of the property made without regard to any such fact if he has not received notice of the fact before the conveyance or distribution.

(3) This section does not prejudice the right of a person to follow the property, or any property representing it, into the hands of another person, other than a purchaser, who has received it.

73 Meaning of disposition—(1) This section applies for the purposes of this Chapter.

(2) A disposition includes the conferring of a power of appointment and any other disposition of an interest in or right over property; and in this subsection a power of appointment includes any discretionary power to transfer a beneficial interest in property without the furnishing of valuable consideration.

(3) This Chapter applies to an oral disposition as if contained in an instrument made when the disposition was made.

(4) The date of death of a testator is the date at which a will or codicil is to be regarded as made.

(5) The provisions of the law of intestate succession applicable to the estate of a deceased person are to be treated as if contained in an instrument executed by him (while of full capacity) immediately before his death.

74 Miscellaneous enactments—(1) Section 67 does not apply for the purposes of—

(a) the table of kindred and affinity in Schedule 1 to the Marriage Act 1949 (c 76), [or

(b) sections 10 and 11 of the Sexual Offences Act 1956 (c 69) (incest), or

[(b) sections 64 and 65 of the Sexual Offences Act 2003 (sex with an adult relative)].

(c) section 54 of the Criminal Law Act 1977 (c 45) (inciting a girl to commit incest).

(2) Section 67 does not apply for the purposes of any provision of—

(a) the British Nationality Act 1981 (c 61),

(b) the Immigration Act 1971 (c 77),

(c) any instrument having effect under an enactment within paragraph (a) or (b), or

(d) any other provision of the law for the time being in force which determines British citizenship, British overseas territories citizenship, the status of a British National (Overseas) or British Overseas citizenship.

Note Sub-s (1): para (b) and word 'or' immediately preceding it substituted, for paras (b), (c) as originally enacted, by the Sexual Offences Act 2003, s 139, Sch 6, para 47 as from 1 May 2004.

75 Pensions Section 67(3) does not affect entitlement to a pension which is payable to or for the benefit of a person and is in payment at the time of the person's adoption.

76 Insurance—(1) Where a child is adopted whose natural parent has effected an insurance with a friendly society or a collecting society or an industrial insurance company for the payment on the death of the child of money for funeral expenses, then—

(a) the rights and liabilities under the policy are by virtue of the adoption transferred to the adoptive parents, and

(b) for the purposes of the enactments relating to such societies and companies, the adoptive parents are to be treated as the person who took out the policy.

(2) Where the adoption is effected by an order made by virtue of section 51(2), the references in subsection (1) to the adoptive parents are to be read as references to the adopter and the other one of the couple.

CHAPTER 5
THE REGISTERS

Adopted Children Register etc

77 Adopted Children Register—(1) The Registrar General must continue to maintain in the General Register Office a register, to be called the Adopted Children Register.

(2) The Adopted Children Register is not to be open to public inspection or search.

(3) No entries may be made in the Adopted Children Register other than entries—

(a) directed to be made in it by adoption orders, or

(b) required to be made under Schedule 1.

(4) A certified copy of an entry in the Adopted Children Register, if purporting to be sealed or stamped with the seal of the General Register Office, is to be received as evidence of the adoption to which it relates without further or other proof.

(5) Where an entry in the Adopted Children Register contains a record—

(a) of the date of birth of the adopted person, or

(b) of the country, or the district and sub-district, of the birth of the adopted person,

a certified copy of the entry is also to be received, without further or other proof, as evidence of that date, or country or district and sub-district, (as the case may be) in all respects as if the copy were a certified copy of an entry in the registers of live-births.

(6) Schedule 1 (registration of adoptions and the amendment of adoption orders) is to have effect.

78 Searches and copies—(1) The Registrar General must continue to maintain at the General Register Office an index of the Adopted Children Register.

(2) Any person may—

(a) search the index,

(b) have a certified copy of any entry in the Adopted Children Register.

(3) But a person is not entitled to have a certified copy of an entry in the Adopted Children Register relating to an adopted person who has not attained the age of 18 years unless the applicant has provided the Registrar General with the prescribed particulars.

'Prescribed' means prescribed by regulations made by the Registrar General with the approval of the Chancellor of the Exchequer.

(4) The terms, conditions and regulations as to payment of fees, and otherwise, applicable under the Births and Deaths Registration Act 1953 (c 20), and the Registration Service Act 1953 (c 37), in respect of—

(a) searches in the index kept in the General Register Office of certified copies of entries in the registers of live-births,

(b) the supply from that office of certified copies of entries in those certified copies,

also apply in respect of searches, and supplies of certified copies, under subsection (2).

79 Connections between the register and birth records—(1) The Registrar General must make traceable the connection between any entry in the registers of live-births or other records which has been marked 'Adopted' and any corresponding entry in the Adopted Children Register.

(2) Information kept by the Registrar General for the purposes of subsection (1) is not to be open to public inspection or search.

(3) Any such information, and any other information which would enable an adopted person to obtain a certified copy of the record of his birth, may only be disclosed by the Registrar General in accordance with this section.

(4) In relation to a person adopted before the appointed day the court may, in exceptional circumstances, order the Registrar General to give any information mentioned in subsection (3) to a person.

(5) On an application made in the prescribed manner by the appropriate adoption agency in respect of an adopted person a record of whose birth is kept by the Registrar General, the Registrar General must give the agency any information relating to the adopted person which is mentioned in subsection (3).

'Appropriate adoption agency' has the same meaning as in section 65.

(6) In relation to a person adopted before the appointed day, Schedule 2 applies instead of subsection (5).

(7) On an application made in the prescribed manner by an adopted person a record of whose birth is kept by the Registrar General and who—

(a) is under the age of 18 years, and

(b) intends to be married,

the Registrar General must inform the applicant whether or not it appears from information contained in the registers of live-births or other records that the applicant and the person whom the applicant intends to marry may be within the prohibited degrees of relationship for the purposes of the Marriage Act 1949 (c 76).

(8) Before the Registrar General gives any information by virtue of this section, any prescribed fee which he has demanded must be paid.

(9) In this section—

'appointed day' means the day appointed for the commencement of sections 56 to 65,

'prescribed' means prescribed by regulations made by the Registrar General with the approval of the Chancellor of the Exchequer.

Adoption Contact Register

80 Adoption Contact Register—(1) The Registrar General must continue to maintain at the General Register Office in accordance with regulations a register in two Parts to be called the Adoption Contact Register.

(2) Part 1 of the register is to contain the prescribed information about adopted persons who have given the prescribed notice expressing their wishes as to making contact with their relatives.

(3) The Registrar General may only make an entry in Part 1 of the register for an adopted person—

(a) a record of whose birth is kept by the Registrar General,

(b) who has attained the age of 18 years, and

(c) who the Registrar General is satisfied has such information as is necessary to enable him to obtain a certified copy of the record of his birth.

(4) Part 2 of the register is to contain the prescribed information about persons who have given the prescribed notice expressing their wishes, as relatives of adopted persons, as to making contact with those persons.

(5) The Registrar General may only make an entry in Part 2 of the register for a person—

(a) who has attained the age of 18 years, and

(b) who the Registrar General is satisfied is a relative of an adopted person and has such information as is necessary to enable him to obtain a certified copy of the record of the adopted person's birth.

(6) Regulations may provide for—

(a) the disclosure of information contained in one Part of the register to persons for whom there is an entry in the other Part,

(b) the payment of prescribed fees in respect of the making or alteration of entries in the register and the disclosure of information contained in the register.

81 Adoption Contact Register: supplementary—(1) The Adoption Contact Register is not to be open to public inspection or search.

(2) In section 80, 'relative', in relation to an adopted person, means any person who (but for his adoption) would be related to him by blood (including half-blood) or marriage.

(3) The Registrar General must not give any information entered in the register to any person except in accordance with subsection (6)(a) of that section or regulations made by virtue of section 64(4)(b).

(4) In section 80, 'regulations' means regulations made by the Registrar General with the approval of the Chancellor of the Exchequer, and 'prescribed' means prescribed by such regulations.

General

82 Interpretation—(1) In this Chapter—

'records' includes certified copies kept by the Registrar General of entries in any register of births,

'registers of live-births' means the registers of live-births made under the Births and Deaths Registration Act 1953 (c 20).

(2) Any register, record or index maintained under this Chapter may be maintained in any form the Registrar General considers appropriate; and references (however expressed) to entries in such a register, or to their amendment, marking or cancellation, are to be read accordingly.

CHAPTER 6
ADOPTIONS WITH A FOREIGN ELEMENT

Bringing children into and out of the United Kingdom

83 Restriction on bringing children in—(1) This section applies where a person who is habitually resident in the British Islands (the 'British resident')—

(a) brings, or causes another to bring, a child who is habitually resident outside the British Islands into the United Kingdom for the purpose of adoption by the British resident, or

(b) at any time brings, or causes another to bring, into the United Kingdom a child adopted by the British resident under an external adoption effected within the period of six months ending with that time.

The references to adoption, or to a child adopted, by the British resident include a reference to adoption, or to a child adopted, by the British resident and another person.

(2) But this section does not apply if the child is intended to be adopted under a Convention adoption order.

(3) An external adoption means an adoption, other than a Convention adoption, of a child effected under the law of any country or territory outside the British Islands, whether or not the adoption is—

(a) an adoption within the meaning of Chapter 4, or
(b) a full adoption (within the meaning of section 88(3)).

(4) Regulations may require a person intending to bring, or to cause another to bring, a child into the United Kingdom in circumstances where this section applies—

(a) to apply to an adoption agency (including a Scottish or Northern Irish adoption agency) in the prescribed manner for an assessment of his suitability to adopt the child, and
(b) to give the agency any information it may require for the purpose of the assessment.

(5) Regulations may require prescribed conditions to be met in respect of a child brought into the United Kingdom in circumstances where this section applies.

(6) In relation to a child brought into the United Kingdom for adoption in circumstances where this section applies, regulations may—

(a) provide for any provision of Chapter 3 to apply with modifications or not to apply,
(b) if notice of intention to adopt has been given, impose functions in respect of the child on the local authority to which the notice was given.

(7) If a person brings, or causes another to bring, a child into the United Kingdom at any time in circumstances where this section applies, he is guilty of an offence if—

(a) he has not complied with any requirement imposed by virtue of subsection (4), or
(b) any condition required to be met by virtue of subsection (5) is not met,

before that time, or before any later time which may be prescribed.

(8) A person guilty of an offence under this section is liable—

(a) on summary conviction to imprisonment for a term not exceeding six months, or a fine not exceeding the statutory maximum, or both,
(b) on conviction on indictment, to imprisonment for a term not exceeding twelve months, or a fine, or both.

(9) In this section, 'prescribed' means prescribed by regulations and 'regulations' means regulations made by the Secretary of State, after consultation with the Assembly.

84 Giving parental responsibility prior to adoption abroad

(1) The High Court may, on an application by persons who the court is satisfied intend to adopt a child under the law of a country or territory outside the British Islands, make an order giving parental responsibility for the child to them.

(2) An order under this section may not give parental responsibility to persons who the court is satisfied meet those requirements as to domicile, or habitual residence, in England and Wales which have to be met if an adoption order is to be made in favour of those persons.

(3) An order under this section may not be made unless any requirements prescribed by regulations are satisfied.

(4) An application for an order under this section may not be made unless at all times during the preceding ten weeks the child's home was with the applicant or, in the case of an application by two people, both of them.

(5) Section 46(2) to (4) has effect in relation to an order under this section as it has effect in relation to adoption orders.

(6) Regulations may provide for any provision of this Act which refers to adoption orders to apply, with or without modifications, to orders under this section.

(7) In this section, 'regulations' means regulations made by the Secretary of State, after consultation with the Assembly.

85 Restriction on taking children out—(1) A child who—

    (a) is a Commonwealth citizen, or

    (b) is habitually resident in the United Kingdom,

must not be removed from the United Kingdom to a place outside the British Islands for the purpose of adoption unless the condition in subsection (2) is met.

    (2) The condition is that—

    (a) the prospective adopters have parental responsibility for the child by virtue of an order under section 84, or

    (b) the child is removed under the authority of an order under section 49 of the Adoption (Scotland) Act 1978 (c 28) or Article 57 of the Adoption (Northern Ireland) Order 1987 (SI 1987/2203 (NI 22)).

(3) Removing a child from the United Kingdom includes arranging to do so; and the circumstances in which a person arranges to remove a child from the United Kingdom include those where he—

    (a) enters into an arrangement for the purpose of facilitating such a removal of the child,

    (b) initiates or takes part in any negotiations of which the purpose is the conclusion of an arrangement within paragraph (a), or

An arrangement includes an agreement (whether or not enforceable).

(4) A person who removes a child from the United Kingdom in contravention of subsection (1) is guilty of an offence.

(5) A person is not guilty of an offence under subsection (4) of causing a person to take any step mentioned in paragraph (a) or (b) of subsection (3) unless it is proved that he knew or had reason to suspect that the step taken would contravene subsection (1).

But this subsection only applies if sufficient evidence is adduced to raise an issue as to whether the person had the knowledge or reason mentioned.

    (6) A person guilty of an offence under this section is liable—

    (a) on summary conviction to imprisonment for a term not exceeding six months, or a fine not exceeding the statutory maximum, or both,

    (b) on conviction on indictment, to imprisonment for a term not exceeding twelve months, or a fine, or both.

    (7) In any proceedings under this section—

    (a) a report by a British consular officer or a deposition made before a British consular officer and authenticated under the signature of that officer is admissible, upon proof that the officer or the deponent cannot be found in the United Kingdom, as evidence of the matters stated in it, and

    (b) it is not necessary to prove the signature or official character of the person who appears to have signed any such report or deposition.

86 Power to modify sections 83 and 85—(1) Regulations may provide for section 83 not to apply if—

    (a) the adopters or (as the case may be) prospective adopters are natural parents, natural relatives or guardians of the child in question (or one of them is), or

(b) the British resident in question is a partner of a parent of the child,
and any prescribed conditions are met.

(2) Regulations may provide for section 85(1) to apply with modifications, or
not to apply, if—

(a) the prospective adopters are parents, relatives or guardians of the child in
question (or one of them is), or

(b) the prospective adopter is a partner of a parent of the child,
and any prescribed conditions are met.

(3) On the occasion of the first exercise of the power to make regulations
under this section—

(a) the statutory instrument containing the regulations is not to be made unless
a draft of the instrument has been laid before, and approved by a resolution
of, each House of Parliament, and

(b) accordingly section 140(2) does not apply to the instrument.

(4) In this section, 'prescribed' means prescribed by regulations and
'regulations' means regulations made by the Secretary of State after consultation
with the Assembly.

Overseas adoptions

87 Overseas adoptions—(1) In this Act, 'overseas adoption'—

(a) means an adoption of a description specified in an order made by the
Secretary of State, being a description of adoptions effected under the law
of any country or territory outside the British Islands, but

(b) does not include a Convention adoption.

(2) Regulations may prescribe the requirements that ought to be met by an
adoption of any description effected after the commencement of the regulations
for it to be an overseas adoption for the purposes of this Act.

(3) At any time when such regulations have effect, the Secretary of State must
exercise his powers under this section so as to secure that subsequently effected
adoptions of any description are not overseas adoptions for the purposes of this
Act if he considers that they are not likely within a reasonable time to meet the
prescribed requirements.

(4) In this section references to this Act include the Adoption Act 1976 (c 36).

(5) An order under this section may contain provision as to the manner in
which evidence of any overseas adoption may be given.

(6) In this section—

'adoption' means an adoption of a child or of a person who was a child at the
time the adoption was applied for,

'regulations' means regulations made by the Secretary of State after consultation
with the Assembly.

Miscellaneous

88 Modification of section 67 for Hague Convention adoptions—(1) If the
High Court is satisfied, on an application under this section, that each of the
following conditions is met in the case of a Convention adoption, it may direct that
section 67(3) does not apply, or does not apply to any extent specified in the
direction.

(2) The conditions are—

(a) that under the law of the country in which the adoption was effected, the
adoption is not a full adoption,

(b) that the consents referred to in Article 4(c) and (d) of the Convention have
not been given for a full adoption or that the United Kingdom is not the
receiving State (within the meaning of Article 2 of the Convention),

(c)   that it would be more favourable to the adopted child for a direction to be given under subsection (1).

(3)   A full adoption is an adoption by virtue of which the child is to be treated in law as not being the child of any person other than the adopters or adopter.

(4)   In relation to a direction under this section and an application for it, sections 59 and 60 of the Family Law Act 1986 (c 55) (declarations under Part 3 of that Act as to marital status) apply as they apply in relation to a direction under that Part and an application for such a direction.

89 Annulment etc of overseas or Hague Convention adoptions—(1) The High Court may, on an application under this subsection, by order annul a Convention adoption or Convention adoption order on the ground that the adoption is contrary to public policy.

(2)   The High Court may, on an application under this subsection—

(a)   by order provide for an overseas adoption or a determination under section 91 to cease to be valid on the ground that the adoption or determination is contrary to public policy or that the authority which purported to authorise the adoption or make the determination was not competent to entertain the case, or

(b)   decide the extent, if any, to which a determination under section 91 has been affected by a subsequent determination under that section.

(3)   The High Court may, in any proceedings in that court, decide that an overseas adoption or a determination under section 91 is to be treated, for the purposes of those proceedings, as invalid on either of the grounds mentioned in subsection (2)(a).

(4)   Subject to the preceding provisions, the validity of a Convention adoption, Convention adoption order or overseas adoption or a determination under section 91 cannot be called in question in proceedings in any court in England and Wales.

90 Section 89: supplementary—(1) Any application for an order under section 89 or a decision under subsection (2)(b) or (3) of that section must be made in the prescribed manner and within any prescribed period.

'Prescribed' means prescribed by rules.

(2)   No application may be made under section 89(1) in respect of an adoption unless immediately before the application is made—

(a)   the person adopted, or

(b)   the adopters or adopter,

habitually reside in England and Wales.

(3)   In deciding in pursuance of section 89 whether such an authority as is mentioned in section 91 was competent to entertain a particular case, a court is bound by any finding of fact made by the authority and stated by the authority to be so made for the purpose of determining whether the authority was competent to entertain the case.

91 Overseas determinations and orders—(1) Subsection (2) applies where any authority of a Convention country (other than the United Kingdom) or of the Channel Islands, the Isle of Man or any British overseas territory has power under the law of that country or territory—

(a)   to authorise, or review the authorisation of, an adoption order made in that country or territory, or

(b)   to give or review a decision revoking or annulling such an order or a Convention adoption.

(2)   If the authority makes a determination in the exercise of that power, the determination is to have effect for the purpose of effecting, confirming or terminating the adoption in question or, as the case may be, confirming its termination.

(3) Subsection (2) is subject to section 89 and to any subsequent determination having effect under that subsection.

CHAPTER 7
MISCELLANEOUS

Restrictions

92 Restriction on arranging adoptions etc—(1) A person who is neither an adoption agency nor acting in pursuance of an order of the High Court must not take any of the steps mentioned in subsection (2).

(2) The steps are—
(a) asking a person other than an adoption agency to provide a child for adoption,
(b) asking a person other than an adoption agency to provide prospective adopters for a child,
(c) offering to find a child for adoption,
(d) offering a child for adoption to a person other than an adoption agency,
(e) handing over a child to any person other than an adoption agency with a view to the child's adoption by that or another person,
(f) receiving a child handed over to him in contravention of paragraph (e),
(g) entering into an agreement with any person for the adoption of a child, or for the purpose of facilitating the adoption of a child, where no adoption agency is acting on behalf of the child in the adoption,
(h) initiating or taking part in negotiations of which the purpose is the conclusion of an agreement within paragraph (g),
(i) causing another person to take any of the steps mentioned in paragraphs (a) to (h).

(3) Subsection (1) does not apply to a person taking any of the steps mentioned in paragraphs (d), (e), (g), (h) and (i) of subsection (2) if the following condition is met.

(4) The condition is that—
(a) the prospective adopters are parents, relatives or guardians of the child (or one of them is), or
(b) the prospective adopter is the partner of a parent of the child.

(5) References to an adoption agency in subsection (2) include a prescribed person outside the United Kingdom exercising functions corresponding to those of an adoption agency, if the functions are being exercised in prescribed circumstances in respect of the child in question.

(6) The Secretary of State may, after consultation with the Assembly, by order make any amendments of subsections (1) to (4), and any consequential amendments of this Act, which he considers necessary or expedient.

(7) In this section—
(a) 'agreement' includes an arrangement (whether or not enforceable),
(b) 'prescribed' means prescribed by regulations made by the Secretary of State after consultation with the Assembly.

93 Offence of breaching restrictions under section 92—(1) If a person contravenes section 92(1), he is guilty of an offence; and, if that person is an adoption society, the person who manages the society is also guilty of the offence.

(2) A person is not guilty of an offence under subsection (1) of taking the step mentioned in paragraph (f) of section 92(2) unless it is proved that he knew or had reason to suspect that the child was handed over to him in contravention of paragraph (e) of that subsection.

(3) A person is not guilty of an offence under subsection (1) of causing a person to take any of the steps mentioned in paragraphs (a) to (h) of section 92(2)

unless it is proved that he knew or had reason to suspect that the step taken would contravene the paragraph in question.

(4) But subsections (2) and (3) only apply if sufficient evidence is adduced to raise an issue as to whether the person had the knowledge or reason mentioned.

(5) A person guilty of an offence under this section is liable on summary conviction to imprisonment for a term not exceeding six months, or a fine not exceeding £10,000, or both.

94 Restriction on reports—(1) A person who is not within a prescribed description may not, in any prescribed circumstances, prepare a report for any person about the suitability of a child for adoption or of a person to adopt a child or about the adoption, or placement for adoption, of a child.

'Prescribed' means prescribed by regulations made by the Secretary of State after consultation with the Assembly.

(2) If a person—

(a) contravenes subsection (1), or

(b) causes a person to prepare a report, or submits to any person a report which has been prepared, in contravention of that subsection,

he is guilty of an offence.

(3) If a person who works for an adoption society—

(a) contravenes subsection (1), or

(b) causes a person to prepare a report, or submits to any person a report which has been prepared, in contravention of that subsection,

the person who manages the society is also guilty of the offence.

(4) A person is not guilty of an offence under subsection (2)(b) unless it is proved that he knew or had reason to suspect that the report would be, or had been, prepared in contravention of subsection (1).

But this subsection only applies if sufficient evidence is adduced to raise an issue as to whether the person had the knowledge or reason mentioned.

(5) A person guilty of an offence under this section is liable on summary conviction to imprisonment for a term not exceeding six months, or a fine not exceeding level 5 on the standard scale, or both.

95 Prohibition of certain payments—(1) This section applies to any payment (other than an excepted payment) which is made for or in consideration of—

(a) the adoption of a child,

(b) giving any consent required in connection with the adoption of a child,

(c) removing from the United Kingdom a child who is a Commonwealth citizen, or is habitually resident in the United Kingdom, to a place outside the British Islands for the purpose of adoption,

(d) a person (who is neither an adoption agency nor acting in pursuance of an order of the High Court) taking any step mentioned in section 92(2),

(e) preparing, causing to be prepared or submitting a report the preparation of which contravenes section 94(1).

(2) In this section and section 96, removing a child from the United Kingdom has the same meaning as in section 85.

(3) Any person who—

(a) makes any payment to which this section applies,

(b) agrees or offers to make any such payment, or

(c) receives or agrees to receive or attempts to obtain any such payment,

is guilty of an offence.

(4) A person guilty of an offence under this section is liable on summary conviction to imprisonment for a term not exceeding six months, or a fine not exceeding £10,000, or both.

96 Excepted payments—(1) A payment is an excepted payment if it is made by virtue of, or in accordance with provision made by or under, this Act, the Adoption (Scotland) Act 1978 (c 28) or the Adoption (Northern Ireland) Order 1987 (SI 1987/2203 (NI 22)).

(2) A payment is an excepted payment if it is made to a registered adoption society by—

(a) a parent or guardian of a child, or

(b) a person who adopts or proposes to adopt a child,

in respect of expenses reasonably incurred by the society in connection with the adoption or proposed adoption of the child.

(3) A payment is an excepted payment if it is made in respect of any legal or medical expenses incurred or to be incurred by any person in connection with an application to a court which he has made or proposes to make for an adoption order, a placement order, or an order under section 26 or 84.

(4) A payment made as mentioned in section 95(1)(c) is an excepted payment if—

(a) the condition in section 85(2) is met, and

(b) the payment is made in respect of the travel and accommodation expenses reasonably incurred in removing the child from the United Kingdom for the purpose of adoption.

97 Sections 92 to 96: interpretation In sections 92 to 96—

(a) 'adoption agency' includes a Scottish or Northern Irish adoption agency,

(b) 'payment' includes reward,

(c) references to adoption are to the adoption of persons, wherever they may be habitually resident, effected under the law of any country or territory, whether within or outside the British Islands.

Information

98 Pre-commencement adoptions: information—(1) Regulations under section 9 may make provision for the purpose of—

(a) assisting persons adopted before the appointed day who have attained the age of 18 to obtain information in relation to their adoption, and

(b) facilitating contact between such persons and their relatives.

(2) For that purpose the regulations may confer functions on—

(a) registered adoption support agencies,

(b) the Registrar General,

(c) adoption agencies.

(3) For that purpose the regulations may—

(a) authorise or require any person mentioned in subsection (2) to disclose information,

(b) authorise or require the disclosure of information contained in records kept under section 8 of the Public Records Act 1958 (c 51) (court records),

and may impose conditions on the disclosure of information, including conditions restricting its further disclosure.

(4) The regulations may authorise the charging of prescribed fees by any person mentioned in subsection (2) or in respect of the disclosure of information under subsection (3)(b).

(5) An authorisation or requirement to disclose information by virtue of subsection (3)(a) has effect in spite of any restriction on the disclosure of information in Chapter 5.

(6) The making of regulations by virtue of subsections (2) to (4) which relate to the Registrar General requires the approval of the Chancellor of the Exchequer.

(7) In this section—

'appointed day' means the day appointed for the commencement of sections 56
  to 65,
'registered adoption support agency' means an adoption support agency in
  respect of which a person is registered under Part 2 of the Care Standards
  Act 2000 (c 14),
'relative', in relation to an adopted person, means any person who (but for his
  adoption) would be related to him by blood (including half-blood) or
  marriage.

Proceedings

99 Proceedings for offences Proceedings for an offence by virtue of section 9
or 59 may not, without the written consent of the Attorney General, be taken by
any person other than *the National Care Standards Commission* [the Commission for
Social Care Inspection] or the Assembly.

Note Words 'the Commission for Social Care Inspection' in square substituted by the Health
and Social Care (Community Health and Standards) Act 2003, s 147, Sch 9, para 32 as from 1
April 2004.

100 Appeals In section 94 of the 1989 Act (appeals under that Act), in
subsections (1)(a) and (2), after 'this Act' there is inserted 'or the Adoption and
Children Act 2002'.

101 Privacy—(1) Proceedings under this Act in the High Court or a County Court
may be heard and determined in private.

(2) In section 12 of the Administration of Justice Act 1960 (c 65) (publication
of information relating to proceedings in private), in subsection (1)(a)(ii), after
'1989' there is inserted 'or the Adoption and Children Act 2002'.

(3) In section 97 of the 1989 Act (privacy for children involved in certain
proceedings), after 'this Act' in subsections (1) and (2) there is inserted 'or the
Adoption and Children Act 2002'.

The Children and Family Court Advisory and Support Service

102 Officers of the Service—(1) For the purposes of—
  (a) any relevant application,
  (b) the signification by any person of any consent to placement or adoption,
rules must provide for the appointment in prescribed cases of an officer of the
Children and Family Court Advisory and Support Service ('the Service').

(2) The rules may provide for the appointment of such an officer in other
circumstances in which it appears to the Lord Chancellor to be necessary or
expedient to do so.

(3) The rules may provide for the officer—
  (a) to act on behalf of the child upon the hearing of any relevant application,
    with the duty of safeguarding the interests of the child in the prescribed
    manner,
  (b) where the court so requests, to prepare a report on matters relating to the
    welfare of the child in question,
  (c) to witness documents which signify consent to placement or adoption,
  (d) to perform prescribed functions.

(4) A report prepared in pursuance of the rules on matters relating to the
welfare of a child must—
  (a) deal with prescribed matters (unless the court orders otherwise), and
  (b) be made in the manner required by the court.
  (5) A person who—

(a) in the case of an application for the making, varying or revocation of a placement order, is employed by the local authority which made the application,

(b) in the case of an application for an adoption order in respect of a child who was placed for adoption, is employed by the adoption agency which placed him, or

(c) is within a prescribed description,

is not to be appointed under subsection (1) or (2).

(6) In this section, 'relevant application' means an application for—

(a) the making, varying or revocation of a placement order,

(b) the making of an order under section 26, or the varying or revocation of such an order,

(c) the making of an adoption order, or

(d) the making of an order under section 84.

(7) Rules may make provision as to the assistance which the court may require an officer of the Service to give to it.

103 Right of officers of the Service to have access to adoption agency records—(1) Where an officer of the Service has been appointed to act under section 102(1), he has the right at all reasonable times to examine and take copies of any records of, or held by, an adoption agency which were compiled in connection with the making, or proposed making, by any person of any application under this Part in respect of the child concerned.

(2) Where an officer of the Service takes a copy of any record which he is entitled to examine under this section, that copy or any part of it is admissible as evidence of any matter referred to in any—

(a) report which he makes to the court in the proceedings in question, or

(b) evidence which he gives in those proceedings.

(3) Subsection (2) has effect regardless of any enactment or rule of law which would otherwise prevent the record in question being admissible in evidence.

Evidence

104 Evidence of consent—(1) If a document signifying any consent which is required by this Part to be given is witnessed in accordance with rules, it is to be admissible in evidence without further proof of the signature of the person by whom it was executed.

(2) A document signifying any such consent which purports to be witnessed in accordance with rules is to be presumed to be so witnessed, and to have been executed and witnessed on the date and at the place specified in the document, unless the contrary is proved.

Scotland, Northern Ireland and the Islands

105 Effect of certain Scottish orders and provisions—(1) A Scottish adoption order or an order under section 25 of the Adoption (Scotland) Act 1978 (c 28) (interim adoption orders) has effect in England and Wales as it has in Scotland, but as if references to the parental responsibilities and the parental rights in relation to a child were to parental responsibility for the child.

(2) An order made under section 18 of the Adoption (Scotland) Act 1978 (freeing orders), and the revocation or variation of such an order under section 20 or 21 of that Act, have effect in England and Wales as they have effect in Scotland, but as if references to the parental responsibilities and the parental rights in relation to a child were to parental responsibility for the child.

(3) Any person who—

   (a) contravenes section 27(1) of that Act (removal where adoption agreed etc), or

   (b) contravenes section 28(1) or (2) of that Act (removal where applicant provided home),

is guilty of an offence and liable on summary conviction to imprisonment for a term not exceeding three months, or a fine not exceeding level 5 on the standard scale, or both.

   (4) Orders made under section 29 of that Act (order to return or not to remove child) are to have effect in England and Wales as if they were orders of the High Court under section 41 of this Act.

106 Effect of certain Northern Irish orders and provisions—(1) A Northern Irish adoption order or an order under Article 26 of the Adoption (Northern Ireland) Order 1987 (SI 1987/2203 (NI 22)) (interim orders) has effect in England and Wales as it has in Northern Ireland.

   (2) An order made under Article 17 or 18 of the Adoption (Northern Ireland) Order 1987 (freeing orders), or the variation or revocation of such an order under Article 20 or 21 of that Order, have effect in England and Wales as they have in Northern Ireland.

   (3) Any person who—

   (a) contravenes Article 28(1) or (2) of the Adoption (Northern Ireland) Order 1987 (removal where adoption agreed etc), or

   (b) contravenes Article 29(1) or (2) of that Order (removal where applicant provided home),

is guilty of an offence and liable on summary conviction to imprisonment for a term not exceeding three months, or a fine not exceeding level 5 on the standard scale, or both.

   (4) Orders made under Article 30 of that Order (order to return or not to remove child) are to have effect in England and Wales as if they were orders of the High Court under section 41 of this Act.

107 Use of adoption records from other parts of the British Islands Any document which is receivable as evidence of any matter—

   (a) in Scotland under section 45(2) of the Adoption (Scotland) Act 1978 (c 28),

   (b) in Northern Ireland under Article 63(1) of the Adoption (Northern Ireland) Order 1987, or

   (c) in the Isle of Man or any of the Channel Islands under an enactment corresponding to section 77(3) of this Act,

is also receivable as evidence of that matter in England and Wales.

108 Channel Islands and the Isle of Man—(1) Regulations may provide—

   (a) for a reference in any provision of this Act to an order of a court to include an order of a court in the Isle of Man or any of the Channel Islands which appears to the Secretary of State to correspond in its effect to the order in question,

   (b) for a reference in any provision of this Act to an adoption agency to include a person who appears to the Secretary of State to exercise functions under the law of the Isle of Man or any of the Channel Islands which correspond to those of an adoption agency and for any reference in any provision of this Act to a child placed for adoption by an adoption agency to be read accordingly,

   (c) for a reference in any provision of this Act to an enactment (including an enactment contained in this Act) to include a provision of the law of the Isle of Man or any of the Channel Islands which appears to the Secretary of State to correspond in its effect to the enactment,

(d) for any reference in any provision of this Act to the United Kingdom to include the Isle of Man or any of the Channel Islands.

(2) Regulations may modify any provision of this Act, as it applies to any order made, or other thing done, under the law of the Isle of Man or any of the Channel Islands.

(3) In this section, 'regulations' means regulations made by the Secretary of State after consultation with the Assembly.

General

109 Avoiding delay—(1) In proceedings in which a question may arise as to whether an adoption order or placement order should be made, or any other question with respect to such an order, the court must (in the light of any rules made by virtue of subsection (2))—

(a) draw up a timetable with a view to determining such a question without delay, and

(b) give such directions as it considers appropriate for the purpose of ensuring that the timetable is adhered to.

(2) Rules may—

(a) prescribe periods within which prescribed steps must be taken in relation to such proceedings, and

(b) make other provision with respect to such proceedings for the purpose of ensuring that such questions are determined without delay.

110 Service of notices etc Any notice or information required to be given by virtue of this Act may be given by post.

PART 2
AMENDMENTS OF THE CHILDREN ACT 1989

111 Parental responsibility of unmarried father—(1) Section 4 of the 1989 Act (acquisition of responsibility by the father of a child who is not married to the child's mother) is amended as follows.

(2) In subsection (1) (cases where parental responsibility is acquired), for the words after 'birth' there is substituted

', the father shall acquire parental responsibility for the child if—

(a) he becomes registered as the child's father under any of the enactments specified in subsection (1A);

(b) he and the child's mother make an agreement (a "parental responsibility agreement") providing for him to have parental responsibility for the child; or

(c) the court, on his application, orders that he shall have parental responsibility for the child.'

(3) After that subsection there is inserted—

'(1A) The enactments referred to in subsection (1)(a) are—

(a) paragraphs (a), (b) and (c) of section 10(1) and of section 10A(1) of the Births and Deaths Registration Act 1953;

(b) paragraphs (a), (b)(i) and (c) of section 18(1), and sections 18(2)(b) and 20(1)(a) of the Registration of Births, Deaths and Marriages (Scotland) Act 1965; and

(c) sub-paragraphs (a), (b) and (c) of Article 14(3) of the Births and Deaths Registration (Northern Ireland) Order 1976.

(1B) The Lord Chancellor may by order amend subsection (1A) so as to add further enactments to the list in that subsection.'

(4) For subsection (3) there is substituted—

'(2A) A person who has acquired parental responsibility under subsection (1) shall cease to have that responsibility only if the court so orders.

(3) The court may make an order under subsection (2A) on the application—

(a) of any person who has parental responsibility for the child; or

(b) with the leave of the court, of the child himself,

subject, in the case of parental responsibility acquired under subsection (1)(c), to section 12(4).'

(5) Accordingly, in section 2(2) of the 1989 Act (a father of a child who is not married to the child's mother shall not have parental responsibility for the child unless he acquires it in accordance with the provisions of the Act), for the words from 'shall not' to 'acquires it' there is substituted 'shall have parental responsibility for the child if he has acquired it (and has not ceased to have it)'.

(6) In section 104 of the 1989 Act (regulations and orders)—

(a) in subsection (2), after 'section' there is inserted '4(1B),', and

(b) in subsection (3), after 'section' there is inserted '4(1B) or'.

(7) Paragraph (a) of section 4(1) of the 1989 Act, as substituted by subsection (2) of this section, does not confer parental responsibility on a man who was registered under an enactment referred to in paragraph (a), (b) or (c) of section 4(1A) of that Act, as inserted by subsection (3) of this section, before the commencement of subsection (3) in relation to that paragraph.

112 Acquisition of parental responsibility by step-parent After section 4 of the 1989 Act there is inserted—

'4A Acquisition of parental responsibility by step-parent—(1) Where a child's parent ('parent A') who has parental responsibility for the child is married to a person who is not the child's parent ('the step-parent')—

(a) parent A or, if the other parent of the child also has parental responsibility for the child, both parents may by agreement with the step-parent provide for the step-parent to have parental responsibility for the child; or

(b) the court may, on the application of the step-parent, order that the step-parent shall have parental responsibility for the child.

(2) An agreement under subsection (1)(a) is also a 'parental responsibility agreement', and section 4(2) applies in relation to such agreements as it applies in relation to parental responsibility agreements under section 4.

(3) A parental responsibility agreement under subsection (1)(a), or an order under subsection (1)(b), may only be brought to an end by an order of the court made on the application—

(a) of any person who has parental responsibility for the child; or

(b) with the leave of the court, of the child himself.

(4) The court may only grant leave under subsection (3)(b) if it is satisfied that the child has sufficient understanding to make the proposed application.'

113 Section 8 orders: local authority foster parents In section 9 of the 1989 Act (restrictions on making section 8 orders)—

(a) in subsection (3)(c), for 'three years' there is substituted 'one year', and

(b) subsection (4) is omitted.

114 Residence orders: extension to age of 18—(1) In section 12 of the 1989 Act (residence orders and parental responsibility), after subsection (4) there is inserted—

'(5) The power of a court to make a residence order in favour of any person who is not the parent or guardian of the child concerned includes power to direct, at the request of that person, that the order continue in force until the child reaches the age of eighteen (unless the order is brought to an end earlier); and any power to vary a residence order is exercisable accordingly.

(6) Where a residence order includes such a direction, an application to vary or discharge the order may only be made, if apart from this subsection the leave of the court is not required, with such leave'.

(2) In section 9 of that Act (restrictions on making section 8 orders), at the beginning of subsection (6) there is inserted 'Subject to section 12(5)'.

(3) In section 91 of that Act (effect and duration of orders), in subsection (10), after '9(6)' there is inserted 'or 12(5)'.

115 Special guardianship—(1) After section 14 of the 1989 Act there is inserted—

'*Special guardianship*

14A Special guardianship orders—(1) A 'special guardianship order' is an order appointing one or more individuals to be a child's 'special guardian' (or special guardians).

(2) A special guardian—

(a) must be aged eighteen or over; and

(b) must not be a parent of the child in question,

and subsections (3) to (6) are to be read in that light.

(3) The court may make a special guardianship order with respect to any child on the application of an individual who—

(a) is entitled to make such an application with respect to the child; or

(b) has obtained the leave of the court to make the application,

or on the joint application of more than one such individual.

(4) Section 9(3) applies in relation to an application for leave to apply for a special guardianship order as it applies in relation to an application for leave to apply for a section 8 order.

(5) The individuals who are entitled to apply for a special guardianship order with respect to a child are—

(a) any guardian of the child;

(b) any individual in whose favour a residence order is in force with respect to the child;

(c) any individual listed in subsection (5)(b) or (c) of section 10 (as read with subsection (10) of that section);

(d) a local authority foster parent with whom the child has lived for a period of at least one year immediately preceding the application.

(6) The court may also make a special guardianship order with respect to a child in any family proceedings in which a question arises with respect to the welfare of the child if—

(a) an application for the order has been made by an individual who falls within subsection (3)(a) or (b) (or more than one such individual jointly); or

(b) the court considers that a special guardianship order should be made even though no such application has been made.

(7) No individual may make an application under subsection (3) or (6)(a) unless, before the beginning of the period of three months ending with the date of the application, he has given written notice of his intention to make the application—

(a) if the child in question is being looked after by a local authority, to that local authority, or

(b) otherwise, to the local authority in whose area the individual is ordinarily resident.

(8) On receipt of such a notice, the local authority must investigate the matter and prepare a report for the court dealing with—
  (a) the suitability of the applicant to be a special guardian;
  (b) such matters (if any) as may be prescribed by the Secretary of State; and
  (c) any other matter which the local authority consider to be relevant.

(9) The court may itself ask a local authority to conduct such an investigation and prepare such a report, and the local authority must do so.

(10) The local authority may make such arrangements as they see fit for any person to act on their behalf in connection with conducting an investigation or preparing a report referred to in subsection (8) or (9).

(11) The court may not make a special guardianship order unless it has received a report dealing with the matters referred to in subsection (8).

(12) Subsections (8) and (9) of section 10 apply in relation to special guardianship orders as they apply in relation to section 8 orders.

(13) This section is subject to section 29(5) and (6) of the Adoption and Children Act 2002.

14B Special guardianship orders: making—(1) Before making a special guardianship order, the court must consider whether, if the order were made—
  (a) a contact order should also be made with respect to the child, and
  (b) any section 8 order in force with respect to the child should be varied or discharged.

(2) On making a special guardianship order, the court may also—
  (a) give leave for the child to be known by a new surname;
  (b) grant the leave required by section 14C(3)(b), either generally or for specified purposes.

14C Special guardianship orders: effect—(1) The effect of a special guardianship order is that while the order remains in force—
  (a) a special guardian appointed by the order has parental responsibility for the child in respect of whom it is made; and
  (b) subject to any other order in force with respect to the child under this Act, a special guardian is entitled to exercise parental responsibility to the exclusion of any other person with parental responsibility for the child (apart from another special guardian).

(2) Subsection (1) does not affect—
  (a) the operation of any enactment or rule of law which requires the consent of more than one person with parental responsibility in a matter affecting the child; or
  (b) any rights which a parent of the child has in relation to the child's adoption or placement for adoption.

(3) While a special guardianship order is in force with respect to a child, no person may—
  (a) cause the child to be known by a new surname; or
  (b) remove him from the United Kingdom,
without either the written consent of every person who has parental responsibility for the child or the leave of the court.

(4) Subsection (3)(b) does not prevent the removal of a child, for a period of less than three months, by a special guardian of his.

(5) If the child with respect to whom a special guardianship order is in force dies, his special guardian must take reasonable steps to give notice of that fact to—
  (a) each parent of the child with parental responsibility; and
  (b) each guardian of the child,
but if the child has more than one special guardian, and one of them has taken

such steps in relation to a particular parent or guardian, any other special guardian need not do so as respects that parent or guardian.

(6) This section is subject to section 29(7) of the Adoption and Children Act 2002.

14D Special guardianship orders: variation and discharge—(1) The court may vary or discharge a special guardianship order on the application of—

(a) the special guardian (or any of them, if there are more than one);

(b) any parent or guardian of the child concerned;

(c) any individual in whose favour a residence order is in force with respect to the child;

(d) any individual not falling within any of paragraphs (a) to (c) who has, or immediately before the making of the special guardianship order had, parental responsibility for the child;

(e) the child himself; or

(f) a local authority designated in a care order with respect to the child.

(2) In any family proceedings in which a question arises with respect to the welfare of a child with respect to whom a special guardianship order is in force, the court may also vary or discharge the special guardianship order if it considers that the order should be varied or discharged, even though no application has been made under subsection (1).

(3) The following must obtain the leave of the court before making an application under subsection (1)—

(a) the child;

(b) any parent or guardian of his;

(c) any step-parent of his who has acquired, and has not lost, parental responsibility for him by virtue of section 4A;

(d) any individual falling within subsection (1)(d) who immediately before the making of the special guardianship order had, but no longer has, parental responsibility for him.

(4) Where the person applying for leave to make an application under subsection (1) is the child, the court may only grant leave if it is satisfied that he has sufficient understanding to make the proposed application under subsection (1).

(5) The court may not grant leave to a person falling within subsection (3)(b)(c) or (d) unless it is satisfied that there has been a significant change in circumstances since the making of the special guardianship order.

14E Special guardianship orders: supplementary—(1) In proceedings in which any question of making, varying or discharging a special guardianship order arises, the court shall (in the light of any rules made by virtue of subsection (3))—

(a) draw up a timetable with a view to determining the question without delay; and

(b) give such directions as it considers appropriate for the purpose of ensuring, so far as is reasonably practicable, that the timetable is adhered to.

(2) Subsection (1) applies also in relation to proceedings in which any other question with respect to a special guardianship order arises.

(3) The power to make rules in subsection (2) of section 11 applies for the purposes of this section as it applies for the purposes of that.

(4) A special guardianship order, or an order varying one, may contain provisions which are to have effect for a specified period.

(5) Section 11(7) (apart from paragraph (c)) applies in relation to special guardianship orders and orders varying them as it applies in relation to section 8 orders.

14F Special guardianship support services—(1) Each local authority must make arrangements for the provision within their area of special guardianship support services, which means—

(a) counselling, advice and information; and

(b) such other services as are prescribed,

in relation to special guardianship.

(2) The power to make regulations under subsection (1)(b) is to be exercised so as to secure that local authorities provide financial support.

(3) At the request of any of the following persons—

(a) a child with respect to whom a special guardianship order is in force;

(b) a special guardian;

(c) a parent;

(d) any other person who falls within a prescribed description,

a local authority may carry out an assessment of that person's needs for special guardianship support services (but, if the Secretary of State so provides in regulations, they must do so if he is a person of a prescribed description, or if his case falls within a prescribed description, or if both he and his case fall within prescribed descriptions).

(4) A local authority may, at the request of any other person, carry out an assessment of that person's needs for special guardianship support services.

(5) Where, as a result of an assessment, a local authority decide that a person has needs for special guardianship support services, they must then decide whether to provide any such services to that person.

(6) If—

(a) a local authority decide to provide any special guardianship support services to a person, and

(b) the circumstances fall within a prescribed description,

the local authority must prepare a plan in accordance with which special guardianship support services are to be provided to him, and keep the plan under review.

(7) The Secretary of State may by regulations make provision about assessments, preparing and reviewing plans, the provision of special guardianship support services in accordance with plans and reviewing the provision of special guardianship support services.

(8) The regulations may in particular make provision—

(a) about the type of assessment which is to be carried out, or the way in which an assessment is to be carried out;

(b) about the way in which a plan is to be prepared;

(c) about the way in which, and the time at which, a plan or the provision of special guardianship support services is to be reviewed;

(d) about the considerations to which a local authority are to have regard in carrying out an assessment or review or preparing a plan;

(e) as to the circumstances in which a local authority may provide special guardianship support services subject to conditions (including conditions as to payment for the support or the repayment of financial support);

(f) as to the consequences of conditions imposed by virtue of paragraph (e) not being met (including the recovery of any financial support provided);

(g) as to the circumstances in which this section may apply to a local authority in respect of persons who are outside that local authority's area;

(h) as to the circumstances in which a local authority may recover from another local authority the expenses of providing special guardianship support services to any person.

(9) A local authority may provide special guardianship support services (or any part of them) by securing their provision by—

    (a) another local authority; or

    (b) a person within a description prescribed in regulations of persons who may provide special guardianship support services,

and may also arrange with any such authority or person for that other authority or that person to carry out the local authority's functions in relation to assessments under this section.

    (10) A local authority may carry out an assessment of the needs of any person for the purposes of this section at the same time as an assessment of his needs is made under any other provision of this Act or under any other enactment.

    (11) Section 27 (co-operation between authorities) applies in relation to the exercise of functions of a local authority under this section as it applies in relation to the exercise of functions of a local authority under Part 3.

14G Special guardianship support services: representations—(1) Every local authority shall establish a procedure for considering representations (including complaints) made to them by any person to whom they may provide special guardianship support services about the discharge of their functions under section 14F in relation to him.

    (2) Regulations may be made by the Secretary of State imposing time limits on the making of representations under subsection (1).

    (3) In considering representations under subsection (1), a local authority shall comply with regulations (if any) made by the Secretary of State for the purposes of this subsection.'

    (2) The 1989 Act is amended as follows.

    (3) In section 1 (welfare of the child), in subsection (4)(b), after 'discharge' there is inserted 'a special guardianship order or'.

    (4) In section 5 (appointment of guardians)—

    (a) in subsection (1)—

        (i) in paragraph (b), for 'or guardian' there is substituted ', guardian or special guardian', and

        (ii) at the end of paragraph (b) there is inserted

'; or

    (c) paragraph (b) does not apply, and the child's only or last surviving special guardian dies.',

    (b) in subsection (4), at the end there is inserted '; and a special guardian of a child may appoint another individual to be the child's guardian in the event of his death', and

    (c) in subsection (7), at the end of paragraph (b) there is inserted 'or he was the child's only (or last surviving) special guardian'.

116 Accommodation of children in need etc—(1) In section 17 of the 1989 Act (provision of services for children in need, their families and others), in subsection (6) (services that may be provided in exercise of the functions under that section) after 'include' there is inserted 'providing accommodation and'.

    (2) In section 22 of that Act (general duty of local authority in relation to children looked after by them), in subsection (1) (looked after children include those provided with accommodation, with exceptions) before '23B' there is inserted '17'.

    (3) In section 24A of that Act (advice and assistance for certain children and young persons aged 16 or over), in subsection (5), for 'or, in exceptional circumstances, cash' there is substituted

'and, in exceptional circumstances, assistance may be given—

    (a) by providing accommodation, if in the circumstances assistance may not be given in respect of the accommodation under section 24B, or

    (b) in cash'.

117 Inquiries by local authorities into representations—(1) In section 24D of the 1989 Act (representations: sections 23A to 24B), after subsection (1) there is inserted—

'(1A) Regulations may be made by the Secretary of State imposing time limits on the making of representations under subsection (1).'

(2) Section 26 of that Act (procedure for considering other representations) is amended as follows.

(3) In subsection (3) (which makes provision as to the persons by whom, and the matters in respect of which, representations may be made), for 'functions under this Part' there is substituted 'qualifying functions'.

(4) After that subsection there is inserted—

'(3A)   The following are qualifying functions for the purposes of subsection (3)—

    (a)   functions under this Part,

    (b)   such functions under Part 4 or 5 as are specified by the Secretary of State in regulations.

(3B)   The duty under subsection (3) extends to representations (including complaints) made to the authority by—

    (a)   any person mentioned in section 3(1) of the Adoption and Children Act 2002 (persons for whose needs provision is made by the Adoption Service) and any other person to whom arrangements for the provision of adoption support services (within the meaning of that Act) extend,

    (b)   such other person as the authority consider has sufficient interest in a child who is or may be adopted to warrant his representations being considered by them,

about the discharge by the authority of such functions under the Adoption and Children Act 2002 as are specified by the Secretary of State in regulations.'

(5) In subsection (4) (procedure to require involvement of independent person), after paragraph (b) there is inserted—

'but this subsection is subject to subsection (5A).'

(6) After that subsection there is inserted—

'(4A) Regulations may be made by the Secretary of State imposing time limits on the making of representations under this section.'

(7) After subsection (5) there is inserted—

'(5A) Regulations under subsection (5) may provide that subsection (4) does not apply in relation to any consideration or discussion which takes place as part of a procedure for which provision is made by the regulations for the purpose of resolving informally the matters raised in the representations.'

118 Review of cases of looked after children—(1) In section 26 of the 1989 Act (review of cases of looked after children, etc), in subsection (2) (regulations as to reviews)—

    (a)   in paragraph (e), 'to consider' is omitted and after 'their care' there is inserted—

        '(i)   to keep the section 31A plan for the child under review and, if they are of the opinion that some change is required, to revise the plan, or make a new plan, accordingly,

        (ii)   to consider',

    (b)   in paragraph (f), 'to consider' is omitted and after the second mention of 'the authority' there is inserted—

        '(i)   if there is no plan for the future care of the child, to prepare one,

        (ii)   if there is such a plan for the child, to keep it under review and, if they are of the opinion that some change is required, to revise the plan or make a new plan, accordingly,

        (iii)   to consider',

(c) after paragraph (j) there is inserted—

'(k) for the authority to appoint a person in respect of each case to carry out in the prescribed manner the functions mentioned in subsection (2A) and any prescribed function'.

(2) After that subsection there is inserted—

'(2A) The functions referred to in subsection (2)(k) are—

(a) participating in the review of the case in question,

(b) monitoring the performance of the authority's functions in respect of the review,

(c) referring the case to an officer of the Children and Family Court Advisory and Support Service, if the person appointed under subsection (2)(k) considers it appropriate to do so.

(2B) A person appointed under subsection (2)(k) must be a person of a prescribed description.

(2C) In relation to children whose cases are referred to officers under subsection (2A)(c), the Lord Chancellor may by regulations—

(a) extend any functions of the officers in respect of family proceedings (within the meaning of section 12 of the Criminal Justice and Court Services Act 2000) to other proceedings,

(b) require any functions of the officers to be performed in the manner prescribed by the regulations.'

119 Advocacy services After section 26 of the 1989 Act there is inserted—

'**26A Advocacy services—**(1) Every local authority shall make arrangements for the provision of assistance to—

(a) persons who make or intend to make representations under section 24D; and

(b) children who make or intend to make representations under section 26.

(2) The assistance provided under the arrangements shall include assistance by way of representation.

(3) The arrangements—

(a) shall secure that a person may not provide assistance if he is a person who is prevented from doing so by regulations made by the Secretary of State; and

(b) shall comply with any other provision made by the regulations in relation to the arrangements.

(4) The Secretary of State may make regulations requiring local authorities to monitor the steps that they have taken with a view to ensuring that they comply with regulations made for the purposes of subsection (3).

(5) Every local authority shall give such publicity to their arrangements for the provision of assistance under this section as they consider appropriate.'

120 Meaning of 'harm' in the 1989 Act In section 31 of the 1989 Act (care and supervision orders), at the end of the definition of 'harm' in subsection (9) there is inserted 'including, for example, impairment suffered from seeing or hearing the ill-treatment of another'.

121 Care plans—(1) In section 31 of the 1989 Act (care and supervision orders), after subsection (3) there is inserted—

'(3A) No care order may be made with respect to a child until the court has considered a section 31A plan.'

(2) After that section there is inserted—

'**31A Care orders: care plans—**(1) Where an application is made on which a care order might be made with respect to a child, the appropriate local authority must, within such time as the court may direct, prepare a plan ('a care plan') for the future care of the child.

(2) While the application is pending, the authority must keep any care plan prepared by them under review and, if they are of the opinion some change is required, revise the plan, or make a new plan, accordingly.

(3) A care plan must give any prescribed information and do so in the prescribed manner.

(4) For the purposes of this section, the appropriate local authority, in relation to a child in respect of whom a care order might be made, is the local authority proposed to be designated in the order.

(5) In section 31(3A) and this section, references to a care order do not include an interim care order.

(6) A plan prepared, or treated as prepared, under this section is referred to in this Act as a 'section 31A plan'.'

(3)   If—

(a) before subsection (2) comes into force, a care order has been made in respect of a child and a plan for the future care of the child has been prepared in connection with the making of the order by the local authority designated in the order, and

(b) on the day on which that subsection comes into force the order is in force, or would be in force but for section 29(1) of this Act,

the plan is to have effect as if made under section 31A of the 1989 Act.

122 Interests of children in proceedings—(1) In section 41 of the 1989 Act (specified proceedings)—

(a) in subsection (6), after paragraph (h) there is inserted—

'(hh)   on an application for the making or revocation of a placement order (within the meaning of section 21 of the Adoption and Children Act 2002);',

(b) after that subsection there is inserted—

'(6A)   The proceedings which may be specified under subsection (6)(i) include (for example) proceedings for the making, varying or discharging of a section 8 order.'

(2) In section 93 of the 1989 Act (rules of court), in subsection (2), after paragraph (b) there is inserted—

'(bb)   for children to be separately represented in relevant proceedings,'.

PART 3
MISCELLANEOUS AND FINAL PROVISIONS

CHAPTER 1
MISCELLANEOUS

Advertisements in the United Kingdom

123 Restriction on advertisements etc—(1) A person must not—

(a) publish or distribute an advertisement or information to which this section applies, or

(b) cause such an advertisement or information to be published or distributed.

(2) This section applies to an advertisement indicating that—

(a) the parent or guardian of a child wants the child to be adopted,

(b) a person wants to adopt a child,

(c) a person other than an adoption agency is willing to take any step mentioned in paragraphs (a) to (e), (g) and (h) and (so far as relating to those paragraphs) (i) of section 92(2),

(d) a person other than an adoption agency is willing to receive a child handed over to him with a view to the child's adoption by him or another, or

(e) a person is willing to remove a child from the United Kingdom for the purposes of adoption.

(3) This section applies to—

(a) information about how to do anything which, if done, would constitute an offence under section 85 or 93, section 11 or 50 of the Adoption (Scotland) Act 1978 (c 28) or Article 11 or 58 of the Adoption (Northern Ireland) Order 1987 (SI 1987/2203 (NI 22)) (whether or not the information includes a warning that doing the thing in question may constitute an offence),

(b) information about a particular child as a child available for adoption.

(4) For the purposes of this section and section 124—

(a) publishing or distributing an advertisement or information means publishing it or distributing it to the public and includes doing so by electronic means (for example, by means of the internet),

(b) the public includes selected members of the public as well as the public generally or any section of the public.

(5) Subsection (1) does not apply to publication or distribution by or on behalf of an adoption agency.

(6) The Secretary of State may by order make any amendments of this section which he considers necessary or expedient in consequence of any developments in technology relating to publishing or distributing advertisements or other information by electronic or electro-magnetic means.

(7) References to an adoption agency in this section include a prescribed person outside the United Kingdom exercising functions corresponding to those of an adoption agency, if the functions are being exercised in prescribed circumstances.

'Prescribed' means prescribed by regulations made by the Secretary of State.

(8) Before exercising the power conferred by subsection (6) or (7), the Secretary of State must consult the Scottish Ministers, the Department of Health, Social Services and Public Safety and the Assembly.

(9) In this section—

(a) 'adoption agency' includes a Scottish or Northern Irish adoption agency,

(b) references to adoption are to the adoption of persons, wherever they may be habitually resident, effected under the law of any country or territory, whether within or outside the British Islands.

124 Offence of breaching restriction under section 123—(1) A person who contravenes section 123(1) is guilty of an offence.

(2) A person is not guilty of an offence under this section unless it is proved that he knew or had reason to suspect that section 123 applied to the advertisement or information.

But this subsection only applies if sufficient evidence is adduced to raise an issue as to whether the person had the knowledge or reason mentioned.

(3) A person guilty of an offence under this section is liable on summary conviction to imprisonment for a term not exceeding three months, or a fine not exceeding level 5 on the standard scale, or both.

Adoption and Children Act Register

125 Adoption and Children Act Register—(1) Her Majesty may by Order in Council make provision for the Secretary of State to establish and maintain a register, to be called the Adoption and Children Act Register, containing—

(a) prescribed information about children who are suitable for adoption and prospective adopters who are suitable to adopt a child,

(b) prescribed information about persons included in the register in pursuance of paragraph (a) in respect of things occurring after their inclusion.

(2) For the purpose of giving assistance in finding persons with whom children may be placed for purposes other than adoption, an Order under this section may—

    (a) provide for the register to contain information about such persons and the children who may be placed with them, and

    (b) apply any of the other provisions of this group of sections (that is, this section and sections 126 to 131), with or without modifications.

(3) The register is not to be open to public inspection or search.

(4) An Order under this section may make provision about the retention of information in the register.

(5) Information is to be kept in the register in any form the Secretary of State considers appropriate.

126 Use of an organisation to establish the register—(1) The Secretary of State may make an arrangement with an organisation under which any function of his under an Order under section 125 of establishing and maintaining the register, and disclosing information entered in, or compiled from information entered in, the register to any person is performed wholly or partly by the organisation on his behalf.

(2) The arrangement may include provision for payments to be made to the organisation by the Secretary of State.

(3) If the Secretary of State makes an arrangement under this section with an organisation, the organisation is to perform the functions exercisable by virtue of this section in accordance with any directions given by the Secretary of State and the directions may be of general application (or general application in any part of Great Britain) or be special directions.

(4) An exercise of the Secretary of State's powers under subsection (1) or (3) requires the agreement of the Scottish Ministers (if the register applies to Scotland) and of the Assembly (if the register applies to Wales).

(5) References in this group of sections to the registration organisation are to any organisation for the time being performing functions in respect of the register by virtue of arrangements under this section.

127 Use of an organisation as agency for payments—(1) An Order under section 125 may authorise an organisation with which an arrangement is made under section 126 to act as agent for the payment or receipt of sums payable by adoption agencies to other adoption agencies and may require adoption agencies to pay or receive such sums through the organisation.

(2) The organisation is to perform the functions exercisable by virtue of this section in accordance with any directions given by the Secretary of State; and the directions may be of general application (or general application in any part of Great Britain) or be special directions.

(3) An exercise of the Secretary of State's power to give directions under subsection (2) requires the agreement of the Scottish Ministers (if any payment agency provision applies to Scotland) and of the Assembly (if any payment agency provision applies to Wales).

128 Supply of information for the register—(1) An Order under section 125 may require adoption agencies to give prescribed information to the Secretary of State or the registration organisation for entry in the register.

(2) Information is to be given to the Secretary of State or the registration organisation when required by the Order and in the prescribed form and manner.

(3) An Order under section 125 may require an agency giving information which is entered on the register to pay a prescribed fee to the Secretary of State or the registration organisation.

(4) But an adoption agency is not to disclose any information to the Secretary of State or the registration organisation—

(a) about prospective adopters who are suitable to adopt a child, or persons who were included in the register as such prospective adopters, without their consent,

(b) about children suitable for adoption, or persons who were included in the register as such children, without the consent of the prescribed person.

(5) Consent under subsection (4) is to be given in the prescribed form.

129 Disclosure of information—(1) Information entered in the register, or compiled from information entered in the register, may only be disclosed under subsection (2) or (3).

(2) Prescribed information entered in the register may be disclosed by the Secretary of State or the registration organisation—

(a) where an adoption agency is acting on behalf of a child who is suitable for adoption, to the agency to assist in finding prospective adopters with whom it would be appropriate for the child to be placed,

(b) where an adoption agency is acting on behalf of prospective adopters who are suitable to adopt a child, to the agency to assist in finding a child appropriate for adoption by them.

(3) Prescribed information entered in the register, or compiled from information entered in the register, may be disclosed by the Secretary of State or the registration organisation to any prescribed person for use for statistical or research purposes, or for other prescribed purposes.

(4) An Order under section 125 may prescribe the steps to be taken by adoption agencies in respect of information received by them by virtue of subsection (2).

(5) Subsection (1) does not apply—

(a) to a disclosure of information with the authority of the Secretary of State, or

(b) to a disclosure by the registration organisation of prescribed information to the Scottish Ministers (if the register applies to Scotland) or the Assembly (if the register applies to Wales).

(6) Information disclosed to any person under subsection (2) or (3) may be given on any prescribed terms or conditions.

(7) An Order under section 125 may, in prescribed circumstances, require a prescribed fee to be paid to the Secretary of State or the registration organisation—

(a) by a prescribed adoption agency in respect of information disclosed under subsection (2), or

(b) by a person to whom information is disclosed under subsection (3).

(8) If any information entered in the register is disclosed to a person in contravention of subsection (1), the person disclosing it is guilty of an offence.

(9) A person guilty of an offence under subsection (8) is liable on summary conviction to imprisonment for a term not exceeding three months, or a fine not exceeding level 5 on the standard scale, or both.

130 Territorial application—(1) In this group of sections, 'adoption agency' means—

(a) a local authority in England,

(b) a registered adoption society whose principal office is in England.

(2) An Order under section 125 may provide for any requirements imposed on adoption agencies in respect of the register to apply—

(a) to Scottish local authorities and to voluntary organisations providing a registered adoption service,

(b) to local authorities in Wales and to registered adoption societies whose principal offices are in Wales, and, in relation to the register, references to adoption agencies in this group of sections include any authorities or societies mentioned in paragraphs (a) and (b) to which an Order under that section applies those requirements.

(3) For the purposes of this group of sections, references to the register applying to Scotland or Wales are to those requirements applying as mentioned in paragraph (a) or, as the case may be, (b) of subsection (2).

(4) An Order under section 125 may apply any provision made by virtue of section 127—

    (a) to Scottish local authorities and to voluntary organisations providing a registered adoption service,

    (b) to local authorities in Wales and to registered adoption societies whose principal offices are in Wales.

(5) For the purposes of this group of sections, references to any payment agency provision applying to Scotland or Wales are to provision made by virtue of section 127 applying as mentioned in paragraph (a) or, as the case may be, (b) of subsection (4).

131 Supplementary—(1) In this group of sections—

    (a) 'organisation' includes a public body and a private or voluntary organisation,

    (b) 'prescribed' means prescribed by an Order under section 125,

    (c) 'the register' means the Adoption and Children Act Register,

    (d) 'Scottish local authority' means a local authority within the meaning of the Regulation of Care (Scotland) Act 2001 (asp 4),

    (e) 'voluntary organisation providing a registered adoption service' has the same meaning as in section 144(3).

(2) For the purposes of this group of sections—

    (a) a child is suitable for adoption if an adoption agency is satisfied that the child ought to be placed for adoption,

    (b) prospective adopters are suitable to adopt a child if an adoption agency is satisfied that they are suitable to have a child placed with them for adoption.

(3) Nothing authorised or required to be done by virtue of this group of sections constitutes an offence under section 93, 94 or 95.

(4) No recommendation to make an Order under section 125 is to be made to Her Majesty in Council unless a draft has been laid before and approved by resolution of each House of Parliament.

(5) If any provision made by an Order under section 125 would, if it were included in an Act of the Scottish Parliament, be within the legislative competence of that Parliament, no recommendation to make the Order is to be made to Her Majesty in Council unless a draft has been laid before, and approved by resolution of, the Parliament.

(6) No recommendation to make an Order under section 125 containing any provision in respect of the register is to be made to Her Majesty in Council if the register applies to Wales or the Order would provide for the register to apply to Wales, unless a draft has been laid before, and approved by resolution of, the Assembly.

(7) No recommendation to make an Order under section 125 containing any provision by virtue of section 127 is to be made to Her Majesty in Council if any payment agency provision applies to Wales or the Order would provide for any payment agency provision to apply to Wales, unless a draft has been laid before, and approved by resolution of, the Assembly.

Other miscellaneous provisions

132 Amendment of Adoption (Scotland) Act 1978: contravention of sections 30 to 36 of this Act After section 29 of the Adoption (Scotland) Act 1978 (c 28) there is inserted—

'29A Contravention of sections 30 to 36 of Adoption and Children Act 2002—(1) A person who contravenes any of the enactments specified in subsection (2) is guilty of an offence and liable on summary conviction to imprisonment for a term not exceeding three months, or a fine not exceeding level 5 on the standard scale, or both.

    (2) Those enactments are—

    (a) section 30(1), (2) and (3) (removal of child placed or who may be placed for adoption),

    (b) sections 32(2)(b), 33(2) and 35(2) (return of child by prospective adopters),

    (c) section 34(1) (removal of child in contravention of placement order),

    (d) section 36(1) (removal of child in non-agency case), and

    (e) section 36(5) (return of child to parent or guardian),

of the Adoption and Children Act 2002.'

133 Scottish restriction on bringing children into or out of United Kingdom—(1) In section 50 of the Adoption (Scotland) Act 1978 (restriction on removal of children for adoption outside Great Britain)—

    (a) in subsection (1), 'not being a parent or guardian or relative of the child' is omitted,

    (b) after subsection (3) there is inserted—

    '(4) The Scottish Ministers may by regulations provide for subsection (1) to apply with modifications, or not to apply, if—

    (a) the prospective adopters are parents, relatives or guardians of the child (or one of them is), or

    (b) the prospective adopter is a step-parent of the child,

and any conditions prescribed by the regulations are met.

    (5) On the occasion of the first exercise of the power to make regulations under subsection (4)—

    (a) the regulations shall not be made unless a draft of the regulations has been approved by a resolution of the Scottish Parliament, and

    (b) accordingly section 60(2) does not apply to the statutory instrument containing the regulations.'

    (2) For section 50A of that Act (restriction on bringing children into the United Kingdom for adoption) there is substituted—

'50A Restriction on bringing children into the United Kingdom—(1) This section applies where a person who is habitually resident in the British Islands (the 'British resident')—

    (a) brings, or causes another to bring, a child who is habitually resident outside the British Islands into the United Kingdom for the purpose of adoption by the British resident; or

    (b) at any time brings, or causes another to bring, into the United Kingdom a child adopted by the British resident under an external adoption effected within the period of six months ending with that time.

    (2) In subsection (1) above the references to adoption, or to a child adopted, by the British resident include a reference to adoption, or to a child adopted, by the British resident and another person.

    (3) This section does not apply if the child is intended to be adopted under a Convention adoption order.

(4) An external adoption means an adoption, other than a Convention adoption, of a child effected under the law of any country or territory outside the British Islands, whether or not the adoption is—

    (a) an adoption within the meaning of Part IV; or

    (b) a full adoption (as defined in section 39(2A)).

(5) Regulations may require a person intending to bring, or to cause another to bring, a child into the United Kingdom in circumstances where this section applies—

    (a) to apply to an adoption agency in the prescribed manner for an assessment of his suitability to adopt the child; and

    (b) to give the agency any information it may require for the purpose of the assessment.

(6) Regulations may require prescribed conditions to be met in respect of a child brought into the United Kingdom in circumstances where this section applies.

(7) In relation to a child brought into the United Kingdom for adoption in circumstances where this section applies, regulations may provide for any provision of Part II of this Act to apply with modifications or not to apply.

(8) If a person brings, or causes another to bring, a child into the United Kingdom at any time in circumstances where this section applies, he is guilty of an offence if—

    (a) he has not complied with any requirement imposed by virtue of subsection (5); or

    (b) any condition required to be met by virtue of subsection (6) is not met,

before that time, or before any later time which may be prescribed.

(9) A person guilty of an offence under this section is liable—

    (a) on summary conviction to imprisonment for a term not exceeding six months, or a fine not exceeding the statutory maximum, or both;

    (b) on conviction on indictment, to imprisonment for a term not exceeding twelve months, or a fine, or both.

(10) Regulations may provide for this section not to apply if—

    (a) the adopters or (as the case may be) prospective adopters are natural parents (whether or not they have parental responsibilities or parental rights in relation to the child), natural relatives or guardians of the child in question (or one of them is), or

    (b) the British resident in question is a step-parent of the child,

and any prescribed conditions are met.

(11) On the occasion of the first exercise of the power to make regulations under subsection (10)—

    (a) the regulations shall not be made unless a draft of the regulations has been approved by a resolution of the Scottish Parliament, and

    (b) accordingly section 60(2) does not apply to the statutory instrument containing the regulations.

(12) In this section, 'prescribed' means prescribed by regulations and 'regulations' means regulations made by the Scottish Ministers.'

(3) In section 65 of that Act (interpretation), in subsection (1), in the definition of 'adoption agency', for 'and 27' there is substituted ', 27 and 50A'.

134 Amendment of Adoption (Scotland) Act 1978: overseas adoptions In section 65 of the Adoption (Scotland) Act 1978 (c 28) (interpretation), for subsection (2) there is substituted—

    '(2) In this Act, 'overseas adoption'—

    (a) means an adoption of a description specified in an order made by the Scottish Ministers, being a description of adoptions effected under the law of any country or territory outside the British Islands, but

    (b) does not include a Convention adoption.

(2A) The Scottish Ministers may by regulations prescribe the requirements that ought to be met by an adoption of any description effected after the commencement of the regulations for it to be an overseas adoption for the purposes of this Act.

(2B) At any time when such regulations have effect, the Scottish Ministers must exercise their power under subsection (2) so as to secure that subsequently effected adoptions of any description are not overseas adoptions for the purposes of this Act if they consider that such adoptions are not likely within a reasonable time to meet the prescribed requirements.

(2C) An order under subsection (2) may contain provision as to the manner in which evidence of any overseas adoption may be given.

(2D) In subsections (2) to (2C), 'adoption' means the adoption of a child or of a person who was a child at the time the adoption was applied for.'

135 Adoption and fostering: criminal records—(1) Part 5 of the Police Act 1997 (c 50) (certificates of criminal records) is amended as follows.

(2) In section 113 (criminal record certificates), in subsection (3A), for 'his suitability' there is substituted 'the suitability of the applicant, or of a person living in the same household as the applicant, to be a foster parent or'.

(3) In section 115 (enhanced criminal record certificates), in subsection (6A), for 'his suitability' there is substituted 'the suitability of the applicant, or of a person living in the same household as the applicant, to be a foster parent or'.

136 Payment of grants in connection with welfare services—(1) Section 93 of the Local Government Act 2000 (c 22) (payment of grants for welfare services) is amended as follows.

(2) In subsection (1) (payment of grants by the Secretary of State), for the words from 'in providing' to the end there is substituted—

'(a) in providing, or contributing to the provision of, such welfare services as may be determined by the Secretary of State, or

(b) in connection with any such welfare services.'

(3) In subsection (2) (payment of grants by the Assembly), for the words from 'in providing' to the end there is substituted—

'(a) in providing, or contributing to the provision of, such welfare services as may be determined by the Assembly, or

(b) in connection with any such welfare services.'

(4) After subsection (6) there is inserted—

'(6A) Before making any determination under subsection (3) or (5) the Secretary of State must obtain the consent of the Treasury.'

137 Extension of the Hague Convention to British overseas territories—(1) Her Majesty may by Order in Council provide for giving effect to the Convention in any British overseas territory.

(2) An Order in Council under subsection (1) in respect of any British overseas territory may, in particular, make any provision corresponding to provision which in relation to any part of Great Britain is made by the Adoption (Intercountry Aspects) Act 1999 (c 18) or may be made by regulations under section 1 of that Act.

(3) The British Nationality Act 1981 (c 61) is amended as follows.

(4) In section 1 (acquisition of British citizenship by birth or adoption)—

(a) in subsection (5), at the end of paragraph (b) there is inserted 'effected under the law of a country or territory outside the United Kingdom',

(b) at the end of subsection (5A)(b) there is inserted 'or in a designated territory',

(c) in subsection (8), the words following 'section 50' are omitted.

(5) In section 15 (acquisition of British overseas territories citizenship)—
(a) after subsection (5) there is inserted—
'(5A) Where—
  (a) a minor who is not a British overseas territories citizen is adopted under a Convention adoption,
  (b) on the date on which the adoption is effected—
    (i) the adopter or, in the case of a joint adoption, one of the adopters is a British overseas territories citizen, and
    (ii) the adopter or, in the case of a joint adoption, both of the adopters are habitually resident in a designated territory, and
  (c) the Convention adoption is effected under the law of a country or territory outside the designated territory,
the minor shall be a British overseas territories citizen as from that date.',
(b) in subsection (6), after 'order' there is inserted 'or a Convention adoption'.
(6) In section 50 (interpretation), in subsection (1)—
(a) after the definition of 'company' there is inserted—
'"Convention adoption" means an adoption effected under the law of a country or territory in which the Convention is in force, and certified in pursuance of Article 23(1) of the Convention',
(b) after the definition of 'Crown service under the government of the United Kingdom' there is inserted—
'"designated territory" means a qualifying territory, or the Sovereign Base Areas of Akrotiri and Dhekelia, which is designated by Her Majesty by Order in Council under subsection (14)'.
(7) After subsection (13) of that section there is inserted—
'(14) For the purposes of the definition of 'designated territory' in subsection (1), an Order in Council may—
  (a) designate any qualifying territory, or the Sovereign Base Areas of Akrotiri and Dhekelia, if the Convention is in force there, and
  (b) make different designations for the purposes of section 1 and section 15;
and, for the purposes of this subsection and the definition of 'Convention adoption' in subsection (1), 'the Convention' means the Convention on the Protection of Children and Co-operation in respect of Intercountry Adoption, concluded at the Hague on 29th May 1993.

An Order in Council under this subsection shall be subject to annulment in pursuance of a resolution of either House of Parliament.'

138 Proceedings in Great Britain Proceedings for an offence by virtue of section 9, 59, 93, 94, 95 or 129—
(a) may not be brought more than six years after the commission of the offence but, subject to that,
(b) may be brought within a period of six months from the date on which evidence sufficient in the opinion of the prosecutor to warrant the proceedings came to his knowledge.
In relation to Scotland, 'the prosecutor' is to be read as 'the procurator fiscal'.

Amendments etc

139 Amendments, transitional and transitory provisions, savings and repeals—(1) Schedule 3 (minor and consequential amendments) is to have effect.
(2) Schedule 4 (transitional and transitory provisions and savings) is to have effect.
(3) The enactments set out in Schedule 5 are repealed to the extent specified.

CHAPTER 2
FINAL PROVISIONS

140 Orders, rules and regulations—(1) Any power to make subordinate legislation conferred by this Act on the Lord Chancellor, the Secretary of State, the Scottish Ministers, the Assembly or the Registrar General is exercisable by statutory instrument.

(2) A statutory instrument containing subordinate legislation made under any provision of this Act (other than section 14 or 148 or an instrument to which subsection (3) applies) is to be subject to annulment in pursuance of a resolution of either House of Parliament.

(3) A statutory instrument containing subordinate legislation—

(a) under section 9 which includes provision made by virtue of section 45(2),

(b) under section 92(6), 94 or 123(6), or

(c) which adds to, replaces or omits any part of the text of an Act,

is not to be made unless a draft of the instrument has been laid before, and approved by resolution of, each House of Parliament.

(4) Subsections (2) and (3) do not apply to an Order in Council or to subordinate legislation made—

(a) by the Scottish Ministers, or

(b) by the Assembly, unless made jointly by the Secretary of State and the Assembly.

(5) A statutory instrument containing regulations under section 63(2) made by the Scottish Ministers is to be subject to annulment in pursuance of a resolution of the Scottish Parliament.

(6) The power of the Department of Health, Social Services and Public Safety to make regulations under section 63(2) is to be exercisable by statutory rule for the purposes of the Statutory Rules (Northern Ireland) Order 1979 (SI 1979/ 1573 (NI 12)); and any such regulations are to be subject to negative resolution within the meaning of section 41(6) of the Interpretation Act (Northern Ireland) 1954 (c 33 (NI)) as if they were statutory instruments within the meaning of that Act.

(7) Subordinate legislation made under this Act may make different provision for different purposes.

(8) A power to make subordinate legislation under this Act (as well as being exercisable in relation to all cases to which it extends) may be exercised in relation to—

(a) those cases subject to specified exceptions, or

(b) a particular case or class of case.

(9) In this section, 'subordinate legislation' does not include a direction.

141 Rules of procedure—(1) *The Lord Chancellor may make rules* [Family Procedure Rules make provision] *in respect of any matter to be prescribed by rules made by virtue of this Act and dealing generally with all matters of procedure.*

(2) *Subsection (1) does not apply in relation to proceedings before magistrates' courts, but the power to make rules conferred by section 144 of the Magistrates' Courts Act 1980 (c 43) includes power to make provision in respect of any of the matters mentioned in that subsection.*

(3) In the case of an application for a placement order, for the variation or revocation of such an order, or for an adoption order, the rules must require any person mentioned in subsection (4) to be notified—

(a) of the date and place where the application will be heard, and

(b) of the fact that, unless the person wishes or the court requires, the person need not attend.

(4) The persons referred to in subsection (3) are—

(a) in the case of a placement order, every person who can be found whose consent to the making of the order is required under subsection (3)(a) of section 21 (or would be required but for subsection (3)(b) of that section) or, if no such person can be found, any relative prescribed by rules who can be found,

(b) in the case of a variation or revocation of a placement order, every person who can be found whose consent to the making of the placement order was required under subsection (3)(a) of section 21 (or would have been required but for subsection (3)(b) of that section),

(c) in the case of an adoption order—

　　(i) every person who can be found whose consent to the making of the order is required under subsection (2)(a) of section 47 (or would be required but for subsection (2)(c) of that section) or, if no such person can be found, any relative prescribed by rules who can be found,

　　(ii) every person who has consented to the making of the order under section 20 (and has not withdrawn the consent) unless he has given a notice under subsection (4)(a) of that section which has effect,

　　(iii) every person who, if leave were given under section 47(5), would be entitled to oppose the making of the order.

(5) Rules made in respect of magistrates' courts may provide—

(a) for enabling any fact tending to establish the identity of a child with a child to whom a document relates to be proved by affidavit, and

(b) for excluding or restricting in relation to any facts that may be so proved the power of a justice of the peace to compel the attendance of witnesses.

Note Sub-s(1): words 'The Lord Chancellor may make rules' in italics repealed and subsequent words in square brackets substituted by the Courts Act 2003, s 109(1), Sch 8, para 413(1), (2) as from a date to be appointed. Sub-s 92) repealed by the Courts Act 2003, s 109(1), (3), Sch 8, para 413(1), (3), Sch 10 as from a date to be appointed.

142 Supplementary and consequential provision—(1) The appropriate Minister may by order make—

(a) any supplementary, incidental or consequential provision,

(b) any transitory, transitional or saving provision,

which he considers necessary or expedient for the purposes of, in consequence of or for giving full effect to any provision of this Act.

(2) For the purposes of subsection (1), where any provision of an order extends to England and Wales, and Scotland or Northern Ireland, the appropriate Minister in relation to the order is the Secretary of State.

(3) Before making an order under subsection (1) containing provision which would, if included in an Act of the Scottish Parliament, be within the legislative competence of that Parliament, the appropriate Minister must consult the Scottish Ministers.

(4) Subsection (5) applies to any power of the Lord Chancellor, the Secretary of State or the Assembly to make regulations, rules or an order by virtue of any other provision of this Act or of Her Majesty to make an Order in Council by virtue of section 125.

(5) The power may be exercised so as to make—

(a) any supplementary, incidental or consequential provision,

(b) any transitory, transitional or saving provision,

which the person exercising the power considers necessary or expedient.

(6) The provision which may be made under subsection (1) or (5) includes provision modifying Schedule 4 or amending or repealing any enactment or instrument.

In relation to an Order in Council, 'enactment' in this subsection includes an enactment comprised in, or in an instrument made under, an Act of the Scottish Parliament.

(7) The power of the Registrar General to make regulations under Chapter 5 of Part 1 may, with the approval of the Chancellor of the Exchequer, be exercised so as to make—

(a) any supplementary, incidental or consequential provision,

(b) any transitory, transitional or saving provision,

which the Registrar General considers necessary or expedient.

143 Offences by bodies corporate and unincorporated bodies—(1) Where an offence under this Act committed by a body corporate is proved to have been committed with the consent or connivance of, or to be attributable to any neglect on the part of, any director, manager, secretary or other similar officer of the body, or a person purporting to act in any such capacity, that person as well as the body is guilty of the offence and liable to be proceeded against and punished accordingly.

(2) Where the affairs of a body corporate are managed by its members, subsection (1) applies in relation to the acts and defaults of a member in connection with his functions of management as it applies to a director of a body corporate.

(3) Proceedings for an offence alleged to have been committed under this Act by an unincorporated body are to be brought in the name of that body (and not in that of any of its members) and, for the purposes of any such proceedings in England and Wales or Northern Ireland, any rules of court relating to the service of documents have effect as if that body were a corporation.

(4) A fine imposed on an unincorporated body on its conviction of an offence under this Act is to be paid out of the funds of that body.

(5) If an unincorporated body is charged with an offence under this Act—

(a) in England and Wales, section 33 of the Criminal Justice Act 1925 (c 86) and Schedule 3 to the Magistrates' Courts Act 1980 (c 43) (procedure on charge of an offence against a corporation),

(b) in Northern Ireland, section 18 of the Criminal Justice Act (Northern Ireland) 1945 (c 15 (NI)) and Schedule 4 to the Magistrates' Courts (Northern Ireland) Order 1981 (SI 1981/1675 (NI 26)) (procedure on charge of an offence against a corporation),

have effect in like manner as in the case of a corporation so charged.

(6) Where an offence under this Act committed by an unincorporated body (other than a partnership) is proved to have been committed with the consent or connivance of, or to be attributable to any neglect on the part of, any officer of the body or any member of its governing body, he as well as the body is guilty of the offence and liable to be proceeded against and punished accordingly.

(7) Where an offence under this Act committed by a partnership is proved to have been committed with the consent or connivance of, or to be attributable to any neglect on the part of, a partner, he as well as the partnership is guilty of the offence and liable to be proceeded against and punished accordingly.

144 General interpretation etc—(1) In this Act—

'appropriate Minister' means—

(a) in relation to England, Scotland or Northern Ireland, the Secretary of State,

(b) in relation to Wales, the Assembly,

and in relation to England and Wales means the Secretary of State and the Assembly acting jointly,

'the Assembly' means the National Assembly for Wales,

'body' includes an unincorporated body,

'by virtue of' includes 'by' and 'under',

'child', except where used to express a relationship, means a person who has not attained the age of 18 years, 'the Convention' means the Convention on Protection of Children and Co-operation in respect of Intercountry Adoption, concluded at the Hague on 29th May 1993,

'Convention adoption order' means an adoption order which, by virtue of regulations under section 1 of the Adoption (Intercountry Aspects) Act 1999 (c 18) (regulations giving effect to the Convention), is made as a Convention adoption order,

'Convention country' means a country or territory in which the Convention is in force,

'court' means, subject to any provision made by virtue of Part 1 of Schedule 11 to the 1989 Act, the High Court, a county court or a magistrates' court,

'enactment' includes an enactment comprised in subordinate legislation,

'fee' includes expenses,

'guardian' has the same meaning as in the 1989 Act and includes a special guardian within the meaning of that Act,

'information' means information recorded in any form,

'local authority' means any unitary authority, or any county council so far as they are not a unitary authority,

'Northern Irish adoption agency' means an adoption agency within the meaning of Article 3 of the Adoption (Northern Ireland) Order 1987 (SI 1987/2203 (NI 22)),

'Northern Irish adoption order' means an order made, or having effect as if made, under Article 12 of the Adoption (Northern Ireland) Order 1987,

'notice' means a notice in writing,

'registration authority' (in Part 1) has the same meaning as in the Care Standards Act 2000 (c 14),

'regulations' means regulations made by the appropriate Minister, unless they are required to be made by the Lord Chancellor, the Secretary of State or the Registrar General,

'relative', in relation to a child, means a grandparent, brother, sister, uncle or aunt, whether of the full blood or half-blood or by marriage,

'rules' means rules made under section 141(1) or made by virtue of section 141(2) under section 144 of the Magistrates' Courts Act 1980 (c 43),

['rules means Family Procedure Rules made by virtue of section 141(1),]

'Scottish adoption order' means an order made, or having effect as if made, under section 12 of the Adoption (Scotland) Act 1978 (c 28),

'subordinate legislation' has the same meaning as in the Interpretation Act 1978 (c 30),

'unitary authority' means—

(a)   the council of any county so far as they are the council for an area for which there are no district councils,

(b)   the council of any district comprised in an area for which there is no county council,

(c)   the council of a county borough,

(d)   the council of a London borough,

(e)   the Common Council of the City of London.

(2) Any power conferred by this Act to prescribe a fee by Order in Council or regulations includes power to prescribe—

(a)   a fee not exceeding a prescribed amount,

(b)   a fee calculated in accordance with the Order or, as the case may be, regulations,

(c)   a fee determined by the person to whom it is payable, being a fee of a reasonable amount.

(3) In this Act, 'Scottish adoption agency' means—

(a)   a local authority, or

(b)   a voluntary organisation providing a registered adoption service;

but in relation to the provision of any particular service, references to a Scottish adoption agency do not include a voluntary organisation unless it is registered in respect of that service or a service which, in Scotland, corresponds to that service.

Expressions used in this subsection have the same meaning as in the Regulation of Care (Scotland) Act 2001 (asp 4) and 'registered' means registered under Part 1 of that Act.

(4) In this Act, a couple means—

(a) a married couple, or

(b) two people (whether of different sexes or the same sex) living as partners in an enduring family relationship.

(5) Subsection (4)(b) does not include two people one of whom is the other's parent, grandparent, sister, brother, aunt or uncle.

(6) References to relationships in subsection (5)—

(a) are to relationships of the full blood or half blood or, in the case of an adopted person, such of those relationships as would exist but for adoption, and

(b) include the relationship of a child with his adoptive, or former adoptive, parents,

but do not include any other adoptive relationships.

(7) For the purposes of this Act, a person is the partner of a child's parent if the person and the parent are a couple but the person is not the child's parent.

Note Sub-s (1): definition 'rules' substituted by the Courts Act 2003, s 109(1), Sch 8, para 414 as from a date to be appointed.

145 Devolution: Wales—(1) The references to the Adoption Act 1976 (c 36) and to the 1989 Act in Schedule 1 to the National Assembly for Wales (Transfer of Functions) Order 1999 (SI 1999/672) are to be treated as referring to those Acts as amended by virtue of this Act.

(2) This section does not affect the power to make further Orders varying or omitting those references.

(3) In Schedule 1 to that Order, in the entry for the Adoption Act 1976, '9' is omitted.

(4) The functions exercisable by the Assembly under sections 9 and 9A of the Adoption Act 1976 (by virtue of paragraphs 4 and 5 of Schedule 4 to this Act) are to be treated for the purposes of section 44 of the Government of Wales Act 1998 (c 38) (parliamentary procedures for subordinate legislation) as if made exercisable by the Assembly by an Order in Council under section 22 of that Act.

146 Expenses There shall be paid out of money provided by Parliament—

(a) any expenditure incurred by a Minister of the Crown by virtue of this Act,

(b) any increase attributable to this Act in the sums payable out of money so provided under any other enactment.

147 Glossary Schedule 6 (glossary) is to have effect.

148 Commencement—(1) This Act (except sections 116 and 136, this Chapter and the provisions mentioned in subsections (5) and (6)) is to come into force on such day as the Secretary of State may by order appoint.

(2) Before making an order under subsection (1) (other than an order bringing paragraph 53 of Schedule 3 into force) the Secretary of State must consult the Assembly.

(3) Before making an order under subsection (1) bringing sections 123 and 124 into force, the Secretary of State must also consult the Scottish Ministers and the Department of Health, Social Services and Public Safety.

(4) Before making an order under subsection (1) bringing sections 125 to 131 into force, the Secretary of State must also consult the Scottish Ministers.

(5) The following are to come into force on such day as the Scottish Ministers may by order appoint—

(a) section 41(5) to (9), so far as relating to Scotland,

(b) sections 132 to 134,

(c) paragraphs 21 to 35 and 82 to 84 of Schedule 3,

(d) paragraphs 15 and 23 of Schedule 4,

(e) the entries in Schedule 5, so far as relating to the provisions mentioned in paragraphs (c) and (d),

(f) section 139, so far as relating to the provisions mentioned in the preceding paragraphs.

(6) Sections 2(6), 3(3) and (4), 4 to 17, 27(3), 53(1) to (3), 54, 56 to 65 and 98, paragraphs 13, 65, 66 and 111 to 113 of Schedule 3 and paragraphs 3 and 5 of Schedule 4 are to come into force on such day as the appropriate Minister may by order appoint.

149 Extent—(1) The amendment or repeal of an enactment has the same extent as the enactment to which it relates.

(2) Subject to that and to the following provisions, this Act except section 137 extends to England and Wales only.

(3) The following extend also to Scotland and Northern Ireland—

(a) sections 63(2) to (5), 65(2)(a) and (b) and (3), 123 and 124,

(b) this Chapter, except sections 141 and 145.

(4) The following extend also to Scotland—

(a) section 41(5) to (9),

(b) sections 125 to 131,

(c) section 138,

(d) section 139, so far as relating to provisions extending to Scotland.

(5) In Schedule 4, paragraph 23 extends only to Scotland.

150 Short title This Act may be cited as the Adoption and Children Act 2002.

SCHEDULE 1   Section 77(6)
REGISTRATION OF ADOPTIONS

Registration of adoption orders

1—(1) Every adoption order must contain a direction to the Registrar General to make in the Adopted Children Register an entry in the form prescribed by regulations made by the Registrar General with the approval of the Chancellor of the Exchequer.

(2) Where, on an application to a court for an adoption order in respect of a child, the identity of the child with a child to whom an entry in the registers of live-births or other records relates is proved to the satisfaction of the court, any adoption order made in pursuance of the application must contain a direction to the Registrar General to secure that the entry in the register or, as the case may be, record in question is marked with the word 'Adopted'.

(3) Where an adoption order is made in respect of a child who has previously been the subject of an adoption order made by a court in England or Wales under Part 1 of this Act or any other enactment—

(a) sub-paragraph (2) does not apply, and

(b) the order must contain a direction to the Registrar General to mark the previous entry in the Adopted Children Register with the word 'Re-adopted'.

(4) Where an adoption order is made, the prescribed officer of the court which

made the order must communicate the order to the Registrar General in the prescribed manner; and the Registrar General must then comply with the directions contained in the order.

'Prescribed' means prescribed by rules.

Registration of adoptions in Scotland, Northern Ireland, the Isle of Man and the Channel Islands

2—(1) Sub-paragraphs (2) and (3) apply where the Registrar General is notified by the authority maintaining a register of adoptions in a part of the British Islands outside England and Wales that an order has been made in that part authorising the adoption of a child.

(2) If an entry in the registers of live-births or other records (and no entry in the Adopted Children Register) relates to the child, the Registrar General must secure that the entry is marked with—

    (a) the word 'Adopted', followed by

    (b) the name, in brackets, of the part in which the order was made.

(3) If an entry in the Adopted Children Register relates to the child, the Registrar General must mark the entry with—

    (a) the word 'Re-adopted', followed by

    (b) the name, in brackets, of the part in which the order was made.

(4) Where, after an entry in either of the registers or other records mentioned in sub-paragraphs (2) and (3) has been so marked, the Registrar General is notified by the authority concerned that—

    (a) the order has been quashed,

    (b) an appeal against the order has been allowed, or

    (c) the order has been revoked,

the Registrar General must secure that the marking is cancelled.

(5) A copy or extract of an entry in any register or other record, being an entry the marking of which is cancelled under sub-paragraph (4), is not to be treated as an accurate copy unless both the marking and the cancellation are omitted from it.

Registration of other adoptions

3—(1) If the Registrar General is satisfied, on an application under this paragraph, that he has sufficient particulars relating to a child adopted under a registrable foreign adoption to enable an entry to be made in the Adopted Children Register for the child he must make the entry accordingly.

(2) If he is also satisfied that an entry in the registers of live-births or other records relates to the child, he must—

    (a) secure that the entry is marked 'Adopted', followed by the name, in brackets, of the country in which the adoption was effected, or

    (b) where appropriate, secure that the overseas registers of births are so marked.

(3) An application under this paragraph must be made, in the prescribed manner, by a prescribed person and the applicant must provide the prescribed documents and other information.

(4) An entry made in the Adopted Children Register by virtue of this paragraph must be made in the prescribed form.

(5) In this Schedule 'registrable foreign adoption' means an adoption which satisfies prescribed requirements and is either—

    (a) adoption under a Convention adoption, or

    (b) adoption under an overseas adoption.

(6) In this paragraph—

    (a) 'prescribed' means prescribed by regulations made by the Registrar General with the approval of the Chancellor of the Exchequer,

   (b) 'overseas register of births' includes—
      (i) a register made under regulations made by the Secretary of State under section 41(1)(g), (h) or (i) of the British Nationality Act 1981 (c 61),
     (ii) a record kept under an Order in Council made under section 1 of the Registration of Births, Deaths and Marriages (Special Provisions) Act 1957 (c 58) (other than a certified copy kept by the Registrar General).

Amendment of orders and rectification of Registers and other records

4—(1) The court by which an adoption order has been made may, on the application of the adopter or the adopted person, amend the order by the correction of any error in the particulars contained in it.

(2) The court by which an adoption order has been made may, if satisfied on the application of the adopter or the adopted person that within the period of one year beginning with the date of the order any new name—
   (a) has been given to the adopted person (whether in baptism or otherwise), or
   (b) has been taken by the adopted person,
either in place of or in addition to a name specified in the particulars required to be entered in the Adopted Children Register in pursuance of the order, amend the order by substituting or, as the case may be, adding that name in those particulars.

(3) The court by which an adoption order has been made may, if satisfied on the application of any person concerned that a direction for the marking of an entry in the registers of live-births, the Adopted Children Register or other records included in the order in pursuance of paragraph 1(2) or (3) was wrongly so included, revoke that direction.

(4) Where an adoption order is amended or a direction revoked under sub-paragraphs (1) to (3), the prescribed officer of the court must communicate the amendment in the prescribed manner to the Registrar General.

'Prescribed' means prescribed by rules.

(5) The Registrar General must then—
   (a) amend the entry in the Adopted Children Register accordingly, or
   (b) secure that the marking of the entry in the registers of live-births, the Adopted Children Register or other records is cancelled,
as the case may be.

(6) Where an adoption order is quashed or an appeal against an adoption order allowed by any court, the court must give directions to the Registrar General to secure that—
   (a) any entry in the Adopted Children Register, and
   (b) any marking of an entry in that Register, the registers of live-births or other records as the case may be, which was effected in pursuance of the order,
is cancelled.

(7) Where an adoption order has been amended, any certified copy of the relevant entry in the Adopted Children Register which may be issued pursuant to section 78(2)(b) must be a copy of the entry as amended, without the reproduction of—
   (a) any note or marking relating to the amendment, or
   (b) any matter cancelled in pursuance of it.

(8) A copy or extract of an entry in any register or other record, being an entry the marking of which has been cancelled, is not to be treated as an accurate copy unless both the marking and the cancellation are omitted from it.

(9) If the Registrar General is satisfied—
   (a) that a registrable foreign adoption has ceased to have effect, whether on annulment or otherwise, or

(b) that any entry or mark was erroneously made in pursuance of paragraph 3
in the Adopted Children Register, the registers of live-births, the overseas
registers of births or other records,

he may secure that such alterations are made in those registers or other records as
he considers are required in consequence of the adoption ceasing to have effect or
to correct the error.

'Overseas register of births' has the same meaning as in paragraph 3.

(10) Where an entry in such a register is amended in pursuance of sub-
paragraph (9), any copy or extract of the entry is not to be treated as accurate
unless it shows the entry as amended but without indicating that it has been
amended.

Marking of entries on re-registration of birth on legitimation

5—(1) Without prejudice to paragraphs 2(4) and 4(5), where, after an entry in
the registers of live-births or other records has been marked in accordance with
paragraph 1 or 2, the birth is re-registered under section 14 of the Births and
Deaths Registration Act 1953 (c 20) (re-registration of births of legitimated
persons), the entry made on the re-registration must be marked in the like
manner.

(2) Without prejudice to paragraph 4(9), where an entry in the registers of live-
births or other records is marked in pursuance of paragraph 3 and the birth in
question is subsequently re-registered under section 14 of that Act, the entry made
on re-registration must be marked in the like manner.

Cancellations in registers on legitimation

6—(1) This paragraph applies where an adoption order is revoked under section
55(1).

(2) The prescribed officer of the court must communicate the revocation in the
prescribed manner to the Registrar General who must then cancel or secure the
cancellation of—

(a) the entry in the Adopted Children Register relating to the adopted person,
and

(b) the marking with the word 'Adopted' of any entry relating to the adopted
person in the registers of live-births or other records.

'Prescribed' means prescribed by rules.

(3) A copy or extract of an entry in any register or other record, being an entry
the marking of which is cancelled under this paragraph, is not to be treated as an
accurate copy unless both the marking and the cancellation are omitted from it.

SCHEDULE 2   Section 79(6)

DISCLOSURE OF BIRTH RECORDS BY REGISTRAR GENERAL

1 On an application made in the prescribed manner by an adopted person—

(a) a record of whose birth is kept by the Registrar General, and

(b) who has attained the age of 18 years,

the Registrar General must give the applicant any information necessary to enable
the applicant to obtain a certified copy of the record of his birth.

'Prescribed' means prescribed by regulations made by the Registrar General
with the approval of the Chancellor of the Exchequer.

2—(1) Before giving any information to an applicant under paragraph 1, the
Registrar General must inform the applicant that counselling services are available
to the applicant—

(a) from a registered adoption society, an organisation within section 144(3)(b) or an adoption society which is registered under Article 4 of the Adoption (Northern Ireland) Order 1987 (SI 1987/2203 (NI 22)),

(b) if the applicant is in England and Wales, at the General Register Office or from any local authority or registered adoption support agency,

(c) if the applicant is in Scotland, from any council constituted under section 2 of the Local Government etc (Scotland) Act 1994 (c 39),

(d) if the applicant is in Northern Ireland, from any Board.

(2) In sub-paragraph (1)(b), 'registered adoption support agency' means an adoption support agency in respect of which a person is registered under Part 2 of the Care Standards Act 2000 (c 14).

(3) In sub-paragraph (1)(d), 'Board' means a Health and Social Services Board established under Article 16 of the Health and Personal Social Services (Northern Ireland) Order 1972 (SI 1972/1265 (NI 14)); but where the functions of a Board are exercisable by a Health and Social Services Trust, references in that sub-paragraph to a Board are to be read as references to the Health and Social Services Trust.

(4) If the applicant chooses to receive counselling from a person or body within sub-paragraph (1), the Registrar General must send to the person or body the information to which the applicant is entitled under paragraph 1.

3—(1) Where an adopted person who is in England and Wales—

(a) applies for information under paragraph 1 or Article 54 of the Adoption (Northern Ireland) Order 1987, or

(b) is supplied with information under section 45 of the Adoption (Scotland) Act 1978 (c 28),

the persons and bodies mentioned in sub-paragraph (2) must, if asked by the applicant to do so, provide counselling for the applicant.

(2) Those persons and bodies are—

(a) the Registrar General,

(b) any local authority,

(c) a registered adoption society, an organisation within section 144(3)(b) or an adoption society which is registered under Article 4 of the Adoption (Northern Ireland) Order 1987.

4—(1) Where a person—

(a) was adopted before 12th November 1975, and

(b) applies for information under paragraph 1,

the Registrar General must not give the information to the applicant unless the applicant has attended an interview with a counsellor arranged by a person or body from whom counselling services are available as mentioned in paragraph 2.

(2) Where the Registrar General is prevented by sub-paragraph (1) from giving information to a person who is not living in the United Kingdom, the Registrar General may give the information to any body which—

(a) the Registrar General is satisfied is suitable to provide counselling to that person, and

(b) has notified the Registrar General that it is prepared to provide such counselling.

SCHEDULE 3   Section 139
MINOR AND CONSEQUENTIAL AMENDMENTS

The Marriage Act 1949 (c 76)

1 Section 3 of the Marriage Act 1949 (marriage of person aged under eighteen) is
amended as follows.

2 In subsection (1), for 'person or persons specified in subsection (1A) of this
section' there is substituted 'appropriate persons'.

3 For subsection (1A) there is substituted—
'(1A) The appropriate persons are—
(a) if none of paragraphs (b) to (h) apply, each of the following—
(i)   any parent of the child who has parental responsibility for him; and
(ii) any guardian of the child;
(b) where a special guardianship order is in force with respect to a child,
each of the child's special guardians, unless any of paragraphs (c) to (g)
applies;
(c) where a care order has effect with respect to the child, the local authority
designated in the order, and each parent, guardian or special guardian
(in so far as their parental responsibility has not been restricted under
section 33(3) of the Children Act 1989), unless paragraph (e) applies;
(d) where a residence order has effect with respect to the child, the persons
with whom the child lives, or is to live, as a result of the order, unless
paragraph (e) applies;
(e) where an adoption agency is authorised to place the child for adoption
under section 19 of the Adoption and Children Act 2002, that agency or,
where a care order has effect with respect to the child, the local authority
designated in the order;
(f) where a placement order is in force with respect to the child, the
appropriate local authority;
(g) where a child has been placed for adoption with prospective adopters,
the prospective adopters (in so far as their parental responsibility has not
been restricted under section 25(4) of the Adoption and Children Act
2002), in addition to those persons specified in paragraph (e) or (f);
(h) where none of paragraphs (b) to (g) apply but a residence order was in
force with respect to the child immediately before he reached the age of
sixteen, the persons with whom he lived, or was to live, as a result of the
order.'

4 For subsection (1B) there is substituted—
'(1B) In this section—
'guardian of a child', 'parental responsibility', 'residence order', 'special
guardian', 'special guardianship order' and 'care order' have the same
meaning as in the Children Act 1989;
'adoption agency', 'placed for adoption', 'placement order' and 'local
authority' have the same meaning as in the Adoption and Children Act
2002;
'appropriate local authority' means the local authority authorised by the
placement order to place the child for adoption.'

5 In subsection (2), for 'The last foregoing subsection' there is substituted
'Subsection (1)'.

The Births and Deaths Registration Act 1953 (c 20)

6 In section 10 of the Births and Deaths Registration Act 1953 (registration of father where parents not married)—
- (a) in subsection (1)(d)(i), for 'a parental responsibility agreement made between them in relation to the child' there is substituted 'any agreement made between them under section 4(1)(b) of the Children Act 1989 in relation to the child',
- (b) in subsection (1)(d)(ii), for 'the Children Act 1989' there is substituted 'that Act',
- (c) in subsection (3), the words following 'the Family Law Reform Act 1987' are omitted.

7 In section 10A of the Births and Deaths Registration Act 1953 (re-registration of father where parents not married)—
- (a) in subsection (1)(d)(i), for 'a parental responsibility agreement made between them in relation to the child' there is substituted 'any agreement made between them under section 4(1)(b) of the Children Act 1989 in relation to the child',
- (b) in subsection (1)(d)(ii), for 'the Children Act 1989' there is substituted 'that Act'.

The Sexual Offences Act 1956 (c 69)

8 In section 28 of the Sexual Offences Act 1956 (causing or encouraging prostitution of, intercourse with, or indecent assault on, girl under sixteen), in subsection (4), the 'or' at the end of paragraph (a) is omitted, and after that paragraph there is inserted—
> '(aa) a special guardianship order under that Act is in force with respect to her and he is not her special guardian; or'.

The Health Services and Public Health Act 1968 (c 46)

9 The Health Services and Public Health Act 1968 is amended as follows.

10 In section 64 (financial assistance by the Secretary of State to certain voluntary organisations), in subsection (3)(a)(xviii), for 'the Adoption Act 1976' there is substituted 'the Adoption and Children Act 2002'.

11 In section 65 (financial and other assistance by local authorities to certain voluntary organisations), in subsection (3)(b), for 'the Adoption Act 1976' there is substituted 'the Adoption and Children Act 2002'.

The Local Authority Social Services Act 1970 (c 42)

12 The Local Authority Social Services Act 1970 is amended as follows.

13 In section 7D (default powers of Secretary of State as respects social services functions of local authorities), in subsection (1), after 'the Children Act 1989' there is inserted 'section 1 or 2(4) of the Adoption (Intercountry Aspects) Act 1999 or the Adoption and Children Act 2002'.

14 In Schedule 1 (enactments conferring functions assigned to social services committee)—
- (a) the entry relating to the Adoption Act 1976 is omitted,
- (b) in the entry relating to the Children Act 1989, after 'Consent to application for residence order in respect of child in care' there is inserted 'Functions relating to special guardianship orders',

(c) in the entry relating to the Adoption (Intercountry Aspects) Act 1999—
  (i) in the first column, for 'Section' there is substituted 'Sections 1 and',
  (ii) in the second column, for 'Article 9(a) to (c) of' there is substituted 'regulations made under section 1 giving effect to' and at the end there is inserted 'and functions under Article 9(a) to (c) of the Convention',

and at the end of the Schedule there is inserted—

'Adoption and Children Act 2002   Maintenance of Adoption Service; functions of local authority as adoption agency.'

The Immigration Act 1971 (c 77)

15 In section 33(1) of the Immigration Act 1971 (interpretation)—
  (a) in the definition of 'Convention adoption', after '1978' there is inserted 'or in the Adoption and Children Act 2002',
  (b) in the definition of 'legally adopted', for 'section 72(2) of the Adoption Act 1976' there is substituted 'section 87 of the Adoption and Children Act 2002'.

The Legitimacy Act 1976 (c 31)

16 The Legitimacy Act 1976 is amended as follows.

17 In section 4 (legitimation of adopted child)—
  (a) in subsection (1), after '1976' there is inserted 'or section 67 of the Adoption and Children Act 2002',
  (b) in subsection (2)—
    (i) in paragraph (a), after '39' there is inserted 'or subsection (3)(b) of the said section 67',
    (ii) in paragraph (b), after '1976' there is inserted 'or section 67, 68 or 69 of the Adoption and Children Act 2002'.

18 In section 6 (dispositions depending on date of birth), at the end of subsection (2) there is inserted 'or section 69(2) of the Adoption and Children Act 2002'.

The Adoption Act 1976 (c 36)

19 In section 38 of the Adoption Act 1976 (meaning of 'adoption' in Part 4), in subsection (2), after '1975' there is inserted 'but does not include an adoption of a kind mentioned in paragraphs (c) to (e) of subsection (1) effected on or after the day which is the appointed day for the purposes of Chapter 4 of Part 1 of the Adoption and Children Act 2002'.

The National Health Service Act 1977 (c 49)

20 In section 124A(3) of the National Health Service Act 1977 (information provided by the Registrar General to the Secretary of State), the 'or' at the end of paragraph (a) is omitted and after that paragraph there is inserted—
  '(aa) entered in the Adopted Children Register maintained by the Registrar General under the Adoption and Children Act 2002; or'.

The Adoption (Scotland) Act 1978 (c 28)

21 The Adoption (Scotland) Act 1978 is amended as follows.

22 In section 11 (restriction on arranging adoptions and placing of children)—

(a) in subsection (2)—
    (i) for paragraph (a) there is substituted—
  '(a) a registered adoption society (within the meaning of section 2(2) of the Adoption and Children Act 2002)'; and
    (ii) for 'section 1' there is substituted 'section 3(1)', and
(b) after subsection (2) there is inserted—
  '(2A) In relation to the provision of any particular service by an adoption society, the reference in subsection (2)(a) to a registered adoption society does not include a voluntary organisation unless it is registered under Part 2 of the Care Standards Act 2000 in respect of that service or a service which, in England, corresponds to that service.'

23 In section 16 (parental agreement to adoption order)—
  (a) in subsection (1), after paragraph (a) there is inserted—
  '(aa) each parent or guardian of the child has consented under section 20 of the Adoption and Children Act 2002 (advance consent to adoption), has not withdrawn the consent and does not oppose the making of the adoption order;
  (ab) subsection (3A) applies and no parent or guardian of the child opposes the making of the adoption order', and
  (b) after subsection (3) there is inserted—
  '(3A) This subsection applies where—
  (a) the child has been placed for adoption by an adoption agency (within the meaning of section 2(1) of the Adoption and Children Act 2002) with the prospective adopters in whose favour the adoption order is proposed to be made; and
  (b) the child was placed for adoption—
    (i) under section 19 of that Act (placing children with parental consent) with the consent of each parent or guardian and the consent of the mother was given when the child was at least six weeks old; or
    (ii) under an order made under section 21 of that Act (placement orders) and the child was at least six weeks old when that order was made.
  (3B) A parent or guardian may not oppose the making of an adoption order under subsection (1)(aa) or (ab) without the leave of the court.
  (3C) The court shall not give leave under subsection (3B) unless satisfied that there has been a change of circumstances since the consent of the parent or guardian was given or, as the case may be, the order under section 21 of that Act was made.
  (3D) The withdrawal of—
  (a) any consent to the placement of a child for adoption—
    (i) under section 19; or
    (ii) under an order made under section 21,
  of the Adoption and Children Act 2002; or
  (b) any consent given under section 20 of that Act,
  is ineffective if it is given after an application for an adoption order is made.'

24 In section 29 (return of children taken away in breach of section 27 or 28)—
  (a) in subsection (1), for 'section 27 or 28 of the Adoption Act 1976' there is substituted 'section 30, 34, 35 or 36 of the Adoption and Children Act 2002', and
  (b) in subsection (2), for 'section 27 or 28 of the Adoption Act 1976', in both places where those words occur, there is substituted 'section 30, 34, 35 or 36 of the Adoption and Children Act 2002'.

25 In section 45 (Adopted Children Register)—
   (a) in subsection (6)(d), for sub-paragraph (ii) there is substituted—
         '(ii) registered under Part II of the Care Standards Act 2000;';
   (b) in subsection (6A)(b), for sub-paragraph (i) there is substituted—
         '(i) Schedule 2 to the Adoption and Children Act 2002;'.

26 In section 47 (annulment etc of overseas adoptions), in subsection (4), for 'section 53 of the Adoption Act 1976' there is substituted 'section 89(2) of the Adoption and Children Act 2002'.

27 In section 50 (restriction on removal of children for adoption outside Great Britain), in subsection (1), for 'section 55 of the Adoption Act 1976' there is substituted 'section 84 of the Adoption and Children Act 2002'.

28 Section 52 (restriction on advertisements) is omitted.

29 In section 53 (effect of determination and orders made in England and Wales and overseas in adoption proceedings), in subsection (2), the words 'England and Wales or' are omitted.

30 After section 53 there is inserted—

'53A Effect of certain orders made in England and Wales—(1) An adoption order (within the meaning of section 46(1) of the Adoption and Children Act 2002) has effect in Scotland as it has in England and Wales but as if any reference to the parental responsibility for the child were to the parental responsibilities and parental rights in relation to the child.
   (2) An order made under section 21 of that Act (placement orders), and the variation or revocation of such an order under section 23 or 24 of that Act, have effect in Scotland as they have in England and Wales but as if any reference to the parental responsibility for the child were to the parental responsibilities and parental rights in relation to the child.

53B Effect of placing for adoption etc under Adoption and Children Act 2002—(1) If—
   (a) a child is placed for adoption under section 19 of the Adoption and Children Act 2002 (placing children with parental consent); or
   (b) an adoption agency is authorised to place a child for adoption under that section,
sections 25 (parental responsibility) and 28(2) to (4) (further consequences of placement) of that Act have effect in Scotland as they have in England and Wales but with the modifications specified in subsection (2).
   (2) Those modifications are—
   (a) in section 25, any reference to the parental responsibility for the child is to be read as a reference to the parental responsibilities and parental rights in relation to the child; and
   (b) in section 28(2), the reference to the court is to be read as a reference to the authorised court.

53C Further consequences of placement and placement orders—(1) Subsection (2) applies where—
   (a) a child is placed for adoption under section 19 of the Adoption and Children Act 2002 (placing children with parental consent); or
   (b) an adoption agency is authorised to place the child for adoption under that section.

(2) No order under subsection (1) of section 11 of the Children (Scotland) Act 1995 (court orders relating to parental responsibilities etc) of a kind referred to in subsection (2)(c) (residence orders) of that section may be made in respect of the child.

(3) On the making of an order under section 21 of the Adoption and Children Act 2002 (a 'placement order') in respect of a child, any order under subsection (1) of section 11 of the Children (Scotland) Act 1995 of a kind referred to in subsection (2)(c) to (f) (residence orders, contact orders, specific issue orders and interdicts in relation to parental responsibilities) of that section in respect of the child ceases to have effect.

(4) Where a placement order is in force—
   (a) no such order as is referred to in subsection (3) of this section; and
   (b) no order under section 55 of the Children (Scotland) Act 1995 (child assessment orders),
may be made in respect of the child.'

31 In section 54 (evidence of adoption in England, Wales and Northern Ireland), in paragraph (a), for 'section 50(2) of the Adoption Act 1976' there is substituted 'section 77(4) and (5) of the Adoption and Children Act 2002'.

32 In section 56 (authorised courts), in subsection (3), for 'Great Britain' there is substituted 'Scotland'.

33 In section 59 (rules of procedure)—
   (a) in subsection (2)—
      (i) for the words from 'in relation to' to 'adoption', where it secondly occurs, there is substituted '(except where an order has been made freeing the child for adoption)'; and
      (ii) for the words from 'every' to 'Act' there is substituted 'any person mentioned in subsection (2A)'; and
   (b) after subsection (2) there is inserted—
   '(2A) The persons referred to in subsection (2) are—
   (a) every person who can be found and whose agreement or consent to the making of the order is required to be given or dispensed with under this Act or, if no such person can be found, any relative prescribed by rules who can be found;
   (b) every person who has consented to the making of the order under section 20 of the Adoption and Children Act 2002 (and has not withdrawn the consent) unless he has given a notice under subsection (4)(a) of that section which has effect;
   (c) every person who, if leave were given under section 16(3B), would be entitled to oppose the making of the order.'

34 In section 60 (orders, rules and regulations), after subsection (3) there is inserted—
   '(3A) An order under section 65(2) shall be subject to annulment in pursuance of a resolution of the Scottish Parliament.'

35 In section 65 (interpretation), in subsection (1)—
   (a) in the definition of 'adoption agency', for 'section 1 of the Adoption Act 1976' there is substituted 'section 2(1) of the Adoption and Children Act 2002',
   (b) in the definition of 'adoption order'—
      (i) in paragraph (b), for 'section 12 of the Adoption Act 1976' there is substituted 'section 46 of the Adoption and Children Act 2002',

(ii)   in paragraph (c), for 'section 55 of the Adoption Act 1976' there is substituted 'section 84 of the Adoption and Children Act 2002', and
(c)   in the definition of 'order freeing a child for adoption', paragraph (a) and the word 'and' immediately following that paragraph are omitted.

The Magistrates' Courts Act 1980 (c 43)

36 The Magistrates' Courts Act 1980 is amended as follows.

37 In section 65 (meaning of family proceedings), in subsection (1), for paragraph (h) there is substituted—
   '(h) the Adoption and Children Act 2002;'.

38 In section 69 (sitting of magistrates' courts for family proceedings), in subsections (2) and (3), for 'the Adoption Act 1976' there is substituted 'the Adoption and Children Act 2002'.

39 In section 71 (newspaper reports of family proceedings)—
   (a)   in subsection (1), '(other than proceedings under the Adoption Act 1976)' is omitted,
   (b)   in subsection (2)—
      (i)   for 'the Adoption Act 1976' there is substituted 'the Adoption and Children Act 2002',
      (ii)   the words following '(a) and (b)' are omitted.

40 In Part 1 of Schedule 6 (fees to be taken by justices' chief executives), in the entry relating to family proceedings—
   (a)   for 'the Adoption Act 1976, except under section 21 of that Act', there is substituted 'the Adoption and Children Act 2002, except under section 23 of that Act',
   (b)   in paragraph (c), for 'section 21 of the Adoption Act 1976' there is substituted 'section 23 of the Adoption and Children Act 2002'.

The Mental Health Act 1983 (c 20)

41 In section 28 of the Mental Health Act 1983 (nearest relative of minor under guardianship, etc), in subsection (3), after "guardian" there is inserted 'includes a special guardian (within the meaning of the Children Act 1989), but'.

The Child Abduction Act 1984 (c 37)

42—(1) Section 1 of the Child Abduction Act 1984 (offence of abduction of child by parent, etc) is amended as follows.
   (2) In subsection (2), after paragraph (c) there is inserted—
   '(ca)   he is a special guardian of the child; or'.
   (3) In subsection (3)(a), after sub-paragraph (iii) there is inserted—
   '(iiia) any special guardian of the child;'.
   (4) In subsection (4), for paragraphs (a) and (b) there is substituted—
   '(a)   he is a person in whose favour there is a residence order in force with respect to the child, and he takes or sends the child out of the United Kingdom for a period of less than one month; or
   (b)   he is a special guardian of the child and he takes or sends the child out of the United Kingdom for a period of less than three months.'
   (5) In subsection (5A), the 'or' at the end of sub-paragraph (i) of paragraph (a) is omitted, and after that sub-paragraph there is inserted—
   '(ia)   who is a special guardian of the child; or'.

(6) In subsection (7)(a), after 'guardian of a child,' there is inserted 'special guardian,'.

43—(1) The Schedule to that Act (modifications of section 1 for children in certain cases) is amended as follows.

(2) In paragraph 3 (adoption and custodianship), for sub-paragraphs (1) and (2) there is substituted—

'(1) This paragraph applies where—
 (a) a child is placed for adoption by an adoption agency under section 19 of the Adoption and Children Act 2002, or an adoption agency is authorised to place the child for adoption under that section; or
 (b) a placement order is in force in respect of the child; or
 (c) an application for such an order has been made in respect of the child and has not been disposed of; or
 (d) an application for an adoption order has been made in respect of the child and has not been disposed of; or
 (e) an order under section 84 of the Adoption and Children Act 2002 (giving parental responsibility prior to adoption abroad) has been made in respect of the child, or an application for such an order in respect of him has been made and has not been disposed of.

(2)   Where this paragraph applies, section 1 of this Act shall have effect as if—
 (a) the reference in subsection (1) to the appropriate consent were—
   (i) in a case within sub-paragraph (1)(a) above, a reference to the consent of each person who has parental responsibility for the child or to the leave of the High Court;
   (ii) in a case within sub-paragraph (1)(b) above, a reference to the leave of the court which made the placement order;
   (iii) in a case within sub-paragraph (1)(c) or (d) above, a reference to the leave of the court to which the application was made;
   (iv) in a case within sub-paragraph (1)(e) above, a reference to the leave of the court which made the order or, as the case may be, to which the application was made;
 (b) subsection (3) were omitted;
 (c) in subsection (4), in paragraph (a), for the words from "in whose favour" to the first mention of "child" there were substituted "who provides the child's home in a case falling within sub-paragraph (1)(a) or (b) of paragraph 3 of the Schedule to this Act"; and
 (d) subsections (4A), (5), (5A) and (6) were omitted.'

(3) In paragraph 5 (interpretation), in sub-paragraph (a), for the words from 'and 'adoption order" to the end there is substituted ', 'adoption order', 'placed for adoption by an adoption agency' and 'placement order' have the same meaning as in the Adoption and Children Act 2002; and'.

The Matrimonial and Family Proceedings Act 1984 (c 42)

44 *In section 40 of the Matrimonial and Family Proceedings Act 1984 (family proceedings rules), in subsection (2), in paragraph (a), after 'the Adoption Act 1968' the 'or' is omitted and after 'the Adoption Act 1976' there is inserted 'or section 141(1) of the Adoption and Children Act 2002'.*

The Child Abduction and Custody Act 1985 (c 60)

45 In Schedule 3 to the Child Abduction and Custody Act 1985 (custody orders), in paragraph 1, the 'and' at the end of paragraph (b) is omitted and after that paragraph there is inserted—

'(bb)   a special guardianship order (within the meaning of the Act of 1989);
and',
and paragraph (c)(v) is omitted.

The Family Law Act 1986 (c 55)

46 The Family Law Act 1986 is amended as follows.

47 In section 1 (orders to which Part 1 applies), in subsection (1), after paragraph
(a) there is inserted—
'(aa)   a special guardianship order made by a court in England and Wales
under the Children Act 1989;
(ab)   an order made under section 26 of the Adoption and Children Act 2002
(contact), other than an order varying or revoking such an order'.

48 In section 2 (jurisdiction: general), after subsection (2) there is inserted—
'(2A)   A court in England and Wales shall not have jurisdiction to make a
special guardianship order under the Children Act 1989 unless the
condition in section 3 of this Act is satisfied.
(2B)   A court in England and Wales shall not have jurisdiction to make an
order under section 26 of the Adoption and Children Act 2002 unless
the condition in section 3 of this Act is satisfied.'

49 In section 57 (declarations as to adoptions effected overseas)—
(a)   for subsection (1)(a) there is substituted—
'(a) a Convention adoption, or an overseas adoption, within the meaning of
the Adoption and Children Act 2002, or',
(b)   in subsection (2)(a), after '1976' there is inserted 'or section 67 of the
Adoption and Children Act 2002'.

The Family Law Reform Act 1987 (c 42)

50 The Family Law Reform Act 1987 is amended as follows.

51 In section 1 (general principle), for paragraph (c) of subsection (3) there is
substituted—
'(c) is an adopted person within the meaning of Chapter 4 of Part 1 of the
Adoption and Children Act 2002'.

52 In section 19 (dispositions of property), in subsection (5), after '1976' there is
inserted 'or section 69 of the Adoption and Children Act 2002'.

The Adoption (Northern Ireland) Order 1987 (SI 1987/2203 (NI 22))

53 In Article 2(2) (interpretation), in the definition of 'prescribed', for 'Articles
54' there is substituted 'Articles 53(3B) and (3D), 54'.

The Children Act 1989 (c 41)

54 The Children Act 1989 is amended as follows.

55 In section 8 (residence, contact and other orders with respect to children), in
subsection (4), for paragraph (d) there is substituted—
'(d) the Adoption and Children Act 2002;'.

56 In section 10 (power of court to make section 8 orders)—
(a)   in subsection (4)(a), for 'or guardian' there is substituted ', guardian or
special guardian',

(b) after subsection (4)(a) there is inserted—
'(aa) any person who by virtue of section 4A has parental responsibility for the child;',
(c) after subsection (5) there is inserted—
'(5A) A local authority foster parent is entitled to apply for a residence order with respect to a child if the child has lived with him for a period of at least one year immediately preceding the application.',
(d) after subsection (7) there is inserted—
'(7A) If a special guardianship order is in force with respect to a child, an application for a residence order may only be made with respect to him, if apart from this subsection the leave of the court is not required, with such leave.'

57 In section 12 (residence orders and parental responsibility), in subsection (3)—
(a) paragraph (a) is omitted,
(b) in paragraph (b), for 'section 55 of the Act of 1976' there is substituted 'section 84 of the Adoption and Children Act 2002'.

58 In section 16 (family assistance orders), in subsection (2)(a), for 'or guardian' there is substituted ', guardian or special guardian'.

59 In section 20 (provision of accommodation for children: general), in subsection (9), the 'or' at the end of paragraph (a) is omitted and after that paragraph there is inserted—
'(aa)   who is a special guardian of the child; or'.

60 In section 24 (persons qualifying for advice and assistance)—
(a) for subsection (1) there is substituted—
'(1) In this Part 'a person qualifying for advice and assistance' means a person to whom subsection (1A) or (1B) applies.
(1A) This subsection applies to a person—
(a) who has reached the age of sixteen but not the age of twenty-one;
(b) with respect to whom a special guardianship order is in force (or, if he has reached the age of eighteen, was in force when he reached that age); and
(c) who was, immediately before the making of that order, looked after by a local authority.
(1B) This subsection applies to a person to whom subsection (1A) does not apply, and who—
(a) is under twenty-one; and
(b) at any time after reaching the age of sixteen but while still a child was, but is no longer, looked after, accommodated or fostered.',
(b) in subsection (2), for 'subsection (1)(b)' there is substituted 'subsection (1B)(b)',
(c) in subsection (5), before paragraph (a) there is inserted—
'(za) in the case of a person to whom subsection (1A) applies, a local authority determined in accordance with regulations made by the Secretary of State;'.

61 In section 24A (advice and assistance for qualifying persons)—
(a) in subsection (2)(b), after 'a person' there is inserted 'to whom section 24(1A) applies, or to whom section 24(1B) applies and',
(b) in subsection (3)(a), after 'if' there is inserted 'he is a person to whom section 24(1A) applies, or he is a person to whom section 24(1B) applies and'.

62 In section 24B (assistance with employment, education and training), in each of subsections (1) and (3)(b), after 'of' there is inserted 'section 24(1A) or'.

63 In section 33 (effect of care order)—
- (a) in subsection (3)(b), for 'a parent or guardian of the child' there is substituted
  '—
  - (i) a parent, guardian or special guardian of the child; or
  - (ii) a person who by virtue of section 4A has parental responsibility for the child,',
- (b) in subsection (5), for 'a parent or guardian of the child who has care of him' there is substituted 'a person mentioned in that provision who has care of the child',
- (c) in subsection (6)(b)—
  - (i) sub-paragraph (i) is omitted,
  - (ii) in sub-paragraph (ii), for 'section 55 of the Act of 1976' there is substituted 'section 84 of the Adoption and Children Act 2002',
- (d) in subsection (9), for 'a parent or guardian of the child' there is substituted 'a person mentioned in that provision'.

64 In section 34 (parental contact etc with children in care)—
- (a) in subsection (1)(b), after 'guardian' there is inserted 'or special guardian', and
- (b) after subsection (1)(b) there is inserted—
  '(ba) any person who by virtue of section 4A has parental responsibility for him;'.

65 In section 80 (inspection of children's homes by persons authorised by Secretary of State), in subsection (1), paragraphs (e) and (f) are omitted.

66 In section 81 (inquiries), in subsection (1), paragraph (b) is omitted.

67 In section 88 (amendments of adoption legislation), subsection (1) is omitted.

68 In section 91 (effect and duration of orders, etc)—
- (a) after subsection (5) there is inserted—
  '(5A) The making of a special guardianship order with respect to a child who is the subject of—
  - (a) a care order; or
  - (b) an order under section 34,
  discharges that order.',
- (b) in subsection (7), after '4(1)' there is inserted '4A(1)',
- (c) in subsection (8)(a), after '4' there is inserted 'or 4A'.

69 In section 102 (power of constable to assist in exercise of certain powers to search for children or inspect premises), in subsection (6), paragraph (c) is omitted.

70 In section 105 (interpretation), in subsection (1)—
- (a) in the definition of 'adoption agency', for 'section 1 of the Adoption Act 1976' there is substituted 'section 2 of the Adoption and Children Act 2002',
- (b) at the appropriate place there is inserted—
  '"section 31A plan" has the meaning given by section 31A(6);',
- (c) in the definition of 'parental responsibility agreement', for 'section 4(1)' there is substituted 'sections 4(1) and 4A(2)',

(d) the definition of 'protected child' is omitted,
(e) after the definition of 'special educational needs' there is inserted—
  '"special guardian" and "special guardianship order" have the meaning given
    by section 14A;'.

71 In Schedule 1 (financial provision for children)—
  (a) in paragraph 1 (orders for financial relief against parents)—
      (i)   in sub-paragraph (1), for 'or guardian' there is substituted ',
           guardian or special guardian', and
      (ii) in sub-paragraph (6), after 'order' there is inserted 'or a special
           guardianship order',
  (b) in paragraph 6 (variation etc of orders for periodical payments), in sub-
       paragraph (8), after 'guardian' there is inserted 'or special guardian',
  (c) in paragraph 8 (financial relief under other enactments), in sub-paragraph
       (1) and in sub-paragraph (2)(b), after 'residence order' there is inserted
       'or a special guardianship order',
  (d) in paragraph 14 (financial provision for child resident in country outside
       England and Wales), in sub-paragraph (1)(b), after 'guardian' there is
       inserted 'or special guardian'.

72 In Schedule 2, in paragraph 19 (arrangements by local authorities to assist
children to live abroad)—
  (a) in sub-paragraph (4) (arrangements to assist children to live abroad), after
       'guardian,' there is inserted 'special guardian,',
  (b) in sub-paragraph (6), for the words from the beginning to 'British subject)'
       there is substituted 'Section 85 of the Adoption and Children Act 2002
       (which imposes restrictions on taking children out of the United
       Kingdom)',
  (c) after sub-paragraph (8) there is inserted—
    '(9) This paragraph does not apply to a local authority placing a child for
adoption with prospective adopters.'

73 In Schedule 8 (privately fostered children), in paragraph 5, for sub-paragraphs
(a) and (b) there is substituted
    'he is placed in the care of a person who proposes to adopt him under
arrangements made by an adoption agency within the meaning of—
    (a)   section 2 of the Adoption and Children Act 2002;
    (b)   section 1 of the Adoption (Scotland) Act 1978; or
    (c)   Article 3 of the Adoption (Northern Ireland) Order 1987'.

74 Part 1 of Schedule 10 is omitted.

75 In Schedule 11 (jurisdiction), in paragraphs 1 and 2, for the words 'the
Adoption Act 1976', wherever they occur, there is substituted 'the Adoption and
Children Act 2002'.

The Human Fertilisation and Embryology Act 1990 (c 37)

76 The Human Fertilisation and Embryology Act 1990 is amended as follows.

77 In section 27 (meaning of mother), in subsection (2), for 'child of any person
other than the adopter or adopters' there is substituted 'woman's child'.

78 In section 28 (meaning of father), in subsection (5)(c), for 'child of any
person other than the adopter or adopters' there is substituted 'man's child'.

79 In section 30 (parental orders in favour of gamete donors), in subsection (10) for 'Adoption Act 1976' there is substituted 'Adoption and Children Act 2002'.

The Courts and Legal Services Act 1990 (c 41)

80 In section 58A of the Courts and Legal Services Act 1990 (conditional fee agreements: supplementary), in subsection (2), for paragraph (b) there is substituted—
    '(b) the Adoption and Children Act 2002;'.

The Child Support Act 1991 (c 48)

81 In section 26 of the Child Support Act 1991 (disputes about parentage), in subsection (3), after '1976' there is inserted 'or Chapter 4 of Part 1 of the Adoption and Children Act 2002'.

The Children (Scotland) Act 1995 (c 36)

82 Section 86 of the Children (Scotland) Act 1995 (parental responsibilities order: general) is amended as follows.

83 In subsection (3), in paragraph (a), for 'section 18 (freeing for adoption) or 55 (adoption abroad) of the Adoption Act 1976' there is substituted 'section 19 (placing children with parental consent) or 84 (giving parental responsibility prior to adoption abroad) of the Adoption and Children Act 2002'.

84 In subsection (6), in paragraph (b), for the words from the beginning to 'Adoption Act 1976' there is substituted—
    '(b) he becomes the subject of an adoption order within the meaning of the Adoption (Scotland) Act 1978;
    (bb) an adoption agency, within the meaning of section 2 of the Adoption and Children Act 2002, is authorised to place him for adoption under section 19 of that Act (placing children with parental consent) or he becomes the subject of an order under section 21 of that Act (placement orders) or under section 84 of that Act (giving parental responsibility prior to adoption abroad)'.

The Family Law Act 1996 (c 27)

85 The Family Law Act 1996 is amended as follows.

86 In section 62 (meaning of 'relevant child' etc)—
    (a) in subsection (2), in paragraph (b), after 'the Adoption Act 1976' there is inserted ', the Adoption and Children Act 2002',
    (b) in subsection (5), for the words from 'has been freed' to '1976' there is substituted 'falls within subsection (7)'.

87 At the end of that section there is inserted—
    '(7) A child falls within this subsection if—
    (a) an adoption agency, within the meaning of section 2 of the Adoption and Children Act 2002, has power to place him for adoption under section 19 of that Act (placing children with parental consent) or he has become the subject of an order under section 21 of that Act (placement orders), or
    (b) he is freed for adoption by virtue of an order made—
        (i) in England and Wales, under section 18 of the Adoption Act 1976,
        (ii) in Scotland, under section 18 of the Adoption (Scotland) Act 1978, or

   (iii) in Northern Ireland, under Article 17(1) or 18(1) of the Adoption
     (Northern Ireland) Order 1987.'

88 In section 63 (interpretation of Part 4)—
 (a) in subsection (1), for the definition of 'adoption order', there is
   substituted—
  '"adoption order" means an adoption order within the meaning of section
    72(1) of the Adoption Act 1976 or section 46(1) of the Adoption and
    Children Act 2002;',
 (b) in subsection (2), after paragraph (h) there is inserted—
  '(i) the Adoption and Children Act 2002.'

The Housing Act 1996 (c 52)

89 Section 178 of the Housing Act 1996 (meaning of associated person) is
amended as follows.

90 In subsection (2), for the words from 'has been freed' to '1976' there is
substituted 'falls within subsection (2A)'.

91 After that subsection there is inserted—
 '(2A) A child falls within this subsection if—
 (a) an adoption agency, within the meaning of section 2 of the Adoption and
   Children Act 2002, is authorised to place him for adoption under section
   19 of that Act (placing children with parental consent) or he has become
   the subject of an order under section 21 of that Act (placement orders),
   or
 (b) he is freed for adoption by virtue of an order made—
  (i) in England and Wales, under section 18 of the Adoption Act 1976,
  (ii) in Scotland, under section 18 of the Adoption (Scotland) Act 1978,
   or
  (iii) in Northern Ireland, under Article 17(1) or 18(1) of the Adoption
    (Northern Ireland) Order 1987.'

92 In subsection (3), for the definition of 'adoption order', there is substituted—
  '"adoption order" means an adoption order within the meaning of section
    72(1) of the Adoption Act 1976 or section 46(1) of the Adoption and
    Children Act 2002;'.

The Police Act 1997 (c 50)

93 In section 115 of the Police Act 1997 (enhanced criminal records), in
subsection (5)(h), for 'section 11 of the Adoption Act 1976' there is substituted
'section 2 of the Adoption and Children Act 2002'.

The Protection of Children Act 1999 (c 14)

94 In section 2B of the Protection of Children Act 1999 (individuals named in the
findings of certain inquiries), in subsection (7), after paragraph (a) there is
inserted—
 '(vi) section 17 of the Adoption and Children Act 2002;'.

The Adoption (Intercountry Aspects) Act 1999 (c 18)

95 The following provisions of the Adoption (Intercountry Aspects) Act 1999
cease to have effect in relation to England and Wales: sections 3, 6, 8, 9 and 11 to
13.

96 Section 2 of that Act (accredited bodies) is amended as follows.

97 In subsection (2A)—
  (a) for the words from the beginning to '2000' there is substituted 'A registered adoption society',
  (b) for 'agency' there is substituted 'society'.

98 For subsection (5) there is substituted—
  '(5) In this section, 'registered adoption society' has the same meaning as in section 2 of the Adoption and Children Act 2002 (basic definitions); and expressions used in this section in its application to England and Wales which are also used in that Act have the same meanings as in that Act.'

99 In subsection (6)—
  (a) the words 'in its application to Scotland' are omitted,
  (b) after 'expressions' there is inserted 'used in this section in its application to Scotland'.

100 Section 14 (restriction on bringing children into the United Kingdom for adoption) is omitted.

101 In section 16(1) (devolution: Wales), the words ', or section 17 or 56A of the 1976 Act,' are omitted.

The Access to Justice Act 1999 (c 22)

102 In Schedule 2 to the Access to Justice Act 1999 (Community Legal Service: excluded services), in paragraph 2(3)(c)—
  (a) for 'section 27 or 28 of the Adoption Act 1976' there is substituted 'section 36 of the Adoption and Children Act 2002',
  (b) for 'an order under Part II or section 29 or 55' there is substituted 'a placement order or adoption order (within the meaning of the Adoption and Children Act 2002) or an order under section 41 or 84'.

The Care Standards Act 2000 (c 14)

103 The Care Standards Act 2000 is amended as follows.

104 In section 4 (basic definitions), in subsection (7), for 'the Adoption Act 1976' there is substituted 'the Adoption and Children Act 2002'.

105 At the end of section 5 (registration authorities) there is inserted—
  '(2) This section is subject to section 36A.'

106 In section 11 (requirement to register), in subsection (3), for 'reference in subsection (1) to an agency does' there is substituted 'references in subsections (1) and (2) to an agency do'.

107 In section 14 (2) (offences conviction of which may result in cancellation of registration), for paragraph (d) there is substituted—
  '(d) an offence under regulations under section 1(3) of the Adoption (Intercountry Aspects) Act 1999,
  (e) an offence under the Adoption and Children Act 2002 or regulations made under it'.

108 In section 16(2) (power to make regulations providing that no application for registration may be made in respect of certain agencies which are unincorporated bodies), 'or a voluntary adoption agency' is omitted.

109 In section 22(10) (disapplication of power to make regulations in the case of voluntary adoption agencies), at the end there is inserted 'or adoption support agencies'.

110 In section 23 (standards), at the end of subsection (4)(d) there is inserted 'or proceedings against a voluntary adoption agency for an offence under section 9(4) of the Adoption Act 1976 or section 9 of the Adoption and Children Act 2002'.

111 In section 31 (inspections by authorised persons), in subsection (3)(b), for 'section 9(2) of the Adoption Act 1976' there is substituted 'section 9 of the Adoption and Children Act 2002'.

112 In section 43 (introductory), in subsection (3)(a)—
  (a) for 'the Adoption Act 1976' there is substituted 'the Adoption and Children Act 2002',
  (b) after 'children' there is inserted 'or the provision of adoption support services (as defined in section 2(6) of the Adoption and Children Act 2002)'.

113 In section 46 (inspections: supplementary), in subsection (7)(c), for 'section 9(3) of the Adoption Act 1976' there is substituted 'section 9 of the Adoption and Children Act 2002'.

114 In section 48 (regulation of fostering functions), at the end of subsection (1) there is inserted—
  '(f) as to the fees or expenses which may be paid to persons assisting local authorities in making decisions in the exercise of such functions'.

115 In section 55(2)(b) (definition of 'social care worker'), for 'or a voluntary adoption agency' there is substituted ', a voluntary adoption agency or an adoption support agency'.

116 In section 121 (general interpretation)—
  (a) in subsection (1), in the definition of 'voluntary organisation', for 'the Adoption Act 1976' there is substituted 'the Adoption and Children Act 2002',
  (b) in subsection (13), in the appropriate place in the table there is inserted—

'Adoption support agency   Section 4'.

117 In Schedule 4 (minor and consequential amendments), paragraph 27(b) is omitted.

The Criminal Justice and Court Services Act 2000 (c 43)

118 In section 12(5) of the Criminal Justice and Court Services Act 2000 (meaning of 'family proceedings' in relation to CAFCASS), paragraph (b) (supervision orders under the 1989 Act) and the preceding 'and' are omitted.

Note Para 44 repealed by the Courts Act 2003, s 10(3), Sch 10 as from a date to be appointed.

SCHEDULE 4   Section 139

TRANSITIONAL AND TRANSITORY PROVISIONS AND SAVINGS

General rules for continuity

1—(1) Any reference (express or implied) in Part 1 or any other enactment, instrument or document to—
   (a)   any provision of Part 1, or
   (b)   things done or falling to be done under or for the purposes of any provision of Part 1,
must, so far as the nature of the reference permits, be construed as including, in relation to the times, circumstances or purposes in relation to which the corresponding provision repealed by this Act had effect, a reference to that corresponding provision or (as the case may be) to things done or falling to be done under or for the purposes of that corresponding provision.
   (2) Any reference (express or implied) in any enactment, instrument or document to—
   (a)   a provision repealed by this Act, or
   (b)   things done or falling to be done under or for the purposes of such a provision,
must, so far as the nature of the reference permits, be construed as including, in relation to the times, circumstances or purposes in relation to which the corresponding provision of Part 1 has effect, a reference to that corresponding provision or (as the case may be) to things done or falling to be done under or for the purposes of that corresponding provision.

General rule for old savings

2—(1) The repeal by this Act of an enactment previously repealed subject to savings does not affect the continued operation of those savings.
   (2) The repeal by this Act of a saving made on the previous repeal of an enactment does not affect the operation of the saving in so far as it is not specifically reproduced in this Act but remains capable of having effect.

Adoption support services

3—*(1) The facilities to be provided by local authorities as part of the service maintained under section 1(1) of the Adoption Act 1976 (c 36) include such arrangements as the authorities may be required by regulations to make for the provision of adoption support services to prescribed persons.*
   (2) Regulations under sub-paragraph (1) may require a local authority—
   (a)   at the request of a prescribed person, to carry out an assessment of his needs for adoption support services,
   (b)   if, as a result of the assessment, the authority decide that he has such needs, to decide whether to provide any such services to him,
   (c)   if the authority decide to provide any such services to a person, and the circumstances fall within a description prescribed by the regulations, to prepare a plan in accordance with which the services are to be provided to him and keep the plan under review.
   (3) Subsections (6) and (7) (except paragraph (a)) of section 4 of this Act apply to regulations under sub-paragraph (1) as they apply to regulations made by virtue of that section.
   (4) Section 57(1) of the Adoption Act 1976 (prohibited payments) does not apply to any payment made in accordance with regulations under sub-paragraph (1).

Regulation of adoption agencies

4—*(1) In section 9 of the Adoption Act 1976—*

(a) for 'Secretary of State' in subsections (2) and (3) there is substituted 'appropriate Minister', and

(b) at the end of that section there is inserted—

'(5) In this section and section 9A, "the appropriate Minister'" means—

(a) in relation to England, the Secretary of State,

(b) in relation to Wales, the National Assembly for Wales,

and in relation to England and Wales, means the Secretary of State and the Assembly acting jointly.'

(2) Until the commencement of the repeal by this Act of section 9(2) of the Adoption Act 1976, section 36A of the Care Standards Act 2000 (c 14) (inserted by section 16 of this Act) is to have effect as if, after '2002', there were inserted 'or under section 9(2) of the Adoption Act 1976'.

Independent review mechanism

5 After section 9 of the Adoption Act 1976 (c 36) there is inserted—

'9A Independent review of determinations—(1) Regulations under section 9 may establish a procedure under which any person in respect of whom a qualifying determination has been made by an adoption agency may apply to a panel constituted by the appropriate Minister for a review of that determination.

(2) The regulations must make provision as to the description of determinations which are qualifying determinations for the purposes of subsection (1).

(3) The regulations may include provision as to—

(a) the duties and powers of a panel (including the power to recover the costs of a review from the adoption agency by which the determination reviewed was made),

(b) the administration and procedures of a panel,

(c) the appointment of members of a panel (including the number, or any limit on the number, of members who may be appointed and any conditions for appointment),

(d) the payment of expenses of members of a panel,

(e) the duties of adoption agencies in connection with reviews conducted under the regulations,

(f) the monitoring of any such reviews.

(4) The appropriate Minister may make an arrangement with an organisation under which functions in relation to the panel are performed by the organisation on his behalf.

(5) If the appropriate Minister makes such an arrangement with an organisation, the organisation is to perform its functions under the arrangement in accordance with any general or special directions given by the appropriate Minister.

(6) The arrangement may include provision for payments to be made to the organisation by the appropriate Minister.

(7) Where the appropriate Minister is the National Assembly for Wales, subsections (4) and (6) also apply as if references to an organisation included references to the Secretary of State.

(8) In this section, 'organisation' includes a public body and a private or voluntary organisation.'

Pending applications for freeing orders

6 Nothing in this Act affects any application for an order under section 18 of the Adoption Act 1976 (freeing for adoption) where—

(a) the application has been made and has not been disposed of immediately before the repeal of that section, and

(b) the child in relation to whom the application is made has his home immediately before that repeal with a person with whom he has been placed for adoption by an adoption agency.

Freeing orders

7—(1) Nothing in this Act affects any order made under section 18 of the Adoption Act 1976 (c 36) and—
    (a) sections 19 to 21 of that Act are to continue to have effect in relation to such an order, and
    (b) Part 1 of Schedule 6 to the Magistrates' Courts Act 1980 (c 43) is to continue to have effect for the purposes of an application under section 21 of the Adoption Act 1976 in relation to such an order.

(2) Section 20 of that Act, as it has effect by virtue of this paragraph, is to apply as if, in subsection (3)(c) after '1989' there were inserted—
    '(iia) any care order, within the meaning of that Act'.

(3) Where a child is free for adoption by virtue of an order made under section 18 of that Act, the third condition in section 47(6) is to be treated as satisfied.

Pending applications for adoption orders

8 Nothing in this Act affects any application for an adoption order under section 12 of the Adoption Act 1976 where—
    (a) the application has been made and has not been disposed of immediately before the repeal of that section, and
    (b) the child in relation to whom the application is made has his home immediately before that repeal with a person with whom he has been placed for adoption by an adoption agency.

Notification of adoption applications

9 Where a notice given in respect of a child by the prospective adopters under section 22(1) of the Adoption Act 1976 is treated by virtue of paragraph 1(1) as having been given for the purposes of section 44(2) in respect of an application to adopt the child, section 42(3) has effect in relation to their application for an adoption order as if for 'six months' there were substituted 'twelve months'.

Adoptions with a foreign element

10 *In section 13 of the Adoption Act 1976 (child to live with adopters before order is made)—*
    (a) in subsection (1)(a), at the beginning there is inserted '(subject to subsection (1A))',
    (b) after subsection (1) there is inserted—
    '(1A) Where an adoption is proposed to be effected by a Convention adoption order, the order shall not be made unless at all times during the preceding six months the child had his home with the applicants or one of them.',
    (c) in subsection (2), after 'subsection (1)' there is inserted 'or (1A)',
    (d) subsection (4) is omitted.

11 *In section 56 of the Adoption Act 1976 (restriction on removal of children for adoption outside Great Britain)—*
    (a) in subsection (1), 'not being a parent or guardian or relative of the child' is omitted,
    (b) at the end of that section there is inserted—
    '(4) Regulations may provide for subsection (1) to apply with modifications, or not to apply, if—
        (a) the prospective adopters are parents, relatives or guardians of the child in question (or one of them is), or
        (b) the prospective adopter is a step-parent of the child,
    and any prescribed conditions are met.
    (5) On the occasion of the first exercise of the power to make regulations under subsection (4)—

(a) the regulations shall not be made unless a draft of the regulations has been approved by a resolution of each House of Parliament, and

(b) accordingly section 67(2) does not apply to the statutory instrument containing the regulations.

(6) In this section, 'prescribed' means prescribed by regulations and 'regulations' means regulations made by the Secretary of State, after consultation with the National Assembly for Wales.'

12 *For section 56A of the Adoption Act 1976 (c 36) there is substituted—*

'56A Restriction on bringing children into the United Kingdom—(1) This section applies where a person who is habitually resident in the British Islands (the 'British resident')—

(a) brings, or causes another to bring, a child who is habitually resident outside the British Islands into the United Kingdom for the purpose of adoption by the British resident, or

(b) at any time brings, or causes another to bring, into the United Kingdom a child adopted by the British resident under an external adoption effected within the period of six months ending with that time.

The references to adoption, or to a child adopted, by the British resident include a reference to adoption, or to a child adopted, by the British resident and another person.

(2) But this section does not apply if the child is intended to be adopted under a Convention adoption order.

(3) An external adoption means an adoption, other than a Convention adoption, of a child effected under the law of any country or territory outside the British Islands, whether or not the adoption is—

(a) an adoption within the meaning of Part IV of this Act, or

(b) a full adoption (within the meaning of section 39(3A)).

(4) Regulations may require a person intending to bring, or to cause another to bring, a child into the United Kingdom in circumstances where this section applies—

(a) to apply to an adoption agency (including an adoption agency within the meaning of section 1 of the Adoption (Scotland) Act 1978 or Article 3 of the Adoption (Northern Ireland) Order 1987) in the prescribed manner for an assessment of his suitability to adopt the child, and

(b) to give the agency any information it may require for the purpose of the assessment.

(5) Regulations may require prescribed conditions to be met in respect of a child brought into the United Kingdom in circumstances where this section applies.

(6) In relation to a child brought into the United Kingdom for adoption in circumstances where this section applies, regulations may provide for any provision of Part II to apply with modifications or not to apply.

(7) If a person brings, or causes another to bring, a child into the United Kingdom at any time in circumstances where this section applies, he is guilty of an offence if—

(a) he has not complied with any requirement imposed by virtue of subsection (4), or

(b) any condition required to be met by virtue of subsection (5) is not met,

before that time, or before any later time which may be prescribed.

(8) A person guilty of an offence under this section is liable—

(a) on summary conviction to imprisonment for a term not exceeding six months, or a fine not exceeding the statutory maximum, or both,

(b) on conviction on indictment, to imprisonment for a term not exceeding twelve months, or a fine, or both.

(9) Regulations may provide for the preceding provisions of this section not to apply if—

(a) the adopters or (as the case may be) prospective adopters are natural parents, natural relatives or guardians of the child in question (or one of them is), or

(b) the British resident in question is a step-parent of the child,

and any prescribed conditions are met.

(10) On the occasion of the first exercise of the power to make regulations under subsection *(9)*—

    (a) the regulations shall not be made unless a draft of the regulations has been approved by a resolution of each House of Parliament, and

    (b) accordingly section 67(2) does not apply to the statutory instrument containing the regulations.

(11) In this section, 'prescribed' means prescribed by regulations and 'regulations' means regulations made by the Secretary of State, after consultation with the National Assembly for Wales.'

13 In section 72 of the Adoption Act 1976 (c 36) (interpretation), subsection (3B) is omitted.

Advertising

14 In section 58 of the Adoption Act 1976 (c 36) (restrictions on advertisements)—

    (a) after subsection (1) there is inserted—

'(1A) Publishing an advertisement includes doing so by electronic means (for example, by means of the internet).',

    (b) in subsection (2), for the words following 'conviction' there is substituted 'to imprisonment for a term not exceeding three months, or a fine not exceeding level 5 on the standard scale, or both'.

15 In section 52 of the Adoption (Scotland) Act 1978 (c 28) (restriction on advertisements)—

    (a) after subsection (1) there is inserted—

'(1A) Publishing an advertisement includes doing so by electronic means (for example, by means of the internet).',

    (b) in subsection (2), for the words following 'conviction' there is substituted 'to imprisonment for a term not exceeding three months, or a fine not exceeding level 5 on the standard scale, or both'.

16—*(1)* The Secretary of State may make regulations providing for the references to an adoption agency in—

    (a) section 58(1)(c) of the Adoption Act 1976, and

    (b) section 52(1)(c) of the Adoption (Scotland) Act 1978,

to include a prescribed person outside the United Kingdom exercising functions corresponding to those of an adoption agency, if the functions are being exercised in prescribed circumstances.

'Prescribed' means prescribed by the regulations.

(2) Before exercising the power conferred by sub-paragraph (1) in relation to the Adoption (Scotland) Act 1978, the Secretary of State must consult the Scottish Ministers.

Status

17—(1) Section 67—

    (a) does not apply to a pre-1976 instrument or enactment in so far as it contains a disposition of property, and

    (b) does not apply to any public general Act in its application to any disposition of property in a pre-1976 instrument or enactment.

(2) Section 73 applies in relation to this paragraph as if this paragraph were contained in Chapter 4 of Part 1; and an instrument or enactment is a pre-1976 instrument or enactment for the purposes of this Schedule if it was passed or made at any time before 1st January 1976.

18 Section 69 does not apply to a pre-1976 instrument.

19 In section 70(1), the reference to Part 3 of the Family Law Reform Act 1987 (c 42) includes Part 2 of the Family Law Reform Act 1969 (c 46).

Registration of adoptions

20—(1) The power of the court under paragraph 4(1) of Schedule 1 to amend an order on the application of the adopter or adopted person includes, in relation to an order made before 1st April 1959, power to make any amendment of the particulars contained in the order which appears to be required to bring the order into the form in which it would have been made if paragraph 1 of that Schedule had applied to the order.

(2) In relation to an adoption order made before the commencement of the Adoption Act 1976 (c 36), the reference in paragraph 4(3) of that Schedule to paragraph 1(2) or (3) is to be read—

  (a) in the case of an order under the Adoption of Children Act 1926 (c 29), as a reference to section 12(3) and (4) of the Adoption of Children Act 1949 (c 98),

  (b) in the case of an order under the Adoption Act 1950 (c 26), as a reference to section 18(3) and (4) of that Act,

  (c) in the case of an order under the Adoption Act 1958 (c 5), as a reference to section 21(4) and (5) of that Act.

The Child Abduction Act 1984 (c 37)

21 Paragraph 43 of Schedule 3 does not affect the Schedule to the Child Abduction Act 1984 in its application to a child who is the subject of—

  (a) an order under section 18 of the Adoption Act 1976 freeing the child for adoption,

  (b) a pending application for such an order, or

  (c) a pending application for an order under section 12 of that Act.

The Courts and Legal Services Act 1990 (c 41)

22 Paragraph 80 of Schedule 3 does not affect section 58A(2)(b) of the Courts and Legal Services Act 1990 in its application to proceedings under the Adoption Act 1976 (c 36).

The Children (Scotland) Act 1995 (c 36)

23 Paragraph 84 of Schedule 3 does not affect section 86(6) of the Children (Scotland) Act 1995 in its application to a child who becomes the subject of an order under section 18 or 55 of the Adoption Act 1976 by virtue of an application made before the repeal of that section.

Note Paras 3-5, 10-16 repealed by s 139(3), Sch 5 hereto as from a date to be appointed.

SCHEDULE 5   Section 139

REPEALS

Short title and chapter	Extent of repeal
Births and Deaths Registration Act 1953 (c 20)	In section 10(3), the words following 'the Family Law Reform Act 1987'.
Sexual Offences Act 1956 (c 69)	In section 28(4), the 'or' at the end of paragraph (a).
Local Authority Social Services Act 1970 (c 42)	In Schedule 1, the entry relating to the Adoption Act 1976.
Adoption Act 1976 (c 36)	The whole Act, except Part 4 and paragraph 6 of Schedule 2.
Criminal Law Act 1977 (c 45)	In Schedule 12, the entries relating to the Adoption Act 1976.
National Health Service Act 1977 (c 49)	In section 124A(3), the 'or' at the end of paragraph (a).
Domestic Proceedings and Magistrates' Courts Act 1978 (c 22)	Sections 73(2), 74(2) and 74(4).
Adoption (Scotland) Act 1978 (c 28)	In section 50, the words 'not being a parent or guardian or relative of the child'.
	Section 52.
	In section 53(2), the words 'England and Wales or'.
	In section 65(1), in the definition of 'order freeing a child for adoption', paragraph (a) and the word 'and' immediately following that paragraph.
Magistrates' Courts Act 1980 (c 43)	In section 71(1) the words '(other than proceedings under the Adoption Act 1976)'.
	In section 71(2) the words following '(a) and (b)'.
	In Schedule 7, paragraphs 141 and 142.
British Nationality Act 1981 (c 61)	In section 1(8), the words following 'section 50'.
Mental Health Act 1983 (c 20)	In Schedule 4, paragraph 45.
Health and Social Services and Social Security Adjudications Act 1983 (c 41)	In Schedule 2, paragraphs 29 to 33, 35 and 36.
	In Schedule 9, paragraph 19.
County Courts Act 1984 (c 28)	In Schedule 2, paragraph 58.
Child Abduction Act 1984 (c 37)	In section 1(5A)(a), the 'or' at the end of sub-paragraph (i).
Matrimonial and Family Proceedings Act 1984 (c 42)	In section 40(2)(a), after 'the Adoption Act 1968', the word 'or'.
	In Schedule 1, paragraph 20.
Child Abduction and Custody Act 1985 (c 60)	In Schedule 3, in paragraph 1, the 'and' at the end of paragraph (b).
	In Schedule 3, in paragraph 1(c), paragraph (v).
Family Law Reform Act 1987 (c 42)	In Schedule 3, paragraphs 2 to 5.
Children Act 1989 (c 41)	Section 9(4).
	Section 12(3)(a).

Short title and chapter	Extent of repeal
	In section 20(9), the 'or' at the end of paragraph (a).
	In section 26(2)(e) and (f), the words 'to consider'.
	Section 33(6)(b)(i).
	Section 80(1)(e) and (f).
	Section 81(1)(b).
	Section 88(1).
	Section 102(6)(c).
	In section 105(1), the definition of 'protected child'.
	In Schedule 10, Part 1.
National Health Service and Community Care Act 1990 (c 19)	In Schedule 9, paragraph 17.
Human Fertilisation and Embryology Act 1990 (c 37)	In Schedule 4, paragraph 4.
Courts and Legal Services Act 1990 (c 41)	In Schedule 16, paragraph 7.
Local Government (Wales) Act 1994 (c 19)	In Schedule 10, paragraph 9.
Health Authorities Act 1995 (c 17)	In Schedule 1, paragraph 101.
Adoption (Intercountry Aspects) Act 1999 (c 18)	In section 2(6), the words 'in its application to Scotland'.
	Section 7(3).
	Section 14.
	In section 16(1), the words ', or section 17 or 56A of the 1976 Act,'.
	In Schedule 2, paragraph 3.
Access to Justice Act 1999 (c 22)	In Schedule 13, paragraph 88.
Care Standards Act 2000 (c 14)	In section 16(2), the words 'or a voluntary adoption agency'.
	In Schedule 4, paragraphs 5 and 27(b).
Local Government Act 2000 (c 22)	In Schedule 5, paragraph 16.
Criminal Justice and Court Services Act 2000 (c 43)	Section 12(5)(b) and the preceding 'and'.
	In Schedule 7, paragraphs 51 to 53.
This Act	In Schedule 4, paragraphs 3 to 5 and 10 to 16.

SCHEDULE 6   Section 147

GLOSSARY

In this Act, the expressions listed in the left-hand column below have the meaning given by, or are to be interpreted in accordance with, the provisions of this Act or (where stated) of the 1989 Act listed in the right-hand column.

Expression	Provision
the 1989 Act	section 2(5)
Adopted Children Register	section 77
Adoption and Children Act Register	section 125
adoption (in relation to Chapter 4 of Part 1)	section 66
adoption agency	section 2(1)
adoption agency placing a child for adoption	section 18(5)
Adoption Contact Register	section 80
adoption order	section 46(1)
Adoption Service	section 2(1)
adoption society	section 2(5)
adoption support agency	section 8
adoption support services	section 2(6)
appointed day (in relation to Chapter 4 of Part 1)	section 66(2)
appropriate Minister	section 144
Assembly	section 144
body	section 144
by virtue of	section 144
care order	section 105(1) of the 1989 Act
child	sections 49(5) and 144
child	assessment order section 43(2) of the 1989 Act
child in the care of a local authority	section 105(1) of the 1989 Act
child looked after by a local authority	section 22 of the 1989 Act
child placed for adoption by an adoption agency	section 18(5)
child to be adopted, adopted child	section 49(5)
consent (in relation to making adoption orders or placing for adoption)	section 52
the Convention	section 144
Convention adoption	section 66(1)(c)
Convention adoption order	section 144
Convention country	section 144
couple	section 144(4)
court	section 144
disposition (in relation to Chapter 4 of Part 1)	section 73
enactment	section 144
fee	section 144
guardian	section 144
information	section 144
interim care order	section 38 of the 1989 Act
local authority	section 144
local authority foster parent	section 23(3) of the 1989 Act
Northern Irish adoption agency	section 144
Northern Irish adoption order	section 144
notice	section 144
notice of intention to adopt	section 44(2)
overseas adoption	section 87
parental responsibility	section 3 of the 1989 Act
partner, in relation to a parent of a child	section 144(7)

Expression	Provision
placement order	section 21
placing, or placed, for adoption	sections 18(5) and 19(4)
prohibited steps order	section 8(1) of the 1989 Act
records (in relation to Chapter 5 of Part 1)	section 82
registered adoption society	section 2(2)
registers of live-births (in relation to Chapter 5 of Part 1)	section 82
registration authority (in Part 1)	section 144
regulations	section 144
relative	section 144, read with section 1(8)
residence order	section 8(1) of the 1989 Act
rules	section 144
Scottish adoption agency	section 144(3)
Scottish adoption order	section 144
specific issue order	section 8(1) of the 1989 Act
subordinate legislation	section 144
supervision order	section 31(11) of the 1989 Act
unitary authority	section 144
voluntary organisation	section 2(5)

COURTS ACT 2003

(2003 c 39)

An Act to make provision about the courts and their procedure and practice; about judges and magistrates; about fines and the enforcement processes of the courts; about periodical payments of damages; and for connected purposes.

[20th November 2003]

Be it enacted by the Queen's most Excellent Majesty, by and with the advice and consent of the Lords Spiritual and Temporal, and Commons, in this present Parliament assembled, and by the authority of the same, as follows:—

*   *   *   *   *

Family proceedings courts and youth courts

49 Family proceedings courts—(1) For section 67 of the 1980 Act (family proceedings courts and panels) substitute—

'**67 Family proceedings courts—**(1) Magistrates' courts—
- (a) constituted in accordance with this section or section 66 of the Courts Act 2003 (judges having powers of District Judges (Magistrates' Courts)), and
- (b) sitting for the purpose of hearing family proceedings,
are to be known as family proceedings courts.

(2) A justice of the peace is not qualified to sit as a member of a family proceedings court to hear family proceedings of any description unless he has an authorisation extending to the proceedings.

(3) He has an authorisation extending to the proceedings only if he has been authorised by the Lord Chancellor or a person acting on his behalf to sit as a member of a family proceedings court to hear—
- (a) proceedings of that description, or
- (b) all family proceedings.

(4) The Lord Chancellor may by rules make provision about—
(a) the grant and revocation of authorisations,
(b) the appointment of chairmen of family proceedings courts, and
(c) the composition of family proceedings courts.
(5) Rules under subsection (4) may confer powers on the Lord Chancellor with respect to any of the matters specified in the rules.
(6) Rules under subsection (4) may be made only after consultation with the Family Procedure Rule Committee.
(7) Rules under subsection (4) are to be made by statutory instrument.
(8) A statutory instrument containing rules under subsection (4) is subject to annulment in pursuance of a resolution of either House of Parliament.'
(2) Omit section 68 of the 1980 Act (combined family panels for two or more petty sessions areas).

50 Youth courts—(1) For section 45 of the 1933 Act (constitution of youth courts) substitute—

'**45 Youth courts**—(1) Magistrates' courts—
(a) constituted in accordance with this section or section 66 of the Courts Act 2003 (judges having powers of District Judges (Magistrates' Courts)), and
(b) sitting for the purpose of—
    (i) hearing any charge against a child or young person, or
    (ii) exercising any other jurisdiction conferred on youth courts by or under this or any other Act,
are to be known as youth courts.
(2) A justice of the peace is not qualified to sit as a member of a youth court for the purpose of dealing with any proceedings unless he has an authorisation extending to the proceedings.
(3) He has an authorisation extending to the proceedings only if he has been authorised by the Lord Chancellor or a person acting on his behalf to sit as a member of a youth court to deal with—
(a) proceedings of that description, or
(b) all proceedings dealt with by youth courts.
(4) The Lord Chancellor may by rules make provision about—
(a) the grant and revocation of authorisations,
(b) the appointment of chairmen of youth courts, and
(c) the composition of youth courts.
(5) Rules under subsection (4) may confer powers on the Lord Chancellor with respect to any of the matters specified in the rules.
(6) Rules under subsection (4) may be made only after consultation with the Criminal Procedure Rule Committee.
(7) Rules under subsection (4) are to be made by statutory instrument.
(8) A statutory instrument containing rules under subsection (4) is subject to annulment in pursuance of a resolution of either House of Parliament.'
(2) Omit Schedule 2 to the 1933 Act (constitution of youth courts).
(3) Omit section 146 of the 1980 Act (rules relating to youth court panels and the composition of youth courts).
(4) 'The 1933 Act' means the Children and Young Persons Act 1933 (c 12).

*   *   *   *   *

Family Procedure Rules and practice directions

75 Family Procedure Rules—(1) There are to be rules of court (to be called 'Family Procedure Rules') governing the practice and procedure to be followed in family proceedings in—

(a)   the High Court,

(b)   county courts, and

(c)   magistrates' courts.

(2) Family Procedure Rules are to be made by a committee known as the Family Procedure Rule Committee.

(3) 'Family proceedings', in relation to a court, means proceedings in that court which are family proceedings as defined by either—

(a)   section 65 of the 1980 Act, or

(b)   section 32 of the Matrimonial and Family Proceedings Act 1984 (c 42).

(4) The power to make Family Procedure Rules includes power to make different provision for different areas, including different provision—

(a)   for a specified court or description of courts, or

(b)   for specified descriptions of proceedings or a specified jurisdiction.

(5) Any power to make or alter Family Procedure Rules is to be exercised with a view to securing that—

(a)   the family justice system is accessible, fair and efficient, and

(b)   the rules are both simple and simply expressed.

76 Further provision about scope of Family Procedure Rules—(1) Family Procedure Rules may not be made in respect of matters which may be dealt with in probate rules made by the President of the Family Division, with the concurrence of the Lord Chancellor, under section 127 of the 1981 Act.

(2) Family Procedure Rules may—

(a)   modify or exclude the application of any provision of the County Courts Act 1984 (c 28), and

(b)   provide for the enforcement in the High Court of orders made in a divorce county court.

(3) Family Procedure Rules may modify the rules of evidence as they apply to family proceedings in any court within the scope of the rules.

(4) Family Procedure Rules may apply any rules of court (including in particular Civil Procedure Rules) which relate to—

(a)   courts which are outside the scope of Family Procedure Rules, or

(b)   proceedings other than family proceedings.

(5) Any rules of court, not made by the Family Procedure Rule Committee, which apply to proceedings of a particular kind in a court within the scope of Family Procedure Rules may be applied by Family Procedure Rules to family proceedings in such a court.

(6) In subsections (4) and (5) 'rules of court' includes any provision governing the practice and procedure of a court which is made by or under an enactment.

(7) Where Family Procedure Rules may be made by applying other rules, the other rules may be applied—

(a)   to any extent,

(b)   with or without modification, and

(c)   as amended from time to time.

(8) Family Procedure Rules may, instead of providing for any matter, refer to provision made or to be made about that matter by directions.

77 Family Procedure Rule Committee—(1) The Family Procedure Rule Committee is to consist of—

(a)   the President of the Family Division, and

(b)   the persons currently appointed by the Lord Chancellor under subsection (2).

(2) The Lord Chancellor must appoint—

(a)   two judges of the Supreme Court, at least one of whom must be a puisne judge attached to the Family Division,

(b)   one Circuit judge,

   (c) one district judge of the principal registry of the Family Division,

   (d) one district judge appointed under section 6 of the County Courts Act 1984 (c 28),

   (e) one District Judge (Magistrates' Courts),

   (f) one lay justice,

   (g) one justices' clerk,

   (h) one person who has—

        (i) a Supreme Court qualification, and

       (ii) particular experience of family practice in the High Court,

   (i) one person who has—

        (i) a Supreme Court qualification, and

       (ii) particular experience of family practice in county courts,

   (j) one person who has—

        (i) a Supreme Court qualification, and

       (ii) particular experience of family practice in magistrates' courts,

   (k) one person who—

        (i) has been granted by an authorised body, under Part 2 of the 1990 Act, the right to conduct litigation in relation to all proceedings in the Supreme Court, and

       (ii) has particular experience of family practice in the High Court,

   (l) one person who—

        (i) has been so granted that right, and

       (ii) has particular experience of family practice in county courts,

   (m) one person who—

        (i) has been so granted that right, and

       (ii) has particular experience of family practice in magistrates' courts,

   (n) one person nominated by CAFCASS, and

   (o) one person with experience in and knowledge of the lay advice sector or the system of justice in relation to family proceedings.

   (3) Before appointing a person under subsection (2), the Lord Chancellor must consult the President of the Family Division.

   (4) Before appointing a person under subsection (2)(a), the Lord Chancellor must consult the Lord Chief Justice.

   (5) Before appointing a person under subsection (2)(h) to (m), the Lord Chancellor must consult any body which—

   (a) has members eligible for appointment under the provision in question, and

   (b) is an authorised body for the purposes of section 27 or 28 of the 1990 Act.

   (6) The Lord Chancellor may reimburse the members of the Family Procedure Rule Committee their travelling and out-of-pocket expenses.

78 Power to change certain requirements relating to Committee—(1) The Lord Chancellor may by order—

   (a) amend section 77(2) (persons to be appointed to Committee by Lord Chancellor), and

   (b) make consequential amendments in any other provision of section 77.

   (2) Before making an order under this section the Lord Chancellor must consult the President of the Family Division.

79 Process for making Family Procedure Rules—(1) The Family Procedure Rule Committee must, before making Family Procedure Rules—

   (a) consult such persons as they consider appropriate, and

   (b) meet (unless it is inexpedient to do so).

   (2) Rules made by the Family Procedure Rule Committee must be—

   (a) signed by a majority of the members of the Committee, and

   (b) submitted to the Lord Chancellor.

(3) The Lord Chancellor may allow, disallow or alter rules so made.

(4) Before altering rules so made the Lord Chancellor must consult the Committee.

(5) Rules so made, as allowed or altered by the Lord Chancellor—

(a) come into force on such day as the Lord Chancellor directs, and

(b) are to be contained in a statutory instrument to which the Statutory Instruments Act 1946 (c 36) applies as if the instrument contained rules made by a Minister of the Crown.

(6) Subject to subsection (7), a statutory instrument containing Family Procedure Rules is subject to annulment in pursuance of a resolution of either House of Parliament.

(7) A statutory instrument containing rules altered by the Lord Chancellor is of no effect unless approved by a resolution of each House of Parliament before the day referred to in subsection (5)(a).

80 Power to amend legislation in connection with the rules—The Lord Chancellor may by order amend, repeal or revoke any enactment to the extent that he considers necessary or desirable—

(a) in order to facilitate the making of Family Procedure Rules, or

(b) in consequence of section 75, 76 or 79 or Family Procedure Rules.

81 Practice directions relating to family proceedings—(1) The President of the Family Division may, with the concurrence of the Lord Chancellor, give directions as to the practice and procedure of—

(a) county courts, and

(b) magistrates' courts,

in family proceedings.

(2) Directions as to the practice and procedure of those courts in family proceedings may not be given by anyone other than the President of the Family Division without the approval of the President of the Family Division and the Lord Chancellor.

(3) The power to give directions under subsection (1) includes power—

(a) to vary or revoke directions as to the practice and procedure of magistrates' courts and county courts (or any of them) in family proceedings, whether given by the President of the Family Division or any other person,

(b) to give directions containing different provision for different cases (including different areas), and

(c) to give directions containing provision for a specific court, for specific proceedings or for a specific jurisdiction.

*　　*　　*　　*　　*

GENDER RECOGNITION ACT 2004

(2004 C 7)

An Act to make provision for and in connection with change of gender.

[1st July 2004]

Be it enacted by the Queen's most Excellent Majesty, by and with the advice and consent of the Lords Spiritual and Temporal, and Commons, in this present Parliament assembled, and by the authority of the same, as follows:—

Applications for gender recognition certificate

1 Applications—(1) A person of either gender who is aged at least 18 may make an application for a gender recognition certificate on the basis of—
 (a) living in the other gender, or
 (b) having changed gender under the law of a country or territory outside the United Kingdom.
 (2) In this Act 'the acquired gender', in relation to a person by whom an application under subsection (1) is or has been made, means—
 (a) in the case of an application under paragraph (a) of that subsection, the gender in which the person is living, or
 (b) in the case of an application under paragraph (b) of that subsection, the gender to which the person has changed under the law of the country or territory concerned.
 (3) An application under subsection (1) is to be determined by a Gender Recognition Panel.
 (4) Schedule 1 (Gender Recognition Panels) has effect.

2 Determination of applications—(1) In the case of an application under section 1(1)(a), the Panel must grant the application if satisfied that the applicant—
 (a) has or has had gender dysphoria,
 (b) has lived in the acquired gender throughout the period of two years ending with the date on which the application is made,
 (c) intends to continue to live in the acquired gender until death, and
 (d) complies with the requirements imposed by and under section 3.
 (2) In the case of an application under section 1(1)(b), the Panel must grant the application if satisfied—
 (a) that the country or territory under the law of which the applicant has changed gender is an approved country or territory, and
 (b) that the applicant complies with the requirements imposed by and under section 3.
 (3) The Panel must reject an application under section 1(1) if not required by subsection (1) or (2) to grant it.
 (4) In this Act 'approved country or territory' means a country or territory prescribed by order made by the Secretary of State after consulting the Scottish Ministers and the Department of Finance and Personnel in Northern Ireland.

3 Evidence—(1) An application under section 1(1)(a) must include either—
 (a) a report made by a registered medical practitioner practising in the field of gender dysphoria and a report made by another registered medical practitioner (who may, but need not, practise in that field), or
 (b) a report made by a chartered psychologist practising in that field and a report made by a registered medical practitioner (who may, but need not, practise in that field).
 (2) But subsection (1) is not complied with unless a report required by that subsection and made by—

(a) a registered medical practitioner, or

(b) a chartered psychologist,

practising in the field of gender dysphoria includes details of the diagnosis of the applicant's gender dysphoria.

(3) And subsection (1) is not complied with in a case where—

(a) the applicant has undergone or is undergoing treatment for the purpose of modifying sexual characteristics, or

(b) treatment for that purpose has been prescribed or planned for the applicant,

unless at least one of the reports required by that subsection includes details of it.

(4) An application under section 1(1)(a) must also include a statutory declaration by the applicant that the applicant meets the conditions in section 2(1)(b) and (c).

(5) An application under section 1(1)(b) must include evidence that the applicant has changed gender under the law of an approved country or territory.

(6) Any application under section 1(1) must include—

(a) a statutory declaration as to whether or not the applicant is married,

(b) any other information or evidence required by an order made by the Secretary of State, and

(c) any other information or evidence which the Panel which is to determine the application may require,

and may include any other information or evidence which the applicant wishes to include.

(7) The Secretary of State may not make an order under subsection (6)(b) without consulting the Scottish Ministers and the Department of Finance and Personnel in Northern Ireland.

(8) If the Panel which is to determine the application requires information or evidence under subsection (6)(c) it must give reasons for doing so.

4 Successful applications—(1) If a Gender Recognition Panel grants an application under section 1(1) it must issue a gender recognition certificate to the applicant.

(2) Unless the applicant is married, the certificate is to be a full gender recognition certificate.

(3) If the applicant is married, the certificate is to be an interim gender recognition certificate.

(4) Schedule 2 (annulment or dissolution of marriage after issue of interim gender recognition certificate) has effect.

(5) The Secretary of State may, after consulting the Scottish Ministers and the Department of Finance and Personnel in Northern Ireland, specify the content and form of gender recognition certificates.

5 Subsequent issue of full certificates—(1) A court which—

(a) makes absolute a decree of nullity granted on the ground that an interim gender recognition certificate has been issued to a party to the marriage, or

(b) (in Scotland) grants a decree of divorce on that ground,

must, on doing so, issue a full gender recognition certificate to that party and send a copy to the Secretary of State.

(2) If an interim gender recognition certificate has been issued to a person and either—

(a) the person's marriage is dissolved or annulled (otherwise than on the ground mentioned in subsection (1)) in proceedings instituted during the period of six months beginning with the day on which it was issued, or

(b) the person's spouse dies within that period,

the person may make an application for a full gender recognition certificate at any time within the period specified in subsection (3) (unless the person is again married).

(3) That period is the period of six months beginning with the day on which the marriage is dissolved or annulled or the death occurs.

(4) An application under subsection (2) must include evidence of the dissolution or annulment of the marriage and the date on which proceedings for it were instituted, or of the death of the spouse and the date on which it occurred.

(5) An application under subsection (2) is to be determined by a Gender Recognition Panel.

(6) The Panel—
(a) must grant the application if satisfied that the applicant is not married, and
(b) otherwise must reject it.

(7) If the Panel grants the application it must issue a full gender recognition certificate to the applicant.

6 Errors in certificates—(1) Where a gender recognition certificate has been issued to a person, the person or the Secretary of State may make an application for a corrected certificate on the ground that the certificate which has been issued contains an error.

(2) If the certificate was issued by a court the application is to be determined by the court but in any other case it is to be determined by a Gender Recognition Panel.

(3) The court or Panel—
(a) must grant the application if satisfied that the gender recognition certificate contains an error, and
(b) otherwise must reject it.

(4) If the court or Panel grants the application it must issue a corrected gender recognition certificate to the applicant.

7 Applications: supplementary—(1) An application to a Gender Recognition Panel under section 1(1), 5(2) or 6(1) must be made in a form and manner specified by the Secretary of State after consulting the Scottish Ministers and the Department of Finance and Personnel in Northern Ireland.

(2) The applicant must pay to the Secretary of State a non-refundable fee of an amount prescribed by order made by the Secretary of State unless the application is made in circumstances in which, in accordance with provision made by the order, no fee is payable; and fees of different amounts may be prescribed for different circumstances.

8 Appeals etc—(1) An applicant to a Gender Recognition Panel under section 1(1), 5(2) or 6(1) may appeal to the High Court or Court of Session on a point of law against a decision by the Panel to reject the application.

(2) An appeal under subsection (1) must be heard in private if the applicant so requests.

(3) On such an appeal the court must—
(a) allow the appeal and issue the certificate applied for,
(b) allow the appeal and refer the matter to the same or another Panel for re-consideration, or
(c) dismiss the appeal.

(4) If an application under section 1(1) is rejected, the applicant may not make another application before the end of the period of six months beginning with the date on which it is rejected.

(5) If an application under section 1(1), 5(2) or 6(1) is granted but the Secretary of State considers that its grant was secured by fraud, the Secretary of State may refer the case to the High Court or Court of Session.

(6) On a reference under subsection (5) the court—

(a) must either quash or confirm the decision to grant the application, and

(b) if it quashes it, must revoke the gender recognition certificate issued on the grant of the application and may make any order which it considers appropriate in consequence of, or otherwise in connection with, doing so.

Consequences of issue of gender recognition certificate etc

9 General—(1) Where a full gender recognition certificate is issued to a person, the person's gender becomes for all purposes the acquired gender (so that, if the acquired gender is the male gender, the person's sex becomes that of a man and, if it is the female gender, the person's sex becomes that of a woman).

(2) Subsection (1) does not affect things done, or events occurring, before the certificate is issued; but it does operate for the interpretation of enactments passed, and instruments and other documents made, before the certificate is issued (as well as those passed or made afterwards).

(3) Subsection (1) is subject to provision made by this Act or any other enactment or any subordinate legislation.

10 Registration—(1) Where there is a UK birth register entry in relation to a person to whom a full gender recognition certificate is issued, the Secretary of State must send a copy of the certificate to the appropriate Registrar General.

(2) In this Act 'UK birth register entry', in relation to a person to whom a full gender recognition certificate is issued, means—

(a) an entry of which a certified copy is kept by a Registrar General, or

(b) an entry in a register so kept,

containing a record of the person's birth or adoption (or, if there would otherwise be more than one, the most recent).

(3) 'The appropriate Registrar General' means whichever of—

(a) the Registrar General for England and Wales,

(b) the Registrar General for Scotland, or

(c) the Registrar General for Northern Ireland,

keeps a certified copy of the person's UK birth register entry or the register containing that entry.

(4) Schedule 3 (provisions about registration) has effect.

11 Marriage—Schedule 4 (amendments of marriage law) has effect.

12 Parenthood—The fact that a person's gender has become the acquired gender under this Act does not affect the status of the person as the father or mother of a child.

13 Social security benefits and pensions—Schedule 5 (entitlement to benefits and pensions) has effect.

14 Discrimination—Schedule 6 (amendments of Sex Discrimination Act 1975 (c 65) and Sex Discrimination (Northern Ireland) Order 1976 (SI 1976/1042 (NI 15))) has effect.

15 Succession etc—The fact that a person's gender has become the acquired gender under this Act does not affect the disposal or devolution of property under a will or other instrument made before the appointed day.

16 Peerages etc—The fact that a person's gender has become the acquired gender under this Act—

(a) does not affect the descent of any peerage or dignity or title of honour, and
(b) does not affect the devolution of any property limited (expressly or not) by a will or other instrument to devolve (as nearly as the law permits) along with any peerage or dignity or title of honour unless an intention that it should do so is expressed in the will or other instrument.

17 Trustees and personal representatives—(1) A trustee or personal representative is not under a duty, by virtue of the law relating to trusts or the administration of estates, to enquire, before conveying or distributing any property, whether a full gender recognition certificate has been issued to any person or revoked (if that fact could affect entitlement to the property).

(2) A trustee or personal representative is not liable to any person by reason of a conveyance or distribution of the property made without regard to whether a full gender recognition certificate has been issued to any person or revoked if the trustee or personal representative has not received notice of the fact before the conveyance or distribution.

(3) This section does not prejudice the right of a person to follow the property, or any property representing it, into the hands of another person who has received it unless that person has purchased it for value in good faith and without notice.

18 Orders where expectations defeated—(1) This section applies where the disposition or devolution of any property under a will or other instrument (made on or after the appointed day) is different from what it would be but for the fact that a person's gender has become the acquired gender under this Act.

(2) A person may apply to the High Court or Court of Session for an order on the ground of being adversely affected by the different disposition or devolution of the property.

(3) The court may, if it is satisfied that it is just to do so, make in relation to any person benefiting from the different disposition or devolution of the property such order as it considers appropriate.

(4) An order may, in particular, make provision for—
(a) the payment of a lump sum to the applicant,
(b) the transfer of property to the applicant,
(c) the settlement of property for the benefit of the applicant,
(d) the acquisition of property and either its transfer to the applicant or its settlement for the benefit of the applicant.

(5) An order may contain consequential or supplementary provisions for giving effect to the order or for ensuring that it operates fairly as between the applicant and the other person or persons affected by it; and an order may, in particular, confer powers on trustees.

19 Sport—(1) A body responsible for regulating the participation of persons as competitors in an event or events involving a gender-affected sport may, if subsection (2) is satisfied, prohibit or restrict the participation as competitors in the event or events of persons whose gender has become the acquired gender under this Act.

(2) This subsection is satisfied if the prohibition or restriction is necessary to secure—
(a) fair competition, or
(b) the safety of competitors,
at the event or events.

(3) 'Sport' means a sport, game or other activity of a competitive nature.

(4) A sport is a gender-affected sport if the physical strength, stamina or physique of average persons of one gender would put them at a disadvantage to average persons of the other gender as competitors in events involving the sport.

(5) This section does not affect—

(a) section 44 of the Sex Discrimination Act 1975 (c 65) (exception from Parts 2 to 4 of that Act for acts related to sport), or

(b) Article 45 of the Sex Discrimination (Northern Ireland) Order 1976 (SI 1976/1042 (NI 15)) (corresponding provision for Northern Ireland).

20 Gender-specific offences—(1) Where (apart from this subsection) a relevant gender-specific offence could be committed or attempted only if the gender of a person to whom a full gender recognition certificate has been issued were not the acquired gender, the fact that the person's gender has become the acquired gender does not prevent the offence being committed or attempted.

(2) An offence is a 'relevant gender-specific offence' if—

(a) either or both of the conditions in subsection (3) are satisfied, and

(b) the commission of the offence involves the accused engaging in sexual activity.

(3) The conditions are—

(a) that the offence may be committed only by a person of a particular gender, and

(b) that the offence may be committed only on, or in relation to, a person of a particular gender,

and the references to a particular gender include a gender identified by reference to the gender of the other person involved.

21 Foreign gender change and marriage—(1) A person's gender is not to be regarded as having changed by reason only that it has changed under the law of a country or territory outside the United Kingdom.

(2) Accordingly, a person is not to be regarded as being married by reason of having entered into a foreign post-recognition marriage.

(3) But if a full gender recognition certificate is issued to a person who has entered into a foreign post-recognition marriage, after the issue of the certificate the marriage is no longer to be regarded as being void on the ground that (at the time when it was entered into) the parties to it were not respectively male and female.

(4) However, subsection (3) does not apply to a foreign post-recognition marriage if a party to it has entered into a later (valid) marriage before the issue of the full gender recognition certificate.

(5) For the purposes of this section a person has entered into a foreign post-recognition marriage if (and only if)—

(a) the person has entered into a marriage in accordance with the law of a country or territory outside the United Kingdom,

(b) before the marriage was entered into the person had changed gender under the law of that or any other country or territory outside the United Kingdom,

(c) the other party to the marriage was not of the gender to which the person had changed under the law of that country or territory, and

(d) by virtue of subsection (1) the person's gender was not regarded as having changed under the law of any part of the United Kingdom.

(6) Nothing in this section prevents the exercise of any enforceable Community right.

Supplementary

22 Prohibition on disclosure of information—(1) It is an offence for a person who has acquired protected information in an official capacity to disclose the information to any other person.

(2) 'Protected information' means information which relates to a person who has made an application under section 1(1) and which—

    (a) concerns that application or any application by the person under section 5(2) or 6(1), or

    (b) if the application under section 1(1) is granted, otherwise concerns the person's gender before it becomes the acquired gender.

(3) A person acquires protected information in an official capacity if the person acquires it—

    (a) in connection with the person's functions as a member of the civil service, a constable or the holder of any other public office or in connection with the functions of a local or public authority or of a voluntary organisation,

    (b) as an employer, or prospective employer, of the person to whom the information relates or as a person employed by such an employer or prospective employer, or

    (c) in the course of, or otherwise in connection with, the conduct of business or the supply of professional services.

(4) But it is not an offence under this section to disclose protected information relating to a person if—

    (a) the information does not enable that person to be identified,

    (b) that person has agreed to the disclosure of the information,

    (c) the information is protected information by virtue of subsection (2)(b) and the person by whom the disclosure is made does not know or believe that a full gender recognition certificate has been issued,

    (d) the disclosure is in accordance with an order of a court or tribunal,

    (e) the disclosure is for the purpose of instituting, or otherwise for the purposes of, proceedings before a court or tribunal,

    (f) the disclosure is for the purpose of preventing or investigating crime,

    (g) the disclosure is made to the Registrar General for England and Wales, the Registrar General for Scotland or the Registrar General for Northern Ireland,

    (h) the disclosure is made for the purposes of the social security system or a pension scheme,

    (i) the disclosure is in accordance with provision made by an order under subsection (5), or

    (j) the disclosure is in accordance with any provision of, or made by virtue of, an enactment other than this section.

(5) The Secretary of State may by order make provision prescribing circumstances in which the disclosure of protected information is not to constitute an offence under this section.

(6) The power conferred by subsection (5) is exercisable by the Scottish Ministers (rather than the Secretary of State) where the provision to be made is within the legislative competence of the Scottish Parliament.

(7) An order under subsection (5) may make provision permitting—

    (a) disclosure to specified persons or persons of a specified description,

    (b) disclosure for specified purposes,

    (c) disclosure of specified descriptions of information, or

    (d) disclosure by specified persons or persons of a specified description.

(8) A person guilty of an offence under this section is liable on summary conviction to a fine not exceeding level 5 on the standard scale.

23 Power to modify statutory provisions—(1) The Secretary of State may by order make provision for modifying the operation of any enactment or subordinate legislation in relation to—

    (a) persons whose gender has become the acquired gender under this Act, or

    (b) any description of such persons.

(2) The power conferred by subsection (1) is exercisable by the Scottish Ministers (rather than the Secretary of State) where the provision to be made is within the legislative competence of the Scottish Parliament.

(3) The appropriate Northern Ireland department may by order make provision for modifying the operation of any enactment or subordinate legislation which deals with a transferred matter in relation to—

(a) persons whose gender has become the acquired gender under this Act, or

(b) any description of such persons.

(4) In subsection (3)—

'the appropriate Northern Ireland department', in relation to any enactment or subordinate legislation which deals with a transferred matter, means the Northern Ireland department which has responsibility for that matter,

'deals with' is to be construed in accordance with section 98(2) and (3) of the Northern Ireland Act 1998 (c 47), and

'transferred matter' has the meaning given by section 4(1) of that Act.

(5) Before an order is made under this section, appropriate consultation must be undertaken with persons likely to be affected by it.

24 Orders and regulations—(1) Any power of the Secretary of State, the Chancellor of the Exchequer, the Scottish Ministers or a Northern Ireland department to make an order under this Act includes power to make any appropriate incidental, supplementary, consequential or transitional provision or savings.

(2) Any power of the Secretary of State, the Chancellor of the Exchequer or the Scottish Ministers to make an order under this Act, and any power of the Registrar General for England and Wales or the Registrar General for Scotland to make regulations under this Act, is exercisable by statutory instrument.

(3) No order may be made under section 2 or paragraph 11 of Schedule 3 unless a draft of the statutory instrument containing the order has been laid before, and approved by a resolution of, each House of Parliament.

(4) A statutory instrument containing an order made by the Secretary of State under section 7, 22 or 23 is subject to annulment in pursuance of a resolution of either House of Parliament.

(5) A statutory instrument containing an order made by the Scottish Ministers under section 22 or 23 is subject to annulment in pursuance of a resolution of the Scottish Parliament.

(6) Any power of a Northern Ireland department to make an order or regulations under this Act is exercisable by statutory rule for the purposes of the Statutory Rules (Northern Ireland) Order 1979 (SI 1979/1573 (NI 12)).

(7) Orders and regulations made by a Northern Ireland department under this Act are subject to negative resolution (within the meaning of section 41(6) of the Interpretation Act (Northern Ireland) 1954 (c 33 (NI))).

25 Interpretation—In this Act—

'the acquired gender' is to be construed in accordance with section 1(2),

'approved country or territory' has the meaning given by section 2(4),

'the appointed day' means the day appointed by order under section 26,

'chartered psychologist' means a person for the time being listed in the British Psychological Society's Register of Chartered Psychologists,

'enactment' includes an enactment contained in an Act of the Scottish Parliament or in any Northern Ireland legislation,

'full gender recognition certificate' and 'interim gender recognition certificate' mean the certificates issued as such under section 4 or 5 and 'gender recognition certificate' means either of those sorts of certificate,

'gender dysphoria' means the disorder variously referred to as gender dysphoria, gender identity disorder and transsexualism,

'Gender Recognition Panel' (and 'Panel') is to be construed in accordance with
  Schedule 1,
'subordinate legislation' means an Order in Council, an order, rules,
  regulations, a scheme, a warrant, bye-laws or any other instrument made
  under an enactment, and
'UK birth register entry' has the meaning given by section 10(2).

26 Commencement—Apart from sections 23 to 25, this section and sections 28
and 29, this Act does not come into force until such day as the Secretary of State
may appoint by order made after consulting the Scottish Ministers and the
Department of Finance and Personnel in Northern Ireland.

27 Applications within two years of commencement—(1) This section applies
where applications are made under section 1(1)(a) during the period of two years
beginning with the appointed day ('the initial period').
  (2) Section 2(1)(a) has effect as if there were inserted at the end 'or has
undergone surgical treatment for the purpose of modifying sexual characteristics,'.
  (3) In the case of an application which—
  (a) is made during the first six months of the initial period, or
  (b) is made during the rest of the initial period and is based on the applicant
      having undergone surgical treatment for the purpose of modifying sexual
      characteristics,
section 2(1)(b) has effect as if for 'two' there were substituted 'six'.
  (4) Subsections (5) and (6) apply in the case of an application to which
subsection (3) applies and in the case of an application—
  (a) made during the rest of the initial period,
  (b) based on the applicant having or having had gender dysphoria, and
  (c) including a statutory declaration by the applicant that the applicant has
      lived in the acquired gender throughout the period of six years ending with
      the date on which the application is made.
  (5) Section 3 has effect as if for subsections (1) to (3) there were substituted—
'(1) An application under section 1(1)(a) must include either—
  (a) a report made by a registered medical practitioner, or
  (b) a report made by a chartered psychologist practising in the field of gender
      dysphoria.
  (2) Where the application is based on the applicant having or having had
gender dysphoria—
  (a) the reference in subsection (1) to a registered medical practitioner is to one
      practising in the field of gender dysphoria, and
  (b) that subsection is not complied with unless the report includes details of the
      diagnosis of the applicant's gender dysphoria.
  (3) Subsection (1) is not complied with in a case where—
  (a) the applicant has undergone or is undergoing treatment for the purpose of
      modifying sexual characteristics, or
  (b) treatment for that purpose has been prescribed or planned for the
      applicant,
unless the report required by that subsection includes details of it.'
  (6) Paragraph 4(2) of Schedule 1 has effect with the omission of paragraph (b).

28 Extent—(1) The following provisions extend only to England and Wales—
  (a) Part 1 of Schedule 2,
  (b) Part 1 of Schedule 3, and
  (c) Part 1 of Schedule 4.
  (2) The following provisions extend only to Scotland—
  (a) section 24(5),
  (b) Part 2 of Schedule 2,

(c) Part 2 of Schedule 3, and

(d) Part 2 of Schedule 4.

(3) The following provisions extend only to England and Wales and Scotland—

(a) paragraphs 12, 14 and 16 of Schedule 5, and

(b) Part 1 of Schedule 6.

(4) The following provisions extend only to Northern Ireland—

(a) section 23(3) and (4),

(b) section 24(6) and (7),

(c) Part 3 of Schedule 2,

(d) Part 3 of Schedule 3,

(e) Part 3 of Schedule 4,

(f) paragraphs 13, 15 and 17 of Schedule 5, and

(g) Part 2 of Schedule 6.

(5) Subject to subsections (1) to (4), this Act extends to Northern Ireland (as well as to England and Wales and Scotland).

29 Short title—This Act may be cited as the Gender Recognition Act 2004.

SCHEDULE 1
GENDER RECOGNITION PANELS

Section 1

List of persons eligible to sit

1 (1) The Lord Chancellor must, after consulting the Scottish Ministers and the Department of Finance and Personnel in Northern Ireland, make appointments to a list of persons eligible to sit as members of Gender Recognition Panels.

(2) The only persons who may be appointed to the list are persons who—

(a) have a relevant legal qualification ('legal members'), or

(b) are registered medical practitioners or chartered psychologists ('medical members').

(3) The following have a relevant legal qualification—

(a) a person who has a 7 year general qualification within the meaning of section 71 of the Courts and Legal Services Act 1990 (c 41),

(b) an advocate or solicitor in Scotland of at least seven years' standing, and

(c) a member of the Bar of Northern Ireland or solicitor of the Supreme Court of Northern Ireland of at least seven years' standing.

President

2 (1) The Lord Chancellor must, after consulting the Scottish Ministers and the Department of Finance and Personnel in Northern Ireland—

(a) appoint one of the legal members to be the President of Gender Recognition Panels ('the President'), and

(b) appoint another of the legal members to be the Deputy President of Gender Recognition Panels ('the Deputy President').

(2) The Deputy President has the functions of the President—

(a) if the President is unavailable, and

(b) during any vacancy in the office of President.

Tenure of persons appointed to list

3 Persons on the list—

(a) hold and vacate their appointments in accordance with the terms on which they are appointed, and

(b) are eligible for re-appointment at the end of their period of appointment.

Membership of Panels

4 (1) The President must make arrangements for determining the membership of Panels.

(2) The arrangements must ensure that a Panel determining an application under section 1(1)(a) includes—

(a) at least one legal member, and

(b) at least one medical member.

5 The arrangements must ensure that a Panel determining an application under section 1(1)(b), 5(2) or 6(1) includes at least one legal member.

Procedure

6 (1) Where a Panel consists of more than one member, either the President or Deputy President or another legal member nominated by the President must preside.

(2) Decisions of a Panel consisting of more than one member may be taken by majority vote (and, if its members are evenly split, the member presiding has a casting vote).

(3) Panels are to determine applications in private.

(4) A Panel must determine an application without a hearing unless the Panel considers that a hearing is necessary.

(5) The President may, after consulting the Council on Tribunals, give directions about the practice and procedure of Panels.

(6) Panels must give reasons for their decisions.

(7) Where a Panel has determined an application, the Secretary of State must communicate to the applicant the Panel's decision and its reasons for making its decision.

Staff and facilities

7 The Secretary of State may make staff and other facilities available to Panels.

Money

8 (1) The Secretary of State may pay sums by way of remuneration, allowances and expenses to members of Panels.

(2) The Secretary of State may pay compensation to a person who ceases to be on the list if the Secretary of State thinks it appropriate to do so because of special circumstances.

Council on Tribunals

9 In Schedule 1 to the Tribunals and Inquiries Act 1992 (c 53) (tribunals under supervision of Council on Tribunals), before paragraph 22 insert—

'Gender Recognition 21AA   Gender Recognition Panels constituted under Schedule 1 to the Gender Recognition Act 2004 (c 7).'

Disqualification

10 In Part 3 of Schedule 1 to the House of Commons Disqualification Act 1975 (c 24) (offices disqualifying person from membership of House of Commons), at the appropriate place insert—

'Person on the list of those eligible to sit as members of a Gender Recognition Panel.'

11

In Part 3 of Schedule 1 to the Northern Ireland Assembly Disqualification Act 1975 (c 25) (offices disqualifying persons from membership of Northern Ireland Assembly), at the appropriate place insert—

'Person on the list of those eligible to sit as members of a Gender Recognition Panel.'

SCHEDULE 2
INTERIM CERTIFICATES: MARRIAGE

Section 4

PART 1
ENGLAND AND WALES

1 The Matrimonial Causes Act 1973 (c 18) is amended as follows.

2 In section 12 (grounds on which a marriage celebrated after 31st July 1971 is voidable), after paragraph (f) insert—
'(g) that an interim gender recognition certificate under the Gender Recognition Act 2004 has, after the time of the marriage, been issued to either party to the marriage;' .

3 In section 13 (bars to relief), after subsection (2) insert—
'(2A) Without prejudice to subsection (1) above, the court shall not grant a decree of nullity by virtue of section 12 above on the ground mentioned in paragraph (g) of that section unless it is satisfied that proceedings were instituted within the period of six months from the date of issue of the interim gender recognition certificate.'

4 (1) Paragraph 11 of Schedule 1 (grounds on which a marriage celebrated before 1st August 1971 is voidable) is amended as follows.
(2) In sub-paragraph (1), after paragraph (d) insert
'or
(e) that an interim gender recognition certificate under the Gender Recognition Act 2004 has been issued to either party to the marriage;' .
(3) After sub-paragraph (3) insert—
'(3A) The court shall not grant a decree of nullity in a case falling within sub-paragraph (1)(e) above unless it is satisfied that proceedings were instituted within six months from the date of issue of the interim gender recognition certificate.'

PART 2
SCOTLAND

5 The Divorce (Scotland) Act 1976 (c 39) is amended as follows.

6 (1) In subsection (1) of section 1 (grounds on which decree of divorce may be granted)—
(a) the words 'the marriage has broken down irretrievably' become paragraph (a), and
(b) after that paragraph insert
'or
(b) an interim gender recognition certificate under the Gender Recognition Act 2004 has, after the date of the marriage, been issued to either party to the marriage.'
(2) Accordingly, the title of that section becomes 'Grounds of divorce'.

7 In section 2(1) (encouragement of reconciliation), for 'in an action for divorce' substitute 'under paragraph (a) of section 1(1)'.

PART 3
NORTHERN IRELAND

8 The Matrimonial Causes (Northern Ireland) Order 1978 (SI 1978/1045 (NI 15)) is amended as follows.

9 In Article 14 (grounds on which a marriage celebrated after the commencement of that Article is voidable), after paragraph (f) insert—
'(g) that an interim gender recognition certificate under the Gender Recognition Act 2004 has, after the time of the marriage, been issued to either party to the marriage;' .

10 In Article 16 (bars to relief), after paragraph (2) insert—
'(2A) Without prejudice to paragraph (1), the court shall not grant a decree of nullity by virtue of Article 14 on the ground mentioned in paragraph (g) of that Article unless it is satisfied that proceedings were instituted within the period of six months from the date of issue of the interim gender recognition certificate.'

11 (1) Paragraph 18 of Schedule 3 (grounds on which a marriage celebrated before the commencement of Article 14 is voidable) is amended as follows.
(2) In sub-paragraph (1), after paragraph (d) insert
'or
(e) that an interim gender recognition certificate under the Gender Recognition Act 2004 has been issued to either party to the marriage;' .
(3) After sub-paragraph (4) insert—
'(4A) The court shall not grant a decree of nullity in a case falling within sub-paragraph (1)(e) unless it is satisfied that proceedings were instituted within six months from the date of issue of the interim gender recognition certificate.'

SCHEDULE 3
REGISTRATION   Section 10

PART 1
ENGLAND AND WALES

Introductory

1 In this Part—
'the Registrar General' means the Registrar General for England and Wales, and
'the 1953 Act' means the Births and Deaths Registration Act 1953 (c 20).

Gender Recognition Register

2 (1) The Registrar General must maintain, in the General Register Office, a register to be called the Gender Recognition Register.
(2) In this Part 'the Gender Recognition Register' means the register maintained under sub-paragraph (1).
(3) The form in which the Gender Recognition Register is maintained is to be determined by the Registrar General.
(4) The Gender Recognition Register is not to be open to public inspection or search.

Entries in Gender Recognition Register and marking of existing birth register entries

3 (1) If the Registrar General receives under section 10(1) a copy of a full gender recognition certificate issued to a person, the Registrar General must—

    (a) make an entry in the Gender Recognition Register containing such particulars as may be prescribed in relation to the person's birth and any other prescribed matter,

    (b) secure that the UK birth register entry is marked in such manner as may be prescribed, and

    (c) make traceable the connection between the entry in the Gender Recognition Register and the UK birth register entry.

(2) Sub-paragraph (1) does not apply if the certificate was issued after an application under section 6(1) and that sub-paragraph has already been complied with in relation to the person.

(3) No certified copy of the UK birth register entry and no short certificate of birth compiled from that entry is to include anything marked by virtue of sub-paragraph (1)(b).

(4) Information kept by the Registrar General for the purposes of sub-paragraph (1)(c) is not to be open to public inspection or search.

(5) 'Prescribed' means prescribed by regulations made by the Registrar General with the approval of the Chancellor of the Exchequer.

Indexing of entries in Gender Recognition Register

4 (1) The Registrar General must make arrangements for each entry made in the Gender Recognition Register to be included in the relevant index kept in the General Register Office.

(2) Any right to search the relevant index includes the right to search entries included in it by virtue of sub-paragraph (1).

(3) Where by virtue of sub-paragraph (1) an index includes entries in the Gender Recognition Register, the index must not disclose that fact.

(4) 'The relevant index', in relation to an entry made in the Gender Recognition Register in relation to a person, means the index of the certified copies of entries in registers, or of entries in registers, which includes the person's UK birth register entry.

Certified copies of entries in Gender Recognition Register

5 (1) Anyone who may have a certified copy of the UK birth register entry of a person issued with a full gender recognition certificate may have a certified copy of the entry made in relation to the person in the Gender Recognition Register.

(2) Any fee which would be payable for a certified copy of the person's UK birth register entry is payable for a certified copy of the entry made in relation to the person in the Gender Recognition Register.

(3) If the person's UK birth register entry is an entry in the Gender Recognition Register, sub-paragraph (1) applies as if the person's UK birth register entry were the most recent entry within section 10(2)(a) or (b) containing a record of the person's birth or adoption which is not an entry in the Gender Recognition Register.

(4) A certified copy of an entry in the Gender Recognition Register must not disclose the fact that the entry is contained in the Gender Recognition Register.

(5) A certified copy of an entry in the Gender Recognition Register must be sealed or stamped with the seal of the General Register Office.

Short certificates of birth compiled from Gender Recognition Register

6 Where a short certificate of birth under section 33 of the 1953 Act is compiled from the Gender Recognition Register, the certificate must not disclose that fact.

Gender Recognition Register: re-registration

7 (1) Section 10A of the 1953 Act (re-registration where parents not married) applies where an entry relating to a person's birth has been made in the Gender Recognition Register as where the birth of a child has been registered under that Act.

(2) In its application by virtue of sub-paragraph (1) section 10A has effect—

(a) as if the reference to the registrar in subsection (1) were to the Registrar General, and

(b) with the omission of subsection (2).

(3) Sections 14 and 14A of the 1953 Act (re-registration in cases of legitimation and after declaration of parentage) apply where an entry relating to a person's birth has been made in the Gender Recognition Register as if the references in those sections to the Registrar General authorising re-registration of the person's birth were to the Registrar General's re-registering it.

Correction etc of Gender Recognition Register

8 (1) Any power or duty of the Registrar General or any other person to correct, alter, amend, mark or cancel the marking of a person's UK birth register entry is exercisable, or falls to be performed, by the Registrar General in relation to an entry in the Gender Recognition Register which—

(a) relates to that person, and

(b) under paragraph 4(1) is included in the index which includes the person's UK birth register entry.

(2) If the person's UK birth register entry is an entry in the Gender Recognition Register, the references in sub-paragraph (1) to the person's UK birth register entry are to the most recent entry within section 10(2)(a) or (b) containing a record of the person's birth or adoption which is not an entry in the Gender Recognition Register.

(3) The Registrar General may correct the Gender Recognition Register by entry in the margin (without any alteration of the original entry) in consequence of the issue of a full gender recognition certificate after an application under section 6(1).

Revocation of gender recognition certificate etc

9 (1) This paragraph applies if, after an entry has been made in the Gender Recognition Register in relation to a person, the High Court or the Court of Session makes an order under section 8(6) quashing the decision to grant the person's application under section 1(1) or 5(2).

(2) The High Court or the Court of Session must inform the Registrar General.

(3) Subject to any appeal, the Registrar General must—

(a) cancel the entry in the Gender Recognition Register, and

(b) cancel, or secure the cancellation, of any marking of an entry relating to the person made by virtue of paragraph 3(1)(b).

Evidence

10 (1) Section 34(5) of the 1953 Act (certified copy of entry in register under that Act deemed to be true copy) applies in relation to the Gender Recognition Register as if it were a register under that Act.

(2) A certified copy of an entry made in the Gender Recognition Register in relation to a person is to be received, without further or other proof, as evidence—

(a) if the relevant index is the index of the Adopted Children Register, of the matters of which a certified copy of an entry in that Register is evidence,

(b) if the relevant index is the index of the Parental Order Register, of the matters of which a certified copy of an entry in that Register is evidence, and

(c) otherwise, of the person's birth.

(3) And any certified copy which is receivable in evidence of any matter in Northern Ireland by virtue of paragraph 31(2)(a) or (b) of this Schedule is also receivable as evidence of that matter in England and Wales.

Regulatory reform

11 The Chancellor of the Exchequer may by order amend this Part in consequence of any order under section 1 of the Regulatory Reform Act 2001 (c 6) which includes provision relating to the system of registration of births and adoptions in England and Wales.

PART 2
SCOTLAND

Introductory

12 In this Part—

'the Registrar General' means the Registrar General for Scotland, and

'the 1965 Act' means the Registration of Births, Deaths and Marriages (Scotland) Act 1965 (c 49).

Gender Recognition Register

13 (1) The Registrar General must maintain, in the General Register Office of Births, Deaths and Marriages in Scotland, a register to be called the Gender Recognition Register.

(2) In this Part 'the Gender Recognition Register' means the register maintained under sub-paragraph (1).

(3) The form in which the Gender Recognition Register is maintained is to be determined by the Registrar General.

(4) The Gender Recognition Register is not to be open to public inspection or search.

Entries in Gender Recognition Register

14 (1) If the Registrar General receives under section 10(1) a copy of a full gender recognition certificate issued to a person, the Registrar General must—

(a) make an entry in the Gender Recognition Register containing such particulars as may be prescribed in relation to the person's birth and any other prescribed matter, and

(b) otherwise than by annotating in any way the birth register, make traceable the connection between the UK birth register entry and the entry in the Gender Recognition Register.

(2) Sub-paragraph (1) does not apply if the gender recognition certificate was issued after an application under section 6(1) and that sub-paragraph has already been complied with in relation to the person.

(3) Information kept by the Registrar General for the purposes of sub-paragraph (1)(b) is not to be open to public inspection or search.

(4) 'Prescribed' means prescribed by regulations made by the Registrar General with the approval of the Scottish Ministers.

Indexing of entries in Gender Recognition Register

15 (1) The Registrar General must make arrangements for each entry made in the Gender Recognition Register to be included in an index of such entries kept in the General Register Office of Births, Deaths and Marriages in Scotland.

(2) Whenever the Registrar General causes a search to be made under subsection (2)(a) of section 38 of the 1965 Act (search of indexes of entries in the registers of births, deaths and marriages) on behalf of any person, he must also, without payment of any fee additional to the fee or fees prescribed under that section—

(a) cause a search to be made of the index of entries in the Gender Recognition Register on behalf of that person, and

(b) issue to that person an extract of any such entry provided that (disregarding, for the purposes of subsection (4)(j) of section 22, this paragraph) disclosure of the entry to the person would not constitute an offence under that section.

Extracts of entries in Gender Recognition Register

16 (1) This paragraph applies in respect of an extract issued under paragraph 15(2)(b).

(2) Except as regards the sex and name of the person to whom it relates, the extract must have the form and content it would have had had it been an extract from the register of births of the entry relating to that person.

(3) The extract must not disclose the fact that the entry is contained in the Gender Recognition Register.

Abbreviated certificates of birth compiled from Gender Recognition Register

17 Where an abbreviated certificate of birth under section 40 of the 1965 Act is compiled from the Gender Recognition Register, the certificate must not disclose that fact.

Gender Recognition Register: correction, re-registration etc

18 Section 18A(2) (decrees of parentage and non-parentage), section 20(1) and (3) (re-registration in certain cases), section 42(1) and (5) (correction of errors), section 43(1), (2) and (5) to (9) (recording change of name or surname) and section 44 (Register of Corrections etc) of the 1965 Act apply in relation to the Gender Recognition Register as they apply in relation to the register of births.

Revocation of gender recognition certificate etc

19 (1) This paragraph applies if, after an entry has been made in the Gender Recognition Register in relation to a person, the High Court or the Court of Session makes an order under section 8(6) quashing the decision to grant the person's application under section 1(1) or 5(2).

(2) The High Court or the Court of Session must inform the Registrar General.

(3) Subject to any appeal, the Registrar General must cancel the entry in the Gender Recognition Register.

Authentication and admissibility

20 Section 41 of the 1965 Act (authentication of extracts etc and their admissibility as evidence) applies in relation to the Gender Recognition Register as in relation to the registers kept under the provisions of that Act.

PART 3
NORTHERN IRELAND

Introductory

21 In this Part—
'the Registrar General' means the Registrar General for Northern Ireland, and
'the 1976 Order' means the Births and Deaths Registration (Northern Ireland)
Order 1976 (SI 1976/1041 (NI 14)).

Gender Recognition Register

22 (1) The Registrar General must maintain, in the General Register Office in Northern Ireland, a register to be called the Gender Recognition Register.

(2) In this Part 'the Gender Recognition Register' means the register maintained under sub-paragraph (1).

(3) The form in which the Gender Recognition Register is maintained is to be determined by the Registrar General.

(4) The Gender Recognition Register is not to be open to public inspection or search.

Entries in Gender Recognition Register and marking of existing birth register entries

23 (1) If the Registrar General receives under section 10(1) a copy of a full gender recognition certificate issued to a person, the Registrar General must—
  (a) make an entry in the Gender Recognition Register containing such particulars as may be prescribed in relation to the person's birth and any other prescribed matter,
  (b) secure that the UK birth register entry is marked in such manner as may be prescribed, and
  (c) make traceable the connection between the entry in the Gender Recognition Register and the UK birth register entry.

(2) Sub-paragraph (1) does not apply if the gender recognition certificate was issued after an application under section 6(1) and that sub-paragraph has already been complied with in relation to the person.

(3) No certified copy of the UK birth register entry and no short certificate of birth compiled from that entry is to include anything marked by virtue of sub-paragraph (1)(b).

(4) Information kept by the Registrar General for the purposes of sub-paragraph (1)(c) is not to be open to public inspection or search.

(5) 'Prescribed' means prescribed by regulations made by the Department of Finance and Personnel.

Indexing of entries in Gender Recognition Register

24 (1) The Registrar General must make arrangements for each entry made in the Gender Recognition Register to be included in the relevant index kept in the General Register Office in Northern Ireland.

(2) Any right to search the relevant index includes the right to search entries included in it by virtue of sub-paragraph (1).

(3) Where by virtue of sub-paragraph (1) an index includes entries in the Gender Recognition Register, the index must not disclose that fact.

(4) 'The relevant index', in relation to an entry made in the Gender Recognition Register in relation to a person, means the index of the entries in registers which includes the UK birth register entry.

Certified copies of entries in Gender Recognition Register

25 (1) Anyone who may have a certified copy of the UK birth register entry of a person issued with a full gender recognition certificate may have a certified copy of the entry made in relation to the person in the Gender Recognition Register.

(2) Any fee which would be payable for a certified copy of the person's UK birth register entry is payable for a certified copy of the entry made in relation to the person in the Gender Recognition Register.

(3) If the person's UK birth register entry is an entry in the Gender Recognition Register, sub-paragraph (1) applies as if the person's UK birth register entry were the most recent entry within section 10(2)(a) or (b) containing a record of the person's birth or adoption which is not an entry in the Gender Recognition Register.

(4) A certified copy of an entry in the Gender Recognition Register must not disclose the fact that the entry is contained in the Gender Recognition Register.

(5) A certified copy of an entry in the Gender Recognition Register must be sealed or stamped with the seal of the General Register Office in Northern Ireland.

Short certificates of birth compiled from Gender Recognition Register

26 Where a short certificate of birth under Article 40 of the 1976 Order is compiled from the Gender Recognition Register, the certificate must not disclose that fact.

Gender Recognition Register: re-registration

27 Articles 18, 19 and 19A of the 1976 Order (re-registration of births) apply where an entry relating to a person's birth has been made in the Gender Recognition Register as if the references in those Articles to the Registrar General authorising re-registration of the person's birth were to the Registrar General's re-registering it.

Correction of errors in Gender Recognition Register

28 (1) Any power or duty of the Registrar General to correct, alter, amend, mark or cancel the marking of a person's UK birth register entry is exercisable, or falls to be performed, by the Registrar General in relation to an entry in the Gender Recognition Register which—

(a) relates to that person, and
(b) under paragraph 24(1) is included in the index which includes the person's UK birth register entry.

(2) If the person's UK birth register entry is an entry in the Gender Recognition Register, the references in sub-paragraph (1) to the person's UK birth register entry are to the most recent entry within section 10(2)(a) or (b) containing a record of the person's birth or adoption which is not an entry in the Gender Recognition Register.

(3) The Registrar General may correct the Gender Recognition Register by entry in the margin (without any alteration of the original entry) in consequence of the issue of a full gender recognition certificate after an application under section 6(1).

Revocation of gender recognition certificate etc

29 (1) This paragraph applies if, after an entry has been made in the Gender Recognition Register in relation to a person, the High Court or the Court of Session makes an order under section 8(6) quashing the decision to grant the person's application under section 1(1) or 5(2).

(2) The High Court or the Court of Session must inform the Registrar General.

(3) Subject to any appeal, the Registrar General must—

(a) cancel the entry in the Gender Recognition Register, and

(b) cancel, or secure the cancellation of, any marking of an entry relating to the person made by virtue of paragraph 23(1)(b).

Change of name

30 Paragraphs (4) to (6) of Article 37 of the 1976 Order (change of name) apply in relation to the Gender Recognition Register as they apply in relation to a register under that Order.

Evidence

31 (1) Article 42 of the 1976 Order (proof of age or death) applies in relation to the Gender Recognition Register as it applies in relation to a register under that Order.

(2) A certified copy of an entry made in the Gender Recognition Register in relation to a person is to be received, without further or other proof, as evidence—

(a) if the relevant index is the index of the Adopted Children Register, of the matters of which a certified copy of an entry in that Register is evidence,

(b) if the relevant index is the index of the Parental Order Register, of the matters of which a certified copy of an entry in that Register is evidence, and

(c) otherwise, of the person's birth.

(3) And any certified copy which is receivable in evidence of any matter in England and Wales by virtue of paragraph 10(2)(a) or (b) of this Schedule is also receivable as evidence of that matter in Northern Ireland.

Fees

32 Article 47 of the 1976 Order (fees for searches, certificates etc) applies in relation to the Gender Recognition Register as it applies in relation to a register under that Order.

SCHEDULE 4

EFFECT ON MARRIAGE   Section 11

PART 1

ENGLAND AND WALES

Marriage Act 1949 (c 76)

1 The Marriage Act 1949 is amended as follows.

2 In section 1 (restrictions on marriage), insert at the end—

'(6) Subsection (5) of this section and Parts 2 and 3 of the First Schedule to this Act have effect subject to the following modifications in the case of a party to a marriage whose gender has become the acquired gender under the Gender Recognition Act 2004 ('the relevant person').

(7) Any reference in those provisions to a former wife or former husband of the relevant person includes (respectively) any former husband or former wife of the relevant person.

(8) And—

(a) the reference in paragraph (b) of subsection (5) of this section to the relevant person's son's mother is to the relevant person's son's father if the relevant person is the son's mother; and

(b) the reference in paragraph (d) of that subsection to the relevant person's daughter's father is to the relevant person's daughter's mother if the relevant person is the daughter's father.'

3 After section 5A insert—

'5B Marriages involving person of acquired gender—(1) A clergyman is not obliged to solemnise the marriage of a person if the clergyman reasonably believes that the person's gender has become the acquired gender under the Gender Recognition Act 2004.

(2) A clerk in Holy Orders of the Church in Wales is not obliged to permit the marriage of a person to be solemnised in the church or chapel of which the clerk is the minister if the clerk reasonably believes that the person's gender has become the acquired gender under that Act.'

Matrimonial Causes Act 1973 (c 18)

4 The Matrimonial Causes Act 1973 is amended as follows.

5 In section 12 (grounds on which a marriage celebrated after 31st July 1971 is voidable), insert at the end—
   '(h) that the respondent is a person whose gender at the time of the marriage had become the acquired gender under the Gender Recognition Act 2004.'

6 In section 13(2), (3) and (4) (bars to relief), for 'or (f)' substitute ', (f) or (h)'.

PART 2
SCOTLAND

Marriage (Scotland) Act 1977 (c 15

7 In section 2 of the Marriage (Scotland) Act 1977 (marriage of related persons), insert at the end—
   '(6) Subsections (1A) and (1B) above and paragraphs 2 and 2A of Schedule 1 to this Act have effect subject to the following modifications in the case of a party to a marriage whose gender has become the acquired gender under the Gender Recognition Act 2004 ('the relevant person').

(7) Any reference in those provisions to a former wife or former husband of the relevant person includes (respectively) any former husband or former wife of the relevant person.

(8) And—
   (a) the reference in paragraph (b) of subsection (1B) above to the relevant person's son's mother is to the relevant person's son's father if the relevant person is the son's mother; and
   (b) the reference in paragraph (d) of that subsection to the relevant person's daughter's father is to the relevant person's daughter's mother if the relevant person is the daughter's father.'

PART 3
NORTHERN IRELAND

Family Law (Miscellaneous Provisions) (Northern Ireland) Order 1984 (SI 1984/1984 (NI 14))

8 In Article 18 of the Family Law (Miscellaneous Provisions) (Northern Ireland) Order 1984 (restrictions on marriage), after paragraph (2D) insert—

'(2DA) Paragraph (2D) and Parts 2 and 3 of the Table in paragraph (1) have effect subject to the following modifications in the case of a party to a marriage whose gender has become the acquired gender under the Gender Recognition Act 2004 ('the relevant person').

(2DB) Any reference in those provisions to a former wife or former husband of the relevant person includes (respectively) any former husband or former wife of the relevant person.

(2DC) And—
  (a) the reference in paragraph (2D)(b) to the relevant person's son's mother is to the relevant person's son's father if the relevant person is the son's mother, and
  (b) the reference in paragraph (2D)(d) to the relevant person's daughter's father is to the relevant person's daughter's mother if the relevant person is the daughter's father.'

Matrimonial Causes (Northern Ireland) Order 1978 (SI 1978/1045 (NI 15))

9 The Matrimonial Causes (Northern Ireland) Order 1978 is amended as follows.

10 In Article 14 (grounds on which a marriage celebrated after the commencement of that Article is voidable), insert at the end—
  '(h) that the respondent is a person whose gender at the time of the marriage had become the acquired gender under the Gender Recognition Act 2004.'

11 In Article 16(2), (3) and (4) (bars to relief), for 'or (f)' substitute ', (f) or (h)'.

SCHEDULE 5
BENEFITS AND PENSIONS

Section 13

PART 1
INTRODUCTORY

1 This Schedule applies where a full gender recognition certificate is issued to a person.

PART 2
STATE BENEFITS

Introductory

2 (1) In this Part of this Schedule 'the 1992 Act' means—
  (a) in England and Wales and Scotland, the Social Security Contributions and Benefits Act 1992 (c 4), and
  (b) in Northern Ireland, the Social Security Contributions and Benefits (Northern Ireland) Act 1992 (c 7).
  (2) In this Part of this Schedule 'the Administration Act' means—
  (a) in England and Wales and Scotland, the Social Security Administration Act 1992 (c 5), and
  (b) in Northern Ireland, the Social Security Administration (Northern Ireland) Act 1992 (c 8).
  (3) Expressions used in this Part of this Schedule and in Part 2 of the 1992 Act have the same meaning in this Part of this Schedule as in Part 2 of the 1992 Act.

Widowed mother's allowance

3 (1) If (immediately before the certificate is issued) the person is, or but for section 1 of the Administration Act would be, entitled to a widowed mother's allowance under section 37 of the 1992 Act (allowance for woman whose husband died before 9th April 2001)—

    (a) the person is not entitled to that allowance afterwards, but

    (b) (instead) subsections (2) to (5) of section 39A of the 1992 Act (widowed parent's allowance) apply in relation to the person.

    (2) If (immediately before the certificate is issued) the person is (actually) entitled to a widowed mother's allowance, the entitlement to widowed parent's allowance conferred by sub-paragraph (1) is not subject to section 1 of the Administration Act.

Widow's pension

4 If (immediately before the certificate is issued) the person is entitled to a widow's pension under section 38 of the 1992 Act (pension for woman whose husband died before 9th April 2001), the person is not entitled to that pension afterwards.

Widowed parent's allowance

5 If (immediately before the certificate is issued) the person is, or but for section 1 of the Administration Act would be, entitled to a widowed parent's allowance by virtue of subsection (1)(b) of section 39A of the 1992 Act (allowance for man whose wife died before 9th April 2001), subsections (2) to (5) of that section continue to apply in relation to the person afterwards.

Long-term incapacity benefit etc

6 If (immediately before the certificate is issued) the person is entitled to incapacity benefit, or a Category A retirement pension, under—

    (a) section 40 of the 1992 Act (long-term incapacity benefit etc for woman whose husband died before 9th April 2001), or

    (b) section 41 of the 1992 Act (long-term incapacity benefit etc for man whose wife died before that date),

the person is not so entitled afterwards.

Category A retirement pension

7 (1) Any question—

    (a) whether the person is entitled to a Category A retirement pension (under section 44 of the 1992 Act) for any period after the certificate is issued, and

    (b) (if so) the rate at which the person is so entitled for the period,

is to be decided as if the person's gender had always been the acquired gender.

    (2) Accordingly, if (immediately before the certificate is issued) the person—

    (a) is a woman entitled to a Category A retirement pension, but

    (b) has not attained the age of 65,

the person ceases to be so entitled when it is issued.

    (3) And, conversely, if (immediately before the certificate is issued) the person—

    (a) is a man who has attained the age at which a woman of the same age attains pensionable age, but

    (b) has not attained the age of 65,

the person is to be treated for the purposes of section 44 of the 1992 Act as attaining pensionable age when it is issued.

    (4) But sub-paragraph (1) does not apply if and to the extent that the decision of any question to which it refers is affected by—

    (a) the payment or crediting of contributions, or the crediting of earnings, in respect of a period ending before the certificate is issued, or

(b) preclusion from regular employment by responsibilities at home for such a
period.

(5) Paragraph 10 makes provision about deferment of Category A retirement
pensions.

Category B retirement pension etc

8 (1) Any question whether the person is entitled to—
   (a) a Category B retirement pension (under section 48A, 48B, 48BB or 51 of
        the 1992 Act), or
   (b) an increase in a Category A retirement pension under section 51A or 52 of
        the 1992 Act (increase in Category A retirement pension by reference to
        amount of Category B retirement pension),
for any period after the certificate is issued is (in accordance with section 9(1)) to
be decided as if the person's gender were the acquired gender (but subject to sub-
paragraph (4)).

(2) Accordingly, if (immediately before the certificate is issued) the person is a
woman entitled to—
   (a) a Category B retirement pension, or
   (b) an increase in a Category A retirement pension under section 51A or 52 of
        the 1992 Act,
the person may cease to be so entitled when it is issued.

(3) And, conversely, if (immediately before the certificate is issued) the
person—
   (a) is a man who has attained the age at which a woman of the same age attains
        pensionable age, but
   (b) has not attained the age of 65,
the person is to be treated for the purposes of sections 48A, 48B and 48BB of the
1992 Act as attaining pensionable age when it is issued.

(4) But a person who is a man (immediately before the certificate is issued) is
not entitled to a Category B retirement pension under section 48B of the 1992 Act
for any period after it is issued if the person—
   (a) attains (or has attained) the age of 65 before 6th April 2010, and
   (b) would not have been entitled to a Category B retirement pension under
        section 51 of the 1992 Act for that period if still a man.

(5) Paragraph 10 makes provision about deferment of Category B retirement
pensions.

Shared additional pension

9 (1) Any question—
   (a) whether the person is entitled to a shared additional pension (under
        section 55A of the 1992 Act) for any period after the certificate is issued,
        and
   (b) (if so) the rate at which the person is so entitled for the period,
is to be decided on the basis of the person attaining pensionable age on the same
date as someone of the acquired gender (and the same age).

(2) Accordingly, if (immediately before the certificate is issued) the person—
   (a) is a woman entitled to a shared additional pension, but
   (b) has not attained the age of 65,
the person ceases to be so entitled when it is issued.

(3) And, conversely, if (immediately before the certificate is issued) the
person—
   (a) is a man who has attained the age at which a woman of the same age attains
        pensionable age, but
   (b) has not attained the age of 65,

the person is to be treated for the purposes of section 55A of the 1992 Act as attaining pensionable age when it is issued.

(4) Paragraph 10 makes provision about deferment of shared additional pensions.

Deferment of pensions

10 (1) The person's entitlement to—

(a) a Category A retirement pension,

(b) a Category B retirement pension, or

(c) a shared additional pension,

is not to be taken to have been deferred for any period ending before the certificate is issued unless the condition in sub-paragraph (2) is satisfied.

(2) The condition is that the entitlement both—

(a) was actually deferred during the period, and

(b) would have been capable of being so deferred had the person's gender been the acquired gender.

Category C retirement pension for widows

11 If (immediately before the certificate is issued) the person is entitled to a Category C retirement pension under section 78(2) of the 1992 Act, the person is not entitled to that pension afterwards.

Graduated retirement benefit: Great Britain

12 (1) The provision that may be made by regulations under paragraph 15 of Schedule 3 to the Social Security (Consequential Provisions) Act 1992 (c 6) (power to retain provisions repealed by Social Security Act 1973 (c 38), with or without modification, for transitional purposes) includes provision modifying the preserved graduated retirement benefit provisions in consequence of this Act.

(2) 'The preserved graduated retirement benefit provisions' are the provisions of the National Insurance Act 1965 (c 51) relating to graduated retirement benefit continued in force, with or without modification, by regulations having effect as if made under that paragraph.

Graduated retirement benefit: Northern Ireland

13 (1) The provision that may be made by regulations under paragraph 15 of Schedule 3 to the Social Security (Consequential Provisions) (Northern Ireland) Act 1992 (c 9) (corresponding power for Northern Ireland) includes provision modifying the Northern Ireland preserved graduated retirement benefit provisions in consequence of this Act.

(2) 'The Northern Ireland preserved graduated retirement benefit provisions' are the provisions of the National Insurance Act (Northern Ireland) 1966 (c 6 (NI)) relating to graduated retirement benefit continued in force, with or without modification, by regulations having effect as if made under that paragraph.

PART 3

OCCUPATIONAL PENSION SCHEMES

Guaranteed minimum pensions etc: Great Britain

14 (1) In this paragraph 'the 1993 Act' means the Pension Schemes Act 1993 (c 48); and expressions used in this paragraph and in that Act have the same meaning in this paragraph as in that Act.

(2) The fact that the person's gender has become the acquired gender does not affect the operation of section 14 of the 1993 Act (guaranteed minimum) in

relation to the person, except to the extent that its operation depends on section 16 of the 1993 Act (revaluation); and sub-paragraphs (3) and (5) have effect subject to that.

(3) If (immediately before the certificate is issued) the person is a woman who is entitled to a guaranteed minimum pension but has not attained the age of 65—

(a) the person is for the purposes of section 13 of the 1993 Act and the guaranteed minimum pension provisions to be treated after it is issued as not having attained pensionable age (so that the entitlement ceases) but as attaining pensionable age on subsequently attaining the age of 65, and

(b) in a case where the person's guaranteed minimum pension has commenced before the certificate is issued, it is to be treated for the purposes of Chapter 3 of Part 4 of the 1993 Act (anti-franking) as if it had not.

(4) But sub-paragraph (3)(a) does not—

(a) affect any pension previously paid to the person, or

(b) prevent section 15 of the 1993 Act (increase of guaranteed minimum where commencement of guaranteed minimum pension postponed) operating to increase the person's guaranteed minimum by reason of a postponement of the commencement of the person's guaranteed minimum pension for a period ending before the certificate is issued.

(5) If (immediately before the certificate is issued) the person is a man who—

(a) has attained the age of 60, but

(b) has not attained the age of 65,

the person is to be treated for the purposes of section 13 of the 1993 Act and the guaranteed minimum pension provisions as attaining pensionable age when it is issued.

(6) If at that time the person has attained the age of 65, the fact that the person's gender has become the acquired gender does not affect the person's pensionable age for those purposes.

(7) The fact that the person's gender has become the acquired gender does not affect any guaranteed minimum pension to which the person is entitled as a widow or widower immediately before the certificate is issued (except in consequence of the operation of the previous provisions of this Schedule).

(8) If a transaction to which section 19 of the 1993 Act applies which is carried out before the certificate is issued discharges a liability to provide a guaranteed minimum pension for or in respect of the person, it continues to do so afterwards.

(9) 'The guaranteed minimum pension provision' means so much of the 1993 Act (apart from section 13) and of any other enactment as relates to guaranteed minimum pensions.

Guaranteed minimum pensions etc: Northern Ireland

15 (1)   In this paragraph 'the 1993 Act' means the Pension Schemes (Northern Ireland) Act 1993 (c 49); and expressions used in this paragraph and in that Act have the same meaning in this paragraph as in that Act.

(2) The fact that the person's gender has become the acquired gender does not affect the operation of section 10 of the 1993 Act (guaranteed minimum) in relation to the person, except to the extent that its operation depends on section 12 of the 1993 Act (revaluation); and sub-paragraphs (3) and (5) have effect subject to that.

(3) If (immediately before the certificate is issued) the person is a woman who is entitled to a guaranteed minimum pension but has not attained the age of 65—

(a) the person is for the purposes of section 9 of the 1993 Act and the guaranteed minimum pension provisions to be treated after it is issued as not having attained pensionable age (so that the entitlement ceases) but as attaining pensionable age on subsequently attaining the age of 65, and

(b) in a case where the person's guaranteed minimum pension has commenced before the certificate is issued, it is to be treated for the purposes of Chapter 3 of Part 4 of the 1993 Act (anti-franking) as if it had not.

(4) But sub-paragraph (3)(a) does not—

(a) affect any pension previously paid to the person, or

(b) prevent section 11 of the 1993 Act (increase of guaranteed minimum where commencement of guaranteed minimum pension postponed) operating to increase the person's guaranteed minimum by reason of a postponement of the commencement of the person's guaranteed minimum pension for a period ending before the certificate is issued.

(5) If (immediately before the certificate is issued) the person is a man who—

(a) has attained the age of 60, but

(b) has not attained the age of 65,

the person is to be treated for the purposes of section 9 of the 1993 Act and the guaranteed minimum pension provisions as attaining pensionable age when it is issued.

(6) If at that time the person has attained the age of 65, the fact that the person's gender has become the acquired gender does not affect the person's pensionable age for those purposes.

(7) The fact that the person's gender has become the acquired gender does not affect any guaranteed minimum pension to which the person is entitled as a widow or widower immediately before the certificate is issued (except in consequence of the operation of the previous provisions of this Schedule).

(8) If a transaction to which section 15 of the 1993 Act applies which is carried out before the certificate is issued discharges a liability to provide a guaranteed minimum pension for or in respect of the person, it continues to do so afterwards.

(9) 'The guaranteed minimum pension provision' means so much of the 1993 Act (apart from section 9) and of any other enactment as relates to guaranteed minimum pensions.

Equivalent pension benefits: Great Britain

16 (1) The provision that may be made by regulations under paragraph 15 of Schedule 3 to the Social Security (Consequential Provisions) Act 1992 (c 6) (power to retain provisions repealed by Social Security Act 1973 (c 38), with or without modification, for transitional purposes) includes provision modifying the preserved equivalent pension benefits provisions in consequence of this Act.

(2) 'The preserved equivalent pension benefits provisions' are the provisions of the National Insurance Act 1965 (c 51) relating to equivalent pension benefits continued in force, with or without modification, by regulations having effect as if made under that paragraph.

Equivalent pension benefits: Northern Ireland

17 (1) The provision that may be made by regulations under paragraph 15 of Schedule 3 to the Social Security (Consequential Provisions) (Northern Ireland) Act 1992 (c 9) (corresponding power for Northern Ireland) includes provision modifying the Northern Ireland preserved equivalent pension benefits provisions in consequence of this Act.

(2) 'The Northern Ireland preserved equivalent pension benefits provisions' are the provisions of the National Insurance Act (Northern Ireland) 1966 (c 6 (NI)) relating to equivalent pension benefits continued in force, with or without modification, by regulations having effect as if made under that paragraph.

SCHEDULE 6
SEX DISCRIMINATION   Section 14

PART 1
GREAT BRITAIN

1 The Sex Discrimination Act 1975 (c 65) is amended as follows.

2 In section 7A (gender reassignment: exception for genuine occupational qualification), insert at the end—
    '(4) Subsection (1) does not apply in relation to discrimination against a person whose gender has become the acquired gender under the Gender Recognition Act 2004.'

3 In section 7B (supplementary exceptions relating to gender reassignment), for subsection (3) substitute—
    '(3) Subsection (2) does not apply in relation to discrimination against a person whose gender has become the acquired gender under the Gender Recognition Act 2004.'

4 In section 9 (discrimination against contract workers), after subsection (3C) insert—
    '(3D) Subsections (3B) and (3C) do not apply in relation to discrimination against a person whose gender has become the acquired gender under the Gender Recognition Act 2004.'

5 In section 11 (partnerships), after subsection (3C) insert—
    '(3D) Subsections (3B) and (3C) do not apply in relation to discrimination against a person whose gender has become the acquired gender under the Gender Recognition Act 2004.'

PART 2
NORTHERN IRELAND

6 The Sex Discrimination (Northern Ireland) Order 1976 (SI 1976/1042 (NI 15)) is amended as follows.

7 In Article 10A (gender reassignment: exception for genuine occupational qualification), insert at the end—
    '(4) Paragraph (1) does not apply in relation to discrimination against a person whose gender has become the acquired gender under the Gender Recognition Act 2004.'

8 In Article 10B (supplementary exceptions relating to gender reassignment), for paragraph (3) substitute—
    '(3) Paragraph (2) does not apply in relation to discrimination against a person whose gender has become the acquired gender under the Gender Recognition Act 2004.'

9 In Article 12 (discrimination against contract workers), after paragraph (3C) insert—
    '(3D) Paragraphs (3B) and (3C) do not apply in relation to discrimination against a person whose gender has become the acquired gender under the Gender Recognition Act 2004.'

10 In Article 14 (partnerships), after paragraph (3C) insert—
    '(3D) Paragraphs (3B) and (3C) do not apply in relation to discrimination against a person whose gender has become the acquired gender under the Gender Recognition Act 2004.'